THE BANTAM NEW COLLEGE FRENCH & ENGLISH DICTIONARY

COMPREHENSIVE: More than 70,000 words and phrases in education, business, travel, science, history, literature, art and music, social sciences, law, medicine, diplomacy, international affairs, and everyday life.

AUTHORITATIVE: Based on reliable spoken and written sources and organized to achieve the utmost clarity, precision, and convenience.

EASY TO USE: All words are found in one single alphabet for each language, including proper names and abbreviations.

A NEW LANDMARK IN FRENCH-ENGLISH DICTIONARIES
FOR THE MODERN USER OF WORDS!

THE BANTAM NEW
COLLEGE DICTIONARY SERIES

Roger J. Steiner, Author

Roger J. Steiner, A.B., A.M., Ph.D., has done extensive linguistic research in France, where he has traveled widely and taught for two years at the University of Bordeaux. Now a member of the French faculty at the University of Delaware, he is the author of a book dealing with the origin and development of bilingual dictionaries, TWO CENTURIES OF SPANISH AND ENGLISH LEXICOGRAPHY (The Hague and Paris, 1970), and has contributed articles and reviews to learned journals.

Edwin B. Williams, General Editor

Edwin B. Williams, A.B., A.M., Ph.D., Doct. d'Univ., LL.D., L.H.D., has been Chairman of the Department of Romance Languages, Dean of the Graduate School, and Provost of the University of Pennsylvania. He is a member of the American Philosophical Society and the Hispanic Society of America and the author of the Holt SPANISH AND ENGLISH DICTIONARY, THE BANTAM NEW COLLEGE SPANISH AND ENGLISH DICTIONARY and many other works on the Spanish, French and Portuguese languages.

THE BANTAM NEW COLLEGE
FRENCH & ENGLISH
DICTIONARY

DICTIONNAIRE
ANGLAIS et FRANÇAIS

BY ROGER J. STEINER
University of Delaware

THE BANTAM NEW COLLEGE
FRENCH & ENGLISH DICTIONARY

A Bantam Book | published April 1972

2nd printing .... July 1973	6th printing .. December 1977
3rd printing ...... January 1974	7th printing ...... March 1979
4th printing . December 1975	8th printing .... April 1980
5th printing .... July 1976	9th printing .... February 1981

ISBN 0–553–14890–7

Published simultaneously in the United States and Canada

Bantam Books are published by Bantam Books, Inc. Its trademark, consisting of the words "Bantam Books" and the portrayal of a bantam, is Registered in U.S. Patent and Trademark
Office and in other countries. Marca Registrada. Bantam
Books, Inc., 666 Fifth Avenue, New York, New York 10103.

PRINTED IN THE UNITED STATES OF AMERICA

18 17 16 15 14 13 12 11 10 9

CONTENTS

CONTENTS

PREFACE

PRÉFACE

Inasmuch as the basic function of a bilingual dictionary is to provide semantic equivalences, syntactical constructions are shown in both the source and target languages on both sides of the Dictionary. In performing this function, a bilingual dictionary must fulfill six purposes. For example, a French and English bilingual dictionary must provide (1) French words which an English-speaking person wishes to use in speaking and writing (by means of the English-French part), (2) English meanings of French words which an English-speaking person encounters in listening and reading (by means of the French-English part), (3) the spelling, pronunciation, and inflection of French words and the gender of French nouns which an English-speaking person needs in order to use French words correctly (by means of the French-English part), (4) English words which a French-speaking person wishes to use in speaking and writing (by means of the French-English part), (5) French meanings of English words which a French-speaking person encounters in listening and reading (by means of the English-French part), and (6) the spelling, pronunciation, and inflection of English words which a French-speaking person needs in order to use English words correctly (by means of the English-French part).

La mission essentielle d'un dictionnaire bilingue étant de fournir à l'usager des équivalences sémantiques, les constructions syntaxiques sont données à la fois dans la langue source et dans la langue cible dans les deux parties de l'ouvrage. En s'acquittant de cette mission, le dictionnaire bilingue doit viser six buts; c'est ainsi qu'un dictionnaire bilingue français et anglais doit donner: (1) dans la partie anglais-français, les mots français que la personne anglophone désire utiliser pour parler et pour écrire; (2) dans la partie français-anglais, les acceptions anglaises des mots français que cette même personne entend dans la langue parlée et rencontre dans la lecture des textes; (3) dans la partie français-anglais, l'orthographe, la prononciation figurée, l'inflexion des mots français et le genre des noms français indispensables à l'anglophone pour l'utilisation correcte de la langue française; (4) dans la partie français-anglais, les mots anglais que la personne francophone désire utiliser pour parler et pour écrire; (5) dans la partie anglais-français, les acceptions françaises des mots anglais que cette même personne entend dans la langue parlée et rencontre dans la lecture des textes; (6) dans la partie anglais-français, l'orthographe, la prononciation figurée et l'inflexion des mots anglais indispensables au francophone pour l'utilisation correcte de la langue anglaise.

It may seem logical to provide the pronunciation and inflection of English words and the pronunciation and inflection of French words and the gender of French nouns where these words appear as target words inasmuch as target words, according to (1) and (4) above, are sought for the purpose of speaking and writing. Thus the user would find not only the words he seeks but all the information he needs about them at one and the same place. But this technique is impractical because target words are not alphabetized and could, therefore, be found only by the

A première vue, il paraît logique que la prononciation et l'inflexion des mots anglais et la prononciation et l'inflexion des mots français et le genre des noms français soient indiqués à la suite des traductions puisqu'on recherche ces traductions, selon (1) et (4) ci-dessus, pour parler et pour écrire. Ainsi, l'usager trouverait au même endroit, non seulement les mots qu'il cherche, mais également tous les renseignements dont il aurait besoin. Cependant, ce procédé n'est pas pratique parce que les traductions ne sont pas présentées dans l'ordre alphabétique et l'on ne pourrait les

roundabout and uncertain way of seeking them through their translations in the other part of the dictionary. And this would be particularly inconvenient for persons using the dictionary for purposes (2) and (5) above. It is much more convenient to provide immediate alphabetized access to pronunciation and inflection where the words appear as source words. Showing the gender of nouns takes so little space that this information is provided with both source and target words.

trouver qu'avec difficulté. Cela entraînerait surtout des inconvénients pour les personnes qui utilisent le dictionnaire dans les cas (2) et (5) ci-dessus. L'ordre alphabétique permet un accès immédiat et plus commode à la prononciation et à l'inflexion quand les mots se présentent comme mots-souches. Néanmoins, l'indication du genre des noms prend si peu de place qu'elle figure aussi bien après les traductions qu'après les mots-souches.

All words are treated in a fixed order according to the parts of speech and the functions of verbs, as follows: article, adjective, substantive, pronoun, adverb, preposition, conjunction, transitive verb, intransitive verb, impersonal verb, auxiliary verb, reflexive verb, impersonal reflexive verb, interjection.

Tous les mots-souches sont traités suivant un ordre fixe—selon les parties du discours et les fonctions des verbes —qui est le suivant: article, adjectif, substantif, pronom, adverbe, préposition, conjonction, verbe transitif, verbe intransitif, verbe impersonnel, verbe auxiliaire, verbe pronominal (réfléchi ou réciproque), verbe à la fois impersonnel et réfléchi, interjection.

Meanings with subject and usage labels come after more general meanings. Subject and usage labels (printed in roman and in parentheses) refer to the preceding entry or phrase (printed in boldface). However, when labels come immediately, i.e., without any intervening punctuation mark, after a target word, they refer to that target word and the preceding word or words separated from it only by commas, e.g.,

Les sens d'un mot suivis des rubriques qui indiquent le sujet ou l'usage du mot viennent à la suite des sens d'emploi normal. Les rubriques qui indiquent le sujet ou l'usage du mot (imprimés en caractères romains et entre parenthèses) s'appliquent au mot-souche ou à la locution précédente (imprimés en caractères gras). Cependant, lorsque la rubrique suit immédiatement la traduction, c'est-à-dire sans aucun signe de ponctuation, elle s'applique à la traduction elle-même ou aux traductions précédentes qui n'en sont séparées que par une virgule, par ex.,

---

optometrist [ɑp'tɑmɪtrɪst] *s* opticien *m*; optométriste *mf* (Canad)

English adjectives are always translated by the French masculine form regardless of whether the translation of the exemplary noun modified would be masculine or feminine, e.g.,

Les adjectifs anglais sont toujours traduits en français au masculin, quel que soit le genre des traductions des noms donnés en exemple et auxquelles ils se rapportent, par ex.,

---

close [klos] *adj* . . . ; *(friendship)* étroit; *(room)* renfermé

In order to facilitate the finding of the meaning and use sought for, changes within a vocabulary entry in part of speech and function of verb, in irregular inflection, in the gender of French nouns, and in the pronunciation of

Afin de faciliter le repérage de l'acception cherchée, les traductions sont groupées selon la partie du discours, la fonction du verbe, l'inflexion irrégulière, le genre du nom français, et la prononciation des mots français et des

viii

French and English words are marked with parallels: ||, instead of the usual semicolons.

Since vocabulary entries are not determined on the basis of etymology, homographs are included in a single entry. When the pronunciation of a homograph changes, this is shown in the proper place after parallels.

Note, however, that plurals and words spelled with capitals are shown as run-on entries. They must be preceded by parallels only when there is a change in part of speech, in pronunciation, or in inflection.

Peculiarities in the pronunciation of the plural of nouns and of run-on entries are generally indicated, e.g.,

mouth [mauθ] *s* (*pl* **mouths** [mauðz])
house [haus] *s* (*pl* **houses** [ˈhauzɪz])
œil [œj] *m* . . . ; **entre quatre yeux** [ɑ̃trəkatzjø]
guet-apens [getapɑ̃] *m* (*pl* **guets-apens** [getapɑ̃])

Periods are omitted after labels and grammatical abbreviations and at the end of vocabulary entries.

Proper nouns and abbreviations are listed in their alphabetical position in the main body of the Dictionary. Thus **Algérie** and **algérien** or **Suède** and **suédois** do not have to be looked up in two different parts of the book. And all subentries are listed in strictly alphabetical order.

The feminine form of a French adjective used as a noun (or a French feminine noun having identical spelling with the feminine form of an adjective) which falls alphabetically in a separate position from the adjective is treated in that position and is listed again as a cross reference under the adjective.

mots anglais. Ces groupes sont séparés par deux barres: ||, au lieu du point-virgule habituel.

Etant donné que l'étymologie n'entre pas dans la séparation des articles, tous les homographes sont incorporés dans le même article. Quand la prononciation d'un homographe change, cette prononciation figurée est placée entre crochets à la suite des deux barres ||.

On remarquera cependant que les pluriels et les mots qui commencent par une majuscule sont présentés parmi les locutions dans l'ordre alphabétique et ne sont séparés de celles-ci que par un point-virgule. Ils ne sont précédés des deux barres || qu'en cas de changement dans la partie du discours, dans la prononciation, ou dans l'inflexion.

Les caractéristiques spéciales de la prononciation du pluriel des noms et des locutions sont généralement indiquées, ex.:

Les points sont omis après les rubriques, les abréviations d'ordre grammatical et à la fin des articles.

Les noms propres et les abréviations se présentent toujours dans l'ordre alphabétique de la nomenclature du Dictionnaire. Par exemple, il n'est pas nécessaire de chercher **Algérie** et **algérien** ou **Suède** et **suédois** dans deux parties du livre. Toutes les locutions se présentent rigoureusement dans l'ordre alphabétique.

Lorsque la forme féminine d'un adjectif français ne suit pas immédiatement la forme masculine alphabétiquement (ou lorsqu'il s'agit d'un nom féminin français qui aurait une orthographe identique à la forme féminine de l'adjectif), et lorsqu'elle est prise substantivement, sa position comme mot-souche substantif est strictement alphabétique; mais un renvoi se trouve alors après le mot-souche adjectif.

cher chère [ʃɛr] adj . . . ‖ ƒ see chère ‖ . . .
chère [ʃɛr] ƒ fare, food and drink; . . .

The centered period is used in vocabulary entries of inflected words to mark off, according to standard orthographic principles in the two languages, the final syllable that has to be detached before the syllable showing the inflection is added, e.g.,

Quand les mots-souches sont des vocables à flexions, on emploie le point centré · pour séparer, selon les principes reconnus de l'orthographe des deux langues, la syllabe finale qui doit être détachée avant que la syllabe de la désinence ne soit attachée, ex.:

heu·reux [œrø] -reuse [røz]
satis·fy ['sætɪs ˌfaɪ] v (pret & pp -fied)

Since the orthographic break coming in French words (a) between the two l's of liquid l, (b) between s and c followed by e, i, or y, and (c) between the two elements of any double consonant pronounced as a single consonant does not correspond to the phonetic break, the centered period is used as usual but the full form of the inflected variant is shown, also with the centered period, and the full phonetic transcription of both forms is shown without a break, e.g.,

Puisque la séparation orthographique qui se trouve dans les mots français (a) entre les deux l de l'l mouillé, (b) entre s et c suivi de e, i, ou y et (c) entre les deux éléments de n'importe quelle consonne doublée prononcée comme simple consonne, ne répond pas à la séparation phonétique, on présente la forme entière de toute variante, imprimée également avec le point centré; et la transcription phonétique complète des deux formes se présente sans séparation, ex.:

(a) merveil·leux [mɛrvejø] merveil·leuse [mɛrvejøz]
(b) évanes·cent [evanesɑ̃] évanes·cente [evanesɑ̃t]
(c) éton·nant [etonɑ̃] éton·nante [etonɑ̃t]
    miel·leux [mjɛlø] miel·leuse [mjɛløz]

Where the orthographic break, according to some authorities,* is not permitted, for example, between a y and a following vowel, the centered period is not used, e.g.,

Lorsque selon l'avis de certains spécialistes,* la séparation orthographique n'est pas permise, par exemple, entre un y et la voyelle suivante, on n'utilisera pas le point centré, ex.:

croyant [krwajɑ̃] croyante [krwajɑ̃t]
métayer [meteje] métayère [metejɛr]

* V. Maurice Grevisse, *Le Bon Usage*, 8th ed., 1964, §89, p. 52.

If the two components of an English solid compound are not separated by an accent mark, a centered period is used to mark off the division between them, e.g., la′dy·bird′.

Dans les cas où les deux éléments d'un mot composé anglais écrit comme mot simple, ne seraient pas séparés par un accent, on utilisera un point centré pour montrer la division entre les deux, par ex., la′dy·bird′.

Numbers referring to the model tables of French verbs (p. 7 ff.) are placed before the abbreviation indicating the part of speech. Numbers referring to the model tables of other French parts of speech (p. 21 ff.) are placed

Les numéros qui renvoient aux tableaux des verbes français à partir de la p. 7, précèdent l'abréviation qui indique la partie du discours. Les numéros qui renvoient aux tableaux des indications grammaticales des autres parties

There are some French transitive verbs which, when used reflexively, take the reflexive pronoun in the dative. As reflexive verbs they may still take a direct object and may, accordingly, be translated by English transitive verbs. And they may in turn be used to translate English transitive verbs. This equation is shown on the French-English side after the abbreviation *ref* by the insertion of (with *dat* of *reflex pron*). It is not shown on the English-French side, as the abbreviation *tr* indicates unmistakably the syntactical relationship.

Il y a certains verbes français transitifs qui sous la forme pronominale régissent le pronom réfléchi comme complément d'attribution. Cependant, sous cette forme pronominale ils sont également transitifs et peuvent se traduire par des verbes transitifs anglais. Inversement, ces verbes pronominaux français peuvent traduire des verbes transitifs anglais. Cette équation est indiquée dans la partie français-anglais à la suite de l'abréviation *ref* par l'insertion de (with *dat* of *reflex pron*). Elle n'est pas indiquée dans la partie anglais-français, puisque l'abréviation *tr* indique nettement la relation syntaxique.

The author wishes to express his gratitude to many persons who helped him in the production of this book and particularly to Dr. Edwin B. Williams, whose efforts were unstinting in the attempt to make this a useful dictionary, to his dear wife Kathryn, whose patience carried through the ten years of research and compilation, and to René Coulet du Gard and to Claud J. Pujolle for their constant help, as well as to the following: Jean Béranger, Brigitte Callay, Paul Dumestre, Maurice Jonas, Marc and Philomena Lampe, Daniel Pralus, Wayne and Paule Ready, and André Vincent.

Labels and Grammatical Abbreviations
Rubriques et abréviations grammaticales

abbr abbreviation—abréviation
(acronym) word formed from the initial letters or syllables of a series of words—mot formé de la suite des lettres initiales ou des syllabes initiales d'une série de mots
adj adjective—adjectif
adv adverb—adverbe
(aer) aeronautics—aéronautique
(agr) agriculture—agriculture
(alg) algebra—algèbre
(anat) anatomy—anatomie
(archaic) archaïque
(archeol) archeology—archéologie
(archit) architecture—architecture
(arith) arithmetic—arithmétique
art article—article
(arti) artillery—artillerie
(astr) astronomy—astronomie
(astrol) astrology—astrologie
(aut) automobile—automobile
aux auxiliary verb—verbe auxiliaire
(bact) bacteriology—bactériologie
(baseball) base-ball
(bb) bookbinding—reliure
(Bib) Biblical—biblique
(billiards) billard
(biochem) biochemistry—biochimie
(biol) biology—biologie
(bk) bookkeeping—comptabilité
(bot) botany—botanique
(bowling) jeu de quilles, jeu de boules
(boxing) boxe
(Brit) British—britannique
(Canad) Canadian—canadien
(*cap*) capital—majuscule
(cards) cartes
(carpentry) charpenterie
(checkers) jeu de dames
(chem) chemistry—chimie
(chess) échecs
(coll) colloquial—familier
(com) commercial—commercial
comp comparative—comparatif
(comp) computers—ordinateurs
(complimentary close) formule de politesse
cond conditional—conditionnel
conj conjunction—conjonction; conjunctive—atone
(culin) cooking—cuisine
dat dative—datif
def definite—défini
dem demonstrative—démonstratif
(dial) dialectal—dialectal
(dipl) diplomacy—diplomatie
disj disjunctive—tonique
(eccl) ecclesiastical—ecclésiastique
(econ) economics—économique
(educ) education—éducation, pédagogie e.g. par ex.
(elec) electricity—électricité
(electron) electronics—électronique
(embryol) embryology—embryologie
(eng) engineering—profession de l'ingénieur, génie
(ent) entomology—entomologie
(equit) horseback riding—équitation
(escr) fencing—escrime
f feminine noun—nom féminin
(fa) fine arts—beaux-arts
fem feminine—féminin
(feudal) feudalism—féodalité
(fig) figurative—figuré
(fishing) pêche
fpl feminine noun plural—nom féminin pluriel
fut future—futur
(game) jeu
(geog) geography—géographie
(geol) geology—géologie
(geom) geometry—géométrie
ger gerund—gérondif
(govt) government—gouvernement
(gram) grammar—grammaire
(gymnastics) gymnastique
(heral) heraldry—héraldique, blason
(hist) history—histoire
(hort) horticulture—horticulture
(hum) humorous—humoristique
(hunting) chasse
(ichth) ichthyology—ichtyologie
i.e. c.-à-d.
imperf imperfect—imparfait
impers impersonal verb—verbe impersonnel
impv imperative—impératif
ind indicative—indicatif
indef indefinite—indéfini
inf infinitive—infinitif
(ins) insurance—assurance
interj interjection—interjection
interr interrogative—interrogatif
intr intransitive—intransitif
invar invariable—invariable
(ironical) ironique
(jewelry) bijouterie
(journ) journalism—journalisme
(Lat) Latin—latin
(law) droit
(*l.c.*) lower case—bas de casse

xii

(letterword) word in the form of an abbreviation which is pronounced by sounding the names of its letters in succession and which functions as a part of speech—mot en forme d'abréviation qu'on prononce en faisant sonner le nom de chaque lettre consécutivement et qui fonctionne comme partie du discours
(lit) literary—littéraire
(logic) logique
m masculine noun—nom masculin
(mach) machinery—machinerie
(mas) masonry—maçonnerie
masc masculine—masculin
(Masonry) franc-maçonnerie
(math) mathematics—mathématiques
(mech) mechanics—mécanique
(med) medicine—médecine
(metallurgy) métallurgie
(meteo) meteorology—météorologie
mf masculine or feminine noun according to sex—nom masculin ou nom féminin selon le sexe
[for *m & f* see abbreviation following (mythol)]
(mil) military—militaire
(min) mining—travail des mines
(mineral) mineralogy—minéralogie
(mountaineering) alpinisme
(mov) moving pictures—cinéma
mpl masculine noun plural—nom masculin pluriel
(mus) music—musique
(mythol) mythology—mythologie
m & f masculine and feminine noun without regard to sex—nom masculin et féminin sans distinction de sexe
(naut) nautical—nautique
(nav) naval—naval
neut neuter—neutre
(nucl) nuclear physics—physique nucléaire
(obs) obsolete—vieilli, vieux
(obstet) obstetrics—obstétrique
(opt) optics—optique
(orn) ornithology—ornithologie
(painting) peinture
(parl) parliamentary procedure—usages parlementaires
(pathol) pathology—pathologie
(pej) pejorative—péjoratif
perf perfect—parfait
pers personal—personnel; person—personne
(pharm) pharmacy—pharmacie
(phila) philately—philatélie
(philos) philosophy—philosophie
(phonet) phonetics—phonétique
(phot) photography—photographie
(phys) physics—physique
(physiol) physiology—physiologie
pl plural—pluriel
(poetic) poetical—poétique

(pol) politics—politique
poss possessive—possessif
pp past participle—participe passé
prep preposition—préposition
pres present—présent
pret preterit—prétérit, passé simple
pron pronoun—pronom
(pros) prosody—métrique, prosodie
(psychoanal) psychoanalytic—psychanalytique
(psychol) psychology—psychologie
(psychopathol) psychopathology—psychopathologie
(public sign) affiche, écriteau
q.ch. or *q.ch.* quelque chose—something
qn or *qn* quelqu'un—someone
(rad) radio—radio
ref reflexive verb—verbe pronominal, réfléchi ou réciproque
reflex reflexive—réfléchi
rel relative—relatif
(rel) religion—religion
(rhet) rhetoric—rhétorique
(rok) rocketry—fusées
(rowing) canotage
(rr) railroad—chemin de fer
s substantive—substantif
(sculp) sculpture—sculpture
(seismol) seismology—sismologie
(sewing) couture
sg singular—singulier
(slang) populaire, argotique
s.o. or *s.o.* someone—quelqu'un
spl substantive plural—substantif pluriel
(sports) sports
s.th. or *s.th.* something—quelque chose
subj subjunctive—subjonctif
super superlative—superlatif
(surg) surgery—chirurgie
(surv) surveying—topographie
(swimming) nage
(taur) bullfighting—tauromachie
(telg) telegraphy—télégraphie
(telp) telephony—téléphonie
(telv) television—télévision
(tennis) tennis
(tex) textile—textile
(theat) theater—théâtre
(theol) theology—théologie
tr transitive verb—verbe transitif
(trademark) marque déposée
(turf) horse racing—courses de chevaux
(typ) printing—imprimerie
(U.S.A.) U.S.A., E.-U.A.
v verb—verbe
var variant—variante
(vet) veterinary medicine—médecine vétérinaire
(vulg) vulgar—grossier
(wrestling) lutte, catch
(zool) zoology—zoologie

PART ONE

French-English

French Pronunciation

The following phonetic symbols represent all the sounds of the French language.

VOWELS

SYMBOL	SOUND	EXAMPLE
[a]	A little more open than the **a** in English **hat**.	**patte** [pat]
[ɑ]	Like **a** in English **father**.	**pâte** [pɑt] **phase** [fɑz]
[ɛ]	Like **e** in English **met**.	**sec** [sɛk] **fer** [fɛr] **fête** [fɛt] **aile** [ɛl] **parallèle** [paralɛl]
[e]	Like **a** in English **fate**, but without the glide the English sound sometimes has.	**été** [ete] **fée** [fe] **et** [e] **créer** [kree]
[ə]	Like **a** in English **comma** or like **o** in English **pardon**.	**le** [lə] **petit** [pəti]
[i]	Like **i** in English **machine** or like **e** in English **she**.	**si** [si]
[ɔ]	A little more open and rounded than **aw** in English **law**.	**donne** [dɔn] **joli** [jɔli]
[o]	Like **o** in English **note** but without the glide the English sound sometimes has.	**mot** [mo] **eau** [o] **faute** [fot]
[u]	Like **u** in English **rude**.	**sou** [su] **four** [fur]
[y]	The lips are rounded for [u] and held without moving while the sound [i] is pronounced.	**su** [sy] **sûr** [syr]
[ø]	The lips are rounded for [o] and held without moving while the sound [e] is pronounced.	**peu** [pø] **eux** [ø] **feutre** [føtr]
[œ]	The lips are rounded for [ɔ] and held without moving while the sound [ɛ] is pronounced.	**peur** [pœr] **seul** [sœl]

NASAL VOWELS

To produce the nasal vowels, sound is emitted through both nose and mouth by means of a lowering of the velum. The orthographic **m** or **n** has no consonantal value.

SYMBOL	SOUND	EXAMPLE
[ɑ̃]	Like **a** in English **father** and nasalized.	**en** [ɑ̃] **tant** [tɑ̃] **temps** [tɑ̃] **paon** [pɑ̃]
[ɔ̃]	More close than **aw** in English **law** and nasalized.	**on** [ɔ̃] **pont** [pɔ̃] **comte** [kɔ̃t]
[ɛ̃]	Like **e** in English **met** and nasalized.	**pin** [pɛ̃] **pain** [pɛ̃] **faim** [fɛ̃] **teint** [tɛ̃]
[œ̃]	Like [œ] of French **bœuf** and nasalized. There has been a tendency in this century to assimilate the nasal sound [œ̃] to the nasal sound [ɛ̃], making **brun** [brœ̃] and **brin** [brɛ̃] much the same.	**un** [œ̃] **parfum** [parfœ̃]

3

DIPHTHONGS

The sounds [j], [ɥ], and [w] are used to form diphthongs.

SYMBOL	SOUND	EXAMPLE
[j]	Like **y** in English **year** or like **y** in English **toy**.	hier [jer] ail [aj]
[ɥ]	Like the letter **u** [y] pronounced with consonantal value preceding a vowel.	lui [lɥi] situation [sitɥasjɔ̃] nuage [nɥaʒ] écuelle [ekɥel]
[w]	Like **w** in English **water**.	oie [wa] jouer [ʒwe] jouir [ʒwir]

CONSONANTS

The speaker of French characteristically keeps the tip of his tongue down behind his lower teeth and arches the back of the tongue at the same time. Thus, sounds such as [t], [d], [n], [s], [z], [l], and [r] must in French be articulated with the tongue tip and blade in the proximity of the back surface of the teeth.

SYMBOL	SOUND	EXAMPLE
[b]	Like **b** in English **baby**.	basse [bɑs]
[d]	Like **d** in English **dead**.	doux [du]
[f]	Like **f** in English **face**.	fou [fu]
[g]	Like **g** in English **go**.	gare [gar]
[k]	Like **k** in English **kill**, but without the aspiration which normally accompanies **k** in English.	cas [kɑ] kiosque [kjɔsk]
[l]	Like **l** in English **like** or in English **slip**—pronounced toward the front of the mouth. Not like **l** in **old**.	lit [li] houle [ul]
[m]	Like **m** in English **more**.	masse [mas]
[n]	Like **n** in English **nest**.	nous [nu]
[ɲ]	Like **ny** in English **canyon** or like **ni** in English **onion**.	signe [siɲ] agneau [aɲo]
[ŋ]	Like **ng** in English **parking**.	parking [parkiŋ]
[p]	Like **p** in English **pen**, but without the aspiration which normally accompanies **p** in English.	passe [pɑs]
[r]	Sometimes the uvular **r** but for some decades now usually a friction **r** with the point of articulation between the rounded back of the tongue and the hard palate. It resembles the Spanish aspirate in **jota**, the German aspirate in **ach**, and the **g** in the modern Greek **gamma** more than it resembles the modern American retroflex **r**. The tip of the tongue must point down near the back of the lower teeth and must not move during the utterance of the French [r].	rire [rir] caractère [karakter] roi [rwa] roue [ru]
[s]	Like **s** in English **send**.	sot [so] leçon [ləsɔ̃] place [plas] lassitude [lasityd] attention [atɑ̃sjɔ̃]
[ʃ]	Like **sh** in English **shall** or **ch** in English **machine**.	cheval [ʃval] mèche [meʃ]
[t]	Like **t** in English **ten**, but without the aspiration which normally accompanies **t** in English.	toux [tu] thé [te]

SYMBOL	SOUND	EXAMPLE
[v]	Like v in English **vest**.	**verre** [ver]
[z]	Like z in English **zeal**.	**zèle** [zɛl]
		oser [oze]
[ʒ]	Like s in English **pleasure**.	**joue** [ʒu]
		rouge [ruʒ]
		mangeur [mãʒœr]

FRENCH STRESS

Stress is not shown on French words in this Dictionary because stress is not a fixed characteristic of the pronunciation of French words. It depends on the position of the word in the sentence and it falls on the last syllable of the word that terminates a rhythmic or sense grouping unless the vowel of that syllable is a mute **e** [ə], in which case it falls on the immediately preceding syllable.

VOWEL LENGTH

Vowel length is not shown in the phonetic transcription of French words in this Dictionary because vowel length, like stress, is not a fixed characteristic of the pronunciation of French words. The following vowel sounds in the positions indicated are long when stressed: 1) all when followed by [r], [z], [v], [ʒ], or [vr]; 2) all spelled with a circumflex accent and followed by a consonant sound; and 3) [ā], [ɔ̃], [ɛ̃], [œ̃], [ɑ], [o], and [ø] followed by a consonant sound. When these conditions are not fulfilled, all vowel sounds are normal in length (or sometimes they may be short in length, even when stressed, if followed by [k], [p], [t], [kt], [rk], [rp], or [rt]).

ELISION AND LIAISON

Elision and liaison are usually made with words beginning with a vowel or a mute **h**. Elision and liaison are made with some words beginning with **y**, such as: **yèbe, yeuse, yeux, Yonne,** and **York**.

However, there are words which begin with a vowel or an **h** with which elision and liaison are not made. Most of these words begin with **h**, called aspirate **h**, although it has not been pronounced for centuries. In this Dictionary these words are indicated by an asterisk placed before the opening bracket of the phonetic symbols, e.g., **hameau** *[amo], **onze** *[ɔ̃z], **a** *[ɑ], **s** *[es].

TABLE OF FRENCH REGULAR VERBS

The letters standing before the names of the tenses in this table correspond to the designation of the tenses shown on the following page. The forms printed in boldface correspond to the key forms described likewise on the following page.

TENSE	FIRST CONJUGATION	SECOND CONJUGATION	THIRD CONJUGATION
inf	**DONNER**	**FINIR**	**VENDRE**
ger	donnant	finissant	vendant
pp	donné	fini	vendu
a) *impv*	donne	finis	vends
	donnons	finissons	vendons
	donnez	finissez	vendez
b) *pres ind*	**donne**	**finis**	**vends**
	donnes	finis	vends
	donne	finit	vend
	donnons	**finissons**	**vendons**
	donnez	finissez	vendez
	donnent	**finissent**	**vendent**
c) *pres subj*	donne	finisse	vende
	donnes	finisses	vendes
	donne	finisse	vende
	donnions	finissions	vendions
	donniez	finissiez	vendiez
	donnent	finissent	vendent
d) *imperf ind*	donnais	finissais	vendais
	donnais	finissais	vendais
	donnait	finissait	vendait
	donnions	finissions	vendions
	donniez	finissiez	vendiez
	donnaient	finissaient	vendaient
e) *fut ind*	**donnerai**	**finirai**	**vendrai**
	donneras	finiras	vendras
	donnera	finira	vendra
	donnerons	finirons	vendrons
	donnerez	finirez	vendrez
	donneront	finiront	vendront
pres cond	donnerais	finirais	vendrais
	donnerais	finirais	vendrais
	donnerait	finirait	vendrait
	donnerions	finirions	vendrions
	donneriez	finiriez	vendriez
	donneraient	finiraient	vendraient
f) *pret ind*	**donnai**	**finis**	**vendis**
	donnas	finis	vendis
	donna	finit	vendit
	donnâmes	finîmes	vendîmes
	donnâtes	finîtes	vendîtes
	donnèrent	finirent	vendirent
imperf subj	donnasse	finisse	vendisse
	donnasses	finisses	vendisses
	donnât	finît	vendît
	donnassions	finissions	vendissions
	donnassiez	finissiez	vendissiez
	donnassent	finissent	vendissent

6

MODEL VERBS

ORDER OF TENSES

(a) imperative
(b) present indicative
(c) present subjunctive

(d) imperfect indicative
(e) future indicative
(f) preterit indicative

In addition to the infinitive, gerund, and past participle, all simple tenses are shown in these tables if they contain one irregular form or more, except the conditional (which can always be derived from the stem of the future indicative) and the imperfect subjunctive (which can always be derived from the preterit indicative). Those forms are considered irregular which deviate morphologically and/or orthographically in root, stem, or ending from the paradigms of regular verbs which appear on page 6. The infinitive is printed in boldface capital letters. And the following forms are printed in boldface: (1) key forms (that is, irregular forms from which other irregular forms can be derived, but not the derived forms), e.g., **buvons**, (2) individual irregular forms which occupy the place of key forms but cannot function as key forms because other irregular forms cannot be derived from them, e.g., **sommes**, and (3) individual irregular forms which cannot be derived from key forms, e.g., **dites**. The names of the key forms and the forms derived from each of them are listed below.

KEY FORM	DERIVED FORMS
1st sg pres ind	*2d & 3d sg pres ind & 2d sg impv**
1st pl pres ind	*2d pl pres ind, 1st & 2d pl pres subj,* whole *imperf ind, 1st & 2d pl impv, &* ger
3d pl pres ind	whole *sg & 3d pl pres subj*
1st sg fut ind	rest of *fut ind & whole conditional*
1st sg pret ind	rest of *pret ind & whole imperf subj*

---

* Some irregular verbs of the third conjugation which end in s, not preceded by d, in the *1st sg pres ind*, end in s also in the *2d sg pres ind* and the *2d sg impv*, and in t in the *3d sg pres ind*, e.g., **crains, crains, craint** and **bois, bois, boit**. And three verbs, namely, **pouvoir, valoir,** and **vouloir,** which end in x in the *1st sg pres ind*, end in x also in the *2d sg pres ind* and the *2d sg impv*, and in t in the *3d sg pres ind*, e.g., **veux, veux, veut**.

7

1st sg pres subj of **faire,**   rest of *pres subj*
  pouvoir, & **savoir**
1st sg pres subj of **aller,**   *2d & 3d sg & 3d pl pres subj*
  valoir, & **vouloir**

§1 ABRÉGER—abrégeant—abrégé   Combination of §10 and §38
- (a) abrège, abrégeons, abrégez
- (b) **abrège,** abrèges, abrège, **abrégeons,** abrégez, **abrègent**
- (c) abrège, abrèges, abrège, abrégions, abrégiez, abrègent
- (d) abrégeais, abrégeais, abrégeait, abrégions, abrégiez, abrégeaient
- (f) **abrégeai,** abrégeas, abrégea, abrégeâmes, abrégeâtes, abrégèrent

§2 ACHETER—achetant—acheté
- (a) achète, achetons, achetez
- (b) **achète,** achètes, achète, achetons, achetez, **achètent**
- (c) achète, achètes, achète, achetions, achetiez, achètent
- (e) **achèterai,** achèteras, achètera, achèterons, achèterez, achèteront

§3 ACQUÉRIR—acquérant—**acquis**
- (a) acquiers, acquérons, acquérez
- (b) **acquiers,** acquiers, acquiert, **acquérons,** acquérez, **acquièrent**
- (c) acquière, acquières, acquière, acquérions, acquériez, acquièrent
- (d) acquérais, acquérais, acquérait, acquérions, acquériez, acquéraient
- (e) **acquerrai,** acquerras, acquerra, acquerrons, acquerrez, acquerront
- (f) **acquis,** acquis, acquit, acquîmes, acquîtes, acquirent

§4 ALLER—allant—allé
- (a) va, allons, allez
- (b) **vais** [ve], **vas, va,** allons, allez, **vont**
- (c) **aille** [aj], ailles, aille, allions, alliez, aillent
- (e) **irai,** iras, ira, irons, irez, iront

§5A ASSEOIR—asseyant—**assis**
- (a) assieds, asseyons, asseyez
- (b) **assieds,** assieds, assied, **asseyons,** asseyez, **asseyent**
- (c) asseye, asseyes, asseye, asseyions, asseyiez, asseyent
- (d) asseyais, asseyais, asseyait, asseyions, asseyiez, asseyaient
- (e) **assiérai,** assiéras, assiéra, assiérons, assiérez, assiéront
- (f) **assis,** assis, assit, assîmes, assîtes, assirent

§5B ASSEOIR—assoyant—**assis**
- (a) assois, assoyons, assoyez
- (b) **assois**, assois, assoit, **assoyons**, assoyez, **assoient**
- (c) assoie, assoies, assoie, assoyions, assoyiez, assoient
- (d) assoyais, assoyais, assoyait, assoyions, assoyiez, assoyaient
- (e) **assoirai**, assoiras, assoira, assoirons, assoirez, assoiront
- (f) **assis**, assis, assit, assîmes, assîtes, assirent

§6 AVOIR—ayant—**eu** [y]
- (a) **aie** [e], **ayons, ayez**
- (b) **ai** [e], **as, a, avons,** avez, **ont**
- (c) **aie, aies, ait, ayons, ayez, aient**
- (d) avais, avais, avait, avions, aviez, avaient
- (e) **aurai**, auras, aura, aurons, aurez, auront
- (f) **eus** [y], eus, eut, eûmes, eûtes, eurent

§7 BATTRE—battant—**battu**
- (a) bats, battons, battez
- (b) **bats**, bats, bat, battons, battez, battent

§8 BOIRE—buvant—**bu**
- (a) bois, buvons, buvez
- (b) bois, bois, boit, **buvons**, buvez, **boivent**
- (c) boive, boives, boive, buvions, buviez, boivent
- (d) buvais, buvais, buvait, buvions, buviez, buvaient
- (f) **bus**, bus, but, bûmes, bûtes, burent

§9 BOUILLIR—bouillant—bouilli
- (a) bous, bouillons, bouillez
- (b) **bous**, bous, bout, **bouillons**, bouillez, **bouillent**
- (c) bouille, bouilles, bouille, bouillions, bouilliez, bouillent
- (d) bouillais, bouillais, bouillait, bouillions, bouilliez, bouillaient

§10 CÉDER—cédant—cédé
- (a) cède, cédons, cédez
- (b) **cède**, cèdes, cède, cédons, cédez, **cèdent**
- (c) cède, cèdes, cède, cédions, cédiez, cèdent

§11 CONCLURE—concluant—**conclu**
- (f) **conclus**, conclus, conclut, conclûmes, conclûtes, conclurent

§12 CONNAÎTRE—connaissant—**connu**
- (a) connais, connaissons, connaissez
- (b) **connais**, connais, connaît, **connaissons**, connaissez, **connaissent**
- (c) connaisse, connaisses, connaisse, connaissions, connaissiez, connaissent

- (d) connaissais, connaissais, connaissait, connaissions, connaissiez, connaissaient
- (f) **connus**, connus, connut, connûmes, connûtes, connurent

§13 COUDRE—cousant—cousu
- (a) couds, cousons, cousez
- (b) couds, couds, coud, **cousons**, cousez, **cousent**
- (c) couse, couses, couse, cousions, cousiez, cousent
- (d) cousais, cousais, cousait, cousions, cousiez, cousaient
- (f) **cousis**, cousis, cousit, cousîmes, cousîtes, cousirent

§14 COURIR—courant—couru
- (a) cours, courons, courez
- (b) **cours**, cours, court, **courons**, courez, **courent**
- (c) coure, coures, coure, courions, couriez, courent
- (d) courais, courais, courait, courions, couriez, couraient
- (e) **courrai**, courras, courra, courrons, courrez, courront
- (f) **courus**, courus, courut, courûmes, courûtes, coururent

§15 CRAINDRE—craignant—craint
- (a) crains, craignons, craignez
- (b) **crains**, crains, craint, **craignons**, craignez, **craignent**
- (c) craigne, craignes, craigne, craignions, craigniez, craignent
- (d) craignais, craignais, craignait, craignions, craigniez, craignaient
- (f) **craignis**, craignis, craignit, cragnîmes, craignîtes, craignirent

§16 CROIRE—croyant—cru
- (a) crois, croyons, croyez
- (b) crois, crois, croit, **croyons**, croyez, croient
- (c) croie, croies, croie, croyions, croyiez, croient
- (d) croyais, croyais, croyait, croyions, croyiez, croyaient
- (f) **crus**, crus, crut, crûmes, crûtes, crurent

§17 CROÎTRE—croissant—crû, crue
- (a) croîs, croissons, croissez
- (b) **croîs**, croîs, croît, **croissons**, croissez, **croissent**
- (c) croisse, croisses, croisse, croissions, croissiez, croissent
- (d) croissais, croissais, croissait, croissions, croissiez, croissaient
- (f) **crûs**, crûs, crût, crûmes, crûtes, crûrent

§18 CUEILLIR—cueillant—cueilli
- (a) cueille, cueillons, cueillez
- (b) **cueille**, cueilles, cueille, **cueillons**, cueillez, **cueillent**
- (c) cueille, cueilles, cueille, cueillions, cueilliez, cueillent

(d) cueillais, cueillais, cueillait, cueillions, cueilliez, cueillaient

(e) **cueillerai**, cueilleras, cueillera, cueillerons, cueillerez, cueilleront

§19 CUIRE—cuisant—**cuit**

(a) cuis, cuisons, cuisez

(b) cuis, cuis, cuit, **cuisons**, cuisez, **cuisent**

(c) cuise, cuises, cuise, cuisions, cuisiez, cuisent

(d) cuisais, cuisais, cuisait, cuisions, cuisiez, cuisaient

(f) **cuisis**, cuisis, cuisit, cuisîmes, cuisîtes, cuisirent

§20 DÉPECER—dépeçant—dépecé   Combination of §2 and §51

(a) dépèce, dépeçons, dépecez

(b) **dépèce**, dépèces, dépèce, **dépeçons**, dépecez, **dépècent**

(c) dépèce, dépèces, dépèce, dépecions, dépeciez, dépècent

(d) dépeçais, dépeçais, dépeçait, dépecions, dépeciez, dépeçaient

(e) **dépècerai**, dépèceras, dépècera, dépècerons, dépècerez, dépèceront

(f) **dépeçai**, dépeças, dépeça, dépeçâmes, dépeçâtes, dépecèrent

§21 DEVOIR—devant—**dû, due**

(a) missing

(b) **dois**, dois, doit, **devons**, devez, **doivent**

(c) doive, doives, doive, devions, deviez, doivent

(d) devais, devais, devait, devions, deviez, devaient

(e) **devrai**, devras, devra, devrons, devrez, devront

(f) **dus**, dus, dut, dûmes, dûtes, durent

§22 DIRE—disant—**dit**

(a) dis, disons, **dites**

(b) dis, dis, dit, **disons, dites, disent**

(c) dise, dises, dise, disions, disiez, disent

(d) disais, disais, disait, disions, disiez, disaient

(f) **dis**, dis, dit, dîmes, dîtes, dirent

§23 DORMIR—dormant—dormi

(a) dors, dormons, dormez

(b) **dors**, dors, dort, **dormons**, dormez, **dorment**

(c) dorme, dormes, dorme, dormions, dormiez, dorment

(d) dormais, dormais, dormait, dormions, dormiez, dormaient

§24 ÉCLORE—éclosant—**éclos**

(a) éclos

(b) éclos, éclos, **éclôt, éclosent**

(c) éclose, écloses, éclose, **éclosions, éclosiez**, éclosent

(d) missing

(f) missing

§25 ÉCRIRE—écrivant—écrit
- (a) écris, écrivons, écrivez
- (b) écris, écris, écrit, **écrivons**, écrivez, **écrivent**
- (c) écrive, écrives, écrive, écrivions, écriviez, écrivent
- (d) écrivais, écrivais, écrivait, écrivions, écriviez, écrivaient
- (f) **écrivis**, écrivis, écrivit, écrivîmes, écrivîtes, écrivirent

§26 ENVOYER—envoyant—envoyé
- (a) envoie, envoyons, envoyez
- (b) **envoie**, envoies, envoie, envoyons, envoyez, **envoient**
- (c) envoie, envoies, envoie, envoyions, envoyiez, envoient
- (e) **enverrai**, enverras, enverra, enverrons, enverrez, enverront

§27 ESSUYER—essuyant—essuyé
- (a) essuie, essuyons, essuyez
- (b) **essuie**, essuies, essuie, essuyons, essuyez, **essuient**
- (c) essuie, essuies, essuie, essuyions, essuyiez, essuient
- (e) **essuierai**, essuieras, essuiera, essuierons, essuierez, essuieront

§28 ÊTRE—étant—été
- (a) sois, soyons, soyez
- (b) suis, es, est, sommes, êtes, sont
- (c) sois, sois, soit, soyons, soyez, soient
- (d) étais, étais, était, étions, étiez, étaient
- (e) serai, seras, sera, serons, serez, seront
- (f) fus, fus, fut, fûmes, fûtes, furent

§29 FAIRE—faisant—fait
- (a) fais, faisons, **faites**
- (b) fais, fais, fait, **faisons**, **faites**, **font**
- (c) **fasse**, fasses, fasse, fassions, fassiez, fassent
- (d) faisais, faisais, faisait, faisions, faisiez, faisaient
- (e) **ferai**, feras, fera, ferons, ferez, feront
- (f) **fis**, fis, fit, fîmes, fîtes, firent

§30 FALLOIR—missing—fallu
- (a) missing
- (b) **faut**
- (c) **faille**
- (d) **fallait**
- (e) **faudra**
- (f) **fallut**

§31 FUIR—fuyant—fui
- (a) fuis, fuyons, fuyez
- (b) fuis, fuis, fuit, **fuyons**, fuyez, **fuient**

12

   (c) fuie, fuies, fuie, fuyions, fuyiez, fuient
   (d) fuyais, fuyais, fuyait, fuyions, fuyiez, fuyaient

§32 GRASSEYER—grasseyant—grasseyé
(regular, unlike other verbs with stem ending in **y**)

§33 HAÏR—haïssant—haï
   (a) hais [ɛ], haïssons, haïssez
   (b) **hais** [ɛ], hais, hait, **haïssons**, haïssez, **haïssent**
   (c) haïsse, haïsses, haïsse, haïssions, haïssiez, haïssent
   (d) haïssais, haïssais, haïssait, haïssions, haïssiez, haïssaient
   (f) haïs, haïs, haït, **haïmes, haïtes,** haïrent

§34 JETER—jetant—jeté
   (a) jette, jetons, jetez
   (b) **jette**, jettes, jette, jetons, jetez, **jettent**
   (c) jette, jettes, jette, jetions, jetiez, jettent
   (e) **jetterai**, jetteras, jettera, jetterons, jetterez, jetteront

§35 JOINDRE—joignant—**joint**
   (a) joins, joignons, joignez
   (b) **joins**, joins, joint, **joignons**, joignez, **joignent**
   (c) joigne, joignes, joigne, joignions, joigniez, joignent
   (d) joignais, joignais, joignait, joignions, joigniez, joignaient
   (f) **joignis**, joignis, joignit, joignîmes, joignîtes, joignirent

§36 LIRE—lisant—**lu**
   (a) lis, lisons, lisez
   (b) lis, lis, lit, **lisons,** lisez, **lisent**
   (c) lise, lises, lise, lisions, lisiez, lisent
   (d) lisais, lisais, lisait, lisions, lisiez, lisaient
   (f) **lus,** lus, lut, lûmes, lûtes, lurent

§37 LUIRE—luisant—**lui**
   (a) luis, luisons, luisez
   (b) luis, luis, luit, **luisons,** luisez, **luisent**
   (c) luise, luises, luise, luisions, luisiez, luisent
   (d) luisais, luisais, luisait, luisions, luisiez, luisaient
   (f) archaic

§38 MANGER—mangeant—mangé
   (a) mange, mangeons, mangez
   (b) mange, manges, mange, **mangeons**, mangez, mangent
   (d) mangeais, mangeais, mangeait, mangions, mangiez, mangeaient
   (f) **mangeai**, mangeas, mangea, mangeâmes, mangeâtes, mangèrent

§39 MAUDIRE—maudissant—**maudit**
- (a) maudis, maudissons, maudissez
- (b) maudis, maudis, maudit, **maudissons**, maudissez, **maudissent**
- (c) maudisse, maudisses, maudisse, maudissions, maudissiez, maudissent
- (d) maudissais, maudissais, maudissait, maudissions, maudissiez, maudissaient
- (f) **maudis**, maudis, maudit, maudîmes, maudîtes, maudirent

§40 MÉDIRE—médisant—**médit**
- (a) médis, médisons, médisez
- (b) médis, médis, médit, **médisons**, médisez, **médisent**
- (c) médise, médises, médise, médisions, médisiez, médisent
- (d) médisais, médisais, médisait, médisions, médisiez, médisaient
- (f) **médis**, médis, médit, médîmes, médîtes, médirent

§41 MENTIR—mentant—**menti**
- (a) mens, mentons, mentez
- (b) **mens**, mens, ment, **mentons**, mentez, **mentent**
- (c) mente, mentes, mente, mentions, mentiez, mentent
- (d) mentais, mentais, mentait, mentions, mentiez, mentaient

§42 METTRE—mettant—**mis**
- (a) mets, mettons, mettez
- (b) **mets**, mets, met, mettons, mettez, mettent
- (f) **mis**, mis, mit, mîmes, mîtes, mirent

§43 MOUDRE—moulant—**moulu**
- (a) mouds, moulons, moulez
- (b) mouds, mouds, moud, **moulons**, moulez, **moulent**
- (c) moule, moules, moule, moulions, mouliez, moulent
- (d) moulais, moulais, moulait, moulions, mouliez, moulaient
- (f) **moulus**, moulus, moulut, moulûmes, moulûtes, moulurent

§44 MOURIR—mourant—**mort**
- (a) meurs, mourons, mourez
- (b) **meurs**, meurs, meurt, **mourons**, mourez, **meurent**
- (c) meure, meures, meure, mourions, mouriez, meurent
- (d) mourais, mourais, mourait, mourions, mouriez, mouraient
- (e) **mourrai**, mourras, mourra, mourrons, mourrez, mourront
- (f) **mourus**, mourus, mourut, mourûmes, mourûtes, moururent

§45 MOUVOIR—mouvant—**mû, mue, mus, mues**
- (a) meus, mouvons, mouvez
- (b) **meus**, meus, meut, **mouvons**, mouvez, **meuvent**

14

(c) meuve, meuves, meuve, mouvions, mouviez, meuvent
(d) mouvais, mouvais, mouvait, mouvions, mouviez, mouvaient
(e) **mouvrai**, mouvras, mouvra, mouvrons, mouvrez, mouvront
(f) **mus**, mus, mut, mûmes, mûtes, murent

§46 NAÎTRE—naissant—**né**
(a) nais, naissons, naissez
(b) **nais**, nais, naît, **naissons**, naissez, **naissent**
(c) naisse, naisses, naisse, naissions, naissiez, naissent
(d) naissais, naissais, naissait, naissions, naissiez, naissaient
(f) **naquis**, naquis, naquit, naquîmes, naquîtes, naquirent

§47 NETTOYER—nettoyant—nettoyé
(a) nettoie, nettoyons, nettoyez
(b) **nettoie**, nettoies, nettoie, nettoyons, nettoyez, **nettoient**
(c) nettoie, nettoies, nettoie, nettoyions, nettoyiez, nettoient
(e) **nettoierai**, nettoieras, nettoiera, nettoierons, nettoierez, nettoieront

§48 PAÎTRE—paissant—**pu**
(a) pais, paissez
(b) **pais**, pais, paît, **paissons**, paissez, **paissent**
(c) paisse, paisses, paisse, paissions, paissiez, paissent
(d) paissais, paissais, paissait, paissions, paissiez, paissaient
(f) missing

§49 PAYER—payant—payé
(a) paie or paye, payons, payez
(b) **paie**, paies, paie, payons, payez, **paient** or
    paye, payes, paye, payons, payez, payent
(c) paie, paies, paie, payions, payiez, paient or
    paye, payes, paye, payions, payiez, payent
(e) **paierai**, paieras, paiera, paierons, paierez, paieront or
    payerai, payeras, payera, payerons, payerez, payeront

§50 PEINDRE—peignant—**peint**
(a) peins, peignons, peignez
(b) **peins**, peins, peint, **peignons**, peignez, **peignent**
(c) peigne, peignes, peigne, peignions, peigniez, peignent
(d) peignais, peignais, peignait, paignions, peigniez, peignaient
(f) **peignis**, peignis, peignit, peignîmes, peignîtes, peignirent

§51 PLACER—plaçant—placé
(a) place, plaçons, placez
(b) place, places, place, **plaçons**, placez, placent
(d) plaçais, plaçais, plaçait, placions, placiez, plaçaient
(f) **plaçai**, plaças, plaça, plaçâmes, plaçâtes, placèrent

§52 PLAIRE—plaisant—**plu**
- (a) plais, plaisons, plaisez
- (b) plais, plais, **plaît**, **plaisons**, plaisez, **plaisent**
- (c) plaise, plaises, plaise, plaisions, plaisiez, plaisent
- (d) plaisais, plaisais, plaisait, plaisions, plaisiez, plaisaient
- (f) **plus**, plus, plut, plûmes, plûtes, plurent

§53 PLEUVOIR—pleuvant—**plu**
- (a) **pleus**, **pleuvons**, **pleuvez** (fig & rare)
- (b) **pleut**, **pleuvent**
- (c) pleuve, pleuvent
- (d) **pleuvait**, **pleuvaient**
- (e) **pleuvra**, **pleuvront**
- (f) **plut**, **plurent**

§54 POURVOIR—pourvoyant—**pourvu**
- (a) pourvois, pourvoyons, pourvoyez
- (b) **pourvois**, pourvois, pourvoit, **pourvoyons**, pourvoyez, **pourvoient**
- (c) pourvoie, pourvoies, pourvoie, pourvoyions, pourvoyiez, pourvoient
- (d) pourvoyais, pourvoyais, pourvoyait, pourvoyions, pourvoyiez, pourvoyaient
- (f) **pourvus**, pourvus, pourvut, pourvûmes, pourvûtes, pourvurent

§55 POUVOIR—pouvant—**pu**
- (a) missing
- (b) **peux** or **puis**, peux, peut, **pouvons**, pouvez, **peuvent**
- (c) **puisse**, puisses, puisse, puissions, puissiez, puissent
- (d) pouvais, pouvais, pouvait, pouvions, pouviez, pouvaient
- (e) **pourrai**, pourras, pourra, pourrons, pourrez, pourront
- (f) **pus**, pus, put, pûmes, pûtes, purent

§56 PRENDRE—prenant—**pris**
- (a) prends, prenons, prenez
- (b) prends, prends, prend, **prenons**, prenez, **prennent**
- (c) prenne, prennes, prenne, prenions, preniez, prennent
- (d) prenais, prenais, prenait, prenions, preniez, prenaient
- (f) **pris**, pris, prit, prîmes, prîtes, prirent

§57 PRÉVOIR—prévoyant—**prévu**
- (a) prévois, prévoyons, prévoyez
- (b) **prévois**, prévois, prévoit, **prévoyons**, prévoyez, **prévoient**
- (c) prévoie, prévoies, prévoie, prévoyions, prévoyiez, prévoient
- (d) prévoyais, prévoyais, prévoyait, prévoyions, prévoyiez, prévoyaient
- (f) **prévis**, prévis, prévit, prévîmes, prévîtes, prévirent

16

§58 RAPIÉCER—rapiéçant—rapiécé Combination of §10 and §51
- (a) rapièce, rapiéçons, rapiécez
- (b) **rapièce**, rapièces, rapièce, **rapiéçons**, rapiécez, **rapiècent**
- (c) rapièce, rapièces, rapièce, rapiécions, rapiéciez, rapiècent
- (d) rapiéçais, rapiéçais, rapiéçait, rapiécions, rapiéciez, rapié-
çaient
- (f) **rapiéçai**, rapiéças, rapiéça, rapiéçâmes, rapiéçâtes, rapiécè-
rent

§59 RECEVOIR—recevant—**reçu**
- (a) reçois, recevons, recevez
- (b) **reçois**, reçois, reçoit, **recevons**, recevez, **reçoivent**
- (c) reçoive, reçoives, reçoive, recevions, receviez, reçoivent
- (d) recevais, recevais, recevait, recevions, receviez, recevaient
- (e) **recevrai**, recevras, recevra, recevrons, recevrez, recevront
- (f) **reçus**, reçus, reçut, reçûmes, reçûtes, reçurent

§60 RÉSOUDRE—résolvant—**résolu; résout** (invar)
- (a) résous, résolvons, résolvez
- (b) **résous**, résous, résout, **résolvons**, résolvez, **résolvent**
- (c) résolve, résolves, résolve, résolvions, résolviez, résolvent
- (d) résolvais, résolvais, résolvait, résolvions, résolviez, résol-
vaient
- (f) **résolus**, résolus, résolut, résolûmes, résolûtes, résolurent

§61 RIRE—riant—**ri**
- (f) **ris**, ris, rit, rîmes, rîtes, rirent

§62 SAVOIR—sachant—**su**
- (a) **sache, sachons, sachez**
- (b) **sais**, sais, sait, **savons**, savez, **savent**
- (c) **sache**, saches, sache, sachions, sachiez, sachent
- (d) savais, savais, savait, savions, saviez, savaient
- (e) **saurai**, sauras, saura, saurons, saurez, sauront
- (f) **sus**, sus, sut, sûmes, sûtes, surent

§63 SERVIR—servant—servi
- (a) sers, servons, servez
- (b) **sers**, sers, sert, **servons**, servez, **servent**
- (c) serve, serves, serve, servions, serviez, servent
- (d) servais, servais, servait, servions, serviez, servaient

§64 SORTIR—sortant—sorti
- (a) sors, sortons, sortez
- (b) **sors**, sors, sort, **sortons**, sortez, **sortent**
- (c) sorte, sortes, sorte, sortions, sortiez, sortent
- (d) sortais, sortais, sortait, sortions, sortiez, sortaient

§65 SOUFFRIR—souffrant—**souffert**
 - (a) souffre, souffrons, souffrez
 - (b) **souffre**, souffres, souffre, **souffrons**, souffrez, **souffrent**
 - (c) souffre, souffres, souffre, souffrions, souffriez, souffrent
 - (d) souffrais, souffrais, souffrait, souffrions, souffriez, souffraient

§66 SUFFIRE—suffisant—**suffi**
 - (a) suffis, suffisons, suffisez
 - (b) suffis, suffis, suffit, **suffisons**, suffisez, **suffisent**
 - (c) suffise, suffises, suffise, suffisions, suffisiez, suffisent
 - (d) suffisais, suffisais, suffisait, suffisions, suffisiez, suffisaient
 - (f) **suffis**, suffis, suffit, suffîmes, suffîtes, suffirent

§67 SUIVRE—suivant—**suivi**
 - (a) suis, suivons, suivez
 - (b) **suis**, suis, suit, suivons, suivez, suivent

§68 TRAIRE—trayant—**trait**
 - (a) trais, trayons, trayez
 - (b) trais, trais, trait, **trayons**, trayez, traient
 - (c) traie, traies, traie, trayions, trayiez, traient
 - (d) trayais, trayais, trayait, trayions, trayiez, trayaient
 - (f) missing

§69 TRESSAILLIR—tressaillant—tressailli
 - (a) tressaille, tressaillons, tressaillez
 - (b) **tressaille**, tressailles, tressaille, **tressaillons**, tressaillez, **tressaillent**
 - (c) tressaille, tressailles, tressaille, tressaillions, tressailliez, tressaillent
 - (d) tressaillais, tressaillais, tressaillait, tressaillions, tressailliez, tressaillaient
 - (e) **tressaillirai**, tressailliras, tressaillira, tressaillirons, tressaillirez, tressailliront, or **tressaillerai**, tressailleras, tressaillera, tressaillerons, tressaillerez, tressailleront

§70 VAINCRE—vainquant—vaincu
 - (a) vaincs [vɛ̃], vainquons, vainquez
 - (b) vaincs, vaincs, vainc, **vainquons**, vainquez, **vainquent**
 - (c) vainque, vainques, vainque, vainquions, vainquiez, vainquent
 - (d) vainquais, vainquais, vainquait, vainquions, vainquiez, vainquaient
 - (f) **vainquis**, vainquis, vainquit, vainquîmes, vainquîtes, vainquirent

§71 VALOIR—valant—**valu**
 - (a) vaux, valons, valez
 - (b) **vaux**, vaux, vaut, **valons**, valez, **valent**

18

(c) **vaille** [vaj], vailles, vaille, valions, valiez, vaillent
(d) valais, valais, valait, valions, valiez, valaient
(e) **vaudrai**, vaudras, vaudra, vaudrons, vaudrez, vaudront
(f) **valus**, valus, valut, valûmes, valûtes, valurent

§72 **VENIR**—venant—**venu**
(a) viens, venons, venez
(b) **viens**, viens, vient, **venons**, venez, **viennent**
(c) vienne, viennes, vienne, venions, veniez, viennent
(e) **viendrai**, viendras, viendra, viendrons, viendrez, viendront
(f) **vins**, vins, vint, vînmes [vɛ̃m], vîntes [vɛ̃t], vinrent [vɛ̃r]

§73 **VÊTIR**—vêtant—**vêtu**
(a) vêts, vêtons, vêtez
(b) **vêts**, vêts, vêt, **vêtons**, vêtez, **vêtent**
(c) vête, vêtes, vête, vêtions, vêtiez, vêtent
(d) vêtais, vêtais, vêtait, vêtions, vêtiez, vêtaient

§74 **VIVRE**—vivant—**vécu**
(a) vis, vivons, vivez
(b) **vis**, vis, vit, vivons, vivez, vivent
(f) **vécus**, vécus, vécut, vécûmes, vécûtes, vécurent

§75 **VOIR**—voyant—**vu**
(a) vois, voyons, voyez
(b) **vois**, vois, voit, **voyons**, voyez, **voient**
(c) voie, voies, voie, voyions, voyiez, voient
(d) voyais, voyais, voyait, voyions, voyiez, voyaient
(e) **verrai**, verras, verra, verrons, verrez, verront
(f) **vis**, vis, vit, vîmes, vîtes, virent

§76 **VOULOIR**—voulant—**voulu**
(a) veux, voulons, voulez
(b) **veux**, veux, veut, **voulons**, voulez, **veulent**
(c) **veuille**, veuilles, veuille, voulions, vouliez, veuillent
(d) voulais, voulais, voulait, voulions, vouliez, voulaient
(e) **voudrai**, voudras, voudra, voudrons, voudrez, voudront
(f) **voulus**, voulus, voulut, voulûmes, voulûtes, voulurent

c) the complement of the verb itself, e.g., les termes dont il se servait the expressions which he used

GRAMMATICAL TABLES

§77 le *art def* the. The following table shows the forms of the definite article, the combination of **le** with **à** and **de**, and the combinations of **les** with **à**, **de**, and **en**.

		masc	*fem*
	sg	le; l' before a vowel or mute h	la; l' before a vowel or mute h
	pl	les	les
with à	sg	au; à l' before a vowel or mute h	à la; à l' before a vowel or mute h
with à	pl	aux	aux
with de	sg	du; de l' before a vowel or mute h	de la; de l' before a vowel or mute h
with de	pl	des	des
with en	pl	ès, e.g., **maître ès arts**	ès, e.g., **docteur ès lettres**

§78 lequel *pron rel* who, whom; which ‖ *pron interr* which, which one. The following table shows all the forms of the word **lequel** and their combinations with the prepositions **à** and **de**.

		masc	*fem*
	sg	lequel	laquelle
	pl	lesquels	lesquelles
with à	sg	auquel	à laquelle
with à	pl	auxquels	auxquelles
with de	sg	duquel	de laquelle
with de	pl	desquels	desquelles

The forms combined with **de** and used as relative pronouns sometimes mean: whose, e.g., **l'étudiant avec la sœur duquel j'ai dansé** the student with whose sister I danced

§79 dont *rel pron* of whom; of which; from which; with which; on which; at which; which; whose. The relative pronoun **dont** may be: a) the complement of the subject of the dependent verb, e.g., **cette malheureuse dont la jambe droite était brisée** that wretched woman whose right leg was broken; b) the complement of the object of the dependent verb, e.g., **sa grande chambre dont on avait fermé les volets** his large bedroom the shutters of which they had closed;

21

c) the complement of the verb itself, e.g., **les termes dont il se servait** the expressions which he used.

If the antecedent is one of point of origin, **d'où** is used, e.g., **la porte d'où il est sorti** the door from which he went out, unless the point of origin is one of ancestry or extraction having to do with a person, e.g., **la famille distinguée dont il sortait** the distinguished family from which he came.

The relative pronoun **dont** cannot be the complement of a noun which is the object of a preposition but must be replaced by a form of **lequel** combined with **de** (see §78), or by **de qui**, e.g., **l'étudiante avec le frère de laquelle** (or **de qui**) **j'ai dansé** the student with whose brother I danced.

§80 quel *adj* what; what sort of; which; what a, e.g., **quelle belle ville!** what a beautiful city!; **n'importe quel** any ‖ *adj interr* what, e.g., **quel est le but de la vie?** what is the purpose of life?; who, e.g., **quel est cet homme?** who is that man? ‖ *adj indef*—**quel que** whoever, e.g., **quel que soit l'homme** whoever the man may be; whatever, e.g., **quelles que soient les difficultés** whatever difficulties there may be; whichever, e.g., **quel que soit le pied sur lequel il s'appuie** whichever foot he leans on. The following table shows all the forms of the word **quel**.

	masc		fem
sg	quel		quelle
pl	quels		quelles

§81 quelqu'un *pron indef* someone, somebody; anyone, anybody; **quelques-uns** some; any, a few. The following table shows all the forms of the word **quelqu'un**.

	masc		fem
sg	quelqu'un		quelqu'une
pl	quelques-uns		quelques-unes

§82A ce *adj dem* this; that; **ces** these; those. The following table shows all the forms of this word.

	masc		fem
sg	ce; cet before a vowel or mute h		cette
pl	ces		ces

This word has two meanings as exemplified by the following example:

cet homme this man; that man

However, the particles **-ci** and **-là** are attached to the noun modified by the forms of **ce** to distinguish what is near the person speaking (i.e., the first person) from what is near the person spoken to (i.e., the second person) or what is remote from both (i.e., the third person), for example:

> **cet homme-ci** this man (*not that man*)
> **cet homme-là** that man (*not this man*)
> **cet homme-là** that man (*yonder*)

---

§82B ce *pron dem*

it, e.g., **c'est un bon livre** it is a good book;

he, e.g., **c'est un bon professeur** he is a good professor;

she, e.g., **c'est une belle femme** she is a beautiful woman;

they, e.g., **ce sont des élèves** they are students

---

§83 celui *pron dem* this one; that one. The following table shows all the forms of the demonstrative pronoun with their translations into English.

	masc	*fem*
sg	**celui** this one; that one; he	**celle** this one; that one; she
pl	**ceux** these; those	**celles** these; those

This word in all its forms is generally used with a following **de** or the relative pronouns **que** and **qui**:

> **celui de** ⎫
> **celle de** ⎬ 's, e.g., **celui de Marie** Mary's
> **ceux de** ⎪
> **celles de** ⎭

celui que	he whom; the one that; the one which	⎫
celle que	she whom; the one that; the one which	whomever;
ceux que	those whom; the ones whom; the ones which	whichever
celles que	those whom; the ones whom; the ones which	⎭
celui qui	he who; the one that; the one which	⎫
celle qui	she who; the one that; the one which	whoever;
ceux qui	those who; the ones who; the ones which	whichever
celles qui	those who; the ones who; the ones which	⎭

§84 celui-ci *pron dem* this one; he; the latter. The particles **-ci** and **-là** are attached to the forms of **celui** to distinguish what is near the person speaking (i.e., the first person) from what is near the person spoken to (i.e., the second person) or remote from both (i.e., the third person). The following table shows all the forms of this word with particles attached and with their translations into English.

	masc	*fem*
sg	**celui-ci** this one	**celle-ci** this one
	celui-là that one	**celle-là** that one
pl	**ceux-ci** these	**celles-ci** these
	ceux-là those	**celles-là** those

23

The forms of **celui-ci** also mean the latter; and the forms of **celui-là**, the former, e.g., **Henri était roi et Catherine était reine. Celle-ci était espagnole et celui-là anglais.** Henry was a king and Catherine was a queen. The former was English and the latter Spanish. (The English word order requires the inversion.)

§85 Disjunctive personal and reflexive pronouns.

This table shows all the forms of the disjunctive personal and reflexive pronouns with their translations into English.

moi	me; myself; I	**nous**	we, us; ourselves
toi	you, thee; yourself	**vous**	you; yourselves
lui	he, him, it; himself	**eux**	they, them *masc*; themselves *masc*
elle	she, her, it; herself	**elles**	they, them *fem*; themselves *fem*
soi	oneself; himself, herself, itself	**soi**	themselves

A) The disjunctive personal pronouns are used:

1) as the object of a preposition, e.g., **Jean a été invité chez elle** John was invited to her house; e.g., **il est très content de lui** he is very satisfied with himself

   Disjunctive pronouns especially as objects of prepositions rarely stand for things. Prepositional phrases which would include them are generally expressed by **y** (see §87), e.g., **je m'y suis avancé** I walked up to it, as contrasted with **je me suis avancé vers lui** I walked up to him; or are expressed by one of the adverbs **là-dessus, là-dessous, là-dedans,** etc., e.g., **voilà mon nom; écrivez le vôtre là-dessous** there is my name; write yours under it, as contrasted with **il n'a pas d'argent sur lui** he has no money with him.

2) after the preposition **à** in phrases which are used to clarify or to stress the meaning of a conjunctive personal pronoun, e.g., **il lui a parlé, à elle** he spoke to her (or, he spoke to *her*)

3) after the preposition **à** in phrases which are used to clarify the meaning of a preceding possessive adjective, e.g., **son chapeau à elle** her hat

4) as predicate pronouns after the verb **être**, especially after **c'est** and **ce sont:**

c'est moi	it is I	**c'est nous**	it is we
c'est toi	it is you, it is thee	**c'est vous**	it is you
c'est lui	it is he	**ce sont eux**	it is they *masc*
c'est elle	it is she	**ce sont elles**	it is they *fem*

5) after **que** (than, as) in comparisons, e.g., **nous y allons plus souvent qu'eux** we go there more often than they; e.g., **nous y allons aussi souvent que vous** we go there as often as you

6) when the verb is not expressed, e.g., **qui a fait cela? Lui** who did that? He did

24

7) to stress the subject or object of the sentence, e.g., **lui, il a raison** he is right
8) in compound subjects and objects, e.g., **lui et moi, nous sommes médecins** he and I are doctors
9) when an adverb separates the subject pronoun from the verb, e.g., **lui toujours arrive en retard** he always arrives late
10) after **être + à** to contrast ownership, e.g., **ce stylo est à lui mais ce papier est à elle** this pen is his but this paper is hers.

B) The disjunctive indefinite reflexive pronoun **soi** corresponds to **on** and is used mainly as the object of a preposition, that is, according to **A**, 1 above, e.g., **on doit parler rarement de soi** one should seldom talk about oneself. But it may also be used in the predicate after the verb **être**, according to **A**, 4 above, e.g., **on a plus confiance quand c'est soi qui conduit** one has more confidence when it is oneself who drives.

§86 The following table shows all the forms of the intensive personal pronouns. They are made by combining the disjunctive personal pronouns with the forms of **même**.

moi-même	myself; I myself	**nous-mêmes**	ourselves; we ourselves
toi-même	yourself, thyself; you yourself	**vous-même**	yourself; you yourself
		vous-mêmes	yourselves; you yourselves
lui-même	himself; he himself; itself		
elle-même	herself; she herself; itself	**eux-mêmes**	themselves; they themselves
soi-même	oneself; itself		
		elles-mêmes	themselves; they themselves

§887 Conjunctive personal and reflexive pronouns.

person	1 subject	2 negative	3 direct & indirect object	4 direct object	5 indirect object
1	Je (j')—I		me (m')—me, to me; myself, to myself		
2	tu—you, thou		te (t')—you, to you; thee, to thee; thyself, to thyself		
3	il—he; it elle—she; it on—one, they	ne (n')—not §90B	se (s')—himself, herself, itself, oneself; to himself, to herself, to itself, to oneself	le (l')—him; it la (l')—her; it	lui—to him; to her
4	nous—we		nous—us, to us; ourselves, to ourselves		
5	vous—you		vous—you, to you; yourself, to yourself; yourselves, to yourselves		
6	ils—they elles—they		se—themselves; to themselves	les—them	leur—to them

This table shows all the forms of the conjunctive personal and reflexive pronouns with their translations into English and their positions (reading horizontally, not vertically) with respect to each other and with respect to the verb; and in negative declarative sentences. All of the elements in this table except the verb and **pas** and **personne** (and the other negative words listed in §90) are unstressed.

In affirmative and negative interrogative sentences, the subject pronouns in column 1 are placed after the verb or auxiliary in column 8 and attached to it with a hyphen. A **t**, preceded and followed by hyphens, is intercalated between third-singular forms ending in a vowel and the subject pronoun. The interrogative forms of the first singular present indicative whose final sound is a nasal vowel or a consonant are not used, while those whose final sound is an oral vowel are, e.g., **où vais-je?** where am I going?; e.g., **que dirai-je?** what shall I say?. And the ending **-e** of the first singular

26

person	6	7	8	9	10	11
	y—there; to it; to them	en—some; of it; of them	VERB or AUXILIARY	*negative*	past participle	*negative*
1						
2						
3						
4						
5						
6				pas—not 890B		personne—no one 890B

present indicative of verbs of the first conjugation is changed to -é, e.g., donné-je? do I give?, but these forms are not in current use in prose. All the forms not used are replaced by the affirmative forms introduced by est-ce que in affirmative interrogative sentences and by n'est-ce pas que in negative interrogative sentences. And est-ce que and n'est-ce pas que may be thus used in any person of any tense of the indicative. The ending -e of the first singular imperfect subjunctive of some verbs is likewise changed to -é in conditional clauses without si in literary usage, e.g., dussé-je if I should.

In affirmative imperative sentences, the subject pronouns are not exrressed and the pronouns in columns 3, 4, 5, 6, and 7 are placed after the verb and attached to it and to each other with hyphens except where elision occurs, and the pronouns in column 4 precede those in column 3. And unless followed by en or y, me is replaced by moi and te is replaced by toi; and moi and toi are stressed.

In negative imperative sentences, the subject pronouns are not expressed either and columns 2, 3, 4, 5, 6, 7, 8, and 9 have the same order as in negative declarative sentences.

A pronoun of column 5 cannot be used with a pronoun of column 3 but is replaced by a disjunctive pronoun preceded by the preposition à.

§88 The following table shows all the forms of possessive adjectives with their translations into English.

masc sg	fem sg	masc & fem pl	
mon	ma*	mes	my
ton	ta*	tes	your, thy, thine
son	sa*	ses	his, her, its
notre	notre	nos	our
votre	votre	vos	your
leur	leur	leurs	their

* The forms **mon, ton,** and **son** are used instead of **ma, ta,** and **sa** respectively before feminine nouns and adjectives beginning with a vowel or mute **h,** e.g., **Marie a fait un cadeau à son aïeule** Mary gave a present to her grandmother; e.g., **elle y est venue avec son aimable tante** she came with her nice aunt.

The possessive adjectives:
1) agree in gender and number with the thing possessed rather than with the possessor, e.g., **Marie lit son livre** Mary is reading her book
2) must be repeated before each noun in a series, e.g., **Marie apporte son stylo et son crayon** Mary is bringing her pen and pencil

§89 The following table shows all the forms of possessive pronouns with their translations into English.

	sg	pl	
masc	le mien	les miens	
fem	la mienne	les miennes	mine
masc	le tien	les tiens	
fem	la tienne	les tiennes	yours, thine
masc	le sien	les siens	
fem	la sienne	les siennes	his, hers, its
masc	le nôtre		
fem	la nôtre	les nôtres	ours
masc	le vôtre		
fem	la vôtre	les vôtres	yours
masc	le leur		
fem	la leur	les leurs	theirs

The possessive pronouns:
1) agree in gender and number with the thing possessed rather than with the possessor, e.g., **donnez votre livre à Marie, elle a perdu le sien** give your book to Mary; she has lost hers
2) are preceded by a definite article, e.g., **tu dois obéir à son ordre et au mien** you must obey his order and mine
3) are sometimes used without antecedent: a) **le mien** mine, my own (*i.e., property*); **le sien** his, his own (*i.e., property*); hers, her own (*i.e., property*); etc.; b) **les miens** my folks, my family;

28

my friends; my men; **les siens** his folks, his family; his friends; his men; her folks, etc.; c) **faire des siennes** (coll) to be up to one's (his, etc.) old tricks.

§90 The adverb **ne** is a conjunctive particle, that is, it always precedes a verb and, like conjunctive pronouns, is unstressed. Because of its weakness, it is generally accompanied by another word, which follows the verb (or auxiliary) in most cases, is stressed, and gives force or added meaning to the negation, e.g., **il n'est pas ici** he is not here.

A) The following table shows **ne** with the various words with which it is associated. (For more detail, see each expression under the second word in the body of the Dictionary, e.g., s.v. **aucun**; e.g., s.v. **aucunement**; etc.)

ne ... aucun	no, none; no one, nobody	ne ... ni ... ni	neither ... nor
ne ... aucunement	by no means	ne ... nul	no, none
ne ... brin (archaic)	not a bit, not a single	ne ... nullement	not at all
		ne ... pas	not, no
ne ... davantage	no more	ne ... pas un	not one
ne ... goutte (archaic)	not a drop, nothing	ne ... personne	no one, nobody
		ne ... plus	no more, no longer
ne ... guère	hardly, scarcely; hardly ever	ne ... plus jamais	never any more
		ne ... plus que	now only
ne ... jamais	never	ne ... point	not, no, not at all
ne ... mie (archaic)	not a crumb, not	ne ... que	only, but
ne ... mot (archaic)	not a word, nothing	ne ... rien	nothing

B) The position of **ne** in the sentence is that of column 2 of §87. The position of **pas** and all the other like words, with the exception of **aucun, ni ... ni, nul, personne,** and **que** is that of column 9. The position of **aucun, nul, personne,** and **que** is that of column 11. And the position of the first **ni** of **ni ... ni** is that of column 11 unless the past participle is one of the correlatives, in which case its position is that of column 9.

Aucun, nul, pas un, personne, and rien may be used as subjects of the verb; they then precede ne and the verb, e.g., **personne n'est ici** no one is here. And **aucun, nul,** and **pas un** may be used as adjectives in the same position, e.g., **nul péril ne l'arrête** no danger stops him.

Usually when an infinitive is in the negative, **pas** immediately follows **ne,** e.g., **il m'a dit de ne pas y aller** he told me not to go there; e.g., **il regrette de ne pas me l'avoir dit** he regrets not having told me it.

C) The adverb **ne** is often used without **pas** or a similar word with the verbs **bouger, cesser, oser, pouvoir,** and **savoir,** e.g., **je ne saurais vous le dire** I can't tell you. And it is not translated (1) with a compound tense after **il y a ... que, voilà ... que,** and **depuis que,** e.g., **il y a trois jours que je ne l'ai vu** it is three days since I saw him or

(2) with the verb of a clause introduced by a) **à moins que, avant que, empêcher ... que**, and **éviter ... que**, e.g., **à moins que je ne sois retenu** unless I am detained; b) **si** meaning unless, e.g., **si je ne me trompe** unless I am mistaken; c) a comparative + **que**, e.g., **vous étiez plus occupé qu'il ne l'était** you were busier than he was; d) a verb or expression of fear such as **avoir peur que, craindre que, redouter que**, e.g., **je crains qu'il ne soit malade** I am afraid that he is sick; e) a negative verb or expression of doubt, denial, despair such as **ne pas désespérer que, ne pas disconvenir que, ne pas douter que, ne pas nier que**, e.g., **je ne doute pas qu'il ne vienne** I do not doubt that he will come.

§91 *adj & adv comp & super* The comparative of superiority of adjectives and adverbs is formed by placing **plus** before the positive, e.g., **heureux** happy, **plus heureux** happier. The superlative of superiority of adjectives and adverbs is the same as the comparative, e.g., **heureux** happy, **plus heureux** happier and happiest. It is to be observed that the superlative is generally used in both French and English with the definite article or the possessive pronoun, e.g., **le plus heureux** the happiest, **son plus heureux** his happiest.

Some adjectives and adverbs have irregular comparatives and superlatives.

ADJECTIVES		ADVERBS	
positive	*comp and super*	*positive*	*comp and super*
bon good	meilleur better; best	beaucoup much	plus more; most
mauvais bad	pire worse; worst	bien well	mieux better; best
petit small	moindre lesser, less; least	mal badly	pis worse; worst
		peu little	moins less; least

30

FRENCH–ENGLISH

A

A, a [ɑ], *[ɑ] *m invar* first letter of the French alphabet

à [a] *prep* to, into; at; by, e.g., **à l'année** by the year; from, e.g., **arracher à** to snatch from; in, e.g., **à l'italienne** in the Italian manner; on, e.g., **à temps** on time; with, e.g., **la jeune fille aux yeux bleus** the girl with the blue eyes

abaisse-langue [abɛslɑ̃g] *m invar* tongue depressor

abaissement [abɛsmɑ̃] *m* lowering; drop; humbling

abaisser [abɛse] *tr* to lower; to humble || *ref* to go down; to humble oneself; to condescend

abandon [abɑ̃dɔ̃] *m* abandon; abandonment; desertion; neglect

abandonner [abɑ̃dɔne] *tr* to abandon; to forsake; to give up || *ref* to neglect oneself, become slovenly; **s'abandonner à** to give way to

abasourdir [abazurdir] *tr* to dumfound, flabbergast; to deafen

abasourdis·sant [abazurdisɑ̃] **abasourdis·sante** [abazurdisɑ̃t] *adj* astounding

abâtardir [abɑtardir] *tr* to debase || *ref* to deteriorate, to degenerate

abâtardissement [abɑtardismɑ̃] *m* debasement; deterioration, degeneration

abat-jour [abaʒur] *m invar* lampshade; eyeshade, sun visor; skylight

abats [aba] *mpl* giblets

abattage [abataʒ] *m* slaughtering (*of animals*); felling (*of trees*); demolition (*of a building*); bag, bagging (*of game*)

abattant [abatɑ̃] *m* drop leaf

abattement [abatmɑ̃] *m* dejection, despondency; prostration; tax deduction

abatteur [abatœr] *m* slaughterer; woodcutter; **abatteur de besogne** hard worker

abattis [abati] *m* felling (*of trees*); clearing (*of woods*); (mil) abatis; **abattis** *mpl* giblets; (slang) arms and legs

abattoir [abatwar] *m* slaughterhouse

abattre [abatr] §7 *tr* to pull down, to demolish; to fell; to slaughter; to overthrow; to discourage; to shoot down, to bring down (*a bird, airplane, etc.*); to lay (*dust*); (cards) to lay down (*one's hand*) || *ref* to abate, subside; to be dejected; to swoop down; to pounce; to crash (*said of airplane*)

abat·tu -tue [abaty] *adj* dejected, downcast

abat-vent [abavɑ̃] *m invar* chimney pot

abbaye [abei] *f* abbey

abbé [abe] *m* abbot; abbé, father

abbesse- [abes] *f* abbess

a b c [abese] *m* (letterword) ABC's; speller

abcès [apsɛ] *m* abscess

abdiquer [abdike] *tr & intr* to abdicate

abdomen [abdɔmɛn] *m* abdomen

abécédaire [abesedɛr] *m* speller

abeille [abɛj] *f* bee

abêtir [abetir] *tr* to make stupid || *intr & ref* to become stupid

abhorrer [abɔre] *tr* to abhor

abîme [abim] *m* abyss; depth

abîmer [abime] *tr* to spoil; to damage || *ref* to sink; to be sunk; to get spoiled

ab·ject -jecte [abʒɛkt] *adj* abject

abjurer [abʒyre] *tr* to abjure

abla·tif [ablatif] **-tive** [tiv] *adj & m* ablative

aboiement [abwamɑ̃] *m* barking; yelp, cry, outcry

abois [abwa] *mpl* desperate straits; **aux abois** at bay; hard pressed

abolir [abɔlir] *tr* to abolish; to annul

abomination [abɔminɑsjɔ̃] *f* abomination

abondamment [abɔ̃damɑ̃] *adv* abundantly

abondance [abɔ̃dɑ̃s] *f* abundance, plenty; wealth; flow (*of words*); **parler d'abondance** to ad-lib

abon·dant [abɔ̃dɑ̃] **-dante** [dɑ̃t] *adj* abundant, plentiful; wordy

abon·né -née [abɔne] *mf* subscriber; season-ticket holder; consumer (*of gas, electricity, etc.*); commuter (*on railroad*)

abonnement [abɔnmɑ̃] *m* subscription

abonner [abɔne] *tr* to take out a subscription for (*s.o.*) || *ref* to subscribe, take out a subscription

abord [abɔr] *m* approach; **abords** outskirts, surroundings; **d'abord** at first; **d'un abord facile** easy to approach; **tout d'abord** first of all

abordable [abɔrdabl] *adj* approachable, accessible; reasonable (*price*)

abordage [abɔrdaʒ] *m* (naut) boarding; (naut) collision

aborder [abɔrde] *tr* to approach, to accost; to board; to collide with, run afoul of || *intr* to land, to go ashore

aborigène [abɔriʒɛn] *adj & m* native, aboriginal

abor·tif [abɔrtif] **-tive** [tiv] *adj* abortive

aboucher [abuʃe] *tr* to join; to bring together || *ref* to have an interview

aboutir [abutir] *intr* to end; to come to an end

aboutissement [abutismã] *m* outcome, result

aboyer [abwaje] §47 *intr* to bark; to bay

abracada-brant [abrakadabrã] **-brante** [brãt] *adj* amazing, breath-taking

abra-sif [abrazif] **-sive** [ziv] *adj & m* abrasive

abrégé [abreʒe] *m* abridgment, summary

abrégement [abreʒmã] *m* abridgment

abréger [abreʒe] §1 *tr* to abridge; to shorten, curtail

abreuvage [abrœvaʒ] *m* watering

abreuver [abrœve] *tr* to water; to soak; to overwhelm, to shower ‖ *ref* to drink

abreuvoir [abrœvwar] *m* drinking trough, watering trough, horsepond

abréviation [abrevjɑsjɔ̃] *f* abbreviation; abridgment, curtailment

abri [abri] *m* shelter, refuge, cover; air-raid shelter; **à l'abri de** protected from

abricot [abriko] *m* apricot

abricotier [abrikɔtje] *m* apricot tree

abri-promenade [abriprɔmnad] *m* hurricane deck, shelter deck

abriter [abrite] *tr* to shelter, protect, shield, screen ‖ *ref* to take shelter

abroger [abrɔʒe] §38 *tr* to abrogate, repeal

a-brupt -brupte [abrypt] *adj* abrupt, steep; rough, crude; blunt

abru-ti -tie [abryti] *adj* sottish

abrutir [abrytir] *tr* to brutalize; to besot; to overwhelm

abrutis-sant [abrytisã] **abrutis-sante** [abrytisãt] *adj* stupefying; deadening

absence [apsãs] *f* absence

ab-sent [apsã] **-sente** [sãt] *adj* absent; absent-minded ‖ *mf* absentee

absenter [apsãte] *ref* to absent oneself, be absent, stay away

abside [apsid] *f* apse

absinthe [apsɛ̃t] *f* absinthe, wormwood; absinthe (*liqueur*)

abso-lu -lue [apsɔly] *adj* absolute

absolument [apsɔlymã] *adv* absolutely

absor-bant [apsɔrbã] **-bante** [bãt] *adj* absorbent; absorbing ‖ *m* absorbent

absorber [apsɔrbe] *tr* to absorb, to soak up; to eat up; to drink ‖ *ref* to become absorbed, be deeply interested

absoudre [apsudr] §60 (*pp* **absous, absoute**; no *pret* or *imperf subj*) *tr* to absolve; to forgive; to acquit

abstenir [apstənir] §72 *ref* to abstain, refrain

absti-nent [apstinã] **-nente** [nãt] *adj* abstinent; abstemious ‖ *mf* moderate eater or drinker

abstraction [apstraksjɔ̃] *f* abstraction; **faire abstraction de** to leave out, to disregard

abstraire [apstrer] §68 (no *pret* or *imperf subj*) *tr* to abstract ‖ *ref* to become engrossed

abs-trait [apstrɛ] **-traite** [trɛt] *adj* abstract

abs-trus [apstry] **-truse** [tryz] *adj* abstruse

absurde [apsyrd] *adj* absurd

absurdité [apsyrdite] *f* absurdity

abus [aby] *m* abuse

abuser [abyze] *tr* to deceive ‖ *intr* to exaggerate; **abuser de** to take advantage of, to impose upon; to indulge unwisely in ‖ *ref* to be mistaken

abu-sif [abyzif] **-sive** [ziv] *adj* abusive, wrong

acacia [akasja] *m* locust tree; **faux acacia** black locust tree

académicien [akademisjɛ̃] *m* academician

académie [akademi] *f* academy

académique [akademik] *adj* academic

acagnarder [akaɲarde] *tr* to make lazy ‖ *ref* to grow lazy; to lounge

acajou [akaʒu] *m* mahogany; mahogany tree; **acajou à pommes** (bot) cashew

acariâtre [akarjɑtr] *adj* grumpy

acca-blant [akablã] **-blante** [blãt] *adj* overwhelming

accabler [akable] *tr* to overwhelm; to weigh down

accalmie [akalmi] *f* lull, standstill

accaparer [akapare] *tr* to corner (*the market*); to monopolize

accéder [aksede] §10 *intr* to accede; to acquiesce; to have access

accéléra-teur [akseleratœr] **-trice** [tris] *adj* accelerating ‖ *m* accelerator

accélérer [akselere] §10 *tr, intr, & ref* to accelerate

accent [aksã] *m* accent; **accent de hauteur** pitch accent; **accent d'insistance** emphasis; **accent d'intensité** stress accent; **accent tonique** tonic accent

accentuer [aksãtɥe] *tr* to accent ‖ *ref* to become more marked

acceptable [akseptabl] *adj* acceptable

acceptation [akseptɑsjɔ̃] *f* acceptance

accepter [aksəpte] *tr* to accept ‖ *intr*—**accepter de** to agree to

acception [aksepsjɔ̃] *f* sense, meaning; preference, partiality

accès [akse] *m* access; outburst; (pathol) attack, bout; **accès aux quais** (public sign) to the docks

accessible [aksesibl] *adj* accessible; susceptible

accession [aksesjɔ̃] *f* accession

accessit [aksesit] *m* honorable mention

accessoire [akseswar] *adj* accessory ‖ **accessoires** *mpl* accessories; (theat) properties

accident [aksidã] *m* accident; unevenness (*of ground*); (mus) accidental

acciden-té -tée [aksidãte] *adj* rough, uneven; bumpy (*road*); eventful (*life*); (coll) wrecked (*car*) ‖ *mf* (coll) casualty, victim

acciden-tel -telle [aksidãtɛl] *adj* accidental

accidenter [aksidãte] *tr* to make uneven; to vary; to injure

accise [aksiz] *f* excise tax

acclamer [aklame] *tr* to acclaim

acclimater [aklimate] *tr* to acclimate ‖ *ref* to become acclimated

accolade [akɔlad] *f* embrace; accolade; (mus, typ) brace

accoler [akɔle] *tr* to hug; to join side by side; to couple (*names*); (typ) to brace

accommo·dant [akɔmɔdã] **-dante** [dãt] *adj* accommodating, obliging

accommodation [akɔmɔdasjɔ̃] *f* accommodation

accommodement [akɔmɔdmã] *m* settlement, compromise; arrangement

accommoder [akɔmɔde] *tr* to accommodate; to conciliate; to arrange (*furniture*); to prepare (*food*)

accompagna·teur [akɔ̃paɲatœr] **-trice** [tris] *mf* accompanist

accompagnement [akɔ̃paɲmã] *m* accompaniment

accompagner [akɔ̃paɲe] *tr* to accompany

accom·pli -plie [akɔ̃pli] *adj* completed; polished; accomplished

accomplir [akɔ̃plir] *tr* to accomplish; to complete; to fulfill (*a promise*) ‖ *ref* to come to pass

accomplissement [akɔ̃plismã] *m* accomplishment, performance

accord [akɔr] *m* accord, agreement, consent; harmony; settlement, bargain; (mus) chord; (mus) tuning; **d'accord** in accord; **d'accord!** O.K.!, check!; **d'un commun accord** by common consent

accordage [akɔrdaʒ] *m* tuning

accordéon [akɔrdeɔ̃] *m* accordion; **en accordéon** squashed; accordion-pleated

accorder [akɔrde] *tr* to grant; to reconcile; (mus, rad) to tune ‖ *intr*—**accorder à qn de** to allow s.o. to ‖ *ref* to harmonize; to tally; to agree

ac·cort [akɔr] **ac·corte** [akɔrt] *adj* sprightly, engaging (*e.g., young lady*)

accoster [akɔste] *tr* to approach ‖ *intr* to dock, to berth

accotement [akɔtmã] *m* shoulder (*of a road*)

accoter [akɔte] *tr* to shore up ‖ *ref* to lean

accouchement [akuʃmã] *m* childbirth

accoucher [akuʃe] *tr* to deliver ‖ *intr* (aux: ÊTRE) to be confined, to be delivered ‖ *intr* (aux: AVOIR)—**accoucher de** to give birth to

accou·cheur [akuʃœr] **-cheuse** [ʃøz] *mf* obstetrician

accouder [akude] *ref* to lean on one's elbows

accoudoir [akudwar] *m* armrest

accouple [akupl] *f* leash

accouplement [akupləmã] *m* coupling; **accouplement consanguin** inbreeding

accoupler [akuple] *tr* to couple; to yoke; to bring together for breeding; to link; (elec) to hook up ‖ *ref* to mate

accourir [akurir] §14 *intr* (aux: AVOIR or ÊTRE) to run up

accoutrement [akutrəmã] *m* togs, get-up

accoutrer [akutre] *tr* to rig out ‖ *ref* to dress ridiculously

accoutu·mé -mée [akutyme] *adj* accustomed; **à l'accoutumée** as usual ‖ *mf* regular customer; frequent visitor

accoutumer [akutyme] *tr* to accustom ‖ *ref* to become accustomed

accouvage [akuvaʒ] *m* artificial incubation

accouver [akuve] *tr* to set (*a hen*) ‖ *intr* to set (*said of a hen*) ‖ *ref* to begin to set

accréditer [akredite] *tr* to accredit; to win a hearing for; **accrédité auprès de** accredited to ‖ *ref* to gain credence or favor

accréditeur [akreditœr] *m* bondsman

accroc [akro] *m* tear (*in a dress*); (fig) snag, hitch

accrochage [akrɔʃaʒ] *m* hanging; hooking; clinch (*in boxing*); collision; (mil) encounter; (rad) receiving; (coll) squabble

accroche [akrɔʃ] *m* hanger

accrocher [akrɔʃe] *tr* to hang, to hang up; to hook; to catch; (mil) to come to grips with; (rad) to pick up; (coll) to buttonhole ‖ *ref* (coll) to come to blows; to cling; to catch; to get caught

accroire [akrwar] (used only in *inf* after **faire**) *tr*—**faire accroire** (with *dat*) to make (*s.o.*) believe ‖ *ref*—**s'en faire accroire** to get a swelled head

accroissement [akrwasmã] *m* growth; accumulation (*of capital*); increment

accroître [akrwatr] §17 (*pp* **accru**; *pres ind* **accrois**; *pret* **accrus**, etc.) *tr* & *ref* to increase

accroupir [akrupir] *ref* to squat, to crouch

accu [aky] *m* storage battery

accueil [akœj] *m* reception, welcome

accueil·lant [akœjã] **accueil·lante** [akœjãt] *adj* hospitable, gracious

accueillir [akœjir] §18 *tr* to welcome; to honor (*a bill*)

acculer [akyle] *tr* to corner

accumulateur [akymylatœr] *m* storage battery

accumuler [akymyle] *tr, intr,* & *ref* to accumulate

accusa·teur [akyzatœr] **-trice** [tris] *adj* incriminating ‖ *mf* accuser

accusatif [akyzatif] *m* accusative

accusation [akyzasjɔ̃] *f* accusation; charge

accu·sé -sée [akyze] *adj* marked; prominent (*features*) ‖ *mf* defendant ‖ *m* acknowledgment (*of receipt*)

accuser [akyze] *tr* to accuse; to acknowledge (*receipt*)

acerbe [aserb] *adj* sour; sharp; caustic (*remark*)

acé·ré -rée [asere] *adj* keen (*edge*); sharp (*tongue*)

acétate [asetat] *m* acetate

acétique [asetik] *adj* acetic

acétone [asetɔn] *f* acetone

achalander [aʃalãde] *tr* to attract customers to ‖ *ref* to get customers

achar·né -née [aʃarne] *adj* fierce; relentless (*pursuit*); inveterate (*gambler*); bitter (*enemy*); **acharné à** bent on, set on

acharnement [aʃarnəmɑ̃] *m* fierceness, fury; stubbornness; eagerness

acharner [aʃarne] *tr* to •set, to sic (*dogs*); to bait (*a trap*) ‖ *ref* to fight bitterly; **s'acharner à** to work away at; to be bent on, to persist in; **s'acharner contre** to attack fiercely; **s'acharner sur** to light into; to swoop down upon; to bear down on; to be dead set against

achat [aʃa] *m* purchase; **achat à terme** installment buying; **aller aux achats** to go shopping

ache [aʃ] *f* wild celery

acheminement [aʃminmɑ̃] *m* forwarding; progress

acheminer [aʃmine] *tr* to direct ‖ *ref* to proceed

acheter [aʃte] §2 *tr* to buy; **acheter à** to buy from, to buy for; **acheter de** to buy from; **acheter pour** to buy for

achèvement [aʃɛvmɑ̃] *m* completion

achever [aʃve] §2 *tr* to complete; to finish off, kill ‖ *intr* to end; to be just finishing ‖ *ref* to come to an end

Achille [aʃil] *m* Achilles

achoppement [aʃɔpmɑ̃] *m* obstacle; impact

achopper [aʃɔpe] *intr & ref* to stumble

achromatique [akrɔmatik] *adj* achromatic

acide [asid] *adj & m* acid; **acide phénique** carbolic acid

acidité [asidite] *f* acidity

acidu•lé -lée [asidyle] *adj* acid; fruit-flavored

aciduler [asidyle] *tr* to acidulate

acier [asje] *m* steel; (fig) sword; **acier inoxydable** stainless steel

aciérie [asjeri] *f* steelworks, steel mill

acmé [akme] *f* acme; (pathol) crisis

acolyte [akɔlit] *m* acolyte; accomplice

acompte [akɔ̃t] *m* installment; deposit, down payment; **acompte provisionnel** payment on estimated income tax

Açores [asɔr] *fpl* Azores

à-côté [akote] *m* (*pl* **-côtés**) sidelight; path (*beside road*); kickback

à-coup [aku] *m* (*pl* **-coups**) jerk; **par à-coups** by fits and starts

acoustique [akustik] *adj* acoustic, acoustical ‖ *f* acoustics

acquéreur [akerœr] *m* buyer

acquérir [akerir] §3 *tr* to acquire, to get

acquiescement [akjɛsmɑ̃] *m* acquiescence

acquiescer [akjese] §51 *intr* to acquiesce

ac•quis [aki] **-quise** [kiz] *adj* established ‖ *m* know-how

acquisition [akizisjɔ̃] *f* acquisition

acquit [aki] *m* receipt; **pour acquit** paid in full

acquit-à-caution [akitakosjɔ̃] *m* (*pl* **acquits-à-caution**) permit to transport in bond

acquittement [akitmɑ̃] *m* acquittal

acquitter [akite] *tr* to acquit; to receipt (*a bill*); to pay, discharge ‖ *ref* to pay one's debts; **s'acquitter de** to fulfill, to perform

âcre [ɑkr] *adj* acrid

acrimo•nieux [akrimɔnjø] **-nieuse** [njøz] *adj* acrimonious

acrobate [akrɔbat] *mf* acrobat

acrobatie [akrɔbasi] *f* acrobatics

acropole [akrɔpɔl] *f* acropolis

acrostiche [akrɔstiʃ] *m* acrostic

acte [akt] *m* action; bill; act; certificate, deed; **acte de présence** personal appearance; **acte de vente** bill of sale; **actes** minutes; **faire acte** to make a declaration; **prendre acte** to take minutes

acteur [aktœr] *m* actor

ac•tif [aktif] **-tive** [tiv] *adj* active; full (*citizen*) ‖ *m* credit side (*of an account*); assets; (gram) active voice

action [aksjɔ̃] *f* action; share (*of stock*); **action de grâces** thanksgiving

actionnaire [aksjɔnɛr] *mf* stockholder

actionner [aksjɔne] *tr* to actuate; to drive; to sue

activer [aktive] *tr* to activate; to hasten ‖ *ref* to hasten

activité [aktivite] *f* activity; active service; **en pleine activité** in full swing

actrice [aktris] *f* actress

actuaire [aktɥɛr] *mf* actuary

actualisation [aktɥalizasjɔ̃] *f* modernization

actualiser [aktɥalize] *tr* to modernize, to bring up to date

actualité [aktɥalite] *f* present condition; **actualités** current events; newsreel; **d'actualité** newsworthy

ac•tuel -tuelle [aktɥɛl] *adj* present, present-day, current

actuellement [aktɥɛlmɑ̃] *adv* now, at the present time

acuité [akɥite] *f* acuity

adage [adaʒ] *m* adage

Adam [adɑ̃] *m* Adam

adapta•teur [adaptatœr] **-trice** [tris] *mf* adapter ‖ *m* (mov) adapter

adaptation [adaptasjɔ̃] *f* adaptation

adapter [adapte] *tr & ref* to adapt

addenda [adɛ̃da] *m invar* addendum

addi•tif [aditif] **-tive** [tiv] *adj & m* additive

addition [adisjɔ̃] *f* addition; check (*for a restaurant meal*)

additionner [adisjɔne] *tr* to add up; to add; to dilute, mix

adénoïde [adenoid] *adj* adenoid

adent [adɑ̃] *m* dovetail

adepte [adɛpt] *mf* adept

adé•quat [adekwa] **-quate** [kwat] *adj* adequate

adhérence [aderɑ̃s] *f* adherence; traction; (pathol) adhesion

adhé•rent [aderɑ̃] **-rente** [rɑ̃t] *adj & mf* adherent

adhérer [adere] §10 *intr* to adhere; to stick; **adhérer à la route** to hold the road

adhé•sif [adezif] **-sive** [ziv] *adj & m* adhesive

adhésion [adezjɔ̃] *f* adhesion

adieu [adjø] *m* (*pl* **adieux**) farewell ‖ *interj* adieu!, bon voyage!; good riddance!; **sans adieu!** see you later!

adja•cent [adʒasɑ̃] **-cente** [sɑ̃t] *adj* adjacent

adjec·tif [adʒɛktif] **-tive** [tiv] *adj & m* adjective

adjoindre [adʒwɛ̃dr] §35 *tr & ref* to join

ad·joint [adʒwɛ̃] **-jointe** [ʒwɛ̃t] *adj & mf* assistant, stand-by

adjudant [adʒydɑ̃] *m* warrant officer; sergeant major; (pej) martinet

adjudication [adʒydikɑsjɔ̃] *f* auction; awarding (*of a contract*)

adjuger [adʒyʒe] §38 *tr* to adjudge, award; to knock down (*at auction*)

admettre [admetr] §42 *tr* to admit

administra·teur [administratœr] **-trice** [tris] *mf* administrator, director

administration [administrɑsjɔ̃] *f* administration; **administration des ponts et chaussées** highway department

administrer [administre] *tr* to administer

admira·teur [admiratœr] **-trice** [tris] *mf* admirer

admira·tif [admiratif] **-tive** [tiv] *adj* admiring; amazed

admiration [admirɑsjɔ̃] *f* admiration; wonder

admirer [admire] *tr* to admire; to wonder at

admissible [admisibl] *adj* admissible; eligible

admission [admisjɔ̃] *f* admission; (aut) intake

admonester [admɔneste] *tr* to admonish

adolescence [adɔlesɑ̃s] *f* adolescence

adoles·cent [adɔlesɑ̃] **adoles·cente** [adɔlesɑ̃t] *adj & mf* adolescent

adonner [adɔne] *ref* to devote oneself; **s'adonner à** to give oneself up to

adopter [adɔpte] *tr* to adopt

adop·tif [adɔptif] **-tive** [tiv] *adj* adopted; adoptive

adoption [adɔpsjɔ̃] *f* adoption

adorable [adɔrabl] *adj* adorable

adora·teur [adɔratœr] **-trice** [tris] *mf* adorer; worshiper

adoration [adɔrɑsjɔ̃] *f* adoration

adorer [adɔre] *tr* to adore, worship

adosser [adɔse] *tr*—**adosser q.ch. à** to turn the back of s.th. against || *ref*—**s'adosser à** to lean back against

adouber [adube] *tr* to dub

adoucir [adusir] *tr* to soften || *ref* to soften; to grow milder

adrénaline [adrenalin] *f* adrenalin

adresse [adres] *f* address; skill, dexterity; neatness; expertness, expertise; **adresse particulière** home address

adresser [adrese] *tr* to address || *ref* to apply

Adriatique [adriatik] *adj & f* Adriatic

a·droit [adrwa] **-droite** [drwat] *adj* adroit, clever; neat

aduler [adyle] *tr* to adulate

adulte [adylt] *adj & mf* adult

adultère [adylter] *adj* adulterous || *m* adultery; adulterer || *f* adulteress

adultérer [adyltere] §10 *tr* to adulterate; to falsify (*a text*)

adulté·rin [adylterɛ̃] **-rine** [rin] *adj* born in adultery

advenir [advənir] §72 (used only in *inf*; *pp*; 3d *pers sg & pl*) *intr* (*aux*: ÊTRE)

to come to pass; **advienne que pourra** come what may

adventice [advɑ̃tis] *adj* adventitious

adverbe [adverb] *m* adverb

adversaire [adverser] *mf* adversary

adverse [advers] *adj* adverse; opposite (*side*)

adversité [adversite] *f* adversity

aérer [aere] §10 *tr* to aerate; to ventilate; to air

aé·rien [aerjɛ̃] **-rienne** [rjɛn] *adj* aerial || *m* elevated railway

aéro [aero] *m* airplane

aérodynamique [aerodinamik] *adj* aerodynamic; streamlined || *f* aerodynamics

aérogare [aerogar] *f* air terminal

aéroglisseur [aeroglisœr] *m* hydrofoil

aérogramme [aerogram] *m* air letter

aérolite or **aérolithe** [aerolit] *m* meteorite, aerolite

aéronef [aeronɛf] *m* aircraft

aérophare [aerofar] *m* air beacon

aéroport [aeropor] *m* airport

aéropor·té **-tée** [aeroporte] *adj* airborne

aéropos·tal **-tale** [aeropostal] *adj* (*pl* **-taux** [to]) air-mail

aérosol [aerosol] *m* aerosol

aérospa·tial **-tiale** [aerospasjal] *adj* (*pl* **-tiaux** [sjo]) aerospace

A.F. *abbr* (**allocations familiales**) family (social security) allotments

affable [afabl] *adj* affable

affadir [afadir] *tr & ref* to stale

affaiblir [afeblir] *tr & ref* to weaken

affaire [afer] *f* affair; job; business; trouble; (law) case; (coll) belongings; **affaire à saisir** bargain; **affaire d'or** (fig) gold mine; **affaire en instance** unfinished business; **affaires** business; **bonne affaire** bargain; **cela fait mon affaire** that is just what I want

affai·ré **-rée** [afere] *adj* busy, bustling

affairiste [aferist] *m* slicker, operator

affaissement [afesmɑ̃] *m* sagging; cave-in, collapse

affaisser [afese] *tr* to weigh down; to depress || *ref* to sag; to cave in, to collapse

affaler [afale] *tr* to haul down || *ref* to drop, sink, flop

affa·mé **-mée** [afame] *adj* famished, starved

affamer [afame] *tr* to starve

affectable [afektabl] *adj* impressionable; mortgageable

affectation [afektɑsjɔ̃] *f* affectation; assignment; allotment

affec·té **-tée** [afekte] *adj* affected; assigned

affecter [afekte] *tr* to affect; to assign; to assume (*various shapes or manners*) || *ref* to grieve

affec·tif [afektif] **-tive** [tiv] *adj* affective, emotional

affection [afeksjɔ̃] *f* affection; mental state; disease, affection

affection·né **-née** [afeksjone] *adj* loving, fond, devoted

affectionner [afɛksjɔne] *tr* to be fond of || *ref* to become attached
affectueusement [afɛktɥøzmɑ̃] *adv* affectionately
affec·tueux [afɛktɥø] **-tueuse** [tɥøz] *adj* affectionate
affé·rent [aferɑ̃] **-rente** [rɑ̃t] *adj* due, accruing
affermer [afɛrme] *tr* to lease, to rent
affermir [afɛrmir] *tr* to strengthen, harden || *ref* to become stronger, sounder
affichage [afiʃaʒ] *m* billposting
affiche [afiʃ] *f* poster, bill; (theat) playbill
afficher [afiʃe] *tr* to post, to post up; to display; (theat) to bill || *ref* to seek the limelight; **s'afficher avec** to hang around with
afficheur [afiʃœr] *m* billposter
affi·lé -lée [afile] *adj* sharpened; sharp (*tongue*) || *adv*—**d'affilée** in a row
affiler [afile] *tr* to sharpen, to whet; to hone, to strop; to set (*a saw*)
affi·lié -liée [afilje] *adj* & *mf* affiliate
affilier [afilje] *tr* & *ref* to affiliate
affiloir [afilwar] *m* sharpener; whetstone; hone, strop
affiner [afine] *tr* to improve; to refine; to sift || *ref* to improve; to mature, ripen
affinité [afinite] *f* affinity; in-law relationship
affirma·tif [afirmatif] **-tive** [tiv] *adj* & *f* affirmative
affirmer [afirme] *tr* to affirm || *ref* to assert oneself; **s'affirmer comme** to take one's place as
affixe [afiks] *m* affix
affleurer [aflœre] *tr* to level; to come up to the level of || *intr* to come to the surface
affliction [afliksjɔ̃] *f* affliction
affli·gé -gée [afliʒe] *adj* sorrowful
affli·geant [afliʒɑ̃] **-geante** [ʒɑ̃t] *adj* sorrowful (*news*)
affliger [afliʒe] §38 *tr* to afflict || *ref* to grieve, to sorrow; **s'affliger de** to sorrow for
affluence [aflyɑ̃s] *f* crowd
af·fluent [aflyɑ̃] **af·fluente** [aflyɑ̃t] *adj* & *m* tributary
affluer [aflye] *intr* to flow; to throng, crowd, flock
afflux [afly] *m* afflux, flow; rush
affo·lé -lée [afole] *adj* panic-stricken
affolement [afɔlmɑ̃] *m* distraction, panic; infatuation; unsteadiness (*of a compass*)
affoler [afole] *tr* to distract, to panic; to infatuate; to disturb (*compass*) || *ref* to be distracted; to stampede; to become infatuated; to spin (*as a compass*)
affran·chi -chie [afrɑ̃ʃi] *adj* emancipated; postpaid || *mf* freethinker
affranchir [afrɑ̃ʃir] *tr* to emancipate, free; to pay the postage for
affranchissement [afrɑ̃ʃismɑ̃] *m* emancipation; payment of postage; cancellation (*of mail*); **affranchissement insuffisant** postage due
affres [afr] *fpl* pangs

affrètement [afrɛtmɑ̃] *m* chartering (*of a boat*)
affréter [afrete] §10 *tr* to charter (*a boat*)
af·freux [afrø] **af·freuse** [afrøz] *adj* frightful
affront [afrɔ̃] *m* affront
affronter [afrɔ̃te] *tr* to confront; to face
affût [afy] *m* hunting blind; mount (*for cannon*); **être à l'affût de** to lie in wait for
affûter [afyte] *tr* to sharpen
afin [afɛ̃] *adv*—**afin de** in order to; **afin que** in order that, so that
afri·cain [afrikɛ̃] **-caine** [kɛn] *adj* African || (*cap*) *mf* African
Afrique [afrik] *f* Africa; **l'Afrique** Africa
agacement [agasmɑ̃] *m* irritation, annoyance
agacer [agase] §51 *tr* to irritate, annoy; to tease; to set on edge
agape [agap] *f* agape; **agapes banquet**
âge [ɑʒ] *m* age; **d'un certain âge** middle-aged; **quel âge avez-vous?** how old are you?
â·gé -gée [aʒe] *adj* old, aged; old, e.g., **âgé de seize ans** sixteen years old
agence [aʒɑ̃s] *f* agency, office, service, bureau; **agence de location** rental service; real-estate office; **agence de voyages** travel bureau; **agence immobilière** real-estate office
agencement [aʒɑ̃smɑ̃] *m* arrangement; furnishing (*of a house*); construction (*of a sentence*); **agencements fixtures**
agencer [aʒɑ̃se] §51 *tr* to arrange
agenda [aʒɛ̃da] *m* engagement book
agenouiller [aʒnuje] *ref* to kneel
agent [aʒɑ̃] *m* agent; policeman; **agent comptable** accountant; **agent de change** stockbroker; **agent de location** realtor
agglomération [aglɔmerasjɔ̃] *f* agglomeration; metropolitan area; built-up area
aggloméré·ré -rée [aglɔmere] *adj* compressed || *m* briquette; adobe
agglomérer [aglɔmere] §10 *tr* & *ref* to agglomerate
aggraver [agrave] *tr* to aggravate || *ref* to become more serious
agile [aʒil] *adj* agile, nimble
agilité [aʒilite] *f* agility
agio·teur [aʒjɔtœr] **-teuse** [tøz] *mf* speculator
agir [aʒir] *intr* to act; to take action || *ref*—**il s'agit de** it is a question of
agis·sant [aʒisɑ̃] **agis·sante** [aʒisɑ̃t] *adj* active
agissements [aʒismɑ̃] *mpl* machinations
agita·teur [aʒitatœr] **-trice** [tris] *mf* agitator (*person*) || *m* stirrer
agi·té -tée [aʒite] *adj* restless; rough (*sea*)
agiter [aʒite] *tr* to agitate; to stir; to wave; to discuss || *ref* to move about
a·gneau [aɲo] *m* (*pl* **-gneaux**) lamb
agnostique [agnɔstik] *adj* & *mf* agnostic
agonie [agɔni] *f* agony, death throes

agrafe [agraf] *f* clasp, pin; paper clip; staple (*for papers*); belt buckle; snap, hook; (med) clamp

agrafer [agrafe] *tr* to clasp, pin; to buckle; to snap; to hook; to fasten, to clip; to staple; (med) to clamp

agrafeuse [agraføz] *f* stapler

agraire [agrer] *adj* agrarian

agrandir [agrɑ̃dir] *tr* to enlarge || *ref* to grow, become larger

agrandissement [agrɑ̃dismɑ̃] *m* enlargement

agréable [agreabl] *adj* agreeable, pleasant; neighborly

agréé agréée [agree] *adj* approved || *m* attorney

agréer [agree] *tr* to accept, approve; **veuillez agréer l'expression de mes sentiments distingués** (complimentary close) sincerely yours || *intr* (with *dat*) to agree with, to please

agrégat [agrega] *m* aggregate

agrégation [agregasjɔ̃] *f* aggregation; admittance (*as a member of an organization*); competitive teacher's examination

agrégé -gée [agreʒe] *adj* aggregate || *mf* one who has passed his *agrégation*

agréger [agreʒe] §1 *tr* to attach, to add || *ref*—**s'agréger** (à) to join

agrément [agremɑ̃] *m* approval; pleasantness; pleasure, pastime; **agréments** adornments

agrès [agre] *mpl* rigging; gym equipment

agresseur [agresœr] *adj* & *m* aggressor

agres·sif [agresif] **agres·sive** [agresiv] *adj* aggressive

agression [agresjɔ̃] *f* aggression; (law) assault

agreste [agrest] *adj* rustic, rural

agricole [agrikɔl] *adj* agricultural

agriculture [agrikyltyr] *f* agriculture

agrumes [agrym] *mpl* citrus fruit

aguerrir [agerir] *tr* to season, inure || *ref* to become seasoned, inured

aguets [age] *mpl* watch, look-out; **être aux aguets** to be on the look-out

agui·chant [agi/ɑ̃] **-chante** [/ɑ̃t] *adj* alluring || *adj fem* sexy

ah [a] *interj* ah!; ah! now then!

ahu·ri -rie [ayri] *adj* dumfounded

ahurir [ayrir] *tr* to dumfound

ahurissement [ayrismɑ̃] *m* stupefaction

aide [ed] *mf* aid, assistant, helper || *f* aid, assistance, help; **aide sociale** welfare department

aider [ede] *tr* to aid, help; **aider** + *inf* to help to + *inf* || *intr* to help || *ref* —**s'aider de** to use

aïe [aj] *interj* ouch!

aïeul aïeule [ajœl] *mf* grandparent || *m* grandfather || *m* (*pl* **aïeux** [ajø]) ancestor || *f* grandmother

aigle [egl] *mf* eagle; **aigle de mer** eagle ray; **aigle pêcheur, grand aigle de mer** osprey, fish hawk; **grand aigle** spread eagle

aiglefin [egləfɛ̃] *m* haddock

ai·glon -glonne [glɔ̃] *mf* eaglet

aigre [egr] *adj* sour, tart, bitter; harsh (*voice*)

aigre-doux [egrədu] **-douce** [dus] *adj* bittersweet

aigrefin [egrəfɛ̃] *m* crook

aigre·let [egrəle] **-lette** [let] *adj* tart

aigrir [egrir] *tr* to turn (*s.th.*) sour || *intr* & *ref* to turn sour

ai·gu -guë [egy] *adj* sharp; acute; shrill, high-pitched || *m* (mus) treble

algue-marine [egmarin] *f* (*pl* **aigues-marines**) aquamarine

aiguille [eguij] *f* needle; peak; spire (*of steeple*); hand (*of clock*); (rr) switch

aiguiller [eguije] *tr* to switch, shunt || *ref* to be switched, shunted

aiguilleur [eguijœr] *m* (aer, rr) towerman

aiguillon [eguijɔ̃] *m* goad; sting

aiguiser [eguize] *tr* to sharpen; to whet (*appetite*)

ail [aj] *m* (*pl* **ails** or **aulx** [o]) garlic

aile [el] *f* wing; flank (*of army*); fender (*of auto*); brim (*of hat*); blade (*of propeller*); vane, arm (*of windmill*); **aile en flèche** (aer) backswept wing

aileron [elrɔ̃] *m* aileron

ailleurs [ajœr] *adv* elsewhere; **d'ailleurs** moreover, besides; from somewhere else; **par ailleurs** furthermore

aimable [emabl] *adj* kind, likeable; **voulez-vous être assez aimable de** will you be good enough to

aimant [emɑ̃] *m* magnet

aimanter [emɑ̃te] *tr* to magnetize

aimer [eme], [eme] *tr* to love; to like; to like to; **aimer à** to like to; **aimer bien** to like, to be fond of; to like to; **aimer mieux** to prefer; to prefer to

aine [en] *f* groin

aî·né -née [ene] *adj* & *mf* elder, eldest, oldest; senior

aînesse [enes] *f* seniority

ainsi [ɛ̃si] *adv* thus; **ainsi de suite** and so forth; **ainsi nommé** so-called; **ainsi que** as well as; **ainsi soit-il** amen

air [er] *m* air; look, appearance; **air de famille** family resemblance; **avoir l'air de** to seem to; **en l'air** empty, idle (*threats, talk*)

airain [erɛ̃] *m* brass; bronze

aire [er] *f* area; threshing floor; eyrie; **aire de lancement** launching pad

airelle [erel] *f* huckleberry; blueberry

aisance [ezɑ̃s] *f* ease, comfort

aise [ez] *adj*—**bien aise** glad, content || *f* ease; **aises** comforts; **à son aise** well-to-do

ai·sé -sée [eze] *adj* easy; natural; well-to-do

aisément [ezemɑ̃] *adv* easily

aisselle [esel] *f* armpit

ajonc [aʒɔ̃] *m* furze

ajou·ré -rée [aʒure] *adj* openwork, perforated

ajourer [aʒure] *tr* to cut openings in

ajournement [aʒurnəmɑ̃] *m* adjournment, postponement; subpoenaing; rejection (*of a candidate*)

ajourner [aʒurne] *tr* to postpone; to subpoena; to reject (*a candidate in an examination*)

ajouter [aʒute] *tr & intr* to add || *ref* to be added

ajus·té -tée [aʒyste] *adj* tight-fitting

ajuster [aʒyste] *tr* to adjust; to arrange; to fit; to aim at

ajusteur [aʒystœr] *m* fitter

alacrité [alakrite] *f* gaiety, vivacity

alambic [alābik] *m* still

alambi·qué -quée [alābike] *adj* finespun, far-fetched

alanguir [alāgir] *tr* to weaken || *ref* to languish

alar·mant [alarmā] **-mante** [māt] *adj* alarming

alarme [alarm] *f* alarm

alarmer [alarme] *tr* to alarm || *ref* to be alarmed

alba·nais [albane] **-naise** [nez] *adj* Albanian || *m* Albanian (*language*) || (*cap*) *mf* Albanian (*person*)

albâtre [albɑtr] *m* alabaster

albatros [albatros] *m* albatross

albi·geois [albiʒwa] **-geoise** [ʒwaz] *adj* Albigensian || (*cap*) *mf* Albigensian

albinos [albinos] *adj & m* albino

album [albɔm] *m* album; scrapbook

albumen [albymen] *m* albumen

alcali [alkali] *m* alkali

alca·lin [alkalɛ̃] **-line** [lin] *adj* alkaline

alchimie [alʃimi] *f* alchemy

alcool [alkɔl] *m* alcohol; **alcool à friction** rubbing alcohol; **alcool dénaturé** denatured alcohol

alcoolique [alkɔɔlik], [alkɔlik] *adj & mf* alcoholic

alcôve [alkov] *f* alcove; **d'alcôve** amatory, gallant

ale [el] *f* ale

aléa [alea] *m* risk

aléatoire [aleatwar] *adj* risky; aleatory

alène [alɛn] *f* awl

alentour [alɑ̃tur] *adv* round about || **alentours** *mpl* neighborhood

alerte [alɛrt] *adj & f* alert; **alerte aérienne** air-raid alarm

alerter [alɛrte] *tr* to alert

alésage [alezaʒ] *m* bore (*of cylinder*)

aléser [aleze] §10 *tr* to ream; to bore

ale·zan [alzã] **-zane** [zan] *adj* chestnut (*colored*)

algarade [algarad] *f* altercation

algèbre [alʒebr] *f* algebra

Alger [alʒe] *m* Algiers

Algérie [alʒeri] *f* Algeria

algé·rien [alʒerjɛ̃] **-rienne** [rjɛn] *adj* Algerian || (*cap*) *mf* Algerian

algé·rois [alʒerwa] **-roise** [rwaz] *adj of* Algiers; Algerian || (*cap*) *mf* native of Algiers; Algerian

algues [alg] *fpl* algae

alias [aljas] *adv* alias

alibi [alibi] *m* (*law*) alibi

alié·né -née [aljene] *adj* alienated; insane || *mf* insane person

aliéner [aljene] §10 *tr* to transfer, alienate || *ref* (with *dat of reflex pron*) to alienate (*s.o.*); (with *dat of reflex pron*) to lose (*e.g., s.o.'s sympathy*)

alignement [aliɲmã] *m* alignment

aligner [aliɲe] *tr* to align; **aligner ses** phrases to choose one's words with care || *ref* to line up

aliment [alimã] *m* aliment, food; **aliments** (*law*) necessities

alimentaire [alimãter] *adj* alimentary; subsistence, e.g., **pension alimentaire** subsistence allowance

alimentation [alimãtasjɔ̃] *f* nourishment; supplying; feeding (*a fire, a machine*)

alimenter [alimãte] *tr* to nourish; to supply; to feed (*a fire, a machine*)

alinéa [alinea] *m* indentation (*of the first line of a paragraph*); paragraph

aliter [alite] *tr* to keep in bed || *ref* to be confined to bed

alizés [alize] *mpl* trade winds

allaiter [alete] *tr* to nurse

al·lant [alã] **al·lante** [alãt] *adj* active || **—allants et venants** passers-by; **beaucoup d'allant** (coll) a lot of pep

allé·chant [aleʃã] **-chante** [ʃãt] *adj* enticing, tempting

allécher [aleʃe] §10 *tr* to allure

allée [ale] *f* walk, path; going; city street, boulevard; aisle (*of theater*)

allégeance [aleʒãs] *f* allegiance; lightening (*of care*); handicapping (*of a race*)

alléger [aleʒe] §1 *tr* to lighten; to alleviate, mitigate, relieve

allégorie [alegɔri] *f* allegory

allègre [alegr] *adj* lively, cheerful

alléguer [alege] §10 *tr* to allege as an excuse; to cite (*an authority*)

Allemagne [almaɲ] *f* Germany; **l'Allemagne** Germany

alle·mand [almã] **-mande** [mãd] *adj* German || *m* German (*language*) || (*cap*) *mf* German (*person*)

aller [ale] *m* going; go; **aller (et) retour** round trip; round-trip ticket; **au pis aller** at the worst || §4 *intr* (*aux:* ÊTRE) to go; to work, function; (with *dat*) to suit, fit, become, e.g., **la robe lui va bien** the dress becomes her; **aller + inf** to be going to + *inf*, e.g., **je vais au magasin acheter des souliers** I am going to the store to buy some shoes; **allez!, allons!, allons donc!** well!, come on!, all right!; **allez-y doucement!** take it easy!; **ça va?, comment allez-vous?** how are you? || *ref*—**s'en aller** to go away || **aux—aller + inf** to be going to + *inf* (to express futurity), e.g., **il va se marier** he is going to get married

allergie [alerʒi] *f* allergy

aller-retour [aleratur] *m*—**faire l'aller-retour** to go and come back

alliage [aljaʒ] *m* alloy

alliance [aljãs] *f* alliance; marriage; wedding ring; **ancienne alliance** Old Covenant; **nouvelle alliance** New Covenant

al·lié -liée [alje] *adj* allied (*by treaty*); united (*in marriage*) || *mf* ally; kin, in-law

allier [alje] *tr* to ally; to alloy || *ref* to become allied, to ally oneself

alligator [aligatɔr] *m* alligator

allô [alo] *interj* hello!

allocation [alləkɑsjɔ̃] *f* allocation, allotment; **allocations familiales** family (social security) allotments

allocution [alləkysjɔ̃] *f* short speech

allonger [alɔ̃ʒe] §38 *tr, intr,* & *ref* to lengthen

allouer [alwe] *tr* to allow, allocate

allumage [alymaʒ] *m* lighting; switching on (*of a light*); kindling (*of a fire*); ignition

allume-feu [alymfø] *m invar* kindling

allumer [alyme] *tr* to ignite; to light (*a cigarette*); to light up (*a room*); to put on, switch on (*a light; a radio; a heater*); to provoke (*anger*) || *ref* to go on (*said of a light*); to light up (*said of eyes*); to catch fire

allumette [alymɛt] *f* match; **allumette de sûreté** safety match

allumette-gaz [alymɛtgɑz] *m* pilot light

allumeur [alymœr] *m* ignition system; **allumeur de réverbères** lamplighter

allumeuse [alymøz] *f* (coll) vamp

allure [alyr] *f* speed, pace; gait, bearing, aspect; **à l'allure de l'escargot** at a snail's pace; **à toute allure** at top speed

allusion [allyzjɔ̃] *f* allusion

almanach [almana] *m* almanac; yearbook

aloès [alɔɛs] *m* aloe

aloi [alwa] *m* legal alloy; quality; **de bon aloi** genuine

alors [alɔr] *adv* then; **alors même que** even though; **alors que** whereas

alose [aloz] *f* shad

alouette [alwɛt] *f* lark, skylark; **alouette sans tête** rolled veal

alourdir [alurdir] *tr* to weigh down, to make heavy || *ref* to become heavy

aloyau [alwajo] *m* (*pl* **aloyaux**) sirloin

Alpes [alp] *fpl*—**les Alpes** the Alps

alphabet [alfabe] *m* alphabet

alpinisme [alpinism] *m* mountain climbing

alpiniste [alpinist] *mf* mountain climber

alpiste [alpist] *m* birdseed

alsa·cien [alzasjɛ̃] **-cienne** [sjɛn] *adj* Alsatian || *m* Alsatian (*dialect*) || (*cap*) *mf* Alsatian (*person*)

alté·rant [alterɑ̃] **-rante** [rɑ̃t] *adj* thirst-provoking

altération [alterɑsjɔ̃] *f* alteration, falsification; deterioration; heavy thirst; (mus) accidental

altérer [altere] §10 *tr* to alter, falsify; to ruin (*one's health*); to weaken, impair; to make thirsty || *ref* to undergo a change for the worse; to become thirsty

alternance [alternɑ̃s] *f* alternation; (agr) rotation

alterna·tif [alternatif] **-tive** [tiv] *adj* alternative; alternating; alternate || *f* alternative, dilemma; alternation

alterne [altern] *adj* alternate (*angles*)

alterner [alterne] *tr* to rotate (*crops*) || *intr* to alternate

al·tier [altje] **-tière** [tjer] *adj* haughty

altitude [altityd] *f* altitude

alto [alto] *m* alto; viola

altruiste [altrɥist] *adj* & *mf* altruist

aluminium [alyminjɔm] *m* aluminum

alun [alœ̃] *m* alum

alunir [alynir] *intr* to land on the moon

alunissage [alynisaʒ] *m* landing on the moon

alvéole [alveɔl] *m* & *f* alveolus; cavity; cell (*of honeycomb*); socket (*of tooth*)

amadou [amadu] *m* punk, tinder

amadouer [amadwe] *tr* to wheedle

amaigrir [amegrir] *tr* to emaciate; to make thin || *ref* to grow thin

amalgame [amalgam] *m* amalgam

amalgamer [amalgame] *tr* & *ref* to amalgamate

aman [amɑ̃] *m*—**demander l'aman** to give in

amande [amɑ̃d] *f* almond; kernel; **amande de Malaga** Jordan almond

amandier [amɑ̃dje] *m* almond tree

a·mant [amɑ̃] **-mante** [mɑ̃t] *mf* lover

amareyeur [amarejœr] *m* oysterman

amariner [amarine] *tr* to season (*a crew*); to impress (*a ship*)

amarre [amar] *f* hawser

amarrer [amare] *tr* & *ref* to moor

amas [ama] *m* mass; heap; cluster (*of stars*); **amas de neige** snowdrift

amasser [amase] *tr* to amass; to gather || *intr* to hoard || *ref* to pile up, to crowd

amateur [amatœr] *adj* amateur || *m* amateur; (coll) prospective buyer

amatir [amatir] *tr* to mat, dull (*metal or glass*)

amazone [amazon] *f* amazon; horsewoman; riding habit; **monter en amazone** to ride sidesaddle || (*cap*) *f* Amazon

ambages [ɑ̃baʒ] *fpl* circumlocutions; **sans ambages** without beating around the bush

ambassade [ɑ̃basad] *f* embassy

ambassadeur [ɑ̃basadœr] *m* ambassador

ambassadrice [ɑ̃basadris] *f* ambassadress; wife of ambassador; emissary

ambiance [ɑ̃bjɑ̃s] *f* environment, milieu; atmosphere, tone

ambidextre [ɑ̃bidekstrə] *adj* ambidextrous || *mf* ambidextrous person

ambi·gu -guë [ɑ̃bigy] *adj* ambiguous || *m* ambiguousness; buffet lunch; odd mixture

ambiguïté [ɑ̃bigɥite] *f* ambiguity

ambi·tieux [ɑ̃bisjø] **-tieuse** [sjøz] *adj* ambitious

ambition [ɑ̃bisjɔ̃] *f* ambition

amble [ɑ̃bl] *m* amble

ambler [ɑ̃ble] *intr* (equit) to amble

ambre [ɑ̃br] *m*—**ambre gris** ambergris; **ambre** (**jaune** *or* **succin**) amber

ambulance [ɑ̃bylɑ̃s] *f* ambulance

ambulan·cier [ɑ̃bylɑ̃sje] **-cière** [sjer] *mf* ambulance driver or attendant

ambu·lant [ɑ̃bylɑ̃] **-lante** [lɑ̃t] *adj* ambulant || *m* railway mail clerk

ambulatoire [ɑ̃bylatwar] *adj* ambulatory; itinerant

âme [ɑm] *f* soul; spirit, heart, mind;

core (*of cable*); bore (*of cannon*); web (*of rail*); sound post (*of violin*); âme damnée evil genius; rendre l'âme to give up the ghost

améliorer [ameljɔre] *tr & ref* to ameliorate, to improve

amen [amen] *m invar* Amen

aménagement [amenaʒmɑ̃] *m* arrangement, equipping; preparation, development (*of land*); adjustment (*of taxes*); aménagements furnishings

aménager [amenaʒe] §38 *tr* to arrange, equip; to remodel; to parcel out; to grade (*a roadbed*); to feed (*a machine*); to harness (*a waterfall*)

amende [amɑ̃d] *f* fine; forfeit (*in a game*); faire amende honorable (coll) to apologize

amendement [amɑ̃dmɑ̃] *m* amendment; fertilizer

amender [amɑ̃de] *tr* to amend; to manure || *ref* to mend one's ways, to amend

amène [amɛn] *adj* pleasant

amener [amne] §2 *tr* to bring; to lead; to bring on; to furnish (*proof*); (naut) to lower; amener pavillon to surrender || *ref* (coll) to arrive; amenez-vous! (slang) get a move on!

aménité [amenite] *f* amenity; aménités cutting remarks

amenuiser [amənɥize] *tr* to whittle || *ref* to be whittled down

a·mer -mère [amer] *adj* bitter || *m* bitters; seamark; gall (*of animal*)

améri·cain -caine [amerikɛ̃] -caine [kɛn] *adj* American || *m* American English || *f* phaeton; bicycle relay || (*cap*) *mf* American (*person*)

américanisme [amerikanism] *m* Americanism; American studies

Amérique [amerik] *f* America; l'Amérique America

amerrir [amerir] *intr* to land, alight on water

amerrissage [amerisaʒ] *m* landing (on water); (rok) splashdown; amerrissage forcé ditching; faire un amerrissage forcé to ditch

amertume [amertym] *f* bitterness

améthyste [ametist] *f* amethyst

ameublement [amœblamɑ̃] *m* furnishings; furniture, suite

ameublir [amœblir] *tr* (agr) to soften, to mellow (*soil*)

ameuter [amøte] *tr* to rouse (*the pack*) || *ref* to riot

a·mi -mie [ami] *adj* friendly || *mf* friend || *f* mistress

amiable [amjabl] *adj* amicable; à l'amiable privately, out of court

amiante [amjɑ̃t] *m* asbestos

amibe [amib] *f* amoeba

ami·bien [amibjɛ̃] -bienne [bjɛn] *adj* amoebic

ami·cal -cale [amikal] *adj* (*pl* -caux [ko]) amicable || *f* professional club

amidon [amidɔ̃] *m* starch

amidonner [amidɔne] *tr* to starch

amincir [amɛ̃sir] *tr* to make more slender, to attenuate || *ref* to grow thinner

ami·ral [amiral] *m* (*pl* -raux [ro]) admiral

amirale [amiral] *f* admiral's wife

amirauté [amirote] *f* admiralty

amitié [amitje] *f* friendship; amitiés (complimentary close) cordially yours; faites mes amitiés à give my regards to; faites-moi l'amitié de do me the favor of

ammo·niac -niaque [amɔnjak] *adj* ammoniacal || *m* ammonia (*gas*) || *f* ammonia (*gas dissolved in water*)

amnésie [amnezi] *f* amnesia

amnistie [amnisti] *f* amnesty

amnistier [amnistje] *tr* to amnesty

amoindrir [amwɛ̃drir] *tr* to lessen || *ref* to diminish

amollir [amɔlir] *tr & ref* to soften

amollissement [amɔlismɑ̃] *m* softening

amonceler [amɔ̃sle] §34 *tr* to pile up, to gather || *ref* to pile up, to gather; to drift (*said of snow*)

amont [amɔ̃] *m* upper waters; en amont upstream; en amont de above

amorçage [amɔrsaʒ] *m* baiting; priming

amorce [amɔrs] *f* bait, lure; fuse, percussion cap; beginning; leader (*of strip of film*); (mov) preview

amorcer [amɔrse] §51 *tr* to bait; to prime; to entice; to begin

amorphe [amɔrf] *adj* amorphous

amortir [amɔrtir] *tr* to absorb (*shock*); to subdue (*color; pain; passions*); to damp (*waves*); to amortize

amortissement [amɔrtismɑ̃] *m* absorption (*of shock, sound, etc.*); amortization

amortisseur [amɔrtisœr] *m* shock absorber

amour [amur] *m* love; love affair; premières amours puppy love || (*cap*) *m* Cupid

amou·reux [amurø] -reuse [røz] *adj* amorous; loving; fond, devoted; amoureux de in love with || *m* lover || *f* sweetheart

amour-propre [amurprɔpr] *m* (*pl* amours-propres) self-esteem; vanity

amovible [amɔvibl] *adj* removable; detachable; (jur) revocable

ampère [ɑ̃per] *m* ampere

ampèremètre [ɑ̃permetr] *m* ammeter

amphibie [ɑ̃fibi] *adj* amphibious, amphibian || *m* amphibian

amphibien [ɑ̃fibjɛ̃] *m* amphibian

amphithéâtre [ɑ̃fiteatr] *m* amphitheater; auditorium (*with raised seats*)

amphitryon [ɑ̃fitrijɔ̃] *m* host at dinner || (*cap*) *m* Amphitryon

ample [ɑ̃pl] *adj* ample; long (*speech*); liberal (*reward*)

amplifica·teur [ɑ̃plifikatœr] -trice [tris] *adj* amplifying || *mf* exaggerator || *m* amplifier; (phot) enlarger

amplifier [ɑ̃plifje] *tr* to amplify, to enlarge

amplitude [ɑ̃plityd] *f* amplitude

ampoule [ɑ̃pul] *f* ampule; (elec) bulb; (pathol) blister

ampu·té -tée [ɑ̃pyte] *mf* amputee

amputer [ɑ̃pyte] *tr* to amputate; to cut (*an article, speech*)

amuïr [amyir] *ref* to become silent

amuïssement [amyismɑ̃] *m* (phonet) silencing

amulette [amylɛt] *f* amulet

amure [amyr] *f* tack (*of sail*)

amuse-gueule [amyzgœl] *m* (*pl* -gueule or -gueules) (coll) appetizer, snack

amusement [amyzmɑ̃] *m* amusement

amuser [amyze] *tr* to amuse; to mislead ‖ *ref* to have a good time; to sow one's wild oats; **s'amuser à** to pass the time by; **s'amuser de** to play with; to make fun of

amygdale [amigdal] *f* tonsil

an [ɑ̃] *m* year; **l'an de grâce** the year of Our Lord

anacarde [anakard] *m* cashew nut

anachronisme [anakrɔnism] *m* anachronism

analogie [analɔʒi] *f* analogy

analogue [analɔg] *adj* analogous; similar

analphabète [analfabɛt] *adj* & *mf* illiterate

analphabétisme [analfabetism] *m* illiteracy

analyse [analiz] *f* analysis; **analyse des renseignements** data processing

analyser [analize] *tr* to analyze

analyseur [analizœr] *m* analyzer, tester

analyste [analist] *mf* analyst

analytique [analitik] *adj* analytic(al)

ananas [anana] *m* pineapple

anarchie [anarʃi] *f* anarchy

anarchiste [anarʃist] *mf* anarchist

anathème [anatɛm] *m* anathema

anatife [anatif] *m* barnacle

anatomie [anatɔmi] *f* anatomy

anatomique [anatɔmik] *adj* anatomic(al)

ances·tral -trale [ɑ̃sɛstral] *adj* (*pl* -traux [tro]) ancestral

ancêtre [ɑ̃sɛtr] *m* ancestor

anche [ɑ̃ʃ] *f* (mus) reed

anchois [ɑ̃ʃwa] *m* anchovy

an·cien -cienne [ɑ̃sjɛ̃] *adj* ancient, old, long-standing; antiquated; antique ‖ (when standing before noun) *adj* former, previous, old; retired (*businessman*); ancient (*Greece, Rome*) ‖ *mf* senior (*in rank*); oldster; **les Anciens** the Ancients

anciennement [ɑ̃sjɛnmɑ̃] *adv* formerly

ancienneté [ɑ̃sjɛnte] *f* antiquity; seniority (*in rank*)

ancre [ɑ̃kr] *f* anchor; **ancres levées** anchors aweigh

ancrer [ɑ̃kre] *tr* & *intr* to anchor ‖ *ref* to become established

andain [ɑ̃dɛ̃] *m* swath; row of shocks

andouille [ɑ̃duj] *f* (coll) fool, sap

andouiller [ɑ̃duje] *m* antler

âne [ɑn] *m* ass, donkey

anéantir [aneɑ̃tir] *tr* to annihilate; to prostrate ‖ *ref* to disappear; to humble oneself (*before God*)

anéantissement [aneɑ̃tismɑ̃] *m* annihilation; prostration

anecdote [anɛgdɔt] *f* anecdote

anémie [anemi] *f* anemia

ânesse [anɛs] *f* she-ass

anesthésie [anɛstezi] *f* anesthesia

anesthésier [anɛstezje] *tr* to anesthetize

anesthésique [anɛstezik] *adj* & *m* anesthetic

anesthésiste [anɛstezist] *mf* anesthetist

anévrisme [anevrism] *m* aneurysm

anfractuosité [ɑ̃fraktɥozite] *f* rough outline (*of coast*); ruggedness, cragginess

ange [ɑ̃ʒ] *m* angel; **ange gardien, ange tutélaire** guardian angel; **être aux anges** to walk on air

angélique [ɑ̃ʒelik] *adj* angelic(al)

angélus [ɑ̃ʒelys] *m* Angelus

angine [ɑ̃ʒin] *f* tonsillitis, quinsy; **angine de poitrine** angina pectoris

an·glais -glaise [ɑ̃glɛ] [glɛz] *adj* English; **à l'anglaise** in the English manner; **filer à l'anglaise** to take French leave ‖ *m* English (*language*) ‖ (*cap*) *m* Englishman; **les Anglais** the English ‖ *f* Englishwoman

angle [ɑ̃gl] *m* angle; corner

Angleterre [ɑ̃glatɛr] *f* England; **l'Angleterre** England

angois·sant [ɑ̃gwasɑ̃] **angois·sante** [ɑ̃gwasɑ̃t] *adj* agonizing

angoisse [ɑ̃gwas] *f* anguish

anguille [ɑ̃gij] *f* eel; **anguille de mer** conger eel

angulaire [ɑ̃gylɛr] *adj* angular

angu·leux -leuse [ɑ̃gylø] [løz] *adj* angular, sharp

anicroche [anikrɔʃ] *f* (coll) hitch, snag

ani·mal -male [animal] *adj* animal (*pl* -maux [mo]) ‖ *m* animal, brute, beast; (coll) blockhead

anima·teur [animatœr] **-trice** [tris] *adj* animating ‖ *mf* animator, moving spirit; master of ceremonies; **animateur de théâtre** theatrical producer

animation [animasjɔ̃] *f* animation

animer [anime] *tr* to animate; to encourage ‖ *ref* to become alive, liven up

animosité [animozite] *f* animosity

anion [anjɔ̃] *m* anion

anis [ani] *m* anise

annales [anal] *fpl* annals

an·neau [ano] *m* (*pl* -neaux) ring

année [ane] *f* year; **année bissextile** leap year; **année de lumière** light-year; **bonne année** Happy New Year

année-lumière [anelymjɛr] *f* (*pl* années-lumière) light-year

annexe [anɛks] *adj* annexed ‖ *f* annex

annexer [anɛkse] *tr* to annex

annexion [anɛksjɔ̃] *f* annexation

annihiler [aniile] *tr* to annihilate

anniversaire [aniversɛr] *adj* & *m* anniversary; **anniversaire de naissance** birthday

annonce [anɔ̃s] *f* announcement; advertisement; (cards) bid; **petites annonces** classified ads

annoncer [anɔ̃se] §51 *tr* to announce; to advertise ‖ *ref* to augur; to promise to be

annonceur [anɔ̃sœr] *m* advertiser

annoncia·teur [anɔ̃sjatœr] **-trice** [tris] *adj* betokening, foreboding ‖ *m* harbinger

annoter [anɔte] *tr* to annotate

annuaire [anɥɛr] *m* annual, yearbook, directory; catalog, bulletin (*e.g., of a school*)

an·nuel -nuelle [anɥɛl] *adj* annual

annuité [anɥite] *f* annuity

annuler [anyle] *tr* to annul

ano·din [anɔdɛ̃] **-dine** [din] *adj & m* anodyne

ânon [anɔ̃] *m* foal of an ass

anonner [anɔne] *tr* to recite in a stumbling manner

anonymat [anɔnima] *m* anonymity

anonyme [anɔnim] *adj* anonymous; incorporated; (fig) colorless, drab || *mf* unidentified person

anor·mal -male [anɔrmal] (*pl* **-maux** [mo]) *adj* abnormal || *mf* abnormal person

anse [ɑ̃s] *f* handle; **faire danser l'anse du panier** to pad the bill

antagonisme [ɑ̃tagɔnism] *m* antagonism

antan [ɑ̃tɑ̃] *m* yesteryear

Antarctique [ɑ̃tarktik] *adj & m* Antarctic || *f* Antarctic (*region*); **l'Antarctique** Antarctica

antécé·dent [ɑ̃tesedɑ̃] **-dente** [dɑ̃t] *adj & m* antecedent

antenne [ɑ̃tɛn] *f* antenna (*feeler; aerial*); outpost; (naut) lateen yard; **porter à l'antenne** to put on the air

antépénultième [ɑ̃tepenyltjɛm] *adj* antepenultimate || *f* antepenult

anté·rieur -rieure [ɑ̃terjœr] *adj* anterior; former; previous, preceding; earlier; front

antériorité [ɑ̃terjɔrite] *f* priority

anthologie [ɑ̃tɔlɔʒi] *f* anthology

anthropoïde [ɑ̃trɔpɔid] *adj & m* anthropoid

anthropophage [ɑ̃trɔpɔfaʒ] *adj & mf* cannibal

antiaé·rien [ɑ̃tiɑerjɛ̃] **-rienne** [rjɛn] *adj* antiaircraft

antialcoolique [ɑ̃tialkɔɔlik] *adj* antialcoholic || *mf* teetotaler; temperance worker

antibiotique [ɑ̃tibjɔtik] *adj & m* antibiotic

antichambre [ɑ̃tiʃɑ̃br] *f* antechamber, anteroom

antichar [ɑ̃tiʃar] *adj* antitank

anticipation [ɑ̃tisipasjɔ̃] *f* anticipation; **anticipations** prophecies (*of science fiction*); **d'anticipation** science fiction (*stories, films, etc.*); **par anticipation** in advance

antici·pé -pée [ɑ̃tisipe] *adj* anticipated, advanced, ahead of time; premature (*e.g., death*)

anticiper [ɑ̃tisipe] *tr* to anticipate; to advance || *intr* to act ahead of time; **anticiper sur** to encroach on; to pay ahead of time; to spend ahead of time

anticléri·cal -cale [ɑ̃tiklerikal] *adj* (*pl* **-caux** [ko]) anticlerical

anticonception·nel -nelle [ɑ̃tikɔ̃sɛpsjɔnɛl] *adj* contraceptive

anticorps [ɑ̃tikɔr] *m* antibody

antidéra·pant [ɑ̃tiderapɑ̃] **-pante** [pɑ̃t] *adj* nonskid || *m* nonskid tire

antidéto·nant [ɑ̃tidetɔnɑ̃] **-nante** [nɑ̃t] *adj & m* antiknock

antidote [ɑ̃tidɔt] *m* antidote

antienne [ɑ̃tjɛn] *f* antiphon, anthem; **chanter toujours la même antienne** to harp on the same subject

antigel [ɑ̃tiʒɛl] *m* antifreeze

antigi·vrant [ɑ̃tiʒivrɑ̃] **-vrante** [vrɑ̃t] *adj* deicing, defrosting || *m* deicer

antigivre [ɑ̃tiʒivr] *m* deicer, defroster

Antilles [ɑ̃tij] *fpl* West Indies

antilope [ɑ̃tilɔp] *f* antelope

antimite [ɑ̃timit] *adj* mothproof || *m* moth killer

antimoine [ɑ̃timwan] *m* antimony

antiparasite [ɑ̃tiparazit] *adj* (rad) static-eliminating || *m* (rad) static eliminator; insecticide

antipathie [ɑ̃tipati] *f* antipathy

antiquaire [ɑ̃tikɛr] *m* antique dealer

antique [ɑ̃tik] *adj* antique, classic; old-fashioned || *m* antique

antiquité [ɑ̃tikite] *f* antiquity; **antiquités** antiques

antisémite [ɑ̃tisemit] *adj* anti-Semitic || *mf* anti-Semite

antisémitique [ɑ̃tisemitik] *adj* anti-Semitic

antiseptique [ɑ̃tisɛptik] *adj & m* antiseptic

antiso·cial -ciale [ɑ̃tisɔsjal] *adj* (*pl* **-ciaux** [sjo]) antisocial

antispor·tif [ɑ̃tispɔrtif] **-tive** [tiv] *adj* unsportsmanlike

antithèse [ɑ̃titɛz] *f* antithesis

antitoxine [ɑ̃titɔksin] *f* antitoxin

antitranspirant [ɑ̃titrɑ̃spirɑ̃] *m* antiperspirant

antonyme [ɑ̃tɔnim] *m* antonym

antre [ɑ̃tr] *m* den, lair; cave

anxiété [ɑ̃ksjete] *f* anxiety

anxieux [ɑ̃ksjø] **anxieuse** [ɑ̃ksjøz] *adj* anxious, worried

aorte [aɔrt] *f* aorta

août [u], [ut] *m* August

A.P. *abbr* (**assistance publique**) welfare department

apache [apaʃ] *m* apache, hoodlum

apaisement [apezmɑ̃] *m* appeasement

apaiser [apeze] *tr* to appease || *ref* to quiet down

apanage [apanaʒ] *m* attribute

aparté [aparte] *m* stage whisper, aside; **en aparté** privately

apathie [apati] *f* apathy

apathique [apatik] *adj* apathetic

apatride [apatrid] *adj* stateless || *mf* stateless person

apercevoir [apersəvwar] §59 *tr* to perceive || *ref* to notice; to realize; **s'apercevoir de** to notice, realize, be aware of

aperçu [apersy] *m* glimpse; view, look; outline

apéri·tif [aperitif] **-tive** [tiv] *adj* appetizing || *m* appetizer

aperture [apertyr] *f* (phonet) aperture

apesanteur [apəzɑ̃tœr] *f* weightlessness

à-peu-près [apøprɛ] *m invar* approximation, rough estimate

apeu·ré -rée [apœre] *adj* frightened

aphorisme [afɔrism] *m* aphorism

aphrodisiaque [afrɔdizjak] *adj* & *m* aphrodisiac

aphte [aft] *m* mouth canker, cold sore

apiculteur [apikyltœr] *m* beekeeper

apiculture [apikyltyr] *f* beekeeping

apitoiement [apitwamã] *m* compassion

apitoyant [apitwajã] **apitoyante** [apitwajãt] *adj* piteous, pitiful

apitoyer [apitwaje] §47 *tr* to move (*s.o.*) to pity || *ref*—**s'apitoyer sur** to feel compassion for

ap. J.-C. *abbr* (après Jésus-Christ) A.D.

aplanir [aplanir] *tr* to even off; to iron out (*difficulties*)

aplatir [aplatir] *tr* to flatten || *ref* to go flat; to grovel

aplomb [aplɔ̃] *m* aplomb; hang (*of gown*); (coll) cheek, rudeness; **aplombs** stand (*of horse*); **d'aplomb** plumb; steadily

apocalyptique [apɔkaliptik] *adj* apocalyptic

apocryphe [apɔkrif] *adj* apocryphal || **Apocryphes** *mpl* Apocrypha

apogée [apɔʒe] *m* apogee

Apollon [apɔllɔ̃] *m* Apollo

apologie [apɔlɔʒi] *f* apology

apophonie [apɔfɔni] *f* ablaut

apoplectique [apɔplektik] *adj* & *mf* apoplectic

apoplexie [apɔpleksi] *f* apoplexy

apostille [apɔstij] *f* endorsement

apostiller [apɔstije] *tr* to endorse

apostolat [apɔstɔla] *m* apostleship

apostrophe [apɔstrɔf] *f* apostrophe; sharp reprimand

apostropher [apɔstrɔfe] *tr* to apostrophize; to reprimand sharply

apothicaire [apɔtiker] *m* apothecary

apôtre [apotr] *m* apostle; **faire le bon apôtre** to play the hypocrite

apparaître [aparetr] §12 *intr* (aux: AVOIR or ÊTRE) to appear, come into view; to become evident

apparat [apara] *m* pomp, ostentation

apparaux [aparo] *mpl* rigging

appareil [aparej] *m* apparatus, machine, appliance; apparel; radio set; airplane; pomp, show, display; camera; telephone; (archit) bond; **à l'appareil!** speaking!; **appareil à sous** slot machine; **appareil plâtré** plaster cast

appareiller [apareje] *tr* to prepare; to bond (*stones*); to pair, match; (naut) to rig || *intr* to set sail

apparemment [aparamã] *adv* apparently

apparence [aparãs] *f* appearance

appa·rent [aparã] **-rente** [rãt] *adj* apparent

apparenter [aparãte] *tr* to relate by marriage || *ref* to become related

apparier [aparje] *tr* to pair off, to match

apparition [aparisjɔ̃] *f* apparition; appearance

apparoir [aparwar] (used only in: *inf*; 3d *sg pres ind* **appert**) *impers*—**il appert de** it follows from; **il appert que** it is evident that

appartement [apartəmã] *m* apartment

appartenance [apartənãs] *f* appurtenance

appartenir [apartənir] §72 *intr*—**appartenir à** to belong to; to pertain to || *impers*—**il appartient à qn de** it behooves s.o. to || *ref* to be one's own master

appas [apɑ] *mpl* charms; bosom

appât [apɑ] *m* bait

appâter [apɑte] *tr* to lure; to fatten up (*fowl*)

appauvrir [apovrir] *tr* to impoverish || *ref* to become impoverished

ap·peau [apo] *m* (*pl* **-peaux**) decoy; bird call

appel [apel] *m* call; appeal; summons; roll call; ring (*on telephone*); (mil) draft; **appel interurbain** long-distance call; **appel nominal** roll call; **faire l'appel** to call the roll

appe·lant [aplã] **-lante** [lãt] *adj* appellant || *mf* appellant || *m* decoy

appelé [aple] *m* draftee

appeler [aple] §34 *tr* to call; to name; to summon; to subpoena; to require; to call up, to draft || *intr* to call; to appeal (*in court*); **en appeler à** to appeal to || *ref* to be named, e.g., **elle s'appelle Marie** she is named Mary, her name is Mary

appendice [apɛ̃dis] *m* appendix

appendicectomie [apɛ̃disektɔmi] *f* appendectomy

appendicite [apɛ̃disit] *f* appendicitis

appentis [apãti] *m* lean-to

appesantir [apzãtir] *tr* to weigh down; to slow down (*e.g., bodily activity*); to make (*a burden*) heavier || *ref* to be weighed down; **s'appesantir sur** to dwell on, to expatiate on

appétis·sant [apetisã] **appétis·sante** [apetisãt] *adj* appetizing, tempting

appétit [apeti] *m* appetite

applaudir [aplodir] *tr* to applaud; **applaudir qn de** to commend, applaud s.o. for || *intr* to applaud; **applaudir à** to approve, commend, applaud || *ref*—**s'applaudir de** to congratulate oneself on, to pat oneself on the back for

applaudissement [aplodismã] *m* round of applause; **applaudissements** applause

applicable [aplikabl] *adj* applicable

application [aplikasjɔ̃] *f* application

applique [aplik] *f* appliqué; sconce

appli·qué **-quée** [aplike] *adj* industrious, studious; applied (*science*)

appliquer [aplike] *tr* to apply || *ref* to apply; to apply oneself

appoint [apwɛ̃] *m* addition; balance; aid, help; **faire l'appoint** to have the right change

appointements [apwɛ̃tmã] *mpl* salary

appointer [apwɛ̃te] *tr* to point, sharpen; to pay a salary to

appontage [apɔ̃taʒ] *m* deck-landing

appontement [apɔ̃tmã] *m* jetty (*landing pier*)

apponter [apɔ̃te] *intr* to deck-land

apport [apɔr] *m* contribution

apporter [apɔrte] *tr* to bring

apposer [apoze] *tr* to affix; to insert (*a clause in a contract*)

appréciable [apresjabl] *adj* appreciable

appréciation [apresjɑsjɔ̃] *f* appreciation, appraisal

apprécier [apresje] *tr* to appreciate

appréhender [apreɑ̃de] *tr* to apprehend; to be apprehensive about

appréhension [apreɑ̃sjɔ̃] *f* apprehension

apprendre [aprɑ̃dr] §56 *tr* to learn; **apprendre à vivre à qn** to teach s.o. manners; **apprendre q.ch. à qn** to inform s.o. of s.th.; to teach s.o. s.th. || *intr* to learn

appren·ti -tie [aprɑ̃ti] *mf* apprentice; beginner, learner

apprentissage [aprɑ̃tisaʒ] *m* apprenticeship

apprêt [apre] *m* preparation, finishing touches; **sans apprêt** unaffectedly

apprêter [aprete] *tr & ref* to prepare

apprivoi·sé -sée [aprivwaze] *adj* tame, domesticated

apprivoiser [aprivwaze] *tr* to tame; to contain (*sorrow*) || *ref* to become tame; to become sociable

approba·teur [aprɔbatœr] **-trice** [tris] *adj* approving || *m* (*slang*) yes man

approbation [aprɔbasjɔ̃] *f* approbation, approval, consent

appro·chant [aprɔʃɑ̃] **-chante** [ʃɑ̃t] *adj* similar || **approchant** *adv* thereabouts

approche [aprɔʃ] *f* approach

approcher [aprɔʃe] *tr* to approach; to draw up (*e.g., a chair*) || *intr* to approach; **approcher de** to approach, approximate || *ref* to approach, to come near; **s'approcher de** to approach, to come near to, to go up to

approfon·di -die [aprɔfɔ̃di] *adj* thorough, deep

approfondir [aprɔfɔ̃dir] *tr* to deepen; to go deep into, get to the bottom of

appropriation [aprɔprijɑsjɔ̃] *f* appropriation; adaptation

appro·prié -priée [aprɔprije] *adj* appropriate

approprier [aprɔprije] *tr* to fit, adapt || *ref* to appropriate, preempt

approuver [apruve] *tr* to approve, to approve of

approvisionnement [aprɔvizjɔnmɑ̃] *m* provisioning, stocking; **approvisionnements** supplies

approvisionner [aprɔvizjɔne] *tr* to provision, to stock || *ref* to lay in supplies

approxima·tif [aprɔksimatif] **-tive** [tiv] *adj* approximate

appui [apɥi] *m* support; endorsement

appui-bras [apɥibra] *m* (*pl* **appuis-bras**) armrest

appui-livres [apɥilivr] *m* (*pl* **appuis-livres**) book end

appui-main [apɥimɛ̃] *m* (*pl* **appuis-main**) maulstick

appui-tête [apɥitet] *m* (*pl* **appuis-tête**) headrest

appuyer [apɥije] §27 *tr* to support; to prop; to rest, lean; to endorse (*a candidate*); **appuyer le doigt sur** to push (*a button, a lever, a switch*) with the finger || *intr*—**appuyer sur** to lean on; to press (*a button*); to move (*a lever*); to pull (*a trigger*); to bear down on (*a pen or pencil*); to stress (*a syllable*) || *ref*—**s'appuyer sur** to lean on; to be based on; to rely on; (*slang*) to put up with

âpre [ɑpr] *adj* harsh, rough; bitter; greedy (*for gain*)

après [apre] *adv* after, afterward; behind; **après que** after || *prep* after; behind; **après Jésus-Christ** (ap. J.-C.) after Christ (A.D.); **d'après** after, from; by, according to

après-demain [apredəmɛ̃] *adv & m* the day after tomorrow

après-guerre [apreger] *m & f* (*pl* **-guerres**) postwar period

après-midi [apremidi] *m & f invar* afternoon

âpreté [ɑprəte] *f* harshness; bitterness

à-propos [aprɔpo] *m* opportuneness, aptness

apte [apt] *adj* apt; **apte à** suitable for

aptitude [aptityd] *f* aptitude; proficiency

apurement [apyrmɑ̃] *m* audit, check

apurer [apyre] *tr* to audit, to check

apyre [apir] *adj* fireproof

aquafortiste [akwafɔrtist] *mf* etcher

aquaplane [akwaplan] *m* aquaplane

aquarelle [akwarel] *f* watercolor

aquarium [akwarjɔm] *m* aquarium

aquatique [akwatik] *adj* aquatic

aqueduc [akdyk] *m* aqueduct

aquilin [akilɛ̃] *adj masc* aquiline

aquilon [akilɔ̃] *m* north wind

ara [ara] *m* (orn) macaw

arabe [arab] *adj* Arabian, Arab || *m* Arabic; Arab (*horse*) || (*cap*) *mf* Arabian, Arab

arachide [araʃid] *f* peanut

araignée [areɲe] *f* spider; grapnel; **araignée de mer** spider crab; **avoir une araignée dans le plafond** (coll) to have bats in the belfry

aratoire [aratwar] *adj* agricultural

arbitrage [arbitraʒ] *m* arbitration

arbitraire [arbitrer] *adj* arbitrary || *m* arbitrariness, despotism

arbitre [arbitr] *m* arbiter; arbitrator; umpire, judge; **libre arbitre** free will

arbitrer [arbitre] *tr & intr* to arbitrate; to umpire

arborer [arbɔre] *tr* to hoist (*a flag*); to show off (*new clothes*)

arbouse [arbuz] *f* arbutus berry

arbousier [arbuzje] *m* arbutus

arbre [arbr] *m* tree; (mach) arbor, shaft; **arbre de Noël** Christmas tree; **arbre généalogique** family tree

arbrisseau [arbriso] *m* (*pl* **-seaux**) bushy tree

arbuste [arbyst] *m* shrub

arc [ark] *m* bow; arch; (elec, geom) arc

arcade [arkad] *f* arcade, archway

arcanes [arkan] *mpl* mysteries, secrets

arcanson [arkɑ̃sɔ̃] *m* rosin

arc-boutant [arkbutɑ̃] *m* (*pl* **arcs-boutants**) flying buttress

arc-en-ciel [arkɑ̃sjel] *m* (*pl* **arcs-en-ciel** [arkɑ̃sjel]) rainbow

archaïque [arkaik] *adj* archaic
archaïsme [arkaism] *m* archaism
archange [arkɑ̃ʒ] *m* archangel
arche [arʃ] *f* arch (*of bridge*); Ark
archéologie [arkeɔlɔʒi] *f* archaeology
archéologue [arkeɔlɔg] *mf* archaeologist
archer [arʃe] *m* archer, bowman
archet [arʃe] *m* bow
archétype [arketip] *m* archetype
archevêque [arʃəvɛk] *m* archbishop
archiduc [arʃidyk] *m* archduke
archipel [arʃipel] *m* archipelago
archiprêtre [arʃipretr] *m* archpriest
architecte [arʃitekt] *m* architect
architecture [arʃitektyr] *f* architecture
archives [arʃiv] *fpl* archives
arçon [arsɔ̃] *m* saddletree
Arctique [arktik] *adj & m* Arctic || *f* Arctic (*region*)
ardemment [ardamɑ̃] *adv* ardently
ar·dent [ardɑ̃] **-dente** [dɑ̃t] *adj* ardent; burning; bright-red (*hair*)
ardeur [ardœr] *f* ardor; intense heat
ardoise [ardwaz] *f* slate
ardoi·sier [ardwazje] **-sière** [zjɛr] *adj* slate || *m* slate-quarry worker || *f* slate quarry
ar·du -due [ardy] *adj* steep; arduous
arène [aren] *f* arena; sand; (fig) arena; **arènes** arena, coliseum, amphitheater
arête [aret] *f* fishbone; beard (*of wheat*); angle, ridge
argent [arʒɑ̃] *m* silver; money; **argent comptant** cash
argenter [arʒɑ̃te] *tr* to silver || *ref* to turn silvery (*i.e., gray*)
argenterie [arʒɑ̃tri] *f* silver plate, silverware
argentier [arʒɑ̃tje] *m* silverware cabinet; (hist) Treasurer
argen·tin [arʒɑ̃tɛ̃] **-tine** [tin] *adj* silvery (*voice*); Argentinian || (cap) *mf* Argentinian (*person*) || **l'Argentine** *f* Argentina
argile [arʒil] *f* clay
argot [argo] *m* slang; jargon, cant
argotique [argotik] *adj* slangy
arguer [argye] (many authorities write: **j'argue, tu argues**, etc.) *tr* to argue, imply; **arguer de faux** to doubt the authenticity of (*a document*) || *intr* to draw a conclusion; **arguer de** to use as a pretext
argument [argymɑ̃] *m* argument
argumentation [argymɑ̃tɑsjɔ̃] *f* argumentation
argumenter [argymɑ̃te] *intr* to argue
argus [argys] *m* look-out, spy; price list, book (*e.g., for used cars*); **argus de la presse** clipping service
aria [arja] *m* (coll) fuss, bother || *f* aria
aride [arid] *adj* arid; (*subject, speaker, etc.*) dry
aridité [aridite] *f* aridity; (fig) dryness, dullness
aristocrate [aristɔkrat] *adj* aristocratic || *mf* aristocrat
aristocratie [aristɔkrasi] *f* aristocracy
Aristote [aristɔt] *m* Aristotle
arithméti·cien [aritmetisjɛ̃] **-cienne** [sjɛn] *mf* arithmetician

arithmétique [aritmetik] *f* arithmetic
arlequin [arləkɛ̃] *m* goulash; wrench || (cap) *m* Harlequin
armateur [armatœr] *m* ship outfitter; shipowner
armature [armatyr] *f* framework; keeper (*of a horseshoe magnet*); (mus) key signature
arme [arm] *f* arm; weapon; **arme blanche** cold steel; steel blade; **armes portatives** small arms; **faire ses premières armes** to make one's début
armée [arme] *f* army
armement [armǝmɑ̃] *m* armament; fire power; (naut) outfitting
armé·nien [armenjɛ̃] **-nienne** [njɛn] *adj* Armenian || *m* Armenian (*language*) || (cap) *mf* Armenian (*person*)
armer [arme] *tr* to arm; to cock (*a gun*); to reinforce (*concrete*); **armer chevalier** to knight || *ref* to arm oneself, to arm
armistice [armistis] *m* armistice
armoire [armwar] *f* wardrobe, closet; **armoire à pharmacie** medicine cabinet; **armoire frigorifique** freezer
armoiries [armwari] *fpl* arms, coat of arms
armoise [armwaz] *f* sagebrush
armorier [armɔrje] *tr* to emblazon
armure [armyr] *f* armor; (tex) weave
aromatique [arɔmatik] *adj* aromatic
arôme [arom] *m* aroma
aronde [arɔ̃d] *f* swallow
arpège [arpeʒ] *m* arpeggio
arpent [arpɑ̃] *m* acre
arpentage [arpɑ̃taʒ] *m* surveying
arpenter [arpɑ̃te] *tr* to survey; (coll) to pace (*the floor*)
arpenteur [arpɑ̃tœr] *m* surveyor
ar·qué -quée [arke] *adj* arched, bowed; cambered (*beam*); hooked (*nose*)
arquer [arke] *tr* to arch, to bow || *ref* to arch, to be bowed
arraché [araʃe] *m* (sports) lift
arrache-clou [araʃklu] *m* (*pl* **-clous**) claw hammer
arrache-pied [araʃpje] *adv*—**d'arrache-pied** at a stretch, without stopping
arracher [araʃe] *tr* to dig up, uproot, tear out, pull out; to wheedle (*money; a confession*); **arracher q.ch. à qn** to take away, snatch, or pry s.th. from s.o.; **arracher q.ch. de q.ch.** to pull s.th. off, from, or out of s.th.; to strip s.th. of s.th.; **arracher qn à** to deliver s.o. from (*evil; temptation; death*); **arracher qn de** to make s.o. get out of (*e.g., bed*) || *ref* to tear oneself away
arra·cheur [araʃœr] **-cheuse** [ʃøz] *mf* puller || *f* (mach) picker
arraisonnement [arezɔnmɑ̃] *m* port inspection
arraisonner [arezɔne] *tr* to inspect (*a ship*)
arrangement [arɑ̃ʒmɑ̃] *m* arrangement
arranger [arɑ̃ʒe] §38 *tr* to arrange; to settle (*a difficulty*); to fix (*to repair; to punish*) || *ref* to be arranged; to get ready; to agree
arrérages [areraʒ] *mpl* arrears
arrestation [arestɑsjɔ̃] *f* arrest

arrêt [arɛ] *m* stop; stopping; arrest; decree; **arrêt complet** standstill; **arrêt facultatif** whistle stop; **mettre aux arrêts** to keep in, to confine to quarters

arrê·té -tée [arete] *adj* stopped, standing; decided, fixed ‖ *m* decree; authorization; (com) closing out (*of an account*); **arrêté de police** police ordinance; **prendre un arrêté** to pass a decree

arrêter [arete] *tr* to stop; to arrest; to fix (*one's gaze*); to settle, decide upon; to hire, engage; to point (*game, as hunting dog does*) ‖ *intr* to stop; to point (*said of hunting dog*) ‖ *ref* to stop; **s'arrêter à** to decide on; **s'arrêter de** + *inf* to stop + *ger*

arrhes [ar] *fpl* deposit, down payment

arriération [arjerasjɔ̃] *f* retardation

arrière [arjer] *adj invar* back, rear; tail (*wind*) ‖ *m* back, rear; stern; **à l'arrière** in back; astern; **en arrière** backward; **en arrière de** behind ‖ *adv* back

arrié·ré -rée [arjere] *adj* backward; delinquent (*in payment*); back (*pay, taxes, etc.*); old-fashioned ‖ *mf* backward child ‖ *m* arrears; back pay; back payment; backlog

arrière-boutique [arjerbutik] *f* (*pl* -boutiques) back room (*of a shop*)

arrière-cour [arjerkur] *f* (*pl* -cours) backyard

arrière-garde [arjergard] *f* (*pl* -gardes) rear guard

arrière-goût [arjergu] *m* (*pl* -goûts) aftertaste

arrière-grand-mère [arjergrɑ̃mɛr] *f* (*pl* -grand-mères) great-grandmother

arrière-grand-père [arjergrɑ̃pɛr] *m* (*pl* -grands-pères) great-grandfather

arrière-pays [arjerpei] *m invar* back country

arrière-pensée [arjerpɑ̃se] *f* (*pl* -pensées) mental reservation, ulterior motive

arrière-plan [arjerplɑ̃] *m* (*pl* -plans) background

arriérer [arjere] §10 *tr* to delay ‖ *ref* to fall behind (*in payment*)

arrière-train [arjertrɛ̃] *m* (*pl* -trains) rear (*of a vehicle*); hindquarters

arrimage [arimaʒ] *m* stowage; docking (*of space vehicle*)

arrimer [arime] *tr* to stow

arrimeur [arimœr] *m* stevedore

arrivage [arivaʒ] *m* arrival (*of goods or ships*)

arrivée [arive] *f* arrival; intake; (sports) finish, goal; **arrivée en douceur** (rok) soft landing

arriver [arive] *intr* (*aux:* ÊTRE) to arrive; to succeed; to happen; **arriver à** to attain, reach; **en arriver à** + *inf* to be reduced to + *ger*

arriviste [arivist] *mf* upstart, parvenu

arrogance [arɔgɑ̃s] *f* arrogance

arro·gant [arɔgɑ̃] **-gante** [gɑ̃t] *adj* arrogant

arroger [arɔʒe] §38 *ref* to arrogate to oneself

arrondir [arɔ̃dir] *tr* to round, round off, round out ‖ *ref* to become round

arrondissement [arɔ̃dismɑ̃] *m* district

arrosage [arozaʒ] *m* sprinkling; irrigation; (mil) heavy bombing

arroser [aroze] *tr* to sprinkle, to water; to irrigate; to flow through (*e.g., a city*); to wash down (*a meal*); (coll) to bribe; (coll) to drink to (*a success*)

arro·seur [arozœr] **-seuse** [zøz] *mf* sprinkler (*person*) ‖ *f* street sprinkler

arrosoir [arozwar] *m* sprinkling can

arse·nal [arsənal] *m* (*pl* -naux [no]) shipyard, navy yard; (fig) storehouse; (archaic) arsenal, armory

arsenic [arsənik] *m* arsenic

art [ar] *m* art; **arts d'agréments** music, drawing, dancing, etc.; **arts ménagers** home economics; **le huitième art** television; **les arts du spectacle** the performing arts; **le septième art** the cinema

artère [arter] *f* artery

arté·riel -rielle [arterjel] *adj* arterial

artériosclé·reux [arterjosklerø] **-reuse** [røz] *adj* & *mf* arteriosclerotic

arté·sien [artezjɛ̃] **-sienne** [zjen] *adj* of Artois; artesian (*well*)

arthrite [artrit] *f* arthritis

artichaut [artiʃo] *m* artichoke

article [artikl] *m* article; entry (*in a dictionary*); **à l'article de la mort** on the point of death; **article de fond** leader; editorial; **article de tête** front-page story; **articles divers** sundries

articuler [artikyle] *tr* & *ref* to articulate

artifice [artifis] *m* artifice; craftsmanship

artifi·ciel -cielle [artifisjel] *adj* artificial

artificier [artifisje] *m* fireworks maker; soldier in charge of ammunition supply

artifi·cieux [artifisjø] **-cieuse** [sjøz] *adj* artful, cunning

artillerie [artijori] *f* artillery

artilleur [artijœr] *m* artilleryman

arti·san [artizɑ̃] **-sane** [zan] *mf* artisan, artificer ‖ *m* craftsman

artiste [artist] *adj* artistic; artist, of art, e.g., **le monde artiste** the world of art ‖ *mf* artist; actor

artistique [artistik] *adj* artistic

ar·yen [arjɛ̃] **-yenne** [jen] *adj* Aryan ‖ (*cap*) *mf* Aryan (*person*)

as [as] *m* ace; **as du volant** speed king

A.S. *abbr* (**assurances sociales**) social security

a/s *abbr* (**aux bons soins de**) c/o

asbeste [asbest] *m* asbestos

ascendance [asɑ̃dɑ̃s] *f* lineal ancestry; rising (*of air; of star*)

ascenseur [asɑ̃sœr] *m* elevator

ascension [asɑ̃sjɔ̃] *f* ascension; **Ascension** *f* Ascension Day

ascèse [asez] *f* asceticism

ascète [aset] *mf* ascetic

ascétique [asetik] *adj* ascetic

ascétisme [asetism] *m* asceticism

aseptique [aseptik] *adj* aseptic

Asie [azi] *f* Asia; **Asie Mineure** Asia Minor; **l'Asie** Asia; **l'Asie Mineure** Asia Minor

asile [azil] *m* asylum, shelter, home
aspect [aspe], [aspek] *m* aspect
asperge [asperʒ] *f* asparagus; **des asperges** asparagus (*stalks and tips used as food*)
asperger [asperʒe] §38 *tr* to sprinkle
aspérité [asperite] *f* roughness; harshness; gruffness
aspersion [aspersjɔ̃] *f* sprinkling
asphalte [asfalt] *m* asphalt
asphyxier [asfiksje] *tr* to asphyxiate ‖ *ref* to be asphyxiated
aspic [aspik] *m* asp
aspi·rant [aspirɑ̃] **-rante** [rɑ̃t] *adj* aspirant, aspiring; suction (*pump*) ‖ *mf* candidate (*for a degree*) ‖ *m* midshipman
aspirateur [aspiratœr] *m* vacuum cleaner; **aspirateur de buée** kitchen fan
aspi·ré -rée [aspire] *adj & m* (phonet) aspirate
aspirer [aspire] *tr* to inhale; to suck in ‖ *intr*—**aspirer à** to aspire to
aspirine [aspirin] *f* aspirin
assagir [asaʒir] *tr* to make wiser ‖ *ref* to become wiser
assail·lant [asajɑ̃] **assail-lante** [asajɑ̃t] *adj* attacking ‖ *mf* assailant
assaillir [asajir] §69 *tr* to assail, to assault
assainir [asenir] *tr* to purify, to clean up; to drain (*a swamp*)
assainissement [asenismɑ̃] *m* purification; draining
assaisonnement [asezɔnmɑ̃] *m* seasoning
assaisonner [asezɔne] *tr* to season, to flavor
assas·sin [asasɛ̃] **assas·sine** [asasin] *adj* murderous ‖ *m* assassin
assassinat [asasina] *m* assassination
assassiner [asasine] *tr* to assassinate; (coll) to bore to death
assaut [aso] *m* assault
assèchement [aseʃmɑ̃] *m* drainage, drying; dryness
assécher [aseʃe] §10 *tr* to drain, to dry up
assemblage [asɑ̃blaʒ] *m* assemblage; assembling (*e.g., of printed pages*); (woodworking) joint, joining
assemblée [asɑ̃ble] *f* assembly, meeting
assembler [asɑ̃ble] *tr* to assemble ‖ *ref* to assemble, convene, meet
assener [asne] §2 *tr* to land (*a blow*)
assentiment [asɑ̃timɑ̃] *m* assent, consent
asseoir [aswar] §5 *tr* to seat, sit, place; to base (*an opinion*) ‖ *ref* to sit down
assermen·té -tée [asermɑ̃te] *adj* under oath
assertion [asersjɔ̃] *f* assertion
asser·vi -vie [aservi] *adj* subservient
asservir [aservir] *tr* to enslave; to subdue (*e.g., passions*) ‖ *ref* to submit (*to convention; to tyranny*)
asservissement [aservismɑ̃] *m* enslavement; subservience
assesseur [asesœr] *adj & m* assistant; associate (*judge*)
assez [ase] *adv* enough; fairly; rather; **assez de** enough; **en voilà assez!**

that's enough!, cut it out! ‖ *interj* enough!, stop!
assi·du -due [asidy] *adj* assiduous; attentive
assidûment [asidymɑ̃] *adv* assiduously
assié·geant [asjeʒɑ̃] **-geante** [ʒɑ̃t] *adj* besieging ‖ *mf* besieger
assiéger [asjeʒe] §1 *tr* to besiege
assiette [asjet] *f* plate, dish; plateful; seat (*of a rider on horseback*); position, condition; **assiette anglaise, assiette de viandes froides** cold cuts; **assiette au beurre** (fig) gravy train; **assiette creuse** soup plate
assignation [asiɲasjɔ̃] *f* assignation; subpoena, summons
assi·gné -gnée [asiɲe] *mf* appointee; **assigné à résidence** permanent appointee; **assigné intérim** temporary appointee
assigner [asiɲe] *tr* to assign, allot; to fix (*a date*); to subpoena, summon
assimilable [asimilabl] *adj* assimilable; comparable
assimilation [asimilasjɔ̃] *f* assimilation
assimiler [asimile] *tr* to assimilate; to compare; to identify with ‖ *ref* to assimilate
as·sis [asi] **as·sise** [asiz] *adj* seated, sitting; firmly established ‖ *f* foundation; stratum; **assises** assizes
assistance [asistɑ̃s] *f* assistance; audience, persons present; presence; **assistance judiciaire** public defender; **assistance publique** welfare department; **assistance sociale** social service
assis·tant [asistɑ̃] **-tante** [tɑ̃t] *adj* assistant ‖ *mf* assistant; bystander, spectator; **assistante sociale** public health nurse
assister [asiste] *tr* to assist, help ‖ *intr*—**assister à** to attend, be present at
association [asɔsjasjɔ̃] *f* association; (sports) soccer; **association des spectateurs** theater club
asso·cié -ciée [asɔsje] *adj & mf* associate
associer [asɔsje] *tr* to associate ‖ *ref* to go into partnership
assoif·fé -fée [aswafe] *adj* thirsty
assolement [asɔlmɑ̃] *m* rotation (*of crops*)
assombrir [asɔ̃brir] *tr & ref* to darken
assom·mant [asɔmɑ̃] **assom·mante** [asɔmɑ̃t] *adj* (coll) boring, fatiguing
assommer [asɔme] *tr* to kill with a heavy blow; to beat up; to stun; (coll) to heckle; (coll) to bore
assommoir [asɔmwar] *m* bludgeon; (coll) gin mill, dive, clip joint
Assomption [asɔ̃psjɔ̃] *f* Assumption
assonance [asɔnɑ̃s] *f* assonance
assor·ti -tie [asɔrti] *adj* assorted (*e.g., cakes*); well-matched (*couple*); stocked, supplied (*store*); to match, e.g., **une cravate assortie** a necktie to match
assortiment [asɔrtimɑ̃] *m* assortment; matching (*of colors*); set (*of dishes*); platter (*of cold cuts*)
assortir [asɔrtir] *tr* to assort, match;

to stock || *ref* to match, harmonize; s'**assortir de** to be accompanied with

assoupir [asupir] *tr* to make drowsy, to lull; to deaden (*pain*) || *ref* to doze off; to lessen (*with time*)

assoupissement [asupismã] *m* drowsiness; lethargy

assouplir [asuplir] *tr* to make supple, flexible; to break in (*a horse*) || *ref* to become supple, manageable

assouplissement [asuplismã] *m* suppleness, flexibility; limbering up; relaxation (*of a rule*)

assourdir [asurdir] *tr* to deafen; to tone down, muffle

assouvir [asuvir] *tr* to assuage, appease, satiate; to satisfy (*e.g.*, *a thirst for vengeance*)

assouvissement [asuvismã] *m* assuagement, appeasement, satisfying

assujet·ti -tie [asyʒeti] *adj* fastened; subject, liable || *mf* taxpayer; contributor (*e.g.*, *to social security*)

assujettir [asyʒetir] *tr* to subjugate; to subject; to fasten, secure || *ref* to submit

assujettis·sant [asyʒetisã] **assujetissante** [asyʒetisãt] *adj* demanding

assujettissement [asyʒetismã] *m* subjugation, subduing; submission (*to a stronger force*); fastening, securing

assumer [asyme] *tr* to assume, take upon oneself

assurance [asyrãs] *f* assurance; insurance; **assurances sociales** social security

assu·ré -rée [asyre] *adj* assured, satisfied; insured || *mf* insured

assurément [asyremã] *adv* assuredly

assurer [asyre] *tr* to assure; to secure; to insure || *ref* to be assured; to make sure; to be insured

astate [astat] *m* astatine

aster [aster] *m* (bot) aster

astérie [asteri] *f* starfish

astérisque [asterisk] *m* asterisk

asthénie [asteni] *f* debility

asthme [asm] *m* asthma

asticot [astiko] *m* maggot

astiquer [astike] *tr* to polish

as·tral -trale [astral] *adj* (*pl* **-traux** [tro]) astral

astre [astrə] *m* star, heavenly body; leading light; **astre de la nuit** moon; **astre du jour** sun

astreindre [astrɛ̃dr] §50 *tr* to force, compel, subject || *ref* to force oneself; to be subjected

astrologie [astrolɔʒi] *f* astrology

astrologue [astrolɔg] *m* astrologer

astronaute [astronot] *mf* astronaut

astronautique [astronotik] *f* astronautics

astronef [astronef] *m* spaceship

astronome [astronɔm] *mf* astronomer

astronomie [astronɔmi] *f* astronomy

astronomique [astronɔmik] *adj* astronomical

astuce [astys] *f* slyness, guile; tricks (*of a trade*)

astu·cieux -cieuse [astysjø] [sjøz] *adj* astute, crafty

atelier [atəlje] *m* studio; workshop

atermolement [atermwamã] *m* procrastination; extension of a loan

athée [ate] *adj* atheistic || *mf* atheist

athéisme [ateism] *m* atheism

Athènes [aten] *f* Athens

athlète [atlet] *mf* athlete

athlétique [atletik] *adj* athletic

athlétisme [atletism] *m* athletics

Atlantique [atlãtik] *adj & m* Atlantic

atlas [atlas] *m* atlas || (*cap*) *m* Atlas

atmosphère [atmosfer] *f* atmosphere

atome [atom] *m* atom

atomique [atomik] *adj* atomic

atomi·sé -sée [atomize] *adj* afflicted with radiation sickness

atomiser [atomize] *tr* to atomize

atone [aton] *adj* dull, expressionless; drab (*life*); (phonet) unaccented

atours [atur] *mpl* finery

atout [atu] *m* trump; **sans atout** no-trump

atrabilaire [atrabiler] *adj & mf* hypochondriac

âtre [ɑtr] *m* hearth

atroce [atrɔs] *adj* atrocious

atrocité [atrosite] *f* atrocity

atrophie [atrofi] *f* atrophy

atrophier [atrofje] *tr & ref* to atrophy

atta·chant [ata/ã] **-chante** [/ãt] *adj* appealing, attractive

attache [ata/] *f* attachment, tie; paper clip; (anat) joint; **attache parisienne** paper clip

attachement [ata/mã] *m* attachment

attacher [ata/e] *tr* to attach; to tie up || *intr* (culin) to stick || *ref* to be fastened, tied; **s'attacher à** to stick to; to become devoted to

attaque [atak] *f* attack; (pathol) stroke; **attaque brusque** or **attaque brusquée** surprise attack; **attaque de nerfs** case of nerves

attaquer [atake] *tr & intr* to attack || *ref*—**s'attaquer à** to attack

attar·dé -dée [atarde] *adj* retarded; behind the times; belated, delayed || *mf* mentally retarded person; lover of the past

attarder [atarde] *tr* to delay, retard || *ref* to be delayed; to stay, remain

atteindre [atɛ̃dr] §50 *tr* to attain; to reach || *intr*—**atteindre à** to attain; to reach; to attain to

at·teint [atɛ̃] **at·teinte** [atɛ̃t] *adj* stricken || *f* reaching; injury; **hors d'atteinte** out of reach; **porter atteinte à** to endanger; **premières atteintes** first signs (*of illness*)

attelage [atlaʒ] *m* harnessing; coupling

atteler [atle] §34 *tr* to harness; to hitch; to couple (*cars on a railroad*) || *ref*—**s'atteler à** (coll) to buckle down to

attelle [atel] *m* splint; **attelles** hames

atte·nant [atənã] **-nante** [nãt] *adj* adjoining

attendre [atɑ̃dr] *tr* to wait for, await; to expect || *intr* to wait || *ref*—**s'attendre à** to expect; to rely on; **s'attendre à + inf** to expect to + *inf*; **s'attendre à ce que + subj** to expect (*s.o.*) to + *inf*, e.g., **il s'attend à ce que je lui raconte toute l'affaire** he expects me to tell him the whole story; **s'y attendre** to expect it or them

attendrir [atɑ̃drir] *tr* to tenderize; to soften || *ref* to become tender; to be deeply touched or moved

attendrissement [atɑ̃drismɑ̃] *m* softening; compassion

atten·du ·due [atɑ̃dy] *adj* expected || **attendus** *mpl* (law) grounds || *adv*— **attendu que** whereas, inasmuch as || **attendu** *prep* in view of

attentat [atɑ̃ta] *m* attempt, assault; outrage (*to decency*); offense (*against the state*)

attente [atɑ̃t] *f* wait; expectation

attenter [atɑ̃te] *intr*—**attenter à** to attempt (*e.g., s.o.'s life*); **attenter à ses jours** to attempt suicide

atten·tif ·tive [atɑ̃tif] -**tive** [tiv] *adj* attentive

attention [atɑ̃sjɔ̃] *f* attention; **attentions** attention, care, consideration || *interj* attention!, be careful!

attention·né ·née [atɑ̃sjone] *adj* considerate

atténuation [atenɥasjɔ̃] *f* attenuation

atténuer [atenɥe] *tr* to subdue, soften (*color; pain; passions*); to attenuate (*words; bacteria*); to extenuate (*a fault*) || *ref* to soften; to lessen

atterrer [atere] *tr* to dismay

atterrir [aterir] *intr* (*aux:* AVOIR or ÊTRE) to land

atterrissage [aterisaʒ] *m* landing; **atterrissage forcé** forced landing; **atterrissage sur le ventre** pancake landing

attestation [atestasjɔ̃] *f* attestation; **attestation d'études** transcript

attester [ateste] *tr* to attest, to attest to; **attester qu de q.ch.** to call s.o. to witness to s.th.

attiédir [atjedir] *tr* & *ref* to cool off; to warm up

attifer [atife] *tr* & *ref* to spruce up

attirail [atiraj] *m* gear, tackle, outfit; (coll) paraphernalia

attirance [atirɑ̃s] *f* attraction, lure, attractiveness

atti·rant [atirɑ̃] -**rante** [rɑ̃t] *adj* appealing, attractive

attirer [atire] *tr* to attract || *ref* to be attracted; to attract each other; to call forth (*criticism*)

attiser [atize] *tr* to stir, stir up, to poke

atti·tré ·trée [atitre] *adj* appointed; regular (*dealer*)

attitude [atityd] *f* attitude

attrac·tif ·tive [atraktif] -**tive** [tiv] *adj* attractive (*force*)

attraction [atraksjɔ̃] *f* attraction; **les attractions** vaudeville

attrait [atre] *m* attraction, attractiveness, appeal; **attraits** charms

attrape [atrap] *f* trap; (coll) trick, joke

attrape-mouche [atrapmuʃ] *m* (*pl* -**mouche** or -**mouches**) flypaper; Venus's-flytrap

attrape-nigaud [atrapnigo] *m* (*pl* -**nigauds**) booby trap

attraper [atrape] *tr* to catch; to snare,

trap; to trick || *ref* to trick each other; to hang on

attrayant [atrejɑ̃] **attrayante** [atrejɑ̃t] *adj* attractive

attribuer [atribɥe] *tr* to ascribe, attribute; to assign (*a share*) || *ref* to claim, assume

attribut [atriby] *m* attribute; predicate

attribu·tif [atribytif] -**tive** [tiv] *adj* (gram) predicative

attribution [atribysjɔ̃] *f* attribution; assignment, assignation

attris·té ·tée [atriste] *adj* sorrowful

attrister [atriste] *tr* to sadden || *ref* to become sad

attrition [atrisjɔ̃] *f* attrition

attroupement [atrupmɑ̃] *m* mob

attrouper [atrupe] *tr* to bring together in a mob || *ref* to flock together in a mob

au [o] §77

aubaine [oben] *f* windfall, godsend, bonanza

aube [ob] *f* dawn

aubépine [obepin] *f* hawthorn

auberge [oberʒ] *f* inn; **auberge de la jeunesse** youth hostel

aubergine [oberʒin] *f* eggplant

au·cun [okɑ̃] -**cune** [kyn] *adj*—**aucun . . . ne** or **ne . . . aucun** §90 no, none, not any || *pron indef*—**aucun ne** §90B no one, nobody; **d'aucuns** some, some people

aucunement [okynmɑ̃] §90 *adv*—**ne . . . aucunement** not at all, by no means

audace [odas] *f* audacity

auda·cieux [odasjø] -**cieuse** [sjøz] *adj* audacious

au-deçà [odəsa] *adv* (obs) on this side; **au-deçà de** (obs) on this side of

au-dedans [odədɑ̃] *adv* inside; **au-dedans de** inside, inside of

au-dehors [odəɔr] *adv* outside; **au-dehors de** outside, outside of

au-delà [odəla] *m*—**l'au-delà** the beyond || *adv* beyond; **au-delà de** beyond

au-dessous [odəsu] *adv* below; **au-dessous de** under

au-dessus [odəsy] *adv* above; **au-dessus de** above

au-devant [odəvɑ̃] *adv*—**aller au-devant de** to go to meet; to anticipate (*s.o.'s wishes*); to court (*defeat*)

audience [odjɑ̃s] *f* audience

audio-fréquence [odjofrekɑ̃s] *f* audio frequency

audiomètre [odjometr] *m* audiometer

audi·teur [oditœr] -**trice** [tris] *mf* listener; auditor (*in class*); **auditeur libre** auditor (*in class*)

audi·tif [oditif] -**tive** [tiv] *adj* auditory

audition [odisjɔ̃] *f* audition; public hearing; musical recital

auditionner [odisjone] *tr* & *intr* to audition

auditoire [oditwar] *m* audience; courtroom

auditorium [oditorjom] *m* auditorium; concert hall; projection room

auge [oʒ] *f* trough

augmentation [ɔgmɑ̃tɑsjɔ̃] *f* augmentation; raise (*in salary*)

augmenter [ɔgmɑ̃te] *tr* to augment; to increase or supplement (*income*); to raise (*prices*); to raise the salary of (*an employee*) || *intr* to augment, increase; **augmenter de** to increase by (*a stated amount*)

augure [ɔgyr] *m* augur; augury

augurer [ɔgyre] *tr & intr* to augur

auguste [ɔgyst] *adj* august

aujourd'hui [oʒurdɥi], [oʒurdɥi] *m & adv* today; **d'aujourd'hui en huit** a week from today; **d'aujourd'hui en quinze** two weeks from today

aumône [omon] *f* alms; **faire l'aumône** to give alms; **faire l'aumône de** (fig) to hand out

aumônier [omonje] *m* chaplain

aune [on] *m* alder || *f* ell

auparavant [oparavɑ̃] *adv* before, previously

auprès [opre] *adv* close by, in the neighborhood; **auprès de** near, close to; at the side of; to, at the side of; to (*a king, a government*); with; compared with

auquel [okel] (*pl* **auxquels**) §78

auréole [ɔreɔl] *f* aureole, halo

auréomycine [ɔreɔmisin] *f* aureomycin

auriculaire [ɔrikyler] *adj* firsthand (*witness*); auricular (*confession*) || *m* little finger

auricule [ɔrikyl] *f* auricle

aurifier [ɔrifje] *tr* to fill (*a tooth*) with gold

aurore [ɔrɔr] *f* aurora, dawn

ausculter [ɔskylte] *tr* to auscultate

auspice [ospis] *m* omen; **sous les auspices de** under the auspices of

aussi [osi] *adv* also, too; therefore, and so; so; **aussi . . . que** as . . . as

aussitôt [osito] *adv* right away, immediately; **aussitôt dit, aussitôt fait** no sooner said than done; **aussitôt que** as soon as

austère [ɔster] *adj* austere

Australie [ɔstrali] *f* Australia; **l'Australie** Australia

austra-lien [ɔstraljɛ̃] **-lienne** [ljen] *adj* Australian || (*cap*) *mf* Australian

autant [otɑ̃] *adv* as much, as many; as far, as long; **autant de** so many; **autant que** as much as, as far as; **d'autant** by so much; **d'autant plus** all the more; **d'autant plus** (or **moins**) . . . **que** . . . plus (or **moins**) all the more (or less) . . . as (or in proportion as) . . . more (or less); **d'autant que** inasmuch as

autel [ɔtel], [otel] *m* altar

auteur [otœr] *adj—une femme auteur** an authoress || *m* author

authentifier [otɑ̃tifje] *tr* to authenticate

authentique [otɑ̃tik] *adj* authentic; genuine (*antique*); notarized

authentiquer [otɑ̃tike] *tr* to notarize

auto [oto], [oto] *f* auto

auto-allumage [otoalymaʒ] *m* preignition

autobiographie [otɔbjɔgrafi] *f* autobiography

auto-buffet [otobyfɛ] *m* drive-in; curb service

autobus [otobys] *m* bus, city bus

autocar [otokar] *m* interurban bus

autochenille [otoʃənij] *f* caterpillar (*tractor*)

autochtone [otɔktɔn] *adj & mf* native

autoclave [otoklav] *m* pressure cooker; autoclave, sterilizer

autocopie [otokopi] *f* duplicating, multicopying; duplicated copy

autocopier [otokopje] *tr* to run off, to duplicate, to ditto

auto-couchette [otokuʃet] *f—en auto-couchette** piggyback

autocrate [otokrat] *mf* autocrat

autocratique [otokratik] *adj* autocratic

autocritique [otokritik] *f* self-criticism

autocuiseur [otokɥizœr] *m* pressure cooker

autodétermination [otodeterminɑsjɔ̃] *f* self-determination

autodidacte [otodidakt] *adj* self-taught || *mf* self-taught person

autodrome [otodrom] *m* race track; test strip

auto-école [otoekɔl] *f* (*pl* **-écoles**) driving school

autogare [otogar] *f* bus station

autographe [otograf] *adj & m* autograph

autographie [otografi] *f* multicopying

autographier [otografje] *tr* to duplicate

autogreffe [otogref] *f* skin grafting

auto-grue [otogry] *f* (*pl* **-grues**) tow truck

autoguidage [otogidaʒ] *m* automatic piloting

auto-intoxication [otoɛ̃tɔksikɑsjɔ̃] *f* autointoxication

automate [otomat] *m* automaton

automation [otomasjɔ̃] *f* automation

automatique [otomatik] *adj* automatic || *m* dial telephone

automatisation [otomatizɑsjɔ̃] *f* automation

automatiser [otomatize] *tr* to automate

automitrailleuse [otomitrajøz] *f* armored car mounting machine guns

autom-nal -nale [otomnal] *adj* (*pl* **-naux** [no]) autumnal

automne [otɔn], [oton] *m* fall, autumn; **à l'automne, en automne** in the fall

automobile [otomɔbil], [otomobil] *adj* automotive || *f* automobile

automobilisme [otomɔbilism] *m* driving, motoring

automobiliste [otomɔbilist] *mf* motorist

automo-teur [otomotœr] **-trice** [tris] *adj* self-propelling, automatic || *m* self-propelled river barge || *f* rail car

autonome [otonom] *adj* autonomous, independent

autonomie [otonomi] *f* autonomy; cruising radius, range (*of ship, plane, or tank*)

autoplastie [otoplasti] *f* plastic surgery

autoportrait [otoportre] *m* self-portrait

auto-propul-sé -sée [otopropylse] *adj* self-propelled

autopsie [otopsi] *f* autopsy

autopsier [otopsje] *tr* to perform an autopsy on

autorail [ɔtɔraj] m rail car

autorisation [ɔtɔrizasjɔ̃] f authorization

autoriser [ɔtɔrize] tr to authorize || ref —s'autoriser de to take as authority, to base one's opinion on

autoritaire [ɔtɔriter] adj authoritarian, bossy

autorité [ɔtɔrite] f authority

autoroute [ɔtɔrut] f superhighway

auto-stop [ɔtɔstɔp] m hitchhiking; faire de l'auto-stop to hitchhike

auto-stop·peur [ɔtɔstɔpœr] -stop·peuse [stɔpøz] mf (pl -stop·peurs -stop·peuses) hitchhiker

autostrade [ɔtɔstrad] f superhighway

autour [otur] m goshawk || adv around; autour de around; about

autre [otr] adj indef other; autre chose (coll) something else; nous autres we, e.g., nous autres Américains we Americans; vous autres you || pron indef other; d'autres others; j'en ai vu bien d'autres I have seen worse than that; un autre another

autrefois [otrəfwa] adv formerly, of old; d'autrefois of yore

autrement [otrəmɑ̃] adv otherwise

Autriche [otriʃ] f Austria; l'Autriche Austria

autri·chien [otriʃjɛ̃] -chienne [ʃjen] adj Austrian || (cap) mf Austrian

autruche [otryʃ] f ostrich

autrui [otrɥi] pron indef others

auvent [ovɑ̃] m canopy (over door); flap (of tent)

aux [o] §77

auxiliaire [oksiljer] adj auxiliary, standby; ancillary || m (gram) auxiliary || f noncombatant unit

aux-quels -quelles [okel] §78

aval [aval] m lower waters; en aval downstream; en aval de below || m (pl avals) endorsement

avalanche [avalɑ̃ʃ] f avalanche

avaler [avale] tr to swallow || intr to go downstream

ava·leur [avalœr] -leuse [løz] mf swallower; avaleur de sabres sword swallower

avaliser [avalize] tr to endorse

avance [avɑ̃s] f advance; en avance fast (clock)

avan·cé -cée [avɑ̃se] adj advanced; overripe; tainted (meat)

avancement [avɑ̃smɑ̃] m advancement

avancer [avɑ̃se] §51 tr, intr, & ref to advance

avanie [avani] f snub, insult; essuyer une avanie to swallow an affront

avant [avɑ̃] adj invar front || m front; (aer) nose; (naut) bow; d'avant previous; en avant forward; en avant de in front of, ahead of || adv before; avant de (with inf) before; avant que before; bien (or très) avant late into; far into; deep into; plus avant farther on || prep before; avant Jésus-Christ (av. J.-C.) before Christ (B.C.)

avantage [avɑ̃taʒ] m advantage; (tennis) add; avantages en nature payment in kind

avanta·geux [avɑ̃taʒø] -geuse [ʒøz] adj advantageous; bargain (price); becoming (e.g., hairdo); conceited (manner)

avant-bras [avɑ̃bra] m invar forearm

avant-cour [avɑ̃kur] f (pl -cours) front yard

avant-coureur [avɑ̃kurœr] (pl -coureurs) adj masc presaging (signs) || m forerunner, precursor, harbinger

avant-goût [avɑ̃gu] m (pl -goûts) foretaste

avant-guerre [avɑ̃ger] m & f (pl -guerres) prewar period

avant-hier [avɑ̃tjer], [avɑ̃jer] adv & m the day before yesterday

avant-port [avɑ̃pɔr] m (pl -ports) outer harbor

avant-poste [avɑ̃pɔst] m (pl -postes) outpost; avant-postes front lines

avant-première [avɑ̃prəmjer] f (pl -premières) review (of a play); premiere (for the drama critics); preview

avant-projet [avɑ̃prɔʒe] m (pl -projets) rough draft; draft (of a law)

avant-propos [avɑ̃prɔpo] m invar foreword

avant-scène [avɑ̃sen] f (pl -scènes) forestage, proscenium

avant-toit [avɑ̃twa] m (pl -toits) eave

avant-train [avɑ̃trɛ̃] m (pl -trains) front end, front assembly (of vehicle)

avant-veille [avɑ̃vej] f (pl -veilles) two days before

avare [avar] adj avaricious, miserly; saving, economical || mf miser

avarice [avaris] f avarice

avari·cieux [avarisjø] -cieuse [sjøz] adj avaricious

avarie [avari] f damage; breakdown; spoilage; (naut) average

avarier [avarje] tr to damage; to spoil || ref to spoil

avatar [avatar] m avatar; avatars vicissitudes

avec [avek] adv (coll) with it; (coll) along, with me, etc. || prep with

aveline [avlin] f filbert

ave·nant [avnɑ̃] -nante [nɑ̃t] adj gracious, charming; à l'avenant in keeping, to match; à l'avenant de in accord with || m (ins) endorsement

avènement [avenmɑ̃] m Advent; accession (to the throne)

avenir [avnir] m future; à l'avenir in the future

Avent [avɑ̃] m Advent

aventure [avɑ̃tyr] f adventure; à l'aventure at random; aimlessly; d'aventure by chance; la bonne aventure fortunetelling; par aventure by chance

aventurer [avɑ̃tyre] tr to venture || ref to take a chance; s'aventurer à to venture to

aventu·reux [avɑ̃tyrø] -reuse [røz] adj adventurous

aventurier [avɑ̃tyrje] m adventurer

aventurière [avɑ̃tyrjer] f adventuress

avenue [avny] f avenue

avé·ré -rée [avere] adj established, authenticated

avérer [avere] §10 tr to aver || ref to prove to be (e.g., difficult)

avers [aver] *m* heads (*of coin*), face (*of medal*)

averse [avers] *f* shower

aversion [aversjɔ̃] *f* aversion

avertir [avertir] *tr* to warn; **avertir qn de** + *inf* to warn s.o. to + *inf*

avertissement [avertismã] *m* warning; notification; foreword

avertisseur [avertisœr] *adj masc* warning ‖ *m* alarm; (aut) horn; (theat) callboy; **avertisseur d'incendie** fire alarm

a•veu [avø] *m* (*pl* -veux) avowal, confession; consent; **sans aveu** unscrupulous

aveu•glant [avœglã] **-glante** [glãt] *adj* blinding

aveugle [avœgl] *adj* blind ‖ *mf* blind person; **en aveugle** without thinking

aveuglement [avœgləmã] *m* (fig) blindness

aveuglément [avœglemã] *adv* blindly

aveugler [avœgle] *tr* to blind; to dazzle; to stop up, to plug; to board up (*a window*) ‖ *ref*—**s'aveugler sur** to shut one's eyes to

aveuglette [avœglet] *adv*—**à l'aveuglette** blindly

aveulir [avølir] *tr* to enervate, deaden ‖ *ref* to become limp, enervated

aveulissement [avølismã] *m* enervation

aviateur [avjatœr] *m* aviator

aviation [avjasjɔ̃] *f* aviation

aviatrice [avjatris] *f* aviatrix

avide [avid] *adj* avid, eager; greedy; voracious; **avide de** avid for

avidité [avidite] *f* avidity, eagerness; greed; voracity

avilir [avilir] *tr* to debase, dishonor; (com) to lower the price of ‖ *ref* to debase oneself; (com) to deteriorate

avilis•sant [avilisã] **avilis•sante** [avilisãt] *adj* debasing

avilissement [avilismã] *m* debasement; (com) depreciation

avi•né -née [avine] *adj* drunk

aviner [avine] *tr* to soak (*a new barrel*) with wine ‖ *ref* (coll) to booze

avion [avjɔ̃] *m* airplane; **avion à réaction** jet; **avion de chasse** fighter plane; **avion long-courrier** long-range plane; **en avion** by plane; **par avion** air mail

avion-cargo [avjɔ̃kargo] *m* (*pl* **avions-cargos**) cargo liner, freighter

avion-taxi [avjɔ̃taksi] *m* (*pl* **avions-taxis**) taxiplane

aviron [avirɔ̃] *m* oar; **aviron de couple** scull

avis [avi] *m* opinion; advice; notice, warning; decision; **à mon avis** in my opinion; **avis au lecteur** note to the reader; **changer d'avis** to change one's mind

avi•sé -sée [avize] *adj* prudent, shrewd; **bien avisé** well-advised

aviser [avize] *tr* to glimpse, descry; to advise, inform, warn ‖ *intr* to decide; **aviser à** to think of, look into; to deal with ‖ *ref*—**s'aviser de** to contrive, to think up; to be on the look-out for; **s'aviser de** + *inf* to take it into one's head to + *inf*

aviso [avizo] *m* dispatch boat, sloop

avivage [avivaʒ] *m* brightening; polishing

aviver [avive] *tr* to revive, to stir up (*fire; passions*); to brighten (*colors*); (med & fig) to open (*a wound*)

av. J.-C. *abbr* (**avant Jésus-Christ**) B.C.

avo•cat [avɔka] **-cate** [kat] *mf* lawyer; advocate; barrister (Brit); **avocat du diable** devil's advocate ‖ *m* avocado

avoine [avwan] *f* oats

avoir [avwar] *m* wealth; credit side (*of ledger*) ‖ §6 *tr* to have; to get; **avoir . . . ans** to be . . . years old, e.g., **mon fils a dix ans** my son is ten years old; **avoir beau** + *inf* to be useless for (*s.o.*) to + *inf*, e.g., **j'ai beau travailler** it is useless for me to work; for expressions like **avoir froid** to be cold, **avoir raison** to be right, see the noun ‖ *intr*—**avoir à** to have to; **en avoir à** or **contre** to be angry with ‖ *impers*—**il y a** there is, there are, e.g., **il n'y a pas d'espoir** there is no hope ‖ *aux* to have, e.g., **j'ai couru trop vite** I have run too fast

avoisiner [avwazine] *tr* to neighbor, to be near

avortement [avɔrtəmã] *m* abortion; miscarriage

avorter [avɔrte] *intr* to abort; to miscarry

avorton [avɔrtɔ̃] *m* runt; (biol) stunt

avoué [avwe] *m* lawyer (*doing notarial work*); solicitor (Brit)

avouer [avwe] *tr* to avow, to admit; to claim, to acknowledge authorship of ‖ *ref* to be admitted; **s'avouer vaincu** to admit defeat

avril [avril] *m* April

axe [aks] *m* axis

axer [akse] *tr* to set on an axis; to orient

axiomatique [aksjɔmatik] *adj* axiomatic

axiome [aksjom] *m* axiom

axonge [aksɔ̃ʒ] *f* lard

ayant-droit [ejãdrwa] *m* (*pl* **ayants-droit**) claimant; beneficiary

azalée [azale] *f* azalea

azimut or **azimuth** [azimyt] *m* azimuth

azote [azɔt] *m* nitrogen

azo•té -tée [azɔte] *adj* nitrogenous

Aztèques [aztek] *mpl* Aztecs

azur [azyr] *adj & m* azure

azyme [azim] *adj* unleavened ‖ *m* unleavened bread

B

B, b [be] *m invar* second letter of the French alphabet

baba [baba] *adj* (coll) flabbergasted, wide-eyed ‖ *m* baba

babeurre [babœr] *m* buttermilk

babil [babil], [babi] *m* babble, chatter; **babil enfantin** baby talk

babillage [babijaʒ] *m* babbling

babil·lard [babijar] **babil·larde** [babijard] *adj* babbling ‖ *mf* babbler ‖ *f* (slang) letter

babiller [babije] *intr* to babble, to chatter

babine [babin] *f* chop (*mouth*); **s'es-suyer** or **se lécher les babines** to lick one's chops

babiole [babjɔl] *f* (coll) bauble

bâbord [babɔr] *m* (naut) pert, port-side; **à bâbord** port; **bâbord armures** port sail

babouche [babuʃ] *f* babouche, slipper

babouin [babwɛ̃] *m* baboon; pimple on the lips; brat

bac [bak] *m* ferryboat; tub, vat; box, bin; tray (*for ice cubes*); drawer (*of refrigerator*); case (*of battery*); (slang) baccalaureate

baccalauréat [bakalɔrea] *m* baccalau-reate, bachelor's degree

bacchanale [bakanal] *f* bacchanal

bâche [baʃ] *f* tarpaulin; hot-water tank

bache·lier [baʃəlje] **-lière** [ljer] *mf* bachelor (*holder of degree*) ‖ *m* (hist) bachelor (*young knight*)

bâcher [baʃe] *tr* to cover with a tar-paulin

bachique [baʃik] *adj* bacchanalian, bacchic; drinking (*song*)

bachot [baʃo] *m* dinghy, punt; (coll) baccalaureate

bachotage [baʃɔtaʒ] *m* (coll) cram-ming (*for an exam*)

bachoter [baʃɔte] *intr* (coll) to cram

bacille [basil] *m* bacillus

bâclage [baklaʒ] *m* blocking up (*of harbor*); (slang) botching (*of work*)

bâcle [bakl] *f* bolt (*of door*)

bâcler [bakle] *tr* to bolt (*a door*); to close up (*a harbor*); (coll) to botch, to hurry through carelessly

bâ·cleur [baklœr] **-cleuse** [kløz] *mf* (coll) botcher

bacon [bakɔ̃] *m* bacon

bactéricide [bakterisid] *adj* bactericid-al ‖ *m* bactericide

bactérie [bakteri] *f* bacterium; **bacté-ries** bacteria

bactériologie [bakterjɔlɔʒi] *f* bacteriol-ogy

ba·daud [bado] **-daude** [dod] *mf* rub-berneck, gawk, idler

badauder [badode] *intr* to stand and stare

badigeon [badiʒɔ̃] *m* whitewash

badigeonner [badiʒɔne] *tr* to white-wash; (med) to paint (*e.g., the throat*)

ba·din [badɛ̃] **-dine** [din] *adj* sprightly, playful, teasing ‖ *mf* tease ‖ *m* (aer) air-speed indicator ‖ *f* cane, switch

badinage [badinaʒ] *m* banter; **badinage amoureux** necking

badiner [badine] *intr* to joke, to tease; to trifle, to be flippant

badinerie [badinri] *f* teasing; child-ishness

bafouer [bafwe] *tr* to heckle, to hu-miliate

bafouiller [bafuje] *intr* (coll) to stam-mer, mumble, babble

bâfrer [bafre] *tr & intr* (slang) to guzzle

bagage [bagaʒ] *m* baggage; **bagages** baggage, luggage; **bagages non ac-compagnés** baggage sent on ahead; **menus bagages** hand luggage; **plier bagage** to pack one's bags; (coll) to scram; (coll) to kick the bucket

bagarre [bagar] *f* brawl, row, riot; **chercher la bagarre** (coll) to be look-ing for a fight

bagarrer [bagare] *intr & ref* to riot; (coll) to brawl, scrap, scuffle

bagar·reur [bagarœr] **bagar·reuse** [ba-garøz] *mf* (coll) rioter, brawler

bagatelle [bagatel] *f* trifle, bagatelle; frivolity ‖ *interj* nonsense!

bagnard [baɲar] *m* convict

bagne [baɲ] *m* penitentiary, penal col-ony; (nav) prison ship; (slang) sweat-shop

bagnole [baɲɔl] *f* (slang) jalopy

bagou [bagu] *m* (coll) gift of gab

bague [bag] *f* ring; cigar band; (mach) collar, sleeve; **bague de fiançailles** engagement ring

baguenauder [bagnode] *intr* to waste time, to fool around ‖ *ref* (coll) to wander about

baguer [bage] *tr* to band (*a tree*); to baste (*cloth*)

baguette [baget] *f* stick, switch, rod; baton; long thin loaf of bread; chop-stick; **baguette de fée** fairy wand; **baguettes de tambour** drumsticks; **mener qn à la baguette** (coll) to lead s.o. by the nose; **passer par les ba-guettes** to run the gauntlet

baguier [bagje] *m* jewel box

bahut [bay] *m* trunk, chest; cupboard; (slang) high school

bai baie [be] *adj* bay (*horse*) ‖ *f* bay; berry; bayberry; bay window

baignade [beɲad] *f* bathing, swim-ming; swimming hole, bathing spot

baigner [beɲe] *tr* to bathe; to wash (*the coast*) ‖ *intr* to be immersed, to soak ‖ *ref* to bathe; to go bathing

bai·gneur [beɲœr] **-gneuse** [ɲøz] *mf* bather; vacationist at a spa or sea-side resort; bathhouse attendant ‖ *m* doll

baignoire [beɲwar] *f* bathtub; (theat) orchestra box

bail [baj] *m* (*pl* **baux** [bo]) lease; **passer un bail** to sign a lease; **pren-dre à bail** to lease

bâillement [bɑjmɑ̃] *m* yawn

bailler [baje] *tr*—**vous me la baillez belle** (coll) you're pulling my leg

bâiller [baje] *intr* to yawn; to be ajar, to be half open

bail·leur [bajœr] **bail·leresse** [bajɛres] *mf* lessor; **bailleur de fonds** lender

bailli [baji] *m* bailiff

baillliage [bajaʒ] *m* bailiwick

bâillon [bajɔ̃] *m* gag, muzzle

bâillonner [bajone] *tr* to gag; (fig) to muzzle

bain [bɛ̃] *m* bath; **bain de soleil** sun bath; **bains** watering place, spa; bathing establishment; **être dans le bain** (coll) to be in hot water

baïonnette [bajonet] *f* bayonet

baiser [beze], [beze] *m* kiss || *tr* (vulgar) to have sex with; (archaic) to kiss

baisoter [bezote] *tr* (coll) to keep on kissing || *ref* (coll) to bill and coo

baisse [bes] *f* fall; **jouer à la baisse** (com) to bear the market

baissement [besmɑ̃] *m* lowering

baisser [bese] *m* lowering; **baisser du rideau** curtain fall || *tr* to lower; to take in (*sail*) || *intr* to fall, drop, sink || *ref* to bend, stoop

baissier [besje] *m* bear (*on the stock exchange*)

bajoue [baʒu] *f* jowl

bal [bal] *m* (*pl* **bals**) ball, dance; **bal travesti** fancy-dress ball

balade [balad] *f* stroll; **balade en auto** joy ride

balader [balade] *ref* to go for a stroll; **se balader en auto** to go joy-riding

bala·deur [baladœr] **-deuse** [døz] *adj* strolling || *mf* stroller || *m* gear || *f* cart (*of street vendor*); lamp with long cord

baladin [baladɛ̃] *m* mountebank, showman; oaf

balafre [balafr] *f* gash, scar

balafrer [balafre] *tr* to gash, to scar

balai [bale] *m* broom; **balai à laver** mop; **balai de sorcière** witches'-broom; **balai électrique** vacuum cleaner; **balai mécanique** carpet sweeper; **donner un coup de balai** to make a clean sweep of (*s.th.*); to kick (*s.o.*) out

balai-éponge [baleepɔ̃ʒ] *m* (*pl* **balais-éponges**) mop

balance [balɑ̃s] *f* balance; scales; **faire la balance de** (bk) to balance

balancement [balɑ̃smɑ̃] *m* swaying, teetering; (fig) indecision, wavering; (fig) harmony (*of phrase*)

balancer [balɑ̃se] §51 *tr* to balance; to move (*arms or legs*) in order to balance; to balance (*an account*); to weigh (*the pros and cons*); to swing, rock; (coll) to fire (*s.o.*) || *intr* to swing, rock; to hesitate, waver || *ref* to swing or to seesaw; to sway, rock; to ride (*at anchor*)

balancier [balɑ̃sje] *m* pendulum; balance wheel; pole (*of tightrope walker*)

balançoire [balɑ̃swar] *f* swing; seesaw, teeter-totter; (slang) nonsense

balayage [balejaʒ] *m* sweeping; (telv) scanning

balayer [baleje], [baleje] §49 *tr* to sweep, to sweep up; to sweep out; to scour (*the sea*); (telv) to scan

balayeur [balejœr] **balayeuse** [balejøz] *mf* sweeper, scavenger || *f* street-cleaning truck

balayures [balejyr] *fpl* sweepings

balbutiement [balbysimɑ̃] *m* stammering, mumbling; initial effort

balbutier [balbysje] *tr* to stammer out || *intr* to stammer, to mumble

balbuzard [balbyzar] *m* osprey, bald buzzard, sea eagle

balcon [balkɔ̃] *m* balcony; (theat) dress circle

baldaquin [baldakɛ̃] *m* canopy, tester

Baléares [balear] *fpl* Balearic Islands

baleine [balen] *f* right whale, whalebone whale; whalebone; rib (*of umbrella*); stay (*of a corset*)

baleinier [balenje] *m* whaling vessel

baleinière [balenjer] *f* whaleboat; lifeboat

balisage [balizaʒ] *m* (aer) ground lights; (naut) buoys

balise [baliz] *f* buoy, marker; ground light, beacon; landing signal

baliser [balize] *tr* to furnish with markers, buoys, landing lights, beacons, or radio signals

balistique [balistik] *adj* ballistic || *f* ballistics

baliverne [balivern] *f* nonsense, humbug

balkanique [balkanik] *adj* Balkan

ballade [balad] *f* ballade

bal·lant [balɑ̃] **bal·lante** [balɑ̃t] *adj* waving, swinging, dangling || *m* oscillation, shaking

balle [bal] *f* ball; bullet; hull, chaff; bale; (tennis) match point; **balle traçante** tracer bullet; **prendre** or **saisir la balle au bond** to seize time by the forelock

ballerine [balrin] *f* ballerina

ballet [bale] *m* ballet

ballon [balɔ̃] *m* balloon; ball; football; soccer ball; round-bottom flask; rounded mountaintop; **ballon d'essai** trial balloon

ballonner [balone] *tr*, *intr*, & *ref* to balloon

ballot [balo] *m* pack; bundle; (slang) blockhead, chump

ballottage [balotaʒ] *m* tossing, shaking; second ballot

ballotter [balote] *tr* & *intr* to toss about

balnéaire [balneer] *adj* seaside

ba·lourd [balur] **-lourde** [lurd] *adj* awkward, lumpish || *mf* blockhead, bumpkin || *m* wobble

balte [balt] *adj* Baltic || (*cap*) *mf* Balt

Baltique [baltik] *f* Baltic (*sea*)

balustrade [balystrad] *f* balustrade, banisters

balustre [balystr] *m* baluster, banister

bal·zan [balzɑ̃] **-zane** [zan] *adj* white-footed (*horse*) || *f* white spot (*on horse's foot*)

bam·bin [bɑ̃bɛ̃] **-bine** [bin] *mf* (coll) babe

bambo·chard [bɑ̃boʃar] **-charde** [ʃard] *adj* (coll) carousing || *mf* (coll) carouser

bamboche [bãbɔʃ] *f* (slang) jag, bender
bambocher [bãbɔʃe] *intr* (coll) to carouse, to go on a spree
bambo·cheur [bãbɔʃœr] **-cheuse** [ʃøz] *adj* (coll) carousing ‖ *mf* (coll) carouser
bambou [bãbu] *m* bamboo
ban [bã] *m* ban; cadenced applause; **ban de mariage** banns; **convoquer le ban et l'arrière-ban** to invite everyone and his brother; **mettre au ban** to banish, to ban
ba·nal -nale [banal] *adj* (*pl* **-nals -nales**) banal, trite, commonplace ‖ *adj* (*pl* **-naux** [no] **-nales**) (archaic) common, public, in common
banaliser [banalize] *tr* to vulgarize, to make commonplace
banalité [banalite] *f* banality; triteness
banane [banan] *f* banana
bananier [bananje] *m* banana tree
banc [bã] *m* bench; shoal; school (*of fish*); pew (*reserved for church officials*); (hist) privy council; **être sur les bancs** to go to high school
bancaire [bãker] *adj* banking, of banks
ban·cal -cale [bãkal] *adj* (*pl* **-cals -cales**) bowlegged, bandy-legged
bandage [bãdaʒ] *m* bandage; bandaging; truss; tire (*of metal or rubber*)
bande [bãd] *f* band; movie film; recording tape; cushion (*in billiards*); wrapper (*of a newspaper*); **bande magnétique** recording tape; tape recording; **bande sonore** or **parlante** sound track; **donner de la bande** to heel, to list; **faire bande à part** to keep to oneself
ban·deau [bãdo] *m* (*pl* **-deaux**) blindfold; headband; bending (*of a bow*); **bandeau royal** diadem; **bandeaux** hair parted in the middle
bander [bãde] *tr* to band, to put a band on; to bandage; to blindfold; to bend (*a bow*); to put a tire on; to draw taut ‖ *ref* to band together; to put up resistance
banderole [bãdrɔl] *f* pennant, streamer; strap (*of gun*)
bandière [bãdjer] *f* battle, e.g., **front de bandière** battle front
bandit [bãdi] *m* bandit
bandoulière [bãduljer] *f* shoulder strap, sling; **en bandoulière** slung over the shoulder
banlieue [bãljø] *f* suburbs; **de banlieue** suburban
banlieu·sard [bãljøzar] **-sarde** [zard] *mf* suburbanite (*especially of a Parisian suburb*)
banne [ban] *f* awning (*of store*)
ban·ni -nie [bani] *adj* banished, exiled ‖ *mf* exile
bannière [banjer] *f* banner, flag
bannir [banir] *tr* to banish
bannissement [banismã] *m* banishment
banque [bãk] *f* bank; **banque des yeux** eye bank; **banque du sang** blood bank; **faire sauter la banque** to break the bank
banqueroute [bãkrut] *f* bankruptcy (*with blame for negligence or fraud*)

banquerou·tier [bãkrutje] **-tière** [tjer] *adj & mf* bankrupt (*with culpability*)
banquet [bãke] *m* banquet
banqueter [bãkte] §34 *intr* to banquet
banquette [bãket] *f* seat (*in a train, bus, automobile*); bank (*of earth or sand*); bunker (*in a golf course*); **banquette arrière** back seat; **banquette de tir** (mil) emplacement for shooting; **jouer devant les banquettes** to play to an empty house
ban·quier [bãkje] **-quière** [kjer] *mf* banker
banquise [bãkiz] *f* pack ice
banquiste [bãkist] *m* charlatan, quack
baptême [batem] *m* baptism; christening; **baptême de la ligne, baptême des tropiques** or **du tropique** polliwog initiation
baptiser [batize] *tr* to baptize; to christen; (slang) to dilute (*wine*) with water
baptis·mal -male [batismal] *adj* (*pl* **-maux** [mo]) baptismal
baptistaire [batister] *adj* baptismal (*certificate*)
baptiste [batist] *mf* Baptist
baptistère [batister] *m* baptistery
baquet [bake] *m* wooden tub, bucket; (aut) bucket seat
bar [bar] *m* bar; (ichth) bass, perch
baragouin [baragwɛ̃] *m* (slang) gibberish
baragouiner [baragwine] *tr* (coll) to murder (*a language*); (coll) to stumble through (*a speech*) ‖ *intr* (coll) to jabber
baraque [barak] *f* booth, stall; shanty, hovel
baraterie [baratri] *f* barratry
baratin [baratɛ̃] *m* (slang) blah-blah, hokum
baratte [barat] *f* churn
baratter [barate] *tr* to churn
Barbade [barbad] *f* Barbados; **la Barbade** Barbados
barbare [barbar] *adj* barbarous, barbaric, savage ‖ *mf* barbarian
barbaresque [barbaresk] *adj* of Barbary
barbarie [barbari] *f* barbarity, barbarism ‖ (*cap*) *f* Barbary
barbarisme [barbarism] *m* barbarism (*in speech or writing*)
barbe [barb] *f* beard; bristle; whiskers (*of an animal*); barbel; **barbes** vane (*of a feather*); deckle edge; **faire q.ch. à la barbe de qn** to do s.th. right under the nose of s.o.; **rire dans sa barbe** to laugh up one's sleeve; **se faire la barbe** to shave ‖ *interj*—**la barbe!** shut up!
bar·beau [barbo] *m* (*pl* **-beaux**) cornflower; (ichth) barbel; (slang) pimp
barbe·lé -lée [barbəle] *adj* barbed ‖ **barbelés** *mpl* barbed wire
bar·bet [barbe] **-bette** [bet] *mf* water spaniel
barbiche [barbiʃ] *f* goatee
barbier [barbje] *m* barber
barbillon [barbijõ] *m* barb
barbiturique [barbityrik] *m* barbiturate
barbon [barbõ] *m* (pej) old fogy

barboter [barbɔte] *intr* to paddle (*like ducks*); to wallow (*like pigs*); to bubble (*like carbonated water*); (coll) to splutter; (slang) to steal

barbo·teur [barbɔtœr] **-teuse** [tøz] *mf* (slang) muddler ‖ *m* duck; wash bottle ‖ *f* rompers

barbouiller [barbuje] *tr* to smear, blur; to daub; (coll) to scribble; **barbouiller le cœur à** to nauseate

barbouil·leur [barbujœr] **barbouil·leuse** [barbujøz] *mf* dauber; messy person; scribbler

bar·bu ·bue [barby] *adj* bearded

bard [bar] *m* handbarrow

bardane [bardan] *f* burdock

barde [bard] *m* bard ‖ *f* blanket of bacon

bar·deau [bardo] *m* (*pl* **-deaux**) shingle; lath

barder [barde] *tr* to carry with a handbarrow; to armor (*a horse*); to blanket (*a roast*)

bardot [bardo] *m* hinny

barème [barɛm] *m* schedule (*of rates, taxes, etc.*)

baréter [barete] §10 *intr* to trumpet (*like an elephant*)

barge [barʒ] *f* barge; haystack; godwit, black-tailed godwit

barguigner [bargiɲe] *intr* to shillyshally, to have trouble deciding

bargui·gneur [barɡiɲœr] **-gneuse** [nøz] *mf* shilly-shallyer, procrastinator

baricaut [bariko] *m* small cask, keg

baril [baril], [bari] *m* small barrel, cask, keg

barillet [barijɛ] *m* small barrel; revolver cylinder; spring case

barlotage [barlɔtaʒ] *m* (coll) motley, mixture of colors

bario·lé ·lée [barjɔle] *adj* speckled, multicolored, variegated

barioler [barjɔle] *tr* to variegate

bariolure [barjɔlyr] *f* clashing colors, motley

bar·man [barman] *m* (*pl* **-men** [mɛn] or **-mans**) bartender

baromètre [barɔmɛtr] *m* barometer

barométrique [barɔmetrik] *adj* barometric

baron [barɔ̃] *m* baron

baronne [barɔn] *f* baroness

baroque [barɔk] *adj* & *m* baroque

barque [bark] *f* boat

barrage [baraʒ] *m* dam; barrage, cordon (*of police*); tollgate; barricade, roadblock, checkpoint; (sports) playoff

barre [bar], [bar] *f* bar; crossbar (*of a t*); tiller, helm; bore (*tidal flood*); **barre de justice** rod to hold shackles; **barre du gouvernail** helm; **barres** (typ) parallels; **jouer aux barres** to play prisoner's base

bar·reau [baro] *m* (*pl* **-reaux**) bar, crossbar, rail; rung (*of ladder or chair*); (law) bar

barrer [bare] *tr* to cross out, strike out, cancel; to cross (*a t; a check in a British bank*); to bar (*the door; the way*); to block off (*a street*); to dam (*a stream*); to steer (*a boat*)

barrette [barɛt], [barɛt] *f* biretta; bar; slide; pin

barreur [barœr] *m* helmsman

barricader [barikade] *tr* to barricade

barricade [barikad] *f* barricade

barrière [barjɛr] *f* barrier; gate (*of a town; of a grade crossing*); tollgate; neighborhood shopping district

barrique [barik] *f* cask; hogshead, large barrel

barrir [barir] *intr* to trumpet (*like an elephant*)

barrot [baro] *m* beam (*of a ship*)

baryton [baritɔ̃] *m* baritone; alto (*saxhorn*)

baryum [barjɔm] *m* barium

bas [bɑ] **basse** [bɑs] *adj* low; base, vile; cloudy (*weather*) ‖ (when standing before noun) *adj* low; base, vile; early (*age*) ‖ *m* stocking; lower part, bottom; **à bas . . . !** down with . . . !; **bas de casse** (typ) lower case; **bas de laine** nest egg, savings; **en bas** at the bottom; downstairs ‖ *f* see **basse** ‖ **bas** *adv* softly; down, low

ba·sal ·sale [bazal] *adj* (*pl* **-saux** [zo]) basic; basal (*metabolism*)

basalte [bazalt] *m* basalt

basa·né ·née [bazane] *adj* tanned, sunburned

basaner [bazane] *tr* to tan, to sunburn

bas-bleu [bablø] *m* (*pl* **-bleus**) bluestocking

bas-côté [bakote] *m* (*pl* **-côtés**) aisle (*of a church*); footpath (*beside a road*)

bascule [baskyl] *f* scale; rocker; seesaw

basculement [baskylmɑ̃] *m* rocking, seesawing, tipping; dimming

basculer [baskyle] *tr* to tip over ‖ *intr* to tip over; to seesaw, rock, swing; **faire basculer** to dim (*the headlights*)

bas-dessus [badəsy] *m* mezzo-soprano

base [baz] *f* base; basis; **à la base** at heart, to the core; **de base** basic

base-ball [bɛzbɔl] *m* baseball

baser [baze] *tr* to base; to ground, found (*an opinion*) ‖ *ref* to be based

bas-fond [bafɔ̃] *m* (*pl* **-fonds**) lowland; shallows; **bas-fonds** dregs, underworld; slums

basilic [bazilik] *m* basil

basilique [bazilik] *f* basilica

basin [bazɛ̃] *m* dimity

basique [bazik] *adj* basic, alkaline

basket [baskɛt] *m* basketball

basoche [bazɔʃ] *f* law, legal profession

basque [bask] *adj* Basque ‖ *m* Basque (*language*) ‖ *f* coattail ‖ (cap) *mf* Basque (*person*)

basse [bas] *f* shoal; tuba; (mus) bass; **basse chiffrée** (mus) figured bass

basse-contre [bɑsk5tr] *f* (*pl* **basses-contre**) basso profundo

basse-cour [baskur] *f* (*pl* **basses-cours**) barnyard, farmyard; barnyard animals; poultry yard

bassesse [bases] *f* baseness; base act

basset [basɛ] *m* basset hound

bassin [basɛ̃] *m* basin; dock; artificial lake; collection plate; pelvis; **bassin**

de lit bedpan; **bassin de radoub** dry dock; **bassin hygiénique** bedpan

bassine [basin] *f* dishpan

bassinoire [basinwar] *f* bedwarmer

basson [basɔ̃] *m* bassoon

baste [bast] *m* ace of clubs; saddle basket ‖ *interj* enough!

bastille [bastij] *f* small fortress

bastion [bastjɔ̃] *m* bastion

bastonnade [bastɔnad] *f* beating

bas-ventre [bavɑ̃tr] *m* abdomen, lower part of the belly

bât [bɑ] *m* packsaddle

bataclan [bataklɑ̃] *m*—**tout le bataclan** (slang) the whole caboodle

bataille [batɑj], [bataj] *f* battle, fight

batailler [batɑje], [bataje] *intr* to battle, to fight

batail·leur [batajœr] batail·leuse [batajøz] *adj* belligerent ‖ *mf* fighter

bataillon [batɑjɔ̃] *m* battalion

bâ·tard [batɑr] -tarde [tard] *adj* & *mf* mongrel; bastard ‖ *m* one-pound loaf of short-length type of bread ‖ *f* cursive handwriting

bâtar·deau [batardo] *m* (*pl* -deaux) cofferdam, caisson

ba·teau [bato] *m* (*pl* -teaux) boat; **bateau automobile** motorboat, motor launch; **bateau à vapeur** steamboat; **bateau à voiles** sailboat; **bateau de guerre** warship; **bateau de pêche** fishing boat; **bateau de sauvetage** lifeboat; **monter un bateau à qn** (slang) to pull s.o.'s leg; **par (le) bateau** by boat

bateau-citerne [batositern] *m* (*pl* bateaux-citernes) tanker

bateau-feu [batofø] *m* (*pl* bateaux-feux) lightship

bateau-maison [batomezɔ̃] *m* (*pl* bateaux-maisons) houseboat

bateau-mouche [batomuʃ] *m* (*pl* bateaux-mouches) excursion boat

bateau-pompe [batopɔ̃p] *m* (*pl* bateaux-pompes) fireboat

batelage [batlaʒ] *m* lighterage; juggling; tumbling

batelée [batle] *f* boatload

bateler [batle] §34 *tr* to lighter ‖ *intr* to juggle; to tumble

bateleur [batlœr] -leuse [løz] *mf* juggler; tumbler

bate·lier [batlje] -lière [ljer] *mf* skipper ‖ *m* boatman; ferryman

batellerie [batelri] *f* lighterage

bâter [bate] *tr* to packsaddle

bath [bat] *adj* (slang) A-one, swell

bâ·ti -tie [bati] *adj* built; **bien bâti** well-built (*person*) ‖ *m* frame; basting (*thread*); basted garment

batifoler [batifole] *intr* (coll) to frolic

bâtiment [batimɑ̃] *m* building; ship

bâtir [batir] *tr* to build; to baste, to tack ‖ *ref* to be built

bâtisse [batis] *f* masonry, construction; building, edifice; ramshackle house

bâtis·seur [batisœr] bâtis·seuse [batisøz] *mf* builder

bâton [batɔ̃] *m* stick; baton; staff, cane; rung (*of a chair*); stroke (*of a pen*); stick (*of gum*); **à bâtons rompus** by fits and starts; impromptu;

(archit) with zigzag molding; **bâton de reprise** (mus) repeat bar; **bâton de rouge à lèvres** lipstick; **bâton de vieillesse** helper or nurse for the aged; **mettre des bâtons dans les roues** to throw a monkey wrench into the works

bâtonner [batɔne] *tr* to cudgel; to cross out

bâtonnet [batɔne] *m* rod (*in the retina*); chopstick

battage [bataʒ] *m* beating; threshing; churning; (slang) ballyhoo

bat·tant [batɑ̃] bat·tante [batɑ̃t] *adj* beating; pelting, driving; swinging (*door*) ‖ *m* flap; clapper (*of bell*); **à deux battants** double (*door*)

batte [bat] *f* mallet, beater; dasher, plunger; bench for beating clothes; wooden sword (*for slapstick comedy*); (sports) bat; **batte de l'or** goldbeating

battement [batmɑ̃] *m* beating, beat; throbbing, pulsing; clapping (*of hands*); dance step; wait (*e.g., between trains*)

batterie [batri] *f* (elec, mil, mus) battery; train service (*in one direction*); ruse, scheming; **batterie de cuisine** kitchen utensils

batteur [batœr] *m* beater; thresher; (sports) batter; **batteur de grève** beachcomber; **batteur de pieux** piledriver; **batteur électrique** electric mixer

batteuse [batøz] *f* threshing machine

battoir [batwar] *m* bat, beetle (*for washing clothes*); tennis racket

battre [batr] §7 *tr* to beat; to clap (*one's hands*); to flap, flutter; to wink; to bang; to pound (*the sidewalk*); to search; to shuffle (*the cards*); **battre la mesure** to beat time; **battre monnaie** to mint money ‖ *intr* to beat ‖ *ref* to fight

bau [bo] *m* (*pl* baux) beam (*of a ship*)

baudet [bode] *m* ass, donkey; stallion ass; sawhorse; (slang) jackass, idiot

baudrier [bodrije] *m* shoulder belt

bauge [boʒ] *f* lair, den; clay and straw mortar; (coll) pigsty

baume [bom] *m* balsam; (*consolation*) balm

ba·vard [bavar] -varde [vard] *adj* talkative, loquacious; tattletale ‖ *mf* chatterer; tattletale; gossip

bavardage [bavardaʒ] *m* chattering, gossiping

bavarder [bavarde] *intr* to chatter; to gossip

bava·rois [bavarwa] -roise [rwaz] *adj* Bavarian ‖ (*cap*) *mf* Bavarian (*person*)

bave [bav] *f* dribble, froth, spittle; (fig) slander

baver [bave] *intr* to dribble, to drool; to run (*like a pen*); **baver sur** to besmirch

bavette [bavet] *f* bib

ba·veux [bavø] -veuse [vøz] *adj* drooling; tendentious, wordy; undercooked

Bavière [bavjɛr] *f* Bavaria; **la Bavière** Bavaria

bavocher [bavɔʃe] *intr* to smear

bavochure [bavɔʃyr] *f* smear

bavure [bavyr] *f* bur (*of metal*); smear

bayer [baje] §49 *intr*—**bayer aux corneilles** to gawk, to stargaze

bazar [bazar] *m* bazaar; five-and-ten; **tout le bazar** (slang) the whole she-bang

béant [beɑ̃] **béante** [beɑ̃t] *adj* gaping, wide-open

béat [bea] **béate** [beat] *adj* smug, complacent, sanctimonious

béatifier [beatifje] *tr* to beatify

béatitude [beatityd] *f* beatitude

beau [bo] (or **bel** [bɛl] before vowel or mute h) **belle** [bɛl] (*pl* **beaux belles**) *adj* beautiful; handsome; **bel et bien** truly, for sure; **de plus belle** more than ever; **il fait beau** it is nice out, we are having fair weather; **tout beau!** steady!, easy does it! || (when standing before noun) *adj* beautiful; handsome; fine, good; considerable, large, long; fair (*weather*); odd-numbered or recto (*page*) || *m* fair one; **faire le beau, faire la belle** to strut, swagger; to sit up and beg (*said of a dog*); **la belle** the deciding match; **la Belle au bois dormant** Sleeping Beauty || *adv*—**il a beau parler** it is no use for him to speak || **belle** *adv*—**la bailler belle** (slang) to tell a whopper; **l'échapper belle** to have a narrow escape

beaucoup [boku] §91 *adv* much, many; **beaucoup de** much, many; **de beaucoup** by far

beau-fils [bofis] *m* (*pl* **beaux-fils**) son-in-law; stepson

beau-frère [bofrɛr] *m* (*pl* **beaux-frères**) brother-in-law

beau-père [bopɛr] *m* (*pl* **beaux-pères**) father-in-law; stepfather

beau-petit-fils [bopətifis] *m* (*pl* **beaux-petits-fils**) son of a stepson or of a stepdaughter

beaupré [bopre] *m* bowsprit

beauté [bote] *f* beauty; **beauté du diable** (coll) bloom of youth; **se faire une beauté** (coll) to doll up

beaux-arts [bozar] *mpl* fine arts

beaux-parents [boparɑ̃] *mpl* in-laws

bébé [bebe] *m* baby

bec [bɛk] *m* beak; nozzle, jet, burner; point (*of a pen*); (mus) mouthpiece; (slang) beak, face, mouth; **avoir bon bec** to be gossipy; **claquer du bec** (coll) to be hungry; **clore, clouer le bec à qn** (coll) to shut s.o. up; **tomber sur un bec** (coll) to encounter an unforeseen obstacle

bécane [bekan] *f* (coll) bike, bicycle

bécarre [bekar] *m* (mus) natural

bécasse [bekas] *f* woodcock; (slang) stupid woman

bécas-seau [bekaso] *m* (*pl* **bécas-seaux**) sandpiper

bec-de-cane [bɛkdəkan] *m* (*pl* **becs-de-cane**) door handle; flat-nosed pliers

bec-de-corbeau [bɛkdəkɔrbo] *m* (*pl* **becs-de-corbeau**) wire cutters

bec-de-corbin [bɛkdəkɔrbɛ̃] *m* (*pl* **becs-de-corbin**) crowbar

bec-de-lièvre [bɛkdəljɛvr] *m* (*pl* **becs-de-lièvre**) harelip

bêche [bɛʃ] *f* spade

bêcher [beʃe] *tr* to dig; (slang) to run (*s.th.*) down, to give (*s.o.*) a dig

bê-cheur [beʃœr] **-cheuse** [ʃøz] *mf* (coll) detractor, critic; (slang) stuffed shirt

béchoir [beʃwar] *m* hoe

bécoter [bekɔte] *tr* to give (*s.o.*) a peck or little kiss on the cheek

becqueter [bekte] §34 *tr* to peck at; (coll) to eat || *ref* to bill and coo

bedaine [bədɛn] *f* paunch, beer belly

bédane [bedan] *m* cold chisel

bé-deau [bedo] *m* (*pl* **-deaux**) beadle

bé-douin [bedwɛ̃] **-douine** [dwin] *adj* Bedouin || (*cap*) *mf* Bedouin (*person*)

bée [be] *adj*—**bouche bée** mouth agape, flabbergasted || *f* penstock

beffroi [befrwa] *m* belfry

bégaiement [begemɑ̃] *m* stammering, stuttering

bégayer [begeje] §49 *tr & intr* to stammer, stutter

bègue [bɛg] *adj* stammering, stuttering || *mf* stammerer

bégueter [begte] §2 *intr* to bleat

bégueule [begœl] *adj* (coll) prudish || *f* (coll) prudish woman

béguin [begɛ̃] *m* hood, cap; sweetheart; (coll) infatuation

béguine [begin] *f* Beguine; sanctimonious woman

beige [bɛʒ] *adj & m* beige

beignet [bɛɲe] *m* fritter

béjaune [beʒon] *m* nestling; greenhorn, novice, ninny

bêlement [bɛlmɑ̃] *m* bleat, bleating

bêler [bele] *intr* to bleat

belette [bəlɛt] *f* weasel

belge [bɛlʒ] *adj* Belgian || (*cap*) *mf* Belgian (*person*)

Belgique [bɛlʒik] *f* Belgium; **la Belgique** Belgium

bélier [belje] *m* ram; battering ram

bélière [beljɛr] *f* sheepbell

bélinogramme [belinɔgram] *m* Wirephoto (*trademark*)

bélinographe [belinɔgraf] *m* Wirephoto transmitter

bélître [belitr] *m* scoundrel

belladone [beladɔn] *f* belladonna

bellâtre [belɑtr] *adj* foppish || *m* fop

belle-dame [bɛldam] *f* belladonna

belle-de-jour [bɛldəʒur] *f* (*pl* **belles-de-jour**) morning glory

belle-de-nuit [bɛldənɥi] *f* (*pl* **belles-de-nuit**) marvel-of-Peru

belle-d'un-jour [bɛldœ̃ʒur] *f* (*pl* **belles-d'un-jour**) day lily

belle-fille [bɛlfij] *f* (*pl* **belles-filles**) daughter-in-law; stepdaughter

belle-mère [bɛlmɛr] *f* (*pl* **belles-mères**) mother-in-law; stepmother

belle-petite-fille [bɛlpətitfij] *f* (*pl* **belles-petites-filles**) daughter of a stepson or of a stepdaughter

belles-lettres [bɛllɛtr] *fpl* belles-lettres, literature

belle-sœur [belsœr] *f* (*pl* belles-sœurs) sister-in-law

belliciste [belisist] *mf* warmonger

belligé·rant [beliʒerɑ̃] **-rante** [rɑ̃t] *adj* & *m* belligerent

belli·queux [belikǿ] **-queuse** [kǿz] *adj* bellicose, warlike

bel·lot [belo] **bel·lote** [belɔt] *adj* pretty, cute; dapper

bémol [bemɔl] *adj invar* & *m* (mus) flat

bémoliser [bemɔlize] *tr* to flat (*a note*); to provide (*a key signature*) with flats

ben [bɛ̃] *interj* (slang) well!

bénédicité [benedisite] *m* grace (*before a meal*)

bénédic·tin [benediktɛ̃] **-tine** [tin] *adj* & *m* Benedictine ‖ (*cap*) *f* Benedictine (*liqueur*)

bénédiction [benediksjɔ̃] *f* benediction; manna from heaven

bénéfice [benefis] *m* profit; benefit; benefice; parsonage, rectory; **à bénéfice** benefit (*performance*); **sous bénéfice d'inventaire** with grave reservations

bénéficiaire [benefisjɛr] *adj* profit, e.g., **marge bénéficiaire** profit margin ‖ *mf* beneficiary

bénéficier [benefisje] *intr* to profit, benefit

benêt [bənɛ] *adj masc* simple-minded ‖ *m* simpleton, numskull

bé·nin [benɛ̃] **-nigne** [niɲ] *adj* benign; mild, slight; benignant, accommodating

béni-oui-oui [beniwiwi] *mpl* yes men

bénir [benir] *tr* to bless, to consecrate

bé·nit [beni] **-nite** [nit] *adj* consecrated (*bread*); holy (*water*)

bénitier [benitje] *m* font (*for holy water*)

benja·min [bɛ̃ʒamɛ̃] **-mine** [min] *mf* baby (*the youngest child*) ‖ (*cap*) *m* Benjamin

benne [bɛn] *f* bucket, bin, hopper; dumper; cage (*in mine*); **benne preneuse** (mach) scoop, jaws (*of crane*)

be·noît [bənwa] **-noîte** [nwat] *adj* indulgent; sanctimonious ‖ (*cap*) *m* Benedict

benzène [bɛ̃zɛn] *m* (chem) benzene

benzine [bɛ̃zin] *f* benzine

béquille [bekij] *f* crutch

béquiller [bekije] *intr* to walk with a crutch or crutches

bercail [berkaj] *m* fold, bosom (*of church or family*)

ber·ceau [berso] *m* (*pl* **-ceaux**) cradle; bower; **berceau de verdure** or **de chèvrefeuille** arbor

bercelonnette [bersəlɔnɛt] *f* bassinet

bercer [berse] §51 *tr* to cradle, rock; to beguile; to assuage (*grief, pain*) ‖ *ref* to rock, swing; to delude oneself (*with vain hopes*)

ber·ceur [bersœr] **-ceuse** [sǿz] *adj* rocking, cradling ‖ *f* rocking chair; cradle song, lullaby

berge [berʒ] *f* bank, steep bank

berger [berʒe] *m* shepherd; shepherd dog

bergère [berʒɛr] *f* shepherdess; wing chair

bergerie [berʒəri] *f* sheepfold; pastoral poem

berle [berl] *f* water parsnip

Berlin [berlɛ̃] *m* Berlin; **Berlin-Est** East Berlin; **Berlin-Ouest** West Berlin

berline [berlin] *f* sedan (*automobile*); berlin (*carriage*)

berlingot [berlɛ̃go] *m* caramel candy; milk carton

berli·nois [berlinwa] **-noise** [nwaz] *adj* Berlin ‖ *mf* Berliner (*person*)

berlue [berly] *f*—**avoir la berlue** (coll) to be blind to what is going on

Bermudes [bermyd] *fpl*—**les Bermudes** Bermuda

bernacle [bernakl] *f* (orn) anatid; (zool) barnacle

berne [bern] *f* hazing; **en berne** at half-mast

berner [berne] *tr* to toss in a blanket; to ridicule; to fool

bernique [bernik] *interj* (coll) shucks!, heck!, what a shame!

berthe [bert] *f* corsage; cape

béryllium [beriljɔm] *m* beryllium

besace [bəzas] *f* beggar's bag; mendicancy

besicles [bəzikl] *fpl* (archaic) spectacles; **prenez donc vos besicles!** (coll) put your specs on!

besogne [bəzɔɲ] *f* work, task; **abattre de la besogne** to accomplish a great deal of work; **aller vite en besogne** to work too hastily

besogner [bəzɔɲe] *intr* to drudge, slave

beso·gneux [bəzɔɲǿ] **-gneuse** [ɲǿz] *adj* needy ‖ *mf* needy person

besoin [bəzwɛ̃] *m* need; poverty, distress; **au besoin** if necessary; **avoir besoin de** to need; **si besoin est** if need be

bes·son [besɔ̃] **bes·sonne** [besɔn] *mf* (dial) twin

bestiaire [bestjɛr] *m* bestiary

bes·tial -tiale [bestjal] (*pl* **-tiaux** [tjo]) *adj* bestial ‖ *mpl* see bestiaux

bestialité [bestjalite] *f* bestiality

bestiaux [bestjo] *mpl* livestock, cattle and horses

bestiole [bestjɔl] *f* bug, vermin

bê·ta [beta] **-tasse** [tas] *adj* (coll) silly ‖ *mf* (coll) sap, dolt

bétail [betaj] *m invar* grazing animals (*on a farm*); **gros bétail** cattle and horses; **menu bétail** or **petit bétail** sheep, goats, pigs, etc.

bête [bɛt] *adj* stupid, foolish ‖ *f* animal; beast; **bête à bon Dieu** (ent) ladybird; **bête de charge**, **bête de somme** pack animal; **bonne bête** harmless fool

bêtifier [betifje], [betifje] *tr* to make stupid ‖ *intr* to play the fool, to talk foolishly

bêtise [betiz], [betiz] *f* foolishness, stupidity, nonsense; trifle; **faire des bêtises** to blunder, do stupid things; to throw money around

béton [betɔ̃] *m* concrete; **béton armé** reinforced concrete

bétonner [betɔne] *tr* to make of concrete

bétonnière [betɔnjer] *f* cement mixer

bette [bet] *f* Swiss chard; **bette à carde** Swiss chard

betterave [betrav] *f* beet; **betterave sucrière** sugar beet

beuglement [bøɡləmɑ̃] *m* bellow, bellowing, lowing

beugler [bøɡle], [bœɡle] *tr* (slang) to bawl out (*a song*) || *intr* to bellow (*like a bull*); to low (*like cattle*)

beurre [bœr] *m* butter; **faire son beurre** (coll) to feather one's nest

beurrée [bœre] *f* slice of bread and butter

beurrer [bœre] *tr* to butter

beur·rier [bœrje] **beur·rière** [bœrjer] *adj* butter || *m* butter dish

beuverie [bœvri] *f* drinking party

bévue [bevy] *f* blunder, slip, boner

biais [bje] **biaise** [bjez] *adj* bias, oblique, slanting; skew (*arch*) || *m* bias, slant; skew (*of an arch*); **de biais** or **en biais** aslant, askew

biaiser [bjeze] *intr* to slant; (fig) to be evasive

bibelot [biblo] *m* curio, trinket, knick-knack

bibeloter [biblɔte] *intr* to buy or collect curios

bibe·ron [bibrɔ̃] **·ronne** [rɔn] *adj* addicted to the bottle || *mf* heavy drinker || *m* nursing bottle

Bible [bibl] *f* Bible

bibliobus [bibliɔbys] *m* bookmobile

bibliographe [bibliɔɡraf] *m* bibliographer

bibliographie [bibliɔɡrafi] *f* bibliography

bibliomane [bibliɔman] *mf* book collector

bibliothécaire [bibliɔteker] *mf* librarian

bibliothèque [bibliɔtɛk] *f* library; bookstand; **bibliothèque vivante** walking encyclopedia

biblique [biblik] *adj* Biblical

biceps [bisɛps] *m* biceps

biche [biʃ] *f* hind; doe; **ma biche** (coll) my darling

bicher [biʃe] *intr* —**ça biche!** (slang) fine!, it's fine!

bichlamar [biʃlamar] *m* pidgin

bichof [biʃɔf] *m* spiced wine

bi·chon [biʃɔ̃] **·chonne** [ʃɔn] *mf* lap dog

bichonner [biʃɔne] *tr* to curl (*one's hair*); to doll up || *ref* to doll up

bicoque [bikɔk] *f* shack, ramshackle house

bicorne [bikɔrn] *adj* two-cornered || *m* cocked hat

bicot [biko] *m* (coll) kid (*goat*); (pej) North African, Arab

bicyclette [bisiklɛt] *f* bicycle

bident [bidɑ̃] *m* two-pronged fork

bidet [bide] *m* bidet; nag (*horse*)

bidon [bidɔ̃] *m* drum (*for liquids*); canteen, water bottle

bidonville [bidɔ̃vil] *m* shantytown

bidule [bidyl] *m* (slang) gadget

bief [bjɛf] *m* millrace; reach, level (*of a stream or canal*)

bielle [bjɛl] *f* connecting rod, tie rod

bien [bjɛ̃] *m* good; welfare; estate, fortune; **biens** property, possessions; **biens consomptibles** consumer goods; **biens immeubles** real estate; **biens meubles** personal property || *adv* **§91** well; rightly, properly, quite; indeed, certainly; fine, e.g., **je vais bien** I'm fine; **bien de** + *art* much, e.g., **bien de l'eau** much water; many, e.g., **bien des gens** many people; **bien entendu** of course; **bien que** although; eh **bien! so!; si bien que** so that; **tant bien que mal** so-so, as well as possible || *interj* good!; all right!; that's enough!

bien-ai·mé ·mée [bjɛ̃neme] *adj* & *mf* beloved, darling

bien-dire [bjɛ̃dir] *m* gracious speech, eloquent delivery; **être sur son bien-dire** to be on one's best behavior

bien-di·sant [bjɛ̃dizɑ̃] **·sante** [zɑ̃t] *adj* smooth-spoken, smooth-tongued

bien-être [bjɛ̃nɛtr] *m* well-being, welfare

bienfaisance [bjɛ̃fəzɑ̃s] *f* charity, beneficence

bienfai·sant [bjɛ̃fəzɑ̃] **·sante** [zɑ̃t] *adj* charitable, beneficent

bienfait [bjɛ̃fɛ] *m* good turn, good deed, favor; **bienfaits** benefits

bienfai·teur [bjɛ̃fɛtœr] **·trice** [tris] *mf* benefactor || *f* benefactress

bien-fondé [bjɛ̃fɔ̃de] *m* cogency

bien-fonds [bjɛ̃fɔ̃] *m* (*pl* **biens-fonds**) real estate

bienheu·reux [bjɛ̃nœrø] **·reuse** [røz] *adj* & *mf* blessed

bien·nal ·nale [bjɛnnal] *adj* (*pl* **-naux** [no]) biennial || *f* biennial exposition

bienséance [bjɛ̃seɑ̃s] *f* propriety

bienséant [bjɛ̃seɑ̃] **bienséante** [bjɛ̃seɑ̃t] *adj* fitting, proper, appropriate

bientôt [bjɛ̃to] *adv* soon; **à bientôt!** so long!

bienveillance [bjɛ̃vejɑ̃s] *f* benevolence, kindness

bienveil·lant [bjɛ̃vejɑ̃] **bienveil·lante** [bjɛ̃vejɑ̃t] *adj* benevolent, kindly, kind

bienvenir [bjɛ̃vnir] *intr*—**se faire bienvenir** to make oneself welcome

bienve·nu ·nue [bjɛ̃vny] *adj* welcome || *m*—**soyez le bienvenu!** welcome! || *f* welcome; **souhaiter la bienvenue à** to welcome

bière [bjer] *f* beer; coffin; **bière à la pression** draft beer

biffer [bife] *tr* to cross out, to cancel, to erase; (slang) to cut (*class*)

biffin [bifɛ̃] *m* (slang) ragman; (slang) doughboy, G.I. Joe

bifo·cal ·cale [bifɔkal] *adj* (*pl* **-caux** [ko]) bifocal

bifteck [biftɛk] *m* beefsteak

bifurquer [bifyrke] *tr* to bifurcate, divide into two branches || *intr* & *ref* to bifurcate, fork; to branch off

bigame [biɡam] *adj* bigamous || *mf* bigamist

bigamie [biɡami] *f* bigamy

bigar·ré -rée [bigare] *adj* mottled, variegated; motley (*crowd*)

bigar·reau [bigaro] *m* (*pl* **-reaux**) white-heart cherry

bigarrer [bigare] *tr* to mottle, to variegate, to streak

bigarrure [bigaryr] *f* variegation, medley, mixture

bigle [bigl] *adj* cross-eyed || *m* beagle

bigler [bigle] *intr* to squint; to be cross-eyed

bigorne [bigɔrn] *f* two-horn anvil

bigorner [bigɔrne] *tr* to form on the anvil; (slang) to smash

bi·got [bigo] **-gote** [gɔt] *adj* sanctimonious || *mf* religious bigot

bigoterie [bigɔtri] *f* religious bigotry

bigoudi [bigudi] *m* hair curler, roller

bihebdomadaire [biebdɔmader] *adj* semiweekly

bi·jou [biʒu] *m* (*pl* **-joux**) jewel

bijouterie [biʒutri] *f* jewelry; jewelry shop; jewelry business

bijou·tier [biʒutje] **-tière** [tjɛr] *mf* jeweler

bilan [bilã] *m* balance sheet; balance; petition of bankruptcy; **faire le bilan** to tabulate the results

bilboquet [bilbɔkɛ] *m* job printing

bile [bil] *f* bile; **se faire de la bile** (coll) to worry, fret

bi·lieux [biljø] **-lieuse** [ljøz] *adj* bilious; irascible, grouchy

bilingue [bilɛ̃g] *adj* bilingual

billard [bijar] *m* billiards; billiard table; billiard room

bille [bij] *f* ball; ball bearing; billiard ball; marble; log; **à bille** ball-point (*pen*)

billet [bije] *m* note; ticket; bill (*currency*); **billet à ordre** promissory note; **billet d'abonnement** season ticket; **billet d'aller et retour** round-trip ticket; **billet de banque** bank note; **billet de correspondance** transfer; **billet de faire-part** announcement, notification (*of birth, wedding, death*); **billet de logement** billet; **billet doux** love letter; **billet simple** one-way ticket

billette [bijɛt] *f* billet

billevesée [bijvəze], [bilvəze] *f* nonsense

billion [biljɔ̃] *m* trillion (U.S.A.); billion (Brit)

billot [bijo] *m* block, chopping block; executioner's block

biloquer [bilɔke] *tr* to plow deeply

bimen·suel -suelle [bimãsɥɛl] *adj* semimonthly

bimes·triel -trielle [bimɛstriɛl] *adj* bimonthly (*every two months*)

bimoteur [bimɔtœr] *adj* twin-motor || *m* twin-motor plane

binaire [binɛr] *adj* binary

biner [bine] *tr* to hoe; to cultivate, to work over (*the soil*) || *intr* to say two masses the same day

binette [binɛt] *f* hoe; (hist) wig; (slang) phiz

bineur [binœr] *m* or **bineuse** [binøz] *f* cultivator (*implement*)

binocle [binɔkl] *m* lorgnette

binoculaire [binɔkylɛr] *adj* & *f* binocular

binôme [binom] *adj* & *m* binomial

biochimie [bjɔʃimi] *f* biochemistry

biographe [bjɔgraf] *mf* biographer

biographie [bjɔgrafi] *f* biography

biographique [bjɔgrafik] *adj* biographical

biologie [bjɔlɔʒi] *f* biology

biologiste [bjɔlɔʒist] *mf* biologist

biophysique [bjɔfizik] *f* biophysics

biopsie [bjɔpsi] *f* biopsy

bioxyde [biɔksid] *m* dioxide

bipar·ti -tie [biparti] *adj* bipartite

bipartisme [bipartism] *m* bipartisanship

bipartite [bipartit] *adj* bipartite; bipartisan

bipède [biped] *adj* & *mf* biped || *m* pair of legs of a horse

biplan [biplã] *m* biplane

bique [bik] *f* nanny goat

bir·man [birmã] **-mane** [man] *adj* Burmese || (*cap*) *mf* Burmese (*person*)

Birmanie [birmani] *f* Burma; **la Birmanie** Burma

bis [bi] **bise** [biz] *adj* gray-brown || [bis] *m*—**un bis au encore** || *f* see **bise** || **bis** [bis] *adv* twice; (mus) repeat; **sept bis** seven A, seven and a half || **bis** [bis] *interj* encore!

bisaïeul bisaïeule [bizajœl] *mf* great-grand-parent || *m* great-grandfather || *f* great-grandmother

bisan·nuel -nuelle [bizanɥɛl] *adj* biennial

bisbille [bisbij] *f* (coll) squabble

biscaïen [biskajɛ̃] **biscaïenne** [biskajɛn] *adj* Biscayan || (*cap*) *mf* Biscayan (*person*)

biscor·nu -nue [biskɔrny] *adj* misshapen, distorted

biscotin [biskɔtɛ̃] *m* hardtack

biscotte [biskɔt] *f* zwieback

biscuit [biskɥi] *m* hardtack; cracker; cookie; unglazed porcelain; **biscuit soda** soda cracker

bise [biz] *f* north wind; (fig) winter; (slang) kiss

bi·seau [bizo] *m* (*pl* **-seaux**) bevel, chamfer; **en biseau** beveled, chamfered

biseauter [bizote] *tr* to bevel, chamfer; to mark (*cards*)

biser [bize] *tr* to redye || *intr* to blacken

bi·son [bizɔ̃] **-sonne** [zɔn] *mf* bison, buffalo

bisque [bisk] *f* bisque

bisquer [biske] *intr* (coll) to be resentful

bissac [bisak] *m* bag, sack

bisser [bise] *tr* to encore; to repeat

bissextile [bisɛkstil] *adj* bissextile, leap, e.g., **année bissextile** leap year

bissexué bissexuée [biseksɥe] *adj* bisexual

bissexuel bissexuelle [biseksɥɛl] *adj* bisexual

bistouri [bisturi] *m* scalpel

bistournage [bisturnaʒ] *m* castration

bistre [bistr] *adj invar* soot-brown || *m* bister, soot-brown

bis·tré -trée [bistre] *adj* swarthy

bisulfate [bisylfat] *m* bisulfate
bisulfite [bisylfit] *m* bisulfite
bitter [biter] *m* bitters
bitume [bitym] *m* bitumen
bitumer [bityme] *tr* to asphalt
bitumi·neux [bityminø] **-neuse** [nøz] *adj* bituminous
bivouac [bivwak] *m* bivouac
bivouaquer [bivwake] *intr* to bivouac
bizarre [bizar] *adj* bizarre, strange
bizutage [bizytaʒ] *m* (slang) initiation, hazing
bizuth [bizyt] *m* (slang) freshman
blackbouler [blakbule] *tr* to blackball; (coll) to flunk
bla·fard [blafar] **-farde** [fard] *adj* pallid, pale, wan; lambent (*flame*)
blague [blag] *f* tobacco pouch; (coll) yarn, tall story, blarney; **blague à part** (coll) all joking aside; **faire une blague** (coll) to play a trick; **sale blague** (coll) dirty trick; **sans blague!** (coll) no kidding!
blaguer [blage] *tr* (coll) to kid; **blaguer qn** (coll) to pull s.o.'s leg || *intr* (coll) to kid, to tell tall stories
bla·gueur [blagœr] **-gueuse** [gøz] *adj* (coll) kidding, tongue-in-cheek || *mf* (coll) kidder, joker
blai·reau [blero] *m* (*pl* **-reaux**) badger; shaving brush
blâmable [blɑmabl] *adj* blameworthy
blâme [blɑm] *m* blame; **s'attirer un blâme** to receive a reprimand
blâmer [blame] *tr* to blame; to disapprove of
blanc [blɑ̃] **blanche** [blɑ̃ʃ] *adj* white; blank; clean; sleepless (*night*); expressionless (*voice*); **blanc comme un linge** white as a sheet || *m* white; blank; white meat; white man; white goods; chalk; bull's-eye; **à blanc** with blank cartridges; **blanc de baleine** spermaceti; **blanc de chaux** whitewash; **en blanc** blank; **en blanc et noir** in black and white
blanc-bec [blɑ̃bɛk] *m* (*pl* **blancs-becs**) (coll) greenhorn, callow youth
blanchâtre [blɑ̃ʃatr] *adj* whitish
blanchir [blɑ̃ʃir] *tr* to whiten; to wash or bleach; to whitewash; to blanch (*almonds*) || *intr* to blanch, whiten; to grow old
blanchissage [blɑ̃ʃisaʒ] *m* laundering; sugar refining
blanchisserie [blɑ̃ʃisri] *f* laundry
blanchis·seur [blɑ̃ʃisœr] **blanchis-seuse** [blɑ̃ʃisøz] *mf* launderer || *m* laundryman || *f* laundress, washerwoman
blanc-manger [blɑ̃mɑ̃ʒe] *m* (*pl* **blancs-manger**) blancmange
blanc-seing [blɑ̃sɛ̃] *m* (*pl* **blancs-seings**) carte blanche
bla·sé -sée [blaze] *adj* blasé, jaded
blaser [blaze] *tr* to cloy, to blunt
blason [blazɔ̃] *m* (heral) blazon
blasonner [blazone] *tr* (heral) to blazon
blasphéma·teur [blasfematœr] **-teuse** [tøz] *adj* blasphemous, blaspheming || *mf* blasphemer
blasphématoire [blasfematwar] *adj* blasphemous
blasphème [blasfem] *m* blasphemy

blasphémer [blasfeme] §10 *tr & intr* to blaspheme
blatte [blat] *f* cockroach
blé [ble] *m* wheat; **blé à moudre** grist; **blé de Turquie** corn; **blé froment** wheat; **blé noir** buckwheat; **manger son blé en herbe** to spend one's money before one has it
bled [bled] *m* (coll) backwoods, hinterland
blême [blem] *adj* pale; livid, sallow, wan; ghastly
blêmir [blemir] *intr* to turn pale or livid, to blanch; to grow dim
blennorragie [blenɔraʒi] *f* gonorrhea
blèse [blez] *adj* lisping || *mf* lisper
blésement [blezmɑ̃] *m* lisping
bléser [bleze] §10 *intr* to lisp
bles·sé -sée [blese] *adj* wounded || *mf* injured person; victim; casualty
blesser [blese], [blɛse] *tr* to wound; to injure
blessure [blesyr] *f* wound; injury
blet blette [ble] [blet] *adj* overripe || *f* chard
blettir [bletir] *intr* to overripen
bleu bleue [blø] (*pl* **bleus bleues**) *adj* blue; fairy (*stories*); violent (*anger*); rare (*meat*) || *m* blue; bluing; bruise; sauce for cooking fish; telegram or pneumatic letter; (coll) raw recruit, greenhorn; **bleu barbeau** light blue; **bleu marine** navy blue; **bleus** coveralls, dungarees; **passer au bleu** to avoid, elude (*a question*); **petit bleu** bad wine
bleuâtre [bløatr] *adj* bluish
bleuet [bløe] *m* bachelor's-button
bleuir [bløir] *tr & intr* to turn blue
bleu·té -tée [bløte] *adj* bluish
blindage [blɛ̃daʒ] *m* armor plate; armor plating; (elec) shield
blin·dé -dée [blɛ̃de] *adj* armored; armor-plated; (elec) shielded || *m* (mil) tank
blinder [blɛ̃de] *tr* to armor-plate; (elec) to shield
bloc [blɔk] *m* block; blocking; tablet, pad (*of paper*); (elec, mach) unit; **à bloc** tight; **en bloc** all together, in a lump; **envoyer** or **mettre au bloc** (slang) to throw (s.o.) in the jug; **serrer le frein à bloc** to jam on the brakes
blocage [blɔkaʒ] *m* blockage, blocking; lumping together; rubble; freezing (*of prices; of wages*); application (*of brakes*)
blocaille [blɔkaj] *f* rubble
bloc-diagramme [blɔkdjagram] *m* (*pl* **blocs-diagrammes**) cross section
bloc-moteur [blɔkmɔtœr] *m* (aut) motor and transmission system
bloc-notes [blɔknɔt] *m* (*pl* **blocs-notes**) scratch pad, note pad
blocus [blɔkys] *m* blockade
blond blonde [blɔ̃] [blɔ̃d] *adj* blond || *m* blond || *f* see **blonde**
blondasse [blɔ̃das] *adj* washed-out blond
blonde [blɔ̃d] *f* blonde; blond lace; **blonde platinée** platinum blonde
blon·din [blɔ̃dɛ̃] **-dine** [din] *adj* fair-

haired || *mf* blond || *m* cableway; hopper for concrete; (obs) fop

blondir [blɔ̃dir] *tr* to bleach || *intr* to turn yellow, become blond

bloquer [blɔke] *tr* to blockade; to block up; to fill with rubble; to jam on (*the brakes*); to stop (*a car*) by jamming on the brakes; to pocket (*a billiard ball*); to run on (*two paragraphs*); to tighten (*a nut or bolt*) as much as possible; to freeze (*wages*)

blottir [blɔtir] *ref* to cower; to curl up

blouse [bluz] *f* smock; billiard pocket

blouser [bluze] *tr* to deceive, take in || *intr* to pucker around the waist || *ref* to be mistaken

blouson [bluzɔ̃] *m* jacket

blouson-noir [bluzɔ̃nwar] *m* (*pl* **blousons-noirs**) juvenile delinquent

blue-jean [bludʒin] *m* blue jeans

bluet [blyɛ] *m* bachelor's-button; (Canad) blueberry

bluette [blyɛt] *f* piece of light fiction; spark, flash

bluffer [blyfe] *tr & intr* to bluff

bluf·feur [blyfœr] **bluf·feuse** [blyføz] *mf* bluffer

blutage [blytaʒ] *m* bolting, sifting; boltings, siftings

bluter [blyte] *tr* to bolt, to sift

blutoir [blytwar] *m* bolter, sifter

B.N. *abbr* (**Bibliothèque Nationale**) National Library

boa [bɔa] *m* boa

bobard [bɔbar] *m* (coll) fish story, tall tale

bobèche [bɔbɛʃ] *f* bobeche (*disk to catch drippings of candle*)

bobine [bɔbin] *f* bobbin; spool, reel; (elec) coil; **bobine d'allumage** (aut) ignition coil

bobiner [bɔbine] *tr* to spool, wind

bocage [bɔkaʒ] *m* grove

boca·ger [bɔkaʒe] **-gère** [ʒɛr] *adj* wooded

bo·cal [bɔkal] *m* (*pl* **-caux** [ko]) jar, bottle, globe; fishbowl

boche [bɔʃ] *adj & mf* (slang & pej) German

bock [bɔk] *m* beer glass (*half pint*); glass of beer; enema; douche

boëte [bwet] *f* fish bait

bœuf [bœf] *m* (*pl* **bœufs** [bø]) beef; head of beef; steer; ox; **bœuf en conserve** corned beef

boggie [bɔʒi] *m* (rr) truck

bogue [bɔgi] *f* chestnut bur

Bohême [bɔɛm] *f* Bohemia; **la Bohême** Bohemia

bohème [bɔɛm] *adj & mf* Bohemian (*artist*) || *f*—**la bohème** Bohemia (*of the artistic world*)

bohé·mien [bɔɛmjɛ̃] **-mienne** [mjɛn] *adj* Bohemian; gypsy || (*cap*) *mf* Bohemian; gypsy

boire [bwar] *m* drink; drinking; **le boire et le manger** food and drink || §8 *tr* to drink; to swallow (*an affront*) || *intr* to drink; **boire à la santé de** to drink to the health of; **boire à** (*même*) to drink out of (*a bottle*); **boire comme un trou** to

drink like a fish; **boire dans** to drink out of (*a glass*)

bois [bwɑ], [bwa] *m* wood; woods; horns, antlers; **bois de chauffage** firewood; **bois de lit** bedstead; **bois flotté** driftwood; **bois fondu** plastic wood; **les bois** (mus) the woodwinds

boisage [bwazaʒ] *m* timbering

boi·sé -sée [bwaze] *adj* wooded; paneled

boiser [bwaze] *tr* to panel, to wainscot; to timber (*a mine*); to reforest

boiserie [bwazri] *f* woodwork, paneling, wainscoting

bois·seau [bwaso] *m* (*pl* **bois·seaux**) bushel

boisson [bwasɔ̃] *f* drink, beverage; **boissons hygiéniques** light wines, beer, and soft drinks

boîte [bwat] *f* box; can; canister; (slang) joint, dump; **boîte aux lettres** mailbox; **boîte de nuit** night club; **boîte d'essieu** (mach) journal box; **boîte de vitesses** transmission-gear box; **boîte postale** post-office box; **en boîte** boxed; canned; **ferme ta boîte!** (slang) shut up!; **mettre en boîte** to box; to can; (slang) to make fun of

boiter [bwate] *intr* to limp

boi·teux [bwatø] **-teuse** [tøz] *adj* lame, limping; unsteady, wobbly (*chair*) || *mf* lame person

boî·tier [bwatje] **-tière** [tjɛr] *mf* box-maker; mail collector (*from mailboxes*) || *m* box, case; kit; medicine kit; (mach) housing; **boîtier de montre** watchcase

boitte [bwat] *f* fish bait

bol [bɔl] *m* bowl, basin; cud; bolus, pellet

bolchevique [bɔlʃevik] *adj* Bolshevik || (*cap*) *mf* Bolshevik

bolcheviste [bɔlʃevist] *adj* Bolshevik || (*cap*) *mf* Bolshevik

bolduc [bɔldyk] *m* colored ribbon

bolée [bɔle] *f* bowlful

bolide [bɔlid] *m* meteorite, fireball; racing car

bombance [bɔ̃bɑ̃s] *f* (coll) feast; **faire bombance** (coll) to have a blowout

bombardement [bɔ̃bardəmɑ̃] *m* bombing; bombardment

bombarder [bɔ̃barde] *tr* to bomb; to bombard; (coll) to appoint at the last minute

bombardier [bɔ̃bardje] *m* bomber; bombardier

bombe [bɔ̃b] *f* bomb; **bombe à hydrogène** hydrogen bomb; **bombe atomique** atomic bomb; **bombe glacée** molded ice cream; **bombe volante** buzz bomb; **faire la bombe** (slang) to go on a spree

bom·bé -bée [bɔ̃be] *adj* convex, bulging

bomber [bɔ̃be] *tr* to bend, to arch; to stick out (*one's chest*); **bomber le torse** (fig) to stick one's nose up || *intr & ref* to bulge

bon [bɔ̃] **bonne** [bɔn] *adj* §91 good; **à quoi bon?** what's the use?; **sentir bon** to smell good; **tenir bon** to hold fast

|| (when standing before noun) *adj* §91 good; fast (*color*) || *m* coupon; **bon de commande** order blank; **pour de bon** or **pour tout de bon** for good, really || *f* see **bonne** || **bon** *interj* good!; what!

bonace [bɔnas] *f* calm (*of the sea*)

bonasse [bɔnas] *adj* simple, naïve

bon-bec [bɔ̃bɛk] *m* (*pl* **bons-becs**) fast talker

bonbon [bɔ̃bɔ̃] *m* bonbon, piece of candy

bonbonne [bɔ̃bɔn] *f* demijohn

bonbonnière [bɔ̃bɔnjɛr] *f* candy dish; candy box

bond [bɔ̃] *m* bound, bounce; leap, jump; **faire faux bond** to miss an appointment; **faux bond** misstep

bonde [bɔ̃d] *f* plug; bunghole; sluice gate

bon-dé -dée [bɔ̃de] *adj* crammed

bondir [bɔ̃dir] *intr* to bound, to bounce; to leap, to jump; **faire bondir** to make (*s.o.*) hit the ceiling

bondissement [bɔ̃dismɑ̃] *m* bouncing, leaping

bondon [bɔ̃dɔ̃] *m* bung

bonheur [bɔnœr] *m* happiness; good luck; **au petit bonheur** by chance, at random; **par bonheur** luckily

bonheur-du-jour [bɔnœrdyʒur] *m* (*pl* **bonheurs-du-jour**) escritoire

bonhomie [bɔnɔmi] *f* good nature; credulity

bonhomme [bɔnɔm] *adj* good-natured, simple-minded || *m* (*pl* **bonshommes** [bɔ̃zɔm]) fellow, guy; old fellow; **bonhomme de neige** snowman; **Bonhomme Hiver** Jack Frost; **faux bonhomme** humbug; **petit bonhomme** little man (*child*)

boni [bɔni] *m* bonus; discount coupon; surplus (*over estimated expenses*)

bonification [bɔnifikasjɔ̃] *f* improvement; discount; bonus; advantage

bonifier [bɔnifje] *tr* to improve; to give a discount to

boniment [bɔnimɑ̃] *m* sales talk, smooth talk

bonimenteur [bɔnimɑ̃tœr] *m* huckster, charlatan

bonjour [bɔ̃ʒur] *m* good day, good morning, good afternoon, hello

bonne [bɔn] *f* maid; **bonne à tout faire** maid of all work

bonne-maman [bɔnmamɑ̃] *f* (*pl* **bonnes-mamans**) grandma

bonnement [bɔnmɑ̃] *adv* honestly, plainly

bonnet [bɔnɛ] *m* bonnet; stocking cap; cup (*of a brassiere*); (mil) undress hat; **bonnet d'âne** dunce cap; **bonnet de nuit** nightcap; **gros bonnet** (coll) VIP

bonneterie [bɔnɛtri] *f* hosiery; knitwear

bon-papa [bɔ̃papa] *m* (*pl* **bons-papas**) grandpa

bonsoir [bɔ̃swar] *m* good evening; (coll) good night

bonté [bɔ̃te] *f* goodness; kindness

booster [bustœr] *m* (rok) booster

borborygme [bɔrbɔrigm] *m* rumbling (*in the stomach*)

bord [bɔr] *m* edge, border; rim, brim; side (*of a ship*); **à bord** on board; **à pleins bords** overflowing; without hindrance; **à ras bords** full to the brim; **être du** (**même**) **bord de** to be of the same mind as; **faux bord** list (*of ship*); **jeter par-dessus bord** to throw overboard

bordage [bɔrdaʒ] *m* edging (*of dress*); planking (*of ship*)

bordé [bɔrde] *m* border, edging

bordée [bɔrde] *f* broadside, volley; (naut) tack; **bordée de bâbord** port watch; **bordée de tribord** starboard watch; **courir une bordée** to go skylarking on shore leave; **tirer une bordée** to jump ship

bordel [bɔrdɛl] *m* (vulgar) brothel

borde-lais -laise [bɔrdəlɛ] *-lɛz] adj* of Bordeaux || *f* Bordeaux cask || (*cap*) *mf* native or inhabitant of Bordeaux

border [bɔrde] *tr* to border; to hem; to sail along (*the coast*); **border un lit** to make a bed

borde-reau [bɔrdəro] *m* (*pl* **-reaux**) itemized account, memorandum

bordure [bɔrdyr] *f* border

bore [bɔr] *m* boron

boréal boréale [bɔreal] *adj* (*pl* **boréaux** [bɔreo] or **boréals**) boreal; northern

borgne [bɔrɲ] *adj* one-eyed; blind in one eye; disreputable (*bar, house, etc.*) || *mf* one-eyed person

borne [bɔrn] *f* landmark; boundary stone; milestone; (elec) binding post, terminal; (slang) kilometer; **bornes** bounds, limits

bor-né -née [bɔrne] *adj* limited, narrow; dull (*mind*)

borner [bɔrne] *tr* to mark out the boundary of; to set limits to || *ref* to restrain oneself

bosquet [bɔskɛ] *m* grove

bosse [bɔs] *f* hump; bump; (coll) flair

bosseler [bɔsle] §34 *tr* to emboss; to dent

bossoir [bɔswar] *m* davit; bow (*of ship*)

bos-su -sue [bɔsy] *adj* hunchbacked || *mf* hunchback; **rire comme un bossu** to split one's sides laughing

botanique [bɔtanik] *adj* botanical || *f* botany

botte [bɔt] *f* boot; bunch (*e.g., of radishes*); sword thrust; **lécher les bottes à qn** (coll) to lick s.o.'s boots

botteler [bɔtle] §34 *tr* to tie in bunches

botter [bɔte] *tr* to boot, to boot out; **cela me botte** that suits me || *ref* to put on one's boots

bottier [bɔtje] *m* custom shoemaker

Bottin [bɔtɛ̃] *m* business directory

bottine [bɔtin] *f* high button shoe

boubouler [bubule] *intr* to hoot like an owl

bouc [buk] *m* billy goat; goatee; **bouc émissaire** scapegoat

boucan [bukɑ̃] *m* smokehouse; (coll) uproar

boucaner [bukane] *tr* to smoke (*meat*)

boucanier [bukanje] *m* buccaneer

boucharde [buʃard] *f* bushhammer

bouche [buʃ] *f* mouth; muzzle (*of gun*); door (*of oven*); entrance (*to subway*); **bouche close!** mum's the word!; **bouche d'incendie** fire hydrant; **bouches** mouth (*of river*); **faire la petite bouche à** to turn up one's nose at

bouchée [buʃe] *f* mouthful; patty; chocolate cream (*candy*)

boucher [buʃe] *m* butcher ‖ *tr* to stop up, to plug; to wall up; to cut off (*the view*); to bung (*a barrel*); to cork (*a bottle*); **bouché à l'émeri** (coll) completely dumb ‖ *ref* to be stopped up

boucherie [buʃri] *f* butcher shop; **boucherie chevaline** horsemeat butcher shop

bouche-trou [buʃtru] *m* (*pl* -**trous**) stopgap

bouchon [buʃ5] *m* cork, stopper; bob (*on a fishline*); **bouchon de circulation** traffic jam

bouclage [buklaʒ] *m* closing of circuit; (mil) encirclement

boucle [bukl] *f* buckle; earring; curl; (aer) loop; **boucler la boucle** to loop the loop

boucler [bukle] *tr* to buckle; to curl (*the hair*); to lock up (*prisoners*); to put a nose ring on (*a bull*); **boucler son budget** (coll) to make ends meet; **la boucler** (slang) to shut up, to button one's lip ‖ *intr* to curl

bouclier [buklije] *m* shield; **bouclier antithermique** heat shield

bouddhisme [budism] *m* Buddhism

bouddhiste [budist] *adj & mf* Buddhist

bouder [bude] *tr* to be distant toward ‖ *intr* to pout, sulk

bou·deur [budœr] -**deuse** [døz] *adj* pouting ‖ *mf* sullen person

boudin [budɛ̃] *m* blood sausage; **à boudin** spiral

boudiner [budine] *tr* to twist

boue [bu] *f* mud

bouée [bwe] *f* buoy; **bouée de sauvetage** life preserver

boueur [bwœr] *m* garbage collector; scavenger

boueux [bwø] **boueuse** [bwøz] *adj* muddy; grimy; (typ) smeary

bouf·fant [bufã] **bouf·fante** [bufãt] *adj* puffed (*sleeves*); baggy (*trousers*)

bouffe [buf] *adj* comic (*opera*) ‖ *f* (slang) grub

bouffée [bufe] *f* puff, gust

bouffer [bufe] *tr* (slang) to gobble up ‖ *intr* to puff out

bouf·fi -fie [bufi] *adj* puffed up or out

bouffir [bufir] *tr & intr* to puff up

bouffissure [bufisyr] *f* swelling

bouf·fon [buf5] **bouf·fonne** [bufɔn] *adj & m* buffoon, comic

bouffonnerie [bufɔnri] *f* buffoonery

bouge [buʒ] *m* bulge; hovel, dive

bougeoir [buʒwar] *m* flat candlestick

bougeotte [buʒɔt] *f* (coll) wanderlust

bouger [buʒe] §38 *tr*—**ne bougez rien!** (coll) don't move a thing! ‖ *intr* to budge, stir

bougie [buʒi] *f* candle; candlepower; spark plug

bou·gon [bug5] -**gonne** [gɔn] *adj* grumbling ‖ *mf* grumbler

bougran [bugrã] *m* buckram

bou·gre [bugr] -**gresse** [gres] *mf* (slang) customer; **bougre d'âne** (slang) perfect ass ‖ *m* (slang) guy; **bon bougre** (slang) swell guy ‖ *f* (slang) wench

bougrement [bugrəmã] *adv* (slang) awfully, darned

bouillabaisse [bujabes] *f* bouillabaisse, fish stew, chowder

bouil·lant [bujã] **bouil·lante** [bujãt] *adj* boiling; fiery, impetuous

bouilleur [bujœr] *m* distiller (*of brandy*); boiler tube; small nuclear reactor

bouilli [buji] *m* beef stew

bouillir [bujir] §9 *tr & intr* to boil; **faire bouillir la marmite** (coll) to bring home the bacon

bouilloire [bujwar] *f* kettle

bouillon [buj5] *m* broth, bouillon; bubble; bubbling; cheap restaurant; **à gros bouillons** gushing; **boire un bouillon** (coll) to gulp water; (coll) to suffer business losses; **bouillon de culture** (bact) broth; **bouillon d'onze heures** poisoned drink; **bouillons** unsold copies, remainders

bouillonnement [bujɔnmã] *m* boiling; effervescence

bouillonner [bujɔne] *tr* to put puffs in (*a dress*) ‖ *intr* to boil up; to have copies left over

bouillotte [bujɔt] *f* hot-water bottle

boulanger [bulãʒe] *m* baker ‖ §38 *intr* to bake bread

boulangerie [bulãʒri] *f* bakery

boule [bul] *f* ball; (slang) nut, head; **boule d'eau chaude** hot-water bottle; **boule de neige** snowball; **boule noire** blackball; **boules** bowling; **en boule** (fig) tied in a knot, on edge; **perdre la boule** (slang) to go off one's rocker; **se mettre en boule** (coll) to get mad

bou·leau [bulo] *m* (*pl* -**leaux**) birch

boule-de-neige [buldəneʒ] *f* (*pl* **boules-de-neige**) guelder-rose; meadow mushroom

bouledogue [buldɔg] *m* bulldog

bouler [bule] *tr* to pad (*a bull's horn*) ‖ *intr* to roll like a ball; **envoyer bouler** (slang) to send (*s.o.*) packing

boulet [bulɛ] *m* cannonball; (coll) cross to bear

boulette [bulɛt] *f* ball, pellet

boulevard [bulvar] *m* boulevard; **boulevard périphérique** belt road

boulevar·dier [bulvardje] -**dière** [djer] *adj* fashionable ‖ *m* boulevardier, man about town

bouleversement [bulversmã] *m* upset

bouleverser [bulverse] *tr* to upset; to overthrow

boulier [bulje] *m* abacus (*for scoring billiards*)

bouline [bulin] *f* (naut) bowline

boulingrin [bulɛ̃grɛ̃] *m* bowling green

bouliste [bulist] *mf* bowler

boulodrome [bulɔdrɔm] *m* bowling alley

boulon [bulɔ̃] *m* bolt; **boulon à œil** eyebolt

boulonner [bulɔne] *tr* to bolt || *intr* (slang) to work

bou·lot [bulo] **-lotte** [lɔt] *adj* (coll) dumpy, squat || *m* (slang) cylindrical loaf of bread; (slang) work

boulotter [bulɔte] *tr* (slang) to eat

boum [bum] *interj* boom!

bouquet [buke] *m* bouquet; clump (*of trees*); prawn; jack rabbit; **c'est le bouquet** (coll) it's tops; (coll) that's the last straw

bouquetière [buktjɛr] *f* flower girl

bouquin [bukɛ̃] *m* (coll) book; (coll) old book

bouquiner [bukine] *intr* to shop around for old books; (coll) to read

bouquinerie [bukinri] *f* secondhand books; secondhand bookstore

bouqui·neur [bukinœr] **-neuse** [nøz] *mf* collector of old books; browser in bookstores

bouquiniste [bukinist] *mf* secondhand bookdealer

bourbe [burb] *f* mire

bour·beux [burbø] **-beuse** [bøz] *adj* miry, muddy

bourbier [burbje] *m* quagmire

bourbillon [burbijɔ̃] *m* core (*of boil*)

bourde [burd] *f* (coll) boner

bourdon [burdɔ̃] *m* bumblebee; big bell; (mus) bourdon; **avoir le bourdon** (slang) to have the blues; **faux bourdon** drone

bourdonnement [burdɔnmɑ̃] *m* buzzing

bourdonner [burdɔne] *tr* (coll) to hum (*a tune*) || *intr* to buzz

bourg [bur] *m* market town

bourgade [burgad] *f* small town

bour·geois [burʒwa] **-geoise** [ʒwaz] *adj* bourgeois, middle-class || *mf* commoner, middle-class person; Philistine; **gros bourgeois** solid citizen || *m* businessman; **en bourgeois** in civies || *f* (slang) old woman (*wife*)

bourgeoisie [burʒwazi] *f* middle class; **haute bourgeoisie** upper middle class; **petite bourgeoisie** lower middle class

bourgeon [burʒɔ̃] *m* bud; pimple

bourgeonnement [burʒɔnmɑ̃] *m* budding

bourgeonner [burʒɔne] *intr* to bud; to break out in pimples

bourgeron [burʒərɔ̃] *m* jumper, overalls; sweat shirt

bourgogne [burgɔɲ] *m* Burgundy (*wine*) || (*cap*) *f* Burgundy (*province*); **la Bourgogne** Burgundy

bourgui·gnon [burgiɲɔ̃] **-gnonne** [ɲɔn] *adj* Burgundian || *m* Burgundian (*dialect*) || (*cap*) *mf* Burgundian

bourlinguer [burlɛ̃ge] *intr* to labor (*in high seas*); (coll) to travel, to venture forth

bourrade [burad] *f* sharp blow; poke

bourrage [buraʒ] *m* cramming; **bourrage de crâne** (coll) ballyhoo

bourre [bur] *f* stuffing, animal hair

bour·reau [buro] *m* (*pl* **-reaux**) executioner; torturer; **bourreau des cœurs** lady-killer; **bourreau de travail** glutton for work

bourrée [bure] *f* fagot of twigs

bourreler [burle] §34 *tr* to torment

bourrelet [burlɛ] *m* weather stripping; roll (*of fat*); contour pillow

bourrer [bure] *tr* to stuff, cram; **bourrer de coups** to pummel, slug; **bourrer le crâne à** (coll) to hand (*s.o.*) a line, to take (*s.o.*) in || *ref* to stuff

bourriche [buriʃ] *f* hamper

bourrique [burik] *f* she-ass; (coll) ass

bour·ru -rue [bury] *adj* rough; grumpy; unfermented (*wine*)

bourse [burs] *f* purse; scholarship, fellowship; stock exchange, bourse; **bourse du travail** labor union hall; **bourses** scrotum

bourse-à-pasteur [bursapastœr] *f* (*pl* **bourses-à-pasteur** [bursapastœr]) (bot) shepherd's-purse

boursicaut or **boursicot** [bursiko] *m* little purse; nest egg

boursicoter [bursikɔte] *intr* to dabble in the stock market

bour·sier [bursje] **-sière** [sjɛr] *adj* scholarship (*student*); stock-market (*operation*) || *mf* scholar (*holder of scholarship*); speculator

boursoufler [bursufle] *tr* to puff up

bousculer [buskyle] *tr* to jostle

bouse [buz] *f*—**bouse de vache** cow dung

bouseux [buzø] *m* (slang) peasant

bousillage [buzijaʒ] *m* cob (*mixture of clay and straw*); (coll) botched job

bousiller [buzije] *tr* (coll) to bungle; (slang) to smash up || *intr* to build with cob

boussole [busɔl] *f* compass; **perdre la boussole** (coll) to go off one's rocker

boustifaille [bustifaj] *f* (slang) feasting; (slang) good food

bout [bu] *m* end; piece, scrap, bit; **à bout** exhausted; **à bout de bras** at arm's length; **à bout portant** point-blank; **à tout bout de champ** at every turn, repeatedly; **au bout du compte** after all; **bout de fil** (telp) (coll) ring, call; **bout de l'an** watch night; **bout d'essai** screen test; **bout d'homme** wisp of a man; **bout filtre** filter tip; **de bout en bout** from start to finish; **montrer le bout de l'oreille** to show one's true colors; **rire du bout des dents** to force a laugh; **sur le bout du doigt** at one's fingertips; **venir à bout de** to succeed in, to triumph over

boutade [butad] *f* sally, quip; whim

bout-dehors [budœɔr] *m* (*pl* **bouts-dehors**) (naut) boom

boute-en-train [butɑ̃trɛ̃] *m invar* life of the party

boute-feu [butfø] *m* (*pl* **-feux**) firebrand

bouteille [butɛj] *f* bottle; **bouteille isolante** vacuum bottle

bouteiller [buteje] *m* (hist) cupbearer

bouterolle [butrɔl] *f* ward (*of lock*); rivet snap

boute-selle [butsɛl] *m* boots and saddies (*trumpet call*)

boutique [butik] *f* shop; stock, goods; workshop; set of tools; **boutique cadeaux, boutique de souvenirs** gift shop; **boutique de modiste** millinery shop; **quelle boutique!** (coll) what a hellhole!, what an awful place!

boutiquier [butikje] *m* shopkeeper

bouton [butɔ̃] *m* button; pimple; doorknob; bud; **bouton de puissance** volume control

bouton-d'argent [butɔ̃darʒɑ̃] *m* (*pl* **boutons-d'argent**) sneezewort

bouton-d'or [butɔ̃dɔr] *m* (*pl* **boutons-d'or**) buttercup

boutonner [butɔne] *tr* to button || *intr* to bud

bouton-neux [butɔnø] **bouton-neuse** [butɔnøz] *adj* pimply

boutonnière [butɔnjɛr] *f* buttonhole

bouton-pression [butɔ̃presjɔ̃] *m* (*pl* **boutons-pression**) snap fastener

bouture [butyr] *f* cutting (*from a plant*)

bouturer [butyre] *tr* to propagate (*plants*) by cuttings || *intr* to shoot suckers

bouverie [buvri] *f* cowshed

bou•vier [buvje] **-vière** [vjɛr] *mf* cowherd

bouvillon [buvijɔ̃] *m* steer, young bullock

bouvreuil [buvrœj] *m* bullfinch; **bouvreuil cramoisi** scarlet grosbeak

box [bɔks] *m* (*pl* **boxes**) stall

boxe [bɔks] *f* boxing

boxer [bɔksœr] *m* boxer (*dog*) || [bɔkse] *tr & intr* to box

boxeur [bɔksœr] *m* (sports) boxer

boy [bɔj] *m* houseboy; chorus boy

boyau [bwajo] *m* (*pl* **boyaux**) intestine, gut; inner tube; (mil) communication trench

boycottage [bɔjkɔtaʒ] *m* boycott

boycotter [bɔjkɔte] *tr* to boycott

boy-scout [bɔjskut] *m* (*pl* **-scouts**) boy scout

b. p. f. *abbr* (**bon pour francs**) value in francs

bracelet [braslɛ] *m* bracelet; wristband; **bracelet de caoutchouc** rubber band; **bracelet de cheville** anklet

bracelet-montre [braslɛmɔ̃tr] *m* (*pl* **bracelets-montres**) wrist watch

braconnage [brakɔnaʒ] *m* poaching

braconner [brakɔne] *intr* to poach

bracon•nier [brakɔnje] **bracon•nière** [brakɔnjɛr] *mf* poacher

brader [brade] *tr* to sell off

braderie [bradəri] *f* clearance sale

braguette [bragɛt] *f* fly (*of trousers*)

brahmane [brɑman] *m* Brahman

brai [brɛ] *m* resin, pitch

braille [brɑj] *m* Braille

brailler [brɑje] *tr & intr* to bawl

brail•leur [brɑjœr] **brail•leuse** [brɑjøz] *adj* loudmouthed || *mf* loudmouth

braiment [brɛmɑ̃] *m* bray

braire [brɛr] §68 (usually used in: *inf*; *ger*; *pp*; 3d *sg & pl*) *intr* to bray

braise [brɛz] *f* embers, coals

braiser [brɛze] *tr* to braise

braisière [brɛzjɛr] *f* braising pan

bramer [brame] *intr* to bell

bran [brɑ̃] *m* bran; (slang) dung; **bran de scie** sawdust

brancard [brɑ̃kar] *m* stretcher; shaft (*of carriage*)

brancardier [brɑ̃kardje] *m* stretcher-bearer

branche [brɑ̃ʃ] *f* branch

brancher [brɑ̃ʃe] *tr* to branch, fork; to hook up, connect; (elec) to plug in || *intr* to perch

brande [brɑ̃d] *f* heather; heath

brandir [brɑ̃dir] *tr* to brandish

brandon [brɑ̃dɔ̃] *m* torch; firebrand; **brandon de discorde** mischief-maker

bran•lant [brɑ̃lɑ̃] **-lante** [lɑ̃t] *adj* shaky, tottering, unsteady

branle [brɑ̃l] *m* oscillation; impetus; **mener le branle** to lead the dance; **mettre en branle** to set in motion

branle-bas [brɑ̃ləba] *m invar* call to battle stations; bustle, commotion

branler [brɑ̃le] *tr* to shake (*the head*) || *intr* to shake; to oscillate; to be loose (*said of tooth*); **branler dans le manche** to be about to fall

braque [brak] *adj* (coll) featherbrained || *mf* (coll) featherbrain || *m* pointer (*dog*)

braquer [brake] *tr* to aim, point; to fix (*the eyes*); to turn (*a steering wheel*); **braquer contre** to turn (*e.g., an audience*) against || *intr* to steer

bras [brɑ] *m* arm; handle; shaft; **à bras raccourcis** violently; **bras de mer** sound (*passage of water*); **bras de pick-up** pickup arm, tone arm; **bras dessus bras dessous** arm in arm; **en bras de chemise** in shirt sleeves; **manquer de bras** to be short-handed

braser [braze] *tr* to braze

brasero [brazero] *m* brazier

brasier [brazje] *m* glowing coals; blaze

bras-le-corps [bralkɔr] *m*—**à bras-le-corps** around the waist

brassage [brasaʒ] *m* brewing

brasse [brɑs], [bras] *f* fathom; breast stroke

brassée [brase] *f* armful; stroke (*in swimming*)

brasser [brase] *tr* to brew

brasserie [brasri] *f* brewery; restaurant, lunchroom

bras•seur [brasœr] **bras•seuse** [brasøz] *mf* brewer; swimmer doing the breast stroke; **brasseur d'affaires** person with many irons in the fire

brassière [brasjɛr] *f* sleeved shirt (*for an infant*); shoulder strap; **brassière de sauvetage** life preserver

bravache [bravaʃ] *adj & m* braggart

bravade [bravad] *f* bravado

brave [brav] *adj* brave || (*when standing before noun*) *adj* worthy, honest || *m* brave man

braver [brave] *tr* to brave

bravoure [bravur] *f* bravery, gallantry

break [brek] *m* station wagon

brebis [brəbi] *f* ewe; sheep, lamb; **brebis galeuse** black sheep

brèche [brɛʃ] *f* breach (*in a wall*); gap (*between mountains*); nick (*e.g., on china*); (fig) dent (*in a fortune*);

battre en brèche to batter; (fig) to disparage; **mourir sur la brèche** to go down fighting

bredouille [brəduj]—**rentrer** or **revenir bredouille** to return empty-handed

bredouiller [brəduje] *tr* to stammer out (*an excuse*) || *intr* to mumble

bref [bref] **brève** [brɛv] *adj* brief, short; curt || *m* papal brief || *f* short syllable; **brèves et longues** dots and dashes || **bref** *adv* briefly, in short

brelan [brəlɑ̃] *m* (cards) three of a kind

breloque [brələk] *f* trinket, charm; **battre la breloque** to sound the all clear; to keep irregular time; (coll) to have a screw loose somewhere

brème [brɛm] *f* (ichth) bream

Brésil [brezil] *m*—**le Brésil** Brazil

brési·lien [breziljɛ̃] **-lienne** [ljɛn] *adj* Brazilian || (*cap*) *mf* Brazilian

Bretagne [brətaɲ] *f* Brittany; **la Bretagne** Brittany

bretelle [brətɛl] *f* strap, sling; access route; **bretelles** suspenders

bre·ton [brətɔ̃] **-tonne** [tɔn] *adj* Breton || *m* Breton (*language*) || (*cap*) *mf* Breton (*person*)

bretteur [brɛtœr] *m* swashbuckler

bretzel [brɛtzel] *m* pretzel

breuvage [brœvaʒ] *m* beverage, drink

brevet [brəve] *m* diploma; license; (mil) commission; **brevet d'invention** patent

breve·té **-tée** [brəvte] *adj* commissioned; patented; **non breveté** noncommissioned || *m* commissioned officer

breveter [brəvte] §34 *tr* to patent

bréviaire [brevjer] *m* (eccl) breviary

bribe [brib] *f* hunk of bread; **bribes** scraps, leavings, fragments

bric [brik] *m*—**de bric et de broc** with odds and ends; somehow

bric-à-brac [brikabrak] *m invar* secondhand merchandise; junk shop

brick [brik] *m* brig (*kind of ship*)

bricolage [brikɔlaʒ] *m* do-it-yourself

bricoler [brikɔle] *intr* to do odd jobs; to putter around

brico·leur [brikɔlœr] **-leuse** [løz] *mf* jack-of-all-trades || *m* handyman

bride [brid] *f* bridle; strap; clamp; **à toute bride** or **à bride abattue** full speed ahead

bridge [bridʒ] *m* (cards, dentistry) bridge

bridger [bridʒe] *intr* to play bridge

brid·geur [bridʒœr] **-geuse** [ʒøz] *mf* bridge player

briefing [brifiŋ] *m* briefing

brièvement [brijevmɑ̃] *adv* briefly

brièveté [brijevte] *f* brevity

brigade [brigad] *f* brigade

brigadier [brigadje] *m* corporal; police sergeant; noncom

brigand [brigɑ̃] *m* brigand

brigantin [brigɑ̃tɛ̃] *m* brigantine

brigue [brig] *f* intrigue, lobbying

briguer [brige] *tr* to influence underhandedly; to lobby for (*s.th.*); to court (*favor, votes*)

brigueur [brigœr] *m* schemer

bril·lant [brijɑ̃] **bril·lante** [brijɑ̃t] *adj* brilliant, bright || *m* brilliancy, luster; fingernail polish

briller [brije] *intr* to shine; to sparkle; **faire briller** to show (*s.o.*) off

brimade [brimad] *f* hazing

brimborion [brɛ̃bɔrjɔ̃] *m* mere trifle

brimer [brime] *tr* to haze

brin [brɛ̃] *m* blade; sprig, shoot; staple (*of hemp, linen*); strand (*of rope*); belt (*of pulley*); (coll) (little) bit, e.g., **un brin d'air** a (little) bit of air; **ne . . . brin** §90 (archaic) not a bit, not a single; **un beau brin de fille** (coll) a fine figure of a girl

brinde [brɛ̃d] *f* (archaic) toast

brindille [brɛ̃dij] *f* twig, sprig

brioche [brijɔʃ] *f* brioche, breakfast roll

brique [brik] *f* brick

briquer [brike] *tr* (coll) to polish up, scour

briquet [brike] *m* lighter

briquetage [briktaʒ] *m* brickwork

briqueter [brikte] §34 *tr* to brick (up)

briqueterie [briketri] *f* brickyard

briqueteur [briktœr] *m* bricklayer

bri·sant [brizɑ̃] *m* breakers; **brisants** surf

brise [briz] *f* breeze

bri·sé **-sée** [brize] *adj* broken; folding (*door*) || *fpl* see **brisées**

brise-bise [brizbiz] *m invar* weather stripping; café curtain

brisées [brize] *fpl* track, footsteps

brise-glace [brizglas] *m invar* (naut) icebreaker

brise-jet [brizʒe] *m invar* (anti)splash attachment (*for water faucet*), spray filter

brise-lames [brizlam] *m invar* breakwater

brisement [brizmɑ̃] *m* breaking

briser [brize] *tr, intr, & ref* to break

brise-tout [briztu] *m invar* (coll) butterfingers, clumsy person

bri·seur [brizœr] **-seuse** [zøz] *mf* breaker (*person*); **briseur de grève** strikebreaker

brise-vent [brizvɑ̃] *m invar* windbreak

brisque [brisk] *f* service stripe

bristol [bristɔl] *m* Bristol board, pasteboard; visiting card

brisure [brizyr] *f* break; joint

britannique [britanik] *adj* British || (*cap*) *mf* Briton

broc [bro] *m* pitcher, jug

brocanter [brɔkɑ̃te] *tr* to buy, sell, or trade (*secondhand articles*) || *intr* to deal in secondhand articles

brocan·teur [brɔkɑ̃tœr] **-teuse** [tøz] *mf* secondhand dealer

brocard [brɔkar] *m* lampoon, brickbat; (zool) brocket; **lancer des brocards** to make sarcastic remarks, to gibe

brocart [brɔkar] *m* brocade

broche [brɔʃ] *f* brooch; pin; (culin) spit, skewer

bro·ché **-chée** [brɔʃe] *adj* paperback, paperbound

brocher [brɔʃe] *tr* to brocade; to sew (*book bindings*); (coll) to hurry through

brochet [brɔʃe] *m* (ichth) pike

brochette [brɔʃɛt] *f* skewer; skewerful; string (*of decorations*)

bro•cheur [brɔʃœr] -cheuse [ʃøz] *mf* bookbinder ‖ *f* stapler

brochure [brɔʃyr] *f* brochure, pamphlet

brocoli [brɔkɔli] *m* broccoli

brodequin [brɔdkɛ̃] *m* buskin

broder [brɔde] *tr & intr* to embroider

broderie [brɔdri] *f* embroidery

brome [brom] *m* (chem) bromine

bromure [bromyr] *m* bromide

bronche [brɔ̃ʃ] *f* bronchial tube

broncher [brɔ̃ʃe] *intr* to stumble; to flinch; to grumble

bronchique [brɔ̃ʃik] *adj* bronchial

bronchite [brɔ̃ʃit] *f* bronchitis

bronze [brɔ̃z] *m* bronze

bron•zé -zée [brɔ̃ze] *adj* bronze; suntanned

bronzer [brɔ̃ze] *tr & ref* to bronze; to sun-tan

brook [bruk] *m* (turf) water jump

broquette [brɔkɛt] *f* brad, tack

brossage [brɔsaʒ] *m* brushing

brosse [brɔs] *f* brush; brosse à cheveux hairbrush; brosse à dents toothbrush; brosse à habits clothesbrush; brosse de chiendent scrubbing brush; brosses shrubs, bushes

brosser [brɔse] *tr* to brush; to paint the broad outlines of (*a picture*); (fig) to sketch; (slang) to beat, conquer ‖ *ref* to brush one's clothes; (coll) to skimp, to scrimp

brouet [brue] *m* gruel, broth

brouette [bruɛt] *f* wheelbarrow

brouetter [bruete] *tr* to carry in a wheelbarrow

brouhaha [bruaa] *m* (coll) babel, hubbub

brouillage [brujaʒ] *m* (rad) jamming

brouillamini [brujamini] *m* (coll) mess

brouillard [brujar] *adj masc* blotting (*paper*) ‖ *m* fog, mist; (com) daybook

brouillasse [brujas] *f* (coll) drizzle

brouillasser [brujase] *intr* (coll) to drizzle

brouille [bruj] *f* discord, misunderstanding

brouiller [bruje] *tr* to mix up; to jam (*a broadcast*); to scramble (*eggs*); brouiller mes (ses, etc.) pistes to cover my (his, etc.) tracks ‖ *ref* to quarrel; to cloud over

brouil•lon [brujɔ̃] brouil•lonne [brujɔn] *adj* crackpot; blundering; at loose ends ‖ *mf* crackpot ‖ *m* scratch pad; draft; outline

broussailles [brusaj] *fpl* underbrush, brushwood; en broussailles disheveled

broussail•leux [brusajø] broussail•leuse [brusajøz] *adj* bushy

broussard [brusar] *m* (coll) bushman, colonist

brousse [brus] *f* veldt, bush

broutage [brutaʒ] *m* grazing (*of animal*); ratatat (*of a machine*)

brouter [brute] *intr* to browze, graze; to jerk, to grab (*said of clutch, cutting tool, brake*)

broutille [brutij] *f* twig; trifle, bauble

broyage [brwajaʒ] *m* grinding, crushing

broyer [brwaje] §47 *tr* to grind, crush; broyer du noir (coll) to be down in the dumps

broyeur [brwajœr] broyeuse [brwajøz] *adj* grinding, crushing ‖ *mf* grinder, crusher ‖ *f* (mach) grinder

bru [bry] *f* daughter-in-law

bruant [bryɑ̃] *m* (orn) bunting; bruant jaune yellowhammer

brucelles [brysɛl] *fpl* tweezers

brugnon [brynɔ̃] *m* nectarine

bruine [brɥin] *f* drizzle

bruiner [brɥine] *intr* to drizzle

bruire [brɥir] (usually used in: *inf*; 3d *sg pres ind* bruit; 3d *sg & pl imperf ind* bruyait or bruissait, bruyaient or bruissaient) *intr* to rustle; to hum, buzz; to splash

bruissement [brɥismɑ̃] *m* rustling

bruit [brɥi] *m* noise; stir, fuss; le bruit court que it is rumored that

bruitage [brɥitaʒ] *m* sound effects

brû•lant [brylɑ̃] -lante [lɑ̃t] *adj* burning; ardent; ticklish (*question*)

brû•lé -lée [bryle] *adj* burned ‖ *m* smell of burning; burned taste ‖ *f* (slang) beating

brûle-gueule [brylgœl] *m invar* (slang) short pipe (*for smoking*)

brûle-parfum [brylparfœ̃] *m invar* incense burner

brûle-pourpoint [brylpurpwɛ̃]—à brûle-pourpoint point-blank

brûler [bryle] *tr* to burn; to burn out (*a fuse*); to go through (*a red light*); to pass (*another car*); to roast (*coffee*); to distill (*liquor*); brûler la cervelle à qn to blow s.o.'s brains out ‖ *intr* to burn, burn up ‖ *ref* to burn up, to be burned

brû•leur [brylœr] -leuse [løz] *mf* arsonist; distiller ‖ *m* (mach) burner; brûleur à café coffee roaster

brûloir [brylwar] *m* roaster

brûlure [brylyr] *f* burn

brume [brym] *f* fog, mist

brumer [bryme] *intr* to be foggy

bru•meux [brymø] -meuse [møz] *adj* foggy, misty

brun [brœ̃] brune [bryn] *adj* darkbrown; dark ‖ *m* brunet; dark brown ‖ *f* see brune

brunâtre [brynɑtr] *adj* brownish

brune [bryn] *f* brunette; twilight

bru•net [brynɛ] -nette [nɛt] *adj* blackhaired ‖ *m* dark-haired man, brunet ‖ *f* brunette

bru•ni -nie [bryni] *adj* burnished, polished ‖ *m* burnishment, polish

brunir [brynir] *tr* to brown; to burnish, polish ‖ *intr* to turn brown

brunissoir [bryniswar] *m* (mach) buffer

brusque [brysk] *adj* brusque; sudden; surprise (*attack*); quick (*movements; decision*)

brusquer [bryske] *tr* to hurry, rush through; to be blunt with

brusquerie [bryskri] *f* brusqueness; suddenness

brut [bry] brute [bryt] *adj* crude, unpolished, unrefined, uncivilized; uncut (*diamond*); raw (*material*); dry (*champagne*); brown (*sugar*); gross (*weight*) ‖ *f* see **brute** ‖ **brut** *adv*—**peser brut** to have a gross weight of

bru·tal -tale [brytal] (*pl* -**taux** [to]) *adj* brutal, rough; outspoken; coarse, beastly ‖ *mf* brute, bully

brutaliser [brytalize] *tr* to bully; to mistreat

brutalité [brytalite] *f* brutality; **brutalité policière** police brutality

brute *f* brute

Bruxelles [brysel] *f* Brussels

bruxel·lois [bryselwa] **bruxel·loise** [bryselwaz] *adj* of Brussels ‖ (*cap*) *mf* native or inhabitant of Brussels

bruyamment [bryijamɑ̃] *adv* noisily

bruyant [bryijɑ̃] **bruyante** [bryijɑ̃t] *adj* noisy

bruyère [bryijɛr] *f* heather; heath

buanderie [byɑ̃dəri] *f* laundry room

buan·dier [byɑ̃dje] **-dière** [djɛr] *mf* laundry worker ‖ *f* laundress

bubonique [bybonik] *adj* bubonic

bûche [byʃ] *f* log; (slang) dunce; **bûche de Noël** yule log; cake decorated as a yule log; **ramasser une bûche** (slang) to take a tumble

bûcher [byʃe] *m* woodshed; pyre; stake (*e.g., for burning witches*) ‖ *tr* to rough-hew; (slang) to bone up on ‖ *intr* (slang) to keep on working; to slave away ‖ *ref* (slang) to fight

bûche·ron [byʃrɔ̃] -**ronne** [rɔn] *mf* woodcutter ‖ *m* lumberjack

bûchette [byʃet] *f* stick of wood

bû·cheur [byʃœr] -**cheuse** [ʃøz] *mf* (coll) eager beaver

budget [bydʒe] *m* budget; **boucler son budget** (coll) to make ends meet

budgétaire [bydʒeter] *adj* budgetary

buée [bɥe] *f* steam; mist

buffet [byfe] *m* buffet; snack bar; station restaurant; **danser devant le buffet** to miss a meal

buf·fle [byfl] **buf·flonne** [byflɔn] *mf* water buffalo; Cape buffalo

bugle [bygl] *m* (mus) saxhorn, bugle ‖ *f* (bot) bugle

building [bildiŋ] *m* large office building, skyscraper

buire [bɥir] *f* ewer

buis [bɥi] *m* boxwood

buisson [bɥisɔ̃] *m* bush

buisson·neux [bɥisɔnø] **buisson·neuse** [bɥisɔnøz] *adj* bushy

buisson·nier [bɥisɔnje] **buisson·nière** [bɥisɔnjɛr] *adj*—**faire l'école buissonnière** (coll) to play hooky

bulbe [bylb] *m* bulb

bul·beux [bylbø] -**beuse** [bøz] *adj* bulbous

bulgare [bylgar] *adj* Bulgarian ‖ *m* Bulgarian (*language*) ‖ (*cap*) *mf* Bulgarian (*person*)

Bulgarie [bylgari] *f* Bulgaria; **la Bulgarie** Bulgaria

bulle [byl] *m* wrapping paper ‖ *f* bubble; blister; (eccl) bull

bulletin [byltɛ̃] *m* bulletin; ballot; **bulletin de bagages** baggage check; **bulletin de commande** order blank;

bulletin de naissance birth certificate; **bulletin scolaire** report card

bul·leux [bylø] **bul·leuse** [byløz] *adj* blistery

bure [byr] *m* mine shaft ‖ *f* drugget, sackcloth

bu·reau [byro] *m* (*pl* -**reaux**) desk; office; **bureau à cylindre** roll-top desk; **bureau ambulant** post-office car; **bureau d'aide sociale** welfare department; **Bureau de l'état civil** Bureau of Vital Statistics; **bureau de location** box office; **bureau de placement** employment agency; **bureau de poste** post office; **bureau des objets trouvés** lost-and-found department; **bureau de tabac** tobacco shop; **bureau directoire** cabinet, committee; **deuxième bureau** intelligence division

bureaucrate [byrokrat] *mf* bureaucrat

bureaucratie [byrokrasi] *f* bureaucracy

bureaucratique [byrokratik] *adj* bureaucratic

burette [byret] *f* cruet; oilcan

burin [byrɛ̃] *m* engraving; burin (*tool*)

burlesque [byrlesk] *adj & m* burlesque

busard [byzar] *m* harrier, marsh hawk

busc [bysk] *m* whalebone

buse [byz] *f* buzzard

business [biznes] *m* (slang) work; (slang) complicated business

bus·qué -quée [byske] *adj* arched

buste [byst] *m* bust

but [by], [byt] *m* mark, goal, target; aim, end, purpose; point (*scored in game*); **aller droit au but** to come straight to the point; **de but en blanc** point-blank

bu·té -tée [byte] *adj* obstinate, headstrong ‖ *f* abutment

buter [byte] *tr* to prop up; (slang) to bump off, kill ‖ *intr*—**buter contre** to bump into, to stumble on ‖ *ref*—**se buter à** to butt up against; (fig) to be dead set on

buteur [bytœr] *m* scorekeeper

butin [bytɛ̃] *m* booty; profits, savings

butiner [bytine] *tr* to pillage; to gather honey from ‖ *intr* to pillage; to gather honey (*said of bees*); **butiner dans** to browse among (*books*)

butoir [bytwar] *m* buffer, stop, catch

bu·tor [bytɔr] -**torde** [tɔrd] *mf* (slang) lout, good-for-nothing

butte [byt] *f* butte, knoll; **butte de tir** butt, mound (*for target practice*); **être en butte à** to be exposed to

butter [byte] *tr* to hill (*plants*)

buttoir [bytwar] *m* (agr) hiller

buty·reux [bytirø] -**reuse** [røz] *adj* buttery

buvable [byvabl] *adj* drinkable; (pharm) to be taken by mouth

buvard [byvar] *adj* blotting (*paper*) ‖ *m* blotter

buvette [byvet] *f* bar, fountain

buvette-buffet [byvetbyfe] *f* (coll) snack bar

bu·veur [byvœr] -**veuse** [vøz] *mf* drinker; **buveur d'eau** abstainer; vacationist at a spa

byzan·tin [bizɑ̃tɛ̃] -**tine** [tin] *adj* Byzantine

C

C, c [se] *m invar* third letter of the French alphabet

C/ *abbr* (**compte**) account

ça [sa] *pron indef* (coll) that; **ah ça non!** no indeed!; **avec ça!** tell me another!; **ça y est** that's that; that's it, that's right; **comment ça!** how so?; **et avec ça?** what else?; **où ça,** where?

çà [sa] *adv*—ah ça! now then! **çà et là** here and there

cabale [kabal] *f* cabal, intrigue

cabaler [kabale] *intr* to cabal, intrigue

caban [kabɑ̃] *m* (naut) peacoat

cabane [kaban] *f* cabin, hut

cabanon [kabanɔ̃] *m* hut; padded cell

cabaret [kabarɛ] *m* tavern; cabaret, night club; liquor closet

cabas [kabɑ] *m* basket

cabestan [kabɛstɑ̃] *m* capstan

cabillaud [kabijo] *m* haddock; (coll) fresh cod

cabine [kabin] *f* cabin (*of ship or airplane*); bathhouse; car (*of elevator*); cab (*of locomotive or truck*); **cabine téléphonique** telephone booth

cabinet [kabinɛ] *m* (ministry) cabinet; study (*of scholar*); office (*of professional man*); clientele; staff (*of a cabinet officer*); toilet; storeroom closet; **cabinet d'aisance** rest room; **cabinet de débarras** storeroom closet; **cabinet de toilette** powder room; **cabinets** rest rooms

câble [kɑbl] *m* cable

câbler [kable] *tr & intr* to cable

câblier [kablije] *m* cable ship

câblogramme [kablɔgram] *m* cablegram

cabo·chard [kabɔʃar] **-charde** [ʃard] *adj* obstinate, pigheaded

caboche [kabɔʃ] *f* hobnail; (coll) noodle (*head*)

cabochon [kabɔʃɔ̃] *m* uncut gem; stud, upholstery nail

cabot [kabo] *m* (ichth) miller's-thumb, bullhead; (coll) ham (*actor*)

cabotage [kabotaʒ] *m* coastal navigation, coasting trade

cabo·tin [kabotɛ̃] **-tine** [tin] *mf* barnstormer; (coll) ham actor; **cabotin de la politique** (coll) corny politician, political orator given to histrionics

cabotinage [kabotinaʒ] *m* barnstorming; (coll) ham acting

cabotiner [kabotine] *intr* to barnstorm; (coll) to play to the grandstand

cabrer [kabre] *tr* to make (*a horse*) rear; to nose up (*a plane*) || *ref* to rear; to kick over the traces; (aer) to nose up

cabri [kabri] *m* (zool) kid

cabriole [kabrijɔl] *f* caper

cabrioler [kabrijɔle] *intr* to caper

cacahouète [kakawɛt] or **cacahuète** [kakaɥɛt] *f* peanut

cacao [kakao] *m* cocoa; cocoa bean

cacaotier [kakaotje] *m* (bot) cacao

cacaoyer [kakaoje] *m* (bot) cacao

cacarder [kakarde] *intr* to cackle

cacatoès [kakatɔɛs] or **cacatois** [kakatwa] *m* cockatoo

cachalot [kaʃalo] *m* sperm whale

cache [kaʃ] *m* masking tape || *f* hiding place

cache-cache [kaʃkaʃ] *m invar* hide-and-seek

cache-col [kaʃkɔl] *m invar* scarf

cachemire [kaʃmir] *m* cashmere

cache-nez [kaʃne] *m invar* muffler

cache-poussière [kaʃpusjɛr] *m invar* duster (*overgarment*)

cacher [kaʃe] *tr* to hide; **cacher q.ch. à qn** to hide s.th. from s.o. || *ref* to hide; **se cacher à** to hide from; **se cacher de q.ch.** to make a secret of s.th.

cache-radiateur [kaʃradjatœr] *m invar* radiator cover

cache-sexe [kaʃseks] *m invar* G-string

cachet [kaʃe] *m* seal; postmark; fee; price of a lesson; meal ticket; (pharm, phila) cachet; (fig) seal; stylishness; **payer au cachet** to pay a set fee

cacheter [kaʃte] §34 *tr* to seal, to seal up; to seal with wax

cachette [kaʃet] *f* hiding place; **en cachette** secretly

cachot [kaʃo] *m* dungeon; prison

cacophonie [kakɔfoni] *f* cacophony

cactier [kaktje] or **cactus** [kaktys] *m* cactus

c.-à-d. *abbr* (**c'est-à-dire**) that is

cadastre [kadastr] *m* land-survey register

cadavre [kadavr] *m* corpse, cadaver; (slang) dead soldier (*bottle*)

ca·deau [kado] *m* (*pl* **-deaux**) gift

cadenas [kadna] *m* padlock

cadenasser [kadnase] *tr* to padlock

cadence [kadɑ̃s] *f* cadence, rhythm, time; output (*of worker, of factory, etc.*); **cadence de tir** rate of firing

cadencer [kadɑ̃se] §51 *tr* to cadence || *intr* to call out cadence

ca·det [kadɛ] **-dette** [det] *adj* younger || *mf* youngest; junior; (sports) player fifteen to eighteen years old; **le cadet de mes soucis** (coll) the least of my worries || *m* caddy; (mil) cadet; younger brother; younger son || *f* younger sister; younger daughter

cadmium [kadmjɔm] *m* cadmium

cadrage [kadraʒ] *m* (mov, telv) framing; (phot) centering

cadran [kadrɑ̃] *m* dial; **cadran d'appel** telephone dial; **cadran solaire** sundial; **faire le tour du cadran** to sleep around the clock

cadre [kadr] *m* frame; framework; setting; outline, framework (*of a literary work*); limits, scope (*of activities or duties*); (mil) cadre; (naut) cot; **cadres** officials; (mil) regulars; **cadres sociaux** memorable dates or events

cadrer [kadre] *tr* to frame (*film*) || *intr* to conform, tally

ca·duc **-duque** [kadyk] *adj* decrepit,

frail; outlived (*custom*); deciduous (*leaves*); lapsed (*insurance policy*); (*law*) null and void

caducée [kadyse] *m* caduceus

C.A.F. *abbr* (coût, assurance, fret) C.I.F. (*cost, insurance, and freight*)

ca·fard [kafar] **-farde** [fard] *adj* sanctimonious || *mf* hypocrite; (coll) squealer || *m* (coll) cockroach; (coll) blues ●

café [kafe] *adj invar* tan || *m* coffee; café; coffeehouse; **café chantant** music hall (*with tables*); **café complet** coffee, hot milk, rolls, butter, and jam; **café nature, café noir** black coffee

café-concert [kafekɔ̃ser] *m* (*pl* **cafés-concerts**) music hall (*with tables*), cabaret

caféier [kafeje] *m* coffee plant

caféière [kafejer] *f* coffee plantation

caféine [kafein] *f* caffeine

cafe·tier [kaftje] **-tière** [tjer] *mf* café owner || *f* coffeepot

cafouiller [kafuje] *intr* (slang) to miss (*said of engine*); (slang) to flounder around

cage [kaʒ] *f* cage; **cage d'un ascenseur** elevator shaft; **cage d'un escalier** stairwell; **cage thoracique** thoracic cavity; **en cage** (coll) in the clink, in the pen

cageot [kaʒo] *m* crate

ca·gnard [kaɲar] **-gnarde** [ɲard] *adj* indolent, lazy || *m* (coll) sunny spot

ca·gneux [kaɲø] **-gneuse** [ɲøz] *adj* knock-kneed; pigeon-toed

cagnotte [kaɲɔt] *f* kitty, pool

ca·got [kago] **-gotte** [gɔt] *adj* hypocritical || *mf* hypocrite

cagoule [kagul] *f* cowl; hood (*with eyeholes*)

cahier [kaje] *m* notebook; **cahier à feuilles mobiles** loose-leaf notebook; **cahier des charges** (com) specifications

cahin-caha [kaẽkaa] *adv* (coll) so-so

cahot [kao] *m* jolt, bump

cahoter [kaɔte] *tr & intr* to jolt

caho·teux [kaɔtø] **-teuse** [tøz] *adj* bumpy (*road*)

cahute [kayt] *f* hut, shack

caille [kaj] *f* quail

cail·lé -lée [kaje] *adj* curdled || *m* curd

caillebotis [kajbɔti] *m* boardwalk; (mil) duckboard; (naut) grating

caillebotte [kajbɔt] *f* curds

caillebotter [kajbɔte] *tr & intr* to curdle

cailler [kaje] *tr & ref* to clot, curdle, curd

caillot [kajo] *m* clot; blood clot

cail·lou [kaju] *m* (*pl* **-loux**) pebble; (coll) bald head; **caillou du Rhin** rhinestone

caillou·teux [kajutø] **-teuse** [tøz] *adj* stony (*road*); pebbly (*beach*)

cailloutis [kajuti] *m* crushed stone, gravel

Cain [kaẽ] *m* Cain

Caire [ker] *m*—**Le Caire** Cairo

caisse [kes] *f* chest, box; case (*for packing; of a clock or piano*); chest-

ful, boxful; till, cash register, coffer, safe; cashier, cashier's window; desk (*in a hotel*); **caisse à eau** water tank; **caisse claire** snare drum; **caisse d'épargne** savings bank; **caisse des écoles** scholarship fund; **grosse caisse** bass drum; bass drummer; **petite caisse** petty cash

caisson [kesɔ̃] *m* caisson

cajoler [kaʒɔle] *tr* to cajole, wheedle

cajolerie [kaʒɔlri] *f* cajolery

cajou [kaʒu] *m* cashew nut

cake [kek] *m* fruit cake

cal [kal] *m* (*pl* **cals**) callus, callosity; **cal vicieux** badly knitted bone

calage [kalaʒ] *m* wedging, chocking; stalling (*of motor*)

calamité [kalamite] *f* calamity

calami·teux [kalamitø] **-teuse** [tøz] *adj* calamitous

calandre [kalɑ̃dr] *f* mangle (*for clothes*); calender (*for paper*); grill (*for car radiator*); (ent) weevil; (orn) lark

calandrer [kalɑ̃dre] *tr* to calender

calcaire [kalker] *adj* calcareous; chalky; hard (*water*) || *m* limestone

calcifier [kalsifje] *tr & ref* to calcify

calciner [kalsine] *tr & ref* to burn to a cinder

calcium [kalsjɔm] *m* calcium

calcul [kalkyl] *m* calculation; (math, pathol) calculus; **calcul biliaire** gallstone; **calcul mental** mental arithmetic; **calcul rénal** kidney stone

calcula·teur [kalkylatœr] **-trice** [tris] *adj* calculating || *mf* calculator (*person*) || *m* (mach) calculator || *f* (mach) computer

calculer [kalkyle] *tr & intr* to calculate

cale [kal] *f* wedge, chock; hold (*of ship*); **cale de construction** stocks; **cale sèche** dry dock

ca·lé -lée [kale] *adj* stalled; (coll) well-informed; (slang) involved, difficult; **calé en** (coll) strong in, up on

calebasse [kalbas] *f* calabash

calèche [kalɛʃ] *f* open carriage

caleçon [kalsɔ̃] *m* drawers, shorts; **caleçon de bain** swimming trunks

calembour [kalɑ̃bur] *m* pun

calendes [kalɑ̃d] *fpl* calends; **aux calendes grecques** (coll) when pigs fly

calendrier [kalɑ̃drije] *m* calendar

calepin [kalpẽ] *m* notebook

caler [kale] *tr* to wedge, to chock; to jam; to stall; to lower (*sail*); (naut) to draw || *intr* to stall (*said of motor*); (coll) to give in || *ref* to stall; to get nicely settled

calfater [kalfate] *tr* to caulk

calfeutrer [kalføtre] *tr* to stop up || *ref* to shut oneself up

calibre [kalibr] *m* caliber

calibrer [kalibre] *tr* to calibrate

calice [kalis] *m* chalice; (bot) calyx

calicot [kaliko] *m* calico; sign, banner; (slang) sales clerk

califat [kalifa] *m* caliphate

calife [kalif] *m* caliph

Californie [kaliforni] *f* California; **la basse Californie** Lower California; **la Californie** California

califourchon [kalifurʃɔ̃]—**à califourchon** astride, astraddle; **s'asseoir à califourchon** to straddle

câ·lin [kɑlɛ̃] **-line** [lin] *adj* coaxing; caressing

câliner [kaline] *tr* to coax; to caress

cal·leux [kalø] **cal·leuse** [kaløz] *adj* callous, calloused

callisthénie [kalisteni] *f* calisthenics

cal·mant [kalmɑ̃] **-mante** [mɑ̃t] *adj* calming ‖ *m* sedative

calmar [kalmar] *m* squid

calme [kalm] *adj & m* calm

calmement [kalməmɑ̃] *adv* calmly

calmer [kalme] *tr* to calm ‖ *ref* to become calm, to calm down

calmir [kalmir] *intr* to abate

calomnie [kalɔmni] *f* calumny, slander

calomnier [kalɔmnje] *tr* to calumniate

calorie [kalɔri] *f* calory

calorifère [kalɔrifɛr] *adj* heating, heat-conducting ‖ *m* heater; **calorifère à air chaud** hot-air heater; **calorifère à eau chaude** hot-water heater

calorifuge [kalɔrifyʒ] *adj* insulating ‖ *m* insulator

calorifuger [kalɔrifyʒe] §38 *tr* to insulate

calorique [kalɔrik] *adj* caloric

calot [kalo] *m* policeman's hat, kepi

calotte [kalɔt] *f* skullcap; dome; (coll) box on the ear; (coll) clergy; **calotte des cieux** vault of heaven; **flanquer une calotte à** (coll) to box on the ear

calotter [kalɔte] *tr* (coll) to box on the ear, to cuff; (slang) to snitch

calque [kalk] *m* tracing; decal; word-for-word correspondence (*between two languages*); slavish imitation; spitting image

calquer [kalke] *tr* to trace; to imitate slavishly

calumet [kalyme] *m* calumet; **calumet de paix** peace pipe

calvados [kalvados] *m* applejack

calvaire [kalvɛr] *m* calvary

calviniste [kalvinist] *adj & mf* Calvinist

calvitie [kalvisi] *f* baldness

camarade [kamarad] *mf* comrade; **camarade de chambre** roommate; **camarade de travail** fellow worker; **camarade d'étude** schoolmate

camaraderie [kamaradri] *f* comradeship; camaraderie, fellowship

ca·mard [kamar] **-marde** [mard] *adj* snub-nosed

cambouis [kɑ̃bwi] *m* axle grease

cambrer [kɑ̃bre] *tr* to curve, arch

cambrioler [kɑ̃brijɔle] *tr* to break into, to burglarize

cambrio·leur [kɑ̃brijɔlœr] **-leuse** [løz] *mf* burglar

cambrure [kɑ̃bryr] *f* curve, arch

cambuse [kɑ̃byz] *f* (naut) storeroom between decks

came [kam] *f* cam

camée [kame] *m* cameo

caméléon [kamelēɔ̃] *m* chameleon

camélia [kamelja] *m* camellia

camelot [kamlo] *m* cheap woolen cloth; huckster; newsboy

camelote [kamlɔt] *f* shoddy merchandise, rubbish, junk

caméra [kamera] *f* (mov, telv) camera

camion [kamjɔ̃] *m* truck; paint bucket; **camion à remorque** trailer (truck); **camion à semi-remorque** semitrailer; **camion d'enregistrement** (mov) sound truck

camion-benne [kamjɔ̃ben] *m* (*pl* **camions-bennes**) dump truck

camion-citerne [kamjɔ̃sitern] *m* (*pl* **camions-citernes**) tank truck

camion-grue [kamjɔ̃gry] *m* (*pl* **camions-grues**) tow truck

camionnage [kamjɔnaʒ] *m* trucking

camionner [kamjɔne] *tr* to truck

camionnette [kamjɔnet] *f* van; **camionnette de police** police wagon; **camionnette sanitaire** mobile health unit

camionneur [kamjɔnœr] *m* trucker; truckdriver, teamster

camisole [kamizɔl] *f* camisole; **camisole de force** strait jacket

camouflage [kamuflaʒ] *m* camouflage

camoufler [kamufle] *tr* to camouflage

camp [kɑ̃] *m* camp

campa·gnard [kɑ̃paɲar] **-gnarde** [ɲard] *adj & mf* rustic

campagne [kɑ̃paɲ] *f* campaign; country

cam·pé **-pée** [kɑ̃pe] *adj* encamped; **bien campé** well-built (*man*); clearly presented (*story*); firmly fixed

campement [kɑ̃pmɑ̃] *m* encampment; camping

camper [kɑ̃pe] *tr* to camp; (coll) to clap (*e.g., one's hat on one's head*); **camper là** *qn* (coll) to run out on *s.o.* ‖ *intr & ref* to camp

cam·peur [kɑ̃pœr] **-peuse** [pøz] *mf* camper

camphre [kɑ̃fr] *m* camphor

camping [kɑ̃piŋ] *m* campground; trailer; camping

campos [kɑ̃po] *m* (coll) vacation, day off

campus [kɑ̃pys] *m* campus

ca·mus [kamy] **-muse** [myz] *adj* snub-nosed, pug-nosed, flat-nosed

Canada [kanada] *m*—**le Canada** Canada

cana·dien [kanadjɛ̃] **-dienne** [djen] *adj* Canadian ‖ *f* sheepskin jacket; station wagon ‖ (*cap*) *mf* Canadian

canaille [kanaj] *adj* vulgar, coarse ‖ *f* rabble, riffraff; scoundrel

ca·nal [kanal] *m* (*pl* **-naux** [no]) canal; tube, pipe; ditch, drain; (rad, telv) channel; **canal de Panama** Panama Canal; **canal de Suez** [sɥez] Suez Canal; **par le canal de** through the good offices of

canapé [kanape] *m* sofa, davenport; (culin) canapé; **canapé à deux places** settee

canapé-lit [kanapeli] *m* (*pl* **canapés-lits**) sofa bed, day bed

canard [kanar] *m* duck; sugar soaked in coffee, brandy, etc.; (mus) false note; (coll) hoax; (coll) rag, paper; **canard mâle** drake; **canard publicitaire** publicity stunt; **canard sauvage** wild duck

canarder [kanarde] *tr* to snipe at ‖ *intr* to snipe

canari [kanari] *m* canary

cancan [kãkã] *m* cancan (*dance*); (coll) gossip

cancaner [kãkane] *intr* to quack; (coll) to gossip

canca-nier [kãkanje] **-nière** [njɛr] *adj* (coll) catty ‖ *mf* (coll) gossip

cancer [kãsɛr] *m* cancer

cancé-reux [kãserø] **-reuse** [røz] *adj* cancerous

cancre [kãkr] *m* (coll) dunce, lazy student; (coll) tightwad; (zool) crab

candélabre [kãdelabr] *m* candelabrum; espaliered fruit tree; cactus; lamppost

candeur [kãdœr] *f* naïveté

candi [kãdi] *adj* candied (*fruit*) ‖ *m* rock candy

candi-dat [kãdida] **-date** [dat] *mf* candidate; nominee

candidature [kãdidatyr] *f* candidacy

candide [kãdid] *adj* naïve

candir [kãdir] *intr—faire candir* to candy, to crystallize (*sugar*) ‖ *ref* to candy, to crystallize

cane [kan] *f* duck, female duck

caner [kane] *intr* (slang) to chicken out

caneton [kãtɔ̃] *m* duckling

canette [kanɛt] *f* female duckling; beer bottle; **canette de bière** can of beer

canevas [kanva] *m* canvas (*cloth*); outline (*of novel, story, etc.*); embroidery netting; (in artillery, in cartography) triangulation

canezou [kanzu] *m* sleeveless lace blouse

caniche [kaniʃ] *m* poodle

canicule [kanikyl] *f* dog days

canif [kanif] *m* penknife, pocketknife

ca-nin [kanɛ̃] **-nine** [nin] *adj* canine ‖ *f* canine (*tooth*)

canitie [kanisi] *f* grayness (*of hair*)

cani-veau [kanivo] *m* (*pl* **-veaux**) gutter; (elec) conduit

cannaie [kane] *f* sugar plantation

canne [kan] *f* cane; reed; cane, walking stick; **canne à pêche** fishing rod; **canne à sucre** sugar cane

canneberge [kanbɛrʒ] *f* cranberry

canneler [kanle] §34 *tr* to groove; to corrugate; to flute (*a column*)

cannelle [kanɛl] *f* cinnamon; spout

cannelure [kanlyr] *f* groove, channel; corrugation; fluting (*of column*)

canner [kane] *tr* to cane (*a chair*)

cannibale [kanibal] *adj* & *mf* cannibal

canoë [kanɔe] *m* canoe

canoéiste [kanɔeist] *mf* canoeist

canon [kanɔ̃] *m* canon; cannon; gun barrel; tube; nozzle; spout; **canon à électrons** electron gun

cañon [kaɲɔ̃] *m* canyon

cano-nial **-niale** [kanɔnjal] *adj* (*pl* **-niaux** [njo]) canonical

canonique [kanɔnik] *adj* canonical

canoniser [kanɔnize] *tr* to canonize

canonnade [kanɔnad] *f* cannonade

canonner [kanɔne] *tr* to cannonade

canonnier [kanɔnje] *m* cannoneer

canonnière [kanɔnjɛr] *f* gunboat; popgun

canot [kano] *m* rowboat, launch; **canot automobile** speedboat, motorboat; **canot de sauvetage** lifeboat

canotage [kanɔtaʒ] *m* boating

canoter [kanɔte] *intr* to go boating

canotier [kanɔtje] *m* rower; skimmer

cant [kã] *m* cant

cantaloup [kãtalu] *m* cantaloupe

cantate [kãtat] *f* cantata

cantatrice [kãtatris] *f* singer

cantilever [kãtilevœr] *adj* & *m* cantilever

cantine [kãtin] *f* canteen (*restaurant*); **cantine d'officier** officer's kit

cantique [kãtik] *m* canticle, ode; **cantique de Noël** (eccl) Christmas carol; **Cantique des Cantiques** (Bib) Song of Songs

canton [kãtɔ̃] *m* canton, district; **Cantons de l'Est** Eastern Townships (*in Canada*)

cantonade [kãtɔnad] *f* (theat) wings; **à la cantonade** (theat) offstage; **crier à la cantonade** to yell out (*s.th.*); **parler à la cantonade** to seem to be talking to oneself; (theat) to speak toward the wings

cantonnement [kãtɔnmã] *m* billeting

cantonner [kãtɔne] *tr* to billet

cantonnier [kãtɔnje] *m* road laborer; (rr) section hand

canular [kanylar] *m* (coll) practical joke, hoax, canard

canule [kanyl] *f* nozzle (*of syringe or injection needle*)

canuler [kanyle] *tr* (slang) to bother

caoutchouc [kautʃu] *m* rubber; **caoutchouc mousse** foam rubber; **caoutchoucs rubbers**, overshoes

caoutchouter [kautʃute] *tr* to rubberize

caoutchou-teux [kautʃutø] **-teuse** [tøz] *adj* rubbery

cap [kap] *m* cape, headland; bow, head (*of ship*); **Cap de Bonne Espérance** Cape of Good Hope; **mettre le cap sur** (coll) to set a course for

capable [kapabl] *adj* capable

capacité [kapasite] *f* capacity; ability

cape [kap] *f* cape; hood; derby; outer leaf, wrapper (*of cigar*); **à la cape** (naut) hove to; **de cape et d'épée** cloak-and-dagger (*novel, movie, etc.*); **rire sous cape** to laugh up one's sleeve; **vendre sous cape** (coll) to sell under the counter

C.A.P.E.S. [kapes] *m* (acronym) (certificat d'aptitude au professorat de l'enseignement du second degré) secondary-school teachers certificate

capillaire [kapilɛr] *adj* capillary ‖ *m* (bot) maidenhair (*fern*)

capitaine [kapiten] *m* captain

capi-tal **-tale** [kapital] (*pl* **-taux** [to] **-tales**) *adj* capital, principal, essential; capital (*city; punishment; crime; letter*); death (*sentence*); deadly (*sins*) ‖ *m* capital, assets; principal (*main sum*); **avec de minces capitaux** on a shoestring; **capitaux** capital ‖ *f* capital (*city; letter*)

capitalisation [kapitalizɑsjɔ̃] f capitalization; hoarding (of money)

capitaliser [kapitalize] tr to capitalize (an income); to compound (interest) || intr to hoard

capitalisme [kapitalism] m capitalism

capitaliste [kapitalist] adj capitalist || mf capitalist; investor

capi·teux [kapitø] **-teuse** [tøz] adj heady (wine, champagne, etc.)

Capitole [kapitɔl] m Capitol

capitonner [kapitɔne] tr to upholster

capituler [kapityle] intr to capitulate; to parley

ca·pon [kapɔ̃] **-ponne** [pɔn] adj cowardly || mf coward; sneak; tattletale

capo·ral [kapɔral] m (pl **-raux** [ro]) corporal; shag, caporal (tobacco); **Caporal a dit ... Simon says ...**

caporalisme [kapɔralism] m militarism; dictatorial government

capot [kapo] adj invar speechless, confused; (cards) trickless || m cover; hood (of automobile); (naut) hatch

capotage [kapɔtaʒ] m overturning

capote [kapɔt] f coat with a hood; hood (of baby carriage); **capote rebattable** (aut) folding top

capoter [kapɔte] intr to capsize; to overturn, upset

câpre [kɑpr] f (bot) caper

caprice [kapris] m caprice, whim

capri·cieux [kaprisjø] **-cieuse** [sjøz] adj capricious, whimsical

capsule [kapsyl] f capsule; bottle cap; percussion cap; (bot) capsule, pod; (rok) capsule; **capsules surrénales** adrenal glands

capsuler [kapsyle] tr to cap

capter [kapte] tr to win over; to harness (a river); to tap (electric current; a water supply); (rad, telv) to receive, pick up

cap·tieux [kapsjø] **-tieuse** [sjøz] adj captious, insidious; specious

cap·tif [kaptif] **-tive** [tiv] adj & mf captive

captiver [kaptive] tr to captivate

captivité [kaptivite] f captivity

capture [kaptyr] f capture

capturer [kaptyre] tr to capture

capuce [kapys] m (eccl) pointed hood

capuchon [kapyʃɔ̃] m hood (of coat); cap (of pen); (aut) valve cap; (eccl) cowl

capucine [kapysin] f nasturtium

caque [kak] f keg, barrel

caquet [kake] m cackle

caqueter [kakte] §34 intr to cackle; to gossip

car [kar] m bus, sightseeing bus, interurban; **car de police** patrol wagon; **car sonore** loudspeaker truck || conj for, because

carabe [karab] m ground beetle

carabine [karabin] f carbine

carabi·né -née [karabine] adj (coll) violent (wind, cold, criticism)

caraco [karako] m loose blouse

caractère [karakter] m character; **caractères gras** boldface

caractériser [karakterize] tr to characterize

caractéristique [karakteristik] adj & f characteristic

carafe [karaf] f carafe; **rester en carafe** (slang) to be left out in the cold

carafon [karafɔ̃] m small carafe

caraïbe [karaib] adj Caribbean, Carib || (cap) mf Carib (person)

carambolage [karɑ̃bolaʒ] m jostling; (coll) bumping (e.g., of autos)

caramboler [karɑ̃bole] tr (coll) to strike, bump into || intr (billiards) to carom

caramel [karamel] m caramel

carapace [karapas] f turtle shell, carapace

carapater [karapate] ref (slang) to beat it

carat [kara] m carat

caravane [karavan] f caravan; house trailer; group (of tourists)

caravaning [karavaniŋ] m trailer camping

caravansérail [karavɑ̃seraj] m caravansary; (fig) world crossroads

caravelle [karavel] f caravel

carbonade [karbɔnad] f see **carbonnade**

carbone [karbɔn] m carbon

carbonique [karbɔnik] adj carbonic

carboniser [karbɔnize] tr to carbonize, char

carbonnade [karbɔnad] f charcoal-grilled steak (ham, etc.); beef and onion stew (in northern France); **à la carbonnade** charcoal-grilled

carburant [karbyrɑ̃] m motor fuel

carburateur [karbyratœr] m carburetor

carbure [karbyr] m carbide

carburéacteur [karbyreaktœr] m jet fuel

carcan [karkɑ̃] m pillory

carcasse [karkas] f skeleton; framework; (coll) carcass

cardan [kardɑ̃] m (mach) universal joint

carde [kard] f card; leaf rib; teasel head

carder [karde] tr to card

cardiaque [kardjak] adj & mf cardiac

cardi·nal -nale [kardinal] adj & m (pl **-naux** [no]) cardinal

cardiogramme [kardjɔgram] m cardiogram

carême [karem] m Lent; **de carême** Lenten

carême-prenant [karemprənɑ̃] m (pl **carêmes-prenants**) Shrovetide

carence [karɑ̃s] f lack, deficiency; failure

carène [karen] f hull

caréner [karene] §10 tr to streamline; (naut) to careen

caren·tiel -tielle [karɑ̃sjel] adj deficiency (disease)

cares·sant [karesɑ̃] **cares·sante** [karesɑ̃t] adj caressing; lovable; nice to pet; soothing (e.g., voice)

caresse [kares] f caress; endearment

caresser [karese] tr to caress; to pet; to nourish (a hope)

cargaison [kargezɔ̃] f cargo

cargo [kargo] m freighter; **cargo mixte** freighter carrying passengers

carl [kari] *m* curry

caricature [karikatyr] *f* caricature; cartoon

caricaturer [karikatyre] *tr* to caricature; cartoon

caricaturiste [karikatyrist] *mf* caricaturist; cartoonist

carie [kari] *f* caries; **carie sèche** dry rot

carillon [karijõ] *m* carillon

carillonner [karijone] *tr & intr* to carillon, to chime

carlingue [karlɛ̃g] *f* (aer) cockpit

carmin [karmɛ̃] *adj & m* carmine

carnage [karnaʒ] *m* carnage

carnas·sier [karnasje] **carnas·sière** [karnasjɛr] *adj* carnivorous || *m* carnivore || *f* game bag

carnation [karnɑsjõ] *f* flesh tint

carna·val [karnaval] *m* (*pl* -vals) carnival; parade dummy

car·né -née [karne] *adj* flesh-colored; meat (*diet*)

carnet [karne] *m* notebook, address book; memo pad; book (*of tickets, checks, stamps, etc.*); **carnet à feuilles mobiles** loose-leaf notebook

carnier [karnje] *m* hunting bag

carotte [karɔt] *f* carrot; (min) core sample; **tirer une carotte à** (coll) to cheat

carotter [karɔte] *tr* (coll) to cheat

carpe [karp] *m* (anat) wrist bones || *f* carp; **être muet comme une carpe** to be still as a mouse

carpette [karpɛt] *f* rug, mat

carquois [karkwa] *m* quiver

carre [kar] *f* thickness (*of board*); crown (*of hat*); edge (*of ice skate*); square toe (*of shoe*); **d'une bonne carre** broad-shouldered (*man*)

car·ré -rée [kare] *adj* square; forthright || *m* square; landing (*of staircase*); patch (*in garden*); (cards) four of a kind; (naut) wardroom || *f* (slang) room, pad

car·reau [karo] *m* (*pl* -reaux) tile, flagstone; windowpane; stall (*in market*); pithead (*of mine*); goose (*of tailor*); quarrel (*square-headed arrow*); (cards) diamond; (cards) diamonds; **à carreaux** checked (*design*); **rester sur le carreaux** (coll) to be left out of the running; **se garder à carreau** (coll) to be on one's guard

carrefour [karfur] *m* crossroads; square (*in a city*)

carrelage [karlaʒ] *m* tiling

carreler [karle] §34 *tr* to tile

carrément [karemã] *adv* squarely, frankly

carrer [kare] *tr* to square || *ref* (coll) to plunk oneself down; (coll) to strut

carrier [karje] *m* quarryman

carrière [karjer] *f* career; course (*e.g., of the sun*); quarry; **donner carrière à** to give free rein to

carriole [karjɔl] *f* light cart, trap; (coll) jalopy

carrossable [karosabl] *adj* passable

carrosse [karos] *m* carriage, coach

carrosserie [karosri] *f* (aut) body

carrossier [karosje] *m* coachmaker

carrousel [karuzel] *m* carrousel; parade ground; tiltyard

carrure [karyr] *f* width (*of shoulders, garment, etc.*); **d'une belle carrure** broad-shouldered (*man*)

cartable [kartabl] *m* briefcase

cartayer [karteje] §49 *intr* to avoid the ruts

carte [kart] *f* card; map, chart; bill (*to pay*); bill of fare, menu; **carte d'abonnement** commutation ticket; season ticket; **carte d'entrée** pass, ticket of admission; **carte des vins** wine list; **carte grise** automobile registration; **carte postale** post card; **cartes truquées** marked cards, stacked deck; **tirer les cartes à qn** to tell s.o.'s fortunes with cards

cartel [kartel] *m* cartel; wall clock; challenge (*to a duel*)

carte-lettre [kartəletr] *f* (*pl* cartes-lettres) gummed letter-envelope

carter [karter] *m* housing; bicycle chain guard; (aut) crankcase

cartilage [kartilaʒ] *m* cartilage, gristle

cartographe [kartograf] *m* cartographer

cartomancie [kartomãsi] *f* fortunetelling with cards

carton [kartõ] *m* pasteboard, cardboard; cardboard box, carton; carton (*of cigarettes*); cartoon (*preliminary sketch*); (typ) cancel; **carton à chapeau** hatbox; **carton à dessin** portfolio for drawings and plans

carton-pâte [kartõpat] *m* papier-mâché

cartouche [kartu/] *m* (archit) cartouche, tablet || *f* cartridge; carton (*of cigarettes*); canister (*of gas mask*); refill (*of pen*); **cartouche à blanc** blank cartridge

cartouchière [kartu/jer] *f* cartridge belt, cartridge case

carvi [karvi] *m* caraway

cas [ka] *m* case; **cas urgent** emergency; **en cas de** in the event of, in a time of; **en cas d'imprévu** in case of emergency; **en cas que, au cas que, au cas où, dans le cas où** in the event that; **faire cas de** to esteem, to make much of; **le cas échéant** should the occasion arise, if necessary; **selon le cas** as the case may be

casa·nier [kazanje] **-nière** [njer] *adj* home-loving || *mf* homebody

casaque [kazak] *f* jockey coat; blouse; **tourner casaque** to be a turncoat

cascade [kaskad] *f* cascade; jerk; spree; **prendre à la cascade** to ad-lib

cascader [kaskade] *intr* to cascade; (slang) to lead a wild life

casca·deur [kaskadœr] **-deuse** [døz] *mf* (mov) double || *m* stunt man || *f* stunt girl

case [kaz] *f* compartment; pigeonhole; square (*e.g., of checkerboard or ledger*); box (*to be filled out on a form*); hut, cabin; **case postale** post-office box

caséine [kazein] *f* casein

caser [kaze] *tr* to put away (*e.g., in a drawer*); to arrange (*e.g., a counter display in a store*); (coll) to place, to find a job for || *ref* (coll) to get settled

caserne [kazɛrn] *f* barracks; **de caserne** off-color (*jokes*); regimented

caserner [kazɛrne] *tr & intr* to barrack

ca·sher -shère [kaʃɛr] *adj* kosher

casier [kasje] *m* rack (*for papers, magazines, letters, bottles*); cabinet; **casier à homards** lobster pot; **casier à tiroirs** music cabinet; **casier judiciaire** police record

casque [kask] *m* helmet; earphones, headset; comb (*of rooster*); **casque à mèche** nightcap; **casque à pointe** spiked helmet; **casque blindé** crash helmet

casquer [kaske] *intr* to fall into a trap; (slang) to shell out

casquette [kaskɛt] *f* cap

cas·sant cas·sante [kɑsɑ̃] [kɑsɑ̃t] *adj* brittle; abrupt, curt

casse [kɑs] *m* (slang) burglarizing || *f* breakage || [kɑs], [kɑs] *f* ladle, scoop; crucible; (bot) cassia; (pharm) senna; (typ) case; (coll) scrap heap, junk

cas·sé -sée [kase] *adj* broken-down; shaky, weak (*voice*)

casse-cou [kasku] *m invar* (coll) daredevil; (coll) stunt man; (coll) danger spot || *interj* look out!

casse-croûte [kaskrut] *m invar* snack

casse-gueule [kasgœl] *adj invar* (slang) risky || *m invar* (coll) risky business

casse-noisettes [kasnwazɛt] *m invar* nutcracker

casse-noix [kasnwa], [kasnwɑ] *m invar* nutcracker

casse-pieds [kaspje] *m invar* (coll) pain in the neck

casser [kase] *tr* to break; to crack, to shatter; (law) to break (*a will*); (mil) to break, to bust; (coll) to split (*one's eardrums*); **casser sa pipe** (coll) to kick the bucket || *ref* to break; (coll) to rack (*one's brains*); **se casser le nez** (coll) to fail

casserole [kasrɔl] *f* saucepan

casse-tête [kastɛt] *m invar* truncheon; din; brain teaser, puzzler; **casse-tête chinois** jigsaw puzzle

cassette [kasɛt], [kasɛt] *f* strongbox, coffer; casket (*for jewels*)

cassis [kasi], [kasis] *m* black currant; cassis (*liqueur*); gutter

cassolette [kasɔlɛt] *f* incense burner

cassonade [kasɔnad] *f* brown sugar

cassoulet [kasule] *m* pork and beans

cassure [kɑsyr] *f* break; crease; rift

castagnettes [kastaɲɛt] *fpl* castanets

caste [kast] *f* caste; **hors caste** outcaste

castil·lan [kastijɑ̃] **castil·lane** [kastijan] *adj* Castilian || *m* Castilian (*language*) || (*cap*) *mf* Castilian (*person*)

Castille [kastij] *f* Castile; **la Castille** Castile

castor [kastɔr] *m* beaver

castrat [kastra] *m* castrato

castrer [kastre] *tr* to castrate

ca·suel -suelle [kazɥɛl] *adj* casual; (coll) brittle || *m* perquisites

cataclysme [kataklism] *m* cataclysm

catacombes [katakɔ̃b] *fpl* catacombs

catafalque [katafalk] *m* catafalque

cataire [katɛr] *f* catnip

Catalogne [katalɔɲ] *f* Catalonia; **la Catalogne** Catalonia

catalogue [katalɔg] *m* catalogue

cataloguer [kataloge] *tr* to catalogue

catalyseur [katalizœr] *m* catalyst

cataplasme [kataplasm] *m* poultice

catapulte [katapylt] *f* catapult

catapulter [katapylte] *tr* to catapult

cataracte [katarakt] *f* cataract

catarrhe [katar] *m* catarrh; bad cold

catastrophe [katastrɔf] *f* catastrophe

catch [katʃ] *m* wrestling

catcheur [katʃœr] *m* wrestler

catéchiser [kateʃize] *tr* to catechize; to reason with

catéchisme [kateʃism] *m* catechism

catégorie [kategɔri] *f* category

catégorique [kategɔrik] *adj* categorical

catgut [katgyt] *m* (surg) catgut

cathédrale [katedral] *f* cathedral

cathéter [kateter] *m* (med) catheter

cathode [katɔd] *f* cathode

catholicisme [katɔlisism] *m* Catholicism

catholicité [katɔlisite] *f* catholicity; Catholicism; Catholics

catholique [katɔlik] *adj* catholic; Catholic; orthodox; **pas très catholique** (coll) questionable || *mf* Catholic

cati [kati] *m* glaze, gloss

catimini [katimini] —**en catimini** (coll) on the sly

catir [katir] *tr* to glaze

cauca·sien [kɔkazjɛ̃] **-sienne** [zjɛn] *adj* Caucasian || (*cap*) *mf* Caucasian

caucasique [kɔkazik] *adj* Caucasian

cauchemar [koʃmar] *m* nightmare

cause [koz] *f* cause; (law) case; **à cause de** because of, on account of, for the sake of; **et pour cause** with good reason; **hors de cause** irrelevant, beside the point; **mettre q.ch. en cause** to question s.th.; **mettre qn en cause** to implicate s.o.

causer [koze] *tr* to cause || *intr* to chat

causerie [kozri] *f* chat; informal lecture

causette [kozɛt] *f*—**faire la causette** (coll) to chat

cau·seur -seuse [kozœr] [zøz] *adj* talkative, chatty || *mf* speaker, conversationalist || *f* love seat

caustique [kostik] *adj* caustic

caute·leux [kotlø] **-leuse** [løz] *adj* crafty, wily; cunning (*mind*)

cautériser [koterize] *tr* to cauterize

caution [kosjɔ̃] *f* security, collateral; guarantor, bondsman; **mettre en liberté sous caution** to let out on bail; **se porter caution pour qn** to put up bail for s.o.; **sujet à caution** unreliable; **verser une caution** to make a deposit

cautionnement [kosjɔnmɑ̃] *m* surety bond, guaranty; bail; deposit

cautionner [kosjɔne] *tr* to bail out; to guarantee

cavalcade [kavalkad] *f* cavalcade

cavalerie [kavalri] *f* cavalry

cava·lier -lière [ljer] *adj* cavalier; bridle (*path*) || *mf* horseback rider; dance partner || *m* cavalier, horseman; escort; (chess) knight || *f* horsewoman

cave [kav] *adj* hollow (*cheeks*) || *f* cellar; liquor cabinet; liquor store; night club; bank (*in game of chance*); stake (*in gambling*); **cave à vin** wine cellar

ca•veau [kavo] *m* (*pl* **-veaux**) small cellar; vault, crypt; rathskeller

caver [kave] *tr* to hollow out || *intr* to ante || *ref* to become hollow (*said of eyes*); to wager

caverne [kavern] *f* cave, cavern; (pathol) cavity (*e.g., in lung*)

caver•neux [kavernø] **-neuse** [nøz] *adj* cavernous; hollow (*voice*)

caviar [kavjar] *m* caviar

caviarder [kavjarde] *tr* to censor

cavité [kavite] *f* cavity, hollow

caw•cher -chère [ka/er] *adj* kosher

Cayes [kaj] *fpl*—**Cayes de la Floride** Florida Keys

C.C.P. *abbr* (**Compte chèques postaux**) postal banking account

ce [sə] (or **cet** [set] before vowel or mute h) **cette** [set] *adj dem* (*pl* **ces** [se]) §82A || **ce** *pron* §82B, §85A4

C.E.A. *abbr* (**Commissariat à l'énergie atomique**) Atomic Energy Commission

céans [seã] *adv* herein

ceci [sesi] *pron dem indef* this, this thing, this matter

cécité [sesite] *f* blindness

céder [sede] §10 *tr* to cede, transfer; to yield, give up; **ne le céder à personne** to be second to none || *intr* to yield, succumb, give way

cédille [sedij] *f* cedilla

cédrat [sedra] *m* citron

cèdre [sedr] *m* cedar

cédule [sedyl] *f* rate, schedule; (law) notification

C.E.E. *abbr* (**Communauté économique européenne**) Common Market

cégétiste [sezetist] *mf* unionist

ceindre [sɛ̃dr] §50 *tr* to buckle on, to gird; to encircle; to wreathe (*one's head*); **ceindre la couronne** to assume the crown || *ref*—**se ceindre de** to gird on

ceinture [sɛ̃tyr] *f* belt; waist, waistline; sash, waistband; girdle; **ceinture de sauvetage** life belt; **ceinture de sécurité** safety belt; **se mettre la ceinture** or **se serrer la ceinture** to tighten one's belt

ceinturer [sɛ̃tyre] *tr* to girdle, to belt; to encircle, to belt; (wrestling) to grip around the waist

cela [səla] *pron dem indef* that, that thing; that matter; **à cela près** with that one exception; **et avec cela?** what else?

célébrant [selebrã] *m* (eccl) celebrant

célébration [selebrasjɔ̃] *f* celebration

célèbre [selebr] *adj* famous

célébrer [selebre] §10 *tr* to celebrate

célébrité [selebrite] *f* celebrity

celer [səle] §2 *tr* to hide, conceal

céleri [selri], [selri] *m* celery

céleste [selest] *adj* celestial

célibat [seliba] *m* celibacy

célibataire [selibater] *adj* single || *m*, celibate || *m* bachelor || *f* spinster

celle [sel] §83

celle-ci [selsi] §84

celle-là [sella] §84

cellier [selje] *m* wine cellar; fruit cellar

cellophane [selofan] *f* cellophane

cellule [selyl], [selyl] *f* cell

celluloïd [selyloid] *m* celluloid

celte [selt] *adj* Celtic || (*cap*) *mf* Celt

celtique [seltik] *adj* & *m* Celtic

celui [səlɥi] **celle** [sel] (*pl* **ceux** [sø] **celles**) §83

celui-ci [səlɥisi] **celle-ci** [selsi] (*pl* **ceux-ci** [søsi] **celles-ci**) §84

celui-là [səlɥila] **celle-là** [sella] (*pl* **ceux-là** [søla] **celles-là**) §84

cémentation [semãtasjɔ̃] *f* casehardening

cendre [sãdr] *f* cinder; **cendres** ashes

cendrée [sãdre] *f* shot; buckshot; (sports) cinder track

cendrer [sãdre] *tr* to cinder

cendrier [sãdrije] *m* ashtray

Cendrillon [sãdrijɔ̃] *f* Cinderella

cène [sen] *f* (eccl) Holy Communion || (*cap*) *f* (eccl) Last Supper

cens [sãs] *m* census; poll tax

cen•sé -sée [sãse] *adj* supposed to, *e.g.*, **je ne suis pas censé le savoir** I am not supposed to know it; reputed to be, *e.g.*, **il est censé juge infaillible** he is reputed to be an infallible judge

censément [sãsemã] *adv* supposedly, apparently, allegedly

censeur [sãsœr] *m* censor; census taker; critic; auditor; proctor

censure [sãsyr] *f* censure; censorship; (psychoanal) censor

censurer [sãsyre] *tr* to censure; to censor

cent [sã] *adj* & *pron* (*pl* **cents** in multiples when standing before modified noun, *e.g.*, **trois cents œufs** three hundred eggs) one hundred, a hundred, hundred; **cent pour cent** one hundred percent; **cent un** [sãœ̃] one hundred and one, a hundred and one, hundred and one; **l'an dix-neuf cent** the year nineteen hundred; **page deux cent** page two hundred || *m* hundred, one hundred || [sɛ̃t] *m* cent

centaine [sãten] *f* hundred; **par centaines** by the hundreds; **une centaine de** about a hundred

centaure [sãtor] *m* centaur

centenaire [sãtner] *adj* centenary || *mf* centenarian || *m* centennial

centen•nal -nale [sãtenal] *adj* (*pl* **-naux** [no]) centennial

centième [sãtjem] *adj*, *pron* (*masc*, *fem*), & *m* hundredth || *f* hundredth performance

centigrade [sãtigrad] *adj* & *m* centigrade

centime [sãtim] *m* centime

centimètre [sãtimetr] *m* centimeter; tape measure

centrage [sãtraz] *m* centering

cen•tral -trale [sãtral] *adj* (*pl* **-traux** [tro]) central; main (*office*) || *m* (telp) central || *f* powerhouse; labor union; **centrale atomique** or **nucléaire** atomic generator

centralisation [sãtralizɑsjɔ̃] ƒ centralization

centraliser [sãtralize] tr & reƒ to centralize

centre [sãtr] m center; **centre commercial** shopping district; **centre de dépression** storm center; **centre de triage** (rr) switchyard; **centre d'études** college; **centre de villégiature** resort; **centre social des étudiants** student center, student union

centrer [sãtre] tr to center

centrifuge [sãtrifyʒ] adj centrifugal

centuple [sãtypl] adj & m hundredfold; **au centuple** hundredfold

cep [sep] m vine stock

cépage [sepaʒ] m (bot) vine

cèpe [sep] ƒ cepe mushroom

cependant [səpãdã] adv meanwhile; however, but, still; **cependant que** while, whereas; **et cependant** and yet

céramique [seramik] adj ceramic ‖ ƒ (art of) ceramics; ceramic piece; **céramiques** ceramics (objects)

cerbère [serber] m (coll) watchdog ‖ (cap) m Cerberus

cer·ceau [serso] m (pl **-ceaux**) hoop; **cerceaux** pinfeathers

cercle [serkl] m circle; circle, club, society; clubhouse; hoop; **en cercle in the cask**

cercler [serkle] tr to ring, encircle; to hoop

cercueil [serkœj] m coffin

céréale [sereal] adj & ƒ cereal

céré·bral -brale [serebral] adj (pl **-braux** [bro]) cerebral

cérémo·nial -niale [seremɔnjal] adj & m ceremonial

cérémonie [seremɔni] ƒ ceremony; **faire des cérémonies** to stand on ceremony

cérémo·niel -nielle [seremɔnjel] adj ceremonial

cérémo·nieux [seremɔnjø] **-nieuse** [njøz] adj ceremonious, formal, stiff

cerf [ser] m deer, red deer; stag, buck

cerf-volant [servɔlã] m (pl **cerfs-volants**) kite

cerisaie [serize] ƒ cherry orchard

cerise [səriz] ƒ cherry

cerisier [sərizje] m cherry tree

cerne [sern] m annual ring (of tree); ring (around moon, black eye, wound)

cer·neau [serno] m (pl **-neaux**) unripe nutmeat

cerner [serne] tr to ring, encircle; to hem in, besiege; to shell (nuts)

cer·tain [sertẽ] **-taine** [ten] adj certain, sure ‖ (when standing before noun) adj certain, some; **certain auteur** a certain author; **depuis un certain temps** for some time; **d'un certain âge** middle-aged ‖ **certains** pron indef pl certain people

certainement [sertenmã] adv certainly

certes [sert] adv indeed, certainly

certificat [sertifika] m certificate

certifier [sertifje] tr to certify

certitude [sertityd] ƒ certainty

cérumen [serymen] m earwax

céruse [seryz] ƒ white lead

cer·veau [servo] m (pl **-veaux**) brain; mind; **cerveau brûlé** (coll) hothead

cervelas [servəla] m salami

cervelet [servəle] m cerebellum

cervelle [servel] ƒ brains; **brûler la cervelle à qn** (coll) to shoot s.o.'s brains out

ces [se] §82A

césa·rien [sezarjẽ] **-rienne** [rjen] adj Caesarean ‖ ƒ Caesarean section

cesse [ses] ƒ cessation, ceasing; **sans cesse** unceasingly, incessantly

cesser [sese] tr to stop, to cease, to leave off (e.g., work) ‖ intr to cease, stop; **cesser de** + inf to stop, cease, quit + ger

cessez-le-feu [seselfø] m invar ceasefire

cession [sesjɔ̃] ƒ ceding, surrender; (law) transfer

c'est-à-dire [setadir] conj that is, namely

césure [sezyr] ƒ caesura

cet [set] §82A

cette [set] §82A

ceux [sø] §83

ceux-ci [søsi] §84

ceux-là [søla] §84

Ceylan [selã] m Ceylon

C.G.T. [seʒete] ƒ (letterword) (**confédération générale du travail**) national labor union ‖ abbr (**Cie Générale transatlantique**) French Line

cha·cal [ʃakal] m (pl **-cals**) jackal

cha·cun [ʃakœ̃] **-cune** [kyn] pron indef each, each one, every one; everybody, everyone; **chacun pour soi** every man for himself; **chacun son goût** every man to his own taste; **tout chacun** (coll) every Tom, Dick, and Harry

chadburn [tʃadbœrn] m (naut) public-address system

chadouf [ʃaduf] m well sweep

cha·grin [ʃagrẽ] **-grine** [grin] adj sad, downcast ‖ m grief, sorrow

chagriner [ʃagrine] tr to grieve, distress; to make into shagreen leather ‖ intr to grieve, worry

chah [ʃa] m shah

chahut [ʃay] m (coll) horseplay, row

chahuter [ʃayte] tr (coll) to upset; (coll) to boo, heckle ‖ intr (coll) to create a disturbance

chai [ʃɛ] m wine cellar

chaîne [ʃen] ƒ chain; warp (of fabric); necklace; (archit) pier; (archit) tie; (naut) cable; (rad, telv) network; (telv) channel; **chaîne de fabrication** or **chaîne de montage** assembly line; **faire la chaîne** to form a bucket brigade

chaînon [ʃenɔ̃] m link

chair [ʃer] ƒ flesh; pulp (of fruits); meat (of animals); **chair de poule** gooseflesh; **chair de sa chair** one's flesh and blood; **chairs** (painting, sculpture) nude parts; **en chair et en os** in the flesh; **ni chair ni poisson** neither fish nor fowl

chaire [ʃer] ƒ pulpit; lectern; chair (held by university professor)

chaise [ʃez] *f* chair; bowline knot; (mach) bracket; **chaise à bascule** rocking chair; **chaise à porteurs** sedan chair; **chaise berceuse** rocking chair; **chaise brisée** folding chair; **chaise d'enfant** high chair; **chaise électrique** electric chair; **chaise percée** commode, toilet; **chaise pliante** folding chair

cha·land [ʃalɑ̃] **-lande** [lɑ̃d] *mf* customer ‖ *m* barge; **chaland de débarquement** (mil) landing craft

châle [ʃɑl] *m* shawl

chalet [ʃale] *m* chalet, cottage, summer home; **chalet de nécessité** public rest room

chaleur [ʃalœr] *f* heat; warmth; **les grandes chaleurs de l'été** the hot weather of summer

chaleu·reux [ʃalœrø] **-reuse** [røz] *adj* warm, heated

châlit [ʃɑli] *m* bedstead

chaloupe [ʃalup] *f* launch

chalu·meau [ʃalymo] *m* (*pl* **-meaux**) reed; blowtorch; (mus) pipe; **chalumeau oxhydrique** or **chalumeau oxyacétylénique** acetylene torch

chalut [ʃaly] *m* trawl

chalutier [ʃalytje] *m* trawler

chamade [ʃamad] *f*—**battre la chamade** to beat wildly (*said of the heart*)

chamailler [ʃamɑje] *ref* to squabble

chamarrer [ʃamare] *tr* to decorate, to ornament; to bedizen, to bedeck; (slang) to cover (*s.o.*) with ridicule

chambarder [ʃɑ̃barde] *tr* (slang) to upset, to turn upside down

chambellan [ʃɑ̃bɛllɑ̃] *m* chamberlain

chambouler [ʃɑ̃bule] *tr* (slang) to upset, to turn topsy-turvy

chambranle [ʃɑ̃brɑ̃l] *m* frame (*of a door or window*); mantelpiece

chambre [ʃɑ̃br] *f* chamber; room; **chambre à air** inner tube; **chambre à coucher** bedroom; **chambre d'ami** guest room; **chambre de compensation** clearing house; **chambre noire** darkroom

chambrée [ʃɑ̃bre] *f* dormitory, barracks; bunkmates

chambrer [ʃɑ̃bre] *tr* to keep under lock and key; to keep (*wine*) at room temperature

cha·meau [ʃamo] **-melle** [mel] *mf* (*pl* **-meaux**) camel ‖ *m* (slang) bitch (*person*)

chamois [ʃamwa] *adj & m* chamois

champ [ʃɑ̃] *m* field; **aux champs** salute (*played on trumpet or drum*); **champ clos** lists, dueling field; **champ de courses** race track; **champ de repos** cemetery; **champ de tir** firing range; **champ libre** clear field; **champs Élysées** Elysian Fields; **Champs-Élysées** Champs Élysées (*street*)

champagne [ʃɑ̃paɲ] *m* champagne; **champagne brut** extra dry champagne; **champagne d'origine** vintage champagne ‖ (*cap*) *f* Champagne; **la Champagne** Champagne

champe·nois [ʃɑ̃pənwa] **-noise** [nwaz] *adj* Champagne ‖ *m* Champagne dialect ‖ (*cap*) *mf* inhabitant of Champagne

champêtre [ʃɑ̃petr] *adj* rustic, rural

champignon [ʃɑ̃piɲɔ̃] *m* mushroom; fungus; (slang) accelerator pedal; **champignon de couche** cultivated mushroom; **champignon vénéneux** toadstool

champignonner [ʃɑ̃piɲɔne] *intr* to mushroom

cham·pion [ʃɑ̃pjɔ̃] **-pionne** [pjɔn] *mf* champion ‖ *f* championess

championnat [ʃɑ̃pjɔna] *m* championship

champlever [ʃɑ̃lve] §2 *tr* to chase out, to gouge out

chan·card [ʃɑ̃sar] **-carde** [sard] *adj* (slang) in luck ‖ *mf* (slang) lucky person

chance [ʃɑ̃s] *f* luck; good luck; **avoir de la chance** to be lucky; **bonne chance** good luck; **chance moyenne** off chance; **chances** chances, risks, probability, possibility

chance·lant [ʃɑ̃slɑ̃] **-lante** [lɑ̃t] *adj* shaky, unsteady, tottering; delicate (*health, constitution*)

chanceler [ʃɑ̃sle] §34 *intr* to stagger, to totter, to teeter; to waver

chancelier [ʃɑ̃səlje] *m* chancellor

chancellerie [ʃɑ̃səlri] *f* chancellery

chan·ceux [ʃɑ̃sø] **-ceuse** [søz] *adj* lucky; risky

chanci [ʃɑ̃si] *m* manure pile for mushroom growing

chancir [ʃɑ̃sir] *intr* to grow moldy

chancre [ʃɑ̃kr] *m* chancre; ulcer, canker

chandail [ʃɑ̃daj] *m* sweater; **chandail à col roulé** turtleneck sweater

chandeleur [ʃɑ̃dlœr] *f*—**la chandeleur** Candlemas

chandelier [ʃɑ̃dəlje] *m* candlestick; chandler

chandelle [ʃɑ̃del] *f* tallow candle; prop, stay (*used in construction*); **chandelle de glace** icicle; **en chandelle** vertically; **voir trente-six chandelles** to see stars (*on account of a blow*)

chanfrein [ʃɑ̃frɛ̃] *m* forehead (*of a horse*); chamfer, beveled edge

chanfreiner [ʃɑ̃frene] *tr* to chamfer, to bevel

change [ʃɑ̃ʒ] *m* exchange; rate of exchange; **de change** in reserve, extra; **donner le change à** to throw off the trail; **prendre le change** to let one self be duped; **rendre le change à qn** to give s.o. a taste of his own medicine

changeable [ʃɑ̃ʒabl] *adj* changeable

chan·geant [ʃɑ̃ʒɑ̃] **-geante** [ʒɑ̃t] *adj* changeable, changing, fickle; iridescent

changement [ʃɑ̃ʒmɑ̃] *m* change; shift, shifting; **changement de propriétaire** under new ownership; **changement de vitesse** gearshift

changer [ʃɑ̃ʒe] §38 *tr* to change; **changer contre** to exchange for ‖ *intr* to change; **changer d'avis** to change one's mind; **changer de place** to change one's seat; **changer de ton**

(coll) to change one's tune; **changer de visage** to blush; to change color || *ref* to change, change clothes

chanoine [ʃanwan] *m* (eccl) canon

hanson [ãsɔ̃] *f* song; **chanson bachique** drinking song; **chanson de geste** medieval epic; **chanson de Noël** Christmas carol; **chanson du terroir** folk song; **chanson sentimentale** torch song

chansonner [ʃãsɔne] *tr* to lampoon in a satirical song

chansonnier [ʃãsɔnœr] *m* lampooner (*who writes satirical songs*)

chanson-nier [ʃãsɔnje] **chanson-nière** [ʃãsɔnjɛr] *mf* songwriter || *m* chansonnier; song book

chant [ʃã] *m* singing; song, chant; canto; crowing (*of rooster*); side (*e.g., of a brick*); **chant du cygne** swan song; **chant de Noël** Christmas carol; **chant national** national anthem; **chants** poetry; **de chant** on end, edgewise

chantage [ʃãtaʒ] *m* blackmail

chan·tant [ʃãtã] **-tante** [tãt] *adj* singable, melodious; singsong (*accent*); musical (*evening*)

chan·teau [ʃãto] *m* (*pl* **-teaux**) chunk (*of bread*); remnant

chantepleure [ʃãtplœr] *f* wine funnel; tap (*of cask*); sprinkler; weep hole

chanter [ʃãte] *tr* to sing || *intr* to sing; to crow (*as a rooster*); to pay blackmail; **chanter faux** to sing out of tune; **chanter juste** to sing in tune; **faire chanter** to blackmail

chanterelle [ʃãtrɛl] *f* first string (*of violin*); decoy bird; mushroom; **appuyer sur la chanterelle** (coll) to rub it in

chan·teur [ʃãtœr] **-teuse** [tøz] *adj* singing; song (*bird*) || *mf* singer; **chanteur de charme** crooner; **chanteur de rythme** jazz singer

chantier [ʃãtje] *m* shipyard; stocks; slip; workshop, yard; gantry, stand (*for barrels*); (public sign) men at work; **chantier de démolition** junkyard, scrap heap; **mettre en or sur le chantier** to start work on

chantilly [ʃãtiji] *m* whipped cream

chantonner [ʃãtɔne] *tr & intr* to hum

chantoung [ʃãtuŋ] *m* shantung

chantourner [ʃãturne] *tr* to jigsaw

chantre [ʃãtr] *m* cantor, chanter; precentor; songster; bard, poet

chanvre [ʃãvr] *m* hemp; **en chanvre** hempen; flaxen (*color*)

chan·vrier [ʃãvrije] **-vrière** [vrijer] *adj* hemp (*industry*) || *mf* dealer in hemp; hemp dresser

chaos [kao] *m* chaos

chaotique [kaɔtik] *adj* chaotic

chaparder [ʃaparde] *tr* (coll) to pilfer, to filch

chape [ʃap] *f* cover, covering; tread (*of tire*); coping (*of bridge*); frame, shell (*of pulley block*); (eccl) cope

cha·peau [ʃapo] *m* (*pl* **-peaux**) hat; head (*of mushroom*); lead (*of magazine or newspaper article*); cap (*of fountain pen; of valve*); cowl (*of*

chimney); **chapeau à cornes** cocked hat; **chapeau bas** hat in hand; **chapeau bas!** hats off!; **chapeau chinois** Chinese bells; **chapeau de roue** hubcap; **chapeau haut de forme** top hat; **chapeau melon** derby; **chapeau mou** fedora

chapeau-cloche [ʃapoklɔʃ] *m* (*pl* **chapeaux-cloches**) cloche (hat)

chapeauter [ʃapote] *tr* (coll) to put a hat on (*e.g., a child*)

chapelain [ʃaplɛ̃] *m* chaplain (*of a private chapel*)

chapeler [ʃaple] §34 *tr* to scrape the crust off of (*bread*)

chapelet [ʃaple] *m* chaplet, rosary; string (*of onions; of islands; of insults*); chain (*of events; of mountains*); series (*e.g., of attacks*); (mil) stick (*of bombs*); **chapelet hydraulique** bucket conveyor; **défiler son chapelet** (coll) to speak one's mind; **dire son chapelet** to tell one's beads; **en chapelet** (elec) in series

chape·lier [ʃaplje] **-lière** [ljer] *mf* hatter || *f* Saratoga trunk

chapelle [ʃapel] *f* chapel; clique, coterie; **chapelle ardente** mortuary chamber lighted by candles; hearse

chapellerie [ʃapelri] *f* hatmaking; millinery; hat shop; millinery shop

chapelure [ʃaplyr] *f* bread crumbs

chaperon [ʃaprɔ̃] *m* chaperon; hood; cape with a hood; coping (*of wall*); **le Petit Chaperon rouge** Little Red Ridinghood

chaperonner [ʃaprɔne] *tr* to chaperon

chapi·teau [ʃapito] *m* (*pl* **-teaux**) capital (*of column*); circus tent

chapitre [ʃapitr] *m* chapter; **commencer un nouveau chapitre** to turn over a new leaf

chapon [ʃapɔ̃] *m* capon; (culin) crust rubbed with garlic

chaque [ʃak] *adj indef* each, every || *pron indef* (coll) each, each one

char [ʃar] *m* chariot; float (*in parade*); (mil) tank; **char d'assaut** or **char de combat** (mil) tank; **char funèbre** hearse

charabia [ʃarabja] *m* gibberish

charançon [ʃarãsɔ̃] *m* weevil

charbon [ʃarbɔ̃] *m* coal; soft coal; charcoal; carbon (*of an electric cell or arc*); cinder (*in the eye*); **charbon ardent** live coal; **charbon de bois** charcoal; **charbon de terre** coal; **être sur les charbons ardents** to be on pins and needles

charbonnage [ʃarbɔnaʒ] *m* coal mining; coal mine

charbonner [ʃarbɔne] *tr* to char; to draw (*a picture*) with charcoal || *intr & ref* to char, to carbonize

charbon·neux [ʃarbɔnø] **charbon·neuse** [ʃarbɔnøz] *adj* sooty; anthrax-carrying

charbon·nier [ʃarbɔnje] **charbon·nière** [ʃarbɔnjer] *adj* coal (*e.g., industry*) || *mf* coal dealer || *m* charcoal burner; coaler || *f* coal scuttle; charcoal kiln; (orn) coal titmouse

charcuter [ʃarkyte] *tr* to butcher, mangle

charcuterie [ʃarkytri] *f* delicatessen; pork butcher shop

charcu·tier [ʃarkytje] **-tière** [tjer] *mf* pork butcher; (coll) sawbones

chardon [ʃardɔ̃] *m* thistle

chardonneret [ʃardɔnre] *m* (orn) goldfinch

charge [ʃarʒ] *f* charge; load, burden; caricature; public office; **à charge de** on condition of, with the proviso of; **à charge de revanche** on condition of getting the same thing in return; **charges de famille** dependents; **être à charge à** to be dependent upon; **être à la charge de** to be supported by; **faire la charge de** to do a takeoff of

char·gé **-gée** [ʃarʒe] *adj* loaded; full; overcast (*sky*); registered (*letter*) || *m* assistant, deputy, envoy; **chargé de cours** assistant professor

chargement [ʃarʒəmã] *m* charging; loading; cargo

charger [ʃarʒe] §38 *tr* to charge; to drive, to take (*s.o. in one's car*) || *intr* (mil) to charge; (naut) to load || *ref* to be loaded; **se charger de** to take charge of; to take up (*a question*)

chargeur [ʃarʒœr] *m* loader; stoker; shipper; clip (*of gun*); (elec) charger

chariot [ʃarjo] *m* wagon, cart; typewriter carriage; **chariot d'enfant** walker; **chariot élévateur** fork-lift truck; **Grand Chariot**, **Chariot de David** Big Dipper; **Petit Chariot** Little Dipper

charitable [ʃaritabl] *adj* charitable

charité [ʃarite] *f* charity; **faire la charité** to give alms; **faites la charité de** or **ayez la charité de** have the goodness to; **par charité** for charity's sake

charlatan [ʃarlatɑ̃] *m* charlatan

charlemagne [ʃarləmaɲ] *m* (cards) king of hearts; **faire charlemagne** to quit while winning

char·mant [ʃarmã] **-mante** [mãt] *adj* charming

charme [ʃarm] *m* charm; (*Carpinus betulus*) hornbeam; **se porter comme un charme** to be fit as a fiddle

charmer [ʃarme] *tr* to charm

char·meur [ʃarmœr] **-meuse** [møz] *adj* charming || *mf* charmer

charmille [ʃarmij] *f* bower, arbor

char·nel **-nelle** [ʃarnel] *adj* carnal

charnière [ʃarnjer] *f* hinge

char·nu **-nue** [ʃarny] *adj* fleshy; plump; pulpy

charogne [ʃarɔɲ] *f* carrion

charpentage [ʃarpãtaʒ] *m* carpentry

charpente [ʃarpãt] *f* framework; scaffolding; frame, build (*of body*)

charpenter [ʃarpãte] *tr* to square (*timber*); to outline, map out, plan (*a novel, speech, etc.*); **être solidement charpenté** to be well built or well constructed || *intr* to carpenter

charpenterie [ʃarpãtri] *f* carpentry; structure (*of building*)

charpentier [ʃarpãtje] *m* carpenter

charpie [ʃarpi] *f* lint; **en charpie** i shreds

charrée [ʃare] *f* lye

charre·tier [ʃartje] **-tière** [tjer] *m* teamster; **jurer comme un charretie** to swear like a trooper

charrette [ʃaret] *f* cart

charriage [ʃarjaʒ] *m* cartage; driftin (*of ice*); (slang) exaggeration

charrier [ʃarje] *tr* to cart, to transport to carry away (*sand, as the rive does*); (slang) to poke fun at || *intr* to be full of ice (*said of river*); (slang) to exaggerate

charroi [ʃarwɑ], [ʃarwa] *m* cartage

charron [ʃarɔ̃], [ʃarɔ̃] *m* wheelwright, cartwright

charroyer [ʃarwaje] §47 *tr* to cart

charrue [ʃary] *f* plow; **mettre la charrue devant les bœufs** to put the cart before the horse

charte [ʃart] *f* charter; title deed; fundamental principle

chas [ʃɑ] *m* eye (*of needle*)

chasse [ʃas] *f* hunt, hunting; hunting song; chase; bag (*game caught*); **aller à la chasse** to go hunting; **chasse à courre** riding to the hounds; **chasse aux appartements** house hunting; **chasse aux fauves** big-game hunting; **chasse d'eau** flush; **chasse gardée** game preserve; **chasse réservée** (public sign) no shooting; **tirer la chasse** to pull the toilet chain

châsse [ʃɑs] *f* reliquary; frame (*e.g., for eyeglasses*) || **châsses** *mpl* (slang) blinkers, eyes

chasse-bestiaux [ʃasbestjo] *m* *invar* cowcatcher

chasse-clou [ʃasklu] *m* (*pl* **-clous**) punch, nail set

chassé-croisé [ʃasekrwaze] *m* (*pl* **chassés-croisés**) futile efforts

chasselas [ʃasla] *m* white table grape

chasse-mouches [ʃasmuʃ] *m* *invar* fly swatter; fly net

chasse-neige [ʃasneʒ] *m* *invar* snowplow

chasse-pierres [ʃaspjer] *m* *invar* (rr) cowcatcher

chasser [ʃase] *tr* to hunt; to chase; to chase away, to put to flight; to drive (*e.g., a herd of cattle*); (coll) to fire (*e.g., a servant*) || *intr* to hunt; to skid; to come, e.g., **le vent chasse du nord** the wind is coming from the north; **chasser de race** (coll) to be a chip off the old block

chasseresse [ʃasres] *f* huntress

chas·seur [ʃasœr] **chas·seuse** [ʃasøz] *mf* hunter; bellhop || *m* chasseur; fighter pilot; **chasseur à réaction** jet fighter; **chasseur d'assaut** fighter plane; **chasseur de chars** antitank tank; **chasseur de sous-marins** submarine chaser

chasseur-bombardier [ʃasœrbɔ̃bardje] *m* fighter-bomber

chassie [ʃasi] *f* gum (*on eyelids*)

chas·sieux [ʃasjø] **chas·sieuse** [ʃasjøz] *adj* gummy (*eyelids*)

châssis [ʃasi] *m* chassis; window frame; chase (*for printing*); **châssis à**

demeure or dormant sealed window frame; **châssis couche** (hort) hotbed; **châssis mobile** movable sash

châssis-presse [ʃasipres] *m* (*pl* **-presses**) printing frame

chaste [ʃast] *adj* chaste

chasteté [ʃastate] *f* chastity

chat [ʃa] **chatte** [ʃat] *mf* cat ‖ *m* tomcat; **à bon chat bon rat** tit for tat; **acheter chat en poche** (coll) to buy a pig in a poke; **appeler un chat un chat** (coll) to call a spade a spade; **chat à neuf queues** cat-o'-nine-tails; **chat dans la gorge** (coll) frog in the throat; **chat de gouttière** alley cat; **chat sauvage** wildcat; **d'autres chats à fouetter** (coll) other fish to fry; **il ne faut pas réveiller le chat qui dort** let sleeping dogs lie; **le Chat botté** Puss in Boots; **mon petit chat!** darling!; **pas un chat** (coll) not a soul ‖ *f* see **chatte**

châtaigne [ʃatɛɲ] *f* chestnut

châtaignier [ʃatɛɲe] *m* chestnut tree

chataire [ʃatɛr] *f* catnip

châ-teau [ʃato] *m* (*pl* **-teaux**) chateau; palace; estate, manor; **château d'eau** water tower; **château de cartes** house of cards; **château fort** castle, fort, citadel; **châteaux en Espagne** castles in the air; **mener une vie de château** to live like a prince

châteaubriand or **châteaubriant** [ʃatobriã] *m* grilled beefsteak

châte-lain [ʃatlɛ̃] **-laine** [lɛn] *mf* proprietor of a country estate ‖ *f* wife of the lord of the manor; bracelet

châtelet [ʃatlɛ] *m* small chateau

chat-huant [ʃayã] *m* (*pl* **chats-huants** [ʃayã]) screech owl

châtier [ʃatje] *tr* to chasten, chastise; to correct; to purify (*style*)

chatière [ʃatjɛr] *f* ventilation hole; cathole

châtiment [ʃatimã] *m* punishment

chatoiement [ʃatwamã] *m* glisten, sparkle; sheen, shimmer; play of colors

chaton [ʃatɔ̃] *m* kitten; setting (*of ring*); (bot) catkin

chatonner [ʃatɔne] *tr* to set (*a gem*) ‖ *intr* to have kittens

chatouillement [ʃatujmã] *m* tickle; tickling sensation

chatouiller [ʃatuje] *tr* to tickle; (fig) to excite, arouse ‖ *intr* to tickle

chatouil-leux [ʃatujø] **chatouil-leuse** [ʃatujøz] *adj* ticklish; touchy

chatoyer [ʃatwaje] §47 *intr* to glisten, to sparkle; to shimmer

chat-pard [ʃapar] *m* (*pl* **chats-pards**) ocelot

châtrer [ʃatre] *tr* to castrate

chatte [ʃat] *adj fem* kittenish ‖ *f* cat, female cat

chatterie [ʃatri] *f* cajoling; sweets

chatterton [ʃatertɔn] *m* friction tape

chaud [ʃo] **chaude** [ʃod] *adj* hot, warm; last-minute (*news flash*); **il fait chaud** it is warm (weather); **pleurer à chaudes larmes** to cry one's eyes out ‖ *m* heat, warmth; **à chaud** emergency (*operation*); (med) in the acute stage; **avoir chaud** to be warm, to be hot (*said of person*); **il a eu chaud** (coll) he had a narrow escape ‖ *adv*—**coûter chaud** (coll) to cost a pretty penny; **servir chaud** to serve (*s.th.*) piping hot

chaudière [ʃodjɛr] *f* boiler

chaudron [ʃodrɔ̃] *m* cauldron

chaudron-nier [ʃodrɔnje] **chaudron-nière** [ʃodrɔnjɛr] *mf* coppersmith; boilermaker

chauffage [ʃofaʒ] *m* heating; stoking; (coll) coaching

chauffard [ʃofar] *m* road hog, Sunday driver

chauffe [ʃof] *f* stoking; furnace

chauffe-assiettes [ʃofasjɛt] *m invar* hot plate

chauffe-bain [ʃofbɛ̃] *m* (*pl* **-bains**) bathroom water heater

chauffe-eau [ʃofo] *m. invar* water heater

chauffe-lit [ʃofli] *m* (*pl* **-lits**) bed-warmer

chauffe-pieds [ʃofpje] *m invar* foot warmer

chauffe-plats [ʃofpla] *m invar* chafing dish

chauffer [ʃofe] *tr* to heat; to warm up; to limber up; (coll) to coach; (slang) to snitch, filch ‖ *intr* to heat up; to get up steam; to overheat; **ça va chauffer!** (coll) watch the fur fly! ‖ *ref* to warm oneself; to heat up

chaufferette [ʃofret] *f* foot warmer; space heater; car heater

chauffeur [ʃofœr] *m* driver; chauffeur; (rr) stoker, fireman

chauffeuse [ʃoføz] *f* fireside chair

chaume [ʃom] *m* stubble; thatch

chaumière [ʃomjɛr] *f* thatched cottage

chaussée [ʃose] *f* pavement, road; causeway

chausse-pied [ʃospje] *m* (*pl* **-pieds**) shoehorn

chausser [ʃose] *tr* to put on (*shoes, skis, glasses, tires, etc.*); to shoe; to fit ‖ *intr* to fit (*said of shoe*); **chausser de** to wear (*a certain size shoe*) ‖ *ref* to put one's shoes on

chausses [ʃos] *fpl* hose (*in medieval dress*); **aux chausses de** on the heels of; **c'est elle qui porte les chausses** (coll) she wears the pants

chausse-trape [ʃostrap] *f* (*pl* **-trapes**) trap

chaussette [ʃosɛt] *f* sock

chausseur [ʃosœr] *m* shoe salesman

chausson [ʃosɔ̃] *m* pump, slipper, savate; **chausson aux pommes** apple turnover

chaussure [ʃosyr] *f* footwear, shoes; shoe; **trouver chaussure à son pied** to find what one needs

chauve [ʃov] *adj* bald

chauve-souris [ʃovsuri] *f* (*pl* **chauves-souris**) (zool) bat

chau-vin [ʃovɛ̃] **-vine** [vin] *adj* chauvinistic ‖ *mf* chauvinist

chauvir [ʃovir] *intr*—**chauvir de l'oreil-le** or **chauvir des oreilles** to prick up the ears (*said of horse, mule, donkey*)

chaux [ʃo] *f* lime

chavirement [ʃavirmã] *m* capsizing, overturning

chavirer [ʃavire] *tr & intr* to tip over, to capsize

chef [ʃɛf] *m* head, chief, leader; boss; scoutmaster; **chef de bande** ringleader, gang leader; **chef de cuisine** chef; **chef de file** leader, standardbearer; **chef de gare** stationmaster; **chef de l'exécutif** chief executive; **chef de musique** bandmaster; **chef de rayon** floorwalker; **chef de tribu** chieftain; **chef d'orchestre** conductor; bandleader; **de son propre chef** by one's own authority, on one's own

chef-d'œuvre [ʃedœvr] *m* (*pl* **chefs-d'œuvre**) masterpiece

chef-lieu [ʃefljø] *m* (*pl* **chefs-lieux**) county seat, capital city

cheftaine [ʃeften] *f* Girl Scout unit leader

cheik [ʃek] *m* sheik

chelem [ʃlɛm] *m* slam (*at bridge*); **être chelem** (*cards*) to be shut out

chemin [ʃmɛ̃] *m* way; road; **chemin battu** beaten path; **chemin de la Croix** (eccl) Way of the Cross; **chemin de fer** railroad; **chemin des écoliers** (coll) long way around; **chemin de table** table runner; **chemin de traverse** side road; shortcut; **chemin de velours** primrose path; **n'y pas aller par quatre chemins** (coll) to come straight to the point

chemineau [ʃmino] *m* (*pl* **-neaux**) hobo, tramp; deadbeat

cheminée [ʃmine] *f* chimney, stack, smokestack; fireplace; (naut) funnel

cheminer [ʃmine] *intr* to trudge, tramp; to make headway

cheminot [ʃmino] *m* railroader

chemise [ʃmiz] *f* shirt; dust jacket (*of book*); folder, file; jacket, shell, metal casing; **chemise de mailles** coat of mail; **chemise de nuit** nightgown

chemiser [ʃmize] *tr* (mach) to case, to jacket

chemiserie [ʃmizri] *f* haberdashery

chemisette [ʃmizet] *f* short-sleeved shirt

chemi·sier [ʃmizje] **-sière** [zjer] *mf* haberdasher || *m* shirtwaist

che·nal [ʃnal] *m* (*pl* **-naux** [no]) channel; millrace

chenapan [ʃnapã] *m* rogue, scoundrel

chêne [ʃen] *m* oak

ché·neau [ʃeno] *m* (*pl* **-neaux**) rain spout

chêne-liège [ʃenljeʒ] *m* (*pl* **chênes-lièges**) cork oak

chenet [ʃne] *m* andiron

chènevis [ʃenvi] *m* hempseed, birdseed

chenil [ʃni] *m* kennel

chenille [ʃnij] *f* caterpillar; chenille; caterpillar tread

chenil·lé -lée [ʃnije] *adj* with a caterpillar tread

che·nu -nue [ʃny] *adj* hoary

cheptel [ʃeptɛl], [ʃetɛl] *m* livestock; **cheptel mort** implements and buildings

chèque [ʃek] *m* check; **chèque de voyage** traveler's check; **chèque sans provision** worthless check; **chèque sans provision** worthless check

chéquier [ʃekje] *m* checkbook

cher chère [ʃer] *adj* expensive, dear || (when standing before noun) *adj* dear, beloved || *f* see **chère** || **cher** *adv* dear(ly); **coûter cher** to cost a great deal

chercher [ʃerʃe] *tr* to look for, search for, seek, hunt; to try to get; **aller chercher** to go and get; **envoyer chercher** to send for || *intr* to search; **chercher à** to try to, to endeavor to || *ref* to look for each other; to feel one's way

cher·cheur [ʃerʃœr] **-cheuse** [ʃøz] *adj* inquiring (*mind*); homing (*device*) || *mf* seeker; researcher, scholar; investigator; prospector (*for gold, uranium, etc.*)

chère [ʃer] *f* fare, food and drink; **faire bonne chère** to live high

ché·ri -rie [ʃeri] *adj & mf* darling

chérir [ʃerir] *tr* to cherish

cherry [ʃeri] *m* cherry cordial

cherté [ʃerte] *f* high price; **cherté de la vie** high cost of living

chérubin [ʃerybɛ̃] *m* cherub

ché·tif -tive [ʃetif], [tiv] *adj* puny, sickly; poor, wretched

che·val [ʃəval] *m* (*pl* **-vaux** [vo]) horse; metric or French horsepower (*735 watts*); **à cheval** on horseback; **à cheval sur** astride; insistent upon; **cheval de bois** or **cheval d'arçons** horse (*for vaulting*); **cheval de course** race horse; **cheval de race** thoroughbred; **cheval de retour** (coll) jailbird; **cheval entier** stallion; **monter sur ses grands chevaux** (fig) to get up on one's high horse

chevalement [ʃvalmã] *m* support, shoring; (min) headframe

chevaler [ʃvale] *tr* to shore up

chevaleresque [ʃvalresk] *adj* knightly, chivalrous

chevalerie [ʃvalri] *f* chivalry

chevalet [ʃvale] *m* easel; sawhorse; stand, frame; bridge (*of violin*)

chevalier [ʃvalje] *m* knight; (orn) sandpiper; **chevalier d'industrie** manipulator, swindler; **chevalier errant** knight-errant; **Chevaliers du tastevin** wine-tasting club

chevalière [ʃvaljer] *f* signet ring

cheva·lin -line [ʃvalɛ̃], [lin] *adj* equine

cheval-vapeur [ʃvalvapœr] *m* (*pl* **chevaux-vapeur**) metric or French horsepower (*735 watts*)

chevauchée [ʃəvoʃe] *f* ride

chevaucher [ʃəvoʃe] *tr* to straddle || *intr* to ride horseback; to overlap

cheve·lu -lue [ʃəvly] *adj* hairy; long-haired

chevelure [ʃəvlyr] *f* hair, head of hair; tail (*of a comet*)

chevet [ʃəve] *m* headboard; bolster; **de chevet** bedside (*lamp, table, book*)

che·veu [ʃəvø] *m* (*pl* **-veux**) hair; **avoir mal aux cheveux** (coll) to have a hangover; **cheveux hair** (*of the head*); hairs; **cheveux en brosse** crew cut; **couper les cheveux en quatre** (coll) to split hairs; **en cheveux** hatless; **faire dresser les cheveux** (coll) to make one's hair stand on end; **ne tenir qu'à un cheveu** (coll) to hang by a thread; **saisir l'occasion aux cheveux** (coll) to take time by the forelock; **se faire des cheveux** (coll) to worry oneself gray; **tiré par les cheveux** (coll) far-fetched

chevillard [ʃəvijar] *m* wholesale cattle dealer or jobber

cheville [ʃəvij] *f* peg; pin; bolt; padding (*of verse*); ankle; **cheville ouvrière** (mach) kingbolt; (fig) mainspring (*of an enterprise*); **être en cheville avec** (coll) to be in cahoots with; **ne pas arriver à la cheville de qn** (coll) not to hold a candle to s.o.

chèvre [ʃɛvr] *f* goat; nanny goat

che·vreau [ʃəvro] *m* (*pl* **-vreaux**) kid

chèvrefeuille [ʃɛvrəfœj] *m* honeysuckle

chevrette [ʃəvrɛt] *f* kid; doe (*roe deer*); shrimp; tripod

chevreuil [ʃəvrœj] *m* roe deer; roebuck

chevron [ʃəvrɔ̃] *m* rafter; chevron, hash mark; **en chevron** in a herringbone pattern

chevron·né -née [ʃəvrɔne] *adj* wearing chevrons; experienced, oldest

chevronner [ʃəvrɔne] *tr* to put rafters on; to give chevrons to

chevroter [ʃəvrɔte] *intr* to bleat; to sing or speak in a quavering voice

chewing-gum [ʃwiŋɡɔm], [tʃuwiŋɡɔm] *m* chewing gum

chez [ʃe] *prep* at the house, home, office, etc., of, e.g., **chez mes amis** at my friends' house; e.g., **chez le boulanger** at the baker's; in the country of, among, e.g., **chez les Français** among the French; in the time of, e.g., **chez les anciens Grecs** in the time of the ancient Greeks; in the work of, e.g., **chez Homère** in Homer's works; with, e.g., **c'est chez lui une habitude** it's a habit with him

chez-soi [ʃeswa] *m invar* home

chialer [ʃjale] *intr* (slang) to cry

chiasse [ʃjas] *f* flyspecks; (metallurgy) dross; (coll) loose bowels

chic [ʃik] *adj invar* stylish, chic; **un chic type** (coll) a good egg ‖ *m* style; skill, knack; (coll) smartness, elegance; (slang) ovation; **de chic** from memory ‖ *interj* (coll) fine!, grand!

chicane [ʃikan] *f* chicanery; shady lawsuit; baffle, baffle plate; **chercher chicane à** to engage in a petty quarrel with; **en chicane** staggered, zigzag; curved (*tube*)

chicaner [ʃikane] *tr* to pick a fight with; **chicaner q.ch. à qn** to quibble over s.th. with s.o. ‖ *intr* to quibble

chicanerie [ʃikanri] *f* chicanery

chiche [ʃiʃ] *adj* stingy; small, dwarf ‖ *interj* (coll) I dare you!

chicon [ʃikɔ̃] *m* (coll) romaine

chicorée [ʃikɔre] *f* chicory; **chicorée frisée** endive

chicot [ʃiko] *m* stump (*of tree*); (coll) stump, stub (*of tooth*)

chien [ʃjɛ̃] **chienne** [ʃjɛn] *mf* dog ‖ *m* hammer (*of gun*); glamour; **à la chien** (coll) with bangs; **chien couchant** setter; (slang) apple polisher; **chien d'arrêt** pointer; **chien d'aveugle** Seeing Eye dog; **chien de or chienne de** (coll) dickens of a; **chien de garde** watchdog; **chien du jardinier** (coll) dog in the manger; **chien savant** performing dog; **de chien** (coll) miserable (*weather, life, etc.*); **en chien de fusil** (coll) curled up (*e.g., to sleep*); **entre chien et loup** (coll) at dusk; **les chiens écrasés** (slang) the accident page (*of newspaper*); **petit chien** pup; **se regarder en chiens de faïence** (coll) to glare at one another ‖ *f* see **chienne**

chiendent [ʃjɛ̃dɑ̃] *m* couch grass; (coll) trouble

chienlit [ʃjɑ̃li] *mf* (vulgar) person who soils his bed ‖ *m* carnival mask; masquerade, fantastic costume

chien-loup [ʃjɛ̃lu] *m* (*pl* **chiens-loups**) wolfhound

chienne [ʃjɛn] *f* bitch

chienner [ʃjɛne] *intr* to whelp

chiennerie [ʃjɛnri] *f* stinginess, meanness

chiffe [ʃif] *f* rag; (coll) weakling

chiffon [ʃifɔ̃] *m* rag; scrap of paper; **chiffons** (coll) fashions

chiffonnade [ʃifɔnad] *f* salad greens

chiffonner [ʃifɔne] *tr* to rumple, crumple; to make (*a dress*); (coll) to ruffle (*tempers*), to bother ‖ *intr* to pick rags; to make dresses

chiffon·nier [ʃifɔnje] **chiffon·nière** [ʃifɔnjɛr] *mf* scavenger, ragpicker ‖ *m* chiffonier

chiffre [ʃifr] *m* figure, number; cipher, code; sum total; combination (*of lock*); monogram; **chiffre d'affaires** turnover; **chiffres romains** roman numerals

chiffrer [ʃifre] *tr* to number; to monogram; to figure the cost of; to cipher, code ‖ *intr* to calculate; to mount up; to cipher, code ‖ *ref*—**se chiffrer par** to amount to

chignole [ʃiɲɔl] *f* breast drill, hand drill; (coll) jalopy

chignon [ʃiɲɔ̃] *m* chignon, bun, knot

Chili [ʃili] *m*—**le Chili** Chile

chimère [ʃimɛr] *f* chimera; **se forger des chimères** to indulge in wishful thinking

chimie [ʃimi] *f* chemistry

chimique [ʃimik] *adj* chemical

chimiste [ʃimist] *mf* chemist

chimpanzé [ʃɛ̃pɑze] *m* chimpanzee

Chine [ʃin] *f* China; **la Chine** China

chi·né -née [ʃine] *adj* mottled, figured

chiner [ʃine] *tr* to mottle (*cloth*); (coll) to make fun of

chi·nois [ʃinwa] **-noise** [nwaz] *adj* Chinese ‖ *m* Chinese (*language*) ‖ (*cap*) *mf* Chinese (*person*)

chinoiserie [ʃinwazri] *f* Chinese curio; **chinoiseries administratives** (coll) red tape

chiot [ʃjo] *m* puppy

chiourme [ʃjurm] *f* chain gang

chiper [ʃipe] *tr* (slang) to swipe

chiple [ʃipl] *f* (coll) shrew

chipoter [ʃipɔte] *intr* to haggle

chips [ʃips] *mpl* potato chips

chique [ʃik] *f* chew, quid (*of tobacco*); (ent) chigger

chiqué [ʃike] *m* (slang) sham, bluff

chiquenaude [ʃiknod] *f* fillip, flick

chiquer [ʃike] *tr* to chew (*tobacco*) || *intr* to chew tobacco

chiromancie [kirɔmɑ̃si] *f* palmistry

chiroman·cien [kirɔmɑ̃sjɛ̃] -**cienne** [sjɛn] *mf* palm reader

chiropracteur [kirɔpraktœr] *m* chiropractor

chirurgi·cal -**cale** [ʃiryrʒikal] *adj* (*pl* -**caux** [ko]) surgical

chirurgie [ʃiryrʒi] *f* surgery

chirur·gien [ʃiryrʒjɛ̃] -**gienne** [ʒjɛn] *mf* surgeon

chirurgien-dentiste [ʃiryrʒjɛ̃dɑ̃tist] *m* (*pl* **chirurgiens-dentistes**) dental surgeon

chiure [ʃjyr] *f* flyspeck

chlore [klɔr] *m* chlorine

chlo·ré -**rée** [klɔre] *adj* chlorinated

chlorhydrique [klɔridrik] *adj* hydrochloric

chloroforme [klɔrɔfɔrm] *m* chloroform

chloroformer [klɔrɔfɔrme] *tr* to chloroform

chlorophylle [klɔrɔfil] *f* chlorophyll

chlorure [klɔryr] *m* chloride; **chlorure de soude** sodium chloride

choc [ʃɔk] *m* shock; clash; bump; clink (*of glasses*)

chocolat [ʃɔkɔla] *adj invar & m* chocolate

chocolaterie [ʃɔkɔlatri] *f* chocolate factory

chœur [kœr] *m* choir, chorus

choir [ʃwar] (usually used only in *inf* and *pp* **chu**; sometimes used in *pres ind* **chois**, etc.; *pret* **chus**, etc.; *fut* **choiral**, etc.) *intr* (*aux:* ÊTRE or AVOIR) to fall; **se laisser choir** to drop, to flop

choi·si -**sie** [ʃwazi] *adj* choice, select; chosen; selected (*works*)

choisir [ʃwazir] *tr & intr* to choose

choix [ʃwa] *m* choice; **au choix** at one's discretion; **de choix** choice

choléra [kɔlera] *m* cholera

cholérique [kɔlerik] *mf* cholera victim

cholestérol [kɔlesterɔl] *m* cholesterol

chômage [ʃomaʒ] *m* unemployment; **en chômage** unemployed

chô·mé -**mée** [ʃome] *adj* closed for business, off, e.g., **jour chômé** day off

chômer [ʃome] *tr* to take (*a day*) off; to observe (*a holiday*) || *intr* to take off (*from work*); to be unemployed

chô·meur [ʃomœr] -**meuse** [møz] *mf* unemployed worker

chope [ʃɔp] *f* stein, beer mug

chopine [ʃɔpin] *f* half-liter measure; (slang) bottle

chopper [ʃɔpe] *intr* to stumble; to blunder

choquer [ʃɔke] *tr* to shock; to bump; to clink (*glasses*); (elec) to shock || *ref* to collide; to take offense

cho·ral -**rale** [kɔral] *adj* (*pl* -**raux** [ro]) choral || *m* (*pl* -**rals**) chorale || *f* choral society, glee club

chorégraphie [kɔregrafi] *f* choreography

choriste [kɔrist] *mf* chorister

chorus [kɔrys] *m*—**faire chorus** to repeat in unison; to chime in; to approve unanimously

chose [ʃoz] *adj invar* (coll) odd; **être tout chose** (coll) to feel funny || *m* thingamajig; **Monsieur Chose** (coll) Mr. what's-his-name || *f* thing || *pron indef masc*—**autre chose** something else; **quelque chose** something

chou [ʃu] **choute** [ʃut] *mf*—**ma choute, mon chou** (coll) sweetheart || *m* (*pl* **choux**) cabbage; **chou à la crème** cream puff; **chou de Bruxelles** Brussels sprouts; **de chou** (coll) of little value; **faire chou blanc** (coll) to draw a blank; **finir dans le chou** (coll) to come in last

choucas [ʃuka] *m* jackdaw

choucroute [ʃukrut] *f* sauerkraut; **choucroute garnie** sauerkraut with ham or sausage

chouette [ʃwet] *adj* (coll) swell; **chouette alors!** (coll) oh boy! || *f* owl; (coll) radio; **chouette épervière** hawk owl

chou-fleur [ʃuflœr] *m* (*pl* **choux-fleurs**) cauliflower

chou-rave [ʃurav] *m* (*pl* **choux-raves**) kohlrabi

chow-chow [ʃuʃu] *m* (*pl* -**chows**) chow (*dog*)

choyer [ʃwaje] §47 *tr* to pamper, coddle; to cherish (*a hope*); to entertain (*an idea*)

chrestomathie [krestɔmati], [krestɔmasi] *f* chrestomathy

chré·tien [kretjɛ̃] -**tienne** [tjɛn] *adj & mf* Christian

chrétiennement [kretjɛnmɑ̃] *adv* in the faith

chrétienté [kretjɛ̃te] *f* Christendom

christ [krist] *m* crucifix || (*cap*) *m* Christ; **le Christ** Christ

christianiser [kristjanize] *tr* to Christianize

christianisme [kristjanism] *m* Christianity

chromatique [krɔmatik] *adj* chromatic

chrome [krom] *m* chrome, chromium

chromer [krome] *tr* to chrome

chromosome [krɔmozom] *m* chromosome

chronique [krɔnik] *adj* chronic || *f* chronicle; column (*in newspaper*); **chronique financière** financial page; **chronique mondaine** society news; **chronique théâtrale** theater page

chroniqueur [krɔnikœr] *m* chronicler; columnist; **chroniqueur dramatique** drama critic

chrono [krɔno] *m*—**faire du 60 chrono** (coll) to do 60 by the clock

chronologie [krɔnɔlɔʒi] *f* chronology

chronologique [krɔnɔlɔʒik] *adj* chronological

chronomètre [krɔnɔmetr] *m* chronometer; stopwatch

chronométrer [krɔnɔmetre] §10 *tr* to clock, to time

chronométreur [krɔnɔmetrœr] *m* time-keeper

chrysalide [krizalid] *f* chrysalis

chrysanthème [krizɑ̃tɛm] *m* chrysan-themum

chuchotement [ʃyʃɔtmɑ̃] *m* whisper, whispering

chuchoter [ʃyʃɔte] *tr & intr* to whisper

chuinter [ʃɥɛ̃te] *intr* to hoot (*said of owl*); to make a swishing sound, to hiss (*said of escaping gas*); to pro-nounce [ʃ] instead of [s] and [ʒ] instead of [z]

chut [ʃyt] *interj* sh!

chute [ʃyt] *f* fall; downfall; drop (*in prices, voltage, etc.*); **chute d'eau** waterfall

chuter [ʃyte] *tr* to hush; to hiss (*an actor*) ‖ *intr* (coll) to fall; (cards) to be down

Chypre [ʃipr] *f* Cyprus

ci [si] *pron indef*—**comme ci comme ça** so-so ‖ *adv*—**entre ci et là** be-tween now and then

-ci [si] §82, §84

ci-après [siapre] *adv* hereafter, below, further on

ci-bas [siba] *adv* below

cible [sibl] *f* target

ciboule [sibul] *f* scallion

ciboulette [sibulɛt] *f* chive, chives

cicatrice [sikatris] *f* scar

cicatriser [sikatrize] *tr* to heal; to scar ‖ *ref* to heal

Cicéron [siserɔ̃] *m* Cicero

cicérone [siserɔn] *m* guide

ci-contre [sikɔ̃tr] *adv* opposite, on the opposite page; in the margin

ci-dessous [sidəsu] *adv* further on, be-low, hereunder

ci-dessus [sidəsy] *adv* above

ci-devant [sidəvɑ̃] *mf invar* (hist) aristocrat; (coll) back number ‖ *adv* previously, formerly

cidre [sidr] *m* cider

Cie *abbr* (**Compagnie**) Co.

ciel [sjɛl] *m* (*pl* **cieux** [sjø]) sky, heav-ens (*firmament*); heaven (*state of great happiness*) ‖ *m* (*pl* **ciels**) heaven (*abode of the blessed*); sky (*upper atmosphere, especially with reference to meteorological condi-tions; representation of sky in a painting*); canopy (*of a bed*) ‖ *m* (*pl* **cieux or ciels**) clime, sky

cierge [sjerʒ] *m* wax candle; cactus; **droit comme un cierge** straight as a ramrod; **en cierge** straight up

cigale [sigal] *f* cicada, grasshopper

cigare [sigar] *m* cigar

cigarette [sigaret] *f* cigarette

ci-gît [siʒi] see **gésir**

cigogne [sigɔɲ] *f* stork

ciguë [sigy] *f* hemlock (*herb and poison*)

ci-in-clus [siɛ̃kly] **-cluse** [klyz] *adj* en-closed ‖ **ci-inclus** *adv* enclosed

ci-joint [siʒwɛ̃] **-jointe** [ʒwɛ̃t] *adj* en-closed ‖ **ci-joint** *adv* enclosed

cil [sil] *m* eyelash; **cils** eyelash (*fringe of hair*)

cilice [silis] *m* hair shirt

ciller [sije] *tr & intr* to blink

cime [sim] *f* summit, top

ciment [simɑ̃] *m* cement; **ciment armé** reinforced concrete

cimentation [simɑ̃tasjɔ̃] *f* cementing

cimenter [simɑ̃te] *tr* to cement

cimeterre [simter] *m* scimitar

cimetière [simtjɛr] *m* cemetery

cinéaste [sineast] *mf* film producer; movie director; scenarist; movie tech-nician

cinégraphiste [sinegrafist] *mf* scenarist

cinéma [sinema] *m* movies; moving-picture theater; cinema; **cinéma auto** drive-in movie; **cinéma d'essai** preview theater; **cinéma muet** silent movie

cinémathèque [sinematek] *f* film li-brary

cinématographique [sinematɔgrafik] *adj* motion-picture, film

cinéphile [sinefil] *mf* movie fan

cinéprojecteur [sineprɔʒektœr] *m* mo-tion-picture projector

ciné-roman [sinerɔmɑ̃] *m* (*pl* **-romans**) published story (*of a film*)

cinétique [sinetik] *adj* kinetic ‖ *f* kinetics

cin-glant [sɛ̃glɑ̃] **-glante** [glɑ̃t] *adj* scathing

cin-glé **-glée** [sɛ̃gle] *adj* (slang) screwy ‖ *mf* (slang) screwball

cingler [sɛ̃gle] *tr* to whip; to cut to the quick ‖ *intr* to go full sail

cinq [sɛ̃(k)] *adj & pron* five; the Fifth, e.g., **Jean cinq** John the Fifth; **cinq heures** five o'clock ‖ *m* five; fifth (*in dates*); **il était moins cinq** (coll) it was a close shave

cinquantaine [sɛ̃kɑ̃tɛn] *f* about fifty; age of fifty, fifty mark, fifties

cinquante [sɛ̃kɑ̃t] *adj, pron, & m* fifty; **cinquante et un** fifty-one; **cinquante et unième** fifty-first

cinquantième [sɛ̃kɑ̃tjɛm] *adj, pron* (*masc, fem*), *& m* fiftieth

cinquième [sɛ̃kjɛm] *adj, pron* (*masc, fem*), *& m* fifth

cintre [sɛ̃tr] *m* arch; coat hanger; bend; **plein cintre** semicircular arch

cin-tré **-trée** [sɛ̃tre] *adj* (slang) crazy

cintrer [sɛ̃tre] *tr* to arch, to bend

cirage [siraʒ] *m* waxing; shoe polish; **dans le cirage** (coll) in the dark

circoncire [sirkɔ̃sir] §66 (*pp* **circoncis**) *tr* to circumcise

circoncision [sirkɔ̃sizjɔ̃] *f* circumcision

circonférence [sirkɔ̃ferɑ̃s] *f* circumfer-ence

circonflexe [sirkɔ̃flɛks] *adj & m* cir-cumflex

circonscription [sirkɔ̃skripsjɔ̃] *f* cir-cumscription; ward, district

circonscrire [sirkɔ̃skrir] §25 *tr* to cir-cumscribe

circons-pect [sirkɔ̃spɛ], [sirkɔ̃spɛk(t)] **-pecte** [pɛkt] *adj* circumspect

circonstance [sirkɔ̃stɑ̃s] *f* circumstance; **circonstances et dépendances** appur-tenances; **de circonstance** proper for the occasion, topical; emergency (*measure*); guest, e.g., **orateur de cir-constance** guest speaker

circonstan•clé -clée [sirkɔ̃stãsje] adj circumstantial, in detail

circonstan•ciel -cielle [sirkɔ̃stãsjel] adj (gram) adverbial

circonvenir [sirkɔ̃vnir] §72 tr to circumvent

circonvoi•sin [sirkɔ̃vwazɛ̃] -sine [zin] adj nearby, neighboring

circuit [sirkɥi] m circuit; circumference; detour; tour

circulaire [sirkyler] adj & f circular

circulation [sirkylɑsjɔ̃] f circulation; traffic; circulation interdite (public sign) no thoroughfare

circuler [sirkyle] intr to circulate

cire [sir] f wax; cire à cacheter sealing wax; cire molle (fig) wax in one's hands

ci•ré -rée [sire] adj waxed || m waterproof garment; raincoat

cirer [sire] tr to wax; to polish

ci•reur [sirœr] -reuse [røz] mf waxer, polisher (person); shoeblack, bootblack || f floor waxer (machine)

ci•reux [sirø] -reuse [røz] adj waxy

ciron [sirɔ̃] m mite

cirque [sirk] m circus; amphitheater

cirrhose [siroz] f cirrhosis

cisaille [sizaj] f metal clippings, scissel; cisailles clippers, shears; wire cutter

cisailler [sizaje] tr to shear

ci•seau [sizo] m (pl -seaux) chisel; ciseau à froid cold chisel; ciseaux scissors; ciseaux à ongles nail scissors; ciseaux à raisin pruning shears; ciseaux à tondre sheep shears

ciseler [sizle] §2 tr to chisel; to chase; to cut, shear; to prune

ciseleur [sizlœr] m chaser, tooler

citadelle [sitadel] f citadel

cita•din [sitadɛ̃] -dine [din] adj urban || mf city dweller

citation [sitɑsjɔ̃] f citation, quotation; citation, summons

cité [site] f housing development; (hist) fortified city, citadel; cité ouvrière low-cost housing development; cité sainte Holy City; cité universitaire university dormitory complex; la Cité the City (district within ancient boundaries)

citer [site] tr to cite, quote; to summon, subpoena

citerne [sitern] f cistern; tank; citerne flottante tanker

cithare [sitar] f cither, zither

citoyen [sitwajɛ̃] citoyenne [sitwajen] mf citizen; (coll) individual, person; citoyens citizenry

citoyenneté [sitwajente] f citizenship; citizenry

citrique [sitrik] adj citric

citron [sitrɔ̃] adj & m lemon

citronnade [sitronad] f lemonade

citron•né -née [sitrone] adj lemon-flavored

citronnelle [sitronel] f citronella

citronner [sitrone] tr to flavor with lemon

citronnier [sitronje] m lemon tree

citrouille [sitruj] f pumpkin, gourd

cive [siv] f scallion

civet [sive] m stew

civette [sivet] f civet; civet cat; chive, chives

civière [sivjer] f stretcher, litter

ci•vil -vile [sivil] adj civil; civilian; secular || m civilian; layman; en civil plain-clothes (man); in cives

civilisation [sivilizɑsjɔ̃] f civilization

civiliser [sivilize] tr to civilize || ref to become civilized

civilité [sivilite] f civility; civilités kind regards; amenities

civique [sivik] adj civic; civil (rights); national (guard)

civisme [sivism] m good citizenship

clabauder [klabode] intr to clamor

claie [kle] f wickerwork; trellis

clair claire [kler] adj clear, bright; evident, plain; light, pale || m light, brightness; clair de lune moonlight; clairs highlights || f oyster bed

clai•ret [klere] -rette [ret] adj light-red; thin, high-pitched (voice) || m light, red wine || f light sparkling wine

claire-voie [klervwa] f (pl claires-voies) latticework, slats; clerestory; à claire-voie with open spaces

clairière [klerjer] f clearing, glade

clairon [klerɔ̃] m bugle; bugler

claironner [klerɔne] tr to announce || intr to sound the bugle

clairse•mé -mée [klersəme] adj scattered, sparse; thin, thinned out

clairvoyance [klervwajɑ̃s] f clear-sightedness, clairvoyance

clairvoyant [klervwajɑ̃] clairvoyante [klervwajɑ̃t] adj clear-sighted, clairvoyant

clamer [klame] tr & intr to cry out

clameur [klamœr] f clamor, outcry

clamp [klɑ̃] m (med) clamp

clampin [klɑ̃pɛ̃] m (mil) straggler

clan [klɑ̃] m clan, clique

clandes•tin [klɑ̃destɛ̃] -tine [tin] adj clandestine

clapet [klape] m valve; ferme ton clapet! (slang) shut your trap!

clapier [klapje] m rabbit hutch

clapoter [klapɔte] intr to splash; to be choppy

claque [klak] m opera hat || f slap, smack; claque, paid applauders

cla•qué -quée [klake] adj dog-tired; sprained

claquement [klakmɑ̃] m clapping; slam (of a door); chattering (of teeth)

claquemurer [klakmyre] tr to shut in || ref to shut oneself up at home

claquer [klake] tr to slap; to clap; to smack (the lips); to slam (the door); to crack (the whip); to click (the heels); to snap (the fingers); (coll) to tire out; (coll) to waste || intr to clap, slam; to crack; (slang) to fail; (slang) to die || ref (with dat of reflex pron) to sprain; (slang) to work oneself to death

claquettes [klaket] fpl tap-dancing

claqueur [klakœr] m applauder, member of a claque

clarifier [klarifje] tr to clarify || ref to become clear

clarine [klarin] f cowbell

clarinette [klarinεt] *f* clarinet

clarté [klarte] *f* clarity; brightness; **clarté du soleil** sunshine

classe [klɑs] *f* class; classroom; **classe de rattrapage** refresher course (*for backward children*); **classe de travaux pratiques** lab class

clas·sé ·sée [klɑse] *adj* pigeonholed, tabled; standard (*literary work*); listed; **non classé** (sports) also-ran

classer [klɑse] *tr* to class; to sort out, to file; to pigeonhole, to table

classeur [klɑsœr] *m* file (*for letters, documents*); filing cabinet

classicisme [klasisism] *m* classicism

classification [klasifikɑsjɔ̃] *f* classification

classifier [klasifje] *tr* to classify; to sort out

classique [klasik] *adj* classic, classical; standard (*author, work*) || *mf* classicist || *m* classic; standard work

claudication [klodikɑsjɔ̃] *f* limping

clause [kloz] *f* clause, stipulation, provision; **clause additionnelle** rider; **clause ambiguë** joker clause; **clause de style** unwritten provision

claustration [klostrɑsjɔ̃] *f* confinement; cloistering

clavecin [klavsε̃] *m* harpsichord

claveciniste [klavsinist] *mf* harpsichordist

clavette [klavεt] *f* pin, cotter pin; key

clavicule [klavikyl] *f* collarbone

clavier [klavje] *m* keyboard; key ring; range (*e.g., of the voice*); **clavier universel** standard keyboard

clayère [klɛjɛr] *f* oyster bed

clé [kle] *f* see **clef**

clef [kle] *adj invar* key || *f* key; wrench; (*wrestling*) lock; **clef anglaise** monkey wrench; **clef à tube** socket wrench; **clef crocodile** alligator wrench; **clef des champs** vacation; **clef de voûte** keystone; **sous clef** under lock and key

clémence [klemɑ̃s] *f* clemency

clé·ment ·mente [klemɑ̃] -[mɑ̃t] *adj* mild, clement

clenche [klɑ̃ʃ] *f* latch

cleptomane [kleptɔman] *mf* kleptomaniac

clerc [klɛr] *m* cleric, clergyman; scholar; clerk

clergé [klɛrʒe] *m* clergy

clergie [klɛrʒi] *f* learning, scholarship; clergy

cléri·cal ·cale [klerikal] *adj & mf* (*pl* -**caux** [ko]) clerical

cliché [kli/e] *m* cliché; (*phot*) negative; (*typ*) plate, stereotype; **prendre un cliché** (*phot*) to make an exposure

clicher [kli/e] *tr* (*typ*) to stereotype

client ·ente [klijɑ̃] -[jɑ̃t] *mf* client; patient; customer; guest (*of a hotel*)

clientèle [klijɑ̃tɛl] *f* clientele; adherents

cligner [kliɲe] *tr* to squint (*one's eyes*) || *intr* to squint, to blink; **cligner de l'œil à** to wink at

cligno·tant ·tante [kliɲɔtɑ̃] -[tɑ̃t] *adj* blinking || *m* (aut) directional signal

clignotement [kliɲɔtmɑ̃] *m* blinking; twinkling; flickering

clignoter [kliɲɔte] *intr* to blink; to twinkle; to flicker

clignoteur [kliɲɔtœr] *m* (aut) directional signal

climat [klima], [klima] *m* climate

climatisation [klimatizɑsjɔ̃] *f* air conditioning

climati·sé ·sée [klimatize] *adj* air-conditioned

climatiseur [klimatizœr] *m* air conditioner

clin [klε̃] *m*—**à clin** (carpentry) overlapping, covering; **clin d'œil** wink; **en un clin d'œil** in the twinkling of an eye

clinicien [klinisjε̃] *adj masc* clinical || *m* clinician

clinique [klinik] *adj* clinical || *f* clinic; private hospital

clinquant [klε̃kɑ̃] *m* foil, tinsel; flashiness, tawdriness

clip [klip] *m* clip, brooch

clique [klik] *f* drum and bugle corps; (coll) gang; **cliques** wooden shoes

cliquet [klikε] *m* (mach) pawl, catch

cliqueter [klikte] §34 *intr* to click, to clink, to clank, to jangle

cliquetis [klikti] *m* click, clink, clank, jangle

cliquette [klikεt] *f* castanets; (fishing) sinker

clisse [klis] *f* draining rack, wicker bottleholder

clivage [klivaʒ] *m* cleavage

cliver [klive] *tr* to cleave; to cut

cloaque [klɔak] *m* cesspool

clo·chard [klɔ/ar] -**charde** [/ard] *mf* beggar, tramp

cloche [klɔ/] *adj* bell (*skirt*) || *f* bell; bell glass; blister (*on skin*); **cloche à plongeurs** diving bell; **cloche de sauvetage** escape hatch (*on submarine*); **déménager à la cloche de bois** (coll) to skip out without paying; **la cloche** (slang) beggars

clochement [klɔ/mɑ̃] *m* limp, limping

cloche-pied [klɔ/pje]—**à cloche-pied** on one foot, hopping

clocher [klɔ/e] *m* steeple; belfry; parish, home town; **de clocher** local (*politics*) || *intr* to limp; **quelque chose cloche** something jars, is not right

clocheton [klɔ/tɔ̃] *m* little steeple

clochette [klɔ/εt] *f* little bell; (bot) bellflower

cloison [klwazɔ̃] *f* partition; division, barrier (*e.g., between classes*); (anat, bot) septum, dividing membrane; (naut) bulkhead; **cloison étanche** (naut) watertight compartment

cloisonner [klwazɔne] *tr* to partition

cloître [klwatr] *m* cloister

cloîtrer [klwatre] *tr* to cloister; to confine

clopin-clopant [klɔpε̃klɔpɑ̃] *adv* (coll) so-so; **aller clopin-clopant** (coll) to go hobbling along

clopiner [klɔpine] *intr* to hobble

cloque [klɔk] *f* blister

cloquer [klɔke] *tr & intr* to blister

clore [klɔr] §24 *tr & intr* to close

clos [klo] **close** [kloz] *adj* closed ‖ *m* enclosure; **clos de vigne** vineyard

clôture [klotyr] *f* fence; wall; cloistered life; closing of an account

clôturer [klotyre] *tr* to enclose, to wall in; to close out (*an account*); to conclude (*a discussion*)

clou [klu] *m* nail; (coll) boil; (coll) jalopy; (coll) feature attraction; (slang) pawnshop; **clou de girofle** clove; **clous** pedestrian crossing; **des clous** (slang) nothing at all!

clouer [klue] *tr* to nail; to immobilize, rivet; **clouer le bec à qn** (coll) to shut s.o.'s mouth

clouter [klute] *tr* to stud; to trim or border with studs, e.g., **passage clouté** pedestrian crossing (bordered with studs)

clown [klun] *m* clown; **faire le clown** to clown (around)

clownerie [klunri] *f* high jinks, clowning

club [klyb] *m* (literary) society; (political) association ‖ [klœb] *m* club (*for social and athletic purposes, etc.*); clubhouse; (golf) club; armchair

clubiste [klybist] *mf* (coll) club member; (coll) joiner

clubman [klœbman] *m* club member

coaccu•sé -sée [kɔakyze] *mf* codefendant

coaguler [kɔagyle] *tr & ref* to coagulate

coaliser [kɔalize] *tr* to form into a coalition ‖ *ref* to form a coalition

coalition [kɔalisjɔ̃] *f* coalition

coassement [kɔasmɑ̃] *m* croak, croaking

coasser [kɔase] *intr* to croak

coasso•cié -ciée [kɔasɔsje] *mf* copartner

coauteur [kɔotœr] *m* coauthor

cobalt [kɔbalt] *m* cobalt

cobaye [kɔbaj] *m* guinea pig

cocaïne [kɔkain] *f* cocaine

cocarde [kɔkard] *f* cockade; rosette of ribbons; **avoir sa cocarde** (coll) to be tipsy; **prendre la cocarde** (coll) to enlist

cocasse [kɔkas] *adj* (coll) funny, ridiculous

coccinelle [kɔksinel] *f* ladybug

coche [kɔʃ] *m* coach, stagecoach; two-door sedan; barge ‖ *f* notch, score; (zool) sow

cocher [kɔʃe] *m* coachman, driver ‖ *tr* to notch, to score; to check off

cochère [kɔʃɛr] *adj* carriage (*entrance*)

co•chon [kɔʃɔ̃] **-chonne** [ʃɔn] *mf* (coll) skunk, slob ‖ *m* pig, hog; **cochon de lait** suckling pig; **cochon de mer** porpoise; **cochon d'Inde** guinea pig

cochonnerie [kɔʃɔnri] *f* (slang) dirty trick; (slang) filthy speech, smut

cocker [kɔker] *m* cocker spaniel

cockpit [kɔkpit] *m* (aer) cockpit

cocktail [kɔktɛl] *m* cocktail; cocktail party

coco [kɔko], [kɔko] *m* coconut; licorice water; **mon coco** (coll) my darling; **un joli coco** (coll) a stinker ‖ *f* (slang) cocaine

cocon [kɔkɔ̃] *m* cocoon

cocorico [kɔkɔriko] *m* cockcrow ‖ *interj* cock-a-doodle-doo!

cocotier [kɔkɔtje] *m* coconut tree

cocotte [kɔkɔt] *f* saucepan; cocotte, floozy; **ma cocotte** (coll) my little chick, my baby doll

co•cu -cue [kɔky] *adj & m* cuckold

cocufier [kɔkyfje] *tr* (slang) to cuckold

code [kɔd] *m* code; **code de la route** traffic regulations; **code pénal** criminal code; **codes** (slang) dimmers; **se mettre en code** to dip one's headlights

codex [kɔdeks] *m* pharmacopoeia

codicille [kɔdisil] *m* codicil

codifier [kɔdifje] *tr* to codify

coéducation [kɔedykasjɔ̃] *f* coeducation

coefficient [kɔefisjɑ̃] *m* coefficient

coéqui•pier -pière [kɔekipje] [pjer] *mf* teammate

coercition [kɔersisjɔ̃] *f* coercion

cœur [kœr] *m* heart; core; courage, spirit; bosom, breast; depth (*of winter*); (cards) heart; (cards) hearts; **à cœur joie** to one's heart's content; **avoir du cœur** to be kind-hearted; **avoir du cœur au ventre** (coll) to have guts; **avoir le cœur sur la main** (coll) to be open-handed; **avoir le cœur sur les lèvres** to wear one's heart on one's sleeve; **cœur de bronze** heart of stone; **de bon cœur** willingly, heartily; **de mauvais cœur** reluctantly; **en avoir le cœur net** to get to the bottom of it; **épancher son cœur à** to open one's heart to; **fendre le cœur à** to break the heart of; **le cœur gros** with a heavy heart; **mal au cœur** or **mal de cœur** stomach ache; nausea; **par cœur** by heart; **prendre à cœur** to take to heart; **se ronger le cœur** to eat one's heart out; **soulever le cœur** to turn the stomach

coexistence [kɔegzistɑ̃s] *f* coexistence

coexister [kɔegziste] *intr* to coexist

coffre [kɔfr] *m* chest; coffer, bin; safe-deposit box; trunk (*of car*); buoy (*for mooring*); cofferdam

coffre-fort [kɔfrəfɔr] *m* (*pl* **coffres-forts**) safe, strongbox, vault

coffret [kɔfre] *m* gift box

cognac [kɔɲak] *m* cognac

cognat [kɔɲa] *m* blood kin

cognée [kɔɲe] *f* ax, hatchet

cogner [kɔɲe] *tr, intr, & ref* to knock, bump

cohabiter [kɔabite] *intr* to cohabit

cohé•rent [kɔerɑ̃] **-rente** [rɑ̃t] *adj* coherent

cohériter [kɔerite] *intr* to inherit jointly

cohéri•tier [kɔeritje] **-tière** [tjer] *mf* coheir

cohésion [kɔezjɔ̃] *f* cohesion

cohorte [kɔɔrt] *f* cohort

cohue [kɔy] *f* crowd, throng, mob

col [kwa] **coite** [kwat] *adj* quiet; demeurer or **se tenir coi** to keep still

coiffe [kwaf] *f* cap; headdress; caul

coif•fé -fée [kwafe] *adj*—**coiffé de** wearing (*a hat*); (fig) crazy about (*a person*); **être coiffé** to be wearing a hairdo; **être né coiffé** (fig) to be lucky

coiffer [kwafe] *tr* to put a hat or cap on (*s.o.*); to dress or do the hair of; (mil) to reach (*an objective*) || *intr*—**coiffer de** to wear (*a certain size hat*) || *ref* to do one's hair; **se coiffer de** (coll) to set one's cap for

coif·feur [kwafœr] **coif·feuse** [kwaføz] *mf* hairdresser; barber; **coiffeur pour dames** coiffeur || *f* dresser, dressing table

coiffure [kwafyr] *f* coiffure; headdress; **coiffure en brosse** crew cut

coin [kwɛ̃] *m* corner; angle; nook; wedge, coin; stamp, die (*for coining money*); (typ) quoin; **le petit coin** (coll) the powder room

coinçage [kwɛ̃saʒ] *m* wedging

coincer [kwɛ̃se] §51 *tr* to wedge, jam; (coll) to pinch, arrest || *ref* to' jam

coïncidence [kɔɛ̃sidɑ̃s] *f* coincidence

coïncider [kɔɛ̃side] *intr* to coincide

coin-coin [kwɛ̃kwɛ̃] *m invar* quack (*of duck*); toot (*of horn*)

coing [kwɛ̃] *m* quince

coït [kɔit] *m* coition

coke [kɔk] *m* coke

cokéfier [kɔkefje] *tr & ref* to coke

col [kɔl] *m* neck (*of bottle; of womb*); collar (*of dress*); mountain pass; (coll) head (*on beer*); **col de fourrure** neckpiece; **col roulé** turtleneck; **faux col** detachable collar

colback [kɔlbak] *m* busby

colère [kɔler] *f* anger; **en colère** angry; **se mettre en colère** to become angry

colé·reux [kɔlerø] **-reuse** [røz] *adj* irascible, choleric

colérique [kɔlerik] *adj* choleric

colibri [kɔlibri] *m* hummingbird

colimaçon [kɔlimasɔ̃] *m* snail; **en colimaçon** spiral

colin [kɔlɛ̃] *m* hake

colin-maillard [kɔlɛ̃majar] *m* blind-man's buff

colique [kɔlik] *f* colic

colis [kɔli] *m* piece of baggage, package, parcel; **colis postal** parcel post

colisée [kɔlize] *m* coliseum

collabora·teur [kɔlaboratœr] **-trice** [tris] *mf* collaborator; contributor

collaborationniste [kɔlaborasjɔnist] *mf* collaborationist

collaborer [kɔlabore] *intr* to collaborate; **collaborer à** to contribute to

collage [kɔlaʒ] *m* pasting, mounting; collage; sizing; clarifying (*of wine*); (coll) common-law marriage

col·lant [kɔlɑ̃] **col·lante** [kɔlɑ̃t] *adj* sticky; tight, close-fitting || *m* tights

collapsus [kɔlapsys] *m* (pathol) collapse

collaté·ral -rale [kɔlateral] (*pl* **-raux** [ro]) *adj* collateral; parallel; intermediate (*points of the compass*) || *mf* collateral (relative) || *m* side aisle of a church

collation [kɔlasjɔ̃] *f* conferring (*of titles, degrees, etc.*); collation (*of texts*) || [kɔlasjɔ̃] *f* snack

collationner [kɔlasjɔne] *tr* to collate,

to compare; **faire collationner un télégramme** to request a copy of a telegram || *intr* to have a snack

colle [kɔl] *f* paste, glue; (coll) brain-teaser, stickler; (slang) detention; (slang) oral exam; (slang) flunking; **colle forte** glue; **poser une colle** (slang) to ask a hard one

collecte [kɔlekt] *f* collection (*for charitable cause*); (eccl) collect

collecteur [kɔlektœr] *adj* main, e.g., **égout collecteur** main sewer || *m* collector; commutator (*of motor or dynamo*); (aut) manifold; **collecteur d'ondes** aerial

collec·tif [kɔlektif] **-tive** [tiv] *adj* collective

collection [kɔleksjɔ̃] *f* collection

collectionner [kɔleksjone] *tr* to collect

collection·neur [kɔleksjɔnœr] **collection-neuse** [kɔleksjɔnøz] *mf* collector

collège [kɔleʒ] *m* high school; preparatory school; college (*of cardinals, electors, etc.*); **collège universitaire** junior college

collé·gial -giale [kɔleʒjal] (*pl* **-giaux** [ʒjo]) *adj* collegiate || *f* collegiate church

collé·gien [kɔleʒjɛ̃] **-gienne** [ʒjen] *adj* high-school || *m* schoolboy || *f* schoolgirl; coed

collègue [kɔleg] *mf* colleague

coller [kɔle] *tr* to paste, stick, glue; to clarify (*wine*); to mat (*e.g., with blood*); (coll) to floor, to stump; (coll) to punish (*a pupil*); (coll) to flunk; (coll) to sock (*e.g., on the jaw*) || *intr* to cling, to fit tightly (*said of dress*); (coll) to stick close; **ça colle!** (slang) O.K.! || *ref* (slang) to have a common-law marriage; **se coller contre** to stand close to; to cling to

collet [kɔle] *m* collar; neck (*of person; of tooth*); neck, scrag (*e.g., of mutton*); cape; snare; stalk and roots; lasso, noose; **collet monté** (coll) stuffed shirt

colleter [kɔlte] §34 *tr* to collar || *ref* to fight, scuffle

collier [kɔlje] *m* necklace; collar; dog collar; horse collar; **à collier** ring-necked; **reprendre le collier** (coll) to get back into harness

colliger [kɔliʒe] §38 *tr* to make a collection of

colline [kɔlin] *f* hill

collision [kɔlizjɔ̃] *f* collision

colloï·dal -dale [kɔlɔidal] *adj* (*pl* **-daux** [do]) colloid, colloidal

colloïde [kɔlɔid] *m* colloid

colloque [kɔlɔk] *m* colloquy, symposium

colloquer [kɔlɔke] *tr* to classify (*creditors' claims*); **colloquer q.ch. à qn** (coll) to palm off s.th. on s.o.

collusion [kɔllyzjɔ̃] *f* collusion

collyre [kɔllir] *m* (med) eyewash

Cologne [kɔlɔɲ] *f* Cologne

Colomb [kɔlɔ̃] *m* Columbus

colombe [kɔlɔ̃b] *f* dove

Colombie [kɔlɔ̃bi] *f* Colombia; **la Colombie** Colombia colombier [kɔlɔ̃bje] m dovecote; large-size paper

colom·bin [kɔlɔ̃bɛ̃] -bine [bin] adj columbine || m stock dove; lead ore || f bird droppings; (bot) columbine

colon [kɔlɔ̃] m colonist; tenant farmer; summer camper

côlon [kolɔ̃] m (anat) colon

colonel [kɔlɔnɛl] m colonel

colonelle [kɔlɔnɛl] f colonel's wife; (theat) performance for the press

colonie [kɔlɔni] f colony; colonie de déportation penal settlement; colonie de vacances summer camp

coloniser [kɔlɔnize] tr to colonize

colonnade [kɔlɔnad] f colonnade

colonne [kɔlɔn] f column; pillar; cinquième colonne fifth column; colonne vertébrale spinal column

colophane [kɔlɔfan] f rosin

colophon [kɔlɔfɔ̃] m colophon

colo·rant [kɔlɔrã] -rante [rãt] adj coloring || m dye, stain

colorer [kɔlɔre] tr & ref to color

colorier [kɔlɔrje] tr to paint, color

coloris [kɔlɔri] m hue; brilliance

colos·sal -sale [kɔlɔsal] adj (pl colos·saux [kɔlɔso]) colossal

colosse [kɔlɔs] m colossus

colporter [kɔlpɔrte] tr to peddle

colporteur [kɔlpɔrtœr] m peddler

coltiner [kɔltine] tr to lug on one's back or on one's head

coma [kɔma] m (pathol) coma

coma·teux [kɔmatø] -teuse [tøz] adj comatose || mf person in a coma

combat [kɔ̃ba] m combat; combat tournoyant (aer) dogfight; hors de combat disabled

comba·tif [kɔ̃batif] -tive [tiv] adj combative

combat·tant [kɔ̃batã] combat·tante [kɔ̃batãt] adj & mf combatant; anciens combattants veterans

combattre [kɔ̃batr] §7 tr & intr to combat

combien [kɔ̃bjɛ̃] adv how much, how many; how far; how long; how, e.g., combien il était brave! how brave he was! || m invar—du combien chaussez-vous? what size shoes do you wear?; du combien coiffez-vous? what size hat do you wear?; le combien? which one (in a series)?; le combien êtes-vous? (coll) what rank do you have?; le combien sommes-nous? (coll) what day of the month is it?; tous les combien? how often?

combinaison [kɔ̃binezɔ̃] f combination; coveralls; slip, undergarment

combi·né -née [kɔ̃bine] adj combined || m French telephone, handset; radio phonograph

combiner [kɔ̃bine] tr to combine; to arrange, group; to concoct (a scheme) || ref (chem) to combine

comble [kɔ̃bl] adj full, packed || m summit; roof, coping; au comble de at the height of; c'est le comble!, c'est un comble! (coll) that's the limit!, that takes the cake!; sous les combles in the attic

combler [kɔ̃ble] tr to heap up; to fill

to the brim; to overwhelm; combler d'honneurs to shower honors upon

combustible [kɔ̃bystibl] adj & m combustible, fuel

combustion [kɔ̃bystjɔ̃] f combustion

comédie [kɔmedi] f comedy; play; sham

comé·dien [kɔmedjɛ̃] -dienne [djɛn] mf comedian; actor; hypocrite; comédien ambulant strolling player || f comedienne; actress

comédon [kɔmedɔ̃] m blackhead

comestible [kɔmɛstibl] adj edible || comestibles mpl foodstuffs

comète [kɔmɛt] f comet

comique [kɔmik] adj & m comic

comité [kɔmite] m committee

comman·dant [kɔmãdã] m commandant, commander; major

commande [kɔmãd] f order (for goods or services); control, command; à la commande (paid) down; de commande postale mail order; de commande operating; (fait) sur commande (made) to order

commandement [kɔmãdəmã] m command, order; commandment

commander [kɔmãde] tr to order (goods or services); to command, order || intr (mil) to command; commander à to control, to have command over; commander à qn de + inf to order s.o. to + inf || ref to control oneself

commanditaire [kɔmãditer] adj sponsoring || mf (com) sponsor, backer

commandite [kɔmãdit] f joint-stock company

commanditer [kɔmãdite] tr to back, to finance; (rad, telv) to sponsor

comme [kɔm] adv as; how; comme ci comme ça so-so || prep as, like || conj as; since

commémorer [kɔmmemɔre] tr to commemorate

commen·çant [kɔmãsã] -çante [sãt] mf beginner

commencement [kɔmãsmã] m beginning

commencer [kɔmãse] §51 tr & intr to begin; commencer à to begin to

comment [kɔmã] m invar how; wherefore || adv how; why; mais comment donc! by all means!; n'importe comment any way || interj what!; indeed!

commentaire [kɔmãter] m commentary; unfriendly comment

commenta·teur [kɔmãtatœr] -trice [tris] mf commentator

commenter [kɔmãte] tr to comment on; to make a commentary on; to criticize

commérage [kɔmeraʒ] m (coll) gossip

commer·çant [kɔmɛrsã] -çante [sãt] adj commercial, business || mf merchant, dealer

commerce [kɔmɛrs] m commerce, trade

commercer [kɔmɛrse] §51 intr to trade

commer·cial -ciale [kɔmɛrsjal] adj (pl -ciaux [sjo] -ciales) commercial || f station wagon

commercialisation [kɔmersjalizɑsjɔ̃] *f* marketing

commercialiser [kɔmersjalize] *tr* to commercialize

commère [kɔmer] *f* (coll) busybody, gossip

commettre [kɔmetr] §42 *tr* to commit; to compromise ‖ *ref* to compromise oneself

commis [kɔmi] *m* clerk; **commis voyageur** traveling salesman

commisération [kɔmizerɑsjɔ̃] *f* commiseration

commissaire [kɔmiser] *m* commissioner; commissary

commissaire-priseur [kɔmiserprizœr] *m* (*pl* **commissaires-priseurs**) appraiser; auctioneer

commissariat [kɔmisarja] *m* commissariat; **commissariat de police** police station

commission [kɔmisjɔ̃] *f* commission; errand; committee

commissionnaire [kɔmisjɔner] *m* agent, broker; messenger

commissionner [kɔmisjɔne] *tr* to commission

commissure [kɔmisyr] *f* corner (*of* lips)

commode [kɔmɔd] *adj* convenient; comfortable; easygoing ‖ *f* chest of drawers, bureau

commodité [kɔmɔdite] *f* comfort, accommodation; **à votre commodité** at your convenience; **commodités** comfort station

commotion [kɔmɔsjɔ̃] *f* commotion; concussion; shock

commotionner [kɔmɔsjɔne] *tr* to shake up, injure, shock

commuer [kɔmɥe] *tr* (law) to commute

com·mun -mune [kɔmœ̃] com·mune [kɔmyn] *adj* common ‖ *m* common run ‖ *f* see **commune**

commu·nal -nale [kɔmynal] (*pl* **-naux** [no]) *adj* communal, common ‖ *mpl* common property, commons

communautaire [kɔmynoter] *adj* communal

communauté [kɔmynote] *f* community; **Communauté économique européenne** Common Market

commune [kɔmyn] *f* commune; **communes** Commons

commu·niant [kɔmynjɑ̃] **-niante** [njɑ̃t] *mf* communicant

communicable [kɔmynikabl] *adj* communicable

communi·cant [kɔmynikɑ̃] **-cante** [kɑ̃t] *adj* communicating

communica·teur [kɔmynikatœr] **-trice** [tris] *adj* connecting (*wire*)

communica·tif [kɔmynikatif] **-tive** [tiv] *adj* communicative; infectious (*laughter*)

communication [kɔmynikɑsjɔ̃] *f* communication; telephone call; (telp) connection; **communication avec avis d'appel** (telp) messenger call; **communication avec préavis** person-to-person call; **communication payable à l'arrivée**, **communication P.C.V.** collect call; **en communication** in touch; **fausse communication** (telp)

wrong number; **vous avez la communication!** (telp) go ahead!

communier [kɔmynje] *intr* to take communion; to have a common bond of sympathy, to be in accord

communion [kɔmynjɔ̃] *f* communion

communiqué [kɔmynike] *m* communiqué

communiquer [kɔmynike] *tr & intr* to communicate

communi·sant [kɔmynizɑ̃] **-sante** [zɑ̃t] *adj* fellow-traveling ‖ *mf* fellow traveler

communisme [kɔmynism] *m* communism

communiste [kɔmynist] *adj & mf* communist

commutateur [kɔmytatœr] *m* (elec) changeover switch, two-way switch

commutation [kɔmytɑsjɔ̃] *f* commutation

commutatrice [kɔmytatris] *f* (elec) rotary converter

com·pact -pacte [kɔ̃pakt] *adj* compact

compagne [kɔ̃paɲ] *f* companion; helpmate

compagnie [kɔ̃paɲi] *f* company; **de compagnie** or **en compagnie** together; **fausser compagnie à** to give (*s.o.*) the slip; **tenir compagnie à** to keep (*s.o.*) company

compagnon [kɔ̃paɲɔ̃] *m* companion; **compagnon d'armes** comrade in arms; **compagnon de jeu** playmate; **compagnon de route** fellow traveler; **compagnon d'infortune** fellow sufferer; **joyeux compagnon** good fellow

comparaison [kɔ̃parezɔ̃] *f* comparison; **en comparaison de** compared to; **par comparaison** in comparison; **sans comparaison** beyond comparison

comparaître [kɔ̃paretr] §12 *intr* (law) to appear (in court)

compara·tif [kɔ̃paratif] **-tive** [tiv] *adj & m* comparative

compa·ré -rée [kɔ̃pare] *adj* comparative

comparer [kɔ̃pare] *tr* to compare

comparoir [kɔ̃parwar] (used only in: *inf*; *ger* **comparant**) *intr* (law) to appear in court

comparse [kɔ̃pars] *mf* (theat) walk-on; (fig) nobody, unimportant person

compartiment [kɔ̃partimɑ̃] *m* compartment

comparution [kɔ̃parysjɔ̃] *f* appearance in court

compas [kɔ̃pa] *m* compasses (*for drawing circles*); calipers; (naut) compass; **avoir le compas dans l'œil** to have a sharp eye

compas·sé -sée [kɔ̃pase] *adj* stiff, studied

compasser [kɔ̃pase] *tr* to measure out, to lay off; **compasser ses discours** to speak like a book

compassion [kɔ̃pasjɔ̃] *f* compassion

compatibilité [kɔ̃patibilite] *f* compatibility

compatir [kɔ̃patir] *intr*—**compatir à** to take pity on, to feel for; to be indulgent toward; to share in (*s.o.'s* *bereavement*); **ne pouvoir compatir** to be unable to agree

compatis·sant [kɔ̃patisɑ̃] **compatis-sante** [kɔ̃patisɑ̃t] *adj* compassionate, sympathetic, indulgent

compatriote [kɔ̃patriɔt] *mf* compatriot

compensa·teur [kɔ̃pɑ̃satœr] **-trice** [tris] *adj* compensating, equalizing

compensation [kɔ̃pɑ̃sɑsjɔ̃] *f* compensation

compenser [kɔ̃pɑ̃se] *tr* to compensate; to compensate for ‖ *ref* to balance each other

compérage [kɔ̃peraʒ] *m* complicity

compère [kɔ̃per] *m* accomplice; comrade; stooge (*for a clown*)

compétence [kɔ̃petɑ̃s] *f* competence, proficiency; (law) jurisdiction

compé·tent [kɔ̃petɑ̃] **-tente** [tɑ̃t] *adj* competent, proficient; (law) having jurisdiction, expert

compéter [kɔ̃pete] §10 *intr*—**compéter à** to belong to by right; to be within the competency of (*a court*)

compéti·teur [kɔ̃petitœr] **-trice** [tris] *mf* rival, competitor

compétition [kɔ̃petisjɔ̃] *f* competition

compilation [kɔ̃pilasjɔ̃] *f* compilation

compiler [kɔ̃pile] *tr* to compile

complainte [kɔ̃plɛ̃t] *f* sad ballad; (law) complaint

complaire [kɔ̃pler] §52 *intr* (with *dat*) to please, gratify ‖ *ref*—**se complaire à** to take pleasure in

complaisance [kɔ̃plezɑ̃s] *f* compliance; courtesy; complacency; **auriez-vous la complaisance de . . . ?** would you be so kind as to . . . ?; **de complaisance** out of kindness

complai·sant [kɔ̃plezɑ̃] **-sante** [zɑ̃t] *adj* complaisant, obliging; complacent

complément [kɔ̃plemɑ̃] *m* complement; (gram) object; **complément d'attribution** (gram) indirect object

com·plet [kɔ̃plɛ] **-plète** [plɛt] *adj* complete, full; **c'est complet!** that's the last straw! ‖ *m* suit (*of clothes*); **au complet** full (*house*); **au grand complet** at full strength

compléter [kɔ̃plete] §10 *tr* to complete ‖ *ref* to be completed; to complement one another

complet-veston [kɔ̃plevestɔ̃] *m* (*pl* **complets-veston**) man's suit

complexe [kɔ̃plɛks] *adj & m* complex; **complexe de culpabilité** guilt complex

complexé complexée [kɔ̃plekse] *adj* (coll) timid, withdrawn ‖ *mf* person with complexes

complexion [kɔ̃pleksjɔ̃] *f* constitution, disposition

complication [kɔ̃plikasjɔ̃] *f* complication

complice [kɔ̃plis] *adj* accessory, abetting ‖ *mf* accomplice; **complice d'adultère** corespondent

complicité [kɔ̃plisite] *f* complicity

compliment [kɔ̃plimɑ̃] *m* compliment

complimenter [kɔ̃plimɑ̃te] *tr* to compliment; to congratulate

complimen·teur [kɔ̃plimɑ̃tœr] **-teuse** [tøz] *adj* complimentary ‖ *mf* flatterer, yes man

compli·qué -quée [kɔ̃plike] *adj* complicated

compliquer [kɔ̃plike] *tr* to complicate ‖ *ref* to become complicated; to have complications

complot [kɔ̃plo] *m* plot, conspiracy

comploter [kɔ̃plɔte] *tr & intr* to plot, conspire

comploteur [kɔ̃plɔtœr] *m* conspirator

comportement [kɔ̃pɔrtəmɑ̃] *m* behavior

comporter [kɔ̃pɔrte] *tr* to permit; to include ‖ *ref* to behave

compo·sant [kɔ̃pozɑ̃] **-sante** [zɑ̃t] *adj* constituent ‖ *m* (chem) component ‖ *f* (mech) component

compo·sé -sée [kɔ̃poze] *adj & m* compound

composer [kɔ̃poze] *tr* to compose; to compound; to dial (*a telephone number*) ‖ *intr* to take an exam; to come to terms ‖ *ref*—**se composer de** to be composed of

composi·teur [kɔ̃pozitœr] **-trice** [tris] *mf* composer; compositor; **amiable compositeur** (law) arbitrator

composition [kɔ̃pozisjɔ̃] *f* composition; compound; dialing (*of telephone number*); term paper; **de bonne composition** easygoing, reasonable; **entrer en composition** to reach an agreement

composteur [kɔ̃pɔstœr] *m* composing stick; dating and numbering machine, dating stamp

compote [kɔ̃pɔt] *f* compote; **compote de pommes** applesauce

compotier [kɔ̃pɔtje] *m* compote (*dish*)

compréhensible [kɔ̃preɑ̃sibl] *adj* comprehensible

compréhen·sif [kɔ̃preɑ̃sif] **-sive** [siv] *adj* understanding; comprehensive

compréhension [kɔ̃preɑ̃sjɔ̃] *f* comprehension, understanding

comprendre [kɔ̃prɑ̃dr] §56 *tr* to understand; to comprehend, to include, to comprise ‖ *intr* to understand ‖ *ref* to be understood; to be included

compresse [kɔ̃prɛs] *f* (med) compress

compresseur [kɔ̃presœr] *m* compressor

compression [kɔ̃presjɔ̃] *f* compression; repression; reduction

compri·mé -mée [kɔ̃prime] *adj* compressed ‖ *m* (pharm) tablet, lozenge

comprimer [kɔ̃prime] *tr* to compress; to repress

com·pris [kɔ̃pri] **-prise** [priz] *adj* understood; included, including, e.g., **la ferme comprise** or **y compris la ferme** the farm included, including the farm

compromet·tant [kɔ̃prɔmetɑ̃] **compromet·tante** [kɔ̃prɔmetɑ̃t] *adj* compromising, incriminating

compromettre [kɔ̃prɔmetr] §42 *tr* to compromise ‖ *intr* to submit to arbitration ‖ *ref* to compromise oneself

compromis [kɔ̃prɔmi] *m* compromise

comptabiliser [kɔ̃tabilize] *tr* (com) to enter into the books

comptabilité [kɔ̃tabilite] *f* bookkeeping, accounting; accounting department, accounts; **comptabilité à partie double** double-entry bookkeeping; **comptabilité simple** single-entry bookkeeping; **tenir la comptabilité** to keep the books

comptable [kɔ̃tabl] *adj* accountable, responsible; accounting (*machine*) ‖ *mf* bookkeeper; **comptable agréé** or **expert comptable** certified public accountant; **comptable contrôleur** auditor

comp·tant [kɔ̃tã] **-tante** [tãt] *adj* spot (*cash*); down, e.g., **argent comptant** cash down ‖ *m*—**au comptant** cash, for cash ‖ **comptant** *adv* cash (down), e.g., **payer comptant** to pay cash

compte [kɔ̃t] *m* account; accounting; (*sports*) count; **à bon compte** cheap; **à ce compte** in that case; **à compte** on account; **au bout du compte** or **en fin de compte** when all is said and done; **compte à rebours** countdown; **compte courant** current account; charge account; **compte de dépôt** checking account; **compte de profits et pertes** profit and loss statement; **compte en banque** bank account; **compte rendu** report, review; **compte rond** round numbers; **donner son compte à** to give the final paycheck to, to discharge; **être en compte à demi** to go fifty-fifty; **loin de compte** wide of the mark; **rendre compte de** to review; **se rendre compte de** to realize, to be aware of; **tenir compte de** to bear in mind

compte-fils [kɔ̃tfil] *m invar* cloth prover

compte-gouttes [kɔ̃tgut] *m invar* dropper; **au compte-gouttes** in driblets

compter [kɔ̃te] *tr* to count; to number, have; **compter** + *inf* to count on + *ger*; **sans compter** not to mention ‖ *intr* to count; **à compter de** starting from; **compter avec** to reckon with; **compter sur** to count on

compte-tours [kɔ̃tatur] *m invar* tachometer, r.p.m. counter

comp·teur [kɔ̃tœr] **-teuse** [tøz] *mf* counter, checker (*person*) ‖ *m* meter; counter; speedometer; **compteur de gaz** gas meter; **compteur de Geiger** Geiger counter; **compteur de stationnement** parking meter; **relever le compteur** to read the meter

compteur-indicateur [kɔ̃tœrɛ̃dikatœr] *m* (*pl* **compteurs-indicateurs**) speedometer

comptine [kɔ̃tin] *f* counting-out rhyme

comptoir [kɔ̃twar] *m* counter; branch bank; bank; **comptoir postal** mail-order house

compulser [kɔ̃pylse] *tr* to go through, examine (*books, papers, etc.*)

computer [kɔ̃pyte] *tr* to compute

comte [kɔ̃t] *m* count

comté [kɔ̃te] *m* county

comtesse [kɔ̃tes] *f* countess

concasser [kɔ̃kase] *tr* to crush, pound

concasseur [kɔ̃kasœr] *adj masc* crushing ‖ *m* (mach) crusher

concave [kɔ̃kav] *adj* concave

concéder [kɔ̃sede] §10 *tr* & *intr* to concede

concen·tré -trée [kɔ̃sãtre] *adj* concentrated; condensed (*milk*); reserved (*person*)

concentrer [kɔ̃sãtre] *tr* to concentrate; to repress, hold back

concentrique [kɔ̃sãtrik] *adj* concentric

concept [kɔ̃sɛpt] *m* concept

conception [kɔ̃sɛpsjɔ̃] *f* conception

concerner [kɔ̃sɛrne] *tr* to concern; **en ce qui concerne** concerning

concert [kɔ̃sɛr] *m* concert; **de concert** together, in concert

concer·tant [kɔ̃sɛrtã] **-tante** [tãt] *adj* performing together ‖ *mf* (mus) performer

concerter [kɔ̃sɛrte] *tr* & *ref* to concert, to plan

concertiste [kɔ̃sɛrtist] *mf* concert performer

concession [kɔ̃sɛsjɔ̃] *f* concession

concessionnaire [kɔ̃sɛsjɔner] *mf* grantee, licensee; dealer (*in automobiles*); agent (*for insurance*)

concetti [kɔ̃tʃeti] *mpl* conceits

concevable [kɔ̃savabl] *adj* conceivable

concevoir [kɔ̃savwar] §59 *tr* to conceive; to compose (*a letter, telegram*)

concierge [kɔ̃sjɛrʒ] *mf* concierge, building superintendent

concile [kɔ̃sil] *m* (eccl) council

concilia·teur [kɔ̃siljatœr] **-trice** [tris] *adj* conciliating ‖ *mf* conciliator

conciliatoire [kɔ̃siljatwar] *adj* conciliatory

concilier [kɔ̃silje] *tr* to reconcile (*two parties, two ideas, etc.*); to win (*e.g., favor*) ‖ *ref* to win over, gain (*e.g., esteem*); to agree

con·cis [kɔ̃si] **-cise** [siz] *adj* concise

concitoyen [kɔ̃sitwajɛ̃] **concitoyenne** [kɔ̃sitwajɛn] *mf* fellow citizen

conclu·ant [kɔ̃klyã] **concluante** [kɔ̃klyãt] *adj* conclusive

conclure [kɔ̃klyr] §11 *tr* to conclude ‖ *intr* to conclude; **conclure à** to decide on, to decide in favor of

conclusion [kɔ̃klyzjɔ̃] *f* conclusion

concombre [kɔ̃kɔ̃br] *m* cucumber

concomi·tant [kɔ̃kɔmitã] **-tante** [tãt] *adj* concomitant

concordance [kɔ̃kɔrdãs] *f* agreement; concordance (*of Bible*)

concorde [kɔ̃kɔrd] *f* concord

concorder [kɔ̃kɔrde] *intr* to agree

concourir [kɔ̃kurir] §14 *intr* to compete; to cooperate; to converge, concur

concours [kɔ̃kur] *m* crowd; cooperation; contest, competition, meet; competitive examination; **concours de beauté** beauty contest; **concours de créanciers** meeting of creditors; **concours hippique** horse show; **hors concours** not competing; in a class by itself

con·cret [kɔ̃krɛ] **-crète** [krɛt] *adj* & *m* concrete

concrétiser [kɔ̃kretize] *tr* to put in concrete form

concubine [kɔ̃kybin] *f* concubine

concurrence [kɔ̃kyrɑ̃s] *f* competition; competitors; **jusqu'à concurrence de** to the amount of; **libre concurrence** free enterprise

concurrencer [kɔ̃kyrɑ̃se] §51 *tr* to rival, to compete with

concur·rent [kɔ̃kyrɑ̃] **concur·rente** [kɔ̃-kyrɑ̃t] *adj* competitive || *mf* competitor; contestant

concurren·tiel -tielle [kɔ̃kyrɑ̃sjɛl] *adj* competitive

concussion [kɔ̃kysjɔ̃] *f* extortion; embezzlement

condamnable [kɔ̃danabl] *adj* blameworthy

condamnation [kɔ̃danɑsjɔ̃] *f* condemnation

condamner [kɔ̃dane] *tr* to condemn; to give up (*an incurable patient*); to forbid the use of; to board up (*a window*); to batten down (*the hatches*)

condensateur [kɔ̃dɑ̃satœr] *m* (elec) condenser

condenser [kɔ̃dɑ̃se] *tr & ref* to condense

condenseur [kɔ̃dɑ̃sœr] *m* condenser

condescendance [kɔ̃desɑ̃dɑ̃s] *f* condescension

condescen·dant [kɔ̃desɑ̃dɑ̃] **-dante** [dɑ̃t] *adj* condescending

condescendre [kɔ̃desɑ̃dr] *intr* to condescend; to yield, comply

condiment [kɔ̃dimɑ̃] *m* condiment

condisciple [kɔ̃disipl] *mf* classmate

condition [kɔ̃disjɔ̃] *f* condition; **à condition, sous condition** conditionally; on approval; **à condition que** on condition that; **dans de bonnes conditions** in good condition; **sans conditions** unconditional

condition·nel -nelle [kɔ̃disjɔnɛl] *adj & m* conditional

conditionner [kɔ̃disjɔne] *tr* to condition; (com) to package

condoléances [kɔ̃dɔleɑ̃s] *fpl* condolence

conduc·teur [kɔ̃dyktœr] **²-trice** [tris] *adj* conducting; driving; (elec) power (line); (elec) lead (*wire*) || *adj masc* (elec, phys) (in predicate after **être**, it may be translated by a noun) conductor, e.g., **les métaux sont bons conducteurs de l'électricité** metals are good conductors of electricity || *mf* guide; leader; driver || *m* motorman; foreman; pressman; (elec, phys) conductor

conduire [kɔ̃dɥir] §19 *tr* to conduct; to lead; to drive; to see (*s.o. to the door*) || *intr* to drive || *ref* to conduct oneself

conduit [kɔ̃dɥi] *m* conduit; **conduit auditif** auditory canal; **conduits lacrymaux** tear ducts

conduite [kɔ̃dɥit] *f* conduct, behavior; management, command; driving (*of a car; of cattle*); pipe line; duct, flue; **avoir de la conduite** to be well behaved; **conduite d'eau** water main; **conduite intérieure** closed car; **faire la conduite à** to escort; **faire une conduite de Grenoble à qn** (coll) to kick s.o. out

cône [kon] *m* cone

confection [kɔ̃feksjɔ̃] *f* manufacture; construction (*e.g., of a machine*); ready-made clothes; **de confection** ready-made (*suit, dress, etc.*)

confectionner [kɔ̃feksjɔne] *tr* to manufacture; to prepare (*a dish*)

confection·neur [kɔ̃feksjɔnœr] **confection·neuse** [kɔ̃feksjɔnøz] *mf* manufacturer (*esp. of ready-made clothes*)

confédération [kɔ̃federɑsjɔ̃] *f* confederation, confederacy

confédérer [kɔ̃federe] §10 *tr & ref* to confederate

conférence [kɔ̃ferɑ̃s] *f* conference; lecture, speech; **conférence au sommet** summit conference; **conférence de presse** press conference

conféren·cier [kɔ̃ferɑ̃sje] **-cière** [sjɛr] *mf* lecturer, speaker

conférer [kɔ̃fere] §10 *tr* to confer, award; to administer (*a sacrament*); to collate, compare || *intr* to confer

confesse [kɔ̃fɛs] *f*—**à confesse** to confession; **de confesse** from confession

confesser [kɔ̃fese] *tr* to confess; (coll) to pump (*s.o.*) || *ref* to confess

confesseur [kɔ̃fesœr] *m* confessor

confession [kɔ̃fesjɔ̃] *f* confession; (eccl) denomination

confessionnal [kɔ̃fesjɔnal] *m* confessional

confession·nel -nelle [kɔ̃fesjɔnɛl] *adj* denominational

confiance [kɔ̃fjɑ̃s] *f* confidence; **confiance en soi** self-confidence; **de confiance** reliable; confidently; **en confiance** with confidence

con·fiant [kɔ̃fjɑ̃] **-fiante** [fjɑ̃t] *adj* confident; confiding, trusting

confidence [kɔ̃fidɑ̃s] *f* confidence, secret

confi·dent [kɔ̃fidɑ̃] **-dente** [dɑ̃t] *mf* confident

confiden·tiel -tielle [kɔ̃fidɑ̃sjɛl] *adj* confidential

confier [kɔ̃fje] *tr* to entrust; to confide, disclose; to commit (*to memory*); to consign; **confier à** to put (*seed*) in (*the ground*) || *ref*—**se confier à** to confide in, to trust; **se confier en** to put one's trust in

confinement [kɔ̃finmɑ̃] *m* imprisonment

confiner [kɔ̃fine] *tr* to confine || *intr*—**confiner à** to border on, to verge on || *ref* to confine oneself; **se confiner dans** to confine oneself to

confins [kɔ̃fɛ] *mpl* confines

confire [kɔ̃fir] §66 (*pp* **confit**) *tr* to preserve; to pickle; to candy; to can (*goose, chicken, etc.*); to dip (*skins*) || *ref* to become immersed (*in work, prayer, etc.*)

confirmer [kɔ̃firme] *tr* to confirm

confiserie [kɔ̃fizri] *f* confectionery

confi·seur [kɔ̃fizœr] **-seuse** [zøz] *mf* confectioner, candymaker

confisquer [kɔ̃fiske] *tr* to confiscate

con·fit [kɔ̃fi] **-fite** [fit] *adj* preserved; pickled; candied; steeped (*e.g., in* *piety);* incrusted (*in bigotry*) ‖ *m* canned chicken, goose, etc.

confiture [kɔ̃fityr] *f* preserves, jam

confitu•rier [kɔ̃fityrje] **-rière** [rjɛr] *mf* manufacturer of jams ‖ *m* jelly glass, jam jar

conflagration [kɔ̃flagrasjɔ̃] *f* conflagration, turmoil

conflit [kɔ̃fli] *m* conflict

confluer [kɔ̃flye] *intr* to meet, come together (*said of two rivers*)

confondre [kɔ̃fɔ̃dr] *tr* to confuse, mix up, mingle; to confound ‖ *ref* to become bewildered, mixed up; **se confondre en excuses** to fall all over oneself apologizing

conforme [kɔ̃fɔrm] *adj* corresponding; certified, e.g., **pour copie conforme** certified copy; **conforme à** conformable to, consistent with; **conforme à l'échantillon** identical with sample; **conforme aux normes** according to specifications; **conforme aux règles** in order

confor•mé -mée [kɔ̃fɔrme] *adj* shaped, built; **bien conformé** well-built; **mal conformé** misshapen

conformément [kɔ̃fɔrmemɑ̃] *adv*—**conformément à** in compliance with

conformer [kɔ̃fɔrme] *tr & ref* to conform

conformiste [kɔ̃fɔrmist] *mf* conformist

conformité [kɔ̃fɔrmite] *f* conformity, conformance

confort [kɔ̃fɔr] *m* comfort; convenience; **pneu confort** balloon tire

confortable [kɔ̃fɔrtabl] *adj* comfortable ‖ *m* comfort; easy chair

confrère [kɔ̃frɛr] *m* confrere, colleague

confrérie [kɔ̃freri] *f* brotherhood

confronter [kɔ̃frɔ̃te] *tr* to confront; to compare, collate

con•fus [kɔ̃fy] **-fuse** [fyz] *adj* confused; vague, blurred; embarrassed

confusion [kɔ̃fyzjɔ̃] *f* confusion

congé [kɔ̃ʒe] *m* leave; vacation; dismissal; **congé libérable** military discharge; **congé payé** vacation with pay; **donner congé à** to lay off; **donner son congé à** to give notice to; **prendre congé de** to take leave of

congédiement [kɔ̃ʒedimɑ̃] *m* dismissal, discharge; paying off (*of crew*)

congédier [kɔ̃ʒedje] *tr* to dismiss

congélateur [kɔ̃ʒelatœr] *m* freezer (*for frozen foods*)

congélation [kɔ̃ʒelasjɔ̃] *f* freezing

congeler [kɔ̃ʒəle] §2 *tr & ref* to freeze; to congeal; **congeler à basse température** to deep-freeze

congéni•tal -tale [kɔ̃ʒenital] *adj* (*pl* **-taux** [to]) congenital

congère [kɔ̃ʒɛr] *f* snowdrift

congestion [kɔ̃ʒestjɔ̃] *f* congestion; **congestion cérébrale** stroke; **congestion pulmonaire** pneumonia

congestionner [kɔ̃ʒestjɔne] *tr & ref* to congest

conglomération [kɔ̃glɔmerasjɔ̃] *f* conglomeration

conglomérer [kɔ̃glɔmere] §10 *tr & ref* to conglomerate

congratulation [kɔ̃gratylasjɔ̃] *f* congratulation

congratuler [kɔ̃gratyle] *tr* to congratulate

congre [kɔ̃gr] *m* conger eel

congréer [kɔ̃gree] *tr* to worm (*rope*)

congrégation [kɔ̃gregasjɔ̃] *f* (eccl) congregation

congrès [kɔ̃grɛ] *m* congress, convention

congressiste [kɔ̃gresist] *mf* delegate ‖ *m* congressman ‖ *f* congresswoman

con•gru -grue [kɔ̃gry] *adj* precise, suitable; scanty; (math) congruent

conifère [kɔnifɛr] *adj* coniferous ‖ *m* conifer

conique [kɔnik] *adj* conical ‖ *f* conic section

conjecture [kɔ̃ʒektyr] *f* conjecture

conjecturer [kɔ̃ʒektyre] *tr & intr* to conjecture, to surmise

conjoindre [kɔ̃ʒwɛ̃dr] §35 *tr* to join in marriage

con•joint [kɔ̃ʒwɛ̃] **-jointe** [ʒwɛ̃t] *adj* united, joint ‖ *mf* spouse, consort

conjoncteur [kɔ̃ʒɔ̃ktœr] *m* automatic switch

conjonction [kɔ̃ʒɔ̃ksjɔ̃] *f* conjunction

conjugaison [kɔ̃ʒygezɔ̃] *f* conjugation

conju•gal -gale [kɔ̃ʒygal] *adj* (*pl* **-gaux** [go]) conjugal, connubial

conjuguer [kɔ̃ʒyge] *tr* to combine (e.g., forces); to conjugate

conjuration [kɔ̃ʒyrasjɔ̃] *f* conjuration; conspiracy; **conjurations** entreaties

conju•ré -rée [kɔ̃ʒyre] *mf* conspirator

conjurer [kɔ̃ʒyre] *tr* to conjure; to conjure away; to conjure up; to conspire for, to plot; **conjurer qn de** + *inf* to entreat s.o. to + *inf* ‖ *intr* to hatch a plot ‖ *ref* to plot together, conspire

connaissance [kɔnesɑ̃s] *f* knowledge; acquaintance; consciousness; attention; **connaissance des temps** nautical almanac; **connaissances** knowledge; **en connaissance de** with full knowledge of; **faire connaissance avec** to become acquainted with; **faire la connaissance de** to meet; **parler en connaissance de cause** to know what one is talking about; **perdre connaissance** to lose consciousness; **sans connaissance** unconscious

connaissement [kɔnesmɑ̃] *m* bill of lading

connais•seur [kɔnesœr] **connais•seuse** [kɔnesøz] *mf* connoisseur; expert

connaître [kɔnɛtr] §12 *tr* to know; to be acquainted with ‖ *intr*—**connaître de** (law) to have jurisdiction over ‖ *ref* to become acquainted; **se connaître à** or **en** to know a lot about; **s'y connaître** to know what one is talking about; **s'y connaître en** to know a lot about

connecter [kɔnekte] *tr* to connect

connétable [kɔnetabl] *m* constable

connexe [kɔneks] *adj* connected

connexion [kɔneksjɔ̃] *f* connection

connexité [kɔneksite] *f* connection

con•nu -nue [kɔny] *adj* well-known ‖ *m*—**le connu** the known

conque [kɔ̃k] *f* conch

conqué•rant [kɔ̃kerɑ̃] **-rante** [rɑ̃t] *adj* (coll) swaggering ‖ *mf* conqueror

conquérir [kɔ̃kerir] §3 *tr* to conquer

conquête [kɔ̃kɛt] *f* conquest

consa•cré -crée [kɔ̃sakre] *adj* accepted, time-honored, stock

consacrer [kɔ̃sakre] *tr* to consecrate; to devote, dedicate (*time, energy, effort*); to give, to spare (*e.g., time*); to sanction, confirm ‖ *ref*—**se consacrer à** to devote or dedicate oneself to

consan•guin [kɔ̃sɑ̃gɛ̃] **-guine** [gin] *adj* consanguineous; on the father's side ‖ *mf* blood relation

consciemment [kɔ̃sjamɑ̃] *adv* consciously

conscience [kɔ̃sjɑ̃s] *f* conscience; conscientiousness; consciousness; **avoir la conscience large** to be broadminded; **en conscience** conscientiously

conscien•cieux [kɔ̃sjɑ̃sjø] **-cieuse** [sjøz] *adj* conscientious

cons•cient [kɔ̃sjɑ̃] **cons•ciente** [kɔ̃sjɑ̃t] *adj* conscious, aware, knowing

conscription [kɔ̃skripsjɔ̃] *f* draft, conscription

conscrit [kɔ̃skri] *m* draftee, conscript

consécration [kɔ̃sekrasjɔ̃] *f* consecration; confirmation

consécu•tif [kɔ̃sekytif] **-tive** [tiv] *adj* consecutive; dependent (*clause*); **consécutif à** resulting from

conseil [kɔ̃sɛj] *m* advice, counsel; counselor; council, board, committee; **conseil d'administration** board of directors; **conseil de guerre** court-martial; staff meeting of top brass; **conseil de prud'hommes** arbitration board; **conseil de révision** draft board; **conseils** advice; **un conseil** a piece of advice

conseil•ler [kɔ̃seje] **conseil•lère** [kɔ̃sejɛr] *mf* councilor; counselor, adviser ‖ *f* councilor's wife; counselor's wife ‖ **conseiller** *tr* to advise, to counsel (*s.o. or s.th.*); **conseiller q.ch. à qn** to recommend s.th. to s.o. ‖ *intr* to advise, to counsel; **conseiller à qn de** + *inf* to advise s.o. to + *inf*

conseil•leur [kɔ̃sejœr] **conseil•leuse** [kɔ̃sejøz] *mf* adviser; know-it-all

consensus [kɔ̃sɛsys] *m* consensus

consentement [kɔ̃sɑ̃tmɑ̃] *m* consent

consentir [kɔ̃sɑ̃tir] §19 *tr* to grant, allow; to accept, recognize; **consentir que** + *subj* to permit (*s.o.*) to + *inf* ‖ *intr* to consent; **consentir à** to consent to, to agree to, to approve of

conséquemment [kɔ̃sekamɑ̃] *adv* consequently; consistently

consé•quence [kɔ̃sekɑ̃s] *f* consequence; consistency; **en conséquence** accordingly

consé•quent [kɔ̃sekɑ̃] **-quente** [kɑ̃t] *adj* consequent; consistent; important ‖ *m* (logic, math) consequent; **par conséquent** consequently

conserva•teur [kɔ̃sɛrvatœr] **-trice** [tris] *adj* conservative ‖ *mf* conservative;

curator, keeper; warden, ranger; registrar

conservation [kɔ̃sɛrvasjɔ̃] *f* conservation, preservation; curatorship; curator's office

conservatisme [kɔ̃sɛrvatism] *m* conservatism

conservatoire [kɔ̃sɛrvatwar] *m* conservatory (*of music*); museum, academy

conserve [kɔ̃sɛrv] *f* canned food, preserves; escort, convoy; **conserves** dark glasses; **conserves au vinaigre** pickles; **mettre en conserve** to can; **voler de conserve avec** to fly alongside of

conserver [kɔ̃sɛrve] *tr* to conserve; to preserve; to keep (*one's health; one's equanimity; a secret*); to escort, to convoy (*a ship*) ‖ *ref* to stay in good shape; to take care of oneself

conserverie [kɔ̃sɛrvəri] *f* canning factory; canning

considérable [kɔ̃siderabl] *adj* considerable; important; large, great

considérant [kɔ̃siderɑ̃] *m* motive, grounds; **considérant que** whereas

considération [kɔ̃siderɑsjɔ̃] *f* consideration

considérer [kɔ̃sidere] §10 *tr* to consider, examine; to esteem, consider

consignataire [kɔ̃siɲatɛr] *m* consignee, trustee

consignation [kɔ̃siɲasjɔ̃] *f* consignment; **en consignation** on consignment

consigne [kɔ̃siɲ] *f* password; baggage room, checkroom; checking fee; confinement to barracks, detention; deposit; (mil) orders, instructions; **en consigne à la douane** held up in customs; **être de consigne** to be on duty; **manquer à la consigne** to disobey orders

consigner [kɔ̃siɲe] *tr* to consign; to check (*baggage*); to put down in writing, to enter in the record; to confine to barracks, to keep (*a student*) in; to put out of bounds (*e.g., for military personnel*); to close (*a port*); **consigner sa** (or **la**) **porte** to be at home to no one

consistance [kɔ̃sistɑ̃s] *f* consistency; stability (*of character*); credit, reality, standing; **en consistance de** consisting of

consis•tant [kɔ̃sistɑ̃] **-tante** [tɑ̃t] *adj* consistent; stable (*character*); **consistant en** consisting of

consister [kɔ̃siste] *intr*—**consister à** + *inf* to consist in + *ger*; **consister dans** or **en** to consist in; to consist of

consistoire [kɔ̃sistwar] *m* consistory

consola•teur [kɔ̃sɔlatœr] **-trice** [tris] *adj* consoling ‖ *mf* comforter

consolation [kɔ̃sɔlasjɔ̃] *f* consolation

console [kɔ̃sɔl] *f* console; console table; bracket

consoler [kɔ̃sɔle] *tr* to console

consolider [kɔ̃sɔlide] *tr* to consolidate; to fund (*a debt*)

consomma•teur [kɔ̃sɔmatœr] **-trice**

[tris] *mf* consumer; customer (*in a restaurant or bar*)

consommation [kɔsɔmasjɔ̃] *f* consummation (*e.g., of a marriage*); perpetration (*e.g., of a crime*); consumption, use; drink (*e.g., in a café*)

consomm·mé -mée [kɔsɔme] *adj* consummate; skilled (*e.g., technician*); consumed, used up ‖ *m* consommé

consommer [kɔsɔme] *tr* to consummate, complete; to perpetrate (*e.g., a crime*); to consume

consomp·tif [kɔsɔptif] -**tive** [tiv] *adj* wasting away

consomption [kɔsɔpsjɔ̃] *f* wasting away, decline

conso·nant [kɔsɔnɑ̃] -**nante** [nɑ̃t] *adj* consonant, harmonious

consonne [kɔsɔn] *f* consonant

consorts [kɔsɔr] *mpl* partners, associates; (pej) confederates

conspira·teur [kɔspiratœr] -**trice** [tris] *mf* conspirator

conspiration [kɔspirasjɔ̃] *f* conspiracy

conspirer [kɔspire] *tr & intr* to conspire

conspuer [kɔspɥe] *tr* to boo, hiss

constamment [kɔstamɑ̃] *adv* constantly

constance [kɔstɑ̃s] *f* constancy

cons·tant [kɔstɑ̃] -**tante** [tɑ̃t] *adj* constant; true; established, evident ‖ *f* constant

constat [kɔsta] *m* affidavit

constatation [kɔstatasjɔ̃] *f* authentication; declaration, claim

constater [kɔstate] *tr* to certify; to find out; to prove, establish

constellation [kɔstellasjɔ̃] *f* constellation

consteller [kɔstelle] *tr* to spangle

consterner [kɔsterne] *tr* to dismay

constipation [kɔstipasjɔ̃] *f* constipation

constiper [kɔstipe] *tr* to constipate

consti·tuant [kɔstitɥɑ̃] -**tuante** [tɥɑ̃t] *adj & m* constituent

constituer [kɔstitɥe] *tr* to constitute; to settle (*a dowry*); to form (*a cabinet*; *a corporation*); to empanel (*a jury*); to appoint (*a lawyer*) ‖ *ref* to be formed; **se constituer prisonnier** to give oneself up

constitu·tif [kɔstitytif] -**tive** [tiv] *adj* constituent

constitution [kɔstitysjɔ̃] *f* constitution; settlement (*of a dowry*); **constitution en société** incorporation

construc·teur [kɔstryktœr] -**trice** [tris] *adj* constructive, building ‖ *mf* constructor, builder

construc·tif [kɔstryktif] -**tive** [tiv] *adj* constructive

construction [kɔstryksjɔ̃] *f* construction; **construction mécanique** mechanical engineering

construire [kɔstrɥir] §19 *tr* to construct, to build; to draw (*e.g., a triangle*); (gram) to construe

consul [kɔsyl] *m* consul

consulaire [kɔsyler] *adj* consular

consulat [kɔsyla] *m* consulate

consul·tant [kɔsyltɑ̃] -**tante** [tɑ̃t] *adj* consulting ‖ *mf* consultant

consulta·tif [kɔsyltatif] -**tive** [tiv] *adj* advisory

consultation [kɔsyltasjɔ̃] *f* consultation; **consultation externe** outpatient clinic; **consultation populaire** poll, referendum

consulte [kɔsylt] *f* (eccl, law) consultation

consulter [kɔsylte] *tr* to consult ‖ *intr* to consult, to give consultations ‖ *ref* to deliberate

consumer [kɔsyme] *tr* to consume, use up, destroy ‖ *ref* to burn out; to waste away; to fail

contact [kɔtakt] *m* contact; **mettre en contact** to put in touch, to connect; **prendre contact** to make contact

contacter [kɔtakte] *tr* (coll) to contact

conta·gieux [kɔtaʒjø] -**gieuse** [ʒjøz] *adj* contagious

contagion [kɔtaʒjɔ̃] *f* contagion

contamination [kɔtaminasjɔ̃] *f* contamination

contaminer [kɔtamine] *tr* to contaminate

conte [kɔt] *m* tale, story; **conte à dormir debout** cock-and-bull story, baloney; **conte de fées** fairy tale

contemplation [kɔtɑ̃plasjɔ̃] *f* contemplation

contempler [kɔtɑ̃ple] *tr* to contemplate

contempo·rain [kɔtɑ̃porɛ̃] -**raine** [ren] *adj & m* contemporary

contemp·teur [kɔtɑ̃ptœr] -**trice** [tris] *mf* scoffer

contenance [kɔtnɑ̃s] *f* capacity; area; countenance; bearing; **faire bonne contenance** to put up a bold front

conte·nant [kɔtnɑ̃] -**nante** [nɑ̃t] *adj* containing ‖ *m* container

contenir [kɔtnir] §72 *tr* to contain; to restrain ‖ *ref* to contain oneself, to hold oneself back

con·tent [kɔtɑ̃] -**tente** [tɑ̃t] *adj* content; happy, glad, pleased; **content de** satisfied with ‖ *m* fill, e.g., **avoir son content** to have one's fill

contentement [kɔtɑ̃tmɑ̃] *m* contentment

contenter [kɔtɑ̃te] *tr* to content, satisfy ‖ *ref* to satisfy one's desires; **se contenter de** to be content or satisfied with

conten·tieux [kɔtɑ̃sjø] -**tieuse** [sjøz] *adj* contentious ‖ *m* contention, litigation; claims department

contention [kɔtɑ̃sjɔ̃] *f* application, intentness

conte·nu -nue [kɔtny] *adj* contained, restrained, stifled ‖ *m* contents

conter [kɔte] *tr* to relate, tell; **en conter à** (coll) to take (*s.o.*) in; **en conter (de belles)** (coll) to tell tall tales ‖ *intr* to narrate, to tell a story

contestation [kɔtestasjɔ̃] *f* argument, dispute; **sans contestation** without opposition

conteste [kɔtest] *f—***sans conteste** incontestably, unquestionably

contester [kɔteste] *tr & intr* to contest

con·teur [kɔtœr] -**teuse** [tøz] *mf* storyteller

contexte [kɔtɛkst] *m* context

conti·gu -guë [kɔ̃tigy] *adj* contiguous; **contigu à** adjoining

continence [kɔ̃tinɑ̃s] *f* continence

conti·nent [kɔ̃tinɑ̃] **-nente** [nɑ̃t] *adj* & *m* continent

continen·tal -tale [kɔ̃tinɑ̃tal] *adj* (*pl* **-taux** [to]) continental

contingence [kɔ̃tɛ̃ʒɑ̃s] *f* contingency

contin·gent [kɔ̃tɛ̃ʒɑ̃] **-gente** [ʒɑ̃t] *adj* contingent || *m* contingent; quota

conti·nu -nue [kɔ̃tiny] *adj* continuous; direct (*current*) || *m* continuum

continuation [kɔ̃tinɥɑsjɔ̃] *f* continuation

conti·nuel -nuelle [kɔ̃tinɥɛl] *adj* continual

continuité [kɔ̃tinɥite] *f* continuity

continûment [kɔ̃tinymɑ̃] *adv* continuously

contorsion [kɔ̃tɔrsjɔ̃] *f* contortion

contour [kɔ̃tur] *m* contour

contourner [kɔ̃turne] *tr* to contour; to go around, to skirt; to get around (*the law*); to twist, distort

contrac·tant -tante [tɑ̃t] *adj* contracting (*parties*) || *mf* contracting party

contracter [kɔ̃trakte] *tr* to contract; to float (*a loan*) || *ref* to contract; to be contracted

contraction [kɔ̃traksjɔ̃] *f* contraction

contradictoire [kɔ̃tradiktwar] *adj* contradictory

contraindre [kɔ̃trɛ̃dr] §15 *tr* to compel, force, constrain; to restrain, to curb || *ref* to restrain oneself

con·traint [kɔ̃trɛ̃] **-trainte** [trɛ̃t] *adj* constrained, forced; stiff (*person*) || *f* constraint; restraint; exigencies (*e.g., of the rhyme*)

contraire [kɔ̃trer] *adj* contrary; opposite (*e.g., direction*); injurious (*e.g., to health*) || *m* contrary, opposite; antonym; **au contraire** on the contrary

contrairement [kɔ̃trermɑ̃] *adv* contrary

contrarier [kɔ̃trarje] *tr* to thwart; to vex, annoy; to contrast (*e.g., colors*)

contrariété [kɔ̃trarjete] *f* vexation, annoyance; clashing (*e.g., of colors*)

contraste [kɔ̃trast] *m* contrast

contraster [kɔ̃traste] *tr* & *intr* to contrast

contrat [kɔ̃tra] *m* contract

contravention [kɔ̃travɑ̃sjɔ̃] *f* infraction; **dresser une contravention** to write out a (traffic) ticket; **recevoir une contravention** to get a ticket

contre [kɔ̃tr] *m* opposite, con; (cards) double; **par contre** on the contrary || *adv* against; nearby; **contre à contre** alongside || *prep* against; contrary to; to, e.g., **dix contre un** ten to one; for, e.g., **échanger contre** to exchange for; e.g., **remède contre la toux** remedy for a cough; (sports) versus; **contre remboursement** (com) collect on delivery

contre-allée [kɔ̃trale] *f* (*pl* **-allées**) parallel walk

contre-amiral [kɔ̃tramiral] *m* (*pl* **-amiraux** [amiro]) rear admiral

contre-appel [kɔ̃trapel] *m* (*pl* **-appels**) second roll call; double-check

contre-attaque [kɔ̃tratak] *f* (*pl* **-attaques**) counterattack

contre-attaquer [kɔ̃tratake] *tr* to counterattack

contrebalancer [kɔ̃trəbalɑ̃se] §51 *tr* to counterbalance

contrebande [kɔ̃trəbɑ̃d] *f* contraband; smuggling; **faire la contrebande** to smuggle

contreban·dier [kɔ̃trəbɑ̃dje] **-dière** [djer] *adj* smuggled, contraband || *mf* smuggler

contrebas [kɔ̃trəba]—**en contrebas** downwards

contrebasse [kɔ̃trəbas] *f* contrabass

contre-biais [kɔ̃trəbje]—**à contre-biais** the wrong way, against the grain

contre-boutant [kɔ̃trəbutɑ̃] *m* (*pl* **-boutants**) shore

contrecarrer [kɔ̃trəkare] *tr* to stymie, to thwart

contre-chant [kɔ̃trəʃɑ̃] *m* (*pl* **-chants**) counter melody

contrecœur [kɔ̃trəkœr] *m* smoke shelf; **à contrecœur** unwillingly

contrecoup [kɔ̃trəku] *m* rebound, recoil, backlash; repercussion

contre-courant [kɔ̃trəkurɑ̃] *m* (*pl* **-courants**) countercurrent; **à contre-courant** upstream; behind the times

contredire [kɔ̃trədir] §40 *tr* to contradict || *ref* to contradict oneself

contrée [kɔ̃tre] *f* region, countryside

contre-écrou [kɔ̃trekru] *m* (*pl* **-écrous**) lock nut

contre-espion [kɔ̃trespjɔ̃] *m* (*pl* **-espions**) counterspy

contre-espionnage [kɔ̃trespjɔnaʒ] *m* (*pl* **-espionnages**) counterespionage

contrefaçon [kɔ̃trəfasɔ̃] *f* infringement (*of patent or copyright*); forgery; counterfeit; plagiarism

contrefacteur [kɔ̃trəfaktœr] *m* forger; counterfeiter; plagiarist

contrefaction [kɔ̃trəfaksjɔ̃] *f* forgery; counterfeiting

contrefaire [kɔ̃trəfer] §29 *tr* to forge; to counterfeit; to imitate, to mimic; to disguise

contre·fait [kɔ̃trəfe] **-faite** [fet] *adj* counterfeit; deformed

contre-fenêtre [kɔ̃trəfnetr] *f* (*pl* **-fenêtres**) inner sash; storm window

contre-feu [kɔ̃trəfø] *m* (*pl* **-feux**) backfire (*in fire fighting*)

contreficher [kɔ̃trəfi/e] *ref* (slang) to not give a rap

contre-fil [kɔ̃trəfil] *m* (*pl* **-fils**) opposite direction, wrong way; **à contre-fil** upstream; against the grain

contre-filet [kɔ̃trəfile] *m* short loin (*club and porterhouse steaks*)

contrefort [kɔ̃trəfɔr] *m* buttress, abutment; foothills

contre-haut [kɔ̃trəo]—**en contre-haut** on a higher level; from top to bottom

contre-interrogatoire [kɔ̃trɛ̃terəgatwar] *m* cross-examination

contre-interroger [kɔ̃trẽterɔʒe] §38 *tr* to cross-examine

contre-jour [kɔ̃trəʒur] *m invar* backlighting; **à contre-jour** against the light

contremaî-tre [kɔ̃trəmetr] **-tresse** [tres] *mf* overseer ‖ *m* foreman; (naut) (hist) boatswain's mate; (nav) petty officer ‖ *f* forewoman

contremander [kɔ̃trəmɑ̃de] *tr* to countermand; to call off

contremarche [kɔ̃trəmarʃ] *f* countermarch; riser (*of stair step*)

contremarque [kɔ̃trəmark] *f* countersign; pass-out check

contremarquer [kɔ̃trəmarke] *tr* to countersign

contre-mesure [kɔ̃trəmzyr] *f* (*pl* **-mesures**) countermeasure

contre-offensive [kɔ̃trɔfɑ̃siv] *f* (*pl* **-offensives**) counteroffensive

contrepartie [kɔ̃trəparti] *f* counterpart; (bk) duplicate entry; **en contrepartie** as against this

contre-pas [kɔ̃trəpɑ] *m invar* half step (*taken in order to get in step*)

contre-pente [kɔ̃trəpɑ̃t] *f* (*pl* **-pentes**) reverse slope

contre-performance [kɔ̃trəperfɔrmɑ̃s] *f* (*pl* **-performances**) unexpected defeat

contrepèterie [kɔ̃trəpetri] *f* spoonerism

contre-pied [kɔ̃trəpje] *m* (*pl* **-pieds**) backtrack; opposite opinion; **à contre-pied** off balance

contre-plaqué [kɔ̃trəplake] *m* (*pl* **-plaqués**) plywood

contre-plaquer [kɔ̃trəplake] *tr* to laminate

contrepoids [kɔ̃trəpwa] *m invar* counterweight, counterbalance

contre-poil [kɔ̃trəpwal] *m* wrong way (*e.g., of fur*); **à contre-poil** the wrong way; at the wrong end

contrepoint [kɔ̃trəpwɛ̃] *m* counterpoint

contre-pointe [kɔ̃trəpwɛ̃t] *f* (*pl* **-pointes**) false edge (*of sword*); tailstock (*of lathe*)

contre-pointer [kɔ̃trəpwɛ̃te] *tr* to quilt

contrepoison [kɔ̃trəpwazɔ̃] *m* antidote

contrer [kɔ̃tre] *tr & intr* (cards) to double; (coll) to counter

contreseing [kɔ̃trəsɛ̃] *m* countersignature

contresens [kɔ̃trəsɑ̃s] *m invar* misinterpretation; mistranslation; wrong way; **à contresens** in the wrong sense; in the wrong direction

contresigner [kɔ̃trəsiɲe] *tr* to countersign

contretemps [kɔ̃trətɑ̃] *m*—**à contretemps** at the wrong moment; syncopated

contre-torpilleur [kɔ̃trətɔrpijœr] *m* (*pl* **-torpilleurs**) (nav) torpedo-boat destroyer

contreve-nant [kɔ̃trəvnɑ̃] **-nante** [nɑ̃t] *mf* lawbreaker, delinquent

contrevenir [kɔ̃trəvnir] §72 *intr* (with *dat*) to contravene, to break (*a law*)

contrevent [kɔ̃trəvɑ̃] *m* shutter, window shutter

contre-voie [kɔ̃trəvwa] *f* (*pl* **-voies**) parallel route; **à contre-voie** in reverse (*of the usual direction*); on the side opposite the platform

contribuable [kɔ̃tribɥabl] *adj* taxpaying ‖ *mf* taxpayer

contribuer [kɔ̃tribɥe] *intr* to contribute

contribution [kɔ̃tribysjɔ̃] *f* contribution; tax

contrister [kɔ̃triste] *tr* to sadden

con-trit [kɔ̃tri] **-trite** [trit] *adj* contrite

contrôlable [kɔ̃trolabl] *adj* verifiable

contrôle [kɔ̃trol] *m* inspection, verification, check; supervision, observation; auditing; inspection booth, ticket window; (mil) muster roll; **contrôle des naissances** birth control; **contrôle de soi** self-control; **contrôle par sondage** spot check

contrôler [kɔ̃trole] *tr* to inspect, verify, check; to supervise, to put under observation; to audit; to criticize ‖ *ref* to control oneself

contrô-leur [kɔ̃trolœr] **-leuse** [løz] *mf* inspector, checker; supervisor, observer; auditor, comptroller; conductor, ticket collector ‖ *m* gauge; **contrôleur de vitesse** speedometer; **contrôleur de vol** flight indicator

controversable [kɔ̃trɔversabl] *adj* controversial

controverse [kɔ̃trɔvers] *f* controversy

controverser [kɔ̃trɔverse] *tr* to controvert

contumace [kɔ̃tymas] *f* contempt of court

con-tus [kɔ̃ty] **-tuse** [tyz] *adj* bruised

contusion [kɔ̃tyzjɔ̃] *f* contusion, bruise

contusionner [kɔ̃tyzjɔne] *tr* to bruise

convain-cant [kɔ̃vɛ̃kɑ̃] **-cante** [kɑ̃t] *adj* convincing

convaincre [kɔ̃vɛ̃kr] §70 *tr* to convince; to convict ‖ *ref* to be satisfied

convain-cu **-cue** [kɔ̃vɛ̃ky] *adj* convinced, dyed-in-the-wool; convicted

convalescence [kɔ̃valesɑ̃s] *f* convalescence

convales-cent [kɔ̃valesɑ̃] **convales-cente** [kɔ̃valesɑ̃t] *adj & mf* convalescent

convenable [kɔ̃vnabl] *adj* suitable, proper; opportune (*moment*)

convenance [kɔ̃vnɑ̃s] *f* suitability, propriety; conformity; **convenances** conventions

convenir [kɔ̃vnir] §72 *intr* to agree; (with *dat*) to fit, suit; **convenir de** to admit, to admit to, to admit the truth of; to agree on ‖ *ref* to agree with one another ‖ *impers*—**il convient** it is fitting, it is appropriate

convention [kɔ̃vɑ̃sjɔ̃] *f* convention

convention-nel **-nelle** [kɔ̃vɑ̃sjɔnel] *adj* conventional

conve-nu **-nue** [kɔ̃vny] *adj* settled; stipulated (*price*); appointed (*time, place*); trite, stereotyped (*language*)

converger [kɔ̃verʒe] §38 *intr* to converge

conversation [kɔ̃versasjɔ̃] *f* conversation

converser [kɔ̃verse] *intr* to converse

conversion [kɔ̃versjɔ̃] *f* conversion; turning

conver·ti -tie [kɔ̃verti] *adj* converted || *mf* convert

convertible [kɔ̃vertibl] *adj* convertible

convertir [kɔ̃vertir] *tr* to convert || *ref* to convert, to be converted; to change one's mind

convertissable [kɔ̃vertisabl] *adj* convertible

convertisseur [kɔ̃vertisœr] *m* converter; (elec) converter

convexe [kɔ̃veks] *adj* convex

conviction [kɔ̃viksjɔ̃] *f* conviction

convier [kɔ̃vje] *tr* to invite

convive [kɔ̃viv] *mf* dinner guest; table companion

convocation [kɔ̃vɔkasjɔ̃] *f* convocation; summoning

convol [kɔ̃vwa] *m* convoy; funeral procession

convoiter [kɔ̃vwate] *tr* to covet

convoi·teur [kɔ̃vwatœr] **-teuse** [tøz] *adj* covetous || *mf* covetous person

convoitise [kɔ̃vwatiz] *f* covetousness, cupidity

convoquer [kɔ̃vɔke] *tr* to convoke; to summon

convoyer [kɔ̃vwaje] §47 *tr* to convoy

convoyeur [kɔ̃vwajœr] *adj* convoying || *m* (mach) conveyor; (nav) escort

convulser [kɔ̃vylse] *tr* to convulse

convulsion [kɔ̃vylsjɔ̃] *f* convulsion

convulsionner [kɔ̃vylsjɔne] *tr* to convulse

coordon·né -née [kɔɔrdɔne] *adj & f* coordinate

coordonner [kɔɔrdɔne] *tr* to coordinate

co·pain [kɔpɛ̃] **-pine** [pin] *mf* (coll) pal, chum

co·peau [kɔpo] *m* (*pl* **-peaux**) chip, shaving

copie [kɔpi] *f* copy; exercise, composition (*at school*); **pour copie conforme** true copy

copier [kɔpje] *tr & intr* to copy

co·pieux [kɔpjø] **-pieuse** [pjøz] *adj* copious

copilote [kɔpilɔt] *m* copilot

copiste [kɔpist] *mf* copyist; copier

coposséder [kɔpɔsede] §10 *tr* to own jointly

copropriété [kɔprɔprijete] *f* joint ownership

copula·tif [kɔpylatif] **-tive** [tiv] *adj* (gram) coordinating

copulation [kɔpylasjɔ̃] *f* copulation

copule [kɔpyl] *f* (gram) copula

coq [kɔk] *adj* bantam || *m* cock rooster; (naut) cook

coq-à-l'âne [kɔkalan] *m invar* cock-and-bull story

coque [kɔk] *f* shell; cocoon; hull; **coque de noix** coconut

coquelicot [kɔkliko] *m* poppy

coqueluche [kɔklyʃ] *f* whooping cough; (coll) rage, vogue

coquemar [kɔkmar] *m* teakettle

coquerie [kɔkri] *f* (naut) galley

coqueriquer [kɔkrike] *intr* to crow

co·quet [kɔke] **-quette** [ket] *adj* coquettish; stylish; considerable (*sum*)

coqueter [kɔkte] §34 *intr* to flirt

coquetier [kɔkətje] *m* eggcup; egg man

coquetterie [kɔketri] *f* coquetry

coquillage [kɔkijaʒ] *m* shellfish; shell

coquille [kɔkij] *f* shell; typographical error (*of transposed letters*); pat (*of butter*); **coquille de noix** nutshell; **coquille Saint-Jacques** scallop

co·quin [kɔkɛ̃] **-quine** [kin] *adj* deceitful; roguish || *mf* scoundrel; rogue

cor [kɔr] *m* horn; corn (*on foot*); prong (*of antler*); horn player; **à cor et à cri** with hue and cry; **cor anglais** English horn; **cor de chasse** hunting horn; **cor d'harmonie** French horn

co·rail [kɔraj] *m* (*pl* **-raux** [ro]) coral

cor·beau [kɔrbo] *m* (*pl* **-beaux**) crow, raven

corbeille [kɔrbej] *f* basket; flower bed; (theat) dress circle; **corbeille à papier** wastebasket; **corbeille de mariage** wedding present

corbillard [kɔrbijar] *m* hearse

corbillon [kɔrbijɔ̃] *m* small basket; word game

cordage [kɔrdaʒ] *m* cordage, rope; (naut) rigging

corde [kɔrd] *f* rope, cord; tightrope; inside track; (geom) chord; **corde à or de boyau** catgut (*for, e.g., violin*); **corde à linge** wash line; **corde à nœuds** knotted rope; **cordes vocales** vocal cords; **être sur la corde raide** to be out on a limb; **les cordes** (mus) the strings; **toucher la corde sensible** to touch a sympathetic chord; **usé jusqu'à la corde** threadbare

cor·dé -dée [kɔrde] *adj* heart-shaped || *f* cord (*of wood*); roped party (*of mountain climbers*)

cor·deau [kɔrdo] *m* (*pl* **-deaux**) tracing line; tracing thread; mine fuse; **tiré au cordeau** in a straight line

cordelier [kɔrdəlje] *m* Franciscan friar

corder [kɔrde] *tr* to twist; to string (a *tennis racket*)

cor·dial -diale [kɔrdjal] *adj & m* (*pl* **-diaux** [djo]) cordial

cordialité [kɔrdjalite] *f* cordiality

cordier [kɔrdje] *m* ropemaker; tailpiece (*of violin*)

cordon [kɔrdɔ̃] *m* cordon; cord; latchstring; **cordon de sonnette** bellpull; **cordon de soulier** shoestring

cordon-bleu [kɔrdɔ̃blø] *m* (*pl* **cordons-bleus**) cordon bleu

cordonnerie [kɔrdɔnri] *f* shoemaking; shoe repairing; shoe store; shoemaker's

cordon·nier [kɔrdɔnje] **cordon·nière** [kɔrdɔnjer] *mf* shoemaker

Corée [kɔre] *f* Korea; **la Corée** Korea

coré·en [kɔreɛ̃] **-éenne** [kɔreen] *adj* Korean || *m* Korean (*language*) || (*cap*) *mf* Korean (*person*)

coriace [kɔrjas] *adj* tough, leathery; (coll) stubborn

coricide [kɔrisid] *m* corn remover

cormoran [kɔrmɔrɑ̃] *m* cormorant

cornac [kɔrnak] *m* mahout

cor·nard [kɔrnar] **-narde** [nard] *adj* horned; (slang) cuckold; (*of horse*) wheezing || *m* (slang) cuckold

corne [kɔrn] *f* horn; dog-ear (*of page*); hoof; shoehorn; **corne d'abondance**

horn of plenty; **faire les cornes à** (coll) to make a face at

cor·né -née [kɔrne] *adj* horny || *f* cornea

corneille [kɔrnej] *f* crow, rook; **corneille d'église** jackdaw

cornemuse [kɔrnəmyz] *f* bagpipe

cornemuseur [kɔrnəmyzœr] *m* bagpiper

corner [kɔrne] *tr* to dog-ear; to give (*s.o.*) the horn; (coll) to trumpet (*news*) about || *intr* to blow the horn, to honk; to ring (*said of ears*); (mus) to blow a horn; **cornez!** sound your horn!

cornet [kɔrne] *m* cornet; horn; dicebox; cornetist; mouthpiece (*of microphone*); receiver (*of telephone*); **cornet acoustique** ear trumpet; **cornet à pistons** cornet; **cornet de glace** ice-cream cone

cornette [kɔrnet] *m* (mil) cornet || *f* (*headdress*) cornet

cornettiste [kɔrnetist] *mf* cornetist

corniche [kɔrni∫] *f* cornice

cornichon [kɔrni∫ɔ̃] *m* pickle, gherkin; (*fool*) (coll) dope, drip

cor·nier -nière [kɔrnje] -nière [njer] *adj* corner || *f* valley (*joining roofs*); angle iron

corniste [kɔrnist] *mf* horn player

Cornouailles [kɔrnwaj] *f* Cornwall

cornouiller [kɔrnuje] *m* dogwood

cor·nu -nue [kɔrny] *adj* horned; preposterous (*ideas*) || *f* (chem) retort

corollaire [kɔrɔller] *m* corollary

coronaire [kɔrɔner] *adj* coronary

coroner [kɔrɔnœr] *m* coroner

corporation [kɔrpɔrɑsjɔ̃] *f* association, guild

corpo·rel -relle [kɔrpɔrel] *adj* corporal, bodily

corps [kɔr] *m* body; corps; **à corps perdu** without thinking; **à mon** (ton, etc.) **corps défendant** in self-defense; reluctantly; **corps à corps** hand-to-hand; in a clinch; **corps céleste** heavenly body; **corps composé** (chem) compound; **corps de garde** guardhouse, guardroom; **corps de logis** main part of the building; **corps du délit** corpus delicti; **corps enseignant** faculty; **corps simple** (chem) simple substance; **prendre corps** to take shape; **saisir au corps** (law) to arrest

corps-à-corps [kɔrakɔr] *m* hand-to-hand combat; (boxing) infighting

corpulence [kɔrpylɑ̃s] *f* corpulence

corpuscule [kɔrpyskyl] *m* (phys) corpuscle

corral [kɔral] *m* corral

cos·su -sue [kɔsy] *adj* rich; well-to-do

cor·rect -recte [kɔrrekt] *adj* correct

correc·teur [kɔrrektœr] **-trice** [tris] *mf* corrector; proofreader

correc·tif [kɔrrektif] **-tive** [tiv] *adj & m* corrective

correction [kɔrreksjɔ̃] *f* correction; correctness; proofreading

corrélation [kɔrrelasjɔ̃] *f* correlation

correspondance [kɔrrespɔ̃dɑ̃s] *f* correspondence; transfer, connection

correspon·dant [kɔrrespɔ̃dɑ̃] **-dante** [dɑ̃t] *adj* corresponding, correspondent || *mf* correspondent; party (*per-*

son who gets a telephone call)

correspondre [kɔrrespɔ̃dr] *intr* to correspond; **correspondre à** to correspond to, to correlate with; **correspondre avec** to correspond with (*a letter writer*); to connect with (*e.g., a train*)

corridor [kɔridɔr] *m* corridor

corriger [kɔriʒe] §38 *tr* to correct; to proofread

corroborer [kɔrrɔbɔre] *tr* to corroborate

corroder [kɔrrɔde] *tr & ref* to corrode; to erode

corrompre [kɔrɔ̃pr] (3d *sg pres ind* **corrompt**) *tr* to corrupt; to rot; to bribe; to seduce; to spoil

corro·sif [kɔrrozif] **-sive** [ziv] *adj & m* corrosive

corrosion [kɔrrosjɔ̃] *f* corrosion; erosion

corroyer [kɔrwaje] §47 *tr* to weld; to plane (*wood*); to prepare (*leather*)

corruption [kɔrrypsjɔ̃] *f* corruption; bribery; seduction

corsage [kɔrsaʒ] *m* blouse, corsage

corsaire [kɔrser] *m* corsair; **corsaire de finance** ruthless businessman, robber baron

corse [kɔrs] *adj* Corsican || *m* Corsican (*language*) || (cap) *f* Corsica; **la Corse** Corsica || (cap) *mf* Corsican (*person*)

cor·sé -sée [kɔrse] *adj* full-bodied, heavy; spicy, racy

corser [kɔrse] *tr* to spike, to give body to (*wine*); to spice up (*a story*) || *ref* to become serious; **ça se corse** the plot thickens

corset [kɔrse] *m* corset

cortège [kɔrteʒ] *m* cortege; parade; **cortège funèbre** funeral procession

cortisone [kɔrtizɔn] *f* cortisone

corvée [kɔrve] *f* chore; forced labor; work party

coryphée [kɔrife] *m* coryphée; (fig) leader

cosaque [kɔzak] *adj* Cossack || (cap) *mf* Cossack

cosmétique [kɔsmetik] *adj* cosmetic || *m* cosmetic; hair set, hair spray || *f* beauty culture

cosmique [kɔsmik] *adj* cosmic

cosmonaute [kɔsmɔnot] *mf* cosmonaut

cosmopolite [kɔsmɔpɔlit] *adj & mf* cosmopolitan

cosmos [kɔsmos] *m* cosmos; outer space

cosse [kɔs] *f* pod; **avoir la cosse** (slang) to be lazy

cos·taud [kɔsto] **-taude** [tod] *adj* (slang) husky, strapping || *m* (slang) muscleman

costume [kɔstym] *m* costume; suit; **costume sur mesure** custom-made or tailor-made suit; **costume tailleur** lady's tailor-made suit

costumer [kɔstyme] *tr & ref* to dress up (*for a fancy-dress ball*); **se costumer en** to come dressed as a

costu·mier [kɔstymje] **-mière** [mjer] *mf* costumer

cote [kɔt] *f* assessment, quota; identification mark, letter, or number; **call number** (*of book*); altitude (*above sea level*); bench mark; book value (*of, e.g., used cars*); racing odds; (telv) rating; **avoir la cote** (coll) to be highly thought of; **cote d'alerte** danger point; **cote d'amour** moral qualifications; **cote de la Bourse** stock-market quotations; **cote mal taillée** rough compromise

côte [kot] *f* rib; chop; coast; slope; **à côtes** ribbed, corded; **aller** or **se mettre à la côte**, **faire côte** to run aground; **avoir les côtes en long** (coll) to feel lazy; **côte à côte** side by side; **côte d'Azur** French Riviera; **côtes découvertes, plates côtes** spareribs; **en côte** uphill; **être à la côte** to be broke; **faire côte** to run aground

co·té -tée [kote] *adj* listed (*on the stock market*); (fig) esteemed

côté [kote] *m* side; **à côté** in the next room; near; **à côté de** beside; **côté cour** (theat) stage right; **côté jardin** (theat) stage left; **d'à côté** next-door; **de côté** sideways; sidelong; aside; **de mon côté** for my part; **donner, passer,** or **toucher à côté** to miss the mark; **du côté de** in the direction of, toward; on the side of; **d'un côté ... de l'autre côté** or **d'un autre côté** on the one hand ... on the other hand; **répondre à côté** to miss the point

co·teau [koto] *m* (*pl* **-teaux**) knoll; slope

Côte-de-l'Or [kotdəlor] *f* Gold Coast

côte·lé -lée [kotle] *adj* ribbed, corded

côtelette [kotlet] *f* cutlet, chop; **côtelettes découvertes** spareribs

coter [kote] *tr* to assess; to mark; to number; to esteem; (com) to quote, to give a quotation on; (geog) to mark the elevations on

coterie [kotri] *f* coterie, clique

cothurne [kotyrn] *m* buskin

cô·tier [kotje] **-tière** [tjer] *adj* coastal

cotir [kotir] *tr* to bruise (*fruit*)

cotisation [kotizɑsjɔ̃] *f* dues; assessment

cotiser [kotize] *tr* to assess (*each member of a group*) ‖ *intr* to pay one's dues ‖ *ref* to club together

coton [kotɔ̃] *m* cotton; **c'est coton** (slang) it's difficult; **coton de verre** glass wool; **coton hydrophile** absorbent cotton; cotton batting; **élever dans le coton** to coddle; **filer un mauvais coton** (coll) to be in a bad way

cotonnade [kotonad] *f* cotton cloth

cotonner [kotone] *tr* to pad or stuff with cotton ‖ *ref* to become fluffy; to become spongy or mealy

cotonnerie [kotonri] *f* cotton field; cotton mill

coton·neux [kotonø] **coton·neuse** [kotonøz] *adj* cottony; spongy, mealy

coton·nier [kotonje] **-nière** [njer] *adj* cotton ‖ *mf* cotton picker ‖ *m* cotton plant

côtoyer [kotwaje] §47 *tr* to skirt (*the edge*); to hug (*the shore*); to border on (*the truth, the ridiculous, etc.*)

cotre [kotr] *m* (naut) cutter

cotte [kot] *f* petticoat; peasant skirt; overalls; **cotte de mailles** coat of mail

cou [ku] *m* neck; **sauter au cou de** to throw one's arms around

couard [kwar] **couarde** [kward] *adj mf* coward

couardise [kwardiz] *f* cowardice

couchage [kuʃaʒ] *m* bedding; bed for the night

cou·chant [kuʃɑ̃] **-chante** [ʃɑ̃t] *adj* setting ‖ *m* west; decline, old age

couche [kuʃ] *f* layer, stratum; coat (*of paint*); diaper; (hort) hotbed; **couche de fond** primer, prime coat; **couches strata**; childbirth, e.g., **une femme en couches** a woman in childbirth; **fausse couche** miscarriage

coucher [kuʃe] *m* setting (*of sun*); going to bed; **coucher du soleil** sunset; **le coucher et la nourriture** room and board ‖ *tr* to put to bed; to put down, lay down; to bend down, flatten; to mention (*in one's will*); **coucher en joue** to aim at; **coucher par écrit** to set down in writing ‖ *intr* to spend the night; (naut) to heel over ‖ *ref* to go to bed, to lie down; to set (*said of sun*); to bend; **allez vous coucher!** (coll) go to blazes!

couchette [kuʃet] *f* berth; crib

couci-couça [kusikusa] or **couci-couci** [kusikusi] *adv* so-so

coucou [kuku] *m* cuckoo; cuckoo clock; (coll) marsh marigold

coude [kud] *m* elbow; angle, bend, turn; **coude à coude** shoulder to shoulder; **jouer des coudes à travers** to elbow one's way through (*a crowd*)

coudée [kude] *f* cubit; **avoir ses coudées franches** to have a free hand; to have elbowroom

cou-de-pied [kudpje] *m* (*pl* **cous-de-pied**) instep

couder [kude] *tr* to bend like an elbow

coudoiement [kudwamɑ̃] *m* elbowing

coudoyer [kudwaje] §47 *tr* to elbow, to jostle; to rub shoulders with

coudraie [kudre] *f* hazel grove

coudre [kudr] §13 *tr & intr* to sew

coudrier [kudrije] *m* hazel tree

couenne [kwan] *f* pigskin; rind, crackling; mole, birthmark

couette [kwet] *f* feather bed; (little) tail; (mach) bearing; **couette de lapin** scut; **couettes** (naut) slip

cougouar or **couguar** [kugwar] *m* cougar

couiner [kwine] *intr* to send Morse code; (coll) to squeak (*said of animal*)

coulage [kulaʒ] *m* flow; leakage; casting (*of metal*); pouring (*of concrete*); (naut) scuttling; (coll) wasting

cou·lant [kulɑ̃] **-lante** [lɑ̃t] *adj* flowing, running; accommodating (*person*) ‖ *m* sliding ring; (bot) runner

coule [kul] *f* cowl; **être à la coule** (slang) to know the ropes

cou·lé -lée [kule] *adj* cast; sunken;

(coll) sunk ‖ *m* (mus) slur ‖ *f* casting; run (*of wild beasts*); **coulée** volcanique outflow of lava

couler [kule] *tr* to pour; to cast (*e.g., a statue*); to scuttle; to pass (*e.g., many happy hours*); (mus) to slur ‖ *intr* to flow; to run; to leak; to sink; to slip (away) ‖ *ref* to slip; slide; (coll) to be done for, to be sunk; **se la couler douce** (coll) to take it easy

couleur [kulœr] *f* color; policy (*of newspaper*); (cards) suit; **de couleur** colored; **les trois couleurs** the tricolor; **sous couleur de** with the pretext of, with a show of

couleuvre [kulœvr] *f* snake; **avaler des couleuvres** (coll) to swallow insults; (coll) to be gullible; **couleuvre à collier** grass snake

coulis [kuli] *m*—**coulis de tomates** tomato sauce

coulisse [kulis] *f* groove; slide (*of trombone*); (com) curb exchange; (pol) lobby; **à coulisse** sliding; **coulisses** (theat) wings; (theat) backstage; **dans les coulisses** behind the scenes, out of sight; **travailler dans les coulisses** to pull strings

coulis-seau [kuliso] *m* (*pl* -seaux) slide, runner

couloir [kulwar] *m* corridor; hallway; lobby

couloire [kulwar] *f* strainer

coup [ku] *m* blow; stroke; blast (*of whistle*); jolt; **à coup de** with the aid of; **à coup sûr** certainly; **après coup** when it is too late; **à tout coup** each time; **boire à petits coups** to sip; **coup de bélier** water hammer (*in pipe*); **coup de coude** nudge; **coup de dés** throw of the dice; risky business; **coup de fer** pressing, ironing; **coup de feu, coup de fusil** shot, gunshot; **coup de fion** (slang) finishing touch; **coup de foudre** thunderbolt; love at first sight; bolt from the blue; **coup de fouet** whiplash; stimulus; **coup de froid** cold snap; **coup de grâce** last straw; deathblow; **coup de Jarnac** [ʒarnak] stab in the back; **coup de patte** expert stroke (*e.g., of the brush*); (coll) dig, insult; **coup de pied** kick; **coup d'épingle** pinprick; **coup de poing** punch; **coup de sang** (pathol) stroke; **coup de semonce** warning shot; **coup de sifflet** whistle, toot; **coup de soleil** sunburn; (coll) sunstroke; **coup de téléphone** telephone call; **coup de tête** butt; sudden impulse; **coup de théâtre** dramatic turn of events; **coup de tonnerre** thunderclap; **coup d'œil** glance, look; **coup manqué, coup raté** miss; **coup monté** put-up job, frame-up; **coups et blessures** assault and battery; **coup sur coup** one right after the other; **donner un coup de main (à)** to lend a helping hand (to); **encore un coup** once again; **en venir aux coups** to come to blows; **être dans le coup** (coll) to be in on it; **faire coup double** to kill two birds with one stone; **faire les quatre coups** (coll) to

live it up, to dissipate; **faire un coup de main** to go on a raid; **manquer son coup** to miss one's chance; **se faire donner un .coup de piston** (coll) to pull wires, to use influence; **sous le coup de** under the (immediate) influence of; **sur le coup** on the spot, outright; **tout à coup** suddenly; **tout d'un coup** at one shot, at once

coupable [kupabl] *adj* guilty ‖ *mf* culprit

cou-pant [kupã] **-pante** [pãt] *adj* cutting, sharp ‖ *m* (cutting) edge

coup-de-poing [kudpwɛ̃] *m* (*pl* coupsde-poing) brass knuckles

coupe [kup] *f* champagne glass; loving cup, trophy; cup competition; cutting; cross section; wood acreage to be cut; cut (*of cloth; of clothes; of playing cards*); division (*of verse*); **coupe claire** cutover forest; **coupe de cheveux** haircut; **coupe sombre** harvested forest; **être sous la coupe de qn** (coll) to be under s.o.'s thumb; **il y a loin de la coupe aux lèvres** there is many a slip between the cup and the lip; **mettre en coupe réglée** (coll) to fleece

cou-pé -pée [kupe] *adj* cut, cut off; interrupted (*sleep*); diluted (*wine*) ‖ *m* coupé ‖ *f* gangway

coupe-circuit [kupsirkɥi] *m invar* (elec) fuse

coupe-coupe [kupkup] *m invar* machete

coupe-feu [kupfφ] *m invar* firebreak

coupe-fil [kupfil] *m invar* wire cutter

coupe-file [kupfil] *m invar* police pass (*for emergency vehicles*)

coupe-gorge [kupgɔrʒ] *m invar* deathtrap, dangerous place

coupe-jarret [kupʒarɛ] *m* (*pl* -jarrets) cutthroat

coupe-ongles [kupɔ̃gl] *m invar* nail clippers

coupe-papier [kuppapje] *m invar* paper knife, letter opener

couper [kupe] *tr* to cut; to cut off; to cut out; to break off, interrupt; to cut, water down; to turn off; to trump; to castrate, geld; **ça te la coupe!** (coll) top that!; **couper la file** (aut) to leave one's lane; **couper la parole à** to interrupt; **couper menu to mince** ‖ *intr* to cut; **couper court à** to cut (*s.o. or s.th.*) short ‖ *ref* to cut oneself; to intersect; (coll) to contradict oneself; (coll) to give oneself away

couperet [kuprɛ] *m* cleaver; guillotine blade

couperose [kuproz] *f* (pathol) acne

cou-peur [kupœr] **-peuse** [pφz] *mf* cutter; **coupeur de bourses** (coll) purse snatcher; **coupeur d'oreilles** (coll) hatchet man, hired thug

couplage [kuplaʒ] *m* (mach) coupling

couple [kupl] *m* couple (*e.g., of friends, cronies, thieves, etc.; man and wife*); pair (*e.g., of pigeons*); (mech) couple, torque; **couple thermo-électrique** thermoelectric couple;

maître couple (naut) midship frame ‖ *f* yoke (*of oxen*); couple; leash

coupler [kuple] *tr* to couple; to pair

coupleur [kuplœr] *m* (mach) coupler

coupole [kupɔl] *f* cupola

coupon [kupɔ̃] *m* coupon; remnant (*of cloth*); theater ticket

coupon-réponse [kupɔ̃repɔ̃s] *m*—**coupon-réponse international** international (postal) reply coupon; **coupon-réponse postal** return-reply post card or letter

coupure [kupyr] *f* cut, incision, slit; cut, deletion; newspaper clipping; small note; interruption, break; drain (*e.g., through a marsh*)

cour [kur] *f* court; courtyard; courtship; **bien en cour** in favor; **cour anglaise** courtyard or court (*of apartment building*); **cour d'appel** appellate court; **cour d'assises** criminal court; **cour de cassation** supreme court of appeals; **cour d'école** school playground; **faire la cour à** to court; **mal en cour** out of favor

courage [kuraʒ] *m* courage; **reprendre courage** to take heart; **travailler avec courage** to work hard ‖ *interj* buck up!, cheer up!

coura·geux [kuraʒø] **-geuse** [ʒøz] *adj* courageous; hard-working

courailler [kuraje] *intr* to gallivant

couramment [kuramã] *adv* currently; fluently, easily

cou·rant [kurã] **-rante** [rãt] *adj* current; running (*water*); present-day (*language, customs, etc.*) ‖ *m* current; flow; shift (*of opinion, population, etc.*); **courant alternatif** alternating current; **courant d'air** draft; **Courant du Golfe** Gulf Stream; **dans le courant du mois** (de la semaine, etc.) in the course of the month (of the week, etc.); **être au courant de** to be informed about

courba·tu -tue [kurbaty] *adj* stiff in the joints, aching all over

courbature [kurbatyr] *f* stiffness, aching

courbaturer [kɔrbatyre] *tr* to make stiff; to exhaust (*the body*)

courbe [kurb] *adj* curved ‖ *f* curve; **courbe de niveau** contour line

cour·bé -bée [kurbe] *adj* curved, bent, crooked

courber [kurbe] *tr* to bend, curve ‖ *intr & ref* to bend, curve; to give in

courbure [kurbyr] *f* curve, curvature; **double courbure** S-curve

courette [kuret] *f* small courtyard

cou·reur [kurœr] **-reuse** [røz] *mf* runner; **coureur cycliste** bicycle racer; **coureur de cotillons** (coll) wolf; **coureur de dot** fortune hunter; **coureur de filles** Casanova, Don Juan; **coureur de girls** stage-door Johnny; **coureur de spectacles** playgoer; **coureur de vitesse** sprinter

courge [kurʒ] *f* gourd, squash

courir [kurir] §14 *tr* to run; to run after; to roam; to frequent ‖ *intr* to run; **le bruit court que** rumor has it

that; **par le temps qui court** at the present time

courlis [kurli] *m* curlew

couronne [kurɔn] *f* crown; wreath; coronet; rim (*of atomic structures*)

couronnement [kurɔnmã] *m* crowning; coronation; coping

couronner [kurɔne] *tr* to crown; to top, cap; to reward ‖ *ref* to be crowned; to be covered (*with flowers*)

courrier [kurje] *m* courier; mail; **courrier du cœur** advice to the lovelorn; **courrier mondain** gossip column; **courrier théâtral** theater section

courriériste [kurjerist] *mf* columnist

courroie [kurwa] *f* strap; belt

courroucer [kuruse] §51 *tr* (lit) to anger

courroux [kuru] *m* (lit) wrath, anger

cours [kur] *m* course; current (*of river*); tree-lined walk; rate (*of exchange*); market quotation; style, vogue; **au cours de** in the course of; **avoir cours** to be in circulation; to be legal tender; to have classes; **cours d'eau** stream, river; **cours d'été** or **cours de vacances** summer school; **cours du soir** night school; **de cours** in length (*said of a river*); **de long cours** long-range; **suivre un cours** to take a course (*in school*)

course [kurs] *f* running; race; errand; trip; ride (*e.g., in a taxi*); course, path; privateering; stroke (*of a piston*); **course à pied** foot race; **course attelée** harness race; **course au trot** trotting race; **course aux armements** arms race; **course de chevaux** horse race; **course de côte** hill climb; **course de taureaux** bullfight; **course de vitesse** sprint; **course d'obstacles** steeplechase; **courses sur route** road racing; **de course** at a run; racing (*car; track; crowd*); (mil) on the double; **en pleine course** in full swing; **faire des courses** to go shopping

cour·sier [kursje] **-sière** [sjer] *mf* messenger ‖ *m* errand boy; steed

coursive [kursiv] *f* (naut) alleyway, gangway (*connecting staterooms*)

court [kur] **courte** [kurt] *adj* short; brief; concise; choppy (*sea*); thick (*sauce, gravy*); **à court** short; **de court** by surprise; **prendre le plus court** to take a shortcut; **tenir de court** to hold on a short leash ‖ (*when standing before noun*) *adj* short, brief (*interval, time, life*) ‖ *m* court (*for tennis*) ‖ *m* court *adv* short; **demeurer court** to forget what one wanted to say; **tourner court** to turn sharp; to stop short, to change the subject; **tout court** simply, merely; plain

courtage [kurtaʒ] *m* brokerage; broker's commission

cour·taud [kurto] **-taude** [tod] *adj* stocky, short and stocky

court-circuit [kursirkɥi] *m* (pl **courts-circuits**) short circuit

court-circuiter [kursirkɥite] *tr* to short-circuit

courtepointe [kurtəpwɛ̃t] *f* counterpane

cour·tier [kurtje] -**tière** [tjer] *mf* broker; agent; **courtier électoral** canvasser

courtisan [kurtizɑ̃] *m* courtier

courtisane [kurtizan] *f* courtesan

courtiser [kurtize] *tr* to court

cour·tois [kurtwa] -**toise** [twaz] *adj* courteous; courtly

courtoisie [kurtwazi] *f* courtesy

court-vê·tu -**tue** [kurvety] *adj* short-skirted

cou·ru -**rue** [kuru] *adj* sought after, popular; **c'est couru** (coll) it's a sure thing

cou·seur [kuzœr] -**seuse** [zøz] *mf* sewer ‖ *f* seamstress; (mach) stitcher

cou·sin [kuzɛ̃] -**sine** [zin] *mf* cousin; **cousin germain** first cousin; **cousins issus de germains** first cousins once removed ‖ *m* mosquito

cousinage [kuzinaʒ] *m* cousinship; (coll) relatives

coussin [kusɛ̃] *m* cushion

coussinet [kusine] *m* little cushion; (mach) bearing

coût [ku] *m* cost; **coût de la vie** cost of living

cou·teau [kuto] *m* (*pl* -**teaux**) knife; **couteau à cran d'arrêt** clasp knife with safety catch; switchblade knife; **couteau à découper** carving knife; **couteau à ressort** switchblade knife; **couteau pliant, couteau de poche** jackknife

coutelas [kutlɑ] *m* cutlass; butcher knife

coutellerie [kutelri] *f* cutlery

coûter [kute] *tr* to cost; **coûte que coûte** cost what it may; **il m'en coûte de** + *inf* it's hard for me to + *inf*

coû·teux [kutø] -**teuse** [tøz] *adj* costly, expensive

coutil [kuti] *m* duck (*cloth*); mattress ticking

coutume [kutym] *f* custom; habit; common law; **de coutume** ordinarily

coutu·mier [kutymje] -**mière** [mjer] *adj* customary; common (*law*); accustomed ‖ *m* book of common law

couture [kutyr] *f* needlework; sewing; seam; suture; scar; **battre qn à plate couture** (coll) to beat s.o. hollow; **examiner sur toutes les coutures** to examine inside and out or from every angle; **haute couture** fashion designing, haute couture; **sans couture** seamless

couturer [kutyre] *tr* to scar

coutu·rier [kutyrje] -**rière** [rjer] *mf* dressmaker ‖ *m* dress designer ‖ *f* seamstress

couvaison [kuvezɔ̃] *f* incubation period

couvée [kuve] *f* brood

couvent [kuvɑ̃] *m* convent; monastery; convent school

couver [kuve] *tr* to brood, hatch ‖ *intr* to brood; to smolder

couvercle [kuverkl] *m* cover, lid

cou·vert [kuver] -**verte** [vert] *adj* covered; dressed, clothed; cloudy (*weather*); wooded (*countryside*) ‖ *m* cover; setting (*of table*); service (*fork and spoon*); cover charge; room, lodging;

authority (*given by a superior*); **à couvert** sheltered; **mettre le couvert** to set the table; **sous le couvert de** under cover of; **sous les couverts** under cover (*of trees*) ‖ *f* glaze

couverture [kuvertyr] *f* cover; coverage; covering; wrapper; blanket; bedspread

couveuse [kuvøz] *f* brood hen; incubator

couvre-chef [kuvrəʃef] *m* (*pl* -**chefs**) (coll) headgear

couvre-feu [kuvrəfø] *m* (*pl* -**feux**) curfew

couvre-lit [kuvrəli] *m* (*pl* -**lits**) bedspread

couvre-livre [kuvrəlivr] *m* (*pl* -**livres**) dust jacket

couvre-pieds [kuvrəpje] *m* invar bedspread; quilt

couvre-plat [kuvrəpla] *m* (*pl* -**plats**) dish cover

couvre-théière [kuvrətejer] *m* (*pl* -**théières**) tea cozy

couvreur [kuvrœr] *m* roofer

couvrir [kuvrir] §65 *tr* to cover ‖ *ref* to cover; to cover oneself; to get cloudy; to put one's hat on

cow-boy [kaubɔj], [kobɔj] *m* (*pl* -**boys**) cowboy

C.P. *abbr* (**case postale**) post-office box

C.R. [seer] *adv* (letterword) (**contre remboursement**) C.O.D.; **envoyez-le-moi C.R.** send it to me C.O.D.

crabe [krab], [krab] *m* crab; caterpillar (tractor)

crachat [kraʃa] *m* sputum, spit

cra·ché -**chée** [kraʃe] *adj* (coll) spitting (*image*)

cracher [kraʃe] *tr* & *intr* to spit

crachin [kraʃɛ̃] *m* light drizzle

crachoir [kraʃwar] *m* spittoon; **tenir le crachoir** (slang) to have the floor, to speak

crachoter [kraʃɔte] *intr* to keep on spitting; to sputter

crack [krak] *m* favorite (*the horse favored to win*); (coll) champion, ace; (coll) crackerjack

cracking [krakiŋ] *m* cracking (*of oil*)

craie [kre] *f* chalk; piece of chalk

crailler [kraje] *intr* to caw

craindre [krɛ̃dr] §15 *tr* to fear, to be afraid of, to dread; to respect ‖ *intr* to be afraid

crainte [krɛ̃t] *f* fear, dread; **dans la crainte que** or **de crainte que** for fear that

crain·tif [krɛ̃tif] -**tive** [tiv] *adj* fearful; timid

cramoi·si -**sie** [kramwazi] *adj* & *m* crimson

crampe [krɑ̃p] *f* cramp (*in a muscle*)

crampon [krɑ̃pɔ̃] *m* clamp; cleat (*on a shoe*); (coll) pest, bore

cramponner [krɑ̃pɔne] *tr* to clamp together; (coll) to pester ‖ *ref* to hold fast, hang on, cling

cran [krɑ̃] *m* notch; cog, catch, tooth; **avoir du cran** (coll) to be game (*for anything*); **baisser un cran** to come down a peg; **être à cran** (coll) to be exasperated, cross

crâne [krɑn] *adj* bold, daring ‖ *m* skull, cranium; **bourrer le crâne à qn** (coll) to hand s.o. a line

crâner [krɑne] *intr* (coll) to swagger

cra·neur [krɑnœr] **-neuse** [nøz] *adj & mf* (coll) braggart

crapaud [krapo] *m* toad; baby grand; flaw (*in diamond*); low armchair; (coll) brat; **avaler un crapaud** (coll) to put up with a lot

crapule [krapyl] *f* underworld; scum; bum, punk; **vivre dans la crapule** to live in debauchery

crapu·leux [krapylø] **-leuse** [løz] *adj* debauched, lewd, filthy

craquage [kraka3] *m* cracking (*of petroleum*)

craquement [krakmɑ̃] *m* crack, crackle

craquer [krake] *intr* to crack; to burst; (coll) to crash, fail

craqueter [krakte] §34 *intr* to crackle

crash [kraʃ] *m* crash landing

crasse [kras] *adj* gross; crass (*ignorance*) ‖ *f* filth, squalor; avarice; dross; **faire une crasse à qn** (slang) to play a dirty trick on s.o.

cras·seux [krasø] **cras·seuse** [krasøz] *adj* filthy, squalid; (coll) stingy

crassier [krasje] *m* slag heap

cratère [krater] *m* crater; ewer

cravache [kravaʃ] *f* riding whip, horsewhip

cravacher [kravaʃe] *tr* to horsewhip

cravate [kravat] *f* necktie, cravat; scarf; sling (*for unloading goods*); **cravate de chanvre** (coll) noose; **cravate de drapeau** pennant

cravater [kravate] *tr* to tie a necktie on (*s.o.*) ‖ *intr* (slang) to tell a fish story

crawl [krol] *m* crawl (*in swimming*)

crayeux [krejø] **crayeuse** [krejøz] *adj* chalky

crayon [krejɔ̃] *m* pencil; **crayon de pastel** wax crayon; **crayon de rouge à lèvres** lipstick

crayonner [krejone] *tr* to crayon, to pencil, to sketch

créance [kreɑ̃s] *f* belief, credence; **créances gelées** frozen assets; **créances véreuses** bad debts

créan·cier [kreɑ̃sje] **-cière** [sjer] *mf* creditor; **créancier hypothécaire** mortgage holder

créa·teur [kreatœr] **-trice** [tris] *adj* creative ‖ *mf* creator; originator

création [kreasjɔ̃] *f* creation

créature [kreatyr] *f* creature

crécelle [kresel] *f* rattle; chatterbox; **de crécelle** rasping

crèche [kreʃ] *f* manger; crèche; day nursery

crédence [kredɑ̃s] *f* buffet, sideboard, credenza

crédibilité [kredibilite] *f* credibility

crédit [kredi] *m* credit; (govt) appropriation

créditer [kredite] *tr* (com) to credit

crédi·teur [kreditœr] **-trice** [tris] *adj* credit (*side, account*) ‖ *mf* creditor

credo [kredo] *m invar* credo, creed

crédule [kredyl] *adj* credulous

créer [kree] *tr* to create

crémaillère [kremajer] *f* pothook;

rack; rack rail; **crémaillère et pignon** rack and pinion; **pendre la crémaillère** to have a housewarming

crémation [kremasjɔ̃] *f* cremation

crématoire [krematwar] *adj & m* crematory

crème [krem] *f* cream; **crème chantilly** whipped cream; **crème de démaquillage** cleansing cream; **crème fouettée** whipped cream; **crème glacée** ice cream

crémer [kreme] §10 *intr* to cream

crémerie [kremri] *f* dairy; milkhouse (*on a farm*); dairy luncheonette

cré·meux [kremø] **-meuse** [møz] *adj* creamy

crémier [kremje] *m* dairyman

crémière [kremjer] *f* dairymaid; cream pitcher

crémone [kremɔn] *f* casement bolt

cré·neau [kreno] *m* (*pl* **-neaux**) crenel; loophole; **créneaux** battlements

créneler [krenle] §34 *tr* to crenelate; to tooth (*a wheel*); to mill (*a coin*)

créole [kreɔl] *adj* Creole ‖ *m* Creole (*language*) ‖ (*cap*) *mf* Creole (*person*)

crêpe [krep] *m* crepe ‖ *f* pancake

crépitation [krepitasjɔ̃] *f* crackle

crépitement [krepitmɑ̃] *m* crackling

crépiter [krepite] *intr* to crackle

cré·pu -pue [krepy] *adj* crimped, frizzly, crinkled

crépuscule [krepyskyl] *m* twilight

cresson [kresɔ̃] *m* cress; **cresson de fontaine** watercress

crête [kret] *f* crest; **crête de coq** cockscomb

Crète [kret] *f* Crete; **la Crète** Crete

crête-de-coq [kretdəkɔk] *f* (*pl* **crêtes-de-coq**) (bot) cockscomb

cré·tin [kretɛ̃] **-tine** [tin] *mf* cretin; (coll) jackass, fathead

cré·tois [kretwa] **-toise** [twaz] *adj* Cretan ‖ (*cap*) *mf* Cretan

creuser [krøze] *tr* to dig, excavate; to hollow out; to furrow; to go into thoroughly ‖ *ref*—**se creuser la tête** (coll) to rack one's brains

creuset [krøze] *m* crucible

creux [krø] **creuse** [krøz] *adj* hollow; concave; sunken, deep-set; empty (*stomach*); deep (*voice*); off-peak (*hours*); **songer creux** to dream idle dreams; **sonner creux** to sound hollow ‖ *m* hollow (*of hand*); hole (*in ground*); pit (*of stomach*); trough (*of wave*); **creux de l'aisselle** armpit; **creux des reins** small of the back

crevaison [krəvezɔ̃] *f* blowout

crevasse [krəvas] *f* crevice; crack (*in skin*); rift (*in clouds*); flaw (*in metal*)

crevasser [krəvase] *tr* to chap ‖ *intr & ref* to crack, to chap

crève-cœur [krevkœr] *m invar* heartbreak, keen disappointment

crever [krəve] §2 *tr* to burst; to work to death (*e.g., a horse*) ‖ *intr* to burst; to split; to burst, go flat (*said of a tire*); (slang) to die, kick the bucket ‖ *ref* to work oneself to death

crevette [krəvet] *f* shrimp; **crevette**

grise shrimp; **crevette rose, crevette bouquet** prawn
C.-R.F. *abbr* (Croix-Rouge française) French Red Cross
cri [kri] *m* cry; shout; whine, squeal; **dernier cri** last word, latest thing
criailler [kriaje] *intr* to honk (*said of goose*); (coll) to whine, complain, grouse; **criailler après, criailler contre** (coll) to nag at
criaillerie [kriɑjri] *f* (coll) shouting; (coll) whining, complaining; (coll) nagging
criant [krijã] **criante** [krijãt] *adj* crying (*shame*); obvious (*truth*); flagrant (*injustice*)
criard [krijar] **criarde** [krijard] *adj* complaining; shrill (*voice*); loud (*color*); pressing (*debts*) || *mf* complainer || *f* scold, shrew
crible [kribl] *m* sieve; **crible à gravier** gravel screen; **crible à minéral** jig; **passer au crible** to sift or screen
cri-blé -blée [krible] *adj* riddled (*with, e.g., debts*); pitted (*by, e.g., smallpox*)
cribler [krible] *tr* to sift, screen; to riddle; **cribler de ridicule** to cover with ridicule
cric [krik] *m* (aut) jack || *interj* crack!, snap!
cricket [kriket] *m* (sports) cricket
cricri [krikri] *m* (ent) cricket
crier [krije] *tr* to cry; to cry out; to shout; to cry for (*revenge*); **crier misère** to complain of being poor; to cry poverty (*said of clothing, furniture, etc.*) || *intr* to cry; to cry out; to shout; to creak, to squeak; to squeal; **crier à** to cry out against (*scandal, injustice, etc.*); to cry for (*help*); **crier après** to yell at, to bawl out; **crier contre** to cry out against; to rail at
crieur [krijœr] **crieuse** [krijøz] *mf* crier; hawker, peddler; **crieur public** town crier
crime [krim] *m* crime; felony
crimi·nel -nelle [kriminel] *adj & mf* criminal
crin [krɛ̃] *m* horsehair (*on mane and tail*); **à tous crins** out-and-out, hardcore (*e.g., revolutionist*)
crinière [krinjer] *f* mane
crique [krik] *f* cove
criquet [krike] *m* locust; weak wine; (coll) shrimp (*person*)
crise [kriz] *f* crisis; **crise d'appendicite** appendicitis attack; **crise de foi** shaken faith; **crise de main-d'œuvre** labor shortage; **crise de nerfs** fit of hysterics; **crise du foie** liver upset; **crise du logement** housing shortage; **crise économique** (com) depression
cris·pant [krispã] **-pante** [pãt] *adj* irritating, annoying
crispation [krispɑsjɔ̃] *f* contraction, shriveling up; (coll) fidgeting
crisper [krispe] *tr* to contract, clench; (coll) to make fidgety || *ref* to contract, to curl up
crisser [krise] *tr* to grind or grit (*one's teeth*) || *intr* to grate, crunch

cris·tal [kristal] *m* (*pl* -taux [to]) crystal; **cristal de roche** rock crystal; **cristal taillé** cut glass; **cristaux** glassware; **cristaux de soude** washing soda
cristal·lin [kristalɛ̃] **cristal·line** [kristalin] *adj* crystalline || *m* crystalline lens (*of the eye*)
cristalliser [kristalize] *tr, intr, & ref* to crystallize
critère [kriter] *m* criterion
critérium [kriterjɔm] *m* championship game
critiquable [kritikabl] *adj* open to criticism, questionable
critique [kritik] *adj* critical || *mf* critic || *f* criticism; critics; **critiques** censure
critiquer [kritike] *tr* to criticize, find fault with || *intr* to find fault
critiqueur [kritikœr] *m* critic, faultfinder
croassement [krɔasmã] *m* croak, caw, croaking (*of raven*)
croasser [krɔase] *intr* to croak, to caw
croate [krɔat] *adj* Croatian || *m* Croat, Croatian (*language*) || (*cap*) *mf* Croatian (*person*)
croc [kro] *m* hook; fang (*of dog*); tusk (*of walrus*)
croc-en-jambe [krɔkɑ̃ʒɑ̃b] *m* (*pl* **crocs-en-jambes** [krɔkɑ̃ʒɑ̃b])—**faire un croc-en-jambe à qn** to trip s.o. up
croche [krɔʃ] *f* (mus) quaver
crochet [krɔʃe] *m* hook; fang (*of snake*); crochet work; crochet needle; picklock; **crochet radiophonique** talent show; **crochets** (typ) brackets; **faire un crochet** to swerve; **vivre aux crochets de** to live on or at the expense of
crocheter [krɔʃte] §2 *tr* to pick (*a lock*)
crocheteur [krɔʃtœr] *m* picklock; porter
cro·chu -chue [krɔʃy] *adj* hooked (*e.g., nose*); crooked; **avoir les mains crochues** to be light-fingered
crocodile [krɔkɔdil] *m* crocodile
crocus [krokys] *m* crocus
croire [krwar] §16 *tr* to believe; **croire + inf** to think that + *ind*; **croire qn + adj** to believe s.o. to be + *adj*; **croire que non** to think not; **croire que oui** to think so; **je crois bien** or **je le crois bien** I should say so || *intr* to believe; **croire à** to believe in; **croire en Dieu** to believe in God; **j'y crois** I believe in it || *ref* to believe oneself to be
croisade [krwazad] *f* crusade
croi·sé -sée [krwaze] *adj* crossed; twilled (*cloth*); double-breasted (*suit*); alternate (*rhymes*) || *m* Crusader || *f* crossing, crossroads
croisement [krwazmã] *m* crossing; intersection; meeting, passing (*of two vehicles*); cross-breeding; **croisement en trèfle** cloverleaf, cloverleaf intersection
croiser [krwaze] *tr* to cross; to fold over; to meet, to pass || *intr* to fold over, to lap; to cruise || *ref* to cross, intersect; to go on a crusade

croiseur [krwazœr] *m* cruiser; **croiseur de bataille** battle cruiser

croisière [krwazjer] *f* cruise; **en croisière** cruising

croissance [krwasɑ̃s] *f* growth

crois·sant [krwasɑ̃] **crois·sante** [krwasɑ̃t] *adj* growing, increasing, rising || *m* crescent; crescent roll; billhook

croître [krwɑtr] §17 *intr* to grow; to increase, to rise

croix [krwɑ] *f* cross; (typ) dagger; **croix gammée** swastika; **en croix** crossed, crosswise

Croix-Rouge [krwɑruʒ] *f* Red Cross

cro·quant [krokɑ̃] **-quante** [kɑ̃t] *adj* crisp, crunchy || *m* wretch

croque-mitaine [krokmiten] *m* (*pl* -**mitaines**) bugaboo, bogeyman

croque-monsieur [krokməsjø] *m invar* grilled ham-and-cheese sandwich

croque-mort [krokmɔr] *m* (*pl* -**morts**) (coll) funeral attendant

croquer [kroke] *tr* to munch; to sketch; to dissipate (*a fortune*) || *intr* to crunch

croquet [kroke] *m* croquet; almond cookie

croquis [kroki] *m* sketch; draft, outline; **croquis coté** diagram, sketch

crosse [kros] *f* crosier; butt (*of gun*); hockey stick; lacrosse stick; golf club; **chercher des crosses à** (slang) to pick a fight with; **mettre la crosse en l'air** to show the white flag, to surrender

crotale [krotal] *m* rattlesnake

crotte [krot] *f* dung; mud; **crotte de chocolat** chocolate cream (candy)

crotter [krote] *tr* to dirty || *ref* to get dirty; to commit a nuisance (*said of dog*)

crottin [krotɛ̃] *m* horse manure

crouler [krule] *intr* to collapse

croup [kru] *m* (pathol) croup

croupe [krup] *f* croup, rump; ridge, brow; **en croupe** behind the rider

croupetons [kruptɔ̃]—**à croupetons** squatting

crou·pi -pie [krupi] *adj* stagnant

croupier [krupje] *m* croupier; financial partner

croupière [krupjer] *f* crupper; **tailler des croupières à** (coll) to make it hard for

croupion [krupjɔ̃] *m* rump

croupir [krupir] *intr* to stagnate; to wallow (*in vice, filth*); to remain (*e.g., in ignorance*)

croustil·lant [krustijɑ̃] **croustil·lante** [krustijɑ̃t] *adj* crisp, crunchy, spicy (*story*)

croustille [krustij] *f* piece of crust; snack; **croustilles** potato chips

croustiller [krustije] *intr* to munch, to nibble

croustil·leux [krustijø] **croustil·leuse** [krustijøz] *adj* spicy (*story*)

croûte [krut] *f* crust; pastry shell (*of meat pie*); scab (*of wound*); (coll) daub, worthless painting; **casser la croûte** (coll) to have a snack

croû·teux [krutø] **-teuse** [tøz] *adj* scabby

croûton [krutɔ̃] *m* crouton; heel (*of bread*); **vieux croûton** (coll) old dodo

croyable [krwajabl], [krwajabl] *adj* believable

croyance [krwajɑ̃s] *f* belief

croy·ant [krwajɑ̃] **croyante** [krwajɑ̃t] *adj* believing || *mf* believer

C.R.S. [seeres] *fpl* (letterword) (Compagnies républicaines de sécurité) state troopers

cru crue [kry] *adj* raw, uncooked; indigestible; crude (*language; art*); glaring, harsh (*light*); hard (*water*); plain (*terms*); **à cru** directly; bareback || *m* region (*in which s.th. is grown*); vineyard; vintage; **de son cru** of his own invention; **du cru local**, at the vineyard || see **crue**

cruauté [kryote] *f* cruelty

cruche [kryʃ] *f* pitcher, jug

cruchon [kryʃɔ̃] *m* small pitcher or jug

cru·cial -ciale [krysjal] *adj* (*pl* -**ciaux** [sjo]) crucial; cross-shaped

crucifiement [krysifimɑ̃] *m* crucifixion

crucifier [krysifje] *tr* to crucify

crucifix [krysifi] *m* crucifix

crucifixion [krysifiksjɔ̃] *f* crucifixion

crudité [krydite] *f* crudity; indigestibility; rawness (*of food*); harshness (*of light*); hardness (*of water*); **crudités** raw fruits and vegetables; off-color remarks

crue [kry] *f* overflow (*of river*); growth

cruel cruelle [kryel] *adj* cruel

cruellement [kryelmɑ̃] *adv* cruelly; sorely

crû·ment [krymɑ̃] *adv* crudely; roughly

crustacé [krystase] *m* crustacean

crypte [kript] *f* crypt

CᵗᵉCᵗ *abbr* (**compte courant**) current account

cubage [kybaʒ] *m* volume

cu·bain [kybɛ̃] **-baine** [ben] *adj* Cuban || (*cap*) *mf* Cuban

cube [kyb] *adj* cubic || *m* cube

cuber [kybe] *tr* to cube

cubique [kybik] *adj* cubic

cueillaison [kœjɛzɔ̃] *f* picking, gathering; harvest time

cueil·leur [kœjœr] **cueil·leuse** [kœjøz] *mf* picker; fruit picker

cueillir [kœjir] §18 *tr* to pick; to pluck; to gather; to win (*laurels*); to steal (*a kiss*); (coll) to nab (*a thief*); (coll) to pick up (*a friend*)

cuiller or **cuillère** [kɥijer] *f* spoon; ladle (*for molten metal*); scoop (*of a dredger*); **cuiller à bouche** tablespoon; **cuiller à café** teaspoon; **cuiller à pot** ladle; **cuiller à soupe** soupspoon; **cuiller et fourchette** fork and spoon

cuillerée [kɥijre] *f* spoonful

cuilleron [kɥijrɔ̃] *m* bowl (*of spoon*)

cuir [kɥir] *m* leather; hide; **cuir chevelu** scalp; **cuir verni** patent leather; **cuir vert** rawhide; **faire des cuirs** to make mistakes in liaison

cuirasse [kɥiras] *f* cuirass, breastplate; armor

cuiras·sé -sée [kɥirase] *adj* armored || *m* battleship

uirasser [kцirase] *tr* to armor || *ref* to steel oneself

cuire [kцir] §19 *tr* to cook; to ripen || *intr* to cook; to sting, smart; **faire cuire** to cook; **il vous en cuira** you'll suffer for it

cul•sant [kцizɑ̃] -**sante** [zɑ̃t] *adj* stinging, smarting

cuisine [kцizin] *f* kitchen; cooking; cuisine; (coll) skulduggery; **cuisine roulante** chuck wagon, field kitchen; **faire la cuisine** to cook

cuisiner [kцizine] *tr* to cook; (coll) to grill (*a suspect*); (coll) to fix (*an election*) || *intr* to cook

cuisi•nier [kцizinje] -**nière** [njɛr] *mf* cook || *f* kitchen stove, cookstove

cuisse [kцis] *f* thigh; (culin) drumstick; **cuisses de grenouille** frogs' legs; **il se croit sorti de la cuisse de Jupiter** (coll) he thinks he is the Lord God Almighty

cuis•seau [kцiso] *m* (*pl* -**seaux**) leg of veal

cuisson [kцisɔ̃] *f* baking, cooking; (fig) burning sensation, smarting; **en cuisson** on the stove, on the grill, in the oven

cuissot [kцiso] *m* leg (*of game*)

cuistre [kцistr] *m* pedant, prig

cuit [kцi] **cuite** [kцit] *adj* cooked; **nous sommes cuits** (coll) our goose is cooked || *f* firing (*in a kiln*); **prendre une cuite** (slang) to get soused

cuivre [kцivr] *m* copper; **cuivre jaune** brass; **les cuivres** (mus) the brasses

cul•vré -**vrée** [kцivre] *adj* copper-colored, bronzed; brassy, metallic (*sound or voice*)

cuivrer [kцivre] *tr* to copper; to bronze, tan; to make (*a sound or one's voice*) brassy or metallic || *ref* to become copper-colored

cul•vreux [kцivrø] -**vreuse** [vrøz] *adj* (chem) cuprous

cul [ky] *m* bottom (*of bottle, bag*); (slang) ass, hind end, rump; **faire cul sec** (slang) to chug-a-lug

culasse [kylas] *f* breechblock; (mach) cylinder head

cul-blanc [kyblɑ̃] *m* (*pl* **culs-blancs**) wheatear, whitetail

culbute [kylbyt] *f* somersault; tumble, bad fall; (coll) failure; (coll) fall (*of a cabinet*); **faire la culbute** to sell at double the purchase price

culbuter [kylbyte] *tr* to overthrow; to overwhelm (*the enemy*) || *intr* to tumble, to fall backwards; to somersault

culbuteur [kylbytœr] *m* (mach) rocker arm

cul-de-basse-fosse [kydbasfos] *m* (*pl* **culs-de-basse-fosse**) dungeon

cul-de-jatte [kydəʒat] *mf* (*pl* **culs-de-jatte**) legless person

cul-de-sac [kydəsak] *m* (*pl* **culs-de-sac**) dead end; (public sign) no outlet

culée [kyle] *f* abutment

culer [kyle] *intr* to back water

culinaire [kyliner] *adj* culinary

culmi•nant [kylminɑ̃] -**nante** [nɑ̃t] *adj* culminating; highest (*point*)

culmination [kylminɑsjɔ̃] *f* (astr) culmination

culminer [kylmine] *intr* to rise high, to tower; (astr) to culminate

culot [kylo] *m* base, bottom; (coll) baby of the family; **avoir du culot** (slang) to have a lot of nerve

culotte [kylot] *f* breeches, pants; forked pipe; panties (*feminine undergarment*); (culin) rump; **culotte de golf** plus fours; **culotte de peau** (slang) old soldier; **culotte de sport** shorts; **porter la culotte** (coll) to wear the pants; **prendre une culotte** (slang) to lose one's shirt; (slang) to have a jag on

culot•té -tée [kylote] *adj* (coll) nervy, fresh

culotter [kylote] *tr* to cure (*a pipe*) || *ref* to put one's pants on

culte [kylt] *m* worship; cult; divine service, ritual; religion, creed; **avoir un culte pour** to worship (*e.g., one's parents*)

cul-terreux [kyterø] *m* (*pl* **culs-terreux**) (coll) clodhopper, hayseed

cultivable [kyltivabl] *adj* arable, tillable

cultiva•teur [kyltivatœr] -**trice** [tris] *adj* farming || *mf* farmer || *m* (mach) cultivator

cultiver [kyltive] *tr* to cultivate; to culture

cultu•ral -**rale** [kyltyral] *adj* (*pl* -**raux** [ro]) agricultural

culture [kyltyr] *f* culture; cultivation

cultu•rel -**relle** [kyltyrel] *adj* cultural

cumula•tif [kymylatif] -**tive** [tiv] *adj* cumulative

cunéiforme [kyneiform] *adj* cuneiform

cupide [kypid] *adj* greedy

cupidité [kypidite] *f* cupidity

Cupidon [kypidɔ̃] *m* Cupid

curage [kyraʒ] *m* cleansing, cleaning out; unstopping (*of a drain*)

curatelle [kyratel] *f* guardianship, trusteeship

cura•teur [kyratœr] -**trice** [tris] *mf* guardian, trustee

cura•tif [kyratif] -**tive** [tiv] *adj* curative

cure [kyr] *f* treatment, cure; vicarage, rectory; parish; sun porch; **n'avoir cure de rien** or **n'en avoir cure** not to care

curé [kyre] *m* parish priest

cure-dent [kyrdɑ̃] *m* (*pl* -**dents**) toothpick

curée [kyre] *f* quarry (*given to the hounds*); scramble, mad race (*for gold, power, recognition, etc.*)

cure-oreille [kyrɔrej] *m* (*pl* -**oreilles**) earpick

cure-pipe [kyrpip] *m* (*pl* -**pipes**) pipe cleaner

curer [kyre] *tr* to clean out; to dredge || *ref* (with *dat* of *reflex pron*) to pick (*one's nails, one's teeth, etc.*)

cu•rieux [kyrjø] -**rieuse** [rjøz] *adj* curious

curiosité [kyrjozite] *f* curiosity; curio; connoisseurs, e.g., **le langage de la curiosité** the jargon of connoisseurs;

curiosités sights; **visiter les curiosités** to go sightseeing

curseur [kyrsœr] *m* slide, runner

cur·sif [kyrsif] **-sive** [siv] *adj* cursory; cursive (*handwriting*) ‖ *f* cursive

cuta·né -née [kytane] *adj* cutaneous

cuticule [kytikyl] *f* cuticle

cuve [kyv] *f* vat, tub, tank

cu·veau [kyvo] *m* (*pl* **-veaux**) small vat or tank

cuver [kyve] *tr* to leave to ferment; **cuver son vin** (coll) to sleep it off ‖ *intr* to ferment in a wine vat

cuvette [kyvet] *f* basin, pan; bulb (*of a thermometer*); (chem, phot) tray

cuvier [kyvje] *m* washtub

C.V. [seve] *m* (letterword) (**cheval-vapeur**) hp, horsepower

cyanamide [sjanamid] *f* cyanamide

cyanose [sjanoz] *f* cyanosis

cyanure [sjanyr] *m* cyanide

cyclable [siklabl] *adj* reserved for bicycles

cycle [sikl] *m* cycle

cyclique [siklik] *adj* cyclic(al)

cycliste [siklist] *mf* cyclist

cyclomoteur [siklomotœr] *m* motorbi‖

cyclone [siklon] *m* cyclone

cyclope [siklɔp] *m* cyclops

cyclotron [siklɔtrɔ̃] *m* cyclotron

cygne [siɲ] *m* swan

cylindrage [silɛ̃draʒ] *m* rolling (o roads, gardens, etc.); calendering mangling

cylindre [silɛ̃dr] *m* cylinder; rolle (e.g., of rolling mill); steam roller

cylindrée [silɛ̃dre] *f* piston displace ment

cylindrer [silɛ̃dre] *tr* to roll (a road, garden, etc.); to calender, to mangle

cylindrique [silɛ̃drik] *adj* cylindrical

cymbale [sɛ̃bal] *f* cymbal

cynique [sinik] *adj & m* cynic

cynisme [sinism] *m* cynicism

cyprès [sipre] *m* cypress

cyrillique [sirilik] *adj* Cyrillic

cytoplasme [sitoplasm] *m* cytoplasm

czar [ksar] *m* czar

czarine [ksarin] *f* czarina

D

D, d [de] *m invar* fourth letter of the French alphabet

d' = **de** before vowel or mute **h**

d'abord [dabor] see **abord**

dactylo [daktilo] *mf* (coll) typist

dactylographe [daktilograf] *mf* typist

dactylographier [daktilografje] *tr* to type

dactyloscopie [daktiloskopi] *f* finger-printing

dada [dada] *m* hobby-horse; hobby, fad, pet subject; **enfourcher son dada** to ride one's hobby

dague [dag] *f* dagger; first antler; tusk

dahlia [dalja] *m* dahlia

daigner [deɲe] *intr*—**daigner** + *inf* to deign to, to condescend to + *inf*; **daignez** please

d'ailleurs [dajœr] see **ailleurs**

daim [dɛ̃] *m* fallow deer; suede

daine [den] *f* doe

dais [de] *m* canopy

dalle [dal] *f* flagstone, slab, paving block; **se rincer la dalle** (slang) to wet one's whistle

daller [dale] *tr* to pave with flagstones

dalto·nien [daltonjɛ̃] **-nienne** [njen] *adj* color-blind ‖ *mf* color-blind person

dam [dɑ̃] *m*—**au dam de** to the detriment of

damas [dama] *m* damask ‖ (cap) [damas] *f* Damascus

damasquiner [damaskine] *tr* to dama-scene

damas·sé -sée [damase] *adj & m* damask

dame [dam] *f* dame; lady; tamp, tamp-er; rowlock; (cards, chess) queen; (checkers) king; **aller à dame** (check-ers) to crown a man king; (chess) to

queen a pawn; **dames** (public sign) ladies ‖ *interj* for heaven's sake!

damer [dame] *tr* to tamp (the earth); (checkers) to crown (a checker); (chess) to queen (a pawn); **damer le pion à qn** to outwit s.o.

damier [damje] *m* checkerboard

damnation [dɑnasjɔ̃] *f* damnation

dam·né -née [dane] *adj & mf* damned

damner [dane] *tr* to damn

damoi·seau [damwazo] **-selle** [zel] *mf* (*pl* **-seaux**) (archaic) young member of the nobility ‖ *m* lady's man ‖ *f* (archaic) damsel

dancing [dɑ̃siɲ] *m* dance hall

dandiner [dɑ̃dine] *tr* to dandle ‖ *ref* to waddle along

dandy [dɑ̃di] *m* dandy

Danemark [danmark] *m*—**le Dane-mark** Denmark

danger [dɑ̃ʒe] *m* danger

dange·reux [dɑ̃ʒrø] **-reuse** [røz] *adj* dangerous

da·nois [danwa] **-noise** [nwaz] *adj* Danish ‖ *m* Danish (*language*) ‖ (cap) *mf* Dane

dans [dɑ̃] *prep* in; into; **boire dans un verre** to drink out of a glass; **dans la suite** later

danse [dɑ̃s] *f* dance; **danse guerrière** war dance

danser [dɑ̃se] *tr & intr* to dance; **faire danser** to mistreat

dan·seur [dɑ̃sœr] **-seuse** [søz] *mf* danc-er; **danseur de corde** tightrope walk-er; **en danseuse** in a standing position (taken by cyclist)

Danube [danyb] *m* Danube

d'après [dapre] see **après**

dard [dar] *m* dart; sting; snake's tongue; harpoon

darder [darde] *tr* to dart, to hurl

dare-dare [dardar] *adv* (coll) on the double

darse [dars] *f* wet dock

date [dat] *f* date; **de fraîche date** recent; **de longue date** of long standing; **en date de** from; **faire date** to mark an epoch; **prendre date** to make an appointment

dater [date] *tr* & *intr* to date; **à dater de** dating from

datif [datif] *m* dative

datte [dat] *f* date

dattier [datje] *m* date palm

daube [dob] *f* braised meat; **en daube** braised

dauber [dobe] *tr* to braise; to heckle; to slander; (coll) to pummel || *intr*—**dauber sur qn** to heckle s.o., to slander s.o.

dau-beur [dobœr] **-beuse** [bøz] *mf* heckler

dauphin [dofɛ̃] *m* dolphin; dauphin

dauphine [dofin] *f* dauphiness

dauphinelle [dofinɛl] *f* delphinium

davantage [davɑ̃taʒ] §90 *adv* more; any more; any longer; **ne . . . davantage** no more; **pas davantage** no longer

de [də] §77, §78, §79 *prep* of, from; with, e.g., **frapper d'une épée** to strike with a sword; (to indicate the agent with the passive voice) by, e.g., **ils sont aimés de tous** they are loved by all; (to indicate the point of departure) from, e.g., **de Paris à Madrid** from Paris to Madrid; (to indicate the point of arrival) for, e.g., **le train de Paris** the train for Paris; (with a following infinitive after certain verbs) to, e.g., **il essaie d'écrire la lettre** he is trying to write the letter; (with a following infinitive after an adjective used with the impersonal expression **il est**) to, e.g., **il est facile de chanter cette chanson** it is easy to sing that song; (after **changer, se souvenir, avoir besoin**, etc.), e.g., **changer de vêtements** to change clothes; (after a comparative and before a numeral) than, e.g., **plus de quarante** more than forty; (to express the indefinite plural or partitive idea), e.g., **de l'eau** water, some water; (to form prepositional phrases with some adverbs), e.g., **auprès de vous** near you; (with the historical infinitive), e.g., **et chacun de pleurer** and everyone cried

dé [de] *m* die (*singular of dice*); thimble; domino; golf tee; **dés** dice

déambuler [deɑ̃byle] *intr* to stroll

débâcle [debɑkl] *m* debacle; breakup (*of ice*)

débâcler [debɑkle] *intr* to break up (*said of ice in a river*)

déballage [debalaʒ] *m* unpacking; cutrate merchandise (*sold by street vendor*)

déballer [debale] *tr* to unpack (*merchandise*); to display (*merchandise*)

débandade [debɑ̃dad] *f* rout, stampede; **à la débandade** in confusion, helter-skelter

débander [debɑ̃de] *tr* to rout, to stampede; to slacken (*s.th. under tension*); to unwind; **débander les yeux à qn** to take the blindfold from s.o.'s eyes || *intr* to flee, to stampede

débaptiser [debatize] *tr* to change the name of, to rename

débarbouiller [debarbuje] *tr* to wash the face of

débarcadère [debarkadɛr] *m* wharf, dock, landing platform

débarder [debarde] *tr* to unload

débardeur [debardœr] *m* stevedore, longshoreman

débar-qué -quée [debarke] *adj* disembarking || *mf* new arrival || *m* disembarkment; **au débarqué** on arrival

débarquement [debarkmɑ̃] *m* disembarkation

débarquer [debarke] *m*—**au débarquer de qn** at the moment of s.o.'s arrival || *tr* to unload; to lower (*a lifeboat, seaplane, etc.*); (coll) to sack (*s.o.*) || *intr* to disembark, get off

débarras [debara] *m* catchall

débarrasser [debarase] *tr* to disencumber, to disentangle; to clear (*the table*); to rid || *ref*—**se débarrasser de** to get rid of

débarrer [debare] *tr* to unbar

débat [deba] *m* debate; dispute; **débats** discussion (*in a meeting*); proceedings (*in a court*)

débâter [debɑte] *tr* to unsaddle

débattre [debatr] §7 *tr* to debate, argue, discuss; to haggle over (*a price*); to question (*items in an account*) || *ref* to struggle; to be debated

débauche [deboʃ] *f* debauch, debauchery; riot (*e.g., of colors*); overeating; striking, quitting work

débaucher [deboʃe] *tr* to debauch; to induce (*a worker*) to strike; to lay off (*workers*); to steal (*a worker*) from another employer || *ref* to become debauched

débile [debil] *adj* weak || *mf* mental defective

débilité [debilite] *f* debility

débiliter [debilite] *tr* to debilitate

débiner [debine] *tr* (slang) to run (*s.o.*) down || *ref* (slang) to fly the coop

débit [debi] *m* debit; retail sale; shop; cutting up (*of wood*); output; way of speaking

débiter [debite] *tr* to debit; to cut up in pieces; to retail; to produce; to speak (*one's part*); to repeat thoughtlessly

débi-teur [debitœr] **-trice** [tris] *adj* debit (*account, balance*); delivery (*spool*) || *mf* debtor || **-teur** [tœr] **-teuse** [tøz] *mf* gossip, talebearer; salesclerk

déblai [deble] *m* excavation; **déblais** rubble, fill

déblaiement [deblemɑ̃] *m* clearing away

déblatérer [deblatere] §10 *tr* to bluster or fling (*threats, abuse*) || *intr*—**déblatérer contre** to rail at

déblayer [debleje] §49 *tr* to clear, to clear away

débloquer [debloke] *tr* to unblock; to unfreeze (*funds, credits, etc.*)

déboire [debwar] *m* unpleasant aftertaste; disappointment

déboisement [debwazmɑ̃] *m* deforestation

déboîter [debwate] *tr* to disconnect (*pipe*); to dislocate (*a shoulder*) || *intr* to move into another lane (*said of automobile*); (naut) to haul (*out of a line*)

débonder [debɔ̃de] *tr* to unbung

débonnaire [debɔnɛr] *adj* good-natured, easygoing; (Bib) meek

débor-dant [debɔrdɑ̃] **-dante** [dɑ̃t] *adj* overflowing

débor-dé -dée [debɔrde] *adj* overwhelmed

déborder [debɔrde] *tr* to extend beyond, to jut out over; to trim the border from; to overwhelm; to untuck (*a bed*); (mil) to outflank || *intr* to overflow; (naut) to shove off

débotté [debɔte] *m*—**au débotté** immediately upon arrival, at once

débouché [debuʃe] *m* outlet; opening (*for trade; of an attack*)

déboucher [debuʃe] *tr* to free from obstruction; to uncork || *intr*—**déboucher dans** to empty into (*said of river*); **déboucher sur** to open onto, to emerge into

déboucler [debukle] *tr* to unbuckle; to take the curls out of

débouler [debule] *tr* to fly down (*e.g., a stairway*) || *intr* to run suddenly out of cover (*said of rabbits*); to dash; **débouler dans** to roll down (*a stairway*)

déboulonner [debulɔne] *tr* to unbolt; (coll) to ruin, have fired; (coll) to debunk

débourber [deburbe] *tr* to clear of mud, to clean

débourrer [debure] *tr* to unhair (*a hide*); to remove the stuffing from (*a chair*); to knock (*a pipe*) clean

débours [debur] *m* disbursement; **rentrer dans ses débours** to recover one's investment

déboursement [debursmɑ̃] *m* disbursing

débourser [deburse] *tr* to disburse

debout [dəbu] *adv* upright, on end; standing; up (*out of bed*)

déboutonner [debutɔne] *tr* to unbutton; **à ventre déboutonné** immoderately || *ref* (coll) to get something off one's chest

débrail-lé -lée [debraje] *adj* untidy, mussed up, unkempt; loose (*morals*); vulgar (*speech*) || *m* untidiness

débrancher [debrɑ̃ʃe] *tr* to switch (*railroad cars*) to a siding; (elec) to disconnect

débrayage [debrejaʒ] *m* (aut) clutch release; (coll) walkout

débrayer [debreje] §49 *tr* to disengage, throw out (*the clutch*) || *intr* to throw out the clutch; (coll) to walk out (*said of strikers*)

débri·dé -dée [debride] *adj* unbridled

débris [debri] *mpl* debris; remains

débrouil·lard [debrujar] **débrouil·lar-** [debrujard] *adj* (coll) resourceful *mf* (coll) smart customer

débrouiller [debruje] *tr* to disentangle, to unravel; to clear up (*a mystery*); to make out (*e.g., a signature*); (coll) to teach (*s.o.*) to be resourceful || *ref* to clear (*said of sky*); (coll) to manage to get along, to take care of oneself; (coll) to extricate oneself (*from a difficult situation*)

débucher [debyʃe] *tr* to flush out (*game*) || *intr* to run out of cover (*said of game*)

débusquer [debyske] *tr* to flush out (*game; the enemy*)

début [deby] *m* debut; beginning, commencement; opening play

débu·tant [debytɑ̃] **-tante** [tɑ̃t] *adj* beginning || *mf* beginner; newcomer (*e.g., to stage or screen*) || *f* débutante

débuter [debyte] *intr* to make one's debut, to begin; to start up a business; to make the opening play

deçà [dəsa] *adv*—**deçà delà** here and there; **en deçà de** on this side of

décacheter [dekaʃte] §34 *tr* to unseal

décade [dekad] *f* period of ten days; (hist, lit) decade

décadence [dekadɑ̃s] *f* decadence

déca·dent [dekadɑ̃] **-dente** [dɑ̃t] *adj* & *mf* decadent

décaféi·né -née [dekafeine] *adj* decaffeinated, caffeine-free

décagénaires [dekaʒenɛr] *mfpl* teenagers

décaisser [dekese] *tr* to uncrate; to disburse, pay out

décalage [dekalaʒ] *m* unkeying; shift; slippage; (aer) stagger

décalcomanie [dekalkɔmani] *f* decal

décaler [dekale] *tr* to unkey; to shift

décalquage [dekalkaʒ] or **décalque** [dekalk] *m* decal

décalquer [dekalke] *tr* to transfer (*a decal*) onto paper, canvas, metal, etc.; **décalquer sur** to transfer (*a decal*) onto (*e.g., paper*)

décamper [dekɑ̃pe] *intr* to decamp

décanat [dekana] *m* deanship

décanter [dekɑ̃te] *tr* to decant

décapant [dekapɑ̃] *m* scouring agent

décaper [dekape] *tr* to scour, scale

décapiter [dekapite] *tr* to behead, to decapitate; to top (*a tree*)

décapotable [dekapɔtabl] *adj* & *f* (aut) convertible

déca·ti -tie [dekati] *adj* haggard, worn-out, faded

décatir [dekatir] *tr* to steam (*cloth*)

décaver [dekave] *tr* (coll) to fleece

décéder [desede] §10 *intr* (aux: ÊTRE) to die (*said of human being*)

décèlement [desɛlmɑ̃] *m* disclosure

déceler [desle] §2 *tr* to uncover, detect; to betray (*confusion*)

décélération [deselerasjɔ̃] *f* deceleration

décembre [desɑ̃br] *m* December

décennie [deseni] *f* decade

dé·cent [desã] -cente [sãt] adj decent

décentraliser [desãtralize] tr to decentralize

déception [desepsjɔ̃] f disappointment

décernement [dɛsɛrnəmã] m awarding

décerner [deserne] tr to award (a prize); to confer (an honor); to issue (a writ)

décès [dɛsɛ] m decease, demise

déce·vant [desvã] -vante [vãt] adj disappointing; deceptive

décevoir [desvwar] §59 tr to disappoint; to deceive

déchaînement [deʃɛnmã] m unchaining, unleashing; outburst, wave

déchaîner [deʃɛne] tr to unchain, let loose || ref to fly into a rage; to break out (said of storm)

déchanter [deʃãte] intr (coll) to sing a different tune

décharge [deʃarʒ] f discharge; drain; rubbish heap, storeroom, shed; à décharge for the defense

déchargement [deʃarʒəmã] m unloading

décharger [deʃarʒe] §38 tr to discharge; to unload; to unburden; to exculpate (a defendant) || ref to vent one's anger; to go off (said of gun); to run down (said of battery); se décharger de q.ch. sur qn to shift the responsibility for s.th. on s.o.

déchargeur [deʃarʒœr] m porter (e.g., in a market); dock hand

déchar·né -née [deʃarne] adj emaciated, skinny, bony

décharner [deʃarne] tr to strip the flesh from; to emaciate || ref to waste away

déchaus·sé -sée [deʃose] adj barefoot

déchausser [deʃose] tr to take the shoes off of (s.o.); to expose the roots of (a tree, a tooth) || ref to take off one's shoes; to shrink (said of gums)

déchéance [deʃeãs] f downfall; lapse, forfeiture (of a right); expiration, term (of a note or loan)

déchet [deʃɛ] m loss, decrease; déchet de route loss in transit; déchets waste products

décheveler [deʃəvle] §34 tr to dishevel, to muss (s.o.'s hair)

déchiffonner [deʃifɔne] tr to iron (wrinkled material)

déchiffrable [deʃifrabl] adj legible; decipherable

déchiffrement [deʃifrəmã] m deciphering, decoding; sight-reading

déchiffrer [deʃifre] tr to decipher; to sight-read (music)

déchif·freur [deʃifrœr] déchif·freuse [deʃifrøz] mf decipherer, decoder; sight-reader

déchique·té -tée [deʃikte] adj jagged, torn

déchiqueter [deʃikte] §34 tr to cut into strips; to shred; to slash

déchi·rant [deʃirã] -rante [rãt] adj heartrending

déchi·ré -rée [deʃire] adj torn; sorry

déchirer [deʃire] tr to tear, to tear up; to split (a country; one's eardrums);

to pick (s.o.'s character) to pieces || ref (with dat of reflex pron) to skin (e.g., one's knee)

déchirure [deʃirur] f tear, rent; sprain

déchoir [deʃwar] (usually used only in: inf; pp déchu; sometimes used in: pres ind déchois, etc.; fut déchoirai, etc.; cond déchoirais, etc.) intr (aux: AVOIR or ÊTRE) to fall (from high estate); to decline, to fall

dé·chu -chue [deʃy] adj fallen; deprived (of rights); expired (insurance policy)

décider [deside] tr to decide, to decide on; décider qn à + inf to persuade s.o. to + inf || intr to decide; décider de to decide, determine the outcome of, e.g., le coup a décidé de la partie the trick decided the (outcome of the) game; décider de + inf to decide to + inf || ref to decide, to make up one's mind, to resolve; se décider à + inf to decide to + inf

déci·mal -male ⌊desimal⌋ adj (pl -maux [mo]) decimal || f decimal

décimer ⌊desime⌋ tr to decimate

déci·sif [desizif] -sive [ziv] adj decisive

décision [desizjɔ̃] f decision; decisiveness

déclama·teur [deklamatœr] -trice [tris] adj bombastic || mf declaimer

déclamatoire ⌊deklamatwar⌋ adj declamatory

déclamer [deklame] tr to declaim || intr to rant; déclamer contre to inveigh against

déclara·tif [deklaratif] -tive [tiv] adj declarative

déclaration [deklarɑsjɔ̃] f declaration; déclaration de revenus income-tax return

déclarer [deklare] tr & intr to declare || ref to declare oneself; to arise, break out, occur

déclassement [deklɑsmã] m disarrangement; drop in social status; transfer to another class (on ship, train, etc.); dismantling; demoting

déclasser [deklɑse] tr to disarrange; to dismantle; to demote

déclenchement [deklãʃmã] m releasing; launching (of an attack)

déclencher [deklãʃe] tr to unlatch, disengage; to release (the shutter); to open (fire); to launch (an attack)

déclencheur [deklãʃœr] m (mach, phot) release

déclic [deklik] m pawl, catch; hair trigger

déclin [deklɛ̃] m decline

déclinaison [deklinɛzɔ̃] f (astr) declination; (gram) declension

décliner [dekline] tr & intr to decline

déclive ⌊dekliv⌋ adj sloping || f slope

déclivité [deklivite] f declivity

dé·clos ⌊deklo⌋ -close [kloz] adj in bloom

décocher [dekɔʃe] tr to let fly; to flash (a smile)

décoder ⌊dekɔde⌋ tr to decode

décoiffer [dekwafe] tr to loosen or muss the hair of; to uncap (a bottle)

|| *ref* to muss one's hair; to take one's hair down

décoincer [dekwɛ̃se] §51 *tr* to unwedge, to loosen (*a jammed part*)

décolérer [dekɔlere] §10 *intr* to calm down

décollage [dekɔlaʒ] *m* unsticking, ungluing; takeoff (*of airplane*)

décoller [dekɔle] *tr* to unstick, detach || *intr* (aer) to take off

décolletage [dekɔltaʒ] *m* low-cut neck; screw cutting; topping

décolle·té -tée [dekɔlte] *adj* décolleté || *m* low-cut neckline; bare neck and shoulders

décolleter [dekɔlte] §34 *tr* to cut the neck of (*a dress*) low; to bare the neck and shoulders of || *ref* to wear a low-necked dress

décoloration [dekɔlɔrasjɔ̃] *f* discoloration

décolorer [dekɔlɔre] *tr & ref* to bleach; to fade

décombres [dekɔ̃br] *mpl* debris, ruins

décommander [dekɔmɑ̃de] *tr* to cancel an order for; to call off (*a dinner*); to cancel the invitation to (*a guest*) || *ref* to cancel a meeting

décompléter [dekɔ̃plete] §10 *tr* to break up (*a set*)

décomposer [dekɔ̃poze] *tr & ref* to decompose

décomposition [dekɔ̃pozisjɔ̃] *f* decomposition

décompression [dekɔ̃presjɔ̃] *f* decompression

décomprimer [dekɔ̃prime] *tr* to decompress

décompte [dekɔ̃t] *m* itemized statement; discount (*to be deducted from total*); disappointment

décompter [dekɔ̃te] *tr* to deduct (*a sum from an account*) || *intr* to strike the wrong hour

déconcerter [dekɔ̃sɛrte] *tr* to disconcert

décon·fit [dekɔ̃fi] **-fite** [fit] *adj* discomfited, baffled, confused

déconfiture [dekɔ̃fityr] *f* discomfiture; downfall, rout; business failure

décongeler [dekɔ̃ʒle] §2 *tr* to thaw; to defrost

décongestionner [dekɔ̃ʒɛstjɔne] *tr* to relieve congestion in

déconseiller [dekɔ̃seje] *tr* to dissuade; **déconseiller q.ch. à qn** to advise s.o. against s.th. || *intr*—**déconseiller à qn de** + *inf* to advise s.o. against + *ger*

déconsidération [dekɔ̃siderasjɔ̃] *f* disrepute

déconsidérer [dekɔ̃sidere] §10 *tr* to bring into disrepute, to discredit

déconsigner [dekɔ̃siɲe] *tr* to take (*one's baggage*) out of the checkroom; to free (*soldiers*) from detention

décontenancer [dekɔ̃tnɑ̃se] §51 *tr* to discountenance, abash || *ref* to lose one's self-assurance

décontrac·té -tée [dekɔ̃trakte] *adj* relaxed, at ease; indifferent

décontracter [dekɔ̃trakte] *tr* to loosen

up (*one's muscles*) || *intr* to stretch one's muscles; to relax

déconvenue [dekɔ̃vny] *f* disappointment, mortification

décor [dekɔr] *m* décor, decoration; (theat) setting; **décor découpé** cutout; **décors** (theat) set, stage setting

décora·teur [dekɔratœr] **-trice** [tris] *mf* interior decorator; stage designer

décora·tif [dekɔratif] **-tive** [tiv] *adj* decorative, ornamental

décoration [dekɔrasjɔ̃] *f* decoration

décorum [dekɔrɔm] *m invar* decorum

découcher [dekuʃe] *intr* to sleep away from home

découdre [dekudr] §13 *tr* to unstitch, to rip up; to gore || *intr*—**en découdre** to cross swords || *ref* to come unsewn, to rip at the seam

découler [dekule] *intr* to trickle; to proceed, arise, be derived

découpage [dekupaʒ] *m* shooting script

découper [dekupe] *tr* to carve (*e.g., a turkey*); to cut out (*a design*); to indent (*the coast*) || *ref*—**se découper sur** to stand out against (*the horizon*)

décou·plé -plée [dekuple] *adj* wellbuilt, brawny

découpler [dekuple] *tr* to unleash

découpure [dekupyr] *f* cutting out; ornamental cutout; indentation (*in coast*)

découragement [dekuraʒmɑ̃] *m* discouragement

décourager [dekuraʒe] §38 *tr* to discourage || *ref* to become discouraged

décours [dekur] *m* wane

décou·su -sue [dekuzy] *adj* unsewn; disjointed, unsystematic; incoherent (*words*); desultory (*remarks*)

décou·vert -verte [dekuver] **-verte** [vert] *adj* uncovered, open, exposed || *m* deficit; overdraft || *f* uncovering, discovery

décou·vreur [dekuvrœr] **-vreuse** [vrøz] *mf* discoverer

découvrir [dekuvrir] §65 *tr* to discover; to discern (*in the distance*); to pick out (*with a searchlight*); to uncover || *intr* to become visible (*said of rocks at low tide*) || *ref* to take off one's hat; to lower one's guard; to clear up (*said of the sky*); to say what one is thinking; to come to light, to be revealed

décrasser [dekrase] *tr* to clean; to polish up

décré·pit [dekrepi] **-pite** [pit] *adj* decrepit

décret [dekre] *m* decree

décrier [dekrije] *tr* to decry, disparage, run down

décrire [dekrir] §25 *tr* to describe

décrocher [dekrɔʃe] *tr* to unhook, take down; (coll) to wangle; **décrocher la timbale** (coll) to hit the jackpot || *intr* to withdraw

décrochez-moi-ça [dekrɔʃemwasa] *m invar* (coll) secondhand clothing store

décroît [dekrwa] *m* last quarter (*of moon*)

décroître [dekrwatr] §17 (*pp* **décru**; *pres ind* **décrois,** etc.; *pret* **décrus,**

etc.) *intr* to decrease; to shorten (*said of days*); to fall (*said of river*)

décrotter [dekrɔte] *tr* to remove mud from; (coll) to teach how to behave

décrotteur [dekrɔtœr] *m* shoeshine boy

décrottoir [dekrɔtwar] *m* doormat; scraper (*for shoes*)

décrue [dekry] *f* fall, drop, subsiding

décrypter [dekripte] *tr* to decipher

déculotter [dekylɔte] *tr* to take the pants off of || *ref* to take off one's pants

décuple [dekypl] *adj & m* tenfold

décupler [dekyple] *tr & intr* to increase tenfold

dédaigner [dedeɲe] *tr* to disdain; to reject (*e.g., an offer*); **dédaigner de** + *inf* not to condescend to + *inf*

dédai·gneux [dedeɲø] **-gneuse** [ɲøz] *adj* disdainful

dédain [dedɛ̃] *m* disdain

dedans [dədɑ̃] *m* inside; **en dedans** inside || *adv* inside, within; **mettre dedans** (coll) to take in, to fool

dédicace [dedikas] *f* dedication

dédicacer [dedikase] §51 *tr* to dedicate, to autograph

dédicatoire [dedikatwar] *adj* dedicatory

dédier [dedje] *tr* to dedicate; to offer (*e.g., a collection to a museum*)

dédire [dedir] §40 *tr*—**dédire qn** to disavow s.o.'s words or actions || *ref* to make a retraction, to back down; **se dédire de** to go back on, to fail to keep

dédit [dedi] *m* penalty (*for breaking a contract*); breach of contract

dédommagement [dedɔmaʒmɑ̃] *m* compensation, damages, indemnity

dédommager [dedɔmaʒe] §38 *tr* to compensate for a loss, to indemnify

dédouaner [dedwane] *tr* to clear through customs; to rehabilitate (*a politician, statesman, etc.*)

dédoublement [dedubləmɑ̃] *m* splitting; subdivision; unfolding

dédoubler [deduble] *tr* to divide or split in two; to remove the lining from; to unfold; to put on another section of (*a train*)

déduction [dedyksjɔ̃] *f* deduction

déduire [dedɥir] §19 *tr* to deduce; to infer; (com) to deduct

déesse [dees] *f* goddess

défaillance [defajɑ̃s] *f* failure, failing; faint; lapse (*of memory*); nonappearance (*of witness*); **défaillance cardiaque** heart failure; **sans défaillance** unflinching

défail·lant [defajɑ̃] **défail·lante** [defajɑ̃t] *adj* failing, faltering

défaillir [defajir] §69 *intr* to fail; to falter, weaken, flag; to faint

défaire [defer] §29 *tr* to undo; to untie, unwrap, unpack; to rearrange; to let down (*one's hair*); to rid; to defeat, to rout; to wear (*s.o.*) down, to tire (*s.o.*) out || *ref* to come undone; **se défaire de** to get rid of

dé·fait [defe] **-faite** [fɛt] *adj* undone, untied; loose; disheveled; drawn

(*countenance*) || *f* defeat; disposal, turnover; (fig) loophole

défaitisme [defetism] *m* defeatism

défaitiste [defetist] *mf* defeatist

défalcation [defalkasjɔ̃] *f* deduction

défalquer [defalke] *tr* to deduct

défaufiler [defofile] *tr* to untack

défausser [defose] *tr* to straighten || *ref*—**se défausser (de)** to discard

défaut [defo] *m* defect, fault; lack (*of knowledge, memory, etc.*); flaw; chink (*in armor*); **à défaut de** in default of, lacking; **faire défaut** to abandon, fail (*e.g., one's friends*); (law) to default; **mettre en défaut** to foil

défaveur [defavœr] *f* disfavor

défavorable [defavɔrabl] *adj* unfavorable

défavoriser [defavɔrize] *tr* to handicap, to put at a disadvantage

défécation [defekasjɔ̃] *f* defecation

défec·tif [defektif] **-tive** [tiv] *adj* (gram) defective

défection [defeksjɔ̃] *f* defection; **faire défection** to defect

défec·tueux [defektɥø] **-tueuse** [tɥøz] *adj* defective, faulty

défectuosité [defektɥozite] *f* imperfection

défen·deur [defɑ̃dœr] **-deresse** [dres] *mf* defendant

défendre [defɑ̃dr] *tr* to defend; to protect (*e.g., against the cold*); **à son corps défendant** in self-defense; against one's will; **défendre q.ch. à qn** to forbid s.o. s.th. || *intr*—**défendre à qn de** + *inf* to forbid s.o. to + *inf* || *ref* to defend oneself; (coll) to hold one's own; **se défendre de** to deny (*e.g., having said s.th.*); to refrain from, to keep from

défen·du -due [defɑ̃dy] *adj* forbidden

défense [defɑ̃s] *f* defense; tusk; **défense passive** civil defense (*against air raids*); (public signs): **défense d'afficher** post no bills; **défense de dépasser** no passing; **défense de déposer des ordures** no dumping, no littering; **défense de doubler** no passing; **défense de faire des ordures** commit no nuisance; **défense de fumer** no smoking; **défense d'entrer** private, keep out, no admittance

défenseur [defɑ̃sœr] *m* defender; lawyer for the defense; stand-by

défen·sif [defɑ̃sif] **-sive** [siv] *adj & f* defensive

déférence [deferɑ̃s] *f* deference

défé·rent [deferɑ̃] **-rente** [rɑ̃t] *adj* deferential

déférer [defere] §10 *tr* to confer, award; to refer (*a case to a court*); **déférer en justice** to haul into court || *intr* to comply; **déférer à** to defer to, to comply with

déferler [deferle] *tr* to unfurl; to set (*the sails of a ship*) || *intr* to spread out (*said of a crowd*); to break (*said of waves*)

défeuiller [defœje] *tr* to defoliate || *ref* to lose its leaves

défi [defi] *m* challenge, dare; **défi à**

l'autorité defiance of authority; porter un défi à to defy; relever un défi to take a dare

défiance [defjãs] *f* distrust

dé•fiant [defjã] -fiante [fjãt] *adj* distrustful

déficeler [defisle] §34 *tr* to untie

déficience [defisjãs] *f* deficiency

défi•cient [defisjã] -ciente [sjãt] *adj* deficient

déficit [defisit] *m* deficit

déficitaire [defisiter] *adj* deficit; meager (*crop*); lean (*year*)

défier [defje] *tr* to challenge; to defy (*death, time,* etc.); défier qn de to dare s.o. to || *ref*—se défier de to mistrust

défiger [defiʒe] §38 *tr* to liquefy

défiguration [defigyrasjɔ̃] *f* disfigurement; defacement

défigurer [defigyre] *tr* to disfigure; to deface; to distort

défilé [defile] *m* defile (*in mountains*); parade, procession, line of march

défilement [defilmã] *m* (mil) defilade, cover

défiler [defile] *tr* to unstring; (mil) to put under cover || *intr* to march by, to parade, to defile || *ref* to come unstrung; to take cover; (coll) to gold-brick

défi•ni -nie [defini] *adj* definite; defined

définir [definir] *tr* to define || *ref* to be defined

définissable [definisabl] *adj* definable

défini•tif [definitif] -tive [tiv] *adj* definitive; standard (*edition*); en définitive in short, all things considered

définition [definisjɔ̃] *f* definition

définitivement [definitivmã] *adv* definitively, for good, permanently

déflation [deflasjɔ̃] *f* deflation (*of currency*); sudden drop (*in wind*)

défleurir [deflœrir] *tr* to deflower, to strip of flowers || *intr* & *ref* to lose its flowers

déflexion [defleksjɔ̃] *f* deflection

défloraison [deflɔrezɔ̃] *f* dropping of petals

déflorer [deflɔre] *tr* to deflower

défon•cé -cée [defɔ̃se] *adj* battered, smashed, crumpled; bumpy

défoncer [defɔ̃se] §51 *tr* to batter in; to stave in (*a cask*); to remove the seat of (*a chair*); to break up (*ground; a road*) || *ref* to be broken up (*said of road*)

déformation [defɔrmasjɔ̃] *f* deformation, distortion; déformation professionnelle narrow professionalism

défor•mé -mée [defɔrme] *adj* out of shape; rough (*road*)

déformer [defɔrme] *tr* to deform, distort || *ref* to become deformed

défoulement [defulmã] *m* (psychoanal) insight, recall; (coll) relief

défrai•chi -chie [defreʃi] *adj* dingy, faded

défraîchir [defreʃir] *tr* to make stale, to fade

défrayer [defreje] §49 *tr* to defray the expenses of (*s.o.*); défrayer la conversation to be the subject of the conversation

défricher [defriʃe] *tr* to reclaim; to clear up (*a puzzler*)

défricheur [defriʃœr] *m* pioneer, explorer

défriser [defrize] *tr* & *ref* to uncurl

défroncer [defrɔ̃se] §51 *tr* to remove the wrinkles from

défroque [defrɔk] *f* piece of discarded clothing

défroquer [defrɔke] *tr* to unfrock || *ref* to give up the frock

dé•funt [defɔ̃] -funte [fɔ̃t] *adj* & *mf* deceased

déga•gé -gée [degaʒe] *adj* breezy, jaunty, nonchalant; free, detached

dégagement [degaʒmã] *m* disengagement; clearing, relieving of congestion; liberation (*e.g., of heat*); exit; retraction (*of promise*); redemption, taking out of hock

dégager [degaʒe] §38 *tr* to disengage; to free, clear, release; to draw, extract (*the moral or essential points*); to give off, liberate; to take back (*one's word*); to redeem, to take out of hock

dégaine [degen] *f* (coll) awkward bearing; ridiculous posture

dégainer [degene] *tr* to unsheathe || *intr* to take up a sword

dégar•ni -nie [degarni] *adj* empty, depleted, stripped

dégarnir [degarnir] *tr* to clear (*a table*); to withdraw soldiers from (*a sector*); to prune || *ref* to thin out

dégât [dega] *m* damage, havoc

dégauchir [degoʃir] *tr* to smooth out the rough edges of (*stone, wood; an inexperienced person*)

dégel [deʒel] *m* thaw

dégeler [deʒle] §2 *tr* to thaw, to defrost; to loosen up, relax || *intr* to thaw out; il dégèle it is thawing

dégéné•ré -rée [deʒenere] *adj* & *mf* degenerate

dégénérer [deʒenere] §10 *intr* to degenerate

dégénérescence [deʒeneresãs] *f* degeneration

dégingan•dé -dée [deʒɛ̃gãde] *adj* gangling, ungainly

dégivrage [deʒivraʒ] *m* defrosting

dégivrer [deʒivre] *tr* to defrost, to de-ice

dégivreur [deʒivrœr] *m* defroster, de-icer

déglacer [deglase] §51 *tr* to deice; to remove the glaze from (*paper*)

dégommer [degɔme] *tr* to ungum; (coll) to fire (*s.o.*)

dégon•flé -flée [degɔ̃fle] *adj* flat (*tire*)

dégonflement [degɔ̃flemã] *m* deflation

dégonfler [degɔ̃fle] *tr* to deflate || *ref* to go flat; to go down, to subside (*said of swelling*); (slang) to lose one's nerve

dégorger [degɔrʒe] §38 *tr* to disgorge; to unstop, open (*a pipe*); to scour (*e.g., wool*) || *intr* to discharge, to overflow

dégour·di -die [degurdi] *adj* limbered up, lively, sharp, adroit || *mf* smart aleck

dégourdir [degurdir] *tr* to remove stiffness or numbness from (*e.g., legs*); to stretch (*one's limbs*); to take the chill off; to teach (*s.o.*) the ropes, to polish (*s.o.*) || *ref* to limber up

dégoût [degu] *m* distaste, dislike

dégoû·tant [degutã] **-tante** [tãt] *adj* disgusting, distasteful

dégoû·té -tée [degute] *adj* fastidious, hard to please || *mf* finicky person

dégoûter [degute] *tr* to disgust; **dégoûter qn de** to make s.o. dislike || *ref* to become fed up

dégoutter [degute] *intr* to drip, trickle

dégradation [degradasjɔ̃] *f* degradation; defacement; shading off, graduation; worsening (*of a situation*); (mil) demotion; **dégradation civique** loss of civil rights

dégrader [degrade] *tr* to degrade, to bring down; to deface; to shade off, to graduate; (mil) to demote, to break || *ref* to debase oneself; to become dilapidated

dégrafer [degrafe] *tr* to unhook, to unclasp

dégraissage [degresaʒ] *m* dry cleaning

dégraisser [degrese] *tr* to remove grease from; to dry-clean

dégrais·seur [degresœr] **dégrais·seuse** [degresøz] *mf* dry cleaner, cleaner and dyer

degré [dəgre] *m* degree; step (*of stairs*); **monter d'un degré** to take a step up (*on the ladder of success*)

dégringolade [degrɛ̃gɔlad] *f* (coll) tumble; (coll) comedown, collapse, downfall

dégringoler [degrɛ̃gɔle] *tr* to bring down (*a government*) || *intr* (coll) to tumble, to tumble down

dégriser [degrize] *tr & ref* to sober up

dégrossir [degrosir] *tr* to rough-hew; to make the preliminary sketches of; to refine or polish (*a hick*)

déguenil·lé -lée [degənije] *adj* ragged, in tatters || *mf* ragamuffin

déguerpir [degerpir] *intr* (coll) to clear out, to beat it; **faire déguerpir** to evict

déguisement [degizmã] *m* disguise

déguiser [degize] *tr* to disguise

dégusta·teur [degystatœr] **-trice** [tris] *mf* winetaster

dégustation [degystasjɔ̃] *f* tasting, art of tasting; consumption (*of beverages*)

déguster [degyste] *tr* to taste discriminatingly; to sip, drink; to consume

déhancher [deɑ̃/e] *tr* to dislocate the hip of || *intr* to swing one's hips

déharnacher [dearna/e] *tr* to unsaddle, unharness || *ref* (coll) to throw off one's heavy clothing

dehors [dəɔr] *m* outside; outward appearance; **du dehors** from without, foreign, external; **en dehors** outside; **en dehors de** outside of; beyond || *adv* outside, out; out-of-doors

déification [deifikasjɔ̃] *f* deification

déifier [deifje] *tr* to deify

déiste [deist] *adj & mf* deist

déité [deite] *f* deity

déjà [deʒa] *adv* already

déjanter [deʒɑ̃te] *tr* to take (*a tire*) off the rim || *ref* to come off

déjection [deʒeksjɔ̃] *f* excretion; volcanic debris

déjeter [deʒte] §34 *tr & ref* to warp, to spring

déjeuner [deʒœne] *m* lunch; breakfast; breakfast set; **petit déjeuner** breakfast || *intr* to have lunch; to have breakfast

déjouer [deʒwe] *tr* to foil, thwart

déjucher [deʒy/e] *tr* to unroost || *intr* to come off the roost (*said of fowl*)

déjuger [deʒyʒe] §38 *ref* to change one's mind

delà [dəla] *adv*—**au delà de** beyond; **par delà** beyond

délabrement [delabrəmã] *m* decay, dilapidation; impairment (*of health*)

délabrer [delabre] *tr* to ruin, wreck || *ref* to become dilapidated

délacer [delase] §51 *tr* to unlace

délai [dele] *m* term, duration, period (*of time*); postponement, extension; **à bref délai** at short notice; **dans le plus bref délai** in the shortest possible time; **dans un délai de** within; **dans un délai record** in record time; **dernier délai** deadline; **sans délai** without delay

délais·sé -sée [delese] *adj* forsaken, forlorn, neglected

délaissement [delesmã] *m* abandonment

délaisser [delese] *tr* to abandon, desert; to relinquish (*a right*)

délassement [delasmã] *m* relaxation

délasser [delase] *tr* to rest, refresh, relax || *ref* to rest up

déla·teur [delatœr] **-trice** [tris] *mf* informer

délation [delasjɔ̃] *f* paid informing

déla·vé -vée [delave] *adj* washed-out, weak

délayer [deleje] §49 *tr* to add water to, to dilute; **délayer un discours** to stretch out a speech

deleatur [deleatyr] *m* dele

délébile [delebil] *adj* erasable

délectable [delektabl] *adj* delectable

délectation [delektasjɔ̃] *f* pleasure

délecter [delekte] *ref*—**se délecter à** to find pleasure in

délégation [delegasjɔ̃] *f* delegation

délé·gué -guée [delege] *adj* delegated || *mf* delegate, spokesman

déléguer [delege] §10 *tr* to delegate

délester [deleste] *tr* to unballast; to unburden, relieve

délétère [deleter] *adj* deleterious

délibération [deliberasjɔ̃] *f* deliberation

délibé·ré -rée [delibere] *adj* deliberate, firm, decided

délibérer [delibere] §10 *tr & intr* to deliberate

déli·cat -cate [delika] *adj* delicate; fine, sensitive (*ear, mind, taste*); touchy; tactful; scrupulous, honest

délicatesse [delikatɛs] *f* delicacy; refinement, fineness; fastidiousness; fragility, weakness

délice [delis] *m* great pleasure || **délices** *fpl* delights, pleasures

déli-cieux [delisjø] **-cieuse** [sjøz] *adj* delicious; delightful, charming

dé-lié -liée [delje] *adj* slender (*figure*); nimble (*mind*); fine (*handwriting*); glib (*tongue*) || *m* upstroke, thin stroke

délier [delje] *tr* to untie, to loosen, to release || *ref* to come loose

délinéament [delineamɑ̃] *m* delineation

délinéer [deline] *tr* to delineate

délinquance [delɛ̃kɑ̃s] *f* delinquency; **délinquance juvénile** juvenile delinquency

délin-quant [delɛ̃kɑ̃] **-quante** [kɑ̃t] *adj & mf* delinquent; **délinquant primaire** first offender

déli-rant [delirɑ̃] **-rante** [rɑ̃t] *adj* delirious, raving

délire [delir] *m* delirium; **en délire** delirious, in a frenzy

délirer [delire] *intr* to be delirious, to rave

délit [deli] *m* offense, wrong, crime; **en flagrant délit** in the act

délivrance [delivrɑ̃s] *f* delivrance; delivery

délivre [delivr] *m* afterbirth, placenta

délivrer [delivre] *tr* to deliver

déloger [deloʒe] §38 *tr* to dislodge; (coll) to oust, to evict || *intr* to move out (*of a house*)

déloyal déloyale [delwajal] *adj* (*pl* **déloyaux** [delwajo]) disloyal; unfair, dishonest

déloyauté [delwajote] *f* disloyalty; disloyal act; dishonesty

delta [delta] *m* delta

déluge [delyʒ] *m* deluge, flood

délu-ré -rée [delyre] *adj* smart, clever; smart-alecky, forward

délurer [delyre] *tr & ref* to wise up

délustrer [delystre] *tr* to take the gloss off of

démagnétiser [demaɲetize] *tr* to demagnetize

démagogie [demagɔʒi] *f* demagogy

démagogique [demagɔʒik] *adj* demagogic

démagogue [demagɔg] *adj* demagogic || *mf* demagogue

démaigrir [demegrir] *tr* to thin down

démailler [demaje] *tr* to unshackle (*a chain*); to unravel (*e.g., a knitted sweater*); to make a run in (*a stocking*) || *ref* to run (*said of stocking*)

démailloter [demajote] *tr* to take the diaper off of

demain [dəmɛ̃] *adv & m* tomorrow; **à demain** until tomorrow; so long; **de demain en huit** a week from tomorrow; **de demain en quinze** two weeks from tomorrow; **demain matin** tomorrow morning

démancher [demɑ̃ʃe] *tr* to remove the handle of; (coll) to dislocate

demande [dəmɑ̃d] *f* request; application (*for a position*); inquiry; demand (*by buyers for goods*)

demander [dəmɑ̃de] *tr* to ask (*a favor; one's way*); to ask for (*a package; a porter*); to require, to need (*attention*); **demander q.ch. à qn** to ask s.o. for s.th. || *intr*—**demander à** or **de + inf** to ask permission to + *inf*; to insist upon + *ger*; **demander après** to ask about, ask for (*s.o.*); **demander à qn de + inf** to ask s.o. to + *inf*; **je ne demande pas mieux** I wish I could || *ref* to be needed; to wonder

deman-deur [dəmɑ̃dœr] **-deuse** [døz] *mf* asker; buyer || **-deur** [dœr] **-deresse** [drɛs] *mf* plaintiff

démangeaison [demɑ̃ʒɛzɔ̃] *f* itch

démanger [demɑ̃ʒe] §38 *tr & intr* to itch || *intr* (with *dat*) to itch; **la langue lui démange** he is itching to speak

démanteler [demɑ̃tle] §2 *tr* to dismantle (*a fort or town*); to uncover (*a spy ring*)

démaquillage [demakijaʒ] *m* removal of paint or make-up

démaquillant [demakijɑ̃] *m* cleansing cream, make-up remover

démaquiller [demakije] *tr & ref* to take the paint or make-up off

démarcation [demarkɑsjɔ̃] *f* demarcation

démarche [demarʃ] *f* gait, step, bearing; method; step, move, action

démarier [demarje] *tr* to thin out (*plants*)

démarque [demark] *f* (com) markdown

démarquer [demarke] *tr* to remove the identification marks from; to plagiarize; to mark down

démarrage [demaraʒ] *m* start

démarrer [demare] *tr* to unmoor || *intr* to cast off (*said of ship*); to start (*said of train or car*); to spurt (*said of racing contestant; said of economy*); **démarrer trop tôt** to jump the gun; **faire démarrer** to start (*a car*); **ne démarrez pas!** don't stir!

démarreur [demarœr] *m* starter (*of car*)

démasquer [demaske] *tr & ref* to unmask

démâter [demɑte] *tr* to dismast || *intr* to lose her masts (*said of ship*)

démêlé [demele] *m* quarrel, dispute; **avoir des démêlés avec** to be at odds with, to run afoul of

démêler [demele] *tr* to disentangle, unravel; to bring to light, uncover (*a plot*); to make out, discern

démembrement [demɑ̃brəmɑ̃] *m* dismemberment

déménagement [demenaʒmɑ̃] *m* moving

déménager [demenaʒe] §38 *tr* to move (*household effects*) to another residence; to move the furniture from (*a house*) || *intr* to move, to change one's residence; (coll) to become childish; **tu déménages!** (coll) you're out of your mind!

déménageur [demenaʒœr] *m* mover

démence [demãs] *f* madness, insanity; **en démence** demented

démener [demne] §2 *ref* to struggle, to be agitated; to take great pains

dé·ment [demã] **-mente** [mãt] *adj* & *mf* lunatic

démenti [demãti] *m* contradiction, denial; proof to the contrary; (coll) shame (*on account of a failure*)

démentir [demãtir] §41 *tr* to contradict, to deny; to give the lie to, to belie ‖ *intr* to go back on one's word; to be inconsistent

démériter [demerite] *intr* to lose esteem, to become unworthy

démesure [deməzyr] *f* lack of moderation, excess

démesu·ré -rée [deməzyre] *adj* measureless, immense; immoderate, excessive

démettre [demetr] §42 *tr* to dismiss (*from a job or position*); to dislocate (*an arm*) ‖ *ref* to resign, retire

démeubler [demœble] *tr* to remove the furniture from

demeurant [dəmœrã]—**au demeurant** all things considered, after all

demeure [dəmœr] *f* home, abode, dwelling; **à demeure** permanently; **dernière demeure** final resting place; **en demeure** in arrears; **mettre qu en demeure de** to oblige s.o. to; **sans plus longue demeure** without further delay

demeurer [dəmœre] *intr* to live, dwell ‖ *intr* (*aux:* ÊTRE) to stay, remain; **en demeurer** to leave off; **en demeurer là** to stop, rest there; **to leave it at that**

demi [dəmi] *m* half; (sports) center; (sports) halfback; **à demi** half; **et demi** and a half, e.g., **un centimètre et demi** a centimeter and a half; (*after* **midi** *or* **minuit**) half past, e.g., **midi et demi** half past twelve

demi-bas [dəmiba] *m* half hose

demi-botte [dəmibɔt] *f* (*pl* -bottes) half boot

demi-cercle [dəmiserkl] *m* (*pl* -cercles) semicircle

demi-clef [dəmikle] *f* (*pl* -clefs) half hitch; **demi-clef à capeler** clove hitch; **deux demi-clefs** two half hitches

demi-congé [dəmikɔ̃ʒe] *m* (*pl* -congés) half-holiday

demi-deuil [dəmidœj] *m* (*pl* -deuils) half mourning

demi-dieu [dəmidjø] *m* (*pl* -dieux) demigod

demie [dəmi] *f* half hour; **et demie** half past, e.g., **deux heures et demie** half past two

demi-finale [dəmifinal] *f* (*pl* -finales) semifinal

demi-frère [dəmifrɛr] *m* (*pl* -frères) half brother; stepbrother

demi-heure [dəmiœr] *f* (*pl* -heures) half-hour; **toutes les demi-heures à la demi-heure juste** every half-hour on the half-hour

demi-jour [dəmiʒur] *m invar* twilight, half-light

demi-journée [dəmiʒurne] *f* (*pl* -journées) half-day; **à demi-journée** halftime

démilitariser [demilitarize] *tr* to demilitarize

demi-longueur [dəmilɔ̃gœr] *f* half-length

demi-lune [dəmilyn] *f* (*pl* -lunes) half-moon

demi-mondaine [dəmimɔ̃dɛn] *f* (*pl* -mondaines) demimondaine

demi-monde [dəmimɔ̃d] *m* demimonde

demi-mot [dəmimo] *m* (*pl* -mots) understatement, euphemism; **comprendre à demi-mot** to get the drift of; to take the hint

déminer [demine] *tr* to clear of mines

demi-pause [dəmipoz] *f* (*pl* -pauses) (mus) half rest

demi-pension [dəmipãsjɔ̃] *f* (*pl* -pensions) breakfast and one meal

demi-place [dəmiplas] *f* (*pl* -places) half fare; half-price seat

demi-reliure [dəmirəljyr] *f* (*pl* -reliures) quarter binding; **demi-reliure à petits coins** half binding

demi-saison [dəmisezɔ̃] *f* in-between season; **de demi-saison** spring-and-fall (*coat*)

demi-sang [dəmisã] *m invar* half-bred horse

demi-sœur [dəmisœr] *f* (*pl* -sœurs) half sister; stepsister

demi-solde [dəmisɔld] *m invar* pensioned officer ‖ *f* (*pl* -soldes) army pension, half pay

demi-soupir [dəmisupir] *m* (*pl* -soupirs) (mus) eighth rest

démission [demisjɔ̃] *f* resignation

démissionnaire [demisjɔner] *adj* outgoing ‖ *mf* former incumbent

démissionner [demisjɔne] *tr* (coll) to fire ‖ *intr* to resign

demi-tasse [dəmitas] *f* (*pl* -tasses) halfcup; small cup, demitasse

demi-teinte [dəmitɛ̃t] *f* (*pl* -teintes) halftone

demi-ton [dəmitɔ̃] *m* (*pl* -tons) (mus) half tone

demi-tour [dəmitur] *m* (*pl* -tours) about-face; half turn; **demi-tour, (à) droite!** about face!; **au demi-tour, à droite!** to the rear!; **faire demi-tour** to do an about-face; to turn back

démobiliser [demobilize] *tr* to demobilize

démocrate [demokrat] *mf* democrat

démocratie [demokrasi] *f* democracy

démocratique [demokratik] *adj* democratic

démo·dé -dée [demode] *adj* old-fashioned, out-of-date, outmoded

démoder [demode] *ref* to be outmoded

demoiselle [dəmwazɛl] *f* single girl, young lady, miss; dragonfly; (slang) girl; **demoiselle de magasin** salesgirl; **demoiselle d'honneur** maid of honor, bridesmaid; lady-in-waiting

démolir [demolir] *tr* to demolish; to overturn (*a cabinet or government*)

démolition [demolisjɔ̃] *f* demolition; **démolitions** scrap, rubble

démon [demɔ̃] *m* demon

démoniaque [demɔnjak] *adj* demonic, demoniac(al) || *mf* demoniac

démonstra·teur [demɔ̃nstratœr] -**trice** [tris] *mf* demonstrator

démonstra·tif [demɔ̃stratif] -**tive** [tiv] *adj & m* demonstrative

démontable [demɔ̃tabl] *adj* collapsible, detachable; knockdown

démonte-pneu [demɔ̃tpnø] *m* (*pl* -pneus) tire iron

démonter [demɔ̃te] *tr* to dismount; to dismantle || *ref* to come apart; to go to pieces (*while taking an exam*)

démontrable [demɔ̃trabl] *adj* demonstrable

démontrer [demɔ̃tre] *tr* to demonstrate

démoraliser [demɔralize] *tr* to demoralize

démouler [demule] *tr* to remove from a mold

dému·ni -**nie** [demyni] *adj* out of money; **démuni de** out of; devoid of

démunir [demynir] *tr* to strip, deprive; to deplete (*a garrison*) || *ref* to deprive oneself

démystifier [demistifje] *tr* to debunk

dénationaliser [denasjɔnalize] *tr* to denationalize

dénaturaliser [denatyralize] *tr* to denaturalize

dénatu·ré -**rée** [denatyre] *adj* denatured; unnatural, perverse

dénaturer [denatyre] *tr* to denature; to pervert; to distort

dénégation [denegasjɔ̃] *f* denial

déni [deni] *m* refusal; (law) denial

dénicher [deniʃe] *tr* to dislodge; to take out of the nest; to make (*s.o.*) move; to search out || *intr* to leave the nest

déni·cheur [deniʃœr] -**cheuse** [ʃøz] *mf* hunter (*of rare books, antiques, etc.*); **dénicheur de vedettes** talent scout

denier [dənje] *m* (fig) penny, farthing; **denier à Dieu** gratuity; **deniers** money, funds; **de ses deniers** with his own money

dénier [denje] *tr* to deny, refuse

dénigrer [denigre] *tr* to disparage

déniveler [denivle] §34 *tr* to make uneven, to change the level of

dénivellation [denivɛllasjɔ̃] *f* or **dénivellement** [denivɛlmɑ̃] *m* unevenness; depression, settling

dénombrement [denɔ̃brəmɑ̃] *m* census, enumeration

dénombrer [denɔ̃bre] *tr* to take a census of, to enumerate

dénomination [denɔminasjɔ̃] *f* denomination, appellation, designation

dénommer [denɔme] *tr* to denominate, to name

dénoncer [denɔ̃se] §51 *tr* to renounce; to indicate, reveal || *ref* to give oneself up

dénonciation [denɔ̃sjasjɔ̃] *f* denunciation; declaration

dénoter [denɔte] *tr* to denote

dénouement [denumɑ̃] *m* outcome, denouement; untying

dénouer [denwe] *tr* to untie; to unravel

dénoyer [denwaje] §47 *tr* to pump out

denrée [dɑ̃re] *f* commodity; **denrées** provisions, products

dense [dɑ̃s] *adj* dense

densité [dɑ̃site] *f* density

dent [dɑ̃] *f* tooth; cog; scallop (*of an edge*); **dent d'éléphant** tusk; **dents de lait** baby teeth; **dents de sagesse** wisdom teeth; **sur les dents** on one's toes

dentaire [dɑ̃ter] *adj* dental

den·tal -**tale** [dɑ̃tal] *adj & f* (*pl* -**taux** [to] -**tales**) dental

dent-de-chien [dɑ̃dəʃjɛ̃] *f* (*pl* **dents-de-chien**) dogtooth violet

dent-de-lion [dɑ̃dəljɔ̃] *f* (*pl* **dents-de-lion**) dandelion

denteler [dɑ̃tle] §34 *tr* to notch, to indent

dentelle [dɑ̃tɛl] *f* lace; lacework

dentelure [dɑ̃tlyr] *f* notching; serration; scalloping; (phila) perforation

denter [dɑ̃te] *tr* to furnish with cogs or teeth

dentier [dɑ̃tje] *m* false teeth, denture

dentifrice [dɑ̃tifris] *m* dentifrice

dentiste [dɑ̃tist] *mf* dentist

denture [dɑ̃tyr] *f* denture; **denture artificielle** false teeth

dénuder [denyde] *tr* to strip, denude

dénuement [denymɑ̃] *m* destitution

dénuer [denɥe] *tr* to deprive, strip

déontologie [deɔ̃tɔlɔʒi] *f* study of ethics; **déontologie médicale** (med) code of medical ethics

dépannage [depanaʒ] *m* emergency service, repairs

dépanner [depane] *tr* to give emergency service to; (coll) to get (*s.o.*) out of a scrape

dépan·neur [depanœr] **dépan·meuse** [depanøz] *adj* repairing || *m* serviceman, repairman || *f* tow truck, wrecker

dépaqueter [depakte] §34 *tr* to unpack, unwrap

dépareil·lé -**lée** [depareje] *adj* incomplete, broken (*set*); odd (*sock*)

dépareiller [depareje] *tr* to break (*a set*)

déparer [depare] *tr* to mar, to spoil the beauty of; to strip of ornaments

déparier [deparje] *tr* to break, split up the pair of

départ [depar] *m* departure; beginning; division; sorting out; **départ usine** F.O.B.; **faux départ** false start

département [departəmɑ̃] *m* (govt) department

départir [departir] §64 (or sometimes like **finir**) *tr* to divide up, to distribute || *ref*—**se départir de** to give up; to depart from

dépassement [depasmɑ̃] *m* passing

dépasser [depase] *tr* to pass, overtake; to go beyond; to overshoot (*the mark*); to exceed; to extend beyond; to be longer than; (coll) to surprise || *intr* to pass; to stick out, to overlap, to show

dépayser [depeize] *tr* to take out of one's familiar surroundings; to bewilder || *ref* to leave one's country

dépecer [depəse] §20 *tr* to carve, to cut up

dépêche [depeʃ] *f* dispatch; telegram

dépêcher [depeʃe] *tr* to dispatch || *ref* to hurry

dépeigner [depeɲe] *tr* to tousle, to muss up (*the hair*)

dépeindre [depɛ̃dr] §50 *tr* to depict

dépendance [depɑ̃dɑ̃s] *f* dependence; **dépendances** outbuildings, annex; dependencies, possessions

dépen‧dant [depɑ̃dɑ̃] **-dante** [dɑ̃t] *adj* dependent

dépendre [depɑ̃dr] *tr* to take down || *intr* to depend; **dépendre de** to depend on; to belong to; **il dépend de vous de** it is for you to

dépens [depɑ̃] *mpl* expenses, costs; **aux dépens de** at the expense of

dépense [depɑ̃s] *f* expense; pantry; dispensary (*of hospital*); flow (*of water*); consumption (*of fuel*)

dépenser [depɑ̃se] *tr* to spend, expend || *ref* to exert oneself, to spend one's energy

dépen‧sier [depɑ̃sje] **-sière** [sjɛr] *adj & mf* spendthrift

dépérir [deperir] *intr* to waste away, decline

dépêtrer [depetre] *tr* to get (*s.o.*) out of a jam

dépeupler [depœple] *tr* to depopulate; to unstock (*a pond*)

dépha‧sé -sée [defaze] *adj* out of phase

dépiauter [depjote] *tr* to skin

dépiécer [depjese] §58 *tr* to dismember

dépiler [depile] *tr* to remove the hair from

dépister [depiste] *tr* to track down

dépit [depi] *m* spite, resentment; **en dépit de** in spite of

dépiter [depite] *tr* to spite, to vex || *ref* to take offense

dépla‧cé -cée [deplase] *adj* displaced (*person*); misplaced, out of place

déplacement [deplasmɑ̃] *m* displacement; movement; travel; transfer (*of an official*); shift (*in votes*); change (*in schedule*); (naut) displacement

déplacer [deplase] §51 *tr* to displace; to move; **déplacer la question** to stray from the subject || *ref* to move

déplaire [depler] §52 *intr* (with *dat*) to displease; (with *dat*) to dislike, e.g., **le lait lui déplaît** he dislikes milk; **ne vous en déplaise** if you have no objection, by your leave || *ref* to be displeased, e.g., **ils se sont déplu** they were displeased; **se déplaire à** not to like it in, e.g., **je me déplais à la campagne** I don't like it in the country

déplai‧sant [deplezɑ̃] **-sante** [zɑ̃t] *adj* unpleasant, disagreeable

déplaisir [deplezir] *m* displeasure

déplanter [deplɑ̃te] *tr* to dig up for transplanting

déplantoir [deplɑ̃twar] *m* garden trowel

dépliant [deplijɑ̃] *m* folder, brochure

déplier [deplie] *tr & ref* to unfold

déplisser [deplise] *tr* to unpleat

déploiement [deplwamɑ̃] *m* unfolding, unfurling; display, array; (mil) deployment

déplorable [deplɔrabl] *adj* deplorable

déplorer [deplɔre] *tr* to deplore; to grieve over

déployer [deplwaje] §47 *tr* to unfold, to unfurl; to display; (mil) to deploy || *ref* (mil) to deploy

déplumer [deplyme] *tr* to pluck (*a chicken*) || *ref* (coll) to lose one's hair

dépolariser [depɔlarize] *tr* to depolarize

dépo‧li -lie [depɔli] *adj* ground (*glass*)

dépolir [depɔlir] *tr* to remove the polish from; to frost (*glass*)

déport [depɔr] *m* disqualifying of oneself; (com) commission; **sans déport** without delay

déportation [depɔrtasjɔ̃] *f* deportation; internment in a concentration camp

dépor‧té -tée [depɔrte] *mf* deported criminal, convict; prisoner in a concentration camp

déportement [depɔrtəmɑ̃] *m* swerve; **déportements** misconduct, immoral conduct, bad habits

déporter [depɔrte] *tr* to deport; to send to a concentration camp; to make (*an automobile*) swerve; to deflect (*an airplane*) from its course || *intr* to swerve

dépo‧sant [depozɑ̃] **-sante** [zɑ̃t] *adj* testifying; depositing || *mf* deponent, witness; depositor

dépose [depoz] *f* removal

déposer [depoze] *tr* to deposit; to depose; to drop, leave off; to register (*a trademark*); to lodge (*a complaint*); to file (*a petition*) || *intr & ref* to depose; to settle, to form a deposit

dépositaire [depoziter] *mf* trustee, holder; dealer

déposséder [deposede] §10 *tr* to dispossess

dépôt [depo] *m* deposit; depository; depot; warehouse; delivery, handing in; **dépôt d'autobus** carbarn; **dépôt de locomotives** roundhouse; **dépôt de mendicité** poorhouse; **dépôt d'épargne** savings account; **dépôt des bagages** baggage room; **dépôt d'essence** filling station; **dépôt de vivres** commissary; **dépôt d'ordures** dump

dépouille [depuj] *f* castoff skin; hide (*taken from animal*); **dépouille mortelle** mortal remains; **dépouilles** spoils (*of war*)

dépouillement [depujmɑ̃] *m* gathering, selection, sifting; despoilment; counting (*of votes*); **dépouillement volontaire** relinquishing

dépouiller [depuje] *tr* to skin; to strip; to gather, select, sift; to count (*votes*) || *ref* to shed one's skin (*said of insects and reptiles*); to strip oneself, to divest oneself

dépour‧vu -vue [depurvy] *adj* destitute; **au dépourvu** unaware; **dépourvu de** devoid of, lacking in

dépoussiérer [depusjere] §10 *tr* to vacuum

dépravation [depravɑsjɔ̃] f depravity

dépraver [deprave] tr to deprave

déprécation [deprekɑsjɔ̃] f supplication

dépréciation [depresjɑsjɔ̃] f depreciation

déprécier [depresje] tr & ref to depreciate

déprédation [depredɑsjɔ̃] f depredation; embezzlement, misappropriation

déprendre [deprɑ̃dr] §56 ref to detach oneself; to come loose; to melt

dépres-sif [depresif] **dépres-sive** [depresiv] adj depressive

dépression [depresjɔ̃] f depression

déprimer [deprime] tr to depress, to lower || ref to be depressed

dépriser [deprize] tr to undervalue

depuis [dəpɥi] adv since; **depuis que** since || prep since, for, e.g., **je suis à Paris depuis trois jours** I have been in Paris for three days; **depuis . . . jusqu'à** from . . . to

dépurer [depyre] tr to purify

députation [depytɑsjɔ̃] f deputation

député [depyte] m deputy

députer [depyte] tr to deputize

der [der] f—**la der des der** (coll) the war to end all wars

déraci-né -née [derasine] adj uprooted || mf uprooted person, wanderer

déraciner [derasine] tr to uproot, to root out; to eradicate

déraillement [derɑjmɑ̃] m derailment

dérailler [deraje] intr to jump the track; (coll) to get off the track

déraison [derezɔ̃] f unreasonableness, irrationality

déraisonnable [derezɔnabl] adj unreasonable

déraisonner [derezɔne] intr to talk nonsense

dérangement [derɑ̃ʒmɑ̃] m derangement; breakdown; disturbance, bother

déranger [derɑ̃ʒe] §38 tr to derange, to put out of order; to disturb, trouble || ref to move, to change jobs; to become disordered, upset; **ne vous dérangez pas!** don't get up!; don't bother!

déraper [derape] intr to skid, to sideslip; to weigh anchor

dératé [derate] m—**courir comme un dératé** to run like a jack rabbit

dératiser [deratize] tr to derat

derby [dɛrbi] m derby (race)

derechef [dərəʃef] adv (lit) once again

déré-glé -glée [deregle] adj out of order; irregular (pulse); disorderly, excessive

dérégler [deregle] §10 tr to put out of order, upset || ref to get out of order; to run wild

dérider [deride] tr to smooth, unwrinkle; to cheer up || ref to cheer up

dérision [derizjɔ̃] f derision

dérisoire [derizwar] adj derisive

dérivation [derivɑsjɔ̃] f derivation; drift; by-pass; diversion (of river, stream, etc.); **en dérivation** shunted (circuit)

dérive [deriv] f drift; (aer) fin; (naut) centerboard; **à la dérive** adrift

déri-vé -vée [derive] adj drifting; shunted (current) || m derivative

dériver [derive] tr to derive; to divert (e.g., a river); to unrivet || intr to derive; to be derived; to result; to drift

dermatologie [dermatɔlɔʒi] f dermatology

der-nier [dernje] **-nière** [njer] adj last; latest; latter; final; last (just elapsed), e.g., **la semaine dernière** last week || (when standing before noun) adj last (in a series), e.g., **la dernière semaine de la guerre** the last week of the war

dernièrement [dernjermɑ̃] adv lately

dernier-né [dernjene] **dernière-née** [dernjerne] mf (pl **-nés -nées**) lastborn child

déro-bé -bée [derobe] adj secret; **à la dérobée** stealthily, on the sly

dérober [derobe] tr to steal; to hide; **dérober à** to steal from; to rescue from (e.g., death) || ref to steal away, disappear; to hide; to shy away, balk; to shirk; to give way (said of knees or one's footing); **se dérober à** to slip away from, to escape from

dérogation [derɔgɑsjɔ̃] f—**dérogation à** departure from (custom); waiving of (principle); deviation from (instructions); **par dérogation à** notwithstanding

déroger [derɔʒe] §38 intr—**déroger à** to depart from (custom); to waive (a principle); to derogate from (dignity, one's rank)

dérouiller [deruje] tr to remove the rust from; to polish (s.o.); (coll) to limber up; (coll) to brush up on || ref to lose its rust; to brush up; to limber up

dérouler [derule] tr & ref to unroll, unfold

dérou-tant [derutɑ̃] **-tante** [tɑ̃t] adj baffling, misleading

déroute [derut] f rout, downfall

dérouter [derute] tr to steer off the course; to reroute; to disconcert, baffle || ref to go astray; to become confused

derrick [derik] m oil derrick

derrière [derjer] m rear, backside || adv & prep behind

derviche [derviʃ] m dervish

des [de] §77

dès [de] prep by (a certain time); from (a certain place); as early as, as far back as; from, beginning with; **dès lors** from that time, ever since; **dès lors que** since, inasmuch as; **dès que** as soon as

désabonner [dezabɔne] tr to cancel the subscription of || ref to cancel one's subscription

désabu-sé -sée [dezabyze] adj disillusioned

désabuser [dezabyze] tr to disabuse, disillusion || ref to have one's eyes opened

désaccord [dezakɔr] *m* disagreement, discord

désaccorder [dezakɔrde] *tr* to put (*an instrument*) out of tune || *ref* to get out of tune

désaccoupler [dezakuple] *tr* to unpair; to uncouple

désaccoutumer [dezakutyme] *tr* to break (*s.o.*) of a habit || *ref* to break oneself of a habit

désaffecter [dezafɛkte] *tr* to turn from its intended use

désagréable [dezagreabl] *adj* disagreeable; unpleasant

désagréger [dezagreʒe] §1 *tr* to break up, to dissolve, to disintegrate

désagrément [dezagremɑ̃] *m* unpleasantness, annoyance

désaimanter [dezemɑ̃te] *tr* to demagnetize

désalté·rant [dezalterɑ̃] **-rante** [rɑ̃t] *adj* thirst-quenching, refreshing

désaltérer [dezaltere] §10 *tr* to quench the thirst of; to refresh with a drink || *ref* to quench one's thirst

désamorcer [dezamɔrse] §51 *tr* to deactivate, to disconnect the fuse of; to unprime

désappointement [dezapwɛ̃tmɑ̃] *m* disappointment

désappointer [dezapwɛ̃te] *tr* to disappoint; to break the point of, to blunt

désapprendre [dezaprɑ̃dr] §56 *tr* to unlearn, to forget

désapproba·teur [dezaprɔbatœr] **-trice** [tris] *adj* disapproving || *mf* critic

désapprouver [dezapruve] *tr* to disapprove of, to disapprove

désarçonner [dezarsɔne] *tr* to unhorse, buck off; (coll) to dumfound

désarmement [dezarməmɑ̃] *m* disarmament; disarming; dismantling (*of ship*)

désarmer [dezarme] *tr* to disarm; to deactivate; to dismantle; to appease || *intr* to disarm; to slacken, let up (*said of hostility*)

désarroi [dezarwa] *m* disorder, disarray, confusion

désarticulation [dezartikylasjɔ̃] *f* dislocation

désassembler [dezasɑ̃ble] *tr* to disassemble

désastre [dezastr] *m* disaster

désas·treux [dezastrø] **-treuse** [trøz] *adj* disastrous

désavantage [dezavɑ̃taʒ] *m* disadvantage

désavantager [dezavɑ̃taʒe] §38 *tr* to put at a disadvantage, to handicap

désavanta·geux [dezavɑ̃taʒø] **-geuse** [ʒøz] *adj* disadvantageous

désa·veu [dezavø] *m* (pl **-veux**) disavowal, denial, repudiation

désavouer [dezavwe] *tr* to disavow, to deny, to repudiate, to disown

désaxé désaxée [dezakse] *adj* unbalanced, out of joint

desceller [desele] *tr* to unseal

descendance [desɑ̃dɑ̃s] *f* descent

descendeur [desɑ̃dœr] *m* ski jumper

descendre [desɑ̃dr], [desɑ̃dr] *tr* to descend, to go down (*a hill, street,*

stairway); to take down, to lower (*a picture*); (coll) to bring down (*an airplane; luggage*); (coll) to drop off, let off at the door || *intr* (aux: ÊTRE) to descend; to go down, to go downstairs; to stay, to stop (*at a hotel*); **descendre + inf** to go down to + *inf*; to stop off to + *inf*; **descendre court** to undershoot (*said of airplane*); **descendre de** to come down from (*a mountain, ladder, tree*); to be descended from

descente [desɑ̃t] *f* descent; invasion, raid; stay (*at a hotel*); stop (*en route*); **descente à terre** (nav) shore leave; **descente de lit** bedside rug

descriptible [deskriptibl] *adj* describable

descrip·tif [deskriptif] **-tive** [tiv] *adj* descriptive

description [deskripsjɔ̃] *f* description

déségrégation [desegregasjɔ̃] *f* desegregation

désempa·ré -rée [dezɑ̃pare] *adj* disconcerted; disabled (*ship*)

désemparer [dezɑ̃pare] *tr* to disable (*a ship*) || *intr*—**sans désemparer** continuously, without intermission

désemplir [dezɑ̃plir] *intr*—**ne pas désemplir** to be always full

désenchaîner [dezɑ̃ʃene] *tr* to unchain

désenchantement [dezɑ̃ʃɑ̃tmɑ̃] *m* disenchantment

désenchanter [dezɑ̃ʃɑ̃te] *tr* to disenchant

désencombrer [dezɑ̃kɔ̃bre] *tr* to disencumber, to clear, to free

désengager [dezɑ̃gaʒe] §38 *tr* to release from a promise

désengorger [dezɑ̃gɔrʒe] §38 *tr* to unstop

désengrener [dezɑ̃grəne] §2 *tr* to disengage, to throw out of gear

désenivrer [dezɑ̃nivre] *tr* & *intr* to sober up

désenlacer [dezɑ̃lase] §51 *tr* to unbind

désennuyer [dezɑ̃nɥije] §27 *tr* to divert, cheer up || *ref* to find relief from boredom

désensabler [dezɑ̃sable] *tr* to free (*a ship*) from the sand; to dredge the sand from (*a canal*)

désensibiliser [desɑ̃sibilize] *tr* to desensitize

désensorceler [dezɑ̃sɔrsəle] §34 *tr* to remove the spell from

désentortiller [dezɑ̃tɔrtije] *tr* to straighten out

désenvelopper [dezɑ̃vlɔpe] *tr* to unwrap

déséquilibre [dezekilibr] *m* mental instability

déséquili·bré -brée [dezekilibre] *adj* mentally unbalanced || *mf* unbalanced person

déséquilibrer [dezekilibre] *tr* to unbalance

dé·sert [dezer] **-serte** [zert] *adj* & *m* desert

déserter [dezerte] *tr* & *intr* to desert

déserteur [dezertœr] *m* deserter

désertion [dezersjɔ̃] *f* desertion

désespérance [dezesperɑ̃s] *f* despair

désespé·ré -rée [dezespere] *adj* desperate, hopeless || *mf* desperate person

désespérer [dezespere] §10 *tr* to be the despair of || *ref* to lose hope

désespoir [dezespwar] *m* despair; **en désespoir de cause** as a last resort

déshabillage [dezabijaʒ] *m* striptease

déshabillé [dezabije] *m* morning wrap

déshabiller [dezabije] *tr & ref* to undress; **déshabiller saint Pierre pour habiller saint Paul** to rob Peter to pay Paul

déshabituer [dezabitɥe] *tr* to break (*s.o.*) of a habit

déshéri·té -tée [dezerite] *adj* underprivileged; **les déshérités** the underprivileged

déshériter [dezerite] *tr* to disinherit; to disadvantage

déshonnête [dezɔnɛt] *adj* improper, immodest

déshonnêteté [dezɔnɛtəte] *f* impropriety, immodesty, indecency

déshonneur [dezɔnœr] *m* dishonor

déshono·rant -rante [dezɔnɔrɑ̃] -**rante** [rɑ̃t] *adj* dishonorable, discreditable

déshonorer [dezɔnɔre] *tr* to dishonor

déshydratation [dezidratasjɔ̃] *f* dehydration

déshydrater [dezidrate] *tr* to dehydrate

désignation [deziɲasjɔ̃] *f* designation; appointment, nomination

dési·gné -gnée [deziɲe] *mf* nominee

désigner [deziɲe] *tr* to designate; to indicate, point out; to appoint, nominate; to signify, mean; to set (*the hour of an appointment*) || *ref*—**se désigner à l'attention de** to bring oneself to the attention of

désillusion [dezillyzjɔ̃] *f* disillusion; disappointment

désillusionner [dezillyzjɔne] *tr* to disillusion; to disappoint

désinence [dezinɑ̃s] *f* (gram) ending

désinfecter [dezɛ̃fɛkte] *tr* to disinfect

désintégration [dezɛ̃tegrasjɔ̃] *f* disintegration

désintégrer [dezɛ̃tegre] §10 *tr & ref* to disintegrate

désintéres·sé -sée [dezɛ̃terese] *adj* disinterested, impartial; unselfish

désintéressement [dezɛ̃teresmɑ̃] *m* disinterestedness, impartiality; payment, satisfaction (*of a debt*); paying off (*of a creditor*)

désintéresser [dezɛ̃terese] *tr* to pay off; to buy out || *ref*—**se désintéresser de** to lose interest in

désintoxication [dezɛ̃tɔksikasjɔ̃] *f* treatment for alcoholism, drug addiction, or poisoning; disintoxication

désinvolte [dezɛ̃vɔlt] *adj* free and easy, casual; offhanded, impertinent

désinvolture [dezɛ̃vɔltyr] *f* free and easy manner, offhandedness; impertinence

désir [dezir] *m* desire

désirable [dezirabl] *adj* desirable

désirer [dezire] *tr* to desire, wish

dési·reux -reuse [dezirø] -**reuse** [røz] *adj* desirous

désister [deziste] *ref* to desist; to withdraw from a runoff election; se dé-

sister de to waive (*a claim*); to drop (*a lawsuit*)

désobéir [dezɔbeir] *intr* to disobey; (*with dat*) to disobey; **être désobéi** to be disobeyed

désobli·geant [dezɔbliʒɑ̃] -**geante** [ʒɑ̃t] *adj* disagreeable, ungracious

désobliger [dezɔbliʒe] §38 *tr* to offend, displease, disoblige

désodori·sant [dezɔdɔrizɑ̃] -**sante** [zɑ̃t] *adj & m* deodorant

désodoriser [dezɔdɔrize] *tr* to deodorize

désœu·vré -vrée [dezœvre] *adj* idle, unoccupied, out of work; **les désœuvrés** the unemployed

désœuvrement [dezœvrəmɑ̃] *m* idleness, unemployment

déso·lant [dezɔlɑ̃] -**lante** [lɑ̃t] *adj* distressing, sad

désolation [dezɔlasjɔ̃] *f* desolation; grief, distress

déso·lé -lée [dezɔle] *adj* desolate; distressed

désoler [dezɔle] *tr* to desolate, destroy; to distress || *ref* to be distressed

désopi·lant [dezɔpilɑ̃] -**lante** [lɑ̃t] *adj* hilarious, sidesplitting

désordon·né -née [dezɔrdɔne] *adj* disordered; untidy; disorderly

désordonner [dezɔrdɔne] *tr* to upset, confuse

désordre [dezɔrdr] *m* disorder, confusion; moral laxity

désorganisa·teur [dezɔrganizatœr] -**trice** [tris] *adj* disorganizing || *mf* troublemaker

désorganisation [dezɔrganizasjɔ̃] *f* disorganization

désorganiser [dezɔrganize] *tr* to disorganize

désorien·té -tée [dezɔrjɑ̃te] *adj* disoriented, bewildered

désorienter [dezɔrjɑ̃te] *tr* to disorient; to mislead; to disconcert || *ref* to become confused; to lose one's bearings

désormais [dezɔrmɛ] *adv* henceforth

désosser [dezɔse] *tr* to bone

despote [dɛspɔt] *m* despot

despotique [dɛspɔtik] *adj* despotic

despotisme [dɛspɔtism] *m* despotism

des-quels -quelles [dekɛl] §78

dessaisir [desezir] *tr* to dispossess; to let go, to release || *ref*—**se dessaisir de** to relinquish

dessalement [desalmɑ̃] *m* desalinization

dessaler [desale] *tr* to desalt, to desalinate || *ref* (coll) to wise up

dessécher [deseʃe] §10 *tr* to dry up, wither; to drain (*a pond*); to dehydrate (*the body*); to sear (*the heart*) || *ref* to dry up; to waste away

dessein [desɛ̃] *m* design, plan, intent; **à dessein** on purpose

desseller [desele] *tr* to unsaddle

desserrer [desere] *tr* to loosen; **ne pas desserrer les dents** to keep mum

dessert [desɛr] *m* dessert, last course

desserte [desɛrt] *f* buffet, sideboard; branch (*of railroad or bus line*); ministry (*of a substituting clergyman*)

dessertir [desertir] *tr* to remove (*a gem*) from its setting

desservant [deservã] *m* parish priest

desservir [deservir] §63 *tr* to clear (*the table*); to be of disservice to, to harm; (aer, aut, rr) to stop at (*a town or station*); (aer, aut, eccl, rr) to serve (*a locality*); (elec) to supply (*a region*)

dessiller [desije] *tr*—**dessiller les yeux à qn** or **de qn** to open s.o.'s eyes, to undeceive s.o.

dessin [desẽ] *m* drawing, sketch, design; profile (*of face*); **dessins animés** (mov) animated cartoons

dessina·teur [desinatœr] **-trice** [tris] *mf* designer; cartoonist

dessiner [desine] *tr* to draw, sketch, design; to delineate, outline || *ref* to stand out, to be outlined

dessoûler or **dessouler** [desule] *tr* & *intr* to sober up

dessous [dəsu] *m* underpart; reverse side, wrong side; coaster (*underneath a glass*); seamy side, machinations behind the scenes; **au dessous de** below; **avoir le dessous** to get the short end of the deal; **du dessous** below; **en dessous** underneath; **les dessous** lingerie, undergarments || *adv* & *prep* under, underneath, below

dessous-de-bouteille [dəsudəbutej] *m invar* coaster

dessous-de-bras [dəsudəbra] *m invar* underarm pad

dessous-de-carafe [dəsudəkaraf] *m invar* coaster

dessous-de-plat [dəsudəpla] *m invar* hot pad

dessous-de-table [dəsudətabl] *m invar* under-the-counter money

dessus [dəsy] *m* upper part; back (*of the hand*); right side (*of material*); (mus) treble part; **au dessus de** beyond, above; **avoir le dessus** to have the upper hand; **le dessus du panier** the cream of the crop || *adv* above || *prep* on, above, over

dessus-de-cheminée [dəsydə/mine] *m invar* mantelpiece

dessus-de-lit [dəsydəli] *m invar* bedspread

dessus-de-porte [dəsydəpɔrt] *m invar* overdoor

dessus-de-table [dəsydətabl] *m invar* table cover

destin [destẽ] *m* destiny, fate

destinataire [destinater] *mf* addressee; payee; **destinataire inconnu** or **absent** (formula stamped on envelope) not at this address

destination [destinasjɔ̃] *f* destination; **à destination de** to, bound for

destinée [destine] *f* destiny

destiner [destine] *tr* to destine; to set aside, to reserve; **destiner q.ch. à qn** to mean or intend s.th. for s.o.

destituer [destitɥe] *tr* to remove from office

destitution [destitysjɔ̃] *f* dismissal, removal from office

destrier [destrije] *m* (hist) steed, charger

destroyer [destrɔjœr] *m* (nav) destroyer

destruc·teur [destryktœr] **-trice** [tris] *adj* destroying, destructive || *mf* destroyer

destruc·tif [destryktif] **-tive** [tiv] *adj* destructive

destruction [destryksjɔ̃] *f* destruction

dé·suet [dezɥe] **-suète** [zɥet] *adj* obsolete, antiquated, out-of-date

désuétude [dezɥetyd] *f* desuetude, disuse

désu·ni **-nie** [dezyni] *adj* at odds, divided against itself; uncoordinated

désunion [dezynjɔ̃] *f* dissension

désunir [dezynir] *tr* to disunite, divide; to estrange

déta·ché **-chée** [deta/e] *adj* detached; clean; spare (*parts*); acting, temporary (*official*); staccato (*note*)

détachement [deta/mã] *m* detachment; (mil) detail

détacher [deta/e] *tr* to detach; to let loose; to clean; to make (*s.th.*) stand out in relief || *ref* to come loose; to break loose; to stand out in relief

détacheur [deta/œr] *m* spot remover

détail [detaj] *m* detail; retail; item (*of an account*); **au détail** at retail; **en détail** detailed

détail·lant [detajã] **détail·lante** [detajãt] *adj* retail || *mf* retailer

détailler [detaje] *tr* to detail; to cut up into pieces; to retail; to itemize (*an account*)

détartrer [detartre] *tr* to remove the scale from (*a boiler*); to remove the tartar from (*teeth*)

détaxation [detaksɑsjɔ̃] *f* lowering or removal of taxes

détaxer [detakse] *tr* to lower or remove the tax from

détecter [detekte] *tr* to detect

détecteur [detektœr] *m* detector; **détecteur de mines** mine detector

détection [deteksjɔ̃] *f* detection

détective [detektiv] *m* detective, private detective; box camera

déteindre [detẽdr] §50 *tr* to fade, bleach || *intr* to fade, run

dételer [detle] §34 *tr* to unharness || *intr* to let up; to settle down

détendre [detãdr] *tr* to relax; to stretch out (*one's legs*); to lower (*the gas*) || *ref* to relax, to enjoy oneself

détenir [detnir] §72 *tr* to detain (*in prison*); to hold, withhold; to own

détente [detãt] *f* trigger; relaxation, easing (*of tension*); relaxation of tension (*in international affairs*)

déten·teur [detãtœr] **-trice** [tris] *mf* holder (*of stock; of a record*); keeper (*of a secret*)

détention [detãsjɔ̃] *f* detention, custody; possession; **détention préventive** pretrial imprisonment, custody

déte·nu **-nue** [detny] *adj* detained, imprisoned || *mf* prisoner

déterger [deterʒe] §38 *tr* to clean

détérioration [deterjɔrɑsjɔ̃] *f* deterioration

détériorer [deterjɔre] *tr* to damage || *intr* to deteriorate

détermination [determinɑsjɔ̃] *f* determination

déterminer [determine] *tr* to determine || *ref* to decide

déter·ré -rée [detere] *adj* disinterred || *mf* (fig) corpse, ghost

déterrer [detere] *tr* to dig up; to exhume

déter·sif [detersif] **-sive** [siv] *adj & m* detergent

détester [deteste] *tr* to detest, to hate

déto·nant [detɔnɑ̃] **-nante** [nɑ̃t] *adj & m* explosive

détoner [detɔne] *intr* to detonate, to explode

détonner [detɔne] *intr* to sing or play off key; to clash (*said of colors*)

détordre [detɔrdr] *tr* to untwist

détortiller [detɔrtije] *tr* to untangle

détour [detur] *m* turn, curve, bend; roundabout way, detour; **sans détour** frankly, honestly

détour·né -née [deturne] *adj* off the beaten track, isolated; indirect, roundabout; twisted (*meaning*)

détourner [deturne] *tr* to divert; to deter; to embezzle; to lead astray; to distort, twist

détrac·teur [detraktœr] **-trice** [tris] *adj* disparaging || *mf* detractor

détra·qué -quée [detrake] *adj* out of order; broken (*in health*); unhinged, deranged || *mf* nervous wreck

détraquer [detrake] *tr* to put out of commission; (coll) to upset, unhinge || *ref* to break down

détrempe [detrɑ̃p] *f* distemper (*painting*); annealing (*of steel*)

détremper [detrɑ̃pe] *tr* to soak; to dilute; to anneal (*steel*)

détresse [detres] *f* distress

détriment [detrimɑ̃] *m* detriment

détritus [detritys] *m* debris, rubbish, refuse

détroit [detrwa] *m* strait, sound

détromper [detrɔ̃pe] *tr* to undeceive, to enlighten

détrôner [detrone] *tr* to dethrone

détrousser [detruse] *tr* to let down (*e.g., one's sleeves*); to hold up (*s.o.*) in the street || *ref* to let down a garment

détrousseur [detrusœr] *m* highwayman

détruire [detrɥir] §19 *tr* to destroy; to put an end to || *ref* (coll) to commit suicide

dette [det] *f* debt; **dette active** asset; **dette passive** liability

deuil [dœj] *m* mourning; grief, sorrow; bereavement; funeral procession; **deuil de veuve** widow's weeds; **faire son deuil de** (coll) to say good-by to

deux [dø] *adj & pron* two; the Second, e.g., **Charles deux** Charles the Second; **deux heures** two o'clock || *m* two; second (*in dates*)

deuxième [døzjem] *adj & m* second

deux-pièces [døpjes] *m invar* two-piece suit

deux-points [døpwɛ̃] *m invar* colon

deux-ponts [døpɔ̃] *m invar* (aer, naut) double-decker

dévaler [devale] *tr* to descend (*a slope*) || *intr* to descend quickly

dévaluation [devalɥɑsjɔ̃] *f* devaluation

dévaluer [devalɥe] *tr* to devaluate

devant [dəvɑ̃] *m* front; **par devant** in front; **prendre les devants** to make the first move; to get ahead; to take precautions || *adv* before, in front || *prep* before, in front of

devanture [dəvɑ̃tyr] *f* show window; display; storefront

dévasta·teur [devastatœr] **-trice** [tris] *adj* devastating

dévastation [devastɑsjɔ̃] *f* devastation

dévaster [devaste] *tr* to devastate

déveine [deven] *f* bad luck

développé [devlɔpe] *m* press (*in weight lifting*)

développement [devlɔpmɑ̃] *m* development; unwrapping (*of package*); expansion

développer [devlɔpe] *tr* to develop; to unwrap (*a package*); to reveal, show (*e.g., a card*); to spread out, open out; to expand (*an algebraic expression*) || *ref* to develop

devenir [dəvnir] §72 *intr* (aux: ÊTRE) to become; **qu'est devenu Robert?** what has become of Robert?

dévergondage [devergɔ̃daʒ] *m* profligacy

dévergon·dé -dée [devergɔ̃de] *adj & mf* profligate

dévergonder [devergɔ̃de] *ref* to become dissolute

dévernir [devernir] *tr* to remove the varnish from

déverrouiller [deveruje] *tr* to unbolt

dé·vers [dever] **-verse** [vers] *adj* warped; out of alignment || *m* inclination, slope; banking

déverser [deverse] *tr* to pour out; to slope, bank || *intr* to pour out; to lean, to become lopsided || *ref* to empty, flow (*said of river*)

dévêtir [devetir] §73 *tr & ref* to undress

déviation [devjɑsjɔ̃] *f* deviation; detour

dévider [devide] *tr* to unwind, to reel off

dévier [devje] *tr* to deflect, to by-pass || *intr* to deviate, to swerve

de·vin [dəvɛ̃] **-vineresse** [vinres] *mf* fortuneteller

deviner [dəvine] *tr* to guess

devinette [dəvinet] *f* riddle

dévirer [devire] *tr* to turn back; to bend back; to feather (*an oar*)

devis [dəvi] *m* estimate

dévisager [devisaʒe] §38 *tr* to stare at, to stare down

devise [dəviz] *f* motto, slogan; heraldic device; name of a ship; currency; **devise forte** strong currency

deviser [dəvize] *intr* to chat

dévisser [devise] *tr* to unscrew

dévitaliser [devitalize] *tr* to kill the nerve of (*a tooth*)

dévoiler [devwale] *tr* to unveil; to straighten (*e.g., a bent wheel*) || *ref* to unveil; to come to light

devoir [dəvwar] *m* duty; exercise,

homework; **devoirs** respects; homework || §21 *tr* to owe || *aux* used to express 1) necessity, e.g., **il doit s'en aller** he must go away; **il devra s'en aller** he will have to go away; **il a dû s'en aller** he had to go away; 2) obligation, e.g., **il devrait s'en aller** he ought to go away, he should go away; **il aurait dû s'en aller** he ought to have gone away, he should have gone away; 3) conjecture, e.g., **il doit être malade** he must be ill; **il a dû être malade** he must have been ill; 4) what is expected or scheduled, e.g., **que dois-je faire maintenant?** what am I to do now?; **le train devait arriver à six heures** the train was to arrive at six o'clock

dévo·lu -lue [devɔly] *adj*—**dévolu à** devolving upon, vested in || *m*—**jeter son dévolu sur** to fix one's choice upon

dévora·teur [devɔratœr] **-trice** [tris] *adj* devouring

dévorer [devore] *tr* to devour, eat up

dévo·reur [devɔrœr] **-reuse** [røz] *mf* devourer; (fig) glutton

dé·vot [devo] **-vote** [vɔt] *adj* devout, pious || *mf* devout, pious person; **faux dévot** hypocrite

dévotion [devosjɔ̃] *f* devotion, devoutness; **à votre dévotion** at your service, at your disposal; **être à la dévotion de qn** to be at s.o.'s beck and call

dé·voué -vouée [devwe] *adj* devoted; **dévoué à vos ordres** (complimentary close) at your service; **votre dévoué** (complimentary close) yours truly

dévouement [devumã] *m* devotion

dévouer [devwe] *tr* to dedicate, sacrifice || *ref* to devote oneself

dévoyé dévoyée [devwaje] *adj* delinquent (*young person*) || *mf* delinquent

dévoyer [devwaje] §47 *tr* to lead astray

dextérité [deksterite] *f* dexterity

dextrose [dekstroz] *m* dextrose

diabète [djabet] *m* diabetes

diabétique [djabetik] *adj & mf* diabetic

diable [djɑbl] *m* devil; hand truck, dolly; (coll) fellow; **à la diable** haphazardly; **c'est là le diable** (coll) there's the rub; **diable à ressort** jack-in-the-box; **du diable** extreme; **en diable** extremely; **faire le diable à quatre** (coll) to raise Cain; **tirer le diable par la queue** (coll) to be hard up

diablerie [djablɘri] *f* deviltry

diabolique [djabɔlik] *adj* diabolic(al)

diaconesse [djakɔnes] *f* deaconess

diacre [djakr] *m* deacon

diacritique [djakritik] *adj* diacritical

diadème [djadem] *m* diadem; (*woman's headdress*) tiara, coronet

diagnose [djagnoz] *f* diagnostics, diagnosis

diagnostic [djagnɔstik] *m* diagnosis

diagnostiquer [djagnɔstike] *tr* to diagnose

diago·nal -nale [djagɔnal] *adj & f* (*pl* **-naux** [no] **-nales**) diagonal

diagonalement [djagɔnalmã] *adv* diagonally, cater-cornered

diagramme [djagram] *m* diagram

dialecte [djalekt] *m* dialect

dialogue [djalɔg] *m* dialogue

diamant [djamã] *m* diamond

diamantaire [djamãter] *adj* diamond-bright || *m* dealer in diamonds

diamé·tral -trale [djametral] *adj* (*pl* **-traux** [tro]) diametric(al)

diamètre [djametr] *m* diameter

diane [djan] *f* reveille

diantre [djãtr] *interj* the dickens!

diapason [djapazɔ̃] *m* range (*of voice or instrument*); pitch, standard pitch; tuning fork

diaphane [djafan] *adj* diaphanous

diaphragme [djafragm] *m* diaphragm

diapo [djapo] *f* (coll) slide

diapositive [djapozitiv] *f* (phot) transparency, slide

diaprer [djapre] *tr* to variegate

diarrhée [djare] *f* diarrhea

diastole [djastɔl] *f* diastole

diathermie [djatermi] *f* diathermy

diatribe [djatrib] *f* diatribe

dichotomie [dikɔtɔmi] *f* dichotomy; split fee (*between physicians*)

dictaphone [diktafɔn] *m* dictaphone

dictateur [diktatœr] *m* dictator

dictature [diktatyr] *f* dictatorship

dictée [dikte] *f* dictation; **écrire sous la dictée de** to take dictation from

dicter [dikte] *tr & intr* to dictate

diction [diksjɔ̃] *f* diction

dictionnaire [diksjɔner] *m* dictionary; **dictionnaire vivant** (coll) walking encyclopedia

dicton [diktɔ̃] *m* saying, proverb

didactique [didaktik] *adj* didactic(al)

dièdre [djedr] *adj & m* dihedral

diérèse [djerez] *f* diaeresis

dièse [djez] *adj & m* (mus) sharp

diesel [dizel] *m* Diesel motor

diéser [djeze] §10 *tr* (mus) to sharp

diète [djet] *f* diet

diététi·cien [djetetisjɛ̃] **-cienne** [sjen] *mf* dietitian

diététique [djetetik] *adj* dietetic || *f* dietetics

dieu [djø] *m* (*pl* **dieux**) god || (*cap*) *m* God; **Dieu merci!** thank heavens!; **mon Dieu!** good gracious!

diffamation [difamasjɔ̃] *f* defamation

diffamer [difame] *tr* to defame

diffé·ré -rée [difere] *adj* deferred; delayed (*action*) || *m* (rad, telv) prerecording; **en différé** (rad, telv) prerecorded

différemment [diferamã] *adv* differently

différence [diferãs] *f* difference; **à la différence de** unlike, contrary to

différencier [diferãsje] *tr & ref* to differentiate

différend [diferã] *m* dispute, disagreement, difference; **partager le différend** to split the difference

diffé·rent [diferã] **-rente** [rãt] *adj* different

différen·tiel -tielle [diferãsjel] *adj* differential || m (mach) differential || f (math) differential

différer [difere] §10 tr to defer, to put off || intr to differ; to disagree

difficile [difisil] adj difficult, hard; hard to please, crotchety; **faire le difficile** to be hard to please

difficulté [difikylte] f difficulty

difforme [diform] adj deformed

difformité [diformite] f deformity

dif·fus [dify] **dif·fuse** [difyz] adj diffuse; verbose, windy

diffuser [difyze] tr to broadcast || ref to diffuse

diffuseur [difyzœr] m spreader (of news); loudspeaker; nozzle

digérer [diʒere] §10 tr & intr to digest || ref to be digested

digeste [diʒɛst] adj (coll) easy to digest || m (law) digest

digestible [diʒɛstibl] adj digestible

diges·tif [diʒɛstif] **-tive** [tiv] adj digestive

digestion [diʒɛstjɔ̃] f digestion

digi·tal **-tale** [diʒital] adj (pl **-taux** [to]) digital || f digitalis, foxglove

digitaline [diʒitalin] f (pharm) digitalis

digne [diɲ] adj worthy; dignified; haughty, uppish

dignitaire [diɲiter] mf dignitary

dignité [diɲite] f dignity

digression [digresjɔ̃] f digression

digue [dig] f dike; breakwater; (fig) barrier

dilacérer [dilasere] §10 tr to lacerate

dilapider [dilapide] tr to squander; to embezzle

dilater [dilate] tr & ref to dilate

dilatoire [dilatwar] adj dilatory

dilemme [dilem] m dilemma

dilettante [diletãt] mf dilettante

diligemment [diliʒamɑ̃] adv diligently

diligence [diliʒɑ̃s] f diligence; **à la diligence de** at the request of

dili·gent [diliʒɑ̃] **-gente** [ʒɑ̃t] adj diligent

diluer [dilɥe] tr to dilute

dilution [dilysjɔ̃] f dilution

dimanche [dimɑ̃ʃ] m Sunday; **du dimanche** (coll) Sunday (driver); (coll) amateur (painter); **le dimanche des Rameaux** Palm Sunday

dîme [dim] f tithe

dimension [dimɑ̃sjɔ̃] f dimension

diminuer [diminɥe] tr & intr to diminish

diminu·tif [diminytif] **-tive** [tiv] adj & m diminutive

dinde [dɛ̃d] f turkey; (culin) turkey; (coll) silly girl

dindon [dɛ̃dɔ̃] m turkey

dindonner [dɛ̃dɔne] tr to dupe, take in

dîner [dine] m dinner; **dîner de garçons** stag dinner; **dîner prié** formal dinner || intr to dine

dînette [dinet] f family meal; children's playtime meal

dî·neur [dinœr] **-neuse** [nøz] mf diner, dinner guest

dinosaure [dinozor] m dinosaur

diocèse [djosez] m diocese

diode [djod] f diode

dionée [djone] f Venus's-flytrap

diphtérie [difteri] f diphtheria

diphtongue [diftɔ̃g] f diphthong

diplomate [diplomat] adj diplomatic || mf diplomat

diplomatie [diplomasi] f diplomacy

diplomatique [diplomatik] adj diplomatic

diplôme [diplom] m diploma

dire [dir] m statement; **au dire de** according to || §22 tr to say, tell, relate; **à l'heure dite** at the appointed time; **à qui le dites-vous?** (coll) you're telling me!; **autrement dit** in other words; **dire que . . .** to think that; **dites-lui bien des choses de ma part** say hello for me; **tu l'as dit!** (coll) you said it! || intr to say; **à vrai dire** to tell the truth; **cela va sans dire** it goes without saying; **c'est beaucoup dire** (coll) that's going rather far; **c'est pas peu dire** (slang) that's saying a lot; **comme on dit** as the saying goes; **dites donc!** hey!, say!; **il n'y a pas à dire** make no mistake about it || ref to be said; to say to oneself or to each other; to claim to be, to call oneself

di·rect **-recte** [dirɛkt] adj direct || m (boxing) solid punch; **en direct** (rad, telv) live

direc·teur [dirɛktœr] **-trice** [tris] adj directing, guiding; principal; driving (rod, wheel) || mf director || f directress

direction [dirɛksjɔ̃] f direction; administration, management, board; head office; (aut) steering

direction·nel **-nelle** [dirɛksjonel] adj directional

directorat [dirɛktora] m directorship

dirigeable [diriʒabl] adj & m dirigible

diri·geant [diriʒɑ̃] **-geante** [ʒɑ̃t] adj governing, ruling || mf ruler, leader, head, executive

diriger [diriʒe] §38 tr to direct, control, manage; to steer || ref to go; to head for; **diriger vers** to head for

dirigisme [diriʒism] m government economic planning and control

discernable [disernabl] adj discernible

discernement [disernamɑ̃] m discernment, perception

discerner [diserne] tr to discern

disciple [disipl] m disciple

disciplinaire [disipliner] adj disciplinary || m military policeman

discipline [disiplin] f discipline; scourge

discipliner [disipline] tr to discipline

disconti·nu **-nue** [diskɔ̃tiny] adj discontinuous

discontinuer [diskɔ̃tinɥe] tr to discontinue

disconvenir [diskɔ̃vnir] §72 tr to deny || intr (with dat) to not suit, displease || intr (aux: ÊTRE)—**ne pas disconvenir de** to admit, not deny

discophile [diskofil] mf record collector

discord [diskor] adj masc out of tune || m instrument out of tune

discordance [diskordɑ̃s] f discordance

discor·dant [diskordɑ̃] **-dante** [dɑ̃t] adj discordant

discorde [diskɔrd] f discord

discorder [diskɔrde] intr to be discordant, to jar

discothèque [diskɔtɛk] f record cabinet; record library; discotheque

discourir [diskurir] §14 intr to discourse

discours [diskur] m discourse; speech

discour·tois [diskurtwa] -toise [twaz] adj discourteous

discourtoisie [diskurtwazi] f discourtesy

discrédit [diskredi] m discredit

discréditer [diskredite] tr to discredit

dis·cret [diskrɛ] -crète [krɛt] adj discreet; discrete

discrétion [diskresjɔ̃] f discretion; à discrétion as much as one wants

discrimination [diskriminasjɔ̃] f discrimination

discriminatoire [diskriminatwar] adj discriminatory

discriminer [diskrimine] tr to discriminate

disculper [diskylpe] tr to clear, exonerate || ref to clear oneself

discur·sif [diskyrsif] -sive [siv] adj discursive

discussion [diskysjɔ̃] f discussion

discuter [diskyte] tr & intr to discuss; to question, debate

di·sert [dizɛr] -serte [zɛrt] adj eloquent, fluent

disertement [dizɛrtəma] adv eloquently, fluently

disette [dizɛt] f shortage, scarcity; famine

di·seur [dizœr] -seuse [zøz] mf talker, speaker; monologuist; **diseuse de bonne aventure** fortuneteller

disgrâce [disgrɑs] f disfavor; misfortune; surliness, gruffness

disgra·cié -ciée [disgrasje] adj out of favor; ill-favored, homely; unfortunate

disgracier [disgrasje] tr to deprive of favor

disgra·cieux [disgrasjø] -cieuse [sjøz] adj awkward; homely, ugly; disagreeable

disjoindre [diszwɛdr] §35 tr to sever, to separate

disjoncteur [diszɔ̃ktœr] m circuit breaker

dislocation [dislokasjɔ̃] f dislocation; separation; dismemberment

disloquer [disloke] tr to dislocate; to disperse; to dismember || ref to break up, disperse

disparaître [disparɛtr] §12 intr to disappear

disparate [disparat] adj incongruous || f incongruity; clash (of colors)

disparité [disparite] f disparity

disparition [disparisjɔ̃] f disappearance

dispa·ru -rue [dispary] adj disappeared; missing (in battle) || mf missing person; **le disparu** the deceased

dispen·dieux [dispɑ̃djø] -dieuse [djøz] adj expensive

dispensaire [dispɑ̃sɛr] m dispensary, outpatient clinic

dispensa·teur [dispɑ̃satœr] -trice [tris] mf dispenser

dispense [dispɑ̃s] f dispensation, exemption

dispenser [dispɑ̃se] tr to dispense; **dispensé du timbrage** (label on envelope) mailing permit

disperser [disperse] tr & ref to disperse

dispersion [dispersjɔ̃] f dispersion, dissipation

disponibilité [disponibilite] f availability; **disponibilités** liquid assets; **en disponibilité** in the reserves

disponible [disponibl] adj available; vacant (seat); (govt, mil) subject to call

dis·pos [dispo] -pose [poz] adj alert, fit, in good condition

dispo·sé -sée [dispoze] adj disposed; arranged; **disposé d'avance** predisposed; **peu disposé** reluctant

disposer [dispoze] tr to dispose || intr to dispose; **disposer de** to dispose of, to have at one's disposal; to have at hand; to make use of; **disposer pour** to provide for (e.g., the future); **vous pouvez disposer** you may leave || ref —**se disposer à** to be disposed to; to plan on

dispositif [dispozitif] m apparatus, device; (mil) disposition

disposition [dispozisjɔ̃] f disposition; disposal; **dispositions** arrangements; aptitude; provisions (of a legal document)

dispropor·tion·né -née [disproporsjone] adj disproportionate, incompatible

dispute [dispyt] f dispute

disputer [dispyte] tr to dispute; (coll) to bawl out || ref to dispute

disquaire [diskɛr] m record dealer

disqualification [diskalifikasjɔ̃] f disqualification

disqualifier [diskalifje] tr & ref to disqualify

disque [disk] m disk; record, disk; (sports) discus; **changer de disque** (coll) to change the subject; **disque de longue durée** long-playing record

dissection [diseksjɔ̃] f dissection

dissemblable [disɑ̃blabl] adj dissimilar

dissemblance [disɑ̃blɑ̃s] f dissimilarity

disséminer [disemine] tr to disseminate

dissension [disɑ̃sjɔ̃] f dissension

dissentiment [disɑ̃tima] m dissent

disséquer [diseke] §10 tr to dissect

dissertation [disɛrtasjɔ̃] f dissertation; (in school) essay; term paper

dissidence [disidɑ̃s] f dissent

dissi·dent [disidɑ̃] -dente [dɑ̃t] adj dissenting || mf dissenter, dissident

dissimiler [disimile] tr (phonet) to dissimilate

dissimulation [disimylasjɔ̃] f dissemblance

dissimuler [disimyle] tr & intr to dissemble; **dissimuler q.ch. à qn** to conceal s.th. from s.o. || ref to hide, skulk

dissipation [disipasjɔ̃] f dissipation

dissi·pé -pée [disipe] adj dissipated; pleasure-seeking; unruly (schoolboy)

dissiper [disipe] tr & ref to dissipate

dissocier [disosje] *tr & ref* to dissociate

disso·lu -lue [disɔly] *adj* dissolute ‖ *mf* profligate

dissolution [disɔlysjɔ̃] *f* dissolution; dissoluteness; rubber cement

dissol·vant [disɔlvɑ̃] **-vante** [vɑ̃t] *adj & m* solvent

dissonance [disɔnɑ̃s] *f* dissonance

dissoudre [disudr] §60 (*pp* **dissous, dissoute**; no *pret* or *imperf subj*) *tr & ref* to dissolve

dissuader [disɥade] *tr* to dissuade

distance [distɑ̃s] *f* distance; **à distance** at a distance

distancer [distɑ̃se] §51 *tr* to outdistance; to distance (*a race horse*)

dis·tant [distɑ̃] **-tante** [tɑ̃t] *adj* distant

distendre [distɑ̃dr] *tr & ref* to distend; to strain (*a muscle*)

distillation [distilasjɔ̃] *f* distillation

distiller [distile] *tr* to distill

distillerie [distilri] *f* distillery; distilling industry

dis·tinct [distɛ̃], [distɛ̃kt] **-tincte** [tɛ̃kt] *adj* distinct

distinc·tif [distɛ̃ktif] **-tive** [tiv] *adj* distinctive

distinction [distɛ̃ksjɔ̃] *f* distinction

distin·gué -guée [distɛ̃ge] *adj* distinguished; famous; sincere, e.g., **veuillez accepter nos sentiments distingués** (complimentary close) please accept our sincere regards

distinguer [distɛ̃ge] *tr* to distinguish ‖ *ref* to be distinguished; to distinguish oneself

distordre [distɔrdr] *tr* to twist, to sprain

dis·tors [distɔr] **-torse** [tɔrs] *adj* twisted

distorsion [distɔrsjɔ̃] *f* sprain; convulsive twist; (electron, opt) distorsion

distraction [distraksjɔ̃] *f* distraction; heedlessness; lapse; embezzlement; appropriation (*of a sum of money*)

distraire [distrer] §68 *tr* to distract, amuse; to separate, set aside (*e.g., part of one's savings*) ‖ *ref* to amuse oneself

dis·trait [distre] **-traite** [tret] *adj* absent-minded

distribuer [distribɥe] *tr* to distribute; to arrange the furnishings of (*an apartment*)

distribu·teur [distribɥtœr] **-trice** [tris] *mf* distributor (*person*) ‖ *m* (mach) distributor; **distributeur automatique** vending machine; **distributeur de musique** jukebox

distribution [distribysjɔ̃] *f* distribution; mail delivery; supply system (*of gas, water, or electricity*); valve gear (*of steam engine*); timing gears (*of internal-combustion engine*); (theat) cast

district [distrik], [distrikt] *m* district

dit [di] **dite** [dit] *adj* agreed upon, stated ‖ *m* saying

dito [dito] *adv* ditto

diva [diva] *f* diva

divaguer [divage] *intr* to ramble

divan [divɑ̃] *m* divan

diverger [diverʒe] §38 *intr* to diverge

di·vers [diver] **-verse** [vers] *adj* changing, varied ‖ **di·vers -verses** *adj pl* diverse, different; several

diversifier [diversifje] *tr & ref* to diversify

diversion [diversjɔ̃] *f* diversion

diversité [diversite] *f* diversity

divertir [divertir] *tr* to divert, amuse ‖ *ref* to be diverted, amused

dividende [dividɑ̃d] *m* dividend

di·vin [divɛ̃] **-vine** [vin] *adj* divine

divination [divinasjɔ̃] *f* divination

divinité [divinite] *f* divinity

diviser [divize] *tr & ref* to divide

diviseur [divizœr] *m* (math) divisor; (fig) troublemaker

divisible [divizibl] *adj* divisible

division [divizjɔ̃] *f* division

divisionnaire [divizjɔner] *adj* divisional ‖ *m* division head

divorce [divɔrs] *m* divorce

divor·cé -cée [divɔrse] *mf* divorced person ‖ *f* divorcee

divorcer [divɔrse] §51 *tr* to divorce (*a married couple*) ‖ *intr* to divorce, to get a divorce; **divorcer avec** to withdraw from (*the world*); **divorcer d'avec** to get a divorce from, to be divorced from, to divorce (*husband or wife*); to withdraw from (*the world*)

divulguer [divylge] *tr* to divulge

dix [di(s)] *adj & pron* ten; the Tenth, e.g., **Jean dix** John the Tenth; **dix heures** ten o'clock ‖ *m* ten; tenth (*in dates*)

dix-huit [dizɥi], [dizɥit] *adj & pron* eighteen; the Eighteenth, e.g., **Jean dix-huit** John the Eighteenth ‖ *m* eighteen; eighteenth (*in dates*)

dix-huitième [dizɥitjem] *adj & m* eighteenth

dixième [dizjem] *adj, pron* (*masc, fem*), *& m* tenth

dix-neuf [diznœf] *adj & pron* nineteen; the Nineteenth, e.g., **Jean dix-neuf** John the Nineteenth ‖ *m* nineteen; nineteenth (*in dates*)

dix-neuvième [diznœvjem] *adj & m* nineteenth

dix-sept [disset] *adj & pron* seventeen; the Seventeenth, e.g., **Jean dix-sept** John the Seventeenth ‖ *m* seventeen; seventeenth (*in dates*)

dix-septième [dissetjem] *adj & m* seventeenth

djinn [dʒin] *m* jinn

d° *abbr* (**dito**) do. (ditto)

docile [dɔsil] *adj* docile

dock [dɔk] *m* dock; warehouse; **dock flottant** floating dry dock

docker [dɔker] *m* dock worker

docte [dɔkt] *adj* learned, scholarly ‖ *mf* scholar ‖ *m* learned man

doc·teur [dɔktœr] **-toresse** [tɔres] *mf* doctor

docto·ral -rale [dɔktɔral] *adj* (*pl* **-raux** [ro]) doctoral

doctorat [dɔktɔra] *m* doctorate

doctrine [dɔktrin] *f* doctrine

document [dɔkymɑ̃] *m* document

documentaire [dɔkymɑ̃ter] *adj & m* documentary

documentation [dɔkymɑ̃tɑsjɔ̃] *f* documentation; literature (*about a region, business, etc.*)

documenter [dɔkymɑ̃te] *tr* to document || *ref* to gather documentary evidence

dodeliner [dɔdline] *tr & intr* to sway, rock

dodo [dodo] *m* (orn) dodo; **aller au dodo** (*baby talk*) to go to bed; **faire dodo** to sleep

do·du -due [dɔdy] *adj* (coll) plump

dogmatique [dɔgmatik] *adj* dogmatic || *mf* dogmatic person || *f* dogmatics

dogmatiser [dɔgmatize] *intr* to dogmatize

dogme [dɔgm] *m* dogma

dogue [dɔg] *m* bulldog

doigt [dwa] *m* finger; **à deux doigts de** a hairbreadth away from; **doigt annulaire** ring finger; **doigt de Dieu** hand of God; **doigt du pied** toe; **mettre le doigt dessus** to hit the nail on the head; **mon petit doigt m'a dit** (coll) a little bird told me; **montrer du doigt** to single out (*for ridicule*); to point at; **petit doigt** little finger; **se mettre le doigt dans l'œil** (coll) to put one's foot in one's mouth; **se mordre les doigts** to be sorry

doigté [dwate] *m* touch; adroitness, skillfulness; fingering

doigter [dwate] *m* fingering || *tr & intr* to finger

doigtier [dwatje] *m* fingerstall

doit [dwa] *m* debit

doléances [dɔleɑ̃s] *fpl* grievances

do·lent -lente [dɔlɑ̃ -lɑ̃t] *adj* doleful

dollar [dɔlar] *m* dollar

domaine [dɔmen] *m* domain

dôme [dom] *m* dome; cathedral

domestication [dɔmestikɑsjɔ̃] *f* domestication

domesticité [dɔmestisite] *f* domestication; staff of servants

domestique [dɔmestik] *adj & mf* domestic

domestiquer [dɔmestike] *tr* to domesticate

domicile [dɔmisil] *m* residence

domicilier [dɔmisilje] *tr* to domicile || *ref* to take up residence

dominance [dɔminɑ̃s] *f* (genetics) dominance

domi·nant -nante [dɔminɑ̃ -nɑ̃t] *adj* dominant || *f* dominating trait; (mus) dominant

domina·teur [dɔminatœr] **-trice** [tris] *adj* domineering, overbearing || *mf* ruler, conqueror

domination [dɔminɑsjɔ̃] *f* domination

dominer [dɔmine] *tr & intr* to dominate || *ref* to control oneself

domini·cal -cale [dɔminikal] *adj* (pl **-caux** [ko]) Sunday; dominical

domino [dɔmino] *m* domino

dommage [dɔmaʒ] *m* loss; injury; **c'est dommage!** that's too bad! **dommages et intérêts** (law) damages; **quel dommage!** what a pity!

dommageable [dɔmaʒabl] *adj* injurious

dommages-intérêts [dɔmaʒɛtera] *mpl* (law) damages

dompter [dɔ̃te] *tr* to tame; to train (*animals*); to subdue

domp·teur [dɔ̃tœr] **-teuse** [tøz] *mf* tamer, trainer; conquerer

don [dɔ̃] *m* gift; don (*Spanish title*)

donataire [dɔnater] *mf* legatee

dona·teur [dɔnatœr] **-trice** [tris] *mf* (law) donor, legator

donation [dɔnɑsjɔ̃] *f* donation, gift, grant

donc [dɔ̃k], [dɔ̃] *adv* therefore, then; thus; now, of course; (often used for emphasis), e.g., **entrez donc!** do come in!

donjon [dɔ̃ʒɔ̃] *m* keep, donjon; (nav) turret

don·nant [dɔnɑ̃] **don·nante** [dɔnɑ̃t] *adj* generous, open-handed; **donnant donnant** tit for tat; cash down; **peu donnant** closefisted

donne [dɔn] *f* (cards) deal; **doña** (*Spanish title*); **fausse donne** misdeal

don·né -née [dɔne] *adj* given; **étant donné que** whereas, since || *f* datum; **données** data, facts

donner [dɔne] *tr* to give; (cards) to deal || *intr* to give; **donner sur** to open onto, to look out on; **donner sur les doigts** to rap one's knuckles

don·neur [dɔnœr] **don·neuse** [dɔnøz] *mf* donor; **donneur universel** type-O blood donor || *m* (cards) dealer

dont [dɔ̃] §79

donzelle [dɔ̃zel] *f* woman of easy virtue

doper [dɔpe] *tr* to dope

doping [dɔpiŋ] *m* dope, pep pill

dorade [dɔrad] *f* gilthead

dorénavant [dɔrenavɑ̃] *adv* henceforth

dorer [dɔre] *tr* to gild; (fig) to sugarcoat

d'ores [dɔr] see **ores**

dorlotement [dɔrlɔtmɑ̃] *m* coddling

dorloter [dɔrlɔte] *tr* to coddle

dor·mant [dɔrmɑ̃] **-mante** [mɑ̃t] *adj* stagnant, immovable || *m* doorframe

dor·meur [dɔrmœr] **-meuse** [møz] *adj* sleeping || *mf* sleeper || *f* earring

dormir [dɔrmir] §23 *intr* to sleep; to lie dormant; **à dormir debout** boring, dull; **dormir debout** to sleep standing up; **dormir sur les deux oreilles** to feel secure

dortoir [dɔrtwar] *m* dormitory

dorure [dɔryr] *f* gilding; gilt; icing

dos [do] *m* back; bridge (*of nose*); **dans le dos de** behind the back of; **en dos d'âne** saddle-backed, hog-backed; **se mettre qn à dos** to make an enemy of s.o.; **voir au dos** see other side

dosage [dozaʒ] *m* dosage

dose [doz] *f* dose

doser [doze] *tr* to dose out, to measure out, to proportion

dossier [dosje] *m* chair back; dossier

dot [dɔt] *f* dowry

dotation [dɔtɑsjɔ̃] *f* endowment

doter [dɔte] *tr* to endow; to dower; to give a dowry to

douaire [dwer] *m* dower

douairière [dwerjer] *f* dowager

douane [dwan] *f* customs, duty; customhouse

doua·nier [dwanje] **-nière** [njer] *adj* customs ‖ *m* customs officer

doublage [dublaʒ] *m* doubling; metal plating of a ship; lining (*act of lining*); dubbing (*on tape or film*)

double [dubl] *adj & adv* double; **à double face** two-faced ‖ *m* double; duplicate, copy; **au double** twice; **double au carbone** carbon copy; **en double** in duplicate

doublement [dubləmã] *m* doubling ‖ *adv* doubly

doubler [duble] *tr* to double; to parallel, to run alongside; to pass (*s.o., s.th. going in the same direction*); to line (*a coat*); to dub (*a film*); to copy, dub (*a sound tape*); to replace (*an actor*); to gain one lap on (*another contestant*); (coll) to cheat ‖ *intr* to double; to pass (*on highway*)

doublure [dublyr] *f* lining; (theat) understudy, replacement

douce-amère [dusamer] *f* (*pl* **douces-amères**) (bot) bittersweet

douceâtre [dusɑtr] *adj* sweetish; mawkish

doucement [dusmã] *adv* softly, slowly ‖ *interj* easy now!, just a minute!

douce·reux [dusrø] **-reuse** [røz] *adj* unpleasantly sweet, cloying; mealy-mouthed

douceur [dusœr] *f* sweetness; softness, gentleness; **douceurs** sweets

douche [duʃ] *f* shower bath; douche; (coll) dressing down; (coll) shock, disappointment

doucher [duʃe] *tr* to give a shower bath to; (coll) to reprimand; (coll) to disappoint ‖ *ref* to take a shower bath

doucir [dusir] *tr* to polish, rub

doué douée [dwe] *adj* gifted, endowed

douer [dwe] *tr* to endow; **douer de** to endow or gift (*s.o.*) with

douille [duj] *f* cartridge case; sconce (*of candlestick*); bushing; (elec) socket

douil·let [duje] **douil·lette** [dujet] *adj* soft, delicate; oversensitive ‖ *f* child's padded coat

douleur [dulœr] *f* pain; sorrow; soreness

doulou·reux [dulurø] **-reuse** [røz] *adj* painful; sad; sore

doute [dut] *m* doubt; **sans doute** no doubt

douter [dute] *tr* to doubt, e.g., **je doute qu'il vienne** I doubt that he will come ‖ *intr* to doubt; **douter de** to doubt beyond a doubt; **douter de** to doubt; to distrust ‖ *ref*—**se douter de** to suspect; **se douter que** to suspect that

dou·teur [dutœr] **-teuse** [tøz] *adj* doubting ‖ *mf* doubter

dou·teux [dutø] **-teuse** [tøz] *adj* doubtful; dubious

Douvres [duvr] Dover

doux [du] **douce** [dus] *adj* sweet; soft; pleasing, suave; quiet; new (*wine*); fresh (*water*); gentle (*slope*); mild

(*weather, climate*); **en douce** on the sly, on the q.t. ‖ **doux** *interj*—**tout doux!** easy there!

douzain [duzɛ̃] *m* twelve-line verse

douzaine [duzen] *f* dozen; **à la douzaine** by the dozen; **une douzaine de** a dozen

douze [duz] *adj & pron* twelve; the Twelfth, e.g., **Jean douze** John the Twelfth ‖ *m* twelve; twelfth (*in dates*)

douzième [duzjem] *adj, pron* (*masc, fem*), *& m* twelfth

doyen [dwajɛ̃] **doyenne** [dwajen] *mf* dean; **doyen d'âge** oldest member

doyenneté [dwajɛnte] *f* seniority

Dr *abbr* (**Docteur**) Dr.

drachme [drakm] *m* drachma; dram

dragage [dragaʒ] *m* dredging

dragée [draʒe] *f* sugar-coated almond; (pharm) pill; (coll) bitter pill; **tenir la dragée haute à qn** to make s.o. pay through the nose; to be high-handed with s.o.

drageon [draʒɔ̃] *m* (bot) sucker

dragon [dragɔ̃] *m* dragon; dragoon; shrew; **dragon de vertu** prude

dragonne [dragon] *f* tassel, sword knot

drague [drag] *f* dredge; minesweeping apparatus

draguer [drage] *tr* to dredge, drag; to sweep for mines

dragueur [dragœr] *adj* minesweeping ‖ *m* dredger; **dragueur de mines** minesweeper

drain [drɛ̃] *m* drainpipe; (med) drain

drainage [drenaʒ] *m* drainage

drainer [drene], [drene] *tr* to drain

draisine [drezin] *f* (rr) handcar

dramatique [dramatik] *adj* dramatic

dramatiser [dramatize] *tr* to dramatize

dramaturge [dramatyrʒ] *mf* playwright

dramaturgie [dramatyrʒi] *f* dramatics

drame [dram] *m* drama; tragic event

drap [dra] *m* cloth; sheet; **être dans de beaux draps** to be in a pretty pickle

dra·peau [drapo] *m* (*pl* **-peaux**) flag; **au drapeau** colors (*bugle call*)!; **drapeau parlementaire** flag of truce; **être sous les drapeaux** to be a serviceman

draper [drape] *tr* to drape ‖ *ref* to drape oneself

draperie [drapri] *f* drapery; drygoods business; textile industry

dra·pier [drapje] **-pière** [pjer] *mf* draper; textile manufacturer

drastique [drastik] *adj* (med) drastic

drêche [dreʃ] *f* draff, residue of malt

drège [drɛʒ] *f* dragnet

drelin [drəlɛ̃] *m* ting-a-ling

dressage [dresaʒ] *m* training (*of animals*); erection

dresser [drese] *tr* to raise, to hold erect; to train; to put up, to erect; to set (*the table; a trap*); to draw up, to draft; to plane, smooth; **dresser l'oreille** to prick up one's ears ‖ *ref* to stand or sit up straight; **se dresser contre** to be dead set against

dressoir [dreswar] *m* sideboard, buffet, dish closet

dribble [dribl] *m* (sports) dribble

dribbler [drible] *tr & intr* (sports) to dribble

drille [drij] *m*—**joyeux drille** gay blade || *f* jeweler's drill brace; **drilles** rags (*for papermaking*)

drisse [dris] *f* halyard, rope

drogue [drɔg] *f* drug; chemical; nostrum, concoction; narcotic; (coll) trash, rubbish

droguer [drɔge] *tr* to drug or dope (*with too much medicine*) || *intr* (coll) to cool one's heels || *ref* to drug or dope oneself

droguerie [drɔgri] *f* drysaltery (Brit)

droguiste [drɔgist] *mf* drysalter (Brit)

droit [drwɑ], [drwa] **droite** [drwat], [drwat] *adj* right; honest, sincere; fair, just || *m* law; right, justice; tax; right angle; **à bon droit** with reason; **de (plein) droit** rightfully, by rights, incontestably; **droit coutumier** common law; **droit de cité** key to the city; acceptability; **droits** duties, customs; rights; **droits civils** rights to manage property; **droits civiques, droits politiques** civil rights; **droits d'auteur** royalty; **droits de reproduction réservés** copyrighted; **tous droits réservés** all rights reserved, copyrighted || *f* right, right-hand side; right hand; straight line; **à droite** to or on the right || **droit** *adv* —**droit au but** straight to the point; **tout droit** straight ahead

droi·tier [drwatje], **[drwatje]** **·tière** [tjɛr] *adj* right-handed || *mf* right-handed person; rightist

droiture [drwatyr], [drwatyr] *f* integrity

drolatique [drɔlatik] *adj* droll, comic

drôle [drol] *adj* droll, funny, strange; **drôle de** funny, e.g., **une drôle d'idée** a funny idea; **drôle de guerre** phony war; **drôle d'homme, de corps, de pistolet,** or **de pierrot** (coll) queer duck || *mf* (coll) queer duck, strange person

drôlerie [drolri] *f* drollery

drôlesse [droles] *f* wench, hussy

dromadaire [drɔmadɛr] *m* dromedary

dronte [drɔ̃t] *m* (orn) dodo

droppage [drɔpaʒ] *m* airdrop

drosser [drɔse] *tr* to drive, carry (*as the wind drives a ship ashore*)

dru drue [dry] *adj* thick, dense; fine (*rain*) || **dru** *adv* thickly, heavily

druide [drɥid] *m* druid

du [dy] §77

dû due [dy] *adj & m* due

duc [dyk] *m* duke; horned owl

ducat [dyka] *m* ducat

duché [dy/e] *m* duchy, dukedom

duchesse [dy/es] *f* duchess

duègne [dɥɛɲ] *f* duenna

duel [dɥel] *m* duel; dual number; **duel oratoire** verbal battle

duelliste [dɥelist] *m* duelist

dulcifier [dylsifje] *tr* to sweeten

dûment [dymɑ̃] *adv* duly

dune [dyn] *f* dune

dunette [dynet] *f* (naut) poop

Dunkerque [dœ̃kɛrk] *f* Dunkirk

duo [dɥo] *m* duet; duo; **duo d'injures** exchange of words, insults

duodénum [dɥodenɔm] *m* duodenum

dupe [dyp] *f* dupe

duper [dype] *tr* to dupe

duperie [dypri] *f* deception, trickery

duplicata [dyplikata] *m* duplicate

duplicateur [dyplikatœr] *m* duplicating machine

duplication [dyplikɑsjɔ̃] *f* duplication

duplicité [dyplisite] *f* duplicity

duquel [dykɛl] §78

dur dure [dyr] *adj* hard; tough; difficult; **coucher sur la dure** to sleep on the bare ground or floor; **dur à la détente** tight-fisted; **dur d'oreille** hard of hearing; **élever un enfant à la dure** to give a child a strict upbringing || *mf* (coll) tough customer || *m* hard material, concrete || **dur** *adv* hard, e.g., **travailler dur** to work hard

durable [dyrabl] *adj* durable

durant [dyrɑ̃] *prep* during; (sometimes stands after noun), e.g., **sa vie durant** during his life

durcir [dyrsir] *tr, intr & ref* to harden

durcissement [dyrsismɑ̃] *m* hardening

durée [dyre] *f* duration; wear

durer [dyre] *intr* to last, endure

dureté [dyrte] *f* hardness; cruelty

durillon [dyrijɔ̃] *m* callus, corn

duvet [dyve] *m* down, fuzz; nap (*of cloth*)

duve·té -tée [dyvte] *adj* downy

duve·teux [dyvtø] **-teuse** [tøz] *adj* fuzzy

dynamique [dinamik] *adj* dynamic || *f* dynamics

dynamite [dinamit] *f* dynamite

dynamiter [dinamite] *tr* to dynamite

dynamo [dinamo] *f* dynamo

dynaste [dinast] *m* dynast

dynastie [dinasti] *f* dynasty

dysenterie [disɑ̃tri] *f* dysentery

dyspepsie [dispepsi] *f* dyspepsia

E

E, e [ə], *[ə] *m invar* fifth letter of the French alphabet

eau [o] *f* (*pl* **eaux**) water; wake (*of ship*); **à l'eau de rose** maudlin; **de la plus belle eau** of the first water; **eau**

calcaire hard water; **eau de cale** bilge water; **eau de Javel** bleach; **eau dentifrice** mouthwash; **eau douce** soft water; fresh water; **eau dure** hard water; **eau lourde** heavy water;

eau oxygénée hydrogen peroxide; **eau vive** running water; **eaux waters;** waterworks; **eaux juvéniles** mineral waters; **eaux thermales** hot springs; **eaux usées, eaux résiduelles** polluted water; **eaux vives** swift current; **être en eau** to sweat; **faire de l'eau** to take in water; **faire eau** to leak; **grandes eaux** fountains; **nager entre deux eaux** to float under the surface; **to play both sides of the street; pêcher en eau trouble** to fish in troubled waters; **porter de l'eau à la rivière** or **à la mer** to carry coals to Newcastle; **tomber à l'eau** to fizzle out

eau-de-vie *f* (*pl* **eaux-de-vie**) brandy; spirits

eau-forte [ofɔrt] *f* (*pl* **eaux-fortes**) aqua fortis; etching

éba·hi -hie [ebai] *adj* dumfounded

ébattre [ebatr] §7 *ref* to frolic, to gambol

ébauche [eboʃ] *f* rough sketch or draft; suspicion (*of a smile*)

ébaucher [eboʃe] *tr* to sketch, to make a rough draft of

ébène [eben] *f* ebony

ébénier [ebenje] *m* ebony (*tree*)

ébéniste [ebenist] *m* cabinetmaker

ébénisterie [ebenistri] *f* cabinetmaking

éberluer [eberlɥe] *tr* to astonish

éblouir [ebluir] *tr* to dazzle, blind

éblouissement [ebluismɑ̃] *m* dazzle; glare; (pathol) dizziness

éboueur [ebwœr] *m* street cleaner, trash man; garbage collector

ébouillanter [ebujɑ̃te] *tr* to scald

éboulement [ebulmɑ̃] *m* cave-in, landslide

ébouler [ebule] *tr* & *ref* to cave in

ébourif·fant [eburifɑ̃] **ébourif·fante** [eburifɑ̃t] *adj* (coll) astounding

ébouriffer [eburife] *tr* to ruffle; (coll) to astound

ébouter [ebute] *tr* to cut off the end of

ébranchage [ebrɑ̃ʃaʒ] *m* pruning

ébrancher [ebrɑ̃ʃe] *tr* to prune

ébranlement [ebrɑ̃lmɑ̃] *m* shaking; shock

ébranler [ebrɑ̃le] *tr* to shake, jar ǁ *ref* to start out; to be shaken

ébrécher [ebreʃe] §10 *tr* to nick; chip; to make a dent in (*e.g., a fortune*) ǁ *ref* to be nicked, chipped; (with *dat* of *reflex pron*) to break off (*a tooth*)

ébriété [ebrijete] *f* inebriation

ébrouer [ebrue] *ref* to snort (*said of horse*); to splash about; to shake the water off oneself

ébruiter [ebrɥite] *tr* to noise about, to blab ǁ *ref* to get around (*said of news*); to leak out (*said of secret*)

ébullition [ebylisjɔ̃] *f* boiling; ebullience, ferment

ébur·né -née [ebyrne] *adj* ivory

écaille [ekaj] *f* scale (*of fish, snake*); shell; tortoise shell

écail·ler [ekaje] **écail·lère** [ekajer] *mf* oyster opener ǁ *m* oysterman ǁ *f* oysterwoman ǁ **écailler.** *tr* & ǁ to scale

écale [ekal] *f* shell, husk, hull

écaler [ekale] *tr* to shell, husk, hull

écarlate [ekarlat] *adj* & *f* scarlet

écarquiller [ekarkije] *tr* (coll) to open wide, to spread apart

écart [ekar] *m* swerve, side step; digression, flight (*of imagination*); difference, gap, spread; error (*in range*); lapse (*in good conduct*); (cards) discard; **à l'écart** aside; aloof; **à l'écart de** far from; **faire le grand écart** to do the splits; **faire un écart** to shy (*said of horse*); to swerve (*said of car*); to step aside (*said of person*)

écar·té -tée [ekarte] *adj* lonely, secluded; wide-apart

écartèlement [ekartɛlmɑ̃] *m* quartering

écarteler [ekartəle] §2 *tr* to quarter

écartement [ekartəmɑ̃] *m* removal, separation; spreading; space between; spark gap; gauge (*of rails*)

écarter [ekarte] *tr* to put aside; to keep away; to ward off; to draw aside; to spread; (cards) to discard ǁ *ref* to turn away; to stray

ecchymose [ekimoz] *f* black-and-blue mark

ecclésiastique [eklezjastik] *adj* & *m* ecclesiastic

écerve·lé -lée [eservəle] *adj* scatterbrained ǁ *mf* scatterbrain

échafaud [eʃafo] *m* scaffold

échafaudage [eʃafodaʒ] *m* scaffolding

échafauder [eʃafode] *tr* to pile up; to lay the groundwork for ǁ *intr* to erect a scaffolding

échalasser [eʃalase] *tr* to stake

échalote [eʃalɔt] *f* shallot

échancrer [eʃɑ̃kre] *tr* to make a V-shaped cut in (*the neck of a dress*); to cut (*a dress*) low in the neck; to indent; to hollow out

échange [eʃɑ̃ʒ] *m* exchange

échanger [eʃɑ̃ʒe] §38 *tr* to exchange; **échanger pour** or **contre** to exchange (*s.th.*) for

échangeur [eʃɑ̃ʒœr] *m* interchange

échanson [eʃɑ̃sɔ̃] *m* cupbearer

échantillon [eʃɑ̃tijɔ̃] *m* sample; **comparer à l'échantillon** to spot-check

échantillonnage [eʃɑ̃tijɔnaʒ] *m* sampling; spot check

échantillonner [eʃɑ̃tijɔne] *tr* to cut samples of; to spot-check; to select (*a sampling to be polled*)

échappatoire [eʃapatwar] *f* loophole, way out

échap·pé -pée [eʃape] *mf* escapee ǁ *f* escape; short period; glimpse; (sports) spurt; **à l'échappée** stealthily

échappement [eʃapmɑ̃] *m* escape, leak; exhaust; escapement (*of watch*); **échappement libre** cutout

échapper [eʃape] *tr*—**l'échapper belle** to have a narrow escape ǁ *intr* to escape; **échapper à** to escape from; **échapper de** to slip out of ǁ *ref* to escape

écharde [eʃard] *f* splinter

écharpe [eʃarp] *f* scarf; sash; sling; **en écharpe** diagonally, crosswise; in a sling; across the shoulder

écharper [eʃarpe] *tr* to slash, cut up

échasse [eʃɑs] f stilt

échauder [eʃode] tr to scald; to whitewash; to gouge (a customer)

échauffement [eʃofmɑ̃] m heating; overexcitement

échauffer [eʃofe] tr to heat; to warm; **échauffer les oreilles à qn** to get s.o.'s dander up || ref to heat up; to become excited

échauffourée [eʃofure] f skirmish; rash undertaking

èche [eʃ] f bait

échéance [eʃeɑ̃s] f due date, expiration

échec [eʃek] m check; chessman; failure; **échec et mat** checkmate; **échecs** [eʃe] chess; chess set; **être échec** to be in check; **jouer aux échecs** to play chess

échelle [eʃɛl] f ladder; scale; **échelle de sauvetage** fire escape; **échelle mobile** sliding scale; **échelle pliante** stepladder; **monter à l'échelle** (coll) to bite, be fooled

échelon [eʃlɔ̃] m echelon; rung (of ladder)

échelonner [eʃlɔne] tr to spread out, to space out

écheniller [eʃnije] tr to remove caterpillars from; to exterminate (pests); to eradicate (corruption)

éche-veau [eʃvo] m (pl -veaux) skein

écheve-lé -lée [eʃəvle] adj disheveled; wild (dance, race)

écheveler [eʃəvle] §34 tr to dishevel

échevin [eʃvɛ̃] m (hist) alderman

échine [eʃin] f spine, backbone; **avoir l'échine souple** (coll) to be a yes man

échiner [eʃine] tr to break the back of; to beat, kill || ref to tire oneself out

échiquier [eʃikje] m chessboard; exchequer

écho [eko] m echo; piece of gossip; **échos** gossip column; **faire écho** to echo

échoir [eʃwar] (usually used only in: inf; ger **échéant**; pp **échu**; 3d sg: pres ind **échoit**; pret **échut**; fut **échoira**; cond **échoirait**) intr (aux: AVOIR or ÊTRE) to fall, devolve; to fall due

échoppe [eʃɔp] f burin; (com) stand, booth; workshop

échopper [eʃɔpe] tr to scoop out

échotier [eʃotje] m gossip columnist, society editor

échouer [eʃwe] tr to ground, to beach || intr to sink; to run aground; to fail || ref to run aground

é-chu -chue [eʃy] adj due, payable

écimer [esime] tr to top

éclaboussement [eklabusmɑ̃] m splash

éclabousser [eklabuse] tr to splash

éclair [ekler] adj lightning (e.g., speed); flash (bulb) || m flash (of light, of lightning, of the eyes, of wit); (culin) éclair; **éclairs** lightning; **éclairs de chaleur** heat lightning; **éclairs en nappe** sheet lightning; **il fait des éclairs** it is lightening; **passer comme un éclair** to flash by

éclairage [ekleraʒ] m lighting; **sous cet éclairage** (fig) in this light

éclaircie [eklersi] f break, clearing; spell of good weather

éclaircissement [eklersismɑ̃] m explanation, clearing up

éclairement [eklermɑ̃] m illumination

éclairer [eklere] tr to light; to enlighten; **éclairer sa lanterne** (fig) to ring a bell for s.o. || intr to light up, to glitter; **il éclaire** it is lightening || ref to be lighted

éclai-reur [eklerœr] -reuse [røz] mf scout || m boy scout || f girl scout

éclat [ekla] m splinter; ray (of sunshine); peal (of thunder); burst (of laughter); brightness, splendor

éclatement [eklatmɑ̃] m explosion; blowout (of tire); (fig) split

éclater [eklate] intr to splinter; to sparkle, glitter; to burst; to break out; to blow up

éclateur [eklatœr] m spark gap (of induction coil)

éclectique [eklɛktik] adj eclectic

éclipse [eklips] f eclipse; **à éclipses** flashing, blinking

éclipser [eklipse] tr to eclipse || ref to be eclipsed; (coll) to vanish; (coll) to sneak off

éclisse [eklis] f splinter; (med) splint; (rr) fishplate

éclisser [eklise] tr to splint

éclo-pé -pée [eklope] adj lame || mf cripple

éclore [eklɔr] §24 intr (aux: ÊTRE) to hatch; to blossom out

éclosion [eklozjɔ̃] f hatching; blooming

écluse [eklyz] f lock (of canal, river, etc.); floodgate

écluser [eklyze] tr to close (a canal) by a lock; to pass (a boat) through a lock

écœurer [ekœre] tr to sicken; to dishearten

école [ekɔl] f school; **école à tir** artillery practice; **école d'application** model school; **école d'arts et métiers** trade school; **école dominicale, école du dimanche** Sunday School; **école libre** private school; **école maternelle** nursery school; **école mixte** coeducational school; **être à bonne école** to be in good hands; **faire école** to set a fashion; to form a school (to set up a doctrine, gain adherents); **faire l'école buissonnière** (coll) to play hooky

éco-lier -lière [ljer] adj schoolboy || mf pupil, scholar; novice || m schoolboy || f schoolgirl

écologie [ekɔlɔʒi] f ecology

éconduire [ekɔ̃dɥir] §19 tr to show out

économat [ekɔnɔma] m comptroller's office; commissary, company or co-op store; **économats** chain stores

écono-me [ekɔnɔm] adj economical || mf treasurer; housekeeper || m bursar

économie [ekɔnɔmi] f economy; **économie de marché** free enterprise; **économies** savings

économique [ekɔnɔmik] adj economic; economical || f economics

économiser [ekɔnɔmize] tr & intr to economize, save

écope [ekɔp] *f* scoop (*for bailing*)

écoper [ekɔpe] *tr* to bail out ‖ *intr* (coll) to get a bawling out

écorce [ekɔrs] *f* bark (*of tree*); peel, rind; crust (*of earth*)

écorcer [ekɔrse] §51 *tr* to peel, to strip off

écorcher [ekɔrʃe] *tr* to peel; to chafe; to fleece, overcharge; to grate on (*the ears*); to burn (*the throat*); to murder (*a language*) ‖ *ref* (with *dat of reflex pron*) to skin (*e.g., one's arm*)

écor·cheur [ekɔrʃœr] **-cheuse** [ʃøz] *mf* skinner; fleecer, swindler

écorchure [ekɔrʃyr] *f* scratch, abrasion

écorner [ekɔrne] *tr* to poll, break the horns of; to dog-ear; to make a hole in (*e.g., a fortune*)

écorni·fler [ekɔrnifle] *tr* to cadge; **écorni·fler un dîner à qn** to bum a dinner off s.o.

écorni·fleur [ekɔrniflœr] **-fleuse** [fløz] *mf* sponger, moocher

écos·sais [ekɔse] **écos·saise** [ekɔsez] *adj* Scotch, Scottish ‖ *m* Scotch, Scottish (*language*); Scotch plaid ‖ (*cap*) *mf* Scot; **les Écossais** the Scotch ‖ *m* Scotchman

Écosse [ekɔs] *f* Scotland; **l'Écosse** Scotland

écosser [ekɔse] *tr* to shell, hull, husk

écot [eko] *m* share; tree stump; **payer son écot** to pay one's share

écoulement [ekulmã] *m* flow; (com) sale, turnover; (pathol) discharge; **écoulement d'eau** drainage

écouler [ekule] *tr* to sell, dispose of ‖ *ref* to run (*said, e.g., of water*); to flow; to drain; to leak; to elapse, go by

écourter [ekurte] *tr* to shorten (*a dress, coat, etc.*); to crop (*the tail, ears, etc.*); to cut short, curtail

écoute [ekut] *f* listening post; monitoring; (naut) sheet; **écoutes** wild boar's ears; **être aux écoutes** to eavesdrop, to keep one's ears to the ground; **se mettre à l'écoute** to listen to the radio

écouter [ekute] *tr* to listen to; **écouter parler** to listen to (*s.o.*) speaking ‖ *intr* to listen; **écouter aux portes** to eavesdrop ‖ *ref* to coddle oneself; **s'écouter parler** to be pleased with the sound of one's own voice

écou·teur [ekutœr] **-teuse** [tøz] *mf* listener; **écouteur aux portes** eavesdropper ‖ *m* telephone receiver; earphone

écoutille [ekutij] *f* hatchway

écouvillon [ekuvijɔ̃] *m* swab, mop

écrabouiller [ekrabuje] *tr* (coll) to squash

écran [ekrã] *m* screen; (phot) filter; **écran de cheminée** fire screen; **écran de protection aérienne** air umbrella; **le petit écran** television screen; **porter à l'écran** to put on the screen

écra·sant [ekrazã] **-sante** [zãt] *adj* crushing

écraser [ekraze] *tr* to crush; to overwhelm; to run over ‖ *ref* to be crushed; to crash

écrémer [ekreme] §10 *tr* to skim; (fig) to skim the cream off

écrémeuse [ekremøz] *f* cream separator

écrevisse [ekrəvis] *f* crayfish

écrier [ekrije] *ref* to cry out, exclaim

écrin [ekrɛ̃] *m* jewel case

écrire [ekrir] §25 *tr* to write; to spell ‖ *intr* to write ‖ *ref* to write to each other; to be written; to be spelled

é·crit [ekri] **-crite** [krit] *adj* written; **c'était écrit** it was fate ‖ *m* writing, written word; written examination; **écrits** writings, works; **par écrit** in writing

écri·teau [ekrito] *m* (*pl* **-teaux**) sign, placard

écritoire [ekritwar] *f* desk set

écriture [ekrityr] *f* handwriting; writing (*style of writing*); **écriture de chat** scrawl; **écritures** accounts; **Écritures** Scriptures; **écritures publiques** government documents

écrivailleur [ekrivajœr] *m* (coll) scribbler, hack writer

écrivain [ekrivɛ̃] *adj*—**femme écrivain** woman writer ‖ *m* writer; **écrivain public** public letter writer

écrivasser [ekrivase] *intr* (coll) to scribble

écrou [ekru] *m* nut (*with internal thread*); register (*on police blotter*); **écrou à oreille** thumb nut

écrouer [ekrue] *tr* to jail, to book

écrouler [ekrule] *ref* to collapse; to crumble; to flop (*in a chair*)

é·cru -crue [ekry] *adj* raw; unbleached

écu [eky] *m* shield; crown (*money*); **écus** money

écubier [ekybje] *m* (naut) hawsehole

écueil [ekœj] *m* reef, sandbank; stumbling block

écuelle [ekɥel] *f* bowl

éculer [ekyle] *tr* to wear down at the heel

écu·mant [ekymã] **-mante** [mãt] *adj* foaming; fuming (*with rage*)

écume [ekym] *f* foam; froth; lather; dross; scum (*on liquids; on metal; of society*); **écume de mer** meerschaum

écumer [ekyme] *tr* to skim, scum; to pick up (*e.g., gossip*); to scour (*the seas*) ‖ *intr* to foam; to scum; to fume (*with anger*)

écu·meur [ekymœr] **-meuse** [møz] *mf* drifter; **écumeur de marmite** hanger-on; **écumeur de mer** pirate

écu·meux [ekymø] **-meuse** [møz] *adj* foamy, frothy

écumoire [ekymwar] *f* skimmer

écurage [ekyraʒ] *m* scouring; cleaning out

écurer [ekyre] *tr* to scour; to clean out

écureuil [ekyrœj] *m* squirrel

écurie [ekyri] *f* stable (*for horses, mules, etc.*); string of horses

écusson [ekysɔ̃] *m* escutcheon; bud (*for grafting*); (mil) identification tag

écuyer [ekɥije] **écuyère** [ekɥijer] *mf* horseback rider ‖ *m* horseman; squire; riding master ‖ *f* horsewoman

eczéma [ɛkzema], [ɛgzema] *m* eczema

edelweiss [edǝlvɑjs], [edɛlvɛs] *m* edelweiss

éden [edɛn] *m* Eden || (*cap*) *m* Garden of Eden

éden·té -tée [edɑte] *adj* toothless

E.D.F. *abbr* (**Electricité de France**) French national electric company

édicter [edikte] *tr* to decree, to promulgate

édicule [edikyl] *m* kiosk; street urinal

édi·fiant [edifjɑ̃] **-fiante** [fjɑ̃t] *adj* edifying

édification [edifikɑsjɔ̃] *f* edification; construction, building

édifice [edifis] *m* edifice, building

édifier [edifje] *tr* to edify; to inform, enlighten; to construct, to build; to found

édit [edi] *m* edict

éditer [edite] *tr* to publish; to edit (*a manuscript*)

édi·teur [editœr] **-trice** [tris] *mf* publisher; editor (*of a manuscript*)

édition [edisjɔ̃] *f* edition; publishing

édito·rial -riale [editɔrjal] *adj & m* (*pl* **-riaux** [rjo]) editorial

édredon [edrǝdɔ̃] *m* eiderdown

éduca·teur [edykatœr] **-trice** [tris] *adj* educational || *mf* educator

éduca·tif [edykatif] **-tive** [tiv] *adj* educational

éducation [edykɑsjɔ̃] *f* education, bringing-up, nurture

éduquer [edyke] *tr* to bring up (*children*); to educate, train

éfaufiler [efofile] *tr* to unravel

effacement [efasmɑ̃] *m* effacement, erasing; self-effacement

effacer [efase] §51 *tr* to efface; to erase || *ref* to efface oneself; to stand aside

effarement [efarmɑ̃] *m* fright, scare

effaroucher [efaruʃe] *tr* to frighten, scare off

effec·tif [efektif] **-tive** [tiv] *adj* actual, real || *m* personnel, manpower; strength (*of military unit*); complement (*of ship*); size (*of class*)

effectivement [efektivmɑ̃] *adv* actually, really, sure enough

effectuer [efektɥe] *tr* to effect

effémi·né -née [efemine] *adj* effeminate

efféminer [efemine] *tr* to make a sissy of; to unman || *ref* to become effeminate

effervescence [efɛrvesɑ̃s] *f* effervescence; excitement, ferment

efferves·cent [efɛrvesɑ̃] **efferves·cente** [efɛrvesɑ̃t] *adj* effervescent

effet [efɛ] *m* effect; (billiards) english; **à cet effet** for that purpose; **en effet** indeed, actually, sure enough; **effet de commerce** bill of exchange; **effets publics** government bonds; **faire de l'effet** to be striking; **faire l'effet de** to give the impression of

effeuillage [efœjaʒ] *m* thinning of leaves

effeuillaison [efœjɛzɔ̃] *f* fall of leaves

effeuiller [efœje] *tr* to thin out the leaves of, to pluck off the petals of || *ref* to shed its leaves

effeuilleuse [efœjøz] *f* (coll) strip-teaser

efficace [efikas] *adj* effective

efficacement [efikasmɑ̃] *adv* effectively

efficacité [efikasite] *f* efficacy, efficiency

efficience [efisjɑ̃s] *f* efficiency

effi·cient [efisjɑ̃] **-ciente** [sjɑ̃t] *adj* efficient

effigie [efiʒi] *f* effigy

effiler [efile] *tr* to unravel; to taper

effilocher [efiloʃe] *tr* to unravel

efflan·qué -quée [eflɑke] *adj* skinny

effleurer [eflœre] *tr* to graze; to touch on

effluve [eflyv] *m* effluvium, emanation

effondrement [efɔ̃drǝmɑ̃] *m* collapse

effondrer [efɔ̃dre] *tr* to break open; to break (*ground*) || *ref* to collapse, cave in; to sink

efforcer [eforse] §51 *ref*—**s'efforcer à** or **de** to try hard to, to strive to

effort [efɔr] *m* effort; (med) hernia, rupture; **effort de rupture** breaking stress; **effort de tension** torque; **faire effort sur soi-même** to get a hold of oneself

effraction [efraksjɔ̃] *f* housebreaking

effraie [efrɛ] *f* screech owl

effranger [efrɑ̃ʒe] §38 *tr & ref* to fray

effrayant [efrejɑ̃] **effrayante** [efrejɑ̃t] *adj* frightful, dreadful

effrayer [efreje] §49 *tr* to frighten || *ref* to be frightened

effré·né -née [efrene] *adj* unbridled

effritement [efritmɑ̃] *m* crumbling

effriter [efrite] *tr & ref* to crumble

effroi [efrwa], [efrwɑ] *m* fright

effron·té -tée [efrɔ̃te] *adj* impudent; shameless; (slang) saucy, sassy

effronterie [efrɔ̃tri] *f* effrontery

effroyable [efrwajabl] *adj* frightful

effusion [efyzjɔ̃] *f* effusion; shedding (*of blood*); (fig) gushing

égailler [egaje] *ref* to scatter

é·gal -gale [egal] (*pl* **-gaux** [go]) *adj* equal; level; (coll) indifferent; **ça m'est égal** (coll) it's all the same to me, it's all right || *mf* equal; **à l'égal de** as much as, no less than

également [egalmɑ̃] *adv* equally, likewise, also

égaler [egale] *tr* to equal, match

égaliser [egalize] *tr* to equalize; to equate

égalitaire [egaliter] *adj & mf* equalitarian

égalité [egalite] *f* equality; evenness; **être à égalité** to be tied

égard [egar] *m* respect; **à l'égard de** with regard to; **à tous (les) égards** in all respects; **eu égard à** in consideration of

éga·ré -rée [egare] *adj* stray, lost

égarement [egarmɑ̃] *m* wandering (*of mind, senses, etc.*); frenzy (*of sorrow, anger, etc.*)

égarer [egare] *tr* to mislead; to misplace; to bewilder || *ref* to get lost, to stray; to be on the wrong track

égayer [egeje] §49 *tr & ref* to cheer up; to brighten

égide [eʒid] *f* aegis

églefin [egləfɛ̃] *m* haddock

église [egliz] *f* church

églogue [eglɔg] *f* eclogue

égoïne [egɔin] *f* handsaw

égoïsme [egɔism] *m* egoism

égoïste [egɔist] *adj* selfish || *mf* egoist

égorgement [egɔrʒəmɑ̃] *m* slaughter

égorger [egɔrʒe] §38 *tr* to cut the throat of; (coll) to overcharge

égosiller [egɔzije] *ref* to shout oneself hoarse

égotisme [egɔtism] *m* egotism

égotiste [egɔtist] *adj* egotistical || *mf* egotist

égout [egu] *m* drainage; sewer; sink, cesspool (*e.g., of iniquity*)

égoutier [egutje] *m* sewer worker

égoutter [egute] *tr* to drain; to let drip || *ref* to drip

égouttoir [egutwar] *m* drainboard

égrapper [egrape] *tr* to pick off from the cluster

égratigner [egratiɲe] *tr* to scratch; to take a dig at, to tease

égratignure [egratiɲyr] *f* scratch; gibe, dig

égrener [egrəne] §2 *tr* to shell (*e.g., peas*); to gin (*cotton*); to pick off (*grapes*); to unstring (*pearls*); to tell (*beads*) || *ref* to drop one by one; to be strung out

égril·lard [egrijar] **égril·larde** [egrijard] *adj* spicy, lewd || *mf* shameless, unblushing person

égrugeoir [egryʒwar] *m* mortar (*for pounding or grinding*)

égruger [egryʒe] §38 *tr* to pound (*in a mortar*)

égueuler [egœle] *tr* to break the neck of (*e.g., a bottle*)

Égypte [eʒipt] *f* Egypt; **l'Égypte** Egypt

égyp·tien [eʒipsjɛ̃] **-tienne** [sjɛn] *adj* Egyptian || (*cap*) *mf* Egyptian

éhon·té -tée [eɔ̃te] *adj* shameless

eider [ejder] *m* eider duck

éjaculation [eʒakylasjɔ̃] *f* ejaculation; (eccl) short, fervent prayer

éjaculer [eʒakyle] *tr & intr* to ejaculate

éjecter [eʒekte] *tr* to eject; (coll) to oust

éjection [eʒeksjɔ̃] *f* ejection

élabo·ré -rée [elabore] *adj* elaborated; prepared, elaborate

élaborer [elabore] *tr* to elaborate; to work out, develop

élaguer [elage] *tr* to prune

élan [elɑ̃] *m* dash; impulse, outburst; spirit, glow; (zool) elk, moose; **avec élan** with enthusiasm

élan·cé -cée [elɑ̃se] *adj* slender, slim

élancement [elɑ̃smɑ̃] *m* throbbing, twinge; yearning (*e.g., for God*)

élancer [elɑ̃se] §51 *intr* to throb, to twinge || *ref* to rush, spring, dash; to spurt out

élargir [elarʒir] *tr* to widen; to broaden; to release (*a prisoner*) || *ref* to widen; to become more lax

élasticité [elastisite] *f* elasticity

élastique [elastik] *adj* elastic || *m* elastic; rubber band

élec·teur [elektœr] **-trice** [tris] *adj* voting || *mf* voter, constituent; (hist) elector; **électeurs** electorate

élec·tif [elektif] **-tive** [tiv] *adj* elective

élection [eleksjɔ̃] *f* election; choice

électorat [elektɔra] *m* right to vote; (hist) electorate

électri·cien [elektrisjɛ̃] **-cienne** [sjɛn] *adj* electrical (*worker*) || *mf* electrician

électricité [elektrisite] *f* electricity

électrifier [elektrifje] *tr* to electrify

électrique [elektrik] *adj* electric(al)

électriser [elektrize] *tr* to electrify

électro [elektro] *m* electromagnet

électro-aimant [elektroɛmɑ̃] *m* (*pl* **-aimants**) electromagnet

électrochoc [elektrɔʃɔk] *m* (med) electric shock treatment

électro-culinaire [elektrokyliner] *adj* electric kitchen (*appliances*)

électrocuter [elektrɔkyte] *tr* to electrocute

électrode [elektrɔd] *f* electrode

électrolyse [elektrɔliz] *f* electrolysis

électrolyte [elektrɔlit] *m* electrolyte

électromagnétique [elektrɔmaɲetik] *adj* electromagnetic

électroména·ger [elektrɔmenaʒe] **-gère** [ʒer] *adj* household-electric

électromo·teur [elektrɔmɔtœr] **-trice** [tris] *adj* electromotive || *m* electric motor

électron [elektrɔ̃] *m* electron

électronique [elektrɔnik] *adj* electronic || *f* electronics

électron-volt [elektrɔ̃vɔlt] *m* (*pl* **électrons-volts**) electron-volt

électrophone [elektrɔfɔn] *m* electric phonograph

électrotype [elektrɔtip] *m* electrotype

électrotyper [elektrɔtipe] *tr* to electrotype

élégance [elegɑ̃s] *f* elegance

élé·gant [elegɑ̃] **-gante** [gɑ̃t] *adj* elegant

élégiaque [eleʒjak] *adj* elegiac || *mf* elegist

élégie [eleʒi] *f* elegy

élément [elemɑ̃] *m* element; (*of an electric battery*) cell, element; (elec, mach) unit; **élément standard** standard part

élémentaire [elemɑ̃ter] *adj* elementary

éléphant [elefɑ̃] *m* elephant

éléphantesque [elefɑ̃tesk] *adj* (coll) gigantic, elephantine

élevage [elvaʒ], [elvaʒ] *m* rearing, raising, breeding; ranch

éléva·teur [elevatœr] **-trice** [tris] *adj* lifting || *m* elevator; hoist

élévation [elevasjɔ̃] *f* elevation; promotion; increase; (rok) lift-off

élève [elev] *mf* pupil, student; **ancien élève** alumnus; **élève externe** day student; **élève interne** boarding student || *f* breeder (*animal*); (hort) seedling

éle·vé -vée [elve] *adj* high, elevated; lofty, noble; **bien élevé** well-bred; **mal élevé** ill-bred

élever [elve] §2 *tr* to raise; to raise,

bring up, nurture; to erect || *ref* to rise; to arise; to be built, to stand

éle·veur [elvœr] **-veuse** [vøz] *mf* breeder, rancher

elfe [elf] *m* elf

élider [elide] *tr* to elide

éligible [eliʒibl] *adj* eligible

élimer [elime] *tr & ref* to wear threadbare

éliminatoire [eliminatwar] *adj* (sports) preliminary || *f* (sports) preliminaries

éliminer [elimine] *tr* to eliminate

élire [elir] §36 *tr* to elect

élision [elizjɔ̃] *f* elision

élite [elit] *f* elite

elle [el] *pron disj* §85 || *pron conj* §87

elle-même [elmɛm] §86

ellipse [elips] *f* (gram) ellipsis; (math) ellipse

elliptique [eliptik] *adj* elliptic(al)

élocution [elɔkysjɔ̃] *f* elocution; choice and arrangement of words

éloge [elɔʒ] *m* eulogy; praise

élo·gieux [elɔʒjø] **-gieuse** [ʒjøz] *adj* full of praise

éloi·gné -gnée [elwaɲe] *adj* distant

éloignement [elwaɲəmɑ̃] *m* remoteness; aversion; postponement

éloigner [elwaɲe] *tr* to move away; to remove; to drive away; to postpone || *ref* to move away; to digress, deviate; to become estranged

élongation [elɔ̃gasjɔ̃] *f* stretching

élonger [elɔ̃ʒe] §38 *tr* to lay (e.g., a cable); **élonger la terre** to skirt the coast

éloquence [elɔkɑ̃s] *f* eloquence

élo·quent [elɔkɑ̃] **-quente** [kɑ̃t] *adj* eloquent

é·lu -lue [ely] *adj* elected || *mf* chosen one; **les élus** the elect

élucider [elyside] *tr* to elucidate

éluder [elyde] *tr* to elude, avoid

éma·cié -ciée [emasje] *adj* emaciated

émacier [emasje] *ref* to become emaciated

é·mail [emaj] *m* (pl **-maux** [mo]) enamel || *m* (pl **-mails**) nail polish; car or bicycle paint

émaillage [emajaʒ] *m* enameling

émailler [emaje] *tr* to enamel; to sprinkle (e.g., with quotations, metaphors, etc.); to dot (e.g., the fields, as flowers do)

émanation [emanasjɔ̃] *f* emanation; manifestation (e.g., of authority)

émanciper [emɑ̃sipe] *tr* to emancipate || *ref* to be emancipated; (coll) to get out of hand

émaner [emane] *intr* to emanate

émarger [emarʒe] §38 *tr* to trim (e.g., a book); to initial (a document) || *intr* to get paid; **émarger à** to be paid from

émasculer [emaskyle] *tr* to emasculate

embâcle [ɑ̃bɑkl] *m* pack ice, ice floe

emballage [ɑ̃balaʒ] *m* packing, wrapping

emballer [ɑ̃bale] *tr* to wrap up, to pack; to race (a motor); (coll) to thrill; (coll) to bawl out || *ref* to bolt, to run away; (mach) to race; (coll) to get worked up

embal·leur [ɑ̃balœr] **embal·leuse** [ɑ̃baløz] *mf* packer

embarbouiller [ɑ̃barbuje] *tr* to besmear; (coll) to muddle, confuse || *ref* (coll) to get tangled up

embarcadère [ɑ̃barkader] *m* wharf; (rr) platform

embarcation [ɑ̃barkasjɔ̃] *f* small boat

embardée [ɑ̃barde] *f* lurch; (aut) swerve; (aer, naut) yaw

embarder [ɑ̃barde] *intr* (aut) to swerve; (aer, naut) to yaw

embargo [ɑ̃bargo] *m* embargo

embarquement [ɑ̃barkəmɑ̃] *m* embarkation; shipping; loading

embarquer [ɑ̃barke] *tr* to embark; to ship (a sea); to load (in car, plane, etc.); (coll) to put in the clink || *ref* to embark; to board; to get into a car

embarras [ɑ̃bara] *m* embarrassment; trouble, inconvenience; encumbrance, obstruction; perplexity; financial difficulties; **embarras de voitures** traffic jam; **embarras du choix** too much to choose from; **faire des embarras** (coll) to put on airs

embarrasser [ɑ̃barase] *tr* to embarrass; to hamper, to obstruct; to stump, to perplex || *ref*—**s'embarrasser de** to take an interest in; to bother with

embaucher [ɑ̃boʃe] *tr* to hire, to sign on; (coll) to entice (soldiers) to desert || *intr* to hire; **on n'embauche pas** (public sign) no help wanted

embauchoir [ɑ̃boʃwar] *m* shoetree

embaumement [ɑ̃boməmɑ̃] *m* embalming; perfuming

embaumer [ɑ̃bome] *tr* to embalm; to perfume || *intr* to smell good

embaumeur [ɑ̃bomœr] *m* embalmer

embellir [ɑ̃belir] *tr* to embellish || *intr* to clear up (said of weather); to improve in looks || *ref* to grow more beautiful

embellissement [ɑ̃belismɑ̃] *m* embellishment

embêtement [ɑ̃bɛtmɑ̃] *m* (coll) annoyance

embêter [ɑ̃bete], [ɑ̃bete] *tr* (coll) to annoy

emblave [ɑ̃blav] *f* grainfield

emblaver [ɑ̃blave] *tr* to sow

emblée [ɑ̃ble]—**d'emblée** then and there, right off; without difficulty

emblématique [ɑ̃blematik] *adj* emblematic(al)

emblème [ɑ̃blɛm] *m* emblem

embobeliner [ɑ̃bɔbline] *tr* (coll) to bamboozle

embobiner [ɑ̃bɔbine] *tr* to wind up (e.g., on a reel); (coll) to bamboozle

emboîter [ɑ̃bwate] *tr* to encase; to nest (boxes, boats, etc.); (mach) to interlock, joint; **emboîter le pas to** fall into step

embolie [ɑ̃bɔli] *f* (pathol) embolism

embonpoint [ɑ̃bɔ̃pwɛ̃] *m* portliness; **prendre de l'embonpoint** to put on flesh

embouche [ɑ̃buʃ] *f* pasture

embou·ché -chée [ãbuʃe] *adj*—**mal embouché** foul-mouthed
emboucher [ãbuʃe] *tr* to blow, sound
embouchoir [ãbuʃwar] *m* mouthpiece
embouchure [ãbuʃyr] *f* mouth (*of a river*); mouthpiece
embourber [ãburbe] *tr* to stick in the mud; to vilify, to implicate
embout [ãbu] *m* tip, ferrule; rubber tip (*for chair*)
embouteillage [ãbutejaʒ] *m* bottling; bottleneck, traffic jam
emboutir [ãbutir] *tr* to stamp, emboss; to smash (*e.g., a fender*) || *ref* to bump
embranchement [ãbrãʃmã] *m* branching (off); branch; branch line; junction (*of roads, track, etc.*)
embrasement [ãbrazmã] *m* conflagration; illumination, glow
embraser [ãbraze] *tr* to set aflame or aglow || *ref* to flame up; to glow
embrassade [ãbrasad] *f* embrace; kissing
embrasse [ãbras] *f* curtain tieback
embrassement [ãbrasmã] *m* embrace
embrasser [ãbrase] *tr* to embrace; to kiss; to join; to undertake; to take in (*at a glance*); to take (*the opportunity*) || *ref* to embrace; to neck
embras·seur [ãbrasœr] **embras·seuse** [ãbrasøz] *mf* smoocher
embrasure [ãbrazyr] *f* embrasure, loophole; opening (*for door or window*)
embrayage [ãbrejaʒ] *m* coupling, engagement; (aut) clutch
embrayer [ãbreje], [ãbreje] §49 *tr* to engage, connect; to throw into gear || *intr* to throw out the clutch in
embrocher [ãbrɔʃe] *tr* to put on a spit
embrouiller [ãbruje] *tr* to embroil || *ref* to become embroiled
embroussail·lé -lée [ãbrusaje] *adj* bushy; tangled; complicated, complex
embru·mé -mée [ãbryme] *adj* foggy, misty
embruns [ãbrœ̃] *mpl* spray
embryologie [ãbrijɔlɔʒi] *f* embryology
embryon [ãbrijɔ̃] *m* embryo
embryonnaire [ãbrijɔner] *adj* embryonic
em·bu -bue [ãby] *adj* lifeless, dull || *m* dull tone (*of a painting*)
embûche [ãbyʃ] *f* snare, trap
embuer [ãbɥe] *tr* to cloud with steam; embué de larmes dimmed with tears
embuscade [ãbyskad] *f* ambush
embus·qué -quée [ãbyske] *adj* in ambush; se tenir embusqué to lie in ambush || *m* (mil) goldbricker, shirker
embusquer [ãbyske] *tr* to ambush, trap || *ref* to lie in ambush; (mil) to get a safe assignment
émé·ché -chée [emeʃe] *adj* (coll) tipsy, high
émender [emãde] *tr* to amend (*a sentence, decree, etc.*)
émeraude [emrod] *f* emerald
émergence [emerʒãs] *f* emergence
émerger [emerʒe] §38 *intr* to emerge
émeri [emri] *m* emery

émerillon [emrijɔ̃] *m* swivel; (orn) merlin
émerillon·né -née [emrijɔne] *adj* lively, gay
émérite [emerit] *adj* experienced; distinguished, remarkable; confirmed (*smoker*); (obs) retired, emeritus
émersion [emersjɔ̃] *f* emersion
émerveillement [emervejmã] *m* wonderment
émerveiller [emerveje] *tr* to astonish, amaze
émétique [emetik] *adj & m* emetic
émet·teur [emetœr] **émet·trice** [emetris] *adj* issuing; transmitting || *mf* maker (*of check, draft*); issuer || *m* broadcasting station; (rad) transmitter
émetteur-récepteur [emetœrreseptœr] *m* (*pl* **émetteurs-récepteurs**) (rad) walkie-talkie
émettre [emetr] §42 *tr* to emit; to express (*an opinion*); to issue (*stamps, bank notes, etc.*); to transmit (*a radio signal*) || *intr* to transmit, broadcast
é·meu [emø] *m* (*pl* **-meus**) (zool) emu
émeute [emøt] *f* riot
émeutier [emøtje] *m* rioter
émietter [emjete] *tr* to crumble; to break up (*an estate*)
émi·grant [emigrã] **-grante** [grãt] *adj & mf* emigrant; migrant
émi·gré -grée [emigre] *adj* emigrating || *mf* emigrant; émigré
émigrer [emigre] *intr* to emigrate; to migrate
émincer [emɛ̃se] §51 *tr* to cut in thin slices
éminemment [eminamã] *adv* eminently
éminence [eminãs] *f* eminence
émi·nent [eminã] **-nente** [nãt] *adj* eminent
émissaire [emiser] *m* emissary; outlet (*of lake, basin, etc.*)
émission [emisjɔ̃] *f* emission; utterance; issue (*of stamps, bank notes, etc.*); (rad) transmission, broadcast
emmagasiner [ãmagazine] *tr* to put in storage; to store up; to stockpile
emmailloter [ãmajɔte] *tr* to swathe; to bandage
emmancher [ãmãʃe] *tr* to put a handle on || *ref* (coll) to begin; s'emmancher bien (coll) to get off to a good start; s'emmancher mal (coll) to get off to a bad start
emmêler [ãmele], [ãmele] *tr* to tangle up; to mix up
emménagement [ãmenaʒmã] *m* moving in; installation
emménager [ãmenaʒe] §38 *tr & intr* to move in
emmener [ãmne] §2 *tr* to take or lead away; to take out (*e.g., to dinner*); to take (*on a visit*)
emmenthal [emɛ̃tal], [emãtal] *m* Swiss cheese
emmiel·lé -lée [ãmjele], [ãmjele] *adj* honeyed (*e.g., words*)
emmitoufler [ãmitufle] *tr & ref* to bundle up (*in warm clothing*)
emmurer [ãmyre] *tr* to wall in, immure

émol [emwa] *m* agitation, alarm

émolument [emɔlymɑ̃] *m* share; **émoluments** emolument, fee, salary

émonder [emɔ̃de] *tr* to prune, trim

émo·tif [emɔtif] **-tive** [tiv] *adj* emotional ‖ *mf* emotional person

émotion [emosjɔ̃] *f* emotion; commotion

émotionnable [emosjɔnabl] *adj* emotional

émotion·nant [emosjɔnɑ̃] **émotionnante** [emosjɔnɑ̃t] *adj* stirring, moving

émotionner [emosjɔne] *tr* to move deeply, thrill, affect ‖ *ref* to get excited, flustered

émoucher [emuʃe] *tr* to chase flies away from

émouchet [emuʃɛ] *m* sparrow hawk

émouchoir [emuʃwar] *m* whisk, fly swatter

émoudre [emudr] §43 *tr* to grind, sharpen

émoulage [emulaʒ] *m* grinding, sharpening

émou·lu·lue [emuly] *adj*—**frais émoulu de** (fig) fresh from, just back from

émous·sé ·sée [emuse] *adj* blunt

émousser [emuse] *tr* to dull, blunt

émoustiller [emustije] *tr* (coll) to exhilarate, to rouse

émouvoir [emuvwar] §45 (*pp* ému) *tr* to move; to excite ‖ *ref* to be moved; to be excited

empailler [ɑ̃paje] *tr* to stuff (*animals*); to cane (*a chair*)

empail·leur [ɑ̃pajœr] **empail·leuse** [ɑ̃pajøz] *mf* taxidermist; caner

empaler [ɑ̃pale] *tr* to impale

empan [ɑ̃pɑ̃] *m* span (*of hand*)

empanacher [ɑ̃panaʃe] *tr* to plume

empaquetage [ɑ̃paktaʒ] *m* packaging; package

empaqueter [ɑ̃pakte] §34 *tr* to package

emparer [ɑ̃pare] *ref*—**s'emparer de** to seize, take hold of

empâter [ɑ̃pate] *tr* to make sticky; to fatten up (*chickens, turkeys, etc.*); to coat (*the tongue*); (typ) to over-ink ‖ *ref* to put on weight; to become coated (*said of tongue*); to become husky (*said of voice*)

empattement [ɑ̃patmɑ̃] *m* foundation, footing; (aut) wheelbase

empaumer [ɑ̃pome] *tr* to catch in the hand; to hit with a racket; to palm (*a card*); (coll) to hoodwink

empêchement [ɑ̃pɛʃmɑ̃] *m* impediment, bar; hindrance, obstacle

empêcher [ɑ̃peʃe] *tr* to hinder; **empêcher qn de** + *inf* to prevent or keep s.o. from + *ger*; **n'empêche que** all the same, e.g., **n'empêche qu'il est très poli** he's very polite all the same ‖ *ref*—**ne pouvoir s'empêcher de** + *inf* not to be able to help + *ger*, e.g., **je n'ai pu m'empêcher de rire** I could not help laughing

empê·cheur [ɑ̃peʃœr] **-cheuse** [ʃøz] *mf*—**empêcheur de danser en rond** (coll) wet blanket

empeigne [ɑ̃pɛɲ] *f* upper (*of shoe*)

empennage [ɑ̃pɛnaʒ] *m* feathers (*of arrow*); fins, vanes; (aer) empennage

empereur [ɑ̃prœr] *m* emperor

emperler [ɑ̃pɛrle] *tr* to ornament with pearls; to cover with drops; **la sueur emperlait son front** his forehead was covered with beads of perspiration

empe·sé ·sée [ɑ̃pəze] *adj* starched; stiff, wooden (*style*)

empeser [ɑ̃pəze] §2 *tr* to starch

empes·té ·tée [ɑ̃peste] *adj* pestilential; stinking, reeking; depraved

empester [ɑ̃peste] *tr* to stink; to corrupt ‖ *intr* to stink

empêtrer [ɑ̃petre] *tr* to hamper; to involve, entangle ‖ *ref* to become involved, entangled

emphase [ɑ̃faz] *f* overemphasis; bombast, pretentiousness

emphatique [ɑ̃fatik] *adj* overemphasized; bombastic, pretentious

emphysème [ɑ̃fizɛm] *m* emphysema

empiècement [ɑ̃pjɛsmɑ̃] *m* yoke (*of shirt, blouse, etc.*)

empierrer [ɑ̃pjere] *tr* to pave with stones; (rr) to ballast

empiétement [ɑ̃pjetmɑ̃] *m* encroachment, incursion

empiéter [ɑ̃pjete] §10 *intr* to encroach

empiffrer [ɑ̃pifre] *tr* (coll) to stuff, fatten ‖ *ref* (coll) to stuff oneself, to guzzle

empiler [ɑ̃pile] *tr* to pile up, stack; (slang) to dupe ‖ *ref* to pile up; **se faire empiler** (slang) to be had

empire [ɑ̃pir] *m* empire; control, supremacy

empirer [ɑ̃pire] *tr* to make worse, to aggravate ‖ *intr* (*aux*: AVOIR or ÊTRE) to grow worse

empirique [ɑ̃pirik] *adj* empiric(al) ‖ *m* empiricist; charlatan, quack

emplacement [ɑ̃plasmɑ̃] *m* emplacement; location, site

emplâtre [ɑ̃platr] *m* patch (*on tire*); (med) plaster; (coll) boob

emplette [ɑ̃plɛt] *f* purchase; **aller faire des emplettes** to go shopping

emplir [ɑ̃plir] *tr & ref* to fill up

emploi [ɑ̃plwa] *m* employment, job; employment, use; (theat) type (*of role*); **double emploi** useless duplication; **emploi du temps** schedule

employé employée [ɑ̃plwaje] *mf* employee; clerk

employer [ɑ̃plwaje] §47 *tr* to employ; to use ‖ *ref* to be employed; **s'employer à** to try to, to do one's best to

employeur [ɑ̃plwajœr] **employeuse** [ɑ̃plwajøz] *mf* employer

empocher [ɑ̃pɔʃe] *tr* (coll) to pocket

empoi·gnant [ɑ̃pwaɲɑ̃] **-gnante** [ɲɑ̃t] *adj* exciting, arresting, thrilling

empoigner [ɑ̃pwaɲe] *tr* to grasp; to collar (*a crook*); to grip, move (*an audience*)

empois [ɑ̃pwa] *m* starch

empoisonnement [ɑ̃pwazɔnmɑ̃] *m* poisoning; **avoir des empoisonnements** (coll) to be annoyed

empoisonner [ɑ̃pwazɔne] *tr* to poison; to infect (*the air*); to corrupt; (coll) to bother || *intr* to reek || *ref* to be poisoned

empoison·neur [ɑ̃pwazɔnœr] **empoison·neuse** [ɑ̃pwazɔnøz] *adj* poisoning || *mf* poisoner; corrupter

empoissonner [ɑ̃pwasɔne] *tr* to stock with fish

empor·té -tée [ɑ̃pɔrte] *adj* quick-tempered, impetuous

emportement [ɑ̃pɔrtəmɑ̃] *m* anger, temper

emporte-pièce [ɑ̃pɔrtəpjɛs] *m* (*pl* **-pièces**) punch; **à l'emporte-pièce** trenchant, cutting, biting (*style, words, etc.*)

emporter [ɑ̃pɔrte] *tr* to take away; to carry off; to remove; **à emporter** to take out, to go (*e.g., said of food to take out of the restaurant*); **l'emporter sur** to have the upper hand over || *ref* to be carried away; to lose one's temper; to run away

empo·té -tée [ɑ̃pɔte] *adj* (coll) clumsy || *mf* (coll) butterfingers

empoter [ɑ̃pɔte] *tr* to pot (*a plant*)

empourprer [ɑ̃purpre] *tr* to set aglow || *ref* to turn crimson; to flush

empoussiérer [ɑ̃pusjere] §10 *tr* to cover with dust

empreindre [ɑ̃prɛ̃dr] §50 *tr* to imprint, stamp

empreinte [ɑ̃prɛ̃t] *f* imprint, stamp; **empreinte des roues** wheel tracks; **empreinte digitale** fingerprint; **empreinte du pied** or **empreinte de pas** footprint

empres·sé -sée [ɑ̃prese] *adj* eager

empressement [ɑ̃presmɑ̃] *m* haste, alacrity; eagerness, readiness

empresser [ɑ̃prese] *ref* to hasten; **s'empresser à** to be anxious to; **s'empresser auprès de** to be attentive to, make a fuss over; to press around; **s'empresser de** to hasten to

emprise [ɑ̃priz] *f* expropriation; control, ascendancy

emprisonnement [ɑ̃prizɔnmɑ̃] *m* imprisonment

emprisonner [ɑ̃prizɔne] *tr* to imprison

emprunt [ɑ̃prœ̃] *m* loan; loan word; **d'emprunt** feigned, assumed

emprunter [ɑ̃prœ̃te] *tr* to borrow; to take (*a road, a route*); to take on (*false appearances*); **emprunter q.ch. à** to borrow s.th. from; to get s.th. from

empuantir [ɑ̃pɥɑ̃tir] *tr* to stink up

empyème [ɑ̃pjɛm] *m* empyema

empyrée [ɑ̃pire] *m* empyrean

é·mu -mue [emy] *adj* moved, touched; tender (*memory*); **ému de** alarmed by

émulation [emylɑsjɔ̃] *f* emulation, rivalry

émule [emyl] *mf* emulator, rival

émulsion [emylsjɔ̃] *f* emulsion

émulsionner [emylsjɔne] *tr* to emulsify

en [ɑ̃] *pron indef & adv* §87 || *prep* in; into; to, e.g., **aller en France** to go to France; e.g., **de mal en pis** from bad to worse; at, e.g., **en mer** at sea; e.g., **en guerre** at war; on, e.g., **en congé** on leave; by, e.g., **en chemin**

de fer by rail; of, made of, e.g., **en bois** (made) of wood

enamourer [ɑ̃namure] *ref* to become enamored, to fall in love

encabaner [ɑ̃kabane] *ref* (Canad) to hole up, to dig in (*e.g., for the winter*)

encablure [ɑ̃kablyr] *f* cable's length (*unit of measure*)

encadrement [ɑ̃kadrəmɑ̃] *m* framing; frame; framework; window frame; doorframe; border, edge; staffing; officering (*furnishing with officers*)

encadrer [ɑ̃kadre] *tr* to frame; to staff (*an organization*); to officer (*troops*); to incorporate (*recruits*) into a unit

encadreur [ɑ̃kadrœr] *m* framer (*person*)

encager [ɑ̃kaʒe] §38 *tr* to cage

encaisse [ɑ̃kɛs] *f* cash on hand, cash balance; **encaisse métallique** bullion

encais·sé -sée [ɑ̃kese] *adj* deeply embanked, sunken

encaissement [ɑ̃kesmɑ̃] *m* cashing (*e.g., of check*); boxing, crating; embankment

encaisser [ɑ̃kese], [ɑ̃kese] *tr* to cash; to box, to crate; to receive (*a blow*); to embank (*a river*); (coll) to put up with || *ref* to be steeply embanked

encaisseur [ɑ̃kesœr] *m* collector; payee; cashier

encan [ɑ̃kɑ̃] *m* auction

encanailler [ɑ̃kanaje] *tr* to debase || *ref* to acquire bad habits; to keep low company

encapuchonner [ɑ̃kapyʃɔne] *tr* to hood

encaquer [ɑ̃kake] *tr* to barrel; to pack (*sardines*); (coll) to pack in like sardines

encart [ɑ̃kar] *m* inset, insert

encarter [ɑ̃karte] *tr* to card (*buttons, pins, etc.*); (bb) to tip in

en-cas [ɑ̃ka] *m invar* snack; reserve, emergency supply

encasernement [ɑ̃kazernəmɑ̃] *m*—**encasernement de conscience** thought control, regimentation

encaserner [ɑ̃kazerne] *tr* to quarter, to barrack (*troops*)

encastrement [ɑ̃kastrəmɑ̃] *m* groove; fitting

encastrer [ɑ̃kastre] *tr & ref* to fit

encaustique [ɑ̃kɔstik] *f* furniture polish; floor wax; encaustic painting

encaustiquer [ɑ̃kɔstike] *tr* to wax

encaver [ɑ̃kave] *tr* to cellar (*wine*)

enceindre [ɑ̃sɛ̃dr] §50 *tr* to enclose, to encircle

enceinte [ɑ̃sɛ̃t] *adj fem* pregnant || *f* enclosure; walls, ramparts; precinct, compass; (boxing) ring

encens [ɑ̃sɑ̃] *m* incense; flattery

encenser [ɑ̃sɑ̃se] *tr* to incense, perfume with incense; to flatter

encensoir [ɑ̃sɑ̃swar] *m* censer

encéphalite [ɑ̃sefalit] *f* encephalitis

encercler [ɑ̃serkle] *tr* to encircle

enchaînement [ɑ̃ʃɛnmɑ̃] *m* chaining up; chain, sequence

enchaîner [ɑ̃ʃene], [ɑ̃ʃene], *tr* to chain; to connect || *intr* to go on speaking || *ref* to be connected

enchan·té -tée [ãʃãte] adj delighted, pleased

enchantement [ãʃãtmã] m enchantment

enchanter [ãʃãte] tr to enchant

enchan·teur [ãʃãtœr] -teresse [tres] adj enchanting, bewitching || m enchanter, magician || f enchantress

enchâsser [ãʃase] tr to enshrine; to insert; to set, chase (a gem)

enchère [ãʃer] f bid, bidding; folle enchère bid that cannot be made good; folly

enchérir [ãʃerir] tr to bid on; to raise the price of || intr to bid; to rise in price; enchérir sur to improve on; to outbid

enchérisseur [ãʃerisœr] m bidder; dernier enchérisseur highest bidder

enchevêtrement [ãʃvetrəmã] m entanglement; network; jumble

enchevêtrer [ãʃvetre] tr to tangle up; to halter (a horse) || ref to become complicated or confused

enchifre·né -née [ãʃifrəne] adj stuffed-up (with a cold)

enclave [ãklav] f enclave

enclaver [ãklave] tr to enclose; to dovetail

enclencher [ãklãʃe] tr & ref to interlock

en·clin [ãklɛ̃] -cline [klin] adj inclined, prone

encliquetage [ãkliktaʒ] m ratchet

encliqueter [ãklikte] §34 tr to cog, to mesh

enclitique [ãklitik] adj & m & f enclitic

enclore [ãklɔr] §24 (has also 1st & 2d pl pres ind enclosons, enclosez) tr to close in, to wall in

enclos [ãklo] m enclosure, close

enclume [ãklym] f anvil; se trouver entre l'enclume et le marteau (coll) to be between the devil and the deep blue sea

encoche [ãkɔʃ] f notch, nick; slot; thumb index

encocher [ãkɔʃe] tr to notch, to nick; to slot

encoignure [ãkɔɲyr] f corner; corner piece; corner cabinet

encollage [ãkɔlaʒ] m gluing; sizing

encoller [ãkɔle] tr to glue; to size

encolure [ãkɔlyr] f collar size; neck line; neck and withers (of horse); gagner par une encolure to win by a neck

encombre [ãkɔ̃br] m—sans encombre without a hitch, without hindrance

encombrement [ãkɔ̃brəmã] m encumbrance, congestion

encombrer [ãkɔ̃bre] tr to encumber; to crowd, congest; to block up, to jam; to litter; to load down || ref—s'encombrer de (coll) to be saddled with

encontre [ãkɔ̃tr]—à l'encontre de counter to, against; contrary to

encore [ãkɔr] adv still, e.g., il est encore ici he is still here; yet, e.g., encore mieux better yet; e.g., pas encore not yet; only, e.g., si encore vous m'en aviez parlé! if only you had told me!; encore que although;

encore une fois once more, once again; en voulez-vous encore? do you want some more? || interj again!, oh no, not again! (expressing impatience or astonishment)

encorner [ãkɔrne] tr to gore, to toss

encouragement [ãkuraʒmã] m encouragement

encourager [ãkuraʒe] §38 tr to encourage

encourir [ãkurir] §14 tr to incur

encrasser [ãkrase] tr to soil, to dirty; to soot (a chimney); to foul (a gun) || ref to get dirty; to stop up, clog; to soot up

encre [ãkr] f ink; encre de Chine India ink; encre sympathique invisible ink

encrer [ãkre] tr to ink

encreur [ãkrœr] adj inking (ribbon, roller) || m ink roller

encrier [ãkrije] m inkwell

encroûter [ãkrute] tr to encrust; to plaster (walls) || ref to become encrusted; to get rusty; to become hidebound, prejudiced

encyclique [ãsiklik] adj & f encyclical

encyclopédie [ãsiklɔpedi] f encyclopedia

encyclopédique [ãsiklɔpedik] adj encyclopedic

endauber [ãdobe] tr to braise

endémie [ãdemi] f endemic

endémique [ãdemik] adj endemic

endenter [ãdãte] tr to tooth, to cog; to mesh (gears); bien endenté (coll) with plenty of teeth; (coll) with a hearty appetite

endetter [ãdete] tr & ref to run into debt

endêver [ãdeve] intr—faire endêver to bedevil, to drive wild

endia·blé -blée [ãdjable] adj devilish, reckless; full of pep

endiguement [ãdigmã] m damming up; embankment

endiguer [ãdige] tr to dam up

endimancher [ãdimãʃe] tr & ref to put on Sunday clothes, to dress up

endive [ãdiv] f endive

endocrine [ãdɔkrin] adj endocrine

endoctriner [ãdɔktrine] tr to indoctrinate; to win over

endolo·ri -rie [ãdɔlɔri] adj painful, sore

endommagement [ãdɔmaʒmã] m damage

endommager [ãdɔmaʒe] §38 tr to damage || ref to suffer damage

endor·mi -mie [ãdɔrmi] adj asleep, sleeping; sluggish, apathetic; dormant; numb (arm or leg)

endormir [ãdɔrmir] §23 tr to put to sleep; to lull, to put off guard || ref to go to sleep; to slack off; to let down one's guard

endos [ãdo] m endorsement

endosse [ãdos] f responsibility

endossement [ãdosmã] m endorsement

endosser [ãdose] tr to endorse; to take on the responsibility of

endosseur [ãdosœr] m endorser

endroit [ãdrwɑ], [ãdrwa] m place, spot; right side (of cloth); à l'endroit right side out; **à l'endroit de** with regard to; **le petit endroit** (coll) the toilet; **mettre à l'endroit** to put on right side out

enduire [ãduir] §19 *tr* to coat, smear

enduit [ãdyi] *m* coat, coating

endurance [ãdyrãs] *f* endurance

endu·rant [ãdyrã] **-rante** [rãt] *adj* untiring; meek, patient

endur·ci -cie [ãdyrsi] *adj* hardened; tough, calloused; inveterate

endurcir [ãdyrsir] *tr* to harden; to inure, to toughen ‖ *ref* to harden; **s'endurcir à** to become accustomed to, to become inured to

endurcissement [ãdyrsismã] *m* hardening

endurer [ãdyre] *tr* to endure

énergétique [enerʒetik] *adj* energy, power

énergie [enerʒi] *f* energy

énergique [enerʒik] *adj* energetic

énergumène [energymɛn] *mf* ranter, wild person, nut

éner·vant [enervã] **-vante** [vãt] *adj* annoying, nerve-racking

énerver [enerve] *tr* to enervate; to unnerve ‖ *ref* to get nervous; to be exasperated

enfance [ãfãs] *f* childhood; infancy; dotage, second childhood; **c'est l'enfance de l'art** (coll) it's child's play; **enfance délinquante** juvenile delinquents; **première enfance** infancy

enfant [ãfã] *adj invar* childish, childlike; **bon enfant** good-natured ‖ *mf* child; **enfant de chœur** altar boy; **enfant de la balle** child who follows in his father's footsteps; **enfant en bas âge** infant; **enfant terrible** (fig) stormy petrel; **enfant trouvé** foundling; **mon enfant!** my boy!; **petit enfant** infant

enfantement [ãfãtmã] *m* childbirth

enfanter [ãfãte] *tr* to give birth to

enfantillage [ãfãtijaʒ] *m* childishness

enfan·tin [ãfãtɛ̃] **-tine** [tin] *adj* childish, infantile

enfari·né -née [ãfarine] *adj* smeared with flour

enfer [ãfer] *m* hell

enfermer [ãferme] *tr* to enclose; to shut up, to lock up ‖ *ref* to shut oneself in; to closet oneself

enferrer [ãfere] *tr* to pierce, to run through ‖ *ref* to run oneself through with a sword; to bite (*said of fish*); (fig) to be caught in one's own trap

enfiévrer [ãfjevre] §10 *tr* to inflame, to make feverish

enfilade [ãfilad] *f* row, string, series; (mil) enfilade; **en enfilade** connecting, e.g., **chambres en enfilade** connecting rooms

enfile-aiguille [ãfilegµij] *m invar* threader, needle threader

enfiler [ãfile] *tr* to pierce; to thread (*a needle*); to string (*beads*); to start down (*a street*); (coll) to put on (*clothes*)

enfin [ãfɛ̃] *adv* finally, at last; in short; after all, anyway

enflam·mé -mée [ãflame], [ãflame] *adj* flaming; bright red; inflamed

enflammer [ãflame], [ãflame] *tr* to inflame ‖ *ref* to be inflamed; to flare up

enfler [ãfle] *tr* to swell; to puff up or out; to exaggerate ‖ *intr & ref* to swell, to puff up

enflure [ãflyr] *f* swelling; (fig) exaggeration

enfon·cé -cée [ãfɔ̃se] *adj* sunken, deep; deep-set; broken (*ribs*); (coll) taken, had (*bested*)

enfoncement [ãfɔ̃smã] *m* driving in; breaking open; hollow, recess

enfoncer [ãfɔ̃se] §51 *tr* to drive in; to push in, break open; (coll) to get the better of ‖ *intr* to sink to the bottom ‖ *ref* to sink, plunge; to give way; to disappear; to penetrate (*said of root, bullet, etc.*)

enforcir [ãforsir] *tr* to reinforce ‖ *intr & ref* to become stronger; to grow

enfouir [ãfwir] *tr* to bury; to hide ‖ *ref* to burrow; to bury oneself (*e.g., in an out-of-the-way locality*)

enfourcher [ãfurʃe] *tr* to stick a pitchfork into; to mount, straddle

enfourchure [ãfur/yr] *f* crotch

enfourner [ãfurne] *tr* to put in the oven; (coll) to gobble down

enfreindre [ãfrɛ̃dr] §50 *tr* to violate, break (*e.g., a law*)

enfuir [ãfµir] §31 *ref* to run away; to escape; to elope

enfu·mé -mée [ãfyme] *adj* blackened; smoky (*color*)

enfumer [ãfyme] *tr* to smoke up, blacken; to smoke out

enfutailler [ãfytaje] *tr* to cask, to barrel

enga·gé -gée [ãgaʒe] *adj* committed; hocked ‖ *m* (mil) enlisted man

engagement [ãgaʒmã] *m* engagement; hocking; obligation; promise; (mil) enlistment; (mil) engagement

engager [ãgaʒe] §38 *tr* to engage; to hock; to enlist, urge, involve; to open, to begin (*negotiations, the conversation, etc.*) ‖ *ref* to commit oneself; to promise, to pledge; to enter a contest; to become engaged to be married; (mil) to enlist; **s'engager dans** to begin (*battle; a conversation*); to plunge into; to fit into

engainer [ãgene], [ãgɛne] *tr* to sheathe, to envelop

engazonner [ãgazɔne] *tr* to sod

engeance [ãʒãs] *f* (pej) breed, brood

engelure [ãʒlyr] *f* chilblain

engendrer [ãʒãdre] *tr* to engender

engin [ãʒɛ̃] *m* device; **engin balistique** ballistic missile; **engin guidé** or **engin spécial** guided missile; **engins de pêche** fishing tackle

englober [ãglɔbe] *tr* to put together, to unite; to embrace, to comprise

engloutir [ãglutir] *tr* to gobble down; to swallow up, to engulf

engluer [ãglye] *tr* to lime (*a trap*); to catch; to take in, hoodwink ‖ *ref* to be caught; to fall into a trap, to be taken in

engommer [ãgɔme] *tr* to gum

engon•cé -cée [ãgɔ̃se] *adj* awkward, stiff (*air*)

engoncer [ãgɔ̃se] §51 *tr* to bundle up; to cramp

engorgement [ãgɔrʒəmã] *m* obstruction, blocking

engorger [ãgɔrʒe] §38 *tr* to obstruct, block

engouement [ãgumã] *m* infatuation; (*pathol*) obstruction

engouer [ãgwe] *tr* to obstruct ‖ *ref*—**s'engouer de** (coll) to be infatuated with, to be wild about

engouffrer [ãgufre] *tr* to engulf; to gobble up; to eat up (*e.g., a fortune*) ‖ *ref* to be swallowed up; to dash; to surge

engour•di -die [ãgurdi] *adj* numb

engourdir [ãgurdir] *tr* to numb; to dull ‖ *ref* to grow numb

engourdissement [ãgurdismã] *m* numbness; dullness, torpidity

engrais [ãgrɛ] *m* fertilizer; manure; fodder; **mettre à l'engrais** to fatten

engraisser [ãgrɛse] [ãgrɛse] *tr* to fatten; to fertilize; to enrich ‖ *intr* (*aux:* AVOIR *or* ÊTRE) to fatten up, to get fat ‖ *ref* to become fat; to become rich

engranger [ãgrãʒe] §38 *tr* to garner; to get in, to put in the barn

engraver [ãgrave] *tr, intr, & ref* to silt up; (*naut*) to run aground

engrenage [ãgrənaʒ] *m* gear; gearing; (coll) mesh, toils; **engrenage à vis sans fin** worm gear; **engrenages de distribution** timing gears

engrener [ãgrəne] §2 *tr* to feed (*a hopper, a thresher; a fowl*); to put into gear, to mesh ‖ *intr & ref* (*mach*) to mesh, engage

engrenure [ãgrənyr] *f* engaging (*of toothed wheels*)

engrumeler [ãgrymle] §34 *tr & ref* to clot, to curdle

engueuler [ãgœle] *tr* (slang) to bawl out

enguirlander [ãgirlãde] *tr* to garland; to adorn; (coll) to bawl out

enhardir [ãardir] *tr* to embolden ‖ *ref*—**s'enhardir à** to be so bold as to

énième [enjɛm] *adj* nth

énigmatique [enigmatik] *adj* enigmatic(al), puzzling

énigme [enigm] *f* enigma, riddle, puzzle

enivrement [ãnivrəmã] *m* intoxication

enivrer [ãnivre] *tr* to intoxicate; to elate ‖ *ref* to get drunk

enjambée [ãʒãbe] *f* stride

enjambement [ãʒãbmã] *m* enjambment

enjamber [ãʒãbe] *tr* to stride over, to span ‖ *intr* to stride along; to run on (*said of line of poetry*); **enjamber sur** to project over; to encroach on

en•jeu [ãʒø] *m* (*pl* -**jeux**) stake, bet

enjoindre [ãʒwɛ̃dr] §35 *tr* to enjoin

enjôler [ãʒole] *tr* (coll) to cajole

enjô•leur [ãʒolœr] -**leuse** [løz] *adj* cajoling ‖ *mf* cajoler, wheedler

enjoliver [ãʒolive] *tr* to embellish

enjoli•veur [ãʒɔlivœr] -**veuse** [vøz] *mf* embellisher ‖ *m* hubcap

en•joué -jouée [ãʒwe] *adj* sprightly

enjouement [ãʒumã] *m* playfulness

enlacement [ãlasmã] *m* embrace, hug; lacing, interweaving

enlacer [ãlase] §51 *tr & ref* to enlace, to entwine; to embrace

enlaidir [ãledir], [ãledir] *tr* to disfigure ‖ *intr* to grow ugly ‖ *ref* to disfigure oneself

enlèvement [ãlɛvmã] *m* removal; kidnaping, abduction

enlever [ãlve] §2 *tr* to take away, take off, remove; to carry off; to lift, lift up; to send up (*a balloon*); (fig) to carry away (*an audience*); **enlever le couvert** to clear the table; **enlever q.ch. à** to take s.th. from, remove s.th. from ‖ *ref* to come off, wear off; to rise; to boil over; (fig) to flare up

enliasser [ãljase] *tr* to tie up in bundles

enliser [ãlize] *ref* to get stuck

enluminer [ãlymine] *tr* to illuminate; to make colorful

enluminure [ãlyminyr] *f* illuminated drawing; (painting) illumination

enneiger [ãneʒe] [ãneʒe] §38 *tr* to cover with snow

enne•mi -mie [enmi] *adj* hostile, inimical; enemy, e.g., **en pays ennemi** in enemy country ‖ *mf* enemy

ennoblir [ãnoblir] *tr* to ennoble

ennui [ãnɥi] *m* ennui, boredom; nuisance, bother; worry, trouble

ennuyer [ãnɥije] §27 *tr* to bore; to bother ‖ *ref* to be bored

énon•cé -cée [enɔ̃se] *m* statement; wording (*of a document*); terms (*of a theorem*)

énoncer [enɔ̃se] §51 *tr* to state, enunciate; to utter

enorgueillir [ãnɔrgœjir] *tr* to make proud or boastful ‖ *ref*—**s'enorgueillir de** to pride oneself on, to boast of, to glory in

énorme [enɔrm] *adj* enormous; (coll) shocking; (coll) outrageous

énormément [enɔrmemã] *adv* enormously, tremendously; (coll) awfully; **énormément de** lots of

énormité [enɔrmite] *f* enormity; (coll) nonsense; (coll) blunder

enquérir [ãkerir] §3 *ref*—**s'enquérir de** to ask or inquire about

enquête [ãkɛt] *f* investigation, inquiry; inquest; inquiry; **enquête par sondage** public-opinion poll

enquêter [ãkete] *intr* to conduct an investigation

enraciner [ãrasine] *tr* to root; to instill ‖ *ref* to take root

enra•gé -gée [ãraʒe] *adj* enraged, hotheaded; mad (*dog*); rabid (*communist*); out-and-out (*socialist*); inveterate (*gambler*); enthusiastic (*sportsman*) ‖ *mf* enthusiast, fan; fanatic, fiend

enrager [ãraʒe] §38 *intr* to be mad; **faire enrager** to enrage

enrayer [ãreje], [ãreje] §49 *tr* to put

spokes to; to jam, lock; to stem, halt || *ref* to jam

enrayure [ārejyr] *f* (mach) skid, shoe

enrégimenter [ārezimāte] *tr* to regiment

enregistrement [ārəʒistrəmā] *m* recording; registration; transcription; checking (*of baggage*); **enregistrement sur bande** or **sur ruban** tape recording

enregistrer [ārəʒistre] *tr* to record; to register; to transcribe; to check (*baggage*)

enregis-treur [ārəʒistrœr] **-treuse** [trøz] *adj* recording || *mf* recorder

enrhumer [āryme] *tr* to give a cold to || *ref* to catch cold

enrichir [āriʃir] *tr* to enrich || *ref* to become rich

enrichissement [āriʃismā] *m* enrichment

enrober [ārɔbe] *tr* to coat; to wrap

enrôlement [ārolmā] *m* enrollment; enlistment

enrôler [ārole] *tr* & *ref* to enroll, enlist

enrouement [ārumā] *m* hoarseness, huskiness

enrouer [ārwe] *tr* to make hoarse || *ref* to become hoarse

enrouiller [āruje] *tr* & *ref* to rust

enroulement [ārulmā] *m* coil; (archit) volute; (elec) winding

enrouler [ārule] *tr* & *ref* to wind, coil; to roll up

ensabler [āsable] *tr* & *ref* to run aground on the sand

ensacher [āsaʃe] *tr* to bag

ensanglanter [āsāglāte] *tr* to stain with blood; to steep in blood

ensei-gnant [āseɲā] **-gnante** [ɲāt] *adj* teaching || *mf* teacher

enseigne [āseɲ] *m* (nav) ensign || *f* flag, ensign; sign (*on tavern, store*)

enseignement [āseɲəmā] *m* teaching, instruction, education; **enseignement confessionnel** parochial school education; **enseignement libre** or **privé** private-school education; **enseignement supérieur** higher education

enseigner [āseɲe] *tr* to teach; to show; **enseigner q.ch. à qn** to teach s.o. s.th. || *intr* to teach; **enseigner à qn à + inf** to teach s.o. to + *inf*

ensemble [āsābl] *m* ensemble; **avec ensemble** in harmony, with one mind; **dans son ensemble** as a whole; **d'ensemble** general, comprehensive, overall; **grand ensemble** housing development || *adv* together

ensemencement [āsmāsmā] *m* sowing

ensemencer [āsmāse] §51 *tr* to seed, sow; to culture (*microorganisms*)

enserrer [āsere] *tr* to enclose; to squeeze, clasp

ensevelir [āsəvlir] *tr* to bury; to shroud

ensevelissement [āsəvlismā] *m* burial; shrouding

ensilage [āsilaʒ] *m* storing in a pit or silo

ensiler [āsile] *tr* to ensilage

ensoleiller [āsɔleje] *tr* to make sunny, to brighten

ensommeil·lé -lée [āsɔmeje], [āsɔmeje] *adj* drowsy

ensorceler [āsɔrsəle] §34 *tr* to bewitch, to enchant

ensorce·leur [āsɔrsəlœr] **-leuse** [løz] *adj* bewitching, enchanting || *m* sorcerer, wizard; charmer || *f* witch; enchantress

ensorcellement [āsɔrselmā] *m* sorcery, enchantment; spell, charm

ensuite [āsɥit] *adv* then, next; afterwards, after; **ensuite?** what then?, what next?; anything else?

ensuivre [āsɥivr] §67 (used only in 3d sg & pl) *ref* to ensue; **il s'ensuit que ... it** follows that . . .

entacher [ātaʃe] *tr* to blemish; **entaché de nullité** null and void

entaille [ātaj] *f* notch, nick; gash

entailler [ātaje] *tr* to notch, to nick; to gash

entame [ātam] *f* top slice, first slice, end slice

entamer [ātame] *tr* to cut the first slice of; to begin; to engage in, to start (*a conversation*); to make a break in (*the skin; a battle line*); to cast a slur upon; to open (*a bottle; negotiations; a card suit*); (coll) to make a dent in (*e.g., one's savings*)

entartrer [ātartre] *tr* & *ref* to scale, fur

entassement [ātasmā] *m* piling up

entasser [ātase] *tr* & *ref* to pile up, to accumulate; to crowd

ente [āt] *f* paintbrush handle; (hort) graft, scion

entendement [ātādmā] *m* understanding; consciousness

entendre [ātādr] *tr* to hear; to understand; to mean; **entendre chanter** to hear (*s.o.*) singing, to hear (*s.o.*) sing; to hear (*s.th.*) sung; **entendre dire que** to hear that; **entendre parler de** to hear of or about; **entendre raison** to listen to reason; **il entend que je le fasse** he expects me to do it, he insists that I do it || *intr* to hear || *ref* to understand one another; to get along; **s'entendre à** to be skilled in, to know

enten·du -due [ātādy] *adj* agreed; **bien entendu** of course; **c'est entendu!** all right!

enténébrer [ātenebre] §10 *tr* to plunge into darkness

entente [ātāt] *f* understanding; agreement, pact; **à double entente** with a double meaning, e.g., **expression à double entente** expression with a double meaning, double entendre; **entente industrielle** (com) combine

entérinement [āterinmā] *m* ratification

entériner [āterine] *tr* to ratify

enterrement [ātermā] *m* burial, interment; funeral procession; funeral; funeral expenses; pigeonholing

enterrer [ātere] *tr* to bury, inter; to pigeonhole, sidetrack; (coll) to attend the funeral services of; **enterrer sa vie de garçon** (coll) to give a farewell stag party || ref to bury oneself; (mil) to dig oneself in

en-tête [ătet] m (pl **-têtes**) headline; chapter heading; letterhead

entê-té -tée [ătete] adj obstinate, stubborn

entêtement [ătetmã] m obstinacy, stubbornness

entêter [ătete] tr to give a headache to; to make giddy || intr to go to one's head || ref to persist

enthousiasme [ătuzjasm] m enthusiasm

enthousiasmer [ătuzjasme] tr & ref to enthuse

enthousiaste [ătuzjast] adj enthusiastic || mf enthusiast, fan, buff

entichement [ătĩ/mã] m infatuation

enticher [ătĩ/e] tr to infatuate || ref to become infatuated

en-tier [ătje] **-tière** [tjer] adj entire, whole, full; obstinate || m whole, entirety; **en entier** in full

entièrement [ătjermã] adv entirely

entité [ătite] f entity, being

entoiler [ătwale] tr to put a backing on, to mount

entomologie [ătɔmɔlɔʒi] f entomology

entonner [ătɔne] tr to barrel; to intone, start off (a song); to sing (s.o.'s praises) || ref to rush up and down (said of wind)

entonnoir [ătɔnwar] m funnel; shell hole

entorse [ătɔrs] f sprain; infringement (of a rule); stretching (of the truth)

entortiller [ătɔrtije] tr & ref to twist

entour [ătur] m—**à l'entour** in the vicinity; **à l'entour de** around; **entours** surroundings

entourage [ăturaʒ] m setting, surroundings; entourage; (mach) casing

entourer [ăture] tr to surround

entourloupette [ăturlupet] f (coll) double cross; **faire une entourloupette à** (coll) to double-cross

entournure [ăturnyr] f armhole; **gêné dans les entournures** ill at ease

entraccuser [ătrakyze] ref to accuse one another

entracte [ătrakt] m intermission

entraide [ătred] f mutual assistance

entrailles [ătraj] fpl entrails; tenderness, pity; bowels (of the earth); **sans entrailles** (fig) heartless

entr'aimer [ătreme], [ătreme] to love each other

entrain [ătrɛ̃] m spirit, gusto, pep

entraînement [ătrenmã] m training; enthusiasm

entraîner [ătrene] tr to carry along or away, to entrain; to involve, entail; to pull (railroad cars); to work (a pump); to train (an athlete) || ref (sports) to train

entraîneur [ătrenœr] m trainer, coach

entraîneuse [ătrenøz] f B-girl

entr'apercevoir [ătrapersəvwar] §59 tr to catch a glimpse of

entrave [ătrav] f shackle; hindrance

entra·vé -vée [ătrave] adj impeded, hampered; checked (vowel)

entraver [ătrave] tr to shackle; to hinder, impede

entre [ătr] prep between; among; in or into, e.g., **entre les mains de** in or into the hands of; **d'entre** among; from among, out of; of, e.g., **l'un d'entre eux** one of them; **entre deux eaux** under the surface of the water

entrebâillement [ătrəbajmã] m chink, slit, crack

entrebâiller [ătrəbaje] tr to leave ajar

entrechat [ătrə/a] m caper; entrechat

entrechoquer [ătrə/ɔke] tr to bump together || ref to clash

entrecôte [ătrəkot] f sirloin steak, loin of beef; top chuck roast

entrecouper [ătrəkupe] tr to interrupt; to intersect || ref to intersect

entrecroiser [ătrəkrwaze] tr & ref to interlace; to intersect

entre-deux [ătrədø] m invar space between; interval; partition; (sports) jump ball

entre-deux-guerres [ătrədøger] m & f invar period between the wars (the First and Second World War)

entrée [ătre] f entrance, entry; admission, admittance; beginning; customs duty; (culin) entree; **avoir ses entrées à, chez, or dans** to have the entree into; **d'entrée** at the start, right off; **entrée de serrure** keyhole; **entrée d'un chapeau** hat size; **entrée interdite** (public sign) keep out, no admittance

entrefaites [ătrəfet] fpl—**sur ces entrefaites** meanwhile

entrefer [ătrəfer] m (elec) air gap

entrefermer [ătrəferme] tr to close part way

entrefilet [ătrəfile] m short feature, special item

entregent [ătrəʒã] m tact, diplomacy, savoir-faire; **avoir de l'entregent** to be a good mixer

entrejambe [ătrəʒãb] m crotch

entrelacer [ătrəlase] §51 tr & ref to interlace, to entwine, intertwine

entrelarder [ătrəlarde] tr to lard; to interlard

entre-ligne [ătrəliɲ] m (pl **-lignes**) space (between the lines); insertion (written between the lines); **à l'entre-ligne** double-spaced

entremêler [ătrəmele] tr to mix, mingle; to intersperse

entremets [ătrəme] m side dish; dessert

entremet·teur [ătrəmetœr] m entremet·teuse [ătrəmetøz] mf go-between || m (pej) pimp

entremettre [ătrəmetr] §42 ref to intervene, to intercede

entremise [ătrəmiz] f intervention; **par l'entremise de** through the medium of

entre-nuire [ătrənɥir] §19 (pp nui) ref (with dat of reflex pron) to hurt each other

entrepont [ătrəpɔ̃] m (naut) betweendecks

entreposer [ătrəpoze] tr to place in a warehouse, to store; to bond

entrepôt [ătrəpo] m warehouse; **en entrepôt** in bond

entrepre·nant [ătrəprənã] **-nante** [năt·

adj enterprising; bold, audacious; gallant

entreprendre [ātrəprādr] §56 *tr* to undertake; to contract for; to enter upon; (coll) to try to win over ‖ *intr*—**entreprendre sur** to encroach upon

entrepre·neur [ātrəprənœr] **-neuse** [nøz] *mf* contractor; **entrepreneur de camionnage** trucker; **entrepreneur de pompes funèbres** undertaker

entreprise [ātrəpriz] *f* undertaking; business, firm; contract

entrer [ātre] *tr* to introduce, bring in ‖ *intr* (*aux*: ÊTRE) to enter; to go in, to come in; **entrer à, dans,** or **en** to enter; to enter into; to begin; **entrer pour** to enter into, to be an ingredient of

entre-rail [ātrəraj] *m* (rr) gauge

entre-regarder [ātrərəgarde] *ref* to exchange glances

entresol [ātrəsɔl] *m* mezzanine

entre-temps [ātrətā] *m invar* interval; **dans l'entre-temps** in the meantime ‖ *adv* meanwhile

entreteneur [ātrətnœr] *m* keeper of a mistress

entretenir [ātrətnir] §72 *tr* to maintain, keep up; to carry on (*a conversation*); to keep (*a mistress*); to entertain, harbor ‖ *ref* to converse, talk

entrete·nu -nue [ātrətny] *adj* kept (*woman*); continuous, undamped (*waves*)

entretien [ātrətjē] *m* maintenance, upkeep; support (*of family, army, etc.*); interview

entretoise [ātrətwaz] *f* strut, brace, crosspiece

entre-tuer [ātrətɥe] *ref* to kill each other, to fight to the death

entre-voie [ātrəvwa] *f* (rr) gauge

entrevoir [ātrəvwar] §75 *tr* to glimpse; to foresee

entre·vu -vue [ātrəvy] *adj* half-seen; vaguely foreseen ‖ *f* interview

entrouvrir [ātruvrir] §65 *tr* & *ref* to open part way

enture [ātyr] *f* splice (*of pieces of wood*)

énumérer [enymere] §10 *tr* to enumerate

envahir [āvair] *tr* to invade

envahissement [āvaismā] *m* invasion

envaser [āvaze] *tr* to fill with mud; to stick in the mud

enveloppe [āvlɔp] *f* envelope; **enveloppe à fenêtre** window envelope

envelopper [āvlɔpe] *tr* to envelop; to wrap up

envenimer [āvnime] *tr* to inflame, make sore; (fig) to envenom, embitter

envergure [āvergyr] *f* span; wingspread; spread of sail; span, scope

envers [āver] *m* wrong side, reverse, back; **à l'envers** inside out; upside down; back to front; topsy-turvy; **mettre à l'envers** to put on backwards ‖ *prep* towards; with regard to; **envers et contre tous** in spite of everyone else

envi [āvi]—**à l'envi** vying with each other; **à l'envi de** vying with

enviable [āvjabl] *adj* enviable

envie [āvi] *f* desire, longing; envy; birthmark; hangnail; **avoir envie de** to feel like, to have a notion to

envier [āvje] *tr* to envy; to desire; **envier q.ch. à qn** to begrudge s.o. s.th.

en·vieux [āvjø] **-vieuse** [vjøz] *adj* envious ‖ *mf* envious person

environ [āvirã] *m* outlying section; **aux environs de** in the vicinity of; around, about; **environs** surroundings ‖ *adv* about, approximately

environnement [āvirɔnmā] *m* environment

environner [āvirɔne] *tr* to surround

envisager [āvizaʒe] §38 *tr* to envisage ‖ *intr*—**envisager + inf** to plan to + *inf*, to expect to + *inf*

envoi [āvwa] *m* consignment; remittance; envoy (*of ballad*)

envol [āvɔl] *m* flight; (aer) takeoff

envolée [āvɔle] *f* flight; (aer) takeoff

envoler [āvɔle] *ref* to fly (*said of time*); (aer) to take off

envoûtement [āvutmā] *m* spell, voodoo

envoûter [āvute] *tr* to cast a spell on

envoyé envoyée [āvwaje] *mf* envoy; messenger; **envoyé spécial** special correspondent (*of newspaper*)

envoyer [āvwaje] §26 *tr* to send; to send out; to throw (*e.g., a stone*); to give (*a kick*); **envoyer promener** to send (*s.o.*) about his business; **en·voyer qn + inf** to send s.o. to + *inf*; **envoyer qn chercher q.ch.** or **qn** to send s.o. for s.th. or s.o. ‖ *intr*—**envoyer chercher** to send for (*s.o.* or *s.th.*) ‖ *ref* (coll) to gulp down

enzyme [āzim] *m* & *f* enzyme

épa·gneul -gneule [epanœl] *mf* spaniel

épais épaisse [epe] [epes] *adj* thick ‖ **épais** *adv* thickly

épaisseur [epesœr] *f* thickness

épaissir [epesir] *tr, intr,* & *ref* to thicken

épanchement [epā/mā] *m* outpouring, effusion; (pathol) discharge

épancher [epā/e] *tr* to pour out; to unburden (*e.g., one's feelings*) ‖ *ref* to pour out; **s'épancher auprès de** to unbosom oneself to; **s'épancher de q.ch.** to get s.th. off one's chest

épandre [epādr] *tr* & *ref* to spread; to scatter

épanouir [epanwir] *tr* to make (*flowers*) bloom; to light up (*the face*) ‖ *ref* to bloom; to beam (*said of face*)

épanouissement [epanwismā] *m* blossoming; brightening up (*of a face*)

épar·gnant -gnante [eparɲā] [ɲāt] *adj* thrifty ‖ *mf* depositor

épargne [eparɲ] *f* saving, thrift; **épargnes** savings

épargner [eparɲe] *tr* to save; to spare; to husband

éparpillement [eparpijmā] *m* scattering

éparpiller [eparpije] *tr* to scatter; to dissipate (*e.g., one's efforts*)

épars [epar] **éparse** [epars] *adj* scattered, sparse; in disorder

épa·tant [epatã] **-tante** [tãt] *adj* (coll) wonderful, terrific

épate [epat] *f*—**faire de l'épate** (slang) to make a big show, to splurge

épa·té **-tée** [epate] *adj* flattened; (slang) flabbergasted

épater [epate] *tr* (coll) to shock, amaze

épaulard [epolar] *m* killer whale

épaule [epol] *f* shoulder; **donner un coup d'épaule à qn** (coll) to give s.o. a hand; **par-dessus l'épaule** (fig) contemptuously

épaulé-jeté [epoleʒte] *m* clean and jerk (in weight lifting)

épaulement [epolmã] *m* breastworks

épauler [epole] *tr* to back, support ‖ *intr* to take aim

épaulette [epolɛt] *f* epaulet

épave [epav] *f* wreck, derelict, stray; **épaves** wreckage

épée [epe] *f* sword

épéiste [epeist] *m* swordsman

épeler [eple] §34 *tr* to spell, to spell out; to read letter by letter

épellation [epɛllasjɔ̃] *f* spelling

éper·du **-due** [eperdy] *adj* bewildered; desperate (*resistance*); mad (*with pain*); wild (*with joy*)

éperdument [eperdymã] *adv* desperately, madly, wildly

éperlan [eperlã] *m* smelt

éperon [eprɔ̃] *m* spur

éperonner [eprone] *tr* to spur

épervier [epervje] *m* sparrow hawk; fish net

éphémère [efemɛr] *adj* ephemeral ‖ *m* mayfly

épi [epi] *m* ear, cob, spike; cowlick

épice [epis] *f* spice

épicéa [episea] *m* Norway spruce

épicer [epise] §51 *tr* to spice

épicerie [episri] *f* grocery store; canned goods

épi·cier [episje] **-cière** [sjer] *mf* grocer

épidémie [epidemi] *f* epidemic

épidémiologie [epidemjɔlɔʒi] *f* epidemiology

épidémique [epidemik] *adj* epidemic; contagious (*e.g., laughter*)

épiderme [epiderm] *m* epidermis

épier [epje] *tr* to spy upon; to be on the lookout for ‖ *intr* to ear, to head

épieu [epjø] *m* (*pl* **épieux**) pike

épiglotte [epiglɔt] *f* epiglottis

épigramme [epigram] *f* epigram

épigraphe [epigraf] *f* epigraph

épilepsie [epilɛpsi] *f* epilepsy

épileptique [epilɛptik] *adj* & *mf* epileptic

épiler [epile] *tr* to pluck (*one's eyebrows*); to remove hair from

épilogue [epilɔg] *m* epilogue

épiloguer [epilɔge] *intr* to split hairs; **épiloguer sur** to carp at

épinard [epinar] *m* spinach; **des épinards** spinach (*leaves used as food*)

épine [epin] *f* thorn; **épine dorsale** backbone; **épine noire** blackthorn; **être sur les épines** to be on pins and needles

épinette [epinet] *f* spinet; hencoop

épi·neux [epinø] **-neuse** [nøz] *adj* thorny; ticklish (*question*)

épingle [epɛ̃gl] *f* pin; **épingle à chapeau** hatpin; **épingle à cheveux** hairpin; **épingle à linge** clothespin; **épingle anglaise** safety pin; **épingle dans une meule de foin** needle in a haystack; **épingle de cravate** stickpin; **épingle de sûreté** safety pin; **monter en épingle** (coll) to make much of; **tiré à quatre épingles** (coll) spic-and-span; (coll) all dolled up; **tirer son épingle du jeu** (coll) to get out by the skin of one's teeth

épingler [epɛ̃gle] *tr* to pin; (coll) to pin down (*s.o.*)

épinière [epinjer] *adj fem* spinal (*cord*)

Épiphanie [epifani] *f* Epiphany, Twelfth-night

épique [epik] *adj* epic

épisco·pal **-pale** [episkɔpal] (*pl* **-paux** [poj]) *adj* episcopal; Episcopalian ‖ *mf* Episcopalian

épisode [epizɔd] *m* episode

épisodique [epizɔdik] *adj* episodic

épisser [epise] *tr* to splice

épissure [episyr] *f* splice

épistémologie [epistemɔlɔʒi] *f* epistemology

épitaphe [epitaf] *f* epitaph

épithète [epitɛt] *f* epithet

épitoge [epitɔʒ] *f* shoulder band (*worn by French lawyers and holders of French degrees*)

épitomé [epitɔme] *m* epitome

épître [epitr] *f* epistle

éplo·ré **-rée** [eplɔre] *adj* in tears

épluchage [eplyʃaʒ] *m* peeling; examination

éplucher [eplyʃe] *tr* to peel, pare; to clean, pick; (fig) to find fault with, to pick holes in

éplu·cheur [eplyʃœr] **-cheuse** [ʃøz] *mf* (coll) faultfinder ‖ *m* potato peeler, orange peeler, peeling knife ‖ *f*— **éplucheuse électrique** electric peeler

épluchure [eplyʃyr] *f* peelings; **épluchure de maïs** cornhusks

épointer [epwɛ̃te] *tr* to dull the point of

éponge [epɔ̃ʒ] *f* sponge

éponger [epɔ̃ʒe] §38 *tr* to sponge off, to mop up

épopée [epɔpe] *f* epic

époque [epɔk] *f* epoch; time; period; **à l'époque de** at the time of; **d'époque** a real antique; **faire époque** to be epoch-making

épouiller [epuje] *tr* to delouse

époumoner [epumɔne] *ref* to shout oneself out of breath

épousailles [epuzaj] *fpl* wedding

épouser [epuze] *tr* to marry; to espouse; **épouser la forme de** to take the exact shape of

époussetage [epustaʒ] *m* dusting

épousseter [epuste] §34 *tr* to dust

époussette [epusɛt] *f* duster

épouvantable [epuvãtabl] *adj* frightful, terrible

épouvantail [epuvãtaj] *m* scarecrow

épouvante [epuvãt] *f* fright, terror

épouvanter [epuvɑ̃te] *tr* to frighten, terrify

époux [epu] **épouse** [epuz] *mf* spouse ‖ *m* husband; **les époux** husband and wife ‖ *f* wife

éprendre [eprɑ̃dr] §56 *ref*—**s'éprendre de** to fall in love with; to hold fast to (*liberty, justice, etc.*)

épreuve [eprœv] *f* proof, test, trial; ordeal; examination; (phot, typ) proof

épris [epri] **éprise** [epriz] *adj* infatuated; **épris de** in love with

éprouver [epruve] *tr* to prove, test, try; to experience, to feel; to put to the test

éprouvette [epruvɛt] *f* test tube; specimen; (med) probe

epsomite [ɛpsɔmit] *f* Epsom salts

épucer [epyse] §51 *tr* to clean of fleas, to delouse

épui·sé **-sée** [epɥize] *adj* exhausted, tired out; sold out

épuisement [epɥizmɑ̃] *m* exhaustion; diminution, draining off

épuiser [epɥize] *tr* to exhaust, use up; to wear out; to tire out ‖ *ref* to run out; to wear out

épuration [epyrasjɔ̃] *f* purification, refining (*e.g., of petroleum*); (pol) purge

épure [epyr] *f* working drawing

épurement [epyrmɑ̃] *m* expurgation

épurer [epyre] *tr* to purify; to expurgate; to weed out, to purge

équanimité [ekwanimite] *f* equanimity

équarrir [ekarir] *tr* to cut up, quarter (*an animal*); to square off

équateur [ekwatœr] *m* equator; **l'Équateur** Ecuador

équation [ekwasjɔ̃] *f* equation

équato·rial **-riale** [ekwatɔrjal] *adj* (*pl* **-riaux** [rjo]) equatorial

équerrage [ekɛraʒ] *m* bevel; beveling

équerre [ekɛr] *f* square (*L- or T-shaped instrument*); **d'équerre** square, true; **mettre d'équerre** to square, to true

équerrer [ekɛre] *tr* to bevel

équestre [ekɛstr] *adj* equestrian

équilaté·ral **-rale** [ekɥilateral] *adj* (*pl* **-raux** [ro]) equilateral

équilibre [ekilibr] *m* equilibrium, balance; equipoise

équilibrer [ekilibre] *tr & ref* to balance

équilibriste [ekilibrist] *mf* balancer, ropedancer

équinoxe [ekinɔks] *m* equinox

équipage [ekipaʒ] *m* crew; retinue; suite; attire

équipe [ekip] *f* team; crew; gang, work party; (naut) train of boats; **équipe de jour** day shift; **équipe de nuit** night shift; **équipe de secours** rescue squad

équipée [ekipe] *f* escapade, lark; crazy project

équipement [ekipmɑ̃] *m* equipment

équiper [ekipe] *tr* to equip

équi·pier **-pière** [pjer] *mf* teammate; crew member

équitable [ekitabl] *adj* equitable

équitation [ekitasjɔ̃] *f* horseback riding

équité [ekite] *f* equity

équiva·lent [ekivalɑ̃] **-lente** [lɑ̃t] *adj & m* equivalent

équivaloir [ekivalwar] §71 *intr*—**équivaloir à** to be equivalent to; to be tantamount to

équivoque [ekivɔk] *adj* equivocal; questionable (*e.g., reputation*) ‖ *f* double entendre; uncertainty; **sans équivoque** without equivocation

équivoquer [ekivɔke] *intr* to equivocate, quibble; to pun

érable [erabl] *m* maple; **érable à sucre** sugar maple

érafler [erafle] *tr* to graze, scratch

éraflure [eraflyr] *f* graze, scratch

érail·lé **-lée** [eraje] *adj* bloodshot (*eyes*); hoarse (*voice*)

érailler [eraje] *tr* to fray

ère [er] *f* era

érection [ereksjɔ̃] *f* erection

érein·té **-tée** [erɛte] *adj* all in, worn out, tired out

éreinter [erɛte] *tr* to exhaust, tire out; (coll) to criticize unmercifully, to run down (*an author, play, etc.*) ‖ *ref* to wear oneself out; to drudge

erg [erg] *m* erg

ergot [ergo] *m* spur (*of rooster*); **monter or se dresser sur ses ergots** (fig) to get up on a high horse

ergotage [ergɔtaʒ] *m* (coll) quibbling

ergoter [ergɔte] *tr* (coll) to quibble

ériger [eriʒe] §38 *tr* to erect ‖ *ref*—**s'ériger en** to set oneself up as

ermitage [ermitaʒ] *m* hermitage

ermite [ermit] *m* hermit

éroder [erɔde] *tr* to erode

érosion [erozjɔ̃] *f* erosion

érotique [erɔtik] *adj* erotic

érotisme [erɔtism] *m* eroticism

er·rant [erɑ̃] **er·rante** [erɑ̃t] *adj* wandering, stray; errant

erratique [eratik] *adj* intermittent, irregular, erratic

erre [er] *f* (naut) headway; **erres** track (*e.g., of deer*)

errements [ermɑ̃] *mpl* ways, methods; (pej) erring ways, bad habits

errer [ere] *intr* to wander; to err; to play (*said of smile*)

erreur [erœr] *f* error, mistake; **erreur de frappe** typing error

erro·né **-née** [erɔne] *adj* erroneous

éructation [eryktasjɔ̃] *f* belch

éructer [erykte] *tr* (fig) to belch forth ‖ *intr* to belch

éru·dit **-dite** [dit] *adj* erudite, learned ‖ *mf* scholar, erudite

érudition [erydisjɔ̃] *f* erudition

éruption [erypsjɔ̃] *f* eruption

ès [es] *prep* §77

esc. *abbr* (**escompte**) discount

esca·beau [eskabo] *m* (*pl* **-beaux**) stool; stepladder

escadre [eskadr] *f* squadron; fleet

escadron [eskadrɔ̃] *m* (mil) squadron

escalade [eskalad] *f* scaling, climbing

escalader [eskalade] *tr* to scale, to climb; to clamber over or up

escalator [eskalatɔr] *m* escalator

escale [eskal] *f* port of call, stop; **faire escale** to make a stop; **sans escale** nonstop

escalier [eskalje] *m* stairway; **escalier à vis** circular stairway; **escalier de sauvetage** fire escape; **escalier en colimaçon** spiral staircase; **escalier mécanique** or **roulant** escalator

escalope [eskalɔp] *f* scallop

escamotable [eskamɔtabl] *adj* retractable (*e.g., landing gear*); concealable (*piece of furniture*)

escamotage [eskamɔtaʒ] *m* sleight of hand; side-stepping, avoiding; theft

escamoter [eskamɔte] *tr* to palm (*a card*); to pick (*a wallet*); to dodge (*a question*); to slur (*a word*); to hush up (*a scandal*); (aer) to retract (*landing gear*)

escamo-teur [eskamɔtœr] **-teuse** [tøz] *mf* prestidigitator; pickpocket

escapade [eskapad] *f* escapade, escape

escarbille [eskarbij] *f* cinder, clinker

escarbot [eskarbo] *m* beetle

escarboucle [eskarbukl] *f* (mineral) carbuncle

escargot [eskargo] *m* snail

escarmouche [eskarmuʃ] *f* skirmish

escarmoucher [eskarmuʃe] *intr* to skirmish

escarpe [eskarp] *m* ruffian, bandit ǁ *f* escarpment (*of a fort*)

escar-pé -pée [eskarpe] *adj* steep

escarpement [eskarpəmɑ̃] *m* escarpment

escarpin [eskarpɛ̃] *m* pump, dancing shoe

escarpolette [eskarpɔlet] *f* swing

escarre [eskar] *f* scab

escarrifier [eskarifje] *tr* to form a scab on

esche [eʃ] *f* bait

Eschyle [eʃil], [eʃil] *m* Aeschylus

escient [esjɑ̃] —**à bon escient** knowingly, wittingly; **à mon** (**ton, ton**, **etc.**) **escient** to my (your, etc.) certain knowledge

esclaffer [esklafe] *ref* to burst out laughing

esclandre [esklɑ̃dr] *m* scandal

esclavage [esklavaʒ] *m* slavery

esclavagiste [esklavaʒist] *adj* pro-slavery ǁ *mf* advocate of slavery

esclave [esklav] *adj* & *mf* slave

escompte [eskɔ̃t] *m* discount, rebate; **escompte de caisse** cash discount; **escompte en dehors** bank discount; **prendre à l'escompte** to discount

escompter [eskɔ̃te] *tr* to discount (*a premature note*); to anticipate

escompteur [eskɔ̃tœr] *adj* discounting (*banker*) ǁ *m* discount broker

escopette [eskɔpet] *f* blunderbuss

escorte [eskɔrt] *f* escort

escorter [eskɔrte] *tr* to escort

escouade [eskwad] *f* infantry section; gang (*of laborers*)

escrime [eskrim] *f* fencing

escrimer [eskrime] *intr* & *ref* to fence; **s'escrimer à** to work with might and main at; **s'escrimer contre** to fence with

escri-meur [eskrimœr] **-meuse** [møz] *mf* fencer

escroc [eskro] *m* crook, swindler

escroquer [eskrɔke] *tr* to swindle

escroquerie [eskrɔkri] *f* swindling, cheating; racket, swindle

ésotérique [ezɔterik] *adj* esoteric

espace [espas] *m* space; room; **espace cosmique** outer space ǁ *f* (typ) space

espacement [espasmɑ̃] *m* spacing

espacer [espase] §51 *tr* to space

espadon [espadɔ̃] *m* swordfish

espadrille [espadrij] *f* tennis shoe; beach sandal; esparto sandal

Espagne [espaɲ] *f* Spain; **l'Espagne** Spain

espa-gnol -gnole [espaɲɔl] *adj* Spanish ǁ *m* Spanish (*language*) ǁ (*cap*) *mf* Spaniard (*person*); **les Espagnols** the Spanish

espagnolette [espaɲɔlet] *f* espagnolette (*door fastener for French casement window*)

espalier [espalje] *m* espalier

espèce [espes] *f* species; sort, kind; **en espèces** in specie; **en l'espèce** in the matter; **espèces sonnantes** hard cash; **sale espèce** cad, bounder ǁ *mf*— **espèce de** (coll) damn, e.g., **cet espèce d'idiot** that damn fool

espérance [esperɑ̃s] *f* hope; **espérances** expectations; prospects

espérer [espere] §10 *tr* to hope, to hope for; (coll) to wait for; **espérer + inf** to hope to + *inf* ǁ *intr* to trust; (coll) to wait

espiègle [espjegl] *adj* mischievous ǁ *mf* rogue

espièglerie [espjegləri] *f* mischievousness; prank

es-pion [espjɔ̃] **-pionne** [pjɔn] *mf* spy ǁ *m* concealed microphone; busybody (*mirror*)

espionnage [espjɔnaʒ] *m* espionage

espionner [espjɔne] *tr* to spy on

espoir [espwar] *m* hope; promise

esprit [espri] *m* spirit; mind; intelligence; wit; spirits (*of wine*); **à l'esprit clair** clearheaded; **avoir l'esprit de l'escalier** to think of what to say too late; **bel esprit** man of letters; **esprit d'équipe** teamwork; **esprit de système** love of order; (pej) pigheadedness; **esprit fort** freethinker; **rendre l'esprit** to give up the ghost

esquif [eskif] *m* skiff

esqui-mau [eskimo] **-maude** [mod] (*pl* **-maux**) *adj* Eskimo ǁ *m* husky, Eskimo dog; Eskimo (*language*) ǁ (*cap*) *mf* Eskimo (*person*)

esquinter [eskɛ̃te] *tr* (coll) to tire out; (coll) to wear out; (coll) to run down, knock, criticize

esquisse [eskis] *f* sketch; outline, draft; beginning (*e.g., of a smile*)

esquisser [eskise] *tr* to sketch; to outline, draft; to begin

esquiver [eskive] *tr* to dodge, to sidestep; **esquiver de la tête** to duck ǁ *ref* to sneak away

essai [ese] *m* essay; trial, test; **à l'essai** on trial; **essais** first attempts (*of artist, writer, etc.*); **faire l'essai de** to try out

essaim [esɛ̃] *m* swarm

essaimer [eseme] *intr* to swarm

essarter [esarte] *tr* to clear (*brush*)

essarts [esar] *mpl* clearings

essayage [esejaʒ] *m* fitting, trying on

essayer [eseje], [eseje] §49 *tr* to try on or try out; to assay (*ore*) || *intr* to try; **essayer de** to try to || *ref*—**s'essayer à** to try one's skill at

essayeur [esejœr] **essayeuse** [esejøz] *mf* assayer

essayiste [esejist] *mf* essayist

esse [es] *f* S-hook; sound hole (*of violin*)

essence [esɑ̃s] *f* essence; gasoline; kind, species; **par essence** by definition

essen·tiel -tielle [esɑ̃sjɛl] *adj & m* essential

esseu·lé -lée [escele] *adj* abandoned

es·sieu [esjø] *m* (*pl* -**sieux**) axle

essor [esɔr] *m* flight; development; boom (*in business*); **donner libre essor à** to give vent to; to give full scope to; **prendre son essor** to take wing

essorer [esɔre] *tr* to spin-dry; to wring; to centrifuge

essoreuse [esɔrøz] *f* spin-drier; wringer; centrifuge

essouf·flé -flée [esufle] *adj* breathless, out of breath

essuie-glace [esɥiglas] *m* (*pl* -**glaces**) windshield wiper

essuie-mains [esɥimɛ̃] *m invar* towel

essuie-plume [esɥiplym] *m* (*pl* -**plumes**) penwiper

essuyer [esɥije], [esɥije] §27 *tr* to wipe; to wipe off; to wipe away; to suffer, endure; to undergo; to weather (*a storm*); **essuyer les plâtres** (coll) to be the first to occupy a house

est [est] *adj invar & m* east

estacade [estakad] *f* breakwater; pier; boom (*barrier of floating logs*); railway trestle

estafette [estafet] *f* messenger

estaminet [estamine] *m* bar, café

estampe [estɑ̃p] *f* print, engraving; (*tool*) stamp

estamper [estɑ̃pe] *tr* to stamp (*with a design*); to engrave; to overcharge, to fleece

estampille [estɑ̃pij] *f* identification mark; trademark; hallmark

ester [estɛr] *m* ester || [este] *intr*—**ester en justice** to go to law, to sue

esthète [estet] *mf* aesthete

esthéti·cien [estetisjɛ̃] -**cienne** [sjɛn] *mf* aesthetician || *f* beautician

esthétique [estetik] *adj* aesthetic || *f* aesthetics

estimable [estimabl] *adj* estimable

estimateur [estimatœr] *m* estimator, appraiser

estimation [estimɑsjɔ̃] *f* estimation, appraisal

estime [estim] *f* esteem; **à l'estime** by guesswork; (naut) by dead reckoning

estimer [estime] *tr* to esteem; to estimate, to assess; **estimer + inf** to think that + *ind*, e.g., **j'estime avoir fait mon devoir** I think that I did my duty

esti·val -vale [estival] *adj* (*pl* -**vaux** [vo]) summer

esti·vant [estivɑ̃] -**vante** [vɑ̃t] *mf* summer vacationist, summer resident

estiver [estive] *intr* to summer

estocade [estɔkad] *f* thrust (*in fencing*); unexpected attack

estomac [estɔma] *m* stomach

estomaquer [estɔmake] *tr* (coll) to astound || *ref* (coll) to be angered

estomper [estɔ̃pe] *tr* to shade off, to rub away (*a drawing*); to blur || *ref* to be blurred

Estonie [estɔni] *f* Estonia; **l'Estonie** Estonia

estrade [estrad] *f* platform

estragon [estragɔ̃] *m* tarragon

estro·pié -piée [estrɔpje] *adj* crippled || *mf* cripple

estuaire [estɥer] *m* estuary

estudian·tin [estydjɑ̃tɛ̃] -**tine** [tin] *adj* student

esturgeon [estyrʒɔ̃] *m* sturgeon

et [e] *conj* and; **et . . . et** both . . . and

Établ. *abbr* (**Établissement**) company, establishment

étable [etabl] *f* stable, cowshed

établer [etable] *tr* to stable

établi [etabli] *m* workbench

établir [etablir] *tr* to establish || *ref* to settle down; to set up headquarters

établissement [etablismɑ̃] *m* establishment

étage [etaʒ] *m* floor, story; tier; level; rank, social level; (rok) stage; **de bas étage** lower-class; **dernier étage** top floor; **premier étage** first floor above ground floor

étager [etaʒe] §38 *tr* to arrange in tiers; to stagger; to perform in stages

étagère [etaʒer] *f* rack, shelf

étai [ete] *m* prop, stay

étain [etɛ̃] *m* tin; pewter

étal [etal] *m* (*pl* **étals** or **étaux** [eto]) stall, stand; butcher's block

étalage [etalaʒ] *m* display

étalager [etalaʒe] §38 *tr* to display

étalagiste [etalaʒist] *mf* window dresser, display artist; demonstrator

étaler [etale] *tr* to display; to spread out || *ref* (coll) to sprawl

étalon [etalɔ̃] *m* stallion; monetary standard

étalonner [etalɔne] *tr* to verify, control; to standardize; to graduate, calibrate

étalon-or [etalɔ̃ɔr] *m* gold standard

étambot [etɑ̃bo] *m* (naut) sternpost

étamer [etame] *tr* to tin-plate; to silver (*a mirror*)

étamine [etamin] *f* stamen; sieve; cheesecloth

étampe [etɑ̃p] *f* stamp, die, punch

étamper [etɑ̃pe] *tr* to stamp, punch

étanche [etɑ̃ʃ] *adj* watertight, airtight

étancher [etɑ̃ʃe] *tr* to check, stanch the flow of; to quench (*one's thirst*); to make watertight or airtight

étang [etɑ̃] *m* pond

étape [etap] *f* stage; stop, halt; day's march; (sports) lap; **brûler les étapes** to go straight through

état [eta] *m* state; statement, record; trade, occupation; government; (hist) estate; **en tout état de cause** at all costs; in any case; **état civil** marital status; **état tampon** buffer state; **être dans tous ses états** to stew; **être en état de** to be in a position to; **faire état de** to take into account; to expect to; **hors d'état** out of order, unfit; **tenir en état** to keep in shape, to repair

étatisation [etatizɑsjɔ̃] *f* nationalization

étatiser [etatize] *tr* to nationalize

étatisme [etatism] *m* statism

état-major [etamaʒɔr] *m* (*pl* **états-majors**) headquarters, staff

état-providence [etaprɔvidɑ̃s] *m* welfare state

États-Unis [etazyni] *mpl* United States

étau [eto] *m* (*pl* **étaux**) vise

étayer [eteje] §49 *tr* to prop, stay

et Cie *abbr* (**et Compagnie**) & Co.

été [ete] *m* summer

éteignoir [etɛɲwar] *m* candle snuffer; (coll) kill-joy, wet blanket

éteindre [etɛ̃dr] §50 *tr* to extinguish, put out; to turn off; to wipe out; to appease (*e.g.*, one's thirst); to dull (a color) || *intr* to put out the light || *ref* to go out; (fig) to die, pass away

éteint [etɛ̃] **éteinte** [etɛ̃t] *adj* extinguished; extinct; dull, dim

étendard [etɑ̃dar] *m* flag, banner

étendoir [etɑ̃dwar] *m* clothesline; drying rack

étendre [etɑ̃dr] *tr* to extend, spread out || *ref* to stretch out; to spread

éten·du **-due** [etɑ̃dy] *adj* outspread; extensive; vast; diluted, adulterated || *f* stretch; range, scope

éter·nel **-nelle** [etɛrnɛl] *adj* eternal

éterniser [etɛrnize] *tr* to perpetuate (a name); to drag out || *ref* (coll) to drag on; **s'éterniser chez qn** (coll) to overstay an invitation

éternité [etɛrnite] *f* eternity

éternuement [etɛrnymɑ̃] *m* sneeze; sneezing

éternuer [etɛrnɥe] *intr* to sneeze

étêter [etete] *tr* to top (a tree); to take the head off (a fish, nail, *etc.*)

éteule [etœl] *f* stubble

éther [etɛr] *m* ether

éthé·ré **-rée** [etere] *adj* ethereal

Éthiopie [etjɔpi] *f* Ethiopia; **l'Éthiopie** Ethiopia

éthio·pien [etjɔpjɛ̃] **-pienne** [pjɛn] *adj* Ethiopian || *m* Ethiopian (*language*) || (*cap*) *mf* Ethiopian (*person*)

éthique [etik] *adj* ethical || *f* ethics

ethnique [etnik] *adj* ethnic(al)

ethnographie [etnɔgrafi] *f* ethnography

ethnologie [etnɔlɔʒi] *f* ethnology

éthyle [etil] *m* ethyl

éthylène [etilɛn] *m* ethylene

étiage [etjaʒ] *m* low-water mark

étince·lant [etɛ̃slɑ̃] **-lante** [lɑ̃t] *adj* sparkling, glittering

étinceler [etɛ̃sle] §34 *intr* to sparkle, glitter

étincelle [etɛ̃sɛl] *f* spark; (fig) flash

étiolement [etjɔlmɑ̃] *m* wilting

étioler [etjɔle] *tr & ref* to wilt

étique [etik] *adj* lean, emaciated

étiqueter [etikte] §34 *tr* to label

étiquette [etikɛt] *f* etiquette; label; **étiquette gommée** sticker

étirer [etire] *tr* to stretch, lengthen, elongate || *ref* (coll) to stretch one's limbs

étoffe [etɔf] *f* stuff; material, fabric; quality, worth

étoile [etwal] *f* star; traffic circle; **à la belle étoile** out of doors; **étoile de mer** starfish; **étoile filante** shooting or falling star; **étoile polaire** pole-star

étoi·lé **-lée** [etwale] *adj* star-spangled, starry

étole [etɔl] *f* stole

éton·nant [etɔnɑ̃] **-nante** [etɔnɑ̃t] *adj* astonishing

étonnement [etɔnmɑ̃] *m* surprise, astonishment; fissure, crack

étonner [etɔne] *tr* to surprise, astonish; to shake or crack (*masonry*) || *ref* to be surprised

étouf·fant [etufɑ̃] **-fante** [etufɑ̃t] *adj* suffocating; sweltering

étouffée [etufe] *f* braising; **cuire à l'étouffée** to braise

étouffer [etufe] *tr*, *intr*, *& ref* to suffocate; to stifle; to choke

étoupe [etup] *f* oakum, tow

étourderie [eturdri] *f* thoughtlessness

étour·di **-die** [eturdi] *adj* scatter-brained || *mf* scatterbrain

étourdir [eturdir] *tr* to stun, daze; to numb; to deafen (*with loud noise*) || *ref* to try to forget, get in a daze

étourdissement [eturdismɑ̃] *m* dizziness; numbing

étour·neau [eturno] *m* (*pl* **-neaux**) starling

étrange [etrɑ̃ʒ] *adj* strange

étran·ger [etrɑ̃ʒe] **-gère** [ʒɛr] *adj* foreign; irrelevant; unknown, strange; **être étranger à** to be unacquainted with || *mf* foreigner; stranger; **à l'étranger** abroad, in a foreign country

étrangeté [etrɑ̃ʒte] *f* strangeness

étrangler [etrɑ̃gle] *tr & intr* to strangle || *ref* to choke; to narrow (*said of passageway, valley, etc.*)

étran·gleur [etrɑ̃glœr] **-gleuse** [gløz] *mf* strangler

étrave [etrav] *f* (naut) stempost; **de l'étrave à l'étambot** from stem to stern

être [etr] *m* being || §28 *intr* to be; **en être pour sa peine** to have nothing for one's trouble; **être à + *pron disj*** to be + *pron poss*, e.g., **le livre est à moi** the book is mine; **n'est-ce pas** see **ne** || *aux* (used with some intransitive verbs and all reflexive verbs) to have, e.g., **elles sont arrivées** they have arrived; (used to form the passive voice) to be, e.g., **il est aimé de tout le monde** he is loved by everybody

étrécir [etresir] *tr & ref* to shrink

étreindre [etrɛ̃dr] §50 *tr* to embrace; to grip, seize

étreinte [etrɛ̃t] *f* embrace; hold, grasp

étrenne [etrɛn] *f* first sale of the day;

avoir l'étrenne de to have the first use of; **étrennes** New-Year gifts

étrenner [etrene] *tr* to put on for the first time; to be the first to wear ǁ *intr* (coll) to be the first to catch it

étrier [etrije] *m* stirrup

étrille [etrij] *f* currycomb

étriller [etrije] *tr* to curry; (coll) to thrash, to tan the hide of; (coll) to overcharge, to fleece

étriper [etripe] *tr* to gut, disembowel

étri-qué -quée [etrike] *adj* skimpy, tight; narrow, cramped

étriquer [etrike] *tr* to make too tight; to shorten (*e.g., a speech*)

étroit [etrwa] **étroite** [etrwat] *adj* narrow; strict; tight; close; **à l'étroit** confined, cramped

étroitesse [etrwates] *f* narrowness; **étroitesse d'esprit** narrow-mindedness

étude [etyd] *f* study; law office; law practice; spadework, planning; **à l'étude** under consideration; **mettre à l'étude** to study; **terminer ses études** to finish one's courses

étu-diant [etydjɑ̃] **-diante** [djɑ̃t] *mf* student

étu-dié -diée [etydje] *adj* studied; set (*speech*); artificial, affected

étudier [etydje] *tr* to study; to practice, rehearse; to learn by heart; to design ǁ *intr* to study ǁ *ref* to be overly introspective; **s'étudier à** to take pains to, to make a point of

étui [etɥi] *m* case, box

étuve [etyv] *f* steam bath or room; drying room; steam sterilizer; incubator (*for breeding cultures*)

étuver [etyve] *tr* to stew; to steam; to dry

étymologie [etimɔlɔʒi] *f* etymology

étymon [etimɔ̃] *m* etymon

eucalyptus [økaliptys] *m* eucalyptus

Eucharistie [økaristi] *f* Eucharist

eunuque [ønyk] *m* eunuch

euphémique [øfemik] *adj* euphemistic

euphémisme [øfemism] *m* euphemism

euphonie [øfɔni] *f* euphony

euphonique [øfɔnik] *adj* euphonic

euphorie [øfɔri] *f* euphoria

Europe [ørɔp] *f* Europe; **l'Europe** Europe

européen [ørɔpeɛ̃] **européenne** [ørɔpeen] *adj* European ǁ (cap) *mf* European

eux [ø] §85

eux-mêmes [ømɛm] §86

évacuer [evakɥe] *tr & ref* to evacuate

éva-dé -dée [evade] *mf* escapee

évader [evade] *ref* to escape, evade

évaluer [evalɥe] *tr* to evaluate, appraise; to estimate

évanes-cent [evanesɑ̃] **évanes-cente** [evanesɑ̃t] *adj* evanescent

évangélique [evɑ̃ʒelik] *adj* evangelic(al)

évangéliste [evɑ̃ʒelist] *m* evangelist

évangile [evɑ̃ʒil] *m* gospel

évanouir [evanwir] *ref* to faint; to lose consciousness; to vanish; (rad) to fade

évanouissement [evanwismɑ̃] *m* fainting; disappearance

évapo-ré -rée [evapɔre] *adj* flighty, fickle, giddy

évaporer [evapɔre] *tr & ref* to evaporate

évaser [evaze] *tr & ref* to widen

éva-sif [evazif] **-sive** [ziv] *adj* evasive

évasion [evazjɔ̃] *f* evasion; escape; **d'évasion** escapist (*literature*)

Ève [ev] *f* Eve; **je ne le connais ni d'Ève ni d'Adam** (coll) I don't know him from Adam

évêché [eveʃe] *m* bishopric

éveil [evej] *m* awakening; alarm, warning

éveil-lé -lée [eveje] *adj* alert, lively; sharp, intelligent

éveiller [eveje] *tr & ref* to wake up

événement [evenmɑ̃], [evenmɑ̃] *m* event; outcome, development; **faire événement** to cause quite a stir

évent [evɑ̃] *m* vent; staleness

éventail [evɑ̃taj] *m* fan; range, spread; screen

éventaire [evɑ̃ter] *m* tray (*carried by flower girl, cigarette girl, etc.*); sidewalk display

éventer [evɑ̃te] *tr* to fan; to ventilate; to get wind of (*a secret*); **éventer la mèche** (coll) to let the cat out of the bag ǁ *ref* to fan oneself; to fade away (*said of odor*); to go stale or flat

éventrer [evɑ̃tre] *tr* to disembowel; to smash open

éventualité [evɑ̃tɥalite] *f* eventuality; possibility

éven-tuel -tuelle [evɑ̃tɥel] *adj* eventual; possible, contingent; forthcoming ǁ *m* eventuality; possibility; possibilities (*e.g., of a job*)

éventuellement [evɑ̃tɥelmɑ̃] *adv* eventually; possibly; if need be

évêque [evek] *m* bishop

évertuer [evertɥe] *ref*—**s'évertuer à** or **pour** + *inf* to strive to + *inf*

éviction [eviksjɔ̃] *f* eviction, removal; **éviction scolaire** quarantine

évidement [evidmɑ̃] *m* hollowing out

évidemment [evidamɑ̃] *adv* evidently

évidence [evidɑ̃s] *f* evidence, obviousness; conspicuousness; **de toute évidence** by all appearances; **se mettre en évidence** to come to the fore

évi-dent [evidɑ̃] **-dente** [dɑ̃t] *adj* evident

évider [evide] *tr* to hollow out

évier [evje] *m* sink

évincer [evɛ̃se] §51 *tr* to evict, to oust; to discriminate against

éviter [evite] *tr* to avoid, escape

évoca-teur [evɔkatœr] **-trice** [tris] *adj* evocative, suggestive

évocation [evɔkasjɔ̃] *f* evocation

évoluer [evɔlɥe] *intr* to evolve; to change one's mind

évolution [evɔlysjɔ̃] *f* evolution

évoquer [evɔke] *tr* to evoke; to recall, to call to mind

exact [egza], [egzakt] **exacte** [egzakt] *adj* exact

exactitude [egzaktityd] *f* exactness; punctuality

exagérer [egzaʒere] §10 *tr* to exaggerate; to overdo

exal-té -tée [egzalte] *adj* impassioned;

high-strung, wrought-up ‖ *mf* hot-head, fanatic

exalter [egzalte] *tr* to exalt; to excite (*e.g., the imagination*) ‖ *ref* to get excited

examen [egzamɛ̃] *m* examination; **à l'examen** under consideration; **on approval; examen de fin d'études** or **examen de fin de classe** final examination; **examen probatoire** placement exam; **libre examen** free inquiry; **se présenter à, passer,** or **subir un examen** to take an examination

examina·teur [egzaminatœr] **-trice** [tris] *mf* examiner

examiner [egzamine] *tr* to examine

exaspération [egzasperasjɔ̃] *f* exasperation; crisis, aggravation

exaspérer [egzaspere] **§10** *tr* to exasperate; to make worse

exaucer [egzose] **§51** *tr* to answer the prayer of; to fulfill (*a wish*)

excava·teur [ekskavatœr] **-trice** [tris] *m & f* excavator, steam shovel

excaver [ekskave] *tr* to excavate

excé·dant [eksedɑ̃] **-dante** [dɑ̃t] *adj* excess; tiresome

excédent [eksedɑ̃] *m* excess, surplus

excédentaire [eksedɑ̃tɛr] *adj* excess

excéder [eksede] **§10** *tr* to exceed; to tire out; to overtax

excellence [ekselɑ̃s] *f* excellence; **Votre Excellence** Your Excellency

exceller [eksele] *intr* to excel

excentricité [eksɑ̃trisite] *f* eccentricity

excentrique [eksɑ̃trik] *adj* eccentric, remote, outlying ‖ *mf* eccentric ‖ *m* (mach) eccentric

excep·té -tée [eksepte] *adj* excepted ‖ **excepté** *adv*—**excepté que** except that ‖ **excepté** *prep* except, except for

exception [eksepsjɔ̃] *f* exception; **à l'exception de** with the exception of

exception·nel -nelle [eksepsjonel] *adj* exceptional

excès [eksɛ] *m* excess; **excès de pose** (phot) overexposure; **excès de vitesse** speeding

exces·sif [eksesif] **exces·sive** [eksesiv] *adj* excessive

exciper [eksipe] *intr*—**exciper de** (law) to offer a plea of, to allege

excitable [eksitabl] *adj* excitable

exci·tant [eksitɑ̃] **-tante** [tɑ̃t] *adj* stimulating ‖ *m* stimulant

exciter [eksite] *tr* to excite, stimulate; to stir, incite; to provoke (*e.g., laughter*)

exclamation [eksklamasjɔ̃] *f* exclamation

exclamer [eksklame] *ref* to exclaim

exclure [eksklyr] **§11** *tr* to exclude

exclu·sif [eksklyzif] **-sive** [ziv] *adj* exclusive

exclusion [eksklyzjɔ̃] *f* exclusion; **à l'exclusion de** exclusive of, excluding

exclusivité [eksklyzivite] *f* exclusiveness; exclusive rights; newsbeat; **en exclusivité** (public sign in front of a theater) exclusive showing

excommunication [ekskɔmynikasjɔ̃] *f* excommunication

excommunier [ekskɔmynje] *tr* to excommunicate

excorier [ekskɔrje] *tr* to scratch, skin

excrément [ekskremɑ̃] *m* excrement

excroissance [ekskrwasɑ̃s] *f* growth, tumor

excursion [ekskyrsjɔ̃] *f* excursion; tour, trip; outing

excursionner [ekskyrsjone] *intr* to go on an excursion

excusable [ekskyzabl] *adj* excusable

excuse [ekskyz] *f* excuse; **des excuses** apologies

excuser [ekskyze] *tr* to excuse ‖ *ref* to excuse oneself, to apologize; **je m'excuse!** (coll) excuse me!

exécrer [egzekre] **§10** *tr* to execrate

exécu·tant [egzekytɑ̃] **-tante** [tɑ̃t] *mf* performer

exécuter [egzekyte] *tr* to execute; to perform; to make (*copies*) ‖ *ref* to comply

exécuteur [egzekytœr] *m*—**exécuteur testamentaire** executor; **exécuteur des hautes œuvres** hangman

exécu·tif [egzekytif] **-tive** [tiv] *adj & m* executive

exécution [egzekysjɔ̃] *f* execution; performance; fulfillment; **mettre à exécution** to carry out

exécutrice [egzekytris] *f* executrix

exemplaire [egzɑ̃plɛr] *adj* exemplary ‖ *m* exemplar, model; sample, specimen; copy (*e.g., of book*); **en double exemplaire** with carbon copy; **exemplaire dédicacé** autographed copy; **exemplaires de passe** extra copies

exemple [egzɑ̃pl] *m* example; **à l'exemple de** after the example of; **par exemple** for example; **par exemple!** the ideal, well I never!; **prêcher d'exemple** to practice what one preaches; **sans exemple** unprecedented

exempt [egzɑ̃] **exempte** [egzɑ̃t] *adj* exempt ‖ *m* (hist) police officer

exempter [egzɑ̃te] *tr* to exempt

exemption [egzɑ̃psjɔ̃] *f* exemption

exer·cé -cée [egzerse] *adj* practiced, experienced

exercer [egzerse] **§51** *tr* to exercise; to exert; to practice (*e.g., medicine*) ‖ *ref* to exercise; to practice, to drill

exercice [egzersis] *m* exercise; drill; practice; **exercice budgétaire** fiscal year

exhalaison [egzalezɔ̃] *f* exhalation (*of gas, vapors, etc.*)

exhalation [egzalasjɔ̃] *f* exhalation (*of air from lungs*)

exhaler [egzale] *tr, intr, & ref* to exhale

exhaure [egzɔr] *f* pumping out (*of a mine*); drain pumps

exhaussement [egzosmɑ̃] *m* raising; rise

exhausser [egzose] *tr* to raise, to increase the height of ‖ *ref* to rise

exhaus·tif [egzostif] **-tive** [tiv] *adj* exhaustive

exhiber [egzibe] *tr* to exhibit; to show (*a ticket, passport, etc.*) || *ref* to make an exhibition of oneself

exhibition [egzibisjɔ̃] *f* exhibition

exhorter [egzɔrte] *tr* to exhort

exhumer [egzyme] *tr* to exhume

exi·geant [egziʒɑ̃] **-geante** [ʒɑ̃t] *adj* exigent, exacting; unreasonable

exigence [egziʒɑ̃s] *f* demand, claim; requirement; unreasonableness; **exigences** exigencies

exiger [egziʒe] §38 *tr* to demand, require, exact

exigible [egziʒibl] *adj* required; due, on demand

exi·gu -guë [egzigy] *adj* tiny; insufficient

exiguïté [egziguite] *f* smallness; insufficiency

exil [egzil] *m* exile

exi·lé -lée [egzile] *adj & mf* exile

exiler [egzile] *tr* to exile

existence [egzistɑ̃s] *f* existence

exister [egziste] *intr* to exist

exode [egzod] *m* exodus; flight (*of capital; of emigrants, refugees, etc.*)

exonération [egzɔnerasjɔ̃] *f* exemption, exoneration

exonérer [egzɔnere] §10 *tr* to exempt, exonerate || *ref* to pay up a debt

exorbi·tant [egzɔrbitɑ̃] **-tante** [tɑ̃t] *adj* exorbitant

exorciser [egzɔrsize] *tr* to exorcise

exotique [egzɔtik] *adj* exotic

expan·sif [ekspɑ̃sif] **-sive** [siv] *adj* expansive

expansion [ekspɑ̃sjɔ̃] *f* expansion; expansiveness; spread (*of a belief*)

expa·trié -triée [ekspatrije] *adj & mf* expatriate

expatrier [ekspatrije] *tr* to expatriate

expectorer [ekspektɔre] *tr & intr* to expectorate

expé·dient [ekspedjɑ̃] **-diente** [djɑ̃t] *adj* expedient || *m* expedient; (coll) makeshift; **expédient provisoire** emergency measure; **vivre d'expédients** to live by one's wits

expédier [ekspedje] *tr* to expedite; to ship; to make a certified copy of; (coll) to dash off, do hurriedly

expédi·teur [ekspeditœr] **-trice** [tris] *adj* forwarding (*station, agency, etc.*) || *mf* sender, shipper

expédi·tif [ekspeditif] **-tive** [tiv] *adj* expeditious

expédition [ekspedisjɔ̃] *f* expedition; shipping; shipment; certified copy

expéditionnaire [ekspedisjɔner] *adj* expeditionary || *mf* sender; clerk

expérience [eksperjɑ̃s] *f* experience; experiment

expérimen·té -tée [eksperimɑ̃te] *adj* experienced

expérimenter [eksperimɑ̃te] *tr* to try out, to test || *intr* to conduct experiments

ex·pert [eksper] **-perte** [pert] *adj* expert || *m* expert; connoisseur; appraiser

expert-comptable [eksperkɔ̃tabl] *m* (*pl* **experts-comptables**) certified public accountant

expertise [ekspertiz] *f* expert appraisal

expertiser [ekspertize] *tr* to appraise

expier [ekspje] *tr* to expiate, to atone for

expirer [ekspire] *tr & intr* to expire; to exhale

explicable [eksplikabl] *adj* explicable, explainable

explica·tif [eksplikatif] **-tive** [tiv] *adj* explanatory

explication [eksplikasjɔ̃] *f* explanation; interpretation (*of a text*); **avoir une explication avec qn** to have it out with s.o.

explicite [eksplisit] *adj* explicit

expliciter [eksplisite] *tr* to make explicit

expliquer [eksplike] *tr* to explain; to give an interpretation of || *ref* to explain oneself; to understand

exploit [eksplwa] *m* exploit; **exploit d'ajournement** subpoena; **signifier un exploit** to serve a summons

exploi·tant [eksplwatɑ̃] **-tante** [tɑ̃t] *adj* operating, working || *mf* operator (*of enterprise*); developer; cultivator; (mov) exhibitor

exploitation [eksplwatasjɔ̃] *f* exploitation; management, development, cultivation; land under cultivation

exploiter [eksplwate] *tr* to exploit; to manage, develop, cultivate || *intr* to serve summonses

explora·teur [eksplɔratœr] **-trice** [tris] *mf* explorer

exploration [eksplɔrasjɔ̃] *f* exploration

explorer [eksplɔre] *tr* to explore; (telv) to scan

exploser [eksploze] *intr* to explode

explosible [eksplozibl] *adj* explosive

explo·sif [eksplozif] **-sive** [ziv] *adj & m* explosive

explosion [eksplozjɔ̃] *f* explosion; **à explosion** internal-combustion (*engine*)

exporta·teur [eksportatœr] **-trice** [tris] *adj* exporting || *mf* exporter

exportation [eksportasjɔ̃] *f* export; exportation

exporter [eksporte] *tr & intr* to export

expo·sant [ekspozɑ̃] **-sante** [zɑ̃t] *mf* exhibitor; petitioner || *m* (math) exponent

exposé [ekspoze] *m* exposition, account, statement; report (*given by a student in class*)

exposer [ekspoze] *tr* to expose; to explain, expound; to exhibit, display

exposition [ekspozisjɔ̃] *f* exposition; exposure (*to one of the points of the compass*); introduction (*of a book*); lying in state; **exposition canine** dog show; **exposition d'horticulture** flower show; **exposition hippique** horse show

ex·près [ekspre] **-presse** [pres] *adj* express || **exprès** *adj invar* special-delivery (*letter, package, etc.*) || *m* express; **par exprès** by special delivery || **exprès** *adv* expressly, on purpose

express [ekspres] *adj & m* express (*train*)

expressément [ɛkspresemã] *adv* expressly

expres·sif [ɛkspresif] **expres·sive** [ɛkspresiv] *adj* expressive

expression [ɛkspresjɔ̃] *f* expression; **d'expression française** native French-speaking

exprimer [ɛksprime] *tr* to express; to squeeze out

exproprier [ɛksprɔprije] *tr* to expropriate

expul·sé ·sée [ɛkspylse] *adj* deported ‖ *mf* deportee

expulser [ɛkspylse] *tr* to expel; to evict; to throw out

expulsion [ɛkspylsjɔ̃] *f* expulsion

expurger [ɛkspyrʒe] §38 *tr* to expurgate

ex·quis [ɛkski] **-quise** [kiz] *adj* exquisite; sharp (*pain*)

exsangue [ɛksãg] *adj* bloodless, anemic

exsuder [ɛksyde] *tr & intr* to exude

extase [ɛkstɑz] *f* ecstasy

exta·sié ·siée [ɛkstɑzje] *adj* enraptured, ecstatic, in ecstasy

extasier [ɛkstɑzje] *ref* to be enraptured

extatique [ɛkstatik] *adj & mf* ecstatic

extempora·né ·née [ɛkstãpɔrane] *adj* (law) unpremeditated; (pharm) ready for use

exten·sif ·sive [ɛkstãsif] **-sive** [siv] *adj* wide (*meaning*); (mech) tensile

extension [ɛkstãsjɔ̃] *f* extension

exténuer [ɛkstenɥe] *tr* to exhaust, tire out ‖ *ref* to tire oneself out

exté·rieur ·rieure [ɛksterjœr] *adj* exterior; external; outer, outside; foreign (*policy*) ‖ *m* exterior; outside; (mov) location shot; **à l'extérieur** outside; abroad; **en extérieur** (mov) on location

extérieurement [ɛksterjœrmã] *adv* externally; superficially; on the outside

extérioriser [ɛksterjɔrize] *tr* to reveal, to show ‖ *ref* to open one's heart

exterminer [ɛkstermine] *tr* to exterminate

externat [ɛksterna] *m* day school

externe [ɛkstern] *adj* external ‖ *m* day student; outpatient; (med) nonresident intern

extinc·teur [ɛkstɛ̃ktœr] **-trice** [tris] *adj* extinguishing ‖ *m* fire extinguisher

extinction [ɛkstɛ̃ksjɔ̃] *f* extinction; extinguishing; loss (*of voice*); **l'extinction des feux** (mil) lights out, taps

extirper [ɛkstirpe] *tr* to extirpate

extorquer [ɛkstɔrke] *tr* to extort

extor·queur [ɛkstɔrkœr] **-queuse** [køz] *mf* extortionist

extorsion [ɛkstɔrsjɔ̃] *f* extortion

extra [ɛkstra] *adj invar* (coll) extra-special, extra ‖ *m invar* extra

extraction [ɛkstraksjɔ̃] *f* extraction

extrader [ɛkstrade] *tr* to extradite

extradition [ɛkstradisjɔ̃] *f* extradition

extra-fin [ɛkstrafɛ̃] **-fine** [fin] *adj* high-quality

extraire [ɛkstrɛr] §68 *tr* to extract; to excerpt; to get out ‖ *ref* to extricate oneself

extrait [ɛkstrɛ] *m* extract; excerpt; abstract; certified copy; **extrait de baptême** baptismal certificate; **extrait de naissance** birth certificate; **extraits** selections (*e.g., in an anthology*)

extra-muros [ɛkstramyros] *adj invar* extramural; suburban ‖ *adv* outside the town

extraordinaire [ɛkstraɔrdiner], [ɛkstrɔrdiner] *adj* extraordinary

extrapoler [ɛkstrapɔle] *tr* to extrapolate

extra-sensoriel ·sensorielle [ɛkstrasãsɔrjel] *adj* extrasensory

extravagance [ɛkstravagãs] *f* extravagance; excess; absurdity, wildness

extrava·gant [ɛkstravagã] **-gante** [gãt] *adj* excessive, extravagant; absurd, wild, eccentric ‖ *mf* eccentric, screwball

extraver·ti ·tie [ɛkstraverti] *adj & mf* extrovert

extrême [ɛkstrem] *adj & m* extreme

extrêmement [ɛkstreməmã] *adv* extremely

extrême-onction [ɛkstrem̃ɔ̃ksjɔ̃] *f* extreme unction

Extrême-Orient [ɛkstremɔrjã] *m* Far East

extrémiste [ɛkstremist] *adj & mf* extremist

extrémité [ɛkstremite] *f* extremity; **en venir à des extrémités** to resort to violence; **être à toute extrémité** to be at death's door

extrinsèque [ɛkstrɛ̃sek] *adj* extrinsic

exubé·rant [ɛgzyberã] **-rante** [rãt] *adj* exuberant

exulter [ɛgzylte] *intr* to exult

ex-voto [ɛksvɔto] *m invar* votive inscription or tablet

F

F, f [ɛf], *[ɛf] m invar* sixth letter of the French alphabet

F *abbr* (franc) franc

fable [fɑbl] *f* fable; laughingstock

fabri·cant [fabrikã] **-cante** [kãt] *mf* manufacturer

fabrica·teur [fabrikatœr] **-trice** [tris] *mf* fabricator (*e.g., of lies*); forger; counterfeiter

fabrication [fabrikasjɔ̃] *f* manufacture; forging; counterfeiting

fabrique [fabrik] *f* factory; factory

workers; mill hands; (obs) church trustees; (obs) church revenue; **fabrique de papier** paper mill

fabriquer [fabrike] *tr* to manufacture; to fabricate; to forge; to counterfeit

fabu·leux [fabylø] **-leuse** [løz] *adj* fabulous

façade [fasad] *f* façade; frontage; **en façade** *sur* facing, overlooking

face [fas] *f* face; side (*of a diamond; of a phonograph record*); surface; heads (*of coin*); **de face** full-faced (*portrait*); **en face (de)** opposite, facing; **faire face à** to face; to face up to; to meet (*an obligation*); **perdre la face** to lose face; **sauver la face** to save face

face-à-main [fasamɛ̃] *m* (*pl* **faces-à-main**) lorgnette

facétie [fasesi] *f* off-color joke; practical joke

facé·tieux [fasesjø] **-tieuse** [sjøz] *adj* droll, funny ‖ *mf* wag

facette [faset] *f* facet

fâ·ché -chée [faʃe] *adj* angry; sorry; **fâché avec** at odds with; **fâché contre** angry with (*a person*); **fâché de** angry at (*a thing*); sorry for

fâcher [faʃe] *tr* to anger ‖ *ref* to get angry; to be sorry

fâ·cheux [faʃø] **-cheuse** [ʃøz] *adj* annoying, tiresome; unfortunate ‖ *mf* nuisance, bore

fa·cial -ciale [fasjal] *adj* (*pl* **-ciaux** [sjo]) facial; face (*value*)

facile [fasil] *adj* easy; easygoing; facile, glib

facilité [fasilite] *f* facility; opportunity (*e.g., to meet s.o.*); **facilités de paiement** installments; easy terms

faciliter [fasilite] *tr* to facilitate

façon [fasɔ̃] *f* fashion; fashioning; way, manner; fit (*of clothes*); **à la façon de** like; **de façon à** so as to; **de façon que** or **de telle façon que** so that, e.g., **parlez de telle façon qu'on vous comprenne** speak so that you can be understood; **de toute façon** in any event; **façons** manners; **faire des façons** to stand on ceremony; **sans façon** informal

faconde [fakɔ̃d] *f* glibness, gift of gab

façonner [fasone] *tr* to fashion, shape; to work (*the land*); to accustom

façon·nier [fasonje] **façon·nière** [fasonjer] *adj* jobbing; fussy ‖ *mf* pieceworker; stuffed shirt

fac-similé [faksimile] *m* (*pl* **-similés**) facsimile

factage [faktaʒ] *m* delivery service; home delivery

facteur [faktœr] *m* factor; mailman; expressman; auctioneer (*at a market*); maker (*of musical instruments*)

factice [faktis] *adj* imitation, artificial

fac·tieux [faksjø] **-tieuse** [sjøz] *adj* factious, seditious ‖ *mf* troublemaker, agitator

faction [faksjɔ̃] *f* faction; **être de faction** to be on sentry duty

factionnaire [faksjoner] *m* sentry

factorerie [faktoreri] *f* trading post

factotum [faktɔtɔm] *m* factotum; meddler; jack-of-all-trades

factum [faktɔm] *m* political pamphlet; (law) brief

facturation [faktyrasjɔ̃] *f* billing, invoicing

facture [faktyr] *f* invoice; bill; workmanship; **établir une facture** to make out an invoice; **suivant facture** as per invoice

facturer [faktyre] *tr* to bill

factu·rier [faktyrje] **-rière** [rjer] *mf* billing clerk ‖ *m* invoice book

faculta·tif [fakyltatif] **-tive** [tiv] *adj* optional

faculté [fakylte] *f* faculty; school, college (*of law, medicine, etc.*); **la Faculté** medical men

fadaise [fadez] *f* piece of nonsense; **fadaises** drivel

fade [fad] *adj* tasteless, flat; insipid, namby-pamby

fader [fade] *tr* (coll) to beat; (coll) to share the swag with; **il est fadé** (coll) he's done for

fadeur [fadœr] *f* insipidity; pointlessness; **fadeurs** platitudes

fagot [fago] *m* faggot; **fagot d'épines** ill-tempered person; **sentir le fagot** to smell of heresy

fagoter [fagote] *tr* to tie up in bundles, to faggot; (coll) to dress like a scarecrow

faible [febl] *adj* feeble, weak; low (*figure; moan*); poor (*harvest*); slight (*difference*) ‖ *mf* weakling ‖ *m* weakness; foible, weak spot; **faible d'esprit** feeble-minded person

faiblesse [febles] *f* feebleness, weakness, frailty

faiblir [feblir] *intr* to weaken; to diminish

faïence [fajɑ̃s] *f* earthenware, pottery

faille [faj] *f* (geol) fault; (tex) faille; (fig) defect; (fig) rift

failli-lie [faji] *adj* & *mf* bankrupt

faillible [fajibl] *adj* fallible

faillir [fajir] *intr* to fail, to go bankrupt ‖ (used only in: *inf*; *ger* **faillant**; *pp* & compound tenses; *pret*; *fut*; *cond*) *intr* to fail; to give way; (with *dat*) to fail, let (*s.o.*) down; **faillir à** to fail in (*a duty*); to fail to keep (*a promise*); **faillir à + inf** to fail to + *inf*; **sans faillir** without fail ‖ (used only in *pret* and *past indef*) *intr*—nearly, almost, e.g., **il a failli être écrasé** he was nearly run over

faillite [fajit] *f* bankruptcy; **faire faillite** to go bankrupt

faim [fɛ̃] *f* hunger; **avoir faim** to be hungry; **avoir une faim de loup** to be hungry as a bear; **manger à sa faim** to eat one's fill

fainéant [feneɑ̃] **fainéante** [feneɑ̃t] *adj* lazy ‖ *mf* loafer, do-nothing

fainéanter [feneɑ̃te] *intr* (coll) to loaf

faire [fer] *m* making, doing ‖ §29 *tr* to make; to do; to give (*an order; a lecture; alms, a gift; thanks*); to take (*a walk; a step*); to pack (*a trunk*); to clean (*the room, the shoes, etc.*); to follow (*a trade*); to keep (*silence*);

to perform (*a play; a miracle*); to play the part of; to charge for, e.g., **combien faites-vous ces souliers?** how much do you charge for these shoes?; to say, e.g., **oui, fit-il** yes, said he; (coll) to estimate the cost of; for expressions like **il fait chaud** it is warm, see the noun; **cela ne fait rien** it doesn't matter; **faire** + *inf* to have + *inf*, e.g., **je le ferai aller** I shall have him go; **faire** + *inf* to make + *inf*, e.g., **je le ferai parler** I will make him talk; **faire** + *inf* to have + *pp*, e.g., **je vais faire faire un complet** I am going to have a suit made; **il n'en fait pas d'autres** that's just like him; **ne faire que** + *inf* to keep on + *ger*, e.g., **il ne fait que crier** he keeps on yelling || *intr* to go, e.g., **la cravate fait bien avec la chemise** the tie goes well with the shirt; to act; **comment faire?** what shall I do?; **faire dans** to make a mess in; **ne faire que de** + *inf* to have just + *pp*, e.g., **il ne fait que d'arriver** he has just arrived || *ref* to become (*a doctor, lawyer, etc.*); to grow (*e.g, old*); to improve; to happen; to pretend to be; **se faire à** to get accustomed to, to adjust to; **s'en faire** to worry, e.g., **ne vous en faites pas!** don't worry!

faire-part [fɛrpar] *m invar* announcement (*of birth, marriage, death*)

faire-valoir [fɛrvalwar] *m invar* turning to account; **faire-valoir direct** farming by the owner

faisable [fəzabl] *adj* feasible

fai·san [fəzɑ̃] **-sane** [zan] or **-sande** [zɑ̃d] *mf* pheasant

faisander [fəzɑ̃de] *tr* to jerk (*game*) || *intr* to become gamy, to get high

fais·ceau [fɛso] *m* (*pl* **-ceaux**) bundle, cluster; beam (*of light*); pencil (*of rays*); **faisceaux** fasces; **faisceaux de preuves** cumulative evidence; **former les faisceaux** to stack or pile arms

fai·seur [fəzœr] **-seuse** [zøz] *mf*—**bon faiseur** first-rate workman; **faiseur de mariages** matchmaker; **faiseur de vers** versifier, poetaster || *m* bluffer; schemer

fait [fɛ] **faite** [fɛt] *adj* well-built, shapely; full-grown; made-up (*with cosmetics*); **fait à la main** hand-made; **tout fait** ready-made || *m* deed, act; fact; **dire son fait à qn** (coll) to give s.o. a piece of one's mind; **prendre fait et cause pour** to take up the cudgels for; **si fait** yes, indeed; **sur le fait** redhanded, in the act; **tout à fait** entirely || [fɛt] *m*—**au fait** to the point; after all; **de fait** *de facto*; **du fait que** owing to the fact that; **en fait** as a matter of fact

faitage [fɛtaʒ] *m* ridgepole; roofs; roofing

fait-divers [fɛdivɛr] *m* (*pl* **faits-divers**) news item

faîte [fɛt] *m* peak; top (*of tree*); ridge (*of roof*)

faîtière [fɛtjɛr] *adj fem* ridge || *f* ridge tile; skylight

fait-tout [fetu] *m invar* stewpan, casserole

faix [fɛ] *m* load, burden; (archit) settling; (physiol) fetus and placenta

falaise [falɛz] *f* cliff, bluff

falla·cieux [falasjø] **-cieuse** [sjøz] *adj* fallacious

falloir [falwar] §30 *impers* to be necessary; **c'est plus qu'il n'en faut** that's more than enough; **comme il faut** proper; properly; the right kind of, e.g., **un chapeau comme il faut** the right kind of hat; **il fallait le dire!** why didn't you say so!; **il faut** + *inf* it is necessary to + *inf*, one must + *inf*; **il faut qu'il** + *subj* it is necessary that he + *subj*, it is necessary for him to + *inf*; he must + *inf* (expressing conjecture), e.g., **il n'est pas venu, il faut qu'il soit malade** he did not come, he must be sick; **il faut qu'il ne** + *subj* + **pas** he must not + *inf*, e.g., **il faut qu'il ne vienne pas** he must not come; **il faut une connaissance des affaires à ce travail** the work requires business experience; **il faut une heure** it takes an hour; **il leur a fallu trois jours** it took them three days; **il leur faut** + *inf* they have to + *inf*, they must + *inf*; **il leur faut du repos** they need rest; **il leur faut sept dollars** they need seven dollars; **il ne faut pas** + *inf* one must not or should not + *inf*, e.g., **il ne faut pas se fier à ce garçon** one must not trust that boy; **il ne faut pas qu'il** + *subj* he must not + *inf*; **que leur faut-il?** what do they need?, what do they require?; **qu'il ne fallait pas** wrong, e.g., **la police a arrêté l'homme qu'il ne fallait pas** the police arrested the wrong man || *ref*— **il s'en faut de beaucoup** not by a long shot, far from it, not by any means; **il s'en faut de dix dollars** there is a shortage of ten dollars; **peu m'en est fallu que . . .** it very nearly happened that . . . ; **peu s'en faut** very nearly; **tant s'en faut que** far from, e.g., **tant s'en faut qu'il soit artiste** he is far from being an artist

fa·lot [falo] **-lotte** [lɔt] *adj* wan, colorless; quaint, droll || *m* lantern

falsification [falsifikɑsjɔ̃] *f* falsification; adulteration; debasement (*of coin*)

falsifier [falsifje] *tr* to falsify; to adulterate; to debase (*coin*)

fa·mé -mée [fame] *adj*—**mal famé** disreputable

famélique [famelik] *adj* famished

fa·meux [famø] **-meuse** [møz] *adj* famous || (when standing before noun) *adj* (coll) notorious; well-known

fami·lial -liale [familjal] *adj* (*pl* **-liaux** [ljo]) family, domestic || *f* station wagon

familiariser [familjarize] *tr* to familiarize || *ref* to become familiar

familiarité [familjarite] *f* familiarity

fami·lier [familje] **-lière** [ljer] *adj*

familiar, intimate; household (*gods*); pet (*animal*) || *mf* familiar, intimate; pet animal

famille [famij] *f* family; **en famille** in the family circle, at home; (Canad) pregnant

famine [famin] *f* famine

fa·nal [fanal] *m* (*pl* **-naux** [no]) lantern; (naut) running light

fanatique [fanatik] *adj* fanatic(al) || *mf* fanatic; enthusiast, fan

fanatisme [fanatism] *m* fanaticism

faner [fane] *tr & ref* to fade

fanfare [fɑ̃far] *f* fanfare; brass band

fanfa·ron [fɑ̃farɔ̃] **-ronne** [rɔn] *adj* bragging || *mf* braggart

fanfaronner [fɑ̃farɔne] *intr* to brag

fange [fɑ̃ʒ] *f* mire, mud; (fig) mire, gutter

fan·geux [fɑ̃ʒø] **-geuse** [ʒøz] *adj* muddy; (fig) dirty, soiled

fanion [fanjɔ̃] *m* pennant, flag

fanon [fanɔ̃] *m* dewlap (*of ox*); whalebone; fetlock; wattle

fantaisie [fɑ̃tezi] *f* imagination; fantasy; fancy, whim; **de fantaisie** fanciful; fancy, e.g., **pain de fantaisie** fancy bread

fantaisiste [fɑ̃tezist] *adj* fantastic, whimsical || *mf* whimsical person; singing comedian

fantasque [fɑ̃task] *adj* fantastic; whimsical, temperamental

fantassin [fɑ̃tasɛ̃] *m* foot soldier

fantastique [fɑ̃tastik] *adj* fantastic

fantoche [fɑ̃tɔʃ] *m* puppet

fantôme [fɑ̃tom] *adj* shadow (*government*) || *m* phantom, ghost

fanum [fanɔm] *m* hallowed ground

faon [fɑ̃] *m* fawn

faonner [fane] *intr* to bring forth young (*said especially of deer*)

faquin [fakɛ̃] *m* rascal

fa·raud [faro] **-raude** [rod] *adj* (coll) swanky || *mf* (coll) fop, bumpkin; **faire le faraud** (coll) to show off

farce [fars] *f* farce; trick, joke; (culin) stuffing

far·ceur [farsœr] **-ceuse** [søz] *mf* practical joker; phony

farcir [farsir] *tr* to stuff

fard [far] *m* make-up; **parler sans fard** to speak plainly, to tell the unvarnished truth; **piquer un fard** (coll) to blush

far·deau [fardo] *m* (*pl* **-deaux**) load, burden; weight (*of years*)

farder [farde] *tr* to make up (*an actor*); to disguise (*the truth*) || *ref* to weigh heavily; (archit) to sink; (theat) to make up

fardier [fardje] *m* dray, cart

farfe·lu -lue [farfəly] *adj* (coll) harebrained, cockeyed, bizarre

farfouiller [farfuje] *tr* (coll) to rummage about in || *intr* (coll) to rummage about; **farfouiller dans** (coll) to rummage about in

farine [farin] *f* flour, meal; **farine de froment** whole-wheat flour; **farine de riz** ground rice; **farine lactée** malted milk

fariner [farine] *tr* (culin) to flour

fari·neux [farinø] **-neuse** [nøz] *adj* white with flour; mealy; starchy

farouche [faruʃ] *adj* wild, savage; unsociable; shy; stubborn (*resistance*); fierce (*look*)

fascicule [fasikyl] *m* fascicle; **fascicule de mobilisation** marching orders

fascina·teur [fasinatœr] **-trice** [tris] *adj* fascinating || *mf* spellbinder

fasciner [fasine] *tr* to fascinate; to spellbind

fascisme [faʃism] *m* fascism

fasciste [faʃist] *adj & mf* fascist

faste [fast] *adj* auspicious; feast (*day*) || *m* pomp; **fastes** annals

fasti·dieux [fastidjø] **-dieuse** [djøz] *adj* tedious, wearisome

fas·tueux [fastɥø] **-tueuse** [tɥøz] *adj* pompous, ostentatious

fat [fat] *adj masc* conceited, foppish || *m* fop

fa·tal -tale [fatal] *adj* (*pl* **-tals**) fatal; fateful; inevitable

fatalisme [fatalism] *m* fatalism

fataliste [fatalist] *adj* fatalistic || *mf* fatalist

fatalité [fatalite] *f* fatality; fatalism; fate; curse, misfortune

fatidique [fatidik] *adj* fateful; prophetic

fati·gant [fatigɑ̃] **-gante** [gɑ̃t] *adj* fatiguing; tiresome (*person*)

fatigue [fatig] *f* fatigue

fati·gué -guée [fatige] *adj* fatigued; worn-out (*clothing*); well-thumbed (*book*)

fatiguer [fatige] *tr* to fatigue; to wear out; to weary || *intr* to strain, labor; to pull (*said of engine*); to bear a heavy strain (*said of beam*) || *ref* to get tired

fatras [fatra] *m* jumble, hodgepodge

fatuité [fatɥite] *f* conceit; foppishness

faubert [fober] *m* (naut) swab

faubourg [fobur] *m* suburb; outskirts; quarter, district (*especially of Paris*)

faubou·rien [foburjɛ̃] **-rienne** [rjɛn] *adj* working-class, vulgar || *mf* resident of the outskirts of a city; local inhabitant

fau·ché -chée [foʃe] *adj* (coll) broke (*without money*)

faucher [foʃe] *tr* to mow, reap; (coll) to swipe

fau·cheur [foʃœr] **-cheuse** [ʃøz] *mf* reaper || *m* (ent) daddy-longlegs || *f* (mach) reaper, mower

faucheux [foʃø] *m* (ent) daddy-longlegs

faucille [fosij] *f* sickle

faucon [fokɔ̃] *m* falcon

fauconnier [fokɔnje] *m* falconer

faufil [fofil] *m* basting thread

faufiler [fofile] *tr* to baste || *ref* to thread one's way, to worm one's way

faune [fon] *m* faun || *f* fauna

faunesse [fones] *f* female faun

faussaire [foser] *mf* forger

fausser [fose] *tr* to falsify, distort; to bend, twist; to warp (*the judgment*); to force (*a lock*); to strain (*the voice*); **fausser compagnie à qn** (coll) to give s.o. the slip || *intr* to sing or play out of tune ‖ *ref* to bend, buckle; to crack (*said of voice*)

fausset [fose] *m* falsetto; plug (*for wine barrel*)

fausseté [foste] *f* falsity; double-dealing

faute [fot] *f* fault; mistake; blame; lack, need, want; (*sports*) foul; (*sports*) error; **faire faute** to be lacking; **faute de** for want of; **faute de copiste** clerical error; **faute de frappe** typing error; **faute d'impression** misprint; **sans faute** without fail

fauter [fote] *intr* (coll) to go wrong (*said of a woman*)

fauteuil [fotœj] *m* armchair, easy chair; seat (*of member of an academy*); chair (*of presiding officer; presiding officer himself*); **fauteuil à bascule** or **à balançoire** rocking chair; **fauteuil à oreilles** wing chair; **fauteuil d'orchestre** orchestra seat; **fauteuil pliant** folding chair; **fauteuil roulant pour malade** wheelchair; **siéger au fauteuil présidentiel** to preside

fau·teur [fotœr] **-trice** [tris] *mf* instigator, agitator

fau·tif [fotif] **-tive** [tiv] *adj* faulty

fauve [fov] *adj* fawn (*color*); musky (*odor*); wild (*beast*) ‖ *m* fawn color; wild beast; **fauves** big game

fauvette [fovet] *f* warbler

faux [fo] **fausse** [fos] *adj* false; counterfeit; wrong, e.g., **fausse date** wrong date; e.g., **fausse note** wrong note ‖ *m* imitation; forgery; **à faux** wrongly ‖ **faux** *f* scythe ‖ **faux** *adv* out of tune, off key

faux-bourdon [foburdɔ̃] *m* (*pl* **-bourdons**) *m* (ent) drone

faux-col [fokɔl] *m* (*pl* **-cols**) collar, detachable collar

faux-filet [fofile] *m* (*pl* **-filets**) sirloin

faux-fuyant [fofɥijɑ̃] *m* (*pl* **-fuyants**) subterfuge, pretext

faux-jour [foʒur] *m* (*pl* **-jours**) half-light

faux-monnayeur [fomɔnejœr] *m* (*pl* **-monnayeurs**) counterfeiter

faux-pas [fopɑ] *m invar* faux pas, slip, blunder

faux-semblant [fosɑ̃blɑ̃] *m* (*pl* **-semblants**) false pretense

faveur [favœr] *f* favor; **à la faveur de** under cover of; **en faveur de** in favor of; on behalf of

favorable [favorabl] *adj* favorable

favo·ri [favori] **-rite** [rit] *adj & mf* favorite ‖ **favoris** *mpl* sideburns ‖ *f* mistress

favoriser [favorize] *tr* to favor; to encourage, promote

F^co or **fco** *abbr* (**franco**) postpaid

fébrile [febril] *adj* feverish

fèces [fes] *fpl* feces

fé·cond [fekɔ̃] **-conde** [kɔ̃d] *adj* fecund, fertile

féconder [fekɔ̃de] *tr* to impregnate

fécondité [fekɔ̃dite] *f* fecundity, fertility

fécule [fekyl] *f* starch; **fécule de maïs** cornstarch

fécu·lent [fekylɑ̃] **-lente** [lɑ̃t] *adj* starchy ‖ *m* starchy food

fédé·ral **-rale** [federal] *adj & m* (*pl* **-raux** [ro]) federal

fédéra·tif [federatif] **-tive** [tiv] *adj* federated, federative

fédération [federasjɔ̃] *f* federation

fédérer [federe] §10 *tr & ref* to federate

fée [fe] *f* fairy; **de fée** fairy; meticulous (*work*); **vieille fée** old hag

féerie [feri] *f* fairyland; fantasy

féerique [ferik] *adj* fairy, magic(al)

feindre [fɛ̃dr] §50 *tr* to feign ‖ *intr* to feign; to limp (*said of horse*)

feinte [fɛ̃t] *f* feint

feinter [fɛ̃te] *tr* (coll) to trick ‖ *intr* to feint

feldspath [feldspat], **felspat**, *m* feldspar

fê·lé **-lée** [fele] *adj* (coll) cracked, crazy

fêler [fele] *tr* to crack

félicitations [felisitasjɔ̃] *fpl* congratulations

féliciter [felisite] *tr* to congratulate; **féliciter qn de** + *inf* to congratulate s.o. for + *ger*; **féliciter qn de** or **pour** to congratulate s.o. for ‖ *ref*—**se féliciter de** to congratulate oneself on, to be pleased with oneself because of

fé·lon [felɔ̃] **-lonne** [lɔn] *adj* disloyal, treasonable

félonie [feloni] *f* disloyalty, treason

fêlure [felyr] *f* crack, chink

femelle [famel] *adj & f* female

fémi·nin [feminɛ̃] **-nine** [nin] *adj & m* feminine

féminisme [feminism] *m* feminism

femme [fam] *f* woman; wife; bride; **bonne femme** (coll) simple, good-natured woman; **femme agent** (*pl* **femmes agents**) policewoman; **femme auteur** (*pl* **femmes auteurs**) authoress; **femme de chambre** chambermaid; **femme de charge** housekeeper; **femme de journée** cleaning woman; **femme de ménage** cleaning woman; **femme d'intérieur** homebody; **femme docteur** woman doctor (*e.g., with Ph.D. degree*); **femme juge** woman judge; **femme médecin** woman doctor (*physician*); **femme pasteur** woman preacher

fendiller [fɑ̃dije] *tr & ref* to crack

fendoir [fɑ̃dwar] *m* cleaver, chopper

fendre [fɑ̃dr] *tr* to crack; to split (*e.g., wood*); to cleave (*e.g., the air*); to break (*one's heart*); to elbow one's way through (*a crowd*) ‖ *ref* to crack; (escr) to lunge

fenêtre [fanetr] *f* window; **fenêtre à battants** casement window, French window; **fenêtre à guillotine** sash window; **fenêtre en saillie** bay window

fenil [fanil], [fani] *m* hayloft

fenouil [fanuj] *m* fennel; **fenouil bâtard** dill

fente [fɑ̃t] *f* crack, split, fissure; notch; slot (*e.g., in a coin telephone*); (escr) lunge

féo·dal -dale [feɔdal] *adj* (*pl* **-daux** [do]) feudal

féodalisme [feɔdalism] *m* feudalism

fer [fer] *m* iron; head (*of tool*); point (*of weapon*); **croiser le fer avec** to cross swords with; **fer à cheval** horseshoe; **fer à friser** curling iron; **fer à marquer** *or* **flétrir** branding iron; **fer à repasser** iron, flatiron; **fer à souder** soldering iron; **fer de fonte** cast iron; **fer forgé** wrought iron; **fers** irons, chains, fetters; **marquer au fer** to brand; **remuer le fer dans la plaie** (coll) to rub it in

ferblanterie [ferblɑ̃tri] *f* tinware; tinwork, sheet-metal work; tinsmith's shop

ferblantier [ferblɑ̃tje] *m* tinsmith

fé·rié -riée [ferje] *adj* feast (*day*)

férir [ferir] *tr—sans coup férir* without striking a blow

ferler [ferle] *tr* (naut) to furl

fermage [fermaʒ] *m* tenant farming; rent

ferme [ferm] *adj* firm || *f* farm, tenant farm; farmhouse || *adv* firmly, fast

fer·mé -mée [ferme] *adj* exclusive, restricted; inscrutable (*countenance*)

ferment [fermɑ̃] *m* ferment

fermenter [fermɑ̃te] *intr* to ferment

fermer [ferme] *tr* to close, to shut; to turn off; **fermer à clef** to lock; **fermer au verrou** to bolt; **la ferme!** (slang) shut up!, shut your trap! || *intr* & *ref* to close, to shut

fermeté [fermǝte] *f* firmness

fermeture [fermǝtyr] *f* closing; fastening; **fermeture éclair** zipper

fer·mier [fermje] **-mière** [mjer] *adj* farming || *m* farmer; tenant farmer; lessee || *f* farmer's wife

fermoir [fermwar] *m* snap, clasp

féroce [ferɔs] *adj* ferocious

férocité [ferɔsite] *f* ferocity

ferraille [feraj] *f* scrap iron; (coll) small change; **mettre à la ferraille** to junk

ferrailleur [ferajœr] *m* dealer in scrap iron; sword rattler

fer·ré -rée [fere] *adj* ironclad; hobnailed (*shoe*); paved (*road*); **ferré sur** well versed in

ferrer [fere] *tr* to shoe (*a horse*)

ferret [fere] *m* tag (*of shoelace*); (geol) hard core

ferronnerie [ferɔnri] *f* ironwork; hardware

ferron·nier [ferɔnje] **ferron·nière** [ferɔnjer] *mf* ironworker; hardware dealer

ferrotypie [ferɔtipi] *f* tintype

ferroviaire [ferɔvjer] *adj* railway

ferrure [feryr] *f* horseshoeing; **ferrures** hardware; metal trim

ferry-boat [feribot] *m* (*pl* **-boats**) train ferry

fertile [fertil] *adj* fertile

fertiliser [fertilize] *tr* to fertilize

fertilité [fertilite] *f* fertility

fé·ru -rue [fery] *adj—féru de* wrapped up in (*an idea, an interest*)

fer·vent [fervɑ̃] **-vente** [vɑ̃t] *adj* fervent || *mf* devotee

ferveur [fervœr] *f* fervor

fesse [fes] *f* buttock

fessée [fese] *f* spanking

fesse-mathieu [fesmatjø] *m* (*pl* **-mathieux**) usurer; skinflint

fesser [fese] *tr* to spank

fes·su -sue [fesy] *adj* broad-bottomed

festin [festɛ̃] *m* feast, banquet

festi·val [festival] *m* (*pl* **-vals**) music festival

festivité [festivite] *f* festivity

feston [festɔ̃] *m* festoon

festonner [festɔne] *tr* to festoon; to scallop

festoyer [festwaye] §47 *tr* to fete, regale || *intr* to feast

fê·tard -tarde [fetar] *mf* merrymaker

fête [fet] *f* festival; feast day, holiday; name day; party, festivity; **être à la fête** (coll) to be very pleased or gratified; **faire fête à** to receive with open arms; **faire la fête** (coll) to carouse; **fête foraine** carnival; **fête légale** *or* **fête nationale** legal holiday; **la fête des Mères** Mother's Day; **la fête des Morts** All Souls' Day; **la fête des Rois** Twelfth-night; **se faire une fête de** to look forward with pleasure to; **souhaiter une bonne fête à qn** to wish s.o. many happy returns

Fête-Dieu [fetdjø] *f* (*pl* **Fêtes-Dieu**)— **la Fête-Dieu** Corpus Christi

fêter [fete] *tr* to fete; to celebrate (*a special event*)

fétiche [fetiʃ] *m* fetish

fétu [fety] *m* straw; trifle

feu feue [fø] *adj* (*pl* **feus**) (standing before noun) late, deceased, e.g., **la feue reine** the late queen || **feu** *adj invar* (standing before article and noun) late, deceased, e.g., **feu la reine** the late queen || *m* (*pl* **feux**) fire; flame; traffic light; burner (*of stove*); **à petit feu** by inches; **du feu a** light (*to ignite a cigar, etc.*); **être sous les feux de la rampe** to be in the limelight; **faire du feu** to light a fire; **faire long feu** to hang fire; to fail; (arti) to miss; **feu d'artifice** fireworks; **feu de joie** bonfire; **feu de paille** (fig) flash in the pan; **feu follet** will-o'-the-wisp; **feux de position**, **feux de stationnement** parking lights; **mettre le feu à** to set on fire; **prendre feu** to catch fire || **feu** *interj* fire! (*command to fire*); **au feu!** fire! (*warning*)

feuillage [fœjaʒ] *m* foliage; **feuillages** fallen branches

feuille [fœj] *f* leaf; sheet; form (*to be filled out*); **feuille de chou** (coll) rag (*newspaper of little value*); **feuille de présence** time sheet; **feuille d'étain** tin foil; **feuille de température** temperature chart; **feuille d'imposition** income-tax blank

feuil·lé feuil·lée [fœje] *adj* leafy, foliaged || *f* bower; **feuillées** (mil) camp latrine

feuiller [fœje] *intr* to leaf

feuille·té -tée [fœjte] *adj* foliated; in flaky layers

feuilleter [fœjte] §34 *tr* to leaf through; to foliate; (culin) to roll into thin layers

feuilleton [fœjtɔ̃] *m* newspaper serial (*printed at bottom of page*); (rad, telv) serial

feuil·lu feuil·lue [fœjy] *adj* leafy ‖ *m* foliage

feuillure [fœjyr] *f* groove

feuler [fœle] *intr* to growl (*said of cat*)

feutre [føtr] *m* felt

feu·tré -trée [føtre] *adj* velvetlike; muffled (*steps*)

feutrer [føtre] *tr* to felt

fève [fɛv] *f* bean; **fève des Rois** bean or figurine baked in the Twelfth-night cake; **fèves au lard** pork and beans

février [fevrie] *m* February

fi [fi] *interj* fie!; **faire fi de** to scorn

fiacre [fjakr] *m* horse-drawn cab

fiançailles [fjɑ̃saj] *fpl* engagement, betrothal

fian·cé -cée [fjɑ̃se] *mf* betrothed ‖ *m* fiancé ‖ *f* fiancée

fiancer [fjɑ̃se] §51 *tr* to betroth ‖ *ref* to become engaged

fiasco [fjasko] *m* (coll) fiasco, failure; **faire fiasco** to flop, fail

fibre [fibr] *f* fiber; (fig) feeling, sensibility; **avoir la fibre sensible** to be easily moved

fi·breux [fibrø] **-breuse** [brøz] *adj* fibrous

ficeler [fisle] §34 *tr* to tie up

ficelle [fisɛl] *adj* (coll) knowing ‖ *f* string; **connaître les ficelles** (fig) to know the ropes; **tenir** or **tirer les ficelles** (fig) to pull strings; **vieille ficelle** (coll) old hand

fiche [fi*ʃ*] *f* peg; slip, form, blank; filing card, index card; membership card; (cards) chip, counter; (elec) plug; **fiche de consolation** booby prize; **fiche femelle** (elec) jack; **fiche perforée** punch card; **fiche scolaire** report card

ficher [fi*ʃ*e] *tr* to drive in (*a stake*); to take down (*information on a form*); to fasten, fix, stick; **ficher qn à la porte** (coll) to kick s.o. out; **ficher une gifle à qn** (coll) to box s.o. on the ear; **fichez-moi le camp!** (slang) beat it! ‖ *ref*—**se ficher de** (slang) to make fun of

fichier [fi*ʃ*je] *m* card catalogue; cabinet, file (*for cards or papers*)

fichtre [fi*ʃ*tra] *interj* (coll) gosh!

fi·chu -chue [fi*ʃ*y] *adj* (coll) wretched, ugly; **fichu de** capable of ‖ *m* scarf, shawl

fic·tif [fiktif] **-tive** [tiv] *adj* fictitious

fiction [fiksjɔ̃] *f* fiction

fidéicommis [fideikɔmi] *m* (law) trust

fidèle [fidɛl] *adj* faithful ‖ *mf* supporter; **les fidèles** (eccl) the congregation, the faithful

fidélité [fidelite] *f* fidelity, faithfulness; **haute fidélité** high fidelity

fief·fé fief·fée [fjefe] *adj* (coll) downright, real, regular (*liar, coward, etc.*)

fiel [fjɛl] *m* bile; gall

fiel·leux [fjelø] **fiel·leuse** [fjeløz] *adj* galling

fiente [fjɑ̃t] *f* droppings

fier fière [fjɛr] *adj* proud; haughty ‖ **fier** [fje] *tr* (archaic) to entrust ‖ *ref*—**se fier à** or **en** to trust, to have confidence in, to rely upon; **se fier à qn de** to entrust s.o. with; **s'y fier** to trust it

fier-à-bras [fjerabra] *m* (*pl* **fier-à-bras** or **fiers-à-bras** [fjerabra]) braggart

fierté [fjerte] *f* pride

fièvre [fjevr] *f* fever; **fièvre aphteuse** foot-and-mouth disease

fifre [fifr] *m* fife; fife player

fi·gé -gée [fiʒe] *adj* curdled; fixed, set; frozen (*smile*); **figé sur place** rooted to the spot

figement [fiʒmɑ̃] *m* clotting, coagulation

figer [fiʒe] §38 *tr* to curdle; to stop dead ‖ *ref* to curdle; to set, to freeze (*said, e.g., of smile*)

fignoler [fiɲɔle] *tr* to work carefully at ‖ *intr* to be finicky

figue [fig] *f* fig; **figue de Barbarie** prickly pear

figuier [figje] *m* fig tree

figu·rant [figyrɑ̃] **-rante** [rɑ̃t] *mf* (theat) supernumerary, extra

figura·tif [figyratif] **-tive** [tiv] *adj* figurative, emblematic

figure [figyr] *f* figure; face (*of a person*); face card; **faire figure** to cut a figure; **figure de proue** (naut) figurehead; **prendre figure** to take shape

figu·ré -rée [figyre] *adj* figurative; figured ‖ *m* figurative sense

figurer [figyre] *tr* to figure ‖ *intr* to figure, take part; (theat) to walk on ‖ *ref* to imagine, believe

fil [fil] *m* thread; wire; edge (*e.g., of knife*); grain (*of wood*); **au fil de l'eau** with the stream; **droit fil** with the grain; **elle lui a donné du fil à retordre** (fig) she gave him more than he bargained for; **fil à plomb** plumb line; **fil de fer barbelé** barbed wire; **fil de lin** yarn; **fil d'or** spun gold; **fils de la vierge** gossamer; **passer au fil de l'épée** to put to the sword; **plein de fils** stringy; **sans fil** wireless

filament [filamɑ̃] *m* filament

filamen·teux [filamɑ̃tø] **-teuse** [tøz] *adj* stringy

filan·dreux [filɑ̃drø] **-dreuse** [drøz] *adj* stringy (*meat*); long, drawn-out

fi·lant [filɑ̃] **-lante** [lɑ̃t] *adj* ropy (*liquid*); shooting (*star*)

filasse [filas] *f* tow, oakum

filature [filatyr] *f* manufacture of thread; spinning mill; shadowing (*of a suspect*)

fil-de-fériste [fildəferist] *mf* tightwire walker

file [fil] *f* file, row, lane; **à la file** one after another, in a row; **file d'attente** waiting line; **marcher en file indienne** to walk Indian file

filer [file] *tr* to spin; to pay out (*rope, cable*); to prolong; to shadow (*a suspect*) ‖ *intr* to ooze; to smoke (*said of lamp*); (coll) to go fast; **filer à**

l'anglaise (coll) to take French leave; **filer doux** (coll) to back down, to give in; **filez!** (coll) get out!

filet [file] *m* net; trickle (*of water*); streak (*of light*); thread (*of screw or nut*); (culin) fillet; (typ) rule; **faux filet** sirloin; **filet à bagage** baggage rack; **filet à cheveux** hair net; **filet à provisions** string bag, mesh bag

fileter [filte] §2 *tr* to thread (*a screw*); to draw (*wire*)

fi·leur [filœr] **-leuse** [løz] *mf* spinner

fi·lial -liale [filjal] *adj* (*pl* **-liaux** [ljo]) filial ‖ *f* (com) branch, subsidiary

filiation [filjɑsjɔ̃] *f* filiation

filière [filjɛr] *f* (mach) die; (mach) drawplate; **filière administrative** official channels; **passer par la filière** (coll) to go through channels; (coll) to work one's way up

filigrane [filigran] *m* filigree; watermark (*in paper*)

filigraner [filigrane] *tr* to filigree

filin [filɛ̃] *m* (naut) rope

fille [fij] *f* daughter; unmarried girl; servant; (pej) tart; **fille de joie, des rues, or de vie, fille publique** prostitute; **fille de salle** nurse's aid; **fille d'honneur** bridesmaid; **jeune fille** girl; **vieille fille** old maid

fillette [fijɛt] *f* young girl, little lass

fil·leul fil·leule [fijœl] *mf* godchild ‖ *m* godson ‖ *f* goddaughter

film [film] *m* film; (fig) train (*of events*); **film sonore** sound film

filmage [filmaʒ] *m* filming

filmer [filme] *tr* to film

filmique [filmik] *adj* film

filon [filɔ̃] *m* vein, lode; (coll) soft job; (coll) bonanza, strike; **filon guide** leader vein

filoselle [filozɛl] *f* floss silk

filou [filu] *m* sneak thief; cheat, sharper

filouter [filute] *tr* (coll) to swindle, cheat; **filouter q.ch. à qn** (coll) to do s.o. out of s.th. ‖ *intr* to cheat at cards

fils [fis] *m* son; (when following proper name) junior; **fils à papa** (coll) rich man's son, playboy; **fils de ses œuvres** (fig) self-made man

filtrage [filtraʒ] *m* filtering; surveillance (*by the police*)

fil·trant [filtrɑ̃] **-trante** [trɑ̃t] *adj* filterable; filter, e.g., **papier filtrant** filter paper

filtre [filtr] *m* filter

filtrer [filtre] *tr & intr* to filter

fin [fɛ̃] **fine** [fin] *adj* fine ‖ (when standing before noun) *adj* clever, sly, smart; secret, hidden ‖ *m* fine linen; smart person; **le fin du fin** the finest of the fine ‖ *f* end; **à la fin** at last; **à seule fin de** for the sole purpose of; **à toutes fins utiles** for your information; **c'est la fin des haricots** (slang) that takes the cake; **en fin de compte** in the end; to get to the point; **fin d'interdiction de dépasser** (public sign) end of no passing; **mot de la fin** clincher; **sans**

fin endless ‖ **fin** *adv* absolutely; finely (*ground*); small, e.g., **écrire fin** to write small

fi·nal -nale [final] (*pl* **-nals** or **-naux** [no]) *adj* final ‖ *m* finale ‖ *f* last syllable or letter; (mus) keynote; (sports) finals

finalement [finalmɑ̃] *adv* finally

finaliste [finalist] *mf* finalist

financement [finɑ̃smɑ̃] *m* financing

financer [finɑ̃se] §51 *tr* to finance

finan·cier [finɑ̃sje] **-cière** [sjɛr] *adj* financial; spicy (*sauce for vol-au-vent*) ‖ *m* financier

finasser [finase] *intr* (coll) to use finesse, to finagle

finasserie [finasri] *f* shrewdness

fi·naud [fino] **-naude** [nod] *adj* wily, sly ‖ *mf* sly fox; smart aleck

finesse [fines] *f* finesse; fineness; **savoir les finesses** to know the fine points or niceties

fi·ni -nie [fini] *adj* finished; finite; ruined (*in health, financially, etc.*); arrant (*rogue*) ‖ *m* finish; finite

finir [finir] *tr & intr* to finish; **en finir avec** to have done with; **finir de** + *inf* to finish + *ger*; **finir par** + *inf* to finish by + *inf*

finissage [finisaʒ] *m* finishing touch, final step

finition [finisjɔ̃] *f* finish; **finitions** finishing touches

finlan·dais [fɛ̃lɑ̃de] **-daise** [dez] *adj* Finnish ‖ *m* Finnish (*language*) ‖ (*cap*) *mf* Finn

Finlande [fɛ̃lɑ̃d] *f* Finland; **la Finlande** Finland

fin·nois [finwa] **fin·noise** [finwaz] *adj* Finnish ‖ *m* Finnish (*language*); Finnic (*branch of Uralic*) ‖ (*cap*) *mf* Finn

fiole [fjɔl] *f* phial

fioriture [fjorityr] *f* flourish, curlicue

firmament [firmamɑ̃] *m* firmament

firme [firm] *f* firm, house, company

fisc [fisk] *m* bureau of internal revenue, tax-collection agency

fis·cal -cale [fiskal] *adj* (*pl* **-caux** [ko]) fiscal; revenue, taxation

fiscaliser [fiskalize] *tr* to subject to tax

fiscalité [fiskalite] *f* tax collections; fiscal policy

fissile [fisil] *adj* fissionable

fission [fisjɔ̃] *f* fission

fissure [fisyr] *f* fissure, crack

fissurer [fisyre] *tr & ref* to fissure

fiston [fistɔ̃] *m* (slang) sonny

fixation [fiksɑsjɔ̃] *f* fixation; fixing

fixe [fiks] *adj* fixed; permanent (*ink*); glassy (*stare*); regular (*time*); set (*price*); standing (*rule*) ‖ *m* fixed income ‖ *interj* (mil) eyes front!

fixe-chaussette [fiksəʃoset] *m* (*pl* **-chaussettes**) garter (*for men's socks*)

fixement [fiksəmɑ̃] *adv* fixedly

fixer [fikse] *tr* to fix; to appoint; (coll) to stare at; **fixer son choix sur** to fix on; **pour fixer les idées** for the sake of argument ‖ *ref* to be fastened; to establish residence; to make up one's mind

flacon [flakɔ̃] *m* small bottle; flask

flageller [flaʒelle] *tr* to flagellate

flageoler [flaʒɔle] *intr* to quiver

flageolet [flaʒɔle] *m* flageolet; kidney bean

flagorner [flagɔrne] *tr* to flatter

fla-grant [flagrɑ̃] **-grante** [grɑ̃t] *adj* flagrant, glaring, obvious

flair [fler] *m* scent, sense of smell; (*discernment*) flair, keen nose

flairer [flere] *tr* to smell, to sniff; to scent, to smell out

fla-mand [flamɑ̃] **-mande** [mɑ̃d] *adj* Flemish ‖ *m* Flemish (*language*) ‖ (*cap*) *mf* Fleming (*person*)

flamant [flamɑ̃] *m* flamingo

flam-bant [flɑ̃bɑ̃] **-bante** [bɑ̃t] *adj* flaming; **flambant neuf** (coll) brand-new

flam-beau [flɑ̃bo] *m* (*pl* **-beaux**) torch; candlestick; large wax candle; (fig) light

flambée [flɑ̃be] *f* blaze

flamber [flɑ̃be] *tr* to singe; to sterilize; **être flambé** (coll) to be all washed up, ruined ‖ *intr* to flame

flamberge [flɑ̃berʒ] *f* (archaic) sword, blade; **mettre flamberge au vent** to unsheathe the sword

flamboiement [flɑ̃bwamɑ̃] *m* glow, flare

flamboyant [flɑ̃bwajɑ̃] **flamboyante** [flɑ̃bwajɑ̃t] *adj* flaming, blazing; (archit) flamboyant

flamboyer [flɑ̃bwaje] §47 *intr* to flame

flamme [flɑm], [flɑm] *f* flame; pennant

flammèche [flameʃ] *f* ember, large spark

flan [flɑ̃] *m* custard; blank (*coin, medal, record*); **à la flan** (slang) happy-go-lucky; botched (*job*); **c'est du flan** (slang) it's ridiculous

flanc [flɑ̃] *m* flank; side (*of ship, mountain, etc.*); **battre du flanc** to pant; **être sur le flanc** (coll) to be laid up; **flancs** (archaic) womb; bosom; **prêter le flanc à** to lay oneself open to; **se battre les flancs** to go to a lot of trouble for nothing; **tirer au flanc** (coll) to gold-brick, to malinger

flancher [flɑ̃ʃe] *intr* (coll) to give in; (coll) to weaken, give way

flanchet [flɑ̃ʃe] *m* flank (*of beef*)

Flandre [flɑ̃dr] *f* Flanders; **la Flandre** Flanders

flanelle [flanel] *f* flannel

flâner [flɑne] *intr* to stroll, saunter; to loaf

flânerie [flɑnri] *f* strolling; loafing

flâ-neur [flɑnœr] **-neuse** [nøz] *mf* stroller; loafer

flanquer [flɑ̃ke] *tr* to flank; (coll) to throw, fling; **flanquer à la porte** (coll) to kick out; **flanquer un coup à** (coll) to take a swing at

fla-pi -pie [flapi] *adj* (coll) tired out, fagged out

flaque [flak] *f* puddle, pool

flash [flaʃ] *m* (*pl* **flashes**) news flash; (phot) flash attachment; (phot) flash bulb

flasque [flask] *adj* flabby ‖ *m* metal trim ‖ *f* flask; powder horn

flatter [flate] *tr* to flatter; to stroke; to delight; to cater to; to delude ‖ *intr* to flatter ‖ *ref*—**se flatter de** to flatter oneself on

flatterie [flatri] *f* flattery

flat-teur [flatœr] **flat-teuse** [flatøz] *adj* flattering ‖ *mf* flatterer

flatulence [flatylɑ̃s] *f* (pathol) flatulence

flatuosité [flatyozite] *f* (pathol) flatulence

fléau [fleo] *m* (*pl* **fléaux**) flail; beam (*of balance*); (fig) scourge, plague

flèche [fleʃ] *f* arrow; spire (*of church*); boom (*of crane*); flitch (*of bacon*); **en flèche** like an arrow; in tandem; **faire flèche de tout bois** to leave no stone unturned; **flèche d'eau** (bot) arrowhead

fléchette [fleʃet] *f* dart (*used in game*)

fléchir [fleʃir] *tr* to bend; to move (*e.g., to pity*) ‖ *intr* to bend, give way; to weaken, to flag; to go down, to sag (*said of prices*)

flegmatique [flegmatik] *adj* phlegmatic, stolid

flegme [flegm] *m* phlegm

flemme [flem] *f* (slang) sluggishness; **tirer sa flemme** (slang) to not lift a finger

flet [fle] *m* flounder

flétan [fletɑ̃] *m* halibut

flétrir [fletrir] *tr & ref* to fade, wither; to weaken

flétrissure [fletrisyr] *f* fading, withering; branding (*of criminals*); blot, stigma

fleur [flœr] *f* flower; blossom; **à fleur de level with, even with; on the surface of; à fleur de peau skin-deep; à fleur de tête bulging (*eyes*); en fleur in bloom; en fleurs in bloom (*said of group of different varieties*); fleur de farine fine white flour; fleur de l'âge prime of life; fleur de lis [flœrdəlis] fleur-de-lis; fleur des pois (coll) pick of the lot; fleurs mold (*on wine, cider, etc.*)

fleurer [flœre] *intr* to exhale or give off an odor; **fleurer bon** to smell good

fleuret [flœre] *m* fencing foil

fleurette [flœret] *f* little flower; **conter fleurette** to flirt

fleu-ri -rie [flœri] *adj* in bloom; flowery; florid (*complexion; style*)

fleurir [flœrir] *tr* to decorate with flowers ‖ *intr* to flower, bloom ‖ *intr* (*ger* **florissant**; *imperf* **florissais**, etc.) to flourish

fleuriste [flœrist] *mf* florist; floral gardener; maker or seller of artificial flowers

fleuron [flœrɔ̃] *m* floret; (archit) finial; **fleuron à sa couronne** feather in his cap

fleuve [flœv] *m* river (*flowing directly to the sea*); (fig) river (*of tears, blood, etc.*)

flexible [fleksibl] *adj* flexible; (fig) pliant

flexion [flɛksjɔ̃] f bending, flexion; (gram) inflection

filibuster [flibyste] tr to rob, to snitch || intr to filibuster

filibustier [flibystje] m filibuster (pirate)

flic [flik] m (slang) copper, fuzz

flirt [flœrt] m flirt; flirtation

flirter [flœrte] intr to flirt

flir·teur [flœrtœr] -teuse [tøz] adj flirtatious || mf flirt

flocon [flɔkɔ̃] m flake; snowflake; tuft (e.g., of wool); **flocons d'avoine** oatmeal; **flocons de maïs** cornflakes; **flocons de neige** snowflakes

floconner [flɔkɔne] intr to form flakes, to become fleecy

flocon·neux [flɔkɔnø] **flocon·neuse** [flɔkɔnøz] adj flaky; fleecy

floraison [flɔrɛzɔ̃] f flowering, blooming

flo·ral -rale [flɔral] adj (pl -raux [ro]) floral

floralies [flɔrali] fpl flower show

flore [flɔr] f flora

floren·tin [flɔrɑ̃tɛ̃] **-tine** [tin] adj Florentine; **à la florentine** with spinach || (cap) mf Florentine (native or inhabitant of Florence)

Floride [flɔrid] f Florida; **la Floride** Florida

florilège [flɔrilɛʒ] m anthology

floris·sant [flɔrisɑ̃] **floris·sante** [flɔrisɑ̃t] adj flourishing

floss [flɔs] m (coll) dental floss

flot [flo] m wave; tide; flood, multitude; **à flot** afloat; **à flots** in torrents, abundantly; **flots** waters (of a lake, the sea, etc.); **flots de** lots of

flottabilité [flɔtabilite] f buoyancy

flottable [flɔtabl] adj buoyant; navigable (for rafts)

flottage [flɔtaʒ] m log driving

flottaison [flɔtɛzɔ̃] f water line

flot·tant [flɔtɑ̃] **flot·tante** [flɔtɑ̃t] adj floating; vacillating, undecided

flotte [flɔt] f fleet; buoy; float (on fishline); (slang) water, rain

flottement [flɔtmɑ̃] m floating; hesitation, vacillation; undulation

flotter [flɔte] intr to float; to waver, hesitate; to fly (said of flag); **il flotte** (slang) it is raining

flotteur [flɔtœr] m log driver; float (of fishline, carburetor, etc.); pontoon, float (of seaplane)

flottille [flɔtij] f flotilla; **flottille de pêche** fishing fleet

flou floue [flu] adj blurred, hazy; fluffy (hair); loose-fitting (dress); light and soft (tones, lines in a painting) || m blur, fuzziness; dressmaking

fluctuation [flyktɥasjɔ̃] f fluctuation

fluctuer [flyktɥe] intr to fluctuate

fluet [flɥɛ] **fluette** [flɥɛt] adj thin, slender

fluide [flɥid] adj & m fluid

fluidifier [flɥidifje] tr to liquefy

fluor [flɥɔr] m fluorine

fluores·cent [flɥɔrɛsɑ̃] **fluores·cente** [flɥɔrɛsɑ̃t] adj fluorescent

fluoridation [flɥɔridasjɔ̃] f fluoridation

fluorider [flɥɔride] tr & intr to fluoridate

fluorure [flɥɔryr] m fluoride

flûte [flyt] f flute; long thin loaf of French bread; tall champagne glass; **flûte à bec** recorder; **flûte de Pan** Pan's pipes; **flûtes** (slang) legs; **grande flûte** concert flute; **jouer** or **se tirer des flûtes** (slang) to run for it; **petite flûte** piccolo || interj shucks!, rats!

flûtiste [flytist] mf flutist

flux [fly] m flow; flood tide; (cards) flush; (chem, elec, med, metallurgy) flux; **flux de sang** flush, blush; dysentery; **flux de ventre** diarrhea; **flux et reflux** ebb and flow

fluxion [flyksjɔ̃] f inflammation

foc [fɔk] m (naut) jib

fo·cal -cale [fɔkal] adj (pl -caux [ko]) focal

fœtus [fetys] m fetus

foi [fwa] f faith; word (of a gentleman); **ajouter foi à** to give credence to; **bonne foi** good faith, sincerity; **de bonne foi** sincere; sincerely; **de mauvaise foi** dishonest; dishonestly; **en foi de quoi** in witness whereof; **faire foi de** to be evidence of; **ma foi!** upon my word; **manquer de foi à** to break faith with; **mauvaise foi** bad faith, insincerity; **sur la foi de** on the strength of

foie [fwa] m liver; **avoir les foies** (slang) to be scared stiff; **foie gras** goose liver

foin [fwɛ̃] m hay; **avoir du foin dans ses bottes** (coll) to be well heeled; **faire du foin** (slang) to kick up a fuss

foire [fwar] f fair; market; (coll) chaos, mess; **foire d'empoigne** free-for-all

foirer [fware] intr (slang) to flop, fail; (slang) to hang fire; (slang) to be stripped (said of screw, nut, etc.)

fois [fwa] f time, e.g., **visiter trois fois par semaine** to visit three times a week; times, e.g., **deux fois deux font quatre** two times two is four; **à la fois** at the same time, together; **deux fois** twice; twofold; **encore une fois** once more, again; **il y avait une fois** once upon a time there was; **maintes et maintes fois** time and time again; **une fois** one time, once; **une fois pour toutes** or **une bonne fois** once and for all

foison [fwazɔ̃] f—**à foison** in abundance

foison·nant [fwazɔnɑ̃] **foison·nante** [fwazɔnɑ̃t] adj abundant, plentiful

foisonner [fwazɔne] intr to abound

folâtre [fɔlɑtr] adj frisky, playful

folâtrer [fɔlɑtre] intr to frolic, romp

folie [fɔli] f madness, insanity; folly, piece of folly; country lodge, hideaway (for romantic trysts); **à la folie** madly, passionately; **faire une folie** to do something crazy; **folie de la persécution** persecution complex

folio [fɔljo] m folio

folioter [fɔljɔte] tr to folio

folle [fɔl] f crazy woman

follement [fɔlmɑ̃] adv madly

fol·let [fɔlɛ] **fol·lette** [fɔlɛt] *adj* merry, playful; elfish

follicule [fɔlikyl] *m* follicle

fomenta·teur [fɔmɑ̃tatœr] **-trice** [tris] *mf* agitator, troublemaker

fomenter [fɔmɑ̃te] *tr* to foment

fon·cé -cée [fɔ̃se] *adj* dark; deep

foncer [fɔ̃se] §51 *tr* to darken; to dig (*a well*); to fit a bottom to (*a cask*) ‖ *intr* to charge, to rush

fon·cier [fɔ̃sje] **-cière** [sjɛr] *adj* landed (*property*); property (*tax*); fundamental, natural ‖ *m* real-estate tax

foncièrement [fɔ̃sjɛrmɑ̃] *adv* fundamentally, naturally

fonction [fɔ̃ksjɔ̃] *f* function; duty; **faire fonction de** to function as

fonctionnaire [fɔ̃ksjɔnɛr] *mf* civil servant; officeholder

fonctionnarisme [fɔ̃ksjɔnarism] *m* bureaucracy

fonction·nel -nelle [fɔ̃ksjɔnɛl] *adj* functional

fonctionner [fɔ̃ksjɔne] *intr* to function, to work

fond [fɔ̃] *m* bottom; back, far end; background; foundation; dregs; core, inner meaning, main issue; **à fond** thoroughly; **à fond de train** at full speed; **au fond, dans le fond,** or **par le fond** actually, really, basically; **de fond** fundamental, main; **de fond en comble** from top to bottom; **faire fond sur** to rely on; **fond sonore** background noise; **râcler les fonds du tiroir** to scrape the bottom of the barrel; **sans fond** bottomless; **y aller au fond** to go the whole way ‖ see **fonds**

fondamen·tal -tale [fɔ̃damɑ̃tal] *adj* (*pl* **-taux** [to]) fundamental, basic

fon·dant -dante [dɑ̃] *adj* melting; juicy, luscious ‖ *m* fondant (*candy*); (metallurgy) flux

fonda·teur [fɔ̃datœr] **-trice** [tris] *mf* founder

fondation [fɔ̃dasjɔ̃] *f* foundation; founding; endowment

fon·dé -dée [fɔ̃de] *adj* founded; justified; authorized; **bien fondé** well-founded ‖ *m*—**fondé de pouvoir** proxy, authorized agent

fondement [fɔ̃dmɑ̃] *m* foundation, basis; (coll) behind; **sans fondement** unfounded

fonder [fɔ̃de] *tr* to found

fonderie [fɔ̃dri] *f* foundry; smelting

fondeur [fɔ̃dœr] *m* founder, smelter

fondre [fɔ̃dr] *tr* to melt, dissolve; to smelt; to cast (*metal*); to blend (*colors*); to merge (*companies*) ‖ *intr* to melt; (coll) to lose weight; **fondre en larmes** to burst into tears; **fondre sur** to pounce on

fondrière [fɔ̃drijɛr] *f* quagmire; mudhole, rut, pothole

fonds [fɔ̃] *m* land (*of an estate*); business, good will; fund; **bon fonds** good nature; **fonds** *mpl* capital; **fonds de commerce** business house; **fonds de prévoyance** reserve fund; **fonds d'État** *mpl* government bonds

fon·du -due [fɔ̃dy] *adj* melted; molten ‖ *m* blending (*of colors*); (mov, telv) dissolve, fade-out

fontaine [fɔ̃tɛn] *f* fountain; spring; well; cistern; **fontaine de Jouvence** Fountain of Youth

fonte [fɔ̃t] *f* melting; casting; cast iron; holster; (typ) font; **venir de fonte avec** to be cast in one piece with

fonts [fɔ̃] *mpl*—**fonts baptismaux** baptismal font

football [futbol] *m* soccer

footing [futiŋ] *m* walking

for [fɔr] *m*—**dans son for intérieur in** his heart of hearts; **for intérieur** conscience

forage [fɔraʒ] *m* drilling

fo·rain [fɔrɛ̃] **-raine** [rɛn] *adj* traveling, itinerant ‖ **forains** *mpl* carnival people

forban [fɔrbɑ̃] *m* pirate

forçage [fɔrsaʒ] *m* (agr) forcing

forçat [fɔrsa] *m* convict; (hist) galley slave; (fig) drudge

force [fɔrs] *f* force; strength; **à force de** by dint of, as a result of; **à toute force** at all costs; **de première force** foremost (*musician, artist, scientist, etc.*); **de toutes ses forces** with all one's might; **force de frappe** striking force; **force m'est de . . .** (lit) I am obliged to . . . ; **force majeure** (law) act of God; **forces** sheep shears; **force vive** (phys) kinetic energy; **la force de l'âge** the prime of life ‖ *adj invar* (archaic) many

forcément [fɔrsemɑ̃] *adv* inevitably, necessarily

force·né -née [fɔrsəne] *adj* frenzied, frantic ‖ *m* madman ‖ *f* crazy woman

forceps [fɔrsɛps] *m* (obstet) forceps

forcer [fɔrse] §51 *tr* to force; to do violence to; to bring to bay; to increase (*the dose*); to strain (*a muscle*); to mark up (*a receipt*); **forcer la main à qn** to force s.o.'s hand; **forcer la note** (coll) to overdo it; **forcer le respect de qn** to compel respect from s.o.; **forcer qn à** or **de + inf** to force s.o. to + *inf* ‖ *ref* to overdo; to do violence to one's feelings

forclore [fɔrklɔr] (used only in *inf* and *pp* **forclos**) *tr* to foreclose

forclusion [fɔrklyziʒ] *f* foreclosure

forer [fɔre] *tr* to drill, to bore

fores·tier [fɔrɛstje] **-tière** [tjɛr] *adj* forest ‖ *m* forester

foret [fɔre] *m* drill

forêt [fɔre] *f* forest

fo·reur [fɔrœr] **-reuse** [røz] *adj* drilling ‖ *mf* driller ‖ *f* drill, machine drill

forfaire [fɔrfɛr] §29 (used only in *inf*; 1st, 2d, & 3d *sg pres ind*; compound tenses) *intr*—**forfaire à** to forfeit (*one's honor*); to fail in (*a duty*)

forfait [fɔrfe] *m* heinous crime; contract; package deal; (turf) forfeit; **à forfait** for a lump sum

forfaitaire [fɔrfeter] *adj* contractual

forfaiture [fɔrfetyr] *f* malfeasance

forfanterie [fɔrfɑ̃tri] *f* bragging

forge [fɔrʒ] *f* forge; steel mill

forger [fɔrʒe] §38 *tr* to forge

forgeron [fɔrʒərɔ̃] *m* blacksmith

forgeur [fɔrʒœr] *m* forger, smith; coiner (*e.g., of new expressions*); fabricator (*of false stories*)

formaliser [fɔrmalize] *ref* to take offense

formaliste [fɔrmalist] *adj* formalistic, conventional ‖ *mf* formalist

formalité [fɔrmalite] *f* formality, convention

format [fɔrma] *m* size, format

formation [fɔrmasjɔ̃] *f* formation; education, training

forme [fɔrm] *f* form; **en forme** fit, in shape; **en forme, en bonne forme,** or **en bonne et due forme,** in order, in due form; **pour la forme** for appearances

for·mel -melle [fɔrmɛl] *adj* explicit; strict; formal, superficial

formellement [fɔrmɛlmɑ̃] *adv* absolutely, strictly

former [fɔrme] *tr & ref* to form

formidable [fɔrmidabl] *adj* formidable; (coll) tremendous, terrific

formulaire [fɔrmylɛr] *m* formulary; form (*with spaces for answers*)

formule [fɔrmyl] *f* formula; form, blank; format; **formule de politesse** complimentary close

formuler [fɔrmyle] *tr* to formulate; to draw up

fort [fɔr] **forte** [fɔrt] *adj* strong; fortified (*city*); **c'est fort!** it's hard to believe! ‖ (when standing before noun) *adj* high (*fever*); large (*sum*); hard (*task*) ‖ *m* fort; strong man; forte; height (*of summer*) ‖ **fort** *adv* exceedingly; loud; hard

forteresse [fɔrtərɛs] *f* fortress, fort

forti·fiant -fiante [fɔrtifjɑ̃] [fjɑ̃t] *adj & m* tonic

fortification [fɔrtifikɑsjɔ̃] *f* fortification

fortifier [fɔrtifje] *tr* to fortify; to confirm (*one's opinions*)

fortin [fɔrtɛ̃] *m* small fort

for·tuit -tuite [fɔrtɥi] [tɥit] *adj* fortuitous, accidental

fortune [fɔrtyn] *f* fortune; **faire fortune** to make a fortune

fortu·né -née [fɔrtyne] *adj* fortunate; rich

fosse [fos] *f* pit; grave; **fosse aux lions** lions' den; **fosse commune** pauper's grave; **fosse d'aisances** cesspool; **fosse septique** septic tank

fossé [fose] *m* ditch, trench; moat; **sauter le fossé** to take the plunge

fossette [fosɛt] *f* dimple

fossile [fosil] *adj & m* fossil ‖ *mf* fossil (*person*)

fossoyeur [foswajœr] *m* gravedigger

fou [fu] or **fol** [fɔl] **folle** [fɔl] (*pl* **fous folles**) *adj* mad, insane; foolish; extravagant; unsteady; loose (*pulley*); (coll) tremendous (*success*); **être fou à lier** to be raving mad; **être fou de** to be wild about; to be wild with (*joy, pain, etc.*) ‖ **fou** *m* madman; fool; jester; (cards) joker; (chess) bishop ‖ *f* see **folle**

foucade [fukad] *f* whim, impulse

foudre [fudr] *m* thunderbolt (*of Zeus*); large cask; **foudre de guerre** great captain; **foudre d'éloquence** powerful orator ‖ *f* lightning; **foudres** displeasure (*e.g., of a prince*); **foudres de l'Église** excommunication

foudroyant [fudrwajɑ̃] **foudroyante** [fudrwajɑ̃t] *adj* lightning-like; crushing, overwhelming

foudroyer [fudrwaje] §47 *tr* to strike with lightning; to strike suddenly; to dumfound; **foudroyer d'un regard** to cast a withering glance at ‖ *intr* to hurl thunderbolts

fouet [fwe] *m* whip; (culin) beater

fouetter [fwete] *tr & intr* to whip

fougère [fuʒɛr] *f* fern

fougue [fug] *f* spirit, ardor

fou·gueux -gueuse [fugø] [gøz] *adj* spirited, fiery, impetuous

fouille [fuj] *f* excavation; search

fouiller [fuje] *tr* to excavate; to search, comb, inspect

fouillis [fuji] *m* jumble, disorder

fouine [fwin] *f* beech marten; pitchfork; harpoon

fouiner [fwine] *intr* (coll) to pry, meddle

fouir [fwir] *tr* to dig, burrow

foulard [fular] *m* scarf, neckerchief

foule [ful] *f* crowd, mob; **en foule** in great numbers

fouler [fule] *tr* to tread on, to press; to sprain ‖ *ref* (with *dat* of *reflex pron*) to sprain; (slang) to put oneself out, to tire oneself out

foulque [fulk] *f* (zool) coot

foulure [fulyr] *f* sprain

four [fur] *m* oven; kiln, furnace; (coll) flop, turkey; **faire cuire au four** to bake; to roast; **faire four** (coll) to flop; **four à briques** brickkiln; **four à chaux** limekiln; **petit four** teacake

fourbe [furb] *adj* deceiving, cheating ‖ *mf* deceiver, cheat

fourberie [furbəri] *f* deceit, cheating

fourbir [furbir] *tr* to furbish, polish

fourbissage [furbisaʒ] *m* furbishing, polishing

four·bu -bue [furby] *adj* broken-down (*horse*); (coll) dead tired, all in

fourche [furʃ] *f* fork; pitchfork; **fourche avant** front fork (*of bicycle*); **fourches patibulaires** (hist) gallows

fourcher [furʃe] *tr & intr* to fork; **la langue lui a fourché** (coll) he made a slip of the tongue

fourchette [furʃɛt] *f* fork; wishbone

four·chu -chue [furʃy] *adj* forked; cloven

fourgon [furgɔ̃] *m* truck; poker; (rr) baggage car; (rr) boxcar; **fourgon bancaire** armored car; **fourgon de queue** caboose; **fourgon funèbre** hearse

fourmi [furmi] *f* ant; **fourmi blanche** white ant, termite

fourmilier [furmilje] *m* anteater

fourmilière [furmiljɛr] *f* ant hill

fourmiller [furmije] *intr* to swarm; to tingle (*said, e.g., of foot*); **fourmiller de** to teem with

fournaise [furnez] *f* furnace; (fig) oven

four‧neau [furno] *m* (*pl* **-neaux**) furnace; cooking stove; **haut fourneau** blast furnace

fournée [furne] *f* batch

four‧ni -nie [furni] *adj* bushy, thick; **bien fourni** well-stocked

fourniment [furnimɑ̃] *m* (mil) kit

fournir [furnir] *tr* to furnish, to supply, to provide; to follow (*a suit in cards*) ‖ *intr* (with *dat*) to supply (*s.o.'s needs*); (with *dat*) to defray (*expenses*); (with *dat*) (cards) to follow (*suit*) ‖ *ref* to grow thick; to be a customer

fournissement [furnismɑ̃] *m* contribution, holdings (*of each shareholder*); statement of holdings

fournisseur [furnisœr] *m* supplier, dealer

fourniture [furnityr] *f* furnishing, supplying; (culin) seasoning; **fournitures** supplies

fourrage [furaʒ] *m* fodder

fourrager [furaʒe] §38 *tr* to forage; to rummage, to rummage through ‖ *intr* to rummage (about), to forage

fourragère [furaʒer] *f* lanyard; tailboard

four‧ré -rée [fure] *adj* lined with fur; furred (*tongue*); stuffed (*dates*); filled (*candies*); sham, hollow (*peace*) ‖ *m* thicket

four‧reau [furo] *m* (*pl* **-reaux**) sheath; scabbard; tight skirt; **coucher dans son fourreau** (coll) to sleep in one's clothes

fourrer [fure] *tr* to line with fur; (coll) to cram, stuff; (coll) to shut up (*in prison*); (coll) to stick, poke ‖ *ref* (coll) to turn, go; (coll) to curl up (*in bed*); **se fourrer dans** (coll) to stick one's nose in

fourre-tout [furtu] *m invar* catchall; duffel bag

fourreur [furœr] *m* furrier

fourrier [furje] *m* quartermaster

fourrière [furjer] *f* pound (*for automobiles; for stray dogs*)

fourrure [furyr] *f* fur

fourvoyer [furvwaje] §47 *tr* to lead astray

fox [fɔks] *m* fox terrier

fox-terrier [fɔksterje] *m* fox terrier

fox-trot [fɔkstrɔt] *m invar* fox trot

foyer [fwaje] *m* foyer, lobby; hearth, fireside; firebox; focus; home; greenroom; center (*of learning; of infection*); **à double foyer** bifocal; **foyer des étudiants** student center; **foyers du soldat** service club; **foyers natifs** native land

frac [frak] *m* cutaway coat

fracas [fraka] *m* crash; roar (*of waves*); peal (*of thunder*)

fracasser [frakase] *tr* & *ref* to break; to shatter, break to pieces

fraction [fraksjɔ̃] *f* fraction; breaking (*e.g., of bread*)

fractionnaire [fraksjɔner] *adj* fractional

fractionnement [fraksjɔnmɑ̃] *m* cracking (*of petroleum*)

fractionner [fraksjɔne] *tr* to divide into fractions

fracture [fraktyr] *f* fracture; breaking open

fracturer [fraktyre] *tr* to fracture; to break open

fragile [fraʒil] *adj* fragile

fragment [fragmɑ̃] *m* fragment

fragmenter [fragmɑ̃te] *tr* to fragment

frai [fre] *m* spawning; spawn, roe

fraîche [freʃ] *f* cool of the day

fraîchement [freʃmɑ̃] *adv* in the open air; recently; (coll) cordially

fraîcheur [freʃœr] *f* coolness; freshness; newness

fraîchir [freʃir] *intr* to become cooler; to freshen (*said of wind*)

frais [fre] **fraîche** [freʃ] *adj* cool; fresh; wet (*paint*); **il fait frais** it is cool out ‖ (when standing before noun) *adj* recent (*date*) ‖ *m* cool place; fresh air; **aux frais de** at the expense of; **de frais** just, freshly; **faire les frais de la conversation** (coll) to take the lead in the conversation; to be the subject of the conversation; **se mettre en frais** (coll) to go to a great deal of expense or trouble ‖ *f* see **fraîche** ‖ **frais** *adv*—**boire frais** to have a cool drink ‖ **frais fraîche** *adv* (agrees with following *pp*) just, freshly, e.g., **garçon frais arrivé de l'école** boy just arrived from school; e.g., **roses fraîches cueillies** freshly gathered roses

fraise [frez] *f* strawberry; wattle (*of turkey*); (mach) countersink

fraiser [freze] *tr* (mach) to countersink

fraisier [frezje] *m* strawberry plant

framboise [frɑ̃bwaz] *f* raspberry

framboisier [frɑ̃bwazje] *m* raspberry bush

franc [frɑ̃] **franche** [frɑ̃ʃ] *adj* free; frank, sincere; complete ‖ (when standing before noun) *adj* arrant (*knave*); downright (*fool*) ‖ **franc franque** [frɑ̃k] *adj* Frankish ‖ *m* franc (*unit of currency*) ‖ (*cap*) *m* Frank (*medieval German*) ‖ **franc** *adv* frankly

fran‧çais [frɑ̃se] **-çaise** [sez] *adj* French ‖ *m* French (*language*); **en bon français** in correct French ‖ (*cap*) *m* Frenchman; **les Français** the French ‖ *f* Frenchwoman

franc-alleu [frɑ̃kalø] *m* (*pl* **francs-alleux** [frɑ̃kalø]) (hist) freehold

France [frɑ̃s] *f* France; **la France** France

franchement [frɑ̃ʃmɑ̃] *adv* frankly, sincerely; without hesitation

franchir [frɑ̃ʃir] *tr* to cross, to go over or through; to jump over; to overcome (*an obstacle*)

franchise [frɑ̃ʃiz] *f* exemption; frankness; freedom; **franchise postale** frank

francique [frɑ̃sik] *m* Frankish

franciser [frɑ̃size] *tr* to make French

franc-maçon [frɑ̃masɔ̃] *m* (*pl* **francs-maçons**) Freemason

franc-maçonnerie [frãmasɔnri] ƒ Free-masonry

franco [frãko] adv free, without shipping costs; **franco de bord** free on board; **franco de port** postpaid

franco-cana-dien [frãkɔkanadjɛ̃] **-dien-ne** [djen] adj French-Canadian ‖ **Franco-Cana-dien -dienne** mƒ French Canadian

francophone [frãkɔfɔn] adj French-speaking ‖ mƒ French speaker

franc-parler [frãparle] m—**avoir son franc-parler** to be free-spoken

franc-tireur [frãtirœr] m (pl **francs-tireurs**) free lance; sniper

frange [frãʒ] ƒ fringe; **à frange** fringed

franger [frãʒe] §38 tr to fringe

franquette [frãket] ƒ—**à la bonne franquette** (coll) simply, without fuss

frap-pant [frapã] **frap-pante** [frapãt] adj striking, surprising

frappe [frap] ƒ minting, striking; stamp (on coins, medals, etc.); touch (in typing)

frap-pé frap-pée [frape] adj struck; iced; (slang) crazy ‖ m (mus) downbeat

frapper [frape] tr to strike, hit, knock; to mint (coin); to stamp (cloth); to ice (e.g., champagne) ‖ intr to strike, hit, knock ‖ ref (coll) to become panic-stricken

frasque [frask] ƒ escapade

frater-nel -nelle [fraternel] adj fraternal, brotherly

fraterniser [fraternize] intr to fraternize

fraternité [fraternite] ƒ fraternity, brotherhood

fraude [frod] ƒ fraud; smuggling; **en fraude** fraudulently; **faire la fraude** to smuggle; **fraude fiscale** tax evasion

fraudu-leux [frodylø] **-leuse** [løz] adj fraudulent

frayer [freje], [freje] §49 tr to mark out (a path) ‖ intr to spawn; **frayer avec** to associate with

frayeur [frejœr] ƒ fright, scare

fredaine [fredɛn] ƒ (coll) escapade, prank, spree

fredon [fredɔ̃] m (cards) three of a kind

fredonnement [fredɔnmã] m hum, humming

fredonner [fredɔne] tr & intr to hum

frégate [fregat] ƒ frigate

frein [frɛ̃] m bit (of bridle); brake (of car); **frein à main** hand brake; **frein à pied** foot brake; **mettre le frein** to put the brake on; **mettre un frein à** to curb, check; **ronger son frein** to champ at the bit

freiner [frene] tr & intr to brake

frelater [frelate] tr to adulterate

frêle [frel] adj frail

frelon [frelɔ̃] m hornet

frémir [fremir] intr to shudder

frémissement [fremismã] m shudder

frêne [fren] m ash tree

frénésie [frenezi] ƒ frenzy

frénétique [frenetik] adj frenzied

fréquemment [frekamã] adv frequently

fréquence [frekãs] ƒ frequency; **basse fréquence** low frequency; **fréquence du pouls** pulse rate; **haute fréquence** high frequency

fré-quent [frekã] **-quente** [kãt] adj frequent; rapid (pulse)

fréquenter [frekãte] tr to frequent; to associate with; (coll) to go steady with (a boy or girl)

frère [frer] m brother; **frère consanguin** half brother (by the father); **frère convers** (eccl) lay brother; **frère de lait** foster brother; **frère germain** whole brother; **frère jumeau** twin brother; **frères siamois** Siamese twins; **frère utérin** half brother (by the mother)

fresque [fresk] ƒ fresco

fret [fre] m freight; chartering; cargo

fréter [frete] §10 tr to charter (a ship); to rent (a car)

fréteur [fretœr] m shipowner

frétiller [fretije] intr to wriggle; to quiver; **frétiller de** to wag (its tail)

fretin [fretɛ̃] m—**le menu fretin** small fry

frette [fret] ƒ hoop, iron ring

freudisme [frødism] m Freudianism

freux [frø] m rook, crow

friand [frijã] **friande** [frijãd] adj tasty; fond (of food, praise, etc.) ‖ m sausage roll

friandise [frijãdiz] ƒ candy, sweet; delicacy, tidbit

fric [frik] m (slang) jack, money

fricasser [frikase] tr to fricassee; to squander

friche [friʃ] ƒ fallow land; **en friche** fallow

friction [friksjɔ̃] ƒ friction; massage

frictionner [friksjɔne] tr to rub, massage

frigide [friʒid] adj frigid

frigidité [friʒidite] ƒ frigidity

frigorifier [frigɔrifje] tr to refrigerate

frigorifique [frigɔrifik] adj refrigerating ‖ m cold-storage plant

fri-leux [frilø] **-leuse** [løz] adj chilly, shivery

frimas [frima] m icy mist, rime

frime [frim] ƒ (coll) sham, fake, hoax

frimousse [frimus] ƒ (coll) little face, cute face

fringale [frɛ̃gal] ƒ (coll) mad hunger

frin-gant [frɛ̃gã] **-gante** [gãt] adj dashing, spirited

fringuer [frɛ̃ge] tr (slang) to dress ‖ intr (obs) to frisk about

fringues [frɛ̃g] fpl (slang) duds

fri-pé -pée [fripe] adj rumpled, mussed, worn, tired (face)

friper [fripe] tr to wrinkle, rumple

friperie [fripri] ƒ secondhand clothes; secondhand furniture

fri-pier [fripje] **-pière** [pjer] mƒ old-clothes dealer; junk dealer

fri-pon [fripɔ̃] **-ponne** [pɔn] adj roguish ‖ mƒ rogue, rascal

friponnerie [fripɔnri] ƒ rascality, cheating

fripouille [fripuj] ƒ (slang) scoundrel

frire [frir] §22 (used in inf; pp; 1st, 2d, 3d sg pres ind; sg imperv; rarely used in *fut; cond*) *tr* to fry; to deep-fry; **être frit** (coll) to be done for || *intr* to fry

frise [friz] *f* frieze

friselis [frizli] *m* soft rustling; gentle lapping (*of water*)

friser [frize] *tr* to curl; to border on; to graze || *intr* to curl

frisoir [frizwar] *m* curling iron

fri·son [frizɔ̃] **-sonne** [zɔn] *adj* Frisian || *m* wave, curl; Frisian (*language*) || (*cap*) *mf* Frisian

fris·quet [friske] **-quette** [ket] *adj* (coll) chilly

frisson [frisɔ̃] *m* shiver; shudder, thrill; **frissons** shivering

frissonner [frisone] *intr* to shiver

frisure [frizyr] *f* curling; curls

frites [frit] *fpl* French fries

frittage [fritaʒ] *m* (metallurgy) sintering

friture [frityr] *f* frying; deep fat; fried fish; (rad, telv) static

frivole [frivɔl] *adj* frivolous, trifling

froc [frɔk] *m* (eccl) frock

froid [frwa] **froide** [frwad] *adj* cold; chilly (*manner*) || *m* cold; coolness (*between persons*); **avoir froid** to be cold; **il fait froid** it is cold; **jeter un froid sur** (fig) to put a damper on

froideur [frwadœr] *f* coldness; coolness

froissement [frwasmɑ̃] *m* bruising; rumpling, crumpling; clash (*of interests*); ruffling (*of feelings*)

froisser [frwase] *tr* to bruise; to rumple, crumple || *ref* to take offense

frôlement [frolmɑ̃] *m* grazing; rustle

frôler [frole] *tr* to graze, to brush against; (coll) to have a narrow escape from

fromage [frɔmaʒ] *m* cheese; (coll) soft job; **fromage blanc** cream cheese; **fromage de tête** headcheese

froma·ger [frɔmaʒe] **-gère** [ʒɛr] *adj* cheese (*industry*) || *m* cheesemaker; (bot) silk-cotton tree

fromagerie [frɔmaʒri] *f* cheese factory; cheese store

froment [frɔmɑ̃] *m* wheat

fronce [frɔ̃s] *f* crease, fold; **à fronces** shirred

froncement [frɔ̃smɑ̃] *m* puckering; **froncement de sourcils** frown

froncer [frɔ̃se] §51 *tr* to pucker; **froncer les sourcils** to frown, to wrinkle one's brow

frondaison [frɔ̃dezɔ̃] *f* foliation; foliage

fronde [frɔ̃d] *f* slingshot

fronder [frɔ̃de] *tr* to scoff at

fron·deur [frɔ̃dœr] **-deuse** [døz] *adj* bantering, irreverent || *mf* scoffer

front [frɔ̃] *m* forehead; impudence; brow (*of hill*); (geog, mil, pol) front; **de front** abreast; frontal; at the same time; **faire front à** to face up to

fronta·lier [frɔ̃talje] **-lière** [ljɛr] *adj* frontier || *m* frontiersman || *f* frontier woman

frontière [frɔ̃tjɛr] *adj* & *f* frontier

frontispice [frɔ̃tispis] *m* frontispiece; title page

frottement [frɔtmɑ̃] *m* rubbing, friction

frotter [frɔte] *tr* to rub; to polish; to strike (*a match*); **frotter les oreilles à qn** (coll) to box s.o.'s ears || *ref*—**se frotter à** (coll) to attack, to challenge; (coll) to rub shoulders with

froufrou [frufru] *m* rustle, swish

frousse [frus] *f* (slang) jitters

fructifier [fryktifje] *intr* to bear fruit

fruc·tueux [fryktɥø] **-tueuse** [tɥøz] *adj* fruitful, profitable

fru·gal **-gale** [frygal] *adj* (*pl* **-gaux** [go]) temperate; frugal (*meal*)

fruit [frɥi] *m* fruit; **des fruits fra**; **fruits civils** income (*from rent, interest, etc.*); **fruits de mer** seafood; **fruit sec** (fig) flop, failure

fruiterie [frɥitri] *f* fruit store

frui·tier [frɥitje] **-tière** [tjɛr] *adj* fruit; fruit-bearing || *mf* fruit vendor

fruste [fryst] *adj* worn; rough, uncouth

frustrer [frystre] *tr* to frustrate, disappoint; to cheat, defraud

fugace [fygas] *adj* fleeting, evanescent

fugi·tif [fyʒitif] **-tive** [tiv] *adj* & *mf* fugitive

fugue [fyg] *f* sudden disappearance; (mus) fugue

fuir [fɥir] §31 *tr* to flee, to run away from || *intr* to flee; to leak; to recede (*said of forehead*)

fuite [fɥit] *f* flight; leak

fulgu·rant [fylgyrɑ̃] **-rante** [rɑ̃t] *adj* flashing; vivid; stabbing (*pain*)

fulguration [fylgyrasjɔ̃] *f* sheet lightning

fulgurer [fylgyre] *intr* to flash

fuligi·neux [fyliʒinø] **-neuse** [nøz] *adj* sooty

fumage [fymaʒ] *m* smoking (*of meat*); manuring (*of fields*)

fume-cigare [fymsigar] *m invar* cigar holder

fume-cigarette [fymsigaret] *m invar* cigarette holder

fumée [fyme] *f* smoke; steam; **fumées** fumes

fumer [fyme] *tr* & *intr* to smoke; to fume; to manure

fumerie [fymri] *f* opium den; smoking room

fumet [fyme] *m* aroma; bouquet (*of wine*)

fu·meur [fymœr] **-meuse** [møz] *mf* smoker; **fumeur à la file** chain smoker

fu·meux [fymø] **-meuse** [møz] *adj* smoky; foggy, hazy (*ideas*)

fumier [fymje] *m* manure; dunghill; (slang) skunk, scoundrel

fumiger [fymiʒe] §38 *tr* to fumigate

fumiste [fymist] *m* heater man; (coll) practical joker

fumisterie [fymistri] *f* heater work; heater shop; (coll) hooey

fumoir [fymwar] *m* smoking room; smokehouse

funambule [fynɑ̃byl] *mf* tightrope walker

funèbre [fynɛbr] *adj* funereal; funeral (*march, procession, service*)

funérailles [fyneraj] *fpl* funeral

funéraire [fynerɛr] *adj* funeral

funeste [fynɛst] *adj* baleful, fatal

funiculaire [fynikylɛr] *adj* & *m* funicular

fur [fyr] *m*—**au fur et à mesure** progressively, gradually; **au fur et à mesure de** in proportion to; **au fur et à mesure que** as, in proportion as

furet [fyrɛ] *m* ferret; snoop; ring-in-the-circle (*parlor game*)

fureter [fyrte] §2 *intr* to ferret

fureur [fyrœr] *f* fury; **à la fureur** passionately; **faire fureur** to be the rage

furi·bond [fyribɔ̃] **-bonde** [bɔ̃d] *adj* furious; withering (*look*) ‖ *mf* irascible individual

furie [fyri] *f* fury; termagant

fu·rieux [fyrjø] **-rieuse** [rjøz] *adj* furious; angry (*wind*)

furoncle [fyrɔ̃kl] *m* boil

fur·tif [fyrtif] **-tive** [tiv] *adj* furtive, stealthy

fusain [fyzɛ̃] *m* charcoal; charcoal drawing; spindle tree

fu·seau [fyzo] *m* (*pl* **-seaux**) spindle; **à fuseau** tapering; **fuseau horaire** time zone (*between two meridians*)

fusée [fyze] *f* rocket; spindleful; spindle (*of axle*); (coll) ripple, burst (*of laughter*); **fusée à retard** delayed-action fuse; **fusée d'artifice** or **fusée volante** skyrocket; **fusée éclairante** flare; **fusée engin** rocket engine; **fusée fusante** time fuse; **fusée percutante** percussion fuse

fuselage [fyzlaʒ] *m* fuselage

fuse·lé **-lée** [fyzle] *adj* spindle-shaped; tapering, slender (*fingers*); streamlined

fuseler [fyzle] §34 *tr* to taper; to streamline

fuser [fyze] *intr* to melt; to run (*said of colors*); to fizz, to spurt; to stream in or out (*said of light*)

fusible [fyzibl] *adj* fusible ‖ *m* fuse

fusil [fyzi] *m* gun, rifle; whetstone; rifleman; **fusil à deux coups** double-barreled gun; **fusil de chasse** shotgun; **fusil mitrailleur** light machine gun; **un bon fusil** a good shot (*person*)

fusillade [fyzijad] *f* fusillade

fusiller [fyzije] *tr* to shoot, to execute by a firing squad

fusion [fyzjɔ̃] *f* fusion

fusionner [fyzjɔne] *tr* & *intr* to blend, to fuse; (com) to merge

fustiger [fystiʒe] §38 *tr* to thrash, flog; to castigate

fût [fy] *m* cask, keg; barrel (*of drum*); stock (*of gun*); trunk (*of tree*); shaft (*of column*); stem (*of candelabrum*)

futaie [fytɛ] *f* stand of timber; **de haute futaie** full-grown

futaille [fytaj] *f* cask, barrel

futaine [fytɛn] *f* fustian

fu·té **-tée** [fyte] *adj* (coll) cunning, shrewd ‖ *f* mastic, filler

futile [fytil] *adj* futile

futilité [fytilite] *f* futility; **futilités** trifles

fu·tur **-ture** [fytyr] *adj* future ‖ *m* future; husband-to-be ‖ *f* future wife

fuyant [fɥijɑ̃] **fuyante** [fɥijɑ̃t] *adj* fleeting; receding (*forehead*)

fuyard [fɥijar] **fuyarde** [fɥijard] *adj* & *mf* runaway

G

G, g [ʒe] *m invar* seventh letter of the French alphabet

gabardine [gabardin] *f* gabardine

gabare [gabar] *f* barge

gabarit [gabari] *m* templet; (rr) maximum structure; (coll) size

gabelle [gabɛl] *f* (hist) salt tax

gâche [gaʃ] *f* catch (*at a door*); trowel; wooden spatula

gâcher [gaʃe] *tr* to mix (*cement*); to spoil, bungle; to squander

gâchette [gaʃɛt] *f* trigger; pawl, spring catch

gâ·cheur [gaʃœr] **-cheuse** [ʃøz] *adj* bungling ‖ *mf* bungler

gâchis [gaʃi] *m* wet cement; mud, slush; (coll) mess, muddle

gaélique [gaelik] *adj* & *m* Gaelic

gaffe [gaf] *f* gaff; (coll) social blunder, faux pas

gaffer [gafe] *tr* to hook with a gaff ‖ *intr* (coll) to make a blunder

gaga [gaga] *adj* (coll) doddering ‖ *mf* (coll) dotard

gage [gaʒ] *m* pledge, pawn; forfeit (*in*

a game); **gages** wage, wages; **prêter sur gages** to pawn

gager [gaʒe] §38 *tr* to wager, to bet; to pay wages to

ga·geur [gaʒœr] **-geuse** [ʒøz] *mf* bettor

gageure [gaʒyr] *f* wager, bet

gagiste [gaʒist] *mf* pledger; wage earner; (theat) extra

ga·gnant [gaɲɑ̃] **-gnante** [ɲɑ̃t] *adj* winning ‖ *mf* winner

gagne-pain [gaɲpɛ̃] *m invar* bread-winner; livelihood, bread and butter

gagne-petit [gaɲpəti] *m invar* cheap-jack, low-salaried worker

gagner [gaɲe] *tr* to gain; to win; to earn; to reach; to save (*time*) ‖ *intr* to improve; to gain; to spread ‖ *ref* to be catching (*said of disease*)

ga·gneur [gaɲœr] **-gneuse** [ɲøz] *mf* winner; earner

gai gaie [ge] *adj* gay; (coll) tipsy

gaiement [gemɑ̃] *adv* gaily

gaieté [gete] *f* gaiety; **de gaieté de cœur** of one's own free will

gail·lard [gajar] **gail·larde** [gajard] *adj*

healthy, hearty; merry; ribald, spicy ‖ *m* sturdy fellow; tricky fellow; **gaillard d'arrière** quarter-deck; **gaillard d'avant** forecastle ‖ *f* bold young lady; husky young woman

gaillardise [gajardiz] *f* cheerfulness; **gaillardises** spicy stories

gain [gɛ̃] *m* gain; earnings; winning (*e.g., of bet*); **avoir gain de cause** to win one's case

gaine [gen] *f* sheath; case, covering; girdle (*corset*); **gaine d'aération** ventilation shaft

gainer [gene] *tr* to sheath, to encase

gaité [gete] *f* gaiety

gala [gala] *m* gala; state dinner

galamment [galamã] *adv* gallantly

ga·lant [galã] **-lante** [lãt] *adj* gallant; amorous; kept (*woman*) ‖ *m* gallant; **vert gallant** gay old blade

galanterie [galãtri] *f* gallantry; libertinism

galaxie [galaksi] *f* galaxy

galbe [galb] *m* curve, sweep, graceful outline

gale [gal] *f* mange; (coll) backbiter, cad

galée [gale] *f* (typ) galley

galéjade [galeʒad] *f* joke, far-fetched story

galère [galer] *f* galley; drudgery; mason's hand truck

galerie [galri] *f* gallery; cornice, rim; baggage rack; **galerie marchande** shopping center

galérien [galerjɛ̃] *m* galley slave

galet [gale] *m* pebble; (mach) roller

galetas [galta] *m* hovel

galette [galet] *f* cake; buckwheat pancake; hardtack; (slang) dough, money; **galette des Rois** twelfth-cake (*eaten at Epiphany*)

ga·leux [galø] **-leuse** [løz] *adj* mangy

galimatias [galimatja] *m* nonsense, gibberish

galion [galjɔ̃] *m* galleon

Galles [gal]—**le pays de Galles** Wales; **prince de Galles** Prince of Wales

gal·lois [galwa] **gal·loise** [galwaz] *adj* Welsh ‖ *m* Welsh (*language*) ‖ (*cap*) *m* Welshman; **les Gallois** the Welsh ‖ (*cap*) *f* Welshwoman

gallon [galɔ̃] *m* gallon (*imperial or American*)

galoche [galɔʃ] *f* clog (*shoe*); **de or en galoche** pointed (*chin*)

galon [galɔ̃] *m* galloon, braid; (mil) stripe, chevron; **prendre du galon** to move up

galonner [galɔne] *tr* to trim with braid

galop [galo] *m* gallop; **petit galop** canter

galoper [galɔpe] *tr & intr* to gallop

galopin [galɔpɛ̃] *m* (coll) urchin

galvaniser [galvanize] *tr* to galvanize

galvauder [galvode] *tr* (coll) to botch; (coll) to waste (*e.g., one's talent*); (coll) to sully (*a name*) ‖ *intr* (slang) to walk the streets ‖ *ref* (slang) to go bad

gambade [gãbad] *f* gambol

gambader [gãbade] *intr* to gambol

gambit [gãbi] *m* gambit

gamelle [gamel] *f* mess kit

ga·min [gamɛ̃] **-mine** [min] *mf* street urchin; youngster

gaminerie [gaminri] *f* mischievousness

gamme [gam] *f* gamut, range; set (*of tools*); (mus) scale, gamut

Gand [gã] *m* Ghent

ganglion [gãglijɔ̃] *m* ganglion

gangrène [gãgren] *f* gangrene

gangrener [gãgrəne] §2 *tr & ref* to gangrene

ganse [gãs] *f* braid, piping

gant [gã] *m* glove; **jeter le gant** to throw down the gauntlet; **prendre des gants pour** to put on kid gloves to; **relever le gant** to take up the gauntlet; **se donner des gants** to take all the credit

gantelet [gãtlε] *m* protective glove

ganter [gãte] *tr* to put gloves on (*s.o.*); to fit, to become (*s.o.; said of gloves*); **cela me gante** (coll) that suits me ‖ *intr*—**ganter de** to wear, to take (*a certain size of glove*) ‖ *ref* to put on one's gloves

garage [garaʒ] *m* garage; turnout

garagiste [garaʒist] *m* garageman, mechanic

ga·rant [garã] **-rante** [rãt] *adj* guaranteeing ‖ *mf* guarantor, warrantor; **se porter garant de** to guarantee ‖ *m* guarantee, warranty

garantie [garãti] *f* guarantee

garantir [garãtir] *tr* to guarantee; to vouch for; to shelter, protect

garce [gars] *f* (coll) wench; (coll) bitch

garçon [garsɔ̃] *m* boy; young man; bachelor; apprentice; waiter; **garçon de courses** errand boy; **garçon de recette** bank messenger; **garçon de salle** orderly; **garçon d'honneur** best man; **garçon manqué** tomboy; **vieux garçon** old bachelor

garçonne [garsɔn] *f* bachelor girl

garçonnet [garsɔnε] *m* little boy

garçon·nier [garsɔnje] **garçon·nière** [garsɔnjεr] *adj* bachelor; tomboyish ‖ *f* bachelor apartment; tomboy

garde [gard] *m* guard, guardsman; keeper, custodian; **garde champêtre** constable; **garde de nuit** night watchman; **garde forestier** ranger ‖ *f* guard; custody; nurse; flyleaf; **de garde** on duty; **garde à vous!** (mil) attention!; **garde civique** national guard; **monter la garde** to go on guard duty; **prendre garde à** to look out for, to take notice of; **prendre garde de** to take care not to; to be careful to; **prendre garde que** to notice that; **prendre garde que . . . ne + subj** to be careful lest, to be careful that . . . not; **sur ses gardes** on one's guard

garde-à-vous [gardavu] *m invar* (*military position*) attention

garde-à-vue [gardavy] *f* custody, imprisonment

garde-barrière [gardəbarjεr] *mf* (*pl* **gardes-barrière** or **gardes-barrières**) crossing guard

garde-bébé [gardəbebe] *mf* (*pl* **-bébés**) baby-sitter

garde-boue [gardəbu] *m invar* mud-guard

garde-chasse [gardəʃas] *m* (*pl* **gardes-chasse** or **gardes-chasses**) game-keeper

garde-corps [gardəkɔr] *m invar* guard-rail; (naut) life line

garde-côte [gardəkot] *m* (*pl* -**côtes**) coast-guard cutter ‖ *m* (*pl* **gardes-côtes**) (obs) coastguardsman; (obs) coast guard

garde-feu [gardəfø] *m invar* fire screen

garde-fou [gardəfu] *m* (*pl* -**fous**) guard-rail

garde-frein [gardəfrɛ̃] *m* (*pl* **gardes-frein** or **gardes-freins**) brakeman

garde-magasin [gardəmagazɛ̃] *m* (*pl* **gardes-magasin** or **gardes-magasins**) warehouseman

garde-malade [gardəmalad] *mf* (*pl* **gardes-malades**) nurse

garde-manger [gardəmɑ̃ʒe] *m invar* icebox; larder

garde-meuble [gardəmœbl] *m* (*pl* -**meuble** or **meubles**) furniture warehouse

garde-nappe [gardənap] *m* (*pl* -**nappe** or **nappes**) table mat, place mat

garde-pêche [gardəpeʃ] *m* (*pl* **gardes-pêche**) fish warden ‖ *m invar* fishery service boat

garder [garde] *tr* to guard; to keep; **garder à vue** to hold in custody; **garder jusqu'à l'arrivée** (formula on envelope) hold for arrival; **garder la chambre** to stay in one's room; **garder la ligne** to keep one's figure ‖ *ref* to keep (*to stay free of deterioration*); **se garder de** to protect oneself from; to watch out for; to take care not to

garde-rats [gardəra] *m invar* rat guard

garderie [gardəri] *f* nursery; forest reserve

garde-robe [gardərɔb] *f* (*pl* -**robes**) wardrobe

gar·deur [gardœr] -**deuse** [døz] *mf* keeper, herder

garde-voie [gardəvwa] *m* (*pl* **gardes-voie** or **gardes-voies**) trackwalker

garde-vue [gardəvy] *m invar* eyeshade, visor

gar·dien [gardjɛ̃] -**dienne** [djen] *adj* guardian (*angel*) ‖ *mf* guard, guardian; keeper; caretaker; attendant (*at a garage*); **gardien de but** goalkeeper; **gardien de la paix** policeman

gare [gar], [gar] *f* station; **gare aérienne** airport; **gare de triage** switch-yard; **gare maritime** port, dock; **gare routière** or **gare d'autobus** bus station ‖ [gar] *interj* look out!

garer [gare] *tr* to park; to put in the garage; (naut) to dock; (rr) to shunt; (coll) to secure (*e.g., a fortune*) ‖ *ref* to get out of the way; to park, park one's car; **se garer de** to look out for

gargariser [gargarize] *ref* to gargle

gargarisme [gargarism] *m* gargle

gargote [gargɔt] *f* (coll) hash house, beanery

gargouille [garguj] *f* gargoyle

gargouillement [gargujmɑ̃] *m* gurgling; rumbling (*in stomach*)

gargouiller [garguje] *intr* to gurgle

garnement [garnəmɑ̃] *m* scamp, bad boy

gar·ni -**nie** [garni] *adj* furnished (*room*) ‖ *m* furnished room; furnished house

garnir [garnir] *tr* to garnish, adorn; to furnish; to strengthen; to line (*a brake*) ‖ *ref* to fill up (*said of crowded room, theater seats, etc.*)

garnison [garnizɔ̃] *f* garrison

garniture [garnityr] *f* garniture, decoration; fittings; accessories; complete set; (culin) garnish; **garniture de feu** fire irons; **garniture de lit** bedding

garrot [garo] *m* garrote (*instrument of torture*); (med) tourniquet; (zool) withers

garrotte [garɔt] *f* garrote (*torture*)

garrotter [garɔte] *tr* to garrote; to pinion

gars [gɑ] *m* (coll) lad

Gascogne [gaskɔɲ] *f* Gascony; **la Gascogne** Gascony

gasconnade [gaskɔnad] *f* gasconade; insincere invitation

gas-oil [gazwal] *m* diesel oil

Gaspésie [gaspezi] *f* Gaspé Peninsula

gaspiller [gaspije] *tr* to waste, squander

gastrique [gastrik] *adj* gastric

gastronomie [gastrɔnɔmi] *f* gastronomy

gâ·teau [gato] *adj invar* (coll) fond (*papa*); (coll) fairy (*godmother*) ‖ *m* (*pl* -**teaux**) cake; (coll) booty, loot; **gâteau de miel** honeycomb; **gâteau des Rois** twelfth-cake

gâte-métier [gatmetje] *m invar* under-cutter

gâte-papier [gatpapje] *m invar* hack writer

gâter [gate] *tr & ref* to spoil

gâte-sauce [gatsos] *m invar* poor cook; kitchen boy

gâ·teux [gatø] -**teuse** [tøz] *adj* (coll) senile ‖ *mf* (coll) dotard

gâtisme [gatism] *m* senility

gauche [goʃ] *adj* left; left-hand; crooked; awkward ‖ *f* left hand; left side; (pol) left wing; **à gauche** to the left; **à gauche, gauche!** (mil) left, face!

gau·cher [goʃe] -**chère** [ʃer] *adj* left-handed ‖ *mf* left-hander

gauchir [goʃir] *tr & intr* to warp

gauchiste [goʃist] *adj & mf* leftist

gaudriole [godrijol] *f* broad joke

gaufre [gofr] *f* waffle; **gaufre de miel** honeycomb

gaufrer [gofre] *tr* to emboss, figure; to flute; to corrugate

gaufrette [gofret] *f* wafer

gaufrier [gofrije] *m* waffle iron

gaule [gol] *f* pole; **la Gaule** Gaul

gauler [gole] *tr* to bring down (*e.g., fruit*) with a pole

gau·lois [golwa] -**loise** [lwaz] *adj* Gaulish, Gallic; broad (*humor*) ‖ *m* Gaulish (*language*) ‖ (*cap*) *mf* Gaul ‖ (*cap*) *f* gauloise (*cigarette*)

gauloiserie [golwazri] *f* racy joking

gaulthérie [goteri] *f* (bot) wintergreen

gausser [gose] *ref*—**se gausser de** (coll) to poke fun at

gaver [gave] *tr & ref* to cram

gavroche [gavrɔʃ] *mf* street urchin

gaz [gɑz] *m* gas; gaslight; gas company; **gaz d'échappement** exhaust; **gaz d'éclairage** illuminating gas; **gaz de combat** poison gas; **gaz en cylindre** bottled gas; **gaz hilarant** laughing gas; **gaz lacrimogène** tear gas; **mettre les gaz** (aut) to step on the gas

gaze [gɑz] *f* gauze; cheesecloth

ga·zé -zée [gɑze] *adj* gassed ‖ *mf* gas casualty

gazéifier [gɑzeifje] *tr* to gasify; to carbonate, charge

gazelle [gɑzɛl] *f* gazelle

gazer [gɑze] *tr* to gas; to cover with gauze; to tone down ‖ *intr* (coll) to go full steam ahead; **ça gaze?** (coll) how goes it?

ga·zeux [gɑzø] **-zeuse** [zøz] *adj* gaseous; carbonated

ga·zier [gɑzje] **-zière** [zjer] *adj* gas ‖ *m* gasman; gas fitter

gazoduc [gɑzodyk] *m* gas pipe line

gazogène [gɑzoʒɛn] *m* gas producer

gazoline [gɑzolin] *f* petroleum ether

gazomètre [gɑzometr] *m* gasholder, gas tank

gazon [gɑzɔ̃] *m* lawn; turf, sod

gazonner [gɑzone] *tr* to sod

gazouiller [gɑzuje] *intr* to chirp, twitter; to warble; to babble

gazouillis [gɑzuji] *m* chirping; warbling; babbling

geai [ʒɛ] *m* jay

géant [ʒeɑ̃] **géante** [ʒeɑ̃t] *adj* gigantic ‖ *m* giant ‖ *f* giantess

Gédéon [ʒedeɔ̃] *m* (Bib) Gideon

gei·gnard [ʒeɲar] **-gnard** [ɲar] *adj* (coll) whining ‖ *mf* (coll) whiner

geignement [ʒeɲmɑ̃] *m* whining, whimper

geindre [ʒɛ̃dr] §50 *intr* to whine, whimper; (coll) to complain

gel [ʒɛl] *m* frost, freezing; (chem) gel

gélatine [ʒelatin] *f* gelatin

gelée [ʒəle] *f* frost; (culin) jelly; **gelée blanche** hoarfrost

geler [ʒəle] §2 *tr, intr & ref* to freeze; to congeal

gelure [ʒəlyr] *f* frostbite

gémi·né -née [ʒemine] *adj* twin; coeducational (*school*)

gémir [ʒemir] *intr* to groan, moan

gémissement [ʒemismɑ̃] *m* groaning, moaning

gemme [ʒɛm] *f* gem; bud; pine resin

gemmer [ʒɛmme] *tr* to tap for resin ‖ *intr* to bud

gê·nant -nante [ʒenɑ̃] [nɑ̃t] *adj* troublesome, embarrassing

gencive [ʒɑ̃siv] *f* (anat) gum

gendarme [ʒɑ̃darm] *m* policeman; rock pinnacle; flaw (*of gem*); (coll) virago; (slang) red herring

gendarmerie [ʒɑ̃darmri] *f* police headquarters

gendre [ʒɑ̃dr] *m* son-in-law

gêne [ʒɛn] *f* discomfort, embarrassment; **être dans la gêne** to be hard up; **être sans gêne** (coll) to be rude, casual

gène [ʒɛn] *m* (biol) gene

généalogie [ʒenealɔʒi] *f* genealogy

gêner [ʒene] *tr* to embarrass; to inconvenience; to hinder; to embarrass financially; to pinch (*the feet*)

géné·ral -rale [ʒeneral] *adj & m* (*pl* **-raux** [ro]) general; **en général** in general; **général de brigade** brigadier general; **général de corps d'armée** lieutenant general; **général de division** major general ‖ *f* general's wife; (theat) opening night; **battre la générale** (mil) to sound the alarm

généralat [ʒenerala] *m* generalship

généraliser [ʒeneralize] *tr & intr* to generalize

généralissime [ʒeneralisim] *m* generalissimo

généralité [ʒeneralite] *f* generality; **la généralité de** the general run of

généra·teur [ʒeneratœr] **-trice** [tris] *adj* generating ‖ *m* boiler ‖ *f* generator

génération [ʒenerasjɔ̃] *f* generation

générer [ʒenere] §10 *tr* to generate

géné·reux [ʒenerø] **-reuse** [røz] *adj* generous; full (*bosom*); rich, full (*wine*)

générique [ʒenerik] *adj* generic ‖ *m* (mov) credit line

générosité [ʒenerozite] *f* generosity; **générosités** acts of generosity

Gênes [ʒɛn] *f* Genoa

genèse [ʒənɛz] *f* genesis

genet [ʒənɛ] *m* jennet (*horse*)

genêt [ʒəne] *m* (bot) broom; **genêt épineux** furze

génétique [ʒenetik] *adj* genetic ‖ *f* genetics

gê·neur [ʒenœr] **-neuse** [nøz] *mf* intruder, spoilsport

Genève [ʒənɛv] *f* Geneva

gene·vois [ʒənvwa], [ʒɛnvwa] **-voise** [vwaz] *adj* Genevan ‖ (*cap*) *mf* Genevan (*person*)

genévrier [ʒənevrije] *m* juniper

gé·nial -niale [ʒenjal] *adj* (*pl* **-niaux** [njo]) brilliant, ingenious; genius-like, of genius

génie [ʒeni] *m* genius; bent, inclination; genie; engineer corps; **génie civil** civil engineering; **génie industriel** industrial engineering; **génie maritime** naval construction

genièvre [ʒənjɛvr] *m* juniper; juniper berry; gin

génisse [ʒenis] *f* heifer

géni·tal -tale [ʒenital] *adj* (*pl* **-taux** [to]) genital

géni·teur [ʒenitœr] **-trice** [tris] *adj* engendering ‖ *m* sire ‖ *f* genetrix

géni·tif [ʒenitif] **-tive** [tiv] *adj & m* genitive

génocide [ʒenɔsid] *m* genocide

gé·nois [ʒenwa] **-noise** [nwaz] *adj* Genoese ‖ (*cap*) *mf* Genoese

ge·nou [ʒənu] *m* (*pl* **-noux**) knee; (mach) joint

genouillère [ʒənujer] *f* kneecap; kneepad

genre [ʒɑ̃r] *m* genre; genus; kind, sort;

manner, way; fashion, taste; (gram) gender; **de genre** (fa) genre; **faire du genre** (coll) to put on airs; **genre humain** humankind

gens [ʒɑ̃] *mpl* (an immediately preceding adjective that varies in its feminine form is put in that form, and so are **certain, quel, tel,** and **tout** that precede that preceding adjective, but the noun remains masculine for that past participles that agree with it, and for adjectives in all other positions, e.g., **toutes ces vieilles gens sont intéressants** all these old people are interesting) people; nations, e.g., **droit des gens** law of nations; men, e.g., **gens de lettres** men of letters; **gens d'affaires** businessmen; **gens d'Église** clergy; **gens de la presse** newsmen; **gens de mer** seamen; **gens de robe** bar; **jeunes gens** young people (*men and women*); young men

gent [ʒɑ̃] *f* (obs) nation, race

gentiane [ʒɑ̃sjan] *f* gentian

gen·til [ʒɑ̃ti] **-tille** [tij] *adj* nice, kind || (*cap*) *m* pagan, gentile

gentilhomme [ʒɑ̃tijɔm] *m* (*pl* **gentils-hommes** [ʒɑ̃tizɔm]) nobleman

gentillesse [ʒɑ̃tijɛs] *f* niceness, kindness; **gentillesses** nice things, kind words

gentil·let [ʒɑ̃tije] **gentil·lette** [ʒɑ̃tijɛt] *adj* rather nice

gentiment [ʒɑ̃timɑ̃] *adv* nicely; gracefully

géographie [ʒeografi] *f* geography

geôle [ʒol] *f* jail

geô·lier [ʒolje] **-lière** [ljɛr] *mf* jailer

géologie [ʒeɔlɔʒi] *f* geology

géologique [ʒeɔlɔʒik] *adj* geologic(al)

géomé·tral **-trale** [ʒeɔmetral] *adj* (*pl* **-traux** [tro]) flat (*projection*)

géométrie [ʒeɔmetri] *f* geometry

géométrique [ʒeɔmetrik] *adj* geometric(al)

géophysique [ʒeofizik] *f* geophysics

géopolitique [ʒeopolitik] *f* geopolitics

Georges [ʒɔrʒ] *m* George

gérance [ʒerɑ̃s] *f* management; board of directors

géranium [ʒeranjɔm] *m* geranium

gé·rant [ʒerɑ̃] **-rante** [rɑ̃t] *mf* manager; **gérant d'une publication** managing editor

gerbe [ʒɛrb] *f* sheaf; spray (*of flowers; of water; of bullets*); shower (*of sparks*)

gerbée [ʒɛrbe] *f* straw

gerber [ʒɛrbe] *tr* to sheave; to stack

gerce [ʒɛrs] *f* crack, split; clothes moth

gercer [ʒɛrse] §51 *tr, intr, & ref* to crack, to chap

gerçure [ʒɛrsyr] *f* crack, chap

gérer [ʒere] §10 *tr* to manage, to run

gériatrie [ʒerjatri] *f* geriatrics

ger·main [ʒɛrmɛ̃] **-maine** [mɛn] *adj* german, first (*cousin*)

germe [ʒɛrm] *m* germ

germer [ʒɛrme] *intr* to germinate

germicide [ʒɛrmisid] *adj* germicidal || *m* germicide

gérondif [ʒerɔ̃dif] *m* gerund

gérontologie [ʒerɔ̃tɔlɔʒi] *f* gerontology

gésier [ʒesje] *m* gizzard

gésir [ʒezir] (used only in *inf*; **ger gisant**; 3d *sg pres ind* **gît**; 1st, 2d, 3d *pl pres ind* **gisons, gisez, gisent**; *imperf ind* **gisais, gisait, gisions, gisiez, gisaient**) *intr* to lie; **ci-gît** here lies (*buried*)

gesse [ʒɛs] *f* vetch; **gesse odorante** sweet pea

gestation [ʒɛstasjɔ̃] *f* gestation

geste [ʒɛst] *m* gesture || *f* medieval epic poem

gesticuler [ʒɛstikyle] *intr* to gesticulate

gestion [ʒɛstjɔ̃] *f* management, administration

gestionnaire [ʒɛstjɔnɛr] *adj* managing || *mf* manager, administrator

geyser [ʒezɛr], [ʒejzɛr] *m* geyser

ghetto [geto], [getto] *m* ghetto

gib·beux [ʒibø] **gib·beuse** [ʒibøz] *adj* humped, hunchbacked

gibecière [ʒibsjɛr] *f* game bag; sack (*for papers, books, etc.*)

gibelotte [ʒiblɔt] *f* rabbit stew

gibet [ʒibe] *m* gibbet, gallows

gibier [ʒibje] *m* game; **gibier à plume** feathered game; **gibier de potence** gallows bird

giboulée [ʒibule] *f* shower; hailstorm

giboyeux [ʒibwajø] **giboyeuse** [ʒibwajøz] *adj* full of game

gibus [ʒibys] *m* opera hat

giclée [ʒikle] *f* spurt

gicler [ʒikle] *intr* to spurt

gicleur [ʒiklœr] *m* atomizer; (aut) spray nozzle (*of carburetor*)

gifle [ʒifl] *f* slap in the face

gifler [ʒifle] *tr* to slap in the face

gigantesque [ʒigɑ̃tɛsk] *adj* gigantic

gigogne [ʒigɔɲ] *adj*—**table gigogne** nest of tables || (*cap*) *f*—**la mère Gigogne** the old woman who lived in a shoe

gigolo [ʒigɔlo] *m* (coll) gigolo

gigot [ʒigo] *m* leg of lamb, leg of mutton; **à gigot** leg-of-mutton (*sleeve*)

gigue [ʒig] *f* jig; haunch (*of venison*); (coll) leg; (slang) long-legged gawky girl

gilet [ʒile] *m* vest; **gilet de sauvetage** life jacket; **gilet pare-balles** bulletproof vest; **pleurer dans le gilet de qn** (coll) to cry on s.o.'s shoulder

gingembre [ʒɛ̃ʒɑ̃br] *m* ginger

girafe [ʒiraf] *f* giraffe

giration [ʒirasjɔ̃] *f* gyration

girl [gœrl] *f* chorus girl

girofle [ʒirɔfl] *m* clove

giroflée [ʒirɔfle] *f* gillyflower

giron [ʒirɔ̃] *m* lap; bosom (*of the Church*)

girouette [ʒirwɛt] *f* weather vane

gisement [ʒizmɑ̃] *m* deposit; lode, seam; (naut) bearing; **gisement de pétrole** oil field

gi·tan [ʒitɑ̃] **-tane** [tan] *adj & mf* gypsy

gîte [ʒit] *m* lodging; lair, cover; deposit (*of ore*); **gîte à la noix** round steak || *f* (naut) list; **donner de la gîte** to heel

gîter [ʒite] *intr* to lodge; to lie, couch;

to perch; (naut) to list, heel || *ref* to find shelter

givre [ʒivr] *m* rime, hoarfrost

givrer [ʒivre] *tr* to frost

glabre [glɑbr] *adj* beardless

glaçage [glasaʒ] *m* icing (on cake)

glace [glas] *f* ice; ice cream; mirror; plate glass; car window; glaze, icing; flaw (of gem); **être de glace** (fig) to be hard as stone; **glace au sirop** sundae; **glace panachée** Neapolitan ice cream; **rompre la glace** (fig) to break the ice

gla·cé -cée [glase] *adj* frozen; iced, chilled; icy, frosty; glazed, glossy

glacer [glase] §51 *tr* to freeze; to chill; to glaze; to ice (a cake)

glacerie [glasri] *f* glass factory

glaciaire [glasjɛr] *adj* glacial

gla·cial -ciale [glasjal] *adj* (*pl* **-cials**) glacial

glacier [glasje] *m* glacier; ice-cream man

glacière [glasjɛr] *f* icehouse; icebox; freezer

glacis [glasi] *m* slope; ramp; (mil) glacis; (painting) glaze

glaçon [glasɔ̃] *m* icicle; ice cube; ice floe; (fig) cold fish, iceberg

glaçure [glasyr] *f* (ceramics) glaze

gladiateur [gladjatœr] *m* gladiator

glaïeul [glajœl] *m* gladiola

glaire [glɛr] *f* white of egg; mucus

glaise [glɛz] *f* clay, loam

glaisière [glezjɛr] *f* clay pit

glaive [glɛv] *m* (lit) sword

gland [glɑ̃] *m* acorn; tassel

glande [glɑ̃d] *f* gland

glane [glan] *f* gleaning; cluster

glaner [glane] *tr* to glean

glanure [glanyr] *f* gleaning

glapir [glapir] *intr* to yelp, yap

glas [glɑ] *m* knell, tolling

glauque [glok] *adj & m* blue-green

glèbe [glɛb] *f* clod (sod); soil (land)

glène [glɛn] *f* (anat) socket; (naut) coil of rope

glissade [glisad] *f* slip; sliding; (dancing) glide; **glissade de terre** landslide; **glissade sur l'aile** (aer) sideslip; **glissade sur la queue** (aer) tail dive

glis·sant [glisɑ̃] **glis·sante** [glisɑ̃t] *adj* slippery

glissement [glismɑ̃] *m* sliding; gliding

glisser [glise] *tr* to slip; to drop (a word into s.o.'s ear) || *intr* to slip; to slide; to skid; to glide || *ref* to slip

glissière [glisjɛr] *f* slide, groove; à **glissière** sliding; zippered

glissoire [gliswar] *f* slide (on ice or snow)

glo·bal -bale [glɔbal] *adj* (*pl* **-baux** [bo]) global; lump (sum)

globe [glɔb] *m* globe; **globe de feu** fireball; **globe de l'œil** eyeball

globule [glɔbyl] *m* globule; (physiol) corpuscle

gloire [glwar] *f* glory; pride; halo; **pour la gloire** for fun, for nothing; **se faire gloire de** to glory in

gloriette [glɔrjɛt] *f* arbor, summerhouse

glo·rieux [glɔrjø] **-rieuse** [rjøz] *adj* glorious; blessed; vain

glorifier [glɔrifje] *tr* to glorify || *ref*— **se glorifier de** to glory in

gloriole [glɔrjɔl] *f* vainglory

glose [gloz] *f* gloss; (coll) gossip

gloser [gloze] *intr* (coll) to gossip

glossaire [glɔsɛr] *m* glossary

glotte [glɔt] *f* glottis

glouglou [gluglu] *m* gurgle, glug; gobble-gobble; coo (of dove)

glouglouter [gluglute] *intr* to gurgle; to gobble (said of turkey)

glousser [gluse] *intr* to cluck; to chuckle

glou·ton [glutɔ̃] **-tonne** [tɔn] *adj* gluttonous || *mf* glutton || *m* (zool) glutton, wolverine

gloutonnerie [glutɔnri] *f* gluttony

glu [gly] *f* birdlime; (coll) trap

gluant [glyɑ̃] **gluante** [glyɑ̃t] *adj* sticky, gummy; (fig) tenacious

glucose [glykoz] *m* glucose

glycérine [gliserin] *f* glycerine

gnognote [ɲɔɲɔt] *f* (coll) junk

gnome [gnom] *m* gnome

gnomon [gnɔmɔ̃] *m* sundial

gnon [ɲɔ̃] *m* (slang) blow, punch

go [go]—**tout de go** (coll) straight off, at once

goal [gol] *m* goalkeeper

gobelet [gɔblɛ] *m* cup, tumbler, mug; **gobelets utilisés** (public sign) used paper drinking cups

gobe-mouches [gɔbmuʃ] *m invar* (zool) flycatcher; (fig) sucker, gull

gober [gɔbe] *tr* to gulp down, to gobble; to suck (an egg); (coll) to swallow, to be a sucker for

goberger [gɔberʒe] §38 *ref* (coll) to guzzle; (coll) to live in comfort

gobeter [gɔbte] §34 *tr* to plaster, to fill in the cracks of

go·beur [gɔbœr] **-beuse** [bøz] *mf* (coll) sucker, gullible person

godet [gɔdɛ] *m* cup; basin; bucket (of water wheel); (bot) calyx; **à godets** flared

godille [gɔdij] *f* scull, oar

godiller [gɔdije] *intr* to scull

godillot [gɔdijo] *m* (slang) clodhopper (shoe)

goéland [gɔelɑ̃] *m* sea gull

goélette [gɔelɛt] *f* (naut) schooner

goémon [gɔemɔ̃] *m* seaweed

gogo [gogo] *m* (coll) sucker, gull; à **gogo** (coll) galore

gogue·nard [gɔgnar] **-narde** [nard] *adj* jeering, mocking

goguenarder [gɔgnarde] *intr* to jeer

goguette [gɔgɛt] *f*—**en goguette** (coll) tipsy

goinfre [gwɛ̃fr] *m* glutton, guzzler

goitre [gwatr] *m* goiter

golf [gɔlf] *m* golf

golfe [gɔlf] *m* gulf

gomme [gɔm] *f* gum; eraser; **gomme à mâcher** chewing gum; **gomme d'épinette** spruce gum; **gomme de sapin** balsam; **gomme élastique** India rubber; **mettre la gomme** (slang) to speed it up

gomme-laque [gɔmlak] *f* (*pl* **gommes-laques**) shellac

gommelaquer [gɔmlake] *tr* to shellac

gommer [gɔme] *tr* to gum; to erase ‖ *intr* to stick, to gum up

gond [gɔ̃] *m* hinge; **sortir de ses gonds** (coll) to fly off the handle

gondole [gɔ̃dɔl] *f* gondola

gondoler [gɔ̃dɔle] *intr & ref* to buckle up

gondolier [gɔ̃dɔlje] *m* gondolier

gonfalon [gɔ̃falɔ̃] *m* pennant

gonflement [gɔ̃fləmɑ̃] *m* swelling

gonfler [gɔ̃fle] *tr* to swell, inflate ‖ *intr* to swell up, puff up ‖ *ref* to become inflated; (coll) to swell up with pride

gonfleur [gɔ̃flœr] *m* tire pump

gong [gɔ̃g] *m* gong

goret [gɔre] *m* piglet; (coll) slob

gorge [gɔrʒ] *f* throat; bust, breasts (*of woman*); gorge; **à pleine gorge or à gorge déployée** at the top of one's voice; **avoir la gorge serrée** to have a lump in one's throat; **faire des gorges chaudes de** (coll) to scoff at; to gloat over; **rendre gorge** to make restitution

gorger [gɔrʒe] §38 *tr & ref* to gorge, stuff

gorille [gɔrij] *m* gorilla; (slang) strong-arm man, bodyguard; (slang) bouncer (*in a night club*)

gosier [gozje] *m* throat, gullet; **à plein gosier** loudly, lustily; **gosier serré** with one's heart in one's mouth; **s'humecter** or **se rincer le gosier** (slang) to wet one's whistle

gosse [gɔs] *mf* (coll) kid, youngster

gothique [gɔtik] *adj* Gothic ‖ *m* Gothic (*language*); Gothic art ‖ *f* black letter, Old English

gouailler [gwaje] *tr* to jeer at ‖ *intr* to jeer

gouape [gwap] *f* (slang) hoodlum, blackguard

gouaper [gwape] *intr* (slang) to lead a disreputable life

goudron [gudrɔ̃] *m* tar

goudronner [gudrɔne] *tr* to tar

gouffre [gufr] *m* gulf, abyss; whirlpool

gouge [guʒ] *f* gouge; harlot

gouger [guʒe] §38 *tr* to gouge

goujat [guʒa] *m* boor, cad

goujon [guʒɔ̃] *m* gudgeon, pin; pintle (*of hinge*); dowel; (ichth) gudgeon; **taquiner le goujon** to go fishing

goulasch [gulaʃ] *m & f* goulash

goule [gul] *f* ghoul

goulet [gule] *m* narrows, sound; **goulet d'étranglement** bottleneck

goulot [gulo] *m* neck (*of bottle*); **boire au goulot** to drink right out of the bottle

gou·lu -lue [guly] *adj* gluttonous

goupil [gupi] *m* (obs) fox

goupille [gupij] *f* pin; **goupille fendue** cotter pin

goupiller [gupije] *tr* to cotter; (slang) to contrive, wangle

goupillon [gupijɔ̃] *m* bottle brush; sprinkler (*for holy water*); **goupillon nettoie-pipes** pipe cleaner

gourd [gur] **gourde** [gurd] *adj* numb (*with cold*) ‖ *adj fem* (coll) dumb ‖

f gourd; canteen, metal flask; (coll) dumbbell

gourdin [gurdɛ̃] *m* cudgel

gourgandine [gurgɑ̃din] *f* (hist) low-necked bodice; (coll) trollop

gour·mand -mande [gurmɑ̃] [mɑ̃d] *adj & mf* gourmand, gourmet

gourmander [gurmɑ̃de] *tr* to bawl out

gourmandise [gurmɑ̃diz] *f* gluttony; love of good food; **gourmandises** delicacies

gourme [gurm] *f* impetigo; **jeter sa gourme** (coll) to sow one's wild oats

gour·mé -mée [gurme] *adj* stiff, stuck-up

gourmet [gurme] *m* gourmet

gourmette [gurmet] *f* curb (*of harness*); curb watch chain

gousse [gus] *f* pod; clove (*of garlic*)

gousset [guse] *m* vest pocket; fob, watch pocket (*in trousers*)

goût [gu] *m* taste; flavor; sense of taste; **au goût du jour** up to date

goûter [gute] *m* afternoon snack ‖ *tr* to taste; to sample; to relish, enjoy ‖ *intr* to have a bite to eat; **goûter à** to sample, try; **goûter de** (coll) to try out (*e.g., a trade*)

goutte [gut] *f* drop, drip; (pathol) gout; **boire la goutte** (coll) to take a nip of brandy; **la goutte d'eau qui a fait déborder le vase** the straw which broke the camel's back; **ne...goutte** §90 (used only with **comprendre, connaître, entendre,** and **voir**) (archaic & hum) not at all, e.g., **je n'y vois goutte** I don't see at all; **tomber goutte à goutte** to drip

goutte-à-goutte [gutagut] *m invar* (med) dropping bottle (*for intravenous drip*)

gouttelette [gutlet] *f* droplet

goutter [gute] *intr* to drip

gouttière [gutjer] *f* eavestrough, gutter; (med) splint

gouvernail [guvernaj] *m* rudder, helm; **gouvernail de profondeur** (aer) elevator

gouver·nant -nante [guvernɑ̃] [nɑ̃t] *adj* governing ‖ **gouvernants** *mpl* powers that be, rulers ‖ *f* governess; housekeeper

gouverne [guvern] *f* guidance; **gouvernes** (aer) controls; **pour votre gouverne** for your guidance

gouvernement [guvernəmɑ̃] *m* government; **gouvernement fantoche** puppet government

gouvernemen·tal -tale [guvernəmɑ̃tal] *adj* (*pl* **-taux** [to]) governmental

gouverner [guverne] *tr* to govern, to control; to steer; to manage with care ‖ *intr* to govern; (naut) to answer to the helm

gouverneur [guvernœr] *m* governor; tutor; director (*e.g., of a bank*)

goyave [gɔjav] *f* guava

goyavier [gɔjavje] *m* guava tree

Graal [gral] *m* Grail

grabat [graba] *m* pallet, straw bed

grâce [gras] *f* grace; **de bonne grâce** willingly; **de grâce** for mercy's sake; **de mauvaise grâce** unwillingly; **faire**

grâce à to pardon; to spare; **faites-moi la grâce de** be kind enough to; **grâce!** mercy!; **grâce à** thanks to

gracier [grasje] *tr* to reprieve

gra·cieux [grasjø] **-cieuse** [sjøz] *adj* gracious; graceful

gracile [grasil] *adj* slender, slim

gradation [gradɑsjɔ̃] *f* gradation

grade [grad] *m* grade; rank; degree (*in school*); **en prendre pour son grade** (coll) to get called down

gra·dé -dée [grade] *adj* noncommissioned ‖ *mf* noncommissioned officer

gradient [gradjã] *m* gradient

gradin [gradɛ̃] *m* tier

graduation [gradɥasjɔ̃] *f* graduation

gra·dué -duée [gradɥe] *adj* graduated (*scale*); graded (*lessons*) ‖ *mf* graduate

gra·duel -duelle [gradɥel] *adj & m* gradual

graduer [gradɥe] *tr* to graduate

grailler [graje] *intr* to speak hoarsely; to sound the horn to recall the dogs

grain [grɛ̃] *m* grain; particle, speck; bean; squall; **grain de beauté** beauty spot, mole; **grain de raisin** grape; **grains** grain, cereals; **veiller au grain** (fig) to be on one's guard

graine [gren] *f* seed; **graine d'anis** aniseed; **mauvaise graine** (coll) shady character; **monter en graine** to run to seed; to soon be on the shelf (*said of young girl*); (coll) to grow; **prendre de la graine de** (coll) to follow the example of

graissage [gresaʒ] *m* (aut) lubrication

graisse [gres] *f* grease; fat; mother (*of wine*)

graisser [grese], [grese] *tr* to grease; to lubricate; to get grease stains on; **graisser la patte à qn** (coll) to grease s.o.'s palm

grais·seux [gresø] **grais·seuse** [gresøz] *adj* greasy

grammaire [gramer] *f* grammar

grammai·rien [gramerjɛ̃] **-rienne** [rjen] *mf* grammarian

grammati·cal -cale [gramatikal] *adj* (*pl* **-caux** [ko]) grammatical

gramme [gram] *m* gram

grand [grã] **grande** [grãd] *adj* tall ‖ (when standing before noun) *adj* large; great; important; high (*priest; mass; society; explosive*); vain, empty (*words*); broad (*daylight*); grand (*dignitary; officer; lady*); main (*road*); (fig) big (*heart*) ‖ *m* adult, grownup, grandee, noble; **en grand** life-size; on a grand scale; enlarged (*copy*); wide (*open*); **grands et petits** young and old ‖ **grand** *adv*—**voir grand** to see big, to envisage great projects

grand-chose [grãʃoz] *mf invar*—**pas grand-chose** (coll) nobody, person of no importance ‖ *adv*—**pas grand-chose** not much

grand-duc [grãdyk] *m* (*pl* **grands-ducs**) grand duke

grand-duché [grãdyʃe] *m* (*pl* **grands-duchés**) grand duchy

Grande-Bretagne [grãdbrətaɲ] *f* Great Britain; **la Grande-Bretagne** Great Britain

grande-duchesse [grãdədyʃes] *f* (*pl* **grandes-duchesses**) grand duchess

grande-let [grãdle] **-lette** [let] *adj* tall for his or her age

grandement [grãdmã] *adv* highly; handsomely; **se tromper grandement** to be very mistaken

grand-erre [grãter] *adv* at full speed

gran·det [grãde] **-dette** [det] *adj* rather big; rather tall

grandeur [grãdœr] *f* size; height; greatness; (astr) magnitude

grandiose [grãdjoz] *adj* grandiose

grandir [grãdir] *tr* to enlarge; to increase ‖ *intr* to grow; to grow up

grandissement [grãdismã] *m* magnification, enlargement; growth

grand-livre [grãlivr] *m* (*pl* **grands-livres**) ledger

grand-maman [grãmamã] *f* (*pl* **-mamans**) grandma

grand-mère [grãmer] *f* (*pl* **-mères** or **grands-mères**) grandmother; (coll) old lady

grand-messe [grãmes] *f* (*pl* **-messes**) high mass

grand-oncle [grãtɔ̃kl] *m* (*pl* **grands-oncles**) granduncle

Grand-Orient [grãtɔrjã] *m* grand lodge

grand-papa [grãpapa] *m* (*pl* **grands-papas**) grandpa

grand-peine [grãpen]—**à grand-peine** with great difficulty

grand-père [grãper] *m* (*pl* **grands-pères**) grandfather

grand-route [grãrut] *f* (*pl* **-routes**) highway

grand-rue [grãry] *f* (*pl* **-rues**) main street

Grands Lacs [grãlak] *mpl* Great Lakes

grands-parents [grãparã] *mpl* grandparents

grand-tante [grãtãt] *f* (*pl* **-tantes**) grandaunt

grange [grãʒ] *f* barn

granit [grani], [granit] *m* granite

granite [granit] *m* granite

granulaire [granyler] *adj* granular

granule [granyl] *m* granule

granu·lé -lée [granyle] *adj* granulated ‖ *m* little pill; medicine in granulated form

granuler [granyle] *tr & ref* to granulate

graphie [grafi] *f* spelling

graphique [grafik] *adj* graphic(al) ‖ *m* graph

graphite [grafit] *m* graphite

grappe [grap] *f* bunch, cluster; string (*of onions*); **une grappe humaine** a bunch of people

grappillage [grapijaʒ] *m* gleaning; (coll) graft

grappiller [grapije] *tr & intr* (in vineyard) to glean; (coll) to pilfer

grappillon [grapijɔ̃] *m* little bunch

grappin [grapɛ̃] *m* grapnel; **jeter or mettre le grappin sur qn** (coll) to get one's hooks into s.o.

gras [grɑ] **grasse** [grɑs] *adj* fat; greasy; rich (*soil*); carnival (*days*); smutty (*stories*); (*typ*) bold-faced ‖ *m* fatty part; calf (*of leg*); foggy weather; **au gras** with meat sauce; **faire gras** to eat meat ‖ **gras** *adv*—**parler gras** to speak with uvular r; to tell smutty stories

gras-double [grɑdubl] *m* (*pl* **-doubles**) tripe

grassement [grɑsmɑ̃] *adv* comfortably; generously

grasseyer [grɑseje] §32 *tr* to make (*one's r's*) uvular ‖ *intr* to speak with uvular r

grassouil·let [grɑsuje] **grassouil·lette** [grɑsujɛt] *adj* (coll) plump, chubby

gratification [gratifikɑsjɔ̃] *f* tip, gratuity

gratifier [gratifje] *tr* to favor, reward; **gratifier qn de q.ch.** to bestow s.th. upon s.o.

gratin [gratɛ̃] *m* (culin) crust; (coll) upper crust; **au gratin** breaded

gratiner [gratine] *tr* to cook au gratin ‖ *intr* to brown, to crisp

gratis [gratis] *adv* gratis

gratitude [gratityd] *f* gratitude

gratte [grat] *f* scraper; (coll) graft

gratte-ciel [gratsjɛl] *m invar* skyscraper

gratte-cul [gratky] *m invar* (bot) hip

gratte-dos [gratdo] *m invar* back scratcher

gratte-papier [gratpapje] *m invar* (coll) pencil pusher, office drudge

gratte-pieds [gratpje] *m invar* shoe-scraper

gratter [grate] *tr* to scratch; to scratch out; to scrape up, scrape together; to itch; (coll) to pocket ‖ *intr* to knock gently ‖ *ref* to scratch; (with *dat* of *reflex pron*) to scratch (*e.g.*, *one's arm*)

grattoir [gratwar] *m* scraper; knife eraser

gra·tuit [gratɥi] **-tuite** [tɥit] *adj* free of charge; gratuitous; unfounded

gratuité [gratɥite] *f* gratuity

grave [grav], [grɑv] *adj* grave; low (*frequency*); (mus) bass; (mus) flat

grave·leux [gravlø] **-leuse** [løz] *adj* gravelly, gritty; smutty, licentious

gravelle [gravɛl] *f* (pathol) gravel

graver [grave] *tr* to engrave; to cut (*a phonograph record*)

graveur [gravœr] *m* engraver; etcher

gravier [gravje] *m* gravel

gravir [gravir] *tr* to climb, climb up

gravitation [gravitɑsjɔ̃] *f* gravitation

gravité [gravite] *f* gravity

graviter [gravite] *intr* to gravitate

gravure [gravyr] *f* engraving; etching; cutting (*of phonograph record*)

gré [gre] *m* will; **à son gré** to one's liking; **bon gré mal gré** willy-nilly; **de bon gré** willingly; **de gré à gré** by mutual consent; **de gré ou de force** willy-nilly; **savoir (bon) gré de** to be grateful for; **savoir mauvais gré de** to be displeased with

grec grecque [grek] *adj* Greek; classic (*profile*) ‖ *m* Greek (*language*) ‖ *f* Greek fret ‖ (*cap*) *mf* Greek

Grèce [gres] *f* Greece; **la Grèce** Greece

gre·din [grədɛ̃] **-dine** [din] *mf* scoundrel

gréement [gremɑ̃] *m* (naut) rigging

gréer [gree] *tr* (naut) to rig

greffe [gref] *m* (jur) office of the court clerk ‖ *f* grafting; (hort, med) graft; **greffe du cœur** heart transplant

greffer [grefe] *tr* to graft; to add ‖ *ref* to be added

greffier [grefje] *m* clerk of court, recorder; court reporter

greffon [grefɔ̃] *m* (hort) graft; (surg) transplant

grégaire [greger] *adj* gregarious

grège [greʒ] *adj* raw (*silk*) ‖ *f* raw silk

grégo·rien [gregɔrjɛ̃] **-rienne** [rjɛn] *adj* Gregorian

grêle [grel] *adj* slender, slim; thin, high-pitched ‖ *f* hail; (fig) shower

grê·lé -lée [grele] *adj* pockmarked

grêler [grele] *tr* to damage by hail; to pockmark ‖ *intr* (fig) to rain down thick; **il grêle** it is hailing

grêlon [grelɔ̃] *m* hailstone

grelot [grəlo] *m* sleigh bell

grelottement [grəlɔtmɑ̃] *m* shivering, trembling; jingle, jingling

grelotter [grəlɔte] *intr* to shiver, tremble; to jingle

grenade [grənad] *f* grenade; (bot) pomegranate; **grenade à main** hand grenade; **grenade éclairante** flare; **grenade lacrymogène** tear bomb; **grenade sous-marine** depth charge

grenadier [grənadje] *m* pomegranate tree; (mil) grenadier

grenadine [grənadin] *f* grenadine

grenaille [grənaj] *f* shot; **grenaille de plomb** buckshot

grenailler [grənaje] *tr* to granulate

grenat [grəna] *adj invar & m* garnet

grenier [grənje] *m* attic, loft; granary

grenouille [grənuj] *f* frog; **grenouille mugissante** or **taureau** bullfrog; **manger la grenouille** (coll) to make off with the money, to abscond

grenouillère [grənujer] *f* marsh

gre·nu -nue [grəny] *adj* full of grain; grainy (*leather*); granular (*marble*) ‖ *m* graininess; granularity

grès [gre] *m* gritstone, sandstone; stoneware; terra cotta (*for drain-pipes*)

grésil [grezil] *m* sleet

grésillement [grezijmɑ̃] *m* sizzling; chirping (*of cricket*)

grésiller [grezije] *tr* to scorch, to shrivel up ‖ *intr* to sizzle, to sputter; **il grésille** it is sleeting

grève [grev] *f* beach; strike; (*armor*) greave; **faire (la) grève** to strike; **faire la grève de la faim** to go on a hunger strike; **grève de solidarité** sympathy strike; **grève du zèle** slowdown (*caused by rigid application of rules*); **grève improvisée, grève inattendue, grève surprise** walkout; **grève perlée** slowdown; **grève sauvage, grève spontanée** wildcat strike; **grève sur le tas** sitdown strike; **grève tournante** strike in one industry at a time or for several hours at a time; **se met-tre en grève** to go on strike

grever [grəve] §2 *tr* to burden; to assess (*property*); **grever de** to burden with

gréviste [grevist] *mf* striker

gribouillage [gribujaʒ] *m* (coll) scribble, scrawl; (coll) daub (*in painting*)

gribouiller [gribuje] *tr* (coll) to scribble off (*a note*) || *intr* (coll) to scribble, scrawl; (coll) to daub

grief [grijef] *m* grievance, complaint; **faire grief de q.ch. à qn** to complain to s.o. about s.th.

grièvement [grijevmɑ̃] *adv* seriously, badly

griffe [grif] *f* claw, talon; signature stamp; (bot) tendril; (mach) hook, grip; **faire ses griffes** to sharpen its claws (*said of cat*); **griffe à papiers** paper clip; **porter la griffe de** to carry the stamp of; **tomber sous la griffe de** (coll) to fall into the clutches of

griffer [grife] *tr* to claw, scratch

griffon [grifɔ̃] *m* griffin

griffonner [grifone] *tr* to scrawl; (coll) to scribble off (*a letter*)

grignoter [griɲɔte] *tr* to nibble on or at; to wear down (*e.g., the enemy*) || *intr* (coll) to make a little profit, to get a cut

gril [gril] *m* gridiron, grid, grill; (theat) upper flies; **être sur le gril** (coll) to be on tenterhooks

grillade [grijad] *f* grilled meat; broiling

grillage [grijaʒ] *m* grating, latticework, trellis; broiling; roasting; toasting; burning out (*of a light bulb*); (tex) singeing

grille [grij] *f* grille; grate, grating; bars; railing; gate; squares (*of crossword puzzle*); grid (*of storage battery and vacuum tube*); **grille des salaires** salary schedule

grille-pain [grijpɛ̃] *m invar* toaster

griller [grije] *tr* to grill, broil; to put a grill on; to roast (*coffee*); to toast (*bread*); to burn out (*a fuse, lamp, electric iron, etc.*); to singe, scorch; to nip (*a bud, as the frost does*) || *intr* to grill; to toast; to burn out; **griller de** to long to

grilloir [grijwar] *m* roaster; (culin) broiler

grillon [grijɔ̃] *m* cricket

grimace [grimas] *f* grimace; **faire des grimaces** to make faces; to smirk, simper; to be full of wrinkles

grimacer [grimase] §51 *intr* to grimace; to make wrong creases

grime [grim] *m* dotard, old fogey

grimer [grime] *tr* to make up (*an actor*) || *ref* to make up

grimper [grɛ̃pe] *tr* to climb || *intr* to climb; **grimper à** or **sur** to climb up on

grimpe·reau [grɛ̃pro] *m* (pl -reaux) (orn) tree creeper

grim·peur [grɛ̃pœr] -peuse [pøz] *adj* climbing || *m* climber

grincement [grɛ̃smɑ̃] *m* grating

grincer [grɛ̃se] §51 *tr* to gnash, grit (*the teeth*) || *intr* to grate, grind, creak; to scratch (*said of pen*)

grin·cheux [grɛ̃ʃø] -cheuse [ʃøz] *adj* grumpy || *mf* grumbler, sorehead

gringa·let [grɛ̃gale] -lette [let] *adj* weak, puny || *m* (coll) weakling, shrimp

griot [grijo] **griotte** [grijɔt] *mf* witch doctor || *m* seconds (*in milling grain*) || *f* sour cherry

grippe [grip] *f* grippe; **prendre en grippe** to take a dislike to

grippeminaud [gripmino] *m* (coll) smoothy, hypocrite

gripper [gripe] *tr* to snatch; (slang) to steal || *intr* (mach) to jam || *ref* to get stuck

grippe-sou [gripsu] *m* (pl -sou or -sous) (coll) tightwad, skinflint

gris [gri] **grise** [griz] *adj* gray; cloudy; brown (*paper*); (coll) tipsy

grisailler [grizaje] *tr* to paint gray || *intr* to turn gray

grisâtre [grizɑtr] *adj* grayish

griser [grize] *tr* to paint gray; (coll) to intoxicate; **les succès l'ont grisé** (coll) success has gone to his head || *ref* to get tipsy; **se griser de** (coll) to revel in

griserie [grizri] *f* intoxication

grisette [grizet] *f* gay working girl

gris-gris [grigri] *m* lucky charm

grisonner [grizone] *intr* to turn gray

grisotte [grizɔt] *f* clock (*in stocking*)

grisou [grizu] *m* firedamp

grive [griv] *f* thrush; **grive mauvis** song thrush; **grive migratoire** (*Turdus migratorius*) robin

grive·lé -lée [grivle] *adj* speckled

grivèlerie [grivelri] *f* sneaking out without paying the check

gri·vois [grivwa] -voise [vwaz] *adj* spicy, off-color

grizzly [grizli] *m* grizzly bear

Groënland [grœnlɑ̃d] *m*—**le Groënland** Greenland

grog [grɔg] *m* grog

gro·gnard [grɔɲar] -gnarde [ɲard] *adj* grumbling || *mf* grumbler

grogner [grɔɲe] *intr* to grunt, to growl; to grumble, to grouch

gro·gnon [grɔɲɔ̃] -gnonne [ɲɔn] *adj* grouchy, grumbling || *mf* grouch, grumbler

grognonner [grɔɲone] *intr* to grunt; to be a complainer, to whine

groin [grwɛ̃] *m* snout; (coll) ugly mug

grommeler [grɔmle] §34 *tr* & *intr* to mutter, grumble; to growl

grondement [grɔ̃dmɑ̃] *m* growl; rumble

gronder [grɔ̃de] *tr* to scold || *intr* to scold; to growl; to grumble

gron·deur [grɔ̃dœr] -deuse [døz] *adj* scolding; grumbling || *mf* grumbler

groom [grum] *m* bellhop, pageboy

gros [gro] **grosse** [gros] *adj* big (*with child*); heavy (*heart*) || (*when standing before noun*) *adj* big, large, bulky; coarse; plain (*common sense*); main (*walls*); high (*stakes*); rich (*merchant*); booming (*voice*); bad (*weather*); heavy, rough (*sea*); swear (*words*) || *m* bulk, main part; **en gros**

wholesale; roughly, without going into detail; **faire le gros et le détail** to deal in wholesale and retail || *f* see **grosse** || **gros** *adv* much, a great deal; (fig) probably

gros-bec [grobɛk] *m* (*pl* -becs) grosbeak

groseille [grozɛj] *f* currant; **groseille à maquereau** gooseberry

groseillier [grozeje] *m* currant bush

Gros-Jean [groʒɑ̃] *m*—**être Gros-Jean comme devant** to be in the same fix again

grosse [gros] *f* fat woman; (com) gross; (law) engrossed copy

grosserie [grosri] *f* silver dishes

grossesse [grosɛs] *f* pregnancy

grosseur [grosœr] *f* size; swelling, tumor

gros·sier [grosje] **-sière** [grosjɛr] *adj* coarse; crude, rude; vulgar, ribald; glaring (*error*)

grossièrement [grosjɛrmɑ̃] *adv* grossly

grossièreté [grosjɛrte] *f* coarseness, grossness, vulgarity

grossir [grosir] *tr* to enlarge; to increase || *intr* to grow larger; to put on weight

grossis·sant [grosisɑ̃] **grossis·sante** [grosisɑ̃t] *adj* swelling; magnifying (*glasses*)

grossiste [grosist] *m* wholesaler, jobber

grotesque [grotɛsk] *adj* grotesque || *mf* grotesque person || *m* grotesque || *f* grotesque (*ornament*)

grotte [grɔt] *f* grotto

grouillement [grujmɑ̃] *m* swarming; rumbling

grouiller [gruje] *intr* to swarm; **grouiller de** to teem with || *ref* (slang) to get a move on

groupe [grup] *m* group; (mach & mil) unit; **groupe franc** (mil) commando; **groupe sanguin** blood type

groupement [grupmɑ̃] *m* grouping; organization

grouper [grupe] *tr* & *ref* to group

gruau [gryo] *m* (*pl* **gruaux**) groats; (culin) gruel; (orn) small crane

grue [gry] *f* crane; (orn) crane; (coll) tart

gruger [gryʒe] §38 *tr* to sponge on, exploit; to crunch

grume [grym] *f* bark; **en grume** rough (*timber*)

gru·meau [grymo] *m* (*pl* -meaux) gob; curd

grumeler [grymle] §34 *intr* to curdle, clot

gruyère [gryjɛr] *m* Gruyère cheese

guatémaltèque [gwatemaltɛk] *adj* Guatemalan || (*cap*) *mf* Guatemalan

gué [ge] *m* ford, crossing; **sonder le gué** (coll) to see how the land lies || *interj* hurrah!

guéable [geabl] *adj* fordable

guéer [gee] *tr* to ford; to water (*a horse*)

guelte [gɛlt] *f* commission, percentage

guenille [gənij] *f* ragged garment; **en guenilles** in tatters

guenon [gənɔ̃] *f* female monkey; long-tailed monkey; (coll) hag, old bag

guépard [gepar] *m* cheetah

guêpe [gɛp] *f* wasp

guère [gɛr] §90 *adv* hardly ever; **ne . . . guère** hardly, scarcely; hardly ever; not very; **ne . . . guère de** hardly any; **ne . . . guère que** hardly any but; hardly anyone but; **ne . . . plus guère** hardly ever any more; not much longer

guères [gɛr] *adv* (poetic) var of **guère**

guéret [gerɛ] *m* fallow land

guéridon [geridɔ̃] *m* pedestal table

guérilla [gerija] *f* guerrilla warfare

guérillero [gerijero] *m* guerrilla

guérir [gerir] *tr* to cure || *intr* to get well; to get better; to heal || *ref* to cure oneself; to recover

guérison [gerizɔ̃] *f* cure, healing; recovery

guérissable [gerisabl] *adj* curable

guéris·seur [gerisœr] **guéris·seuse** [gerisøz] *mf* healer; quack

guérite [gerit] *f* sentry box; (rr) signal box; **guérite téléphonique** call box

guerre [gɛr] *f* war; **de guerre lasse** for the sake of peace and quiet; **être de bonne guerre** to be fair, to be cricket; **guerre à outrance** all-out war; **Guerre de Troie** Trojan War; **guerre d'usure** war of attrition; **guerre éclair** blitzkrieg; **guerre froide** cold war; **guerre presse-bouton** push-button war

guer·rier [gɛrje] **guer·rière** [gɛrjɛr] *adj* warlike, martial || *m* warrior || *f* amazon

guerroyant [gɛrwajɑ̃] **guerroyante** [gɛrwajɑ̃t] *adj* warlike, bellicose

guerroyer [gɛrwaje] §47 *intr* to make war

guerroyeur [gɛrwajœr] **guerroyeuse** [gɛrwajøz] *adj* fighting (*spirit*) || *mf* fighter

guet [gɛ] *m* watch, lookout

guet-apens [gɛtapɑ̃] *m* (*pl* **guets-apens** [gɛtapɑ̃]) ambush, trap

guêtre [gɛtr] *f* gaiter, legging

guêtrer [gɛtre] *tr* & *ref* to put gaiters on

guetter [gete] *tr* to watch; to watch for; (coll) to lie in wait for

guetteur [getœr] *m* lookout, sentinel

gueu·lard [gœlar] **-larde** [lard] *adj* (slang) loud-mouthed; (slang) fond of good eating || *mf* gourmet; (slang) loud-mouth || *m* mouth (*of blast furnace; of cannon*); (naut) megaphone

gueule [gœl] *f* mouth (*of animal; of furnace, cannon, etc.*); (slang) mouth, mug (*of person*); **avoir de la gueule** (coll) to have a certain air; **avoir la gueule de bois** (coll) to have a hangover; **fine gueule** (coll) gourmet; **gueule cassée** (coll) disabled veteran; **gueule noire** (coll) miner; **ta gueule!** (slang) shut up!

gueule-de-loup [gœldəlu] *f* (*pl* **gueules-de-loup**) (bot) snapdragon

gueuler [gœle] *tr* & *intr* (slang) to bellow

gueuleton [gœltɔ̃] *m* (slang) big feed

gueux [gø] **gueuse** [gøz] *adj* beggarly, wretched || *mf* beggar; scamp || *f* pig iron; pig (*mold*); woolen jacket; (coll) whore; **courir la gueuse** (coll) to go whoring

gugusse [gygys] *m* clown

gui [gi] *m* mistletoe; (naut) boom

guichet [gi∫e] *m* window (*in post office, bank, box office, etc.*); counter (*e.g., in bank*); wicket

guidage [gidaʒ] *m* (rok) guidance

guide [gid] *m* guide; guidebook ‖ *f* rein; **mener la vie à grandes guides** to live extravagantly

guide-âne [gidɑn] *m* (*pl* -âne or -ânes) manual, guide

guider [gide] *tr* to guide

guidon [gidɔ̃] *m* handlebars; sight, bead (*of gun*); (naut) pennant

guigne [giɲ] *f* heart cherry; (coll) jinx

guigner [giɲe] *tr* to steal a glance at; (coll) to covet ‖ *intr* to peep

guignol [giɲɔl] *m* Punch (*puppet*); Punch and Judy show; (aer) king post

guignolet [giɲɔle] *m* cherry brandy

guillaume [gijom] *m* rabbet plane; **Guillaume** William

guilledou [gijdu] *m*—**courir le guilledou** (coll) to make the rounds

guillemet [gijme] *m* quotation mark; **fermer les guillemets** to close quotes; **ouvrir les guillemets** to quote

guillemeter [gijməte] §34 *tr* to put in quotes

guiller [gije] *intr* to ferment

guille·ret [gijre] -**rette** [ret] *adj* chipper, lively, gay

guillotine [gijɔtin] *f* guillotine; **à guillotine** sliding; sash (*window*)

guillotiner [gijɔtine] *tr* to guillotine

guimauve [gimov] *f* (bot) marshmallow

guimbarde [gɛ̃bard] *f* (mus) jew's-harp; (coll) jalopy

guimpe [gɛ̃p] *f* wimple

guin·dé -dée [gɛ̃de] *adj* affected, stiff

guin·deau [gɛ̃do] *m* (*pl* -deaux) windlass

guinder [gɛ̃de] *tr* to hoist ‖ *ref* to put on airs

guinée [gine] *f* guinea (*coin*); **Guinée** Guinea; **la Guinée** Guinea

guingan [gɛ̃gɑ̃] *m* gingham

guingois [gɛ̃gwa] *m*—**de guingois** askew; lopsidedly

guinguette [gɛ̃get] *f* roadside inn, roadside park

guipage [gipaʒ] *m* wrapping, lapping

guiper [gipe] *tr* to wind; to cover (*a wire*)

guipure [gipyr] *f* pillow lace

guirlande [girlɑ̃d] *f* garland, wreath

guirlander [girlɑ̃de] *tr* to garland

guise [giz] *f* manner; **à sa guise** as one pleases; **en guise de** by way of

guitare [gitar] *f* guitar

guitariste [gitarist] *mf* guitarist

guppy [gypi] *m* guppy

gustation [gystɑsjɔ̃] *f* tasting; drinking

guttu·ral -rale [gytyral] (*pl* -raux [ro] -rales) *adj & f* guttural

Guyane [gɥijan] *f* Guiana; **la Guyane** Guiana

gymnase [ʒimnɑz] *m* gymnasium

gymnaste [ʒimnast] *mf* gymnast

gymnote [ʒimnɔt] *m* electric eel

gynécologie [ʒinekɔlɔʒi] *f* gynecology

gypse [ʒips] *m* gypsum

gyrocompas [ʒirokɔ̃pa] *m* gyrocompass

gyroscope [ʒirɔskɔp] *m* gyroscope

H

H, h [a∫], *[a∫] *m* invar eighth letter of the French alphabet

habile [abil] *adj* skillful; clever

habileté [abilte] *f* skill; cleverness

habiliter [abilite] *tr* to qualify, entitle

habillement [abijmɑ̃] *m* clothing; clothes

habiller [abije] *tr* to dress; to clothe; to put together ‖ *intr* to be becoming, e.g., **robe qui habille bien** becoming dress ‖ *ref* to dress; to get dressed; **s'habiller chez** to buy one's clothes at or from

habit [abi] *m* dress suit; habit, frock; **habit de cérémonie** or **soirée, habit à queue de pie, habit à queue de morue** tails; **habits** clothes

habitacle [abitakl] *m* (aer) cockpit; (naut) binnacle; (poetic) dwelling

habi·tant [abitɑ̃] -**tante** [tɑ̃t] *mf* inhabitant

habitat [abita] *m* habitat; living conditions, housing

habitation [abitɑsjɔ̃] *f* habitation; dwelling; residence; **habitation à bon marché** or **à loyer modéré** low-rent apartment

habi·té -tée [abite] *adj* inhabited; (rok) manned

habiter [abite] *tr* to live in, to inhabit ‖ *intr* to live, reside

habitude [abityd] *f* habit, custom; **comme d'habitude** as usual; **d'habitude** usually

habi·tuel -tuelle [abitɥel] *adj* habitual

habituer [abitɥe] *tr* to accustom

hâbler *[able] *intr* to brag, to boast

hâblerie *[abləri] *f* bragging

hâ·bleur *[ablœr] -**bleuse** [bløz] *adj* boastful ‖ *mf* braggart, boaster

hache *[a∫] *f* ax, hatchet

ha·ché -chée *[a∫e] *adj* ground, chopped; hachured; choppy (*sea*); jerky (*style*); dotted (*line*)

hacher *[a∫e] *tr* to hack; to grind, chop up; **hacher menu** to mince

hache·reau *[a∫ro] *m* (*pl* -reaux) hatchet

hachette *[aʃet] f hatchet
hachis *[aʃi] m hash, forcemeat
hachisch *[aʃiʃ] m hashish
hachoir *[aʃwar] m cleaver; chopping board
hachure *[aʃyr] f shading
hachurer *[aʃyre] tr to shade, hatch
haddock *[adɔk] m finnan haddie
ha-gard *[agar] -garde [gard] adj haggard
haie *[e] f hedge; hurdle; line, row
haïe *[aj] interj giddap!
haillon *[ajɔ̃] m old piece of clothing; en haillons in rags and tatters
haillon-neux *[ajɔnø] haillon-neuse *[ajɔnøz] adj ragged, tattered
haine *[en] f hate
hai-neux *[ɛnø] -neuse [nøz] adj full of hate, spiteful, malevolent
haïr *[air] §33 tr to hate, to detest || intr—haïr de to hate to
haire *[ɛr] f hair shirt
haïssable *[aisabl] adj hateful
Haïti [aiti] f Haiti
haï-tien *[aisjɛ̃] -tienne [sjen] adj Haitian || (cap) mf Haitian
halcyon [alsjɔ̃] m (orn) kingfisher
hâle *[al] m sun tan
haleine *[alen] f breath; avoir l'haleine courte to be short-winded; (fig) to have little inspiration: de longue haleine hard, arduous (work); en haleine in good form; hors d'haleine out of breath perdre haleine to get out of breath reprendre haleine to catch one's breath; tenir en haleine to hold (e.g., an audience) breathless
halenée [alne] f whiff; strong breath
haler *[ale] tr to haul, to tow
hâler *[ale] tr to tan
hale-tant *[altã] -tante [tãt] adj breathless, panting
haleter *[alte] §2 intr to pant, puff
hall *[ol] m lobby; hall, auditorium
halle *[al] f market, marketplace; exchange
hallebarde *[albard] f halberd; il pleut des hallebardes (coll) it's raining cats and dogs
hallier *[alje] m thicket
hallucination [allysinasjɔ̃] f hallucination
halo *[alo] m halo
halogène [alɔʒɛn] m halogen
halte *[alt] f halt; stop; (rr) flag stop, way station faire faire halte à to halt || interj halt!
halte-là *[altla] interj (mil) halt!
haltère *[alter m dumbbell
haltérophile [alterɔfil] m weight lifter
haltérophilie [alterɔfili] f weight lifting
hamac *[amak] m hammock
ha-meau *[amo] m (pl -meaux) hamlet
hameçon [amsɔ̃] m hook, fishhook; (fig) bait
hammam *[ammam] m Turkish bath
hampe *[ãp] f staff, pole; shaft; downstroke; (culin) flank
hamster *[amster] m hamster
han *[ã], [hã] m grunt
hanap *[anap] m hanap, goblet
hanche *[ãʃ] f hip; haunch

hancher *[ãʃe] intr to lean on one leg || ref to stand at ease
handball *[ãbol] m handball
handicap *[ãdikap] m handicap
handicaper *[ãdikape] tr to handicap
hangar *[ãgar] m hangar; shed
hanneton *[antɔ̃] m June bug, chafer
hanter *[ãte] tr to haunt
hantise *[ãtiz] f obsession
happe *[ap] f crucible tongs; (carp) cramp, staple
happer *[ape] tr to snap up; (coll) to nab || intr to stick
haquenée *[akne] f palfrey
haquet *[ake] m dray; haquet à main pushcart
harangue *[arãg] f harangue
haranguer *[arãge] tr & intr to harangue
haras *[ara] m stud farm
harasser *[arase] tr to tire out
harceler *[arsəle] §2 or §34 tr to harass, to harry; to pester; to dun
harde *[ard] f herd; leash; set (of dogs); hardes old clothes
har-di -die *[ardi] adj bold || hardi interj up and at them!
hardiesse *[ardjes] f boldness
harem *[arem] m harem
hareng *[arã] m herring; hareng fumé kipper; hareng saur red herring; see comme un hareng (coll) long and thin; serrés comme des harengs (coll) packed like sardines
harengère *[arãʒer] f fishwife; (coll) shrew
harenguet *[arãge] m sprat
hargne *[arɲ] f bad temper
har-gneux *[arɲø] -gneuse [ɲøz] adj bad-tempered, peevish, surly
haricot *[ariko] m bean; haricot beurre lima bean, butter bean; haricot de Lima lima bean; haricot de mouton haricot (stew); haricot de Soissons kidney bean; haricot vert string bean
harmonica [armɔnika] m mouth organ
harmonie [armɔni] f harmony; (mus) band
harmo-nieux [armɔnjø] -nieuse [njøz] adj harmonious
harmonique [armɔnik] adj harmonic
harmoniser [armɔnize] tr & ref to harmonize
harnachement *[arnaʃmã] m harness; harnessing
harnacher *[arnaʃe] tr to harness; to rig out
harnais *[arne] m harness
haro *[aro] m—crier haro sur (coll) to make a hue and cry against
harpagon [arpagɔ̃] m scrooge
harpe *[arp] f harp
harpie *[arpi] f harpy
harpiste *[arpist] mf harpist
harpon *[arpɔ̃] m harpoon
harponner *[arpɔne] tr to harpoon; (coll) to nab (e.g., a thief)
hart *[ar] f noose
hasard *[azar] m hazard, chance; à tout hasard just in case, come what may; au hasard at random; par hasard by chance

hasar·dé -dée * [azarde] *adj* hazardous
hasar·deux * [azardø] -deuse [døz] *adj* risky, uncertain
hase * [az] *f* doe hare
hâte * [αt] *f* haste; **à la hâte** hastily; **avoir hâte** de to be eager to; **en hâte**, **en toute hâte** posthaste
hâter * [αte] *tr & ref* to hasten
hâ·tif * [αtif] -tive [tiv] *adj* premature; (hort) early
hauban * [obα] *m* (naut) shroud; (naut) guy
haubert * [ober] *m* coat of mail
hausse * [os] *f* rise, increase; block, wedge, prop; (mil) elevation, range; **jouer à la hausse** to bull the market
haussement * [osmα] *m* shrug
hausser * [ose] *tr* to raise, to lift; to shrug (*one's shoulders*) || *intr* to rise
haussier * [osje] *m* bull (*on the stock exchange*)
haussière * [osjer] *f* (naut) hawser
haut * [o] haute * [ot] *adj* high; loud; high and mighty || (*when standing before noun*) *adj* high; loud; upper, higher; early (*pay*); early (*antiquity*, *Middle Ages, etc.*) || *m* top; height; **de haut en bas** from top to bottom, **en haut** up; upst. irs; **haut de casse** (typ) upper case, **haut des côtes** sparerib; **le prendre de haut** to get on one's high horse; **traiter de haut en bas** to high-hat || *f see* **haute** || **haut** *adv* high; up high; loudly; **haut les bras!** start working!; **haut les cœurs!** lift up your hearts!; **haut les mains!** hands up!
hau·tain * [otɛ̃] -taine [ten] *adj* haughty
hautbois * [obwa] *m* oboe
haut-de-chausses * [odə∫os] *m* (*pl* hauts-de-chausses) trunk hose, breeches
haut-de-forme * [odəform] *m* (*pl* hauts-de-forme) top hat
haute * [ot] *f* high society
hautement * [otmα] *adv* loudly; openly, clearly; highly (*qualified*); proudly
hauteur * [otœr] *f* height; hill, upland; altitude; nobility; haughtiness; (phys) pitch (*of sound*); **à la hauteur de** equal to, up to; (naut) off
haut-fond * [of∫] *m* (*pl* hauts-fonds) shoal, shallows
haut-le-cœur * [oləkœr] *m invar* nausea
haut-le-corps * [oləkɔr] *m invar* jump, sudden start
haut-parleur * [oparlœr] *m* (*pl* haut-parleurs) loudspeaker
hautu·rier * [otyrje] -rière [rjer] *adj* deep-sea
havage * [avaʒ] *m* (min) cutting
havane * [avan] *adj invar* tan, brown || *m* Havana cigar || (*cap*) *f—La* Havane Havana
hâve * [αv] *adj* haggard, peaked
havir * [avir] *tr* (culin) to sear
havre * [αvr] *m* haven, harbor
havresac * [αvrəsak] *m* haversack, knapsack; tool bag
hawaïen *or* hawaiien [awajɛ̃], [avajɛ̃],
hawaïenne *or* hawaiienne [awajen],

[avajen] *adj* Hawaiian || (*cap*) *m*) Hawaiian
Haye * [e] *f—La Haye* The Hague
H.B.M. [a∫beem] *f* (letterword) (**habitation à bon marché**) low-rent apartment
he * [e], [he] *interj* hey!
heaume * [om] *m* helmet
hebdomadaire [ebdɔmader] *adj & m* weekly
héberger [eberʒe] §38 *tr* to lodge
hébé·té -tée [ebete] *adj* dazed
hébéter [ebete] §10 *tr* to daze, stupefy
hébraïque [ebraik] *adj* Hebrew
hébraï·sant [ebraizα̃] -sante [zα̃t] *mf* Hebraist
hébraïser [ebraize] *tr & intr* to Hebraize
hé·breu [ebrø] (*pl* -breux) *adj masc* Hebrew || *m* Hebrew (*language*); **c'est de l'hébreu pour moi** it's Greek to me || (*cap*) *m* Hebrew (*man*)
hécatombe [ekatɔ̃b] *f* hecatomb
hein * [ɛ̃] *interj* (coll) eh!, what!
hélas * [elas] *interj* alas!
Hélène [elen *f* Helen
héler * [ele] §10 *tr* to hail, to call
hélice [elis] *f* (aer) propeller; (math) helix spiral; (naut) screw
hélicoptère [elikɔpter] *m* helicopter
héliport [elipɔr *m* heliport
hélium [eljɔm] *m* helium
hélix [eliks] *m* helix
hellène [elen] *adj* Hellenic || (*cap*) *mf* Hellene
helvétique [elvetik] *adj* Swiss
hématie [emati] *f* red blood corpuscle
hémisphere [emisfer] *m* hemisphere
hémistiche [emisti∫] *m* hemistich
hémoglobine [emɔglɔbin] *f* hemoglobin
hémophilie [emɔfili] *f* hemophilia
hémorragie [emɔraʒi] *f* hemorrhage
hémorroïdes [emɔrɔid] *fpl* hemorrhoids
hémostatique [emɔstatik] *adj* hemostatic || *m* hemostat, hemostat
henné [enne] *m* henna
hennir * [enir] *intr* to neigh, whinny
hennissement * [enismα̃] *m* neigh, whinny
Henri [α̃ri], * [α̃ri] *m* Henry
héraldique [eraldik] *adj* heraldic
héraut * [ero] *m* herald
herbe [erb] *f* grass; lawn; herb; **couper l'herbe sous le pied de qn** (coll) to pull the rug from under s.o.'s feet; **en herbe** unripe; budding; **fines herbes** herbs for seasoning; **herbe à la puce** (Canad) poison ivy; **herbe aux chats** catnip; **herbes médicinales** *or* **officinales** (pharm) herbs; **herbes potagères** potherbs; **mauvaise herbe** weed
her·beux [erbø] -beuse [bøz] *adj* grassy
herboristerie [erbɔristri] *f* herb shop
her·bu -bue [erby] *adj* grassy
herculéen [erkyleɛ̃] herculéenne [erkyleen] *adj* herculean
hère * [er] *m* wretch
héréditaire [erediter] *adj* hereditary
hérédité [eredite] *f* heredity
hérésie [erezi] *f* heresy
hérétique [eretik] *adj & mf* heretic

héris·sé héris·sée *[erise] *adj* bristly; shaggy; prickly; surly

hérisser *[erise] *tr & intr* to bristle

hérisson *[eris5] *m* hedgehog

héritage [erita3] *m* heritage; inheritance

hériter [erite] *tr* to inherit || *intr* to inherit; **hériter de** to become the heir of; to inherit, to come into

héri·tier [eritje] **-tière** [tjɛr] *mf* heir || *f* heiress

hermétique [ermetik] *adj* hermetic(al), airtight; (fig) obscure

hermine [ermin] *f* ermine

herminette [erminɛt] *f* adze

hernie *[ɛrni] *f* hernia

her·nieux *[ɛrnjø] **-nieuse** [njøz] *adj* ruptured

héroïne [erɔin] *f* heroine; *(drug)* heroin

héroïque [erɔik] *adj* heroic

héroïsme [erɔism] *m* heroism

héron *[erɔ̃] *m* heron

héros *[ero] *m* hero

herse *[ɛrs] *f* harrow; portcullis; **les herses** (theat) stage lights

herser *[ɛrse] *tr* to harrow

hési·tant [ezitɑ̃] **-tante** [tɑ̃t] *adj* hesitant

hésitation [ezitasjɔ̃] *f* hesitation

hésiter [ezite] *intr* to hesitate

hétéroclite [eterɔklit] *adj* unusual, odd

hétérodoxe [eterɔdɔks] *adj* heterodox

hétérodyne [eterɔdin] *adj* heterodyne

hétérogène [eterɔʒɛn] *adj* heterogeneous

hêtre *[ɛtr] *m* beech, beech tree

heur [œr] *m* pleasure; **heur et malheur** joys and sorrows

heure [œr] *f* hour; time *(of day)*; o'clock; **à la bonne heure!** fine!; **à l'heure** on time; by the hour, per hour; **à l'heure juste, à l'heure sonnante** on the hour; **à tout à l'heure!** see you later!; **à toute heure** at any time; **de bonne heure** early; **heure d'été** daylight-saving time; **heure H** zero hour; **heure légale** twelve-month daylight time (standard time); **heure militaire** sharp, e.g., **huit heures, heure militaire** eight sharp; **heures d'affluence** rush hours; **heures de consultation** office hours; **heures de pointe** rush hours; **heures d'ouverture** business hours; **heures supplémentaires** overtime; **l'heure du déjeuner** lunch hour; **tout à l'heure in a little while; a little while ago

heu·reux [œrø], [ørø] **-reuse** [røz] *adj* happy, pleased; lucky, fortunate

heurt *[œr] *m* knock, bump; clash; bruise; **sans heurt** without a hitch

heur·té -tée *[œrte] *adj* clashing *(colors)*; abrupt *(style)*

heurter *[œrte] *tr* to knock against, to bump into; to antagonize || *intr*—**heurter contre** to bump into || *ref* to clash, to collide; **se heurter à** to come up against

heurtoir *[œrtwar] *m* door knocker; (rr) buffer

hi *[i] *m invar*—**hi hi hi!** ho ho ho!;

pousser des hi et des ha to sputter in amazement

hiatus [jatys], *[jatys] *m* hiatus

hiberner [iberne] *intr* to hibernate

hibiscus [ibiskys] *m* hibiscus

hi·bou *[ibu] *m (pl* **-boux)** owl

hic *[ik] *m*—**voilà le hic!** (coll) there's the rub!

hi·deux *[idø] **-deuse** [døz] *adj* hideous

hie *[i] *f* pile driver

hièble [jɛbl] *f* (bot) elder

hié·mal -male [jemal] *adj (pl* **-maux** [mo]) winter

hier [jɛr] *adv & m* yesterday; **hier soir** last evening, last night

hiérarchie *[jerarʃi] *f* hierarchy

hiéroglyphe [jerɔglif] *m* hieroglyphic

hiéroglyphique [jerɔglifik] *adj* hieroglyphic

hila·rant [ilarɑ̃] **-rante** [rɑ̃t] *adj* hilarious; laughing *(gas)*

hilare [ilar] *adj* hilarious

hin·dou -doue [ɛ̃du] *adj* Hindu || *(cap)* *mf* Hindu

hippique [ipik] *adj* horse (race, show)

hippisme [ipism] *m* horse racing

hippodrome [ipɔdrom] *m* hippodrome, race track

hippopotame [ipɔpotam] *m* hippopotamus

hirondelle [irɔ̃dɛl] *f* (orn) swallow; (coll) bicycle cop

hispanique [ispanik] *adj* Hispanic

hispani·sant [ispanizɑ̃] **-sante** [zɑ̃t] *mf* Hispanist

hisser *[ise] *tr* to hoist, to raise

histoire [istwar] *f* history; story; **faire des histoires à** (coll) to make trouble for; **histoire à dormir debout** (coll) tall tale; **histoire de rire** (coll) just for fun; **histoire de s'informer** (coll) out of curiosity; **pas d'histoires** (coll) no fuss

histologie [istɔlɔʒi] *f* histology

histo·rien [istɔrjɛ̃] **-rienne** [rjɛn] *mf* historian

historier [istɔrje] *tr* to illustrate, adorn

historique [istɔrik] *adj* historic(al) || *m* historical account

histrion [istrijɔ̃] *m* ham actor

hiver [ivɛr] *m* winter

hiver·nal -nale [ivɛrnal] *adj (pl* **-naux** [no]) winter

hiverner [ivɛrne] *intr* to winter

H.L.M. a/elem] *m* (letterword) (habitation à loyer modéré) low-rent apartment

ho *[o], [ho] *interj* hey there!; what!

hobe·reau *[ɔbro] *m (pl* **-reaux)** (orn) hobby; (coll) squire

hoche *[ɔʃ] *f* nick on a blade

hochement *[ɔʃmɑ̃] *m* shake, toss

hochepot *[ɔʃpo] *m* (culin) hotchpotch

hochequeue *[ɔʃkø] *m* (orn) wagtail

hocher *[ɔʃe] *tr* to shake; to nod

hochet *[ɔʃɛ] *m* rattle (toy); bauble

hockey *[ɔkɛ] *m* hockey; **hockey sur glace** ice hockey

hoirie [wari] *f* legacy

holà *[ɔla], [hɔla] *m invar*—**mettre le**

holà à (coll) to put a stop to || *interj* hey!; stop!

holding *[ɔldiŋ] *m* holding company

hold-up *[ɔldœp] *m invar* holdup

hollan·dais *[ɔlɑ̃dɛ] **-daise** [dɛz] *adj* Dutch || *m* Dutch (*language*) || (*cap*) *mf* Hollander (*person*)

hollande *[ɔlɑ̃d] *m* Edam cheese || *f* Holland (*linen*) || (*cap*) *f* Holland; **la Hollande** Holland

holocauste [ɔlɔkost] *m* holocaust

homard *[ɔmar] *m* lobster

home *[om] *m* home

homélie [ɔmeli] *f* homily

homéopathie [ɔmeɔpati] *f* homeopathy

homicide [ɔmisid] *adj* homicidal || *mf* homicide (*person*) || *m* homicide (*act*)

hommage [ɔmaʒ] *m* homage; **hommage de l'auteur** (formula in presenting complimentary copies) with the compliments of the author; **hommages** respects, compliments

hommasse [ɔmas] *adj* mannish (*woman*)

homme [ɔm] *m* man; **brave homme** fine man, honest man; **être homme à** to be the man to, to be capable of; **homme à tout faire** jack-of-all-trades; handyman; **homme d'affaires** businessman; **homme d'armes** man-at-arms; **homme de droite** rightist; **homme de gauche** leftist; **homme d'église** churchman; **homme de guerre** or **d'épée** military man; **homme de la rue** man in the street, first comer; **homme de l'espace** spaceman; **homme de lettres** man of letters; **homme de paille** figurehead, stooge; **homme de peine** workingman; **homme des bois** orang-utan; **homme d'État** statesman; **homme de troupe** (*pl* **hommes des troupes)** (mil) enlisted man, private; **homme d'expédition** go-getter; **homme d'intérieur** homebody; **homme du monde** man of the world; **homme galant** ladies' man; **hommes de bien** men of good will; **honnête homme** upright man; man of culture, gentleman; **jeune homme** young man; teen-age boy; **le vieil homme** (Bib) the old Adam; **un homme à la mer!** man overboard!

homme-grenouille [ɔmgrənuj] *m* (*pl* **hommes-grenouilles)** frogman

homme-sandwich [ɔmsɑ̃dwitʃ], [ɔmsɑ̃dwiʃ] *m* (*pl* **hommes-sandwichs)** sandwich man

homogène [ɔmɔʒɛn] *adj* homogeneous

homogénéiser [ɔmɔʒeneize] *tr* to homogenize

homologation [ɔmɔlɔgasjɔ̃] *f* validation

homologue [ɔmɔlɔg] *adj* homologous || *mf* (fig) opposite number

homologuer [ɔmɔlɔge] *tr* to confirm, endorse; to probate (*e.g., a will*)

homonyme [ɔmɔnim] *adj* homonymous || *m* homonym; namesake

homosexuel homosexuelle [ɔmɔseksɥɛl] *adj & mf* homosexual

hongre *[ɔ̃gr] *adj* gelded || *m* gelding

hongrer *[ɔ̃gre] *tr* to geld

Hongrie *[ɔ̃gri] *f* Hungary; **la Hongrie** Hungary

hon·grois *[ɔ̃grwa] **-groise** [grwaz] *adj* Hungarian || *m* Hungarian (*language*) || (*cap*) *mf* Hungarian (*person*)

honnête [ɔnɛt] *adj* honest, honorable

honnêteté [ɔnɛtte] *f* honesty, uprightness

honneur [ɔnœr] *m* honor; **faire honneur à sa parole** to keep one's word

honnir *[ɔnir] *tr* to shame

honorabilité [ɔnɔrabilite] *f* respectability

honorable [ɔnɔrabl] *adj* honorable

honoraire [ɔnɔrɛr] *adj* honorary, emeritus || **honoraires** *mpl* honorarium, fee

honorer [ɔnɔre] *tr* to honor || *ref* **s'honorer de** to pride oneself on

honorifique [ɔnɔrifik] *adj* honorific

honte *[ɔ̃t] *f* shame; **avoir honte** to be ashamed; **faire honte à qn** to make s.o. ashamed; **faire honte à ses parents** to be a disgrace to one's parents; **fausse honte** bashfulness; **sans honte** unashamedly

hon·teux *[ɔ̃tø] **-teuse** [tøz] *adj* ashamed; shameful

hop *[ɔp] *interj* go!, off with you!

hôpi·tal [ɔpital] *m* (*pl* **-taux** [to]) hospital; charity hospital

hoquet *[ɔke] *m* hiccough

hoqueter *[ɔkte] §34 *intr* to hiccough

horaire [ɔrɛr] *adj* hourly, by hour || *m* timetable; schedule

horde *[ɔrd] *f* horde

horion *[ɔrjɔ̃] *m* punch, clout

horizon [ɔrizɔ̃] *m* horizon

horizon·tal -tale [ɔrizɔ̃tal] (*pl* **-taux** [to] **-tales**) *adj & f* horizontal

horloge [ɔrlɔʒ] *f* clock

horlo·ger [ɔrlɔʒe] **-gère** [ʒɛr] *adj* clockmaking, watchmaking || *mf* clockmaker, watchmaker

horlogerie [ɔrlɔʒri] *f* clockmaking, watchmaking; **d'horlogerie** clockwork

hormis *[ɔrmi] *prep* (lit) except for

hormone [ɔrmɔn] *f* hormone

horoscope [ɔrɔskɔp] *m* horoscope; **tirer l'horoscope de qn** to cast s.o.'s horoscope

horreur [ɔrœr] *f* horror; **avoir horreur de** to have a horror of; **commettre des horreurs** to commit atrocities; **dire des horreurs** to say obscene things; **dire des horreurs de** to say shocking things about

horrible [ɔribl] *adj* horrible

horrifier [ɔrifje] *tr* to horrify

horripi·lant *[ɔrripilɑ̃] **-lante** [lɑ̃t] (coll) *adj* hair-raising

horripilation [ɔrripilasjɔ̃] *f* gooseflesh; (coll) exasperation

horripiler *[ɔrripile] *tr* to give gooseflesh to; (coll) to exasperate

hors *[ɔr] *prep* out, beyond, outside; except, except for, save; **hors de** out of, outside of; **hors de soi** beside oneself, frantic; **hors d'ici!** get out!; **hors tout** overall

hors-bord *[ɔrbɔr] m invar* outboard (*motor or motorboat*)

hors-caste *[ɔrkast] mf invar* outcaste

hors-concours *[ɔrkɔ̃kur] adj invar* excluded from competition ‖ *m invar* contestant excluded from competition

hors-d'œuvre *[ɔrdœvr] m invar* hors-d'œuvre

hors-jeu *[ɔrjø] m invar* offside position

hors-la-loi *[ɔrlalwa] m invar* outlaw

hors-ligne *[ɔrliɲ] adj invar* (coll) exceptional ‖ *m invar* roadside

hors-texte [ɔrtɛks] *m invar* (bb) insert

hortensia [ɔrtɑ̃sja] *m* hydrangea

horticole [ɔrtikɔl] *adj* horticultural

horticulture [ɔrtikyltyr] *f* horticulture

hospice [ɔspis] *m* hospice; home (*for the old, infirm, orphaned, etc.*)

hospita·lier [ɔspitalje] **-lière** [ljɛr] *adj* hospitable; hospital ‖ *mf* hospital employee

hospitaliser [ɔspitalize] *tr* to hospitalize

hospitalité [ɔspitalite] *f* hospitality

hostie [ɔsti] *f* (eccl) Host

hostile [ɔstil] *adj* hostile

hostilité [ɔstilite] *f* hostility

hôte [ot] *m* host; guest

hôtel [otel], [ɔtɛl] *m* hotel; mansion; **hôtel des Monnaies** mint; **hôtel des Postes** main post office; **hôtel de ville** city hall; **hôtel meublé** rooming house, residential hotel

hôtel-Dieu [oteldjø], [ɔteldjø] *m* (*pl* **hôtels-Dieu**) city hospital

hôte·lier [otalje], [ɔtalje] **-lière** [ljɛr] *adj* hotel (*business*) ‖ *mf* hotel manager

hôtellerie [otelri], [ɔtelri] *f* hotel business; fine restaurant; hostelry, hostel

hôtesse [otes] *f* hostess; **hôtesse de l'air** air hostess, stewardess

hotte *[ɔt] f* basket (*carried on back*); hod (*of mason*); hood (*of chimney*)

hou *[u] interj* oh no!

houache *[wa] f* wake (*of ship*)

houblon *[ubl3] m* hop (*vine*); hops (*dried flowers*)

houe *[u] f* hoe

houer *[we] tr* to hoe

houille *[uj] f* coal; **houille blanche** water power; **houille bleue** tide power; **houille d'or** energy from the sun; **houille grasse** or **collante** soft coal; **houille incolore** wind power; **houille maigre** or **éclatante** hard coal; **houille rouge** energy from the heat of the earth

houil·ler *[uje]* **houil·lère** *[ujer] adj* coal-bearing, carboniferous; coal (*industry*) ‖ *f* coal mine

houilleur *[ujœr] m* coal miner

houle *[ul] f* swell

houlette *[ulet] f* crook (*of shepherd*); (hort) trowel

hou·leux *[ulø]* **-leuse** [løz] *adj* swelling (*sea*); (fig) stormy, turbulent

houp *[up], [hup] interj* go to it!

houppe *[up] f* tuft; crest; tassel; **houppe à poudre** powder puff

houppelande *[uplɑ̃d] f* greatcoat

houppette *[upet] f* tuft; powder puff

hourra *[ura], [hura] m*—**pousser trois hourras** to give three cheers ‖ *interj* hurrah!

hourvari *[urvari] m* call to the hounds; (coll) uproar

houspiller *[uspije] tr* to jostle, knock around; to rake over the coals, to tell off

housse *[us] f* slipcover; cover (*e.g., for typewriter*); garment bag; housing, horsecloth; (aut) seat cover

housser *[use] tr* to dust (*with feather duster*)

houssine *[usin] f* rug beater; switch

houssoir *[uswar] m* feather duster; whisk broom

houx *[u] m* holly

hoyau *[wajo] m* (*pl* **hoyaux**) mattock; pickax

hublot *[yblo] m* porthole

huche *[yʃ] f* hutch; bin

hucher *[yʃe] tr* to call, to shout to

hue *[y] interj* gee!; gee up! **tirer à hue et à dia** (fig) to pull in opposite directions

huée *[ye] f* hoot, boo

huer *[ye] tr & intr* to hoot, to boo

hugue·not *[ygno]* **-note** [nɔt] *adj* Huguenot ‖ *f* pipkin ‖ (cap) *mf* Huguenot (*person*)

huile *[ɥil] f* oil; big shot; **d'huile** calm, e.g., **mer d'huile** calm sea; **huile de coude** elbow grease; **huile de foie de morue** cod-liver oil; **huile de freins** brake fluid; **huile de ricin** castor oil; **huile lourde** diesel fuel; **huile solaire** suntan oil; **les huiles** (coll) the VIP's; **sentir l'huile** (fig) to smell of midnight oil; **verser de l'huile sur le feu** (fig) to add fuel to the fire

huiler [ɥile] *tr* to oil; to grease

hui·leux [ɥilø] **-leuse** [løz] *adj* oily; greasy

huis *[ɥi] m* (archaic) door; **à huis clos** behind closed doors; (law) in camera; **à huis ouvert** spectators admitted ‖ *[ɥi] m*—**demander le huis clos** to request a closed-door session

huisserie [ɥisri] *f* doorframe

huissier [ɥisje] *m* doorman; usher (*before a person of rank*); **huissier audiencier** bailiff; **huissier exploitant** process server

huit *[ɥi(t)] adj & pron* eight; the Eighth, e.g., **Jean huit** John the Eighth; **huit heures** eight o'clock ‖ *m* eight; eighth (*in dates*); **faire des huit** to cut figures of eight (*in figure skating*)

huitain *[ɥitɛ̃] m* eight-line verse

huitaine *[ɥiten] f* (grouping of) eight; week; **à huitaine** the same day next week; **une huitaine** of about eight

huitième *[ɥitjem] adj, pron (masc, fem), & m* eighth

huître [ɥitrə] *f* oyster

huit-reflets *[ɥirəfle] m invar* top hat

huî·trier [ɥitrije] **-trière** [trijer] *adj* oyster (*industry*) ‖ *m* (orn) oyster-catcher ‖ *f* oyster bed

hulotte *[ylɔt] *f* hoot owl
hululer *[ylyle] *intr* to hoot
hum *[œm], [hœm] *interj* hum!
hu·main [ymɛ̃] **-maine** [men] *adj* human; humane
humaniste [ymanist] *adj & m* humanist
humanitaire [ymaniter] *adj & mf* humanitarian
humanité [ymanite] *f* humanity; **humanités (classiques)** humanities (*Greek & Latin classics*); **humanités modernes** humanities, belles-lettres; **humanités scientifiques** liberal studies (*concerned with the observation and classification of facts*)
humble [œ̃bl] *adj* humble
humecter [ymɛkte] *tr* to moisten || *ref* to become damp; **s'humecter le gosier** (slang) to wet one's whistle
humer *[yme] *tr* to suck, to suck up; to sip; to inhale, to breathe in
humérus [ymerys] *m* humerus
humeur [ymœr] *f* humor, body fluid; humor, mood, spirits; **avec humeur** testily; **avoir de l'humeur** to be in a bad mood; **être de bonne humeur** to be in a good humor
humide [ymid] *adj* humid, damp; wet
humidifier [ymidifje] *tr* to humidify
humidité [ymidite] *f* humidity
humi·liant [ymiljɑ̃] **-liante** [ljɑ̃t] *adj* humiliating
humiliation [ymiljɑsjɔ̃] *f* humiliation
humilier [ymilje] *tr* to humiliate, to humble || *ref* to humble oneself
humilité [ymilite] *f* humility
humoriste [ymɔrist] *adj* humorous (*writer*) || *mf* humorist
humoristique [ymɔristik] *adj* humorous
humour [ymur] *m* humor; **humour noir** macabre humor, sick humor
humus [ymys] *m* humus
hune *[yn] *f* (naut) top; **hune de vigie** (naut) crow's-nest
huppe *[yp] *f* tuft, crest (*of bird*); (orn) hoopoe
hup·pé -pée *[ype] *adj* tufted, crested; (coll) smart, stylish
hure *[yr] *f* head (*of boar, salmon, etc.*); (culin) headcheese
hurlement *[yrlmɑ̃] *m* howl, roar; howling, roaring (*e.g., of wind*)
hurler *[yrle] *tr* to cry out, yell || *intr* to howl, to roar
hur·leur *[yrlœr] **-leuse** [løz] *adj* howling || *mf* howler || *m* (zool) howler
hurluberlu [yrlyberly] *m* (coll) scatterbrain
hu·ron [yrɔ̃] **-ronne** [rɔn] *adj* (coll) boorish, uncouth || *mf* (coll) boor
hurricane *[urikan], *[œriken] *m* hurricane
hutte *[yt] *f* hut, cabin
hyacinthe [jasɛ̃t] *f* hyacinth (*stone*)
hya·lin [jalɛ̃] **-line** [lin] *adj* glassy
hybride [ibrid] *adj & m* hybrid
hydrate [idrat] *m* hydrate
hydrater [idrate] *tr & ref* to hydrate

hydraulique [idrolik] *adj* hydraulic || *f* hydraulics
hydravion [idravjɔ̃] *m* hydroplane
hydre [idr] *f* hydra
hydrocarbure [idrɔkarbyr] *m* hydrocarbon
hydro-électrique [idrɔelɛktrik] *adj* hydroelectric
hydrofoil [idrɔfɔjl] *m* hydrofoil
hydrofuge [idrɔfyʒ] *adj* waterproof
hydrofuger [idrɔfyʒe] §38 *tr* to waterproof
hydrogène [idrɔʒen] *m* hydrogen
hydroglisseur [idrɔglisœr] *m* speedboat
hydromètre [idrɔmetr] *m* hydrometer || *f* (ent) water spider
hydrophile [idrɔfil] *adj* absorbent || *m* —**hydrophile brun** (ent) water devil
hydrophobie [idrɔfɔbi] *f* hydrophobia
hydropisie [idrɔpizi] *f* dropsy
hydroscope [idrɔskɔp] *m* dowser
hydroxyde [idrɔksid] *m* hydroxide
hyène [jen] *f* hyena
hygiène [iʒjɛn] *f* hygiene
hygiénique [iʒjenik] *adj* hygienic
hymnaire [imner] *m* hymnal
hymne [imnə], [im] *m* hymn, ode, anthem; **hymne national** national anthem || *f* (eccl) hymn, canticle
hyperacidité [iperasidite] *f* hyperacidity
hyperbole [iperbɔl] *f* (math) hyperbola; (rhet) hyperbole
hypersensible [ipersɑ̃sibl] *adj* hypersensitive, supersensitive
hypersensi·tif [ipersɑ̃sitif] **-tive** [tiv] *adj* hypersensitive, supersensitive
hypertension [ipertɑ̃sjɔ̃] *f* high blood pressure, hypertension
hypnose [ipnoz] *f* hypnosis
hypnotique [ipnɔtik] *adj & m* hypnotic
hypnotiser [ipnɔtize] *tr* to hypnotize || *ref* —**s'hypnotiser sur** (fig) to be hypnotized by
hypnoti·seur [ipnɔtizœr] **-seuse** [zøz] *m* hypnotist
hypnotisme [ipnɔtism] *m* hypnotism
hypocondriaque [ipɔkɔ̃drijak] *adj & mf* hypochondriac
hypocrisie [ipɔkrizi] *f* hypocrisy
hypocrite [ipɔkrit] *adj* hypocritical || *mf* hypocrite
hypodermique [ipɔdermik] *adj* hypodermic
hyposulfite [ipɔsylfit] *m* hyposulfite
hypotension [ipɔtɑ̃sjɔ̃] *f* low blood pressure
hypoténuse [ipɔtenyz] *f* hypotenuse
hypothèque [ipɔtek] *f* mortgage; **prendre une hypothèque sur** to put a mortgage on; **purger une hypothèque** to pay off a mortgage
hypothéquer [ipɔteke] §10 *tr* to mortgage
hypothèse [ipɔtez] *f* hypothesis
hypothétique [ipɔtetik] *adj* hypothetic(al)
hystérie [isteri] *f* hysteria
hystérique [isterik] *adj* hysteric(al)

I

I, i [i], *[I] *m invar* ninth letter of the French alphabet
iambique [jābik] *adj* iambic
ibé·rien [iberjɛ̃] -**rienne** [rjen] *adj* Iberian || (*cap*) *mf* Iberian
ibérique [iberik] *adj* Iberian
iceberg [isberg] *m* iceberg
ichtyologie [iktjɔlɔʒi] *f* ichthyology
ici [isi] *adv* here; this is, e.g., **ici Paris** (rad, telv) this is Paris; **ici Robert** (telp) this is Robert; **d'ici** hereabouts; from today; **d'ici demain** before tomorrow; **d'ici là** between now and then, in the meantime; **d'ici peu** before long; **jusqu'ici** up to now, hitherto; **par ici** this way, through here
ici-bas [isiba] *adv* here below, on earth
icône [ikon] *f* icon
iconoclaste [ikɔnɔklast] *adj* iconoclastic || *mf* iconoclast
iconographie [ikɔnografi] *f* iconography; pictures, pictorial material
iconoscope [ikɔnɔskɔp] *m* iconoscope
ictère [ikter] *m* jaundice
ictérique [ikterik] *adj* jaundiced
idéal idéale [ideal] *adj & m* (*pl* **idéaux** [ideo] or **idéals**) ideal
idéaliser [idealize] *tr* idealize
idéaliste [idealist] *adj & mf* idealist
idée [ide] *f* idea; mind, head; opinion, esteem; (coll) shade, touch; **changer d'idée** to change one's mind
identification [idātifikasjɔ̃] *f* identification
identifier [idātifje] *tr* to identify
identique [idātik] *adj* identic(al)
identité [idātite] *f* identity
idéologie [ideɔlɔʒi] *f* ideology; (pej) utopianism
idéologique [ideɔlɔʒik] *adj* ideologic(al); conceptual
ides [id] *fpl* ides
idiomatique [idjɔmatik] *adj* idiomatic
idiome [idjom] *m* idiom, language
idiosyncrasie [idjɔsɛ̃krazi] *f* idiosyncrasy
i·diot [idjo] -**diote** [djɔt] *adj* idiotic || *mf* idiot
idiotie [idjɔsi] *f* idiocy
idiotisme [idjɔtism] *m* idiom, idiomatic expression
idolâtrer [idɔlatre] *tr* to idolize
idolâtrie [idɔlatri] *f* idolatry
idole [idɔl] *f* idol
idylle [idil] *f* idyll; romance, love affair
idyllique [idilik] *adj* idyllic
if [if] *m* yew
IGAME [igam] *m* (acronym) (**I**nspecteur **G**énéral de l'**A**dministration en **M**ission **E**xtraordinaire) head prefect
igname [iɲam], [iŋam] *f* yam
ignare [iɲar] *adj* ignorant
ig·né -**née** [igne] *adj* igneous
ignifuge [ignifyʒ] *adj* fireproof || *m* fireproofing
ignifuger [ignifyʒe] §38 *tr* to fireproof

ignition [ignisjɔ̃] *f* ignition; red heat (of metal)
ignoble [iɲɔbl] *adj* ignoble; disgusting
ignomi·nieux [iɲɔminjø] -**nieuse** [njøz] *adj* ignominious
ignorance [iɲɔrɑ̃s] *f* ignorance
igno·rant [iɲɔrɑ̃] -**rante** [rɑ̃t] *adj* ignorant || *mf* ignoramus
ignorer [iɲɔre] *tr* not to know, to be ignorant of; to be unacquainted with
il [il] §87
île [il] *f* island, isle; **les îles Normandes** the Channel Islands
illé·gal -**gale** [illegal] *adj* (*pl* -**gaux** [go]) illegal
illégitime [illeʒitim] *adj* illegitimate; unjustified
illet·tré -**trée** [illetre] *adj & mf* illiterate
illicite [illisit] *adj* illicit; foul (*blow*)
illimi·té -**tée** [illimite] *adj* unlimited
illisible [illizibl] *adj* illegible; unreadable (*book*)
illogique [illɔʒik] *adj* illogical
illumination [illyminasjɔ̃] *f* illumination
illumi·né -**née** [illymine] *adj & mf* fanatic, visionary
illuminer [illymine] *tr* to illuminate
illusion [illyzjɔ̃] *f* illusion; **illusion de la vue** optical illusion; **se faire des illusions** to indulge in wishful thinking
illusionner [illyzjɔne] *tr* to delude || *ref* to delude oneself
illusionniste [illyzjɔnist] *mf* magician
illusoire [illyzwar] *adj* illusory, illusive
illustra·teur [illystratœr] *m* illustrator
illustration [illystrasjɔ̃] *f* illustration; glorification; glory; celebrity
illustre [illystr] *adj* illustrious, renowned
illus·tré -**trée** [illystre] *adj* illustrated || *m* illustrated magazine
illustrer [illystre] *tr* to illustrate || *ref* to distinguish oneself
îlot [ilo] *m* small island, isle; block (of houses)
ils [il] §87
image [imaʒ] *f* image; picture; **images** imagery
imager [imaʒe] §38 *tr* to embellish with metaphors, to color
imagerie [imaʒri] *f*—**imagerie d'Épinal** cardboard cutouts
imaginaire [imaʒiner] *adj* imaginary
imagination [imaʒinasjɔ̃] *f* imagination
imaginer [imaʒine] *tr* to imagine; to invent || *intr* to imagine; **imaginer de** + *inf* to have the idea of + *ger* || *ref* to imagine oneself; (with *dat* of *reflex pron*) to imagine
imbattable [ɛ̃batabl] *adj* unbeatable
imbat·tu -**tue** [ɛ̃baty] *adj* unbeaten
imbécile [ɛ̃besil] *adj & mf* imbecile
imbécillité [ɛ̃besilite] *f* imbecility
imberbe [ɛ̃berb] *adj* beardless
imbiber [ɛ̃bibe] *tr & ref* to soak; **s'imbiber de** to soak up; to be imbued with

imbri·qué -quée [ɛbrike] adj overlapping

imbrisable [ɛbrizabl] adj unbreakable

imbrûlable [ɛbrylabl] adj fireproof

im·bu -bue [ɛby] adj—imbu de imbued with, steeped in

imita·teur [imitatœr] -trice [tris] mf imitator

imitation [imitasjɔ̃] f imitation

imiter [imite] tr to imitate

immacu·lé -lée [immakyle] adj immaculate

immangeable [ɛmɑ̃ʒabl] adj inedible

immanquable [ɛmɑ̃kabl] adj infallible; inevitable

immaté·riel -rielle [immaterjel] adj immaterial

immatriculation [immatrikylasjɔ̃] f registration; enrollment

immatriculer [immatrikyle] tr to register

immature [immatyr] adj unmatured

immé·diat [immedja] -diate [djat] adj immediate

immédiatement [immedjatmɑ̃] adv immediately

immémo·rial -riale [immemorjal] adj (pl -riaux [rjo]) immemorial

immense [immɑ̃s] adj immense

immensurable [immɑ̃syrabl] adj immeasurable, immensurable

immerger [immerʒe] §38 tr to immerse, to dip; to throw overboard; to lay (a cable)

imméri·té -tée [immerite] adj undeserved

immersion [immersjɔ̃] f immersion

immettable [ɛmetabl] adj unwearable

immeuble [immœbl] adj real, e.g., biens immeubles real estate || m building, apartment building

immi·grant [immigrɑ̃] -grante [grɑ̃t] adj & mf immigrant

immigration [immigrasjɔ̃] f immigration

immi·gré -grée [immigre] adj & mf immigrant

immigrer [immigre] intr to immigrate

immi·nent [imminɑ̃] -nente [nɑ̃t] adj imminent, impending

immiscer [immise] §51 ref—s'immiscer dans to interfere with, to meddle with

immixtion [immiksjɔ̃] f interference

immobile [immobil] adj motionless; immobile (resolute); dead (typewriter key)

immobi·lier [immobilje] -lière [ljer] adj real-estate, property; real, e.g., biens immobiliers real estate

immobiliser [immobilize] tr to immobilize; to tie up || ref to come to a stop

immodé·ré -rée [immodere] adj immoderate

immonde [immɔ̃d] adj foul, filthy; (eccl) unclean

immondices [immɔ̃dis] fpl garbage, refuse

immo·ral -rale [immoral] adj (pl -raux [ro]) immoral

immortaliser [immortalize] tr to immortalize

immor·tel -telle [immortel] adj & mf immortal || f (bot) everlasting

immoti·vé -vée [immotive] adj groundless

immuable [immɥabl] adj changeless

immuniser [immynize] tr to immunize

immunité [immynite] f immunity

im·pair -paire [ɛper] adj odd, uneven || m (coll) blunder

impardonnable [ɛpardonabl] adj unpardonable

impar·fait [ɛparfe] -faite [fet] adj & m imperfect

imparité [ɛparite] f inequality, disparity

impar·tial -tiale [ɛparsjal] adj (pl -tiaux [sjo]) impartial

impartir [ɛpartir] tr to grant

impasse [ɛpas] f blind alley, dead-end street; impasse, deadlock; (cards) finesse; faire l'impasse à (cards) to finesse

impassible [ɛpasibl] adj impassible; impassive (look, face, etc.)

impatience [ɛpasjɑ̃s] f impatience; impatiences (coll) attack of nerves

impa·tient [ɛpasjɑ̃] -tiente [sjɑ̃t] adj impatient

impatienter [ɛpasjɑ̃te] tr to make impatient || ref to lose patience

impatroniser [ɛpatronize] ref to take charge; to take hold

impavide [ɛpavid] adj fearless

impayable [ɛpejabl] adj (coll) priceless, very funny

impa·yé -yée [ɛpeje] adj unpaid

impeccable [ɛpekabl] adj impeccable

impénétrable [ɛpenetrabl] adj impenetrable

impéni·tent [ɛpenitɑ̃] -tente [tɑ̃t] adj impenitent, obdurate, inveterate

impensable [ɛpɑ̃sabl] adj unthinkable

imper [ɛper] m (coll) raincoat

impéra·tif [ɛperatif] -tive [tiv] adj & m imperative

impératrice [ɛperatris] f empress

imperceptible [ɛperseptibl] adj imperceptible; negligible

imperdable [ɛperdabl] adj unlosable

imperfection [ɛperfeksjɔ̃] f imperfection, defect

impé·rial -riale [ɛperjal] adj (pl -riaux [rjo]) imperial || f goatee; upper deck (of bus, coach, etc.)

impérialiste [ɛperjalist] adj & mf imperialist

impé·rieux [ɛperjø] -rieuse [rjøz] adj imperious, haughty; imperative, urgent

impérissable [ɛperisabl] adj imperishable

impéritie [ɛperisi] f incompetence

imperméabiliser [ɛpermeabilize] tr to waterproof

imperméable [ɛpermeabl] adj waterproof; impervious || m raincoat

imperson·nel -nelle [ɛpersonel] adj impersonal; commonplace; ordinary

imperti·nent [ɛpertinɑ̃] -nente [nɑ̃t] adj impertinent || mf impertinent person

impé·trant [ɛpetrɑ̃] -trante [trɑ̃t] mf holder (of a title or degree)

impé·tueux [ɛ̃petɥø] **-tueuse** [tɥøz] *adj* impetuous

impie [ɛ̃pi] *adj* impious, ungodly; blasphemous || *mf* unbeliever; blasphemer

impiété [ɛ̃pjete] *f* impiety; disrespect

impitoyable [ɛ̃pitwajabl] *adj* unmerciful

implanter [ɛ̃plɑ̃te] *tr* to implant; to introduce || *ref* to take root; **s'implanter chez** (coll) to thrust oneself upon

implication [ɛ̃plikɑsjɔ̃] *f* implication

implicite [ɛ̃plisit] *adj* implicit

impliquer [ɛ̃plike] *tr* to implicate; to imply

implorer [ɛ̃plɔre] *tr* to implore

imployable [ɛ̃plwajabl] *adj* pitiless; inflexible

impo·li -lie [ɛ̃pɔli] *adj* impolite

impolitique [ɛ̃pɔlitik] *adj* ill-advised

impondérable [ɛ̃pɔ̃derabl] *adj & m* imponderable

impopulaire [ɛ̃pɔpyler] *adj* unpopular

impopularité [ɛ̃pɔpylarite] *f* unpopularity

importance [ɛ̃pɔrtɑ̃s] *f* importance; size; **d'importance** large, of consequence; thoroughly, very hard

impor·tant [ɛ̃pɔrtɑ̃] **-tante** [tɑ̃t] *adj* important; large, considerable || *m* main thing; **faire l'important** (coll) to act big

importa·teur [ɛ̃pɔrtatœr] **-trice** [tris] *mf* importer

importer [ɛ̃pɔrte] *tr* to import || *intr* to matter; to be important; **n'importe** no matter, never mind; **n'importe comment** any way; **n'importe où** anywhere; **n'importe quand** anytime; **n'importe quel . . .** any . . . ; **n'importe qui** anybody; **n'importe quoi** anything; **peu m'importe** it doesn't matter to me; **qu'importe?** what does it matter?

impor·tun [ɛ̃pɔrtœ̃] **-tune** [tyn] *adj* bothersome || *mf* pest, nuisance

importuner [ɛ̃pɔrtyne] *tr* to importune

imposable [ɛ̃pozabl] *adj* taxable

impo·sant [ɛ̃pozɑ̃] **-sante** [zɑ̃t] *adj* imposing

impo·sé -sée [ɛ̃poze] *adj* taxed; fixed (*price*) || *mf* taxpayer

imposer [ɛ̃poze] *tr* to impose; to levy a tax on || *intr*—**en imposer à** to make an impression on; to impose on || *ref* to assert oneself; to be indispensable; **s'imposer à** to force itself upon; **s'imposer chez** to foist oneself upon

imposition [ɛ̃pozisjɔ̃] *f* imposition; taxation; laying on, levying

impossible [ɛ̃pɔsibl] *adj* impossible

imposte [ɛ̃pɔst] *f* transom; (archit) impost

imposteur [ɛ̃pɔstœr] *m* impostor

imposture [ɛ̃pɔstyr] *f* imposture

impôt [ɛ̃po] *m* tax; **impôt du sang** military duty; **impôt foncier** property tax; **impôt indirect** sales tax; **impôt retenu à la source** withholding tax; **impôt sur le revenu** income tax

impotence [ɛ̃pɔtɑ̃s] *f* lameness, infirmity

impo·tent [ɛ̃pɔtɑ̃] **-tente** [tɑ̃t] *adj* crippled; bedridden || *mf* cripple

impraticable [ɛ̃pratikabl] *adj* impracticable; impassable (*e.g., road*)

impré·cis [ɛ̃presi] **-cise** [siz] *adj* vague, hazy

imprégner [ɛ̃preɲe] §10 *tr* to impregnate

imprenable [ɛ̃prənabl] *adj* impregnable

impréparation [ɛ̃preparɑsjɔ̃] *f* unpreparedness

impresario [ɛ̃presarjo] *m* impresario

impression [ɛ̃presjɔ̃] *f* impression; printing

impression·nant [ɛ̃presjɔnɑ̃] **impression·nante** [ɛ̃presjɔnɑ̃t] *adj* impressive

impressionner [ɛ̃presjɔne] *tr* to impress, to affect; (phot) to expose

imprévisible [ɛ̃previzibl] *adj* unforeseeable

imprévision [ɛ̃previzjɔ̃] *f* lack of foresight

imprévoyant [ɛ̃prevwajɑ̃] **imprévoyante** [ɛ̃prevwajɑ̃t] *adj* improvident, shortsighted

impré·vu -vue [ɛ̃prevy] *adj & m* unforeseen, unexpected; **sauf imprévu** unless something unforeseen happens

impri·mé -mée [ɛ̃prime] *adj* printed || *m* print, calico; printed work, book; printing (*as opposed to script*); **imprimés** printed matter

imprimer [ɛ̃prime] *tr* to print; to imprint; to impress; to impart (*e.g., movement*)

imprimerie [ɛ̃primri] *f* printing; printing office, print shop

imprimeur [ɛ̃primœr] *m* printer

imprimeur-éditeur [ɛ̃primœreditœr] *m* (*pl* **imprimeurs-éditeurs**) printer and publisher

imprimeur-libraire [ɛ̃primœrlibrer] *m* (*pl* **imprimeurs-libraires**) printer and publisher

imprimeuse [ɛ̃primøz] *f* printing press

improbable [ɛ̃prɔbabl] *adj* improbable

improba·tif [ɛ̃prɔbatif] **-tive** [tiv] *adj* disapproving

improbité [ɛ̃prɔbite] *f* dishonesty

improduc·tif [ɛ̃prɔdyktif] **-tive** [tiv] *adj* unproductive

impromp·tu -tue [ɛ̃prɔ̃pty] *adj* impromptu || *m* impromptu play; (mus) impromptu || **impromptu** *adv* impromptu

impropre [ɛ̃prɔpr] *adj* improper (*not right*); **impropre à** unfit for

impropriété [ɛ̃prɔprjete] *f* incorrectness

improviser [ɛ̃prɔvize] *tr & intr* to improvise

improviste [ɛ̃prɔvist]—**à l'improviste** unexpectedly, impromptu; **prendre à l'improviste** to catch napping

impru·dent -dente [ɛ̃prydɑ̃] **-dente** [dɑ̃t] *adj* imprudent

impubère [ɛ̃pyber] *adj* under the age of puberty

impubliable [ɛ̃pybljabl] *adj* unpublishable, not fit to print

impu·dent -dente [ɛ̃pydɑ̃] **-dente** [dɑ̃t] *adj* impudent

impudeur [ɛ̃pydœr] *f* immodesty

impudicité [ɛ̃pydisite] f indecency

impudique [ɛ̃pydik] adj immodest

impuissance [ɛ̃pɥisɑ̃s] f impotence; être dans l'impuissance de faire q.ch. to be powerless to do s.th.

impuis·sant [ɛ̃pɥisɑ̃] impuis·sante [ɛ̃pɥisɑ̃t] adj impotent, powerless, helpless; (pathol) impotent

impul·sif [ɛ̃pylsif] -sive [siv] adj impulsive || mf impulsive person

impulsion [ɛ̃pylsjɔ̃] f impulse; donner l'impulsion à to give an impetus to; sous l'impulsion du moment on the spur of the moment

impunément [ɛ̃pynemɑ̃] adv with impunity

impu·ni -nie [ɛ̃pyni] adj unpunished

impunité [ɛ̃pynite] f impunity

im·pur -pure [ɛ̃pyr] adj impure

impureté [ɛ̃pyrte] f impurity

imputation [ɛ̃pytasjɔ̃] f imputation; (com) charge; (com) deduction

imputer [ɛ̃pyte] tr to impute, ascribe; (com) imputer q.ch. à to charge s.th. to

inaccessible [inaksesibl] adj inaccessible

inac·tif [inaktif] -tive [tiv] adj inactive

inaction [inaksjɔ̃] f inaction

inactivité [inaktivite] f inactivity

inadaptation [inadaptasjɔ̃] f maladjustment

inadap·té -tée [inadapte] adj maladjusted || mf misfit

inadvertance [inadvertɑ̃s] f—par inadvertance inadvertently

inalté·ré -rée [inaltere] adj unspoiled

inani·mé -mée [inanime] adj inanimate

inappréciable [inapresjabl] adj inappreciable, imperceptible; invaluable

inapprivoisable [inaprivwazabl] adj untamable

inapte [inapt] adj inept; inapte à unfit for, unsuitable for || mf dropout, washout; les inaptes the unfit; the unemployable

inaptitude [inaptityd] f unfitness

inarticu·lé -lée [inartikyle] adj inarticulate

inassou·vi -vie [inasuvi] adj unsatisfied

inattaquable [inatakabl] adj unquestionable; unassailable; inattaquable par unaffected by, resistant to

inatten·du -due [inatɑ̃dy] adj unexpected

inatten·tif [inatɑ̃tif] -tive [tiv] adj inattentive; careless

inattention [inatɑ̃sjɔ̃] f inattentiveness, carelessness

inaudible [inodibl] adj inaudible

inaugu·ral -rale [inogyral] adj (pl -raux [ro]) inaugural

inauguration [inogyrasjɔ̃] f inauguration

inaugurer [inogyre] tr to inaugurate; to unveil (a statue)

inauthentique [inotɑ̃tik] adj unauthentic

inavouable [inavuabl] adj shameful

ina·voué -vouée [inavwe] adj unacknowledged

inca [ɛ̃ka] adj invar Inca || (cap) m Inca

incandes·cent [ɛ̃kɑ̃desɑ̃] incandes·cente [ɛ̃kɑ̃desɑ̃t] adj incandescent; wild, stirred up (crowd)

incapable [ɛ̃kapabl] adj incapable; (law) incompetent || mf (law) incompetent person

incapacité [ɛ̃kapasite] f incapacity; disability

incarcérer [ɛ̃karsere] §10 tr to incarcerate

incar·nat [ɛ̃karna] -nate [nat] adj flesh-colored; rosy || m flesh color

incarnation [ɛ̃karnasjɔ̃] f incarnation

incar·né -née [ɛ̃karne] adj incarnate; ingrowing (nail)

incarner [ɛ̃karne] tr to incarnate, to embody || ref to become incarnate; (pathol) to become ingrown; s'incarner dans to become the embodiment of

incartade [ɛ̃kartad] f indiscretion; prank

incassable [ɛ̃kasabl] adj unbreakable

incendiaire [ɛ̃sɑ̃djɛr] adj & mf incendiary

incendie [ɛ̃sɑ̃di] m fire, conflagration; incendie volontaire arson

incen·dié -diée [ɛ̃sɑ̃dje] adj burnt down || mf fire victim

incendier [ɛ̃sɑ̃dje] tr to set on fire; to burn down; (fig) to fire, inflame; (slang) to give a tongue-lashing to

incer·tain [ɛ̃sɛrtɛ̃] -taine [ten] adj uncertain; indistinct; unsettled (weather)

incertitude [ɛ̃sɛrtityd] f incertitude, uncertainty; doubt; dans l'incertitude in doubt

incessamment [ɛ̃sesamɑ̃] adv incessantly; without delay, at any moment

inces·sant [ɛ̃sesɑ̃] inces·sante [ɛ̃sesɑ̃t] adj incessant

inceste [ɛ̃sest] m incest

inces·tueux [ɛ̃sestɥø] -tueuse [tɥøz] adj incestuous

inchan·gé -gée [ɛ̃ʃɑ̃ʒe] adj unchanged

incidemment [ɛ̃sidamɑ̃] adv incidentally

incidence [ɛ̃sidɑ̃s] f incidence

inci·dent [ɛ̃sidɑ̃] -dente [dɑ̃t] adj & m incident

incinérer [ɛ̃sinere] §10 tr to incinerate; to cremate

incirconcis [ɛ̃sirkɔ̃si] adj masc uncircumcised

inciser [ɛ̃size] tr to make an incision in; to tap (a tree); (med) to lance

inci·sif [ɛ̃sizif] -sive [ziv] adj incisive || f incisor

incision [ɛ̃sizjɔ̃] f incision

incitation [ɛ̃sitasjɔ̃] f incitement

inciter [ɛ̃site] tr to incite

inci·vil -vile [ɛ̃sivil] adj uncivil

incivili·sé -sée [ɛ̃sivilize] adj uncivilized

inclassable [ɛ̃klasabl] adj unclassifiable

inclé·ment -mente [ɛ̃klemɑ̃ -mɑ̃t] adj inclement

inclinaison [ɛ̃klinezɔ̃] f inclination; slope

inclination [ɛ̃klinasjɔ̃] f inclination; bow; love, affection

incliner [ɛ̃kline] tr & ref to incline; to bend; to bow

inclure [ɛklyr] §11 (*pp* **inclus**) *tr* to include; to enclose

in•clus [ɛkly] **-cluse** [klyz] *adj* including, e.g., **jusqu'à la page dix incluse** up to and including page ten; inclusive, e.g., **de mercredi à samedi inclus** from Wednesday to Saturday inclusive

inclu•sif [ɛklyzif] **-sive** [ziv] *adj* inclusive

inclusivement [ɛklyzivmɑ] *adv* inclusively, inclusive

incognito [ɛkɔnito] *m & adv* incognito

incohé•rent [ɛkoerɑ] **-rente** [rɑt] *adj* incoherent; inconsistent, illogical

incolore [ɛkolɔr] *adj* colorless

incomber [ɛkɔbe] *intr*—**incomber à** to devolve on, to fall upon; **il incombe à qn de** it behooves s.o. to

incombustible [ɛkɔbystibl] *adj* incombustible; fireproof

incommode [ɛkomɔd] *adj* inconvenient; unwieldy

incommoder [ɛkomɔde] *tr* to inconvenience

incommodité [ɛkomɔdite] *f* inconvenience

incomparable [ɛkɔparabl] *adj* incomparable

incompatible [ɛkɔpatibl] *adj* incompatible; conflicting

incompétence [ɛkɔpetɑs] *f* incompetence; lack of jurisdiction

incompé•tent [ɛkɔpetɑ] **-tente** [tɑt] *adj* incompetent; lacking jurisdiction

incom•plet [ɛkɔplɛ] **-plète** [plɛt] *adj* incomplete

incompréhensible [ɛkɔpreɑsibl] *adj* incomprehensible

incom•pris [ɛkɔpri] **-prise** [priz] *adj* misunderstood

inconcevable [ɛkɔsvabl] *adj* inconceivable

inconciliable [ɛkɔsiljabl] *adj* irreconcilable

incondition•nel -nelle [ɛkɔdisjonɛl] *adj* unconditional

inconduite [ɛkɔdɥit] *f* misconduct

inconfort [ɛkɔfor] *m* discomfort

incon•gru -grue [ɛkɔgry] *adj* incongruous

incon•nu -nue [ɛkɔny] *adj* unknown; **inconnu à cette adresse** address unknown || *mf* unknown (*person*) || *m* unknown (*what is not known*) || *m* (math) unknown

inconsciemment [ɛkɔsjamɑ] *adv* subconsciously, unconsciously

inconscience [ɛkɔsjɑs] *f* unconsciousness; unawareness

incons•cient [ɛkɔsjɑ] **incons•ciente** [ɛkɔsjɑt] *adj* unconscious, unaware, oblivious; thoughtless; subconscious || *mf* dazed person || *m* unconscious

inconséquence [ɛkɔsekɑs] *f* inconsistency; thoughtlessness, inconsiderateness

inconsé•quent [ɛkɔsekɑ] **-quente** [kɑt] *adj* inconsistent; thoughtless, inconsiderate

inconsidé•ré -rée [ɛkɔsidere] *adj* inconsiderate

inconsistance [ɛkɔsistɑs] *f* inconsistency; flimsiness, instability

inconsis•tant [ɛkɔsistɑ] **-tante** [tɑt] *adj* inconsistent; flimsy, unstable

inconsolable [ɛkɔsolabl] *adj* inconsolable

incons•tant [ɛkɔstɑ] **-tante** [tɑt] *adj* inconstant

inconstitution•nel -nelle [ɛkɔstitysjonɛl] *adj* unconstitutional

inconti•nent [ɛkɔtinɑ] **-nente** [nɑt] *adj* incontinent || **incontinent** *adv* at once, forthwith

incontrôlable [ɛkɔtrolabl] *adj* unverifiable

incontrô•lé -lée [ɛkɔtrole] *adj* unverified; unchecked, spontaneous

inconvenance [ɛkɔvnɑs] *f* impropriety

inconve•nant [ɛkɔvnɑ] **-nante** [nɑt] *adj* improper, indecent

inconvénient [ɛkɔvenjɑ] *m* inconvenience, disadvantage; **voir un inconvénient à** to have an objection to

incorporation [ɛkɔrporasjɔ] *f* incorporation; (mil) induction

incorpo•ré -rée [ɛkɔrpore] *adj* built-in

incorpo•rel -relle [ɛkɔrporel] *adj* incorporeal; intangible (*property*)

incorporer [ɛkɔrpore] *tr* to incorporate; (mil) to induct || *ref* to incorporate

incor•rect -recte [ɛkɔrekt] *adj* incorrect; unfair

incrédule [ɛkredyl] *adj* incredulous; unbelieving || *mf* unbeliever, freethinker

incrédulité [ɛkredylite] *f* incredulity; disbelief

increvable [ɛkrəvabl] *adj* punctureproof; (slang) untiring

incriminer [ɛkrimine] *tr* to incriminate

incrochetable [ɛkrɔʃtabl] *adj* burglarproof (*lock*)

incroyable [ɛkrwajabl] *adj* unbelievable

incroyant [ɛkrwajɑ] **incroyante** [ɛkrwajɑt] *adj* unbelieving || *mf* unbeliever

incrustation [ɛkrystasjɔ] *f* incrustation; inlay; (sewing) insert

incruster [ɛkryste] *tr* to incrust; to inlay || *ref* to take root, to become ingrained

incubateur [ɛkybatœr] *m* incubator

incuber [ɛkybe] *tr* to incubate

inculpation [ɛkylpasjɔ] *f* indictment; **sous l'inculpation de** on a charge of

incul•pé -pée [ɛkylpe] *adj* indicted; **inculpé de** charged with, accused of || *mf* accused, defendant

inculper [ɛkylpe] *tr* to indict, to charge

inculquer [ɛkylke] *tr* to inculcate

inculte [ɛkylt] *adj* uncultivated; uncouth

incunables [ɛkynabl] *mpl* incunabula

incurable [ɛkyrabl] *adj & mf* incurable

incurie [ɛkyri] *f* carelessness

incursion [ɛkyrsjɔ] *f* incursion, foray

Inde [ɛd] *f* India; **Indes Occidentales** West Indies; **Indes Orientales Néerlandaises** Dutch East Indies; **l'Inde** India

indébrouillable [ɛdebrujabl] *adj* inextricable, hopelessly involved

indécence [ɛ̃desɑ̃s] *f* indecency

indé·cent [ɛ̃desɑ̃] **-cente** [sɑ̃t] *adj* indecent

indéchiffrable [ɛ̃de/ifrabl] *adj* undecipherable; incomprehensible; illegible

indé·cis [ɛ̃desi] **-cise** [siz] *adj* indecisive; uncertain, undecided; blurred

indéclinable [ɛ̃deklinabl] *adj* indeclinable

indécrottable [ɛ̃dekrɔtabl] *adj* (coll) incorrigible, hopeless

indéfectible [ɛ̃defektibl] *adj* everlasting; unfailing

indéfendable [ɛ̃defɑ̃dabl] *adj* indefensible

indéfi·ni -nie [ɛ̃defini] *adj* indefinite

indéfinissable [ɛ̃definisabl] *adj* indefinable

indéfrisable [ɛ̃defrizabl] *adj* permanent (wave) ‖ *f* permanent wave

indélébile [ɛ̃delebil] *adj* indelible

indéli·cat [ɛ̃delika] **-cate** [kat] *adj* indelicate; dishonest

indémaillable [ɛ̃demajabl] *adj* runproof

indemne [ɛ̃demn] *adj* undamaged, unharmed

indemnisation [ɛ̃demnizasjɔ̃] *f* indemnification, compensation

indemniser [ɛ̃demnize] *tr* to compensate

indemnité [ɛ̃demnite] *f* indemnity; allowance, grant; compensation; **indemnité journalière** workmen's compensation; **indemnité parlementaire** salary of members (of parliamentary body)

indéniable [ɛ̃denjabl] *adj* undeniable

indépendance [ɛ̃depɑ̃dɑ̃s] *f* independence

indépen·dant [ɛ̃depɑ̃dɑ̃] **-dante** [dɑ̃t] *adj & mf* independent

indéréglable [ɛ̃dereglabl] *adj* foolproof

indescriptible [ɛ̃deskriptibl] *adj* indescribable

indésirable [ɛ̃dezirabl] *adj* undesirable

indestructible [ɛ̃destryktibl] *adj* indestructible

indétermi·né -née [ɛ̃determine] *adj* indeterminate

indétraquable [ɛ̃detrakabl] *adj* foolproof

index [ɛ̃deks] *m* index; forefinger; index number; Index (eccl) Index

indica·teur [ɛ̃dikatœr] **-trice** [tris] *adj* indicating ‖ *mf* informer ‖ *m* gauge; indicator, pointer; timetable; road sign; guidebook; street guide

indica·tif [ɛ̃dikatif] **-tive** [tiv] *adj* indicative, suggestive ‖ *m* (gram) indicative; (rad) station identification; **indicatif d'appel** (rad, telg) call letters or number

indication [ɛ̃dikasjɔ̃] *f* indication; **fausse indication** wrong piece of information; **indications** directions; **sauf indication contraire** unless otherwise directed; **sur l'indication de** at the suggestion of

indice [ɛ̃dis] *m* indication, sign; clue; **indice des prix** price index; **indice d'octane** octane number; **indice du coût de la vie** cost-of-living index

indicible [ɛ̃disibl] *adj* inexpressible

in·dien [ɛ̃djɛ̃] **-dienne** [djen] *adj* Indian ‖ *f* calico, chintz ‖ (cap) *mf* Indian

indifféremment [ɛ̃diferamɑ̃] *adv* indiscriminately

indiffé·rent [ɛ̃diferɑ̃] **-rente** [rɑ̃t] *adj* indifferent; unimportant; **cela m'est indifférent** it's all the same to me

indigence [ɛ̃diʒɑ̃s] *f* indigence, poverty

indigène [ɛ̃diʒen] *adj* indigenous, native ‖ *mf* native

indi·gent [ɛ̃diʒɑ̃] **-gente** [ʒɑ̃t] *adj* indigent ‖ *mf* pauper; **les indigents** the poor

indigeste [ɛ̃diʒest] *adj* indigestible; heavy, stodgy; undigested, mixed up

indigestion [ɛ̃diʒestjɔ̃] *f* indigestion

indignation [ɛ̃diɲasjɔ̃] *f* indignation

indigne [ɛ̃diɲ] *adj* unworthy; shameful

indi·gné -gnée [ɛ̃diɲe] *adj* indignant

indigner [ɛ̃diɲe] *tr* to outrage ‖ *ref* to be indignant

indignité [ɛ̃diɲite] *f* unworthiness; indignity, outrage

indigo [ɛ̃digo] *adj invar & m* indigo

indi·qué -quée [ɛ̃dike] *adj* advisable, appropriate; **être tout indiqué pour** to be just the thing for; to be just the man for

indiquer [ɛ̃dike] *tr* to indicate; to name; **indiquer du doigt** to point to, to point out

indi·rect -recte [ɛ̃direkt] *adj* indirect

indisciplinable [ɛ̃disiplinabl] *adj* unruly

indiscipline [ɛ̃disiplin] *f* lack of discipline, disobedience

indiscipli·né -née [ɛ̃disipline] *adj* undisciplined

indis·cret -crète [ɛ̃diskre] [kret] *adj* indiscreet

indiscrétion [ɛ̃diskresjɔ̃] *f* indiscretion; **sans indiscrétion . . . if** I may ask . . .

indiscutable [ɛ̃diskytabl] *adj* unquestionable

indiscu·té -tée [ɛ̃diskyte] *adj* unquestioned

indispensable [ɛ̃dispɑ̃sabl] *adj & m* indispensable, essential

indisponible [ɛ̃disponibl] *adj* unavailable; out of commission (said of car, machine, etc.)

indispo·sé -sée [ɛ̃dispoze] *adj* indisposed (slightly ill); ill-disposed

indisposer [ɛ̃dispoze] *tr* to indispose

indissoluble [ɛ̃disolybl] *adj* indissoluble

indis·tinct [ɛ̃distɛ̃], [ɛ̃distɛ̃kt] **-tincte** [tɛ̃kt] *adj* indistinct

indistinctement [ɛ̃distɛ̃ktəmɑ̃] *adv* indistinctly; indiscriminately

individu [ɛ̃dividy] *m* individual; (coll) fellow, guy

individualiser [ɛ̃dividyalize] *tr* to individualize

individualité [ɛ̃dividyalite] *f* individuality

indivi·duel -duelle [ɛ̃dividyel] *adj* individual; separate

indi·vis [ɛ̃divi] **-vise** [viz] *adj* joint; **par indivis** jointly

indivisible [ɛ̃divizibl] *adj* indivisible

Indochine [ɛ̃doʃin] *f* Indochina; **l'Indochine** Indochina

indocile [ɛ̃dɔsil] *adj* rebellious, unruly

indo-européen [ɛ̃doørɔpeɛ̃] **-européenne** [ørøpeen] *adj* Indo-European || *m* Indo-European (*language*) || (*cap*) *mf* Indo-European

indo·lent [ɛ̃dɔlɑ̃] **-lente** [lɑ̃t] *adj* indolent; apathetic; painless (*e.g., tumor*) || *mf* idler

indolore [ɛ̃dɔlɔr] *adj* painless

indomptable [ɛ̃dɔ̃tabl] *adj* indomitable

indomp·té -tée [ɛ̃dɔ̃te] *adj* untamed

Indonésie [ɛ̃dɔnezi] *f* Indonesia; l'**Indonésie** Indonesia

indoné·sien [ɛ̃dɔnezjɛ̃] **-sienne** [zjɛn] *adj* Indonesian || *m* Indonesian (*language*) || (*cap*) *mf* Indonesian (*person*)

in-douze [ɛ̃dux] *adj invar & m invar* duodecimo

in·du -due [ɛ̃dy] *adj* unseemly (*e.g., hour*); undue (*haste*); unwarranted (*remark*) || *m* something not due

inducteur [ɛ̃dyktœr] *m* (elec) field

induction [ɛ̃dyksjɔ̃] *f* (elec, logic) induction

induire [ɛ̃dɥir] §19 *tr* to induce; **induire en** to lead into (*temptation, error, etc.*)

in·duit -duite [ɛ̃dɥi] *adj* induced || *m* (elec) armature

indulgence [ɛ̃dylʒɑ̃s] *f* indulgence

indul·gent [ɛ̃dylʒɑ̃] **-gente** [ʒɑ̃t] *adj* indulgent

indûment [ɛ̃dymɑ̃] *adv* unduly

indurer [ɛ̃dyre] *tr & ref* to harden

industrialiser [ɛ̃dystrijalize] *tr* to industrialize || *s ref* to become industrialized

industrie [ɛ̃dystri] *f* industry; trickery; (obs) occupation. trade; l'**industrie du spectacle** show business

industrie-clef [ɛ̃dystrikle] *f* (*pl* industries-clefs*) key industry

indus·triel -trielle [ɛ̃dystrijel] *adj* industrial || *m* industrialist

indus·trieux [ɛ̃dystrijø] **-trieuse** [trijøz] *adj* industrious; skilled

inébranlable [inebrɑ̃labl] *adj* unshakable

inéchangeable [ineʃɑ̃ʒabl] *adj* unexchangeable

iné·dit [inedi] **-dite** [dit] *adj* unpublished; new, novel

inéducable [inedykabl] *adj* unteachable

ineffable [inefabl] *adj* ineffable

ineffaçable [inefasabl] *adj* indelible

inefficace [inefikas] *adj* ineffective, inefficient

iné·gal -gale [inegal] *adj* (*pl* -gaux [go]) unequal; uneven

inégalité [inegalite] *f* inequality; unevenness

inéligible [ineliʒibl] *adj* ineligible

inéluctable [inelyktabl] *adj* unavoidable

inénarrable [inenarabl] *adj* beyond words, too funny for words

inepte [inept] *adj* inept, inane

ineptie [inepsi] *f* ineptitude, inanity; inane remark

inépuisable [inepɥizabl] *adj* inexhaustible

inerme [inerm] *adj* thornless

inertie [inersi] *f* inertia

inescomptable [ineskɔ̃tabl] *adj* not subject to discount

inespé·ré -rée [inespere] *adj* unhoped-for, unexpected

inévitable [inevitabl] *adj* inevitable

inexact inexacte [inegzakt] *adj* inexact, inaccurate; unpunctual

inexactitude [inegzaktityd] *f* inexactness, inaccuracy; unpunctuality

inexau·cé -cée [inegzose] *adj* unfulfilled, unanswered

inexcitable [ineksitabl] *adj* unexcitable

inexcusable [inekskyzabl] *adj* inexcusable

inexécutable [inegzekytabl] *adj* impracticable

inexécution [inegzekysjɔ̃] *f* nonfulfillment

inexer·cé -cée [inegzerse] *adj* untried; untrained

inexhaustible [inegzostibl] *adj* inexhaustible

inexigible [inegziʒibl] *adj* uncollectable

inexis·tant [inegzistɑ̃] **-tante** [tɑ̃t] *adj* nonexistent

inexorable [inegzorabl] *adj* inexorable

inexpérience [ineksperjɑ̃s] *f* inexperience

inexpérimen·té -tée [ineksperimɑ̃te] *adj* inexperienced; untried

inex·pié -piée [inekspje] *adj* unexpiated

inexplicable [ineksplikabl] *adj* inexplicable, unexplainable

inexpli·qué -quée [ineksplike] *adj* unexplained

inexploi·té -tée [ineksplwate] *adj* untapped

inexplo·ré -rée [ineksplɔre] *adj* unexplored

inexpres·sif [inekspresif] **inexpres·sive** [inekspresiv] *adj* expressionless

inexprimable [ineksprimabl] *adj* inexpressible

inexpri·mé -mée [ineksprime] *adj* unexpressed

inexpugnable [inekspygnabl] *adj* impregnable

inextinguible [inekstɛ̃gibl], [inekstɛ̃gɥibl] *adj* inextinguishable; uncontrollable; unquenchable

infaillible [ɛ̃fajibl] *adj* infallible

infaisable [ɛ̃fazabl] *adj* unfeasible

infa·mant [ɛ̃famɑ̃] **-mante** [mɑ̃t] *adj* opprobrious

infâme [ɛ̃fɑm] *adj* infamous; squalid

infamie [ɛ̃fami] *f* infamy; dire des **infamies à** to hurl insults at; noter d'**infamie** to brand as infamous

infant [ɛ̃fɑ̃] *m* infante

infante [ɛ̃fɑ̃t] *f* infanta

infanterie [ɛ̃fɑ̃tri] *f* infantry; **infanterie de l'air, infanterie aéroportée** parachute troops; **infanterie de marine** overseas troops; **infanterie portée, infanterie motorisée** motorized troops

infantile [ɛ̃fɑ̃til] *adj* infantile

infatigable [ɛ̃fatigabl] *adj* indefatigable

infatuation [ɛ̃fatɥasjɔ̃] *f* conceit, false pride

infa·tué -tuée [ɛ̃fatɥe] *adj* infatuated with oneself, conceited

infé·cond [ɛ̃fekɔ̃] **-conde** [kɔ̃d] *adj* sterile, barren

in·fect -fecte [ɛ̃fɛkt] *adj* stinking; foul, vile

infecter [ɛ̃fɛkte] *tr* to infect; to pollute; to stink up

infec·tieux [ɛ̃fɛksjø] **-tieuse** [sjøz] *adj* infectious

infection [ɛ̃fɛksjɔ̃] *f* infection; stench

inférer [ɛ̃fere] §10 *tr* to infer, conclude

infé·rieur -rieure [ɛ̃ferjœr] *adj* lower; inferior; **inférieur à** below; less than || *mf* subordinate, inferior

infériorité [ɛ̃ferjorite] *f* inferiority

infer·nal -nale [ɛ̃fɛrnal] *adj* (*pl* **-naux** [no]) infernal

infester [ɛ̃fɛste] *tr* to infest

infidèle [ɛ̃fidɛl] *adj* infidel; unfaithful || *mf* infidel || *m* unfaithful husband || *f* unfaithful wife

infidélité [ɛ̃fidelite] *f* infidelity; inaccuracy, unfaithfulness

infiltration [ɛ̃filtrɑsjɔ̃] *f* infiltration

infiltrer [ɛ̃filtre] *ref* to infiltrate; to seep, percolate; **s'infiltrer à travers or dans** to infiltrate

infime [ɛ̃fim] *adj* very small, infinitesimal; very low; trifling, negligible

infi·ni -nie [ɛ̃fini] *adj* infinite || *m* infinite; (math) infinity; **à l'infini** infinitely

infiniment [ɛ̃finimɑ̃] *adv* infinitely; (coll) greatly, deeply, terribly

infinité [ɛ̃finite] *f* infinity

infini·tif [ɛ̃finitif] **-tive** [tiv] *adj* & *m* infinitive

infirme [ɛ̃firm] *adj* infirm, crippled, disabled || *mf* invalid, cripple

infirmer [ɛ̃firme] *tr* (law) to invalidate

infirmerie [ɛ̃firməri] *f* infirmary; (nav) sick bay

infir·mier [ɛ̃firmje] **-mière** [mjɛr] *mf* nurse; **infirmière bénévole** volunteer nurse; **infirmière diplômée** registered nurse || *m* male nurse; orderly, attendant

infirmière-major [ɛ̃firmjɛrmaʒɔr] *f* head nurse

infirmité [ɛ̃firmite] *f* infirmity

infixe [ɛ̃fiks] *m* infix

inflammable [ɛ̃flamabl] *adj* inflammable

inflammation [ɛ̃flamɑsjɔ̃] *f* inflammation

inflammatoire [ɛ̃flamatwar] *adj* inflammatory

inflation [ɛ̃flɑsjɔ̃] *f* inflation

inflationniste [ɛ̃flɑsjɔnist] *adj* inflationary

infléchir [ɛ̃fle/ir] *tr* to inflect, bend || *ref* to bend, curve

inflexible [ɛ̃flɛksibl] *adj* inflexible

inflexion [ɛ̃flɛksjɔ̃] *f* inflection; change; bend, curve; metaphory

infliger [ɛ̃fliʒe] §38 *tr* to inflict; **infliger q.ch. à** to inflict s.th. on

influence [ɛ̃flyɑ̃s] *f* influence

influencer [ɛ̃flyɑ̃se] §51 *tr* to influence

influent [ɛ̃flyɑ̃] **influente** [ɛ̃flyɑ̃t] *adj* influential

influenza [ɛ̃flyɑ̃za] *f* influenza

influer [ɛ̃flye] *intr*—**influer sur** to influence

in-folio [ɛ̃foljo] *adj* & *m* (*pl* **-folio** or **-folios**) folio

informa·teur [ɛ̃formatœr] **-trice** [tris] *mf* informant

information [ɛ̃formɑsjɔ̃] *f* information; piece of information; (law) investigation; **aller aux informations** to make inquiries; **information génétique** genetic characteristics; **informations** news; information; **informations de presse** press reports

informatique [ɛ̃formatik] *adj* informational || *f* information storage

informe [ɛ̃form] *adj* formless, shapeless

informer [ɛ̃forme] *tr* to inform, advise || *intr*—**informer contre** to inform on || *ref* to inquire, to keep oneself informed

infortune [ɛ̃fortyn] *f* misfortune

infortu·né -née [ɛ̃fortyne] *adj* unfortunate

infraction [ɛ̃fraksjɔ̃] *f* infraction

infranchissable [ɛ̃frɑ̃/isabl] *adj* insuperable; impassable (*e.g.*, *mountain*)

infrarouge [ɛ̃fraruʒ] *adj* & *m* infrared

infrason [ɛ̃frasɔ̃] *m* infrasonic vibration

infrastructure [ɛ̃frastryktyr] *f* infrastructure; (rr) roadbed

infroissable [ɛ̃frwasabl] *adj* creaseless, wrinkleproof

infruc·tueux [ɛ̃fryktɥø] **-tueuse** [tɥøz] *adj* unfruitful, fruitless

in·fus [ɛ̃fy] **-fuse** [fyz] *adj* inborn, innate, intuitive

infuser [ɛ̃fyze] *tr* to infuse; to brew; **infuser un sang nouveau à** to put new blood or life into || *intr* to steep

infusion [ɛ̃fyzjɔ̃] *f* steeping; brew

ingambe [ɛ̃gɑ̃b] *adj* spry, nimble, alert

ingénier [ɛ̃ʒenje] *ref* to strive hard

ingénierie [ɛ̃ʒeniri] or **ingéniérie** [ɛ̃ʒenjeri] *f* engineering

ingénieur [ɛ̃ʒenjœr] *m* engineer; **ingénieur des ponts et chaussées** civil engineer

ingé·nieux [ɛ̃ʒenjø] **-nieuse** [njøz] *adj* ingenious

ingéniosité [ɛ̃ʒenjozite] *f* ingenuity

ingé·nu -nue [ɛ̃ʒeny] *adj* ingenuous, artless || *mf* naïve person || *f* ingénue

ingénuité [ɛ̃ʒenɥite] *f* ingenuousness

ingérer [ɛ̃ʒere] §10 *tr* to ingest || *ref* to meddle

ingouvernable [ɛ̃guvɛrnabl] *adj* unruly, unmanageable

in·grat [ɛ̃gra] **-grate** [grat] *adj* ungrateful; disagreeable; thankless (*task*); unprofitable (*work*); barren (*soil*); awkward (*age*) || *mf* ingrate

ingratitude [ɛ̃gratityd] *f* ingratitude

ingrédient [ɛ̃gredjɑ̃] *m* ingredient

inguérissable [ɛ̃gerisabl] *adj* & *mf* incurable

ingurgiter [ɛ̃gyrʒite] *tr* to swallow; to gulp down

inhabile [inabil] *adj* unskilled; unfitted, unqualified

inhabileté [inabilte] *f* inability; clumsiness; unfitness

inhabitable [inabitabl] *adj* uninhabitable

inhabi·té -tée [inabite] *adj* uninhabited

inhabi·tuel -tuelle [inabityɛl] *adj* unusual

inhé·rent [inerɑ̃] **-rente** [rɑ̃t] *adj* inherent

inhiber [inibe] *tr* to inhibit

inhibition [inibisjɔ̃] *f* inhibition

inhospita·lier [inɔspitalje] **-lière** [ljer] *adj* inhospitable

inhu·main [inymɛ̃] **-maine** [men] *adj* inhuman

inhumanité [inymanite] *f* inhumanity

inhumation [inymasjɔ̃] *f* burial

inhumer [inyme] *tr* to bury, to inter

inimitié [inimitje] *f* enmity

inintelli·gent [inɛ̃teliʒɑ̃] **-gente** [ʒɑ̃t] *adj* unintelligent

inintéres·sant [inɛ̃teresɑ̃] **inintéres·sante** [inɛ̃teresɑ̃t] *adj* uninteresting

ininterrom·pu -pue [inɛ̃terɔ̃py] *adj* uninterrupted

inique [inik] *adj* iniquitous, unjust

iniquité [inikite] *f* iniquity

ini·tial -tiale [inisjal] (*pl* **-tiaux** [sjo] **-tiales**) *adj* & *f* initial

initia·teur [inisjatœr] **-trice** [tris] *adj* initiating ‖ *mf* initiator

initiation [inisjasjɔ̃] *f* initiation

initiative [inisjativ] *f* initiative

initier [inisje] *tr* to initiate; to introduce ‖ *ref* to become initiated

injecter [ʒɛkte] *tr* to inject; to impregnate ‖ *ref* to become bloodshot

injec·teur [ʒɛktœr] **-trice** [tris] *adj* injecting ‖ *m* injector; nozzle (*in motor*)

injection [ʒɛksjɔ̃] *f* injection; impregnation; redness (*of eyes*); (geog) intrusion

injonction [ʒɔ̃ksjɔ̃] *f* injunction, order

injouable [ʒwabl] *adj* unplayable

injure [ʒyr] *f* insult; wrong; **l'injure des ans** the ravages of time

injurier [ʒyrje] *tr* to insult, to abuse

inju·rieux [ʒyrjø] **-rieuse** [rjøz] *adj* insulting, abusive; harmful, offensive

injuste [ʒyst] *adj* unjust

injustice [ʒystis] *f* injustice

injusti·fié -fiée [ʒystifje] *adj* unjustified

inlassable [ɛ̃lasabl] *adj* untiring

in·né -née [inne] *adj* innate, inborn

innocence [inɔsɑ̃s] *f* innocence

inno·cent [inɔsɑ̃] **-cente** [sɑ̃t] *adj* & *mf* innocent

innocenter [inɔsɑ̃te] *tr* to exonerate

innocuité [inɔkɥite] *f* innocuousness

innombrable [inɔ̃brabl] *adj* innumerable

innova·teur [inɔvatœr] **-trice** [tris] *adj* innovating ‖ *mf* innovator

innovation [inɔvasjɔ̃] *f* innovation

innover [inɔve] *tr* & *intr* to innovate

inoccu·pé -pée [inɔkype] *adj* unoccupied; unemployed, idle ‖ *mf* idler

in-octavo [inɔktavo] *adj* & *m* (*pl* **-octavo** or **-octavos**) octavo

inoculation [inɔkylasjɔ̃] *f* inoculation

inoculer [inɔkyle] *tr* to inoculate

inodore [inɔdɔr] *adj* odorless

inoffen·sif [inɔfɑ̃sif] **-sive** [siv] *adj* inoffensive

inondation [inɔ̃dɑsjɔ̃] *f* flood

inonder [inɔ̃de] *tr* to flood

inopi·né -née [inɔpine] *adj* unexpected

inoppor·tun [inɔpɔrtœ̃] **-tune** [tyn] *adj* untimely, inconvenient

inopportunité [inɔpɔrtynite] *f* untimeliness

inorganique [inɔrganik] *adj* inorganic

inorgani·sé -sée [inɔrganize] *adj* unorganized (*workers*), nonunion

inoubliable [inublijabl] *adj* unforgettable

inouï inouïe [inwi] *adj* unheard-of

inoxydable [inɔksidabl] *adj* inoxidizable, stainless, rustproof

inqualifiable [ɛ̃kalifjabl] *adj* unspeakable

in·quiet [ɛ̃kje] **-quiète** [kjet] *adj* anxious, worried, uneasy; restless

inquié·tant [ɛ̃kjetɑ̃] **-tante** [tɑ̃t] *adj* disquieting, worrisome

inquiéter [ɛ̃kjete], §10 *tr* & *intr* to worry

inquiétude [ɛ̃kjetyd] *f* uneasiness, worry

inquisi·teur [ɛ̃kizitœr] **-trice** [tris] *adj* inquisitorial; searching (*e.g.,* **look**) ‖ *m* inquisitor

inquisition [ɛ̃kizisjɔ̃] *f* inquisition; investigation

inracontable [ɛ̃rakɔ̃tabl] *adj* untellable

insaisissable [ɛ̃sezisabl] *adj* hard to catch; elusive

insalubre [ɛ̃salybr] *adj* unhealthy

insane [ɛ̃san] *adj* insane, crazy

insanité [ɛ̃sanite] *f* insanity; piece of folly

insatiable [ɛ̃sasjabl] *adj* insatiable

insatisfaction [ɛ̃satisfaksjɔ̃] *f* dissatisfaction

inscription [ɛ̃skripsjɔ̃] *f* inscription; registration, enrollment; **inscription de or en faux** (law) plea of forgery; **prendre ses inscriptions** to register at a university

inscrire [ɛ̃skrir] §25 *tr* to inscribe; to register; to record ‖ *ref* to register, enroll; **s'inscrire à** to join; **s'inscrire en faux contre** to deny; **s'inscrire pour** to sign up for

ins·crit [ɛ̃skri] **-crite** [krit] *adj* inscribed; registered, enrolled ‖ *mf* registered student; (sports) entry; **inscrit maritime** naval recruit

insecte [ɛ̃sekt] *m* insect, bug

insecticide [ɛ̃sektisid] *adj* insecticidal ‖ *m* insecticide

insen·sé -sée [ɛ̃sɑ̃se] *adj* senseless, insane, crazy ‖ *m* madman ‖ *f* madwoman

insensible [ɛ̃sɑ̃sibl] *adj* insensitive; imperceptible

inséparable [ɛ̃separabl] *adj* inseparable ‖ *m* lovebird

insérer [ɛ̃sere] §10 *tr* to insert

insertion [ɛ̃sersjɔ̃] *f* insertion

insi·dieux [ɛ̃sidjø] **-dieuse** [djøz] *adj* insidious

insigne [ɛ̃siɲ] *adj* signal, noteworthy; notorious ‖ *m* badge, mark; **insignes** insignia

insigni·fiant [ɛ̃siɲifjɑ̃] **-fiante** [fjɑ̃t] *adj* insignificant

insincère [ɛ̃sɛ̃ser] *adj* insincere

insinuation [ɛ̃sinɥɑsjɔ̃] *f* insinuation

insinuer [ɛ̃sinɥe] *tr* to insinuate; to

hint, hint at; to work in, introduce || *ref—s'insinuer dans* to worm one's way into

insipide [ɛ̃sipid] *adj* insipid, tasteless; insipid, dull

insister [ɛ̃siste] *intr* to insist; (coll) to continue, persevere; **insister pour** to insist on; **insister sur** to stress

insociable [ɛ̃sɔsjabl] *adj* unsociable

insolation [ɛ̃sɔlɑsjɔ̃] *f* exposure to the sun; sunstroke

insolence [ɛ̃sɔlɑ̃s] *f* insolence

inso•lent [ɛ̃sɔlɑ̃] **-lente** [lɑ̃t] *adj* insolent; extraordinary, unexpected

insolite [ɛ̃sɔlit] *adj* bizarre

insoluble [ɛ̃sɔlybl] *adj* insoluble

insolvabilité [ɛ̃sɔlvabilite] *f* insolvency

insolvable [ɛ̃sɔlvabl] *adj* insolvent

insomnie [ɛ̃sɔmni] *f* insomnia

insondable [ɛ̃sɔ̃dabl] *adj* unfathomable

insonore [ɛ̃sɔnɔr] *adj* soundproof; noiseless

insonoriser [ɛ̃sɔnɔrize] *tr* to soundproof

insouciance [ɛ̃susjɑ̃s] *f* carefreeness; indifference, carelessness

insou•ciant [ɛ̃susjɑ̃] **-ciante** [sjɑ̃t] *adj* carefree, unconcerned

insou•cieux [ɛ̃susjø] **-cieuse** [sjøz] *adj* carefree, unmindful

insou•mis [ɛ̃sumi] **-mise** [miz] *adj* unruly; unsubjugated || *mf* rebel || *m* (mil) A.W.O.L.

insoumission [ɛ̃sumisjɔ̃] *f* insubordination, rebellion; (mil) absence without leave

insoupçonnable [ɛ̃supsɔnabl] *adj* above suspicion

insoupçon•né **-née** [ɛ̃supsɔne] *adj* unsuspected

insoutenable [ɛ̃sutnabl] *adj* untenable; unbearable

inspecter [ɛ̃spekte] *tr* to inspect

inspec•teur [ɛ̃spektœr] **-trice** [tris] *mf* inspector

inspection [ɛ̃speksjɔ̃] *f* inspection; inspectorship

inspiration [ɛ̃spirɑsjɔ̃] *f* inspiration

inspirer [ɛ̃spire] *tr* to inspire; to breathe in; **inspirer à qn de** to inspire s.o. to; **inspirer q.ch. à qn** to inspire s.o. with s.th. || *ref—s'inspirer de* to be inspired by

instable [ɛ̃stabl] *adj* unstable

installateur [ɛ̃stalatœr] *m* heater man; fitter, plumber

installation [ɛ̃stalɑsjɔ̃] *f* installation; equipment, outfit; appointments, fittings

installer [ɛ̃stale] *tr* to install; to equip, furnish; **être bien installé** to be comfortably settled || *ref* to settle down, to set up shop; **s'installer chez** to foist oneself on

instamment [ɛ̃stamɑ̃] *adv* urgently, earnestly

instance [ɛ̃stɑ̃s] *f* insistence; **avec instance** earnestly; **en instance** pending; **en instance de** on the point of; **en seconde instance** on appeal; **instances** entreaties; **introduire une instance** to start proceedings

ins•tant [ɛ̃stɑ̃] **-tante** [tɑ̃t] *adj* urgent, pressing || *m* instant, moment; **à cha-** que instant, **à tout instant** continually; **à l'instant** at once, right away, just now; **at the moment; par instant** from time to time

instanta•né **-née** [ɛ̃stɑ̃tane] *adj* instantaneous || *m* snapshot

instantanément [ɛ̃stɑ̃tanemɑ̃] *adv* instantaneously; instantly

instar [ɛ̃star]—**à l'instar de** in the manner of

instauration [ɛ̃stɔrɑsjɔ̃] *f* establishment

instaurer [ɛ̃stɔre] *tr* to establish

instigation [ɛ̃stigɑsjɔ̃] *f* instigation

instiller [ɛ̃stile] *tr* to instill

instinct [ɛ̃stɛ̃] *m* instinct; **d'instinct, par instinct** by instinct

instinc•tif [ɛ̃stɛ̃ktif] **-tive** [tiv] *adj* instinctive

instituer [ɛ̃stitɥe] *tr* to found; to institute (*e.g.,* proceedings)

institut [ɛ̃stity] *m* institute; **institut de beauté** beauty parlor; **institut de coupe** tonsorial parlor; **institut dentaire** dental school

institu•teur [ɛ̃stitytœr] **-trice** [tris] *mf* schoolteacher; founder

institution [ɛ̃stitysjɔ̃] *f* institution

instructeur [ɛ̃stryktœr] *m* instructor

instruc•tif [ɛ̃stryktif] **-tive** [tiv] *adj* instructive

instruction [ɛ̃stryksjɔ̃] *f* instruction; education; **instruction judiciaire** (law) preliminary investigation; **instructions permanentes** standing orders

instruire [ɛ̃strɥir] §19 *tr* to instruct; **instruire qn de** to inform s.o. of || *ref* to improve one's mind

instrument [ɛ̃strymɑ̃] *m* instrument; **instrument à anche** reed instrument; **instrument à cordes** stringed instrument; **instrument à vent** wind instrument; **instrument en bois** woodwind; **instrument en cuivre** brass

instrumen•tal -tale [ɛ̃strymɑ̃tal] *adj* (*pl* **-taux** [to]) instrumental

instrumenter [ɛ̃strymɑ̃te] *tr* to instrument

instrumentiste [ɛ̃strymɑ̃tist] *mf* instrumentalist

insu [ɛ̃sy] *m*—**à l'insu de** unknown to; **à mon insu** unknown to me

insubmersible [ɛ̃sybmɛrsibl] *adj* unsinkable

insubordon•né **-née** [ɛ̃sybɔrdɔne] *adj* insubordinate

insuccès [ɛ̃syksɛ] *m* failure

insuffi•sant [ɛ̃syfizɑ̃] **-sante** [zɑ̃t] *adj* insufficient

insulaire [ɛ̃syler] *adj* insular || *mf* islander

insuline [ɛ̃sylin] *f* insulin

insulte [ɛ̃sylt] *f* insult

insulter [ɛ̃sylte] *tr* to insult || *intr* (with *dat*) to offend, outrage

insupportable [ɛ̃sypɔrtabl] *adj* unbearable

insur•gé -gée [ɛ̃syrʒe] *adj & mf* insurgent

insurger [ɛ̃syrʒe] §38 *ref* to revolt, rebel

insurmontable [ɛ̃syrmɔ̃tabl] *adj* insurmountable

insurrection [ɛ̃syreksjɔ̃] *f* insurrection

in·tact -tacte [ɛ̃takt] *adj* intact, untouched

intangible [ɛ̃tɑ̃ʒibl] *adj* intangible

intarissable [ɛ̃tarisabl] *adj* inexhaustible

inté·gral -grale [ɛ̃tegral] *adj* (*pl* **-graux** [gro]) integral; complete (*e.g.*, *edition*); full (*e.g.*, *payment*) || *f* complete works; (math) integral

inté·grant [ɛ̃tegrɑ̃] **-grante** [grɑ̃t] *adj* integral

intégration [ɛ̃tegrasjɔ̃] *f* integration

intègre [ɛ̃tɛgr] *adj* honest, upright

intégrer [ɛ̃tegre] §10 *tr* to integrate || *ref* to form an integral part; (slang) to be accepted (*at an exclusive school*)

intégrité [ɛ̃tegrite] *f* integrity

intellect [ɛ̃telɛkt] *m* intellect

intellec·tuel -tuelle [ɛ̃telɛktɥɛl] *adj & mf* intellectual

intelligence [ɛ̃teliʒɑ̃s] *f* intelligence; intellect (*person*); **en bonne intelligence avec** on good terms with; **être d'intelligence** to be in collusion

intelli·gent [ɛ̃teliʒɑ̃] **-gente** [ʒɑ̃t] *adj* intelligent

intelligible [ɛ̃teliʒibl] *adj* intelligible

intempé·rant [ɛ̃tɑ̃perɑ̃] **-rante** [rɑ̃t] *adj* intemperate

intempéries [ɛ̃tɑ̃peri] *fpl* bad weather

intempes·tif [ɛ̃tɑ̃pɛstif] **-tive** [tiv] *adj* untimely

intenable [ɛ̃tnabl] *adj* untenable

intendance [ɛ̃tɑ̃dɑ̃s] *f* stewardship; controllership, office of bursar; **Intendance** (mil) Quartermaster Corps

inten·dant [ɛ̃tɑ̃dɑ̃] **-dante** [dɑ̃t] *mf* steward, superintendent; controller, bursar; **intendant militaire** quartermaster

intense [ɛ̃tɑ̃s] *adj* intense

inten·sif [ɛ̃tɑ̃sif] **-sive** [siv] *adj* intensive

intensifier [ɛ̃tɑ̃sifje] *tr & ref* to intensify

intensité [ɛ̃tɑ̃site] *f* intensity

intenter [ɛ̃tɑ̃te] *tr* to start (*a suit*); to bring (*an action*)

intention [ɛ̃tɑ̃sjɔ̃] *f* intention, intent; **à l'intention de** for (the sake of)

intention·né -née [ɛ̃tɑ̃sjone] *adj* motivated; **bien intentionné** well-meaning; **mal intentionné** ill-disposed

intention·nel -nelle [ɛ̃tɑ̃sjonɛl] *adj* intentional

inter [ɛ̃tɛr] *m* (coll) long distance

interaction [ɛ̃teraksjɔ̃] *f* interaction, interplay

intercaler [ɛ̃tɛrkale] *tr* to intercalate; to insert, to sandwich

intercéder [ɛ̃tɛrsede] §10 *intr* to intercede

intercepter [ɛ̃tɛrsɛpte] *tr* to intercept

intercepteur [ɛ̃tɛrsɛptœr] *m* interceptor

interchangeable [ɛ̃tɛrʃɑ̃ʒabl] *adj* interchangeable

interclasse [ɛ̃tɛrklas] *m* (educ) break between classes

intercourse [ɛ̃tɛrkurs] *f* (naut) free entry

interdépen·dant [ɛ̃tɛrdepɑ̃dɑ̃] **-dante** [dɑ̃t] *adj* interdependent

interdiction [ɛ̃tɛrdiksjɔ̃] *f* interdiction; suspension; **interdiction de séjour** forbidden entry

interdire [ɛ̃tɛrdir] §40 *tr* to prohibit, to forbid; to confound, to abash; to interdict; to suspend; **interdire q.ch. à qn** to forbid s.o. s.th.

inter·dit [ɛ̃tɛrdi] **-dite** [dit] *adj* prohibited, forbidden; dumfounded, abashed; deprived of rights; (mil) off limits || *m* interdict

intéres·sant [ɛ̃teresɑ̃] **intéres·sante** [ɛ̃teresɑ̃t] *adj* interesting; attractive (*offer*)

intéres·sé -sée [ɛ̃terese] *adj* interested; self-seeking || *mf* interested party

intéresser [ɛ̃terese] *tr* to interest; to involve || *ref*—**s'intéresser à** or **dans** to be interested in

intérêt [ɛ̃terɛ] *m* interest; **intérêts composés** compound interest

interférence [ɛ̃tɛrferɑ̃s] *f* interference

interférer [ɛ̃tɛrfere] §10 *intr* (phys) to interfere || *ref* to interfere with each other

inté·rieur -rieure [ɛ̃terjœr] *adj* interior, inner, inside || *m* interior; inside; house, home

intérieurement [ɛ̃terjœrmɑ̃] *adv* inwardly, internally; to oneself

intérim [ɛ̃terim] *m invar* interim; **dans l'intérim** in the meantime; **par intérim** acting, pro tem, interim

intérimaire [ɛ̃terimɛr] *adj* temporary, acting

interjection [ɛ̃tɛrʒeksjɔ̃] *f* interjection

interligne [ɛ̃tɛrliɲ] *m* space between the lines; writing in the space between the lines; **à double interligne** double-spaced || *f* lead

interligner [ɛ̃tɛrliɲe] *tr* to interline; (typ) to lead out

interlocu·teur [ɛ̃tɛrlɔkytœr] **-trice** [tris] *mf* interlocutor; intermediary; party (*with whom one is conversing*)

interlope [ɛ̃tɛrlɔp] *adj* illegal, shady || *m* (naut) smuggling vessel

interloquer [ɛ̃tɛrlɔke] *tr* to disconcert

interlude [ɛ̃tɛrlyd] *m* interlude

intermède [ɛ̃tɛrmɛd] *m* (theat & fig) interlude

intermédiaire [ɛ̃tɛrmedjɛr] *adj* intermediate, intermediary || *mf* intermediary || *m* (com) middleman; **par l'intermédiaire de** by means of, by the medium of

interminable [ɛ̃tɛrminabl] *adj* interminable

intermit·tent [ɛ̃tɛrmitɑ̃] **intermit·tente** [ɛ̃tɛrmitɑ̃t] *adj* intermittent

internat [ɛ̃tɛrna] *m* boarding school; boarding-school life; (med) internship

internatio·nal -nale [ɛ̃tɛrnasjonal] *adj* (*pl* **-naux** [no]) international

interne [ɛ̃tɛrn] *adj* inner; (math) interior || *mf* boarder (*at a school*); (med) intern

inter·né -née [ɛ̃tɛrne] *mf* internee

internement [ɛ̃tɛrnəmɑ̃] *m* internment; confinement (*of a mental patient*)

interner [ɛterne] *tr* to intern

interpeller [ɛterpele] *tr* to question, to interrogate; to yell at; to heckle

interphone [ɛterfɔn] *m* intercom

interplanétaire [ɛterplaneter] *adj* interplanetary

interpoler [ɛterpɔle] *tr* to interpolate

interposer [ɛterpoze] *tr* to interpose

interprétation [ɛterpretɑsjɔ̃] *f* interpretation

interprète [ɛterpret] *mf* interpreter

interpréter [ɛterprete] §10 *tr* to interpret; **mal interpréter** to misinterpret

interrogation [ɛterɔgɑsjɔ̃] *f* interrogation

interroger [ɛterɔʒe] §38 *tr* to interrogate, to question

interrompre [ɛterɔ̃pr] (3d *sg pres ind* **interrompt** [ɛterɔ̃]) *tr* to interrupt; to heckle || *ref* to break off, to be interrupted

interrup·teur [ɛteryptœr] **-trice** [tris] *adj* interrupting, circuit-breaking || *m* switch, **interrupteur à couteau** knife switch **interrupteur à culbuteur** or **à bascule** toggle switch; **interrupteur d'escalier** two-way switch; **interrupteur encastré** flush switch; **interrupteur olive** pea switch

interruption [ɛterypsjɔ̃] *f* interruption

intersection [ɛterseksjɔ̃] *f* intersection

intersigne [ɛtersiɲ] *m* omen, portent

interstellaire [ɛtersteler] *adj* interstellar

interstice [ɛterstis] *m* interstice

interur·bain [ɛteryrbɛ̃] **-baine** [ben] *adj* interurban; (telp) long-distance || *m* (telp) long distance

intervalle [ɛterval] *m* interval

intervenir [ɛtervnir] §72 (*aux:* ÊTRE) *intr* to intervene; to take place, happen; (med) to operate; **faire intervenir** to call in

intervention [ɛtervɑ̃sjɔ̃] *f* intervention; (med) operation

intervertir [ɛtervertir] *tr* to invert, to transpose

interview [ɛtervju] *f* (journ) interview

interviewer [ɛtervjuvœr] *m* interviewer || [ɛtervjuve] *tr* to interview

intestat [ɛtesta] *adj & mf invar* intestate

intes·tin [ɛtestɛ̃] **-tine** [tin] *adj* intestine, internal || *m* intestine; **gros intestin** large intestine; **intestin grêle** small intestine

intimation [ɛtimɑsjɔ̃] *f* (law) summons

intime [ɛtim] *adj & mf* intimate

inti·mé -mée [ɛtime] *mf* (law) defendant

intimer [ɛtime] *tr* to notify; to give (*an order*)

intimider [ɛtimide] *tr* to intimidate

intimité [ɛtimite] *f* intimacy; privacy; depths (*of one's being*)

intituler [ɛtityle] *tr* to entitle

intolérable [ɛtɔlerabl] *adj* intolerable

intolé·rant [ɛtɔlerɑ̃] **-rante** [rɑ̃t] *adj* intolerant

intonation [ɛtɔnɑsjɔ̃] *f* intonation

intouchable [ɛtu/abl] *adj & mf* untouchable

intoxication [ɛtɔksikɑsjɔ̃] *f* poisoning

intoxiquer [ɛtɔksike] *tr* to poison

intraitable [ɛtretabl] *adj* intractable

intransi·geant [ɛtrɑ̃ziʒɑ̃] **-geante** [ʒɑ̃t] *adj* intransigent || *mf* diehard, standpatter

intransi·tif [ɛtrɑ̃zitif] **-tive** [tiv] *adj* intransitive

intravei·neux [ɛtravenø] **-neuse** [nøz] *adj* intravenous

intrépide [ɛtrepid] *adj* intrepid; persistent

intri·gant [ɛtrigɑ̃] **-gante** [gɑ̃t] *adj* intriguing || *mf* plotter, schemer

intrigue [ɛtrig] *f* intrigue, plot; love affair; **intrigues de couloir** lobbying

intriguer [ɛtrige] *tr & intr* to intrigue

intrinsèque [ɛtrɛ̃sek] *adj* intrinsic

introduction [ɛtrɔdyksjɔ̃] *f* introduction; admission

introduire [ɛtrɔdɥir] §19 *tr* to introduce, to bring in; to show in; to interject (*e.g., a remark*) || *ref* to be introduced; **s'introduire dans** to slip in

intronisation [ɛtrɔnizɑsjɔ̃] *f* investiture, inauguration

introniser [ɛtrɔnize] *tr* to enthrone

introspec·tif [ɛtrɔspektif] **-tive** [tiv] *adj* introspective

introuvable [ɛtruvabl] *adj* unfindable

introver·ti -tie [ɛtrɔverti] *adj & mf* introvert

in·trus [ɛtry] **-truse** [tryz] *adj* intruding || *mf* intruder

intrusion [ɛtryzjɔ̃] *f* intrusion

intuition [ɛtɥisjɔ̃] *f* intuition

inusable [inyzabl] *adj* durable, wearproof

inusi·té -tée [inyzite] *adj* obsolete

inutile [inytil] *adj* useless, unnecessary

inutilement [inytilmɑ̃] *adv* in vain, uselessly; unnecessarily

inutilité [inytilite] *f* uselessness

invain·cu -cue [ɛ̃vɛ̃ky] *adj* unconquered

invalide [ɛ̃valid] *adj* invalid || *mf* invalid, cripple; **invalide de guerre** disabled veteran

invalider [ɛ̃valide] *tr* to invalidate

invalidité [ɛ̃validite] *f* invalidity; disability

invariable [ɛ̃variabl] *adj* invariable

invasion [ɛ̃vazjɔ̃] *f* invasion

invective [ɛ̃vektiv] *f* invective

invectiver [ɛ̃vektive] *tr* to rail at || *intr* to inveigh

invendable [ɛ̃vɑ̃dabl] *adj* unsalable

inven·du -due [ɛ̃vɑ̃dy] *adj* unsold || *m* —**les invendus** the unsold copies; the unsold articles

inventaire [ɛ̃vɑ̃ter] *m* inventory

inventer [ɛ̃vɑ̃te] *tr* to invent

inven·teur [ɛ̃vɑ̃tœr] **-trice** [tris] *mf* inventor; (law) finder

inven·tif [ɛ̃vɑ̃tif] **-tive** [tiv] *adj* inventive

invention [ɛ̃vɑ̃sjɔ̃] *f* invention

inventorier [ɛ̃vɑ̃tɔrje] *tr* to inventory

inversable [ɛ̃versabl] *adj* untippable, uncapsizable

inverse [ɛ̃vers] *adj & m* inverse; **faire l'inverse de** to do the opposite of

inverser [ɛ̃verse] *tr* to invert, to reverse || *intr* (elec) to reverse

inverseur [ɛ̃versœr] *m* reversing device; **inverseur des phares** (aut) dimmer

inversion [ɛ̃versjɔ̃] *f* inversion

inverté·bré -brée [ɛ̃vertebre] *adj & m* invertebrate

inver·ti -tie [ɛ̃verti] *mf* invert

invertir [ɛ̃vertir] *tr* to invert, reverse

investiga·teur [ɛ̃vestigatœr] **-trice** [tris] *adj* investigative; searching ‖ *mf* investigator

investigation [ɛ̃vestigɑsjɔ̃] *f* investigation

investir [ɛ̃vestir] *tr* to invest; to vest; **investir qn de sa confiance** to place one's confidence in s.o.

investissement [ɛ̃vestismɑ̃] *m* investment

investiture [ɛ̃vestityr] *f* investiture; nomination *(as a candidate for election)*

invété·ré -rée [ɛ̃vetere] *adj* inveterate

invétérer [ɛ̃vetere] *ref* to become inveterate

invincible [ɛ̃vɛ̃sibl] *adj* invincible

invisible [ɛ̃vizibl] *adj* invisible; (coll) hiding, keeping out of sight

invitation [ɛ̃vitɑsjɔ̃] *f* invitation

invite [ɛ̃vit] *f* invitation, inducement; **répondre à l'invite de qn** (cards) to return s.o.'s lead; (fig) to respond to s.o.'s advances

invi·té -tée [ɛ̃vite] *adj* invited ‖ *mf* guest

inviter [ɛ̃vite] *tr* to invite

involontaire [ɛ̃vɔlɔ̃ter] *adj* involuntary

invoquer [ɛ̃vɔke] *tr* to invoke

invraisemblable [ɛ̃vresɑ̃blabl] *adj* improbable, unlikely, hard to believe; (coll) strange, weird

invraisemblance [ɛ̃vresɑ̃blɑ̃s] *f* improbability, unlikelihood; (coll) queerness

invulnérable [ɛ̃vylnerabl] *adj* invulnerable

iode [jɔd] *m* iodine

iodure [jɔdyr] *m* iodide

ion [jɔ̃] *m* ion

ioniser [jɔnize] *tr* to ionize

iota [jɔta] *m* iota

Irak [irak] *m*—**l'Irak** Iraq

ira·kien [irakjɛ̃] **-kienne** [kjen] *adj* Iraqi ‖ *(cap) mf* Iraqi

Iran [irɑ̃] *m*—**l'Iran** Iran

ira·nien [iranjɛ̃] **-nienne** [njen] *adj* Iranian ‖ *m* Iranian *(language)* ‖ *(cap) mf* Iranian *(person)*

iris [iris] *m* iris

irlan·dais [irlɑ̃de] **-daise** [dez] *adj* Irish ‖ *m* Irish *(language)* ‖ *(cap)* Irishman; **les Irlandais** the Irish ‖ *(cap) f* Irishwoman

Irlande [irlɑ̃d] *f* Ireland; **l'Irlande** Ireland

ironie [irɔni] *f* irony

ironique [irɔnik] *adj* ironic(al)

ironiser [irɔnize] *tr* to say ironically ‖ *intr* to speak ironically, to jeer

irradier [iradje] *tr & ref* to irradiate

irraison·né -née [irezɔne] *adj* unreasoning

irration·nel -nelle [irasjɔnel] *adj* irrational

irréalisable [irealizabl] *adj* impractical, unattainable

irréalité [irealite] *f* unreality

irrécouvrable [irekuvrabl] *adj* uncollectible

irrécupérable [irekyperabl] *adj* irretrievable

irrécusable [irekyzabl] *adj* unimpeachable, incontestable, indisputable

irréel irréelle [ireel] *adj* unreal

irréfléchi -chie [irefleʃi] *adj* rash, thoughtless

irréfutable [irefytabl] *adj* irrefutable

irrégu·lier [iregylje] **-lière** [ljer] *adj & m* irregular

irréli·gieux [irelizjø] **-gieuse** [ʒjøz] *adj* irreligious

irrémédiable [iremedjabl] *adj* irremediable

irremplaçable [irɑ̃plasabl] *adj* irreplaceable

irréparable [ireparabl] *adj* irreparable; irretrievable *(loss, mistake, etc.)*

irrépressible [irepresibl] *adj* irrepressible

irréprochable [ireprɔʃabl] *adj* irreproachable

irrésistible [irezistibl] *adj* irresistible

irréso·lu -lue [irezɔly] *adj* irresolute

irrespect [irespe] *m* disrespect

irrespec·tueux [irespektɥø] **-tueuse** [tɥøz] *adj* disrespectful

irrespirable [irespirabl] *adj* unbreathable

irresponsable [irespɔ̃sabl] *adj* irresponsible

irrétrécissable [iretresisabl] *adj* preshrunk, unshrinkable

irrévéren·cieux [ireverɑ̃sjø] **-cieuse** [sjøz] *adj* irreverent

irréversible [ireversibl] *adj* irreversible

irrévocable [irevɔkabl] *adj* irrevocable

irrigation [irigɑsjɔ̃] *f* irrigation

irriguer [irige] *tr* to irrigate

irri·tant -tante [iritɑ̃] **-tante** [tɑ̃t] *adj* irritating ‖ *m* irritant

irritation [iritɑsjɔ̃] *f* irritation

irriter [irite] *tr* to irritate ‖ *ref* to become irritated

irruption [irypsjɔ̃] *f* irruption; invasion; **faire irruption** to burst in

isabelle [izabel] *m* dun or light-bay horse ‖ *(cap) f* Isabel

Isaïe [izai] *m* Isaiah

Islam [islam] *m*—**l'Islam** Islam

islan·dais [islɑ̃de] **-daise** [dez] *adj* Icelandic ‖ *m* Icelandic *(language)* ‖ *(cap) mf* Icelander

Islande [islɑ̃d] *f* Iceland; **l'Islande** Iceland

isocèle [izɔsel] *adj* isosceles

iso·lant [izɔlɑ̃] **-lante** [lɑ̃t] *adj* insulating ‖ *m* insulator

isolateur [izɔlatœr] *m* insulator

isolation [izɔlɑsjɔ̃] *f* insulation; **isolation phonique** soundproofing

isolationniste [izɔlɑsjɔnist] *adj & mf* isolationist

iso·lé -lée [izɔle] *adj* isolated; independent; insulated

isolement [izɔlmɑ̃] *m* isolation; insulation

isolément [izɔlemɑ̃] *adv* separately, independently

isoler [izɔle] *tr* to isolate; to insulate ‖ *ref* to cut oneself off

isoloir [izɔlwar] *m* polling booth

isotope [izɔtɔp] *m* isotope

Israël [israel] *m*—l'Israël Israel

israé•lien [israeljɛ̃] **-lienne** [ljen] *adj* Israeli ‖ (*cap*) *mf* Israeli

israélite [israelit] *adj* Israelite ‖ (*cap*) *mf* Israelite

is•su is•sue [isy] *adj*—**issu de** descended from, born of ‖ *f* exit, way out; outlet; outcome, issue; **à l'issue de** on the way out from; at the end of; **issues** sharps, middlings (*in milling flour*); offal (*in butchering*); **sans issue** without exit; without any way out

isthme [ism] *m* isthmus

Italie [itali] *f* Italy; **l'Italie** Italy

ita•lien [italjɛ̃] **-lienne** [ljen] *adj* Italian ‖ *m* Italian (*language*) ‖ (*cap*) *mf* Italian (*person*)

italique [italik] *adj* Italic; (*typ*) italic ‖ *m* (*typ*) italics

item [item] *m* question (*in a test*) ‖ *adv* ditto

itinéraire [itinerer] *adj* & *m* itinerary

itiné•rant [itinerɑ̃] **-rante** [rɑ̃t] *adj* & *mf* itinerant

itou [itu] *adv* (slang) also, likewise

ivoire [ivwar] *m* ivory

ivraie [ivre] *f* darnel, cockle; (Bib) tares

ivre [ivr] *adj* drunk, intoxicated

ivresse [ivres] *f* drunkenness; ecstasy, rapture

ivrogne [ivrɔɲ] *adj* hard-drinking ‖ *m* drunkard

ivrognerie [ivrɔɲri] *f* drunkenness

ivrognesse [ivrɔɲes] *f* drinking woman

J

J, j [ʒi] *m invar* tenth letter of the French alphabet

jabot [ʒabo] *m* jabot; crop (*of bird*)

jabotage [ʒabotaʒ] *m* jabbering

jaboter [ʒabote] *tr* & *intr* to jabber

jacasse [ʒakas] *f* magpie; chatterbox

jacasser [ʒakase] *intr* to chatter, to jabber

jacasserie [ʒakasri] *f* chatter, jabber

jachère [ʒa/er] *f* fallow ground

jacinthe [ʒasɛ̃t] *f* hyacinth; **jacinthe des bois** bluebell

Jacques [ʒɑk] *m* James, Jacob; **Jacques Bonhomme** the typical Frenchman

jactance [ʒaktɑ̃s] *f* bragging

jade [ʒad] *m* jade

jadis [ʒadis] *adv* formerly, of yore

jaguar [ʒagwar] *m* jaguar

jaillir [ʒajir] *intr* to gush, to burst forth

jaillissement [ʒajismɑ̃] *m* gush

jais [ʒe] *m* jet

jalon [ʒalɔ̃] *m* stake; landmark; surveying staff

jalonner [ʒalone] *tr* to stake out; to mark (*a way, a channel*)

jalousie [ʒaluzi] *f* jealousy; awning; Venetian blind

ja•loux [ʒalu] **-louse** [luz] *adj* jealous

jamais [ʒame] *adv* ever; never; **jamais de la vie!** not on your life!; **jamais plus** never again; **ne . . . jamais** §90 never; **pour jamais** forever

jambe [ʒɑ̃b] *f* leg. **à toutes jambes** as fast as possible; **prendre ses jambes à son cou** to take to one's heels

jambon [ʒɑ̃bɔ̃] *m* ham; **jambon d'York** boiled ham

jambon•neau [ʒɑ̃bono] *m* (*pl* **-neaux**) ham knuckle

jamboree [ʒɑ̃bore], [dʒambori] *m* jamboree

jante [ʒɑ̃t] *f* felloe; rim (*of auto wheel*)

janvier [ʒɑ̃vje] *m* January

Japon [ʒapɔ̃] *m*—**le Japon** Japan

japo•nais [ʒapone] **-naise** [nez] *adj* Japanese ‖ *m* Japanese (*language*) ‖ (*cap*) *mf* Japanese (*person*)

japper [ʒape] *intr* to yap, to yelp

jaquemart [ʒakmar] *m* jack (*figurine striking the time on a bell*)

jaquette [ʒaket] *f* coat, jacket; cutaway coat, morning coat; book jacket

jardin [ʒardɛ̃] *m* garden; **jardin d'acclimatation** zoo; **jardin d'enfants** kindergarten; **jardin d'hiver** greenhouse

jardiner [ʒardine] *tr* to clear out, to trim ‖ *intr* to garden

jardi•nier [ʒardinje] **-nière** [njer] *adj* garden ‖ *mf* gardener ‖ *m* flower stand; mixed vegetables; spring wagon ‖ *f* kindergartner (*teacher*)

jargon [ʒargɔ̃] *m* jargon

jarre [ʒar] *f* earthenware jar

jarret [ʒare] *m* hock, gambrel; shin (*of beef or veal*); back of the knee

jarretelle [ʒartel] *f* garter

jarretière [ʒartjer] *f* garter

jars [ʒar] *m* gander

jaser [ʒaze] *intr* to babble, prattle; to blab, gossip

jasmin [ʒasmɛ̃] *m* jasmine

jaspe [ʒasp] *m* jasper; (bb) marbling

jasper [ʒaspe] *tr* to marble, speckle

jatte [ʒat] *f* bowl

jauge [ʒoʒ] *f* gauge; dipstick; (agr) trench; (naut) tonnage

jauger [ʒoʒe] §38 *tr* to gauge, measure; (naut) to draw

jaunâtre [ʒonɑtr] *adj* yellowish; sallow

jaune [ʒon] *adj* yellow ‖ *mf* yellow

person (*Oriental*) ‖ *m* yellow; yolk (*of egg*); scab, strikebreaker
jaunir [ʒonir] *tr* & *intr* to yellow
jaunisse [ʒonis] *f* jaundice
Javel [ʒavɛl] *f*—**eau de Javel** bleach
javelle [ʒavɛl] *f* swath (*of grain*); bunch (*of twigs*)
javelliser [ʒavelize] *tr* to chlorinate (*water*)
javelot [ʒavlo] *m* javelin
jazz [dʒaz] *m* jazz
je [ʒə] §87
Jean [ʒɑ̃] *m* John
Jeanne [ʒan] *f* Jane, Jean, Joan
jeannette [ʒanɛt] *f* gold cross (*ornament*); sleeveboard
Jeannot [ʒano] *m* (coll) Johnny, Jack
jeep [dʒip] *f* jeep
Jéhovah [ʒeova] *m* Jehovah
je-m'en-fichisme [ʒmɑ̃fiʃism] *m* (slang) what-the-hell attitude
je-ne-sais-quoi [ʒənsekwa] *m* *invar* what-you-call-it
Jérôme [ʒerom] *m* Jerome
jerrycan [dʒerikan] *m* gasoline can
jersey [ʒerse] *m* jersey, sweater
Jérusalem [ʒeryzalem] *f* Jerusalem
Jésuite [ʒezɥit] *m* Jesuit
Jésus [ʒezy] *m* Jesus
Jésus-Christ [ʒezykri] *m* Jesus Christ
jet [ʒe] *m* throw, cast; jet; spurt, gush; flash (*of light*); **du premier jet** at the first try; **jet à la mer** jettison; **jet d'eau** fountain; **jet de pierre** stone's throw
jetée [ʒəte] *f* breakwater, jetty
jeter [ʒəte] §34 *tr* to throw; to throw away; to throw down; to hurl, fling; to toss; to cast (*a glance*); to shed (*the skin*); to pour forth; to utter; to drop (*anchor*); to lay (*the foundations*) ‖ *intr* to sprout ‖ *ref* to throw oneself; to rush; to empty (*said of a river*)
jeton [ʒətɔ̃] *m* token, counter; slug
jeu [ʒø] *m* (*pl* **jeux**) play, game, sport; gambling; pack, deck (*of cards*); set (*of chessmen; of tools*); playing; acting; execution, performance; **en jeu** in gear; at stake; **franc jeu** fair play; **gros jeu** high stakes; **jeu d'eau** dancing waters; **jeu de dames** checkers; **jeu de hasard** game of chance; **jeu de massacre** hit-the-baby (*game at fair*); **jeu de mots** pun, play on words; **jeu d'enfant** child's play; **jeu de patience** jigsaw puzzle; **jeu de puce** tiddlywinks; **jeu de société** parlor game; **jeu d'orgue** organ stop; **jouer un jeu d'enfer** to play for high stakes; **vieux jeu** old hat
jeudi [ʒødi] *m* Thursday; **jeudi saint** Maundy Thursday
jeun [ʒœ̃]—**à jeun** fasting; on an empty stomach
jeune [ʒœn] *adj* young; youthful; junior, younger ‖ *m* young man; **jeunes délinquants** juvenile delinquents; **les jeunes** young people; the young (*of an animal*)
jeûne [ʒøn] *m* fast, fasting

jeûner [ʒøne] *intr* to fast; to abstain; to eat sparingly
jeunesse [ʒœnes] *f* youth; youthfulness; boyhood, girlhood; **jeunesse dorée** young people of wealth and fashion
jeu-net [ʒœne] **-nette** [net] *adj* youngish
jeû-neur [ʒønœr] **-neuse** [nøz] *mf* faster
joaillerie [ʒoajri] *f* jewelry; jewelry business; jewelry shop
joail-lier [ʒoaje] **joail-lière** [ʒoajer] *mf* jeweler
jobard [ʒobar] *m* (coll) dupe
jobarderie [ʒobardri] *f* gullibility
jockey [ʒoke] *m* jockey
jodler [ʒodle] *tr* & *intr* to yodel
joie [ʒwa] *f* joy; **joies** pleasures
joindre [ʒwɛ̃dr] §35 *tr* to join; to add; to adjoin; to catch up with; **joindre les deux bouts** to make both ends meet ‖ *intr* to join ‖ *ref* to join, unite; to be adjacent, to come together
joint [ʒwɛ̃] **jointe** [ʒwɛ̃t] *adj* joined; joint (*effort*); **joint à** added to ‖ *m* joint; **joint de cardan** (mach) universal joint; **joint de culasse** (aut) gasket (*of cylinder head*); **joint de dilatation thermique** expansion joint; **trouver le joint** (coll) to hit on the solution
jointure [ʒwɛ̃tyr] *f* knuckle; joint
joker [ʒokɛr] *m* joker
jo-li -lie [ʒoli] *adj* pretty; tidy (*income*)
joliment [ʒolimɑ̃] *adv* nicely; (coll) extremely, awfully
Jonas [ʒonas], [ʒonɑ] *m* Jonah
jonc [ʒɔ̃] *m* rush; **jonc d'Inde** rattan
jonchée [ʒɔ̃ʃe] *f* litter (*things strewn about*); cottage cheese
joncher [ʒɔ̃ʃe] *tr* to strew; to litter
jonction [ʒɔ̃ksjɔ̃] *f* junction
jongler [ʒɔ̃gle] *intr* to juggle
jonglerie [ʒɔ̃gləri] *f* jugglery
jongleur [ʒɔ̃glœr] *m* juggler; jongleur
jonque [ʒɔ̃k] *f* (naut) junk
jonquille [ʒɔ̃kij] *adj invar* pale-yellow ‖ *m* pale yellow ‖ *f* jonquil
Jordanie [ʒordani] *f* Jordan; **la Jordanie** Jordan
joue [ʒu] *f* cheek; **se caler les joues** (slang) to stuff oneself
jouer [ʒwe] *tr* to play; to gamble away; to feign; to act (*a part*) ‖ *intr* to play; to gamble; to feign; **faire jouer** to spring (*a lock*); **jouer à** to play (*a game*); **jouer à la baisse** to bear the market; **jouer à la hausse** to bull the market; **jouer de** to play (*a musical instrument*) ‖ *ref* to frolic; **se jouer de** to make fun of; to be independent of; to make light of
jouet [ʒwe] *m* toy, plaything
joueur [ʒwœr] **joueuse** [ʒwøz] *mf* player (*of games; of musical instruments*); gambler; **beau joueur** good sport; **joueur à la baisse** bear; **joueur à la hausse** bull; **mauvais joueur** poor sport
jouf-flu -flue [ʒufly] *adj* chubby
joug [ʒu] *m* yoke

jouir [ʒwir] *intr* to enjoy oneself, enjoy life; **jouir de** to enjoy

jouissance [ʒwisɑ̃s] *f* enjoyment; use, possession

jouis·seur [ʒwisœr] **jouis·seuse** [ʒwisøz] *adj* pleasure-loving ‖ *mf* pleasure lover

jou·jou [ʒuʒu] *m* (*pl* **-joux**) toy, plaything

jour [ʒur] *m* day; daylight; light, window, opening; **à jour** openwork; up to date; **de nos jours** nowadays; **grand jour** broad daylight; **huit jours** a week; **il fait jour** it is getting light; **jour chômé** day off; **jour de ma fête** my birthday; **jour férié** legal holiday; **jour ouvrable** workday; **le jour de l'An** New Year's day; **le jour J** D-Day; **quinze jours** two weeks; **sous un faux jour** in a false light; **vivre au jour le jour** to live from hand to mouth

Jourdain [ʒurdɛ̃] *m* Jordan (*river*)

jour·nal [ʒurnal] *m* (*pl* **-naux** [no]) newspaper; journal; diary; (naut) logbook, journal; **journal parlé** newscast; **journal télévisé** telecast

journa·lier [ʒurnalje] **-lière** [ljɛr] *adj* daily ‖ *m* day laborer

journalisme [ʒurnalism] *m* journalism

journaliste [ʒurnalist] *mf* journalist

journée [ʒurne] *f* day; day's journey; day's pay; day's work; **journée d'accueil** open house; **toute la journée** all day long

journellement [ʒurnɛlmɑ̃] *adv* daily

joute [ʒut] *f* joust

jouter [ʒute] *intr* to joust

jo·vial [ʒɔvjal] *adj* (*pl* **-vials** or **-viaux** [vjo] **-viales**) jovial, jocose

joyau [ʒwajo] *m* (*pl* **joyaux**) jewel

joyeux [ʒwajø] **joyeuse** [ʒwajøz] *adj* joyful, cheerful; jocose

jubi·lant [ʒybilɑ̃] **-lante** [lɑ̃t] *adj* jubilant

jubilé [ʒybile] *m* jubilee; golden-wedding anniversary

jucher [ʒyʃe] *tr & intr* to perch ‖ *ref* to go to roost

judaïque [ʒydaik] *adj* Jewish

judaïsme [ʒydaism] *m* Judaism

judas [ʒyda] *m* peephole ‖ (*cap*) *m* Judas

judicature [ʒydikatyr] *f* judiciary

judiciaire [ʒydisjɛr] *adj* legal, judicial

judi·cieux [ʒydisjø] **-cieuse** [sjøz] *adj* judicious, judicial

juge [ʒyʒ] *m* judge; umpire; **juge assesseur** associate judge

jugement [ʒyʒmɑ̃] *m* judgment

juger [ʒyʒe] §38 *tr & intr* to judge

jugulaire [ʒygylɛr] *adj* jugular ‖ *f* chin strap

juif [ʒɥif] **juive** [ʒɥiv] *adj* Jewish ‖ (*cap*) *mf* Jew

juillet [ʒɥijɛ] *m* July

juin [ʒɥɛ̃] *m* June

Jules [ʒyl] *m* Julius; (coll) Mack; (slang) pimp; (slang) chamber pot

ju·lien [ʒyljɛ̃] **-lienne** [ljen] *adj* Julian ‖ *f* (*soup*) julienne; (bot) rocket

ju·meau [ʒymo] **-melle** [mɛl] (*pl* **-meaux** **-melles**) *adj & mf* twin ‖ see **jumelles**

jumelage [ʒymlaʒ] *m* twinning

jume·lé [ʒymle] **-lée** *adj* double; twin (*cities*); semidetached (*house*); bilingual (*text*)

jumeler [ʒymle] §34 *tr* to couple, to join; to pair

jumelles [ʒymɛl] *fpl* opera glasses; field glasses; **jumelles de manchettes** cuff links

jument [ʒymɑ̃] *f* mare

jungle [ʒœ̃gl] *f* jungle

jupe [ʒyp] *f* skirt

jupon [ʒypɔ̃] *m* petticoat

juré [ʒyre] *m* juror; member of an examining board

jurer [ʒyre] *tr* to swear ‖ *intr* to swear; to blaspheme

juridiction [ʒyridiksjɔ̃] *f* jurisdiction

juridique [ʒyridik] *adj* legal, judicial

juriste [ʒyrist] *m* writer on legal matters

juron [ʒyrɔ̃] *m* oath

jury [ʒyri] *m* jury; examining board

jus [ʒy] *m* juice; gravy; (slang) drink (*body of water*)

jusqu'au-boutiste [ʒyskobutist] *mf* (coll) bitterender, diehard

jusque [ʒysk(ə)] *adv* even; **jusqu'à** as far as, down to, up to; until; even; **jusqu'à ce que** until; **jusqu'après** until after; **jusqu'à quand** how long ‖ *prep* as far as; until; **jusques et y compris** [ʒyskazeikɔ̃pri] up to and including; **jusqu'ici** this far; until now; **jusqu'où** how far

jusque-là [ʒyskəla] *adv* that far; until then

jusquiame [ʒyskjam] *f* henbane

juste [ʒyst] *adj* just, righteous; accurate; just enough; sharp, e.g., **à six heures justes** at six o'clock sharp; (mus) in tune, on key ‖ *adv* justly; correctly, exactly

justement [ʒystəmɑ̃] *adv* just; justly; exactly; as it happens

juste-milieu [ʒystəmiljø] *m* happy medium, golden mean

justesse [ʒystes] *f* justness; precision, accuracy; **de justesse** barely

justice [ʒystis] *f* justice; **faire justice de** to mete out just punishment to; to make short work of

justiciable [ʒystisjabl] *adj*—**justiciable de** accountable to; subject to

justifier [ʒystifje] *tr* to justify ‖ *intr*—**justifier de** to account for, to prove ‖ *ref* to clear oneself

jute [ʒyt] *m* jute

ju·teux [ʒytø] **-teuse** [tøz] *adj* juicy

juvénile [ʒyvenil] *adj* juvenile, youthful

juxtaposer [ʒykstapoze] *tr* to juxtapose

K

K, k [ka] *m invar* eleventh letter of the French alphabet
kaki [kaki] *adj invar* & *m* khaki
kaléidoscope [kaleidɔskɔp] *m* kaleidoscope
kangourou [kãguru] *m* kangaroo
keepsake [kipsɛk] *m* giftbook, keepsake
képi [kepi] *m* kepi
kermesse [kɛrmɛs] *f* charity bazaar
kérosène [kerozɛn] *m* kerosene
ketchup [kɛt/œp] *m* ketchup
khan [kã] *m* khan
kidnapper [kidnape] *tr* to kidnap
kidnap·peur [kidnapœr] **kidnap·peuse** [kidnapøz] *mf* kidnaper
kif [kif] *m* (coll) pot, marijuana
kif-kif [kifkif] *adj invar* (coll) all the same; **c'est kif-kif** (coll) it's fifty-fifty
kilo [kilo] *m* kilo, kilogram
kilocycle [kilosikl] *m* kilocycle
kilogramme [kilɔgram] *m* kilogram
kilomètre [kilɔmetr] *m* kilometer, kilo
kilowatt [kilɔwat] *m* kilowatt
kilowatt-heure [kilɔwatœr] *m* (*pl* kilowatts-heures) kilowatt-hour

kilt [kilt] *m* kilt
kimono [kimɔno] *m* kimono
kinescope [kineskɔp] *m* kinescope
kiosque [kjɔsk] *m* newsstand; bandstand; summerhouse
kipper [kipœr], [kiper] *m* kipper
klaxon [klaksɔn] *m* (aut) horn
klaxonner [klaksɔne] *intr* to sound the horn
kleptomane [kleptɔman] *adj* & *mf* kleptomaniac
km/h *abbr* (**kilomètres-heure, kilomètres à l'heure**) kilometers per hour
knock-out [nɔkaut], [knkut] *adj invar* (boxing) knocked out, groggy ‖ *m* (boxing) knockout
k.o. [kao] (letterword) (**knock-out**) *adj* k.o., knocked out; **mettre k.o.** to knock out ‖ *m* k.o., knockout
kraft [kraft] *m* strong wrapping paper
krak [krak] *m* crash (*e.g., on stock market*)
kyrielle [kirjel] *f* rigmarole, string
kyste [kist] *m* cyst

L

L, l [ɛl], *[ɛl] *m invar* twelfth letter of the French alphabet
la [la] *art §77* ‖ *m* (mus) la ‖ *pron §87*
là [la] *adv* there; here, e.g., **je suis là** I am here; in, e.g., **est-il là?** is he in?; **il n'était pas là** he was out; **là, là!** there, there! (*it's not as bad as that!*)
-là [la] *§82, §84*
là-bas [laba] *adv* yonder, over there
label [label] *m* union label
labeur [labœr] *m* labor, toil
la·bial -biale [labjal] (*pl* -biaux [bjo] -biales) *adj* & *f* labial
laboran·tin [labɔrãtɛ̃] -tine [tin] *mf* laboratory assistant
laboratoire [labɔratwar] *m* laboratory
labo·rieux [labɔrjø] -rieuse [rjøz] *adj* laborious; arduous; industrious; working (*classes*); **c'est laborieux!** (coll) it's endless!
labour [labur] *m* tilling, plowing
labourable [laburabl] *adj* arable, tillable
labourer [labure] *tr* to till, to plow; to furrow (*the brow*); to scratch
laboureur [laburœr] *m* farm hand, plowman
Labrador [labradɔr] *m—le* **Labrador** Labrador
labyrinthe [labirɛ̃t] *m* labyrinth, maze
lac [lak] *m* lake; **Grands Lacs** Great Lakes
lacer [lase] *§51 tr* to lace; to tie (*one's shoes*)

lacération [laserasjɔ̃] *f* tearing
lacérer [lasere] *§10 tr* to lacerate; to tear up
lacet [lase] *m* lace; snare, noose; bowstring (*for strangling*); hairpin curve; **en lacet** winding (*road*); **lacet de soulier** shoelace
lâche [laʃ] *adj* slack, loose; lax, careless; cowardly ‖ *mf* coward
lâcher [laʃe] *tr* to loosen; to let go, to release; to turn loose; to blurt out (*a word*); to fire (*a shot*); (coll) to drop (*one's friends*); **lâcher pied** to give ground; **lâcher prise** to let go
lâcheté [laʃte] *f* cowardice
lâ·cheur [laʃœr] **-cheuse** [ʃøz] *mf* fickle friend, turncoat
lacis [lasi] *m* network (*of threads, nerves*)
laconique [lakɔnik] *adj* laconic
lacrymogène [lakrimɔʒen] *adj* tear (*gas*)
lacs [la] *m* noose, snare; **lacs d'amour** love knot
lac·té -tée [lakte] *adj* milky; milk (*diet*)
lacune [lakyn] *f* lacuna, gap, blank
lad [lad] *m* stableboy
là-dedans [ladədɑ̃] *§85A adv* in it, within, in that, in there
là-dessous [ladəsu] *§85A adv* under it, under that, under there
là-dessus [ladəsy] *§85A adv* on it, on that; thereupon

ladre [lɑdr] *adj* stingy, niggardly ‖ *mf* miser

ladrerie [lɑdrəri] *f* miserliness

lagon [lagɔ̃] *m* lagoon

lagune [lagyn] *f* lagoon

lai laie [lɛ] *adj* lay ‖ *m* lay (*poem*) ‖ *f* see **laie**

laïc laïque [laik] *adj* lay, secular ‖ *mf* layman ‖ *f* laywoman

laiche [lɛʃ] *f* (bot) sedge, reed grass

laïcisation [laisizɑsjɔ̃] *f* secularization

laïciser [laisize] *tr* to secularize

laid [lɛ] **laide** [lɛd] *adj* ugly; plain, homely; mean, low-down

laide-ron [lɛdrɔ̃] **-ronne** [rɔn] *adj* homely, ugly ‖ **laideron** *m* or *f* ugly wench

laideur [lɛdœr] *f* ugliness; meanness

laie [lɛ] *f* (zool) wild sow

lainage [lɛnaʒ] *m* woolens

laine [lɛn] *f* wool; **laine d'acier** steel wool; **manger or tondre la laine sur le dos à** (fig) to fleece

lainer [lɛne] *tr* to teasel, to nap

lai-neux [lɛnø] **-neuse** [nøz] *adj* wooly; downy

lai-nier [lɛnje] **-nière** [njɛr] *adj* wool (*industry*) ‖ *mf* dealer in wool; worker in wool

laïque [laik] *adj* lay, secular ‖ *mf* layman ‖ *f* laywoman

laisse [lɛs] *f* leash; foreshore; laisse

laissé-pour-compte laissée-pour-compte [lesepurkɔ̃t] *adj* returned (*merchandise*) ‖ *m* (*pl* **laissés-pour-compte**) reject; leftover merchandise

laisser [lese], [lɛse] *tr* to leave, to quit; to let, to allow; to let go (*at a low price*); to let have, e.g., **il me l'a laissé pour trois dollars** he let me have it for three dollars; **laisser** + *inf* + **qn** to let s.o. + *inf*, e.g., **il a laissé Marie aller au théâtre** he let Mary go to the theater; e.g., **il me l'a laissé peindre or il m'a laissé le peindre** he let me paint it ‖ *intr*—**ne pas laisser de** to not fail to, to not stop ‖ *ref* to let oneself, e.g., **se laisser aller** to let oneself go; **se laisser aller à** to give way to

laisser-aller [leseale] *m* abandon, easygoingness; slovenliness, negligence

laisser-passer [lesepase] *m invar* permit, pass

lait [lɛ] *m* milk; **lait de chaux** whitewash; **lait de poule** eggnog; **lait écrémé** skim milk; **se mettre au lait** to go on a milk diet

laitage [lɛtaʒ] *m* dairy products

laitance [lɛtɑ̃s] *f* milt

laiterie [lɛtri] *f* dairy, creamery; dairy farming

lai-tier [lɛtje] **-tière** [tjɛr] *adj* dairy; milch (*cow*) ‖ *m* milkman; (metallurgy) slag, dross ‖ *f* dairymaid; milch cow

laiton [lɛtɔ̃] *m* brass

laitonner [lɛtone] *tr* to plate with brass

laitue [lɛty] *f* lettuce; **laitue romaine** romaine

laïus [lajys] *m* (coll) speech, impromptu remarks; (coll) hot air

laïus-seur [lajyscœr] **laïus-seuse** [lajysøz] *mf* (coll) windbag

laize [lɛz] *f* width (*of cloth*)

lamanage [lamanaʒ] *m* harborage

lamaneur [lamancœr] *m* harbor pilot

lam-beau [lɑbo] *m* (*pl* **-beaux**) scrap, bit; rag; **en lambeaux** in tatters, in shreds

lam-bin [lɑ̃bɛ̃] **-bine** [bin] *adj* (coll) slow ‖ *mf* (coll) slowpoke

lambiner [lɑ̃bine] *intr* (coll) to dawdle

lambris [lɑ̃bri] *m* paneling, wainscoting; plaster (*of ceiling*); **lambris dorés** (fig) palatial home

lambrisser [lɑ̃brise] *tr* to panel, to wainscot; to plaster

lame [lam] *f* blade; slat (*of blinds*); runner (*of skate*); wave; lamina, thin plate; sword; (fig) swordsman; **lame de fond** ground swell

la-mé -mée [lame] *adj* gold-trimmed, silver-trimmed, spangled ‖ *m*—**de lamé**, e.g., **une robe de lamé** a spangled dress

lamelle [lamɛl] *f* lamella, thin strip; slide (*of microscope*)

lamentable [lamɑ̃tabl] *adj* lamentable

lamentation [lamɑ̃tɑsjɔ̃] *f* lamentation, lament

lamenter [lamɑ̃te] *intr & ref* to lament

laminer [lamine] *tr* to laminate; to roll (*a metal*)

laminoir [laminwar] *m* rolling mill; calender

lampadaire [lɑ̃padɛr] *m* lamppost; floor lamp

lampe [lɑ̃p] *f* lamp; (electron) tube; **lampe à pétrole** kerosene lamp; **lampe à rayons ultraviolets** sun lamp; **lampe à souder** blowtorch; **lampe au néon** neon light; **lampe de chevet** bedlamp; **lampe de poche** flashlight; **lampe survoltée** photoflood bulb; **s'en mettre plein la lampe** (slang) to fill one's belly

lampée [lɑ̃pe] *f* (coll) gulp, swig

lamper [lɑ̃pe] *tr* (coll) to gulp down, to guzzle

lampe-tempête [lɑ̃ptɑ̃pɛt] *f* (*pl* **lampes-tempête**) hurricane lamp

lampion [lɑ̃pjɔ̃] *m* Chinese lantern

lampiste [lɑ̃pist] *m* lightman; (coll) scapegoat; (coll) underling

lamproie [lɑ̃prwa] *f* lamprey

lampyre [lɑ̃pir] *m* glowworm

lance [lɑ̃s] *f* lance; nozzle (*of hose*); **rompre une lance avec** to cross swords with

lan-cé -cée [lɑ̃se] *adj* flying (*start*); in the swim

lance-bombes [lɑ̃sbɔ̃b] *m invar* trench mortar; (aer) bomb release

lancée [lɑ̃se] *f* impetus

lance-flammes [lɑ̃sflam] *m invar* flamethrower

lance-fusées [lɑ̃sfyze] *m invar* rocket launcher

lancement [lɑ̃smɑ̃] *m* launching, throwing; (*of ship; of new product on the market*) launching; (aer) airdrop; (aer) release; (baseball) pitching

lance-mines [lɑ̃smin] *m invar* minelayer

lance-pierres [lãspjer] *m invar* slingshot

lancer [lãse] §51 *tr* to throw, fling, cast; to launch (*e.g., a ship, a new product*); to issue (*e.g., an appeal*); (baseball) to pitch || *ref* to rush, dash; **se lancer dans** to launch out into, to take up

lance-roquettes [lãsrɔkɛt] *m invar* (arti) bazooka

lance-torpilles [lãstɔrpij] *m invar* torpedo tube

lancette [lãsɛt] *f* (surg) lancet

lan·ceur [lãsœr] **-ceuse** [søz] *mf* promoter; (baseball) pitcher; (sports) hurler, thrower || *m* (rok) booster

lanci·nant [lãsinã] **-nante** [nãt] *adj* shooting, throbbing (*pain*); gnawing (*regret*)

lanciner [lãsine] *tr* to torment || *intr* to shoot; to throb

lan·dau [lãdo] *m* (*pl* **-daus**) landau; baby carriage

lande [lãd] *f* moor, heath

landier [lãdje] *m* kitchen firedog with pothangers

langage [lãgaʒ] *m* language, speech

lange [lãʒ] *m* diaper

langer [lãʒe] §38 *tr* to swaddle, diaper

langou·reux [lãgurø] **-reuse** [røz] *adj* languorous

langouste [lãgust] *f* spiny lobster, crayfish

langous·tier [lãgustje] **-tière** [tjɛr] *m & f* lobster net || *m* lobster boat

langoustine [lãgustin] *f* prawn

langue [lãg] *f* tongue; language, speech; **avoir la langue bien pendue** (coll) to have the gift of gab; **donner sa langue au chat** (coll) to give up; **langue cible** target language; **langue source** source language; **langues vivantes** modern languages; **langue verte** slang; **mauvaise langue** backbiter, gossip; **prendre langue avec** to open up a conversation with; **tirer la langue à** to stick out one's tongue at

langue-de-chat [lãgdəʃa] *f* (*pl* **langues-de-chat**) (culin) ladyfinger

languette [lãgɛt] *f* tongue (*e.g., of shoe*); pointer (*of scale*); flap, strip

langueur [lãgœr] *f* languor

languir [lãgir] *intr* to languish; to pine away

languis·sant [lãgisã] **languis·sante** [lãgisãt] *adj* languid; languishing; longdrawn-out, tiresome

lanière [lanjɛr] *f* strap, strip, thong

lanoline [lanɔlin] *f* lanolin

lanterne [lãtɛrn] *f* lantern; (aut) parking light; (obs) street lamp; **conter des lanternes** (coll) to talk nonsense; **lanterne d'agrandissement** (phot) enlarger; **lanterne de projection, lanterne à projections** slide projector, filmstrip projector; **lanterne rouge** (slang) tail end, last to arrive; **lanterne sourde** dark lantern; **lanterne vénitienne** Japanese lantern; **oublier d'éclairer** or **d'allumer sa lanterne** (coll) to leave out the most important point

lanterner [lãterne] *tr* (coll) to string along, to put off || *intr* to loaf around, to dawdle; **faire lanterner qn** to keep s.o. waiting

lapider [lapide] *tr* to stone; to vilify

la·pin [lapɛ̃] **-pine** [pin] *mf* rabbit; **lapin de garenne** wild rabbit; **lapin russe** albino rabbit; **poser un lapin à qn** (coll) to stand s.o. up

la·pon [lapõ] **-pone** [pɔn] *adj* Lappish || *m* Lapp, Lappish (*language*) || (cap) *mf* Lapp, Laplander (*person*)

Laponie [lapɔni] *f* Lapland; **la Laponie** Lapland

lapsus [lapsys] *m* slip (*of tongue, pen, etc.*)

laquais [lakɛ] *m* lackey, footman

laque [lak] *m & f* lacquer || *m* lacquer ware || *f* lac; shellac; hair spray

laquelle [lakɛl] §78

laquer [lake] *tr* to shellac; to lacquer

larcin [larsɛ̃] *m* petty larceny; plagiarism

lard [lar] *m* bacon, side pork; (coll) fat (*of a person*); (slang) fat slob; **se faire du lard** (coll) to get fat

larder [larde] *tr* to lard; to pierce, riddle

large [larʒ] *adj* wide, broad; generous; ample; large, e.g., **pour une large part** to a large extent || *m* width, breadth; open sea; room, e.g., **donner du large à qn** to give s.o. room; **au large** in the offing; **au large de** off, e.g., **au large du Havre** off Le Havre; **prendre le large** (coll) to shove off || *adv* boldly; **calculer large** to figure roughly; **habiller large** to dress in loose-fitting clothes; **il n'en mène pas large** (fig) he gets rattled in a tight spot; **voir large** (fig) to think big

largement [larʒəmã] *adv* widely; abundantly; fully; plenty, e.g., **vous avez largement le temps** you have plenty of time

largesse [larʒɛs] *f* largess

largeur [larʒœr] *f* width, breadth; (naut) beam

larguer [large] *tr* to let go, to release

larme [larm] *f* tear; (coll) drop; **fondre en larmes** to burst into tears; **pleurer à chaudes larmes** to shed bitter tears

larmoyant [larmwajã] **larmoyante** [larmwajãt] *adj* tearful; watery (*eyes*)

larmoyer [larmwaje] §47 *intr* to water (*said of eyes*); to snivel, to blubber

lar·ron [larõ] **lar·ronnesse** [larɔnes] *mf* thief; **s'entendre comme larrons en foire** to be as thick as thieves

larve [larv] *f* larva

laryn·gé -gée [larɛ̃ʒe] *adj* laryngeal

laryn·gien [larɛ̃ʒjɛ̃] **-gienne** [ʒjen] *adj* laryngeal

laryngite [larɛ̃ʒit] *f* laryngitis

laryngoscope [larɛ̃gɔskɔp] *m* laryngoscope

larynx [larɛ̃ks] *m* larynx

las [lɑ] **lasse** [lɑs] *adj* weary || **las** [lɑs], [la] *interj* alas!

las·cif [lasif] **las·cive** [lasiv] *adj* lascivious

lasciveté [lasivte] *f* lasciviousness

laser [lazer] *m* laser

las·sant [lɑsɑ̃] las·sante [lɑsɑ̃t] *adj* tiring, tedious

lasser [lɑse] *tr* to tire, to weary; to wear out (*s.o.'s patience*) ‖ *ref*— sans se lasser unceasingly; se lasser de + *inf* to tire of + *ger*; to tire oneself out + *ger*

lassitude [lɑsityd] *f* lassitude, weariness

lasso [lɑso] *m* lasso

latence [latɑ̃s] *f* latency

la·tent [latɑ̃] -tente [tɑ̃t] *adj* latent

laté·ral -rale [lateral] *adj* (*pl* -raux) lateral

la·tin [latɛ̃] -tine [tin] *adj* Latin ‖ *m* Latin (*language*) ‖ (*cap*) *mf* Latin (*person*)

latino-améri·cain [latinoamerikɛ̃] -caine [ken] (*pl* -américains) *adj* Latin-American ‖ (*cap*) *mf* Latin American

latitude [latityd] *f* latitude

latrines [latrin] *fpl* latrine

latte [lat] *f* lath; broadsword

latter [late] *tr* to lath

lattis [lati] *m* lathing, laths

laudanum [lodanɔm] *m* laudanum

lauda·tif [lodatif] -tive [tiv] *adj* laudatory

lauréat [lɔrea] lauréate [lɔreat] *adj* laureate ‖ *mf* winner, laureate

laurier [lɔrje] *m* laurel, sweet bay; laurier rose rosebay; s'endormir sur ses lauriers to rest on one's laurels

lavable [lavabl] *adj* washable

lavabo [lavabo] *m* washbowl; washroom; lavabos toilet, lavatory

lavage [lavaʒ] *m* washing; lavage de cerveau (coll) brainwashing; lavage des titres wash sale; lavage de tête (coll) dressing down

lavallière [lavaljer] *f* loosely tied bow

lavande [lavɑ̃d] *f* lavender

lavandière [lavɑ̃djer] *f* washerwoman

lave [lav] *f* lava

lave-glace [lavglas] *m* (*pl* -glaces) (aut) windshield washer

lavement [lavmɑ̃] *m* enema

laver [lave] *tr* to wash; laver le cerveau à (coll) to brainwash ‖ *intr* to wash ‖ *ref* to wash oneself, wash; (with *dat* of *reflex pron*) to wash (*e.g., one's hands*)

laverie [lavri] *f* (min) washery; laverie automatique, laverie libre-service self-service laundry

lavette [lavet] *f* dishcloth

la·veur [lavœr] -veuse [vøz] *mf* washer; laveur de vaisselle dishwasher (*person*); laveur de vitres window washer (*person*) ‖ *f* washerwoman; washing machine

lavoir [lavwar] *m* place for washing clothes

lavure [lavyr] *f* dishwater; (coll) swill, hogwash

laxa·tif [laksatif] -tive [tiv] *adj & m* laxative

layer [leje] §49 *tr* to blaze a trail through; to blaze (*trees to mark a trail*)

layette [lejet] *f* layette; packing case

lazzi [lazi] *mpl* jeers

le [lə] *art* §77 ‖ *pron* §87

leader [lidœr] *m* leader

lèche [leʃ] *f* (coll) thin slice (*e.g., of bread*); faire de la lèche à qn (slang) to lick s.o.'s boots

lèche-carreaux [leʃkaro] *m invar* (slang) window-shopping

lèchefrite [leʃfrit] *f* dripping pan

lécher [leʃe] §10 *tr* to lick; to overpolish (*one's style*)

lé·cheur [leʃœr] -cheuse [ʃøz] *mf* (coll) bootlicker, flatterer

lèche-vitrines [leʃvitrin] *m invar* window-shopping; faire du lèche-vitrines to go window-shopping

leçon [ləsɔ̃] *f* lesson; reading (*of manuscript*); faire la leçon à to lecture, sermonize; to prime on what to say

lec·teur [lektœr] -trice [tris] *mf* reader; lecturer (*of university rank*) ‖ *m* playback

lecture [lektyr] *f* reading; playback; lecture sur les lèvres lip reading

ledit [lədi] ladite [ladit] *adj* (*pl* lesdits [ledi] lesdites [ledit]) the aforesaid

lé·gal -gale [legal] *adj* (*pl* -gaux [go]) legal; statutory

légaliser [legalize] *tr* to legalize

légalité [legalite] *f* legality

légat [lega] *m* papal legate

légataire [legater] *mf* legatee; légataire universel residual heir

légation [legasjɔ̃] *f* legation

légendaire [leʒɑ̃der] *adj* legendary

légende [leʒɑ̃d] *f* legend; caption

lé·ger [leʒe] -gère [ʒer] *adj* light; slight (*accent, difference, pain, mistake, etc.*); faint (*sound, tint, etc.*); delicate (*odor, perfume, etc.*); mild, weak (*drink*); scanty (*dress*); graceful (*figure*); empty (*stomach*); agile, active; frivolous, carefree; à la légère lightly; without due consideration

légèreté [leʒerte] *f* lightness; gracefulness; frivolity; fickleness

leggings [legiŋs] *mpl & fpl* leggings

leghorn [legɔrn] *f* leghorn (*chicken*)

légiférer [leʒifere] §10 *intr* to legislate

légion [leʒjɔ̃] *f* legion

législa·teur [leʒislatœr] -trice [tris] *mf* legislator

législa·tif [leʒislatif] -tive [tiv] *adj* legislative

législation [leʒislasjɔ̃] *f* legislation

législature [leʒislatyr] *f* legislative session; legislature

légiste [leʒist] *m* jurist

légitime [leʒitim] *adj* legitimate ‖ *f* (slang) lawful spouse; ma légitime (slang) my better half

légitimer [leʒitime] *tr* to legitimate; to justify

légitimité [leʒitimite] *f* legitimacy

legs [le], [leg] *m* legacy

léguer [lege] §10 *tr* to bequeath

légume [legym] *m* vegetable; legume (*pod*) ‖ *f*—grosse légume (slang) bigwig, big wheel

légu·mier [legymje] -mière [mjer] *adj* vegetable (*garden, farming, etc.*) ‖ *m* vegetable dish

lendemain [lɑ̃dmɛ̃] *m* next day; results,

outcome, e.g., **avoir d'heureux lendemains** to have happy results or a happy outcome; **au lendemain de** the day after; **le lendemain matin** the next morning; **sans lendemain** short-lived

lénifier [lenifje] *tr* (med) to soothe
lent [lã] **lente** [lãt] *adj* slow || *f* nit
lentement [lãtmã] *adv* slowly; deliberately
lenteur [lãtœr] *f* slowness, sluggishness; **lenteurs** delays, dilatoriness
lentille [lãtij] *f* lens; (bot) lentil; **lentilles freckles**
léopard [leopar] *m* leopard
lèpre [lɛpr] *f* leprosy
lé•preux [leprø] **-preuse** [prøz] *adj* leprous || *mf* leper
lequel [ləkɛl] §78
les [le] *art* §77 || *pron* §87 || *prep* near (*in place names*)
les•bien [lɛsbjɛ̃] **-bienne** [bjɛn] *adj* Lesbian || *f* lesbian || (*cap*) *mf* Lesbian
lèse-majesté [lɛzmaʒɛste] *f*—**crime de lèse-majesté** lese majesty, high treason
léser [leze] §10 *tr* to injure
lésine [lezin] *f* stinginess
lésiner [lezine] *intr* to haggle, to be stingy
lésion [lezjɔ̃] *f* lesion; wrong, damage
les•quels -quelles [lekɛl] §78
lessivage [lesivaʒ] *m* washing; **lessivage de crâne** (coll) brainwashing
lessive [lesiv] *f* washing (*of clothes*); wash; washing soda, lye; **faire la lessive** to do the wash
lessiver [lesive] *tr* to wash; to scrub (*with a cleaning agent*); (slang) to clean out (*e.g., another poker player*); **être lessivé** (slang) to be exhausted
lessiveuse [lesivøz] *f* washing machine
lest [lɛst] *m* ballast
leste [lɛst] *adj* nimble, quick; suggestive, broad, flippant
lestement [lɛstəmã] *adv* nimbly, deftly
lester [lɛste] *tr* to ballast; (coll) to fill (*one's stomach, pockets, etc.*) || *ref* (coll) to stuff oneself
léthargie [letarʒi] *f* lethargy
léthargique [letarʒik] *adj* lethargic || *mf* lethargic person
Lettonie [lɛtɔni] *f* Latvia; **la Lettonie** Latvia
lettrage [letraʒ] *m* lettering
lettre [lɛtr] *f* letter; **à la lettre, au pied de la lettre** to the letter; **avant la lettre** before complete development; **en toutes lettres** in full; in so many words; **lettre de change** bill of exchange; **lettre de faire-part** announcement; **lettre de voiture** bill of lading; **lettre d'imprimerie** printed letter; **lettre majuscule** capital letter; **lettres numérales** roman numerals; **mettre une lettre à la poste** to mail a letter
let•tré -trée [letre] *adj* lettered, literate || *mf* learned person
lettre-morte [letrəmɔrt] *f* letter returned to sender

lettrine [letrin] *f* catchword; initial letter
leu [lø] *m*—**à la queue leu leu** in single file
leucémie [løsemi] *f* leukemia
leucorrhée [løkɔre] *f* leucorrhea
leur [lœr] *adj poss* §88 || *pron poss* §89 || *pron pers* §87
leurre [lœr] *m* lure; delusion
leurrer [lœre] *tr* to lure; to trick, delude || *ref* to be deceived
levain [ləvɛ̃] *m* leaven
levant [ləvã] *adj masc* rising (*sun*) || *m* east || (*cap*) *m* Levant
levan•tin [ləvãtɛ̃] **-tine** [tin] *adj* Levantine || (*cap*) *mf* Levantine
le•vé -vée [ləve] *adj* rising (*sun*); raised (*e.g., hand*); up, e.g., **le soleil est levé** the sun is up || *m* (mus) upbeat; (surv) survey || *f* levee, embankment; collection (*of mail*); levying (*of troops, taxes, etc.*); raising (*of siege*); lifting (*of embargo*); striking (*of camp*); breaking (*of seals*); upstroke (*of piston*); **faire une levée** (cards) to take a trick; **levée de boucliers** public protest, outcry; **levée d'écrou** discharge (*from prison*); **levée de séance** adjournment; **levée du corps** removal of the body; funeral service (*in front of the coffin*); **levées manquantes** (cards) undertricks
lever [ləve] *m* rising; (surv) survey; **lever du rideau** rise of the curtain; curtain raiser; **lever du soleil** sunrise || §2 *tr* to lift; to raise; to collect, to pick up (*the mail*); to levy (*troops, taxes, etc.*); to strike (*camp*); to adjourn (*a meeting*); to weigh (*anchor*); to relieve (*a guard*); to remit (*a punishment*); to flush (*e.g., a partridge*); to effect (*a survey*); to break (*the seals*) || *intr* to come up (*said of plants*); to rise (*said of dough*) || *ref* to get up; to stand up; to rise; to heave (*said of sea*); to clear up (*said of weather*)
léviathan [levjatã] *m* leviathan
levier [ləvje] *m* lever; crowbar; **être aux leviers de commande** (aer) to be at the controls; (fig) to be in control; **levier de changement de vitesse** gearshift lever
lévitation [levitasjɔ̃] *f* levitation
levraut [ləvro] *m* young hare, leveret
lèvre [lɛvr] *f* lip; rim; **du bout des lèvres** half-heartedly, guardedly; **embrasser sur les lèvres** to kiss; **serrer les lèvres** to purse one's lips
lévrier [levrije] *m* greyhound
levure [ləvyr] *f* yeast; **levure anglaise** or **chimique** baking powder; **levure de bière** brewer's yeast
lexi•cal -cale [lɛksikal] *adj* (*pl* **-caux** [ko]) lexical
lexicographe [lɛksikɔgraf] *mf* lexicographer
lexicographie [lɛksikɔgrafi] *f* lexicography
lexicographique [lɛksikɔgrafik] *adj* lexicographic(al)
lexicologie [lɛksikɔlɔʒi] *f* lexicology

lexique [leksik] *m* lexicon, vocabulary; abridged dictionary

lez [le] *prep* near (*in place names*)

lézard [lezar] *m* lizard; **faire le lézard** (coll) to sun oneself, to loaf

lézarde [lezard] *f* crack, split, crevice; gimp (*of furniture*); braid; (mil) gold braid

lézarder [lezarde] *tr & ref* to crack, to split || *intr* (coll) to bask in the sun

liaison [ljezɔ̃] *f* liaison

liant [ljɑ̃] **liante** [ljɑ̃t] *adj* flexible, supple; sociable, affable || *m* flexibility; sociability; binder, binding material; **avoir du liant** to be a good mixer

liard [ljar] *m* (fig) farthing

liasse [ljas] *f* packet, bundle (*e.g., of letters*); wad (*of bank notes*)

Liban [libɑ̃] *m*—**le Liban** Lebanon

liba-nais [libane] **-naise** [nez] *adj* Lebanese || (*cap*) *mf* Lebanese

libation [libasjɔ̃] *f* libation

libelle [libel] *m* lampoon

libellé [libele] *m* wording

libeller [libele], [libɛle] *tr* to word; to draw up (*e.g., a contract*); to make out (*a check*)

libellule [libellyl] *f* dragonfly

libé-ral -rale [liberal] *adj & mf* (*pl* **-raux** [ro]) liberal

libéralisme [liberalism] *m* liberalism

libéralité [liberalite] *f* liberality

libéra-teur [liberatœr] **-trice** [tris] *adj* liberating || *mf* liberator

libération [liberasjɔ̃] *f* liberation

libérer [libere] §10 *tr* to liberate || *ref* to free oneself; to pay up

liberté [liberte] *f* liberty, freedom; **liberté d'association** or **liberté de réunion** right of assembly; **liberté de langage** freedom of speech; **liberté de la presse** freedom of the press; **liberté de la propriété** right to own private property; **liberté du commerce et de l'industrie** free enterprise; **liberté du culte** freedom of worship

liber-tin [libertɛ̃] **-tine** [tin] *adj* libertine; (archaic) freethinking || *mf* libertine; (archaic) freethinker

libidi-neux [libidinø] **-neuse** [nøz] *adj* libidinous

libido [libido] *f* libido

libraire [librer] *mf* bookseller; publisher

libraire-éditeur [librereditœr] *m* (*pl* **libraires-éditeurs**) publisher and bookseller

librairie [libreri] *f* bookstore; book trade; publishing house

libre [libr] *adj* free; **je suis libre de mon temps** my time is my own; **libre arbitre** free will; **libre de** free to, at liberty to

libre-échange [libre/ɑ̃ʒ] *m* free trade

libre-échangiste [libre/ɑ̃ʒist] *m* (*pl* **-échangistes**) free trader

libre-pen-seur [librepɑ̃sœr] **-seuse** [søz] *mf* (*pl* **libres-penseurs**) freethinker

libre-service [librəservis] *m* (*pl* **libres-services**) self-service; self-service store

lice [lis] *f* enclosure or fence (*of race track, fairground, tiltyard, etc.*); (zool) hound bitch; **de basse lice** (tex) low-warp; **de haute lice** (tex) high-warp; **entrer en lice** to enter the lists

licence [lisɑ̃s] *f* license; **licence ès lettres** advanced liberal-arts degree, master of arts; **prendre des licences avec** to take liberties with

licen-cié -ciée [lisɑ̃sje] *mf* holder of a master's degree

licenciement [lisɑ̃simɑ̃] *m* discharge, layoff

licencier [lisɑ̃sje] *tr* to discharge, lay off

licen-cieux [lisɑ̃sjø] **-cieuse** [sjøz] *adj* licentious

lichen [liken] *m* lichen

licher [li/e] *tr* (slang) to gulp down

licite [lisit] *adj* lawful, licit

licorne [likɔrn] *f* unicorn

licou [liku] *m* halter

lie [li] *f* dregs, lees; (fig) dregs, scum

lie-de-vin [lidvɛ̃] *adj invar* maroon

liège [ljɛʒ] *m* cork

lien [ljɛ̃] *m* tie, bond, link

lier [lje] *tr* to tie, to bind, to link || *ref* to bind together; to make friends; **lier conversation avec** to fall into conversation with; **se lier d'amitié avec** to become friends with

lierre [ljer] *m* ivy

liesse [ljes] *f*—**en liesse** in festive mood, gay

lieu [ljø] *m* (*pl* **lieux**) place; **au lieu de** instead of, in lieu of; **avoir lieu** to take place; **avoir lieu de** to have reason to; **donner lieu à** to give rise to; **en aucun lieu** nowhere; **en dernier lieu** finally; **en haut lieu** high up, in responsible circles; **en premier lieu** first of all; **en quelque lieu que** wherever; **en tous lieux** everywhere; **il y a lieu à** there is room for; **lieu commun** commonplace; platitude; **lieu de villégiature** resort; **lieu géométrique** locus; **lieux premiers**; **lieux d'aisances** rest rooms; **lieux payants** comfort station, public lavatory; **sur les lieux** on the spot; on the premises; **tenir lieu** to take place; **tenir lieu de** to take the place of

lieu-dit [ljødi] *m* (*pl* **lieux-dits**)—**le lieu-dit . . .** the place called . . .

lieue [ljø] *f* league

lieur [ljœr] **lieuse** [ljøz] *mf* binder || *f* (mach) binder

lieutenant [ljøtnɑ̃] *m* lieutenant; (merchant marine) mate; **lieutenant de port** harbor master; **lieutenant de vaisseau** (nav) lieutenant commander

lieutenant-colonel [ljøtnɑ̃kolonel] *m* (*pl* **lieutenants-colonels**) lieutenant colonel

lièvre [ljevr] *m* hare; **c'est là que gît le lièvre** there's the rub; **lever un lièvre** (fig) to raise an embarrassing question; **prendre le lièvre au gîte** (fig) to catch s.o. napping

ligament [ligamɑ̃] *m* ligament

ligature [ligatyr] *f* ligature

ligaturer [ligatyre] *tr* to tie up

ligne [liɲ] *f* line; figure, waistline; (*of an automobile*) lines; **aller à la ligne** to begin a new paragraph; **avoir de la ligne** to have a good figure; **en première ligne** of the first importance; on the firing line; **garder sa ligne** to keep one's figure; **grande ligne** (rr) main line; **grandes lignes** broad outline; **hors ligne** unrivaled, outstanding; **ligne à postes groupés** (telp) party line; **ligne de changement de date** international date line; **ligne de flottaison** water line; **ligne de mire** (arti) line of sight; **ligne de partage des eaux** watershed; **ligne partagée** (telp) party line; **ligne pointillée** or **hachée** dotted line

lignée [liɲe] *f* lineage, offspring

li•gneux [liɲø] **-gneuse** [ɲøz] *adj* woody

lignifier [liɲifje] *tr & ref* to turn into wood

ligot [ligo] *m* firewood (*in tied bundle*)

ligoter [ligɔte] *tr* to tie up, to bind

ligue [lig] *f* league

liguer [lige] *tr & ref* to league

lilas [lila] *adj invar & m* lilac

li•lial -liale [liljal] *adj* (*pl* **-liaux** [ljo]) lily-white, lily-like

lillipu•tien [lilipysjɛ̃] **-tienne** [sjɛn] *adj & mf* Lilliputian

limace [limas] *f* (zool) slug; (coll) slowpoke; (slang) shirt

limaçon [limasɔ̃] *m* snail; **en limaçon** spiral

limaille [limaj] *f* filings

limbe [lɛ̃b] *m* (astr, bot) limb; **limbes** limbo

lime [lim] *f* file; (*Citrus limetta*) sweet lime; **dernier coup de lime** finishing touches; **enlever à la lime** to file off; **lime à ongles** nail file; **lime émeri** emery board

limer [lime] *tr* to file; to fray; (fig) to polish

limette [limɛt] *f* (*Citrus limetta*) sweet lime

limier [limje] *m* bloodhound; (coll) sleuth

liminaire [liminɛr] *adj* preliminary

limitation [limitasjɔ̃] *f* limitation

limite [limit] *f* limit; maximum, e.g., **vitesse limite** maximum speed; **dernière limite** deadline

limiter [limite] *tr* to limit || *ref* to be limited; to limit oneself

limitrophe [limitrɔf] *adj* frontier; **limitrophe de** adjacent to

limogeage [limɔʒaʒ] *m* (coll) removal from office

limoger [limɔʒe] §38 *tr* (coll) to remove from office, to relieve of a command

limon [limɔ̃] *m* silt; clay; mud; shaft (*of wagon*)

limonade [limɔnad] *f* lemon soda

limona•dier [limɔnadje] **-dière** [djɛr] *mf* soft-drink manufacturer; café manager

limo•neux [limɔnø] **-neuse** [nøz] *adj* silty; muddy

limousine [limuzin] *f* heavy cloak; (aut) limousine

limpide [lɛ̃pid] *adj* limpid

lin [lɛ̃] *m* flax; linen

linceul [lɛ̃sœl] *m* shroud; cover (*of snow*)

linéament [lineamɑ̃] *m* lineament

linge [lɛ̃ʒ] *m* linen (*sheets, tablecloths, underclothes, etc.*); piece of linen; **laver le linge** to do the wash; **linge de corps** underclothes

lingère [lɛ̃ʒɛr] *f* linen maid; linen closet

lingerie [lɛ̃ʒri] *f* linen (*sheets, tablecloths, underclothes, etc.*); linen closet; **lingerie de dame** lingerie; **lingerie d'homme** men's underwear

lingot [lɛ̃go] *m* ingot

lin•gual -guale [lɛ̃gwal] (*pl* **-guaux** [gwo] **-guales**) *adj & f* lingual

linguiste [lɛ̃gɥist] *mf* linguist

linguistique [lɛ̃gɥistik] *adj* linguistic || *f* linguistics

liniment [linimɑ̃] *m* liniment

linoléum [linɔleɔm] *m* linoleum

linon [linɔ̃] *m* lawn (*sheer linen*)

linotte [linɔt] *f* (orn) linnet

linotype [linɔtip] *f* linotype

linotypiste [linɔtipist] *mf* linotype operator

lin•teau [lɛ̃to] *m* (*pl* **-teaux**) lintel

lion [ljɔ̃] **lionne** [ljɔn] *mf* lion || *f* lioness

lion•ceau [ljɔ̃so] *m* (*pl* **-ceaux**) lion cub

lippe [lip] *f* thick lower lip, blubber lip

lip•pu -pue [lipy] *adj* thick-lipped

liquéfier [likefje] *tr* to liquefy

liqueur [likœr] *f* liqueur; liquid; (chem, pharm) liquor

liquidation [likidasjɔ̃] *f* liquidation; settlement; clearance sale

liquide [likid] *adj & m* liquid || *f* liquid (*consonant*)

liquider [likide] *tr* to liquidate; to settle (*a score*); to wind up (*a piece of business*); (coll) to get rid of; to put an end to

liquidité [likidite] *f* liquidity

liquo•reux [likɔrø] **-reuse** [røz] *adj* sweet

lire [lir] §36 *tr & intr* to read; **lire à haute voix** to read aloud; **lire à vue** to sight-read; **lire sur les lèvres** to lip-read || *ref* to read; to show, e.g., **la surprise se lit sur votre visage** your face shows surprise

lis [lis] *m* lily; **lis blanc** lily; **lis jaune** day lily

Lisbonne [lizbɔn] *f* Lisbon

liséré [lizre] or **liseré** [lizere] *m* braid, border, strip

li•seur [lizœr] **-seuse** [zøz] *mf* reader || *f* bookmark; reading lamp; book jacket; bed jacket

lisibilité [lizibilite] *f* legibility

lisible [lizibl] *adj* legible; readable

lisière [lizjɛr] *f* edge, border; list, selvage; **tenir en lisières** to keep in leading strings

lisse [lis] *adj* smooth, polished, sleek || *f* (naut) handrail

lisser [lise] *tr* to smooth, to polish, to

sleek; to glaze (*paper*) ‖ *ref* to become smooth; **se lisser les plumes** to preen its feathers

liste [list] *f* list

lit [li] *m* bed; layer; stratum; **dans le lit de la marée** in the tideway; **dans le lit du vent** in the wind's eye; **du premier lit** by or of the first marriage; **lit de mort** deathbed; **lit d'époque** period bed; **lit de sangle**, **lit de camp** folding cot, camp bed; **lit en portefeuille** apple-pie bed; **lit pliant**, **lit escamotable**, **lit à rabattement** foldaway bed; **lits jumeaux** twin beds

litanie [litani] *f* litany; tale of woe

lit-cage [likaʒ] *m* (*pl* **lits-cages**) foldaway bed

litée [lite] *f* litter (*of animals*)

literie [litri] *f* bedding, bedclothes

lithine [litin] *f* lithia

lithium [litjɔm] *m* lithium

lithographe [litɔgraf] *mf* lithographer

lithographie [litɔgrafi] *f* lithography; lithograph

lithographier [litɔgrafje] *tr* to lithograph

litière [litjɛr] *f* litter (*bedding for animals*); **faire litière de** to trample

litige [litiʒ] *m* litigation

litigieux [litiʒjø] **-gieuse** [ʒjøz] *adj* litigious

litre [litr] *m* liter

littéraire [literɛr] *adj* literary ‖ *mf* teacher of literature; belletrist

littéral -rale [literal] *adj* (*pl* **-raux** [ro]) literal; literary, written

littérature [literatyr] *f* literature

littoral -rale [litɔral] *adj* (*pl* **-raux** [ro]) *adj* littoral, coastal ‖ *m* coast, coastline

Lituanie [lituani] *f* Lithuania; **la Lituanie** Lithuania

lituanien [lituanjɛ̃] **-nienne** [njɛn] *adj* Lithuanian ‖ *m* Lithuanian (*language*) ‖ (*cap*) *mf* Lithuanian (*person*)

liturgie [lityrʒi] *f* liturgy

liturgique [lityrʒik] *adj* liturgic(al)

livide [livid] *adj* livid

Livourne [livurn] *f* Leghorn

livrable [livrabl] *adj* ready for delivery

livraison [livrɛzɔ̃] *f* delivery; installment; **livraison contre remboursement** cash on delivery

livre [livr] *m* book; **à livre ouvert** at sight; **faire un livre** to write a book; (racing) to make book; **feuilleter un livre** to glance through a book; **grand livre** (bk) ledger; **livre de bord** (aer, naut) logbook; **livre de classe** textbook; **livre de cuisine**, **livre de recettes** cookbook; **livre d'or** blue book; testimonial volume; **livre jaune** white book; **petit livre** (bk) journal, day book; **porter au grand livre** (bk) to post ‖ *f* pound (*weight; currency*)

livrée [livre] *f* livery; appearances; coat (*of horse, deer, etc.*)

livrer [livre] *tr* to deliver; to surrender; to betray ‖ *ref*—**se livrer à** to surrender oneself to; to give way to; to indulge in

livresque [livrɛsk] *adj* bookish

livret [livre] *m* booklet; (mus) libretto; **livret de caisse d'épargne** bankbook; **livret de famille** marriage certificate; **livret militaire** military record; **livret scolaire** transcript (*of grades*)

livreur [livrœr] **-vreuse** [vrøz] *mf* deliverer (*of parcels, packages, etc.*) ‖ *m* deliveryman ‖ *f* woman who makes deliveries; delivery truck

lobe [lɔb] *m* lobe

local -cale [lɔkal] (*pl* **-caux** [ko]) *adj* local ‖ *m* place, premises, quarters; headquarters; **locaux** (sports) home team; **locaux commerciaux** office space

localiser [lɔkalize] *tr* to locate; to localize

localité [lɔkalite] *f* locality

locataire [lɔkatɛr] *mf* tenant, renter

location [lɔkasjɔ̃] *f* rental; reservation

loch [lɔk] *m* (naut) log (*to determine speed*)

locomotive [lɔkɔmɔtiv] *f* locomotive; (fig) mover

locuste [lɔkyst] *f* (ent) locust

locuteur [lɔkytœr] **-trice** [tris] *mf* speaker

locution [lɔkysjɔ̃] *f* locution; phrase

lof [lɔf] *m* windward side; **aller or venir au lof** to sail into the wind

logarithme [lɔgaritm] *m* logarithm

loge [lɔʒ] *f* lodge; circus cage; concierge's room; chamber, cell; (theat) dressing room; (theat) box

logeabilité [lɔʒabilite] *f* spaciousness

logeable [lɔʒabl] *adj* livable, inhabitable

logement [lɔʒmã] *m* lodging, lodgings

loger [lɔʒe] §38 *tr*, *intr*, & *ref* to lodge

logeur [lɔʒœr] **-geuse** [ʒøz] *mf* proprietor of a boardinghouse ‖ *m* landlord ‖ *f* landlady

logicien [lɔʒisjɛ̃] **-cienne** [sjɛn] *mf* logician

logique [lɔʒik] *adj* logical ‖ *f* logic

logis [lɔʒi] *m* abode

logistique [lɔʒistik] *adj* logistic(al) ‖ *f* logistics

loi [lwa] *f* law; **faire des lois** to legislate; **faire la loi** to lay down the law; **loi exceptionnelle** emergency legislation

loin [lwɛ̃] *adv* far; far away, far off; **au loin** in the distance; **d'aussi loin que**, **du plus loin que** as soon as; as far back as; **de loin** from afar; far from; far be it from (*e.g., me*); **de loin en loin** now and then; **il y a loin de** it is a far cry from

lointain -taine [lwɛ̃tɛn] *adj* faraway, distant, remote; early (*e.g., memories*) ‖ *m* distance, background; **le lointain** (theat) upstage

loir [lwar] *m* dormouse; **dormir comme un loir** to sleep like a log

loisible [lwazibl] *adj*—**il m'est** (**lui est**, etc.) **loisible de** I am (he is, etc.) free to or entitled to, it is open for me (him, etc.) to loisir [lwazir] *m* leisure, spare time; loisirs diversions

lolo [lolo] *m* (coll) milk (*in baby talk*)

lombes [lɔ̃b] *mpl* loins

londo·nien [lɔ̃dɔnjɛ̃] -nienne [njɛn] *adj* London || (*cap*) *mf* Londoner

Londres [lɔ̃dr] *m* London

londrès [lɔ̃drɛs] *m* Havana cigar

long [lɔ̃] longue [lɔ̃g] *adj* long; lengthy (*speech*); long (*syllable, vowel*); thin, weak (*sauce, gravy*); slow (*to understand, to decide*) || (*when standing before noun*) *adj* long; de longue main of ˉlong standing || *m* length; extent; au long at length; de long lengthwise; de long en large up and down, back and forth; le long de along || *f* see longue || long *adv* much; en dire long to talk a long time; to speak volumes; en savoir long sur to know a great deal about; en savoir plus long to know more about it

longanimité [lɔ̃ganimite] *f* long-suffering

long-courrier [lɔ̃kurje] (*pl* -courriers) *adj* long-range || *m* airliner; liner, ocean liner

longe [lɔ̃ʒ] *f* tether, leash; (culin) loin

longer [lɔ̃ʒe] §38 *tr* to walk along, to go beside; to extend along, to skirt

longeron [lɔ̃ʒrɔ̃] *m* crossbeam, girder

longévité [lɔ̃ʒevite] *f* longevity

longitude [lɔ̃ʒityd] *f* longitude

longtemps [lɔ̃tɑ̃] *m* a long time; avant longtemps before long; depuis longtemps for a long time; long since; ne . . . plus longtemps no . . . longer || *adv* long; for a long time

longue [lɔ̃g] *f* long syllable; long vowel; long suit (*in cards*); à la longue in the long run

longuement [lɔ̃gmɑ̃] *adv* at length, a long time

lon·guet [lɔ̃gɛ] -guette [gɛt] *adj* (coll) longish, rather long

longueur [lɔ̃gœr] *f* length; lengthiness; de longueur, dans la longueur lengthwise; d'une longueur by a length, by a head; longueur d'onde wavelength

longue-vue [lɔ̃gvy] *f* (*pl* longues-vues) telescope, spyglass

looping [lupiŋ] *m* loop-the-loop

lopin [lɔpɛ̃] *m* patch of ground, plot

loquace [lɔkwas] [lɔkas] *adj* loquacious

loque [lɔk] *f* rag; être comme une loque to feel like a dishrag; être en loques to be in tatters

loquet [lɔkɛ] *m* latch

loque·teux [lɔktø] -teuse [tøz] *adj* in tatters || *mf* tatterdemalion

lorgner [lɔrɲe] *tr* to cast a sidelong glance at; to ogle; to have one's eyes on (*a job, an inheritance, etc.*)

lorgnette [lɔrɲet] *f* opera glasses

lorgnon [lɔrɲɔ̃] *m* pince-nez; lorgnette

loriot [lɔrjo] *m* golden oriole

lorry [lɔri] *m* lorry, small flatcar

lors [lɔr] *adv*—lors de at the time of; lors même que even if

lorsque [lɔrsk] *conj* when

losange [lɔzɑ̃ʒ] *m* (geom) lozenge; en losange diamond-shaped; oval-shaped

lot [lo] *m* lot; prize (*e.g., in lottery*); gagner le gros lot to hit the jackpot

loterie [lɔtri] *f* lottery

lo·ti -tie [lɔti] *adj*—bien loti well off; mal loti badly off

lotion [losjɔ̃] *f* lotion; lotion capillaire hair tonic

lotionner [losjɔne] *tr* to bathe (*a wound*)

lotir [lɔtir] *tr* to parcel out; lotir qn de q.ch. to allot s.th. to s.o.

lotissement [lɔtismɑ̃] *m* allotment, apportionment; building lot

louable [lwabl] *adj* praiseworthy; for hire

louage [lwaʒ] *m* hire

louange [lwɑ̃ʒ] *f* praise; à la louange de in praise of

louanger [lwɑ̃ʒe] §38 *tr* to praise, extol

louan·geur [lwɑ̃ʒœr] -geuse [ʒøz] *adj* laudatory, flattering

louche [luʃ] *adj* ambiguous; suspicious, shady; cross-eyed; cloudy (*e.g., wine*) || *f* ladle; basting spoon

loucher [luʃe] *intr* to be cross-eyed, to squint; faire loucher qn de jalousie (coll) to turn s.o. green with envy; loucher sur (coll) to cast longing eyes at

louchet [luʃe] *m* spade (*for digging*)

louer [lwe] *tr* to rent, hire; to reserve (*a seat*); to praise || *ref* to be rented; to hire oneself out; se louer de to be satisfied with

loueur [lwœr] loueuse [lwøz] *mf* operator of a rental service; flatterer

loufoque [lufɔk] *adj* (slang) cracked || *m* (slang) crackpot

lougre [lugr] *m* (naut) lugger

Louisiane [lwizjan] *f* Louisiana; la Louisiane Louisiana

lou·lou [lulu] -loute [lut] *mf* (coll) darling, pet || *m*—loulou de Poméranie Pomeranian, spitz

loup [lu] *m* wolf; mask; flaw; avoir vu le loup to have lost one's innocence; crier au loup to cry wolf; loup de mer (ichth) wolf eel; (coll) old salt; mon petit loup (coll) my pet

loup-cervier [luservje] *m* (*pl* loups-cerviers) lynx

loupe [lup] *f* magnifying glass; gnarl (*on tree*); (pathol) wen

lou·pé -pée [lupe] *adj* bungled; defective || *m* defect

louper [lupe] *tr* (coll) to goof up, to muff; (coll) to miss (*e.g., one's train*) || *intr* (coll) to fail, to goof

loup-garou [lugaru] *m* (*pl* loups-garous) werewolf

lou·piot [lupjo] -piotte [pjɔt] *mf* (coll) kid, child; loupiots (coll) small fry

lourd [lur] lourde [lurd] *adj* heavy; hefty; clumsy; sultry (*weather*); off-color (*joke*); dull (*mind*); (agr) hard to cultivate || (*when standing before noun*) *adj* heavy; grave; clumsy (*e.g., compliments*); off-color (*joke*) || lourd *adv* heavy, heavily

lour·daud [lurdo] -**daude** [dod] *adj* clumsy, loutish, dull ‖ *mf* lout, oaf

lourdement [lurdəmã] *adv* heavily; clumsily; **avancer** or **rouler lourdement** to lumber along

lourdeur [lurdœr] *f* heaviness; clumsiness; sultriness; dullness

loustic [lustik] *m* wag, clown; (coll) screwball, character

loutre [lutr] *f* otter

louve [luv] *f* she-wolf

louve·teau [luvto] *m* (*pl* -**teaux**) wolf cub; cub scout

louvoyer [luvwaje] §47 *intr* to be evasive; (naut) to tack

lovelace [lɔvlas] *m* seducer, Don Juan

lover [lɔve] *tr & ref* to coil

loyal loyale [lwajal] *adj* (*pl* **loyaux** [lwajo]) loyal; honest; fair, just

loyaliste [lwajalist] *mf* loyalist

loyauté [lwajote] *f* loyalty; honesty; fairness

loyer [lwaje] *m* rent

lubie [lybi] *f* whim

lubricité [lybrisite] *f* lubricity, lewdness

lubri·fiant [lybrifjã] -**fiante** [fjãt] *adj & m* lubricant

lubrifier [lybrifje] *tr* to lubricate

lucarne [lykarn] *f* dormer window; skylight

lucide [lysid] *adj* lucid

luciole [lysjɔl] *f* firefly

lucra·tif [lykratif] -**tive** [tiv] *adj* lucrative

lucre [lykr] *m* lucre

luette [lɥɛt] *f* uvula

lueur [lɥœr] *f* glimmer, gleam; flash, blink

luge [lyʒ] *f* sled

lugubre [lygybr] *adj* gloomy

lui [lɥi] *pron disj* §85 ‖ *pron conj* §87

lui-même [lɥimɛm] §86

luire [lɥir] §37 *intr* to shine; to gleam, glow, glisten; to dawn

lui-sant [lɥizã] -**sante** [zãt] *adj* shining

lulu [lyly] *m* (orn) tree pipit

lumbago [lɔ̃bago] *m* lumbago

lumière [lymjɛr] *f* light; aperture; (person) luminary; **avoir des lumières de** to have knowledge of

lumignon [lymiɲɔ̃] *m* feeble light

luminaire [lyminɛr] *m* luminary

lumines·cent [lyminɛsã] **lumines·cente** [lyminɛsãt] *adj* luminescent

lumi·neux [lyminø] -**neuse** [nøz] *adj* luminous; light (*e.g.*, spot); bright (idea)

lunaire [lynɛr] *adj* lunar ‖ *f* (bot) honesty

lunatique [lynatik] *adj* whimsical, eccentric ‖ *mf* whimsical person, eccentric

lunch [lœntʃ], [lœ̃ʃ] *m* buffet lunch

lundi [lœ̃di] *m* Monday

lune [lyn] *f* moon; **être dans la lune** to be daydreaming; **lune de miel** honeymoon; **lune des moissons** harvest moon; **vieilles lunes** good old days, bygone days

lu·né -**née** [lyne] *adj* moon-shaped;

bien luné in a good mood; **mal luné** in a bad mood

lune·tier [lyntje] -**tière** [tjɛr] *mf* optician

lunette [lynɛt] *f* telescope, spyglass; toilet seat; hole (*in toilet seat*); wishbone (*of turkey, chicken*); (archit) lunette; (aut) rear window; **lunettes** eyeglasses, spectacles; goggles; **lunettes de lecture**, **lunettes pour lire** reading glasses; **lunettes de soleil** sunglasses; **lunettes noires** dark glasses

lurette [lyrɛt] *f*—**il y a belle lurette** (coll) ages ago

luron [lyrɔ̃] *m* (coll) playboy

luronne [lyrɔn] *f* (coll) hussy

lustre [lystr] *m* luster; five-year period; chandelier

lus·tré -**trée** [lystre] *adj* lustrous, glossy

lustrine [lystrin] *f* cotton satin

lut [lyt] *m* (chem) lute

luth [lyt] *m* (mus) lute

lutherie [lytri] *f* violin making

luthé·rien [lyterjɛ̃] -**rienne** [rjɛn] *adj* Lutheran ‖ (*cap*) *mf* Lutheran

luthier [lytje] *m* violin maker

lu·tin [lytɛ̃] -**tine** [tin] *adj* impish ‖ *m* imp

lutiner [lytine] *tr* to tease

lutrin [lytrɛ̃] *m* lectern

lutte [lyt] *f* struggle, fight; wrestling; **de bonne lutte** aboveboard; **de haute lutte** by force; in open competition; hard-won; **lutte à la corde de traction** tug of war; **lutte libre** catch-as-catch-can

lutter [lyte] *intr* to fight, to struggle; to wrestle

lut·teur [lytœr] **lut·teuse** [lytøz] *mf* wrestler; (fig) fighter

luxation [lyksasjɔ̃] *f* dislocation

luxe [lyks] *m* luxury

Luxembourg [lyksãbur] *m*—**le Luxembourg** Luxembourg

luxer [lykse] *tr* to dislocate

luxueux [lyksɥø] **luxueuse** [lyksɥøz] *adj* luxurious

luxure [lyksyr] *f* lechery, lust

luxu·riant [lyksyrjã] -**riante** [rjãt] *adj* luxuriant

luxu·rieux [lyksyrjø] -**rieuse** [rjøz] *adj* lecherous, lustful

luzerne [lyzɛrn] *f* alfalfa

lycée [lise] *m* high school; lyceum

lycéen [liseɛ̃] **lycéenne** [liseɛn] *mf* high-school student

lymphatique [lɛ̃fatik] *adj* lymphatic

lymphe [lɛ̃f] *f* lymph

lynchage [lɛ̃ʃaʒ] *m* lynching

lyncher [lɛ̃ʃe] *tr* to lynch

lynx [lɛ̃ks] *m* lynx

Lyon [ljɔ̃] *m* Lyons

lyon·nais [ljonɛ] **lyon·naise** [ljonɛz] *adj* Lyonese; **à la lyonnaise** lyonnaise

lyre [lir] *f* lyre

lyrique [lirik] *adj* lyric(al) ‖ *m* lyric poet ‖ *f* lyric poetry

lyrisme [lirism] *m* lyricism

lys [lis] *m* lily; **lys blanc** lily; **lys jaune** day lily

lysimaque [lizimak] *f* loosestrife

M

M, m [em], *[em] *m invar* thirteenth letter of the French alphabet

M. *abbr* (**Monsieur**) Mr.

ma [ma] §88

ma·boul -boule [mabul] *adj* (slang) nuts, balmy || *mf* (slang) nut

macabre [makabr] *adj* macabre

macadam [makadam] *m* macadam

macadamiser [makadamize] *tr* to macadamize

macaron [makarɔ̃] *m* macaroon

macchabée [makabe] *m* (slang) stiff (*corpse*)

macédoine [masedwan] *f* macédoine, medley; **macédoine de fruits** fruit salad; **macédoine de légumes** mixed vegetables

macérer [masere] §10 *tr* to macerate; to mortify (*the flesh*); to soak, to steep || *intr* to soak, to steep

mâchefer [maʃfer] *m* clinker

mâcher [maʃe] *tr* to chew; **mâcher la besogne à qn** to do all one's work for one. **ne pas mâcher ses mots** to not mince words

machin [maʃɛ̃] *m* (coll) what-do-you-call-it; (coll) what's-his-name, so-and-so

machi·nal -nale [maʃinal] *adj* (*pl* -naux [no]) mechanical

machination [maʃinasjɔ̃] *f* machination

machine [maʃin] *f* machine; engine; **faire machine arrière** to go into reverse; **machine à calculer** adding machine; **machine à coudre** sewing machine. **machine à écrire** typewriter; **machine à laver** washing machine. **machine à laver la vaisselle** dishwasher **machine à vapeur** steam engine; **machines** machinery

machine-outil [maʃinuti] *f* (*pl* **machines-outils**) machine tool

machinerie [maʃinri] *f* machinery; engine room

machiniste [maʃinist] *m* (theat) stage-hand

mâchoire [maʃwar] *f* jaw; jawbone; lower jaw

mâchonner [maʃɔne] *tr* to chew, munch; to mumble (*e.g., the end of a sentence*)

mâchurer [maʃyre] *tr* to crush; to smudge

maçon [masɔ̃] *m* mason

maçonner [masɔne] *tr* to mason, to wall up

maçonnerie [masɔnri] *f* masonry

macule [makyl] *f* spot, blotch; inkblot; birthmark

maculer [makyle] *tr* to soil, spot; (typ) to smear

madame [madam] *f* (*pl* **mesdames** [medam]) madam; Mrs.; (not translated), e.g., **madame votre femme** your wife

Madeleine [madlɛn] *f* Madeleine, Magdalen; sponge cake; **pleurer comme une Madeleine** to weep bitterly

mademoiselle [madmwazɛl] *f* (*pl* **mesdemoiselles** [medmwazɛl]) Miss; eldest daughter; (not translated), e.g., **mademoiselle votre fille** your daughter

Madone [madɔn] *f* Madonna

ma·dré -drée [madre] *adj* sly, cagey || *mf* sly one

madrier [madrije] *m* beam

maf·flu -flue [mafly] *adj* heavy-jowled

magasin [magazɛ̃] *m* store; warehouse; magazine (*of gun or camera; for munitions or powder*). **avoir en magasin** to have in stock; **grands magasins** department store; **magasin à libre service** self-service store; **magasin à succursales multiples** chain store; **magasin d'antiquités** antique shop; **magasin de modes** dress shop

magasinage [magazinaʒ] *m* storage, warehousing; storage charges; (Canad) shopping

magasinier [magazinje] *m* warehouseman

magazine [magazin] *m* magazine; (mov, telv) hour, program, e.g., **magazine féminin** woman's hour

mages [maʒ] *mpl* Magi

magi·cien [maʒisjɛ̃] **-cienne** [sjɛn] *mf* magician

magie [maʒi] *f* magic

magique [maʒik] *adj* magic

magis·tral -trale [maʒistral] *adj* (*pl* -traux [tro]) masterful, masterly; magisterial; (pharm) magistral

magistrat [maʒistra] *m* magistrate

magnanime [maɲanim] *adj* magnanimous

magnat [magna] *m* magnate

magnésium [maɲezjɔm] *m* magnesium

magnétique [maɲetik] *adj* magnetic; hypnotic

magnétiser [maɲetize] *tr* to magnetize; to hypnotize; to spellbind

magnétisme [maɲetism] *m* magnetism

magnéto [maɲeto] *f* magneto

magnétophone [maɲetɔfɔn] *m* tape recorder

magnétoscope [maɲetɔskɔp] *m* video tape recorder; video tape recording

magnifier [maɲifje] *tr* to extol, glorify

magnifique [maɲifik] *adj* magnificent; lavishly generous

magnitude [maɲityd] *f* (astr) magnitude

magot [mago] *m* Barbary ape; figurine; (coll) hoard, pile (*of money*)

Mahomet [maɔmɛ] *m* Mahomet

mahomé·tan [maɔmetɑ̃] **-tane** [tan] *adj & m* Mohammedan

mai [mɛ] *m* May; Maypole

maie [mɛ] *f* bread bin; kneading trough

maigre [megr] *adj* lean; thin; meager; meatless (*day*); **faire maigre** to abstain from meat

maigreur [megrœr] *f* leanness; meagerness

maigri·chon [megriʃɔ̃] **-chonne** [ʃɔn] *adj* (coll) skinny

maigrir [megrir] *tr* to slim; to make (*s.o.*) look thinner || *intr* to lose weight

mail [maj] *m* mail

maille [maj] *f* link; stitch; mesh, loop; **avoir maille à partir avec qn** to have a bone to pick with s.o.; **mailles mail**

maillet [maje] *m* mallet

maillon [mɑjɔ̃] *m* link (*of a chain*)

maillot [majo] *m* swimming suit; jersey; **maillot de bain** swimming suit; **maillot de corps** undershirt; **maillot de danseur** tights; **maillot des acrobates** tights

main [mɛ̃] *f* hand; quire; **à la main** by hand; **à main levée** in one stroke; **avoir la haute main sur** to control; **avoir la main, être la main** (cards) to be the dealer; **battre des mains** to applaud; **de la main à la main** privately; **de longue main** carefully; for a long time; **de main à main** from one person to another; **de première main** firsthand; **donner les mains à q.ch.** to be in favor of s.th.; **en venir aux mains** to come to blows; **faire main basse sur** to grab, to steal; **haut les mains!** hands up!; **passer la main dans** le dos à qn to soft-soap s.o.; **serrer la main à** to shake hands with; **sous main** secretly; **tout main** handmade

main-d'œuvre [mɛ̃dœvr] *f* (*pl* **mains-d'œuvre**) labor; laborers, manpower

maint [mɛ̃] **mainte** [mɛ̃t] *adj* many a; **à maintes reprises** time and again

maintenant [mɛ̃tnɑ̃] *adv* now

maintenir [mɛ̃tnir] §72 *intr* to maintain; to hold up || *ref* to keep on; to keep up

maintien [mɛ̃tjɛ̃] *m* maintenance; bearing

maire [mer] *m* mayor

mairesse [meres] *f* (coll) mayor's wife

mairie [meri] *f* town hall, city hall

mais [me] *m* but || *adv* why, well; **mais non** certainly not || *conj* but

maïs [mais] *m* corn, maize

maison [mezɔ̃] *f* house; home; household, family, house, firm, business; **à la maison** at home, home; **fait à la maison** homemade; **maison centrale** state or federal prison; **maison close, borgne, publique, mal famée, de débauche, de passe, de rendez-vous, de tolérance** house of ill fame; **maison d'accouchement** lying-in hospital; **maison d'antiquités, de meubles d'époque,** or **d'originaux** antique shop; **maison de commerce** firm; **maison de confiance** (com) trustworthy firm; **maison de correction** reform school; **maison de couture** dressmaking establishment **maison de fous** madhouse; **maison de jeux** gambling house; **maison de plaisance** or **de campagne** cottage, summer home; **maison de rapport** apartment house; **maison de repos** rest home; **maison de retraite** old-people's home; **maison de santé** nursing home; **maison jumelée** semi-detached house; **maison mère** head office; **maison**

mortuaire home of the deceased; **maison religieuse** convent

maisonnée [mezone] *f* household

maisonnette [mezɔnet] *f* little house, cottage

maî·tre [metr] **-tresse** [tres] *adj* expert, capable; basic, key; main (*beam, girder*); utter (*fool*); arrant (*knave*); high (*card*) || *m* master; Mr. (*when addressing a lawyer*); (naut) mate; (naut) petty officer; **être passé maître en** to be a past master of or in; **maître chanteur** blackmailer; **maître d'armes** fencing master; **maître de chapelle** choirmaster; **maître d'école** schoolmaster; **maître de conférences** associate professor; **maître de forges** ironmaster; **maître de maison** man of the house, householder; **maître d'équipage** boatswain; **maître d'études** monitor, supervisor; **maître d'hôtel** headwaiter; butler; **maître d'œuvre** foreman; **maître Jacques** jack-of-all-trades; **maître mécanicien** chief engineer; **maître mineur** mine foreman; **maître queue** chef; **passer maître** to know one's trade § *f* see **maîtresse**

maître-autel [metrotel] *m* (*pl* **maîtres-autels**) high altar

maîtresse [metres] *f* mistress; **maîtresse d'école** schoolmistress; **maîtresse de maison** lady of the house

maîtrise [metriz] *f* mastery, command; master's degree; **maîtrise de soi** self-control

maîtriser [metrize] *tr* to master, control; to subdue

maj. *abbr* (**majuscule**) cap.

majesté [maʒeste] *f* majesty

majes·tueux [maʒestɥø] **-tueuse** [tɥøz] *adj* majestic

ma·jeur **-jeure** [maʒœr] *adj* & *m* major

major [maʒɔr] *m* regimental quartermaster; army doctor; **être le major de sa promotion** to be at the head of one's class

majordome [maʒɔrdom] *m* major-domo

majorer [maʒɔre] *tr* to increase the price of; to overprice; to raise (*the price*)

majoritaire [maʒɔriter] *adj* majority

majorité [maʒɔrite] *f* majority

Majorque [maʒɔrk] *f* Majorca

major·quin [maʒɔrkɛ̃] **-quine** [kin] *adj* Majorcan || (*cap*) *mf* Majorcan

majuscule [maʒyskyl] *adj* capital (*letter*) || *f* capital letter

mal [mal] *adj*—**de mal** bad, e.g., **dire q.ch. de mal** to say s.th. bad; **pas mal** not bad, quite good-looking || *m* (*pl* **maux** [mo]) evil; trouble; hurt; pain; wrong; **avoir du mal à** + *inf* to have a hard time + *ger*; to have difficulty in + *ger*; **avoir mal à la tête** to have a headache; **avoir mal au cœur** to be nauseated; **avoir mal aux dents** to have a toothache; **avoir mal de gorge** to have a sore throat; **dire du mal de qn** to speak ill of s.o.; **faire mal à, faire du mal à** to hurt, to harm; **le Mal** Evil; **mal aux reins**

backache; **mal blanc** whitlow; **mal de l'air** airsickness; **mal de la route** carsickness; **mal de mer** seasickness; **mal des rayons** radiation sickness; **mal du pays** homesickness; **mal du siècle** Weltschmerz, romantic melancholy; **se donner du mal** to take pains || *adv* §91 badly, bad; **de mal en pis** from bad to worse; **être mal avec qn** to be on bad terms with s.o.; **pas mal** not bad; **pas mal de** a lot of, quite a few

malade [malad] *adj* sick, ill || *mf* patient, sick person

maladie [maladi] *f* disease, sickness; distemper; **elle va en faire une maladie** (coll) she'll be terribly upset over it; **maladie de carence** or **par carence** deficiency disease; **maladie de cœur** heart trouble; **maladie des caissons** bends; **maladie diplomatique** malingering; **revenir de maladie** to convalesce

mala·dif [maladif] **-dive** [div] *adj* sickly; morbid

maladresse [maladrɛs] *f* awkwardness; blunder

mala·droit [maladrwa] **-droite** [drwat] *adj* clumsy, awkward

ma·lais [malɛ] **-laise** [lɛz] *adj* Malay || *m* Malay (*language*) || see **malaise** *m* || (*cap*) *mf* Malay (*person*)

malaise [malɛz] *m* malaise, discomfort

malai·sé ·sée [maleze] *adj* difficult

malap·pris [malapri] **malap·prise** [malapriz] *adj* uncouth, ill-bred || *mf* ill-bred person

malard [malar] *m* (orn) mallard

malaria [malarja] *f* malaria

malavi·sé ·sée [malavize] *adj* ill-advised, indiscreet

malaxer [malakse] *tr* to knead; to churn (*butter*); to massage

malaxeur [malaksœr] *m* churn; (mach) mixer

malchance [malʃɑ̃s] *f* bad luck; **par malchance** unluckily; **une malchance** a piece of bad luck

malchan·ceux [malʃɑ̃sø] **-ceuse** [søz] *adj* unlucky

malcommode [malkɔmɔd] *adj* inconvenient; unsuitable, impracticable

maldonne [maldɔn] *f* misdeal

mâle [mal] *adj* male; energetic, virile || *m* male

malédiction [malediksjɔ̃] *f* curse

maléfice [malefis] *m* evil spell

maléfique [malefik] *adj* baleful

malencon·treux [malɑ̃kɔ̃trø] **-treuse** [trøz] *adj* untimely, unfortunate

malentendu [malɑ̃tɑ̃dy] *m* misunderstanding

malfaçon [malfasɔ̃] *f* defect

malfai·sant [malfəzɑ̃] **-sante** [zɑ̃t] *adj* mischievous, harmful

malfaiteur [malfɛtœr] *m* malefactor

malfa·mé ·mée [malfame] *adj* ill-famed

malgra·cieux [malgrasjø] **-cieuse** [sjøz] *adj* ungracious

malgré [malgre] *prep* in spite of; **malgré que** in spite of the fact that, although

malhabile [malabil] *adj* inexperienced, clumsy

malheur [malœr] *m* misfortune; unhappiness; bad luck; **faire un malheur** to commit an act of violence; **jouer de malheur** to be unlucky

malheu·reux [malœrø] **-reuse** [røz] *adj* unfortunate; unhappy; unlucky; paltry || *m* poor man, wretch; **les malheureux** the unfortunate || *f* poor woman, wretch

malhonnête [malɔnɛt] *adj* dishonest; (slang) rude, uncivil

malhonnêteté [malɔnɛtte] *f* dishonesty

malice [malis] *f* mischievousness

mali·cieux [malisjø] **-cieuse** [sjøz] *adj* malicious, mischievous

malignité [maliɲite] *f* malignancy

ma·lin [malɛ̃] **-line** [lin] *adj* cunning, sly, smart; mischievous; malignant (*e.g., tumor*); **ce n'est pas malin** (coll) it's easy || *mf* sly one; **Le Malin** the Evil One

malingre [malɛ̃gr] *adj* weakly, puny

malintention·né ·née [malɛ̃tɑ̃sjɔne] *adj* evil-minded, ill-disposed

mal-jugé [malʒyʒe] *m* miscarriage (*of justice*)

malle [mal] *f* trunk; mailboat; **faire ses malles** to pack

malléable [maleabl] *adj* malleable; compliant, pliable

mallette [malɛt] *f* suitcase; small trunk

malmener [malməne] §2 *tr* to rough up

malodo·rant [malɔdɔrɑ̃] **-rante** [rɑ̃t] *adj* malodorous; bad (*breath*)

malo·tru ·true [malɔtry] *adj* coarse, uncouth || *mf* ill-bred person, oaf

malpropre [malprɔpr] *adj* dirty; improper; crude, clumsy (*workmanship*)

mal·sain [malsɛ̃] **-saine** [sɛn] *adj* unhealthy

malséant [malseɑ̃] **malséante** [malseɑ̃t] *adj* improper

malson·nant [malsɔnɑ̃] **malson·nante** [malsɔnɑ̃t] *adj* offensive, objectionable

malt [malt] *m* malt

maltraiter [maltrete] *tr* to mistreat

malveil·lant [malvejɑ̃] **malveil·lante** [malvejɑ̃t] *adj* malevolent

malve·nu ·nue [malvəny] *adj* ill-advised, out of place; poorly developed

malversation [malvɛrsasjɔ̃] *f* embezzlement

maman [mamɑ̃] *f* mamma

mamelle [mamɛl] *f* breast; udder

mamelon [mamlɔ̃] *m* nipple, teat; knoll

mamie [mami] *f* (coll) my dear

mammifère [mamifɛr] *adj* mammalian || *m* mammal

mammouth [mamut] *m* mammoth

mamours [mamur] *mpl* (coll) caresses

mam'selle or **mam'zelle** [mamzɛl] *f* (coll) Miss

manant [manɑ̃] *m* hick, yokel

manche [mɑ̃ʃ] *m* handle; stick, stock; neck (*of violin*); (culin) knuckle; **branler au manche** or **dans le manche** to be shaky; **manche à balai** broomstick; (aer) joy stick; **manche à gigot** holder (*for carving*) || *f* sleeve; hose; channel; game, heat, round; shaft, chute; (baseball) inning; (bridge) game; (tennis) set; **en manches de chemise** in shirt sleeves; **la Manche** the English Channel; **manche à air** windsock; **manche à manche** neck and neck, even up; **manches à gigot** leg-of-mutton sleeves

manchette [mɑ̃ʃɛt] *f* cuff; (journ) headline

manchon [mɑ̃ʃɔ̃] *m* muff; (of gaslight) mantle; (mach) casing, sleeve

man·chot [mɑ̃ʃo] **-chote** [ʃɔt] *adj* one-armed; one-handed; (coll) clumsy || *mf* one-armed person; one-handed person || *m* (orn) penguin

mandarine [mɑ̃darin] *f* mandarin orange

mandat [mɑ̃da] *m* mandate; term of office; money order; power of attorney; proxy; **mandat d'arrêt** warrant; **mandat de perquisition** search warrant

mandataire [mɑ̃dater] *mf* representative; proxy; defender

mandat-carte [mɑ̃dakart] *m* (pl **mandats-carte**) postal-card money order

mandat-poste [mɑ̃dapɔst] *m* (pl **mandats-poste**) postal money order

Mandchourie [mɑ̃t/uri] *f* Manchuria; **la Mandchourie** Manchuria

mander [mɑ̃de] *tr* to summon

mandoline [mɑ̃dɔlin] *f* mandolin

mandragore [mɑ̃dragɔr] *f* mandrake

mandrin [mɑ̃drɛ̃] *m* (mach) punch; (mach) chuck

manécanterie [manekɑ̃tri] *f* choir school

manège [manɛʒ] *m* horsemanship; riding school; trick, little game; **manège de chevaux de bois** merry-go-round

mânes [mɑn] *mpl* shades, spirits (of ancestors)

maneton [mantɔ̃] *m* crank handle; pin (of crankshaft)

manette [manet] *f* lever, switch

manganèse [mɑ̃ganɛz] *m* manganese

mangeable [mɑ̃ʒabl] *adj* edible; barely fit to eat

mangeaille [mɑ̃ʒaj] *f* swill; (coll) grub, chow

mangeotter [mɑ̃ʒɔte] *tr* to pick at (one's food)

manger [mɑ̃ʒe] *m* food, e.g., **le boire et le manger** food and drink; (slang) meal || **§38** *tr* to eat; to eat up; to mumble (one's words); **manger du bout des lèvres** to nibble at || *intr* to eat

mangerie [mɑ̃ʒri] *f* (coll) big meal

mange-tout [mɑ̃ʒtu] *m invar* sugar pea

man·geur [mɑ̃ʒœr] **-geuse** [ʒøz] *mf* eater; wastrel, spendthrift; **mangeur d'hommes** man-eater

mangouste [mɑ̃gust] *f* mongoose

maniable [manjabl] *adj* maneuverable, easy to handle, supple

maniaque [manjak] *adj & mf* maniac

manie [mani] *f* mania

maniement [manimɑ̃] *m* handling

manier [manje] *tr* to handle || *ref* (coll) to get a move on

manière [manjer] *f* manner; **à la ma-**

nière de in the manner of; **de manière à** so as to; **de manière que** so that; **de toute manière** in any case; **d'une manière ou d'une autre** one way or another; **en aucune manière** by no means; **faire des manières** to pretend to be indifferent, to want to be coaxed; **manière de voir** point of view; **manières** manners

manié·ré -rée [manjere] *adj* mannered, affected

maniérisme [manjerism] *m* mannerism

ma·nieur [manjœr] **-nieuse** [njøz] *mf* handler; **grand manieur d'argent** tycoon

manifes·tant [manifestɑ̃] **-tante** [tɑ̃t] *mf* demonstrator

manifestation [manifestasjɔ̃] *f* demonstration, manifestation

manifeste [manifest] *adj* manifest || *m* manifesto; (naut) manifest

manifester [manifeste] *tr* to manifest || *intr* to demonstrate || *ref* to reveal oneself

manigance [manigɑ̃s] *f* trick, intrigue

manipuler [manipyle] *tr* to manipulate; to handle (e.g., packages); to arrange (equipment) for an experiment

manitou [manitu] *m* manitou; (coll) bigwig

manivelle [manivel] *f* crank

manne [man] *f* manna

mannequin [mankɛ̃] *m* mannequin; scarecrow

manœuvre [manœvr] *m* hand, laborer || *f* maneuver; (naut) handling, maneuvering; (rr) shifting; **fausse manœuvre** wrong move; **manœuvres** rigging

manœuvrer [manœvre] *tr & intr* to maneuver; (rr) to shift

manoir [manwar] *m* manor, manor house

man·quant [mɑ̃kɑ̃] **-quante** [kɑ̃t] *adj* missing || *mf* absentee || *m* missing article; **manquants** shortages

manque [mɑ̃k] *m* lack, shortage; insufficiency; **manque de gagner** lost opportunity; **manque de parole** breach of faith; **par manque de** for lack of || *f*—**à la manque** (coll) rotten, poor, dud

man·qué -quée [mɑ̃ke] *adj* missed, unsuccessful; broken (engagement); (with abilities which were not professionally developed), e.g., **le docteur est un cuisinier manqué** the doctor could have been a cook by profession

manquement [mɑ̃kmɑ̃] *m* breach, lapse

manquer [mɑ̃ke] *tr* to miss; to flunk || *intr* to misfire; to be missing, e.g., **il en manque trois** three are missing; to be missed, e.g., **vous lui manquez beaucoup** you are very much missed by him, he misses you very much; to be short, e.g., **il lui manque cinq francs** he is five francs short; **manquer à** to break (one's word); to disobey (an order); to fail to observe (a rule); to fail, e.g., **le cœur lui a manqué** his heart failed him; **manquer de** to lack, to be short of, to run out of; **manquer de** + *inf* to nearly + *inf*, e.g., **il a manqué de se noyer** he nearly drowned; **sans manquer without fail** || *ref* to miss each other; to fail

mansarde [mɑ̃sard] *f* mansard roof; mansard

manse [mɑ̃s] *m & f* (hist) small manor

mante [mɑ̃t] *f* mantle; **mante religieuse** (ent) praying mantis

man•teau [mɑ̃to] *m* (*pl* **-teaux**) overcoat; mantle, cloak; mantelpiece; **sous le manteau** sub rosa

mantille [mɑ̃tij] *f* mantilla

manucure [manykyr] *mf* manicurist

ma•nuel -nuelle [manɥel] *adj* manual || *mf* laborer, blue-collar worker || *m* manual, handbook

manufacture [manyfaktyr] *f* factory, plant

manufacturer [manyfaktyre] *tr* to manufacture

manus•crit [manyskri] **-crite** [krit] *adj & m* manuscript

manutention [manytɑ̃sjɔ̃] *f* handling (*of merchandise*)

manutentionner [manytɑ̃sjɔne] *tr* to handle (*merchandise*)

mappemonde [mapmɔ̃d] *f* world map; **mappemonde céleste** map of the heavens

maque•reau [makro] **-relle** [rel] (*pl* **-reaux -relles**) *mf* (slang) procurer || *m* mackerel; (slang) pimp || *f* (slang) madam (*of a brothel*)

maquette [maket] *f* maquette, model; dummy (*of book*); rough sketch

maquignon [makiɲɔ̃] *m* horse trader; wholesale cattle dealer; (coll) go-between

maquignonnage [makiɲɔnaʒ] *m* horse trading

maquignonner [makiɲɔne] *intr* to horse-trade

maquillage [makijaʒ] *m* make-up; fakery

maquiller [makije] *tr* to make up; to fake, to distort || *ref* to make up

maquil•leur [makijœr] **maquil•leuse** [makijøz] *mf* make-up artist || *m* make-up man

maquis [maki] *m* bush; maquis; **prendre le maquis** to go underground

maraî•cher [mareʃe] **-chère** [ʃer] *adj* truck-farming || *mf* truck farmer

marais [mare] *m* marsh; truck farm; **marais salant** saltern

marasme [marasm] *m* depression; doldrums, standstill

marathon [maratɔ̃] *m* marathon

marâtre [marɑtr] *f* stepmother; cruel mother

maraude [marod] *f* marauding; **en maraude** cruising (*taxi*)

marauder [marode] *intr* to maraud; to cruise (*said of taxi*)

marau•deur [marodœr] **-deuse** [døz] *adj* marauding || *mf* marauder

marbre [marbr] *m* marble; (typ) stone

marbrer [marbre] *tr* to marble; to mottle, vein; to bruise, blotch

marc [mar] *m* mark (*old coin*); marc, pulp; **marc de café** coffee grounds;

marc de thé tea leaves || [mark] (*cap*) *m* Mark

marcassin [markasɛ̃] *m* young wild boar

mar•chand [marʃɑ̃] **-chande** [ʃɑ̃d] *adj* marketable; sale (*value*); trading (*center*); wholesale (*price*); merchant (*marine*) || *mf* merchant; **marchand ambulant** peddler; **marchand de canons** munitions maker; **marchand de couleurs** paint dealer, dealer in household articles; **marchand de ferraille** junk dealer; **marchand de journaux** newsdealer; **marchand des quatre-saisons** fruit vendor; **marchand forain** hawker || *f* **—marchande d'amour** or **de plaisir** prostitute

marchandage [marʃɑ̃daʒ] *m* bargaining; haggling; deal, underhanded arrangement

marchander [marʃɑ̃de] *tr* to bargain over; to haggle over; to be stingy with (*e.g., one's compliments*) || *intr* to haggle

marchan•deur [marʃɑ̃dœr] **-deuse** [døz] *mf* bargainer; haggler

marchandise [marʃɑ̃diz] *f* merchandise; **marchandises** goods

mar•chant [marʃɑ̃] **-chante** [ʃɑ̃t] *adj* marching; militant (*wing of political party*); (mil) wheeling (*flank*)

marche [marʃ] *f* march; step (*of stairway*); walking; movement; progress, course; (aut) gear; **à dix minutes de marche** ten minutes walk from here; **attention à la marche!** watch your step!; **en marche** in motion, running, operating; **faire marche arrière** to back up, to reverse; **fermer la marche** to bring up the rear; **marche funèbre** funeral march; **ouvrir la marche** to lead off the procession

marché [marʃe] *m* market; marketing, shopping; deal, bargain; **à bon marché** cheap; cheaply; **à meilleur marché** cheaper; more cheaply; **bon marché** cheapness; cheap; cheaply; **faire bon marché de** to set little store by; **faire son marché** to do the marketing; **lancer, mettre,** or **vendre sur le marché** to market; **marché noir** black market; **par-dessus le marché** into the bargain

marchepied [marʃəpje] *m* footstool; little stepladder; running board; (fig) stepping stone

marcher [marʃe] *intr* to walk; to run, operate; to march; **marcher à grands pas** to stride; **marcher au pas** to walk in step; **marcher dans l'espace** to take a space walk; **marcher sur** to tread on, to walk on; **marchez au pas** (public sign) drive slowly

mar•cheur [marʃœr] **-cheuse** [ʃøz] *mf* walker

mardi [mardi] *m* Tuesday; **mardi gras** Shrove Tuesday; Mardi gras

mare [mar] *f* pool, pond

marécage [marekaʒ] *m* marsh, swamp

maréca•geux [marekaʒø] **-geuse** [ʒøz] *adj* marshy, swampy

maré•chal [mareʃal] *m* (*pl* **-chaux**

[/o]) marshal; blacksmith; **maréchal des logis** artillery or cavalry sergeant
maréchale [mareʃal] *f* marshal's wife
maréchal-ferrant [mareʃalferɑ̃] *m* (*pl* **maréchaux-ferrants**) blacksmith, farrier
marée [mare] *f* tide; fresh seafood; **marée descendante** ebb tide; **marée montante** flood tide
marelle [marel] *f* hopscotch
marémo-teur [maremɔtœr] **-trice** [tris] *adj* tide-driven
margarine [margarin] *f* margarine
marge [marʒ] *f* margin; border, edge; leeway, room; **en marge de** on the fringe of; a footnote to; **marge bénéficiaire** margin of profit; **marge de sécurité** margin of safety
margelle [marʒel] *f* curb, edge (*of well, fountain, etc.*)
margeur [marʒœr] *m* margin stop
margi-nal -nale [marʒinal] *adj* (*pl* **-naux** [no]) marginal
margot [margo] *f* (coll) magpie; (coll) chatterbox; **Margot** (coll) Maggie
margotin [margotɛ̃] *m* kindling
margouillis [marguji] *m* (coll) rotten stinking mess
margou-lin [margulɛ̃] **-line** [lin] *mf* sharpster, shyster
marguerite [margərit] *f* daisy; **Marguerite** Margaret
marguillier [margije] *m* churchwarden
mari [mari] *m* husband
mariable [marjabl] *adj* marriageable
mariage [marjaʒ] *m* marriage; wedding; blend, combination
Marianne [marjan] *f* Marian; Marianne (*symbol of the French Republic*)
ma-rié -riée [marje] *adj* married ‖ *m* bridegroom; **jeunes mariés** newlyweds; **les mariés** the bride and groom ‖ *f* bride
marier [marje] *tr* to marry, join in wedlock; to marry off; to blend, harmonize ‖ *ref* **se marier** to get married; **se marier avec** to marry
marie-salope [marisalɔp] *f* (*pl* **maries-salopes**) dredger; (slang) slut
ma-rieur [marjœr] **-rieuse** [rjøz] *mf* (coll) matchmaker
marihuana [mariɥana] or **marijuana** [mariɥana] *f* marijuana
ma-rin [marɛ̃] **-rine** [rin] *adj* marine; seagoing; sea, e.g., **brise marine** sea breeze ‖ *m* sailor, seaman; sailor suit ‖ *f* navy; seascape; **marine marchande** merchant marine
mariner [marine] *tr & intr* to marinate
mari-nier [marinje] **-nière** [njer] *adj* naval; petty (*officer*); **à la marinière** cooked in gravy with onions ‖ *m* waterman ‖ *f* blouse; (swimming) sidestroke
marionnette [marjɔnet] *f* marionette; (fig) puppet
mari-tal -tale [marital] *adj* (*pl* **-taux** [to]) of the husband
maritime [maritim] *adj* maritime
maritorne [maritɔrn] *f* slut
marivaudage [marivodaʒ] *m* playful flirting; sophisticated conversation
marjolaine [marʒɔlen] *f* marjoram

marlou [marlu] *m* (slang) pimp
marmaille [marmaj] *f* (coll) brats
marmelade [marməlad] *f* marmalade; (coll) mess
marmite [marmit] *f* pot, pan; (geol) pothole; (mil) shell, heavy shell; **marmite autoclave**, **marmite sous pression** pressure cooker; **marmite norvégienne** double boiler
marmiton [marmitɔ̃] *m* cook's helper
marmonner [marmɔne] *tr & intr* to mumble
marmot [marmo] *m* (coll) lad; (coll) grotesque figurine (*on knocker*); **croquer le marmot** (coll) to cool one's heels; **marmots** (coll) urchins, kids
marmotte [marmɔt] *f* woodchuck; **dormir comme une marmotte** to sleep like a log; **marmotte d'Amérique** groundhog; **marmotte de commis voyageur** traveling salesman's sample case
marmouset [marmuze] *m* grotesque figurine; little man
marner [marne] *tr* to marl
marner [marne] *tr* to marl
Maroc [marɔk] *m*—**le Maroc** Morocco
maro-cain [marɔkɛ̃] **-caine** [ken] *adj* Moroccan ‖ (*cap*) *mf* Moroccan
maronner [marɔne] *intr* (coll) to grumble
maroquin [marɔkɛ̃] *m* morocco leather
maroquinerie [marɔkinri] *f* leather goods
marotte [marɔt] *f* fad; whim; dummy head (*of milliner*); jester's staff
mar-quant [markɑ̃] **-quante** [kɑ̃t] *adj* remarkable, outstanding; purple (*passages*)
marque [mark] *f* mark; brand, make; hallmark; token, sign; **de marque** distinguished; **marque déposée** trademark
marquer [marke] *tr* to mark; to brand; to score; to indicate, show ‖ *intr* to make a mark, to leave an impression
marqueterie [markətri], [marketri] *f* marquetry, inlay
mar-queur [markœr] **-queuse** [køz] *mf* marker ‖ *m* scorekeeper; scorer ‖ *f* (mach) stenciler
marquis [marki] *m* marquis
marquise [markiz] *f* marchioness, marquise; marquee, awning; (rr) roof (*over platform*)
marraine [maren] *f* godmother, sponsor; christener; **marraine de guerre** war mother
mar-rant [marɑ̃] **-rante** [marɑ̃t] *adj* (slang) sidesplitting; (slang) funny, queer
marre [mar] *adv*—**en avoir marre** (coll) to be fed up
marrer [mare] *ref* (slang) to have a good laugh
mar-ron [marɔ̃] **-ronne** [marɔn] *adj* quack (*doctor*); shyster (*lawyer*) ‖ **marron** *adj invar* reddish-brown, chestnut ‖ *m* chestnut; **marron d'Inde** horse chestnut
marronnier [marɔnje] *m* chestnut tree; **marronnier d'Inde** horse-chestnut tree

mars [mars] *m* March; **Mars** Mars
Marseille [marsej] *f* Marseilles
marsouin [marswɛ̃] *m* porpoise
marte [mart] *f* (zool) marten
mar-teau [marto] (*pl* **-teaux**) *adj* (coll) cracked; balmy ‖ *m* hammer; (ichth) hammerhead; **marteau de porte** knocker
marteau-pilon [martopilɔ̃] *m* (*pl* **marteaux-pilons**) drop hammer
marteler [martəle] §2 *tr* to hammer; to hammer out
Marthe [mart] *f* Martha
mar-tial -tiale [marsjal] *adj* (*pl* **-tiaux** [sjo]) martial
martinet [martinɛ] *m* triphammer; scourge, cat-o'-nine-tails; (orn) martin, swift
martin-pêcheur [martɛ̃peʃœr] *m* (*pl* **martins-pêcheurs**) (orn) kingfisher
martre [martr] *f* (zool) marten
mar-tyr -tyre [martir] *adj & mf* martyr ‖ **martyre** *m* martyrdom
martyriser [martirize] *tr* to martyr
marxiste [marksist] *adj & mf* Marxist
maryland [marilɑ̃] *m* choice tobacco ‖ (*cap*) *m*—le Maryland Maryland
mas [ma], [mas] *m* farmhouse or farm (*in Provence*)
mascarade [maskarad] *f* masquerade
mascaret [maskarɛ] *m* bore
mascaron [maskarɔ̃] *m* mask, mascaron
mascotte [maskɔt] *f* mascot
mascu-lin [maskylɛ̃] **-line** [lin] *adj & m* masculine
masque [mask] *m* mask; **masque à gaz** gas mask; **masque mortuaire** death mask
masquer [maske] *tr & ref* to mask
massacre [masakr] *m* massacre; botched job
massacrer [masakre] *tr* to massacre; to botch
massage [masaʒ] *m* massage
masse [mas] *f* mass; sledge hammer; mace; pool, common fund; (elec) ground (*e.g., of an automobile*); **masse d'air froid** cold front; **mettre à la masse** (elec) to ground; **une masse de** (coll) a lot of
massepain [maspɛ̃] *m* marzipan
masser [mase] *tr* to mass; to massage ‖ *ref* to mass; to massage oneself
massette [masɛt] *f* sledge hammer (*of stonemason*); (bot) bulrush
mas-seur [masœr] **mas-seuse** [masøz] *mf* masseur ‖ *m* massager (*instrument*)
mas-sif [masif] **mas-sive** [masiv] *adj* massive; heavyset; solid (*e.g., gold*) ‖ *m* massif, high plateau; clump (*of flowers, trees, etc.*)
massue [masy] *f* club, bludgeon
mastic [mastik] *m* putty
mastiquer [mastike] *tr* to masticate; to putty
mastoc [mastɔk] *adj invar* heavy, massive
masturber [mastyrbe] *tr & ref* to masturbate
m'as-tu-vu -vue [matyvy] (*pl* **-vu -vue**) *adj* (coll) stuck-up ‖ *mf* (coll) show-

off, smart aleck; (coll) bragging actor
masure [mazyr] *f* hovel, shack, shanty
mat mate [mat] *adj* dull, flat ‖ **mat** *adj invar* checkmated ‖ *m* checkmate ‖ **mat** *adv* dull
mât [ma] *m* mast; pole
matamore [matamɔr] *m* braggart
match [matʃ] *m* match, contest, game
matelas [matla] *m* mattress; (coll) roll (*of bills*)
matelasser [matlase] *tr* to pad, to cushion
matelot [matlo] *m* sailor, seaman
matelote [matlɔt] *f* fish stew in wine
mater [mate] *tr* to dull; to checkmate; to subdue
matérialiser [materjalize] *ref* to materialize
matérialiste [materjalist] *adj* materialistic ‖ *mf* materialist
maté-riau [materjo] *m* (*pl* **-riaux**) material
maté-riel -rielle [materjɛl] *adj* material; materialistic ‖ *m* material; equipment; (mil) matériel; **matériel roulant** (rr) rolling stock ‖ *f* (slang) living
mater-nel -nelle [maternɛl] *adj* maternal ‖ *f* nursery school
maternité [maternite] *f* maternity; maternity hospital
math or **maths** [mat] *fpl* (coll) math
mathémati-cien [matematisjɛ̃] **-cienne** [sjen] *mf* mathematician
mathématique [matematik] *adj* mathematical ‖ **mathématiques** *fpl* mathematics
matière [matjer] *f* matter; subject matter; material; **matière première** raw material
matin [matɛ̃] *m* morning; early part of the morning; **au petit matin** in the wee hours of the morning; **de bon matin, de grand matin** very early; **du matin** in the morning, A.M., e.g., **onze heures du matin** eleven o'clock in the morning, eleven A.M. ‖ *adv* early
mâ-tin [matɛ̃] **-tine** [tin] *mf* (coll) sly one ‖ *m* (zool) mastiff ‖ **mâtin** *adv* indeed!, well I'll be!
mati-nal -nale [matinal] *adj* (*pl* **-naux** [no]) morning; early-rising
mâti-né -née [matine] *adj* crossbred; **mâtiné de** mixed with, crossbred with
matinée [matine] *f* morning; matinée; **faire la grasse matinée** to sleep late
mâtiner [matine] *tr* to crossbreed
matines [matin] *fpl* matins
matité [matite] *f* dullness
ma-tois -toise [matwa] *adj* sly, cunning ‖ *mf* sly dog
matou [matu] *m* tomcat
matraque [matrak] *f* bludgeon; club, billy
matraquer [matrake] *tr* to club, bludgeon
matriarcat [matrijarka] *m* matriarchy
matrice [matris] *f* matrix
matricide [matrisid] *mf* matricide (*person*) ‖ *m* matricide (*action*)
matricule [matrikyl] *adj* serial (*num-*

ber) || *m* serial number || *f* roll, register

matrimo·nial -niale [matrimɔnjal] *adj* (*pl* **-niaux** [njo]) matrimonial, marital

matrone [matrɔn] *f* matron; matriarch; old hag; midwife; abortionist

mâture [matyr] *f* masts (*of ship*)

maudire [modir] §39 *tr* to curse, to damn

mau·dit [modi] **-dite** [dit] *adj* cursed

maugréer [mogree] *intr* to grumble, gripe

maure [mɔr] *adj* Moorish || (*cap*) *m* Moor

mauresque [mɔresk] *adj* Moorish || (*cap*) *f* Moorish woman

mausolée [mozɔle] *m* mausoleum

maussade [mosad] *adj* sullen, gloomy

mau·vais [mɔve], [move] **-vaise** [vez] *adj* §91 bad; evil; wrong; **il fait mauvais** the weather is bad; **sentir mauvais** to smell bad; **sentir mauvais** to smell bad || *mf* wicked person; **le Mauvais** the Evil One || *m* evil

mauve [mov] *adj* mauve || *f* (bot) mallow

mauviette [movjet] *f* (orn) lark; (coll) milquetoast

mauvis [movi] *m* (orn) redwing

maxillaire [maksiler] *m* jawbone

maxime [maksim] *f* maxim

maximum [maksimɔm] *adj & m* maximum

mayonnaise [majɔnez] *f* mayonnaise

mazette [mazet] *f* duffer || *interj* gosh!

mazout [mazut] *m* fuel oil

mazouter [mazute] *intr* to fuel up

Mᵉ *abbr* (**Maître**) Mr.

me [mə] §87

méandre [meãdr] *m* meander

mec [mek] *m* (slang) guy; (slang) tough egg

mécanicien [mekanisjẽ] *m* mechanic; machinist; engineer (*of locomotive*)

mécanicienne [mekanisjen] *f* sewing-machine operator

mécanique [mekanik] *adj* mechanical || *f* mechanism; mechanics

mécaniser [mekanize] *tr* to mechanize

mécanisme [mekanism] *m* mechanism

mécano [mekano] *m* (coll) mechanic

Mécène [mesen] *m* patron, Maecenas

méchanceté [meʃãste] *f* malice, wickedness; nastiness

mé·chant [meʃã] **-chante** [ʃãt] *adj* malicious, wicked; nasty; naughty (*child*) || *mf* mean person; **faire le méchant** to threaten; (coll) to strike back; **les méchants** the wicked; **méchant!** naughty boy!

mèche [meʃ] *f* wick; fuse; lock (*of hair*); bit (*of drill*); **être de mèche avec** (coll) to be in cahoots with; **éventer** or **découvrir la mèche** to discover the plot; **il n'y a pas mèche** (coll) it's no go, nothing doing; **vendre la mèche** (coll) to let the cat out of the bag

mécompte [mekɔ̃t] *m* miscalculation; disappointment

méconnaissable [mekɔnesabl] *adj* unrecognizable

méconnaître [mekɔnetr] §12 *tr* to ignore; to underestimate

mécon·nu -nue [mekɔny] *adj* underestimated, misunderstood

mécon·tent [mekɔ̃tã] **-tente** [tãt] *adj* dissatisfied, displeased || *mf* grumbler

mécontentement [mekɔ̃tãtmã] *m* dissatisfaction, displeasure

mécontenter [mekɔ̃tãte] *tr* to displease

Mecque [mek] *f*—**La Mecque** Mecca

mécréant [mekreã] **mécréante** [mekreãt] *adj* unbelieving || *mf* unbeliever

médaille [medaj] *f* medal

médaillon [medajɔ̃] *m* medallion; locket; thin round slice (*e.g., of meat*); pat (*of butter*)

médecin [medsẽ], [metsẽ] *m* doctor; **femme médecin** woman doctor

médecine [medsin], [metsin] *f* medicine (*science and art*)

mé·dian [medjã] **-diane** [djan] *adj & f* median

média·teur [medjatœr] **-trice** [tris] *mf* mediator

médiation [medjɑsjɔ̃] *f* mediation

médi·cal -cale [medikal] *adj* (*pl* **-caux** [ko]) medical

médicament [medikamã] *m* (pharm) medicine

médicamenter [medikamãte] *tr* to dose

médicamen·teux [medikamãtø] **-teuse** [tøz] *adj* medicinal

médici·nal -nale [medisinal] *adj* (*pl* **-naux** [no]) medicinal

médié·val -vale [medjeval] *adj* (*pl* **-vaux** [vo]) medieval

médiéviste [medjevist] *mf* medievalist

médiocre [medjɔkr] *adj* mediocre, poor; average

médiocrité [medjɔkrite] *f* mediocrity

médire [medir] §40 *intr* to backbite; **médire de** to run down, to disparage

médisance [medizãs] *f* disparagement, backbiting

médi·sant [medizã] **-sante** [zãt] *adj* disparaging, backbiting || *mf* slanderer

méditation [meditɑsjɔ̃] *f* meditation

méditer [medite] *tr & intr* to meditate

méditerra·né -née [mediterane] *adj* Mediterranean; inland || (*cap*) *f* **Médi·terr·anéan** (Sea)

méditerranéen [mediteraneẽ] **méditerranéenne** [mediteraneen] *adj* Mediterranean

médium [medjɔm] *m* medium (*in spiritualism*); range (*of voice*)

médiumnique [medjɔmnik] *adj* psychic

médius [medjys] *m* middle finger

méduse [medyz] *f* jellyfish, medusa || (*cap*) *f* Medusa

méduser [medyze] *tr* to petrify (*with terror*)

meeting [mitiŋ] *m* rally, meet, meeting

méfait [mefe] *m* misdeed; **méfaits** ravages

méfiance [mefjãs] *f* mistrust

mé·fiant [mefjã] **-fiante** [fjãt] *adj* mistrustful

méfier [mefje] *ref* to beware; **se méfier de** to guard against, to mistrust

mégacycle [megasikl] *m* megacycle

mégaphone [megafɔn] *m* megaphone

mégarde [megard] *f*—**par mégarde** inadvertently

mégère [meʒer] *f* shrew

mégohm [megom] *m* megohm

mégot [mego] *m* butt (*of cigarette or cigar*)

meil·leur -leure §91 *adj comp & super* better; best; **meilleur marché** cheaper

mélancolie [melɑ̃kɔli] *f* melancholy, melancholia

mélancolique [melɑ̃kɔlik] *adj* melancholy

mélange [melɑ̃ʒ] *m* mixing, blending; mixture, blend

mélanger [melɑ̃ʒe] §38 *tr* to mix, to blend

mélan·geur [melɑ̃ʒœr] **-geuse** [ʒøz] *m & f* mixer

mélasse [melas] *f* molasses; **dans la mélasse** (coll) in the soup

mê·lé -lée [mele] *adj* mixed ‖ *f* melee

mêler [mele] *tr* to mix; to tangle; to shuffle (*the cards*) ‖ *ref* to mix; **se mêler à** to mingle with; to join in; **se mêler de** to meddle with, to interfere with

mélèze [melez] *m* (bot) larch

mélodie [melɔdi] *f* melody

mélo·dieux [melɔdjø] **-dieuse** [djøz] *adj* melodious

mélodique [melɔdik] *adj* melodic

mélodramatique [melɔdramatik] *adj* melodramatic

mélomane [melɔman] *adj* music-loving ‖ *mf* music lover

melon [məlɔ̃] *m* melon; derby; **melon d'eau** watermelon

mélopée [melɔpe] *f* singsong, chant

membrane [mɑ̃bran] *f* membrane; **membrane vibrante** (elec) diaphragm

membre [mɑ̃br] *m* member; limb, member; **membre de phrase** clause

membrure [mɑ̃bryr] *f* frame, limbs

même [mem] *adj indef* very, e.g., **le jour même** on that very day ‖ (when standing before noun) *adj indef* same, e.g., **en même temps** at the same time ‖ *pron indef* same, same one; **à même de** + *inf* up to + *ger*, in a position to + *inf*; **à même le** (la, etc.) straight out of the (*e.g., bottle*); flush with the (*e.g., pavement*); next to one's (*e.g., skin*); on the bare (*ground, sand, etc.*); **cela revient au même** that amounts to the same thing; **de même** likewise; **de même que** in the same way as; **tout de même** nevertheless ‖ *adv* even; **même quand** even when; **même si** even if

-même [mem] §86

mémento [memɛ̃to] *m* memento; memo book

mémère [memer] *f* (coll) granny; (coll) blowsy dame

mémoire [memwar] *m* memorandum; statement, account; term paper; treatise; petition; **mémoires** memoirs ‖ *f* memory; **de mémoire** from memory; **de mémoire d'homme** within memory; **pour mémoire** for the record

mémorandum [memɔrɑ̃dɔm] *m* memorandum; **mémorandum de combat** battle orders

mémo·rial [memɔrjal] *m* (*pl* **-riaux** [rjo]) memorial; (dipl) memorandum; memoirs

menace [mənas] *f* menace, threat

menacer [mənase] §51 *tr & intr* to menace, to threaten

ménage [menaʒ] *m* household; family; married couple; furniture; **de ménage** homemade; **faire bon ménage** to get along well; **faire des ménages** to do housework (*for hire*); **faire le ménage** to do the housework; **se mettre en ménage** to set up housekeeping; (coll) to live together (*without being married*)

ménagement [menaʒmɑ̃] *m* discretion; consideration

ména·ger [menaʒe] **-gère** [ʒer] *adj* household; thrifty; **ménager de** thrifty with ‖ *f* housewife, homemaker; silverware; silverware case ‖ **ménager** §38 *tr* to be careful with, to spare; to save (*money; one's strength*); to husband (*one's resources, one's strength*); to be considerate of, to handle with kid gloves; to arrange, to bring about; to install, to provide; to make (*e.g., a hole*) ‖ *intr* to save ‖ *ref* to take good care of oneself

ménagerie [menaʒri] *f* menagerie

men·diant [mɑ̃djɑ̃] **-diante** [djɑ̃t] *adj & mf* beggar; **des mendiants** dessert (*of dried fruits and nuts*)

mendier [mɑ̃dje] *tr & intr* to beg

menées [məne] *fpl* intrigues, schemes

mener [məne] §2 *tr* to lead; to take; to manage; to draw (*e.g., a line*) ‖ *intr* to lead

ménestrel [menestrel] *m* wandering minstrel

ménétrier [menetrije] *m* fiddler

me·neur [mənœr] **-neuse** [nøz] *mf* leader; ringleader; **meneur de jeu** master of ceremonies; narrator; moving spirit

menotte [mənɔt] *f* tiny hand; **menottes** handcuffs; **mettre** or **passer les menottes à** to handcuff

mensonge [mɑ̃sɔ̃ʒ] *m* lie; **pieux mensonge** white lie

menson·ger [mɑ̃sɔ̃ʒe] **-gère** [ʒer] *adj* lying, false; illusory, deceptive

menstrues [mɑ̃stry] *fpl* menses

mensualité [mɑ̃sɥalite] *f* monthly installment; monthly salary

men·suel -suelle [mɑ̃sɥel] *adj* monthly

men·tal -tale [mɑ̃tal] *adj* (*pl* **-taux** [to]) mental

mentalité [mɑ̃talite] *f* mentality

men·teur [mɑ̃tœr] **-teuse** [tøz] *adj* lying ‖ *mf* liar

menthe [mɑ̃t] *f* mint; **menthe poivrée** peppermint; **menthe verte** spearmint

mention [mɑ̃sjɔ̃] *f* mention; **avec mention** with honors; **biffer les mentions inutiles** to cross out the questions which do not apply; **être reçu sans mention** to receive just a passing grade

mentionner [mɑ̃sjɔne] *tr* to mention

mentir [mãtir] §41 *intr* to lie

menton [mãtɔ̃] *m* chin

mentonnière [mãtɔnjɛr] *f* chin rest; chin strap

me·nu -nue [məny] *adj* small, little; tiny, fine || *m* menu; minute detail

menuet [mənɥɛ] *m* minuet

menuiserie [mənɥizri] *f* carpentry; woodwork

menuisier [mənɥizje] *m* carpenter

méprendre [meprãdr] §56 *ref* to be mistaken; **à s'y méprendre** enough to take one for the other; **il n'y a pas à s'y méprendre** there's no mistake about it

mépris [mepri] *m* contempt, scorn

méprisable [meprizabl] *adj* contemptible, despicable

mépri·sant [meprizã] **-sante** [zãt] *adj* contemptuous, scornful

méprise [mepriz] *f* mistake

mépriser [meprize] *tr* to despise, scorn

mer [mɛr] *f* sea; **basse mer** low tide; **de haute mer** seagoing; **haute mer, pleine mer** high seas; **high tide; mer des Indes** Indian Ocean; **sur mer** afloat

mercanti [mɛrkãti] *m* profiteer

mercantile [mɛrkãtil] *adj* profiteering, mercenary

mercenaire [mɛrsənɛr] *adj & mf* mercenary

mercerie [mɛrsəri] *f* notions

merci [mɛrsi] *m* thanks, thank you; **merci de** + *inf* thank you for + *ger*; **merci de** or **pour** thank you for || *f*— **à la merci de** at the mercy of; **Dieu merci!** thank heavens! || *interj* thanks!, thank you!; no thanks!, no thank you!

mercredi [mɛrkrədi] *m* Wednesday; **mercredi des Cendres** Ash Wednesday

mercure [mɛrkyr] *m* mercury

mercuriale [mɛrkyrjal] *f* reprimand; market quotations; mercury (*weed*)

merde [mɛrd] *f* excrement; **merde alors!** (coll) well I'll be!

mère [mɛr] *f* mother; **la mère Gigogne** the old woman who lived in a shoe

méri·dien [meridjɛ̃] **-dienne** [djɛn] *adj & m* meridian || *f* meridian line; couch, sofa; siesta

méridio·nal -nale [meridjɔnal] (*pl* **-naux** [no]) *adj* meridional, southern || (*cap*) *mf* inhabitant of the Midi

meringue [mərɛ̃g] *f* meringue

merise [məriz] *f* wild cherry

merisier [mərizje] *m* wild cherry (tree)

méri·tant [meritã] **-tante** [tãt] *adj* deserving, worthy

mérite [merit] *m* merit

mériter [merite] *tr* to merit, to deserve; to win, earn || *intr*—**mériter bien de** to deserve the gratitude of

méritoire [meritwar] *adj* deserving, meritorious

merlan [mɛrlã] *m* (ichth) whiting

merle [mɛrl] *m* (orn) blackbird; **merle blanc** (fig) rara avis; **vilain merle** (fig) dirty dog

merlin [mɛrlɛ̃] *m* ax; poleax; (naut) marline

merluche [mɛrlyʃ] *f* (ichth) hake, cod

merveille [mɛrvɛj] *f* marvel, wonder; **à merveille** marvelously, wonderfully

merveil·leux [mɛrvejø] **merveil·leuse** [mɛrvejøz] *adj* marvelous, wonderful

mes [me] §88

mésalliance [mezaljãs] *f* misalliance, mismatch

mésallier [mezalje] *tr* to misally || *ref* to marry beneath one's station

mésange [mezãʒ] *f* (orn) chickadee, titmouse

mésaventure [mezavãtyr] *f* misadventure

mésentente [mezãtãt] *f* misunderstanding

mésestimer [mezɛstime] *tr* to underestimate

mésintelligence [mezɛ̃teliʒãs] *f* misunderstanding, discord

mes·quin [mɛskɛ̃] **-quine** [kin] *adj* mean; stingy; petty

mess [mɛs] *m* officer's mess

message [mesaʒ] *m* message

messa·ger [mesaʒe] **-gère** [ʒɛr] *mf* messenger

messagerie [mesaʒri] *f* express; messageries express company

messe [mɛs] *f* (eccl) Mass; **dire** or **faire des messes basses** (coll) to speak in an undertone; **messe basse, petite messe** Low Mass; **première messe, messe du début** early Mass

Messie [mesi] *m* Messiah

messieurs-dames [mesjødam] *interj* ladies and gentlemen!

mesure [məzyr] *f* measure; measurement; (mus, poetic) measure; **à mesure** successively, one by one; **à mesure que** as; according as, proportionately as; **battre la mesure** to keep time; **dans la mesure de** insofar as; **dans une certaine mesure** to a certain extent; **être en mesure de** to be in a position to; **faire sur mesure** to make (*clothing*) to order; (fig) to tailor-make; **mesure de circonstance** emergency measure; **mesure en ruban** tape measure; **prendre des mesures** de to take measures to; **prendre la mesure de** to size up; **prendre les mesures de** to measure

mesurer [məzyre] *tr* to measure; to measure off or out || *ref* to measure; **se mesurer avec** to measure swords with

métairie [meteri] *f* farm (*of a sharecropper*)

mé·tal [metal] *m* (*pl* **-taux** [to]) metal

métallique [metalik] *adj* metallic

métalloïde [metalɔid] *m* nonmetal

métallurgie [metalyrʒi] *f* metallurgy

métamorphose [metamɔrfoz] *f* metamorphosis

métaphore [metafɔr] *f* metaphor

métaphorique [metafɔrik] *adj* metaphorical

métathèse [metatɛz] *f* metathesis

métayage [metejaʒ] *m* sharecropping, tenant farming

métayer [meteje] **métayère** [metejer] *mf* sharecropper méteil [metej] *m* wheat and rye

météo [meteo] *adj invar* meteorological ‖ *m* weatherman ‖ *f* meteorology; weather bureau; weather report

météore [meteɔr] *m* meteor (*atmospheric phenomenon*)

météorite [meteɔrit| *m* & *f* meteorite

météorologie [meteɔrɔlɔʒi] *f* meteorology; weather bureau; weather report

métèque [metek] *m* (pej) foreigner

méthane [metan] *m* methane

méthode [metɔd] *f* method

méthodique [metɔdik] *adj* methodic(al)

méthodiste [metɔdist] *adj* & *mf* Methodist

méticu-leux [metikylø] -leuse [løz] *adj* meticulous

métier [metje] *m* trade, craft; loom; faites votre métier! mind your own business!; sur le métier on the stocks

mé-tis -tisse [metis] *adj* & *mf* half-breed

métisser [metise] *tr* to crossbreed

métrage [metraʒ] *m* length in meters; length (*of remnant, film, etc.*); (mov) length of film in meters (*in English*: footage, *i.e., length of film in feet*); court métrage (mov) short subject, short; long métrage (mov) full-length movie, feature

mètre [metr] *m* meter; mètre à ruban tape measure; mètre pliant folding rule

métrer [metre] §10 *tr* to measure out by the meter

métrique [metrik] *adj* metric(al) ‖ *f* metrics

métro [metro] *m* subway

métronome [metrɔnɔm] *m* metronome

métropole [metrɔpɔl] *f* metropolis; mother country

métropoli-tain [metrɔpɔlitɛ̃] -taine [ten] *adj* metropolitan ‖ *m* subway; (eccl) metropolitan

mets [me] *m* dish, food

mettable [metabl] *adj* wearable

met-teur [metœr] met-teuse [metøz] *mf*—metteur au point mechanic; metteur en œuvre setter; (fig) promoter; metteur en ondes (rad) director, producer; metteur en pages (typ) make-up man; metteur en scène (mov, theat) director, producer

mettre [metr] §42 *tr* to put, lay, place; to put on (*clothes*); to set (*the table*); to take (*time*); mettre à feu (rok) to fire; mettre au point to carry out, complete; to tune up, adjust; (opt) to focus; (rad) to tune; mettre au rancart to pigeonhole; mettre en accusation to indict; mettre en marche to start; mettre en œuvre to put into action; mettre en valeur to develop, improve; to set off, enhance; mettre en vigueur to enforce; mettre feu à to set fire to; mettre que (coll) to suppose that ‖ *intr*—mettre bas (zool) to litter ‖ *ref* to sit or stand; to go; se mettre à to begin to; se mettre à table to sit down to eat; (slang) to confess; se mettre en colère to get angry; se

mettre en route to set out; se mettre mal avec to quarrel with

meuble [mœbl] *adj* uncemented; loose (*ground*); personal (*property*) ‖ *m* piece of furniture; meubles furniture; meubles d'occasion secondhand furniture

meubler [mœble] *tr* to furnish

meuglement [mœɡləmɑ̃] *m* lowing (*of cow*)

meugler [mœɡle] *intr* to low

meule [mœl] *f* millstone; grindstone; stack (*e.g., of hay*)

meuler [mœle] *tr* to grind

meu-nier [mønje] -nière [njer] *adj* milling (*e.g., industry*) ‖ *m* miller ‖ *f* miller's wife; à la meunière sautéed in butter

meurt-de-faim [mœrdəfɛ̃] *mf invar* starveling; de meurt-de-faim starvation (*wages*)

meurtre [mœrtr] *m* manslaughter; (fig) shame, crime; meurtre commis avec préméditation murder

meur-trier [mœrtrije] -trière [trijer] *adj* murderous, deadly ‖ *m* murderer ‖ *f* murderess; gun slit, loophole

meurtrir [mœrtrir] *tr* to bruise

meute [møt] *f* pack, band

mévente [mevɑ̃t] *f* slump (*in sales*)

mexi-cain |meksikɛ̃ -caine [ken] *adj* Mexican ‖ (cap) *mf* Mexican

Mexico [meksiko] Mexico City

Mexique [meksik] *m*—le Mexique Mexico

mezzanine [medzanin] *m* & *f* (theat) mezzanine ‖ *f* mezzanine; mezzanine window

miaou [mjau] *m* meow

miaulement [mjolmɑ̃] *m* meow; caterwauling; catcall

miauler [mjole] *intr* to meow

mi-bas [miba] *m invar* half hose

mica [mika] *m* mica

miche [mi∫] *f* round loaf of bread

mi-chemin [mi/mɛ̃] *m*—à mi-chemin halfway

mi-clos [miklo] -close [kloz] *adj* (pl -clos -closes) half-shut

micmac [mikmak] *m* (coll) underhand dealing

mi-corps [mikɔr] *m*—à mi-corps to the waist

mi-côte [mikot]—à mi-côte halfway up the hill

microbe [mikrɔb] *m* microbe

microbicide [mikrɔbisid] *adj* & *m* germicide

microbiologie [mikrɔbjɔlɔʒi] *f* microbiology

microfilm [mikrɔfilm] *m* microfilm

microfilmer [mikrɔfilme] *tr* to microfilm

micro-onde [mikrɔɔd] *f* (pl -ondes) microwave

microphone [mikrɔfɔn] *m* microphone

microscope [mikrɔskɔp] *m* microscope

microscopique [mikrɔskɔpik] *adj* microscopic

microsillon [mikrɔsijɔ̃] *adj* & *m* microgroove

midi [midi] *m* noon; south; twelve, e.g., midi dix ten minutes after twelve; **chercher midi à quatorze heures** (fig) to look for difficulties where there are none; **Midi** south of France

midinette [midinɛt] *f* dressmaker's assistant; working girl

mie [mi] *f* soft part, crumb; female friend; **ne . . . mie** §90 (archaic) not a crumb, not, e.g., **je n'en veux mie** I don't want any

miel [mjɛl] *m* honey

miel·leux [mjɛlø] **miel·leuse** [mjɛløz] *adj* honeyed, unctuous

mien [mjɛ̃] **mienne** [mjɛn] §89

miette [mjɛt] *f* crumb

mieux [mjø] §91 *adv comp & super* better; **aimer mieux** to prefer; **à qui mieux mieux** trying to outdo each other; **de mieux en mieux** better and better; **être mieux, aller mieux** to feel better; **tant mieux** so much the better; **valoir mieux** to be better

mieux-être [mjøzetr] *m* improved well-being

mièvre [mjɛvr] *adj* dainty, affected

mi-figue [mifig] *f*—**mi-figue mi-raisin** half one way half the other; half in jest half in earnest

mi·gnard [miɲar] **-gnarde** [ɲard] *adj* affected, mincing

mi·gnon [miɲɔ̃] **-gnonne** [ɲɔn] *adj* cute, darling ‖ *mf* darling

mignon·net [miɲɔnɛ] **mignon·nette** [miɲɔnɛt] *adj* dainty ‖ *f* fine lace; pepper; (bot) pink

mignoter [miɲɔte] *tr* (coll) to pet (*a child*)

migraine [migrɛn] *f* migraine; headache

migratoire [migratwar] *adj* migratory

mi-jambe [miʒɑ̃b] *f*—**à mi-jambe** up to one's knee

mijoter [miʒɔte] *tr* to simmer; (coll) to cook up, to brew ‖ *intr* to simmer

mil [mil] *adj* one thousand, e.g., **l'an mil neuf cent soixante-six** the year one thousand nine hundred and sixty-six ‖ *m* Indian club; millet

milan [milɑ̃] *m* (orn) kite

milice [milis] *f* militia

mi·lieu [miljø] *m* (*pl* **-lieux**) middle; milieu; **milieu de table** centerpiece

militaire [militɛr] *adj* military ‖ *m* soldier; **le militaire** the military

mili·tant [militɑ̃] **-tante** [tɑ̃t] *adj & mf* militant

militariser [militarize] *tr* to militarize

militarisme [militarism] *m* militarism

militer [milite] *intr* to militate

mille [mil] *adj & pron* thousand ‖ *m* thousand; mile; **mettre dans le mille** to hit the bull's-eye; **mille marin** international nautical mile

millefeuille [milfœj] *m* napoleon (*pastry*)

mille-feuille [milfœj] *f* (*pl* **-feuilles**) (bot) yarrow

millénaire [milener] *adj* millennial ‖ *m* millennium

mille-pattes [milpat] *m invar* centipede

millésime [milezim] *m* date, vintage

millet [mije] *m* millet; birdseed

milliard [miljar] *m* billion

milliardaire [miljarder] *mf* billionaire

millième [miljɛm] *adj, pron* (*masc, fem*) thousandth ‖ *m* thousandth; mill (*thousandth part of a dollar*)

millier [milje] *m* thousand; about a thousand; **par milliers** by the thousands; **un millier de** a thousand

milligramme [miligram] *m* milligram

millimètre [milimɛtr] *m* millimeter

million [miljɔ̃] *m* million; **un million de** a million

millionième [miljɔnjɛm] *adj, pron* (*masc, fem*), *& m* millionth

millionnaire [miljɔnɛr] *adj & m* millionaire

mime [mim] *mf* mime; mimic

mimer [mime] *tr & intr* to mime; to mimic

mimique [mimik] *adj* sign (*language*) ‖ *f* mimicry

minable [minabl] *adj* wretched, shabby; (coll) pitiful (*performance, existence, etc.*) ‖ *mf* unfortunate

minaret [minarɛ] *m* minaret

minauder [minode] *intr* to simper, smirk

minau·dier [minodje] **-dière** [djɛr] *adj* mincing

mince [mɛ̃s] *adj* thin, slim, slight; **mince!** or **mince alors!** golly!

mine [min] *f* mine; lead (*of pencil*); look, face; looks; (fig) mine (*of information*); **avoir bonne mine** to look well; **avoir la mine d'être** to look to be; **avoir mauvaise mine** to look badly; **faire bonne mine à** to be nice to; **faire des mines** to simper; **faire la mine à** to pout at; **faire mauvaise mine à** to be unpleasant to; **faire mine de** to make as if to

miner [mine] *tr* to mine; to undermine; to wear away

minerai [minrɛ] *m* ore

miné·ral -rale [mineral] (*pl* **-raux** [ro]) *adj & m* mineral

minéralogie [mineralɔʒi] *f* mineralogy

mi·net [minɛ] **-nette** [nɛt] *mf* (coll) kitty, pussy; (coll) darling

mi·neur -neure [minœr] *adj & mf* minor ‖ *m* miner

miniature [minjatyr] *f* miniature

miniaturisation [minjatyrizasjɔ̃] *f* miniaturization

miniaturiser [minjatyrize] *tr* to miniaturize

minijupe [miniʒyp] *f* miniskirt

mini·mal -male [minimal] *adj* (*pl* **-maux** [mo]) minimum (*temperature*)

minime [minim] *adj* tiny; derisory (*salary*)

minimiser [minimize] *tr* to minimize

minimum [minimɔm] *adj & m* minimum; **minimum vital** minimum wage

ministère [minister] *m* ministry; **ministère des Affaires étrangères** Department of State

ministé·riel -rielle [ministerjɛl] *adj* ministerial

ministre [ministr] *m* minister; **ministre des Affaires étrangères** secretary of state; **premier ministre** premier, prime minister

minium [minjɔm] *m* red lead

minois [minwa] *m* (coll) pretty little face

minoritaire [minɔriter] *adj* minority

minorité [minɔrite] *f* minority

Minorque [minɔrk] *f* Minorca

minoterie [minɔtri] *f* flour mill; flour industry

minotier [minɔtje] *m* miller

minuit [minɥi] *m* midnight; twelve, e.g., **minuit et demi** twelve thirty

minuscule [minyskyl] *adj* tiny; small (*letter*) || *f* small letter

minus habens [minysabɛ̃s] *mf invar* (coll) moron; idiot

minutage [minytaʒ] *m* timing

minute [minyt] *f* minute, moment, instant; **à la minute** that very moment || *interj* (coll) just a minute!

minuter [minyte] *tr* to itemize; to time

minuterie [minytri] *f* delayed-action switch, (mach) timing mechanism

minutie [minysi] *f* minute detail; great care; **minuties** minutiae

minu-tieux [minysjø] **-tieuse** [sjøz] *adj* meticulous, thorough

mioche [mjɔʃ] *mf* (coll) brat

mi-pente [mipɑ̃t] – **à mi-pente** halfway up or halfway down

mirabilis [mirabilis] *m* (bot) marvel-of-Peru

miracle [mirakl] *m* miracle; wonder, marvel; miracle play; **crier au miracle** to go into ecstasies

miracu-leux [mirakylø] **-leuse** [løz] *adj* miraculous; wonderful, marvelous

mirador [miradɔr] *m* watchtower

mirage [miraʒ] *m* mirage

mire [mir] *f* sight (*of gun*); surveyor's pole; (telv) test pattern

mire-œufs [mirø] *m invar* candler

mirer [mire] *tr* to candle (*eggs*) || *ref* to look at oneself; to be reflected

mirifique [mirifik] *adj* (coll) marvelous

mirobo-lant [mirɔbɔlɑ̃] **-lante** [lɑ̃t] *adj* (coll) astounding

miroir [mirwar] *m* mirror; **miroir à alouettes** decoy

miroiter [mirwate] *intr* to sparkle, gleam; **faire miroiter q.ch. à qn** to lure s.o. with s.th.

miroton [mirɔtɔ̃] *m* Irish stew

misaine [mizɛn] *f* foresail

misanthrope [mizɑ̃trɔp] *mf* misanthrope

miscellanées [miselane], [misellane] *fpl* miscellany

mise [miz] *f* placing, putting; dress, attire; (cards) stake, ante; **de mise** acceptable, proper; **mise à feu** firing (*e.g., of missile*); **mise à l'eau** launching; **mise à prix** opening bid; **mise au point** carrying out, completion, tuning up, adjustment; (opt) focusing; (rad) tuning; **mis-** au **rancart** pigeonholing, **mise bas** delivery (*of litter*); **mise de fonds** investment; **mise en accusation** indictment; **mise en demeure** (law) injunction; **mise en marche** starting; **mise en œuvre** putting into action; **mise en scène** (theat) direction; (theat & fig) staging; **mise**

en valeur development, improvement; **mise en vigueur** enforcement

miser [mize] *tr & intr* to ante; to stake, bet; to bid (*e.g., at auction*)

misérable [mizerabl] *adj* miserable || *mf* wretch

misère [mizer] *f* misery, wretchedness; poverty; worry, (coll) trifle; **crier misère** to make a poor mouth; to look forsaken; **faire des misères à** to pester

misé-reux [mizerø] **-reuse** [røz] *adj* destitute, wretched || *mf* pauper

miséricorde [mizerikɔrd] *f* mercy

miséricor-dieux [mizerikɔrdjø] **-dieuse** [djøz] *adj* merciful

missel [misel] *m* missal

missile [misil] *m* guided missile

mission [misjɔ̃] *f* mission

missionnaire [misjoner] *adj & m* missionary

missive [misiv] *adj & f* missive

mitaine [miten] *f* mitt

mite [mit] *f* (ent) mite; (ent) clothes moth

mi-té-tée [mite] *adj* moth-eaten; (coll) shabby

mi-temps [mitɑ̃] *f invar* (sports) half time; **à mi-temps** half time

miter [mite] *ref* to become moth-eaten

mi-teux [mitø] **-teuse** [tøz] *adj* shabby || *mf* (coll) shabby-looking person

mitiger [mitiʒe] §38 *tr* to mitigate

mitonner [mitone] *tr* to simmer; to pamper, (coll) to contrive, devise || *intr* to simmer

mitoyen [mitwajɛ̃] **mitoyenne** [mitwajɛn] *adj* midway, intermediate, dividing; jointly owned, common

mitraille [mitraj] *f* scrap iron; grapeshot; artillery fire

mitrailler [mitraje] *tr* to machine-gun; to pepper (*with gunfire, flash bulbs, etc.*)

mitraillette [mitrajet] *f* submachine gun, Tommy gun

mitrail-leur [mitrajœr] **mitrail-leuse** [mitrajøz] *adj* repeating, automatic (*firearm*) || *m* machine gunner || *f* machine gun

mitre [mitr] *f* miter; chimney pot

mitron [mitrɔ̃] *m* baker's boy

mi-voix [mivwa] – **à mi-voix** in a low voice, under one's breath

mixte [mikst] *adj* mixed; coeducational; composite; joint (*e.g., commission*); (rr) freight-and-passenger

mixtion [mikstjɔ̃] *f* mixing; mixture

mixture [mikstyr] *f* mixture

Mlle *abbr* (Mademoiselle) Miss

MM *abbr* (Messieurs) Messrs.

Mme *abbr* (Madame) Mrs.; Mme.

mobile [mɔbil] *adj* mobile || *m* motive; (fa) mobile

mobi-lier [mɔbilje] **-lière** [ljer] *adj* personal || *m* furniture

mobilisable [mɔbilizabl] *adj* (mil) subject to call

mobilisation [mɔbilizasjɔ̃] *f* mobilization

mobiliser [mɔbilize] *tr & intr* to mobilize

mobilité [mɔbilite] *f* mobility

moche [mɔʃ] *adj* (coll) ugly; (coll) lousy

modalité [mɔdalite] *f* modality, manner, method; **modalités** terms

mode [mɔd] *m* kind, method, mode; (gram) mood; (mus) mode; **mode d'emploi** directions for use || *f* fashion; **à la mode** in style, fashionable; **à la mode de** in the manner of; **modes** fashions; millinery

modèle [mɔdɛl] *adj* & *m* model

modeler [mɔdle] §2 *tr* to model; to shape, mold || *ref*—**se modeler sur** to take as a model

modéliste [mɔdelist] *mf* model-airplane designer, etc.; dress designer

modéra•teur [mɔderatœr] **-trice** [tris] *adj* moderating || *mf* moderator; regulator; moderator (*for slowing down neutrons*); **modérateur de son** volume control

modé•ré -rée [mɔdere] *adj* moderate

modérer [mɔdere] §10 *tr* & *ref* to moderate

moderne [mɔdɛrn] *adj* modern

moderniser [mɔdɛrnize] *tr* to modernize

modeste [mɔdɛst] *adj* modest

modestie [mɔdɛsti] *f* modesty

modicité [mɔdisite] *f* paucity (*of resources*); lowness (*of price*)

modifica•teur [mɔdifikatœr] **-trice** [tris] *adj* modifying || *m* modifier

modifier [mɔdifje] *tr* to modify

modique [mɔdik] *adj* moderate, reasonable

modiste [mɔdist] *f* milliner

modulation [mɔdylasjɔ̃] *f* modulation; **modulation d'amplitude** amplitude modulation; **modulation de fréquence** frequency modulation

module [mɔdyl] *m* module; **module lunaire** (rok) lunar module

moduler [mɔdyle] *tr* & *intr* to modulate

moelle [mwal] *f* marrow; (bot) pith; **moelle épinière** spinal cord

moel•leux [mwalø] **moel•leuse** [mwaløz] *adj* soft; mellow; flowing (*brush stroke*)

moellon [mwalɔ̃] *m* building stone

mœurs [mœr], [mœrs] *fpl* customs, habits; morals

mohair [mɔɛr] *m* mohair

moi [mwa] §85, §87

moignon [mwaɲɔ̃] *m* stump

moi-même [mwamɛm] §86

moindre [mwɛ̃dr] §91 *adj comp* & *super* less; lesser; least, slightest

moine [mwan] *m* monk

moi•neau [mwano] *m* (*pl* **-neaux**) sparrow

moins [mwɛ̃] *m* less; minus; **au moins** or **du moins** at least; **(le) moins** (the) least; **moins de** fewer || *adv comp* & *super* §91 less; fewer; **à moins de** + *inf* without + *ger*, unless + *inf*; **à moins que** unless; **de moins en moins** less and less; **en moins de rien** in no time at all; **moins de** (followed by numeral) less than; **moins que** less than; **rien moins que** anything but ||

prep minus; to, e.g., **dix heures moins le quart** a quarter to ten

moire [mwar] *f* moire; **moire de soie** watered silk

moi•ré -rée [mware] *adj* watered (*silk*) || *m* wavy sheen

mois [mwa] *m* month

Moïse [mɔiz] *m* Moses

moi•si -sie [mwazi] *adj* moldy || *m* mold; **sentir le moisi** to have a musty smell

moisir [mwazir] *tr* to mold || *intr* to become moldy, to mold; (fig) to vegetate || *ref* to mold

moisissure [mwazisyr] *f* mold

moisson [mwasɔ̃] *f* harvest

moissonner [mwasɔne] *tr* to harvest, reap

moisson•neur [mwasɔnœr] **moisson•neuse** [mwasɔnøz] *mf* reaper || *f* (mach) reaper

moite [mwat] *adj* moist, damp; clammy

moiteur [mwatœr] *f* moistness, dampness; **moiteur froide** clamminess

moitié [mwatje] *f* half; (coll) better half (*wife*); **à moitié, la moitié** half; **à moitié chemin** halfway; **à moitié prix** at half price; **de moitié** by half || *adv* half

moka [mɔka] *m* mocha coffee; mocha cake

molaire [mɔlɛr] *adj* & *f* molar

môle [mol] *m* mole, breakwater || *f* (ichth) sunfish

molécule [mɔlekyl] *f* molecule

moleskine [mɔlɛskin] *f* (*fabric*) moleskin; imitation leather

molester [mɔlɛste] *tr* to molest

moleter [mɔlte] §34 *tr* to knurl, to mill

mollas•son [mɔlasɔ̃] **mollas•sonne** [mɔlasɔn] *mf* (coll) softy

mollement [mɔlmɑ̃] *adv* flabbily; listlessly

mollesse [mɔlɛs] *f* flabbiness; apathy; softness (*of contour*); mildness (*of climate*)

mol•let [mɔlɛ] **mol•lette** [mɔlɛt] *adj* soft, downy; soft-boiled (*egg*) || *m* (anat) calf

molletière [mɔltjɛr] *f* puttee, legging

molleton [mɔltɔ̃] *m* flannel

mollir [mɔlir] *intr* to weaken

mollusque [mɔlysk] *m* mollusk

molosse [mɔlɔs] *m* watchdog

molybdène [mɔlibdɛn] *m* molybdenum

môme [mom] *adj* (slang) little || *mf* (coll) kid || *f* (slang) babe

moment [mɔmɑ̃] *m* moment; **à aucun moment** at no time; **à ce moment-là** then, at that time; **à tout moment, à tous moments** continually; **au moment où** just when; **c'est le moment** now is the time; **d'un moment à l'autre** at any moment; **en ce moment** now; at this moment; **par moments** now and then; **sur le moment** at the very moment; **un petit moment** a little while

momenta•né -née [mɔmɑ̃tane] *adj* momentary

momerie [mɔmri] *f* mummery

momie [mɔmi] *f* mummy

mon [mɔ̃] §88

M^{on} *abbr* (**Maison**) (com) House

mona·cal -cale [mɔnakal] *adj* (*pl* **-caux** [ko]) monastic, monkish

monachisme [mɔnaʃism], [mɔnakism] *m* monasticism

monarchique [mɔnarʃik] *adj* monarchic

monarque [mɔnark] *m* monarch

monastère [mɔnaster] *m* monastery

monastique [mɔnastik] *adj* monastic

mon·ceau [mɔ̃so] *m* (*pl* **-ceaux**) heap, pile

mon·dain [mɔ̃dɛ̃] **-daine** [den] *adj* worldly; social (*life, functions, etc.*); sophisticated || *mf* worldly-minded person; socialite

mondanité [mɔ̃danite] *f* worldliness; **mondanités** social events; (journ) social news

monde [mɔ̃d] *m* world; people; **avoir du monde chez soi** to have company; **il y a du monde, il y a un monde fou** there is a big crowd; **le beau monde, le grand monde** high society, fashionable society; **mettre au monde** to give birth to; **tout le monde** everybody, everyone

monder [mɔ̃de] *tr* to hull; to blanch; to stone

mon·dial -diale [mɔ̃djal] *adj* (*pl* **-diaux** [djo]) world; world-wide

monétaire [mɔneter] *adj* monetary

mon·gol -gole [mɔ̃gɔl] *adj* Mongol || *m* Mongol (*language*) || (*cap*) *mf* Mongol (*person*)

moni·teur [mɔnitœr] **-trice** [tris] *mf* coach, trainer, instructor; monitor (*at school*)

monnaie [mɔne] *f* change, small change; money (*legal tender of a country*); **fausse monnaie** counterfeit money; **la Monnaie** the Mint; **monnaie forte** hard currency; **payer en monnaie de singe** to give lip service to

monnayer [mɔneje] §49 *tr* to mint, to coin; to convert into cash; to cash in on

monnayeur [mɔnejœr] *m*—**faux monnayeur** counterfeiter

monocle [mɔnɔkl] *m* monocle

monogamie [mɔnɔgami] *f* monogamy

monogramme [mɔnɔgram] *m* monogram

monographie [mɔnɔgrafi] *f* monograph

monolithique [mɔnɔlitik] *adj* monolithic

monologue [mɔnɔlɔg] *m* monologue

monologuer [mɔnɔlɔge] *tr* to soliloquize

monomanie [mɔnɔmani] *f* monomania

monôme [mɔnom] *m* single file (*of students*); (math) monomial

monoplan [mɔnɔplɑ̃] *m* monoplane

monopole [mɔnɔpɔl] *m* monopoly

monopoliser [mɔnɔpɔlize] *tr* to monopolize

monorail [mɔnɔraj] *m* monorail

monosyllabe [mɔnɔsilab] *m* monosyllable

monothéiste [mɔnɔteist] *adj* & *mf* monotheist

monotone [mɔnɔtɔn] *adj* monotonous

monotonie [mɔnɔtɔni] *f* monotony

monotype [mɔnɔtip] *adj* monotypic ||

m monotype || *f* Monotype (*machine to set type*)

monseigneur [mɔ̃seɲœr] *m* (*pl* **messeigneurs** [mesɛɲœr]) monseigneur

monsieur [masjø] *m* (*pl* **messieurs** [mesjø]) gentleman; sir; mister; Mr.

monstre [mɔ̃str] *adj* huge, monster || *m* monster; freak; **monstres sacrés** (fig) sacred cows, idols

mons·trueux [mɔ̃stryø] **-trueuse** [tryøz] *adj* monstrous

mont [mɔ̃] *m* mount; mountain; **par monts et par vaux** over hill and dale; **passer les monts** to cross the Alps

montage [mɔ̃taʒ] *m* hoisting; setting up (*of a machine*); (elec) hookup; (mov) cutting, editing

monta·gnard [mɔ̃taɲar] **-gnarde** [ɲard] *adj* mountain || *mf* mountaineer

montagne [mɔ̃taɲ] *f* mountain; **montagnes russes** roller coaster

monta·gneux [mɔ̃taɲø] **-gneuse** [ɲøz] *adj* mountainous

mon·tant [mɔ̃tɑ̃] **-tante** [tɑ̃t] *adj* rising, ascending; uphill; vertical; high-necked (*dress*) || *m* upright, riser; gatepost; total (*sum*); allure; (culin) tang; **montants** goal posts; (slang) pair of trousers

mont-de-piété [mɔ̃dpjete] *m* (*pl* **monts-de-piété**) pawnshop

mon·té -tée [mɔ̃te] *adj* mounted; organized; equipped, well-provided; worked-up, angry || *f* climb; slope

monte-charge [mɔ̃tʃarʒ] *m invar* freight elevator

monte-plats [mɔ̃tpla] *m invar* dumbwaiter

monter [mɔ̃te] *tr* to go up, to climb; to mount; to set up; to carry up, take up, bring up || *intr* (*aux:* ÊTRE) to go up, to come up; to come upstairs; to rise; to come in (*said of tide*); **monter + inf** to go up to + *inf*; **monter à en** to go up, to climb, to ascend, to mount; **monter sur** to mount (*the throne*); to go on (*the stage*) || *ref*—**se monter à** to amount to; **se monter en** to lay in a supply of; **se monter la tête** to get excited

montre [mɔ̃tr] *f* show, display; watch; **en montre** in the window, on display; **faire montre de** to show off, to parade; **montre à remontoir** stemwinder; **montre à répétition** repeater

montre-bracelet [mɔ̃trəbrasle] *f* (*pl* **montres-bracelets**) wrist watch

montrer [mɔ̃tre] *tr* to show; **montrer du doigt** to point out or at || *ref* to appear; to show oneself to be (*e.g., patient*)

mon·treur [mɔ̃trœr] **-treuse** [trøz] *mf* showman, exhibitor

mon·tueux [mɔ̃tɥø] **-tueuse** [tɥøz] *adj* rolling, hilly

monture [mɔ̃tyr] *f* mounting; assembling; mount (*e.g., horse*)

monument [mɔnymɑ̃] *m* monument; **monument aux morts** memorial monument

moquer [mɔke] *tr* & *ref* to mock; **se moquer de** to make fun of, to laugh at

moquerie [mɔkri] *f* mockery

moquette [mɔkɛt] *f* pile carpet

mo•ral -rale [mɔral] (*pl* **-raux** [ro]) *adj* moral || *m* morale || *f* ethics; moral (*of a fable*); **faire la morale à qn** to lecture s.o.

moralité [mɔralite] *f* morality; moral (*e.g., of a fable*)

morasse [mɔras] *f* final proof (*of newspaper*)

moratoire [mɔratwar] *m* moratorium

moratorium [mɔratɔrjɔm] *m* moratorium

morbide [mɔrbid] *adj* morbid

morbleu [mɔrblø] *interj* (obs) zounds!

mor•ceau [mɔrso] *m* (*pl* **-ceaux**) piece, bit; morsel; **bas morceaux** (culin) cheap cuts; **en morceaux in cubes** (*of sugar*); **morceaux choisis** selected passages

morceler [mɔrsəle] §34 *tr* to parcel out

morcellement [mɔrsɛlmɑ̃] *m* parceling out, division

mordancer [mɔrdɑ̃se] §51 *tr* to size

mor•dant [mɔrdɑ̃] **-dante** [dɑ̃t] *adj* mordant, caustic || *m* mordant; cutting edge; fighting spirit; (mus) mordent

mordicus [mɔrdikys] *adv* (coll) stoutly, tenaciously

mordiller [mɔrdije] *tr & intr* to nibble; to nip

mordo•ré -rée [mɔrdɔre] *adj* golden-brown, bronze-colored

mordre [mɔrdr] *tr* to bite || *intr* to bite; **mordre à** to bite on; to take to, to find easy; **mordre dans** to bite into; **mordre sur** to encroach upon || *ref* to bite

mor•du -due [mɔrdy] *adj* bitten; smitten || *mf* (coll) fan (*person*)

morelle [mɔrɛl] *f* nightshade

morfondre [mɔrfɔ̃dr] *tr* to chill to the bone || *ref* to be bored waiting

morgue [mɔrg] *f* morgue; haughtiness

mori•caud [mɔriko] **-caude** [kod] *adj* (coll) dark-skinned, dusky

morigéner [mɔriʒene] §10 *tr* to scold

morillon [mɔrijɔ̃] *m* rough emerald; duck; **morillon à dos blanc** canvasback

mor•mon [mɔrmɔ̃] **-mone** [mɔn] *adj & mf* Mormon

morne [mɔrn] *adj* dismal, gloomy || *m* hillock, knoll

mornifle [mɔrnifl] *f* (coll) slap

morose [mɔroz] *adj* morose

morphine [mɔrfin] *f* morphine

morphologie [mɔrfɔlɔʒi] *f* morphology

morpion [mɔrpjɔ̃] *m* tick-tack-toe; (*youngster*) (slang) squirt; (*Phthirius pubis*) (slang) crab louse

mors [mɔr] *m* bit; jaw (*of vise*)

morse [mɔrs] *m* Morse code; walrus

morsure [mɔrsyr] *f* bite

mort [mɔr] **morte** [mɔrt] *adj* dead; spent (*bullet*); (aut) neutral || *mf* dead person, corpse || *m* (bridge) dummy; **faire le mort** to play dead || *mort f* death; **attraper la mort** to catch one's death of cold

mortadelle [mɔrtadɛl] *f* bologna

mortaise [mɔrtɛz] *f* mortise

mortaiser [mɔrteze] *tr* to mortise

mortalité [mɔrtalite] *f* mortality

mort-aux-rats [mɔrtora], [mɔrora] *f invar* rat poison

mort-bois [mɔrbwa] *m* deadwood

morte-eau [mɔrto] *f* (*pl* **mortes-eaux** [mɔrtazo]) low tide

mor•tel -telle [mɔrtɛl] *adj & mf* mortal

morte-saison [mɔrtəsɛzɔ̃] *f* (*pl* **mortes-saisons**) off-season

mortier [mɔrtje] *m* mortar; round judicial cap

mortifier [mɔrtifje] *tr* to mortify; to tenderize (*meat*)

mort-né -née [mɔrne] (*pl* **-nés**) *adj* stillborn || *mf* stillborn child

mortuaire [mɔrtɥɛr] *adj* mortuary; funeral (*e.g., service*); death (*notice*)

morue [mɔry] *f* cod

morve [mɔrv] *f* snot

mor•veux [mɔrvø] **-veuse** [vøz] *adj* snotty || *mf* (coll) young snot, brat, whippersnapper

mosaïque [mɔzaik] *adj* mosaic; Mosaic || *f* mosaic

Moscou [mɔsku] *m* Moscow

mosquée [mɔske] *f* mosque

mot [mo] *m* word; answer (*to riddle*); **à mots couverts guardedly; au bas mot** at least; **avoir toujours le mot pour rire** to be always cracking jokes; **bon mot** witticism; **gros mots** foul words; **le mot à mot** the word-for-word translation; **mot à double sens double entendre; mot de passe** password; **mot d'ordre** slogan; **mot pour mot** word for word; **mots croisés** crossword puzzle; **ne . . . mot** §90 (archaic) not a word, nothing; **placer un mot** to put in a word; **prendre qn au mot** to take s.o. at his word; **sans mot dire** without a word

motard [mɔtar] *m* (coll) motorcyclist; (coll) motorcycle cop

mot-clé [mɔkle] *m* (*pl* **mots-clés**) key word

motel [mɔtɛl] *m* motel

mo•teur [mɔtœr] **-trice** [tris] *adj* driving (*wheel*); drive (*shaft*); motive (*power*); power (*brake*); motor (*nerve*) || *m* motor, engine; prime mover; instigator; **moteur à deux temps** two-cycle engine; **moteur à explosion** internal-combustion engine; **moteur à quatre temps** four-cycle engine; **moteur à réaction** jet engine; **moteur hors bord** outboard motor

moteur-fusée *m* (*pl* **moteurs-fusées**) rocket engine

motif [mɔtif] *m* motive; (fa, mus) motif

motion [mosjɔ̃] *f* (parl) motion

motiver [mɔtive] *tr* to motivate

moto [mɔto] *f* motorcycle

motoriser [mɔtɔrize] *tr* to motorize

mot-outil [mɔuti] *m* (*pl* **mots-outils**) link word

mot-piège [mɔpjɛʒ] *m* (*pl* **mots-pièges**) tricky word

mots-croisés [mokrwaze] *mpl* crossword puzzle

mot-souche [mosuʃ] *m* (*pl* **mots-souches**) entry word; (typ) catchword

motte [mɔt] *f* clod, lump; slab (*of butter*); **motte de gazon** turf

motus [mɔtys] *interj* mum's the word!

mou [mu] (*or* **mol** [mɔl] before vowel or mute *h*) **molle** [mɔl] (*pl* **mous molles**) *adj* soft; limp, flabby, slack; spineless, listless || *m* slack; lights, lungs; (coll) softy

mou·chard [muʃar] **-charde** [ʃard] *mf* (coll) stool pigeon, squealer

moucharder [muʃarde] *tr* (coll) to spy on; (coll) to squeal on || *intr* (coll) to squeal

mouche [muʃ] *f* fly; beauty spot; **faire d'une mouche un éléphant** to make a mountain out of a molehill; **faire la mouche** to fly into a rage; **faire mouche** to hit the bull's-eye; **mouche à miel** honeybee; **mouche d'Espagne** (pharm) Spanish fly; **mouche du coche** busybody

moucher [muʃe] *tr* to blow (*one's nose*); to snuff, to trim; (coll) to scold || *ref* to blow one's nose

moucherolle [muʃrɔl] *f* (orn) flycatcher

moucheron [muʃrɔ̃] *m* gnat; snuff (*of candle*)

moucheter [muʃte] §34 *tr* to speckle

mouchoir [muʃwar] *m* handkerchief

moudre [mudr] §43 *tr* to grind

moue [mu] *f* wry face; **faire la moue** to pout

mouette [mwɛt] *f* gull, sea gull; **mouette rieuse** black-headed gull

mouffette [mufɛt] *f* skunk

moufle [mufl] *m & f* pulley block || *f* mitten

mouillage [mujaʒ] *m* anchorage; wetting; watering, diluting

mouil·lé -lée [muje] *adj* wet; at anchor; palatalized; liquid (*l*)

mouiller [muje] *tr* to wet; to water, dilute; to palatalize; to drop (*anchor*) || *intr* to drop anchor || *ref* to get wet; to water; (coll) to become involved

moulage [mulaʒ] *m* molding, casting; mold, cast; grinding, milling

moule [mul] *m* mold, form || *f* mussel; (slang) fleabrain; (slang) jellyfish

mouler [mule] *tr* to mold; to outline, e.g., **corsage qui moule le buste** blouse which outlines the bosom

moulin [mulɛ̃] *m* mill; **moulin à café** coffee grinder; **moulin à paroles** (coll) windbag; **moulin à vent** windmill

moulinet [muline] *m* winch; reel (*of casting rod*); turnstile; pinwheel (*child's toy*); **faire le moulinet avec** to twirl

moult [mult] *adv* (obs) much, many

mou·lu -lue [muly] *adj* ground; (coll) done in

moulure [mulyr] *f* molding

mou·rant [murɑ̃] **-rante** [rɑ̃t] *adj* dying || *mf* dying person

mourir [murir] §44 *intr* (*aux*: ÊTRE) to die || *ref* to be dying

mouron [murɔ̃] *m* (bot) starwort, stitchwort; (bot) pimpernel

mousquetaire [muskəter] *m* musketeer

mousse [mus] *adj* dull || *m* cabin boy || *f* moss; froth, foam; lather, suds; whipped cream

mousseline [muslin] *f* muslin; **mousseline de soie chiffon**

mousser [muse] *intr* to froth, to foam; to lather; **faire mousser** (coll) to crack up, to build up; (slang) to enrage

mous·seux [musø] **mous·seuse** [musøz] *adj* mossy; frothy, foamy; sudsy; sparkling (*wine*)

mousson [musɔ̃] *f* monsoon

moustache [mustaʃ] *f* moustache; **moustaches** whiskers (*of, e.g., cat*); **moustaches en croc** handle-bar moustache

moustiquaire [mustiker] *f* mosquito net

moustique [mustik] *m* mosquito

moût [mu] *m* must; wort

moutard [mutar] *m* (slang) kid

moutarde [mutard] *f* mustard

moutier [mutje] *m* (obs) monastery

mouton [mutɔ̃] *m* sheep; mutton; (slang) stool pigeon; **doux comme un mouton** gentle as a lamb; **moutons** whitecaps; **moutons de Panurge** (fig) chameleons, yes men; **revenons à nos moutons** let's get back to our subject

mouton·né -née [mutɔne] *adj* fleecy; frothy (*sea*); mackerel (*sky*)

moutonner [mutɔne] *tr* to curl || *intr* to break into whitecaps

mouton·neux [mutɔnø] **mouton·neuse** [mutɔnøz] *adj* frothy; fleecy (*e.g., cloud*)

mouture [mutyr] *f* grinding; mixture of wheat, rye, and barley; (fig) reworking

mouvement [muvmɑ̃] *m* movement; motion; **mouvement d'horlogerie** clockwork; **mouvement d'humeur** fit of bad temper; **mouvement ondulatoire** wave motion

mouvemen·té -tée [muvmɑ̃te] *adj* lively; eventful; hilly, broken (*terrain*)

mouvementer [muvmɑ̃te] *tr* to enliven

mouvoir [muvwar] §45 *tr* to move; to set in motion; to drive || *ref* to move, stir

moyen [mwajɛ̃] **moyenne** [mwajen] *adj* average; ordinary; middle, intermediate; medium || *m* way, manner; **au moyen de** by means of; **moyens** means || *f* average; mean; passing mark; **en moyenne** on an average

moyen-âge [mwajenaʒ] *m* Middle Ages

moyen-courrier [mwajɛ̃kurje] *m* (*pl* **moyens-courriers**) medium-range plane

moyennant [mwajenɑ̃] *prep* in exchange for || *conj* provided that

Moyen-Orient [mwajenɔrjɑ̃] *m* Middle East

moyeu [mwajø̃] *m* (*pl* **moyeux**) hub
mû mue [my] *adj* driven, propelled ‖ *f*
see **mue**
mucosité ⎸mykozite⎸ *f* mucus
mucus ⎸mykys⎸ *m* mucus
mue ⎸my⎸ *f* molt, shedding
muer ⎸mɥe⎸ *intr* to molt; to shed;
(*said of voice*) to break, change
muet ⎸mɥɛ⎸ **muett**- ⎸mɥɛt⎸ *adj* mute;
silent; non-speaking (*rôle*); blank;
dead (*key*) ‖ *mf* mute ‖ *m* silent
movie
mufle [myfl] *m* muzzle, snout; (coll)
cad, skunk
mugir ⎸myʒir⎸ *intr* to bellow
mugissement [myʒismã] *m* bellow
muguet ⎸mygɛ⎸ *m* lily of the valley
mulâ·tre ⎸mylɑtr⎸ **-tresse** [trɛs] *mf*
mulatto
mule ⎸myl⎸ *f* mule
mulet ⎸mylɛ⎸ *m* mule; (ichth) mullet
mule·tier ⎸myltje⎸ **-tière** [tjer] *adj* mule
(*e.g., trail*) ‖ *mf* muleteer
mulette ⎸mylɛt⎸ *f* fresh-water clam
mulot ⎸mylo⎸ *m* field mouse
multilaté·ral -ral- ⎸myltilateral⎸ *adj* (*pl*
-raux ⎸ro⎸) multilateral
multiple ⎸myltipl⎸ *adj & m* multiple
multiplicité ⎸myltiplisite⎸ *f* multiplicity
multiplier ⎸myltiplije⎸ *tr & ref* to multiply
multitude ⎸myltityd⎸ *f* multitude
munici·pal -pale ⎸mynisipal⎸ *adj* (*pl*
-paux ⎸po⎸) municipal
municipalité ⎸mynisipalite⎸ *f* munici-
pality; city officials; city hall ·
munifi·cent ⎸mynifisã⎸ **-cente** [sãt] *adj*
munificent
munir ⎸mynir⎸ *tr* to provide, equip ‖
ref—**se munir de** to provide oneself
with
munitions ⎸mynisjɔ̃⎸ *fpl* munitions
mu·queux ⎸mykø⎸ **-queuse** [køz] *adj*
mucous ‖ *f* mucous membrane
mur [myr] *m* wall; **mettre au pied du
mur** to corner; **mur de soutènement**
retaining wall; **mur sonique, mur du
son** sound barrier
mûr mûre [myr] *adj* ripe, mature ‖ *f*
see **mûre**
muraille ⎸myrɑj⎸ *f* wall, rampart
mu·ral -rale ⎸myral⎸ *adj* (*pl* **-raux**
⎸ro⎸) mural
mûre ⎸myr⎸ *f* mulberry; blackberry
murer ⎸myre⎸ *tr* to wall up or in ‖ *ref*
to shut oneself up
mûrier ⎸myrje⎸ *m* mulberry tree
mûrir ⎸myrir⎸ *tr & intr* to ripen, mature
murmure ⎸myrmyr⎸ *m* murmur
murmurer ⎸myrmyre⎸ *tr & intr* to murmur
musaraigne ⎸myzarɛɲ⎸ *f* (zool) shrew
musarder ⎸myzarde⎸ *intr* to dawdle
musc [mysk] *m* musk
muscade [myskad] *f* nutmeg; **passez
muscade!** presto!
muscardin ⎸myskardɛ̃⎸ *m* dormouse
muscat [myska] *m* muscatel
muscle [myskl] *m* muscle

mus·clé -clée ⎸myskle⎸ *adj* muscular;
(coll) powerful (*e.g., drama*); (slang)
difficult
musculaire [myskyler] *adj* muscular
muscu·leux ⎸myskylø⎸ **-leuse** [løz] *adj*
muscular
muse ⎸myz⎸ *f* muse; **les Muses** the
Muses
mu·seau [myzo] *m* (*pl* **-seaux**) snout;
(coll) mug, face
musée ⎸myze⎸ *m* museum
museler ⎸myzle⎸ §34 *tr* to muzzle
muselière [myzəljer] *f* muzzle
muser ⎸myze⎸ *intr* to dawdle
musette ⎸myzɛt⎸ *f* feed bag; kit bag;
haversack
muséum [myzeɔm] *m* museum of natural history
musi·cal -cale ⎸myzikal⎸ *adj* (*pl* **-caux**
⎸ko⎸) musical
music-hall ⎸myzikol⎸ *m* (*pl* **-halls**)
vaudeville; vaudeville house; music
hall (Brit)
musi·cien ⎸myzisjɛ̃⎸ **-cienne** [sjen] *mf*
musician
musicologie ⎸myzikɔlɔʒi⎸ *f* musicology
musique ⎸myzik⎸ *f* music; band; **toujours la même musique** (coll) the
same old song
mus·qué -quée ⎸myske⎸ *adj* musk-
scented
musul·man -mane ⎸myzylmã⎸ **-mane** [man]
adj & mf Mussulman
mutation ⎸mytasjɔ̃⎸ *f* mutation; transfer; (biol) mutation, sport
muter ⎸myte⎸ *tr* to transfer
muti·lé -lée ⎸mytile⎸ *mf* disabled veteran
mutiler ⎸mytile⎸ *tr* to mutilate; to deface; to disable; to garble (*e.g., the
truth*)
mu·tin ⎸mytɛ̃⎸ **-tine** [tin] *adj* roguish ‖
mf mutineer
muti·né -née ⎸mytine⎸ *adj* mutinous ‖
mf mutineer
mutiner ⎸mytine⎸ *ref* to mutiny
mutualité ⎸mytɥalite⎸ *f* mutual insurance
mu·tuel -tuelle ⎸mytɥel⎸ *adj* mutual ‖
f mutual benefit association
myope ⎸mjɔp⎸ *adj* near-sighted ‖ *mf*
near-sighted person
myriade ⎸mirjad⎸ *f* myriad
myrrhe ⎸mir⎸ *f* myrrh
myrte ⎸mirt⎸ *m* myrtle
myrtille ⎸mirtij⎸ *f* blueberry
mystère ⎸mister⎸ *m* mystery
mysté·rieux ⎸misterjø⎸ **-rieuse** [rjøz]
adj mysterious
mysticisme ⎸mistisism⎸ *m* mysticism
mystification ⎸mistifikasjɔ̃⎸ *f* mystification; hoax
mystifier ⎸mistifje⎸ *tr* to mystify; to
hoax
mystique ⎸mistik⎸ *adj & mf* mystic
mythe ⎸mit⎸ *m* myth
mythique ⎸mitik⎸ *adj* mythical
mythologie ⎸mitɔlɔʒi⎸ *f* mythology
mythologique ⎸mitɔlɔʒik⎸ *adj* mythological

N

N, n [en], *[en] *m invar* fourteenth letter of the French alphabet

na·bot [nabo] **-bote** [bɔt] *adj* dwarfish ‖ *mf* dwarf, midget

nacelle [nasɛl] *f* (aer) nacelle; (naut) wherry, skiff; (fig) boat

nacre [nakr] *f* mother-of-pearl

na·cré -crée [nakre] *adj* pearly

nage [naʒ] *f* swimming; rowing, paddling; **être (tout) en nage** to be wet with sweat; **nage à la pagaie** paddling; **nage de côté** sidestroke; **nage en couple** sculling; **nage en grenouille** breaststroke

nagée [naʒe] *f* swimming stroke

nageoire [naʒwar] *f* fin; flipper (*of seal*); float (*for swimmers*)

nager [naʒe] §38 *intr* to swim; to float; to row; **nager à culer** (naut) to back water; **nager debout** to tread water; to row standing up; **nager entre deux eaux** to swim under water; (fig) to carry water on both shoulders

na·geur [naʒœr] **-geuse** [ʒøz] *adj* swimming; floating ‖ *mf* swimmer; rower

naguère or **naguères** [nager] *adv* lately, just now

naïf [naif] **naïve** [naiv] *adj* naïve ‖ *mf* simple-minded person

nain [nɛ̃] **naine** [nɛn] *adj & mf* dwarf

naissain [nesɛ̃] *m* seed oysters

naissance [nesɑ̃s] *f* birth; lineage; descent; beginning; (archit) springing line; **de basse naissance** lowborn; **de haute naissance** highborn; **de naissance** by birth; **donner naissance à** to give birth to; to give rise to; **naissance de la gorge** bosom, throat; **naissance des cheveux** hairline; **naissance du jour** daybreak; **prendre naissance** to arise, originate

nais·sant [nesɑ̃] **nais·sante** [nesɑ̃t] *adj* nascent, rising, budding

naître [netr] §46 *intr* (aux: ÊTRE) to be born; to bud; to arise, originate; to dawn; **faire naître** to give birth to; to give rise to

naïveté [naivte] *f* naïveté; artlessness

nanan [nanɑ̃], [nɑ̃nɑ̃] *m* (coll) goody; **du nanan** (coll) nice

nantir [nɑ̃tir] *tr* to give security or a pledge to; **nantir de** to provide with ‖ *intr* to stock up; to feather one's nest ‖ *ref*—**se nantir de** to provide oneself with

nantissement [nɑ̃tismɑ̃] *m* security

napée [nape] *f* wood nymph

napel [napel] *m* monkshood, wolfsbane

naphte [naft] *m* naphtha

napoléo·nien [napɔleɔnjɛ̃] **-nienne** [njɛn] *adj* Napoleonic

nappage [napaʒ] *m* table linen

nappe [nap] *f* tablecloth; sheet (*of water, flame*); net (*for fishing; for bird catching*); **mettre la nappe** to set the table; **nappe d'autel** altar cloth; **ôter la nappe** to clear the table

napperon [naprɔ̃] *m* tablecloth cover; **petit napperon** doily

narcisse [narsis] *m* narcissus; **narcisse des bois** daffodil; **Narcisse** Narcissus

narcotique [narkɔtik] *adj & m* narcotic

narcotiser [narkɔtize] *tr* to dope

nargue [narg] *f* scorn, contempt; **faire nargue de** to defy; **nargue de . . . !** fie on . . . !

narguer [narge] *tr* to flout, to snap one's fingers at

marguilé [nargile] *m* hookah

narine [narin] *f* nostril

nar·quois [narkwa] **-quoise** [kwaz] *adj* sly, cunning; sneering

narra·teur [naratœr] **-trice** [tris] *mf* narrator, storyteller

narra·tif [naratif] **-tive** [tiv] *adj* narrative

narration [narɑsjɔ̃] *f* narration; narrative

narrer [nare] *tr* to narrate, relate

na·sal -sale [nazal] *adj* (*pl* **-saux** [zo]) nasal ‖ *f* nasal (*vowel*)

nasaliser [nazalize] *tr & intr* to nasalize

nasarde [nazard] *f* fillip on one's nose (*in contempt*); snub, insult

na·seau [nazo] *m* (*pl* **-seaux**) nostril (*of horse, etc.*); **naseaux** (coll) snout

nasil·lard [nazijar] **nasil·larde** [nazijard] *adj* nasal

nasiller [nazije] *intr* to talk through one's nose; to squawk, quack

nasse [nas] *f* fish trap; (sports) basket

na·tal -tale [natal] *adj* (*pl* **-tals**) natal, of birth, native

natalité [natalite] *f* birth rate

natation [natɑsjɔ̃] *f* swimming

na·tif [natif] **-tive** [tiv] *adj & mf* native

nation [nɑsjɔ̃] *f* nation; **Nations Unies** United Nations

natio·nal -nale [nɑsjɔnal] *adj & mf* (*pl* **-naux** [no] **-nales**) national

nationaliser [nɑsjɔnalize] *tr* to nationalize

nationalité [nɑsjɔnalite] *f* nationality

nativité [nativite] *f* nativity; nativity scene; **Nativité** Nativity

natte [nat] *f* mat, matting; braid

natter [nate] *tr* to weave; to braid

naturalisation [natyralizɑsjɔ̃] *f* naturalization

naturaliser [natyralize] *tr* to naturalize

naturalisme [natyralism] *m* naturalism

naturaliste [natyralist] *adj & mf* naturalist

nature [natyr] *adj invar* raw; black (*coffee*) ‖ *f* nature; **nature morte** (painting) still life

natu·rel -relle [natyrel] *adj* natural; native ‖ *m* naturalness; native, citizen

naturellement [natyrelmɑ̃] *adv* naturally; of course

naufrage [nofraʒ] *m* shipwreck

naufra·gé -gée [nofraʒe] *adj* shipwrecked ‖ *mf* shipwrecked person

nauséa·bond [nozeabɔ̃] **-bonde** [bɔ̃d] *adj* nauseating

nausée [noze] *f* nausea

nauséeux [nozeø] **nauséeuse** [nozeøz] *adj* nauseous

nautique [notik] *adj* nautical

nautisme [notism] *m* yachting

nauto·nier [notɔnje] **-nière** [njer] *mf* pilot

na·val -vale [naval] *adj* (*pl* **-vals**) naval; nautical, maritime

navel [navɛl] *f* navel orange

navet [navɛ] *m* turnip

navette [navɛt] *f* shuttle; shuttle train; **faire la navette** to shuttle, to ply back and forth

navigable [navigabl] *adj* navigable (*river*); seaworthy (*ship*)

naviga·teur [navigatœr] **-trice** [tris] *adj* seafaring || *m* navigator

navigation [navigasjɔ̃] *f* navigation; sailing; **navigation de plaisance** (sports) sailing

naviguer [navige] *intr* to navigate, sail; **naviguer sur** to navigate, sail (*the sea*)

navire [navir] *m* ship; **navire de débarquement** landing craft; **navire marchand** merchantman

navire-citerne [navirsitern] *m* (*pl* **navires-citernes**) tanker

navire-école [navirekɔl] *m* (*pl* **navires-écoles**) training ship

navire-jumeau [navirʒymo] *m* (*pl* **navires-jumeaux**) sister ship

na·vrant [navrɑ̃] **-vrante** [vrɑ̃t] *adj* distressing, heartrending

na·vré -vrée [navre] *adj* sorry, grieved

navrer [navre] *tr* to distress, grieve

nazaréen [nazareɛ̃] **nazaréenne** [nazareen] *adj* Nazarene || (*cap*) *mf* Nazarene

N.-D. *abbr* (**Notre-Dame**) Our Lady

ne [nə] **887, 890**; **n'est-ce pas?** isn't that so? La traduction précédente est généralement remplacée par diverses locutions. Si l'énoncé est négatif, la question qui équivaut à **n'est-ce pas?** sera affirmative, par ex., **Vous ne travaillez pas. N'est-ce pas?** You are not working. Are you? Si l'énoncé est affirmatif, la question sera négative, par ex., **Vous travaillez. N'est-ce pas?** You are working. Are you not? ou Aren't you? Si l'énoncé contient un auxiliaire, la question contiendra cet auxiliaire moins l'infinitif ou moins le participe passé, par ex., **Il arrivera demain. N'est-ce pas?** He will arrive tomorrow. Won't he? par ex., **Paul est déjà arrivé. N'est-ce pas?** Paul has already arrived. Hasn't he? Si l'énoncé ne contient un auxiliaire ni forme de la copule "to be", la question contiendra l'auxiliaire "do" ou "did" moins l'infinitif, par ex., **Marie parle anglais. N'est-ce pas?** Mary speaks English. Doesn't she?

né née [ne] *adj* born; by birth; **bien né** highborn; **né** pour cut out for

néanmoins [neãmwɛ̃] *adv* nevertheless

néant [neã] *m* nothing, nothingness; worthlessness; obscurity; none (*as a response on the appropriate blank of an official form*)

nébu·leux [nebylø] **-leuse** [løz] *adj* nebulous; gloomy (*facial expression*); worried (*brow*) || *f* nebula

nécessaire [neseser] *adj* necessary, needful; **nécessaire à** required for || *m* necessities; kit, dressing case

nécessairement [nesesermã] *adv* necessarily

nécessité [nesesite] *f* necessity; need; **nécessité préalable** prerequisite

nécessiter [nesesite] *tr* to necessitate

nécessi·teux [nesesitø] **-teuse** [tøz] *adj* needy || *mf* needy person; **les nécessiteux** the needy

nécrologie [nekrɔlɔʒi] *f* necrology, obituary

nectar [nektar] *m* nectar

néerlan·dais [neerlãde] **-daise** [dez] *adj* Dutch || *m* Dutch (*language*) || (*cap*) *mf* Netherlander

nef [nef] *f* nave; (archaic) ship; **nef latérale** aisle

néfaste [nefast] *adj* ill-starred, unlucky

nèfle [nefl] *f* medlar

néflier [neflije] *m* medlar tree

néga·teur [negatœr] **-trice** [tris] *adj* negative

néga·tif [negatif] **-tive** [tiv] *adj* negative || *m* (phot) negative || *f* negative (*side of a question*)

négation [negasjɔ̃] *f* negation; (gram) negative

négli·gé -gée [negliʒe] *adj* careless; unadorned, unstudied || *m* carelessness; negligee, dressing gown

négligeable [negliʒabl] *adj* negligible

négligence [negliʒãs] *f* negligence; **avec négligence** slovenly

négli·gent [negliʒã] **-gente** [ʒãt] *adj* negligent || *mf* careless person

négliger [negliʒe] **§38** *tr* to neglect || *ref* to neglect oneself

négoce [negɔs] *m* trade, commerce; (com) company

négociable [negɔsjabl] *adj* negotiable

négo·ciant [negɔsjã] **-ciante** [sjãt] *mf* wholesaler, dealer

négocia·teur [negɔsjatœr] **-trice** [tris] *mf* negotiator

négociation [negɔsjasjɔ̃] *f* negotiation

négocier [negɔsje] *tr* to negotiate || *intr* to negotiate; to deal

nègre [negr] *adj* Negro; dark brown || *m* Negro; ghost writer; **petit nègre** pidgin, Creole

négrerie [negrəri] *f* slave quarters

négrier [negrije] *adj* masc slave || *m* slave driver; slave ship

neige [neʒ] *f* snow

neiger [neʒe] **§38** *intr* to snow

Némésis [nemezis] *f* Nemesis

nenni [nani], [neni], [neni] *adv* (archaic) no, not

nénuphar [nenyfar] *m* water lily

néologisme [neɔlɔʒism] *m* neologism

néon [neɔ̃] *m* neon

néophyte [neɔfit] *mf* neophyte, convert

neptunium [neptynjɔm] *m* neptunium

nerf [ner] *m* nerve; tendon, sinew; (archit, bb) rib; (fig) backbone, sinew; **avoir du nerf** to have nerves of steel; **avoir les nerfs à fleur de peau** to be on edge; **nerf de bœuf**

scourge; **porter sur les nerfs à qn** to get on s.o.'s nerves

Néron [nerɔ̃] *m* Nero

ner•veux [nervø] **-veuse** [vøz] *adj* nervous; nerve; jittery; sinewy, muscular; forceful (*style*)

nervure [nervyr] *f* rib

net **nette** [nɛt] *adj* clean; clear, sharp, distinct; net; **net d'impôt** tax-exempt ‖ *m*—**mettre au net** to make a fair copy of ‖ **net** *adv* flatly, point-blank, outright

netteté [nɛtəte] *f* neatness; clearness, sharpness

nettoiement [netwamɑ̃] *m* cleaning

nettoyage [netwaja3] *m* cleaning; **nettoyage à sec** dry cleaning

nettoyer [netwaje] §47 *tr* to clean; to wash up or out; **nettoyer à sec** to dry-clean ‖ *ref* to wash up, to clean oneself

nettoyeur [netwajœr] **nettoyeuse** [netwajøz] *mf* cleaner

neuf [nœf] **neuve** [nœv] *adj* new; **flambant neuf, tout neuf** brand-new ‖ **neuf** *adj & pron* nine; the Ninth, e.g., **Jean neuf** John the Ninth; **neuf heures** nine o'clock ‖ *m* nine; ninth (*in dates*)

neutraliser [nøtralize] *tr* to neutralize

neutralité [nøtralite] *f* neutrality

neutre [nøtr] *adj & m* neuter; neutral

neuvième [nœvjem] *adj, pron* (*masc, fem*), *& m* ninth

ne•veu [nəvø] *m* (*pl* -**veux**) nephew; **nos neveux** our posterity

névralgie [nevral3i] *f* neuralgia

névrose [nevroz] *f* neurosis

névro•sé -sée [nevroze] *adj & mf* neurotic

New York [nujɔrk], [nœjɔrk] *m* New York

newyor•kais [nœjorke] **-kaise** [kez] *adj* New York ‖ (*cap*) *mf* New Yorker

nez [ne] *m* nose; cape, headland; **nez à nez** face to face

ni [ni] §90 *conj*—**ne . . . ni . . . ni** neither . . . nor, e.g., **elle n'a ni papier ni stylo** she has neither paper nor pen; **ni . . . ni** neither . . . nor; **ni . . . non plus** nor . . . either

niable [njabl] *adj* deniable

niais [nje] **niaise** [njez] *adj* foolish, silly, simple-minded ‖ *mf* fool, simpleton

niaiserie [njezəri] *f* foolishness, silliness, simpleness

niche [niʃ] *f* niche; alcove; prank; **niche à chien** doghouse

nichée [niʃe] *f* brood

nicher [niʃe] *tr* to niche, to lodge ‖ *intr* to nestle; to nest; to hide ‖ *ref* to nest

nickeler [nikle] §34 *tr* to nickel-plate

nickelure [niklyr] *f* nickel plate

nicotine [nikotin] *f* nicotine

nid [ni] *m* nest; **en nid d'abeilles** honeycombed; **nid de pie** crow's-nest

nièce [njes] *f* niece

nième [njem] *adj* nth

nier [nje] *tr* to deny ‖ *intr* to plead not guilty

ni•gaud [nigo] **-gaude** [god] *adj* silly ‖ *mf* nincompoop

nigauderie [nigodri] *f* silliness

nihilisme [niilism] *m* nihilism

Nil [nil] *m* Nile

nimbe [nɛ̃b] *m* halo, nimbus

nimber [nɛ̃be] *tr* to halo

nimbus [nɛ̃bys] *m* (meteo) nimbus

nipper [nipe] *tr* (coll) to tog ‖ *ref* (coll) to tog oneself out

nippes [nip] *fpl* (coll) worn-out clothes; (slang) duds

nique [nik] *f*—**faire la nique à** to turn up one's nose at

nitrate [nitrat] *m* nitrate

nitre [nitr] *m* niter, nitrate

ni•treux [nitrø] **-treuse** [trøz] *adj* nitrous

nitrière [nitrijer] *f* saltpeter bed

nitrique [nitrik] *adj* nitric

nitrogène [nitroʒen] *m* nitrogen

nitroglycérine [nitrogliserin] *f* nitroglycerin

ni•veau [nivo] *m* (*pl* -**veaux**) level; **au niveau de** on a par with; **niveau à bulle d'air** spirit level; **niveau à lunettes** surveyor's level; **niveau d'essence** gasoline gauge; **niveau de vie** standard of living; **niveau d'huile** oil gauge; **niveau mental** I.Q.

niveler [nivle] §34 *tr* to level; to survey

nive•leur [nivlœr] **-leuse** [løz] *mf* leveler ‖ *m* harrow ‖ *f* (agr) leveler

nivellement [nivelmɑ̃] *m* leveling; surveying

No, **n°** *abbr* (**numéro**) no.

noble [nobl] *adj & mf* noble

noblesse [nobles] *f* nobility; nobleness

noce [nos] *f* wedding; wedding party; **faire la noce** to go on a spree; **ne pas être à la noce** to be in trouble; **noces** wedding

no•ceur [nosœr] **-ceuse** [søz] *adj* (coll) bacchanalian, reveling ‖ *mf* (coll) reveler, debauchee

no•cif [nosif] **-cive** [siv] *adj* noxious

noctambule [noktɑ̃byl] *mf* nighthawk; sleepwalker

nocturne [noktyrn] *adj* nocturnal; night; nightly ‖ *m* (mus) nocturne ‖ *f* open night (*of store*)

nodosité [nodozite] *f* nodule (*of root*); node, wart

Noé [noe] *m* Noah

noël [noel] *m* Christmas carol; (coll) Christmas present; **Noël** Christmas

nœud [nø] *m* knot; rosette; finger joint; Adam's apple; tie, alliance; crux (*of question, plot, crisis*); node; (naut) knot; **nœud de vache** granny knot; **nœud plat** square knot; **nœuds** coils (*of snake*); **nœud vital** nerve center

noir noire [nwar] *adj* black; **noir comme poix** pitch-black ‖ *mf* Negro ‖ *m* black; bruise; **broyer du noir** to be blue, down in the dumps; **noir de fumée** lampblack ‖ *f* (mus) quarter note

noirâtre [nwarɑtr] *adj* blackish

noi•raud [nwaro] **-raude** [rod] *adj* swarthy

noirceur [nwarsœr] *f* blackness; black spot

noircir [nwarsir] *tr* to blacken || *intr* & *ref* to burn black; to turn dark

noircissure [nwarsisyr] *f* black spot, smudge

noise [nwaz] *f* squabble; **chercher noise à** to pick a quarrel with

noisetier [nwaztje] *m* hazelnut tree

noisette [nwazet] *adj invar* reddish-brown || *f* hazelnut

noix [nwa], [nwa] *f* walnut; nut; **à la noix** (slang) trifling; **noix d'acajou, noix de cajou** cashew nut; **noix du Brésil** Brazil nut; **noix de coco** coconut; **noix de galle** nutgall; **noix de muscade** nutmeg; **noix de veau** round of veal

nolis [noli] *m* freight

noliser [nolize] *tr* to charter (*a ship*)

nom [nɔ̃] *m* name; noun; **de nom** by name; **nom à rallonges, nom à tiroirs** (coll) word made up of several parts; **nom commercial** trade name; **nom de baptême** baptismal name, Christian name; **nom de demoiselle** maiden name; **nom de famille** surname; **nom de guerre** fictitious name, assumed name; **nom de jeune fille** maiden name; **nom d'emprunt** assumed name; **nom de théâtre** stage name; **nom marchand** trade name; **petit nom** first name; **petit nom d'amitié** pet name; **sans nom** nameless; **sous le nom de** by the name of

nomade [nomad] *adj* & *mf* nomad

nombre [nɔ̃br] *m* number, quantity

nombrer [nɔ̃bre] *tr* to number

nom‧breux [nɔ̃brø] **-breuse** [brøz] *adj* numerous; rhythmic, harmonious (*e.g., prose*)

nombril [nɔ̃bri] *m* navel

nomenclature [nomãklatyr] *f* nomenclature; vocabulary; body (*of dictionary*)

nomi‧nal -nale [nominal] *adj* (*pl* **-naux** [no]) nominal; **appel nominal** roll call

nomina‧tif [nominatif] **-tive** [tiv] *adj* nominative; registered (*stocks, bonds, etc.*) || *m* nominative

nomination [nominasjɔ̃] *f* appointment

nom‧mé -mée [nome] *adj* named; appointed; called || *m*—**le nommé . . .** the man called . . .

nommément [nomemã] *adv* namely, particularly

nommer [nome] *tr* to name, call; to appoint || *ref* to be named, e.g., **je me nomme . . .** my name is . . .

non [nɔ̃] *m invar* no || *adv* no, not; **non pas** not so; **non plus** neither, not, nor . . . either, e.g., **moi non plus nor I** either; **non point!** by no means!; **que non!** no indeed!

non-belligé‧rant [nɔ̃beliʒerã] **-rante** [rãt] *adj* & *mf* nonbelligerent

nonce [nɔ̃s] *m* nuncio

noncha‧lant [nɔ̃ʃalã] **-lante** [lãt] *adj* nonchalant

non-combat‧tant [nɔ̃kɔ̃batã] **non-combat‧tante** [nɔ̃kɔ̃batãt] *adj* & *mf* noncombatant

non-conformiste [nɔ̃kɔ̃fɔrmist] *adj* & *mf* nonconformist

non-enga‧gé -gée [nɔ̃nãgaʒe] *adj* unaligned, uncommitted

nonnain [nonɛ̃] *f* (pej) nun

nonne [non] *f* nun

nonobstant [nonopstã] *adv* notwithstanding; **nonobstant que** although || *prep* in spite of

non-pesanteur [nɔ̃pəzãtœr] *f* weightlessness

non-rési‧dent [nɔ̃rezidã] **-dente** [dãt] *adj* & *mf* nonresident

non-réussite [nɔ̃reysit] *f* failure

non-sens [nɔ̃sãs] *m* absurdity, nonsense

non-usage [nonyzaʒ] *m* disuse

non-violence [nɔ̃vjolãs] *f* nonviolence

nord [nor] *adj invar* north, northern || *m* north; **du nord** northern; **faire le nord** to steer northward; **vers le nord** northward

nord-est [norest] *adj invar* & *m* northeast

nord-ouest [norwest] *adj invar* & *m* northwest

nor‧mal -male [normal] *adj* (*pl* **-maux** [mo]) normal; regular, standard; perpendicular || *f* normal; perpendicular

norma‧lien [normaljɛ̃] **-lienne** [ljen] *mf* student at a teachers college

nor‧mand [normã] **-mande** [mãd] *adj* Norman || *m* Norman (*dialect*) || (*cap*) *mf* Norman (*person*)

Normandie [normãdi] *f* Normandy; **la Normandie** Normandy

norme [norm] *f* norm; specifications

nor‧rois [norwa] **nor‧roise** [norwaz] *adj* Norse || *m* Norse (*language*) || (*cap*) *m* Norseman

Norvège [norveʒ] *f* Norway; **la Norvège** Norway

norvé‧gien [norveʒjɛ̃] **-gienne** [ʒjen] *adj* Norwegian || *m* Norwegian (*language*) || *f* round-stemmed rowboat || (*cap*) *mf* Norwegian (*person*)

nos [no] §88

nostalgie [nostalʒi] *f* nostalgia, homesickness

nostalgique [nostalʒik] *adj* nostalgic, homesick

notable [notabl] *adj* notable, noteworthy || *m* notable

notaire [noter] *m* notary; lawyer

notamment [notamã] *adv* especially

notation [notasjɔ̃] *f* notation

note [not] *f* note; bill (*to be paid*); grade, mark (*in school*); footnote; **être dans la note** to be in the swing of things; **note de rappel** reminder; **prendre note de** to note down

noter [note] *tr* to note; to note down; to notice; to mark (*a student*); to write down (*a tune*)

notice [notis] *f* notice (*review, sketch*)

notification [notifikasjɔ̃] *f* notification, notice

notifier [notifje] *tr* to report on; to serve (*a summons*)

notion [nosjɔ̃] *f* notion

notoire [notwar] *adj* well-known

notoriété [notorjete] *f* fame

notre [nɔtr] §88
nôtre [notr] §89; **serez-vous des nô-tres?** will you join us?
noue [nu] *f* pasture land; roof gutter
noué nouée [nwe] *adj* afflicted with rickets
nouer [nwe] *tr* to knot; to tie; to form; to cook up (*a plot*) ‖ *ref* to form knots; to be tied; (*hort*) to set
noueux [nwø] **noueuse** [nwøz] *adj* knotty, gnarled
nouille [nuj] *f* noodle
nounou [nunu] *f* nanny
nour·ri -rie [nuri] *adj* heavy, sustained; rich (*style*)
nourrice [nuris] *f* wet nurse; can; (*aut*) reserve tank
nourricerie [nurisri] *f* baby farm; stock farm; silkworm farm
nourri·cier [nurisje] **-cière** [sjer] *adj* nutritive; nourishing; foster
nourrir [nurir] *tr* to nourish; to suckle; to feed (*a fire*); to nurse (*plants; hopes*) ‖ *intr* to be nourishing ‖ *ref* to feed; to thrive
nourrisseur [nurisœr] *m* stock raiser, dairyman
nourrisson [nurisɔ̃] *m* nursling, suckling; foster child
nourriture [nurityr] *f* nourishment, food; nourishing; nursing, breast-feeding; **nourriture du feu** firewood
nous [nu] §85, §87; **nous autres Américains** we Americans
nous-mêmes [numem] §86
nou·veau [nuvo] (or **-vel** [vel] before vowel or mute *h*) **-velle** [vel] (*pl* **-veaux -velles**) *adj* new (*recent*) ‖ (when standing before noun) *adj* new (*other, additional, different*) ‖ *m* freshman; **à nouveau** anew; **de nouveau** again; **du nouveau** something new; **le nouveau** the new ‖ *f* see **nouvelle**
nouveau-né -née [nuvone] *adj & mf* (*pl* -nés) newborn
nouveauté [nuvote] *f* newness, novelty
nouvelle [nuvel] *f* piece of news; novelette, short story; **donnez-moi de vos nouvelles** let me hear from you; **nouvelles** news
Nouvelle-Angleterre [nuvelɑ̃glətɛr] *f* New England; **la Nouvelle-Angleterre** New England
Nouvelle-Écosse [nuvelekɔs] *f* Nova Scotia; **la Nouvelle-Écosse** Nova Scotia
Nouvelle-Orléans [nuvelɔrleɑ̃] *f—***la Nouvelle-Orléans** New Orleans
nouvelliste [nuvelist] *mf* short-story writer
nova·teur [nɔvatœr] **-trice** [tris] *adj* innovating ‖ *mf* innovator
novembre [nɔvɑ̃br] *m* November
novice [nɔvis] *adj* inexperienced, new ‖ *mf* novice, neophyte
noviciat [nɔvisja] *m* novitiate
novocaïne [nɔvɔkaïn] *f* novocaine
noyade [nwajad] *f* drowning
noyau [nwajo] *m* (*pl* **noyaux**) nucleus; stone, kernel; pit (*of fruit*); core (*of electromagnet*); newel; hub; (*fig*) cell (*of conspirators*); (*fig*) bunch (*of*

card players); **noyau d'atome** atomic nucleus
noyautage [nwajotaʒ] *m* infiltration (*e.g., of communists*)
noyer [nwaje] *m* walnut tree; **en noyer** in walnut (*wood*) ‖ §47 *tr & ref* to drown
nu nue [ny] *adj* naked, nude; bare; barren; uncarpeted; unharnassed, unsaddled (*horse*); (*aut*) stripped ‖ *m* nude; **à nu** exposed; bareback ‖ *f* see **nue**
nuage [nɥaʒ] *m* cloud
nua·geux [nɥaʒø] **-geuse** [ʒøz] *adj* cloudy
nuance [nɥɑ̃s] *f* hue, shade, tone, nuance
nucléaire [nykleer] *adj* nuclear
nucléole [nykleɔl] *m* nucleolus
nucléon [nykleɔ̃] *m* nucleon
nudiste [nydist] *adj & mf* nudist
nudité [nydite] *f* nakedness; nudity; plainness (*of style*); nude
nue [ny] *f* clouds; sky; **mettre** or **porter aux nues** to praise to the skies
nuée [nɥe] *f* cloud, storm cloud; flock
nuire [nɥir] §19 (*pp* **nui**) *intr* (with *dat*) to harm, to injure
nuisible [nɥizibl] *adj* harmful
nuit [nɥi] *f* night; **à la nuit close** after dark; **bonne nuit** good night; **cette nuit** last night; **nuit blanche** sleepless night
nuitamment [nɥitamɑ̃] *adv* at night
nu-jambes [nyʒɑ̃b] *adj invar* bare-legged
nul nulle [nyl] *adj indef* no; **ne . . . nul** or **nul . . . ne** §90 no; **nul et non avenu** [nylenɔnavny] null and void ‖ *f* dummy word or letter ‖ **nul** *pron indef*—**nul ne** §90B no one, nobody
nullement [nylmɑ̃] §90 *adv* not at all
nullité [nyllite] *f* nonentity, nobody
nûment [nymɑ̃] *adv* candidly, frankly
numé·ral -rale [nymeral] *adj & m* (*pl* **-raux** [ro]) numeral
numération [nymerasjɔ̃] *f* numeration; **numération globulaire** blood count
numérique [nymerik] *adj* numerical
numéro [nymero] *m* numeral; number; issue, number (*of a periodical*), e.g., **dernier numéro** current issue; e.g., **numéro ancien** back number; (slang) queer duck; **faire un numéro** to dial; **numéro de vestiaire** check (*of checkroom*); **numéro d'ordre** serial number
numéroter [nymerɔte] *tr* to number
numismatique [nymismatik] *adj* numismatic ‖ *f* numismatics
nu-pieds [nypje] *adj invar* barefooted
nup·tial -tiale [nypsjal] *adj* (*pl* **-tiaux** [sjo]) nuptial
nuque [nyk] *f* nape, scruff
nurse [nœrs] *f* children's nurse
nu-tête [nytɛt] *adj invar* bareheaded
nutri·tif [nytritif] **-tive** [tiv] *adj* nutritive; nutritious
nutrition [nytrisjɔ̃] *f* nutrition
nylon [nilɔ̃] *m* nylon
nymphe [nɛ̃f] *f* nymph

O

O, o [o], *[o] *m invar* fifteenth letter
of the French alphabet
oasis [ɔazis] *f* oasis
obéir [ɔbeir] *intr* to obey; (with *dat*)
to obey, yield to; (with *dat*) to be
subject to; **être obéi** to be obeyed;
obéir au doigt et à l'œil to obey
blindly
obéissance [ɔbeisɑ̃s] *f* obedience
obéis•sant [ɔbeisɑ̃] **obéis•sante** [ɔbei-
sɑ̃t] *adj* obedient
obélisque [ɔbelisk] *m* obelisk
obérer [ɔbere] §10 *tr* to burden with
debt || *ref* to run into debt
obèse [ɔbez] *adj* obese
obésité [ɔbezite] *f* obesity
objecter [ɔbʒɛkte] *tr* to object, e.g.,
objecter que . . . to object that . . . ;
to bring up, e.g., **objecter q.ch. à qn**
to bring up s.th against s.o.; to put
forward (*in opposition*), e.g., **objecter de bonnes raisons à** or **contre un
argument** to put forward good rea-
sons against an argument
objecteur [ɔbʒɛktœr] *m*—**objecteur de
conscience** conscientious objector
objec•tif [ɔbʒɛktif] **-tive** [tiv] *adj* ob-
jective || *m* objective; object lens;
(mil) target
objection [ɔbʒɛksjɔ̃] *f* objection; **faire
des objections** to object
objectivité [ɔbʒɛktivite] *f* objectivity
objet [ɔbʒɛ] *m* object; **menus objets**
notions; **objet d'art** work of art;
objet de risée laughingstock; **objets
de première nécessité** articles of
everyday use; **remplir son object** to
attain one's end
obligation [ɔbligasjɔ̃] *f* obligation;
(com) bond, debenture; **être dans
l'obligation de** to be obliged to
obligatoire [ɔbligatwar] *adj* required,
obligatory; (coll) inevitable
obli•gé -gée [ɔbliʒe] *adj* obliged, com-
pelled; necessary, indispensable; **bien
obligé** much obliged; **c'est obligé**
(coll) it has to be; **être obligé de** to
be obliged to
obli•geant [ɔbliʒɑ̃] **-geante** [ʒɑ̃t] *adj*
obliging
obliger [ɔbliʒe] §38 *tr* to oblige || *ref*—
s'obliger à + *inf* to undertake to +
inf; **s'obliger pour qn** to stand surety
for s.o.
oblique [ɔblik] *adj* oblique
oblitération [ɔbliterasjɔ̃] *f* obliteration;
cancellation (*of postage stamp*);
(pathol) occlusion
oblitérer [ɔblitere] §10 *tr* to obliterate;
to cancel (*a postage stamp*); to obstruct (*e.g., a vein*)
o•blong [ɔblɔ̃] **-blongue** [blɔ̃g] *adj*
oblong
obnubiler [ɔbnybile] *tr* to cloud, befog
obole [ɔbɔl] *f* widow's mite
obscène [ɔpsɛn] *adj* obscene
obscénité [ɔpsenite] *f* obscenity
obs•cur -cure [ɔpskyr] *adj* obscure
obscurcir [ɔpskyrsir] *tr* to obscure; to
dim || *ref* to grow dark; to grow dim

obscurité [ɔpskyrite] *f* obscurity
obséder [ɔpsede] §10 *tr* to obsess; to
importune, to harass
obsèques [ɔpsek] *fpl* obsequies, funeral
rites
obsé•quieux [ɔpsekjø] **-quieuse** [kjøz]
adj obsequious
observance [ɔpsɛrvɑ̃s] *f* observance
observa•teur [ɔpsɛrvatœr] **-trice** [tris]
adj observant || *mf* observer
observation [ɔpsɛrvasjɔ̃] *f* observation
observatoire [ɔpsɛrvatwar] *m* observa-
tory
observer [ɔpsɛrve] *tr* to observe || *ref*
to watch oneself; to watch each other
obsession [ɔpsesjɔ̃] *f* obsession
obsolète [ɔpsolet] *adj* obsolete
obstacle [ɔpstakl] *m* obstacle
obstétrique [ɔpstetrik] *adj* obstetrical
|| *f* obstetrics
obstination [ɔpstinasjɔ̃] *f* obstinacy
obsti•né -née [ɔpstine] *adj* obstinate
obstruction [ɔpstryksjɔ̃] *f* obstruction;
(sports) blocking; **faire de l'obstruction** (pol) to filibuster; **obstruction
systématique** filibustering
obstruer [ɔpstrye] *tr* to obstruct
obtempérer [ɔptɑ̃pere] §10 *intr* (with
dat) to comply with, to obey
obtenir [ɔptənir] §72 *tr* to obtain, get
obtention [ɔptɑ̃sjɔ̃] *f* obtaining
obtura•teur [ɔptyratœr] **-trice** [tris]
adj stopping, closing || *m* (mach)
stopcock; (phot) shutter
obturation [ɔptyrasjɔ̃] *f* stopping up;
filling (*of tooth*); **obturation des
lumières** blackout
obturer [ɔptyre] *tr* to stop up; to fill
(*a tooth*)
ob•tus [ɔpty] **-tuse** [tyz] *adj* obtuse
obus [ɔby] *m* (mil) shell; plunger (*of
tire valve*); **obus à balles** shrapnel;
obus à mitraille shrapnel; **obus de
rupture** armor-piercing shell
obvier [ɔbvje] *intr* (with *dat*) to obviate, to prevent
oc [ɔk] *adv* (Old Provençal) yes
occasion [ɔkazjɔ̃], [ɔkazjɔ̃] *f* occasion;
opportunity; bargain; **à l'occasion** on
occasion; **à l'occasion de** for (*e.g.,
s.o.'s birthday*); **d'occasion** secondhand (*clothing*); used (*car*)
occasion•nel -nelle [ɔkazjɔnel] *adj* occasional; chance (*meeting*); deter-
mining (*cause*)
occasionnellement [ɔkazjɔnelmɑ̃] *adv*
occasionally; by chance, accidentally
occasionner [ɔkazjɔne] *tr* to occasion
occident [ɔksidɑ̃] *m* occident, west
occiden•tal -tale [ɔksidɑtal] *adj & mf*
(*pl* **-taux** [to]) occidental
occlu•sif [ɔklyzif] **-sive** [ziv] *adj & f*
occlusive
occlusion [ɔklyzjɔ̃] *f* occlusion
occulte [ɔkylt] *adj* occult
occu•pant [ɔkypɑ̃] **-pante** [pɑ̃t] *adj*
occupying || *mf* occupant
occupation [ɔkypasjɔ̃] *f* occupation
occu•pé -pée [ɔkype] *adj* occupied; **occupé** (public sign) in use

occuper [ɔkype] *tr* to occupy || *ref* to find something to do; **s'occuper de** to be occupied with, to be busy with; to take care of, to handle

occurrence [ɔkyrãs] *f* occurrence; **en l'occurrence** under the circumstances; **être en occurrence** to occur; **selon l'occurrence** as the case may be

océan [ɔseã] *m* ocean; **océan glacial arctique** Arctic Ocean; **océan Indien** Indian Ocean

océanique [ɔseanik] *adj* oceanic

ocre [ɔkr] *f* ochre

octane [ɔktan] *m* octane

octave [ɔktav] *f* octave

octa·von [ɔktavɔ̃] -**vonne** [vɔn] *mf* octoroon

octobre [ɔktɔbr] *m* October

octroi [ɔktrwa] *m* granting (*of a favor*); tax on provisions being brought into town

octroyer [ɔktrwaje] §47 *tr* to grant, concede; to bestow

oculaire [ɔkylɛr] *adj* ocular, eye || *m* ocular, eyepiece

oculariste [ɔkylarist] *mf* optician (*who specializes in glass eyes*)

oculiste [ɔkylist] *mf* oculist

ode [ɔd] *f* ode

odeur [ɔdœr] *f* odor, scent

o·dieux [ɔdjø] -**dieuse** [djøz] *adj* odious || *m* odium, odiousness

odo·rant [ɔdɔrã] -**rante** [rãt] *adj* fragrant

odorat [ɔdɔra] *m* (sense of) smell

Odyssée [ɔdise] *f* Odyssey

œcuménique [ekymenik] *adj* ecumenical

œdème [edɛm] *m* (pathol) edema

Œdipe [edip] *m* Oedipus

œil [œj] *m* (*pl* yeux [jø]) les yeux [lezjø]) eye; typeface, font; bud; **avoir l'œil (américain)** (coll) to be observant; **coûter les yeux de la tête** (coll) to cost a fortune; **donner de l'œil à** to give a better appearance to; **entre quatre yeux** [ãtrəkatzjø] (coll) between you and me; **faire les gros yeux à** (coll) to glare at; **faire les yeux doux à** to make eyes at; **ne pas avoir les yeux dans la poche** (coll) to keep one's eyes peeled; (coll) to be no shrinking violet; **œil au beurre noir** (coll) black eye; **œil de pie** (naut) eyelet; **œil de verre** glass eye; **œil électrique** electric eye; **pocher un œil à qn** to give s.o. a black eye; **sale œil** disapproving or dirty look; **sauter aux yeux, crever les yeux** to be obvious; **se mettre le doigt dans l'œil** (coll) to put one's foot in one's mouth; **se rincer l'œil** (slang) to get an eyeful; **taper dans l'œil à** or **de qn** (coll) to take s.o.'s fancy; **voir d'un mauvais œil** to take a dim view of

œil-de-bœuf [œjdəbœf] *m* (*pl* œils-de-bœuf) bull's-eye, small oval window

œil-de-chat [œjdəʃa] *m* (*pl* œils-de-chat) cat's-eye (*gem*)

œil-de-perdrix [œjdəpɛrdri] *m* (*pl* œils-de-perdrix) (pathol) soft corn

œillade [œjad] *f* glance, leer, wink;

lancer, jeter, or décocher une œillade à to ogle

œillère [œjɛr] *f* eyecup; blinker; **avoir des œillères** to be biased

œillet [œjɛ] *m* eyelet; eyelet hole; carnation, clove pink; **œillet d'Inde** (*Tagetes*) marigold

œilleton [œjtɔ̃] *m* eye, bud; eyepiece; sight (*of rifle, camera, etc.*)

œillette [œjɛt] *f* opium poppy

œnologie [enɔlɔʒi] *f* science of viniculture, oenology

œsophage [ezɔfaʒ] *m* esophagus

œstres [ɛstr] *mpl* botflies, nose flies

œuf [œf] *m* (*pl* œufs [ø]) egg; **marcher sur des œufs** to walk on thin ice; **œuf à la coque** soft-boiled egg; **œuf à repriser** darning egg; **œuf de Colomb** ingenious, though obvious, solution to a problem; **œuf de Pâques** or **œuf rouge** Easter egg; **œuf dur** hard-boiled egg; **œuf mollet** soft-boiled egg; **œuf poché** poached egg; **œufs** spawn, roe; **œufs au lait** custard; **œufs au miroir** fried eggs; **œufs brouillés** scrambled eggs; **œuf sur le plat** fried egg; **plein comme un œuf** chock-full; **tondre un œuf** to squeeze blood out of a turnip; **tuer, écraser, or étouffer dans l'œuf** to nip in the bud

œuvre [œvr] *m* works (*of a painter*); dans œuvre inside (*measurements*); hors d'œuvre out of alignment; **le grand œuvre** the philosopher's stone; **le gros œuvre** (archit) the foundation, walls, and roof || *f* work; piece of work; **bonnes œuvres** good works; **mettre en œuvre** to implement, to use; **mettre qn à l'œuvre** to set s.o. to work; **mettre tout en œuvre** to leave no stone unturned; **œuvres complètes** collected works; **œuvres mortes** (naut) topsides; **œuvre pie** good deed, good work; **œuvres vives** (naut) hull below water line; **se mettre à l'œuvre** to get to work

offen·sant [ɔfãsã] -**sante** [sãt] *adj* offensive

offense [ɔfãs] *f* offense; **faire offense à qn** to offend s.o.; **soit dit sans offense** with all due respect

offenser [ɔfãse] *tr* to offend || *ref* to be offended

offen·sif [ɔfãsif] -**sive** [siv] *adj & f* offensive

office [ɔfis] *m* office; (eccl) office, service; **d'office** ex officio; **faire l'office de** to act as; **office d'ami** friendly turn; **remplir son office** (fig) to do its job || *f* pantry

offi·ciel -**cielle** [ɔfisjɛl] *adj & mf* official

officier [ɔfisje] *m* officer; (naut) mate; **officier de service** (mil) officer of the day; **officier ministériel** notary public; **officier supérieur** (mil) field officer || *intr* to officiate

offi·cieux [ɔfisjø] -**cieuse** [sjøz] *adj* unofficial, off-the-cuff; zealous; well-meant (*lie*); **faire l'officieux** to be officious

offrant [ɔfrɑ̃] *m*—**le plus offrant** the highest bidder

offre [ɔfr] *f* offer; **l'offre et la demande** supply and demand; **offres d'emploi** (formula in want ads) help wanted

offrir [ɔfrir] §65 *tr* to offer ‖ *ref* to offer oneself; to offer itself, to occur

offset [ɔfsɛt] *m invar* offset

offusquer [ɔfyske] *tr* to obfuscate, obscure; to irritate, displease ‖ *ref*— **s'offusquer de** to take offense at

ogive [ɔʒiv] *f* ogive; (rok) nose cone

ogre [ɔgr] **ogresse** [ɔgrɛs] *mf* ogre; **manger comme un ogre** (coll) to eat like a horse

ohé [ɔe] *interj* hey!; **ohé du navire!** ship ahoy!

ohm [om] *m* ohm

oie [wa] *f* goose; simpleton; **oie blanche** simple little goose (*naïve girl*); **oie sauvage** wild goose

oignon [ɔɲɔ̃] *m* onion; (hort) bulb; (pathol) bunion; (coll) turnip, pocket watch; **aux petits oignons** (coll) perfect; **occupe-toi de tes oignons** (coll) mind your own business

oïl [ɔil], [ɔj] *adv* (Old French) yes

oindre [wɛ̃dr] §35 *tr* to anoint

oi•seau [wazo] *m* (*pl* -**seaux**) bird; hod (*of mason*); (coll) character; **être comme l'oiseau sur la branche** to be here today and gone tomorrow; **oiseau de paradis, oiseau des îles** bird of paradise; **oiseau des tempêtes** stormy petrel; **oiseaux domestiques, oiseaux de basse-cour** poultry

oiseau-mouche [wazomuʃ] *m* (*pl* -**mouches**) hummingbird

oiseler [wazle] §34 *tr* to train (*hawks*) ‖ *intr* to trap birds

oiselet [wazlɛ] *m* little bird

oiseleur [wazlœr] *m* fowler

oise•lier [wazəlje] -**lière** [ljer] *mf* bird fancier

oi•seux [wazø] -**seuse** [zøz] *adj* useless

oi•sif [wazif] -**sive** [ziv] *adj* idle ‖ *mf* idler

oisillon [wazijɔ̃] *m* fledgling

oisiveté [wazivte] *f* idleness

oison [wazɔ̃] *m* gosling; (coll) ninny

O.K. [oke] *interj* (letterword) O.K.!

oléagi•neux [ɔleaʒinø] -**neuse** [nøz] *adj* oily

olfac•tif [ɔlfaktif] -**tive** [tiv] *adj* olfactory

olibrius [ɔlibrijys] *m* pedant; pest; braggart (*in medieval plays*)

oligarchie [ɔligar/i] *f* oligarchy

olivaie [ɔlive] *f* olive grove

olivâtre [ɔlivɑtr] *adj* olive (*complexion*)

olive [ɔliv] *adj invar & f* olive

olivette [ɔlivɛt] *f* olive grove

olivier [ɔlivje] *m* olive tree; olive wood; **Olivier** Oliver

olympiade [ɔlɛ̃pjad] *f* olympiad

olym•pien [ɔlɛ̃pjɛ̃] -**pienne** [pjɛn] *adj* Olympian

olympique [ɔlɛ̃pik] *adj* Olympic

ombilic [ɔ̃bilik] *m* umbilicus

ombili•cal -cale [ɔ̃bilikal] *adj* (*pl* -**caux** [ko]) umbilical

ombrage [ɔ̃braʒ] *m* shade; **porter om-** brage à to offend; **prendre ombrage (de)** to take offense (at)

ombrager [ɔ̃braʒe] §38 *tr* to shade

ombra•geux [ɔ̃braʒø] -**geuse** [ʒøz] *adj* shy, skittish; touchy; distrustful

ombre [ɔ̃br] *f* shadow; shade; **ombres (chinoises)** shadow play, shadowgraph; **une ombre au tableau** (coll) a fly in the ointment

ombrelle [ɔ̃brɛl] *f* parasol; (aer) umbrella

ombrer [ɔ̃bre] *tr* to shade; to apply eye shadow to

om•breux [ɔ̃brø] -**breuse** [brøz] *adj* shady

omelette [ɔmlɛt] *f* omelet

omettre [ɔmɛtr] §42 *tr* to omit

omission [ɔmisjɔ̃] *f* omission

omnibus [ɔmnibys] *adj* omnibus; local (*train*) ‖ *m* omnibus; local (train)

omnipo•tent [ɔmnipɔtɑ̃] -**tente** [tɑ̃t] *adj* omnipotent

omnis•cient [ɔmnisjɑ̃] **omnis•ciente** [ɔmnisjɑ̃t] *adj* omniscient

omnium [ɔmnjɔm] *m* (com) holding company, general trading company; (sports) open race

omnivore [ɔmnivɔr] *adj* omnivorous

omoplate [ɔmɔplat] *f* shoulder blade

on [ɔ̃] §87 *pron indef* one, they, people; (coll) we, e.g., **y va-t-on?** are we going there?; (coll) I, e.g., **on est fatigué** I am tired; (often translated by passive forms), e.g., **on sait que** it is generally known that

once [ɔ̃s] *f* ounce

oncle [ɔ̃kl] *m* uncle

onction [ɔ̃ksjɔ̃] *f* unction; eloquence

onc•tueux [ɔ̃ktɥø] -**tueuse** [tɥøz] *adj* unctuous; greasy; bland

onde [ɔ̃d] *f* wave; watering (*of silk*); (poetic) water; **les petites ondes** (rad) shortwave; **mettre en ondes** to put on the air; **onde de choc** (aer) shock wave; **onde porteuse** (rad) carrier wave; **ondes amorties** (rad) damped waves; **ondes entretenues** (rad) continuous waves; **ondes radiophoniques** airwaves; **onde sonore** sound wave

ondée [ɔ̃de] *f* shower

on-dit [ɔ̃di] *m invar* gossip, scuttlebutt

ondoyant [ɔ̃dwajɑ̃] **ondoyante** [ɔ̃dwajɑ̃t] *adj* undulating, wavy; wavering (*person*)

ondoyer [ɔ̃dwaje] §47 *tr* to baptize in an emergency ‖ *intr* to undulate, wave

ondulation [ɔ̃dylasjɔ̃] *f* undulation, waving; flowing (*e.g., of drapery*); wave (*of hair*); **à ondulations** rolling (*ground*); **ondulation permanente** permanent wave

ondu•lé -lée [ɔ̃dyle] *adj* wavy; corrugated

onduler [ɔ̃dyle] *tr* to wave (*hair*) ‖ *intr* to wave, to undulate

oné•reux [ɔnerø] -**reuse** [røz] *adj* onerous

ongle [ɔ̃gl] *m* nail, fingernail; **jusqu'au bout des ongles** to or at one's fingertips; **ongle des pieds** toenail

onglée [ɔ̃gle] *f* numbness in the fingertips

onglet [ɔ̃glɛ] *m* nail hole, groove (*in blade*); thimble; **à onglets** thumb-indexed; **monter sur onglet** (bb) to insert (*a page*)

onguent [ɔ̃gɑ̃] *m* ointment, salve

O.N.U. [ɔny] (acronym) or [ɔeny] (letterword) (**Organisation des Nations Unies**) *f* UN

onyx [ɔniks] *m* onyx

onzain *[ɔ̃zɛ̃] m* eleven-line verse

onze *[ɔ̃z] adj & pron* eleven; the Eleventh, e.g., **Jean onze** John the Eleventh; **onze heures** eleven o'clock || *m* eleven; eleventh (*in dates*), e.g., **le onze mai** the eleventh of May

onzième *[ɔ̃zjɛm] adj, pron (masc, fem), & m* eleventh

opale [ɔpal] *f* opal

opaque [ɔpak] *adj* opaque

opéra [ɔpera] *m* opera; opera house; **grand opéra, opéra sérieux** grand opera; **opéra bouffe** comic opera, **opéra bouffe**

opéra-comique [ɔperakɔmik] *m* (*pl* **opéras-comiques**) light opera

opéra·teur [ɔperatœr] **-trice** [tris] *mf* operator || *m* cameraman

opération [ɔperasjɔ̃] *f* operation

opé·ré -rée [ɔpere] *mf* surgical patient

opérer [ɔpere] §10 *tr* to operate on; **opérer à chaud** to perform an emergency operation on (*s.o.*); **opérer qn de q.ch.** (med) to operate on s.o. for s.th. || *intr* to operate; to work || *ref* to occur, take place

opérette [ɔperɛt] *f* operetta, musical comedy

opia·cé -cée [ɔpjase] *adj* opiate

opiner [ɔpine] *intr* to opine; **opiner du bonnet** (coll) to be a yes man

opiniâtre [ɔpinjɑtr] *adj* stubborn

opiniâtreté [ɔpinjɑtrəte] *f* stubbornness

opinion [ɔpinjɔ̃] *f* opinion; public opinion; **avoir bonne opinion de** to think highly of; **avoir une piètre opinion de** to take a dim view of

opium [ɔpjɔm] *m* opium

oponce [ɔpɔ̃s] *m* prickly pear

opossum [ɔpɔsɔm] *m* opossum

oppor·tun [ɔpɔrtœ̃] **-tune** [tyn] *adj* opportune, timely, expedient

opportuniste [ɔpɔrtynist] *adj* opportunistic || *mf* opportunist

opportunité [ɔpɔrtynite] *f* opportuneness

oppo·sant [ɔpozɑ̃] **-sante** [zɑ̃t] *adj* opposing || *mf* opponent

oppo·sé -sée [ɔpoze] *adj & m* opposite, contrary; **à l'opposé de** contrary to

opposer [ɔpoze] *tr* to raise (*an objection*); **opposer q.ch. à** to set up s.th. against; to place s.th. opposite; to contrast s.th. with || *ref*—**s'opposer à** to oppose, object to

opposite [ɔpozit] *m*—**à l'opposite (de)** opposite

opposition [ɔpozisjɔ̃] *f* opposition; contrast

oppresser [ɔprese] *tr* to oppress; to impede (*respiration*); to weigh upon (*one's heart*)

oppresseur [ɔpresœr] *m* oppressor

oppres·sif [ɔpresif] **oppres·sive** [ɔpresiv] *adj* oppressive

oppression [ɔpresjɔ̃] *f* oppression; difficulty in breathing

opprimer [ɔprime] *tr* to oppress

opprobre [ɔprɔbr] *m* opprobrium, shame

opter [ɔpte] *intr* to opt, to choose

opticien [ɔptisjɛ̃] *m* optician

optimisme [ɔptimism] *m* optimism

optimiste [ɔptimist] *adj* optimistic || *mf* optimist

option [ɔpsjɔ̃] *f* option

optique [ɔptik] *adj* optic(al) || *f* optics; perspective; **sous cette optique** from that point of view

opu·lent [ɔpylɑ̃] **-lente** [lɑ̃t] *adj* opulent

opuscule [ɔpyskyl] *m* opuscule, treatise; brochure, pamphlet

or [ɔr] *m* gold; **rouler sur l'or** to be rolling in money || *adv* now; therefore

oracle [ɔrakl] *m* oracle

orage [ɔraʒ] *m* storm

ora·geux [ɔraʒø] **-geuse** [ʒøz] *adj* stormy

oraison [ɔrezɔ̃] *f* prayer; **oraison dominicale** Lord's Prayer; **oraison funèbre** funeral oration; **prononcer l'oraison funèbre de** (coll) to write off (*a custom, institution, etc.*)

o·ral -rale [ɔral] *adj* (*pl* **-raux** [ro]) oral

orange [ɔrɑ̃ʒ] *adj invar* orange (*color*) || *m* orange (*color*) || *f* orange (*fruit*)

oran·gé -gée [ɔrɑ̃ʒe] *adj & m* orange (*color*)

orangeade [ɔrɑ̃ʒad] *f* orangeade

oranger [ɔrɑ̃ʒe] *m* orange tree

orangerale [ɔrɑ̃ʒre] *f* orange grove

orangerie [ɔrɑ̃ʒri] *f* orangery; orange grove

orang-outan [ɔrɑ̃utɑ̃] *m* (*pl* **orangs-outans**) orang-outang

ora·teur [ɔratœr] **-trice** [tris] *mf* orator; speaker

oratoire [ɔratwar] *adj* oratorical || *m* (eccl) oratory

oratorio [ɔratɔrjo] *m* oratorio

orbite [ɔrbit] *f* orbit; socket (*of eye*); **placer sur son orbite, mettre en orbite** to orbit; **sur orbite** in orbit

orchestre [ɔrkestr] *m* orchestra; band; **orchestre de typique** rumba band

orchestrer [ɔrkestre] *tr* to orchestrate

orchidée [ɔrkide] *f* orchid

ordalie [ɔrdali] *f* (hist) ordeal

ordinaire [ɔrdiner] *adj* ordinary || *m* ordinary; regular bill of fare; (mil) mess; **d'ordinaire, à l'ordinaire** ordinarily

ordi·nal -nale [ɔrdinal] *adj & m* (*pl* **-naux** [no]) ordinal

ordinateur [ɔrdinatœr] *m* (electron) computer

ordination [ɔrdinasjɔ̃] *f* ordination

ordonnance [ɔrdɔnɑ̃s] *f* ordinance; order, arrangement; (pharm) prescription

ordonna·teur [ɔrdɔnatœr] **-trice** [tris]

mf organizer; marshal; **ordonnateur des pompes funèbres** funeral director

ordon·né -née [ɔrdɔne] *adj* orderly

ordonner [ɔrdɔne] *tr* to arrange, put in order; to order; to prescribe (*e.g., medicine*); (eccl) to ordain; **ordonner à qn de** + *inf* to order s.o. to + *inf*; **ordonner q.ch. à qn** to order s.o. to do s.th.

ordre [ɔrdr] *m* order; **avoir de l'ordre** to be neat, orderly; **à vos ordres at your service; dans l'ordre d'entrée en scène** (theat) in order of appearance; **en ordre** in order; **jusqu'à nouvel ordre** until further notice; as things stand; **les ordres** (eccl) orders; **ordre du jour** (mil) order of the day; (parl) agenda; **ordre public** law and order; **payez à l'ordre de** (com) pay to the order of; **sous les ordres de** under the command of

ordure [ɔrdyr] *f* rubbish, filth; **ordures ménagères** garbage

ordu·rier -rière [ɔrdyrje] [rjɛr] *adj* lewd, filthy

orée [ɔre] *f* edge (*of a forest*)

oreille [ɔrej] *f* ear; **avoir l'oreille basse** to be humiliated; **dormir sur les deux oreilles** to sleep soundly; **dresser or tendre l'oreille** to prick up one's ears; **échauffer les oreilles à qn** to rile s.o. up; **faire la sourde oreille** to turn a deaf ear; **rompre les oreilles à qn** (coll) to talk s.o.'s head off; **se faire tirer l'oreille** (coll) to play hard to get

oreiller [ɔreje] *m* pillow

oreillette [ɔrejɛt] *f* earflap (*of cap*); (anat) auricle

oreillons [ɔrejɔ̃] *mpl* mumps

ores [ɔr] *adv*—**d'ores et déjà** [dɔrzedeʒa] from now on

Orfée [ɔrfe] *m* Orpheus

orfèvre [ɔrfɛvr] *m* goldsmith; silversmith; **être orfèvre en la matière** (coll) to know one's onions

orfèvrerie [ɔrfɛvrari] *f* goldsmith's shop; goldsmith's trade; gold plate; gold or silver jewelry

orfraie [ɔrfrɛ] *f* osprey, fish hawk

organdi [ɔrgɑ̃di] *m* organdy

organe [ɔrgan] *m* organ; part (*of a machine*)

organique [ɔrganik] *adj* organic

organisa·teur [ɔrganizatœr] **-trice** [tris] *adj* organizing ‖ *mf* organizer

organisation [ɔrganizasjɔ̃] *f* organization

organiser [ɔrganize] *tr* to organize

organisme [ɔrganism] *m* organism; organization

organiste [ɔrganist] *mf* organist

orgasme [ɔrgasm] *m* orgasm

orge [ɔrʒ] *f* barley

orgelet [ɔrʒəlɛ] *m* (pathol) sty

orgie [ɔrʒi] *f* orgy

orgue [ɔrg] *m* organ; **orgue de Barbarie** hand organ; **orgue de cinéma** theater organ ‖ *f*—**les grandes orgues** the pipe organ

orgueil [ɔrgœj] *m* pride, conceit; **avoir l'orgueil de** to take pride in

orgueil·leux [ɔrgœjø] **orgueil·leuse** [ɔrgœjøz] *adj* proud, haughty

orient [ɔrjɑ̃] *m* orient; east; **Orient** Orient, East

orien·tal -tale [ɔrjɑtal] (*pl* **-taux** [to]) *adj* oriental; eastern, east ‖ (*cap*) *mf* Oriental (*person*)

orientation [ɔrjɑtɑsjɔ̃] *f* orientation; **orientation professionnelle** vocational guidance

orienter [ɔrjɑte] *tr* to orient; to guide ‖ *ref* to take one's bearings

orien·teur [ɔrjɑtœr] **-teuse** [tøz] *mf* guidance counselor

orifice [ɔrifis] *m* orifice, hole, opening

origan [ɔrigɑ̃] *m* marjoram

originaire [ɔriziner] *adj* native; original, first

origi·nal -nale [ɔriʒinal] *adj* (*pl* **-naux** [no]) original; eccentric, peculiar ‖ *m* antique (*piece of furniture*); eccentric, card (*person*); (typ) copy, original

originalité [ɔriʒinalite] *f* originality; eccentricity

origine [ɔriʒin] *f* origin

origi·nel -nelle [ɔriʒinɛl] *adj* original (*sin; meaning*); primitive, early

ori·gnal [ɔriɲal] *m* (*pl* **-gnaux** [ɲo]) moose, elk

orillon [ɔrijɔ̃] *m* ear, handle; (archit) projection

ori·peau [ɔripo] *m* (*pl* **-peaux**) tinsel; **orip·eaux** cheap finery

Orléans [ɔrleɑ̃] *f* Orléans; **la Nouvelle Orléans** New Orleans

orme [ɔrm] *m* elm; **attendez-moi sous l'orme** (coll) I won't be there

or·né -née [ɔrne] *adj* ornate

ornement [ɔrnəmɑ̃] *m* ornament

ornemen·tal -tale [ɔrnəmɑtal] *adj* (*pl* **-taux** [to]) ornamental

orner [ɔrne] *tr* to ornament, to adorn

ornière [ɔrnjɛr] *f* rut, groove

ornithologie [ɔrnitɔlɔʒi] *f* ornithology

orphe·lin [ɔrfəlɛ̃] **-line** [lin] *adj* & *mf* orphan

orphelinat [ɔrfəlina] *m* orphanage (*asylum*)

orphéon [ɔrfeɔ̃] *m* male choir, glee club; brass band

orteil [ɔrtɛj] *m* toe; big toe; **gros orteil** big toe

O.R.T.F. [oɛrteɛf] *m* (letterword) (**office de radio-télévision française**) French radio and television system

orthodoxe [ɔrtɔdɔks] *adj* orthodox

orthographe [ɔrtɔgraf] *f* spelling, orthography

orthographier [ɔrtɔgrafje] *tr* to spell

ortie [ɔrti] *f* nettle

orviétan [ɔrvjetɑ̃] *m* nostrum

os [ɔs] *m* (*pl* **os** [o]) bone; **à gros os** big-boned; **os à moelle** marrowbone; **trempé jusqu'aux os** soaked to the skin

osciller [ɔsile] *intr* to oscillate; to waver, hesitate

o·sé -sée [oze] *adj* daring, bold; risqué, off-color

oseille [ozɛj] *f* sorrel; (slang) dough

oser [oze] *tr* & *intr* to dare

osier [ozje] *m* osier; **d'osier** wicker

o.mose [ɔsmoz] f osmosis

ossature [ɔsatyr] f bone structure; framework, skeleton

ossements [ɔsmɑ̃] mpl bones, remains

os-seux [ɔsø] os-seuse [ɔsøz] adj bony

ossifier [ɔsifje] tr & ref to ossify

os-su -sue [ɔsy] adj bony; big-boned

ostensible [ɔstɑ̃sibl] adj conspicuous, ostensible; ostentatious

ostensoir [ɔstɑ̃swar] m monstrance

ostentatoire [ɔstɑ̃tatwar] adj ostentatious

ostracisme [ɔstrasism] m ostracism

otage [ɔtaʒ] m hostage

otalgie [ɔtalʒi] f earache

O.T.A.N. or OTAN [ɔtan], [ɔtɑ̃], [ɔtɑ̃] f (acronym) (Organisation du traité de l'Atlantique Nord)—l'O.T.A.N. NATO

otarie [ɔtari] f sea lion

OTASE [ɔtaz] f (acronym) (Organisation du traité de l'Asie du Sud-Est)—l'OTASE SEATO

ôter [ote] tr to remove, to take away; to take off; to tip (one's hat); ôter q.ch. à qn to remove or take away s.th. from s.o.; ôter q.ch. de q.ch. to take s.th. away from s.th. || ref to withdraw; to get out of the way

otto-man [ɔtɔmɑ̃] -mane [man] adj Ottoman || m ottoman (corded fabric) || f ottoman (divan) || (cap) mf Ottoman (person)

ou [u] conj or; ou . . . ou either . . . or

où [u] adv where; d'où from where, whence; où que wherever; par où which way || conj where; when; d'où from where, whence; par où through which; partout où wherever

ouailles [waj] fpl (eccl) flock

ouais [we] interj (coll) oh yeah!

ouate *[wat] f cotton batting, wadding

ouater *[wate] tr to pad, to wad

oubli [ubli] m forgetfulness; omission, oversight; tomber dans l'oubli to fall into oblivion

oublier [ublije] tr & intr to forget || ref to forget oneself; to be forgotten

oubliettes [ublijet] fpl dungeon of oblivion

ou-blieux [ublijø] -blieuse [blijøz] adj forgetful, oblivious, unmindful

ouche [uʃ] f orchard; vegetable garden

ouest [west] adj invar & m west

ouest-alle-mand [westalmɑ̃] -mande [mɑ̃d] adj West German || (cap) mf West German

ouf *[uf] interj whew!

oui *[wi] m invar yes; les oui l'emportent the ayes have it || adv yes; je crois que oui I think so; oui madame yes ma'am; oui monsieur yes sir; oui mon capitaine (mon général, etc.) yes sir

oui-dire [widir] m invar hearsay; simples ouï-dire (law) hearsay evidence

ouïe [wi] f hearing; être tout ouïe [tutwi] to be all ears; ouïes gills; sound holes (of violin) || interj oh my!

ouïr [wir] (used only in: inf, compound tenses with pp ouï, and 2d pl impv

oyez) tr to hear; oyez . . . ! hear ye . . . !

ouragan [uragɑ̃] m hurricane

ourdir [urdir] tr to warp (cloth before weaving); to hatch (e.g., a plot)

ourler [urle] tr to hem; ourler à jour to hemstitch

ourlet [urle] m hem; ourlet de la jupe hemline

ours [urs] m bear; (fig) lone wolf; ours en peluche teddy bear; ours mal léché unmannerly boor; ours marin (zool) seal; vendre la peau de l'ours avant de l'avoir tué to count one's chickens before they are hatched

ourse [urs] f she-bear; la Grande Ourse the Big Dipper, the Great Bear; la Petite Ourse the Little Dipper, the Little Bear

oursin [ursɛ̃] m sea urchin

ourson [ursɔ̃] m bear cub

ouste [ust] interj (coll) out!, out you go!

outarde [utard] f (orn) bustard

outil [uti] m tool, implement

outillage [utijaʒ] m tools; equipment

outil-lé -lée [utije] adj equipped with tools; tooled-up (factory)

outiller [utije] tr to equip with tools; to tool up (a factory) || ref to supply oneself with equipment; to tool up

outilleur [utijœr] m toolmaker

outrage [utraʒ] m outrage, affront; ravages (of time); contempt of court; faire outrage à qn to outrage s.o.; outrage aux bonnes mœurs traffic in pornography; outrage public à la pudeur indecent exposure

outrager [utraʒe] §38 tr to outrage, to affront

outra-geux [utraʒø] -geuse [ʒøz] adj outrageous, insulting

outrance [utrɑ̃s] f excess; exaggeration; à outrance to the limit

outran-cier [utrɑ̃sje] -cière [sjer] adj extreme, excessive, out-and-out || mf extremist, out-and-outer

outre [utr] f goatskin canteen || adv further; d'outre en d'outre right through; en outre besides, moreover; passer outre à to ignore (e.g., an order) || prep in addition to, apart from; beyond

ou-tré -trée [utre] adj overdone, exaggerated; exasperated

outrecui-dant [utrəkɥidɑ̃] -dante [dɑ̃t] adj self-satisfied; insolent, presumptuous

outre-Manche [utrəmɑ̃ʃ] adv across the Channel

outremer [utrəmer] m ultramarine, lapis lazuli (color)

outre-mer [utrəmer] adv overseas

outre-monts [utrəmɔ̃] adv over the mountains (i.e., the Alps)

outrepasser [utrəpase] tr to go beyond, to exceed

outrer [utre] tr to overdo, to exaggerate; to exasperate

outre-tombe [utratɔ̃b] adv—d'outre-tombe posthumous

ou-vert [uver] -verte [vert] adj open;

exposed; frank, candid; on (said of meter, gas, etc.)

ouverture [uvertyr] f opening; hole, gap; (mus) overture; (phot) aperture

ouvrable [uvrabl] adj working, e.g., jour ouvrable working day

ouvrage [uvraʒ] m work, handiwork; piece of work; work, treatise

ouvrager [uvraʒe] §38 tr to work (e.g., iron); to turn (wood)

ou·vré -**vrée** [uvre] adj worked, wrought; finished (product)

ouvre-boîtes [uvrəbwat] m invar can opener

ouvre-bouteilles [uvrəbutej] m invar bottle opener

ouvreur [uvrœr] m opener (in poker)

ouvreuse [uvrøz] f usher

ou·vrier [uvrije] -**vrière** [vrijer] adj working, worker; worker's, workingman's || mf worker || m workman, laborer; workingman || f workingwoman

ouvrir [uvrir] §65 tr to open; to turn on (the light; the radio or television; the gas); **ouvrir boutique** to set up shop || intr to be open; to open (said of store, school, etc.; said of card player) || ref to open; to be opened; **s'ouvrir à** to open up to, confide in

ouvroir [uvrwar] m workroom

ovaire [over] m ovary

ovale [oval] adj & m oval

ovation [ovasjɔ̃] f ovation

ovationner [ovasjone] tr to give an ovation to

Ovide [ovid] m Ovid

oxford [oksfor] m oxford cloth

oxyde [oksid] m oxide

oxyder [okside] tr & ref to oxidize

oxygène [oksiʒen] m oxygen

oxygéner [oksiʒene] §10 tr to oxygenate; to bleach (hair) || ref—**s'oxygéner les poumons** (coll) to fill one's lungs full of ozone

oxyton [oksitɔ̃] adj & m oxytone

ozone [ozon] m ozone

P

P, p [pe] m invar sixteenth letter of the French alphabet

pacage [pakaʒ] m pasture

pacifica·teur [pasifikatœr] -**trice** [tris] mf pacifier

pacifier [pasifje] tr to pacify

pacifique [pasifik] adj pacific || **Pacifique** adj & m Pacific

pacifisme [pasifism] m pacifism

pacifiste [pasifist] mf pacifist

pacotille [pakotij] f junk; **de pacotille** shoddy; junky

pacte [pakt] m pact, covenant

pactiser [paktize] intr to compromise; to traffic (with the enemy)

paf [paf] adj (slang) tipsy, tight || interj bang!

pagaie [page] f paddle

pagaïe or pagaille [pagaj] f disorder; **en pagaïe** (coll) in great quantity; (coll) in a mess

paganisme [paganism] m paganism

pagayer [pageje] §49 tr & intr to paddle

page [paʒ] m page || f page (of a book); **être à la page** to be up to date

paginer [paʒine] tr to page

pagne [paɲ] m loincloth

paie [pe] f pay, wages

paiement [pemɑ̃] m payment

païen [pajɛ̃] **païenne** [pajɛn] adj & mf pagan

pail·lard [pajar] **pail·larde** [pajard] adj ribald || mf debauchee

paillasse [pajas] m buffoon || f straw mattress; (slang) whore

paillasson [pajasɔ̃] m doormat

paille [paj] f straw; flaw; (Bib) mote; **paille de fer** iron shavings

pail·lé -**lée** [paje] adj rush-bottomed (chair)

pailler [paje] m straw stack || tr to bottom (a chair) with straw; to mulch

pailleter [pajte] §34 tr to spangle

paillette [pajet] f spangle; flake (of mica; of soap); grain (of gold); flaw (in a diamond)

pain [pɛ̃] m bread; loaf (of bread, of sugar); cake (of soap); pat (of butter); **avoir du pain sur la planche** (coll) to have a lot to do; **pain à cacheter** sealing wafer; **pain aux raisins** raisin roll; **pain bis** brown bread; **pain complet** whole-wheat bread; **pain de fantaisie** bread sold by the loaf (instead of by weight); **pain de mie** sandwich bread; **pain d'épice** gingerbread; **pain grillé** toast; **pain perdu** French toast; **petit pain** roll; **se vendre comme des petits pains** (coll) to sell like hot cakes

pair paire [per] adj even (number) || m peer; equal; (com) par; **hors de pair, hors pair** unrivaled; **marcher de pair avec** to keep abreast of; **travailler au pair** (coll) to work for one's keep; **au pair at par** || f pair; couple; brace (of dogs, pistols, etc.); yoke (of oxen)

pairesse [peres] f peeress

pairie [peri], [peri] f peerage

paisible [pezibl] adj peaceful

paître [petr] §48 tr & intr to graze; **envoyer paître** (coll) to send packing

paix [pe] f peace

Pakistan [pakistɑ̃] m—**le Pakistan** Pakistan

pakista·nais [pakistane] -**naise** [nez] adj Pakistani || (cap) mf Pakistani

pal [pal] *m* (*pl* **paux** [po] or **pals**)
  pale, stake
palabre [palabr] *m & f* palaver
palace [palas] *m* luxury hotel
palais [pale] *m* palace; palate; court-
  house, law courts
palan [palɑ̃] *m* block and tackle
palanque [palɑ̃k] *f* stockade
pala·tal -tale [palatal] (*pl* **-taux** [to]
  -tales) *adj & f* palatal
pale [pal] *f* blade (*of, e.g., oar*); stake;
  sluice gate; (eccl) pall
pâle [pal] *adj* pale
palefrenier [palfrənje] *m* groom; (coll)
  hick, oaf
palefroi [palfrwa] *m* palfrey
paleron [palrɔ̃] *m* bottom chuck roast
palet [palɛ] *m* disk, flat stone; puck
paletot [palto] *m* topcoat
palette [palɛt] *f* palette; paddle
pâleur [palœr] *f* pallor; paleness
palier [palje] *m* landing (*of stairs*);
  plateau (*of curve of a graph*); (mach)
  bearing; **en palier** on the level; **palier
  à billes** ball bearing; **par paliers**
  graduated (*e.g., tax*)
pâlir [palir] *tr & intr* to pale, turn pale
palis [pali] *m* picket fence
palissade [palisad] *f* palisade; fence
palissandre [palisɑ̃dr] *m* rosewood
pallier [palje] *tr* to palliate; to mitigate
  || *intr* (with *dat*) to mitigate
palmarès [palmares] *m* list of winners
palme [palm] *f* (bot) palm
palmeraie [palmərɛ] *f* palm grove
palmier [palmje] *m* palm tree
palmipède [palmiped] *adj* webfooted ||
  m webfoot
palombe [palɔ̃b] *f* ringdove
palourde [palurd] *f* clam
palpable [palpabl] *adj* palpable; plain,
  obvious
palper [palpe] *tr* to feel; to palpate;
  (coll) to pocket (*money*)
palpiter [palpite] *intr* to palpitate
palsambleu [palsɑ̃blø] *interj* zounds!
paltoquet [paltɔkɛ] *m* nonentity
palu·déen -déenne [palydeɛ̃] **-déenne** [deen] *adj*
  marsh (*plant*); swamp (*fever*)
paludisme [palydism] *m* malaria
pâmer [pame] *ref* to swoon
pâmoison [pamwazɔ̃] *f* swoon
pamphlet [pɑ̃flɛ] *m* lampoon
pamplemousse [pɑ̃pləmus] *m & f*
  grapefruit
pan [pɑ̃] *m* tail (*of shirt or coat*); section; side, face; patch (*of sky*); **Pan**
  Pan || *interj* bang!
panacée [panase] *f* panacea
panachage [pana/aʒ] *m* mixing; **faire
  du panachage** to split one's vote
panache [pana/] *m* plume; wreath (*of
  smoke*); **aimer le panache** to be fond
  of show; **avoir son panache** (coll) to
  be tipsy; **faire panache** to somersault, to turn over
pana·ché -chée [pana/e] *adj* variegated; mixed (*salad*); motley (*crowd*)
panacher [pana/e] *tr* to variegate; to
  plume; to split (*one's vote*) || *ref* to
  become variegated
panais [panɛ] *m* parsnip
panama [panama] *m* panama hat; le

Panama Panama; **Panama** Panama
  City
panaris [panari] *m* (pathol) whitlow,
  felon
pancarte [pɑ̃kart] *f* placard; poster,
  sign
panchromatique [pɑ̃krɔmatik] *adj* panchromatic
pancréas [pɑ̃kreas] *m* pancreas
pandémonium [pɑ̃demɔnjɔm] *m* den of
  iniquity; pandemonium
pa·né -née [pane] *adj* breaded
panetière [pantjer] *f* breadbox
panier [panje] *m* basket; hoop (*of
  skirt*); creel (*trap*); **être dans le
  même panier** to be in the same boat;
  panier à ouvrage work basket; **panier à papier** wastepaper basket; **panier à provisions** shopping basket;
  panier à salade wire salad washer;
  (coll) paddy wagon; **panier percé**
  spendthrift
panier-repas [panjerəpa] *m* (*pl* **pa-
  niers-repas**) box lunch
panique [panik] *adj & f* panic
panne [pan] *f* breakdown, trouble;
  plush; fat (*of pig*); peen (*of hammer*); tip (*of soldering iron*); bank
  (*of clouds*); purlin (*of roof*); daub;
  (theat) small part; (en) **panne sèche**
  (public sign) out of gas; **être dans la
  panne** (coll) to be hard up; **être en
  panne** (coll) to be unable to continue; **être en panne de** (coll) to be
  deprived of; **laisser en panne** to leave
  in the lurch; **mettre en panne** (naut)
  to heave to; **panne fendue** claw (*of
  hammer*); **rester en panne** to come
  to a standstill; **tomber en panne** to
  have a breakdown
pan·né -née [pane] *adj* (slang) hard up
pan·neau [pano] *m* (*pl* **-neaux**) panel;
  snare, net; **condamner les panneaux**
  (naut) to batten down the hatches;
  donner dans le panneau to walk into
  the trap; **panneau d'affichage** bill-
  board; **panneau de tête** headboard
  (*of bed*); **panneaux** paneling; **panneaux de signalisation** traffic signs;
  tomber or **donner dans le panneau**
  to be taken in, to fall into a trap
panoplie [panɔpli] *f* panoply
panorama [panɔrama] *m* panorama
panoramiquer [panɔramike] *intr* (mov,
  telv) to pan
panse [pɑ̃s] *f* belly; rumen, first stomach
pansement [pɑ̃smɑ̃] *m* (surg) dressing
panser [pɑ̃se] *tr* to dress, bandage; to
  groom (*an animal*)
pan·su -sue [pɑ̃sy] *adj* potbellied
pantalon [pɑ̃talɔ̃] *m* trousers, pair of
  trousers, panties; slacks; **pantalon à
  pattes d'éléphant** bell-bottomed trousers; **pantalon corsaire** pedal pushers;
  pantalon de coutil ducks; blue jeans;
  pantalon de golf knickers; **pantalon
  de ski** ski pants
pante [pɑ̃t] *m* (slang) guy
panteler [pɑ̃tle] §34 *intr* to pant
panthéisme [pɑ̃teism] *m* pantheism
panthéon [pɑ̃teɔ̃] *m* pantheon
panthère [pɑ̃ter] *f* panther

pantin [pɑ̃tɛ̃] *m* puppet; jumping jack; **pantin articulé** string puppet

pantomime [pɑ̃tɔmim] *f* pantomime

pantou·flard [pɑ̃tuflar] **-flarde** [flard] *mf* (coll) homebody

pantoufle [pɑ̃tufl] *f* slipper

pantoufler [pɑ̃tufle] *intr* to leave government service

paon [pɑ̃] *m* peacock, peafowl; peacock butterfly

paonne [pan] *f* peahen

papa [papa] *m* papa; **à la papa** (coll) cautiously; **papa** (coll) outmoded; **papa gâteau** (coll) sugar daddy

papas [papɑs] *m* pope (*in Orthodox Church*)

papauté [papote] *f* papacy

pape [pap] *m* pope

pape·lard [paplar] **-larde** [lard] *adj* hypocritical ‖ *mf* hypocrite ‖ *m* scrap of paper

paperasse [papras] *f* old paper

paperasserie [paprasri] *f* red tape

paperas·sier [paprasje] **paperas·sière** [paprasjɛr] *adj* fond of red tape ‖ *mf* bureaucrat

papeterie [paptri] *f* paper mill; stationery store

pape·tier [paptje] **-tière** [tjɛr] *mf* stationer

papier [papje] *m* paper; newspaper article; document; piece of paper; **être dans les petits papiers de** (coll) to be in the good graces of; **gratter du papier** to scribble; **papier à calquer**, **papier végétal** tracing paper; **papier à en-tête** letterhead; **papier à lettres** writing paper; **papier à machine** typewriter paper; **papier à musique** staff paper; **papier bible**, **indien**, *or* **pelure** Bible paper, onionskin; **papier buvard** blotting paper; **papier carbone** carbon paper; **papier collant** Scotch tape; **papier d'emballage** wrapping paper; **papier de soie** tissue paper; **papier d'étain** tin foil; **papier de verre** sandpaper; **papier hygiénique** toilet paper; **papier journal** newsprint; **papier kraft** cardboard (*for packing*); **papier mâché** papier-maché; **papier ministre** foolscap; **papier paraffiné** wax paper; **papier peint** wallpaper; **papier rayé** lined paper; **papier sensible** photographic paper; **papier tue-mouches** flypaper; **rayez cela de vos papiers!** (coll) don't count on it!

papier-filtre [papjefiltrə] *m* filter paper

papier-monnaie [papjemɔnɛ] *m* paper money

papier-pierre [papjepjɛr] *m* (*pl* **papiers-pierre**) papier-mâché

papille [papij], [papil] *f* papilla; **papille gustative** taste bud

papillon [papijɔ̃] *m* butterfly; flier, handbill; inset; form, application; thumbscrew, wing nut; butterfly valve; rider (*to document*); (coll) parking ticket; **papillon de nuit** moth; **papillons noirs** gloomy thoughts

papillonner [papijɔne] *intr* to flit about

papillote [papijɔt] *f* curlpaper; (culin) paper wrapper

papilloter [papijɔte] *intr* to blink; to flicker

papoter [papɔte] *intr* to chitchat

paprika [paprika] *m* paprika

papyrus [papirys] *m* papyrus

pâque [pɑk] *f* Passover; **la pâque russe** Russian Easter; **Pâque** Passover

paquebot [pakbo] *m* liner

pâquerette [pɑkrɛt] *f* white daisy

Pâques [pɑk] *m* Easter ‖ *fpl* Easter; **faire ses pâques** *or* **Pâques** to take Easter Communion; **Pâques fleuries** Palm Sunday

paquet [pakɛ] *m* packet, bundle; package; parcel; pack (*of cigarettes*); dressing down; **être un paquet d'os** [dɔs] to be nothing but skin and bones; **faire son paquet** (coll) to pack up; **mettre le paquet** (coll) to shoot the works; **paquet de mer** heavy sea; **petit paquet** parcel (*under a kilogram*); **petits paquets** parcel post; **un paquet de** a lot of

par [par] *prep* by; through; out of, e.g., **par la fenêtre** out of the window; per, a, e.g., **huit dollars par jour** eight dollars per day, eight dollars a day; on, e.g., **par une belle matinée** on a beautiful morning; in, e.g., **par temps de brume** in foggy weather; **de par la loi** in the name of the law; **par avion** (formula on envelope) air mail; **par delà** beyond; **par derrière** at the back, the back way; **par devant** in front, before; **par exemple** for example; **par ici** this way; **par là** that way; **par où?** which way?

para [para] *m* (coll) paratrooper

parabole [parabɔl] *f* parable; (*curve*) parabola

parachever [paraʃve] §2 *tr* to finish off

parachutage [paraʃytaʒ] *m* airdrop, airdropping

parachute [paraʃyt] *m* parachute

parachuter [paraʃyte] *tr* to airdrop; (coll) to appoint in haste

parachutisme [paraʃytism] *m* parachuting; (sports) skydiving

parachutiste [paraʃytist] *mf* parachutist; (sports) skydiver ‖ *m* paratrooper

parade [parad] *f* show; parry; sudden stop (*of horse*); come-on (*in front of sideshow*); (mil) inspection, parade; **à la parade** on parade; **faire parade de** to show off, to display

parader [parade] *intr* to show off

paradis [paradi] *m* paradise; (theat) peanut gallery

paradoxal paradoxale [paradɔksal] *adj* (*pl* **paradoxaux** [paradɔkso]) paradoxical

paradoxe [paradɔks] *m* paradox

parafe [paraf] *m* flourish; initials

parafer [parafe] *tr* to initial

paraffine [parafin] *f* paraffin

paraffiner [parafine] *tr* to paraffin

parages [paraʒ] *mpl* region, vicinity; **dans ces parages** in these parts

paragraphe [paragraf] *m* paragraph

Paraguay [paragε] *m*—le **Paraguay** Paraguay

paraguayen [paragεjɛ̃] **paraguayenne** [paragεjεn] *adj* Paraguayan || (*cap*) *mf* Paraguayan

paraître [parεtr] §12 *intr* to appear; to seem; to come out; to show off; **à ce qu'il paraît** from all appearances; **faire paraître** to publish; **vient de paraître** just out

parallèle [paralεl] *adj* parallel || *m* parallel, comparison; (geog) parallel || *f* (geom) parallel

paralyser [paralize] *tr* to paralyze

paralysie [paralizi] *f* paralysis

paralytique [paralitik] *adj & mf* paralytic

parangon [parɑ̃gɔ̃] *m* paragon

paranoïaque [paranɔjak] *adj & mf* paranoiac

parapet [parapε] *m* railing, parapet; (mil) parapet

paraphe [paraf] *m* flourish; initials

parapher [parafe] *tr* to initial

paraphrase [parafrɑz] *f* circumlocution, paraphrase; commentary

paraphraser [parafraze] *tr* to paraphrase

parapluie [paraplɥi] *m* umbrella

parasite [parazit] *adj* parasitic(al) || *m* parasite; **parasites** (rad) static

parasiter [parazite] *tr* to live as a parasite on or in (*a host*); (fig) to sponge on

parasol [parasɔl] *m* parasol; beach umbrella

paratonnerre [paratɔnεr] *m* lightning rod

parâtre [parɑtr] *m* stepfather; cruel father

paravent [paravɑ̃] *m* folding screen

parbleu [parblø] *interj* rather!, by Jove!, you bet!

parc [park] *m* park; sheepfold; corral, pen; playpen; grounds, property; (mil) supply depot; (rr) rolling stock; **parc à huîtres** oyster bed; **parc automobile** motor pool; **parc de stationnement (payant)** parking lot

parcage [parkaʒ] *m* parking

parcelle [parsεl] *f* particle; plot

parce que [pars(ə)kə] *conj* because

parchemin [parʃəmɛ̃] *m* parchment; (coll) sheepskin (*diploma*)

parchemi-né -née [parʃəmine] *adj* wrinkled

parcheminer [parʃəmine] *tr* to parchmentize || *ref* to shrivel up

par-ci [parsi] *adv*—**par-ci par-là** here and there

parcimo-nieux [parsimɔnjø] **-nieuse** [njøz] *adj* parsimonious

parcomètre [parkɔmεtr] *m* parking meter

parcourir [parkurir] §14 *tr* to travel through, to tour; to wander about; to cover (*a distance*); to scour (*the country*); to glance through

parcours [parkur] *m* run, trip; route, distance covered; round (*e.g., of golf*); stroke (*of piston*)

par-delà [pardəla] *adv & prep* beyond

par-derrière [pardεrjεr] *adv & prep* behind

par-dessous [pardəsu] *adv & prep* underneath

pardessus [pardəsy] *m* overcoat

par-dessus [pardəsy] *adv* on top, over || *prep* on top of, over

par-devant [pardəvɑ̃] *adv* in front || *prep* in front of, before

par-devers [pardəvεr] *prep* in the presence of; **par-devers soi** in one's own possession

pardi [pardi] *interj* (coll) of course!

pardon [pardɔ̃] *m* pardon; Breton pilgrimage || *adv* (to contradict a negative statement or question) yes, e.g., **Vous ne parlez pas français, n'est-ce pas? Pardon, je le parle très bien** You don't speak French, do you? Yes, I speak it very well || *interj* pardon me!; (slang) oh boy!

pardonnable [pardɔnabl] *adj* pardonable

pardonner [pardɔne] *tr* to pardon; **pardonner q.ch. à qn** to pardon s.o. for s.th. || *intr* (with *dat*) to pardon, to forgive; **ne pas pardonner** to be fatal (*said of illness, mistake, etc.*)

pare-balles [parbal] *adj invar* bulletproof

pare-boue [parbu] *m invar* mudguard

pare-brise [parbriz] *m invar* windshield

pare-chocs [parʃɔk] *m invar* (aut) bumper

pare-étincelles [paretɛ̃sεl] *m invar* fire screen

pa-reil -reille [parεj] *adj* identical, the same; such, such a || *mf* equal, match; **sans pareil, sans pareille** without parallel, unequaled || *m*—**c'est du pareil au même** (coll) it's six of one and half dozen of the other || *f* same (thing); **rendre la pareille à qn** to pay s.o. back in his own coin

pareillement [parεjmɑ̃] *adv* likewise

parement [parmɑ̃] *m* cuff; facing; trimming; (eccl) parament

pa-rent [parɑ̃] **-rente** [rɑ̃t] *adj* like || *mf* relative; **parents** parents; relatives; ancestors; **plus proche parent** next of kin

parenté [parɑ̃te] *f* relationship; relations

parenthèse [parɑ̃tεz] *f* parenthesis; **entre parenthèses** in parentheses

parer [pare] *tr* to adorn; to parry; to prepare || *intr*—**parer à** to provide for || *ref* to show off

pare-soleil [parsɔlεj] *m invar* sun visor

paresse [parεs] *f* laziness

paresser [parese] *intr* (coll) to loaf

pares-seux [parεsø] **pares-seuse** [parεsøz] *adj* lazy || *mf* lazy person, lazybones; malingerer || *m* (zool) sloth

par ex. *abbr* (**par exemple**) e.g.

parfaire [parfεr] §29 *tr* to perfect; to make up (*e.g., a sum of money*)

par-fait [parfε] **-faite** [fεt] *adj & m* perfect || **parfait** *interj* fine!, excellent!

parfaitement [parfεtmɑ̃] *adv* perfectly; completely; certainly, of course

parfois [parfwa] *adv* sometimes

parfum [parfœ̃] *m* perfume; aroma; bouquet (*of wines*); flavor (*of ice cream*)

parfumer [parfyme] *tr* to perfume; to flavor || *ref* to use perfume

pari [pari] *m* bet, wager

paria [parja] *m* pariah

parier [parje] *tr & intr* to bet, wager

Paris [pari] *m* Paris

pari·sien [parizjɛ̃] **-sienne** [zjɛn] *adj* Parisian || (*cap*) *mf* Parisian

parité [parite] *f* parity; likeness; evenness (*of numbers*)

parjure [parʒyr] *adj* perjured || *mf* perjurer || *m* perjury

parking [parkiŋ] *m* parking lot

par·lant [parlɑ̃] **-lante** [lɑ̃t] *adj* speaking; talking (*e.g., picture*); eloquent, expressive

parlement [parləmɑ̃] *m* parliament

parlementaire [parləmɑ̃ter] *adj* parliamentary || *mf* peace envoy; member of a parliament, legislator

parlementer [parləmɑ̃te] *intr* to parley

parler [parle] *m* speech, way of speaking; dialect || *tr & intr* to speak, to talk

par·leur [parlœr] **-leuse** [løz] *mf*—**beau parleur** good talker; windbag

parloir [parlwar] *m* reception room

parlote [parlɔt] *f* (coll) talk, gossip, rumor

parmi [parmi] *prep* among

Parnasse [parnas] *m*—**le Parnasse** Parnassus (*poetry*); Mount Parnassus

parodie [parɔdi] *f* parody, travesty

parodier [parɔdje] *tr* to parody, to travesty

paroi [parwa] *f* partition, wall; inner side; (anat) wall

paroisse [parwas] *f* parish

parois·sial -siale [parwasjal] *adj* (*pl* **parois·siaux** [parwasjo]) parochial, parish

parois·sien [parwasjɛ̃] **parois·sienne** [parwasjɛn] *mf* parishioner || *m* prayer book; (coll) fellow

parole [parɔl] *f* word; speech; word, promise; **avoir la parole** to have the floor; **donner la parole à** to recognize, to give the floor to; **sur parole** on one's word

paro·lier [parɔlje] **-lière** [ljer] *mf* lyricist; librettist

parpaing [parpɛ̃] *m* concrete block; building block

parquer [parke] *tr* to park; to pen in || *intr* to be penned in || *ref* to park

Parques [park] *fpl* Fates

parquet [parke] *m* parquet, floor; floor (*of stock exchange*); public prosecutor's office

parqueter [parkəte] §34 *tr* to parquet, to floor

parrain [parɛ̃] *m* godfather; sponsor

parricide [parisid] *mf* parricide, patricide (*person*) || *m* parricide, patricide (*act*)

parsemer [parsəme] §2 *tr* to sprinkle; to spangle

part [par] *m* newborn child; dropping (*of young by animal in labor*) || *f* part, share; **aller quelque part** (coll) to go to the toilet; **à part** aside; aside from; **à part entière** with full privileges; **autre part** elsewhere; **avoir part au gâteau** (coll) to have a slice in the pie; **d'autre part** besides; **de la part de** on the part of, from; **de part en part** through and through; **de toutes parts** on all sides; **d'une part . . . d'autre part**; on the one hand . . . on the other hand; **faire la part de** to make allowance for; **faire part** de to announce; **faire part de q.ch.** à qn to inform s.o. of s.th.; **nulle part** nowhere; **nulle part ailleurs** nowhere else; **pour ma part** as for me, for my part; **prendre en bonne part** to take good-naturedly; **prendre en mauvaise part** to take offense at; **prendre part à** to take part in; **quelque part** somewhere

partage [partaʒ] *m* division, partition; sharing; share; tie vote; **échoir en partage à qn** to fall to s.o.'s lot

partager [partaʒe] §38 *tr* to share; to divide

partance [partɑ̃s] *f* departure; **en partance** leaving; **en partance pour** bound for

partant [partɑ̃] *m* (sports) starter; **partants** departing guests, departing travelers, etc. || *adv* (lit) consequently

partenaire [partəner] *mf* partner; sparring partner

parterre [parter] *m* orchestra circle; flower bed

parti [parti] *m* party; side; match, good catch; **faire un mauvais parti à** to rough up, to mistreat; **parti pris** fixed opinion; prejudice; **prendre le parti de** to decide to; **prendre le parti de qn** to take s.o.'s side; **prendre parti** to take sides; **prendre son parti** to make up one's mind; **prendre son parti de** to resign oneself to; **tirer parti de** to take advantage of

par·tial -tiale [parsjal] *adj* (*pl* **-tiaux** [sjo]) partial, biased

partici·pant [partisipɑ̃] **-pante** [pɑ̃t] *adj & mf* participant

participation [partisipɑsjɔ̃] *f* participation

participe [partisip] *m* participle

participer [partisipe] *intr*—**participer à** to participate in; **participer de** to partake of

particulariser [partikylarize] *tr* to specify || *ref* to make oneself conspicuous

particularité [partikylarite] *f* peculiarity; detail

particule [partikyl] *f* particle

particu·lier [partikylje] **-lière** [ljer] *adj* particular; special; private || *mf* private citizen; (coll) odd person || *m* particular

partie [parti] *f* part; line; specialty; game, winning score; contest; party (*diversion*); (law) party; **avoir partie liée avec** to be in league with; **faire partie de** to belong to; **faire partie intégrante de** to be part and parcel of; **partie civile** plaintiff; **partie de chasse** hunting party; **partie de plai-**

sir outing, picnic; **partie nulle** tie game; **prendre à partie** to take to task

par·tiel -tielle [parsjɛl] *adj* partial

partir [partir] (used only in *inf*) *tr*— **avoir maille à partir** to have a bone to pick || §64 *intr* (*aux*: ÊTRE) to leave; to go off (*said of firearm*); to begin; **à partir de** from; from . . . on, e.g., **à partir de maintenant** from now on; **faire partir** to send off; to remove (*a spot*); to set off (*an explosive*); to fire (*a gun*); **partir + inf** to leave in order to + *inf*; **partir de** to come from; to start with; **partir pour** or **à** to leave for

parti·san [partizɑ̃] **-sane** [zan] *adj* & *mf* partisan

partition [partisjɔ̃] *f* (mus) score

partout [partu] *adv* everywhere; **partout ailleurs** anywhere else; every-where else; **partout où** wherever; everywhere

parure [paryr] *f* ornament; set; finery; necklace

parution [parysjɔ̃] *f* appearance, pub-lication

parvenir [parvənir] §72 *intr* (*aux*: ÊTRE) —**parvenir à** to reach; **parvenir à + inf** to succeed in + *ger*

parve·nu -nue [parvəny] *adj* & *mf* up-start

parvis [parvi] *m* square (*in front of a church*)

pas [pɑ] *m* step; pace; footprint; foot-fall; pass; straits; pitch (*of screw*); **allonger le pas** to quicken one's pace; to put one's best foot forward; **à pas comptés** with measured tread; **à pas de loup, à pas feutrés** stealth-ily; **à pas de tortue** at a snail's pace; **à quatre pas** nearby; **au pas** at a walk; **céder le pas (à)** to stand aside (for); to keep clear (*in front of a driveway*); **de ce pas** at once; **être au pas** to be in step; **faire le premier pas** to make the first move; **faire les cent pas** to come and go; **faux pas** misstep; blunder; **marcher sur les pas de** to follow in the footsteps of; **marquer le pas** to mark time; mau-vais pas tight squeeze, fix; **pas à pas** little by little, cautiously; **pas d'armes** passage at arms; **Pas de Calais** Straits of Dover; **pas de cheval** hoof-beat; **pas de clerc** blunder; **pas de deux** two-step; **pas de la porte** door-step; **pas de l'oie** goosestep; **pas de porte** (com) price paid for good will; **prendre le pas sur** to get ahead of || *adv*—**ne . . . pas** §90 not, e.g., **je ne sais pas** I do not know; e.g., **ne pas signer** to not sign; (used with **non**), e.g., **non pas** no; (used without **ne**) (slang) not, e.g., **je fais pas de politi-que** I don't meddle in politics; **n'est-ce pas?** see **ne**; **pas?** (coll) not so?; **pas de** no; **pas du tout** not at all; **pas encore** not yet

pas·cal -cale [paskal] *adj* (*pl* **-caux** [ko]) Passover; Easter

passable [pasabl] *adj* passable, fair; mediocre, so-so

passade [pasad] *f* passing fancy

passage [pasaʒ] *m* passage; crossing; pass; **barrer le passage** to block the way; **livrer passage à** to let through; **passage à niveau** grade crossing; **passage au-dessous de la voie, pas-sage souterrain** underpass; **passage au-dessus de la voie** overpass; pas-sage **clouté, passage zébré** pedestrian crossing; **passage de vitesses** gear shifting; **passage interdit** (public sign) do not enter; (public sign) no thoroughfare; **passage protégé** arte-rial crossing (*vehicles intersecting highway must stop*)

passa·ger [pasaʒe] **-gère** [ʒɛr] *adj* passing, fleeting; migratory; busy (*road*) || *mf* passenger; **passager clandestin, passager de cale** stow-away; **passager d'entrepont** steerage passenger

pas·sant [pasɑ̃] **-sante** [pasɑ̃t] *adj* busy (*street*) || *mf* passer-by

passation [pasasjɔ̃] *f* handing over

passavant [pasavɑ̃] *m* permit; (naut) gangway

passe [pɑs] *m* master key || *f* pass; channel; **être en bonne passe de** to be in a fair way to; **être en passe de** to be about to; **mauvaise passe** tight spot

pas·sé -sée [pase] *adj* past; faded; overripe; last (*week*) || *m* past; past tense || **passé** *prep* past, beyond, after

passe-bouillon [pasbujɔ̃] *m invar* soup strainer

passe-droit [pasdrwa] *m* (*pl* **-droits**) illegal favor; injustice

passe-lacet [paslase] *m* (*pl* **-lacets**) bodkin

passe-lait [pasle] *m invar* milk strainer

passe-lettres [pasletr] *m* (*pl* **-lettres**) letter drop

passement [pasmɑ̃] *m* braid, trimming

passementer [pasmɑ̃te] *tr* to trim

passementerie [pasmɑ̃tri] *f* trimmings

passe-montagne [pasmɔ̃taɲ] *m* (*pl* **-montagnes**) storm hood, ski mask

passe-partout [paspartu] *m invar* mas-ter key; slip mount

passe-passe [paspas] *m invar* legerde-main

passepoil [paspwal] *m* piping, braid

passeport [paspɔr] *m* passport

passer [pase] *tr* to pass; to ferry; to get across (*e.g., a river*); to spend; to pass (*e.g., the evening*); to take (*an exam*); to slip on (*e.g., a dressing gown*); to show (*a film*); to make (*a telephone call*); to go on (*one's way*); **passer q.ch. à qn** to hand or lend s.o. s.th.; to forgive s.o. s.th. || *intr* (*aux*: AVOIR or ÊTRE) to pass; to pass away; to become; **en passer par là** to knuckle under; **faire passer** to get (*e.g., a message*) through; to while away (*the time*); **passer à** to pass over to; **passer chez** or **passer voir** to drop in on; **passer outre à** to over-ride; **passer par** to pass through, to go through; **passer pour** to pass for or as; **passons!** let's skip it! || *ref* to happen; to take place; **se passer de** to do without

passe•reau [pɑsro] *m* (*pl* **-reaux**) sparrow

passerelle [pɑsrɛl] *f* footbridge; gangplank; (naut) bridge

passe-temps [pɑstɑ̃] *m invar* pastime, hobby

passe-thé [pɑste] *m invar* tea strainer

pas•seur [pɑsœr] **pas•seuse** [pɑsøz] *mf* smuggler || *m* ferryman

passible [pɑsibl] *adj*—**passible de** liable for, subject to

pas•sif [pɑsif] **pas•sive** [pɑsiv] *adj* passive || *m* passive; debts, liabilities

passiflore [pɑsiflɔr] *f* passionflower

passion [pɑsjɔ̃], [pɑsjɔ̃] *f* passion

passion•nant [pɑsjɔnɑ̃] **passion•nante** [pɑsjɔnɑ̃t] *adj* thrilling, fascinating

passion•né -née [pɑsjone] *adj* passionate; impassioned; **passionné de** or **pour** passionately fond of || *mf* enthusiast, fan

passion•nel -nelle [pɑsjonɛl] *adj* of passion, of jealousy

passionner [pɑsjone] *tr* to excite the interest of, to arouse || *ref*—**se passionner pour** or **à** to be passionately fond of

passoire [pɑswar] *f* colander; strainer; (fig) sieve

pastel [pɑstɛl] *m* pastel; (bot) woad

pastèque [pɑstɛk] *f* watermelon

pasteur [pɑstœr] *m* pastor, minister; shepherd

pasteuriser [pɑstœrize] *tr* to pasteurize

pastiche [pɑstiʃ] *m* pastiche; parody

pastille [pɑstij] *f* lozenge, drop; tire patch; polka dot; **pastille pectorale** cough drop

pasto•ral -rale [pɑstoral] (*pl* **-raux** [ro] **-rales**) *adj & f* pastoral

pastorat [pɑstora] *m* pastorate

pat [pat] *adj invar* (chess) in stalemate; **faire pat** to stalemate || *m* (chess) stalemate

patache [pataʃ] *f* police boat; (coll) rattletrap

patachon [pataʃɔ̃] *m*—**mener une vie de patachon** to lead a wild life

patapouf [patapuf] *m* (coll) roly-poly || *interj* flop!

pataquès [patakɛs] *m* faulty liaison; blooper, goof

patate [patat] *f* sweet potato; (coll) spud

patati [patati]—**et patati et patata!** (coll) and so on and on!

patatras [patatra] *interj* bang!, crash!

pa•taud [pato] **-taude** [tod] *adj* clumsy, loutish || *mf* lout

patauger [patoʒe] §38 *intr* to splash; (coll) to flounder

pâte [pat] *f* paste; dough, batter; **en pâte** (typ) pied; **mettre la main à la pâte** to put one's shoulder to the wheel; **pâte à papier** wood pulp; **pâte brisée**, **pâte feuilletée** puff paste; **pâte dentifrice** toothpaste; **pâte molle** spineless person; **pâtes alimentaires** pastas (*macaroni*, *noodles*, *spaghetti*, *etc.*); **peindre à la pâte** to paint with a full brush; **une bonne pâte d'homme** (coll) a good sort

pâté [pate] *m* blot, splotch; (typ) pi;

pâté de foie gras minced goose livers; **pâté de maisons** block of houses; **pâté en croûte** meat or fish pie; **pâté maison** chef's-special pâté

pâtée [pate] *f* dog food, cat food; chicken feed

pate•lin [patlɛ̃] **-line** [lin] *adj* fawning, wheedling || *m* wheedler; (coll) native village

patenôtre [patnotr] *f* prayer; (archaic) mumbo jumbo

pa•tent [patɑ̃] **-tente** [tɑ̃t] *adj* patent || *f* license; tax; **patente (de santé)** (naut) bill of health

paten•té -tée [patɑ̃te] *adj* licensed || *mf* licensed dealer

patenter [patɑ̃te] *tr* to license

Pater [pater] *m invar* Lord's Prayer

patère [pater] *f* clothes hook; curtain hook

paterne [patern] *adj* mawkish, mealy-mouthed

pater•nel -nelle [paternɛl] *adj* paternal; fatherly || *m* (slang) pop, dad

paternité [paternite] *f* paternity; fatherhood; authorship

pâ•teux [patø] **-teuse** [tøz] *adj* pasty; thick; coated (*tongue*)

pathétique [patetik] *adj* pathetic || *m* pathos

pathologie [patolɔʒi] *f* pathology

pathos [patos] *m* bathos

patibulaire [patibyler] *adj* hangdog (*look*)

patience [pasjɑ̃s] *f* patience

pa•tient [pasjɑ̃] **-tiente** [sjɑ̃t] *adj & mf* patient

patienter [pasjɑ̃te] *intr* to be patient

patin [patɛ̃] *m* skate; runner; sill, sleeper; (sole) patten; (aer) skid; (rr) base, flange (*of rails*); **patin à glace** ice skate; **patin à roulettes** roller skate; **patin de frein** brake shoe

patiner [patine] *intr* to skate; to slide; to skid

patinette [patinɛt] *f* scooter

pati•neur [patinœr] **-neuse** [nøz] *mf* skater

patinoire [patinwar] *f* skating rink

patio [patjo], [pasjo] *m* patio

pâtir [patir] *intr*—**pâtir de** to suffer from

pâtisserie [patisri] *f* pastry; pastry shop; pastry making

pâtis•sier [patisje] **pâtis•sière** [patisjer] *mf* pastry cook; proprietor of a pastry shop

patoche [patoʃ] *f* (coll) hand, paw

patois [patwa] *m* patois; jargon, lingo

patouiller [patuje] *tr* (coll) to paw, maul || *intr* (coll) to splash

patraque [patrak] *adj* in bad shape || *f* (coll) turnip (*old watch*)

pâtre [patr] *m* herdsman

patriarche [patrijarʃ] *m* patriarch

patrice [patris] *m* patrician; **Patrice** Patrick

patri•cien [patrisjɛ̃] **-cienne** [sjɛn] *adj & mf* patrician

patrie [patri] *f* native land, fatherland

patrimoine [patrimwan] *m* patrimony

patrio•tard [patrijɔtar] **-tarde** [tard] *adj* flag-waving, chauvinistic

patriote [patrijɔt] *adj* patriotic ‖ *mf* patriot

patriotique [patrijɔtik] *adj* patriotic

patriotisme [patrijɔtism] *m* patriotism

pa·tron [patrɔ̃] **-tronne** [trɔn] *mf* patron saint; proprietor; boss; sponsor ‖ *m* pattern, model; captain, skipper; coxswain; master, lord; medium size; **grand patron** large size; **patron à jours** stencil; **patron de thèse** thesis sponsor ‖ *f* mistress of the house; (slang) better half

patronage [patrɔnaʒ] *m* patronage, protection; sponsorship; (eccl) social center

patronat [patrɔna] *m* management

patronner [patrɔne] *tr* to patronize, to protect; to sponsor; to stencil

patrouille [patruj] *f* patrol

patrouiller [patruje] *intr* to patrol

patte [pat] *f* paw; foot (*of bird*); leg (*of insect*); flap, tab; hook; (coll) hand, foot, or leg (*of person*); **à pattes d'éléphant** bell-bottom (*trousers*); **à quatre pattes** on all fours; **faire patte de velours** (coll) to pull in one's claws; **graisser la patte à** (coll) to grease the palm of; **patte d'épaule** shoulder strap; **pattes de mouche** (coll) scrawl

patte-d'oie [patdwa] *f* (*pl* **pattes-d'oie**) crow's-foot; crossroads; (bot) goosefoot

pattemouille [patmuj] *f* damp cloth

pâturage [pɑtyraʒ] *m* pasture; pasturage; pasture rights

pâture [pɑtyr] *f* fodder; pasture; (fig) food

paume [pom] *f* palm; (archaic) tennis

pau·mé -mée [pome] *adj* (coll) lost

paupière [popjɛr] *f* eyelid

pause [poz] *f* pause; (mus) full rest; **pause café** coffee break

pauvre [povr] *adj* poor; **pauvre de moi!** woe is me!; **pauvre d'esprit** (coll) dim-witted ‖ (when standing before noun) *adj* poor, wretched; late (*deceased*) ‖ *mf* pauper; **les pauvres** the poor

pauvreté [povrəte] *f* poverty

P.A.V. [peave] *adj* (letterword) (**payable avec préavis**) person-to-person (*telephone call*)

pavaner [pavane] *ref* to strut

pavé [pave] *m* pavement, street; paving stone; paving block; (culin) slab; **sur le pavé** pounding the streets, out of work

pavement [pavmɑ̃] *m* paving (*act*); mosaic or marble flooring

paver [pave] *tr* to pave

pavillon [pavijɔ̃] *m* pavilion; tent, canopy; lodge, one-story house; wing, pavilion; flag; bell (*of trumpet*); **amener son pavillon** to strike one's colors; **baisser pavillon** to knuckle under

pavois [pavwa] *m* shield; **élever sur le pavois** to extol

pavoiser [pavwaze] *tr* to deck out with bunting, to decorate

pavot [pavo] *m* poppy

payable [pejabl] *adj* payable

payant [pejɑ̃] **payante** [pejɑ̃t] *adj* paying

paye [pɛj] *f* pay, wages

payement [pɛjmɑ̃] *m* payment

payer [peje] §49 *tr* to pay; to pay for; **payer comptant** to pay cash for; **payer de retour** to pay back; **payer q.ch. à qn** to pay s.o. for s.th.; to pay for s.th. for s.o.; **payer qn de q.ch.** to pay s.o. for s.th.; **payer rubis sur l'ongle** to pay down on the nail ‖ *intr* to pay ‖ *ref* to treat oneself to; to take what is due; **pouvoir se** (*dat*) **payer** to be able to afford; **se payer de** to be satisfied with

pays [pei] *m* country; region; town; (coll) fellow countryman; **du pays** local; **le pays de** the land of; **pays de cocagne** land of milk and honey

paysage [peizaʒ] *m* landscape, scenery; (painting) landscape

paysagiste [peizaʒist] *m* landscape painter

pay·san [peizɑ̃] **-sane** [zan] *adj* & *mf* peasant

Pays-Bas [peibɑ], [peibɑ] *mpl*—**les Pays-Bas** The Netherlands

payse [peiz] *f* countrywoman

P.C. [pese] *m* (letterword) (**parti communiste**) Communist party; (**poste de commandement**) command post

P.c.c. *abbr* (**pour copie conforme**) certified copy

p.c.v. or **P.C.V.** [peseve] *m* (letterword) (**payable chez vous**) or (**à percevoir**)—**téléphoner en p.c.v.** to telephone collect

péage [peaʒ] *m* toll

peau [po] *f* (*pl* **peaux**) skin; pelt; hide; film (*on milk*); (slang) bag, whore; **entrer dans la peau d'un personnage** (theat) to get right inside a part; **faire peau neuve** to turn over a new leaf; **la peau!** (slang) nothing doing!; **peau d'âne** (coll) sheepskin; **peau de tambour** drumhead; **vendre la peau de l'ours avant de l'avoir tué** to count one's chickens before they are hatched

peau-rouge [poruʒ] *mf* (*pl* **peaux-rouges**) redskin

pêche [pɛʃ] *f* peach; fishing; **pêche à la mouche noyée** fly casting; **pêche au coup** fishing with hook, line, and pole; **pêche au lancer** casting; **pêche sous-marine** deep-sea fishing; **pêche sportive** fishing with a fly rod or casting rod

péché [peʃe] *m* sin

pécher [peʃe] §10 *intr* to sin

pêcher [peʃe] *m* peach tree ‖ *tr* to fish, fish for; (coll) to get ‖ *intr* to fish; **pêcher à la mouche** to fly-fish

pêcherie [peʃri] *f* fishery

pé·cheur [peʃœr] **-cheresse** [ʃres] *mf* sinner

pê·cheur [peʃœr] **-cheuse** [ʃøz] *mf* fisher; **pêcheur de perles** pearl diver ‖ *m* fisherman

pécore [pekɔr] *f* (coll) silly goose

pecque [pek] *f* (coll) silly affected woman

péculat [pekyla] *m* embezzlement

pécule [pekyl] *m* nest egg

pédagogie [pedagɔʒi] *f* pedagogy, education

pédagogue [pedagɔg] *adj* pedagogical ‖ *mf* pedagogue; teacher

pédale [pedal] *f* pedal; treadle; (vulg) pederast; pédale d'embrayage (aut) clutch pedal

pédaler [pedale] *intr* to pedal

pédalier [pedalje] *m* pedal keyboard; pedal and sprocket-wheel assembly

pédalo [pedalo] *m* water bicycle

pé·dant [pedã] -dante [dãt] *adj* pedantic ‖ *mf* pedant

pédanterie [pedãtri] *f* pedantry

pédantesque [pedãtɛsk] *adj* pedantic

pédestre [pedɛstr] *adj* on foot

pédiatrie [pedjatri] *f* pediatrics

pédicure [pedikyr] *mf* chiropodist

pedigree [pedigri] *m* pedigree

Pégase [pegaz] *m* Pegasus

pègre [pɛgr] *f* underworld

peigne [pɛɲ] *m* comb; card (*for wool*); reed (*of loom*); (zool) scallop

peigner [peɲe] *tr* to comb; to card ‖ *ref* to comb one's hair

peignoir [peɲwar] *m* bathrobe; dressing gown, peignoir

peindre [pɛdr] §50 *tr & intr* to paint

peine [pen] *f* pain; trouble; difficulty; penalty; à peine hardly, scarcely; en être pour sa peine to have nothing to show for one's trouble; faire (de la) peine à to grieve; faire peine à voir to be pathetic; peine capitale capital punishment; peine de cœur heartache; peine de mort death penalty; peine pécuniaire financial distress; purger sa peine to serve one's sentence; valoir la peine to be worth while; veuillez vous donner la peine de please be so kind as to

peiner [pene] *tr* to pain, grieve; to fatigue ‖ *intr* to labor

peintre [pɛtr] *m* painter

peinture [pɛtyr] *f* paint; painting; attention à la peinture (public sign) wet paint; je ne peux pas le voir en peinture (coll) I can't stand him

peinturer [pɛtyre] *tr* to lay a coat of paint on; to daub

peinturlurer [pɛtyrlyre] *tr* (coll) to paint in all the colors of the rainbow

péjora·tif [peʒɔratif] -tive [tiv] *adj & m* pejorative

pékin [pekɛ] *m* pekin; en pékin (slang) in civies; Pékin Peking

péki·nois [pekinwa] -noise [nwaz] *adj* Pekingese ‖ *m* Pekingese (*language; dog*) ‖ (*cap*) *mf* Pekingese (*inhabitant*)

pelage [pəlaʒ] *m* coat (*of animal*)

pe·lé -lée [pəle] *adj* bald; bare

pêle-mêle [pɛlmɛl] *m invar* jumble ‖ *adv* pell-mell

peler [pəle] §2 *tr, intr, & ref* to peel, to peel off

pèle·rin [pɛlrɛ] -rine [rin] *mf* pilgrim ‖ *m* peregrine falcon; basking shark ‖ *f* see pèlerine

pèlerinage [pɛlrinaʒ] *m* pilgrimage

pèlerine [pɛlrin] *f* pelerine, cape; hooded cape

péliade [peljad] *f* adder

pélican [pelikã] *m* pelican

pellagre [pelagr] *f* pellagra

pelle [pel] *f* shovel; scoop; pelle à poussière dustpan; pelle à vapeur steam shovel; pelle mécanique power-er shovel; ramasser à la pelle to shovel, to shovel up

pelletée [pelte] *f* shovelful

pelleter [pelte] §34 *tr* to shovel

pelleterie [peltri] *f* fur trade; skin, pelt

pelleteuse [peltøz] *f* power shovel

pellicule [pelikyl], [pellikyl] *f* film; pellicle; speck of dandruff; (phot) film; pellicules dandruff

pelote [plɔt] *f* ball (*of string, of snow, etc.*); faire sa pelote (coll) to make one's pile; pelote basque pelota; pelote d'épingles pincushion

peloter [plɔte] *tr* to wind into a ball; (fig) to flatter; (slang) to feel up, to paw ‖ *intr* to bat the ball back and forth

pelo·teur [plɔtœr] -teuse [tøz] *adj* flattering, ingratiating; (coll) fresh, amorous, spoony ‖ *mf* (coll) masher, spooner

peloton [plɔtɔ̃] *m* little ball (*e.g., of wool*); group (*of racers*); (mil) platoon, troop, detachment; peloton d'exécution firing squad

pelotonner [plɔtɔne] *tr* to wind into a ball ‖ *ref* to curl up, to snuggle

pelouse [pluz] *f* lawn; (golf) green

peluche [plyʃ] *f* plush

pelure [plyr] *f* peel, peeling, skin; rind; (coll) coat

pénaliser [penalize] *tr* to penalize

pénalité [penalite] *f* penalty

pe·naud [pəno] -naude [nod] *adj* bashful, shy; shamefaced; crestfallen

penchant [pãʃã] *m* penchant, bent

pen·ché -chée [pãʃe] *adj* leaning, stooping, bent over

pencher [pãʃe] *tr, intr, & ref* to lean, to bend, to incline; se pencher sur to make a close study of

pendable [pãdabl] *adj* outrageous; (archaic) hangable

pendaison [pãdezɔ̃] *f* hanging

pen·dant [pãdã] -dante [dãt] *adj* hanging; pending ‖ *m* pendant; counterpart; pendant d'oreille eardrop; se faire pendant to make a pair ‖ pendant *adv*—pendant que while ‖ pendant *prep* during

pendeloque [pãdlɔk] *f* pendant; jewel (*of eardrop*)

pendentif [pãdãtif] *m* pendant; eardrop; lavaliere

penderie [pãdri] *f* clothes closet

pendoir [pãdwar] *m* meat hook

pendre [pãdr] *tr* to hang; to hang up; être pendu à to hang on (*e.g., the telephone*) ‖ *intr* to hang; to hang down; to sag; ça lui pend au nez he's got it coming to him ‖ *ref* to hang oneself; se pendre à to hang on to

pen·du -due [pãdy] *adj* hanging; hanged ‖ *mf* hanged person

pendule [pãdyl] *m* pendulum ‖ *f* clock; pendule à pile battery clock

pêne [pen] *m* bolt; latch

pénétration [penetrɑsjɔ̃] *f* penetration; permeation

pénétrer [penetre] §10 *tr* to penetrate, to permeate ‖ *intr* to penetrate; to enter ‖ *ref* to mix; **se pénétrer de** to become imbued with

pénible [penibl] *adj* hard, painful

péniche [peni∫] *f* barge; houseboat; **péniche de débarquement** landing craft

pénicilline [penisilin] *f* penicillin

péninsulaire [penɛ̃syler] *adj* peninsular

péninsule [penɛ̃syl] *f* large peninsula

pénitence [penitɑ̃s] *f* penitence; penalty (*in games*); punishment; **en pénitence** in disgrace; **faire pénitence** to do penance

pénitencier [penitɑ̃sje] *m* penitentiary; penal colony

péni·tent [penitɑ̃] **-tente** [tɑ̃t] *adj & mf* penitent

penne [pen] *f* quill, feather

Pennsylvanie [pensilvani] *f* Pennsylvania; **la Pennsylvanie** Pennsylvania

pénombre [penɔ̃br] *f* penumbra; half-light; **dans la pénombre** out of the limelight

pense-bête [pɑ̃sbet] *m* (*pl* **-bêtes**) (coll) reminder

pensée [pɑ̃se] *f* thought; thinking; (bot) pansy

penser [pɑ̃se] *tr* to think; **penser de** to think of (*to have as an opinion of*); **penser** + *inf* to intend to + *inf* ‖ *intr* to think; **penser à** to think of (*to direct one's thoughts toward*); **y penser** to think of it, e.g., **pendant que j'y pense** while I think of it

penseur [pɑ̃sœr] *m* thinker

pen·sif [pɑ̃sif] **-sive** [siv] *adj* pensive; absent-minded

pension [pɑ̃sjɔ̃] *f* pension (*annuity; room and board; boardinghouse*); **avec pension complète** with three meals; **pension de famille** residential hotel; **pension de retraite**, **pension viagère** annuity; **prendre pension** to board; **sans pension** without meals

pensionnaire [pɑ̃sjɔner] *mf* boarder; guest (*in hotel*); resident student ‖ *f* naïve girl

pensionnat [pɑ̃sjɔna] *m* boarding school

pension·né **-née** [pɑ̃sjɔne] *adj* pensioned ‖ *mf* pensioner

pensionner [pɑ̃sjɔne] *tr* to pension

pensum [pɛ̃sɔm] *m* thankless task

Pentagone [pɛ̃tagɔn] *m* Pentagon

pente [pɑ̃t] *f* slope; inclination; bent; fall (*of river*); **en pente** sloping

Pentecôte [pɑ̃tkot] *f*—**la Pentecôte** Pentecost, Whitsunday

pénultième [penyltjem] *adj* next to the last ‖ *f* penult

pénurie [penyri] *f* lack, shortage

pépé [pepe] *m* (slang) grandpa

pépée [pepe] *f* (slang) doll; (slang) doll

pépère [peper] *adj* (coll) easygoing ‖ *m* grandpa; (coll) old duffer; (coll) overgrown boy

pépètes [pepɛt] *fpl* (slang) dough

pépie [pepi] *f* (vet) pip; **avoir la pépie** (coll) to be thirsty

pépiement [pepimɑ̃] *m* chirp

pépier [pepje] *intr* to chirp

pépin [pepɛ̃] *m* pip, seed; (coll) umbrella; **avoir un pépin** (coll) to strike a snag

pépinière [pepinjer] *f* (hort) nursery; (fig) training school; (fig) hotbed

pépiniériste [pepinjerist] *m* nurseryman

pépite [pepit] *f* nugget

péque·naud [peknɔ] **-naude** [nod] *adj & mf* (slang) peasant

péquenot [peknɔ] *m* (slang) peasant

perçage [persaʒ] *m* drilling, boring

per·çant [persɑ̃] **-çante** [sɑ̃t] *adj* piercing, penetrating

perce [pers] *f* drill, bore; **en perce** on tap

perce-neige [persəneʒ] *m invar* (bot) snowdrop

percepteur [perseptœr] *m* tax collector

perception [persepsjɔ̃] *f* perception; tax collection; tax; tax department, bureau of internal revenue

percer [perse] §51 *tr* to pierce; to drill; to tap (*a barrel*); to break through ‖ *intr* to come through or out; to burst (*said, e.g., of abscess*); to make a name for oneself

perceuse [persøz] *f* drill; machine drill

percevoir [persəvwar] §59 *tr* to perceive; to collect

perche [per∫] *f* pole; (ichth) perch; (coll) beanpole; **perche à sauter** vaulting pole; **perche à son microphone stand**; **tendre la perche à** to lend a helping hand to

percher [per∫e] *tr* to perch ‖ *intr* to perch, to roost

perchoir [per∫war] *m* perch

per·clus [perkly] **-cluse** [klyz] *adj* crippled, paralyzed

percolateur [perkɔlatœr] *m* large coffee maker

percuter [perkyte] *tr* to strike; to crash into; to percuss ‖ *intr* to crash

percuteur [perkytœr] *m* firing pin

per·dant [perdɑ̃] **-dante** [dɑ̃t] *adj* losing ‖ *mf* loser

perdition [perdisjɔ̃] *f* perdition; **en perdition** (naut) in distress

perdre [perdrə] *tr* to lose; to ruin ‖ *intr* to lose; to leak; to deteriorate ‖ *ref* to get lost; to disappear

per·dreau [perdro] *m* (*pl* **-dreaux**) young partridge

perdrix [perdri] *f* partridge

per·du -due [perdy] *adj* lost; spare (*time*); stray (*bullet*); remote (*locality*); advance (*sentry*)

père [per] *m* father; senior, e.g., **M. Martin père** Mr. Martin, senior; **père de famille** head of the household; **père spirituel** father confessor

péréquation [perekwasjɔ̃] *f* equalizing

perfection [perfeksjɔ̃] *f* perfection

perfectionner [perfeksjɔne] *tr* to perfect ‖ *ref* to improve

perfide [perfid] *adj* perfidious ‖ *mf* treacherous person

perfidie [perfidi] *f* perfidy

perforation [perfɔrɑsjɔ̃] *f* perforation
perforatrice [perfɔratris] *f* pneumatic drill; perforator; keypunch (machine)
perforer [perfɔre] *tr* to perforate; to drill, bore; to punch (*a card*)
performance [perfɔrmɑ̃s] *f* (sports) performance
péricliter [periklite] *intr* to fail
péril [peril] *m* peril
péril·leux [perijø] **péril·leuse** [perijøz] *adj* perilous
péri·mé -mée [perime] *adj* expired, elapsed; out-of-date
périmer [perime] *intr & ref* to lapse
période [perjɔd] *f* period; (phys) cycle
périodique [perjɔdik] *adj* periodic(al)
péripétie [peripesi] *f* vicissitude
périphérie [periferi] *f* periphery
périphérique [periferik] *adj* peripheral
périple [peripl] *m* journey
périr [perir] *intr* to perish
périscope [periskɔp] *m* periscope
périssable [perisabl] *adj* perishable
perle [perl] *f* pearl; bead
perler [perle] *tr* to pearl; to do to perfection || *intr* to form beads
permanence [permanɑ̃s] *f* permanence; headquarters, station; en permanence at all hours
perma·nent [permanɑ̃] **-nente** [nɑ̃t] *adj* permanent; standing; continuous, nonstop || *f* permanent
perme [perm] *f* (coll) furlough
permettre [permetr] §42 *tr* to permit; **permettre q.ch. à qn** to allow s.o. s.th. || *intr*—**permettez!** excuse me!; **permettre à qn de** + *inf* to permit s.o. to or let s.o. + *inf*; **vous permettez?** may I? || *ref*—**se permettre de** to take the liberty of
permis [permi] *m* permit, license; **permis de conduire** driver's license
permission [permisjɔ̃] *f* permission; (mil) furlough, leave
permissionnaire [permisjɔner] *m* soldier on leave
permutation [permytɑsjɔ̃] *f* permutation; exchange of posts; transposition
permuter [permyte] *tr* to permute; to exchange || *intr* to change places
perni·cieux [pernisjø] **-cieuse** [sjøz] *adj* pernicious
péroné [perɔne] *m* (anat) fibula
pérorer [perɔre] *intr* to hold forth
Pérou [peru] *m*—**le Pérou** Peru
peroxyde [perɔksid] *m* peroxide
perpendiculaire [perpɑ̃dikyler] *adj & f* perpendicular
perpète [perpet]—**à perpète** (slang) forever
perpétrer [perpetre] §10 *tr* to perpetrate
perpé·tuel -tuelle [perpetɥel] *adj* perpetual; life (*imprisonment*); constant, continual
perpétuer [perpetɥe] *tr* to perpetuate || *ref* to be perpetuated
perpétuité [perpetɥite] *f* perpetuity; à perpétuité forever; for life

perplexe [perpleks] *adj* perplexed; **rendre perplexe** to perplex
perplexité [perpleksite] *f* perplexity
perquisition [perkizisjɔ̃] *f* search
perquisitionner [perkizisjɔne] *intr* to make a search
perron [perɔ̃] *m* front-entrance stone steps
perroquet [perɔke] *m* parrot
perruche [peryʃ] *f* parakeet; hen parrot
perruque [peryk] *f* wig; **vieille perruque** (coll) old fogey
per·san [persɑ̃] **-sane** [san] *adj* Persian || *m* Persian (*language*) || (*cap*) *mf* Persian (*person*)
perse [pers] *adj* Persian || (*cap*) *mf* Persian || (*cap*) *f* Persia; **la Perse** Persia
persécuter [persekyte] *tr* to persecute
persécution [persekysjɔ̃] *f* persecution
persévérer [persevere] §10 *intr* to persevere
persienne [persjen] *f* Persian blind, slatted shutter
persil [persi] *m* parsley
persis·tant [persistɑ̃] **-tante** [tɑ̃t] *adj* persistent
persister [persiste] *intr* to persist; **persister à** to persist in
personnage [persɔnaʒ] *m* personage; (theat) character
personnalité [persɔnalite] *f* personality
personne [persɔn] *f* person; self; appearance; lady, e.g., **belle personne** beautiful lady; e.g., **jolie personne** pretty lady; **grande personne** grown-up; **par personne** per person; **payer de sa personne** to not spare one's efforts; **s'assurer de la personne de** to arrest; **une tierce personne** a third party || *pron indef* no one, nobody; **personne ne** or **ne . . . personne** §90B no one, nobody, not anyone
person·nel -nelle [persɔnel] *adj* personal || *m* personnel
personnifier [persɔnifje] *tr* to personify
perspective [perspektiv] *f* perspective; outlook; **en perspective** in view
perspicace [perspikas] *adj* perspicacious
persuader [persɥade] *tr* to persuade; **persuader q.ch. à qn** or **persuader qn de q.ch.** to persuade s.o. of s.th. || *intr*—**persuader à qn de** to persuade s.o. to || *ref* to be convinced
persuasion [persɥazjɔ̃] *f* persuasion
perte [pert] *f* loss; ruin, downfall; **à perte de vue** as far as the eye can see; **en pure perte** uselessly
perti·nent [pertinɑ̃] **-nente** [nɑ̃t] *adj* pertinent
perturba·teur [pertyrbatœr] **-trice** [tris] *adj* disturbing || *mf* troublemaker
perturber [pertyrbe] *tr* to perturb
péru·vien [peryvjɛ̃] **-vienne** [vjen] *adj* Peruvian || (*cap*) *mf* Peruvian
pervenche [pervɑ̃ʃ] *f* periwinkle
per·vers [perver] **-verse** [vers] *adj* perverted || *mf* pervert
perversion [perversjɔ̃] *f* perversion

perversité [perversite] *f* perversity, depravity

pervertir [pervertir] *tr* to pervert

pesage [pəzaʒ] *m* weigh-in; paddock

pe·sant [pəzã] **-sante** [zãt] *adj* heavy ‖ *m*—**valoir son pesant d'or** to be worth one's weight in gold

pesanteur [pəzãtœr] *f* heaviness; weight; (phys) gravity

pèse-bébé [pezbebe] *m* (*pl* **-bébés**) baby scale

pesée [pəze] *f* weighing; leverage

pèse-lettre [pezletr] *m* (*pl* **-lettres**) letter scale

pèse-personne [pezpersɔn] *m* (*pl* **-personnes**) bathroom scale

peser [pəze] §2 *tr* to weigh ‖ *intr* to weigh; **peser à** to hang heavy on; **peser sur** to bear down on; to lie down on; to lie heavy on; to stress ‖ *ref* to weigh oneself; to weigh in

peson [pəzɔ̃] *m* spring scale

pessimisme [pesimism] *m* pessimism

pessimiste [pesimist] *adj* pessimistic ‖ *mf* pessimist

peste [pest] *f* plague; pest, nuisance ‖ *interj* gosh!

pester [peste] *intr* to grouse; **pester contre** to rail at

pestiféré -rée [pestifere] *adj* plagueridden ‖ *mf* victim of the plague

pestilence [pestilɑ̃s] *f* pestilence

pet [pe] *m* (slang) scandal; (vulgar) wind; **ça ne vaut pas un pet (de lapin)** (coll) it's not worth a wooden nickel ‖ *interj* (coll) look out!

pétale [petal] *m* petal

pétarade [petarad] *f* series of explosions; backfire

pétard [petar] *m* firecracker; blast; (slang) gat, revolver; (slang) backside; **faire du pétard** (coll) to kick up a fuss; **lancer un pétard** (coll) to drop a bombshell

pet-de-loup [pedlu] *m* (*pl* **pets-de-loup**) absent-minded professor

pet-de-nonne [pednɔn] *m* (*pl* **pets-de-nonne**) fritter

pet-en-l'air [petãler] *m invar* short jacket

péter [pete] §10 *tr*—**péter du feu** (coll) to be a live wire ‖ *intr* (coll) to go bang; (vulg) to break wind

pètesec [petsek] *adj invar* (coll) bossy, despotic ‖ *m invar* (coll) martinet, bossy fellow

pétil·lant [petijã] **pétil·lante** [petijãt] *adj* crackling; sparkling

pétiller [petije] *intr* to crackle; to sparkle

pe·tiot [pətjo] **-tiote** [tjɔt] *adj* (coll) tiny, wee ‖ *mf* (coll) tot

pe·tit [pəti] **-tite** [tit] *adj* §91 small, little; short; minor, lower; **en petit** shortened; miniature; **petit à petit** little by little, bit by bit ‖ *mf* youngster; young (*of an animal*); poor little thing ‖ *m* little boy ‖ *f* little girl

petit-beurre [pətibœr] *m* (*pl* **petits-beurre**) cookie

petit-cou·sin [pətikuzɛ̃] **-sine** [zin] *mf* (*pl* **petits-cousins**) second cousin

petite-fille [pətitfij] *f* (*pl* **petites-filles**) granddaughter

petite-nièce [pətitnjes] *f* (*pl* **petites-nièces**) great-niece

petitesse [pətites] *f* smallness

petit-fils [pətifis] *m* (*pl* **petits-fils**) grandson; grandchild

petit-gris [pətigri] *m* (*pl* **petits-gris**) miniver; snail

pétition [petisjɔ̃] *f* petition; **faire une pétition de principe** to beg the question

petit-lait [pətile] *m* (*pl* **petits-laits**) whey

petit-neveu [pətinvø] *m* (*pl* **petits-neveux**) great-nephew

petits-enfants [pətizãfã] *mpl* grandchildren

petit-suisse [pətisɥis] *m* (*pl* **petits-suisses**) cream cheese

peton [pətɔ̃] *m* (coll) tiny foot

pétoncle [petɔ̃kl] *m* scallop

Pétrarque [petrark] *m* Petrarch

pétrifier [petrifje] *tr & ref* to petrify

pétrin [petrɛ̃] *m* kneading trough; (coll) mess, jam

pétrir [petrir] *tr* to knead; to mold

pétrole [petrɔl] *m* petroleum; **à pétrole** kerosene (*lamp*); **pétrole brut** crude oil; **pétrole lampant** kerosene

pétro-lier [petrɔlje] **-lière** [ljer] *adj* oil ‖ *m* tanker; oil baron

P et T [peete] *fpl* (letterword) (**Postes et télécommunications**) post office, telephone, and telegraph

pétu·lant [petylã] **-lante** [lãt] *adj* lively, frisky

peu [pø] *m* bit, little; **peu de** few; not much; not many; **peu de chose** not much ‖ *adv* §91 little; not very; **à peu près** about, practically; **depuis peu** of late; **peu ou prou** more or less; **peu probable** improbable; **peu s'en faut** very nearly; **pour peu que, si peu que** however little; **quelque peu** somewhat; **sous peu** before long; **tant soit peu** ever so little

peuplade [pœplad] *f* tribe

peuple [pœpl] *adj* plebeian, common ‖ *m* people

peuplement [pœpləmã] *m* populating; planting; stocking (*e.g., with fish*)

peupler [pœple] *tr* to people; to plant; to stock ‖ *intr* to multiply, to breed

peuplier [pøplje] *m* poplar

peur [pœr] *f* fear; **avoir peur (de)** to be afraid (of); **de peur que** lest, for fear that; **une peur bleue** (coll) an awful fright

peu·reux [pœrø] **-reuse** [røz] *adj* fearful, timid

peut-être [pøtetr] *adv* perhaps; **peut-être que non** perhaps not

p. ex. *abbr* (**par exemple**) e.g.

phalange [falãʒ] *f* phalanx

phalène [falen] *m & f* moth

Pharaon [faraɔ̃] *m* Pharaoh

phare [far] *m* lighthouse; beacon; (aut) headlight; **phares code** dimmers

phari·sien [farizjɛ̃] **-sienne** [zjen] *adj* pharisaic ‖ *mf* pharisee

pharmaceutique [farmasøtik] *adj* pharmaceutical || *f* pharmaceutics

pharmacie [farmasi] *f* drugstore, pharmacy; medicine chest; drugs

pharma·cien [farmasjɛ̃] **-cienne** [sjɛn] *mf* pharmacist

pharynx [farɛ̃ks] *m* pharynx

phase [faz] *f* phase

Phébé [febe] *f* Phoebe

Phénicie [fenisi] *f* Phoenicia; **la Phénicie** Phoenicia

phéni·cien [fenisjɛ̃] **-cienne** [sjɛn] *adj* Phoenician || *(cap) mf* Phoenician

phénix [feniks] *m* phoenix

phénomé·nal -nale [fenomenal] *adj (pl* **-naux** [no]) phenomenal

phénomène [fenomɛn] *m* phenomenon; (coll) monster, freak

philanthrope [filɑ̃trɔp] *mf* philanthropist

philanthropie [filɑ̃trɔpi] *f* philanthropy

philatélie [filateli] *f* philately

philatéliste [filatelist] *mf* philatelist

philip·pin [filipɛ̃] **-pine** [pin] *adj* Philippine || *(cap) mf* Filipino

Philippines [filipin] *fpl* Philippines

philistin [filistɛ̃] *adj masc & m* Philistine

philologie [filɔlɔʒi] *f* philology

philologue [filɔlɔg] *mf* philologist

philosophe [filɔzɔf] *adj* philosophic || *mf* philosopher

philosophie [filɔzɔfi] *f* philosophy

philosophique [filɔzɔfik] *adj* philosophic(al)

philtre [filtr] *m* philter

phlébite [flebit] *f* phlebitis

phobie [fobi] *f* phobia

phonétique [fɔnetik] *adj* phonetic || *f* phonetics

phoniatrie [fɔnjatri] *f* speech therapy

phono [fɔno] *m* (coll) phonograph

phonographe [fɔnɔgraf] *m* phonograph

phonologie [fɔnɔlɔʒi] *f* phonology

phonothèque [fɔnɔtek] *f* record library

phoque [fɔk] *m* seal

phosphate [fɔsfat] *m* phosphate

phosphore [fɔsfɔr] *m* phosphorus

phosphores·cent [fɔsfɔresɑ̃] **phosphores·cente** [fɔsfɔresɑ̃t] *adj* phosphorescent

photo [fɔto] *f* photo, snapshot

photocopier [fɔtɔkɔpje] *tr* to photocopy, to photostat

photogénique [fɔtɔʒenik] *adj* photogenic

photographe [fɔtɔgraf] *mf* photographer

photographie [fɔtɔgrafi] *f* photography; photograph

photographier [fɔtɔgrafje] *tr* to photograph

photogravure [fɔtɔgravyr] *f* photoengraving

photostat [fɔtɔsta] *m* photostat

phrase [frɑz] *f* sentence; (mus) phrase; **phrase de choc** punch line

phrénologie [frenɔlɔʒi] *f* phrenology

physi·cien [fizisjɛ̃] **-cienne** [sjɛn] *mf* physicist

physiologie [fizjɔlɔʒi] *f* physiology

physiologique [fizjɔlɔʒik] *adj* physiological

physionomie [fizjɔnɔmi] *f* physiognomy

physique [fizik] *adj* physical; material || *m* physique; appearance || *f* physics

piaffer [pjafe] *intr* to paw the ground; to fidget, fume

piailler [pjaje] *intr* (coll) to cheep; (coll) to squeal

pianiste [pjanist] *mf* pianist

piano [pjano] *m* piano; **piano à queue** grand piano; **piano droit** upright piano || *adv* (coll) quietly

pianoter [pjanɔte] *intr* to strum; to drum, to thrum; to rattle away

piastre [pjastr] *f* (Canad) dollar

piauler [pjole] *intr* to peep; to screech *(said of pulley)*; (coll) to whine

pic [pik] *m* peak; *(tool)* pick; (orn) woodpecker; **à pic** sheer, steep; (coll) in the nick of time; **couler à pic** to sink like a stone

picaillons [pikajɔ̃] *mpl* (slang) dough

picaresque [pikaresk] *adj* picaresque

piccolo [pikɔlo] *m* piccolo

pichet [pi/e] *m* pitcher, jug

pick-up [pikœp] *m invar* pickup; record player; pickup truck

picoler [pikɔle] *intr* (slang) to get pickled

picorer [pikɔre] *tr & intr* to peck

picoter [pikɔte] *tr* to prick; to peck at; to sting

picotin [pikɔtɛ̃] *m* peck *(measure)*

pictu·ral -rale [piktyral] *adj (pl* **-raux** [ro]) pictorial

pie [pi] *adj invar* piebald || *f* magpie

pièce [pjes] *f* piece; patch; room; play; document; coin; wine barrel; **à la pièce** separately; **donner la pièce** to tip; **faire pièce à** to play a trick on; to put a check on; **inventé de toutes pièces** made up out of the whole cloth; **la pièce** apiece; **pièce à conviction** (law) exhibit; **pièce comptable** voucher; **pièce d'eau** ornamental pond; **pièce de rechange, pièce détachée** spare part; **pièce de résistance** pièce de résistance; (culin) entree; **tout d'une pièce** in one piece; (coll) rigid; (coll) stiffly || *adv* apiece

pied [pje] *m* foot; foothold; **à pied** on foot; **au pied de la lettre** literally; **au pied levé** offhand; **de pied en cap** from head to toe; **faire le pied de grue** (coll) to cool one's heels, to stand around waiting; **faire les pieds à** (coll) to give what's coming to; **faire un pied de nez** (coll) to thumb one's nose; **lever le pied** to abscond; **mettre à pied** to dismiss, fire; **mettre les pieds dans le plat** (coll) to put one's foot in one's mouth; **mettre pied à terre** to dismount; **pied équin** clubfoot; **travailler comme un pied** (coll) to botch one's work

pied-à-terre [pjetater] *m invar* hangout, temporary base

pied-bot [pjebo] *m (pl* **pieds-bots**) clubfooted person

pied-d'alouette [pjedalwɛt] *m* (*pl* **pieds-d'alouette**) delphinium

pied-droit [pjedrwa] *m* (*pl* **pieds-droits**) (archit) pier

piédes·tal -tale [pjedestal] *m* (*pl* **-taux** [to]) pedestal

pied-noir [pjenwar] *m* (*pl* **pieds-noirs**) Algerian of European descent

piège [pjɛʒ] *m* trap, snare

piéger [pjeʒe] §11 *tr* to trap, to snare; to booby-trap

pie-grièche [pigrijɛʃ] *f* (*pl* **pies-grièches**) shrike; shrew

pierraille [pjɛrɑj] *f* rubble

pierre [pjɛr] *f* stone; **faire d'une pierre deux coups** to kill two birds with one stone; **Pierre** Peter; **pierre à aiguiser** whetstone; **pierre à briquet** flint; **pierre à chaux, pierre à plâtre** gypsum; **pierre à feu, pierre à fusil** gunflint; **pierre angulaire** cornerstone; **pierre à rasoir** hone; **pierre calcaire** limestone; **pierre d'achoppement** stumbling block; **pierre de gué** stepping stone; **pierre de touche** touchstone; **pierre tombale** tombstone

pierreries [pjɛrri] *fpl* precious stones

pier·reux -reuse [pjɛrø] [pjɛrøz] *adj* stony || *f* (coll) streetwalker

pierrot [pjɛro] *m* clown; sparrow; (coll) oddball; (coll) greenhorn

piété [pjete] *f* piety; devotion

piéter [pjete] §10 *intr* to toe the line || *ref* to stand firm

piétiner [pjetine] *tr* to trample on || *intr* to stamp; to mark time

piéton [pjetɔ̃] *m* pedestrian

piètre [pjɛtr] *adj* poor, wretched

pieu [pjø] *m* (*pl* **pieux**) post, stake; (archit) pile

pieuvre [pjœvr] *f* octopus; (coll) leech

pieux pieuse [pjø] [pjøz] *adj* pious; dutiful; white (*lie*)

pif [pif] *m* (slang) snout (*nose*) || *interj* bang!

pige [piʒ] *f* (slang) year; **à la pige** (journ) so much a line; **faire la pige à** (slang) to outdo

pigeon [piʒɔ̃] *m* pigeon; **pigeon voyageur** homing pigeon

pigeonner [piʒɔne] *tr* (coll) to dupe

pigeonnier [piʒɔnje] *m* dovecote

piger [piʒe] §38 *tr* (slang) to look at; (slang) to get || *intr*—**tu piges?** (slang) do you get it?

pigment [pigmɑ̃] *m* pigment

pignocher [piɲɔʃe] *intr* to pick at one's food

pignon [piɲɔ̃] *m* gable; (mach) pinion; **avoir pignon sur rue** (coll) to have a home of one's own; (coll) to be well off; **pignon de chaîne** sprocket wheel

pile [pil] *f* stack, pile; pier; (elec) battery (*primary cell*); (coll) thrashing; **pile atomique** atomic pile; **pile ou face** heads or tails; **pile sèche** dry cell || *adv* (coll) short; (coll) exactly

piler [pile] *tr* to grind, to crush

pilier [pilje] *m* pillar; **pilier de cabaret** barfly

pillage [pijaʒ] *m* looting

pil·lard [pijar] **pil·larde** [pijard] *adj* looting || *mf* looter

piller [pije] *tr* & *intr* to loot; to plagiarize

pil·leur [pijœr] **pil·leuse** [pijøz] *mf* pillager

pilon [pilɔ̃] *m* pestle; (coll) drumstick (*of chicken*); (coll) wooden leg; **pilon à vapeur** steam hammer

pilonnage [pilɔnaʒ] *m* crushing; **pilonnage aérien** saturation bombing

pilonner [pilɔne] *tr* to crush; to bomb

pilori [pilɔri] *m* pillory

pilot [pilo] *m* pile (*in piling*); rags (*for paper*)

pilotage [pilɔtaʒ] *m* piloting; **pilotage sans visibilité** blind flying

pilote [pilɔt] *m* pilot; **pilote de ligne** airline pilot; **pilote d'essai** test pilot

piloter [pilɔte] *tr* to pilot; to guide; to drive piles into || *intr* to pilot; to be a guide

pilotis [piloti] *m* piles

pilule [pilyl] *f* pill; (coll) bitter pill; **dorer la pilule** to gild the lily

piment [pimɑ̃] *m* allspice (*berry*); (fig) spice; **piment doux** sweet pepper; **piment rouge** red or hot pepper

pimenter [pimɑ̃te] *tr* to season with red pepper; (fig) to spice

pim·pant -pante [pɛ̃pɑ̃] [pɑ̃t] *adj* smart, spruce

pin [pɛ̃] *m* pine; **pin de Weymouth** (*Pinus strobus*) white pine; **pin sylvestre** (*Pinus sylvestris*) Scotch pine

pinacle [pinakl] *m* pinnacle

pince [pɛ̃s] *f* tongs; pliers; forceps; crowbar; gripper; grip; pleat; claw (*of crab*); **aller à pinces** (slang) to hoof it; **petites pinces, pince à épiler** tweezers; **pince à linge** clothespin; **pince à sucre** sugar tongs; **pince hémostatique** hemostat; **pinces tongs**; pincers, pliers; **pinces de cycliste** bicycle clips; **serrer la pince à** (slang) to shake hands with

pin·cé -cée [pɛ̃se] *adj* prim, tight-lipped; thin, pinched || *f* see **pincée**

pin·ceau [pɛ̃so] *m* (*pl* **-ceaux**) paintbrush; pencil (*of light*)

pincée [pɛ̃se] *f* pinch

pincement [pɛ̃smɑ̃] *m* pinching; plucking

pince-monseigneur [pɛ̃smɔ̃seɲœr] *f* (*pl* **pinces-monseigneur**) jimmy

pince-nez [pɛ̃sne] *m invar* nose glasses

pincer [pɛ̃se] §51 *tr* to pinch; to grip; to nip off; to pluck; to top (*plants*); to purse (*the lips*); to pleat; (coll) to nab, to catch || *intr* to bite (*said of cold*); **en pincer pour** (slang) to have a crush on; **pincer de** (mus) to strum on

pince-sans-rire [pɛ̃sɑ̃rir] *adj invar* deadpan || *mf invar* deadpan comic

pincette [pɛ̃sɛt] *f* tweezers; **pincettes** tweezers; fire tongs

pinçon [pɛ̃sɔ̃] *m* bruise (*from pinch*)

pinède [pined] *f* pine grove

pingouin [pɛ̃gwɛ̃] *m* (*family*: Alcidae) auk

pingre [pɛ̃gr] *adj* (coll) stingy ‖ *mf* (coll) tightwad

pinson [pɛ̃sɔ̃] *m* (orn) finch

pintade [pɛ̃tad] *f* guinea fowl

pin up [pinœp] *f invar* (coll) pinup girl

pioche [pjɔʃ] *f* pickax

piocher [pjɔʃe] *tr & intr* to dig, to pick; (coll) to cram

pio·cheur [pjɔʃœr] **-cheuse** [ʃøz] *mf* digger; (coll) grind ‖ *f* (mach) cultivator

piolet [pjɔlɛ] *m* ice ax

pion [pjɔ̃] *m* (checkers) man; (chess & fig) pawn; (slang) proctor; **damer le pion à** (coll) to get the better of

pionnier [pjɔnje] *m* pioneer

pipe [pip] *f* pipe; **casser sa pipe** (slang) to kick the bucket

pi·peau [pipo] *m* (*pl* **-peaux**) bird call; shepherd's pipe; lime twig

piper [pipe] *tr* to snare, to catch; to load (*the dice*); to mark (*the cards*) ‖ *intr*—**ne pipe pas!** (coll) not a peep out of you!

pi·quant [pikɑ̃] **-quante** [kɑ̃t] *adj* piquant, intriguing; racy, spicy ‖ *m* sting; prickle; quill (*of porcupine*); piquancy, pungency; point (*of story*); (fig) bite

pique [pik] *m* (cards) spade; (cards) spades ‖ *f* pike; pique

pi·qué -quée [pike] *adj* stung; sour; (mus) staccato; (coll) batty; **piqué de** studded with ‖ *m* quilt; **descendre en piqué** to nose-dive

pique-assiette [pikasjɛt] *mf* (*pl* **-assiettes**) (coll) sponger

pique-feu [pikfø] *m invar* poker

pique-nique [piknik] *m* (*pl* **-niques**) picnic

pique-niquer [piknike] *intr* to picnic

piquer [pike] *tr* to sting; to prick; to pique; to stimulate; to quilt; to spur; to give a shot to; (mus) to play staccato; (slang) to filch; (slang) to pinch, to nab ‖ *intr* to turn sour; (aer) to nose-dive ‖ *ref* to be piqued; to spot; to give oneself a shot; se **piquer de** to take pride in; se **piquer pour** to take a fancy to

piquet [pikɛ] *m* peg, stake; picket; **piquet de grève** picket line

piqueter [pikte] §34 *tr* to stake out; to spot, dot

piquette [pikɛt] *f* poor wine; (coll) crushing defeat

pi·queur [pikœr] **-queuse** [køz] *mf* stitcher ‖ *m* huntsman; outrider

piqûre [pikyr] *f* sting, bite; prick; injection, shot; stitching; puncture; **piqûre de ver** moth hole

pirate [pirat] *m* pirate; **pirate de l'air** hijacker

pirater [pirate] *intr* to pirate

piraterie [piratri] *f* piracy; **piraterie aérienne** hijacking

pire [pir] §91 *adj comp & super* worse; worst ‖ *m* (the) worst

pirouette [pirwɛt] *f* pirouette

pirouetter [pirwete] *intr* to pirouette

pis [pi] *adj comp & super* worse;

worst ‖ *m* udder; **au pis aller** at worst; **de pis en pis** worse and worse; **(le) pis** (the) worst; **qui pis est** what's worse; **tant pis** so much the worse ‖ *adv comp & super* §91 worse; worst

pis-aller [pizale] *m invar* makeshift

piscine [pisin] *f* swimming pool

pissenlit [pisãli] *m* dandelion

pisser [pise] *tr* (coll) to spout (*water*); (coll) to leak; (slang) to pass (*e.g., blood*); **pisser de la copie** (slang) to be a hack writer ‖ *intr* (slang) to urinate

pisse-vinaigre [pisvinegr] *m invar* (coll) skinflint

pissotière [pisɔtjɛr] *f* (coll) street urinal

pistache [pistaʃ] *f* pistachio

piste [pist] *f* track; trail; ring (*of, e.g., circus*); rink; lane (*of highway*); à **double piste** four-lane (*highway*); **piste cavalière** bridle path; **piste cyclable** bicycle path; **piste d'atterrissage** landing strip; **piste de danse** dance floor; **piste d'envoi** runway; **piste pour skieurs** ski run; **piste sonore** sound track

pister [piste] *tr* to track, trail

pistolet [pistɔlɛ] *m* pistol; spray gun; (coll) card; **pistolet à bouchon** popgun; **pistolet d'arçon** horse pistol; **pistolet mitrailleur** submachine gun

piston [pistɔ̃] *m* piston; (coll) pull

pistonner [pistɔne] *tr* (coll) to push, to back

pitance [pitãs] *f* ration; food

pi·teux [pitø] **-teuse** [tøz] *adj* pitiful, sorry, sad

pitié [pitje] *f* pity; **à faire pitié** (coll) very badly; **par pitié!** for pity's sake!; **quelle pitié!** how awful!

piton [pitɔ̃] *m* screw eye; peak

pitou [pitu] *m* (Canad) dog; (Canad) tyke

pitoyable [pitwajabl] *adj* pitiful

pitre [pitr] *m* clown

pittoresque [pitɔresk] *adj* picturesque

pivoine [pivwan] *f* peony

pivot [pivo] *m* pivot

pivoter [pivɔte] *intr* to pivot

P.J. [peʒi] *f* (letterword) (**police judiciaire**) (coll) police (*dealing with criminal cases*)

placage [plakaʒ] *m* veneering; plating

placard [plakar] *m* cupboard; closet; placard, poster; (typ) galley

placarder [plakarde] *tr* to placard; (typ) to print in galleys

place [plas] *f* place; city square; room; seat; job, position; fare; **sur place** on the spot

placement [plasmã] *m* placement; investment; **de placement** employment (*agency*)

placer [plase] §51 *tr* to place; to invest; to slip in ‖ *ref* to seat oneself; to rank; to get a job; to take place

pla·ceur [plasœr] **-ceuse** [søz] *mf* employment agent ‖ *m* usher

placide [plasid] *adj* placid

pla·cier [plasje] **-cière** [sjɛr] *mf* agent, representative

plafond [plafɔ̃] *m* ceiling

plafonner [plafɔne] *intr*—**plafonner (à)** to hit the top (at)

plafonnier [plafɔnje] *m* ceiling light; (aut) dome light

plage [plaʒ] *f* beach; band (*of record*); (poetic) clime

plagiaire [plaʒjɛr] *mf* plagiarist

plagiat [plaʒja] *m* plagiarism

plagier [plaʒje] *tr & intr* to plagiarize

plagiste [plaʒist] *mf* beach concessionaire

plaider [plede] *tr* to argue (*a case*); to plead (*e.g., ignorance*) ‖ *intr* to plead; to go to law

plai·deur [pledœr] **-deuse** [døz] *mf* litigant

plaidoirie [pledwari] *f* pleading

plaidoyer [pledwaje] *m* appeal (*of lawyer to judge or jury*)

plaie [ple] *f* wound, sore; plague; **plaie en séton** flesh wound

plai·gnant [pleɲɑ̃] **-gnante** [ɲɑ̃t] *mf* plaintiff

plain [plɛ̃] *m* high tide

plaindre [plɛ̃dr] §15 *tr* to pity ‖ *ref* to complain

plaine [plen] *f* plain

plain-pied [plɛ̃pje] *m*—**de plain-pied** on the same floor; (fig) on an equal footing

plainte [plɛ̃t] *f* complaint; moan

plain·tif [plɛ̃tif] **-tive** [tiv] *adj* plaintive

plaire [plɛr] §52 *intr* (with *dat*) to please; (with *dat*) to like, e.g., **le lait lui plaît** he likes milk; **s'il vous plaît** please ‖ *ref* to be pleased; to enjoy oneself; to like one another; **se plaire à** to like it in, e.g., **je me plais à la campagne** I like it in the country

plaisance [plezɑ̃s] *f*—**de plaisance** pleasure (*e.g., boat*)

plai·sant [plezɑ̃] **-sante** [zɑ̃t] *adj* pleasant; funny ‖ *m*—**mauvais plaisant** practical joker

plaisanter [plezɑ̃te] *tr* to poke fun at ‖ *intr* to joke

plaisanterie [plezɑ̃tri] *f* joke; joking

plaisantin [plezɑ̃tɛ̃] *adj masc* roguish, waggish ‖ *m* wag

plaisir [plezir] *m* pleasure; **à plaisir** without cause; at one's pleasure; **au plaisir (de vous revoir)** good-by; **faire plaisir à** to please, give pleasure to

plan [plɑ̃] **plane** [plan] *adj* even, flat; plane (*angle*) ‖ *m* plan; design; (geom) plane; **au deuxième plan** in the background; **au premier plan** in the foreground; downstage; **au troisième plan** far in the background; **gros plan** (mov) close-up; **laisser en plan** (coll) to leave stranded; (coll) to put off, delay; **lever un plan** to survey; **plan de travail** work schedule; **rester en plan** (coll) to remain in suspense; **sur le plan de** from the point of view of ‖ *f* see **plane**

planche [plɑ̃ʃ] *f* board; plank; (hort) bed; (typ) plate; (slang) blackboard; **faire la planche** to float on one's back; **planche de bord** instrument panel; **planche de débarquement** gangplank; **planche de salut** sheet anchor

planchéier [plɑ̃ʃeje] *tr* to floor; to board

plancher [plɑ̃ʃe] *m* floor; **le plancher des vaches** (coll) terra firma

plane [plan] *f* drawknife

planer [plane] *tr* to plane ‖ *intr* to hover; to glide; to float; **planer sur** to overlook, to sweep (*e.g., a landscape with one's eyes*); (fig) to hover over

planète [planɛt] *f* planet

planeur [planœr] *m* glider

planeuse [planøz] *f* planing machine

planification [planifikɑsjɔ̃] *f* planning

planifier [planifje] *tr* to plan

planning [planiŋ] *m* detailed plan; **planning familial** birth control

plan-plan [plɑ̃plɑ̃] *adv* (coll) quietly, without hurrying

planque [plɑ̃k] *f* (coll) soft job; (slang) hideout

planquer [plɑ̃ke] *tr* to hide ‖ *ref* (mil) to take cover; (slang) to hide out

plant [plɑ̃] *m* planting; bed, patch; seedling, sapling

plantation [plɑ̃tɑsjɔ̃] *f* planting; plantation; **plantation de cheveux** hairline; head of hair

plante [plɑ̃t] *f* plant; sole

plan·té -tée [plɑ̃te] *adj* set, situated

planter [plɑ̃te] *tr* to plant; to set; **planter là** to give the slip to ‖ *ref* to stand

planteur [plɑ̃tœr] *m* planter

plantoir [plɑ̃twar] *m* (hort) dibble

planton [plɑ̃tɔ̃] *m* (mil) orderly

plantu·reux [plɑ̃tyrø] **-reuse** [røz] *adj* abundant; fertile; (coll) buxom

plaque [plak] *f* plate; plaque; splotch; **plaque à crêpes** pancake griddle; **plaque croûteuse** scab; **plaque d'immatriculation**, **plaque minéralogique** (aut) license plate; **plaque tournante** (rr) turntable; (fig) hub (*of a city*)

plaquer [plake] *tr* to plate; to veneer; to plaster down (*one's hair*); to strike (*a chord*); (football) to tackle; (coll) to jilt; **plaquer à l'électricité** to electroplate ‖ *ref* to lie flat; (aer) to pancake

plaquette [plakɛt] *f* plaque; pamphlet; (histology) platelet

plastic [plastik] *m* plastic bomb

plastique [plastik] *adj* plastic ‖ *m* plastics ‖ *f* plastic art

plastron [plastrɔ̃] *m* shirt front; breastplate; hostile contingent (*in war games*)

plastronner [plastrɔne] *intr* (fig) to throw out one's chest

plat [pla] **plate** [plat] *adj* flat; even; smooth (*sea*); dead (*calm*); corny (*joke*); **à plat** run-down; flat ‖ *m* dish; platter; course (*of meal*); flat (*of hand*); blade (*of oar*); face (*of hammer*); **plat cuisiné** platter, short-order meal; **plat de côtes** sparerib; **plat du jour** today's special, chef's special; **plat principal, plat de résistance** entree; **plats** (bb) boards

platane [platan] *m* plane tree; **faux platane** sycamore

pla·teau [plato] *m* (*pl* -**teaux**) plateau; tray; shelf; platform; plate; pan (*of scale*); (mov, telv) set; (rr) flatcar; (theat) stage; **plateau porte-disque** turntable (*of phonograph*); **plateau tournant** revolving stage

plate-bande [platbãd] *f* (*pl* **plates-bandes**) flower bed

plate-forme [platfɔrm] *f* (*pl* **plates-formes**) platform; (rr) flatcar

platine [platin] *m* platinum || *f* plate; platen; lock (*of gun*); stage (*of microscope*)

plati·né -**née** [platine] *adj* platinum-plated; platinum

platitude [platityd] *f* platitude; flatness; obsequiousness

Platon [platɔ̃] *m* Plato

plâtre [platr] *m* plaster; plaster cast; **essuyer les plâtres** to be the first occupant of a new house; **plâtre à mouler** plaster of Paris

plâtrer [platre] *tr* to plaster; to put in a cast; to fertilize || *ref* (coll) to pile on the make-up or face powder

plausible [plozibl] *adj* plausible

plébéien [plebejɛ̃] **plébéienne** [plebe-jɛn] *adj* & *mf* plebeian

plein pleine [plɛ̃ [plɛn] *adj* full; round, plump; solid (*bar, wheel, wire, etc.*); continuous (*line*); heavy (*heart*); in foal, with calf, etc.; (coll) drunk; **plein aux as** (coll) well-heeled; **plein de** full of; covered with; preoccupied with; **plein de soi** self-centered || (when standing before *noun*) *adj* full; high (*tide*); **en plein** + *noun* in the midst of the + *noun*, right in the + *noun*; at the height of the (*season*); in the open (*air*); out at (*sea*), on the high (*seas*); in broad (*daylight*); in the dead of (*winter*) || *m* full (*of the moon*); bull's-eye; downstroke; **battre son plein** to be in full swing; **en plein** plumb, plump, squarely; **faire le plein (de)** to fill up the tank (with) || **plein** *adv* full; **tout plein** very much

plein-emploi [plenãplwa] *m* full employment

pleu·rard [plœrar] -**rarde** [rard] *adj* (coll) whimpering || *mf* (coll) whimperer

pleurer [plœre] *tr* to weep over; **pleurer misère** to complain of being poor || *intr* to cry, weep; **pleurer à chaudes larmes** to weep bitterly

pleurésie [plœrezi] *f* pleurisy

pleu·reur [plœrœr] -**reuse** [røz] *adj* weeping || *f* paid mourner

pleurnicher [plœrniʃe] *intr* to whimper, snivel

pleurs [plœr] *mpl* tears

pleutre [pløtr] *adj* (coll) cowardly || *m* (coll) coward

pleuvasser [pløvase] *intr* (coll) to drizzle

pleuvoir [pløvwar] §53 *intr* & *impers* to rain; **pleuvoir à verse, à flots,** or **à seaux** to rain buckets

pli [pli] *m* fold; pleat; bend (*of arm or leg*); hollow (*of knee*); letter; envelope; undulation (*of ground*); (cards) trick; **faux pli** crease, wrinkle; **petit pli** tuck; **sous ce pli** enclosed, herewith; **sous pli cacheté** in a sealed envelope; **sous pli distinct** or **séparé** under separate cover

pliage [plijaʒ] *m* folding

pliant [plijã] **pliante** [plijãt] *adj* folding; collapsible; **pliant** || *m* campstool, folding chair

plier [plije] *tr* to fold; to bend; to force || *intr* to fold; to bend; to yield; **ne pas plier, s.v.p.** (formula on envelope) please do not bend || *ref* to fold; to yield; to fall back (*said of army*)

plisser [plise] *tr* to pleat; to crease; to wrinkle; to squint (*the eyes*) || *intr* to fold || *ref* to wrinkle; to pucker up (*said of mouth*)

plomb [plɔ̃] *m* lead; shot; seal; plumb; sinker (*of fishline*); (elec) fuse; **à plomb** plumb, vertical; straight down, directly; **faire sauter un plomb** to burn or blow out a fuse

plombage [plɔ̃baʒ] *m* filling (*of tooth*); sealing (*e.g., at customs*)

plombagine [plɔ̃baʒin] *f* graphite

plom·bé -**bée** [plɔ̃be] *adj* leaden; in bond, sealed; filled (*tooth*); livid (*hue*)

plomber [plɔ̃be] *tr* to cover with lead; to seal; to plumb; to fill (*a tooth*); to make livid; to roll (*the ground*)

plomberie [plɔ̃bri] *f* plumbing; plumbing-supply store; leadwork

plombeur [plɔ̃bœr] *m* (mach) roller

plombier [plɔ̃bje] *m* plumber; worker in lead

plonge [plɔ̃ʒ] *f* dishwashing

plon·geant [plɔ̃ʒã] -**geante** [ʒãt] *adj* plunging; from above

plongée [plɔ̃ʒe] *f* plunge; dive; dip, slope; **en plongée** submerged

plongeoir [plɔ̃ʒwar] *m* diving board

plongeon [plɔ̃ʒɔ̃] *m* plunge; dive; (football) tackle; **plongeon de haut vol** high dive

plonger [plɔ̃ʒe] §38 *tr* to plunge; to thrust, to stick || *intr* to plunge; to dive; (coll) to have a good view; **plonger raide** to crash-dive || *ref*—**se plonger dans** to immerse oneself in; to give oneself over to

plon·geur [plɔ̃ʒœr] -**geuse** [ʒøz] *mf* diving || *mf* diver; dishwasher (*in restaurant*) || *m* (mach) plunger; (orn) diver

plot [plo] *m* (elec) contact point

ployer [plwaje] §47 *tr* & *intr* to bend

pluches [plyʃ] *fpl* (mil) K.P.

pluie [plɥi] *f* rain; shower; **pluies radioactives** fallout

plumage [plymaʒ] *m* plumage

plumard [plymar] *m*—aller au plumard (slang) to hit the hay

plume [plym] *f* feather; pen; penpoint

plu-meau [plymo] *m* (*pl* -meaux) feather duster

plumer [plyme] *tr* to pluck; (coll) to fleece ‖ *intr* to feather one's oar

plumet [plyme] *m* plume

plu-meux [plymø] -meuse [møz] *adj* feathery

plumier [plymje] *m* pencil box

plupart [plypar] *f*—la plupart most; the most; for the most part; la plupart de most; the most; most of, the majority of; la plupart d'entre nous (eux) most of us (them); pour la plupart for the most part

plu-riel -rielle [plyrjɛl] *adj & m* plural; au pluriel in the plural

plus [ply] ([plyz] before vowel; [plys] in final position) *m* plus; au plus, tout au plus at the most, at best; at the latest; at the outside; d'autant plus all the more so; de plus more; moreover, besides; de plus en plus more and more; en plus extra; en plus de in addition to, besides; le plus, la plus, les plus (the) most; le plus de the most; le plus que as much as, as fast as; ni . . . non plus nor . . . either, e.g., ni moi non plus nor I either; ni plus ni moins neither more nor less; non plus neither, not . . . either; plus de more, e.g., plus de chaleur more heat; no more, e.g., plus de potage no more soup; qui plus est what is more, moreover ‖ *adv comp & super* §91 more; plus + *adj* most + *adj*, extremely + *adj*; (le) plus . . . (the) most . . ., e.g., ce que j'aime le plus what I like (the) most; le (or son, etc.) plus + *adj* the (or his, etc.) most; ne . . . plus §90 no more, no longer; ne . . . plus que §90 now only, e.g., il n'y a plus que mon oncle there is now only my uncle; on ne peut plus + *adj* or *adv* extremely + *adj* or *adv*; plus de (followed by numeral) more than; plus jamais never more; plus . . . plus (or moins) the more . . . the more (or the less); plus que more than; plus tôt sooner ‖ *prep* plus

plusieurs [plyzjœr] *adj & pron indef* several

plus-que-parfait [plyskəparfɛ] *m* pluperfect

plus-value [plyvaly] *f* (*pl* -values) appreciation; increase; surplus; extra cost; surplus value (*in Marxian economics*)

Plutarque [plytark] *m* Plutarch

Pluton [plytɔ̃] *m* Pluto

plutonium [plytɔnjɔm] *m* plutonium

plutôt [plyto] *adv* rather; instead; plutôt . . . que rather . . . than

pluvier [plyvje] *m* (orn) plover

plu-vieux [plyvjø] -vieuse [vjøz] *adj* rainy

pneu [pnø] *m* (*pl* pneus) tire; express letter (*by Parisian tube*); pneu ballon or confort balloon tire; pneu de secours spare tire

pneumatique [pnømatik] *adj* pneumatic ‖ *m* tire; express letter (*by Parisian tube*)

pneumonie [pnømɔni] *f* pneumonia

pochade [pɔʃad] *f* sketch

po-chard [pɔʃar] -charde [ʃard] *mf* (coll) boozer, guzzler

poche [pɔʃ] *f* pocket; bag, pouch; crop (*of bird*)

po-ché -chée [pɔʃe] *adj* poached; black (*eye*)

pocher [pɔʃe] *tr* to poach; to dash off (*a sketch*)

pochette [pɔʃɛt] *f* folder; book (*of matches*); kit; fancy handkerchief; pochette à disque record jacket; pochette surprise surprise package

pocheuse [pɔʃøz] *f* egg poacher

pochoir [pɔʃwar] *m* stencil

poêle [pwal] *m* stove; pall; canopy ‖ *f* frying pan

poêlon [pwalɔ̃] *m* saucepan

poème [pɔɛm] *m* poem; poème symphonique tone poem

poésie [pɔezi] *f* poetry; poem

poète [pɔɛt] *mf* poet

poétesse [pɔetɛs] *f* poetess

poétique [pɔetik] *adj* poetic(al) ‖ *f* poetics

pogrom [pɔgrɔm] *m* pogrom

poids [pwa], [pwɑ] *m* weight; poids lourd truck

poi-gnant [pwaɲɑ̃] -gnante [ɲɑ̃t] *adj* poignant

poignard [pwaɲar] *m* dagger

poignarder [pwaɲarde] *tr* to stab

poigne [pwaɲ] *f* grip, grasp; à poigne strong, energetic

poignée [pwaɲe] *f* handful; handle; grip; hilt; poignée de main handshake

poignet [pwaɲe] *m* wrist; cuff; poignet mousquetaire French cuff

poil [pwal] *m* hair; bristle; nap, pile; coat (*of animals*); à poil naked; bareback; au poil (slang) peachy; avoir un poil dans la main (coll) to be lazy; de mauvais poil (coll) in a bad mood; de tout poil (coll) of every shade and hue; poil follet down; reprendre du poil de la bête (coll) to be one's own self again; se mettre à poil to strip to the skin

poi-lu -lue [pwaly] *adj* hairy ‖ *m* (mil) doughboy

poinçon [pwɛ̃sɔ̃] *m* punch; stamp; hallmark; poinçon à glace ice pick

poinçonner [pwɛ̃sɔne] *tr* to punch; to stamp; to prick; to hallmark

poinçonneuse [pwɛ̃sɔnøz] *f* stamping machine; ticket punch

poindre [pwɛ̃dr] §35 *intr* to dawn; to sprout

poing [pwɛ̃] *m* first; dormir à poings fermés to sleep like a log

point [pwɛ̃] *m* point; stitch; period (*used also in French to mark the divisions of whole numbers*); hole (*in a strap*); mark (*on a test*); (aer, naut) position; (typ) point; **à point** at the right moment; to a turn, medium; **à point nommé** in the nick of time; **à tel point que** to such a degree that; **au dernier point** to the utmost degree; **de point en point** exactly to the letter; **de tout point, en tout point** entirely; **deux points** colon; **faire le point** to take stock, to get one's bearings; **mettre au point** to focus; to adjust, to tune up; to develop, to perfect; **mettre les points sur les i** to dot one's i's; **point d'appui** fulcrum; base of operations; **point de bâti** (sewing) tack; **point de départ** starting point; **point de repère** point of reference, guide; (surv) bench mark; (fig) landmark; **point d'estime** dead reckoning; **point d'exclamation** exclamation point; **point d'interrogation** question mark; **point d'orgue** (mus) pause; **point du jour** break of day; **point et virgule** semicolon; **point mort** dead center; (aut) neutral; **points et traits** dots and dashes ‖ *adv*—**ne . . . point** §90 not; not at all

pointage [pwɛtaʒ] *m* checking; check mark; aiming

pointe [pwɛt] *f* point; tip; peak; head (*of* arrow); tine (*e.g., of bullet*); toe (*of* shoe); twinge (*of* pain); dash (*of, e.g.,* vanilla); suggestion, touch; witty phrase, quip; (geog) cape, point; (mil) spearhead; **à pointes** spiked (*shoes*); **de pointe** peak (*e.g., hours*); **discuter sur les pointes d'épingle** to split hairs; **en pointe** tapering; **faire des pointes** to toe-dance; **pointe d'aiguille** needlepoint; **pointe de Paris** wire nail; **pointe de vitesse** spurt; **pointe du jour** daybreak; **sur la pointe des pieds** on tiptoe

poin·teau [pwɛto] *m* (*pl* **-teaux**) checker; needle

pointer [pwɛtœr] *m* pointer (*dog*) ‖ [pwɛte] *tr* to check off; to check in; to prick up (*the ears*); to dot ‖ *intr* to rise, to soar skywards; to stand out; to sprout ‖ *ref* to check in, to show up

poin·teur [pwɛtœr] **-teuse** [tøz] *mf* checker; scorer; timekeeper; gunner; (*dog*) pointer

pointillé [pwɛtije] *m* perforated line

pointil·leux [pwɛtijø] **pointil·leuse** [pwɛtijøz] *adj* punctilious; touchy; captious

poin·tu ·tue [pwɛty] *adj* pointed; shrill; (fig) touchy

pointure [pwɛtyr] *f* size

poire [pwar] *f* pear; bulb (*of camera, syringe, horn, etc.*); (slang) mug; (slang) sucker, sap; **couper la poire en deux** to split the difference; **garder une poire pour la soif** to put something aside for a rainy day; **poire à poudre** powder flask; **poire électrique** pear-shaped switch

poi·reau [pwaro] *m* (*pl* **-reaux**) (bot) leek

poirée [pware] *f* (bot) Swiss chard

poirier [pwarje] *m* pear tree

pois [pwa], [pwɑ] *m* pea; polka dot; **petits pois, pois verts** peas; **pois cassés** split peas; **pois chiche** chickpea; **pois de senteur** sweet pea

poison [pwazɔ̃] *m* poison

pois·sard [pwasar] **pois·sarde** [pwasard] *adj* vulgar ‖ *f* fishwife

poisser [pwase] *tr* to coat with wax or pitch ‖ *intr* to be sticky

pois·seux [pwasø] **pois·seuse** [pwasøz] *adj* sticky

poisson [pwasɔ̃] *m* fish; **poisson d'avril** April Fool (*joke, trick*); **poisson rouge** goldfish

poisson-chat [pwasɔ̃ʃa] *m* (*pl* **poissons-chats**) catfish

poissonnerie [pwasɔnri] *f* fish market

poisson·nier [pwasɔnje] **poisson·nière** [pwasɔnjɛr] *mf* dealer in fish ‖ *f* fishwife; fish kettle

poitrail [pwatraj] *m* breast

poitrinaire [pwatrinɛr] *adj & mf* (pathol) consumptive

poitrine [pwatrin] *f* chest; breast; bosom

poivre [pwavr] *m* pepper

poivrer [pwavre] *tr* to pepper

poivrier [pwavrije] *m* pepper plant; pepper shaker

poivrière [pwavrijɛr] *f* pepper shaker; pepper plantation

poivron [pwavrɔ̃] *m* pepper; sweet pepper plant

poix [pwa], [pwɑ] *f* pitch; **poix sèche** resin

poker [pɔkɛr] *m* poker; four of a kind

polaire [pɔlɛr] *adj* pole, polar

polariser [pɔlarize] *tr* to polarize

pôle [pol] *m* pole

po·li ·lie [pɔli] *adj* polished; polite ‖ *m* polish, gloss

police [pɔlis] *f* police; policy; **police d'assurance** insurance policy

policer [pɔlise] §51 *tr* to civilize; (obs) to police

Polichinelle [pɔliʃinɛl] *m* Punch; **de polichinelle** open (*secret*)

poli·cier [pɔlisje] **-cière** [sjɛr] *adj* police (*investigation, dog, etc.*); detective (*e.g., story*) ‖ *m* plain-clothes man, detective

polio [pɔljo] *mf* (coll) polio victim ‖ *f* (coll) polio

polir [pɔlir] *tr* to polish

polissoir [pɔliswar] *m* polisher

polis·son [pɔlisɔ̃] **polis·sonne** [pɔlisɔn] *adj* smutty ‖ *mf* scamp, rascal

politesse [pɔlites] *f* politeness; **politesses** civilities, compliments

politicard [pɔlitikar] *m* unscrupulous politician

politi·cien [pɔlitisjɛ̃] **-cienne** [sjɛn] *adj* short-sighted; insincere ‖ *mf* politician

politique [pɔlitik] *adj* political; prudent, wise ‖ *m* politician; statesman ‖ *f* politics; policy; cunning, shrewdness

pollen [pɔllɛn] *m* pollen

polluer [pɔllɥe] *tr* to pollute

polo [pɔlo] *m* polo

Pologne [pɔlɔɲ] *f* Poland; **la Pologne** Poland

polo·nais [pɔlɔnɛ] **-naise** [nɛz] *adj* Polish || *m* Polish (*language*) || (*cap*) *mf* Pole

polonium [pɔlɔnjɔm] *m* polonium

pol·tron [pɔltrɔ̃] **-tronne** [trɔn] *adj* cowardly || *mf* coward

polycopie [pɔlikɔpi] *f* mimeographing; tiré à la **polycopie** mimeographed

polycopié [pɔlikɔpje] *m* mimeographed university lectures

polycopier [pɔlikɔpje] *tr* to mimeograph

polygame [pɔligam] *adj* polygamous || *mf* polygamist

polyglotte [pɔliglɔt] *adj* polyglot || *mf* polyglot, linguist

polygone [pɔligɔn] *m* polygon; shooting range

polynôme [pɔlinom] *m* polynomial

polype [pɔlip] *m* polyp

polythéiste [pɔliteist] *adj* polytheistic || *mf* polytheist

pom [pɔ̃] *interj* bang!

pommade [pɔmad] *f* pomade; **passer de la pommade à** (coll) to soft-soap

pomme [pɔm] *f* apple; ball, knob; head (*of lettuce*); **pomme de discorde** bone of contention; **pomme de pin** pine cone; **pomme de terre** potato; **pommes chips** potato chips; **pommes de terre au four** baked potatoes; **pommes de terre en robe de chambre** *en* **robe des champs**, or **en chemise** potatoes in their jackets; **pommes de terre sautées** fried potatoes; **pommes frites** French fried potatoes; **pommes soufflées** potato puffs; **pommes vapeur** boiled potatoes; **steamed potatoes**

pom·meau [pɔmo] *m* (*pl* **-meaux**) pommel; butt (*of fishing pole*)

pomme·lé [pɔmle] *adj* dappled; fleecy (*clouds*); mackerel (*sky*)

pommette [pɔmɛt] *f* cheekbone

pommier [pɔmje] *m* apple tree

pompe [pɔ̃p] *f* pomp; pump; **à la pompe** on draught; **pompe à incendie** fire engine; **pompe aspirante** suction pump; **pompes funèbres** funeral

pomper [pɔ̃pe] *tr* to pump; to suck in

pompette [pɔ̃pɛt] *adj* (coll) tipsy

pom·peux [pɔ̃pø] **-peuse** [pøz] *adj* pompous; high-flown

pom·pier [pɔ̃pje] **-pière** [pjɛr] *adj* conventional; pretentious || *mf* fitter || *m* fireman

pompiste [pɔ̃pist] *mf* filling-station attendant

pomponner [pɔ̃pɔne] *tr & ref* to dress up

ponçage [pɔ̃saʒ] *m* sandpapering; pumicing

ponce [pɔ̃s] *f* pumice stone

pon·ceau [pɔ̃so] (*pl* **-ceaux**) *adj* poppy-red || *m* rude bridge; culvert

poncer [pɔ̃se] §51 *tr* to sandpaper; to pumice

poncho [pɔ̃tʃo] *m* poncho

poncif [pɔ̃sif] *m* banality

ponctualité [pɔ̃ktɥalite] *f* punctuality

ponctuation [pɔ̃ktɥasjɔ̃] *f* punctuation

ponc·tuel -tuelle [pɔ̃ktɥɛl] *adj* punctual

ponctuer [pɔ̃ktɥe] *tr* to punctuate

pondération [pɔ̃derasjɔ̃] *f* balance; weighting

pondé·ré -rée [pɔ̃dere] *adj* moderate, well-balanced; weighted

pondérer [pɔ̃dere] §10 *tr* to balance; to weight

pondeuse [pɔ̃døz] *f* layer (*hen*); (coll) prolific woman

pondre [pɔ̃dr] *tr* to lay (*an egg*); (coll) to turn out (*a book*); (slang) to bear (*a child*) || *intr* to lay

poney [pɔnɛ] *m* pony

pont [pɔ̃] *m* bridge; (naut) deck; **faire le pont** (coll) to take the intervening day or days off; **pont aérien** airlift; **pont arrière** (aut) rear-axle assembly; **pont cantilever**, **pont à consoles** cantilever bridge; **ponts et chaussées** [pɔ̃ze/ose] highway department; **pont suspendu** suspension bridge

ponte [pɔ̃t] *f* egg laying; eggs

pontet [pɔ̃tɛ] *m* trigger guard

pontife [pɔ̃tif] *m* pontiff

pont-levis [pɔ̃lvi] *m* (*pl* **ponts-levis**) drawbridge

ponton [pɔ̃tɔ̃] *m* pontoon; landing stage

pont-promenade [pɔ̃prɔmnad] *m* (*pl* **ponts-promenades**) promenade deck

pool [pul] *m* pool (*combine*)

pope [pɔp] *m* Orthodox priest

popeline [pɔplin] *f* poplin

popote [pɔpɔt] *adj invar* (coll) stay-at-home || *f* (mil) mess; (coll) cooking; **faire la popote** (coll) to do the cooking oneself

populace [pɔpylas] *f* populace, rabble

populaire [pɔpylɛr] *adj* popular; vulgar, common

populariser [pɔpylarize] *tr* to popularize

popularité [pɔpylarite] *f* popularity

population [pɔpylasjɔ̃] *f* population

popu·leux [pɔpylø] **-leuse** [løz] *adj* populous; crowded

populo [pɔpylo] *m* (coll) rabble

porc [pɔr] *m* pig, hog; pork

porcelaine [pɔrsəlɛn] *f* porcelain; china

porcelet [pɔrsəlɛ] *m* piglet

porc-épic [pɔrkepik] *m* (*pl* **porcs-épics** [pɔrkepik]) porcupine

porche [pɔrʃ] *m* porch, portico

porcher [pɔrʃe] *m* swineherd

porcherie [pɔrʃəri] *f* pigpen

pore [pɔr] *m* pore

po·reux [pɔrø] **-reuse** [røz] *adj* porous

pornographie [pɔrnɔgrafi] *f* pornography

porphyre [pɔrfir] *m* porphyry

port [pɔr] *m* port; carrying; wearing; bearing; shipping charges; **arriver à bon port** to arrive safe; **port d'attache** home port; **port d'escale** port of call; **port franc** duty-free; **free port; port payé** postpaid

portable [pɔrtabl] *adj* portable; wearable

portail [pɔrtaj] *m* portal, gate

por·tant [pɔrtã] **-tante** [tãt] *adj* bearing; lifting; **être bien portant** to be in good health ‖ *m* handle

porta·tif [pɔrtatif] **-tive** [tiv] *adj* portable

porte [pɔrt] *f* door; doorway; gate; **fausse porte** blind door; **porte à deux battants** double door; **porte à tambour** revolving door; **porte battante** swinging door; **porte cochère** covered carriage entrance

porte-à-faux [pɔrtafo] *m invar*—**en porte-à-faux** out of line; (fig) in an untenable position

porte-aiguilles [pɔrtegɥi] *m invar* needle case

porte-allumettes [pɔrtalymet] *m invar* matchbox

porte-assiette [pɔrtasjet] *m* (*pl* **-assiette** or **-assiettes**) place mat

porte-avions [pɔrtavjɔ̃] *m invar* aircraft carrier

porte-bagages [pɔrtbagaʒ] *m invar* baggage rack

porte-bannière [pɔrtbanjer] *mf* (*pl* **-bannière** or **-bannières**) colorbearer

porte-bonheur [pɔrtbɔnœr] *m invar* good-luck charm

porte-carte [pɔrtəkart] *m* (*pl* **-carte** or **-cartes**) card case

porte-chapeaux [pɔrtʃapo] *m invar* hatrack

porte-cigarette [pɔrtsigaret] *m invar* cigarette holder

porte-cigarettes [pɔrtsigaret] *m invar* cigarette case

porte-clés or **porte-clefs** [pɔrtəkle] *m invar* key ring

porte-disques [pɔrtdisk] *m invar* record case

porte-documents [pɔrtdɔkymã] *m invar* letter case, portfolio

porte-drapeau [pɔrtdrapo] *m* (*pl* **-drapeau** or **-drapeaux**) standard-bearer

portée [pɔrte] *f* range, reach; import, significance; litter; (mus) staff; **à la portée de** within reach of; **à portée de la voix** within speaking distance; **à portée de l'oreille** within hearing distance; **hors de la portée de** out of reach of

portefaix [pɔrtəfe] *m* porter; dock hand

porte-fenêtre [pɔrtfənetr], [pɔrtəfnetr] *f* (*pl* **portes-fenêtres**) French window, French door

portefeuille [pɔrtəfœj] *m* portfolio; wallet, billfold

porteman·teau [pɔrtmãto] *m* (*pl* **-teaux**) clothes tree; **en portemanteau** square (*shoulders*)

porte-mine [pɔrtəmin] *m* (*pl* **-mine** or **mines**) mechanical pencil

porte-monnaie [pɔrtmɔne] *m invar* change purse

porte-parapluies [pɔrtparaplɥi] *m invar* umbrella stand

porte-parole [pɔrtparɔl] *m invar* spokesman, mouthpiece

porte-plume [pɔrtəplym] *m invar* penholder; **porte-plume réservoir** fountain pen

porter [pɔrte] *tr* to carry; to bear; to wear; to propose (*a toast*); **être porté sur** to have a weakness for; **porter à l'écran** (mov) to put on the screen ‖ *intr* to carry; **porter sur** to bear down on, to emphasize; to be aimed at ‖ *ref* to be worn: to proceed, to go; to be, e.g., **comment vous portez-vous?** how are you?; **se porter à** to indulge in; **se porter candidat** to run as a candidate

porte-savon [pɔrtsavɔ̃] *m* (*pl* **-savon** or **-savons**) soap dish

porte-serviettes [pɔrtservjet] *m invar* towel rack

por·teur [pɔrtœr] **-teuse** [tøz] *mf* porter; bearer; holder

porte-vêtement [pɔrtəvetmã] *m invar* clothes hanger

porte-voix [pɔrtəvwa] *m invar* megaphone; **mettre les mains en porte-voix** to cup one's hands

por·tier [pɔrtje] **-tière** [tjer] *mf* concierge ‖ *m* doorman ‖ *f* door (*of car*); portiere

portillon [pɔrtijɔ̃] *m* gate; (rr) side gate (*at crossing*); **refouler du portillon** (slang) to have bad breath

portion [pɔrsjɔ̃] *f* portion; share

portique [pɔrtik] *m* portico

porto [pɔrto] *m* port wine

portori·cain [pɔrtɔrikɛ̃] **-caine** [ken] *adj* Puerto Rican ‖ (*cap*) *mf* Puerto Rican

Porto Rico [pɔrtoriko] *f* Puerto Rico

portrait [pɔrtre] *m* portrait; **être tout le portrait de** to be the very image of; **portrait à mi-corps** half-length portrait; **portrait de face** full-faced portrait

portraitiste [pɔrtretist] *mf* portrait painter

portu·gais [pɔrtyge] **-gaise** [gez] *adj* Portuguese ‖ *m* Portuguese (*language*) ‖ (*cap*) *mf* Portuguese (*person*)

Portugal [pɔrtygal] *m*—**le Portugal** Portugal

pose [poz] *f* pose; laying, setting in place; (phot) exposure

po·sé **-sée** [poze] *adj* poised, steady, trained (*voice*)

posément [pozemã] *adv* calmly, steadily, carefully

posemètre [pozmetr] *m* (phot) light meter, exposure meter

poser [poze] *tr* to place; to arrange; to ask (*a question*); to set up (*a principle*) ‖ *intr* to pose ‖ *ref* to pose; to alight; to land; **se poser en** to set oneself up as

po·seur [pozœr] **-seuse** [zøz] *mf* layer; poseur; phony; **poseur d'affiches** billposter

posi·tif [pozitif] **-tive** [tiv] *adj & m* positive

position [pozisjɔ̃] *f* position

posséder [pɔsede] §10 *tr* to possess, own; to have a command of, to know perfectly ‖ *ref* to control oneself

possession [pɔsesjɔ̃] *f* possession

possibilité [pɔsibilite] f possibility

possible [pɔsibl] adj & m possible

postage [pɔstaʒ] m mailing

pos·tal -tale [pɔstal] adj (pl **-taux** [to]) postal

postdate [pɔstdat] f postdate

postdater [pɔstdate] tr to postdate

poste [pɔst] m post; station; set; position, job; **poste de douane** port of entry; **poste d'émetteur** broadcasting station; **poste de radio** radio set; **poste de repérage** tracking station; **poste de secours** first-aid station; **poste des malades** (nav) sick bay; **poste d'essence** gas station; **poste d'incendie** fire station; **poste supplémentaire** (telp) extension || f post, mail; **mettre à la poste** to mail; **poste restante** general delivery; **postes** post office department

poster [pɔste] tr to post || ref to lie in wait

postérité [pɔsterite] f posterity

posthume [pɔstym] adj posthumous

postiche [pɔstiʃ] adj false; detachable || m toupee; switch, false hair

pos·tier [pɔstje] **-tière** [tjɛr] mf postal clerk

postscolaire [pɔstskɔler] adj adult (education); extension (courses)

post-scriptum [pɔstskriptɔm] m invar postscript

postu·lant [pɔstylɑ̃] **-lante** [lɑ̃t] mf applicant, candidate; postulant

postuler [pɔstyle] tr to apply for || intr to apply; **postuler pour** to represent (a client)

posture [pɔstyr] f posture; situation

pot [po] m pot; pitcher, jug; jar; can; **découvrir le pot aux roses** (coll) to discover the secret; **payer les pots cassés** (coll) to pay the piper; **pot à bière** beer mug; **pot à fleurs** flowerpot; **pot d'échappement** (aut) muffler; **pot de noir** cloudy weather; **pot d'étain** pewter tankard; **tourner autour du pot** (coll) to beat about the bush

potable [pɔtabl] adj drinkable; (coll) acceptable, passable

potache [pɔtaʃ] m (coll) schoolboy

potage [pɔtaʒ] m soup; **potage de maïs** hominy; **pour tout potage** (lit) all told

pota·ger [pɔtaʒe] **-gère** [ʒɛr] adj vegetable || m vegetable garden

potasse [pɔtas] f potash

potasser [pɔtase] tr (coll) to bone up on || intr (coll) to grind away

potas·seur [pɔtasœr] **potas·seuse** [pɔtasøz] mf (coll) grind

potassium [pɔtasjɔm] m potassium

pot-au-feu [pɔtofø] adj invar (coll) home-loving || m invar beef stew

pot-de-vin [pɔdvɛ̃] m (pl **pots-de-vin**) bribe, money under the table

po·teau [pɔto] m (pl **-teaux**) post, pole; **poteau de but** goal post; **poteau indicateur** signpost

pote·lé -lée [pɔtle] adj chubby

potence [pɔtɑ̃s] f gallows; bracket

potentat [pɔtɑ̃ta] m potentate

poten·tiel -tielle [pɔtɑ̃sjel] adj & m potential

poterie [pɔtri] f pottery; metalware; **poterie mordorée** lusterware

poterne [pɔtern] f postern

potiche [pɔtiʃ] f large Oriental vase; (fig) figurehead

potin [pɔtɛ̃] m piece of gossip; racket; **faire du potin** (coll) to raise a row; **potins** gossip

potiner [pɔtine] intr to gossip

potion [posjɔ̃] f potion

potiron [pɔtirɔ̃] m pumpkin; **potiron lumineux** jack-o'-lantern

pou [pu] m (pl **poux**) louse

poubelle [pubel] f garbage can

pouce [pus] m thumb; big toe; inch; **manger sur le pouce** (coll) to eat on the run

poudre [pudr] f powder; face powder; **en poudre** powdered; granulated (sugar); **il n'a pas inventé la poudre** (coll) he's not so smart; **jeter de la poudre aux yeux de** to deceive; **poudre dentifrice** tooth powder; **se mettre de la poudre** to powder one's nose

poudrer [pudre] tr to powder

poudrerie [pudrəri] f powder mill

pou·dreux [pudrø] **-dreuse** [drøz] adj powdery; dusty || f sugar shaker

poudrier [pudrije] m compact

poudrière [pudrijer] f powder magazine; (fig) powder keg

poudroyer [pudrwaje] §47 intr to raise the dust; to shine through the dust

pouf [puf] m hassock, pouf || interj plop!; **faire pouf** (slang) to flop

pouffer [pufe] intr to burst out laughing

pouil·leux [pujø] **pouil·leuse** [pujøz] adj lousy; sordid || mf person covered with lice

pouillot [pujo] m (orn) warbler

poulailler [pulaje] m henhouse; (theat) peanut gallery

poulain [pulɛ̃] m colt, foal

poule [pul] f hen; chicken; (in games) pool; jackpot; (turf) sweepstakes; (coll) skirt, dame; (slang) tart, mistress; **ma poule** (coll) my pet; **poule au pot** chicken stew; **poule d'Inde** turkey hen; **poule mouillée** (coll) milksop; **tuer la poule aux œufs d'or** to kill the goose that lays the golden eggs

poulet [pule] m chicken; (coll) love letter; **mon petit poulet** (coll) my pet; **poulet d'Inde** turkey cock

poulette [pulet] f pullet; (coll) gal; **ma poulette** (coll) darling

pouliche [puliʃ] f filly

poulie [puli] f pulley; block

poulpe [pulp] m octopus

pouls [pu] m pulse; **tâter le pouls à** to feel the pulse of

poumon [pumɔ̃] m lung

poupe [pup] f (naut) stern, poop

poupée [pupe] f doll; dummy; sore finger; (mach) headstock

pou·pon [pupɔ̃] **-ponne** [pɔn] mf baby; chubby-faced youngster

pouponnière [pupɔnjer] *f* nursery

pour [pur] *m*—le pour et le contre the pros and the cons ‖ *adv*—pour lors then; pour peu que however little; pour que in order that; pour . . . que however, e.g., pour charmante qu'elle soit however charming she may be ‖ *prep* for; in order to; pour ainsi dire so to speak; pour cent per cent

pourboire [purbwar] *m* tip

pour·ceau [purso] *m* (*pl* -ceaux) swine, hog, pig

pourcentage [pursɑ̃taʒ] *m* percentage

pourchasser [purʃase] *tr* to hound

pourlécher [purleʃe] §10 *ref* to smack one's lips

pourparlers [purparle] *mpl* talks, parley, conference

pourpoint [purpwɛ̃] *m* doublet

pourpre [purpr] *adj* purple ‖ *m* purple (*violescent*) ‖ *f* purple (*deep red, crimson*)

pourquoi [purkwa] *m* why; le pourquoi et le comment the why and the wherefore ‖ *adv & conj* why; pourquoi pas? why not?

pour·ri -rie [puri] *adj* rotten; spoiled ‖ *m* rotten part

pourrir [purir] *tr, intr, & ref* to rot; to spoil; to corrupt

pourriture [purityr] *f* rot; decay; corruption

poursuite [pursɥit] *f* pursuit; (law) action, suit; (coll) spotlight

poursui·vant -vante [pursɥivɑ̃] -[vɑ̃t] *mf* pursuer; (law) plaintiff

poursuivre [pursɥivr] §67 *tr* to pursue, chase; to proceed with; to persecute; to sue ‖ *intr* to continue ‖ *ref* to be continued

pourtant [purtɑ̃] *adv* however, nevertheless, yet

pourtour [purtur] *m* circumference

pourvoi [purvwa] *m* (law) appeal

pourvoir [purvwar] §54 *tr*—pourvoir de to supply with, to provide with; to favor with ‖ *intr*—pourvoir à to provide for, to attend to ‖ *ref* (law) to appeal

pourvoyeur [purvwajœr] **pourvoyeuse** [purvwajøz] *mf* provider, supplier; caterer; pourvoyeurs gun crew

pourvu que [purvykə] *conj* provided that

pousse [pus] *f* shoot, sprout

pous·sé -sée [puse] *adj* elaborate; searching, exhaustive ‖ *f* push, shove; thrust; rise; pressure; (rok) thrust

pousse-café [puskafe] *m invar* liqueur

pousser [puse] *tr* to push, to shove, to egg on, to urge; to utter (*a cry*); to heave (*a sigh*); pousser plus loin to carry further ‖ *intr* to push, shove; to grow; to push on ‖ *ref* to push oneself forward

poussette [puset] *f* baby carriage

poussier [pusje] *m* coal dust

poussière [pusjer] *f* dust; powder; poussière d'eau spray; une pous-

sière a trifle; une poussière de a lot of

poussié·reux [pusjerø] -reuse [røz] *adj* dusty; powdery

pous·sif [pusif] **pous·sive** [pusiv] *adj* wheezy

poussin [pusɛ̃] *m* chick

poussoir [puswar] *m* push button

poutre [putr] *f* beam; joist; girder

poutrelle [putrel] *f* small girder

pouvoir [puvwar] *m* power; pouvoir d'achat purchasing power ‖ §55 *tr* to be able to do; je n'y puis rien I can't or cannot help it, I can do nothing about it ‖ *intr* to be able; on ne peut mieux couldn't be better; on ne peut plus I (we, they, etc.) can do no more; I'm (we're, they're, etc.) all in ‖ *aux* used to express 1) ability, e.g., elle peut prédire l'avenir she is able to predict the future; she can predict the future; 2) permission, e.g., vous pouvez partir you may go; e.g.; puis-je partir? may I go?; 3) possibility, e.g., il peut pleuvoir it may rain; e.g., il a pu oublier son parapluie he may have forgotten his umbrella; 4) optative, e.g., puisse-t-il venir! may he come! ‖ *impers ref*—il se peut que it is possible that, e.g., il se peut qu'il vienne ce soir it is possible that he may come this evening, he may come this evening; il se pourrait bien que it might well be that, e.g., il se pourrait bien qu'il vînt ce soir it might well be that he will come this evening, he may come this evening ‖ *ref* to be possible; cela ne se peut pas that is not possible

pragmatique [pragmatik] *adj* pragmatic(al)

prairie [preri], [preri] *f* meadow; les Prairies the prairie

praticable [pratikabl] *adj* practicable; passable ‖ *m* practicable stage property; (mov, telv) camera platform

prati·cien [pratisjɛ̃] -cienne [sjen] *mf* practitioner

prati·quant -quante [pratikɑ̃] -[kɑ̃t] *adj* practicing (*e.g., Catholic*); churchy ‖ *mf* churchgoer

pratique [pratik] *adj* practical ‖ *f* practice; contact, company; customer; libre pratique freedom of worship; (naut) freedom from quarantine

pratiquement [pratikmɑ̃] *adv* practically, in practice

pratiquer [pratike] *tr* to practice; to cut, make (*e.g., a hole*); to frequent; to read a great deal of ‖ *intr* to practice (*said, e.g., of doctor*); to practice one's religion ‖ *ref* to be practiced, done; to rule, prevail (*said of prices*)

pré [pre] *m* meadow; sur le pré on the field of honor (*dueling ground*)

préalable [prealabl] *adj* previous; preliminary ‖ *m* prerequisite; au préalable before, in advance

préambule [preɑ̃byl] *m* preamble

préau [preo] *m* (*pl* préaux) yard

préavis [preavi] *m* advance warning;

avec **préavis** person-to-person (*telephone call*)
précaire [preker] *adj* precarious
précaution [prekosjɔ̃] *f* precaution
précautionner [prekosjone] *tr* to caution || *intr* to be on one's guard
précaution‧neux [prekosjønø] **précaution‧neuse** [prekosjønøz] *adj* precautious
précé‧dent [presedã] **-dente** [dãt] *adj* preceding || *m* precedent
précéder [presede] §10 *tr* & *intr* to precede
précepte [presept] *m* precept
précep‧teur [preseptœr] **-trice** [tris] *mf* tutor
prêche [preʃ] *m* sermon
prêcher [preʃe] *tr* to preach; to preach to || *intr* to preach; **prêcher d'exemple** to practice what one preaches
prê‧cheur [preʃœr] **-cheuse** [ʃøz] *adj* preaching || *mf* sermonizer
pré‧cieux [presjø] **-cieuse** [sjøz] *adj* precious; valuable; affected
préciosité [presjozite] *f* preciosity (*French literary style corresponding to English euphuism*)
précipice [presipis] *m* precipice
précipi‧té **-tée** [presipite] *adj* hurried, precipitous || *m* precipitate
précipiter [presipite] *tr* to hurl || *ref* to hurl oneself; to precipitate; to hurry, rush
pré‧cis [presi] **-cise** [siz] *adj* precise; sharp, e.g., **trois heures précises** three o'clock sharp || *m* abstract, summary
préciser [presize] *tr* to specify || *intr* to be precise || *ref* to become clear; to take shape, to jell
précision [presizjɔ̃] *f* precision; **précisions** data
préci‧té **-tée** [presite] *adj* aforementioned
précoce [prekɔs] *adj* precocious; (bot) early
précon‧çu **-çue** [prekɔsy] *adj* preconceived
préconiser [prekɔnize] *tr* to advocate, recommend
précur‧seur [prekyrsœr] *adj masc* precursory || *m* forerunner, harbinger
prédateur [predatœr] *adj masc* predatory || *m* predatory animal
prédécesseur [predesesœr] *m* predecessor
prédicateur [predikatœr] *m* preacher
prédiction [prediksjɔ̃] *f* prediction
prédire [predir] §40 *tr* to predict
prédisposer [predispoze] *tr* to predispose
prédomi‧nant [predominã] **-nante** [nãt] *adj* predominant
préémi‧nent [preeminã] **-nente** [nãt] *adj* preeminent
préfabri‧qué **-quée** [prefabrike] *adj* prefabricated
préface [prefas] *f* preface
préfacer [prefase] §51 *tr* to preface
préfecture [prefektyr] *f* prefecture; **préfecture de police** police headquarters
préférable [preferabl] *adj* preferable

préférence [preferãs] *f* preference
préférer [prefere] §10 *tr* to prefer
préfet [prefe] *m* prefect; **préfet de police** police commissioner
préfixe [prefiks] *m* prefix
préfixer [prefikse] *tr* to prefix
préhistorique [preistorik] *adj* prehistoric
préjudice [preʒydis] *m* prejudice, detriment; **porter préjudice à** to injure, to harm; **sans préjudice de** without affecting
préjudiciable [preʒydisjabl] *adj* detrimental
préjudicier [preʒydisje] *intr* (with *dat*) to harm, damage
préjugé [preʒyʒe] *m* prejudice
préjuger [preʒyʒe] §38 *tr* to foresee || *intr*—**préjuger de** to prejudge
préjart [prelar] *m* tarpaulin
prélasser [prelɑse] *ref* to lounge
prélat [prela] *m* prelate
prélèvement [prelevmã] *m* deduction; sample; levy
prélever [prelve] §2 *tr* to set aside, deduct; to take (*a sample*); to levy; **prélever à** to take from
préliminaire [preliminer] *adj* & *m* preliminary
prélude [prelyd] *m* prelude
préluder [prelyde] *intr* to warm up (*said of singer, musician, etc.*); **préluder à** to prelude
prématu‧ré **-rée** [prematyre] *adj* premature
préméditer [premedite] *tr* to premeditate
prémices [premis] *fpl* first fruits; beginning
pre‧mier [prəmje] **-mière** [mjer] *adj* first; raw (*materials*); prime (*number*); the First, e.g., **Jean premier** John the First || (*when standing before noun*) *adj* first; prime (*minister*); maiden (*voyage*); early (*infancy*) || *m* first; **jeune premier** leading man; **premier de cordée** leader || *f* first; first class; (theat) première; **jeune première** leading lady || *pron* (*masc* & *fem*) first
premier-né [prəmjene] **première-née** [prəmjerne] (*pl* **premiers-nés**) *adj* & *mf* first-born
prémisse [premis] *f* premise
prémonition [premonisjɔ̃] *f* premonition
prémunir [premynir] *tr* to forewarn || *ref*—**se prémunir contre** to protect oneself against
pre‧nant [prənã] **-nante** [nãt] *adj* sticky; winning, pleasing
prendre [prãdr] §56 *tr* to take; to take on; to take up; to catch; to get (*to obtain and bring*); to steal (*a kiss*); to buy (*a ticket*); to make (*an appointment*); **à tout prendre** all things considered; **prendre de l'âge** to be getting old; **prendre la mer** to take to sea; **prendre l'eau** to leak; **prendre le large** to take to the open sea; **prendre q.ch. à qn** to take s.th. from s.o.; to charge s.o. s.th. (*i.e., a cer-*

tain sum of money); **prendre son temps** to take one's time || *intr* to catch (*said of fire*); to take root; to form (*said of ice*); to set (*said of mortar*); to stick (*to a pan or dish*); to catch on (*said of a style*); to turn (*right or left*); **prendre à droite** to bear to the right; **qu'est-ce qui lui prend?** what's come over him? || *ref* to get caught, to catch (*e.g.*, *on a nail*); to congeal; to clot; to curdle; to jam; to take from each other; **pour qui se prend-il?** who does he think he is?; **s'en prendre à qn de q.ch.** to blame s.o. for s.th.; **se prendre à** to begin to; **se prendre d'amitié** to strike up a friendship; **se prendre de vin** to get drunk; **s'y prendre** to go about it

pre·neur [prənœr] **-neuse** [nøz] *mf* taker; buyer; payee; lessee

prénom [prenɔ̃] *m* first name

prénommer [prenɔme] *tr* to name || *ref* **—il** (**elle**, etc.) **se prénomme** his (her, etc.) first name is

préoccupation [preɔkypɑsjɔ̃] *f* preoccupation

préoccuper [preɔkype] *tr* to preoccupy || *ref*—**se préoccuper de** to pay attention to; to be concerned about

prépara·teur [preparatœr] **-trice** [tris] *mf* laboratory assistant

préparatifs [preparatif] *mpl* preparations

préparation [preparɑsjɔ̃] *f* preparation; notice, warning

préparatoire [preparatwar] *adj* preparatory

préparer [prepare] *tr, intr, & ref* to prepare

prépondé·rant [prepɔ̃derɑ̃] **-rante** [rɑ̃t] *adj* preponderant

prépo·sé -sée [prepoze] *mf* employee, clerk; **préposé de la douane** customs officer; **préposé au vestiaire** hatcheck girl

préposer [prepoze] *tr*—**préposer qn à q.ch.** to put s.o. in charge of s.th.

préposition [prepozisjɔ̃] *f* preposition

prérogative [prerɔgativ] *f* prerogative

près [pre] *adv* near; **à beaucoup près** by far; **à cela près except for that; **à peu d'exceptions près** with few exceptions; **à peu près** about, practically; **à . . . près** except for; within, *e.g.*, **je peux vous dire l'heure à cinq minutes près** I can tell you what time it is within five minutes; **au plus près** to the nearest point; **de près** close; closely; **ici près** near here; **près de** near; nearly, about; alongside, at the side of; **près de** + *inf* about to + *inf*; **tout près** nearby, right here || *prep* near; to, at

présage [prezaʒ] *m* presage, foreboding

présager [prezaʒe] §38 *tr* to presage, forebode; to anticipate

pré-salé -salée [presale] *m* (*pl* **prés-salés**) salt-meadow sheep; salt-meadow mutton

presbyte [presbit] *adj* far-sighted || *mf* far-sighted person

presbytère [presbiter] *m* presbytery

presbyté·rien [presbiterjɛ̃] **-rienne** [rjɛn] *adj* & *mf* Presbyterian

presbytie [presbisi] *f* far-sightedness

prescription [preskripsjɔ̃] *f* prescription

prescrire [preskrir] §25 *tr* to prescribe || *ref* to be prescribed

préséance [preseɑ̃s] *f* precedence

présence [prezɑ̃s] *f* presence; attendance; **en présence** face to face

pré·sent -sente [prezɑ̃] **-sente** [zɑ̃t] *adj* present || *m* present, gift; (*gram*) present; **les présents** those present

présentable [prezɑ̃tabl] *adj* presentable

présenta·teur [prezɑ̃tatœr] **-trice** [tris] *mf* (*rad*) announcer; **présentateur de disques** disk jockey

présentation [prezɑ̃tɑsjɔ̃] *f* presentation; introduction; appearance; look, form (*of a new product*)

présentement [prezɑ̃tmɑ̃] *adv* right now

présenter [prezɑ̃te] *tr* to present; to introduce; to offer; to pay (*one's respects*) || *ref* to present oneself; to present itself; **se présenter à** to be a candidate for

présérie [preseri] *f* (*com*) trial run, sample run

préservatif [prezervatif] *m* preventive; condom

préserver [prezerve] *tr* to preserve

présidence [prezidɑ̃s] *f* presidency; chairmanship; presidential mansion

prési·dent [prezidɑ̃] **-dente** [dɑ̃t] *mf* president; chairman; presiding judge || *f* president's wife; chairwoman; **madame la présidente** madam chairman

présiden·tiel -tielle [prezidɑ̃sjɛl] *adj* presidential

présider [prezide] *tr* to preside over || *intr* to preside; **présider à** to preside over

présomp·tif [prezɔ̃ptif] **-tive** [tiv] *adj* presumptive, presumed

présomption [prezɔ̃psjɔ̃] *f* presumption

présomp·tueux [prezɔ̃ptɥø] **-tueuse** [tɥøz] *adj* presumptuous

presque [presk(ə)] *adv* almost, nearly; **presque jamais** hardly ever; **presque personne** scarcely anybody

presqu'île [preskil] *f* peninsula

pres·sant [presɑ̃] **-sante** [sɑ̃t] *adj* pressing, urgent

presse [pres] *f* press; hurry, rush; crowd; hand screw, clamp; **mettre sous presse** to go to press

pres·sé -sée [prese] *adj* pressed; pressing, urgent; squeezed

presse-bouton [presbutɔ̃] *adj invar* push-button (*warfare*)

presse-citron [presitrɔ̃] *m invar* lemon squeezer

pressentiment [presɑ̃timɑ̃] *m* presentiment, foreboding

pressentir [presɑ̃tir] §41 *tr* to have a foreboding of; to sound out

presse-papiers [prespapje] *m invar* paperweight

presse-purée [prespyre] *m invar* potato masher

presser [prese], [prese] *tr* to press; to squeeze; to hurry, hasten || *intr* to be urgent || *ref* to hurry; **se presser à** to crowd around

pressing [presiŋ] *m* dry cleaner's, tailor shop

pression [presjɔ̃] *f* pressure; snap fastener; **à la pression** on draught; **pression artérielle** blood pressure

pressoir [preswar] *m* press

pressurer [presyre] *tr* to press, squeeze; to bleed white, to wring money out of

pressuriser [presyrize] *tr* to pressurize

prestance [prestɑ̃s] *f* commanding appearance, dignified bearing

prestation [prestasjɔ̃] *f* taking (*of oath*); tax; allotment, allowance, benefit

preste [prest] *adj* nimble

prestidigita·teur [prestidiʒitatœr] **-trice** [tris] *mf* magician

prestidigitation [prestidiʒitasjɔ̃] *f* sleight of hand, legerdemain

prestige [prestiʒ] *m* prestige; illusion, magic

presti·gieux [prestiʒjø] **-gieuse** [ʒjøz] *adj* prestigious, famous; marvelous

présumer [prezyme] *tr* to presume; to presume to be || *intr* to presume; **présumer de** to presume upon

présupposer [presypoze] *tr* to presuppose

présure [prezyr] *f* rennet

prêt [pre] **prête** [pret] *adj* ready; **prêt à porter** ready-to-wear, ready-made; **prêt à tout** ready for anything || *m* loan

prêt-à-porter [pretaporte] *m* (*pl* **prêts-à-porter** [pretaporte]) ready-to-wear, ready-made clothes

prêt-bail [prebaj] *m invar* lend-lease

préten·dant [pretɑ̃dɑ̃] **-dante** [dɑ̃t] *mf* pretender || *m* suitor

prétendre [pretɑ̃dr] *tr* to claim; to require || *intr*—**prétendre à** to aspire to; to lay claim to

préten·du -due [pretɑ̃dy] *adj* so-called, alleged || *m* fiancé || *f* fiancée

prête-nom [pretnɔ̃] *m* (*pl* **-noms**) dummy, figurehead, straw man

prétentaine [pretɑ̃ten] *f*—**courir la prétentaine** (coll) to be on the loose; (coll) to have many love affairs

préten·tieux [pretɑ̃sjø] **-tieuse** [sjøz] *adj* pretentious

prétention [pretɑ̃sjɔ̃] *f* pretention, pretense; claim, pretensions

prêter [prete], [prete] *tr* to lend; to give (*e.g., help*); to pay (*attention*); to take (*an oath*); to impart (*e.g., luster*); to attribute, ascribe || *intr* to lend; to stretch; **prêter à** to lend itself to || *ref*—**se prêter à** to lend itself to; to be a party to, to countenance; to indulge in

prê·teur [pretœr] **-teuse** [tøz] *mf* lender; **prêteur sur gages** pawnbroker

prétexte [pretekst] *m* pretext

prétexter [pretekste] *tr* to give as a pretext

prétonique [pretɔnik] *adj* pretonic

prêtre [pretr] *m* priest

prêtresse [pretres] *f* priestess

prêtrise [pretriz] *f* priesthood

preuve [prœv] *f* proof, evidence

preux [prø] *adj masc* valiant || *m* doughty knight

prévaloir [prevalwar] §71 (*subj* **prévale**, etc.) *intr* to prevail || *ref*—**se prévaloir de** to avail oneself of; to pride oneself on

prévarication [prevarikasjɔ̃] *f* breach of trust

prévariquer [prevarike] *intr* to betray one's trust

prévenance [prevnɑ̃s] *f* kindness, thoughtfulness

préve·nant [prevnɑ̃] **-nante** [nɑ̃t] *adj* attentive, considerate; prepossessing

prévenir [prevnir] §72 *tr* to anticipate; to avert, forestall; to ward off, to prevent; to notify, inform; to bias, to prejudice

préven·tif [prevɑ̃tif] **-tive** [tiv] *adj* preventive; pretrial (*detention*)

prévention [prevɑ̃sjɔ̃] *f* bias, prejudice; custody, imprisonment; prevention (*of accidents*); **prévention routière** traffic police; road safety

préve·nu -nue [prevny] *adj* biased, prejudiced; forewarned; accused || *mf* prisoner, accused, defendant

prévision [previzjɔ̃] *f* anticipation, estimate; **prévision du temps** weather forecast; **prévisions** expectations

prévoir [prevwar] §57 *tr* to foresee, anticipate; to forecast

prévoyance [prevwajɑ̃s] *f* foresight

prévo·yant [prevwajɑ̃] **prévoyante** [prevwajɑ̃t] *adj* far-sighted, provident

prie-dieu [pridjø] *m invar* prie-dieu *f* praying mantis

prier [prije] *tr* to ask, to beg; to pray (*God*); **je vous en prie!** I beg your pardon!; by all means!; you are welcome!; please have some!; **je vous prie!** please!; **prier qn de** + *inf* to ask, to beg s.o. to + *inf* || *intr* to pray

prière [prijer] *f* prayer; **prière de . . .** please . . . ; **prière d'insérer** publisher's insert for reviewers

primaire [primer] *adj* primary; first (*offender*); (coll) narrow-minded || *m* (elec) primary; (coll) primitive

primat [prima] *m* (eccl) primate

primate [primat] *m* (zool) primate

primauté [primote] *f* supremacy

prime [prim] *adj* early (*youth*); (math) prime || *f* premium; bonus; free gift; (eccl) prime; **prime de transport** traveling expenses

primer [prime] *tr* to excel; to take priority over; to award a prize to

primerose [primroz] *f* hollyhock

primesau·tier [primsotje] **-tière** [tjer] *adj* impulsive, quick

primeur [primœr] *f* freshness; first fruit; early vegetable; (journ) beat, scoop; **primeurs** fruits and vegetables out of season

primevère [primver] *f* primrose

primi·tif [primitif] **-tive** [tiv] *adj* primitive; original, early; primary (*colors; tense*) ‖ *mf* primitive

primo [primo] *adv* firstly

primor·dial **-diale** [primɔrdjal] *adj* (*pl* **-diaux** [djo]) primordial; fundamental, prime, primary

prince [prɛ̃s] *m* prince; **prince de Galles** Prince of Wales

princesse [prɛ̃ses] *f* princess

prin·cier [prɛ̃sje] **-cière** [sjer] *adj* princely

princi·pal **-pale** [prɛ̃sipal] *adj & m* (*pl* **-paux** [po]) principal, chief

principauté [prɛ̃sipote] *f* principality

principe [prɛ̃sip] *m* principle; beginning; source

printa·nier [prɛ̃tanje] **-nière** [njer] *adj* spring; springlike

printemps [prɛ̃tɑ̃] *m* spring; springtime; **au printemps** in the spring

priorité [prijɔrite] *f* priority; right of way; **de priorité** preferred (*stock*); main (*road*); **priorité à droite, priorité à gauche** (public sign) yield

pris [pri] **prise** [priz] *adj* set, frozen; **être pris** to be busy; **pris de vin** drunk ‖ *f* capture, seizure; taking; hold; setting; tap, faucet; (*med*) dose; (*naut*) prize; **donner prise à** to lay oneself open to; **être aux prises avec** to be struggling with; **hors de prise** out of gear; **lâcher prise** to let go; **prise d'air** ventilator; **prise d'antenne** (rad) lead-in; **prise d'armes** military parade; **prise d'eau** water faucet; hydrant; **prise de bec** (coll) quarrel; **prise de conscience** awakening, awareness; **prise de courant** (elec) plug; (elec) tap, outlet; **prise de position** statement of opinion; **prise de sang** blood specimen; **prise de son** recording; **prise de tabac** pinch of snuff; **prise de terre** (elec) ground connection; **prise de vue(s)** (phot) shot, picture taking; **prise de vue directe** (telv) live broadcast; **prise directe** high gear

prisée [prize] *f* appraisal

priser [prize] *tr* to value; to snuff up ‖ *intr* to take snuff

pri·seur [prizœr] **-seuse** [zøz] *mf* snuffer ‖ *m* appraiser

prisme [prism] *m* prism

prison [prizɔ̃] *f* prison

prison·nier [prizɔnje] **prison·nière** [prizɔnjer] *mf* prisoner

privautés [privote] *fpl* liberties

pri·vé **-vée** [prive] *adj* private; tame, pet ‖ *m* private life

priver [prive] *tr* to deprive ‖ *ref* to deprive oneself; **se priver de** to do without, to abstain from

privilège [privilɛʒ] *m* privilege

privilé·gié **-giée** [privileʒje] *adj* privileged; preferred (*stock*)

prix [pri] *m* price; prize; value; **à aucun prix** not at any price; by no means; **à tout prix** at all costs; **au**

prix de at the price of; at the rate of; compared with; **dans mes prix** within my means; **grand prix** championship race; **hors de prix** at a prohibitive cost; **prix courant** list price; **prix de départ** upset price; **prix de détail** retail price; **prix de fabrique** factory price; **prix de gros** wholesale price; **prix de la vie** cost of living; **prix de location** rent; **prix de revient** cost price; **prix de vente** selling price; **prix fixe** table d'hôte

probabilité [prɔbabilite] *f* probability

probable [prɔbabl] *adj* probable, likely

pro·bant [prɔbɑ̃] **-bante** [bɑ̃t] *adj* convincing; conclusive (*evidence*)

probe [prɔb] *adj* honest, upright

problème [prɔblɛm] *m* problem

procédé [prɔsede] *m* process; procedure; tip (*of cue*); **procédés** proceedings; behavior

procéder [prɔsede] §10 *intr* to proceed; (with *dat*) to perform, carry out; **procéder de** to arise from

procédure [prɔsedyr] *f* procedure; proceedings

procès [prɔse] *m* lawsuit, case; trial; **intenter un procès à** to sue; to prosecute; **sans autre forme de procès** then and there, without appeal

proces·sif [prɔsesif] **proces·sive** [prɔsesiv] *adj* litigious

procession [prɔsesjɔ̃] *f* procession

processus [prɔsesys] *m* process

procès-verbal [prɔseverbal] *m* (*pl* **-verbaux** [verbo]) report; minutes; ticket (*e.g., for speeding*)

pro·chain [prɔʃɛ̃] **-chaine** [ʃen] *adj* next; impending; (lit) nearest, immediate; **la prochaine semaine** the next week; **la semaine prochaine** next week ‖ *m* neighbor, fellow-man ‖ *f*—**à la prochaine!** (coll) so long!

prochainement [prɔʃenmɑ̃] *adv* shortly

proche [prɔʃ] *adj* near; nearby; close (*relative*) ‖ **proches** *mpl* close relatives ‖ *adv*—**de proche en proche** little by little

proclamer [prɔklame] *tr* to proclaim

proclitique [prɔklitik] *adj & m* proclitic

procuration [prɔkyrasjɔ̃] *f* power of attorney; **par procuration** by proxy

procurer [prɔkyre] *tr & ref* to procure, to get

procureur [prɔkyrœr] *m* attorney; **procureur de la république** district attorney; **procureur général** attorney general

prodige [prɔdiʒ] *m* prodigy; wonder

prodi·gieux [prɔdiʒjø] **-gieuse** [ʒjøz] *adj* prodigious, wonderful; terrific

prodigue [prɔdig] *adj* prodigal, lavish ‖ *mf* prodigal, spendthrift

prodiguer [prɔdige] *tr* to squander, waste; to lavish ‖ *ref* to not spare oneself; to show off

prodrome [prɔdrom] *m* harbinger; introduction

produc·teur [prɔdyktœr] **-trice** [tris] *adj* productive ‖ *mf* producer

produc·tif [prɔdyktif] ·**tive** [tiv] *adj* productive; producing

production [prɔdyksjɔ̃] *f* production

produire [prɔdɥir] §19 *tr* to produce; to create; to introduce || *ref* to take place; to be produced; to show up

produit [prɔdɥi] *m* product; proceeds; offspring; **produit de luxe** luxury item; **produit pharmaceutique** patent medicine, drug; **produits agricoles** agricultural produce; **produits de beauté** cosmetics

proémi·nent [prɔeminã] ·**nente** [nãt] *adj* prominent, protuberant

profane [prɔfan] *adj* profane; lay, uninformed || *mf* profane; layman

profaner [prɔfane] *tr* to profane; (fig) to prostitute

proférer [prɔfere] §10 *tr* to utter

professer [prɔfese] *tr* to profess; to teach || *intr* to teach

professeur [prɔfesœr] *m* teacher; professor

profession [prɔfesjɔ̃] *f* profession; occupation, trade

profession·nel ·**nelle** [prɔfesjɔnɛl] *adj* & *mf* professional

profil [prɔfil] *m* profile; side face; cross section; skyline (*of city*)

profi·lé ·**lée** [prɔfile] *adj* streamlined, aerodynamic

profiler [prɔfile] *tr* to profile || *ref*— se **profiler sur** to stand out against

profit [prɔfi] *m* profit; **mettre à profit** to take advantage of; **profits et pertes** profit and loss

profitable [prɔfitabl] *adj* profitable

profiter [prɔfite] *intr* to profit; to grow; (with *dat*) to profit; **profiter à, dans,** or **en** to profit from

profi·teur [prɔfitœr] ·**teuse** [tøz] *mf* profiteer

pro·fond [prɔfɔ̃] ·**fonde** [fɔ̃d] *adj* profound; deep; low (*bow; voice*); **peu profond** shallow || *m* depths || *f* (slang) pocket || **profond** *adv* deep

profondément [prɔfɔ̃demã] *adv* profoundly, deeply; soundly; deep

profondeur [prɔfɔ̃dœr] *f* depth

progéniture [prɔʒenityr] *f* progeny; offspring, child

programma·teur [prɔgramatœr] ·**trice** [tris] *mf* (mov, rad, telv) programmer

programmation [prɔgramɑsjɔ̃] *f* programming

programme [prɔgram] *m* program; **programme de prévoyance** retirement program; **programme des études** curriculum

programmer [prɔgrame] *tr* to program

program·meur [prɔgramœr] **program·meuse** [prɔgramøz] *mf* (comp) programmer

progrès [prɔgrɛ] *m* progress; **faire des progrès** to make progress

progresser [prɔgrese] *intr* to progress

progres·sif [prɔgresif] **progres·sive** [prɔgresiv] *adj* progressive

progressiste [prɔgresist] *adj* & *mf* progressive

prohiber [prɔibe] *tr* to prohibit

prohibition [prɔibisjɔ̃] *f* prohibition

proie [prwa], [prwɑ] *f* prey; **de proie** predatory; **en proie à** a prey to

projecteur [prɔʒɛktœr] *m* projector; searchlight; (mov) projection machine

projectile [prɔʒɛktil] *m* projectile; **projectile téléguidé** guided missile

projection [prɔʒɛksjɔ̃] *f* projection

projet [prɔʒɛ] *m* project; draft; sketch; plan; **faire des projets** to make plans; **projet de loi** bill

projeter [prɔʒte] §34 *tr* to project; to pour forth (*smoke*); to cast (*a shadow*); to plan || *intr* to plan

prolétaire [prɔletɛr] *m* proletarian

prolétariat [prɔletarja] *m* proletariat

proléta·rien [prɔletarjɛ̃] ·**rienne** [rjɛn] *adj* proletarian

proliférer [prɔlifere] §10 *intr* to proliferate

prolifique [prɔlifik] *adj* prolific

prolixe [prɔliks] *adj* prolix

prologue [prɔlɔg] *m* prologue; preface

prolonger [prɔlɔ̃ʒe] §38 *tr* to prolong; to extend || *ref* to be prolonged; to continue, extend

promenade [prɔmnad] *f* promenade; walk; ride; drive; sail; **faire une promenade** (en auto, à cheval, à motocyclette, en bateau, etc.) to take a ride

promener [prɔmne] §2 *tr* to take for a walk or drive; to walk (*e.g., a dog*); to take along; **envoyer promener qn** (coll) to send s.o. packing; **promener . . . sur** to run (*e.g., one's hand, eyes*) over || *ref* to stroll; to go for a walk, ride, drive, or sail; **allez vous promener!** get out of here!

prome·neur [prɔmnœr] ·**neuse** [nøz] *mf* walker, stroller

promenoir [prɔmnwar] *m* ambulatory, cloister; (theat) standing room

promesse [prɔmɛs] *f* promise

promettre [prɔmɛtr] §42 *tr* to promise; **promettre q.ch. à qn** to promise s.th. to s.o. || *intr* to look promising; **promettre à qn de** + *inf* to promise s.o. to + *inf* || *ref* to promise oneself; (with *dat* of *reflex pron*) to promise oneself (*e.g., a vacation*); **se promettre de** to resolve to

pro·mis [prɔmi] ·**mise** [miz] *adj* promised; **promis à** headed for

promiscuité [prɔmiskɥite] *f* indiscriminate mixture; lack of privacy

promontoire [prɔmɔ̃twar] *m* promontory

promo·teur [prɔmɔtœr] ·**trice** [tris] *mf* promoter; originator

promotion [prɔmɔsjɔ̃] *f* promotion; uplift; class (*in school*)

promouvoir [prɔmuvwar] §45 (*pp* **promu**) *tr* to promote

prompt [prɔ̃] **prompte** [prɔ̃t] *adj* prompt, ready, quick

promptitude [prɔ̃tityd] *f* promptness

promulguer [prɔmylge] *tr* to promulgate

prône [pron] *m* homily

prôner [prone] *tr* to extol

pronom [prɔnɔ̃] *m* pronoun

pronomi·nal ·**nale** [prɔnɔminal] *adj* (*pl*

-naux [no]) pronominal; reflexive (*verb*)

pronon·cé -cée [prɔnɔ̃se] *adj* marked; sharp (*curve*); prominent (*nose*)

prononcer [prɔnɔ̃se] §51 *tr* to pronounce; to utter; to deliver (*a speech*); to pass (*judgment*) || *intr* to decide || *ref* to be pronounced; to express an opinion

prononciation [prɔnɔ̃sjasjɔ̃] *f* pronunciation

pronostic [prɔnɔstik] *m* prognosis

pronostiquer [prɔnɔstike] *tr* to prognosticate

propagande [prɔpagɑ̃d] *f* propaganda; publicity, advertising

propager [prɔpaʒe] §38 *tr* to propagate; to spread || *ref* to be propagated; to spread

propédeutique [prɔpedøtik] *f* (*educ*) preliminary study

propension [prɔpɑ̃sjɔ̃] *f* propensity

prophète [prɔfɛt] *m* prophet

prophétesse [prɔfetes] *f* prophetess

prophétie [prɔfesi] *f* prophecy

prophétiser [prɔfetize] *tr* to prophesy

prophylactique [prɔfilaktik] *adj* prophylactic

propice [prɔpis] *adj* propitious; lucky (*star*)

proportion [prɔpɔrsjɔ̃] *f* proportion; en proportion de in proportion to

proportion·né -née [prɔpɔrsjɔne] *adj* proportionate

proportion·nel -nelle [prɔpɔrsjɔnel] *adj* proportional

proportionner [prɔpɔrsjɔne] *tr* to proportion

propos [prɔpo] *m* remark; purpose; à ce propos in this connection; à propos by the way; timely, fitting; at the right moment; à propos de with regard to, concerning; à tout propos at every turn; changer de propos to change the subject; de propos délibéré on purpose; des propos en l'air idle talk; hors de propos out of place; irrelevant

proposer [prɔpoze] *tr* to propose; to nominate; to recommend (*s.o.*) || *ref* to have in mind; to apply (*for a job*); se proposer de to intend to

proposition [prɔpozisjɔ̃] *f* proposition; proposal; clause

propre [prɔpr] *adj* clean, neat; original (*meaning*); proper (*name*); literal (*meaning*); propre à fit for, suited to || (when standing before noun) *adj* own || *m* characteristic; au propre in the literal sense; c'est du propre! (coll) what a dirty trick!; en propre in one's own right

pro·pret -prette [pret] *adj* (coll) clean, bright

propreté [prɔprəte] *f* cleanliness, neatness

propriétaire [prɔprijeter] *mf* proprietor, owner; landowner || *m* landlord || *f* proprietress; landlady

propriété [prɔprijete] *f* property; propriety, appropriateness

propulseur [prɔpylsœr] *m* engine, motor; outboard motor; (rok) booster

propulsion [prɔpylsjɔ̃] *f* propulsion; propulsion à réaction jet propulsion

prorata [prɔrata] *m invar*—au prorata de in proportion to

proroger [prɔrɔʒe] §38 *tr* to postpone; to extend; to adjourn || *ref* to be adjourned

prosaïque [prozaik] *adj* prosaic

prosateur [prozatœr] *m* prose writer

proscrire [prɔskrir] §25 *tr* to proscribe; to banish, outlaw

pros·crit [prɔskri] -crite [krit] *adj* banished || *mf* outlaw

prose [proz] *f* prose; (coll) style (*of writing*)

prosélyte [prɔzelit] *mf* proselyte

prosodie [prɔzɔdi] *f* prosody

prospecter [prɔspekte] *tr & intr* to prospect

prospec·teur [prɔspektœr] -trice [tris] *mf* prospector

prospectus [prɔspektys] *m* prospectus; handbill

prospère [prɔsper] *adj* prosperous

prospérer [prɔspere] §10 *intr* to prosper, to thrive

prospérité [prɔsperite] *f* prosperity

prosternation [prɔsternasjɔ̃] *f* prostration; groveling

prosterner [prɔsterne] *tr* to bend over || *ref* to prostrate oneself; to grovel

prostituée [prɔstitɥe] *f* prostitute

prostituer [prɔstitɥe] *tr* to prostitute

prostration [prɔstrasjɔ̃] *f* prostration

pros·tré -trée [prɔstre] *adj* prostrate

protagoniste [prɔtagɔnist] *m* protagonist

prote [prɔt] *m* (typ) foreman

protection [prɔteksjɔ̃] *f* protection; protection civile civil defense

proté·gé -gée [prɔteʒe] *adj* guarded; arterial (*crossing*) || *mf* protégé, dependent; pet

protège-cahier [prɔteʒkaje] *m* (*pl* -cahiers) notebook cover

protège-livre [prɔteʒlivr] *m* (*pl* -livres) dust jacket

protéger [prɔteʒe] §1 *tr* to protect; to be a patron of

protéine [prɔtein] *f* protein

protes·tant [prɔtestɑ̃] -tante [tɑ̃t] *adj & mf* Protestant; protestant

protestation [prɔtestasjɔ̃] *f* protest

protester [prɔteste] *tr & intr* to protest; protester de to protest

protêt [prɔtɛ] *m* (com) protest

protocole [prɔtɔkɔl] *m* protocol

proton [prɔtɔ̃] *m* proton

protoplasme [prɔtɔplasm] *m* protoplasm

prototype [prɔtɔtip] *m* prototype

protozoaire [prɔtɔzɔer] *m* protozoan

protubérance [prɔtyberɑ̃s] *f* protuberance

proue [pru] *f* prow, bow

prouesse [prɥes] *f* prowess

prouver [pruve] *tr* to prove

provenance [prɔvnɑ̃s] *f* origin; en provenance de from

proven·çal -çale [prɔvɑ̃sal] (*pl* -çaux [so]) *adj* Provençal || *m* Provençal (*language*) || (*cap*) *mf* Provençal (*person*)

provenir [prɔvnir] §72 *intr* (*aux*: ÊTRE) —**provenir de** to come from

proverbe [prɔvɛrb] *m* proverb

providence [prɔvidɑ̃s] *f* providence

providen·tiel -tielle [prɔvidɑ̃sjɛl] *adj* providential

province [prɔvɛ̃s] *adj invar* (coll) provincial ‖ *f* province; **la province** the provinces (*all of France outside of Paris*)

proviseur [prɔvizœr] *m* headmaster

provision [prɔvizjɔ̃] *f* stock, store; deposit; **aller aux provisions** to go shopping; **faire provision de** to stock up on; **provisions** provisions, foodstuffs; **sans provision** bad (*check*)

provisoire [prɔvizwar] *adj* provisional, temporary; emergency

provo·cant -cante [prɔvɔkɑ̃ -kɑ̃t] *adj* provocative

provoquer [prɔvɔke] *tr* to provoke; to cause, bring about; to arouse

proxénète [prɔksenɛt] *mf* procurer ‖ *m* pimp

proximité [prɔksimite] *f* proximity; **à proximité de** near

prude [pryd] *adj* prudish ‖ *f* prude

prudence [prydɑ̃s] *f* prudence

pru·dent -dente [prydɑ̃ -dɑ̃t] *adj* prudent

pruderie [prydri] *f* prudery

prud'homme [prydɔm] *m* arbitrator; (obs) solid citizen

prudhommesque [prydɔmɛsk] *adj* pompous

pruine [prɥin] *f* bloom

prune [pryn] *f* plum; **des prunes!** (slang) nuts!; **pour des prunes** (coll) for nothing

pru·neau [pryno] *m* (*pl* **-neaux**) prune; (slang) bullet

prunelle [prynɛl] *f* pupil (*of eye*); sloe; sloe gin; **jouer de la prunelle** (coll) to ogle; **prunelle de ses yeux** apple of his (one's, etc.) eye

prunellier [prynelje] *m* sloe, blackthorn

prunier [prynje] *m* plum tree

prus·sien [prysjɛ̃] **prus·sienne** [prysjɛn] *adj* Prussian ‖ (*cap*) *mf* Prussian

P.-S. [pees] *m* (letterword) (*postscriptum*) P.S.

psalmodier [psalmɔdje] *tr & intr* to speak in a singsong

psaume [psom] *m* psalm

psautier [psotje] *m* psalter

pseudonyme [psødɔnim] *adj* pseudonymous ‖ *m* pseudonym; nom de plume

psitt [psit] *interj* (coll) hist!

P.S.V. [peesve] *m* (letterword) (*pilotage sans visibilité*) blind flying

psychanalyse [psikanaliz] *f* psychoanalysis

psychanalyser [psikanalize] *tr* to psychoanalyze

psyché [psi/e] *f* psyche; cheval glass

psychiatre [psikjatr] *mf* psychiatrist

psychiatrie [psikjatri] *f* psychiatry

psychique [psi/ik] *adj* psychic

psychologie [psikɔlɔʒi] *f* psychology

psychologique [psikɔlɔʒik] *adj* psychologic(al)

psychologue [psikɔlɔg] *mf* psychologist

psychopathe [psikɔpat] *mf* psychopath

psychose [psikoz] *f* psychosis

psychotique [psikɔtik] *adj & mf* psychotic

ptomaïne [ptɔmain] *f* ptomaine

P.T.T. [petete] *fpl* (letterword) (*Postes, télégraphes, et téléphones*) post office, telephone, and telegraph

puant -ante [pɥɑ̃ -ɑ̃t] *adj* stinking

puanteur [pɥɑ̃tœr] *f* stench, stink

puberté [pybɛrte] *f* puberty

pu·blic -blique [pyblik] *adj* public; notorious ‖ *m* public; audience

publication [pyblikasjɔ̃] *f* publication; proclamation

publicitaire [pyblisiter] *adj* advertising ‖ *m* advertising man

publicité [pyblisite] *f* publicity; advertising; **publicité aérienne** skywriting

publier [pyblije] *tr* to publish; to publicize, proclaim

puce [pys] *f* flea; **mettre la puce à l'oreille à qn** (fig) to put a bug in s.o.'s ear

pu·ceau [pyso] **-celle** [sɛl] (*pl* **-ceaux**) *adj & mf* (coll) virgin ‖ *f* maid

puceron [pysrɔ̃] *m* plant louse

pudding [pudriŋ] *m* plum pudding

puddler [pydle] *tr* to puddle

pudeur [pydœr] *f* modesty

pudi·bond [pydibɔ̃] **-bonde** [bɔ̃d] *adj* prudish

pudibonderie [pydibɔ̃dri] *f* false modesty

pudique [pydik] *adj* modest, chaste

puer [pɥe] *tr* to reek of ‖ *intr* to stink

pué·ril -rile [pɥeril] *adj* puerile

puérilité [pɥerilite] *f* puerility

pugilat [pyʒila] *m* fight, brawl

pugiliste [pyʒilist] *m* pugilist

pugnace [pygnas] *adj* pugnacious

puî·né -née [pɥine] *adj* younger ‖ *mf* younger child

puis [pɥi] *adv* then; next; et **puis** besides; **et puis après?** (coll) what next?

puisard [pɥizar] *m* drain, cesspool; sump

puisatier [pɥizatje] *m* well digger

puiser [pɥize] *tr* to draw (*water*); **puiser à** or **dans** to draw (*s.th.*) from ‖ *intr*—**puiser à** or **dans** to draw from or on; to dip or reach into

puisque [pɥisk(ə)] *conj* since, as, seeing that

puissamment [pɥisamɑ̃] *adv* powerfully; exceedingly

puissance [pɥisɑ̃s] *f* power

puis·sant [pɥisɑ̃] **puis·sante** [pɥisɑ̃t] *adj* powerful

puits [pɥi] *m* well; pit; (min) shaft; (naut) locker; **puits absorbant, puits perdu** cesspool; **puits de pétrole** oil well; **puits de science** fountain of knowledge

pull-over [pulɔvœr], [pylɔver] *m* (*pl* **-overs**) sweater, pullover

pulluler [pylyle] *intr* to swarm, to teem

pulmonaire [pylmɔner] *adj* pulmonary ‖ *f* (bot) lungwort pulpe [pylp] *f* pulp

pulsation [pylsɑsjɔ̃] *f* pulsation, beat; pulse

pulsion [pylsjɔ̃] *f* (psychoanal) impulse

pulvérisateur [pylverizatœr] *m* spray, atomizer

pulvériser [pylverize] *tr* to pulverize; to spray

punaise [pynez] *f* bug; bedbug; thumbtack

punch [pɔ̃ʃ] *m* punch (*drink*) ‖ [pœnʃ] *m* (boxing) punch

punching-ball [pœnʃiŋbol] *m* punching bag

punir [pynir] *tr & intr* to punish

punition [pynisjɔ̃] *f* punishment

pupille [pypil], [pypij] *mf* ward ‖ *f* pupil (*of eye*)

pupitre [pypitr] *m* desk; stand, rack; lectern; console, controls; **pupitre à musique** music stand

pur pure [pyr] *adj* pure ‖ *mf* diehard; **les purs** the pure in heart

purée [pyre] *f* purée; mashed potatoes; (coll) wretch; **être dans la purée** (coll) to be broke; **purée de pois** (culin, fig) pea soup ‖ *interj* (slang) how awful!

pureté [pyrte] *f* purity

purga·tif [pyrgatif] -tive [tiv] *adj & m* purgative

purgatoire [pyrgatwar] *m* purgatory

purge [pyrʒ] *f* purge

purger [pyrʒe] §38 *tr* to purge; to pay off (*e.g., a mortgage*); to serve (*a sentence*)

purifier [pyrifje] *tr* to purify

puri·tain [pyritɛ̃] -taine [ten] *adj & mf* puritan; Puritan

pur-sang [pyrsɑ̃] *adj & m invar* thoroughbred

pus [py] *m* pus

pusillanime [pyzilanim] *adj* pusillanimous

pustule [pystyl] *f* pimple

putain [pytɛ̃] *adj invar* (coll) amiable, agreeable ‖ *f* (vulg) whore

putois [pytwa] *m* skunk, polecat

putréfier [pytrefje] *tr & ref* to decompose, to rot

putride [pytrid] *adj* putrid

puy [pɥi] *m* volcanic peak

puzzle [pœzl] *m* jigsaw puzzle

p.-v. [peve] *m* (letterword) (**procès-verbal**) (coll) ticket, e.g., **attraper un p.-v.** to get a ticket

pygargue [pigarg] *m* osprey, fish hawk

pygmée [pigme] *m* pygmy

pygméen [pigmeɛ̃] pygméenne [pigmeen] *adj* pygmy

pyjama [piʒama] *m* pajamas; **un pyjama** a pair of pajamas

pylône [pilon] *m* pylon; tower

pyramide [piramid] *f* pyramid

Pyrénées [pirene] *fpl* Pyrenees

pyrite [pirit] *f* pyrites

pyrotechnie [pirɔtekni] *f* pyrotechnics

pyrotechnique [pirɔteknik] *adj* pyrotechnical

python [pitɔ̃] *m* python

pythonisse [pitɔnis] *f* pythoness

pyxide [piksid] *f* pyx

Q

Q, q [ky] *m invar* seventeenth letter of the French alphabet

quadrant [kwadrɑ̃], [kadrɑ̃] *m* (math) quadrant

quadrilatère [kwadrilater] *m* quadrilateral

quadrupède [kwadryped] *m* quadruped

quadruple [kwadrypl] *adj & m* quadruple

quadrupler [kwadryple] *tr & intr* to quadruple

quadru·plés -plées [kwadryple] *mfpl* quadruplets

quai [ke] *m* quay, wharf; platform (*e.g., in a railroad station*); embankment, levee; **amener à quai** to berth; **le Quai d'Orsay** the French foreign office

qua·ker [kwekœr], [kwaker] -keresse [kres] *mf* Quaker

qualifiable [kalifjabl] *adj* describable

quali·fié -fiée [kalifje] *adj* qualified; qualifying; aggravated (*crime*)

qualifier [kalifje] *tr & intr* to qualify

qualité [kalite] *f* quality; title, capacity; **avoir qualité pour** to be authorized to; **en qualité de** in the capacity of

quand [kɑ̃] *adv* when; how soon; **n'importe quand** anytime; **quand même** though, just the same ‖ *conj* when; **quand même** even if

quant [kɑ̃] *adv*—**quant à** as for, as to, as far as; **quant à cela** for that matter

quant-à-soi [kɑ̃taswa] *m* dignity, reserve; **rester** or **se tenir sur son quant-à-soi** to keep one's distance

quantique [kwɑ̃tik] *adj* quantum

quantité [kɑ̃tite] *f* quantity

quan·tum [kwɑ̃tɔm] *m* (*pl* -ta [ta]) quantum

quarantaine [karɑ̃ten] *f* age of forty, forty mark, forties; quarantine; **une quarantaine de** about forty

quarante [karɑ̃t] *adj, pron, & m* forty; **quarante et un** forty-one; **quarante et unième** forty-first

quarante-deux [karɑ̃tdø] *adj, pron, & m* forty-two

quarante-deuxième [karɑ̃tdøzjem] *adj, pron (masc, fem), & m* forty-second

quarantième [karɑ̃tjem] *adj, pron (masc, fem), & m* fortieth

quart [kar] *m* quarter; fourth (*in fractions*); quarter of a pound; quarter of a liter; **bon quart!** (naut) all's well!; **passer un mauvais quart d'heure** to have a trying time; **petit quart** (naut) dogwatch; **prendre le quart** (naut) to come on watch; **quart de cercle** quadrant; **quart de soupir** (mus) sixteenth-note rest; **quart d'heure de Rabelais** day of reckoning; **tous les quarts d'heure au quart d'heure juste** every quarter-hour on the quarter-hour; **un petit quart d'heure** a quarter of an hour or so

quarte [kart] *adj* quartan (*fever*) || *f* half-gallon; (escr) quarte; (mus) fourth

quarte-ron [kartərɔ̃] **-ronne** [rɔn] *mf* quadroon || *m* handful (*e.g., of people*)

quartette [kwartet] *m* combo (*foursome*)

quartier [kartje] *m* quarter; neighborhood; section (*of orange*); portion; **à quartier** aloof; apart; **avoir quartier libre** (mil) to have a pass; to be off duty; **les beaux quartiers** the upper-class residential district; **mettre en quartiers** to dismember; **quartier d'affaires** business district; **quartier général** (mil) headquarters; **quartier réservé** red-light district; **quartiers** quarters, barracks

quartier-maître [kartjemetr] *m* (*pl* **quartiers-maîtres**) quartermaster

quartz [kwarts] *m* quartz

quasar [kwazar], [kazar] *m* quasar

quasi [kazi] *m* butt (*of a loin cut*) || *adv* almost

quasiment [kazimã] *adv* (coll) almost

quatorze [katɔrz] *adj & pron* fourteen; **the Fourteenth**, *e.g.,* **Jean quatorze** John the Fourteenth || *m* fourteen; fourteenth (*in dates*)

quatorzième [katɔrzjem] *adj, pron* (*masc, fem*), *& m* fourteenth

quatrain [katrɛ̃] *m* quatrain

quatre [katr] *adj & pron* four; **the Fourth**, *e.g.,* **Jean quatre** John the Fourth; **quatre à quatre** four at a time; **quatre heures four o'clock** || *m* four; fourth (*in dates*); **se mettre en quatre pour** to fall all over oneself for; **se tenir à quatre** to keep oneself under control

quatre-épices [katrepis] *m & f invar* allspice (*plant*); **des quatre-épices** allspice (*spice*)

quatre-saisons [katrəsɛzɔ̃], [katsɛzɔ̃] *f invar* everbearing small strawberry

quatre-temps [katrətã] *mpl* Ember days

quatre-vingt-dix [katrəvɛ̃di(s)], *adj, pron, & m* ninety

quatre-vingt-dixième [katrəvɛ̃dizjem] *adj, pron* (*masc, fem*), *& m* ninetieth

quatre-vingtième [katrəvɛ̃tjem] *adj, pron* (*masc, fem*), *& m* eightieth

quatre-vingt-onze [katrəvɛ̃ɔ̃z] *adj, pron, & m* ninety-one

quatre-vingt-onzième [katrəvɛ̃ɔ̃zjem] *adj, pron* (*masc, fem*), *& m* ninety-first

quatre-vingts [katrəvɛ̃] *adj & pron*

eighty; **quatre-vingt** eighty, *e.g.,* **page quatre-vingt** page eighty || *m* eighty

quatre-vingt-un [katrəvɛ̃œ̃] *adj, pron, & m* eighty-one

quatre-vingt-unième [katrəvɛ̃ynjem] *adj, pron* (*masc, fem*), *& m* eighty-first

quatrième [katrijem] *adj, pron* (*masc, fem*), *& m* fourth

quatuor [kwatuɔr] *m* (mus) quartet

que [kə] (or qu' [k] before a vowel or mute h) *pron rel* whom; which, that; **ce que** that which, what || *pron interr* what; **qu'est-ce que . . . ?** what (as direct object) . . . ?; **qu'est-ce qui . . . ?** what (as subject) . . . ? || *adv* why, *e.g.,* **qu'avez-vous besoin de tant de livres?** why do you need so many books?; how!, *e.g.,* **que cette femme est belle!** how beautiful that woman is!; **que de** what a lot of, *e.g.,* **que de difficultés!** what a lot of difficulties! || *conj* that; when, *e.g.,* **un jour que je suis allé chez le dentiste** once when I went to the dentist; since, *e.g.,* **il y a trois jours qu'il est arrivé** it is three days since he came; until, *e.g.,* **attendez qu'il vienne** wait until he comes; than, *e.g.,* **plus grand que moi** taller than I; as, *e.g.,* **aussi grand que moi** as tall as I; but, *e.g.,* **personne que vous** no one but you; whether, *e.g.,* **qu'il parte ou qu'il reste** whether he leaves or stays; (in a conditional sentence without **si**, to introduce the conditional in a dependent clause which represents the main clause of the corresponding sentence in English), *e.g.,* **il ferait faillite que cela ne m'étonnerait pas** if he went bankrupt it would not surprise me; (as a repetition of another conjunction), *e.g.,* **si elle chante et que la salle soit comble** if she sings and there is a full house; *e.g.,* **comme il avait soif et que le vin était bon** as he was thirsty and the wine was good; (in a prayer or exhortation), *e.g.,* **que Dieu vous bénisse!** may God bless you!, God bless you!; (in a command), *e.g.,* **qu'il parle** (aille, parte, etc.) let him speak (go, leave, etc.); **ne . . . que** §90 only, but

quel quelle [kɛl] §80

quelconque [kɛlkɔ̃k] *adj indef* any; any, whatever; any at all, some kind of || (when standing before noun) *adj indef* some, some sort of || *adj* ordinary, nondescript, mediocre

quelque [kɛlkə] *adj indef* some, any; **quelque chose** (always *masc*) something; **quelque chose de bon** something good; **quelque part** somewhere; **quelque . . . qui** or **quelque . . . que** whatever . . . ; whichever . . . ; **quelques** a few || *adv* some, about; **quelque peu** somewhat; **quelque** + *adj* or *adv* . . . **que** however + *adj* or *adv*

quelquefois [kɛlkəfwa] *adv* sometimes

quel-qu'un [kɛlkœ̃] **-qu'une** [kyn] §81

quémander [kemãde] *tr* to beg for || *intr* to beg

qu'en-dira-t-on [kɑ̃diratɔ̃] *m invar*
what other people will say, gossip
quenotte [kənɔt] *f* (coll) baby tooth
quenouille [kənuj] *f* distaff; distaff
side
querelle [kərɛl] *f* quarrel; **chercher
querelle à** to pick a quarrel with; **une
querelle d'Allemand, une mauvaise
querelle** a groundless quarrel
quereller [kərɛle] *tr* to nag, scold ||
ref to quarrel
querel·leur [kərɛlœr] **querel·leuse**
[kərɛløz] *adj* quarrelsome || *mf*
wrangler || *f* shrew
quérir [kerir] (used only in *inf*) *tr* to
go for, to fetch
question [kɛstjɔ̃] *f* question
questionnaire [kɛstjɔnɛr] *m* questionnaire
questionner [kɛstjɔne] *tr* to question
question·neur [kɛstjɔnœr] **question·
neuse** [kɛstjɔnøz] *adj* inquisitive ||
mf inquisitive person || *m* (rad, telv)
quizmaster
quête [kɛt] *f* quest; **faire la quête** to
take up the collection
quêter [kete] *tr* to beg or fish for
(*votes, praise, etc.*); to hunt for
(*game*); to collect (*contributions*) ||
intr to take up a collection
quetsche [kwetʃ] *f* quetsch
queue [kø] *f* tail; queue; billiard cue;
train (*of dress*); handle (*of pan*); bottom (*of class*); stem, stalk; **à la
queue leu leu** in single file; **faire la
queue** to line up, to queue up; **fausse
queue** miscue; **queue de cheval** (bot)
horsetail; **queue de loup** (bot) purple
foxglove; **queue de poisson** (aut)
fishtail; **queue de vache** cat's-tail
(*cirrus*); **sans queue ni tête** without
head or tail; **venir en queue** to bring
up the rear
queue-d'aronde [kødarɔ̃d] *f* (*pl* **queues-
d'aronde**) dovetail; **assembler à
queue-d'aronde** to dovetail
queue-de-morue [kødmɔry] *f* (*pl*
queues-de-morue) tails, swallow-
tailed coat; (painting) flat brush
queue-de-rat [kødəra] *f* (*pl* **queues-de-
rat**) rat-tail file; taper
qui [ki] *pron rel* who, whom; which,
that; **ce qui** that which, what; **n'importe qui** anyone; **qui que** anyone,
no one; whoever, e.g., **qui que vous
soyez** whoever you are || *pron interr*
who, whom; **qui est-ce que . . . ?**
whom . . . ?; **qui est-ce qui . . . ?**
who . . . ?
quia [kɥija]—**mettre** or **réduire qn à
quia** (obs) to stump or floor s.o.
quiconque [kikɔ̃k] *pron indef* whoever,
whosoever; whomever; anyone
quidam [kɥidam], [kidam] *m* individual, person
quiétude [kɥijetyd], [kjetyd] *f* peace of
mind; quiet, calm
quignon [kiɲɔ̃] *m* hunk (*of bread*)
quille [kij] *f* keel; pin (*for bowling*);
quilles ninepins
quincaillerie [kɛ̃kajri] *f* hardware;
hardware store

quincail·lier [kɛ̃kaje] **quincail·lière**
[kɛ̃kajɛr] *mf* hardware dealer
quinconce [kɛ̃kɔ̃s] *m* quincunx; **en
quinconce** quincuncially
quinine [kinin] *f* quinine
quinquen·nal ·nale [kɥɛ̃kɥennal] *adj*
(*pl* **-naux** [no]) five-year
quinquet [kɛ̃kɛ] *m*—**allume tes quin-
quets!** (slang) open your eyes!
quinquina [kɛ̃kina] *m* cinchona
quin·tal [kɛ̃tal] *m* (*pl* **-taux** [to]) hun-
dredweight; one hundred kilograms
quinte [kɛ̃t] *f* whim; (cards) sequence
of five; (mus) fifth; **quinte de toux**
fit of coughing
quintes·sence [kɛ̃tesɑ̃s] *f* quintessence
quintette [kɥɛ̃tɛt], [kɛ̃tɛt] *m* (mus)
quintet; (coll) five-piece combo;
quintette à cordes string quintet
quin·teux [kɛ̃tø] **-teuse** [tøz] *adj*
crotchety, fitful, restive
quintu·plés ·plées [kɛ̃typle] *mfpl* quintuplets
quinzaine [kɛ̃zɛn] *f* (group of) fifteen;
two weeks, fortnight; **une quinzaine
de** about fifteen
quinze [kɛ̃z] *adj & pron* fifteen; the
Fifteenth, e.g., **Jean quinze** John the
Fifteenth || *m* fifteen; fifteenth (*in
dates*)
quinzième [kɛ̃zjem] *adj, pron* (*masc,
fem*), & *m* fifteenth
quiproquo [kiproko] *m* mistaken identity, misunderstanding
quiscale [kɥiskal] *m* (orn) purple
grackle
quittance [kitɑ̃s] *f* receipt
quitte [kit] *adj* free (*from obligation*);
clear (*of debts*); (en) **être quitte pour**
to get off with; **être quitte to be**
quits; **tenir qn quitte de** to release
s.o. from || *m*—**quitte (à) quitte ou
double** to play double or nothing ||
adv—**quitte à** even if one has to, e.g.,
**commençons par en rire, quitte à en
pleurer plus tard** let us begin by
laughing, even if we have to cry later
on
quitter [kite] *tr* to leave; to take off
(*e.g., a coat*) || *intr* to leave, go away;
ne quittez pas! (telp) hold the line! ||
ref to part, separate
quitus [kɥitys] *m* discharge, acquit-
tance
qui-vive [kiviv] *m invar*—**sur le qui-
vive** on the qui vive || *interj* (mil)
who goes there?
quoi [kwa] *pron indef* what; **à
quoi bon?** what's the use?; **de quoi
enough; **moyennant quoi** in exchange
for which; **n'importe quoi** anything;
quoi que whatever; **quoi qu'il en soit**
be that as it may; **sans quoi** otherwise
quoique [kwakə] *conj* although, though
quolibet [kɔlibe] *m* gibe, quip
quorum [kwɔrɔm], [kɔrɔm] *m* quorum
quota [kwɔta], [kɔta] *m* quota
quote-part [kɔtpar] *f invar* quota, share
quoti·di·n ·dienne [djen] *adj*
daily || *m* daily newspaper
quotient [kɔsjɑ̃] *m* quotient
quotité [kɔtite] *f* share, amount

R

R, r [er], *[er] m invar* eighteenth letter of the French alphabet

rabâcher [rabɑʃe] *tr* to harp on ǁ *intr* to harp on the same thing

rabais [rabe] *m* reduction, discount

rabaisser [rabese] *tr* to lower; to disparage

rabat [raba] *m* flap (*vestment*)

rabat-joie [rabaʒwa] *m invar* kill-joy

rabattre [rabatr] §7 *tr* to lower; to discount; to turn down; to fold up; to pull down; to cut back; to flush (*game*) ǁ *intr* to turn; **en rabattre** to come down a peg or two; **rabattre de** to reduce (*a price*) ǁ *ref* to fold; to drop down; to turn the other way; **se rabattre sur** to fall back on

rabat·tu -tue [rabaty] *adj* turndown

rabbin [rabɛ̃] *m* rabbi

rabibocher [rabibɔʃe] *tr* (coll) to patch up ǁ *ref* (coll) to make up

rabiot [rabjo] *m* overtime; extra bit; (mil) extra service; (coll) graft

rabioter [rabjɔte] *tr & intr* to graft

râ·blé -blée [rable] *adj* husky

rabot [rabo] *m* plane

raboter [rabɔte] *tr* to plane

rabo·teux -teuse [rabɔtø] -teuse [tøz] *adj* rough, uneven ǁ *f* (mach) planer

rabou·gri -grie [rabugri] *adj* scrub, scrawny

rabrouer [rabrue] *tr* to snub

racaille [rakaj] *f* riffraff

raccommodage [rakɔmɔdaʒ] *m* mending; darning; patching

raccommodement [rakɔmɔdmɑ̃] *m* (coll) reconciliation

raccommoder [rakɔmɔde] *tr* to mend; to darn; to patch; (coll) to patch up

raccompagner [rakɔ̃paɲe] *tr* to see back, to see home

raccord [rakɔr] *m* connection; coupling; joint; adapter; **faire un raccord à** to touch up

raccordement [rakɔrdəmɑ̃] *m* connecting, linking, joining

raccorder [rakɔrde] *tr & ref* to connect

raccour·ci -cie [rakursi] *adj* shortened; abridged; squat, dumpy; bobbed (*hair*) ǁ *m* abridgment; shortcut, cutoff; foreshortening; **en raccourci** in miniature; in a nutshell

raccourcir [rakursir] *tr* to shorten; to abridge; to foreshorten ǁ *intr* to grow shorter

raccourcissement [rakursismɑ̃] *m* shortening; abridgment; shrinking

raccroc [rakro] *m* fluke

raccrocher [rakrɔʃe] *tr & intr* to hang up ǁ *ref*—**se raccrocher à** to hang on to

race [ras] *f* race; **de race** thoroughbred

ra·cé -cée [rase] *adj* thoroughbred

rachat [raʃa] *m* repurchase; redemption; ransom

racheter [raʃte] §2 *tr* to buy back; to redeem; to ransom

rachitique [raʃitik] *adj* rickety

rachitisme [raʃitism] *m* rickets

ra·cial -ciale [rasjal] *adj* (*pl* -ciaux [sjo]) race, racial

racine [rasin] *f* root; **racine carrée** square root; **racine cubique** cube root

racket [raket] *m* (coll) racket

racketter or **racketteur** [raketœr] *m* racketeer

raclée [rakle] *f* beating

racler [rakle] *tr* to scrape

raclette [raklet] *f* scraper; hoe; (phot) squeegee

racloir [raklwar] *m* scraper

raclure [raklyr] *f* scrapings

racolage [rakɔlaʒ] *m* soliciting

racoler [rakɔle] *tr* (coll) to solicit; (archaic) to shanghai

raco·leur [rakɔlœr] **-leuse** [løz] *mf* recruiter ǁ *f* (coll) hustler, streetwalker

racontar [rakɔ̃tar] *m* (coll) gossip

raconter [rakɔ̃te] *tr* to tell, narrate; to describe

racon·teur [rakɔ̃tœr] **-teuse** [tøz] *mf* storyteller

racornir [rakɔrnir] *tr & intr* to harden; to shrivel

radar [radar] *m* radar

rade [rad] *f* roadstead; **en rade** (coll) abandoned

ra·deau [rado] *m* (*pl* -deaux) raft

ra·diant [radjɑ̃] **-diante** [djɑ̃t] *adj* (astr, phys) radiant

radiateur [radjatœr] *m* radiator

radiation [radjɑsjɔ̃] *f* radiation; striking off

radi·cal -cale [radikal] *adj & mf* (*pl* -caux [ko]) radical ǁ *m* (chem, gram, math) radical

radier [radje] *tr* to cross out, to strike out or off

ra·dieux [radjø] **-dieuse** [djøz] *adj* radiant

radin [radɛ̃] *adj mdsc & fem* (slang) stingy

radio [radjo] *m* radiogram; radio operator ǁ *f* radio; radio set; X ray

radioac·tif [radjoaktif] **-tive** [tiv] *adj* radioactive

radio-crochet [radjokrɔʃe] *m* (*pl* -crochets) talent show

radiodiffuser [radjodifyze] *tr* to broadcast

radiodiffusion [radjodifyzjɔ̃] *f* broadcasting

radiofréquence [radjɔfrekɑ̃s] *f* radiofrequency

radiogramme [radjɔgram] *m* radiogram

radiographier [radjɔgrafje] *tr* to X-ray

radio-journal [radjɔʒurnal] *m* (*pl* -journaux [ʒurno]) radio newscast

radiologie [radjɔlɔʒi] *f* radiology

radiophare [radjɔfar] *m* radio beacon

radioreportage [radjɔrəpɔrtaʒ] *m* news broadcast; sports broadcast

radioscopie [radjɔskɔpi] *f* radioscopy, fluoroscopy

radiotélévi·sé -sée [radjɔtelevize] *adj* broadcast over radio and television

radis [radi] *m* radish

radium [radjɔm] *m* radium

radius [radjys] *m* (anat) radius
radotage [radɔtaʒ] *m* drivel, twaddle
radoter [radɔte] *intr* to talk nonsense, to ramble
radoub [radu] *m* (naut) graving
radouber [radube] *tr* (naut) to grave
radoucir [radusir] *tr* & *ref* to calm down
rafale [rafal] *f* squall, gust; burst of gunfire
raffermir [rafermir] *tr* & *ref* to harden
raffinage [rafinaʒ] *m* refining
raffinement [rafinmã] *m* refinement
raffiner |rafine| *tr* to refine || *intr* to be subtle; **raffiner sur** to overdo
raffinerie |rafinri| *f* refinery
raffoler |rafɔle| *intr*—**raffoler de** to dote on, to be wild about
raffut [rafy] *m* (coll) uproar
rafistolage [rafistɔlaʒ] *m* (coll) patching up
rafistoler [rafistɔle] *tr* (coll) to patch up
rafle [rɑfl] *f* raid, mass arrest; stalk; corncob
rafler [rɑfle] *tr* (coll) to carry away, to make a clean sweep of
rafraîchir [rafreʃir] *tr* to cool; to refresh; to freshen up; to trim (*the hair*) || *intr* to cool || *ref* to cool off; to refresh oneself
rafraîchissement [rafreʃismɑ̃] *m* refreshment; cooling off
ragaillardir |ragajardir| *tr* to cheer up
rage [raʒ] *f* rabies; **à la rage** madly; **faire rage** to rage
rager [raʒe] §38 *intr* (coll) to be enraged
ra·geur [raʒœr] **-geuse** [ʒøz] *adj* bad-tempered
ragot [rago] *m* (coll) gossip
ragoût [ragu] *m* stew, ragout; (obs) spice, relish
ragoû·tant |ragutɑ̃| **-tante** [tɑ̃t] *adj* tempting, inviting; pleasing; **peu ragoûtant** not very appetizing
rai [re] *m* ray; spoke
raid [red] *m* raid; air raid; endurance test
raide [red] *adj* stiff; tight, taut; steep; (coll) incredible || *adv* suddenly
raideur [redœr] *f* stiffness
raidillon [redijɔ̃] *m* short steep path
raidir [redir] *tr* & *ref* to stiffen
raie [re] *f* stripe, streak; stroke; line (*of spectrum*); part (*of hair*); (ichth) ray, skate
raifort [refɔr] *m* horseradish
rail [rɑj] *m* rail; **rail conducteur** third rail; **remettre sur les rails** (fig) to put back on the track; **sortir des rails** to jump the track
railler |rɑje| *tr* to make fun of || *intr* to joke || *ref*—**se railler de** to make fun of
raillerie |rɑjri| *f* raillery, banter
rail·leur [rɑjœr] **rail·leuse** [rɑjøz] *adj* teasing, bantering || *mf* teaser
rainette [renet] *f* tree frog
rainure [renyr] *f* groove
raisin [rezɛ̃] *m* grapes; grape; **raisin d'ours** (bot) bearberry; **raisins de Corinthe** currants; **raisins de mer**

cuttlefish eggs; **raisins de Smyrne** seedless raisins; **raisins secs** raisins
raisiné [rezine] *m* grape jelly; (slang) blood
raison ˹rezɔ̃˺ *f* reason; ratio, rate; **à raison de** at the rate of; **avoir raison** to be right; **avoir raison de** to get the better of; **donner raison à** to back, support; **en raison de** because of; **raison sociale** trade name; **se faire une raison** to resign oneself
raisonnable [rezɔnabl] *adj* reasonable; rational
raison·né -née [rezɔne] *adj* rational; detailed
raisonnement [rezɔnmɑ̃] *m* reasoning; argument
raisonner [rezɔne] *tr* to reason out; to reason with || *intr* to reason; to argue || *ref* to reason with oneself
raison·neur [rezɔnœr] **raison·neuse** [rezɔnøz] *adj* rational; argumentative || *mf* reasoner; arguer
rajeunir [raʒœnir] *tr* to rejuvenate || *intr* to grow young again || *ref* to pretend to be younger than one is
rajeunissement [raʒœnismɑ̃] *m* rejuvenation
rajouter [raʒute] *tr* to add again; (coll) to add more
rajuster [raʒyste] *tr* to readjust; to adjust || *ref* to adjust one's clothes
râle [rɑl] *m* rale; death rattle; (orn) rail
ralen·ti -tie [ralɑ̃ti] *adj* slow || *m* slowdown; **au ralenti** slowdown (*work*); go-slow (*policy*); slow-motion (*moving picture*); idling (*motor*); **tourner au ralenti** (aut) to idle
ralentir |ralɑ̃tir| *tr, intr,* & *ref* to slow down; **ralentir** (public sign) slow
ralliement [ralimɑ̃] *m* rally
rallier |ralje| *tr* & *ref* to rally
rallonge [ralɔ̃ʒ] *f* extra piece; leaf (*of table*); (coll) under-the-table payment; **à rallonges** extension (*table*)
rallonger [ralɔ̃ʒe] §38 *tr* & *intr* to lengthen
rallumer [ralyme] *tr* to relight; (fig) to rekindle || *intr* to put on the lights again || *ref* to be rekindled
rallye [rali] *m* rallye
ramage [ramaʒ] *m* floral design; warbling
ramas [ramɑ] *m* heap; pack (*e.g., of thieves*)
ramassage [ramɑsaʒ] *m* gathering; **ramassage scolaire** school-bus service
ramas·sé -sée [ramɑse] *adj* stocky; compact (*style*)
ramasser .[ramɑse] *tr* to gather; to gather together; to pick up; (coll) to catch (*a scolding; a cold*) || *ref* to gather; to gather oneself together
rambarde [rɑ̃bard] *f* handrail
rame [ram] *f* prop, stick; oar, pole; ream (*of paper*); string (*e.g., of barges*); (rr) train, section; **rame de métro** subway train
ra·meau [ramo] *m* (*pl* **-meaux**) branch; sprig
ramée [rame] *f* boughs

ramener [ramne] §2 *tr* to lead back; to bring back; to reduce; to restore

ramer [rame] *tr* to stake (*a plant*) || *intr* to row

ra·meur [ramœr] **-meuse** [møz] *mf* rower

ramier [ramje] *m* wood pigeon

ramifier [ramifje] *tr & ref* to ramify, to branch out

ramol·li -lie [ramɔli] *adj* sodden; (coll) half-witted || *mf* (coll) half-wit

ramollir [ramɔlir] *tr & ref* to soften

ramoner [ramɔne] *tr* to sweep (*a chimney*)

ramoneur [ramɔnœr] *m* chimney sweep

ram·pant [rãpã] **-pante** [pãt] *adj* crawling, creeping; (hum) ground (*crew*)

rampe [rãp] *f* ramp; grade, gradient; banister; flight (*of stairs*); (aer) runway lights; (theat) footlights; **rampe de lancement** launching pad

ramper [rãpe] *intr* to crawl; to grovel; (bot) to creep

ramure [ramyr] *f* branches; antlers

rancart [rãkar] *m* (slang) rendezvous; **mettre au rancart** (coll) to scrap, to shelve

rance [rãs] *adj* rancid

ranch [rãtʃ] *m* ranch

rancir [rãsir] *intr & ref* to turn rancid

rancœur [rãkœr] *f* rancor

rançon [rãsɔ̃] *f* ransom

rançonner [rãsɔne] *tr* to ransom

rancune [rãkyn] *f* grudge

rancu·nier [rãkynje] **-nière** [njer] *adj* vindictive

randonnée [rãdɔne] *f* long walk; long ride

rang [rã] *m* rank; **au premier rang** in the first row; ranking; **en rang d'oignons** in a line

ran·gé -gée [rãʒe] *adj* orderly; pitched (*battle*); steady (*person*)

ranger [rãʒe] §38 *tr* to range; to rank || *ref* to take one's place; to get out of the way; to mend one's ways; **se ranger à** to adopt, take (*e.g., a suggestion*)

ranimer [ranime] *tr & ref* to revive

raout [raut] *m* reception

rapace [rapas] *adj* rapacious || *m* bird of prey

rapatriement [rapatrimã] *m* repatriation

rapatrier [rapatrije] *tr* to repatriate

râpe [rɑp] *f* rasp; grater

râ·pé -pée [rɑpe] *adj* grated; threadbare || *m* (coll) grated cheese

râper [rɑpe] *tr* to rasp, to grate

rapetasser [raptase] *tr* (coll) to patch up

rapetisser [raptise] *tr, intr, & ref* to shrink, shorten

râ·peux [rɑpø] **-peuse** [pøz] *adj* raspy, grating

ra·piat [rapja] **-piate** [pjat] *adj* (coll) stingy || *mf* (coll) skinflint

ṛapide [rapid] *adj* rapid; steep || *m* rapids; (rr) express; **rapides** rapids

ṛapidité [rapidite] *f* rapidity; steepness

rapiéçage [rapjesaʒ] *m* patching

rapiécer [rapjese] §58 *tr* to patch

rapière [rapjer] *f* rapier

rapin [rapɛ̃] *m* dauber; (coll) art student

rapine [rapin] *f* rapine, pillage

rappel [rapel] *m* recall; reminder; call-up; recurrence; booster (*shot*); (theat) curtain call; **battre le rappel** to call to arms; **rappel au règlement** point of order; **rappel de chariot** backspacer

rappeler [raple] §34 *tr* to recall; to remind; to call back; to call up || *ref* to remember

rapport [rapɔr] *m* yield, return; report; connection, bearing; (math) ratio; **en rapport avec** in touch with; in keeping with; **par rapport à** in comparison with; **rapports** relations; sexual relations; **sous tous les rapports** in all respects

rapporter [rapɔrte] *tr* to bring back; to yield; to report; to relate; to repeal, call off; to attach; to retrieve (*game*); (bk) to post || *intr* to yield; (coll) to squeal || *ref*—**s'en rapporter à** to leave it up to; **se rapporter à** to be related to, to refer to

rappor·teur [rapɔrtœr] **-teuse** [tøz] *mf* tattletale || *m* recorder; (geom) protractor

rapprochement [raprɔʃmã] *m* bringing together; parallel; rapprochement

rapprocher [raprɔʃe] *tr* to bring closer; to reconcile; to compare || *ref* to draw closer, to approach; **se rapprocher de** to approximate, to resemble

rapt [rapt] *m* kidnapping

raquette [raket] *f* racket; snowshoe; tennis player; (bot) prickly pear

rare [rar] *adj* rare; scarce; sparse, thin (*hair*)

rarement [rarmã] *adv* rarely, seldom

rareté [rarte] *f* rarity; scarcity; rareness

ras [rɑ] **rase** [rɑz] *adj* short (*hair, nap, etc.*); level; close-cropped; close-shaven; open (*country*) || *m*—**à ras de, au ras de** flush with; **ras d'eau** water line; **ras du cou** crew neck; **voler au ras du sol** to skim along the ground

rasade [rɑzad] *f* bumper, glassful

rasage [rɑzaʒ] *m* shearing; shaving

ra·sant [rɑzã] **-sante** [zãt] *adj* level; grazing; close to the ground; (coll) boring

rase-mottes [rɑzmɔt] *m invar*—**faire du rase-mottes** or **voler en rase-mottes** to hedgehop

raser [rɑze] *tr* to shave; to raze; to graze || *ref* to shave

ra·seur [rɑzœr] **-seuse** [zøz] *adj* (coll) boring || *mf* (coll) bore

rasoir [rɑzwar] *adj invar* (slang) boring || *m* razor; (slang) bore; **rasoir à manche** straight razor; **rasoir de sûreté** safety razor

rassasiement [rasazimã] *m* satiation

rassasier [rasazje] *tr* to satisfy; to satiate || *ref* to have one's fill

rassemblement [rasãbləmã] *m* assembling; crowd; muster; (*trumpet call*) assembly; **rassemblement!** (mil) fall in!

rassembler [rasᾶmble] *tr & ref* to gather together

rasseoir |raswar] §5 *tr* to reseat; to set in place again || *ref* to sit down again

rasséréner [raserene] §10 *tr & ref* to calm down

rassir [rasir] *intr & ref* (coll) to get stale

ras·sis [rasi] **ras·sise** [rasiz] *adj* level-headed; stale (*bread*)

rassortir |rasərtir] *tr* to restock || *ref* to lay in a new stock

rassurer [rasyre] *tr* to reassure || *ref* to be reassured

rastaquouère [rastakwεr] *m* (coll) flashy stranger

rat [ra] *m* rat; (coll) tightwad; **fait comme un rat** caught like a rat in a trap; **mon rat** (coll) my turtledove; **rat à bourse** gopher; **rat de bibliothèque** bookworm; **rat de cale** stowaway; **rat de cave** thin candle; tax collector; **rat d'égout** sewer rat; **rat des champs** field mouse; **rat d'hôtel** hotel thief; **rat d'Opéra** ballet girl; **rat musqué** muskrat

ratatiner [ratatine] *ref* to shrivel up

ratatouille [ratatuj] *f* (coll) stew; (coll) bad cooking; (coll) blows

rate [rat] *f* spleen; female rat

ra·té -tée [rate] *adj* miscarried; bad (*shot, landing, etc.*) || *mf* failure, dropout

râ·teau [rɑto] *m* (*pl* -teaux) rake

râteler [ratle] §34 *tr* to rake

râtelier [ratəlje] *m* rack; set of false teeth; **manger à deux râteliers** (coll) to play both sides of the street; **râtelier d'armes** gun rack

rater [rate] *tr* to miss || *intr* to miss, to misfire; to fail

ratiboiser [ratibwaze] *tr* (coll) to take to the cleaners; **ratiboiser q.ch. à qn** (coll) to clean s.o. out of s.th.

ratifier |ratifje] *tr* to ratify

ration |rɑsjɔ̃] *f* ration

ration·nel -nelle [rasjɔnɛl] *adj* rational

rationnement [rasjɔnmɑ̃] *m* rationing

rationner [rasjɔne] *tr* to ration

ratisser [ratise] *tr* to rake; to rake in; to search with a fine-tooth comb; (coll) to fleece

ratissoire [ratiswar] *f* hoe

raton [ratɔ̃] *m* little rat; **raton laveur** raccoon

rattacher [rataʃe] *tr* to tie again; to link; to unite || *ref* to be connected

rattrapage [ratrapaʒ] *m* catch-up; (typ) catchword

rattraper [ratrape] *tr* to catch up to; to recover; to recapture || *ref* to catch up; **se rattraper à** to catch hold of; **se rattraper de** to make good, to recoup

rature [ratyr] *f* erasure

raturer [ratyre] *tr* to cross out

rauque [rok] *adj* hoarse, raucous

ravage [ravaʒ] *m* ravage

ravager [ravaʒe] §38 *tr* to ravage

ravalement [ravalmɑ̃] *m* trimming down; resurfacing; disparagement

ravaler [ravale] *tr* to choke down; to disparage; to drag down; to resurface; to eat (*one's words*) || *ref* to lower oneself

ravaudage [ravodaʒ] *m* mending; darning; (fig) patchwork

ravauder [ravode] *tr* to mend; to darn

ravier [ravje] *m* hors-d'oeuvre dish

ravigoter [ravigote] *tr* (coll) to revive

ravilir [ravilir] *tr* to debase

ravin [ravɛ̃] *m* ravine

ravine [ravin] *f* mountain torrent

raviner [ravine] *tr* to furrow

ravir [ravir] *tr* to ravish; to kidnap, abduct; to delight, entrance; **ravir q.ch. à qn** to snatch or take s.th. from s.o. || *intr*—**à ravir** marvelously

raviser [ravize] *ref* to change one's mind

ravis·sant [ravisɑ̃] **ravis·sante** [ravisɑ̃t] *adj* ravishing, entrancing

ravis·seur [ravisœr] **ravis·seuse** [ravisøz] *mf* kidnaper

ravitaillement [ravitɑjmɑ̃] *m* supplying; supplies

ravitailler [ravitaje] *tr* to supply; to fill up the gas tank of (*a vehicle*) || *ref* to lay in supplies; to fill up (*to get gas*)

raviver [ravive] *tr* to revive; to brighten up; to reopen (*an old wound*) || *ref* to revive; to break out again

ravoir [ravwar] (used only in *inf*) *tr* to get back again

rayer [reje] §49 *tr* to cross out, to strike out; to rule, to line; to stripe; to rifle (*a gun*)

rayon [rejɔ̃] *m* ray; radius; spoke; shelf; honeycomb; department (*in a store*); point (*of star*); **ce n'est pas mon rayon** (coll) that's not in my line; **rayon de lune** moonbeam; **rayons X** X rays; **rayon visuel** line of sight

rayon·nant [rejɔnɑ̃] **rayon·nante** [rejɔnɑ̃t] *adj* radiant; radiating; radioactive; (rad) transmitting

rayonne [rejɔn] *f* rayon

rayonner [rejɔne] *intr* to radiate

rayure [rejyr] *f* stripe; scratch; rifling

raz [rɑ] *m* race (*channel and current of water*); **raz de marée** tidal wave; landslide (*in an election*)

razzia [razja] *f* raid

razzier [razje] *tr* to raid

réacteur [reaktœr] *m* reactor; **réacteur nucléaire** nuclear reactor

réactif [reaktif] *m* (chem) reagent

réaction [reaksjɔ̃] *f* reaction; kick (*of rifle*); **à réaction** jet; **réaction en chaîne** chain reaction

réactionnaire [reaksjɔner] *adj & mf* reactionary

réadaptation [readaptasjɔ̃] *f* rehabilitation; **réadaptation fonctionnelle** occupational therapy

réadapter [readapte] *tr* to rehabilitate || *ref* to be rehabilitated

réaffirmer [reafirme] *tr* to reaffirm

réagir [reaʒir] *intr* to react

réalisable [realizabl] *adj* feasible; (com) saleable

réalisa·teur [realizatœr] **-trice** [tris]

adj producing || *mf* achiever; producer || *m* (mov, rad, telv) director

réalisation [realizɑsjɔ̃] *f* accomplishment; work; (mov, rad, telv) production; (com) liquidation

réaliser [realize] *tr* to realize; to accomplish; to sell out; (mov) to produce || *ref* to come to pass, to be realized

réalisme [realism] *m* realism

réaliste [realist] *adj* realistic || *mf* realist

réalité [realite] *f* reality

réanimer [reanime] *tr* to revive

réapparaître [reaparetr] §12 *intr* to reappear

réapparition [reaparisjɔ̃] *f* reappearance

réarmement [rearmǝmã] *m* rearmament

réassortir [reasɔrtir] *tr* to restock || *ref* to lay in a new stock

réassurer [reasyre] *tr* to reinsure

rébarba·tif [rebarbatif] **-tive** [tiv] *adj* forbidding, repulsive

rebâtir [rǝbatir] *tr* to rebuild

rebattre [rǝbatr] §7 *tr* to beat; to reshuffle; to repeat over and over again

rebat·tu -tue [rǝbaty] *adj* hackneyed

rebelle [rǝbɛl] *adj* rebellious || *mf* rebel

rebeller [rǝbele], [rǝbɛlle] *ref* to rebel

rébellion [rebeljɔ̃] *f* rebellion

rebiffer [rǝbife] *ref* to kick over the traces

reboisement [rǝbwazmã] *m* reforestation

rebond [rǝbɔ̃] *m* rebound

rebon·di -die [rǝbɔ̃di] *adj* plump, buxom; paunchy

rebondir [rǝbɔ̃dir] *intr* to bounce; (fig) to come up again

rebord [rǝbɔr] *m* edge, border; sill, ledge; hem; brim (*of hat*); rim (*of saucer*); lip (*of cup*)

reboucher [rǝbuʃe] *tr* to recork; to stop up || *ref* to be stopped up

rebours [rǝbur] *m*—**à rebours** backwards; against the grain; the wrong way; backhanded (*compliment*); **à** or **au rebours de** contrary to

rebouter [rǝbute] *tr* to set (*a bone*)

rebrousse-poil [rǝbruspwal]—**à rebrousse-poil** against the grain, the wrong way

rebrousser [rǝbruse] *tr* to brush up; rebrousser chemin to turn back; rebrousser qn (coll) to rub s.o. the wrong way || *ref* to turn up, to bend back

rebuffade [rǝbyfad] *f* rebuff; essuyer une rebuffade to be snubbed

rebut [rǝby] *m* castoff; waste; scum (*of society*); rebuff; de rebut castoff; waste; unclaimed (*letter*); mettre au rebut to discard

rebu·tant [rǝbytã] **-tante** [tãt] *adj* dull, tedious; repugnant

rebuter [rǝbyte] *tr* to rebuff; to bore; to be repulsive to

recaler [rǝkale] *tr* (coll) to flunk

récapitulation [rekapitylɑsjɔ̃] *f* recapitulation

recéder [rǝsede] §10 *tr* to give or sell back

recel [rǝsɛl] *m* concealment (*of stolen goods; of criminals*)

receler [rǝsle] §2 or **recéler** [rǝsele] §10 *tr* to conceal; to receive (*stolen goods*); to harbor (*a criminal*) || *intr* to hide

rece·leur [rǝslœr] **-leuse** [løz] *mf* fence, receiver of stolen goods

récemment [resamã] *adv* recently, lately

recensement [rǝsãsmã] *m* census; recensement du contingent draft registration

recenser [rǝsãse] *tr* to take the census of; to take a count of

recenseur [rǝsãsœr] *m* census taker

ré·cent [resã] **-cente** [sãt] *adj* recent

récépissé [resepise] *m* receipt

réceptacle [reseptakl] *m* receptacle

récep·teur [reseptœr] **-trice** [tris] *adj* receiving || *m* receiver

récep·tif [reseptif] **-tive** [tiv] *adj* receptive

réception [resepsjɔ̃] *f* reception; receipt; approval; admission (*to a club*); registration desk (*of hotel*); landing (*of, e.g., a parachutist*); (sports) catch; accuser réception de to acknowledge receipt of

réceptionnaire [resepsjɔner] *mf* consignee; chief receptionist

récession [resesjɔ̃] *f* recession

recette [rǝsɛt] *f* receipt; collection (*of debts, taxes, etc.*); (culin) recipe; faire recette to be a box-office attraction; recettes de métier tricks of the trade

recevable [rǝsvabl] *adj* acceptable; admissible

rece·veur [rǝsvœr] **-veuse** [vøz] *mf* collector; conductor (*of bus, streetcar, etc.*); blood recipient; receveur des postes postmaster; receveur universel recipient of blood from a universal donor

recevoir [rǝsvwar] §59 *tr* to receive; to accommodate; to admit (*to a school, club, etc.*); être reçu to be admitted; to pass || *intr* to receive

rechange [rǝʃãʒ] *m* replacement, change; de rechange spare (*e.g., parts*)

rechaper [rǝʃape] *tr* to recap, to retread

réchapper [reʃape] *intr*—en réchapper to get away with it; to get well; réchapper à or de to escape from

recharge [rǝʃarʒ] *f* refill; recharging; reloading

recharger [rǝʃarʒe] §38 *tr* to recharge; to refill; to reload; to ballast (*a roadbed*)

réchaud [reʃo] *m* hot plate

réchauffer [reʃofe] *tr & ref* to warm up

rêche [rɛʃ] *adj* rough, harsh

recherche [rǝʃɛrʃ] *f* search; quest; investigation, piece of research; refinement; recherches research

recher·ché -chée [rǝʃɛrʃe] *adj* sought-after, in demand; elaborate; studied; affected

rechercher [rəʃerʃe] *tr* to seek, to look for

rechigner [rəʃiɲe] *intr*—**rechigner à** to balk at

rechute [rəʃyt] *f* relapse

rechuter [rəʃyte] *intr* to relapse

récidive [residiv] *f* recurrence; second offense

récidiver [residive] *intr* to recur; to relapse

récif [resif] *m* reef

récipiendaire [resipjāder] *m* new member, inductee; recipient

récipient [resipjā] *m* recipient, vessel

réciprocité [resiprɔsite] *f* reciprocity

réciproque [resiprɔk] *adj* reciprocal || *f* converse

récit [resi] *m* recital, account

réci·tal -tale [resital] *m* (*pl* -tals) recital

récitation [resitɑsjɔ̃] *f* recitation

réciter [resite] *tr* to recite

récla·mant [reklamā] -mante [māt] *mf* claimant

réclamation [reklamɑsjɔ̃] *f* complaint; demand

réclame [reklam] *f* advertising; advertisement; (theat) cue; (typ) catchword; **faire de la réclame** to advertise, to ballyhoo; **réclame à éclipse** flashing sign; **réclame lumineuse** illuminated sign

réclamer [reklame] *tr* to claim; to clamor for; to demand || *intr* to lodge a complaint; to intercede || *ref* —**se réclamer de** to appeal to; to claim kinship with; **se réclamer de qn** to use s.o.'s name as a reference

reclassement [rəklɑsmā] *m* reclassification

reclasser [rəklɑse] *tr* to reclassify

re·clus [rəkly] -cluse [klyz] *adj & mf* recluse

recoin [rəkwɛ̃] *m* nook, cranny

récollection [rekɔleksjɔ̃] *f* religious meditation

recoller [rəkɔle] *tr* to paste again

récolte [rekɔlt] *f* harvest

récolter [rekɔlte] *tr* to harvest

recommander [rəkɔmāde] *tr* to recommend; to register (*a letter*) || *ref*—**se recommander à** to seek the protection of; **se recommander de** to ask (*s.o.*) for a reference

recommencer [rəkɔmāse] §51 *tr & intr* to begin again

récompense [rekɔ̃pās] *f* recompense, reward; award

récompenser [rekɔ̃pāse] *tr* to recompense

réconcilier [rekɔ̃silje] *tr* to reconcile

reconduire [rəkɔ̃dɥir] §19 *tr* to escort; (coll) to kick out, to send packing

réconfort [rekɔ̃fɔr] *m* comfort

réconfor·tant [rekɔ̃fɔrtā] -tante [tāt] *adj* consoling; stimulating

réconforter [rekɔ̃fɔrte] *tr* to comfort; to revive || *ref* to recuperate; to cheer up

reconnaissance [rəkɔnesās] *f* recognition; gratitude; (mil) reconnaissance; **aller en reconnaissance** to recon-

noiter; **reconnaissance de** or **pour** gratitude for

reconnais·sant [rəkɔnesā] **reconnais·sante** [rəkɔnesāt] *adj* grateful; **être reconnaissant de** + *inf* to be grateful for + *ger*; **être reconnaissant de** or **pour** to be grateful for

reconnaître [rəkɔnetr] §12 *tr* to recognize; (mil) to reconnoiter || *ref* to recognize oneself; to know where one is; to acknowledge oneself (*e.g.*, *guilty*); **s'y reconnaître** to know where one is

reconquérir [rəkɔ̃kerir] §3 *tr* to reconquer

reconquête [rəkɔ̃ket] *f* reconquest

reconsidérer [rəkɔ̃sidere] §10 *tr* to reconsider

reconstituant [rəkɔ̃stitɥā] *m* tonic

reconstituer [rəkɔ̃stitɥe] *tr* to reconstruct; to restore

reconstruire [rəkɔ̃strɥir] §19 *tr* to reconstruct

record [rəkɔr] *adj invar & m* record

recordman [rəkɔrdman] *m* record holder

recoudre [rəkudr] §13 *tr* to sew up

recouper [rəkupe] *tr* to cut again; to blend (*wines*)

recourir [rəkurir] §14 *intr* to run again; **recourir à** to resort to; to appeal to

recours [rəkur] *m* recourse; **recours en grâce** petition for pardon

recouvrement [rəkuvrəmā] *m* recovery

recouvrer [rəkuvre] *tr* to recover

recouvrir [rəkuvrir] §65 *tr* to cover; to cover up; to mask; to resurface (*e.g.*, *a road*) || *ref* to overlap

récréation [rekreɑsjɔ̃] *f* recreation; recess (*at school*)

recréer [rəkree] *tr* to re-create

récréer [rekree] *tr & ref* to relax

récrier [rekrije] *ref* to cry out

récrire [rekrir] §25 *tr* to rewrite; to write again

recroquevil·lé -lée [rəkrɔkvije] *adj* shriveled up, curled up; huddled up

recroqueviller [rəkrɔkvije] *tr & ref* to shrivel up, to curl up

re·cru -crue [rəkry] *adj* exhausted

recrue [rəkry] *f* recruit

recruter [rəkryte] *tr* to recruit || *ref* to be recruited

rectangle [rektāgl] *m* rectangle

rectificateur [rektifikatœr] *m* rectifier

rectifier [rektifje] *tr* to rectify; to true up; to grind (*a cylinder*)

rectum [rektɔm] *m* rectum

reçu [rəsy] *m* receipt

recueil [rəkœj] *m* collection; compilation

recueillement [rəkœjmā] *m* meditation

recueillir [rəkœjir] §18 *tr* to collect, to gather; to take in (*a needy person*); to receive (*a legacy*) || *ref* to collect oneself, to meditate

recuire [rəkɥir] §19 *tr* to anneal, to temper; to cook over again || *intr* (fig) to stew

recul [rəkyl] *m* backing, backward movement; kick, recoil; **être en recul** to be losing ground; **prendre du recul** to consider in perspective

reculer [rəkyle] *tr* to move back; to put off (*e.g., a decision*) ‖ *intr* to move back; to back out; to recoil; **reculer devant** to shrink from ‖ *ref* to move back

reculons [rəkylɔ̃]—**à reculons** backwards

récupération [rekyperasjɔ̃] *f* recovery

récupérer [rekypere] §10 *tr* to salvage, to recover; to recuperate; to make up (*e.g., lost hours*); to find another job for ‖ *intr* to recuperate

récurer [rekyre] *tr* to scour

récur·rent [rekyrɑ̃] **récur·rente** [rekyrɑ̃t] *adj* recurrent

récuser [rekyze] *tr* to take exception to ‖ *ref* to refuse to give one's opinion

rédac·teur [redaktœr] **-trice** [tris] *mf* editor; **rédacteur en chef** editor in chief; **rédacteur gérant** managing editor; **rédacteur publicitaire** copywriter; **rédacteur sportif** sports editor

rédaction [redaksjɔ̃] *f* editorial staff; editorial office; edition; editing

reddition [redisjɔ̃] *f* surrender

redécouvrir [rədekuvrir] §65 *tr* to rediscover

rédemp·teur [redɑ̃ptœr] **-trice** [tris] *adj* redemptive ‖ *mf* redeemer

rédemption [redɑ̃psjɔ̃] *f* redemption

redevable [rədvabl] *adj* indebted

redevance [rədvɑ̃s] *f* dues, fees; rent; tax (*on radio sets*)

rédiger [rediʒe] §38 *tr* to edit; to draft; to write up

redingote [rədɛ̃gɔt] *f* frock coat

redire [rədir] §22 *tr* to repeat; to give away (*a secret*) ‖ *intr*—**trouver à redire à** to find fault with

redon·dant [rədɔ̃dɑ̃] **-dante** [dɑ̃t] *adj* redundant

redoutable [rədutabl] *adj* frightening

redoute [rədut] *f* redoubt

redouter [rədute] *tr* to dread

redressement [rədresmɑ̃] *m* straightening out; redress; (elec) rectifying

redresser [rədrese] *tr* to straighten; to hold up (*e.g., the head*); to redress; (elec) to rectify ‖ *ref* to straighten up

redresseur [rədresœr] *m* (elec) rectifier; **redresseur de torts** knight-errant; (coll) reformer

réduction [redyksjɔ̃] *f* reduction

réduire [reduir] §19 *tr* to reduce; to set (*a bone*)

réduit [redui] *m* retreat, nook; redoubt

rééditer [reedite] *tr* to reedit

réel réelle [reel] *adj & m* real, actual

réélection [reeleksjɔ̃] *f* reelection

réellement [reelmɑ̃] *adv* really

réescompte [reeskɔ̃t] *m* rediscount

réexamen [reegzamɛ̃] *m* reexamination

réexpédier [reekspedje] *tr* to reship; to return to sender

réexpédition [reekspedisjɔ̃] *f* reshipment; return

refaire [rəfɛr] §29 *tr* to redo ‖ *intr*—**à refaire** to be done over; to be dealt over ‖ *ref* to recover; to make good one's losses

référence [referɑ̃s] *f* reference

référendum or referendum [referɛ̃dɔm] *m* referendum

référer [refere] §10 *intr*—**en référer à** to appeal to ‖ *ref*—**s'en référer à** to leave it up to; **se référer à** to refer to

refermer [rəfɛrme] *tr & ref* to close again, to close

refiler [rəfile] *tr*—**refiler à qn** (slang) to palm off on s.o.

réfléchir [refleʃir] *tr & intr* to reflect ‖ *ref* to be reflected

reflet [rəflɛ] *m* reflection; glint, gleam

refléter [rəflete] §10 *tr* to reflect ‖ *ref* to be mirrored

réflexe [reflɛks] *adj & m* reflex

réflexion [refleksjɔ̃] *f* reflection

refluer [rəflye] *intr* to ebb

reflux [rəfly] *m* ebb

refonte [rəfɔ̃t] *f* recasting

réforma·teur [reformatœr] **-trice** [tris] *mf* reformer

réformation [reformasjɔ̃] *f* reformation

réforme [reform] *f* reform; **la Réforme** the Reformation

réfor·mé -mée [reforme] *adj* (eccl) Reformed; (mil) disabled

reformer [rəforme] *tr & ref* to regroup

réformer [reforme] *tr* to reform; (mil) to discharge ‖ *ref* to reform

refou·lé -lée [rəfule] *adj* (coll) inhibited

refoulement [rəfulmɑ̃] *m* driving back; (psychoanal) repression

refouler [rəfule] *tr* to drive back; to choke back (*a sob*); to sail against (*the current*); to compress, stem; (psychoanal) to repress ‖ *intr* to flow back

réfractaire [refraktɛr] *adj* refractory; rebellious ‖ *mf* insubordinate

réfraction [refraksjɔ̃] *f* refraction

refrain [rəfrɛ̃] *m* refrain; hum; **le même refrain** the same old tune

réfréner [refrene] §10 *tr* to curb

réfrigérateur [refriʒeratœr] *m* refrigerator

réfrigérer [refriʒere] §10 *tr* to refrigerate; (coll) to chill to the bone

refroidir [rəfrwadir] *tr* to cool; (slang) to rub out ‖ *intr* to cool ‖ *ref* to cool; to catch cold

refroidissement [rəfrwadismɑ̃] *m* cooling

refuge [rəfyʒ] *m* refuge; shelter; safety zone

réfu·gié -giée [refyʒje] *mf* refugee

réfugier [refyʒje] *ref* to take refuge

refus [rəfy] *m* refusal; **refus seulement** regrets only (*to invitation*)

refuser [rəfyze] *tr* to refuse; to refuse to recognize; to flunk; to decline ‖ *intr* to refuse; **refuser de or à** to refuse to ‖ *ref* to be refused; **se refuser à** to refuse to accept

réfuter [refyte] *tr* to refute

regagner [rəgaɲe] *tr* to regain

regain [rəgɛ̃] *m* second growth; (fig) aftermath; **regain de** new lease on

ré·gal [regal] *m* (*pl* **-gals**) treat

régaler [regale] *tr* to treat; to level ‖ *intr* to treat

regard [rəgar] *m* look, glance; **couver du regard** to gloat over; to look fondly at; to look greedily at; **en regard** facing, opposite

regar·dant [rəgardã] **-dante** [dãt] *adj*
(coll) penny-pinching

regarder [rəgarde] *tr* to look at; to
face; to concern || *intr* to look; **re-
garder à** to pay attention to; to watch
(*one's money*); to mind (*the price*);
y regarder à deux fois to watch one's
step, think twice || *ref* to face each
other

régate [regat] *f* regatta

régence [reʒãs] *f* regency

régénérer [reʒenere] §10 *tr & ref* to
regenerate

ré·gent [reʒã] **-gente** [ʒãt] *mf* regent

régenter [reʒãte] *tr & intr* to boss

régicide [reʒisid] *mf* regicide (*person*)
|| *m* regicide (*act*)

régie [reʒi] *f* commission, administration; excise tax; stage management;
en régie state owned or operated

regimber [rəʒɛ̃be] *intr & ref* to revolt;
to balk

régime [reʒim] *m* government, form of
government; administration; system;
diet; performance, working conditions; rate (*of speed; of flow; of
charge or discharge of a storage battery*); bunch, cluster; stem (*of
bananas*); (gram) complement;
(gram) government; **en régime permanent** under steady working conditions

régiment [reʒimã] *m* regiment

régimentaire [reʒimãter] *adj* regimental

région [reʒjɔ̃] *f* region

régir [reʒir] *tr* to govern

régisseur [reʒisœr] *m* manager; stage
manager

registre [rəʒistr] *m* register; damper;
throttle valve

réglable [reglabl] *adj* adjustable

réglage [reglaʒ] *m* setting, adjusting;
lines (*on paper*); (mach, rad, telv)
tuning

règle [regl] *f* rule; ruler; **en règle** in
order; **en règle générale** as a general
rule; **règle à calcul** slide rule; **règles**
menstrual period

ré·glé -glée [regle] *adj* regulated; ad-
justed, tuned; well-behaved, orderly;
ruled (*paper*); finished, decided

règlement [regləmã] *m* regulation, rule;
settlement; **règlement intérieur** by-
laws

réglementaire [regləmãter] *adj* regular;
regulation

réglementer [regləmãte] *tr* to regulate,
to control

régler [regle] §10 *tr* to regulate, to put
in order; to set (*a watch*); to settle
(*an account*); to rule (*paper*); (aut,
rad, telv) to tune || *intr* to pay

réglisse [reglis] *m & f* licorice

règne [rɛɲ] *m* reign; (biol) kingdom

régner [reɲe] §10 *intr* to reign

regorger [rəgɔrʒe] §38 *intr* to overflow; **regorger de** to abound in

regratter [rəgrate] *tr* to scrape || *intr*
to pinch pennies

regret [rəgrɛ] *m* regret; **à regret** regret-
fully

regrettable [rəgretabl] *adj* regrettable

regretter [rəgrete] *tr* to regret; to long
for, to miss || *intr* to be sorry

régulariser [regylarize] *tr* to regularize;
to adjust, regulate

régularité [regylarite] *f* regularity

régula·teur [regylatœr] **-trice** [tris] *adj*
regulating || *m* (mach) governor

régulation [regylɑsjɔ̃] *f* regulation

régu·lier [regylje] **-lière** [ljɛr] *adj* regu-
lar; (coll) aboveboard, fair || *m* reg-
ular

réhabiliter [reabilite] *tr* to rehabilitate

rehausser [rəose] *tr* to heighten; to enhance

Reims [rɛ̃s] *m* Rheims

rein [rɛ̃] *m* kidney

réincarnation [reɛ̃karnɑsjɔ̃] *f* reincarnation

reine [rɛn] *f* queen

reine-claude [rɛnklod] *f* (*pl* **-claudes** or
reines-claudes) greengage

reine-des-prés [rɛndepre] *f* (*pl* **reines-
des-prés**) meadowsweet

reine-marguerite [rɛnmargərit] *f* (*pl*
reines-marguerites) aster

réintégrer [reɛ̃tegre] §10 *tr* to reinstate;
to return to

réitérer [reitere] §10 *tr* reiterate

rejaillir [rəʒajir] *intr* to spurt out; to
bounce; to splash; **rejaillir sur** to reflect on

rejet [rəʒɛ] *m* casting up; rejection;
enjambment; (bot) shoot

rejeter [rəʒte] §34 *tr* to reject; to throw
back; to throw up; to shift (*responsi-
bility*) || *ref* to fall back

rejeton [rəʒtɔ̃] *m* shoot; offshoot, offspring; (coll) child

rejoindre [rəʒwɛ̃dr] §35 *tr* to rejoin;
to overtake || *ref* to meet

réjouir [reʒwir] *tr* to gladden, cheer ||
ref to rejoice, to be delighted

réjouissance [reʒwisãs] *f* rejoicing;
réjouissances festivities

réjouis·sant [reʒwisã] **réjouis·sante**
[reʒwisãt] *adj* cheery; amusing

relâche [rəlɑʃ] *m & f* respite, letup || *f*
(naut) stop; **faire relâche** (naut) to
make a call; (theat) to close (*for a
day or two*); **relâche** (public sign) no
performance today

relâ·ché -chée [rəlɑʃe] *adj* lax; loose

relâchement [rəlɑʃmã] *m* relaxation;
letting up

relâcher [rəlɑʃe] *tr* to loosen; to relax;
to release || *intr* (naut) to make a call
|| *ref* to loosen; to become lax

relais [rəlɛ] *m* relay; shift

relance [rəlãs] *f* raise (*e.g., in poker*);
outbreak

relancer [rəlãse] §51 *tr* to start up
again; to harass, to hound; to return
(*the ball*); to raise (*the ante*) || *intr*
(cards) to raise

re·laps -lapse [rəlaps] *mf* backslider

relater [rəlate] *tr* to relate

rela·tif [rəlatif] **-tive** [tiv] *adj* relative

relation [rəlɑsjɔ̃] *f* relation; **en relation
avec, en relations avec** in touch with;
relations connections

relativité [rəlativite] *f* relativity

relaxation [rəlaksɑsjɔ̃] *f* relaxation

relaxer [rəlakse] *tr* to relax; to free ‖ *ref* to relax

relayer [rəleje] §49 *tr* to relay; to relieve ‖ *ref* to work in relays or shifts

reléguer [rəlege] §10 *tr* to relegate

relent [rəlɑ̃] *m* musty smell

relève [rəlɛv] *f* relief; change (*of the guard*); **prendre la relève** to take over

rele·vé -vée [rəlve] *adj* lofty, elevated; turned up; graded (*curve*); spicy ‖ *m* check list; tuck (*in dress*); (culin) next course; **faire le relevé de** to survey; to check off; **relevé de compte** bank statement; **relevé de compteur** meter reading; **relevé de notes des écoles** transcript of grades

relèvement [rəlɛvmɑ̃] *m* raising; recovery, improvement; picking up (*e.g., of wounded*); (naut) bearing

relever [rəlve] §2 *tr* to raise; to turn up; to restore; to relieve, enhance; to pick out; to take a reading of; to season; (mil) to relieve ‖ *intr*—**relever de** to recover from; to depend on ‖ *ref* to rise; to recover; to right itself; to take turns

relief [rəljɛf] *m* relief; **en relief** in relief; **reliefs** leavings

relier [rəlje] *tr* to bind; to link

re·lieur [rəljœr] **-lieuse** [ljøz] *mf* bookbinder

reli·gieux [rəliʒjø] **-gieuse** [ʒjøz] *adj* religious ‖ *m* monk ‖ *f* nun; cream puff

religion [rəliʒjɔ̃] *f* religion

reliquat [rəlika] *m* remainder

relique [rəlik] *f* relic

relire [rəlir] §36 *tr* to read again; to read over again

reliure [rəljyr] *f* binding; bookbinding

reloger [rəlɔʒe] §38 *tr* to find a new home for, to relocate

reluire [rəlɥir] §37 *intr* to shine, gleam, sparkle

relui·sant [rəlɥizɑ̃] **-sante** [zɑ̃t] *adj* shiny, gleaming; **peu reluisant** unpromising, not brilliant

reluquer [rəlyke] *tr* to have an eye on

remâcher [rəmɑʃe] *tr* (coll) to stew over

remailler [rəmaje] *tr* to mend the meshes of

remanier [rəmanje] *tr* to revise, revamp; to reshuffle

remarier [rəmarje] *tr & ref* to remarry

remarquable [rəmarkabl] *adj* remarkable

remarquer [rəmarke] *tr & intr* to remark, to notice; **faire remarquer** to point out ‖ *ref*—**se faire remarquer** to make oneself conspicuous

remballer [rɑ̃bale] *tr* to repack

rembarquer [rɑ̃barke] *tr, intr, & ref* to reembark

rembarrer [rɑ̃bare] *tr* to snub, rebuff

remblai [rɑ̃blɛ] *m* fill; embankment

remblayer [rɑ̃bleje] §49 *tr* to fill

rembobiner [rɑ̃bɔbine] *tr* to rewind

remboîter [rɑ̃bwate] *tr* to reset (*a bone*); to recase (*a book*)

rembourrer [rɑ̃bure] *tr* to upholster; to stuff; to pad

rembourrure [rɑ̃buryr] *f* stuffing

remboursement [rɑ̃bursəmɑ̃] *m* reimbursement

rembourser [rɑ̃burse] *tr* to reimburse

rembrunir [rɑ̃brynir] *tr* to darken; to sadden ‖ *ref* to cloud over

remède [rəmɛd] *m* remedy

remédier [rəmedje] *intr* (with *dat*) to remedy

remembrement [rəmɑ̃brəmɑ̃] *m* regrouping

remémorer [rəmemɔre] *tr*—**remémorer q.ch. à qn** to remind s.o. of s.th. ‖ *ref* to remember

remerciement [rəmɛrsimɑ̃] *m* thanking; **remerciements** thanks; **mille remerciements de** or **pour** a thousand thanks for

remercier [rəmɛrsje] *tr* to thank; to dismiss (*an employee*); to refuse with thanks; **remercier qn de** + *inf* to thank s.o. for + *ger*; **remercier qn de** or **pour** to thank s.o. for

remettre [rəmɛtr] §42 *tr* to remit, to deliver; to put back; to put back on; to give back; to put off; to reset ‖ *ref* to resume; to recover; to pull oneself together; (*said of weather*) to clear; **s'en remettre à** to leave it up to, to depend on

remise [rəmiz] *f* remittance; discount; delivery; postponement; surrender, return; garage; cover (*for game*); **de remise** rented (*car*)

remiser [rəmize] *tr* to put away; to park ‖ *ref* to take cover

rémission [remisjɔ̃] *f* remission

remmailler [rɑ̃maje] *tr* to darn

remmener [rɑ̃mne] §2 *tr* to take back

remon·tant [rəmɔ̃tɑ̃] **-tante** [tɑ̃t] *adj* fortifying; remontant (*rose*) ‖ *m* tonic

remonte [rəmɔ̃t] *f* ascent

remontée [rəmɔ̃te] *f* climb; surfacing; comeback

remonte-pente [rəmɔ̃tpɑ̃t] *m* (*pl* **-pentes**) ski lift

remonter [rəmɔ̃te] *tr* to remount; to pull up; to wind (*a clock*); to pep up; (theat) to put on again ‖ *intr* (aux: ÊTRE) to go up again; to date back ‖ *ref* to pep up

remontoir [rəmɔ̃twar] *m* knob (*of stem-winder*)

remontrance [rəmɔ̃trɑ̃s] *f* remonstrance

remontrer [rəmɔ̃tre] *tr* to show again; to point out ‖ *intr*—**en remontrer à** to outdo, to best

remords [rəmɔr] *m* remorse

remorque [rəmɔrk] *f* tow rope; trailer; **à la remorque** in tow

remorquer [rəmɔrke] *tr* to tow; to haul

remorqueur [rəmɔrkœr] *m* tugboat

rémouleur [remulœr] *m* knife grinder, scissors grinder

remous [rəmu] *m* eddy; wash (*of boat*); agitation

rempailler [rɑ̃paje] *tr* to cane

rempart [rɑ̃par] *m* rampart

remplaçable [rɑ̃plasabl] *adj* replaceable

rempla·çant [rɑ̃plasɑ̃] **-çante** [sɑ̃t] *mf* replacement, substitute

remplacement [rãplasmã] *m* replacement

remplacer [rãplase] §51 *tr* to replace; to take the place of; **remplacer par** to replace with

rem·pli -plie [rãpli] *adj* full || *m* tuck

remplir [rãplir] *tr* to fill; to fill up; to fill out or in; to fulfill || *ref* to fill up

remplissage [rãplisaʒ] *m* filling up

remplumer [rãplyme] *ref* (coll) to put on flesh again; (coll) to make a comeback

remporter [rãpɔrte] *tr* to take back; to carry off; to win

remue-ménage [rəmymenaʒ] *m invar* stir, bustle, to-do

remuer [rəmɥe] *tr* to move; to stir; to remove (*e.g., a piece of furniture*) || *intr* to move || *ref* to move; to hustle

rémunération [remynerasjɔ̃] *f* remuneration

renâcler [rənakle] *intr* to snort; **renâcler à** (coll) to shrink from, to bridle at

renaissance [rənesɑ̃s] *f* renascence, rebirth; renaissance

renais·sant [rənesɑ̃] **renais·sante** [rənesɑ̃t] *adj* renascent, reviving; Renaissance

renaître [rənetr] §46 *tr* to be reborn; to revive; to grow again

re·nard [rənar] **-narde** [nard] *mf* fox

renché·ri -rie [rãʃeri] *adj* fastidious

renchérir [rãʃerir] *tr* to make more expensive || *intr* to go up in price; **renchérir sur** to improve on

rencontre [rãkɔ̃tr] *f* meeting, encounter; clash; collision; **aller à la rencontre de** to go to meet

rencontrer [rãkɔ̃tre] *tr* to meet, encounter || *ref* to meet; to collide; to occur

rendement [rãdmã] *m* yield; (mech) output, efficiency

rendez-vous [rãdevu] *m* appointment, date; rendezvous; **sur rendez-vous** by appointment

rendre [rãdr] *tr* to render; to yield; to surrender; to make; to translate; to vomit || *intr* to bring in, yield || *ref* to surrender; **se rendre à** to go to; **se rendre compte de** to realize

ren·du -due [rãdy] *adj* arrived; translated; all in, exhausted || *m* rendering; returned article

rêne [ren] *f* rein

réné·gat [renega] **-gate** [gat] *mf* renegade

renfer·mé -mée [rãferme] *adj* close-mouthed, stand-offish || *m* close smell; **sentir le renfermé** to smell stuffy

renfermer [rãferme] *tr* to contain; to include || *ref*—**se renfermer dans** to withdraw into; to confine oneself to

renfler [rãfle] *ref* to swell up

renflouer [rãflue] *tr* to keep afloat; to salvage

renfoncement [rãfɔ̃smã] *m* recess; hollow; dent

renfoncer [rãfɔ̃se] §51 *tr* to recess; to dent; to pull down (*e.g., one's hat*) || *ref* to recede; to draw back

renforcement [rãfɔrsəmã] *m* reinforcement

renforcer [rãfɔrse] §51 *tr* to reinforce

renforcir [rãfɔrsir] *tr* (slang) to strengthen || *intr* (slang) to grow stronger

renfort [rãfɔr] *m* reinforcement

renfro·gné -gnée [rãfrɔɲe] *adj* sullen, glum

renfrogner [rãfrɔɲe] *ref* to scowl

rengager [rãgaʒe] §38 *tr* to rehire || *intr & ref* to reenlist

rengaine [rãgen] *f*—**la même rengaine** the same old story; **vieille rengaine** old refrain

rengorger [rãgɔrʒe] §38 *ref* to strut

reniement [rənimã] *m* denial

renier [rənje] *tr* to deny; to repudiate

renifler [rənifle] *tr & intr* to sniff

renne [ren] *m* reindeer

renom [rənɔ̃] *m* renown, fame

renom·mé -mée [rənɔme] *adj* renowned, well-known || *f* fame; reputation

renommer [rənɔme] *tr* to reelect; to reappoint

renoncement [rənɔ̃smã] *m* renunciation

renoncer [rənɔ̃se] §51 *tr* to renounce, repudiate || *intr* to give up; (cards) to renege; (with *dat*) to renounce; (with *dat*) to give up, to abandon; **y renoncer** to give it up

renonciation [rənɔ̃sjasjɔ̃] *f* renunciation; waiver

renoncule [rənɔ̃kyl] *f* buttercup; **renoncule double** bachelor's-button; **renoncule langue** spearwort

renouer [rənwe] *tr* to tie again; to resume (*e.g., a conversation*) || *intr* to renew a friendship

renou·veau [rənuvo] *m* (*pl* **-veaux**) springtime; revival

renouvelable [rənuvlabl] *adj* renewable

renouveler [rənuvle] §34 *tr & ref* to renew

renouvellement [rənuvelmã] *m* renewal

rénover [renɔve] *tr* to renew; to renovate

renseignement [rãseɲmã] *m* piece of information; **de renseignements** (mil) intelligence; **renseignements** information

renseigner [rãseɲe] *tr* to inform || *ref* to find out; **se renseigner auprès de qn** to inquire of s.o.

rentable [rãtabl] *adj* profitable

rente [rãt] *f* revenue, income; annuity; dividend, return; **rente viagère** life annuity

ren·té -tée [rãte] *adj* well-off

renter [rãte] *tr* to endow

ren·tier [rãtje] **-tière** [tjer] *mf* person of independent means

ren·tré -trée [rãtre] *adj* sunken (*eyes*); suppressed (*feelings*) || *f* return; reopening (*of school*); yield

rentrer [rãtre] *tr* to bring in or back; to put in; to hold back (*e.g., one's tears*); to draw in (*claws*) || *intr* (*aux:* ÊTRE) to return, to reenter; to go or come home; to be paid or collected; **rentrer dans** to fit into; to come back to; to get back, recover; **rentrer en soi-même** to take stock of oneself

renverse [rãvɛrs] *f* shift, turn; **à la renverse** backwards

renversement [rãvɛrsəmã] *m* reversal, shift; upset, overturn; overthrow

renverser [rãvɛrse] *tr* to reverse; to overthrow ‖ *intr & ref* to capsize

renvoi [rãvwa] *m* dismissal; postponement; reference; return; belch

renvoyer [rãvwaje] §26 *tr* to dismiss; to fire (*an employee*); to postpone; to refer; to send back

réorganiser [reɔrganize] *tr & ref* to reorganize

réouverture [reuvɛrtyr] *f* reopening

repaire [rəpɛr] *m* den

repaître [rəpɛtr] §12 *tr* to graze; **repaître de** to feast (*e.g., one's eyes*) on ‖ *ref* to eat one's fill (*said of only animals*); **se repaître de** to indulge in, to wallow in

répandre [repãdr] *tr* to spread; to strew, scatter; to spill; to shed ‖ *ref* to spread; **se répandre en** to be profuse in

répan·du -due [repãdy] *adj* widespread; widely known

reparaître [rəparɛtr] §12 *intr* to reappear

répara·teur [reparatœr] **-trice** [tris] *adj* restorative ‖ *m* repairman

réparation [reparasjõ] *f* repair; reparation; restoration

réparer [repare] *tr* to repair; to mend, patch; to make up (*a loss*); to redress (*a wrong*); to restore (*one's strength*)

repartie [rəparti], [reparti] *f* repartee

repartir [rəpartir] §64 *tr* to retort ‖ *intr* (*aux:* ÊTRE) to start again; to leave again

répartir [repartir] *tr* to distribute

répartiteur [repartitœr] *m* distributor; assessor

répartition [repartisjõ] *f* distribution; apportionment; range (*of words*)

repas [rəpa] *m* meal, repast; **dernier repas** (rel) last supper; **repas champêtre** picnic; **repas de noce** wedding breakfast; **repas froid** cold snack; **repas sur le pouce** takeout meal

repassage [rəpasaʒ] *m* recrossing; ironing; stropping; whetting

repasser [rəpase] *tr* to pass again; to go over, to review; to iron; to strop; to whet ‖ *intr* to pass by again; to drop in again

repêcher [rəpeʃe] *tr* to fish out; to give another chance to; (coll) to get (*s.o.*) out of a scrape

repentance [rəpãtãs] *f* repentance

repen·tant [rəpãtã] **-tante** [tãt] *adj* repentant

repen·ti -tie [rəpãti] *adj* repentant

repentir [rəpãtir] *m* repentance ‖ §41 *ref* to repent; **se repentir de** to be sorry for, to repent

repérage [reperaʒ] *m* spotting, locating; tracking; marking with a reference mark; (mov) synchronization

répercussion [reperkysjõ] *f* repercussion

répercuter [reperkyte] *tr* to reflect ‖ *ref* to reverberate; to have repercussions

repère [rəpɛr] *m* mark, reference

repérer [repere] §10 *tr* to locate, spot; to mark with a reference mark; (mov) to synchronize

répertoire [repɛrtwar] *m* repertory; index; **répertoire à onglets** thumb index; **répertoire d'adresses** address book; **répertoire vivant** walking encyclopedia

répéter [repete] §10 *tr & ref* to repeat

répéti·teur [repetitœr] **-trice** [tris] *mf* assistant teacher; coach, tutor

répétition [repetisjõ] *f* repetition; private lesson, tutoring; rehearsal; **répétition des couturières** next to last dress rehearsal; **répétition générale** final dress rehearsal

repeupler [rəpœple] *tr* to repeople; to restock

repiquer [rəpike] *tr* to plant out (*seedlings*); to repave; to restitch; to rerecord; (phot) to retouch ‖ *intr*— **repiquer à** (slang) to come back to

répit [repi] *m* respite, letup

replacement [rəplasmã] *m* replacement; reinvestment

replacer [rəplase] §51 *tr* to replace; to find a new job for; to reinvest ‖ *ref* to find a new job

replâtrage [rəplɑtraʒ] *m* replastering; makeshift; (fig) patchwork

re·plet [rəplɛ] **-plète** [plɛt] *adj* fat, plump

repli [rəpli] *m* crease, fold; dip, depression; (mil) falling back

replier [rəplije] *tr* to refold; to turn up; to close (*e.g., an umbrella*) ‖ *ref* to curl up, to coil up; (mil) to fall back

réplique [replik] *f* reply, retort; replica; **donner la réplique à qn** to answer s.o.; (theat) to give s.o. his cue; (theat) to play the straight man or stooge for s.o.

répliquer [replike] *tr & intr* to reply

replonger [rəplõʒe] §38 *tr* to plunge again ‖ *intr* to dive again ‖ *ref*—**se replonger dans** to get back into

répon·dant [repõdã] **-dante** [dãt] *mf* guarantor; (eccl) server; **avoir du répondant** (coll) to have money behind one

répondre [repõdr] *tr* to answer (*e.g., yes or no*); to assure ‖ *intr* to answer, reply; to answer back, be saucy; to reecho; **répondre à** to answer (*e.g., a question, a letter*); to correspond to; **répondre de** to answer for (*a person*); to guarantee (*a thing*) ‖ *ref* to answer each other; to correspond to each other; to be in harmony

réponse [repõs] *f* answer, response; **réponse normande** evasive answer

report [rəpɔr] *m* carrying forward or over; carry-over

reportage [rəpɔrtaʒ] *m* reporting

reporter [rəpɔrter] *m* reporter ‖ [rəpɔrte] *tr* to carry back; to postpone; (math) to carry forward ‖ *intr* (com) to carry stock; **à reporter** carried forward ‖ *ref*—**se reporter à** to be carried back to (e.g., *childhood days*); to refer to

reporteur [rəpɔrtœr] *m* broker

repos [rəpo] *m* rest, repose; **au repos** not running, still; **de tout repos** reliable; **en repos** at rest; **repos!** (mil) at ease!

repo·sé -sée [rəpoze] *adj* refreshed, relaxed

reposer [rəpoze] *tr* to rest ‖ *intr* to rest; **ici repose . . . here lies . . .** ‖ *ref* to rest; **s'en reposer sur** to rely on

repous·sant [rəpusã] **repous·sante** [rəpusãt] *adj* repulsive

repousser [rəpuse] *tr* to push, shove; to repulse, repel; to reject, refuse; to postpone; to emboss ‖ *intr* to grow again; to be offensive; (arti) to recoil

repoussoir [rəpuswar] *m* foil; contrast; (mach) driving bolt

reprendre [rəprãdr] §56 *tr* to take back; to resume; to regain (*consciousness*); to find fault with; to take in (e.g., *a dress*); to catch (*one's breath*); (theat) to put on again ‖ *intr* to start again; to pick up, to improve; to criticize ‖ *ref* to pull oneself together; to correct oneself in speaking

représailles [rəprezaj] *fpl* reprisal

représentant [rəprezãtã] *m* representative

représenta·tif [rəprezãtatif] **-tive** [tiv] *adj* representative

représentation [rəprezãtasjɔ̃] *f* representation; performance; remonstrance

représenter [rəprezãte] *tr* to represent; to put on, to perform ‖ *intr* to make a good showing

répression [represjɔ̃] *f* repression

réprimande [reprimãd] *f* reprimand

réprimander [reprimãde] *tr* to reprimand

réprimer [reprime] *tr* to repress

re·pris [rəpri] **-prise** [priz] *adj* recaptured; **être repris de** to suffer from a recurrence of ‖ *m*—**repris de justice** hardened criminal, habitual offender ‖ *f* see **reprise**

reprisage [rəprizaʒ] *m* darning

reprise [rəpriz] *f* recapture; resumption; darning; pickup (*acceleration of motor*); (theat) revival; **à plusieurs reprises** several times; **faire une reprise à** to darn; **par reprises** a little at a time

repriser [rəprize] *tr* to darn; to mend

réproba·teur [reprɔbatœr] **-trice** [tris] *adj* reproving

reproche [rəprɔʃ] *m* reproach

reprocher [rəprɔʃe] *tr* to reproach; to begrudge; (law) to take exception to (*a witness*); **reprocher q.ch. à qn** to reproach s.o. for s.th.; to begrudge s.o. s.th.; to remind s.o. reproachfully of s.th.

reproduction [rəprɔdyksjɔ̃] *f* reproduction

reproduire [rəprɔdɥir] §19 *tr & ref* to reproduce

réprou·vé -vée [repruve] *adj & mf* outcast; damned

réprouver [repruve] *tr* to disapprove

reptile [reptil] *m* reptile

re·pu -pue [rəpy] *adj* satiated

républi·cain [repyblikɛ̃] **-caine** [ken] *adj & mf* republican

république [repyblik] *f* republic

répudier [repydje] *tr* to repudiate

répu·gnant [repynã] **-gnante** [nãt] *adj* repugnant

répugner [repyne] *intr* (with *dat*) to disgust; to balk at; **répugner à** + *inf* to be loath to + *inf*

répul·sif [repylsif] **-sive** [siv] *adj* repulsive

réputation [repytasjɔ̃] *f* reputation

répu·té -tée [repyte] *adj* of high repute; **être réputé** to be reputed to be

requérir [rakerir] §3 *tr* to demand; to ask; to require; to summon; to requisition

requête [rəket] *f* petition, appeal

requiem [rekɥijɛm] *m* requiem

requin [rəkɛ̃] *m* shark

réquisition [rekizisjɔ̃] *f* requisition

réquisitionner [rekizisjone] *tr* to requisition

réquisitoire [rekizitwar] *m* indictment

res·capé -capée [reskape] *adj* rescued ‖ *mf* survivor

rescinder [resɛ̃de] *tr* to rescind

rescousse [reskus] *f* rescue

ré·seau [rezo] *m* (*pl* **-seaux**) net; network, system; **réseau de barbelés** barbed wire entanglement

réséda [rezeda] *m* mignonette

réservation [rezervasjɔ̃] *f* reservation

réserve [rezerv] *f* reserve; reservation; **de réserve** emergency, reserve (*rations, fund, etc.*); **sous réserve que** on condition that; **sous toutes réserves** without committing oneself

réserver [rezerve] *tr* to reserve; to set aside ‖ *ref* to set aside for oneself; to wait and see, to hold off

réserviste [rezervist] *m* reservist

réservoir [rezervwar] *m* reservoir, tank; **réservoir de bombes** bomb bay

résidence [rezidãs] *f* residence

rési·dent [rezidã] **-dente** [dãt] *mf* alien, foreigner; (dipl) resident

résiden·tiel -tielle [rezidãsjel] *adj* residential

résider [rezide] *intr* to reside

résidu [rezidy] *m* residue; refuse

résignation [rezinasjɔ̃] *f* resignation

résigner [rezine] *tr* to resign ‖ *ref* to be or become resigned

résilier [rezilje] *tr* to cancel

résille [rezij] *f* hair net

résine [rezin] *f* resin

résistance [rezistãs] *f* resistance

résis·tant [rezistã] **-tante** [tãt] *adj* resistant; strong; fast (*color*)

résister [reziste] *intr* to be fast, not run (*said of colors or dyes*); (with *dat*) to resist, to withstand, to hold out against; (with *dat*) to weather (e.g., *a storm*); **résister à** + *inf* to resist + *inf*

réso·lu -lue [rezɔly] *adj* resolute, resolved

résolution [rezɔlysjɔ̃] *f* resolution; canceling

résonance [rezɔnɑ̃s] *f* resonance

résonner [rezɔne] *intr* to resound; to re-echo

résorber [rezɔrbe] *tr* to absorb || *ref* to become absorbed

résoudre [rezudr] §60 *tr* to resolve; to decide; to solve; to persuade; to cancel; **être résolu à** to be resolved to || *intr*—**résoudre de** to decide to || *ref*—**se résoudre à** to decide to; to reconcile oneself to; **se résoudre en** to turn into

respect [respe] *m* respect; **présenter ses respects (à)** to pay one's respects (to); **respect de soi** or **soi-même** self-respect; **respect humain** [respekymɛ̃] fear of what people might say; **sauf votre (mon,** etc.**) respect** with all due respect; pardon the language

respectable [respektabl] *adj* respectable

respecter [respekte] *tr* to respect || *ref* to keep one's self-respect

respec·tif [respektif] **-tive** [tiv] *adj* respective

respec·tueux [respektɥø] **-tueuse** [tɥøz] *adj* respectful

respirer [respire] *tr* to breathe || *intr* to breathe; to catch one's breath

resplendis·sant [resplɑ̃disɑ̃] **resplendis·sante** [resplɑ̃disɑ̃t] *adj* resplendent

responsabilité [respɔ̃sabilite] *f* responsibility

responsable [respɔ̃sabl] *adj* responsible; **responsable de** responsible for; **responsable envers** accountable to || *mf* person responsible, person in charge

resquiller [reskije] *tr* (coll) to obtain by fraud || *intr* (coll) to crash the gate

resquil·leur [reskijœr] **resquil·leuse** [reskijøz] *mf* (coll) gate-crasher

ressac [rəsak] *m* surf; undertow

ressaisir [rəsezir] *tr* to recapture || *ref* to regain one's self-control

ressasser [rəsase] *tr* to go over and over again

ressaut [rəso] *m* projection; sharp rise

ressemblance [rəsɑ̃blɑ̃s] *f* resemblance

ressembler [rəsɑ̃ble] *intr* (with *dat*) to resemble, look like || *ref* to resemble one another; to be alike, to look alike

ressemeler [rəsəmle] §34 *tr* to resole

ressentiment [rəsɑ̃timɑ̃] *m* resentment

ressentir [rəsɑ̃tir] §41 *tr* to feel keenly, to be hurt by (*an insult*); to experience (*joy, pain, surprise*) || *ref*—**se ressentir de** to feel the aftereffects of

resserre [rəser] *f* shed, storeroom

resserrer [rəsere] *tr* to tighten; to contract; to close; to lock up (*e.g., valuables*) again || *ref* to tighten; to contract

ressort [rəsɔr] *m* spring; springiness; motive; **du ressort de** within the jurisdiction of; **en dernier ressort** without appeal; as a last resort; **ressort à boudin** coil spring; **sans ressort** slack

ressortir [rəsɔrtir] *intr*—**ressortir à** to come under the jurisdiction of; to

fall under the head of || §64 *intr* (*aux:* ÊTRE) to go out again; to stand out, to be evident; **faire ressortir** to set off; **il ressort de** it follows from; **il ressort que** it follows that

ressortis·sant [rəsɔrtisɑ̃] **ressortis·sante** [rəsɔrtisɑ̃t] *adj*—**ressortissant à** under the jurisdiction of || *mf* national

ressource [rəsurs] *f* resource

ressouvenir [rəsuvnir] §72 *ref* to reminisce; **se ressouvenir de** to recall

ressusciter [resysite] *tr* to resuscitate; to resurrect || *intr* (*aux:* ÊTRE) to rise from the dead; to get well

res·tant [restɑ̃] **-tante** [tɑ̃t] *adj* remaining || *m* remainder

restaurant [restɔrɑ̃] *m* restaurant; **restaurant libre-service** self-service restaurant

restauration [restɔrɑsjɔ̃] *f* restoration; restaurant business

restaurer [restɔre] *tr* to restore || *ref* (coll) to take some nourishment

reste [rest] *m* rest, remainder; remnant; relic; **au reste, du reste** moreover; **de reste** spare; **restes** remains; leftovers

rester [reste] *intr* (*aux:* ÊTRE) to remain, to stay; to be left over; **en rester** to stop, to leave off; **en rester là** to stop right there; **il me (te, leur,** etc.**) reste q.ch.** I (you, they, etc.) have s.th. left

restituer [restitɥe] *tr* to restore; to give back

restitution [restitysjɔ̃] *f* restitution; restoration

restoroute [restɔrut] *m* drive-in restaurant

restreindre [restrɛ̃dr] §50 *tr* to restrict; to curtail || *ref* to become limited; to cut down expenses

res·treint [restrɛ̃] **-treinte** [trɛ̃t] *adj* limited

restriction [restriksjɔ̃] *f* restriction

résultat [rezylta] *m* result

résulter [rezylte] *intr* to result; **il en résulte que** it follows that

résumé [rezyme] *m* summary, recapitulation; **en résumé** in short, in a word

résumer [rezyme] *tr* to summarize || *ref* to be summed up

résurrection [rezyreksjɔ̃] *f* resurrection

rétablir [retablir] *tr* to restore || *ref* to recover

rétablissement [retablismɑ̃] *m* restoration; recovery

retailler [rətaje] *tr* to resharpen

retape [rətap] *f* (slang) streetwalking

retaper [rətape] *tr* (coll) to straighten up; (coll) to give a lick and a promise to || *ref* (coll) to perk up

retard [rətar] *m* delay; **en retard** late; slow (*clock*); **en retard sur** behind

retardataire [rətardater] *adj* tardy; retarded || *mf* latecomer, straggler

retarder [rətarde] *tr* to delay; to put off; to set back || *intr* to go slow, to be behind

retenir [rətnir] §72 *tr* to hold or keep back; to detain; to remember, note; to reserve; to retain (*a lawyer*); to carry (*a number*) || *ref*—**se retenir à** to cling to; **se retenir de** to refrain from

retentir [rətãtir] *intr* to resound

rete·nu -nue [rətny] *adj* reserved; held back || *f* withholding; reserve; **retenue à la source** withholding tax

réticence [retisãs] *f* evasiveness, concealment; hesitation; reservation, misgiving

réti·cent -cente [retisã] *-cente* [sãt] *adj* evasive; hesitant; reserved, withdrawn

réticule [retikyl] *m* handbag

ré·tif [retif] *-tive* [tiv] *adj* restive

rétine [retin] *f* retina

retirement [rətirmã] *m* contraction

retirer [rətire] *tr* to withdraw; to take off; to fire again || *intr* to fire again || *ref* to withdraw; to retire

retombée [rətɔ̃be] *f* fall; hang (*of cloth*); **retombées radioactives** fallout

retomber [rətɔ̃be] *intr* (*aux*: ÊTRE) to fall again; to fall; to fall back; to hang, hang down; to relapse

retordre [rətərdrə] *tr* to twist; to wring out

rétorquer [retorke] *tr* to retort

re·tors [rətɔr] *-torse* [tɔrs] *adj* twisted; wily; curved (*beak*) || *mf* rascal

retouche [rətuʃ] *f* retouch; (phot) retouching; **retouches** alterations

retoucher [rətuʃe] *tr* to retouch; to make alterations on

retour [rətur] *m* return; turn, bend; reversal (*e.g., of opinion*); **en retour d'équerre** at right angles; **être de retour** to be back; **par retour du courrier** by return mail; **retour à la masse** (elec) ground (*on chassis of auto, radio, etc.*); **retour à la terre** (elec) ground; **retour d'âge** change of life; **retour de flamme** backfire; **retour de manivelle** kick (of the crank); (fig) backlash; **retour en arrière** flashback

retourner [rəturne] *tr* to send back, to return; to upset; to turn over (*e.g., the soil*); to turn inside out || *intr* (*aux*: ÊTRE) to go back, to return || *ref* to turn around, to look back; to turn over; (fig) to veer, to shift; **s'en retourner** to go back; **se retourner contre** to turn against

retracer [rətrase] §51 *tr* to retrace; to bring to mind, to recall || *ref* to come to mind again; to recall

rétracter [retrakte] *tr & ref* to retract

rétraction [retraksjɔ̃] *f* contraction

retrait [rətre] *m* withdrawal; shrinkage; running out (*of tide*); **en retrait** set back, recessed; (typ) indented; **retrait de permis** suspension of driver's license

retraite [rətret] *f* retreat; retirement; pension; **battre en retraite** to retreat; **en retraite** retired; **prendre sa retraite** to retire; **toucher sa retraite** to draw one's pension

retrai·té -tée [rətrete] *adj* pensioned, retired || *mf* pensioner

retranchement [rətrãʃmã] *m* retrenchment; cutting out

retrancher [rətrãʃe] *tr* to cut off or out, to retrench || *ref* to become entrenched

retransmettre [rətrãsmetr] §42 *tr* to retransmit; to rebroadcast

retransmission [rətrãsmisjɔ̃] *f* retransmission; rebroadcast

rétré·ci -cie [retresi] *adj* narrow; shrunk

rétrécir [retresir] *tr* to shrink; to take in (*a garment*) || *intr & ref* to shrink; to narrow

retremper [rətrãpe] *tr* to soak again; to retemper; to give new strength or life to || *ref* to take another dip; to get new vigor

rétribuer [retribɥe] *tr* to remunerate

rétribution [retribysjɔ̃] *f* retribution; salary, fee

rétroaction [retroaksjɔ̃] *f* feedback; retroaction

rétrofusée [retrofyze] *f* retrorocket

rétrograder [retrograde] *intr* to retrogress

rétrospection [retrospeksjɔ̃] *f* retrospection

retrousser [rətruse] *tr* to roll up, to turn up; to curl up (*one's lip*) || *ref* to turn up or pull up one's clothes

retrouver [rətruve] *tr* to find again; to recover || *ref* to be back again; to meet again; to get one's bearings

rétroviseur [retrovizœr] *m* rear-view mirror

rets [re] *m*—**prendre dans des rets** to snare

réunification [reynifikasjɔ̃] *f* reunification

réunion [reynjɔ̃] *f* reunion; meeting

réunir [reynir] *tr* to unite, join; to reunite; to call together, convene || *ref* to meet; to reunite

réus·si -sie [reysi] *adj* successful

réussir [reysir] *tr* to make a success of, to be good at || *intr* to succeed; **réussir à** to succeed in; to pass (*an exam*)

réussite [reysit] *f* success; **faire une réussite** (cards) to play solitaire

revaloir [rəvalwar] §71 *tr*—**revaloir q.ch. à qn** to pay s.o. back for s.th.

revan·chard [rəvãʃar] *-charde* [ʃard] *adj* (coll) vengeful || *mf* (coll) avenger

revanche [rəvãʃ] *f* revenge; return bout or engagement, return match; **en revanche** on the other hand; **prendre sa revanche sur** to get even with

revancher [rəvãʃe] *ref* to get even

rêvasser [revase] *intr* to daydream

rêvasserie [revasri] *f* fitful dreaming; daydreaming

rêve [rev] *m* dream

revêche [rəveʃ] *adj* sullen, crabbed

réveil [revej] *m* awakening; alarm clock; (mil) reveille

réveille-matin [revejmatɛ̃] *m invar* alarm clock

réveiller [reveje] *tr & ref* to wake up

réveillon [revejɔ̃] *m* Christmas Eve supper; New Year's Eve party

réveillonner [revejone] *intr* to celebrate Christmas Eve or New Year's Eve

révéla·teur [revelatœr] *-trice* [tris] *adj*

revealing; telltale || *mf* informer || *m* (phot) developer

révélation [revelasjɔ̃] *f* revelation

révéler [revele] §10 *tr* to reveal; (phot) to develop

revenant [rəvnɑ̃] *m* ghost

reven-deur [rəvɑ̃dœr] **-deuse** [døz] *mf* retailer; secondhand dealer

revendication [rəvɑ̃dikɑsjɔ̃] *f* claim

revendiquer [rəvɑ̃dike] *tr* to claim; to insist upon; to assume (*a responsibility*)

revendre [rəvɑ̃dr] *tr* to resell

revenez-y [rəvnezi] *m invar* (coll) return; **un goût de revenez-y** (coll) a taste like more

revenir [rəvnir] §72 *intr* (aux: ÊTRE) to return, come back; (with *dat*) to suit, to please; **en revenir** to have a narrow escape; **faire revenir** (culin) to brown; **n'en pas revenir** to not get over it; **revenir à** to come to, to amount to; to come to (*e.g.*, *mind*); **revenir à soi** to come to; **revenir bredouille** to come back empty-handed; **revenir de** to recover from; to realize (*a mistake*); **revenir de loin** to have been at death's door; **revenir sur** to go back on (*e.g.*, *one's word*) || *ref*—**s'en revenir** to come back

revente [rəvɑ̃t] *f* resale

revenu [rəvny] *m* revenue, income

revenue [rəvny] *f* new growth (*of trees*)

rêver [reve] *tr* to dream || *intr* to dream; **rêver à** to dream of (*think about*); **rêver de** to dream of (*in sleep; to long to*)

réverbère [reverber] *m* streetlight

réverbérer [reverbere] §10 *tr* to reflect (*light, heat, etc.*) || *ref* to be reflected

reverdir [rəverdir] *tr* to make green || *intr* to grow green; to become young again

révérence [reverɑ̃s] *f* reverence; curtsy; **révérence parler** (coll) pardon the language; **tirer sa révérence** to bow out

révéren-cieux [reverɑ̃sjø] **-cieuse** [sjøz] *adj* obsequious

révé-rend [reverɑ̃] **-rende** [rɑ̃d] *adj & m* reverend

révérer [revere] §10 *tr* to revere

rêverie [revri] *f* reverie

revers [rəver] *m* reverse; lapel; (tennis) backhand; **à revers** from behind; **revers de main** slap with the back of the hand

reverser [rəverse] *tr* to pour back; to pour out again

réversible [reversibl] *adj* reversible

revêtement [rəvetmɑ̃] *m* surfacing; facing; lining; casing

revêtir [rəvetir] §73 *tr* to put on; to clothe, to dress up; to invest; to surface; to line; to face; to assume (*a form; an aspect*)

rê-veur [rəvœr] **-veuse** [vøz] *adj* dreamy || *mf* dreamer; **cela me laisse rêveur** that leaves me puzzled

revirement [rəvirmɑ̃] *m* sudden reversal; (naut) tack

réviser [revize] *tr* to revise; to review; to overhaul; to recondition

réviseur [revizœr] *m* proofreader

révision [revizjɔ̃] *f* revision; review; overhauling; proofreading

révisionniste [revizjɔnist] *adj & mf* revisionist

revivre [rəvivr] §74 *tr* to live again, relive || *intr* to live again

révocation [revokɑsjɔ̃] *f* dismissal; revocation

revoici [rəvwasi] *prep*—**me** (**vous**, etc.) **revoici** (coll) here I am (you are, etc.) again

revoilà [rəvwala] *prep*—**le** (**la**, etc.) **voilà** (coll) there it, he (she, etc.) is again

revoir [rəvwar] *m*—**au revoir** good-by || §75 *tr* to see again; to review; to revise || *ref* to meet again

révol-tant [revoltɑ̃] **-tante** [tɑ̃t] *adj* revolting

révolte [revolt] *f* revolt, rebellion

révol-té [revolte] **-tée** [revolte] *adj & mf* rebel

révolter [revolte] *tr & ref* to revolt; **se révolter devant** to be revolted by

révo-lu [revoly] **-lue** [revoly] *adj* completed; elapsed; bygone

révolution [revolysjɔ̃] *f* revolution

révolutionnaire [revolysjɔner] *adj & mf* revolutionary

revolver [revolver] *m* revolver

révoquer [revoke] *tr* to revoke; to countermand; to dismiss; to recall

re-vu **-vue** [rəvy] *adj* revised || *f* see revue

revue [rəvy] *f* review; magazine, journal; (theat) revue; **passer en revue** to review (*past events; troops*)

rez-de-chaussée [red/ose] *m invar* first floor, ground floor

R.F. *abbr* (**République Française**) French Republic

rhabiller [rabije] *tr* to repair; to dress again; to refurbish || *ref* to change one's clothes; **va te rhabiller!** (pej) get out!

rhapsodie [rapsodi] *f* rhapsody

Rhénanie [renani] *f* Rhineland

rhéostat [reosta] *m* rheostat

rhétorique [retorik] *adj* rhetorical || *f* rhetoric

Rhin [rɛ̃] *m* Rhine

rhinocéros [rinoseros] *m* rhinoceros

rhubarbe [rybarb] *f* rhubarb

rhum [rom] *m* rum

rhumati-sant [rymatizɑ̃] **-sante** [zɑ̃t] *adj & mf* rheumatic

rhumatis-mal **-male** [rymatismal] *adj* (*pl* **-maux** [mo]) rheumatic

rhumatisme [rymatism] *m* rheumatism

rhume [rym] *m* cold; **rhume des foins** hay fever

riant [rijɑ̃] **riante** [rijɑ̃t] *adj* smiling; cheerful, pleasant

ribambelle [ribɑ̃bel] *f* (coll) long string, swarm, lot

ri-baud [ribo] **-baude** [bod] *adj* licentious || *mf* camp follower; debauchee

ricanement [rikanmɑ̃] *m* snicker

ricaner [rikane] *intr* to snicker

ri-chard [ri/ar] **-charde** [/ard] *mf* (coll) moneybags

riche [ri/] *adj* rich || *m* rich man; **nouveaux riches** newly rich

riche·lieu [riʃəljø] *m* (*pl* **-lieu** or **-lieus**) oxford

richesse [riʃɛs] *f* wealth; richness; **richesses** riches; **richesses naturelles** natural resources

ricin [risɛ̃] *m* castor-oil plant; castor bean

ricocher [rikɔʃe] *intr* to ricochet, rebound

ricochet [rikɔʃɛ] *m* ricochet; **faire des ricochets** to play ducks and drakes; **par ricochet** indirectly

rictus [riktys] *m* rictus; grin

ride [rid] *f* wrinkle; ripple

ri·deau [rido] *m* (*pl* **-deaux**) curtain; **rideau d'arbres** line of trees; **rideau de fer** iron curtain; safety blind (*of a store*); (theat) fire curtain; **rideau de feu** (mil) cover of artillery fire; **rideau de fumée** smoke screen

ridelle [ridɛl] *f* rave, side rails (*of wagon*)

rider [ride] *tr* to wrinkle; to ripple

ridicule [ridikyl] *adj* ridiculous ‖ *m* ridicule

ridiculiser [ridikylize] *tr* to ridicule

rien [rjɛ̃] *m* trifle; **comme un rien** with no trouble at all; **un rien de** just a little (bit) of; **un rien de temps** no time at all ‖ *pron indef*—**de rien** don't mention it, you're welcome; of no importance; **il n'en est rien** such is not the case; **rien ne** or **ne . . . rien** §90B nothing, not anything; **rien de moins (que)** nothing less (than); **rien que** nothing but

rieur [rjœr] **rieuse** [rjøz] *adj* laughing ‖ *mf* laugher, mocker ‖ *f* (orn) black-headed gull

riflard [riflar] *m* coarse file; jack plane; paring chisel

rigide [riʒid] *adj* rigid; stiff; strict

rigolade [rigolad] *f* (coll) good time, fun; (coll) big joke

rigole [rigol] *f* drain; ditch

rigoler [rigole] *intr* (slang) to laugh, to joke

rigo·lo [rigolo] **-lote** [lɔt] *adj* (coll) comical; (coll) queer, funny ‖ *mf* (coll) card ‖ *m* (slang) rod, gat

rigou·reux [rigurø] **-reuse** [røz] *adj* rigorous; severe

rigueur [rigœr] *f* rigor, strictness; **à la rigueur** to the letter; as a last resort; **de rigueur** compulsory, de rigueur

rillons [rijɔ̃] *mpl* cracklings

rimail·leur [rimajœr] **rimail·leuse** [rimajøz] *mf* (coll) rhymester

rime [rim] *f* rhyme; **rimes croisées** alternate rhymes; **rimes plates** couplets of alternate masculine and feminine rhymes

rimer [rime] *tr & intr* to rhyme

rinçage [rɛ̃saʒ] *m* rinse

rince-bouche [rɛ̃sbuʃ] *m invar* mouthwash

rince-bouteilles [rɛ̃sbutɛj] *m invar* (mach) bottle-washing machine

rince-doigts [rɛ̃sdwa] *m invar* fingerbowl

rincer [rɛ̃se] §51 *tr* to rinse; (slang) to ruin, to take to the cleaners

rinçure [rɛ̃syr] *f* rinsing water

ring [riŋ] *m* ring (*for, e.g., boxing*)

ringard [rɛ̃gar] *m* poker (*for fire*)

ripaille [ripaj] *f* (coll) blowout; **faire ripaille** (coll) to carouse

ripe [rip] *f* scraper

riper [ripe] *tr* to scrape; (naut) to slip ‖ *intr* to slip; to skid

riposte [ripɔst] *f* riposte, retort

riposter [ripɔste] *tr* to riposte, to retort

rire [rir] *m* laugh; laughter; laughing ‖ §61 *intr* to laugh; to joke; to smile; **pour rire** for fun, in jest; **rire dans sa barbe, rire sous cape** to laugh up one's sleeve; **rire de** to laugh at or over; **rire du bout des lèvres, rire du bout des dents** to titter; **rire jaune** to force a laugh ‖ *ref*—**se rire de** to laugh at

ris [ri] *m* (naut) reef; (obs) laughter; **ris d'agneau** or **de veau** sweetbread

risée [rize] *f* scorn; laughingstock; light squall

risible [rizibl] *adj* laughable

risque [risk] *m* risk

ris·qué -quée [riske] *adj* risky; risqué

risquer [riske] *tr* to risk; to hasard (*e.g., a remark*) ‖ *intr*—**risquer de** + *inf* to risk + *ger*; to have a good chance of + *ger*

risque-tout [riskətu] *mf invar* daredevil

rissoler [risole] *tr & intr* to brown

ristourne [risturn] *f* rebate, refund; dividend

ristourner [risturne] *tr* to refund

ritournelle [riturnɛl] *f*—**c'est toujours la même ritournelle** it's always the same old story; **ritournelle publicitaire** advertising jingle or slogan

ri·tuel -tuelle [ritɥɛl] *adj & m* ritual

rivage [rivaʒ] *m* shore; bank

ri·val -vale [rival] (*pl* **-vaux** [vo] **-vales**) *adj & mf* rival

rivaliser [rivalize] *intr* to compete; **rivaliser avec** to compete with, to rival

rivalité [rivalite] *f* rivalry

rive [riv] *f* shore; bank

river [rive] *tr* to rivet

rive·rain [rivrɛ̃] **-raine** [rɛn] *adj* waterfront; bordering ‖ *mf* riversider; dweller along a street or road

riveraineté [rivrɛnte] *f* riparian rights

rivet [rivɛ] *m* rivet

rivière [rivjɛr] *f* river, stream, tributary; (turf) water jump; **rivière de diamants** diamond necklace

rixe [riks] *f* brawl

riz [ri] *m* rice; **riz au lait** rice pudding; **riz glacé** polished rice

rizière [rizjɛr] *f* rice field

robe [rɔb] *f* dress; gown; robe; wrapper (*of cigar*); skin (*of onion, sausage, etc.*); husk (*of, e.g., bean*); **robe de chambre** dressing gown; **robe d'intérieur** housecoat

rober [rɔbe] *tr* to husk, to skin; to wrap (*a cigar*)

roberts [rɔbɛr] *mpl* (slang) breasts

robin [rɔbɛ̃] *m* (coll) judge; (pej) shyster

robinet [rɔbinɛ] *m* faucet, tap; cock;

robinet d'eau tiède (coll) bore; **robinet mélangeur** mixing faucet

robinier [rɔbinje] *m* (bot) locust tree

robot [rɔbo] *m* robot

robre [rɔbr] *m* rubber (*in bridge*)

robuste [rɔbyst] *adj* robust; firm

roc [rɔk] *m* rock

rocaille [rɔkaj] *adj* rococo ‖ *f* stones; rocky ground; stonework

rocail·leux [rɔkajø] **rocail·leuse** [rɔkajøz] *adj* rocky, stony; harsh

roche [rɔʃ] *f* rock; boulder

rocher [rɔʃe] *m* rock; crag

rochet [rɔʃe] *m* ratchet; bobbin

ro·cheux [rɔʃø] **-cheuse** [ʃøz] *adj* rocky

rodage [rɔdaʒ] *m* grinding; breaking in; **en rodage** being broken in, new

roder [rɔde] *tr* to grind (*a valve*); to break in (*a new car*); to polish up (*a new play*)

rôder [rode] *intr* to prowl

rô·deur [rodœr] **-deuse** [døz] *adj* prowling ‖ *mf* prowler

rogatons [rɔgatõ] *mpl* (coll) scraps

rogne [rɔɲ] *f* (coll) anger; **mettre qn en rogne** (coll) to make s.o. see red

rogner [rɔɲe] *tr* to pare, to trim

rognon [rɔɲõ] *m* kidney

rogomme [rɔgɔm] *m*—**de rogomme** (coll) husky, beery (*voice*)

rogue [rɔg] *adj* arrogant

roi [rwa], [rwa] *m* king; **tirer les rois** to gather to eat the Twelfth-night cake

roitelet [rwatlɛ] *m* kinglet; (orn) kinglet

rôle [rol] *m* role; roll, muster

ro·main [rɔmɛ̃] **-maine** [mɛn] *adj* Roman; roman (*type*); romaine (*lettuce*) ‖ *m* (typ) roman ‖ *f* romaine (lettuce) ‖ (*cap*) *mf* Roman (*person*)

ro·man [rɔmɑ̃] **-mane** [man] *adj* Romance (*language*); (archit) Romanesque ‖ *m* novel; **roman d'anticipation** science-fiction novel; **roman policier** detective story

romance [rɔmɑ̃s] *f* ballad

romanche [rɔmɑ̃ʃ] *m* Romansh

roman·cier [rɔmɑ̃sje] **-cière** [sjɛr] *mf* novelist; **romancier d'anticipation** science-fiction writer

ro·mand [rɔmɑ̃] **-mande** [mɑ̃d] *adj* French-speaking (*Switzerland*)

romanesque [rɔmanɛsk] *adj* romanesque, romantic, fabulous

roman-feuilleton [rɔmɑ̃fœjtõ] *m* (*pl* **romans-feuilletons**) newspaper serial

roman-fleuve [rɔmɑ̃flœv] *m* (*pl* **romans-fleuves**) saga novel

romani·chel **-chelle** [rɔmaniʃel] *mf* gypsy, vagrant

romantique [rɔmɑ̃tik] *adj & mf* romantic

romantisme [rɔmɑ̃tism] *m* romanticism

romarin [rɔmarɛ̃] *m* (bot) rosemary

Rome [rɔm] *f* Rome

rompre [rõpr] (3d *sg pres ind* **rompt** [rõ]) *tr* to break; to burst; to break in, train; to break off ‖ *intr & ref* to break

romsteck [rɔmstɛk] *m* rump steak

ronce [rõs] *f* bramble; curly grain (*of wood*); **en ronces artificielles** barbed-wire (*fence*)

ronchonner [rõʃɔne] *intr* (coll) to bellyache, grumble

rond [rõ] **ronde** [rõd] *adj* round; rounded; plump; straightforward; (slang) tight, drunk ‖ *m* ring, circle; round slice; (coll) dough, money; **en rond** in a circle; **rond de fumée** smoke ring; **rond de serviette** napkin ring ‖ *f* round; beat, round; round dance; radius; round hand; (mus) whole note; **à la ronde** around; **s'amuser à la ronde, faire la ronde** to go ring-around-a-rosy ‖ **rond** *adv* —**tourner rond** to work or go smoothly

rond-de-cuir [rõdkɥir] *m* (*pl* **ronds-de-cuir**) leather seat; (pej) bureaucrat

ron·deau [rõdo] *m* (*pl* **-deaux**) rondeau; field roller

ronde·let [rõdlɛ] **-lette** [lɛt] *adj* plump; tidy (*sum*)

rondelle [rõdɛl] *f* disk; slice; washer (*of faucet, bolt, etc.*)

rondement [rõdmɑ̃] *adv* briskly; **mener rondement** to make short work of; **parler rondement** to be blunt

rondeur [rõdœr] *f* roundness; plumpness; frankness

rond-point [rõpwɛ̃] *m* (*pl* **ronds-points**) intersection, crossroads; traffic circle; circus, roundabout (Brit)

ronéo [rɔneo] *f* Mimeograph machine

ronéotyper [rɔneotipe] *tr* to mimeograph

ron·flant [rõflɑ̃] **-flante** [flɑ̃t] *adj* snoring; roaring; whirring, humming; (pej) high-sounding, pretentious

ronflement [rõfləmɑ̃] *m* snore; roar; whirr, hum

ronfler [rõfle] *intr* to snore; to roar; to whirr, to hum

ron·fleur [rõflœr] **-fleuse** [fløz] *mf* snorer ‖ *m* vibrator (*replacing bell*)

ronger [rõʒe] §38 *tr* to gnaw, nibble; to eat away; to bite (*one's nails*); to corrode; to torment ‖ *ref* to be worn away; to be eaten away; to eat one's heart out, to fret

ron·geur [rõʒœr] **-geuse** [ʒøz] *adj* gnawing ‖ *m* rodent

ronron [rõrõ] *m* purr; drone

ronronnement [rõrɔnmɑ̃] *m* purring

ronronner [rõrɔne] *intr* to purr

roquer [rɔke] *intr* (chess) to castle

roquet [rɔkɛ] *m* cur, yapper; (*breed of dog*) pug

roquette [rɔkɛt] *f* (*plant; missile*) rocket

rosace [rɔzas] *f* rose window; (archit) rosette

rosa·cé -cée [rɔzase] *adj* roselike ‖ *f* skin eruption

rosaire [rɔzɛr] *m* rosary

rosâtre [rɔzatr] *adj* dusty-pink

rosbif [rɔsbif] *m* roast beef

rose [roz] *adj & m* rose, pink (*color*) ‖ *f* rose; rose window; **dire la rose** to box the compass; **rose des vents** compass card; **rose d'Inde** (*Tagetes*) marigold

ro·sé -sée [roze] *adj* rose, rose-colored ‖ *m* rosé wine ‖ *f* see **rosée**

ro•seau [rozo] m (pl -seaux) reed

rosée [roze] f dew

roséole [rozeɔl] f rash; rose rash

roseraie [rozrɛ] f rose garden

rosette [rozɛt] f bowknot; rosette; red ink; red chalk

rosier [rozje] m rosebush; rosier églantier sweetbrier

rosse [rɔs] adj nasty, mean; strict, stern; cynical || f (coll) beast, stinker; (coll) nag; sale rosse (coll) dirty bitch

rossée [rase] f (coll) thrashing

rosser [rase] tr to beat up, thrash; (coll) to beat, to best

rossignol [rosiɲɔl] m skeleton key; (orn) nightingale; (coll) piece of junk, drug on the market

rot [ro] m (slang) burp, belch

rota•tif [rɔtatif] -tive [tiv] adj rotary || f rotary press

rotation [rɔtɑsjɔ̃] f rotation; turnover (of merchandise)

rotatoire [rɔtatwar] adj rotary

roter [rote] intr (slang) to burp

rô•ti -tie [roti] adj roasted || m roast || f piece of toast; rôtie à l'anglaise Welsh rarebit

rotin [rɔtɛ̃] m rattan; de or en rotin cane (chair); pas un rotin! not a penny!

rôtir [rotir] tr, intr, & ref to roast; to toast; to scorch

rôtisserie [rotisri] f rotisserie shop (where roasted fowl is sold); grill-room (restaurant)

rôtissoire [rotiswar] f rotisserie

rotonde [rɔtɔ̃d] f rotunda; (rr) round-house

rotor [rɔtɔr] m rotor

rotule [rɔtyl] f kneecap

roture [rɔtyr] f common people

rotu•rier [rɔtyrje] -rière [rjɛr] adj plebeian, of the common people || mf commoner

rouage [rwaʒ] m cog; rouages movement (of a watch)

rou•blard [rublar] -blarde [blard] adj (coll) wily || mf (coll) schemer

roublardise [rublardiz] f (coll) cunning

roucoulement [rukulmɑ̃] m cooing; billing and cooing

roucouler [rukule] tr & intr to coo

roue [ru] f wheel; faire la roue to turn cartwheels; to strut; roue de secours spare wheel (with tire)

roué rouée [rwe] adj slick; knocked out || mf slicker || m rake

rouelle [rwɛl] f fillet (of veal)

rouer [rwe] tr to break upon the wheel; rouer de coups to thrash, beat up

rouerie [ruri] f trickery; trick

rouet [rwe] m spinning wheel

rouge [ruʒ] adj red || m red; rouge; blush; porter au rouge to heat red-hot; rouge à lèvres lipstick || adv red

rou•geaud [ruʒo] -geaude [ʒod] adj ruddy || mf ruddy-faced person

rouge-gorge [ruʒgɔrʒ] m (pl rouges-gorges) robin (Erithacus rubecula)

rougeole [ruʒɔl] f measles

rougeur [ruʒœr] f redness; blush; rougeurs red spots

rougir [ruʒir] tr to redden || intr to turn red; to blush

rouille [ruj] f rust

rouil•lé -lée [ruje] adj rusty; (out of practice; blighted) rusty

rouiller [ruje] tr, intr, & ref to rust

roulade [rulad] f trill; (mus) run

rou•lant [rulɑ̃] -lante [lɑ̃t] adj rolling; (coll) funny

rou•leau [rulo] m (pl -leaux) roller; roll; spool; rolling pin; rouleau compresseur road roller

roulement [rulmɑ̃] m roll; rotation; rattle, clatter; exchange; par roulement in rotation; roulement à billes ball bearing

rouler [rule] tr to roll; (coll) to take in, cheat || intr to roll; to roll along; rouler sur to roll in (wealth); to turn on || ref to roll; to roll up; to toss and turn; (with dat of reflex pron) to twiddle (one's thumbs); se les rouler (coll) to not turn a hand

roule-ta-bille [rultabij] m invar (coll) rolling stone

roulette [rulɛt] f small wheel; castor; roulette; aller comme sur des roulettes to go well, to work smoothly

rou•leur [rulœr] -leuse [løz] mf drifter (from one job to another) || m freight handler || f streetwalker

roulis [ruli] m (naut) roll

roulotte [rulɔt] f trailer; gypsy wagon

rou•main [rumɛ̃] -maine [mɛn] adj Rumanian || m Rumanian (language) || (cap) mf Rumanian (person)

roupiller [rupije] intr to take a snooze

rou•quin [rukɛ̃] -quine [kin] adj (coll) red-headed; || mf (coll) redhead || m (slang) red wine; Rouquin Red (nickname)

rouspéter [ruspete] §10 intr (coll) to bellyache, to kick

rouspé•teur [ruspetœr] -teuse [tøz] mf (coll) bellyacher, complainer

roussâtre [rusatr] adj auburn

rousse [rus] f redhead, auburn-haired woman; (slang) cops

rousseur [rusœr] f reddishness; freckle

roussir [rusir] tr to scorch; to singe || intr to become brown; faire roussir (culin) to brown

route [rut] f road; route, itinerary; bonne route! happy motoring!; en route! let's go!; faire fausse route to take the wrong road; (fig) to be on the wrong track; mettre en route to start; route déformée rough road; route déviée detour

rou•tier [rutje] -tière [tjɛr] adj road (e.g., map) || m trucker; bicycle racer; Explorer, Rover (boy scout); (naut) track chart; vieux routier veteran, old hand

routine [rutin] f routine

routi•nier [rutinje] -nière [njɛr] adj routine; one-track (mind)

rouvieux [ruvjø] adj masc mangy || m mange

rouvrir [ruvrir] §65 tr & intr to reopen

roux [ru] rousse [rus] adj russet, red-

dish; red, auburn (*hair*); browned
(*butter*) || *mf* redhead || *m* russet,
reddish brown, auburn (*color*);
brown sauce || *f* see **rousse**
royal royale ⌊rwajal⌋ *adj* (*pl* **royaux**
[rwajo]) royal || *f* imperial, goatee
royaliste ⌊rwajalist⌋ *adj & mf* royalist
royaume ⌊rwajom⌋ *m* kingdom
royauté ⌊rwajote⌋ *f* royalty
R.S.V.P. ⌊eresvepe⌋ *m* (letterword)
(**répondez, s'il vous plaît**) R.S.V.P.
R.T.F. ⌊erteef⌋ *f* (letterword) (**radio-
diffusion-télévision française**) French
radio and television
ruade ⌊ryad⌋ *f* kick, buck
ruban ⌊rybã⌋ *m* ribbon; tape; **ruban
adhésif** adhesive tape; **ruban adhésif
transparent** transparent tape; **ruban
de chapeau** hatband; **ruban de frein**
brake lining; **ruban encreur** typewriter ribbon; **ruban magnétique** recording tape
rubéole ⌊rybeol⌋ *f* German measles
rubis ⌊rybi⌋ *m* ruby; jewel (*of watch*);
payer rubis sur l'ongle to pay down
on the nail
rubrique ⌊rybrik⌋ *f* rubric; caption,
heading; label (*in a dictionary*)
ruche ⌊ry∫⌋ *f* beehive
rude ⌊ryd⌋ *adj* rude, rough; rugged;
hard; steep; (coll) amazing
rudement ⌊rydmã⌋ *adv* roughly; (coll)
awfully, mighty
rudesse ⌊rydes⌋ *f* rudeness, roughness;
harshness
rudiment ⌊rydimã⌋ *m* rudiment
rudoyer ⌊rydwaje⌋ §47 *tr* to bully,
browbeat; to abuse, treat roughly
rue ⌊ry⌋ *f* street; **rue barrée** (public
sign) no thoroughfare; (public sign)
closed for repairs; **rue sans issue**
(public sign) no outlet
ruée ⌊rqe⌋ *f* rush; **ruée vers l'or** gold
rush
ruelle ⌊rqel⌋ *f* alley, lane; space between bed and wall
ruer ⌊rqe⌋ *intr* to kick, to buck; **ruer
dans les brancards** to kick over the
traces || *ref*—**se ruer sur** to rush at
rugir ⌊ryʒir⌋ *intr* to roar, bellow

rugissement ⌊ryʒismã⌋ *m* roar
ru·gueux ⌊rygø⌋ **-gueuse** ⌊gøz⌋ *adj*
rough, rugged
ruine ⌊rqin⌋ *f* ruin
ruiner ⌊rqine⌋ *tr* to ruin
ruis·seau ⌊rqiso⌋ *m* (*pl* **-seaux**) stream,
brook; (fig) gutter
ruisseler ⌊rqisle⌋ §34 *intr* to stream; to
drip, to trickle
ruisselet ⌊rqisle⌋ *m* little stream
ruissellement ⌊rqiselmã⌋ *m* streaming;
(*e.g., of light*) flood
rumeur ⌊rymœr⌋ *f* rumor; hum (*e.g., of
voices*); roar (*of the sea*); **rumeur
publique** public opinion
ru·pin ⌊rypɛ̃⌋ **-pine** ⌊pin⌋ *adj* (slang)
rich || *mf* (slang) swell
rupiner ⌊rypine⌋ *tr & intr* (coll) to do
well
rupteur ⌊ryptœr⌋ *m* (elec) contact
breaker
rupture ⌊ryptyr⌋ *f* rupture; breach;
break; breaking off
ru·ral -rale ⌊ryral⌋ (*pl* **-raux** [ro]) *adj*
rural || *mf* farmer; **ruraux** country
people
ruse ⌊ryz⌋ *f* ruse
ru·sé -sée ⌊ryze⌋ *adj* cunning, crafty ||
mf sly one
russe ⌊rys⌋ *adj* Russian || *m* Russian
(*language*) || (*cap*) *mf* Russian (*per-
son*)
Russie ⌊rysi⌋ *f* Russia; **la Russie** Russia
rus·taud ⌊rysto⌋ **-taude** ⌊tod⌋ *adj* rus-
tic, clumsy || *mf* bumpkin
rustique ⌊rystik⌋ *adj* rustic; hardy
rustre ⌊rystr⌋ *adj* oafish || *m* bumpkin,
oaf; (obs) peasant
rut ⌊ryt⌋ *m* (zool) rut
ruti·lant ⌊rytilã⌋ **-lante** ⌊lãt⌋ *adj* bright-
red; gleaming
rutiler ⌊rytile⌋ *intr* to gleam, to glow
rythme ⌊ritm⌋ *m* rhythm; rate (*of production*)
ryth·mé -mée ⌊ritme⌋ *adj* rhyth-
mic(al); cadenced
rythmer ⌊ritme⌋ *tr* to cadence; to mark
with a rhythm
rythmique ⌊ritmik⌋ *adj* rhythmic(al)

S

S, s ⌊es⌋, *⌊es⌋ *m invar* nineteenth
letter of the French alphabet
S. *abbr* (**saint**) St.
sa ⌊sa⌋ §88
S.A. ⌊esa⌋ *f* (letterword) (**Société
anonyme**) Inc.
sabbat ⌊saba⌋ *m* Sabbath; witches'
Sabbath; racket, uproarious gaiety;
sabbat des chats caterwauling
sabir ⌊sabir⌋ *m* pidgin
sable ⌊sabl⌋ *m* sand; sable; **sable
mouvant** quicksand
sabler ⌊sable⌋ *tr* to sandblast; to drink

in one gulp; to toss off (*some champagne*)
sa·bleux ⌊sablø⌋ **-bleuse** ⌊bløz⌋ *adj*
sandy || *f* sandblast; sandblaster
sablier ⌊sablije⌋ *m* hourglass; (*for drying ink*) sandbox; dealer in sand
sablière ⌊sablijer⌋ *f* sandpit; wall plate;
(rr) sandbox
sablon·neux ⌊sablɔnø⌋ **sablon·neuse**
⌊sablɔnøz⌋ *adj* sandy
sablonnière ⌊sablɔnjer⌋ *f* sandpit
sabord ⌊sabɔr⌋ *m* porthole
saborder ⌊sabɔrde⌋ *tr* to scuttle

sabot [sabo] *m* wooden shoe; hoof; whipping top; bungled work; ferrule; caster cup; **dormir comme un sabot** to sleep like a top; **sabot de frein** brake shoe; **sabot d'enrayage** wedge, block, scotch

sabotage [sabɔtaʒ] *m* sabotage

saboter [sabɔte] *tr* to sabotage; to bungle || *intr* (coll) to make one's wooden shoes clatter

sabo-teur [sabɔtœr] **-teuse** [tøz] *mf* saboteur, bungler

sabo-tier [sabɔtje] **-tière** [tjɛr] *mf* maker and seller of wooden shoes || *f* clog dance

sabre [sabr] *m* saber

sabrer [sabre] *tr* to saber; (coll) to botch; (coll) to cut, condense

sac [sak] *m* sack, bag; **être un sac d'os** [dos] to be nothing but skin and bones; **sac à main** handbag; **sac à malice** bag of tricks; **sac à provisions** shopping bag; **sac de couchage** sleeping bag

saccade [sakad] *f* jerk

sacca-dé -dée [sakade] *adj* jerky

saccager [sakaʒe] §38 *tr* to sack; (coll) to upset, to turn topsy-turvy

saccha-rin [sakarɛ̃] **-rine** [rin] *adj* saccharine || *f* saccharin

saccharose [sakaroz] *m* sucrose

sacerdoce [saserdɔs] *m* priesthood

sacerdo-tal -tale [saserdɔtal] *adj* (*pl* **-taux** [to]) sacerdotal, priestly

sachet [saʃɛ] *m* sachet; packet (*of needles, medicine, etc.*); powder charge

sacoche [sakɔʃ] *f* satchel

sacramen-tel -telle [sakramɑ̃tɛl] *adj* sacramental

sacre [sakr] *m* crowning, consecration

sa-cré -crée [sakre] *adj* sacred; (anat) sacral || (when standing before noun) *adj* (coll) darned, blasted

sacrement [sakramɑ̃] *m* sacrament

sacrer [sakre] *tr* to crown, to consecrate || *intr* to curse

sacrifice [sakrifis] *m* sacrifice

sacrifier [sakrifje] *tr* to sacrifice

sacrilège [sakrilɛʒ] *adj* sacrilegious || *mf* sacrilegious person || *m* sacrilege

sacristain [sakristɛ̃] *m* sexton

sadique [sadik] *adj* sadistic || *mf* sadist

safran [safrɑ̃] *m* saffron

sagace [sagas] *adj* sagacious, shrewd

sage [saʒ] *adj* wise; well-behaved, modest (*woman*); good (*child*); **soyez sage!** be good! || *mf* sage

sage-femme [saʒfam] *f* (*pl* **sages-femmes**) midwife

sagesse [saʒɛs] *f* wisdom; good behavior

sai-gnant [sɛɲɑ̃] **-gnante** [ɲɑ̃t] *adj* bleeding; (*wound*) fresh; (*meat*) rare

saignée [seɲe] *f* bloodletting; bend of the arm, small of the arm; (fig) drain on the purse

saignement [sɛɲmɑ̃] *m* bleeding; **saignement de nez** nosebleed

saigner [sɛɲe], [seɲe] *tr & intr* to bleed; **saigner à blanc, saigner aux quatre veines** to bleed white

sail-lant [sajɑ̃] **sail-lante** [sajɑ̃t] *adj* prominent, salient; projecting; high (*cheekbones*)

saillie [saji] *f* projection; spurt; sally, outburst; **faire saillie** to jut out, project

saillir [sajir] (used only in *inf, ger,* & 3d *sg & pl*) *tr* (agr) to cover || §69 *intr* to protrude, to project; to spurt

sain [sɛ̃] **saine** [sɛn] *adj* healthy; **sain d'esprit** sane; **sain et sauf** safe and sound

saindoux [sɛ̃du] *m* lard

sainement [sɛnmɑ̃] *adv* soundly

saint [sɛ̃] **sainte** [sɛ̃t] *adj* saintly; sacred, holy || *mf* saint

sainteté [sɛ̃tte] *f* holiness

saisie [sezi] *f* seizure; foreclosure

saisie-arrêt [seziarɛ] *f* (*pl* **-arrêts**) attachment, garnishment

saisir [sezir] *tr* to seize; to sear (*meat*); to grasp (*to understand*); to strike, startle; to overcome; **saisir un tribunal de** to lay before a court || *ref* **—se saisir de** to take possession of

saisissement [sezismɑ̃] *m* chill; shock

saison [sezɔ̃] *f* season

salace [salas] *adj* salacious

salade [salad] *f* salad; (fig) mess; **salade russe** mixed vegetable salad with mayonnaise

saladier [saladje] *m* salad bowl

salaire [salɛr] *m* salary, wage; recompense, punishment

salariat [salarja] *m* salaried workers, employees; salary (*fixed wage*)

sala-rié -riée [salarje] *adj* salaried, hired || *mf* wage earner; employee

sa-laud [salo] **-laude** [lod] *adj* (coll) slovenly || *mf* (slang) skunk, scoundrel

sale [sal] *adj* dirty; dull (*color*) || *mf* dirty person

sa-lé -lée [sale] *adj* salty, salted; dirty (*joke*); padded (*bill*); (slang) exaggerated || *m* salt pork

saler [sale] *tr* to salt

saleté [salte] *f* dirtiness; piece of dirt; (slang) dirty trick; (slang) dirt

salière [saljer] *f* saltcellar

salir [salir] *tr & ref* to soil

salive [saliv] *f* saliva

salle [sal] *f* room; hall; auditorium; ward (*in a hospital*); (theat) audience, house; **salle à manger** dining room; **salle d'armes** fencing room; **salle d'attente** waiting room; **salle de bains** bathroom; **salle d'écoute** language laboratory; **salle de police** (mil) guardhouse; **salle des accouchées** maternity ward; **salle de séjour** living room; **salle des machines** engine room; **salle des pas perdus** lobby, waiting room; **salle de rédaction** city room; **salle de spectacle** movie house; **salle des ventes** salesroom, showroom; **salle de travail** delivery room; **salle d'exposition** showroom

salon [salɔ̃] *m* living room, parlor; exposition; saloon (*ship's lounge*); **salon de beauté** beauty parlor; **salon de l'automobile** automobile show; **salon de thé** tearoom

salon·nard [salɔnar] **salon·narde** [salɔnard] *mf* sycophant

saloperie [salɔpri] *f* (slang) trash

salopette [salɔpet] *f* coveralls, overalls; bib; smock

salpêtre [salpetr] *m* saltpeter

salsepareille [salsəparej] *f* sarsaparilla

saltimbanque ｜saltɛ̃bɑ̃k] *mf* tumbler; mounteband, charlatan

salubre [salybr] *adj* salubrious, healthful

saluer [salɥe] *tr* to salute; to greet, to bow to, to wave to

salut [saly] *m* health; safety; salvation; salute; greeting, bow; nod; salut! (coll) hi!, howdy!; **salut les gars!, salut les copains!** hi, fellows!

salutation [salytɑsjɔ̃] *f* greeting; **salutations distinguées,** or **sincères salutations** (complimentary close) yours truly

salve [salv] *f* salvo, salute

samari·tain [samaritɛ̃] **-taine** [ten] *adj* Samaritan ‖ (*cap*) *mf* Samaritan

samedi [samdi] *m* Saturday

sanatorium ｜sanatɔrjɔm] *m* sanitarium

sanctifier ｜sɑ̃ktifje] *tr* to sanctify

sanction [sɑ̃ksjɔ̃] *f* sanction; penalty

sanctionner [sɑ̃ksjɔne] *tr* to sanction; to penalize

sanctuaire [sɑ̃ktɥer] *m* sanctuary

sandale ｜sɑ̃dal] *f* sandal; gym shoe

sandwich [sɑ̃dwitʃ], [sɑ̃dwiʃ] *m* (*pl* **sandwiches, sandwichs**) sandwich

sang [sɑ̃] *m* blood; **avoir le sang chaud** (coll) to be a go-getter; **bon sang!** (coll) darn it it!; **sang et tripes** blood and guts; **se faire du mauvais sang** to get all stewed up

sang-froid [sɑ̃frwa], [sɑ̃frwɑ] *m* self-control

san·glant [sɑ̃glɑ̃] **-glante** [glɑ̃t] *adj* bloody; cruel

sangle [sɑ̃gl] *f* cinch

sanglier [sɑ̃glije] *m* wild boar

sanglot [sɑ̃glo] *m* sob

sangloter [sɑ̃glɔte] *intr* to sob

sang-mêlé [sɑ̃mele] *m invar* half-breed

sangsue [sɑ̃sy] *f* bloodsucker, leech

san·guin [sɑ̃gɛ̃] **-guine** [gin] *adj* sanguine ‖ *f* (fa) sanguine

sanitaire [saniter] *adj* sanitary; hospital, e.g., **avion sanitaire** hospital plane

sans [sɑ̃] *adv*—**sans que** without; **sans quoi** or else ‖ *prep* without; **sans cesse** ceaselessly; **sans façon** informally; **sans fil** wireless

sans-abri [sɑ̃zabri] *mf invar* homeless person

sans-cœur [sɑ̃kœr] *mf invar* heartless person

sans-filiste [sɑ̃filist] *mf* (*pl* **-filistes**) radio operator; radio amateur

sans-gêne [sɑ̃ʒɛn] *adj invar* offhanded ‖ *mf invar* offhanded person ‖ *m* offhandedness

sansonnet [sɑ̃sɔne] *m* starling; blackbird

sans-travail [sɑ̃travaj] *mf invar* unemployed worker

san·tal [sɑ̃tal] *m* (*pl* **-taux** [to]) (bot) sandalwood

santé [sɑ̃te] *f* health; sanity; **santé publique** public health service

sape [sap] *f* sap (*undermining*)

saper ｜sape] *tr* to sap, to undermine

sapeur [sapœr] *m* (mil) sapper; **fumer comme un sapeur** (coll) to smoke like a chimney

sapeur·pompier [sapœrpɔ̃pje] *m* (*pl* **sapeurs-pompiers**) fireman; **sapeurs-pompiers** fire department

saphir ｜safir] *m* sapphire; sapphire needle

sapin [sapɛ̃] *m* fir

sapristi [sapristi] *interj* hang it!

saquer [sake] *tr* (slang) to fire, to sack

sarbacane [sarbakan] *f* blowgun

sarcasme [sarkasm] *m* sarcasm

sarcler ｜sarkle] *tr* to weed, root out

sarcloir [sarklwar] *m* hoe

Sardaigne [sardeɲ] *f* Sardinia; **la Sardaigne** Sardinia

sarde [sard] *adj* Sardinian ‖ *m* Sardinian (*language*) ‖ (*cap*) *mf* Sardinian (*person*)

sardine ｜sardin] *f* sardine

S.A.R.L. *abbr* (**Société à responsabilité limitée**) corporation

sarment [sarmɑ̃] *m* vine; vine shoot

sarra·sin [sarazɛ̃] **-sine** [zin] *adj* Saracen ‖ *m* buckwheat ‖ *f* portcullis ‖ (*cap*) *mf* Saracen

sar·rau [saro] *m* (*pl* **-raus**) smock

sarriette [sarjet] *f* (bot) savory

sas [sɑ], [sɑs] *m* sieve; lock (*of canal, submarine, etc.*); air lock (*of caisson, spaceship, etc.*); **sas d'évacuation** (aer) escape hatch

sasser ｜sɑse] *tr* to sift, screen; to pass through a lock

satelliser [satelize] *tr* to make a satellite of; (rok) to put into orbit

satellite [satelit] *adj & m* satellite

satin ｜satɛ̃] *m* satin

satinette [satinet] *f* sateen

satire [satir] *f* satire

satirique [satirik] *adj* satiric(al)

satiriser [satirize] *tr* to satirize

satisfaction [satisfaksjɔ̃] *f* satisfaction

satisfaire [satisfer] §29 *tr* to satisfy ‖ *intr* to satisfy; (with *dat*) to fulfill; (with *dat*) to meet (*a need*) ‖ *ref* to be satisfied

satisfai·sant [satisfəzɑ̃] **-sante** [zɑ̃t] *adj* satisfactory; satisfying

saturer [satyre] *tr* to saturate

Saturne [satyrn] *m* Saturn

saturnisme [satyrnism] *m* lead poisoning

sauce [sos] *f* sauce; gravy; drawing pencil; (tech) solution

saucer [sose] §51 *tr* to dip in sauce or gravy; (coll) to soak to the skin; (coll) to reprimand severely

saucière ｜sosjer] *f* gravy bowl

saucisse ｜sosis] *f* sausage; frankfurter

saucisson [sosisɔ̃] *m* bologna, sausage

sauf [sof] **sauve** [sov] *adj* safe ‖ **sauf** *prep* save, except; barring; subject to (*e.g., correction*)

sauf-conduit [sofkɔ̃dɥi] *m* (*pl* **-conduits**) safe-conduct

sauge [soʒ] *f* (bot) sage, salvia

saugre•nu -nue [sogrəny] *adj* absurd, silly

saule [sol] *m* willow

saumâtre [somɑtr] *adj* brackish

saumon [somɔ̃] *m* salmon; pig (*of crude metal*)

saumure [somyr] *f* brine

sauner [sone] *intr* to make salt

saupoudrer [sopudre] *tr* to sprinkle (*with powder, sugar; citations*)

saurer [sɔre] *tr* to kipper

saut [so] *m* leap, jump; falls, waterfall; **au saut du lit** on getting out of bed; **faire le saut** to take the fatal step; **faire un saut chez** to drop in on; **par sauts et par bonds** by fits and starts; **saut à la perche** pole vault; **saut de carpe** jackknife; **saut de l'ange** swan dive; **saut en chute libre** skydiving; **saut périlleux** somersault

saut-de-lit [sodli] *m invar* wrap

saut-de-mouton [sodmut5] *m* (*pl* **sauts-de-mouton**) cloverleaf (*intersection*)

saute [sot] *f* change in direction, shift

saute-mouton [sotmut5] *m* leapfrog

sauter [sote] *tr* to leap over; to skip || *intr* to leap, jump; to blow up; **faire sauter** to sauté; to flip (*a pancake*); to fire (*an employee*); **sauter à cloche-pied** to hop on one foot; **sauter à pieds joints** to do a standing jump; **sauter aux nues** to get mad

sauterelle [sotrɛl] *f* grasshopper

sauterie [sotri] *f* (coll) hop (*dancing party*)

sau•teur [sotœr] **-teuse** [tøz] *adj* jumping || *mf* jumper || *m* jumper, jumping horse || *f* frying pan

sautiller [sotije] *intr* to hop

sautoir [sotwar] *m* St. Andrew's cross; **en sautoir** crossways

sauvage [sovaʒ] *adj* savage; wild; shy || *mf* savage

sauvagerie [sovaʒri] *f* savagery; wildness; shyness

sauvegarde [sovgard] *f* safeguard

sauvegarder [sovgarde] *tr* to safeguard

sauve-qui-peut [sovkipø] *m invar* panic, stampede, rout

sauver [sove] *tr* to save; to rescue || *intr—***sauve qui peut!** every man for himself! || *ref* to run away; to escape; (theat) to exit; **sauve-toi!** (coll) scram!

sauvetage [sovtaʒ] *m* salvage; lifesaving, rescue

sauveteur [sovtœr] *adj masc* lifesaving || *m* lifesaver

sauveur [sovœr] *adj masc* Saviour || *m* savior; **Le Sauveur** the Saviour

savamment [savamɑ̃] *adv* knowingly; skillfully

savane [savan] *f* prairie, savanna

sa•vant [savɑ̃] **-vante** [vɑ̃t] *adj* scholarly, learned || *mf* scientist, scholar, savant; **savant atomiste** nuclear physicist

savate [savat] *f* old slipper; foot boxing; (coll) butterfingers; **traîner la savate** to be down at the heel

saveur [savœr] *f* savor, taste

savoir [savwar] *m* learning || §62 *tr* & *intr* to know; to know how to; à

savoir namely, to wit; **à savoir que** with the understanding that; **en savoir long** to know all about it; **pas que je sache** not that I know of

savoir-faire [savwarfer] *m invar* know-how

savon [savɔ̃] *m* soap; (slang) sharp reprimand; **savon en paillettes** soap flakes

savonnage [savonaʒ] *m* soaping

savonner [savone] *tr* to soap

savonnerie [savonri] *f* soap factory

savonnette [savonet] *f* toilet soap

savon•neux [savonø] **savon•neuse** [savonøz] *adj* soapy

savourer [savure] *tr* to savor

savou•reux [savurø] **-reuse** [røz] *adj* savory, tasty

saxon [saks5] **saxonne** [saksɔn] *adj* Saxon || *m* Saxon (*language*) || (*cap*) *mf* Saxon (*person*)

saxophone [saksofɔn] *m* saxophone

saynète [senet] *f* sketch, playlet

sca•bieux [skabjø] **-bieuse** [bjøz] *adj* scabby || *f* scabious

sca•breux [skabrø] **-breuse** [brøz] *adj* rough (*road*); risky (*business*); scabrous (*remark*)

scalpel [skalpel] *m* scalpel

scalper [skalpe] *tr* to scalp

scandale [skɑdal] *m* scandal; disturbance

scanda•leux [skɑdalø] **-leuse** [løz] *adj* scandalous

scandaliser [skɑdalize] *tr* to lead astray; to scandalize || *ref* to take offense

scander [skɑde] *tr* to scan (*verses*)

scandinave [skɑdinav] *adj* Scandinavian || *m* Scandinavian (*language*) || (*cap*) *mf* Scandinavian (*person*); **Scandinaves** Scandinavian countries

scaphandre [skafɑdr] *m* diving suit; spacesuit; **scaphandre autonome** aqualung

scaphandrier [skafɑdrije] *m* diver

scarlatine [skarlatin] *f* scarlet fever

scarole [skarɔl] *f* escarole

sceau [so] *m* (*pl* **seaux**) seal

scélé•rat [selera] **-rate** [rat] *adj* villainous || *mf* villain

scellé [sele] *m* seal

sceller [sele] *tr* to seal

scénario [senarjo] *m* scenario

scène [sen] *f* scene; stage; theater

scénique [senik] *adj* scenic

scepticisme [septisism] *m* skepticism

sceptique [septik] *adj* & *mf* skeptic

sceptre [septr] *m* scepter

schah [ʃa] *m* shah

schelem [ʃlem] *m* slam (*at bridge*)

schéma [ʃema] *m* diagram

schisme [ʃism] *m* schism

schizophrène [skizofren] *adj* & *mf* schizophrenic

schlague [ʃlag] *f* flogging

schooner [skunœr], [ʃunœr] *m* schooner

sciatique [sjatik] *adj* sciatic || *f* (pathol) sciatica

scie [si] *f* saw; (coll) bore, nuisance; **scie à découper** jig saw

sciemment [sjamɑ̃] *adv* knowingly

science [sjãs] *f* science; learning, knowledge

science-fiction [sjãsfiksjɔ̃] *f* science fiction

scientifique [sjãtifik] *adj* scientific ‖ *mf* scientist

scier [sje] *tr* to saw; (coll) to bore ‖ *intr* (naut) to row backwards

scierie [siri] *f* sawmill

scieur [sjœr] *m* sawyer

scinder [sɛ̃de] *tr* to divide ‖ *ref* to be divided

scintil·lant [sɛ̃tijɑ̃] **scintil·lante** [sɛ̃tijɑ̃t] *adj* scintillating; twinkling

scintillation [sɛ̃tijɑ̃sjɔ̃] *f* twinkling, twinkle; (phys) scintillation

scintillement [sɛ̃tijmɑ̃] *m* twinkling

scintiller [sɛ̃tije] *intr* to scintillate; to twinkle

scion [sjɔ̃] *m* scion; tip (*of fishing rod*)

scission [sisjɔ̃] *f* schism; (biol & phys) fission

sciure [sjyr] *f* sawdust

sclérose [skleroz] *f* sclerosis

scolaire [skɔler] *adj* school

scolastique [skɔlastik] *adj & m* scholastic ‖ *f* scholasticism

sconse [skɔ̃s] *m* skunk fur; skunk

scories [skɔri] *fpl* slag, dross

scorpion [skɔrpjɔ̃] *m* scorpion

scout scoute [skut] *adj & m* scout

scoutisme [skutism] *m* scouting

scribe [skrib] *m* scribe

script [skript] *m* scrip; (typ) script

scripturaire [skriptyrer] *adj* Scriptural ‖ *m* fundamentalist

scrofule [skrɔfyl] *f* scrofula

scrotum [skrɔtɔm] *m* scrotum

scrupule [skrypyl] *m* scruple

scrupu·leux [skrypylø] **-leuse** [løz] *adj* scrupulous

scruter [skryte] *tr* to scrutinize

scrutin [skrytɛ̃] *m* ballot; balloting; voting, poll; **dépouiller le scrutin** to count the votes; **scrutin de ballottage** runoff election

scrutiner [skrytine] *intr* to ballot

sculpter [skylte] *tr* to sculpture; to carve (*wood*)

sculpteur [skyltœr] *m* sculptor

sculpture [skyltyr] *f* sculpture

s.d. *abbr* (**sans date**) n.d.

S.D.N. [esdeen] *f* (letterword) (**Société des Nations**) League of Nations

se [sə] §87

séance [seɑ̃s] *f* session, sitting; seat (*in an assembly*); performance, showing; **séance tenante** on the spot

séant [seɑ̃] **séante** [seɑ̃t] *adj* fitting, decent; sitting (*as a king or a court in session*) ‖ *m* buttocks, bottom; **se mettre sur son séant** to sit up (*in bed*)

seau [so] *m* (*pl* **seaux**) bucket, pail; **il pleut à seaux** it's raining cats and dogs; **seau à charbon** coal scuttle

sébile [sebil] *f* wooden bowl

sec [sɛk] **sèche** [seʃ] *adj* dry; sharp; rude; unguarded (*card*); total (*loss*); **en cinq sec** in a jiffy; **sec comme un hareng** (coll) long and thin; **tout sec** and nothing more ‖ *m* dryness; **à sec** dry; (coll) broke ‖ *f see* **sèche** ‖ **sec** *adv*—**aussi sec** (slang) on the spot;

boire sec to drink one's liquor straight; **frapper sec** to land a hard fast punch; **parler sec** to talk tough

sécession [sesesjɔ̃] *f* secession

sèche [seʃ] *f* (slang) fag, cigarette

sèche-cheveux [seʃʃəvø] *m invar* hair drier

sécher [seʃe] §10 *tr* to dry; to season; to cut (*a class*) ‖ *intr* to become dry

sécheresse [seʃres] *f* dryness; drought; baldness (*of style*); curtness; (fig) coldness

séchoir [seʃwar] *m* drier; drying room; clotheshorse

se·cond [səgɔ̃] **-conde** [gɔ̃d] *adj & pron* second; **en second** next in rank ‖ *m* second ‖ *f see* **seconde**

secondaire [səgɔ̃der] *adj & m* secondary

seconde [səgɔ̃d] *f* second (*in time; musical interval; of angle*); second class

seconder [səgɔ̃de] *tr* to help, second

secouable [səkurabl] *adj* helpful

secourir [səkurir] §14 *tr* to help, aid

secourisme [səkurism] *m* first aid

secouriste [səkurist] *mf* first-aider; first-aid worker

secours [səkur] *m* help, aid; **au secours!** help!; **de secours** emergency; spare (*tire*); **des secours** supplies, relief

secousse [səkus] *f* shake, jolt; (elec) shock

se·cret [səkre] **-crète** [kret] *adj* secret; secretive ‖ *m* secret; secrecy; **au secret** in solitary confinement ‖ *f see* **secrète**

secrétaire [səkreter] *mf* secretary ‖ *m* secretary (*desk*)

secrète [səkret] *f* central intelligence

sécréter [sekrete] §10 *tr* to secrete

sectaire [sekter] *adj & mf* sectarian

secte [sekt] *f* sect

secteur [sektœr] *m* sector; (elec) house current, local supply circuit; **secteur postal** postal zone; (mil) A.P.O. number

section [seksjɔ̃] *f* section; cross section

sectionner [seksjɔne] *tr* to section; to cut ‖ *ref* to break apart

séculaire [sekyler] *adj* secular

sécu·lier [sekylje] **-lière** [ljer] *adj & m* secular

sécurité [sekyrite] *f* security

séda·tif [sedatif] **-tive** [tiv] *adj & m* sedative

sédation [sedasjɔ̃] *f* sedation

sédentaire [sedɑ̃ter] *adj* sedentary

sédiment [sedimɑ̃] *m* sediment

sédi·tieux [sedisjø] **-tieuse** [sjøz] *adj* seditious

sédition [sedisjɔ̃] *f* sedition

séduc·teur [sedyktœr] **-trice** [tris] *adj* seducing, bewitching ‖ *mf* seducer ‖ *f* vamp

séduction [sedyksjɔ̃] *f* seduction

séduire [sedɥir] §19 *tr* to seduce; to charm, to bewitch; to bribe

sédui·sant [sedɥizɑ̃] **-sante** [zɑ̃t] *adj* seductive, tempting

segment [sɛgmã] *m* segment; **segment de piston** piston ring

ségrégation [segregasjɔ̃] *f* segregation

ségrégationniste [segregasjɔnist] *adj* segregationist

seiche [sɛʃ] *f* cuttlefish

séide [seid] *m* henchman

seigle [sɛgl] *m* rye

seigneur [sɛɲœr] *m* lord

sein [sɛ̃] *m* breast; bosom; womb; **au sein de** in the heart of

seine [sɛn] *f* dragnet

seing [sɛ̃] *m* signature; **sous seing privé** privately witnessed

seize [sɛz] *adj & pron* sixteen; the Sixteenth, e.g., **Jean seize** John the Sixteenth || *m* sixteen; sixteenth (*in dates*)

seizième [sɛzjɛm] *adj, pron* (*masc, fem*), & *m* sixteenth

séjour [seʒur] *m* stay, visit

séjourner [seʒurne] *intr* to reside; to stay, to visit

sel [sɛl] *m* salt; **gros sel** coarse salt; (*fig*) dirty joke; **sel ammoniac** sal ammoniac; **sel gemme** rock salt

sélec·tif [selɛktif] **-tive** [tiv] *adj* selective

sélection [selɛksjɔ̃] *f* selection

sélectionner [selɛksjɔne] *tr* to select

self [sɛlf] *f* (elec) coil, spark coil

self-service [selfsɛrvis] *m* self-service

selle [sɛl] *f* saddle; seat (*of bicycle, motorcycle, etc.*); sculptor's tripod; stool, movement; (culin) saddle; **aller à la selle** to go to the toilet

seller [sɛle] *tr* to saddle

sellier [sɛlje] *m* saddler

selon [səlɔ̃] *adv*—**c'est selon** that depends; **selon que** according as || *prep* according to; after (*e.g., my own heart*)

semailles [səmaj] *fpl* sowing, seeding

semaine [səmɛn] *f* week; week's wages; set of seven; **à la petite semaine** day-to-day, hand-to-mouth; short-sighted; **de semaine** on duty during the week; **la semaine des quatre jeudis** (coll) never; **semaine anglaise** five-day workweek

semai·nier [səmənje] **-nière** [njɛr] *mf* week worker || *m* highboy; office calendar

sémantique [semãtik] *adj* semantic || *f* semantics

sémaphore [semafor] *m* semaphore

semblable [sãblabl] *adj* similar, like || *m* fellow-man, equal

semblant [sãblã] *m* semblance, appearance; **faire semblant** to pretend

sembler [sãble] *intr* to seem; to seem to

semelle [səmɛl] *f* sole; foot (*of stocking*); tread (*of tire*); bed (*of concrete*)

semence [səmãs] *f* seed; semen; brad; **semence de perles** seed pearls

semer [səme] §2 *tr* to seed, to sow; to scatter, strew; to lay (*mines*); (slang) to outdistance; (slang) to drop (*an acquaintance*)

semestre [səmɛstr] *m* semester; six-month period

semes·triel -trielle [səmestrijɛl] *adj* six-month; semester

se·meur [səmœr] **-meuse** [møz] *mf* sower; spreader of gossip || *f* seeder, drill

semi-chenillé [səmi/nije] *m* half-track

semi-conduc·teur [səmikɔ̃dyktœr] **-trice** [tris] *adj* semiconductive || *m* semiconductor

semifi·ni -nie [səmifini] *adj* unfinished

sémil·lant [semijã] **sémil·lante** [semijãt] *adj* sprightly, lively

séminaire [seminɛr] *m* seminary; seminar; conference

semi-remorque [səmirəmɔrk] *f* (*pl* -**remorques**) semitrailer

semis [səmi] *m* sowing; seedling; seedbed

sémite [semit] *adj* Semitic || (*cap*) *mf* Semite

sémitique [semitik] *adj* Semitic

semoir [səmwar] *m* seeder, drill

semonce [səmɔ̃s] *f* reprimand; (naut) order to heave to

semoncer [səmɔ̃se] §51 *tr* to reprimand; (naut) to order to heave to

semoule [səmul] *f* (culin) semolina

sénat [sena] *m* senate

sénateur [senatœr] *m* senator

sénile [senil] *adj* senile

sens [sãs] *m* sense, meaning; opinion; direction; **en sens inverse** in the opposite direction; **sens dessus dessous** [sãdəsydəsu] upside down; **sens devant derrière** [sãdəvãderjɛr] back to front; **sens interdit** (public sign) no entry; **sens obligatoire** (public sign) right way, this way; **sens unique** (public sign) one way

sensation [sãsasjɔ̃] *f* sensation

sensation·nel -nelle [sãsasjɔnel] *adj* sensational

sen·sé -sée [sãse] *adj* sensible

sensibiliser [sãsibilize] *tr* to sensitize

sensibilité [sãsibilite] *f* sensibility; sensitivity

sensible [sãsibl] *adj* sensitive; sensible; appreciable, perceptible

sensi·tif -tive [sãsitif] **-tive** [tiv] *adj* sensory; sensitive, touchy

senso·riel -rielle [sãsɔrjɛl] *adj* sensory

sen·suel -suelle [sãsɥɛl] *adj* sensual

sent-bon [sãbɔ̃] *m invar* odor, perfume

sentence [sãtãs] *f* proverb; (law) sentence

senteur [sãtœr] *f* odor, perfume

sentier [sãtje] *m* path; **hors des sentiers battus** off the beaten track

sentiment [sãtimã] *m* sentiment, feeling

sentimen·tal -tale [sãtimãtal] *adj* (*pl* -**taux** [to]) sentimental

sentine [sãtin] *f* bilge

sentinelle [sãtinel] *f* sentinel

sentir [sãtir] §41 *tr* to feel; to smell; to smell like, smell of; to taste of; to have all the earmarks of; to show the effects of; **ne pas pouvoir sentir qn** to be unable to stand s.o. || *intr* to smell; to smell bad || *ref* to feel; to be felt; **se sentir de** to feel the effects of

seoir [swar] §5A (3d *pl pres ind* **siéent**;

used only in 3d *sg & pl* of most simple tenses) *intr* (with *dat*) to be suitable to, to become; to be fitting to, to be proper for ‖ (used only in *inf* and 2d *sg & pl* and 1st *pl impv*) *ref* (coll & poetic) to sit down, have a seat

séparation [separasjɔ̃] *f* separation

séparer [separe] *tr & ref* to separate, to divide

sept [set] *adj & pron* seven; the Seventh, e.g., **Jean sept** John the Seventh; **sept heures** seven o'clock ‖ *m* seven; seventh (*in dates*)

septembre [septɑ̃br] *m* September

septième [setjɛm] *adj, pron* (*masc, fem*), *& m* seventh

septique [septik] *adj* septic

sépulcre [sepylkr] *m* sepulcher

sépulture [sepyltyr] *f* grave, tomb, burial place; burial

séquelle [sekɛl] *f* gang; (pathol) complications; **séquelles** aftermath

séquence [sekɑ̃s] *f* sequence; (*in poker*) straight

séquestrer [sekɛstre] *tr* to sequester

séraphin [serafɛ̃] *m* seraph; (coll) angel

serbe [sɛrb] *adj* Serb ‖ (*cap*) *mf* Serb

se-rein [sərɛ̃] **-reine** [rɛn] *adj* serene ‖ *m* night dew

sérénade [serenad] *f* serenade

sérénité [serenite] *f* serenity

serf [sɛr], [sɛrf] **serve** [sɛrv] *mf* serf

serge [sɛrʒ] *f* serge

sergent [sɛrʒɑ̃] *m* sergeant

série [seri] *f* series, string, set; (elec) series; **de série** standard; stock (*car*); **en série** in (a) series; mass, e.g., **fabrication en série** mass production; **hors série** outsize (*wearing apparel*); discontinued (*as an item of manufacture*); custom-built; almost unheard of; **série noire** run of bad luck

sé-rieux [serjø] **-rieuse** [rjøz] *adj* serious

serin [sərɛ̃] *m* canary; (coll) simpleton

seringa [sərɛ̃ga] *m* mock orange

seringue [sərɛ̃g] *f* syringe; (hort) spray gun; **seringue à graisse** grease gun; **seringue à injections** hypodermic syringe; **seringue à instillations** nasal spray

serment [sɛrmɑ̃] *m* oath; **prêter serment** to take oath

sermon [sɛrmɔ̃] *m* sermon

sermonner [sɛrmɔne] *tr* to sermonize

serpe [sɛrp] *f* billhook

serpent [sɛrpɑ̃] *m* snake, serpent; **serpent à sonnettes** rattlesnake; **serpent caché sous les fleurs** snake in the grass

serpenter [sɛrpɑ̃te] *intr* to wind

serpen-tin [sɛrpɑ̃tɛ̃] **-tine** [tin] *adj* serpentine ‖ *m* coil; worm (*of still*); paper streamer

serpillière [sɛrpijɛr] *f* floorcloth; sacking, burlap

serpolet [sɛrpɔle] *m* thyme

serre [sɛr] *f* greenhouse; **serres** claws, talons

ser-ré -rée [sɛre] *adj* tight; narrow; compact; close ‖ **serré** *adv*—**jouer serré** to play it close to the vest

serre-fils [sɛrfil] *m invar* (elec) binding post

serre-freins [sɛrfrɛ̃] *m invar* brakeman

serre-livres [sɛrlivr] *m invar* book end

serrement [sɛrmɑ̃] *m* squeezing, pressing; (min) partition (*to keep out water*); (pathol) pang; **serrement de cœur** heaviness of heart; **serrement de main** handshake

serrer [sɛre] *tr* to press; to squeeze; to wring; to tighten; to close up (*ranks*); to clasp, shake, e.g., **serrer la main** à to shake hands with; to grit (*one's teeth*); to put on (*the brakes*) ‖ *intr*—**serrer à droite** (public sign) squeeze to right ‖ *ref* to squeeze together, to be close together

serre-tête [sɛrtɛt] *m invar* headband; kerchief; crash helmet; (telp) headset

serrure [sɛryr] *f* lock; **serrure de sûreté** safety lock

serrurier [sɛryrje] *m* locksmith

sertir [sɛrtir] *tr* to set (*a stone*)

sérum [serɔm] *m* serum

servage [sɛrvaʒ] *m* serfdom

ser-veur [sɛrvœr] **-veuse** [vøz] *mf* (tennis) server ‖ *m* waiter; barman ‖ *f* waitress; barmaid; extra maid; (mach) coffee maker

serviable [sɛrvjabl] *adj* obliging

service [sɛrvis] *m* service; agency; **être de service** to be on duty; **service compris** tip included; **service de garde** twenty-four-hour service; **service des abonnés absents** telephone answering service; **service des renseignements téléphoniques** information; **service sanitaire** ambulance corps

serviette [sɛrvjɛt] *f* napkin; towel; brief case; **serviette de bain** bath towel; **serviette éponge** washcloth; Turkish towel; **serviette hygiénique** sanitary napkin

servile [sɛrvil] *adj* servile

servir [sɛrvir] §63 *tr* to serve; to deal (*cards*) ‖ *intr* to serve; **servir à** to be useful for, to serve as; **servir à qu de** to serve s.o. as; **servir de** to serve as, to function as ‖ *ref* to help oneself; **se servir chez** to patronize; **se servir de** to use

serviteur [sɛrvitœr] *m* servant

servitude [sɛrvityd] *f* servitude; (law) easement

servofrein [sɛrvɔfrɛ̃] *m* power brake

ses [se] §88

sésame [sezam] *m* sesame

session [sesjɔ̃] *f* session

seuil [sœj] *m* threshold

seul seule [sœl] *adj* alone; lonely ‖ (when standing before noun) *adj* sole, single, only ‖ *pron indef* single one, only one; single person, only person ‖ **seul** *adv* alone

seulement [sœlmɑ̃] *adv* only, even ‖ *conj* but

sève [sɛv] *f* sap; vim

sévère [sever] *adj* severe; stern; strict

sévices [sevis] *mpl* cruelty, brutality

sévir [sevir] *intr* to rage

sevrage [səvraʒ] *m* weaning

sevrer [səvre] §2 *tr* to wean
sexe [seks] *m* sex; le beau sexe the fair sex; le sexe fort the sterner sex
sextant [sekstã] *m* sextant
sextuor [sekstɥɔr] *m* (mus) sextet
sexuel sexuelle [seksɥel] *adj* sexual
seyant [sejã] seyante [sejãt] *adj* becoming
shampooing [ʃãpwɛ̃] *m* shampoo
shérif [ʃerif] *m* sheriff
short [ʃɔrt] *m* shorts
si [si] *m invar* if; des si et des car ifs and buts || *adv* so; as; (to contradict a negative statement or question) yes, e.g., Vous ne le saviez pas. Si! You didn't know. Yes, I did!; si bien que so that, with the result that; si peu que so little that; si peu que ce soit however little it may be; si + *adj* or *adv* + que + *subj* however + *adj* or *adv* + *ind*, e.g., si vite qu'il s'en aille however fast he goes away || *conj* if; whether; si . . . ne unless, e.g., si je ne me trompe unless I am mistaken; si ce n'est unless; si tant est que if it is true that
sia-mois [sjamwa] -moise [mwaz] *adj* Siamese || (*cap*) *mf* Siamese
sibé-rien [siberjɛ̃] -rienne [rjen] *adj* Siberian || (*cap*) *mf* Siberian
sibylle [sibil] *f* sibyl
Sicile [sisil] *f* Sicily; la Sicile Sicily
sici-lien [sisiljɛ̃] -lienne [ljen] *adj* Sicilian || (*cap*) *mf* Sicilian
sidé-ral -rale [sideral] *adj* (*pl* -raux [ro]) sidereal
sidérer [sidere] §10 *tr* (coll) to flabbergast
sidérurgie [sideryrʒi] *f* iron-and-steel industry
sidérurgique [sideryrʒik] *adj* iron-and-steel
siècle [sjekl] *m* century; age; (eccl) world
siège [sjeʒ] *m* seat; headquarters; (eccl) see; (mil) siege; siège à glissière glider; siège baquet (*pl* sièges baquets) bucket seat; siège éjectable ejection seat
siéger [sjeʒe] §1 *intr* to sit, to be in session; (*said of malady*) to be seated
sien [sjɛ̃] sienne [sjen] §89
sieste [sjest] *f* siesta; faire la sieste to take a siesta
sifflement [sifləmã] *m* whistle; hiss; swish, whiz
siffler [sifle] *tr* to whistle (*e.g., a tune*); to hiss, boo; to whistle to || *intr* to whistle; to hiss; to swish, to whiz
sifflet [sifle] *m* whistle
sif-fleur [siflœr] sif-fleuse [sifløz] *mf* whistler
sigle [sigl] *m* abbreviation; word formed by literation; acronym
si-gnal [sinal] *m* (*pl* -gnaux [no]) signal; sign; (telp) busy signal
signa-lé -lée [sinale] *adj* signal, noteworthy
signalement [sinalmã] *m* description
signaler [sinale] *tr* to signal; to point out || *ref* to distinguish oneself
signalisation [sinalizasjɔ̃] *f* signs
signataire [sinater] *adj* & *mf* signatory

signature [sinatyr] *f* signature; signing
signe [sin] *m* sign; faire signe à to motion to, to signal; signe de ponctuation punctuation mark; signe de tête nod
signer [sine] *tr* to sign || *ref* to cross oneself
signet [sine], [sine] *m* bookmark
significa-tif [sinifikatif] -tive [tiv] *adj* significant
signifier [sinifje] *tr* to signify; to mean
silence [silãs] *m* silence
silen-cieux [silãsjø] -cieuse [sjøz] *adj* silent || *m* (aut) muffler
silex [sileks] *m* flint
silhouette [silwet] *f* silhouette
silhouetter [silwete] *tr* to silhouette
silicium [silisjɔm] *m* silicon
silicone [silikon] *f* silicone
sillage [sijaʒ] *m* wake
sillet [sije] *m* (mus) nut
sillon [sijɔ̃] *m* furrow; groove; sillon sonore sound track
sillonner [sijone] *tr* to furrow; to groove; to cross, to streak
silo [silo] *m* silo
silure [silyr] *m* catfish
simagrée [simagre] *f* pretense
similaire [similer] *adj* similar
similigravure [similigravyr] *f* halftone
similitude [similityd] *f* similarity
similor [similɔr] *m* ormolu
simple [sɛ̃pl] *adj* simple; passer en simple police to go to police court; simple particulier private citizen; simple soldat private || *mf* simpleminded person || *m* simple (*herb*); (tennis) singles
sim-plet [sɛ̃ple] -plette [plet] *adj* artless
simplifier [sɛ̃plifje] *tr* to simplify
simpliste [sɛ̃plist] *adj* oversimple
simulacre [simylakr] *m* sham; simulacre de combat sham battle
simuler [simyle] *tr* to simulate
simulta-né -née [simyltane] *adj* simultaneous
sinapisme [sinapism] *m* mustard plaster
sincère [sɛ̃ser] *adj* sincere
sincérité [sɛ̃serite] *f* sincerity
sinécure [sinekyr] *f* sinecure
singe [sɛ̃ʒ] *m* monkey; (slang) boss; grimacer comme un vieux singe to grin like a Cheshire cat
singer [sɛ̃ʒe] §38 *tr* to ape
singerie [sɛ̃ʒri] *f* monkeyshine; grimace; monkey cage
singulariser [sɛ̃gylarize] *tr* to draw attention to || *ref* to stand out
singu-lier [sɛ̃gylje] -lière [ljer] *adj* & *m* singular
sinistre [sinistr] *adj* sinister || *m* disaster
sinis-tré -trée [sinistre] *adj* damaged, ruined; homeless; shipwrecked || *mf* victim
sinon [sinɔ̃] *adv* if not; perhaps even; sinon que except for the fact that || *prep* except for, except to || *conj* except, unless; or else, else, otherwise
si-nueux [sinɥø] -nueuse [nɥøz] *adj* sinuous, winding
sinus [sinys] *m* sinus; (trig) sine

sionisme [sjɔnism] *m* Zionism

siphon [sifɔ̃] *m* siphon; siphon bottle; trap (*double-curved pipe*)

siphonner [sifone] *tr* to siphon

sirène [siren] *f* siren; foghorn

sirop [siro] *m* syrup; **sirop pectoral** cough syrup

siroter [sirote] *tr & intr* (coll) to sip

sis [si] **sise** [siz] *adj* located

sismographe [sismɔgraf] *m* seismograph

sismologie [sismɔlɔʒi] *f* seismology

site [sit] *m* site; lay of the land

sitôt [sito] *adv* immediately; **sitôt dit, sitôt fait** no sooner said than done; **sitôt que** as soon as

sittelle [sitel] *f* (orn) nuthatch

situation [situɑsjɔ̃] *f* situation; **situation sans issue** deadlock, impasse

situer [situe] *tr* to situate, to locate

six [si(s)] *adj & pron* six; the Sixth, e.g., **Jean six** John the Sixth; **six heures** six o'clock || *m* six; sixth (*in dates*)

sixième [sizjem] *adj, pron (masc, fem), & m* sixth

six-quatre-deux [siskatdø]—**à la six-quatre-deux** (coll) slapdash

sizain [sizɛ̃] *m* six-line verse; pack (*of cub scouts*)

sizerin [sizrɛ̃] *m* (orn) redpoll

ski [ski] *m* ski; skiing; **faire du ski** to go skiing; **ski nautique** water-skiing

skier [skje] *intr* to ski

skieur [skjœr] **skieuse** [skjøz] *mf* skier

slalom [slalɔm] *m* slalom

slave [slav] *adj* Slav; Slavic || *m* Slavic (*language*) || (*cap*) *mf* Slav (*person*)

slogan [slɔgɑ̃] *m* (com) slogan

slovaque [slɔvak] *adj* Slovak || *m* Slovak (*language*) || (*cap*) *mf* Slovak (*person*)

smoking [smɔkiŋ] *m* tuxedo

snack [snak] *m* snack bar

S.N.C.F. [esenseef] *f* (letterword) (Société nationale des Chemins de fer français) French railroad

snob [snɔb] *adj invar* snobbish || *mf* (*pl* snob *or* snobs) snob

snober [snɔbe] *tr* to snub

snobisme [snɔbism] *m* snobbery

sobre [sɔbr] *adj* sober, moderate; simple (*ornamentation*)

sobriété [sɔbrijete] *f* sobriety; moderation (*in eating, speaking*)

sobriquet [sɔbrike] *m* nickname

soc [sɔk] *m* plowshare

sociable [sɔsjabl] *adj* sociable, neighborly; social (*creature*)

so•cial -ciale [sɔsjal] *adj* (*pl* -ciaux [sjo]) social

sociali•sant -sante [sɔsjalizɑ̃] -sɑ̃t] *adj* socialistic || *mf* socialist sympathizer

socialiser [sɔsjalize] *tr* to socialize

socialisme [sɔsjalism] *m* socialism

socialiste [sɔsjalist] *adj & mf* socialist

sociétaire [sɔsjeter] *mf* stockholder; member (*e.g., of an acting company*)

société [sɔsjete] *f* society; company; firm, partnership; **société anonyme** stock company, corporation; **société de prévoyance** benefit society; **Société des Nations** League of Nations

sociologie [sɔsjɔlɔʒi] *f* sociology

socle [sɔkl] *m* pedestal; footing, socle

socque [sɔk] *m* clog, sabot; (theat) comedy

socquette [sɔket] *f* anklet

Socrate [sɔkrat] *m* Socrates

soda [sɔda] *m* soda water

sodium [sɔdjɔm] *m* sodium

sœur [sœr] *f* sister; **et ta sœur!** (slang) knock it off!; **ma sœur** (eccl) sister

sofa [sɔfa] *m* sofa

soi [swa] §85, §85B; **à part soi** to oneself (himself, etc.); **de soi, en soi** in itself

soi-disant [swadizɑ̃] *adj invar* so-called, self-styled || *adv* supposedly

soie [swa] *f* silk; bristle

soierie [swari] *f* silk goods; silk factory

soif [swaf] *f* thirst; **avoir soif** to be thirsty

soi•gné -gnée [swaɲe] *adj* well-groomed, trim; polished (*speech*)

soigner [swaɲe] *tr* to nurse, take care of; to groom; to polish (*one's style*)

soigneur [swaɲœr] *m* (sports) trainer

soi•gneux -gneuse [swaɲø] -ɲøz] *adj* careful, meticulous

soi-même [swamɛm] §86

soin [swɛ̃] *m* care, attention; treatment; **aux bons soins de** in care of (*c/o*); **être aux petits soins auprès de** to wait on (*s.o.*) hand and foot; **premiers soins** first aid; **soins d'urgence** first aid

soir [swar] *m* evening, night; **hier soir** last night; **le soir** in the evening, at night

soirée [sware] *f* evening; evening party; **en soirée** evening (*performance*); **soirée dansante** dance

soit [swa], [swat] *conj* take for instance, e.g., **soit quatre multiplié par deux** take for instance four multiplied by two; say, e.g., **bien des hommes étaient perdus, soit un million** many men were lost, say a million; **soit . . soit** either . . . or, whether . . . or; **soit que . . . soit que** whether . . . or || [swat] *interj* so be it!, all right!

soixante [swasɑ̃t] *adj, pron, & m* sixty; **soixante et onze** seventy-one; **soixante et onzième** seventy-first; **soixante et un** sixty-one; **soixante et unième** sixty-first

soixante-dix [swasɑ̃tdi(s)] *adj, pron, & m* seventy

soixante-dixième [swasɑ̃tdizjem] *adj, pron (masc, fem), & m* seventieth

soixantième [swasɑ̃tjem] *adj, pron (masc, fem), & m* sixtieth

soja [sɔʒa] *m* soybean

sol [sɔl] *m* soil; ground; floor

solaire [sɔler] *adj* solar

soldat [sɔlda] *m* soldier

soldatesque [sɔldatesk] *adj* barrackroom (*humor; manners*) || *f* rowdies

solde [sɔld] *m* balance (*of an account*); remnant; clearance sale; **en solde** reduced (*in price*) || *f* (mil) pay

solder [sɔlde] *tr* to settle (*an account*); to sell out; (mil) to pay || *intr* to sell out

sol·deur [sɔldœr] **-deuse** [døz] *mf* dealer in seconds and remnants

sole [sɔl] *f* sole (*fish*); field (*used for crop rotation*)

soleil [sɔlej] *m* sun; sunshine, sunlight; sunflower; pinwheel; **il fait du soleil** or **il fait soleil** it is sunny

solen·nel -nelle [sɔlanel] *adj* solemn

solénoïde [sɔlenɔid] *m* solenoid

solfège [sɔlfeʒ] *m* sol-fa

solidage [sɔlidaʒ] *f* goldenrod

solidaire [sɔlider] *adj* interdependent; jointly binding; **solidaire de responsible for**; answerable to; integral with, in one piece with

solidariser [sɔlidarize] *ref* to join together

solidarité [sɔlidarite] *f* solidarity, interdependence

solide [sɔlid] *adj & m* solid

solidité [sɔlidite] *f* solidity; soundness; strength (*e.g., of a fabric*)

soliloque [sɔlilɔk] *m* soliloquy

soliste [sɔlist] *mf* soloist

solitaire [sɔliter] *adj* solitary; lonely ‖ *m* solitary, anchorite; old wild boar; solitaire

solitude [sɔlityd] *f* solitude

solive [sɔliv] *f* joist

soli·veau [sɔlivo] *m* (*pl* **-veaux**) small joist; (coll) nobody

solliciter [sɔllisite] *tr* to solicit; to apply for; to incite; to attract (*attention; iron*); to induce ‖ *intr* to seek favors

sollici·teur [sɔllisitœr] **-teuse** [tøz] *mf* solicitor, office seeker, petitioner, lobbyist

solo [sɔlo] *adj invar & m* solo

solstice [sɔlstis] *m* solstice

soluble [sɔlybl] *adj* soluble; solvable

solution [sɔlysjɔ̃] *f* solution

solutionner [sɔlysjɔne] *tr* to solve

solvabilité [sɔlvabilite] *f* solvency

solvable [sɔlvabl] *adj* solvent

solvant [sɔlvɑ̃] *m* solvent

sombre [sɔ̃br] *adj* somber; sullen

sombrer [sɔ̃bre] *intr* to sink; to vanish (*as a fortune*)

sommaire [sɔmer] *adj & m* summary

sommation [sɔmasjɔ̃] *f* summons; sentry challenge; **faire les trois sommations** to read the riot act

somme [sɔm] *m* nap ‖ *f* sum; **en somme, somme toute** in short, when all is said and done

sommeil [sɔmej] *m* sleep; **avoir sommeil** to be sleepy

sommeiller [sɔmeje] *intr* to doze; to lie dormant

sommelier [sɔmalje] *m* wine steward

sommer [sɔme] *tr* to add up; to summon, to issue a legal writ to

sommet [sɔme] *m* summit, top; apex (*of a triangle*); vertex (*of an angle*); (fig) acme

sommier [sɔmje] *m* bedspring; ledger; crossbeam; (archaic) pack animal; **sommier élastique** spring mattress

sommité [sɔmite] *f* pinnacle, crest; leader, authority

somnambule [sɔmnɑ̃byl] *adj* sleepwalking ‖ *mf* sleepwalker

somnifère [sɔmnifer] *adj & m* soporific

somnolence [sɔmnɔlɑ̃s] *f* drowsiness; indolence, laziness

somno·lent [sɔmnɔlɑ̃] **-lente** [lɑ̃t] *adj* somnolent, drowsy; indolent

somnoler [sɔmnɔle] *intr* to doze

somptuaire [sɔ̃ptɥer] *adj* luxury (*tax*)

somp·tueux [sɔ̃ptɥø] **-tueuse** [tɥøz] *adj* sumptuous

son [sɔ̃] *adj poss* §88 ‖ *m* sound; bran

sonate [sɔnat] *f* sonata

sondage [sɔ̃daʒ] *m* sounding, probing; **sondage de l'opinion** public-opinion poll; **sondage d'exploration** wildcat (*well*)

sonde [sɔ̃d] *f* lead, probe; borer, drill

sonder [sɔ̃de] *tr* to sound, probe, bore, fathom; to explore, reconnoiter; to poll (*e.g., public opinion*); to sound out (*s.o.*)

son·deur [sɔ̃dœr] **-deuse** [døz] *mf* prober, sounder

songe [sɔ̃ʒ] *m* dream

songe-creux [sɔ̃ʒkrø] *m invar* visionary, pipe dreamer

songer [sɔ̃ʒe] §38 *tr* to dream up ‖ *intr* to dream; to think; to intend to; **songer à** to think of; to imagine, to dream of; **songez-y!** think it over!

songerie [sɔ̃ʒri] *f* reverie, daydreaming

son·geur [sɔ̃ʒœr] **-geuse** [ʒøz] *adj* dreamy, preoccupied ‖ *mf* daydreamer

sonique [sɔnik] *adj* sonic, of sound

sonnaille [sɔnaj] *f* cowbell, sheepbell

sonnailler [sɔnaje] *m* bellwether ‖ *intr* to ring often and without cause

son·nant [sɔnɑ̃] **son·nante** [sɔnɑ̃t] *adj* striking (*clock*); metal (*money*); at the stroke of, e.g., **à huit heures sonnantes** at the stroke of eight

son·né -née [sɔne] *adj* past, e.g., **deux heures sonnées** past two o'clock; over, e.g., **il a soixante ans sonnés** he is over sixty; (slang) cuckoo, nuts; (slang) stunned

sonner [sɔne] *tr* to ring; to ring for; to sound ‖ *intr* to ring; to strike; to sound

sonnerie [sɔnri] *f* chimes, chiming; set of bells, carillon; fanfare; ring (*of a telephone, doorbell, etc.*); alarm or striking mechanism (*of clock*)

sonnet [sɔne] *m* sonnet

sonnette [sɔnet] *f* doorbell; pile driver

sonneur [sɔnœr] *m* bellringer; trumpeter

sonore [sɔnɔr] *adj* sonorous; sound (*wave, track*); echoing (*hall, cathedral, etc.*); (phonet) voiced ‖ *f* voiced consonant

sonoriser [sɔnɔrize] *tr* to record sound effects on (*a film*); to equip (*an auditorium*) with loudspeakers

sonorité [sɔnɔrite] *f* sonority, resonance

sonotone [sɔnɔtɔn] *m* hearing aid

sophistication [sɔfistikasjɔ̃] *f* adulteration

sophisti·qué -quée [sɔfistike] *adj* adulterated; artificial, counterfeit

sophistiquer [sɔfistike] *tr* to adulterate; to subtilize

Sophocle [sɔfɔkl] *m* Sophocles

sopraniste [sɔpranist] *m* male soprano

sopra·no [sɔprano] *mf* (*pl* **-ni** [ni] *or* **-nos**) soprano || *m* soprano (*voice*)

sorbet [sɔrbe] *m* sherbet

sorbetière [sɔrbətjer] *f* ice-cream freezer

sorbon·nard [sɔrbɔnar] **sorbon·narde** [sɔrbɔnard] *mf* (coll) Sorbonne student; (coll) Sorbonne professor

sorcellerie [sɔrselri] *f* sorcery

sor·cier [sɔrsje] **-cière** [sjer] *adj* sorcerer's; **cela n'est pas sorcier** there's no trick to that || *m* sorcerer, wizard || *f* sorceress, witch; **vieille sorcière** old hag

sordide [sɔrdid] *adj* sordid

sornette [sɔrnet] *f* nonsense

sort [sɔr] *m* fate, destiny; fortune, lot; spell, charm

sortable [sɔrtabl] *adj* suitable, acceptable; presentable

sor·tant [sɔrtã] **-tante** [tãt] *adj* retiring (*congressman*); winning (*number*) || *mf* person leaving

sorte [sɔrt] *f* sort, kind; state, condition; way, manner; **de la sorte** this way, thus; **de sorte que** so that, with the result that; **en quelque sorte** in a certain way; **en sorte que** in such a way that

sortie [sɔrti] *f* exit, way out; outing, jaunt; quitting time; outburst, tirade; (mil) sortie; **sortie de bain** bathrobe; **sortie de bal** evening wrap; **sortie de secours** emergency exit; **sortie de voiture(s)** driveway

sortilège [sɔrtilɛʒ] *m* spell, charm

sortir [sɔrtir] §64 *tr* to take out, to bring out; to publish || *intr* (*aux:* ÊTRE) to go out, to come out; to come forth; to stand out; **au sortir de** on coming out of; **sortir de** + *inf* (coll) to have just + *pp*

S.O.S. [esoes] *m* (letterword) S.O.S.

sosie [sozi] *m* double

sot [so] **sotte** [sɔt] *adj* stupid, silly || *mf* fool, simpleton

sottise [sɔtiz] *f* stupidity, silliness, foolishness

sou [su] *m* sou; (fig) penny, farthing; **sans le sou** penniless; **sou à sou** *or* **sou par sou** a penny at a time

soubassement [subasmã] *m* subfoundation, infrastructure

soubresaut [subrəso] *m* sudden start, jerk; palpitation, jump (*of the heart*)

soubrette [subret] *f* (theat) soubrette; (coll) attractive chambermaid

souche [suʃ] *f* stump; stock; stack (*of fireplace*); strain (*of virus*); (coll) dolt

souci [susi] *m* care; marigold; **sans souci** carefree

soucier [susje] *ref* to care, concern oneself

soucieusement [susjøzmã] *adv* uneasily, anxiously; with concern

sou·cieux [susjø] **-cieuse** [sjøz] *adj* solicitous, concerned; uneasy, anxious

soucoupe [sukup] *f* saucer; **soucoupe volante** flying saucer

soudage [sudaʒ] *m* soldering; welding

sou·dain [sudɛ̃] **-daine** [den] *adj* sudden || **soudain** *adv* suddenly

soudainement [sudenmã] *adv* suddenly

soudaineté [sudente] *f* suddenness

souda·nais [sudane] **-naise** [nez] *adj* Sudanic || *m* Sudanic (*language*) || (*cap*) *mf* Sudanese (*person*)

soude [sud] *f* (chem) soda

souder [sude] *tr* to solder; to weld || *ref* to knit (*as bones do*)

soudeur [sudœr] *m* welder

soudoyer [sudwaje] §47 *tr* to bribe; to hire (*assassins*)

soudure [sudyr] *f* solder; soldering; soldered joint; knitting (*of bones*); **faire la soudure** to bridge the gap; **soudure autogène** welding

soue [su] *f* pigsty

soufflage [suflaʒ] *m* blowing; glass blowing

souffle [sufl] *m* breath; breathing

souf·flé -flée [sufle] *adj* puffed up || *m* soufflé

souffler [sufle] *tr* to blow; to blow out (*a candle*); to blow up (*a balloon*); to prompt (*an actor*); to huff (*a checker*); to suggest (*an idea*); **ne pas souffler mot** to not breathe a word; **souffler à l'oreille** to whisper; **souffler q.ch. à qn** to take s.th. from s.o. || *intr* to blow; to pant, puff; to take a breather, to catch one's breath

soufflerie [sufləri] *f* bellows; wind tunnel

soufflet [sufle] *m* slap in the face; affront, insult; bellows; gore (*of dress*); (rr) flexible cover (*between two cars*)

souffleter [sufləte] §34 *tr* to slap in the face; to affront

souf·fleur [suflœr] **souf·fleuse** [sufløz] *mf* (theat) prompter || *m* glass blower || *f* (mach) blower

soufflure [suflyr] *f* blister, bubble

souffrance [sufrãs] *f* suffering; **en souffrance** unfinished (*business*); outstanding (*bill*); unclaimed (*parcel*); at a standstill, suspended

souf·frant [sufrã] **souf·frante** [sufrãt] *adj* suffering; sick, ailing

souffre-douleur [sufrədulœr] *m invar* butt (*of a joke*), laughingstock

souffre·teux [sufrətø] **-teuse** [tøz] *adj* sickly; destitute, half-starved

souffrir [sufrir] §65 *tr* to suffer; to stand, bear, tolerate; to permit || *intr* to suffer || *ref* to put up with each other

soufre [sufr] *m* sulfur

soufrer [sufre] *tr* to sulfurate

souhait [swe] *m* wish; **à souhait** to one's liking, to perfection; **à vos souhaits!** (salutation) gesundheit!; **souhaits** good wishes; **souhaits de bonne année** New Year's greetings

souhaitable [swetabl] *adj* desirable

souhaiter [swete] *tr* to wish; to wish for; to wish to; **je vous la souhaite bonne et heureuse** I wish you a happy New Year

souille [suj] *f* wallow

souiller [suje] *tr* to dirty, spot, stain, soil, sully

souillon [sujɔ̃] *f* (coll) scullery maid

souillure [sujyr] *f* spot, stain

soûl [su] **soûle** [sul] *adj* drunk; sottish || *m* fill, e.g., **manger son soûl** to eat one's fill

soulagement [sulaʒmɑ̃] *m* relief; comfort

soulager [sulaʒe] §38 *tr* to relieve; to comfort

soûler [sule] *tr* (slang) to cram down one's throat; (slang) to get (*s.o.*) drunk || *ref* (fig) to have one's fill; (slang) to get drunk

soulèvement [sulɛvmɑ̃] *m* upheaval; uprising; surge; **soulèvement de cœur** nausea

soulever [sulve] §2 *tr* to raise, heave, lift (up); to stir up || *ref* to rise; to raise oneself; to revolt

soulier [sulje] *m* shoe

soulignement [sulinəmɑ̃] *m* underlining

souligner [suliɲe] *tr* to underline; to emphasize

soulte [sult] *f* balance due

soumettre [sumɛtr] §42 *tr* to submit; to subject; to overcome, subdue || *ref* to submit, surrender

sou·mis [sumi] **-mise** [miz] *adj* submissive, subservient; subject; amenable (*to a law*)

soumission [sumisjɔ̃] *f* submission, surrender; bid (*to perform a service*); guarantee

soumissionnaire [sumisjɔnɛr] *mf* bidder

soupape [supap] *f* valve; **soupape à réglage** or **à papillon** damper; **soupape de sûreté** safety valve; **soupape électrique** rectifier

soupçon [supsɔ̃] *m* suspicion; misgiving; dash, touch (*small amount*)

soupçonner [supsɔne] *tr & intr* to suspect

soupçon·neux [supsɔnø] **soupçon·neuse** [supsɔnøz] *adj* suspicious

soupe [sup] *f* vegetable soup; sop (*bread*); (mil) mess; **de soupe** on K.P.; **soupe au lait** (coll) meantempered person; **soupe populaire** soup kitchen; **trempé comme une soupe** soaking wet

soupente [supɑ̃t] *f* attic

souper [supe] *m* supper || *intr* to have supper

soupeser [supəze] §2 *tr* to heft, to weigh (*e.g., a package*) in one's hand

soupière [supjɛr] *f* soup tureen

soupir [supir] *m* sigh; breath; (mus) quarter rest

soupi·rail [supiraj] *m* (*pl* **-raux** [ro]) cellar window

soupirant [supirɑ̃] *m* suitor

soupirer [supire] *intr* to sigh; **soupirer après** or **pour** to long for

souple [supl] *adj* supple; flexible, pliant; versatile, adaptable

souplesse [suples] *f* suppleness, flexibility

souquer [suke] *tr* to haul taut || *intr* to pull hard (*on the oars*)

source [surs] *f* source; spring, fountain; **source de pétrole** oil well; **source jaillissante** gusher

sourcier [sursje] *m* dowser

sourcil [surci] *m* eyebrow

sourciller [sursije] *intr* to knit one's brows; **sans sourciller** without batting an eye

sourcil·leux [sursijø] **sourcil·leuse** [sursijøz] *adj* supercilious

sourd [sur] **sourde** [surd] *adj* deaf; quiet; dull (*sound, color*); deep (*voice*); undeclared (*war*); (phonet) unvoiced; **sourd comme un pot** (coll) stone-deaf || *mf* deaf person || *f* unvoiced consonant

sourdement [surdəmɑ̃] *adv* secretly; heavily; dully

sourdine [surdin] *f* (mus) mute; **à la sourdine** muted; **en sourdine** on the sly

sourd-muet [surmɥɛ] **sourde-muette** [surdəmɥɛt] (*pl* **sourds-muets**) *adj* deaf and dumb, deaf-mute || *mf* deaf-mute

sourdre [surdr] (used in: *inf*; 3d *sg & pl pres and* **sourd, sourdent**) *intr* to spring, well up

souricier [surisje] *m* mouser

souricière [surisjɛr] *f* mousetrap; (fig) trap

sourire [surir] *m* smile || §61 *intr* to smile; **sourire à** to smile at; to smile on; to look good to

souris [suri] *m* (obs) smile || *f* mouse

sour·nois [surnwa] **-noise** [nwaz] *adj* sly, cunning, artful

sous [su] *prep* under; on (*a certain day; certain conditions*); **sous caoutchouc** rubber-covered; **sous clef** under lock and key; **sous la main** at hand; **sous les drapeaux** in the army; **sous main** underhandedly; **sous peu** shortly; **sous un certain angle** from a certain point of view

sous-alimentation [suzalimɑ̃tasjɔ̃] *f* dernourishment

sous-bois [subwa] *m* underbrush, undergrowth

sous-chef [suʃɛf] *m* (*pl* **-chefs**) assistant (*to the head man*), deputy, second-in-command

souscripteur [suskriptœr] *m* subscriber (*to a loan or charity*); signer (*of a commercial paper*)

souscription [suskripsjɔ̃] *f* signature; subscription; **souscription de soutien** sustaining membership

souscrire [suskrir] §25 *tr & intr* to subscribe

sous-cuta·né **-née** [sukytane] *adj* subcutaneous

sous-dévelop·pé **-pée** [sudevlope] *adj* underdeveloped

sous-diacre [sudjakr] *m* subdeacon

sous-direc·teur [sudirektœr] **-trice** [tris] *mf* (*pl* **-directeurs**) second-in-command

sous-entendre [suzɑ̃tɑ̃dr] *tr* to understand (*what is not expressed*); to imply

sous-entendu [suzɑ̃tɑ̃dy] *m* inference, implication, innuendo, double meaning, double entendre

sous-entente [suzɑ̃tɑ̃t] *f* mental reservation; hidden, cryptic meaning

sous-entrepreneur [suzɑ̃trəprənœr] *m* (*pl* -entrepreneurs) subcontractor

sous-estimer [suzestime] *tr* to underestimate

sous-fifre [sufifr] *m* (*pl* -fifres) (coll) underling

sous-garde [sugard] *f* trigger guard

sous-lieutenant [suljøtnɑ̃] *m* (*pl* -lieutenants) second lieutenant

sous-location [sulokasjɔ̃] *f* sublease

sous-louer [sulwe] *tr* to sublet, sublease

sous-main [sumɛ̃] *m invar* desk blotter; **en sous-main** underhandedly

sous-marin [sumarɛ̃] **-marine** [marin] *adj & m* (*pl* -marins) submarine

sous-marinier [sumarinje] *m* (*pl* -mariniers) submarine crewman

sous-mentonnière [sumɑ̃tɔnjɛr] *f* (*pl* -mentonnières) chin strap

sous-nappe [sunap] *f* (*pl* -nappes) table pad

sous-off [suzɔf] *m* (*pl* -offs) noncom

sous-officier [suzɔfisje] *m* (*pl* -officiers) noncommissioned officer

sous-ordre [suzɔrdr] *m* (*pl* -ordres) underling, subordinate; (biol) suborder; **en sous-ordre** subordinate; subordinately

sous-production [suprɔdyksjɔ̃] *f* underproduction

sous-produit [suprɔdɥi] *m* (*pl* -produits) by-product

sous-secrétaire [suskreter] *m* (*pl* -secrétaires) undersecretary

sous-secrétariat [suskretarja] *m* undersecretaryship

sous-seing [susɛ̃] *m invar* privately witnessed document

soussi-gné -gnée [susiɲe] *adj & mf* undersigned

sous-sol [susɔl] *m* (*pl* -sols) subsoil; basement

sous-titre [sutitr] *m* (*pl* -titres) subtitle

sous-titrer [sutitre] *tr* to subtitle

soustraction [sustraksjɔ̃] *f* subtraction; (law) purloining

soustraire [sustrer] §68 *tr* to remove; take away; to subtract; to deduct; **soustraire de** to subtract from; **soustraire q.ch. à qn** to take s.th. away from s.o.; to steal s.th. from s.o. || *ref* to withdraw; **se soustraire à** to escape from

sous-traitant [sutretɑ̃] *m* (*pl* -traitants) subcontractor; sublessee

sous-traité [sutrete] *m* (*pl* -traités) subcontract

sous-traiter [sutrete] *tr & intr* to subcontract

sous-ventrière [suvɑ̃trijer] *f* (*pl* -ventrières) girth

sous-verre [suver] *m invar* passe-partout; coaster

sous-vêtement [suvetmɑ̃] *m* (*pl* -vêtements) undergarment

soutache [sutaʃ] *f* braid

soutacher [sutaʃe] *tr* to trim with braid

soutane [sutan] *f* soutane, cassock

soutanelle [sutanel] *f* frock coat; choir robe

soute [sut] *f* (naut) storeroom; **soute à charbon** coal bunker

soutenable [sutnabl] *adj* supportable, tenable

soutenance [sutnɑ̃s] *f* defense (*of an academic thesis*)

soutènement [sutenmɑ̃] *m* support

souteneur [sutnœr] *m* pimp

soutenir [sutnir] §72 *tr* to support, bear; to sustain; to insist, claim; to defend (*a thesis*) || *ref* to stand up; to keep afloat

soute-nu -nue [sutny] *adj* sustained; elevated (*style*); steady (*market*); true (*colors*)

souter-rain [suterɛ̃] **souter-raine** [suterɛn] *adj* subterranean, underground; underhanded || *m* tunnel, subway (*for pedestrians*)

soutien [sutjɛ̃] *m* support; stand-by

soutien-gorge [sutjɛ̃gɔrʒ] *m* (*pl* soutiens-gorge) brassiere

soutirage [sutiraʒ] *m* racking

soutirer [sutire] *tr* to rack (*wine*); **soutirer q.ch. à qn** to get s.th. out of s.o., to sponge on s.o. for s.th.

souvenir [suvnir] *m* memory, remembrance; souvenir || §72 *intr*—**faire souvenir qn de q.ch.** to remind s.o. of s.th. || *ref* to remember; **se souvenir de** to remember

souvent [suvɑ̃] *adv* often

souve-rain -raine [ren] *adj & mf* sovereign || *m* sovereign (*coin*)

souveraineté [suvrente] *f* sovereignty

soviet [sɔvjet] *m* soviet

soviétique [sɔvjetik] *adj* Soviet || (*cap*) *mf* Soviet Russian

soya [sɔja] *m* soybean

soyeux [swajø] **soyeuse** [swajøz] *adj* silky

S.P. *abbr* (**sapeurs-pompiers**) fire department

spa-cieux [spasjø] **-cieuse** [sjøz] *adj* spacious, roomy

spadassin [spadasɛ̃] *m* hatchet man, hired thug

spaghetti [spagetti] *m* spaghetti

sparadrap [sparadra] *m* adhesive tape

spartiate [sparsjat] *adj* Spartan || (*cap*) *mf* Spartan

spasme [spasm] *m* spasm

spasmodique [spasmɔdik] *adj* spasmodic; (pathol) spastic

spath [spat] *m* (mineral) spar

spa-tial -tiale [spasjal] *adj* (*pl* -tiaux [sjo]) spatial

spatule [spatyl] *f* spatula; (orn) spoonbill

spea-ker [spikœr] **-kerine** [krin] *mf* (rad, telv) announcer || *m* speaker (*presiding officer*)

spé-cial -ciale [spesjal] *adj* (*pl* -ciaux [sjo]) special

spécialiser [spesjalize] *tr & ref* to specialize

spécialiste [spesjalist] *mf* specialist; expert

spécialité [spesjalite] *f* specialty; specialization; patent medicine

spé-cieux [spesjø] **-cieuse** [sjøz] *adj* specious

spécifier [spesifje] *tr* to specify

spécifique [spesifik] *adj & m* specific

spécimen [spesimen] *adj & m* specimen

spectacle [spektakl] *m* spectacle, sight; show; play; **à grand spectacle** spectacular (*production*)

specta·teur [spektatœr] **-trice** [tris] *mf* spectator

spectre [spektr] *m* ghost; spectrum; (fig) specter

spécula·teur [spekylatœr] **-trice** [tris] *mf* speculator

spéculer [spekyle] *tr* to speculate

spéléologie [speleɔlɔʒi] *f* speleology

sperme [sperm] *m* sperm

sphère [sfer] *f* sphere

sphérique [sferik] *adj* spherical

sphinx [sfɛ̃ks] *m* sphinx

spider [spider] *m* (aut) rumble seat

spi·nal -nale [spinal] *adj* (*pl* **-naux** [no]) spinal

spi·ral -rale [spiral] (*pl* **-raux** [ro]) *adj* spiral || *m* hairspring (*of watch*) || *f* spiral; **en spirale** spiral

·ire [spir] *f* turn (*in a wire*); whorl (*of a shell*)

spirée [spire] *f* (bot) spirea

spirite [spirit] *adj & mf* spiritualist

spiri·tuel -tuelle [spiritɥel] *adj* spiritual; sacred (*music*); witty || *m* ecclesiastical power

spiri·tueux [spiritɥø] **-tueuse** [tɥøz] *adj* spirituous || *m* spirituous liquor

spleen [splin] *m* boredom, melancholy

splendeur [splɑ̃dœr] *f* splendor

splendide [splɑ̃did] *adj* splendid; bright, brilliant

spolia·teur [spɔljatœr] **-trice** [tris] *adj* despoiling || *mf* despoiler

spolier [spɔlje] *tr* to despoil

spon·gieux [spɔ̃ʒjø] **-gieuse** [ʒjøz] *adj* spongy

sponta·né -née [spɔ̃tane] *adj* spontaneous

sporadique [spɔradik] *adj* sporadic(al)

sport [spɔr] *adj invar* sport, sporting; sportsmanlike || *m* sport

spor·tif [spɔrtif] **-tive** [tiv] *adj* sport, sporting || *mf* athlete, player || *m* sportsman

spot [spɔt] *m* spotlight; (radar) blip

spoutnik [sputnik] *m* sputnik

spu·meux [spymø] **-meuse** [møz] *adj* frothy, foamy

squale [skwal] *m* (ichth) dogfish

squelette [skəlɛt] *m* skeleton

squelettique [skəletik] *adj* skeletal

S.R. *abbr* (Service de renseignements) information desk or bureau

stabiliser [stabilize] *tr* to stabilize

stabilité [stabilite] *f* stability

stable [stabl] *adj* stable

stade [stad] *m* stadium; (fig) stage (*of development*)

stage [staʒ] *m* probationary period, apprenticeship

stagiaire [staʒjer] *adj & mf* apprentice

stag·nant [stagnɑ̃] **-nante** [nɑ̃t] *adj* stagnant

stalle [stal] *f* stall

stance [stɑ̃s] *f* stanza

stand [stɑ̃d] *m* stands; shooting gallery; pit (*for motor racing*)

standard [stɑ̃dar] *adj invar* standard || *m* standard; switchboard

standardiser [stɑ̃dardize] *tr* to standardize

standardiste [stɑ̃dardist] *mf* switchboard operator, telephone operator

standing [stɑ̃diŋ] *m* status, standing; standard of living; **de grand standing** luxury (*apartments*)

star [star] *f* (mov, theat) star

starter [starter], [startœr] *m* (aut) choke; (sports) starter

station [stasjɔ̃] *f* station; resort; (rr) flag station; **station d'écoute** monitoring station; **station d'émission** broadcasting station; **station de repérage** tracking station; **station de taxis** taxi stand; **station orbitale** space station

stationnaire [stasjɔner] *adj* stationary || *m* gunboat

stationnement [stasjɔnmɑ̃] *m* parking; **stationnement interdit** (public sign) no parking

stationner [stasjɔne] *intr* to stop; to park

station-service [stasjɔ̃servis] *f* (*pl* **stations-service**) service station

statique [statik] *adj* static

statisti·cien [statistisjɛ̃] **-cienne** [sjen] *mf* statistician

statistique [statistik] *adj* statistical || *f* statistics

statuaire [statɥer] *adj* statuary || *mf* sculptor || *f* statuary

statue [staty] *f* statue

statuer [statɥe] *tr* to hand down (*a ruling*) || *intr* to hand down a ruling

statu quo [statykwo], [statuko] *m* status quo

stature [statyr] *f* stature

statut [staty] *m* statute; legal status

statutaire [statyter] *adj* statutory

Ste *abbr* (**Sainte**) St. (*female saint*)

Sté *abbr* (**Société**) Inc.

sténo [steno] *f* stenographer; stenography

sténodactylo [stenɔdaktilo] *f* shorthand typist; shorthand typing

sténogramme [stenɔgram] *m* shorthand notes

sténographe [stenɔgraf] *mf* stenographer

sténographie [stenɔgrafi] *f* stenography

sténographier [stenɔgrafje] *tr* to take down in shorthand

stéréo [stereo] *adj invar* stereo || *f*—**en stéréo** (electron) in stereo

stéréophonie [stereɔfɔni] *f* stereophonic sound system; **en stéréophonie** stereophonic (*e.g., broadcast*)

stéréoscopique [stereɔskɔpik] *adj* stereo, stereoscopic

stéréoty·pé -pée [stereɔtipe] *adj* stereotyped

stérile [steril] *adj* sterile

stériliser [sterilize] *tr* to sterilize

stérilité [sterilite] *f* sterility

sterling [sterliŋ] *adj invar* sterling

stéthoscope [stetɔskɔp] *m* stethoscope

stick [stik] *m* walking stick

stigmate [stigmat] *m* stigma

stigmatiser [stigmatize] *tr* to stigmatize

stimu·lant [stimylã] **-lante** [lãt] *adj* & *m* stimulant

stimuler [stimyle] *tr* to stimulate

stimu·lus [stimylys] *m* (*pl* **-li** [li]) (physiol) stimulus

stipendier [stipãdje] *tr* to hire (*e.g., an assassin*); to bribe

stipuler [stipyle] *tr* to stipulate

stock [stɔk] *m* goods, stock; hoard

stocker [stɔke] *tr* & *intr* to stockpile

stockiste [stɔkist] *m* authorized dealer (*carrying parts, motors, etc.*)

stoï·cien [stɔisjɛ̃] **-cienne** [sjɛn] *adj* & *mf* Stoic

stoïque [stɔik] *adj* stoical ‖ *mf* Stoic

stop [stɔp] *m* stop; stoplight; **du stop** (coll) hitchhiking ‖ *interj* stop!

stoppage [stɔpaʒ] *m* reweaving, invisible mending

stopper [stɔpe] *tr* to reweave; to stop ‖ *intr* to stop

store [stɔr] *m* blind; window awning; outside window shade

strabique [strabik] *adj* squint-eyed

strabisme [strabism] *m* squint

strapontin [strapɔ̃tɛ̃] *m* jump seat; (theat) attached folding seat

strass [stras] *m* paste (*jewelry*)

stratagème [strataʒɛm] *m* stratagem

strate [strat] *f* (geol) stratum

stratège [strateʒ] *m* strategist

stratégie [strateʒi] *f* strategy

stratégique [strateʒik] *adj* strategic(al)

stratégiste [strateʒist] *m* strategist

stratifier [stratifje] *tr* & *ref* to stratify

stratosphère [stratɔsfer] *f* stratosphere

strict stricte [strikt] *adj* strict

stri·dent [stridã] **-dente** [dãt] *adj* strident

strie [stri] *f* streak; stripe

strier [strije] *tr* to streak; to score, groove

strontium [strɔ̃sjɔm] *m* strontium

strophe [strɔf] *f* verse, stanza; strophe

structu·ral -rale [stryktyral] *adj* (*pl* **-raux** [ro]) structural

structure [stryktyr] *f* structure

strychnine [striknin] *f* strychnine

stuc [styk] *m* stucco; **enduire de stuc** to stucco

stu·dieux [stydjø] **-dieuse** [djøz] *adj* studious

studio [stydjo] *m* studio

stupé·fait [stypefe] **-faite** [fet] *adj* dumfounded, amazed

stupé·fiant [stypefjã] **-fiante** [fjãt] *adj* astounding ‖ *m* drug, narcotic

stupéfier [stypefje] *tr* to astound; to stupefy (*as with a drug*)

stupeur [stypœr] *f* stupor; amazement

stupide [stypid] *adj* stupid

stupidité [stypidite] *f* stupidity

stuquer [styke] *tr* to stucco

style [stil] *m* style; stylus

styler [stile] *tr* to train

stylet [stile] *m* stiletto

styliser [stilize] *tr* to stylize

stylo [stilo] *m* pen, fountain pen; **stylo à bille** ball-point pen

styptique [stiptik] *adj* & *m* styptic

suaire [sɥer] *m* shroud, winding sheet

suave [sɥav] *adj* sweet (*perfume, music, etc.*); bland (*food*); suave

subcons·cient [sypkɔ̃sjã] **subcons·ciente** [sypkɔ̃sjãt] *adj* & *m* subconscious

subdiviser [sybdivize] *tr* to subdivide

subir [sybir] *tr* to submit to; to undergo; to feel, experience; to take (*an exam*); to serve (*a sentence*)

su·bit [sybi] **-bite** [bit] *adj* sudden

subjec·tif [sybʒektif] **-tive** [tiv] *adj* subjective

subjonc·tif [sybʒɔ̃ktif] **-tive** [tiv] *adj* & *m* subjunctive

subjuguer [sybʒyge] *tr* to dominate; to spellbind

sublime [syblim] *adj* sublime

sublimer [syblime] *tr* to sublimate

submerger [sybmerʒe] §38 *tr* to submerge

submersible [sybmersibl] *adj* & *m* submersible

submersion [sybmersjɔ̃] *f* submersion

subodorer [sybodɔre] *tr* to scent (*game*); (fig) to scent (*a plot*)

subordon·né -née [sybɔrdɔne] *adj* & *mf* subordinate

subordonner [sybɔrdɔne] *tr* to subordinate

suborner [sybɔrne] *tr* to bribe

subrécargue [sybrekarg] *m* supercargo

subreptice [sybreptis] *adj* surreptitious

subsé·quent [sypsekã] **-quente** [kãt] *adj* subsequent

subside [sypsid], [sybzid] *m* subsidy

subsidiaire [sypsidjer] *adj* subsidiary

subsistance [sybzistãs], [sypsistãs] *f* subsistence; (mil) rations

subsister [sybziste], [sypsiste] *intr* to subsist

substance [sypstãs] *f* substance; **en substance** briefly

substan·tiel -tielle [sypstãsjel] *adj* substantial

substan·tif [sypstãtif] **-tive** [tiv] *adj* & *m* substantive

substituer [sypstitɥe] *tr*—**substituer qn** or **q.ch. à** to substitute s.o. or s.th. for, e.g., **une biche fut substituée à Iphigénie** a hind was substituted for Iphigenia ‖ *ref*—**se substituer à** to take the place of

substitut [sypstity] *m* substitute

substitution [sypstitysjɔ̃] *f* substitution

substrat [sypstra] *m* substratum

subterfuge [sypterfyʒ] *m* subterfuge

sub·til -tile [syptil] *adj* subtle; fine (*powder, dust, etc.*); quick (*poison*); delicate (*scent*); clever (*crook*)

subtiliser [syptilize] *tr* to pick (*a purse*) ‖ *intr* to split hairs

subtilité [syptilite] *f* subtlety

subur·bain -baine [sybyrbɛ̃] **-baine** [ben] *adj* suburban

subvenir [sybvənir] §72 *intr* (with *dat*) to supply, provide, satisfy

subvention [sybvãsjɔ̃] *f* subsidy, subvention

subventionner [sybvãsjɔne] *tr* to subsidize

subver·sif [sybversif] **-sive** [siv] *adj* subversive

subvertir [sybvertir] *tr* to subvert

suc [syk] *m* juice; sap; (fig) essence

succéda•né -née [syksedane] *adj & m* substitute

succéder [syksede] §10 *intr* to happen; (with *dat*) to succeed, follow; **succéder à** to succeed to (*the throne, a fortune*) ‖ *réf* to follow one after the other, to follow one another

succès [sykse] *m* success; outcome; **avoir du succès** to be a success

succes•sif [syksesif] **succes•sive** [syksesiv] *adj* successive

succession [syksesjɔ̃] *f* succession; inheritance; heirs

suc•cinct [syksɛ̃] **-cincte** [sɛ̃t] *adj* succinct; scanty; meager

succion [syksjɔ̃] *f* suction

succomber [sykɔ̃be] *intr* to succumb

succursale [sykyrsal] *f* branch

sucer [syse] §51 *tr* to suck

sucette [syset] *f* pacifier; lollipop, sucker

su•ceur [sysœr] **-ceuse** [søz] *adj* sucking ‖ *m* nozzle

suçoter [sysote] *tr* to suck away at

sucre [sykr] *m* sugar; **sucre brut** brown sugar; **sucre candi** rock candy; **sucre de canne** cane sugar; **sucre glace** confectioners' sugar

su•cré -crée [sykre] *adj* sugary; with sugar, e.g., **du café sucré** coffee with sugar ‖ *f*—**faire la sucrée** to be mealy-mouthed

sucrer [sykre] *tr* to sugar; (slang) to take away, to cut out ‖ *réf* (slang) to grab the lion's share

sucrerie [sykrəri] *f* sugar refinery; **sucreries** candy

su•crier [sykrije] **-crière** [krijer] *adj* sugar ‖ *m* sugar bowl

sud [syd] *adj invar & m* south

sud-améri•cain [sydamerikɛ̃] **-caine** [ken] *adj* South American ‖ (*cap*) *mf* (*pl* **Sud-Américains**) South American

sudation [sydasjɔ̃] *f* sweating

sud-est [sydest] *adj invar & m* southeast

sudiste [sydist] *mf* Southerner (*in U.S.A.*)

sud-ouest [sydwest] *adj invar & m* southwest

sud-vietna•mien [sydvjetnamjɛ̃] **-mienne** [mjen] *adj* South Vietnamese ‖ (*cap*) *mf* (*pl* **Sud-Vietnamiens**) South Vietnamese

suède [sɥed] *m* suede ‖ (*cap*) *f* Sweden; **la Suède** Sweden

své•dois [sɥedwa] **-doise** [dwaz] *adj* Swedish ‖ *m* Swedish (*language*) ‖ (*cap*) *mf* Swede

suée [sɥe] *f* sweating

suer [sɥe] *tr & intr* to sweat

sueur [sɥœr] *f* sweat

suffire [syfir] §66 *intr* to suffice; (with *dat*) to suffice; **il suffit de** + *inf* it suffices to + *inf*; **suffire à** + *inf* to suffice to + *inf*; **suffit!** enough! ‖ *réf* to be self-sufficient

suffisance [syfizɑ̃s] *f* sufficiency; self-sufficiency, smugness

suffi•sant [syfizɑ̃] **-sante** [zɑ̃t] *adj* sufficient; smug, sophomoric; impudent ‖ *mf* prig

suffixe [syfiks] *m* suffix

suffoquer [syfoke] *tr & intr* to suffocate, choke, stifle, smother

suffrage [syfraʒ] *m* suffrage, vote; public approval; **au suffrage universel** by popular vote; **suffrage capacitaire** suffrage contingent upon literacy tests; **suffrage censitaire** suffrage upon payment of taxes

suggérer [sygʒere] §10 *tr* to suggest

sugges•tif [sygʒestif] **-tive** [tiv] *adj* suggestive

suggestion [sygʒestjɔ̃] *f* suggestion

suggestionner [sygʒestjone] *tr* to influence by means of suggestion

suicide [sɥisid] *adj* suicidal ‖ *m* suicide (*act*)

suici•dé -dée [sɥiside] *adj* dead by suicide ‖ *mf* suicide (*person*)

suicider [sɥiside] *réf* to commit suicide

suie [sɥi] *f* soot

suif [sɥif] *m* tallow

suint [sɥɛ̃] *m* wool fat, wool grease

suinter [sɥɛ̃te] *intr* to seep, to ooze; to sweat (*said of wall*); to run (*said of wound*)

suisse [sɥis] *adj* Swiss; **faire suisse** to eat or drink by oneself; to go Dutch ‖ *m* Swiss guard; uniformed usher; **petit suisse** cream cheese ‖ (*cap*) *f* Switzerland; **la Suisse** Switzerland ‖ **Suisse Suissesse** [sɥises] *mf* Swiss (*person*)

suite [sɥit] *f* suite; consequence; continuation, sequel (*of literary work*); sequence, series; **à la suite de** after; **de suite** in succession; in a row; **par la suite** later on; **par suite** consequently; **par suite de** because of

sui•vant [sɥivɑ̃] **-vante** [vɑ̃t] *adj* next, following, subsequent ‖ *mf* follower; next (person) ‖ *f* servant, confidante ‖ **suivant** *adv*—**suivant que** according as ‖ **suivant** *prep* according to

sui•veur [sɥivœr] **-veuse** [vøz] *adj* follow-up (*e.g., car*) ‖ *mf* follower

sui•vi -vie [sɥivi] *adj* connected, coherent; popular

suivre [sɥivr] §67 *tr* to follow; to take (*a course in school*); **suivre la mode** (fig) to follow suit ‖ *intr* to follow; **à suivre** to be continued ‖ *réf* to follow in succession; to follow one after the other

su•jet [syʒe] **-jette** [ʒet] *adj* subject; apt, liable; inclined ‖ *mf* subject (*of a government*); **mauvais sujet** ne'er-do-well ‖ *m* subject, topic; (gram) subject; **au sujet de** about, concerning

sujétion [syʒesjɔ̃] *f* subjection

sulfamide [sylfamid] *m* sulfa drug

sulfure [sylfyr] *m* sulfide

sulfurique [sylfyrik] *adj* sulfuric

sultan [syltɑ̃] *m* sultan

sumac [symak] *m* sumac; **sumac véneux** poison ivy

super [syper] *m* (coll) high-test gas

superbe [syperb] *adj* superb; proud ‖ *m* proud person ‖ *f* pride

supercarburant [syperkarbyrã] *m* high-test gasoline

supercherie [syper/əri] *f* hoax, swindle

superfétatoire [syperfetatwar] *adj* redundant

superficie [syperfisi] *f* surface, area

superfi·ciel ·cielle [syperfisjɛl] *adj* superficial

super·flu ·flue [syperfly] *adj* superfluous ‖ *m* superfluity, excess

supé·rieur ·rieure [syperjœr] *adj* superior; higher; upper (*e.g.*, *story*); supérieur à above; more than ‖ *mf* superior

supérieurement [syperjœrmã] *adv* superlatively, exceptionally

supériorité [syperjorite] *f* superiority

superla·tif ·tive [syperlatif] [tiv] *adj & m* superlative; au superlatif superlatively; in the superlative

supermarché [sypermar/e] *m* supermarket

superposer [syperpoze] *tr* to superimpose ‖ *ref* to intervene

supersonique [sypersɔnik] *adj* supersonic

supersti·tieux [syperstisjø] **·tieuse** [sjøz] *adj* superstitious

superstition [syperstisjɔ̃] *f* superstition

superstrat [syperstra] *m* superstratum

superviser [sypervize] *tr* to inspect; to revise; to correct; to supervise

supplanter [syplɑ̃te] *tr* to supplant

suppléance [sypleɑ̃s] *f* substituting; temporary post

suppléant [sypleɑ̃] **suppléante** [sypleɑ̃t] *adj* substituting ‖ *mf* substitute (*e.g.*, *a teacher, judge*)

suppléer [syplee] *tr* to supply; to take the place of; to make up for (*what is lacking*); to fill in (*the gaps*); to substitute for (*s.o.*); to fill (*a vacancy*) ‖ *intr*—**suppléer à** to make up for (*s.th.*)

supplément [syplemã] *m* supplement

supplé·tif ·tive [sypletif] [tiv] *adj & m* (mil) auxiliary

suppliant [syplijã] **suppliante** [syplijãt] *adj & mf* suppliant, supplicant

supplice [syplis] *m* torture; punishment; être au supplice to be in agony

supplicier [syplisje] *tr* to torture to death; to torment

supplier [syplije] *tr* to beseech, implore, supplicate; **je vous en supplie** I beg you; **supplier qn de** to implore s.o. to

supplique [syplik] *f* petition

support [sypɔr] *m* support, prop, pillar, bracket, strut; standard (*e.g.*, *for a lamp*)

support-chaussette [sypɔr/oset] *m* (pl **supports-chaussette**) garter (*for men*)

supporter [sypɔrtœr], [sypɔrter] *m* fan, devotee, supporter, partisan ‖ [sypɔrte] *tr* to support, to prop up; to bear, to endure; to stand, to tolerate, to put up with ‖ *intr*—**supporter de** + *inf* to tolerate or stand

for + *ger* ‖ *ref* to be tolerated; to put up with each other

suppo·sé ·sée [sypoze] *adj* supposed, admitted; spurious, assumed ‖ **supposé** *prep* supposing, admitting, granting

supposer [sypoze] *tr* to suppose; to imply; **à supposer que . . .** suppose that . . . ; **supposer un testament** to palm off a forged will

supposition [sypozisjɔ̃] *f* supposition; forgery, fraudulent substitution or alteration; supposition de part or supposition d'enfant false claim of maternity and maternal rights

suppositoire [sypozitwar] *m* suppository

suppôt [sypo] *m* henchman, tool, agitator, hireling; **suppôt de Bacchus** drunkard; **suppôt du diable** imp

suppression [sypresjɔ̃] *f* suppression; elimination (*of a job*); discontinuance (*of a festival*); killing (*of a person*); **suppression de part** or **suppression d'enfant** concealment of a child's birth or death

supprimer [syprime] *tr* to suppress, to cancel, to abolish; to cut out, to omit; (slang) to eliminate, liquidate ‖ *ref* to kill oneself

suppurer [sypyre] *intr* to suppurate

supputation [sypytasjɔ̃] *f* calculation, evaluation, reckoning

supputer [sypyte] *tr* to calculate (*e.g.*, *forthcoming profits, expenses*)

suprême [syprem] *adj* supreme; last

sur sure [syr] *adj* sour ‖ **sur** *prep* on, over; about, concerning; with (*on the person of*); out of, in, e.g., **un jour sur quatre** one day out of four, one day in four; after, e.g., **page sur page** page after page; **sur ce, sur quoi** whereupon; **sur le fait** in the act

sûr sûre [syr] *adj* sure; trustworthy; safe; certain; **à coup sûr, pour sûr** for sure, without fail

surabon·dant [syrabɔ̃dɑ̃] **·dante** [dɑ̃t] *adj* superabundant

surabonder [syrabɔ̃de] *intr* to superabound; **surabonder de** or **en** to be glutted with

surajouter [syraʒute] *tr* to add on

suralimentation [syralimɑ̃tasjɔ̃] *f* forced feeding; (aut) supercharging

suran·né ·née [syrane] *adj* outmoded, out-of-date, superannuated; expired (*driver's license, passport, etc.*)

surboum [syrbum] *f* (slang) dance, hop

surcharge [syr/arʒ] *f* surcharge; overwriting; (sports) handicap (*of weight on a horse*)

surcharger [syr/arʒe] §38 *tr* to surcharge; to write a word over (*another word*); to write a word over a crossed-out word on (*a document*)

surchauffe [syr/of] *f* superheating; overheating (*of the economy*)

surchauffer [syr/ofe] *tr* to superheat (*steam; an oven*); to overheat (*an oven, iron, etc.*)

surchoix [syr/wa] *m* finest quality

surclasser [syrklɑse] *tr* to outclass

surcompo-sé -sée [syrkɔ̃poze] *adj* (gram) double-compound

surcompression [syrkɔ̃presjɔ̃] *f* pressurization, high compression

surcompri-mé -mée [syrkɔ̃prime] *adj* high-compression (*engine*)

surcomprimer [syrkɔ̃prime] *tr* to supercharge; to pressurize

surcontrer [syrkɔ̃tre] *tr* (cards) to redouble

surcouper [syrkupe] *tr* (cards) to overtrump

surcroît [syrkrwɑ], [syrkrwa] *m* addition, increase; **de surcroît** or **par surcroît** in addition, extra

surdi-mutité [syrdimųtite] *f* deaf-muteness

surdité [syrdite] *f* deafness

su-reau [syro] *m* (*pl* -reaux) elderberry

surélévation [syrelevasjɔ̃] *f* escalation, excessive increase; extra story (*added to a building*)

surélever [syrelve] §2 *tr* to raise, raise up; to drive up; to jack up

surenchère [syrɑ̃ʃer] *f* higher bid; **surenchère électorale** campaign promise, political outbidding

surenchérir [syrɑ̃ʃerir] *intr* to make a higher bid; **surenchérir sur qn** to outbid s.o.

surestimer [syrestime] *tr* to overestimate

su-ret [syre] **-rette** [ret] *adj* tart

sûreté [syrte] *f* safety, security; sureness (*of touch; of taste*); surety; **en sûreté** out of harm's way; in custody, confined (*e.g., in prison*); **sûreté individuelle** legal protection (*e.g., against arbitrary arrest*); **Sûreté nationale** or **la Sûreté** central intelligence; **sûretés** precautions; guarantees, security (*for a loan*)

surévaluer [syrevalųe] *tr* to overvalue

surexciter [syreksite] *tr* to overexcite

surexposer [syrekspoze] *tr* (phot) to overexpose

surexposition [syrekspozisjɔ̃] *f* (phot) overexposure

surface [syrfas] *f* surface; financial backing; **faire surface** to surface (*said of a submarine*)

surfaire [syrfer] §29 *tr & intr* to overprice; to overrate

sur-fin [syrfɛ̃] **-fine** [fin] *adj* superfine

surge-lé -lée [syrʒəle] *adj* frozen (*foods*)

surgeon [syrʒɔ̃] *m* offshoot, sucker

surgir [syrʒir] *intr* to spring up; arise, appear; to arrive, reach port

surglacer [syrglase] §51 *tr* to glaze; to ice (*cake*)

surhaussement [syrosmɑ̃] *m* heightening, raising; banking (*of road*)

surhausser [syrose] *tr* to heighten, to raise; to force up (*prices*); to force up the price of (*s.th.*); to bank (*a road*)

surhomme [syrɔm] *m* superman

surhu-main [syrymɛ̃] **-maine** [men] *adj* superhuman

surimpression [syrɛ̃presjɔ̃] *f* superimposition; (mov) montage

surintendant [syrɛ̃tɑ̃dɑ̃] *m* superintendent, administrator

surir [syrir] *intr* to turn sour

sur-le-champ [syrlʃɑ̃] *adv* on the spot, immediately

surlendemain [syrlɑ̃dmɛ̃] *m*—**le surlendemain** the second day after, two days later

surlier [syrlje] *tr* to whip (*a rope*)

surmenage [syrmənaʒ] *m* overworking, fatigue

surmener [syrməne] §2 *tr & ref* to overwork

sur-moi [syrmwa] *m* superego

surmonter [syrmɔ̃te] *tr* to surmount ‖ *intr* to come to the top (*said of oil in water*)

surmouler [syrmule] *tr* to cast from another mold

surmultiplication [syrmyltiplikasjɔ̃] *f* (aut) overdrive

surnager [syrnaʒe] §38 *intr* to float; to survive

surnatu-rel -relle [syrnatyrel] *adj & m* supernatural

surnom [syrnɔ̃] *m* nickname, sobriquet

surnombre [syrnɔ̃br] *m* excess number; **en surnombre** supernumerary; spare; **rester en surnombre** to be odd man; **surnombre des habitants** overpopulation

surnommer [syrnɔme] *tr* to name, call, nickname

surnuméraire [syrnymerer] *adj* supernumerary, extra ‖ *mf* substitute, supernumerary

suroffre [syrɔfr] *f* better or higher offer

suroît [syrwa] *m* southwest wind

surpasser [syrpɑse] *tr* to surpass; to astonish ‖ *ref* to outdo oneself

surpaye [syrpej] *f* extra pay

surpayer [syrpeje] §49 *tr* to pay too much to; to pay too much for

surpeu-plé -plée [syrpœple] *adj* overpopulated

surpeuplement [syrpœpləmɑ̃] *m* overpopulation

surplis [syrpli] *m* surplice

surplomber [syrplɔ̃be] *tr & intr* to overhang

surplus [syrply] *m* surplus; **au surplus** moreover

surpopulation [syrpɔpylasjɔ̃] *f* overpopulation

surprendre [syrprɑ̃dr] §56 *tr* to surprise; to come upon by chance; to detect; to overtake, catch

surprise [syrpriz] *f* surprise

surprise-party or **surprise-partie** [syrprizparti] *f* (*pl* **surprises-parties**) private dancing party

surproduction [syrprɔdyksjɔ̃] *f* overproduction

surréalisme [syrealism] *m* surrealism

sursaut [syrso] *m* sudden start; **en sursaut** with a start

sursauter [syrsote] *intr* to give a jump, to start, to jerk

surseoir [syrswar] §5B (fut surseoirai, etc.) tr to postpone, defer, put off ‖ intr—surseoir (with dat) to stay (an investigation; an execution)

sursis [syrsi] m suspension (of penalty); postponement, deferment, stay; en sursis, avec sursis suspended (sentence)

surtaxe [syrtaks] f surtax, surcharge; surtaxe postale postage due

surtaxer [syrtakse] tr to surtax

surtension [syrtɑ̃sjɔ̃] f (elec) surge

surtout [syrtu] m topcoat; centerpiece, epergne ‖ adv especially, particularly

surveillance [syrvejɑ̃s] f supervision; (by the police) surveillance

surveil·lant [syrvejɑ̃] surveil·lante [syrvejɑ̃t] mf supervisor, superintendent, overseer; surveillant d'études studyhall proctor

surveiller [syrveje] tr to inspect, to put under surveillance; to supervise, watch over, monitor

survenir [syrvənir] §72 intr (aux: ÊTRE) to arrive unexpectedly, to happen suddenly, to crop up

survenue [syrvəny] f unexpected arrival

survêtement [syrvetmɑ̃] m track suit, sweat shirt

survie [syrvi] f survival; afterlife; (law) survivorship

survivance [syrvivɑ̃s] f survival

survi·vant [syrvivɑ̃] -vante [vɑ̃t] adj surviving ‖ mf survivor

survivre [syrvivr] §74 intr to survive; (with dat) to survive, outlive

survoler [syrvɔle] tr to fly over; to skim over (e.g., a problem)

survol·té -tée [syrvɔlte] adj electrified, charged with emotion

sus [sys], [sy] adv—en sus de in addition to ‖ interj up and at it (them)!

susceptible [syseptibl] adj susceptible; susceptible de capable of

susciter [sysite] tr to stir up, evoke, rouse; (lit) to raise up

sus·dit [sysdi] -dite [dit] adj aforesaid

susmention·né -née [sysmɑ̃sjɔne] adj aforementioned

sus·pect [syspe], [syspɛkt] -pecte [pɛkt] adj suspect, suspicious ‖ mf suspect

suspecter [syspɛkte] tr to suspect

suspendre [syspɑ̃dr] tr to suspend; to hang, to hang up; être suspendu aux lèvres de qn to hang on s.o.'s every word ‖ ref to be hung; to hang on

suspen·du -due [syspɑ̃dy] adj suspended; hanging

suspens [syspɑ̃] m suspense; en suspens suspended; in abeyance; outstanding

suspension [syspɑ̃sjɔ̃] f suspension

suspi·cieux [syspisjø] -cieuse [sjøz] adj suspicious

suspicion [syspisjɔ̃] f suspicion

sustenter [systɑ̃te] tr to sustain ‖ ref to sustain oneself

susurrer [sysyre] tr & intr to murmur, to whisper

susvi·sé -sée [sysvize] adj above-mentioned

suture [sytyr] f suture

suturer [sytyre] tr to suture

suze·rain [syzrɛ̃] -raine [rɛn] adj & mf suzerain

svastika [svastika] m swastika

svelte [svelt] adj slender, lithe, willowy

S.V.P. [esvepe] m (letterword) (s'il vous plaît) if you please, please

sweater [switœr] m sweater

sycophante [sikɔfɑ̃t] m informer

syllabe [silab] f syllable

syllogisme [silɔʒism] m syllogism

sylphe [ailf] m sylph

sylvestre [silvestr] adj sylvan

symbole [sɛ̃bɔl] m symbol; Symbole des apôtres Apostles' Creed

symbolique [sɛ̃bɔlik] adj symbolic(al)

symboliser [sɛ̃bɔlize] tr to symbolize

symbolisme [sɛ̃bɔlism] m symbolism

symétrie [simetri] f symmetry

symétrique [simetrik] adj symmetric(al)

sympathie [sɛ̃pati] f fondness, liking; sympathy

sympathique [sɛ̃patik] adj likable, attractive; sympathetic

sympathi·sant [sɛ̃patizɑ̃] -sante [zɑ̃t] adj sympathetic ‖ mf sympathizer

sympathiser [sɛ̃patize] intr to get along well; sympathiser avec to be drawn toward

symphonie [sɛ̃fɔni] f symphony

symptôme [sɛ̃ptom] m symptom

synagogue [sinagɔg] f synagogue

synchrone [sɛ̃krɔn] adj synchronous

synchroniser [sɛ̃krɔnize] tr to synchronize

syncope [sɛ̃kɔp] f faint, swoon, syncope; syncopation

syndicat [sɛ̃dika] m labor union; syndicat d'initiative chamber of commerce; syndicat patronal employers' association

syndicats-patrons [sɛ̃dikapatrɔ̃] adj invar labor-management

syndiquer [sɛ̃dike] tr & ref to syndicate

synonyme [sinɔnim] adj synonymous ‖ m synonym

synopsis [sinɔpsis] m & f (mov) synopsis

syntaxe [sɛ̃taks] f syntax

synthèse [sɛ̃tez] f synthesis

synthétique [sɛ̃tetik] adj synthetic

synthétiser [sɛ̃tetize] tr to synthesize

syntonisation [sɛ̃tɔnizasjɔ̃] f tuning (of radio)

syntoniser [sɛ̃tɔnize] tr to tune in

syphilis [sifilis] f syphilis

Syrie [siri] f Syria; la Syrie Syria

sy·rien [sirjɛ̃] -rienne [rjen] adj Syrian ‖ (cap) mf Syrian (person)

systématique [sistematik] adj systematic

systématiser [sistematize] tr to systematize

système [sistem] m system; courir, porter, or taper sur le système à qn (slang) to get on s.o.'s nerves; système D (coll) resourcefulness

systole [sistɔl] f systole

T

T, t [te] *m invar* twentieth letter of the French alphabet

t. *abbr* (tome) vol.

ta [ta] §88

tabac [taba] *m* tobacco; tobacco shop; **avoir le gros tabac** (slang) to be a hit; **passer qn à tabac** (coll) to give s.o. the third degree; **tabac à chiquer** chewing tobacco; **tabac à priser** snuff

tabagie [tabaʒi] *f* smoke-filled room

tabasser [tabase] *tr* (slang) to give a licking to, to shellac

tabatière [tabatjɛr] *f* snuffbox; skylight, dormer window

tabernacle [tabɛrnakl] *m* tabernacle

table [tabl] *f* table; **aimer la table** to like good food; **à table!** dinner is served!; **dresser** or **mettre la table** to set the table; **faire table rase** to make a clean sweep. **sainte table** altar rail; **se mettre à table** (slang) to tell all, to confess, to squeal; **table à abattants** gate-leg table; **table à ouvrage** worktable; **table à rallonges** extension table, **table de chevet**, **table de nuit** bedside table; **table d'écoute** wiretap; **table de jeu** card table; **table des matières** table of contents; **table de toilette** dressing table; **table d'hôte** table d'hôte; chef's special; **table d'opération** operating table; **table gigogne** nest of tables; **table interurbaine** long-distance switchboard; **table roulante** serving cart; **tenir table ouverte** to keep open house

ta·bleau [tablo] *m* (*pl* **-bleaux**) painting, picture; scoreboard; board; table, catalogue; panel (*of jurors*); **tableau d'affichage** bulletin board; **tableau d'avancement** seniority list; **tableau de bord** dashboard; instrument panel; **tableau de distribution** switchboard; **tableau d'honneur** honor roll; **tableau noir** blackboard; **tableau vivant** tableau

tabler [table] *intr*—**tabler sur** to count on; to use as a base

tablette [tablet] *f* shelf; mantelpiece; bar (*e.g., of chocolate*); **rayez cela de vos tablettes** don't count on it; **tablettes** pocket notebook

table-valise [tablavaliz] *f* (*pl* **tables-valises**) folding table

tablier [tablije] *m* apron; roadway (*of bridge*); hood (*of chimney*); **tablier de fer** protective shutter (*on store window*)

ta·bou -bou or **boue** [tabu] *adj* & *m* taboo

tabouret [taburɛ] *m* stool; footstool

tabulaire [tabylɛr] *adj* tabular

tabulateur [tabylatœr] *m* tabulator

tac [tak] *m* click, clack; **du tac au tac** tit for tat; **tac tac tac tac!** rat-a-tat-tat!

tache [taʃ] *f* spot, stain; blemish, flaw; blot, smear; speck; **faire tache** to be out of place; **faire tache d'huile** to

spread; **sans tache** spotless, unblemished; **tache de rousseur, tache de son** freckle; **tache de vin** birthmark; **tache originelle** original sin; **tache solaire** sunspot

tâche [taʃ] *f* task, job; **prendre à tâche de** to try to; **travailler à la tâche** to do piecework

tacher [taʃe] *tr* & *ref* to spot, stain

tâcher [taʃe] *tr*—**tâcher que** to see to it that || *intr*—**tâcher de** to try to; **y tâcher** to try

tâcheron [taʃrɔ̃] *m* small jobber; pieceworker; hard worker; wage slave

tacheter [taʃte] §34 *tr* to spot, to speckle

tacite [tasit] *adj* tacit

taciturne [tasityrn] *adj* taciturn

tacot [tako] *m* (coll) jalopy

tact [takt] *m* tact; sense of touch

tacticien [taktisjɛ̃] *m* tactician

tactique [taktik] *adj* tactical || *f* tactics

taffetas [tafta] *m* taffeta; **taffetas gommé** adhesive tape

Tage [taʒ] *m* Tagus

taïaut [tajo] *interj* tallyho!

taie [te] *f* (pathol) leukoma; **avoir une taie sur l'œil** (fig) to be blinded by prejudice; **taie d'oreiller** pillowcase

taillader [tajade] *tr* & *ref* to slash, cut

taille [taj] *f* cutting (*e.g., of diamond*); trimming (*e.g., of hedge*); height, stature; waist, waistline; size; cut (*of garment*); **à la taille de, de la taille de** to the measure of, suitable for; **avoir la taille fine** to have a slim waist; **de taille** big enough, strong enough; (coll) big; **être de taille à** to be up to, to be big enough to; **taille de guêpe** wasp waist; **taille en dessous** next size smaller; **taille en dessus** next size larger

tail·lé -lée [taje] *adj* cut; trimmed; **bien taillé** well-built; **taillé pour** cut out for

taille-crayon [tajkrɛjɔ̃] *m* (*pl* **-crayon** or **-crayons**) pencil sharpener

taille-douce [tajdus] *f* (*pl* **tailles-douces**) copperplate

taille-pain [tajpɛ̃] *m invar* bread knife; bread slicer

tailler [taje] *tr* to cut; to sharpen (*a pencil*); to prune, trim (*a tree*); to carve (*stone*); to clip (*hair*) || *intr* (cards) to deal || *ref* to carve out (*a path; a career*); (coll) to beat it

tailleur [tajœr] *m* tailor; woman's suit; (cards) dealer; **en tailleur** squatting (*while tailoring*); **tailleur de diamants** diamond cutter; **tailleur de pierre** stonecutter, **tailleur sur mesure** lady's tailor-made suit

taillis [taji] *m* thicket, copse

tain [tɛ̃] *m* silvering (*of mirror*)

taire [tɛr] §52 (3d *sg pres ind* **tait**) *tr* to hush up, to hide; **la tairas-tu?** (slang) will you shut your trap?; **taire q.ch. à qn** to keep s.th. from s.o. || *intr*—**faire taire** to silence || *ref* to keep quiet, keep still; **se taire sur** to say nothing about; **tais-toi!** shut up!

talent [talɑ̃] *m* talent

talen·tueux [talɑ̃tyø] **-tueuse** [tyøz] *adj* talented

taloche [talɔʃ] *f* plastering trowel; (coll) clout, smack

talon [talɔ̃] *m* heel; stub

talonner [talɔne] *tr* to tail; to harass; to dig one's spurs into ‖ *intr* to bump

talus [taly] *m* slope; embankment

tambour [tɑ̃bur] *m* drum; drummer; entryway; spool (*of reel*); **tambour battant** (coll) roughly; (coll) quickly; **tambour cylindrique** revolving door; **tambour de basque** tambourine; **tambour de freins** brake drum; **tambour de ville** town crier

tambouriner [tɑ̃burine] *tr* to drum; to broadcast far and wide ‖ *intr* to beat a tattoo; to drum

tambour-major [tɑ̃burmaʒɔr] *m* (*pl* **tambours-majors**) drum major

tamis [tami] *m* sieve; **passer au tamis** to sift; **tamis à farine** flour sifter

Tamise [tamiz] *f* Thames

tamiser [tamize] *tr & intr* to sift

tampon [tɑ̃pɔ̃] *m* plug; bung; swab; rubber stamp; buffer; cancellation, postmark; (surg) tampon; **tampon buvard** hand blotter; **tampon encreur** stamp pad

tamponner [tɑ̃pɔne] *tr* to swab, to dab; to bump, to bump into; (surg) to tampon

tan [tɑ̃] *adj invar* tan ‖ *m* tanbark

tancer [tɑ̃se] §51 *tr* to scold

tandem [tɑ̃dem] *m* tandem; **en tandem** tandem

tandis que [tɑ̃dikə], [tɑ̃diskə] *conj* while; whereas

tangage [tɑ̃gaʒ] *m* (naut) pitching

Tanger [tɑ̃ʒe] *m* Tangier

tangible [tɑ̃ʒibl] *adj* tangible

tanguer [tɑ̃ge] *intr* to pitch (*said of ship*)

tanière [tanjɛr] *f* den, lair

tanker [tɑ̃kɛr] *m* oil tanker

tan·nant [tɑ̃nɑ̃] **tan·nante** [tɑ̃nɑ̃t] *adj* (coll) boring

tanne [tan] *f* spot (*on leather*); blackhead

tanner [tane] *tr* to tan; (coll) to pester

tannerie [tanri] *f* tannery

tanneur [tanœr] *m* tanner

tan-sad [tɑ̃sad] *m* (*pl* **-sads**) rear seat (*of motorcycle*)

tant [tɑ̃] *adv* so, so much; so long; **en tant que** as; in so far as; **si tant est que** if it is true that; **tant bien que mal** somehow or other; **tant de** so many; so much; **tant mieux** so much the better; **tant pis** so much the worse; never mind; **tant qu'à faire** while we're (you've, etc.) at it; **tant que** as well as; as long as; **tant s'en faut** far from it; **tant soit peu** ever so little; **vous m'en direz tant** (coll) you've just said a mouthful

tante [tɑ̃t] *f* aunt; (slang) fairy; **ma tante** (coll) the hockshop

tantième [tɑ̃tjem] *m* percentage

tantine [tɑ̃tin] *f* (coll) auntie

tantôt [tɑ̃to] *m* (coll) afternoon ‖ *adv* in a little while; a little while ago; (coll) in the afternoon; **à tantôt** see you soon; **tantôt . . . tantôt** sometimes . . . sometimes

taon [tɑ̃] *m* horsefly

tapage [tapaʒ] *m* uproar

tapa·geur [tapaʒœr] **-geuse** [ʒøz] *adj* loud

tape [tap] *f* tap, slap

ta·pé -pée [tape] *adj* dried (*fruit*); rotten in spots; (coll) crazy; (slang) worn (*with age or fatigue*); **bien tapé** (coll) well done; (coll) nicely served; (coll) to the point

tape-à-l'œil [tapalœj] *adj* gaudy, showy ‖ *m invar* mere show

taper [tape] *tr* to tap, to slap; to type; (coll) to hit (*s.o. for money*) ‖ *intr* to tap, to slap; to type; (coll) to go to the head (*said of wine*); **ça tape ici** (slang) it hurts here; **taper dans** (coll) to use; **taper dans le mille** (coll) to succeed; **taper dans l'œil de qn** (coll) to make a hit with s.o.; **taper de** to hit (*e.g., 100 m.p.h.*); **taper des pieds** to stamp one's feet; **taper sur** (coll) to get on (*s.o.'s nerves*); **taper sur le ventre de qn** (coll) to give s.o. a poke in the ribs; **taper sur qn** (coll) to run down s.o., to give s.o. a going-over

tapette [tapet] *f* carpet beater; fly swatter; handball; (slang) fairy; **avoir une fière tapette** (coll) to be a chatterbox

tapin [tapɛ̃] *m* (coll) drummer boy; (slang) solicitation (*by a prostitute*)

tapinois [tapinwa] **—en tapinois** stealthily

tapir [tapir] *ref* to crouch, to squat; to hide

tapis [tapi] *m* carpet; rug; game of chance; **mettre sur le tapis** to bring up for discussion; **tapis de bain** bath mat; **tapis de sol** ground cloth; **tapis de table** table covering; **tapis roulant** conveyor belt; moving sidewalk

tapis-brosse [tapibrɔs] *m* (*pl* **-brosses**) doormat

tapisser [tapise] *tr* to upholster; to tapestry; to wallpaper

tapisserie [tapisri] *f* upholstery; tapestry; **faire tapisserie** to be a wallflower

tapis·sier [tapisje] **tapis·sière** [tapisjer] *mf* upholsterer; tapestry maker; paperhanger

tapoter [tapote] *tr & intr* to tap

taquet [take] *m* wedge, peg; (mach) tappet; (naut) cleat; **taquet d'arrêt** (rr) scotch, wedge

ta·quin [takɛ̃] **-quine** [kin] *adj* teasing ‖ *mf* tease

taquiner [takine] *tr* to tease

taquinerie [takinri] *f* teasing

taraud [taro] *m* (mach) tap

tarauder [tarode] *tr* (mach) to tap; (coll) to pester

taraudeuse [tarodøz] *f* tap wrench

tard [tar] *m*—**sur le tard** late in the day; late in life ‖ *adv* late; **pas plus tard que** no later than; **plus tard** later on

tarder [tarde] *intr* to delay; **tarder à** to be long in ‖ *impers*—**il tarde** (with *dat*) **de** long to, e.g., **il lui tarde de vous voir** he longs to see you

tar·dif [tardif] **-dive** [div] *adj* late; backward; tardy

tardivement [tardivmɑ̃] *adv* belatedly

tare [tar] *f* defect, blemish; taint; loss in value; tare (*weight*)

tarer [tare] *tr* to damage; to taint; to tare ‖ *ref* to spoil

targette [tarʒɛt] *f* latch

targuer [targe] *ref*—**se targuer de** to pride oneself on

tarière [tarjɛr] *f* auger, drill

tarif [tarif] *m* price list; rate, tariff; **plein tarif** full fare; **tarifs postaux** postal rates

tarifaire [tarifɛr] *adj* tariff

tarifer [tarife] *tr* to price; to rate

tarir [tarir] *tr* to drain, exhaust, dry up ‖ *intr* to dry up, to run dry; **ne pas tarir** to never run out ‖ *ref* to dry up; to be exhausted

tarse [tars] *m* tarsus; instep

tartare [tartar] *adj* tartar (*sauce*); Tartar ‖ (*cap*) *mf* Tartar

tarte [tart] *adj* (coll) silly, stupid; (coll) ugly ‖ *f* pie, tart; (slang) slap

tartine [tartin] *f* slice of bread and butter or jam; (coll) long-winded speech; (coll) rambling article

tartiner [tartine] *tr* to spread

tartre [tartr] *m* tartar; scale

tartuferie [tartyfri] *f* hypocrisy

tas [tɑ] *m* heap, pile; **mettre en tas** to pile up; **prendre sur le tas** to catch red-handed; **tas de foin** haystack; **un tas de** (coll) a lot of

tasse [tas] *f* cup; **tasse à café** coffee cup; **tasse à thé** teacup; **tasse de café** cup of coffee

tas·seau [taso] *m* (*pl* **-seaux**) bracket; cleat; lug (*on casting*)

tasser [tase] *tr* to cram; to tamp; **bien tassé** (coll) brimful ‖ *intr* to grow thick ‖ *ref* to settle; to huddle; (coll) to go back to normal

taste-vin [tastavɛ̃] *m invar* wine taster (*cup*); sampling tube

tata [tata] *f* (slang) auntie

tâter [tate] *tr* to feel, to touch; to test, to feel out; **tâter le pouls à qn** to feel s.o.'s pulse ‖ *intr*—**tâter de** to taste; to experience; to try one's hand at ‖ *ref* to stop to think, to ponder

tâte-vin [tatvɛ̃] *m invar* wine taster (*cup*); sampling tube

tatil·lon [tatijɔ̃] **tatil·lonne** [tatijɔn] *adj* fussy, hairsplitting ‖ *mf* hairsplitter

tâtonner [tatɔne] *intr* to grope

tâtons [tatɔ̃]—**à tâtons** gropingly

tatouage [tatwaʒ] *m* tattoo

tatouer [tatwe] *tr* to tattoo

taudis [todi] *m* hovel; **taudis** *mpl* slums

taule [tol] *f* (slang) fleabag; **faire de la taule** (slang) to do a stretch

taupe [top] *f* mole; moleskin

taupin [topɛ̃] *m* (mil) sapper; (coll) engineering student

taupinière [topinjɛr] *f* molehill

tau·reau [toro] *m* (*pl* **-reaux**) bull

taux [to] *m* rate; **taux d'escompte** discount rate

taveler [tavle] §34 *tr* to spot ‖ *ref* to become spotted

taverne [tavɛrn] *f* inn, tavern

taxation [taksɑsjɔ̃] *f* fixing (*of prices, wages, etc.*); assessment; taxation

taxe [taks] *f* fixed price; rate; tax; **taxe à la valeur ajoutée** value-added tax; **taxe de luxe** luxury tax; **taxe de séjour** nonresident tax; **taxe directe** sales tax; **taxe perçue** postage paid; **taxe supplémentaire** postage due; **taxe sur les spectacles** entertainment tax

taxer [takse] *tr* to fix the price of; to regulate the rate of; to assess; to tax; **taxer qn de** to tax or charge s.o. with ‖ *ref* to set an offering price; **se taxer de** to accuse oneself of

taxi [taksi] *m* taxi; (coll) cabdriving; **hep taxi! taxi!** ‖ *mf* (coll) cabdriver

taxidermie [taksidɛrmi] *f* taxidermy

taxiphone [taksifɔn] *m* pay phone

Tchécoslovaquie [tʃekɔslɔvaki] *f* Czechoslovakia; **la Tchécoslovaquie** Czechoslovakia

tchèque [tʃɛk] *adj* Czech ‖ *m* Czech (*language*) ‖ (*cap*) *mf* Czech (*person*)

te [tə] §87

techni·cien [teknisjɛ̃] **-cienne** [sjɛn] *mf* technician; engineer

technique [teknik] *adj* technical ‖ *f* technique; engineering

teck [tɛk] *m* teak

teigne [tɛɲ] *f* moth; ringworm; (fig) pest, nuisance

teindre [tɛ̃dr] §50 *tr* to dye; to tint ‖ *ref* to be tinted; to dye or tint one's hair; (with *dat* of *reflex pron*) to dye or tint (*one's hair*)

teint [tɛ̃] **teinte** [tɛ̃t] *adj* dyed; with dyed hair ‖ *m* dye; complexion; **bon teint** fast color ‖ *f* tint, shade; (fig) tinge

teinter [tɛ̃te] *tr* to tint; to tinge

teinture [tɛ̃tyr] *f* dye; dyeing; tincture; (fig) smattering; **teinture d'iode** (pharm) iodine

teinturerie [tɛ̃tyrri] *f* dry cleaner's; dyer's; dyeing

teintu·rier [tɛ̃tyrje] **-rière** [rjɛr] *mf* dry cleaner; dyer

tel **telle** [tɛl] *adj* such; like, e.g., **père tel fils** like father like son; **de telle sorte que** so that; **tel ou tel** such and such a; **tel que** such as, the same as, as; **tel quel** as is ‖ *mf*—**un tel** or **une telle** so-and-so ‖ *pron* such a one, such

télé [tele] *f* (coll) TV; (coll) TV set

télécommander [telekɔmɑ̃de] *tr* to operate by remote control; (fig) to inspire, influence

téléférique [teleferik] *m* skyride, cableway

télégramme [telegram] *m* telegram

télégraphe [telegraf] *m* telegraph

télégraphier [telegrafje] *tr & intr* to telegraph

télégraphiste [telegrafist] *mf* telegrapher

téléguider [telegide] *tr* to guide (*e.g.*, *a missile*); (coll) to influence

téléimprimeur [teleɛ̃primœr] *m* teletype, teleprinter

télémètre [telemetr] *m* telemeter; range finder

téléobjectif [teleobʒektif] *m* telephoto lens

télépathie [telepati] *f* telepathy

téléphérique [teleferik] *m* skyride, cableway

téléphone [telefɔn] *m* telephone

téléphoner [telefone] *tr & intr* to telephone

téléphoniste [telefɔnist] *mf* telephone operator ‖ *m* lineman ‖ *f* telephone girl

télescope [teleskɔp] *m* telescope

télescoper [teleskɔpe] *tr & ref* to telescope

télescopique [teleskɔpik] *adj* telescopic

téléscripteur [teleskriptœr] *m* teletype, teletypewriter

télésiège [telesjeʒ] *m* chair lift

téléski [teleski] *m* ski lift

téléspecta·teur [telespektatœr] **-trice** [tris] *mf* (television) viewer

télétype [teletip] *m* teletype

téléviser [televize] *tr* to televise

téléviseur [televizœr *m* television set; **téléviseur à servo-réglage** remote-control television set

télévision [televizjɔ̃] *f* television; (coll) television set

télévi·suel -suelle [televizɥel] *adj* television

tellement [telmɑ̃] *adv* so much, so; **tellement de** so much, so many; **tellement que** to such an extent that

téméraire [temerer] *adj* rash, reckless, foolhardy

témérité [temerite] *f* temerity, rashness

témoignage [temwaɲaʒ] *m* testimony, witness; **en témoignage de quoi** in witness whereof; **rendre témoignage à** or **pour** to testify in favor of

témoigner [temwaɲe] *tr* to show; to testify ‖ *intr* to testify; **témoigner de** to give evidence of; to bear witness to

témoin [temwɛ̃] *adj invar* type, model; pilot ‖ *m* witness, control (*in scientific experiment*); second (*in duel*) **prendre à témoin** to call to witness; **témoin à charge** witness for the prosecution; **témoin à décharge** witness for the defense; **témoin oculaire** eyewitness

tempe [tɑ̃p] *f* (anat) temple

tempérament [tɑ̃peramɑ̃] *m* temperament; amorous nature; **à tempérament** on the installment plan

tempérance [tɑ̃perɑ̃s] *f* temperance

tempé·rant [tɑ̃perɑ̃] **-rante** [rɑ̃t] *adj* temperate

température [tɑ̃peratyr] *f* temperature

tempé·ré -rée [tɑ̃pere] *adj* temperate; tempered; restrained

tempérer [tɑ̃pere] §10 *tr* to temper ‖ *ref* to moderate

tempête [tɑ̃pet] *f* tempest, storm; **affronter la tempête** (fig) to face the music; **tempête dans un verre d'eau** tempest in a teapot; **tempête de neige**

blizzard; **tempête de poussière** dust storm; **tempête de sable** sandstorm

tempêter [tɑ̃pete] *intr* to storm

tempé·tueux [tɑ̃petɥø] **-tueuse** [tɥøz] *adj* tempestuous

temple [tɑ̃pl] *m* temple; chapel, church

tempo [tempo], [tɛ̃po] *m* tempo

temporaire [tɑ̃pɔrer] *adj* temporary

tempo·ral -rale [tɑ̃pɔral] *adj* (*pl* **-raux** [ro]) (anat) temporal

tempo·rel -relle [tɑ̃pɔrel] *adj* temporal

temporiser [tɑ̃pɔrize] *intr* to temporize, to stall

temps [tɑ̃] *m* time; times; cycle (*of internal-combustion engine*); position, movement (*in gymnastics, fencing, carrying of arms*); weather, e.g., **quel temps fait-il?** what is the weather like?; (gram) tense; (mus) beat, measure; **à temps** in time; **avoir fait son temps** to have seen better days; **dans le temps** formerly; **de temps en temps** from time to time; **en même temps** at the same time; **en temps et lieu** in due course; **en temps utile** in due course; **faire son temps** to do time (*in prison*); **gagner du temps** to save time; **le bon vieux temps** the good old days; **Le Temps** Father Time; **temps atomique** atomic era; **temps d'arrêt** pause, halt

tenable [tənabl] *adj*—**pas tenable** unbearable; unbearable

tenace [tənas] *adj* tenacious

ténacité [tenasite] *f* tenacity

tenailler [tənɑje] *tr* to torture

tenailles [tənɑj] *fpl* pincers

tenan·cier [tənɑ̃sje] **-cière** [sjer] *mf* sharecropper; lessee; keeper (*e.g.*, *of a dive*)

te·nant [tənɑ̃] **-nante** [nɑ̃t] *adj* attached (*collar*) ‖ *mf* (sports) holder (*of a title*) ‖ *m* champion, supporter; **connaître les tenants et les aboutissants** to know the ins and outs; **d'un seul tenant** in one piece

tendance [tɑ̃dɑ̃s] *f* tendency

tendan·cieux [tɑ̃dɑ̃sjø] **-cieuse** [sjøz] *adj* tendentious, slanted

ten·deur [tɑ̃dœr] **-deuse** [døz] *mf* paperhanger; layer (*of traps*) ‖ *m* stretcher

tendoir [tɑ̃dwar] *m* clothesline

tendon [tɑ̃dɔ̃] *m* tendon

tendre [tɑ̃dr] *adj* tender ‖ *tr* to stretch; to hang; to bend (*a bow*); to lay (*a trap*); to strain (*one's ear*); to hold out, to reach out ‖ *intr*—**tendre à** to aim at; to tend toward ‖ *ref* to become strained

tendresse [tɑ̃dres] *f* tenderness, love, affection; (coll) partiality; **mille tendresses** (*closing of letter*) fondly

tendreté [tɑ̃drəte] *f* tenderness

ten·du -due [tɑ̃dy] *adj* tense, taut; strained; stretched out; **tendu de** hung with

ténèbres [tenebr] *fpl* darkness

téné·breux [tenebrø] **-breuse** [brøz] *adj* dark; somber (*person*); shady (*deal*); obscure (*style*)

te·neur [tənœr] **-neuse** [nøz] *mf* holder; **teneur de livres** bookkeeper

‖ **teneur** *f* tenor, gist; text; grade (*e.g., of ore*)

ténia [tenja] *m* tapeworm

tenir [tənir] §72 *tr* to hold; to keep; to take up (*space*); **être tenu à** to be obliged to; **être tenu de** to be responsible for ‖ *intr* to hold; **il me tient qu'à vous** it's up to you; **tenez!** here!; **tenir à** to insist upon; to care for, to value; to be caused by; **tenir de** to take after, to resemble; **tenir debout** (fig) to hold water, to ring true; **tenir q.ch. de qn** to have s.th. from s.o., to learn s.th. from s.o.; **tiens!** well!, hey! ‖ *ref* to stay, remain; to sit up; to stand up; to behave; to contain oneself; **à quoi s'en tenir** what to believe; **s'en tenir à** to limit oneself to; to abide by

tennis [tenis] *m* tennis; tennis court

ténor [tenɔr] *adj masc* tenor ‖ *m* tenor; star performer

tension [tɑ̃sjɔ̃] *f* tension; blood pressure; **avoir la tension** to have high blood pressure; **haute tension** (elec) high tension; **tension artérielle** blood pressure

tentacule [tɑ̃takyl] *m* tentacle

tenta·teur [tɑ̃tatœr] **-trice** [tris] *mf* tempter

tentation [tɑ̃tɑsjɔ̃] *f* temptation

tentative [tɑ̃tativ] *f* attempt

tente [tɑ̃t] *f* tent; awning

tente-abri [tɑ̃tabri] *f* (*pl* **tentes-abris** [tɑ̃tabri]) pup tent

tenter [tɑ̃te] *tr* to tempt; to attempt ‖ *intr*—**tenter de** to attempt to

tenture [tɑ̃tyr] *f* drape; hangings; wallpaper

te·nu -nue [təny] *adj* firm (*securities, market, etc.*); **bien tenu** well-kept ‖ *f* see **tenue**

té·nu -nue [teny] *adj* tenuous; thin

tenue [təny] *f* holding; managing; upkeep, maintenance; behavior; bearing; dress, costume; uniform; session; (mus) hold; **avoir de la tenue** to have good manners; **avoir une bonne tenue** (horsemanship) to have a good seat; **en tenue** in uniform; **grande tenue** (mil) full dress; **petite tenue** (mil) undress; **tenue des livres** bookkeeping; **tenue de soirée** evening clothes; **tenue de ville** street clothes

térébenthine [terebɑ̃tin] *f* turpentine

tergiverser [tɛrʒivɛrse] *intr* to duck, equivocate, vacillate

terme [tɛrm] *m* term; end, limit; (econ) quarterly payment; **avant terme** prematurely; **terme fatal** last day of grace

terminaison [tɛrminɛzɔ̃] *f* ending, termination

termi·nal -nale [tɛrminal] *adj* (*pl* **-naux** [no]) terminal

terminer [tɛrmine] *tr & ref* to terminate

terminus [tɛrminys] *m* terminal ‖ *interj* the end has come!

termite [tɛrmit] *m* termite

terne [tɛrn] *adj* dull, drab

ternir [tɛrnir] *tr & ref* to tarnish

terrain [tɛrɛ̃] *m* ground; terrain; playing field; dueling field; **ne pas être**

sur son terrain to be out of one's depth; **tâter le terrain** to find out the lay of the land; **terrain à bâtir** or **à lotir** building plot; **terrain brûlant** (fig) unsafe ground; **terrain d'atterrissage** landing field; **terrain d'aviation** airfield; **terrain de courses** race track; **terrain de jeux** playground; **terrain de manœuvres** parade ground; **terrain vague** vacant lot

terrasse [teras] *f* terrace; sidewalk café; **terrasse en plein air** outdoor café

terrasser [terase] *tr* to embank; to floor, to knock down

terre [tɛr] *f* earth; land; (elec) ground; **descendre à terre** to go ashore; **la Terre Sainte** the Holy Land; **mettre pied à terre** to dismount; **par terre** on the floor; on the ground; **terre cuite** terra cotta; **Terre de Feu** Tierra del Fuego; **terre ferme** terra firma; **terre franche** loam

ter·reau [tero] *m* (*pl* **-reaux**) compost

terre-neuve [tɛrnœv] *m invar* Newfoundland dog ‖ —**Terre-Neuve** *f* Newfoundland

terre-plein [tɛrplɛ̃] *m* (*pl* **-pleins**) median, divider (*of road*); fill, embankment; earthwork, rampart; terrace; (rr) roadbed

terrer [tere] *tr* to earth up (*e.g., a tree*); to earth over (*seed*) ‖ *ref* to burrow; to entrench oneself

terrestre [terɛstr] *adj* land; terrestrial

terreur [terœr] *f* terror; **la Terreur** the Reign of Terror

ter·reux [terø] **ter·reuse** [terøz] *adj* earthy; dirty; sallow (*complexion*)

terrible [teribl] *adj* terrible; terrific

ter·rien [terjɛ̃] **ter·rienne** [terjen] *adj* landed (*gentry*) ‖ *mf* landowner; landlubber ‖ *m* earthman

terrier [terje] *m* hole, burrow; (dog) terrier

terrifier [terifje] *tr* to terrify

terrir [terir] *intr* to come close to shore (*said of fish*)

territoire [teritwar] *m* territory

terroir [tɛrwar] *m* soil; homeland

terroriser [tɛrɔrize] *tr* to terrorize

tertiaire [tɛrsjɛr] *adj* tertiary

tertre [tɛrtr] *m* mound, knoll

tes [te] §88

tesson [tesɔ̃] *m* shard; broken glass

test [tɛst] *m* test; (zool) shell; **test de niveau** placement test

testament [tɛstamɑ̃] *m* testament; will

testa·teur [tɛstatœr] **-trice** [tris] *mf* testator

tester [tɛste] *tr* to test ‖ *intr* to make one's will

testicule [tɛstikyl] *m* testicle

tétanos [tetanos] *m* tetanus

têtard [tetar] *m* tadpole; (bot) pollard

tête [tɛt] *f* head; heading (*e.g., of chapter*); **à la tête de** in charge of, at the head of; **à tête reposée** at (one's) leisure; **avoir la tête près du bonnet** (coll) to be quick-tempered; **avoir une bonne tête** to have a pleasant look or expression; **de tête** in one's mind's eye, mentally; capable, *e.g.*, **une femme de tête** a capable woman;

en avoir par-dessus la tête (coll) to be fed up with it; en tête foremost, at the front, leading; en tête à tête avec alone with; faire la tête à to frown at, to give a dirty look to; faire une tête to wear a long face; forte tête strong-minded person; jeter à la tête à qn (fig) to cast in s.o.'s face; la tête en bas head downwards, upside down; la tête la première headfirst, headlong; laver la tête à qn (coll) to give s.o. a dressing down; mauvaise tête troublemaker; monter à la tête de qn to go to s.o.'s head; n'en faire qu'à sa tête to be a law unto oneself; par tête per capita, per head; piquer une tête to take a header, to dive; saluer de la tête to nod; se mettre en tête de to take it into one's head to; se payer la tête de qn (coll) to pull s.o.'s leg; tenir tête à to face up to, to stand up to; tête baissée headlong, heedless; tête brûlée daredevil; tête chercheuse homing head (of missile); tête d'affiche (theat) headliner; tête de bois blockhead; tête de cuvée choice wine; tête de lecture (elec) playback head; tête de ligne truck terminal; tête de linotte scatterbrain; tête de pont (mil) bridgehead, beachhead; tête de Turc butt, scapegoat, fall guy; tête montée excitable person; tête morte et tibias skull and crossbones; tomber sur la tête (coll) to be off one's rocker

tête-à-queue [tetakø] m invar about-face, slue

tétée [tete] f sucking; feeding time

téter [tete] §10 tr & intr to suck

tétine [tetin] f nipple; teat

téton [tetɔ̃] m (coll) tit

tétras [tetra] m grouse

tette [tet] f (coll) tit

tê·tu -tue [tety] adj stubborn

teuf-teuf [tœftœf] m (pl teuf-teuf or teufs-teufs) (coll) jalopy || interj chug!, chug!

tévé [teve] f (acronym) (télévision) TV

texte [tekst] m text; apprendre son texte (theat) to learn one's lines

textile [tekstil] adj & m textile

tex·tuel -tuelle [tekstɥel] adj textual; verbatim

texture [tekstyr] f texture

thaï [tai] adj invar & m Thai

thaïlan·dais [tajlɑ̃dɛ] **-daise** [dɛz] adj Thai || (cap) mf Thai

Thaïlande [tajlɑ̃d] f Thailand

thaumaturge [tomatyrʒ] m miracle worker, magician

thé [te] m tea

théâ·tral -trale [teatral] adj (pl -traux [tro]) theatrical

théâtre [teatr] m theater; stage, boards; scene (e.g., of the crime)

théier [teje] **théière** [tejer] adj tea || m tea (shrub) || f see théière

théière [tejer] f teapot

thème [tem] m theme; translation (into a foreign language)

théologie [teɔlɔʒi] f theology

théorème [teɔrɛm] m theorem

théorie [teɔri] f theory; procession

théorique [teɔrik] adj theoretical

thérapeutique [terapøtik] adj therapeutic || f therapeutics

thérapie [terapi] f therapy

Thérèse [terɛz] f Theresa

ther·mal -male [termal] adj (pl -maux [mo]) thermal

thermique [termik] adj thermal

thermocouple [termɔkupl] m thermocouple

thermodynamique [termɔdinamik] adj thermodynamic || f thermodynamics

thermomètre [termɔmetr] m thermometer

thermonucléaire [termɔnykleer] adj thermonuclear

Thermopyles [termɔpil] fpl—les Thermopyles Thermopylae

thermos [termɔs] f thermos bottle

thermosiphon [termɔsifɔ̃] m hot-water heater

thermostat [termɔsta] m thermostat

thésauriser [tezorize] tr & intr to hoard

thésauri·seur [tezorizœr] **-seuse** [zøz] mf hoarder

thèse [tez] f thesis

thon [tɔ̃] m tuna

thorax [tɔraks] m thorax

thrène [tren] m threnody

thuriféraire [tyriferer] m incense bearer; flatterer

thym [tɛ̃] m thyme

thyroïde [tirɔid] adj & f thyroid

tiare [tjar] f tiara (papal miter); papacy

tibia [tibja] m tibia; shin; tibias croisés et tête de mort skull and crossbones

tic [tik] m (pathol) tic; **tic tac** ticktock

ticket [tike] m ticket (of bus, subway, etc.); check (for article in baggage room); ration stamp; sans tickets unrationed; ticket de quai platform ticket

tic-tac [tiktak] m invar tick

tiède [tjed] adj lukewarm; mild

tiédeur [tjedœr] f lukewarmness; mildness

tiédir [tjedir] tr to take the chill off || intr to become lukewarm

tien [tjɛ̃] **tienne** [tjen] §89

tiens [tjɛ̃] interj well!, hey!

tiers [tjer] **tierce** [tjers] adj third; tertian (fever) || m third (in fractions); le tiers a third; the third party; le tiers et le quart (coll) everybody and anybody || f (typ) press proof

tige [tiʒ] f stem; trunk; shaft; shank; piston rod; leg (of boot); stock (of genealogy)

tignasse [tiɲas] f shock, mop (of hair)

tigre [tigr] m tiger

ti·gré -grée [tigre] adj striped; speckled, spotted

tigresse [tigres] f tigress

tillac [tijak] m top deck (of old-time ships)

tilleul [tijœl] m linden

timbale [tɛ̃bal] f metal cup, mug; (culin) mold; (mus) kettledrum; décrocher la timbale (coll) to carry off the prize

timballer [tɛ̃balje] m kettledrummer

timbrage [tɛbraʒ] *m* stamping; cancellation (*of mail*)

timbre [tɛbr] *m* bell; doorbell; buzzer; seal, stamp; postage stamp; postmark; snare (*of drum*); (phonet, phys) timbre

tim·bré -brée [tɛbre] *adj* stamped; ringing (*voice*); (coll) cracked, crazy

timbre-poste [tɛbrəpɔst] *m* (*pl* **timbres-poste**) postage stamp

timbrer [tɛbre] *tr* to stamp; to postmark

timbres-prime [tɛmbrəprim] *mpl* trading stamps

timide [timid] *adj* timid, shy

timon [timɔ̃] *m* pole (*of carriage*); beam (*of plow*); (naut) helm

timonier [timɔnje] *m* helmsman; wheel horse

timo·ré -rée [timɔre] *adj* timorous

tin [tɛ̃] *m* chock

tinette [tinet] *f* firkin (*tub*); bucket (*for fecal matter*)

tintamarre [tɛ̃tamar] *m* uproar

tintement [tɛ̃tmɑ̃] *m* tolling (*of bell*); tinkle (*of bell*); ringing (*in ears*)

tinter [tɛ̃te] *tr* to toll || *intr* to toll; to tinkle; to jingle, to clink; to ring (*said of ears*)

tintin [tɛ̃tɛ̃] *m*—**faire tintin** (slang) to do without || *interj* (slang) nothing doing!

tintouin [tɛ̃twɛ̃] *m* (coll) trouble

tique [tik] *f* (ent) tick

tiquer [tike] *intr* to twitch; (coll) to wince; **sans tiquer** (coll) without turning a hair

tir [tir] *m* shooting; firing; aim; shooting gallery; **tir à la cible** target practice; **tir à l'arc** archery; **tir au fusil** gunnery; **tir au pigeon** trapshooting

tirade [tirad] *f* (theat) long speech

tirage [tiraʒ] *m* drawing; towing; draft (*of chimney*); printing; circulation (*of newspaper*); (coll) tension, friction; **tirage à part** offprint; **tirage au sort** lottery drawing; **tirage de luxe** deluxe edition

tiraillement [tirɑjmɑ̃] *m* pain, cramp; conflict, tension

tirailler [tirɑje] *tr* to pull about, to tug at; to pester || *intr* to blaze away; **tirailler sur** to snipe at || *ref* to have a misunderstanding

tirailleur [tirɑjœr] *m* sharpshooter; sniper; (fig) free lance

tirant [tirɑ̃] *m* string; strap; **tirant d'eau** draft (*of ship*)

tire [tir] *f* (heral) row (*of vair*); (slang) car, auto; (Canad) taffy pull

ti·ré -rée [tire] *adj* drawn; printed || *m* shooting preserve; payee; **tiré à part** offprint

tire-au-flanc [tiroflɑ̃] *m invar* malingerer, shirker

tire-botte [tirbɔt] *m* (*pl* **-bottes**) bootjack

tire-bouchon [tirbuʃɔ̃] *m* (*pl* **-bouchons**) corkscrew; corkscrew curl

tire-bouchonner [tirbuʃɔne] *tr* to twist in a spiral

tire-bouton [tirbutɔ̃] *m* (*pl* **-boutons**) buttonhook

tire-clou [tirklu] *m* (*pl* **-clous**) nail puller

tire-d'aile [tirdɛl]—**à tire-d'aile** with wings outspread, swiftly

tire-fond [tirfɔ̃] *m invar* spike; screw eye

tire-larigot [tirlarigo]—**boire à tire-larigot** to drink like a fish

tire-ligne [tirliɲ] *m* (*pl* **-lignes**) ruling pen

tirelire [tirlir] *f* piggy bank; (face) (coll) mug; (head) (coll) noggin; (slang) belly

tire-l'œil [tirlœj] *m invar* eye catcher

tirer [tire] *tr* to draw; to pull, to tug; to shoot, to fire; to run off, to print; to take out; to take, to get; to stick out (*one's tongue*); **tirer au clair** to bring out into the open; **tirer parti de** to turn to account || *intr* to pull; to shoot; to draw (*e.g., to a close*); to draw (*said of chimney*); **tirer à, vers,** or **sur** to border on || *ref* to extricate oneself; **s'en tirer** to manage; **se tirer d'affaire** to pull through, to get along

tiret [tire] *m* dash; blank (*to be filled in*)

tirette [tiret] *f* slide (*of desk*); damper (*of chimney*)

tireur [tirœr] *m* marksman; drawer; payer (*of check*); printer; **tireur de bois flotté** log driver; **tireur d'élite** sharpshooter; **tireur d'épée** fencer; **tireur isolé** sniper

tireuse [tirøz] *f* markswoman; **tireuse de cartes** fortuneteller

tiroir [tirwar] *m* drawer; (mach) slide valve; **à tiroirs** episodic (*play, novel, etc.*)

tiroir-caisse [tirwarkɛs] *m* (*pl* **tiroirs-caisses**) cash register

tisane [tizan] *f* tea, infusion; (coll) bad champagne; (slang) slap

tison [tizɔ̃] *m* ember; (fig) firebrand

tisonner [tizɔne] *tr* to poke

tisonnier [tizɔnje] *m* poker

tissage [tisaʒ] *m* weaving

tisser [tise] *tr* & *intr* to weave

tisse·rand [tisrɑ̃] **-rande** [rɑ̃d] *mf* weaver

tis·seur [tisœr] **tis·seuse** [tisøz] *mf* weaver

tissu [tisy] *m* tissue; cloth; fabric, material; pack (*of lies*)

tissu-éponge [tisyepɔ̃ʒ] *m* (*pl* **tissus-éponges**) toweling, terry cloth

tissure [tisyr] *f* texture; (fig) framework

titane [titan] *m* titanium

titi [titi] *m* (slang) street urchin

Titien [tisjɛ̃] *m*—**le Titien** Titian

titre [titr] *m* title; title page; heading; fineness (*of coinage*); claim, right; concentration (*of a solution*); **à juste titre** rightly so; **à titre de** in the capacity of; by virtue of; **à titre d'emprunt** as a loan; **à titre d'essai** on trial; **à titre gratuit** or **gracieux** free of charge; **titres** qualifications; (com) securities

titrer [titre] *tr* to title; to subtitle (*films*)

tituber [titybe] *intr* to stagger

titulaire [tityler] *adj* titular ‖ *mf* incumbent; holder (*of passport, license, degree, post*)

titulariser [titylarize] *tr* to confirm the appointment of

toast [tost] *m* toast; **porter un toast à** to toast

toboggan [tɔbɔgɑ̃] *m* toboggan; toboggan run; slide, chute

toc [tɔk] *adj invar* (coll) worthless; (coll) crazy ‖ *m* (mach) chuck; (coll) imitation; **en toc** (coll) worthless; **toc, toc!** knock, knock!

tohu-bohu [tɔybɔy] *m* hubbub

toi [twa] §85, §87

toile [twal] *f* cloth; linen; canvas, painting; (theat) curtain; **toile à coton** calico; **toile à laver** dishrag; **toile à matelas** ticking; **toile à voile** sailcloth; **toile cirée** oilcloth; **toile d'araignée** cobweb; **toile de fond** backdrop

toilette [twalet] *f* toilet; dressing table; dress, outfit (*of a woman*); **aimer la toilette** to be fond of clothing; **faire la toilette de** to lay out (*a corpse*)

toi-même [twamem] §86

toise [twaz] *f* fathom; **passer à la toise** to measure the height of

toiser [twaze] *tr* to size up

toison [twazɔ̃] *f* fleece; mop (*of hair*); **Toison d'or** Golden Fleece

toit [twa] *m* roof; rooftop; home, house; **crier sur les toits** to shout from the housetops

toiture [twatyr] *f* roofing

tôle [tol] *f* sheet metal; tole (*decorative metalware*); **tôle de blindage** armor plate; **tôle étamée** tin plate; **tôle galvanisée** galvanized iron; **tôle noire** sheet iron; **tôle ondulée** corrugated iron

tolérable [tɔlerabl] *adj* tolerable, bearable

tolérance [tɔlerɑ̃s] *f* tolerance

tolérer [tɔlere] §10 *tr* to tolerate

tôlerie [tolri] *f* sheet metal; rolling mill

tolet [tɔle] *m* oarlock

tomaison [tɔmezɔ̃] *f* volume number

tomate [tɔmat] *f* tomato

tombe [tɔ̃b] *f* tomb; grave; tombstone

tom-beau [tɔ̃bo] *m* (*pl* **-beaux**) tomb; **à tombeau couvert** lickety-split

tombée [tɔ̃be] *f* fall (*of rain, snow, etc.*); **tombée de la nuit** nightfall

tomber [tɔ̃be] *tr* to throw (*a wrestler*); (coll) to remove (*a piece of clothing*); (slang) to seduce (*a woman*) ‖ *intr* (*aux:* ÊTRE) to fall, to drop; **tomber amoureux** to fall in love; **tomber bien** to happen just in time; **tomber en panne** to have a breakdown; **tomber sur** to run into, chance upon; to turn to (*said of conversation*)

tombe-reau [tɔ̃bro] *m* (*pl* **-reaux**) dump truck; dumpcart; load

tombola [tɔ̃bɔla] *m* raffle

tome [tɔm] *m* tome, volume

ton [tɔ̃] *adj poss* §88 ‖ *m* tone; (mus) key

tonal -nale [tɔnal] *adj* (*pl* **-nals**) tonal

ton-deur -deuse [tɔ̃dœr] -**deuse** [døz] *mf* shearer ‖ *f* shears; **tondeuse à cheveux** hair clippers; **tondeuse à gazon** lawn mower; **tondeuse (à gazon) à moteur** power mower; **tondeuse électrique** electric clippers; **tondeuse mécanique** cropper; power mower

tondre [tɔ̃dr] *tr* to clip; to shear; to mow

toni-fiant -fiante [tɔnifjɑ̃] -**fiante** [fjɑ̃t] *adj & m* tonic

tonifier [tɔnifje] *tr* to tone up

tonique [tɔnik] *adj & m* tonic

toni-truant -truante [tɔnitryɑ̃] -**truante** [tryɑ̃t] *adj* (coll) thunderous

tonne [tɔn] *f* ton; tun

ton-neau [tɔno] *m* (*pl* **-neaux**) barrel; cart; roll (*of automobile, airplane, etc.*); (naut) ton; **au tonneau on draught**; **tonneau de poudre** powder keg

tonnelet [tɔnle] *m* keg

tonnelier [tɔnəlje] *m* cooper

tonnelle [tɔnel] *f* arbor

tonner [tɔne] *intr* to thunder

tonnerre [tɔner] *m* thunder

tonte [tɔ̃t] *f* clipping; shearing; mowing

tonton [tɔ̃tɔ̃] *m* (slang) uncle

top [tɔp] *m* beep

topaze [tɔpaz] *f* topaz

toper [tɔpe] *intr* to shake hands on it; **tope là!** it's a deal!

topinambour [tɔpinɑ̃bur] *m* Jerusalem artichoke

topique [tɔpik] *adj* local, regional

topographie [tɔpɔgrafi] *f* topography

toquade [tɔkad] *f* (coll) infatuation

toquante [tɔkɑ̃t] *f* (coll) ticker (*watch*)

toque [tɔk] *f* toque; cap (*of chef; of judge*)

to-qué -quée [tɔke] *adj* (coll) crazy, cracked ‖ *mf* (coll) nut

toquer [tɔke] *tr* to infatuate ‖ *intr* (coll) to rap, tap ‖ *ref*—**se toquer de** to be infatuated with

torche [tɔrʃ] *f* torch; **se mettre en torche** to fail to open (*said of parachute*); **torche électrique** flashlight

torcher [tɔrʃe] *tr* to wipe clean; to rush through, to botch; to daub with clay and straw

torchère [tɔrʃer] *f* candelabrum; floor lamp

torchis [tɔrʃi] *m* adobe

torchon [tɔrʃɔ̃] *m* dishcloth; rag; (coll) scribble; **le torchon brûle** they're squabbling

torchonner [tɔrʃɔne] *tr* (coll) to botch

tor-dant -dante [tɔrdɑ̃] -**dante** [dɑ̃t] *adj* (coll) sidesplitting

tord-boyaux [tɔrbwajo] *m invar* (coll) rotgut

tordeuse [tɔrdøz] *f* moth

tordoir [tɔrdwar] *m* wringer; rope-making machine

tordre [tɔrdr] *tr* to twist; to wring ‖ *ref* to twist; to writhe; **se tordre de rire** to split one's sides laughing

tornade [tɔrnad] *f* tornado

toron [tɔrɔ̃] *m* strand (*of rope*)

torpédo [tɔrpedo] *f* (archaic) open touring car

torpeur [tɔrpœr] *f* torpor
torpille [tɔrpij] *f* torpedo; (arti) mine
torpiller [tɔrpije] *tr* to torpedo
torpilleur [tɔrpijœr] *m* torpedo boat; torpedoman
torque [tɔrk] *f* coil of wire; twist (*of tobacco*)
torréfaction [tɔrefaksjɔ̃] *f* roasting
torréfier [tɔrefje] *tr* to roast
torrent [tɔrɑ̃] *m* torrent
torride [tɔrid] *adj* torrid
tors [tɔr] **torse** [tɔrs] *adj* twisted; crooked || *m* twist || see **torse** *m*
torsade [tɔrsad] *f* twisted cord; coil (*of hair*); **à torsades** fringed
torsader [tɔrsade] *tr* to twist
torse [tɔrs] *m* torso, trunk
torsion [tɔrsjɔ̃] *f* twisting, torsion
tort [tɔr] *m* wrong; harm; **à tort** wrongly; **à tort et à travers** at random, wildly; carelessly, inconsiderately; **à tort ou à raison** rightly or wrongly; **avoir tort** to be wrong; **donner tort à** to lay the blame on; **faire tort à** to wrong
torticolis [tɔrtikɔli] *m* stiff neck
tortillard [tɔrtijar] *adj masc* knotty || *m* (coll) jerkwater train
tortiller [tɔrtije] *tr* to twist, to twirl; (slang) to gulp down || *intr* to wriggle; (coll) to beat about the bush || *ref* to wriggle, squirm; to writhe, twist
tor·tu -tue [tɔrty] *adj* crooked || *f* turtle, tortoise
tor·tueux [tɔrtɥø] **-tueuse** [tɥøz] *adj* winding; devious, underhanded
torture [tɔrtyr] *f* torture
torturer [tɔrtyre] *tr* to torture
torve [tɔrv] *adj* menacing
tos·can [tɔskɑ̃] **-cane** [kan] *adj* Tuscan || *m* Tuscan (*dialect*) || (*cap*) *mf* Tuscan (*person*)
tôt [to] *adv* soon; early; **au plus tôt** as soon as possible; at the earliest; **le plus tôt possible** as soon as possible; **pas de si tôt** not soon; **tôt ou tard** sooner or later
to·tal -tale [tɔtal] *adj & m* (*pl* **-taux** [to]) total
totaliser [tɔtalize] *tr* to total
totalitaire [tɔtaliter] *adj* totalitarian
totem [tɔtem] *m* totem
toton [tɔtɔ̃] *m* teetotum
toubib [tubib] *m* (coll) medical officer; (coll) doctor, physician
tou·chant [tuʃɑ̃] **-chante** [ʃɑ̃t] *adj* touching || **touchant** *prep* touching, concerning
touche [tuʃ] *f* touch; key (*of piano or typewriter*); stop (*of organ*); fret (*of guitar*); fingerboard (*of violin*); hit (*in fencing*); bite (*on fishline*); goad (*for cattle*); tab (*of file index*); thumb index; (elec) contact; (coll) look, appearance; **touche de blocage** shift lock; **touche de manœuvre** shift key
touche-à-tout [tuʃatu] *m invar* (coll) busybody
toucher [tuʃe] *m* touch, sense of touch || *tr* to touch; to concern; to cash (*a check*); to draw out (*money*); to goad

(*cattle*); (mus) to pluck (*the strings*) || *intr* to touch; **toucher à** to touch (*one's food, capital, etc.*); to touch on; to call at (*a port*); to be about to achieve (*one's aim*); **toucher de** to play (*e.g., the piano*) || *ref* to touch
touer [twe] *tr* to warp, to kedge
touffe [tuf] *f* tuft; clump (*of trees*)
touffeur [tufœr] *f* suffocating heat
touf·fu -fue [tufy] *adj* bushy; (fig) dense
touille [tuj] *m* dogfish, shark
touiller [tuje] *tr* (coll) to stir; (coll) to mix; (coll) to shuffle
toujours [tuʒur] *adv* always; still; anyhow; **M. Toujours** (coll) yes man; **pour toujours** forever
toupet [tupe] *m* tuft (*of hair*); forelock (*of horse*); (coll) nerve, brass
toupie [tupi] *f* top; molding board; silly woman
tour [tur] *m* turn; tour; trick; lathe; **à tour de bras** with all one's might; **à tour de rôle** in turn; **en un tour de main** in a jiffy; **faire le tour de** to tour, to visit; to walk or ride around; **faire un tour de** to take a walk or ride in; **tour à tour** by turns; **tour de bâton** (coll) rake-off, killing; **tour de main**, **tour d'adresse** sleight of hand; **tour de poitrine** chest size; **tour de taille** waist measurement; **tour de tête** hat size; **tours et retours** twists and turns || *f* tower; (chess) castle, rook; (mil) turret; **tour de contrôle** control tower; **tour de guet** lookout tower
tourbe [turb] *f* peat; mob
tourbillon [turbijɔ̃] *m* whirl; whirlpool; whirlwind
tourbillonner [turbijɔne] *intr* to whirl, to swirl
tourelle [turel] *f* turret
tourillon [turijɔ̃] *m* axle; trunnion
touriste [turist] *adj & mf* tourist
tourment [turmɑ̃] *m* torment
tourmente [turmɑ̃t] *f* storm
tourmenter [turmɑ̃te] *tr* to torment || *ref* to fret
tour·nant [turnɑ̃] **-nante** [nɑ̃t] *adj* turning, revolving || *m* turn; turning point; water wheel
tourne-à-gauche [turnagoʃ] *m invar* wrench; saw set; diestock
tournebroche [turnəbrɔʃ] *m* roasting jack, turnspit
tourne-disque [turnədisk] *m* (*pl* **-disques**) record player
tournedos [turnado] *m* filet mignon
tournée [turne] *f* round; **en tournée** (theat) on tour; **faire une tournée** to take a trip; **tournée électorale** political campaign
tournemain [turnəmɛ̃]—**en un tournemain** in a split second
tourne-pierre [turnəpjer] *m* (*pl* **-pierres**) (orn) turnstone
tourner [turne] *tr* to turn; to turn over; to shoot (*a moving picture; a scene*); to outflank; **tourner et retourner** to turn over and over || *intr* to turn; (mov) to shoot a picture; (theat) to tour; **la tête me (lui, etc.) tourne** my

(his, etc.) head is turning, I feel (he feels, etc.) dizzy; **silence, on tourne!** quiet on the set!; **tourner à** or en to turn into; **tourner autour du pot** (coll) to beat about the bush; **tourner bien** to turn out well; **tourner en rond** to go around in circles, to spin; **tourner mal** to go bad || *ref* to turn

tournesol [turnəsɔl] *m* litmus; sunflower

tournevis [turnəvis] *m* screwdriver

tourniquet [turnike] *m* turnstile; revolving door; revolving display stand; (surg) tourniquet; **passer au tourniquet** (slang) to be courtmartialed

tournoi [turnwa] *m* tournament

tournoyer [turnwaje] §47 *intr* to turn, to wheel; to twirl; to tourney

tournure [turnyr] *f* turn, course (*of events*); wording, phrasing, turn (*of phrase*); expression; shape, figure

tourte [turt] *adj* (slang) stupid || *f* (coll) dolt; **tourte à la viande** meat pie

tour·teau [turto] *m* (*pl* -**teaux**) oil cake; crab

tourte·reau [turtəro] *m* (*pl* -**reaux**) turtledove, young lover

tourterelle [turtərɛl] *f* turtledove

tourtière [turtjɛr] *f* pie pan

toussailler [tusaje] *intr* to keep on coughing

Toussaint [tusɛ̃] *f* All Saints' Day; **la Toussaint** All Saints' Day

tousser [tuse] *intr* to cough; to clear one's throat

tousserie [tusri] *f* constant coughing

toussotement [tusɔtmɑ̃] *m* slight coughing

toussoter [tusɔte] *intr* to cough slightly

tout [tu] **toute** [tut] (*pl* **tous toutes**) *adj* any, every, all; **tous les** all, all of, e.g., **tous les hommes** all men, all of the men; whole, entire, e.g., **toute la journée** the whole day; **à tout coup** every time; **à toute heure** at any time; **tous les deux** both || *m* (*pl* **touts**) whole, all; everything; sum; **du tout** (coll) not at all; **en tout** wholly, in all; **pas du tout** not at all || **tout toute** (*pl* **tous** [tus] **toutes**) *pron* all, everything, anything; **à tout prendre** on the whole; **tout compté** all things considered || **tout** *adv* all, quite, completely; very, e.g., **un des tout premiers** one of the very foremost; **tout à côté de** right next to; **tout à coup** suddenly; **tout à fait** quite; **tout à l'heure** in a little while; a little while ago; **tout au plus** at most; **tout de même** however, all the same; **tout de suite** at once, immediately; **tout en** while, e.g., **tout en parlant** while talking; **tout éveillé** wide awake; **tout fait** ready-made; **tout haut** aloud; **tout neuf** brand-new; **tout nu** stark-naked; **tout près** nearby; **tout . . . que** despite the fact that, e.g., **tout vieux qu'il était** despite the fact that he was old || **toute toutes** *adv* (before a feminine word beginning with a

consonant or an aspirate **h**) all, quite, completely, e.g., **elles sont toutes seules** they are all (or quite or completely) alone

tout-à-l'égout [tutalegu] *m invar* sewerage

toute-épice [tutepis] *f* (*pl* **toutes-épices** [tutepis]) allspice (*berry*)

toutefois [tutfwa] *adv* however

toute-puissance [tutpɥisɑ̃s] *f* omnipotence

toutou [tutu] *m* (coll) doggie

Tout-Paris [tupari] *m invar* high society, smart set (*in Paris*)

tout-petit [tupəti] *m* (*pl* -**petits**) toddler

tout-puissant [tupɥisɑ̃] **toute-puissante** [tutpɥisɑ̃t] (*pl* **tout-puissants toutes-puissantes**) *adj* almighty || **le Tout-Puissant** the Almighty

tout-venant [tuvnɑ̃] *m invar* all comers; run-of-the-mine coal; run-of-the-mill product; ordinary run of people

toux [tu] *f* cough

toxicomane [tɔksikɔman] *adj* addicted || *mf* drug addict

toxicomanie [tɔksikɔmani] *f* drug addiction

toxique [tɔksik] *adj* toxic || *m* poison

trac [trak] *m* (coll) stage fright; **avoir le trac** (coll) to lose one's nerve; **tout à trac** without thinking

tracas [traka] *m* worry, trouble

tracasser [trakase] *tr & ref* to worry

tracasserie [trakasri] *f* bother; **tracasseries** interference

tracassin [trakasɛ̃] *m* (coll) worry

trace [tras] *f* trace; track, trail; sketch; footprint; **marcher sur les traces de** to follow in the footsteps of

tracé [trase] *m* tracing; **faire le tracé de** to lay out; (math) to plot

tracer [trase] §51 *tr* to trace, draw

tra·ceur [trasœr] -**ceuse** [søz] *mf* tracer || *m* tracer (*radioactive substance*)

trachée [traʃe] *f* trachea, windpipe

trachée-artère [traʃe/arter] *f* (*pl* **trachées-artères**) windpipe

tract [trakt] *m* tract

tractation [traktɑsjɔ̃] *f* underhanded deal

tracteur [traktœr] *m* tractor

traction [traksjɔ̃] *f* traction; **faire des tractions** to do chin-ups; **traction avant** front-wheel drive

tradition [tradisjɔ̃] *f* tradition

tradition·nel -**nelle** [tradisjɔnɛl] *adj* traditional

traduc·teur [tradyktœr] -**trice** [tris] *mf* translator

traduction [tradyksjɔ̃] *f* translation

traduire [tradɥir] §19 *tr* to translate; **traduire en justice** to haul into court

trafic [trafik] *m* traffic, trade; **trafic d'influence** influence peddling; **trafic routier** highway traffic

trafi·quant [trafikɑ̃] -**quante** [kɑ̃t] *mf* racketeer; **trafiquant en stupéfiants** dope peddler

trafiquer [trafike] *tr* to traffic in || *intr* to traffic; **trafiquer de** to traffic in or on

trafi·queur [trafikœr] -**queuse** [køz] *mf* racketeer

tragédie [traʒedi] f tragedy

tragé·dien [traʒedjɛ̃] **-dienne** [djɛn] mf tragedian

tragique [traʒik] adj tragic

trahir [trair] tr to betray

trahison [traizɔ̃] f betrayal; treason

train [trɛ̃] m pace, speed; manner, way; series; raft (of logs); (rr) train; (coll) row, racket; **être en train de** + inf to be in the act or process of + ger; (translated by a progressive form of the verb), e.g., **je suis en train d'écrire** I am writing; **mettre en train** to start; **train arrière** (aut) rear-axle assembly; (rr) rear car; **train avant** (aut) front-axle assembly; **train d'atterrissage** landing gear; **train de banlieue** suburban train; **train de marchandises** freight train; **train de vie** way of life; standard of living; **train direct** through train; **train omnibus** local train; **train sanitaire** military hospital train

traî·nant [trenɑ̃] **-nante** [nɑ̃t] adj trailing; creeping; drawling; languid

traî·nard [trenar] **-narde** [nard] mf straggler

traîne [tren] f train (of dress); dragnet; **à la traîne** dragging; straggling; in tow

traî·neau [treno] m (pl **-neaux**) sleigh; sled; sledge; dragnet

traînée [trene] f trail, train; (coll) streetwalker

traîner [trene] tr to drag, to lug; to drawl; to shuffle (the feet) || intr to drag; to straggle; to lie around || ref to crawl; to creep; to limp

traî·neur [trenœr] **-neuse** [nøz] mf straggler; loiterer

train-train [trɛ̃trɛ̃] m routine

traire [trer] §68 tr to milk

trait [tre] m arrow, dart; dash; stroke; feature (of face); trait, characteristic; trace (of harness); **avoir trait à** to refer to; **de trait** draft (horse); **d'un trait** in one gulp; **partir comme un trait** to be off like a shot; **tracer à grands traits** to trace in broad outlines; **trait d'esprit** witticism; **trait d'héroïsme** heroic deed; **trait d'union** hyphen; **trait pour trait** exactly

traitable [tretabl] adj tractable

traite [tret] f trade, traffic; milking; (com) draft; **tout d'une traite** at a single stretch

traité [trete] m treatise; treaty

traitement [tretmɑ̃] m treatment; salary; **mauvais traitements** affront, mistreatment

traiter [trete] tr to treat; to receive; **traiter qn de** to call s.o. (a name) || intr to negotiate; **traiter de** to deal with

traiteur [tretœr] m caterer; (obs) restaurateur

traî·tre [tretr] **-tresse** [tres] adj traitorous; treacherous; (coll) single || mf traitor; (theat) villain || f traitress

traîtrise [tretriz] f treachery

trajectoire [traʒɛktwar] f trajectory

trajet [traʒe] m distance, trip, passage; (aer) flight

tralala [tralala] m (coll) fuss

trame [tram] f weft; web (of life); conspiracy

tramer [trame] tr to weave; to hatch (a plot) || ref to be plotted

traminot [tramino] m traction-company employee

tramontane [tramɔ̃tan] f north wind; **perdre la tramontane** to lose one's bearings

tramp [trãp] m tramp steamer

tramway [tramwe] m streetcar

tran·chant [trɑ̃/ɑ̃] **-chante** [/ɑ̃t] adj cutting; glaring; trenchant || m cutting edge; knife; side (of hand); **à double tranchant** or **à deux tranchants** two-edged

tranche [trɑ̃/] f slice; section; portion, installment; group (of figures); cross section; **doré sur tranches** (bb) gilt-edged; (coll) gilded (e.g., youth); **une tranche de vie** a slice of life

tranchée [trɑ̃/e] f trench; **tranchées** colic

trancher [trɑ̃/e] tr to cut off; to slice; to decide, settle || intr to decide once and for all; to stand out; **trancher avec** to contrast with; **trancher dans le vif** to cut to the quick; (fig) to take drastic measures; **trancher · de** (lit) to affect the manners of

tranquille [trɑ̃kil] adj quiet, tranquil; **laissez-moi tranquille** leave me alone; **soyez tranquille** don't worry

tranquilli·sant [trɑ̃kilizɑ̃] **-sante** [zɑ̃t] adj tranquilizing || m tranquilizer

tranquilliser [trɑ̃kilize] tr to tranquilize; to reassure || ref to calm down

tranquillité [trɑ̃kilite] f tranquility

transaction [trɑ̃zaksjɔ̃] f transaction; compromise

transat [trɑ̃zat] m (coll) transatlantic liner; (coll) deck chair || **la Transat** (coll) the French Line

transatlantique [trɑ̃zatlɑ̃tik] adj & m transatlantic

transbordement [trɑ̃sbɔrdəmɑ̃] m transshipment, transfer

transborder [trɑ̃sbɔrde] tr to transship, to transfer

transbordeur [trɑ̃sbɔrdœr] m transporter bridge

transcender [trɑ̃sɑ̃de] tr & ref to transcend

transcription [trɑ̃skripsjɔ̃] f transcription

transcrire [trɑ̃skrir] §25 tr to transcribe; **transcrire en clair** to decode

transe [trɑ̃s] f apprehension, anxiety; trance; **être dans des transes** to be quaking in one's boots

transept [trɑ̃sɛpt] m transept

transférer [trɑ̃sfere] §10 tr to transfer; to convey

transfert [trɑ̃sfɛr] m transfer, transference

transfo [trɑ̃sfo] m (coll) transformer

transforma·teur [trɑ̃sfɔrmatœr] **-trice** [tris] adj (elec) transforming || m (elec) transformer; **transformateur abaisseur (de tension)** step-down transformer; **transformateur de sonnerie** doorbell transformer; **transfor-**

mateur **élévateur** (de tension) step-up transformer

transformer [trɑ̃sfɔrme] *tr & ref* to transform

transfuge [trɑ̃sfyʒ] *m* turncoat

transfuser [trɑ̃sfyze] *tr* to transfuse; to instill

transfusion [trɑ̃sfyzjɔ̃] *f* transfusion

transgresser [trɑ̃sgrese] *tr* to transgress

transgression [trɑ̃sgresjɔ̃] *f* transgression

transhumer [trɑ̃zyme] *tr & intr* to move from winter to summer pasture

tran·si -sie [trɑ̃zi], [trɑ̃si] *adj* chilled to the bone; numb, transfixed (*with fright*)

transiger [trɑ̃ziʒe] §38 *intr* to compromise

transistor [trɑ̃zistɔr] *m* transistor

transit [trɑ̃zit] *m* transit

transi·tif -tive [trɑ̃zitif] *adj* transitive

transition [trɑ̃zisjɔ̃] *f* transition

transitoire [trɑ̃zitwar] *adj* transitory; transitional

translation [trɑ̃slɑsjɔ̃] *f* transfer, translation

translitérer [trɑ̃slitere] §10 *tr* to transliterate

translucide [trɑ̃slysid] *adj* translucent

transmetteur [trɑ̃smetœr] *adj masc* transmitting ‖ *m* (telg, telp) transmitter; **transmetteur d'ordres** (naut) engine-room telegraph

transmettre [trɑ̃smetr] §42 *tr* to transmit; to transfer; (sports) to pass

transmission [trɑ̃smisjɔ̃] *f* transmission; broadcast; **transmission en différé** recorded broadcast; **transmission en direct** live broadcast; **transmissions** (mil) signal corps

transmuer [trɑ̃smɥe] *tr* to transmute

transmuter [trɑ̃smyte] *tr* to transmute

transparaître [trɑ̃sparetr] §12 *intr* to show through

transpa·rent -rente [trɑ̃sparɑ̃] -[rɑ̃t] *adj* transparent

transpercer [trɑ̃sperse] §51 *tr* to transfix

transpiration [trɑ̃spirɑsjɔ̃] *f* perspiration

transpirer [trɑ̃spire] *tr* to sweat ‖ *intr* to sweat, perspire; to leak out (*said of news*)

transplanter [trɑ̃splɑ̃te] *tr* to transplant

transport [trɑ̃spɔr] *m* transport; transportation; **transport au cerveau** cerebral hemorrhage

transpor·té -tée [trɑ̃spɔrte] *adj* enraptured, carried away

transporter [trɑ̃spɔrte] *tr* to transport

transposer [trɑ̃spoze] *tr* to transpose

transver·sal -sale [trɑ̃sversal] *adj* (*pl* -saux* [so]) transversal; cross (*street*)

trapèze [trapez] *m* trapeze; trapezoid

trappe [trap] *f* trap door; pitfall, trap; **Trappist** monastery; **Trappe** Trappist order

trappeur [trapœr] *m* trapper

tra·pu -pue [trapy] *adj* stocky, squat

traque [trak] *f* driving of game

traquenard [traknar] *m* trap, booby trap, pitfall

traquer [trake] *tr* to hem in, to bring to bay

traumatique [tromatik] *adj* traumatic

tra·vail [travaj] *m* (*pl* -vaux* [vo]) work; workmanship; **en travail** in labor; **Travail** Labor; **travail à la pièce**, **travail à la tâche** piecework; **travail d'équipe** teamwork; **travail de Romain** herculean task; **travaux forcés** hard labor; **travaux ménagers** housework ‖ *m* (*pl* -vails*) stocks (*for horses*)

travail·lé -lée [travaje] *adj* finely wrought, elaborate; labored

travailler [travaje] *tr* to work; to worry ‖ *intr* to work; to warp (*said of wood*)

travail·leur [travajœr] **travail·leuse** [travajøz] *adj* hardworking ‖ *mf* worker, toiler

travailliste [travajist] *adj & mf* Labourite (Brit)

travée [trave] *f* span (*of bridge*); row of seats; (archit) bay

traveling [travliŋ] *m* (mov, telv) dolly (*for camera*)

travers [traver] *m* breadth; fault, failing; **à travers** across, through; **de travers** awry; **en travers de** across; **par le travers de** abreast of

traverse [travers] *f* crossbeam; cross street; setback; rung (*of ladder*); (rr) tie; **de traverse** cross (*e.g., street*); **mettre à la traverse de** to oppose

traversée [traverse] *f* crossing

traverser [traverse] *tr* to cross; to cut across

traver·sier -sière [traversje] *adj* cross, crossing

traversin [traversɛ̃] *m* bolster (*of bed*)

traves·ti -tie [travesti] *adj* disguised; costume (*ball*) ‖ *m* fancy costume, disguise; transvestite; female impersonator

travestir [travestir] *tr* to travesty; to disguise

travestissement [travestismɑ̃] *m* travesty; disguise

trébucher [trebyʃe] *intr* to stumble

tréfiler [trefile] *tr* to wiredraw

trèfle [trefl] *m* clover; trefoil; cloverleaf (*intersection*); (cards) club; (cards) clubs

tréfonds [trefɔ̃] *m* secret depths

treillage [trejaʒ] *m* trellis

treillager [trejaʒe] §38 *tr* to trellis

treille [trej] *f* grape arbor

treillis [treji] *m* latticework; iron grating; denim; **treillis métallique** wire netting

treillisser [trejise] *tr* to trellis

treize [trez] *adj & pron* thirteen; the Thirteenth, e.g., **Jean treize** John the Thirteenth ‖ *m* thirteen; thirteenth (*in dates*); **treize à la douzaine** baker's dozen

treizième [trezjem] *adj, pron* (*masc, fem*), *& m* thirteenth

tréma [trema] *m* dieresis

tremble [trɑ̃bl] *m* aspen (*tree*)

tremblement [trɑ̃bləmɑ̃] *m* trembling; **tremblement de terre** earthquake

trembler [trɑ̃ble] *intr* to tremble

trembleur [trɑ̃blœr] *m* vibrator, buzzer; (rel) Shaker; (rel) Quaker

trembloter [trɑ̃blɔte] *intr* to quiver; to quaver

trémie [tremi] *f* hopper

trémoussement [tremusmɑ̃] *m* fluttering, flutter; jiggling, jiggle

trémousser [tremuse] *ref* to flutter; to jiggle; (coll) to bustle

trempage [trɑ̃paʒ] *m* soaking

trempe [trɑ̃p] *f* temper; soaking; (slang) scolding

trempée [trɑ̃pe] *f* tempering

tremper [trɑ̃pe] *tr* to temper; to dilute; to dunk ‖ *intr* to soak; to become involved (*in, e.g., a scandal*)

trempette [trɑ̃pet] *f*—**faire la trempette** to dunk; **faire trempette** to take a dip

tremplin [trɑ̃plɛ̃] *m* springboard, diving board; trampoline; ski jump; (fig) springboard

trentaine [trɑ̃ten] *f* age of thirty; **une trentaine de** about thirty

trente [trɑ̃t] *adj & pron* thirty; **sur son trente et un** (coll) all spruced up; **trente et un** thirty-one; **trente et unième** thirty-first ‖ *m* thirty; thirtieth (*in dates*); **trente et un** thirty-one; **thirty-first** (*in dates*); **trente et unième** thirty-first

trente-deux [trɑ̃tdø] *adj, pron, & m* thirty-two

trente-deuxième [trɑ̃tdøzjem] *adj, pron* (*masc, fem*), *& m* thirty-second

trente-six [trɑ̃tsi(s)] *adj, pron, & m* thirty-six; **tous les trente-six du mois** (coll) once in a blue moon

trentième [trɑ̃tjem] *adj, pron* (*masc, fem*), *& m* thirtieth

trépas [trepa] *m* (lit) death; **passer de vie à trépas** (lit) to pass away

trépasser [trepase] *intr* (lit) to die

trépied [trepje] *m* tripod

trépigner [trepiɲe] *intr* to stamp one's feet

très [tre] *adv* very; **le très honorable** the Right Honorable

trésor [trezɔr] *m* treasure; **Trésor** Treasury

trésorerie [trezɔrri] *f* treasury

tréso·rier [trezɔrje] **-rière** [rjer] *mf* treasurer

tressaillement [tresajmɑ̃] *m* start, quiver

tressaillir [tresajir] §69 *intr* to give a start, to quiver

tressauter [tresote] *intr* to start

tresse [tres] *f* tress

tresser [trese] *tr* to braid, to plait; to weave (*e.g., a basket*)

tré·teau [treto] *m* (*pl* **-teaux**) trestle; **sur les tréteaux** (theat) on the boards

treuil [trœj] *m* windlass; winch

trêve [trev] *f* truce; respite; **trêve de ... that's enough ...**

tri [tri] *m* sorting

triage [trijaʒ] *m* sorting, selection; classification; (rr) shifting

triangle [trijɑ̃gl] *m* triangle

tribord [tribɔr] *m* starboard

tribu [triby] *f* tribe

tribu·nal [tribynal] *m* (*pl* **-naux** [no]) tribunal, court; **en plein tribunal** in

open court; **tribunal de police** police court; **tribunaux pour enfants** juvenile courts

tribune [tribyn] *f* rostrum, tribune; gallery; grandstand; **monter à la tribune** to take the floor; **tribune des journalistes** press box; **tribune d'orgue** organ loft; **tribune libre** open forum

tribut [triby] *m* tribute

tributaire [tribyter] *adj & m* tributary; **être tributaire de** to be dependent upon

tricher [triʃe] *tr & intr* to cheat

tricherie [triʃri] *f* cheating

tri·cheur [triʃœr] **-cheuse** [ʃøz] *mf* cheater; **tricheur professionnel** card-sharper

tricolore [trikɔlɔr] *adj & m* tricolor

tricot [triko] *m* knitting; knitted garment

tricotage [trikɔtaʒ] *m* knitting

tricoter [trikɔte] *tr & intr* to knit

trier [trije] *tr* to pick out, to screen; **trier sur le volet** to hand-pick

trieur [trijœr] **trieuse** [trijøz] *mf* sorter ‖ *m & f* (mach) sorter

trigonométrie [trigɔnɔmetri] *f* trigonometry

trille [trij] *m* trill

triller [trije] *tr & intr* to trill

trillion [triljɔ̃] *m* quintillion (U.S.A.); trillion (Brit)

trilogie [trilɔʒi] *f* trilogy

trimbaler [trɛ̃bale] *tr* to cart around

trimer [trime] *intr* to slave

trimestre [trimestr] *m* quarter (*of a year*); quarter's salary; quarter's rent; (educ) term

tringle [trɛ̃gl] *f* rod; **tringle de rideau** curtain rod

trinité [trinite] *f* trinity

trinquer [trɛ̃ke] *intr* to clink glasses, to toast; (slang) to drink; **trinquer avec** to hobnob with

trio [trijo] *m* trio

triom·phant [trijɔ̃fɑ̃] **-phante** [fɑ̃t] *adj* triumphant

triomphe [trijɔ̃f] *m* triumph; **faire triomphe à** to welcome in triumph

tripar·ti -tie [triparti] *adj* tripartite

tripartite [tripartit] *adj* tripartite

tripatouiller [tripatuje] *tr* (coll) to tamper with

tripette [tripet] *f*—**ça ne vaut pas tripette** it's not worth a wooden nickel

triple [tripl] *adj & m* triple

tri·plé -plée [triple] *mf* triplet

tripler [triple] *tr & intr* to triple

triplicata [triplikata] *m invar* triplicate

tripot [tripo] *m* gambling den; house of ill repute

tripoter [tripote] *tr* to finger, toy with ‖ *intr* to dabble, to potter around; to rummage

trique [trik] *f* (coll) cudgel

triste [trist] *adj* sad

tristesse [tristes] *f* sadness, sorrow

triturer [trityre] *tr* to pulverize, to grind ‖ *ref*—**se triturer la cervelle** to rack one's brain

tri·vial -viale [trivjal] *adj* (*pl* **-viaux** [vjo]) trivial; vulgar, coarse

trivialité [trivjalite] *f* triviality; vulgarity, coarseness

troc [trɔk] *m* barter; swap; **troc pour troc** even up

troglodyte [trɔglɔdit] *m* cave dweller; (orn) wren

trognon [trɔɲɔ̃] *m* core; (slang) darling, pet

Troie [trwa], [trwa] *f* Troy

trois [trwa] *adj & pron* three; the Third, e.g., **Jean trois** John the Third; **trois heures** three o'clock || *m* three; third (*in dates*)

troisième [trwazjɛm] *adj, pron* (*masc, fem*), *& m* third

trolley [trɔle] *m* trolley

trolleybus [trɔlebys] *m* trackless trolley

trombe [trɔ̃b] *f* waterspout; **entrer en trombe** to dash in; **trombe d'eau** deluge

trombone [trɔ̃bɔn] *m* trombone; paper clip

trompe [trɔ̃p] *f* horn; trunk (*of elephant*); beak (*of insect*); **trompe d'Eustache** Eustachian tube

trompe-la-mort [trɔ̃plamɔr] *mf invar* daredevil

trompe-l'œil [trɔ̃plœj] *m invar* dummy effect; (coll) bluff, fake; **en trompe-l'œil** in perspective

tromper [trɔ̃pe] *tr* to deceive, to cheat || *ref* to be wrong; **se tromper de** to be mistaken about

tromperie [trɔ̃pri] *f* deceit; fraud; illusion

trompeter [trɔ̃pte] §34 *tr & intr* to trumpet

trompette [trɔ̃pɛt] *m* trumpeter || *f* trumpet; **en trompette** turned up

trom·peur [trɔ̃pœr] **-peuse** [pøz] *adj* false, lying || *mf* deceiver

tronc [trɔ̃] *m* trunk; (slang) head; **tronc des pauvres** poor box

tronche [trɔ̃ʃ] *f* (slang) noodle

tronçon [trɔ̃sɔ̃] *m* stump; section (*e.g., of track*)

trône [tron] *m* throne

trôner [trone] *intr* to sit in state || *ref* —**se trôner sur** to lord it over

tronquer [trɔ̃ke] *tr* to truncate, to cut off; to mutilate

trop [tro] *m* excess; too much; **de trop** too much; to excess; in the way, e.g., **il est de trop ici** he is in the way here; **par trop** altogether, excessively; **trop de . . .** too much . . . ; too many . . . || *adv* too; too much; **trop lourd** overweight

trophée [trofe] *m* trophy

tropi·cal -cale [trɔpikal] *adj* (*pl* -caux [ko]) tropical

trop-plein [troplɛ̃] *m* (*pl* -pleins) overflow

troquer [trɔke] *tr* to barter; **troquer contre** to swap for

trot [tro] *m* trot; **au trot** at a trot; (coll) on the double, quickly

trotte [trɔt] *f* (coll) quite a distance to walk

trotter [trɔte] *intr* to trot

trot·teur [trɔtœr] **trot·teuse** [trɔtøz] *mf* (turf) trotter || *f* second hand; **trotteuse centrale** sweep-second

trottin [trɔtɛ̃] *m* errand girl

trottinette [trɔtinet] *f* scooter

trottoir [trɔtwar] *m* sidewalk; **faire le trottoir** to walk the streets (*said of prostitute*); **trottoir roulant** escalator

trou [tru] *m* hole; pothole; eye (*of needle*); gap; jerkwater town; **faire son trou** to feather one's nest; **faire un trou à la lune** to fly the coop; **trou d'air** air pocket; **trou de clef** keyhole (*of clock*); **trou de la serrure** keyhole; **trou d'obus** shell hole; **trou du souffleur** prompter's box; **trou individuel** (mil) foxhole

trouble [trubl] *adj* muddy, cloudy, turbid (*liquid*); murky (*sky*); misty (*glass*); blurred (*image; sight*); dim (*light*); vague, disquieting || *m* disquiet; unrest; trouble (*illness*)

trouble-fête [trubləfet] *mf invar* wet blanket, kill-joy

troubler [truble] *tr* to upset, trouble; to make muddy; to disturb; to make cloudy; to blur || *ref* to become muddy or cloudy; to lose one's composure

trouée [true] *f* gap, breach; (mil) breakthrough

trouille [truj] *f*—**avoir la trouille** (slang) to get cold feet

troupe [trup] *f* troop; band, party; (theat) troupe

trou·peau [trupo] *m* (*pl* -peaux) flock; herd; **attention aux troupeaux** (public sign) cattle crossing

troupier [trupje] *m* (coll) soldier; **jurer comme un troupier** to swear like a trooper

trousse [trus] *f* case, kit; **avoir qn à ses trousses** to have s.o. at one's heels; **trousse de première urgence** first-aid kit

trous·seau [truso] *m* (*pl* -seaux) trousseau; outfit; bunch (*of keys*)

troussequin [truskɛ̃] *m* cantle

trousser [truse] *tr* to turn up; to tuck up; to polish off; (culin) to truss || *ref* to lift one's skirts

trouvaille [truvaj] *f* find

trouver [truve] *tr* to find || *ref* to be found; to find oneself; to be, e.g., **où se trouve-t-il?** where is he?; **il se trouve que . . .** it happens that . . . ; **se trouver mal** to feel ill

troyen [trwajɛ̃] **troyenne** [trwajɛn] *adj* Trojan || (*cap*) *mf* Trojan

truand [tryɑ̃] **truande** [tryɑ̃d] *adj & m* good-for-nothing

truc [tryk] *m* gadget, device; (coll) trick, gimmick; (coll) thing; (coll) what's-his-name

truchement [tryʃmɑ̃] *m* spokesman; interpreter; **par le truchement de** thanks to, through

trucu·lent [trykylɑ̃] **-lente** [lɑ̃t] *adj* truculent

truelle [tryel] *f* trowel

truffe [tryf] *f* truffle

truie [trɥi] *f* sow

truisme [trɥism] *m* truism

truite [trɥit] *f* trout

tru·meau [trymo] *m* (*pl* -meaux) trumeau (*mirror with painting above in same frame*)

truquage [tryka3] *m* faking

truquer [tryke] *tr* to fake; to cook (*the accounts*); to stack (*the deck*); to load (*the dice*); to fix (*the outcome of a fight*) ‖ *intr* to resort to fakery

trust [trœst] *m* trust, holding company

T.S.F. [teesef] *f* (letterword) (**télégraphie sans fil**) wireless; radio

t. s. v. p. *abbr* (**tournez s'il vous plaît**) over (*please turn the page*)

tu [ty] §87; **être à tu et à toi avec to** hobnob with

T.U. [tey] *m* (letterword) (**temps universel**) universal time, Greenwich Mean Time

tube [tyb] *m* tube; pipe; (anat) duct; (slang) hit

tubercule [tyberkyl] *m* tubercle; tuber

tuberculose [tyberkyloz] *f* tuberculosis

tue-mouches [tymu] *m invar* flypaper

tuer [tɥe] *tr* to kill ‖ *ref* to be killed; to kill oneself

tuerie [tyri] *f* slaughter

tue-tête [tytɛt]—**à tue-tête** at the top of one's voice

tuile [tɥil] *f* tile; (coll) nasty blow

tuilerie [tɥilri] *f* tileworks

tulipe [tylip] *f* tulip

tumeur [tymœr] *f* tumor

tumulte [tymylt] *m* tumult, hubbub

tungstène [tœksten] *m* tungsten

tunique [tynik] *f* tunic

tunnel [tynel] *m* tunnel; **passer sous un tunnel** to go through a tunnel; **tunnel aérodynamique** wind tunnel

turban [tyrbã] *m* turban

turbine [tyrbin] *f* turbine

turbu·lent [tyrbylã] **-lente** [lãt] *adj* turbulent

turc turque [tyrk] *adj* Turkish ‖ *m* Turkish (*language*) ‖ (*cap*) *mf* Turk (*person*)

turf [tyrf] *m*—**le turf** the turf, the track

turfiste [tyrfist] *m* turfman, racegoer

turlututu [tyrlytyty] *interj* fiddlesticks!, nonsense!

Turquie [tyrki] *f* Turkey; **la Turquie** Turkey

turquoise [tyrkwaz] *m* turquoise (*color*) ‖ *f* turquoise (*stone*)

tutelle [tytel] *f* guardianship, tutelage; trusteeship

tu·teur [tytœr] **-trice** [tris] *mf* guardian ‖ *m* (hort) stake, prop

tutoyer [tytwaje] §47 *tr* to thou, to address familiarly ‖ *ref* to thou each other, to be on a first-name basis

tuyau [tɥijo], [tyjo] *m* (*pl* **tuyaux**) pipe, tube; fluting; (coll) tip; **tuyau d'arrosage** garden hose; **tuyau d'échappement** exhaust; **tuyau d'incendie** fire hose

tuyauter [tɥijote], [tyjote] *tr* to flute; (coll) to tip off ‖ *intr* (coll) to crib

tuyauterie [tɥijotri] *f* pipe mill; piping; (aut) manifold; **tuyauterie d'admission** intake manifold; **tuyauterie d'échappement** exhaust manifold

tympan [tẽpã] *m* eardrum; (archit, mus) tympanum

type [tip] *m* type; (coll) fellow, character

typer [tipe] *tr* to type

typhoïde [tifoid] *adj* & *f* typhoid

typhon [tifɔ̃] *m* typhoon

typique [tipik] *adj* typical; South American (*music*)

typographie [tipɔgrafi] *f* typography

typographique [tipɔgrafik] *adj* typographic(al)

tyran [tirã] *m* tyrant; (orn) kingbird

tyrannie [tirani] *f* tyranny

tyrannique [tiranik] *adj* tyrannic(al)

U

U, u [y], **[y] *m invar* twenty-first letter of the French alphabet

Ukraine [ykren] *f* Ukraine

ukrai·nien [ykrenjẽ] **-nienne** [njen] *adj* Ukrainian ‖ *m* Ukrainian (*language*) ‖ (*cap*) *mf* Ukrainian (*person*)

ulcère [ylser] *m* ulcer, sore

ulcérer [ylsere] §10 *tr* to ulcerate; to embitter ‖ *ref* to ulcerate; to fester

ulté·rieur -rieure [ylterjœr] *adj* ulterior; subsequent

ultimatum [yltimatɔm] *m* ultimatum

ultime [yltim] *adj* ultimate, final

ultra-court [yltrakur] **-courte** [kurt] *adj* (electron) ultrashort

ultravio·let [yltravjɔle] **-lette** [let] *adj* & *m* ultraviolet

ululer [ylyle] *intr* to hoot

un [œ̃] **une** [yn] *adj* & *pron* one; **l'un à l'autre** to each other, to one another; **l'un et l'autre** both; **l'un l'autre** each other, one another; **ni**

l'un ni l'autre neither, neither one; **un à un** one by one; **une heure** one o'clock ‖ *art indef* a ‖ *m* one ‖ *f*—**la une** the front page

unanime [ynanim] *adj* unanimous

unanimité [ynanimite] *f* unanimity

Unesco [ynesko]·*f* (acronym) (**Organisation des Nations Unies pour l'Éducation, la Science et la Culture**)—**l'Unesco** UNESCO

u·ni -nie [yni] *adj* united; smooth, level; uneventful; plain; solid (*color*); together (*said, e.g., of the hands of a clock*) ‖ *m* plain cloth

unicorne [ynikɔrn] *m* unicorn

unification [ynifikasjɔ̃] *f* unification

unifier [ynifje] *tr* to unify ‖ *ref* to consolidate, merge; to become unified

uniforme [ynifɔrm] *adj* & *m* uniform

uniformiser [ynifɔrmize] *tr* to make uniform

uniformité [ynifɔrmite] *f* uniformity

unijambiste [yniʒãbist] *adj* one-legged ‖ *mf* one-legged person

unilaté·ral -rale [ynilateral] *adj (pl -raux* [ro]) unilateral

union [ynjɔ̃] *f* union; **union libre** common-law marriage

unique [ynik] *adj* only, single; unique

unir [ynir] *tr & ref* to unite

unisson [ynisɔ̃] *m* unison

unitaire [yniter] *adj* unit

unité [ynite] *f* unity; unit; battleship; (coll) one million old francs

univers [yniver] *m* universe

univer·sel -selle [yniversel] *adj & m* universal

universitaire [yniversiter] *adj* university

université [yniversite] *f* university

uranium [yranjom] *m* uranium

ur·bain -baine [yrbɛ̃] [ben] *adj* urban; urbane

urbaniser [yrbanize] *tr* to urbanize

urbanisme [yrbanism] *m* city planning

urbaniste [yrbanist] *adj* zoning (*ordinance*) ‖ *mf* city planner

urbanité [yrbanite] *f* urbanity

urètre [yretr] *m* urethra

urgence [yrʒãs] *f* urgency; emergency; emergency case; **d'urgence** emergency (*e.g., hospital ward*); right away, without delay

ur·gent -gente [yrʒã] [ʒãt] *adj* urgent; emergency (*case*); (formula on letter or envelope) rush ‖ *m* urgent matter

urinaire [yriner] *adj* urinary

uri·nal [yrinal] *m* (*pl* **-naux** [no]) urinal (*for use in bed*)

urine [yrin] *f* urine

uriner [yrine] *tr & intr* to urinate

urinoir [yrinwar] *m* urinal (*place*)

urne [yrn] *f* urn; ballot box; **aller aux urnes** to go to the polls

urologie [yrɔlɔʒi] *f* urology

U.R.S.S. [yreses] *f* (letterword) (**Union des Républiques Socialistes Soviétiques**) U.S.S.R.

Ursse [yrs] *f* (acronym) (**Union des Républiques Socialistes Soviétiques**) U.S.S.R.

urticaire [yrtiker] *f* hives

urubu [yryby] *m* turkey vulture

us [ys] *mpl—***les us et (les) coutumes** the manners and customs

U.S. [ys] *adj* (letterword) (**United States**) U.S., e.g., **l'aviation U.S.** U.S. aviation

U.S.A. [yesa] *mpl* (letterword) (**United States of America**) U.S.A.

usage [yzaʒ] *m* usage; custom; use; **faire de l'usage** to wear well; **hors d'usage** outmoded; (gram) obsolete; **manquer d'usage** to lack good breeding; **usage du monde** good breeding, savoir-vivre

usa·gé -gée [yzaʒe] *adj* secondhand; worn-out, used

usa·ger -gère [yzaʒe] [ʒer] *mf* user

usant [yzã] **usante** [yzãt] *adj* exhausting, wearing

u·sé -sée [yze] *adj* worn-out; trite, commonplace

user [yze] *tr* to wear out; to wear away; to ruin (*e.g., health*) ‖ *intr*— **en user bien avec** to treat well; **user de** to use ‖ *ref* to wear out

usine [yzin] *f* factory, mill, plant; **usine à gaz** gasworks

usiner [yzine] *tr* to machine, to tool

usi·nier [yzinje] **-nière** [njer] *adj* manufacturing; factory (*town*) ‖ *m* manufacturer

usi·té -tée [yzite] *adj* used, in use; **peu usité** out of use, rare

ustensile [ystãsil] *m* utensil, implement

u·suel -suelle [yzɥel] *adj* usual

usure [yzyr] *f* usury; wear; wear and tear

usurper [yzyrpe] *tr* to usurp

utérus [yterys] *m* uterus, womb

utilisable [ytilizabl] *adj* usable

utilisa·teur [ytilizatœr] **-trice** [tris] *mf* user

utilitaire [ytiliter] *adj* utilitarian; utility (*vehicle, goods, etc.*)

utilité [ytilite] *f* utility, usefulness, use; (theat) support; (theat) supporting rôle; **jouer les utilités** (fig) to play second fiddle; **utilités** (theat) small parts

utopique [ytɔpik] *adj* utopian

utopiste [ytɔpist] *mf* utopian

V

V, v [ve] *m invar* twenty-second letter of the French alphabet

v. *abbr* (**voir**) see; (**volume**) vol.

vacance [vakãs] *f* vacancy, opening; **vacances** vacation

vacancier [vakãsje] *m* vacationist

va·cant [vakã] **-cante** [kãt] *adj* vacant

vacarme [vakarm] *m* din, racket

vacation [vakasjɔ̃] *f* investigation; **vacations** fee; recess

vaccin [vaksɛ̃] *m* vaccine

vaccination [vaksinasjɔ̃] *f* vaccination

vaccine [vaksin] *f* cowpox

vacciner [vaksine] *tr* to vaccinate

vache [vaʃ] *adj* embarrassing (*question*); cantankerous (*person*) ‖ *f* cow; cowhide; (*woman*) (slang) bitch; (*man*) (slang) swine, rat; (*policeman*) (slang) flatfoot, bull; **en vache** leather (*e.g., suitcase*); **manger de la vache enragée** (coll) not to have a red cent to one's name; **oh, la vache!** damn it!; **parler français comme une vache espagnole** (coll) to murder the French language; **vache à eau** canvas bucket (*for camping*); **vache à lait** milch cow; (coll) gull, sucker

vachement [vaʃmɑ̃] *adv* (slang) tremendously

va·cher [vaʃe] **-chère** [ʃɛr] *mf* cowherd

vacherie [vaʃri] *f* cowshed; dairy farm; (coll) dirty trick

vachette [vaʃɛt] *f* young calf; calf (*leather*)

vaciller [vasije] *intr* to vacillate, waver; to flicker; to totter

vacuité [vakɥite] *f* vacuity, emptiness

vacuum [vakɥɔm] *m* vacuum

vade-mecum [vademekɔm] *m invar* handbook, vade mecum

vadrouille [vadruj] *f* (naut) mop, swab; (slang) bender, spree

vadrouiller [vadruje] *intr* (slang) to ramble around, to gad about

vadrouil·leur [vadrujœr] **vadrouil·leuse** [vadrujøz] *mf* (slang) rounder

va-et-vient [vaevjɛ̃] *m invar* backward-and-forward motion; hurrying to and fro; comings and goings; ferryboat; (elec) two-way switch

vaga·bond [vagabɔ̃] **-bonde** [bɔ̃d] *adj* vagabond || *mf* vagabond, tramp

vagabondage [vagabɔ̃daʒ] *m* vagrancy; **vagabondage interdit** (public sign) no loitering, no begging

vagabonder [vagabɔ̃de] *intr* to wander about, to roam, to tramp

vagir [vaʒir] *intr* to cry, wail

vague [vag] *adj* vague; vacant (*look; lot*); waste (*land*) || *m* vagueness; (fig) space, thin air || *f* wave; **la nouvelle vague** the wave of the future; **vague de fond** ground swell

vaguemestre [vagmɛstr] *m* (mil, nav) mail clerk

vaguer [vage] *intr* to wander

vaillance [vajɑ̃s] *f* valor

vail·lant [vajɑ̃] **vail·lante** [vajɑ̃t] *adj* valiant; up to scratch

vain [vɛ̃] **vaine** [vɛn] *adj* vein; **en vain** in vain

vaincre [vɛ̃kr] §70 *tr* to defeat, conquer; to overcome (*fear, instinct, etc.*) || *intr* to conquer || *ref* to control oneself

vain·cu **-cue** [vɛ̃ky] *adj* defeated, beaten, conquered || *mf* loser

vainqueur [vɛ̃kœr] *adj masc* victorious || *m* victor, winner

vairon [vɛrɔ̃] *adj masc* whitish (*eye*); **vairons de different colors** (*said of eyes*) || *m* (ichth) minnow

vais·seau [veso] *m* (*pl* **-seaux**) vessel; nave (*of church*); **vaisseau amiral** flagship; **vaisseau sanguin** blood vessel; **vaisseau spatial** spaceship

vaisseau-école [vesoekɔl] *m* (*pl* **vaisseaux-écoles**) (nav) training ship

vaisselier [vesəlje] *m* china closet

vaisselle [vesɛl] *f* dishes; **faire la vaisselle** to wash the dishes; **vaisselle plate** plate (*of gold or silver*)

val [val] *m* (*pl* **vaux** [vo] or **vals**) (obs) valley; **à val** going down the valley; **à val de** (obs) down from

valable [valabl] *adj* valid; worthwhile (*e.g., experience*)

valence [valɑ̃s] *f* (chem) valence

valen·tin [valɑ̃tɛ̃] **-tine** [tin] *mf* valentine (*sweetheart*)

valet [vale] *m* valet; holdfast, clamp; (cards) jack; **valet de chambre** valet; **valet de ferme** hired man; **valet de pied** footman

valeur [valœr] *f* value, worth, merit; valor; (*person, thing, or quality worth having*) asset; (com) security, stock; **de valeur** able; valuable; (Canad) too bad, unfortunate; **envoyer en valeur déclarée** to insure (*a package*); **mettre en valeur** to develop (*e.g., a region*); to set off, enhance

valeu·reux [valœrø] **-reuse** [røz] *adj* valorous, brave

validation [validasjɔ̃] *f* validation

valide [valid] *adj* valid; fit, able-bodied

valider [valide] *tr* to validate

validité [validite] *f* validity

valise [valiz] *f* suitcase; **faire ses valises** to pack, to pack one's bags; **valise diplomatique** diplomatic pouch

vallée [vale] *f* valley

vallon [valɔ̃] *m* vale, dell

valoir [valwar] §71 *tr* to equal; **un service en vaut un autre** one good turn deserves another; **valoir q.ch. à qn** to get or bring s.o. s.th., e.g., **cela lui a valu une amélioration** that got him a raise; e.g., **la condamnation lui a valu cinq ans de prison** the verdict brought him five years in prison || *intr* to be worth; **autant vaut y renoncer** might as well give up; **cela ne vaut rien** it's worth nothing; **faire valoir** to set off to advantage; to use to advantage; to develop (*one's land*); to invest (*funds, capital*); to put forward (*one's reasons*); **faire valoir que . . .** to argue that . . . || *impers*—**il vaut mieux** it would be better to, e.g., **il vaut mieux attendre** it would be better to wait; **mieux vaut tard que jamais** better late than never || *ref*—**les deux se valent** one is as good as the other

valse [vals] *f* waltz

valser [valse] *tr & intr* to waltz

valve [valv] *f* (aut, bot, zool) valve; (elec) vacuum tube

valvule [valvyl] *f* valve

vamp [vãp] *f* vamp

vamper [vãpe] *tr* (coll) to vamp

vampire [vãpir] *m* vampire

van [vã] *m* van (*for moving horses*)

vandale [vãdal] *adj* vandal; Vandal || *m* vandal || (*cap*) *mf* Vandal

vandalisme [vãdalism] *m* vandalism

vanille [vanij] *f* vanilla

vani·teux [vanitø] **-teuse** [tøz] *adj* vain, conceited

vanne [van] *f* sluice gate, floodgate; butterfly valve; (slang) gibe

van·neau [vano] *m* (*pl* **-neaux**) (orn) lapwing

vanner [vane] *tr* to winnow; to tire out

vannerie [vanri] *f* basketry

vannier [vanje] *m* basket maker

van·tail [vãtaj] *m* (*pl* **-taux** [to]) leaf (*of door, shutter, sluice gate, etc.*)

van·tard [vãtar] -tarde [tard] adj
bragging, boastful || mf braggart

vantardise [vãtardiz] f bragging, boasting

vanter [vãte] tr to praise; to boost, to
push (a product on the market) || ref
to brag, to boast

va-nu-pieds [vanypje] mf invar (coll)
tramp

vapeur [vapœr] m steamship || f steam;
vapor, mist; à la vapeur steamed
(e.g., potatoes); under steam; (coll)
at full speed; à vapeur steam (e.g.,
engine); vapeurs low spirits

vaporisateur [vaporizatœr] m atomizer,
spray

vaporiser [vaporize] tr & ref to vapor-
ize; to spray

vaquer [vake] intr to take a recess;
vaquer à to attend to || impers—il
vaque there is vacant

varappe [varap] f cliff; rock climbing

varech [varek] m wrack, seaweed

vareuse [varøz] f (mil) blouse; (nav)
peacoat

variable [varjabl] adj & f variable

va·riant [varjã] -riante [rjãt] adj & f
variant

variation [varjasjɔ̃] f variation

varice [varis] f varicose veins

varicelle [varisel] f chicken pox

va·rié -riée [varje] adj varied

varier [varje] tr & intr to vary

variété [varjete] f variety; variétés selections (from literary works); vaudeville

variole [varjɔl] f smallpox

vari·queux [varikø] -queuse [køz] adj
varicose

Varsovie [varsɔvi] f Warsaw

vase [vaz] m vase; vessel; en vase clos
shut up; in an airtight chamber; vase
de nuit chamber pot || f mud, slime

vaseline [vazlin] f vaseline

va·seux [vazø] -seuse [zøz] adj muddy,
slimy; (coll) all in, tired; (coll) fuzzy,
obscure

vasistas [vazistas] m transom

vasouiller [vazuje] tr (coll) to make a
mess of || intr (coll) to go badly

vasque [vask] f basin (of fountain)

vas·sal -sale [vasal] (pl vas·saux
[vaso] -sales) adj & mf vassal

vaste [vast] adj vast

vastement [vastəmã] adv (coll) very

Vatican [vatikã] m Vatican

vaticane [vatikan] adj fem Vatican

va-tout [vatu] m—jouer son va-tout to
stake one's all

vaudeville [vodvil] m vaudeville (light
theatrical piece interspersed with
songs); (obs) satirical song

vaudou [vodu] adj invar & m voodoo

vau-l'eau [volo]—à vau-l'eau down-
stream; s'en aller à vau-l'eau (fig)
to go to pot

vau-rien [vorjɛ̃] -rienne [rjen] mf
good-for-nothing

vautour [votur] m vulture

vautrer [votre] ref to wallow

veau [vo] m (pl veaux) calf; veal; calf-
skin; (coll) lazybones, dope; pleurer

comme un veau to cry like a baby;
veau marin seal

vé·cu -cue [veky] adj true to life

vedette [vədet] f patrol boat; scout;
lead, star; en vedette in the limelight;
mettre en vedette to headline, to
highlight; vedette de l'écran movie
star; vedette du petit écran television
star

végé·tal -tale [vezetal] (pl -taux [to])
adj vegetable, vegetal || m vegetable

végéta·rien [vezetarjɛ̃] -rienne [rjen]
adj & mf vegetarian

végétation [vezetasjɔ̃] f vegetation;
végétations (adénoïdes) adenoids

végéter [vezete] §10 intr to vegetate

véhémence [veemɑ̃s] f vehemence

véhé·ment [veemɑ̃] -mente [mɑ̃t] adj
vehement

véhicule [veikyl] m vehicle

veille [vej] f watch, vigil; wakefulness;
à la veille de on the eve of; just before; on the verge or point of; la
veille de the eve of; the day before;
la Veille de Noël Christmas Eve; la
Veille du Jour de l'An New Year's
Eve; veilles sleepless nights, late
nights; night work

veillée [veje] f evening; social evening;
veillée funèbre, veillée du corps wake

veiller [veje] tr to sit up with, to watch
over || intr to sit up, to stay up; to
keep watch; veiller à to look after, to
see to

veil·leur [vejœr] veil·leuse [vejøz] mf
watcher || m watchman; veilleur de
nuit night watchman || f see veilleuse

veilleuse [vejøz] f night light; rush-
light; pilot light; mettre en veilleuse
to turn down low; to dim (the headlights); to slow down (production in
a factory)

vei·nard [venar] -narde [nard] adj
(coll) lucky || mf (coll) lucky person

veine [ven] f vein; luck; veine alors!
(coll) swell

veiner [vene] tr to vein

vei·neux [venø] -neuse [nøz] adj
veined; venous

vélaire [veler] adj & f velar

vêler [vele] intr to calve

vélin [velɛ̃] m vellum

velléitaire [veleiter] adj & mf erratic

velléité [veleite] f stray impulse, fancy;
velléité de sourire slight smile

vélo [velo] m bike; faire du vélo to go
bicycle riding

vélocité [velosite] f velocity; speed;
agility

vélomoteur [velomotœr] m motorbike

velours [vəlur] m velvet; velours côtelé corduroy

velou·té -tée [vəlute] adj velvety || m
velvetiness

velouter [vəlute] tr to make velvety

ve·lu -lue [vəly] adj hairy

vélum [velɔm] m awning

velvet [velvet] m velveteen

venaison [venezɔ̃] f venison

ve·nant [vənɑ̃] -nante [nɑ̃t] adj com-
ing; thriving || mf comer; à tout ve-
nant to all comers

vendange [vãdãʒ] f grape harvest; vintage
vendanger [vãdãʒe] §38 tr to pick (the grapes) || intr to harvest grapes
ven·deur [vãdœr] **-deuse** [døz] mf seller, vendor; salesclerk; **vendeur ambulant** peddler || m salesman || f salesgirl, saleslady
vendre [vãdr] tr to sell; to sell out, to betray; **à vendre** for sale; **vendre au détail** to retail; **vendre aux enchères** to auction off; **vendre en gros** to wholesale || ref to sell; to sell oneself, to sell out
vendredi [vãdrədi] m Friday; **vendredi saint** Good Friday
ven·du -due [vãdy] adj sold; corrupt || mf traitor
véné·neux [venenø] **-neuse** [nøz] adj poisonous
vénérable [venerabl] adj venerable
vénérer [venere] §10 tr to venerate
véné·rien [venerjɛ̃] **-rienne** [rjɛn] adj venereal || mf person with venereal disease
vengeance [vãʒãs] f vengeance, revenge
venger [vãʒe] §38 tr to avenge || ref to get revenge
ven·geur [vãʒœr] **-geuse** [ʒøz] adj avenging || mf avenger
veni·meux [vənimø] **-meuse** [møz] adj venomous
venin [vənɛ̃] m venom
venir [vənir] §72 intr to come; **à venir** forthcoming; **faire venir** to send for; **où voulez-vous en venir?** what are you getting at?; **venez avec** (coll) come along; **venir de** to have just, e.g., **il vient de partir** he has just left || impers—**il me** (nous, etc.) **vient à l'esprit que** it occurs to me (to us, etc.) that
Venise [vəniz] f Venice
véni·tien [venisjɛ̃] **-tienne** [sjɛn] adj Venetian || (cap) mf Venetian
vent [vã] m wind; **avoir le vent en poupe** to be in luck; **avoir vent de** to get wind of; **contre vents et marées** through thick and thin; **en plein vent** in the open air; **être dans le vent** to be up to date; **il fait du vent** it is windy; **les vents** (mus) the woodwinds; **vent arrière** tailwind; **vent coulis** draft; **vent debout** headwind; **vent en poupe** (naut) tailwind
vente [vãt] f sale; felling (of timber); **en vente** on sale; **en vente libre** (pharm) on sale without a prescription; **jeunes ventes** new overgrowth; **vente amiable** private sale; **vente à tempérament** installment selling; **vente à terme** sale on time; **vente au détail** retailing; **vente en gros** wholesaling
ventilateur [vãtilatœr] m ventilator; fan; electric fan
ventiler [vãtile] tr to ventilate; to value separately; (bk) to apportion
ventouse [vãtuz] f sucker; suction cup; suction grip; nozzle (of vacuum cleaner); vent
ventre [vãtr] m belly; stomach; womb;

à plat ventre prostrate; **à ventre déboutonné** (coll) excessively; (coll) with all one's might; **avoir q.ch. dans le ventre** (coll) to have s.th. on the ball; **bas ventre** (fig) genitals; **ventre à terre** (coll) lickety-split
ventricule [vãtrikyl] m ventricle
ventriloque [vãtrilɔk] mf ventriloquist
ventriloquie [vãtrilɔki] f ventriloquism
ventripo·tent [vãtripɔtã] **-tente** [tãt] adj (coll) potbellied
ven·tru -true [vãtry] adj potbellied
ve·nu -nue [vəny] adj—**bien venu** successful; welcome || mf—**le premier venu** the first comer; just anyone; **les nouveaux venus** the newcomers || f coming, advent
Vénus [venys] f Venus
vénusté [venyste] f charm, grace
vêpres [vepr] fpl vespers
ver [ver] m worm; **tirer les vers du nez à** to worm secrets out of, to pump; **ver à soie** silkworm; **ver de terre** earthworm; **ver luisant** glowworm
véracité [verasite] f veracity
véranda [verãda] f veranda
ver·bal -bale [verbal] adj (pl **-baux** [bo]) verbal; (gram) verb
verbaliser [verbalize] intr to write out a report or summons; **verbaliser contre qn** to give s.o. a ticket (e.g., for speeding)
verbe [verb] m verb; **avoir le verbe haut** to talk loud; **Verbe** (eccl) Word
ver·beux [verbø] **-beuse** [bøz] adj verbose, wordy
verbiage [verbjaʒ] m verbiage
verdâtre [verdatr] adj greenish
verdeur [verdœr] f greenness; vigor, spryness; crudeness (of speech)
verdict [verdikt], [verdik] m verdict
verdir [verdir] tr & intr to turn green
verdoyer [verdwaje] §47 intr to become green
verdure [verdyr] f verdure; greens
vé·reux [verø] **-reuse** [røz] adj wormy
verge [verʒ] f rod; shank (of anchor); penis
verger [verʒe] m orchard
verglas [vergla] m glare ice; sleet
vergogne [vergɔɲ] f—**sans vergogne** immodest, brazen; immodestly, brazenly
véridique [veridik] adj veracious
vérifica·teur [verifikatœr] **-trice** [tris] mf inspector, examiner; **vérificateur comptable** auditor
vérification [verifikasjɔ̃] f verification; auditing; ascertainment
vérifier [verifje] tr to verify; to audit; to ascertain
véritable [veritabl] adj veritable; real, genuine
vérité [verite] f truth; **à la vérité** to tell the truth; **dire à qn ses quatre vérités** (coll) to give s.o. a piece of one's mind; **en vérité** truly, in truth
ver·meil -meille [vermej] adj rosy
vermillon [vermijɔ̃] adj invar & m vermilion
vermine [vermin] f vermin

vermou·lu -lue [vermuly] *adj* worm-eaten

vermout or **vermouth** [vermut] *m* vermouth

vernaculaire [vernakyler] *adj* vernacular

vernir [vernir] *tr* to varnish; **être verni** (coll) to be lucky

vernis [verni] *m* varnish; (fig) veneer

vernissage [vernisaʒ] *m* varnishing; private viewing (*of pictures*)

vernisser [vernise] *tr* to glaze

vérole [verɔl] *f* (slang) syphilis; **petite vérole** smallpox

verre [ver] *m* glass; crystal (*of watch*); **verre à vitre** windowpane; **verre consigné** bottle with deposit; **verre de contact** contact lens; **verre de lamp** lamp chimney; **verre dépoli** frosted glass; **verre perdu** disposable bottle (*no deposit*); **verres** eyeglasses; **verres de soleil** sunglasses; **verres grossissants** magnifying glasses; **verre taillé** cut glass

verrière [verjer] *f* stained-glass window

verrou [veru] *m* bolt; **être sous les verrous** to be locked up

verrouiller [veruje] *tr* to bolt; to lock up || *ref* to lock oneself in

verrue [very] *f* wart

vers [ver] *m* verse; **les vers** verse, poetry || *prep* toward; about, e.g., **vers les cinq heures** about five o'clock

Versailles [versaj] *f* Versailles

versant [versã] *m* slope, side

versatile [versatil] *adj* fickle

verse [vers] *f*—**pleuvoir à verse** to pour

ver·sé -sée [verse] *adj*—**versé dans** versed in

versement [versəmã] *m* deposit; installment; **versement anticipé** payment in advance

verser [verse] *tr* to pour; to upset; to tip over; to deposit || *intr* to overturn

verset [verse] *m* (Bib) verse

versification [versifikasjɔ̃] *f* versification

versifier [versifje] *tr & intr* to versify

version [versjɔ̃] *f* version; translation from a foreign language

verso [verso] *m* verso; **au verso** on the back

vert [ver] **verte** [vert] *adj* green; verdant; vigorous (*person*); new (*wine*); raw (*leather*); sharp (*scolding*); spicy (*story*); **ils sont trop verts!** sour grapes || *m* green; greenery; **mettre au vert** to put out to pasture; **se mettre au vert** to take a rest in the country

vert-de-gris [verdəgri] *m invar* verdigris

vertèbre [vertebr] *f* vertebra

verté·bré -brée [vertebre] *adj & m* vertebrate

verti·cal -cale [vertikal] (*pl* **-caux** [ko] **-cales**) *adj* vertical || *m* (astr) vertical circle || *f* vertical

vertige [vertiʒ] *m* vertigo, dizziness

vertigo [vertigo] *m* staggers (*of horse*); caprice

vertu [verty] *f* virtue

ver·tueux [vertyø] **-tueuse** [tyøz] *adj* virtuous

verve [verv] *f* verve

ver·veux [vervø] **-veuse** [vøz] *adj* lively, animated || *m* fishnet

vésanie [vezani] *f* madness

vesce [ves] *f* vetch

vésicule [vezikyl] *f* vesicle; blister; **vésicule biliaire** gall bladder

vespasienne [vespazjen] *f* street urinal

vessie [vesi] *f* bladder; **vessie à glace** ice bag

veste [vest] *f* coat, suit coat; **remporter une veste** (coll) to suffer a setback; **retourner sa veste** (coll) to do an about-face; **veste croisée** double-breasted coat; **veste de pyjama** pajama top; **veste de sport** sport coat; **veste d'intérieur**, **veste d'appartement** lounging robe; **veste droite** single-breasted coat

vestiaire [vestjer] *m* checkroom, cloak-room

vestibule [vestibyl] *m* vestibule

vestige [vestiʒ] *m* vestige; footprint

veston [vestɔ̃] *m* coat

Vésuve [vezyv] *m*—**le Vésuve** Vesuvius

vêtement [vetmã] *m* garment; **vêtements** clothes

vétéran [veterã] *m* veteran

vétérinaire [veteriner] *adj & mf* veterinary

vétille [vetij] *f* trifle

vétiller [vetije] *intr* to split hairs

vêtir [vetir] §73 *tr & ref* to dress

veto [veto] *m* veto; **mettre or opposer son veto à** to veto

vétuste [vetyst] *adj* decrepit, rickety

veuf [vœf] **veuve** [vœv] *adj* widowed || *m* widower || *f* see **veuve**

veule [vøl] *adj* (coll) feeble, weak

veuvage [vœvaʒ] *m* widowhood; widowerhood

veuve [vœv] *f* widow

vexation [veksasjɔ̃] *f* vexation

vexer [vekse] *tr* to vex

via [vja] *prep* via

viaduc [vjadyk] *m* viaduct

via·ger [vjaʒe] **-gère** [ʒer] *adj* life, for life || *m* life annuity

viande [vjãd] *f* meat; **amène ta viande!** (slang) get over here!

vibration [vibrasjɔ̃] *f* vibration

vibrer [vibre] *intr* to vibrate

vicaire [viker] *m* vicar

vice [vis] *m* vice; defect; **vice de conformation** physical defect; **vice de forme** (law) irregularity, flaw; **vice versa** vice versa

vice-amiral [visamiral] *m* (*pl* **-amiraux** [amiro]) vice-admiral

vice-président [visprezidã] **-présidente** [prezidãt] *mf* (*pl* **-présidents**) vice-president

vice-roi [visrwa] *m* (*pl* **-rois**) viceroy

vice-versa [viseversa], [visversa] *adv* vice versa

vi·cié -ciée [visje] *adj* foul, polluted; poor, thin (*blood*)

vicier [visje] *tr* to foul, to pollute; to taint, to spoil

vi·cieux [visjø] **-cieuse** [sjøz] *adj* vicious; wrong (*use*)

vici·nal -nale [visinal] *adj* (*pl* -**naux** [no]) local, side (*road*)

vicissitude [visisityd] *f* vicissitude

vicomte [vikɔ̃t] *m* viscount

victime [viktim] *f* victim

victoire [viktwar] *f* victory

victo·rieux [viktɔrjø] -**rieuse** [rjøz] *adj* victorious

victuailles [viktɥaj] *fpl* victuals, foods

vidange [vidɑ̃ʒ] *f* draining; night soil; drain (*of pipe, sink, etc.*)

vidanger [vidɑ̃ʒe] §38 *tr* to drain

vide [vid] *adj* empty; blank; vacant || *m* emptiness, void; vacuum

vi·dé -dée [vide] *adj* cleaned (*fish, fowl, etc.*); played out, exhausted

vide-bouteille [vidbutej] *m* (*pl* -**bouteilles**) siphon

vide-cave [vidkav] *m invar* sump pump

vide-citron [vidsitrɔ̃] *m* (*pl* -**citrons**) lemon squeezer

vide-gousset [vidguse] *m* (*pl* -**goussets**) (hum) thief

vide-ordures [vidɔrdyr] *m invar* garbage shoot

vide-poches [vidpɔʃ] *m invar* dresser; pin tray; (aut) glove compartment

vider [vide] *tr* to empty; to drain; to clean (*fish, fowl, etc.*); to settle (*a question*); **se faire vider de** (coll) to get thrown out of; to be fired from; to be expelled from

vi·deur [vidœr] -**deuse** [døz] *mf* (coll) bouncer (*in a night club*)

viduité [vidɥite] *f* widowhood

vidure [vidyr] *f* guts (*e.g., of cleaned fish*); **vidures de poubelle** garbage

vie [vi] *f* life; livelihood, living; **à vie** for life; **de ma** (**sa**, *etc.*) **vie** in my (his, *etc.*) life, *e.g.*, **je ne l'ai jamais vu de ma vie** I have never seen it in my life; **jamais de la vie!** not on your life!; **vie de bâton de chaise** disorderly life; **vie de château** life of ease

vieillard [vjejar] *m* old man; **les vieillards** old people

vieille [vjej] *f* old woman

vieilleries [vjejri] *fpl* old things; old ideas

vieillesse [vjejes] *f* old age

vieill·li -lie [vjeji] *adj* aged; out-of-date, antiquated

vieillir [vjejir] *tr* to age; to make (*s.o.*) look older || *intr* to age, to grow old || *ref* to make oneself look older

vieil·lot [vjejo] **vieil·lotte** [vjejɔt] *adj* (coll) oldish, quaint

vielle [vjel] *f* (hist) hurdy-gurdy

Vienne [vjen] *f* Vienna; **Vienne** (*city in France*)

vien·nois [vjenwa] **vien·noise** [vjennwaz] *adj* Viennese || (*cap*) *mf* Viennese

vierge [vjerʒ] *adj* virginal; virgin; blank; unexposed (*film*) || *f* virgin

Vietnam [vjetnam] *m*—**le Vietnam** Vietnam

vietna·mien [vjetnamjɛ̃] -**mienne** [mjen] *adj* Vietnamese || (*cap*) *mf* Vietnamese

vieux [vjø] (or **vieil** [vjej] before vowel or mute h) **vieille** [vjej] *adj* old (*wine*) || (when standing before

noun) *adj* old; old-fashioned; obsolete (*word, meaning, etc.*) || *mf* old person || *m* old man; **les vieux** old people; **mon vieux** (coll) my boy || *f* see **vieille**

vif [vif] **vive** [viv] *adj* alive, living, lively, quick; bright, intense; hearty, heartfelt; sharp (*criticism*); keen (*pleasure*); spring (*water*) || *m* quick; **couper dans le vif** to take drastic measures; **entrer dans le vif de** to get to the heart of; **peindre au vif** to paint from life; **piqué au vif** stung to the quick

vif-argent [vifarʒɑ̃] *m* quicksilver; (*person*) live wire

vigie [viʒi] *f* lookout

vigilance [viʒilɑ̃s] *f* vigilance

vigi·lant [viʒilɑ̃] -**lante** [lɑ̃t] *adj* vigilant || *m* night watchman

vigile [viʒil] *m* night watchman || *f* (eccl) vigil

vigne [viɲ] *f* vine; vineyard; **vigne blanche** clematis; **vigne de Judas** bittersweet; **vigne vierge** Virginia creeper

vigne·ron [viɲrɔ̃] -**ronne** [rɔn] *mf* vinegrower; vintner

vignette [viɲet] *f* vignette; tax stamp; gummed tab

vignoble [viɲɔbl] *m* vineyard

vigou·reux [vigurø] -**reuse** [røz] *adj* vigorous

vigueur [vigœr] *f* vigor; **entrer en vigueur** to go into effect

vil vile [vil] *adj* vile; cheap

vi·lain [vilɛ̃] -**laine** [len] *adj* nasty; ugly; naughty || *mf* nasty person

vilebrequin [vilbrəkɛ̃] *m* brace (*of brace and bit*); crankshaft

vilenie [vilni] *f* villainy; abuse

villa [villa] *f* villa; cottage, small one-story home

village [vilaʒ] *m* village

villa·geois [vilaʒwa] -**geoise** [ʒwaz] *mf* villager

ville [vil] *f* city; town; **aller en ville** to go downtown; **la Ville Lumière** the City of Light (*Paris*); **ville champignon** boom town; **ville satellite** suburban town; **villes jumelées** twin cities; **villes réunies** twin cities

villégiature [vileʒjatyr] *f* vacation

vin [vɛ̃] *m* wine; **avoir le vin gai** to be hilariously drunk; **être entre deux vins** to be tipsy; **vin d'honneur** reception (*at which toasts are offered*); **vin d'orange sangaree**; **vin mousseux** sparkling wine; **vin ordinaire** table wine

vinaigre [vinegr] *m* vinegar

vinaigrette [vinegret] *f* French dressing, vinaigrette sauce

vindica·tif [vɛ̃dikatif] -**tive** [tiv] *adj* vindictive

vingt [vɛ̃] *adj & pron* twenty; the Twentieth, *e.g.*, **Jean vingt** John the Twentieth; **vingt et un** [vɛ̃teœ̃] twenty-one; twenty-first, *e.g.*, **Jean vingt et un** John the Twenty-first; **vingt et unième** twenty-first || *m* twenty; twentieth (*in dates*); **vingt et**

un twenty-one; twenty-first (*in dates*); **vingt et unième** twenty-first
vingtaine [vẽtεn] *f* score; **une vingtaine de** about twenty
vingt-deux [vẽtdø] *adj & pron* twenty-two; the Twenty-second, e.g., **Jean vingt-deux** John the Twenty-second ‖ *m* twenty-two; twenty-second (*in dates*) ‖ *interj* (slang) beware!; cheese it!
vingt-deuxième [vẽtdøzjem] *adj, pron* (*masc, fem*), & *m* twenty-second
vingt-et-un [vẽteœ̃] *m* (cards) twenty-one
vingtième [vẽtjem] *adj, pron* (*masc, fem*), & *m* twentieth
vinyle [vinil] *m* vinyl
viol [vjɔl] *m* rape
violation [vjɔlasjɔ̃] *f* violation
violence [vjɔlɑ̃s] *f* violence
vio·lent [vjɔlɑ̃] **-lente** [lɑ̃t] *adj* violent
violenter [vjɔlɑ̃te] *tr* to do violence to
violer [vjɔle] *tr* to violate; to break (*the faith*); to rape, ravish
vio·let [vjɔle] **-lette** [let] *adj & m* violet (*color*) ‖ *f* (bot) violet
violon [vjɔlɔ̃] *m* violin; (slang) calaboose, jug; **payer les violons** (coll) to pay the piper; **violon d'Ingres** hobby
violoncelle [vjɔlɔ̃sel] *m* violoncello
violoniste [vjɔlɔnist] *mf* violinist
vipère [viper] *f* viper
virage [viraʒ] *m* turning; turn, e.g., **pas de virage à gauche** no left turn; (aer) bank; (phot) toning; **virage en épingle à cheveux** hairpin curve; **virage** (public sign) winding road; **virage sur place** U-turn
virago [virago] *f* mannish woman
virée [vire] *f* (coll) spin (*in a car*); (coll) round (*of bars*)
virement [virmɑ̃] *m* transfer (*of funds*); (naut) tacking
virer [vire] *tr* to transfer (*funds*); (phot) to tone ‖ *intr* to turn; (aer) to bank; **virer à** to turn (*sour, red, etc.*); **virer de bord** (naut) to tack
virevolte [virvɔlt] *f* turn; about-face
virevolter [virvɔlte] *intr* to make an about-face; to go hither and thither
virginité [virʒinite] *f* virginity, maidenhood
virgule [virgyl] *f* (gram) comma; (*used in French to set off the decimal fraction from the integer*) decimal point
virilité [virilite] *f* virility
virole [virɔl] *f* ferrule
virologie [virɔlɔʒi] *f* virology
vir·tuel -tuelle [virtɥel] *adj* potential; (mech, opt, phys) virtual
virtuose [virtɥoz] *mf* virtuoso
virtuosité [virtɥozite] *f* virtuosity
virulence [virylɑ̃s] *f* virulence
viru·lent -lente [lɑ̃t] *adj* virulent
virus [virys] *m* virus
vis [vis] *f* screw; thread (*of screw*); spiral staircase; **fermer à vis** to screw shut; **serrer la vis à** (fig) to put the screws on; **vis à métaux** machine screw; **vis de blocage** setscrew
visa [viza] *m* visa; (fig) approval

visage [vizaʒ] *m* face; **à deux visages** two-faced; **faire bon visage à** to pretend to be friendly to; **trouver visage de bois** to find the door closed; **visages pâles** palefaces; **voir qn sous son vrai visage** to see s.o. in his true colors
visagiste [vizaʒist] *mf* beautician
vis-à-vis [vizavi] *adv* vis-à-vis; **vis-à-vis de** vis-à-vis; towards; in the presence of ‖ *m* vis-à-vis; **en vis-à-vis** facing
viscère [viser] *m* organ; **viscères** viscera
visée [vize] *f* aim
viser [vize] *tr* to aim; to aim at; to concern; to visa ‖ *intr* to aim; **viser à** to aim at; to aim to
viseur [vizœr] *m* viewfinder; sight (*of gun*); **viseur de lancement** bombsight
visibilité [vizibilite] *f* visibility; **sans visibilité** blind (*flying*)
visible [vizibl] *adj* visible; obvious; (coll) at home, free; (coll) open to the public
visière [vizjer] *f* visor; sight (*of gun*); **rompre en visière à** to take a stand against
vision [vizjɔ̃] *f* vision
visionnaire [vizjɔner] *adj & mf* visionary
visionner [vizjɔne] *tr* to view, inspect
visionneuse [vizjɔnøz] *f* viewer
visite [vizit] *f* visit; inspection; **en, de visite** visiting; **faire, rendre visite à** to visit
visiter [vizite] *tr* to visit; to inspect
visi·teur [vizitœr] **-teuse** [tøz] *adj* visiting (*e.g., nurse*) ‖ *mf* visitor; inspector
vison [vizɔ̃] *m* mink
vis·queux [viskø] **-queuse** [køz] *adj* viscous
visser [vise] *tr* to screw; to screw on; (coll) to put the screws on
visualiser [vizɥalize] *tr* to visualize
vi·suel -suelle [vizɥel] *adj* visual
vi·tal -tale [vital] *adj* (*pl* **-taux** [to]) vital
vitaliser [vitalize] *tr* to vitalize
vitalité [vitalite] *f* vitality
vitamine [vitamin] *f* vitamin
vite [vit] *adj* fast, swift ‖ *adv* fast, quickly; **faites vite!** hurry up!
vitesse [vites] *f* speed, velocity; rate; **à toute vitesse** at full speed; **changer de vitesse** (aut) to shift gears; **en grande vitesse** (rr) by express; **en petite vitesse** (rr) by freight; **en première** (**seconde**, etc.) **vitesse** (aut) in first (second, etc.) gear; **vitesse acquise** momentum
viticole [vitikɔl] *adj* wine
vitrage [vitraʒ] *m* glasswork; small window curtain; sash; glazing
vi·trail [vitraj] *m* (*pl* **-traux** [tro]) stained-glass window
vitre [vitr] *f* windowpane, pane (aut) window; **casser les vitres** (coll) to kick up a fuss
vi·tré -trée [vitre] *adj* glazed; vitreous (*humor*); glassed-in

vi·treux [vitrø] **-treuse** [trøz] *adj* glassy; vitreous

vitrier [vitrije] *m* glazier

vitrine [vitrin] *f* show window; showcase; glass cabinet; **lécher les vitrines** (coll) to go window-shopping

vitupérer [vitypere] §10 *tr* to vituperate, abuse || *intr*—**vitupérer contre** (coll) to vituperate

vivace [vivas] *adj* hardy, vigorous; long-lived; (bot) perennial

vivacité [vivasite] *f* vivacity

vivan·dier [vivɑ̃dje] **-dière** [djer] *mf* sutler || *f* camp follower

vi·vant [vivɑ̃] **-vante** [vɑ̃t] *adj* living, alive; lively; modern (*language*) || *m*—**bon vivant** high liver, jolly companion; **du vivant de** during the lifetime of; **les vivants et les morts** the quick and the dead

vivat [viva] *m* viva || *interj* viva!

vivement [vivmɑ̃] *adv* quickly; warmly; deeply; sharply, briskly

viveur [vivœr] *m* pleasure seeker, rounder

vivier [vivje] *m* fish preserve, fishpond

vivifier [vivifje] *tr* to vivify, vitalize

vivisection [vivisɛksj5] *f* vivisection

vivoir [vivwar] *m* (Canad) living room

vivoter [vivɔte] *intr* (coll) to live from hand to mouth

vivre [vivr] *m*—**le vivre et le couvert** room and board; **le vivre et le vêtement** food and clothing; **vivres provisions;** (mil) rations, supplies || §74 *tr* to live (*one's life, faith, art*); to live through, to experience || *intr* to live; **être difficile à vivre** to be difficult to live with; **qui vive?** (mil) who is there?; **qui vivra verra** time will tell; **vive!, vivent!** viva!, long live!; **vivre au jour le jour** to live from hand to mouth; **vivre de** to live on

vizir [vizir] *m* vizier

vlan [vlɑ̃] *interj* whack!

vocable [vɔkabl] *m* word

vocabulaire [vɔkabylɛr] *m* vocabulary

vo·cal -cale [vɔkal] *adj* (*pl* **-caux** [ko]) vocal

vocaliser [vɔkalize] *tr, intr, & ref* to vocalize

vocatif [vɔkatif] *m* vocative

vocation [vɔkɑsj5] *f* vocation, calling; **vocation pédagogique** teaching career

vociférer [vɔsifere] §10 *tr* to shout (*e.g., insults*) || *intr* to vociferate

vœu [vø] *m* (*pl* **vœux**) vow; wish; resolution; **meilleurs vœux!** best wishes!; **tous mes vœux!** my best wishes!

vogue [vɔg] *f* vogue, fashion; **en vogue** in vogue, in fashion

voguer [vɔge] *intr* to sail; **vogue la galère!** let's chance it, here goes!

voici [vwasi] *prep* here is, here are; for, e.g., **voici quatre jours qu'elle est partie** she has been gone for four days; **le voici** here he is; **nous voici** here we are; **que voici** here, e.g., **mon frère que voici va vous accompagner** my brother here is going to accompany you

voie [vwa] *f* way; road; lane (*of high-*

way); (anat) tract; (rr) track; **en voie de** on the road to, nearing; **être en bonne voie** to be doing well; **voie d'eau** leak; **voie de garage** driveway; **voie d'évitement** siding; **Voie lactée** Milky Way; **voie maritime** seaway; **voie(s) de fait** (law) assault and battery; **voie surface** surface mail

voilà [vwala] *prep* there is, there are; here is, here are; that's, e.g., **voilà pourquoi** that's why; ago, e.g., **voilà quatre jours qu'elle est partie** she left four days ago; **voilà, monsieur** there you are, sir

voile [vwal] *m* veil; (phot) fog (*on negative*); **voile du palais** soft palate; **voile noir** (pathol) blackout || *f* sail; sailboat; **faire voile sur** to set sail for

voi·lé -lée [vwale] *adj* veiled; overcast; muffled; warped; husky (*voice*); (phot) fogged; **peu voilé** thinly veiled; broad (*e.g., hint*)

voiler [vwale] *tr* to veil; (phot) to fog || *ref* to cloud over; to become warped

voi·lier [vwalje] **-lière** [ljer] *adj* sailing || *m* sailboat; sailmaker; migratory bird

voilure [vwalyr] *f* sails; warping

voir [vwar] §75 *tr* to see; **faire voir** to show; **voir jouer** to see (*s.o.*) playing, to see (*s.o.*) play; to see (*s.th.*) played; **voir qn qui vient** to see s.o. coming, to see s.o. come; **voir venir qn** to see s.o. coming, to see s.o. come; (fig) to see through s.o. || *intr* to see; **faites voir!** let's see it!, let me see it!; **j'en ai vu bien d'autres** I have seen worse than that; **n'avoir rien à voir avec, à,** or **dans** to have nothing to do with; **voir à** + *inf* to see that + *ind*, e.g., **voir à nous loger** to see that we are housed; **voir au dos** see other side, turn the page; **voyons!** see here!, come now! || *ref* to see oneself; to see one another; to be obvious; to be seen, to be found

voire [vwar] *adv* nay, indeed; **voire même** or even, and even

voirie [vwari] *f* highway department; garbage collection; dump

voi·sé -sé [vwaze] *adj* voiced

voi·sin [vwaz5] **-sine** [zin] *adj* neighboring; adjoining; **voisin de** near || *mf* neighbor

voisinage [vwazinaʒ] *m* neighborhood; neighborliness

voisiner [vwazine] *intr* to visit one's neighbors; **voisiner avec** to be placed next to

voiture [vwatyr] *f* vehicle; carriage; (aut, rr) car; **en voiture!** all aboard!; **petite voiture** (coll) wheelchair; **voiture à bras** handcart; **voiture d'enfant** baby carriage; **voiture de pompier** fire engine; **voiture de remise** rented car; **voiture de série** stock car; **voiture de tourisme** pleasure car; **voiture d'infirme** wheelchair; **voiture d'occasion** used car

voiture-bar [vwatyrbar] *f* (*pl* **voitures-bars**) club car

voiture-lit [vwatyrli] *f* (*pl* **voitures-lits**) sleeping car

voiturer [vwatyre] *tr* to transport, to convey

voiture-restaurant [vwatyrrestɔrɑ̃] *f* (*pl* **voitures-restaurants**) dining car

voiture-salon [vwatyrsalɔ̃] *f* (*pl* **voitures-salons**) parlor car

voix [vwa], [vwɑ] *f* voice; vote; **à haute voix** aloud; in a loud voice; **à pleine voix** at the top of one's voice; **à voix basse** in a low voice; **à voix haute** in a loud voice; **de vive voix** by word of mouth; **voix de tête, voix de fausset** falsetto

vol [vɔl] *m* theft, robbery; flight; flock; **au vol** in flight; in passing; **à vol d'oiseau** as the crow flies; **de haut vol** high-flying; big-time (*crook*); **vol avec effraction** burglary; **vol cosmique** space flight; **vol plané** vol-plane; **vol sans visibilité** blind flying

volage [vɔlaʒ] *adj* fickle, changeable

volaille [vɔlɑj] *f* fowl; (slang) hens (*women*); (slang) gal

vo·lant [vɔlɑ̃] **-lante** [lɑ̃t] *adj* flying ‖ *m* steering wheel; flywheel; shuttlecock; sail (*of windmill*); flounce (*of dress*); leaf (*attached to stub*); **volant de sécurité** safety margin, reserve

vola·til -tile [vɔlatil] *adj* volatile ‖ *m* bird; fowl

volatiliser [vɔlatilize] *tr & ref* to volatilize

volcan [vɔlkɑ̃] *m* volcano

volcanique [vɔlkanik] *adj* volcanic

vole [vɔl] *f*—**faire la vole** to take all the tricks

volée [vɔle] *f* volley; flight (*of birds*; *of stairs*); flock; **à la volée** on the wing; at random; **à toute volée** loud and clear; **de haute volée** upperclass; **de la première volée** first-class, crack; **sonner à toute volée** to peal out

voler [vɔle] *tr* to rob; to steal; to fly at; **ne l'avoir pas volé** to deserve all that is coming; **voler à** to steal from ‖ *intr* to rob; to steal; to fly

volet [vɔle] *m* shutter; inside flap; end paper; (aer) flap; **trier sur le volet** to choose with care

voleter [vɔlte] §34 *intr* to flutter

vo·leur -leuse [lœz] *adj* thievish ‖ *mf* thief; **au voleur!** stop thief!; **voleur à la tire** pickpocket; **voleur à l'étalage** shoplifter; **voleur de grand chemin** highwayman

volition [vɔlisjɔ̃] *f* volition

volley-ball [vɔlebol] *m* volleyball

volontaire [vɔlɔ̃ter] *adj* voluntary; headstrong, willful; determined (*chin*) ‖ *mf* volunteer

volonté [vɔlɔ̃te] *f* will; wishes; **à volonté** at will; **bonne volonté** good will; **faire ses quatre volontés** (coll) to do just as one pleases; **mauvaise volonté** ill will

volontiers [vɔlɔ̃tje] *adv* gladly, willingly

volt [vɔlt] *m* volt

voltage [vɔltaʒ] *m* voltage

volte-face [vɔltafas] *f invar* volte-face

voltige [vɔltiʒ] *f* acrobatics

voltiger [vɔltiʒe] §38 *intr* to flit about; to flutter

voltmètre [vɔltmetr] *m* voltmeter

volubile [vɔlybil] *adj* voluble

volume [vɔlym] *m* volume; **faire du volume** (coll) to put on airs

volumi·neux [vɔlyminø] **-neuse** [nøz] *adj* voluminous

volupté [vɔlypte] *f* voluptuousness, ecstasy

volup·tueux [vɔlyptɥø] **-tueuse** [tɥøz] *adj* voluptuous ‖ *mf* voluptuary

vomir [vɔmir] *tr & intr* to vomit

vomissure [vɔmisyr] *f* vomit

vorace [vɔras] *adj* voracious

voracité [vɔrasite] *f* voracity

vos [vo] §88

vo·tant [vɔtɑ̃] **-tante** [tɑ̃t] *mf* voter

vote [vɔt] *m* vote; **passer au vote** to vote on; **vote affirmatif** yea; **vote négatif** nay; **vote par correspondance** absentee ballot; **vote par procuration** proxy

voter [vɔte] *tr* to vote; to vote for ‖ *intr* to vote; **voter à mains levées** to vote by show of hands; **voter par assis et levé** to give one's vote by standing or by remaining seated

vo·tif [vɔtif] **-tive** [tiv] *adj* votive

votre [vɔtr] §88

vôtre [votr] §89

vouer [vwe] *tr* to vow, to dedicate; to doom, to condemn; **voué à** headed for; doomed to ‖ *ref*—**se vouer à** to dedicate oneself to

vouloir [vulwar] *m* will ‖ §76 *tr* to want, to wish; to require; **je voudrais** I would like; **j'aimerais** I would like to; **veuillez + inf** please + inf; **voulez-vous vous taire?** will you be quiet?; **vouloir bien** to be glad to, to be willing to; **vouloir dire** to mean ‖ *intr*—**en vouloir à** to bear a grudge against; **je veux!** (slang) and how!; **je veux bien** I'm quite willing; **si vous voulez bien** if you don't mind ‖ *ref*—**s'en vouloir** to have it in for each other

vou·lu -lue [vuly] *adj* required; deliberate

vous [vu] §85, §87; **vous autres Américains** you Americans

vous-même [vumem] §86

voussoir [vuswar] *m* (archit) arch stone

voussure [vusyr] *f* arch, arching

voûte [vut] *f* vault; **voûte céleste** canopy of heaven

voûter [vute] *tr* to vault; to bend ‖ *ref* to become round-shouldered

vouvoyer [vuvwaje] §47 *tr* to address with the pronoun **vous** (*instead of* **tu**)

voy. *abbr* (**voyez**) see

voyage [vwajaʒ] *m* trip, journey, voyage; ride (*in car, train, plane, etc.*); **voyage à forfait** all-expense tour; **voyage aller et retour** round trip; **voyage de noces** honeymoon

voyager [vwajaʒe] §38 *intr* to travel

voya·geur [vwajaʒœr] **-geuse** [ʒøz] *mf* traveler; passenger

voyance [vwajɑ̃s] *f* clairvoyance

voyant [vwajɑ̃] **voyante** [vwajɑ̃t] *adj* loud, gaudy ‖ *mf* clairvoyant ‖ *m* signal; (aut) gauge ‖ *f* fortuneteller

voyelle [vwajel] *f* vowel

voyeur [vwajœr] **voyeuse** [vwajøz] *mf* voyeur ‖ *m* Peeping Tom

voyou [vwaju] **voyoute** [vwajut] *adj* gutter (*e.g., language*) ‖ *mf* gutter-snipe; brat; hoodlum

vrac [vrak]—**en vrac** unpacked, loose; in bulk; in disorder

vrai vraie [vre], [vre] *adj* true, real, genuine ‖ *m* truth; **à vrai dire** to tell the truth; **pour vrai** (coll) for good

vraiment [vremã] *adv* truly, really

vraisemblable [vresãblabl] *adj* probable, likely; true to life, realistic (*play, novel*)

vraisemblance [vresãblãs] *f* probability, likelihood; realism

vrille [vrij] *f* drill; (aer) spin; (bot) tendril

vriller [vrije] *tr* to bore ‖ *intr* to go into a tailspin

vrombir [vrɔ̃bir] *intr* to throb; to buzz; to hum; to purr (*said of motor*)

vu vue [vy] *adj* seen, regarded; **bien vu de** in favor with; **mal vu de** out of favor with ‖ *m*—**au vu de** upon presentation of; **au vu et au su de tout le monde** openly ‖ *f* view; sight; eyesight; **avoir à vue** to have in mind; **à vue in sight**; (com) on demand; **à vue de nez** at first sight; **à vue d'œil** visibly; quickly; **de vue** by sight; **en vue** in evidence; in sight; **en vue de** in order to; **garder à vue** to keep under observation, to keep locked up; **perdre qn de vue** to lose sight of s.o.; to get out of touch with s.o.; **vue à vol d'oiseau** bird's-eye view; **vues sur** designs on ‖ *vu prep* considering, in view of; **vu que** whereas

vulcaniser [vylkanize] *tr* to vulcanize

vulgaire [vylger] *adj* common, vulgar; ordinary, everyday; vernacular ‖ *m* common herd; vernacular

vulgariser [vylgarize] *tr* to popularize; to make vulgar

vulgarité [vylgarite] *f* vulgarity

vulnérable [vylnerabl] *adj* vulnerable

Vve *abbr* (**veuve**) widow

W

W, w [dublǝve] *m invar* twenty-third letter of the French alphabet

wagon [vagɔ̃] *m* (rr) car, coach; (coll) big car; **un wagon** (coll) a lot; **wagon à bagages** baggage car; **wagon à bestiaux** cattle car; **wagon couvert** boxcar; **wagon de marchandises** freight car; **wagon frigorifique** or **réfrigérant** refrigerator car; **wagon plat** flat car

wagon-bar [vagɔ̃bar] *m* (*pl* **wagons-bars**) club car

wagon-citerne [vagɔ̃sitern] *m* (*pl* **wagons-citernes**) tank car

wagon-lit [vagɔ̃li] *m* (*pl* **wagons-lits**) sleeping car

wagon-poste [vagɔ̃pɔst] *m* (*pl* **wagons-poste**) mail car

wagon-réservoir [vagɔ̃rezervwar] *m* (*pl* **wagons-réservoirs**) tank car

wagon-restaurant [vagɔ̃restɔrã] *m* (*pl* **wagons-restaurants**) dining car

wagon-salon [vagɔ̃salɔ̃] *m* (*pl* **wagons-salons**) parlor car

wagon-tombereau [vagɔ̃tɔ̃bro] *m* (*pl* **wagons-tombereaux**) dump truck

wallace [valas] *f* drinking fountain

wal-lon [walɔ̃] **wal-lonne** [walɔn] *adj* Walloon ‖ *m* Walloon (*dialect*) ‖ (*cap*) *mf* Walloon

warrant [warã], [varã] *m* receipt

water-polo [waterpolo] *m* water polo

waterproof [waterpruf] *adj invar* waterproof ‖ *m invar* raincoat

waters [water], [vater] *mpl* toilet

watt [wat] *m* watt

watt-heure [watœr] *m* (*pl* **watts-heures**) watt-hour

wattman [watman] *m* motorman

wattmètre [watmetr] *m* wattmeter

week-end [wikend] *m* (*pl* **-ends**) weekend

whisky [wiski] *m* whiskey; **whisky écossais** Scotch

wolfram [vɔlfram] *m* wolfram

X

X, x [iks], *[iks] *m invar* twenty-fourth letter of the French alphabet

Xavier [gzavje] *m* Xavier

xénon [ksenɔ̃] *m* xenon

xénophobe [ksenɔfɔb] *adj* xenophobic ‖ *mf* xenophobe

Xérès [keres], [gzeres] *m* Jerez; sherry

Xerxès [gzerses] *m* Xerxes

xylophone [ksilɔfɔn] *m* xylophone

Y

Y, y [igrɛk], *[igrɛk] *m invar* twenty-fifth letter of the French alphabet

y [i] *pron pers* §87 to it, to them; at it, at them; in it, in them; by it, by them; of it, of them, e.g., **j'y pense** I am thinking of it or them; (untranslated with certain verbs), e.g., **je n'y vois.pas** I don't see; e.g., **il s'y connaît** (coll) he's an expert, he knows what he's talking about; him, her, e.g., **je m'y fie** I trust him; **allez-y!** go ahead!, start!; **ça y est!** that's it!; **je n'y suis pour personne** I am not at home for anybody; **je n'y suis pour rien** I have nothing to do with it; **j'y suis!** I've got it! || *adv* there; here, in, e.g., **Monsieur votre père y est-il?** is your father here?, is your father in?

yacht [jɔt], [jak] *m* yacht; **yacht à glace** iceboat

yacht-club [jɔtklœb] *m* yacht club

yankee [jɑ̃ki] *adj masc* Yankee || (*cap*) *mf* Yankee

yèble [jɛbl] *f* (bot) elder; **l'yèble** the elder

yeoman [jɔman] *m* yeoman

yeuse [jøz] *f* holm oak; **l'yeuse** the holm oak

yeux [jø] *mpl* see **œil**

yé-yé [jeje] (*pl -yés*) *adj & mf* jitterbug

yiddish [jidiʃ] *adj invar & m* Yiddish

yogourt [jɔgur] *m* yogurt

yole [jɔl] *f* yawl

Yonne [jɔn] *f* Yonne; **l'Yonne** the Yonne

yougoslave [jugɔslav] *adj* Yugoslav || (*cap*) *mf* Yugoslav

Yougoslavie [jugɔslavi] *f* Yugoslavia; **la Yougoslavie** Yugoslavia

youyou [juju] *m* dinghy

Z

Z, z [zɛd] *m invar* twenty-sixth letter of the French alphabet

za·zou -zoue [zazu] *adj* (coll) jazzy || *m* (coll) zoot suiter

zèbre [zɛbr] *m* zebra; (slang) guy

zébrer [zebre] §10 *tr* to stripe; **le soleil zèbre** the sun casts streaks of light on

zébrure [zebryr] *f* stripe

zéla·teur [zelatœr] **-trice** [tris] *mf* zealot

zèle [zɛl] *m* zeal

zénith [zenit] *m* zenith

zéphyr [zefir] *m* zephyr

zeppelin [zɛplɛ̃] *m* zeppelin

zéro [zero] *m* zero

zest [zɛst] *m*—**entre le zist et le zest** (coll) betwixt and between || *interj* tush!

zeste [zɛst] *m* peel (*of citrus fruit*); dividing membrane (*of nut*); **pas un zeste** (fig) not a particle of difference

Zeus [zøs] *m* Zeus

zézaiement [zezɛmɑ̃] *m* lisp

zézayer [zezeje] §49 *intr* to lisp

zibeline [ziblin] *f* sable

zieuter [zjøte] *tr* (slang) to get a load of

zigzag [zigzag] *m* zigzag

zigzaguer [zigzage] *intr* to zigzag

zinc [zɛ̃g] *m* zinc; (coll) bar

zizanie [zizani] *f* wild rice; tare; **semer la zizanie** to sow discord

zodiaque [zɔdjak] *m* zodiac

zone [zon] *f* zone; **zone bleu** center city with limited parking

zoo [zoo] *m* zoo

zoologie [zɔɔlɔʒi] *f* zoology

zoologique [zɔɔlɔʒik] *adj* zoologic(al)

zouave [zwav] *m* Zouave; **faire le zouave** (coll) to play the fool

zut [zyt] *interj* heck!, hang it!

PART TWO

Anglais-Français

La prononciation de l'anglais

Les signes suivants représentent à peu près tous les sons de la langue anglaise.

VOYELLES

SIGNE	SON	EXEMPLE
[æ]	Plus fermé que a dans patte.	hat [hæt]
[ɑ]	Comme a dans pâte.	father ['fɑðər] proper ['prɑpər]
[ɛ]	Comme e dans sec.	met [mɛt]
[e]	Comme e dans récit. Surtout en position finale, [e] se prononce comme s'il était suivi de [ɪ].	fate [fet] they [ðe]
[ə]	C'est e muet, par ex., e dans gouvernement.	heaven ['hevən] pardon ['pardən]
[i]	Comme i dans mine.	she [ʃi] machine [mə'ʃin]
[ɪ]	Moins fermé que i dans mirage.	fit [fɪt] beer [bɪr]
[o]	Comme au dans haut. Surtout en position finale, [o] se prononce comme s'il était suivi de [ʊ].	nose [noz] road [rod] row [ro]
[ɔ]	Un peu plus fermé que o dans donne.	bought [bɔt] law [lɔ]
[ʌ]	Plus ou moins comme eu dans peur.	cup [kʌp] come [kʌm] mother ['mʌðər]
[ʊ]	Moins fermé que ou dans doublage.	pull [pʊl] book [bʊk] wolf [wʊlf]
[u]	Comme ou dans doublage.	move [muv] tomb [tum]

DIPHTONGUES

SIGNE	SON	EXEMPLE
[aɪ]	Comme aï dans aïl.	night [naɪt] eye [aɪ]
[au]	Comme aou dans caoutchouc.	found [faund] cow [kau]
[ɔɪ]	Comme oy dans boy.	voice [vɔɪs] oil [ɔɪl]

CONSONNES

SIGNE	SON	EXEMPLE
[b]	Comme b dans bébé.	bed [bed] robber ['rɑbər]
[d]	Comme d dans don.	dead [ded] add [æd]

3

SIGNE	SON	EXEMPLE
[dʒ]	Comme dj dans djinn.	gem [dʒem] jail [dʒel]
[ð]	Comme la consonne castillane d intervocalique de moda.	this [ðɪs] father ['faðər]
[f]	Comme f dans fin.	face [fes] phone [fon]
[g]	Comme g dans gallois.	go [go] get [get]
[h]	Comme la consonne allemande h de Haus ou comme la consonne espagnole j de jota mais moins aspiré.	hot [hɑt] alcohol ['ælkə‚hɔl]
[j]	Comme i dans hier ou comme y dans yod.	yes [jes] unit ['junɪt]
[k]	Comme k dans kiosque ou comme c dans cote, mais accompagné d'une aspiration.	cat [kæt] chord [kɔrd] kill [kɪl]
[l]	Comme l ou ll dans pulluler.	late [let] allow [ə'laʊ]
[m]	Comme m dans mère.	more [mɔr] command [kə'mænd]
[n]	Comme n dans note.	nest [nest] manner ['mænər]
[ŋ]	Comme ng dans parking.	king [kɪŋ] conquer ['kaŋkər]
[p]	Comme p dans père, mais accompagné d'une aspiration.	pen [pen] cap [kæp]
[r]	Le r le plus commun dans une grande partie de l'Angleterre et dans la plus grande partie des Etats-Unis et du Canada, c'est le r rétroflexe, une semi-voyelle dont l'articulation se produit par la pointe de la langue élevée vers la voûte du palais. Cette consonne est très faible dans la position intervocalique ou à la fin de la syllabe et, par conséquent, elle y est très peu audible. L'articulation de cette consonne tend à colorier le son des voyelles voisines.	run [rʌn] far [fɑr] art [ɑrt] carry ['kæri]
	Le r, précédé des sons [ʌ] ou [ə], donne sa propre couleur à ces sons et disparaît complètement en tant que son consonant.	burn [bʌrn] learn [lʌrn] weather ['weðər]
[s]	Comme ss dans classe.	send [send] cellar ['selər]
[ʃ]	Comme ch dans chose.	shall [ʃæl] machine [mə'ʃin] nation ['neʃən]
[t]	Comme t dans table, mais accompagné d'une aspiration.	ten [ten] dropped [drɑpt]
[tʃ]	Comme tch dans caoutchouc.	child [tʃaɪld] much [mʌtʃ] nature ['netʃər]
[θ]	Comme la consonne castillane c de cinco.	think [θɪŋk] truth [truθ]
[v]	Comme v dans veuve.	vest [vest] over ['ovər] of [ɑv]
[w]	Comme w dans watt; comme le [w] produit en prononçant le mot bois.	work [wark] tweed [twid] queen [kwin]
[z]	Comme s dans rose ou comme z dans zèbre.	zeal [zil] busy ['bɪzi] his [hɪz] winds [wɪndz]
[ʒ]	Comme j dans jardin.	azure ['eʒər] measure ['meʒər]

4

L'accent tonique principal, indiqué par le signe graphique ˈ , et l'accent secondaire, indiqué par le signe graphique ˌ , précèdent la syllabe à laquelle ils s'appliquent, par ex., **fascinate** [ˈfæsɪ ˌnet].

La prononciation des mots composés

Dans la partie anglais-français du Dictionnaire la prononciation figurée de tous les mots anglais simples est indiquée selon une nouvelle adaptation de la méthode de l'Association phonétique internationale, et placée entre crochets à la suite du mot-souche.

Il y a trois genres de mots composés en anglais: (1) les mots dont les éléments composants sont soudés en un mot simple, par ex., **steamboat** vapeur, (2) les mots dont les éléments composants sont reliés entre eux par un trait d'union, par ex., **short-circuit** court-circuiter, et (3) les mots dont les éléments composants restent graphiquement indépendants, par ex., **post card** carte postale. La prononciation des mots composés anglais n'est pas indiquée dans ce Dictionnaire lorsque celle des éléments composants a déjà été indiquée à la suite de ces éléments là où ils apparaissent comme mots-souches. Néanmoins, les accents principaux et secondaires sont indiqués dans l'écriture de ces mots composés, ex.: **steamˈboat**, **shortˈ-cirˈcuit**, **postˈ cardˈ**, **eyeˈ of the mornˈing**.

En ce qui concerne les éléments composants qui se terminent par **-ing** [ɪŋ] dans les mots composés, l'accent seul est précisé lorsque ces éléments se présentent également comme mots-souches suivis de la prononciation figurée, par ex., **playˈing cardˈ**.

Dans les noms dans lesquels les éléments composants **-man** et **-men** portent l'accent secondaire, les voyelles de ces éléments se prononcent comme dans les mots simples **man** et **men**, par ex., **mailman** [ˈmel ˌmæn] et **mailmen** [ˈmel ˌmen]. Dans les noms dans lesquels ces éléments composants sont inaccentués, les voyelles se prononcent dans les deux formes comme e muet, par ex., **policeman** [pəˈlismən] et **policemen** [pəˈlismən]. Il y a des noms dans lesquels ces éléments composants se prononcent des deux façons, c'est-à-dire, avec l'accent secondaire ou sans accent, par ex., **doorman** [ˈdor ˌmæn] ou [ˈdormən] et **doormen** [ˈdor ˌmen] ou [ˈdormən]. Dans ce Dictionnaire la transcription phonétique de ces mots est omise si le premier élément composant se présente ailleurs comme mot-souche suivi de la prononciation figurée. Cependant, l'accentuation de ces mots est indiquée dans ce mot-souche même:

> **mailˈman** *s* (*pl* **-men**)
> **policeˈman** *s* (*pl* **-men**)
> **doorˈman** or **doorˈman** *s* (*pl* **-men** or **-men**)

La prononciation des participes passés

Lorsqu'un mot a pour désinence **-ed** (ou **-d** après un e muet), et une prononciation conforme aux principes énoncés plus bas, celle-ci ne figurera pas dans ce Dictionnaire, si elle est indiquée quand la forme du mot sans cette désinence se présente comme mot-souche.

La désinence **-ed** (ou **-d** après un **e** muet) du prétérit, du participe passé, et de certains adjectifs possède trois prononciations différentes selon le son de la dernière consonne du radical.

1) Si le radical se termine par le son d'une consonne sonore (sauf [d]), que voici: [b], [g], [l], [m], [n], [ŋ], [r], [v], [z], [ð], [ʒ], ou [dʒ] ou par le son d'une voyelle, -ed se prononce [d].

SON DU RADICAL	INFINITIF	PRÉTÉRIT ET PARTICIPE PASSÉ
[b]	ebb [eb] rob [rɑb] robe [rob]	ebbed [ebd] robbed [rɑbd] robed [robd]
[g]	egg [eg] sag [sæg]	egged [egd] sagged [sægd]
[l]	mail [mel] scale [skel]	mailed [meld] scaled [skeld]
[m]	storm [stɔrm] bomb [bɑm] name [nem]	stormed [stɔrmd] bombed [bɑmd] named [nemd]
[n]	tan [tæn] sign [saɪn] mine [maɪn]	tanned [tænd] signed [saɪnd] mined [maɪnd]
[ŋ]	hang [hæŋ]	hanged [hæŋd]
[r]	fear [fɪr] care [ker]	feared [fɪrd] cared [kerd]
[v]	rev [rev] save [sev]	revved [revd] saved [sevd]
[z]	buzz [bʌz] fuse [fjuz]	buzzed [bʌzd] fused [fjuzd]
[ð]	smooth [smuð] bathe [beð]	smoothed [smuðd] bathed [beðd]
[ʒ]	massage [məˈsɑʒ]	massaged [məˈsɑʒd]
[dʒ]	page [pedʒ]	paged [pedʒd]
son de voyelle	key [ki] sigh [saɪ] paw [pɔ]	keyed [kid] sighed [saɪd] pawed [pɔd]

2) Si le radical se termine par le son d'une consonne sourde (sauf [t]), que voici: [f], [k], [p], [s], [θ], [ʃ], ou [tʃ], -ed se prononce [t].

SON DU RADICAL	INFINITIF	PRÉTÉRIT ET PARTICIPE PASSÉ
[f]	loaf [lof] knife [naɪf]	loafed [loft] knifed [naɪft]
[k]	back [bæk] bake [bek]	backed [bækt] baked [bekt]
[p]	cap [kæp] wipe [waɪp]	capped [kæpt] wiped [waɪpt]
[s]	hiss [hɪs] mix [mɪks]	hissed [hɪst] mixed [mɪkst]
[θ]	lath [læθ]	lathed [læθt]
[ʃ]	mash [mæʃ]	mashed [mæʃt]
[tʃ]	match [mætʃ]	matched [mætʃt]

3) Si le radical se termine par le son d'une dentale, que voici: [t] ou [d], -ed se prononce [ɪd] ou [əd].

SON DU RADICAL	INFINITIF	PRÉTÉRIT ET PARTICIPE PASSÉ
[t]	wait [wet] mate [met]	waited [ˈwetɪd] mated [ˈmetɪd]
[d]	mend [mend] wade [wed]	mended [ˈmendɪd] waded [ˈwedɪd]

6

Notez que le redoublement orthographique de la consonne finale après une voyelle simple accentuée n'altère pas la prononciation de la désinence -ed: **batted** ['bætɪd], **dropped** [drɑpt], **robbed** [rɑbd].

Ces règles s'appliquent aussi aux adjectifs composés qui se terminent par **-ed**. On n'indique que l'accent de ces adjectifs lorsque les éléments composants (le dernier, bien entendu, sans la désinence **-ed**) se présentent ailleurs comme mots-souches suivis de la prononciation figurée, par ex., **flat'-nosed'**.

Cependant, le **-ed** de quelques adjectifs formés sur un radical qui se termine par un son consonantique en plus de ceux qui se terminent par [d] et [t], est prononcé [ɪd] et cette irrégularité s'indique en donnant la prononciation figurée complète, par ex., **blessed** ['blesɪd], **crabbed** ['kræbɪd].

A

A, a [e] *s* I1ère lettre de l'alphabet
a *art indef* un
aback [ə'bæk] *adv* avec le vent dessus; **taken aback** déconcerté
abandon [ə'bændən] *s* abandon *m* ‖ *tr* abandonner
abase [ə'bes] *tr* abaisser, humilier
abasement [ə'besmənt] *s* abaissement *m*
abash [ə'bæʃ] *tr* décontenancer
abashed *adj* confus, confondu
abate [ə'bet] *tr* diminuer, réduire; (*part of price*) rabattre ‖ *intr* se calmer; (*said of wind*) tomber
abbess ['æbɪs] *s* abbesse *f*
abbey ['æbɪ] *s* abbaye *f*
abbot ['æbət] *s* abbé *m*
abbreviate [ə'brivɪ,et] *tr* abréger
abbreviation [ə,brivɪ'eʃən] *s* abréviation *f*
A B C's [,e,bi'siz] *spl* (*letterword*) a b c m
abdicate ['æbdɪ,ket] *tr & intr* abdiquer
abdomen ['æbdəmən], [æb'domən] *s* abdomen *m*
abduct [æb'dʌkt] *tr* enlever, ravir
abeam [ə'bim] *adv* par le travers
abed [ə'bed] *adv* au lit
abet [ə'bet] *v* (*pret & pp* **abetted;** *ger* **abetting**) *tr* encourager
abettor [ə'betər] *s* complice *mf*
abeyance [ə'be-əns] *s* suspension *f*; **in abeyance** en suspens
ab·hor [æb'hɔr] *v* (*pret & pp* **-horred;** *ger* **-horring**) *tr* abhorrer, détester
abhorrent [æb'hɑrənt], [æb'hɔrənt] *adj* détestable, répugnant
abide [ə'baɪd] *v* (*pret & pp* **abode** or **abided**) *tr* attendre ‖ *intr* demeurer, continuer, persister; **to abide by** s'en tenir à; rester fidèle à
abili·ty [ə'bɪlɪtɪ] *s* (*pl* **-ties**) capacité *f*, habileté *f*; talent *m*
abject [æb'dʒekt] *adj* abject
ablative ['æblətɪv] *adj & s* ablatif *m*
ablaut ['æblaut] *s* apophonie *f*
ablaze [ə'blez] *adj* enflammé; (*colorful*) resplendissant ‖ *adv* en feu
able ['ebəl] *adj* capable, habile; **to be able to** pouvoir
a'ble-bod'ied *adj* robuste, vigoureux; (*seaman*) breveté
abloom [ə'blum] *adj & adv* en fleur
abnormal [æb'nɔrməl] *adj* anormal
abnormali·ty [,æbnɔr'mælɪtɪ] *s* (*pl* **-ties**) anomalie *f*, irrégularité *f*; (*of body*) difformité *f*
aboard [ə'bord] *adv* à bord; **all aboard!** en voiture!; **to go aboard** s'embarquer ‖ *prep* à bord de
abode [ə'bod] *s* demeure *f*, résidence *f*

abolish [ə'balɪʃ] *tr* abolir
A-bomb ['e,bam] *s* bombe *f* atomique
abomination [ə,bamɪ'neʃən] *s* abomination *f*
aborigines [,æbə'rɪdʒɪ,niz] *spl* aborigènes *mpl*
abort [ə'bɔrt] *intr* avorter
abortion [ə'bɔrʃən] *s* avortement *m*
abound [ə'baund] *intr* abonder
about [ə'baut] *adv* à la ronde, tout autour; (*almost*) presque; (*here and there*) çà et là; **to be about to** être sur le point de ‖ *prep* autour de, aux environs de; (*approximately*) environ; au sujet de; vers, e.g., **about six o'clock** vers six heures; **it is about ... il s'agit de ...**
about'-face' or **about'-face'** *s* volte-face *f*; (*mil*) demi-tour *m* ‖ **about'-face'** *intr* faire volte-face
above [ə'bʌv] *adv* en haut; au-dessus, ci-dessus ‖ *prep* au-dessus de; plus que, outre; (*another point on the river*) en amont de; **above all** surtout
above'-men'tioned *adj* susmentionné
abrasive [ə'bresɪv], [ə'brezɪv] *adj & s* abrasif *m*
abreast [ə'brest] *adj & adv* de front; **three abreast** par rangs de trois; **to be abreast of** or **with** être en ligne avec; **to keep abreast of** se tenir au courant de
abridge [ə'brɪdʒ] *tr* abréger
abridgment [ə'brɪdʒmənt] *s* abrégé *m*, résumé *m*; réduction *f*
abroad [ə'brod] *adv* au loin; (*in foreign parts*) à l'étranger
abrogate ['æbrə,get] *tr* abroger
abrupt [ə'brʌpt] *adj* (*steep; impolite*) abrupt; (*hasty*) brusque, précipité
abscess ['æbses] *s* abcès *m*
abscond [æb'skand] *intr* s'enfuir, déguerpir; **to abscond with** lever le pied avec
absence ['æbsəns] *s* absence *f*
absent ['æbsənt] *adj* absent ‖ [æb'sent] *tr*—**to absent oneself** s'absenter
absentee [,æbsən'ti] *s* absent *m*
ab'sent-mind'ed *adj* absent, distrait
absolute ['æbsə,lut] *adj & s* absolu *m*
absolutely ['æbsə,lutli] *adv* absolument ‖ [,æbsə'lutli] *adv* (coll) absolument
absolve [æb'salv] *tr* absoudre
absorb [æb'sɔrb] *tr* absorber; **to be** or **become absorbed in** s'absorber dans
absorbent [æb'sɔrbənt] *adj* absorbant; (*cotton*) hydrophile ‖ *s* absorbant *m*
absorbing [æb'sɔrbɪŋ] *adj* absorbant
abstain [æb'sten] *intr* s'abstenir

abstemious [æb'stimɪ‑əs] *adj* abstinent, sobre

abstinent ['æbstɪnənt] *adj* abstinent

abstract ['æbstrækt] *adj* abstrait ‖ *s* abrégé *m*, résumé *m* ‖ *tr* résumer ‖ [æb'strækt] *tr* abstraire; *(to remove)* soustraire

abstractedly [æb'stræktɪdli] *adv* d'un œil distrait

abstruse [æb'strus] *adj* abstrus

absurd [æb'sʌrd], [æb'zʌrd] *adj* absurde

absurdi‑ty [æb'sʌrdɪti], [æb'zʌrdɪti] *s* (*pl* ‑ties) absurdité *f*

abundance [ə'bʌndəns] *s* abondance *f*

abundant [ə'bʌndənt] *adj* abondant

abuse [ə'bjus] *s* abus *m*; (*mistreatment*) maltraitement *m*; (*insulting words*) insultes *fpl* ‖ [ə'bjuz] *tr* abuser de; maltraiter; insulter

abusive [ə'bjusɪv] *adj* (*insulting*) injurieux; (*wrong*) abusif

abut [ə'bʌt] *v* (*pret & pp* abutted; *ger* abutting) *intr*—to abut on border, confiner

abutment [ə'bʌtmənt] *s* (*of wall*) contrefort *m*; (*of bridge*) culée *f*; (*of arch*) pied-droit *m*

abyss [ə'bɪs] *s* abîme *m*

A.C. ['e'si] *s* (letterword) (**alternating current**) courant *m* alternatif

academic [,ækə'demɪk] *adj* académique; théorique ‖ *s* étudiant *m* or professeur *m* de l'université

academical [,ækə'demɪkəl] *adj* académique; théorique ‖ **academicals** *spl* costume *m* académique

academician [ə,kædə'mɪʃən] *s* académicien *m*

acade‑my [ə'kædəmi] *s* (*pl* ‑mies) académie *f*; (*preparatory school*) collège *m*

accede [æk'sid] *intr* acquiescer; **to accede to** accéder à; (*the throne*) monter sur

accelerate [æk'selə,ret] *tr & intr* accélérer

accelerator [æk'selə,retər] *s* accélérateur *m*

accent ['æksent] *s* accent *m* ‖ ['æksent], [æk'sent] *tr* accentuer

accentuate [æk'sent/ʊ,et] *tr* accentuer

accept [æk'sept] *tr* accepter

acceptable [æk'septəbəl] *adj* acceptable

acceptance [æk'septəns] *s* acceptation *f*; (*approval*) approbation *f*

acceptation [,æksep'teʃən] *s* acceptation *f*; (*meaning*) acception *f*

access ['ækses] *s* accès *m*

accessible [æk'sesɪbəl] *adj* accessible

accession [æk'seʃən] *s* accession *f*

accesso‑ry [æk'sesəri] *adj* accessoire ‖ *s* (*pl* ‑ries) accessoire *m*; (*to a crime*) complice *mf*

ac'cess route' *s* voie *f* de raccordement, bretelle *f*

accident ['æksɪdənt] *s* accident *m*; **by accident** par accident

accidental [,æksɪ'dentəl] *adj* accidentel ‖ *s* (mus) accident *m*

ac'cident-prone' *adj* prédisposé aux accidents

acclaim [ə'klem] *tr* acclamer

acclimate ['æklɪ,met] *tr* acclimater

accommodate [ə'kamə,det] *tr* accommoder; (*to oblige*) rendre service à; (*to lodge*) loger

accommodating [ə'kamə,detɪŋ] *adj* accommodant, serviable

accommodation [ə,kamə'deʃən] *s* accommodation *f*; **accommodations** commodités *fpl*; (*in a train*) place *f*; (*in a hotel*) chambre *f*; (*room and board*) le vivre et le couvert

accompaniment [ə'kʌmpənɪmənt] *s* accompagnement *m*

accompanist [ə'kʌmpənɪst] *s* accompagnateur *m*

accompa‑ny [ə'kʌmpəni] *v* (*pret & pp* ‑nied) *tr* accompagner

accomplice [ə'kamplɪs] *s* complice *mf*

accomplish [ə'kamplɪʃ] *tr* accomplir

accomplishment [ə'kamplɪʃmənt] *s* accomplissement *m*, réalisation *f*; (*thing itself*) œuvre *f* accomplie; **accomplishments** arts *mpl* d'agrément, talents *mpl*

accord [ə'kɔrd] *s* accord *m*; **in accord** d'accord; **of one's own accord** de son plein gré ‖ *tr* accorder ‖ *intr* se mettre d'accord

accordance [ə'kɔrdəns] *s* accord *m*; **in accordance with** conformément à

according [ə'kɔrdɪŋ] *adj*—**according as** selon que; **according to** selon, d'après, suivant; **according to expert advice** au dire d'experts

accordingly [ə'kɔrdɪŋli] *adv* en conséquence

accordion [ə'kɔrdɪ‑ən] *s* accordéon *m*

accost [ə'kɔst], [ə'kast] *tr* accoster

account [ə'kaunt] *s* compte *m*; profit *m*, calcul *m*; (*narration*) récit *m*; (*report*) compte rendu; (*explanation*) explication *f*; **of no account** sans importance; **on account of** à cause de; **on no account** en aucune façon; **to call to account** demander des comptes à ‖ *intr*—**to account for** expliquer; (*money*) rendre compte de

accountable [ə'kauntəbəl] *adj* responsable; (*explainable*) explicable

accountant [ə'kauntənt] *s* comptable *mf*

account' book' *s* registre *m* de comptabilité

accounting [ə'kauntɪŋ] *s* règlement *m* de comptes; (*profession*) comptabilité *f*

accouterments [ə'kutərmənts] *spl* équipement *m*

accredit [ə'kredɪt] *tr* accréditer

accretion [ə'kriʃən] *s* accroissement *m*

accrue [ə'kru] *intr* s'accroître; **to accrue from** dériver de; **to accrue to** échoir à

accumulate [ə'kjumjə,let] *tr* accumuler ‖ *intr* s'accumuler

accuracy ['ækjərəsi] *s* exactitude *f*

accurate ['ækjərɪt] *adj* exact; (*aim*) juste; (*translation*) fidèle

accursed [ə'kʌrsɪd], [ə'kʌrst] *adj* maudit

accusation [,ækjə'zeʃən] *s* accusation *f*

accusative [ə'kjuzətɪv] *adj & s* accusatif *m*

accuse [ə'kjuz] *tr* accuser

accused *s* accusé *m*, inculpé *m*

accustom [ə'kʌstəm] *tr* accoutumer; **to become accustomed** s'accoutumer

ace [es] *s* as *m*; **to have an ace up one's sleeve** avoir un atout dans la manche

acetate ['æsɪ‚tet] *s* acétate *m*

ace'tic ac'id [ə'sitɪk] *s* acide *m* acétique

acetone ['æsɪ‚ton] *s* acétone *f*

acet'ylene torch' [ə'setɪ‚lin] *s* chalumeau *m* oxyacétylénique

ache [ek] *s* douleur *f* || *intr* faire mal; **my head aches** j'ai mal à la tête; **to be aching to** (coll) brûler de

achieve [ə't∫iv] *tr* accomplir, atteindre; (*a victory*) remporter

achievement [ə't∫ivmənt] *s* accomplissement *m*, réalisation *f*; (*thing itself*) œuvre *f* remarquable, réussite *f*; (*heroic deed*) exploit *m*

Achil'les' heel' [ə'kɪliz] *s* talon *m* d'Achille

acid ['æsɪd] *adj & s* acide *m*

acidi-ty [ə'sɪdɪti] *s* (*pl* **-ties**) acidité *f*

ac'id test' [s] (fig) épreuve *f* définitive

acknowledge [æk'nɑlɪdʒ] *tr* reconnaître; **to acknowledge receipt of** accuser réception de

acknowledgment [æk'nɑlɪdʒmənt] *s* reconnaissance *f*; (*of a letter*) accusé *m* de réception; (*receipt*) récépissé *m*

acme ['ækmi] *s* comble *m*, sommet *m*

acolyte ['ækə‚laɪt] *s* enfant *m* de chœur; (*priest*) acolyte *m*; assistant *m*

acorn ['ekɔrn], ['ekərn] *s* gland *m*

acoustic [ə'kustɪk] *adj* acoustique || **acoustics** *s & spl* acoustique *f*

acquaint [ə'kwent] *tr* informer; **to be acquainted** se connaître; **to be acquainted with** connaître

acquaintance [ə'kwentəns] *s* connaissance *f*

acquiesce [‚ækwi'ɛs] *intr* acquiescer

acquiescence [‚ækwi'ɛsəns] *s* acquiescement *m*, consentement *m*

acquire [ə'kwaɪr] *tr* acquérir; (*friends; a reputation*) s'acquérir

acquirement [ə'kwaɪrmənt] *s* acquisition *f*

acquisition [‚ækwɪ'zɪ∫ən] *s* acquisition *f*

acquisitive [ə'kwɪzɪtɪv] *adj* âpre au gain, avide

acquit [ə'kwɪt] *v* (*pret & pp* **acquitted**; *ger* **acquitting**) *tr* acquitter; **to acquit oneself** se comporter

acquittal [ə'kwɪtəl] *s* acquittement *m*

acre ['ekər] *s* acre *f*

acrid ['ækrɪd] *adj* âcre

acrimonious [‚ækrɪ'moni-əs] *adj* acrimonieux

acrobat ['ækrə‚bæt] *s* acrobate *mf*

acrobatic [‚ækrə'bætɪk] *adj* acrobatique || **acrobatics** *s* (*profession*) acrobatie *f*; **acrobatics** *spl* (*stunts*) acrobaties

acronym ['ækrənɪm] *s* sigle *m*

acropolis [ə'krɑpəlɪs] *s* acropole *f*

across [ə'krɔs], [ə'krɑs] *adv* en travers, à travers; (*sidewise*) en largeur || *prep* en travers de; (*e.g., the street*) de l'autre côté de; **across country** à travers champs; **to come across** rencontrer par hasard; **to go across** traverser

acrostic [ə'krɔstɪk], [ə'krɑstɪk] *s* acrostiche *m*

act [ækt] *s* action *f*, acte *m*; (circus, rad, telv) numéro *m*; (govt) loi *f*; (law, theat) acte; (coll) allure *f* affectée, comédie *f*; **in the act** sur le fait, en flagrant délit || *tr* jouer; **to act the fool** faire le pitre || *intr* agir; se conduire; (theat) jouer; **to act as** servir de; **to act on** influer sur

acting ['æktɪŋ] *adj* intérimaire || *s* (*actor's art*) jeu *m*; (*profession*) théâtre *m*

action ['æk∫ən] *s* action *f*; (law) acte *m*; (mach) jeu *m*; (theat) intrigue *f*; **out of action** hors de service; **to go into action** (mil) aller au feu; **to suit the action to the word** joindre le geste à la parole; **to take action** prendre des mesures

activate ['æktɪ‚vet] *tr* activer

active ['æktɪv] *adj* actif

activi-ty [æk'tɪvɪti] *s* (*pl* **-ties**) activité *f*

actor ['æktər] *s* acteur *m*

actress ['æktrɪs] *s* actrice *f*

actual ['ækt∫u-əl] *adj* véritable, réel, effectif

actually ['ækt∫u-əli] *adv* réellement, en réalité, effectivement

actuar-y ['ækt∫u‚ɛri] *s* (*pl* **-ies**) actuaire *m*

actuate ['ækt∫u‚et] *tr* actionner; (*to motivate*) animer

acuity [ə'kju-ɪti] *s* acuité *f*

acumen [ə'kjumən] *s* finesse *f*

acute [ə'kjut] *adj* aigu; (fig) avisé

acutely [ə'kjutli] *adv* profondément

A.D. ['e'di] *adj* (letterword) (**Anno Domini**) ap. J.-C.

ad [æd] *s* (coll) annonce *f*

adage ['ædɪdʒ] *s* adage *m*

Adam ['ædəm] *s* Adam *m*; **I don't know him from Adam** (coll) je ne le connais ni d'Ève ni d'Adam

adamant ['ædəmənt] *adj* inflexible

Ad'am's ap'ple *s* pomme *f* d'Adam

adapt [ə'dæpt] *tr* adapter

adaptation [‚ædæp'te∫ən] *s* adaptation *f*

adapter [ə'dæptər] *s* adaptateur *m*, raccord *m*; (phot) bague *f* porte-objectif

add [æd] *tr* ajouter; **to add up** additionner || *intr* additionner; **to add up to** s'élever à

adder ['ædər] *s* (zool) vipère *f*

addict ['ædɪkt] *s* toxicomane *mf*; (sports) fanatique *mf* || [ə'dɪkt] *tr* atteindre de toxicomanie; **to be addicted to** (*to enjoy*) s'adonner à

addiction [ə'dɪk∫ən] *s* toxicomanie *f*; **addiction to** penchant *m* pour

add'ing machine' *s* machine *f* à calculer, additionneuse *f*

addition [ə'dɪʃən] s addition f; **in addition to** en plus de

additive ['ædɪtɪv] adj & s additif m

addle ['ædəl] tr brouiller

address [ə'dres], ['ædres] s adresse f || [ə'dres] s discours m; **to deliver an address** prononcer un discours || tr adresser; s'adresser à; (an audience) faire un discours à

address' book' s carnet m d'adresses

addressee [,ædre'si] s destinataire mf

adduce [ə'd(j)us] tr alléguer; (proof) fournir

adenoids ['ædə,nɔɪdz] spl végétations fpl adénoïdes

adept [ə'dept] adj habile || s adepte mf

adequate ['ædɪkwɪt] adj suffisant, adéquat; **adequate to** à la hauteur de, proportionné à

adhere [æd'hɪr] intr adhérer

adherence [æd'hɪrəns] s adhérence f

adherent [æd'hɪrənt] adj & s adhérent m

adhesion [æd'hiʒən] s adhésion f; (pathol) adhérence f

adhesive [æd'hisɪv], [æd'hizɪv] adj & s adhésif m

adhe'sive tape' s sparadrap m

adieu [ə'd(j)u] s (pl **adieus** or **adieux**) adieu m || interj adieu!

ad infinitum [,æd,ɪnfɪ'naɪtəm] adv sans fin

adjacent [ə'dʒesənt] adj adjacent

adjective ['ædʒɪktɪv] adj & s adjectif m

adjoin [ə'dʒɔɪn] tr avoisiner || intr être contigu

adjoining [ə'dʒɔɪnɪŋ] adj contigu

adjourn [ə'dʒʌrn] tr (to postpone) remettre, reporter; (a meeting, a session) lever; (sine die; for resumption at another time or place) ajourner || intr s'ajourner; lever la séance

adjournment [ə'dʒʌrnmənt] s suspension f de séance

adjudge [ə'dʒʌdʒ] tr adjuger; (a criminal) condamner

adjudicate [ə'dʒudɪ,ket] tr & intr juger

adjunct ['ædʒʌŋkt] adj & s adjoint m; **adjuncts** accessoires mpl

adjust [ə'dʒʌst] tr ajuster || intr s'adapter

adjustable [ə'dʒʌstəbəl] adj réglable

adjustment [ə'dʒʌstmənt] s ajustage m, réglage m; (arrangement) ajustement m, règlement m; (telv) mise f au point

adjutant ['ædʒətənt] s adjutant m

ad-lib [,æd'lɪb] adj improvisé || v (pret & pp -**libbed**; ger -**libbing**) tr & intr improviser (en cascade)

administer [æd'mɪnɪstər] tr administrer; **to administer an oath** faire prêter serment || intr—**to administer to** pourvoir à, aider, assister

administration [æd,mɪnɪs'treʃən] s administration f; gouvernement m

administrator [æd'mɪnɪs,tretər] s administrateur m

admiral ['ædmɪrəl] s amiral m

admiral·ty ['ædmɪrəlti] s (pl -**ties**) amirauté f; ministère m de la marine

admiration [,ædmɪ'reʃən] s admiration f

admire [æd'maɪr] tr admirer

admirer [æd'maɪrər] s admirateur m; (suitor) soupirant m

admission [æd'mɪʃən] s admission f; (price) entrée f; (confession) aveu m

ad·mit [æd'mɪt] v (pret & pp -**mitted**; ger -**mitting**) tr admettre; (e.g., a mistake) avouer; **admit bearer** laisser passer

admittance [æd'mɪtəns] s entrée f

admittedly [æd'mɪtɪdli] adv manifestement

admonish [æd'monɪʃ] tr admonester

ad nauseam [æd'nɔʃɪ·əm], [æd'nɔsɪəm] adv jusqu'au dégoût

ado [ə'du] s agitation f; **much ado about nothing** beaucoup de bruit pour rien; **without further ado** sans plus de façons

adolescence [,ædə'lesəns] s adolescence f

adolescent [,ædə'lesənt] adj & s adolescent m

adopt [ə'dɑpt] tr adopter

adoption [ə'dɑpʃən] s adoption f

adoptive [ə'dɑptɪv] adj adoptif

adorable [ə'dorəbəl] adj adorable

adoration [,ædə'reʃən] s adoration f

adore [ə'dor] tr adorer

adorn [ə'dɔrn] tr orner, parer

adornment [ə'dɔrnmənt] s parure f

adre'nal glands' ['ædrɪnəl], [ə'drinəl] spl (capsules) surrénales fpl

adrenalin [ə'drenəlɪn] s adrénaline f

Adriatic [,edrɪ'ætɪk], [,ædrɪ'ætɪk] adj & s Adriatique f

adrift [ə'drɪft] adj & adv à la dérive

adroit [ə'drɔɪt] adj adroit, habile

adulate ['ædʒə,let] tr aduler

adult [ə'dʌlt], ['ædʌlt] adj & s adulte mf

adulterate [ə'dʌltə,ret] tr frelater

adulteration [ə,dʌltə'reʃən] s frelatage m

adulterer [ə'dʌltərər] s adultère m

adulteress [ə'dʌltərɪs] s adultère f

adulterous [ə'dʌltərəs] adj adultère

adulter·y [ə'dʌltəri] s (pl -**ies**) adultère m

adumbrate [æd'ʌmbret], ['ædəm,bret] tr ébaucher; (to foreshadow) présager

advance [æd'væns], [æd'vɑns] s avance f; **advances** propositions fpl; propositions malhonnêtes; **in advance** d'avance; en avance || tr avancer || intr avancer, s'avancer; (said of prices) augmenter; (said of stocks) monter

advancement [æd'vænsmənt], [æd'vɑnsmənt] s avancement m

advance' pay'ment s versement m anticipé

advantage [æd'ventɪdʒ], [æd'vɑntɪdʒ] s avantage m; **to take advantage of** profiter de

advent ['ædvent] s venue f; **Advent** (eccl) Avent m

adventitious [,ædven'tɪʃəs] adj adventice

adventure [æd'ventʃər] s aventure f

adventurer [æd'ventʃərər] s aventurier m

adventuress [æd'ventʃərɪs] s aventurière f

adventurous [æd'ventʃərəs] adj aventureux

adverb ['ædvʌrb] s adverbe m

adversar·y ['ædvərˌseri] s (pl -ies) adversaire mf

adverse [æd'vʌrs], ['ædvʌrs] adj adverse

adversi·ty [æd'vʌrsɪti] s (pl -ties) adversité f

advertise ['ædvərˌtaɪz], [ˌædvər'taɪz] tr & intr annoncer

advertisement [ˌædvər'taɪzmənt], [æd-'vʌrtɪzmənt] s annonce f

advertiser ['ædvərˌtaɪzər], [ˌædvər-'taɪzər] s annonceur m

advertising ['ædvərˌtaɪzɪŋ] s réclame f

ad'vertising a'gency s agence f de publicité

ad'vertising man' s entrepreneur m de publicité

advice [æd'vaɪs] s conseil m; conseils; a piece of advice un conseil

advisable [æd'vaɪzəbəl] adj opportun, recommandable

advise [æd'vaɪz] tr conseiller; (to inform) aviser; to advise against déconseiller; to advise s.o. to + inf conseiller à qn de + inf

advisedly [æd'vaɪzɪdli] adv en connaissance de cause

advisement [æd'vaɪzmənt] s conseils mpl; to take under advisement mettre en délibération

adviser [æd'vaɪzər] s conseiller m

advisory [æd'vaɪzəri] adj consultatif

advocacy ['ædvəkəsi] s plaidoyer m

advocate ['ædvəˌket] s partisan m; (lawyer) avocat m || tr préconiser

Aege'an Sea' [ɪ'dʒiːən] s mer f Égée, mer de l'Archipel

aegis ['idʒɪs] s égide f

aerate ['eret] tr aérer

aerial ['erɪ.əl] adj aérien || s antenne f

aerodynamic [ˌerodaɪ'næmɪk] adj aérodynamique || aerodynamics s aérodynamique f

aeronautic [ˌero'nɔtɪk] adj aéronautique || aeronautics s aéronautique f

aerosol ['erəˌsɔl] s aérosol m

aerospace ['erəˌspes] adj aérospatial

Aeschylus ['eskɪləs] s Eschyle m

aesthete ['esθit] s esthète mf

aesthetic [es'θetɪk] adj esthétique || aesthetics s esthétique f

afar [ə'fɑr] adv au loin

affable ['æfəbəl] adj affable

affair [ə'fer] s affaire f; (of lovers) affaire de cœur

affect [ə'fekt] tr affecter

affectation [ˌæfek'teʃən] s affectation f

affected adj affecté, maniéré

affection [ə'fekʃən] s affection f

affectionate [ə'fekʃənɪt] adj affectueux

affidavit [ˌæfɪ'devɪt] s déclaration f sous serment

affiliate [ə'fɪlɪˌet] s (com) société f affiliée || tr affilier || intr s'affilier

affini·ty [ə'fɪnɪti] s (pl -ties) affinité f; (inlawry) alliance f

affirm [ə'fʌrm] tr & intr affirmer

affirmative [ə'fʌrmətɪv] adj affirmatif || s affirmative f

affix ['æfɪks] s affixe m || [ə'fɪks] tr annexer; (a signature) apposer; (guilt) attribuer; (on the wall) afficher

afflict [ə'flɪkt] tr affliger

affliction [ə'flɪkʃən] s (sorrow) affliction f; (disorder) infirmité f

affluence ['æflu.əns] s affluence f de biens, richesse f

afford [ə'ford] tr fournir; se permettre, avoir de quoi payer

affront [ə'frʌnt] s affront m || tr insulter

Afghanistan [æf'gænɪˌstæn] s l'Afghanistan m

afire [ə'faɪr] adj & adv en feu

aflame [ə'flem] adj & adv en flammes

afloat [ə'flot] adj & adv à flot; (rumor) en circulation; to keep afloat on the water se tenir sur l'eau

afoot [ə'fut] adj & adv à pied; (underway) en œuvre

aforesaid [ə'forˌsed] adj susdit; ci-dessus mentionné

afraid [ə'fred] adj effrayé; to be afraid avoir peur

afresh [ə'freʃ] adv à nouveau

Africa ['æfrɪkə] s Afrique f; l'Afrique

African ['æfrɪkən] adj africain || s Africain m

after ['æftər], ['ɑftər] adj suivant, postérieur || adv après, plus tard || prep après, à la suite de; (in the manner or style of) d'après; (not translated in expressions of time), e.g., eight minutes after ten dix heures huit || conj après que

af'ter-din'ner adj d'après dîner

af'ter-effect' s contrecoup m; aftereffects (pathol) séquelles fpl

af'ter-glow' s lueur f du coucher

af'ter-im'age s image f consécutive

af'ter-life' s survie f

af'ter-noon' s après-midi m & f; good afternoon! bonjour!

af'ter-shav'ing lo'tion s eau f de Cologne pour la barbe

af'ter-taste' s arrière-goût m

af'ter-thought' s réflexion f après coup

afterward ['æftərwərd], ['ɑftərwərd] adv après, ensuite

again [ə'gen] adv encore, de plus; de nouveau, encore une fois; now and again de temps en temps

against [ə'genst] prep contre; against the grain à rebrousse-poil; over against en face de; par contraste avec

age [edʒ] s âge m; (about a hundred years) siècle m; for ages depuis longtemps; of age majeur; to come of age atteindre sa majorité; under age mineur || tr & intr vieillir

aged [edʒd] adj (wine, cheese, etc.)

vieilli; (of the age of) âgé de ||
['edʒɪd] adj âgé, vieux

agen‧cy ['edʒənsɪ] s (pl -cies) agence
f; (means) action f

agenda [ə'dʒendə] s ordre m du jour

agent ['edʒənt] s agent m; (means)
moyen m; (com) commissionnaire m

agglomeration [ə‚glamə'reʃən] s agglomération f

aggrandizement [ə'grændɪzmənt] s
agrandissement m

aggravate ['ægrə‚vet] tr aggraver;
(coll) exaspérer

aggregate ['ægrɪ‚get] adj global || s
agrégat m || tr rassembler; (coll)
s'élever à

aggression [ə'greʃən] s agression f

aggressive [ə'gresɪv] adj agressif; (live-
wire) entreprenant

aggressor [ə'gresər] s agresseur m

aghast [ə'gæst], [ə'gast] adj abasourdi

agile ['ædʒɪl] adj agile

agility [ə'dʒɪlɪtɪ] s agilité f

agitate ['ædʒɪ‚tet] tr agiter

agitator ['ædʒɪ‚tetər] s agitateur m

aglow [ə'glo] adj & adv rougeoyant

agnostic [æg'nastɪk] adj & s agnostique mf

ago [ə'go] adv il y a, e.g., two days
ago il y a deux jours

agog [ə'gag] adj & adv en émoi

agonizing ['ægə‚naɪzɪŋ] adj angoissant

ago‧ny ['ægənɪ] s (pl -nies) angoisse f;
(death struggle) agonie f

agrarian [ə'grerɪ‧ən] adj agraire; (law)
agrairien || s agrairien m

agree [ə'gri] intr être d'accord, s'accorder; agreed! d'accord!; to agree
to consentir à

agreeable [ə'gri‧əbəl] adj agréable,
sympathique; (consenting) d'accord

agreement [ə'grimənt] s accord m;
contrat m

agriculture ['ægrɪ‚kʌltʃər] s agriculture f

aground [ə'graund] adj (naut) échoué
|| adv—to run aground échouer

ague ['egju] s fièvre f intermittente;
accès m de frisson

ahead [ə'hed] adj & adv en avant;
ahead of avant; devant; straight
ahead tout droit; to get ahead of
devancer

ahem [ə'hem] interj hum!

ahoy [ə'hɔɪ] interj—ship ahoy! ohé
du navire!

aid [ed] s (assistance) aide f; (assist-
ant) aide mf || tr aider

aide-de-camp ['eddə'kæmp] s (pl
aides-de-camp) officier m d'ordonnance, aide m de camp

ail [el] tr affliger; what ails you?
qu'avez-vous? || intr être souffrant

ailment ['elmənt] s indisposition f,
maladie f

aim [em] s but m, objectif m; (of gun)
pointage m || tr diriger; (a blow) al-
longer; (a telescope, cannon, etc.)
pointer, viser || intr viser

air [er] s air m; on the air à la radio,
à la télévision, à l'antenne; to put on
airs prendre des airs; to put on the

air radiodiffuser; to walk on air ne
pas toucher terre; up in the air con-
fondu, sidéré; (angry) très monté ||
tr aérer; (a question) ventiler; (feelings) donner libre cours à

air-borne ['er‚born] adj aéroporté

air′ brake′ s frein m à air comprimé

air′-condi′tion tr climatiser

air′ condi′tioner s climatiseur m

air′ condi′tioning s climatisation f

air′craft′ s aéronef m, appareil m
d'aviation

air′craft car′rier s porte-avions m

air′drop′ s parachutage m || tr para-
chuter

air′field′ s terrain m d'aviation, aéro-
drome m

air′ force′ s forces fpl aériennes

air′ gap′ s (elec) entrefer m

air′ let′ter s aérogramme m

air′lift′ s pont m aérien

air′line′ s ligne f aérienne

air′line pi′lot s pilote m de ligne

air′li′ner s avion m de transport

air′mail′ adj aéropostal || s poste f
aérienne; by airmail par avion

air′plane′ s avion m

air′ pock′et s trou m d'air

air′ pollu′tion s pollution f de l'air

air′port′ s aéroport m

air′ raid′ s attaque f aérienne

air′-raid drill′ s exercice m d'alerte
aérienne

air′-raid shel′ter s abri m

air′-raid ward′en s chef m d'îlot

air′-raid warn′ing s alarme f aérienne

air′sick′ adj atteint du mal de l'air

air′sick′ness s mal m de l'air

air′ sleeve′ or sock′ s manche f à air

air′strip′ s piste f

air′ term′inal s aérogare f

air′tight′ adj hermétique

air′waves′ spl ondes fpl radiophoniques

air′way′ s route f aérienne

air-y ['erɪ] adj (comp -ier; super -iest)
aérien; gracieux; (coll) maniéré

aisle [aɪl] s (through rows of seats)
passage m central, allée f; (in a
train) couloir m; (long passageway
in a church) nef f latérale

ajar [ə'dʒar] adj entrebâillé

akimbo [ə'kɪmbo] adj & adv—with
arms akimbo les poings sur les
hanches

akin [ə'kɪn] adj apparenté

alabaster ['ælə‚bæstər], ['ælə‚bastər]
s albâtre m

alacrity [ə'lækrɪtɪ] s vivacité f, empressement m

alarm [ə'larm] s alarme f; (of clock)
sonnerie f || tr alarmer

alarm′ clock′ s réveille-matin m, réveil
m

alarming [ə'larmɪŋ] adj alarmant

alas [ə'læs], [ə'las] interj hélas!

Albanian [æl'benɪ‧ən] adj albanais || s
(language) albanais m; (person)
Albanais

albatross ['ælbə‚trɔs], ['ælbə‚tras] s
albatros m

albi‧no [æl'baɪno] adj albinos || s (pl
-nos) albinos m

album ['ælbəm] *s* album *m*

albumen [æl'bjumən] *s* albumen *m*

alchemy ['ælkɪmɪ] *s* alchimie *f*

alcohol ['ælkə,hɔl], ['ælkə,hal] *s* alcool *m*

alcoholic [,ælkə'hɔlɪk], [,ælkə'halɪk] *adj & s* alcoolique *mf*

alcove ['ælkov] *s* niche *f*; *(for a bed)* alcôve *f*

alder ['ɔldər] *s* aune *m*

alder-man ['ɔldərmən] *s* (*pl* **-men**) conseiller *m* municipal

ale [el] *s* ale *f*

alembic [ə'lembɪk] *s* alambic *m*; (*fig*) creuset *m*

alert [ə'lʌrt] *adj & s* alerte *f* ‖ *tr* alerter

alfalfa [æl'fælfə] *s* luzerne *f*

algebra ['ældʒɪbrə] *s* algèbre *f*

Algeria [æl'dʒɪrɪ·ə] *s* Algérie *f*

Algerian [æl'dʒɪrɪ·ən] *adj* (*of Algeria*) algérien; (*of Algiers, the Barbary state*) algérois ‖ *s* Algérien *m*; Algérois *m*

Algiers [æl'dʒɪrz] *s* Alger *m*

alias ['elɪ·əs] *s* nom *m* d'emprunt ‖ *adv* alias, autrement dit

ali-bi ['ælɪ,baɪ] *s* (*pl* **-bis**) excuse *f*; (*law*) alibi *m*

alien ['eljən] *adj & s* étranger *m*

alienate ['eljə,net], ['elɪ·ə,net] *tr* s'aliéner; (*to transfer*) aliéner

alight [ə'laɪt] *adj* allumé ‖ *v* (*pret & pp* **alighted** or **alit** [ə'lɪt]) *intr* descendre, se poser; (aer) (*on land*) atterrir; (aer) (*on sea*) amerrir

align [ə'laɪn] *tr* aligner ‖ *intr* s'aligner

alike [ə'laɪk] *adj* pareils, e.g., **these books are alike** ces livres sont pareils; **to look alike** se ressembler ‖ *adv* de la même façon

alimony ['ælɪ,monɪ] *s* pension *f* alimentaire après divorce

alive [ə'laɪv] *adj* vivant; vif; **alive to** sensible à

alka-li ['ælkə,laɪ] *s* (*pl* **-lis** or **-lies**) alcali *m*

alkaline ['ælkə,laɪn], ['ælkəlɪn] *adj* alcalin

all [ɔl] *adj indef* tout; tout le ‖ *s* tout *m* ‖ *pron indef* tout; tous; **all of** tout le; **first of all** tout d'abord; **is that all?** c'est tout?; (*ironically*) ce n'est que ça?; **not at all** pas du tout ‖ *adv* tout; **all at once** tout à coup; **all but** presque; **all in** (coll) éreinté; **all in all** à tout prendre; **all off** (slang) abandonné; **all right** bon, ça va, très bien; **all's well!** (naut) bon quart!; **all the better** tant mieux; **all told** en tout; **fifteen (thirty, etc.) all** (tennis) égalité à quinze (trente, etc.); **to be all for** ne demander mieux que

allay [ə'le] *tr* apaiser

all'-clear' *s* fin *f* d'alerte

allege [ə'ledʒ] *tr* alléguer; déclarer sous serment; affirmer sans preuve

alleged *adj* présumé, prétendu, censé

allegedly [ə'ledʒɪdlɪ] *adv* prétendument, censément

allegiance [ə'lidʒəns] *s* allégeance *f*

allegoric(al) [,ælɪ'gɑrɪk(əl)], [,ælɪ-'gɔrɪk(əl)] *adj* allégorique

allego-ry ['ælɪ,gorɪ] *s* (*pl* **-ries**) allégorie *f*

aller-gy ['ælərdʒɪ] *s* (*pl* **-gies**) allergie *f*

alleviate [ə'livɪ,et] *tr* soulager, alléger

alley ['ælɪ] *s* ruelle *f*; **that is up my alley** (slang) cela est dans mes cordes

al'ley cat' *s* chat *m* de gouttière

alliance [ə'laɪ·əns] *s* alliance *f*

alligator ['ælɪ,getər] *s* alligator *m*

al'ligator pear' *s* poire *f* d'avocat

al'ligator wrench' *s* clef *f* à machoires dentées

alliteration [ə,lɪtə'reʃən] *s* allitération *f*

all'-know'ing *adj* omniscient

allocate ['ælə,ket] *tr* allouer, assigner

allot [ə'lɑt] *v* (*pret & pp* **allotted**; *ger* **allotting**) *tr* répartir

allotment [ə'lɑtmənt] *s* allocation *f*; (*from social security*) prestation *f*

all'-out' *adj* total

allow [ə'laʊ] *tr* permettre; (*a fact; a privilege*) accorder; (*as an allocation*) allouer ‖ *intr*—**to allow for** tenir compte de

allowance [ə'laʊ·əns] *s* allocation *f*, indemnité *f*; concession *f*; tolérance *f*

alloy ['ælɔɪ], [ə'lɔɪ] *s* alliage *m* ‖ [ə'lɔɪ] *tr* allier

all' right! *interj* bon!, très bien!, ça va!; (*agreed!*) c'est entendu!, d'accord!

all'-round' *adj* (*athlete*) complet; (*man*) universel; total, global

All' Saints'' Day' *s* la Toussaint

All' Souls'' Day' *s* la fête des Morts

all'spice' *s* (*plant*) quatre-épices *f*; (*berry*) toute-épice *f*; piment *m*

all'-time' *adj* record

allude [ə'lud] *intr*—**to allude to** faire allusion à

allure [ə'lʊr] *tr* séduire, tenter

allurement [ə'lʊrmənt] *s* charme *m*

alluring [ə'lʊrɪŋ] *adj* séduisant

all' wet' *adj* (coll) fichu, erroné

al-ly ['ælaɪ], [ə'laɪ] *s* (*pl* **-lies**) allié *m* ‖ [ə'laɪ] *v* (*pret & pp* **-lied**) *tr* allier

almanac ['ɔlmə,næk] *s* almanach *m*

almighty [ɔl'maɪtɪ] *adj* omnipotent

almond ['amənd], ['æmənd] *s* amande *f*

al'mond tree' *s* amandier *m*

almost ['ɔlmost], [ɔl'most] *adv* presque; **I almost fell** j'ai failli tomber

alms [amz] *s & spl* aumône *f*

alms'house' *s* hospice *m*

aloe ['ælo] *s* aloès *m*

aloft [ə'lɔft], [ə'laft] *adv* en l'air; (aer) en vol; (naut) en haut

alone [ə'lon] *adj* seul, e.g., **my arm alone suffices** mon bras seul suffit; e.g., **the metropolis alone** la seule métropole; **let alone . . .** sans compter . . . ; **to leave alone** laisser tranquille ‖ *adv* seulement

along [ə'lɔŋ], [ə'laŋ] *adv* avec; **all along** tout le temps; **come along!** venez donc!; **to get along** s'en aller; se porter, faire des progrès ‖ *prep* le long de; sur

along'side' *adv* à côté ‖ *prep* à côté de

aloof [ə'luf] *adj* isolé, peu abordable || *adv* à l'écart, à distance

aloud [ə'laud] *adv* à haute voix

alpenstock ['ælpən,stɑk] *s* bâton ☞ ferré

alphabet ['ælfə,bet] *s* alphabet *m*

alpine ['ælpaɪn] *adj* alpin

Alps [ælps] *spl*—the Alps les Alpes *fpl*

already [ɔl'redɪ] *adv* déjà

Alsatian [æl'seʃən] *adj* alsacien || *s* (*dialect*) alsacien *m*; (*person*) Alsacien *m*

also ['ɔlso] *adv* aussi, également

altar ['ɔltər] *s* autel *m*

al'tar boy' *s* enfant *m* de chœur

al'tar cloth' *s* nappe *f* d'autel

al'tar-piece' *s* rétable *m*

al'tar rail' *s* grille *f* du chœur

alter ['ɔltər] *tr* altérer; (*a suit of clothes*) retoucher, faire des retouches à; (*an animal*) châtrer || *intr* se modifier

alteration [,ɔltə'reʃən] *s* altération *f*; (*in a building*) modification *f*; alterations (*in clothing*) retouches *fpl*

alternate ['ɔltərnɪt], ['æltərnɪt] *adj* alternatif; (*angle*) alterne; (*rhyme*) croisé || ['ɔltər,net], ['æltər,net] *tr* faire alternance à || *intr* alterner

al'ternating cur'rent *s* courant *m* alternatif

alternative [ɔl'tʌrnətɪv], [æl'tʌrnətɪv] *adj* & *s* alternatif *m*

although [ɔl'ðo] *conj* bien que, quoique

altitude ['æltɪ,t(j)ud] *s* altitude *f*

al·to ['ælto] *s* (*pl* -tos) alto *m*

altogether [,ɔltə'geðər] *adv* ensemble; entièrement; tout compris

altruist ['æltru·ɪst] *adj* & *s* altruiste *mf*

alum ['æləm] *s* alun *m*

aluminum [ə'luminəm] *s* aluminium *m*

alum·nus [ə'lʌmnəs] *s* (*pl* -ni [naɪ]) diplômé *m*, ancien étudiant *m*

alveo·lus [æl'vi·ələs] *s* (*pl* -li [,laɪ]) alvéole *m*

always ['ɔlwɪz], ['ɔlwez] *adv* toujours

A.M. ['e'em] *adv* (letterword) (*ante meridiem*) du matin

amalgam [ə'mælgəm] *s* amalgame *m*

amalgamate [ə'mælgə,met] *tr* amalgamer || *intr* s'amalgamer

amass [ə'mæs] *tr* amasser

amateur ['æmətʃər] *adj* & *s* amateur ☞

amaze [ə'mez] *tr* étonner

amazing [ə'mezɪŋ] *adj* étonnant

amazon ['æmə,zɑn], ['æməzən] *s* amazone *f*; **Amazon** Amazone *f*; (*river*) fleuve *m* des Amazones

ambassador [æm'bæsədər] *s* ambassadeur *m*

ambassadress [æm'bæsədrɪs] *s* ambassadrice *f*, ambassadeur *m*

amber ['æmbər] *adj* ambré || *s* ambre *m* jaune, ambre *m* succin

ambidextrous [,æmbɪ'dekstrəs] *adj* ambidextre

ambigui·ty [,æmbɪ'gju·ɪti] *s* (*pl* -ties) ambiguïté *f*

ambition [æm'bɪʃən] *s* ambition *f*

ambitious [æm'bɪʃəs] *adj* ambitieux

amble ['æmbəl] *s* amble *m* || *intr* (*to stroll*) déambuler; (*equit*) ambler

ambulance ['æmbjələns] *s* ambulance *f*

am'bulance corps' *s* service *m* sanitaire

am'bulance driv'er *s* ambulancier *m*

ambulatory ['æmbjələ,tori] *adj* ambulatoire

ambush ['æmbuʃ] *s* embuscade *f* || *tr* embusquer

ameliorate [ə'miljə,ret] *tr* améliorer || *intr* s'améliorer

amen ['e'men], ['ɑ'men] *s* amen *m* || *interj* ainsi soit-il!

amenable [ə'minəbəl], [ə'menəbəl] *adj* docile; amenable to (*a court*) justiciable de; (*a fine*) passible de; (*a law*) soumis à; (*persuasion*) disposé à; (*a superior*) responsable envers

amend [ə'mend] *tr* amender || *intr* s'amender

amendment [ə'mendmənt] *s* amendement *m*

amends [ə'mendz] *spl* dédommagement *m*; to make amends to dédommager

ameni·ty [ə'minɪti], [ə'menɪti] *s* (*pl* -ties) aménité *f*; amenities agréments *mpl*; civilités *fpl*

America [ə'merɪkə] *s* Amérique *f*; l'Amérique

American [ə'merɪkən] *adj* américain || *s* Américain *m*

Amer'ican Eng'lish *s* anglais *m* d'Amérique, américain *m*

Amer'ican In'dian *s* amérindien *m*

Americanism [ə'merɪkə,nɪzəm] *s* (*word*) américanisme *m*; patriotisme *m* américain

Amer'ican plan' *s* pension *f* complète

Amer'ican way of life' *s* mode *m* de vie américain

amethyst ['æmɪθɪst] *s* améthyste *f*

amiable ['emɪ·əbəl] *adj* aimable

amicable ['æmɪkəbəl] *adj* amical

amid [ə'mɪd] *prep* au milieu de

amid'ships *adv* au milieu du navire

amidst [ə'mɪdst] *prep* au milieu de

amiss [ə'mɪs] *adj* détraqué; **not amiss** pas mal; **something amiss** quelque chose qui manque, quelque chose qui cloche || *adv* de travers; **to take amiss** prendre en mauvaise part

ami·ty ['æmɪti] *s* (*pl* -ties) amitié *f*

ammeter ['æm,mitər] *s* ampèremètre *m*

ammonia [ə'monɪ·ə] *s* (*gas*) ammoniac *m*; (*gas dissolved in water*) ammoniaque *f*

ammunition [,æmjə'nɪʃən] *s* munitions *fpl*

amnesia [æm'niʒɪ·ə], [æm'niʒə] *s* amnésie *f*

amnes·ty ['æmnɪsti] *s* (*pl* -ties) amnistie *f* || *v* (*pret* & *pp* -tied) *tr* amnistier

amoeba [ə'mibə] *s* amibe *f*

among [ə'mʌŋ] *prep* entre, parmi

amorous ['æmərəs] *adj* amoureux

amorphous [ə'mɔrfəs] *adj* amorphe

amortize ['æmər,taɪz] *tr* amortir

amount [ə'maunt] *s* montant *m*, quantité *f* || *intr*—to amount to s'élever à

ampere ['æmpɪr] *s* ampère *m*

amphibian [æm'fɪbɪ·ən] *adj & s* amphibie *mf*; amphibien *m*
amphibious [æm'fɪbɪ·əs] *adj* amphibie
amphitheater ['æmfɪ,θi·ətər] *s* amphithéâtre *m*
ample ['æmpəl] *adj* ample; *(speech)* satisfaisant; *(reward)* suffisant
amplifier ['æmplɪ,faɪ·ər] *s* amplificateur *m*
ampli·fy ['æmplɪ,faɪ] *v (pret & pp -fied) tr* amplifier
amplitude ['æmplɪ,t(j)ud] *s* amplitude *f*
am'plitude modula'tion *s* modulation *f* d'amplitude
amputate ['æmpjə,tet] *tr* amputer
amputee [,æmpjə'ti] *s* amputé *m*
amuck [ə'mʌk] *adv*—**to run amuck** s'emballer
amulet ['æmjəlɪt] *s* amulette *f*
amuse [ə'mjuz] *tr* amuser
amusement [ə'mjuzmənt] *s* amusement *m*
amusing [ə'mjuzɪŋ] *adj* amusant
an [æn], [ən] *art indef* (devant un son vocalique) un
anachronism [ə'nækrə,nɪzəm] *s* anachronisme *m*
analogous [ə'næləgəs] *adj* analogue
analo·gy [ə'nælədʒɪ] *s (pl -gies)* analogie *f*
analy·sis [ə'nælɪsɪs] *s (pl -ses* [,siz])* analyse *f*
analyst ['ænəlɪst] *s* analyste *mf*
analytic(al) [,ænə'lɪtɪk(əl)] *adj* analytique
analyze ['ænə,laɪz] *tr* analyser
anarchist ['ænərkɪst] *s* anarchiste *mf*
anarchy ['ænərkɪ] *s* anarchie *f*
anathema [ə'næθɪmə] *s* anathème *m*
anatomic(al) [,ænə'tɑmɪk(əl)] *adj* anatomique
anato·my [ə'nætəmɪ] *s (pl -mies)* anatomie *f*
ancestor ['ænsestər] *s* ancêtre *m*
ances·try ['ænsestrɪ] *s (pl -tries)* ancêtres *mpl*, aïeux *mpl*; *(line)* ascendance *f*
anchor ['æŋkər] *s* ancre *f*; **anchors aweigh!** ancres levées!; **to cast anchor** jeter l'ancre, mouiller l'ancre; **to weigh anchor** lever l'ancre || *tr & intr* ancrer
ancho·vy ['æntʃovi] *s (pl -vies)* anchois *m*
ancient ['enʃənt] *adj* ancien
and [ænd] *conj* et; **and/or** et/ou; **and so forth** et ainsi de suite
andiron ['ænd,aɪ·ərn] *s* chenet *m*
anecdote ['ænɪk,dot] *s* anecdote *f*
anemia [ə'nimɪ·ə] *s* anémie *f*
anesthesia [,ænɪs'θiʒə] *s* anesthésie *f*
anesthetic [,ænɪs'θetɪk] *adj & s* anesthésique *m*
anesthetist [æ'nesθɪtɪst] *s* anesthésiste *mf*
anesthetize [æ'nesθɪ,taɪz] *tr* anesthésier
aneurysm ['ænjə,rɪzəm] *s* anévrisme *m*
anew [ə'n(j)u] *adv* à (or de) nouveau
angel ['endʒəl] *s* ange *m*; *(financial backer)* (coll) bailleur *m* de fonds

angelic(al) [æn'dʒelɪk(əl)] *adj* angélique
anger ['æŋgər] *s* colère *f* || *tr* mettre en colère, fâcher
angina pectoris [æn'dʒaɪnə'pektərɪs] *s* angine *f* de poitrine
angle ['æŋgəl] *s* angle *m* || *tr* (journ) présenter sous un certain angle || *intr* pêcher à la ligne; **to angle for** essayer d'attraper; *(a compliment)* quêter
angler ['æŋglər] *s* pêcheur *m* à la ligne; *(schemer)* intrigant *m*
an·gry ['æŋgri] *adj (comp -grier; super -griest)* fâché; **angry at** fâché de; **angry with** fâché contre; **to become angry** se mettre en colère
anguish ['æŋgwɪʃ] *s* angoisse *f*
angular ['æŋgjələr] *adj* angulaire; *(features)* anguleux
animal ['ænɪməl] *adj & s* animal *m*
animate ['ænɪmɪt] *adj* animé || ['ænɪ,met] *tr* animer
an'imated cartoon' *s* dessins *mpl* animés
animation [,ænɪ'meʃən] *s* animation *f*
animosi·ty [,ænɪ'mɑsɪtɪ] *s (pl -ties)* animosité *f*
animus ['ænɪməs] *s* animosité *f*; intention *f*
anion ['æn,aɪ·ən] *s* anion *m*
anise ['ænɪs] *s* anis *m*
aniseed ['ænɪ,sid] *s* graine *f* d'anis
ankle ['æŋkəl] *s* cheville *f*
anklet ['æŋklɪt] *s* socquette *f*; bracelet *m* de cheville
annals ['ænəlz] *spl* annales *fpl*
anneal [ə'nil] *tr* recuire, détremper
annex ['æneks] *s* annexe *f* || [ə'neks] *tr* annexer, rattacher
annexation [,æneks'eʃən] *s* annexion *f*, rattachement *m*
annihilate [ə'naɪ·ɪ,let] *tr* annihiler
annihilation [ə,naɪ·ɪ'leʃən] *s* anéantissement *m*
anniversa·ry [,ænɪ'vʌrsərɪ] *adj* anniversaire || *s (pl -ries)* anniversaire *m*
annotate ['ænə,tet] *tr* annoter
announce [ə'naʊns] *tr* annoncer
announcement [ə'naʊnsmənt] *s* annonce *f*, avis *m*
announcer [ə'naʊnsər] *s* annonceur *m*; (rad) présentateur *m*, speaker *m*
annoy [ə'nɔɪ] *tr* ennuyer, tourmenter
annoyance [ə'nɔɪ·əns] *s* ennui *m*
annoying [ə'nɔɪ·ɪŋ] *adj* ennuyeux
annual ['ænju·əl] *adj* annuel || *s* annuaire *m*; plante *f* annuelle
annui·ty [ə'n(j)u·ɪtɪ] *s (pl -ties) (annual payment)* annuité *f*; *(of a retired person)* pension *f* de retraite, pension viagère
an·nul [ə'nʌl] *v (pret & pp -nulled; ger -nulling) tr* annuler; abolir
anode ['ænod] *s* anode *f*
anodyne ['ænə,daɪn] *adj & s* anodin *m*
anoint [ə'nɔɪnt] *tr* oindre
anon [ə'nɑn] *adv* tout à l'heure
anonymity [,ænə'nɪmɪtɪ] *s* anonymat *m*
anonymous [ə'nɑnɪməs] *adj* anonyme
another [ə'nʌðər] *adj & pron indef* un autre; *(an additional)* encore un; **many another** beaucoup d'autres

answer ['ænsər], ['ɑnsər] s réponse *f*; (math) solution *f* ‖ *tr* (e.g., *yes or no*) répondre; (*a question, a letter*) répondre à ‖ *intr* répondre; **to answer for** répondre de

an'swer book' s livre *m* du maître

an'swering ser'vice s (telp) service *m* des abonnés absents

ant [ænt] s fourmi *f*

antagonism [æn'tægə,nɪzəm] s antagonisme *m*

antagonize [æn'tægə,naɪz] *tr* contrarier; (*a friend*) s'aliéner

Antarctic [ænt'ɑrktɪk] *adj* & *s* Antarctique *f*

Antarctica [ænt'ɑrktɪkə] s l'Antarctique *f*

Antarc'tic O'cean s Océan *m* glacial antarctique

ante ['ænti] s mise *f* ‖ *tr* miser ‖ *intr* miser, caver; **ante up!** misez!

anteater ['ænt,itər] s fourmilier *m*

antecedent [,æntɪ'sidənt] *adj* & *s* antécédent *m*

antechamber ['æntɪ,tʃembər] s antichambre *f*

antelope ['æntɪ,lop] s antilope *f*

anten-na [æn'tenə] s (*pl* -nae [ni]) (ent) antenne *f* ‖ s (*pl* -nas) (rad) antenne *f*

antepenult [,æntɪ'pinʌlt] s antépénultième *f*

anterior [æn'tɪrɪ-ər] *adj* antérieur

anthem ['ænθəm] s hymne *m*; (eccl) antienne *f*, hymne *f*

ant' hill' s fourmilière *f*

antholo-gy [æn'θɑlədʒi] s (*pl* -gies) anthologie *f*

anthropoid ['ænθro,pɔɪd] *adj* & *s* anthropoïde *m*

antiaircraft [,æntɪ'er,kræft], [,ænti'er,krɑft] *adj* antiaérien, contre-avions

antibiotic [,æntɪbaɪ'ɑtɪk] *adj* & *s* antibiotique *m*

antibod-y ['æntɪ,bɑdi] s (*pl* -ies) anticorps *m*

anticipate [æn'tɪsɪ,pet] *tr* anticiper; (*to expect*) s'attendre à

anticipation [æn,tɪsɪ'peʃən] s anticipation *f*

anticlimax [,æntɪ'klaɪmæks] s chute *f* dans le trivial, désillusion *f*

antics ['æntɪks] *spl* bouffonnerie *f*

antidote ['æntɪ,dot] s antidote *m*

antifreeze [,æntɪ'friz] s antigel *m*

antiglare [,æntɪ'gler] *adj* antiaveuglant

antiknock [,æntɪ'nɑk] *adj* & *s* antidétonant *m*

an'timis'sile mis'sile [,æntɪ'mɪsəl] s missile *m* antimissile

antimony ['æntɪ,moni] s antimoine *m*

antipa-thy [æn'tɪpəθi] s (*pl* -thies) antipathie *f*

antiperspirant [,æntɪ'pʌrspərənt] s antitranspirant *m*

antiphon ['æntɪ,fɑn] s antienne *f*

antiquated ['æntɪ,kwetɪd] *adj* vieilli, démodé

antique [æn'tik] *adj* antique; ancien ‖ s (*piece of furniture*) original *m*; **antiques meubles** *mpl* d'époque

antique' deal'er s antiquaire *m*

antique' shop' s magasin *m* d'antiquités, maison *f* de meubles d'époque

antiqui-ty [æn'tɪkwɪti] s (*pl* -ties) antiquité *f*; (*oldness*) ancienneté *f*

anti-Semitic [,æntɪsɪ'mɪtɪk] *adj* antisémite, antisémitique

antiseptic [,æntɪ'septɪk] *adj* & *s* antiseptique *m*

an'titank' gun' [,æntɪ'tæŋk] s canon *m* antichar

antithe-sis [æn'tɪθɪsɪs] s (*pl* -ses [,siz]) antithèse *f*

antitoxin [,æntɪ'tɑksɪn] s antitoxine *f*

antiwar [,æntɪ'wɔr] *adj* antimilitariste

antler ['æntlər] s andouiller *m*

antonym ['æntənɪm] s antonyme *m*

anvil ['ænvɪl] s enclume *f*

anxie-ty [æŋ'zaɪ-əti] s (*pl* -ties) anxiété *f*, inquiétude *f*

anxious ['æŋk/əs] *adj* inquiet, soucieux; **to be anxious to** avoir envie de, tenir beaucoup à

any ['eni] *adj indef* quelque, du; aucun; **any day** n'importe quel jour; **any place** n'importe où; **any time** n'importe quand, à tout moment; **any way** n'importe comment, de toute façon ‖ *pron indef* quiconque; quelques-uns §81; **not . . . any** ne . . . aucun §90; ne . . . en . . . pas, e.g., **I will not give him any** je ne lui en donnerai pas ‖ *adv* un peu

an'y•bod'y *pron indef* quelqu'un §81; n'importe qui; **not . . . anybody** ne . . . personne

an'y•how' *adv* en tout cas; cependant

an'y•one' *pron indef* quelqu'un §81; n'importe qui; quiconque; **not . . . anyone** ne . . . personne, e.g., **I don't see anyone** je ne vois personne

an'y•thing' *pron indef* quelque chose; n'importe quoi; **anything at all** quoi que ce soit, si peu que ce soit; **anything but** rien de moins que; **anything else?** et avec ça?, ensuite?; **not . . . anything** ne . . . rien

an'y•way' *adv* en tout cas

an'y•where' *adv* n'importe où; **not . . . anywhere** ne . . . nulle part

aor-ta [e'ɔrtə] s (*pl* -tas or -tae [ti]) aorte *f*

apace [ə'pes] *adv* vite, rapidement

apache [ə'pɑʃ], [ə'pæʃ] s apache *m* ‖ **Apache** [ə'pætʃi] s apache *m*

apart [ə'pɑrt] *adj* séparé ‖ *adv* à part, à l'écart; **apart from** en dehors de

apartment [ə'pɑrtmənt] s appartement *m*

apart'ment house' s maison *f* de rapport, immeuble *m* d'habitation

apathetic [,æpə'θetɪk] *adj* apathique

apa•thy ['æpəθi] s (*pl* -thies) apathie *f*

ape [ep] s singe *m* ‖ *tr* singer

aperture ['æpərt/ər] s ouverture *f*; (phonet) aperture *f*

apex ['epeks] s (*pl* apexes or apices ['æpɪ,siz]) sommet *m*; (astr) apex *m*

aphid ['efɪd], ['æfɪd] s puceron *m*

aphorism ['æfə,rɪzəm] s aphorisme *m*

aphrodisiac [,æfrə'dɪzɪ,æk] *adj* & *s* aphrodisiaque *m*

apiar·y ['epɪ‚ɛrɪ] s (pl -ies) rucher m
apiece [ə'pis] adv la pièce, chacun
apish ['epɪʃ] adj simiesque; (fig) imitateur
aplomb [ə'plɑm], [ə'plɔm] s aplomb m
apocalyptic(al) [ə‚pɑkə'lɪptɪk(əl)] adj apocalyptique
Apocrypha [ə'pɑkrɪfə] s apocryphes mpl
apogee ['æpə‚dʒi] s apogée m
Apollo [ə'pɑlo] s Apollon m
apologetic [ə‚pɑlə'dʒɛtɪk] adj prêt à s'excuser, humble, penaud
apologize [ə'pɑlə‚dʒaɪz] intr faire des excuses, s'excuser
apolo·gy [ə'pɑlədʒi] s (pl -gies) excuse f; (makeshift) semblant m, prétexte m; (apologia) apologie f
A.P.O. number [‚e'pi'o‚nʌmbər] (letterword) (Army Post Office) secteur m postal
apoplectic [‚æpə'plɛktɪk] adj & s apoplectique mf
apoplexy ['æpə‚plɛksi] s apoplexie f
apostle [ə'pɑsəl] s apôtre m
Apos'tles' Creed' s symbole m des apôtres
apos'tle·ship' s apostolat m
apostrophe [ə'pɑstrəfi] s apostrophe f
apothecar·y [ə'pɑθɪ‚kɛri] s (pl -ies) apothicaire m
appall [ə'pɔl] tr épouvanter, effrayer, consterner
appalling [ə'pɔlɪŋ] adj épouvantable
appara·tus [‚æpə'retəs], [‚æpə'rætəs] s (pl -tus or -tuses) appareil m, dispositif m
appar·el [ə'pærəl] s (equipment; clothes) appareil m; (clothes) habillement m || v (pret & pp -eled or -elled) ger -eling or -elling) tr habiller, vêtir; parer
apparent [ə'pærənt], [ə'pɛrənt] adj apparent; (heir) présomptif
apparition [‚æpə'rɪʃən] s apparition f
appeal [ə'pil] s appel m, recours m; charme m, attrait m; (law) pourvoi m || tr (a case) faire appeler || intr séduire, charmer; s'adresser, recourir; (law) appeler, pourvoir en cassation
appealing [ə'pilɪŋ] adj séduisant, attrayant, sympathique
appear [ə'pɪr] intr (to come into view; to be published; to seem) paraître; (to come into view) apparaître
appearance [ə'pɪrəns] s (look) apparence f, aspect m; (act of showing up) apparition f; (in print) parution f; to all appearances selon toute vraisemblance; to make one's appearance faire acte de présence
appease [ə'piz] tr apaiser
appeasement [ə'pizmənt] s apaisement m
appeaser [ə'pizər] s conciliateur m, pacificateur m
appel'late court' [ə'pɛlɪt], [ə'pɛlet] s tribunal m d'appel; **highest appellate court** cour f de cassation
append [ə'pɛnd] tr apposer, ajouter

appendage [ə'pɛndɪdʒ] s dépendance f, accessoire m
appendecto·my [‚æpən'dɛktəmi] s (pl -mies) appendicectomie f
appendicitis [ə‚pɛndɪ'saɪtɪs] s appendicite f
appen·dix [ə'pɛndɪks] s (pl -dixes or -dices [dɪ‚siz]) appendice m
appertain [‚æpər'ten] intr se rapporter
appetite ['æpɪ‚taɪt] s appétit m
appetizer ['æpɪ‚taɪzər] s apéritif m
appetizing ['æpɪ‚taɪzɪŋ] adj appétissant
applaud [ə'plɔd] tr applaudir; (to approve) applaudir à; **to applaud s.o. for** applaudir qn de || intr applaudir
applause [ə'plɔz] s applaudissements mpl
apple ['æpəl] s pomme f; (tree) pommier m
ap'ple·jack' s calvados m
ap'ple of the eye' s prunelle f des yeux
ap'ple or'chard s pommeraie f, verger m à pommes
ap'ple pie' s tarte f aux pommes
ap'ple pol'isher s (coll) chien m couchant, flagorneur m
ap'ple-sauce' s compote f de pommes; (slang) balivernes fpl
ap'ple tree' s pommier m
ap'ple turn'over s chausson m (aux pommes)
appliance [ə'plaɪ·əns] s appareil m; application f; **appliances** accessoires mpl
applicable ['æplɪkəbəl] adj applicable
applicant ['æplɪkənt] s candidat m, postulant m
application [‚æplɪ'keʃən] s application f; (for a job) demande f, sollicitation f
applica'tion blank' s formule f
applied' arts' spl arts mpl industriels
ap·ply [ə'plaɪ] v (pret & pp -plied) tr appliquer || intr s'appliquer; **to apply for** solliciter, postuler; **to apply to s.o.** s'adresser à qn
appoint [ə'pɔɪnt] tr nommer, désigner; (obs) équiper
appointed adj désigné; (time) convenu, dit
appointment [ə'pɔɪntmənt] s (engagement) rendez-vous m; (to a position) désignation f, nomination f; **appointments** (of a room) aménagements mpl; **by appointment** sur rendez-vous
apportion [ə'pɔrʃən] tr répartir; (com) ventiler
appraisal [ə'prezəl] s appréciation f, estimation f, évaluation f; (by an appraiser) expertise f
appraise [ə'prez] tr priser, estimer, évaluer; faire l'expertise de
appraiser [ə'prezər] s priseur m, estimateur m, évaluateur m; expert m, commissaire-priseur m
appreciable [ə'priʃɪ·əbəl] adj appréciable, sensible
appreciate [ə'priʃɪ‚et] tr apprécier; (to be grateful for) reconnaître; (to be aware of) être sensible à, s'apercevoir de || intr augmenter, hausser

appreciation [ə͵priʃɪ'eʃən] s appréciation f; reconnaissance f, gratitude f; (rise in value) plus-value f

appreciative [ə'priʃɪ͵etɪv] adj reconnaissant

apprehend [͵æprɪ'hend] tr comprendre; (to seize; to fear) appréhender

apprehension [͵æprɪ'henʃən] s appréhension f

apprehensive [͵æprɪ'hensɪv] adj craintif

apprentice [ə'prentɪs] s apprenti m

appren'tice-ship' s apprentissage m

apprise [ə'praɪz] tr prévenir, informer, mettre au courant

approach [ə'protʃ] s approche f; **to make approaches** to faire des avances à || tr approcher, approcher de, s'approcher de || intr approcher, s'approcher

approachable [ə'protʃəbəl] adj abordable, accessible

approbation [͵æprə'beʃən] s approbation f

appropriate [ə'proprɪ͵ɪt] adj approprié || [ə'proprɪ͵et] tr (to take for oneself) s'approprier; (to assign) affecter

appropriation [ə͵proprɪ'eʃən] s appropriation f; (assigning) affectation f; (govt) crédit m budgétaire

approval [ə'pruvəl] s approbation f, consentement m; **on approval** à l'essai, à condition

approve [ə'pruv] tr approuver || intr être d'accord; **to approve of** approuver

approximate [ə'praksɪmɪt] adj approximatif || [ə'praksɪ͵met] tr se rapprocher de

appurtenance [ə'pʌrtɪnəns] s appartenance f; attirail m; **appurtenances** dépendances fpl

apricot ['eprɪ͵kɑt], ['æprɪ͵kɑt] s abricot m; (tree) abricotier m

April ['eprɪl] s avril m

A'pril fool' s (joke) poisson m d'avril; (victim) dupe f, dindon m

A'pril Fools'' Day' s le jour du poisson d'avril

apron ['eprən] s tablier m; (aer) aire f de manœuvre

apropos [͵æprə'po] adj opportun || adv opportunément; **apropos of** quant à, à l'égard de

apse [æps] s abside f

apt [æpt] adj apte; bien à propos; **apt to** enclin à, porté à

aptitude ['æptɪ͵t(j)ud] s aptitude f

aquacade ['ækwə͵ked] s féerie f sur l'eau, spectacle m aquatique

aqualung ['ækwə͵lʌŋ] s scaphandre m autonome

aquamarine [͵ækwəmə'rin] s aiguemarine f

aquaplane ['ækwə͵plen] s aquaplane m

aquari-um ['ækwerɪ͵əm] s (pl -ums or -a [ə]) aquarium m

aquatic [ə'kwætɪk], [ə'kwɑtɪk] adj aquatique || **aquatics** spl sports mpl nautiques

aqueduct ['ækwə͵dʌkt] s aqueduc m

aquiline ['ækwɪ͵laɪn] adj aquilin

Arab ['ærəb] adj arabe || s (horse) arabe m; (person) Arabe mf

Arabian [ə'rebɪ͵ən] adj arabe || s Arabe mf

Arabic ['ærəbɪk] adj arabique || s (language) arabe m

Ar'abic nu'meral s chiffre m arabe

arbiter ['ɑrbɪtər] s arbitre m

arbitrary ['ɑrbɪ͵treri] adj arbitraire

arbitrate ['ɑrbɪ͵tret] tr & intr arbitrer

arbitration [͵ɑrbɪ'treʃən] s arbitrage m

arbitrator ['ɑrbɪ͵tretər] s arbitre m; (law) amiable compositeur m

arbor ['ɑrbər] s berceau m, charmille f; (mach.) arbre m

arbore·tum [͵ɑrbə'ritəm] s (pl -tums or -ta [tə]) jardin m botanique d'arbres

arbutus [ɑr'bjutəs] s arbousier m

arc [ɑrk] s (elec, geom) arc m

arcade [ɑr'ked] s arcade f; galerie f

arcane [ɑr'ken] adj mystérieux

arch [ɑrtʃ] s insigne; espiègle || s (of a building, cathedral, etc.) arc m; (of bridge) arche f; (of vault) voûte f || tr voûter; (the back) arquer || intr se voûter; s'arquer

archaic [ɑr'ke·ɪk] adj archaïque

archaism ['ɑrke͵ɪzəm], ['ɑrkɪ͵ɪzəm] s archaïsme m

archangel ['ɑrk͵endʒəl] s archange m

arch'bish'op s archevêque m

arch'duke' s archiduc m

arched [ɑrtʃt] adj voûté, courbé, arqué

archeologist [͵ɑrkɪ'ɑlədʒɪst] s archéologue mf

archeology [͵ɑrkɪ'ɑlɪdʒɪ] s archéologie f

archer ['ɑrtʃər] s archer m

archery ['ɑrtʃərɪ] s tir m à l'arc

archetype ['ɑrkɪ͵taɪp] s archétype m

archipela·go [͵ɑrkɪ'peləgo] s (pl -gos or -goes) archipel m

architect ['ɑrkɪ͵tekt] s architecte m

architecture ['ɑrkɪ͵tektʃər] s architecture f

archives ['ɑrkaɪvz] spl archives fpl

arch'priest' s archiprêtre m

arch'way' s voûte f, arcade f

Arctic ['ɑrktɪk] adj & s (ocean) Arctique m; (region) Arctique f

arc' weld'ing s soudure f à l'arc

ardent ['ɑrdənt] adj ardent

ardor ['ɑrdər] s ardeur f

arduous ['ɑrdʒʊ·əs], ['ɑrdju·əs] adj ardu, difficile

area ['erɪ·ə] s aire f, surface f; territoire m; (mil) secteur m, zone f

arena [ə'rinə] s arène f

Argentina [͵ɑrdʒen'tinə] s Argentine f; l'Argentine

argue ['ɑrgju] tr (a question) discuter; (a case) plaider; (a point) soutenir; (to imply) arguer; **to argue s.o. into** + ger persuader à qn de + inf || intr discuter, argumenter; plaider

argument ['ɑrgjəmənt] s (proof; reason; theme) argument m; discussion f, argumentation f; dispute f

argumentative [͵ɑrgjə'mentətɪv] adj disposé à argumenter, raisonneur

aria ['ɑrɪ·ə], ['erɪ·ə] s aria f

arid [ˈærɪd] *adj* aride

aridity [əˈrɪdɪti] *s* aridité *f*

arise [əˈraɪz] *v* (*pret* **arose** [əˈroz]; *pp* **arisen** [əˈrɪzən]) *intr* (*to rise*) se lever; (*to originate*) provenir, prendre naissance; (*to occur*) se produire; (*to be raised, as objections*) s'élever

aristocra·cy [ˌærɪsˈtɑkrəsi] *s* (*pl* -**cies**) aristocratie *f*

aristocrat [əˈrɪstəˌkræt] *s* aristocrate *mf*

aristocratic [əˌrɪstəˈkrætɪk] *adj* aristocrate

Aristotle [ˈærɪˌstɑtəl] *s* Aristote *m*

arithmetic [əˈrɪθmətɪk] *s* arithmétique *f*

arithmetician [əˌrɪθməˈtɪʃən] *s* arithméticien *m*

ark [ɑrk] *s* arche *f*

arm [ɑrm] *s* bras *m*; (mil) arme *f*; **arm in arm** bras dessus bras dessous; **at arm's length** à bout de bras; **under my** (**your, etc.**) **arm** sous mon (ton, etc.) aisselle; **up in arms** en rébellion ouverte ‖ *tr* armer ‖ *intr* s'armer

armada [ɑrˈmɑdə], [ɑrˈmedə] *s* armada *f*, grande flotte *f*

armadil·lo [ˌɑrməˈdɪlo] *s* (*pl* -**los**) tatou *m*

armament [ˈɑrməmənt] *s* armement *m*

armature [ˈɑrməˌtʃər] *s* (elec) induit *m*

arm/band/ *s* brassard *m*

arm/chair/ *s* fauteuil *m*

Armenian [ɑrˈminɪ·ən] *adj* arménien ‖ *s* (*language*) arménien *m*; (*person*) Arménien

armful [ˈɑrmˌful] *s* brassée *f*

arm/hole/ *s* emmanchure *f*, entournure *f*

armistice [ˈɑrmɪstɪs] *s* armistice *m*

armor [ˈɑrmər] *s* (*personal*) armure *f*; (*on ships, tanks, etc.*) cuirasse *f*, blindage *m* ‖ *tr* cuirasser, blinder ‖ *intr* se mettre à l'armure

ar/mored car/ *s* fourgon *m* blindé

ar/mor plate/ *s* plaque *f* de blindage

ar/mor-plate/ *tr* cuirasser, blinder

armor·y [ˈɑrməri] *s* (*pl* -**ies**) ateliers *mpl* d'armes, salle *f* d'armes

arm/pit/ *s* aisselle *f*

arm/rest/ *s* appui-bras *m*, accoudoir *m*

arms/ race/ *s* course *f* aux armements

ar·my [ˈɑrmi] *adj* militaire ‖ *s* (*pl* -**mies**) armée *f*

aroma [əˈromə] *s* arôme *m*

aromatic [ˌærəˈmætɪk] *adj* aromatique

around [əˈraund] *adv* autour, alentour; de tous côtés ‖ *prep* autour de; **around 1950** (coll) vers 1950

arouse [əˈrauz] *tr* éveiller; (*from sleep*) réveiller

arpeg·gio [ɑrˈpedʒo] *s* (*pl* -**gios**) arpège *m*

arraign [əˈren] *tr* accuser; (law) mettre en accusation

arrange [əˈrendʒ] *tr* arranger ‖ *intr* s'arranger

arrangement [əˈrendʒmənt] *s* arrangement *m*

array [əˈre] *s* ordre *m*; (*display*) étalage *m*; (*adornment*) parure *f*; (mil) rangée *f*, rangs *mpl* ‖ *tr* ranger, disposer; (*to adorn*) parer

arrearage [əˈrɪrɪdʒ] *s* arriéré *m*

arrears [əˈrɪrz] *spl* arriéré *m*; **in arrears** arriéré

arrest [əˈrest] *s* (*capture*) arrestation *f*; (*halt*) arrêt *m* ‖ *tr* arrêter; fixer; (*attention*) retenir

arrival [əˈraɪvəl] *s* arrivée *f*; (*of goods or ships*) arrivage *m*

arrive [əˈraɪv] *intr* arriver

arrogance [ˈærəgəns] *s* arrogance *f*

arrogant [ˈærəgənt] *adj* arrogant

arrogate [ˈærəˌget] *tr*—**to arrogate to oneself** s'arroger

arrow [ˈæro] *s* flèche *f*

ar/row·head/ *s* tête *f* de flèche; (bot) sagittaire *m*

arsenal [ˈɑrsənəl] *s* ateliers *mpl* d'armes; manufacture *f* d'armes

arsenic [ˈɑrsɪnɪk] *s* arsenic *m*

arson [ˈɑrsən] *s* incendie *m* volontaire

arsonist [ˈɑrsənɪst] *s* incendiaire *mf*

art [ɑrt] *s* art *m*

arterial [ɑrˈtɪrɪ·əl] *adj* artériel

arteriosclerotic [ɑrˌtɪrɪ·osklɪˈrɑtɪk] *adj* artérioscléreux

arter·y [ˈɑrtəri] *s* (*pl* -**ies**) artère *f*

arte/sian well/ [ɑrˈtiʒən] *s* puits *m* artésien

artful [ˈɑrtfəl] *adj* ingénieux; (*crafty*) artificieux, sournois; artificiel

arthritis [ɑrˈθraɪtɪs] *s* arthrite *f*

artichoke [ˈɑrtɪˌtʃok] *s* artichaut *m*

article [ˈɑrtɪkəl] *s* article; **article of clothing** objet *m* d'habillement

articulate [ɑrˈtɪkjəlɪt] *adj* articulé; (*expressing oneself clearly*) clair, expressif; (*speech*) intelligible; (*creature*) doué de la parole ‖ [ɑrˈtɪkjəˌlet] *tr* articuler ‖ *intr* s'articuler

artifact [ˈɑrtɪˌfækt] *s* artefact *m*

artifice [ˈɑrtɪfɪs] *s* artifice *m*

artificial [ˌɑrtɪˈfɪʃəl] *adj* artificiel

artificiali·ty [ˌɑrtɪˌfɪʃɪˈælɪti] *s* (*pl* -**ties**) manque *m* de naturel

artillery [ɑrˈtɪləri] *s* artillerie *f*

artil/lery·man [ɑrˈtɪləri] *s* (*pl* -**men**) artilleur *m*

artisan [ˈɑrtɪzən] *s* artisan *m*

artist [ˈɑrtɪst] *s* artiste *mf*

artistic [ɑrˈtɪstɪk] *adj* artistique, artiste

artistry [ˈɑrtɪstri] *s* art *m*, habileté *f*

artless [ˈɑrtlɪs] *adj* naturel; ingénu, naïf; sans art

arts/ and crafts/ *spl* arts et métiers *mpl*

Aryan [ˈerɪ·ən], [ˈɑrjən] *adj* aryen ‖ *s* (*person*) Aryen *m*

as [æz], [əz] *pron rel* que, e.g., **the same as** le même que ‖ *adv* aussi, e.g., **as ... as** aussi ... que; **as for** quant à; **as is** tel quel; **as of** (*a certain date*) en date du; **as regards** en ce qui concerne; **as soon as** aussitôt que; **as though** comme si; **as yet** jusqu'ici ‖ *prep* comme ‖ *conj* puisque; comme; que

asbestos [æsˈbestəs] *s* amiante *m*, asbeste *m*

ascend [əˈsend] *tr* (*a ladder*) monter à; (*a mountain*) gravir; (*a river*) remonter ‖ *intr* monter, s'élever

ascendancy [əˈsendənsi] *s* supériorité *f*, domination *f*

ascension [əˈsenʃən] *s* ascension *f*

Ascen/sion Day/ *s* Ascension *f*

ascent [ə'sent] s ascension f

ascertain [,æsər'ten] tr vérifier

ascertainment [,æsər'tenmənt] s constatation f

ascetic [ə'setɪk] adj ascétique || s ascète mf

asceticism [ə'setɪ,sɪzəm] s ascétisme m, ascèse f

ascorbic acid [ə'skɔrbɪk] s acide m ascorbique

ascribe [ə'skraɪb] tr attribuer, imputer

aseptic [ə'septɪk], [e'septɪk] adj aseptique

ash [æ/] s cendre f; (tree) frêne m

ashamed [ə'/emd] adj honteux; to be ashamed avoir honte

ash'can' s poubelle f

ashen ['æ/ən] adj cendré

ashore [ə'/or] adv à terre; to go ashore débarquer

ash'tray' s cendrier m

Ash' Wednes'day s le mercredi des Cendres

Asia ['eʒə], ['e/ə] s Asie f; l'Asie

A'sia Mi'nor s Asie f Mineure; l'Asie Mineure

aside [ə'saɪd] s aparté m || adv de côté, à part; (aloof, at a distance) à l'écart; aside from en dehors de, à part; to step aside s'écarter; (fig) quitter la partie

asinine ['æsɪ,naɪn] adj stupide

ask [æsk], [ɑsk] tr (a favor; one's way) demander; (a question) poser; to ask s.o. about s.th. interroger qn au sujet de q.ch.; to ask s.o. for s.th. demander q.ch. à qn; to ask s.o. to + inf demander à qn de' + inf, prier qn de + inf || intr—to ask about s'enquérir de; to ask for (a package; a porter) demander; (to inquire about) demander après; you asked for it (you're in for it) (coll) c'est bien fait pour vous

askance [ə'skæns] adv de côté; to look askance at regarder de travers

askew [ə'skju] adj & adv de travers, en biais, de biais

asleep [ə'slip] adj endormi; to fall asleep s'endormir

asp [æsp] s aspic m

asparagus [ə'spærəgəs] s asperge f; (stalks and tips used as food) des asperges

aspect ['æspekt] s aspect m

aspen ['æspən] s tremble m

aspersion [ə'spʌrʒən], [ə'spʌr/ən] s (sprinkling) aspersion f; (slander) calomnie f

asphalt ['æsfɔlt], ['æsfælt] s asphalte m

asphyxiate [æs'fɪksɪ,et] tr asphyxier

aspirate ['æspɪrɪt] adj & s (phonet) aspiré m || ['æspɪ,ret] tr aspirer

aspire [ə'spaɪr] intr—to aspire to aspirer à

aspirin ['æspɪrɪn] s aspirine f

ass [æs] s âne m

assail [ə'sel] tr assaillir

assailant [ə'selənt] s assaillant m

assassin [ə'sæsɪn] s assassin m

assassinate [ə'sæsɪ,net] tr assassiner

assassination [ə,sæsɪ'ne/ən] s assassinat m

assault [ə'sɔlt] s assaut m; (rape) viol m; (law) voie f de fait || tr assaillir

assault' and bat'tery s (law) voies fpl de fait

assay [ə'se], ['æse] s essai m; métal m titré || [ə'se] tr essayer; titrer

assayer [ə'se-ər] s essayeur m

as'say val'ue s teneur f

assemblage [ə'semblɪdʒ] s assemblage m

assemble [ə'sembəl] tr assembler || intr s'assembler, se réunir

assem•bly [ə'semblɪ] s (pl -blies) (meeting) assemblée f, réunion f; (assembling) assemblage m, montage m

assem'bly hall' s salle f de conférences; (educ) grand amphithéâtre m

assem'bly line' s chaîne f de fabrication, chaîne de montage

assem'bly room' s salle f de réunion; (mach) atelier m de montage

assent [ə'sent] s assentiment m || intr assentir

assert [ə'sʌrt] tr affirmer; (one's rights) revendiquer; to assert oneself imposer le respect, s'imposer

assertion [ə'sʌr/ən] s assertion f

assess [ə'ses] tr (damages, taxes, etc.) évaluer; (value of property) coter; (property for tax purposes) grever

assessment [ə'sesmənt] s évaluation f; cote f; charge f, taxe f

assessor [ə'sesər] s répartiteur m d'impôts

asset ['æset] s avantage m; possession f; assets biens mpl, avoirs mpl, actif m

assiduous [ə'sɪdʒʊ-əs], [ə'sɪdju-əs] adj assidu

assign [ə'saɪn] tr assigner; (mil) affecter

assignation [,æsɪg'ne/ən] s assignation f; rendez-vous m illicite

assignment [ə'saɪnmənt] s attribution f; (schoolwork) devoirs mpl; (law) assignation f, transfer m; (mil) affectation f

assimilate [ə'sɪmɪ,let] tr assimiler || intr s'assimiler

assimilation [ə,sɪmɪ'le/ən] s assimilation f

assist [ə'sɪst] tr assister, aider, secourir || intr être assistant

assistance [ə'sɪstəns] s assistance f, aide f, secours m

assistant [ə'sɪstənt] adj & s assistant m, adjoint m

assizes [ə'saɪzɪz] spl assises fpl

associate [ə'so/ɪ-ɪt], [ə'so/ɪ,et] adj associé f s associé m || [ə'so/ɪ,et] tr associer || intr s'associer

association [ə,so/ɪ'e/ən] s association f

assonance ['æsənəns] s assonance f

assort [ə'sɔrt] tr assortir || intr s'associer

assorted adj assorti

assortment [ə'sɔrtmənt] s assortiment m

assuage [ə'swedʒ] tr assouvir; soulager, apaiser

assume [ə's(j)um] tr supposer; (various

forms) affecter; (*a fact*) présumer; (*a name*) emprunter; (*duties*) assumer, se charger de

assumed *adj* supposé; (*borrowed*) d'emprunt, emprunté; (*feigned*) feint

assumed′ name′ *s* nom *m* d'emprunt, nom de guerre

assuming [ə'ʃ(j)umɪŋ] *adj* prétentieux

assumption [ə'sʌmpʃən] *s* présomption *f*, hypothèse *f*; (*of virtue*) affectation *f*; (*of power*) appropriation *f*; **Assumption** (eccl) Assomption *f*

assurance [ə'ʃʊrəns] *s* assurance *f*, confiance *f*; promesse *f*

assure [ə'ʃʊr] *tr* assurer, garantir

astatine [ˈæstəˌtin] *s* astate *m*

aster [ˈæstər] *s* aster *m*; (*China aster*) reine-marguerite *f*

asterisk [ˈæstəˌrɪsk] *s* astérisque *m*

astern [əˈstʌrn] *adv* à l'arrière

asthma [ˈæzmə], [ˈæsmə] *s* asthme *m*

astonish [əˈstɑnɪʃ] *tr* étonner

astonishing [əˈstɑnɪʃɪŋ] *adj* étonnant

astonishment [əˈstɑnɪʃmənt] *s* étonnement *m*

astound [əˈstaʊnd] *tr* stupéfier, ahurir, étonner

astounding [əˈstaʊndɪŋ] *adj* étonnant, abasourdissant; (*success*) foudroyant

astraddle [əˈstrædəl] *adv* à califourchon

astray [əˈstre] *adv*—to go astray s'égarer; to lead astray égarer

astride [əˈstraɪd] *adv* à califourchon || *prep* à califourchon sur

astrologer [əˈstrɑlədʒər] *s* astrologue *m*

astrology [əˈstrɑlədʒi] *s* astrologie *f*

astronaut [ˈæstrəˌnɔt] *s* astronaute *mf*

astronautics [ˌæstrəˈnɔtɪks] *s* astronautique *f*

astronomer [əˈstrɑnəmər] *s* astronome *m*

astronomic(al) [ˌæstrəˈnɑmɪk(əl)] *adj* astronomique

as′tronom′ical year′ *s* année *f* solaire, année tropique

astronomy [əˈstrɑnəmi] *s* astronomie *f*

astute [əˈst(j)ut] *adj* astucieux, fin

asunder [əˈsʌndər] *adj* séparé || *adv* en deux

asylum [əˈsaɪləm] *s* asile *m*

at [æt], [ət] *prep* à, e.g., at Paris à Paris; chez, e.g., at John's chez Jean; en, e.g., at the same time en même temps

atheism [ˈeθiˌɪzəm] *s* athéisme *m*

atheist [ˈeθi-ɪst] *s* athée *mf*

atheistic [ˌeθiˈɪstɪk] *adj* athée

Athens [ˈæθɪnz] *s* Athènes *f*

athlete [ˈæθlit] *s* athlète *m*, sportif *m*

ath′lete's foot′ *s* pied *m* d'athlète

athletic [æθˈlɛtɪk] *adj* athlétique || **athletics** *s* athlétisme *m*

athwart [əˈθwɔrt] *adv* par le travers

Atlantic [ætˈlæntɪk] *adj* & *s* Atlantique *m*

atlas [ˈætləs] *s* atlas *m*

atmosphere [ˈætməsˌfɪr] *s* atmosphère *f*

atmospheric [ˌætməsˈfɛrɪk] *adj* atmosphérique || **atmospherics** *spl* parasites *mpl* atmosphériques

atom [ˈætəm] *s* atome *m*

atomic [əˈtɑmɪk] *adj* atomique

atom′ic bomb′ *s* bombe *f* atomique

atom′ic nuc′leus *s* noyau *m* d'atome

atom′ic pile′ *s* pile *f* atomique

atom′ic struc′ture *s* édifice *m* atomique

atomize [ˈætəˌmaɪz] *tr* atomiser

atomizer [ˈætəˌmaɪzər] *s* atomiseur *m*, vaporisateur *m*

atone [əˈton] *intr*—to atone for expier

atonement [əˈtonmənt] *s* expiation *f*

atrocious [əˈtroʃəs] *adj* atroce

atrocity [əˈtrɑsɪti] *s* (*pl* -ties) atrocité *f*

atrophy [ˈætrəfi] *s* atrophie *f* || *v* (*pret* & *pp* -phied) *tr* atrophier || *intr* s'atrophier

attach [əˈtætʃ] *tr* attacher; (*property*) saisir; (*salary*) mettre opposition sur; to be attached to s'attacher à

attachment [əˈtætʃmənt] *s* attache *f*; (*of the sentiments*) attachement *m*; (law) opposition *f*, saisie-arrêt *f*

attack [əˈtæk] *s* attaque *f* || *tr* attaquer; s'attaquer à || *intr* attaquer

attacker [əˈtækər] *s* assaillant *m*

attain [əˈten] *tr* atteindre

attainment [əˈtenmənt] *s* acquisition *f*, réalisation *f*; **attainments** connaissances *fpl*

attar [ˈætər] *s* essence *f*

attempt [əˈtɛmpt] *s* tentative *f*, essai *m*; (*assault*) attentat *m* || *tr* tenter; (*s.o.'s life*) attenter à

attend [əˈtɛnd] *tr* (*a performance*) assister à; (*a sick person*) soigner; (*a person*) servir; to attend classes suivre des cours || *intr*—to attend to vaquer à, s'occuper de

attendance [əˈtɛndəns] *s* assistance *f*; présence *f*; (med) soins *mpl*

attendant [əˈtɛndənt] *adj* concomitant || *s* assistant *m*; (*to royalty*) serviteur *m*; attendants suite *f*

attention [əˈtɛnʃən] *s* attention *f*; attention: Mr. Doe à l'attention de M. Dupont; attentions égards *mpl* || *interj* attention!; (mil) garde à vous!

attentive [əˈtɛntɪv] *adj* attentif

attenuate [əˈtɛnjuˌet] *tr* amincir; (*words; bacteria*) atténuer

attest [əˈtɛst] *tr* attester || *intr*—to attest to attester

Attic [ˈætɪk] *adj* attique || (*l.c.*) *s* mansarde *f*, grenier *m*, soupente *f*

attire [əˈtaɪr] *s* vêtement *m*, parure *f* || *tr* habiller, vêtir; parer

attitude [ˈætɪˌt(j)ud] *s* attitude *f*

attorney [əˈtʌrni] *s* avoué *m*, avocat *m*

attor′ney gen′eral *s* procureur *m* général, ministre *m* de justice

attract [əˈtrækt] *tr* attirer

attraction [əˈtrækʃən] *s* attraction *f*; attrait *m*, attirance *f*

attractive [əˈtræktɪv] *adj* attirant, attrayant; (*said, e.g., of a force*) attractif

attribute [ˈætrɪˌbjut] *s* attribut *m* || [əˈtrɪbjut] *tr* attribuer

attrition [əˈtrɪʃən] *s* attrition *f*, usure *f*

attune [əˈt(j)un] *tr* accorder

auburn [ˈɔbərn] *adj* auburn, brun rougeâtre

auction ['ɔkʃən] s vente f aux enchè-res || tr vendre aux enchères

auctioneer [ˌɔkʃən'ɪr] s adjudicateur m, commissaire-priseur m || tr & intr vendre aux enchères

audacious [ɔ'deʃəs] adj audacieux

audacity [ɔ'dæsɪti] s audace f

audience ['ɔdɪəns] s (hearing; formal interview) audience f; (assembly of hearers or spectators) assistance f, salle f, auditoire m; (those who fol-low what one says or writes) public m

au'dio fre'quency ['ɔdɪˌo] s audio-fréquence f

audiometer [ˌɔdɪ'ɑmɪtər] s audiomè-tre m

audit ['ɔdɪt] s apurement m || tr apurer; to audit a class assister à la classe en auditeur libre

audition [ɔ'dɪʃən] s audition f || tr & intr auditionner

auditor ['ɔdɪtər] s (com) comptable m agréé, expert comptable m; (educ) auditeur m libre

auditorium [ˌɔdɪ'torɪəm] s auditorium m, salle f, amphithéâtre m

auditory ['ɔdɪˌtorɪ] adj auditif

auger ['ɔgər] s tarière f

aught [ɔt] s zéro m || pron indef—for aught I know autant que je sache || adv du tout

augment [ɔg'mɛnt] tr & intr augmenter

augur ['ɔgər] s augure m || tr & intr augurer; to augur well être de bon augure

augu·ry ['ɔgjəri] s (pl -ries) augure m

august [ɔ'gʌst] adj auguste || **August** ['ɔgəst] s août m

auk [ɔk] s guillemot m

aunt [ænt], [ɑnt] s tante f

aureomycin [ˌɔrɪ·o'maɪsɪn] s (pharm) auréomycine f

auricle ['ɔrɪkəl] s auricule f, oreil-lette f

aurora [ə'rɔrə] s aurore f

auscultate ['ɔskəlˌtet] tr ausculter

auspices ['ɔspɪsɪz] spl auspices mpl

auspicious [ɔs'pɪʃəs] adj propice, favorable

austere [ɔs'tɪr] adj austère

Australia [ɔ'streljə] s Australie f; l'Australie

Australian [ɔ'streljən] adj australien || s (person) Australien m

Austria ['ɔstrɪə] s Autriche f; l'Au-triche

Austrian ['ɔstrɪən] adj autrichien || s (person) Autrichien m

authentic [ɔ'θɛntɪk] adj authentique

authenticate [ɔ'θɛntɪˌket] tr authenti-fier, constater l'authenticité de

author ['ɔθər] s auteur m

authoress ['ɔθərɪs] s femme f auteur

authoritarian [ɔˌθɑrɪ'tɛrɪən], [ɔˌθɔrɪ-'tɛrɪən] adj autoritaire || s homme m autoritaire

authoritative [ɔ'θɑrɪˌtetɪv], [ɔ'θɔrɪ-ˌtetɪv] adj autorisé; (dictatorial) au-toritaire

authori·ty [ɔ'θɑrɪti], [ɔ'θɔrɪti] s (pl -ties) autorité f; on good authority de bonne part

authorize ['ɔθəˌraɪz] tr autoriser

au'thor·ship' s paternité f

au·to ['ɔto] s (pl -tos) (coll) auto f, voiture f

autobiogra·phy [ˌɔtobaɪ'ɑgrəfi], [ˌɔto-bɪ'ɑgrəfi] s (pl -phies) autobiogra-phie f

autocrat ['ɔtəˌkræt] s autocrate mf

autocratic(al) [ˌɔtə'krætɪk(əl)] adj au-tocratique

autograph ['ɔtəˌgræf], ['ɔtəˌgraf] s autographe m || tr écrire l'autogra-phe sur, dédicacer

au'tographed cop'y s exemplaire m dédicacé

au'to·intox'ica'tion s auto-intoxication f

automat ['ɔtəˌmæt] s restaurant m li-bre service

automate ['ɔtəˌmet] tr automatiser

automatic [ˌɔtə'mætɪk] adj automa-tique || s revolver m

automat'ic transmis'sion s changement m de vitesse automatique

automation [ˌɔtə'meʃən] s automatisa-tion f, automation f

automa·ton [ɔ'tɑməˌtɑn] s (pl -tons or -ta [tə]) automate m

automobile [ˌɔtəmo'bil], [ˌɔtə'mobɪl] s automobile f

automobile' show' s salon m de l'au-tomobile

automotive [ˌɔtə'motɪv] adj automo-bile; automoteur

autonomous [ɔ'tɑnəməs] adj autonome

autonomy [ɔ'tɑnəmi] s autonomie f

autop·sy ['ɔtɑpsi] s (pl -sies) autopsie f

autumn ['ɔtəm] s automne m

autumnal [ɔ'tʌmnəl] adj automnal, d'automne

auxilia·ry [ɔg'zɪljəri] adj auxiliaire || s (pl -ries) auxiliaire mf; auxiliaries (mil) troupes fpl auxiliaires

avail [ə'vel] s utilité f || tr profiter à; to avail oneself of avoir recours à, profiter de || intr être utile, servir

available [ə'veləbəl] adj disponible; (e.g., train) accessible; to make avail-able to mettre à la disposition de

avalanche ['ævəˌlæntʃ], ['ævəˌlɑntʃ] s avalanche f

avarice ['ævərɪs] s avarice f

avaricious [ˌævə'rɪʃəs] adj avaricieux

avenge [ə'vɛndʒ] tr venger

avenger [ə'vɛndʒər] s vengeur m

avenue ['ævəˌn(j)u] s avenue f

aver [ə'vʌr] v (pret & pp averred; ger averring) tr avérer, affirmer

average ['ævərɪdʒ] adj moyen || s moyenne f; on the average en moyen-ne || tr prendre la moyenne de || intr atteindre une moyenne

averse [ə'vʌrs] adj—averse to hostile à, opposé à, ennemi de

aversion [ə'vʌrʒən] s aversion f

avert [ə'vʌrt] tr détourner, écarter; empêcher, éviter

aviar·y ['evɪˌɛri] s (pl -ies) volière f

aviation [ˌevɪ'eʃən] s aviation f

aviator ['evɪˌetər] s aviateur m

avid ['ævɪd] adj avide; avid for avide de

avidity [ə'vɪdɪti] *s* avidité *f*

avoca-do [,ævo'kɑdo] *s* (*pl* -dos) avocat *m*

avocation [,ævə'keʃən] *s* occupation *f*, profession *f*; distraction *f*

avoid [ə'vɔɪd] *tr* éviter

avoidable [ə'vɔɪdəbəl] *adj* évitable

avoidance [ə'vɔɪdəns] *s* dérobade *f*

avow [ə'vau] *tr* avouer

avowal [ə'vau·əl] *s* aveu *m*

avowedly [ə'vau·ɪdli] *adv* ouvertement, franchement

await [ə'wet] *tr* attendre

awake [ə'wek] *adj* éveillé || *v* (*pret & pp* awoke [ə'wok] *or* awaked) *tr* éveiller || *intr* s'éveiller

awaken [ə'wekən] *tr* éveiller, réveiller || *intr* se réveiller

awakening [ə'wekənɪŋ] *s* réveil *m*; (*disillusionment*) désabusement *m*

award [ə'wɔrd] *s* prix *m*; (*law*) dommages et intérêts *mpl* || *tr* décerner; accorder

aware [ə'wer] *adj* conscient; **to become aware of** se rendre compte de

awareness [ə'wernɪs] *s* conscience *f*

away [ə'we] *adj* absent || *adv* au loin, loin; **away from** éloigné de, loin de; **to do away with** abolir; **to get away** s'absenter; (*to escape*) échapper; **to go away** s'en aller; **to make away with** (*to steal*) dérober; **to run away** se sauver; **to send away** renvoyer; **to take away** enlever || *interj* hors d'ici!; **away with!** à bas!

awe [ɔ] *s* crainte *f* révérentielle || *tr* inspirer de la crainte à

awesome ['mɔsəm] *adj* impressionnant

awful ['ɔfəl] *adj* terrible; (*coll*) terrible, affreux

awfully ['ɔfəli] *adv* terriblement; (*coll*) joliment, rudement

awhile [ə'hwaɪl] *adv* quelque temps, un peu, un moment

awkward ['ɔkwərd] *adj* gauche, maladroit; (*moment*) embarrassant

awl [ɔl] *s* alène *f*

awning ['ɔnɪŋ] *s* tente *f*; (*in front of store*) banne *f*

A.W.O.L. ['e'dʌbəl,ju'o'ɛl] (letter-word ['ewɔl] (acronym) *s* (**absent without leave**) absence *f* illégale; **to be A.W.O.L.** être absent sans permission

awry [ə'raɪ] *adv* de travers

ax [æks] *s* hache *f*

axiom ['æksɪ·əm] *s* axiome *m*

axiomatic [,æksɪ·ə'mætɪk] *adj* axiomatique

axis ['æksɪs] *s* (*pl* axes ['æksiz]) axe *m*

axle ['æksəl] *s* essieu *m*

ax'le grease' *s* cambouis *m*

ay *or* **aye** [aɪ] *s* oui *m*; **aye aye, sir!** oui, commandant!, bien, capitaine!; **the ayes have it** les oui l'emportent [e] *adv* toujours

azalea [ə'zeljə] *s* azalée *f*

azimuth ['æzɪməθ] *s* azimut *m*

Azores [ə'zorz], ['ezorz] *spl* Açores *fpl*

Aztecs ['æztɛks] *spl* Aztèques *mpl*

azure ['æʒər], ['eʒər] *adj* azuré, d'azur || *s* azur *m* || *tr* azurer

---

B

A, b [bi] *s* IIe lettre de l'alphabet

babble ['bæbəl] *s* babil *m* || *tr* (*secrets*) dire à tort et à travers || *intr* babiller; (*said of birds*) jaser; (*said of brook*) murmurer

babbling ['bæblɪŋ] *adj* (*gossiper*) babillard; (*brook*) murmurant || *s* babillage *m*

babe [beb] *s* bébé *m*, bambin *m*; (*naive person*) (coll) enfant *mf*; (*pretty girl*) (coll) pépée *f*, môme *f*

babel ['bebəl] *s* brouhaha *m*, vacarme *m*

baboon [bæ'bun] *s* babouin *m*

ba-by ['bebi] *s* (*pl* -bies) bébé *m*; (*youngest child*) cadet *m*, benjamin *m*; **baby!** (*honey!*) (coll) ma choute! || *v* (*pret & pp* -bied) *tr* traiter en bébé, dorloter; (*e.g., a machine*) traiter avec soin

ba'by car'riage *s* voiture *f* d'enfant, poussette *f*; (*with hood*) landau *m*

ba'by grand' *s* piano *m* demi-queue

ba'by-sit'ter *s* gardienne *f* d'enfants, garde-bébé *mf*

ba'by talk' *s* babil *m* enfantin

ba'by teeth' *spl* dents *fpl* de lait

baccalaureate [,bækə'lɔrɪ·ɪt] *s* baccalauréat *m*

bacchanal ['bækənəl] *adj* bachique || *s* bacchanale *f*; (*person*) noceur *m*

bachelor ['bætʃələr] *s* célibataire *m*; (*graduate*) bachelier *m*

bach'elor apart'ment *s* garçonnière *f*

bach'elor girl' *s* garçonne *f*

bach'elor-hood' *s* célibat *m*

bach'elor's-but'ton *s* (bot) bluet *m*, barbeau *m*

bach'elor's degree' *s* baccalauréat *m*

bacil-lus [bə'sɪləs] *s* (*pl* -li [laɪ]) bacille *m*

back [bæk] *adj* postérieur || *s* dos *m*; (*of house; of head or body*) derrière *m*; (*of house; of car*) arrière *m*; (*of room*) fond *m*; (*of fabric*) envers *m*; (*of seat*) dossier *m*; (*of medal; of hand*) revers *m*; (*of page*) verso *m*; (sports) arrière; **back to back** dos à dos; **with one's back to the wall** poussé au pied du mur, aux abois || *adv* en arrière, à l'arrière; **as far back as** déjà en, dès; **back and forth**

de long en large; **back of** derrière; **back to front** sens devant derrière; **in back** par derrière; **some weeks back** il y a quelques semaines; **to be back** être de retour; **to come back** revenir; **to go back** retourner; **to go back home** rentrer; **to go back on** (coll) abandonner; **to go back to** (*to hark back to*) remonter à; **to make one's way back** s'en retourner ‖ *tr* faire faire marche arrière à; (*e.g., a car*) faire reculer; (*to support*) appuyer, soutenir; (*to reinforce*) renforcer; (*e.g., a racehorse*) parier pour; **to back s.o. up** soutenir qn; **to back water** nager à culer ‖ *intr* reculer; faire marche arrière; **to back down** (fig) se rétracter, se retirer; **to back out of** (*e.g., an agreement*) se dédire de, se soustraire à; **to back up** reculer

back'ache' *s* mal *m* de dos

back'bite' *v* (pret -**bit**; pp -**bitten** or **bit**) *tr* médire de ‖ *intr* médire

back'bit'er *s* médisant *m*

back'bone' *s* colonne *f* vertébrale, épine *f* dorsale, échine *f*; (*of a fish*) grande arête *f*; (*of an enterprise*) colonne *f*, appui *m*; (fig) caractère *m*, cran *m*; **to have no backbone** (fig) avoir l'échine souple

back'break'ing *adj* éreintant, dur

back'door' *adj* (fig) secret, clandestin

back' door' *s* porte *f* de derrière; (fig) petite porte

back'down' *s* (coll) palinodie *f*

back'drop' *s* toile *f* de fond

backer ['bækər] *s* (*of team, party, etc.*) supporter *m*; (com) bailleur *m* de fonds, commanditaire *m*

back'fire' *s* retour *m* de flamme, pétarade *f*; (*for firefighting*) contre-feu *m*; (mach) contre-allumage *m* ‖ *intr* donner des retours de flamme; (fig) produire un résultat imprévu

backgammon [bæk,gæmən], [,bæk-'gæmən] *s* trictrac *m*, jacquet *m*

back'ground' *s* fond *m*; (*of person*) origines *fpl*, éducation *f*; (*music, sound effects, etc.*) fond sonore

back'hand' *s* (tennis) revers *m*

back'hand'ed *adj* de revers; (*compliment*) à rebours, équivoque

backing ['bækɪŋ] *s* (support) appui *m*, soutien *m*; (reinforcement) renforcement *m*; (backing up) recul *m*

back' in'terest *s* arrérage *m*; arrérages *mpl*

back'lash' *s* contrecoup *m*

back'light'ing *s* contre-jour *m*

back'log' *s* arriéré *m*, accumulation *f*

back' num'ber *s* (*of newspaper, magazine*) vieux numéro *m*; (coll) vieux jeu *m*

back' pay' *s* salaire *m* arriéré; (mil) arriéré *m* de solde

back' pay'ment *s* arriéré *m*

back' scratch'er *s* gratte-dos *m*; (slang) lèche-bottes *m*

back' seat' *s* banquette *f* arrière; **to take a back seat** (fig) aller au second plan

back'side' *s* derrière *m*, postérieur *m*

back'slide' *intr* récidiver

back'slid'er *s* récidiviste *mf*, relaps *m*

back'space key' *s* rappel *m* de chariot

back'spac'er *s* rappel *m* de chariot

back'spin' *s* (*of ball*) coup *m* en bas, effet *m*

back'stage' *adv* dans les coulisses

back'stairs' *adj* caché, indirect

back' stairs' *spl* escalier *m* de service

back'stitch' *s* point *m* arrière

back'stop' *s* (baseball) attrapeur *m* ‖ *v* (pret & pp -**stopped**; ger -**stopping**) *tr* (coll) soutenir

back'stroke' *s* (*of piston*) course *f* de retour; (swimming) brasse *f* sur le dos

back'swept wing' *s* aile *f* en flèche

back' talk' *s* réplique *f* impertinente

back' tax'es *spl* impôts *mpl* arriérés

back'track' *intr* rebrousser chemin

back'up' *s* appui *m*, soutien *m*

back'up light' *s* phare *m* de recul

backward ['bækwərd] *adj* (*in direction*) en arrière, rétrograde; (*in time*) en retard; (*in development*) arriéré, attardé ‖ *adv* en arrière; (*opposite to the normal*) à rebours; (*walking*) à reculons; (*flowing*) à contre-courant; (*stroking of the hair*) à contre-poil; **backward and forward** de long en large; **to go backward and forward** aller et venir

back'ward-and-for'ward mo'tion *s* va-et-vient *m*

backwardness ['bækwərdnɪs] *s* retard *m*, lenteur *f*

backwards ['bækwərdz] *adv* var of **backward**

back'wash' *s* remous *m*

back'wa'ter *s* (*of river*) bras *m* mort; (*e.g., of water wheel*) remous *m*; (fig) endroit *m* isolé, trou *m*

back' wheel' *s* roue *f* arrière

back'woods' *spl* forêts *fpl* de l'intérieur; bled *m*, brousse *f*

back'woods'man *s* (pl -**men**) défricheur *m* de forêts, coureur *m* des bois

back'yard' *s* derrière *m* (de la maison)

bacon ['bekən] *s* lard *m*, bacon *m*; (slang) butin *m*; **to bring home the bacon** (coll) remporter la timbale

bacteria [bæk'tɪrɪ-ə] *spl* bactéries *fpl*

bacteriology [bæk,tɪrɪ'alədʒɪ] *s* bactériologie *f*

bacteri-um [bæk'tɪrɪ-əm] *s* (pl -**a** [ə]) bactérie *f*

bad [bæd] *adj* mauvais §91; (*wicked*) méchant; (*serious*) grave; **from bad to worse** de mal en pis; **too bad!** c'est dommage!

bad' breath' *s* haleine *f* forte

bad' com'pany *s* mauvaises fréquentations *fpl*

bad' debt' *s* mauvaise créance *f*

bad' egg' *s* (slang) mauvais sujet *m*

bad' exam'ple *s* exemple *m* pernicieux

badge [bædʒ] *s* insigne *m*, plaque *f*

badger ['bædʒər] *s* blaireau *m* ‖ *tr* harceler, ennuyer

bad' lot' *s* voyous *mpl*, racaille *f*

badly ['bædli] *adv* mal §91; *(seriously)* gravement; **to want badly** avoir grande envie de

bad'man' *s (pl -men')* bandit *m*

badness ['bædnɪs] *s* mauvaise qualité *f*; *(of character)* méchanceté *f*

bad'-tem'pered *adj* susceptible, méchant; *(e.g., horse)* vicieux, rétif

baffle ['bæfəl] *s* déflecteur *m*, chicane *f* || *tr* déconcerter, confondre

baffling ['bæflɪŋ] *adj* déconcertant

bag [bæg] *s* sac *m*; *(suitcase)* valise *f*; *(of game)* chasse *f* || *v (pret & pp* **bagged**; *ger* **bagging**) *tr* ensacher, mettre en sac; *(game)* abattre, tuer || *intr (said of clothing)* faire poche

bagful ['bæg,ful] *s* sachée *f*

baggage ['bægɪdʒ] *s* bagage *m*, bagages

bag'gage car' *s (rr)* fourgon *m* à bagages

bag'gage check' *s* bulletin *m* de bagages

bag'gage room' *s* bureau *m* de gare expéditeur; *(checkroom)* consigne *f*

bag'gage truck' *s* chariot *m* à bagages; *(hand truck)* diable *m*

bag·gy ['bægi] *adj (comp* **-gier;** *super* **-giest)** bouffant

bag' of tricks' *s* sac *m* à malice

bag'pipe' *s* cornemuse *f*

bail [bel] *s* caution *f*; **to be out on bail** être libre sous caution; **to put up bail** se porter caution || *tr* cautionner; **to bail out** se porter caution pour; *(a boat)* écoper || *intr*—**to bail out** *(aer)* sauter en parachute

bailiff ['belɪf] *s (of a court)* huissier *m*, bailli *m*; *(on a farm)* régisseur *m*

bailiwick ['belɪwɪk] *s* bailliage *m*, rayon *m*; *(fig)* domaine *m*

bait [bet] *s* appât *m*, amorce *f* || *tr* appâter, amorcer; *(to harass)* harceler

bake [bek] *tr* faire cuire au four; **to bake bread** boulanger, faire le pain || *intr* cuire au four

baked' pota'toes *spl* pommes *fpl* de terre au four

bakelite ['bekə,laɪt] *s* bakélite *f*

baker ['bekər] *s* boulanger *m*

bak'er's doz'en *s* treize *m* à la douzaine

baker·y ['bekəri] *s (pl* **-ies)** boulangerie *f*

baking ['bekɪŋ] *s* cuisson *f* au four

bak'ing pow'der *s* levure *f* anglaise

bak'ing so'da *s* bicarbonate *m* de soude

balance ['bæləns] *s* balance *f*, équilibre *m*; *(scales)* balance *f*; *(what is left)* reste *m*; *(com)* solde *m*, report *m* || *tr* balancer; *(an account)* solder || *intr* se balancer; se solder

bal'ance of pay'ments *s* balance *f* des comptes

bal'ance of pow'er *s* équilibre *m* politique

bal'ance of trade' *s* balance du commerce

bal'ance sheet' *s* bilan *m*

bal'ance wheel' *s* balancier *m*

balancing ['bælənsɪŋ] *s* balancement

m; équilibrage *m*; ajustement *m*; *(com)* règlement *m* des comptes

balco·ny ['bælkəni] *s (pl* **-nies)** balcon *m*; *(in a theater)* galerie *f*

bald [bɔld] *adj* chauve; *(fact, statement, etc.)* simple, net, carré

balderdash ['bɔldər,dæʃ] *s* galimatias *m*, fatras *m*

baldness ['bɔldnɪs] *s* calvitie *f*

bale [bel] *s* balle *f* || *tr* emballer

Balear'ic Is'lands [,bælɪ'ærɪk] *spl* Baléares *fpl*

baleful ['belfəl] *adj* funeste, fatal; triste

balk [bɔk] *s* déception *f*, contretemps *m*; *(beam)* poutre *f*; *(agr)* billon *m* || *tr* frustrer || *intr* regimber

Balkan ['bɔlkən] *adj* balkanique

balk·y ['bɔki] *adj (comp* **-ier;** *super* **-iest)** regimbé, rétif

ball [bɔl] *s* balle *f*; *(in billiards; in bearings)* bille *f*; *(spherical body)* boule *f*; *(dance)* bal *m*; *(sports)* ballon *m*; **to be on the ball** (slang) être toujours là pour le coup; **to have s.th. on the ball** (slang) avoir q.ch. dans le ventre; **to play ball** jouer au ballon; (slang) coopérer; **(to be in cahoots)** (slang) être en tandem || *tr*—**to ball up** (slang) bousiller, embrouiller

ballad ['bæləd] *s (song)* romance *f*, complainte *f*; *(poem)* ballade *f*

ball' and chain' *s* boulet *m*; (slang) femme *f*, épouse *f*

ball'-and-sock'et joint' *s* joint *m* à rotule

ballast ['bæləst] *s (aer, naut)* lest *m*; *(rr)* ballast *m* || *tr* lester; ballaster

ball' bear'ing *s* bille *f*, roulement *m* à billes

ball' cock' *s* robinet *m* à flotteur

ballerina [,bælə'rinə] *s* ballerine *f*

ballet ['bæle] *s* ballet *m*

ballistic [bə'lɪstɪk] *adj* balistique || **ballistics** *s* balistique *f*

ballis'tic mis'sile *s* engin *m* balistique

balloon [bə'lun] *s* ballon *m* || *tr* ballonner || *intr* ballonner, se ballonner

ballot ['bælət] *s* scrutin *m*; *(individual ballot)* bulletin *m* || *intr* scrutiner, voter

bal'lot box' *s* urne *f*; **to stuff the ballot boxes** bourrer les urnes

balloting ['bælətɪŋ] *s* scrutin *m*

ball'-point pen' *s* stylo *m* à bille

ball'room' *s* salon *m* de bal, salle *f* de danse

ballyhoo ['bælɪ,hu] *s* publicité *f* tapageuse || *tr* faire de la réclame pour

balm [bam] *s* baume *m* || *tr* parfumer

balm·y ['bami] *adj (comp* **-ier;** *super* **-iest)** embaumé; (slang) toqué

baloney [bə'loni] *s (culin)* mortadelle *fpl*; (slang) fadaises *fpl*

balsam ['bɔlsəm] *s* baume *m*

bal'sam fir' *s* sapin *m* baumier

bal'sam pop'lar *s* peuplier *m* baumier

Balt [bɔlt] *s* Balte *mf*

Bal'timore o'riole [,bɔltɪ,mor] *s* loriot *m* de Baltimore

baluster ['bæləstər] *s* balustre *m*

balustrade [ˌbæləsˈtred] s balustrade f, rampe f

bamboo [bæmˈbu] s bambou m

bamboozle [bæmˈbuzəl] tr (slang) mystifier

ban [bæn] s ban m, interdiction f; **bans** bans mpl ‖ v (pret & pp **banned**; ger **banning**) tr mettre au ban

banal [ˈbenəl], [bəˈnæl] adj banal

banali·ty [bəˈnæliti] s (pl -ties) banalité f

banana [bəˈnænə] s banane f

banan′a tree′ s bananier m

band [bænd] s bande f, lien m; musique f, fanfare f; (dance band) orchestre m; (strip of color) raie f; **to beat the band** (slang) sans pareille; (hastily) vivement ‖ tr entourer de bandes; (a bird) marquer de bandes ‖ intr—**to band together** se grouper

bandage [ˈbændɪdʒ] s (dressing) pansement m; (holding the dressing in place) bandage m ‖ tr panser; bander

band′box′ s carton m de modiste

bandit [ˈbændɪt] s bandit m

band′mas′ter s chef m de musique

band′ saw′ s scie f à ruban

band′stand′ s kiosque m

band′wag′on s char m de la victoire; **to jump on the bandwagon** suivre la majorité victorieuse

ban·dy [ˈbændi] adj tortu ‖ v (pret & pp -died) tr renvoyer, échanger; **to bandy words** se renvoyer des paroles ‖ intr se disputer

ban′dy-leg′ged adj bancal

bane [ben] s poison m; ruine f

baneful [ˈbenfəl] adj funeste, nuisible

bang [bæŋ] s coup m; (of a door) claquement m; (of fireworks; of a gun) détonation f; **bangs** frange f; **to go off with a bang** détoner; (slang) réussir ‖ tr frapper; (a door) faire claquer; **to bang down** (e.g., a lid) abattre violemment; **to bang up** (slang) rosser, cogner ‖ intr claquer avec fracas; **to bang against** cogner; **to bang on** frapper à ‖ interj pan!; pom!

bang′-up′ adj (slang) de premier ordre, à la hauteur

banish [ˈbænɪʃ] tr bannir, exiler

banishment [ˈbænɪʃmənt] s bannissement m

banister [ˈbænɪstər] s balustre m; **banisters** balustrade f, rampe f

bank [bæŋk] s banque f; (of river) rive f, bord m; (shoal) banc m; (slope) talus m, terrasse f; (in a gambling game) cave f; (aer) virage m incliné; **to break the bank** faire sauter la banque ‖ tr terrasser; (money) déposer; (an airplane) incliner ‖ intr (aer) virer, virer sur l'aile, s'incliner; **to bank on** compter sur

bank′ account′ s compte m en banque

bank′book′ s carnet m de banque

banked adj incliné

banker [ˈbæŋkər] s banquier m

banking [ˈbæŋkɪŋ] adj bancaire

bank′ note′ s billet m de banque

bank′roll′ s paquet m de billets, liasse f de billets

bankrupt [ˈbæŋkrʌpt] adj & s failli m; (with guilt) banqueroutier m; **to go bankrupt** faire banqueroute ‖ tr mettre en faillite

bankrupt·cy [ˈbæŋkrʌptsi] s (pl -cies) banqueroute f

bank′ vault′ s chambre f forte

banner [ˈbænər] s bannière f

ban′ner cry′ s cri m de guerre

ban′ner year′ s année f record

banquet [ˈbæŋkwɪt] s banquet m ‖ intr banqueter

bantam [ˈbæntəm] adj nain ‖ s poulet m nain, poulet de Bantam

ban′tam-weight′ s poids m bantam

banter [ˈbæntər] s badinage m ‖ tr & intr badiner

bantering [ˈbæntərɪŋ] adj railleur, goguenard

baptism [ˈbæptɪzəm] s baptême m

baptismal [bæpˈtɪzməl] adj baptismal

baptis′mal certif′icate s extrait m baptême, bulletin m de naissance

baptis′mal font′ s fonts mpl baptismaux

Baptist [ˈbæptɪst] s baptiste mf

baptister·y [ˈbæptɪstəri] s (pl -ies) baptistère m

baptize [bæpˈtaɪz], [ˈbæptaɪz] tr baptiser

bar [bar] s barre f, barreau m; (obstacle) barrière f, empêchement m; (barroom; counter) bar m; (profession of law) barreau; (of public opinion) tribunal m; (of chocolate) tablette f; (mus) mesure f; (phys) bar; **behind bars** sous les barreaux ‖ prep —**bar none** sans exception ‖ v (pret & pp **barred**; ger **barring**) tr barrer

barb [barb] s barbillon m; dent f d'une flèche; (in metalwork) barbe f ‖ tr garnir de barbillons

Barbados [barˈbedoz] s la Barbade

barbarian [barˈberiən] adj & s barbare mf

barbaric [barˈbærɪk] adj barbare

barbarism [ˈbarbəˌrɪzəm] s barbarie f; (in speech or writing) barbarisme m

barbari·ty [barˈbæriti] s (pl -ties) barbarie f

barbarous [ˈbarbərəs] adj barbare

barbecue [ˈbarbɪˌkju] s grillade f en plein air ‖ tr griller à la sauce piquante

bar′becue pit′ s rôtisserie f en plein air

barbed adj barbelé, pointu

barbed′ wire′ s fil m de fer barbelé

barbed′-wire entan′glement s réseau m de barbelés

barber [ˈbarbər] s coiffeur m; (who shaves) barbier m

bar′ber pole′ s enseigne f de barbier

bar′ber-shop′ s salon m de coiffure

bar′ber-shop quartet′ s ensemble m harmonique de chanteurs amateurs

barbiturate [barˈbɪtʃəˌret], [ˌbarbɪˈtʃuret] adj & s barbiturique m

bard [bard] s barde m

bare [ber] adj nu; découvert; simple ‖ tr mettre à nu

bare'back' adv à nu
bare'faced' adj éhonté, effronté, sans déguisement
bare'foot' adj nu-pieds
bare'head'ed adj nu-tête
bare'leg'ged adj nu-jambes
barely ['berli] adv à peine
bareness ['bernis] s nudité f, dénuement m; (of style) pauvreté f
bar'fly' s (pl -flies) (slang) pilier m de cabaret
bargain ['bargin] s (deal) marché m, affaire f; (cheap purchase) solde m, occasion f; into the bargain par-dessus le marché || tr—to bargain away vendre à perte || intr entrer en négociations; she gave him more than he bargained for (fig) elle lui a donné du fil à retordre; to bargain over marchander; to bargain with traiter avec
bar'gain count'er s rayon m des soldes
bar'gain sale' s vente f de soldes
barge [bardʒ] s barge f, chaland m, péniche f || intr—to barge into entrer sans façons
baritone ['bærɪ,ton] adj de baryton || s baryton m
barium ['berɪ-əm] s baryum m
bark [bark] s (of tree) écorce f; (of dog) aboiement m; (boat) trois-mâts m; his bark is worse than his bite il fait plus de bruit que de mal || tr—to bark out dire d'un ton sec || intr aboyer; to bark up the wrong tree suivre une mauvaise piste
bar'keep'er s barman m
barker ['barkər] (coll) s bonimenteur m, barnum m
barley ['barli] s orge f
bar'maid' s fille f de comptoir, demoiselle f de comptoir, serveuse f
barn [barn] s (for grain) grange f; (for horses) écurie f; (for livestock) étable f
barnacle ['barnəkəl] s (on a ship) anatife m, patelle f; (goose) bernacle f
barn'owl' s (Tyto alba) effraie f
barn'storm' intr aller en tournée
barn'yard' s basse-cour f
barometer [bə'ramɪtər] s baromètre m
barometric [,bærə'metrɪk] adj barométrique
baron ['bærən] s baron m; (of steel, coal, lumber) (coll) magnat m
baroness ['bærənɪs] s baronne f
baroque [bə'rok] adj & s baroque m
bar'rack-room' adj (humor; manners) soldatesque, de caserne || s chambrée f
barracks ['bærəks] spl caserne f
barrage [bə'raʒ] s barrage m
barred adj barré; (excluded) exclu
barrel ['bærəl] s tonneau m, fût m; large barrel barrique f; small barrel baril m, baricaut m, barillet m
bar'rel or'gan s orgue m de Barbarie
barren ['bærən] adj stérile; (bare) nu; (of style) aride, sec
barricade [,bærɪ'ked] s barricade f || tr barricader

barrier ['bærɪ-ər] s barrière f
bar'rier reef' s récif-barrière m
barring ['barɪŋ] prep sauf
barrister ['bærɪstər] s (Brit) avocat m
bar'room' s cabaret m, bar m, bistrot m
bar'tend'er s barman m
barter ['bartər] s échange m, troc m || tr échanger
ba'sal metab'olism ['besəl] s métabolisme m basal
basalt [bə'sɔlt], ['bæsɔlt] s basalte m
base [bes] adj bas, vil || s base f; fondement m, ligne f d'appui, principe m; (pedestal) socle m || tr baser; fonder
base'ball' s base-ball m
base'board' s moulure f de base
basement ['besmənt] s sous-sol m, cave f
base'ment win'dow s soupirail m
bash [bæʃ] tr cogner, assommer
bashful ['bæʃfəl] adj timide
basic ['besɪk] adj fondamental, de base, essentiel; (alkaline) basique
basil ['bæzəl] s basilic m
basilica [bə'sɪlɪkə] s basilique f
basin ['besɪn] s bassin m; (washbasin) cuvette f; (bowl) bol m
ba·sis ['besɪs] s (pl -ses [siz]) base f, fondement m; on the basis of sur la base de
bask [bæsk], [bask] intr se chauffer
basket ['bæskɪt], ['baskɪt] s panier m; (with a handle) corbeille f; (carried on the back) hotte f
bas'ket-ball' s basket-ball m, basket m
bas'ket lunch' s panier-repas m
bas'ket-mak'er s vannier m
bas'ket-work' s vannerie f
Basque [bæsk] adj basque || s (language) basque m; (person) Basque mf
bass [bes] adj grave, bas || s (mus) basse f || [bæs] s (ichth) bar m
bass' drum' [bes] s grosse caisse f
bassinet [,bæsɪ'net], ['bæsɪ,net] s bercelonnette f
bassoon [bə'sun] s basson m
bass' viol' ['bes'vaɪ-əl] s basse f de viole
basswood ['bæs,wud] s tilleul m
bastard ['bæstərd] adj & s bâtard m
baste [best] tr (to thrash) rosser; (to scold) éreinter; (culin) arroser; (sewing) faufiler, baguer, bâtir
bastion ['bæstʃən], ['bæstɪ-ən] s bastion m
bat [bæt] s bâton m; (for cricket) bat m; (sports) batte f; (zool) chauve-souris f; (blow) (coll) coup m; to be at bat tenir la batte; to go to bat for (coll) intervenir au profit de; to have bats in the belfry (coll) avoir une araignée dans le plafond || v (pret & pp batted; ger batting) tr battre
batch [bætʃ] s (of papers) liasse f; (coll) fournée f, lot m
bated ['betɪd] adj—with bated breath en baissant la voix, dans un souffle
bath [bæθ], [baθ] s bain m; (bathroom) salle f de bains; to take a bath prendre un bain, se baigner
bathe [beð] tr baigner || intr se baigner

bather ['beðər] s baigneur m
bath'house' s établissement m de bains; (*at the seashore*) cabine f
bath'ing suit' s costume m de bain
bath'ing trunks' s slip m de bain
bath' mat' s tapis m de bain
bath'robe' s peignoir m
bath'room' s salle f de bains
bath'room fix'tures spl appareils mpl sanitaires
bath'room scale' s pèse-personne m
bath' tow'el s serviette f de bain
bath'tub' s baignoire f
baton [bæ'tɑn], ['bætən] s baguette f, bâton m de chef d'orchestre
battalion [bə'tæljən] s bataillon m
batten ['bætən] tr—to batten down the hatches condamner les panneaux
batter ['bætər] s (culin) pâte f; (sports) batteur m || tr battre
bat'tering ram' s bélier m
batter-y ['bætəri] s (pl -ies) (elec, mil, mus) batterie f; (*primary cell*) pile f; (*secondary cell or cells*) accumulateur m, accu m
battle ['bætəl] s bataille f; to do battle livrer combat || tr & intr combattre
bat'tle-ax' s hache f d'armes; (*shrew*) (slang) harpie f, mégère f
bat'tle cruis'er s croiseur m de bataille
bat'tle cry' s cri m de guerre
bat'tle-field' s champ m de bataille
bat'tle-front' s front m de bataille
bat'tle line' s ligne f de feu
battlement ['bætəlmənt] s créneau m; battlements parapet m, rempart m
bat'tle roy'al s mêlée f générale
bat'tle-ship' s cuirassé m, navire m de guerre
bat-ty ['bæti] adj (comp -tier; super -tiest) (slang) dingo, maboul, braque
bauble ['bɔbəl] s babiole f, bagatelle f; (*of jester*) marotte f
Bavaria [bə'vɛrɪ-ə] s la Bavière
Bavarian [bə'vɛrɪ-ən] adj bavarois || s Bavarois m
bawd-y ['bɔdi] adj (comp -ier; super -iest) obscène, impudique
bawl [bɔl] tr—to bawl out (slang) engueuler || intr gueuler; (*to cry*) sangloter
bawl'ing out' s (slang) engueulade f
bay [be] adj & s baie f; at bay aux abois || intr aboyer, hurler
bay'ber'ry s (pl -ries) baie f
bay'berry tree' s laurier m
bayonet ['be-ənɪt] s baïonnette f || tr percer d'un coup de baïonnette
bayou ['baɪ-u], ['baɪ-o] s anse f
bay' rum' s eau f de toilette au laurier
bay' win'dow s fenêtre f en saillie; (slang) bedaine f, gros ventre m
bazaar [bə'zɑr] s bazar m; (*social event*) kermesse f
B.C. ['bi'si] adv (letterword) (before Christ) av. J.-C.
be [bi] v (*pres am* [æm], is [ɪz], are [ɑr]; *pret was* [wɑz] or [wʌz], were [wʌr]; pp been [bɪn]) intr être; avoir, e.g., to be five years old avoir cinq ans; e.g., to be ten feet long

avoir dix pieds de long; e.g., what is the matter with you? qu'avez-vous?; here is or here are voici; how are you? comment allez-vous?, ça va?, comment vous portez-vous?; how much is that? combien coûte cela?, c'est combien ça?; so be it ainsi soit-il; there is or there are il y a; (in directing the attention) voilà; for expressions like it is warm il fait chaud or I am cold j'ai froid, see the noun || aux (to form the passive voice) être, e.g., he is loved by everybody il est aimé de tout le monde; (progressive not expressed in French), e.g., he is eating il mange; to be to + inf devoir + inf, e.g., I am to give a speech je dois prononcer un discours
beach [bit∫] s plage f, bord m de la mer; grève f, rivage m || tr & intr échouer
beach'comb'er s batteur m de grève
beach'head' s (mil) tête f de pont
beach' umbrel'la s parasol m de plage
beacon ['bikən] s signal m, phare m || tr éclairer || intr briller
bead [bid] s perle f, grain m; (*of a gun*) guidon m; beads collier m; (*of sweat*) gouttes fpl; (eccl) chapelet m; to draw a bead on viser; to tell one's beads égrener son chapelet
beadle ['bidəl] s bedeau m, appariteur m
beagle ['bigəl] s beagle m, briquet m
beak [bik] s bec m; (*nose*) (slang) pif m; (slang) grand nez m crochu
beaker ['bikər] s coupe f, vase m à bec, verre m à expérience
beam [bim] s poutre f; (*plank*) madrier m; (*of roof*) solive f; (*of ship*) bau m, barrot m; (*of light; of hope*) rayon m; (rad) faisceau m; on the beam (slang) sur la bonne piste; to be off the beam (slang) faire fausse route || tr (*light, waves, etc.*) émettre; to beam a broadcast faire une émission || intr rayonner
bean [bin] s haricot m; fève f; (slang) caboche f; to spill the beans (coll) vendre la mèche
beaner-y ['binəri] s (pl -ies) (slang) gargote f
bean'pole' s perche f à fèves; (*person*) (slang) asperge f
bean'stalk' s tige f de fève, tige de haricot
bear [bɛr] s ours m; (*in the stock market*) baissier m || v (pret bore [bor]; pp borne [born]) tr porter; (*a child*) enfanter; (*interest on money*) rapporter; (*to put up with*) souffrir, supporter; to bear the market jouer à la baisse || intr porter; to bear down appuyer; to bear up against résister à; to bear upon avoir du rapport à; to bring to bear mettre en jeu
bearable ['bɛrəbəl] adj supportable
bear' cub' s ourson m
beard [bɪrd] s barbe f || tr braver, narguer
bearded adj barbu

beardless ['bɪrdlɪs] *adj* imberbe, sans barbe

bearer ['berər] *s* porteur *m*

bearing ['berɪŋ] *s* port *m*, maintien *m*; (mach) roulement *m*, coussinet *m*; (naut) relèvement *m*; **to get one's bearings** se retrouver; **to have a bearing on** s'appliquer à; **to take bearings** (naut) faire le point

bear' mar'ket *s* marché *m* à la baisse

bear'skin' *s* peau *f* d'ours; colback *m*

beast [bist] *s* bête *f*, animal *m*; (person) brute *f*, animal *m*

beast·ly ['bistli] *adj* (*comp* **-lier**; *super* **-liest**) brutal, bestial; (coll) abominable, détestable

beast' of bur'den *s* bête *f* de somme, bête de charge

beat [bit] *s* battement *m*; (*of policeman*) ronde *f*; (mus) mesure *f*, temps *m* || *v* (*pret* **beat**; *pp* **beat** or **beaten**) *tr* battre; (*to defeat*) vaincre, battre; **that beats me!** (slang) ça me dépasse!; **to beat back** or **down** rabattre; **to beat in** enfoncer; **to beat it** (slang) filer, décamper; **to beat s.o. hollow** (coll) battre qn à plate couture; **to beat s.o. out of money** (slang) escroquer qn; **to beat time** battre la mesure; **to beat up** (slang) rosser || *intr* battre; **to beat around the bush** (coll) tourner autour du pot

beater ['bitər] *s* batteur *m*; (culin) fouet *m*

beati·fy [bɪ'ætɪ‚faɪ] *v* (*pret* & *pp* **-fied**) *tr* béatifier

beating ['bitɪŋ] *s* battement *m*; (*blows*) bastonnade *f*, rossée *f*; (*defeat*) (coll) raclée *f*

beatitude [bɪ'ætɪ‚t(j)ud] *s* béatitude *f*

beau [bo] *s* (*pl* **beaus** or **beaux** [boz]) beau *m*, galant *m*

beautician [bju'tɪʃən] *s* coiffeur *m*, coiffeuse *f*, esthéticienne *f*

beautiful ['bjutɪfəl] *adj* beau

beautifully ['bjutɪfəli] *adv* admirablement

beauti·fy ['bjutɪ‚faɪ] *v* (*pret* & *pp* **-fied**) *tr* embellir

beau·ty ['bjuti] *s* (*pl* **-ties**) beauté *f*

beau'ty con'test *s* concours *m* de beauté

beau'ty par'lor or **beau'ty shop'** *s* salon *m* or institut *m* de beauté

beau'ty queen' *s* reine *f* de beauté

beau'ty sleep' *s* sommeil *m* avant minuit

beau'ty spot' *s* (*place*) coin *m* délicieux; (*on face*) grain *m* de beauté

beaver ['bivər] *s* castor *m*

becalm [bɪ'kɑm] *tr* calmer, apaiser; (naut) abriter

because [bɪ'kɔz] *conj* parce que; **because of** à cause de, par suite de

beck [bek] *s*—**to be at s.o.'s beck and call** obéir à qn au doigt et à l'œil

beckon ['bekən] *tr* faire signe à, appeler || *intr* appeler

be·come [bɪ'kʌm] *v* (*pret* **-came**; *pp* **-come**) *tr* convenir à, aller à, seoir à || *intr* devenir; se faire, e.g., **to become a doctor** se faire médecin; e.g., **to become known** se faire connaître;

to become accustomed s'accoutumer; **to become old** vieillir; **what has become of him?** qu'est-ce qu'il est devenu?

becoming [bɪ'kʌmɪŋ] *adj* convenable, seyant

bed [bed] *s* lit *m*; couche *f*; **to go to bed** se coucher; **to put to bed** coucher

bed' and board' *s* le vivre et le couvert

bed'bug' *s* punaise *f* (des lits)

bed'clothes' *spl* couvertures *fpl* et draps *mpl*

bedding ['bedɪŋ] *s* literie *f*

bedeck [bɪ'dek] *tr* parer, orner, chamarrer; **to bedeck oneself** s'attifer

bed'fast' *adj* cloué au lit

bed'fel'low *s* camarade *m* de lit

bedizen [bɪ'daɪzən], [bɪ'dɪzən] *tr* attifer, chamarrer

bed'jack'et *s* liseuse *f*

bedlam ['bedləm] *s* pétaudière *f*, tumulte *m*

bed'lamp' *s* lampe *f* de chevet

bed' lin'en *s* literie *f*, draps *mpl* en toile de fil

bed'pan' *s* bassin *m* (de lit)

bed'post' *s* pied *m* de lit

bedraggled [bɪ'drægəld] *adj* crotté, échevelé

bedridden ['bed‚rɪdən] *adj* alité, cloué au lit

bed'rock' *s* roche *f* de fond; tuf *m*; (fig) fondement *m*

bed'room' *s* chambre *f* à coucher

bed'room lamp' *s* lampe *f* de chevet

bed'side' *s* bord *m* du lit, chevet *m*

bed'side book' *s* livre *m* de chevet

bed'sore' *s* escarre *f*

bed'spread' *s* dessus-de-lit *m*

bed'spring' *s* sommier *m*

bed'stead' *s* bois *m* de lit

bed' tick' *s* coutil *m*

bed'time' *s* l'heure *f* du coucher

bed' warm'er *s* chauffe-lit *m*

bed'wet'ting *s* énurésie *f*

bee [bi] *s* abeille *f*; (*get-together*) réunion *f*; (*contest*) concours *m*

beech [bitʃ] *s* hêtre *m*

beech' mar'ten *s* (zool) fouine *f*

beech'nut' *s* faîne *f*

beef [bif] *s* bœuf *m* || *tr*—**beef up** (coll) renforcer || *intr* (slang) rouspéter

beef' cat'tle *s* bœufs *mpl* de boucherie

beef'steak' *s* bifteck *m*

beef' stew' *s* ragoût *m* de bœuf

bee'hive' *s* ruche *f*

bee'keep'er *s* apiculteur *m*

bee'keep'ing *s* apiculture *f*

bee'line' *s*—**to make a beeline for** aller en droite ligne à

beer [bɪr] *s* bière *f*

beer' bot'tle *s* canette *f* (de bière)

bees'wax' *s* cire *f* d'abeille

beet [bit] *s* betterave *f*

beetle ['bitəl] *s* scarabée *m*, escarbot *m*

bee'tle-browed' *adj* à sourcils épais, à sourcils fournis

be·fall [bɪ'fɔl] *v* (*pret* **-fell**; *pp* **-fallen**) *tr* arriver à || *intr* arriver

befitting [bɪ'fɪtɪŋ] *adj* convenable, seyant

before [bɪ'for] *adv* avant, auparavant || *prep* avant; (*in front of*) devant; **before** + *ger* avant de + *inf* || *conj* avant que

before'hand' *adv* d'avance, préalablement, auparavant

befriend [bɪ'frɛnd] *tr* venir en aide à

befuddle [bɪ'fʌdəl] *tr* embrouiller

beg [bɛg] *v* (*pret & pp* **begged**; *ger* **begging**) *tr* mendier; (*to entreat*) prier || *intr* mendier; (*said of dog*) faire le beau; **I beg of you** je vous en prie; **to beg for** solliciter; **to beg off** s'excuser; **to go begging** (fig) rester pour compte

be·get [bɪ'gɛt] *v* (*pret* **-got**; *pp* **-gotten** or **-got**; *ger* **-getting**) *tr* engendrer

beggar ['bɛgər] *s* mendiant *m*

beggarly ['bɛgərlɪ] *adj* chétif, misérable

be·gin [bɪ'gɪn] *v* (*pret* **-gan** ['gæn]; *pp* **-gun** ['gʌn]; *ger* **-ginning**) *tr & intr* commencer; **beginning with** à partir de; **to begin to** commencer à

beginner [bɪ'gɪnər] *s* débutant *m*, commençant *m*; (*tyro*) blanc-bec *m*, novice *m*, béjaune *m*; (mil) bleu *m*

beginning [bɪ'gɪnɪŋ] *s* commencement *m*, début *m*

begrudge [bɪ'grʌdʒ] *tr* donner à contrecœur; **to begrudge s.o. s.th.** envier q.ch. à qn

beguile [bɪ'gaɪl] *tr* charmer, tromper

behalf [bɪ'hæf], [bɪ'hɑf] *s*—**on behalf of** de la part de, au nom de

behave [bɪ'hev] *intr* se comporter, se conduire; se comporter bien

behavior [bɪ'hevjər] *s* comportement *m*, conduite *f*

behead [bɪ'hɛd] *tr* décapiter

beheading [bɪ'hɛdɪŋ] *s* décapitation *f*

behest [bɪ'hɛst] *s* ordre *m*, demande *f*

behind [bɪ'haɪnd] *s* derrière *m* || *adv* derrière, par derrière; **to be behind** être en retard; **to fall behind** traîner en arrière || *prep* derrière; en arrière de; **behind the back of** dans le dos de; **behind time** en retard

be·hold [bɪ'hold] *v* (*pret & pp* **-held** ['hɛld]) *tr* contempler || *interj* voyez!, voici!

behoove [bɪ'huv] *impers*—**it behooves him to** il lui appartient de; **it does not behoove him to** mal lui sied de

being ['bi·ɪŋ] *adj*—**for the time being** pour le moment || *s* être *m*

belabor [bɪ'lebər] *tr* rosser; (fig) trop insister sur

belated [bɪ'letɪd] *adj* attardé, tardif

belch [bɛltʃ] *s* éructation *f*; rot *m* (slang) || *tr & intr* éructer

bel·fry ['bɛlfrɪ] *s* (*pl* **-fries**) beffroi *m*, clocher *m*

Belgian ['bɛldʒən] *adj* belge || *s* Belge *mf*

Belgium ['bɛldʒəm] *s* Belgique *f*; la Belgique

be·lie [bɪ'laɪ] *v* (*pret & pp* **-lied** ['laɪd]; *ger* **-lying** ['laɪ·ɪŋ]) *tr* démentir

belief [bɪ'lif] *s* croyance *f*

believable [bɪ'livəbəl] *adj* croyable

believe [bɪ'liv] *tr & intr* croire; **to believe in** croire à or en; **to make believe** faire semblant, feindre

believer [bɪ'livər] *s* croyant *m*

belittle [bɪ'lɪtəl] *tr* rabaisser

bell [bɛl] *s* cloche *f*; (*of a clock or gong*) timbre *m*; (*small bell*) sonnette *f*, clochette *f*; (*big bell*) bourdon *m*; (*on animals*) grelot *m*, clarine *f*, sonnaille *f*; (*of a trumpet*) pavillon *m*; **bells** sonnerie *f* || *tr* attacher un grelot à

belladonna [,bɛlə'dɑnə] *s* belladone *f*

bell'-bot'tom trou'sers *spl* pantalon *m* à pattes d'éléphant

bell'boy' *s* chasseur *m*, garçon *m* d'hôtel

bell' glass' *s* globe *m* *f*, garde-poussière *m*

bell'hop' *s* chasseur *m*, garçon *m* d'hôtel

bellicose ['bɛlɪ,kos] *adj* belliqueux

belligerent [bə'lɪdʒərənt] *adj & s* belligérant *m*

bell' jar' *s* var of **bell glass**

bellow ['bɛlo] *s* mugissement *m*; **bellows** (*of camera; of fireplace*) soufflet *m*; (*of organ; of forge*) soufflerie *f* || *intr* mugir, beugler

bell'pull' *s* cordon *m* de sonnette

bell' ring'er *s* sonneur *m*; carillonneur *m*

bell'-shaped' *adj* en forme de cloche

bell' tow'er *s* clocher *m*, campanile *m*

beliwether ['bɛl,wɛðər] *s* sonnailler *m*

bel·ly ['bɛlɪ] *s* (*pl* **-lies**) ventre *m* || *v* (*pret & pp* **-lied**) *intr*—**to belly out** s'enfler

bel'ly-ache' *s* (coll) mal *m* de ventre || *intr* (slang) rouspéter

bel'ly-but'ton *s* (coll) nombril *m*

bel'ly dance' *s* (coll) danse *f* du ventre

bel'ly flop' *s* plat ventre *m* (acrobatique)

bellyful ['bɛlɪ,fʊl] *s* (slang) ventrée *f*

bel'ly-land' *intr* (aer) aterrir sur le ventre

belong [bɪ'lɔŋ], [bɪ'lɑŋ] *intr* (*to have the proper qualities*) aller bien; **to belong in** devoir être dans, e.g., **this chair belongs in that corner** cette chaise doit être dans ce coin-là; **to belong to** appartenir à; **to belong together** aller ensemble

belongings [bɪ'lɔŋɪŋz], [bɪ'lɑŋɪŋz] *spl* biens *mpl*, effets *mpl*

beloved [bɪ'lʌvɪd], [bɪ'lʌvd] *adj & s* bien-aimé *m*

below [bɪ'lo] *adv* dessous, au-dessous, en bas; (*as follows, following*) ci-dessous, ci-après || *prep* sous, au-dessous de; (*another point on the river*) en aval de

belt [bɛlt] *s* ceinture *f*; zone *f*; (*of a machine*) courroie *f*; **to tighten one's belt** se serrer la ceinture || *tr* ceindre; (slang) cogner

belt' buck'le *s* boucle *f* de ceinturon

belt' convey'or *s* tapis *m* roulant

belted *adj* à ceinture

belt'way' *s* route *f* de ceinture, boulevard *m* périphérique

bemoan [bɪˈmon] *tr* déplorer

bemuse [bɪˈmjuz] *tr* stupéfier, hébéter

bench [bentʃ] *s* banc *m*; (law) siège *m*

bench' mark' *s* repère *m*

bend [bend] *s* courbure *f*; (of road) tournant *m*; (of river) sinuosité *f*; **bends** mal *m* des caissons ‖ *v* (*pret & pp* **bent** [bent]) *tr* courber; (elbow; a person to one's will) plier; (the knee) fléchir ‖ *intr* courber; plier; **do not bend** (label) ne pas plier; **to bend down** se courber

bender [ˈbendər] *s*—**to go on a bender** (slang) faire la bombe

beneath [bɪˈniθ] *adv* dessous, au-dessous, en bas ‖ *prep* sous, au-dessous de

benediction [ˌbenɪˈdɪkʃən] *s* bénédiction *f*

benefactor [ˈbenɪˌfæktər], [ˌbenɪˈfæktər] *s* bienfaiteur *m*

beneficence [bɪˈnefɪsəns] *s* bienfaisance *f*

beneficent [bɪˈnefɪsənt] *adj* bienfaisant, avantageux; (remedy) salutaire

beneficial [ˌbenɪˈfɪʃəl] *adj* profitable, avantageux; (remedy) salutaire

beneficiar·y [ˌbenɪˈfɪʃɪˌerɪ] *s* (*pl* **-ies**) bénéficiaire *mf*, ayant droit *m*

benefit [ˈbenɪfɪt] *s* profit *m*; (theat) bénéfice *m*; **benefits** bienfaits *mpl*, avantages *mpl*; **for the benefit of** au profit de ‖ *tr* profiter (with *dat*) ‖ *intr* bénéficier

ben'efit soci'ety *s* société *f* de prévoyance

benevolent [bɪˈnevələnt] *adj* bienveillant, bienfaisant, bénévole

benign [bɪˈnaɪn] *adj* bénin

bent [bent] *adj* courbé, plié; (person's back) voûté; (determined) résolu; **bent over** (shoulders) voûté; (figure, person) courbé; **to be bent on** être acharné à ‖ *s* penchant *m*; **to have a bent for** avoir du goût pour

benzene [ˈbenzin] *s* (chem) benzène *m*

benzine [ˈbenzin] *s* benzine *f*

bequeath [bɪˈkwið], [bɪˈkwiθ] *tr* léguer

bequest [bɪˈkwest] *s* legs *m*

berate [bɪˈret] *tr* gronder

be·reave [bɪˈriv] *v* (*pret & pp* **-reaved** or **-reft** [ˈreft]) *tr* priver; (to cause sorrow to) affliger

bereavement [bɪˈrivmənt] *s* privation *f*; (sorrow) deuil *m*, affliction *f*

Berlin [bərˈlɪn] *adj* berlinois ‖ *s* Berlin *m*

Berliner [bərˈlɪnər] *s* berlinois *m*

Bermuda [bərˈmjudə] *s* les Bermudes *fpl*

ber·ry [ˈberɪ] *s* (*pl* **-ries**) baie *f*; (seed) grain *m*

berserk [bərˈsɑrk], [bərˈzɑrk] *adv* frénétiquement; **to go berserk** frapper à tort et à travers

berth [bɑrθ] *s* couchette *f*; (at a dock) emplacement *m*; (space to move about) évitage *m*; (fig) poste *m*, situation *f* ‖ *tr* (a ship) accoster

beryllium [bəˈrɪlɪəm] *s* béryllium *m*

be·seech [bɪˈsitʃ] *v* (*pret & pp* **-sought** [ˈsɔt] or **-seeched**) *tr* supplier

be·set [bɪˈset] *v* (*pret & pp* **-set**; *ger* **-setting**) *tr* assiéger, assaillir

beside [bɪˈsaɪd] *prep* à côté de, auprès de; **to be beside oneself** être hors de soi; **to be beside oneself with** (e.g., joy) être transporté de

besides [bɪˈsaɪdz] *adv* en outre, de plus; (otherwise) d'ailleurs ‖ *prep* en sus de, en plus de, outre

besiege [bɪˈsidʒ] *tr* assiéger

besmear [bɪˈsmɪr] *tr* barbouiller

besmirch [bɪˈsmɜrtʃ] *tr* souiller

best [best] *adj super* (le) meilleur §91 ‖ *s* (le) meilleur *m*; **at best** au mieux; **to do one's best** faire de son mieux; **to get the best of it** avoir le dessus; **to make the best of** s'accommoder de ‖ *adv super* (le) mieux §91 ‖ *tr* l'emporter sur

bestial [ˈbestʃəl], [ˈbestʃəl] *adj* bestial, brutal

best' man' *s* garçon *m* d'honneur

bestow [bɪˈsto] *tr* accorder, conférer

bestowal [bɪˈsto·əl] *s* don *m*, dispensation *f*

best' sell'er *s* livre *m* à succès, succès *m* de librairie

bet [bet] *s* pari *m*, gageure *f*; **make your bets!** faites vos jeux! ‖ *v* (*pret & pp* **bet** or **betted**; *ger* **betting**) *tr & intr* parier; **you bet!** (slang) je vous crois!, tu parles!

be·take [bɪˈtek] *v* (*pret* **-took**; *pp* **-taken**) *tr*—**to betake oneself** se rendre

betray [bɪˈtre] *tr* trahir

betrayal [bɪˈtre·əl] *s* trahison *f*

betrayer [bɪˈtre·ər] *s* traître *m*

betroth [bɪˈtroð], [bɪˈtrɔθ] *tr*—**to be betrothed** se fiancer

betrothal [bɪˈtroðəl], [bɪˈtrɔθəl] *s* fiançailles *fpl*

better [ˈbetər] *adj comp* meilleur §91; **better than** meilleur que ‖ *adv comp* mieux §91; **better than** mieux que; (followed by numeral) plus de; **it is better to** il vaut mieux de; **so much the better** tant mieux; **to be better** (in better health) aller mieux; **to be better to** valoir mieux; **to get better** s'améliorer; **to get the better of** l'emporter sur; **to think better** se raviser ‖ *tr* améliorer ‖ *intr* s'améliorer

bet'ter half' *s* (coll) chère moitié *f*

bet'ting odds' *spl* cote *f* (des paris)

bettor [ˈbetər] *s* parieur *m*, gageur *m*

between [bɪˈtwin] *adv* au milieu; dans l'intervalle ‖ *prep* entre; **between friends** dans l'intimité

between'-decks' *s* (naut) entrepont *m*

bev·el [ˈbevəl] *adj* biseauté, taillé en biseau ‖ *s* (instrument) équerre *f*; (sloping part) biseau *m* ‖ *v* (*pret & pp* **-eled** or **-elled**; *ger* **-eling** or **-elling**) *tr* biseauter, chanfreiner, équerrer

beverage [ˈbevərɪdʒ] *s* boisson *f*

bev·y [ˈbevɪ] *s* (*pl* **-ies**) bande *f*

bewail [bɪˈwel] *tr* lamenter, pleurer

beware [bɪˈwer] *tr* se bien garder de ‖ *intr* prendre garde; **to beware of**

prendre garde à ‖ *interj* gare!, prenez garde!

bewilder [bɪˈwɪldər] *tr* confondre, ahurir

bewilderment [bɪˈwɪldərmənt] *s* confusion *f*, ahurissement *m*

bewitch [bɪˈwɪtʃ] *tr* ensorceler

bewitching [bɪˈwɪtʃɪŋ] *adj* enchanteur

beyond [bɪˈjɑnd] *s*—**the beyond** l'au-delà *m* ‖ *adv* au-delà ‖ *prep* au-delà de; **beyond a doubt** hors de doute; **it's beyond me** (coll) je n'y comprends rien; **to go beyond** dépasser

biannual [barˈænju·əl] *adj* semi-annuel

bias [ˈbaɪ·əs] *adj* biais ‖ *s* biais *m*; (fig) prévention *f*, préjugé *m* ‖ *tr* prédisposer, prévenir, rendre partial

bib [bɪb] *s* bavette *f*

Bible [ˈbaɪbəl] *s* Bible *f*

Biblical [ˈbɪblɪkəl] *adj* biblique

bibliographer [ˌbɪblɪˈɑgrəfər] *s* bibliographe *m*

bibliography [ˌbɪblɪˈɑgrəfi] *s* (*pl* -phies) bibliographie *f*

biceps [ˈbaɪseps] *s* biceps *m*

bicker [ˈbɪkər] *intr* se quereller, se chamailler

bickering [ˈbɪkərɪŋ] *s* bisbille *f*

bicuspid [baɪˈkʌspɪd] *s* prémolaire *f*

bicycle [ˈbaɪsɪkəl] *s* bicyclette *f*, vélo *m* ‖ *intr* faire de la bicyclette, aller à bicyclette

bi′cycle path′ *s* piste *f* cyclable

bicyclist [ˈbaɪsɪklɪst] *s* cycliste *mf*

bid [bɪd] *s* enchère *f*, offre *f*, mise *f*; (*e.g.*, *to build a school*) soumission *f*; (cards) demande *f* ‖ *v* (*pret* **bade** [bæd] or **bid**; *ger* **bidden** [ˈbɪdən]) *tr* inviter; (*to order*) commander; (cards) demander; **to bid ten thousand on** mettre une enchère de dix mille sur ‖ *intr*—**to bid on** mettre une enchère sur

bidder [ˈbɪdər] *s* enchérisseur *m*, offrant *m*; (*person who submits an estimate*) soumissionnaire *m*

bidding [ˈbɪdɪŋ] *s* enchères *fpl*; **at s.o.'s bidding** aux ordres de qn

bide [baɪd] *tr*—**to bide one's time** attendre l'heure or le bon moment

biennial [baɪˈenɪ·əl] *adj* biennal

bier [bɪr] *s* (*frame or stand*) catafalque *m*; (*coffin*) cercueil *m*

biff [bɪf] *s* (slang) gnon *m*, beigne *f* ‖ *tr* (slang) gifler, cogner

bifocal [baɪˈfokəl] *adj* bifocal ‖ **bifocals** *spl* lunettes *fpl* bifocales

big [bɪg] *adj* (*comp* **bigger**; *super* **biggest**) gros, grand; (*man*) de grande taille ‖ *adv*—**to grow big** grossir, grandir; **to talk big** (slang) se vanter

bigamist [ˈbɪgəmɪst] *s* bigame *mf*

bigamous [ˈbɪgəməs] *adj* bigame

bigamy [ˈbɪgəmi] *s* bigamie *f*

big′-boned′ *adj* ossu, à gros os

big′ busi′ness *s* (pej) les grosses affaires *fpl*

Big′ Dip′per *s* Grande Ourse *f*

big′ game′ *s* fauves *mpl*, gros gibier *m*

big′-heart′ed *adj* généreux, cordial

big′mouth′ *s* (slang) gueulard *m*

bigot [ˈbɪgət] *s* bigot *m*

bigoted [ˈbɪgətɪd] *adj* bigot

bigotry [ˈbɪgətri] *s* (*pl* -ries) bigoterie *f*

big′ shot′ *s* (slang) grand manitou *m*, gros bonnet *m*

big′ splash′ *s* (slang) sensation *f* à tout casser

big′ stiff′ *s* (slang) personnage *m* guindé

big′ talk′ *s* (slang) vantardise *f*

big′-time′ op′erator *s* (slang) gros trafiquant *m*

big′ toe′ *s* orteil *m*, gros orteil

big′ top′ *s* (*circus tent*) chapiteau *m*

big′ wheel′ *s* (slang) gros bonnet *m*, grand manitou *m*, grosse légume *f*

big′wig′ *s* (coll) gros bonnet *m*, grand manitou *m*, grosse légume *f*

bike [baɪk] *s* (coll) bécane *f*, vélo *m*

bile [baɪl] *s* bile *f*

bilge [bɪldʒ] *s* sentine *f*, cale *f*

bilge′ wa′ter *s* eau *f* de cale

bilingual [baɪˈlɪŋgwəl] *adj* bilingue

bilious [ˈbɪljəs] *adj* bilieux

bilk [bɪlk] *s* tromperie *f*, escroquerie *f* ‖ *tr* tromper, escroquer

bill [bɪl] *s* (*invoice*) facture *f*, mémoire *m*; (*in a hotel*) note *f*; (*in a restaurant*) addition *f*; (*currency*) billet *m*; (*of a bird*) bec *m*; (*posted*) affiche *f*, placard *m*, écriteau *m*; (*in a legislature*) projet *m* de loi; **post no bills** (public sign) défense d'afficher; **to head the bill** (theat) avoir la vedette ‖ *tr* facturer

bill′board′ *s* tableau *m* d'affichage, panneau *m* d'affichage

billet [ˈbɪlɪt] *s* (*order*) billet *m* de logement; (*of metal or wood*) billette *f* ‖ *tr* loger, cantonner

bill′fold′ *s* portefeuille *m*

billiard ball′ *s* bille *f*

billiards [ˈbɪljərdz] *s* & *spl* billard *m*

bil′liard ta′ble *s* billard *m*

billion [ˈbɪljən] *s* (U.S.A.) milliard *m*; (Brit) billion *m*

billionaire [ˌbɪljənˈer] *s* milliardaire *mf*

bill′ of exchange′ *s* lettre *f* de change, traite *f*

bill′ of fare′ *s* carte *f* du jour

bill′ of health′ *s* patente *f* de santé

bill′ of lad′ing *s* connaissement *m*

bill′ of rights′ *s* déclaration *f* des droits de l'homme

bill′ of sale′ *s* acte *m* de vente

billow [ˈbɪlo] *s* flot *m*, grosse vague *f* ‖ *intr* ondoyer

billowy [ˈbɪlo·i] *adj* onduleux, ondoyant

bill′post′er *s* colleur *m* d'affiches, afficheur *m*

bil·ly [ˈbɪli] *s* (*pl* -lies) bâton *m*

bil′ly goat′ *s* (coll) bouc *m*

bimonthly [baɪˈmʌnθli] *adj* bimestriel

bin [bɪn] *s* huche *f*, coffre *m*

binary [ˈbaɪnəri] *adj* binaire

binaural [baɪˈnɔrəl], [bɪnˈɔrəl] *adj* stéréophonique; à deux oreilles

bind [baɪnd] *v* (*pret* & *pp* **bound** [baʊnd]) *tr* lier, attacher; (*a book*) relier; (*s.o. to an agreement*) obliger

binder ['baɪndər] s (*person*) lieur m; (*of books*) relieur m; (*agreement*) conventions fpl; (mach) lieuse f

binder·y ['baɪndəri] s (pl -ies) atelier m de reliure

binding ['baɪndɪŋ] adj obligatoire; (med) astringent; **binding on all concerned** solidaire || s reliure f

bind'ing post' s (elec) borne f

binge [bɪndʒ] s (coll) noce f, bombe f

bingo ['bɪŋgo] s loto m

binocular [bɪ'nɑkjələr] adj & s binoculaire m; **binoculars** jumelles fpl

binomial [baɪ'nomɪ·əl] adj & s binôme m

biochemistry [‚baɪ·o'kɛmɪstri] s biochimie f

biographer [baɪ'ɑgrəfər] s biographe m

biographic(al) [‚baɪ·ə'græfɪk(əl)] adj biographique

biogra·phy [baɪ'ɑgrəfi] s (pl -phies) biographie f

biologist [baɪ'ɑlədʒɪst] s biologiste mf

biology [baɪ'ɑlədʒi] s biologie f

biophysics [‚baɪ·ə'fɪzɪks] s biophysique f

biop·sy ['baɪ·ɑpsi] s (pl -sies) biopsie f

bipartisan [baɪ'pɑrtɪzən] adj bipartite

bipartite [baɪ'pɑrtaɪt] adj biparti

biped ['baɪpɛd] adj & s bipède m

biplane ['baɪ‚plen] s biplan m

birch [bɑrtʃ] s bouleau m; (*for whipping*) verges fpl || tr battre à coups de verges

birch' rod' s verges fpl

bird [bɑrd] s oiseau m; (slang) type m, individu m; **a bird in the hand is worth two in the bush** un "tiens" vaut mieux que deux "tu l'auras"; **to give s.o. the bird** (slang) envoyer qn promener; **to kill two birds with one stone** faire d'une pierre deux coups

bird' bath' s baignoire f pour oiseaux, bain m pour oiseaux

bird' cage' s cage f d'oiseau

bird' call' s appeau m, pipeau m

bird' dog' s chien m pour la plume

bird' fan'cier s oiselier

birdie ['bɑrdi] s oiselet m, oisillon m

bird' lime' s glu f

bird' of pas'sage s oiseau m de passage

bird' of prey' s oiseau m de proie

bird' seed' s alpiste m, chènevis m

bird's'-eye' s (*pattern*) œil-de-perdrix m

bird's'-eye view' s vue f à vol d'oiseau, tour m d'horizon, vue d'ensemble

biretta [bɪ'rɛtə] s barette f

birth [bɑrθ] s naissance f; **by birth** de naissance; **to give birth to** donner naissance à

birth' certif'icate s acte m de naissance, bulletin m de naissance

birth' control' s contrôle m des naissances, procréation f dirigée

birth'day' s anniversaire m; **happy birthday!** heureux anniversaire!

birth'day cake' s gâteau m d'anniversaire

birth'day pres'ent s cadeau m d'anniversaire

birth'mark' s tache f, envie f

birth'place' s lieu m de naissance

birth' rate' s natalité f, taux m de natalité

birth'right' s droit m de naissance; droit d'aînesse

biscuit ['bɪskɪt] s petit pain m, crêpe f au beurre, gâteau m feuilleté

bisect [baɪ'sɛkt] tr couper en deux, diviser en deux

bisexual [baɪ'sɛk/ʊ·əl] adj bissexuel

bishop ['bɪʃəp] s évêque m; (chess) fou m

bishopric ['bɪʃəprɪk] s évêché m

bison ['baɪsən], ['baɪzən] s bison m

bisulfate [baɪ'sʌlfet] s bisulfate m

bisulfite [baɪ'sʌlfaɪt] s bisulfite m

bit [bɪt] s morceau m, bout m, brin m; (*of a bridle*) mors m; (*of a drill*) mèche f; **bit by bit** petit à petit

bitch [bɪtʃ] s (*dog*) chienne f; (*fox*) renarde f; (*wolf*) louve f; (vulgar) vache f

bite [baɪt] s (*of food*) bouchée f; (*by an animal*) morsure f; (*by an insect*) piqûre f; (*by a fish on a hook*) touche f || v (*pret* **bit** [bɪt]; *pp* **bit** or **bitten** ['bɪtən]) tr mordre; (*said of an insect or snake*) piquer

biting ['baɪtɪŋ] adj mordant; (*cold*) piquant; (*wind*) coupant

bit' play'er s figurant m

bitter ['bɪtər] adj amer; (*cold*) âpre, noir; (*fight*) acharné; (*style*) mordant || **bitters** spl bitter m

bit'ter end' s—**to the bitter end** jusqu'au bout

bit'ter-end'er s (coll) intransigeant m, jusqu'au-boutiste mf

bitterness ['bɪtərnɪs] s amertume f; (*of winter*) âpreté f; (fig) aigreur f

bit'ter-sweet' adj aigre-doux || s douce-amère f

bitumen [bɪ't(j)umən] s bitume m

bivou·ac ['bɪvu‚æk], ['bɪvwæk] s bivouac m, cantonnement m || v (*pret & pp* -acked; *ger* -acking) intr bivouaquer

biweekly [baɪ'wikli] adj bimensuel || adv bimensuellement

biyearly [baɪ'jɪrli] adj semestriel || adv semestriellement

bizarre [bɪ'zɑr] adj bizarre

blab [blæb] v (*pret & pp* **blabbed**; *ger* **blabbing**) tr ébruiter || intr jaser

blabber ['blæbər] intr jaser

blab'ber-mouth' s (slang) jaseur m

black [blæk] adj & s noir m || tr noircir; **to black out** faire le black-out dans

black'-and-blue' adj meurtri

black'-and-white' adj en blanc et noir

black'ball' tr blackbouler

black'ber'ry s (pl -ries) mûre f, mûre de ronce

black'berry bush' s mûrier m sauvage

black'bird' s (*Turdus merula*) merle m

black'board' s tableau m noir

black'board eras'er s éponge f, chiffon m

black' cur'rant s cassis m

black' damp' s mofette f

blacken ['blækən] *tr* noircir

black' eye' *s* œil *m* poché; **to give s.o. a black eye** pocher l'œil à qn; (fig) ruiner la réputation de qn

black'-eyed Su'san ['suzən] *s* marguerite *f* américaine

blackguard ['blægɑrd] *s* vaurien *m*, salaud *m*

black'head' *s* comédon *m*, tanne *f*

black'-headed gull' *s* mouette *f* rieuse

blacking ['blækɪŋ] *s* cirage *m* noir

blackish ['blækɪʃ] *adj* noirâtre

black'jack' *s* assommoir *m*; (cards) vingt-et-un *m* ‖ *tr* assommer

black' lead' [led] *s* mine *f* de plomb

black' let'ter *s* caractère *m* gothique

black' list' *s* liste *f* noire

black'-list' *tr* mettre à l'index, mettre en quarantaine

black' lo'cust *s* (bot) faux acacia *m*

black' mag'ic *s* magie *f* noire

black'mail' *s* chantage *m* ‖ *tr* faire chanter ‖ *intr* faire du chantage

blackmailer ['blæk‚melər] *s* maître *m* chanteur

black' mark' *s* (of censure) tache *f*

black' mar'ket *s* marché *m* noir

black' marketeer' [‚mɑrkɪ'tir] *s* trafiquant *m* du marché noir

black'out' *s* black-out *m*; (of aviator) cécité *f* temporaire

black' pep'per *s* poivre *m* noir

black' sheep' *s* (fig) brebis *f* galeuse

black'smith' *s* forgeron *m*, maréchal-ferrant *m*

bladder ['blædər] *s* vessie *f*

bladderwort ['blædər‚wʌrt] *s* utriculaire *f*

blade [bled] *s* lame *f*; (of grass) brin *m*; (of propeller) aile *f*, pale *f*; (of oar) plat *m*; (young man) gaillard *m*; (mach) ailette *f*, palette *f*, aube *f*

blah [blɑ] *s* (slang) sornettes *fpl*, fadaises *fpl*, bêtises *fpl*

blah-blah ['blɑ'blɑ] *s* baratin *m*

blamable ['blemǝbǝl] *adj* blâmable, coupable

blame [blem] *s* blâme *m*; reproches *mpl* ‖ *tr* blâmer; reprocher; s'en prendre à

blameless ['blemlɪs] *adj* sans reproche

blame'wor'thy *adj* blâmable

blanch [blæntʃ], [blɑntʃ] *tr & intr* blanchir

bland [blænd] *adj* doux, suave; (with dissimulation) narquois

blandish ['blændɪʃ] *tr* flatter, cajoler

blandishment ['blændɪʃmǝnt] *s* flatterie *f*; attrait *m*, charme *m*

blank [blæŋk] *adj* blanc; (check; form) en blanc; (mind) confondu, déconcerté ‖ *s* blanc *m*; trou *m*, vide *m*, lacune *f*; (metal mold) flan *m*; (form to be filled out) fiche *f*, formule *f*, feuille *f*; (space to be filled in) tiret *m* ‖ *tr*—**to blank out** effacer ‖ *intr*—**to blank out** (coll) s'évanouir

blank' check' *s* chèque *m* en blanc; (fig) chèque en blanc

blanket ['blæŋkɪt] *adj* général ‖ *s* couverture *f* ‖ *tr* envelopper; traiter sous une rubrique générale

blank' verse' *s* vers *mpl* blancs

blare [bler] *s* bruit *m*; (of trumpet) sonnerie *f* ‖ *tr* faire retentir; (like a trumpet) sonner ‖ *intr* retentir

blarney ['blɑrni] *s* (coll) flagornerie *f* ‖ *tr* (coll) flagorner

blaspheme [blæs'fim] *tr & intr* blasphémer

blasphemous ['blæsfɪmǝs] *adj* blasphématoire, blasphémateur

blasphe·my ['blæsfɪmi] *s* (pl -mies) blasphème *m*

blast [blæst], [blɑst] *s* rafale *f*, souffle *m*; explosion *f*; (of dynamite) charge *f*; (of whistle) coup *m*; (of trumpet) sonnerie *f*; **at full blast** à toute allure ‖ *tr* (to blow up) faire sauter; (hopes) ruiner; (a plant) flétrir ‖ *intr* (said of plant) se faner; **to blast off** (said of rocket) se mettre à feu

blast' fur'nace *s* haut fourneau *m*

blasting ['blæstɪŋ], ['blɑstɪŋ] *s* abattage *m* à la poudre; (of hopes) anéantissement *m*; (coll) abattage *m*, verte semonce *f*

blast'ing cap' *s* capsule *f* fulminante

blast'off' *s* mise *f* à feu

blatant ['bletǝnt] *adj* criard; (injustice) criant

blaze [blez] *s* flamme *f*, flambée *f*; (e.g., blazing house) incendie *m*; **to run like blazes** (slang) courir furieusement ‖ *tr*—**to blaze the trail** frayer la piste ‖ *intr* flamboyer, s'embraser

blazing ['blezɪŋ] *adj* embrasé, en feu; (sun) flamboyant

blazon ['blezǝn] *s* (heral) blason *m* ‖ *tr* célébrer; exalter; (heral) blasonner; **to blazon out** proclamer

bleach [blitʃ] *s* décolorant *m*, eau *f* de Javel; (for hair) eau oxygénée ‖ *tr* blanchir, décolorer

bleachers ['blitʃǝrz] *spl* gradins *mpl*, tribune *f*

bleak [blik] *adj* froid, morne, nu

blear-eyed ['blɪr'ɑɪd] *adj* chassieux, larmoyant; (dull) d'un esprit épais

blear·y ['blɪri] *adj* (comp -ier; super -iest) (eyes) chassieux; (prospect) voilé, incertain

bleat [blit] *s* bêlement *m* ‖ *intr* bêler, bégueter

bleed [blid] *v* (pret & pp bled [bled]) *tr & intr* saigner; **to bleed white** saigner à blanc

bleeding ['blidɪŋ] *adj* saignant ‖ *s* saignement *m*; (bloodletting) saignée *f*

blemish ['blemɪʃ] *s* défaut *m*, tache *f* ‖ *tr* défigurer; (a reputation) souiller

blench [blentʃ] *intr* pâlir; (to draw back) broncher

blend [blend] *s* mélange *m* ‖ *v* (pret & pp blended or blent [blent]) *tr* mêler, mélanger; fondre, marier ‖ *intr* se fondre, se marier

bless [bles] *tr* bénir

blessed ['blesɪd] *adj* béni, saint; (happy) bienheureux

blessing ['blesɪŋ] *s* bénédiction *f*; (at meals) bénédicité *m*

blight [blaɪt] *s* rouille *f*, nielle *f*; (*of peaches*) cloque *f*; (*of potatoes; of vines*) brunissure *f*; (fig) flétrissure *f* ‖ *tr* rouiller, nieller; (*hopes, aspirations*) flétrir, frustrer

blimp [blɪmp] *s* vedette *f* (aérienne)

blind [blaɪnd] *adj* aveugle; **blind by birth** aveugle-né; **blind in one eye** borgne; **blind person** aveugle *m* ‖ *s* store *m*; (*for hunting*) guet-apens *m*; (fig) feinte *f*; (*cards*) talon *m* ‖ *tr* aveugler; (*by dazzling*) éblouir

blind′ al′ley *s* cul-de-sac *m*, impasse *f*

blinder ['blaɪndər] *s* œillère *f*

blind′ flight′ *s* vol *m* à l'aveuglette

blind′ fly′ing *s* (aer) pilotage *m* sans visibilité

blind′fold *adj* les yeux bandés ‖ *s* bandeau *m* ‖ *tr* bander les yeux de

blindly ['blaɪndli] *adv* aveuglément

blind′ man′ *s* aveugle *m*

blind′man's buff′ *s* colin-maillard *m*

blindness ['blaɪndnɪs] *s* cécité *f*; (fig) aveuglement *m*

blind′ spot′ *s* côté *m* faible

blink [blɪŋk] *s* clignotement *m* ‖ *tr* faire clignoter ‖ *intr* clignoter

blinker ['blɪŋkər] *s* feu *m* clignotant; (*for horses*) œillère *f*; (*for signals*) projecteur *m* clignotant

blink′er light′ *s* feu *m* à éclipses

blip [blɪp] *s* spot *m*

bliss [blɪs] *s* félicité *f*, béatitude *f*

blissful ['blɪsfəl] *adj* bienheureux

blister ['blɪstər] *s* ampoule *f*, bulle *f* ‖ *tr* couvrir d'ampoules; (*paint*) boursoufler ‖ *intr* se couvrir d'ampoules; se boursoufler

blithe [blaɪð], [blaɪθ] *adj* gai, joyeux

blitzkrieg ['blɪts‚krig] *s* guerre *f* éclair

blizzard ['blɪzərd] *s* tempête *f* de neige

bloat [blot] *tr* boursoufler, enfler ‖ *intr* se boursoufler, enfler

blob [blɑb] *s* motte *f*; (*of color*) tache *f*; (*of ink*) pâté *m*

block [blɑk] *s* bloc *m*; (*toy*) cube *m*; (*of shares*) tranche *f*; (*of houses*) pâté *m*, îlot *m* ‖ *tr* (*a project*) contrecarrer; (*a wall*) condamner, murer; **to block up** boucher, bloquer

blockade [blɑ'ked] *s* blocus *m*; **to run the blockade** forcer le blocus ‖ *tr* bloquer

block′ and tac′kle *s* palan *m*

block′head′ *s* sot *m*, niais *m*

blond [blɑnd] *adj* & *s* blond *m*

blonde [blɑnd] *adj* & *s* blonde *f*

blood [blʌd] *s* sang *m*; parenté *f*, race *f*; **in cold blood** de sang-froid; **to put new blood into** infuser un sang nouveau à

blood′ and guts′ *spl* sang *m* et tripes

blood′ bank′ *s* banque *f* du sang

blood′ count′ *s* numération *f* globulaire

blood′curd′ling *adj* horripilant

blood′hound′ *s* limier *m*

bloodless ['blʌdlɪs] *adj* exsangue; (*revolution*) sans effusion de sang

bloodletting ['blʌd‚letɪŋ] *s* saignée *f*; (fig) effusion *f* de sang

blood′ or′ange *s* sanguine *f*

blood′ plas′ma *s* plasma *m* sanguin

blood′ poi′soning *s* septicémie *f*, empoisonnement *m* du sang

blood′ pres′sure *s* tension *f* artérielle

blood′shed′ *s* effusion *f* de sang

blood′shot′ *adj* injecté, éraillé

blood′ spec′imen *s* prise *f* de sang

blood′stained′ *adj* taché de sang

blood′stream′ *s* circulation *f* du sang

blood′suck′er *s* sangsue *f*

blood′ test′ *s* examen *m* du sang

blood′thirst′y *adj* sanguinaire

blood′ transfu′sion *s* transfusion *f* de sang, transfusion sanguine

blood′ type′ *s* groupe *m* de sang

blood′ ves′sel *s* vaisseau *m* sanguin

blood·y ['blʌdi] *adj* (*comp* **-ier**; *super* **-iest**) sanglant

bloom [blum] *s* fleur *f*; fraîcheur *f*; (*of a fruit*) velouté *m*, duvet *m*; **in bloom** en fleur ‖ *intr* fleurir

bloomers ['blumərz] *spl* culotte *f* de femme

blooper ['blupər] *s* (coll) gaffe *f*, bévue *f*; (rad) poste *m* brouilleur

blossom ['blɑsəm] *s* fleur *f*; **in blossom** en fleur ‖ *intr* fleurir; **to blossom out** s'épanouir

blot [blɑt] *s* tache *f*; (*of ink*) pâté *m* ‖ *v* (*pret* & *pp* **blotted**; *ger* **blotting**) *tr* tacher, barbouiller; (*ink*) sécher; **to blot out** rayer ‖ *intr* (*said of ink*) boire

blotch [blɑtʃ] *s* tache *f*; (*on face*) pustule *f* ‖ *tr* couvrir de taches; (*the skin*) marbrer

blotch·y ['blɑtʃi] *adj* (*comp* **-ier**; *super* **-iest**) brouillé, tacheté

blotter ['blɑtər] *s* buvard *m*

blot′ting pa′per *s* papier *m* buvard

blouse [blaʊs] *s* corsage *m*; (*children's*) chemise *f*; (mil) vareuse *f*

blow [blo] *s* coup *m*; **to come to blows** en venir aux coups ‖ *v* (*pret* **blew** [blu]; *pp* **blown**) *tr* souffler; **to blow one's nose** se moucher; **to blow out** (*a candle*) éteindre; **to blow up** faire sauter; (*a photograph*) agrandir; (*a balloon*) gonfler ‖ *intr* souffler; (slang) décamper en vitesse; **to blow out** (*said of a tire*) éclater; **to blow over** passer; **to blow up** éclater; (slang) se mettre en colère

blower ['blo‚ər] *s* soufflerie *f*; (mach) ventilateur *m*

blow′fly′ *s* (*pl* **-flies**) mouche *f* à viande

blow′gun′ *s* sarbacane *f*

blow′hard′ *s* (slang) hâbleur *m*

blow′hole′ *s* (*of tunnel*) ventilateur *m*; (*of whale*) évent *m*

blowing ['blo·ɪŋ] *s* soufflage *m*; (*of the wind*) soufflement *m*

blow′out′ *s* (*of a tire*) éclatement *m*; (*orgy*) (slang) gueuleton *m*

blow′pipe′ *s* chalumeau *m*

blow′torch′ *s* lampe *f* à souder

blubber ['blʌbər] *s* graisse *f* de baleine ‖ *tr* bredouiller ‖ *intr* pleurer comme un veau

bludgeon ['blʌdʒən] *s* matraque *f* ‖ *tr* assommer

blue [blu] *adj* bleu; **to be blue** (coll) broyer du noir, avoir le cafard ‖ *s* bleu *m; from out of the blue* du ciel, à l'improviste; *the blues* le cafard, l'humeur *f* noire || *tr* bleuir

blue/bell/ *s* jacinthe *f* des bois

blue/ber/ry *s* (*pl* **-ries**) myrtille *f*

blue/bird/ *s* oiseau *m* bleu

blue/-black/ *adj* noir tirant sur le bleu

blue/ blood/ *s* sang *m* royal; aristocrate *mf*

blue/bot/tle *s* bluet *m*, barbeau *m*

blue/ cheese/ *s* roquefort *m* américain

blue/ chip/ *s* valeur-vedette *f*, valeur *f* de tout repos

blue/-gray/ *adj* gris bleuté, gris-bleu

blue/jay/ *s* geai *m* bleu

blue/ jeans/ *spl* blue-jean *m*

blue/ moon/ *s—once in a blue moon* tous les trente-six du mois

blue/nose/ *s* puritain *m*, collet *m* monté

blue/-pen/cil *v* (*pret & pp* **-ciled** or **-cilled**; *ger* **-ciling** or **-cilling**) *tr* corriger au crayon bleu; couper, censurer

blue/print/ *s* dessin *m* négatif, photocalque *m*; (fig) plan *m*, schéma *m* || *tr* planifier

blue/stock/ing *s* (coll) bas-bleu *m*

bluff [blʌf] *adj* abrupt; (*cliff*) escarpé; (*person*) brusque || *s* (*cliff*) falaise *f*, cap *m* à pic; (*deception*) bluff *m*; *to call s.o.'s bluff* relever un défi || *tr & intr* bluffer

bluffer [ˈblʌfər] *s* bluffeur *m*

bluish [ˈbluɪʃ] *adj* bleuté, bleuâtre

blunder [ˈblʌndər] *s* bévue *f*, gaffe *f* || *intr* faire une bévue, gaffer; *to blunder into* se heurter contre; *to blunder upon* découvrir par hasard; tomber sur

blunt [blʌnt] *adj* (*blade*) émoussé; (*point*) épointé; (*person*) brusque || *tr* émousser; épointer

bluntly [ˈblʌntli] *adv* brusquement, sans façons; carrément, sans ménagements

blur [blʌr] *s* barbouillage *m* || *v* (*pret & pp* **blurred**; *ger* **blurring**) *tr* embrouiller, voiler

blurb [blʌrb] *s* annonce *f*; publicité *f* au protège-livre

blurt [blʌrt] *tr—to blurt out* laisser échapper, lâcher

blush [blʌʃ] *s* rougeur *f*; *at first blush* au premier abord || *intr* rougir

bluster [ˈblʌstər] *s* rodomontade *f*, fanfaronnade *f* || *intr* (*of wind*) souffler en rafales; (*of person*) faire du fracas

blustery [ˈblʌstəri] *adj* (*wind*) orageux; (*person*) bravache, fanfaron

boar [bor] *s* (*male swine*) verrat *m*; (*wild hog*) sanglier *m*

board [bord] *s* planche *f*; (e.g., *of directors*) conseil *m*, commission *f*; (*meals*) le couvert; *above board* cartes sur table; *on board* à bord || *tr* (*a ship*) monter à bord de; (*paying guests*) nourrir || *intr* monter à bord; (*said of paying guest*) prendre pension

board/ and room/ *s* pension *f* et chambre *f*

boarder [ˈbordər] *s* pensionnaire *mf*; (*student*) interne *mf*

board/ing-house/ *s* pension *f* (de famille)

board/ of direc/tors *s* conseil *m* d'administration, gérance *f*

board/ of trade/ *s* association *f* des industriels et commerçants

board/ of trustees/ *s* comité *m* administrateur (e.g., *of a university*)

board/walk/ *s* promenade *f* planchéiée au bord de la mer; (*over mud*) caillebotis *m*

boast [bost] *s* vanterie *f* || *intr* se vanter

boastful [ˈbostfəl] *adj* vantard

boasting [ˈbostɪŋ] *s* jactance *f*

boat [bot] *s* bateau *m*; (*small boat*) embarcation *f*; *to miss the boat* (coll) manquer le coche

boat/ hook/ *s* gaffe *f*

boat/house/ *s* hangar *m* à bateaux or à canots

boating [ˈbotɪŋ] *s* canotage *m*; *to go boating* faire du canotage

boat/load/ *s* batelée *f*

boat/man *s* (*pl* **-men**) batelier *m*

boat/ race/ *s* régate *f*

boatswain [ˈbosən], [ˈbot ˌswen] *s* maître *m* d'équipage

bob [bab] *s* plomb *m*; (*of hair*) chignon *m* || *v* (*pret & pp* **bobbed**; *ger* **bobbing**) *intr* s'agiter, danser

bobbin [ˈbabɪn] *s* bobine *f*

bob/by pin/ *s* épingle *f* à cheveux

bob/by-socks/ *spl* (coll) socquettes *fpl*, chaussettes *fpl* basses

bobbysoxer [ˈbabɪˌsaksər] *s* (coll) zazou *m*, jeune lycéenne *f*

bob/sled/ *s* bobsleigh *m*

bob/tail/ *adj* à queue écartée || *tr* couper court

bode [bod] *tr & intr* présager

bodily [ˈbadɪli] *adj* corporel, physique || *adv* corporellement, en corps

bod·y [ˈbadi] *s* (*pl* **-ies**) corps *m*; (*dead body*) cadavre *m*; (*solidity*) consistance *f*; (*flavor of wine*) sève *f*, générosité *f*; (aer) fuselage *m*; (aut) carrosserie *f*; *to come in a body* venir en corps

bod/y-guard/ *s* garde *m* du corps; (*group*) garde *f* du corps

bog [bag] *s* marécage *m*, fondrière *f* || *v* (*pret & pp* **bogged**; *ger* **bogging**) *intr—to bog down* s'enliser

bogey-man [ˈbogi ˌmæn] *s* (*pl* **-men**) croque-mitaine *m*

bogus [ˈbogəs] *adj* faux, simulé

Bohemia [boˈhimɪə] *s* (*country*) Bohême *f*, la Bohême; (*of artistic world*) la bohème

Bohemian [boˈhimɪən] *adj* bohémien; (*unconventional, arty*) bohème, de bohème || *s* (*person living in the country of Bohemia*) Bohémien *m*; (*artist*) bohème *mf*

boil [bɔɪl] *s* ébullition *f*; (*on the skin*) furoncle *m*, clou *m* || *tr* faire bouillir || *intr* bouillir

boiled/ din/ner *s* pot-au-feu *m*

boiled/ ham/ *s* jambon *m* d'York

boiled/ pota/toes *spl* pommes *fpl* bouillies, pommes vapeur

boiler ['bɔɪlər] s chaudière f
boi'ler-mak'er s chaudronnier m
boiling ['bɔɪlɪŋ] adj bouillonnant || s
ébullition f, bouillonnement m
boisterous ['bɔɪstərəs] adj bruyant,
débordant
bold [bold] adj hardi, osé, téméraire;
(headland) à pic; (look) assuré
bold'face' s (typ) caractères mpl gras
bold'-faced' adj (forward) effronté
boldness ['boldnɪs] s hardiesse f; effronterie f
boll' wee'vil [bol] s anthonome m du
coton, charançon m du coton
bologna [bə'lona], [bə'lonjə] s mortadelle f, gros saucisson m
Bolshevik ['bɑl/əvɪk], ['bɔl/əvɪk] adj
bolcheviste, bolchevique || s Bol-
cheviste mf, Bolchevique mf
bolster ['bolstər] s traversin m || tr
soutenir
bolt [bolt] s verrou m; (with a thread
at one end) boulon m; (of cloth)
rouleau m || tr verrouiller; (food)
gober; (e.g., a political party) lâcher
|| intr décamper
bomb [bɑm] s bombe f || tr bombarder
bombard [bɑm'bɑrd] tr bombarder
bombardier [,bɑmbər'dɪr] s bombardier m
bombardment [bɑm'bɑrdmənt] s bombardement m
bombast ['bɑmbæst] s boursouflure f
bombastic [bɑm'bæstɪk] adj bour-
souflé
bomb' bay' s (aer) soute f à bombes
bomb' cra'ter s entonnoir m, trou m
d'obus
bomber ['bɑmər] s avion m de bombardement, bombardier m
bombing ['bɑmɪŋ] s bombardement m
bomb'proof' adj à l'épreuve des bombes
bomb'shell' s obus m; to fall like a
bombshell tomber comme une bombe
bomb' shel'ter s abri m à l'épreuve des
bombes
bomb'sight' s viseur m de bombardement
bona fide ['bonə,faɪd] adj & adv de
bonne foi
bonanza [bo'nænzə] s aubaine f, filon
m
bonbon ['bɑn,bɑn] s bonbon m
bond [bɑnd] s lien m; (com) obliga-
tion f; in bond en entrepôt || tr
(com) entreposer, mettre en entrepôt
bondage ['bɑndɪdʒ] s esclavage m
bond'hold'er s obligataire mf
bone [bon] s os m; (of a fish) arête f;
to have a bone to pick avoir maille à
partir || tr (meat or fish) désosser ||
intr—to bone up on (a subject)
(slang) potasser, piocher
bone'head' s (slang) ignorant m
boneless ['bonlɪs] adj sans os; sans
arêtes
bone' of conten'tion s pomme f de
discorde
boner ['bonər] s (coll) bourde f
bonfire ['bɑn,faɪr] s feu m de joie;
(for burning trash) feu de jardin

bonnet ['bɑnɪt] s bonnet m; chapeau
m à brides; (fig) chapeau
bonus ['bonəs] s boni m, prime f
bon-y ['boni] adj (comp -ier; super
-iest) osseux; (thin) décharné
boo [bu] s huée f, sifflement m; not to
say boo ne pas souffler mot || tr &
intr huer, siffler
boob [bub] s (coll) emplâtre m
boo-by ['bubi] s (pl -bies) (coll) nigaud m
boo'by hatch' s (slang) asile m d'aliénés; (prison) (slang) violon m
boo'by prize' s fiche f de consolation
boo'by trap' s engin m piégé; (fig) attrape-nigaud m
boo'by-trap' v (pret & pp -trapped; ger
-trapping) tr piéger
book [buk] s livre m; (of tickets) carnet m; (libretto) livret m; by the
book d'après le texte, selon les règles; to make book (sports) inscrire
les paris || tr (a seat or room) re-
tenir, réserver
book'bind'er s relieur m
book'bind'er-y s (pl -ies) atelier m de
reliure
book'case' s bibliothèque f, étagère f
book' end' s serre-livres m, appui-
livres m
booking ['bukɪŋ] s réservation f;
(theat) location f
bookish ['bukɪ/] adj livresque; (person) studieux
book'keep'er s comptable mf, teneur
m de livres
book'keep'ing s comptabilité f
book' learn'ing s science f livresque
booklet ['buklɪt] s livret m; (notebook) cahier m; (pamphlet) brochure f
book'lov'er s bibliophile mf
book'mark' s signet m
bookmobile ['bukmo,bil] s bibliobus m
book'plate' s ex-libris m
book'rack' s étagère f
book' review' s compte m rendu
book'sell'er s libraire mf
book'shelf' s (pl -shelves) rayon m,
étagère f
book'stand' s étalage m de livres; (in
a station) bibliothèque f
book'store' s librairie f
book' val'ue s (com) valeur f comptable
book'worm' s ciron m; (fig) rat m de
bibliothèque
boom [bum] s retentissement m,
grondement m; (rapid rise or growth)
vague f de prospérité, boom m; (naut)
bout-dehors m || intr retentir; (com)
prospérer || interj boum!
boomerang ['bumə,ræŋ] s boomerang
m
boom' town' s ville f champignon
boon [bun] s bienfait m, avantage m;
(archaic) don m, faveur f
boon' compan'ion s joyeux compagnon
m
boor [bur] s rustre m, goujat m
boost [bust] s relèvement m; (help)

aide f || tr soulever par derrière; (prices) hausser; (to praise) faire la réclame pour

booster ['bustər] s (enthusiastic backer) réclamiste mf; (go-getter) homme m d'expédition, lanceur m d'affaires; (elec) survolteur m; (rok) booster m, propulseur m

boost'er rock'et s fusée f de lancement

boost'er shot' s piqûre f de rappel

boot [but] s botte f, bottine f; **to boot** en sus; **to lick s.o.'s boots** (coll) lécher les bottes à qn || tr botter

boot'black' s cireur m de bottes

booth [buθ] s (at fair) baraque f; (e.g., for telephoning) cabine f

boot'leg' adj (slang) clandestin, de contrebande || v (pret & pp -legged; ger -legging) tr (slang) faire la contrebande de || intr (slang) faire la contrebande

bootlegger ['but,legər] s (slang) contrebandier m; (slang) contrebandier m d'alcool, bootlegger m

boot'leg'ging s contrebande f

boot'lick' tr (coll) lécher les bottes à

boo-ty ['buti] s (pl -ties) butin m

booze [buz] s (coll) boisson f alcoolique || intr (coll) s'adonner à la boisson

border ['bordər] s bord m, bordure f; (of field and forest; of a piece of cloth) lisière f; (of a road) marge f; (of a country) frontière f; (edging) galon m, bordé m || tr border; (a handkerchief) liséré || intr—**to border on** confiner à, toucher à; (a color) tirer sur

bor'der-line' adj indéterminé || s ligne f de démarcation

bore [bor] s trou m; (of gun) calibre m; (of cannon) âme f; (of cylinder) alésage m; (nuisance) ennui m; (person) raseur m || tr percer; (a cylinder) aléser; (to annoy) ennuyer

boreal ['bori·əl] adj boréal

boredom ['bordəm] s ennui m

boring ['borɪŋ] adj ennuyeux, rasant, rasoir || s perçage m, percement m

born [bɔrn] adj né; **to be born** naître

borough ['bʌro] s (town) bourg m; circonscription f électorale

borrow ['baro], ['bɔro] tr emprunter; **to borrow from** emprunter à

borrower ['baro·ər], ['bɔro·ər] s emprunteur m

bor'rower's card' s bulletin m de prêt

borrowing ['baro·ɪŋ], ['bɔro·ɪŋ] s emprunt m

borzoi ['bɔrzɔɪ] s lévrier m russe

bosom ['buzəm] s sein m, poitrine f; (of the Church) giron m

boss [bɔs], [bɑs] s patron m, chef m; (foreman) contremaître m || tr diriger

boss-y ['bɔsi], ['bɑsi] adj (comp -ier; super -iest) autoritaire; **to be bossy** jordonner

botanical [bə'tænɪkəl] adj botanique

botanist ['batənɪst] s botaniste mf

botany ['batəni] s botanique f

both [boθ] adj deux, e.g., **with both hands** à deux mains; les deux, e.g.,

both books les deux livres || pron les deux, tous les deux || conj à la fois; **both . . . and** aussi bien . . . que, e.g., **both in England and France** aussi bien en Angleterre qu'en France

bother ['baðər] s ennui m || tr ennuyer, déranger || intr se déranger

bothersome ['baðərsəm] adj importun

bottle ['batəl] s bouteille f || tr mettre en bouteille, embouteiller

bot'tle cap' s capsule f

bot'tled gas' s gaz m en cylindre

bot'tle-neck' s goulot m; (fig) embouteillage m

bot'tle o'pener s ouvre-bouteilles m

bottler ['batlər] s metteur m en bouteilles

bottling ['batlɪŋ] s mise f en bouteilles

bottom ['batəm] s fond m; **at the bottom of** au fond de; (the page) en bas de; **to reach the bottom of the barrel** (coll) être à fond de cale

bot'tom dol'lar s dernier sou m

bottomless ['batəmlɪs] adj sans fond

bough [bau] s rameau m

boulder ['boldər] s bloc m, rocher m

boulevard ['bulə,vard] s boulevard m

bounce [bauns] s (elasticity) bond m; (of a ball) rebond m || tr faire rebondir; (slang) flanquer à la porte || intr rebondir

bouncer ['baunsər] s (in night club) (coll) videur m, gorille m

bound [baund] adj (tied) lié; (obliged) obligé, tenu; **bound for** en partance pour || s bond m, saut m; **bounds** fpl bornes fpl, limites fpl; **out of bounds** hors jeu; (prohibited) défendu || tr borner, limiter || intr bondir

bounda-ry ['baundəri] s (pl -ries) borne f, limite f

boun'dary stone' s borne f

boundless ['baundlɪs] adj sans bornes

boun-ty ['baunti] s (pl -ties) largesse f; (award) prime f

bouquet [bu'ke], [bo'ke] s bouquet m

bout [baut] s rencontre f; (e.g., of fever) accès m; (sports) match m

bow [bau] s inclination f, révérence f; (of ship) avant m, proue f || tr incliner, courber || intr s'incliner, se courber; **to bow down** se prosterner; **to bow out** se retirer; **to bow to** saluer || [bo] s (weapon) arc m; (bowknot) nœud m; (of violin) archet m || intr (mus) tirer l'archet

bowdlerize ['baudlə,raɪz] tr expurger

bowel ['bau·əl] s intestin m, boyau m; **bowels** entrailles fpl

bow'el move'ment s selle f; **to have a bowel movement** aller à la selle

bower ['bau·ər] s berceau m, tonnelle f

bow'ie knife' ['bo·ɪ], ['bu·ɪ] s couteau-poignard m

bowknot ['bo,nat] s nœud m en forme de rose, rosette f

bowl [bol] s bol m, jatte f; (of pipe) fourneau m; (of spoon) cuilleron m; **bowls** (sports) boules fpl || tr rouler, lancer; **to bowl over** (to overturn) (coll) renverser; (slang) déconcerter

|| *intr*—**to bowl along** rouler rapide-ment

bowlegged ['bo͵legd], ['bo͵legɪd] *adj* aux jambes arquées

bowler ['bolər] *s* (*hat*) chapeau *m* melon; (*in cricket*) lanceur *m*; (*in bowling*) joueur *m* de boules

bowling ['bolɪŋ] *s* jeu *m* de boules, jeu de quilles

bowl′ing al′ley *s* boulodrome *m*

bowl′ing green′ *s* boulingrin *m*

bowl′ing pin′ *s* quille *f*

bowsprit ['bausprɪt], ['bosprɪt] *s* beaupré *m*

bow′ tie′ [bo] *s* nœud *m* papillon

box [bɑks] *s* boîte *f*; (*law*) barre *f*; (*theat*) loge *f*, baignoire *f*; **box on the ear** claque *f* || *tr* emboîter; (*to hit*) boxer; **to box the compass** réciter la rose des vents || *intr* (*sports*) boxer

box′car′ *s* (rr) wagon *m* couvert

boxer ['bɑksər] *s* (*person*) boxeur *m*; (*dog*) boxer *m*

boxing ['bɑksɪŋ] *s* emboîtage *m*; (*sports*) boxe *f*

box′ of′fice *s* bureau *m* de location

box′-office flop′ *s* (slang) four *m*

box′-office hit′ *s* pièce *f* à succès

box′wood′ *s* buis *m*

boy [bɔɪ] *s* garçon *m*; (*little boy*) garçonnet *m*

boycott ['bɔɪkɑt] *s* boycottage *m* || *tr* boycotter

boy′ friend′ *s* ami *m*, camarade *m*; (*of a girl*) bon ami *m*

boyhood ['bɔɪhud] *s* enfance *f*, jeu-nesse *f*, adolescence *f*

boyish ['bɔɪ·ɪʃ] *adj* de garçon

boy′ scout′ *s* boy-scout *m*

bra [brɑ] *s* (coll) soutien-gorge *m*

brace [bres] *s* attache *f*, lien *m*; (*of game birds*) couple *f*; (*of pistols*) paire *f*; (*to impart a rotary move-ment to a bit*) vilebrequin *m*; (aer, aut) entretoise *f*; (mus, typ) accolade *f* || *tr* ancrer, entretoiser; (*to tone up*) fortifier, remonter || *intr*—**to brace up** prendre courage

brace′ and bit′ *s* vilebrequin *m*

bracelet ['breslɪt] *s* bracelet *m*

bracer ['bresər] *s* tonique *m*

bracing ['bresɪŋ] *adj* tonique, forti-fiant

bracket ['brækɪt] *s* console *f*; (*group-ing*) niveau *m*; (mach) chaise *f*; (typ) crochet *m* || *tr* grouper; (typ) mettre entre crochets

brackish ['brækɪʃ] *adj* saumâtre

brad [bræd] *s* semence *f*, clou *m* (sans tête)

brag [bræg] *s* (*pret & pp* **bragged**; *ger* **bragging**) *intr* se vanter

braggadoci·o [͵brægə'doʃɪ͵o] *s* (*pl* -**os**) fanfaronnade *f*; (*person*) fanfaron *m*

braggart ['brægərt] *s* vantard *m*

bragging ['brægɪŋ] *s* vanterie *f*

Brah·man ['brɑmən] *s* (*pl* -**mans**) brahmane *m*

braid [bred] *s* tresse *f*, passement *m*; (mil) galon *m*; **to trim with braid** soutacher || *tr* passementer; (*the hair*) tresser

braille [brel] *s* braille *m*

brain [bren] *s* cerveau *m*; **brains** cer-velle *f*; (fig) intelligence *f*, cerveau; **to rack one's brains** se creuser la cer-velle || *tr* casser la tête à

brain′ child′ *s* idée *f* de génie

brainless ['brenlɪs] *adj* sans cervelle

brain′storm′ *s* accès *m* de folie; (coll) confusion *f* mentale; (coll) trouvaille *f*, bonne idée *f*

brain′wash′ *tr* (*by use of torture, drugs, etc.*) faire un lavage de cerveau à; (*by means of commercials, sales talk, etc.*) bourrer le crâne de

brain′wash′ing *s* lavage *m* de cerveau; bourrage *m* de crâne

brain′work′ *s* travail *m* intellectuel

brain·y ['breni] *adj* (*comp* -ier; *super* -iest) (coll) intelligent, à l'esprit vif

braise [brez] *tr* braiser, endauber

brais′ing pan′ *s* braisière *f*

brake [brek] *s* frein *m*; **to put on the brakes** serrer les freins || *tr & intr* freiner

brake′ drum′ *s* tambour *m* de frein

brake′ light′ *s* (aut) feu *m* de freinage

brake′ lin′ing *s* garniture *f* de frein

brake′man *s* (*pl* -**men**) serre-freins *m*

brake′ ped′al *s* pédale *f* de frein

brake′ shoe′ *s* sabot *m* de frein

bramble ['bræmbəl] *s* ronce *f*

bran [bræn] *s* son *m*, bran *m*

branch [bræntʃ] *s* branche *f*; (*of tree*) rameau *m*, branche; (*of a business*) succursale *f*, filiale *f* || *intr*—**to branch off** s'embrancher, se bifur-quer; **to branch out** se ramifier

branch′ line′ *s* embranchement *m*

branch′ of′fice *s* succursale *f*; bureau *m* de quartier

branch′ road′ *s* embranchement *m*

brand [brænd] *s* (*trademark*) marque *f*; (*torch*) brandon *m*; (*coal*) tison *m*; (*on a criminal*) flétrissure *f*; (*on cat-tle*) marque || *tr* marquer au fer rouge, flétrir

brand′ing i′ron *s* fer *m* à flétrir

brandish ['brændɪʃ] *tr* brandir

brand′-new′ *adj* tout neuf, flambant neuf

bran·dy ['brændi] *s* (*pl* -**dies**) eau-de-vie *f*

brash [bræʃ] *adj* impertinent

brass [bræs], [brɑs] *s* laiton *m*; (mil) (coll) officiers *mpl* supérieurs, galon-nard *m*; (slang) toupet *m*, culot *m*; **big brass** (slang) grosses légumes *fpl*; **the brasses** (mus) les cuivres

brass′ band′ *s* fanfare *f*, musique *f*

brassiere [brə'zɪr] *s* soutien-gorge *m*

brass′ knuck′les *spl* coup-de-poing *m*

brass′ tack′ *s* semence *f* (de tapissier); **to get down to brass tacks** (coll) en venir aux faits

brat [bræt] *s* (coll) gamin *m*, gosse *mf*

brava·do [brə'vado] *s* (*pl* -**does** or -**dos**) bravade *f*

brave [brev] *adj* brave || *s* guerrier *m* peau-rouge || *tr* braver

bravery ['brevəri] *s* bravoure *f*

bra·vo ['brɑvo] *s* (*pl* -**vos**) bravo *m* || *interj* bravo!

brawl [brɔl] s bagarre f, querelle f ||
   intr se bagarrer, se quereller
brawler ['brɔlər] s bagarreur m
brawn [brɔn] s muscle m; muscles bien
   développés; (culin) fromage m de
   cochon
brawn·y ['brɔni] adj (comp -ier; super
   -iest) bien découplé, musclé
bray [bre] s braiment m || intr braire
braze [brez] tr braser
brazen ['brezən] adj effronté || tr—to
   brazen through mener à bonne fin
   avec une effronterie audacieuse
Brazil [brə'zɪl] s le Brésil
Brazilian [brə'zɪljən] adj brésilien || s
   (person) Brésilien m
Brazil' nut' s noix f du Brésil
breach [brit/] s (in a wall) brèche f;
   (violation) infraction f || tr ouvrir
   une brèche dans
breach' of con'tract s rupture f de
   contrat
breach' of prom'ise s rupture f de
   fiançailles
breach' of the peace' s attentat m contre l'ordre public
breach' of trust' s abus m de confiance
bread [brɛd] s pain m || tr paner,
   gratiner
bread' and but'ter s (fig) gagne-pain m
bread'bas'ket s panier m à pain, corbeille f à pain
bread'board' s planche f à pain
bread' crumbs' spl chapelure f
breaded adj (culin) au gratin
bread'ed veal' cut'let s escalope f
   panée de veau
bread'fruit' s fruit m à pain; (tree)
   arbre m à pain, jacquier m
bread' knife' s couteau m à pain
breadth [brɛdθ] s largeur f
bread'win'ner s soutien m de famille
break [brek] s rupture f; (of an object)
   brisure f, cassure f; (in time or
   space) trou m, pause f; (slang)
   chance f || s (pret **broke** [brok]; pp
   broken) tr rompre, briser, casser; (a
   law) violer; (the heart) fendre; (one's
   word) manquer à; (a will; a soldier
   by reducing his rank) casser; to
   break bread rompre le pain; to **break
   down** (for analysis) analyser; to
   break in (a door) enfoncer; (a new
   car) roder || intr rompre, briser, se
   briser; (said of clouds) se dissiper;
   (said of waves) déferler; to **break
   down** avoir une panne
breakable ['brekəbəl] adj fragile
breakage ['brekɪdʒ] s casse f
break'down' s (stoppage) arrêt m;
   (disaster) débâcle f; (of health)
   épuisement m; (of negotiations) rupture f; (for analysis) analyse f, ventilation f; (mach) panne f
breaker ['brekər] s brisant m
breakfast ['brɛkfəst] s petit déjeuner
   m || intr prendre le petit déjeuner
break'fast food' s céréales fpl (pour le
   petit déjeuner)
break'neck' adj vertigineux; at **break-
   neck speed** à tombeau ouvert
break' of day' s point m du jour

break'through' s (mil) percée f; (fig)
   découverte f sensationnelle
break'up' s dissolution f; écroulement
   m; (in health) abattement m
break'wa'ter s digue f, brise-lames m
breast [brɛst] s sein m; (of cooked
   chicken) blanc m; to **make a clean
   breast of** it se déboutonner
breast'bone' s sternum m; (of fowl)
   bréchet m
breast' feed'ing s allaitement m
breast'plate' s (of high priest) pectoral
   m; (of armor) plastron m
breast'stroke' s brasse f
breast'work' s (mil) parapet m
breath [brɛθ] s haleine f, souffle m;
   last breath dernier soupir m; out of
   breath hors d'haleine
breathe [brið] tr & intr respirer, souffler; **not to breathe a word** ne pas
   souffler mot
breathing ['briðɪŋ] s souffle m
breath'ing space' s répit m
breathless ['brɛθlɪs] adj haletant, hors
   d'haleine; inanimé
breath'tak'ing adj émouvant, sensationnel
breech [brit/] s culasse f
breech'es bu'oy s (naut) bouée-culotte f
breed [brid] s race f || v (pret & pp
   bred [brɛd]) tr engendrer; (e.g., cat-
   tle) élever || intr se reproduire
breeder ['bridər] s éleveur m
breeding ['bridɪŋ] s (of animals) élevage m; **good breeding** savoir-vivre m
breeze [briz] s brise f
breez·y ['brizi] adj (comp -ier; super
   -iest) aéré; (coll) désinvolte, dégagé
brethren ['brɛðrɪn] spl frères mpl
Breton ['brɛtən] adj breton || s (lan-
   guage) breton m; (person) Breton m
breviar·y ['brivɪˌɛri], ['brɛvɪˌɛri] s (pl
   -ies) (eccl) bréviaire m
brevi·ty ['brɛvɪti] s (pl -ties) brièveté f
brew [bru] s breuvage m, infusion f ||
   tr infuser; (beer) brasser || intr s'in-
   fuser
brewer ['bru·ər] s brasseur m
brew'er's yeast' s levure f de bière
brewer·y ['bru·əri] s (pl -ies) brasserie f
brewing ['bru·ɪŋ] s brassage m
bribe [braɪb] s pot-de-vin m || tr
   corrompre, suborner, soudoyer
briber·y ['braɪbəri] s (pl -ies) corruption f, subornation f
brick [brɪk] s brique f || tr briqueter
brick'bat' s brocard m; to **hurl brick-
   bats** lancer des brocards
brick'lay'er s briqueteur m
brick'work' s briquetage m
brick'yard' s briqueterie f
bridal ['braɪdəl] adj nuptial
bride [braɪd] s (nouvelle) mariée f
bride'groom' s (nouveau) marié m
brides'maid' s demoiselle f d'honneur
bride'-to-be' s future femme f
bridge [brɪdʒ] s pont m; (cards, dentistry) bridge m; (naut) passerelle f;
   to **burn one's bridges** couper les
   ponts || tr construire un pont sur; to
   bridge a gap combler une lacune

bridge'head' s (mil) tête f de pont

bridle ['braɪdəl] s bride f; (fig) frein m ‖ tr brider; (fig) freiner ‖ intr se raidir

bri'dle path' s piste f cavalière

brief [brif] adj bref ‖ s résumé m; (law) dossier m; **briefs** slip m; **to hold a brief for** plaider pour ‖ tr mettre au courant

brief' case' s serviette f

briefing ['brifɪŋ] s briefing m, renseignements mpl tactiques

briefly ['brifli] adv bref, brièvement, en substance

brier ['braɪ.ər] s ronce f

brig [brɪg] s prison f navale; (ship) brick m

brigade [brɪ'ged] s brigade f

brigadier [,brɪgə'dɪr] s général m de brigade

brigand ['brɪgənd] s brigand m

brigantine ['brɪgən,tin], ['brɪgən-,taɪn] s brigantin f

bright [braɪt] adj brillant; (day) clair; (color) vif; (person) (fig) brillant

brighten ['braɪtən] tr faire briller; égayer, réjouir ‖ intr s'éclaircir

bright' ide'a s (coll) idée f lumineuse

brightness ['braɪtnɪs] s éclat m, clarté f; (of mind) vivacité f

brilliance ['brɪljəns] or **brilliancy** ['brɪljənsi] s brillant m, éclat m

brilliant ['brɪljənt] adj & s brillant m

brim [brɪm] s bord m ‖ v (pret & pp **brimmed**; ger **brimming**) intr—to **brim over** (with) déborder (de)

brimful ['brɪm,ful] adj à ras bords

brim'stone' s soufre m

brine [braɪn] s saumure f

bring [brɪŋ] v (pret & pp **brought** [brɔt]) tr apporter; (a person) amener, conduire; **to bring back** rapporter; (a person) ramener; **to bring down** (baggage) descendre; (with a gun) abattre; **to bring in** entrer, introduire; **to bring out** faire ressortir; (e.g., a book) publier; **to bring together** réunir; **to bring to pass** causer, opérer; **to bring up** éduquer, élever; (baggage) monter

bring'ing-up' s éducation f

brink [brɪŋk] s bord m

brisk [brɪsk] adj vif, actif, animé

brisket ['brɪskɪt] s (culin) poitrine f

bristle ['brɪsəl] s soie f; (of brush) poil m ‖ tr hérisser ‖ intr se hérisser

bristling ['brɪslɪŋ] adj hérissé

Bris'tol board' ['brɪstəl] s bristol m

Britain ['brɪtən] s Grande-Bretagne f; **la Grande-Bretagne**

British ['brɪtɪʃ] adj britannique ‖ **the British** les Britanniques

Britisher ['brɪtɪʃər] s Britannique mf

Briton ['brɪtən] s Britannique mf

Brittany ['brɪtəni] s Bretagne f; la Bretagne

brittle ['brɪtəl] adj fragile, cassant

broach [brotʃ] s broche f; (for tapping casks) mèche f à percer ‖ tr (e.g., a keg of beer) mettre en perce; (a subject) entamer

broad [brɔd] adj (wide) large; (immense) vaste; (mind, views) libéral, tolérant; (accent) fort, prononcé; (use, sense) répandu, général; (daylight) plein; (joke, story) grossier, salé

broad'-backed' adj d'une belle carrure

broad'brimmed' adj à larges bords

broad'cast' adj diffusé; (rad) radiodiffusé ‖ s (rad) radiodiffusion f, émission f ‖ v (pret & pp **-cast**) tr diffuser, répandre ‖ (pret & pp **-cast** or **-casted**) tr radiodiffuser ‖ intr (rad) émettre

broad'casting sta'tion s station f d'émission

broad'cloth' s popeline f

broaden ['brodən] tr élargir ‖ intr s'élargir

broad'-gauge' adj à voie large

broad' jump' s saut m en longueur

broad'-mind'ed adj à l'esprit large

broad'side' s bordée f; (typ) placard m

brocade [bro'ked] s brocart m ‖ tr brocher

broccoli ['brakəli] s brocoli m

brochure [bro'ʃur] s brochure f

brogue [brog] s accent m irlandais; (shoe) soulier m grossier

broil [brɔɪl] s grillade f; (quarrel) rixe f ‖ tr & intr griller

broiler ['brɔɪlər] s gril m

broke [brok] adj (slang) fauché

broken ['brokən] adj brisé, cassé; (promise, ranks; beam) rompu

brok'en-down' adj délabré; en panne

bro'ken-heart'ed adj au cœur brisé

broker ['brokər] s courtier m

brokerage ['brokərɪdʒ] s courtage m

bromide ['bromaɪd] s bromure m; (coll) platitude f

bromine ['bromin] s brome m

bronchial ['braŋkɪ.əl] adj bronchique

bron'chial tube' s bronche f

bronchitis [braŋ'kaɪtɪs] s bronchite f

bron·co ['braŋko] s (pl **-cos**) cheval m sauvage

bronze [branz] adj bronzé ‖ s bronze m ‖ tr bronzer ‖ intr se bronzer

brooch [brotʃ], [brutʃ] s broche f

brood [brud] s couvée f; (of children) nichée f ‖ intr couver; (to sulk) broyer du noir; **to brood over** songer sombrement à

brood' hen' s couveuse f

brood'mare' s poulinière f

brook [bruk] s ruisseau m ‖ tr—to **brook no** ne pas tolérer

brooklet ['bruklɪt] s ruisseau m

broom [brum], [brum] s balai m; (bot) genêt m

broom'stick' s manche m à balai

broth [brɔθ], [braθ] s bouillon m, consommé m

brothel ['braθəl], ['brɔθəl] s bordel m

brother ['brʌðər] s frère m

broth'er-hood' s fraternité f

broth'er-in-law' s (pl **brothers-in-law**) beau-frère m

brotherly ['brʌðərli] adj fraternel ‖ adv fraternellement

brow [brau] s (forehead) front m;

(*eyebrow*) sourcil *m*; **to knit one's brow** froncer le sourcil

brow/beat/ *v* (*pret* -**beat**; *pp* -**beaten**) *tr* rabrouer, brusquer

brown [braun] *adj* marron; (*paper*) gris; (*bread*) bis; (*shoes*) jaune; (*butter*) roux, noir; (*hair*) brun, châtain || *tr* brunir; (culin) rissoler, dorer

brownish ['braunɪʃ] *adj* brunâtre

brown/ stud/y *s*—**in a brown study** absorbé dans des méditations

brown/ sug/ar *s* cassonade *f*, sucre *m* brut

browse [brauz] *intr* (*said of animals*) brouter; (*said of booklovers*) butiner; (*said of customers for secondhand books*) bouquiner

bruise [bruz] *s* (*on body or fruit*) meurtrissure *f*; (*on body*) contusion *f* || *tr* meurtrir, contusionner

bruiser ['bruzər] *s* (coll) costaud *m*

bruit [brut] *tr* ébruiter; **to bruit about** répandre

brunette [bru'nɛt] *adj* & *s* brune *f*, brunette *f*

brunt [brʌnt] *s* choc *m*, assaut *m*; **to bear the brunt of** (fig) faire tous les frais de

brush [brʌʃ] *s* brosse *f*; (*countryside*) brousse *f*; (elec) balai *m* || *tr* brosser; **to brush aside** écarter || *intr*—**to brush against** frôler; **to brush up on** repasser, rafraîchir

brush/-off/ *s* (slang) affront *m*; **to give a brush-off to** (slang) expédier avec rudesse

brush/wood/ *s* broussailles *fpl*, brindilles *fpl*

brusque [brʌsk] *adj* brusque

Brussels ['brʌsəlz] *s* Bruxelles *f*

Brus/sels sprouts/ *mpl* chou *m* de Bruxelles

brutal ['brutəl] *adj* brutal

brutali-ty [bru'tælɪti] *s* (*pl* -**ties**) brutalité *f*

brute [brut] *adj* brutal || *s* bête *f*, animal *m*; (*person*) brute *f*, animal *m*

brutish ['brutɪʃ] *adj* grossier, brut, brutal

bubble ['bʌbəl] *s* bulle *f* || *intr* bouillonner; (*said of drink*) pétiller; **to bubble over** déborder

bub/ble gum/ *s* gomme *f* à claquer

bub-bly ['bʌbli] *adj* (*comp* -**blier**; *super* -**bliest**) bouillonnant, gazeux

bubon/ic plague/ [bju'bɑnɪk] *s* peste *f* bubonique

buccaneer [,bʌkə'nɪr] *s* boucanier *m*

buck [bʌk] *s* (*red deer*) cerf *m*; (*fallow deer*) daim *m*; (*roebuck*) chevreuil *m*; (slang) dollar *m*; the male of many animals such as: (*goat*) bouc *m*; (*rabbit*) lapin *m*; (*hare*) lièvre *m*; **to pass the buck** (coll) renvoyer la balle || *tr*—**to buck off** (*a rider*) désarçonner; **to buck up** (coll) remonter le courage de || *intr*—**to buck up** (coll) reprendre courage

bucket ['bʌkɪt] *s* seau *m*; **to kick the bucket** (slang) casser sa pipe

buck/et seat/ *s* siège *m* à baquet

buckle ['bʌkəl] *s* boucle *f* || *tr* boucler || *intr* arquer, gauchir; **to buckle down** s'appliquer

buck/ pri/vate *s* simple soldat *m*

buckram ['bʌkrəm] *s* bougran *m*

buck/saw/ *s* scie *f* à bûches

buck/shot/ *s* gros plomb *m*

buck/tooth/ *s* (*pl* -**teeth**) dent *f* saillante

buck/wheat/ *s* sarrasin *m*

buck/wheat cake/ *s* crêpe *f* de sarrasin

bud [bʌd] *s* bouton *m*, bourgeon *m* || *v* (*pret & pp* budded; *ger* budding) *intr* boutonner, bourgeonner

Buddhism ['budɪzəm] *s* bouddhisme *m*

Buddhist ['budɪst] *adj* & *s* bouddhiste *mf*

budding ['bʌdɪŋ] *adj* en bouton; (*beginning*) en germe, naissant

bud-dy ['bʌdi] *s* (*pl* -**dies**) (coll) copain *m*

budge [bʌdʒ] *tr* faire bouger || *intr* bouger

budget ['bʌdʒɪt] *s* budget *m* || *tr* comptabiliser, inscrire au budget

budgetary ['bʌdʒɪ,tɛri] *adj* budgétaire

buff [bʌf] *adj* (*color*) chamois || *s* (coll) fanatique *mf*, enthousiaste *mf* || *tr* polir, émeuler

buffa-lo ['bʌfə,lo] *s* (*pl* -**loes** or -**los**) bison *m*; (*water buffalo; Cape buffalo*) buffle *m*

buffer ['bʌfər] *s* (mach) brunissoir *m*; (rr) (*on cars*) tampon *m*; (rr) (*at end of track*) butoir *m*

buff/er state/ *s* état *m* tampon

buff/er zone/ *s* zone *f* tampon

buffet [bu'fe] *s* buffet *m* || ['bʌfɪt] *tr* frapper (violemment)

buffet/ lunch/ [bu'fe] *s* lunch *m*

buffoon [bə'fun] *s* bouffon *m*

buffooner-y [bə'funəri] *s* (*pl* -**ies**) bouffonnerie *f*

bug [bʌg] *s* insecte *m*; (*germ*) microbe *m*; (*in a mechanical device*) vice *m*, défaut *m*; (coll) idée *f* fixe, lutin *m*; (Brit) punaise *f*; **he's a bug for . . .** (coll) il est fou de . . . || *v* (*pret & pp* bugged; *ger* bugging) *tr* (slang) installer une table d'écoute dans; installer un microphone dans; (*to annoy*) (slang) embêter, emmerder

bug/bear/ *s* épouvantail *m*, croquemitaine *m*; (*pet peeve*) bête *f* noire

bug/-eyed/ *adj* (slang) aux yeux saillants

bug-gy ['bʌgi] *adj* (*comp* -**gier**; *super* -**giest**) infesté d'insectes; infesté; (slang) fou || *s* (*pl* -**gies**) buggy *m* à quatre roues; (*two-wheeled*) buggy, boguet *m*

bug/house/ *s* (slang) cabanon *m*

bugle ['bjugəl] *s* (bot) bugle *f*; (mus) clairon *m* || *tr* & *intr* claironner

bu/gle call/ *s* sonnerie *f* de clairon

bugler ['bjuglər] *s* clairon *m*

build [bɪld] *s* structure *f*; (*of human body*) taille *f*, charpente *f* || *v* (*pret & pp* built [bɪlt]) *tr* bâtir, construire

builder ['bɪldər] *s* constructeur *m*; (*of bridges, roads, etc.*) entrepreneur *m*

building ['bɪldɪŋ] *s* immeuble *m*, bâtiment *m*, édifice *m*

build'ing and loan' associa'tion *s* société *f* de prêt à la construction

build'ing lot' *s* terrain *m* à bâtir

built'-in' *adj* incorporé

built'-up' *adj* aggloméré; (*heel*) renforcé; (*land*) bâti

bulb [bʌlb] *s* bulbe *m*; (*of vaporizer*) poire *f*; (bot) oignon *m*; (elec) ampoule *f*

bulbous ['bʌlbəs] *adj* bulbeux

Bulgaria [bʌl'gɛrɪ·ə] *s* Bulgarie *f*; la Bulgarie

Bulgarian [bʌl'gɛrɪ·ən] *adj* bulgare ‖ *s* (*language*) bulgare *m*; (*person*) Bulgare *mf*

bulge [bʌldʒ] *s* bosse *f*, bombement *m*; (mil) saillant *m* ‖ *tr* bourrer, gonfler ‖ *intr* faire une bosse, bomber

bulk [bʌlk] *s* masse *f*, volume *m*; **in bulk** en bloc; (com) en vrac ‖ *tr* entasser (en vrac) ‖ *intr* tenir de la place; **to bulk large** devenir important

bulk'head' *s* (naut) cloison *f*

bulk·y ['bʌlki] *adj* (*comp* **-ier**; *super* **-iest**) volumineux

bull [bul] *s* taureau *m*; (*on the stock exchange*) haussier *m*, spéculateur *m* à la hausse; (eccl) bulle *f*; (*policeman*) (slang) flic *m*, vache *f*; (*exaggeration*) (slang) blague *f*, boniment *m*, chiqué *m*; **like a bull in a china shop** comme un éléphant dans un magasin de porcelaine; **to take the bull by the horns** (fig) prendre le taureau par les cornes ‖ *tr*—**to bull the market** jouer à la hausse

bull'dog' *s* bouledogue *m*

bull'doze' *tr* passer au bulldozer; (coll) intimider

bulldozer ['bul,dozər] *s* chasse-terre *m*, bulldozer *m*

bullet ['bulɪt] *s* balle *f*

bulletin ['bulɪtɪn] *s* bulletin *m*; (*e.g., of a university*) annuaire *m*

bul'letin board' *s* tableau *m* d'affichage

bul'let-proof' *adj* à l'épreuve des balles ‖ *tr* blinder

bul'let-proof vest' *s* gilet *m* pare-balles

bull'fight' *s* course *f* de taureaux

bull'fight'er *s* torero *m*

bull'fight'ing *s* tauromachie *f*

bull'finch' *s* bouvreuil *m*

bull'frog' *s* grenouille *f* d'Amérique

bull'head' *s* (ichth) chabot *m*, cabot *m*; (*miller's-thumb*) meunier *m*

bull'head'ed *adj* entêté

bullion ['buljən] *s* (*of gold*) or *m*; (*of silver*) argent *m*; encaisse *f* métallique, lingots *mpl* d'or, lingots d'argent; (*on uniform*) cordonnet *m* d'or, cordonnet d'argent

bull' mar'ket *s* marché *m* à la hausse

bullock ['bulək] *s* bœuf *m*

bull' pen' *s* toril *m*; (*jail*) poste *m* de détention préventive

bull'ring' *s* arène *f*, arène pour les courses de taureaux

bull's'-eye' *s* mouche *f*; **to hit the bull's-eye** faire mouche

bull's'-eye win'dow *s* œil-de-bœuf *m*

bull'ter'rier *s* bull-terrier *m*

bul·ly ['buli] *adj* (coll) épatant ‖ *s* (*pl* **-lies**) brute *f*, brutal *m*; (*at school*) brimeur *m*, tyranneau *m* ‖ *v* (*pret* & *pp* **-lied**) *tr* brutaliser, malmener; (*at school*) brimer, tyranniser

bulrush ['bul,rʌʃ] *s* jonc *m* des marais

bulwark ['bulwərk] *s* rempart *m*; (naut) pavois *m* ‖ *tr* garnir de remparts; (fig) protéger

bum [bʌm] *adj* (slang) moche, de camelote ‖ *s* (slang) clochard *m* ‖ *v* (*pret* & *pp* **bummed**; *ger* **bumming**) *tr* & *intr* (slang) écornifler

bumble ['bʌmbəl] *tr* bâcler ‖ *intr* (*to stumble*) trébucher; (*in speaking*) bafouiller; (*said of bee*) bourdonner

bum'ble·bee' *s* bourdon *m*

bump [bʌmp] *s* choc *m*; (*protuberance*) bosse *f*; (*of car on rough road*) cahot *m* ‖ *tr* cogner, tamponner, heurter; **to bump off** (*to kill*) (slang) buter ‖ *intr* se cogner; **to bump along** (*said of car*) cahoter; **to bump into** buter contre, choquer

bumper ['bʌmpər] *adj* exceptionnel ‖ *s* (aut) pare-chocs *m*; (rr) tampon *m*

bumpkin ['bʌmpkɪn] *s* péquenot *m*, rustre *m*

bumptious ['bʌmpʃəs] *adj* outrecuidant

bump·y ['bʌmpi] *adj* (*comp* **-ier**; *super* **-iest**) bosselé; (*road*) cahoteux

bun [bʌn] *s* brioche *f*, petit pain *m*; (*hair*) chignon *m*

bunch [bʌntʃ] *s* botte *f*; (*of bananas*) régime *m*; (*of flowers*) bouquet *m*; (*of grapes*) grappe *f*; (*of keys*) trousseau *m*; (*of people*) groupe *m*, bande *f*; (*of ribbons*) flot *m*; (*of twigs*) paquet *m*; (*on body*) bosse *f* ‖ *tr* grouper ‖ *intr* se serrer

buncombe ['bʌŋkəm] *s* (coll) balivernes *fpl*, sornettes *fpl*

bundle ['bʌndəl] *s* paquet *m*; (*of banknotes, papers, etc.*) liasse *f* ‖ *tr* empaqueter, mettre en paquet; **to bundle up** (*in warm clothing*) emmitoufler ‖ *intr*—**to bundle up** s'emmitoufler

bung [bʌŋ] *s* bonde *f* ‖ *tr* mettre une bonde à

bungalow ['bʌŋgə,lo] *s* bungalow *m*

bung'hole' *s* bonde *f*

bungle ['bʌŋgəl] *s* gâchis *m*, bousillage *m* ‖ *tr* saboter, bousiller ‖ *intr* saboter

bungler ['bʌŋglər] *s* gâcheur *m*, bousilleur *m*

bungling ['bʌŋglɪŋ] *adj* gauche, maladroit ‖ *s* maladresse *f*

bunion ['bʌnjən] *s* oignon *m* (au pied)

bunk [bʌŋk] *s* couchette *f*; (slang) balivernes *fpl*, sornettes *fpl* ‖ *intr* (coll) se coucher

bunk' bed' *s* (naut) cadre *m*

bunker ['bʌŋkər] *s* (golf) banquette *f*; (naut) soute *f*

bun·ny ['bʌni] *s* (*pl* **-nies**) petit lapin *m*

bunting ['bʌntɪŋ] *s* drapeaux *mpl*; (*cloth*) étamine *f*; (orn) bruant *m*

buoy [bɔɪ], ['bu·i] *s* bouée *f* ‖ *tr*—**to buoy up** faire flotter; (fig) soutenir

buoyancy ['bɔɪ-ənsi], ['bujənsi] s flottabilité f

buoyant ['bɔɪ-ənt], ['bujənt] adj flottant; (cheerful) plein d'allant, plein de ressort

bur [bʌr] s (of chestnut) bogue f; (ragged metal edge) bavure f, barbe f

burble ['bʌrbəl] s murmure m ‖ intr murmurer

burden ['bʌrdən] s fardeau m, charge f; (mus) refrain m ‖ tr charger

burdensome ['bʌrdənsəm] adj onéreux

burdock ['bʌrdɑk] s bardane f

bureau ['bjʊro] s commode f, chiffonier m; (office) bureau m

bureaucracy [bju'rɑkrəsi] s (pl -cies) bureaucratie f

bureaucrat ['bjʊrə,kræt] s bureaucrate mf

bureaucratic [,bjʊrə'krætɪk] adj bureaucratique

bu'reau of vi'tal statis'tics s bureau m de l'état civil

burg [bʌrg] s (coll) hameau m, patelin m; (coll) ville f

burglar ['bʌrglər] s cambrioleur m

bur'glar alarm' s signalisateur m antivol, sonnette f d'alarme

burglarize ['bʌrglə,raɪz] tr cambrioler

bur'glar-proof' adj incrochetable

burglar·y ['bʌrgləri] s (pl -ies) cambriolage m

Burgundian [bər'gʌndɪ-ən] adj bourguignon ‖ s (dialect) bourguignon m; (person) Bourguignon m

Burgundy ['bʌrgəndi] s Bourgogne f; la Bourgogne ‖ **burgun·dy** s (-dies) (wine) bourgogne m

burial ['berɪ-əl] s enterrement m, inhumation f

bur'ial ground' s cimetière m

burlap ['bʌrlæp] s toile f d'emballage, serpillière f

burlesque [bər'lesk] adj & s burlesque m ‖ tr parodier

burlesque' show' s music-hall m

bur·ly ['bʌrli] adj (comp -lier; super -liest) solide, costaud

Burma ['bʌrmə] s Birmanie f; la Birmanie

Bur·mese [bər'miz] adj birman ‖ s (pl -mese) (language) birman m; (person) Birman m

burn [bʌrn] s brûlure f ‖ v (pret & pp burned or burnt [bʌrnt]) tr & intr brûler; **to burn out** (elec) griller

burner ['bʌrnər] s brûleur m; (using gas) bec m; (of a stove) feu m

burning ['bʌrnɪŋ] adj brûlant; (in flames) en feu ‖ s brûlure f; (fire) incendie m

burnish ['bʌrnɪʃ] tr brunir, polir

burrow ['bʌro] s terrier m ‖ tr creuser ‖ intr se terrer

bursar ['bʌrsər] s économe m

burst [bʌrst] s éclat m, explosion f ‖ v (pret & pp burst) intr faire éclater; (a balloon) crever; (a boiler; one's buttons) faire sauter ‖ intr éclater, exploser; (said of tire) crever; **to burst into tears** fondre en larmes; **to burst out laughing** éclater de rire

bur·y ['beri] v (pret & pp -ied) tr enterrer, ensevelir; (e.g., pirate treasure) enfouir

bus [bʌs] s (pl busses or buses) autobus m; (interurban or sightseeing) car m, autocar m ‖ v (pret & pp bused or bussed; ger busing or bussing) tr transporter en autobus

bus'boy' s aide-serveur m

bush [bʊʃ] s buisson m; (shrub) arbuste m; (in Africa and Australia) brousse f; **to beat around the bush** tourner autour du pot, tortiller

bushed [bʊʃt] adj (coll) éreinté

bushel ['bʊʃəl] s boisseau m

bushing ['bʊʃɪŋ] s manchon m, douille f, bague f, coussinet m

bush·y ['bʊʃi] adj (comp -ier; super -iest) (countryside) buissonneux; (hair) touffu; (eyebrows) broussailleux

business ['bɪznɪs] adj commercial ‖ s affaires fpl; (subject) sujet m; (theat) jeux mpl de scène; **it's none of your business** cela ne vous regarde pas; **mind your own business!** occupez-vous de vos affaires!, faites votre métier!; **to mean business** (coll) ne pas plaisanter; **to send about one's business** envoyer paître

busi'ness dis'trict s quartier m commerçant

busi'ness hours' s heures fpl d'ouverture

busi'ness house' s maison f de commerce

busi'ness·like' adj pratique; (manner, transaction) sérieux

busi'ness·man' s (pl -men') homme m d'affaires; **big businessman** grand industriel m, chef m d'industrie

busi'ness man'ager s directeur m commercial

busi'ness reply' card' s carte f postale avec réponse payée

busi'ness suit' s complet m veston

busi'ness·wom'an s (pl -wom'en) femme f d'affaires

buskin ['bʌskɪn] s brodequin m

bus' sta'tion s gare f routière

bus' stop' s arrêt m d'autobus

bust [bʌst] s buste m; (of woman) gorge f, buste; (slang) faillite f ‖ tr (mil) limoger; (slang) casser ‖ intr (slang) échouer

busting ['bʌstɪŋ] s (mil) cassation f

bustle ['bʌsəl] s remue-ménage m, affairement m, branle-bas m ‖ intr se remuer, s'affairer

bustling ['bʌslɪŋ] adj affairé

bus·y ['bɪzi] adj (comp -ier; super -iest) occupé ‖ v (pret & pp -ied) tr —**to busy oneself with** s'occuper de

bus'y·bod'y s (pl -ies) officieux m

bus'y sig'nal s (telp) signal m de ligne occupée

but [bʌt] adv seulement; ne . . . que, e.g., **to have nothing but trouble** n'avoir que des ennuis; **but for** sans; **but for that** à part cela ‖ prep sauf, excepté; **all but** presque ‖ conj mais

butcher ['bʊtʃər] s boucher m ‖ tr (an

animal for meat) abattre, dépecer; (*to massacre; to bungle*) massacrer

butch'er knife' s couperet m, coutelas m (de boucher)

butch'er shop' s boucherie f

butler ['bʌtlər] s maître m d'hôtel, intendant m

butt [bʌt] s bout m; (*cask*) futaille f; (*of a gun*) crosse f; (*of a cigarette*) mégot m; (*of a joke*) souffre-douleur m, plastron m; (*blow*) coup m de tête, coup de corne; (slang) postérieur m, derrière m || tr (*like a goat*) donner un coup de corne à || intr—to butt up against buter contre; to butt in (coll) intervenir sans façon

butte [bjut] s butte f, tertre m, puy m

butt' end' s gros bout m

butter ['bʌtər] s beurre m || tr beurrer; to butter up (coll) passer de la pommade à, pateliner

but'ter-cup' s renoncule f, bouton-d'or m

but'ter dish' s beurrier m, beurrière f

but'ter-fat' s crème f

but'ter-fin'gered adj maladroit

but'ter-fin'gers s brise-tout m

but'ter-fly' s (pl -flies) papillon m

but'ter knife' s couteau m à beurre

but'ter-milk' s babeurre m

but'ter-scotch' s caramel m au beurre

buttocks ['bʌtəks] spl fesses fpl

button ['bʌtən] s bouton m || tr boutonner

but'ton-hole' s boutonnière f || tr (coll) retenir (qqn) par le pan de sa veste

but'ton-hook' s tire-bouton m

buttress ['bʌtrɪs] s contrefort m || tr arc-bouter; (fig) étayer

buxom ['bʌksəm] adj plantureuse

buy [baɪ] s—a good buy (coll) une bonne affaire || v (pret & pp bought [bɔt]) tr acheter; (*a ticket*) prendre; to buy a drink for payer un verre à; to buy back racheter; to buy from acheter à or de; to buy out (*a part-*

ner) désintéresser; to buy s.o. off se débarrasser de qn, racheter qn; to buy up accaparer

buyer ['baɪ·ər] s acheteur m

buzz [bʌz] s bourdonnement m; to give s.o. a buzz (*on the telephone*) (coll) passer un coup de fil à || tr (aer) survoler à basse altitude || intr bourdonner

buzzard ['bʌzərd] s buse f

buzz' bomb' s bombe f volante

buzzer ['bʌzər] s trembleur m

buzz' saw' s scie f circulaire

by [baɪ] adv près, auprès; (*aside*) de côté; by and by tout à l'heure, sous peu; by and large généralement parlant || prep par; (*near*) près de; by a head (*taller*) d'une tête; by day pendant la journée; by far de beaucoup; by Monday d'ici à lundi; by profession de profession; by the way à propos; to be followed (loved, etc.) by être suivi (aimé, etc.) de

by-and-by ['baɪ·ən'baɪ] s proche avenir m; in the sweet by-and-by à la Saint-Glinglin

by'gone' adj d'autrefois, passé

by'law' s ordonnance f, règlement m

by'-line' s signature f de journaliste

by'-pass' s déviation f; (elec) dérivation f || tr éviter, contourner; (mach) amener or placer en dérivation

by'-play' s (theat) jeu m en aparté

by'-prod'uct s sous-produit m

by'-road' s chemin m détourné

bystander ['baɪˌstændər] s spectateur m, assistant m

by'way' s chemin m écarté, voie f indirecte

by'word' s dicton m, proverbe m; objet m de dérision

Byzantine ['bɪzənˌtin], [bɪ'zæntin] adj & s byzantin m

Byzantium [bɪ'zænʃɪ·əm], [bɪ'zæntɪ·əm] s Byzance f

C

C, c [si] s IIIᵉ lettre de l'alphabet

cab [kæb] s taxi m; (*of locomotive or truck*) cabine f; (*hansom*) fiacre m, cab m

cabaret [ˌkæbə're] s boîte f de nuit, cabaret m

cabbage ['kæbɪdʒ] s chou m

cab'driv'er s chauffeur m de taxi

cabin ['kæbɪn] s case f, cabane f; (*of ship or airplane*) cabine f

cab'in boy' s (naut) mousse m

cabinet ['kæbɪnɪt] s cabinet m; (*cupboard; radio cabinet*) meuble m; (*of professional men*) étude f, cabinet; (*of officers*) cabinet, bureau m directoire, comité m, conseil m

cab'inet-mak'er s ébéniste m, menuisier m

cab'inet mem'ber s ministre m

cable ['kebəl] s câble m || tr & intr câbler

ca'ble car' s funiculaire m, téléférique m

ca'ble-gram' s câblogramme m

ca'ble ship' s câblier m

ca'ble's length' s encablure f

caboose [kə'bus] s (naut) coquerie f; (rr) fourgon m de queue, wagon m du personnel

cab'stand' s station f de taxi

cache [kæʃ] s cachette f, cache f || tr mettre dans une cachette, cacher

cachet [kæ'ʃe] s cachet m

cackle ['kækəl] *s* caquet *m* ‖ *intr* caqueter; (*said of goose*) cacarder

cacopho·ny [kə'kɑfənɪ] *s* (*pl* -nies) cacophonie *f*

cac·tus ['kæktəs] *s* (*pl* -tuses or -ti [taɪ]) cactus *m*

cad [kæd] *s* malotru *m*

cadaver [kə'dævər] *s* cadavre *m*

cad·dy ['kædɪ] *s* (*pl* -dies) boîte *f* à thé; (*person*) cadet *m*, caddie *m*

cadence ['kedəns] *s* cadence *f*

cadet [kə'dɛt] *s* cadet *m*

cadmium ['kædmɪ·əm] *s* cadmium *m*

Caesar'ean opera'tion [sɪ'zɛrɪ·ən] *s* césarienne *f*

café [kæ'fe] *s* cabaret *m*; caférestaurant *m*

ca'fé soci'ety ['kædmɪ·əm] *s* gens *mpl* chic des cabarets à la mode

cafeteria [ˌkæfə'tɪrɪ·ə] *s* caféteria *f*, restaurant *m* de libre-service

caffeine [kæ'fin], ['kæfin], ['kæfi·ɪn] *s* caféine *f*

cage [kedʒ] *s* cage *f* ‖ *tr* mettre en cage

ca·gey ['kedʒɪ] *adj* (*comp* -gier; *super* -giest) (coll) rusé, fin

cahoots [kə'huts] **—in cahoots** (slang) de mèche

Cain [ken] *s* Caïn *m*; **to raise Cain** (coll) faire le diable à quatre

Cairo ['kaɪro] *s* Le Caire

caisson ['kesən] *s* caisson *m*

cais'son disease' *s* maladie *f* des caissons

cajole [kə'dʒol] *tr* cajoler, enjôler

cajoler·y [kə'dʒolərɪ] *s* (*pl* -ies) cajolerie *f*, enjôlement *m*

cake [kek] *s* gâteau *m*; (*one-layer cake*) galette *f*; (*pastry*) pâtisserie *f*; (*of soap, wax*) pain *m*; (*of ice*) bloc *m*; (*crust*) croûte *f*; **to sell like hot cakes** (coll) se vendre comme des petits pains; **to take the cake** (coll) être la fin des haricots ‖ *tr* couvrir d'une croûte ‖ *intr* s'agglutiner, faire croûte

calabash ['kælə,bæʃ] *s* calebasse *f*; (*tree*) calebassier *m*

calaboose ['kælə,bus] *s* (coll) violon *m*, tôle *f*

calamitous [kə'læmɪtəs] *adj* calamiteux

calami·ty [kə'læmɪtɪ] *s* (*pl* -ties) calamité *f*

calci·fy ['kælsɪ,faɪ] *v* (*pret & pp* -fied) *tr* calcifier ‖ *intr* se calcifier

calcium ['kælsɪ·əm] *s* calcium *m*

calculate ['kælkjə,let] *tr & intr* calculer

calculating ['kælkjə,letɪŋ] *adj* calculateur

calculation [ˌkælkjə'leʃən] *s* calcul *m*

calcu·lus ['kælkjələs] *s* (*pl* -luses or -li [,laɪ]) (math, pathol) calcul *m*

caldron ['kɔldrən] *s* (culin) chaudron *m*; (mach) chaudière *f*

calendar ['kæləndər] *s* calendrier *m*

cal'endar year' *s* année *f* civile

calender ['kæləndər] *s* calandre *f* ‖ *tr* calandrer, cylindrer

calf [kæf], [kɑf] *s* (*pl* calves [kævz], [kɑvz]) veau *m*; (*of leg*) mollet *m*

calf'skin' *s* veau *m*, peau *f* de veau

calf's' liv'er *s* foie *m* de veau

caliber ['kælɪbər] *s* calibre *m*

calibrate ['kælɪ,bret] *tr* calibrer

cali·co ['kælɪ,ko] *s* (*pl* -coes or -cos) calicot *m*, indienne *f*

California [ˌkælɪ'fɔrnɪ·ə] *s* Californie *f*; la Californie

calipers ['kælɪpərz] *spl* compas *m* à calibrer

caliph ['kelɪf], ['kælɪf] *s* calife *m*

caliphate ['kælɪ,fet] *s* califat *m*

calisthenic [ˌkælɪs'θɛnɪk] *adj* callisthénique ‖ **calisthenics** *spl* callisthénie *f*

calk [kɔk] *s* crampon *m* à glace ‖ *tr* calfater

call [kɔl] *s* appel *m*; (*cry*) cri *m*; (*visit*) visite *f*; (*at a port*) escale *f*; **to have no call to** n'avoir aucune raison de ‖ *tr* appeler; (*e.g., the doctor*) faire venir; (*a meeting*) convoquer; **to call aside** prendre à part; **to call back** rappeler; **to call down** (*from upstairs*) faire descendre; (*the wrath of the gods*) invoquer; (*to scold*) (coll) gronder; **to call off** (*a dog*) rappeler; (coll) annuler, décommander; **to call the roll** faire l'appel; **to call to mind** rappeler; **to call to order** rappeler à l'ordre; **to call up** (coll) passer un coup de fil à; (mil) mobiliser ‖ *intr* appeler, crier; (*to visit*) faire une visite; (naut) faire escale; **to call upon** faire appel à; **to call upon s.o. to speak** inviter qn à prendre la parole

call' bell' *s* sonnette *f*

call' box' *s* guérite *f* téléphonique

call' boy' *s* (*in a hotel*) chasseur *m*; (theat) avertisseur *m*

caller ['kɔlər] *s* visiteur *m*

call' girl' *s* call-girl *f*

calling ['kɔlɪŋ] *s* vocation *f*, profession *f*; (*of a meeting*) convocation *f*

cal'ling card' *s* carte *f* de visite

call' let'ter *s* (telg, rad) indicatif *m* d'appel

call' mon'ey *s* prêts *mpl* au jour le jour

callous ['kæləs] *adj* (*foot, hand, etc.*) calleux; (*unfeeling*) endurci, insensible

callow ['kælo] *adj* inexpérimenté, novice

cal'low youth' *s* blanc-bec *m*

callus ['kæləs] *s* (*on skin*) cal *m*, durillon *m*, callosité *f*; (bot) cal *m*

calm [kɑm] *adj & s* calme *m* ‖ *tr* calmer; **to calm down** pacifier ‖ *intr* **—to calm down** se calmer; (*said of wind or sea*) calmir

calorie ['kælərɪ] *s* calorie *f*

calum·ny ['kæləmnɪ] *s* (*pl* -nies) calomnie *f*

calva·ry ['kælvərɪ] *s* (*pl* -ries) calvaire *m*; Calvary le Calvaire

calve [kæv], [kɑv] *intr* vêler

cam [kæm] *s* came *f*

cambric ['kembrɪk] *s* batiste *f*

camel ['kæməl] *s* chameau *m*

camellia [kə'miljə] *s* camélia *m*

came·o ['kæmɪ,o] *s* (*pl* -os) camée *m*

camera ['kæmərə] s appareil m (photographique)

cam'era-man' s (pl -men') photographe m

camouflage ['kæmə,flɑʒ] s camouflage m || tr camoufler

camp [kæmp] s camp m || intr camper; to go camping faire du camping

campaign [kæm'pen] s campagne f || intr faire campagne

campaigner [kæm'penər] s propagandiste m f; vétéran m

camp' bed' s lit m de camp, lit de sangle

camp' chair' s chaise f pliante

camper ['kæmpər] s campeur m

camp'fire' s feu m de camp

camp'ground' s camping m

camphor ['kæmfər] s camphre m

camping ['kæmpɪŋ] s camping m

camp'stool' s pliant m

campus ['kæmpəs] s campus m, terrain m universitaire

cam'shaft' s arbre m à cames

can [kæn] s boîte f; (e.g., for gasoline) bidon m || v (pret & pp canned; ger canning) tr mettre en boîte, conserver; (to dismiss) (slang) dégommer || v (pret & cond could [kud] aux—Albert can't do it Albert ne peut (pas) le faire; can he swim? sait-il nager?

Canada ['kænədə] s le Canada

Canadian [kə'nedɪ-ən] adj canadien || s (person) Canadien m

canal [kə'næl] s canal m

canary [kə'neri] s (pl -ies) canari m, serin m

can-cel ['kænsəl] v (pret & pp -celed or -celled; ger -celing or -celling) tr annuler; (a word) biffer, rayer; (a contract) résilier; (a postage stamp) oblitérer; to cancel an invitation décommander les invités; to cancel each other out s'annuler, se détruire

cancellation [,kænsə'leʃən] s annulation f; (of postage stamp) oblitération f; (of contract) résiliation f

cancer ['kænsər] s cancer m

cancerous ['kænsərəs] adj cancéreux

candela-brum [,kændə'lebrəm] s (pl -bra [brə] or -brums) candélabre m

candid ['kændɪd] adj franc

candida-cy ['kændɪdəsi] s (pl -cies) candidature f

candidate ['kændɪ,det] s candidat m

candied adj candi

candied' fruit' s fruit m candi

candle ['kændəl] s bougie f; (of tallow) chandelle f; (eccl) cierge m

can'dle-hold'er s bougeoir m

can'dle-light' s lumière f de bougie

can'dle-pow'er s (phys) bougie f

can'dle-stick' s chandelier m, bougeoir m

can'dle ta'ble s guéridon m

candor ['kændər] s franchise f, loyauté f

can-dy ['kændi] s (pl -dies) confiserie f, bonbons mpl; candies douceurs fpl; piece of candy bonbon m || v (pret & pp -died) tr glacer, faire candir || intr se candir

can'dy box' s boîte f à bonbons

can'dy corn' s grains mpl de maïs soufflés et sucrés

can'dy dish' s bonbonnière

can'dy store' s confiserie f

cane [ken] s canne f; (bot) canne || tr canner, rempailler

cane' chair' s chaise f cannée

cane' sug'ar s sucre m de canne

canine ['kenaɪn] adj canin || s (tooth) canine f

canister ['kænɪstər] s boîte f métallique; (mil) boîte à mitraille

canker ['kæŋkər] s chancre m; (in fruit; in society) ver m rongeur || tr ronger; (society) corrompre

canned' goods' spl conserves fpl, aliments mpl conservés

canned' mu'sic s (coll) musique f enregistrée

canner-y ['kænəri] s (pl -ies) conserverie f

cannibal ['kænɪbəl] adj & s cannibale mf

canning ['kænɪŋ] s conservation f

can'ning fac'tory s conserverie f

cannon ['kænən] s canon m

cannonade [,kænə'ned] s canonnade f || tr canonner

can'non-ball' s boulet m (de canon)

can'non fod'der s chair f à canon

can-ny ['kæni] adj (comp -nier; super -niest) prudent, circonspect; rusé, malin

canoe [kə'nu] s canoë m

canoeist [kə'nu-ɪst] s canoéiste mf

canon ['kænən] s canon m

canonical [kə'nɑnɪkəl] adj canonique, canonial || canonicals spl vêtements mpl sacerdotaux

canonize ['kænə,naɪz] tr canoniser

can' o'pener s ouvre-boîtes m

cano-py ['kænəpi] s (pl -pies) dais m; (over an entrance) marquise f

cant [kænt] s cant m, cafardise f; (argot) jargon m || tr (to tip) incliner || intr (to tip) s'incliner; (to be hypocritical) papelarder

cantaloupe ['kæntə,lop] s cantaloup m

cantankerous [kæn'tæŋkərəs] adj revêche, acariâtre

cantata [kən'tɑtə] s cantate f

canteen [kæn'tin] s (shop) cantine f; (water flask) bidon m; (service club) foyer m du soldat, du marin, etc.

canter ['kæntər] s petit galop m || intr aller au petit galop

canticle ['kæntɪkəl] s cantique m, hymne f

cantilever ['kæntɪ,livər] adj & s cantilever m

can'tilever bridge' s pont m cantilever, pont à consoles

canton [kæn'tɑn] s canton m

canvas ['kænvəs] s (cloth) canevas m; (picture) toile f

canvass ['kænvəs] s enquête f, sondage m; (pol) tournée f électorale || tr (a voter) solliciter la voix de; (a district) faire une tournée électorale dans; (com) prospecter || intr (com) faire la place; to canvass for (a candidate) faire une campagne électorale en faveur de

canyon ['kænjən] s cañon m

cap [kæp] s (*with visor*) casquette f; (*without brim*) bonnet m; (*to wear with academic gown*) toque f, mortier m; (*of bottle*) capsule f; (*of cartridge*) amorce f, capsule; (*of fountain pen*) capuchon m, chapeau m; (*of valve; to cover photographic lens*) chapeau; **to set one's cap for** chercher à captiver ∥ v (*pret & pp* **capped;** *ger* **capping**) tr coiffer; (*a bottle*) capsuler; (*a cartridge*) amorcer; (*a success*) couronner; (*to outdo*) (coll) surpasser

cap. *abbr* (**capital letter**) maj.

capable ['kepəbəl] *adj* capable

capacious [kə'peʃəs] *adj* spacieux, vaste, ample

capaci-ty [kə'pæsɪti] s (*pl* **-ties**) capacité f; **filled to capacity** comble; **in the capacity of** en tant que, en qualité de, à titre de

cap' and gown' s costume m académique, toge f et mortier m; **in cap and gown** en toque et en toge

cape [kep] s (*clothing*) cape f, pèlerine f; (geog) cap m, promontoire m

Cape' of Good Hope' s Cap m de Bonne Espérance

caper ['kepər] s cabriole f, gambade f; (bot) câpre f ∥ tr cabrioler, gambader

Cape'town' s Le Cap

capital ['kæpɪtəl] *adj* capital; excellent ∥ s (*city*) capitale f; (archit) chapiteau m; (com) capital m; (typ) majuscule f, capitale; **small capital** petite capitale

cap'ital let'ter s majuscule f

cap'ital and la'bor *spl* le capital et le travail

capitalism ['kæpɪtə,lɪzəm] s capitalisme m

capitalist ['kæpɪtəlɪst] *adj & s* capitaliste mf

capitalize ['kæpɪtə,laɪz] tr & intr capitaliser; (typ) écrire avec une majuscule; **to capitalize on** miser sur, tourner à son profit, tirer parti de

capitol ['kæpɪtəl] s capitole m

capitulate [kə'pɪtʃə,let] intr capituler

capon ['kepən] s chapon m

caprice [kə'pris] s caprice m

capricious [kə'prɪʃəs] *adj* capricieux

capsize ['kæpsaɪz] tr faire chavirer ∥ intr chavirer, capoter

capstan ['kæpstən] s cabestan m

capsule ['kæpsəl] s capsule f; (bot, rok) capsule

captain ['kæptən] s capitaine m; chef m; (sports) chef d'équipe ∥ tr commander, diriger

captain·cy ['kæptənsi] s (*pl* **-cies**) direction f, commandement m; grade m de capitaine

caption ['kæpʃən] s légende f; (mov) sous-titre m ∥ tr intituler, donner un sous-titre à

captious ['kæpʃəs] *adj* pointilleux, chicaneux; (*insidious*) captieux

captivate ['kæptɪ,vet] tr captiver

captive ['kæptɪv] *adj & s* captif m

captivi-ty [kæp'tɪvɪti] s (*pl* **-ties**) captivité f

captor ['kæptər] s ravisseur m; (naut) auteur m d'une prise

capture ['kæptʃər] s capture f, prise f ∥ tr capturer

car [kar] s auto f, voiture f; (*of elevator*) cabine f; (rr) wagon m, voiture; (*for mail, baggage, etc.*) (rr) fourgon m

carafe [kə'ræf] s carafe f

caramel ['kærəməl], ['karməl] s caramel m

carat ['kærət] s carat m

caravan ['kærə,væn] s caravane f

caravansa·ry [,kærə'vænsəri] s (*pl* **-ries**) caravansérail m

caraway ['kærə,we] s carvi m

car'away seed' s graine f de carvi

car'barn' s dépôt m de tramways

carbide ['karbaɪd] s carbure m

carbine ['karbaɪn] s carabine f

carbol'ic ac'id [kar'balɪk] s acide m phénique

carbon ['karbən] s (*chemical element*) carbone m; (*part of arc light or battery*) charbon m; (*in auto cylinder*) calamine f; papier m carbone

car'bonated wa'ter ['karbə,netɪd] s eau f gazeuse, soda m

car'bon cop'y s double m au carbone; (fig) calque m; (*person*) (fig) sosie m

car'bon diox'ide s gaz m carbonique

car'bon monox'ide s oxyde m de carbone

car'bon pa'per s papier m carbone

carbuncle ['karbʌŋkəl] s furoncle m

carburetor ['karbə,retər] s carburateur m

carcass ['karkəs] s (*dead body*) cadavre m; (*without offal*) carcasse f

card [kard] s carte f; (*for filing*) fiche f; (*for carding*) carde f; (coll) original m, numéro m, type m; **to put one's cards on the table** jouer cartes sur table ∥ tr carder, peigner

card'board' s carton m

card' case' s porte-cartes m

card' cat'alogue s fichier m

cardiac ['kardɪ,æk] *adj* cardiaque ∥ s (*patient*) (coll) cardiaque mf

cardinal ['kardɪnəl] *adj & s* cardinal m

card' in'dex s fichier m

cardiogram ['kardɪ·o,græm] s cardiogramme m

card'sharp' s tricheur m

card' ta'ble s table f de jeu

card' trick' s tour m de cartes

care [ker] s (*attention*) soin m; (*anxiety*) souci m; (*responsibility*) charge f; (*upkeep*) entretien m; **in care of** aux bons soins de, à l'attention de; **take care!** faites attention!; **to take care not to** se garder de; **to take care of** se charger de; (*a sick person*) soigner; **to take care to** avoir soin de ∥ *intr*—**I don't care** ça m'est égal; **to care about** se soucier de, se préoccuper de; **to care for** (*s.o.*) avoir de la sympathie pour; (*s.th.*) trouver plaisir à; (*a sick person*) soigner; **to care to** désirer, vouloir

areen [kə'rin] *tr* faire coucher sur le côté || *intr* donner de la bande, s'incliner

areer [kə'rɪr] *s* carrière *f*

are/free/ *adj* sans souci, insouciant

areful ['kɛrfəl] *adj* soigneux, attentif; **be careful!** soyez prudent!

areless ['kɛrlɪs] *adj* (*neglectful*) négligent; (*nonchalant*) insouciant

arelessness ['kɛrlɪsnɪs] *s* négligence *f*

aress [kə'rɛs] *s* caresse *f* || *tr* caresser

aret ['kærət] *s* guidon *m* de renvoi

care/tak/er *s* concierge *mf*, gardien *m*

care/tak/er gov/ernment *s* gouvernement *m* intérimaire

care/worn/ *adj* rongé par les soucis

car/fare/ *s* prix *m* du trajet, place *f*; **to pay carfare** payer le parcours

car-go ['kargo] *s* (*pl* **-goes** or **-gos**) cargaison *f*

car/ heat/er *s* chauffage *m* de voiture

Car·ibbe/an Sea/ [,kærɪ'bi·ən], [kə-'rɪbɪ·ən] *s* Mer *f* des Caraïbes, Mer des Antilles

caricature ['kærɪkət/ər] *s* caricature *f* || *tr* caricaturer

caricaturist ['kærɪkət/ərɪst] *s* caricaturiste *mf*

caries ['kɛriz], ['kɛrɪ ,iz] *s* carie *f*

carillon ['kærɪ ,lan], [kə'rɪljən] *s* carillon *m* || *tr & intr* carillonner

car/load/ *s* voiturée *f*

carnage ['karnɪdʒ] *s* carnage *m*

carnal ['karnəl] *adj* charnel; sexuel

car/nal sin/ *s* péché *m* de la chair

carnation [kar'ne/ən] *s* œillet *m*

carnival ['karnɪvəl] *s* carnaval *m*; fête *f*

car·ol ['kærəl] *s* chanson *f*, cantique *m*; (*Christmas carol*) noël *m* || *v* (*pret & pp* **-oled** or **-olled**; *ger* **-oling** or **-olling**) *tr & intr* chanter

carom ['kærəm] *s* carambolage *m* || *intr* caramboler

carouse [kə'rauz] *intr* faire la bombe

carp [karp] *s* carpe *f* || *intr* se plaindre

carpenter ['karpəntər] *s* charpentier *m*; (*joiner*) menuisier *m*

carpentry ['karpəntri] *s* charpenterie *f*

carpet ['karpɪt] *s* tapis *m* || *tr* recouvrir d'un tapis

car/pet sweep/er *s* balai *m* mécanique

car/port/ *s* abri *m* pour auto

car/-rent/al serv/ice *s* entreprise *f* de location de voitures

carriage ['kærɪdʒ] *s* voiture *f*; (*used to transport royalty*) carrosse *m*; (*bearing*) port *m*, maintien *m*; (*cost of transport*) frais *mpl* de port; (*of typewriter; of rocket*) chariot *m*; (*of gun*) affût *m*

carrier ['kærɪ·ər] *s* (*person*) porteur *m*; (*e.g., a teamster*) camionneur *m*, voiturier *m*; (*vehicle*) transporteur *m*

car/rier pig/eon *s* pigeon *m* voyageur

car/rier wave/ *s* onde *f* porteuse

carrion ['kærɪ·ən] *s* charogne *f*

carrot ['kærət] *s* carotte *f*

carrousel [,kærə'zɛl] *s* (*merry-go-round*) manège *m* de chevaux de bois; (*hist*) carrousel *m*

car-ry ['kæri] *v* (*pret & pp* **-ried**) *tr* porter; (*in adding numbers*) retenir; **to be carried** (*parl*) être voté, être adopté; **to be carried away** (*e.g., with enthusiasm*) être entraîné, s'importer; **to carry away** or **off** emporter, enlever; **to carry back** rapporter; **to carry down** descendre; **to carry forward** avancer; (bk) reporter; **to carry on** continuer; (*e.g., a conversation*) soutenir; **to carry oneself straight** se tenir droit; **to carry out** (*a plan*) exécuter; **to carry over** (bk) reporter; **to carry through** mener à bonne fin; **to carry up** monter; **to carry with one** (*e.g., an audience*) entraîner || *intr* (*said of voice or sound*) porter; **to carry on** continuer; (*in a ridiculous manner*) (coll) faire des espiègleries; (*angrily*) (coll) s'emporter

car/ sick/ness *s* mal *m* de la route

cart [kart] *s* charrette *f*; **to put the cart before the horse** mettre la charrue devant les bœufs || *tr* charrier; (*to truck*) camionner

cartel [kar'tɛl] *s* cartel *m*

cartilage ['kartɪlɪdʒ] *s* cartilage *m*

cartographer [kar'tagrəfər] *s* cartographe *m*

carton ['kartən] *s* carton *m*, boîte *f*

cartoon [kar'tun] *s* dessin *m* humoristique; caricature *f*; (*comic strip*) bande *f* dessinée; (*mov*) dessin animé || *tr* caricaturer

cartoonist [kar'tunɪst] *s* caricaturiste *mf*

cartridge ['kartrɪdʒ] *s* cartouche *f*; capsule *f* enregistreuse de pick-up

car/tridge belt/ *s* cartouchière *f*

car/tridge case/ *s* cartouchière *f*

cart/wheel/ *s* roue *f*; **to turn cartwheels** faire la roue

carve [karv] *tr & intr* sculpter; (culin) découper

carver ['karvər] *s* sculpteur *m*; (culin) découpeur *m*

carv/ing knife/ *s* couteau *m* à découper

cascade [kæs'ked] *s* cascade *f* || *intr* cascader

case [kes] *s* (*instance, example*) cas *m*; (*for packing; of clock or piano*) caisse *f*; (*for cigarettes, eyeglasses, cartridges*) étui *m*; (*for jewels, silver, etc.*) écrin *m*; (*for watch*) boîtier *m*; (*for pillow*) taie *f*; (*for surgical instruments*) trousse *f*; (*for sausage*) peau *f*; (*showcase*) vitrine *f*; (*covering*) enveloppe *f*, couverture *f*; (law) cause *f*; (typ) casse *f*; **as the case may be** selon le cas; **in any case** en tout cas; **in case** au cas où; **in case of emergency** en cas d'imprévu; **in no case** en aucun cas; **just in case** à tout hasard; **to win one's case** avoir gain de cause || *tr* (*to put into a case*) encaisser; (*to package*) envelopper; (*to observe*) (slang) observer, épier

case'hard'en *tr* aciérer, cémenter; (fig) endurcir

casein ['kesɪ·ɪn] *s* caséine *f*

casement ['kesmənt] *s* croisée *f*

cash [kæʃ] *s* espèces *fpl*; **cash down** argent comptant; **cash offer** offre *f* réelle; **cash on delivery** livraison contre remboursement; **cash on hand** fonds *mpl* en caisse; **in cash** en numéraire || *tr* toucher, encaisser || *intr* —**to cash in on** (coll) tirer parti de

cash' and car'ry *s* achat *m* au comptant et à emporter

cash' bal'ance *s* solde *m* de caisse

cash' dis'count *s* escompte *m* au comptant

cashew ['kæʃu] *s* noix *f* d'acajou, anacarde *m*; (*tree*) anacardier *m*

cash'ew nut' *s* noix *f* d'acajou

cashier [kæ'ʃɪr] *s* caissier *m*

cashmere ['kæʃmɪr] *s* cachemire *m*

cash' reg'ister *s* caisse *f* enregistreuse

casing ['kesɪŋ] *s* enveloppe *f*, chemise *f*, coffrage *m*; (*of door or window*) chambranle *m*

cask [kæsk], [kɑsk] *s* tonneau *m*, fût *m*

casket ['kæskɪt], ['kɑskɪt] *s* (*for jewels*) écrin *m*, cassette *f*; (*for interment*) cercueil *m*

casserole ['kæsə‚rol] *s* terrine *f*

cassock ['kæsək] *s* soutane *f*

east [kæst], [kɑst] *s* (*mold*) moule *m*; (*of metal*) fonte *f*; (*of fish line*) lancer *m*; (*throw*) jet *m*; (*for broken limb*) plâtre *m*; (*squint*) léger strabisme *m*; (*theat*) distribution *f* || *v* (*pret & pp* **cast**) *tr* fondre, jeter en moule; (*to throw*) lancer; (*a glance*) jeter; (*a play*) distribuer les rôles de; **to be cast in one piece with** venir de fonte avec; **to cast aside** mettre de côté; **to cast lots** tirer au sort; **to cast off** rejeter; **to cast out** mettre à la porte; (*a spell*) exorciser || *intr* (fishing) lancer la canne; **to cast about for** chercher; **to cast off** (naut) larguer les amarres

castanets [‚kæstə'nets] *spl* castagnettes *fpl*

cast'away' *adj & s* naufragé *m*

caste [kæst], [kɑst] *s* caste *f*

caster ['kæstər], ['kɑstər] *s* (*wheel*) roulette *f*; (*cruet stand*) huilier *m*; (*shaker*) saupoudreuse *f*

castigate ['kæstɪ‚get] *tr* châtier, corriger

Castile [kæs'til] *s* Castille *f*; la Castille

Castilian [kæs'tɪljən] *adj* castillan || *s* (*language*) castillan *m*; (*person*) Castillan *m*

casting ['kæstɪŋ] *s* fonte *f*; (*thing cast*) pièce *f* fondue; (*act*) lancement *m*; (fishing) pêche *f* au lancer; (theat) distribution *f*

cast'ing rod' *s* canne *f* à lancer

cast' i'ron *s* fonte *f*

cast'-i'ron *adj* en fonte

cast'-iron stom'ach *s* estomac *m* d'autruche

castle ['kæsəl], ['kɑsəl] *s* château *m*; (*fortified castle*) château fort; (chess) tour *f* || *tr & intr* (chess) roquer

cast'off' *adj & s* rejeté *m*

cas'tor oil' ['kæstər], ['kɑstər] *s* huile *f* de ricin

castrate ['kæstret] *tr* castrer

casual ['kæʒʊ·əl] *adj* casuel; (*indifferent*) insouciant, désinvolte

casually ['kæʒʊ·əli] *adv* nonchalamment, avec désinvolture; (*by chance*) fortuitement

casual·ty ['kæʒʊ·əlti] *s* (*pl* **-ties**) accident *m*; (*person*) accidenté *m*; **casualties** (mil) pertes *fpl*

cas'ualty list' *s* état *m* des pertes

cat [kæt] *s* (*tomcat*) chat *m*; (*female cat*) chatte *f*; (naut) capon *m*; (*shrew*) (coll) cancanière *f*, chipie *f*; **a cat may look at a queen** un chien regarde bien un évêque; **to let the cat out of the bag** (coll) vendre or éventer la mèche; **to rain cats and dogs** (coll) pleuvoir à seaux

cataclysm ['kætə‚klɪzəm] *s* cataclysme *m*

catacombs ['kætə‚komz] *spl* catacombes *fpl*

catalogue ['kætə‚lɔg], ['kætə‚lɑg] *s* catalogue *m*; (*university*) annuaire *m* || *tr* cataloguer, classer

Catalonia [‚kætə'lonɪ·ə] *s* Catalogne *f*; la Catalogne

catalyst ['kætəlɪst] *s* catalyseur *m*

catapult ['kætə‚pʌlt] *s* catapulte *f* || *tr* catapulter

cataract ['kætə‚rækt] *s* cataracte *f*

catarrh [kə'tar] *s* catarrhe *m*

catastrophe [kə'tæstrəfi] *s* catastrophe *f*

cat'call' *s* huée *f*; (theat) coup *m* de sifflet || *tr & intr* (theat) siffler

catch [kætʃ] *s* prise *f*; (*on door*) loquet *m*; (*on buckle*) ardillon *m*; (*caught by fisherman*) pêche *f*; (mach) cliquet *m*, chien *m*; **there's a catch to it** (coll) c'est une attrape || *v* (*pret & pp* **caught** [kɔt]) *tr* attraper; (*a train; a fish; fire*) prendre; (*a word or sound*) saisir; (*e.g., one's coat*) accrocher; **caught like a rat in a trap** fait comme un rat; **to catch hold of** saisir, s'accrocher à; **to catch s.o. in the act** prendre qn sur le fait; **to catch up** (*in a mistake*) surprendre || *intr* prendre; (*said of fire*) s'allumer, s'enflammer, se prendre; **to catch on** (*a nail, thorn, etc.*) s'accrocher à; (*to understand*) (coll) comprendre; (*to become popular*) (coll) devenir célèbre, devenir populaire; **to catch up to** rattraper; **to catch up with** rattraper

catch'all' *s* débarras *m*, fourre-tout *m*

catching ['kætʃɪŋ] *adj* contagieux; (*e.g., smile*) communicatif

catch' ques'tion *s* (coll) colle *f*

catch'word' *s* mot *m* de ralliement, slogan *m*; (*cliché*) rengaine *f*, scie *f*; (*at the bottom of page*) réclame *f*; (theat) réplique *f*; (typ) mot-souche *m*

catch·y ['kætʃi] *adj* (*comp* **-ier**; *super* **-iest**) (*tune*) facile à retenir, entraînant; (*question*) insidieux, à traquenard

catechism ['kætɪ‚kɪzəm] *s* catéchisme *m*

categorical [ˌkætɪˈgɑrɪkəl], [ˌkætɪˈgɔrɪkəl] *adj* catégorique

catego·ry [ˈkætɪˌgori] *s (pl* -ries) catégorie *f*

cater [ˈketər] *tr (e.g., a wedding)* fournir le buffet de || *intr* être fournisseur; **to cater to** pourvoir à; *(to favor)* entourer de prévenances

cat'er-cor•nered [ˈkætər ˌkɔrnərd] *adj* diagonal || *adv* diagonalement

caterer [ˈketərər] *s* fournisseur *m*, traiteur *m*

caterpillar [ˈkætər ˌpɪlər] *s* chenille *f*

cat'erpillar trac'tor *s* autochenille *f*

cat'fish' *s* poisson-chat *m*

cat'gut' *s* boyau *m* de chat; *(string)* corde *f* à boyau, boyau; *(surg)* cat-gut *m*

cathedral [kəˈθidrəl] *s* cathédrale *f*

catheter [ˈkæθɪtər] *s (med)* cathéter *m*

catheterization [ˌkæθɪtərɪˈzeʃən] *s (surg)* cathétérisme *m*

cathode [ˈkæθod] *s* cathode *m*

catholic [ˈkæθəlɪk] *adj (universal)* catholique; tolérant, large, e.g., **he has a catholic mind** il a l'esprit large, il est fort tolérant || *(cap) adj & s* catholique *mf*

Catholicism [kəˈθɑlɪˌsɪzəm] *s* catholicisme *m*

catholicity [ˌkæθəˈlɪsɪti] *s* catholicité *f*, universalité *f*; *(tolerance)* largeur *f* d'esprit, tolérance *f*

catkin [ˈkætkɪn] *s (bot)* chaton *m*

cat'nap' *s* petit somme *m*

cat'nip' *s* herbe-aux-chats *f*, cataire *f*

cat-o'-nine-tails [ˌkætəˈnain ˌtelz] *s* chat *m* à neuf queues

cat's'-paw' *s (naut)* risée *f*; *(coll)* dupe *f*

catsup [ˈkætsəp], [ˈkætʃəp] *s* sauce *f* tomate

cattle [ˈkætəl] *s* bœufs *mpl*; *(including horses)* gros bétail *m*, bestiaux *mpl*

cat'tle car' *s* fourgon *m* à bestiaux

cat'tle cross'ing *s* passage *m* de troupeaux

cat'tle-man *s (pl* -men) éleveur *m* de bétail

cat'tle thief' *s* voleur *m* de bétail

cat-ty [ˈkæti] *adj (comp* -tier; *super* -tiest) *(coll)* cancanier, méchant

cat'ty-cor'ner *adj (coll)* diagonal || *adv (coll)* diagonalement

cat'walk' *s* passerelle *f*

Caucasian [kɔˈkeʒən], [kɔˈkeʃən] *adj* caucasien || *s* Caucasien *m*

caucus [ˈkɔkəs] *s* comité *m* électoral || *intr* se grouper en comité électoral

cauliflower [ˈkɔlɪ ˌflauər] *s* chou-fleur *m*

caulk [kɔk] *tr* calfater

cause [kɔz] *s* cause *f*; **to have cause to** avoir lieu de || *tr* causer; **to cause to** + *inf* faire + *inf*, e.g., **he caused him to stumble** il l'a fait trébucher

cause'way' *s* chaussée *f*

caustic [ˈkɔstɪk] *adj* caustique

cauterize [ˈkɔtə ˌraɪz] *tr* cautériser

caution [ˈkɔʃən] *s* prudence *f*, précaution *f*; *(warning)* avertissement *m* || *tr* mettre en garde, avertir

cautious [ˈkɔʃəs] *adj* prudent, circonspect

cavalcade [ˌkævəlˈked], [ˈkævəl ˌked] *s* cavalcade *f*

cavalier [ˌkævəˈlɪr] *adj & s* cavalier *m*

caval•ry [ˈkævəlri] *s (pl* -ries) cavalerie *f*

cav'alry-man or **cav'alry-man** *s (pl* -men' or -men) cavalier *m*

cave [kev] *s* caverne *f* || *intr*—**to cave in** s'effondrer

cave'-in' *s* effondrement *m*

cavern [ˈkævərn] *s* caverne *f*

caviar [ˈkævɪ ˌar], [ˈkɑvɪ ˌar] *s* caviar *m*

cav•il [ˈkævɪl] *v (pret & pp* -iled or -illed; *ger* -iling or -illing) *intr* ergoter, chicaner

cavi•ty [ˈkævɪti] *s (pl* -ties) cavité *f*

cavort [kəˈvɔrt] *intr* gambader, caracoler

caw [kɔ] *s* croassement *m* || *intr* croasser, crailler

cease [sis] *s* cessation *f*; **without cease** sans cesse || *tr & intr* cesser; **to cease fire** cesser le feu

cease'-fire' *s* cessez-le-feu *m*

ceaseless [ˈsislɪs] *adj* incessant, continuel

cedar [ˈsidər] *s* cèdre *m*

cede [sid] *tr & intr* céder

cedilla [sɪˈdɪlə] *s* cédille *f*

ceiling [ˈsilɪŋ] *s* plafond *m*; **to hit the ceiling** *(coll)* sortir de ses gonds

ceil'ing lamp' *s* plafonnier *m*

ceil'ing price' *s* prix *m* maximum

celebrant [ˈsɛlɪbrənt] *s (eccl)* célébrant *m*

celebrate [ˈsɛlɪ ˌbret] *tr* célébrer

celebrated *adj* célèbre

celebration [ˌsɛlɪˈbreʃən] *s* célébration *f*, fête *f*

celebri•ty [sɪˈlɛbrɪti] *s (pl* -ties) célébrité *f*; *(e.g., movie star)* vedette *f*

celery [ˈsɛləri] *s* céleri *m*

celestial [sɪˈlɛstʃəl] *adj* céleste

celiba•cy [ˈsɛlɪbəsi] *s (pl* -cies) célibat *m*

celibate [ˈsɛlɪ ˌbet], [ˈsɛlɪbɪt] *adj & s* célibataire *mf*

cell [sɛl] *s* cellule *f*; *(of electric battery)* élément *m*

cellar [ˈsɛlər] *s (basement; wine cellar)* cave *f*; *(often partly above ground)* sous-sol *m*

cellist or **'cellist** [ˈtʃɛlɪst] *s* violoncelliste *mf*

cel•lo or **'cel•lo** [ˈtʃɛlo] *s (pl* -los) violoncelle *m*

cellophane [ˈsɛlə ˌfen] *s* cellophane *f*

celluloid [ˈsɛljə ˌlɔɪd] *s* celluloïd *m*

Celt [sɛlt], [kɛlt] *s* Celte *mf*

Celtic [ˈsɛltɪk], [ˈkɛltɪk] *adj* celte, celtique || *s* celtique *m*

cement [sɪˈmɛnt] *s* ciment *m* || *tr* cimenter

cement' mix'er *s* bétonnière *f*

cemeter•y [ˈsɛmɪ ˌtɛri] *s (pl* -ies) cimetière *m*

censer [ˈsɛnsər] *s* encensoir *m*

censor [ˈsɛnsər] *s* censeur *m* || *tr* censurer

cen'sor·ship' s censure f
censure ['sɛnʃər] s blâme m ‖ tr blâmer
census ['sɛnsəs] s recensement m, dénombrement m; (in Roman Empire)
cens m
cen'sus tak'er s recenseur m; (in ancient Rome) censeur m
cent [sɛnt] s cent m; not to have a red
cent to one's name n'avoir pas un
sou vaillant
centaur ['sɛntɔr] s centaure m
centenarian [ˌsɛntɪ'nɛrɪ·ən] s centenaire mf
centennial [sɛn'tɛnɪ·əl] adj centennal ‖
s centenaire m
center ['sɛntər] adj central ‖ s centre
m; (middle) milieu m ‖ tr centrer
‖ intr—to center on concentrer sur
centering ['sɛntərɪŋ] s centrage m;
(phot) cadrage m
cen'ter·piece' s surtout m; milieu m de
table
centigrade ['sɛntɪˌgred] adj & s centigrade m
centimeter ['sɛntɪˌmitər] s centimètre
m
centipede ['sɛntɪˌpid] s mille-pattes m,
myriapodes m
central ['sɛntrəl] adj & s central m
Cen'tral Amer'ica s l'Amérique f centrale
Cen'tral Intel'ligence s la Sûreté, la
Sûreté nationale
centralize ['sɛntrəˌlaɪz] tr centraliser ‖
intr se centraliser
centrifugal [sɛn'trɪfjʊgəl] adj centrifuge
centrifuge ['sɛntrɪˌfjudʒ] s essoreuse f
‖ tr essorer
centu·ry ['sɛntʃəri] s (pl -ries) siècle m
cen'tury-old' adj séculaire
ceramic [sɪ'ræmɪk] adj céramique ‖
ceramics s (art) céramique f; spl (objects) céramiques
cereal ['sɪrɪ·əl] adj céréalier ‖ s (grain)
céréale f; (oatmeal) flocons mpl
d'avoine; (cornflakes) flocons de
maïs; (cooked cereal) bouillie f,
gruau m
cerebral ['sɛrɪbrəl] adj cérébral
ceremonial [ˌsɛrɪ'monɪ·əl] adj cérémonial; (e.g., tribal rites) cérémoniel ‖
s cérémonial m
ceremonious [ˌsɛrɪ'monɪ·əs] adj cérémonieux
ceremo·ny ['sɛrɪˌmoni] s (pl -nies)
cérémonie f; to stand on ceremony
faire des cérémonies
certain ['sʌrtən] adj certain; a certain
certain; certain people certains; for
certain pour sûr, à coup sûr; to make
certain of s'assurer de
certainly ['sʌrtənli] adv certainement
certain·ty ['sʌrtənti] s (pl -ties) certitude f
certificate [sər'tɪfɪkɪt] s certificat m;
(of birth, of marriage, etc.) bulletin
m, acte m, extrait m; (proof) attestation f
cer'tified cop'y s extrait m; (formula
used on documents) pour copie conforme

cer'tified pub'lic account'ant s expert-
comptable m, comptable m agréé
certi·fy ['sʌrtɪˌfaɪ] v (pret & pp -fied)
tr certifier
cervix ['sʌrvɪks] s (pl cervices [sər-
'vaɪsiz]) nuque f
cessation [sɛ'seʃən] s cessation f, cesse f
cesspool ['sɛsˌpul] s fosse f d'aisance,
cloaque m
Ceylon [sɪ'lɑn] s Ceylan m
Ceylo·nese [ˌsilə'niz] adj cingalais ‖ s
(pl -nese) Cingalais m
chafe [tʃef] tr écorcher, irriter ‖ intr
s'écorcher, s'irriter
chaff [tʃæf], [tʃɑf] s balle f; (banter)
raillerie f ‖ tr railler, persifler
chaf'ing dish' s réchaud m de table,
chauffe-plats m
chagrin [ʃə'grɪn] s mortification f,
humiliation f ‖ tr mortifier, humilier
chain [tʃen] s chaîne f ‖ tr enchaîner
chain' gang' s forçats mpl à la chaîne
chain' reac'tion s (phys) réaction f en
chaîne
chain' smok'er s fumeur m à la file
chain'stitch' s point m de chaînette
chain' store' s magasin m à succursales
multiples, économat m
chair [tʃɛr] s chaise f; (held by university professor) chaire f; (of presiding officer; presiding officer himself) fauteuil m; to take a chair prendre un siège, s'asseoir; to take the
chair occuper le fauteuil, présider une
assemblée ‖ tr présider
chair' lift' s télé-siège m
chair'man s (pl -men) président m
chair'man·ship' s présidence f
chair'wom'an s (pl -wom'en) prési-
dente f
chalice ['tʃælɪs] s calice m
chalk [tʃɔk] s craie f; a piece of chalk
une craie, un morceau de craie ‖ tr
marquer avec de la craie, écrire à la
craie
chalk·y ['tʃɔki] adj (comp -ier; super
-iest) crayeux
challenge ['tʃælɪndʒ] s défi m; (objection) contestation f; (mil) qui-vive
m; (sports) challenge m ‖ tr défier;
(to question) mettre en question, contester; (mil) crier qui-vive à
chamber ['tʃembər] s chambre f
chamberlain ['tʃembərlɪn] s chambellan m
cham'ber·maid' s femme f de chambre
cham'ber mu'sic s musique f de chambre
Cham'ber of Com'merce s syndicat m
d'initiative
chameleon [kə'mili·ən] s caméléon m
chamfer ['tʃæmfər] s chanfrein m ‖ tr
chanfreiner
cham·ois ['ʃæmi] s (pl -ois) chamois
m
champ [tʃæmp] s mâchonnement m ‖
tr mâcher bruyamment; to champ the
bit ronger le frein
champagne [ʃæm'pen] s champagne m
‖ (cap) adj champenois ‖ (cap) s
Champagne f; la Champagne
champion ['tʃæmpɪ·ən] s champion m
‖ tr se faire le champion de, défendre

cham'pion·ship' *s* championnat *m*

chance [tʃɑns], [tʃɑns] *adj* fortuit, de rencontre ‖ *s* hasard *m*; risque *m*; (*opportunity*) occasion *f*; **by chance** par hasard, fortuitement; **chances** chances *fpl*, sort *m*; **to take a chance** encourir un risque; acheter un billet de loterie; **to take chances** jouer gros jeu ‖ *tr* hasarder, risquer ‖ *intr*—**to chance** to venir à, avoir l'occasion de; **to chance upon** rencontrer de hasard

chancel [tʃɑnsəl], [tʃɑnsəl] *s* chœur *m*, sanctuaire *m*

chancell·er·y [tʃɑnsələri], [tʃɑnsələri] *s* (*pl* -**ies**) chancellerie *f*

chancellor [tʃɑnsələr], [tʃɑnsələr] *s* chancelier *m*, ministre *m*

chancre [ʃæŋkər] *s* chancre *m*

chandelier [ˌʃændəˈlɪr] *s* lustre *m*

change [tʃendʒ] *s* changement *m*; (*coins*) monnaie *f*; **change in the wind** saute *f* de vent; **change of address** changement de domicile; **change of clothes** vêtements *mpl* de rechange; **for a change** comme distraction; pour changer ‖ *tr* changer; changer de, e.g., **to change religions** changer de culte; **to change sides** tourner casaque ‖ *intr* changer; (*said of voice at puberty*) muer; **to change over** (*e.g., from one system to another*) passer

changeable [tʃendʒəbəl] *adj* changeable; (*weather*) variable; (*character*) changeant, mobile

changeless [tʃendʒlɪs] *adj* immuable

change' of life' *s* retour *m* d'âge

change' of voice' *s* mue *f*

change'o'ver *s* changement *m*, renversement *m*, relève *f*

change' purse' *s* porte-monnaie *m*

chan·nel [tʃænəl] *s* (*body of water joining two others*) canal *m*; (*bed of river*) chenal *m*; (*means of communication*) voie *f*, canal; (*passage*) conduit *m*; (*groove*) cannelure *f*; (*strait*) bras *m* de mer; (*for trade*) débouché *m*; (*rad*) canal; (*rad, telv*) chaîne *f*; (*telv*) canal (Canad); **through channels** par la voie hiérarchique ‖ *v* (*pret & pp* -**neled** or -**nelled**; *ger* -**neling** or -**nelling**) *tr* creuser, canneler

Chan'nel Is'lands *spl* îles *fpl* Anglo-Normandes

chant [tʃænt], [tʃɑnt] *s* chant *m*; (*song sung in a monotone*) plain-chant *m*, psalmodie *f* ‖ *tr & intr* psalmodier

chanter [tʃæntər], [tʃɑntər] *s* chantre *m*

chantey [ʃænti], [tʃænti] *s* chanson *f* de bord

chaos [keˈɑs] *s* chaos *m*

chaotic [keˈɑtɪk] *adj* chaotique

chap [tʃæp] *s* crevasse *f*, gerçure *f*; (*coll*) type *m*, individu *m* ‖ *v* (*pret & pp* **chapped**; *ger* **chapping**) *tr* crevasser, gercer ‖ *intr* se crevasser, se gercer

chapel [tʃæpəl] *s* chapelle *f*; (*in a house*) oratoire *m*; (*Protestant chapel*) temple *m*

chaperon [ʃæpəˌron] *s* chaperon *m*, duègne *f* ‖ *tr* chaperonner

chaplain [tʃæplɪn] *s* aumônier *m*

chaplet [tʃæplɪt] *s* chapelet *m*

chapter [tʃæptər] *s* chapitre *m*; (*of an association*) bureau *m* régional

char [tʃɑr] *v* (*pret & pp* **charred**; *ger* **charring**) *tr & intr* charbonner; **to become charred** se charbonner, se carboniser

character [kærɪktər] *s* caractère *m*; (*theat*) personnage *m*; (*coll*) type *m*, sujet *m*

characteristic [ˌkærɪktəˈrɪstɪk] *adj & s* caractéristique *f*

characterize [ˈkærɪktəˌraɪz] *tr* caractériser

char'acter ref'erence *s* certificat *m* de moralité

char'coal' *s* charbon *m* de bois

char'coal burn'er *s* charbonnier *m*

char'coal pen'cil *s* charbon *m*, crayon *m* de fusain

charge [tʃɑrdʒ] *s* charge *f*; prix *m*; (*against a defendant*) chef *m* d'accusation; (*made to a jury*) résumé *m*; **on a charge of** sous l'inculpation de; **to reverse the charges** téléphoner en p.c.v.; **to take charge of** se charger de; **without charge** gratis ‖ *tr* charger; **to charge s.o. s.th.** prendre or demander q.ch. à qn pour q.ch.; **to charge to s.o.'s account** mettre sur le compte de qn ‖ *intr* (*mil*) charger; **to charge down on** foncer sur

charge' account' *s* compte *m* courant

charger [tʃɑrdʒər] *s* cheval *m* de bataille; (*elec*) chargeur *m*

chariot [tʃærɪ·ət] *s* char *m*

charitable [tʃærɪtəbəl] *adj* charitable

chari·ty [tʃærɪti] *s* (*pl* -**ties**) charité *f*; (*alms*) bienfaisance *f*, aumônes *fpl*; (*institution*) société *f* or œuvre *f* de bienfaisance; **for charity's sake** par charité

charlatan [ʃɑrlətən] *s* charlatan *m*

charm [tʃɑrm] *s* charme *m*; (*e.g., on a bracelet*) breloque *f*, porte-bonheur *m* ‖ *tr* charmer

charming [tʃɑrmɪŋ] *adj* charmeur, charmant

charnel [tʃɑrnəl] *adj* de charnier ‖ *s* charnier *m*, ossuaire *m*

chart [tʃɑrt] *s* (*map*) carte *f*; (*graph*) dessin *m* graphique; (*diagram*) diagramme *m*; (*table*) tableau *m* ‖ *tr* inscrire sur un dessin graphique; (*naut*) porter sur une carte, dresser la carte de

charter [tʃɑrtər] *s* charte *f*; (*of band*) privilège *m*; (*naut*) affrètement *m* ‖ *tr* accorder une charte à; (*a ship*) affréter, noliser; (*a bus*) louer

char'ter mem'ber *s* membre *m* fondateur

char'wom'an *s* (*pl* -**wom'en**) nettoyeuse *f*

chase [tʃes] s chasse f, poursuite f; (for printing) châssis m || tr chasser; (a gem) enchâsser; (gold) ciseler; (metal) repousser; **to chase away** chasser || intr—**to chase after** pourchasser, poursuivre

chaser ['tʃesər] s chasseur m; (of women) (coll) coureur m; (taken after an alcoholic drink) (coll) rince-gueule m

chasm ['kæzəm] s abîme m

chas·sis ['tʃæsi] s (pl -sis [siz]) châssis m

chaste [tʃest] adj chaste

chasten ['tʃesən] tr châtier

chastise [tʃæs'taɪz] tr châtier, corriger

chastisement ['tʃæstɪzmənt], [tʃæs-'taɪzmənt] s châtiment m

chastity ['tʃæstɪti] s chasteté f

chat [tʃæt] s causerie f, causette f || v (pret & pp chatted; ger chatting) intr causer, bavarder

chattel ['tʃætəl] s bien m meuble, objet m mobiliaire

chatter ['tʃætər] s bavardage m, caquetage m || intr bavarder, caqueter; (said of teeth) claquer

chat'ter-box' s bavard m, babillard m

chauffeur ['ʃofər], [ʃo'fʌr] s chauffeur m

chauvinistic [,ʃovɪ'nɪstɪk] adj chauvin

cheap [tʃip] adj bon marché; (coll) honteux; **to get off cheap** (coll) en être quitte à bon compte

cheapen ['tʃipən] tr baisser le prix de; diminuer la valeur de

cheap'skate' s (slang) rat m

cheat [tʃit] s tricheur m, fraudeur m || tr tricher, frauder || intr (e.g., at cards) tricher; (e.g., in an examination) frauder

cheating ['tʃitɪŋ] s tricherie f, fraude f

check [tʃek] s (stopping) arrêt m; (brake) frein m; (supervision) contrôle m, vérification f; (in a restaurant) addition f; (drawn on a bank) chèque m; (e.g., of a chessboard) carreau m; (of the king in chess) échec m; (for baggage) bulletin m; (pass-out check) contremarque f; (chip, counter) jeton m; **in check** en échec || tr arrêter, freiner; contrôler, vérifier; (baggage) faire enregistrer; (e.g., one's coat) mettre au vestiaire; (the king in chess) faire échec à; **to check off** pointer, cocher || intr s'arrêter; **to check in** (at a hotel) s'inscrire sur le registre; **to check out** (of a hotel) régler sa note; **to check up on** contrôler, examiner

check'book' s carnet m de chèques, chéquier m

checked adj (checkered) à carreaux; (syllable) entravé

checker ['tʃekər] s (inspector) contrôleur m; (piece used in game) pion m; (square of checkerboard) carreau m; **checkers** jeu m de dames || tr quadriller; (to divide in squares) quadriller; (to scatter here and there) diaprer

check'er-board' s damier m

checkered adj (divided into squares) quadrillé, à carreaux; (varied) varié, accidenté; (career, life) plein de vicissitudes, mouvementé

check' girl' s préposée f au vestiaire

check'ing account' s compte m en banque

check' list' s liste f de contrôle

check' mark' s trait m de repère, repère m, coche f

check'mate' s échec et mat m; (fig) échec m || tr faire échec et mat à, mater || intr faire échec et mat, mater || interj échec et mat!

check'-out count'er s caisse f de supermarché

check'point' s contrôle m de police

check'room' s (cloakroom) vestiaire m; (baggage room) consigne f

check'up' s vérification f, examen m

cheek [tʃik] s joue f; (coll) aplomb m, toupet m

cheek'bone' s pommette f

cheep [tʃip] intr piauler

cheer [tʃɪr] s bonne humeur f, gaieté f; encouragement m, e.g., **word of cheer** parole f d'encouragement; **cheers** acclamations fpl, bravos mpl, vivats mpl; **three cheers for...!** vive...!; **to give three cheers** pousser trois hourras || tr (to cheer up) encourager, égayer; (to applaud) acclamer, applaudir || intr pousser des vivats, applaudir; **cheer up!** courage!

cheerful ['tʃɪrfəl] adj de bonne humeur, gai; (place) d'aspect agréable

cheerfully ['tʃɪrfəli] adv gaiement; (willingly) de bon cœur

cheer'lead'er s chef m de claque

cheerless ['tʃɪrlɪs] adj morne, triste

cheese [tʃiz] s fromage m || tr—**cheese it, the cops!** (slang) vingt-deux, les flics!

cheese'cake' s (slang) les pin up fpl

cheese' cake' s soufflé m au fromage, tarte f au fromage

cheese'cloth' s gaze f

chees·y ['tʃizi] adj (comp -ier; super -iest) caséeux; (slang) miteux

cheetah ['tʃitə] s guépard m

chef [ʃef] s chef m de cuisine, maître queux m

chemical ['kemɪkəl] adj chimique || s produit m chimique

chemist ['kemɪst] s chimiste mf

chemistry ['kemɪstri] s chimie f

cherish ['tʃerɪʃ] tr chérir; (an idea) nourrir; (a hope) caresser

cher·ry ['tʃeri] s (pl -ries) cerise f; (tree) cerisier m

cher'ry or'chard s cerisaie f

cher'ry tree' s cerisier m

cher·ub ['tʃerəb] s (pl -ubim [əbɪm]) chérubin m || s (pl -ubs) (fig) chérubin m

chess [tʃes] s échecs mpl; **to play chess** jouer aux échecs

chess'board' s échiquier m

chess'man' s (pl -men') pièce f du jeu d'échecs

chess' set' s échecs mpl

chest [tʃest] s caisse f; (of drawers)

'commode *f*; (anat) poitrine *f*; **to get s.th. off one's chest** (coll) se déboutonner, dire ce qu'on a sur le cœur

chestnut ['tʃɛsnət] *adj* (*color*) châtain ‖ *s* (*color*) châtain *m*; (*nut*) châtaigne *f*; (*tree*) châtaignier *m*

chest' of drawers' *s* commode *f*, chiffonnier *m*

cheval' glass' [ʃəˈvæl] *s* psyché *f*

chevron ['ʃɛvrən] *s* chevron *m*

chew [tʃu] *tr* mâcher; (*tobacco*) chiquer

chewing ['tʃu·ɪŋ] *s* mastication *f*

chew'ing gum' *s* gomme *f* à mâcher, chewing-gum *m*

chicaner-y [ʃɪˈkɛnəri] *s* (*pl* -ies) truc *m*, ruse *f*, artifice *m*

chick [tʃɪk] *s* poussin *m*; (*girl*) (slang) tendron *m*

chickadee ['tʃɪkəˌdi] *s* (*Parus atricapillus*) mésange *f* boréale

chicken ['tʃɪkən] *s* poulet *m*; **to be chicken** (slang) avoir la frousse ‖ *intr*—**to chicken out** (slang) caner

chick'en coop' *s* poulailler *m*

chick'en-heart'ed *adj* froussard, poltron

chick'en pox' *s* varicelle *f*

chick'en stew' *s* poule-au-pot *m*

chick'en wire' *s* treillis *m* métallique

chick'pea' *s* pois *m* chiche

chico-ry ['tʃɪkəri] *s* (*pl* -ries) chicorée *f*

chide [tʃaɪd] *v* (*pret* **chided** or **chid** [tʃɪd]; *pp* **chided**, **chid**, or **chidden** ['tʃɪdən]) *tr* & *intr* gronder

chief [tʃif] *adj* principal, en chef ‖ *s* chef *m*; (*boss*) (coll) patron *m*

chief' exec'utive *s* chef *m* de l'exécutif

chief' jus'tice *s* président *m* de la Cour suprême

chiefly ['tʃifli] *adv* principalement

chief' of police' *s* préfet *m* de police

chief' of staff' *s* chef *m* d'état-major

chief' of state' *s* chef *m* d'État

chieftain ['tʃiftən] *s* chef *m*

chiffon [ʃɪˈfɑn] *s* mousseline *f* de soie

chiffonier [ˌʃɪfəˈnɪr] *s* chiffonnier *m*

chilblain ['tʃɪlˌblen] *s* engelure *f*

child [tʃaɪld] *s* (*pl* **children** ['tʃɪldrən]) enfant *mf*; **with child** enceinte

child'birth' *s* accouchement *m*

child'hood *s* enfance *f*

childish ['tʃaɪldɪʃ] *adj* enfantin, puéril

child' la'bor *s* travail *m* des enfants

child'like' *adj* enfantin, d'enfant

child's' play' *s* jeu *m* d'enfant; **it's child's play** c'est l'enfance de l'art

child' wel'fare *s* protection *f* de l'enfance

Chile ['tʃɪli] *s* le Chili

chil'i pep'per ['tʃɪli] *s* piment *m*

chill [tʃɪl] *adj* & *s* froid *m*; **sudden chill** saisissement *m*, coup *m* de froid; **to take the chill off** faire tiédir ‖ *tr* refroidir; (*a person*) transir, faire frissonner; (*wine*) frapper

chill-y ['tʃɪli] *adj* (*comp* -**ler**; *super* -**iest**) froid; (*sensitive to cold*) frileux; **it is chilly** il fait frisquet

chime [tʃaɪm] *s* coup *m* de son; **chimes** (*at doorway*) sonnerie *f*; (*in bell tower*) carillon *m* ‖ *tr* & *intr* carillonner

chimera [kaɪˈmɪrə], [kɪˈmɪrə] *s* chimère *f*

chiming ['tʃaɪmɪŋ] *s* carillonnement *m*, sonnerie *f*

chimney ['tʃɪmni] *s* cheminée *f*; (*of lamp*) verre *m*

chim'ney pot' *s* abat-vent *m*, mitre *f*

chim'ney sweep' *s* ramoneur *m*

chimpanzee [tʃɪmˈpænzi], [ˌtʃɪmpænˈzi] *s* chimpanzé *m*

chin [tʃɪn] *s* menton *m*

china ['tʃaɪnə] *s* porcelaine *f* de Chine; **China** Chine *f*; la Chine

chi'na clos'et *s* vitrine *f*

chi'na·ware' *s* porcelaine *f*

Chi-nese [tʃaɪˈniz] *adj* chinois ‖ *s* (*language*) chinois *m* ‖ *s* (*pl* -**nese**) Chinois *m* (*person*)

Chi'nese lan'tern *s* lanterne *f* vénitienne, lampion *m*

chink [tʃɪŋk] *s* fente *f*, crevasse *f*; **chink in one's armor** (coll) défaut *m* de la cuirasse

chin' strap' *s* sous-mentonnière *f*, jugulaire *f*

chip [tʃɪp] *s* copeau *m*, éclat *m*; (*in gambling*) jeton *m*; **to be a chip off the old block** (coll) chasser de race, être un rejeton de la vieille souche ‖ *v* (*pret* & *pp* **chipped**; *ger* **chipping**) *tr* enlever un copeau à ‖ *intr* s'écailler; **to chip in** contribuer

chipmunk ['tʃɪpˌmʌŋk] *s* tamias *m* rayé

chipper ['tʃɪpər] *adj* (coll) en forme, guilleret

chiropodist [kaɪˈrɑpədɪst], [kɪˈrɑpədɪst] *s* pédicure *mf*

chiropractor ['kaɪrəˌpræktər] *s* chiropracteur *m*

chirp [tʃʌrp] *s* gazouillis *m*, pépiement *m* ‖ *intr* gazouiller, pépier

chis-el ['tʃɪzəl] *s* ciseau *m* ‖ *v* (*pret* & *pp* -**eled** or -**elled**; *ger* -**eling** or -**elling**) *tr* ciseler; (*a person*) (slang) escroquer; **to chisel s.o. out of s.th.** (slang) escroquer q.ch. à qn

chiseler ['tʃɪzələr] *s* ciseleur *m*; (slang) escroc *m*

chit [tʃɪt] *s* note *f*, ticket *m*; (coll) gamin *m*

chit'-chat' *s* bavardage *m*

chivalrous ['ʃɪvəlrəs] *adj* honorable, courtois; (lit) chevaleresque

chivalry ['ʃɪvəlri] *s* (*of Middle Ages*) chevalerie *f*; (*politeness*) courtoisie *f*, galanterie *f*

chive [tʃaɪv] *s* ciboulette *f*, civette *f*

chloride ['klɔraɪd] *s* chlorure *m*

chlorinate ['klɔrɪˌnet] *tr* (*water*) verduniser

chlorination [ˌklɔrɪˈneʃən] *s* verdunisation *f*

chlorine ['klɔrɪn] *s* chlore *m*

chloroform ['klɔrəˌfɔrm] *s* chloroforme *m* ‖ *tr* chloroformer

chlorophyll ['klɔrəfɪl] *s* chlorophylle *f*

chock [tʃɑk] *s* cale *f*; (naut) poulie *f* ‖ *tr* caler

chock'-full' *adj* bondé, comble, bourré

chocolate ['tʃɔkəlɪt], ['tʃɑkəlɪt] *adj* & *s* chocolat *m*

choc'olate bar' s tablette f de chocolat
choice [tʃɔɪs] adj de choix, choisi ‖ m choix m; **by choice** par goût, volontairement
choir [kwaɪr] s chœur m
choir'boy' s enfant m de chœur
choir'mas'ter s chef m de chœur; (eccl) maître m de chapelle
choir' robe' s soutanelle f
choke [tʃok] s (aut) starter m ‖ tr étouffer; (to obstruct) obstruer, boucher; **to choke back, down,** or **off** étouffer; **to choke up** obstruer, engorger ‖ intr étouffer; **to choke up** (e.g., with tears) étouffer
choke' coil' s (elec) bobine f de réactance
choker [ˈtʃokər] s (scarf) foulard m; (necklace) collier m court
choking [ˈtʃokɪŋ] s étouffement m
cholera [ˈkɑlərə] s choléra m
choleric [ˈkɑlərɪk] adj coléreux
cholesterol [kəˈlɛstəˌrol], [kəˈlɛstəˌral] s cholestérol m
choose [tʃuz] v (pret **chose** [tʃoz]; pp **chosen** [ˈtʃozən]) tr & intr choisir
choos•y [ˈtʃuzi] adj (comp **-ier**; super **-iest**) (coll) difficile à plaire, chipoteur
chop [tʃɑp] s coup m de hache; (culin) côtelette f; **to lick one's chops** (coll) se lécher or s'essuyer les babines ‖ v (pret & pp **chopped**; ger **chopping**) tr hacher, couper; **to chop down** abattre; **to chop off** trancher, couper; **to chop up** couper en morceaux, hacher ‖ intr (said of waves) clapoter
chopper [ˈtʃɑpər] s (of butcher) couperet m; (coll) hélicoptère m; **choppers** (slang) les dents fpl
chop'ping block' s billot m, hachoir m
chop•py [ˈtʃɑpi] adj (comp **-pier**; ger **-piest**) agité; (waves) clapoteux
chop'stick' s baguette f, bâtonnet m
choral [ˈkorəl] adj choral
chorale [koˈral] s choral m
cho'ral soci'ety s chorale f
chord [kɔrd] s accord m; (geom) corde f
chore [tʃor] s devoir m; (burdensome chore) corvée f, besogne f
choreography [ˌkorɪˈɑgrəfi] s chorégraphie f
chorister [ˈkɑrɪstər], [ˈkɔrɪstər] s choriste m/f
chortle [ˈtʃɔrtəl] intr glousser
chorus [ˈkorəs] s chœur m, chorale f; (of song) refrain m; (of protest) concert m ‖ tr répéter en chœur, faire chorus
cho'rus boy' s boy m
cho'rus girl' s girl f
cho'sen few' [ˈtʃozən] s élite f
chow [tʃaʊ] s (dog) chow-chow m; (mil) boustifaille f, mangeaille f
chow'-chow' s (culin) macédoine f assaisonnée
chowder [ˈtʃaʊdər] s soupe f au poisson
Christ [kraɪst] s Christ m; **le Christ**
christen [ˈkrɪsən] tr baptiser
Christendom [ˈkrɪsəndəm] s chrétienté f

christening [ˈkrɪsənɪŋ] s baptême m
Christian [ˈkrɪstʃən] adj & s chrétien m
Christianity [ˌkrɪstʃɪˈænɪti] s christianisme m
Christianize [ˈkrɪstʃəˌnaɪz] tr christianiser
Christian name' s nom m de baptême
Christmas [ˈkrɪsməs] adj de Noël ‖ s Noël m; **Merry Christmas!** Joyeux Noël!
Christ'mas card' s carte f de Noël
Christ'mas car'ol s chanson f de Noël, chant m de Noël; (eccl) cantique m de Noël
Christ'mas Day' s le jour de Noël
Christ'mas Eve' s la veille de Noël
Christ'mas gift' s cadeau m de Noël
Christ'mas tree' s arbre m de Noël
Christ'mas tree' lights' spl guirlandes fpl
chromatic [kroˈmætɪk] adj chromatique
chrome [krom] adj chromé ‖ s acier m chromé; (color) jaune m; (chem) chrome m ‖ tr chromer
chromium [ˈkromɪəm] s chrome m
chromosome [ˈkromə,som] s chromosome m
chronic [ˈkrɑnɪk] adj chronique
chronicle [ˈkrɑnɪkəl] s chronique f ‖ tr faire la chronique de
chronicler [ˈkrɑnɪklər] s chroniqueur m
chronologic(al) [ˌkrɑnəˈlɑdʒɪk(əl)] adj chronologique
chronolo•gy [krəˈnɑlədʒi] s (pl **-gies**) chronologie f
chronometer [krəˈnɑmɪtər] s chronomètre m
chrysanthemum [krɪˈsænθɪməm] s chrysanthème m
chub•by [ˈtʃʌbi] adj (comp **-bier**; super **-biest**) joufflu, potelé, dodu
chuck [tʃʌk] s (tap, blow, etc.) petite tape f; (under the chin) caresse f sous le menton; (of lathe) mandrin m; (bottom chuck and chuck rib) paleron m; (top chuck roast and chuck rib) entrecôte f ‖ tr tapoter; **to chuck away** jeter
chuckle [ˈtʃʌkəl] s gloussement m, petit rire m ‖ intr glousser, rire tout bas
chum [tʃʌm] s (coll) copain m ‖ v (pret & pp **chummed**; ger **chumming**) intr—**to chum around with** (coll) fraterniser avec
chum•my [ˈtʃʌmi] adj (comp **-mier**; super **-miest**) intime, familier
chump [tʃʌmp] s (slang) ballot m, lourdaud m
chunk [tʃʌŋk] s gros morceau m; (e.g., of wood) bloc m
church [tʃʌrtʃ] s église f
church'go'er s pratiquant m
church'man s (pl **-men**) (clergyman) ecclésiastique m; (layman) membre m d'une église, fidèle m/f, paroissien m
church' mem'ber s fidèle m/f
church' ser'vice s office m, culte m
church'yard' s cimetière m
churlish [ˈtʃʌrlɪʃ] adj rustre, grossier; (out of sorts) grincheux
churn [tʃʌrn] s baratte f ‖ tr (cream)

baratter; (e.g., water) agiter; **to churn butter** battre le beurre || intr bouillonner

chute [ʃut] s glissière f; parachute m; (of river) rapide m, chute f d'eau

Cicero [ˈsɪsəˌro] s Cicéron m

cider [ˈsaɪdər] s cidre m

cigar [sɪˈgɑr] s cigare m

cigarette [ˌsɪgəˈrɛt] s cigarette f

cigarette' butt' s mégot m

cigarette' case' s étui m à cigarettes

cigarette' fiend' s fumeur m enragé

cigarette' hold'er s fume-cigarette m

cigarette' light'er s briquet m

cigar' hold'er s fume-cigare m

cigar' store' s bureau m de tabac

cinch [sɪntʃ] s (of saddle) sangle f; **it's a cinch** (coll) c'est couru d'avance || tr sangler; (to make sure of) (slang) assurer

cinder [ˈsɪndər] s cendre f

Cinderella [ˌsɪndəˈrɛlə] s la Cendrillon f

cin'der track' s piste f cendrée

cinema [ˈsɪnəmə] s cinéma m

cinnamon [ˈsɪnəmən] s cannelle f

cipher [ˈsaɪfər] s zéro m; (code) chiffre m; **in cipher** en chiffres || tr & intr chiffrer

circle [ˈsʌrkəl] s cercle m; (coterie) milieu m, monde m; **to have circles around the eyes** avoir les yeux cernés || tr ceindre, entourer; (to travel around) faire le tour de

circuit [ˈsʌrkɪt] s circuit m; (of judge) tournée f

cir'cuit break'er s (elec) disjoncteur m

cir'cuit court' s cour f d'assises

circuitous [sərˈkjuɪtəs] adj détourné, indirect

circular [ˈsʌrkjələr] adj & s circulaire f

circulate [ˈsʌrkjəˌlet] tr faire circuler || intr circuler

circulation [ˌsʌrkjəˈleʃən] s circulation f; (of newspaper) tirage m

circumcise [ˈsʌrkəmˌsaɪz] tr circoncire

circumcision [ˌsʌrkəmˈsɪʒən] s circoncision f

circumference [sərˈkʌmfərəns] s circonférence f

circumflex [ˈsʌrkəmˌflɛks] adj & s circonflexe m

circumlocution [ˌsʌrkəmloˈkjuʃən] s circonlocution f

circumscribe [ˌsʌrkəmˈskraɪb] tr circonscrire

circumspect [ˈsʌrkəmˌspɛkt] adv circonspect

circumstance [ˈsʌrkəmˌstæns] s circonstance f; (pomp) cérémonie f; **in easy circumstances** aisé; **under no circumstance** sous aucun prétexte; **under the circumstances** dans ces conditions

circumstantial [ˌsʌrkəmˈstænʃəl] adj (derived from circumstances) circonstanciel; (detailed) circonstancié

cir'cumstan'tial ev'idence s preuves fpl indirectes

circumvent [ˌsʌrkəmˈvɛnt] tr circonvenir

circus [ˈsʌrkəs] s cirque m; (Brit) rond-point m

cirrhosis [sɪˈrosɪs] s cirrhose f

cistern [ˈsɪstərn] s citerne f

citadel [ˈsɪtədəl] s citadelle f

citation [saɪˈteʃən] s citation f; (award) présentation f, mention f

cite [saɪt] tr citer

cither [ˈsɪθər] s cithare f

citified [ˈsɪtɪˌfaɪd] adj urbain

citizen [ˈsɪtɪzən] s citoyen m

citizen-ry [ˈsɪtɪzənri] s (pl -ries) citoyens mpl

cit'izen-ship' s citoyenneté f

citric [ˈsɪtrɪk] adj citrique

citron [ˈsɪtrən] s cédrat m; (tree) cédratier m

citronella [ˌsɪtrəˈnɛlə] s citronnelle f

cit'rus fruit' [ˈsɪtrəs] s agrumes mpl

cit-y [ˈsɪti] s (pl -ies) ville f; **the City** (district within ancient boundaries) la Cité

cit'y coun'cil s conseil m municipal

cit'y hall' s hôtel m de ville

cit'y plan'ner s urbaniste mf

cit'y plan'ning s urbanisme m

civ'et cat' [ˈsɪvɪt] s civette f

civic [ˈsɪvɪk] adj civique; **civics** instruction f civique

civies [ˈsɪviz] spl (coll) vêtements mpl civils; **in civies** en civil, en bourgeois

civil [ˈsɪvɪl] adj civil; (courteous) poli

civ'il defense' s protection f civile

civ'il engineer'ing s génie m civil

civilian [sɪˈvɪljən] adj & s civil m

civ'il ian life' s vie f civile

civili-ty [sɪˈvɪlɪti] s (pl -ties) civilité f

civilization [ˌsɪvɪlɪˈzeʃən] s civilisation f

civilize [ˈsɪvɪˌlaɪz] tr civiliser

civ'il rights' spl droits mpl civiques, droits politiques

civ'il serv'ant s fonctionnaire mf

civ'il serv'ice s fonction f publique

civ'il war' s guerre f civile; **Civil War** (of the United States) Guerre de Sécession

clack [klæk] s claquement m || intr claquer

clad [klæd] adj vêtu, habillé

claim [klem] s demande f; (to a right) revendication f; (in prospecting) concession f || tr (a right) réclamer, revendiquer; (to require) exiger, demander; **to claim that . . .** prétendre que . . .; **to claim to** prétendre

claimant [ˈklemənt] s prétendant m, ayant droit m

clairvoyance [klerˈvɔɪəns] s voyance f, seconde vue f; (keen insight) clairvoyance f

clairvoyant [klerˈvɔɪənt] adj clairvoyant || s voyante f; voyant m

clam [klæm] s palourde f || v (pret & pp clammed; ger clamming) intr—**to clam up** (slang) se taire

clam'bake' s pique-nique m aux palourdes

clamber [ˈklæmbər] intr grimper; **to clamber over** or **up** escalader

clam-my [ˈklæmi] adj (comp -mier; super -miest) moite; (clinging) collant

clamor [ˈklæmər] s clameur f || intr vociférer; **to clamor for** réclamer

clamorous ['klæmərəs] *adj* bruyant
clamp [klæmp] *s* crampon *m*, agrafe *f*; (*med*) clamp *m* || *tr* fixer, attacher; **to clamp together** cramponner || *intr* —**to clamp down on** (coll) visser
clan [klæn] *s* clan *m*
clandestine [klæn'destɪn] *adj* clandestin
clang [klæŋ] *s* bruit *m* métallique, choc *m* retentissant, cliquetis *m* || *tr* faire résonner || *intr* résonner
clank [klæŋk] *s* bruit *m* sec, bruit métallique, cliquetis *m* || *tr* faire résonner || *intr* résonner
clannish ['klænɪʃ] *adj* partisan
clap [klæp] *s* coup *m*; (*with hand*) tape *f*; (*with the hands*) battement *m* || *v* (*pret & pp* clapped; *ger* clapping) *tr* battre; (*into jail*) (coll) fourrer; **to clap the hands** claquer or battre les mains || *intr* applaudir, claquer
clapper ['klæpər] *s* applaudisseur *m*; (*of bell*) battant *m*
claque [klæk] *s* (*paid clappers*) claque *f*; (*crush hat*) claque *m*
claret ['klærɪt] *s* bordeaux *m*
clari·fy ['klærɪ,faɪ] *v* (*pret & pp* -fied) *tr* clarifier
clarinet [,klærɪ'nɛt] *s* clarinette *f*
clarity ['klærɪti] *s* clarté *f*
clash [klæʃ] *s* choc *m*; (*conflict*) dispute *f*; (*of colors*) disparate *f* || *intr* se heurter, s'entre-choquer; (*said of colors*) former une disparate
clasp [klæsp], [klɑsp] *s* agrafe *f*, fermoir *m*; (*embrace*) étreinte *f* || *tr* agrafer; (*to embrace*) étreindre
clasp' knife' *s* couteau *m* pliant
class [klæs], [klɑs] *s* classe *f* || *tr* classer
classic ['klæsɪk] *adj & s* classique *m*
classical ['klæsɪkəl] *adj* classique
classicism ['klæsɪ,sɪzəm] *s* classicisme *m*
classicist ['klæsɪsɪst] *s* classique *mf*
classification [,klæsɪfɪ'keʃən] *s* classification *f*, classement *m*
classified *adj* classifié, classé; (*documents*) secret, confidentiel
clas'sified advertise'ments *spl* petites annonces *fpl*
classi·fy ['klæsɪ,faɪ] *v* (*pret & pp* -fied) *tr* classifier
class'mate' *s* camarade *mf* de classe
class'room' *s* salle *f* de classe, classe *f*
class·y ['klæsi] *adj* (*comp* -ier; *super* -iest) (slang) chic
clatter ['klætər] *s* fracas *m* || *intr* faire un fracas
clause [klɔz] *s* clause *f*, article *m*; (gram) proposition *f*
clavicle ['klævɪkəl] *s* clavicule *f*
claw [klɔ] *s* (*of animal*) griffe *f*; (*of crab*) pince *f*; (*of hammer*) panne *f* fendue || *tr* griffer, déchirer
clay [kle] *s* argile *f*, glaise *f*
clay' pig'eon *s* pigeon *m* d'argile
clay' pipe' *s* pipe *f* en terre
clay' pit' *s* argilière *f*, glaisière *f*
clean [klin] *adj* propre, net; (*precise*) net *m* adv net; tout à fait || *tr* nettoyer; (*fish*) vider; (*streets*) balayer; **to clean out** curer; (*a person*) (slang)

mettre à sec, décaver; **to clean up** nettoyer || *intr* faire le nettoyage
clean'-cut' *adj* bien délimité, net; (*e.g., athlete*) bien découplé
cleaner ['klinər] *s* nettoyeur *m*, dégraisseur *m*; **to be taken to the cleaners** (slang) se faire rincer
cleaning ['klinɪŋ] *s* nettoyage *m*
clean'ing wom'an *s* femme *f* de ménage
cleanliness ['klɛnlɪnɪs] *s* propreté *f*, netteté *f*
cleanse [klɛnz] *tr* nettoyer, écurer; (*e.g., a wound*) assainir; (*e.g., one's thoughts*) purifier
cleanser ['klɛnzər] *s* produit *m* de nettoyage; (*soap*) détersif *m*
clean'-shav'en *adj* rasé de frais
cleans'ing cream' *s* crème *f* de démaquillage
clean'up' *s* nettoiement *m*
clear [klɪr] *adj* clair; (*sharp*) net; (*free*) dégagé, libre; (*unmortgaged*) franc d'hypothèque; **to become clear** s'éclaircir; **to keep clear of** éviter || *tr* (*to brighten*) éclaircir; (*e.g., a fence*) franchir; (*obstacles*) dégager; (*land*) défricher; (*goods in customs*) dédouaner; (*an account*) solder; **to clear away** écarter, enlever; **to clear oneself** se disculper; **to clear out** (*e.g., a garden*) jardiner; **to clear the table** desservir, enlever le couvert, ôter la nappe; **to clear up** éclaircir || *intr* (*said of weather*) s'éclaircir; **to clear out** (coll) filer, se sauver
clearance ['klɪrəns] *s* permis *m*, laissez-passer *m*, autorisation *f*; (*between two objects*) espace *m* libre; (com) compensation *f*; (mach) espace *m* mort, jeu *m*
clear'ance sale' *s* vente *f* de soldes
clear'-cut' *adj* net, tranché; (*case*) absolu
clear'-head'ed *adj* lucide, perspicace
clearing ['klɪrɪŋ] *s* (*in clouds*) éclaircie *f*; (*in forest*) clairière *f*, trouée *f*
clear'ing house' *s* (com) comptoir *m* de règlement, chambre *f* de compensation
clearness ['klɪrnɪs] *s* clarté *f*, netteté *f*
clear'-sight'ed *adj* perspicace, clairvoyant
cleat [klit] *s* taquet *m*
cleavage ['klivɪdʒ] *s* clivage *m*
cleave [kliv] *v* (*pret & pp* cleft [klɛft] *or* cleaved) *tr* fendre || *intr* se fendre; **to cleave to** s'attacher à, adhérer à
cleaver ['klivər] *s* couperet *m*, hachoir *m*
clef [klɛf] *s* (mus) clef *f*
cleft [klɛft] *adj* fendu || *s* fente *f*, crevasse *f*
cleft' pal'ate *s* palais *m* fendu, fissure *f* palatine
clemen·cy ['klɛmənsi] *s* (*pl* -cies) clémence *f*
clement ['klɛmənt] *adj* clément
clench [klɛntʃ] *tr* serrer, crisper
cler·gy ['klɜrdʒi] *s* (*pl* -gies) (*members*) clergé *m*; (*profession*) clergie *f*
cler'gy·man *s* (*pl* -men) ecclésiastique *m*, clerc *m*

cleric ['klerɪk] s clerc m, ecclésiastique m

clerical ['klerɪkəl] adj clerical; de bureau ‖ s clerical m; **clericals** habit m ecclésiastique

cler'ical er'ror s faute f de copiste, faute de sténographe

cler'ical work' s travail m de bureau

clerk [klʌrk] s (clerical worker) employé m de bureau, commis m; (in lawyer's office) clerc m; (in store) vendeur m; (in bank) comptable mf; (of court) greffier m; (eccl) clerc

clever ['klevər] adj habile, adroit

cliché [kli'ʃe] s cliché m, expression f consacrée

click [klɪk] s cliquetis m, clic m; (of heels) bruit m sec; (of tongue) claquement m; (of a machine) déclic m ‖ tr cliqueter, faire un déclic; (to succeed) (coll) réussir; (to get along well) (coll) s'entendre à merveille

client ['klaɪ‧ənt] s client m

clientele [ˌklaɪ‧ən'tɛl] s clientèle f

cliff [klɪf] s falaise f, talus m raide

climate ['klaɪmɪt] s climat m

climax ['klaɪmæks] s point m culminant, comble m

climb [klaɪm] s montée f, ascension f ‖ tr & intr monter, gravir; grimper; **to climb down** descendre

climber ['klaɪmər] s grimpeur m; (bot) plante f grimpante; (social climber) parvenu m, arriviste mf

climbing ['klaɪmɪŋ] s montée f, escalade f

clinch [klɪntʃ] s crampon m, rivet m; (boxing) corps-à-corps m ‖ tr river; (a bargain) boucler ‖ intr se prendre corps à corps

clincher ['klɪntʃər] s (coll) argument m sans réplique

cling [klɪŋ] v (pret & pp clung [klʌŋ]) intr s'accrocher, se cramponner; **to cling to** (a person) se serrer contre; (a belief) adhérer à

cling'stone peach' s alberge f

clinic ['klɪnɪk] s clinique f

clinical ['klɪnɪkəl] adj clinique

clinician [klɪ'nɪ‧ʃən] s clinicien m

clink [klɪŋk] s cliquetis m; (e.g., of glasses) tintement m, choc m ‖ tr (glasses, in a toast) choquer; **to clink glasses with** trinquer avec ‖ intr tinter, cliqueter

clip [klɪp] s attache f; (brooch) agrafe f, clip m; (of gun) chargeur m; (blow) (coll) taloche f; (fast pace) (coll) pas m rapide ‖ v (pret & pp clipped; ger clipping) tr (to fasten) attacher; (hair) rafraîchir; (sheep) tondre; (one's words) avaler

clipper ['klɪpər] s (aer) clipper m; (naut) voilier m de course; **clippers** tondeuse f

clipping ['klɪpɪŋ] s tondage m; (of sheep) tonte f; (of one's hair) taille f; (of newspaper) coupure f (de presse); **clippings** (cuttings, shavings, etc.) rognures fpl, chutes fpl

clip'ping ser'vice s argus m

clique [klik] s coterie f, clan m, chapelle f

cloak [klok] s manteau m ‖ tr masquer

cloak'-and-dag'ger adj (e.g., story) de cape et d'épée

cloak'room' s vestiaire m; (rr) consigne f

clock [klɑk] s pendule f; (e.g., in a tower) horloge f; **to turn back the clock** retarder l'horloge; (fig) revenir en arrière ‖ tr chronométrer

clock'mak'er s horloger m

clock'tow'er s tour f de l'horloge

clock'wise' adj & adv dans le sens des aiguilles d'une montre

clock'work' s mouvement m d'horlogerie; **like clockwork** (coll) comme une horloge

clod [klɑd] s motte f; (person) rustre mf

clod'hop'per s cul-terreux m; (shoe) godillot m

clog [klɑg] s (shoe) galoche f, socque m; (hindrance) entrave f ‖ v (pret & pp clogged; ger clogging) tr (e.g., a pipe) boucher; (e.g., traffic) entraver ‖ intr se boucher

cloister ['klɔɪstər] s cloître m ‖ tr cloîtrer

close [klos] adj proche, tout près; (game; weave; formation, order) serré; (friend) intime; (friendship) étroit; (room) renfermé, étouffant; (translation) fidèle; **close to** près de ‖ adv près, de près ‖ [kloz] s (enclosure) clos m; (end) fin f; (closing) fermeture f ‖ tr fermer; (to end) conclure, terminer; (an account) régler, clôturer; (ranks) serrer, resserrer; (a meeting) lever; **close quotes** fermez les guillemets; **to close in** enfermer; **to close out** (com) liquider, solder ‖ intr se fermer; finir, se terminer; (on certain days) (theat) faire relâche; **to close in on** (the enemy) aborder

close' call' [klos] s—**to have a close call** (coll) l'échapper belle

close-cropped ['klos'krɑpt] adj coupé ras

closed [klozd] adj fermé; (road) barré; (e.g., pipe) obturé, bouché; (ranks) serré; (public sign in front of theater) relâche; **with closed eyes** les yeux clos

closed' car' s conduite f intérieure

closed'-cir'cuit tel'evision s télévision f en circuit fermé

closed' sea'son s fermeture f de la chasse, fermeture de la pêche

closefisted ['klos'fɪstəd] adj ladre, avare

close-fitting ['klos'fɪtɪŋ] adj collant, ajusté, qui moule le corps

close-grained ['klos'grend] adj serré

closely ['klosli] adv (near) de près, étroitement; (exactly) exactement

close-mouthed ['klos'maʊðd] adj peu communicatif, économe de mots

closeness ['klosnɪs] s (nearness) proximité f; (accuracy) exactitude f; (stinginess) avarice f; (of weather) lourdeur f; (of air) manque m d'air

close′ shave′ [klos] *s*—to have a close shave se faire raser de près; (coll) échapper à un cheveu près

closet [′klɑzɪt] *s* placard *m*

clos′et dra′ma *s* spectacle *m* dans un fauteuil

close-up [′klos‚ʌp] *s* premier plan *m*, gros plan

closing [′klozɪŋ] *adj* dernier, final ‖ *s* fermeture *f*; (*of account; of meeting*) clôture *f*

clos′ing-out′ sale′ *s* soldes *mpl* des fins de séries

clos′ing price′ *s* dernier cours *m*

clot [klɑt] *s* caillot *m* ‖ *v* (*pret & pp* **clotted;** *ger* **clotting**) *tr* cailler ‖ *intr* se cailler

cloth [klɔθ], [klɑθ] *s* étoffe *f*; (*fabric*) tissu *m*; (*of wool*) drap *m*; (*of cotton or linen*) toile *f*; **cloths** (*for cleaning*) chiffons *mpl*, torchons *mpl*, linge *m*; **the cloth** le clergé

clothe [kloð] *v* (*pret & pp* **clothed** or **clad** [klæd]) *tr* habiller, vêtir; (*e.g., with authority*) revêtir, investir

clothes [kloz], [kloðz] *spl* vêtements *mpl*, habits *mpl*; (*underclothes, shirts, etc.; wash*) linge *m*; **in plain clothes** en civil; **to put on one's clothes** s'habiller; **to take off one's clothes** se déshabiller

clothes′ bas′ket *s* panier *m* à linge

clothes′ brush′ *s* brosse *f* à habits

clothes′ clos′et *s* garde-robe *f*, penderie *f*, placard *m*

clothes′ dry′er *s* séchoir *m* à linge

clothes′ hang′er *s* cintre *m*

clothes′ horse′ *s* séchoir-chevalet *m*

clothes′ line′ *s* corde *f* à linge, étendoir *m*

clothes′ moth′ *s* gerce *f*

clothes′ pin′ *s* pince *f* à linge

clothes′ rack′ *s* patère *f*

clothier [′kloðjər] *s* confectionneur *m*, marchand *m* de confections

clothing [′kloðɪŋ] *s* vêtements *mpl*

cloud [klaʊd] *s* nuage *m*; (*heavy cloud; multitude*) nuée *f*; **in the clouds** dans les nues ‖ *tr* couvrir de nuages; (phot) voiler ‖ *intr* (phot) se voiler; **to cloud over** or **up** se couvrir de nuages

cloud′burst′ *s* averse *f*, rafale *f* de pluie

cloud′ cham′ber *s* (phys) chambre *f* d'ionisation

cloudless [′klaʊdlɪs] *adj* sans nuages

cloud-y [′klaʊdi] *adj* (*comp* **-ier;** *super* **-iest**) nuageux; (phot) voilé

clout [klaʊt] *s* (coll) gifle *f* ‖ *tr* (coll) gifler

clove [klov] *s* clou *m* de girofle, girofle *m*; (*of garlic*) gousse *f*; (bot) giroflier *m*

clove′ hitch′ *s* demi-clef *f* à capeler

clo′ven hoof′ [′kloven] *s* pied *m* fourchu; **to show the cloven hoof** (coll) montrer le bout de l'oreille

clover [′klovər] *s* trèfle *m*; **to be in clover** (coll) être sur le velours

clo′ver-leaf′ *s* (*pl* **-leaves**) feuille *f* de trèfle; (*intersection*) croisement *m* en trèfle, saut-de-mouton *m*

clown [klaʊn] *s* clown *m*, pitre *m*, bouffon *m* ‖ *intr* faire le pitre

clownish [′klaʊnɪʃ] *adj* bouffon; (*clumsy*) empoté, rustre

cloy [klɔɪ] *tr* rassasier

club [klʌb] *s* massue *f*, gourdin *m*, assommoir *m*; cercle *m*, amicale *f*, club *m*; (cards) trèfle *m*; (golf) crosse *f*, club *m* ‖ *v* (*pret & pp* **clubbed;** *ger* **clubbing**) *tr* (*to strike*) assommer; (*to pool*) mettre en commun ‖ *intr*—**to club together** s'associer; se cotiser

club′ car′ *s* voiture-salon *f*

club′ foot′ *s* (*pl* **-feet**) pied *m* équin, pied bot

club′ foot′ed *adj*—**to be clubfooted** avoir le pied bot, être pied-bot

club′ house′ *s* club *m*, cercle *m*

club′ man *s* (*pl* **-men**) clubman *m*

club′ room′ *s* salle *f* de réunion

club′ steak′ *s* aloyau *m* de bœuf

club′ wom′an *s* (*pl* **-wom′en**) cercleuse *f*

cluck [klʌk] *s* gloussement *m* ‖ *intr* glousser

clue [klu] *s* indice *m*, indication *f*; **to find the clue** trouver la clef; **to give s.o. a clue** mettre qn sur la piste; **to have the clue** tenir le bout du fil

clump [klʌmp] *s* (*of earth*) bloc *m*, masse *f*; (*of trees*) bouquet *m*; (*of shrubs or flowers*) massif *m*; (*gait*) pas *m* lourd ‖ *intr*—**to clump along** marcher lourdement

clum-sy [′klʌmzi] *adj* (*comp* **-sier;** *super* **-siest**) (*worker*) maladroit, gauche; (*work*) bâclé, grossier

cluster [′klʌstər] *s* bouquet *m*, massif *m*; (*of grapes*) grappe *f*; (*of pears*) glane *f*; (*of bananas*) régime *m*; (*of diamonds*) épi *m*, nœud *m*; (*of stars*) amas *m* ‖ *tr* grouper ‖ *intr*—**to cluster around** se rassembler; **to cluster together** se congloméer

clutch [klʌtʃ] *s* (*grasp, grip*) griffe *f*, serre *f*; (aut) embrayage *m*; (aut) pédale *f* d'embrayage; **to fall into the clutches of** tomber sous la patte de; **to let in the clutch** embrayer; **to throw out the clutch** débrayer ‖ *tr* saisir, empoigner ‖ *intr*—**to clutch at** se raccrocher à

clutter [′klʌtər] *s* encombrement *m* ‖ *tr*—**to clutter up** encombrer

Co. *abbr* (**Company**) Cᶦᵉ

c/o *abbr* (**in care of**) a/s (aux soins de)

coach [kotʃ] *s* coche *m*, carrosse *f*; (bus) autocar *m*, car *m*; (*two-door sedan*) coche *m*; (rr) voiture *f*; (sports) entraîneur *m*, moniteur *m* ‖ *tr* donner des leçons particulières à; entraîner; (*for an exam*) préparer à un examen, chauffer; (*an actor*) faire répéter

coach′-and-four′ *s* carrosse *f* à quatre chevaux

coach′ box′ *s* siège *m* du cocher

coach′ house′ *s* remise *f*

coaching [′kotʃɪŋ] *s* leçons *fpl* particulières, chauffage *m*, répétitions *fpl*; (sport) entraînement *m*

coach′ man *s* (*pl* **-men**) cocher *m*

coagulate [ko'ægjə,let] *tr* coaguler ‖ *intr* se coaguler

coal [kol] *adj* charbonnier, houiller ‖ *s* houille *f*, charbon *m*; **coals** (*embers*) tisons *mpl*, charbons ardents; **to carry coals to Newcastle** porter de l'eau à la rivière

coal'bin' *s* coffre *m* à charbon

coal' bunk'er *s* soute *f* à charbon

coal' car' *s* wagon-tombereau *m*

coal'deal'er *s* charbonnier *m*

coalesce [,ko·ə'lɛs] *intr* s'unir, se combiner, fusionner

coal' field' *s* bassin *m* houiller

coalition [,ko·ə'lɪ/ən] *s* coalition *f*; **to form a coalition** se coaliser

coal' mine' *s* houillère *f*

coal' oil' *s* pétrole *m* lampant

coal' scut'tle *s* seau *m* à charbon

coal' tar' *s* goudron *m* de houille

coal'yard' *s* charbonnerie *f*

coarse [kors] *adj* (*in manners*) grossier; (*composed of large particles*) gros; (*hair, skin*) rude

coarse'-grained' *adj* à gros grain; (*wood*) à gros fil

coarseness ['korsnɪs] *s* grossièreté *f*; (*of hair, skin*) rudesse *f*

coast [kost] *s* côte *f*; **the coast is clear** la route est libre ‖ *intr* caboter; (*said of automobile*) aller au débrayé; (*said of bicycle*) aller en roue libre; **to coast along** continuer sur sa lancée

coastal ['kostəl] *adj* côtier

coaster ['kostər] *s* dessous-de-verre *m*, sous-verre *m*; (*naut*) caboteur *m*

coast'er brake' *s* frein *m* à contre-pédalage

coast' guard' *s* service *m* de guet le long des côtes

coast'-guard cut'ter *s* garde-côte *m*

coast'guards'man *s* (*pl* -men) soldat *m* chargé de la garde des côtes

coasting ['kostɪŋ] *s* (*e.g., on a cycle*) descente *f* en roue libre

coast'ing trade' *s* cabotage *m*

coast'line' *s* littoral *m*

coast'wise' *adj* côtier ‖ *adv* le long de la côte

coat [kot] *s* (*jacket*) veste *f*; (*suitcoat*) veston *m*; (*topcoat*) manteau *m*; (*of an animal*) robe *f*, pelage *m*, livrée *f*; (*of paint*) couche *f* ‖ *tr* enduire; (*with chocolate*) enrober; (*a pill*) dragéifier

coat' hang'er *s* cintre *m*, portemanteau *m*

coating ['kotɪŋ] *s* enduit *m*, couche *f*

coat' of arms' *s* écu *m* armorial; (*bearings*) blason *m*, armoiries *fpl*

coat' of mail' *s* cotte *f* de mailles

coat'rack' *s* portemanteau *m*

coat'room' *s* vestiaire *m*

coat'tail' *s* basque *f*

coauthor [ko'ɔθər] *s* coauteur *m*

coax [koks] *tr* cajoler, amadouer

cob [kab] *s* (*of corn*) épi *m* de maïs; (*horse*) cob *m*; (*swan*) cygne *m* mâle

cobalt ['kobɔlt] *s* cobalt *m*

cobbler ['kablər] *s* cordonnier *m*; (*cake*) tourte *f* aux fruits; (*drink*) boisson *f* glacée

cobble·stone ['kabəl,ston] *s* pavé *m*

cob'web' *s* toile *f* d'araignée

cocaine [ko'ken] *s* cocaïne *f*

cock [kak] *s* coq *m*; (*faucet*) robinet *m*; (*of gun*) chien *m* ‖ *tr* (*one's ears*) dresser, redresser; (*one's hat*) mettre sur l'oreille, retrousser; (*a rifle*) armer

cockade [ka'ked] *s* cocarde *f*

cock-a-doodle-doo ['kakə,dudəl'du] *interj* cocorico!

cock'-and-bull' sto'ry *s* coq-à-l'âne *m*

cock'crow' *s* cocorico *m*

cocked' hat' *s* chapeau *m* à cornes; **to knock into a cocked hat** (slang) démolir, aplatir

cock'er span'iel ['kakər] *s* cocker *m*

cock'eyed' *adj* (coll) de travers, de biais; (slang) insensé

cock'fight' *s* combat *m* de coqs

cockle ['kakəl] *s* (bot) nielle *f*; (zool) bucarde *f*, clovisse *f*

cock'pit' *s* (aer) cockpit *m*, carlingue *f*

cock'roach' *s* blatte *f*, cafard *m*

cockscomb ['kaks,kom] *s* crête *f* de coq; (bot) crête-de-coq *f*

cock'sure' *adj* (coll) sûr et certain

cock'tail' *s* cocktail *m*

cock'tail dress' *s* robe *f* de cocktail

cock'tail par'ty *s* cocktail *m*

cock'tail shak'er *s* shaker *m*

cock·y ['kaki] *adj* (*comp* -ier; *super* -iest) (coll) effronté, suffisant

cocoa ['koko] *s* cacao *m*; (*drink*) chocolat *m*

co'coa bean' *s* cacao *m*

coconut ['kokə,nʌt] *s* noix *f* de coco, coco *m*

co'conut palm' *s* cocotier *m*

cocoon [kə'kun] *s* cocon *m*

cod [kad] *s* (ichth) morue *f*

C.O.D. ['si'o'di] *s* (letterword) (**Collect on Delivery**) C.R., contre remboursement, e.g., **send it to me C.O.D.** envoyez-le-moi C.R.

coddle ['kadəl] *tr* dorloter, gâter

code [kod] *s* code *m*; (*secret code*) chiffre *m* ‖ *tr* chiffrer

code' word' *s* mot *m* convenu

codex ['kodeks] *s* (*pl* **codices** ['kodɪ,siz], ['kadɪ,siz]) manuscrit *m* ancien

cod'fish' *s* morue *f*

codger ['kadʒər] *s*—**old codger** (coll) vieux bonhomme *m*

codicil ['kadısɪl] *s* (*of will*) codicille *m*; (*of contract, treaty, etc.*) avenant *m*

codi·fy ['kadɪ,faɪ], ['kodɪ,faɪ] *v* (*pret & pp* -fied) *tr* codifier

cod'-liv'er oil' *s* huile *f* de foie de morue

coed ['ko,ed] *s* collégienne *f*, étudiante *f* universitaire

coeducation [,ko·edʒə'ke/ən] *s* co-éducation *f*

co'educa'tional school' [,ko·edʒə'ke-/ənəl] *s* école *f* mixte

coefficient [,ko·ı'fɪ/ənt] *s* coefficient *m*

coerce [ko'ʌrs] *tr* contraindre, forcer

coercion [ko'ʌr/ən] *s* coercition *f*

coexist [ˌkoˈɪgˈzɪst] *intr* coexister

coexistence [ˌkoˈɪgˈzɪstəns] *s* coexistence *f*

coffee [ˈkɔfi], [ˈkafi] *s* café *m*; **black coffee** café noir, café nature; **ground coffee** café moulu; **roasted coffee** café brûlé, café torréfié

coffee and rolls *s* café *m* complet

cof'fee bean' *s* grain *m* de café

cof'fee break' *s* pause-café *f*

cof'fee-cake' *s* gimblette *f* (qui se prend avec le café)

cof'fee cup' *s* tasse *f* à café

cof'fee grind'er *s* moulin *m* à café

cof'fee grounds' *s* marc *m* de café

cof'fee mak'er *s* percolateur *m*

cof'fee mill' *s* moulin *m* à café

cof'fee planta'tion *s* caféière *f*

cof'fee-pot' *s* cafetière *f*; (*for pouring*) verseuse *f*

cof'fee roast'er *s* brûloir *m*

cof'fee shop' *s* (*of hotel*) hôtel-restaurant *m*; (*in station*) buffet *m*

cof'fee tree' *s* caféier *m*

coffer [ˈkɔfər], [ˈkafər] *s* coffre *m*, caisse *f*; (*archit*) caisson *m*; **coffers** trésor *m*, fonds *mpl*

cof'fer-dam' *s* coffre *m*, bâtardeau *m*

coffin [ˈkɔfɪn], [ˈkafɪn] *s* cercueil *m*, bière *f*

cog [kɑg] *s* dent *f*; (*cogwheel*) roue *f* dentée; **to slip a cog** (coll) avoir des absences

cogency [ˈkodʒənsi] *s* force *f* (de persuasion)

cogent [ˈkodʒənt] *adj* puissant, convaincant

cogitate [ˈkɑdʒɪ.tet] *tr & intr* méditer

cognac [ˈkonjæk], [ˈkɑnjæk] *s* cognac *m*

cognate [ˈkɑgnet] *adj* congénère, apparenté ‖ *s* congénère *mf*; (*word*) mot *m* apparenté

cognizance [ˈkɑgnɪzəns], [ˈkɑnɪzəns] *s* connaissance *f*

cognizant [ˈkɑgnɪzənt], [ˈkɑnɪzənt] *adj* informé

cog'wheel' *s* roue *f* dentée

cohabit [koˈhæbɪt] *intr* cohabiter

coheir [koˈer] *s* cohéritier

cohere [koˈhɪr] *intr* s'agglomérer, adhérer; (*said of reasoning or style*) se suivre logiquement, correspondre

coherent [koˈhɪrənt] *adj* cohérent

cohesion [koˈhiʒən] *s* cohésion *f*

coiffeur [kwaˈfʌr] *s* coiffeur *m* pour dames

coiffure [kwaˈfjur] *s* coiffure *f* ‖ *tr* coiffer

coil [kɔɪl] *s* (*something wound in a spiral*) rouleau *m*; (*single turn of spiral*) tour *m*; (*of a still*) serpentin *m*; (*of hair*) boucle *f*; (elec) bobine *f*; **coils** (*of snake*) nœuds *mpl* ‖ *tr* enrouler; (naut) lover, gléner ‖ *intr* s'enrouler; (*said of snake or stream*) serpenter

coil' spring' *s* ressort *m* en spirale, ressort à boudin

coin [kɔɪn] *s* monnaie *f*; (*single coin*) pièce *f* de monnaie; (*wedge*) coin *m*; **in coin** en espèces, en numéraire; **to pay back s.o. in his own coin** rendre à qn la monnaie de sa pièce; **to toss a coin** jouer à pile ou face ‖ *tr* (*a new word; a story or lie*) forger, inventer; **to coin money** frapper de la monnaie; (coll) faire des affaires d'or, s'enrichir à vue d'œil

coinage [ˈkɔɪnɪdʒ] *s* monnayage *m*; (fig) invention *f*

coincide [ˌkoˈɪnˈsaɪd] *intr* coïncider

coincidence [koˈɪnsɪdəns] *s* coïncidence *f*

coition [koˈɪʃən] or **coitus** [ˈkoˈɪtəs] *s* coït *m*

coke [kok] *s* coke *m* ‖ *tr* cokéfier ‖ *intr* se cokéfier

colander [ˈkʌləndər], [ˈkɑləndər] *s* passoire *f*

cold [kold] *adj* froid; **it is cold** (*said of weather*) il fait froid; **to be cold** (*said of person*) avoir froid ‖ *s* froid *m*; (*indisposition*) rhume *m*; **to be left out in the cold** (slang) rester en carafe; **to catch a cold** attraper un rhume, s'enrhumer

cold' blood' *s*—**in cold blood** de sang-froid

cold'-blood'ed *adj* insensible; (*sensitive to cold*) frileux; (zool) à sang froid

cold' chis'el *s* ciseau *m* à froid

cold' com'fort *s* maigre consolation *f*

cold' cream' *s* cold-cream *m*

cold' cuts' *spl* viandes *fpl* froides, assiette *f* anglaise

cold' feet' [fit] *spl*—**to have cold feet** (coll) avoir froid aux yeux

cold' front' *s* front *m* froid

cold'-heart'ed *adj* au cœur dur, insensible

coldness [ˈkoldnɪs] *s* froideur *f*; (*in the air*) froidure *f*

cold' shoul'der *s*—**to give s.o. the cold shoulder** (coll) battre froid à qn

cold' snap' *s* coup *m* de froid

cold' stor'age *s* entrepôt *m* frigorifique; **in cold storage** en glacière

cold'-stor'age *adj* frigorifique

cold' war' *s* guerre *f* froide

cold' wave' *s* vague *f* de froid

coleslaw [ˈkolˌslɔ] *s* salade *f* de chou

colic [ˈkɑlɪk] *s* colique *f*

coliseum [ˌkɑlɪˈsiˑəm] *s* colisée *m*

collaborate [kəˈlæbəˌret] *intr* collaborer

collaborationist [kəˌlæbəˈreʃənɪst] *s* collaborationniste *mf*

collaborator [kəˈlæbəˌretər] *s* collaborateur *m*

collapse [kəˈlæps] *s* écroulement *m*, effondrement *m*; (*of prices; of government*) chute *f*; (*of prices; of a beam*) fléchissement *m*; (pathol) collapsus *m* ‖ *intr* s'écrouler, s'effondrer; (*said of government*) tomber; (*said of structure or prices*) s'effondrer; (*said of balloon*) se dégonfler

collapsible [kəˈlæpsɪbəl] *adj* démontable, rabattable, pliant

collar [ˈkɑlər] *s* (*of dress, shirt*) collet *m*, col *m*; (*worn by dog; on pigeon*) collier *m*; (mach) collier ‖ *tr* colleter; (coll) empoigner

col·lar·band' s pied m de col (d'une chemise)

col·lar·bone' s clavicule f

collate [kə'let], ['kalet] tr collationner, conférer

collateral [kə'lætərəl] adj accessoire; correspondant; (kin) collatéral || s (kin) collatéral m; (com) nantissement m

collation [kə'leʃən] s collation f

colleague ['kalig] s collègue mf

collect ['kalekt] s (eccl) collecte f || [kə'lekt] tr rassembler; (taxes) percevoir, lever; (stamps, antiques) collectionner; (eggs, classroom papers; tickets) ramasser; (mail) faire la levée de; (debts) recouvrer; (gifts, money) collecter; (one's thoughts; anecdotes) recueillir; **to collect oneself** se reprendre, se remettre || intr (for the poor) quêter; (to gather together) se rassembler, se réunir; (to pile up) s'amasser || adv en p.c.v., e.g., **to telephone collect** téléphoner en p.c.v.

collect' call' s (telp) communication f P.C.V.

collected adj recueilli, maître de soi

collection [kə'lekʃən] s collection f; (of taxes) perception f, levée f, recouvrement m; (of mail) levée; (of verses) recueil m

collec'tion plate' s plateau m de quête

collective [kə'lektɪv] adj collectif

collector [kə'lektər] s (of stamps, antiques) collectionneur m; (of taxes) percepteur m, receveur m, collecteur m; (of tickets) contrôleur m

college ['kalɪdʒ] s (of cardinals, electors, etc.) collège m; (school in a university) faculté f; (U.S.A.) école f des arts et sciences

collegian [kə'lidʒɪ·ən] s étudiant m

collegiate [kə'lidʒɪ·ɪt] adj collégial, de l'université, universitaire

collide [kə'laɪd] intr se heurter, se tamponner; **to collide with** se heurter à or contre, heurter contre

collier ['kaljər] s houilleur m; (ship) charbonnier m

collier·y ['kaljərɪ] s (pl -ies) houillère f

collision [kə'lɪʒən] s collision f

collocate ['kalo,ket] tr disposer en rapport; (creditors) colloquer

colloid ['kalɔɪd] adj colloïdal || s colloïde m

colloquial [kə'lokwɪ·əl] adj familier

colloquialism [kə'lokwɪ·ə,lɪzəm] s expression f familière

collo·quy ['kaləkwi] s (pl -quies) colloque m

collusion [kə'luʒən] s collusion f; **to be in collusion with** être d'intelligence avec

cologne [kə'lon] s eau f de Cologne

Colombia [kə'lʌmbɪ·ə] s Colombie f; la Colombie

colon ['kolən] s (anat) côlon m; (gram) deux points mpl

colonel ['kʌrnəl] s colonel m

colonial [kə'lonɪ·əl] adj & s colonial m

colonist ['kalənɪst] s colon m

colonize ['kalə,naɪz] tr & intr coloniser

colonnade [,kalə'ned] s colonnade f

colo·ny ['kalənɪ] s (pl -nies) colonie f

colophon ['kalə,fan] s colophon m

color ['kʌlər] s couleur f; **the colors** les couleurs, le drapeau; **to call to the colors** appeler sous les drapeaux; **to give or lend color to** colorer; (fig) rendre vraisemblable; **to show one's true colors** se révéler sous son vrai jour; **under color of** sous couleur de; **with flying colors** enseignes déployées || tr colorer; (e.g., a drawing) colorier; (to exaggerate) donner de l'éclat à, imager; (to dye) teindre || intr se colorer; (to blush) rougir

col'or-bear'er s porte-drapeau m

col'or-blind' adj daltonien, aveugle des couleurs

colored adj coloré; (person) de couleur; (drawing) colorié

colorful ['kʌlərfəl] adj (striking) coloré; (unusual) pittoresque

col'or guard' s garde f d'honneur du drapeau

coloring ['kʌlərɪŋ] adj colorant || s colorant m; (of painting, complexion, style) coloris m

colorless ['kʌlərlɪs] adj incolore

col'or photog'raphy s photographie f en couleurs

col'or salute' s (mil) salut m au drapeau, salut aux couleurs

col'or ser'geant s sergent-chef m, sergent-major m

col'or tel'evision s télévision f en couleurs

colossal [kə'lasəl] adj colossal

colossus [kə'lasəs] s colosse m

colt [kolt] s poulain m

Columbus [kə'lʌmbəs] s Colomb m

column ['kaləm] s colonne f; (journ) rubrique f, chronique f, courrier m; (mil) colonne

columnar [kə'lʌmnər] adj en colonne

columnist ['kaləmnɪst] s chroniqueur m, courriériste mf

coma ['komə] s (pathol) coma m

comb [kom] s peigne m; (currycomb) étrille f; (of rooster; of wave) crête f; (filled with honey) rayon m || tr peigner; explorer minutieusement, fouiller; **to comb out** démêler || intr (said of waves) déferler

com·bat ['kambæt], ['kambət] s combat m || ['kambæt], [kəm'bæt] v (pret & pp -bated or -batted; ger -bating or -batting) tr & intr combattre

combatant ['kambətənt] adj & s combattant m

com'bat du'ty s service m de combat, service au front

combination [,kambɪ'neʃən] s combinaison f

combine ['kambaɪn] s trust m, combinaison f financière, entente f industrielle; (agr) moissonneuse-batteuse f || [kəm'baɪn] tr combiner || intr se liguer, fusionner; (chem) se combiner

combin'ing form' s élément m de composition

combo ['kambo] s (of four musicians) quartette f

combustible [kəm'bʌstɪbəl] adj & s combustible m

combustion [kəm'bʌstʃən] s combustion f

come [kʌm] v (pret came [kem]; pp come) intr venir; come in! entrez!; to come after succéder à, suivre; (to come to get) venir chercher; to come apart se séparer, se défaire; to come around (to snap back) se rétablir; (to give in) céder; to come at (to attack) se jeter sur; to come back revenir; (coll) revenir en vogue; to come before précéder; (e.g., a legislature) se mettre devant; to come between s'interposer entre; to come by (to get) obtenir; (to pass) passer; to come down descendre; to come downstairs descendre (en bas); to come down with tomber malade avec; to come for venir chercher; to come from provenir de, dériver de; (said of wind) chasser de; to come in entrer; entrer dans; (said of tide) monter; (said of style) entrer en vogue; to come in for avoir part à; (e.g., an inheritance) succéder à; (e.g., sympathy) s'attirer; to come off se détacher; (to take place) avoir lieu; en sortir, e.g., to come off victorious en sortir vainqueur; to come out sortir; (said of sun, stars; said of book) paraître; (said of buds) éclore; (said of news) se divulguer; (said of debutante) débuter; to come out for se prononcer pour; to come over se laisser persuader; arriver, e.g., what's come over him? qu'est-ce qui lui est arrivé?; to come through (e.g., fields) passer par, passer à travers; (e.g., a wall) pénétrer; (an illness) surmonter; se tirer indemne; to come to revenir à soi; to come together s'assembler, se réunir; to come true se réaliser; to come up monter; (to occur) se présenter; to come upstairs monter (en haut); to come up to monter jusqu'à, venir à; to come up with proposer

come'-and-go' s va-et-vient m

come'back' s (of style) (coll) retour m en vogue; (of statesman) (coll) retour m au pouvoir; (slang) réplique f, riposte f; to stage a comeback (coll) se réhabiliter, faire une belle remontée

comedian [kə'mɪdɪ-ən] s comique m; (on the legitimate stage) comédien m; auteur m comique

comedienne [kə,mɪdɪ'ɛn] s comédienne f

come'down' s humiliation f, déchéance f

come·dy ['kamədi] s (pl -dies) comédie f

come·ly ['kʌmli] adj (comp -lier; super -liest) (attractive) avenant, gracieux; (decorous) convenable, bienséant

come'-on' s (slang) leurre m, attrape f

comet ['kamɪt] s comète f

comfort ['kʌmfərt] s confort m; consolation f; (person) consolateur m;

comforts commodités fpl, agréments mpl || tr consoler, réconforter

comfortable ['kʌmfərtəbəl] adj confortable; (in a state of comfort) bien; (well-off) à l'aise

comforter ['kʌmfərtər] s consolateur m; (bedcover) couvre-pieds m piqué; (of wool) cache-nez m; (for baby) tétine f, sucette f

comforting ['kʌmfərtɪŋ] adj consolateur, réconfortant

com'fort sta'tion s chalet m de nécessité, lieux mpl d'aisances, toilette f

comic ['kamɪk] adj & s comique m; comics (cartoons) dessins mpl humoristiques

com'ic op'era s opéra m bouffe

com'ic strip' s bande f humoristique

coming ['kʌmɪŋ] adj qui vient; (future) d'avenir, de demain || s arrivée f, venue f; comings and goings allées et venues

com'ing out' s (of stocks, bonds, etc.) émission f; (of a book) parution f; (of a young lady) début m

comma ['kamə] s virgule f; (in French a period or sometimes a small space is used to mark the divisions of whole numbers) point m

command [kə'mænd], [kə'mand] s (leadership) gouvernement m; (order, direction) commandement m, ordre m; (e.g., of a foreign language) maîtrise f; to be at s.o.'s command être aux ordres de qn; to have a command of (a language) posséder; to have at one's command avoir à sa disposition || tr commander, ordonner; (respect) inspirer; (to look out over) dominer; (a language) connaître || intr (mil) commander, donner les ordres

commandant [,kamən'dænt], [,kamən'dant] s commandant m

commandeer [,kamən'dɪr] tr réquisitionner

commander [kə'mændər], [kə'mandər] s commandant m

comman'der in chief' s commandant m en chef

commanding [kə'mændɪŋ], [kə'mandɪŋ] adj imposant; (in charge) d'autorité

commemorate [kə'mɛməret] tr commémorer, célébrer

commence [kə'mɛns] tr & intr commencer

commencement [kə'mɛnsmənt] s commencement m; (educ) jour m de la distribution des prix, jour de la collation des grades

commence'ment ex'ercise s cérémonie f de remise des diplômes

commend [kə'mɛnd] tr (to praise) louer; (to entrust) confier, recommander

commendable [kə'mɛndəbəl] adj louable

commendation [,kamən'deʃən] s louange f, éloge m; (mil) citation f

comment ['kamɛnt] s remarque f, observation f, commentaire m || intr faire des observations; **to comment on** commenter

commentar·y ['kɑmən‚teri] s (pl **-ies**) commentaire m

commentator ['kɑmən‚tetər] s commentateur m

commerce ['kɑmərs] s commerce m, négoce m

commercial [kə'mʌrʃəl] adj commercial, commerçant ‖ s annonce f publicitaire

commercialize [kə'mʌrʃə‚laɪz] tr commercialiser

commiserate [kə'mɪzə‚ret] intr—to **commiserate with** compatir aux malheurs de

commiseration [kə‚mɪzə're/ən] s commisération f

commissar [‚kɑmɪ'sɑr] s commissaire m

commissar·y ['kɑmɪ‚seri] s (pl **-ies**) (person) commissaire m; (canteen) cantine f

commission [kə'mɪ/ən] s commission f; (board, council) conseil m; (com) guelte f; (mil) brevet m; **out of commission** hors de service; (naut) désarmé ‖ tr commissionner; (mil) promouvoir

commis'sioned of'ficer s breveté m

commissioner [kə'mɪ/ənər] s commissaire m

com·mit [kə'mɪt] v (pret & pp **-mitted**; ger **-mitting**) tr (an error, crime, etc.) commettre; (one's soul, one's money, etc.) confier; (one's word) engager; (to a mental hospital) interner; **to commit to memory** apprendre par cœur; **to commit to prison** envoyer en prison; **to commit to writing** coucher par écrit

commitment [kə'mɪtmənt] s (act of committing) perpétration f; (to a mental institution) internement m; (to prison) emprisonnement m; (to a cause) engagement m

committal [kə'mɪtəl] s (of a crime) perpétration f; (of a task) délégation f; **committal to prison** mise en prison

commit'tal ser'vice s (eccl) prières fpl au bord de la tombe

committee [kə'mɪti] s comité m, commission f

commode [kə'mod] s (toilet) chaise f percée; (dressing table) grande table f de nuit

commodious [kə'modɪ·əs] adj spacieux, confortable

commodi·ty [kə'mɑdɪti] s (pl **-ties**) denrée f, marchandise f

common ['kɑmən] adj commun ‖ s terrain m communal; **commons** communaux mpl; (of school) réfectoire m; **the Commons** (Brit) les communes fpl

com'mon car'rier s entreprise f de transports

commoner ['kɑmənər] s homme m du peuple, roturier m; (Brit) membre m de la Chambre des communes

com'mon law' s droit m coutumier, coutume f

com'mon-law mar'riage s union f libre, collage m

Com'mon Mar'ket s Marché m Commun

com'mon noun' s nom m commun

com'mon-place' adj banal ‖ s banalité f

com'mon sense' s sens m commun

com'mon-sense' adj sensé

com'mon stock' s action f ordinaire, actions ordinaires

commonweal ['kɑmən‚wil] s bien m public

com'mon-wealth' s état m, république f

commotion [kə'mo/ən] s commotion f

commune [kə'mjun] intr s'entretenir; (eccl) communier

communicant [kə'mjunɪkənt] s informateur m; (eccl) communiant m

communicate [kə'mjunɪ‚ket] tr & intr communiquer

communicating [kə'mjunɪ‚ketɪŋ] adj communicant

communication [kə‚mjunɪ'ke/ən] s communication f

communicative [kə'mjunɪ‚ketɪv] adj communicatif

communion [kə'mjunjən] s communion f; **to take communion** communier

communism ['kɑmjə‚nɪzəm] s communisme m

communist ['kɑmjənɪst] adj & s communiste mf

communi·ty [kə'mjunɪti] s (pl **-ties**) (locality) voisinage m; (group of people living together) communauté f

commu'nity chest' s caisse f de secours

commutation [‚kɑmjə'te/ən] s commutation f

commuta'tion tick'et s carte f d'abonnement

commutator ['kɑmjə‚tetər] s (elec) collecteur m

commute [kə'mjut] tr échanger; (e.g., a prison term) commuer ‖ intr s'abonner au chemin de fer; voyager avec carte d'abonnement

commuter [kə'mjutər] s abonné m au chemin de fer

compact [kəm'pækt] adj compact ‖ ['kɑmpækt] s (agreement) pacte m; (for cosmetics) poudrier m, boîte f à poudre

companion [kəm'pænjən] s compagnon m; (female companion) compagne f

companionable [kəm'pænjənəbəl] adj sociable

compan'ion-ship' s camaraderie f

compan'ion-way' s escalier m des cabines

compa·ny ['kʌmpəni] s (pl **-nies**) compagnie f; (com) société f, compagnie; (naut) équipage m; (theat) troupe f; **to have company** avoir du monde; **to keep bad company** fréquenter la mauvaise compagnie; **to keep company** sortir ensemble; **to keep s.o. company** tenir compagnie à qn; **to part company** se séparer

comparative [kəm'pærətɪv] adj comparatif; (anatomy, literature, etc.) comparé ‖ s comparatif m

compare [kəm'per] *s*—**beyond compare** incomparablement, sans égal || *tr* comparer; **compared to** en comparaison de; **to be compared to** se comparer à

comparison [kəm'pærɪsən] *s* comparaison *f*

compartment [kəm'pɑrtmənt] *s* compartiment *m*

compass ['kʌmpəs] *s* (*for showing direction*) boussole *f*; (*range, reach*) portée *f*; (*for drawing circles*) compas *m*; **to box the compass** réciter la rose des vents || *tr*—**to compass about** entourer

com'pass card' *s* rose *f* des vents

compassion [kəm'pæʃən] *s* compassion *f*

compassionate [kəm'pæʃənɪt] *adj* compatissant

compatibility [kəm,pætɪ'bɪlɪti] *s* compatibilité *f*, convenance *f*

com·pel [kəm'pel] *v* (*pret & pp* -**pelled**; *ger* -**pelling**) *tr* contraindre, obliger; (*respect, silence*) imposer

compelling [kəm'pelɪŋ] *adj* irrésistible; (*motive*) impérieux

compendious [kəm'pendɪ·əs] *adj* abrégé, succinct

compensate ['kampən,set] *tr* compenser; **to compensate s.o. for** dédommager qn de || *intr*—**to compensate for** compenser

compensation [,kampən'seʃən] *s* compensation *f*

compete [kəm'pit] *intr* concourir

competence ['kampɪtəns] or **competency** ['kampɪtənsi] *s* compétence *f*

competent ['kampɪtənt] *adj* compétent

competition [,kampɪ'tɪʃən] *s* concurrence *f*, compétition *f*; (*contest*) concours *m*; (*sports*) compétition, épreuve *f*

competitive [kəm'petɪtɪv] *adj* compétitif

compet'itive exam'ination *s* concours *m*

competitor [kəm'petɪtər] *s* concurrent *m*

compilation [,kampɪ'leʃən] *s* compilation *f*

compile [kəm'paɪl] *tr* compiler

complacency [kəm'plesənsi] *s* complaisance *f*; (*self-satisfaction*) suffisance *f*

complacent [kəm'plesənt] *adj* complaisant; content de soi, suffisant

complain [kəm'plen] *intr* se plaindre

complainant [kəm'plenənt] *s* plaignant *m*

complaint [kəm'plent] *s* plainte *f*; (*grievance*) grief *m*; (*illness*) maladie *f*, mal *m*

complaisant [kəm'plezənt], ['kamplɪ,zænt] *adj* complaisant

complement ['kamplɪmənt] *s* complément *m*; (*mil*) effectif *m* || ['kamplɪ,mənt] *tr* compléter

complete [kəm'plit] *adj* complet || *tr* compléter

complex [kəm'pleks], ['kampleks] *adj* complexe || ['kampleks] *s* complexe *m*

complexion [kəm'plekʃən] *s* (*texture* of skin, especially of face*) teint *m*; (*general aspect*) caractère *m*; (*constitution*) complexion *f*

compliance [kəm'plaɪ·əns] *s* complaisance *f*; soumission *f*, conformité *f*; **in compliance with** conformément à

complicate ['kamplɪ,ket] *tr* compliquer

complicated *adj* compliqué

complication [,kamplɪ'keʃən] *s* complication *f*

complici·ty [kəm'plɪsɪti] *s* (*pl* -**ties**) complicité *f*

compliment ['kamplɪmənt] *s* compliment *m*; **compliments** (*kind regards*) civilités *fpl*; **to pay a compliment to** faire un compliment à; **with the compliments of the author** hommage de l'auteur || *tr* complimenter

com'plimen'tary cop'y [,kamplɪ'mentəri] *s* exemplaire *m* en hommage; **to give a complimentary copy of a book** faire hommage d'un livre

com'plimen'tary tick'et *s* billet *m* de faveur

com·ply [kəm'plaɪ] *v* (*pret & pp* -**plied**) *intr*—**to comply with** se conformer à, acquiescer à

component [kəm'ponənt] *adj* composant || *s* (chem) composant *m*; (mech, math) composante *f*

comportment [kəm'portmənt] *s* comportement *m*

compose [kəm'poz] *tr* composer; **to be composed of** se composer de; **to compose oneself** se calmer

composed *adj* paisible, tranquille

composer [kəm'pozər] *s* compositeur *m*

compos'ing stick' *s* compositeur *m*

composite [kəm'pazɪt] *adj & s* composé *m*

composition [,kampə'zɪʃən] *s* composition *f*

compositor [kəm'pazɪtər] *s* compositeur *m*

compost ['kampost] *s* compost *m*

composure [kəm'pozər] *s* calme *m*, sang-froid *m*

compote ['kampot] *s* (*stewed fruits*) compote *f*; (*dish*) compotier *m*

compound ['kampaund] *adj* composé || *s* composé *m*; (gram) mot *m* composé; (math) complexe *m*; (mil) enceinte *f* || [kam'paund] *tr* composer, combiner; (*interest*) capitaliser

comprehend [,kamprɪ'hend] *tr* comprendre

comprehensible [,kamprɪ'hensɪbəl] *adj* compréhensible

comprehension [,kamprɪ'henʃən] *s* compréhension *f*

comprehensive [,kamprɪ'hensɪv] *adj* compréhensif, étendu; (*study, view, measure*) d'ensemble

compress ['kampres] *s* (med) compresse *f* || [kəm'pres] *tr* comprimer

compression [kəm'preʃən] *s* compression *f*

comprise [kəm'praɪz] *tr* comprendre, renfermer

compromise ['kamprə,maɪz] *s* compromis *m*; *(with one's conscience)* transaction *f*; **rough compromise** cote *f* mal taillée ‖ *tr* (*e.g.,* one's honor) compromettre ‖ *intr* (*to make concessions*) transiger

comptroller [kən'trolər] *s* vérificateur *m*, contrôleur *m*

compulsive [kəm'pʌlsɪv] *adj* obligatoire; (psychol) compulsif

compulsory [kəm'pʌlsəri] *adj* obligatoire, forcé

compute [kəm'pjut] *tr* computer, calculer, supputer ‖ *intr* calculer

computer [kəm'pjutər] *s* ordinateur *m*

comrade ['kɑmræd], ['kɑmrɪd] *s* camarade *mf*

com′rade in arms′ *s* compagnon *m* d'armes

com′rade-ship′ *s* camaraderie *f*

con [kɑn] *s* contre *m* ‖ *v* (*pret & pp* **conned**; *ger* **conning**) *tr* étudier; (naut) gouverner; (slang) escroquer

concave ['kɑnkev], [kɑn'kev] *adj* concave

conceal [kən'sil] *tr* dissimuler

concealment [kən'silmənt] *s* dissimulation *f*; *(place)* cachette *f*

concede [kən'sid] *tr & intr* concéder

conceit [kən'sit] *s* (*vanity*) vanité *f*; (*witty expression*) saillie *f*, mot *m*; **conceits** concetti *mpl*

conceited *adj* vaniteux, vain

conceivable [kən'sivəbəl] *adj* concevable

conceive [kən'siv] *tr & intr* concevoir

concentrate [kɑnsən,tret] *tr* concentrer ‖ *intr* se concentrer

concentra′tion camp′ [,kɑnsən'treʃən] *s* camp *m* de concentration

concentric [kən'sɛntrɪk] *adj* concentrique

concept ['kɑnsɛpt] *s* concept *m*

conception [kən'sɛpʃən] *s* conception *f*

concern [kən'sʌrn] *s* (*business establishment*) maison *f*, compagnie *f*; (*worry*) inquiétude *f*; (*relation, reference*) intérêt *m*; (*matter*) affaire *f* ‖ *tr* concerner; **as concerns** quant à; **persons concerned** intéressés *mpl*; **to be concerned** être inquiet; **to be concerned about** se préoccuper de; **to concern oneself with** s'intéresser à; **to whom it may concern** à qui de droit

concerning [kən'sʌrnɪŋ] *prep* concernant, en ce qui concerne, touchant

concert ['kɑnsərt] *s* concert *m*; **in concert** de concert ‖ [kən'sʌrt] *tr* concerter ‖ *intr* se concerter

con′cert-mas′ter *s* premier violon *m* soliste

concerto [kən't∫ɛrto] *s* (*pl* **-tos** *or* **-ti** [ti]) concerto *m*

concession [kən'sɛʃən] *s* concession *f*

conciliate [kən'sɪlɪ,et] *tr* concilier

conciliatory [kən'sɪlɪ-ə,tori] *adj* conciliatoire

concise [kən'sais] *adj* concis

conclude [kən'klud] *tr & intr* conclure

conclusion [kən'kluʒən] *s* conclusion *f*

conclusive [kən'klusɪv] *adj* concluant

concoct [kən'kɑkt] *tr* confectionner; (*a story*) inventer; (*a plan*) machiner

concoction [kɑn'kɑkʃən] *s* confection *f*; (*mixture*) mélange *m*; (pej) drogue *f*

concomitant [kən'kɑmɪtənt] *adj* concomitant ‖ *s* accompagnement *m*

concord ['kɑnkɔrd] *s* concorde *f*; (gram) concordance *f*; (mus) accord *m*

concordance [kən'kɔrdəns] *s* concordance *f*

concourse ['kɑnkɔrs] *s* (*of people*) concours *m*, foule *f*; (*road*) boulevard *m*; (*of railroad station*) hall *m*, salle *f* des pas perdus

concrete ['kɑnkrit], [kɑn'krit] *adj* concret; de béton ‖ *s* concret *m*; (*for construction*) béton *m* ‖ *tr* (*a sidewalk*) bétonner

con′crete block′ *s* parpaing *m*

con′crete mix′er *s* bétonnière *f*

concubine ['kɑŋkjə,bain] *s* concubine *f*

con-cur [kən'kʌr] *v* (*pret & pp* **-curred**; *ger* **-curring**) *intr* (*said of events*) concourir; (*said of persons*) s'accorder

concurrence [kən'kʌrəns] *s* concours *m*

concurrent [kən'kʌrənt] *adj* concourant

concussion [kən'kʌʃən] *s* secousse *f*, ébranlement *m*; (pathol) commotion *f*

condemn [kən'dɛm] *tr* condamner

condemnation [,kɑndɛm'neʃən] *s* condamnation *f*

condense [kən'dɛns] *tr* condenser ‖ *intr* se condenser

condenser [kən'dɛnsər] *s* condenseur *m*; (elec) condensateur *m*

condescend [,kɑndɪ'sɛnd] *intr* condescendre

condescending [,kɑndɪ'sɛndɪŋ] *adj* condescendant

condescension [,kɑndɪ'sɛnʃən] *s* condescendance *f*

condiment ['kɑndɪmənt] *s* condiment *m*

condition [kən'dɪʃən] *s* condition *f*; **on condition that** à condition que ‖ *tr* conditionner

conditional [kən'dɪʃənəl] *adj & s* conditionnel *m*

condole [kən'dol] *intr*—**to condole with** offrir ses condoléances à

condolence [kən'doləns] *s* condoléances *fpl*

condone [kən'don] *tr* pardonner, tolérer

conducive [kən'd(j)usɪv] *adj* favorable

conduct ['kɑndʌkt] *s* conduite *f*, comportement *m* ‖ [kən'dʌkt] *tr* conduire

conductor [kən'dʌktər] *s* (*on bus or streetcar*) receveur *m*; (mus) chef *m* d'orchestre; (rr) chef de train; (elec, phys) conducteur *m*; (elec, phys) (in predicate after **to be**, it may be translated by an adjective) conducteur, *e.g.,* **metals are good conductors of electricity** les métaux sont bons conducteurs de l'électricité

conduit ['kɑndɪt], ['kɑndu-ɪt] *s* conduit *m*; (elec) caniveau *m* cone [kon] s cône m; (for popcorn, ice cream) cornet m, plaisir m

confection [kən'fek/ən] s confiserie f

confectioner [kən'fek/ənər] s confiseur m

confec/tioners' sug/ar s sucre m glace

confectioner·y [kən'fek/ə,neri] s (pl -ies) confiserie f

confedera·cy [kən'fədərəsi] s (pl -cies) confédération f; (for unlawful purposes) conspiration f, entente f

confederate [kən'fedərit] adj confédéré || s complice mf; Confederate (hist) Confédéré m || [kən'fedə,ret] tr confédérer || intr se confédérer

con·fer [kən'fʌr] v (pret & pp -ferred; ger -ferring) tr & intr conférer

conference ['kɑnfərəns] s conférence f; (interview) entretien m; (sports) groupement m (d'équipes)

conferment [kən'fʌrmənt] s (of degrees) collation f

confess [kən'fes] tr confesser || intr se confesser

confession [kən'feʃən] s confession f

confessional [kən'feʃənəl] s confessional m

confessor [kən'fesər] s confesseur m

confidant [,kɑnfɪ'dænt], ['kɑnfɪ,dænt] s confident m

confide [kən'faɪd] tr confier || intr—to confide in se confier à

confidence ['kɑnfɪdəns] s confiance f; (secret) confidence f; in strict confidence sous toute réserve; to have confidence in se confier à

confident ['kɑnfɪdənt] adj confiant || s confident m

confidential [,kɑnfɪ'denʃəl] adj confidentiel

confiden/tial sec/retary s secrétaire m particulier, secrétaire f particulière

confine ['kɑnfaɪn] s (obs) confinement m; the confines les confins mpl || [kən'faɪn] tr confiner, enfermer; (to keep within limits) limiter; to be confined (said of woman) accoucher; to be confined to bed être alité

confinement [kən'faɪnmənt] s limitation f; (in prison) emprisonnement m; (in childbirth) accouchement m

confirm [kən'fʌrm] tr confirmer

confirmed adj (reassured) confirmé; (bachelor) endurci; (drunkard) fieffé; (drinker) invétéré; (smoker) émérite

confiscate ['kɑnfɪs,ket] tr confisquer

conflagration [,kɑnflə'greʃən] s conflagration f, incendie m

conflict ['kɑnflɪkt] s conflit m || [kən'flɪkt] intr être en contradiction, se heurter

conflicting [kən'flɪktɪŋ] adj contradictoire; (events, class hours, etc.) incompatible

con/flict of in/terest s conflit m d'intérêts, conflit des intérêts

conform [kən'fɔrm] tr conformer || intr se conformer, s'accommoder

conformist [kən'fɔrmɪst] s conformiste mf

conformi·ty [kən'fɔrmɪti] s (pl -ties)

conformité f; in conformity with conformément à

confound [kən'faʊnd] tr confondre || ['kɑn'faʊnd] tr maudire; confound it! diable!

confounded adj confus; (damned) sacré

confrere ['kɑnfrer] s confrère m

confront [kən'frʌnt] tr (to face boldly) affronter, faire face à; (witnesses, documents) confronter; to be confronted by se trouver en face de

confuse [kən'fjuz] tr confondre; to get confused devenir confus, s'embrouiller

confusing [kən'fjuzɪŋ] adj déroutant, embrouillant

confusion [kən'fjuʒən] s confusion f

confute [kən'fjut] tr réfuter

congeal [kən'dʒil] tr congeler || intr se congeler

congenial [kən'dʒinjəl] adj sympathique, agréable; compatible; congenial to or with apparenté à, conforme au tempérament de

congenital [kən'dʒenɪtəl] adj congénital

con/ger eel/ ['kɑŋgər] s congre m, anguille f de mer

congest [kən'dʒest] tr congestionner || intr se congestionner

congestion [kən'dʒestʃən] s congestion f

conglomeration [kən,glɑmə'reʃən] s conglomération f

congratulate [kən'grætʃə,let] tr féliciter, congratuler; to congratulate s.o. for féliciter qn de or pour; to congratulate s.o. for + ger féliciter qn de + inf

congratulations [kən,grætʃə'leʃənz] spl félicitations fpl

congregate ['kɑŋgrɪ,get] tr rassembler || intr se rassembler

congregation [,kɑŋgrɪ'geʃən] s rassemblement m; (parishioners) fidèles mfpl; (Protestant parishioners; committee of Roman Catholic prelates) congrégation f

congress ['kɑŋgrɪs] s congrès m

congressional [kən'greʃənəl] adj parlementaire

con/gress·man s (pl -men) congressiste m, parlementaire m

con/gress·wom/an s (pl -wom/en) congressiste f, parlementaire f

congruent ['kɑŋgru·ənt] adj (math) congru

conical ['kɑnɪkəl] adj conique

conjecture [kən'dʒektʃər] s conjecture f || tr & intr conjecturer

conjugal ['kɑndʒəgəl] adj conjugal

conjugate ['kɑndʒə,get] tr conjuguer

conjugation [,kɑndʒə'geʃən] s conjugaison f

conjunction [kən'dʒʌŋkʃən] s conjonction f

conjuration [,kɑndʒə'reʃən] s conjuration f

conjure [kən'dʒur] tr (to appeal to solemnly) conjurer || ['kɑndʒər], ['kɑndʒər] tr (to exorcise, drive away) conjurer; to conjure up évoquer || intr faire de la sorcellerie

connect [kə'nɛkt] *tr* relier, joindre; (*e.g.*, *two parties on the telephone*) mettre en communication; (*a pipe, an electrical device*) brancher, connecter || *intr* se lier, se joindre; **to connect with** (*said of train*) correspondre avec

connected *adj* (*related*) connexe; (*logical*) suivi

connecting [kə'nɛktɪŋ] *adj* de liaison; (*wire*) de connexion; (*pipe*) de raccord; (*street*) communiquant

connect′ing tow′er *s* bielle *f*

connection [kə'nɛkʃən] *s* connexion *f*, liaison *f*; (*between two causes*) connexité *f*; (*in families*) parenté *f*, parent *m*; (*by telephone*) communication *f*; (*of trains*) correspondance *f*; (*elec*) connexion; **connections** (*in the business world*) clientèle *f*, relations *fpl*; (*in families*) alliés *mpl*, consanguins *mpl*; **in connection with** à propos de

con′ning tow′er [ˈkɑnɪŋ] *s* (*e.g.*, *on battleship*) poste *m* or tourelle *f* de commandement; (*on sub*) kiosque *m*

conniption [kə'nɪpʃən] *s* (coll) rogne *f*

connive [kə'naɪv] *intr* être de connivence, être complice

connote [kə'not] *tr* (*to signify*) signifier, vouloir dire; (*to imply*) suggérer, sous-entendre

connubial [kə'n(j)ubɪəl] *adj* conjugal

conquer [ˈkɑŋkər] *tr* conquérir

conqueror [ˈkɑŋkərər] *s* conquérant

conquest [ˈkɑŋkwɛst] *s* conquête *f*

conscience [ˈkɑnʃəns] *s* conscience *f*; **in all conscience** en conscience; **to have on one′s conscience** avoir sur la conscience

conscientious [ˌkɑnʃɪ'ɛnʃəs] *adj* consciencieux

conscien′tious objec′tor [əb'dʒɛktər] *s* objecteur *m* de conscience

conscious [ˈkɑnʃəs] *adj* conscient; **to be conscious** (*not unconscious*) avoir connaissance; **to be conscious of** avoir conscience de

consciousness [ˈkɑnʃəsnɪs] *s* (*not sleep or coma*) connaissance *f*; (*awareness*) conscience *f*

conscript [ˈkɑnskrɪpt] *s* (mil) conscrit *m*; (nav) inscrit *m* maritime || [kən'skrɪpt] *tr* (mil) enrôler; (nav) inscrire

conscription [kən'skrɪpʃən] *s* conscription *f*

consecrate [ˈkɑnsɪˌkrɛt] *tr* consacrer; (*e.g.*, *bread*) bénir; (*a king or bishop*) sacrer

consecration [ˌkɑnsɪ'krɛʃən] *s* consécration *f*; (*to a task*) dévouement *m*; (*of a king or bishop*) sacre *m*

consecutive [kən'sɛkjətɪv] *adj* de suite, consécutif

consensus [kən'sɛnsəs] *s* consensus *m*

consent [kən'sɛnt] *s* consentement *m*; **by common consent** d'un commun accord || *intr* consentir

consequence [ˈkɑnsɪˌkwɛns] *s* conséquence *f*

consequential [ˌkɑnsɪ'kwɛnʃəl] *adj* conséquent, logique

consequently [ˈkɑnsɪˌkwɛntli] *adv* conséquemment, par conséquent

conservation [ˌkɑnsər'vɛʃən] *s* conservation *f*

conservatism [kən'sʌrvəˌtɪzəm] *s* conservatisme *m*

conservative [kən'sʌrvətɪv] *adj & s* conservateur *m*; **at a conservative estimate** au bas mot, au moins

conservato•ry [kən'sʌrvəˌtori] *s* (*pl* -ries) (*of music*) conservatoire *m*; (*greenhouse*) serre *f*

conserve [kən'sʌrv] *tr* conserver

consider [kən'sɪdər] *tr* considérer

considerable [kən'sɪdərəbəl] *adj* considérable

considerate [kən'sɪdərɪt] *adj* prévenant, plein d'égards

consideration [kən,sɪdə'rɛʃən] *s* considération *f*; (*remuneration*) rétribution *f*; (*favor*) indulgence *f*; **to take into consideration** tenir compte de; **under consideration** à l'étude

considering [kən'sɪdərɪŋ] *prep* eu égard à; **considering that** vu que

consign [kən'saɪn] *tr* consigner

consignee [ˌkɑnsaɪ'ni] *s* consignataire *m*

consignment [kən'saɪnmənt] *s* consignation *f*, livraison *f*

consist [kən'sɪst] *intr*—**to consist in** consister dans or en; **to consist in** + *ger* consister à + *inf*; **to consist of** consister dans or en

consisten•cy [kən'sɪstənsi] *s* (*pl* -cies) (*logical connection*) conséquence *f*; (*firmness, amount of firmness*) consistance *f*

consistent [kən'sɪstənt] *adj* (*agreeing with itself or oneself*) conséquent; (*holding firmly together*) consistant; **consistent with** compatible avec

consisto•ry [kən'sɪstəri] *s* (*pl* -ries) consistoire *m*

consolation [ˌkɑnsə'lɛʃən] *s* consolation *f*

console [ˈkɑnsol] *s* console *f* || [kən'sol] *tr* consoler

con′sole ta′ble *s* console *f*

consolidate [kən'sɑlɪˌdɛt] *tr* consolider

consonant [ˈkɑnsənənt] *adj* (*in sound*) consonant; **consonant with** d'accord avec || *s* consonne *f*

consort [ˈkɑnsɔrt] *s* compagnon *m*; (*husband*) conjoint *m*; (*wife*) conjointe *f*; **prince m consort**; (*convoy*) conserve *f* || [kən'sɔrt] *tr* unir || *intr* s'associer; (*to harmonize*) s'accorder; **to consort with** s'associer à or avec

conspicuous [kən'spɪkjuəs] *adj* apparent, frappant; (*attracting special attention*) voyant; **to make oneself conspicuous** se faire remarquer

conspira•cy [kən'spɪrəsi] *s* (*pl* -cies) conspiration *f*, conjuration *f*

conspirator [kən'spɪrətər] *s* conspirateur *m*, conjuré *m*

conspire [kən'spaɪr] *intr* conspirer

constable [ˈkɑnstəbəl], [ˈkʌnstəbəl] *s* garde *m* champêtre; juge *m* de paix

constancy ['kɒnstənsɪ] s constance f
constant ['kɒnstənt] adj constant ‖ s constante f
constantly ['kɒnstəntlɪ] adv constamment
constellation [,kɒnstə'leʃən] s constellation f
constipate ['kɒnstɪ,pet] tr constiper
constipation [,kɒnstɪ'peʃən] s constipation f
constituen-cy [kən'stɪtʃu·ənsɪ] s (pl -cies) électeurs mpl, commettants mpl; circonscription f électorale
constituent [kən'stɪtʃu·ənt] adj constituant, constitutif ‖ s élément m, constituant m; (voter, client) électeur m, commettant m
constitute ['kɒnstɪ,t(j)ut] tr constituer
constitution [,kɒnstɪ't(j)uʃən] s constitution f
constrain [kən'stren] tr contraindre
constraint [kən'strent] s contrainte f; (restraint) retenue f; (uneasiness) gêne f
constrict [kən'strɪkt] tr resserrer
construct [kən'strʌkt] tr construire
construction [kən'strʌkʃən] s construction f; interprétation f
constructive [kən'strʌktɪv] adj constructif, constructeur
construe [kən'stru] tr expliquer, interpréter; (gram) construire
consul ['kɒnsəl] s consul m
consular ['kɒns(j)ələr] adj consulaire
consulate ['kɒns(j)əlɪt] s consulat m
consult [kən'sʌlt] tr consulter ‖ intr consulter; se consulter
consultant [kən'sʌltənt] s conseiller m, consultant m
consultation [,kɒnsəl'teʃən] s consultation f; (eccl, law) consulte f
consume [kən's(j)um] tr (to make use of, use up) consommer; (to use up entirely; to destroy) consumer, épuiser
consumer [kən's(j)umər] s consommateur m; (of gas, electricity, etc.) abonné m
consum'er goods' spl denrées fpl de consommation
consummate [kən'sʌmɪt] adj consommé ‖ ['kɒnsə,met] tr consommer
consumption [kən'sʌmpʃən] s consommation f; (pathol) tuberculose f pulmonaire
consumptive [kən'sʌmptɪv] adj destructeur; (pathol) poitrinaire ‖ s (pathol) poitrinaire mf
contact ['kɒntækt] s contact m; to put in contact mettre en contact ‖ tr (coll) prendre contact avec, contacter ‖ intr prendre contact
con'tact lens' s verre m de contact, lentille f de contact
contagion [kən'tedʒən] s contagion f
contagious [kən'tedʒəs] adj contagieux
contain [kən'ten] tr contenir; (one's sorrow) apprivoiser
container [kən'tenər] s boîte f, contenant m, récipient m
containment [kən'tenmənt] s refoulement m, retenue f

contaminate [kən'tæmɪ,net] tr contaminer
contamination [kən,tæmɪ'neʃən] s contamination f
contemplate ['kɒntəm,plet] tr & intr contempler; (e.g., a trip) projeter; to contemplate + ger penser + inf
contemplation [,kɒntəm'pleʃən] s contemplation f
contemporaneous [kən,tɛmpə'renɪ·əs] adj contemporain
contemporar-y [kən'tɛmpə,rɛrɪ] adj contemporain ‖ s (pl -ies) contemporain m
contempt [kən'tɛmpt] s mépris m, nargue f; (law) contumace f; to hold in contempt mépriser
contemptible [kən'tɛmptɪbəl] adj méprisable
contempt' of court' s outrage m à la justice
contemptuous [kən'tɛmptʃu·əs] adj méprisant
contend [kən'tɛnd] tr prétendre ‖ intr combattre; to contend with lutter contre
contender [kən'tɛndər] s concurrent m, compétiteur m
content [kən'tɛnt] adj & s content m ‖ ['kɒntɛnt] s contenu m; contents contenu; (of table of contents) matières fpl ‖ [kən'tɛnt] tr contenter
contented [kən'tɛntɪd] adj content, satisfait
contention [kən'tɛnʃən] s (strife) dispute f, différend m; (point argued for) point m discuté, argument m; (law) contentieux m
contentious [kən'tɛnʃəs] adj contentieux
contentment [kən'tɛntmənt] s contentement m
contest ['kɒntɛst] s (struggle, fight) lutte f, dispute f; (competition) concours m, compétition f ‖ [kən'tɛst] tr & intr contester
contestant [kən'tɛstənt] s concurrent m
context ['kɒntɛkst] s contexte m
contiguous [kən'tɪgju·əs] adj contigu
continence ['kɒntɪnəns] s continence f
continent ['kɒntɪnənt] adj & s continent m
continental [,kɒntɪ'nɛntəl] adj continental
contingen-cy [kən'tɪndʒɛnsɪ] s (pl -cies) contingence f
contingent [kən'tɪndʒənt] adj & s contingent m
continual [kən'tɪnju·əl] adj continuel
continuation [kən,tɪnju'eʃən] s continuation f; (e.g., of a story) suite f
continue [kən'tɪnju] tr & intr continuer; continued on page two (three, etc.) suite page deux (trois, etc.); to be continued à suivre
continui-ty [,kɒntɪ'n(j)u·ɪtɪ] s (pl -ties) continuité f; (mov, rad, telv) découpage m, scénario m
continuous [kən'tɪnju·əs] adj continu
contin'uous show'ing s (mov) spectacle m permanent

contin'uous waves' *spl* ondes *fpl* entretenues

contortion [kən'tɔrʃən] *s* contorsion *f*

contour ['kɑntur] *s* contour *m* || *tr* contourner

con'tour line' *s* courbe *f* de niveau

contraband ['kɑntrə,bænd] *adj* contrebandier || *s* contrebande *f*

contrabass ['kɑntrə,bes] *s* contrebasse *f*

contraceptive [,kɑntrə'sɛptɪv] *adj & s* contraceptif *m*

contract ['kɑntrækt] *s* contrat *m* || ['kɑntrækt], [kən'trækt] *tr* contracter || *intr* se contracter

contraction [kən'trækʃən] *s* contraction *f*

contractor [kən'træktər] *s* entrepreneur *m*

contradict [,kɑntrə'dɪkt] *tr* contredire

contradiction [,kɑntrə'dɪkʃən] *s* contradiction *f*

contradictory [,kɑntrə'dɪktəri] *adj* contradictoire

contral·to [kən'trælto] *s* (*pl* -tos) contralto *m*

contraption [kən'træpʃən] *s* (coll) machin *m*, truc *m*

contra·ry ['kɑntreri] *adj* contraire || *adv* contrairement || [kən'treri] *adj* (coll) obstiné, têtu || ['kɑntreri] *s* (*pl* -ries) contraire *m*; **on the contrary** au contraire, par contre

contrast ['kɑntræst] *s* contraste *m* || [kən'træst] *tr & intr* contraster

contravene [,kɑntrə'vin] *tr* contredire; (*a law*) contrevenir (with *dat*)

contribute [kən'trɪbjut] *tr* (e.g., *a sum of money*) contribuer pour || *intr* contribuer; (*to a newspaper, conference, etc.*) collaborer

contribution [,kɑntrɪ'bjuʃən] *s* contribution *f*, apport *m*; (e.g., *for charity*) souscription *f*; (*to a newspaper, conference, etc.*) collaboration *f*

contributor [kən'trɪbjutər] *s* (*donor*) donneur *m*; (e.g., *to a charitable cause*) souscripteur *m*; (*to a newspaper, conference, etc.*) collaborateur *m*

contrite ['kɑn'traɪt] *adj* contrit

contrition [kən'trɪʃən] *s* contrition *f*

contrivance [kən'traɪvəns] *s* invention *f*, expédient *m*; (*gadget*) dispositif *m*

contrive [kən'traɪv] *tr* inventer || *intr* s'arranger; **to contrive to** trouver moyen de

con·trol [kən'trol] *s* direction *f*, autorité *f*; (*mastery*) maîtrise *f*; (*surveillance*) contrôle *m*; **controls** commandes *fpl* || *v* (*pret & pp* -trolled; *ger* -trolling) *tr* diriger; maîtriser; (*to give surveillance to*) contrôler; (*to handle the controls of*) commander; **to control oneself** se contrôler

controller [kən'trolər] *s* contrôleur *m*, appareil *m* de contrôle; (elec) contrôleur *m*

control' pan'el *s* (aer) planche *f* de bord, tableau *m* de bord

control' stick' *s* (aer) manche *m* à balai

control' tow'er *s* poste-vigie *m*, tourelle *f* de commandement

controversial [,kɑntrə'vʌrʃəl] *adj* controversable

controver·sy ['kɑntrə,vʌrsi] *s* (*pl* -sies) controverse *f*; dispute *f*, querelle *f*

controvert ['kɑntrə,vʌrt], [,kɑntrə'vʌrt] *tr* controverser; contredire

contumacious [,kɑnt(j)u'meʃəs] *adj* rebelle, récalcitrant

contume·ly ['kɑnt(j)umɪli] *s* (*pl* -lies) injure *f*, outrage *m*, mépris *m*

contusion [kən't(j)uʒən] *s* contusion *f*

conundrum [kə'nʌndrəm] *s* devinette *f*, énigme *f*

convalesce [,kɑnvə'lɛs] *intr* guérir, se remettre, se rétablir

convalescence [,kɑnvə'lɛsəns] *s* convalescence *f*

convalescent [,kɑnvə'lɛsənt] *adj & s* convalescent *m*

convales'cent home' *s* maison *f* de repos

convene [kən'vin] *tr* assembler, convoquer || *intr* s'assembler

convenience [kən'vinjəns] *s* commodité *f*; (e.g., *in the home*) confort *m*; **at your earliest convenience** aussitôt que possible

convent ['kɑnvɛnt] *s* couvent *m* (de religieuses)

convention [kən'vɛnʃən] *s* assemblée *f*, congrès *m*; (*agreement*) convention *f*; (*accepted usage*) convention sociale; **conventions** convenances *fpl*, bienséances *fpl*

conventional [kən'vɛnʃənəl] *adj* conventionnel; (*in conduct*) respectueux des convenances; (*everyday*) usuel; (*model, type*) traditionnel

converge [kən'vʌrdʒ] *intr* converger

conversant [kən'vʌrsənt] *adj* familier, versé

conversation [,kɑnvər'seʃən] *s* conversation *f*

conversational [,kɑnvər'seʃənəl] *adj* de conversation

converse ['kɑnvʌrs] *adj & s* contraire *m*, inverse *m*, réciproque *f* || [kən'vʌrs] *intr* converser

conversion [kən'vʌrʒən] *s* conversion *f*

convert ['kɑnvʌrt] *s* converti *m* || [kən'vʌrt] *tr* convertir || *intr* se convertir

converter [kən'vʌrtər] *s* convertisseur *m*

convertible [kən'vʌrtɪbəl] *adj* (*person*) convertissable; (*thing; security*) convertible; (aut) décapotable *f* || *s* (aut) décapotable *f*

convex ['kɑnvɛks], [kɑn'vɛks] *adj* convexe, bombé

convey [kən've] *tr* transporter; (e.g., *a message*) communiquer; (e.g., *property*) transmettre; (law) céder

conveyance [kən've·əns] *s* transport *m*; (*vehicle*) moyen *m* de transport, voiture *f*; (*of message*) communication *f*; (*transfer*) transmission *f*; (law) transfert *m*, cession *f*

conveyor [kən've·ər] *s* transporteur *m*, convoyeur *m*

convey'or belt' *s* tapis *m* roulant

convict ['kɑnvɪkt] *s* condamné *m*, for-

çat *m* ‖ [kən'vɪkt] *tr* condamner, convaincre
conviction [kən'vɪkʃən] *s* condamnation *f*; (*certainty*) conviction *f*
convince [kən'vɪns] *tr* convaincre
convincing [kən'vɪnsɪŋ] *adj* convaincant
convivial [kən'vɪvɪ·əl] *adj* jovial, plein d'entrain
convocation [,kɑnvə'keʃən] *s* (*calling together*) convocation *f*; (*meeting*) assemblée *f*
convoke [kən'vok] *tr* convoquer
convolution [,kɑnvə'luʃən] *s* (*of brain*) circonvolution *f*
convoy ['kɑnvɔɪ] *s* convoi *m*, conserve *f*, e.g., **to sail in convoy** naviguer de conserve ‖ *tr* convoyer
convulse [kən'vʌls] *tr* convulsionner, convulser; **to be convulsed with laughter** se tordre de rire
coo [ku] *intr* roucouler
cooing ['ku·ɪŋ] *s* roucoulement *m*
cook [kʊk] *s* cuisinier *m*, chef *m*; (*female cook*) cuisinière *f* ‖ *tr* cuisiner, faire cuire; **to cook up** (*a plot*) machiner, tramer ‖ *intr* faire la cuisine, cuisiner; (*said of food*) cuire
cook'book' *s* livre *m* de cuisine
cooker ['kʊkər] *s* réchaud *m*, cuisinière *f*
cookery ['kʊkəri] *s* cuisine *f*
cookie ['kʊki] *s* var of **cooky**
cooking ['kʊkɪŋ] *s* cuisine *f*; (*e.g., of meat*) cuisson *f*
cook'ing uten'sils *spl* batterie *f* de cuisine
cook'stove' *s* cuisinière *f*
cook·y ['kʊki] *s* (*pl* **-ies**) biscuit *m*, gâteau *m* sec
cool [kul] *adj* frais; (*e.g., to an idea*) indifférent; **it is cool out** il fait frais; **to keep cool** tenir au frais; se tenir tranquille ‖ *s* fraîcheur *f* ‖ *tr* rafraîchir, refroidir; **to cool one's heels** (coll) se morfondre ‖ *intr* se refroidir, se rafraîchir; **to cool down** se calmer; **to cool off** se refroidir
cooler ['kulər] *s* frigorifique *m*; (*prison*) (slang) violon *m*, tôle *f*
cool'-head'ed *adj* imperturbable, de sang-froid
coolness ['kulnɪs] *s* fraîcheur *f*; (*of disposition*) sang-froid *m*, calme *m*; (*stand-offishness*) froideur *f*
coon [kun] *s* raton *m* laveur
coop [kup] *s* poulailler *m*; **to fly the coop** (slang) débiner, décamper ‖ *tr* enfermer dans un poulailler; **to coop up** claquemurer
co-op ['ko·ɑp], [ko'ɑp] *s* entreprise *f* coopérative
cooper ['kupər] *s* tonnelier *m*
cooperate [ko'ɑpə,ret] *intr* coopérer; (*to be helpful*) faire preuve de bonne volonté
cooperation [ko,ɑpə'reʃən] *s* coopération *f*
cooperative [ko'ɑpə,retɪv] *adj* coopératif
coordinate [ko'ɔrdɪnɪt] *adj* coordonné

‖ *s* coordonnée *f* ‖ [ko'ɔrdɪ,net] *tr* coordonner
coot [kut] *s* foulque *f*; **old coot** (coll) vieille baderne *f*
cootie ['kuti] *s* (slang) pou *m*
cop [kɑp] *s* (slang) flic *m* ‖ *v* (*pret* & *pp* **copped**; *ger* **copping**) *tr* (slang) dérober
copartner [ko'pɑrtnər] *s* coassocié *m*, coparticipant *m*; (*in crime*) complice *m/f*
cope [kop] *intr*—**to cope with** faire face à, tenir tête à
cope'stone' *s* couronnement *m*
copier ['kɑpɪ·ər] *s* (*person who copies*) copiste *mf*, imitateur *m*; (*apparatus*) appareil *m* à copier
copilot ['ko,paɪlət] *s* copilote *m*
coping ['kopɪŋ] *s* faîte *m*, comble *m*; (*of bridge*) chape *f*
copious ['kopɪ·əs] *adj* copieux
copper ['kɑpər] *adj* de cuivre, en cuivre; (*color*) cuivré ‖ *s* cuivre *m*; (*coin*) petite monnaie *f*; (slang) flic *m*
cop'per·smith' *s* chaudronnier *m*
coppery ['kɑpəri] *adj* cuivreux
coppice ['kɑpɪs] *s* taillis *m*
copulate ['kɑpjə,let] *intr* s'accoupler
copulation [,kɑpjə'leʃən] *s* copulation *f*, accouplement *m*
cop·y ['kɑpi] *s* (*pl* **-ies**) copie *f*; (*of a book*) exemplaire *m*; (*of a magazine*) numéro *m*; (*for printer*) original *m*; **to make copies** exécuter des doubles ‖ *v* (*pret* & *pp* **-ied**) *tr* & *intr* copier
cop'y·book' *s* cahier *m*
cop'y·cat' *s* (coll) imitateur *m*, singe *m*
cop'y·right' *s* propriété *f* artistique or littéraire, droit *m* de l'artiste or de l'auteur, copyright *m*; (formula on printed matter) dépôt *m* légal ‖ *tr* réserver les droits de publication de
cop'y·right'ed *adj* (formula used on printed material) droits de reproduction réservés
cop'y·writ'er *s* rédacteur *m* d'annonces publicitaires
co·quet [ko'ket] *v* (*pret* & *pp* **-quetted**; *ger* **-quetting**) *intr* coqueter
coquetry ['kokətri], [ko'ketri] *s* (*pl* **-ries**) coquetterie *f*
coquette [ko'ket] *s* coquette *f* ‖ *intr* coqueter
coquettish [ko'ketɪʃ] *adj* coquet
coral ['kɑrəl], ['kɔrəl] *adj* de corail, en corail ‖ *s* corail *m*
cor'al reef' *s* récif *m* de corail
cord [kɔrd] *s* corde *f*; (*string*) ficelle *f*; (*attached to a bell*) cordon *m*; (elec) fil *m* ‖ *tr* corder
cordage ['kɔrdɪdʒ] *s* cordage *m*
cordial ['kɔrdʒəl] *adj* & *s* cordial *m*
cordiali·ty [kɔr'dʒælɪti] *s* (*pl* **-ties**) cordialité *f*
corduroy ['kɔrdə,rɔɪ] *s* velours *m* côtelé; **corduroys** pantalon *m* en velours côtelé
core [kor] *s* cœur *m*; (elec) noyau *m*; **rotten to the core** pourri à la base ‖ *tr* vider
corespondent [,korɪs'pɑndənt] *s* complice *mf* d'adultère

cork [kɔrk] s liège m; (of bottle) bouchon m; to take the cork out of déboucher ‖ tr boucher

corking ['kɔrkɪŋ] adj (coll) épatant

cork/ oak/ s chêne-liège m

cork/screw/ s tire-bouchon m

cork/-tipped/ adj à bout de liège

cormorant ['kɔrmərənt] s cormoran m

corn [kɔrn] s (in U.S.A.) maïs m; (in England) blé m; (in Scotland) avoine f; (single seed) grain m; (on foot) cor m, durillon m; (whiskey) (coll) eau-de-vie f de grain; (slang) platitude f, banalité f

corn/ bread/ s pain m de maïs

corn/cob/ s épi m de maïs; (without the grain) rafle f

corn/cob pipe/ s pipe f en rafle de maïs

corn/crib/ s dépôt m de maïs

cornea ['kɔrnɪ-ə] s cornée f

corned/ beef/ s bœuf m salé

corner ['kɔrnər] adj cornier ‖ s coin m, angle m; (of room) encoignure f; (of lips) commissure f; around the corner au tournant; in a corner (fig) au pied du mur, à l'accul: to cut a corner close prendre un virage à la corde; to cut corners (in spending) rogner les dépenses; (in work) bâcler un travail ‖ tr coincer, acculer; (the market) accaparer

cor/ner cup/board/ s encoignure f

cor/ner room/ s pièce f d'angle

cor/ner-stone/ s pierre f angulaire

cornet [kɔr'nɛt] s cornet m; (head-dress) cornette f; (mil) cornette m; (mus) cornet à pistons

corn/ exchange/ s bourse f des céréales

corn/field/ s (in U.S.A.) champ m de maïs; (in England) champ de blé; (in Scotland) champ d'avoine

corn/flakes/ spl paillettes fpl de maïs

corn/ flour/ s farine f de maïs

corn/flow/er s bluet m, barbeau m

corn/ frit/ter s crêpes fpl de maïs

corn/husk/ s enveloppe f de l'épi de maïs

cornice ['kɔrnɪs] s corniche f

corn/ meal/ s farine f de maïs

corn/ on the cob/ s maïs m en épi

corn/ pad/ s bourrelet m coricide

corn/ pone/ s pain m de maïs

corn/ pop/per s appareil m pour faire éclater le maïs

corn/ remov/er s coricide m

corn/ silk/ s barbe f de maïs

corn/stalk/ s tige f de maïs

corn/starch/ s fécule f de maïs

cornucopia [,kɔrnə'kopɪ-ə] s corne f d'abondance

Cornwall ['kɔrn,wɔl], ['kɔrnwəl] s la Cornouailles

corn/y ['kɔrni] adj (comp -ier; super -iest) (slang) banal, trivial, fade

corollar-y ['kɑrə,lɛri], ['kɔrə,lɛri] s (pl -ies) corollaire m

coronary ['kɑrə,nɛri], ['kɔrə,nɛri] adj coronaire

coronation [,kɑrə'neʃən], [kɔrə'neʃən] s couronnement m, sacre m

cor/oner's in/quest ['kɑrənərz], ['kɔrənərz] s enquête f judiciaire par-devant jury (en cas de mort violente ou suspecte)

coronet ['kɑrə,nɛt], ['kɔrə,nɛt] s diadème m; (worn by members of nobility) couronne f; (worn by earl or baron) tortil m

corporal ['kɔrpərəl] adj corporel ‖ s (mil) caporal m

corporate ['kɔrpərɪt] adj incorporé

corporation [,kɔrpə'reʃən] s société f anonyme, compagnie f anonyme

corporeal [kɔr'porɪ-əl] adj corporel, matériel

corps [kor] s (pl corps [korz]) corps m; (mil) corps d'armée

corpse [kɔrps] s cadavre m

corps/man s (pl -men) (mil) infirmier m

corpulent ['kɔrpjələnt] adj corpulent

corpuscle ['kɔrpəsəl] s (phys) corpuscule m; (physiol) globule m

corpus delicti ['kɔrpəsdɪ'lɪktaɪ] s (law) corps m du délit

cor·ral [kə'ræl] s corral m, enclos m ‖ v (pret & pp -ralled; ger -ralling) tr enfermer dans un corral; (fig) saisir

correct [kə'rɛkt] adj correct ‖ tr corriger

correction [kə'rɛkʃən] s correction f

corrective [kə'rɛktɪv] adj & s correctif m

correc/tive lens/es spl verres mpl correcteurs

correctness [kə'rɛktnɪs] s correction f

correlate ['kɑrə,let], ['kɔrə,let] tr mettre en corrélation ‖ intr correspondre; to correlate with correspondre à

correlation [,kɑrə'leʃən], [,kɔrɪ'leʃən] s corrélation f

correspond [,kɑrɪ'spand], [,kɔrɪ'spand] intr correspondre

correspondence [,kɑrɪ'spandəns], [,kɔrɪ'spandəns] s correspondance f

correspondent [,kɑrɪ'spandənt], [,kɔrɪ'spandənt] adj & s correspondant m

corresponding [,kɑrɪ'spandɪŋ], [,kɔrɪ'spandɪŋ] adj correspondant

corridor ['kɑrɪdər], ['kɔrɪdər] s corridor m, couloir m

corroborate [kə'rabə,ret] tr corroborer

corrode [kə'rod] tr corroder ‖ intr se corroder

corrosion [kə'roʒən] s corrosion f

corrosive [kə'rosɪv] adj & s corrosif m

corrugated ['kɑrə,getɪd], ['kɔrə,getɪd] adj ondulé

corrupt [kə'rʌpt] adj corrompu ‖ tr corrompre

corruption [kə'rʌpʃən] s corruption f

corsage [kɔr'saʒ] s bouquet m

corsair ['kor,sɛr] s corsaire m

corset ['kɔrsɪt] s corset m

Corsica ['kɔrsɪkə] s Corse f; la Corse

Corsican ['kɔrsɪkən] adj corse ‖ s (dialect) corse m; (person) Corse mf

cortege [kɔr'tɛʒ] s cortège m

cor·tex ['kɔr,tɛks] s (pl -tices [tɪ,siz]) cortex m

cortisone ['kɔrtɪ,son] s cortisone f

coruscate ['kɑrəs,ket], ['kɔrəs,ket] intr scintiller

cosmetic [kaz'metɪk] *adj & s* cosmétique *m*

cosmic ['kazmɪk] *adj* cosmique

cosmonaut ['kazmə‚nɔt] *s* cosmonaute *mf*

cosmopolitan [‚kazmə'palɪtən] *adj & s* cosmopolite *mf*

cosmos ['kazməs] *s* cosmos *m*

Cossack ['ka‚sæk] *adj* cosaque ‖ *s* Cosaque *mf*

cost [kɔst], [kast] *s* coût *m*; (*price*) prix *m*; **at all costs** à tout prix, coûte que coûte; **at cost** au prix coûtant; **costs** frais *mpl*; (*law*) dépens *mpl* ‖ *v* (*pret & pp* **cost**) *intr* coûter

cost′ account′ing *s* comptabilité *f* industrielle

costliness ['kɔstlɪnɪs], ['kastlɪnɪs] *s* cherté *f*, haut prix *m*

cost·ly ['kɔstli], ['kastli] *adj* (*comp* **-lier**; *super* **-liest**) coûteux, cher

cost′ of liv′ing *s* coût *m* de la vie

cost′ price′ *s* prix *m* coûtant; (*net price*) prix de revient

costume ['kast(j)um] *s* costume *m*

cos′tume ball′ *s* bal *m* costumé

cos′tume jew′elry *s* bijoux *mpl* en toc

costumer [kas't(j)umər] *s* costumier *m*

cot [kat] *s* lit *m* de sangle

coterie ['kotəri] *s* coterie *f*

cottage ['katɪdʒ] *s* chalet *m*, cabanon *m*, villa *f*; (*with a thatched roof*) chaumière *f*

cot′tage cheese′ *s* lait *m* caillé, caillé *m*, jonchée *f*

cot′ter pin′ ['katər] *s* goupille *f* fendue, clavette *f*

cotton ['katən] *adj* cotonnier, de coton ‖ *s* coton *m* ‖ *intr*—**to cotton up to** (coll) éprouver de la sympathie pour

cot′ton bat′ting *s* coton *m* or ouate *f* hydrophile

cot′ton field′ *s* cotonnerie *f*

cot′ton gin′ *s* égreneuse *f*

cot′ton mill′ *s* filature *f* de coton, cotonnerie *f*

cot′ton pick′er *s* cotonnier *m*

cot′ton pick′ing *s* récolte *f* du coton

cot′tonseed′ *s* graine *f* de coton

cot′tonseed oil′ *s* huile *f* de coton

cot′ton waste′ *s* déchets *mpl* or bourre *f* de coton

cot′ton-wood′ *s* peuplier *m* de Virginie

cottony ['katəni] *adj* cotonneux

couch [kautʃ] *s* (*without back*) divan *m*; (*with back*) sofa *m*, canapé *m* ‖ *tt* (*a demand, a letter*) rédiger ‖ *intr* (*to lie in wait*) se tapir

cougar ['kugər] *s* couguar *m*, cougouar *m*

cough [kɔf], [kaf] *s* toux *f* ‖ *tr*—**to cough up** cracher en toussant; (slang) (*money*) cracher ‖ *intr* tousser

cough′ drop′ *s* pastille *f* pectorale, pastille pour la toux

cough′ syr′up *s* sirop *m* pectoral, sirop contre la toux

could [kud] *aux*—**he could not come** il ne pouvait pas venir; **he couldn′t do it** il n′a (pas) pu le faire; **he couldn′t do it if he wanted to** il ne pourrait

(pas) le faire s′il le voulait, il ne saurait (pas) le faire s′il le voulait

council ['kaunsəl] *s* conseil *m*; (eccl) concile *m*

coun′cil·man *s* (*pl* **-men**) conseiller *m* municipal

councilor ['kaunsələr] *s* conseiller *m*

coun·sel ['kaunsəl] *s* conseil *m*, avis *m*; (*lawyer*) avocat *m* ‖ *v* (*pret & pp* **-seled** or **-selled**; *ger* **-seling** or **-selling**) *tr & intr* conseiller; **to counsel s.o. to** + *inf* conseiller à qn de + *inf*

counselor ['kaunsələr] *s* conseiller *m*, conseil *m*; (*lawyer*) avocat *m*

count [kaunt] *s* compte *m*; (*nobleman*) comte *m* ‖ *tr* compter; **to count the votes** dépouiller le scrutin ‖ *intr* compter; **count off!** (mil) comptez-vous!; **to count for** valoir; **to count on** (*to have confidence in*) compter sur (*s.o. or s.th.*); **to count on** + *ger* compter + *inf*

countable ['kauntəbəl] *adj* comptable

count′down′ *s* compte *m* à rebours

countenance ['kauntɪnəns] *s* mine *f*, contenance *f*; **to give countenance to** appuyer; **to keep one′s countenance** garder son sérieux; **to lose countenance** perdre contenance ‖ *tr* soutenir, approver

counter ['kauntər] *adj* contraire ‖ *s* compteur *m*; (*piece of wood or metal for keeping score*) jeton *m*; (*board in shop over which business is transacted*) comptoir *m*; (*in a bar or café*) zinc *m*; **under the counter** en dessous de table, sous le comptoir, sous cape ‖ *adv* contrairement; en sens inverse; **to run counter to** aller à l′encontre de ‖ *tr* contrarier, contrecarrer; (*a move, e.g., in chess*) contrer; (*an opinion*) prendre le contre-pied de ‖ *intr* parer le coup, parer un coup; **to counter with** riposter par

coun′ter·act′ *tr* contrebattre

coun′ter·attack′ *s* contre-attaque *f* ‖ **coun′ter·attack′** *tr* contre-attaquer

coun′ter·bal′ance *s* contrepoids *m* ‖ **coun′ter·bal′ance** *tr* contrebalancer

coun′ter·clock′wise′ *adj & adv* en sens inverse des aiguilles d′une montre

coun′ter·cur′rent *s* contre-courant *m*

coun′ter·es′pionage *s* contre-espionnage *m*

counterfeit ['kauntərfɪt] *adj* contrefait; (*beauty*) sophistiqué ‖ *s* contrefaction *f*, contrefaçon *f*; (*money*) fausse monnaie *f* ‖ *tr* contrefaire; (*e.g., an illness*) feindre

counterfeiter ['kauntər‚fɪtər] *s* contrefacteur *m*; (*of money*) faux-monnayeur *m*

coun′terfeit mon′ey *s* fausse monnaie *f*, faux billets *mpl*

coun′ter·ir′ritant *adj & s* révulsif *m*

countermand ['kauntər‚mænd], ['kauntər‚mand] *s* contre-ordre *m* ‖ *tr* contremander

coun′ter·march′ *s* contremarche *f* ‖ *intr* faire une contremarche

coun′ter·meas′ure *s* contre-mesure *f*

coun′ter·offen′sive *s* contre-offensive *f*

coun'ter·pane' *s* courtepointe *f*
coun'ter·part' *s* contrepartie *f*, homologue *m*
coun'ter·point' *s* contrepoint *m*
coun'ter·poise' *s* contrepoids *m* ‖ *tr* faire équilibre à
coun'ter·rev'olu'tionar·y *adj* contrerévolutionnaire ‖ *s* (*pl* -ies) contrerévolutionnaire *mf*
coun'ter·sign' *s* contremarque *f*; (*signature*) contreseing *m*; (mil) mot *m* d'ordre ‖ *tr* contresigner
coun'ter·sig'nature *s* contreseing *m*
coun'ter·sink' *s* fraise *f* ‖ *v* (*pret & pp* -sunk*) *tr* fraiser
coun'ter·spy' *s* (*pl* -spies) contre-espion *m*
coun'ter·stroke' *s* contrecoup *m*
coun'ter·weight' *s* contrepoids *m*
countess ['kaʊntɪs] *s* comtesse *f*
countless ['kaʊntlɪs] *adj* innombrable
countrified ['kʌntrɪ,faɪd] *adj* provincial, campagnard
coun·try ['kʌntri] *s* (*pl* -tries) (*territory of a nation*) pays *m*; (*land of one's birth*) patrie *f*; (*region*) contrée *f*; (*not the city*) campagne *f*
coun'try club' *s* club *m* privé situé hors des agglomérations
coun'try es'tate *s* domaine *m*
coun'try·folk' *s* campagnards *mpl*
coun'try gen'tleman *s* châtelain *m*, propriétaire *m* d'un château
coun'try house' *s* maison *f* de campagne
coun'try·man *s* (*pl* -men) (*of the same country*) compatriote *mf*; (*rural*) compagnard *m*
coun'try·side' *s* paysage *m*, campagne *f*
coun'try town' *s* petite ville *f* de province
coun'try-wide' *adj* national
coun'try·wom'an *s* (*pl* -wom'en) (*of the same country*) compatriote *f*; (*rural*) campagnarde *f*
coun·ty ['kaʊnti] *s* (*pl* -ties) comté *m*
coun'ty seat' *s* chef-lieu *m* de comté
coupé [kupe] *s* coupé *m*
couple ['kʌpəl] *s* (*man and wife; male and female; friends*) couple *m*, paire *f*; (*of eggs, cakes, etc.*) couple *f*; (elec, mech) couple *m* ‖ *tr* coupler, accoupler; (mach) embrayer ‖ *intr* s'accoupler
coupler ['kʌplər] *s* (mach) coupleur *m*
coupling ['kʌplɪŋ] *s* accouplement *m*; (mach) couplage *m*
coupon ['k(j)upɑn] *s* coupon *m*, bon *m*
courage ['kʌrɪdʒ] *s* courage *m*
courageous [kə'redʒəs] *adj* courageux
courier ['kʌrɪ·ər], ['kʊrɪ·ər] *s* courrier *m*; (*on horseback*) estafette *f*
course [kors] *s* cours *m*; carrière *f*, voie *f*, course *f*; (*of a meal*) service *m*, plat *m*; (*of a stream*) parcours *m*, cours *m*; (*direction*) route *f*, chemin *m*; **in due course** en temps voulu; **in the course of** au cours de; **in the course of time** avec le temps; **of course!** naturellement!, bien entendu!; **to give a course** faire un cours; **to set a course for** (naut) mettre le

cap sur; **to take a course** suivre un cours ‖ *tr & intr* courir
court [kort] *s* cour *f*; (*of law*) tribunal *m*, cour; (sports) terrain *m*, court *m*; **out of court** à l'amiable ‖ *tr* courtiser, faire la cour à; (*favor, votes*) briguer, solliciter; (*danger*) aller audevant de
courteous ['kʌrtɪ·əs] *adj* poli, courtois
courtesan ['kʌrtɪzən], ['kortɪzən] *s* courtisane *f*
courte·sy ['kʌrtɪsi] *s* (*pl* -sies) politesse *f*, courtoisie *f*; **through the courtesy of** avec la gracieuse permission de
court'house' *s* palais *m* de justice
courtier ['kortɪ·ər] *s* courtisan *m*
court' jest'er *s* bouffon *m* du roi
court·ly ['kortli] *adj* (*comp* -lier; *super* -liest) courtois, élégant
court'-mar'tial *s* (*pl* **courts-martial**) conseil *m* de guerre ‖ *v* (*pret & pp* -tialed or -tialled; *ger* -tialing or -tialling) *tr* traduire en conseil de guerre; **to be court-martialed** passer en conseil de guerre
court' plas'ter *s* taffetas *m* gommé, sparadrap *m*
court'room' *s* salle *f* du tribunal
court'ship *s* cour *f*
court'yard' *s* cour *f*
cousin ['kʌzɪn] *s* cousin *m*
cove [kov] *s* anse *f*, crique *f*
covenant ['kʌvənənt] *s* contrat *m*, accord *m*, pacte *m*; (Bib) alliance *f*
cover ['kʌvər] *s* couverture *f*; (*lid*) couvercle *m*; (*for furniture*) housse *f*; (*of wild game*) remise *f*, gîte *m*; (com) couverture *f*, provision *f*, marge *f*; (mach) chape *f*; (phila) enveloppe *f*; **from cover to cover** de la première à la dernière; **to take cover** se mettre à l'abri; **under cover** (e.g., *of trees*) sous les couverts; (*safe from harm*) à couvert; **under cover of** sous le couvert de, dissimulé dans; **under separate cover** sous pli distinct ‖ *tr* couvrir; (*a certain distance*) parcourir; (*a newspaper story*) faire le reportage de; (*one's tracks*) brouiller; (*with, e.g., chocolate*) enrober; **to cover up** recouvrir ‖ *intr* se couvrir; (*to brood*) couver
coverage ['kʌvərɪdʒ] *s* (*amount or space covered*) portée *f*; (*of news*) reportage *m*; (*insurance*) assurance *f*, couverture *f* d'assurance
cov'er·alls' *spl* salopette *f*, bleus *mpl*
cov'er charge' *s* couvert *m*
cov'ered wag'on *s* chariot *m* couvert
cov'er girl' *s* cover-girl *f*, pin up *f*
covering ['kʌvərɪŋ] *s* couverture *f*, recouvrement *m*
covert ['kʌvərt] *adj* couvert, caché
cov'er-up' *s* subterfuge *m*; (*reply*) réponse *f* évasive
covet ['kʌvɪt] *tr* convoiter
covetous ['kʌvɪtəs] *adj* cupide, avide
covetousness ['kʌvɪtəsnɪs] *s* convoitise *f*, cupidité *f*

covey ['kʌvi] s couvée f; (*in flight*) volée f

cow [kau] s vache f; (*of seal, elephant*) femelle f || tr (coll) intimider

coward ['kau·ərd] s lâche mf

cowardice ['kau·ərdɪs] s lâcheté f

cowardly ['kau·ərdli] adj lâche || adv lâchement, peureusement

cow'bell' s grelot m, clarine f

cow'boy' s cow-boy m

cow'catch'er s (rr) chasse-bestiaux m

cower ['kau·ər] intr se tapir

cow'herd' s vacher m, bouvier m

cow'hide' s vache f, peau f de vache; fouet m || tr fouetter

cowl [kaul] s capuchon m, cagoule f; (*of chimney*) chapeau m; (aer, aut) capot m

cow'lick' s mèche f rebelle

cow'pox' s (pathol) vaccine f

coxcomb ['kaks‚kom] s (*conceited person*) petit-maître m, fat m; (bot) crête-de-coq f

coxswain ['kaksən], ['kak‚swen] s patron m de chaloupe; (*rowing*) barreur m

coy [kɔɪ] adj réservé, modeste

co·zy ['kozi] adj (comp -zier; super -ziest) douillet, intime || s (pl -zies) couvre-théière m

C.P.A. ['si'pi'e] s (letterword) (certified public accountant) expert-comptable m, comptable m agréé

crab [kræb] s crabe m; (*grouch*) grincheux m || v (pret & pp crabbed; ger crabbing) intr (coll) se plaindre

crab' ap'ple s pomme f sauvage

crabbed ['kræbɪd] adj acariâtre; (*handwriting*) de chat; (*author*) hermétique; (*style*) entortillé

crab·by ['kræbi] adj (comp -bier; super -biest) (coll) revêche, grognon

crack [kræk] s (*of troops*) d'élite; (coll) expert, de premier ordre || s (*noise*) bruit m sec, craquement m; (*of whip*) claquement m; (*fissure*) fente f; (*e.g., in a dish*) fêlure f; (*e.g., in a wall*) lézarde f; (*in skin*) gerçure f; (*joke*) bon mot m; **crack of dawn** pointe f du jour || tr (*one's fingers; petroleum*) faire craquer; (*a whip*) claquer; (*to split*) fendre; (*e.g., a dish*) fêler; (*e.g., a wall*) lézarder; (*the skin*) gercer; (*nuts*) casser; **to crack a joke** (slang) faire or lâcher une plaisanterie; **to crack up** (*to praise*) (coll) vanter, prôner; (*to crash*) (coll) écraser || intr (*to make a noise*) craquer; (*said of whip*) claquer; (*to be split*) se fendre; (*said of dish*) se fêler; (*said of wall*) se lézarder; (*said of skin*) se gercer; **to crack up** (*to crash*) (coll) s'écraser; (*to break down*) (coll) craquer, s'effondrer

crack'-brained' adj timbré; **to be crack-brained** avoir le cerveau fêlé

crack'down' s (coll) répression f

cracked adj (*split*) fendu, fêlé; (*foolish*) (coll) timbré, toqué, cinglé

cracker ['krækər] s biscuit m sec

crack'er-bar'rel adj (coll) en chambre, au petit pied

crack'er-jack' adj (slang) expérimenté, remarquable || s (slang) crack m

cracking ['krækɪŋ] s (*of petroleum*) cracking m

crackle ['krækəl] s crépitation f || intr crépiter, pétiller

crack'le-ware' s porcelaine f craquelée

crackling ['kræklɪŋ] s crépitement m, pétillement m; (culin) couenne f rissolée; **cracklings** cretons mpl

crack'pot' adj & s (slang) original m, excentrique mf

crack' shot' s (coll) fin tireur m

crack'-up' s (*collision*) (coll) écrasement m; (*breakdown*) (coll) effondrement m

cradle ['kredəl] s berceau m || tr bercer

cra'dle-song' s berceuse f

craft [kræft], [krɑft] s métier m; (*trickery*) artifice m; (naut) embarcation f, barque f

craftiness ['kræftɪnɪs], ['krɑftɪnɪs] s ruse f, astuce f

crafts'man s (pl -men) artisan m

crafts'man·ship' s habileté f technique; exécution f

craft·y ['kræfti], ['krɑfti] adj (comp -ier; super -iest) rusé

crag [kræg] s rocher m escarpé

cram [kræm] v (pret & pp crammed; ger cramming) tr (*with food*) bourrer, gaver; (*with people*) bonder; (*for an exam*) (coll) chauffer || intr se bourrer, se gaver; (*for an exam*) (coll) potasser

cramp [kræmp] s (*metal bar; clamp*) crampon m; (*in a muscle*) crampe f; (carpentry) serre-joint m || tr cramponner, agrafer; presser, serrer; (*one's movements, style, or manner of living*) gêner

cranber·ry ['kræn‚beri] s (pl -ries) (*Vaccinium oxycoccus or V. uliginosum*) canneberge f, airelle f canneberge

crane [kren] s (mach, orn) grue f || tr (*one's neck*) allonger, tendre || intr allonger le cou

crani·um ['kreni·əm] s (pl -a [ə]) crâne m

crank [kræŋk] s manivelle f; (*person*) (coll) excentrique mf || tr (*a motor*) faire partir à la manivelle

crank' case' s carter m

crank'shaft' s vilebrequin m

crank·y ['kræŋki] adj (comp -ier; super -iest) revêche, grincheux; (*not working well*) détraqué; (*queer*) excentrique

cran·ny ['kræni] s (pl -nies) fente f, crevasse f; (*corner*) coin m

crape [krep] s crêpe m

crape'hang'er s (slang) rabat-joie m

craps [kræps] s (slang) jeu m de dés; **to shoot craps** (slang) jouer aux dés

crash [kræʃ] s fracas m, écroulement m; (*of thunder*) coup m; (*e.g., of airplane*) écrasement m; (*e.g., on stock market*) krach m || tr briser, fracasser; (*e.g., an airplane*) écraser || intr retentir; (*said of airplane*) s'écraser; (*to fail*) craquer; **to crash into** emboutir, tamponner; **to crash through** enfoncer

crash′ dive′ s brusque plongée f

crash′ hel′met s casque m

crash′-land′ing s crash m, atterrissage m violent

crass [kræs] adj grossier; (*ignorance*) crasse

crate [kret] s caisse f à claire-voie, cageot m ‖ tr emballer dans une caisse à claire-voie

crater [′kretər] s cratère m

cravat [krə′væt] s cravate f

crave [krev] tr désirer ardemment; implorer; requérir, e.g., **the problem craves serious consideration** le problème requiert une considération sérieuse; **to crave s.o.'s pardon** demander pardon à qn ‖ intr—**to crave for** désirer ardemment; implorer

craven [′krevən] adj & s poltron m

craving [′krevɪŋ] s désir m ardent, désir obsédant

craw [krɔ] s jabot m

crawl [krɔl] s rampement m; (swimming) crawl m ‖ intr ramper; **to be crawling with** fourmiller de, grouiller de; **to crawl along** se traîner; **to crawl on one's hands and knees** aller à quatre pattes; **to crawl over** escalader; **to crawl up** grimper

crayon [′kre-ən] s crayon m de pastel, pastel m ‖ tr crayonner

craze [krez] s manie f, toquade f ‖ tr rendre fou

cra·zy [′krezi] adj (comp -**zier**; super -**ziest**) fou; (*rickety*) délabré; **to be crazy about** (coll) être fou de, être toqué de; **to drive crazy** rendre fou, affoler

cra′zy bone′ s nerf m du coude

cra′zy quilt′ s courtepointe f multicolore

creak [krik] s cri m, grincement m ‖ intr crier, grincer

creak·y [′kriki] adj (comp -**ier**; super -**iest**) criard

cream [krim] s crème f; **creams** (with chocolate coating) chocolats mpl fourrés f ‖ tr écrémer; (*butter and sugar together*) mélanger ‖ intr crémer

cream′ cheese′ s fromage m à la crème, fromage blanc, petit suisse m

creamer·y [′kriməri] s (pl -**ies**) laiterie f; compagnie f laitière

cream′ of tar′tar s crème f de tartre

cream′ pitch′er s crémière f

cream′ puff′ s chou m à la crème

cream′ sep′arator [′sepə‚retər] s écrémeuse f

cream·y [′krimi] adj (comp -**ier**; super -**iest**) crémeux

crease [kris] s pli m, faux pli m ‖ tr & intr plisser

create [kri′et] tr créer

creation [kri′eʃən] s création f

creative [kri′etɪv] adj créateur, inventif

creator [kri′etər] s créateur m

creature [′kritʃər] s créature f

credence [′kridəns] s créance f, croyance f, foi f

credentials [krɪ′denʃəlz] spl papiers mpl, pièces fpl justificatives, lettres fpl de créance

credibility [‚kredɪ′bɪlɪti] s crédibilité f

credible [′kredɪbəl] adj croyable, digne de foi

credit [′kredɪt] s crédit m; (*belief*; *claim*) créance f; **on credit** à crédit; **to be a credit to** faire honneur à; **to take credit for** s'attribuer le mérite de ‖ tr croire, ajouter foi à; (com) créditer, porter au crédit

creditable [′kredɪtəbəl] adj estimable, honorable

cred′it card′ s carte f de crédit

creditor [′kredɪtər] s créditeur m, créancier m

cre·do [′krido], [′kredo] s (pl -**dos**) credo m

credulous [′kredʒələs] adj crédule

creed [krid] s credo m; (*denomination*) foi f

creek [krik] s ruisseau m

creep [krip] v (pret & pp **crept** [krept]) intr ramper; (*stealthily*) se glisser; (*slowly*) se traîner, se couler; (*to climb*) grimper; (*with a sensation of insects*) fourmiller; **to creep up on s.o.** s'approcher de qn à pas lents

creeper [′kripər] s plante f rampante

creeping [′kripɪŋ] adj lent, traînant; (*plant*) rampant ‖ s rampement m

creep·y [′kripi] adj (comp -**ier**; super -**iest**) (coll) mystérieux· **to feel creepy** fourmiller

cremate [′krimet] tr incinérer

cremation [krɪ′meʃən] s crémation f, incinération f

cremato·ry [′krimə‚tori] adj crématoire ‖ s (pl -**ries**) crématoire m, four m crématoire

Creole [′kri-ol] adj créole ‖ s (*language*) créole m; (*person*) Créole mf

crepe [krep] s crêpe m; (*pancake*) crêpe f

crepe′ pa′per s papier m crêpe

crescent [′kresənt] s croissant m

cress [kres] s cresson m

crest [krest] s crête f

crested [′krestɪd] adj à crête; (*with feathers*) huppé

crest′fall′en adj abattu, découragé

Cretan [′kritən] adj crétois f ‖ s Crétois m

Crete [krit] s Crète f; la Crète

cretin [′kritən] s crétin m

crevice [′krevɪs] s crevasse f, fente f

crew [kru] s équipe f; (*of a ship*) équipage m; (*group, especially of armed men*) bande f, troupe f

crew′ cut′ s cheveux mpl en brosse

crew′ mem′ber s équipier m

crib [krɪb] s lit m d'enfant; crèche f, mangeoire f; (*for grain*) coffre m; (*student's pony*) corrigé m employé subrepticement ‖ v (pret & pp **cribbed**; ger **cribbing**) tr & intr (coll) copier à la dérobée

cricket [′krɪkɪt] s (ent) grillon m; (sports) cricket m; (coll) franc jeu m, jeu loyal; **to be cricket** être de bonne guerre

crier ['kraɪ·ər] s crieur m
crime [kraɪm] s crime m; (misdemeanor) délit m
criminal ['krɪmɪnəl] adj & s criminel m
crim′inal code′ s code m pénal
crim′inal court′ s cour f d'assises
crim′inal law′ s loi f pénale
crimp [krɪmp] s (in cloth) pli m; (in hair) frisure f; (recruiter) racoleur m; **to put a crimp in** (coll) mettre obstacle à ‖ tr (cloth) plisser; (hair) friser, crêper; (metal) onduler
crimson ['krɪmzən] adj & s cramoisi m
cringe [krɪndʒ] intr s'humilier, s'abaisser
cringing ['krɪndʒɪŋ] adj craintif, servile ‖ s crainte f, servilité f
crinkle ['krɪŋkəl] s pli m, ride f ‖ tr froisser, plisser ‖ intr se froisser
cripple ['krɪpəl] s estropié m; (lame person) boiteux m ‖ tr estropier; (a machine) disloquer; (business or industry) paralyser; (a ship) désemparer
cri·sis ['kraɪsɪs] s (pl -ses [siz]) crise f
crisp [krɪsp] adj croustillant; (tone) tranchant, brusque; (air) vif, frais
crisscross ['krɪs,krɔs], ['krɪs,krɑs] adj entrecroisé, treillissé ‖ s entrecroisement m; (e.g., of wires) enchevêtrement m ‖ adv en forme de croix ‖ tr entrecroiser ‖ intr s'entrecroiser
criteri·on [kraɪ'tɪrɪ·ən] s (pl -a [ə] or -ons) critère m
critic ['krɪtɪk] s critique mf; (faultfinder) critiqueur m, désapprobateur m
critical ['krɪtɪkəl] adj critique
critically ['krɪtɪkəli] adv en critique; **critically ill** gravement malade
criticism ['krɪtɪ,sɪzəm] s critique f
criticize ['krɪtɪ,saɪz] tr & intr critiquer
croak [krok] s (of raven) croassement m; (of frog) coassement m ‖ intr (said of raven) croasser; (said of frog) coasser; (to die) (slang) mourir
Croat ['kro·æt] s (language) croate m; (person) Croate mf
Croatian [kro'eʃən] adj croate ‖ s (language) croate m; (person) Croate mf
cro·chet [kro'ʃe] s crochet m ‖ v (pret & pp -cheted ['ʃed]; ger -cheting ['ʃe·ɪŋ]) tr & intr tricoter au crochet
crochet′ nee′dle s crochet m
crock [krɑk] s pot m de terre
crockery ['krɑkəri] s faïence f, poterie f
crocodile ['krɑkə,daɪl] s crocodile m
croc′odile tears′ spl larmes fpl de crocodile
crocus ['krokəs] s crocus m
crone [kron] s vieille femme f au visage parcheminé
cro·ny ['kroni] s (pl -nies) copain m
crook [krʊk] s (hook) croc m; (of shepherd) houlette f; (of bishop) crosse f; (in road) courbure f; (person) (coll) escroc m ‖ tr courber ‖ intr se courber
crooked ['krʊkɪd] adj courbé, crochu; (path; conduct) tortueux; (tree; nose; legs) tortu; (person) (coll) malhonnête, fourbe

croon [krun] intr chanter des chansons sentimentales
crooner ['krunər] s chanteur m de charme
crop [krɑp] s récolte f; (head of hair) cheveux mpl ras; (of bird) jabot m; (whip) fouet m; (of whip) manche m; (of appointments, promotions, heroes, discoveries) moisson f ‖ v (pret & pp cropped; ger cropping) tr tondre; (head of hair) couper, tailler; (ears of animal) essoriller ‖ intr—**to crop up** (coll) surgir, s'élever brusquement
croquet [kro'ke] s croquet m
crosier ['kroʒər] s crosse f
cross [krɔs], [krɑs] adj transversal, oblique; (breed) croisé; (ill-humored) maussade ‖ s croix f; (of races or breeds; of roads) croisement m ‖ tr croiser; (the sea; a street) traverser; (breeds) croiser, métisser; (the threshold) franchir; (said of one road with respect to another) couper; (the letter t) barrer; (e.g., s.o.'s plans) (coll) contrecarrer; **to cross oneself** (eccl) se signer; **to cross out** biffer, rayer ‖ intr se croiser, passer; **to cross over** passer de l'autre côté
cross′bones′ spl tibias mpl croisés
cross′bow′ s arbalète f
cross′breed′ v (pret & pp -bred) tr croiser, métisser
cross′-coun′try adj à travers champs
cross′cur′rent s contre-courant m; tendance f contraire
cross′-exami·na′tion s contre-interrogatoire m
cross′-exam′ine tr contre-interroger, contre-examiner
cross′-eyed′ adj louche
crossing ['krɔsɪŋ], ['krɑsɪŋ] s croisement m; (of ocean) traversée f; (of river, mountain, etc.) passage m; (rr) passage m à niveau
cross′ing gate′ s barrière f d'un passage à niveau
cross′patch′ s (coll) grincheux m, grognon m
cross′piece′ s entretoise f
cross′ ref′erence s renvoi m
cross′road′ s voie f transversale, chemin m de traverse; **crossroads** carrefour m, croisement m
cross′ sec′tion s coupe f transversale; (e.g., of building) section f; (of opinion) sondage m, groupe m représentatif; tranche f de vie
cross′-sec′tion tr couper transversalement
cross′ street′ s rue f de traverse, rue transversale
cross′wise′ adv en croix, en sautoir
cross′word puz′zle s mots mpl croisés
crotch [krɑtʃ] s (forked piece) fourche f; (between legs) entrejambe f, enfourchure f
crotchet ['krɑtʃɪt] s (mus) noire f; (coll) lubie f
crotchety ['krɑtʃɪti] adj capricieux, fantasque

crouch [krautʃ] *s* accroupissement *m* || *intr* s'accroupir, se blottir

croup [krup] *s* (*of horse*) croupe *f*; (pathol) croup *m*

croupier ['krupɪ·ər] *s* croupier *m*

crouton ['krutɑn] *s* croûton *m*

crow [kro] *s* corbeau *m*; (*rook*) corneille *f*, freux *m*; **as the crow flies** à vol d'oiseau; **to eat crow** (coll) avaler des couleuvres || *intr* (*said of cock*) chanter; (*said of babies*) gazouiller; **to crow over** chanter victoire sur, triompher bruyamment de

crow'bar' *s* levier *m*; (*for forcing doors*) pince-monseigneur *f*

crowd [kraud] *s* foule *f*; (*large flock of people*) affluence *f*, presse *f*; (*mob, common people*) populace *f*, vulgaire *m*; (*clique, set*) bande *f*, monde *m*; **a crowd** (*of people*) du monde, beaucoup de monde || *tr* serrer, entasser; (*to push*) pousser; (*a debtor*) presser; **to crowd out** ne pas laisser de place à || *intr* affluer, s'amasser; **to crowd around** se presser autour de; **to crowd in** s'attrouper

crowded [kraudɪd] *adj* encombré, bondé

crow'foot' *s* renoncule *f*, bouton *m* d'or

crowing ['kro·ɪŋ] *s* chant *m* de coq, cocorico *m*; (*of babies*) gazouillement *m*

crown [kraun] *s* couronne *f*; (*of hat*) calotte *f* || *tr* couronner, sacrer; (checkers) damer; **to crown s.o.** (slang) flanquer un coup sur la tête à qn

crowning ['kraunɪŋ] *s* couronnement *m*

crown' prince' *s* prince *m* héritier

crown' prin'cess *s* princesse *f* héritière

crow's'-foot' *s* (*pl* -feet) patte-d'oie *f*

crow's'-nest' *s* (naut) nid *m* de pie, tonneau *m* de vigie

crucial ['kru·əl] *adj* crucial

crucible ['krusɪbəl] *s* creuset *m*

crucifix ['krusɪfɪks] *s* crucifix *m*, christ *m*

crucifixion [ˌkrusɪ'fɪkʃən] *s* crucifixion *f*

cruci·fy ['krusɪˌfaɪ] *v* (*pret & pp* -fied) *tr* crucifier

crude [krud] *adj* (*raw, unrefined*) cru, brut; (*lacking culture*) fruste, grossier; (*unfinished*) informe, grossier, mal développé; (*oil*) brut

crudi·ty ['krudɪti] *s* (*pl* -ties) crudité *f*; (*of person*) grossièreté *f*

cruel ['kru·əl] *adj* cruel

cruel·ty ['kru·əlti] *s* (*pl* -ties) cruauté *f*

cruet ['kru·ɪt] *s* burette *f*

cru'et stand' *s* huilier *m*

cruise [kruz] *s* croisière *f* || *intr* croiser

cruiser ['kruzər] *s* croiseur *m*

cruising ['kruzɪŋ] *adj* en croisière; (*taxi*) en maraude

cruis'ing range' *s* autonomie *f*

cruis'ing speed' *s* vitesse *f* de route

cruller ['krʌlər] *s* beignet *m*

crumb [krʌm] *s* miette *f*; (*soft part of bread*) mie *f* || *tr* (*cutlets, etc.*) paner

crumble ['krʌmbəl] *tr* émietter, réduire en miettes; (*e.g., stone*) effriter || *intr* s'émietter; s'effriter; (*to fall to pieces*) s'écrouler

crum·my ['krʌmi] *adj* (*comp* -mier; *super* -miest*) (slang) sale, minable

crumple ['krʌmpəl] *tr* friper, froisser; (*a fender*) mettre en accordéon || *intr* se friper, se froisser

crunch [krʌntʃ] *tr* croquer, broyer || *intr* (*said of snow*) craquer

crupper ['krʌpər] *s* croupière *f*

crusade [kru'sed] *s* croisade *f* || *intr* se croiser, prendre part à une croisade

crush [krʌʃ] *s* écrasement *m*; (*of people*) presse *f*, foule *f*; **to have a crush on** (slang) avoir un béguin pour || *tr* écraser; (*e.g., stone*) broyer, concasser; (*to oppress, grieve*) accabler, aplatir

crush' hat' *s* claque *m*, gibus *m*

crust [krʌst] *s* croûte *f*

crustacean [krʌs'teʃən] *s* crustacé *m*

crust·y ['krʌsti] *adj* (*comp* -ier; *super* -iest) croustillant; (*said of person*) bourru, hargneux

crutch [krʌtʃ] *s* béquille *f*

crux [krʌks] *s* nœud *m*

cry [kraɪ] *s* (*pl* cries) cri *m*; (*of wolf*) hurlement *m*; (*of bull*) mugissement *m*; **to cry one's eyes out** pleurer à chaudes larmes; **to have a good cry** donner libre cours aux larmes || *v* (*pret & pp* cried) *tr* crier; **to cry out** crier || *intr* crier; (*to weep*) pleurer; **to cry for** crier à; **to cry for joy** pleurer de joie; **to cry out** pousser des cris, s'écrier; **to cry out against** crier à

cry'ba·by *s* (*pl* -bies) pleurard *m*

crypt [krɪpt] *s* crypte *f*

cryptic(al) ['krɪptɪk(əl)] *adj* secret, occulte; (*silence*) énigmatique

crystal ['krɪstəl] *s* cristal *m*

crys'tal ball' *s* boule *f* de cristal

crystalline ['krɪstəlɪn], ['krɪstəˌlaɪn] *adj* cristallin

crystallize ['krɪstəˌlaɪz] *tr* cristalliser; (*sugar*) candir || *intr* cristalliser; (*said of sugar*) se candir; (*said of one's thoughts*) (fig) se cristalliser

cub [kʌb] *s* petit *m*; (*of bear*) ourson *m*; (*of fox*) renardeau *m*; (*of lion*) lionceau *m*; (*of wolf*) louveteau *m*

Cuban ['kjubən] *adj* cubain || *s* Cubain *m*

cubbyhole ['kʌbɪˌhol] *s* retraite *f*; (*in wall*) placard *m*; (*in furniture*) case *f*

cube [kjub] *adj & s* cube *m*; **in cubes** (*said of sugar*) en morceaux || *tr* cuber

cube' root' *s* racine *f* cubique

cubic ['kjubɪk] *adj* cubique, cube

cu'bic me'ter *s* mètre *m* cube

cub' report'er *s* reporter *m* débutant

cub' scout' *s* louveteau *m*

cuckold ['kʌkəld] *adj & s* cocu *m*, cornard *m* || *tr* cocufier

cuckoo ['kuku] *adj* (slang) niais, benêt || *s* coucou *m*

cuck'oo clock' *s* coucou *m*

cucumber ['kjukəmbər] *s* concombre *m*

cud [kʌd] *s* bol *m* alimentaire; **to chew the cud** ruminer

cuddle ['kʌdəl] *tr* serrer doucement dans les bras || *intr* (*said of lovers*) s'étreindre; **to cuddle up** se pelotonner

cudg·el ['kʌdʒəl] *s* gourdin *m*, trique *f*; **to take up the cudgels for** prendre fait et cause pour || *v* (*pret & pp* -eled *or* -elled; *ger* -eling *or* -elling) *tr* bâtonner, rosser

cue [kju] *s* avis *m*; (*hint*) mot *m*; (*rod used in billiards; persons in line*) queue *f*; (*mus*) indication *f* de rentrée; (*theat*) réclame *f*; **to give s.o. the cue** faire la leçon à qn, donner le mot à qn; **to take one's cue from** se conformer à

cuff [kʌf] *s* (*of shirt*) poignet *m*, manchette *f*; (*of coat or trousers*) parement *m*; (*blow*) taloche *f*, manchette *f* || *tr* talocher, flanquer une taloche à

cuff′ link′ *s* bouton *m* de manchette

cuirass [kwɪ′ræs] *s* cuirasse *f*

cuisine [kwɪ′zin] *s* cuisine *f*

culinary ['kjulɪˌnɛri] *adj* culinaire

cull [kʌl] *tr* choisir; (*to gather, pluck*) cueillir; **to cull from** recueillir dans

culm [kʌlm] *s* chaume *m*; (*coal dust*) charbonnaille *f*

culminate ['kʌlmɪˌnet] *intr* (*astr*) culminer; **to culminate in** finir par, se terminer en

culmination [ˌkʌlmɪ′neʃən] *s* point *m* culminant; (*astr*) culmination *f*

culottes [k(j)u′lɑts] *spl* pantalon *m* de plage

culpable ['kʌlpəbəl] *adj* coupable

culprit ['kʌlprɪt] *s* coupable *mf*; (*accused*) accusé *m*, prévenu *m*

cult [kʌlt] *s* culte *m*

cultivate ['kʌltɪˌvet] *tr* cultiver

cultivation [ˌkʌltɪ′veʃən] *s* culture *f*

cultivator ['kʌltɪˌvetər] *s* (*person*) cultivateur *m*, exploitant *m* agricole; (*mach*) cultivateur *m*, scarificateur *m*

cultural ['kʌltʃərəl] *adj* culturel

culture ['kʌltʃər] *s* culture *f* || *tr* cultiver

cultured *adj* (*learned*) cultivé, lettré

cul′tured pearl′ *s* perle *f* de culture

culvert ['kʌlvərt] *s* ponceau *m*, cassis *m*

cumbersome ['kʌmbərsəm] *adj* incommode, encombrant; (*clumsy*) lourd, difficile à manier

cummerbund ['kʌmərˌbʌnd] *s* ceinture *f* d'étoffe

cumulative ['kjumjəˌletɪv] *adj* croissant, cumulatif

cunning ['kʌnɪŋ] *adj* (*sly*) astucieux, rusé; (*clever*) habile, fin; (*attractive*) gentil || *s* (*slyness*) astuce *f*, ruse *f*; (*cleverness*) habileté *f*, finesse *f*

cup [kʌp] *s* tasse *f*; (*of metal*) gobelet *m*, timbale *f*; (*bot, eccl*) calice *m*; (*mach*) godet *m* graisseur; (*sports*) coupe *f* || *v* (*pret & pp* cupped; *ger* cupping) *tr* (surg) ventouser

cupboard ['kʌbərd] *s* armoire *f*; (*in wall*) placard *m*

Cupid ['kjupɪd] *s* Cupidon *m*

cupidity [kju′pɪdɪti] *s* cupidité *f*

cupola ['kjupələ] *s* coupole *f*

cur [kʌr] *s* chien *m* métis, roquet *m*; (*despicable person*) mufle *m*

curate ['kjurɪt] *s* vicaire *m*

curative ['kjurətɪv] *adj* curatif

curator [kju′retər] *s* conservateur *m*

curb [kʌrb] *s* bordure *f* de pavés, bord *m* de trottoir; (*of well*) margelle *f*; (*of bit*) gourmette *f*; (*market*) coulisse *f*; (*check, restraint*) frein *m* || *tr* (*a horse*) gourmer; (*passions, anger, desires*) réprimer, refréner; **curb your dog** (*public sign*) faites faire votre chien dans le ruisseau

curb′ serv′ice *s* restoroute *m*

curb′stone′ *s* garde-pavé *m*; **curbstones** bordure *f* de pavés

curd [kʌrd] *s* caillé *m*; **curds** caillebotte *f* || *tr* cailler, caillebotter || *intr* se cailler, se caillebotter

curdle ['kʌrdəl] *tr* cailler; (*the blood*) figer || *intr* se cailler; se figer

curds′ and whey′ *spl* lait *m* caillé sucré

cure [kjur] *s* guérison *f*; (*treatment*) cure *f*; (*remedy*) remède *m* || *tr* guérir; (*meat, leather*) saler; (*a pipe*) culotter

cure′-all′ *s* panacée *f*

curfew ['kʌrfju] *s* couvre-feu *m*

curi·o ['kjurɪˌo] *s* (*pl* -os) bibelot *m*

curiosi·ty [ˌkjurɪ′ɑsɪti] *s* (*pl* -ties) curiosité *f*

curious ['kjurɪ·əs] *adj* curieux

curl [kʌrl] *s* boucle *f*, frisure *f*; (*spiral-shaped*) volute *f*; (*of smoke*) spirale *f* || *tr* boucler, friser; (*to coil, to roll up*) enrouler, tire-bouchonner; **to curl one's lip** faire la moue || *intr* boucler, friser; (*said of smoke*) s'élever en spirales; (*said of waves*) onduler, déferler; **to curl up** (*said of leaves, paper, etc.*) se recroqueviller; (*in bed*) se rouler en boule

curlew ['kʌrl(j)u] *s* courlis *m*

curlicue ['kʌrlɪˌkju] *s* paraphe *m*

curl′ing i′ron *s* fer *m* à friser

curl′pa′per *s* papillote *f*

curl·y ['kʌrli] *adj* (*comp* -ier; *super* -iest) bouclé, frisé

curmudgeon [kər′mʌdʒən] *s* (*cross-patch*) bourru *m*, sale bougre *m*; (*miser*) ladre *mf*

currant ['kʌrənt] *s* groseille *f*

curren·cy ['kʌrənsi] *s* (*pl* -cies) circulation *f*; (*legal tender*) monnaie *f*, devises *fpl*; **to give currency to** donner cours à

current ['kʌrənt] *adj* courant; (*month*) en cours; (*accepted*) admis, reçu; (*present-day*) actuel || *s* courant *m*; (*stream*) courant, cours *m*

cur′rent account′ *s* compte *m* courant

cur′rent events′ *spl* actualités *fpl*

cur′rent fail′ure *s* panne *f* de secteur

cur′rent is′sue *s* dernier numéro *m*

curricu·lum [kə′rɪkjələm] *s* (*pl* -lums *or* -la [lə]) programme *m* scolaire, plan *m* d'études

cur·ry ['kʌri] *s* (*pl* -ries) cari *m* || *v* (*pret & pp* -ried) *tr* (*a horse*) étriller; (*culin*) apprêter au cari; **to curry favor with** faire la cour à

cur′ry·comb′ *s* étrille *f* || *tr* étriller

cur'ry pow'der *s* cari *m*

curse [kʌrs] *s* malédiction *f*; (*oath*) juron *m* ‖ *tr* maudire ‖ *intr* jurer, sacrer

cursed ['kʌrsɪd], [kʌrst] *adj* maudit, exécrable, sacré

cursive ['kʌrsɪv] *adj* cursif ‖ *s* cursive *f*

cursory ['kʌrsəri] *adj* superficiel, précipité

curt [kʌrt] *adj* brusque, court

curtail [kər'tel] *tr* amoindrir, diminuer; (*expenses*) restreindre; (*rights*) enlever

curtailment [kʌr'telmənt] *s* diminution *f*; (*of expenses*) restriction *f*; (*of rights*) privation *f*

curtain ['kʌrtən] *s* rideau *m* ‖ *tr* garnir de rideaux; (*to hide*) cacher sous des rideaux; **to curtain off** séparer par un rideau

cur'tain call' *s* rappel *m*

cur'tain rais'er *s* (*play*) lever *m* de rideau

cur'tain ring' *s* anneau *m* de rideau

cur'tain rod' *s* tringle *f* de rideau

curt·sy ['kʌrtsi] *s* (*pl* -sies) révérence *f* ‖ *v* (*pret & pp* -sied) *intr* faire la révérence

curvature ['kʌrvətʃər] *s* courbure *f*; (*of spine*) déviation *f*

curve [kʌrv] *s* courbe *f*; (*of road*) virage *m*; (*curvature*) courbure *f* ‖ *tr* courber ‖ *intr* se courber

curved *adj* courbe, courbé

cushion ['kʊʃən] *s* coussin *m* ‖ *tr* (*a chair*) rembourrer; (*a shock*) amortir

cuspidor ['kʌspɪ,dɔr] *s* crachoir *m*

cuss [kʌs] *s* (*person*) (coll) vaurien *m*, chenapan *m* ‖ *tr* (coll) maudire ‖ *intr* (coll) jurer, sacrer

cuss'word' *s* (coll) juron *m*

custard ['kʌstərd] *s* flan *m*, œufs *mpl* au lait, crème *f* caramel

custodian [kʌs'todɪ·ən] *s* gardien *m*; concierge *mf*

custo·dy ['kʌstədi] *s* (*pl* -dies) garde *f*; emprisonnement *m*; **in custody** en sûreté; **to take into custody** mettre en état d'arrestation

custom ['kʌstəm] *s* coutume *f*; (*customers*) clientèle *f*; **customs** douane *f*; (*duties*) droits *mpl* de douane

customary ['kʌstə,meri] *adj* coutumier, ordinaire, habituel

custom-built ['kʌstəm'bɪlt] *adj* hors série, fait sur commande

customer ['kʌstəmər] *s* client *m*, chaland *m*; (coll) individu *m*, type *m*; **customers** clientèle *f*, achalandage *m*

cus'tom·house' *adj* douanier ‖ *s* douane *f*

custom-made ['kʌstəm'med] *adj* fait sur commande; (*clothes*) sur mesure

cus'toms clear'ance *s* expédition *f* douanière

cus'toms of'ficer *s* douanier *m*

cus'toms u'nion *f* douane *f*

cus'tom tai'lor *s* tailleur *m* à façon

cut [kʌt] *adj* coupé; **cut out** taillé, e.g., **he is not cut out for that** il n'est pas taillé pour cela; e.g., **your work is cut out for you** voilà votre besogne

taillée ‖ *s* coupe *f*; (*piece cut off*) tranche *f*, morceau *m*; (*slash*) coupure *f*; (*with knife, whip, etc.*) coup *m*; (*in prices, wages, etc.*) réduction *f*, baisse *f*; (*of a garment*) coupe; (typ) gravure *f*, planche *f*; (*absence from school*) (coll) séchage *m*; (*in winnings, earnings, etc.*) (slang) part *f*; **the cheap cuts** les bas morceaux *mpl* ‖ *v* (*pret & pp* cut; *ger* cutting) *tr* couper; (*meat, bread*) trancher; (*prices*) réduire, baisser; (*e.g., a hole*) pratiquer; (*glass, diamonds*) tailler; (*fingernails*) rogner; (*an article, play, speech*) sabrer, faire des coupures à; (*a phonograph record*) enregistrer; (*a class*) (coll) sécher; **to cut down** faucher, abattre; (*expenses*) réduire; **to cut off, out,** or **up** découper, couper; **to cut short** couper court à ‖ *intr* couper; trancher; **to cut in** (*a conversation*) s'immiscer dans; (coll) enlever la danseuse d'un autre; **to cut off** (*debate*) clore; **to cut up** (slang) faire le pitre

cut'-and-dried' *adj* décidé d'avance, tout fait; monotone, rasoir

cutaneous [kju'tenɪ·əs] *adj* cutané

cut'away' *s* frac *m*

cut'back' *s* réduction *f*; (mov) retour *m* en arrière

cute [kjut] *adj* (coll) mignon; (*shrewd*) (coll) rusé

cut' glass' *s* cristal *m* taillé

cuticle ['kjutɪkəl] *s* cuticule *f*

cutlass ['kʌtləs] *s* coutelas *m*

cutlery ['kʌtləri] *s* coutellerie *f*

cutlet ['kʌtlɪt] *s* côtelette *f*; (*without bone*) escalope *f*

cut'off' *s* point *m* de coupure; (*road*) raccourci *m*; (*of river*) bras *m* mort; (*of cylinder*) obturateur *m*

cut'out' *s* (aut) échappement *m* libre; (elec) coupe-circuit *m*; (mov) décor *m* découpé

cut'-rate' *adj* à prix réduit

cutter ['kʌtər] *s* (naut) cotre *m*

cut'throat' *s* coupe-jarret *m*

cutting ['kʌtɪŋ] *adj* tranchant; (*tone, remark*) mordant, cinglant ‖ *s* coupe *f*; (*from a newspaper*) coupure *f*; (*e.g., of prices*) réduction *f*; (hort) bouture *f*; (mov) découpage *m*

cuttlefish ['kʌtəl,fɪʃ] *s* seiche *f*

cut'wa'ter *s* (naut) étrave *f*; (*of bridge*) bec *m*

cyanamide [saɪ'ænə,maɪd] *s* cyanamide *f*

cyanide ['saɪ·ə,naɪd] *s* cyanure *m*

cyanosis [,saɪ·ə'nosɪs] *s* cyanose *f*

cycle ['saɪkəl] *s* cycle *m*; (*of internal-combustion engine*) temps *m*; (phys) période *f* ‖ *intr* faire de la bicyclette

cyclic(al) ['saɪklɪk(əl)], ['sɪklɪk(əl)] *adj* cyclique

cyclist ['saɪklɪst] *s* cycliste *mf*

cyclone ['saɪklon] *s* cyclone *m*

cyclops ['saɪklɑps] *s* cyclope *m*

cyclotron ['saɪklo,trɑn], ['sɪklo,trɑn] *s* cyclotron *m*

cylinder ['sɪlɪndər] *s* cylindre *m*; (*of revolver*) barillet *m*

cyl′inder block′ s cylindre m
cyl′inder bore′ s alésage m
cyl′inder head′ s culasse f
cylindric(al) [sɪ'lɪndrɪk(əl)] adj cylindrique
cymbal ['sɪmbəl] s cymbale f
cynic ['sɪnɪk] adj & s cynique m
cynical ['sɪnɪkəl] adj cynique
cynicism ['sɪnɪ ,sɪzəm] s cynisme m
cynosure ['saɪnə ,ʃʊr], ['sɪnə ,ʃʊr] s guide m, exemple m, norme f; (center of attention) clou m; (astr) cynosure f
cypress ['saɪprəs] s cyprès m

Cyprus ['saɪprəs] s Chypre f
Cyrillic [sɪ'rɪlɪk] adj cyrillique
cyst [sɪst] s kyste m; (on the skin) vésicule f
czar [zɑr] s tsar m, czar m
czarina [zɑ'rinə] s tsarine f, czarine f
Czech [tʃek] adj tchèque ‖ s (language) tchèque m; (person) Tchèque mf
Czecho-Slovak ['tʃeko'slovæk] adj tchécoslovaque ‖ s Tchécoslovaque mf
Czecho-Slovakia [,tʃekoslo'væki-ə] s Tchécoslovaquie f; la Tchécoslovaquie

D

D, d [di] s IVᵉ lettre de l'alphabet
dab [dæb] s touche f; (of ink) tache f; (of butter) petit morceau m ‖ (pret & pp dabbed; ger dabbing) tr essuyer légèrement; (to pat) tapoter
dabble ['dæbəl] tr humecter ‖ intr barboter; **to dabble in** se mêler de; **to dabble in the stock market** boursicoter
dad [dæd] s (coll) papa m
dad-dy ['dædi] s (pl -dies) papa m
dad′dy-long′legs′ s (pl -legs) faucheux m
daffodil ['dæfədɪl] s jonquille f des prés, narcisse m des bois
daff-y ['dæfi] adj (comp -ier; supér -iest) (coll) timbré, toqué
dagger ['dægər] s poignard m, dague f; (typ) croix f, obel m; **to look daggers at** foudroyer du regard
dahlia ['dæljə] s dahlia m
dai-ly ['deli] adj quotidien, journalier ‖ s (pl -lies) quotidien m ‖ adv journellement
dain-ty ['denti] adj (comp -tier; super -tiest) délicat ‖ s (pl -ties) friandise f
dair-y ['deri] s (pl -ies) laiterie f; (shop) crémerie f; (farm) vacherie f
dair′y farm′ s vacherie f
dair′y-man s (pl -men) laitier m
dais ['de-ɪs] s estrade f
dai-sy ['dezi] s (pl -sies) marguerite f
dal-ly ['dæli] v (pret & pp -lied) intr badiner; (to delay) s'attarder
dam [dæm] s barrage m; (female quadruped) mère f ‖ v (pret & pp dammed; ger damming) tr contenir, endiguer
damage ['dæmɪdʒ] s dommage m, dégâts mpl; (to engine, ship, etc.) avaries fpl; (to one's reputation) tort m; **damages** (law) dommages-intérêts mpl ‖ tr endommager; (merchandise; a machine) avarier; (a reputation) faire du tort à
damaging ['dæmɪdʒɪŋ] adj dommageable, préjudiciable
damascene ['dæmə ,sin], [,dæmə'sin]

adj damasquiné ‖ s damasquinage m ‖ tr damasquiner
Damascus [də'mæskəs] s Damas f
dame [dem] s dame f; (coll) jupon m
damn [dæm] s juron m, gros mot m; **I don't give a damn** (slang) je m'en fiche; **that's not worth a damn** (slang) ça ne vaut pas un pet de lapin, ça ne vaut pas chipette ‖ tr condamner; (to criticize harshly) éreinter; (to curse) maudire; **damn it!** oh, la vache!; **to damn with faint praise** assommer avec des fleurs ‖ intr maudire
damnation [dæm'neʃən] s damnation f
damned [dæmd] adj damné m; **the damned** les damnés ‖ adv (slang) diablement, bigrement
damp [dæmp] adj humide, moite ‖ s humidité f; (firedamp) grisou m ‖ tr (to dampen) humecter, mouiller; (a furnace) étouffer; (sound; electromagnetic waves) amortir
dampen ['dæmpən] tr humecter; (enthusiasm) refroidir; (to muffle) amortir
damper ['dæmpər] s (of chimney) registre m; (of stovepipe) soupape f de réglage; (of piano) étouffoir m; **to put a damper on** (fig) jeter un froid sur
damsel ['dæmzəl] s demoiselle f
dance [dæns], [dɑns] s danse f; bal m, soirée f dansante ‖ tr & intr danser
dance′ band′ s orchestre m de danse
dance′ floor′ s piste f de danse
dance′ hall′ s dancing m, salle f de danse
dance′ pro′gram s carnet m de bal
dancer ['dænsər], ['dɑnsər] s danseur m
danc′ing part′ner s danseur m
dandelion ['dændɪ ,laɪ-ən] s pissenlit m
dandruff ['dændrəf] s pellicules fpl
dan-dy ['dændi] adj (comp -dier; super -diest) (coll) chic, chouette ‖ s (pl -dies) dandy m, élégant m
Dane [den] s Danois m
danger ['dendʒər] s danger m

dangerous [ˈdendʒərəs] *adj* dangereux

dangle [ˈdæŋgəl] *tr* faire pendiller ‖ *intr* pendiller

Danish [ˈdenɪʃ] *adj & s* danois *m*

dank [dæŋk] *adj* humide, moite

Danube [ˈdænjub] *s* Danube *m*

dapper [ˈdæpər] *adj* fringant, élégant

dappled [ˈdæpəld] *adj* tacheté, (*sky*) pommelé, (*horse*) moucheté, miroité

dare [der] *s* défi *m*; **to take a dare** relever un défi ‖ *tr* défier; **to dare s.o. to** + *inf* défier qn de + *inf* ‖ *intr* oser; **to dare** + *inf* oser + *inf*

dare/dev/il *s* risque-tout *mf*

daring [ˈderɪŋ] *adj* audacieux, hardi ‖ *s* audace *f*, hardiesse *f*

dark [dark] *adj* sombre, obscur; (*color*) foncé; (*complexion*) basané, brun; **it is dark** il fait noir, il fait nuit ‖ *s* obscurité *f*, ténèbres *fpl*

Dark/ Ag/es *spl* âge *m* des ténèbres

darken [ˈdarkən] *tr* assombrir; (*the complexion*) brunir; (*a color*) foncer ‖ *intr* s'assombrir; (*said of forehead*) se rembrunir

dark/ horse/ *s* (pol) candidat *m* obscur; (sports) outsider *m*

darkly [ˈdarkli] *adv* obscurément; (*mysteriously*) ténébreusement; (*threateningly*) d'un air menaçant

dark/ meat/ *s* viande *f* brune; (*of game*) viande noire

darkness [ˈdarknɪs] *s* obscurité *f*

dark/room/ *s* (phot) chambre *f* noire

darling [ˈdarlɪŋ] *adj & s* chéri *m*, bien-aimé *m*; **my darling** mon chou

darn [darn] *s* reprise *f*, raccommodage *m* ‖ *tr* repriser, raccommoder ‖ *interj* zut!

darn/ing egg/ *s* œuf *m* à repriser

darn/ing nee/dle *s* aiguille *f* à repriser

dart [dart] *s* dard *m*; (*small missile used in a game*) fléchette *f* ‖ *intr* se précipiter, aller comme une flèche

dash [dæʃ] *s* trait *m*; (*small amount*) soupçon *m*, petit brin *m*; (*of color*) pointe *f*, touche *f*; (*splash*) choc *m*, floc *m*; (*spirit*) élan *m*, fougue *f*; (*in printing, writing*) tiret *m*; (*in telegraphy*) trait *m*, longue *f* ‖ *tr* (*quickly*) précipiter; (*violently*) heurter; (*hopes*) abattre; **to dash off** écrire d'un trait, esquisser; **to dash to pieces** fracasser ‖ *intr* se précipiter; **to dash against** se heurter contre; **to dash by** filer à grand train; **to dash in** entrer en trombe; **to dash off or out** s'élancer, s'élancer dehors

dash/board/ *s* tableau *m* de bord

dashing [ˈdæʃɪŋ] *adj* impétueux, fougueux; (*elegant*) brillant & franc

dastard [ˈdæstərd] *adj & s* lâche *mf*

data [ˈdetə], [ˈdætə] *spl* données *fpl*

da/ta proc/essing *s* analyse *f* des renseignements, étude *f* des données

date [det] *s* (*time*) date *f*; (*on books, on coins*) millésime *m*; (*palm*) dattier *m*; (*fruit*) datte *f*; (*of note, of loan*) terme *m*, échéance *f*; (*appointment*) rendez-vous *m*; **out of date** suranné, périmé; **to date** à ce jour; **up to date** à la page, au courant ‖ *tr* dater;

(e.g., *a work of art*) assigner une date à; (coll) fixer un rendez-vous avec ‖ *intr* (*to be outmoded*) dater; **to date from** dater de, remonter à

date/ line/ *s* ligne *f* de changement de date

date/ palm/ *s* dattier *m*

dative [ˈdetɪv] *s* datif *m*

daub [dɔb] *s* barbouillage *m* ‖ *tr* barbouiller

daughter [ˈdɔtər] *s* fille *f*

daugh/ter-in-law/ *s* (*pl* **daughters-in-law**) belle-fille *f*, bru *f*

daunt [dɔnt] *tr* intimider, abattre

dauntless [ˈdɔntlɪs] *adj* intrépide

dauphin [ˈdɔfɪn] *s* dauphin *m*

davenport [ˈdævən‚port] *s* canapé-lit *m*

daw [dɔ] *s* choucas *m*

dawdle [ˈdɔdəl] *intr* flâner, muser

dawn [dɔn] *s* aube *f*, aurore *f* ‖ *intr* poindre; **to dawn on** venir à l'esprit à

day [de] *adj* (*work*) diurne; (*worker*) de journée ‖ *s* jour *m*; (*of travel, work, worry*) journée *f*; (*of the month*) quantième *m*; **a day** (*per day*) par jour; **by the day** à la journée; **day by day** au jour le jour, jour par jour; **every day** tous les jours, chaque jour; **every other day** tous les deux jours; **from day to day** de jour en jour; **good old days** bon vieux temps; **in less than a day** du jour au lendemain; **in these days** de nos jours; **in those days** à ce moment-là, à cette époque; **one fine day** un beau jour; **the day after** le lendemain; **the day after tomorrow** après-demain; l'après-demain *m*; **the day before** la veille; la veille de; **the day before yesterday** avant-hier; l'avant-hier *m*

day/ bed/ *s* canapé-lit *m*

day/break/ *s* pointe *f* du jour, lever *m* du jour; **at daybreak** au jour levant

day/ coach/ *s* (rr) voiture *f*

day/dream/ *s* rêvasserie *f*, rêverie *f* ‖ *intr* rêvasser, rêver creux

day/dream/er *s* songe-creux *m*, songeur *m*

day/dream/ing *s* rêvasserie *f*

day/ la/borer *s* journalier *m*

day/light/ *s* jour *m*; **in broad daylight** en plein jour; **to see daylight** (coll) comprendre; (coll) voir la fin d'une tâche difficile

day/light-sav/ing time/ *s* heure *f* d'été

day/ lil/y *s* lis *m* jaune, belle-d'un-jour *f*

day/ nurs/ery *s* garderie *f* d'enfants, crèche *f*

day/ off/ *s* jour *m* de congé, jour chômé

day/ of reck/oning *s* jour *m* de règlement; (*last judgment*) jour d'expiation

day/ shift/ *s* équipe *f* de jour

day/ stu/dent *s* externe *mf*

day/time/ *s* jour *m*, journée *f*

daze [dez] *s* étourdissement *m*; **in a daze** hébété ‖ *tr* étourdir

dazzle [ˈdæzəl] *s* éblouissement *m* ‖ *tr* éblouir

dazzling [ˈdæzlɪŋ] *adj* éblouissant

D.C. [ˈdiˈsi] *s* (letterword) (**District of**

Columbia) le district de Columbia; *(direct current)* le courant continu

D'-day' s le jour J

deacon [ˈdikən] s diacre m

deaconess [ˈdikənɪs] s diaconesse f

dead [ded] *adj* mort; *(tired)* épuisé; *(color)* terne; *(business)* stagnant; *(sleep)* profond; *(calm)* plat; *(loss)* sec; *(typewriter key)* immobile; **on a dead level** à franc niveau || *s*—**in the dead of night** au milieu de la nuit; **the dead** les morts; **the dead of winter** le cœur de l'hiver || *adv* absolument; **to stop dead** s'arrêter net

dead'beat' s (slang) écornifleur m

dead' bolt' s pêne m dormant

dead' calm' s calme m plat

dead' cen'ter s point m mort

dead'-drunk' *adj* ivre mort

deaden [ˈdedən] *tr* amortir; *(sound)* assourdir

dead' end' s cul-de-sac m, impasse f

dead' latch' s pêne m dormant

dead'-let'ter of'fice s bureau m des rebuts

dead'line' s dernier délai m, date f limite

dead'lock' s serrure f à pêne dormant; (fig) impasse f || *tr* faire aboutir à une impasse

dead-ly [ˈdedli] *adj* (*comp* -**lier**; *super* -**liest**) mortel; *(sin)* capital

dead' pan' s (slang) visage m sans expression

dead' reck'oning s estime f; *(position)* point m d'estime

dead' ring'er s (coll) portrait m vivant

dead' sol'dier s *(bottle)* (slang) cadavre m

dead' weight' s poids m lourd

dead'wood' s bois m mort; (fig) objet m or individu m inutile

deaf [def] *adj* sourd; **to turn a deaf ear** faire la sourde oreille

deaf'-and-dumb' *adj* sourd-muet

deafen [ˈdefən] *tr* assourdir

deafening [ˈdefənɪŋ] *adj* assourdissant

deaf'-mute' *adj & s* sourd-muet m

deafness [ˈdefnɪs] s surdité f

deal [dil] s affaire f; *(cards)* main f, donne f; **a good deal (of)** or **a great deal (of)** beaucoup (de); **to think a great deal of s.o.** estimer qn || *v (pret & pp* **dealt** [delt]) *tr (a blow)* donner, porter; *(cards)* donner, distribuer; **to deal out** *(e.g., gifts)* distribuer, répartir; *(alms)* dispenser; *(justice)* rendre || *intr* négocier; *(cards)* faire la donne; **to deal in** faire le commerce de; **to deal with** *(a person)* traiter avec; *(a subject)* traiter de

dealer [ˈdilər] s marchand m, négociant m; *(of cards)* donneur m; *(middleman, e.g., in selling automobiles)* concessionnaire m, stockiste m

dean [din] s doyen m

dean'ship s doyenné m, décanat m

dear [dɪr] *adj* cher; **dear me!** mon Dieu!; **Dear Sir** *(salutation in a letter)* Monsieur || s chéri m

dearie [ˈdɪri] s (coll) petite, chérie f

dearth [dʌrθ] s disette f, pénurie f

death [deθ] s mort f; **at death's door** à deux doigts de la mort; **to bore to death** raser; **to put to death** mettre à mort; **to starve to death** mourir de faim; faire mourir de faim

death'bed' s lit m de mort

death'blow' s coup m mortel

death' certif'icate s constatation f de décès, extrait m mortuaire

death' house' s quartier m de la mort

death' knell' s glas m funèbre

deathless [ˈdeθlɪs] *adj* immortel

deathly [ˈdeθli] *adj* mortel || *adv* mortellement, comme la mort

death' mask' s masque m mortuaire

death' pen'alty s peine f capitale

death' rate' s mortalité f, taux m de mortalité

death' rat'tle s râle m de la mort

death' war'rant s ordre m d'exécution

death'watch' s veillée f funèbre

deb [deb] s (slang) débutante f

debacle [deˈbakəl] s débâcle m

de-bar [dɪˈbar] *v (pret & pp* -**barred**; *ger* -**barring**) *tr* exclure; empêcher

debark [dɪˈbark] *tr & intr* débarquer

debarkation [ˌdɪbarˈkeʃən] s débarquement m

debase [dɪˈbes] *tr* avilir, abaisser; *(e.g., money)* altérer

debatable [dɪˈbetəbəl] *adj* discutable

debate [dɪˈbet] s débat m; **under debate** en discussion || *tr & intr* discuter

debauch [dɪˈbɔtʃ] s débauche f || *tr* débaucher, corrompre

debauchee [ˌdebɔˈʃi], [ˌdebɔˈtʃi] s débauché m

debaucher-y [dɪˈbɔtʃəri] s *(pl* -**ies**) débauche f

debenture [dɪˈbentʃər] s *(bond)* obligation f; *(voucher)* reçu m

debilitate [dɪˈbɪlɪˌtet] *tr* débiliter

debili-ty [dɪˈbɪlɪti] s *(pl* -**ties**) débilité f

debit [ˈdebɪt] s débit m; *(entry on debit side)* article m au débit || *tr* débiter, porter au débit

deb'it bal'ance s solde m débiteur

debonair [ˌdebəˈner] *adj* gai, jovial; élégant, charmant

debris [dəˈbri], [ˈdebri] s débris mpl, détritus m; *(from ruined buildings)* décombres mpl

debt [det] s dette f; **to run into debt** s'endetter

debtor [ˈdetər] s débiteur m

debut [deˈbju], [ˈdebju] s début m || *intr* débuter

debutante [ˌdebjuˈtant], [ˈdebjəˌtænt] s débutante f

decade [ˈdeked] s décennie f, décade f

decadence [dɪˈkedəns] s décadence f

decadent [dɪˈkedənt] *adj & s* décadent m

decal [ˈdikæl], [dɪˈkæl], [ˈdekəl] s décalcomanie f

decamp [dɪˈkæmp] *intr* décamper

decanter [dɪˈkæntər] s carafe f

decapitate [dɪˈkæpɪˌtet] *tr* décapiter

decay [dɪˈke] s *(rotting)* pourriture f; *(decline)* décadence f; *(falling to pieces)* délabrement m; *(of teeth)*

carie *f* ‖ *tr* pourrir; (*teeth*) carier ‖
intr pourrir, se gâter; (*said of teeth*)
se carier; tomber en décadence or
ruine; délabrer
decease [dɪ'sis] *s* décès *m* ‖ *intr* décéder
deceit [dɪ'sit] *s* tromperie *f*
deceitful [dɪ'sitfəl] *adj* trompeur
deceive [dɪ'siv] *tr & intr* tromper
decelerate [dɪ'sɛlə‚ret] *tr & intr* ralentir
December [dɪ'sɛmbər] *s* décembre *m*
decen·cy [di'sɪnsi] *s* (*pl* -**cies**) décence
f; **decencies** convenances *fpl*
decent [di'sɪnt] *adj* décent
decentralize [dɪ'sɛntrə‚laɪz] *tr* décentraliser
deception [dɪ'sɛpʃən] *s* tromperie *f*
deceptive [dɪ'sɛptɪv] *adj* trompeur
decide [dɪ'saɪd] *tr* décider; (*the outcome*) décider de ‖ *intr* décider, se
décider; **to decide to** + *inf* décider
de + *inf*, se décider à + *inf*; **to decide upon a day** fixer un jour
deciduous [dɪ'sɪdʒʊ‚əs], [dɪ'sɪdjʊ‚əs]
adj caduc
decimal [dɛsɪməl] *adj* décimal ‖ *s*
décimale *f*
dec′imal point′ *s* (*in French the comma
is used to separate the decimal fraction from the integer*) virgule *f*
decimate [dɛsɪ‚met] *tr* décimer
decipher [dɪ'saɪfər] *tr* déchiffrer
decision [dɪ'sɪʒən] *s* décision *f*
decisive [dɪ'saɪsɪv] *adj* décisif
deck [dɛk] *s* (*of cards*) jeu *m*, paquet
m; (*of ship*) pont *m*; **between decks**
(naut) dans l'entrepont ‖ *tr*—**to deck
out** parer, orner
deck′ chair′ *s* transatlantique *m*, tran-
sat *m*, chaise *f* longue de bord
deck′ hand′ *s* matelot *m* de pont
deck′-land′ *intr* apponter
deck′-land′ing *s* appontage *m*
deck′le edge′ [dɛkəl] *s* barbes *fpl*,
bords *mpl* baveux
declaim [dɪ'klem] *tr & intr* déclamer
declaration [‚dɛklə'reʃən] *s* déclaration *f*
declarative [dɪ'klærətɪv] *adj* déclaratif
declare [dɪ'klɛr] *tr & intr* déclarer
declension [dɪ'klɛnʃən] *s* (gram) déclinaison *f*
declination [‚dɛklɪ'neʃən] *s* (astr, geog)
déclinaison *f*
decline [dɪ'klaɪn] *s* déclin *m*, décca-
dence *f*; (*in prices*) baisse *f* ‖ *tr &
intr* décliner
decliv·i·ty [dɪ'klɪvɪti] *s* (*pl* -**ties**) déclivité *f*, pente *f*
decode [dɪ'kod] *tr* décoder, déchiffrer
decompose [‚dikəm'poz] *tr* décomposer ‖ *intr* se décomposer
decomposition [‚dikɑmpə'zɪʃən] *s* décomposition *f*
decompression [‚dikəm'prɛʃən] *s* décompression *f*
decontamination [‚dikən‚tæmɪ'neʃən]
s décontamination *f*
decorate [dɛkə‚ret] *tr* décorer
decoration [‚dɛkə'reʃən] *s* décoration *f*
decorator [dɛkə‚retər] *s* décorateur *m*

decorous [dɛkərəs], [dɪ'korəs] *adj*
convenable, correct, bienséant
decorum [dɪ'korəm] *s* décorum *m*
decoy [dɪ'kɔɪ], [dikɔɪ] *s* leurre *m*, appât *m*; (*bird*) appeau *m* ‖ *tr* [dɪ'kɔɪ]
tr leurrer
decrease [dikris], [dɪ'kris] *s* diminution *f* ‖ [dɪ'kris] *tr & intr* diminuer
decree [dɪ'kri] *s* décret *m*, arrêté *m*;
(*of divorce*) ordonnance *f* ‖ *tr* décréter, arrêter, ordonner
decrepit [dɪ'krɛpɪt] *adj* décrépit
de·cry [dɪ'kraɪ] *v* (*pret & pp* -**cried**)
tr décrier, dénigrer
dedicate [dɛdɪ‚ket] *tr* dédier
dedication [‚dɛdɪ'keʃən] *s* consécration
f; (*e.g., in a book*) dédicace *f*
dedicatory [dɛdɪkə‚tori] *adj* dédicatoire
deduce [dɪ'd(j)us] *tr* déduire, inférer
deduct [dɪ'dʌkt] *tr* déduire
deduction [dɪ'dʌkʃən] *s* déduction *f*
deed [did] *s* action *f*, acte *m*; (law)
acte, titre *m*, contrat *m*; **deed of val-
or** haut fait *m*; **good deed** bonne
action; **in deed** dans le fait ‖ *tr* transférer par un acte
deem [dim] *tr* estimer, juger, croire ‖
intr penser
deep [dip] *adj* profond; (*sound*) grave;
(*color*) foncé; de profondeur, e.g.,
to be twenty feet deep avoir vingt
pieds de profondeur; **deep in debt**
criblé de dettes; **deep in thought**
plongé dans la méditation ‖ *adv* profondément; **deep into the night** très
avant dans la nuit
deepen [dipən] *tr* approfondir ‖ *intr*
s'approfondir
deep′-freeze′ *v* (*pret* -**froze**; *pp* -**frozen**)
tr congeler à basse température
deep′-laid′ *adj* habilement ourdi
deep′ mourn′ing *s* grand deuil *m*
deep′-root′ed *adj* profondément enraciné
deep′-sea fish′ing *s* grande pêche *f* au
large, pêche maritime
deer [dɪr] *s* (*red deer*) cerf *m*; (*fallow
deer*) daim *m*; (*roe deer*) chevreuil *m*
deer′skin′ *s* peau *f* de daim
deface [dɪ'fes] *tr* défigurer
de facto [di'fækto] *adv* de fait, de facto
defamation [‚dɛfə'meʃən], [‚difə'me-
ʃən] *s* diffamation *f*, injures *fpl*
defame [dɪ'fem] *tr* diffamer
default [dɪ'fɔlt] *s* manque *m*, défaut
m; (*on an obligation*) carence *f*; **by
default** par défaut; (sports) par forfait; **in default of** à défaut de ‖ *tr* (*a
debt*) manquer de s'acquitter de ‖
intr ne pas tenir ses engagements;
(sports) perdre par forfait
defeat [dɪ'fit] *s* défaite *f*; **unexpected
defeat** contre-performance *f* ‖ *tr*
vaincre, battre, défaire
defeatism [dɪ'fitɪzəm] *s* défaitisme *m*
defeatist [dɪ'fitɪst] *adj & s* défaitiste
mf
defecate [dɛfɪ‚ket] *intr* déféquer
defect [dɪ'fɛkt], [difɛkt] *s* défaut *m*,
imperfection *f*, vice *m* ‖ [dɪ'fɛkt]
intr faire défection, déserter

defection [dɪˈfekʃən] *s* défection *f*
defective [dɪˈfektɪv] *adj* défectueux, vicieux; (gram) défectif
defend [dɪˈfend] *tr* défendre
defendant [dɪˈfendənt] *s* (law) défendeur *m*, intimé *m*
defense [dɪˈfens] *s* défense *f*
defenseless [dɪˈfenslɪs] *adj* sans défense
defensive [dɪˈfensɪv] *adj* défensif ‖ *s* défensive *f*
de·fer [dɪˈfʌr] *v* (pret & pp -ferred; ger -ferring) *tr* différer; (mil) mettre en sursis ‖ *intr*—**to defer to** déférer à
deference [ˈdefərəns] *s* déférence *f*
deferential [ˌdefəˈrenʃəl] *adj* déférent
deferment [dɪˈfʌrmənt] *s* ajournement *m*, remise *f*; (extension of time) délai *m*; (mil) sursis *m* d'appel
defiance [dɪˈfaɪəns] *s* défi *m*, provocation *f*, nargue *f*; **in defiance of** au mépris de, en dépit de
defiant [dɪˈfaɪənt] *adj* provocant, hostile, de défi
deficien·cy [dɪˈfɪʃənsi] *s* (pl -cies) déficience *f*, insuffisance *f*; (of vitamins or minerals) carence *f*; (com) déficit *m*
deficient [dɪˈfɪʃənt] *adj* déficient, insuffisant
deficit [ˈdefɪsɪt] *adj* déficitaire ‖ *s* déficit *m*
defile [dɪˈfaɪl], [ˈdifaɪl] *s* défilé *m* ‖ [dɪˈfaɪl] *tr* souiller ‖ *intr* défiler
defilement [dɪˈfaɪlmənt] *s* souillure *f*
define [dɪˈfaɪn] *tr* définir
definite [ˈdefɪnɪt] *adj* défini; (opinions, viewpoints) décidé
definitely [ˈdefɪnɪtli] *adv* décidément, nettement
definition [ˌdefɪˈnɪʃən] *s* définition *f*
definitive [dɪˈfɪnɪtɪv] *adj* définitif
deflate [dɪˈflet] *tr* dégonfler; (currency) amener la déflation de ‖ *intr* se dégonfler
deflation [dɪˈfleʃən] *s* dégonflement *m*; (of prices) déflation *f*
deflect [dɪˈflekt] *tr & intr* dévier
deflower [dɪˈflaʊər] *tr* déflorer; (to strip of flowers) défleurir
deforest [diˈfarɪst], [diˈfɔrɪst] *tr* déboiser
deform [dɪˈfɔrm] *tr* déformer
deformed *adj* contrefait, difforme
deformi·ty [dɪˈfɔrmɪti] *s* (pl -ties) difformité *f*
defraud [dɪˈfrɔd] *tr* frauder
defray [dɪˈfre] *tr* payer, supporter
defrost [diˈfrɔst], [diˈfrast] *tr* décongeler, dégivrer
defroster [diˈfrɔstər], [diˈfrastər] *s* dégivreur *m*, dégivreur *m*
defrosting [diˈfrɔstɪŋ], [diˈfrastɪŋ] *s* dégèlement *m*, dégivrage *m*
deft [deft] *adj* adroit, habile; (hand) exerce, preste
defunct [dɪˈfʌŋkt] *adj* défunt; (practice, style, etc.) tombé en désuétude
de·fy [dɪˈfaɪ] *v* (pret & pp -fied) *tr* défier, braver, porter un défi à
degeneracy [dɪˈdʒenərəsi] *s* dégénérescence *f*

degenerate [dɪˈdʒenərɪt] *adj & s* dégénéré *m* ‖ [dɪˈdʒenəˌret] *intr* dégénérer
degrade [dɪˈgred] *tr* dégrader
degrading [dɪˈgredɪŋ] *adj* dégradant
degree [dɪˈgri] *s* degré *m*; (from a university) grade *m*; (of humidity) titre *m*; **to take a degree** obtenir ses diplômes, obtenir ses titres universitaires
dehumidi·fy [ˌdihjuˈmɪdɪˌfaɪ] *v* (pret & pp -fied) *tr* déshumidifier
dehydrate [diˈhaɪdret] *tr* déshydrater; (the body) dessécher
deice [diˈaɪs] *tr* déglacer, dégivrer
deicer [diˈaɪsər] *s* dégivreur *m*, antigivrant *m*
dei·fy [ˈdi·ɪˌfaɪ] *v* (pret & pp -fied) *tr* déifier
deign [den] *intr*—**to deign to** daigner
dei·ty [ˈdi·ɪti] *s* (pl -ties) divinité *f*; (mythol) déité *f*; **the Deity** Dieu *m*
dejected [dɪˈdʒektɪd] *adj* abattu, découragé
dejection [dɪˈdʒekʃən] *s* abattement *m*
delay [dɪˈle] *s* retard *m*; (postponement) sursis *m*, remise *f*; **without delay** sans délai; **without further delay** sans plus tarder ‖ *tr* retarder; (to put off) remettre, différer ‖ *intr* tarder, s'attarder
delayed′-ac′tion *adj* à action différée
delayed′-ac′tion switch′ *s* minuterie *f* d'escalier
delayed′-time′ switch′ *s* coupe-circuit *m* à action différée
dele [ˈdili] *s* (typ) deleatur *m*
delectable [dɪˈlektəbəl] *adj* délectable
delegate [ˈdelɪˌget], [ˈdelɪgɪt] *s* délégué *m*; (at a convention) congressiste *mf*, délégué *f* ‖ [ˈdelɪˌget] *tr* déléguer
delegation [ˌdelɪˈgeʃən] *s* délégation *f*
delete [dɪˈlit] *tr* supprimer
deletion [dɪˈliʃən] *s* suppression *f*; (the deleted part) passage *m* supprimé
deliberate [dɪˈlɪbərɪt] *adj* (premeditated) délibéré, réfléchi; (cautious) circonspect; (slow) lent ‖ [dɪˈlɪbəˌret] *tr & intr* délibérer
deliberately [dɪˈlɪbərɪtli] *adv* (on purpose) exprès, de propos délibéré; (without hurrying) posément, sans hâte
deliberation [dɪˌlɪbəˈreʃən] *s* délibération *f*; (slowness) lenteur *f*
delica·cy [ˈdelɪkəsi] *s* (pl -cies) délicatesse *f*; (choice food) friandise *f*, gourmandise *f*
delicate [ˈdelɪkɪt] *adj* délicat
delicatessen [ˌdelɪkəˈtesən] *s* charcuterie *f*
delicious [dɪˈlɪʃəs] *adj* délicieux
delight [dɪˈlaɪt] *s* délice *m*, délices *fpl*, plaisir *m* ‖ *tr* enchanter, ravir ‖ *intr*—**to delight in** se délecter à
delighted *adj* enchanté, ravi, content
delightful [dɪˈlaɪtfəl] *adj* délicieux, ravissant, enchanteur
delineate [dɪˈlɪnɪˌet] *tr* esquisser
delinquen·cy [dɪˈlɪŋkwənsi] *s* (pl -cies) délit *m*, faute *f*; (e.g., of juveniles) délinquance *f*

delinquent [dɪˈlɪŋkwənt] *adj* négligent, coupable; (*in payment*) arriéré; (*in guilt*) délinquant || *s* délinquant *m*; créancier *m* en retard

delirious [dɪˈlɪrɪ·əs] *adj* délirant

deliri·um [dɪˈlɪrɪ·əm] *s* (*pl* **-ums** or **-a** [ə]) délire *m*

deliver [dɪˈlɪvər] *tr* délivrer; (*e.g., laundry*) livrer; (*mail*) distribuer; (*a blow*) asséner; (*an opinion*) exprimer; (*a speech*) prononcer; (*energy*) débiter, fournir; **to be delivered of a child** accoucher d'un enfant

deliver·y [dɪˈlɪvəri] *s* (*pl* **-ies**) *s* remise *f*; (*e.g., of a package*) livraison *f*; (*of mail*) distribution *f*; (*of a speech*) of electricity) débit *m*; (*of a woman in childbirth*) accouchement *m*, délivrance *f*; **free delivery** livraison franco

deliv'ery-man *s* (*pl* **-men**) livreur *m*

deliv'ery room' *s* salle *f* d'accouchement, salle de travail

deliv'ery truck' *s* fourgon *m* à livraison

dell [del] *s* vallon *m*

delouse [diˈlaʊs], [diˈlaʊz] *tr* épouiller

delphinium [delˈfɪnɪ·əm] *s* dauphinelle *f*, pied-d'alouette *m*

delta [ˈdeltə] *s* delta *m*

delude [dɪˈlud] *tr* duper, tromper

deluge [ˈdeljudʒ] *s* déluge *m* || *tr* inonder

delusion [dɪˈluʒən] *s* illusion *f*, tromperie *f*; **delusions** (psychopathol) hallucinations *fpl*; **delusions of grandeur** folie *f* des grandeurs

delusive [dɪˈlusɪv] or **delusory** [dɪˈlusəri] *adj* trompeur

de luxe [dɪˈlʊks], [dɪˈlʌks] *adj & adv* de luxe

delve [delv] *intr*—**to delve into** fouiller dans, approfondir

demagnetize [diˈmægnɪ·taɪz] *tr* démagnétiser, désaimanter

demagogue [ˈdeməˌgag] *s* démagogue *mf*

demand [dɪˈmænd], [dɪˈmɑnd] *s* exigence *f*; (*of the buying public*) demande *f*; **demands** exigences, **in great demand** très recherché; **on demand** sur demande || *tr* exiger

demanding [dɪˈmændɪŋ], [dɪˈmɑndɪŋ] *adj* exigeant

demarcate [dɪˈmɑrket], [ˈdɪmɑrˌket] *tr* délimiter

demean [dɪˈmin] *tr* dégrader; **to demean oneself** se conduire

demeanor [dɪˈminər] *s* conduite *f*, tenue *f*

demented [dɪˈmentɪd] *adj* aliéné, fou

demerit [diˈmerɪt] *s* démérite *m*

demigod [ˈdemɪˌgad] *s* demi-dieu *m*

demijohn [ˈdemɪˌdʒan] *s* dame-jeanne *f*

demilitarize [diˈmɪlɪtəˌraɪz] *tr* démilitariser

demise [dɪˈmaɪz] *s* décès *m*

demitasse [ˈdemɪˌtæs], [ˈdemɪˌtɑs] *s* petite tasse *f* à café; (*contents*) café *m* noir

demobilize [diˈmobɪˌlaɪz] *tr* démobiliser

democra·cy [dɪˈmɑkrəsi] *s* (*pl* **-cies**) démocratie *f*

democrat [ˈdeməˌkræt] *s* démocrate *mf*

democratic [ˌdeməˈkrætɪk] *adj* démocratique

demolish [dɪˈmɑlɪʃ] *tr* démolir

demolition [ˌdeməˈlɪʃən], [ˌdiməˈlɪʃən] *s* démolition *f*

demon [ˈdimən] *s* démon *m*

demoniac [dɪˈmonɪˌæk] *adj & s* démoniaque *mf*

demonic [dɪˈmɑnɪk] *adj* démoniaque

demonstrate [ˈdemənˌstret] *tr* démontrer || *intr* (*to show feelings in public gatherings*) manifester

demonstration [ˌdemənˈstreʃən] *s* démonstration *f*; (*public show of feeling*) manifestation *f*

demonstrative [dɪˈmɑnstrətɪv] *adj* démonstratif

demonstrator [ˈdemənˌstretər] *s* (*salesman*) démonstrateur *m*; (*agitator*) manifestant *m*

demoralize [dɪˈmɑrəˌlaɪz], [dɪˈmɔrəˌlaɪz] *tr* démoraliser

demote [dɪˈmot] *tr* rétrograder

demotion [dɪˈmoʃən] *s* rétrogradation *f*

de·mur [dɪˈmʌr] *v* (*pret & pp* **-murred**; *ger* **-murring**) *intr* faire des objections

demure [dɪˈmjʊr] *adj* modeste, posé

demurrage [dɪˈmʌrɪdʒ] *s* (naut) surestarie *f*

den [den] *s* (*of animals; of thieves*) repaire *m*, retraite *f*; (*of wild beasts*) antre *m*; (*of lions*) tanière *f*; (*room in a house*) cabinet *m* de travail, fumoir *m*; (Cub Scouts) sizaine *f*

denaturalize [diˈnætʃərəˌlaɪz] *tr* dénaturaliser

denial [dɪˈnaɪ·əl] *s* (*contradiction*) dénégation *f*, démenti *m*; (*refusal*) refus *m*, déni *m*

denim [ˈdenɪm] *s* coutil *m*

denizen [ˈdenɪzən] *s* habitant *m*

Denmark [ˈdenmɑrk] *s* le Danemark

denomination [dɪˌnɑmɪˈneʃən] *s* dénomination *f*; (*of coin or stamp*) valeur *f*; (eccl) secte *f*, confession *f*, communion *f*

denote [dɪˈnot] *tr* dénoter

denounce [dɪˈnaʊns] *tr* dénoncer

dense [dens] *adj* dense; (*stupid*) bête

densi·ty [ˈdensɪti] *s* (*pl* **-ties**) densité *f*

dent [dent] *s* marque *f* de coup, creux *m*; (*in a knife; in a fortune*) brèche *f*; **to make a dent in** faire une brèche à || *tr* ébrécher

dental [ˈdentəl] *adj* dentaire; (phonet) dental || *s* dentale *f*

den'tal floss' *s* fil *m* dentaire

den'tal sur'geon *s* chirurgien-dentiste *m*

dentifrice [ˈdentɪfrɪs] *s* dentifrice *m*

dentist [ˈdentɪst] *s* dentiste *m*

dentistry [ˈdentɪstri] *s* odontologie *f*

denture [ˈdentʃər] *s* (*set of teeth*) denture *f*; (*set of artificial teeth*) dentier *m*, râtelier *m*

denunciation [dɪˌnʌnsɪˈeʃən], [dɪˌnʌnʃɪˈeʃən] *s* dénonciation *f*

de·ny [dɪˈnaɪ] *v* (*pret & pp* **-nied**) *tr* nier, démentir; **to deny oneself** se refuser, se priver

deodorant [di'odərənt] *adj* & *s* désodorisant *m*

deodorize [di'odə‚raɪz] *tr* désodoriser

depart [dɪ'pɑrt] *intr* partir; **to depart from** se départir de

departed *adj* (dead) mort, défunt

department [dɪ'pɑrtmənt] *s* département *m*; (of hospital) service *m*; (of agency) bureau *m*; (of store) rayon *m*, comptoir *m*; (of university) section *f*

Depart'ment of State' *s* ministère *m* des affaires étrangères

depart'ment store' *s* grands magasins *mpl*, galerie *f*

departure [dɪ'pɑrtʃər] *s* départ *m*

depend [dɪ'pend] *intr* dépendre; **to depend on or upon** dépendre de

dependable [dɪ'pendəbəl] *adj* sûr; (person) digne de confiance

dependence [dɪ'pendəns] *s* dépendance *f*; **dependence on** dépendance de; (trust in) confiance en

dependen·cy [dɪ'pendənsi] *s* (pl -cies) dépendance *f*; (country, territory) possession *f*, colonie *f*

dependent [dɪ'pendənt] *adj* dépendant; **dependent on** dépendant de; (s.o. for family support) à la charge de ‖ *s* charge *f* de famille

depend'ent clause' *s* proposition *f* subordonnée

depict [dɪ'pɪkt] *tr* dépeindre, décrire

depiction [dɪ'pɪkʃən] *s* peinture *f*

deplete [dɪ'plit] *tr* épuiser

depletion [dɪ'pliʃən] *s* épuisement *m*

deplorable [dɪ'plorəbəl] *adj* déplorable

deplore [dɪ'plor] *tr* déplorer

deploy [dɪ'plɔɪ] *tr* (mil) déployer ‖ *intr* (mil) se déployer

deployment [dɪ'plɔɪmənt] *s* (mil) déploiement *m*

depolarize [di'polə‚raɪz] *tr* dépolariser

depopulate [di'pɑpjə‚let] *tr* & *intr* dépeupler

deport [dɪ'port] *tr* déporter; **to deport oneself** se comporter

deportation [‚dipor'teʃən] *s* déportation *f*

deportee [‚dipor'ti] *s* déporté *m*

deportment [dɪ'portmənt] *s* comportement *m*, tenue *f*, manières *fpl*

depose [dɪ'poz] *tr* & *intr* déposer

deposit [dɪ'pɑzɪt] *s* dépôt *m*; (as pledge) cautionnement *m*, arrhes *fpl*, gage *m*; **no deposit** (bottle) perdu; **to pay a deposit** verser une provision, un acompte, or une caution; **with deposit** (on a bottle) consigné ‖ *tr* déposer; laisser comme provision

depos'it account' *s* compte *m* courant

depositor [dɪ'pɑzɪtər] *s* déposant *m*

deposito·ry [dɪ'pɑzɪ‚tori] *s* (pl -ries) dépôt *m*; (person) dépositaire *mf*

depot ['dipo], ['depo] *s* dépôt *m*; (rr) gare *f*

depraved [dɪ'prevd] *adj* dépravé

depravi·ty [dɪ'prævɪti] *s* (pl -ties) dépravation *f*

deprecate ['deprɪ‚ket] *tr* désapprouver

depreciate [dɪ'priʃɪ‚et] *tr* déprécier ‖ *intr* se déprécier

depreciation [dɪ‚priʃɪ'eʃən] *s* dépréciation *f*

depredation [‚deprɪ'deʃən] *s* déprédation *f*

depress [dɪ'pres] *tr* déprimer; (prices) abaisser

depressing [dɪ'presɪŋ] *adj* attristant

depression [dɪ'preʃən] *s* dépression *f*

deprive [dɪ'praɪv] *tr* priver

depth [depθ] *s* profondeur *f*; (in sound) gravité *f*; **depths** abîme *m*; **in the depth of winter** en plein hiver; **to go beyond one's depth** perdre pied; sortir de sa compétence

depth' bomb' *s* bombe *f* sous-marine

depth' charge' *s* grenade *f* sous-marine

deputation [‚depjə'teʃən] *s* députation *f*

deputize ['depjə‚taɪz] *tr* députer

depu·ty ['depjəti] *s* (pl -ties) député *m*

derail [dɪ'rel] *tr* faire dérailler ‖ *intr* dérailler

derailment [dɪ'relmənt] *s* déraillement *m*

derange [dɪ'rendʒ] *tr* déranger

derangement [dɪ'rendʒmənt] *s* dérangement *m*; (of mind) aliénation *f*

der·by ['dɑrbi] *s* (pl -bies) (race) derby *m*; (hat) chapeau *m* melon

derelict ['derɪlɪkt] *adj* abandonné, délaissé; (in one's duty) négligent ‖ *s* épave *f*

dereliction [‚derɪ'lɪkʃən] *s* abandon *m*, renoncement *m*

deride [dɪ'raɪd] *tr* tourner en dérision, ridiculiser

derision [dɪ'rɪʒən] *s* dérision *f*

derisive [dɪ'raɪsɪv] *adj* dérisoire

derivation [‚derɪ'veʃən] *s* dérivation *f*

derivative [dɪ'rɪvətɪv] *adj* & *s* dérivé *m*

derive [dɪ'raɪv] *tr* & *intr* dériver

dermatology [‚dɑrmə'tɑlədʒi] *s* dermatologie *f*

derogatory [dɪ'rɑgə‚tori] *adj* péjoratif

derrick ['derɪk] *s* grue *f*; (for extracting oil) derrick *m*

dervish ['dʌrvɪʃ] *s* derviche *m*

desalinization [di‚selɪnɪ'zeʃən] *s* dessalement *m*

desalt [di'sɔlt] *tr* dessaler

descend [dɪ'send] *tr* descendre ‖ *intr* descendre; (said of rain) tomber; **to be descended from** descendre de; **to descend on** s'abattre sur

descendant [dɪ'sendənt] *adj* & *s* descendant *m*

descendent [dɪ'sendənt] *adj* descendant

descent [dɪ'sent] *s* descente *f*; (drop in temperature) chute *f*; (lineage) descendance *f*, naissance *f*

describe [dɪ'skraɪb] *tr* décrire

description [dɪ'skrɪpʃən] *s* description *f*

descriptive [dɪ'skrɪptɪv] *adj* descriptif

de·scry [dɪ'skraɪ] *v* (pret & pp -scried) *tr* découvrir, apercevoir

desecrate ['desɪ‚kret] *tr* profaner

desegregate [di'segrɪ‚get] *intr* supprimer la ségrégation raciale

desegregation [di‚segrɪ'geʃən] *s* déségrégation *f*

desensitize [di'sensɪ‚taɪz] *tr* désensibiliser

desert ['dezərt] *adj & s* désert *m* ‖ [dɪ'zʌrt] *s* mérite *m*; **to get one's just deserts** recevoir son salaire, recevoir sa juste punition ‖ *tr & intr* déserter

deserted *adj* (*person*) abandonné; (*place*) désert, nu

deserter [dɪ'zʌrtər] *s* déserteur *m*

desertion [dɪ'zʌrʃən] *s* désertion *f*

deserve [dɪ'zʌrv] *tr & intr* mériter

deservedly [dɪ'zʌrvɪdli] *adv* à juste titre, dignement

deserving [dɪ'zʌrvɪŋ] *adj* méritoire, digne

design [dɪ'zaɪn] *s* (*combination of details; art of designing; work of art*) dessin *m*; (*plan, scheme*) dessein *m*, projet *m*, plan *m*; (*model, outline*) modèle *m*, type *m*, grandes lignes *fpl*; **to have designs on** avoir des desseins sur ‖ *tr* inventer, projeter; (*e.g., a dress*) dessiner; (*a secret plan*) combiner; **designed for** destiné à

designate ['dezɪɡ,net] *tr* désigner

designer [dɪ'zaɪnər] *s* dessinateur *m*

designing [dɪ'zaɪnɪŋ] *adj* artificieux, intrigant ‖ *s* dessin *m*

desirable [dɪ'zaɪrəbəl] *adj* désirable

desire [dɪ'zaɪr] *s* désir *m* ‖ *tr* désirer

desirous [dɪ'zaɪrəs] *adj* désireux

desist [dɪ'zɪst] *intr* cesser

desk [desk] *s* bureau *m*; (*in schoolroom*) pupitre *m*; (*of cashier*) caisse *f*

desk′ blot′ter *s* sous-main *m*

desk′ clerk′ *s* réceptionnaire *mf*

desk′ set′ *s* écritoire *f*

desolate ['desəlɪt] *adj* désert; (*sad*) désolé; (*alone*) abandonné ‖ ['desə,let] *tr* désoler

desolation [,desə'leʃən] *s* désolation *f*

despair [dɪ'sper] *s* désespoir *m*, désespérance *f* ‖ *intr* désespérer

despairing [dɪ'sperɪŋ] *adj* désespéré

despera•do [,despə'redo], [,despə'rado] *s* (*pl* -**does** or -**dos**) hors-la-loi *m*

desperate ['despərɪt] *adj* capable de tout, poussé à bout; (*bitter, excessive*) acharné, à outrance; (*hopeless*) désespéré; (*remedy*) héroïque

desperation [,despə're′ən] *s* désespoir *m*; (*recklessness*) témérité *f*

despicable ['despɪkəbəl] *adj* méprisable, mesquin

despise [dɪ'spaɪz] *tr* mépriser, dédaigner

despite [dɪ'spaɪt] *prep* en dépit de, malgré

despoil [dɪ'spɔɪl] *tr* dépouiller

desponden•cy [dɪ'spandənsi] *s* (*pl* -**cies**) abattement *m*, accablement *m*

despondent [dɪ'spandənt] *adj* abattu, accablé, déprimé

despot ['despat] *s* despote *m*, tyran *m*

despotic [des'patɪk] *adj* despotique

despotism ['despə,tɪzəm] *s* despotisme *m*

dessert [dɪ'zʌrt] *s* dessert *m*

dessert′ spoon′ *s* cuiller *f* à dessert

destination [,destɪ'neʃən] *s* destination *f*

destine ['destɪn] *tr* destiner

desti•ny ['destɪni] *s* (*pl* -**nies**) destin *m*, destinée *f*

destitute ['destɪ,t(j)ut] *adj* indigent; dépourvu

destitution [,destɪ't(j)uʃən] *s* dénuement *m*, indigence *f*

destroy [dɪ'strɔɪ] *tr* détruire

destroyer [dɪ'strɔɪ•ər] *s* destructeur *m*; (*nav*) destroyer *m*

destruction [dɪ'strʌkʃən] *s* destruction *f*

destructive [dɪ'strʌktɪv] *adj* destructeur, destructif

desultory ['desəl,tori] *adj* décousu, sans suite; (*conversation*) à bâtons rompus

detach [dɪ'tætʃ] *tr* détacher

detachable [dɪ'tætʃəbəl] *adj* détachable, démontable; (*collar*) faux

detached *adj* détaché

detachment [dɪ'tætʃmənt] *s* détachement *m*

detail [dɪ'tel], ['ditel] *s* détail *m*; (*mil*) extrait *m* de l'ordre du jour; (*mil*) détachement *m* ‖ [dɪ'tel] *tr* détailler

detailed′ state′ment *s* bordereau *m*

detain [dɪ'ten] *tr* retenir, retarder; (*in prison*) détenir

detect [dɪ'tekt] *tr* déceler, détecter

detection [dɪ'tekʃən] *s* détection *f*

detective [dɪ'tektɪv] *adj* (*device*) détecteur; (*film, novel*) policier ‖ *s* détective *m*, agent *m* de la sûreté

detec′tive sto′ry *s* roman *m* policier

detector [dɪ'tektər] *s* détecteur *m*

detention [dɪ'tenʃən] *s* détention *f*

de•ter [dɪ'tʌr] *s* (*pret & pp* -**terred**) *ger* -**terring**) *tr* détourner

detergent [dɪ'tʌrdʒənt] *adj & s* détersif *m*

deteriorate [dɪ'tɪrɪ•ə,ret] *tr* détériorer ‖ *intr* se détériorer

determination [dɪ,tʌrmɪ'neʃən] *s* détermination *f*

determine [dɪ'tʌrmɪn] *tr* déterminer

determined *adj* déterminé, résolu

deterrent [dɪ'tʌrənt] *adj & s* préventif *m*

detest [dɪ'test] *tr* détester

dethrone [dɪ'θron] *tr* détrôner

detonate ['detə,net], ['ditə,net] *tr* faire détoner, faire éclater ‖ *intr* détoner

detour ['ditur], [dɪ'tur] *s* déviation *f*; (*indirect manner*) détour *m* ‖ *tr & intr* dévier

detract [dɪ'trækt] *tr* diminuer ‖ *intr* — **to detract from** amoindrir

detractor [dɪ'træktər] *s* détracteur *m*

detriment ['detrɪmənt] *s* détriment *m*

detrimental [,detrɪ'mentəl] *adj* préjudiciable, nuisible

deuce [d(j)us] *s* deux *m*; **what the deuce!** (*coll*) diantre!, que diable!

devaluate [di'vælju,et] *tr* dévaluer

devaluation [di,vælju'eʃən] *s* dévaluation *f*

devastate ['devəs,tet] *tr* dévaster

devastating ['devəs,tetɪŋ] *adj* dévastateur; (*coll*) écrasant, accablant

devastation [,devəs'teʃən] *s* dévastation *f*

develop [dɪ'veləp] *tr* développer; (*a mine*) exploiter; (*e.g., a fever*) contracter; (phot) révéler, développer ‖ *intr* se développer; (*to become evident*) se produire, se manifester

developer [dɪˈvɛləpər] *s* entrepreneur *m*; (*builder*) maître *m* d'œuvre; (phot) révélateur *m*

development [dɪˈvɛləpmənt] *s* développement *m*; (*event*) événement *m* récent; (*of housing*) cité *f*, grand ensemble *m*

deviate [ˈdivɪ‚et] *s* perverti *m* ‖ *tr* faire dévier ‖ *intr* dévier

deviation [‚divɪˈeʃən] *s* déviation *f*

device [dɪˈvaɪs] *s* appareil *m*, dispositif *m*; (*trick*) stratagème *m*, ruse *f*; (*motto*) emblème *m*, devise *f*; **to leave s.o. to his own devices** abandonner qn à ses propres moyens

dev·il [ˈdɛvəl] *s* diable *m*; **speak of the devil!** (coll) je vois un loup!; **to be between the devil and the deep blue sea** (coll) se trouver entre l'enclume et le marteau; **to raise the devil** (slang) faire le diable à quatre ‖ *v* (*pret* & *pp* **-iled** or **-illed;** *ger* **-iling** or **-illing**) *tr* épicer fortement; (coll) tourmenter

devilish [ˈdɛvəlɪʃ] *adj* diabolique; (*roguish*) coquin

dev'il-may-care' *adj* insouciant, étourdi

devilment [ˈdɛvəlmənt] *s* (*mischief*) diablerie *f*; (*evil*) méchanceté *f*

devil·try [ˈdɛvəltri] *s* (*pl* **-tries**) méchanceté *f*, cruauté *f*; (*mischief*) espièglerie *f*

devious [ˈdivɪ‚əs] *adj* (*straying*) détourné, dévié; (*roundabout; shifty*) tortueux

devise [dɪˈvaɪz] *tr* combiner, inventer; (law) léguer

devoid [dɪˈvɔɪd] *adj* dépourvu, vide, dénué

devolve [dɪˈvɑlv] *intr*—**to devolve on, to,** or **upon** échoir à

devote [dɪˈvot] *tr* consacrer

devoted [dɪˈvotɪd] *adj* dévoué; **devoted to** voué à, dévoué à, attaché à

devotee [‚devəˈti] *s* dévot *m*, adepte *mf*; (sports) fervent *m*, fanatique *mf*

devotion [dɪˈvoʃən] *s* dévotion *f*; (*to study, work, etc.*) dévouement *m*; **devotions** dévotions, prières *fpl*

devour [dɪˈvaʊr] *tr* dévorer

devout [dɪˈvaʊt] *adj* dévot, pieux

dew [d(j)u] *s* rosée *f*

dew'lap' *s* fanon *m*, double menton *m*

dew·y [ˈd(j)u‚i] *adj* (*comp* **-ier;** *super* **-iest**) couvert de rosée

dexterity [deksˈterɪti] *s* dextérité *f*, adresse *f*

diabetes [‚daɪ‚əˈbitɪs], [‚daɪ‚əˈbitiz] *s* diabète *m*

diabetic [‚daɪ‚əˈbɛtɪk], [‚daɪ‚əˈbitɪk] *adj* & *s* diabétique *mf*

diabolic(al) [‚daɪ‚əˈbɑlɪk(əl)] *adj* diabolique

diacritical [‚daɪ‚əˈkrɪtɪkəl] *adj* diacritique

diadem [ˈdaɪ‚ə‚dɛm] *s* diadème *m*

diaere·sis [daɪˈerɪsɪs] *s* (*pl* **-ses** [‚siz]) diérèse *f*; (*mark*) tréma *m*

diagnose [‚daɪ‚əgˈnos], [‚daɪ‚əgˈnoz] *tr* diagnostiquer

diagno·sis [‚daɪ‚əgˈnosɪs] *s* (*pl* **-ses** [siz]) diagnostic *m*

diagonal [daɪˈægənəl] *adj* diagonal ‖ *s* diagonale *f*

dia·gram [ˈdaɪ‚ə‚græm] *s* diagramme *m*, croquis *m* coté ‖ *v* (*pret* & *pp* **-gramed** or **-grammed;** *ger* **-graming** or **-gramming**) *tr* représenter schématiquement

di·al [ˈdaɪ‚əl], [daɪl] *s* cadran *m* ‖ *v* (*pret* & *pp* **-aled** or **-alled;** *ger* **-aling** or **-alling**) *tr* (*a telephone number*) composer ‖ *intr* faire un numéro

dialect [ˈdaɪ‚ə‚lɛkt] *s* dialecte *m*

dialing [ˈdaɪ‚əlɪŋ] *s* (telp) composition *f* du numéro

dialogue [ˈdaɪ‚ə‚lɔg], [ˈdaɪ‚ə‚lɑg] *s* dialogue *m*

di'al tel'ephone *s* téléphone *m* automatique, automatique *m*

di'al tone' *s* (telp) tonalité *f*

diameter [daɪˈæmɪtər] *s* diamètre *m*

diametric(al) [‚daɪ‚əˈmɛtrɪk(əl)] *adj* diamétral

diamond [ˈdaɪmənd] *s* diamant *m*; (*figure of a rhombus*) losange *m*; (baseball) petit champ *m*; (cards) carreau *m*

diaper [ˈdaɪ‚əpər] *s* lange *m*, couche *f* ‖ *tr* (*to variegate*) diaprer

diaphanous [daɪˈæfənəs] *adj* diaphane

diaphragm [ˈdaɪ‚ə‚fræm] *s* diaphragme *m*

diarrhea [‚daɪ‚əˈri‚ə] *s* diarrhée *f*

dia·ry [ˈdaɪ‚əri] *s* (*pl* **-ries**) journal *m*

diastole [daɪˈæstəli] *s* diastole *f*

diathermy [ˈdaɪ‚ə‚θɑrmi] *s* diathermie *f*

diatribe [ˈdaɪ‚ə‚traɪb] *s* diatribe *f*

dice [daɪs] *spl* dés *mpl*; **no dice!** (slang) pas moyen!; **to load the dice** piper les dés ‖ *tr* couper en cubes

dice'box' *s* cornet *m* à dés

dichoto·my [daɪˈkɑtəmi] *s* (*pl* **-mies**) dichotomie *f*

dictaphone [ˈdɪktə‚fon] *s* (trademark) dictaphone *m*

dictate [ˈdɪktet] *s* précepte *m*, règle *f* ‖ *tr* & *intr* dicter

dictation [dɪkˈteʃən] *s* dictée *f*; **to take dictation from** écrire sous la dictée de

dictator [ˈdɪktetər], [dɪkˈtetər] *s* dictateur *m*

dic'tator·ship' *s* dictature *f*

diction [ˈdɪkʃən] *s* diction *f*

dictionar·y [ˈdɪkʃən‚eri] *s* (*pl* **-ies**) dictionnaire *m*

dic·tum [ˈdɪktəm] *s* (*pl* **-ta** [tə]) dicton *m*; (law) opinion *f*, arrêt *m*

didactic(al) [daɪˈdæktɪk(əl)], [dɪˈdæktɪk(əl)] *adj* didactique

die [daɪ] *s* (*pl* **dice** [daɪs]) dé *m*; **the die is cast** le dé en est jeté ‖ *s* (*pl* **dies**) (*for stamping coins, medals, etc.*) coin *m*; (*for cutting threads*) filière *f*; (*key pattern*) jeu *m* ‖ *v* (*pret* & *pp* **died;** *ger* **dying**) *intr* mourir; **to be dying** se mourir; **to be dying to** (coll) mourir d'envie de; **to die away**

s'éteindre; **to die laughing** (coll) mourir de rire

die'hard' *adj* intransigeant ‖ *s* intransigeant *m*, jusqu'au-boutiste *mf*

die'sel en'gine ['dizəl] *s* diesel *m*, moteur *m* diesel

die'sel oil' *s* gas-oil *m*

die'stock' *s* porte-filière *m*

diet ['dai·ət] *s* nourriture *f*; (*congress; abstention from food*) diète *f*; (*special menu*) régime *m* ‖ *intr* être or se mettre au régime, suivre un régime

dietetic [,dai·ə'tetik] *adj* diététique ‖ **dietetics** *s* diététique *f*

dietician [,dai·ə'trɪʃən] *s* diététicien *m*

differ ['dɪfər] *intr* différer; **to differ with** être en désaccord avec

difference ['dɪfərəns] *s* différence *f*; (*controversy*) différend *m*; **to make no difference** ne rien faire; **to split the difference** partager le différend

different ['dɪfərənt] *adj* différent

differential [,dɪfə'renʃəl] *adj* différentiel ‖ *s* (mach) différentiel *m*; (math) différentielle *f*

differentiate [,dɪfə'renʃɪ,et] *tr* différencier ‖ *intr* se différencier

difficult ['dɪfɪ,kʌlt] *adj* difficile

difficul·ty ['dɪfɪ,kʌlti] *s* (*pl* -ties) difficulté *f*

diffident ['dɪfɪdənt] *adj* défiant, timide

diffuse [dɪ'fjus] *adj* diffus ‖ [dɪ'fjuz] *tr* diffuser ‖ *intr* se diffuser

dig [dɪg] *s*—**to give s.o. a dig** (coll) lancer un trait à qn ‖ *v* (*pret & pp* **dug** [dʌg]; *ger* **digging**) *tr* bêcher, creuser; **to dig up** déterrer ‖ *intr* bêcher

digest ['daidʒest] *s* abrégé *m*, résumé *m*; (*publication*) digest *m*, sélection *f*; (law) digeste *m* ‖ [dɪ'dʒest], [dai-'dʒest] *tr & intr* digérer

digestible [dɪ'dʒestɪbəl], [dai'dʒestɪbəl] *adj* digestible

digestion [dɪ'dʒest/ən], [dai'dʒest/ən] *s* digestion *f*

digestive [dɪ'dʒestɪv], [dai'dʒestɪv] *adj* digestif

diges'tive tract' *s* appareil *m* digestif

digit ['dɪdʒɪt] *s* chiffre *m*; (*finger*) doigt *m*; (*toe*) doigt du pied

digitalis [,dɪdʒɪ'telɪs], [,dɪdʒɪ'telɪs] *s* (bot) digitale *f*; (pharm) digitaline *f*

dignified ['dɪgnɪ,faid] *adj* (*air*) digne

digni·fy ['dɪgnɪ,fai] *v* (*pret & pp* -**fied**) *tr* glorifier, honorer

dignitar·y ['dɪgnɪ,teri] *s* (*pl* -ies) dignitaire *mf*

digni·ty ['dɪgnɪti] *s* (*pl* -ties) dignité *f*; **to stand on one's dignity** rester sur son quant-à-soi, le prendre de haut

digress [dɪ'gres], [dai'gres] *intr* faire une digression

digression [dɪ'greʃən], [dai'greʃən] *s* digression *f*

dihedral [dai'hidrəl] *adj & s* dièdre *m*

dike [daɪk] *s* digue *f*

dilapidated [dɪ'læpɪ,detɪd] *adj* délabré, déglingué

dilate [dai'let] *tr* dilater ‖ *intr* se dilater

dilatory ['dɪlə,tori] *adj* lent, tardif; (*strategy, answer*) dilatoire

dilemma [dɪ'lemə] *s* dilemme *m*

dilettan·te [,dɪlɪ'tænti] *adj* dilettante ‖ *s* (*pl* -**tes** or -**ti** [ti]) dilettante *mf*

diligence ['dɪlɪdʒəns] *s* diligence *f*

diligent ['dɪlɪdʒənt] *adj* diligent

dill [dɪl] *s* fenouil *m* bâtard, aneth *m*

dillydal·ly ['dɪlɪ,dæli] *v* (*pret & pp* -**lied**) *intr* traînasser

dilute [dɪ'lut], [dai'lut] *adj* dilué ‖ [dɪ'lut] *tr* diluer, délayer

dilution [dɪ'luʃən] *s* dilution *f*

dim [dɪm] *adj* faible, indistinct; (*forebodings*) obscur; (*memory*) effacé; (*color*) terne; (*idea of what is going on*) obtus, confus; **to take a dim view of** envisager sans enthousiasme ‖ *v* (*pret & pp* **dimmed**; *ger* **dimming**) *tr* affaiblir, obscurcir; (*beauty*) ternir; (*the headlights*) baisser, mettre en code ‖ *intr* s'affaiblir, s'obscurcir; (*said of color, beauty, etc.*) se ternir

dime [daim] *s* monnaie *f* de dix cents américains

dimension [dɪ'menʃən] *s* dimension *f*

diminish [dɪ'mɪnɪ/] *tr & intr* diminuer

diminutive [dɪ'mɪnjətɪv] *adj & s* diminutif *m*

dimi·ty ['dɪmɪti] *s* (*pl* -ties) basin *m*, brillanté *m*

dimly ['dɪmli] *adv* indistinctement

dimmers ['dɪmərz] *spl* (aut) feux *mpl* code, feux de croisement; **to put on the dimmers** se mettre en code

dimple ['dɪmpəl] *s* fossette *f*

dim'wit' *s* (slang) sot *m*, niais *m*

din [dɪn] *s* tapage *m*, fracas *m* ‖ *v* (*pret & pp* **dinned**; *ger* **dinning**) *tr* assourdir; répéter sans cesse ‖ *intr* sonner bruyamment

dine [dain] *tr* fêter par un dîner ‖ *intr* dîner; **to dine out** dîner en ville

diner ['dainər] *s* dîneur *m*; (*short-order restaurant*) plats-cuisinés *m*; (rr) wagon-restaurant *m*

dinette [dai'net] *s* coin-repas *m*

ding-dong ['dɪŋ,dɔŋ], ['dɪŋ,dɑŋ] *s* tintement *m*, digue-din-don *m*

din·ghy ['dɪŋgi] *s* (*pl* -**ghies**) canot *m*, youyou *m*

din·gy ['dɪndʒi] *adj* (*comp* -**gier**; *super* -**giest**) défraîchi, terne

din'ing car' *s* wagon-restaurant *m*

din'ing hall' *s* salle *f* à manger; (*of university*) réfectoire *m*

din'ing-room' *s* salle *f* à manger

din'ing-room suite' *s* salle *f* à manger

dinner ['dinər] *s* dîner *m*

din'ner coat' *s* smoking *m*

din'ner dance' *s* dîner *m* suivi de bal

din'ner guest' *s* convive *mf*, invité *m*

din'ner jack'et *s* smoking *m*

din'ner pail' *s* potager *m*

din'ner set' *s* service *m* de table

din'ner time' *s* heure *f* du dîner

dinosaur ['dainə,sɔr] *s* dinosaure *m*

dint [dɪnt] *s*—**by dint of** à force de

diocese ['dai·ə,sis], ['dai·əsɪs] *s* diocèse *m*

diode ['dai·od] *s* diode *f*

dioxide [dai'ɑksaid] *s* bioxyde *m*

dip [dɪp] *s* (*immersion*) plongeon *m*; (*swim*) baignade *f*; (*slope*) pente *f*; (*of magnetic needle*) inclinaison *f* ‖ *v* (*pret* & *pp* **dipped**; *ger* **dipping**) *tr* plonger; (*a flag*) marquer ‖ *intr* plonger; (*said of magnetic needle*) incliner; (*said of scale*) pencher; **to dip into** (*a book*) feuilleter; (*one's capital*) prendre dans

diphtheria [dɪfˈθɪrɪ·ə] *s* diphtérie *f*

diphthong [ˈdɪfθɒŋ], [ˈdɪfθaŋ] *s* diphtongue *f*

diphthongize [ˈdɪfθɒŋˌgaɪz], [ˈdɪfθaŋ- ˌgaɪz] *tr* diphtonguer ‖ *intr* se diphtonguer

diploma [dɪˈplomə] *s* diplôme *m*

diploma·cy [dɪˈploməsi] *s* (*pl* **-cies**) diplomatie *f*

diplomat [ˈdɪpləˌmæt] *s* diplomate *mf*

diplomatic [ˌdɪpləˈmætɪk] *adj* diplomatique, diplomate

dip'lomat'ic pouch' *s* valise *f* diplomatique

dipper [ˈdɪpər] *s* louche *f*, cuiller *f* à pot

dip'stick' *s* jauge *f*

dire [daɪr] *adj* affreux, terrible

direct [dɪˈrɛkt], [daɪˈrɛkt] *adj* direct, franc, sincère ‖ *tr* diriger; (*to order*) ordonner; (*a letter, question, etc.*) adresser; (*to point out*) indiquer; (*theat*) mettre en scène

direct' cur'rent *s* courant *m* continu

direct' di'aling *s* (*telp*) automatique *m* interurbain

direct' hit' *s* coup *m* or tir *m* direct

direction [dɪˈrɛkʃən], [daɪˈrɛkʃən] *s* direction *f*; (*e.g., of a street*) sens *m*; (*theat*) mise *f* en scène; **directions** instructions *fpl*; (*for use*) mode *m* d'emploi

directional [dɪˈrɛkʃənəl], [daɪˈrɛkʃən- əl] *adj* directionnel

direc'tional sig'nal *s* clignotant *m*

directive [dɪˈrɛktɪv], [daɪˈrɛktɪv] *s* ordre *m*, avis *m*

direct' ob'ject *s* (*gram*) complément *m* direct

director [dɪˈrɛktər], [daɪˈrɛktər] *s* directeur *m*, administrateur *m*, chef *m*; (*of a board*) membre *m* du conseil, votant *m*; (*theat*) metteur *m* en scène

direc'tor·ship' *s* direction *f*, directorat *m*

directo·ry [dɪˈrɛktəri], [daɪˈrɛktəri] *s* (*pl* **-ries**) (*board of directors*) conseil *m* d'administration; (*e.g., of telephone*) annuaire *m*; (*e.g., of genealogy*) almanach *m*; (*eccl*) directoire *m*

dirge [dʌrdʒ] *s* hymne *f* or chant *m* funèbre

dirigible [ˈdɪrɪdʒɪbəl] *adj* & *s* dirigeable *m*

dirt [dʌrt] *s* saleté *f*, ordure *f*; (*on clothes, skin, etc.*) crasse *f*; (*mire*) crotte *f*, boue *f*; (*earth*) terre *f*

dirt'-cheap' *adj* vendu à vil prix

dirt' road' *s* chemin *m* de terre

dirt·y [ˈdʌrti] *adj* (*comp* **-ier**; *super* **-iest**) sale, malpropre; (*clothes, skin, etc.*) crasseux; (*muddy*) crotté, boueux; (*mean*) méchant, vilain

dir'ty lin'en *s* linge *m* sale; **don't wash your dirty linen in public** il faut laver son linge sale en famille

dir'ty trick' *s* (*slang*) sale tour *m*

disabili·ty [ˌdɪsəˈbɪlɪti] *s* (*pl* **-ties**) incapacité *f*, invalidité *f*

disabil'ity pen'sion *s* pension *f* d'invalidité

disable [dɪsˈebəl] *tr* rendre incapable, mettre hors de combat; (*to hurt the limbs of*) estropier, mutiler

disabled *adj* (*serviceman*) invalide; (*ship*) désemparé

disa'bled vet'eran *s* invalide *m*, réformé *m*

disabuse [ˌdɪsəˈbjuz] *tr* désabuser

disadvantage [ˌdɪsədˈvæntɪdʒ], [ˌdɪs- əd'vantɪdʒ] *s* désavantage *m* ‖ *tr* désavantager

disadvantageous [dɪsˌædvənˈtedʒəs] *adj* désavantageux

disagree [ˌdɪsəˈgri] *intr* différer; **to disagree with** (*to cause discomfort to*) ne pas convenir à; (*to dissent from*) donner tort à

disagreeable [ˌdɪsəˈgri·əbəl] *adj* désagréable; (*mood, weather, etc.*) maussade

disagreement [ˌdɪsəˈgrimənt] *s* désaccord *m*, différend *m*

disallow [ˌdɪsəˈlau] *tr* désapprouver, rejeter

disappear [ˌdɪsəˈpɪr] *intr* disparaître; (*phonet*) s'amuïr

disappearance [ˌdɪsəˈpɪrəns] *s* disparition *f*; (*phonet*) amuïssement *m*

disappoint [ˌdɪsəˈpɔɪnt] *tr* décevoir, désappointer

disappointed *adj* déçu

disappointment [ˌdɪsəˈpɔɪntmənt] *s* déception *f*, désappointement *m*

disapproval [ˌdɪsəˈpruvəl] *s* désapprobation *f*

disapprove [ˌdɪsəˈpruv] *tr* & *intr* désapprouver

disarm [dɪsˈɑrm] *tr* & *intr* désarmer

disarmament [dɪsˈɑrməmənt] *s* désarmement *m*

disarming [dɪsˈɑrmɪŋ] *adj* désarmant

disarray [ˌdɪsəˈre] *s* désarroi *m*, désordre *m*; **in disarray** (*said of apparel*) à demi vêtu ‖ *tr* mettre en désarroi

disassemble [ˌdɪsəˈsɛmbəl] *tr* démonter, désassembler

disassociate [ˌdɪsəˈsoʃɪˌet] *tr* dissocier

disaster [dɪˈzæstər], [dɪˈzɑstər] *s* désastre *m*

disastrous [dɪˈzæstrəs], [dɪˈzɑstrəs] *adj* désastreux

disavow [ˌdɪsəˈvau] *tr* désavouer

disavowal [ˌdɪsəˈvau·əl] *s* désaveu *m*

disband [dɪsˈbænd] *tr* licencier, congédier ‖ *intr* se débander, se disperser

dis·bar [dɪsˈbɑr] *v* (*pret* & *pp* **-barred**; *ger* **-barring**) *tr* (*law*) rayer du barreau

disbelief [ˌdɪsbɪˈlif] *s* incroyance *f*

disbelieve [ˌdɪsbɪˈliv] *tr* & *intr* ne pas croire

disburse [dɪsˈbʌrs] *tr* débourser

disbursement [dɪsˈbʌrsmənt] *s* déboursement *m*; **disbursements** débours *mpl*

disc [dɪsk] *s* disque *m*

discard [dɪsˈkɑrd] *s* rebut *m*; (cards) écart *m*; **discards** marchandises *fpl* de rebut || *tr* mettre de côté, jeter; (cards) écarter || *intr* (cards) se défausser

discern [dɪˈzʌrn], [dɪˈsʌrn] *tr* discerner, percevoir

discernible [dɪˈzʌrnɪbəl], [dɪˈsʌrnɪbəl] *adj* discernable

discerning [dɪˈzʌrnɪŋ], [dɪˈsʌrnɪŋ] *adj* judicieux, pénétrant, éclairé

discernment [dɪˈzʌrnmənt], [dɪˈsʌrnmənt] *s* discernement *m*

discharge [dɪsˈtʃɑrdʒ] *s* décharge *f*; (of a prisoner) élargissement *m*; (from a job) congé *m*, renvoi *m*; (from the armed forces) libération *f*; (from the armed forces for unfitness) réforme *f*; (from a wound) suppuration *f* || *tr* décharger; (a prisoner) élargir; (an employee) congédier, renvoyer, licencier; (a soldier) libérer, réformer || *intr* se décharger; (pathol) suppurer

disciple [dɪˈsaɪpəl] *s* disciple *m*

disciplinarian [ˌdɪsɪplɪˈnɛrɪ·ən] *s* partisan *m* d'une forte discipline; personne *f* qui impose une forte discipline

disciplinary [ˈdɪsɪplɪˌnɛri] *adj* disciplinaire

discipline [ˈdɪsɪplɪn] *s* discipline *f* || *tr* discipliner

disclaim [dɪsˈklem] *tr* désavouer, renier

disclaimer [dɪsˈklemər] *s* désaveu *m*

disclose [dɪsˈkloz] *tr* découvrir, révéler

disclosure [dɪsˈkloʒər] *s* découverte *f*, révélation *f*

discolor [dɪsˈkʌlər] *tr* décolorer || *intr* se décolorer

discoloration [dɪsˌkʌləˈreʃən] *s* décoloration *f*

discomfit [dɪsˈkʌmfɪt] *tr* décontenancer, bafouer

discomfiture [dɪsˈkʌmfɪtʃər] *s* déconfiture *f*, déconvenue *f*

discomfort [dɪsˈkʌmfərt] *s* malaise *m*; (inconvenience) gêne *f* || *tr* gêner

disconcert [ˌdɪskənˈsʌrt] *tr* déconcerter

disconnect [ˌdɪskəˈnɛkt] *tr* désunir, séparer; (a mechanism) débrayer; (a plug) débrancher; (current) couper

disconsolate [dɪsˈkɑnsəlɪt] *adj* désolé, inconsolable

discontent [ˌdɪskənˈtɛnt] *adj* mécontent || *s* mécontentement *m* || *tr* mécontenter

discontented *adj* mécontent

discontinue [ˌdɪskənˈtɪnju] *tr* discontinuer

discontinuous [ˌdɪskənˈtɪnju·əs] *adj* discontinu

discord [ˈdɪskɔrd] *s* discorde *f*, désaccord *m*; (mus) discordance *f*

discordance [dɪsˈkɔrdəns] *s* discordance *f*

discotheque [ˈdɪskəˌtɛk] *s* discothèque *f*

discount [ˈdɪskaunt] *s* escompte *m*, remise *f*, rabais *m* || [ˈdɪskaunt], [dɪsˈkaunt] *tr* escompter, rabattre

dis'count rate' *s* taux *m* d'escompte

discourage [dɪsˈkʌrɪdʒ] *tr* décourager

discouragement [dɪsˈkʌrɪdʒmənt] *s* découragement *m*

discourse [ˈdɪskors], [dɪsˈkors] *s* discours *m* || [dɪsˈkors] *intr* discourir

discourteous [dɪsˈkʌrtɪ·əs] *adj* impoli, discourtois

discourte·sy [dɪsˈkʌrtəsi] *s* (pl -sies) impolitesse *f*, discourtoisie *f*

discover [dɪsˈkʌvər] *tr* découvrir

discoverer [dɪsˈkʌvərər] *s* découvreur *m*

discover·y [dɪsˈkʌvəri] *s* (pl -ies) découverte *f*

discredit [dɪsˈkrɛdɪt] *s* discrédit *m* || *tr* discréditer

discreditable [dɪsˈkrɛdɪtəbəl] *adj* déshonorant, peu honorable

discreet [dɪsˈkrit] *adj* discret

discrepan·cy [dɪsˈkrɛpənsi] *s* (pl -cies) désaccord *m*, différence *f*

discretion [dɪsˈkrɛʃən] *s* discrétion *f*

discriminate [dɪsˈkrɪmɪˌnet] *tr & intr* discriminer; **to discriminate against** défavoriser

discrimination [dɪsˌkrɪmɪˈneʃən] *s* discrimination *f*

discriminatory [dɪsˈkrɪmɪnəˌtori] *adj* discriminatoire

discus [ˈdɪskəs] *s* (sports) disque *m*, palet *m*

discuss [dɪsˈkʌs] *tr & intr* discuter

discussion [dɪsˈkʌʃən] *s* discussion *f*

disdain [dɪsˈden] *s* dédain *m* || *tr* dédaigner

disdainful [dɪsˈdenfəl] *adj* dédaigneux

disease [dɪˈziz] *s* maladie *f*

diseased *adj* malade

disembark [ˌdɪsɛmˈbɑrk] *tr & intr* débarquer

disembarkation [dɪsˌɛmbɑrˈkeʃən] *s* débarquement *m*

disembow·el [ˌdɪsɛmˈbau·əl] *v* (pret & pp -eled or -elled; ger -eling or -elling) *tr* éventrer

disenchant [ˌdɪsɛnˈtʃænt], [ˌdɪsɛnˈtʃɑnt] *tr* désenchanter

disenchantment [ˌdɪsɛnˈtʃæntmənt], [ˌdɪsɛnˈtʃɑntmənt] *s* désenchantement *m*

disengage [ˌdɪsɛnˈgedʒ] *tr* dégager; (toothed wheels) désengrener; (a motor) débrayer || *intr* se dégager

disengagement [ˌdɪsɛnˈgedʒmənt] *s* dégagement *m*, détachement *m*

disentangle [ˌdɪsɛnˈtæŋgəl] *tr* démêler, débrouiller

disentanglement [ˌdɪsɛnˈtæŋgəlmənt] *s* démêlage *m*, débrouillement *m*

disestablish [ˌdɪsɛsˈtæblɪʃ] *tr* (the Church) séparer de l'État

disfavor [dɪsˈfevər] *s* défaveur *f* || *tr* défavoriser

disfigure [dɪsˈfɪgjər] *tr* défigurer, enlaidir

disfigurement [dɪsˈfɪgjərmənt] *s* défiguration *f*

disfranchise [dɪsˈfrænt/aɪz] *tr* priver de ses droits civiques

disgorge [dɪsˈgɔrdʒ] *tr* & *intr* dégorger

disgrace [dɪsˈgres] *s* déshonneur *m* || *tr* déshonorer; (*to deprive of favor*) disgracier; **to disgrace oneself** se déshonorer

disgraceful [dɪsˈgresfəl] *adj* déshonorant, honteux

disgruntled [dɪsˈgrʌntəld] *adj* contrarié, de mauvaise humeur

disguise [dɪsˈgaɪz] *s* déguisement *m* || *tr* déguiser

disgust [dɪsˈgʌst] *s* dégoût *m* || *tr* dégoûter

disgusting [dɪsˈgʌstɪŋ] *adj* dégoûtant

dish [dɪʃ] *s* plat *m*; (*food*) mets *m*, plat; **to wash the dishes** faire la vaisselle || *tr*—**to dish up** servir

dish' clos'et *s* étagère *f* à vaisselle

dish'cloth' *s* lavette *f*

dishearten [dɪsˈhɑrtən] *tr* décourager

dishev•el [dɪˈʃɛvəl] *v* (*pret* & *pp* **-eled** or **-elled**; *ger* **-eling** or **-elling**) *tr* écheveler

dishonest [dɪsˈɑnɪst] *adj* malhonnête, déloyal

dishones•ty [dɪsˈɑnɪsti] *s* (*pl* **-ties**) malhonnêteté *f*, déloyauté *f*, improbité *f*

dishonor [dɪsˈɑnər] *s* déshonneur *m* || *tr* déshonorer

dishonorable [dɪsˈɑnərəbəl] *adj* déshonorant

dish'pan' *s* bassine *f*

dish' rack' *s* égouttoir *m*

dish'rag' *s* lavette *f*

dish'tow'el *s* torchon *m*

dish'wash'er *s* machine *f* à laver la vaisselle, lave-vaisselles *f*; (*person*) plongeur *m*

dish'wa'ter *s* eau *f* de vaisselle

disillusion [ˌdɪsɪˈluʒən] *s* désillusion *f* || *tr* désillusionner

disillusionment [ˌdɪsɪˈluʒənmənt] *s* désillusionnement *m*

disinclination [dɪsˌɪnklɪˈneʃən] *s* répugnance *f*, aversion *f*

disinclined [ˌdɪsɪnˈklaɪnd] *adj* indisposé

disinfect [ˌdɪsɪnˈfɛkt] *tr* désinfecter

disinfectant [ˌdɪsɪnˈfɛktənt] *adj* & *s* désinfectant *m*

disingenuous [ˌdɪsɪnˈdʒɛnjuˌəs] *adj* insincère, sans franchise

disinherit [ˌdɪsɪnˈhɛrɪt] *tr* déshériter

disintegrate [dɪsˈɪntɪˌgret] *tr* désagréger; (*nucl*) désintégrer || *intr* se désagréger; (*nucl*) se désintégrer

disintegration [dɪsˌɪntɪˈgreʃən] *s* désagrégation *f*; (*nucl*) désintégration *f*

disin•ter [ˌdɪsɪnˈtʌr] *v* (*pret* & *pp* **-terred**; *ger* **-terring**) *tr* déterrer

disinterested [dɪsˈɪntəˌrɛstɪd], [dɪsˈɪntrɪstɪd] *adj* désintéressé

disjointed [dɪsˈdʒɔɪntɪd] *adj* désarticulé; (*e.g., style*) décousu

disjunctive [dɪsˈdʒʌŋktɪv] *adj* disjonctif; (*pronoun*) tonique

disk [dɪsk] *s* disque *m*

disk' jock'ey *s* présentateur *m* de disques

dislike [dɪsˈlaɪk] *s* aversion *f*; **to take a dislike for** prendre en aversion || *tr* ne pas aimer

dislocate [ˈdɪsloˌket] *tr* disloquer; (*a joint*) luxer

dislodge [dɪsˈlɑdʒ] *tr* déplacer; (*e.g., the enemy*) déloger

disloyal [dɪsˈlɔɪ•əl] *adj* déloyal

disloyal•ty [dɪsˈlɔɪ•əlti] *s* (*pl* **-ties**) déloyauté *f*

dismal [ˈdɪzməl] *adj* sombre, triste

dismantle [dɪsˈmæntəl] *tr* démanteler; (*a machine*) démonter; (*a ship*) désarmer

dismay [dɪsˈme] *s* consternation *f* || *tr* consterner

dismember [dɪsˈmɛmbər] *tr* démembrer

dismiss [dɪsˈmɪs] *tr* congédier; (*a servant*) renvoyer; (*an employee*) licencier; (*a government official*) destituer; (*a class in school*) terminer

dismissal [dɪsˈmɪsəl] *s* congédiement *m*; (*from a job*) congé *m*, renvoi *m*; (*of an appeal*) (law) rejet *m*

dismount [dɪsˈmaunt] *tr* démonter || *intr* descendre

disobedience [ˌdɪsəˈbidɪ•əns] *s* désobéissance *f*

disobedient [ˌdɪsəˈbidɪ•ənt] *adj* désobéissant

disobey [ˌdɪsəˈbe] *tr* désobéir (with *dat*); **to be disobeyed** être désobéi || *intr* désobéir

disorder [dɪsˈɔrdər] *s* désordre *m* || *tr* désordonner

disorderly [dɪsˈɔrdərli] *adj* désordonné, déréglé; (*crowd*) turbulent, effervescent

disor'derly con'duct *s* conduite *f* désordonnée

disor'derly house' *s* maison *f* de prostitution; maison de jeu

disorganize [dɪsˈɔrgəˌnaɪz] *tr* désorganiser

disoriented [dɪsˈɔrɪˌɛntɪd] *adj* désorienté

disown [dɪsˈon] *tr* désavouer, renier

disparage [dɪˈspærɪdʒ] *tr* dénigrer, déprécier

disparagement [dɪˈspærɪdʒmənt] *s* dénigrement *m*, dépréciation *f*

disparate [ˈdɪspərɪt] *adj* disparate

dispari•ty [dɪˈspærɪti] *s* (*pl* **-ties**) disparité *f*

dispassionate [dɪsˈpæ/ənɪt] *adj* calme; impartial

dispatch [dɪˈspæt/] *s* dépêche *f*; (*shipment*) envoi *m*, expédition *f*; (*promptness*) promptitude *f* || *tr* dépêcher; (coll) expédier

dis•pel [dɪˈspɛl] *v* (*pret* & *pp* **-pelled**; *ger* **-pelling**) *tr* dissiper, disperser

dispensa•ry [dɪˈspɛnsəri] *s* (*pl* **-ries**) dispensaire *m*

dispensation [ˌdɪspɛnˈse/ən] (*dispensing*) dispensation *f*; (*exemption*) dispense *f*

dispense [dɪˈspɛns] *tr* dispenser, distribuer || *intr*—**to dispense with** se passer de; se défaire de

dispenser [dɪˈspɛnsər] *s* dispensateur *m*; (*automatic*) distributeur *m*

disperse [dɪ'spʌrs] *tr* disperser ‖ *intr* se disperser

dispersion [dɪ'spʌrʒən], [dɪ'spʌrʃən] *s* dispersion *f*

dispirit [dɪ'spɪrɪt] *tr* décourager

displace [dɪs'ples] *tr* déplacer; (*to take the place of*) remplacer

displaced' per'son *s* personne *f* déplacée

displacement [dɪs'plesmənt] *s* déplacement *m*; (*substitution*) remplacement *m*

display [dɪ'sple] *s* exposition *f*, étalage *m*; (*of emotion*) manifestation *f* ‖ *tr* exposer, étaler; (*anger, courage, etc.*) manifester; (*ignorance*) révéler

display' cab'inet *s* vitrine *f*

display' win'dow *s* vitrine *f*, devanture *f*

displease [dɪs'pliz] *tr* déplaire (with *dat*)

displeasing [dɪs'plizɪŋ] *adj* déplaisant

displeasure [dɪs'plɛʒər] *s* déplaisir *m*, mécontentement *m*

disposable [dɪ'spozəbəl] *adj* (*available*) disponible; (*made to be disposed of*) à jeter; (*container*) perdu, e.g., disposable bottle verre perdu

disposal [dɪ'spozəl] *s* disposition *f*; (*of a question*) résolution *f*; (*of trash, garbage, etc.*) destruction *f*

dispose [dɪ'spoz] *tr* disposer ‖ *intr* disposer; **to dispose of** disposer de; (*to get rid of*) se défaire de; (*a question*) résoudre, trancher

disposed *adj*—**to be disposed to** se disposer à, être porté à

disposition [ˌdɪspə'zɪʃən] *s* disposition *f*; (*mental outlook*) naturel *m*; (mil) dispositif *m*

dispossess [ˌdɪspə'zɛs] *tr* déposséder; expulser

disproof [dɪs'pruf] *s* réfutation *f*

disproportionate [ˌdɪsprə'porʃənɪt] *adj* disproportionné

disprove [dɪs'pruv] *tr* réfuter

dispute [dɪs'pjut] *s* dispute *f*; **beyond dispute** incontestable ‖ *tr* disputer ‖ *intr* se disputer

disqual•i•fy [dɪs'kwɑlɪˌfaɪ] *v* (*pret & pp* -**fied**) *tr* disqualifier

disquiet [dɪs'kwaɪ•ət] *s* inquiétude *f* ‖ *tr* inquiéter

disquisition [ˌdɪskwɪ'zɪʃən] *s* essai *m*, traité *m* considérable

disregard [ˌdɪsrɪ'gɑrd] *s* indifférence *f*; **disregard for** manque *m* d'égards envers ‖ *tr* ne pas faire cas de, passer sous silence

disrepair [ˌdɪsrɪ'per] *s* délabrement *m*

disreputable [dɪs'repjətəbəl] *adj* déshonorant, suspect; (*shabby*) débraillé, râpé

disrepute [ˌdɪsrɪ'pjut] *s* discrédit *m*

disrespect [ˌdɪsrɪ'spɛkt] *s* irrévérence *f*; manque *m* de respect, irrespect *m*

disrespectful [ˌdɪsrɪ'spɛktfəl] *adj* irrévérencieux, irrespectueux; **to be disrespectful to** manquer de respect à

disrobe [dɪs'rob] *tr* déshabiller ‖ *intr* se déshabiller

disrupt [dɪs'rʌpt] *tr* rompre; (*to throw into disorder*) bouleverser

disruption [dɪs'rʌpʃən] *s* rupture *f*; (*disorganization*) bouleversement *m*

dissatisfaction [ˌdɪssætɪs'fækʃən] *s* mécontentement *m*

dissatisfied *adj* mécontent

dissatis•fy [dɪs'sætɪsˌfaɪ] *v* (*pret & pp* -**fied**) *tr* mécontenter

dissect [dɪ'sɛkt] *tr* disséquer

dissection [dɪ'sɛkʃən] *s* dissection *f*

dissemble [dɪ'sɛmbəl] *tr & intr* dissimuler

disseminate [dɪ'sɛmɪˌnet] *tr* disséminer

dissension [dɪ'sɛnʃən] *s* dissension *f*

dissent [dɪ'sɛnt] *s* dissentiment *m*; (*nonconformity*) dissidence *f* ‖ *intr* différer

dissenter [dɪ'sɛntər] *s* dissident *m*

dissertation [ˌdɪsər'teʃən] *s* dissertation *f*; (*for a degree*) thèse *f*; (*speech*) discours *m*

disservice [dɪs'sʌrvɪs] *s* mauvais service *m*, tort *m*

dissidence [ˈdɪsɪdəns] *s* dissidence *f*

dissident [ˈdɪsɪdənt] *adj & s* dissident *m*

dissimilar [dɪ'sɪmɪlər] *adj* dissemblable

dissimilate [dɪ'sɪmɪˌlet] *tr* (phonet) dissimiler

dissimulate [dɪ'sɪmjəˌlet] *tr & intr* dissimuler

dissipate [ˈdɪsɪˌpet] *tr* dissiper; (*energy, heat, etc.*) disperser ‖ *intr* se dissiper

dissipated *adj* dissipé; débauché

dissipation [ˌdɪsɪ'peʃən] *s* dissipation *f*; (*of energy, heat, etc.*) dispersion *f*

dissociate [dɪ'soʃɪˌet] *tr* dissocier ‖ *intr* se dissocier

dissolute [ˈdɪsəˌlut] *adj* dissolu •

dissolution [ˌdɪsə'luʃən] *s* dissolution *f*

dissolve [dɪ'zɑlv] *tr* dissoudre ‖ *intr* se dissoudre

dissonance [ˈdɪsənəns] *s* dissonance *f*

dissuade [dɪ'swed] *tr* dissuader

distaff [ˈdɪstæf], [ˈdɪstɑf] *s* quenouille *f*

dis'taff side' *s* côté *m* maternel

distance [ˈdɪstəns] *s* distance *f*; **at a distance** à distance; **in the distance** au loin, dans le lointain ‖ *tr* distancer

distant [ˈdɪstənt] *adj* distant; (*uncle, cousin, etc.*) éloigné

distaste [dɪs'test] *s* dégoût *m*, aversion *f*

distasteful [dɪs'testfəl] *adj* dégoûtant, répugnant

distemper [dɪs'tempər] *s* (*of dog*) roupie *f*; (*painting*) détrempe *f* ‖ *tr* peindre en détrempe

distend [dɪ'stend] *tr* distendre ‖ *intr* se distendre

distension [dɪ'stenʃən] *s* distension *f*

distill [dɪ'stɪl] *tr* distiller

distillation [ˌdɪstɪ'leʃən] *s* distillation *f*

distiller•y [dɪs'tɪləri] *s* (*pl* -**ies**) distillerie *f*

distinct [dɪ'stɪŋkt] *adj* distinct; (*unusual*) insigne

distinction [dɪs'tɪŋkʃən] *s* distinction *f*

distinctive [dɪs'tɪŋktɪv] *adj* distinctif

distinguish [dɪs'tɪŋgwɪʃ] *tr* distinguer; **to distinguish oneself** se distinguer, se faire remarquer

distinguished *adj* distingué

distort [dɪs'tɔrt] tr déformer
distortion [dɪs'tɔrʃən] s déformation f; (of meaning) sens m forcé; (phot, rad) distorsion f
distract [dɪ'strækt] tr (to amuse) distraire; (to bewilder) bouleverser
distracted adj bouleversé, éperdu
distraction [dɪ'strækʃən] s (amusement) distraction f; (madness) folie f
distraught [dɪ'strɔt] adj bouleversé
distress [dɪ'stres] s détresse f || tr affliger
distress' call' s signal m de détresse
distressing [dɪ'stresɪŋ] adj affligeant, pénible
distribute [dɪ'strɪbjut] tr distribuer
distribution [,dɪstrə'bjuʃən] s distribution f
distributor [dɪ'strɪbjətər] s distributeur m; (for a product) concessionnaire mf
district ['dɪstrɪkt] s contrée f, région f; (of a city) quartier m; (administrative division) district m, circonscription f || tr diviser en districts
dis'trict attor'ney s procureur m de la République, procureur général
distrust [dɪs'trʌst] s défiance f, méfiance f || tr se défier de, se méfier de
distrustful [dɪs'trʌstfəl] adj défiant
disturb [dɪs'tɜrb] tr déranger, troubler; (the peace) perturber
disturbance [dɪs'tɜrbəns] s dérangement m, trouble m; (riot) bagarre f, émeute f; (in the atmosphere or magnetic field) perturbation f
disuse [dɪs'jus] s désuétude f
ditch [dɪtʃ] s fossé m; to the last ditch jusqu'à la dernière extrémité || tr fossoyer; (slang) se défaire de || intr (aer) faire un amerrissage forcé
ditch' reed' s (bot) laîche f
dither ['dɪðər] s agitation f; to be in a dither (coll) s'agiter sans but
dit•to ['dɪto] s (pl -tos) le même; (on a duplicating machine) copie f, duplicata m || adv dito, de même, idem || tr copier, reproduire
dit•ty ['dɪti] s (pl -ties) chansonnette f; **old ditty** (coll) vieux refrain m
diva ['divə] s diva f
divan [dɪ'væn], [dɪ'væn] s divan m
dive [daɪv] s plongeon m; (of a submarine) plongée f; (aer) piqué m; (coll) gargote f, cabaret m borgne || v (pret & pp dived or dove [dov]) intr plonger; (said of submarine) plonger, effectuer une plongée; (aer) piquer; to dive for (e.g., pearls) pêcher; to dive into (coll) piquer une tête dans
dive'-bomb' tr & intr bombarder en piqué
dive' bomb'er s bombardier m à piqué
dive' bomb'ing s bombardement m en piqué, piqué m
diver ['daɪvər] s plongeur m; (person who works under water) scaphandrier m; (orn) plongeon m
diverge [dɪ'vʌrdʒ], [daɪ'vʌrdʒ] intr diverger

divers ['daɪvərz] adj divers
diverse [dɪ'vʌrs], [daɪ'vʌrs], ['daɪvʌrs] adj divers
diversi•fy [dɪ'vʌrsɪ,faɪ], [daɪ'vʌrsɪ,faɪ] v (pret & pp -fied) tr diversifier || intr se diversifier
diversion [dɪ'vʌrʒən], [daɪ'vʌrʒən] s diversion f
diversi•ty [dɪ'vʌrsɪti], [daɪ'vʌrsɪti] s (pl -ties) diversité f
divert [dɪ'vʌrt], [daɪ'vʌrt] tr détourner; (to entertain) distraire, divertir
diverting [dɪ'vʌrtɪŋ], [daɪ'vʌrtɪŋ] adj divertissant
divest [dɪ'vest], [daɪ'vest] tr dépouiller; to divest oneself of se défaire de; (property, holdings) se déposséder de
divide [dɪ'vaɪd] s (geog) ligne f de partage || tr diviser || intr se diviser
dividend ['dɪvɪ,dend] s dividende m
dividers [dɪ'vaɪdərz] spl compas m de mesure
dividing [dɪ'vaɪdɪŋ] s division f; **dividing up** répartition f, partage m
divination [,dɪvɪ'neʃən] s divination f
divine [dɪ'vaɪn] adj divin || s ecclésiastique mf || tr deviner
diviner [dɪ'vaɪnər] s devin m
diving ['daɪvɪŋ] s plongeon m
div'ing bell' s cloche f à plongeur
div'ing board' s plongeoir m, tremplin m
div'ing suit' s scaphandre m
div'ing rod' [dɪ'vaɪnɪŋ] s baguette f divinatoire
divini•ty [dɪ'vɪnɪti] s (pl -ties) divinité f; (subject of study) théologie f; **the Divinity** Dieu m
divisible [dɪ'vɪzɪbəl] adj divisible
division [dɪ'vɪʒən] s division f
divisor [dɪ'vaɪzər] s diviseur m
divorce [dɪ'vors] s divorce m; to get a divorce divorcer; to get a divorce from (husband or wife) divorcer d'avec || tr (the married couple) divorcer; (husband or wife) divorcer d'avec || intr divorcer
divorcee [dɪvor'si] s divorcée f
divulge [dɪ'vʌldʒ] tr divulguer
dizziness ['dɪzɪnɪs] s vertige m
diz•zy ['dɪzi] adj (comp -zier; super -ziest) vertigineux; (coll) étourdi, farfelu; to feel dizzy avoir le vertige; to make dizzy étourdir
do [du] v (3d pers does [dʌz]; pret did [dɪd]; pp done [dʌn]; ger doing ['du·ɪŋ]) tr faire; (homage; justice; a good turn) rendre; to do over refaire; to do up emballer, envelopper || intr faire; **how do you do?** enchanté de faire votre connaissance; comment allez-vous?; **that will do** c'est bien; en voilà assez; **that will never do** cela n'ira jamais; **to do away with** supprimer; **to do without** se passer de; **will I do?** suis-je bien comme ça?; **will it do?** ça va-t-il comme ça? || aux used in English but not specifically expressed in French: 1) in questions, e.g., **do you speak French?** parlez-vous français?; 2) in negative sentences, e.g., **I do not speak French**

je ne parle pas français; 3) as a substitute for another verb in an elliptical question, e.g., **I saw him. Did you?** je l'ai vu. L'avez-vous vu?; 4) for emphasis, e.g., **I do believe what you told me** je crois bien ce que vous m'avez dit; 5) in inversions after certain adverbs, e.g., **hardly did we finish when . . .** à peine avions-nous fini que . . .; 6) in an imperative entreaty, e.g., **do come in!** entrez donc!

do. *abbr* (ditto) d°

docile ['dɑsɪl] *adj* docile

dock [dɑk] *s* embarcadère *m*, quai *m*; *(area including piers and waterways)* bassin *m*, dock *m*; (bot) oseille *f*, patience *f*; (law) banc *m* des prévenus ‖ *tr* faire entrer au bassin; *(an animal)* couper la queue à; *(s.o.'s salary)* retrancher ‖ *intr* (naut) s'amarrer au quai

docket ['dɑkɪt] *s* (law) rôle *m*; **on the docket** pendant, non jugé; **to put on the docket** (coll) prendre en main

dock′ hand′ *s* docker *m*

docking ['dɑkɪŋ] *s* (rok) arrimage *m*

dock′ work′er *s* docker *m*

dock′yard′ *s* chantier *m*

doctor ['dɑktər] *s* docteur *m*; *(woman)* femme *f* docteur; (med) docteur, médecin *m*; (med) doctoresse *f*; **Doctor Curie** *(professor, Ph.D., etc.)* Monsieur Curie; Madame Curie ‖ *tr* soigner; *(e.g., a chipped vase)* réparer; *(e.g., the facts)* falsifier ‖ *intr* pratiquer la médecine; (coll) être en traitement; (coll) prendre des médicaments

doctorate ['dɑktərɪt] *s* doctorat *m*

Doc′tor of Laws′ *s* docteur *m* en droit

doctrine ['dɑktrɪn] *s* doctrine *f*

document ['dɑkjəmənt] *s* document *m* ‖ ['dɑkjə‚ment] *tr* documenter

documenta·ry [‚dɑkjə'mentəri] *adj* documentaire ‖ *s* (*pl* -ries) documentaire *m*

documentation [‚dɑkjəmen'teʃən] *s* documentation *f*

doddering ['dɑdərɪŋ] *adj* tremblotant, gâteux

dodge [dɑdʒ] *s* écart *m*, esquive *f*; (coll) ruse *f*, truc *m* ‖ *tr* esquiver; *(a question)* éluder ‖ *intr* s'esquiver

do·do ['dodo] *s* (*pl* -dos or -does) (orn) dronte *m*, dodo *m*; (coll) vieux fossile *m*, innocent *m*

doe [do] *s* *(of fallow deer)* daine *f*; *(hind)* biche *f*; *(roe doe)* chevrette *f*; *(of hare)* hase *f*; *(of rabbit)* lapine *f*

doe′skin′ *s* peau *f* de daim

doff [dɑf], [dɔf] *tr* ôter

dog [dɑg], [dɔg] *s* chien *m*; **let sleeping dogs lie** il ne faut pas réveiller le chat qui dort; **to go to the dogs** (coll) se débaucher; *(said of business)* (coll) aller à vau-l'eau; **to put on the dog** (coll) faire de l'épate ‖ *v* (pret & pp **dogged**; ger **dogging**) *tr* poursuivre

dog′catch′er *s* employé *m* de la fourrière

dog′ days′ *spl* canicule *f*

doge [dodʒ] *s* doge *m*

dog′face′ *s* (slang) troufion *m*

dog′fight′ *s* (aer) combat *m* aérien tournoyant et violent; (coll) bagarre *f*

dogged ['dɔgɪd], ['dɑgɪd] *adj* tenace, obstiné

doggerel ['dɔgərəl], ['dɑgərəl] *s* vers *mpl* de mirliton

dog·gy ['dɔgi], ['dɑgi] *adj* (*comp* -gier; *super* -giest) canin, de chien ‖ *s* (*pl* -gies) toutou *m*

dog′house′ *s* niche *f* à chien; **in the doghouse** (slang) en disgrâce

dog′ in the man′ger *s* chien *m* du jardinier

dog′ Lat′in *s* latin *m* de cuisine

dogma ['dɔgmə], ['dɑgmə] *s* dogme *m*

dogmatic [dɔg'mætɪk], [dɑg'mætɪk] *adj* dogmatique ‖ **dogmatics** *s* dogmatique *f*

dog′ pound′ *s* fourrière *f*

dog′ rac′ing *s* courses *fpl* de lévriers

dog′ rose′ *s* rose *f* des haies

dog's′-ear′ *s* corne *f* ‖ *tr* corner

dog′ show′ *s* exposition *f* canine

dog′ sled′ or **dog′ sledge′** *s* traîneau *m* à chiens

dog's′ life′ *s* vie *f* de chien

Dog′ Star′ *s* Canicule *f*

dog′ tag′ *s* (mil) plaque *f* d'identité

dog′-tired′ *adj* éreinté, fourbu

dog′tooth′ *s* (*pl* -teeth) dent *f* de chien, canine *f*; (archit, bot, mach) dent-de-chien *f*

dog′tooth vi′olet *s* dent-de-chien *f*

dog′trot′ *s* petit-trot *m*

dog′watch′ *s* (naut) petit quart *m*

dog′wood′ *s* cornouiller *m*

doi·ly ['dɔɪli] *s* (*pl* -lies) napperon *m*; *(underplate)* garde-nappe *m*

doings ['duɪŋz] *spl* actions *fpl*, œuvres *fpl*, faits et gestes *mpl*

do-it-yourself [‚duɪt jər'sɛlf] *adj* de bricolage ‖ *s* bricolage *m*

doldrums ['doldrəmz], ['dɑldrəmz] *spl* marasme *m*; (naut) zone *f* des calmes

dole [dol] *s* aumône *f*; indemnité *f* de chômage ‖ *tr*—**to dole out** distribuer parcimonieusement

doleful ['dolfəl] *adj* morne

doll [dɑl] *s* poupée *f* ‖ *tr*—**to be dolled up** (coll) être tiré à quatre épingles ‖ *intr*—**to doll up** (coll) se parer, s'endimancher

dollar ['dɑlər] *s* dollar *m*

dol·ly ['dɑli] *s* (*pl* -lies) *(low movable frame)* chariot *m*; *(hand truck)* diable *m*; *(child's doll)* poupée *f*; (mov, telv) travelling *m*

dolphin ['dɑlfɪn] *s* dauphin *m*

dolt [dolt] *s* nigaud *m*, lourdaud *m*

doltish ['doltɪʃ] *adj* nigaud, lourdaud

domain [do'men] *s* domaine *m*; *(private estate)* terres *fpl*, propriété *f*

dome [dom] *s* dôme *m*, coupole *f*

dome′ light′ *s* (aut) plafonnier *m*

domestic [də'mestɪk] *adj* & *s* domestique *mf*

domesticate [də'mestɪ‚ket] *tr* domestiquer

domesticity [ˌdɔmes'tɪsɪti] s caractère m casanier; vie f familiale

domicile ['dɑmɪsɪl], ['dɑmɪˌsaɪl] s domicile m || tr domicilier

dominance ['dɑmɪnəns] s prédominance f; (genetics) dominance f

dominant ['dɑmɪnənt] adj prédominant, dominant || s (mus) dominante f

dominate ['dɑmɪˌnet] tr & intr dominer

dominating ['dɑmɪˌnetɪŋ] adj dominateur

domination [ˌdɑmɪ'neʃən] s domination f

domineer [ˌdɑmɪ'nɪr] intr se montrer tyrannique

domineering [ˌdɑmɪ'nɪrɪŋ] adj tyrannique, autoritaire

dominion [də'mɪnjən] s domination f; (of British Commonwealth) dominion m

domi·no ['dɑmɪˌno] s (pl -noes or -nos) domino m; **dominoes** sg (game) les dominos

don [dɑn] s (tutor) précepteur m || v (pret & pp **donned**; ger **donning**) tr mettre, enfiler

donate ['donet] tr faire un don de

donation [do'neʃən] s don m, cadeau m

done [dʌn] adj fait; **are you done?** en avez-vous fini?; **it is done** (it is finished) c'en est fait; **to be done** (e.g., beefsteak) être cuit; **to have done with** en finir avec; **well done!** très bien!, bravo!, à la bonne heure!

done' for' adj (tired out) (coll) fourbu; (ruined) (coll) abattu; (out of the running) (coll) hors de combat; (dead) (coll) estourbi

donkey ['dɑŋki], ['dʌŋki] s âne m, baudet m

donor ['donər] s donneur m; (law) donateur m

doodle ['dudəl] tr & intr griffonner

doom [dum] s condamnation f; destin m funeste || tr condamner

dooms'day' s jugement m dernier

door [dor] s porte f; (of a carriage or automobile) portière f; (one part of a double door) battant m; **behind closed doors** à huis clos; **to see to the door** conduire à la porte; **to show s.o. the door** éconduire qn, mettre qn à la porte

door'bell' s timbre m, sonnette f

door'bell transform'er s transformateur m de sonnerie

door'bell wire' s fil m sonnerie

door' check' s arrêt m de porte

door'frame' s chambranle m, huisserie f, dormant m

door'head' s linteau m

door'jamb' s jambage m

door'knob' s bouton m de porte

door'knock'er s heurtoir m, marteau m de porte

door' latch' s loquet m

door'man s (pl -men) portier m

door'mat' s essuie-pieds m, paillasson m

door'nail' s clou m de porte; **dead as a doornail** (coll) bien mort

door'post' s montant m de porte

door' scrap'er ['skrepər] s décrottoir m, grattepieds m

door'sill' s seuil m, traverse f

door'step' s seuil m, pas m

door'stop' s entrebâilleur m, butoir m

door'-to-door' adj porte-à-porte

door'way' s porte f, portail m

dope [dop] s enduit m; (slang) narcotique m, stupéfiant m; (information) (slang) renseignements mpl; (fool) (slang) cornichon m || tr enduire; (slang) doper, stupéfier; **to dope out** (slang) deviner, déchiffrer

dope' fiend' s (slang) toxicomane mf

dope' ped'dler s trafiquant m de stupéfiants

dormant ['dɔrmənt] adj endormi, assoupi; latent; **to lie dormant** dormir

dor'mer win'dow ['dɔrmər] s lucarne f

dormi·to·ry ['dɔrmɪˌtori] s (pl -ries) (room) dortoir m; (building) pavillon m des étudiants, maison f de résidence

dor'mitory com'plex s cité f universitaire

dor·mouse ['dɔrˌmaus] s (pl -mice) loir m

dosage ['dosɪdʒ] s dosage m

dose [dos] s dose f || tr donner en doses; donner un médicament à

dossier ['dɑsɪˌe] s dossier m

dot [dɑt] s point m; **on the dot** (coll) à l'heure tapante; pile, e.g., **at noon on the dot** à midi pile || v (pret & pp **dotted**; ger **dotting**) tr (to make with dots) pointiller; **to dot one's i's** mettre les points sur les i

dotage ['dotɪdʒ] s radotage m

dotard ['dotərd] s gâteux m, gaga m

dote [dot] intr radoter; **to dote on** raffoler de

doting ['dotɪŋ] adj radoteur; (loving to excess) qui aime follement

dots' and dash'es spl (telg) points et traits mpl

dot'ted line' s ligne f pointillée, ligne hachée; **to sign on the dotted line** signer aveuglément

double ['dʌbəl] adj & adv double, en deux, deux fois || s double m; (cards) contre m; (stunt man) (mov) cascadeur m; **doubles** (tennis) double m; **on the double!** (coll) dare-dare!, au trot! || v tr doubler; (cards) contrer; **to double up** plier en deux || intr doubler; (cards) contrer; **to double back** faire un crochet; **to double up** se plier, se tordre

dou'ble-act'ing adj à double effet

dou'ble-bar'reled adj (gun) à deux coups

dou'ble bass' [bes] s contrebasse f

dou'ble bed' s grand lit m, lit à deux places

dou'ble boil'er s bain-marie m

dou'ble-breast'ed adj croisé

dou'ble chin' s double menton m

dou'ble cross' s (slang) entourloupette f, double jeu m

dou'ble-cross' tr (coll) doubler, rouler, faire une entourloupette à dou'ble-cross'er *s* (slang) personne *f* double, faux jeton *m*

dou'ble date' *s* partie *f* carrée, sortie *f* à quatre

dou'ble-deal'er *s* personne *f* double, homme *m* à deux visages

dou'ble-deal'ing *adj* hypocrite ‖ *s* duplicité *f*

dou'ble-deck'er *s* (*bed*) lits *mpl* superposés, lits gigognes, lit à deux étages; (*bus*) autobus *m* à deux étages; (*sandwich*) double sandwich *m*; (aer, naut) deux-ponts *m*

dou'ble-edged' *adj* à deux tranchants, à double tranchant

double entendre ['dubələn'tandrə] *s* expression *f* à double entente, mot *m* à double sens

dou'ble-en'try *adj* en partie double

dou'ble-faced' *adj* à double face

dou'ble fea'ture *s* (mov) deux grands films *mpl*, double programme *m*

dou'ble-joint'ed *adj* désarticulé

dou'ble-lock' *tr* fermer à double tour

dou'ble-park' *tr* faire stationner en double file ‖ *intr* stationner en double file

dou'ble room' *s* chambre *f* à deux lits

dou'ble-spaced' *adj* à l'interligne

dou'ble stand'ard *s* code *m* de morale à deux aspects; **to have a double standard** avoir deux poids et deux mesures

doublet ['dʌblɪt] *s* (*close-fitting jacket*) pourpoint *m*; (*counterfeit stone; each of two words having the same origin*) doublet *m*

dou'ble-talk' *s* (coll) non-sens *m*; (coll) paroles *fpl* creuses or ambiguës, mots *mpl* couverts

dou'ble time' *s* (*for work*) salaire *m* double; (mil) pas *m* redoublé

doubleton ['dʌbəltən] *s* deux cartes *fpl* d'une couleur

dou'ble track' *s* double piste *f*

doubling ['dʌblɪŋ] *s* doublement *m*

doubly ['dʌblɪ] *adv* doublement

doubt [daut] *s* doute *m*; **beyond a doubt** à n'en pas douter; **no doubt** sans doute ‖ *tr* douter de; **to doubt that** douter que; **to doubt whether** douter si ‖ *intr* douter

doubter ['dautər] *s* douteur *m*

doubtful ['dautfəl] *adj* douteux; indécis, hésitant

doubtless ['dautlɪs] *adv* sans doute

douche [duʃ] *s* douche *f*; (*instrument*) seringue *f* à lavement ‖ *tr* doucher ‖ *intr* se doucher

dough [do] *s* pâte *f*; (slang) fric *m*; **big dough** (slang) grosse galette *f*

dough'boy' *s* (coll) troufion *m*, biffin *m*; (*in the first World War*) poilu *m*

dough'nut' *s* beignet *m*

dough·ty ['dautɪ] *adj* (*comp* -tier; *super* -tiest) vaillant, preux

dough·y ['do·ɪ] *adj* (*comp* -ier; *super* -iest) pâteux

dour [daur], [dur] *adj* (*severe*) austère; (*obstinate*) buté; (*gloomy*) mélancolique

douse [daus] *tr* tremper, arroser; (slang) éteindre

dove [dʌv] *s* colombe *f*

dovecote ['dʌv,kot] *s* pigeonnier *m*, colombier *m*

Dover ['dovər] *s* Douvres

dove'tail' *s* queue-d'aronde *f*, adent *m* ‖ *tr* assembler à queue-d'aronde, adenter; (fig) raccorder, opérer le raccord entre ‖ *intr* se raccorder

dove'tailed' *adj* à queue-d'aronde

dowager ['dau·adʒər] *s* douairière *f*

dow·dy ['daudɪ] *adj* (*comp* -dier; *super* -diest) gauche, fagoté, mal habillé

dow·el ['dau·əl] *s* goujon *m* ‖ *v* (*pret* & *pp* -eled or -elled; *ger* -eling or -elling) *tr* goujonner

dower ['dau·ər] *s* (*widow's portion*) douaire *m*; (*marriage portion*) dot *f*; (*natural gift*) don *m* ‖ *tr* assigner un douaire à; doter

down [daun] *adj* bas; (*train*) descendant; (*storage battery*) épuisé; (*tire*) à plat; (*sun*) couché; (*wind, sea, etc.*) calmé; (*blinds; prices*) baissé; (*stocks*) en moins-value; (*sad*) abattu, triste ‖ *s* duvet *m*; (*sand hill*) dune *f* ‖ *adv* en bas, au bas, vers les bas; à terre; (*south*) au sud; **down!** (*in elevator*) on descend!, pour la descente!; **down from** du haut de; **down there** là-bas; **down to** jusqu'à; **down under** aux antipodes; **down with . . . !** à bas . . . !; for expressions like **to go down** descendre or **to pay down** payer comptant, see the verb ‖ *prep* en bas de; (*along*) le long de; (*a stream*) en descendant ‖ *tr* descendre, abattre; (*to swallow*) (coll) avaler

down'-and-out' *adj* décavé

down'beat' *s* (mus) temps *m* fort, frappé *m*, premier accent *m*

down'cast' *adj* abattu, baissé

down'fall' *s* chute *f*, ruine *f*

down'grade' *adj* (coll) descendant ‖ *s* descente *f*; **to be on the downgrade** déchoir ‖ *adv* en déclin ‖ *tr* déclasser

down'heart'ed *adj* abattu, découragé

down'hill' *adj* descendant ‖ *adv*—**to go downhill** aller en descendant; (fig) décliner

down' pay'ment *s* acompte *m*

down'pour' *s* déluge *m*, averse *f*

down'right' *adj* absolu, véritable ‖ *adv* tout à fait, absolument

down'stairs' *adj* rez-de-chaussée *m* ‖ *adv* en bas; **to go downstairs** descendre

down'stream' *adv* en aval

down'stroke' *s* (*of piston*) course *f* descendante; (*in writing*) jambage *m*

down'town' *adj* du centre ‖ *s* centre *m* ‖ *adv* en ville

down'trend' *s* tendance *f* à la baisse

downtrodden ['daun,tradən] *adj* opprimé

downward ['daunwərd] *adj* descendant ‖ *adv* en bas, en descendant

downwards ['daunwərdz] *adv* en bas, en descendant

down'wash' *s* (aer) air *m* déplacé

down·y ['daunɪ] *adj* (*comp* -ier; *super*

-lest) duveteux; (velvety) velouté; (soft) mou, moelleux

dow·ry |'dauri| s (pl -ries) dot f

dowser |'dauzər| s sourcier m, hydroscope m

doze |doz| s petit somme m || intr sommeiller; **to doze off** s'assoupir

dozen |'dʌzən| s douzaine f; **a dozen . . .** une douzaine de . . .; **by the dozen** à la douzaine

D.P. abbr (displaced person) personne f déplacée

Dr. abbr (Doctor) Dr

drab |dræb| adj (comp drabber; super drabbest) gris || s gris m

drach·ma |'drækmə| s (pl -mas or -mae [mi]) drachme f

draft |dræft|, |drɑft| s courant m d'air; (pulling; current of air in chimney) tirage m; (sketch, outline) ébauche f; (of a letter, novel, etc.) brouillon m, premier jet m; (of a bill in Congress) projet m; (of a law) avant-projet m; (drink) trait m, gorgée f; (com) mandat m, traite f; (mil) conscription f; (naut) tirant m d'eau, draft; (game) dames fpl; **on draft** à la pression; **to be exempted from the draft** être exempté du service militaire || tr (a document) rédiger, faire le brouillon de; (a bill in Congress) dresser; (a recruit) appeler sous les drapeaux; **to be drafted** être appelé sous les drapeaux

draft′ beer′ s bière f pression

draft′ board′ s conseil m de révision, commission f locale des conscriptions

draft′ call′ s appel m sous les drapeaux

draft·ee |ˌdræf'ti|, |ˌdrɑf'ti| s appelé m (sous les drapeaux), conscrit m

draft′ horse′ s cheval m de trait

drafting |'dræftɪŋ|, |'drɑftɪŋ| s dessin m industriel

draft′ing room′ s bureau m d'études

drafts·man s (pl -men) dessinateur m; (man who draws up documents) rédacteur m

draft·y |'dræfti|, |'drɑfti| adj (comp -ier; super -iest) plein de courants d'air

drag |dræg| s (net) drège f; (sledge or sled) traîneau m; (stone drag) fardier m; (brake) enrayure f; (impediment) entrave f; (aer) résistance f à l'avancement || v (pret & pp dragged, ger dragging) tr traîner; (one feet) traînasser; (a net) draguer; (a field) herser; **to drag down** entraîner; **to drag in** introduire de force; **to drag out** faire sortir de force || intr traîner à terre; se traîner

drag′net′ s traîneau m, chalut m

dragon |'drægən| s dragon m

drag′on-fly′ s (pl -flies) demoiselle f, libellule f

dragoon |drə'gun| s dragon m || tr tyranniser; forcer, contraindre

drain |dren| s (sewer) égout m; (pipe) tuyau m d'égout; (ditch) tranchée f d'écoulement; (source of continual expense) saignée f; (med) drain m ||

tr (wet ground) drainer; (a glass or cup) vider entièrement; (a crankcase) vidanger; (s.o. of strength) épuiser; (med) drainer || intr s'égoutter, s'écouler

drainage |'drenɪdʒ| s drainage m

drain′board′ s égouttoir m

drain′ cock′ s purgeur m

drain′pipe′ s tuyau m d'écoulement, drain m

drain′ plug′ s bouchon m de vidange

drake |drek| s canard m mâle

dram |dræm| s (weight) drachme m; (drink) petit verre f, goutte f

drama |'drɑmə|, |'dræmə| s drame m

dra′ma crit′ic s chroniqueur m dramatique

dra′ma review′ s avant-première f

dramatic |drə'mætɪk| adj dramatique || dramatics s dramaturgie f, art m dramatique

dramatist |'dræmətɪst| s auteur m dramatique, dramaturge mf

dramatize |'dræməˌtaɪz| tr dramatiser

drape |drep| s rideau m; (hang of a curtain, skirt, etc.) drapement m || tr draper, tendre; se draper dans

draper·y |'drepəri| s (pl -ies) draperie f; draperies rideaux mpl, tentures fpl

drastic |'dræstɪk| adj énergique, radical; (laxative) drastique

draught |dræft|, |drɑft| s (of fish) coup m de filet; (drink) trait m, gorgée f; (naut) tirant m d'eau; draughts (game) dames fpl; **on draught** à la pression

draught′ beer′ s bière f pression

draught′board′ s damier m

draw |drɔ| s tirage m; (in a game or other contest) partie f nulle, match m nul || v (pret drew |dru|; pp drawn |drɔn|) tr tirer; (a crowd) attirer; (a design) dessiner; (a card) tirer; (trumps) faire tomber; (a bow) bander, tendre; (water) puiser; **to draw a conclusion** tirer une conséquence; **to draw aside** prendre à l'écart; **to draw blood** faire saigner; **to draw interest** porter intérêt; **to draw lots** tirer au sort; **to draw off** (e.g., a liquid) soutirer; **to draw out** (a person) faire parler; (an activity) prolonger, traîner; **to draw up** (a list) dresser; (a plan) rédiger; (naut) jauger || intr tirer; dessiner; faire partie nulle, faire match nul; **to draw away** s'éloigner; **to draw back** reculer, se retirer; **to draw near** approcher; s'approcher de

draw′back′ s désavantage m, inconvénient m

draw′bridge′ s pont-levis m

drawee |drɔ'i| s tiré m, accepteur m

drawer |'drɔ·ər| s dessinateur m; (com) tireur m |drɔr| s tiroir m; drawers caleçon m

drawing |'drɔ·ɪŋ| s dessin m; (in a lottery) tirage m

draw′ing board′ s planche f à dessin

draw′ing card′ s attrait m, attraction f

draw′ing room′ s salon m

draw′knife′ s (pl -knives) plane f

drawl [drɔl] *s* voix *f* traînante ‖ *tr* dire d'une voix traînante ‖ *intr* traîner la voix en parlant

drawn' but'ter [drɔn] *s* beurre *m* fondu; sauce *f* blanche

drawn' work' *s* broderie *f* à fils tirés

dray [dre] *s* haquet *m*, charrette *f*; (*sledge*) fardier *m*, schlitte *f*

drayage ['dre-ɪdʒ] *s* charriage *m*, charroi *m*; frais *mpl* de transport

dray' horse' *s* cheval *m* de trait

dray'man *s* (*pl* -men) haquetier *m*

dread [drɛd] *adj* redoutable, terrible ‖ *s* terreur *f*, crainte *f* ‖ *tr* & *intr* redouter, craindre

dreadful ['drɛdfəl] *adj* épouvantable

dream [drim] *s* rêve *m*, songe *m*; (*fancy, illusion*) rêverie *f*, songerie *f* ‖ *v* (*pret* & *pp* **dreamed** or **dreamt** [drɛmt]) *tr*—**to dream up** rêver ‖ *intr* rêver, songer; **to dream of** (*future plans*) rêver à; (*s.o.*) rêver de

dreamer ['drimər] *s* rêveur *m*

dream'land' *s* pays *m* des songes

dream' world' *s* monde *m* des rêves

dream-y ['drimi] *adj* (*comp* -**ier**; *super* -**iest**) rêveur; (*slang*) épatant

drear-y ['drɪri] *adj* (*comp* -**ier**; *super* -**iest**) triste, morne; monotone

dredge [drɛdʒ] *s* drague *f* ‖ *tr* draguer

dredger ['drɛdʒər] *s* dragueur *m*; (*mach*) drague *f*

dredging ['drɛdʒɪŋ] *s* dragage *m*

dregs [drɛgz] *spl* lie *f*

drench [drɛntʃ] *tr* tremper, inonder

dress [drɛs] *s* habillement *m*, costume *m*; (*woman's attire*) toilette *f*, mise *f*; (*woman's dress*) robe *f* ‖ *tr* habiller, vêtir; (*to apply a dressing to*) panser; (*culin*) garnir; **to dress down** (*coll*) passer un savon à, chapitrer; **to dress up** parer; (*ranks*) (mil) aligner; **to get dressed** s'habiller ‖ *intr* s'habiller, se vêtir; (mil) s'aligner; **to dress up** se parer

dress' ball' *s* bal *m* paré

dress' cir'cle *s* corbeille *f*, premier balcon *m*

dress' coat' *s* frac *m*

dresser ['drɛsər] *s* coiffeuse *f*; commode *f* à miroir; (*sideboard*) dressoir *m*; **to be a good dresser** être recherché dans sa mise

dress' form' *s* mannequin *m*

dress' goods' *spl* étoffes *fpl* pour costumes

dressing ['drɛsɪŋ] *s* toilette *f*; (*for food*) assaisonnement *m*, sauce *f*; (*stuffing for fowl*) farce *f*; (*fertilizer*) engrais *m*; (*for a wound*) pansement *m*

dress'ing down' *s* (coll) savon *m*, verte réprimande *f*, algarade *f*

dress'ing gown' *s* peignoir *m*, robe *f* de chambre

dress'ing room' *s* cabinet *m* de toilette; (theat) loge *f*

dress'ing sta'tion *s* poste *m* de secours

dress'ing ta'ble *s* coiffeuse *f*, toilette *f*

dress'mak'er *s* couturière *f*

dress'mak'ing *s* couture *f*

dress'making estab'lishment *s* maison *f* de couture

dress' rehear'sal *s* répétition *f* en costume; **final dress rehearsal** répétition générale

dress' shield' *s* dessous-de-bras *m*

dress' shirt' *s* chemise *f* à plastron

dress' shop' *s* magasin *m* de modes

dress' suit' *s* habit *m* de cérémonie, tenue *f* de soirée

dress' tie' *s* cravate *f* de smoking, cravate-plastron *f*

dress' u'niform *s* (mil) grande tenue *f*

dress-y ['drɛsi] *adj* (*comp* -**ier**; *super* -**iest**) (coll) élégant, chic

dribble ['drɪbəl] *s* dégouttement *m*; (*of child*) bave *f*; (sports) dribble *m* ‖ *tr* (sports) dribbler ‖ *intr* dégoutter; (*said of child*) baver; (sports) dribbler

driblet ['drɪblɪt] *s* chiquet *m*; **in driblets** au compte-gouttes

dried' ap'ple [draɪd] *s* pomme *f* tapée

dried' beef' *s* viande *f* boucanée

dried' fig' *s* figue *f* sèche

dried' fruit' *s* fruit *m* sec

dried' pear' *s* poire *f* tapée

drier ['draɪ-ər] *s* (*for clothes*) séchoir *m*, sécheuse *f*; (*for paint*) siccatif *m*; (mach) sécheur *m*

drift [drɪft] *s* dérive *f*; (*of sand, snow*) amoncellement *m*; (*of meaning*) sens *m*, direction *f* ‖ *intr* aller à la dérive; (*said of snow*) s'amonceler; (aer, naut) dériver; (fig) se laisser aller, flotter

drift' ice' *s* glaces *fpl* flottantes

drift'wood' *s* bois *m* flotté

drill [drɪl] *s* foret *m*; (*machine*) perforatrice *f*; (*fabric*) coutil *m*, treillis *m*; (*furrow*) sillon *m*; (*agricultural implement*) semoir *m*; (*in school; on the drill ground*) exercice *m* ‖ *tr* instruire; (*e.g., students*) former, entraîner; (mach) forer; (mil) faire faire l'exercice à; **to drill s.th. into s.o.** seriner q.ch. à qn ‖ *intr* faire l'exercice; forer

driller ['drɪlər] *s* foreur *m*

drill' field' or **drill' ground'** *s* terrain *m* d'exercice

drill'mas'ter *s* moniteur *m*; (mil) instructeur *m*

drill' press' *s* foreuse *f* à colonnes

drink [drɪŋk] *s* boisson *f*, breuvage *m*; boire *m*, e.g., **food and drink** le boire et le manger ‖ *v* (*pret* **drank** [dræŋk]; *pp* **drunk** [drʌŋk]) *tr* boire; (*e.g., with a meal*) prendre; **to drink down** boire d'un trait ‖ *intr* boire; **to drink out of** (*a glass*) boire dans; (*a bottle*) boire à; **to drink to the health of** boire à la santé de

drinkable ['drɪŋkəbəl] *adj* buvable, potable

drinker ['drɪŋkər] *s* buveur *m*

drink'ing cup' *s* tasse *f* à boire, gobelet *m*

drink'ing foun'tain *s* fontaine *f* à boire, borne-fontaine *f*

drink'ing song' *s* chanson *f* à boire

drink'ing trough' *s* abreuvoir *m*

drink'ing wa'ter s eau f potable

drip [drɪp] s (drop) goutte f; (dripping) égout m, dégouttement m; (person) (slang) cornichon m || v (pret & pp dripped; ger dripping) intr dégoutter, goutter

drip' cof'fee s café-filtre m

drip' cof'fee mak'er s cafetière f à filtre

drip'-dry' adj à séchage rapide; (label on shirt) repassage inutile

dripolator ['drɪpə‚letər] s filtre m à café

drip' pan' s égouttoir m

dripping ['drɪpɪŋ] s ruissellement m; drippings graisse f de rôti

drive [draɪv] s (in an automobile) promenade f; (road) chaussée f; (vigor) énergie f, initiative f; (fund-raising) campagne f; (push forward) propulsion f; (aut) (point of power application to roadway) traction f; (golf) crossée f; (mach) transmission f; to go for a drive faire une promenade en auto || v (pret drove [drov]; pp driven ['drɪvən]) tr (an automobile, locomotive, etc.; an animal; a person in an automobile) conduire (a nail) enfoncer; (a bargain) conclure; (the ball in a game) renvoyer, chasser; (to push, force) pousser, forcer; (to overwork) surmener; to drive away chasser; to drive back repousser; (e.g., in a car) reconduire; to drive crazy rendre fou; to drive in enfoncer; to drive out chasser; to drive to despair conduire au désespoir || intr conduire; drive slowly (public sign) marcher au pas; to drive away partir, démarrer; to drive back rentrer en auto; to drive on continuer sa route; to drive out sortir

drive'-in' s (motion-picture theater) cinéma m auto; (restaurant) restoroute m

driv•el ['drɪvəl] s (slobber) bave f; (nonsense) bêtises fpl || v (pret -eled or -elled; ger -eling or -elling) intr baver; (to talk nonsense) radoter

driver ['draɪvər] s chauffeur m, conducteur m; (of a carriage) cocher m; (of a locomotive) mécanicien m; (of pack animals) toucheur m

driv'er's li'cense s permis m de conduire

drive' shaft' s arbre m d'entraînement

drive'way' s voie f de garage, sortie f de voiture

drive' wheel' s roue f motrice, roue de transmission

driv'ing school' s auto-école f

drizzle ['drɪzəl] s pluie f fine, bruine f || intr bruiner, brouillasser

droll [drol] adj drôle, drolatique

dromedar•y ['drɑmə‚deri] s (pl -ies) dromadaire m

drone [dron] s bourdonnement m; (of plane or engine) vrombissement m, ronron m; (idler) fainéant m; (aer) avion m téléguidé, avion sans pilote; (ent) faux bourdon m || intr bourdonner, ronronner

drool [drul] intr baver

droop [drup] s inclinaison f || intr se baisser; (to lose one's pep) s'alanguir; (bot) languir

drooping ['drupɪŋ] adj languissant

drop [drɑp] s goutte f; (fall) chute f; (slope) précipice m; (de, th of drop) hauteur f de chute; (in price, in temperature) baisse f; (lozenge) pastille f; (of supplies from an airplane) droppage m; a drop in the bucket une goutte d'eau dans la mer || s (pret & pp dropped; ger dropping) tr laisser tomber; (a curtain; the eyes, voice) baisser; (from an airplane) lâcher; (e.g., a name from a list) omettre, supprimer; (a remark) glisser; (a conversation; relations; negotiations) cesser; (anchor) jeter, mouiller; (an idea, a habit, etc.) renoncer à; to drop off déposer || intr tomber; se laisser tomber; baisser; cesser; to drop in entrer en passant; to drop in on faire un saut chez; to drop off se détacher; s'endormir; to drop out of (to quit) renoncer à, abandonner

drop' cur'tain s rideau m d'entracte

drop' ham'mer s marteau-pilon m

drop' kick' s coup m tombé

drop' leaf' s abattant m

drop'light' s lampe f suspendue

drop'out' s raté m; to become a drop-out abandonner les études

dropper ['drɑpər] s compte-gouttes m

dropsy ['drɑpsi] s hydropisie f

drop' ta'ble s table f à abattants

dross [drɔs], [drɑs] s scories mpl, écume f

drought [draut] s sécheresse f

drove [drov] s troupeau m; (multitude) foule f, flots mpl; in droves par bandes

drover ['drovər] s bouvier m

drown [draun] tr noyer; to drown out couvrir || intr se noyer

drowse [drauz] intr somnoler, s'assoupir

drow•sy ['drauzi] adj (comp -sier; super -siest) somnolent

drub [drʌb] v (pret & pp drubbed; ger drubbing) tr flanquer une raclée à, rosser

drudge [drʌdʒ] s homme m de peine, piocheur m; harmless drudge (e.g., who compiles dictionaries) gratte-papier m inoffensif

drudger•y ['drʌdʒəri] s (pl -ies) corvée f, travail m pénible

drug [drʌg] s drogue f, stupéfiant m, produit m pharmaceutique; drug on the market rossignol m || v (pret & pp drugged; ger drugging) tr (a person) donner un stupéfiant à, stupéfier; (food or drink) ajouter un stupéfiant à

drug' ad'dict s toxicomane mf

drug' addic'tion s toxicomanie f

druggist ['drʌgɪst] s pharmacien m

drug' hab'it s toxicomanie f, vice m des stupéfiants

drug′store′ s pharmacie-bazar f, pharmacie f

drug′ traf′fic s trafic m des stupéfiants

druid ['dru·ɪd] s druide m

drum [drʌm] s (cylinder; instrument of percussion) tambour m; (container for oil, gasoline, etc.) bidon m; **to play the drum** battre du tambour ‖ v (pret & pp **drummed;** ger **drumming**) tr (e.g., a march) tambouriner; rassembler au son du tambour; **to drum into** fourrer dans; **to drum up customers** racoler des clients ‖ intr jouer du tambour; (with the fingers) tambouriner; (on the piano) pianoter

drum′ and bu′gle corps′ s clairons et tambours mpl, clique f

drum′ beat′ s coup m de tambour

drum′fire′ s (mil) tir m nourri, feu m roulant

drum′head′ s peau f de tambour; (naut) noix f

drum′ ma′jor s tambour-major m

drummer ['drʌmər] s tambour m; (salesman) (coll) commis m voyageur

drum′stick′ s baguette f de tambour; (of chicken) cuisse f, pilon m

drunk [drʌŋk] adj ivre, soûl; **to get drunk** s'enivrer; **to get s.o. drunk** enivrer qn ‖ s (person) (coll) ivrogne m; (state) ivresse f; **to go on a drunk** (coll) se soûler

drunkard ['drʌŋkərd] s ivrogne m

drunken ['drʌŋkən] adj enivré

drunk′en driv′ing s conduite f en état d'ivresse

drunkenness ['drʌŋkənnɪs] s ivresse f

dry [draɪ] adj (comp **drier;** super **driest**) sec; (thirsty) assoiffé; (boring) aride ‖ s (pl **drys**) (prohibitionist) antialcoolique mf ‖ v (pret & pp **dried**) tr sécher; (the dishes) essuyer ‖ intr sécher; **to dry up** se dessécher; (slang) se taire

dry′ bat′tery s pile f sèche; (number of dry cells) batterie f de piles

dry′ cell′ s pile f sèche

dry′-clean′ tr nettoyer à sec

dry′ clean′er s nettoyeur m à sec, teinturier m

dry′ clean′er's s teinturerie f

dry′ clean′ing s nettoyage m à sec

dry′ dock′ s cale f sèche, bassin m de radoub

dry′-eyed′ adj d'un œil sec

dry′ goods′ spl tissus mpl, étoffes fpl

dry′ ice′ s glace f sèche

dry′ land′ s terre f ferme

dry′ meas′ure s mesure f à grains

dryness ['draɪnɪs] s sécheresse f; (e.g., of a speaker) aridité f

dry′ nurse′ s nourrice f sèche

dry′ rot′ s carie f sèche

dry′ run′ s exercice m simulé, répétition f, examen m blanc

dry′ sea′son s saison f sèche

dry′ wash′ s blanchissage m sans repassage

dual ['d(j)u·əl] adj double ‖ s duel m

dub [dʌb] s (slang) balourd m ‖ v (pret & pp **dubbed;** ger **dubbing**) tr (to nickname) donner un sobriquet à; (to

knight) donner l'accolade à, adouber; (a tape recording or movie film) doubler

dubbing ['dʌbɪŋ] s (mov) doublage m

dubious ['d(j)ubɪ·əs] adj (undecided) hésitant; (questionable) douteux

ducat ['dʌkət] s ducat m

duchess ['dʌtʃɪs] s duchesse f

duch·y ['dʌtʃi] s (pl **-ies**) duché m

duck [dʌk] s canard m; (female) cane f; (motion) esquive f; **ducks** (trousers) pantalon m de coutil ‖ tr (the head) baisser ‖ intr se baisser; **to duck out** (coll) s'esquiver

ducking ['dʌkɪŋ] s plongeon m, bain m forcé

duckling ['dʌklɪŋ] s caneton m; (female) canette f

ducks′ and drakes′ s—**to play at ducks and drakes** faire des ricochets sur l'eau; (fig) jeter son argent par les fenêtres

duct [dʌkt] s conduit m, canal m

duct′less glands′ ['dʌktlɪs] spl glandes fpl closes

duct′work′ s tuyauterie f, canalisation f

dud [dʌd] s (slang) obus m qui a raté; (slang) raté m, navet m; **duds** (clothes) (coll) frusques fpl, nippes fpl

dude [d(j)ud] s poseur m, gommeux m

dude′ ranch′ s ranch m d'opérette

due [d(j)u] adj dû; (note) échéant; (bill) exigible; (train, bus, person) attendu; **due to** par suite de; **in due form** en bonne forme, en règle; **to fall due** venir à l'échéance; **when is the train due?** à quelle heure doit arriver le train? ‖ s dû m; **dues** cotisation f; **to pay one's dues** cotiser ‖ adv droit vers, e.g., **due north** droit vers le nord

due′ date′ s échéance f

duel ['d(j)u·əl] s duel m; **to fight a duel** se battre en duel ‖ v (pret & pp **dueled** or **duelled;** ger **dueling** or **duelling**) intr se battre en duel

duelist or **duellist** ['d(j)u·əlɪst] s duelliste m

duenna [d(j)u·'enə] s duègne f

dues′-pay′ing adj cotisateur

duet [d(j)u·'et] s duo m

duke [d(j)uk] s duc m

dukedom ['d(j)ukdəm] s duché m

dull [dʌl] adj (not sharp) émoussé; (color) terne; (sound; pain) sourd; (stupid) lourd; (business) lent; (boring) ennuyeux; (flat) fade, insipide; **to become dull** s'émousser; (said of senses) s'engourdir ‖ tr (a knife) émousser; (color) ternir; (sound; pain) amortir; (spirits) hébéter, engourdir ‖ intr s'émousser; se ternir; s'amortir; s'engourdir

dullard ['dʌlərd] s lourdaud m, hébété m

dullness ['dʌlnɪs] s (of knife) émoussement m; (e.g., of wits) lenteur f

duly ['d(j)uli] adv dûment, justement

dumb [dʌm] adj (lacking the power to speak) muet; (coll) gourde, imbécile;

completely **dumb** (coll) bouché à l'émeri; **to play dumb** (coll) feindre l'innocence

dumb'bell' s (sports) haltère m; (slang) gourde f, imbécile mf

dumb' crea'ture s animal m, brute f

dumb'wait'er s monte-plats m; (serving table) table f roulante

dumfound ['dʌm,faund] tr abasourdir, ébahir

dum•my ['dʌmi] adj faux, factice || s (pl -mies) (dress form) mannequin; (in card games) mort m; (figurehead, straw man) prête-nom m, homme m de paille; (skeleton copy of a book or magazine) maquette f; (object put in place of the real thing) simulacre m; (slang) bêta m, ballot m

dump [dʌmp] s (pile of rubbish) amas m, tas m; (place) dépotoir m; (mil) dépôt m; (slang) taudis m; **to be down in the dumps** (coll) avoir le cafard || tr décharger, déverser; (on rubbish pile) jeter au rebut; (com) vendre en faisant du dumping

dumping ['dʌmpɪŋ] s (com) dumping m

dumpling ['dʌmplɪŋ] s dumpling m, boulette f

dump' truck' s tombereau m

dump•y ['dʌmpi] adj (comp -ier; super -iest) (short and fat) courtaud, trapu; (shabby) râpé, minable

dun [dʌn] adj isabelle || s créancier m importun; (demand for payment) demande f pressante || v (pret & pp dunned; ger dunning) tr (for payment) importuner, poursuivre

dunce [dʌns] s âne m, cancre m

dunce' cap' s bonnet m d'âne

dune [d(j)un] s dune f

dung [dʌŋ] s fumier m

dungarees [,dʌŋgə'riz] spl pantalon m de treillis, treillis m, bleu m

dungeon ['dʌndʒən] s cachot m, cul-de-basse-fosse m; (keep of castle) donjon m

dung'hill' s tas m de fumier

dunk [dʌŋk] tr & intr tremper

du•o ['d(j)u•o] s (pl -os) duo m

duode•num [,d(j)u•ə'dinəm] s (pl -na [nə]) duodénum m

dupe [d(j)up] s dupe f, dindon m de la farce || tr duper

duplex ['d(j)upleks] adj double, duplex || s maison f double

du'plex house' s maison f double

duplicate ['d(j)uplɪkɪt] adj double || s duplicata m, polycopie f; **in duplicate** en double, en duplicata || ['d(j)upli,ket] tr faire le double de, reproduire; (on a machine) polycopier, ronéocopier

du'plicating machine' s duplicateur m

duplici•ty [d(j)u'plɪsɪti] s (pl -ties) duplicité f

durable ['d(j)urəbəl] adj durable

duration [d(j)u'reʃən] s durée f

duress ['d(j)ures], [d(j)u'res] s contrainte f; emprisonnement m

during ['d(j)urɪŋ] prep pendant

dusk [dʌsk] s crépuscule m; **at dusk** entre chien et loup

dust [dʌst] s poussière f || tr (to free of dust) épousseter; (to sprinkle with dust) saupoudrer; **to dust off** épousseter

dust' bowl' s région f dénudée

dust'cloth' s chiffon m à épousseter

dust' cloud' s nuage m de poussière

duster ['dʌstər] s (made of feathers) plumeau m; (made of cloth) chiffon m; (overgarment) cache-poussière m

dust' jack'et s protège-livre m, couvre-livre m, liseuse f

dust'pan' s pelle f à ordures

dust' rag' s chiffon m à épousseter

dust•y ['dʌsti] adj (comp -ier; super -iest) poussiéreux; (color) cendré

Dutch [dʌtʃ] adj hollandais, néerlandais; (slang) allemand || s (language) hollandais m, néerlandais m; (slang) allemand m; **in Dutch** (slang) en disgrâce; **the Dutch** les Hollandais mpl, les Néerlandais mpl; (slang) les Allemands mpl; **we will go Dutch** (coll) chacun paiera son écot

Dutch'man s (pl -men) Hollandais m, Néerlandais m; (slang) Allemand m

Dutch' treat' s—**to have a Dutch treat** (coll) faire suisse, payer son écot

dutiable ['d(j)uti•əbəl] adj soumis aux droits de douane

dutiful ['d(j)utɪfəl] adj respectueux, soumis, plein d'égards

du•ty ['d(j)uti] s (pl -ties) devoir m; **duties fonctions** fpl; (taxes, customs) droits mpl; **to be off duty** ne pas être de service, avoir quartier libre; **to be on duty** être de service, être de garde

du'ty-free' adj exempt de droits

dwarf [dwɔrf] adj & s nain m || tr & intr rapetisser

dwell [dwel] v (pret & pp dwelled or dwelt [dwelt]) intr demeurer; **to dwell on** appuyer sur

dwelling ['dwelɪŋ] s demeure f, habitation f

dwell'ing house' s maison f d'habitation

dwindle ['dwɪndəl] intr diminuer; **to dwindle away** s'affaiblir

dye [daɪ] s teinture f || v (pret & pp dyed; ger dyeing) tr teindre

dyed'-in-the-wool' adj intransigeant

dyeing ['daɪ•ɪŋ] s teinture f

dyer ['daɪ•ər] s teinturier m

dying ['daɪ•ɪŋ] adj mourant, moribond

dynamic [daɪ'næmɪk], [dɪ'næmɪk] adj dynamique || **dynamics** s dynamique f

dynamite ['daɪnə,maɪt] s dynamite f || tr dynamiter

dyna•mo ['daɪnə,mo] s (pl -mos) dynamo f

dynast ['daɪnæst] s dynaste m

dynas•ty ['daɪnəsti] s (pl -ties) dynastie f

dysentery ['dɪsən,teri] s dysenterie f

dyspepsia [dɪs'pepsɪ•ə], [dɪs'pep/ə] s dyspepsie f

E

E, e [i] *s* V^e lettre de l'alphabet

each [it∫] *adj indef* chaque ‖ *pron indef* chacun; **each other** nous, se; l'un l'autre; **to each other** l'un à l'autre ‖ *adv* chacun; *(apiece)* pièce, la pièce

eager ['igər] *adj* ardent, empressé; **eager for** avide de; **to be eager to** brûler de, désirer ardemment

ea'ger bea'ver *s* bûcheur *m*, mouche *f* du coche

eagerness ['igərnɪs] *s* ardeur *f*, empressement *m*

eagle ['igəl] *s* aigle *m*

ea'gle-eyed' *adj* à l'œil d'aigle

ea'gle ray' *s* (ichth) aigle *m* de mer

eaglet ['iglɪt] *s* aiglon *m*

ear [ɪr] *s* oreille *f*; *(of corn or wheat)* épi *m*; **to box s.o.'s ears** frotter les oreilles à qn; **to prick up one's ears** dresser l'oreille; **to turn a deaf ear** faire la sourde oreille ‖ *intr (said of grain)* épier

ear'ache' *s* douleur *f* d'oreille

ear'drop' *s* pendant *m* d'oreille

ear'drum' *s* tympan *m*

ear'flap' *s* lobe *m* de l'oreille; *(on a cap)* protège-oreilles *m*

earl [ʌrl] *s* comte *m*

earldom ['ʌrldəm] *s* comté *m*

ear·ly ['ʌrli] *(comp* **-lier;** *super* **-liest)** *adj* primitif; *(first in a series)* premier; *(occurring in the near future)* prochain; *(in the morning)* matinal; *(ahead of time)* en avance; **at an early age** dès l'enfance ‖ *adv* de bonne heure, tôt; anciennement; **as early as** dès

ear'ly bird' *s* matinal *m*

ear'ly mass' *s* première messe *f*

ear'ly-morn'ing *adj* matinal

ear'ly ris'er *s* matinal *m*

ear'ly-ris'ing *adj* matineux, matinal

ear'mark' *s* marque *f*, cachet *m* ‖ *tr (animals)* marquer à l'oreille; *(e.g., money)* spécialiser; **to earmark for** affecter à, assigner à

ear'muff' *s* couvre-oreille *m*

earn [ʌrn] *tr* gagner; **(to get as one's due)** mériter; *(interest)* rapporter

earnest ['ʌrnɪst] *adj* sérieux; **in earnest** sérieusement ‖ *s* gage *m*; (com) arrhes *fpl*

earnings ['ʌrnɪŋz] *spl (wages)* gages *mpl*; *(profits)* profit *m*, bénéfices *mpl*

ear'phone' *s* écouteur *m*; **earphones** casque *m*, écouteurs

ear'ring' *s* boucle *f* d'oreille

ear'split'ting *adj* assourdissant

earth [ʌrθ] *s* terre *f*; **to come down to earth** retomber des nues; **where on earth . . . ?** où diable . . . ?

earthen ['ʌrθən] *adj* de terre, en terre

ear'then·ware' *s* faïence *f*

earthly ['ʌrθli] *adj* terrestre

earth'man' or **earth'man** *s (pl* **men'** or **men)** terrien *m*

earth'quake' *s* tremblement *m* de terre

earth'work' *s* terrassement *m*

earth'worm' *s* lombric *m*, ver *m* de terre

earth·y ['ʌrθi] *adj (comp* **-ier;** *super* **-iest)** terreux; *(worldly)* mondain; *(unrefined)* grossier, terre à terre

ear' trum'pet *s* cornet *m* acoustique

ease [iz] *s* aise *f*; *(readiness, naturalness)* désinvolture *f*; *(comfort, well-being)* bien-être *m*, tranquillité *f*; **at ease** tranquille; (mil) au repos; **to take one's ease** prendre ses aises; **with ease** facilement ‖ *tr* faciliter; *(a burden)* alléger; *(e.g., one's mind)* calmer, apaiser; *(to let up on)* ralentir ‖ *intr* se calmer, s'apaiser

easel ['izəl] *s* chevalet *m*

easement ['izmənt] *s* (law) servitude *f*

easily ['izɪli] *adv* facilement, aisément; *(certainly)* sans doute

easiness ['izɪnɪs] *s* facilité *f*; *(of manner)* désinvolture *f*, insouciance *f*

east [ist] *adj & s* est *m* ‖ *adv* à l'est, vers l'est

Easter ['istər] *s* Pâques *m*; **Happy Easter!** Joyeuses Pâques!

East'er egg' *s* œuf *m* de Pâques

East'er Mon'day *s* lundi *m* de Pâques

eastern ['istərn] *adj* oriental, de l'est

East'ern Stand'ard Time' *s* l'heure *f* de l'Est

East'ern Town'ships *spl (in Canada)* Cantons *mpl* de l'Est

eastward ['istwərd] *adv* vers l'est

eas·y ['izi] *adj (comp* **-ier;** *super* **-iest)** facile; *(easygoing)* aisé, désinvolte ‖ *adv* (coll) facilement; (coll) lentement; **to take it easy** (coll) en prendre à son aise

eas'y chair' *s* fauteuil *m*, bergère *f*

eas'y·go'ing *adj* insouciant, nonchalant, commode à vivre

eas'y mark' *s* jobard *m*

eas'y pay'ments *spl* facilités *fpl* de paiement

eat [it] *v (pret* **ate** [et]; *pp* **eaten** ['itən]) *tr* manger; **to eat away** ronger ‖ *intr* manger

eatable ['itəbəl] *adj* comestible

eaves [ivz] *spl* avant-toits *mpl*

eaves'drop' *v (pret & pp* **-dropped;** *ger* **-dropping)** *intr* écouter à la porte

ebb [eb] *s* reflux *m*, baisse *f* ‖ *intr* refluer, baisser; **to ebb and flow** monter et baisser, fluer et refluer

ebb' and flow' *s* flux et reflux *m*

ebb' tide' *s* marée *f* descendante, jusant *m*

ebon·y ['ebəni] *s (pl* **-ies)** ébène *f*; *(tree)* ébénier *m*

ebullient [ɪ'bʌljənt] *adj* bouillonnant; (fig) enthousiaste, exubérant

eccentric [ek'sentrik] *adj* excentrique ‖ *s (odd person)* excentrique *mf*; *(device)* excentrique *m*

eccentrici·ty [ˌeksen'trɪsɪti] s (pl -ties) excentricité f

ecclesiastic [ɪˌklizɪ'æstɪk] adj & s ecclésiastique m

echelon ['eʃəˌlan] s échelon m ‖ tr (mil) échelonner

ech·o ['eko] s (pl -oes) écho m ‖ tr répéter ‖ intr faire écho

eclectic [ek'lektɪk] adj & s éclectique mf

eclipse [ɪ'klɪps] s éclipse f ‖ tr éclipser

eclogue ['eklɔg], ['eklag] s églogue f

ecology [ɪ'kalədʒi] s écologie f

economic [ˌikə'namɪk], [ˌekə'namɪk] adj économique ‖ **economics** s économique f

economical [ˌikə'namɪkəl], [ˌekə-'namɪkəl] adj économe

economize [ɪ'kanəˌmaɪz] tr & intr économiser

econo·my [ɪ'kanəmi] s (pl -mies) économie f

ecsta·sy ['ekstəsi] s (pl -sies) extase f

ecstatic [ek'stætɪk] adj & s extatique mf

Ecuador ['ekwəˌdɔr] s l'Équateur m

ecumenic(al) [ˌekjə'menɪk(əl)] adj œcuménique

eczema ['eksɪmə], [eg'zimə] s eczéma m

ed·dy ['edi] s (pl -dies) tourbillon m ‖ v (pret & pp -died) intr tourbillonner

edelweiss ['edəlˌvaɪs] s edelweiss m, fleur f de neige

Eden ['idən] s (fig) éden m

edge [edʒ] s bord m; (of a knife, sword, etc.) fil m, tranchant m; (of a field, forest, etc.; of a strip of cloth) lisière f; (slang) avantage m; **on edge** de chant; (nervous) énervé, crispé; **to be on edge** avoir les nerfs à fleur de peau; **to have the edge on** (coll) enfoncer; **to set the teeth on edge** agacer les dents ‖ tr border; (to sharpen) affiler, aiguiser ‖ intr s'avancer de biais; **to edge away** s'écarter peu à peu; **to edge in** se glisser parmi or dans

edge'ways' adv de côté, de biais

edging ['edʒɪŋ] s bordure f

edg·y ['edʒi] adj (comp -ier; super -iest) (nervous) crispé, irritable

edible ['edɪbəl] adj comestible

edict ['idɪkt] s édit m

edification [ˌedɪfɪ'keʃən] s édification f

edifice ['edɪfɪs] s édifice m

edi·fy ['edɪˌfaɪ] v (pret & pp -fied) tr édifier

edifying ['edɪˌfaɪ·ɪŋ] adj édifiant

edit ['edɪt] tr préparer la publication de; (e.g., a newspaper) diriger, rédiger; (a text) éditer

edition [ɪ'dɪʃən] s édition f

editor ['edɪtər] s (of newspaper or magazine) rédacteur m; (of manuscript) éditeur m; (of feature or column) chroniqueur m, courriériste mf

editorial [ˌedɪ'tɔrɪ·əl] adj & s éditorial m

edito'rial of'fice s rédaction f

edito'rial pol'icy s ligne f politique

edito'rial staff s rédaction f

ed'itor in chief' s rédacteur m en chef

educate ['edʒʊˌket] tr instruire, éduquer

educated adj cultivé, instruit

education [ˌedʒʊ'keʃən] s éducation f, instruction f

educational [ˌedʒʊ'keʃənəl] adj éducatif, éducateur

educator ['edʒʊˌketər] s éducateur m

eel [il] s anguille f

ee·rie or **ee·ry** ['iri] adj (comp -rier; super -riest) mystérieux, spectral

efface [ɪ'fes] tr effacer

effect [ɪ'fekt] s effet m; **in effect** en fait, effectivement; **to be in effect** être en vigueur; **to feel the effects of** se ressentir de; **to go into effect, to take effect** prendre effet; (said of law) entrer en vigueur ‖ tr effectuer, mettre à exécution

effective [ɪ'fektɪv] adj efficace; (actually in effect) en vigueur; (striking) impressionnant; **to become effective** produire son effet; (to go into effect) entrer en vigueur

effectual [ɪ'fektʃʊ·əl] adj efficace

effectuate [ɪ'fektʃʊˌet] tr effectuer

effeminacy [ɪ'femɪnəsi] s effémination f

effeminate [ɪ'femɪnɪt] adj efféminé; **to become effeminate** s'efféminer

effervesce [ˌefər'ves] intr être en effervescence

effervescent [ˌefər'vesənt] adj effervescent

effete [ɪ'fit] adj stérile, épuisé

efficacious [ˌefɪ'keʃəs] adj efficace

efficacy ['efɪkəsi] s efficacité f

efficien·cy [ɪ'fɪʃənsi] s (pl -cies) efficacité f; (of business) efficience f; (of machine) rendement m; (of person) compétence f

effi'ciency ex'pert s ingénieur m en organisation

efficient [ɪ'fɪʃənt] adj efficace; (of machine) efficient, de bon rendement; (of person) efficient, compétent

effi·gy ['efɪdʒi] s (pl -gies) effigie f

effort ['efərt] s effort m

effronter·y [ɪ'frʌntəri] s (pl -ies) effronterie f

effusion [ɪ'fjuʒən] s effusion f

effusive [ɪ'fjusɪv] adj démonstratif; **to be effusive in** se répandre en

e.g. abbr (Lat: exempli gratia for example) par ex., ex.

egg [eg] s œuf m ‖ tr—**to egg on** pousser, inciter

egg'beat'er s fouet m, batteur m à œufs

egg'cup' s coquetier m

egg'head' s (slang) intellectuel m

eggnog ['egˌnag] s lait m de poule

egg'plant' s aubergine f

egg' poach'er s pocheuse f

egg'shell' s coquille f d'œuf

egg' white' s blanc m d'œuf

egoism ['egoˌɪzəm], ['igoˌɪzəm] s égoïsme m

egoist ['ego·ɪst], ['igo·ɪst] s égoïste mf

egotism ['ego‚tɪzəm], ['igo‚tɪzəm] s égotisme m

egotist ['egotɪst], ['igotɪst] s égotiste mf

egregious [ɪ'gridʒəs] adj insigne, notoire

egress ['igres] s sortie f, issue f

egret ['igret] s aigrette f

Egypt ['idʒɪpt] s Égypte f; l'Égypte

Egyptian [ɪ'dʒɪp/ən] adj égyptien || s Égyptien m

ei'der down' ['aɪdər] s édredon m

ei'der duck' s eider m

eight [et] adj & pron huit || s huit m; (group of eight) huitaine f; about eight une huitaine de; eight o'clock huit heures

eight'ball' s—behind the eightball (coll) dans le pétrin

eighteen ['et'tin] adj, pron, & s dix-huit m

eighteenth ['et'tinθ] adj & pron dix-huitième (masc, fem); the Eighteenth dix-huit, e.g., John the Eighteenth Jean dix-huit || s dix-huitième m; the eighteenth (in dates) le dix-huit

eighth [etθ] adj & pron huitième (masc, fem); the Eighth huit, e.g., John the Eighth Jean huit || s huitième m; the eighth (in dates) le huit

eightieth ['eti·tθ] adj & pron quatre-vingtième (masc, fem) || s quatre-vingtième m

eigh·ty ['eti] adj & pron quatre-vingts || s (pl -ties) quatre-vingts m

eighty-first' adj & pron quatre-vingt-unième (masc, fem) || s quatre-vingt-unième m

eighty-one' adj, pron, & s quatre-vingt-un m

either ['iðər], ['aɪðər] adj & pron indef l'un ou l'autre; l'un et l'autre; on either side de chaque côté || adv—not either non plus || conj—either . . . or ou . . . ou, soit . . . soit, ou bien . . . ou bien

ejaculate [ɪ'dʒækjə‚let] tr & intr crier; (physiol) éjaculer

eject [ɪ'dʒekt] tr éjecter; (to evict) expulser, chasser

ejection [ɪ'dʒek/ən] s éjection f; (eviction) expulsion f

ejec'tion seat' s (aer) siège m éjectable

eke [ik] tr—to eke out gagner avec difficulté

elaborate [ɪ'læbərɪt] adj élaboré, soigné; (ornate) orné, travaillé; (involved) compliqué, recherché || [ɪ'læbə‚ret] tr élaborer || intr—to elaborate on or upon donner des détails sur

elapse [ɪ'læps] intr s'écouler

elastic [ɪ'læstɪk] adj & s élastique m

elasticity [ɪ‚læs'tɪsɪti], [‚ilæs'tɪsɪti] s élasticité f

elated [ɪ'letɪd] adj transporté, exalté

elation [ɪ'le/ən] s transport m, exultation f

elbow ['elbo] s coude m; at one's elbow à portée de la main; to rub

elbows with coudoyer || tr coudoyer; to elbow one's way se frayer un chemin à coups de coude || intr jouer des coudes

el'bow grease' s (coll) huile f de coude

el'bow·room' s espace m; to have elbowroom avoir ses coudées franches

elder ['eldər] adj aîné, plus âgé || s aîné m; (senior) doyen m; (bot) sureau m; (eccl) ancien m

el'der·ber'ry s (pl -ries) sureau m; (berry) baie f de sureau

elderly ['eldərli] adj vieux, âgé

eld'er states'man s vétéran m de la politique

eldest ['eldɪst] adj (l')aîné, (le) plus âgé

elect [ɪ'lekt] adj élu || s—the elect les élus mpl || tr élire

election [ɪ'lek/ən] s élection f

electioneer [ɪ‚lek/ə'nɪr] intr faire la campagne électorale, solliciter des voix

elective [ɪ'lektɪv] adj électif; (optional) facultatif || s matière f à option

elec'toral col'lege [ɪ'lektərəl] s collège m électoral

electorate [ɪ'lektərɪt] s corps m électoral, électeurs mpl, votants mpl

electric(al) [ɪ'lektrɪk(əl)] adj électrique

elec'trical engineer' s ingénieur m électricien

elec'trical engineer'ing s technique f électrique

elec'tric blan'ket s couverture f chauffante

elec'tric chair' s chaise f électrique

elec'tric clothes' dri'er s séchoir m électrique

elec'tric eel' s gymnote m

elec'tric eye' s cellule f photo-électrique

elec'tric fan' s ventilateur m électrique

elec'tric heat'er s radiateur m électrique

electrician [ɪ‚lek'trɪ/ən], [‚elek'trɪ/ən] s électricien m

electricity [ɪ‚lek'trɪsɪti], [‚elek'trɪsɪti] s électricité f

elec'tric light' s lampe f électrique

elec'tric me'ter s compteur m de courant

elec'tric mix'er s batteur m électrique

elec'tric per'colator s cafetière f électrique

elec'tric range' s cuisinière f électrique

elec'tric shav'er s rasoir m électrique

elec'tric shock' treat'ment s (med) électrochoc m

electri·fy [ɪ'lektrɪ‚faɪ] v (pret & pp -fied) tr (to provide with electric power) électrifier; (to communicate electricity to; to thrill) électriser

elec·tro [ɪ'lektro] s (pl -tros) électrotype m

electrocute [ɪ'lektrə‚kjut] tr électrocuter

electrode [ɪ'lektrod] s électrode f

electrolysis [ɪ‚lek'trɑlɪsɪs], [‚elek'trɑlɪsɪs] s électrolyse f

electrolyte [ɪ'lektrə‚laɪt] s électrolyte m

electromagnet [ɪ‚lektrə'mægnɪt] s électro-aimant m

electromagnetic [ɪ‚lektrəmæg'netɪk] adj électromagnétique

electron [ɪ'lektrən] s électron m

elec'tron gun' s canon m à électrons

electronic [ɪ‚lek'trɑnɪk], [‚elek'trɑn‑ɪk] adj électronique || electronics s électronique f

elec'tron mi'croscope s microscope m électronique

electroplate [ɪ'lektrə‚plet] tr galvaniser

electrotype [ɪ'lektrə‚taɪp] s électrotype m || tr électrotyper

elegance ['elɪgəns] s élégance f

elegant ['elɪgənt] adj élégant

elegiac [‚elɪ'dʒaɪ‑æk] [ɪ'lidʒɪ‚æk] adj élégiaque

ele‑gy ['elɪdʒi] s (pl -gies) élégie f

element ['elɪmənt] s élément m

elementary [‚elɪ'mentəri] adj élémentaire

elephant ['elɪfənt] s éléphant m

elevate ['elɪ‚vet] tr élever

elevated rail'way s métro m aérien

elevation [‚elɪ've/ən] s élévation f

elevator ['elɪ‚vetər] s ascenseur m; (for freight) monte-charge m; (for hoisting grain) élévateur m; (warehouse for storing grain) silo m à céréales; (aer) gouvernail m d'altitude, gouvernail de profondeur

eleven [ɪ'levən] adj & pron onze || s onze m; eleven o'clock onze heures

eleventh [ɪ'levənθ] adj & pron onzième (masc, fem); the Eleventh onze, e.g., John the Eleventh Jean onze || s onzième m; the eleventh (in dates) le onze

elev'enth hour' s dernier moment m

elf [elf] s (pl elves [elvz]) elfe m

elicit [ɪ'lɪsɪt] tr (e.g., a smile) provoquer, faire sortir; (e.g., help) obtenir

elide [ɪ'laɪd] tr élider

eligible ['elɪdʒɪbəl] adj éligible; (e.g., bachelor) sortable

eliminate [ɪ'lɪmɪ‚net] tr éliminer

elision [ɪ'lɪʒən] s élision f

elite [e'lit] s élite f

elk [elk] s élan m

ellipse [ɪ'lɪps] s (geom) ellipse f

ellip‑sis [ɪ'lɪpsɪs] s (pl -ses [siz]) ellipse f; (punctuation) points mpl de suspension

elliptic(al) [ɪ'lɪptɪk(əl)] adj elliptique

elm [elm] s orme m

elongate [ɪ'lɔŋget], [ɪ'lɑŋget] tr allonger, prolonger

elope [ɪ'lop] intr s'enfuir avec un amant

elopement [ɪ'lopmənt] s enlèvement m consenti

eloquence ['eləkwəns] s éloquence f

eloquent ['eləkwənt] adj éloquent

else [els] adj—nobody else personne d'autre; nothing else rien d'autre; somebody else quelqu'un d'autre, un autre; something else autre chose; what else quoi encore; who else qui encore; who's else de qui d'autre || adv d'une autre façon, autrement; how(ever) else de toute autre façon;

nowhere else nulle part ailleurs; or else sinon, ou bien, sans quoi; somewhere else ailleurs, autre part; when else quand encore; where else où encore

else'where' adv ailleurs, autre part encore

elucidate [ɪ'lusɪ‚det] tr élucider

elude [ɪ'lud] tr éluder, se soustraire à; (a pursuer) échapper à

elusive [ɪ'lusɪv] adj évasif, fuyant; (baffling) insaisissable, déconcertant

emaciated [ɪ'me/ɪ‚etɪd] adj émacié; to become emaciated s'émacier

emanate ['emə‚net] intr émaner

emancipate [ɪ'mænsɪ‚pet] tr émanciper

embalm [em'bɑm] tr embaumer

embalming [em'bɑmɪŋ] s embaumement m

embankment [em'bæŋkmənt] s (of river) digue f; (of road) remblai m

embar‑go [em'bɑrgo] s (pl -goes) embargo m || tr mettre un embargo sur

embark [em'bɑrk] intr s'embarquer

embarkation [‚embɑr'ke/ən] s embarquement m

embarrass [em'bærəs] tr faire honte à; (to make difficult) embarrasser

embarrassment [em'bærəsmənt] s honte f; (difficulty) embarras m

embas‑sy ['embəsi] s (pl -sies) ambassade f

em‑bed [em'bed] v (pret & pp -bedded; ger -bedding) tr encastrer

embellish [em'belɪ/] tr embellir

embellishment [em'belɪ/mənt] s embellissement m

ember ['embər] s tison 'm; embers braise f

Em'ber days' spl quatre-temps mpl

embezzle [em'bezəl] tr détourner, s'approprier || intr commettre des détournements

embezzler [em'bezlər] s détourneur m de fonds

embitter [em'bɪtər] tr aigrir

emblazon [em'blezən] tr embellir; exalter, célébrer

emblem ['embləm] s emblème m

emblematic(al) [‚emblə'mætɪk(əl)] adj emblématique

embodiment [em'bɑdɪmənt] s personnification f, incarnation f

embod‑y [em'bɑdi] v (pret & pp -ied) tr personnifier, incarner; (to include) incorporer

embolden [em'boldən] tr enhardir

embolism ['embə‚lɪzəm] s embolie f

emboss [em'bɔs], [em'bɑs] tr (to raise in relief) graver en relief; (metal) bosseler; (e.g., leather) gaufrer, repousser

embouchure [‚ɑmbu'/ur] s embouchure f; (mus) position f des lèvres

embrace [em'bres] s étreinte f, embrassement m || tr étreindre, embrasser || intr s'étreindre, s'embrasser

embroider [em'brɔɪdər] tr broder

embroider‑y [em'brɔɪdəri] s (pl -ies) broderie f

embroil [em'brɔɪl] tr (to throw into confusion) embrouiller; (to involve in contention) brouiller

embroilment [em'brɔɪlmənt] *s* embrouillage *m*, brouillamini *m*, imbroglio *m*

embry·o ['ɛmbrɪ͵o] *s* (*pl* -os) embryon *m*

embryology [͵ɛmbrɪ'ɑlədʒɪ] *s* embryologie *f*

embryonic [͵ɛmbrɪ'ɑnɪk] *adj* embryonnaire

emend [ɪ'mɛnd] *tr* corriger

emendation [͵imɛn'deʃən] *s* correction *f*

emerald ['ɛmərəld] *s* émeraude *f*

emerge [ɪ'mʌrdʒ] *intr* émerger

emergence [ɪ'mʌrdʒəns] *s* émergence *f*

emergen·cy [ɪ'mʌrdʒənsɪ] *adj* urgent, d'urgence; (*exit*) de secours || *s* (*pl* -cies) cas *m* urgent

emer'gency brake' *s* frein *m* de secours

emer'gency ex'it *s* sortie *f* de secours

emer'gency land'ing *s* atterrissage *m* forcé

emer'gency opera'tion *s* (med) opération *f* à chaud

emer'gency ra'tions *spl* vivres *mpl* de réserve

emer'gency ward' *s* salle *f* d'urgence

emeritus [ɪ'mɛrɪtəs] *adj* honoraire, d'honneur

emersion [ɪ'mʌrʒən], [ɪ'mʌrʃən] *s* émersion *f*

emery ['ɛmərɪ] *s* émeri *m*

em'ery cloth' *s* toile *f* d'émeri

em'ery wheel' *s* meule *f* en émeri

emetic [ɪ'mɛtɪk] *adj & s* émétique *m*

emigrant ['ɛmɪgrənt] *adj & s* émigrant *m*

emigrate ['ɛmɪ͵gret] *intr* émigrer

eminence ['ɛmɪnəns] *s* éminence *f*

eminent ['ɛmɪnənt] *adj* éminent; **most eminent** (eccl) éminentissime

emissar·y ['ɛmɪ͵sɛrɪ] *s* (*pl* -ies) émissaire *m*

emit [ɪ'mɪt] *v* (*pret & pp* emitted; *ger* emitting) *tr* émettre; (*a gas, an odor, etc.*) exhaler

emolument [ɪ'mɑljəmənt] *s* émoluments *mpl*

emotion [ɪ'moʃən] *s* émotion *f*

emotional [ɪ'moʃənəl] *adj* émotif, émotionnable

emperor ['ɛmpərər] *s* empereur *m*

empha·sis ['ɛmfəsɪs] *s* (*pl* -ses [͵siz]) accentuation *f*, mise *f* en relief; énergie *f*, force *f*; (*on word or phrase*) accent *m* d'insistance; **to place emphasis on** insister vivement sur; **with emphasis on** en insistant particulièrement sur

emphasize ['ɛmfə͵saɪz] *tr* accentuer, mettre en relief; appuyer sur, souligner

emphatic [ɛm'fætɪk] *adj* accentué, énergique

emphysema [͵ɛmfɪ'simə] *s* emphysème *m*

empire ['ɛmpaɪr] *s* empire *m*

empiric(al) [ɛm'pɪrɪk(əl)] *adj* empirique

empiricist [ɛm'pɪrɪsɪst] *s* empirique *m*

emplacement [ɛm'plesmənt] *s* emplacement *m*

employ [ɛm'plɔɪ] *s* service *m* || *tr* employer

employee [ɛm'plɔɪ·i], [͵ɛmplɔɪ'i] *s* employé *m*

employer [ɛm'plɔɪ·ər] *s* employeur *m*, patron *m*, chef *m*

employment [ɛm'plɔɪmənt] *s* emploi *m*

employ'ment a'gency *s* bureau *m* de placement

empower [ɛm'pau·ər] *tr* autoriser

empress ['ɛmprɪs] *s* impératrice *f*

emptiness ['ɛmptɪnɪs] *s* vide *m*

emp·ty ['ɛmptɪ] *adj* (*comp* -tier; *super* -tiest) vide; (*hollow*) creux, vain; (coll) affamé || *v* (*pret & pp* -tied) *tr* vider || *intr* se vider; (*said of river*) se jeter; (*said of auditorium*) se dégarnir

emp'ty-hand'ed *adj & adv* les mains vides

emp'ty-head'ed *adj* écervelé

empye·ma [͵ɛmpɪ'imə] *s* (*pl* -mata [mətə]) empyème *m*

empyrean [͵ɛmpɪ'ri·ən] *s* empyrée *m*

emu ['imju] *s* (zool) émeu *m*

emulate ['ɛmjə͵let] *tr* chercher à égaler, imiter || *intr* rivaliser

emulator ['ɛmjə͵letər] *s* émule *mf*

emulsi·fy [ɪ'mʌlsɪ͵faɪ] *v* (*pret & pp* -fied) *tr* émulsionner

emulsion [ɪ'mʌlʃən] *s* émulsion *f*

enable [ɛn'ebəl] *tr*—**to enable to** rendre capable de, mettre à même de

enact [ɛn'ækt] *tr* (*to decree*) décréter, arrêter; (theat) représenter

enactment [ɛn'æktmənt] *s* loi *f*; (*establishing*) établissement *m*; (govt) promulgation *f*; (law) décret *m*; (theat) représentation *f*

enam·el [ɪ'næməl] *s* émail *m* || *v* (*pret & pp* -eled or -elled; *ger* -eling or -elling) *tr* émailler

enameling [ɪ'næməlɪŋ] *s* émaillage *m*

enam'el·ware' *s* ustensiles *mpl* en fer émaillé

enamor [ɛn'æmər] *tr* rendre amoureux; **to become enamored with** s'énamourer de

encamp [ɛn'kæmp] *tr & intr* camper

encampment [ɛn'kæmpmənt] *s* campement *m*

encase [ɛn'kes] *tr* mettre en caisse; enfermer, envelopper

encephalitis [ɛn͵sɛfə'laɪtɪs] *s* encéphalite *f*

enchain [ɛn't ʃen] *tr* enchaîner

enchant [ɛn't ʃænt], [ɛn't ʃɑnt] *tr* enchanter

enchanting [ɛn't ʃæntɪŋ], [ɛn't ʃɑntɪŋ] *adj* charmant, ravissant; (*casting a spell*) enchanteur

enchantment [ɛn't ʃæntmənt], [ɛn't ʃɑntmənt] *s* enchantement *m*

enchantress [ɛn't ʃæntrɪs], [ɛn't ʃɑntrɪs] *s* enchanteresse *f*

encircle [ɛn'sʌrkəl] *tr* encercler, cerner; (*a word*) entourer d'un cercle

enclitic [ɛn'klɪtɪk] *adj & s* enclitique *m*

enclose [ɛn'kloz] *tr* enclore, entourer; (*in a letter*) inclure, joindre

enclosed *adj* (*in a letter*) ci-joint, ci-inclus

enclosure [ɛn'kloʒər] s clôture f, enceinte f, enclos m; (e.g., in a letter) pièce f jointe, pièce annexée

encomi·um [ɛn'komɪ·əm] s (pl -ums or -a [ə]) panégyrique m, éloge m

encompass [ɛn'kʌmpəs] tr entourer, renfermer

encore ['ankor] s rappel m, bis m || tr bisser || interj bis!

encounter [ɛn'kaʊntər] s rencontre f || tr rencontrer || intr se rencontrer, combattre

encourage [ɛn'kʌrɪdʒ] tr encourager

encouragement [ɛn'kʌrɪdʒmənt] s encouragement m

encroach [ɛn'krotʃ] intr—to encroach on or upon empiéter sur; abuser de

encumber [ɛn'kʌmbər] tr encombrer, embarrasser; (with debts) grever

encumbrance [ɛn'kʌmbrəns] s encombrement m, embarras m; (law) charge f

encyclical [ɛn'sɪklɪkəl], [ɛn'saɪklɪkəl] adj & s encyclique f

encyclopedia [ɛn,saɪklə'pidɪ·ə] s encyclopédie f

encyclopedic [ɛn,saɪklə'pidɪk] adj encyclopédique

end [ɛnd] s (in time) fin f; (in space; small piece) bout m; (purpose) but m; (end of set period of time) terme m; at loose ends en pagaille; at the end, in the end à la fin; to be at the end of one's rope être au bout de son rouleau; to bring to an end mettre fin à; to come to an end prendre fin; to make both ends meet joindre les deux bouts; to stand on end (said of hair) se dresser; to this end à cet effet || tr achever, terminer || intr s'achever, se terminer; to end up by finir par

endanger [ɛn'dendʒər] tr mettre en danger

endear [ɛn'dɪr] tr faire aimer; to endear oneself to se faire aimer de

endeavor [ɛn'dɛvər] s effort m, tentative f || intr—to endeavor to s'efforcer de, tâcher de

endemic [ɛn'dɛmɪk] adj endémique

ending ['ɛndɪŋ] s fin f, terminaison f; (gram) désinence f

endive ['ɛndaɪv] s (blanched type) endive f; (Cichorium endivia) chicorée f frisée

endless ['ɛndlɪs] adj sans fin

end·most adj extrême

endocrine ['ɛndo,kraɪn], ['ɛndokrɪn] adj endocrine

endorse [ɛn'dɔrs] tr endosser; (a candidate) appuyer; (a plan) souscrire à

endorsement [ɛn'dɔrsmənt] s endos m, endossement m; (approval) appui m, approbation f

endorser [ɛn'dɔrsər] s endosseur m

endow [ɛn'daʊ] tr doter, fonder

endowment [ɛn'daʊmənt] s dotation f, fondation f; (talent) don m

endow·ment fund s caisse f de dotation

end' pa'per s pages fpl de garde

endurance [ɛn'd(j)ʊrəns] s endurance f

endur'ance test' s épreuve f d'endurance

endure [ɛn'd(j)ʊr] tr endurer || intr durer

enduring [ɛn'd(j)ʊrɪŋ] adj durable

enema ['ɛnəmə] s lavement m

enemy ['ɛnəmi] adj ennemi || s (pl -mies) ennemi m

energetic [,ɛnər'dʒɛtɪk] adj énergique

energy ['ɛnərdʒi] s (pl -gies) énergie f

en'ergy bal'ance s (nucl) bilan m énergétique

enervate ['ɛnər,vet] tr énerver

enfeeble [ɛn'fibəl] tr affaiblir

enfold [ɛn'fold] tr envelopper, enrouler; (to embrace) embrasser

enforce [ɛn'fɔrs] tr (a law) faire exécuter, mettre en vigueur; (one's rights, one's point of view) faire valoir, appuyer; (e.g., obedience) imposer

enforcement [ɛn'fɔrsmənt] s contrainte f; (of a law) exécution f, mise f en vigueur

enfranchise [ɛn'fræntʃaɪz] tr affranchir; donner le droit de vote à

engage [ɛn'gedʒ] tr engager; (to hire) engager, embaucher; (to reserve) retenir, réserver, louer; (s.o.'s attention) fixer, attirer; (the clutch) embrayer; (toothed wheels) engrener; to be engaged in s'occuper de; to be engaged to be married être fiancé; to engage s.o. in conversation entamer une conversation avec qn || intr s'engager; (mach) engrener; to engage in s'embarquer dans, entrer en or dans

engaged adj (to be married) fiancé; (busy) occupé, pris; (mach) en prise; (mil) aux prises, aux mains

engagement [ɛn'gedʒmənt] s engagement m; (betrothal) fiançailles fpl; (appointment) rendez-vous m; (mach) embrayage m, engrenage m; (mil) engagement, combat m

engage'ment ring' s bague f or anneau m de fiançailles

engaging [ɛn'gedʒɪŋ] adj engageant, attirant

engender [ɛn'dʒɛndər] tr engendrer

engine ['ɛndʒɪn] s machine f; (of automobile) moteur m

engineer [,ɛndʒə'nɪr] s ingénieur m; (engine driver) mécanicien m || tr diriger or construire en qualité d'ingénieur; (coll) manigancer, machiner

engineering [,ɛndʒə'nɪrɪŋ] s génie m

en'gine house' s dépôt m de pompes à incendie

en'gine·man' or **en'gine·man** s (pl -men' or -men) mécanicien m

en'gine room' s chambre f des machines

en'gine-room' tel'egraph s (naut) transmetteur m d'ordres

en'gine trou'ble s panne f de moteur

England ['ɪŋglənd] s Angleterre f; l'Angleterre

English ['ɪŋglɪʃ] adj anglais || s (language) anglais m; (billiards) effet m; the English les Anglais

Eng'lish Chan'nel s Manche f

Eng/lish dai/sy s marguerite f des champs

Eng/lish horn/ s cor m anglais

Eng/lish·man s (pl -men) Anglais m

Eng/lish-speak/ing adj anglophone, d'expression anglaise; (country) de langue anglaise

Eng/lish·wom/an s (pl -wom/en) Anglaise f

engraft [ɛnˈgræft], [ɛnˈgrɑft] tr greffer; (fig) implanter

engrave [ɛnˈgrev] tr graver

engraver [ɛnˈgrevər] s graveur m

engraving [ɛnˈgrevɪŋ] s gravure f

engross [ɛnˈgros] tr absorber, occuper; (a document) grossoyer

engrossing [ɛnˈgrosɪŋ] adj absorbant

engulf [ɛnˈgʌlf] tr engouffrer, engloutir

enhance [ɛnˈhæns], [ɛnˈhɑns] tr rehausser, relever

enhancement [ɛnˈhænsmənt], [ɛnˈhɑnsmənt] s rehaussement m

enigma [ɪˈnɪgmə] s énigme f

enigmatic(al) [ˌɪnɪgˈmætɪk(əl)] adj énigmatique

enjoin [ɛnˈdʒɔɪn] tr enjoindre; (to forbid) interdire

enjoy [ɛnˈdʒɔɪ] tr jouir de; **to enjoy +** ger prendre plaisir à + inf; **to enjoy oneself** s'amuser, se divertir

enjoyable [ɛnˈdʒɔɪ·əbəl] adj agréable, plaisant; (show, party, etc.) divertissant

enjoyment [ɛnˈdʒɔɪmənt] s (pleasure) plaisir m; (pleasurable use) jouissance f

enkindle [ɛnˈkɪndəl] tr allumer

enlarge [ɛnˈlɑrdʒ] tr agrandir, élargir; (phot) agrandir || intr s'agrandir, s'élargir; **to enlarge on** or **upon** discourir longuement sur, amplifier

enlargement [ɛnˈlɑrdʒmənt] s agrandissement m

enlighten [ɛnˈlaɪtən] tr éclairer

enlightenment [ɛnˈlaɪtənmənt] s éclaircissements mpl; **the Enlightenment** le siècle des lumières

enlist [ɛnˈlɪst] tr enrôler || intr s'enrôler, s'engager

enlist/ed man/ s homme m de troupe

enlistment [ɛnˈlɪstmənt] s enrôlement m, engagement m

enliven [ɛnˈlaɪvən] tr animer, égayer

enmesh [ɛnˈmɛʃ] tr prendre dans les rets; (e.g., in an evil design) empêtrer; (mach) engrener

enmi·ty [ˈɛnmɪti] s (pl -ties) inimitié f

ennoble [ɛnˈnobəl] tr ennoblir; (to confer a title of nobility upon) anoblir

ennui [ˈɑnwi] s ennui m

enormous [ɪˈnɔrməs] adj énorme

enormously [ɪˈnɔrməsli] adv énormément

enough [ɪˈnʌf] adj, s, & adv assez; **more than enough** plus qu'il n'en faut; **that's enough!** en voilà assez!; **to be intelligent enough** être assez intelligent; **to have enough to live on** avoir de quoi vivre || interj assez!, ça suffit!

enounce [ɪˈnaʊns] tr énoncer

enrage [ɛnˈredʒ] tr faire enrager, rendre furieux; **to be enraged** enrager

enrapture [ɛnˈræptʃər] tr ravir, transporter

enrich [ɛnˈrɪtʃ] tr enrichir

enrichment [ɛnˈrɪtʃmənt] s enrichissement m

enroll [ɛnˈrol] tr enrôler; (a student) inscrire; (to wrap up) enrouler || intr s'enrôler; (said of student) prendre ses inscriptions, se faire inscrire

enrollment [ɛnˈrolmənt] s enrôlement m; (of a student) inscription f; (wrapping up) enroulement m

ensconce [ɛnˈskɑns] tr cacher; **to ensconce oneself** s'installer

ensemble [ɑnˈsɑmbəl] s ensemble m

ensign [ˈɛnsaɪn] s enseigne f || [ˈɛnsən], [ˈɛnsaɪn] s (nav) enseigne m de deuxième classe

ensilage [ˈɛnsɪlɪdʒ] s fourrage m d'un silo américain || tr ensiler

enslave [ɛnˈslev] tr asservir, réduire en esclavage

enslavement [ɛnˈslevmənt] s asservissement m

ensnare [ɛnˈsnɛr] tr prendre au piège, attraper

ensue [ɛnˈs(j)u] intr s'ensuivre, résulter

ensuing [ɛnˈs(j)u·ɪŋ] adj suivant

ensure [ɛnˈʃʊr] tr assurer, garantir

entail [ɛnˈtel] tr occasionner, entraîner

entangle [ɛnˈtæŋgəl] tr embrouiller

entanglement [ɛnˈtæŋgəlmənt] s embrouillement m, embarras m

enter [ˈɛntər] tr (a room, a house, etc.) entrer dans; (a school, the army, etc.) entrer à; (e.g., a period of convalescence) entrer en; (a highway, a public square, etc.) déboucher sur; (e.g., a club) devenir membre de; (a request) enregistrer, consigner par écrit; (a student, a contestant, etc.) admettre, faire inscrire; (in the customhouse) déclarer; (to make a record of) inscrire, porter; **to enter one's name for** se faire inscrire à or pour || intr entrer; (theat) entrer en scène; **to enter into** entrer à, dans, or en; (to be an ingredient of) entrer pour; **to enter on** or **upon** entreprendre, débuter dans

enterprise [ˈɛntərˌpraɪz] s (undertaking) entreprise f; (spirit, push) esprit m d'entreprise, allant m, entrain m

enterprising [ˈɛntərˌpraɪzɪŋ] adj entreprenant

entertain [ˌɛntərˈten] tr (to distract) amuser, divertir; (to show hospitality to) recevoir; (at a meal) régaler; (a hope) entretenir, nourrir; (an idea) concevoir || intr recevoir

entertainer [ˌɛntərˈtenər] s (host) hôte m, amphitryon m; amuseur m; (comedian) comique mf

entertaining [ˌɛntərˈtenɪŋ] adj amusant, divertissant

entertainment [ˌɛntərˈtenmənt] s (distraction) amusement m, divertissement m; (show) spectacle m; (as a guest) accueil m, hospitalité f en'tertain'ment tax' *s* taxe *f* sur les spectacles

enthrall [ɛn'θrɔl] *tr* (*to charm*) captiver, charmer; (*to enslave*) asservir, rendre esclave

enthrone [ɛn'θron] *tr* introniser

enthuse [ɛn'θ(j)uz] *tr* (coll) enthousiasmer ǁ *intr* (coll) s'enthousiasmer

enthusiasm [ɛn'θ(j)uzɪ‚æzəm] *s* enthousiasme *m*

enthusiast [ɛn'θ(j)uzɪ‚æst] *s* enthousiaste *mf*; (*camera fiend, sports fan, etc.*) fanatique *mf*, enragé *m*

enthusiastic [ɛn‚θ(j)uzɪ'æstɪk] *adj* enthousiaste; (*for sports, music, a hobby*) fanatique, enragé

entice [ɛn'taɪs] *tr* attirer, séduire; (*to evil*) tenter, chercher à séduire

enticement [ɛn'taɪsmənt] *s* attrait *m*, appât *m*; tentation *f*, séduction *f*

entire [ɛn'taɪr] *adj* entier

entirely [ɛn'taɪrli] *adv* entièrement, en entier; (*absolutely*) tout à fait, absolument

entire·ty [ɛn'taɪrti] *s* (*pl* -ties) totalité *f*, entier *m*; in its entirety dans sa totalité

entitle [ɛn'taɪtəl] *tr* (*to name*) intituler; (*to qualify*) donner le droit à; to be entitled to avoir droit à

enti·ty ['ɛntɪti] *s* (*pl* -ties) entité *f*

entomb [ɛn'tum] *tr* ensevelir

entombment [ɛn'tummənt] *s* ensevelissement *m*

entomology [‚ɛntə'mɑlədʒi] *s* entomologie *f*

entourage [‚antu'raʒ] *s* entourage *m*

entrails ['ɛntrelz], ['ɛntrəlz] *spl* entrailles *fpl*

entrain [ɛn'tren] *tr* faire prendre le train, embarquer; (*to carry along*) entraîner ǁ *intr* embarquer, s'embarquer

entrance ['ɛntrəns] *s* entrée *f*; (theat) entrée en scène; entrance to . . . (*public sign*) accès à . . . ǁ [ɛn'træns], [ɛn'trans] *tr* enchanter, ensorceler; to be entranced s'extasier

en'trance examina'tion *s* examen *m* d'entrée

en'trance fee' *s* droits *mpl* d'entrée

entrancing [ɛn'trænsɪŋ], [ɛn'transɪŋ] *adj* enchanteur, ensorceleur

entrant ['ɛntrənt] *s* inscrit *m*; (*in a competition*) concurrent *m*, participant *m*

en·trap [ɛn'træp] *v* (*pret & pp* -trapped*; ger* -trapping) *tr* attraper

entreat [ɛn'trit] *tr* supplier, prier, conjurer

entreat·y [ɛn'triti] *s* (*pl* -ies) supplication *f*, prière *f*

entree ['antre] *s* (*entrance; course preceding the roast*) entrée *f*; (*main dish*) plat *m* de résistance

entrench [ɛn'trɛntʃ] *tr* retrancher; to be entrenched se retrancher ǁ *intr* to entrench on *or* upon empiéter sur

entrust [ɛn'trʌst] *tr*—to entrust s.o. with s th., to entrust s.th. to s.o. confier q.ch. à qn

en·try ['ɛntri] *s* (*pl* -tries) entrée *f*; (*in a dictionary*) article *m*, entrée; (*on a register*) inscription *f*; (*in a competition*) concurrent *m*, participant *m*; (*thing entered for judging in a competition*) objet *m* exposé

en'try blank' *s* feuille *f* d'inscription

entwine [ɛn'twaɪn] *tr* entrelacer, enlacer ǁ *intr* s'entrelacer, s'enlacer

enumerate [ɪ'n(j)umə‚ret] *tr* énumérer

enunciate [ɪ'nʌnsɪ‚et], [ɪ'nʌnʃɪ‚et] *tr* énoncer, déclarer; (*to articulate*) articuler, prononcer

envelop [ɛn'vɛləp] *tr* envelopper

envelope ['ɛnvə‚lop], ['ɑnvə‚lop] *s* enveloppe *f*; in an envelope sous enveloppe, sous pli

envenom [ɛn'vɛnəm] *tr* envenimer, empoisonner

enviable ['ɛnvɪ‚əbəl] *adj* enviable, digne d'envie

envious ['ɛnvɪ‚əs] *adj* envieux

environment [ɛn'vaɪrənmənt] *s* environnement *m*, milieu *m*

environs [ɛn'vaɪrənz] *spl* environs *mpl*

envisage [ɛn'vɪzɪdʒ] *tr* envisager

envoi ['ɛnvɔɪ] *s* envoi *m*

envoy ['ɛnvɔɪ] *s* envoyé *m*, émissaire *m*; (*of poem*) envoi *m*

en·vy ['ɛnvi] *s* (*pl* -vies) envie *f* ǁ (*pret & pp* -vied) *tr* envier

enzyme ['ɛnzaɪm], ['ɛnzɪm] *s* enzyme *m & f*

epaulet ['ɛpə‚let] *s* épaulette *f*

epergne [ɪ'pʌrn], [e'pern] *s* surtout *m*

ephemeral [ɪ'fɛmərəl] *adj* éphémère

epic ['ɛpɪk] *adj* épique ǁ *s* épopée *f*

epicure ['ɛpɪ‚kjur] *s* gourmet *m*, gastronome *m*

epidemic [‚ɛpɪ'dɛmɪk] *adj* épidémique ǁ *s* épidémie *f*

epidemiology [‚ɛpɪ‚dimɪ'ɑlədʒi] *s* épidémiologie *f*

epidermis [‚ɛpɪ'dʌrmɪs] *s* épiderme *m*

epiglottis [‚ɛpɪ'glɑtɪs] *s* épiglotte *f*

epigram ['ɛpɪ‚græm] *s* épigramme *f*

epilepsy ['ɛpɪ‚lɛpsi] *s* épilepsie *f*

epileptic [‚ɛpɪ'lɛptɪk] *adj & s* épileptique *mf*

epilogue ['ɛpɪ‚lɔg], ['ɛpɪ‚lag] *s* épilogue *m*

episcopal [ɪ'pɪskəpəl] *adj* épiscopal

Episcopalian [ɪ‚pɪskə'pelɪ‚ən] *adj* épiscopal ǁ *s* épiscopal *m*

episode ['ɛpɪ‚sod] *s* épisode *m*

episodic [‚ɛpɪ'sɑdɪk] *adj* épisodique

epistle [ɪ'pɪsəl] *s* épître *f*

epitaph ['ɛpɪ‚tæf] *s* épitaphe *f*

epithet ['ɛpɪ‚θet] *s* épithète *f*

epitome [ɪ'pɪtəmi] *s* (*abridgment*) épitomé *m*; (*representative of a class*) modèle *m*, personnification *f*

epitomize [ɪ'pɪtə‚maɪz] *tr* abréger; personnifier

epoch ['ɛpək], ['ipak] *s* époque *f*

epochal ['ɛpəkəl] *adj* mémorable

ep'och-mak'ing *adj* qui fait époque

Ep'som salts' ['ɛpsəm] *spl* epsomite *f*, sels *mpl* d'Epsom

equable ['ɛkwəbəl], ['ikwəbəl] *adj* uniforme, égal; tranquille

equal ['ikwəl] *adj* égal; to be equal to égaler, valoir; (*e.g., the occasion*) être à la hauteur de; **to be equal to** + ger être de force à + inf, être à même de + inf; **to get equal with** (coll) se venger de || s égal m, pareil m || v (pret & pp **equaled** or **equalled**) ger **equaling** or **equalling**) tr égaler

equali·ty [ɪˈkwɑlɪti] s (pl **-ties**) égalité f

equalize [ˈikwəˌlaɪz] tr égaliser

equally [ˈikwəli] adv également

equanimity [ˌikwəˈnɪmɪti] s équanimité f, égalité f d'âme

equate [iˈkwet] tr égaliser, mettre en équation

equation [iˈkweʒən], [iˈkweʃən] s équation f

equator [iˈkwetər] s équateur m

equatorial [ˌikwəˈtoriəl] adj équatorial

equestrian [iˈkwestriˌ ən] adj équestre || s cavalier m, écuyer m

equilateral [ˌikwiˈlætərəl] adj équilatéral

equilibrium [ˌikwiˈlibriˌ əm] s équilibre m

equinoctial [ˌikwiˈnɑkʃəl] adj équinoxial

equinox [ˈikwiˌnɑks] s équinoxe m

equip [iˈkwɪp] v (pret & pp **equipped**; ger **equipping**) tr équiper, outiller; **to equip with** munir de

equipment [iˈkwɪpmənt] s équipement m, matériel m

equipoise [ˈikwiˌpɔɪz], [ˈɛkwiˌpɔɪz] s équilibre m || tr équilibrer

equitable [ˈɛkwɪtəbəl] adj équitable

equi·ty [ˈɛkwɪti] s (pl **-ties**) équité f; (com) part f résiduaire

equivalent [iˈkwɪvələnt] adj & s équivalent m

equivocal [iˈkwɪvəkəl] adj équivoque

equivocate [iˈkwɪvəˌket] intr équivoquer

equivocation [iˌkwɪvəˈkeʃən] s tergiversation f, équivoque f

era [ˈɪrə], [ˈirə] s ère f, époque f

eradicate [iˈrædiˌket] tr déraciner, extirper

erase [iˈres] tr effacer, biffer

eraser [iˈresər] s gomme f à effacer; brosse f

erasure [iˈreʃər] s effacement m, rature f

ere [ɛr] prep (poetic) avant || conj (poetic) avant que

erect [iˈrɛkt] adj droit, debout || tr (to set in an upright position) dresser, élever; (a building) ériger, édifier; (a machine) monter

erection [iˈrɛkʃən] s érection f

erg [ʌrg] s erg m

ermine [ˈʌrmɪn] s hermine f

erode [iˈrod] tr éroder

erosion [iˈroʒən] s érosion f

erotic [iˈrɑtɪk] adj érotique

err [ʌr] intr se tromper, faire erreur, errer; (to do wrong) s'égarer, pécher

errand [ˈɛrənd] s commission f, course f; **to go on** or **to run an errand** faire une course

er'rand boy' s coursier m, garçon de courses

erratic [iˈrætɪk] adj variable; capricieux, excentrique

erroneous [iˈroniˌəs] adj erroné

error [ˈɛrər] s erreur f

erudite [ˈɛr(j)uˌdaɪt] adj érudit

erudition [ˌɛr(j)uˈdɪʃən] s érudition f

erupt [iˈrʌpt] intr faire éruption

eruption [iˈrʌpʃən] s éruption f

escalate [ˈɛskəˌlet] intr faire éruption

escalation [ˌɛskəˈleʃən] s escalade f

escalator [ˈɛskəˌletər] s escalator m, escalier m mécanique or roulant

escallop [ɛsˈkæləp] s coquille f Saint-Jacques, peigne m, pétoncle m; (culin) coquille au gratin || tr (the edges) denteler, découper; (culin) gratiner et cuire au four et à la crème

escapade [ˌɛskəˈped] s fredaine f, frasque f; (getting away) escapade f

escape [ɛsˈkep] s (getaway) évasion f, fuite f; (from responsibilities, duties, etc.) évasion, escapade f; (of gas, liquid, etc.) échappement m, fuite; (of a clock) échappement; **to have a narrow escape** l'échapper belle; **to make one's escape** se sauver, s'échapper || tr échapper à, éviter || intr échapper, s'échapper, s'évader; **to escape from** échapper à

escape' clause' s échappatoire f m

escapee [ˌɛskəˈpi] s évadé m, échappé m

escape' hatch' s (aer) sas m d'évacuation

escape' lit'erature s littérature f d'évasion

escapement [ɛsˈkepmənt] s issue f, débouché m; (mach) échappement m

escape' wheel' s roue f de rencontre

escarole [ˈɛskəˌrol] s scarole f

escarpment [ɛsˈkɑrpmənt] s escarpement m

eschew [ɛsˈtʃu] tr éviter, s'abstenir de

escort [ˈɛskɔrt] s escorte f; (gentleman escort) cavalier m || [ɛsˈkɔrt] tr escorter

escutcheon [ɛsˈkʌtʃən] s écusson m

Eski·mo [ˈɛskiˌmo] s (pl **-mos** or **-mo**) (language; dog) esquimau m; (person) Esquimo m, Esquimau m

Es'kimo wom'an s Esquimaude f, femme f esquimau

esophagus [iˈsɑfəgəs] s (pl **-gi** [ˌdʒaɪ]) œsophage m

esoteric [ˌɛsoˈtɛrɪk] adj ésotérique

especial [ɛsˈpɛʃəl] adj spécial

especially [ɛsˈpɛʃəli] adv surtout, particulièrement

espionage [ˈɛspiˌənɪdʒ], [ˌɛspiˈənaʒ] s espionnage m

espousal [ɛsˈpauzəl] s épousailles f; **espousal of** (a cause) adoption de, adhésion à

espouse [ɛsˈpauz] tr épouser; (to advocate, adopt) adopter, embrasser

Esq. abbr (**Esquire**)—**John Smith, Esq.** Monsieur Jean Smith

esquire [ɛsˈkwaɪr], [ˈɛskwaɪr] s (hist) écuyer m

essay [ˈɛse] s essai m || tr essayer

essayist [ˈɛseˌɪst] s essayiste mf

essence ['ɛsəns] s essence f

essential [e'sen/əl] adj & s essentiel m

establish [es'tæbliʃ] tr établir

establishment [es'tæbliʃmənt] s établissement m

estate [es'tet] s (landed property) domaine m, propriété f, terres fpl; (a person's possessions) biens mpl, possessions fpl; (left by a decedent) héritage m, succession f; (social status) rang m, condition f; (hist) état m

esteem [es'tim] s estime f || tr estimer

esthete ['ɛsθit] s esthète mf

esthetic [es'θetɪk] adj esthétique || esthetics s esthétique f

estimable ['estɪməbəl] adj estimable

estimate ['ɛstɪ,met], ['ɛstɪmɪt] s évaluation f, appréciation f; (appraisal) estimation f || ['ɛstɪ,met] tr (to judge, deem) apprécier, estimer; (the cost) estimer, évaluer

estimation [,ɛstɪ'meʃən] s (opinion) jugement m; (esteem) estime f; (appraisal) estimation f; in my estimation à mon avis

Estonia [es'toni·ə] s Estonie f; l'Estonie

estrangement [es'trendʒmənt] s éloignement m; (a becoming unfriendly) désaffection f

estuar·y ['ɛst/u,eri] s (pl -ies) estuaire m

etch [ɛt/] tr & intr graver à l'eau-forte

etcher ['ɛt/ər] s aquafortiste m

etching ['ɛt/ɪŋ] s eau-forte f

eternal [ɪ'tʌrnəl] adj éternel

eterni·ty [ɪ'tʌrnɪti] s (pl -ties) éternité f

ether ['iθər] s éther m

ethereal [ɪ'θɪrɪ·əl] adj éthéré

ethical ['ɛθɪkəl] adj éthique

ethics ['ɛθɪks] s (branch of philosophy) étique f, morale f; spl (one's conduct, one's moral principles) morale

Ethiopia [,iθɪ'opɪ·ə] s Éthiopie f; l'Éthiopie

Ethiopian [,iθɪ'opɪ·ən] adj éthiopien f; s (language) éthiopien m; (person) Éthiopien m

ethnic(al) ['ɛθnɪk(əl)] adj ethnique

ethnography [ɛθ'nɑgrəfi] s ethnographie f

ethnology [ɛθ'nɑlədʒi] s ethnologie f

ethyl ['ɛθɪl] s éthyle m

ethylene ['ɛθɪ,lin] s éthylène m

etiquette ['ɛtɪ,kɛt] s étiquette f

etymolo·gy [,ɛtɪ'mɑlədʒi] s (pl -gies) étymologie f

ety·mon [ˈɛtɪ,mɑn] s (pl -mons or -ma [mə]) étymon m

eucalyp·tus [,jukə'lɪptəs] s (pl -tuses or -ti [taɪ]) eucalyptus m

Eucharist ['jukərɪst] s Eucharistie f

euchre ['jukər] s euchre m || tr (coll) l'emporter sur

eulogize ['julə,dʒaɪz] tr faire l'éloge de

eulo·gy ['julədʒi] s (pl -gies) éloge m

eunuch ['junək] s eunuque m

euphemism ['jufɪ,mɪzəm] s euphémisme m

euphemistic [,jufɪ'mɪstɪk] adj euphémique

euphonic [ju'fɑnɪk] adj euphonique

eupho·ny ['jufəni] s (pl -nies) euphonie f

euphoria [ju'forɪ·ə] s euphorie f

euphuism ['jufju,ɪzəm] s euphuisme m; préciosité f

Europe ['jurəp] s Europe f; l'Europe

European [,jurə'pi·ən] adj européen m; s Européen m

euthanasia [,juθə'neʒə] s euthanasie f

evacuate [ɪ'vækju,et] tr évacuer || intr s'évacuer

evade [ɪ'ved] tr échapper à, éviter, esquiver || intr s'évader

evaluate [ɪ'vælju,et] tr évaluer

Evangel [ɪ'vændʒəl] s évangile m

evangelic(al) [,ɪvæn'dʒelɪk(əl)], [,ɛvən'dʒelɪk(əl)] adj évangélique

evangelist [ɪ'vændʒəlɪst] s évangéliste m

evaporate [ɪ'væpə,ret] tr évaporer || intr s'évaporer

evasion [ɪ've3ən] s évasion f; subterfuge m, détour m

evasive [ɪ'vesɪv] adj évasif

eve [iv] s veille f; (poetic) soir m; on the eve of à la veille de; Eve Ève f

even ['ivən] adj (smooth) uni; (number) pair; (equal, uniform) égal; (temperament) calme, rassis, égal; even with à fleur de; to be even (to get even) quitte; (cards, sports) être manche à manche or point à point; to get even with (coll) rendre la pareille à || adv même; even + comp encore + comp, e.g., even better encore mieux; even so quand même || tr aplanir, égaliser

evening ['ivnɪŋ] adj du soir || s soir m; all evening toute la soirée; every evening tous les soirs; in the evening le soir; the evening before la veille au soir

eve'ning clothes' s tenue f de soirée; (for women) toilette f de soirée; (for men) habit m de soirée

eve'ning damp' s serein m

eve'ning prim'rose s onagraire f

eve'ning star' s étoile f du soir, étoile du berger

eve'ning wrap' s sortie f de bal

e'ven·song' s (eccl) vêpres fpl

event [ɪ'vent] s événement m; at all events or in any event en tout cas; in the event that dans le cas où

eventful [ɪ'ventfəl] adj mouvementé; mémorable

eventual [ɪ'vent/u·əl] adj final

eventuali·ty [ɪ,vent/u'ælɪti] s (pl -ties) éventualité f

eventually [ɪ'vent/u·əli] adv finalement, à la longue

eventuate [ɪ'vent/u,et] intr—to eventuate in se terminer par, aboutir à

ever ['ɛvər] adv (at all times) toujours; (at any time) jamais; ever since dès lors, depuis; for ever and ever à tout jamais; hardly ever presque jamais

ev'er·glade' s région f marécageuse

ev'er·green' adj toujours vert || s arbre m vert; evergreens plantes fpl vertes, verdure f décorative ev'er·last'ing adj éternel; (continual) sempiternel, perpétuel

ev'er·more' adv toujours; for evermore à jamais

every ['ɛvri] adj tous les; (each) chaque, tout; (coll) tout, e.g., every bit as good as tout aussi bon que; every man for himself sauve qui peut; every now and then de temps en temps; every once in a while de temps à autre; every other day tous les deux jours; every other one un sur deux; every which way (coll) de tous côtés; (coll) en désordre

ev'ery·bod'y pron indef tout le monde

ev'ery·day' adj de tous les jours

ev'ery·man' s Monsieur Tout-le-monde

ev'ery·one' or ev'ery one' pron indef chacun, tous, tout le monde

ev'ery·thing' pron indef tout

ev'ery·where' adv partout, de toutes parts; partout où; everywhere else partout ailleurs

evict [ɪ'vɪkt] tr évincer, expulser

eviction [ɪ'vɪkʃən] s éviction f

evidence ['ɛvɪdəns] s évidence f; (proof) preuve f, témoignage m || tr manifester, démontrer

evident ['ɛvɪdənt] adj évident

evidently ['ɛvɪdəntli], [,ɛvɪ'dɛntli] adv évidemment

evil ['ivəl] adj mauvais, méchant || s mal m, méchanceté f

evildoer ['ivəl,du·ər] s malfaisant m, méchant m

e'vil·do'ing s malfaisance f

e'vil eye' s mauvais œil m

e'vil-mind'ed adj malintentionné, malin

E'vil One' s Esprit m malin

evince [ɪ'vɪns] tr montrer, manifester

evocative [ɪ'vɑkətɪv] adj évocateur

evoke [ɪ'vok] tr évoquer

evolution [,ɛvə'luʃən] s évolution f

evolve [ɪ'vɑlv] tr développer, élaborer || intr évoluer

ewe [ju] s brebis f

ewer ['ju·ər] s aiguière f

exact [ɛg'zækt] adj exact || tr exiger

exacting [ɛg'zæktɪŋ] adj exigeant

exactly [ɛg'zæktli] adv exactement; (sharp, on the dot) précisément, justement

exactness [ɛg'zæktnɪs] s exactitude f

exaggerate [ɛg'zædʒə,ret] tr exagérer

exalt [ɛg'zɔlt] tr exalter

exam [ɛg'zæm] s (coll) examen m

examination [ɛg,zæmɪ'neʃən] s examen m; to take an examination se présenter à, passer, or subir un examen

examine [ɛg'zæmɪn] tr examiner

examiner [ɛg'zæmɪnər] s inspecteur m, vérificateur m; (in a school) examinateur m

example [ɛg'zæmpəl], [ɛg'zampəl] s exemple m; for example par exemple

exasperate [ɛg'zæspə,ret] tr exaspérer

exasperation [ɛg,zæspə'reʃən] s exaspération f

excavate ['ɛkskə,vet] tr excaver

exceed [ɛk'sid] tr excéder

exceedingly [ɛk'sidɪŋli] adv extrêmement

excel [ɛk'sɛl] v (pret & pp -celled; ger -celling) tr surpasser || intr exceller; to excel in exceller dans; to excel in + ger exceller à + inf

excellence ['ɛksələns] s excellence f

excellen·cy ['ɛksələnsi] s (pl -cies) excellence f; Your Excellency Votre Excellence

excelsior [ɛk'sɛlsɪ·ər] s copeaux mpl d'emballage

except [ɛk'sɛpt] adv—except for excepté; except that excepté que || prep excepté || tr excepter

exception [ɛk'sɛpʃən] s exception f; to take exception to trouver à redire à; with the exception of à l'exception de

exceptional [ɛk'sɛpʃənəl] adj exceptionnel

excerpt ['ɛksʌrpt], [ɛk'sʌrpt] s extrait m, citation f || [ɛk'sʌrpt] tr extraire

excess [ɛk'sɛs], [ɛk'sɛs] adj excédentaire || [ɛk'sɛs] s (amount or degree) excédent m, excès m; (excessive amount; immoderate indulgence) excès m; in excess of en plus de

ex'cess bag'gage s excédent m de bagages

ex'cess fare' s supplément m

excessive [ɛk'sɛsɪv] adj excessif

ex'cess-prof'its tax' s contribution f sur les bénéfices extraordinaires

ex'cess weight' s excédent m de poids

exchange [ɛks'tʃendʒ] s échange m; (barter) troc m; (com) bourse f; (telp) central m || tr échanger; (to barter) troquer; to exchange compliments échanger des politesses; to exchange for échanger contre, échanger pour

exchequer [ɛks'tʃɛkər], ['ɛkstʃɛkər] s trésor m public; ministère m des finances; (hist) échiquier m

excise [ɛk'saɪz], ['ɛksaɪz] s contributions fpl indirectes || tr effacer, rayer; (surg) exciser

excitable [ɛk'saɪtəbəl] adj excitable

excite [ɛk'saɪt] tr exciter

excitement [ɛk'saɪtmənt] m agitation f, excitation f

exciting [ɛk'saɪtɪŋ] adj émotionnant, entraînant, passionnant

exclaim [ɛks'klem] tr s'écrier, e.g., "All is lost!" he exclaimed "Tout est perdu!" s'écria-t-il || intr s'exclamer, se récrier

exclamation [,ɛkskle'meʃən] s exclamation f

exclama'tion mark' s point m d'exclamation

exclude [ɛks'klud] tr exclure

excluding [ɛks'kludɪŋ] prep à l'exclusion de, sans compter

exclusion [ɛks'kluʒən] s exclusion f

exclusive [ɛks'klusɪv] adj exclusif; (expensive; fashionable) (coll) choisi, select; exclusive of à l'exclusion de

exclu'sive rights' spl exclusivité f

exclu'sive show'ing s (public sign in front of a theater) en exclusivité

excommunicate [,ɛkskə'mjunɪ,ket] tr excommunier

excommunication [ˌekskə‚mjunɪˈke-ʃən] *s* excommunication *f*

excoriate [eksˈkɔrɪ‚et] *tr* (fig) vitupérer

excrement [ˈekskrəmənt] *s* excrément *m*

excruciating [eksˈkruɪ‚etɪŋ] *adj* affreux, atroce

exculpate [ˈekskʌl‚pet], [eksˈkʌlpet] *tr* disculper

excursion [eksˈkʌrʒən], [eksˈkʌrʃən] *s* excursion *f*

excusable [eksˈkjuzəbəl] *adj* excusable

excuse [eksˈkjus] *s* excuse *f* ‖ [eksˈkjuz] *tr* excuser; **excuse me!** pardon!, je m'excuse!, **to excuse oneself** s'excuser

execrate [ˈeksɪ‚kret] *tr* exécrer; (*to curse*) maudire

execute [ˈeksɪ‚kjut] *tr* exécuter

execution [ˌeksɪˈkjuʃən] *s* exécution *f*

executioner [ˌeksɪˈkjuʃənər] *s* bourreau *m*

executive [egˈzekjɪtɪv] *adj* (*powers*) exécutif; (*position*) administratif ‖ *s* exécutif *m*; (*of school, business, etc.*) directeur *m*, administrateur *m*

Exec′utive Man′sion *s* (U.S.A.) demeure *f* du Président

executor [egˈzekjətər] *s* exécuteur *m* testamentaire

executrix [egˈzekjətrɪks] *s* exécutrice *f* testamentaire

exemplary [egˈzempləri], [ˈegzəm‚pleri] *adj* exemplaire

exempli•fy [egˈzemplɪ‚faɪ] *v* (*pret & pp* **-fied**) *tr* démontrer par des exemples; (*to be a model of*) servir d'exemple à

exempt [egˈzempt] *adj* exempt ‖ *tr* exempter

exemption [egˈzempʃən] *s* exemption *f*; **exemptions** (*from taxes*) déductions *fpl*

exercise [ˈeksər‚saɪz] *s* exercice *m*; **exercises** cérémonies *fpl* ‖ *tr* exercer ‖ *intr* s'exercer, s'entraîner

exert [egˈzʌrt] *tr* exercer; **to exert oneself** faire des efforts

exertion [egˈzʌrʃən] *s* effort *m*; (*e.g., of power*) exercice *m*

exhalation [ˌeks‚hə‚leʃən] *s* (*of air*) expiration *f*; (*of gas, vapors, etc.*) exhalaison *f*

exhale [eksˈhel], [egˈzel] *tr* (*air from lungs*) expirer; (*gas, vapor*) exhaler ‖ *intr* expirer; s'exhaler

exhaust [egˈzɔst] *s* échappement *m*; gaz *mpl* d'échappement ‖ *tr* épuiser; faire le vide dans

exhaust′ fan′ *s* ventilateur *m* aspirant

exhaustion [egˈzɔstʃən] *s* épuisement *m*

exhaustive [egˈzɔstɪv] *adj* exhaustif

exhaust′ man′ifold *s* tuyauterie *f* or collecteur *m* d'échappement

exhaust′ pipe′ *s* tuyau *m* d'échappement

exhaust′ valve′ *s* soupape *f* d'échappement

exhibit [egˈzɪbɪt] *s* exhibition *f*; (*of art*) exposition *f*; (law) document *m* à l'appui, pièce *f* à conviction ‖ *tr*

exhiber; (*e.g., pictures*) exposer ‖ *intr* faire une exposition

exhibition [ˌeksɪˈbɪʃən] *s* exhibition *f*

exhibitor [egˈzɪbɪtər] *s* exposant *m*

exhilarate [egˈzɪlə‚ret] *tr* égayer, animer

exhort [egˈzɔrt] *tr* exhorter

exhume [eksˈhjum], [egˈzjum] *tr* exhumer

exigen•cy [ˈeksɪdʒənsi] *s* (*pl* **-cies**) exigence *f*

exigent [ˈeksɪdʒənt] *adj* exigeant

exile [ˈegzaɪl], [ˈeksaɪl] *s* exil *m*; (*person*) exilé *m* ‖ *tr* exiler

exist [egˈzɪst] *intr* exister

existence [egˈzɪstəns] *s* existence *f*

exit [ˈegzɪt], [ˈeksɪt] *s* sortie *f* ‖ *intr* sortir

exodus [ˈeksədəs] *s* exode *m*

exonerate [egˈzɑnə‚ret] *tr* (*to free from blame*) disculper; (*to free from an obligation*) exonérer, dispenser

exorbitant [egˈzɔrbɪtənt] *adj* exorbitant

exorcize [ˈeksɔr‚saɪz] *tr* exorciser

exotic [egˈzɑtɪk] *adj* exotique

expand [eksˈpænd] *tr* (*a gas, metal, etc.*) dilater; (*to enlarge, develop*) élargir, développer; (*to unfold, stretch out*) étendre, déployer; (*the chest*) gonfler; (math) développer ‖ *intr* se dilater; s'élargir, se développer; s'étendre, se déployer; se gonfler

expanse [eksˈpæns] *s* étendue *f*

expansion [eksˈpænʃən] *s* expansion *f*

expan′sion joint′ *s* joint *m* de dilatation thermique

expansive [eksˈpænsɪv] *adj* expansif; (*broad*) large, étendu

expatiate [eksˈpeʃɪ‚et] *intr* discourir, s'étendre

expatriate [eksˈpetrɪ‚ɪt] *adj & s* expatrié *m* ‖ [eksˈpetrɪ‚et] *tr* expatrier

expect [eksˈpekt] *tr* (*to await the coming of*) attendre; (*to look for as likely*) s'attendre à: **to expect it** s'y attendre; **to expect s.o. to** *inf* s'attendre à ce que qn -∣ *subj*; **to expect to** + *inf* s'attendre à + *inf*

expectan•cy [eksˈpektənsi] *s* (*pl* **-cies**) attente *f*, expectative *f*

expect′ant moth′er [eksˈpektənt] *s* future mère *f*

expectation [ˌekspekˈteʃən] *s* expectative *f*, espérance *f*

expectorate [eksˈpektə‚ret] *tr & intr* expectorer

expedien•cy [eksˈpidɪ‚ənsi] *s* (*pl* **-cies**) convenance *f*, opportunité *f*; opportunisme *m*, débrouillage *m*

expedient [eksˈpidɪ‚ənt] *adj* expédient; (*looking out for oneself*) débrouillard ‖ *s* exrédient *m*

expedite [ˈekspɪ‚daɪt] *tr* expédier

expedition [ˌekspɪˈdɪʃən] *s* expédition *f*; célérité *f*, promptitude *f*

expeditionary [ˌekspɪˈdɪʃən‚eri] *adj* expéditionnaire

expeditious [ˌekspɪˈdɪʃəs] *adj* expéditif

ex•pel [eksˈpel] *v* (*pret & pp* **-pelled**; *ger* **-pelling**) *tr* expulser; (*from school*) renvoyer

expend [eks'pend] *tr* (*to pay out*) dépenser; (*to use up*) consommer

expendable [eks'pendəbəl] *adj* non récupérable; (*soldier*) sacrifiable

expenditure [eks'pendɪtʃər] *s* dépense *f*; consommation *f*

expense [eks'pens] *s* dépense *f*; **at the expense of** aux dépens de; **expenses** frais *mpl*; (*for which a person will be reimbursed*) indemnité *f*; **to meet expenses** faire face aux dépenses

expense' account' *s* état *m* de frais, note *f* de frais

expensive [eks'pensɪv] *adj* cher, couteux; (*tastes*) dispendieux

experience [eks'pɪrɪ·əns] *s* expérience *f* || *tr* éprouver

experienced *adj* expérimenté

experiment [eks'perɪmənt] *s* expérience *f* || [eks'perɪ,ment] *intr* faire des expériences, expérimenter

expert ['ekspərt] *adj* & *s* expert *m*

expertise [,ekspər'tiz] *s* maîtrise *f*

expiate ['ekspɪ,et] *tr* expier

expire [eks'paɪr] *tr* & *intr* expirer

expired *adj* (*lease*; *passport*) expiré; (*note*; *permit*) périmé; (*e.g.*, *driver's license*) suranné; (*insurance policy*) déchu

explain [eks'plen] *tr* expliquer; **to explain oneself** s'expliquer || *intr* expliquer

explainable [eks'plenəbəl] *adj* explicable

explanation [,eksplə'neʃən] *s* explication *f*

explanatory [eks'plænə,tori] *adj* explicatif

explicit [eks'plɪsɪt] *adj* explicite

explode [eks'plod] *tr* faire sauter; (*a theory*, *opinion*, *etc.*) discréditer || *intr* exploser, éclater, sauter

exploit [eks'plɔɪt], ['eksplɔɪt] *s* exploit *m* || [eks'plɔɪt] *tr* exploiter

exploitation [,eksplɔɪ'reʃən] *s* exploitation *f*

exploration [,eksplə'reʃən] *s* exploration *f*

explore [eks'plor] *tr* explorer

explorer [eks'plorər] *s* explorateur *m*; (*boy scout*) routier *m*

explosion [eks'ploʒən] *s* explosion *f*

explosive [eks'plosɪv] *adj* explosif; (*mixture*) explosible || *s* explosif *m*

exponent [eks'ponənt] *s* interprète *mf*; (*math*) exposant *m*

export ['eksport] *s* exportation *f* || [eks'port], ['eksport] *tr* & *intr* exporter

exportation [,ekspor'teʃən] *s* exportation *f*

exporter ['eksportər], [eks'portər] *s* exportateur *m*

expose [eks'poz] *tr* exposer; (*to unmask*) démasquer, dévoiler; (*phot*) impressionner

exposé [,ekspo'ze] *s* dévoilement *m*, révélation *f*, mise *f* en lumière

exposition [,ekspə'zɪʃən] *s* exposition *f*

expostulate [eks'pastʃə,let] *intr* faire des remontrances; **to expostulate with** faire des remontrances à

exposure [eks'poʒər] *s* exposition *f*; (*unmasking*) dévoilement *m*; (*phot*) exposition *f*; (*phot*) durée *f* d'exposition

expound [eks'paund] *tr* exposer

express [eks'pres] *adj* exprès, formel; (*train*; *gun*) express || *s* (*merchandise*) messagerie *f*; (*train*) express *m*, rapide *m*; **by express** (rr) en grande vitesse || *adv* (rr) en grande vitesse || *tr* exprimer; (*merchandise*) envoyer en grande vitesse; (*through the express company*) expédier par les messageries; **to express oneself** s'exprimer

express' com'pany *s* messageries *fpl*

express' high'way *s* autoroute *f*

expression [eks'preʃən] *s* expression *f*

expressive [eks'presɪv] *adj* expressif

expressly [eks'presli] *adv* exprès

express'man *s* (*pl* **-men**) entrepreneur *m* de messageries; facteur *m*, agent *m* d'un service de messageries

express' train' *s* train *m* express

express'way' *s* autoroute *f*

expropriate [eks'propri,et] *tr* exproprier

expulsion [eks'pʌlʃən] *s* expulsion *f*; (*from schools*) renvoi *m*

expunge [eks'pʌndʒ] *tr* effacer, supprimer, rayer

expurgate ['ekspər,get] *tr* expurger

exquisite ['ekskwɪzɪt], [eks'kwɪzɪt] *adj* exquis

ex-service-man [,eks'sʌrvɪs,mæn] *s* (*pl* **-men'**) ancien combattant *m*

extant ['ekstənt], [eks'tænt] *adj* existant, subsistant

extemporaneous [eks ,tempə'reni·əs] *adj* improvisé, impromptu

extemporaneously [eks ,tempə'reni·əsli] *adv* à l'impromptu, d'abondance

extempore [eks'tempəri] *adj* improvisé || *adv* d'abondance, à l'impromptu

extemporize [eks'tempə,raɪz] *tr* & *intr* improviser

extend [eks'tend] *tr* étendre; (*a period of time*; *a street*; *a line*) prolonger; (*a treaty*; *a session*; *a right*; *a due date*) proroger; (*a helping hand*) tendre || *intr* s'étendre

extended *adj* étendu, prolongé

extension [eks'tenʃən] *s* extension *f*; prolongation *f*; (*board for a table*) rallonge *f*; (*to building*) annexe *f*; (*telp*) poste *m*

exten'sion cord' *s* cordon *m* prolongateur, prolongateur *m*

exten'sion lad'der *s* échelle *f* à coulisse

exten'sion ta'ble *s* table *f* à rallonges

extensive [eks'tensɪv] *adj* vaste, étendu

extent [eks'tent] *s* étendue *f*; **to a certain extent** dans une certaine mesure; **to a great extent** en grande partie, considérablement; **to the full extent** dans toute la mesure

extenuate [eks'tenju,et] *tr* atténuer; minimiser

exterior [eks'tɪrɪ·ər] *adj* & *s* extérieur *m*

exterminate [eks'tʌrmɪ,net] *tr* exterminer

external [ɛks'tʌrnəl] *adj* extérieur; (pharm, med) externe || **externals** *spl* dehors *mpl*, apparences *fpl*; (*superficialities*) choses *fpl* secondaires

extinct [ɛks'tɪŋkt] *adj* (*volcano*) éteint; disparu; tombé en désuétude

extinction [ɛks'tɪŋkʃən] *s* extinction *f*

extinguish [ɛks'tɪŋwɪʃ] *tr* éteindre

extinguisher [ɛks'tɪŋwɪʃər] *s* (*for candles*) éteignoir *m*; (*for fires*) extincteur *m*

extirpate ['ɛkstər‚pet], [ɛks'tʌrpet] *tr* extirper

ex-tol [ɛks'tol], [ɛks'tɑl] *v* (*pret & pp -tolled; ger -tolling*) *tr* exalter, vanter

extort [ɛks'tɔrt] *tr* extorquer

extortion [ɛks'tɔrʃən] *s* extorsion *f*

extortionist [ɛks'tɔrʃənɪst] *s* extorqueur *m*

extra ['ɛkstrə] *adj* supplémentaire; (*of high quality*) extra, extra-fin; (*spare*) de rechange || *s* extra *m*; (*of a newspaper*) édition *f* spéciale; (mov, theat) figurant *m* || *adv* en plus, en sus; (*not on the bill*) non compris

ex'tra board' *s* (*for extension table*) rallonge *f*

ex'tra charge' *s* supplément *m*

extract ['ɛkstrækt] *s* extrait *m* || [ɛks'trækt] *tr* extraire

extraction [ɛks'trækʃən] *s* extraction *f*

extracurricular [‚ɛkstrəkə'rɪkjələr] *adj* extra-scolaire

extradite ['ɛkstrə‚daɪt] *tr* extrader

extradition [‚ɛkstrə'dɪʃən] *s* extradition *f*

ex'tra-dry' *adj* (*champagne*) très sec

ex'tra fare' *s* supplément *m* de billet

extramural [‚ɛkstrə'mjurəl] *adj* à l'extérieur de la ville; à l'extérieur de l'université

extraneous [ɛks'trenɪ‐əs] *adj* étranger

extraordinary [ɛks'trɔrdɪ‚nerɪ], [‚ɛkstrə'ɔrdɪ‚nerɪ] *adj* extraordinaire

extrapolate [ɛks'træpə‚let] *tr & intr* extrapoler

extrasensory [‚ɛkstrə'sensərɪ] *adj* extrasensoriel

ex'tra-spe'cial *adj* extra

extravagance [ɛks'trævəgəns] *s* (*lavishness*) prodigalité *f*, gaspillage *m*; (*folly*) extravagance *f*

extravagant [ɛks'trævəgənt] *adj* (*person*) dépensier, prodigue; (*price*) exorbitant; (*e.g., praise*) outré; (*e.g., claims*) exagéré, extravagant

extreme [ɛks'trim] *adj & s* extrême *m*; **in the extreme, to extremes** à l'extrême

extremely [ɛks'trimlɪ] *adv* extrêmement

extreme' unc'tion *s* extrême-onction *f*

extremist [ɛks'trimɪst] *adj & s* extrémiste *mf*

extremi-ty [ɛks'tremɪtɪ] *s* (*pl* -**ties**) extrémité *f*; **extremities** extrémités

extricate ['ɛkstrɪ‚ket] *tr* dégager; (*a gas*) libérer; **to extricate oneself from** se tirer de, se dépêtrer de

extrinsic [ɛks'trɪnsɪk] *adj* extrinsèque

extrovert ['ɛkstrə‚vʌrt] *adj & s* extraverti *m*

extrude [ɛks'trud] *intr* faire saillie, dépasser

exuberant [ɛg'z(j)ubərənt] *adj* exubérant

exude [ɛg'zud], [ɛk'sud] *tr & intr* exsuder

exult [ɛg'zʌlt] *intr* exulter

exultant [ɛg'zʌltənt] *adj* triomphant

eye [aɪ] *s* œil *m*; (*of needle*) chas *m*, trou *m*; (*of hook and eye*) porte *f*; **to catch s.o.'s eye** tirer l'œil à qn; **to lay eyes on** jeter les yeux sur; **to make eyes at** (coll) faire les yeux doux à; **to see eye to eye with s.o.** voir les choses du même œil que qn; **with an eye to** en vue de; **without batting an eye** (coll) sans sourciller || *v* (*pret & pp* **eyed**; *ger* **eying** or **eyeing**) *tr* toiser, reluquer

eye'ball' *s* globe *m* oculaire

eye' bank' *s* banque *f* des yeux

eye'bolt' *s* boulon *m* à œil

eye'brow' *s* sourcil *m*

eye' cup' *s* œillère *f*

eye' drops' *spl* collyre *m*

eyeful ['aɪful] *s* vue *f*, coup *m* d'œil; **to get an eyeful** (coll) s'en mettre plein la vue, se rincer l'œil

eye'glass' *s* (*of optical instrument*) oculaire *m*; (*eyecup*) œillère *f*; **eyeglasses** lunettes *fpl*

eye'lash' *s* cil *m*; (*fringe of hair*) cils

eyelet ['aɪlɪt] *s* œillet *m*; (*of sail*) œil *m* de pie

eye'lid' *s* paupière *f*

eye' of the morn'ing *s* astre *m* du jour

eye' o'pener ['opənər] *s* révélation *f*; (coll) goutte *f* de bonne heure

eye'piece' *s* oculaire *m*

eye'shade' *s* visière *f*, abat-jour *m*

eye' shad'ow *s* fard *m* à paupière

eye'shot' *s* portée *f* de la vue

eye'sight' *s* vue *f*; (*eyeshot*) portée *f* de la vue

eye' sock'et *s* orbite *f* de l'œil

eye'sore' *s* objet *m* déplaisant

eye'strain' *s* fatigue *f* des yeux; **to suffer from eyestrain** avoir les yeux fatigués

eye'-test chart' *s* tableau *m* de lecture pour la vision

eye'tooth' *s* (*pl* -**teeth**) dent *f* œillère or canine; **to cut one's eyeteeth** (coll) ne pas être un blanc-bec; **to give one's eyeteeth for** (coll) donner la prunelle de ses yeux pour

eye'wash' *s* collyre *m*; (slang) de l'eau bénite de cour, de la poudre aux yeux

eye'wit'ness *s* témoin *m* oculaire

ey-rie or **ey-ry** ['erɪ] *s* (*pl* -**ries**) aire *f* (de l'aigle); (fig) nid *m* d'aigle

F

F, f [ef] s VIe lettre de l'alphabet
fable ['febəl] s fable f
fabric ['fæbrɪk] s tissu m, étoffe f
fabricate ['fæbrɪ‚ket] tr fabriquer
fabrication [‚fæbrɪ'keʃən] s fabrication f; (lie) mensonge m
fabulous ['fæbjələs] adj fabuleux
façade [fə'sad] s façade f
face [fes] s visage m, figure f; (side) face f; (of the earth) surface f; (appearance, expression) mine f, physionomie f; about face! (mil) demitour! to keep a straight face montrer un front sérieux; to lose face perdre la face; to make a face faire une grimace; to set one's face against faire front à || tr faire face à; (a wall) revêtir; (a garment) mettre un revers à || intr—to face about faire demi-tour; to face up to faire face à, affronter
face'card' s figure f
face' lift'ing s ridectomie f
face' pow'der s poudre f de riz
facet ['fæsɪt] s facette f
facetious [fə'siʃəs] adj plaisant
face' tow'el s serviette f de toilette
face' val'ue s valeur f, faciale, valeur nominale
facial ['feʃəl] adj facial || s massage m esthétique
fa'cial tis'sue s serviette f à démaquiller
facilitate [fə'sɪlɪ‚tet] tr faciliter
facili-ty [fə'sɪlɪti] s (pl -ties) facilité f; facilities installations fpl
facing ['fesɪŋ] s revêtement m; (of garment) revers m
facsimile [fæk'sɪmɪli] s fac-similé m
fact [fækt] s fait m; in fact en fait, de fait; the fact is that c'est que
faction ['fækʃən] s faction f
factor ['fæktər] s facteur m || tr résoudre or décomposer en facteurs
facto-ry ['fæktəri] s (pl -ries) usine f, fabrique f
fac'tory price' s prix m de facture
factual ['fæktʃʊ‚əl] adj vrai, réel
facul-ty ['fækəlti] s (pl -ties) faculté f; (teaching staff) corps m enseignant
fad [fæd] s mode f, marotte f; latest fad dernier cri m
fade [fed] tr déteindre, décolorer || intr déteindre, se décolorer; (to lose vigor, freshness) se faner; to fade in apparaître graduellement; to fade out disparaître graduellement
fade'-in' s (mov) apparition f en fondu
fade'-out' s (mov) fondu m
fag [fæg] s (slang) cibiche f || v (pret & pp fagged; ger fagging) tr—to fag out éreinter
fagot ['fægət] s fagot m; (for filling up trenches) fascine f || tr fagoter
fail [fel] s—without fail sans faute || intr manquer à; (a student) refuser; (an examination) échouer à or dans

|| intr manquer, faire défaut; (to not succeed) échouer, rater; (said of motor) tomber en panne; (to weaken) baisser, faiblir; to fail in faillir à; to fail to manquer de, faillir à; to fail to do or to keep manquer or faillir à
failing ['felɪŋ] s défaillant || s défaut m || prep à défaut de
failure ['feljər] s insuccès m, échec m; (lack) manque m, défaut m; (person) raté m; (com) faillite f
faint [fent] adj faible; to feel faint se sentir mal || s évanouissement m || intr s'évanouir
faint'-heart'ed adj timide, peureux
fair [fer] adj juste, équitable; (honest) loyal, honnête; (average) moyen, passable; (clear) clair; (beautiful) beau; (pleasing) agréable, plaisant; (of hair) blond; (complexion) blanc; to be fair (to be just) être de bonne guerre || s foire f, fête f; (bazaar) kermesse f || adv impartialement; to bid fair to avoir des chances de; to play fair jouer franc jeu
fair' cop'y s copie f au net
fair'ground' s champ m de foire
fairly ['ferli] adv impartialement, loyalement; assez
fair'-mind'ed adj impartial
fairness ['fernɪs] s impartialité f, justice f; (of complexion) clarté f
fair' play' s franc jeu m
fair' sex' s beau sexe m
fair'way' s (golf) parcours m normal; (naut) chenal m
fair'-weath'er adj (e.g., friend) des beaux jours
fair-y ['feri] adj féerique || s (pl -ies) fée f; (homosexual) (coll) tante f
fair'y god'moth'er s marraine f fée; (coll) marraine gâteau
fair'y-land' s royaume m des fées
fair'y tale' s conte m de fées
faith [feθ] s foi f; to break faith with manquer de foi à; to keep faith with tenir ses engagements envers; to pin one's faith on mettre tout son espoir en
faithful ['feθfəl] adj fidèle || s—the faithful les fidèles mpl
faithless ['feθlɪs] adj infidèle
fake [fek] adj (coll) faux || s faux m, article m truqué || tr truquer
faker ['fekər] s truqueur m
falcon ['fɔkən], ['fɔlkən] s faucon m
falconer ['fɔkənər], ['fɔlkənər] s fauconnier m
fall [fɔl] adj automnal || s chute f; (of prices) baisse f; (season) automne m & f; falls chute d'eau || v (pret fell [fel]; pp fallen ['fɔlən]) intr tomber; (said of prices) baisser; fall in! (mil) rassemblement!; fall out! (mil) rompez les rangs!; to fall down (said of person) tomber par terre; (said of building) s'écrouler; to fall for (coll)

se laisser prendre à; (*to fall in love with*) (coll) tomber amoureux de; **to fall in** s'effondrer; (mil) former des rangs; **to fall into the trap** donner dans le piège; **to fall off** tomber de; (*to decline*) baisser, diminuer; **to fall out** (*to disagree*) se brouiller; **to fall over oneself to** (coll) se mettre en quatre pour

fallacious [fəˈleʃəs] *adj* fallacieux

falla·cy [ˈfæləsi] *s* (*pl* -cies) erreur *f*, fausseté *f*

fall' guy' *s* (slang) tête *f* de Turc

fallible [ˈfælɪbəl] *adj* faillible

fall'ing star' *s* étoile *f* filante

fall'out' *s* pluies *fpl* radioactives, retombées *fpl* radioactives

fall'out shel'ter *s* abri *m* antiatomique

fallow [ˈfælo] *adj* en friche, en jachère || *s* friche *f*, jachère *f* || *tr* laisser en friche or en jachère

false [fɔls] *adj* faux; artificiel, simulé; (*hair*) postiche || *adv* faussement; **to play false** tromper

false' alarm' *s* fausse alerte *f*

false' bot'tom *s* double fond *m*

false' cog'nate *s* faux ami *m*

false' eye'lashes *spl* cils *mpl* postiches

false' face' *s* masque *m*

false'-heart'ed *adj* perfide, traître

false'hood *s* mensonge *m*

false' pretens'es *spl* faux-semblants *mpl*

false' return' *s* fausse déclaration *f* d'impôts

false' step' *s* faux-pas *m*

false' teeth' [ˈtiθ] *spl* fausses dents *fpl*

falset·to [fɔlˈseto] *s* (*pl* -tos) fausset *m*, voix *f* de tête; (*person*) fausset *m*

falsi·fy [ˈfɔlsɪˌfaɪ] *v* (*pret & pp* -fied) *tr* falsifier, fausser

falsi·ty [ˈfɔlsɪti] *s* (*pl* -ties) fausseté *f*

falter [ˈfɔltər] *s* vacillation *f*, hésitation *f*; (*of speech*) balbutiement *m* || *intr* vaciller, hésiter; balbutier

fame [fem] *s* renom *m*, renommée *f*

famed *adj* renommé, célèbre

familiar [fəˈmɪljər] *adj & s* familier *m*; **to become familiar with** se familiariser avec

familiari·ty [fəˌmɪliˈærti] *s* (*pl* -ties) familiarité *f*

familiarize [fəˈmɪljəˌraɪz] *tr* familiariser

fami·ly [ˈfæmɪli] *adj* familial; **in a or the family way** (coll) dans une position intéressante; (coll) en famille (Canad) || *s* (*pl* -lies) famille *f*

fam'ily man' *s* (*pl* **men'**) père *m* de famille; (*stay-at-home*) homme *m* casanier, pantouflard *m*

fam'ily name' *s* nom *m* de famille

fam'ily physi'cian *s* médecin *m* de famille

fam'ily tree' *s* arbre *m* généalogique

famine [ˈfæmɪn] *s* famine *f*

famish [ˈfæmɪʃ] *tr* affamer, priver de vivres || *intr* souffrir de la faim

famished *adj* affamé, famélique; **to be famished** (coll) mourir de faim

famous [ˈfeməs] *adj* renommé, célèbre

fan [fæn] *s* éventail *m*; (mach) ventilateur *m*; (coll) fanatique *mf*, enragé

m || *v* (*pret & pp* **fanned**; *ger* **fanning**) *tr* éventer; (*to winnow*) vanner; (*e.g., passions*) exciter || *intr*—**to fan out** se déployer en éventail

fanatic [fəˈnætɪk] *adj & s* fanatique *mf*

fanatical [fəˈnætɪkəl] *adj* fanatique

fanaticism [fəˈnætɪˌsɪzəm] *s* fanatisme *m*

fan' belt' *s* (aut) courroie *f* de ventilateur

fancied *adj* imaginaire, supposé

fanciful [ˈfænsɪfəl] *adj* fantaisiste, capricieux

fan·cy [ˈfænsi] *adj* (*comp* -cier; *super* -ciest) ornemental; (*goods, clothes, bread*) de fantaisie; (*high-quality*) fin, extra, de luxe || *s* (*pl* -cies) fantaisie *f*, caprice *m*; **to take a fancy to** prendre du goût pour; (*a loved one*) prendre en affection || *v* (*pret & pp* -cied) *tr* s'imaginer, se figurer; **to fancy oneself** s'imaginer; **to fancy that** imaginer que

fan'cy dress' *s* costume *m* de fantaisie, travesti *m*

fan'cy dress' ball' *s* bal *m* costumé, bal travesti

fan'cy foods' *spl* comestibles *mpl* de fantaisie

fan'cy-free' *adj* libre, gai, sans amour

fan'cy jew'elry *s* bijouterie *f* de fantaisie

fan'cy skat'ing *s* patinage *m* de fantaisie

fan'cy-work' *s* broderie *f*, ouvrage *m* d'agrément

fanfare [ˈfænfɛr] *s* fanfare *f*

fang [fæŋ] *s* croc *m*; (*of snake*) crochet *m*

fantastic(al) [fænˈtæstɪk(əl)] *adj* fantastique

fanta·sy [ˈfæntəzi], [ˈfæntəsi] *s* (*pl* -sies) fantaisie *f*

far [fɑr] *adj* lointain; **on the far side of** à l'autre côté de || *adv* loin; **as far as** autant que; (*up to*) jusqu'à; **as far as I am concerned** quant à moi; **as far as I know** pour autant que je sache; **by far** de beaucoup; **far and wide** partout; **far away** au loin; **far from** loin de; **far from it** tant s'en faut; **far into the night** fort avant dans la nuit; **far into the woods** avant dans le bois; **far off** au loin; **how far?** jusqu'où?; **how far is it from . . . ?** combien y a-t-il de . . . ?; **in so far as** dans la mesure où; **so far or thus far** jusqu'ici; **to go far to** contribuer pour beaucoup à

far'away' *adj* éloigné, distant

farce [fɑrs] *s* farce *f*

farcical [ˈfɑrsɪkəl] *adj* grotesque, ridicule

fare [fɛr] *s* prix *m*, tarif *m*; (*cost of taxi*) course *f*; (*passenger in taxi*) client *m*; (*passenger in bus*) voyageur *m*; (culin) chère *f*, ordinaire *m*; **fares, please!** vos places, s'il vous plaît! || *intr* se porter; **how did you fare?** comment ça s'est-il passé?

Far' East' *s* Extrême-Orient *m*

fare'well' s adieu m; **to bid s.o. fare-well** dire adieu à qn

far'-fetched' adj tiré par les cheveux

far-flung [ˈfarˈflʌŋ] adj étendu, vaste, d'une grande envergure

farm [farm] s ferme f; (sharecropper's farm) métairie f || tr cultiver, exploiter; **to farm out** donner à ferme; (work) donner en exploitation à l'extérieur || intr faire de la culture

farmer [ˈfarmər] s fermier m

farm' hand' s valet m de ferme

farm'house' s ferme f, maison f de ferme

farming [ˈfarmɪŋ] s agriculture f, exploitation f agricole

farm'yard' s cour f de ferme

Far' North' s Grand Nord m

far'-off' adj lointain, éloigné

far'-reach'ing adj à longue portée

far'sight'ed adj prévoyant; (physiol) presbyte

farther [ˈfarðər] adj plus éloigné || adv plus loin

farthest [ˈfarðɪst] adj (le) plus éloigné || adv le plus loin; au plus

farthing [ˈfarðɪŋ] s liard m

fascinate [ˈfæsɪˌnet] tr fasciner

fascinating [ˈfæsɪˌnetɪŋ] adj fascinateur, fascinant

fascism [ˈfæʃɪzəm] s fascisme m

fascist [ˈfæʃɪst] adj & s fasciste mf

fashion [ˈfæʃən] s mode f, vogue f; (manner) façon f, manière f; **after a fashion** tant bien que mal; **in fashion** à la mode, en vogue; **out of fashion** démodé || tr façonner

fashionable [ˈfæʃənəbəl] adj à la mode, élégant, chic

fash'ion design'ing s haute couture f

fash'ion plate' s gravure f de mode; (person) (coll) élégant m

fash'ion show' s présentation f de collection

fast [fæst], [fast] adj rapide; (fixed) solide, fixe; (clock) en avance; (friend) fidèle; (color) grand, bon, e.g., **fast color** grand teint, bon teint; (person) (slang) dévergondé; **to make fast** fixer, fermer || s jeûne m; **to break one's fast** rompre le jeûne || adv vite, rapidement; (firmly) solidement, ferme; (asleep) profondément; **to hold fast** tenir bon; **to live fast** (coll) faire la noce, mener la vie à grandes guides; **to stand fast against** tenir tête à || intr jeûner

fast' day' s jour m de jeûne, jour maigre

fasten [ˈfæsən], [ˈfasən] tr attacher, fixer; (e.g., a belt) ajuster || intr s'attacher, se fixer

fastener [ˈfæsənər], [ˈfasənər] s attache f, agrafe f

fastidious [fæsˈtɪdɪˌəs] adj délicat, dégoûté, difficile

fasting [ˈfæstɪŋ], [ˈfastɪŋ] s jeûne m

fat [fæt] adj (comp fatter; super fattest) (plump; greasy) gras; (large) gros; (soil) riche; (spark) nourri; **to get fat** engraisser || s graisse f; (of meat) gras m

fatal [ˈfetəl] adj fatal

fatalism [ˈfetəˌlɪzəm] s fatalisme m

fatalist [ˈfetəlɪst] s fataliste mf

fatali·ty [fəˈtælɪti] s (pl -ties) fatalité f; (in accidents, war, etc.) mort f, accident m mortel

fate [fet] s sort m, destin m; **the Fates** les Parques fpl

fated [ˈfetɪd] adj destiné, voué

fateful [ˈfetfəl] adj fatal; (prophetic) fatidique

fat'head' s (coll) crétin m, sot m

father [ˈfaðər] s père m; **Father** (salutation given a priest) Monsieur l'abbé || tr servir de père à; (to beget) engendrer; (an idea, project) inventer

fa'ther-hood' s paternité f

fa'ther-in-law' s (pl **fathers-in-law**) beau-père m

fa'ther-land' s patrie f

fatherless [ˈfaðərlɪs] adj sans père, orphelin de père

fatherly [ˈfaðərli] adj paternel

Fa'ther Time' s le Temps

fathom [ˈfæðəm] s brasse f || tr sonder

fathomless [ˈfæðəmlɪs] adj insondable

fatigue [fəˈtig] s fatigue f; **fatigues** (mil) bleus mpl

fatigue' clothes' spl tenue f de corvée

fatigue' du'ty s (mil) corvée f

fatten [ˈfætən] tr & intr engraisser

fat·ty [ˈfæti] adj (comp -tier; super -tiest) gras, grassieux; (tissue) adipeux; (chubby) (coll) potelé, dodu || s (pl -ties) (coll) bon gros m

fatuous [ˈfætʃ·uˌəs] adj sot, idiot

faucet [ˈfɔsɪt] s robinet m

fault [fɔlt] s faute f; (geol) faille f; **to a fault** à l'excès; **to find fault with** trouver à redire à

fault'find'er s critiqueur m, éplucheur m

fault'find'ing adj chicaneur || s chicanerie f, critique f

faultless [ˈfɔltlɪs] adj sans défaut

fault·y [ˈfɔlti] adj (comp -ier; super -iest) fautif, défectueux

faun [fɔn] s faune m

fauna [ˈfɔnə] s faune f

favor [ˈfevər] s faveur f; **do me the favor to** faites-moi le plaisir de; **to be in favor of** être partisan de; **to be in favor with** jouir de la faveur de; **to decide in s.o.'s favor** donner gain de cause à qn || tr favoriser; (to look like) (coll) tenir de; (e.g., a sore leg) (coll) ménager

favorable [ˈfevərəbəl] adj favorable

favorite [ˈfevərɪt] adj & s favori m

fawn [fɔn] s (color) fauve f || s faon m || intr—**to fawn upon** (said of dog) faire des caresses à; (said of person) faire le chien couchant auprès de

faze [fez] tr (coll) affecter, troubler

FBI [ˌɛfˌbiˈaɪ] s (letterword) (**Federal Bureau of Investigation**) Sûreté f nationale, Sûreté (the French equivalent)

fear [fɪr] s crainte f, peur f || tr craindre, avoir peur de || intr craindre, avoir peur

fearful [ˈfɪrfəl] adj (frightened) peureux, effrayé; *(frightful)* effrayant; (coll) énorme, effrayant

fearless [ˈfɪrlɪs] *adj* sans peur

feasible [ˈfɪzɪbəl] *adj* faisable

feast [fist] *s* festin *m*, régal *m* ‖ *tr* régaler ‖ *intr* faire bonne chère; **to feast on** se régaler de

feast′ day′ *s* fête *f*, jour *m* de fête

feat [fit] *s* exploit *m*, haut fait *m*

feather [ˈfeðər] *s* plume *f*; **feather in one′s cap** (coll) fleuron *m* à sa couronne; **in fine feather** (coll) plein d′entrain ‖ *tr* emplumer; *(an oar)* ramener à plat; **to feather one′s nest** (coll) faire son beurre

feath′er bed′ *s* lit *m* de plumes, couette *f*

feath′er-bed′ding *s* emploi *m* de plus d′ouvriers qu′il n′en faut

feath′er-brained′ *adj* braque, étourdi

feath′er dust′er *s* plumeau *m*

feath′er-edge′ *s* *(of board)* biseau *m*; *(of tool)* morfil *m*

feath′er-weight′ *s* poids-plume *m*

feathery [ˈfeðəri] *adj* plumeux

feature [ˈfitʃər] *s* trait *m*, caractéristique *f*; (mov) long métrage *m*, grand film *m* ‖ *tr* caractériser; offrir comme attraction principale

fea′ture writ′er *s* rédacteur *m*

February [ˈfebruˌɛri] *s* février *m*

feces [ˈfisiz] *spl* fèces *fpl*

feckless [ˈfeklɪs] *adj* veule, faible

federal [ˈfedərəl] *adj & s* fédéral *m*

federate [ˈfedəˌret] *adj* fédéré ‖ *tr* fédérer ‖ *intr* se fédérer

federation [ˌfedəˈreʃən] *s* fédération *f*

fedora [frˈdorə] *s* chapeau *m* mou

fed′ up′ [ˈfed] *adj*—**to be fed up** (coll) en avoir marre; **to be fed up with** (coll) avoir plein le dos de

fee [fi] *s* honoraires *mpl*, cachet *m*; **for a nominal fee** pour une somme symbolique

feeble [ˈfibəl] *adj* faible

fee′ble-mind′ed *adj* imbécile; obtus, à l′esprit lourd

feed [fid] *s* nourriture *f*, pâture *f*; (mach) alimentation *f*; (slang) grand repas *m* ‖ *v* *(pret & pp* **fed** [fed]) *tr* nourrir, donner à manger à; *(a machine)* alimenter ‖ *intr* manger; **to feed upon** se nourrir de

feed′back′ *s* réalimentation *f*, régénération *f*, contre-réaction *f*

feed′ bag′ *s* musette-mangeoire *f*; **to put on the feed bag** (slang) casser la croûte

feeder [ˈfidər] *s* alimenteur *m*; (elec) canal *m* d′amenée

feed′ pump′ *s* pompe *f* d′alimentation

feed′ trough′ *s* mangeoire *f*, auge *f*

feed′ wire′ *s* (elec) fil *m* d′amenée

feel [fil] *s* sensation *f* ‖ *v* *(pret & pp* **felt** [felt]) *tr* sentir, éprouver; *(the pulse)* tâter; *(to examine)* palper; **to feel one′s way** avancer à tâtons ‖ *intr* *(sick, tired, etc.)* se sentir; **feel for** tâtonner, chercher à tâtons; *(to sympathize with)* (coll) être plein de pitié pour; **to feel like** avoir envie de

feeler [ˈfilər] *s* (ent) antenne *f*; **to put out a feeler** (coll) tâter le terrain

feeling [ˈfilɪŋ] *s* *(with senses)* toucher *m*, tact *m*; *(with hands)* tâtage *m*; *(impression, emotion)* sentiment *m*; **feelings** sensibilité *f*

feign [fen] *tr & intr* feindre

feint [fent] *s* feinte *f* ‖ *intr* feinter

feldspar [ˈfeldˌspar] *s* feldspath *m*

felicitate [fəˈlɪsɪˌtet] *tr* féliciter

felicitous [fəˈlɪsɪtəs] *adj* heureux, à propos

fell [fel] *adj* cruel, féroce ‖ *tr* abattre

felloe [ˈfelo] *s* jante *f*

fellow [ˈfelo] *s* *(of a society)* membre *m*; *(holder of a fellowship)* boursier *m*; *(friend, neighbor, etc.)* homme *m*, compagnon *m*; (coll) type *m*, bonhomme *m*, gars *m*; **poor fellow!** (coll) pauvre garçon!

fel′low cit′izen *s* concitoyen *m*

fel′low coun′tryman *s* compatriote *mf*

fel′low crea′ture *s* semblable *mf*

fel′low-man′ *s* *(pl -men′)* semblable *m*, prochain *m*

fel′low mem′ber *s* confrère *m*

fel′low-ship′ *s* camaraderie *f*; *(scholarship)* bourse *f*; *(organization)* association *f*

fel′low stu′dent *s* condisciple *m*

fel′low trav′eler *s* compagnon *m* de voyage; (pol) compagnon de route

felon [ˈfelən] *s* criminel *m*; (pathol) panaris *m*

felo-ny [ˈfeləni] *s* *(pl -nies)* crime *m*

felt [felt] *s* feutre *m* ‖ *tr* feutrer

female [ˈfimel] *adj* *(sex)* féminin; *(animal, plant, piece of a device)* femelle ‖ *s* *(person)* femme *f*; *(plant, animal)* femelle *f*

feminine [ˈfemɪnɪn] *adj & s* féminin *m*

feminism [ˈfemɪˌnɪzəm] *s* féminisme *m*

fen [fen] *s* marécage *m*

fence [fens] *s* barrière *f*, clôture *f*; palissade *f*; *(for stolen goods)* receleur *m*; **on the fence** (coll) indécis, en balance ‖ *tr* clôturer ‖ *intr* faire de l′escrime

fencing [ˈfensɪŋ] *s* *(enclosure)* clôture *f*; *(sports)* escrime *f*

fenc′ing acad′emy *s* salle *f* d′armes

fenc′ing mas′ter *s* maître *m* d′armes

fenc′ing match′ *s* assaut *m* d′armes

fend [fend] *tr*—**to fend off** parer ‖ *intr*—**to fend for oneself** (coll) se débrouiller, se tirer d′affaire

fender [ˈfendər] *s* *(mudguard)* aile *f*, garde-boue *m*; *(of locomotive)* chasse-pierres *m*; *(of fireplace)* garde-feu *m*

fennel [ˈfenəl] *s* fenouil *m*

ferment [ˈfɜrment] *s* ferment *m* ‖ [fərˈment] *tr* faire fermenter; *(wine)* cuver ‖ *intr* fermenter

fern [fɜrn] *s* fougère *f*

ferocious [fəˈroʃəs] *adj* féroce

feroci·ty [fəˈrɑsɪti] *s* *(pl -ties)* férocité *f*

ferret [ˈfɛrɪt] *s* furet *m* ‖ *tr*—**to ferret out** dénicher ‖ *intr* fureter

Fer′ris wheel′ [ˈfɛrɪs] *s* grande roue *f*

fer-ry [ˈfɛri] *s* *(pl -ries)* bac *m*; *(to transport trains)* ferry-boat *m* ‖ *v* (*pret* & *pp* **-ried**) *tr* & *intr* passer en bac

fer'ry·boat' *s* bac *m*; (*to transport trains*) ferry-boat *m*

fer'ry-man *s* (*pl* **-men**) passeur *m*

fertile [ˈfʌrtɪl] *adj* fertile, fécond

fertilize [ˈfʌrtɪˌlaɪz] *tr* fertiliser; (*to impregnate*) feconder

fertilizer [ˈfʌrtɪˌlaɪzər] *s* engrais *m*, amendement *m*; (*bot*) fécondateur *m*

fervent [ˈfʌrvənt] *adj* fervent

fervid [ˈfʌrvɪd] *adj* fervent

fervor [ˈfʌrvər] *s* ferveur *f*

fester [ˈfɛstər] *s* ulcère *m* ‖ *tr* ulcérer ‖ *intr* s'ulcérer

festival [ˈfɛstɪvəl] *adj* de fête ‖ *s* fête *f*; (*mov*, *mus*) festival *m*

festive [ˈfɛstɪv] *adj* de fête, gai

festivi·ty [fɛsˈtɪvɪti] *s* (*pl* **-ties**) festivité *f*

festoon [fɛsˈtun] *s* feston *m* ‖ *tr* festonner

fetch [fɛtʃ] *tr* aller chercher; (*a certain price*) se vendre à

fetching [ˈfɛtʃɪŋ] *adj* (coll) séduisant

fete [fɛt] *s* fête *f* ‖ *tr* fêter

fetish [ˈfɛtɪʃ], [ˈfitɪʃ] *s* fétiche *m*

fetlock [ˈfɛtlɑk] *s* boulet *m*; (*tuft of hair*) fanon *m*

fetter [ˈfɛtər] *s* lien *m*; **fetters** fers *mpl*, chaînes *fpl* ‖ *tr* enchaîner, entraver

fettle [ˈfɛtəl] *s* condition *f*, état *m*; **in fine fettle** en pleine forme

fetus [ˈfitəs] *s* fœtus *m*

feud [fjud] *s* querelle *f*, vendetta *f* ‖ *intr* être à couteaux tirés

feudal [ˈfjudəl] *adj* féodal

feudalism [ˈfjudəˌlɪzəm] *s* féodalisme *m*

fever [ˈfivər] *s* fièvre *f*

fe'ver blis'ter *s* bouton *m* de fièvre

feverish [ˈfivərɪʃ] *adj* fiévreux

few [fju] *adj* peu de; **a few . . .** quelques **. . .** ; **quite a few** pas mal de; **the few . . .** les rares **. . .** ‖ *pron indef* peu; **a few** quelques-uns §81; **quite a few** beaucoup

fiancé [ˌfi·ɑnˈse] *s* fiancé *m*

fiancée [ˌfi·ɑnˈse] *s* fiancée *f*

fias·co [fiˈæsko] *s* (*pl* **-cos** or **-coes**) fiasco *m*, échec *m*

fiat [ˈfaɪət], [ˈfaɪæt] *s* ordonnance *f*, autorisation *f*

fib [fɪb] *s* (coll) petit mensonge *m*, blague *f* ‖ *v* (*pret* & *pp* **fibbed**; *ger* **fibbing**) *intr* (coll) blaguer

fiber [ˈfaɪbər] *s* fibre *f*

fibrous [ˈfaɪbrəs] *adj* fibreux

fickle [ˈfɪkəl] *adj* inconstant, volage

fiction [ˈfɪkʃən] *s* fiction *f*; (*branch of literature*) ouvrages *mpl* d'imagination, romans *mpl*

fictional [ˈfɪkʃənəl] *adj* romanesque, d'imagination

fictionalize [ˈfɪkʃənəˌlaɪz] *tr* romancer

fictitious [fɪkˈtɪʃəs] *adj* fictif

fiddle [ˈfɪdəl] *s* violon *m* ‖ *tr*—**to fiddle away** (coll) gaspiller ‖ *intr* jouer du violon; **to fiddle around** or **with** (coll) tripoter

fiddler [ˈfɪdlər] *s* (coll) violoneux *m*

fid'dle·stick' *s* (coll) archet *m*; **fiddlesticks!** (coll) quelle blague!

fiddling [ˈfɪdlɪŋ] *adj* (coll) musard

fideli·ty [faɪˈdɛlɪti], [fɪˈdɛlɪti] *s* (*pl* **-ties**) fidélité *f*

fidget [ˈfɪdʒɪt] *intr* se trémousser; **to fidget with** tripoter

fidgety [ˈfɪdʒɪti] *adj* nerveux

fiduciar·y [fɪˈd(j)uʃɪˌɛri] *adj* fiduciaire ‖ *s* (*pl* **-ies**) fiduciaire *m*

fie [faɪ] *interj* fi!; **fie on . . . !** nargue de . . . !

field [fild] *s* champ *m*; (*area*, *activity*) domaine *m*, aire *f*; (*aer*, *sports*) terrain *m*; (*elec*) champ; (*of motor or dynamo*) (elec) inducteur *m*; (mil) aire *f*, théâtre *m*

field' day' *s* (*cleanup*) (mil) manœuvres *fpl* de garnison; (sports) manifestation *f* sportive

fielder [ˈfildər] *s* (baseball) chasseur *m*, homme *m* de champ

field' glass'es *spl* jumelles *fpl*

field' hock'ey *s* hockey *m* sur gazon

field' hos'pital *s* ambulance *f*, formation *f* sanitaire

field' mag'net *s* aimant *m* inducteur

field' mar'shal *s* maréchal *m*

field' mouse' *s* mulot *m*

field'piece' *s* pièce *f* de campagne

fiend [find] *s* démon *m*; (*mischief-maker*) (coll) espiègle *mf*; (*enthusiast*) (coll) mordu *m*; (*addict*) (coll) toxicomane *mf*

fiendish [ˈfindɪʃ] *adj* diabolique

fierce [fɪrs] *adj* féroce, farouche; (*wind*) furieux; (coll) très mauvais

fierceness [ˈfɪrsnɪs] *s* férocité *f*

fier·y [ˈfaɪri], [ˈfaɪ·əri] *adj* (*comp* **-ier**; *super* **-iest**) ardent; (*speech*) enflammé; (*horse*, *person*, *etc.*) fougueux

fife [faɪf] *s* fifre *m*

fifteen [ˈfɪfˈtin] *adj*, *pron*, & *s* quinze *m*; **about fifteen** une quinzaine de

fifteenth [ˈfɪfˈtinθ] *adj* & *pron* quinzième (*masc*, *fem*); **the Fifteenth** quinze, e.g., **John the Fifteenth** Jean quinze ‖ *s* quinzième *m*; **the fifteenth** (*in dates*) le quinze

fifth [fɪfθ] *adj* & *pron* cinquième (*masc*, *fem*); **the Fifth** cinq, e.g., **John the Fifth** Jean cinq ‖ *s* cinquième *m*; (mus) quinte *f*; **the fifth** (*in dates*) le cinq

fifth' col'umn *s* cinquième colonne *f*

fiftieth [ˈfɪftɪ·θ] *adj* & *pron* cinquantième (*masc*, *fem*) ‖ *s* cinquantième *m*

fif·ty [ˈfɪfti] *adj* & *pron* cinquante ‖ *s* (*pl* **-ties**) cinquante *m*; **about fifty** une cinquantaine *f*; **fifties** (*years of the decade*) années *fpl* cinquante

fif'ty-fif'ty *adv*—**to go fifty-fifty** (coll) être de moitié, être en compte à demi

fig [fɪg] *s* figue *f*; (*tree*) figuier *m*; **a fig for . . . !** (coll) nargue de . . . !

fight [faɪt] *s* combat *m*, bataille *f*; (*spirit*) cœur *m*; **to pick a fight with** chercher querelle à ‖ *v* (*pret* & *pp* **fought** [fɔt]) *tr* combattre, se battre contre; **to fight off** repousser ‖ *intr* combattre, se battre; **to fight shy of** se défier de

fighter ['faɪtər] s combattant m; (game person) batailleur m; (aer) chasseur m, avion m de chasse

fight'er pi'lot s chasseur m

fig' leaf' s feuille f de figuier; (on statues) feuille de vigne

figment ['fɪgmənt] s fiction f, invention f

figurative ['fɪgjərətɪv] adj figuratif; (meaning) figuré

figure ['fɪgjər] s figure f; (bodily form) taille f; (math) chiffre m; **to be good at figures** être bon en calcul; **to have a good figure** avoir de la ligne; **to keep one's figure** garder sa ligne || tr figurer; (to embellish) orner de motifs; (to imagine) se figurer, s'imaginer; **to figure out** calculer; (coll) déchiffrer || intr figurer; **to figure on** compter sur

fig'ured bass' [bes] s (mus) basse f chiffrée

fig'ured silk' s soie f à dessin

fig'ure-head' s prête-nom m, homme m de paille; (naut) figure f de proue

fig'ure of speech' s figure f de rhétorique

fig'ure skat'ing s patinage m de fantaisie

filament ['fɪləmənt] s filament m

filbert ['fɪlbərt] s noisette f, aveline f; (tree) noisetier m, avelinier m

filch [fɪltʃ] tr chaparder, chiper

file [faɪl] s (tool) lime f; (for papers) classeur m; (for cards) fichier m; (personal record) dossier m; (line) file f; **in single file** en file indienne, à la queue leu leu; **to form single file** dédoubler les rangs || tr limer; classer, ranger; (a petition) déposer; **to file down** enlever à la lime || intr—**to file off** défiler; **to file out** sortir un à un

file' case' s fichier m

file' clerk' s employé m, commis m

file' num'ber s (e.g., used in answering a letter) référence f

filial ['fɪlɪəl], ['fɪljəl] adj filial

filiation [,fɪlɪ'eʃən] s filiation f

filibuster ['fɪlɪ,bʌstər] s (use of delaying tactics) obstruction f; (legislator) obstructionniste mf; (pirate) flibustier m || tr (legislation) obstruer || intr faire de l'obstruction

filigree ['fɪlɪ,gri] adj filigrané || s filigrane m || tr filigraner

filing ['faɪlɪŋ] s (of documents) classement m; (with a tool) limage m; **filings** limaille f, grains mpl de limaille

fil'ing cab'inet s classeur m

fil'ing card' s fiche f

Filipi·no [,fɪlɪ'pino] adj philippin || s (pl -nos) Philippin m

fill [fɪl] s suffisance f; (earth, stones, etc.) remblai m; **to have one's fill of** avoir tout son soûl de || tr remplir; (a prescription) exécuter; (a tooth) plomber; (a cylinder with gas) charger; (a hollow or gap) combler; (a job) occuper; **to fill in** remblayer,

combler; **to fill out** (a questionnaire) remplir || intr se remplir; **to fill out** se gonfler; (said of sail) s'enfler; **to fill up** se combler; (to fill the tank full) faire le plein

filler ['fɪlər] s remplissage m; (of cigar) tripe f; (sizing) apprêt m, mastic m; (in notebook) papier m; (journ) pesée f

fillet ['fɪlɪt] s bande f; (for hair) bandeau m; (archit) moulure f || ['fɪle], ['fɪlɪt] s (culin) filet m || tr couper en filets

filling ['fɪlɪŋ] adj (food) rassasiant || s (of job) occupation f; (of tooth) plombage m; (e.g., of turkey) farce f; (of cigar) tripe f

fill'ing sta'tion s poste m d'essence

fill'ing-station attend'ant s pompiste mf

fillip ['fɪlɪp] s tonique m, stimulant m; (with finger) chiquenaude f || tr donner une chiquenaude à

fil·ly ['fɪlɪ] s (pl -lies) pouliche f; (coll) fillette f

film [fɪlm] s film m; (in a roll) pellicule f, film || tr filmer

filming ['fɪlmɪŋ] s filmage m

film' li'brary s cinémathèque f

film' mak'er s cinéaste mf

film' star' s vedette f du cinéma

film' strip' s film m fixe

film·y ['fɪlmɪ] adj (comp -ier; super -iest) diaphane, voilé

filter ['fɪltər] s filtre m || tr & intr filtrer

filtering ['fɪltərɪŋ] s filtrage m; (of water) filtration f

fil'ter pa'per s papier-filtre m

fil'ter tip' adj à bout-filtre || s bout-filtre m, bout-filtrant m

filth [fɪlθ] s saleté f, ordure f; (fig) obscénité f

filth·y ['fɪlθɪ] adj (comp -ier; super -iest) sale, immonde

filth·y lu'cre ['lukər] s (coll) lucre m

fin [fɪn] s nageoire f

final ['faɪnəl] adj final; (last in a series) ultime, définitif || s examen final; (sports) finale f

finale [fɪ'nalɪ] s (mus) final m

finalist ['faɪnəlɪst] s finaliste mf

finally ['faɪnəli] adv finalement, enfin

finance [fɪ'næns], ['faɪnæns] s finance f || tr financer

financial [fɪ'nænʃəl], [faɪ'nænʃəl] adj financier; (interest; distress) pécuniaire

financier [,fɪnən'sɪr], [,faɪnən'sɪr] s financier m

financing [fɪ'nænsɪŋ], ['faɪnænsɪŋ] s financement m

finch [fɪntʃ] s pinson m

find [faɪnd] s trouvaille f || v (pret & pp found [faʊnd]) tr trouver; **to find out** apprendre || intr (law) déclarer; **to find out** (about) se renseigner (sur), se mettre au courant (de); **find out!** à vous de trouver!

finder ['faɪndər] s (of camera) viseur m; (of optical instrument) chercheur m

finding ['faɪndɪŋ] s découverte f; (law) décision f; **findings** conclusions fpl

fine [faɪn] adj fin; (weather) beau; (person, manners, etc.) distingué, excellent; **that's fine!** bien!, parfait! || s amende f || tr mettre à l'amende

fine' arts' spl beaux-arts mpl

fineness ['faɪnnɪs] s finesse f; (of metal) titre m

fine' print' s petits caractères mpl

finer-y ['faɪnəri] s (pl -ies) parure f

finespun ['faɪn,spʌn] adj ténu; (fig) subtil

finesse [fɪ'nɛs] s finesse f; (in bridge) impasse f; **to use finesse** finasser || tr faire l'impasse à

fine'-toothed comb' s peigne m aux dents fines, peigne fin

finger ['fɪŋgər] s doigt m; (slang) mouchard m, indicateur m; **not to lift a finger** (fig) ne pas remuer le petit doigt; **to burn one's fingers** (fig) se faire échauder; **to put one's finger on the spot** (fig) mettre le doigt dessus; **to slip between the fingers** glisser entre les doigts; **to snap one's fingers at** (fig) faire la figue à, narguer; **to twist around one's little finger** (coll) mener par le bout du nez, faire tourner comme un toton || tr toucher du doigt, manier; (mus) doigter; (slang) espionner; (slang) identifier

fin'ger board' s (of guitar) touche f; (of piano) clavier m

fin'ger bowl' s rince-doigts m

fin'ger dexter'ity s (mus) doigté m

fingering ['fɪŋgərɪŋ] s maniement m; (mus) doigté m

fin'ger-nail' s ongle m

fin'gernail pol'ish s brillant m

fin'ger-print' s empreinte f digitale || tr prendre les empreintes digitales de

fin'ger-tip' s bout m du doigt; **to have at one's fingertips** tenir sur le bout du doigt

finicky ['fɪnɪki] adj méticuleux

finish ['fɪnɪʃ] s (perfection) achevé m, fini m; (elegance) finesse f; (conclusion) fin f; (gloss, coating, etc.) fini m || tr & intr finir; **to finish +** ger finir de + inf; **to finish by +** ger finir par + inf

fin'ishing touch' s dernière main f

finite ['faɪnaɪt] adj & s fini m

Finland ['fɪnlənd] s Finlande f; **la Finlande**

Finlander ['fɪnləndər] s Finlandais m

Finn [fɪn] s (member of a Finnish-speaking group of people) Finnois m; (native or inhabitant of Finland) Finlandais m

Finnish ['fɪnɪʃ] adj & s finnois m

fir [fʌr] s sapin m

fire [faɪr] s feu m; (destructive burning) incendie m; **to catch fire** prendre feu; **to set on fire** mettre le feu à || tr mettre le feu à; (e.g., passions) enflammer; (a weapon) tirer; (a rocket) lancer; (an employee) (coll) renvoyer || interj (warning) au feu!; (command to fire) feu!

fire' alarm' s avertisseur m d'incendie; (box) poste m avertisseur d'incendie

fire'arm' s arme f à feu

fire'ball' s globe m de feu; (mil) grenade f incendiaire

fire'bird' s loriot m d'Amérique

fire'boat' s bateau-pompe m

fire'box' s boîte f à feu; (rr) foyer m

fire'brand' s tison m; (coll) brandon m de discorde

fire'break' s tranchée f garde-feu, pare-feu m

fire'brick' s brique f réfractaire

fire' brigade' s corps m de sapeurs-pompiers

fire'bug' s (coll) incendiaire mf

fire' chief' s capitaine m des pompiers

fire' com'pany s corps m de sapeurs-pompiers; (insurance company) compagnie f d'assurance contre l'incendie

fire'crack'er s pétard m

fire'damp' s grisou m

fire' depart'ment s service m des incendies, sapeurs-pompiers mpl

fire'dog' s chenet m, landier m

fire' drill' s exercices mpl de sauvetage en cas d'incendie

fire' en'gine s pompe f à incendie

fire' escape' s échelle f de sauvetage, escalier m de secours

fire' extin'guisher s extincteur m

fire'fly' s (pl -flies) luciole f

fire'guard' s (before hearth) pare-étincelles m; (in forest) pare-feu m

fire' hose' s manche f d'incendie

fire'house' s caserne f de pompiers, poste m de pompiers

fire' hy'drant s bouche f d'incendie

fire' insur'ance s assurance f contre l'incendie

fire' i'rons spl garniture f de foyer

fire'less cook'er ['faɪrlɪs] s marmite f norvégienne

fire'man s (pl -men) (man who stokes fires) chauffeur m; (man who extinguishes fires) sapeur-pompier m, pompier m

fire'place' s cheminée f, foyer m

fire'plug' s bouche f d'incendie

fire'pow'er s puissance f de feu

fire'proof' adj ignifuge; (dish) apyre f || tr ignifuger

fire' sale' s vente f après incendie

fire' screen' s écran m de cheminée, garde-feu m

fire' ship' s brûlot m

fire' shov'el s pelle f à feu

fire'side' s coin m du feu

fire'trap' s édifice m qui invite l'incendie

fire' wall' s coupe-feu m

fire'ward'en s garde m forestier, vigie f

fire'wa'ter s (slang) gnole f, whisky m

fire'wood' s bois m de chauffage

fire'works' spl feu m d'artifice

firing ['faɪrɪŋ] s (of furnace) chauffe f; (of bricks, ceramics, etc.) cuite f; (of gun) tir m, feu m; (by a group of soldiers) fusillade f; (of an internal-combustion engine) allumage m; (of an employee) (coll) renvoi m

fir'ing line' s ligne f de feu, chaîne f de combat

fir'ing or'der s rythme m d'allumage

fir'ing pin' s percuteur m, aiguille f

fir'ing squad' s peloton m d'exécution; *(for ceremonies)* piquet m d'honneurs funèbres

firm [fʌrm] *adj & adv* ferme; **to stand firm** tenir bon ‖ s maison f de commerce, firme f

firmament ['fʌrməmənt] s firmament m

firm' name' s nom m commercial

firmness ['fʌrmnɪs] s fermeté f

first [fʌrst] *adj, pron, & s* premier m; **at first** au commencement, au début; **first come first served** les premiers vont devant; **from the first** depuis le premier jour; **John the First** Jean premier ‖ *adv* premièrement, d'abord; **first and last** en tout et pour tout; **first of all, first off** tout d'abord, de prime abord

first' aid' s premiers soins mpl, premiers secours mpl

first'-aid' kit' s boîte f à pansements, trousse f de première urgence

first'-aid' sta'tion s poste m de secours

first'-born' *adj & s* premier-né m

first'-class' *adj* de première classe, de premier ordre ‖ *adv* en première classe

first' cous'in s cousin m germain

first' draft' s brouillon m, premier jet m

first' fin'ger s index m

first' floor' s rez-de-chaussée m

first' fruits' spl prémices fpl

first'hand' *adj & adv* de première main

first' lieuten'ant s lieutenant m en premier

firstly ['fʌrstli] *adv* en premier lieu, d'abord

first' mate' s (naut) second m

first' name' s prénom m, petit nom m

first' night' s (theat) première f

first-nighter [ˌfʌrst'naɪtər] s (theat) habitué m des premières

first' offend'er s délinquant m primaire

first' of'ficer s (naut) officier m en second

first' prize' s (in a lottery) gros lot m; **to win first prize** remporter le prix

first' quar'ter s (of the moon) premier quartier m

first'-rate' *adj* de premier ordre, de première qualité; (coll) excellent ‖ *adv* (coll) très bien, à merveille

first'-run mov'ie s film m en exclusivité

fiscal ['fɪskəl] *adj* fiscal

fis'cal year' s exercice m budgétaire

fish [fɪʃ] s poisson m; **to be like a fish out of water** être comme un poisson sur la paille; **to be neither fish nor fowl** être ni chair ni poisson; **to drink like a fish** boire comme un trou; **to have other fish to fry** avoir d'autres chiens à fouetter ‖ *tr* pêcher; (rr) éclisser; **to fish out or up** repêcher ‖ *intr* pêcher; **to fish for compliments** quêter des compliments; **to go fishing** aller à la pêche; **to take fishing** emmener à la pêche

fish'bone' s arête f

fish'bowl' s bocal m

fisher ['fɪʃər] s pêcheur m; (zool) martre f

fish'er·man s (pl -men) pêcheur m

fisher·y ['fɪʃəri] s (pl -ies) (activity; business) pêche f; (grounds) pêcherie f

fish' hawk' s aigle m pêcheur

fish'hook' s hameçon m

fishing ['fɪʃɪŋ] *adj* pêcheur, de pêche ‖ s pêche f

fish'ing ground' s pêcherie f

fish'ing reel' s moulinet m

fish'ing rod' s canne f à pêche

fish'ing tack'le s attirail m de pêche

fish'line' s ligne f de pêche

fish' mar'ket s poissonnerie f

fish'plate' s (rr) éclisse f

fish'pool' s vivier m

fish' spear' s foëne f, fouëne f

fish' sto'ry s hâblerie f, blague f

fish'tail' s queue f de poisson; (aer) embardée f ‖ *intr* (aer) embarder

fish'wife' s (pl -wives') poissonnière f; (foul-mouthed woman) poissarde f

fish'worm' s asticot m

fish·y ['fɪʃi] *adj* (comp -ier; super -iest) (eyes) (coll) vitreux; (coll) véreux, louche

fission ['fɪʃən] s (biol) scission f; (nucl) fission f

fissionable ['fɪʃənəbəl] *adj* fissible, fissile

fissure ['fɪʃər] s fissure f, fente f ‖ *tr* fissurer ‖ *intr* se fissurer

fist [fɪst] s poing m; (typ) petite main f; **to shake one's fist at** menacer du poing

fist'fight' s combat m à coup de poings

fistful ['fɪstful] s poignée f

fisticuffs ['fɪstɪˌkʌfs] spl empoignade f or rixe f à coups de poing; (sports) boxe f

fit [fɪt] *adj* (comp fitter; super fittest) bon, convenable; capable, digne; (in good health) en forme, sain; **fit to be tied** (coll) en colère; **fit to drink** buvable; **fit to eat** mangeable; **to feel fit** être frais et dispos ‖ s ajustement m; (of clothes) coupe f, façon f; (of fever, rage, coughing) accès m; **by fits and starts** par accès; **fit of coughing** quinte f de toux ‖ v (pret & pp fitted; ger fitting) *tr* ajuster; (s.th. in s.th) emboîter; **to fit for** (e.g., a task) préparer à; **to fit out or up** aménager; **to fit out with** garnir de ‖ *intr* s'emboîter; **to fit in with** s'accorder avec, convenir à

fitful ['fɪtfəl] *adj* intermittent

fitness ['fɪtnɪs] s convenance f; (for a task) aptitude f; (good shape) bonne forme f

fitter ['fɪtər] s ajusteur m; (of machinery) monteur m; (of clothing) essayeur m

fitting ['fɪtɪŋ] *adj* convenable, approprié, à propos ‖ s ajustage m; (of a garment) essayage m; **fittings** aménagements mpl; (of metal) ferrures fpl

five [faɪv] *adj* & *pron* cinq || *s* cinq *m*; **five o'clock** cinq heures

five'-year plan' *s* plan *m* quinquennal

fix [fɪks] *s* (coll) mauvais pas *m*; **to be in a fix** (coll) être dans le pétrin || *tr* réparer; (*e.g., a date; a photographic image; prices; one's eyes*) fixer; (slang) donner son compte à

fixedly ['fɪksɪdli] *adv* fixement

fixing ['fɪksɪŋ] *s* fixation *f*; (phot) fixage *m*; **fixings** (slang) collation *f*, des mets *mpl*

fix'ing bath' *s* bain *m* de fixage, fixateur *m*

fixture ['fɪkstʃər] *s* accessoire *m*, garniture *f*; **fixtures** meubles *mpl* à demeure

fizz [fɪz] *s* pétillement *m* || *intr* pétiller

fizzle ['fɪzəl] *s* (coll) avortement *m* || *intr* (coll) avorter; **to fizzle out** (coll) tomber à l'eau, échouer

flabbergasted ['flæbər,gæstɪd] *adj* (coll) éberlué, épaté

flab•by ['flæbɪ] *adj* (comp -bier; super -biest) mou, flasque

flag [flæg] *s* drapeau *m* || *v* (pret & pp flagged; ger flagging) *tr*—to flag s.o. transmettre des signaux à qn en agitant un fanion || *intr* faiblir, se relâcher

flag' cap'tain *s* (nav) capitaine *m* de pavillon

flag'man *s* (pl -men) signaleur *m*; (rr) garde-voie *m*

flag' of truce' *s* drapeau *m* parlementaire

flag'pole' *s* hampe *f* de drapeau; (naut) mât *m* de pavillon; (surv) jalon *m*

flagrant ['flegrənt] *adj* scandaleux; (*e.g., injustice*) flagrant

flag'ship' *s* (nav) vaisseau *m* amiral

flag'staff' *s* hampe *f* de drapeau

flag'stone' *s* dalle *f*

flag' stop' *s* (rr) halte *f*, arrêt *m* facultatif

flag'-wav'ing *adj* cocardier || *s* patriotisme *m* de façade

flail [flel] *s* fléau *m* || *tr* (agr) battre au fléau; (fig) éreinter

flair [fler] *s* flair *m*; aptitude *f*

flak [flæk] *s* tir *m* contre-avions

flake [flek] *s* (of snow; of cereal) flocon *m*; (of soap; of mica) paillette *f*; (of paint) écaille *f* || *intr* tomber en flocons; **to flake off** s'écailler

flak•y ['flekɪ] *adj* (comp -ier; super -iest) floconneux, lamelleux

flamboyant [flæm'bɔɪ-ənt] *adj* fleuri, orné, coloré; (archit) flamboyant

flame [flem] *s* flamme *f*; (coll) amant *m*, amante *f* || *tr* flamber || *intr* flamber, flamboyer

flamethrower ['flem,θro-ər] *s* lance-flammes *m*

flaming ['flemɪŋ] *adj* flambant

flamin•go [flə'mɪŋgo] *s* (pl -gos or -goes) flamant *m*

flammable ['flæməbəl] *adj* inflammable

Flanders ['flændərz] *s* Flandre *f*; la Flandre

flange [flændʒ] *s* rebord *m*, saillie *f*; (of wheel) jante *f*; (of rail) patin *m*

flank [flæŋk] *s* flanc *m* || *tr* flanquer

flannel ['flænəl] *s* flanelle *f*

flap [flæp] *s* (part that can be folded under) rabat *m*; (fold in clothing) pan *m*; (of a cap) couvre-nuque *m*; (of a pocket; of an envelope) patte *f*; (of wings) coup *m*, battement *m*; (of a table) battant *m*; (of a sail, flag, etc.) claquement *m*; (slang) tape *f*; (aer) volet *m* || *v* (pret & pp flapped; ger flapping) *tr* (wings, arms, etc.) battre; (to slap) taper || *intr* battre; (said of sail, flag, etc.) claquer; (said of curtain) voltiger; (to hang down) pendre

flap'jack' *s* (coll) crêpe *f*

flare [fler] *s* éclat *m* vif; (e.g., of skirt; of pipe or funnel) évasement *m*; (for signaling) fusée *f* éclairante || *tr* évaser || *intr* flamboyer; (to spread outward) s'évaser; **to flare up** s'enflammer; (to reappear) se produire de nouveau; (to become angry) s'emporter

flare'-up' *s* flambée *f* soudaine; (of illness) recrudescence *f*; (of anger) accès *m* de colère

flash [flæʃ] *s* éclair *m*; (of hope) lueur *f*, rayon *m*; (of wit) trait *m*; (of genius) éclair; (brief moment) instant *m*; (ostentation) (coll) tape-à-l'œil *m*; (last-minute news) (coll) nouvelle *f* éclair; **flash in the pan** (coll) feu *m* de paille; **in a flash** en un clin d'œil || *tr* projeter; (a gem) faire étinceler; (to show off) faire parade de; (a message) répandre, transmettre || *intr* jeter des éclairs; (said of gem, eyes, etc.) étinceler; **to flash by** passer comme un éclair

flash'back' *s* (mov) retour *m* en arrière, rappel *m*

flash' bulb' *s* ampoule *f* flash, flash *m*

flash' flood' *s* crue *f* subite

flashing ['flæʃɪŋ] *adj* éclatant; (light) à éclats; (signal) clignotant || *s* bande *f* de solin

flash'light' *s* lampe *f* torche, lampe de poche; (phot) lampe éclair

flash'light bat'tery *s* pile *f* torche

flash•y ['flæʃɪ] *adj* (comp -ier; super -iest) (coll) tapageur, criard

flask [flæsk], [flɑsk] *s* flacon *m*, gourde *f*; (in lab) ballon *m*, flacon

flat [flæt] *adj* (comp flatter; super flattest) plat, uni; (nose) aplati; (refusal) net; (beer) éventé; (tire) dégonflé; (dull, tasteless) fade, terne; (mus) bémol *m*; (flat tire) crevaison *f*; (of sword) plat *m*; (mus) bémol *m*; (theat) châssis *m* || *adv* (outright) (coll) nettement, carrément; **to fall flat** tomber à plat; (fig) manquer son effet; **to sing flat** chanter faux

flat'boat' *s* plate *f*

flat-broke ['flæt'brok] *adj* (coll) complètement fauché, à la côte

flat'car' *s* plate-forme *f*

flat'foot' s (slang) flic m

flat'-foot'ed adj aux pieds plats; (coll) franc, brutal

flat'i'ron s fer m à repasser

flatly ['flætli] adv net, platement

flat'-nosed' adj camard, camus

flatten ['flætən] tr aplatir, aplanir; (metallurgy) laminer ‖ intr s'aplatir, s'aplanir; **to flatten out** (aer) se redresser

flatter ['flætər] tr & intr flatter

flatterer ['flætərər] s flatteur m

flattering ['flætərɪŋ] adj flatteur

flatter•y ['flætəri] s (pl -ies) flatterie f

flat'tire' s pneu m dégonflé, à plat, or crevé, crevaison f

flat'top' s (nav) porte-avions m

flatulence ['flætʃələns] s boursouflure f; (pathol) flatulence f

flat'ware' s couverts mpl; (plates) assiettes fpl

flaunt [flɔnt], [flɑnt] tr faire étalage de

flautist ['flɔtɪst] s flûtiste mf

flavor ['flevər] s saveur f, goût m; (ice cream) parfum m ‖ tr assaisonner, parfumer

flavoring ['flevərɪŋ] s assaisonnement m; (lemon, rum, etc.) parfum m

flaw [flɔ] s défaut m, tache f; (crack) fêlure f; (in metal) paille f; (in diamond) crapaud m

flawless ['flɔlɪs] adj sans défaut, sans tache

flax [flæks] s lin m

flaxen ['flæksən] adj de lin, blond

flax'seed' s graine f de lin

flay [fle] tr écorcher; (to criticize) rosser, fustiger

flea [fli] s puce f

flea'bite' s piqûre f de puce; (trifle) vétille f

fleck [flek] s tache f; (particle) particule f ‖ tr tacheter

fledgling ['fledʒlɪŋ] adj (lawyer, teacher) en herbe, débutant ‖ s oisillon m; (novice) débutant m, béjaune m

flee [fli] v (pret & pp fled [fled]) tr & intr fuir

fleece [flis] s toison f ‖ tr tondre; (to strip of money) (coll) écorcher, plumer

fleec•y ['flisi] adj (comp -ier; super -iest) laineux; (snow, wool) floconneux; (hair) moutonneux; (clouds) moutonné

fleet [flit] adj rapide ‖ s flotte f

fleet'-foot'ed adj au pied léger

fleeting ['flitɪŋ] adj passager, fugitif

Fleming ['flemɪŋ] s Flamand m

Flemish ['flemɪʃ] adj & s flamand m

flesh [fleʃ] s chair f; **in the flesh** en chair et en os; **to lose flesh** perdre de l'embonpoint; **to put on flesh** prendre de l'embonpoint, s'empâter

flesh' and blood' s nature f humaine; (relatives) famille f, parenté f

flesh'-col'ored adj couleur f de chair, carné

flesh'pot' s (pot for cooking meat) pot-au-feu m; **fleshpots** (high living) luxe m, grande chère f; (evil places) mai-

sons fpl de débauche, mauvais lieux mpl

flesh' wound' [wund] s blessure f en séton, blessure superficielle

flesh•y ['fleʃi] adj (comp -ier; super -iest) charnu

flex [fleks] tr & intr fléchir

flexible ['fleksɪbəl] adj flexible

flick [flɪk] s (with finger) chiquenaude f; (with whip) petit coup m; **flicks** (coll) ciné m ‖ tr faire une chiquenaude à; (a whip) faire claquer

flicker ['flɪkər] s petite lueur f vacillante; (of eyelids) battement m; (of emotion) frisson m ‖ intr trembloter, vaciller; (said of eyelids) ciller

flier ['flaɪ•ər] s aviateur m; (coll) spéculation f au hasard; (rr) rapide m; (handbill) (coll) prospectus m

flight [flaɪt] s fuite f; (of airplane) vol m; (of birds) volée f; (of stairs) volée; (of fancy) élan m; **to put to flight** mettre en fuite; **to take flight** prendre la fuite

flight' deck' s (nav) pont m d'envol

flight' record'er s enregistreur m en vol

flight•y ['flaɪti] adj (comp -ier; super -iest) volage, léger; braque, écervelé

flim·flam ['flɪm,flæm] s (coll) baliverne f; (fraud) (coll) escroquerie f ‖ v (pret & pp -flammed; ger -flamming) tr (coll) escroquer

flims•y ['flɪmzi] adj (comp -ier; super -iest) léger; (e.g., cloth) fragile; (e.g., excuse) frivole

flinch [flɪntʃ] intr reculer, fléchir; **without flinching** sans broncher, sans hésiter

fling [flɪŋ] s jet m; **to go on a fling** faire la noce; **to have a fling at** tenter; **to have one's fling** jeter sa gourme ‖ v (pret & pp flung [flʌŋ]) tr lancer; (on the floor, out the window; in jail) jeter; **to fling open** ouvrir brusquement

flint [flɪnt] s silex m; (of lighter) pierre f

flint'lock' s fusil m à pierre

flint•y ['flɪnti] adj (comp -ier; super -iest) siliceux; (heart) de pierre, insensible

flip [flɪp] adj (comp flipper; super flippest) (coll) mutin, moqueur ‖ s chiquenaude f; (somersault) culbute f; (aer) petit tour m de vol ‖ v (pret & pp flipped; ger flipping) tr donner une chiquenaude à; (a page) tourner rapidement; **to flip a coin** jouer à pile ou face; **to flip over** (a phonograph record) retourner

flippancy ['flɪpənsi] s désinvolture f

flippant ['flɪpənt] adj désinvolte

flipper ['flɪpər] s nageoire f

flirt [flʌrt] s flirteur m, flirt m ‖ intr flirter; (said only of a man) conter fleurette

flit [flɪt] v (pret & pp flitted; ger flitting) intr voleter; **to flit away** passer rapidement; **to flit here and there** voltiger

float [flot] s (raft) radeau m; (on fish line; in carburetor; on seaplane) flotteur *m*; (*on fish line or net*) flotte *f*; (*of mason*) aplanissoire *f*; (*in parade*) char *m* de cavalcade, char de Carnaval || *tr* faire flotter; (*a loan*) émettre, contracter || *intr* flotter, nager; (*on one's back*) faire la planche

floater ['flotər] *s* vagabond *m*; (*illegal voter*) faux électeur *m*

floating ['flotɪŋ] *adj* flottant; (*free*) libre || *s* flottement *m*; (*of loan*) émission *f*

float'ing is'land *s* (culin) œufs *mpl* à la neige

flock [flɑk] *s* (*of birds*) volée *f*; (*of sheep*) troupeau *m*; (*of people*) foule *f*, bande *f*; (*of nonsense*) tas *m*; (*of faithful*) ouailles *fpl* || *intr* s'assembler; **to flock in** entrer en foule; **to flock together** s'attrouper

floe [flo] *s* banquise *f*; (*floating piece of ice*) glaçon *m* flottant

flog [flɑg] *v* (*pret & pp* **flogged**; *ger* **flogging**) *tr* fouetter, flageller

flogging ['flɑgɪŋ] *s* fouet *m*

flood [flʌd] *s* inondation *f*; (*caused by heavy rain*) déluge *m*; (*sudden rise of river*) crue *f*; (*of tide*) flot *m*; (*of words, tears, light*) flots *mpl*, déluge || *tr* inonder; (*to overwhelm*) submerger, inonder; (*a carburetor*) noyer || *intr* (*said of river*) déborder; (aut) se noyer

flood'gate' *s* (*of a dam*) vanne *f*; (*of a canal*) porte *f* d'écluse

flood'light' *s* phare *m* d'éclairage, projecteur *m* de lumière || *tr* illuminer par projecteurs

flood' tide' *s* marée *f* montante, flux *m*

floor [flor] *s* (*inside bottom surface of room*) plancher *m*, parquet *m*; (*story of building*) étage *m*; (*of swimming pool, the sea, etc.*) fond *m*; (*of assembly hall*) enceinte *f*, parquet; (*of the court*) prétoire *m*, parquet; (naut) varangue *f*; **to ask for the floor** réclamer la parole; **to give s.o. the floor** donner la parole à qn; **to have the floor** avoir la parole; **to take the floor** prendre la parole || *tr* parqueter; (*an opponent*) terrasser; (*to disconcert*) (coll) désarçonner

flooring ['florɪŋ] *s* planchéiage *m*, parquetage *m*

floor' lamp' *s* lampe *f* à pied, lampadaire *m*

floor' mop' *s* brosse *f* à parquet

floor' show' *s* spectacle *m* de cabaret

floor' tim'ber *s* (naut) varangue *f*

floor'walk'er *s* chef *m* de rayon

floor' wax' *s* cire *f* à parquet, encaustique *f*

flop [flɑp] *s* (coll) insuccès *m*, échec *m*; (*literary work or painting*) (coll) navet *m*; (*play*) (coll) four *m*; **to take a flop** (coll) faire patapouf || *v* (*pret & pp* **flopped**; *ger* **flopping**) *intr* tomber lourdement; (*to fail*) (coll) échouer, rater

flora ['florə] *s* flore *f*

floral ['florəl] *adj* floral

florescence [flo'rɛsəns] *s* floraison *f*

florid ['flɑrɪd], ['florɪd] *adj* fleuri, flamboyant; (*complexion*) rubicond

Florida ['flɑrɪdə], ['florɪdə] *s* Floride *f*; la Floride

Flor'ida Keys' *spl* Cayes *fpl* de la Floride

floss [flɑs], [flas] *s* bourre *f*; (*of corn*) barbe *f*

floss' silk' *s* bourre *f* de soie, filoselle *f*

floss·y ['flɑsi], ['flasi] *adj* (*comp* -**ier**; *super* -**iest**) soyeux; (slang) pimpant, tapageur

flotsam ['flɑtsəm] *s* épave *f*

flot'sam and jet'sam *s* choses *fpl* de flot et de mer, épaves *fpl*

flounce [flauns] *s* volant *m* || *tr* garnir de volants || *intr* s'élancer avec emportement

flounder ['flaundər] *s* flet *m*; (*plaice*) carrelet *m*, plie *f* || *intr* patauger

flour [flaur] *s* farine *f* || *tr* fariner

flourish ['flʌrɪʃ] *s* fioriture *f*; (*on a signature*) paraphe *m*; (*of trumpets*) fanfare *m*; (*brandishing*) brandissement *m* || *tr* brandir; (*to wave*) agiter || *intr* fleurir, prospérer

flourishing ['flʌrɪʃɪŋ] *adj* florissant

flour' mill' *s* moulin *m*, minoterie *f*

floury ['flaurɪ] *adj* farineux

flout [flaut] *tr* se moquer de, narguer || *intr* se moquer

flow [flo] *s* écoulement *m*; (*of tide, blood, words*) flot *m*, flux *m*; (*of blood to the head*) afflux *m*; (*rate of flow*) débit *m*; (*current*) courant *m* || *intr* écouler; (*said of tide*) monter; (*said of blood in the body*) circuler; (fig) couler; **to flow into** déboucher dans, se verser dans; **to flow over** déborder

flower ['flau·ər] *s* fleur *f* || *tr & intr* fleurir

flow'er bed' *s* plate-bande *f*, parterre *m*; (*round flower bed*) corbeille *f*

flow'er gar'den *s* jardin *m* de fleurs, jardin d'agrément

flow'er girl' *s* bouquetière *f*; (*at a wedding*) fille *f* d'honneur

flow'er·pot' *s* pot *m* à fleurs

flow'er shop' *s* boutique *f* de fleuriste

flow'er show' *s* exposition *f* horticole, floralies *fpl*

flow'er stand' *s* jardinière *f*

flowery ['flau·əri] *adj* fleuri

flu [flu] *s* (coll) grippe *f*

fluctuate ['flʌktʃu‚et] *intr* fluctuer

flue [flu] *s* tuyau *m*

fluency ['flu·ənsi] *s* facilité *f*

fluent ['flu·ənt] *adj* disert, facile; (*flowing*) coulant

fluently ['flu·əntli] *adv* couramment

fluff [flʌf] *s* (*velvety cloth*) peluche *f*; (*tuft of fur, dust, etc.*) duvet *m*; (*boner made by actor*) (coll) loup *m* || *tr* lainer, rendre pelucheux; (*one's entrance*) (coll) louper; (*one's lines*) (coll) bouler || *intr* pelucher

fluff·y ['flʌfi] *adj* (*comp* -**ier**; *super* -**iest**) duveteux; (*hair*) flou

fluid ['flu·ɪd] *adj & s* fluide *m*

fluke [fluk] *s* (*of anchor*) patte *f*; (billiards) raccroc *m*, coup *m* de veine

flume [flum] s canalisation f, ravin m
flunk [flʌŋk] tr (a student) (coll) recaler, coller; (an exam) rater ‖ intr être recalé, se faire coller
flunk·y [ˈflʌŋki] s (pl -ies) laquais m
fluorescent [ˌfluˑəˈrɛsənt] adj fluorescent
fluoridate [ˈflɔrɪˌdet], [ˈflʊrɪˌdet] tr & intr fluorider
fluoridation [ˌflɔrɪˈdeʃən], [ˌflʊrɪˈdeʃən] s fluoridation f
fluoride [ˈfluˑəˌraɪd] s fluorure m
fluorine [ˈfluˑəˌrin] s fluor m
fluoroscopy [ˌfluˑəˈrɑskəpi] s radioscopie f
fluorspar [ˈfluˑəˌspɑr] s spath m fluor
flur·ry [ˈflʌri] s (pl -ries) agitation f; (of wind, snow, etc.) rafale f ‖ v (pret & pp -ried) tr agiter
flush [flʌʃ] adj (level) à ras; (well-provided) bien pourvu; (healthy) vigoureux; **flush** with au ras de, au niveau de ‖ s (of light) éclat m; (in the cheeks) rougeur f; (of joy) transport m; (of toilet) chasse f d'eau; (in poker) flush m; **in the first flush of** dans l'ivresse ou le premier éclat de ‖ adv à ras, de niveau; (directly) droit ‖ tr (a bird) lever; **to flush a toilet** tirer la chasse d'eau; **to flush out** (e.g., a drain) laver à grande eau ‖ intr (to blush) rougir
flush′ switch′ s interrupteur m encastré
flush′ tank′ s réservoir m de chasse
flush′ toi′let s water-closet m à chasse d'eau
fluster [ˈflʌstər] s agitation f; **in a fluster** en émoi ‖ tr agiter
flute [flut] s flûte f ‖ tr (a column) canneler; (a dress) tuyauter
flutist [ˈflutɪst] s flûtiste mf
flutter [ˈflʌtər] s battement m; **all of a flutter** (coll) tout agité ‖ intr voleter; (said of pulse) battre fébrilement; (said of heart) palpiter
flux [flʌks] s flux m; (for fusing metals) acide m à souder; **to be in flux** être dans un état indécis
fly [flaɪ] s (pl flies) mouche f; (for fishing) mouche artificielle; (of trousers) braguette f; (of tent) auvent m; **flies** (theat) cintres mpl; **fly in the ointment** (fig) ombre f au tableau; **on the fly** au vol ‖ v (pret flew [flu]; pp flown [flon]) tr (a kite) faire voler; (an airplane) piloter; (freight or passengers) transporter en avion; (e.g. the Atlantic) survoler; (to flee from) fuir ‖ intr voler; (to flee) fuir; (said of flag) flotter; **to fly blind** voler à l'aveuglette; **to fly by** voler; **to fly in the face of** porter un défi à; **to fly off** s'envoler; **to fly off the handle** (coll) sortir de ses gonds; **to fly open** s'ouvrir brusquement; **to fly over** survoler
fly′blow′ s œufs mpl de mouche
fly′-by-night′ adj mal financé, indigne de confiance ‖ s financier m qui lève le pied
fly′ cast′ing s pêche f à la mouche noyée

fly′catch′er s attrape-mouches m; (bot) dionée f, attrape-mouches; (orn) gobe-mouches m
fly′-fish′ intr pêcher à la mouche
flying [ˈflaɪˑɪŋ] adj volant; rapide; court, passager ‖ s aviation f; vol m
fly′ing but′tress s arc-boutant m
fly′ing col′ors—with flying colors drapeau m déployé; brillamment
fly′ing field′ s champ m d'aviation
fly′ing-fish′ s poisson m volant
fly′ing sau′cer s soucoupe f volante
fly′ing start′ s départ m lancé
fly′ing time′ s heures fpl de vol
fly′leaf′ s (pl -leaves) feuille f de garde, garde f
fly′ net′ s (for a bed) moustiquaire f; (for a horse) chasse-mouches m
fly′pa′per s papier m tue-mouches
fly′ rod′ s canne f à mouche
fly′speck′ s chiure f, chiasse f
fly′ swat′ter [ˌswatər] s chasse-mouches m, émouchoir m
fly′trap′ s attrape-mouches m
fly′wheel′ s volant m
foal [fol] s poulain m ‖ intr mettre bas
foam [fom] s écume f; (on beer) mousse f ‖ intr écumer, mousser
foam′ rub′ber s caoutchouc m mousse
foam·y [ˈfomi] adj (comp -ier; super -iest) écumeux, mousseux
fob [fab] s (pocket) gousset m; (ornament) breloque f ‖ v (pret & pp fobbed; ger fobbing) tr—**to fob off s.th. on s.o.** refiler q.ch. à qn
f.o.b. or **F.O.B.** [ˌɛfˌoˈbi] adv (letter-word) (free on board) franco de bord, départ usine
focal [ˈfokəl] adj focal
fo·cus [ˈfokəs] s (pl -cuses or -ci [saɪ]) foyer m; **in focus** au point; **out of focus** non réglé, hors du point focal ‖ v (pret & pp -cused or -cussed; ger -cusing or -cussing) tr mettre au point, faire converger; (a beam of electrons) focaliser; (e.g., attention) concentrer ‖ intr converger; **to focus on** se concentrer sur
fodder [ˈfadər] s fourrage m
foe [fo] s ennemi m, adversaire mf
fog [fag], [fɔg] s brouillard m; (naut) brume f; (phot) voile m ‖ v (pret & pp fogged; ger fogging) tr embrumer; (phot) voiler ‖ intr s'embrumer; (phot) se voiler
fog′ bank′ s banc m de brume
fog′ bell′ s cloche f de brume
fog′bound′ adj arrêté par le brouillard, pris dans le brouillard
fog·gy [ˈfagi], [ˈfɔgi] adj (comp -gier; super -giest) brumeux; (phot) voilé; (fig) confus, flou; **it is foggy** il fait du brouillard
fog′horn′ s sirène f, corne f, or trompe f de brume
foible [ˈfɔɪbəl] s faible m, marotte f
foil [fɔɪl] s (thin sheet of metal) feuille f, lame f; (of mirror) tain m; (sword) fleuret m; (person whose personality sets off another's) repoussoir m ‖ tr déjouer, frustrer

foil'-wrapped' *adj* ceint de papier d'argent

foist [fɔɪst] *tr*—to foist oneself upon s'imposer chez; to foist s.th. on s.o. imposer q.ch. à qn

fold [fold] *s* pli *m*, repli *m*; (*for sheep*) parc *m*, bergerie *f*; (*of fat*) bourrelet *m*; (*of the faithful*) bercail *m* ‖ *tr* plier, replier; (*one's arms*) se croiser; to fold in (culin) incorporer; to fold up replier ‖ *intr* se replier; to fold up (theat) faire four; (coll) s'effondrer

folder ['foldər] *s* (*covers for holding papers*) chemise *f*; (*pamphlet*) dépliant *m*; (*person folding newspapers*) plieur *m*

folderol ['faldə‚ral] *s* sottise *f*; (*piece of foolishness*) bagatelle *f*

folding ['foldɪŋ] *adj* pliant, repliant, rabattable

fold'ing cam'era *s* appareil *m* pliant

fold'ing chair' *s* chaise *f* pliante, chaise brisée

fold'ing cot' *s* lit *m* pliant or escamotable

fold'ing door' *s* porte *f* à deux battants

fold'ing rule' *s* mètre *m* pliant

fold'ing screen' *s* paravent *m*

fold'ing seat' *s* strapontin *m*

foliage ['folɪ‚ɪdʒ] *s* feuillage *m*, feuillu *m*

foli•o ['folɪ‚o] *adj* in-folio ‖ *s* (*pl* -os) (*sheet*) folio *m*; (*book*) in-folio *m* ‖ *tr* folioter, paginer

folk [fok] *adj* populaire, traditionnel, du peuple ‖ *s* (*pl* folk or folks) peuple *m*, race *f*; folks (coll) gens *mpl*, personnes *fpl*; my folks (coll) les miens *mpl*, ma famille

folk' dance' *s* danse *f* folklorique

folk'lore' *s* folklore *m*

folk' mu'sic *s* musique *f* populaire

folk' song' *s* chanson *f* du terroir

folk•sy ['foksi] *adj* (*comp* -sier; *super* -siest) (coll) sociable, liant; (*like common people*) (coll) du terroir

folk'ways' *spl* coutumes *fpl* traditionnelles

follicle ['falɪkəl] *s* follicule *m*

follow ['falo] *tr* suivre; (*to come after*) succéder (with *dat*); (*to understand*) comprendre; (*a profession*) embrasser; to follow up poursuivre; (*e.g., a success*) exploiter ‖ *intr* suivre; (*one after the other*) se suivre; as follows comme suit; it follows that il s'ensuit que

follower ['falo•ər] *s* suivant *m*; partisan *m*, disciple *m*

following ['falo•ɪŋ] *adj* suivant ‖ *s* (*of a prince*) suite *f*; (*followers*) partisans *mpl*, disciples *mpl*

fol'low the lead'er *s* jeu *m* de la queue leu leu

fol'low-up' *adj* de continuation, complémentaire; (*car*) suiveur ‖ *s* soins *mpl* post-hospitaliers

fol•ly ['fali] *s* (*pl* -lies) sottise *f*; (*madness*) folie *f*; follies spectacle *m* de music-hall, folies *fpl*

foment [fo'ment] *tr* fomenter

fond [fand] *adj* affectueux, tendre; to become fond of s'attacher à

fondle ['fandəl] *tr* caresser

fondness ['fandnɪs] *s* affection *f*, tendresse *f*; (*appetite*) goût *m*, penchant *m*

font [fant] *s* source *f*; (*for holy water*) bénitier *m*; (*for baptism*) fonts *mpl*; (typ) fonte *f*

food [fud] *adj* alimentaire ‖ *s* nourriture *f*, aliments *mpl*; food for thought matière *f* à réflexion; good food bonne cuisine *f*

food' and cloth'ing *s* le vivre et le vêtement

food' and drink' *s* le boire et le manger

food'stuffs' *spl* denrées *fpl* alimentaires, vivres *mpl*

fool [ful] *s* sot *m*; (*jester*) fou *m*; (*person imposed on*) innocent *m*, niais *m*; to make a fool of se moquer de; to play the fool faire le pitre ‖ *tr* mystifier, abuser; to fool away gaspiller sottement ‖ *intr* faire la bête; to fool around (coll) gâcher son temps; to fool with (coll) tripoter

fooler•y ['fuləri] *s* (*pl* -ies) sottise *f*, ânerie *f*

fool'har'dy *adj* (*comp* -dier; *super* -diest) téméraire

fooling ['fulɪŋ] *s* tromperie *f*; no fooling! sans blague!

foolish ['fulɪʃ] *adj* sot, niais; ridicule, absurde

fool'proof' *adj* à toute épreuve; infaillible

fools'cap' *s* papier *m* ministre

fool's' er'rand *s*—to go on a fool's errand y aller pour des prunes

foot [fut] *s* (*pl* feet [fit]) pied *m*; (*of cat, dog, bird*) patte *f*; on foot à pied; to drag one's feet aller à pas de tortue; to have one foot in the grave avoir un pied dans la tombe; to put one's best foot forward (coll) partir du bon pied; to put one's foot down faire acte d'autorité; to put one's foot in it (coll) mettre les pieds dans le plat; to stand on one's own feet voler de ses propres ailes; to tread under foot fouler aux pieds ‖ *tr* (*the bill*) payer; to foot it aller à pied

footage ['futɪdʒ] *s* (mov, telv) (in French) métrage *m*, i.e., *length of film in meters*) longueur *f* d'un film en pieds

foot'-and-mouth' disease' *s* (vet) fièvre *f* aphteuse

foot'ball' *s* football *m* américain; (*ball*) ballon *m*

foot' brake' *s* frein *m* à pédale

foot'bridge' *s* passerelle *f*

foot'fall' *s* pas *m* léger, bruit *m* de pas

foot'hills' *spl* contreforts *mpl*, collines *fpl* basses

foot'hold' *s*—to gain a foothold prendre pied

footing ['futɪŋ] *s* équilibre *m*; (archit) empattement *m*, base *f*, socle *m*; to be on a friendly footing être en bons termes; to be on an equal footing être sur un pied d'égalité; **to lose one's footing** perdre pied

foot′lights′ *spl* (theat) rampe *f*

foot′lock′er *s* (mil) cantine *f*

foot′loose′ *adj* libre, sans entraves

foot′man *s* (pl **-men**) valet *m* de pied

foot′mark′ *s* empreinte *f* de pied

foot′note′ *s* note *f* au bas de la page

foot′pad′ *s* voleur *m* de grand chemin

foot′path′ *s* sentier *m* pour piétons

foot′print′ *s* empreinte *f* de pas, trace *f*

foot′ race′ *s* course *f* à pied

foot′rest′ *s* cale-pied *m*, repose-pied *m*

foot′ sol′dier *s* fantassin *m*

foot′sore′ *adj* aux pieds endoloris, éclopé

foot′step′ *s* pas *m*; **to follow in s.o.'s footsteps** suivre les traces de qn

foot′stone′ *s* pierre *f* tumulaire (au pied d'une tombe); (archit) première pierre

foot′stool′ *s* tabouret *m*

foot′ warm′er *s* chauffe-pieds *m*

foot′wear′ *s* chaussures *fpl*

foot′work′ *s* jeu *m* de jambes

foot′worn′ *adj* usé; (*person*) aux pieds endoloris

fop [fɑp] *s* petit-maître *m*, bellâtre *m*

for [fɔr], [fər] *prep* pour; de, e.g., **to thank s.o.** for remercier qn de; e.g., **time for dinner** l'heure du dîner; e.g., **to cry for joy** pleurer de joie; e.g., **request for money** demande d'argent; à, e.g., **for sale** à vendre; e.g., **to sell for a high price** vendre à un prix élevé; e.g., **it is for you to decide** c'est à vous de décider; par, e.g., **famous for** célèbre par; e.g., **for example** par exemple; e.g., **for pity's sake** par pitié; contre, e.g., **a remedy for** un remède contre; as for quant à; for + *ger* pour + *perf inf*, e.g., **he was punished for stealing** il fut puni pour avoir volé; **for all that** malgré tout cela; **for short** en abrégé; **he has been in Paris for a week** il est à Paris depuis une semaine, il y a une semaine qu'il est à Paris; **he was in Paris for a week** il était à Paris pendant une semaine; **to be for** (*to be in favor of*) être en faveur de, être partisan de or pour; **to use s.th. for s.th.** employer q.ch. comme q.ch., **to use coal for fuel** employer le charbon comme combustible ‖ *conj* car, parce que

forage ['fɑrɪdʒ], ['fɔrɪdʒ] *s* fourrage *m* ‖ *tr & intr* fourrager

foray ['fɑre], ['fɔre] *s* incursion *f* ‖ *tr* saccager, fourrager ‖ *intr* faire une incursion

for·bear [fɔr'bɛr] *v* (pret **-bore**; pp **-borne**) *tr* s'abstenir de ‖ *intr* se montrer patient

forbearance [fɔr'bɛrəns] *s* abstention *f*; patience *f*

for·bid [fɔr'bɪd] *v* (pret **-bade** or **-bad** ['bæd]; pp **-bidden**; ger **-bidding**) *tr* défendre, interdire; **God forbid!** qu'à Dieu ne plaise!; **to forbid s.o. s.th.** défendre q.ch. à qn; **to forbid s.o. to** défendre à qn de

forbidden [fɔr'bɪdən] *adj* défendu

forbidding [fɔr'bɪdɪŋ] *adj* rebutant, rébarbatif, sinistre

force [fɔrs] *s* force *f*; (*of a word*) signification *f*, valeur *f*; **in force** en vigueur; **in full force** en force; **the allied forces** les puissances alliées ‖ *tr* forcer; **to force back** repousser; (*air; water*) refouler; **to force in** (e.g., *a door*) enfoncer; **to force one's way into** (e.g., *a house*) pénétrer de force dans; **to force s.o.'s hand** forcer la main à qn; **to force s.o. to** + *inf* forcer qn à or de + *inf*; **to force s.th. into s.th.** faire q.ch. dans q.ch.; **to force up** (e.g., *prices*) faire monter

forced′ draft′ *s* tirage *m* forcé

forced′ land′ing *s* atterrissage *m* forcé

forced′ march′ *s* marche *f* forcée

force′-feed′ *tr* (pret & pp **-fed**) gaver, suralimenter

force′-feed′ing *s* suralimentation *f*

forceful ['fɔrsfəl] *adj* énergique

for·ceps ['fɔrseps] *s* (pl **-ceps** or **-cipes** [sɪ,piz]) (dent, surg) pince *f*; (obstet) forceps *m*

force′ pump′ *s* pompe *f* foulante

forcible ['fɔrsɪbəl] *adj* énergique, vigoureux; (*convincing*) convaincant; (*imposed*) forcé

ford [fɔrd] *s* gué *m* ‖ *tr* franchir à gué

fore [fɔr] *adj* antérieur; (naut) de l'avant ‖ *s* (naut) avant *m*; **to the fore** en vue, en vedette ‖ *adv* à l'avant ‖ *interj* (golf) gare devant!

fore′ and aft′ *adv* de l'avant à l'arrière

fore′arm′ *s* avant-bras *m* ‖ **fore·arm′** *tr* prémunir; (*to warn*) avertir

fore′bear′ *s* ancêtre *m*

foreboding [fɔr'bodɪŋ] *s* (*sign*) présage *m*; (*feeling*) pressentiment *m*

fore′cast′ *s* prévision *f* ‖ *v* (pret & pp **-cast** or **-casted**) *tr* pronostiquer

forecastle ['fɔksəl], ['fɔr,kæsəl], ['for,kəsəl] *s* gaillard *m* d'avant

fore·close′ *tr* exclure; (law) forclore; **to foreclose the mortgage** saisir l'immeuble hypothéqué

foreclosure [fɔr'kloʒər] *s* saisie *f*, forclusion *f*

fore·doom′ *tr* condamner par avance

fore′ edge′ *s* (bb) tranche *f*

fore′fa′ther *s* aïeul *m*, ancêtre *m*

fore′fin′ger *s* index *m*

fore′foot′ *s* (pl **-feet**) patte *f* de devant

fore′front′ *s* premier rang *m*; **in the forefront** en première ligne

fore·go′ *v* (pret **-went**; pp **-gone**) *tr* (*to give up*) renoncer à

foregoing ['fɔr,goɪŋ], [fɔr'go·ɪŋ] *adj* précédent, antérieur; (*facts, text, etc. already cited*) déjà cité, ci-dessus

fore′gone′ *adj* inévitable; (*anticipated*) décidé d'avance, prévu

fore′ground′ *s* premier plan *m*

fore′hand′ed *adj* prévoyant; (*thrifty*) ménager

forehead ['fɑrɪd], ['fɔrɪd] *s* front *m*

foreign ['fɑrɪn], ['fɔrɪn] *adj* étranger

for′eign affairs′ *spl* affaires *fpl* étrangères

foreigner ['fɑrɪnər], ['fɔrɪnər] *s* étranger *m*

for'eign exchange' *s* change *m* étranger; (*currency*) devises *fpl*

for'eign min'ister *s* ministre *m* des affaires étrangères

for'eign of'fice *s* ministère *m* des affaires étrangères

for'eign serv'ice *s* (dipl) service *m* diplomatique; (mil) service *m* à l'étranger

for'eign trade' *s* commerce *m* extérieur

fore'leg' *s* jambe *f* de devant

fore'lock' *s* mèche *f* sur le front; (*of horse*) toupet *m*; **to take time by the forelock** saisir l'occasion par les cheveux

fore'man *s* (pl **-men**) chef *m* d'équipe; (*in machine shop, factory*) contremaître *m*; (*of jury*) premier juré *m*

foremast ['formæst], ['for,mæst], ['for,mɑst] *s* mât *m* de misaine

fore'most' *adj* premier, principal || *adv* au premier rang

fore'noon' *s* matinée *f*

fore'part' *s* avant *m*, devant *m*, partie *f* avant

fore'paw' *s* patte *f* de devant

fore'quar'ter *s* quartier *m* de devant

fore'run'ner *s* précurseur *m*, avant-coureur *m*, avant-coureur *m*; (*sign*) signe *m* avant-coureur

foresail ['forsəl], ['for,sel], *s* misaine *f*, voile *f* de misaine

fore·see' *v* (pret **-saw**; pp **-seen**) *tr* prévoir

foreseeable [for'si·əbəl] *adj* prévisible

fore·shad'ow *tr* présager, préfigurer

fore'short'en *tr* dessiner en raccourci

fore'short'ening *s* raccourci *m*

fore'sight' *s* prévision *f*, prévoyance *f*

fore'sight'ed *adj* prévoyant

fore'skin' *s* prépuce *m*

forest ['fɑrɪst], ['fɔrɪst] *adj* forestier || *s* forêt *f*

fore'stage' *s* (theat) avant-scène *f*

fore·stall' *tr* anticiper, devancer

for'est rang'er *s* garde *m* forestier

forestry ['fɑrɪstrɪ], ['fɔrɪstrɪ] *s* sylviculture *f*

fore'taste' *s* avant-goût *m*

fore·tell' *v* (pret & pp **-told**) *tr* prédire

fore'thought' *s* prévoyance *f*; (law) préméditation *f*

for·ev'er *adv* pour toujours, à jamais

fore·warn' *tr* avertir, prévenir

fore'word' *s* avant-propos *m*, avis *m* au lecteur

forfeit ['fɔrfɪt] *adj* perdu || *s* (*pledge*) dédit *m*, gage *m*; (*fine*) amende *f*; **to play at forfeits** jouer aux gages || *tr* être déchu de, être privé de

forfeiture ['fɔrfɪtʃər] *s* perte *f*; (*fine*) amende *f*, confiscation *f*

forge [fordʒ] *s* forge *f* || *tr* forger; (*e.g., documents*) contrefaire, falsifier

forger ['fordʒər] *s* forgeur *m*; (*e.g., of documents*) faussaire *mf*

forger·y ['fordʒərɪ] *s* (pl **-ies**) contrefaçon *f*; (*of a document, a painting, etc.*) faux *m*

for·get' [fər'gɛt] *v* (pret **-got**; pp **-got** or **-gotten**; ger **-getting**) *tr & intr* oublier; **forget it!** n'y pensez plus!; **to forget to** + *inf* oublier de + *inf*

forgetful [fər'gɛtfəl] *adj* oublieux

forget'-me-not' *s* myosotis *m*, ne-m'oubliez-pas *m*

forgivable [fər'gɪvəbəl] *adj* pardonnable

for·give [fər'gɪv] *v* (pret **-gave**; pp **-given**) *tr & intr* pardonner

forgiveness [fər'gɪvnɪs] *s* pardon *m*

forgiving [fər'gɪvɪŋ] *adj* indulgent, miséricordieux

for·go [fər'go] *v* (pret **-went**; pp **-gone**) *tr* renoncer à, s'abstenir de

fork [fork] *s* fourche *f*; (*of road, tree, stem*) fourche *f*, bifurcation *f*; (*at table*) fourchette *f* || *tr & intr* fourcher, bifurquer

forked *adj* fourchu

forked' light'ning *s* éclairs *mpl* en zigzag

fork'lift truck' *s* chariot *m* élévateur

forlorn [fər'lɔrn] *adj* (*destitute*) abandonné; (*hopeless*) désespéré; (*wretched*) misérable

forlorn' hope' *s* tentative *f* désespérée

form [fɔrm] *s* forme *f*; (*paper to be filled out*) formule *f*, fiche *f*, feuille *f*; (*construction to give shape to cement*) coffrage *m* || *tr* former || *intr* se former

formal ['fɔrməl] *adj* cérémonieux, officiel; (*formalistic*) formaliste; (*superficial*) formel, de pure forme

for'mal attire' *s* tenue *f* de cérémonie

for'mal call' *s* visite *f* de politesse

for'mal din'ner *s* dîner *m* de cérémonie, dîner prié

formal·ity [fɔr'mælɪti] *s* (pl **-ties**) formalité *f*; (*stiffness*) raideur *f*; (*polite conventions*) cérémonie *f*, étiquette *f*

for'mal par'ty *s* soirée *f* de gala

for'mal speech' *s* discours *m* d'apparat

format ['fɔrmæt] *s* format *m*

formation [fɔr'meʃən] *s* formation *f*

former ['fɔrmər] *adj* antérieur, précédent; (*long past*) ancien; (*first of two things mentioned*) premier || *pron*—**the former** celui-là §84; le premier

formerly ['fɔrmərlɪ] *adv* autrefois, anciennement, jadis

form'fit'ting *adj* ajusté, moulant

formidable ['fɔrmɪdəbəl] *adj* formidable

formless ['fɔrmlɪs] *adj* informe

form' let'ter *s* lettre *f* circulaire

formu·la ['fɔrmjələ] *s* (pl **-las** or **-lae** [,li]) formule *f*

formulate ['fɔrmjə,let] *tr* formuler

for·sake [fər'sek] *v* (pret **-sook** ['suk]; pp **-saken** ['sekən]) *tr* abandonner, délaisser

fort [fort] *s* fort *m*, forteresse *f*; **hold the fort!** (coll) je vous confie la maison!

forte [fort] *s* fort *m*

forth [forθ] *adv* en avant; **and so forth** et ainsi de suite; **from this day forth** à partir de ce jour; **to go forth** sortir, se mettre en route

forth'com'ing *adj* à venir, à paraître

forth'right' adj net, direct || adv droit, carrément; (*immediately*) tout de suite

forth'with' adv sur-le-champ

fortieth ['fortɪ·ɪθ] adj & pron quarantième (*masc, fem*) || s quarantième m

fortification [ˌfortɪfɪ'keʃən] s fortification f

forti·fy ['fortɪˌfaɪ] v (*pret & pp* -**fied**) tr fortifier; (*wine*) viner

fortitude ['fortɪˌt(j)ud] s force f d'âme

fortnight ['fort,naɪt], ['fortnɪt] s quinze jours mpl, quinzaine f

fortress ['fortrɪs] s forteresse f

fortuitous [for't(j)u·ɪtəs] adj (*accidental*) fortuit; (*lucky*) fortuné

fortunate ['fortʃənɪt] adj heureux

fortune ['fortʃən] s fortune f; **to make a fortune** faire fortune; **to tell s.o. his fortune** dire la bonne aventure à qn

for'tune hunt'er s coureur m de dots

for'tune·tel'ler s diseuse f de bonne aventure

for·ty ['fortɪ] adj & pron quarante || s (*pl* -**ties**) quarante m; **about forty** une quarantaine

fo·rum ['forəm] s (*pl* -**rums** or -**ra** [rə]) forum m; (*e.g., of public opinion*) tribunal m; **open forum** tribune f libre

forward ['forwərd] adj de devant; (*precocious*) avancé, précoce; (*bold*) audacieux, effronté || s (sports) avant m || adv en avant; **to bring forward** (bk) reporter; **to come forward** s'avancer; **to look forward to** compter sur, se faire une fête de || tr envoyer, expédier; (*a letter*) faire suivre; (*a project*) avancer, favoriser

for'warding address' s adresse f d'expédition, adresse d'envoi

fossil ['fasɪl] adj & s fossile m

foster ['fastər], ['fostər] adj de lait, nourricier || tr encourager, entretenir

fos'ter broth'er s frère m de lait

fos'ter fa'ther s père m nourricier

foul [faul] adj immonde; (*air*) vicié; (*wind*) contraire; (*weather*) gros, sale; (*breath*) fétide; (*language*) ordurier; (*water*) bourbeux; (*ball*) hors jeu || s (baseball) faute f; (boxing) coup m bas || adv déloyalement || tr (sports) commettre une faute contre || intr (*said of anchor, propeller, rope, etc.*) s'engager

foul-mouthed ['faul'mauðd], ['faul-'mauθt] adj mal embouché

foul' play' s malveillance f; (sports) jeu m déloyal

found [faund] tr fonder, établir; (*metal*) fondre

foundation [faun'deʃən] s (*basis; masonry support*) fondement m; (*act of endowing*) dotation f; (*endowment*) fondation f

founder ['faundər] s fondateur m; (*in foundry*) fondeur m || intr (*said of horse*) boiter bas; (*said of building*) s'effondrer; (naut) sombrer

foundling ['faundlɪŋ] s enfant m trouvé

found'ling hos'pital s hospice m des enfants trouvés

found·ry ['faundri] s (*pl* -**ries**) fonderie f

found'ry·man s (*pl* -**men**) fondeur m

fount [faunt] s source f

fountain ['fauntən] s fontaine f

foun'tain·head' s source f, origine f

Foun'tain of Youth' s fontaine f de Jouvence

foun'tain pen' s stylo m

four [for] adj & pron quatre || s quatre m; **four o'clock** quatre heures; **on all fours** à quatre pattes

four'-cy'cle adj (mach) à quatre temps

four'-cyl'inder adj (mach) à quatre cylindres

four'-flush' intr (coll) bluffer, faire le fanfaron

fourflusher ['for,flʌʃər] s (coll) bluffeur m

four'-foot'ed adj quadrupède

four' hun'dred adj & pron quatre cents || s quatre cents m; **the Four Hundred** la haute société; le Tout Paris

four'-in-hand' s (tie) cravate-plastron f; (*team*) attelage m à quatre

four'-lane' adj à quatre voies

four'-leaf clo'ver s trèfle m à quatre feuilles

four'-motor plane' s quadrimoteur m

four'-o'clock' s (*Mirabilis jalapa*) belle-de-nuit f

four' of a kind' s (cards) un carré

four'-post'er s lit m à colonnes

four'score' adj quatre-vingts

foursome ['forsəm] s partie f double

fourteen ['for'tin] adj, pron, & s quatorze m

fourteenth ['for'tinθ] adj & pron quatorzième (*masc, fem*); **the Fourteenth** quatorze, e.g., **John the Fourteenth** Jean quatorze || s quatorze m; **the fourteenth** (*in dates*) le quatorze

fourth [forθ] adj & pron quatrième (*masc, fem*); **the Fourth** quatre, e.g., **John the Fourth** Jean quatre || s quatrième m; (*in fractions*) quart m; **the fourth** (*in dates*) le quatre

fourth' estate' s quatrième pouvoir m

fowl [faul] s volaille f

fox [faks] s renard m || tr (coll) mystifier

fox'glove' s digitale f

fox'hole' s renardière f; (mil) gourbi m, abri m de tranchée

fox'hound' s fox-hound m

fox' hunt' s chasse f au renard

fox' ter'rier s fox-terrier m

fox' trot' s (*of animal*) petit trot m; (*dance*) fox-trot m

fox·y ['faksi] adj (*comp* -**ier**; *super* -**iest**) rusé, madré

foyer ['foɪ·ər] s (*lobby*) foyer m; (*entrance hall*) vestibule m

fracas ['frekəs] s bagarre f, rixe f

fraction ['frækʃən] s fraction f

fractional ['frækʃənəl] adj fractionnaire

frac'tional cur'rency s monnaie f divisionnaire

fracture ['fræktʃər] s fracture f; **to set**

a fracture réduire une fracture || *tr* fracturer

fragile ['frædʒɪl] *adj* fragile

fragment ['frægmənt] *s* fragment *m* || *tr* fragmenter

fragrance ['fregrəns] *s* parfum *m*

fragrant ['fregrənt] *adj* parfumé

frail [frel] *adj* frêle; (*e.g., virtue*) fragile, faible || *s* (*basket*) couffe *f*

frail·ty ['frelti] *s* (*pl* **-ties**) fragilité *f*; (*weakness*) faiblesse *f*

frame [frem] *s* (*of picture, mirror*) cadre *m*; (*of glasses*) monture *f*; (*of window, car*) châssis *m*; (*of window, motor*) bâti *m*; (*support, stand*) armature *f*; (*structure*) charpente *f*; (*for embroidering*) métier *m*; (*of comic strip*) cadre, dessin *m*; (*mov, telv*) image *f* || *tr* former, charpenter; (*a picture*) encadrer; (*film*) cadrer; (*an answer*) formuler; (*slang*) monter une accusation contre

frame′ house′ *s* maison *f* en bois

frame′ of mind′ *s* disposition *f* d'esprit

frame′-up′ *s* (slang) coup *m* monté

frame′work′ *s* charpente *f*, squelette *m*

framing ['fremɪŋ] *s* (mov, phot) cadrage *m*

France [fræns], [frɑns] *s* France *f*; la France

franchise ['fræntʃaɪz] *s* concession *f*, privilège *m*; droit *m* de vote

frank [fræŋk] *adj* franc || *s* franchise *f* postale; **Frank** (*medieval German person*) Franc *m*; (*masculine name*) François *m* || *tr* affranchir

frankfurter ['fræŋkfərtər] *s* saucisse *f* de Francfort

frankincense ['fræŋkɪn,sens] *s* oliban *m*

Frankish ['fræŋkɪʃ] *adj* franc || *s* francique *m*

frankness ['fræŋknɪs] *s* franchise *f*

frantic ['fræntɪk] *adj* frénétique

fraternal [frə'tʌrnəl] *adj* fraternel

fraterni·ty [frə'tʌrnɪti] *s* (*pl* **-ties**) fraternité *f*; (*association*) confrérie *f*; (*at a university*) club *m* d'étudiants, amicale *f* estudiantine

fraternize ['frætər,naɪz] *intr* fraterniser

fraud [frɔd] *s* fraude *f*; (*person*) imposteur *m*, fourbe *mf*

fraudulent ['frɔdjələnt] *adj* frauduleux, en fraude

fraught [frɔt] *adj*—**fraught with** chargé de

fray [fre] *s* bagarre *f* || *tr* érailler || *intr* s'érailler

freak [frik] *s* (*sudden fancy*) caprice *m*; (*anomaly*) curiosité *f*; (*person, animal*) monstre *m*

freakish ['frikɪʃ] *adj* capricieux, bizarre; (*grotesque*) monstrueux

freckle ['frekəl] *s* tache *f* de rousseur, éphélide *f*

freckly ['frekli] *adj* couvert de taches de rousseur

free [fri] *adj* (*comp* **freer** ['fri·ər]; *super* **freest** ['fri·ɪst]) libre; (*without charge*) gratuit; (*without extra charge*) franc, exempt; (*e.g., end of a*

rope) dégagé; (*with money, advice, etc.*) libéral, généreux; (*manner, speech, etc.*) franc, ouvert; **to set free** libérer, affranchir || *adv* franco, gratis, gratuitement; (naut) largue, e.g., **running free** courant largue || *v* (*pret & pp* **freed** [frid]; *ger* **freeing** ['fri·ɪŋ]) *tr* libérer; (*a prisoner*) affranchir, élargir; (*to disengage*) dégager; (*from an obligation*) exempter

free′ and eas′y *adj* désinvolte, dégagé

freebooter ['fri,butər] *s* flibustier *m*, maraudeur *m*

free′ com′peti′tion *s* libre concurrence *f*

freedom ['fridəm] *s* liberté *f*

free′dom of speech′ *s* liberté *f* de la parole

free′dom of the press′ *s* liberté *f* de la presse

free′dom of the seas′ *s* liberté *f* des mers

free′dom of thought′ *s* liberté *f* de la pensée

free′dom of wor′ship *s* liberté *f* du culte, libre pratique *f*

free′-for-all′ *s* foire *f* d'empoigne, mêlée *f*

free′ hand′ *s* carte *f* blanche

free′-hand draw′ing *s* dessin *m* à main levée

free′hand′ed *adj* libéral, généreux

free′hold′ *s* (law) propriété *f* foncière perpétuelle; (hist) franc-alleu *m*

free′ lance′ *s* franc-tireur *m*

free′man *s* (*pl* **-men**) homme *m* libre; (*citizen*) citoyen *m*

Free′ma′son *s* franc-maçon *m*

Free′ma′sonry *s* franc-maçonnerie *f*

free′ of charge′ *adj & adv* gratis, exempt de frais

free′ on board′ *adv* franco de bord, départ usine

free′ port′ *s* port *m* franc

free′ speech′ *s* liberté *f* de la parole

free′-spo′ken *adj* franc; **to be free-spoken** avoir son franc-parler

free′think′er *s* libre penseur *m*

free′ thought′ *s* libre pensée *f*

free′ tick′et *s* billet *m* de faveur

free′ trade′ *s* libre-échange *m*

free′ trad′er *s* libre-échangiste *mf*

free′way′ *s* autoroute *f*

free′will′ *adj* volontaire, de plein gré

free′ will′ *s* libre arbitre *m*; **of one's own free will** de son propre gré

freeze [friz] *s* congélation *f* || *v* (*pret* **froze** [froz]; *pp* **frozen**) *tr* geler, congeler; (*assets, credits, etc.*) geler, bloquer; (*e.g., meat*) congeler || *intr* geler; **it is freezing** il gèle

freezer ['frizər] *s* (*for making ice cream*) sorbetière *f*; (*for foods*) congélateur *m*

freight [fret] *s* fret *m*, chargement *m*; (*cost*) fret, prix *m* du transport; **by freight** (rr) en petite vitesse || *tr* transporter; (*a ship, truck, etc.*) charger

freight′ car′ *s* wagon *m* de marchandises, wagon à caisse

freighter ['fretər] *s* cargo *m*

freight' plat'form *s* quai *m* de déchargement

freight' sta'tion *s* gare *f* de marchandises

freight' train' *s* train *m* de marchandises

freight' yard' *s* (rr) cour *f* de marchandises

French [frɛntʃ] *adj* français || *s* (*language*) français *m*; **the French** les Français

French' Cana'dian *s* Franco-Canadien *m*

French'-Cana'dian *adj* franco-canadien

French' chalk' *s* craie *f* de tailleur, stéatite *f*

French' cuff' *s* poignet *m* mousquetaire

French' door' *s* porte-fenêtre *f*

French' dress'ing *s* vinaigrette *f*

French' fries' *spl* frites *fpl*

French' horn' *s* (mus) cor *m* d'harmonie

French' horse'power *s* (*735 watts*) cheval-vapeur *m*, cheval *m*

French' leave' *s*—**to take French leave** filer à l'anglaise

French'man *s* (*pl* **-men**) Français *m*

French' roll' *s* petit pain *m*

French'-speak'ing *adj* francophone; (*country*) de langue française

French' tel'ephone *s* combiné *m*

French' toast' *s* pain *m* perdu

French' win'dow *s* porte-fenêtre *f*

French'wom'an *s* (*pl* **-wom'en**) Française *f*

frenzied ['frɛnzɪd] *adj* frénétique

fren·zy ['frɛnzi] *s* (*pl* **-zies**) frénésie *f*

frequen·cy ['frikwənsi] *s* (*pl* **-cies**) fréquence *f*

fre'quency modula'tion *s* modulation *f* de fréquence

frequent ['frikwənt] *adj* fréquent [frɪ'kwɛnt], ['frikwənt] *tr* fréquenter

frequently ['frikwəntli] *adv* fréquemment

fres·co ['frɛsko] *s* (*pl* **-coes** or **-cos**) fresque *f* || *tr* peindre à fresque

fresh [frɛʃ] *adj* frais; (*water*) doux; (*e.g., idea*) nouveau; (*wound*) saignant; (*cheeky*) (coll) osé, impertinent; **fresh paint!** (public sign) attention, peinture fraîche! || *adv* nouvellement; **fresh in** (coll) récemment arrivé; **fresh out** (coll) récemment épuisé

freshen ['frɛʃən] *tr* rafraîchir || *intr* se rafraîchir; (*said of wind*) fraîchir

freshet ['frɛʃɪt] *s* crue *f*

fresh'man *s* (*pl* **-men**) étudiant *m* de première année, bizut *m*

freshness ['frɛʃnɪs] *s* fraîcheur *f*; (*sauciness*) impudence *f*, impertinence *f*

fresh'-wa'ter *adj* d'eau douce

fret [frɛt] *s* (*interlaced design*) frette *f*; (*uneasiness*) inquiétude *f*; (mus) touchette *f* || *v* (*pret & pp* **fretted**; *ger* **fretting**) *tr* ajourer || *intr* s'inquiéter, geindre

fretful ['frɛtfəl] *adj* irritable, boudeur

fret'work' *s* ajour *m*, ornementation *f* ajourée

Freudianism ['frɔɪdɪ·ə‚nɪzəm] *s* freudisme *m*

friar ['fraɪ·ər] *s* moine *m*

fricassee [‚frɪkə'si] *s* fricassée *f*

friction ['frɪkʃən] *s* friction *f*

fric'tion tape' *s* chatterton *m*, ruban *m* isolant

Friday ['fraɪdi] *s* vendredi *m*

fried [fraɪd] *adj* frit

fried' egg' *s* œuf *m* sur le plat

friend [frɛnd] *s* ami *m*; **to make friends with** se lier d'amitié avec

friend·ly ['frɛndli] *adj* (*comp* **-lier**; *super* **-liest**) amical, sympathique

friendship ['frɛndʃɪp] *s* amitié *f*

frieze [friz] *s* (archit) frise *f*

frigate ['frɪgɪt] *s* frégate *f*

fright [fraɪt] *s* frayeur *f*, effroi *m*; (*grotesque or ridiculous person*) (coll) épouvantail *m*; **to take fright at** s'effrayer de

frighten ['fraɪtən] *tr* effrayer; **to frighten away** effaroucher, faire fuir

frightful ['fraɪtfəl] *adj* effroyable; (coll) affreux; (*huge*) (coll) énorme

frigid ['frɪdʒɪd] *adj* frigide; (*zone*) glacial

frigidity [frɪ'dʒɪdɪti] *s* frigidité *f*

frill [frɪl] *s* (*on shirt front*) jabot *m*; (*frippery*) falbala *m*

fringe [frɪndʒ] *s* frange *f*; (*border*) bordure *f*; (opt) frange; **on the fringe of** en marge de || *tr* franger

fringe' ben'efits *spl* supplément *m* de solde, bénéfices *mpl* marginaux

fripper·y ['frɪpəri] *s* (*pl* **-ies**) (*flashiness*) clinquant *m*; (*inferior goods*) camelote *f*

frisk [frɪsk] *tr* (slang) fouiller, palper || *intr*—**to frisk about** gambader, folâtrer

frisk·y ['frɪski] *adj* (*comp* **-ier**; *super* **-iest**) vif, folâtre; (*horse*) fringant

fritter ['frɪtər] *s* beignet *m* || *tr*—**fritter away** gaspiller

frivolous ['frɪvələs] *adj* frivole

frizzle ['frɪzəl] *s* frisure *f* || *tr* frisotter; (culin) faire frire || *intr* frisotter; (culin) grésiller

friz·zly ['frɪzli] *adj* (*comp* **-zlier**; *super* **-zliest**) crépu, crépelu

fro [fro] *adv*—**to and fro** de long en large; **to go to and fro** aller et venir

frock [frɑk] *s* robe *f*; (*overalls, smock*) blouse *f*; (eccl) froc *m*

frock' coat' *s* redingote *f*

frog [frɑg], [frɔg] *s* grenouille *f*; (*in throat*) chat *m*

frog'man' *s* (*pl* **-men'**) homme-grenouille *m*

frogs'' legs' *spl* cuisses *fpl* de grenouille *f*

frol·ic ['frɑlɪk] *s* gaieté *f*, ébats *mpl* || *v* (*pret & pp* **-icked**; *ger* **-icking**) *intr* s'ébattre, folâtrer

frolicsome ['frɑlɪksəm] *adj* folâtre

from [frʌm], [frɑm], [frəm] *prep* de; de la part de, e.g., **greetings from your friend** compliments de la part de votre ami; (*since*) a, **a shelter from the rain** un abri contre la pluie; **from a certain angle** sous un certain angle; **from . . . to** depuis . . .

jusqu'à; **from what I hear** d'après ce que j'apprends; **the flight from** le vol en provenance de; **to drink from** (a glass) boire dans; (a bottle) boire à; **to learn from a book** apprendre dans un livre; **to steal from** voler à

front [frʌnt] adj antérieur, de devant || s devant m; (first place) premier rang m; (aut) avant m; (geog, mil, pol) front m; (figurehead) (coll) prête-nom m; **in front** par devant; **in front of** en face de, devant; **to put up a bold front** (coll) faire bonne contenance || tr (to face) donner sur; (to confront) affronter || intr—**to front on** donner sur

frontage [ˈfrʌntɪdʒ] s façade f; (along a street, lake, etc.) largeur f

front′ door′ s porte f d'entrée

front′ drive′ s (aut) traction f avant

frontier [frʌnˈtɪr] adj frontalier || s frontière f; (hist) front m de colonisation, front pionnier

frontiers′man s (pl -men) frontalier m, broussard m

frontispiece [ˈfrʌntɪsˌpis] s frontispice m; (archit) façade f principale

front′ lines′ spl avant-postes mpl

front′ mat′ter s (of book) feuilles fpl liminaires

front′ of′fice s direction f

front′ porch′ s porche m

front′ room′ s chambre f sur la rue

front′ row′ s premier rang m

front′ seat′ s siège m avant; (aut) banquette f avant

front′ steps′ spl perron m

front′ view′ s vue f de face

front′ yard′ s devant m de la maison

frost [frɔst], [frɑst] s (freezing) gelée f; (frozen dew) givre m || tr (to freeze) geler; (to cover with frost) givrer; (culin) glacer

frost′bite′ s engelure f

frost′ed glass′ s verre m dépoli

frosting [ˈfrɔstɪŋ], [ˈfrɑstɪŋ] s (on glass) dépolissage m; (culin) fondant m

frost·y [ˈfrɔsti], [ˈfrɑsti] adj (comp -ier; super -iest) couvert de givre; (reception, welcome) glacé, glacial

froth [frɔθ], [frɑθ] s écume f; (on soap, beer, chocolate) mousse f; (frivolity) futilité f || intr mousser; (at the mouth) écumer

froth·y [ˈfrɔθi], [ˈfrɑθi] adj (comp -ier; super -iest) écumeux; (soap, beer, chocolate) mousseux; (frivolous) creux, futile

froward [ˈfrowərd] adj obstiné, revêche

frown [fraun] s froncement m de sourcils || intr froncer les sourcils; **to frown at** or **on** être contraire à, désapprouver

frows·y or **frowz·y** [ˈfrauzi] adj (comp -ier; super -iest) malpropre, négligé, peu soigné; (smelling bad) malodorant

fro′zen as′sets spl fonds mpl gelés

fro′zen foods′ spl aliments mpl surgelés

frugal [ˈfrugəl] adj sobre, modéré; (meal) frugal

fruit [frut] adj fruitier || s fruit m; les fruits, e.g., **I like fruit** j'aime les fruits

fruit′ cake′ s cake m

fruit′ cup′ s coupe f de fruits

fruit′ fly′ s mouche f du vinaigre

fruitful [ˈfrutfəl] adj fructueux, fécond

fruition [fruˈɪʃən] s réalisation f; **to come to fruition** fructifier

fruit′ juice′ s jus m de fruits

fruitless [ˈfrutlɪs] adj stérile, vain

fruit′ sal′ad s macédoine f de fruits, salade f de fruits

fruit′ stand′ s étalage m de fruits

fruit′ store′ s fruiterie f

frumpish [ˈfrʌmpɪʃ] adj fagoté, négligé

frustrate [ˈfrʌstret] tr frustrer

fry [fraɪ] s (pl fries) (culin) friture f; (ichth) fretin m || v (pret & pp fried) tr faire frire; (to sauté) faire sauter || intr frire

fry′ing pan′ s poêle f à frire; **to jump from the frying pan into the fire** sauter de la poêle dans le feu

fudge [fʌdʒ] s fondant m de chocolat; (humbug) blague f

fuel [ˈfjuəl] s combustible m; (aut) carburant m; (fig) aliment m || v (pret & pp fueled or fuelled; ger fueling or fuelling) tr pourvoir en combustible

fu′el gauge′ s jauge f de combustible

fu′el line′ s conduite f de combustible

fu′el oil′ s mazout m, fuel-oil m, fuel m

fu′el tank′ s réservoir m de carburant; (aut) réservoir à essence

fugitive [ˈfjudʒɪtɪv] adj & s fugitif m

ful·crum [ˈfʌlkrəm] s (pl -crums or -cra [krə]) point m d'appui

fulfill [fulˈfɪl] tr accomplir; (an obligation) s'acquitter de, remplir

fulfillment [fulˈfɪlmənt] s accomplissement m

full [ful] adj plein; (dress, garment) ample, bouffant; (schedule) chargé; (lips) gros, fort; (brother, sister) germain; (having no more room) complet; **full to overflowing** plein à déborder || s plein m; **in full** intégralement, entièrement; (to spell in full) en toutes lettres; **to the full** complètement || adv complètement; **full in the face** en pleine figure; **full many a** bien des; **full well** parfaitement || tr (cloth) fouler

full′ blast′ adv (coll) en pleine activité

full′-blood′ed adj robuste; (thoroughbred) pur sang

full-blown [ˈfulˈblon] adj achevé, développé; en pleine fleur

full′-bod′ied adj (e.g., wine) corsé

full′ dress′ s grande tenue f

full′-dress coat′ s frac m

full′-faced′ adj (portrait) de face

full-fledged [ˈfulˈfledʒd] adj véritable, rien moins que

full-grown [ˈfulˈgron] adj (plant) mûr; (tree) de haute futaie; (person) adulte

full′ house′ s (poker) main f pleine; (theat) salle f comble
full′-length′ adj (portrait) en pied
full′-length mir′ror s psyché f
full′-length mov′ie s long métrage m
full′ load′ s plein chargement m
full′ meas′ure s mesure f comble
full′ moon′ s pleine lune f
full′ name′ s nom m et prénoms mpl
full′ pow′ers spl pleins pouvoirs mpl
full′ rest′ s (mus.) pause f
full′ sail′ adv toutes voiles dehors
full′ ses′sion s assemblée f plénière
full′-sized′ adj de grandeur nature
full′ speed′ s toute vitesse f
full′ stop′ s (gram) point m final; **to come to a full stop** s'arrêter net
full′ swing′ s—**in full swing** en pleine activité, en train
full′ tilt′ adv à toute vitesse
full′ time′ adv à pleines journées
full′-time′ adj à temps plein
full′ view′ s—**in full view** à la vue de tous
full′ weight′ s poids m juste
fully ['fʊli], ['fʊlɪ] adv entièrement, pleinement
fulsome ['fʊlsəm], ['fʌlsəm] adj écœurant, bas, servile
fumble ['fʌmbəl] tr manier maladroitement; (the ball) ne pas attraper, laisser tomber || intr tâtonner
fume [fjum] s (bad humor) rage f; **fumes** fumées fpl, vapeurs fpl || tr & intr fumer
fumigate ['fjumɪ‚get] tr fumiger
fun [fʌn] s amusement m, gaieté f; (badinage) plaisanterie f; **in fun** pour rire; **to have fun** s'amuser; **to make fun of** se moquer de
function ['fʌŋkʃən] s fonction f; (meeting) cérémonie f || intr fonctionner; **to function as** faire fonction de
functional ['fʌŋkʃənəl] adj fonctionnel
functionar·y ['fʌŋkʃə‚nɛri] s (pl -ies) fonctionnaire mf
fund [fʌnd] s fonds m; **funds** fonds mpl || tr (a debt) consolider
fundamental [‚fʌndə'mɛntəl] adj fondamental || s principe m, base f
fundamentalist [‚fʌndə'mɛntəlɪst] s (rel) scripturaire m
funeral ['fjunərəl] adj (march, procession, ceremony) funèbre; (expenses) funéraire || s funérailles fpl
fu′neral direc′tor s entrepreneur m de pompes funèbres
fu′neral home′ or **par′lor** s chapelle f mortuaire; salon m mortuaire (Canad); (business) entreprise f de pompes funèbres
fu′neral proces′sion s convoi m funèbre, enterrement m, deuil m
fu′neral serv′ice s office m des morts
funereal [fju'nɪrɪ‚əl] adj funèbre
fungus ['fʌŋgəs] s (pl **funguses** or **fungi** ['fʌndʒaɪ]) (bot) champignon m; (pathol) fongus m
funicular [fju'nɪkjələr] adj & s funiculaire m
funk [fʌŋk] s (coll) frousse f

fun·nel ['fʌnəl] s entonnoir m; (smokestack) cheminée f; (tube for ventilation) tuyau m || v (pret & pp -neled or -nelled; ger -neling or -nelling) tr verser avec un entonnoir; (to channel) concentrer
funnies ['fʌniz] spl pages fpl comiques
fun·ny ['fʌni] adj (comp -nier; super -niest) comique; amusant, drôle; (coll) bizarre, curieux; **to strike s.o. as funny** paraître drôle à qn
fun′ny pa′per s pages fpl comiques
fur [fʌr] s fourrure f; (on tongue) empâtement m; **furs** pelleteries fpl
furbish ['fʌrbɪʃ] tr fourbir; **to furbish up** remettre à neuf
furious ['fjʊrɪ‚əs] adj furieux
furl [fʌrl] tr (naut) ferler
fur′-lined′ adj doublé de fourrure
furlough ['fʌrlo] s permission f; **on furlough** en permission || tr donner une permission à
furnace ['fʌrnɪs] s (to heat a house) calorifère m; (to produce steam) chaudière f; (e.g., to smelt ores) fourneau m; (rr) foyer m; (fig) fournaise f
furnish ['fʌrnɪʃ] tr fournir; (a house) meubler
fur′nished apart′ment s garni m, appartement m meublé
furnishings ['fʌrnɪʃɪŋz] spl ameublement m; (things to wear) articles mpl d'habillement
furniture ['fʌrnɪtʃər] s meubles mpl; **a piece of furniture** un meuble; **a suite of furniture** un mobilier
fur′niture deal′er s marchand m de meubles
fur′niture pol′ish s encaustique f
fur′niture store′ s maison f d'ameublement
fur′niture ware′house s garde-meuble m
furor ['fjʊror] s fureur f
furrier ['fʌrɪ‚ər] s fourreur m, pelletier m
furrow ['fʌro] s sillon m || tr sillonner
fur·ry ['fʌri] adj (comp -rier; super -riest) fourré, à fourrure
further ['fʌrðər] adj additionnel, supplémentaire || adv plus loin; (besides) en outre, de plus || tr avancer, favoriser
furtherance ['fʌrðərəns] s avancement m
fur′ther·more′ adv de plus, d'ailleurs
furthest ['fʌrðɪst] adj (le) plus éloigné || adv le plus loin
furtive ['fʌrtɪv] adj furtif
fu·ry ['fjʊri] s (pl -ries) furie f
furze [fʌrz] s genêt m épineux, ajonc m d'Europe
fuse [fjuz] s (tube or wick filled with explosive material) étoupille f, mèche f; (device for exploding a bomb or projectile) fusée f; (elec) fusible m, plomb m de sûreté, plomb fusible m; **to burn** or **blow out a fuse** faire sauter un plomb || tr fondre; étoupiller || intr se fondre
fuse′ box′ s boîte f à fusibles

fuselage ['fjuzəlɪdʒ], [ˌfjuzə'laʒ] *s* fuselage *m*

fusible ['fjuzɪbəl] *adj* fusible

fusillade [ˌfjuzɪ'led] *s* fusillade *f*

fusion ['fjuʒən] *s* fusion *f*

fuss [fʌs] *s* fracas *m*; (*dispute*) bagarre *f*; **to kick up a fuss** (coll) faire un tas d'histoires; **to make a fuss over** faire grand cas de || *intr* faire des embarras, simagrées, or chichis; **to fuss over** être aux petits soins auprès de

fuss·y ['fʌsi] *adj* (*comp* **-ier**; *super* **-iest**) tracassier, tatillon; (*in dress*) pomponné

fustian ['fʌstʃən] *s* (*cloth*) futaine *f*; (*bombast*) grandiloquence *f*

futile ['fjutɪl] *adj* futile

future ['fjutʃər] *adj* futur, d'avenir || *s* avenir *m*; (gram) futur *m*; **futures** (com) valeurs *fpl* négociées à terme; **in the future** à l'avenir; **in the near future** à brève échéance

fuzz [fʌz] *s* (*on a peach*) duvet *m*; (*on a blanket*) peluche *f*; (*in pockets and corners*) bourre *f*

fuzz·y ['fʌzi] *adj* (*comp* **-ier**; *super* **-iest**) pelucheux; (*hair*) crépelu; (*indistinct*) flou

G

G, g [dʒi] *s* VIIᵉ lettre de l'alphabet

gab [gæb] *s* (coll) bavardage *m*, langue *f* || *v* (*pret & pp* **gabbed**; *ger* **gabbing**) *intr* (coll) bavarder

gabardine ['gæbər,din] *s* gabardine *f*

gabble ['gæbəl] *s* jacasserie *f* || *intr* jacasser

gable ['gebəl] *s* (*of roof*) pignon *m*; (*over a door or window*) gable *m*

ga'ble end' *s* pignon *m*

ga'ble roof' *s* comble *m* sur pignon, toit *m* à deux pentes

gad [gæd] *v* (*pret & pp* **gadded**; *ger* **gadding**) *intr*—**to gad about** courir la prétantaine, vadrouiller

gad'about' *s* vadrouilleur *m*

gad'fly' *s* (*pl* **-flies**) taon *m*

gadget ['gædʒɪt] *s* dispositif *m*; (*unnamed article*) machin *m*, truc *m*

Gaelic ['gelɪk] *adj & s* gaélique *m*

gaff [gæf] *s* gaffe *f*; **to stand the gaff** (slang) ne pas broncher

gaffer ['gæfər] *s* (coll) vieux bonhomme *m*

gag [gæg] *s* bâillon *m*; (*interpolation by an actor*) gag *m*; (*joke*) blague *f* || *v* (*pret & pp* **gagged**; *ger* **gagging**) *tr* bâillonner || *intr* avoir des haut-le-cœur

gage [gedʒ] *s* (*pledge*) gage *m*; (*challenge*) défi *m*

gaie·ty ['ge·ti] *s* (*pl* **-ties**) gaieté *f*

gaily ['geli] *adv* gaiement

gain [gen] *s* gain *m*; (*increase*) accroissement *m* || *tr* gagner; (*to reach*) atteindre, gagner || *intr* gagner du terrain; (*said of invalid*) s'améliorer; (*said of watch*) avancer; **to gain on** prendre de l'avance sur

gainful ['genfəl] *adj* profitable

gain'say' *v* (*pret & pp* **-said** [ˌsed], [ˌsed]) *tr* (*to deny*) nier; (*to contradict*) contredire; **not to gainsay** ne pas disconvenir de

gait [get] *s* démarche *f*, allure *f*

gaiter ['getər] *s* guêtre *f*

gala ['gælə], ['gelə] *adj* de gala || *s* gala *m*

galax·y ['gæləksi] *s* (*pl* **-ies**) galaxie *f*

gale [gel] *s* gros vent *m*; **gales of laughter** éclats *mpl* de rire; **to weather a gale** étaler un coup de vent

gall [gɔl] *s* bile *f*, fiel *m*; (*something bitter*) (fig) fiel *m*, amertume *f*; (*audacity*) (coll) toupet *m* || *tr* écorcher par le frottement; (fig) irriter

gallant ['gælənt] *adj* (*spirited, daring*) vaillant, brave; (*stately, grand*) fier, noble; (*showy, gay*) élégant, superbe, de fête *f*; ['gælənt], [gə'lænt] *adj* galant || *s* galant *m*; vaillant *m* || [gə'lænt] *intr* faire le galant

gallant·ry ['gæləntri] *s* (*pl* **-ries**) galanterie *f*; (*bravery*) vaillance *f*

gall' blad'der *s* vésicule *f* biliaire

gall' duct' *s* conduit *m* biliaire

galleon ['gælɪ·ən] *s* (naut) galion *m*

galler·y ['gæləri] *s* (*pl* **-ies**) galerie *f*; (*cheapest seats in theater*) poulailler *m*; **to play to the gallery** poser pour la galerie

galley ['gæli] *s* (*ship*) galère *f*; (*ship's kitchen*) coquerie *f*; (*typ*) galée *f*

gal'ley proof' *s* placard *m*, épreuve *f* en placard

gal'ley slave' *s* galérien *m*

Gallic ['gælɪk] *adj* gaulois

Gal'lic wit' *s* esprit *m* gaulois

galling ['gɔlɪŋ] *adj* irritant, blessant

gallivant ['gælɪ,vænt] *intr* courailler

gall'nut' *s* noix *f* de galle

gallon ['gælən] *s* gallon *m* américain

galloon [gə'lun] *s* galon *m*

gallop ['gæləp] *s* galop *m* || *tr* faire galoper || *intr* galoper

gal·lows ['gæloz] *s* (*pl* **-lows** or **-lowses**) gibet *m*, potence *f*

gal'lows bird' *s* (coll) gibier *m* de potence

gall'stone' *s* calcul *m* biliaire

galore [gə'lor] *adv* à foison, à gogo

galoshes [gə'lɑʃɪz] *spl* caoutchoucs *mpl*

galvanize ['gælvə,naɪz] *tr* galvaniser

gal'vanized i'ron *s* tôle *f* galvanisée

gambit ['gæmbɪt] *s* gambit *m*

gamble ['gæmbəl] *s* risque *m*, affaire *f* de chance || *tr* jouer; **to gamble away**

perdre au jeu || *intr* jouer; jouer à la Bourse; (fig) prendre des risques

gambler ['gæmblər] *s* joueur *m*

gambling ['gæmblɪŋ] *s* jeu *m*

gam'bling den' *s* tripot *m*

gam'bling house' *s* maison *f* de jeu

gam'bling ta'ble *s* table *f* de jeu

gam·bol ['gæmbəl] *s* gambade *f* || *v* (*pret & pp* -**boled** or -**bolled**; *ger* -**boling** or -**bolling**) *intr* gambader

gambrel ['gæmbrəl] *s* (*hock*) jarret *m*; (*in butcher shop*) jambier *m*

gam'brel roof' *s* toit *m* en croupe

game [gem] *adj* crâne, résolu; (*leg*) boiteux || *s* jeu *m*; (*contest*) match *m*; (*score necessary to win*) partie *f*; (*animal or bird*) gibier *m*; **to make game of** tourner en dérision

game'bag' *s* carnassière *f*, gibecière *f*

game' bird' *s* oiseau *m* que l'on chasse

game'cock' *s* coq *m* de combat

game'keep'er *s* garde-chasse *m*

game' of chance' *s* jeu *m* de hasard

game' preserve' *s* chasse *f* gardée

game' war'den *s* garde-chasse *m*

gamut ['gæmət] *s* gamme *f*

gam·y ['gemi] *adj* (*comp* -**ier**; *super* -**iest**) (*having flavor of uncooked game*) faisandé; (*plucky*) crâne

gander ['gændər] *s* jars *m*

gang [gæŋ] *adj* multiple || *s* (*of workmen*) équipe *f*, brigade *f*; (*of thugs*) bande *f*; (*of wrongdoers*) séquelle *f*, clique *f* || *intr*—**to gang up** se concerter; **to gang up on** se liguer contre

gangling ['gæŋglɪŋ] *adj* dégingandé

gangli·on ['gæŋglɪ·ən] *s* (*pl* -**ons** or -**a** [ə]) ganglion *m*

gang'plank' *s* passerelle *f*, planche *f* de débarquement

gangrene ['gæŋgrin] *s* gangrène *f* || *tr* gangrener || *intr* se gangrener

gangster ['gæŋstər] *s* bandit *m*, gangster *m*

gang'way' *s* (*passageway*) passage *m*, coursive *f*; (*gangplank*) planche *f* de débarquement; (*in ship's side*) coupée *f* || *interj* rangez-vous!, dégagez!

gan·try ['gæntri] *s* (*pl* -**tries**) (*for barrels*) chantier *m*; (*for crane*) portique *m*; (rr) pont *m* à signaux

gan'try crane' *s* grue *f* à portique

gap [gæp] *s* lacune *f*; (*in wall*) brèche *f*; (*between mountains*) col *m*, gorge *f*; (*between two points of view*) abîme *m*, gouffre *m*

gape [gep], [gæp] *s* ouverture *f*, brèche *f*; (*yawn*) bâillement *m*; (*look of astonishment*) badauderie *f* || *intr* (*to yawn*) bâiller; (*to look with astonishment*) badauder; **to gape at** regarder bouche bée

garage [ɡə'raʒ] *s* garage *m*

garb [ɡarb] *s* costume *m* || *tr* vêtir

garbage ['ɡarbɪdʒ] *s* ordures *fpl*

gar'bage can' *s* poubelle *f*

gar'bage collec'tor *s* boueur *m*

gar'bage dispos'al *s* destruction *f* des ordures ménagères

gar'bage truck' *s* benne *f* à ordures

garble ['ɡarbəl] *tr* mutiler, tronquer

garden ['ɡardən] *s* jardin *m*; (*of vege-*

tables) potager *m*; (*of flowers*) parterre *m* || *intr* jardiner

gar'den cit'y *s* cité-jardin *f*

gardener ['ɡardnər] *s* jardinier *m*

gardening ['ɡardnɪŋ] *s* jardinage *m*

gar'den par'ty *s* garden-party *f*

gargle [ˈɡarɡəl] *s* gargarisme *m* || *intr* se gargariser

gargoyle ['ɡarɡɔɪl] *s* gargouille *f*

garish ['ɡerɪ], ['ɡærɪ] *adj* cru, rutilant, criard

garland ['ɡarlənd] *s* guirlande *f* || *tr* guirlander

garlic ['ɡarlɪk] *s* ail *m*

garment ['ɡarmənt] *s* vêtement *m*

gar'ment bag' *s* housse *f* à vêtements

garner [ˈɡarnər] *tr* (*to gather, collect*) amasser; (*cereals*) engranger

garnet ['ɡarnɪt] *adj & s* grenat *m*

garnish ['ɡarnɪ] *s* garniture *f* || *tr* garnir; (law) effectuer une saisie-arrêt sur

garret ['ɡærɪt] *s* grenier *m*; (*dormer room*) mansarde *f*

garrison ['ɡærɪsən] *s* garnison *f* || *tr* (*troops*) mettre en garnison; (*a city*) mettre les troupes en garnison dans

garrote [ɡə'rat], [ɡə'rot] *s* (*method of execution*) garrotte *f*; (*iron collar used for such an execution*) garrot *m* || *tr* garrotter

garrulous ['ɡær(j)ələs] *adj* bavard

garter ['ɡartər] *s* jarretelle *f*, jarretière *f*; (*for men's socks*) support-chaussette *m*, fixe-chaussette *m*

garth [ɡarθ] *s* cour *f* intérieure d'un cloître

gas [ɡæs] *s* gaz *m*; (coll) essence *f*; (*empty talk*) (coll) bavardage *m*; **out of gas** en panne sèche || *v* (*pret & pp* **gassed**; *ger* **gassing**) *tr* gazer, asphyxier || *intr* dégager des gaz; (*to talk nonsense*) (coll) bavarder

gas'bag' *s* enveloppe *f* à gaz; (coll) blagueur *m*, baratineur *m*

gas' burn'er *s* bec *m* de gaz

gas' cham'ber *s* chambre *f* à gaz

Gascony ['ɡæskəni] *s* Gascogne *f*; la Gascogne

gas' en'gine *s* moteur *m* à gaz

gaseous ['ɡæsɪ·əs] *adj* gazeux

gas' gen'erator *s* gazogène *m*

gash [ɡæ] *s* entaille *f*; (*on face*) balafre *f* || *tr* entailler; balafrer

gas' heat' *s* chauffage *m* au gaz

gas' heat'er *s* (*for hot water*) chauffe-eau *m* à gaz; (*for house heat*) calorifère *m* à gaz

gas'hold'er *s* gazomètre *m*

gasi·fy ['ɡæsɪˌfaɪ] *v* (*pret & pp* -**fied**) *tr* gazéifier || *intr* se gazéifier

gas' jet' *s* bec *m* de gaz

gasket ['ɡæskɪt] *s* joint *m*

gas'light' *s* éclairage *m* au gaz

gas' main' *s* conduite *f* de gaz

gas' mask' *s* masque *m* à gaz

gas' me'ter *s* compteur *m* à gaz

gasoline ['ɡæsəˌlin], [ˌɡæsə'lin] *s* essence *f*

gas'oline can' *s* bidon *m* d'essence

gas'oline gauge' *s* voyant *m* d'essence

gas'oline pump' *s* pompe *f* à essence

gasp [gæsp], [gɑsp] s halètement m; (of surprise; of death) hoquet m || tr —to gasp out (a word) dire dans un souffle || intr haleter

gas' pipe' s conduite f de gaz

gas' produc'er s gazogène m

gas' range' s fourneau m à gaz, cuisinière f à gaz

gas' sta'tion s poste m d'essence

gas' stove' s cuisinière f à gaz, réchaud m à gaz

gas' tank' s gazomètre m; (aut) réservoir m d'essence

gastric ['gæstrɪk] adj gastrique

gastronomy [gæs'trɑnəmi] s gastronomie f

gas' works' spl usine f à gaz

gate [get] s porte f; (in fence or wall) grille f; (main gate) portail f; (of sluice) vanne f; (number paying admission; amount paid) entrée f; (rr) barrière f; to crash the gate resquiller

gate-crasher ['get,kræʃər] s (coll) resquilleur m

gate' keep'er s portier m; (rr) garde-barrière mf

gate'-leg ta'ble s table f à abattants

gate' post' s montant m

gate' way' s passage m, entrée f; (main entrance) portail m

gather ['gæðər] tr amasser, rassembler; (the harvest) rentrer; (fruits, flowers, etc.) cueillir, ramasser; (one's thoughts) recueillir; (bb) rassembler; (sewing) froncer; (to deduce) (fig) conclure; to gather dust s'encrasser; to gather oneself together se ramasser || intr se réunir, s'assembler; (said of clouds) s'amonceler

gathering ['gæðərɪŋ] s réunion f, rassemblement m; (of harvest) récolte f; (of fruits, flowers, etc.) cueillette f; (bb) assemblage m; (sewing) froncis m

gaud·y ['gɔdi] adj (comp -ier; super -iest) criard, voyant

gauge [gedʒ] s jauge f, calibre m; (of liquid in a container) niveau m; (of gasoline, oil, etc.) indicateur m; (of carpenter) trusquin m; (rr) écartement m || tr jauger, calibrer; (a person; s.o.'s capacities; a distance) juger de, jauger

gauge' glass' s indicateur m de niveau

Gaul [gɔl] s Gaule f; la Gaule

Gaulish ['gɔlɪʃ] adj & s gaulois m

gaunt [gɔnt], [gɑnt] adj décharné, étique, efflanqué

gauntlet ['gɔntlɪt], ['gɑntlɪt] s gantelet m; to run the gauntlet passer par les baguettes; to take up the gauntlet relever le gant; to throw down the gauntlet jeter le gant

gauze [gɔz] s gaze f

gavel ['gævəl] s marteau m

gawk [gɔk] s (coll) godiche mf || intr (coll) bayer aux corneilles; to gawk at (coll) regarder bouche bée

gawk·y ['gɔki] adj (comp -ier; super -iest) godiche

gay [ge] adj gai

gay' blade' s (coll) joyeux drille m

gaze [gez] s regard m fixe || intr regarder fixement

gazelle [gə'zel] s gazelle f

gazette [gə'zet] s gazette f; journal m officiel

gazetteer [,gæzə'tɪr] s dictionnaire m géographique

gear [gɪr] s attirail m, appareil m; (of transmission, steering, etc.) mécanisme m; (adjustment of automobile transmission) marche f, vitesse f; (two or more toothed wheels meshed together) engrenage m; out of gear débrayé; to throw into gear embrayer; to throw out of gear débrayer; (fig) disloquer || tr & intr engrener

gear' box' s (aut) boîte f de vitesses

gear' shift' s changement m de vitesse

gear' shift lev'er s levier m de changement de vitesse

gear' wheel' s roue f d'engrenage

gee [dʒi] interj sapristi!; (to the right) hue!; gee up! hue!

Gei'ger count'er s compteur m de Geiger

gel [dʒel] s (chem) gel m

gelatine ['dʒelətin] s gélatine f

geld [geld] v (pret & pp gelded or gelt [gelt]) tr châtrer

gelding ['geldɪŋ] s hongre m

gem [dʒem] s gemme f; (fig) bijou m

gender ['dʒendər] s (gram) genre m; (coll) sexe m

gene [dʒin] s (biol) gène m

geneal·o·gy [,dʒeni'ælədʒi], [,dʒini-'ælədʒi] s (pl -gies) généalogie f

general ['dʒenərəl] adj & s général m; in general en général

gen'eral deliv'ery s poste f restante

generalissi·mo [,dʒenərə'lɪsɪmo] s (pl -mos) généralissime m

generali·ty [,dʒenə'rælɪti] s (pl -ties) généralité f

generalize ['dʒenərə,laɪz] tr & intr généraliser

generally ['dʒenərəli] adj généralement

gen'eral practi'tioner s médecin m de médecine générale

gen'eral·ship' s tactique f; (office) généralat m

gen'eral staff' s état-major m

generate ['dʒenə,ret] tr générer; (to beget) engendrer; (geom) engendrer

gen'erating sta'tion s usine f génératrice, centrale f

generation [,dʒenə'reʃən] s génération f

generator ['dʒenə,retər] s (chem) gazogène m; (elec) génératrice f

generic [dʒɪ'nerɪk] adj générique

generosi·ty [,dʒenə'rɑsɪti] s (pl -ties) générosité f

generous ['dʒenərəs] adj généreux

gene·sis ['dʒenɪsɪs] s (pl -ses [,siz]) genèse f; Genesis (Bib) La Genèse

genetic [dʒɪ'netɪk] adj génétique; genetics s génétique f

Geneva [dʒɪ'nivə] s Genève f

genial ['dʒini·əl] adj affable

genie ['dʒini] s génie m

genital ['dʒenɪtəl] *adj* génital || **genitals** *spl* organes *mpl* génitaux

genitive ['dʒenɪtɪv] *s* génitif *m*

genius ['dʒinjəs], ['dʒinɪ·əs] *s* (*pl* **geniuses**) génie *m* || *s* (*pl* **genii** ['dʒinɪˌaɪ]) génie *m*

Genoa ['dʒenoə] *s* Gênes *f*

genocide ['dʒenəˌsaɪd] *s* génocide *m*

genteel [dʒen'til] *adj* distingué, de bon ton; élégant, chic

gentian ['dʒenʃən] *s* gentiane *f*

gentile ['dʒentaɪl] *s* non-juif *m*, chrétien *m*

gentili·ty [dʒen'tɪlɪti] *s* (*pl* -**ties**) (*birth*) naissance *f* distinguée; (*breeding*) politesse *f*

gentle ['dʒentəl] *adj* doux; (*in birth*) noble, bien né; (*e.g., tap on the shoulder*) léger

gen'tle·folk' *s* gens *mpl* de bonne naissance

gen·tle·man *s* (*pl* -**men**) monsieur *m*; (*man of independent means*) rentier *m*; (*hist*) gentilhomme *m*

gentlemanly ['dʒentəlmənli] *adj* bien élevé, de bon ton

gen'tleman's agree'ment *s* engagement *m* sur parole, contrat *m* verbal

gen'tle sex' *s* sexe *m* faible

gentry ['dʒentri] *s* gens *mpl* de bonne naissance; (*Brit*) petite noblesse *f*

genuine ['dʒenju·ɪn] *adj* véritable, authentique; (*person*) sincère, franc

genus ['dʒinəs] *s* (*pl* **genera** ['dʒenərə] or **genuses**) genre *m*

geogra·phy [dʒɪ'ɑgrəfi] *s* (*pl* -**phies**) géographie *f*

geologic(al) [ˌdʒi·ə'lɑdʒɪk(əl)] *adj* géologique

geolo·gy [dʒɪ'ɑlədʒi] *s* (*pl* -**gies**) géologie *f*

geometric(al) [ˌdʒi·ə'metrɪk(əl)] *adj* géométrique

geome·try [dʒɪ'ɑmɪtri] *s* (*pl* -**tries**) géométrie *f*

geophysics [ˌdʒi·ə'fɪzɪks] *s* géophysique *f*

geopolitics [ˌdʒi·ə'pɑlɪtɪks] *s* géopolitique *f*

George [dʒɔrdʒ] *s* Georges *m*

geranium [dʒɪ'renɪ·əm] *s* géranium *m*

geriatrics [ˌdʒerɪ'ætrɪks] *s* gériatrie *f*

germ [dʒʌrm] *s* germe *m*

German ['dʒʌrmən] *adj* allemand || *s* (*language*) allemand *m*; (*person*) Allemand *m*

germane [dʒer'men] *adj* à propos, pertinent; **germane to** se rapporter à

Ger'man mea'sles *s* rubéole *f*

Ger'man sil'ver *s* maillechort *m*, argentan *m*

Germa·ny ['dʒʌrməni] *s* (*pl* -**nies**) Allemagne *f*; l'Allemagne

germicidal [ˌdʒʌrmɪ'saɪdəl] *adj* germicide

germicide ['dʒʌrmɪˌsaɪd] *s* germicide *m*

germinate ['dʒʌrmɪˌnet] *intr* germer

germ' war'fare *s* guerre *f* bactériologique

gerontology [ˌdʒerən'tɑlədʒi] *s* gérontologie *f*

gerund ['dʒerənd] *s* gérondif *m*

gestation [dʒes'teʃən] *s* gestation *f*

gesticulate [dʒes'tɪkjəˌlet] *intr* gesticuler

gesture ['dʒestʃər] *s* geste *m* || *intr* faire des gestes; **to gesture to** faire signe à

get [get] *v* (*pret* **got** [gɑt]; *pp* **got** or **gotten** ['gɑtən]; *ger* **getting**) *tr* obtenir, procurer; (*to receive*) avoir, recevoir; (*to catch*) attraper; (*to seek*) chercher, aller chercher; (*to reach*) atteindre; (*to find*) trouver, rencontrer; (*to obtain and bring*) prendre; (*e.g., dinner*) faire; (*rad*) avoir, prendre, accrocher; (*to understand*) (*coll*) comprendre; **to get across** faire accepter; faire comprendre; **to get a kick out of** (*coll*) prendre plaisir à; **to get back** ravoir, se faire rendre; **to get down** descendre; (*to swallow*) avaler; **to get in** rentrer; **to get s.o. to** + *inf* persuader à qn de + *inf*; **to get s.th. done** faire faire q.ch. || *intr* (*to become*) devenir, se faire; (*to arrive*) arriver, parvenir; **get up!** (*said to an animal*) hue!; **to get about** (*said of news*) se répandre; (*said of convalescent*) être de nouveau sur pied; **to get accustomed to** se faire à; **to get across** traverser; **to get along** circuler; **to get along without** se passer de; **to get along with** s'accorder avec; **to get angry** se fâcher; **to get away** s'évader; **to get away with** s'en aller avec; (*coll*) s'en tirer avec; **to get back** reculer; (*to return*) rentrer; **to get back at** (*coll*) rendre la pareille à, se venger sur; **to get by** passer; (*to manage, to shift*) (*coll*) s'en tirer sans peine; **to get dark** faire nuit; **to get down** descendre; **to get going** se mettre en marche; **to get in** or **into** entrer dans; **to get off with** en être quitte pour; **to get on** monter sur; (*a car*) monter dans; continuer; (*to succeed*) faire des progrès; **to get out** sortir; **to get rid of** se défaire de; **to get to** arriver à; (*to have an opportunity to*) avoir l'occasion de; **to get up** se lever; **to not get over it** (*coll*) ne pas en revenir

get'away' *s* démarrage *m*; (*flight*) fuite *f*

get'-togeth'er *s* réunion *f*

get'up' *s* (*style*) (*coll*) présentation *f*; (*outfit*) (*coll*) affublement *m*

geyser ['gaɪzər] *s* geyser *m* || ['gizər] *s* (*Brit*) chauffe-eau *m* à gaz

ghast·ly ['gæstli], ['gɑstli] *adj* (*comp* -**lier**; *super* -**liest**) livide, blême; horrible, affreux

Ghent [gent] *s* Gand *m*

gherkin ['gʌrkɪn] *s* cornichon *m*

ghet·to ['geto] *s* (*pl* -**tos**) ghetto *m*

ghost [gost] *s* revenant *m*; (*shade, semblance*) ombre *f*; **not the ghost of a chance** pas la moindre chance; **to give up the ghost** rendre l'âme, rendre l'esprit

ghost·ly ['gostli] *adj* (*comp* -**lier**; *super* -**liest**) spectral, fantomatique

ghost' sto'ry *s* histoire *f* de revenants

ghost' town' s ville f morte

ghost' writ'er s nègre m

ghoul [gul] s goule f; (body snatcher) déterreur m de cadavres

ghoulish ['gulɪʃ] adj vampirique

GI ['dʒi'aɪ] (letterword) (General Issue) adj fourni par l'armée || s (pl GI's) soldat m américain, simple soldat

giant ['dʒaɪ-ənt] adj & s géant m

giantess ['dʒaɪ-əntɪs] s géante f

gibberish ['dʒɪbərɪʃ], ['gɪbərɪʃ] s baragouin m

gibbet ['dʒɪbɪt] s gibet m, potence f

gibe [dʒaɪb] s raillerie f, moquerie f || tr & intr railler; **to gibe at** se moquer de, railler

giblets ['dʒɪblɪts] spl abattis m, abats mpl

gid-dy ['gɪdi] adj (comp **-dier**; super **-diest**) étourdi; (height) vertigineux; (foolish) léger, frivole

Gideon ['gɪdɪ-ən] s (Bib) Gédéon m

gift [gɪft] s cadeau m; (natural ability) don m, talent m || tr douer

gifted adj doué

gift' horse' s—**never look a gift horse in the mouth** à cheval donné on ne regarde pas à la bride

gift' of gab' s (coll) bagou m, faconde f

gift' shop' s boutique f de souvenirs, magasin m de nouveautés

gift'-wrap' v (pret & pp **-wrapped**; ger **-wrapping**) tr faire un paquet cadeau de

gigantic [dʒaɪ'gæntɪk] adj gigantesque

giggle ['gɪgəl] s petit rire m || intr pousser des petits rires, glousser

gigo-lo ['dʒɪgə,lo] s (pl **-los**) gigolo m

GI' Joe' s [,dʒi,aɪ'dʒo] s le troufion

gild [gɪld] v (pret & pp **gilded** or **gilt** [gɪlt]) tr dorer

gilding ['gɪldɪŋ] s dorure f

gill [gɪl] s (of cock) fanon m; **gills** (of fish) ouïes fpl, branchies fpl

gilt [gɪlt] adj & s doré m

gilt'-edged' adj (e.g., book) doré sur tranche; (securities) de premier ordre, de tout repos

gimcrack ['dʒɪm,kræk] adj de pacotille, de camelote || s babiole f

gimlet ['gɪmlɪt] s vrille f, perçoir m

gimmick ['gɪmɪk] s (coll) truc m, machin m; (trick) tour m

gin [dʒɪn] s (alcoholic liquor) gin m, genièvre m; (for cotton, corn, etc.) égreneuse f; (snare) trébuchet m || v (pret & pp **ginned**; ger **ginning**) tr égrener

ginger ['dʒɪndʒər] s gingembre m; (fig) entrain m, allant m

gin'ger ale' s boisson f gazeuse au gingembre

gin'ger-bread' s pain m d'épice; ornement m de mauvais goût

gingerly ['dʒɪndʒərlɪ] adj précautionneux || adv tout doux, avec précaution

gin'ger-snap' s gâteau m sec au gingembre

gingham ['gɪŋəm] s guingan m

giraffe [dʒɪ'ræf], [dʒɪ'rɑf] s girafe f

gird [gɑrd] v (pret & pp **girt** [gʌrt] or **girded**) tr ceindre; **to gird on** se ceindre de; **to gird oneself for** se préparer à

girder ['gɑrdər] s poutre f

girdle ['gɑrdəl] s ceinture f || tr ceindre, entourer

girl [gɑrl] s jeune fille f; (little girl) petite fille f; (servant) bonne f

girl' friend' s (sweetheart) petite amie f, bonne amie f; (female friend) amie f, camarade f

girl'hood s enfance f, jeunesse f d'une femme

girlish ['gɑrlɪʃ] adj de jeune fille, de petite fille

girl' scout' s éclaireuse f, guide f

girls' school' s école f de filles

girth [gɑrθ] s (band) sangle f; (measure around) circonférence f; (of person) tour m de taille

gist [dʒɪst] s fond m, essence f

give [gɪv] s élasticité f || v (pret **gave** [gev]; pp **given** ['gɪvən]) tr donner; (a speech, a lecture, a class; a smile) faire; **to give away** donner, distribuer; **to give back** rendre, remettre; **to give forth** or **off** émettre; **to give oneself up** se rendre; **to give up** renoncer à, abandonner || intr donner; **to give in** se rendre; **to give out** manquer; (to become exhausted) s'épuiser; **to give way** faire place, reculer

give'-and-take' s compromis m; échange m de propos plaisants

give'away' s (coll) révélation f involontaire; (coll) trahison f; **to play give-away** jouer à qui perd gagne

given ['gɪvən] adj donné; **given that** vu que, étant donné que

giv'en name' s prénom m

giver ['gɪvər] s donneur m, donateur m

gizzard ['gɪzərd] s gésier m

glacial ['gleʃəl] adj glacial; (chem) en cristaux; (geol) glaciaire

glacier ['gleʃər] s glacier m

glad [glæd] adj (comp **gladder**; super **gladdest**) content, heureux; **to be glad to** être content or heureux de

gladden ['glædən] tr réjouir

glade [gled] s clairière f, éclaircie f

glad' hand' s (coll) accueil m chaleureux

gladiator ['glædɪ,etər] s gladiateur m

gladiola [,glædɪ'olə], [glə'daɪ-ələ] s glaïeul m

gladly ['glædlɪ] adv volontiers, avec plaisir

gladness ['glædnɪs] s joie f, plaisir m

glad' rags' spl (slang) frusques fpl des grands jours

glamorous ['glæmərəs] adj ravissant, éclatant

glamour ['glæmər] s charme m, éclat m

glam'our girl' s ensorceleuse f

glance [glæns], [glɑns] s coup m d'œil; **at a glance** d'un seul coup d'œil; **at first glance** à première vue || intr jeter un regard; **to glance at** jeter un coup d'œil sur; **to glance off** ricocher, dévier; **to glance through a book**

feuilleter un livre; **to glance up** lever les yeux

gland [glænd] s glande f

glanders ['glændərz] spl (vet) morve f

glare [gler] s lumière f éblouissante; (*look*) regard m irrité ‖ intr éblouir, briller; **to glare at** lancer un regard méchant à, foudroyer du regard

glare/ ice/ s verglas m

glaring ['glerɪŋ] adj éblouissant; (*mistake, fact*) évident, qui saute aux yeux; (*blunder, abuse*) grossier, scandaleux

glass [glæs], [glɑs] s verre m; (*mirror*) glace f; **glasses** lunettes fpl

glass/ blow/er ['blo-ər] s verrier-souffleur m

glass/ case/ s vitrine f

glass/ cut/ter s (*tool*) diamant m; (*workman*) vitrier m

glass/ door/ s porte f vitrée

glassful ['glæsful], ['glɑsful] s verre m

glass/ house/ s serre f; (fig) maison f de verre

glass/ware/ s verrerie f

glass/ wool/ s laine f de verre

glass/works/ s verrerie f, glacerie f

glass-y ['glæsi], ['glɑsi] adj (comp -ier; super -iest) vitreux; (*smooth*) lisse

glaze [glez] s (ceramics) vernis m; (culin) glace f; (tex) lustre m ‖ tr (to cover with a glossy coating) glacer; (to fit with glass) vitrer

glazier ['glezər] s vitrier m

gleam [glim] s rayon m; (of hope) lueur f ‖ intr rayonner, reluire

glean [glin] tr glaner

glee [gli] s allégresse f, joie f

glee/ club/ s orphéon m, société f chorale

glen [glen] s vallon m, ravin m

glib [glɪb] adj (comp glibber; super glibbest) facile; (*tongue*) délié

glide [glaɪd] s glissement m; (aer) vol m plané; (mus) port m de voix; (phonet) son m transitoire ‖ intr glisser, se glisser; (aer) planer

glider ['glaɪdər] s (porch seat) siège m à glissière; (aer) planeur m

glimmer ['glɪmər] s faible lueur f ‖ intr jeter une faible lueur

glimmering ['glɪmərɪŋ] adj faible, vacillant ‖ s faible lueur f, miroitement m; soupçon m, indice m

glimpse [glɪmps] s aperçu m; **to catch a glimpse of** entrevoir, aviser ‖ tr entrevoir

glint [glɪnt] s reflet m, éclair m ‖ intr jeter un reflet, étinceler

glisten ['glɪsən] s scintillement m ‖ intr scintiller

glitter ['glɪtər] s éclat m, étincellement m ‖ intr étinceler

gloaming ['glomɪŋ] s crépuscule m, jour m crépusculaire

gloat [glot] intr éprouver un malin plaisir; **to gloat over** faire de gorges chaudes de; (*e.g., one's victim*) couver du regard

global ['globəl] adj sphérique; mondial

globe [glob] s globe m

globe/-trot/ter s globe-trotter m

globule ['glɑbjul] s globule m

gloom [glum] s obscurité f, ténèbres fpl; tristesse f

gloom-y ['glumi] adj (comp -ier; super -iest) sombre, lugubre; (*ideas*) noir

glori-fy ['glorɪ,faɪ] v (pret & pp -fied) tr glorifier

glorious ['glorɪəs] adj glorieux

glo-ry ['glori] s (pl -ries) gloire f; **to be in one's glory** être aux anges; **to go to glory** (slang) aller à la ruine ‖ v (pret & pp -ried) intr—**to glory in** se glorifier de

gloss [glɔs], [glɑs] s lustre m; (on cloth) cati m; (on floor) brillant m; (note, commentary) glose f; **to take off the gloss from** décatir ‖ tr lustrer; **to gloss over** maquiller, farder

glossa-ry ['glɑsəri] s (pl -ries) glossaire m

gloss-y ['glɔsi], ['glɑsi] adj (comp -ier; super -iest) lustré, brillant

glot/tal stop/ ['glɑtəl] s coup m de glotte

glottis ['glɑtɪs] s glotte f

glove [glʌv] s gant m ‖ tr ganter

glove/ compart/ment s boîte f à gants

glow [glo] s rougeoiement m ‖ intr rougeoyer

glower ['glau-ər] s grise mine f ‖ intr avoir l'air renfrogné

glowing ['glo-ɪŋ] adj rougeoyant, incandescent; (healthy) rayonnant; (cheeks) vermeil; (reports) enthousiaste, élogieux

glow/worm/ s ver m luisant

glucose ['glukos] s glucose m

glue [glu] s colle f ‖ tr coller

glue/pot/ s pot m à colle

gluey ['glu·i] adj (comp gluier; super gluiest) gluant

glum [glʌm] adj (comp glummer; super glummest) maussade, renfrogné

glut [glʌt] s surabondance f; (on the market) engorgement m ‖ v (pret & pp glutted; ger glutting) tr (with food) rassasier; (the market) inonder, engorger

glutton ['glʌtən] s glouton m

gluttonous ['glʌtənəs] adj glouton

glutton-y ['glʌtəni] s (pl -ies) gloutonnerie f

glycerine ['glɪsərɪn] s glycérine f

G.M.T. abbr (Greenwich mean time temps moyen de Greenwich) T.U., temps m universel

gnarl [nɑrl] s (bot) nœud m ‖ tr tordre ‖ intr grogner

gnarled adj noueux

gnash [næʃ] tr—**to gnash the teeth** grincer des dents or les dents

gnat [næt] s moucheron m, moustique m

gnaw [nɔ] tr ronger

gnome [nom] s gnome m

go [go] s (pl goes) aller m; **a lot of go** (slang) beaucoup d'allant; **it's no go** (coll) ça ne marche pas, pas mèche; **to have a go at** (coll) essayer; **to make a go of** (coll) réussir à ‖ v (*pret* went [wɛnt]; *pp* gone [gɔn], [gɑn]) *tr*—to go it alone le faire tout seul ‖ *intr* aller; (*to work, operate*) marcher; y aller, e.g., **did you go?** y êtes-vous allé?; devenir, e.g., **to go crazy** devenir fou; faire, e.g., **to go quack-quack** faire couin-couin; **going, going, gone!** une fois, deux fois, adjugé!; **go to it!** allez-y!; **to be going to** or **to go to** + *inf* aller + *inf*, e.g., **I am going to the store to buy some shoes** je vais au magasin acheter des souliers; (to express futurity from the point of view of the present or past) aller + *inf*, e.g., **he is going to get married** il va se marier; (*he was going to get married*) il allait se marier; **to go** (*to take out*) (coll) à emporter; **to go against** contrarier; **to go ahead of** dépasser; **to go away** s'en aller; **to go back** retourner; (*to return home*) rentrer; (*to back up*) reculer; (*to date back*) remonter; **to go by** passer; (*a rule, model, etc.*) agir selon; **to go down** descendre; (*said of sun*) se coucher; (*said of ship*) sombrer; **to go fishing** aller à la pêche; **to go for** or **to go get** aller chercher; **to go in** entrer; entrer dans; (*to fit into*) tenir dans; **to go in for** se consacrer à; **to go in with** s'associer à or avec, se joindre à; **to go off** (*said of bomb, gun, etc.*) partir; **to go on** + *ger* continuer à + *inf*; **to go out** sortir; (*said of light, fire, etc.*) s'éteindre; **to go over** (*to examine*) parcourir, repasser; **to go through** (*e.g., a door*) passer par; (*e.g., a city*) traverser; (*a fortune*) dissiper, dilapider; **to go together** (*said, e.g., of colors*) s'assortir; (*said of lovers*) être très liés; **to go under** succomber; (*said, e.g., of submarine*) plonger; (*a false name*) être connu sous; **to go up** monter; **to go with** accompagner; (*a color, dress, etc.*) s'assortir avec; **to go without** se passer de; **to let go of** lâcher

goad [god] *s* aiguillon *m* ‖ *tr* aiguillonner

go'-ahead' *adj* (coll) entreprenant ‖ *s* (coll) signal *m* d'aller en avant

goal [gol] *s* but *m*

goal'keep'er *s* goal *m*, gardien *m* de but

goal' line' *s* ligne *f* de but

goal' post' *s* montant *m*, poteau *m* de but

goat [got] *s* chèvre *f*; (*male goat*) bouc *m*; (coll) dindon *m*; **to get the goat of** (slang) exaspérer, irriter

goatee [go'ti] *s* barbiche *f*

goat'herd' *s* chevrier *m*

goat'skin' *s* peau *f* de chèvre

goat'suck'er *s* (orn) engoulevent *m*

gob [gɑb] *s* (coll) grumeau *m*; (coll) marin *m*

gobble ['gɑbəl] *s* glouglou *m* ‖ *tr* engloutir, bâfrer ‖ *intr* bâfrer; (*said of turkey*) glouglouter

gobbledegook ['gɑbəldɪ ˌguk] *s* (coll) palabre *m* & *f*, charabia *m*

go'-between' *s* intermédiaire *mf*; (*in shady love affairs*) entremetteur *m*

goblet ['gɑblɪt] *s* verre *m* à pied

goblin ['gɑblɪn] *s* lutin *m*

go'-by' *s* (coll) affront *m*; **to give s.o. the go-by** (coll) brûler la politesse à qn

go'cart' *s* chariot *m*; (*baby carriage*) poussette *f*; (*handcart*) charrette *f* à bras

god [gɑd] *s* dieu *m*; **God forbid** qu'à Dieu ne plaise; **God grant** plût à Dieu; **God willing** s'il plaît à Dieu

god'child' *s* (*pl* -children) filleul *m*

god'daugh'ter *s* filleule *f*

goddess ['gɑdɪs] *s* déesse *f*

god'fa'ther *s* parrain *m*

God'-fear'ing *adj* dévot, pieux

God'forsak'en *adj* abandonné de Dieu; (coll) perdu, misérable

god'head' *s* divinité *f*; **Godhead** Dieu *m*

godless ['gɑdlɪs] *adj* athée, impie

god-ly ['gɑdlɪ] *adj* (*comp* -lier; *super* -liest) dévot, pieux

god'moth'er *s* marraine *f*

God's' a'cre *s* le champ de repos

god'send' *s* aubaine *f*

god'son' *s* filleul *m*

God'speed' *s* bonne chance *f*, bon voyage *m*

go-getter ['go ˌgɛtər] *s* (coll) homme *m* d'expédition, lanceur *m* d'affaires

goggle ['gɑgəl] *intr* rouler de gros yeux; (*to open the eyes wide*) écarquiller les yeux

gog'gle-eyed' *adj* aux yeux saillants

goggles ['gɑgəlz] *spl* lunettes *fpl* protectrices

going ['go·ɪŋ] *adj* en marche; **going on two o'clock** presque deux heures ‖ *s* départ *m*; **good going!** bien joué!

go'ing concern' *s* maison *f* en pleine activité

go'ings on' *spl* (coll) chahut *m*, tapage *m*; (coll) événements *mpl*

goiter ['gɔɪtər] *s* goitre *m*

gold [gold] *adj* d'or, en or ‖ *s* or *m*

gold'beat'er *s* batteur *m* d'or

gold'beater's skin' *s* baudruche *f*

gold'crest' *s* roitelet *m* à tête dorée

golden ['goldən] *adj* d'or; (*gilt*) doré; (*hair*) d'or, d'un blond doré; (*opportunity*) favorable, magnifique

gold'en age' *s* âge *m* d'or

gold'en calf' *s* veau *m* d'or

Gold'en Fleece' *s* Toison *f* d'or

gold'en mean' *s* juste-milieu *m*

gold'en plov'er *s* pluvier *m* doré

gold'en-rod' *s* solidage *f*, gerbe *f* d'or

gold'en rule' *s* règle *f* de la charité chrétienne

gold'en wed'ding *s* noces *fpl* d'or, jubilé *m*

gold'-filled' *adj* (*tooth*) aurifié

gold'finch' *s* chardonneret *m*

gold'fish' *s* poisson *m* rouge

goldilocks ['goldɪ ˌlɑks] *s* jeune fille *f* aux cheveux d'or

gold' leaf' *s* feuille *f* d'or

gold' mine' *s* mine *f* d'or; **to strike a gold mine** (fig) dénicher le bon filon, faire des affaires d'or

gold' plate' s vaisselle f d'or
gold'-plate' tr plaquer d'or
gold' rush' s ruée f vers l'or
gold'smith' s orfèvre m
gold' stan'dard s étalon-or m
golf [galf] s golf m ‖ intr jouer au golf
golf' club' s crosse f de golf, club m;
(association) club m de golf
golfer ['galfər] s joueur m de golf
golf' links' spl terrain m de golf
gondola ['gɑndələ] s gondole f
gondolier [ˌgɑndə'lɪr] s gondolier m
gone [gɔn], [gɑn] adj parti, disparu;
(used up) épuisé; (ruined) ruiné,
fichu; (dead) mort; **far gone** avancé;
gone on (in love with) (coll) entiché
de, épris de
gong [gɔŋ], [gɑŋ] s gong m
gonorrhea [ˌgɑnə'ri·ə] s blennorragie f
goo [gu] s (slang) matière f collante
good [gud] adj (comp **better**; super
best) bon §91; (child) sage; (meals)
soigné; **good for you!** bien fait!; **to
be good at** être fort en, être expert à;
to make good prospérer; (a loss)
compenser; (a promise) tenir; **will
you be good enough to** voulez-vous
être assez aimable de ‖ s bien m; **for
good** pour de bon, définitivement;
goods biens mpl; (com) marchandises
fpl; **to catch with the goods** (slang)
prendre la main dans le sac; **to the
good** de gagné, e.g., **all** or **so much
to the good** autant de gagné ‖ interj
bon!, bien!, à la bonne heure!; **very
good!** parfait!
good' after·noon' s bonjour m
good'-by' or **good'-bye'** s adieu m ‖
interj au revoir!; (before a long journey) adieu!
good' cit'izenship s civisme m
good' day' s bonjour m
good' deed' s bonne action f
good' egg' s (slang) chic type m
good' eve'ning s bonsoir m
good' fel'low s brave garçon m, brave
type m
good' fel'lowship s camaraderie f
good'-for-noth'ing adj inutile m ‖ s
bon m à rien
Good' Fri'day s le Vendredi saint
good' grac'es spl bonnes grâces fpl
good'-heart'ed adj au cœur généreux
good'-hu'mored adj de bonne humeur
good'-look'ing adj beau, joli
good' looks' spl belle mine f
good' luck' s bonne chance f
good·ly ['gudli] adj (comp **-lier**; super
-liest) considérable, important; (quality) bon; (appearance) beau
good' morn'ing s bonjour m
good'-na'tured adj aimable, accommodant
goodness ['gudnis] s bonté f; **for goodness' sake!** pour l'amour de Dieu!;
goodness knows Dieu seul sait ‖
interj mon Dieu!
good' night' s bonne nuit f
good' sense' s bon sens m
good'-sized' adj de grandeur moyenne,
assez grand

good' speed' s succès m, bonne chance f
good'-tem'pered adj de caractère facile, d'humeur égale
good' time' s bon temps m; **to have a
good time** prendre du bon temps,
bien s'amuser; **to make good time**
arriver en peu de temps
good' turn' s bienfait m, service m
good' will' s bonne volonté f; (com)
achalandage m
good' works' spl bonnes œuvres fpl
good·y ['gudi] adj (coll) d'une piété
affectée ‖ s (coll) petit saint
m; **goodies** friandises fpl ‖ interj
chouette!; chic!
gooey ['gu·i] adj (comp **gooier**; super
gooiest) (slang) gluant; (sentimental)
(slang) à l'eau de rose
goof [guf] s (slang) toqué m ‖ intr—
to goof off (slang) tirer au flanc
goof·y ['gufi] adj (comp **-ier**; super
-iest) (slang) toqué, maboul
goon [gun] s (roughneck) (coll) dur m;
(coll) terroriste m professionnel;
(slang) niais m
goose [gus] s (pl **geese** [gis]) oie f;
**to kill the goose that lays the golden
eggs** tuer la poule aux œufs d'or ‖ s
(pl **gooses**) (of tailor) carreau m
goose'ber'ry s (pl **-ries**) groseille f
verte
goose' egg' s œuf m d'oie; (slang) zéro
m
goose' flesh' s chair f de poule
goose'neck' s col m de cygne
goose' pim'ples spl chair f de poule
goose' step' s (mil) pas m de l'oie
goose'-step' v (pret & pp **-stepped**; ger
-stepping) intr marcher au pas de
l'oie
gopher ['gofər] s citelle m
gore [gor] s (blood) sang m caillé;
(sewing) soufflet m ‖ tr percer d'un
coup de corne; (sewing) tailler en
pointe
gorge [gɔrdʒ] s gorge f ‖ tr gorger ‖
intr se gorger
gorgeous ['gɔrdʒəs] adj magnifique
gorilla [gə'rɪlə] s gorille m
gorse [gɔrs] s (bot) genêt m épineux
gor·y ['gori] adj (comp **-ier**; super
-iest) ensanglanté, sanglant
gosh [gɑʃ] interj (coll) sapristi!, mon
Dieu!
goshawk ['gɑs,hɔk] s autour m
gospel ['gɑspəl] s évangile m; **Gospel**
Évangile
gos'pel truth' s parole f d'Évangile
gossamer ['gɑsəmər] adj ténu ‖ s toile
f d'araignée, fils mpl de la Vierge;
(gauze) gaze f
gossip ['gɑsɪp] s commérage m, cancan
m; (person) commère f; **piece of gossip** potin m, racontar m ‖ intr cancaner
gos'sip col'umnist s échotier m
Gothic ['gɑθɪk] adj & s gothique m
gouge [gaudʒ] s gouge f ‖ tr gouger;
(to swindle) empiler
goulash ['gulɑʃ] s goulasch m & f
gourd [gord], [gurd] s gourde f

gourmand ['gurmənd] *s* gourmand *m*; (*glutton*) glouton *m*

gourmet ['gurme] *s* gourmet *m*

gout [gaut] *s* goutte *f*

govern ['gʌvərn] *tr* gouverner; (gram) régir ‖ *intr* gouverner

governess ['gʌvərnɪs] *s* institutrice *f*, gouvernante *f*

government ['gʌvərnmənt] *s* gouvernement *m*

governmental [,gʌvərn'mentəl] *adj* gouvernemental

governor ['gʌvərnər] *s* gouverneur *m*; (mach) régulateur *m*

gown [gaun] *s* robe *f*

grab [græb] *s* prise *f*; (coll) vol *m*, coup *m* ‖ *v* (*pret & pp* grabbed; *ger* grabbing) *tr* empoigner, saisir ‖ *intr* —to grab at s'agripper à

grab′ bag′ *s* sac *m* à surprises

grace [gres] *s* grâce *f*; (*prayer at table before meals*) bénédicité *m*; (*prayer at table after meals*) grâces; (*extension of time*) délai *m* de grâce ‖ *tr* orner; honorer

graceful ['gresfəl] *adj* gracieux

grace′ note′ *s* note *f* d'agrément, appoggiature *f*

gracious ['greʃəs] *adj* gracieux; (*compassionate*) miséricordieux

grackle ['grækəl] *s* (*myna*) mainate *m*; (*purple grackle*) quiscale *m*

gradation [gre'deʃən] *s* gradation *f*

grade [gred] *s* (*rank*) grade *m*; (*of oil*) grade; qualité *f*; (*school class*) classe *f*, année *f*; (*mark in school*) note *f*; (*slope*) pente *f*; **to make the grade** réussir ‖ *tr* classer; (*a school paper*) noter; (*land*) niveler

grade′ cross′ing *s* (rr) passage *m* à niveau

grade′ school′ *s* école *f* primaire

gradient ['gredɪ-ənt] *adj* montant ‖ *s* pente *f*; (phys) gradient *m*

gradual ['grædʒʊ-əl] *adj & s* graduel *m*

gradually ['grædʒʊ-əli] *adv* graduellement, peu à peu

graduate ['grædʒʊ-ɪt] *s* diplômé *m* ‖ ['grædʒʊ,et] *tr* conférer un diplôme à, décerner des diplômes à; (*to mark with degrees*) graduer ‖ *intr* recevoir son diplôme

grad′uate school′ *s* faculté *f* des hautes études

grad′uate stu′dent *s* étudiant *m* avancé, étudiant de maîtrise, de doctorat

grad′uate work′ *s* études *fpl* avancées

grad′uat′ing class′ *s* classe *f* sortante

graduation [,grædʒʊ'eʃən] *s* collation *f* des grades; (*e.g., marking on beaker*) graduation *f*

graft [græft], [grɑft] *s* (hort, surg) greffe *f*; (coll) gratte *f*, grattage *m* ‖ *tr & intr* (hort, surg) greffer; (coll) gratter

grafter ['græftər], ['grɑftər] *s* (hort) greffeur *m*; (coll) homme *m* véreux, concussionnaire *mf*

gra′ham bread′ ['gre-əm] *s* pain *m* entier

gra′ham flour′ *s* farine *f* entière

grain [gren] *s* (*small seed; tiny particle of sand, etc.; small unit of weight; small amount*) grain *m*; (*cereal seeds*) grains *mpl*, céréales *fpl*; (*in stone*) fil *m*; (*in wood*) fibres *fpl*; **against the grain** à contre-fil, à rebrousse-poil ‖ *tr* grener; (*wood, etc.*) veiner

grain′ el′evator *s* dépôt *m* et élévateur *m* à grains

grain′field′ *s* champ *m* de blé

graining ['grenɪŋ] *s* grenage *m*; (*of painting*) veinage *m*

gram [græm] *s* gramme *m*

grammar ['græmər] *s* grammaire *f*

grammarian [grə'merɪ-ən] *s* grammairien *m*

gram′mar school′ *s* école *f* primaire

grammatical [grə'mætɪkəl] *adj* grammatical

grana·ry ['grænəri] *s* (*pl* -ries) grenier *m*

grand [grænd] *adj* magnifique; (*person*) grand; (coll) formidable

grand′aunt′ *s* grand-tante *f*

grand′child′ *s* (*pl* -chil′dren) petit-fils *m*; petite-fille *f*; **grandchildren** petits-enfants *mpl*

grand′daugh′ter *s* petite-fille *f*

grand′ duch′ess *s* grande-duchesse *f*

grand′ duch′y *s* grand-duché *m*

grand′ duke′ *s* grand-duc *m*

grandee [græn'di] *s* grand *m* d'Espagne

grand′fa′ther *s* grand-père *m*

grand′father's clock′ *s* pendule *f* à gaine, horloge *f* comtoise

grandiose ['grændɪ,os] *adj* grandiose; pompeux

grand′ ju′ry *s* jury *m* d'accusation

grand′ lar′ceny *s* grand larcin *m*

grand′ lodge′ *s* grand orient *m*

grandma ['grænd,mɑ], ['grænd,mɑ], ['græmə] *s* (coll) grand-maman *f*

grand′moth′er *s* grand-mère *f*

grand′neph′ew *s* petit-neveu *m*

grand′niece′ *s* petite-nièce *f*

grand′ op′era *s* grand opéra *m*

grandpa ['grænd,pɑ], ['græn,pɑ], ['græmpɑ] *s* (coll) grand-papa *m*

grand′par′ent *s* grand-père *m*; grand-mère *f*; **grandparents** grands-parents *mpl*

grand′ pian′o *s* piano *m* à queue

grand′ slam′ *s* grand chelem *m*

grand′son′ *s* petit-fils *m*

grand′stand′ *s* tribune *f*, gradins *mpl*

grand′ to′tal *s* total *m* global

grand′un′cle *s* grand-oncle *m*

grand′ vizier′ *s* grand vizir *m*

grange [grendʒ] *s* ferme *f*; syndicat *m* d'agriculteurs

granite ['grænɪt] *s* granite *m*, granit *m*

gran·ny ['græni] *s* (*pl* -nies) (coll) grand-mère *f*

gran′ny knot′ *s* nœud *m* de vache

grant [grænt], [grɑnt] *s* concession *f*; (*subsidy*) subvention *f*; (*scholarship*) bourse *f* ‖ *tr* concéder, accorder; (*a wish*) exaucer; (*e.g., a charter*) octroyer; (*a degree*) décerner; **to take for granted** escompter, tenir pour évident; traiter avec indifférence

grantee [græn'ti], [grɑn'ti] *s* donataire *mf*

grantor [græn'tɔr], [grɑn'tɔr] s donateur m

granular ['grænjələr] adj granulaire

granulate ['grænjə‚let] tr granuler ‖ intr se granuler

gran′ulated sug′ar s sucre m cristallisé

granule ['grænjul] s granule m, granulé m

grape [grep] s (fruit) raisin m; (vine) vigne f; (single grape) grain m de raisin

grape′ ar′bor s treille f

grape′fruit′ s (fruit) pamplemousse m & f; (tree) pamplemoussier m

grape′ juice′ s jus m de raisin

grape′shot′ s mitraille f

grape′vine′ s vigne f; (chain of gossip) source f de canards

graph [græf], [grɑf] s graphique m; (gram) graphie f

graphic(al) ['græfɪk(əl)] adj graphique; (fig) vivant m

graphite ['græfaɪt] s graphite m

graph′ pa′per s papier m quadrillé

grapnel ['græpnəl] s grappin m

grapple ['græpəl] s grappin m; (fight) corps à corps m ‖ tr saisir au grappin; (a person) empoigner à bras le corps ‖ intr (to fight) lutter corps à corps; **to grapple with** en venir aux prises avec, s'attaquer à

grap′pling i′ron s grappin m

grasp [græsp], [grɑsp] s prise f; **to have a good grasp of** avoir une profonde connaissance de; **within one's grasp** à sa portée ‖ tr saisir ‖ intr—**to grasp at** tâcher de saisir; saisir avidement

grasping ['græspɪŋ], ['grɑspɪŋ] adj avide, rapace

grass [græs], [grɑs] s herbe f; (pasture) herbage m; (lawn) gazon m; **keep off the grass** (public sign) ne marchez pas sur le gazon; **to go to grass** (fig) s'étaler par terre

grass′hop′per s sauterelle f

grass′-roots′ adj populaire, du peuple

grass′ seed′ s graine f fourragère; (for lawns) graine f pour gazon

grass′ snake′ s (Tropidonotus natrix) couleuvre f à collier

grass′ wid′ow s demi-veuve f

grass·y ['græsɪ], ['grɑsɪ] adj (comp -ier; super -iest) herbeux

grate [gret] s grille f, grillage m ‖ tr (to put a grate on) griller; (e.g., cheese) râper; **to grate the teeth** grincer des dents ‖ intr grincer; **to grate on** écorcher

grateful ['gretfəl] adj reconnaissant; agréable; **to be grateful for** être reconnaissant de or pour

grater ['gretər] s râpe f

grati·fy ['grætɪ‚faɪ] v (pret & pp -fied) tr faire plaisir à, satisfaire

gratifying ['grætɪ‚faɪ‧ɪŋ] adj agréable, satisfaisant

grating ['gretɪŋ] adj grinçant ‖ s grillage m, grille f

gratis ['gretɪs], ['grætɪs] adj gratuit, gracieux ‖ adv gratis, gratuitement

gratitude ['grætɪ‚t(j)ud] s gratitude f, reconnaissance f; **gratitude for** reconnaissance de or pour

gratuitous [grə't(j)u‧ɪtəs] adj gratuit

gratu·ity [grə't(j)u‧ɪti] s (pl -ties) gratification f, pourboire m

grave [grev] adj grave ‖ s fosse f, tombe f

gravedigger ['grev‚dɪgər] s fossoyeur m

gravel ['grævəl] s gravier m; (pathol) gravelle f

grav′en im′age ['grevən] s image f taillée

grave′stone′ s pierre f tombale

grave′yard′ s cimetière m

gravitate ['grævɪ‚tet] intr graviter

gravitation [‚grævɪ'te‧ʃən] s gravitation f

gravi·ty [ˈgrævɪti] s (pl -ties) gravité f; (phys) pesanteur f, gravité

gra·vy ['grevi] s (pl -vies) (juice from cooking meat) jus m; (sauce made with this juice) sauce f; (slang) profit m facile, profit supplémentaire

gra′vy boat′ s saucière f

gra′vy train′ s (slang) assiette f au beurre

gray [gre] adj gris; (gray-haired) gris, chenu; **to turn gray** grisonner ‖ s gris m ‖ intr grisonner

gray′beard′ s barbon m, ancien m

gray′-haired′ adj gris, chenu

gray′hound′ s lévrier m; (female) levrette f

grayish ['gre‧ɪʃ] adj grisâtre

gray′ mat′ter s substance f grise

graze [grez] tr (to touch lightly) frôler, effleurer; (to scratch lightly in passing) érafler; (to pasture) faire paître ‖ intr paître

grease [gris] s graisse f ‖ [gris], [griz] tr graisser

grease′ cup′ [gris] s godet m graisseur

grease′ gun′ [gris] s graisseur m, seringue f à graisse

grease′ paint′ [gris] s fard m, grimage m

greas·y ['grisi], ['grizi] adj (comp -ier; super -iest) graisseux, gras

great [gret] adj grand; (coll) excellent, formidable; **a great deal, a great many** beaucoup

great′-aunt′ s grand-tante f

Great′ Bear′ s Grande Ourse f

Great′ Brit′ain s Grande Bretagne f; la Grande Bretagne

great′coat′ s capote f

Great′ Dane′ s danois m

Great′er Lon′don s le Grand Londres

Great′er New′ York′ s le Grand New York

great′-grand′child′ s (pl -chil′dren) arrière-petit-fils m; arrière-petite-fille f; **great-grandchildren** arrière-petits-enfants mpl

great′-grand′daugh′ter s arrière-petite-fille f

great′-grand′fa′ther s arrière-grand-père m, bisaïeul m

great′-grand′moth′er s arrière-grand-mère f, bisaïeule f

great'-grand'par'ents *spl* arrière-grands-parents *mpl*

great'-grand'son *s* arrière-petit-fils *m*

greatly ['gretli] *adv* grandement, fort, beaucoup

great'-neph'ew *s* petit-neveu *m*

greatness ['gretnɪs] *s* grandeur *f*

great'-niece' *s* petite-nièce *f*

great'-un'cle *s* grand-oncle *m*

Great' War' *s* Grande Guerre *f*

Grecian ['griʃən] *adj* grec ‖ *s* (*person*) Grec *m*

Greece [gris] *s* Grèce *f*; la Grèce

greed [grid] *s* avidité *f*

greed·y ['gridi] *adj* (*comp* **-ier**; *super* **-iest**) avide

Greek [grik] *adj* grec ‖ *s* (*language*) grec *m*; (*unintelligible language*) (coll) hébreu *m*, e.g., **it's Greek to me** (coll) c'est de l'hébreu pour moi; (*person*) Grec *m*

Greek' fire' *s* feu *m* grégeois

green [grin] *adj* vert; inexpérimenté, novice ‖ *s* vert *m*; (*lawn*) gazon *m*; (*golf*) pelouse *f* d'arrivée; **greens** légumes *mpl* verts

green'back' *s* (U.S.A.) billet *m* de banque

greener·y ['grinəri] *s* (*pl* **-ies**) verdure *f*

green'-eyed' *adj* aux yeux verts; (*envious*) jaloux

green'gage' *s* (bot) reine-claude *f*

green'gro'cer·y *s* (*pl* **-ies**) fruiterie *f*

green'horn' *s* blanc-bec *m*, bleu *m*

green'house' *s* serre *f*

greenish ['grinɪʃ] *adj* verdâtre

Greenland ['grinlənd] *s* le Groënland

green' light' *s* feu *m* vert, voie *f* libre

greenness ['grinnɪs] *s* verdure *f*; (*unripeness*) verdeur *f*; inexpérience *f*, naïveté *f*

green' pep'per *s* poivron *m* vert

green'room' *s* (theat) foyer *m*

greensward ['grin‚swɔrd] *s* pelouse *f*

green' thumb' *s*—**to have a green thumb** avoir la main verte

greet [grit] *tr* saluer; (*to welcome*) accueillir

greeting ['gritɪŋ] *s* salutation *f*; (*welcome*) accueil *m*; **greetings** (*on greeting card*) vœux *mpl* ‖ **greetings** *interj* salut!

greet'ing card' *s* carte *f* de vœux

gregarious [grɪ'gɛrɪ-əs] *adj* grégaire

Gregorian [grɪ'gorɪ-ən] *adj* grégorien

grenade [grɪ'ned] *s* grenade *f*

grey [gre] *adj*, *s*, & *intr* var of **gray**

grey'hound' *s* var of **grayhound**

grid [grɪd] *s* (*of storage battery and vacuum tube*) grille *f*; (*on map*) quadrillage *m*; (culin) gril *m*

griddle ['grɪdəl] *s* plaque *f* chauffante

grid'dle-cake' *s* crêpe *f*

grid'i'ron *s* gril *m*; (sports) terrain *m* de football

grid' leak' *s* résistance *f* de fuite de la grille

grid' line' *s* ligne *f* de quadrillage

grief [grif] *s* chagrin *m*, affliction *f*; **to come to grief** finir mal

grief'-strick'en *adj* affligé, navré

grievance ['grivəns] *s* grief *m*

grieve [griv] *tr* chagriner, affliger ‖ *intr* se chagriner, s'affliger

grievous ['grivəs] *adj* grave, douloureux

griffin ['grɪfɪn] *s* griffon *m*

grill [grɪl] *s* gril *m*; (*grating*) grille *f* ‖ *tr* griller; (*an accused person*) (coll) cuisiner

grille [grɪl] *s* grille *f*; (aut) calandre *f*

grilled' beef'steak' *s* châteaubriand *m*

grill'room' *s* grill-room *m*

grim [grɪm] *adj* (*comp* **grimmer**; *super* **grimmest**) (*fierce*) menaçant; (*repellent*) macabre; (*unyielding*) implacable; (*stern-looking*) lugubre

grimace ['grɪməs], [grɪ'mes] *s* grimace *f* ‖ *intr* grimacer

grime [graɪm] *s* crasse *f*, saleté *f*

grim·y ['graɪmi] *adj* (*comp* **-ier**; *super* **-iest**) crasseux, sale

grin [grɪn] *s* grimace *f*; (*smile*) large sourire *m* ‖ *v* (*pret* & *pp* **grinned**; *ger* **grinning**) *intr* avoir un large sourire, rire à belles dents

grind [graɪnd] *s* (*of coffee*) moulure *f*; (*job*) (coll) boulot *m*, collier *m*; (*student*) (coll) bûcheur *m*; **daily grind** (coll) train-train *m* quotidien ‖ *v* (*pret* & *pp* **ground** [graʊnd]) *tr* (*coffee, flour*) moudre; (*food*) broyer; (*meat*) hacher; (*a knife*) aiguiser; (*the teeth*) grincer; (*valves*) roder ‖ *intr* grincer; **to grind away at** (coll) bûcher

grinder ['graɪndər] *s* (*for coffee, pepper, etc.*) moulin *m*, broyeur *m*; (*for meat*) hachoir *m*; (*for tools*) repasseur *m*; (*back tooth*) molaire *f*

grind'stone' *s* meule *f*, pierre *f* à aiguiser

grip [grɪp] *s* prise *f*; (*with hand*) poigne *f*; (*handle*) poignée *f*; (*handbag*) sac *m* de voyage; (*understanding*) compréhension *f*; **to come to grips** en venir aux prises; **to lose one's grip** lâcher prise ‖ *v* (*pret* & *pp* **gripped**; *ger* **gripping**) *tr* serrer, saisir fortement; (*e.g., a theater audience*) empoigner

gripe [graɪp] *s* (coll) rouspétance *f* ‖ *intr* (coll) rouspéter, ronchonner

grippe [grɪp] *s* grippe *f*

gripping ['grɪpɪŋ] *adj* passionnant

gris·ly ['grɪzli] *adj* (*comp* **-lier**; *super* **-liest**) horrible, macabre

grist [grɪst] *s* blé *m* à moudre

gristle ['grɪsəl] *s* cartilage *m*

gris·tly ['grɪsli] *adj* (*comp* **-tlier**; *super* **-tliest**) cartilagineux

grist'mill' *s* moulin *m* à blé

grit [grɪt] *s* grès *m*, sable *m*; (*courage*) cran *m*; **grits** gruau *m* ‖ *v* (*pret* & *pp* **gritted**; *ger* **gritting**) *tr* (*one's teeth*) grincer

grit·ty ['grɪti] *adj* (*comp* **-tier**; *super* **-tiest**) sablonneux; (fig) plein de cran

griz·zly ['grɪzli] *adj* (*comp* **-zlier**; *super* **-zliest**) grisonnant ‖ *s* (*pl* **-zlies**) ours *m* gris

griz'zly bear' *s* ours *m* gris

groan [gron] *s* gémissement *m* ‖ *intr* gémir

grocer ['grosər] s épicier m

grocer-y ['grosəri] s (pl -ies) épicerie f; groceries denrées fpl

gro'cery store' s épicerie f

grog [grɑg] s grog m

grog-gy ['grɑgi] adj (comp -gier; super -giest) (coll) vacillant; (shaky, e.g., from a blow) (coll) étourdi; (drunk) (coll) gris, ivre

groin [grɔɪn] s (anat) aine f; (archit) arête f

groom [grum] s (bridegroom) marié m; (stableboy) palefrenier m || tr soigner, astiquer; (horses) panser; (a politician, a starlet, etc.) dresser, préparer

grooms'man s (pl -men) garçon m d'honneur

groove [gruv] s rainure f; (of pulley) gorge f; (of phonograph record) sillon m; (mark left by wheel) ornière f; (of window, door, etc.) feuillure f; in the groove (coll) comme sur des roulettes; to get into a groove (coll) devenir routinier || tr rainer, canneler

grope [grop] intr tâtonner; to grope for chercher à tâtons

gropingly ['gropɪŋli] adv à tâtons

grosbeak ['gros,bik] s gros-bec m

gross [gros] adj gros; (fat, burly) gras, épais; (crass, vulgar) grossier; (weight; receipts) brut; (displacement) global || s invar recette f brute; (twelve dozen) grosse f || tr produire en recette brute, produire brut, e.g., the business grossed a million dollars l'entreprise a produit un million de dollars, brut

gross' na'tional prod'uct s produit m national brut

grotesque [gro'tesk] adj grotesque || s grotesque m; (ornament) grotesque f

grot-to ['grɑto] s (pl -toes or -tos) grotte f

grouch [graʊtʃ] s (coll) humeur f grognon; (person) (coll) grognon m || intr (coll) grogner

grouch-y ['graʊtʃi] adj (comp -ier; super -iest) (coll) grognon, maussade

ground [graʊnd] s terre f; (piece of land) terrain m; (basis, foundation) fondement m, base f; (reason) motif m, cause f; (elec) terre f; (body of automobile corresponding to ground) (elec) masse f; ground for complaint grief m; grounds parc m, terrain; fondement, cause; (of coffee) marc m; on the ground of pour raison de, sous prétexte de; to be losing ground être en recul; to break ground donner le premier coup de pioche; to have grounds for avoir matière à; to stand one's ground tenir bon or ferme; to yield ground lâcher pied || tr fonder, baser; (elec) mettre à terre; grounded (aer) interdit de vol, gardé au sol; to ground s.o. in s.th. enseigner à fond q.ch. à qn

ground' connec'tion s prise f de terre

ground' crew' s équipe f au sol, personnel m rampant

ground' floor' s rez-de-chaussée m

ground' glass' s verre m dépoli

ground' hog' s marmotte f d'Amérique

grounding ['graʊndɪŋ] s (aer) interdiction f de vol; (elec) mise f à la masse

ground' installa'tions spl (aer) infrastructure f

ground' lead' [lid] s (elec) conduite f à terre

groundless ['graʊndlɪs] adj sans fondement

ground' meat' s viande f hachée

ground' plan' s plan m de base; (archit) plan horizontal

ground' speed' s (aer) vitesse f par rapport au sol

ground' swell' s lame f de fond

ground' troops' spl (mil) effectifs mpl terrestres

ground' wire' s (elec) fil m de terre, fil de masse

ground'work' s fondement m, fond m

group [grup] s groupe m || tr grouper || intr se grouper

grouse [graʊs] s coq m de bruyère || intr (slang) grogner

grove [grov] s bocage m, bosquet m

grov-el ['grɑvəl], ['grʌvəl] v (pret & pp -eled or -elled; ger -eling or -elling) intr se vautrer; (before s.o.) ramper

grow [gro] v (pret grew [gru]; pp grown [gron]) tr cultiver, faire pousser; (a beard) laisser pousser || intr croître; (said of plants) pousser; (said of seeds) germer; (to become) devenir; to grow angry se mettre en colère; to grow old vieillir; to grow out of se développer de; (e.g., a suit of clothes) devenir trop grand pour; to grow up grandir, profiter

growl [graʊl] s grondement m, grognement m || tr & intr gronder, grogner

grown'-up' adj adulte || s (pl grown-ups) adulte mf; grown-ups grandes personnes fpl

growth [groθ] s croissance f, développement m; (increase) accroissement m; (of trees, grass, etc.) pousse f; (pathol) excroissance f, grosseur f

grub [grʌb] s asticot m; (person) homme m de peine; (food) (coll) boustifaille f || v (pret & pp grubbed; ger grubbing) tr défricher || intr fouiller

grub-by ['grʌbi] adj (comp -bier; super -biest) sale, malpropre

grudge [grʌdʒ] s rancune f; to have a grudge against garder rancune à || donner à contre-cœur

grudgingly ['grʌdʒɪŋli] adv à contre-cœur

gruel ['gru-əl] s gruau m, bouillie f

grueling ['gru-əlɪŋ] adj éreintant

gruesome ['grusəm] adj macabre

gruff [grʌf] adj bourru, brusque; (voice) rauque, gros

grumble ['grʌmbəl] s grognement m || intr grogner, grommeler

grump-y ['grʌmpi] adj (comp -ier; super -iest) maussade, grognon

grunt [grʌnt] s grognement m || intr grogner

G'-string' s (loincloth) pagne m; (worn by women entertainers) cache-sexe m; (mus) corde f de sol

guarantee [ˌgærən'ti] s garantie f; (guarantor) garant m, répondant m; (security) caution f || tr garantir

guarantor ['gærən͵tor] s garant m

guaran-ty ['gærənti] s (pl -ties) garantie f || v (pret & pp -tied) tr garantir

guard [gard] s garde f; (person) garde m; on guard en garde; (on duty) de garde; (mil) en faction, de faction; on one's guard sur ses gardes; to mount guard monter la garde; under guard gardé à vue || to guard || intr être de faction; to guard against se garder de

guard' du'ty s service m de garde

guard'house' s guérite f, corps-de-garde m; prison f militaire

guardian ['gardi·ən] adj gardien || s gardien m; (of a ward) tuteur m

guard'ian an'gel s ange m gardien, ange tutélaire

guard'ian·ship' s garde f; (law) tutelle f

guard'rail' s garde-fou m, parapet m

guard'room' s corps-de-garde m, salle f de police; (prison) bloc m, tôle f

guards'man s (pl -men) garde m

Guatemalan [ˌgwatɪ'malən] adj guatémaltèque || s Guatémaltèque mf

guava ['gwavə] s goyave f; (tree) goyavier m

guerrilla [gə'rɪlə] s guérillero m; guerrillas (band) guérilla f

guerril'la war'fare s guérilla f

guess [ges] s conjecture f || tr & intr conjecturer; (a secret, riddle, etc.) deviner; (coll) supposer, penser; I guess so je crois que oui; to guess right bien deviner

guess'work' s supposition f; by guesswork au jugé

guest [gest] s invité m, hôte mf; (in a hotel) client m, hôte

guest' room' s chambre f d'ami

guest' speak'er s orateur m de circonstance

guffaw [gə'fɔ] s gros rire m || to intr dire avec un gros rire || intr rire bruyamment

Guiana [gɪ'anə], [gɪ'ænə] s Guyane f; la Guyane

guidance ['gaɪdəns] s gouverne f; (guiding) conduite f; (in choosing a career) orientation f; (of rocket) guidage m; for your guidance pour votre gouverne

guid'ance coun'selor s orienteur m

guide [gaɪd] s guide m || tr guider

guide'book' s guide m

guid'ed mis'sile s engin m téléguidé

guide' dog' s chien m d'aveugle

guide' line' s (fig) norme f, règle f; guide lines (for writing straight lines) transparent m, guide-âne m

guide'post' s poteau m indicateur

guide' word' s lettrine f

guild [gɪld] s association f, corporation f; (eccl) confrérie f; (hist) guilde f

guild'hall' s hôtel m de ville

guile [gaɪl] s astuce f, artifice m

guileful ['gaɪlfəl] adj astucieux, artificieux

guileless ['gaɪllɪs] adj candide, innocent

guillotine ['gɪlə͵tin] s guillotine f || tr guillotiner

guilt [gɪlt] s culpabilité f

guiltless ['gɪltlɪs] adj innocent

guilt-y ['gɪlti] adj (comp -ier; super -iest) coupable; found guilty reconnu coupable

guimpe [gɪmp], [gæmp] s empiècement m

guinea ['gɪni] s guinée f; Guinea Guinée f; la Guinée

guin'ea fowl' or **hen'** s poule f de Guinée, pintade f

guin'ea pig' s cobaye m

guise [gaɪz] s apparences fpl, déguisement m; under the guise of sous un semblant de, sous le masque de

guitar [gɪ'tar] s guitare f

guitarist [gɪ'tarɪst] s guitariste mf

gulch [gʌltʃ] s ravin m

gulf [gʌlf] s golfe m; (fig) gouffre m

Gulf' of Mex'ico s Golfe m du Mexique

Gulf' Stream' s Courant m du Golfe

gull [gʌl] s mouette f, goéland m; (coll) gogo m, jobard m || tr escroquer, duper

gullet ['gʌlɪt] s gosier m

gullible ['gʌlɪbəl] adj crédule, naïf

gul·ly ['gʌli] s (pl -lies) ravin m; (channel) rigole f

gulp [gʌlp] s gorgée f, lampée f; at one gulp d'un trait || tr—to gulp down avaler à grandes bouchées, lamper; (e.g., tears) ravaler, refouler || intr avoir la gorge serrée

gum [gʌm] s gomme f; (on eyelids) chassie f; (anat) gencive f || v (pret & pp gummed) tr gommer; er gumming) tr gommer; to gum up encrasser; (coll) bousiller

gum' ar'abic s gomme f arabique

gum'boil' s phlegmon m, fluxion f

gum' boot' s botte f de caoutchouc

gum'drop' s boule f de gomme, pâte f de fruits

gum·my ['gʌmi] adj (comp -mier; super -miest) gommeux; (eyelids) chassieux

gumption ['gʌmpʃən] s (coll) initiative f, cran m

gum'shoe' s caoutchouc m; (coll) détective m || intr rôder en tapinois, marcher furtivement

gun [gʌn] s fusil m; (for spraying) pistolet m; to stick to one's guns (coll) ne pas en démordre || v (pret & pp gunned; ger gunning) tr—to gun down tuer d'un coup de fusil; to gun the engine (slang) appuyer sur le champignon || intr—to gun for (game) chasser; (an enemy) pourchasser

gun' bar'rel s canon m

gun'boat' s cannonière f

gun' car'riage s affût m de canon

gun'cot'ton s fulmicoton m

gun′ crew′ s peloton m de pièce, servants mpl de canon

gun′fire′ s canonnade f, coups mpl de feu

gun′man s (pl -men) bandit m

gun′ met′al s métal m bleui

gunner ['gʌnər] s canonnier m, artilleur m; (aer) mitrailleur m

gunnery ['gʌnəri] s tir m, canonnage m

gunnysack ['gʌni‚sæk] s sac m de serpillière

gun′pow′der s poudre f à canon

gun′run′ning s contrebande f d'armes

gun′shot′ s coup m de feu, coup de fusil

gun′smith′ s armurier m

gun′stock′ s fût m

gunwale ['gʌnəl] s (naut) plat-bord m

gup·py ['gʌpi] s (pl -pies) guppy m

gurgle ['gʌrgəl] s glouglou m, gargouillement m || intr glouglouter, gargouiller

gush [gʌʃ] s jaillissement m || intr jaillir; to gush over (coll) s'attendrir sur

gusher ['gʌʃər] s puits m jaillissant

gush·y ['gʌʃi] adj (comp -ier; super -iest) (coll) démonstratif, expansif

gusset ['gʌsɪt] s (in garment) soufflet m; (mach) gousset m

gust [gʌst] s bouffée f, coup m

gusto ['gʌsto] s goût m, entrain m

gust·y ['gʌsti] adj (comp -ier; super -iest) venteux; (wind) à rafales

gut [gʌt] s boyau m; guts (coll) cran m || v (pret & pp gutted; ger gutting) tr raser à l'intérieur; (to take out the guts of) vider

gutter ['gʌtər] s (on side of road) caniveau m; (in street) ruisseau m; (of roof) gouttière f; (ditch formed by rain water) rigole f

gut′ter·snipe′ s (coll) voyou m

guttural ['gʌtərəl] adj guttural || s gutturale f

guy [gaɪ] s câble m tenseur; (naut) hauban m; (coll) type m, gars m || tr haubaner; (coll) se moquer de

guy′ wire′ s câble m tenseur; (naut) hauban m

guzzle ['gʌzəl] tr & intr boire avidement

guzzler ['gʌzlər] s soiffard m

gym [dʒɪm] s (coll) gymnase m

gymnasi·um [dʒɪm'nezi·əm] s (pl -ums or -a [ə]) gymnase m

gymnast ['dʒɪmnæst] s gymnaste mf

gynecology [‚gaɪnə'kalədʒi], [‚dʒaɪnə'kalədʒi] s gynécologie f

gyp [dʒɪp] s (slang) escroquerie f; (person) (slang) aigrefin m || v (pret & pp gypped; ger gypping) tr (slang) tirer une carotte à, refaire, gruger

gypsum ['dʒɪpsəm] s gypse m

gyp·sy ['dʒɪpsi] adj bohémien || s (pl -sies) bohémien m; Gypsy (language) tsigane m, romanichel m; (person) gitan m, tsigane mf, romanichel m

gyp′sy moth′ s zigzag m

gyrate ['dʒaɪret] intr tournoyer

gyrocompass ['dʒaɪro‚kʌmpəs] s gyrocompas m

gyroscope ['dʒaɪrə‚skop] s gyroscope m

H

H, h [etʃ] s VIIIᵉ lettre de l'alphabet

haberdasher ['hæbər‚dæʃər] s chemisier m

haberdasher·y ['hæbər‚dæʃəri] s (pl -ies) chemiserie f, confection f pour hommes

habit ['hæbɪt] s habitude f; (dress) habit m, costume m; to get into the habit of s'habituer à

habitual [hə'bɪtʃu·əl] adj habituel

habituate [hə'bɪtʃu‚et] tr habituer

hack [hæk] s (notch) entaille f; (cough) toux f sèche; (hackney) voiture f de louage; (old nag) rosse f; (writer) écrivassier m || tr hacher

hackney ['hækni] s voiture f de louage

hackneyed ['hæknid] adj banal, battu

hack′saw′ s scie f à métaux

haddock ['hædək] s églefin m

hag [hæg] s (ugly woman) guenon f; (witch) sorcière f; old hag vieille fée f

haggard ['hægərd] adj décharné, hâve; (wild-looking) hagard, farouche

haggle ['hægəl] intr marchander; to haggle over marchander

Hague [heg] s—**The Hague** La Haye

hail [hel] s (frozen rain) grêle f; within hail à portée de la voix || tr saluer; (a ship, taxi, etc.) héler || intr grêler; to hail from venir de || interj salut!

Hail′ Mar′y s Ave Maria m

hail′stone′ s grêlon m

hail′storm′ s tempête f de grêle

hair [hɛr] s poil m; (of person) cheveu m; (head of human hair) cheveux mpl; against the hair à rebrousse-poil, à contre-poil; hairs cheveux; to a hair à un cheveu près; to get in s.o.'s hair (slang) porter sur les nerfs à qn; to let one's hair down (slang) en prendre à son aise; to make s.o.'s hair stand on end faire dresser les cheveux à qn; to not turn a hair ne pas tiquer; to split hairs fendre or couper les cheveux en quatre

hair′breadth′ s épaisseur f d'un cheveu; to escape by a hairbreadth l'échapper belle

hair′brush′ s brosse f à cheveux

hair′cloth′ s thibaude f; (for furniture) tissu-crin m

hair′ curl′er [ˌkʌrlər] s frisoir m; (pin) bigoudi m

hair′cut′ s coupe f de cheveux; **to get a haircut** se faire couper les cheveux

hair′do′ s (pl -dos) coiffure f

hair′dress′er s coiffeur m pour dames; coiffeuse f

hair′dress′ing s cosmétique m

hair′ dri′er s sèche-cheveux m, séchoir m à cheveux

hair′ dye′ s teinture f des cheveux

hair′line′ s (on face of type) délié m; (along the upper forehead) naissance f des cheveux, plantation f des cheveux

hair′ net′ s résille f

hair′pin′ s épingle f à cheveux

hair′pin turn′ s lacet m

hair′-rais′ing adj (coll) horripilant

hair′ rib′bon s ruban m à cheveux

hair′ set′ s mise f en plis

hair′ shirt′ s haire f, cilice m

hair′split′ting adj vétilleux, trop subtil ‖ s ergotage m

hair′ spray′ s (for setting hair) laque f, fixatif m

hair′spring′ s spiral m

hair′ style′ s coiffure f

hair′ ton′ic s lotion f capillaire

hair′ trig′ger s détente f douce

hair·y [ˈheri] adj (comp -ier; super -iest) poilu, velu; (on head) chevelu

Haiti [ˈheti] s Haïti f

Haitian [ˈhetɪ·ən], [ˈheʃən] adj haïtien ‖ s Haïtien m

halberd [ˈhælbərd] s hallebarde f

hal′cyon days′ [ˈhælsɪ·ən] spl jours mpl alcyoniens, jours sereins

hale [hel] adj vigoureux, sain; **hale and hearty** frais et gaillard ‖ tr haler

half [hæf], [hɑf] adj demi ‖ s (pl halves [hævz], [hɑvz]) moitié f, la moitié; (of the hour) demi m; **by half** de moitié, à demi; **half an hour** une demi-heure; **in half** en deux; **to go halves** être de moitié ‖ adv moitié, à moitié; **half . . . half** moitié . . . moitié; **half past** et demie, e.g., **half past three** trois heures et demie

half′-and-half′ adj & adv moitié l'un moitié l'autre, en parties égales ‖ s (for coffee) mélange m de lait et de crème; (beer) mélange de bière et porter

half′back′ s (football) demi-arrière m, demi f

half′-baked′ adj à moitié cuit; (person) inexpérimenté; (plan) prématuré, incomplet

half′ bind′ing s (bb) demi-reliure f à petit coins

half′-blood′ s métis m; demi-frère m

half′ boot′ s demi-botte f

half′-bound′ adj (bb) en demi-reliure à coins

half′-breed′ s métis m, sang-mêlé m; (e.g., horse) demi-sang m

half′ broth′er s demi-frère m

half′-cocked′ adv (coll) avec trop de hâte

half′-day′ s demi-journée f

half′-doz′en s demi-douzaine f

half′ fare′ s demi-tarif m, demi-place f

half′-full′ adj à moitié plein

half′-heart′ed adj sans entrain, hésitant

half′-hol′iday s demi-congé m

half′ hose′ s chaussettes fpl

half′-hour′ s demi-heure f; **every half-hour on the half-hour** toutes les demi-heures à la demi-heure juste; **on the half-hour** à la demie

half′ leath′er s (bb) demi-reliure f à petit coins

half′-length′ s demi-longueur f

half′-length por′trait s portrait m en buste

half′-light′ s demi-jour m

half′-mast′ s—**at half-mast** en berne, à mi-mât

half′ moon′ s demi-lune f

half′ mourn′ing s demi-deuil m

half′ note′ s (mus) blanche f

half′ pay′ s demi-solde f

halfpen·ny ‖ [ˈhepəni], [ˈhepni] s (pl -nies) demi-penny m; (fig) sou m

half′ pint′ s demi-pinte f; (little runt) (slang) petit culot m

half′-seas o′ver adj—**to be half-seas over** avoir du vent dans les voiles

half′ shell′ s (either half of a bivalve) écaille f; **on the half shell** dans sa coquille

half′ sis′ter s demi-sœur f

half′ sole′ s demi-semelle f

half′-staff′ s—**at half-staff** à mi-mât

half′-tim′bered adj à demi-boisage

half′ time′ s (sports) mi-temps m

half′-time′ adj à demi-journée

half′ ti′tle s faux titre m, avant-titre m

half′tone′ s (painting, phot) demi-teinte f; (typ) similigravure f

half′ tone′ s (mus) demi-ton m

half′-track′ s semi-chenillé m

half′-truth′ s demi-vérité f

half′turn′ s demi-tour m; (of wheel) demi-révolution f

half′way′ adj & adv à mi-chemin; **halfway through** à moitié de; **halfway up** à mi-côte; **to meet s.o. halfway** couper la poire en deux avec qn

half′-wit′ted adj à moitié idiot

halibut [ˈhælɪbət] s flétan m

halitosis [ˌhælɪˈtosɪs] s mauvaise haleine f

hall [hɔl] s (passageway) corridor m, couloir m; (entranceway) entrée f, vestibule m; (large meeting room) salle f, hall m; (assembly room of a university) amphithéâtre m; (building of a university) bâtiment m

halleluiah or **hallelujah** [ˌhælɪˈlujə] s alléluia m ‖ interj alléluia!

hall′mark′ s estampille f, poinçon m; (fig) cachet m, marque f

hal·lo [həˈlo] s (pl -los) holà m ‖ intr huer ‖ interj holà!, ohé!; (hunting) taïaut!

hallow [ˈhælo] tr sanctifier

hallowed adj sanctifié, saint

Halloween or **Hallowe′en** [ˌhæloˈin] s la veille de la Toussaint

hallucination [həˌlusɪˈneʃən] s hallucination f

hall′way′ s corridor m, couloir m
ha·lo [′helo] s (pl -los or -loes) (meteo) auréole f, halo m; (around a head) auréole
halogen [′hæləʤən] s halogène m
halt [hɔlt] adj boiteux, estropié ‖ s halte f, arrêt m; **to come to a halt** faire halte ‖ tr faire faire halte à ‖ intr faire halte ‖ interj halte!; (mil) halte-là!
halter [′hɔltər] s licou m; (noose) corde f
halting [′hɔltɪŋ] adj boiteux; hésitant
halve [hæv], [hɑv] tr diviser or partager en deux; réduire de moitié
halyard [′hæljərd] s (naut) drisse f
ham [hæm] s (part of leg behind knee) jarret m; (thigh and buttock) fesse f; (culin) cuisse f; (cured) (culin) jambon m; (rad) radio amateur m; (theat) cabotin m; **hams** fesses
hamburger [′hæm,bɑrɡər] s sandwich m à la hambourgeoise, hamburger m; (Hamburg steak) biftek m haché
hamlet [′hæmlɪt] s hameau m
hammer [′hæmər] s marteau m; (of gun) chien m, percuteur m ‖ tr marteler; **to hammer out** étendre au marteau; (to resolve) résoudre ‖ intr—**to hammer away at** (e.g., a job) travailler d'arrache-pied à
hammock [′hæmək] s hamac m
hamper [′hæmpər] s manne f ‖ tr embarrasser, gêner, empêcher
hamster [′hæmstər] s hamster m
ham′string′ v (pret & pp -strung) tr couper le jarret à; (fig) couper les moyens à
hand [hænd] adj à main, à la main, manuel ‖ s main f; (workman) manœuvre m, ouvrier m; (way of writing) écriture f; (clapping of hands) applaudissements mpl; (of clock or watch) aiguille f; (a round of play) coup m, partie f, main; (of God) doigt m; (measure) palme f; (cards) jeu m; **at hand** sous la main; (said of approaching event) proche, prochain; **by hand** à la main; **hands off!** n'y touchez pas!; **hands up!** haut les mains!; **hand to hand** corps à corps; **on every hand** de toutes parts, de tous côtés; **on the one hand . . . on the other hand** d'une part . . . d'autre part; **to live from hand to mouth** vivre au jour le jour; **to shake hands with** serrer la main à; **to wait on hand and foot** être aux petits soins pour; **to win hands down** gagner dans un fauteuil; **under the hand and seal of** signé et scellé de ‖ tr donner, présenter; (e.g., food at table) passer; **to hand down** (e.g., property) léguer; (a verdict) prononcer; **to hand in** remettre; **to hand on** transmettre; **to hand out** distribuer; **to hand over** céder, livrer
hand′bag′ s sac m à main
hand′ bag′gage s menus bagages mpl
hand′ball′ s pelote f; (game) handball m
hand′bill′ s prospectus m

hand′book′ s manuel m
hand′ brake′ s frein m à main
hand′car′ s (rr) draisine f
hand′cart′ s voiture f à bras
hand′clasp′ s poignée f de main
hand′ control′ s commande f à main
hand′cuff′ s menotte f ‖ tr mettre les menottes à
handful [′hænd,ful] s poignée f
hand′ glass′ s miroir m à main; (magnifying glass) loupe f à main
hand′ grenade′ s grenade f à main
handi·cap [′hændɪ,kæp] s handicap m ‖ v (pret & pp -capped; ger -capping) tr handicaper
handicraft [′hændɪ,kræft], [′hændɪ,krɑft] s habileté f manuelle; métier m; **handicrafts** produits mpl d'artisanat
handiwork [′hændɪ,wɑrk] s ouvrage m, travail m manuel; (fig) œuvre f
handkerchief [′hæŋkərtʃɪf], [′hæŋkər,tʃif] s mouchoir m
handle [′hændəl] s (of basket, crock, pitcher) anse f; (of shovel, broom, knife) manche m; (of umbrella, sword, door) poignée f; (of frying pan) queue f; (of pump) brimbale f; (of handcart) brancard m; (of wheelbarrow) bras m; (opportunity, pretext) prétexte m; (mach) manivelle f, manette f; **to fly off the handle** (coll) sortir de ses gonds ‖ tr manier; (with one's hands) palper, tâter; **handle with care** (shipping label) fragile; **to handle roughly** malmener ‖ intr—**to handle well** (mach) avoir de bonnes réactions
han′dle·bars′ spl guidon m
handler [′hændlər] s (sports) entraîneur m
handling [′hændlɪŋ] s (e.g., of tool) maniement m; (e.g., of person) traitement m; (of merchandise) manutention f
hand′made′ adj fait à la main
hand′maid′ or **hand′maid′en** s servante f; (fig) auxiliaire mf
hand′-me-down′ s (coll) vêtement m de seconde main
hand′ or′gan s orgue m de Barbarie
hand′out′ s (notes) (coll) documentation f; (slang) aumône f
hand′-picked′ adj trié sur le volet
hand′rail′ s main f courante, rampe f
hand′saw′ s égoïne f, scie f à main
hand′set′ s combiné m
hand′shake′ s poignée f de main
handsome [′hænsəm] adj beau; (e.g., fortune) considérable
hand′spring′ s—**to do a handspring** prendre appui sur les mains pour faire la culbute
hand′-to-hand′ adj corps-à-corps
hand′-to-mouth′ adj—**to lead a hand-to-mouth existence** vivre au jour le jour
hand′ truck′ s bard m, diable m
hand′work′ s travail m à la main
hand′writ′ing s écriture f
handwritten [′hænd,rɪtən] adj manuscrit, autographe

hand·y ['hændi] *adj* (*comp* **-ier**; *super* **-iest**) (*easy to handle*) maniable; (*within easy reach*) accessible, sous la main; (*skillful*) adroit, habile; **to come in handy** être très à propos

hand'y·man' *s* (*pl* **-men'**) homme *m* à tout faire, bricoleur *m*

hang [hæŋ] *s* (*of dress, curtain, etc.*) retombée *f*, drapé *m*; (*skill; insight*) adresse *f*, sens *m*; **I don't give a hang!** (coll) je m'en moque pas mal!; **to get the hang** (coll) saisir le truc, attraper le chic || *v* (*pret & pp* **hung** [hʌŋ]) *tr* pendre; (*laundry*) étendre; (*wallpaper*) coller; (*one's head*) baisser; **hang it all!** zut alors!; **to hang up** suspendre, accrocher; (telp) raccrocher || *intr* pendre, être accroché; **to hang around** flâner, rôder; **to hang on** se cramponner à, s'accrocher à; (*to depend on*) dépendre de; (*to stay put*) tenir bon; **to hang out** pendre dehors; (slang) demeurer, loger; **to hang over** (*to threaten*) peser sur, menacer; **to hang together** rester unis; **to hang up** (telp) raccrocher || *v* (*pret & pp* **hung** or **hanged**) *tr* (*to execute by hanging*) pendre || *intr* se pendre

hangar ['hæŋər], ['hæŋgər] *s* hangar *m*

hang'dog' *adj* (*look*) patibulaire

hanger ['hæŋər] *s* crochet *m*; (*coathanger*) cintre *m*, portemanteau *m*

hang'er-on' *s* (*pl* **hangers-on**) parasite *m*, pique-assiette *m*

hanging ['hæŋɪŋ] *adj* pendant, suspendu || *s* pendaison *f*; **hangings** tentures *fpl*

hang'man *s* (*pl* **-men**) bourreau *m*

hang'nail' *s* envie *f*

hang'out' *s* (coll) repaire *m*

hang'o'ver *s* (coll) gueule *f* de bois

hank [hæŋk] *s* écheveau *m*

hanker ['hæŋkər] *intr*—**to hanker after** or **for** désirer vivement, être affamé de

Hannibal ['hænɪbəl] *s* Annibal *m*

haphazard [,hæp'hæzərd] *adj* fortuit, imprévu; au petit bonheur || *adv* à l'aventure, au hasard

hapless ['hæplɪs] *adj* malheureux, malchanceux

happen ['hæpən] *intr* arriver, se passer; (*to be the case by chance*) survenir; **happen what may** advienne que pourra; **how does it happen that . . . ?** comment se fait-il que . . . ?, d'où vient-il que . . . ?; **to happen on** tomber sur; **to happen to** + *inf* se trou·ver +, venir à + *inf*

happening ['hæpənɪŋ] *s* événement *m*

happily ['hæpɪli] *adv* heureusement

happiness ['hæpɪnɪs] *s* bonheur *m*

hap·py ['hæpi] *adj* (*comp* **-pier**; *super* **-piest**) heureux; (*pleased*) content; (*hour*) propice; **to be happy to** être heureux or content de

hap'py-go-luck'y *adj* sans souci, insouciant || *adv* (archaic) à l'aventure

hap'py me'dium *s* juste-milieu *m*

Hap'py New' Year' *interj* bonne année!

harangue [hə'ræŋ] *s* harangue *f* || *tr & intr* haranguer

harass ['hærəs], [hə'ræs] *tr* harceler; tourmenter

harbinger ['hɑrbɪndʒər] *s* avant-coureur *m*, précurseur *m*

harbor ['hɑrbər] *s* port *m*; || *tr* héberger, donner asile à; (*a criminal, stolen goods, etc.*) receler; (*suspicions; a hope*) entretenir, nourrir; (*a grudge*) garder

har'bor mas'ter *s* capitaine *m* de port

hard [hɑrd] *adj* dur; (*difficult*) difficile; (*water*) cru, calcaire; (*work*) assidu, dur; **to be hard on** (*to treat severely*) être dur or sévère envers; (*to wear out fast*) user || *adv* dur, fort; (*firmly*) ferme; **hard upon** de près, tout contre; **to rain hard** pleuvoir fort; **to try hard** bien essayer

hard'-and-fast' *adj* strict, inflexible, établi

hard-bitten ['hɑrd'bɪtən] *adj* tenace, dur à cuire

hard'-boiled' *adj* (*egg*) dur; (coll) dur, inflexible

hard' can'dy *s* bonbons *mpl*; **piece of hard candy** bonbon *m*

hard' cash' *s* espèces *fpl* sonnantes

hard' ci'der *s* cidre *m*

hard' coal' *s* houille *f* éclatante, anthracite *m*

hard' drink' *s* boissons *fpl* alcooliques, liqueurs *fpl* fortes

hard' drink'er *s* grand buveur *m*

hard'-earned' *adj* péniblement gagné

harden ['hɑrdən] *tr* durcir, endurcir || *intr* se durcir, s'endurcir

hardening ['hɑrdənɪŋ] *s* durcissement *m*; (fig) endurcissement *m*

hard' fact' *s* fait *m* brutal; **hard facts** réalités *fpl*

hard-fought ['hɑrd'fɔt] *adj* acharné, chaudement disputé

hard'-head'ed *adj* positif, à la tête froide

hard'-heart'ed *adj* dur, sans compassion

hardihood ['hɑrdɪ,hʊd] *s* endurance *f*; courage *m*; audace *f*

hardiness ['hɑrdɪnɪs] *s* vigueur *f*

hard' la'bor *s* travaux *mpl* forcés

hard' luck' *s* guigne *f*, malchance *f*

hardly ['hɑrdli] *adv* guère; à peine; ne . . . guère, e.g., **he hardly thinks of anything else** à peine pense-t-il à autre chose, il ne pense guère à autre chose; **hardly ever** presque jamais

hardness ['hɑrdnɪs] *s* dureté *f*

hard' of hear'ing *adj* dur d'oreille

hard'-pressed' *adj* aux abois, gêné

hard' rub'ber *s* caoutchouc *m* durci, ébonite *f*

hard'-shell' *adj* (*clam*) à carapace dure; (coll) opiniâtre

hard'ship' *s* peine *f*; **hardships** privations *fpl*; fatigues *fpl*

hard'tack' *s* biscuit *m*, biscotin *m*

hard' times' *spl* difficultés *fpl*, temps *mpl* difficiles

hard' to please' *adj* difficile à contenter, exigeant

hard' up' *adj* (coll) à court d'argent;
to be hard up for (coll) être à court
de

hard'ware' *s* quincaillerie *f*; (*trim-mings*) ferrure *f*

hard'ware'man *s* (*pl* **-men**) quincaillier *m*

hard'ware store' *s* quincaillerie *f*

hard-won ['hɑrd,wʌn] *adj* chèrement
disputé, conquis de haute lutte

hard'wood' *s* bois *m* dur; arbre *m* de
bois dur

hard'wood floor' *s* parquet *m*

har-dy ['hɑrdi] *adj* (*comp* **-dier**; *super*
-diest) vigoureux, robuste; (*rash*)
hardi; (*hort*) résistant

hare [her] *s* lièvre *m*

hare'brained' *adj* écervelé, farfelu

hare'lip' *s* bec-de-lièvre *m*

harem ['herəm] *s* harem *m*

hark [hɑrk] *intr* écouter; **to hark back
to** en revenir à || *interj* écoutez!

harken ['hɑrkən] *intr*—**to harken to**
écouter

harlequin ['hɑrləkwin] *s* arlequin *m*

harlot ['hɑrlət] *s* prostituée *f*, fille *f*
publique

harm [hɑrm] *s* mal *m*, dommage *m* || *tr*
nuire (with *dat*), faire du mal (with
dat)

harmful ['hɑrmfəl] *adj* nuisible

harmless ['hɑrmlis] *adj* inoffensif

harmonic [hɑr'mɑnɪk] *adj* harmonique

harmonica [hɑr'mɑnɪkə] *s* harmonica
m

harmonious [hɑr'monɪ-əs] *adj* harmonieux

harmonize ['hɑrmə,naɪz] *tr* harmoniser || *intr* s'harmoniser

harmo·ny ['hɑrmoni] *s* (*pl* **-nies**) harmonie *f*

harness ['hɑrnis] *s* harnais *m*, harnachement *m*; **to die in the harness**
(coll) mourir sous le harnais, mourir
debout; **to get back in the harness**
(coll) reprendre le collier || *tr* harnacher; (*e.g., a river*) aménager,
capter

har'ness ma'ker *s* bourrelier *m*, harnacheur *m*

har'ness race' *s* course *f* attelée

harp [hɑrp] *s* harpe *f* || *intr*—**to harp
on** rabâcher

harpist ['hɑrpɪst] *s* harpiste *mf*

harpoon [hɑr'pun] *s* harpon *m* || *tr*
harponner

harpsichord ['hɑrpsɪ,kɔrd] *s* clavecin *m*

har·py ['hɑrpi] *s* (*pl* **-pies**) harpie *f*

harrow ['hæro] *s* (agr) herse *f* || *tr*
tourmenter; (agr) herser

harrowing ['hæro-ɪŋ] *adj* horripilant

har·ry ['hæri] *v* (*pret & pp* **-ried**) *tr*
harceler; (*to devastate*) ravager

harsh [hɑrʃ] *adj* (*life, treatment, etc.*)
sévère, dur; (*to the touch*) rude; (*to
the taste*) âpre; (*to the ear*) discordant

harshness ['hɑrʃnɪs] *s* dureté *f*, rudesse
f; âpreté *f*

hart [hɑrt] *s* cerf *m*

harum-scarum ['herəm'skerəm] *adj & s*
écervelé || *adv* en casse-cou

harvest ['hɑrvɪst] *s* récolte *f*; (*of grain*)
moisson *f* || *tr* récolter, moissonner ||
intr faire la récolte or moisson

harvester ['hɑrvɪstər] *s* moissonneur *m*;
(mach) moissonneuse *f*

har'vest home' *s* fin *f* de la moisson;
fête *f* de la moisson

har'vest moon' *s* lune *f* des moissons

has-been ['hæz,bɪn] *s* (coll) vieille
croûte *f*

hash [hæʃ] *s* hachis *m* || *tr* hacher

hash' house' *s* (slang) gargote *f*

hashish ['hæʃɪʃ] *s* hachisch *m*

hasp [hæsp], [hɑsp] *s* moraillon *m*

hassle ['hæsəl] *s* (coll) querelle *f*, accrochage *m*

hassock ['hæsək] *s* pouf *m*

haste [hest] *s* hâte *f*; **in haste** à la hâte;
to make haste se hâter

hasten ['hesən] *tr* hâter || *intr* se hâter

hast·y ['hesti] *adj* (*comp* **-ier**; *super*
-iest) hâtif, précipité; (*rash*) inconsidéré, emporté

hat [hæt] *s* chapeau *m*; **hat in hand**
chapeau bas; **hats off to . . . !** chapeau bas devant . . . !; **to keep under
one's hat** (coll) garder strictement
pour soi; **to talk through one's hat**
(coll) parler à tort et à travers; **to
throw one's hat in the ring** (coll)
descendre dans l'arène

hat'band' *s* ruban *m* de chapeau

hat' block' *s* forme *f* à chapeaux

hat'box' *s* carton *m* à chapeaux

hatch [hætʃ] *s* (brood) éclosion *f*; (*trap
door*) trappe *f*; (*lower half of door*)
demi-porte *f*; (*opening in ship's deck*)
écoutille *f*; (*hood over hatchway*)
capot *m*; (*lid for opening in ship's
deck*) panneau *m* de descente || *tr*
(eggs) couver, faire éclore; (*a plot*)
ourdir, manigancer; (*to hachure*)
hachurer || *intr* éclore; (*said of
chicks*) sortir de la coquille

hat'check girl' *s* préposée *f* au vestiaire

hatchet ['hætʃɪt] *s* hachette *f*; **to bury
the hatchet** faire la paix

hatch'way' *s* écoutille *f*

hate [het] *s* haine *f* || *tr* haïr, détester;
to hate to haïr de

hateful ['hetfəl] *adj* haïssable

hat'pin' *s* épingle *f* à chapeau

hat'rack' *s* porte-chapeaux *m*

hatred ['hetrɪd] *s* haine *f*

hat' shop' *s* chapellerie *f*

hatter ['hætər] *s* chapelier *m*

haughtiness ['hɔtɪnɪs] *s* hauteur *f*

haugh·ty ['hɔti] *adj* (*comp* **-tier**; *super*
-tiest) hautain, altier

haul [hɔl] *s* (pull, tug) effort *m*;
(*amount caught*) coup *m* de filet,
prise *f*; (*distance covered*) parcours
m, distance *f* de transport || *tr* (*to
tug*) tirer; (com) transporter

haulage ['hɔlɪdʒ] *s* transport *m*; (*cost*)
frais *m* de transport

haunch [hɔntʃ], [hɑntʃ] *s* (hip) hanche
f; (*hind quarter of an animal*) quartier *m*; (*leg of animal used for food*)
cuissot *m*

haunt [hɔnt], [hɑnt] *s* lieu *m* fréquenté, rendez-vous *m*; (*e.g., of criminals*) repaire *m* ‖ *tr* (*to obsess*) hanter; (*to frequent*) fréquenter

haunt/ed house/ *s* maison *f* hantée par les fantômes

Havana [hə'vænə] *s* La Havane

have [hæv] *s*—the haves and the have-nots les riches et les pauvres ‖ *v* (3d *pers* has [hæz]; *pret* & *pp* had [hæd]) *tr* avoir; to have + *inf* aller + *inf*, e.g., I shall have him go je le ferai aller; to have + *pp* faire + *inf*, e.g., I am going to have a suit made je vais faire faire un complet; to have nothing to do with n'avoir rien à voir avec; to have on (*clothing*) porter; to have s.th. to + *inf* avoir q.ch. à + *inf*, e.g., I have a lot of work to do j'ai beaucoup de travail à faire ‖ *intr*—to have to avoir à de-voir; falloir, e.g., I have to go il me faut aller; falloir que, e.g., I have to read him the letter il faut que je lui lise la lettre ‖ *aux* (to form compound past tenses) avoir, e.g., I have run too fast j'ai couru trop vite; (to form compound past tenses with some in-transitive verbs and all reflexive verbs) être, e.g., they have arrived elles sont arrivées; to have just + *pp* venir de + *inf*, e.g., they have just returned ils viennent de rentrer; e.g., they had just returned ils venaient de rentrer

have/lock *s* couvre-nuque *m*

haven ['hevən] *s* havre *m*, asile *m*

haversack ['hævər,sæk] *s* havresac *m*

havoc ['hævək] *s* ravage *m*; to play havoc with causer des dégâts à

haw [hɔ] *s* (bot) cenelle *f* ‖ *tr* & *intr* tourner à gauche ‖ *interj* dia!, à gauche!

Hawaiian [hə'warjən] *adj* hawaïen ‖ *s* Hawaïen *m*

Hawai/ian Is/lands *spl* îles *fpl* Hawaii

haw/-haw/ *s* rire *m* bête ‖ *intr* rire bêtement ‖ *interj* heu!

hawk [hɔk] *s* faucon *m*; (*mortarboard*) taloche *f*; (*sharper*) (coll) vautour *m* ‖ *tr* colporter; to hawk up expectorer ‖ *intr* chasser au faucon; (*to hawk up phlegm*) graillonner

hawker ['hɔkər] *s* colporteur *m*

hawk/ owl/ *s* chouette *f* épervière

hawks/bill tur/tle *s* caret *m*, caouane *f*

hawse [hɔz] *s* (*hole*) écubier *m*; (*prow*) nez *m*; (*distance*) évitage *m*

hawse/hole/ *s* écubier *m*

hawser ['hɔzər] *s* haussière *f*

haw/thorn/ *s* aubépine *f*

hay [he] *s* foin *m*; to hit the hay (slang) aller au plumard; to make hay faire les foins

hay/ fe/ver *s* rhume *m* des foins

hay/field/ *s* pré *m* à foin

hay/fork/ *s* fourche *f* à foin

hay/loft/ *s* fenil *m*, grenier *m* à foin

hay/mak/er *s* (boxing) coup *m* de poing en assommoir

haymow ['he,mau] *s* fenil *m*; approvisionnement *m* de foin

hay/rack/ *s* râtelier *m*

hay/ride/ *s* promenade *f* en charrette de foin

hay/seed/ *s* graine *f* de foin; (coll) cul-terreux *m*

hay/stack/ *s* meule *f* de foin

hay/wire/ *adj* (slang) en pagaille; to go haywire (slang) perdre la boussole ‖ *s* fil *m* de fer à lier le foin

hazard ['hæzərd] *s* risque *m*, danger *m*; (golf) obstacle *m*; at all hazards à tout hasard ‖ *tr* hasarder, risquer

hazardous ['hæzərdəs] *adj* hasardé

haze [hez] *s* brume *f*; (fig) obscurité *f* ‖ *tr* brimer

hazel ['hezəl] *adj* couleur de noisette, brun clair ‖ *s* (*tree*) noisetier *m*, avelinier *m*

ha/zel-nut/ *s* noisette *f*, aveline *f*

hazing ['hezɪŋ] *s* brimade *f*; (at university) bizutage *m*

ha/zy ['hezi] *adj* (*comp* -zier; *super* -ziest) brumeux; (*notion*) nébuleux, vague

H/-bomb/ *s* bombe *f* H

he [hi] *pron pers* il §87; lui §85; ce §82B; he who celui qui §83

head [hɛd] *s* tête *f*; (*of bed*) chevet *m*; (*of boil*) tête; (*on glass of beer*) mousse *f*; (*of drum*) peau *f*; (*of cane*) pomme *f*; (*of coin*) face *f*; (*of barrel, cylinder, etc.*) fond *m*; (*of cylinder of automobile engine*) culasse *f*; (*of celery*) pied *m*; (*of ship*) avant *m*; (*of spear, ax, etc.*) fer *m*; (*of arrow*) pointe *f*; (*of business, department, etc.*) chef *m*, directeur *m*; (*of school*) directeur, principal *m*; (*of stream*) source *f*; (*of lake; of the table*) bout *m*, haut bout; (*caption*) titre *m*; (*decisive point*) point *m* culminant, crise *f*; at the head of à la tête de; from head to foot des pieds à la tête; head downwards la tête en bas; head of cattle bœuf *m*; head over heels in love (with) éperdument amoureux (de); heads or tails pile ou face; over one's head (*beyond reach*) hors de la portée de qn; (*going to a higher authority*) sans tenir compte de qn; to be out of one's head (coll) être tim-bré ou fou; to go to one's head mon-ter à la tête de qn; to keep one's head garder son sang-froid; to keep one's head above water se tenir à flot; to not make head or tail of it n'y comprendre rien; to put heads together prendre conseil; to take it into one's head to avoir l'idée de, se mettre en tête de; to win by a head gagner d'une tête ‖ *tr* (*to direct*) diriger; (*a procession*) conduire, me-ner; (*an organization; a class in school*) être en tête de; (*a list*) venir en tête de; to head off détourner ‖ *intr* (*said of grain*) épier; to head for or towards se diriger vers

head/ache/ *s* mal *m* de tête

head/band/ *s* bandeau *m*

head/board/ *s* panneau *m* de tête

head/cheese/ *s* fromage *m* de tête

head/ cold/ *s* rhume *m* de cerveau

head/dress/ *s* coiffure *f*

head'first' *adv* la tête la première; (*impetuously*) précipitamment

head'frame' *s* (min) chevalement *m*

head'gear' *s* garniture *f* de tête, couvre-chef *m*; (*for protection*) casque *m*

head'hunt'er *s* chasseur *m* de têtes

heading [ˈhɛdɪŋ] *s* titre *m*; (*of letter*) en-tête *m*; (*of chapter*) tête *f*

headland [ˈhɛdlənd] *s* promontoire *m*

headless [ˈhɛdlɪs] *adj* sans tête; (*leaderless*) sans chef

head'light' *s* (aut) phare *m*; (naut) fanal *m*; (rr) feu *m* d'avant

head'line' *s* (*of newspaper*) manchette *f*; (*of article*) titre *m*; **to make the headlines** apparaître aux premières pages des journaux ‖ *tr* mettre en vedette

head'lin'er *s* (slang) tête *f* d'affiche

head'long' *adj* précipité ‖ *adv* précipitamment

head'man' *s* (*pl* -men') chef *m*

head'mas'ter *s* principal *m*, directeur *m*

head'most' *adj* de tête, premier

head' of'fice *s* bureau *m* central; (*director's office*) direction *f*; (*of a corporation*) siège *m* social

head' of hair' *s* chevelure *f*

head'-on' *adj* & *adv* de front, face à face

head'phones' *spl* écouteurs *mpl*, casque *m*

head'piece' *s* (*any covering for head*) casque *m*; (*headset*) écouteur *m*; (*brains, judgment*) tête *f*, caboche *f*; (typ) vignette *f*, en-tête *m*

head'quar'ters *s* bureau *m* central; commissariat *m* de police; (mil) quartier *m* général; (*staff headquarters*) (mil) état-major *m*

head'rest' *s* appui-tête *m*

head'set' *s* casque *m*, écouteurs *mpl*

heads'man *s* (*pl* -men) bourreau *m*

head'stone' *s* pierre *f* tumulaire (à la tête d'une tombe); (*cornerstone*) pierre angulaire

head'strong' *adj* têtu, entêté

head'wait'er *s* maître *m* d'hôtel, steward *m*

head'wa'ters *spl* cours *m* supérieur d'une rivière

head'way' *s* progrès *m*, marche *f* avant; (*between buses*) intervalle *m*; (naut) erre *f*; **to make headway** progresser, aller de l'avant

head'wear' *s* garniture *f* de tête

headwind [ˈhɛd‚wɪnd] *s* vent *m* contraire, vent debout

head'work' *s* travail *m* mental, travail de tête

head-y [ˈhɛdi] *adj* (*comp* -ier; *super* -iest) (*wine*) capiteux; (*conduct*) emporté; (*news*) excitant; (*perfume*) entêtant

heal [hil] *tr* guérir; (*a wound*) cicatriser ‖ *intr* guérir

healer [ˈhilər] *s* guérisseur *m*

healing [ˈhilɪŋ] *s* guérison *f*

health [hɛlθ] *s* santé *f*; **to be in good health** se porter bien, être en bonne santé; **to be in poor health** se porter mal, être en mauvaise santé; **to drink to the health of** boire à la santé de; **to enjoy radiant health** avoir une santé florissante; **to your health!** à votre santé!

healthful [ˈhɛlθfəl] *adj* sain; (*air, climate, etc.*) salubre; (*recreation, work, etc.*) salutaire

health·y [ˈhɛlθi] *adj* (*comp* -ier; *super* -iest) sain; (*air, climate, etc.*) salubre; (*person*) bien portant; (*appetite*) robuste

heap [hip] *s* tas *m*, amas *m* ‖ *tr* entasser, amasser; **to heap** (*honors, praise, etc.*) **on s.o.** combler qn de; **to heap** (*insults*) **on s.o.** accabler qn de

hear [hɪr] *v* (*pret* & *pp* **heard** [hʌrd]) *tr* entendre, ouïr; **to hear it said** l'entendre dire; **to hear s.o. sing, to hear s.o. singing** entendre chanter qn, entendre qn qui chante; **to hear s.th. sung** entendre chanter q.ch. ‖ *intr* entendre; **hear! hear!** très bien!, bravo!; **hear ye! oyez!; to hear about** entendre parler de; **to hear from** avoir des nouvelles de; **to hear of** entendre parler de; **to hear tell of** (coll) entendre parler de; **to hear that** entendre dire que

hearer [ˈhɪrər] *s* auditeur *m*; **hearers** auditoire *m*

hearing [ˈhɪrɪŋ] *s* (*sense*) l'ouïe *f*; (*act; opportunity to be heard*) audition *f*; (law) audience *f*; **in the hearing of** en la présence de, devant; **within hearing** à portée de la voix

hear'ing aid' *s* sonotone *m*, microvibrateur *m*, appareil *m* de correction auditive

hear'say' *s* ouï-dire *m*

hear'say ev'idence *s* simples ouï-dire *mpl*

hearse [hʌrs] *s* corbillard *m*, char *m* funèbre

heart [hɑrt] *s* cœur *m*; (cards) cœur *m*; **after one's heart** selon son cœur; **at heart** au fond; **by heart** par cœur; **heart and soul corps et âme; lift up your hearts!** haut les cœurs!; **to break the heart of** fendre le cœur à; **to die of a broken heart** mourir de chagrin; **to eat one's heart out** se ronger le cœur; **to eat to one's heart's content** manger tout son soûl; **to get to the heart of the matter** entrer dans le vif de la question; **to have one's heart in one's work** avoir le cœur à l'ouvrage; **to have one's heart in the right place** avoir le cœur bien placé; **to lose heart** perdre courage; **to open one's heart to** épancher son cœur à; **to take heart** prendre courage; **to take to heart** prendre à cœur; **to wear one's heart on one's sleeve** avoir le cœur sur les lèvres; **with a heavy heart** le cœur gros; **with all one's heart** de tout son cœur; **with one's heart in one's mouth** le gosier serré

heart'ache' *s* peine *f* de cœur

heart' attack' *s* crise *f* cardiaque

heart'beat' *s* battement *m* du cœur

heart'break' *s* crève-cœur *m*

heartbroken ['hɑrt,brokən] adj navré, chagriné

heart'burn' s pyrosis m

heart' cher'ry s guigne f

heart' disease' s maladie f de cœur

hearten ['hɑrtən] tr encourager

heart' fail'ure s arrêt m du cœur

heartfelt ['hɑrt,fɛlt] adj sincère, cordial, bien senti

hearth [hɑrθ] s foyer m, âtre m

hearth'stone' s pierre f de cheminée

heartily ['hɑrtɪli] adv de bon cœur, sincèrement

heartless ['hɑrtlɪs] adj sans cœur

heart' of stone' s (fig) cœur m de bronze

heart'-rend'ing adj désolant, navrant

heart'sick' adj désolé, chagrin

heart'strings' spl fibres fpl, replis mpl du cœur

heart'-to-heart' adj franc, ouvert; sérieux || adv à cœur ouvert

heart' trans'plant s greffe f du cœur, transplantation f cardiaque

heart' trou'ble s maladie f de cœur

heart'wood' s bois m de cœur

heart·y ['hɑrti] adj (comp -ier; super -iest) cordial, sincère, (meal) copieux; (laugh) sonore; (eater) gros

heat [hit] s chaleur f; (heating) chauffage m; (rut of animals) rut m; (in horse racing) éliminatoire f; in heat en rut || tr échauffer; (e.g., a house) chauffer || intr s'échauffer; to heat up chauffer

heated adj chauffé; (fig) chaud, échauffé

heater ['hitər] s (for food) réchaud m; (for heating house) calorifère m

heath [hiθ] s bruyère f

hea·then ['hiðən] adj païen || s (pl -then or -thens) païen m

heathendom ['hiðəndəm] s paganisme m

heather ['hɛðər] s bruyère f

heating ['hitɪŋ] adj échauffant || s chauffage m

heat' light'ning s éclairs mpl de chaleur

heat' shield' s (rok) bouclier m contre la chaleur, bouclier antithermique

heat'stroke' s insolation f, coup m de chaleur

heat' wave' s vague f de chaleur; (phys) onde f calorifique

heave [hiv] s soulèvement m; **heaves** (vet) pousse f || v (pret & pp heaved or hove [hov]) tr soulever; (to throw) lancer; (a sigh) pousser; (the anchor) lever || intr se soulever; faire des efforts pour vomir; (said of bosom) palpiter

heaven ['hɛvən] s ciel m; **for heaven's sake** pour l'amour de Dieu; **Heaven** le ciel; **heavens** cieux mpl, ciel

heavenly ['hɛvənli] adj céleste

heav'enly bod'y s corps m céleste

heav·y ['hɛvi] adj (comp -ier; super -iest) lourd, pesant; (heart; crop; eater; baggage; rain, sea, weather) gros; (meal) copieux; (sleep) profond; (work) pénible; (book, reading, etc.) indigeste; (parts) (theat) tra-

gique, sombre || adv lourd, lourdement; **to hang heavy on** peser sur

heav'y drink'er s fort buveur m

heav'y-du'ty adj extra-fort

heav'y-heart'ed adj au cœur lourd

heav'y-set' adj de forte carrure, costaud

heav'y-weight' s (boxing) poids m lourd

Hebraist ['hibre·ɪst] s hébraïsant m

Hebrew ['hibru] adj hébreu, hébraïque || s (language) hébreu m, langue f hébraïque; (man) Hébreu m; (woman) Juive f

hecatomb ['hɛkə,tom] s hécatombe f

heckle ['hɛkəl] tr interrompre bruyamment, chahuter; (on account of trifles) asticoter, harceler

heckler ['hɛklər] s interrupteur m impertinent, interpellateur m

hectic ['hɛktɪk] adj fou, bouleversant

hedge [hɛdʒ] s haie f || tr entourer d'une haie; **to hedge in** entourer de tous côtés || intr chercher des échappatoires, hésiter; (com) faire la contrepartie

hedge'hog' s hérisson m; (porcupine) porc-épic m

hedge'hop' v (pret & pp -hopped; ger -hopping) intr (aer) voler en rase-mottes

hedgerow ['hɛdʒ,ro] s bordure f de haies, haie f vive

heed [hid] s attention f, soin m; **to take heed** prendre garde || tr faire attention à, prendre garde à || intr faire attention, prendre garde

heedful ['hidfəl] adj attentif

heedless ['hidlɪs] adj inattentif

heehaw ['hi,hɔ] s hi-han m || intr pousser des hi-hans

heel [hil] s talon m; (slang) goujat m; **to be at the heel** traîner la savate; **to cool one's heels** (coll) croquer le marmot, faire le pied de grue

heft·y ['hɛfti] adj (comp -ier; super -iest) costaud; (heavy) pesant

heifer ['hɛfər] s génisse f

height [haɪt] s hauteur f; (e.g., of folly) comble m

heighten ['haɪtən] tr rehausser; (to increase the amount of) augmenter; (to set off, bring out) relever || intr se rehausser; augmenter

heinous ['henəs] adj odieux, atroce

heir [ɛr] s héritier m; **to become the heir of** hériter de

heir' appar'ent s (pl **heirs apparent**) héritier m présomptif

heiress ['ɛrɪs] s héritière f

heir'loom' s meuble m, bijou m, or souvenir m de famille

Helen ['hɛlən] s Hélène f

helicopter ['hɛlɪ,kɑptər] s hélicoptère m

heliport ['hɛlɪ,pɔrt] s héliport m

helium ['hilɪəm] s hélium m

helix ['hilɪks] s (pl **helixes** or **helices** ['hɛlɪ,siz]) hélice f; (anat) hélix m

hell [hɛl] s enfer m

hell'bent' adj (slang) hardi; **hellbent on** (slang) acharné en diable à

hell'cat' s (*bad-tempered woman*) harpie *f*; (*witch*) sorcière *f*

Hellene ['helin] s Hellène *mf*

Hellenic [he'lenɪk], [he'linɪk] *adj* hellène

hell'fire' s feu *m* de l'enfer

hellish ['helɪʃ] *adj* infernal

hel·lo [he'lo] s (*pl* -los) bonjour *m* ‖ *interj* bonjour!; (*on telephone*) allô!

helm [helm] s gouvernail *m*

helmet ['helmɪt] s casque *m*

helms'man s (*pl* -men) homme *m* de barre

help [help] s aide *f*, secours *m*; (*workers*) main-d'œuvre *f*; (*office workers*) employés *mpl*; (*domestic servants*) domestiques *mfpl*; **help wanted** (*public sign*) offres d'emploi, on embauche; **there's no help for it** il n'y a pas de remède ‖ *tr* aider, secourir; **so help me God!** que Dieu me juge!; **to help down** aider à descendre; **to help oneself** se défendre; (*to food*) se servir; **to not be able to help** ne pouvoir s'empêcher de ‖ *intr* aider ‖ *interj* au secours!

helper ['helpər] s aide *mf*, assistant *m*

helpful ['helpfəl] *adj* utile; (*person*) serviable, secourable

helping ['helpɪŋ] s (*of food*) portion *f*

helpless ['helplɪs] *adj* (*weak*) faible; (*powerless*) impuissant; (*penniless*) sans ressource; (*confused*) désemparé; (*situation*) sans recours

helter-skelter ['heltər'skeltər] *adj* désordonné ‖ s débandade *f* ‖ *adv* pêlemêle

hem [hem] s ourlet *m*, bord *m* ‖ *v* (*pret & pp* hemmed; *ger* hemming) *tr* ourler, border; **to hem in** entourer, cerner ‖ *intr* faire un ourlet; **to hem and haw** ânonner; (*fig*) tourner autour du pot ‖ *interj* hum!

hemisphere ['hemɪ,sfɪr] s hémisphère *m*

hemistich ['hemɪ,stɪk] s hémistiche *m*

hem'line' s ourlet *m* de la jupe

hem'lock' s (*Tsuga canadensis*) sapin *m* du Canada, pruche *f*; (*herb and poison*) ciguë *f*

hemoglobin [,hemə'globɪn], [,himə'globɪn] s hémoglobine *f*

hemophilia [,hemə'fɪlɪ·ə], [,himə'fɪlɪ·ə] s hémophilie *f*

hemorrhage ['hemərɪdʒ] s hémorragie *f*

hemorrhoids ['hemə,rɔɪdz] *spl* hémorroïdes *fpl*

hemostat ['hemə,stæt], ['himə,stæt] s hémostatique *m*

hemp [hemp] s chanvre *m*

hem'stitch' s ourlet *m* à jour ‖ *tr* ourler à jour ‖ *intr* faire un ourlet à jour

hen [hen] s poule *f*

hence [hens] *adv* d'ici; (*therefore*) d'où, donc

hence'forth' *adv* désormais, dorénavant

hench·man ['hentʃmən] s (*pl* -men) partisan *m*, acolyte *m*, complice *mf*

hen'coop' s cage *f* à poules, épinette *f*

hen'house' s poulailler *m*

henna ['henə] s henné *m* ‖ *tr* teindre au henné

hen'peck' *tr* mener par le bout du nez

Henry ['henri] s Henri *m*

hep [hep] (*slang*) à la page, dans le train; **to be hep to** (*slang*) être au courant de

her [hʌr] *adj poss* son §88 ‖ *pron pers* elle §85; la §87; lui §87

herald ['herəld] s héraut *m*; (*fig*) avant-coureur *m* ‖ *tr* annoncer; **to herald in** introduire

herald·ry ['herəldri] s (*pl* -ries) héraldique *f*, blason *m*

herb [ʌrb], [hʌrb] s herbe *f*; (*pharm*) herbe médicinale ou officinale; **herbs for seasoning** fines herbes

herculean [,hʌr'kjulɪ·ən], [,hʌrkju'lɪ·ən] *adj* herculéen

herd [hʌrd] s troupeau *m* ‖ *tr* rassembler en troupeau ‖ *intr*—**to herd together** s'attrouper

herds'man s (*pl* -men) pâtre *m*; (*of sheep*) berger *m*; (*of cattle*) bouvier *m*

here [hɪr] *adv* ici; **from here to there** d'ici là; **here and there** çà et là, parci par-là; **here below** ici-bas; **here or here are** voici; **here lies** ci-gît; **that's neither here nor there** ça n'a rien à y voir ‖ *interj* tenez!; (*answering roll call*) présent!

hereabouts ['hɪrə,bauts] *adv* près d'ici

here·af'ter s—**the hereafter** l'autre monde ‖ *adv* désormais, à l'avenir; (*farther along*) ci-après

hereditary [hɪ'redɪ,teri] *adj* héréditaire

heredi·ty [hɪ'redɪti] s (*pl* -ties) hérédité *f*

here·in' *adv* ici; (*on this point*) en ceci; (*in this writing*) ci-inclus

here·of' *adv* de ceci, à ce sujet

here·on' *adv* là-dessus

here·sy ['herəsi] s (*pl* -sies) hérésie *f*

heretic ['heretɪk] *adj & s* hérétique *mf*

heretical [hɪ'retɪkəl] *adj* hérétique

heretofore [,hɪrtʊ'for] *adv* jusqu'ici

here·upon' *adv* là-dessus

here·with' *adv* ci-joint, avec ceci

heritage ['herɪtɪdʒ] s héritage *m*

hermetic(al) [hʌr'metɪk(əl)] *adj* hermétique

hermit ['hʌrmɪt] s ermite *m*

hermitage ['hʌrmɪtɪdʒ] s ermitage *m*

herni·a ['hʌrnɪ·ə] s (*pl* -as or -ae [,i]) hernie *f*

he·ro ['hɪro] s (*pl* -roes) héros *m*

heroic [hɪ'ro·ɪk] *adj* héroïque ‖ **heroics** *spl* (*verse*) vers *m* héroïque; (*language*) grandiloquence *f*

heroin ['hero·ɪn] s héroïne *f*

heroine ['hero·ɪn] s héroïne *f*

heroism ['hero,ɪzəm] s héroïsme *m*

heron ['herən] s héron *m*

herring ['herɪŋ] s hareng *m*

her'ring·bone' s (*in fabrics*) point *m* de chausson; (*in hardwood floors*) parquet *m* à bâtons rompus; (*in design*) arête *f* de hareng

hers [hʌrz] *pron poss* le sien §89

her·self' *pron pers* elle §85; soi §85; elle-même §86; se §87

hesitan·cy ['hezɪtənsɪ] *s* (*pl* **-cies**) hésitation *f*

hesitant ['hezɪtənt] *adj* hésitant

hesitate ['hezɪ ˌtet] *intr* hésiter

hesitation [ˌhezɪ'teʃən] *s* hésitation *f*

heterodox ['hetərə ˌdɑks] *adj* hétérodoxe

heterodyne ['hetərə ˌdaɪn] *adj* hétérodyne

heterogeneous [ˌhetərə'dʒɪnɪ·əs] *adj* hétérogène

hew [hju] *v* (*pret* **hewed**; *pp* **hewed** or **hewn**) *tr* tailler, couper; **to hew down** abattre ‖ *intr*—**to hew close to the line** (coll) agir dans les règles, être très méticuleux

hex [heks] *s* porte-guigne *m* ‖ *tr* porter la guigne à

hey [he] *interj* hé!; attention!

hey'day' *s* meilleure période *f*, fleur *f*

hi [haɪ] *interj* salut!

hia·tus [haɪ'etəs] *s* (*pl* **-tuses** or **-tus**) (*gap*) lacune *f*; (*in a text; in verse*) hiatus *m*

hibernate ['haɪbər ˌnet] *intr* hiberner

hibiscus [hɪ'bɪskəs], [haɪ'bɪskəs] *s* hibiscus *m*, ketmie *f*

hiccough or **hiccup** ['hɪkəp] *s* hoquet *m* ‖ *intr* hoqueter

hick [hɪk] (coll) *adj & s* rustaud *m*

hicko·ry ['hɪkərɪ] *s* (*pl* **-ries**) hickory *m*

hidden ['hɪdən] *adj* caché, dérobée; (*mysterious*) occulte

hide [haɪd] *s* peau *f*, cuir *m* ‖ *v* (*pret* **hid** [hɪd]; *pp* **hid** or **hidden** ['hɪdən]) *tr* cacher; **to hide s.th. from** cacher q.ch. à ‖ *intr* se cacher; **to hide from** se cacher à

hide'-and-seek' *s* cache-cache *m*

hide'bound' *adj* à l'esprit étroit

hideous ['hɪdɪ·əs] *adj* hideux

hide'-out' *s* (coll) repaire *m*, planque *f*

hiding ['haɪdɪŋ] *s* dissimulation *f*; (*punishment*) (coll) raclée *f*, rossée *f*; **in hiding** caché

hid'ing place' *s* cachette *f*

hierar·chy ['haɪ·ə ˌrɑrkɪ] *s* (*pl* **-chies**) hiérarchie *f*

hieroglyphic [ˌhaɪ·ərə'glɪfɪk] *adj* hiéroglyphique ‖ *s* hiéroglyphe *m*

hi-fi ['haɪ'faɪ] *adj* (coll) de haute fidélité ‖ *s* (coll) haute fidélité *f*

hi'-fi' fan' *s* (coll) fanatique *mf* de la haute fidélité

high [haɪ] *adj* haut; (*river, price, rate, temperature, opinion*) élevé; (*fever, wind*) fort; (*sea, wind*) gros; (*cheekbones*) saillant; (*sound*) aigu; (coll) gris; (culin) avancé; **high and dry** à sec; **high and mighty** prétentieux; **to be high** (coll) avoir son pompon ‖ *s* (aut) prise *f* directe; **on high** en haut, dans le ciel ‖ *adv* haut; à un prix élevé; **high and low** partout; **to aim high** viser haut; **to come high** se vendre cher

high' al'tar *s* maître-autel *m*

high'ball' *s* whisky *m* à l'eau

high' blood' pres'sure *s* hypertension *f*

high'born' *adj* de haute naissance

high'boy' *s* chiffonnier *m* semainier

high'brow' *adj & s* (slang) intellectuel *m*

high' chair' *s* chaise *f* d'enfant

high' command' *s* haut commandement *m*

high' cost of liv'ing *s* cherté *f* de la vie

high'er educa'tion ['haɪ·ər] *s* enseignement *m* supérieur

high'er-up' *s* (coll) supérieur *m* hiérarchique

high'est bid'der ['haɪ·ɪst] *s* dernier enchérisseur *m*

high' explo'sive *s* haut explosif *m*, explosif puissant

highfalutin [ˌhaɪfə'lutən] *adj* (coll) pompeux, ampoulé

high' fidel'ity *s* haute fidélité *f*

high' fre'quency *s* haute fréquence *f*

high' gear' *s* (aut) prise *f* directe

high'-grade' *adj* de qualité supérieure

high'-hand'ed *adj* autoritaire, arbitraire

high' hat' *s* chapeau *m* haut de forme

high'-hat' *adj* (coll) snob, poseur ‖ **high'-hat'** *v* (*pret & pp* **-hatted**; *ger* **-hatting**) *tr* (coll) traiter de haut en bas

high'-heeled' *adj* à talons hauts

high' horse' *s* raideur *f* hautaine; **to get up on one's high horse** monter sur ses grands chevaux

high' jinks' [ˌdʒɪŋks] *s* (slang) clownerie *f*, drôlerie *f*

high' jump' *s* saut *m* en hauteur

high'-key' *adj* (phot) lumineux

highland ['haɪlənd] *s* pays *m* de montagne; **highlands** hautes terres *fpl*

high' life' *s* grand monde *m*

high'light' *s* (*big moment*) clou *m*; **highlights** (*in a picture*) clairs *mpl* ‖ *tr* mettre en vedette

highly ['haɪlɪ] *adv* hautement; (*very*) extrêmement, fort; haut, e.g., **highly colored** haut en couleur; **to think highly of** avoir une bonne opinion de

High' Mass' *s* grand-messe *f*

high'-mind'ed *adj* magnanime, noble

highness ['haɪnɪs] *s* hauteur *f*; **Highness** Altesse *f*

high' noon' *s* plein midi *m*

high'-oc'tane *adj* à indice d'octane élevé

high'-pitched' *adj* aigu; (*roof*) à forte pente

high'-powered' *adj* de haute puissance

high'-pres'sure *adj* à haute pression; (fig) dynamique, persuasif ‖ *tr* (coll) gonfler à bloc

high'-priced' *adj* de prix élevé

high' priest' *s* grand prêtre *m*; (fig) pontife *m*

high'road' *s* grand-route *f*; (fig) bonne voie *f*

high' school' *s* école *f* secondaire publique; (*in France*) lycée *m*

high'-school stu'dent *s* lycéen *m*; collégien *m*

high' sea' *s* houle *f*, grosse mer *f*; **high seas** haute mer

high' soci'ety *s* la haute société, le beau monde

high'-sound'ing *adj* pompeux, prétentieux

high'-speed' *adj* à grande vitesse

high'-spir'ited *adj* fougueux, plein
d'entrain

high' spir'its *spl* gaieté *f*, entrain *m*

high' stakes' *spl*—to play for high
stakes jouer gros jeu

high-strung ['haɪ'strʌŋ] *adj* tendu,
nerveux

high'-test' gas'oline *s* supercarburant *m*

high' tide' *s* marée *f* haute, haute
marée

high' time' *s* heure *f*, e.g., it is high
time for you to go c'est certainement
l'heure de votre départ; (slang) bombance *f*, bombe *f*

high' trea'son *s* haute trahison *f*

high' volt'age *s* haute tension *f*

high wa'ter *s* marée *f* haute, hautes
eaux *fpl*

high'way' *s* grand-route *f*

high'way commis'sion *s* administration
f des ponts et chaussées

high'way'man *s* (*pl* -men) voleur *m* de
grand chemin

high'way map' *s* carte *f* routière

hijack ['haɪ,dʒæk] *tr* (coll) arrêter et
voler du butin (coll) saisir de
force; (*an airplane*) (coll) détourner

hijacker ['haɪ,dʒækər] *s* (coll) bandit
m, bandit de grand chemin; (coll)
pirate *m* de l'air, pirate aérien

hijacking ['haɪ,dʒækɪŋ] *s* (coll) piraterie *f* aérienne, détournement *m*

hike [haɪk] *s* excursion *f* à pied,
voyage *m* pédestre; (*e.g., in rent*)
hausse *f* || *tr* hausser, faire monter ||
intr faire de longues promenades à
pied

hiker ['haɪkər] *s* excursionniste *mf* à
pied, touriste *mf* pédestre

hilarious [hɪ'lɛrɪ·əs], [haɪ'lɛrɪ·əs] *adj*
hilare, gai; (*joke*) hilarant

hill [hɪl] *s* colline *f*, coteau *m*; (*incline*)
côte *f*; (mil) cote *f*; over hill and
dale par monts et par vaux || *tr* (*a
plant*) butter, chausser

hill'bil'ly *s* (*pl* -lies) montagnard *m*
rustique

hillock ['hɪlək] *s* tertre *m*, butte *f*

hill'side' *s* versant *m*, coteau *m*

hill·y ['hɪlɪ] *adj* (*comp* -ier; *super* -iest)
montueux, accidenté; (*steep*) en
pente, à fortes pentes

hilt [hɪlt] *s* poignée *f*; up to the hilt
jusqu'à la garde

him [hɪm] *pron pers* lui §85, §87; le
§87

him·self' *pron* lui §85; soi §85; lui-
même §86; se §87

hind [haɪnd] *adj* postérieur, de derrière
|| *s* biche *f*

hinder ['hɪndər] *tr* empêcher

hind'most' *adj* dernier, ultime

hind'quar'ter *s* arrière-train *m*, train *m*
de derrière; (*of horse*) arrière-main *m*

hindrance ['hɪndrəns] *s* empêchement
m

hind'sight' *s* (*of firearm*) hausse *f*;
compréhension *f* tardive

Hindu ['hɪndu] *adj* hindou || *s* Hindou
m

hinge [hɪndʒ] *s* charnière *f*, gond *m*;
(*of mollusk*) charnière; (bb) onglet *m*
|| *intr*—to hinge on axer sur, dé-
pendre de

hin·ny ['hɪnɪ] *s* (*pl* -nies) bardot *m*

hint [hɪnt] *s* insinuation *f*; (*small quantity*) soupçon *m*; to take the hint
comprendre à demi-mot, accepter le
conseil || *tr* insinuer || *intr* procéder
par insinuation; to hint at laisser entendre

hinterland ['hɪntər,lænd] *s* arrière-pays
m

hip [hɪp] *adj* (slang) à la page, dans le
train; to be hip to (slang) être au
courant de || *s* hanche *f*; (*of roof*)
arête *f*

hip'bone' *s* os *m* coxal, os de la hanche

hipped *adj*—to be hipped on (coll)
avoir la manie de

hippety-hop ['hɪpɪtɪ'hap] *adv* (coll)
en sautillant

hip·po ['hɪpo] *s* (*pl* -pos) (coll) hippopotame *m*

hippopota·mus [,hɪpə'patəməs] *s* (*pl*
-muses or -mi [,maɪ]) hippopotame
m

hip' roof' *s* toit *m* en croupe

hire [haɪr] *s* (*salary*) gages *mpl*; (*rent-
ing*) louage *m*; for hire à louer; in
the hire of aux gages de || *tr* (*a per-
son*) engager, embaucher; (*to rent*)
louer, prendre en location || *intr*—to
hire out (*said of person*) se louer,
entrer en service

hired' girl' *s* servante *f*, servante de
ferme

hired' man' *s* (*pl* men') *s* (coll) valet *m*
de ferme, garçon *m* de ferme

hireling ['haɪrlɪŋ] *adj & s* mercenaire *mf*

hiring ['haɪrɪŋ] *s* embauchage *m*

his [hɪz] *adj poss* son §88 || *pron poss*
le sien §89

Hispanic [hɪs'pænɪk] *adj* hispanique

Hispanist ['hɪspənɪst], [hɪs'pænɪst] *s*
hispanisant *m*

hiss [hɪs] *s* sifflement *m* || *tr & intr*
siffler

hist [hɪst] *interj* psitt!, pst!

histology [hɪs'talədʒi] *s* histologie *f*

historian [hɪs'tɔrɪ·ən] *s* historien *m*

historic(al) [hɪs'tɔrɪk(əl)], [hɪs'tɔrɪk-
(əl)] *adj* historique

histo·ry ['hɪstəri] *s* (*pl* -ries) histoire *f*

histrionic [,hɪstrɪ'anɪk] *adj* théâtral;
histrionics *s* art *m* du théâtre; (fig)
attitude *f* spectaculaire

hit [hɪt] *s* coup *m*; (*blow that hits its
mark*) coup au but, coup heureux;
(*sarcastic remark*) coup de patte,
trait *m* satirique; (*on the hit parade*)
tube *m*; (baseball) coup de batte;
(theat) succès *m*, spectacle *m* très
couru; (coll) réussite *f*; to make a hit
(coll) faire sensation || *v* (*pret & pp*
hit; *ger* hitting) *tr* frapper; (*the
mark*) atteindre; (*e.g., a car*) heurter,
heurter contre; (*to move the emotions of*) toucher; to hit it off (coll)

s'entendre, se trouver d'accord || *intr* frapper; to hit on tomber sur, trouver

hit'-and-run' driv'er *s* chauffard *m* qui abandonne la scène d'un accident, qui prend la fuite

hitch [hɪtʃ] *s* saccade *f*, secousse *f*; obstacle *m*, difficulté *f*; (*knot*) nœud *m*, e.g., **timber hitch** nœud de bois; **without a hitch** sans accroc || *tr* accrocher; (*naut*) nouer; **to hitch up** (*e.g., a horse*) atteler

hitch'hike' *intr* (coll) faire de l'auto-stop

hitch'hik'er *s* auto-stoppeur *m*

hitch'hik'ing *s* auto-stop *m*

hitch'ing post' *s* poteau *m* d'attache

hither ['hɪðər] *adv* ici; **hither and thither** çà et là

hith'er-to' *adv* jusqu'ici, jusqu'à présent

hit'-or-miss' *adj* capricieux, éventuel

hit' parade' *s* (coll) chansons *fpl* populaires du moment

hit' rec'ord *s* (coll) disque *m* à succès

hive [haɪv] *s* ruche *f*; **hives** (pathol) urticaire *f*

hoard [hord] *s* entassement *m*, trésor *m* || *tr* accumuler secrètement, thésauriser || *intr* accumuler, entasser, thésauriser

hoarding ['hordɪŋ] *s* accumulation *f* secrète, thésaurisation *f*

hoarfrost ['hor,frɔst] *s* givre *m*, gelée *f* blanche

hoarse [hors] *adj* enroué, rauque

hoarseness ['horsnɪs] *s* enrouement *m*

hoar·y ['hori] *adj* (*comp* **-ier;** *super* **-iest**) chenu, blanchi

hoax [hoks] *s* mystification *f*, canard *m* || *tr* mystifier

hob [hɑb] *s* (*of fireplace*) plaque *f*; **to play hob** (coll) causer des ennuis; **to play hob with** (coll) bouleverser

hobble ['hɑbəl] *s* (*limp*) boitillement *m*; (*rope used to tie the legs of animal*) entrave *f* || *tr* faire boiter; (*e.g., a horse*) entraver || *intr* boiter, clocher

hob·by ['hɑbi] *s* (*pl* **-bies**) distraction *f*, violon *m* d'Ingres; (orn) hobereau *m*; **to ride one's hobby** enfourcher son dada

hob'by·horse' *s* cheval *m* de bois

hob'gob'lin *s* lutin *m*; (*bogy*) épouvantail *m*

hob'nail' *s* caboche *f*

hob·nob ['hɑb,nɑb] *v* (*pret & pp* **-nobbed;** *ger* **-nobbing**) *intr* trinquer ensemble; **to hobnob with** être à tu et à toi avec

ho·bo ['hobo] *s* (*pl* **-bos** or **-boes**) chemineau *m*, vagabond *m*

hock [hɑk] *s* (*of horse*) jarret *m*; (*wine*) vin *m* du Rhin; (*pawn*) (coll) gage *m*; **in hock** (coll) au clou; (*in prison*) (coll) au bloc || *tr* couper le jarret à; (*to pawn*) (coll) mettre en gage, mettre au clou

hockey ['hɑki] *s* hockey *m*

hock'shop' *s* (slang) mont-de-piété *m*, clou *m*

hocus-pocus ['hokəs'pokəs] *s* tour *m* de passe-passe; (*meaningless formula*) abracadabra *m*

hod [hɑd] *s* oiseau *m*, auge *f*

hod' car'rier *s* aide-maçon *m*

hodgepodge ['hɑdʒ,pɑdʒ] *s* salmigondis *m*, méli-mélo *m*

hoe [ho] *s* houe *f*, binette *f* || *tr* houer, biner

hog [hɑg], [hɔg] *s* pourceau *m*, porc *m*; (*pig*) cochon *m* || *v* (*pret & pp* **hogged;** *ger* **hogging**) *tr* (slang) s'emparer de, saisir avidement

hog'back' *s* dos *m* d'âne

hoggish ['hɑgɪʃ], ['hɔgɪʃ] *adj* glouton

hogs'head' *s* barrique *f*

hog'wash' *s* eaux *fpl* grasses; vinasse *f*; (fig) boniments *mpl* à la noix de coco

hoist [hɔɪst] *s* monte-charge *m*, grue *f*; (*shove*) poussée *f* vers le haut || *tr* lever, guinder; (*a flag, sail, boat, etc.*) hisser

hoity-toity ['hɔɪtɪ'tɔɪtɪ] *adj* hautain; **to be hoity-toity** le prendre de haut

hokum ['hokəm] *s* (coll) boniments *mpl*, fumisterie *f*

hold [hold] *s* prise *f*; (*handle*) poignée *f*, manche *m*; (*domination*) pouvoir *m*, autorité *f*; (mus) point *m* d'orgue; (naut) cale *f*; **hold for arrival** (formula on envelope) garder jusqu'à l'arrivée; **to take hold of** empoigner, saisir || *v* (*pret & pp* **held** [held]) *tr* tenir; (*one's breath; s.o.'s attention*) retenir; (*to contain*) contenir; (*a job; a title*) avoir, posséder; (*e.g., a university chair*) occuper; (*a fort*) défendre; (*a note*) (mus) tenir, prolonger; **to be held to be . . .** passer pour . . . ; **to hold back** or **in** retenir; **to hold one's own** rivaliser, se défendre; **to hold out** tendre, offrir; **to hold over** continuer, remettre; **to hold s.o. to . . .** tenir qn pour . . . ; **to hold s.o. to his word** obliger qn à tenir sa promesse; **to hold up** (*to delay*) retarder; (*to keep from falling*) retenir, soutenir; (*to rob*) (coll) voler à main armée. || *intr* (*to hold good*) rester valable, rester en vigueur; **hold on!** (telp) restez en ligne!; **to hold back** se retenir, hésiter; **to hold forth** disserter; **to hold off** se tenir à distance; **to hold on** or **out** tenir bon; **to hold on to** s'accrocher à, se cramponner à; **to hold out for** insister pour

holder ['holdər] *s* possesseur *m*; (*of stock*) porteur *m*; (*of stock; of a record*) détenteur *m*; (*of degree, fellowship, etc.*) impétrant *m*; (*for a cigarette*) porte-cigarettes *m*; (*of a post, a right, etc.*) titulaire *mf*; (*for holding, e.g., a hot dish*) poignée *f*

holding ['holdɪŋ] *s* possession *f*; **holdings** valeurs *fpl*; (*of an investor*) portefeuille *m*; (*of a landlord*) propriétés *fpl*

hold'ing com'pany *s* holding trust *m*, holding *m*

hold'up' *s* (*stop, delay*) arrêt *m*; (coll) attaque *f* à main armée, hold-up *m*; **what's the holdup?** (coll) qu'est-ce qu'on attend?

hole [hol] *s* trou *m*; **in the hole** (coll)

dans l'embarras; **to burn a hole in s.o.'s pocket** (coll) brûler la poche à qn; **to get s.o. out of a hole** (coll) tirer qn d'un mauvais pas; **to pick holes in** (coll) trouver à redire à, démolir; **to wear holes in** (e.g., a garment) trouer || intr—**to hole up se** terrer

holiday ['hɑlɪ,de] s jour m de fête, jour férié; (vacation) vacances fpl

holiness ['holɪnɪs] s sainteté f; **His Holiness** Sa Sainteté

holla ['hɑlə], [hə'lɑ] interj holà!

Holland ['hɑlənd] s Hollande f; **la Hollande**

Hollander ['hɑləndər] s Hollandais m

hollow ['hɑlo] adj & s creux m || adv —**to beat all hollow** (coll) battre à plate couture || tr creuser

hol·ly ['hɑli] s (pl -lies) houx m

hol'ly-hock' s primerose f, rose f trémière

holm' oak' [hom] s yeuse f

holocaust ['hɑlə,kɔst] s (sacrifice) holocauste m; (disaster) sinistre m

holster ['holstər] s étui m; (on saddle) fonte f

ho·ly ['holi] adj (comp -lier; super -liest) saint; (e.g., water) bénit

Ho'ly Ghost' s Saint-Esprit m

ho'ly or'ders spl ordres mpl sacrés

Ho'ly Scrip'ture s l'Écriture f Sainte

Ho'ly See' s Saint-Siège m

Ho'ly Sep'ulcher s Saint Sépulcre m

ho'ly wa'ter s eau f bénite

Ho'ly Writ' s l'Écriture f Sainte

homage ['hɑmɪdʒ], ['ɑmɪdʒ] s hommage m

home [hom] adj domestique; national, natal || s foyer m, chez-soi m, domicile m; (house) maison f; (of the arts; native land) patrie f; (for the sick, poor, etc.) asile m, foyer, hospice m; **at home** à la maison; (at ease) à l'aise; **make yourself at home** faites comme chez vous || adv à la maison; **to see s.o. home** raccompagner qn jusqu'à chez lui; **to strike home** frapper juste, toucher au vif

home' address' s adresse f personnelle

home·bod·y s (pl -ies) casanier m, pantouflard m

homebred ['hom,brɛd] adj élevé à la maison; du pays, indigène

home'-brew' s boisson f faite à la maison

home'com'ing s retour m au foyer; (at university, church, etc.) journée f or semaine f des anciens

home' coun'try s pays m natal

home' deliv'ery s livraison f à domicile

home' econom'ics s économie f domestique; (instruction) enseignement m ménager

home' front' s théâtre m d'opérations à l'intérieur du pays

home'land' s patrie f, pays m natal

homeless ['homlɪs] adj sans foyer

home' life' s vie f familiale

home'like' adj familial, comme chez soi

home'-lov'ing adj casanier

home·ly ['homli] adj (comp -lier; super -liest) (not good-looking) laid, vilain; (not elegant) sans façons

home'made' adj fait à la maison, de ménage

home'mak'er s maîtresse f de maison, ménagère f

home' of'fice s siège m social

homeopathy [,homɪ'ɑpəθi], [,hɑmɪ'ɑpəθi] s homéopathie f

home'own'er s propriétaire mf

home' plate' s (baseball) marbre m (Canad)

home' port' s port m d'attache

home' rule' s autonomie f, gouvernement m autonome

home'sick' adj nostalgique; **to be homesick** avoir le mal du pays

home'sick'ness s mal m du pays, nostalgie f

homespun ['hom,spʌn] adj filé à la maison; (fig) simple, sans apprêt

home'stead' s bien m de famille, ferme f

home'stretch' s fin f de course, dernière étape f

home' team' s locaux mpl, équipe f qui reçoit

home'town' s ville f natale

homeward ['homwərd] adj de retour || adv vers la maison; vers son pays

home'work' s travail m à la maison; devoirs mpl

homey ['homi] adj (comp homier; super homiest) (coll) familial, intime

homicidal [,hɑmɪ'saɪdəl] adj homicide

homicide ['hɑmɪ,saɪd] s (act) homicide m; (person) homicide mf

hom·i·ly ['hɑmɪli] s (pl -lies) homélie f

hom'ing head' s (of missile) tête f chercheuse

hom'ing pi'geon s pigeon m voyageur

hominy ['hɑmɪni] s semoule f de maïs

homogeneous [,homə'dʒɪnɪ-əs], [,hɑmə'dʒɪnɪ-əs] adj homogène

homogenize [hə'mɑdʒə,naɪz] tr homogénéiser

homonym ['hɑmənɪm] s homonyme m

homonymous [hə'mɑnɪməs] adj homonyme

homosexual [,homə'sɛkʃʊ-əl] adj & s homosexuel m

hone [hon] s pierre f à aiguiser || tr aiguiser, affiler

honest ['ɑnɪst] adj honnête; (money) honnêtement acquis

honesty ['ɑnɪsti] s honnêteté f; (bot) monnaie f du pape

hon·ey ['hʌni] s miel m || v (pret & pp -eyed or -ied) tr emmieller

hon'ey-bee' s abeille f à miel

hon'ey-comb' s rayon m, gâteau m de cire; (anything like a honeycomb) nid m d'abeilles || tr cribler

honeyed adj emmiellé

hon'ey-moon' s lune f de miel; voyage m de noces || intr passer la lune de miel

hon'ey-suck'le s chèvrefeuille m

honk [hɑŋk], [hɔŋk] s (aut) klaxon m || tr (the horn) sonner || intr klaxonner

honkytonk ['haŋki,taŋk], ['hɔŋki-
,tɔŋk] s (slang) boui-boui m
honor ['anər] s honneur m; (award)
distinction f; honors honneurs || tr
honorer
honorable ['anərəbəl] adj honorable
hon'orable dis'charge s (mil) démobi-
lisation f honorable
honorari·um [,anə'reri·əm] s (pl -ums
or -a [ə]) s honoraires mpl
honorary ['anə,reri] adj honoraire
honorific [,anə'rifik] adj honorifique
|| s formule f de politesse
hood [hud] s capuchon m, chaperon
m; (of chimney) hotte f; (academic
hood) capuce m; (aut) capot m;
(slang) gangster m || tr capoter
hoodlum ['hudləm] s (coll) chenapan m
hoodoo ['hudu] s (bad luck) guigne f;
(rites) vaudou m || tr porter la
guigne à
hood'wink' tr tromper, abuser
hooey ['hu·i] s (slang) blague f
hoof [huf], [huf] s sabot m; on the
hoof sur pied || tr—to hoof it (coll)
aller à pied
hoof'beat' s pas m de cheval
hook [huk] s crochet m; (for fishing)
hameçon m; (to join two things) croc
m; (boxing) crochet m; by hook or
by crook (coll) de bric ou de broc,
coûte que coûte; hook line and
sinker (coll) tout à fait, avec tout le
bataclan; to get one's hooks on to
(coll) mettre le grappin sur || tr ac-
crocher; (e.g., a dress) agrafer; (e.g.,
a boat) crocher, gaffer; (slang)
amorcer, attraper; to hook up agrafer; (e.g., a loudspeaking system)
monter || intr s'accrocher
hookah ['hukə] s narguilé m
hook' and eye' s agrafe f et porte f
hook' and lad'der s camion m équipé
d'une échelle d'incendie
hooked' rug' s tapis m à points noués
hook'up' s (diagram) (rad, telv) montage m; (network) (rad, telv) chaîne f
hook'worm' s ankylostome m
hooky ['huki] s—to play hooky (coll)
faire l'école buissonnière
hooligan ['huligən] s voyou m
hooliganism ['huligən,izəm] s voyou-
terie f
hoop [hup], [hup] s cerceau m; (of
cask) cercle m || tr cercler, entourer
hoop' skirt' s crinoline f
hoot [hut] s huée f; (of owl) ululement
m || tr huer || intr huer; (said of owl)
ululer; to hoot at huer
hoot' owl' s chat-huant m, hulotte f
hop [hap] s saut m; (dance) (coll) sauterie f, surboum f; (coll) vol m en
avion, étape f; hops (bot) houblon
m || v (pret & pp hopped) ger hop-
ping) tr sauter, franchir; (e.g., a taxi)
(coll) prendre || intr sauter, sautiller;
to hop on one foot sauter à cloche-
pied; to hop over sauter
hope [hop] s (feeling of hope) espérance f; (instance of hope) espoir m;
(person or thing one puts one's hope
in) espérance, espoir || tr & intr

espérer; to hope for espérer; to hope
to + inf espérer + inf
hope' chest' s trousseau m
hopeful ['hopfəl] adj (feeling hope)
plein d'espoir; (giving hope) promet-
teur
hopeless ['hoplis] adj sans espoir
hopper ['hapər] s (funnel-shaped container) trémie f; (of blast furnace)
gueulard m
hop'per car' s wagon-trémie m
hop'scotch' s marelle f
horde [hord] s horde f
horehound ['hor,haund] s (bot) mar-
rube m
horizon [hə'raizən] s horizon m
horizontal [,hari'zantəl], [,hɔri'zan-
təl] adj horizontal || s horizontale f
hor'izon'tal hold' s (telv) commande
f de stabilité horizontale
hormone ['hɔrmon] s hormone f
horn [hɔrn] s (bony projection on head
of certain animals) corne f; (of anvil)
bigorne f; (of auto) klaxon m; (of
snail; of insect) antenne f; (mus) cor
m; (French horn) (mus) cor d'harmonie; (of deer) bois m; to
blow one's own horn (coll) se vanter,
exalter son propre mérite; to draw in
one's horns (fig) rentrer les cornes;
to toot the horn corner || intr—to
horn in (slang) intervenir sans façon
horn'beam' s (bot) charme m
horned' owl' s duc m
hornet ['hɔrnit] s frelon m
hor'net's nest' s guêpier m
horn' of plen'ty s corne f d'abondance
horn'pipe' s chalumeau m; (dance)
matelote f
horn'rimmed' glas'ses spl lunettes fpl
à monture en corne
horn·y ['hɔrni] adj (comp -ier; super
-iest) corné, en corne; (callous) calleux; (horned) cornu
horoscope ['harə,skop], ['hɔrə,skop]
s horoscope m; to cast s.o.'s horoscope tirer l'horoscope de qn
horrible ['haribəl], ['hɔribəl] adj horrible; (coll) horrible, détestable
horrid ['harid], ['hɔrid] adj affreux;
(coll) affreux, très désagréable
horri·fy ['hari,fai], ['hɔri,fai] v (pret
& pp -fied) tr horrifier
horror ['harər], ['hɔrər] s horreur f;
to have a horror of avoir horreur de
hors d'oeuvre [ɔr'dʌrv] s (pl hors
d'oeuvres [ɔr'dʌrvz]) hors-d'œuvre m
horse [hɔrs] s cheval m; (of carpenter)
chevalet m; hold your horses! (coll)
arrêtez un moment!; to back the
wrong horse (coll) miser sur le mauvais cheval; to be a horse of another
color (coll) être une autre paire de
manches; to eat like a horse (coll)
manger comme un ogre; to ride a
horse monter à cheval || intr—to
horse around (slang) muser, se baguenauder
horse'back' s—on horseback à cheval
|| adv—to ride horseback monter à
cheval

horse/back rid/ing s équitation f, exercice m à cheval

horse/ blan/ket s couverture f de cheval

horse/ break/er s dompteur m de chevaux

horse/car/ s tramway m à chevaux

horse/ chest/nut s (tree) marronnier m d'Inde; (nut) marron m d'Inde

horse/cloth/ s housse f

horse/ coll/ar s collier m de cheval

horse/ deal/er s marchand m de chevaux

horse/ doc/tor s (coll) vétérinaire m

horse/ fly/ s (pl flies) taon m

horse/hair/ s crin m

horse/hide/ s peau f or cuir m de cheval

horse/laugh/ s gros rire m bruyant

horse/less car/riage ['hɔrslɪs] s voiture f sans chevaux

horse/man s (pl -men) cavalier m; (at race track) turfiste m

horsemanship ['hɔrsmən,ʃɪp] s équitation f

horse/ meat/ s viande f de cheval

horse/ op/era s (coll) western m

horse/ pis/tol s pistolet m d'arçon

horse/play/ s jeu m de mains, clownerie f

horse/pow/er s (746 watts) cheval-vapeur anglais

horse/ race/ s course f de chevaux

horse/rad/ish s raifort m

horse/ sense/ s (coll) gros bon sens m

horse/shoe/ s fer m à cheval

horse/shoe/ing s ferrure f, ferrage m

horse/shoe mag/net s aimant m en fer à cheval

horse/ show/ s exposition f de chevaux, concours m hippique

horse/tail/ s queue f de cheval; (bot) prèle f

horse/ thief/ s voleur m de chevaux

horse/ trad/er s maquignon m

horse/ trad/ing s maquignonnage m

horse/whip/ s cravache f ‖ v (pret & pp -whipped; ger -whipping) tr cravacher

horse/wom/an s (pl -wom/en) cavalière f, amazone f

hors·y ['hɔrsi] adj (comp -ier; super -iest) chevalin; (coll) hippomane; (awkward in appearance) (coll) maladroit

horticultural [,hɔrtɪ'kʌlt/ərəl] adj horticole

horticulture ['hɔrtɪ,kʌlt/ər] s horticulture f

hose [hoz] s (flexible tube) tuyau m ‖ s (pl hose) (stocking) bas m; (sock) chaussette f

hosier ['hoʒər] s bonnetier m

hosiery ['hoʒəri] s la bonneterie f; (stockings) les bas mpl

hospice ['haspɪs] s hospice m

hospitable ['haspɪtəbəl], [has'pɪtəbəl] adj hospitalier

hospital ['haspɪtəl] s hôpital m, clinique f, maison f de santé

hospitali·ty [,haspɪ'tælɪti] s (pl -ties) hospitalité f

hospitalize ['haspɪtə,laɪz] tr hospitaliser

hos/pital plane/ s avion m sanitaire

hos/pital ship/ s navire-hôpital m

hos/pital train/ s train m sanitaire

host [host] s hôte m; (who entertains dinner guests) amphitryon m; (multitude) foule f, légion f; (army) armée f; Host (eccl) hostie f

hostage ['hastɪdʒ] s otage m

hostel ['hastəl] s hôtellerie f; (youth hostel) auberge f de la jeunesse

hostel·ry ['hastəlri] s (pl -ries) hôtellerie f

hostess ['hostɪs] s hôtesse f; (taxi dancer) entraîneuse f

hostile ['hastɪl] adj hostile

hostili·ty [has'tɪlɪti] s (pl -ties) hostilité f

hostler ['haslər], ['aslər] s palefrenier m, valet m d'écurie

hot [hat] adj (comp hotter; super hottest) chaud; (spicy) piquant; (fight, pursuit, etc.) acharné; (in rut) en chaleur; (radioactive) (coll) fortement radioactif; hot off (e.g., the press) (coll) sortant tout droit de; to be hot (said of person) avoir chaud; (said of weather) faire chaud; to get hot under the collar (coll) s'emporter; to make it hot for (coll) rendre la vie intenable à, harceler

hot/ air/ s (slang) hâblerie f, discours mpl vides

hot/-air/ fur/nace s calorifère m à air chaud

hot/ and cold/ run/ning wa/ter s eau f courante chaude et froide

hot/bed/ s (hort) couche f, couche de fumier; (e.g., of vice) foyer m; (e.g., of intrigue) officine f

hot/-blood/ed adj au sang fougueux

hot/box/ s (rr) coussinet m échauffé

hot/ cake/ s crêpe f; to sell like hot cakes (coll) se vendre comme des petits pains

hot/ dog/ s saucisse f de Francfort, saucisse chaude

hotel [ho'tel] adj hôtelier ‖ s hôtel m

hotel/keep/er s hôtelier m

hot/foot/ adv (coll) à toute vitesse ‖ tr —to hotfoot it after (coll) s'élancer à la poursuite de

hot/head/ed adj exalté, fougueux

hot/house/ s serre f chaude

hot/ pad/ s (for plates at table) garde-nappe m, dessous-de-plat m

hot/ pep/per s piment m rouge

hot/ plate/ s réchaud m

hot/ rod/ s (slang) bolide m

hot/ rod/der [,radər] s (slang) bolide m, casse-cou m

hot/ springs/ spl sources fpl thermales

hot/-temp/ered adj coléreux, irascible

hot/ wa/ter s (coll) mauvaise passe f; to be in hot water (coll) être dans le pétrin

hot/-wa/ter boil/er s chaudière f à eau chaude

hot/-wa/ter bot/tle s bouillotte f

hot/-wa/ter heat/er s calorifère m à eau

chaude; (with instantaneous delivery of hot water) chauffe-eau m

hot'-wa'ter heat'ing s chauffage m par eau chaude

hot'-wa'ter tank' s réservoir m d'eau chaude, bâche f

hound [haund] s chien m de chasse, chien courant; to follow the hounds or to ride to hounds chasser à courre || tr poursuivre avec ardeur, pourchasser

hour [aur] s heure f; by the hour à l'heure; on the hour à l'heure sonnante; to keep late hours se coucher tard

hour'glass' s sablier m

hour'-glass fig'ure s taille f de guêpe

hour' hand' s petite aiguille f, aiguille des heures

hourly ['aurli] adj à l'heure, horaire || adv toutes les heures; (hour by hour) d'heure en heure

house [haus] s (pl houses ['hauzız]) maison f; (legislative body) chambre f; (theat) salle f, e.g., full house salle comble; to be on the house (coll) être au frais du patron; to bring down the house (theat) faire crouler la salle sous les applaudissements; to keep house for tenir la maison de; to put one's house in order (fig) mettre de l'ordre dans ses affaires || [hauz] tr loger, abriter

house' arrest' s—under house arrest en résidence surveillée

house'boat' s bateau-maison m

house'boy' s boy m

house'break'er s cambrioleur m

house'break'ing s effraction f, cambriolage m

housebroken ['haus,brokən] adj (dog or cat) dressé à la propreté

house' clean'ing s grand nettoyage m de la maison

house'coat' s peignoir m

house' cur'rent s courant m de secteur, secteur m

house'fly' s (pl -flies) mouche f domestique

houseful ['hausˌful] s pleine maison f

house' fur'nishings spl ménage m

house'hold' adj domestique, du ménage || s ménage m, maisonnée f

house'hold'er s chef m de famille, maître m de maison

house' hunt'ing s chasse f aux appartements

house'keep'er s ménagère f; (employee) femme f de charge; (for a bachelor) gouvernante f

house'keep'ing s le ménage, l'économie f domestique; to set up housekeeping se mettre en ménage

house'maid' s bonne f

house'moth'er s maîtresse f d'internat

house' of cards' s château m de cartes

House' of Com'mons s Chambre f des communes

house' of ill' repute' s maison f mal famée, maison borgne

House' of Represen'tatives s Chambre f des Représentants

house' paint'er s peintre m en bâtiments

house' physi'cian s (in hospital) interne m; (e.g., in hotel) médecin m

house'top' s toit m; to shout from the housetops (coll) crier sur les toits

house' trail'er s caravane f

house'warm'ing s—to have a housewarming pendre la crémaillère

house'wife' s (pl -wives') maîtresse f de maison, ménagère f

house'work' s travaux mpl ménagers; to do the housework faire le ménage

housing ['hauzıŋ] s logement m, habitation f; (horsecloth) housse f; (mach) enchâssure f, carter m

hous'ing devel'opment s (houses) grand ensemble m, habitations fpl neuves; (apartments) cité f

hous'ing short'age s crise f du logement

hovel ['hʌvəl], ['hɑvəl] s bicoque f, masure f; (shed for cattle, tools, etc.) appentis m, cabane f

hover ['hʌvər], ['hɑvər] intr planer, voltiger; (to move to and fro near a person) papillonner; (to hang around threateningly) rôder; (said of smile on lips) errer; hésiter

how [hau] s comment m; the how, the when, and the wherefore (coll) tous les détails || adv comment; how + adj quel + adj, e.g., how beautiful a morning! quelle belle matinée!; comme + c'est + adj, e.g., how beautiful it is! comme c'est beau!; que + c'est + adj, e.g., how beautiful it is! que c'est beau!; how are you? comment allez-vous?, ça va?; how early quand, à quelle heure; how else de quelle autre manière; how far jusqu'où; à quelle distance, e.g., how far is it? à quelle distance est-ce?; how long (in time) jusqu'à quand, combien de temps; how long is the stick? quelle est la longueur du bâton?; how many combien; how much combien; (at what price) à combien; how often combien de fois; how old are you? quel âge avez-vous?; how soon quand, à quelle heure; to know how to savoir

how-do-you-do ['haudəjə'du] s—that's a fine how-do-you-do! (coll) en voilà une affaire!

how'ev'er adv cependant, pourtant, toutefois; however little it may be si peu que ce soit; however much or many it may be autant que ce soit; however pretty she may be quelque jolie qu'elle soit; however that may be quoi qu'il en soit || conj comme, e.g., do it however you want faites-le comme vous voudrez

howitzer ['hau-ıtsər] s obusier m

howl [haul] s hurlement m || tr hurler; to howl down faire taire en poussant des huées || intr hurler; (said of wind) mugir

howler ['haulər] s hurleur m; (coll) grosse gaffe f, bourde f, bévue f

hoyden ['hɔıdən] s petite coquine f

H.P. or **hp** *abbr* (**horsepower**) CV
hub [hʌb] *s* moyeu *m*; (fig) centre *m*
hubbub ['hʌbəb] *s* vacarme *m*, tumulte *m*
hub'cap' *s* enjoliveur *m*, chapeau *m* de roue
huckster ['hʌkstər] *s* (*peddler*) camelot *m*; (*adman*) publicitaire *mf*
huddle ['hʌdəl] *s* (coll) conférence *f* secrète; **to go into a huddle** (coll) entrer en conclave ‖ *intr* s'entasser, se presser
hue [hju] *s* teinte *f*, nuance *f*
hue' and cry' *s* clameur *f* de haro; **with hue and cry** à cor et à cri
huff [hʌf] *s* accès *m* de colère; **in a huff** vexé, offensé
hug [hʌg] *s* étreinte *f* ‖ *v* (*pret & pp* **hugged**; *ger* **hugging**) *tr* étreindre; (*e.g., the coast*) serrer; (*e.g., the wall*) raser ‖ *intr* s'étreindre
huge [hjudʒ] *adj* énorme, immense
huh [hʌ] *interj* hein!, hé!
hulk [hʌlk] *s* (*body of an old ship*) carcasse *f*; (*old ship used as warehouse, prison, etc.*) ponton *m*; (*heavy, unwieldy person*) mastodonte *m*
hull [hʌl] *s* (*of certain vegetables*) cosse *f*; (*of nuts*) écale *f*; (*of ship or hydroplane*) coque *f* ‖ *tr* (*e.g., peas*) écosser; (*e.g., almonds*) écaler
hullabaloo ['hʌləbə‚lu], [‚hʌləbə'lu] *s* (coll) boucan *m*, brouhaha *m*
hum [hʌm] *s* (*e.g., of bee*) bourdonnement *m*; (*e.g., of motor*) vrombissement *m*; (*of singer*) fredonnement *m* ‖ *v* (*pret & pp* **hummed**; *ger* **humming**) *tr* (*a melody*) fredonner, chantonner ‖ *intr* (*said of bee*) bourdonner; (*said of machine*) vrombir; (*said of singer*) fredonner, chantonner; (*to be active*) (coll) aller rondement ‖ *interj* hum!
human ['hjumən] *adj* humain
hu'man be'ing *s* être *m* humain
humane [hju'men] *adj* humain, compatissant
humanist ['hjumənɪst] *adj & s* humaniste *m*
humanitarian [hju‚mænɪ'terɪ‚ən] *adj & s* humanitaire *mf*
humani·ty [hju'mænɪti] *s* (*pl* **-ties**) humanité *f*; **humanities** (*Greek and Latin classics*) humanités classiques; (*belles-lettres*) humanités modernes
hu'man·kind' *s* genre *m* humain
humble ['hʌmbəl], ['ʌmbəl] *adj* humble ‖ *tr* humilier; **to humble oneself** s'humilier
hum'ble pie' *s*—**to eat humble pie** faire amende honorable, s'humilier
hum'bug' *s* blague *f*; (*person*) imposteur *m* ‖ *v* (*pret & pp* **-bugged**; *ger* **-bugging**) *tr* mystifier
hum'drum' *adj* monotone, banal
humer·us ['hjumərəs] *s* (*pl* **-i** [‚aɪ]) humérus *m*
humid ['hjumɪd] *adj* humide, moite
humidifier [hju'mɪdɪ‚faɪ·ər] *s* humidificateur *m*
humidi·fy [hju'mɪdɪ‚faɪ] *v* (*pret & pp* **-fied**) *tr* humidifier

humidity [hju'mɪdɪti] *s* humidité *f*
humiliate [hju'mɪlɪ‚et] *tr* humilier
humiliating [hju'mɪlɪ‚etɪŋ] *adj* humiliant
humili·ty [hju'mɪlɪti] *s* (*pl* **-ties**) humilité *f*
hum'ming·bird' *s* oiseau-mouche *m*, colibri *m*
humor ['hjumər], ['jumər] *s* (*comic quality*) humour *m*; (*frame of mind; fluid*) humeur *f*; **out of humor** maussade, grognon; **to be in the humor to** être d'humeur à ‖ *tr* ménager, satisfaire; (*s.o.'s fancies*) se plier à, accéder à
humorist ['hjumərɪst], ['jumərɪst] *s* humoriste *mf*, comique *mf*
humorous ['hjumərəs], ['jumərəs] *adj* humoristique; (*writer*) humoriste
hump [hʌmp] *s* bosse *f*
hump'back' *s* bossu *m*; (*whale*) mégaptère *m*
humus ['hjuməs] *s* humus *m*
hunch [hʌntʃ] *s* bosse *f*; (*premonition*) (coll) pressentiment *m* ‖ *tr* arrondir, voûter ‖ *intr* s'accroupir
hunch'back' *s* bossu *m*
hundred ['hʌndrəd] *adj* cent ‖ *s* cent *m*, centaine *f*; **about a hundred** une centaine; **a hundred or one hundred** cent; une centaine; **by the hundreds** par centaines
hun'dred·fold' *adj & s* centuple *m*; **to increase a hundredfold** centupler ‖ *adv* au centuple
hundredth ['hʌndrədθ] *adj, pron, & s* centième *m*
hun'dred·weight' *s* quintal *m*
Hungarian [hʌŋ'gerɪ·ən] *adj* hongrois ‖ *s* (*language*) hongrois *m*; (*person*) Hongrois *m*
Hungary ['hʌŋgəri] *s* Hongrie *f*; **la Hongrie**
hunger ['hʌŋgər] *s* faim *f* ‖ *intr* avoir faim; **to hunger for** être affamé de
hun'ger march' *s* marche *f* de la faim
hun'ger strike' *s* grève *f* de la faim
hun·gry ['hʌŋgri] *adj* (*comp* **-grier**; *super* **-griest**) affamé; **to be hungry** avoir faim
hunk [hʌŋk] *s* gros morceau *m*
hunt [hʌnt] *s* (*act of hunting*) chasse *f*; (*hunting party*) équipage *m* de chasse; **on the hunt for** à la recherche de ‖ *tr* chasser; (*to seek, look for*) chercher; **to hunt down** donner la chasse à, traquer; **to hunt out** faire la chasse à ‖ *intr* chasser; (*with dogs*) chasser à courre; **to go hunting** aller à la chasse; **to hunt for** chercher; **to take hunting** emmener à la chasse
hunter ['hʌntər] *s* chasseur *m*
hunting ['hʌntɪŋ] *adj* de chasse ‖ *s* chasse *f*
hunt'ing dog' *s* chien *m* de chasse
hunt'ing ground' *s* terrain *m* de chasse, chasse *f*
hunt'ing horn' *s* cor *m* de chasse
hunt'ing jack'et *s* paletot *m* de chasse
hunt'ing knife' *s* couteau *m* de chasse

hunt′ing li′cense s permis m de chasse
hunt′ing lodge′ s pavillon m de chasse
hunt′ing sea′son s saison f de la chasse
huntress [ˈhʌntrɪs] s chasseuse f
hunts′man s (pl -men) chasseur m
hurdle [ˈhʌrdəl] s (hedge over which horses jump) haie f; (wooden frame over which runners jump) barrière f; (fig) obstacle m; **hurdles** course f d'obstacles || tr sauter
hur′dle race′ s course f d'obstacles; (turf) course de haies
hurdy-gur·dy [ˈhʌrdiˌgɑrdi] s (pl -dies) orgue m de Barbarie
hurl [hʌrl] s lancée f || tr lancer; **to hurl back** repousser, refouler
hurrah [hʌˈrɑ] or **hurray** [huˈre] s hourra m || interj hourra!; **hurrah for . . . !** vive . . . !
hurricane [ˈhʌriˌken] s ouragan m, hurricane m
hurried [ˈhʌrid] adj pressé, précipité; (hasty) hâtif, fait à la hâte
hur·ry [ˈhʌri] s (pl -ries) hâte f; **to be in a hurry** être pressé || v (pret & pp -ried) tr hâter, presser || intr se hâter, se presser; **to hurry after** courir après; **to hurry away** s'en aller bien vite; **to hurry back** revenir vite; **to hurry over** venir vite; **to hurry up** se dépêcher
hurt [hʌrt] adj blessé || s blessure f; (pain) douleur f || v (pret & pp hurt) tr faire mal à || intr faire mal, e.g., **does that hurt?** ça fait mal?; avoir mal, e.g., **my head hurts** j'ai mal à la tête
hurtful [ˈhʌrtfəl] adj nuisible
hurtle [ˈhʌrtəl] intr se précipiter
husband [ˈhʌzbənd] s mari m, époux m || tr ménager, économiser
hus′band-man s (pl -men) cultivateur m
husbandry [ˈhʌzbəndri] s agriculture f; (raising of livestock) élevage m
hush [hʌ/] s silence m, calme m || tr faire taire; **to hush up** (e.g., a scandal) étouffer || intr se taire || interj chut!
hushaby [ˈhʌ/əˌbaɪ] interj fais dodo!
hush′-hush′ adj très secret
hush′ mon′ey s prix m du silence
husk [hʌsk] s peau f; (of certain vegetables) cosse f, gousse f; (of nuts) écale f; (of corn) enveloppe f; (of oats) balle f; (of onion) pelure f || tr (grain) vanner; (vegetables) éplucher; (peas) écosser; (nuts) écaler
husk′ing bee′ s réunion f pour l'épluchage du maïs
husk·y [ˈhʌski] adj (comp -ier; super -iest) costaud; (voice) enroué || s (pl -ies) (dog) chien m esquimau
hus·sy [ˈhʌzi], [ˈhʌsi] s (pl -sies) (coll) garce f; (coll) coquine f
hustle [ˈhʌsəl] s (coll) bousculade f, énergie f, allant m || tr pousser, bousculer || intr se dépêcher, se presser; (to work hard) (coll) se démener, s'activer
hustler [ˈhʌslər] s (go-getter) homme m d'action; (swindler) (slang) filou

m; (streetwalker) (slang) traînée f, grue f
hut [hʌt] s hutte f, cabane f; (mil) baraque f
hutch [hʌt/] s (for rabbits) clapier m; (used by baker) huche f, pétrin m
hyacinth [ˈhaɪəsɪnθ] s (stone) hyacinthe f; (flower) jacinthe f
hybrid [ˈhaɪbrɪd] adj & s hybride m
hy-dra [ˈhaɪdrə] s (pl -dras or -drae [dri]) hydre f
hydrant [ˈhaɪdrənt] s prise f d'eau; (faucet) robinet m; (fire hydrant) bouche f d'incendie
hydrate [ˈhaɪdret] s hydrate m || tr hydrater || intr s'hydrater
hydraulic [haɪˈdrɔlɪk] adj hydraulique || **hydraulics** s hydraulique f
hydrau′lic ram′ s bélier m hydraulique
hydrocarbon [ˌhaɪdrəˈkɑrbən] s hydrocarbure m
hy′drochlo′ric ac′id [ˌhaɪdrəˈklorɪk] s acide m chlorhydrique
hydroelectric [ˌhaɪdro-ɪˈlektrɪk] adj hydro-électrique
hydrofoil [ˈhaɪdrəˌfoɪl] s hydrofoil m
hydrogen [ˈhaɪdrədʒən] s hydrogène m
hy′drogen bomb′ s bombe f à hydrogène
hy′drogen perox′ide s eau f oxygénée
hy′drogen sul′fide s hydrogène m sulfuré
hydrometer [haɪˈdrɑmɪtər] s aréomètre m, hydromètre m
hydrophobia [ˌhaɪdrəˈfobɪ-ə] s hydrophobie f
hydroplane [ˈhaɪdrəˌplen] s hydravion m
hydroxide [haɪˈdrɑksaɪd] s hydroxyde m
hyena [haɪˈinə] s hyène f
hygiene [ˈhaɪdʒin], [ˈhaɪdʒɪˌin] s hygiène f
hygienic [ˌhaɪdʒɪˈenɪk], [haɪˈdʒinɪk] adj hygiénique
hymn [hɪm] s hymne m; (eccl) hymne f, cantique m
hymnal [ˈhɪmnəl] s livre m d'hymnes
hyperacidity [ˌhaɪpərəˈsɪdɪti] s hyperacidité f
hyperbola [haɪˈpʌrbələ] s hyperbole f
hyperbole [haɪˈpʌrbəli] s hyperbole f
hypersensitive [ˌhaɪpərˈsensɪtɪv] adj hypersensible, hypersensitif
hypertension [ˌhaɪpərˈten/ən] s hypertension f
hyphen [ˈhaɪfən] s trait m d'union
hyphenate [ˈhaɪfəˌnet] tr joindre avec un trait d'union
hypno·sis [hɪpˈnosɪs] s (pl -ses [siz]) hypnose f
hypnotic [hɪpˈnɑtɪk] adj & s hypnotique m
hypnotism [ˈhɪpnəˌtɪzəm] s hypnotisme m
hypnotist [ˈhɪpnətɪst] s hypnotiseur m
hypnotize [ˈhɪpnəˌtaɪz] tr hypnotiser
hypochondriac [ˌhaɪpəˈkɑndrɪˌæk], [ˌhɪpəˈkɑndrɪˌæk] adj & s hypocondriaque mf

hypocri·sy [hɪ'pɑkrəsɪ] *s* (*pl* **-sies**) hypocrisie *f*

hypocrite ['hɪpəkrɪt] *s* hypocrite *mf*

hypocritical [ˌhɪpə'krɪtɪkəl] *adj* hypocrite

hypodermic [ˌhaɪpə'dʌrmɪk] *adj* hypodermique

hyposulfite [ˌhaɪpə'sʌlfaɪt] *s* hyposulfite *m*

hypotenuse [haɪ'pɑtɪˌn(j)us] *s* hypoténuse *f*

hypothe·sis [haɪ'pɑθɪsɪs] *s* (*pl* **-ses** [ˌsiz]) hypothèse *f*

hypothetic(al) [ˌhaɪpə'θetɪk(əl)] *adj* hypothétique

hysteria [hɪs'tɪrɪ·ə] *s* agitation *f*, frénésie *f*; (pathol) hystérie *f*

hysteric [hɪs'terɪk] *adj* hystérique || **hysterics** *spl* crise *f* de nerfs, crise de larmes, fou rire *m*

hysterical [hɪs'terɪkəl] *adj* hystérique

I

I, i [aɪ] *s* IXe lettre de l'alphabet

I *pron* je §87; moi §85

iambic [aɪ'æmbɪk] *adj* ïambique

Iberian [aɪ'bɪrɪ·ən] *adj* ibérien, ibérique || *s* Ibérien *m*

ibex ['aɪbeks] *s* (*pl* **ibexes** or **ibices** ['ɪbɪˌsiz]) bouquetin *m*

ice [aɪs] *s* glace *f*; **to break the ice** (fig) rompre la glace; **to cut no ice** (coll) ne rien casser, ne pas prendre; **to skate on thin ice** (coll) s'engager sur un terrain dangereux || *tr* glacer; (e.g., champagne) frapper; (e.g., melon) rafraîchir || *intr* geler; **to ice up** (said of windshield, airplane wings, etc.) se givrer

ice/ age/ *s* époque *f* glaciaire

ice/ bag/ *s* sac *m* à glace

ice/ bank/ *s* banquise *f*

iceberg ['aɪsˌbʌrg] *s* banquise *f*, iceberg *m*; (person) (coll) glaçon *m*

ice/boat/ *s* (*icebreaker*) brise-glace *m*; (*for sport*) bateau *m* à patins

icebound ['aɪsˌbaʊnd] *adj* pris dans les glaces

ice/box/ *s* glacière *f*

ice/break/er *s* brise-glace *m*

ice/cap/ *s* calotte *f* glaciaire

ice/ cream/ *s* glace *f*

ice/-cream/ cone/ *s* cornet *m* de glace, glace *f* en cornet

ice/-cream/ freez/er *s* sorbetière *f*

ice/ cube/ *s* glaçon *m*

ice/-cube/ tray/ *s* bac *m* à glaçons

iced/ tea/ *s* thé *m* glacé

ice/ floe/ *s* banquise *f*

ice/ hock/ey *s* hockey *m* sur glace

ice/ jam/ *s* embâcle *m*

Iceland ['aɪslənd] *s* Islande *f*; l'Islande

Icelander ['aɪsˌləndər], ['aɪslændər] *s* Islandais *m*

Icelandic [aɪs'lændɪk] *adj & s* islandais *m*

ice/man/ *s* (*pl* **-men/**) glacier *m*

ice/ pack/ *s* (*pack ice*) embâcle *m*; (med) vessie *f* de glace

ice/ pail/ *s* seau *m* à glace

ice/ pick/ *s* poinçon *m* à glace; (of mountain climber) piolet *m*

ice/ skate/ *s* patin *m* à glace

ice/ wa/ter *s* eau *f* glacée *f*

ichthyology [ˌɪkθɪ'ɑlədʒɪ] *s* ichtyologie *f*

icicle ['aɪsɪkəl] *s* glaçon *m*, chandelle *f* de glace

icing ['aɪsɪŋ] *s* (on cake) glaçage *m*; (aer) givrage *m*

icon ['aɪkɑn] *s* icône *f*

iconoclast [aɪ'kɑnəˌklæst] *s* iconoclaste *mf*

iconoclastic [aɪˌkɑnə'klæstɪk] *adj* iconoclaste

iconoscope [aɪ'kɑnəˌskop] *s* (trademark) iconoscope *m*

icy ['aɪsɪ] *adj* (comp **icier**; super **iciest**) glacé; (slippery) glissant; (fig) froid, glacial

idea [aɪ'di·ə] *s* idée *f*; **the very idea!** par exemple!

ideal [aɪ'di·əl] *adj & s* idéal *m*

idealist [aɪ'di·əlɪst] *adj & s* idéaliste *mf*

idealistic [aɪˌdi·ə'lɪstɪk] *adj* idéaliste

idealize [aɪ'di·əˌlaɪz] *tr* idéaliser

identic(al) [aɪ'dentɪk(əl)] *adj* identique

identification [aɪˌdentɪfɪ'keʃən] *s* identification *f*

identifica/tion card/ *s* carte *f* d'identité

identifica/tion tag/ *s* plaque *f* d'identité

identi·fy [aɪ'dentɪˌfaɪ] *v* (pret & pp **-fied**) *tr* identifier

identi·ty [aɪ'dentɪtɪ] *s* (*pl* **-ties**) identité *f*

ideolo·gy [ˌaɪdɪ'ɑlədʒɪ], [ˌɪdɪ'ɑlədʒɪ] *s* (*pl* **-gies**) idéologie *fpl*

ides [aɪdz] *spl* ides *fpl*

idio·cy ['ɪdɪ·əsɪ] *s* (*pl* **-cies**) idiotie *f*

idiom ['ɪdɪəm] *s* (phrase, expression) idiotisme *m*; (language, style) idiome *m*

idiomatic [ˌɪdɪ·ə'mætɪk] *adj* idiomatique

idiosyncra·sy [ˌɪdɪ·ə'sɪnkrəsɪ] *s* (*pl* **-sies**) idiosyncrasie *f*

idiot ['ɪdɪ·ət] *s* idiot *m*

idiotic [ˌɪdɪ'ɑtɪk] *adj* idiot

idle ['aɪdəl] *adj* oisif, désœuvré; (futile) oiseux; **to run idle** marcher au ralenti || *tr*—**to idle away** (time) passer à ne rien faire || *intr* fainéanter; (mach) tourner au ralenti

idleness ['aɪdəlnɪs] *s* oisiveté *f*

idler ['aɪdlər] *s* oisif *m*

idling ['aɪdlɪŋ] *s* (of motor) ralenti *m*

idol ['aɪdəl] s idole f

idola-try [aɪ'dɒlətrɪ] s (pl **-tries**) idolâtrie f

idolize ['aɪdə,laɪz] tr idolâtrer

idyll ['aɪdəl] s idylle f

idyllic [aɪ'dɪlɪk] adj idyllique

if [ɪf] s—**ifs and buts** des si et des mais || conj si; **even if** quand même; **if it is true** that si tant est que; **if not** sinon; **if so** dans ce cas, s'il en est ainsi

ignis fatuus ['ɪgnɪs'fætʃuːəs] s (pl **ignes fatui** ['ɪgniːz'fætʃuː,aɪ]) feu m follet

ignite [ɪg'naɪt] tr allumer || intr prendre feu

ignition [ɪg'nɪʃən] s ignition f; (aut) allumage m

igni'tion coil' s (aut) bobine f d'allumage

igni'tion switch' s (key) (aut) clé f de contact; (button) (aut) bouton m de contact

ignoble [ɪg'nobəl] adj ignoble

ignominious [,ɪgnə'mɪnɪ·əs] adj ignominieux

ignoramus [,ɪgnə'reməs] s ignorant m

ignorance ['ɪgnərəns] s ignorance f

ignorant ['ɪgnərənt] adj ignorant; **to be ignorant of** ignorer

ignore [ɪg'nor] tr ne pas tenir compte de, ne pas faire attention à; (a suggestion) passer outre à; (to snub) faire semblant de ne pas voir, ignorer à dessein

ilk [ɪlk] s espèce f; **of that ilk** de cet acabit

ill [ɪl] adj (comp **worse** [wʌrs]; super **worst** [wʌrst]) malade, souffrant || adv mal; **to take ill** prendre en mauvaise part; (to get sick) tomber malade

ill'-advised' adj (person) malavisé; (action) peu judicieux

ill-bred ['ɪl'brɛd] adj mal élevé

ill'-consid'ered adj peu réfléchi, hâtif

ill'-disposed' adj mal disposé, malintentionné

illegal [ɪ'ligəl] adj illégal

illegible [ɪ'lɛdʒɪbəl] adj illisible

illegitimate [,ɪlɪ'dʒɪtɪmɪt] adj illégitime

ill'-famed' adj mal famé

ill'-fat'ed adj malheureux, infortuné

ill-gotten ['ɪl'gɑtən] adj mal acquis

ill' health' s mauvaise santé f

ill'-hu'mored adj de mauvaise humeur, maussade

illicit [ɪ'lɪsɪt] adj illicite

illitera-cy [ɪ'lɪtərəsɪ] s (pl **-cies**) ignorance f; analphabétisme m

illiterate [ɪ'lɪtərɪt] adj (uneducated) ignorant, illettré; (unable to read or write) analphabète || s analphabète mf

ill'-man'nered adj malappris, mal élevé

ill'-na'tured adj désagréable, méchant

illness ['ɪlnɪs] s maladie f

illogical [ɪ'lɑdʒɪkəl] adj illogique

ill-spent ['ɪl'spɛnt] adj gaspillé

ill'-starred' adj néfaste, de mauvais augure

ill'-tem'pered adj désagréable, de mauvais caractère

ill'-timed' adj intempestif, mal à propos

ill'-treat' tr maltraiter, rudoyer

illuminate [ɪ'lumɪ,net] tr illuminer; (a manuscript) enluminer

illu'minating gas' s gaz m d'éclairage

illumination [ɪ'lumɪ'neʃən] s illumination f; (in manuscript) enluminure f

illusion [ɪ'luʒən] s illusion f

illusive [ɪ'lusɪv] adj illusoire, trompeur

illusory [ɪ'lusərɪ] adj illusoire

illustrate ['ɪləs,tret], [ɪ'lʌstret] tr illustrer

illustration [,ɪləs'treʃən] s illustration f; (explanation) explication f, éclaircissement m

illustrative [ɪ'lʌstrətɪv] adj explicatif, éclairant

illustrator ['ɪləs,tretər] s illustrateur m, dessinateur m

illustrious [ɪ'lʌstrɪ·əs] adj illustre

ill' will' s rancune f

image ['ɪmɪdʒ] s image f

image-ry ['ɪmɪdʒrɪ], ['ɪmɪdʒərɪ] s (pl **-ries**) images fpl

imaginary [ɪ'mædʒɪ,nɛrɪ] adj imaginaire

imagination [ɪ,mædʒɪ'neʃən] s imagination f

imagine [ɪ'mædʒɪn] tr imaginer, s'imaginer || intr imaginer; **imagine!** figurez-vous!

imbecile ['ɪmbɪsɪl] adj & s imbécile mf

imbecili-ty [,ɪmbɪ'sɪlɪtɪ] s (pl **-ties**) imbécillité f

imbibe [ɪm'baɪb] tr absorber || intr boire, lever le coude

imbue [ɪm'bju] tr imprégner, pénétrer; **imbued with** imbu de

imitate ['ɪmɪ,tet] tr imiter

imitation [,ɪmɪ'teʃən] adj d'imitation || s imitation f

imitator ['ɪmɪ,tetər] s imitateur m

immaculate [ɪ'mækjəlɪt] adj immaculé

immaterial [,ɪmə'tɪrɪ·əl] adj immatériel; (pointless) sans conséquence; **it's immaterial to me** cela m'est égal

immature [,ɪmə'tjur] adj pas mûr, peu mûr; pas adulte

immeasurable [ɪ'mɛʒərəbəl] adj immensurable

immediacy [ɪ'midɪ·əsɪ] s caractère m immédiat, imminence f

immediate [ɪ'midɪ·ɪt] adj immédiat

immediately [ɪ'midɪ·ɪtlɪ] adv immédiatement

immemorial [,ɪmɪ'morɪ·əl] adj immémorial

immense [ɪ'mɛns] adj immense

immerse [ɪ'mʌrs] tr immerger, plonger

immersion [ɪ'mʌrʃən], [ɪ'mʌrʒən] s immersion f

immigrant ['ɪmɪgrənt] adj & s immigrant m

immigrate ['ɪmɪ,gret] intr immigrer

immigration [,ɪmɪ'greʃən] s immigration f

imminent ['ɪmɪnənt] adj imminent, très prochain

immobile [ɪ'mobɪl], [ɪ'mobɪl] *adj* immobile

immobilize [ɪ'mobɪ,laɪz] *tr* immobiliser

immoderate [ɪ'madərɪt] *adj* immodéré

immodest [ɪ'madɪst] *adj* impudique

immoral [ɪ'marəl], [ɪ'mɔrəl] *adj* immoral

immortal [ɪ'mɔrtəl] *adj & s* immortel *m*

immortalize [ɪ'mɔrtə,laɪz] *tr* immortaliser

immune [ɪ'mjun] *adj* dispensé, exempt; (med) immunisé

immunize ['ɪmjə,naɪz], [ɪ'mjunaɪz] *tr* immuniser

imp [ɪmp] *s* suppôt *m* du diable; (*child*) diablotin *m*, polisson *m*

impact ['ɪmpækt] *s* impact *m*

impair [ɪm'per] *tr* endommager, affaiblir; (*health, digestion*) délabrer

impan·el [ɪm'pænəl] *v* (*pret & pp* -eled or -elled; *ger* -eling or -elling) *tr* appeler à faire partie de; (*a jury*) dresser la liste de

impart [ɪm'part] *tr* imprimer, communiquer; (*to make known*) communiquer

impartial [ɪm'parʃəl] *adj* impartial

impassable [ɪm'pæsəbəl], [ɪm'pasəbəl] *adj* (*road*) impraticable; (*mountain*) infranchissable

impassible [ɪm'pæsɪbəl] *adj* impassible

impassioned [ɪm'pæʃənd] *adj* passionné

impassive [ɪm'pæsɪv] *adj* insensible; (*look, face*) impassible, composé

impatience [ɪm'peʃəns] *s* impatience *f*

impatient [ɪm'peʃənt] *adj* impatient

impeach [ɪm'pitʃ] *tr* accuser; (*s.o.'s honor, veracity*) attaquer

impeachment [ɪm'pitʃmənt] *s* accusation *f*; (*of honor, veracity*) attaque *f*

impeccable [ɪm'pekəbəl] *adj* impeccable

impecunious [,ɪmpɪ'kjunɪ·əs] *adj* besogneux, impécunieux

impede [ɪm'pid] *tr* entraver, empêcher

impediment [ɪm'pedɪmənt] *s* obstacle *m*, empêchement *m*

im·pel [ɪm'pel] *v* (*pret & pp* -pelled; *ger* -pelling) *tr* pousser, forcer

impending [ɪm'pendɪŋ] *adj* imminent

impenetrable [ɪm'penətrəbəl] *adj* impénétrable

impenitent [ɪm'penɪtənt] *adj* impénitent *m*

imperative [ɪm'perɪtɪv] *adj & s* impératif *m*

imperceptible [,ɪmpər'septɪbəl] *adj* imperceptible

imperfect [ɪm'pʌrfɪkt] *adj & s* imparfait *m*

imperfection [,ɪmpər'fek/ən] *s* imperfection *f*

imperial [ɪm'pɪrɪ·əl] *adj* impérial

imperialist [ɪm'pɪrɪ·əlɪst] *adj & s* impérialiste *mf*

imper·il [ɪm'perɪl] *v* (*pret & pp* -iled or -illed; *ger* -iling or -illing) *tr* mettre en péril, exposer au danger

imperious [ɪm'pɪrɪ·əs] *adj* impérieux

imperishable [ɪm'perɪ/əbəl] *adj* impérissable

impersonal [ɪm'pʌrsənəl] *adj* impersonnel

impersonate [ɪm'pʌrsə,net] *tr* contrefaire, singer; jouer le rôle de

impertinent [ɪm'pʌrtɪnənt] *adj* impertinent

impetuous [ɪm'pet/u·əs] *adj* impétueux

impetus ['ɪmpɪtəs] *s* impulsion *f*; (mech) force *f* impulsive; (fig) élan *m*

impie·ty [ɪm'paɪ·əti] *s* (*pl* -ties) impiété *f*

impinge [ɪm'pɪndʒ] *intr*—to impinge on or upon empiéter sur; (*to violate*) enfreindre

impious ['ɪmpɪ·əs] *adj* impie

impish ['ɪmpɪʃ] *adj* espiègle

implant [ɪm'plænt] *tr* implanter

implement ['ɪmplɪmənt] *s* outil *m*, ustensile *m* || *tr* mettre en œuvre, réaliser; (*to provide with implements*) outiller

implicate ['ɪmplɪ,ket] *tr* impliquer

implicit [ɪm'plɪsɪt] *adj* implicite

implied [ɪm'plaɪd] *adj* implicite, sousentendu

implore [ɪm'plor] *tr* implorer, supplier, solliciter

im·ply [ɪm'plaɪ] *v* (*pret & pp* -plied) *tr* impliquer

impolite [,ɪmpə'laɪt] *adj* impoli

import ['ɪmport] *s* importance *f*; (*meaning*) sens *m*, signification *f*; (*extent*) portée *f*; (com) article *m* d'importation; imports importations *fpl* || [ɪm'port], ['ɪmport] *tr* importer; (*to mean*) signifier, vouloir dire

importance [ɪm'portəns] *s* importance *f*

important [ɪm'portənt] *adj* important

importer [ɪm'portər] *s* importateur *m*

importune [,ɪmpor't(j)un] *tr* importuner, harceler

impose [ɪm'poz] *tr* imposer || *intr*—to impose on or upon en imposer à, abuser de

imposing [ɪm'pozɪŋ] *adj* imposant

imposition [,ɪmpə'zɪ/ən] *s* (*laying on of a burden or obligation*) imposition *f*; (*rudeness, taking unfair advantage*) abus *m*

impossible [ɪm'pasɪbəl] *adj* impossible

impostor [ɪm'pastər] *s* imposteur *m*

imposture [ɪm'pastʃər] *s* imposture *f*

impotence [ɪm'potəns] *s* impuissance *f*

impotent ['ɪmpotənt] *adj* impuissant

impound [ɪm'paund] *tr* confisquer, saisir; (*a dog, an auto, etc.*) mettre en fourrière

impoverish [ɪm'pavərɪ/] *tr* appauvrir

impracticable [ɪm'præktɪkəbəl] *adj* impraticable, inexécutable

impractical [ɪm'præktɪkəl] *adj* peu pratique; (*plan*) impraticable

impregnable [ɪm'pregnəbəl] *adj* imprenable, inexpugnable

impregnate [ɪm'pregnet] *tr* imprégner; (*to make pregnant*) féconder

impresari·o [,ɪmprɪ'sarɪ,o] *s* (*pl* -os) imprésario *m*

impress [ɪm'pres] *tr* (*to have an effec*

on the mind or emotions of) impressionner; (to mark by using pressure)
imprimer; (on the memory) graver;
(mil) enrôler de force; **to impress s.o.
with** pénétrer qn de

impression [ɪm'preʃən] s impression f

impressive [ɪm'presɪv] adj impressionnant

imprint ['ɪmprɪnt] s empreinte f; (typ)
rubrique f, griffe f || [ɪm'prɪnt] tr
imprimer

imprison [ɪm'prɪzən] tr emprisonner

imprisonment [ɪm'prɪzənmənt] s emprisonnement m

improbable [ɪm'prɑbəbəl] adj improbable

impromptu [ɪm'prɑmpt(j)u] adj & adv
impromptu || s (mus) impromptu m

impromp'tu speech' s improvisation f,
discours m improvisé

improper [ɪm'prɑpər] adj (not the
right) impropre; (contrary to good
taste or decency) inconvenant

improve [ɪm'pruv] tr améliorer, per-
fectionner || intr s'améliorer, se per-
fectionner

improvement [ɪm'pruvmənt] s amélioration f, perfectionnement m

improvident [ɪm'prɑvɪdənt] adj imprévoyant

improvise ['ɪmprə,vaɪz] tr & intr improviser

imprudent [ɪm'prudənt] adj imprudent

impudent ['ɪmpjədənt] adj impudent,
effronté

impugn [ɪm'pjun] tr contester, mettre
en doute

impulse ['ɪmpʌls] s impulsion f

impulsive [ɪm'pʌlsɪv] adj impulsif

impunity [ɪm'pjunɪti] s impunité f

impure [ɪm'pjur] adj impur

impurity [ɪm'pjurɪti] s (pl -ties) impureté f

impute [ɪm'pjut] tr imputer

in [ɪn] adv en dedans, à l'intérieur; (at
home) à la maison, chez soi; (pol) au
pouvoir; **all in** (tired) (coll) éreinté;
in here ici, par ici; **in there** là-dedans,
là || prep dans; en; (inside) en de-
dans de, à l'intérieur de; (in ratios)
sur, e.g., **one in a hundred** un sur
cent; **in that** du fait que || s (coll)
entrée f, e.g., **to have an in with**
avoir ses entrées chez

inability [,ɪnə'bɪlɪti] s incapacité f,
impuissance f

inaccessible [,ɪnæk'sesɪbəl] adj inaccessible

inaccuracy [ɪn'ækjərəsi] s (pl -cies)
inexactitude f, infidélité f

inaccurate [ɪn'ækjərɪt] adj inexact, infidèle

inaction [ɪn'ækʃən] s inaction f

inactive [ɪn'æktɪv] adj inactif

inactivity [,ɪnæk'tɪvɪti] s inactivité f

inadequate [ɪn'ædɪkwɪt] adj insuffisant

inadvertent [,ɪnəd'vʌrtənt] adj distrait,
étourdi; commis par inadvertance

inadvisable [,ɪnəd'vaɪzəbəl] adj imprudent, peu sage

inane [ɪn'en] adj inepte, absurde

inanimate [ɪn'ænɪmɪt] adj inanimé

inappropriate [,ɪnə'proprɪ·ɪt] adj inap-
proprié; (word) impropre

inarticulate [,ɪnɑr'tɪkjəlɪt] adj inarti-
culé; (person) muet, incapable de
s'exprimer

inartistic [,ɪnɑr'tɪstɪk] adj peu artistique; (person) peu artiste

inasmuch as [,ɪnəz'mʌtʃ ,æz] conj attendu que, vu que

inattentive [,ɪnə'tentɪv] adj inattentif

inaudible [ɪn'ɔdɪbəl] adj inaudible

inaugural [ɪn'ɔgjərəl] adj inaugural || s
discours m d'inauguration

inaugurate [ɪn'ɔgjə,ret] tr inaugurer

inauguration [ɪn,ɔgjə'reʃən] s inauguration f; (investiture) installation f

inborn ['ɪn,bɔrn] adj inné, infus

in'breed'ing s croisement m consanguin

Inc. abbr (Incorporated) S.A.

incandescent [,ɪnkən'desənt] adj incandescent

incapable [ɪn'kepəbəl] adj incapable

incapacitate [,ɪnkə'pæsɪ,tet] tr rendre
incapable

incarcerate [ɪn'kɑrsə,ret] tr incarcérer

incarnate [ɪn'kɑrnɪt], [ɪn'kɑrnet] adj
incarné || [ɪn'kɑrnet] tr incarner

incarnation [,ɪnkɑr'neʃən] s incarnation f

incendiary [ɪn'sendɪ,erɪ] adj incen-
diaire || s (pl -ies) incendiaire mf

incense ['ɪnsens] s encens m || tr (to
burn incense before) encenser ||
[ɪn'sens] tr exaspérer, irriter

in'cense burn'er s brûle-parfum m

incentive [ɪn'sentɪv] adj & s stimulant
m

inception [ɪn'sepʃən] s début m

incessant [ɪn'sesənt] adj incessant

incest ['ɪnsest] s inceste m

incestuous [ɪn'sestʃʊ·əs] adj incestueux

inch [ɪntʃ] s pouce m; **by inches** peu à
peu, petit à petit; **not to give way an
inch** ne pas reculer d'une semelle;
within an inch of à deux doigts de ||
intr—**to inch along** se déplacer im-
perceptiblement; **to inch forward**
avancer peu à peu

incidence ['ɪnsɪdəns] s incidence f;
(range of occurrence) portée f

incident ['ɪnsɪdənt] adj & s incident m

incidental [,ɪnsɪ'dentəl] adj accidentel,
fortuit; (expenses) accessoire || inci-
dentals s faux frais mpl

incidentally [,ɪnsɪ'dentəli] adv incidemment, à propos

incinerate [ɪn'sɪnə,ret] tr incinérer

incipient [ɪn'sɪpɪ·ənt] adj naissant

incision [ɪn'sɪʒən] s incision f

incisive [ɪn'saɪsɪv] adj incisif

incisor [ɪn'saɪzər] s incisive f

incite [ɪn'saɪt] tr inciter

inclement [ɪn'klemənt] adj inclément

inclination [,ɪnklɪ'neʃən] s inclination
f; (slope) inclinaison f

incline ['ɪnklaɪn], [ɪn'klaɪn] s incli-
naison f, pente f || [ɪn'klaɪn] tr incli-
ner || intr s'incliner

include [ɪn'klud] tr comprendre, comporter; (to contain) renfermer; (e.g.,
in a letter) inclure

including [ɪn'kludɪŋ] prep y compris;

up to and including page ten jusqu'à la page dix incluse

inclusive [ɪnˈkluːsɪv] *adj* global; (*including everything*) tout compris; **from Wednesday to Saturday inclusive** de mercredi à samedi inclus; **inclusive of . . .** qui comprend . . . || *adv* inclusivement

incognito [ɪnˈkɒɡnɪˌtoʊ] *adj & adv* incognito || *s* (*pl* -tos) incognito *m*

incoherent [ˌɪnkoʊˈhɪərənt] *adj* incohérent

incombustible [ˌɪnkəmˈbʌstɪbəl] *adj* incombustible

income [ˈɪnkʌm] *s* revenu *m*, revenus *mpl*; (*annual income*) rentes *fpl*

in′come tax′ *s* impôt *m* sur le revenu

in′come-tax return′ *s* déclaration *f* de revenus

in′com′ing *adj* entrant, rentrant; (*tide*) montant || *s* arrivée *f*

incomparable [ɪnˈkɒmpərəbəl] *adj* incomparable

incompatible [ˌɪnkəmˈpætɪbəl] *adj* incompatible

incompetent [ɪnˈkɒmpɪtənt] *adj & s* incompétent *m*, incapable *mf*

incomplete [ˌɪnkəmˈpliːt] *adj* incomplet

incomprehensible [ˌɪnkɒmprɪˈhensɪbəl] *adj* incompréhensible

inconceivable [ˌɪnkənˈsiːvəbəl] *adj* inconcevable

inconclusive [ˌɪnkənˈkluːsɪv] *adj* peu concluant, non concluant

incongruous [ɪnˈkɒŋɡruːəs] *adj* incongru, impropre; disparate

inconsequential [ɪnˌkɒnsɪˈkwenʃəl] *adj* sans importance

inconsiderate [ˌɪnkənˈsɪdərɪt] *adj* inconsidéré

inconsisten·cy [ˌɪnkənˈsɪstənsi] *s* (*pl* -cies) (*lack of coherence; instability*) inconsistance *f*; (*lack of logical connection or uniformity*) inconséquence *f*

inconsistent [ˌɪnkənˈsɪstənt] *adj* (*lacking coherence of parts; unstable*) inconsistant; (*not agreeing with itself or oneself*) inconséquent

inconspicuous [ˌɪnkənˈspɪkjuːəs] *adj* peu apparent; peu impressionnant

inconstant [ɪnˈkɒnstənt] *adj* inconstant

incontinent [ɪnˈkɒntɪnənt] *adj* incontinent

incontrovertible [ˌɪnkɒntrəˈvɜːtɪbəl] *adj* incontestable

inconvenience [ˌɪnkənˈviːnɪəns] *s* incommodité *f* || *tr* incommoder, gêner

inconvenient [ˌɪnkənˈviːnɪənt] *adj* incommode, gênant; (*time*) inopportun

incorporate [ɪnˈkɔːrpəˌreɪt] *tr* incorporer; (*com*) constituer en société anonyme || *intr* s'incorporer; (*com*) se constituer en société anonyme

incorporation [ɪnˌkɔːrpəˈreɪʃən] *s* incorporation *f*; (*of company*) constitution *f* en société anonyme; (*of town*) érection *f* en municipalité

incorrect [ˌɪnkəˈrekt] *adj* incorrect

increase [ˈɪnkriːs] *s* augmentation *f*; **on the increase** en voie d'accroissement || [ɪnˈkriːs] *tr & intr* augmenter

increasingly [ɪnˈkriːsɪŋli] *adv* de plus en plus

incredible [ɪnˈkredɪbəl] *adj* incroyable

incredulous [ɪnˈkredʒələs] *adj* incrédule

increment [ˈɪnkrɪmənt] *s* augmentation *f*

incriminate [ɪnˈkrɪmɪˌneɪt] *tr* incriminer

incrust [ɪnˈkrʌst] *tr* incruster

incubate [ˈɪnkjəˌbeɪt] *tr* incuber, couver || *intr* couver

incubator [ˈɪnkjəˌbeɪtər] *s* incubateur *m*

inculcate [ɪnˈkʌlkeɪt], [ˈɪnkʌlˌkeɪt] *tr* inculquer

incumben·cy [ɪnˈkʌmbənsi] *s* (*pl* -cies) charge *f*; période *f* d'exercice

incumbent [ɪnˈkʌmbənt] *adj*—**to be incumbent on** incomber (with *dat*) || *s* titulaire *mf*

incunabula [ˌɪnkjuˈnæbjələ] *spl* origines *fpl*; (*books*) incunables *mpl*

in·cur [ɪnˈkɜːr] *v* (*pret & pp* -curred; *ger* -curring) *tr* encourir; (*a debt*) contracter

incurable [ɪnˈkjʊərəbəl] *adj & s* incurable *mf*, inguérissable *mf*

incursion [ɪnˈkɜːʒən], [ɪnˈkɜːʃən] *s* incursion *f*

indebted [ɪnˈdetɪd] *adj* endetté; **indebted to s.o. for** redevable à qn de

indecen·cy [ɪnˈdiːsənsi] *s* (*pl* -cies) indécence *f*, impudeur *f*

indecent [ɪnˈdiːsənt] *adj* indécent, impudique

inde′cent expo′sure *s* attentat *m* à la pudeur

indecisive [ˌɪndɪˈsaɪsɪv] *adj* indécis

indeclinable [ˌɪndɪˈklaɪnəbəl] *adj* (*gram*) indéclinable

indeed [ɪnˈdiːd] *adv* en effet; (*truly*) en vérité || *interj* vraiment!

indefatigable [ˌɪndɪˈfætɪɡəbəl] *adj* infatigable

indefensible [ˌɪndɪˈfensɪbəl] *adj* indéfendable

indefinable [ˌɪndɪˈfaɪnəbəl] *adj* indéfinissable

indefinite [ɪnˈdefɪnɪt] *adj* indéfini

indelible [ɪnˈdelɪbəl] *adj* indélébile

indelicate [ɪnˈdelɪkɪt] *adj* indélicat

indemnification [ɪnˌdemnɪfɪˈkeɪʃən] *s* indemnisation *f*

indemni·fy [ɪnˈdemnɪˌfaɪ] *v* (*pret & pp* -fied) *tr* indemniser

indemni·ty [ɪnˈdemnɪti] *s* (*pl* -ties) indemnité *f*

indent [ɪnˈdent] *tr* denteler; (*to recess*) renfoncer; (*typ*) mettre en alinéa, rentrer || *intr* (*typ*) faire un alinéa

indentation [ˌɪndenˈteɪʃən] *s* dentelure *f*; (*notch*) entaille *f*; (*recess*) renfoncement *m*; (*typ*) alinéa *m*

indented *adj* (*typ*) en alinéa

indenture [ɪnˈdentʃər] *s* contrat *m* d'apprentissage || *tr* mettre en apprentissage

independence [ˌɪndɪˈpendəns] *s* indépendance *f*

independen·cy [ˌɪndɪˈpendənsi] *s* (*pl* -cies) indépendance *f*; nation *f* indépendante

independent [ˌɪndɪˈpɛndənt] *adj & s* indépendant *m*

indescribable [ˌɪndɪˈskraɪbəbəl] *adj* indescriptible, indicible

indestructible [ˌɪndɪˈstrʌktɪbəl] *adj* indestructible

index [ˈɪndɛks] *s (pl* **indexes** or **indices** [ˈɪndɪˌsiz]) index *m; (of prices)* indice *m; (typ)* main *f;* **Index** Index ‖ *tr* répertorier; *(a book)* faire un index à

in′dex card′ *s* fiche *f*

in′dex fin′ger *s* index *m*

in′dex tab′ *s* onglet *m*

India [ˈɪndɪə] *s* Inde *f;* l'Inde

In′dia ink′ *s* encre *f* de Chine

Indian [ˈɪndɪən] *adj* indien ‖ *s* Indien *m*

In′dian club′ *s* mil *m,* massue *f*

In′dian corn′ *s* maïs *m*

In′dian file′ *s* file *f* indienne ‖ *adv* en file indienne, à la queue leu leu

In′dian O′cean *s* mer *f* des Indes, océan *m* Indien

In′dian sum′mer *s* été *m* de la Saint-Martin

In′dia rub′ber *s* caoutchouc *m,* gomme *f*

indicate [ˈɪndɪˌket] *tr* indiquer

indication [ˌɪndɪˈkeʃən] *s* indication *f*

indicative [ɪnˈdɪkətɪv] *adj & s* indicatif *m*

indicator [ˈɪndɪˌketər] *s* indicateur *m*

indict [ɪnˈdaɪt] *tr* (law) inculper

indictment [ɪnˈdaɪtmənt] *s* inculpation *f,* mise *f* en accusation

indifferent [ɪnˈdɪfərənt] *adj* indifférent; *(poor)* médiocre

indigenous [ɪnˈdɪdʒɪnəs] *adj* indigène

indigent [ˈɪndɪdʒənt] *adj* indigent

indigestible [ˌɪndɪˈdʒɛstɪbəl] *adj* indigeste

indigestion [ˌɪndɪˈdʒɛstʃən] *s* indigestion *f*

indignant [ɪnˈdɪgnənt] *adj* indigné

indignation [ˌɪndɪgˈneʃən] *s* indignation *f*

indigni•ty [ɪnˈdɪgnɪti] *s (pl* **-ties**) indignité *f*

indi•go [ˈɪndɪˌgo] *adj* indigo ‖ *s (pl* **-gos** or **-goes**) indigo *m*

indirect [ˌɪndɪˈrɛkt], [ˌɪndaɪˈrɛkt] *adj* indirect

in′direct dis′course *s* discours *m* indirect, style *m* indirect

indiscreet [ˌɪndɪsˈkrit] *adj* indiscret

indispensable [ˌɪndɪsˈpɛnsəbəl] *adj* indispensable

indispose [ˌɪndɪsˈpoz] *tr* indisposer

indisposed *adj* indisposé; *(disinclined)* peu enclin, peu disposé

indissoluble [ˌɪndɪˈsɑljəbəl] *adj* indissoluble

indistinct [ˌɪndɪˈstɪŋkt] *adj* indistinct

individual [ˌɪndɪˈvɪdʒʊ-əl] *adj* individuel ‖ *s* individu *m*

individuali•ty [ˌɪndɪˌvɪdʒʊˈælɪti] *s (pl* **-ties**) individualité *f*

indivisible [ˌɪndɪˈvɪzɪbəl] *adj* indivisible

Indochina [ˈɪndoˈtʃaɪnə] *s* Indochine *f;* l'Indochine

indoctrinate [ɪnˈdɑktrɪˌnet] *tr* endoctriner, catéchiser

Indo-European [ˈɪndoˌjʊrəˈpi-ən] *adj* indo-européen ‖ *s (language)* indo-européen *m; (person)* Indo-Européen *m*

indolent [ˈɪndələnt] *adj* indolent

Indonesia [ˌɪndoˈniʒə], [ˌɪndoˈniʒə] *s* Indonésie *f;* l'Indonésie

Indonesian [ˌɪndoˈniʒən], [ˌɪndoˈniʒən] *adj* indonésien ‖ *s (language)* indonésien *m; (person)* Indonésien *m*

indoor [ˈɪnˌdor] *adj* d'intérieur; *(homeloving)* casanier; *(tennis)* couvert; *(swimming pool)* fermé

indoors [ˈɪnˈdorz] *adv* à l'intérieur

induce [ɪnˈd(j)us] *tr (to bring about)* provoquer; **to induce s.o. to** porter qn à

induced *adj* provoqué; *(elec)* induit

inducement [ɪnˈd(j)usmənt] *s* encouragement *m,* mobile *m,* invite *f*

induct [ɪnˈdʌkt] *tr* installer; *(mil)* incorporer

inductee [ˌɪnˈdʌkti] *s* appelé *m*

induction [ɪnˈdʌkʃən] *s* installation *f;* (elec, logic) induction *f;* (mil) incorporation *f*

induc′tion coil′ *s* bobine *f* d'induction

indulge [ɪnˈdʌldʒ] *tr* favoriser; *(s.o.'s desires)* donner libre cours à; *(a child)* tout passer à ‖ *intr* (coll) boire; (coll) fumer; **to indulge in** se livrer à

indulgence [ɪnˈdʌldʒəns] *s* indulgence *f;* **indulgence in** jouissance de

indulgent [ɪnˈdʌldʒənt] *adj* indulgent

industrial [ɪnˈdʌstri-əl] *adj* industriel

industrialist [ɪnˈdʌstri-əlɪst] *s* industriel *m*

industrialize [ɪnˈdʌstri-əˌlaɪz] *tr* industrialiser

industrious [ɪnˈdʌstri-əs] *adj* industrieux, appliqué, assidu

indus•try [ˈɪndəstri] *s (pl* **-tries**) industrie *f; (zeal)* assiduité *f*

inebriation [ɪnˌibriˈeʃən] *s* ébriété *f*

inedible [ɪnˈɛdɪbəl] *adj* incomestible

ineffable [ɪnˈɛfəbəl] *adj* ineffable

ineffective [ˌɪnɪˈfɛktɪv] *adj* inefficace; *(person)* incapable

ineffectual [ˌɪnɪˈfɛktʃʊ-əl] *adj* inefficace

inefficient [ˌɪnɪˈfɪʃənt] *adj* inefficace; *(person)* incapable

ineligible [ɪnˈɛlɪdʒɪbəl] *adj* inéligible

inept [ɪnˈɛpt] *adj* inepte

inequali•ty [ˌɪnɪˈkwɑlɪti] *s (pl* **-ties**) inégalité *f*

inequi•ty [ɪnˈɛkwɪti] *s (pl* **-ties**) injustice *f*

inertia [ɪnˈʌrʃə] *s* inertie *f*

inescapable [ˌɪnesˈkepəbəl] *adj* inéluctable

inevitable [ɪnˈɛvɪtəbəl] *adj* inévitable

inexact [ˌɪnɛgˈzækt] *adj* inexact

inexcusable [ˌɪnɛksˈkjuzəbəl] *adj* inexcusable

inexhaustible [ˌɪnɛgˈzɔstɪbəl] *adj* inexhaustible, inépuisable

inexorable [ɪnˈɛksərəbəl] *adj* inexorable

inexpedient [,ınek'spidı·ənt] *adj* inopportun, peu expédient

inexpensive [,ınek'spensıv] *adj* pas cher, bon marché

inexperience [,ınek'spırı·əns] *s* inexpérience *f*

inexperienced *adj* inexpérimenté

inexplicable [ın'eksplıkəbəl] *adj* inexplicable

inexpressible [,ınek'spresıbəl] *adj* inexprimable, indicible

infallible [ın'fælıbəl] *adj* infaillible

infamous ['ınfəməs] *adj* infâme

infa·my ['ınfəmi] *s* (*pl* -mies) infamie *f*

infan·cy ['ınfənsi] *s* (*pl* -cies) première enfance *f*; (fig) enfance *f*

infant ['ınfənt] *adj* infantile; (*in the earliest stage*) (fig) débutant ‖ *s* nourrisson *m*, bébé *m*; enfant *mf* en bas âge

infantile ['ınfən,taıl], ['ınfəntıl] *adj* infantile; (*childish*) enfantin

in'fantile paral'ysis *s* paralysie *f* infantile

infan·try ['ınfəntri] *s* (*pl* -tries) infanterie *f*

in'fantry·man *s* (*pl* -men) militaire *m* de l'infanterie, fantassin *m*

infatuated [ın'fætʃu,etıd] *adj* entiché, épris; **infatuated with oneself** infatué; **to be infatuated** s'engouer

infect [ın'fekt] *tr* infecter

infection [ın'fekʃən] *s* infection *f*

infectious [ın'fekʃəs] *adj* infectieux; (*laughter*) communicatif, contagieux

in·fer [ın'fʌr] *v* (*pret & pp* -ferred; *ger* -ferring) inférer

inferior [ın'fırı·ər] *adj & s* inférieur *m*

inferiori·ty [ın ,fırı'arıti] *s* infériorité *f*

inferior'ity com'plex *s* complexe *m* d'infériorité

infernal [ın'fʌrnəl] *adj* infernal

infest [ın'fest] *tr* infester

infidel ['ınfıdəl] *adj & s* infidèle *mf*

infideli·ty [,ınfı'delıti] *s* (*pl* -ties) infidélité *f*

in'field *s* (baseball) petit champ *m*

infiltrate [ın'fıltret], ['ınfıl,tret] *tr* s'infiltrer dans, pénétrer; (*with conspirators*) noyauter ‖ *intr* s'infiltrer

infinite ['ınfınıt] *adj & s* infini *m*

infinitely ['ınfınıtli] *adv* infiniment

infinitive [ın'fınıtıv] *adj & s* infinitif *m*

infini·ty [ın'fınıti] *s* (*pl* -ties) infinité *f*; (math) infini *m*

infirm [ın'fʌrm] *adj* infirme, maladif

infirma·ry [ın'fʌrməri] *s* (*pl* -ries) infirmerie *f*

infirmi·ty [ın'fʌrmıti] *s* (*pl* -ties) infirmité *f*

in'fix *s* infixe *m*

inflame [ın'flem] *tr* enflammer ‖ *intr* s'enflammer

inflammable [ın'flæməbəl] *adj* inflammable

inflammation [,ınflə'meʃən] *s* inflammation *f*

inflammatory [ın'flæmə,tori] *adj* incendiaire, provocateur; (pathol) inflammatoire

inflate [ın'flet] *tr* gonfler ‖ *intr* se gonfler

inflation [ın'fleʃən] *s* gonflement *m*; (com) inflation *f*

inflationary [ın'fleʃən,eri] *adj* inflationniste

inflect [ın'flekt] *tr* infléchir; (*e.g., a noun*) décliner; (*a verb*) conjuguer; (*the voice*) moduler

inflection [ın'flekʃən] *s* inflexion *f*

inflexible [ın'fleksıbəl] *adj* inflexible

inflict [ın'flıkt] *tr* infliger

influence ['ınflu·əns] *s* influence *f* ‖ *tr* influencer, influer sur

in'fluence ped'dling *s* trafic *m* d'influence

influential [,ınflu'enʃəl] *adj* influent

influenza [,ınflu'enzə] *s* influenza *f*

in'flux *s* afflux *m*

inform [ın'fɔrm] *tr* informer, renseigner; **keep me informed** tenez-moi au courant ‖ *intr*—**to inform on** informer contre, dénoncer

informal [ın'fɔrməl] *adj* sans cérémonie; (*person; manners*) familier; (*unofficial*) officieux

infor'mal dance' *s* sauterie *f*

informant [ın'fɔrmənt] *s* informateur *m*; (*in, e.g., language study*) source *f* d'informations

information [,ınfər'meʃən] *s* information *f*, renseignements *mpl*; (telp) service *m* des renseignements téléphoniques; **piece of information** information, renseignement

informational [,ınfər'meʃənəl] *adj* instructif, documentaire; (comp) informatique

informa'tion bu'reau *s* bureau *m* de renseignements

informative [ın'fɔrmətıv] *adj* instructif, édifiant

informed' sour'ces *spl* sources *fpl* bien informées

informer [ın'fɔrmər] *s* délateur *m*, dénonciateur *m*; (*police spy*) indicateur *m*, mouchard *m*

infraction [ın'frækʃən] *s* infraction *f*

infrared [,ınfrə'red] *adj & s* infrarouge *m*

infrequent [ın'frikwənt] *adj* peu fréquent, rare

infringe [ın'frındʒ] *tr* enfreindre; (*a patent*) contrefaire ‖ *intr*—**to infringe on** empiéter sur, enfreindre

infringement [ın'frındʒmənt] *s* infraction *f*; (*on patent rights*) contrefaçon *f*

infuriate [ın'fjurı,et] *tr* rendre furieux

infuse [ın'fjuz] *tr* infuser

infusion [ın'fjuʒən] *s* infusion *f*

ingenious [ın'dʒinjəs] *adj* ingénieux

ingenui·ty [,ındʒı'n(j)u·ıti] *s* (*pl* -ties) ingéniosité *f*

ingenuous [ın'dʒenju·əs] *adj* ingénu, naïf

ingenuousness [ın'dʒenju·əsnıs] *s* ingénuité *f*, naïveté *f*

ingest [ın'dʒest] *tr* ingérer

ingot ['ıngət] *s* lingot *m*

in·grained' *adj* imprégné; (*habit*) invétéré; (*prejudice*) enraciné

ingrate ['ıngret] *adj & s* ingrat *m*

ingratiate [ɪnˈgreʃɪˌet] *tr*—to ingratiate oneself (with) se faire bien voir (de)

ingratiating [ɪnˈgreʃɪˌetɪŋ] *adj* insinuant, persuasif

ingratitude [ɪnˈgrætɪˌt(j)ud] *s* ingratitude *f*

ingredient [ɪnˈgridɪ·ənt] *s* ingrédient *m*

in'growing nail' *s* ongle *m* incarné

ingulf [ɪnˈgʌlf] *tr* engouffrer

inhabit [ɪnˈhæbɪt] *tr* habiter

inhabitant [ɪnˈhæbɪtənt] *s* habitant *m*

inhale [ɪnˈhel] *tr* inhaler, aspirer; (*smoke*) avaler || *intr* (*while smoking*) avaler

inherent [ɪnˈhɪrənt] *adj* inhérent

inherit [ɪnˈhɛrɪt] *tr* (*e.g., money*) hériter; (*e.g., money to become the heir or successor of*) hériter de; **to inherit s.th. from s.o.** hériter q.ch. de qn

inheritance [ɪnˈhɛrɪtəns] *s* héritage *m*

inher'itance tax' *s* droits *mpl* de succession

inheritor [ɪnˈhɛrɪtər] *s* héritier *m*

inhibit [ɪnˈhɪbɪt] *tr* inhiber

inhibition [ˌɪnɪˈbɪʃən] *s* inhibition *f*

inhospitable [ɪnˈhɒspɪtəbəl], [ˌɪnhɒsˈpɪtəbəl] *adj* inhospitalier

inhuman [ɪnˈhjumən] *adj* inhumain

inhumane [ˌɪnhjuˈmen] *adj* inhumain, insensible

inhumani·ty [ˌɪnhjuˈmænɪti] *s* (*pl* -ties) inhumanité *f*

inimical [ɪˈnɪmɪkəl] *adj* inamical

iniqui·ty [ɪˈnɪkwɪti] *s* (*pl* -ties) iniquité *f*

ini·tial [ɪˈnɪʃəl] *adj* initial || *s* initiale *f*; **initials** parafe *m*, initiales || *v* (*pret* -tialed or -tialled; *ger* -tialing or -tialling) *tr* signer de ses initiales, parafer

initiate [ɪˈnɪʃɪˌet] *s* initié *m* || *tr* initier; (*a project*) commencer

initiation [ɪˌnɪʃɪˈeʃən] *s* initiation *f*

initiative [ɪˈnɪʃɪ·ətɪv], [ɪˈnɪʃ/ətɪv] *s* initiative *f*

inject [ɪnˈdʒɛkt] *tr* injecter; (*a remark or suggestion*) introduire

injection [ɪnˈdʒɛkʃən] *s* injection *f*

injudicious [ˌɪndʒuˈdɪʃəs] *adj* peu judicieux

injunction [ɪnˈdʒʌŋkʃən] *s* injonction *f*; (*law*) mise *f* en demeure

injure [ˈɪndʒər] *tr* (*to harm*) nuire (with *dat*); (*to wound*) blesser; (*to offend*) faire tort à, léser

injurious [ɪnˈdʒʊrɪ·əs] *adj* nuisible, préjudiciable; (*offensive*) blessant, injurieux

inju·ry [ˈɪndʒəri] *s* (*pl* -ries) blessure *f*, lésion *f*; (*harm*) tort *m*; injure *f*, offense *f*

injustice [ɪnˈdʒʌstɪs] *s* injustice *f*

ink [ɪŋk] *s* encre *f* || *tr* encrer

ink' blot' *s* pâté *m*, macule *f*

inkling [ˈɪŋklɪŋ] *s* soupçon *m*, pressentiment *m*

ink' pad' *s* tampon *m* encreur

ink'stand' *s* encrier *m*

ink'well' *s* encrier *m* de bureau

ink·y [ˈɪŋki] *adj* (*comp* -ier; *super* -iest) noir foncé; taché d'encre

inlaid [ˈɪnˌled], [ˌɪnˈled] *adj* incrusté

inland [ˈɪnlənd] *adj* & *s* intérieur *m* || *adv* à l'intérieur, vers l'intérieur

in'-law' *s* (coll) parent *m* par alliance; **the in-laws** (coll) la belle-famille, les beaux-parents *mpl*

in·lay [ˈɪnˌle] *s* incrustation *f* || [ɪnˈle], [ˈɪnˌle] *v* (*pret* & *pp* -laid) *tr* incruster

in'let' *s* bras *m* de mer, crique *f*; (*e.g., of air*) arrivée *f*

in'mate' *s* habitant *m*; (*of an institution*) pensionnaire *mf*

inn [ɪn] *s* auberge *f*

innate [ɪˈnet], [ˈɪnet] *adj* inné, infus

inner [ˈɪnər] *adj* intérieur; (*e.g., ear*) interne; intime, secret

in'ner·spring' mat'tress *s* sommier *m* à ressorts internes

in'ner tube' *s* chambre *f* à air

inning [ˈɪnɪŋ] *s* manche *f*, tour *m*

inn'keep'er *s* aubergiste *mf*

innocence [ˈɪnəsəns] *s* innocence *f*

innocent [ˈɪnəsənt] *adj* & *s* innocent *m*

innocuous [ɪˈnɒkju·əs] *adj* inoffensif

innovate [ˈɪnəˌvet] *tr* & *intr* innover

innovation [ˌɪnəˈveʃən] *s* innovation *f*

innuen·do [ˌɪnjuˈɛndo] *s* (*pl* -does) allusion *f*, sous-entendu *m*

innumerable [ɪˈn(j)umərəbəl] *adj* innombrable

inoculate [ɪnˈɒkjəˌlet] *tr* inoculer

inoculation [ɪnˌɒkjəˈleʃən] *s* inoculation *f*

inoffensive [ˌɪnəˈfɛnsɪv] *adj* inoffensif

inopportune [ɪnˌɒpərˈt(j)un] *adj* inopportun, mal choisi

inordinate [ɪnˈɔrdɪnɪt] *adj* désordonné, déréglé; (*unrestrained*) démesuré

inorganic [ˌɪnɔrˈgænɪk] *adj* inorganique

in'put' *s* consommation *f*; (elec) prise *f*, entrée *f*

inquest [ˈɪnkwɛst] *s* enquête *f*

inquire [ɪnˈkwaɪr] *tr* s'informer de, e.g., **to inquire the price of** s'informer du prix de || *intr* s'enquérir; **to inquire about** s'enquérir de, se renseigner sur; **to inquire into** faire des recherches sur

inquir·y [ɪnˈkwaɪri], [ˈɪnkwɪri] *s* (*pl* -ies) investigation *f*, enquête *f*; (*question*) demande *f*; **to make inquiries** s'informer

inquisition [ˌɪnkwɪˈzɪʃən] *s* inquisition *f*

inquisitive [ɪnˈkwɪzɪtɪv] *adj* curieux, questionneur

in'road' *s* incursion *f*, empiètement *m*

ins' and outs' *spl* tours et détours *mpl*

insane [ɪnˈsen] *adj* dément, fou; (*unreasonable*) insensé, insane

insane' asy'lum *s* asile *m* d'aliénés

insani·ty [ɪnˈsænɪti] *s* (*pl* -ties) démence *f*, aliénation *f*

insatiable [ɪnˈseʃəbəl] *adj* insatiable

inscribe [ɪnˈskraɪb] *tr* inscrire; (*a book*) dédier

inscription [ɪnˈskrɪpʃən] *s* inscription *f*; (*of a book*) dédicace *f*

inscrutable [ɪn'skrutəbəl] *adj* impénétrable, fermé

insect ['ɪnsekt] *s* insecte *m*

insecticide [ɪn'sektɪ,saɪd] *adj & s* insecticide *m*

insecure [,ɪnsɪ'kjur] *adj* peu sûr; (*nervous*) inquiet

insensitive [ɪn'sensɪtɪv] *adj* insensible

inseparable [ɪn'sepərəbəl] *adj* inséparable

insert ['ɪnsʌrt] *s* (sewing) incrustation *f*; (typ) hors-texte *m*, encart *m* ‖ [ɪn-'sʌrt] *tr* insérer, introduire; (typ) encarter

insertion [ɪn'sʌrʃən] *s* insertion *f*; (sewing) incrustation *f*

in-set ['ɪn,set] *s* (*map, picture, etc.*) médaillon *m*; (sewing) incrustation *f*; (typ) hors-texte *m*, encart *m* ‖ [ɪn'set], ['ɪn,set] *v* (*pret & pp* -set; *ger* -setting) *tr* insérer; (*a page or pages*) encarter

in'shore' *adj* côtier ‖ *adv* près de la côte

in'side' *adj* d'intérieur, interne; secret ‖ *s* intérieur *m*, dedans *m*; **insides** (coll) entrailles *fpl* ‖ *adv* à l'intérieur; **inside and out** au-dedans et au-dehors; **inside of** à l'intérieur de; **inside out** à l'envers; **to turn inside out** (*e.g., a coat*) retourner ‖ *prep* à l'intérieur de, dans

in'side informa'tion *s* tuyau *m*, tuyaux *mpl*

insider [ɪn'saɪdər] *s* initié *m*

in'side track' *s*—**to have the inside track** prendre à la corde; (fig) avoir un avantage

insidious [ɪn'sɪdɪ·əs] *adj* insidieux

in'sight' *s* pénétration *f*; (psychol) défoulement *m*

insigni·a [ɪn'sɪgnɪ·ə] *s* (*pl* -a or -as) insigne *m*

insignificant [,ɪnsɪg'nɪfɪkənt] *adj* insignifiant

insincere [,ɪnsɪn'sɪr] *adj* insincère, peu sincère

insinuate [ɪn'sɪnju,et] *tr* insinuer

insipid [ɪn'sɪpɪd] *adj* insipide

insist [ɪn'sɪst] *intr* insister; **to insist on** insister sur; **to insist on** + *ger* insister pour + *inf*

insofar as [,ɪnso'fɑrəz] *conj* pour autant que, dans la mesure où

insolence ['ɪnsələns] *s* insolence *f*

insolent ['ɪnsələnt] *adj* insolent

insoluble [ɪn'saljəbəl] *adj* insoluble

insolven·cy [ɪn'salvənsi] *s* (*pl* -cies) insolvabilité *f*

insolvent [ɪn'salvənt] *adj* insolvable

insomnia [ɪn'samnɪ·ə] *s* insomnie *f*

insomuch [,ɪnso'mʌtʃ] *adv*—**insomuch as** vu que; **insomuch that** à tel point que

inspect [ɪn'spekt] *tr* inspecter

inspection [ɪn'spekʃən] *s* inspection *f*

inspector [ɪn'spektər] *s* inspecteur *m*

inspiration [,ɪnspɪ'reʃən] *s* inspiration *f*

inspire [ɪn'spaɪr] *tr* inspirer

inspiring [ɪn'spaɪrɪŋ] *adj* inspirant

install [ɪn'stɔl] *tr* installer

installment [ɪn'stɔlmənt] *s* installation *f*; (*delivery*) livraison *f*; (*serial story*)

feuilleton *m*; (*partial payment*) acompte *m*, versement *m*; **in installments** par acomptes, par tranches

install'ment plan' *s* vente *f* à tempérament or à crédit; **on the installment plan** avec facilités de paiement

instance ['ɪnstəns] *s* cas *m*, exemple *m*; **for instance** par exemple

instant ['ɪnstənt] *adj* imminent, immédiat; **on the fifth instant** le cinq courant ‖ *s* instant *m*, moment *m*

instantaneous [,ɪnstən'tenɪ·əs] *adj* instantané

instantly ['ɪnstəntli] *adv* à l'instant

instead [ɪn'sted] *adv* plutôt, au contraire; à ma (votre, sa, etc.) place; **instead of** au lieu de

in'step' *s* cou-de-pied *m*

instigate ['ɪnstɪ,get] *tr* inciter

instigation [,ɪnstɪ'geʃən] *s* instigation *f*

instill [ɪn'stɪl] *tr* instiller

instinct ['ɪnstɪŋkt] *s* instinct *m*

instinctive [ɪn'stɪŋktɪv] *adj* instinctif

institute ['ɪnstɪ,t(j)ut] *s* institut *m* ‖ *tr* instituer

institution [,ɪnstɪ't(j)uʃən] *s* institution *f*

instruct [ɪn'strʌkt] *tr* instruire

instruction [ɪn'strʌkʃən] *s* instruction *f*

instructive [ɪn'strʌktɪv] *adj* instructif

instructor [ɪn'strʌktər] *s* instructeur *m*

instrument ['ɪnstrəmənt] *s* instrument *m* ‖ ['ɪnstrə,ment] *tr* instrumenter

instrumental [,ɪnstrə'mentəl] *adj* instrumental; **to be instrumental in** contribuer à

instrumentalist [,ɪnstrə'mentəlɪst] *s* instrumentiste *mf*

instrumentali·ty [,ɪnstrəmən'tælɪti] *s* (*pl* -ties) intermédiaire *m*, intervention *f*

in'strument board' *s* tableau *m* de bord

in'strument fly'ing *s* radio-navigation *f*, vol *m* aux instruments

in'strument land'ing *s* atterrissage *m* aux instruments

in'strument pan'el *s* tableau *m* de bord

insubordinate [,ɪnsə'bɔrdɪnɪt] *adj* insubordonné

insufferable [ɪn'sʌfərəbəl] *adj* insupportable, intolérable

insufficient [,ɪnsə'fɪʃənt] *adj* insuffisant

insular ['ɪnsələr], ['ɪnsjulər] *adj* insulaire

insulate ['ɪnsə,let] *tr* insoler

in'sulating tape' *s* ruban *m* isolant, chatterton *m*

insulation [,ɪnsə'leʃən] *s* isolation *f*

insulator ['ɪnsə,letər] *s* isolant *m*

insulin ['ɪnsəlɪn] *s* insuline *f*

insult ['ɪnsʌlt] *s* insulte *f* ‖ [ɪn'sʌlt] *tr* insulter

insulting [ɪn'sʌltɪŋ] *adj* insultant, injurieux

insurance [ɪn'ʃurəns] *s* assurance *f*

insure [ɪn'ʃur] *tr* assurer

insurer [ɪn'ʃurər] *s* assureur *m*

insurgent [ɪn'sʌrdʒənt] *adj & s* insurgé *m*

insurmountable [ˌɪnsərˈmauntəbəl] *adj* insurmontable

insurrection [ˌɪnsəˈrekʃən] *s* insurrection *f*

intact [ɪnˈtækt] *adj* intact

in'take' *s* (*place*) entrée *f*; (*act or amount*) prise *f*; (*mach*) admission *f*

in'take man'ifold *s* tubulure *f* d'admission, collecteur *m* d'admission

in'take valve' *s* soupape *f* d'admission

intangible [ɪnˈtændʒɪbəl] *adj* intangible

integer [ˈɪntɪdʒər] *s* nombre *m* entier

integral [ˈɪntɪgrəl] *adj* intégral; (*part*) intégrant; **integral with** solidaire de ‖ *s* intégrale *f*

integrate [ˈɪntɪˌgret] *tr* intégrer

integration [ˌɪntɪˈgreʃən] *s* intégration *f*

integrity [ɪnˈtegrɪti] *s* intégrité *f*

intellect [ˈɪntəˌlekt] *s* intellect *m*; (*person*) intelligence *f*

intellectual [ˌɪntəˈlektʃʊ·əl] *adj & s* intellectuel *m*

intelligence [ɪnˈtelɪdʒəns] *s* intelligence *f*

intel'ligence bu'reau *s* deuxième bureau *m*, service *m* de renseignements

intel'ligence quo'tient *s* quotient *m* intellectuel

intel'ligence test' *s* test *m* d'habileté mentale

intelligent [ɪnˈtelɪdʒənt] *adj* intelligent

intelligible [ɪnˈtelɪdʒɪbəl] *adj* intelligible

intemperate [ɪnˈtempərɪt] *adj* intempérant

intend [ɪnˈtend] *tr* destiner; signifier; vouloir dire; **to intend to** avoir l'intention de, penser; **to intend to become** se destiner à

intended *adj & s* (*coll*) futur *m*

intense [ɪnˈtens] *adj* intense

intensi·fy [ɪnˈtensɪˌfaɪ] *v* (*pret & pp* **-fied**) *tr* intensifier ‖ *intr* s'intensifier

intensi·ty [ɪnˈtensɪti] *s* (*pl* **-ties**) intensité *f*

intensive [ɪnˈtensɪv] *adj* intensif

intent [ɪnˈtent] *adj* attentif; (*look, gaze*) fixe, intense; **intent on** résolu à ‖ *s* intention *f*; **to all intents and purposes** en fait, pratiquement

intention [ɪnˈtenʃən] *s* intention *f*

intentional [ɪnˈtenʃənəl] *adj* intentionnel, délibéré

intentionally [ɪnˈtenʃənəli] *adv* exprès, à dessein

in·ter [ɪnˈtʌr] *v* (*pret & pp* **-terred**; *ger* **-terring**) *tr* enterrer

interact [ˌɪntərˈækt] *intr* agir réciproquement

interaction [ˌɪntərˈækʃən] *s* interaction *f*

inter·breed [ˌɪntərˈbrid] *v* (*pret & pp* **-bred**) *tr* croiser ‖ *intr* se croiser

intercalate [ɪnˈtʌrkəˌlet] *tr* intercaler

intercede [ˌɪntərˈsid] *intr* intercéder

intercept [ˌɪntərˈsept] *tr* intercepter

interceptor [ˌɪntərˈseptər] *s* intercepteur *m*

interchange [ˈɪntərˌtʃendʒ] *s* échange *m*, permutation *f*; (*transfer point*) correspondance *f*; (*on highway*)

échangeur *m* ‖ [ˌɪntərˈtʃendʒ] *tr* échanger, permuter ‖ *intr* permuter

intercollegiate [ˌɪntərkəˈlidʒɪ·ɪt] *adj* interuniversitaire, entre universités

intercom [ˈɪntərˌkɑm] *s* (coll) interphone *m*

intercourse [ˈɪntərˌkors] *s* relations *fpl*, rapports *mpl*; (*copulation*) copulation *f*, coït *m*

intercross [ˌɪntərˈkrɔs], [ˌɪntərˈkrɑs] *tr* entrecroiser ‖ *intr* s'entrecroiser

interdict [ˈɪntərˌdɪkt] *s* interdit *m* ‖ [ˌɪntərˈdɪkt] *tr* interdire; **to interdict s.o. from** + *ger* interdire à qn de + *inf*

interest [ˈɪntərɪst], [ˈɪntrɪst] *s* intérêt *m*; **the interests** les gens influents; **to pay back with interest** rendre avec usure ‖ [ˈɪntərɪst], [ˈɪntrɪst], [ˈɪntəˌrest] *tr* intéresser

interested *adj* intéressé; **to be interested in** s'intéresser à or dans

interesting [ˈɪntrɪstɪŋ], [ˈɪntəˌrestɪŋ] *adj* intéressant

interfere [ˌɪntərˈfɪr] *intr* (*to meddle*) s'ingérer; (*phys*) interférer; **to interfere with** intervenir dans, se mêler de; (*to come into opposition with*) gêner, entraver; **to interfere with each other** interférer (entre eux)

interference [ˌɪntərˈfɪrəns] *s* interférence *f*, intervention *f*; (*phys*) interférence; (*jamming*) (rad) brouillage *m*

interim [ˈɪntərɪm] *adj* provisoire, par intérim ‖ *s* intérim *m*

interior [ɪnˈtɪrɪ·ər] *adj & s* intérieur *m*

inte'rior dec'orator *s* décorateur *m* d'intérieurs

interject [ˌɪntərˈdʒekt] *tr* interposer; (*questions*) lancer

interjection [ˌɪntərˈdʒekʃən] *s* intervention *f*; (gram) interjection *f*

interlard [ˌɪntərˈlɑrd] *tr* entrelarder

interline [ˌɪntərˈlaɪn] *tr* interligner

interlining [ˈɪntərˌlaɪnɪŋ] *s* doublure *f* intermédiaire

interlock [ˌɪntərˈlɑk] *tr* emboîter, engager ‖ *intr* s'emboîter, s'engager

interloper [ˈɪntərˌlopər] *s* intrus *m*

interlude [ˈɪntərˌlud] *s* (mov, mus, telv) interlude *m*; (theat, fig) intermède *m*

intermediar·y [ˌɪntərˈmidɪˌɛri] *adj* intermédiaire ‖ *s* (*pl* **-ies**) intermédiaire *mf*

intermediate [ˌɪntərˈmidɪ·ɪt] *adj* intermédiaire

interment [ɪnˈtʌrmənt] *s* enterrement *m*, sépulture *f*

interminable [ɪnˈtʌrmɪnəbəl] *adj* interminable

intermingle [ˌɪntərˈmɪŋgəl] *tr* entremêler ‖ *intr* s'entremêler

intermission [ˌɪntərˈmɪʃən] *s* relâche *m*, pause *f*; (theat) entracte *m*

intermittent [ˌɪntərˈmɪtənt] *adj* intermittent

intermix [ˌɪntərˈmɪks] *tr* entremêler ‖ *intr* s'entremêler

intern [ˈɪntʌrn] *s* interne *mf* ‖ [ɪnˈtʌrn] *tr* interner

internal [ɪn'tɜrnəl] *adj* interne

inter'nal-combus'tion en'gine *s* moteur *m* à explosion

inter'nal rev'enue *s* recettes *fpl* fiscales

international [,ɪntər'næʃənəl] *adj* international; *(exposition)* universel

in'terna'tional date' line' *s* ligne *f* de changement de date

in'terna'tional time' zone' *s* fuseau *m* horaire international

internecine [,ɪntər'nisɪn] *adj* domestique, intestin; *(war)* sanguinaire, d'extermination

internee [,ɪntɜr'ni] *s* interné *m*

internment [ɪn'tɜrnmənt] *s* internement *m*

in'tern·ship' *s* internat *m*

interpellate [,ɪntər'pɛlet], [ɪn'tɜrpɪ,let] *tr* interpeller

interplanetary [,ɪntər'plænə,tɛri] *adj* interplanétaire

interplan'etary trav'el *s* voyages *mpl* interplanétaires

interplay ['ɪntər,ple] *s* interaction *f*

interpolate [ɪn'tɜrpə,let] *tr* interpoler

interpose [,ɪntər'poz] *tr* interposer

interpret [ɪn'tɜrprɪt] *tr* interpréter

interpretation [ɪn,tɜrprɪ'teʃən] *s* interprétation *f*

interpreter [ɪn'tɜrprɪtər] *s* interprète *mf*

interrogate [ɪn'tɛrə,get] *tr* interroger

interrogation [ɪn,tɛrə'geʃən] *s* interrogation *f*

interroga'tion mark' *s* point *m* d'interrogation

interrupt [,ɪntə'rʌpt] *tr* interrompre

interruption [,ɪntə'rʌpʃən] *s* interruption *f*

intersect [,ɪntər'sɛkt] *tr* entrecouper || *intr* s'entrecouper

intersection [,ɪntər'sɛkʃən] *s* intersection *f*

intersperse [,ɪntər'spʌrs] *tr* entremêler

interstellar [,ɪntər'stɛlər] *adj* interstellaire

interstice [ɪn'tɜrstɪs] *s* interstice *m*

intertwine [,ɪntər'twaɪn] *tr* entrelacer || *intr* s'entrelacer

interval ['ɪntərvəl] *s* intervalle *m*

intervene [,ɪntər'vin] *intr* intervenir

intervening [,ɪntər'vinɪŋ] *adj (period)* intermédiaire; *(party)* intervenant

intervention [,ɪntər'vɛnʃən] *s* intervention *f*

interview ['ɪntər,vju] *s* entrevue *f*; *(journ)* interview *f* || *tr* avoir une entrevue avec; *(journ)* interviewer

inter·weave [,ɪntər'wiv] *v (pret* -wove or -weaved; *pp* -wove, woven or weaved) *tr* entrelacer; *(to intermingle)* entremêler

intestate [ɪn'tɛstet], [ɪn'tɛstɪt] *adj & s* intestat *m*

intestine [ɪn'tɛstɪn] *adj & s* intestin *m*

intima·cy ['ɪntɪməsi] *s (pl* -cies) intimité *f*; rapports *mpl* sexuels

intimate ['ɪntɪmɪt] *adj & s* intime *mf* || ['ɪntɪ,met] *tr* donner à entendre

intimation [,ɪntɪ'meʃən] *s* suggestion *f*, insinuation *f*

intimidate [ɪn'tɪmɪ,det] *tr* intimider

into ['ɪntu], ['ɪntu] *prep* dans, en

intolerant [ɪn'talərənt] *adj* intolérant

intonation [,ɪnto'neʃən] *s* intonation *f*

intone [ɪn'ton] *tr (to begin to sing)* entonner; *(to sing or recite in a monotone)* psalmodier || *intr* psalmodier

intoxicant [ɪn'taksɪkənt] *s* boisson *f* alcoolique

intoxicate [ɪn'taksɪ,ket] *tr* enivrer; *(to poison)* intoxiquer

intoxication [ɪn,taksɪ'keʃən] *s* ivresse *f*; *(poisoning)* intoxication *f*; *(fig)* enivrement *m*

intractable [ɪn'træktəbəl] *adj* intraitable

intransigent [ɪn'trænsɪdʒənt] *adj* intransigeant

intransitive [ɪn'trænsɪtɪv] *adj* intransitif

intravenous [,ɪntrə'vinəs] *adj* intraveineux

intrepid [ɪn'trɛpɪd] *adj* intrépide

intricate ['ɪntrɪkɪt] *adj* compliqué

intrigue [ɪn'trig], ['ɪntrig] *s* intrigue *f* || [ɪn'trig] *tr & intr* intriguer

intrinsic(al) [ɪn'trɪnsɪk(əl)] *adj* intrinsèque

introduce [,ɪntrə'd(j)us] *tr* introduire; *(to make acquainted)* présenter

introduction [,ɪntrə'dʌkʃən] *s* introduction *f*; *(of one person to another or others)* présentation *f*

introductory [,ɪntrə'dʌktəri] *adj* préliminaire; *(text)* liminaire; *(speech, letter, etc.)* de présentation

introduc'tory of'fer *s* offre *f* de présentation

introspective [,ɪntrə'spɛktɪv] *adj* introspectif; *(person)* méditatif

introvert ['ɪntrə,vʌrt] *adj & s* introverti *m*

intrude [ɪn'trud] *intr* s'ingérer, s'immiscer; **to intrude on s.o.** déranger qn

intruder [ɪn'trudər] *s* intrus *m*

intrusion [ɪn'truʒən] *s* intrusion *f*

intrusive [ɪn'trusɪv] *adj* importun

intuition [,ɪnt(j)u'ɪʃən] *s* intuition *f*

inundate ['ɪnən,det] *tr* inonder

inundation [,ɪnən'deʃən] *s* inondation *f*

inure [ɪn'jur] *tr* aguerrir, endurcir || *intr* entrer en vigueur; **to inure to** rejaillir sur

invade [ɪn'ved] *tr* envahir

invader [ɪn'vedər] *s* envahisseur *m*

invalid [ɪn'vælɪd] *adj* invalide, nul || ['ɪnvəlɪd] *adj & s* malade *mf*, invalide *mf*

invalidate [ɪn'vælɪ,det] *tr* invalider

invalidity [,ɪnvə'lɪdɪti] *s* invalidité *f*

invaluable [ɪn'væljʊ-əbəl] *adj* inappréciable, inestimable

invariable [ɪn'vɛri-əbəl] *adj* invariable

invasion [ɪn'veʒən] *s* invasion *f*

invective [ɪn'vɛktɪv] *s* invective *f*

inveigh [ɪn've] *intr*—**to inveigh against** invectiver contre

inveigle [ɪn'vegəl], [ɪn'vigəl] *tr* séduire, enjôler; **to inveigle s.o. into** + *ger* entraîner qn à + *inf*

invent [ɪn'vɛnt] *tr* inventer

invention [ɪn'vɛnʃən] *s* invention *f*

inventive [ɪn'ventɪv] *adj* inventif
inventiveness [ɪn'ventɪvnɪs] *s* esprit *m* inventif
inventor [ɪn'ventər] *s* inventeur *m*
inven·to·ry ['ɪnvən,torɪ] *s* (*pl* -ries) inventaire *m* || *v* (*pret & pp* -ried) *tr* inventorier
inverse [ɪn'vʌrs] *adj & s* inverse *m*
inversion [ɪn'vʌrʒən], [ɪn'vʌrʃən] *s* interversion *f*, inversion *f*
invert ['ɪnvʌrt] *adj & s* inverti *m* || [ɪn'vʌrt] *tr* inverser; (*an image*) invertir
invertebrate [ɪn'vʌrtɪ,bret], [ɪn'vʌrtɪ-brɪt] *adj & s* invertébré *m*
invest [ɪn'vest] *tr* investir; (*money*) investir, placer; to invest with investir de || *intr* investir or placer de l'argent
investigate [ɪn'vestɪ,get] *tr* examiner, rechercher
investigation [ɪn,vestɪ'geʃən] *s* investigation *f*
investigator [ɪn'vestɪ,getər] *s* investigateur *m*, chercheur *m*
investment [ɪn'vestmənt] *s* investissement *m*, placement *m*; (*with an office or dignity*) investiture *f*; (*siege*) investissement
investor [ɪn'vestər] *s* capitaliste *mf*
inveterate [ɪn'vetərɪt] *adj* invétéré
invidious [ɪn'vɪdɪ·əs] *adj* odieux
invigorate [ɪn'vɪgə,ret] *tr* vivifier, fortifier
invigorating [ɪn'vɪgə,retɪŋ] *adj* vivifiant, fortifiant
invincible [ɪn'vɪnsɪbəl] *adj* invincible
invisible [ɪn'vɪzɪbəl] *adj* invisible
invis·ible ink' *s* encre *f* sympathique
invitation [,ɪnvɪ'teʃən] *s* invitation *f*
invite [ɪn'vaɪt] *tr* inviter
inviting [ɪn'vaɪtɪŋ] *adj* invitant
invoice ['ɪnvɔɪs] *s* facture *f*; as per invoice suivant facture || *tr* facturer
invoke [ɪn'vok] *tr* invoquer
involuntary [ɪn'vɑlən,terɪ] *adj* involontaire
involve [ɪn'vɑlv] *tr* impliquer, entraîner, engager
invulnerable [ɪn'vʌlnərəbəl] *adj* invulnérable
inward ['ɪnwərd] *adj* intérieur || *adv* intérieurement, en dedans
iodide ['aɪ·ə,daɪd] *s* iodure *m*
iodine ['aɪ·ə,dɪn] *s* (chem) iode *m* || ['aɪ·ə,daɪn] *s* (pharm) teinture *f* d'iode
ion ['aɪ·ən], ['aɪ·ɑn] *s* ion *m*
ionize ['aɪ·ə,naɪz] *tr* ioniser
I.O.U. ['aɪ,o'ju] *s* (letterword) (I owe you) reconnaissance *f* de dette
I.Q. ['aɪ'kju] *s* (letterword) (intelligence quotient) quotient *m* intellectuel
Iran [ɪ'ran], [aɪ'ræn] *s* l'Iran *m*
Iranian [aɪ'renɪ·ən] *adj* iranien || *s* (*language*) iranien *m*; (*person*) Iranien *m*
Iraq [ɪ'rak] *s* l'Irak *m*
Ira·qi [ɪ'rakɪ] *adj* irakien || *s* (*pl* -qis) Irakien *m*
irate ['aɪret], [aɪ'ret] *adj* irrité
ire [aɪr] *s* courroux *m*, colère *f*

Ireland ['aɪrlənd] *s* Irlande *f*; l'Irlande *m*
iris ['aɪrɪs] *s* iris *m*
Irish ['aɪrɪʃ] *adj* irlandais || *s* (*language*) irlandais *m*; the Irish les Irlandais
I'rish·man *s* (*pl* -men) Irlandais *m*
I'rish stew' *s* ragoût *m* irlandais
I'rish·wom'an *s* (*pl* -wom'en) Irlandaise *f*
irk [ʌrk] *tr* ennuyer, fâcher
irksome ['ʌrksəm] *adj* ennuyeux
iron ['aɪ·ərn] *s* fer *m*; (*for pressing clothes*) fer à repasser; irons (*fetters*) fers; to have too many irons in the fire courir deux lièvres à la fois; to strike while the iron is hot battre le fer tant qu'il est chaud || *tr* (*clothes*) repasser; to iron out (*a difficulty*) aplanir
I'ron and steel' in'dustry *s* sidérurgie *f*
i'ron-bound' *adj* cerclé; (*unyielding*) inflexible; (*rock-bound*) plein de récifs
ironclad ['aɪ·ərn,klæd] *adj* blindé, cuirassé; (*e.g., contract*) infrangible
i'ron cur'tain *s* rideau *m* de fer
i'ron diges'tion *s* estomac *m* d'autruche
i'ron horse' *s* coursier *m* de fer
ironic(al) [aɪ'ranɪk(əl)] *adj* ironique
ironing ['aɪ·ərnɪŋ] *s* repassage *m*
i'roning board' *s* planche *f* à repasser
i'ron lung' *s* poumon *m* d'acier
i'ron ore' *s* minerai *m* de fer
i'ron·ware' *s* quincaillerie *f*, ferblanterie *f*
i'ron will' *s* volonté *f* inflexible
i'ron·work' *s* ferrure *f*, ferronnerie *f*
i'ron·work'er *s* ferronnier *m*
iro·ny ['aɪrənɪ] *s* (*pl* -nies) ironie *f*
irradiate [ɪ'redɪ,et] *tr & intr* irradier
irrational [ɪ'ræʃənəl] *adj* irrationnel
irredeemable [,ɪrɪ'diməbəl] *adj* irrémédiable; (*bonds*) non remboursable
irrefutable [,ɪrɪ'fjutəbəl], [ɪ'refjutə-bəl] *adj* irréfutable
irregular [ɪ'regjələr] *adj & s* irrégulier *m*
irrelevant [ɪ'reləvənt] *adj* non pertinent, hors de propos
irreligious [,ɪrɪ'lɪdʒəs] *adj* irréligieux
irremediable [,ɪrɪ'midɪ·əbəl] *adj* irrémédiable
irreparable [ɪ'repərəbəl] *adj* irréparable
irreplaceable [,ɪrɪ'plesəbəl] *adj* irremplaçable
irrepressible [,ɪrɪ'presɪbəl] *adj* irrépressible, irrésistible
irreproachable [,ɪrɪ'protʃəbəl] *adj* irréprochable
irresistible [,ɪrɪ'zɪstɪbəl] *adj* irrésistible
irrespective [,ɪrɪ'spektɪv] *adj*—irrespective of indépendant de
irresponsible [,ɪrɪ'spansɪbəl] *adj* irresponsable
irretrievable [,ɪrɪ'trivəbəl] *adj* irréparable; (*lost*) irrécupérable
irreverent [ɪ'revərənt] *adj* irrévérencieux
irrevocable [ɪ'revəkəbəl] *adj* irrévocable
irrigate ['ɪrɪ,get] *tr* irriguer

irrigation [,ɪrɪ'geʃən] *s* irrigation *f*

irritant ['ɪrɪtənt] *adj & s* irritant *m*

irritate ['ɪrɪ,tet] *tr* irriter

irritation [,ɪrɪ'teʃən] *s* irritation *f*

irruption [ɪ'rʌpʃən] *s* irruption *f*

Isaiah [aɪ'zeə] *s* Isaïe *m*

isinglass ['aɪzɪŋ,glæs], ['aɪzɪŋ,glɑs] *s* gélatine *f*, colle *f* de poisson; (mineral) mica *m*

Islam ['ɪsləm], [ɪs'lɑm] *s* l'Islam *m*

island ['aɪlənd] *adj* insulaire || *s* île *f*

islander ['aɪləndər] *s* insulaire *mf*

isle [aɪl] *s* île *f*; (poetic) île *f*

isolate ['aɪsə,let], ['ɪsə,let] *tr* isoler

isolation [,aɪsə'leʃən], [,ɪsə'leʃən] *s* isolement *m*

isolationist [,aɪsə'leʃənɪst], [,ɪsə'leʃənɪst] *adj & s* isolationniste *mf*

isosceles [aɪ'sɑsə,liz] *adj* isocèle

isotope ['aɪsə,top] *s* isotope *m*

Israel ['ɪzrɪəl] *s* l'Israël *m*

Israe-li [ɪz'reli] *adj* israélien || *s* (*pl* -lis [liz]) Israélien *m*

Israelite ['ɪzrɪə,laɪt] *adj* israélite || *s* Israélite *mf*

issuance ['ɪʃʊəns] *s* émission *f*

issue ['ɪʃʊ] *s* (*way out*) sortie *f*, issue *f*; (*outcome*) issue; (*of a magazine*) numéro *m*; (*offspring*) descendance *f*; (*of banknotes, stamps, etc.*) émission *f*; (*under discussion*) point *m* à discuter; (pathol) écoulement *m*; **at issue** en jeu, en litige; **to take issue with** être en désaccord avec; **without issue** sans enfants || *tr* (*a book, a magazine*) publier; (*banknotes, stamps, etc.*) émettre; (*a summons*) lancer; (*an order*) donner; (*a procla-*

mation) faire; (*a verdict*) rendre || *intr* sortir, déboucher

isthmus ['ɪsməs] *s* isthme *m*

it [ɪt] *pron pers* ce §82B, §85; il §87; le §87; y §87; en §87

Italian [ɪ'tæljən] *adj* italien || *s* (*language*) italien *m*; (*person*) Italien *m*

italic [ɪ'tælɪk] *adj* (typ) italique; **Italic** italique || *italics spl* italique *m*

italicize [ɪ'tælɪ,saɪz] *tr* mettre en italique

Italy ['ɪtəli] *s* Italie *f*; l'Italie

itch [ɪtʃ] *s* démangeaison *f*; (pathol) gale *f* || *tr* démanger (*with dat*) || *intr* (*said of part of body*) démanger; (*said of person*) avoir une démangeaison; **to itch to** (fig) avoir une démangeaison de

itch-y ['ɪtʃi] *adj* (*comp* -ier; *super* -iest) piquant; (pathol) galeux

item ['aɪtəm] *s* article *m*; (*in a list*) point *m*; (*piece of news*) nouvelle *f*

itemize ['aɪtə,maɪz] *tr* spécifier, énumérer

itinerant [aɪ'tɪnərənt], [ɪ'tɪnərənt] *adj & s* itinérant *m*

itinerar-y [aɪ'tɪnə,reri], [ɪ'tɪnə,reri] *adj* itinéraire *m* || *s* (*pl* -ies) itinéraire *m*

its [ɪts] *adj poss* son §88 || *pron poss* le sien §89

it'self' *pron pers* soi §85; lui-même §86; se §87

ivied ['aɪvid] *adj* couvert de lierre

ivo-ry ['aɪvəri] *adj* d'ivoire, en ivoire || *s* (*pl* -ries) ivoire *m*; **to tickle the ivories** (slang) taquiner l'ivoire

i'vory tow'er *s* (fig) tour *f* d'ivoire

ivy ['aɪvi] *s* (*pl* ivies) lierre *m*

J

J, j [dʒe] *s* Xᵉ lettre de l'alphabet

jab [dʒæb] *s* (*with a sharp point; with a penknife; with the elbow*) coup *m*; (*with a needle*) piqûre *f*; (*with the fist*) coup sec || *v* (*pret & pp* jabbed; *ger* jabbing) *tr* donner un coup de coude à; piquer; donner un coup sec à; (*a knife*) enfoncer

jabber ['dʒæbər] *tr & intr* jaboter

jack [dʒæk] *s* (aut) cric *m*; (cards) valet *m*; (elec) jack *m*, prise *f*; (coll) fric *m*; **Jack** Jeannot *m* || *tr—to jack up** soulever au cric; (*prices*) faire monter

jackal ['dʒækəl] *s* chacal *m*

jack'ass' *s* baudet *m*

jack'daw' *s* choucas *m*

jacket ['dʒækɪt] *s* (*of a woman; of a book*) jaquette *f*; (*of a man's suit*) veston *m*; (*metal casing*) chemise *f*

Jack' Frost' *s* le Bonhomme Hiver

jack'-in-the-box' *s* diable *m* à ressort, boîte *f* à surprise

jack'knife' *s* (*pl* -knives) couteau *m* de poche, couteau pliant; (*fancy dive*) saut *m* de carpe

jack'-of-all'-trades' *s* bricoleur *m*

jack-o'-lantern ['dʒækə,læntərn] *s* potiron *m* lumineux

jack'pot' *s* gros lot *m*, poule *f*; **to hit the jackpot** décrocher la timbale

jack' rab'bit *s* lièvre *m* des prairies

Jacob ['dʒekəb] *s* Jacques *m*

jade [dʒed] *s* (*stone; color*) jade *m*; (*horse*) haridelle *f*; (*woman*) coquine *f*, friponne *f*

jaded *adj* éreinté, excédé; blasé

jag [dʒæg] *s* dentelure *f*; **to have a jag on** (slang) être paf

jagged ['dʒægɪd] *adj* dentelé

jaguar ['dʒægwɑr] *s* jaguar *m*

jail [dʒel] *s* prison *f* || *tr* emprisonner

jail'bird' *s* cheval *m* de retour

jailer ['dʒelər] *s* geôlier *m*

jalop-y [dʒə'lɑpi] *s* (*pl* -ies) bagnole *f*, tacot *m*, guimbarde *f*, clou *m*

jam [dʒæm] *s* confiture *f*; **to be in a jam** (coll) être dans le pétrin || *v* (*pret & pp* jammed; *ger* jamming) *tr* coincer || *intr* se coincer

jamboree [,dʒæmbə'ri] *s* (*of boy scouts*) jamboree *m*; (slang) bombance *f*

James [dʒemz] *s* Jacques *m*

jamming ['dʒæmɪŋ] s (rad) brouillage m

Jane [dʒen] s Jeanne f

jangle ['dʒæŋgəl] s cliquetis m || tr faire cliqueter; (nerves) mettre en boule § intr cliqueter

janitor ['dʒænɪtər] s concierge m

janitress ['dʒænɪtrɪs] s concierge f

January ['dʒænju͵erɪ] s janvier m

ja·pan [dʒə'pæn] s laque m du Japon; **Japan** le Japon || v (pret & pp -panned; ger -panning) tr laquer

Japa·nese [͵dʒæpə'niz] adj japonais m; s (language) japonais m; s (pl -nese) (person) Japonais m

Jap'anese bee'tle s cétoine f

Jap'anese lan'tern s lanterne f vénitienne

jar [dʒɑr] s pot m, bocal m; secousse f || v (pret & pp jarred; ger jarring) tr ébranler, secouer § intr trembler, vibrer; (said of sounds, colors, opinions) discorder; **to jar on the nerves** taper sur les nerfs

jargon ['dʒɑrgən] s jargon m

jasmine ['dʒæsmɪn], ['dʒæzmɪn] s jasmin m

jasper ['dʒæspər] s jaspe m

jaundice ['dʒɔndɪs], ['dʒɑndɪs] s jaunisse f, ictère m

jaundiced adj ictérique; (fig) amer

jaunt [dʒɔnt], [dʒɑnt] s excursion f

jaun·ty ['dʒɔntɪ], ['dʒɑntɪ] adj (comp -tier; super -tiest) vif, dégagé; (smart) chic

javelin ['dʒævlɪn], ['dʒævəlɪn] s javelot m

jaw [dʒɔ] s mâchoire f; (of animal) gueule f; **jaws** (e.g., of death) griffes fpl || tr (slang) engueuler § intr (to gossip) (slang) bavarder

jaw'bone' s mâchoire f, maxillaire m

jay [dʒe] s geai m

jay'walk' intr traverser la rue en dehors des clous

jay'walk'er s piéton m distrait

jazz [dʒæz] s jazz m || tr—**to jazz up** (coll) animer, égayer

jazz' band' s orchestre m de jazz

jazz' sing'er s chanteur m de rythme

jealous ['dʒeləs] adj jaloux

jealous·y ['dʒeləsɪ] s (pl -ies) jalousie f

jean [dʒin] s treillis m; **Jean** Jeanne f; **jeans** pantalon m de treillis

jeep [dʒip] s jeep f

jeer [dʒɪr] s raillerie f || intr railler; **to jeer at** se moquer de

Jehovah [dʒɪ'hovə] s Jéhovah m

jell [dʒel] s gelée f || intr se convertir en gelée; (to take hold) prendre forme, se préciser

jel·ly ['dʒelɪ] s (pl -lies) gelée f || v (pret & pp -lied) tr convertir en gelée || intr se convertir en gelée

jel'ly-fish' s méduse f; (person) chiffe f

jeopardize ['dʒepər͵daɪz] tr mettre en danger, compromettre

jeopardy ['dʒepərdɪ] s danger m

jerk [dʒʌrk] s saccade f, secousse f;

(slang) mufle m || tr tirer brusquement, secouer || intr se mouvoir brusquement

jerk'water town' s trou m, petite ville f de province

jerk'water train' s tortillard m

jerk·y ['dʒʌrkɪ] adj (comp -ier; super -iest) saccadé

Jerome [dʒə'rom] s Jérôme m

jersey ['dʒʌrzɪ] s jersey m

Jerusalem [dʒɪ'rusələm] s Jérusalem f

jest ['dʒest] s plaisanterie f; **in jest** en plaisantant || intr plaisanter

jester ['dʒestər] s plaisantin m; (medieval clown) bouffon m

Jesuit ['dʒeʒu͵ɪt], ['dʒezju͵ɪt] adj jésuite, jésuitique || s Jésuite m

Jesus ['dʒizəs] s Jésus m

Je'sus Christ' s Jésus-Christ m

jet [dʒet] s (color; mineral) jais m; (of water, gas, etc.) jet m; avion m à réaction || v (pret & pp jetted; ger jetting) intr gicler, jaillir; voyager en jet

jet'-black' adj noir de jais

jet' en'gine s moteur m à réaction

jet' fight'er s chasseur m à réaction

jet' fu'el s carburéacteur m

jet'lin'er s avion m de ligne à réaction

jet' plane' s avion m à réaction

jet' propul'sion s propulsion f par réaction

jetsam ['dʒetsəm] s marchandise f jetée à la mer

jettison ['dʒetɪsən] s jet m à la mer || tr jeter à la mer; (fig) mettre au rebut, rejeter

jet·ty ['dʒetɪ] s (pl -ties) (wharf) appontement m; (breakwater) jetée f

Jew [dʒu] s Juif m; (rel) juif m

jewel ['dʒu·əl] s joyau m, bijou m; (of a watch) rubis m; (person) bijou

jew'el case' s écrin m

jeweler or **jeweller** ['dʒu·ələr] s horloger-bijoutier m, bijoutier m

jewelry ['dʒu·əlrɪ] s joaillerie f

jew'elry store' s bijouterie f; (for watches) horlogerie f

Jewess ['dʒu·ɪs] s Juive f; (rel) juive f

Jewish ['dʒu·ɪʃ] adj juif, judaïque

Jews'-harp or **jew's-harp** ['dʒuz͵hɑrp] s guimbarde f

jib [dʒɪb] s (mach) flèche f; (naut) foc m

jibe [dʒaɪb] s moquerie f || intr (coll) concorder; **to jibe at** se moquer de

jif·fy ['dʒɪfɪ] s (pl -fies)—**in a jiffy** (coll) en un clin d'œil

jig [dʒɪg] s (dance) gigue f; **the jig is up** (slang) il n'y a pas mèche, tout est dans le lac

jigger ['dʒɪgər] s mesure f qui contient une once et demie; (for fishing) leurre m; (tackle) palan m; (flea) puce f; (for separating ore) crible m; (naut) tapecul m; (gadget) (coll) machin m

jiggle ['dʒɪgəl] s petite secousse f || tr agiter, secouer || intr se trémousser

jig'saw' tr chantourner

jig' saw' s scie f à chantourner

jig'saw puz'zle *s* casse-tête *m* chinois, puzzle *m*

jilt [dʒɪlt] *tr* lâcher, repousser

jim·my ['dʒɪmi] *s* (*pl* -mies) pince-monseigneur *f* ‖ *v* (*pret & pp* -mied) *tr* forcer à l'aide d'une pince-monseigneur

jingle ['dʒɪŋgəl] *s* (*small bell*) grelot *m*; (*sound*) grelottement *m*; (*poem*) rimes *fpl* enfantines; slogan *m* à rimes; (*rad*) réclame *f* chantée ‖ *tr* faire grelotter ‖ *intr* grelotter

jin·go ['dʒɪŋgo] *adj* chauvin ‖ *s* (*pl* -goes) chauvin *m*; **by jingo!** (*coll*) sapristi!

jingoism ['dʒɪŋgo͵ɪzəm] *s* chauvinisme *m*

jinx [dʒɪŋks] *s* guigne *f* ‖ *tr* (*coll*) porter la guigne à

jitters ['dʒɪtərz] *spl* (*coll*) frousse *f*, trouille *f*; **to give the jitters to** (*coll*) flanquer la trouille à

jittery ['dʒɪtəri] *adj* froussard

Joan [dʒon] *s* Jeanne *f*

job [dʒab] *s* (*piece of work*) travail *m*; (*chore*) besogne *f*, tâche *f*; (*employment*) emploi *m*; (*work done by contract*) travail à forfait; (*slang*) vol *m*; **bad job** (*fig*) mauvaise affaire *f*; **by the job** à la pièce; **on the job** faisant un stage; (*slang*) attentif; **soft job** (*coll*) filon *m*, fromage *m*; **to be out of a job** être en chômage; **to lie down on the job** (*slang*) tirer au flanc

jobber ['dʒabər] *s* grossiste *m*; (*pieceworker*) ouvrier *m* à la tâche; (*dishonest official*) agioteur *m*

job'hold'er *s* employé *m*; (*in the government*) fonctionnaire *m*

job' lot' *s* solde *m* de marchandises

job' print'ing *s* bilboquet *m*

jockey ['dʒaki] *s* jockey *m* ‖ *tr* (*coll*) manœuvrer

jockstrap ['dʒak͵stræp] *s* suspensoir *m*

jocose [dʒo'kos] *adj* jovial, joyeux

jocular ['dʒakjələr] *adj* facétieux

jog [dʒag] *s* saccade *f* ‖ *v* (*pret & pp* jogged; *ger* jogging) *tr* secouer; (*the memory*) rafraîchir ‖ *intr*—**to jog along** aller au petit trot

John [dʒan] *s* Jean *m*; **john** (*slang*) toilettes *fpl*

John' Bull' *s* l'Anglais *m* typique

John' Doe' *s* M. Dupont, M. Durand

Johnny ['dʒani] *s* (*coll*) Jeannot *m*

john'ny-cake' *s* galette *f* de farine de maïs

John'ny-come'-late'ly *s* (*coll*) nouveau venu *m*

join [dʒɔɪn] *tr* joindre; (*to meet*) rejoindre; (*a club, a church*) se joindre à, entrer dans; (*a political party*) s'affilier à; (*the army*) s'engager dans; **to join s.o. in** + *ger* se joindre à qn pour + *inf* ‖ *intr* se joindre

joiner ['dʒɔɪnər] *s* menuisier *m*; (*coll*) clubiste *mf*

joint [dʒɔɪnt] *adj* joint, combiné ‖ *s* joint *m*; (*culin*) rôti *m*; (*slang*) boîte *f*; **out of joint** disloqué; (*fig*) de travers

joint' account' *s* compte *m* indivis

joint' commit'tee *s* commission *f* mixte

joint' own'er *s* copropriétaire *mf*

joint'-stock' com'pany *s* société *f* par actions

joist [dʒɔɪst] *s* solive *f*, poutre *f*

joke [dʒok] *s* plaisanterie *f*; **to play a joke on** faire une attrape à ‖ *intr* plaisanter

joker ['dʒokər] *s* farceur *m*, blagueur *m*; (*cards*) joker *m*, fou *m*; (*coll*) clause *f* ambiguë

jol·ly ['dʒali] *adj* (*comp* -lier; *super* -liest) joyeux, enjoué ‖ *adv* (*coll*) rudement

jolt [dʒolt] *s* cahot *m*, secousse *f* ‖ *tr* cahoter, secouer ‖ *intr* cahoter

Jonah ['dʒona] *s* Jonas *m*

jonquil ['dʒaŋkwɪl] *s* jonquille *f*

Jordan ['dʒɔrdən] *s* (*country*) Jordanie *f*; la Jordanie; (*river*) Jourdain *m*

josh [dʒaʃ] *tr & intr* (*coll*) blaguer

jostle ['dʒasəl] *tr* bousculer ‖ *intr* se bousculer

jot [dʒat] *s*—**not a jot** pas un iota ‖ *v* (*pret & pp* jotted; *ger* jotting) *tr*—**to jot down** prendre note de

journal ['dʒʌrnəl] *s* journal *m*; (*magazine*) revue *f*; (*mach*) tourillon *m*; (*naut*) journal de bord

jour'nal box' *s* boîte *f* d'essieu

journalism ['dʒʌrnə͵lɪzəm] *s* journalisme *m*

journalist ['dʒʌrnəlɪst] *s* journaliste *mf*

journey ['dʒʌrni] *s* voyage *m*; trajet *m*, parcours *m* ‖ *intr* voyager

jour'ney·man *s* (*pl* -men) compagnon *m*

joust [dʒast], [dʒust], [dʒaust] *s* joute *f* ‖ *intr* jouter

Jove [dʒov] *s* Jupiter *m*; **by Jove!** parbleu!

jovial ['dʒovɪ·əl] *adj* jovial

jowl [dʒaul] *s* bajoue *f*

joy [dʒɔɪ] *s* joie *f*

joyful ['dʒɔɪfəl] *adj* joyeux

joyless ['dʒɔɪlɪs] *adj* sans joie

joyous ['dʒɔɪ·əs] *adj* joyeux

joy' ride' *s* (*coll*) balade *f* en auto

joy' stick' *s* manche *m* à balai

Jr. *abbr* (**junior**) fils, e.g., **Mr. Martin, Jr.** M. Martin fils

jubilant ['dʒubɪlənt] *adj* jubilant

jubilee ['dʒubɪ͵li] *s* jubilé *m*

Judaism ['dʒude͵ɪzəm] *s* judaïsme *m*

judge [dʒʌdʒ] *s* juge *m* ‖ *tr & intr* juger; **judging by** à en juger par

judge' ad'vocate *s* commissaire *m* du gouvernement

judgment ['dʒʌdʒmənt] *s* jugement *m*

judg'ment day' *s* jour *m* du jugement dernier

judicial [dʒu'dɪʃəl] *adj* judiciaire; (*legal*) juridique

judiciar·y [dʒu'dɪʃɪ͵eri] *adj* judiciaire ‖ *s* (*pl* -ies) pouvoir *m* judiciaire; (*judges*) judicature *f*

judicious [dʒu'dɪʃəs] *s* judicieux

jug [dʒʌg] *s* (*of earthenware*) cruche *f*; (*of metal*) broc *m*; (*jail*) (*slang*) bloc *m*

juggle ['dʒʌgəl] *tr* jongler avec; **to juggle away** escamoter ‖ *intr* jongler

juggler ['dʒʌglər] *s* jongleur *m*; imposteur *m*, mystificateur *m*

jugglery ['dʒʌgləri] or **juggling** ['dʒʌglɪŋ] *s* jonglerie *f*; (*trickery*) passe-passe *m*

Jugoslavia ['jugo'slɑvɪ-ə] *s* Yougoslavie *f*; **la Yougoslavie**

jugular ['dʒʌgjələr], ['dʒugjələr] *adj & s* jugulaire *f*

juice [dʒus] *s* jus *m*; (coll) courant *m* électrique

juic·y ['dʒusi] *adj* (*comp* **-ier**; *super* **-iest**) juteux; (fig) savoureux

jukebox ['dʒuk,bɑks] *s* pick-up *m* électrique à sous, distributeur *m* de musique

July [dʒu'laɪ] *s* juillet *m*

jumble ['dʒʌmbəl] *s* fouillis *m*, enchevêtrement *m* ‖ *tr* brouiller

jumbo ['dʒʌmbo] *adj* (coll) géant

jump [dʒʌmp] *s* saut *m*, bond *m*; (*nervous start*) sursaut *m*; (sports) saut *m*; (sports) obstacle *m* ‖ *tr* sauter; **to jump ship** tirer une bordée; **to jump the gun** démarrer trop tôt; **to jump the track** dérailler ‖ *intr* sauter, bondir; **to jump at the chance** sauter sur l'occasion

jump' ball' *s* (sports) entre-deux *m*

jump'ing jack' *s* pantin *m*

jump' rope' *s* corde *f* à sauter

jump' seat' *s* strapontin *m*

jump·y ['dʒʌmpi] *adj* (*comp* **-ier**; *super* **-iest**) nerveux

junction ['dʒʌŋkʃən] *s* jonction *f*; (*of railroads, roads*) embranchement *m*

juncture ['dʒʌŋktʃər] *s* jointure *f*; (*occasion*) conjoncture *f*; **at this juncture** en cette occasion

June [dʒun] *s* juin *m*

jungle ['dʒʌŋgəl] *s* jungle *f*

jun'gle war'fare *s* guerre *f* de la brousse

junior ['dʒunjər] *adj* cadet; **Bobby Watson, Junior** le jeune Bobby Watson; **Martin, Junior** Martin fils ‖ *s* cadet *m*; (educ) étudiant *m* de troisième année

jun'ior of'ficer *s* officier *m* subalterne

juniper ['dʒunɪpər] *s* genévrier *m*

ju'niper ber'ry *s* genièvre *m*

junk [dʒʌŋk] *s* (*old metal*) ferraille *f*; (*worthless objects*) bric-à-brac *m*; (*cheap merchandise*) camelote *f*, pacotille *f*; (coll) gnognote *f*; (naut) jonque *f* ‖ *tr* mettre au rebut

junk' deal'er *s* fripier *m*; marchand *m* de ferraille

junket ['dʒʌŋkɪt] *s* excursion *f*; voyage *m* officiel aux frais de la princesse

junk'man *s* (*pl* **-men'**) ferrailleur *m*; chiffonnier *m*

junk' shop' *s* boutique *f* de bric-à-brac et friperie; marchand *m* de bric-à-brac *m*

junk'yard' *s* cimetière *m* de ferraille

jurisdiction [,dʒurɪs'dɪk/ən] *s* juridiction *f*; **within the jurisdiction of** du ressort de

jurist ['dʒurɪst] *s* légiste *m*

juror ['dʒurər] *s* juré *m*

ju·ry ['dʒuri] *s* (*pl* **-ries**) jury *m*

just [dʒʌst] *adj* juste ‖ *adv* seulement; justement; **just as** à l'instant où; (*in the same way that*) de même que; **just as it is** tel quel; **just out** vient de paraître; **to have just** venir de

justice ['dʒʌstɪs] *s* justice *f*; (*judge*) juge *m*

jus'tice of the peace' *s* juge *m* de paix

justi·fy ['dʒʌstɪ,faɪ] *v* (*pret & pp* **-fied**) *tr* justifier

justly ['dʒʌstli] *adv* justement

jut [dʒʌt] *v* (*pret & pp* **jutted**; *ger* **jutting**) *intr*—**to jut out** faire saillie

jute [dʒut] *s* jute *m*

juvenile ['dʒuvənɪl], ['dʒuvə,naɪl] *adj* juvénile, adolescent; (*e.g., books*) pour la jeunesse ‖ *s* adolescent *m*

ju'venile delin'quency *s* délinquance *f* juvénile

ju'venile delin'quent *s* délinquant *m* juvénile; **juvenile delinquents** jeunes délinquants *mpl*

juxtapose [,dʒʌkstə'poz] *tr* juxtaposer

K

K, k [ke] *s* XIᵉ lettre de l'alphabet

kale [kel] *s* chou *m* frisé

kaleidoscope [kə'laɪdə,skop] *s* kaléidoscope *m*

kangaroo [,kæŋgə'ru] *s* kangourou *m*

kan'garoo court' *s* tribunal *m* bidon

Kashmir ['kæ/mɪr] *s* le Cachemire

kash'mir shawl' *s* châle *m* de cachemire

keel [kil] *s* quille *f* ‖ *intr*—**to keel over** (naut) chavirer; (coll) tomber dans les pommes

keen [kin] *adj* (*having a sharp edge*) aiguisé, affilé; (*sharp, cutting*) mordant, pénétrant; (*sharp-witted*) perçant, perspicace; (*eager, much interested*) enthousiaste, vif; (slang) formidable; **keen on** engoué de, passionné de

keep [kip] *s* entretien *m*; (*of medieval castle*) donjon *m*; **for keeps** (*for good*) (coll) pour de bon; (*forever*) (coll) à tout jamais; **to earn one's keep** (coll) gagner sa nourriture, gagner sa vie; **to play for keeps** (coll) jouer le tout pour le tout ‖ *v* (*pret & pp* **kept** [kept]) *tr* garder, conserver; (*one's word or promise; accounts, a diary*) tenir; (*animals*) élever; (*a garden*) cultiver; (*a hotel, a school, etc.*) diriger; (*an appointment*) ne pas manquer à; *(a holiday)* observer; *(a person)* avoir à sa charge, entretenir; **keep it up!** ne flanchez pas!, continuez!; **to keep away** éloigner; **to keep back** retenir; **to keep down** baisser; *(prices)* maintenir bas; *(a revolt)* réprimer; **to keep in** retenir; *(a student after school)* garder en retenue; *(dust, fire, etc.)* entretenir; **to keep off** éloigner; **to keep out** tenir éloigné, empêcher d'entrer; **to keep quiet** faire taire; **to keep running** laisser marcher; **to keep score** marquer les points; **to keep servants** avoir des domestiques; **to keep s.o. busy** occuper qn; **to keep s.o. clean (cool, warm, etc.)** tenir qn propre (au frais, au chaud, etc.); **to keep s.o. or s.th. from** + *ger* empêcher qn or q.ch. de + *inf*; **to keep s.o. informed about** mettre or tenir qn au courant de; **to keep s.o. waiting** faire attendre qn; **to keep up** maintenir; *(e.g., all night)* faire veiller ‖ *intr* rester, se tenir; *(in good shape)* demeurer, se conserver; *(e.g., from rotting)* se garder; **keep out** *(public sign)* entrée interdite; **that can keep** (coll) ça peut attendre; **to keep** + *ger* continuer à + *inf*; **to keep away** s'éloigner, se tenir à l'écart; **to keep from** + *ger* s'abstenir de + *inf*; **to keep in with** rester en bons termes avec; **to keep on** + *ger* continuer à + *inf*; **to keep out** rester dehors; **to keep out of** ne pas se mêler de; **to keep quiet** rester tranquille, se taire; **to keep to** *(e.g., the right)* garder *(e.g., la droite)*; **to keep up** tenir bon, tenir ferme; **to keep up with** aller de pair avec

keeper ['kipər] *s* gardien *m*, garde *m*; *(of a game preserve)* garde forestier; *(of a horseshoe magnet)* armature *f*

keeping ['kipiŋ] *s* garde *f*, surveillance *f*; *(of a holiday)* observance *f*; **in keeping with** en accord avec; **in safe keeping** sous bonne garde; **out of keeping with** en désaccord avec

keep'sake' *s* souvenir *m*, gage *m* d'amitié

keg [keg] *s* tonnelet *m*; *(of herring)* caque *f*

ken [ken] *s*—**beyond the ken of** hors de la portée de

kennel ['kenəl] *s* chenil *m*

kep·i ['kepi], ['kepi] *s* (*pl* **-is**) képi *m*

kept' wom'an [kept] *s* (*pl* **wom'en**) femme *f* entretenue

kerchief ['kʌrtʃɪf] *s* fichu *m*

kernel ['kʌrnəl] *s* *(inner part of a nut or fruit stone)* amande *f*; *(of wheat or corn)* grain *m*; *(fig)* noyau *m*, cœur *m*

kerosene ['kerə,sin], [,kerə'sin] *s* kérosène *m*, pétrole *m* lampant

ker'osene lamp' *s* lampe *f* à pétrole

kerplunk [,kʌr'plʌŋk] *interj* patatras!

ketchup ['ketʃəp] *s* sauce *f* tomate, ketchup *m*

kettle ['ketəl] *s* chaudron *m*, marmite *f*; *(teakettle)* bouilloire *f*

ket'tle·drum' *s* timbale *f*

key [ki] *adj* clef, clé ‖ *s* clef *f*, clé *f*; *(of piano, typewriter, etc.)* touche *f*; *(wedge or cotter used to lock parts together)* cheville *f*, clavette *f*; *(reef or low island)* caye *f*; *(answer book)* livre *m* du maître; *(tone of voice)* ton *m*; *(to a map)* légende *f*; *(bot)* samare *f*; *(mus)* tonalité *f*; *(telg)* manipulateur *m*; **key to the city** droit *m* de cité; **off key** faux; **on key** juste ‖ *tr* claveter, coincer; **to be keyed up** être surexcité, être tendu

key'board' *s* clavier *m*

key'hole' *s* trou *m* de la serrure; *(of clock)* trou de clef

key'man' *s* (*pl* **-men'**) pivot *m*, homme *m* indispensable

key'note' *s* (mus) tonique *f*; (fig) dominante *f*

key'note speech' *s* discours *m* d'ouverture

key'punch' *s* (mach) perforatrice *f*

key'ring' *s* porte-clefs *m*

key' sig'nature *s* (mus) armature *f* de la clé

key'stone' *s* clef *f* de voûte

key' word' *s* mot-clé *m*

kha·ki ['kɑki], ['kæki] *adj* kaki ‖ *s* (*pl* **-kis**) kaki *m*

khan [kɑn] *s* khan *m*

kibitz ['kɪbɪts] *intr* (coll) faire la mouche du coche

kibitzer ['kɪbɪtsər] *s* (coll) casse-pieds *mf*, curieux *m*

kick [kɪk] *s* coup *m* de pied; *(e.g., of a horse)* ruade *f*; *(of a gun)* recul *m*; *(complaint)* (slang) plainte *f*; *(thrill)* (slang) effet *m*, frisson *m*; **to get a kick out of** (slang) s'en payer une tranche de ‖ *tr* donner un coup de pied à; *(a ball)* botter; **to kick out** (coll) chasser à coups de pied; **to kick s.o. in the pants** (coll) botter le derrière à qn; **to kick the bucket** (coll) casser sa pipe, passer l'arme à gauche; **to kick up a row** (slang) déclencher un chahut ‖ *intr* donner un coup de pied; *(said of gun)* reculer; *(said of horse)* ruer; (sports) botter; **to kick against** regimber contre; **to kick off** (football) donner le coup d'envoi

kick'back' *s* contrecoup *m*; (slang) ristourne *f*

kick'off' *s* (sports) coup *m* d'envoi

kid [kɪd] *s* chevreau *m*; (coll) gosse *mf*, mioche *mf* ‖ *v* (*pret & pp* **kidded**; *ger* **kidding**) *tr & intr* (slang) blaguer; **to kid oneself** (slang) se faire des illusions

kidder ['kɪdər] *s* (slang) blagueur *m*

kidding ['kɪdɪŋ] *s* (slang) blague *f*; **no kidding!** (slang) sans blague!

kid' gloves' *spl* gants *mpl* de chevreau; **to handle with kid gloves** traiter avec douceur, ménager

kid'nap *v* (*pret & pp* **-naped** or **-napped**; *ger* **-naping** or **-napping**) *tr* kidnapper

kidnaper or **kidnapper** ['kɪdnæpər] *s* kidnappeur *m*

kidnaping or **kidnapping** ['kɪdnæpɪŋ] *s* kidnappage *m*

kidney ['kɪdni] *s* rein *m*; (culin) rognon *m*

kid'ney bean' *s* haricot *m* de Soissons

kid'ney-shaped' *adj* réniforme

kid'ney stone' *s* calcul *m* rénal

kill [kɪl] *s* mise *f* à mort; (*bag of game*) gibier *m* tué ‖ *tr* tuer; (*an animal*) abattre; (*a bill, amendment, etc.*) mettre son veto à, faire échouer

killer ['kɪlər] *s* assassin *m*

kill'er whale' *s* épaulard *m*, orque *f*

killing ['kɪlɪŋ] *adj* meurtrier; (*exhausting; ridiculous*) crevant ‖ *s* tuerie *f*; to make a killing (coll) réussir un beau coup

kill'-joy' *s* rabat-joie *m*, trouble-fête *mf*

kiln [kɪl], [kɪln] *s* four *m*

kil·o ['kilo], ['kɪlo] *s* (*pl* -os) kilo *m*, kilogramme *m*; kilomètre *m*

kilocycle ['kɪlə,saɪkəl] *s* kilocycle *m*

kilogram ['kɪlə,græm] *s* kilogramme *m*

kilometer ['kɪlə,mitər], [kɪ'lɑmɪtər] *s* kilomètre *m*

kilowatt ['kɪlə,wɑt] *s* kilowatt *m*

kilowatt-hour ['kɪlə,wɑt'aur] *s* (*pl* -hours) kilowatt-heure *m*

kilt [kɪlt] *s* kilt *m*

kilter ['kɪltər] *s*—to be out of kilter (coll) être détraqué

kimo·no [kɪ'monə], [kɪ'mono] *s* (*pl* -nos) kimono *m*

kin [kɪn] *s* (*family relationship*) parenté *f*; (*relatives*) les parents *mpl*; **of kin** apparenté; **the next of kin** le plus proche parent, les plus proches parents

kind [kaɪnd] *adj* bon, bienveillant; **kind to** bon pour; **to be so kind as to** être assez aimable pour ‖ *s* espèce *f*, genre *m*, sorte *f*, classe *f*; **all kinds of** (coll) quantité de; **kind of** (coll) plutôt, en quelque sorte; **of a kind** semblable, de même nature; **to pay in kind** payer en nature

kindergarten ['kɪndər,gɑrtən] *s* jardin *m* d'enfants

kindergartner ['kɪndər,gɑrtnər] *s* élève *mf* de jardin d'enfants; (*teacher*) jardinière *f*

kind'-heart'ed *adj* bon, bienveillant

kindle ['kɪndəl] *tr* allumer ‖ *intr* s'allumer

kindling ['kɪndlɪŋ] *s* allumage *m*; (*wood*) bois *m* d'allumage

kin'dling wood' *s* bois *m* d'allumage

kind·ly ['kaɪndli] *adj* (*comp* -lier; *super* -liest) (*kind-hearted*) bon, bienveillant; (*e.g., climate*) doux; (*e.g., terrain*) favorable ‖ *adv* avec bonté, avec bienveillance; **to take kindly** prendre en bonne part; **to take kindly to** prendre en amitié

kindness ['kaɪndnɪs] *s* bonté *f*, obligeance *f*

kindred ['kɪndrɪd] *adj* apparenté, de même nature ‖ *s* parenté *f*, famille *f*; parenté, ressemblance *f*

kinescope ['kɪnɪ,skop] *s* (*trademark*) kinescope *m*

kinetic [kɪ'netɪk], [kaɪ'netɪk] *adj* cinétique ‖ **kinetics** *s* cinétique *f*

kinet'ic en'ergy *s* énergie *f* cinétique

king [kɪŋ] *s* roi *m*; (*cards, chess, & fig*) roi; (*checkers*) pion *m* doublé, dame *f* ‖ *tr* (*checkers*) damer

king'bolt' *s* cheville *f* maîtresse

kingdom ['kɪŋdəm] *s* royaume *m*; (*one of three divisions of nature*) règne *m*

king'fish'er *s* martin-pêcheur *m*

king·ly ['kɪŋli] *adj* (*comp* -lier; *super* -liest) royal, de roi, digne d'un roi ‖ *adv* en roi, de roi, comme un roi

king'pin' *s* cheville *f* ouvrière; (bowling) quille *f* du milieu; (coll) ponte *m*, pontife *m*

king'post' *s* poinçon *m*

kingship ['kɪŋʃɪp] *s* royauté *f*

king'-size' *adj* grand format, géant

king's' ran'som *s* rançon *f* de roi

kink [kɪŋk] *s* (*twist, e.g., in a rope*) nœud *m*; (*in a wire*) faux pli *m*; (*in hair*) frisette *f*, bouclette *f*; (*soreness in neck*) torticolis *m*; (*flaw, difficulty*) point *m* faible; (*mental twist*) lubie *f*; (naut) coque *f* ‖ *tr* nouer, entortiller ‖ *intr* se nouer, s'entortiller

kink·y ['kɪŋki] *adj* (*comp* -ier; *super* -iest) crépu, bouclé

kinsfolk ['kɪnz,fok] *spl* parents *mpl*

kin'ship *s* parenté *f*

kins·man ['kɪnzmən] *s* (*pl* -men) parent *m*

kins·woman ['kɪnz,wumən] *s* (*pl* -wom'en) parente *f*

kipper ['kɪpər] *s* kipper *m* ‖ *tr* saurer

kiss [kɪs] *s* baiser *m* ‖ *tr* embrasser, donner un baiser à ‖ *intr* s'embrasser

kit [kɪt] *s* nécessaire *m*; (*tub*) tonnelet *m*; (*of traveler*) trousse *f* de voyage; (mil) équipement *m*, sac *m*; **the whole kit and caboodle** (coll) tout le saint-frusquin

kitchen ['kɪtʃən] *s* cuisine *f*

kitch'en cup'board *s* vaisselier *m*

kitchenette [,kɪtʃə'nɛt] *s* petite cuisine *f*

kitch'en gar'den *s* jardin *m* potager

kitch'en-maid' *s* fille *f* de cuisine

kitch'en police' *s* (mil) corvée *f* de cuisine

kitch'en range' *s* cuisinière *f*

kitch'en sink' *s* évier *m*

kitch'en-ware' *s* ustensiles *mpl* de cuisine

kite [kaɪt] *s* cerf-volant *m*; (orn) milan *m*; **to fly a kite** lancer or enlever un cerf-volant

kith' and kin' [kɪθ] *spl* amis et parents *mpl*, cousinage *m*

kitten ['kɪtən] *s* chaton *m*, petit chat *m*

kittenish ['kɪtənɪʃ] *adj* enjoué, folâtre; (*woman*) coquette, chatte

kit·ty ['kɪti] *s* (*pl* -ties) minet *m*, minou *m*; (*in card games*) cagnotte *f*, poule *f*; **kitty, kitty, kitty!** minet, minet, minet!

kleptomaniac [,kleptə'meni,æk] *adj & s* kleptomane *mf*

knack [næk] *s* adresse *f*, chic *m*

knapsack ['næp,sæk] s sac m à dos, havresac m

knave [nev] s fripon m; (cards) valet m

knaver·y ['nevəri] s (pl -ies) friponnerie f

knead [nid] tr pétrir; (to massage) masser

knee [ni] s genou m; **to bring s.o. to his knees** mettre qn à genoux; **to go down on one's knees** se mettre à genoux

knee' breech'es spl culotte f courte

knee'cap' s rotule f; (protective covering) genouillère f

knee'-deep' adj jusqu'aux genoux

knee'-high' adj à la hauteur du genou

knee'hole' s trou m, évidement m pour l'entrée des genoux

knee' jerk' s réflexe m rotulien

kneel [nil] v (pret & pp knelt [nɛlt] or kneeled) intr s'agenouiller, se mettre à genoux

knee'pad' s genouillère f

knee'pan' s rotule f

knee' swell' s (of organ) genouillère f

knell [nɛl] s glas m; **to toll the knell of** sonner le glas de || intr sonner le glas

knickers ['nɪkərz] spl pantalons mpl de golf, knickerbockers mpl

knickknack ['nɪk,næk] s colifichet m

knife [naɪf] s (pl knives [naɪvz]) couteau m; (of paper cutter or other instrument) couperet m, lame f; **to go under the knife** (coll) monter or passer sur le billard || tr poignarder

knife' sharp'ener s fusil m, affiloir m

knife' switch' s (elec) interrupteur m à couteau

knight [naɪt] s chevalier m; (chess) cavalier m || tr créer or faire chevalier

knight-errant ['naɪt'ɛrənt] s (pl knights-errant) chevalier m errant

knighthood ['naɪthʊd] s chevalerie f

knightly ['naɪtli] adj chevaleresque

knit [nɪt] v (pret & pp knitted or knit; ger knitting) tr tricoter; (one's brows) froncer; **to knit together** lier, unir || intr tricoter; (said of bones) se souder

knit' goods' spl tricot m, bonneterie f

knitting ['nɪtɪŋ] s (action) tricotage m; (product) tricot m

knit'ting machine' s tricoteuse f

knit'ting nee'dle s aiguille f à tricoter

knit'wear' s tricot m

knob [nɑb] s (lump) bosse f; (of a door, drawer, etc.) bouton m, poignée f; (of a radio) bouton

knock [nɑk] s coup m, heurt m; (of an internal-combustion engine) cognement m; (slang) éreintement m, dénigrement m || tr frapper; (repeatedly) cogner à, contre, or sur; (slang) éreinter, dénigrer; **to knock about** bousculer; **to knock against** heurter contre; **to knock down** (with a blow, punch, etc.) renverser; (at the highest bidder) adjuger; **to knock in** enfoncer; **to knock off** faire tomber; **to knock out** faire sortir en cognant; (boxing) mettre knock-out; (to fatigue) (coll) claquer, fatiguer || intr

frapper; (said of internal-combustion engine) cogner; **to knock about** vagabonder, se balader; **to knock against** se heurter contre; **to knock at** or **on** (e.g., a door) heurter à, frapper à; **to knock off** (to stop working) (coll) débrayer

knock'down' adj (dismountable) démontable || s (blow) coup m d'assommoir; (discount) escompte m

knocked' out' adj éreinté; (boxing) knock-out

knocker ['nɑkər] s (on a door) heurtoir m, marteau m; (critic) (coll) éreinteur m

knock-kneed ['nɑk,nid] adj cagneux

knock'out' s (boxing) knock-out m; (person) (coll) type m renversant; (thing) (coll) chose f sensationnelle

knock'out drops' spl (slang) narcotique m

knoll [nol] s mamelon m, tertre m

knot [nɑt] s nœud m; (e.g., of people) groupe m; (naut) nœud m, mille m marin à l'heure; (loosely) (naut) mille marin; **to tie a knot** faire un nœud; **to tie the knot** (coll) prononcer le conjungo || v (pret & pp knotted; ger knotting) tr nouer; **to knot one's brow** froncer le sourcil || intr se nouer

knot'hole' s trou m de nœud

knot·ty ['nɑti] adj (comp -tier; super -tiest) noueux; (e.g., question) épineux

know [no] s—**to be in the know** (coll) être au courant, être à la page || v (pret knew [n(j)u]; pp known) tr & intr (by reasoning or learning) savoir; (by the senses or by perception; through acquaintance or recognition) connaître; **as far as I know** autant que je sache; **to know about** être informé de, savoir; **to know best** être le meilleur juge; **to know how to** + inf savoir + inf; **to let s.o. know about** faire part à qn de; **you ought to know better** vous devriez avoir honte; **you ought to know better than to . . .** vous devriez vous bien garder de . . . ; **you wouldn't know s.o. from . . .** on prendrait qn pour . . .

knowable ['noəbəl] adj connaissable

know'-how' s technique f, savoir-faire m

knowing ['no·ɪŋ] adj avisé; (look, smile) entendu

knowingly ['no·ɪŋli] adv sciemment, en connaissance de cause; (on purpose) exprès

know'-it-all' adj (coll) omniscient || s (coll) Monsieur Je-sais-tout m

knowledge ['nɑlɪdʒ] s (faculty) science f, connaissances fpl, savoir m; (awareness, familiarity) connaissance f; **not to my knowledge** pas que je sache; **to have a thorough knowledge of** posséder une connaissance approfondie de; **to my knowledge**, **to the best of my knowledge** à ma connaissance, autant que je sache; **without my knowledge** à mon insu

knowledgeable ['nɑlɪdʒəbəl] *adj* (coll) intelligent, bien informé

know'-noth'ing *s* ignorant *m*

knuckle ['nʌkəl] *s* jointure *f* or articulation *f* du doigt; (*of a quadruped*) jarret *m*; (*mach*) joint *m* en charnière; **knuckle of ham** jambonneau *m*; **to rap s.o. over the knuckles** donner sur les doigts or ongles à qn ‖ *intr*—**to knuckle down** se soumettre; (*to work hard*) s'y mettre sérieusement

knurl [nʌrl] *s* molette *f* ‖ *tr* moleter

k.o. ['ke'ʊ] (letterword) (**knockout**) *s* k.o. *m* ‖ *tr* mettre k.o.

Koran [ko'rɑn], [ko'ræn] *s* Coran *m*

Korea [ko'ri-ə] *s* Corée *f*; **la Corée**

Korean [ko'ri-ən] *adj* coréen ‖ *s* (*language*) coréen; (*person*) Coréen *m*

kosher ['koʃər] *adj* casher, cawcher; (coll) convenable

kowtow ['kau'tau], ['ko'tau] *intr* se prosterner à la chinoise; **to kowtow to** faire des courbettes à or devant

K.P. ['ke'pi] *s* (letterword) (**kitchen police**) (mil) corvée *f* de cuisine; **to be on K.P. duty** (mil) être de soupe

kudos ['k(j)udɑs] *s* (coll) gloire *f*, éloges *mpl*, flatteries *fpl*

L

L, l [el] *s* XIIᵉ lettre de l'alphabet

la‧bel ['lebəl] *s* étiquette *f*; (*brand*) marque *f*; (*in a dictionary*) rubrique *f*, référence *f* ‖ *v* (*pret & pp* **-beled** or **-belled**) *ger* **-beling** or **-belling**) *tr* étiqueter

labial ['lebɪ-əl] *adj* labial ‖ *s* labiale *f*

labor ['lebər] *adj* ouvrier ‖ *s* travail *m*; (*toil*) labeur *m*, peine *f*; (*job, task*) tâche *f*, besogne *f*; (*manual work involved in an undertaking; the wages for such work*) main-d'œuvre *f*; (*wage-earning worker as contrasted with capital and management*) le salariat, le travail; (*childbirth*) couches *fpl*, travail; **to be in labor** être en couches ‖ *tr* (*a point, subject, etc.*) insister sur; (*one's style*) travailler, élaborer ‖ *intr* travailler; (*to toil*) travailler dur, peiner; (*to exert oneself*) s'efforcer; (*said of ship*) fatiguer, bourlinguer; **to labor under** être victime de; (*a hill, slope, etc.*) gravir; **to labor up** (*a hill, slope, etc.*) gravir; **to labor uphill** peiner en côte; **to labor with child** être en travail d'enfant

la'bor and man'agement *spl* la classe ouvrière et le patronat

laborato‧ry ['læbərə,tori] *s* (*pl* -ries) laboratoire *m*

lab'oratory class' *s* classe *f* de travaux pratiques

labored ['lebərd] *adj* travaillé, trop élaboré; (*e.g., breathing*) pénible

laborer ['lebərər] *s* travailleur *m*, ouvrier *m*; (*unskilled worker*) journalier *m*, manœuvre *m*

laborious [lə'borɪ-əs] *adj* laborieux

la'bor move'ment *s* mouvement *m* syndicaliste

la'bor un'ion *s* syndicat *m*, syndicat ouvrier

Labourite ['lebə,raɪt] *adj & s* (Brit) travailliste *mf*

La'bour Par'ty ['lebər] *adj* (Brit) travailliste ‖ *s* parti *m* travailliste

Labrador ['læbrə,dor] *s* le Labrador

laburnum [lə'bʌrnəm] *s* cytise *m*

labyrinth ['læbɪrɪnθ] *s* labyrinthe *m*

lace [les] *s* dentelle *f*; (*string to tie shoe, corset, etc.*) lacet *m*, cordon *m*; (*braid*) broderies *fpl* ‖ *tr* garnir or border de dentelles; (*shoes, corset, etc.*) lacer; (*to braid*) entrelacer; (coll) flanquer une rossée à, rosser

lace' trim'ming *s* passementerie *f*

lace'work' *s* dentelles *fpl*, passementerie *f*

lachrymose ['lækrɪ,mos] *adj* larmoyant

lacing ['lesɪŋ] *s* lacet *m*, cordon *m*; (*trimming*) galon *m*, passement *m*; (coll) rossée *f*

lack [læk] *s* manque *m*, défaut *m*; (*lack of necessities*) pénurie *f*; **for lack of** faute de ‖ *tr* manquer de, être dépourvu de ‖ *intr* (*to be lacking*) manquer

lackadaisical [,lækə'dezɪkəl] *adj* languissant, apathique

lackey ['læki] *s* laquais *m*

lacking ['lækɪŋ] *prep* dépourvu de, dénué de

lack'lus'ter *adj* terne, fade

laconic [lə'kɑnɪk] *adj* laconique

lacquer ['lækər] *s* laque *m & f* ‖ *tr* laquer

lac'quer ware' *s* laques *mpl*, objets *mpl* d'art en laque

lacrosse [lə'krɔs], [lə'krɑs] *s* crosse *f*, jeu *m* de crosse; **to play lacrosse** jouer à la crosse

lacu‧na [lə'kjunə] *s* (*pl* -nas or -nae [ni]) lacune *f*

lac‧y ['lesi] *adj* (*comp* -ier; *super* -iest) de dentelle; (fig) fin, léger

lad [læd] *s* garçon *m*, gars *m*

ladder ['lædər] *s* échelle *f*; (*stepping stone*) (fig) marchepied *m*, échelon *m*; (*stepladder*) marchepied, escabeau *m*; (*run in stocking*) (Brit) démaillage *m*; (*stairway*) (naut) escalier *m*

lad'der truck' *s* fourgon-pompe *m* à échelle

la'dies' room' *s* toilettes *fpl* pour dames, lavabos *mpl* pour dames

ladle ['ledəl] *s* louche *f* || *tr* servir à la louche

la·dy ['ledɪ] *s* (*pl* -dies) dame *f*; **ladies** (public sign) dames; **ladies and gentlemen!** (formula used in addressing an audience) mesdames, mesdemoiselles, messieurs!; messieurs dames! (coll)

la'dy·bird' *or* **la'dy·bug'** *s* coccinelle *f*, bête *f* à bon Dieu

la'dy·fin'ger *s* biscuit *m* à la cuiller

la'dy-in-wait'ing *s* (*pl* **ladies-in-waiting**) demoiselle *f* d'honneur

la'dy·kil'ler *s* bourreau *m* des cœurs, tombeur *m* de femmes

la'dy·like' *adj* de bon ton, de dame

la'dy·love' *s* bien-aimée *f*, dulcinée *f*

la'dy of the house' *s* maîtresse *f* de maison

la'dy's maid' *s* camériste *f*

la'dy's man' *s* homme *m* à succès

lag [læg] *s* retard *m* || *v* (*pret & pp* **lagged**; *ger* **lagging**) *intr* traîner; **to lag behind** rester en arrière

la'ger beer' ['lɑgər] *s* bière *f* de fermentation basse, lager *m*

laggard ['lægərd] *adj* tardif || *s* traînard *m*

lagoon [lə'gun] *s* lagune *f*

laid' pa'per [led] *s* papier *m* vergé

laid' up' *adj* mis en réserve; (naut) mis en rade; (coll) alité, au lit

lair [ler] *s* tanière *f*; (fig) repaire *m*

laity ['le·ɪtɪ] *s* profanes *mfpl*; (eccl) laïques *mfpl*

lake [lek] *adj* lacustre || *s* lac *m*

lamb [læm] *s* agneau *m*

lambaste [læm'best] *tr* (*to thrash*) (coll) flanquer une rossée à; (*to reprimand harshly*) (coll) passer un savon à

lamb' chop' *s* côtelette *f* d'agneau

lambkin ['læmkɪn] *s* agnelet *m*

lamb'skin' *s* peau *f* d'agneau; (*dressed with its wool*) mouton *m*, agnelin *m*

lame [lem] *adj* boiteux; (*sore*) endolori; (*e.g., excuse*) faible, piètre || *tr* estropier, rendre boiteux

lament [lə'ment] *s* lamentation *f*; (*dirge*) complainte *f* || *tr* déplorer || *intr* lamenter, se lamenter

lamentable ['læməntəbəl] *adj* lamentable

lamentation [,læmən'tefən] *s* lamentation *f*

laminate ['læmɪ,net] *tr* laminer

lamp [læmp] *s* lampe *f*

lamp'black' *s* noir *m* de fumée

lamp' chim'ney *s* verre *m* de lampe

lamp'light' *s* lumière *f* de lampe

lamp'light'er *s* allumeur *m* de réverbères

lampoon [læm'pun] *s* libelle *m*, pasquinade *f* || *tr* faire des libelles contre

lamp'post' *s* réverbère *m*, poteau *m* de réverbère

lamprey ['læmprɪ] *s* lamproie *f*

lamp'shade' *s* abat-jour *m*

lamp'wick' *s* mèche *f* de lampe

lance [læns], [lɑns] *s* lance *f*; (surg) lancette *f*, bistouri *m* || *tr* percer d'un coup de lance; (surg) donner un coup de lancette or bistouri à

lancet ['lænsɪt], ['lɑnsɪt] *s* (surg) lancette *f*, bistouri *m*

land [lænd] *adj* terrestre, de terre || *s* terre *f*; **land of milk and honey** pays de cocagne; **to make land** toucher terre; **to see how the land lies** sonder or tâter le terrain || *tr* débarquer, mettre à terre; (*an airplane*) atterrir; (*a fish*) amener à terre; (*e.g., a job*) (coll) décrocher; (*a blow*) (coll) flanquer || *intr* débarquer, descendre à terre; (*said of airplane*) atterrir; **to land on one's feet** retomber sur ses pieds; **to land on the moon** alunir; **to land on the water** amerrir

land' breeze' *s* brise *f* de terre

landed *adj* (*owning land*) terrien; (*real-estate*) immobilier

land'ed prop'erty *s* propriété *f* foncière

land'fall' *s* (*sighting land*) abordage *m*; (*landing of ship or plane*) atterrissage *m*; (*landslide*) glissement *m* de terrain

landing ['lændɪŋ] *s* (*of plane*) atterrissage *m*; (*of ship*) mise *f* à terre, débarquement *m*; (*place where passengers and goods are landed*) débarcadère *m*; (*of stairway*) palier *m*; (*on the moon*) alunissage *m*

land'ing bea'con *s* (aer) radiophare *m* d'atterrissage

land'ing craft' *s* (nav) péniche *f* de débarquement

land'ing field' *s* (aer) terrain *m* d'atterrissage

land'ing force' *s* (nav) détachement *m* de débarquement

land'ing gear' *s* (aer) train *m* d'atterrissage

land'ing par'ty *s* (nav) détachement *m* de débarquement

land'ing stage' *s* débarcadère *m*

land'ing strip' *s* (aer) piste *f* d'atterrissage

land'la'dy *s* (*pl* -dies) (*e.g., of an apartment*) logeuse *f*, propriétaire *f*; (*of a lodging house*) patronne *f*; (*of an inn*) aubergiste *f*

land'locked' *adj* entouré de terre

land'lord' *s* (*e.g., of an apartment*) logeur *m*, propriétaire *m*; (*of a lodging house*) patron *m*; (*of an inn*) aubergiste *m*

landlubber ['lænd,lʌbər] *s* marin *m* d'eau douce

land'mark' *s* point *m* de repère, borne *f*; (*important event*) étape *f* importante; (naut) amer *m*

land' of'fice *s* bureau *m* du cadastre

land'own'er *s* propriétaire *m* foncier

landscape ['lænd,skep] *s* paysage *m* || *tr* aménager en jardins

land'scape ar'chitect *s* architecte *m* paysagiste

land'scape gar'dener *s* jardinier *m* paysagiste

land'scape paint'er *s* paysagiste *mf*

landscapist ['lænd,skepɪst] *s* paysagiste *mf*

land'slide' s glissement m de terrain, éboulement m; (in an election) raz m de marée

landward ['lændwərd] adv du côté de la terre, vers la terre

land' wind' [wɪnd] s vent m de terre

lane [len] s (narrow street or passage) ruelle f; (in the country) sentier m; (of an automobile highway) voie f; (line of cars) file f; (of an air or ocean route) route f de navigation

langsyne ['læŋ'saɪn] s (Scotch) le temps jadis ‖ adv (Scotch) au temps jadis

language ['læŋgwɪdʒ] s langage m; (e.g., of a nation) langue f

languid ['læŋgwɪd] adj languissant

languish ['læŋgwɪʃ] intr languir

languor ['læŋgər] s langueur f

languorous ['læŋgərəs] adj langoureux

lank [læŋk] adj efflanqué, maigre; (hair) plat, e.g., **lank hair** cheveux plats

lank·y ['læŋki] adj (comp -ier; super -iest) grand et maigre

lanolin ['lænəlɪn] s lanoline f

lantern ['læntərn] s lanterne f

lan'tern slide' s diapositive f

lanyard ['lænjərd] s (around the neck) cordon m; (arti) tire-feu m; (naut) ride f

lap [læp] s (of human body or clothing) genoux mpl, giron m; (of garment) genoux, pan m; (with the tongue) coup m de langue; (of the waves) clapotis m; (in a race) (sports) tour m; **last lap** dernière étape f ‖ v (pret & pp lapped; ger lapping) tr (with the tongue) laper; **to lap up** laper; (coll) gober ‖ intr laper; (said of waves) clapoter; **to lap over** déborder

lap' dog' s bichon m, chien m de manchon

lapel [lə'pel] s revers m

Lap'land' s Laponie f; la Laponie

Laplander ['læp,lændər] s Lapon m

Lapp [læp] s (language) lapon m; (person) Lapon m

lap' robe' s couverture f de voyage

lapse [læps] s (passing of time) laps m; (slipping into guilt or error) faute f, écart m; (fall, decline) chute f; (e.g., of an insurance policy) expiration f, échéance f; (of memory) absence f, défaillance f ‖ intr (to elapse) s'écouler, passer; (to err) manquer à ses devoirs; (to decline) déchoir; (said, e.g., of a right) périmer, tomber en désuétude; (said, e.g., of a legacy) devenir caduc; (said, e.g., of an insurance policy) cesser d'être en vigueur

lap'wing' s (orn) vanneau m huppé

larce·ny ['lɑrsəni] s (pl -nies) larcin m, vol m

larch [lɑrtʃ] s (bot) mélèze m

lard [lɑrd] s saindoux m ‖ tr larder

larder ['lɑrdər] s garde-manger m

large [lɑrdʒ] adj grand; **at large** en liberté

large' intes'tine s gros intestin m

largely ['lɑrdʒli] adv principalement

largeness ['lɑrdʒnɪs] s grandeur f

large'-scale' adj sur une large échelle, de grande envergure

lariat ['lærɪ·ət] s (for catching animals) lasso m; (for tying grazing animals) longe f

lark [lɑrk] s alouette f; (prank) espièglerie f; **to go on a lark** (coll) faire la bombe

lark'spur' s (rocket larkspur) pied-d'alouette m; (field larkspur) consoude f royale

lar·va ['lɑrvə] s (pl -vae [vi]) larve f

laryngeal [lə'rɪndʒɪ·əl], [,lærɪn'dʒi·əl] adj laryngé, laryngien

laryngitis [,lærɪn'dʒaɪtɪs] s laryngite f

laryngoscope [lə'rɪŋgə,skop] s laryngoscope m

larynx ['lærɪŋks] s (pl larynxes or larynges [lə'rɪndʒiz]) larynx m

lascivious [lə'sɪvɪ·əs] adj lascif

lasciviousness [lə'sɪvɪ·əsnɪs] s lasciveté f

laser ['lezər] s (acronym) (light amplification by stimulated emission of radiation) laser m

lash [læʃ] s (cord on end of whip) mèche f; coup m; (splatter of rain on window) fouettement m; (eyelash) cil m ‖ tr fouetter, cingler; (to bind, tie) lier; (naut) amarrer ‖ intr fouetter; **to lash out** at cingler

lashing ['læʃɪŋ] s fouettée f; (rope) amarre f; (naut) amarrage m

lass [læs] s jeune fille f, jeunesse f; bonne amie f

lassitude ['læsɪ,t(j)ud] s lassitude f

las·so ['læso], [læ'su] s (pl -sos or -soes) lasso m

last [læst], [lɑst] adj (in a series) dernier (before noun), e.g., **the last week of the war** la dernière semaine de la guerre; (just elapsed) dernier (after noun), e.g., **last week** la semaine dernière; **before last** avant-dernier, e.g., **the time before last** l'avant-dernière fois; **the last two** les deux derniers ‖ s dernier m; (the end) fin f, bout m; (for holding shoe) forme f; **at last** enfin, à la fin; **at long last** à la fin des fins; **the last of the month** la fin du mois; **to the last** jusqu'à la fin, jusqu'au bout ‖ intr durer; (to hold out) tenir

last' eve'ning adv hier soir

lasting ['læstɪŋ], ['lɑstɪŋ] adj durable

lastly ['læstli], ['lɑstli] adv pour finir, en dernier lieu, enfin

last'-min'ute news' s nouvelles fpl de dernière heure

last' name' s nom m, nom de famille

last' night' adv hier soir; cette nuit

last' quar'ter s dernier quartier m

last' sleep' s sommeil m de la mort

last' straw' s—that's the last straw! c'est le comble!

Last' Sup'per s (eccl) Cène f

last will' and test'ament s testament m, acte m de dernière volonté

last' word' s dernier mot m; (latest style) (coll) dernier cri m

latch [læt/] s loquet m ‖ tr fermer au loquet

latch'key' s clef f de porte d'entrée

latch'string' s cordon m de loquet

late [let] adj (happening after the usual time) tardif; (person; train, bus, etc.) en retard; (e.g., art) de la dernière époque; (events) dernier, récent; (news) de la dernière heure; (incumbent of an office) ancien; (deceased) défunt, feu; at a late hour in (the night, the day) bien avant dans, à une heure avancée de; in the late seventeenth century (eighteenth century, etc.) vers la fin du dix-septième siècle (dix-huitième siècle, etc.); it is late il est tard; of late dernièrement, récemment, depuis peu; to be late être en retard; to be late in + ger tarder à + inf ‖ adv tard, tardivement; (after the appointed time) en retard; late in (the afternoon, the season, the week, the month) vers la fin de; late in life sur le tard; very late in (the night, the day) bien avant dans, à une heure avancée de

late-comer ['let ˌkʌmər] s (newcomer) nouveau venu m; (one who arrives late) retardataire mf

lateen' sail' [læ'tin] s voile f latine

lateen' yard' s antenne f

lately ['letli] adv dernièrement, récemment, depuis peu

latency ['letənsi] s latence f

latent ['letənt] adj latent

later ['letər] adj comp plus tard, plus tardif; (event) subséquent, plus récent; (kings, luminaries, etc.) derniers en date; later than postérieur à ‖ adv comp plus tard; later on plus tard, par la suite; see you later (coll) à tout à l'heure

lateral ['lætərəl] adj latéral

lath [læθ], [lɑθ] s latte f ‖ tr latter

lathe [leð] s (mach) tour m; to turn on a lathe façonner au tour

lather ['læðər] s (of soap) mousse f; (of horse) écume f ‖ tr savonner ‖ intr (said of soap) mousser; (said of horse) être couvert d'écume

lathing ['læðɪŋ], ['lɑθɪŋ] s lattage m

Latin ['lætɪn], ['lætən] adj latin ‖ s (language) latin m; (person) Latin m

Lat'in Amer'ica s l'Amérique f latine

Lat'in-Amer'ican adj latino-américain ‖ s Latino-américain m

latitude ['lætɪ ˌt(j)ud] s latitude f

latrine [lə'trin] s latrines fpl

latter ['lætər] adj dernier; the latter part of (e.g., a century) la fin de ‖ pron—the latter celui-ci §84; le dernier

lattice ['lætɪs] adj treillissé ‖ s treillis m ‖ tr treillisser

lat'tice gird'er s poutre f à croisillons

lat'tice-work' s treillis m, grillage m

laud [lɔd] tr louer

laudable ['lɔdəbəl] adj louable

laudanum ['lɔdənəm], ['lɔdnəm] s laudanum m

laudatory ['lɔdə ˌtori] adj laudatif, élogieux

laugh [læf], [lɑf] s rire m ‖ tr—to laugh away chasser en riant; to laugh off tourner en plaisanterie ‖ intr rire; to laugh at rire de

laughable ['læfəbəl], ['lɑfəbəl] adj risible

laughing ['læfɪŋ], ['lɑfɪŋ] adj riant, rieur; it's no laughing matter il n'y a pas de quoi rire ‖ s rire m

laugh'ing gas' s gaz m hilarant

laugh'ing-stock' s risée f, fable f

laughter ['læftər], ['lɑftər] s rire m

launch [lɔnt/], [lɑnt/] s (open motorboat) canot m automobile, vedette f; (naut) chaloupe f ‖ tr lancer; (an attack) déclencher ‖ intr—to launch into, to launch out on se lancer dans

launching ['lɔnt/ɪŋ], ['lɑnt/ɪŋ] s lancement m

launch'ing pad' s rampe f de lancement, aire f de lancement

launder ['lɔndər], ['lɑndər] tr blanchir

launderer ['lɔndərər], ['lɑndərər] s blanchisseur m, buandier m

laundering ['lɔndərɪŋ], ['lɑndərɪŋ] s blanchissage m

laundress ['lɔndrɪs], ['lɑndrɪs] s blanchisseuse f, buandière f

laun-dry ['lɔndri], ['lɑndri] s (pl -dries) linge m à blanchir, lessive f; (room) buanderie f; (business) blanchisserie f

laun'dry-man s (pl -men) blanchisseur m, buandier m

laun'dry room' s buanderie f

laun'dry-wom'an s (pl -wom'en) blanchisseuse f, buandière f

laureate ['lɔrɪ ɪt] adj & s lauréat m

lau-rel ['lɔrəl], ['lɑrəl] s laurier m; to rest on one's laurels s'endormir sur ses lauriers ‖ v (pret & pp -reled or -relled) ger -reling or -relling) tr couronner de lauriers

lava ['lɑvə], ['lævə] s lave f

lavaliere [ˌlævə'lɪr] s pendentif m

lavato-ry ['lævə ˌtori] s (pl -ries) (room equipped for washing hands and face; bowl with running water) lavabo m; (toilet) lavabos

lavender ['lævəndər] s lavande f

lav'ender wa'ter s eau f de lavande

lavish ['lævɪ/] adj prodigue; (reception, dinner, etc.) somptueux, magnifique ‖ tr prodiguer

law [lɔ] s (of man, of nature, of science) loi f; (branch of knowledge concerned with law; body of laws; study of law, profession of law) droit m; to go to law recourir à la justice; to go to law with s.o. citer qn en justice; to lay down the law faire la loi; to practice law exercer le droit; to read law étudier le droit, faire son droit

law'-abid'ing adj soumis aux lois, respectueux des lois

law' and or'der s ordre m public; to maintain law and order maintenir or faire régner l'ordre

law'break'er s transgresseur m de la loi

law' court' s cour f de justice, tribunal m

lawful ['lɔfəl] *adj* légal, légitime

lawless ['lɔlɪs] *adj* sans loi; *(unbridled)* sans frein, déréglé

law'mak'er *s* législateur *m*

lawn [lɔn] *s* pelouse *f*, gazon *m*; *(fabric)* batiste *f*, linon *m*

lawn' mow'er *s* tondeuse *f* de gazon

law' of'fice *s* étude *f* (d'avocat)

law' of na'tions *s* loi *f* des nations

law' of the jun'gle *s* loi *f* de la jungle

law' stu'dent *s* étudiant *m* en droit

law'suit' *s* procès *m*

lawyer ['lɔjər] *s* avocat *m*

lax [læks] *adj* (in morals, discipline, etc.) relâché, négligent; *(loose, not tense)* lâche; *(vague)* vague, flou

laxative ['læksətɪv] *adj & s* laxatif *m*

lay [le] *adj (not belonging to clergy)* laïc or laïque; *(not having special training)* profane *s* situation *f*; *(poem)* lai *m* ‖ *v (pret & pp* laid [led]) *tr* poser, mettre; *(a trap)* tendre; *(eggs)* pondre; *(e.g., bricks)* ranger; *(a foundation)* jeter, établir; *(a cable)* poser; *(a mine)* (naut) mouiller; **to be laid in Rome** (in France, etc.) *(said, e.g., of scene)* se passer à Rome (en France, etc.); **to lay aside, away,** or **by** mettre de côté; **to lay down** *(one's life)* sacrifier; *(one's weapons)* déposer; *(conditions)* imposer; **to lay down the law to s.o.** (coll) rappeler qn à l'ordre; **to lay in** *(supplies)* faire provision de; **to lay into s.o.** (coll) sauter dessus qn; **to lay it on thick** (coll) y aller fort; **to lay low** *(to overwhelm)* abattre, terrasser; **to lay off** *(an employee)* congédier; *(to mark the boundaries of)* tracer; *(to stop bothering)* (coll) laisser tranquille; **to lay on** *(paint)* appliquer; *(hands; taxes)* imposer; **to lay open** mettre à nu; **to lay out** arranger; *(to display)* étaler; *(to outline)* tracer; *(money)* débourser; *(a corpse)* faire la toilette de; *(a garden)* aménager; **to lay up** *(to stock up on)* amasser; *(to injure)* aliter; *(a boat)* mettre en rade ‖ *intr (said of hen)* pondre; **to lay about** frapper de tous côtés; **to lay for** être à l'affût de, guetter; **to lay into** (slang) rosser, battre; **to lay off** (coll) cesser; **to lay off smoking** (coll) renoncer au tabac; **to lay over** faire escale; **to lay to** (naut) se mettre à la cape

lay' broth'er *s* frère *m* lai, frère convers

layer ['le·ər] *s* couche *f*; *(hen)* pondeuse *f* ‖ *tr* (hort) marcotter

lay'er cake' *s* gâteau *m* sandwich

layette [le'et] *s* layette *f*

lay' fig'ure *s* mannequin *m*

laying ['le·ɪŋ] *s* pose *f*; *(of foundation)* assise *f*; *(of eggs)* ponte *f*

lay'man *s (pl -men) (person who is not a clergyman)* laïc *m* or laïque *mf*; *(person who has no special training)* profane *mf*

lay'off' *s (discharge)* renvoi *m*; *(unemployment)* chômage *m*

lay' of the land' *s* configuration *f* du terrain; (fig) aspect *m* de l'affaire

lay'out' *s* plan *m*, dessin *m*, tracé *m*; *(of tools)* montage *m*; *(organization)* disposition *f*; *(banquet)* (coll) festin *m*

lay'o'ver *s* arrêt *m* en cours de route

lay' sis'ter *s* sœur *f* laie, sœur converse

laziness ['lezinɪs] *s* paresse *f*

la·zy ['lezi] *adj (comp* -zier; *super* -ziest) paresseux

la'zy-bones' *s* (coll) flemmard *m*, fainéant *m*

lb. *abbr* **(pound)** livre *f*

lea [li] *s (meadow)* pâturage *m*, prairie *f*

lead [led] *adj* en plomb, de plomb [led] *s* plomb *m*; *(of lead pencil)* mine *f* (de plombagine); *(for sounding depth)* (naut) sonde *f*; (typ) interligne *f* ‖ [led] *v (pret & pp* leaded; *ger* leading) *tr* plomber; (typ) interligner ‖ [lid] *s (foremost place)* avance *f*; *(guidance)* direction *f*, conduite, *f*; *(leash)* laisse *f*; *(of a newspaper article)* article *m* de fond; *(leading role)* premier rôle *m*; *(leading man)* jeune premier *m*; (elec) câble *m* de canalisation, conducteur *m*; (elec, mach) avance; (min) filon *m*; **to follow s.o.'s lead** suivre l'exemple de qn; **to have the lead** (cards) avoir la main; **to return the lead** (cards) rejouer la couleur; **to take the lead** prendre le pas ‖ [lid] *v (pret & pp* led [led]) *tr* conduire, mener; *(to command)* commander, diriger; *(to be foremost in)* être à la tête de; *(e.g., an orchestra)* diriger; *(a good or bad life)* mener; *(a certain card)* attaquer de; *(a certain card suit)* attaquer; (elec, mach) canaliser; **to lead away** or **off** emmener; **to lead off** *(to start)* commencer; **to lead on** encourager; **to lead s.o. to believe** mener qn à croire ‖ *intr* aller devant, tenir la tête; (cards) avoir la main; **to lead to** conduire à, mener à; *(another street, a certain result, etc.)* aboutir à; **to lead up to** *(a great work)* préluder à *(un grand ouvrage)*; *(a subject)* amener *(un sujet)*

leaden ['ledən] *adj (of lead; like lead)* de plomb, en plomb; *(heavy as lead)* pesant; *(sluggish)* alangui; *(complexion)* plombé

leader ['lidər] *s* chef *m*, guide *mf*; *(ringleader)* tête *f*; chef d'orchestre; *(in a dance; among animals)* meneur *m*; *(in a newspaper)* article *m* de fond; *(of a reel of tape or film)* amorce *f*; *(bargain)* article réclame; *(vein of ore)* filon *m*

leadership ['lidər‚ʃɪp] *s* direction *f*; don *m* de commandement

leading ['lidɪŋ] *adj* principal, premier

lead'ing edge' *s* (aer) bord *m* d'attaque

lead'ing la'dy *s* vedette *f*, étoile *f*, jeune première *f*

lead'ing man' *s (pl* men') jeune premier *m*

lead'ing ques'tion *s* question *f* tendancieuse

lead'-in wire' ['lid ‚ɪn] *s* (rad, telv) fil *m* d'amenée

lead/ pen/cil [led] *s* crayon *m* (à mine de graphite)

lead/ poi/soning [led] *s* saturnisme *m*

leaf [lif] *s* (*pl* **leaves** [livz]) feuille *f*; (*inserted leaf of table*) rallonge *f*; (*hinged leaf of door or table top*) battant *m*; **to shake like a leaf** trembler comme une feuille; **to turn over a new leaf** tourner la page, faire peau neuve || *intr*—**to leaf through** feuilleter

leaf/less ['liflɪs] *adj* sans feuilles, dénudé

leaf/let ['liflɪt] *s* dépliant *m*, papillon *m*, feuillet *m*; (bot) foliole *f*

leaf/stalk/ *s* (bot) pétiole *m*

leaf-y ['lifi] *adj* (*comp* -ier; *super* -lest) feuillu, touffu

league [lig] *s* (*unit of distance*) lieue *f*; (*association, alliance*) ligue *f* || *tr* liguer || *intr* se liguer

League/ of Na/tions *s* Société *f* des Nations

leak [lik] *s* fuite *f*; (*in a ship*) voie *f* d'eau; (*of electricity, heat, etc.*) perte *f*, fuite; (*of news, secrets, money, etc.*) fuite; **to spring a leak** avoir une fuite; (naut) faire une voie d'eau || *tr* faire couler; (*gas, steam; secrets, news*) laisser échapper || *intr* fuire, s'écouler; (naut) faire eau; **to leak away** se perdre; **to leak out** (*said of news, secrets, etc.*) transpirer, s'ébruiter

leakage ['likɪdʒ] *s* fuite *f*; (elec) perte *f*

leak-y ['liki] *adj* (*comp* -ier; *super* -lest) percé, troué; qui a des fuites; (*shoes*) qui prennent l'eau; (coll) indiscret

lean [lin] *adj* maigre; (*gasoline mixture*) pauvre || *s* inclinaison *f*; (*of meat*) maigre *m* || *v* (*pret & pp* **leaned** or **leant** [lent]) *tr* incliner; **to lean s.th. against s.th.** appuyer q.ch. contre q.ch. || *intr* s'incliner, pencher; **to lean against** s'appuyer contre; **to lean forward** s'incliner or se pencher en avant; **to lean out of** (*e.g., a window*) se pencher par; **to lean over** se pencher sur; (*e.g., s.o.'s shoulder*) se pencher sur; **to lean toward** (fig) incliner à or vers, pencher pour or vers

leaning ['linɪŋ] *adj* penché || *s* inclinaison *f*; (fig) inclination *f*, penchant *m*

lean/-to/ *s* (*pl* -tos) appentis *m*

lean/ years/ *spl* années *fpl* maigres

leap [lip] *s* saut *m*, bond *m*; **by leaps and bounds** par sauts et par bonds; **leap in the dark** saut à l'aveuglette || *v* (*pret & pp* **leaped** or **leapt** [lept]) *tr* sauter, franchir || *intr* sauter, bondir; **to leap across** or **over** sauter; **to leap up** sursauter; (*said, e.g., of flame*) jaillir

leap/ day/ *s* jour *m* intercalaire

leap/frog/ *s* saute-mouton *m*

leap/ year/ *s* année *f* bissextile

learn [lʌrn] *v* (*pret & pp* **learned** or **learnt** [lʌrnt]) *tr* apprendre || *intr* apprendre; **to learn to** apprendre à

learned ['lʌrnɪd] *adj* savant, érudit

learn/ed jour/nal *s* revue *f* d'une société savante

learn/ed profes/sion *s* profession *f* libérale

learn/ed soci/ety *s* société *f* savante

learn/ed word/ *s* mot *m* savant

learner ['lʌrnər] *s* élève *mf*; (*beginner*) débutant *m*, apprenti *m*

learn/er's per/mit *s* (aut) permis *m* de conduire (*d'un élève chauffeur*)

learning ['lʌrnɪŋ] *s* (*act and time devoted*) étude *f*; (*scholarship*) savoir *m*, érudition *f*, science *f*

lease [lis] *s* bail *m*; **to give a new lease on life** donner un regain de vie || *tr* (*in the role of landlord*) donner or louer à bail; (*in the role of tenant*) prendre à bail

lease/hold/ *adj* tenu à bail || *s* tenure *f* à bail

leash [liʃ] *s* laisse *f*; **on the leash** en laisse, à l'attache; **to strain at the leash** (fig) ruer dans les brancards || *tr* tenir en laisse

least [list] *adj super* (le) moindre §91 || *s* (le) moins *m*; **at least** du moins; **at the very least** tout au moins; **not in the least** pas le moins du monde, nullement || *adv super* (le) moins §91

leather ['leðər] *s* cuir *m*

leath/er-back tur/tle *s* luth *m*

leath/er-neck/ *s* (slang) fusilier *m* marin

leathery ['leðəri] *adj* (*e.g., steak*) (coll) coriace

leave [liv] *s* permission *f*; **by your leave** ne vous en déplaise; **on leave** en congé; (mil) en permission; **to give leave to s.o. to** permettre or accorder à qn de; **to take leave of** (de), faire ses adieux (à) || *v* (*pret & pp* **left** [left]) *tr* (*to let stay; to stop, give up; to disregard*) laisser; (*to go away from*) partir de, quitter; (*to bequeath*) léguer, laisser; (*a wife*) quitter, abandonner; **to be left** rester, e.g., **the letter was left unanswered** la lettre est restée sans réponse; e.g., **there are three dollars left** il reste trois dollars; **to be left for s.o.** être à qn de; **to be left over** rester; **to leave about** (*without putting away*) laisser traîner; **to leave alone** laisser tranquille; **to leave it up to** s'en remettre à, s'en rapporter à; **to leave no stone unturned** faire flèche de tout bois, mettre tout en œuvre; **to leave off** (*a piece of clothing*) ne pas mettre; (*a passenger*) déposer; **to leave off + ger** cesser de + *inf*, renoncer à + *inf*; **to leave out** omettre || *intr* partir, s'en aller; **where did we leave off?** où en sommes-nous restés?

leaven ['levən] *s* levain *m* || *tr* faire lever; (fig) transformer, modifier

leavening ['levənɪŋ] *adj* transformateur || *s* levain *m*

leave/ of ab/sence *s* congé *m*

leave/-tak/ing *s* congé *m*, adieux *mpl*

leavings ['livɪŋz] *spl* restes *mpl*, reliefs *mpl*

Leba·nese [ˌlɛbəˈniz] *adj* libanais *|| s* (*pl* -nese) Libanais *m*

Lebanon ['lebənən] *s* le Liban

lecher ['letʃər] *s* débauché *m*, libertin *m* || *intr* vivre dans la débauche

lecherous ['letʃərəs] *adj* lubrique, lascif

lechery ['letʃəri] *s* lubricité *f*, lasciveté *f*

lectern ['lektərn] *s* lutrin *m*

lecture ['lektʃər] *s* conférence *f*; *(tedious reprimand)* sermon *m* || *tr* faire une conférence à; *(to rebuke)* sermonner || *intr* faire une conférence or des conférences

lecturer ['lektʃərər] *s* conférencier *m*

ledge [ledʒ] *s* saillie *f*, corniche *f*; *(projection in a wall)* corniche *f*

ledger ['ledʒər] *s* (slab) pierre *f* tombale; (com) grand livre *m*

ledg'er line' *s* (mus) ligne *f* supplémentaire

lee [li] *s* (shelter) (naut) abri *m*; *(quarter toward which wind blows)* côté *m* sous le vent; lee lies *f*

leech [litʃ] *s* sangsue *f*; to stick like a leech to s.o. s'accrocher à qn

leek [lik] *s* poireau *m*

leer [lɪr] *s* regard *m* lubrique, œillade *f* || *intr* lancer or jeter une œillade; to leer at lorgner

leer·y ['lɪri] *adj* (comp -ier; super -iest) (coll) soupçonneux, méfiant

leeward ['liwərd], ['lu·ərd] *adj & adv* sous le vent || *s* côté *m* sous le vent; to pass to leeward of passer sous le vent de

Lee'ward Is'lands ['liwərd] *spl* îles *fpl* Sous-le-Vent

lee'way' *s* (aer, naut) dérive *f*; *(of time, money)* (coll) marge *f*; *(for action)* (coll) champ *m*, liberté *f*

left [left] *adj* gauche; *(left over)* de surplus || *s* (left hand) gauche *f*; (boxing) gauche *m*; on the left, to the left à gauche; the Left (pol) la gauche; to make a left tourner à gauche || *adv* à gauche

left' field' *s* (baseball) gauche *f* du grand champ

left'-hand' drive' *s* conduite *f* à gauche

left'-hand'ed *adj* gaucher; *(clumsy)* gauche; *(counterclockwise)* à gauche, en sens inverse des aiguilles d'une montre; *(e.g., compliment)* douteux, ambigu

leftish ['leftɪʃ] *adj* gauchisant

leftism ['leftɪzəm] *s* gauchisme *m*

leftist ['leftɪst] *adj & s* gauchiste *mf*

left'o'ver *adj* de surplus, restant || **left'overs** *mpl* restes *mpl*

left'-wing' *adj* gauchiste, gauchisant

left-winger ['left'wɪŋər] *s* (coll) gauchiste *mf*

left·y ['lefti] *adj* (coll) gaucher || *s* (pl -ies) (coll) gaucher *m*

leg [leg] *s* jambe *f*; *(of boot or stocking)* tige *f*; *(of fowl, of frogs)* cuisse *f*; *(of journey)* étape *f*; to be on one's last legs n'avoir plus de jambes; to pull the leg of (coll) se payer la tête de, faire marcher

lega·cy ['legəsi] *s* (pl -cies) legs *m*

legal ['ligəl] *adj* légal; *(practice)* juridique

le'gal hol'iday *s* jour *m* férié

legali·ty [lɪ'gælɪti] *s* (pl -ties) légalité *f*

legalize ['ligə,laɪz] *tr* légaliser

le'gal ten'der *s* cours *m* légal, monnaie *f* libératoire

legate ['legɪt] *s* ambassadeur *m*, envoyé *m*; (eccl) légat *m*

legatee [,legə'ti] *s* légataire *mf*

legation [lɪ'geʃən] *s* légation *f*

legend ['ledʒənd] *s* légende *f*

legendary ['ledʒən,deri] *adj* légendaire

legerdemain [,ledʒərdɪ'men] *s* escamotage *m*, passe-passe *m*

leggings ['legɪŋz] *spl* jambières *fpl*, guêtres *fpl*, leggings *fpl*

leg-gy ['legi] *adj* (comp -gier; super -giest) (awkward) dégingandé; *(attractive)* aux longues jambes élégantes

leg'horn' *s* (hat) chapeau *m* de paille d'Italie; (chicken) leghorn *f*; **Leghorn** Livourne *f*

legibility [,ledʒɪ'brlɪti] *s* lisibilité *f*

legible ['ledʒɪbəl] *adj* lisible

legion ['lidʒən] *s* légion *f*

legislate ['ledʒɪs,let] *tr* imposer à force de loi || *intr* faire des lois, légiférer

legislation [,ledʒɪs'leʃən] *s* législation *f*

legislative ['ledʒɪs,letɪv] *adj* législatif

legislator ['ledʒɪs,letər] *s* législateur *m*

legislature ['ledʒɪs,letʃər] *s* assemblée *f* législative, législature *f*

legitimacy [lɪ'dʒɪtɪməsi] *s* légitimité *f*

legitimate [lɪ'dʒɪtɪmɪt] *adj* légitime || [lɪ'dʒɪtɪ,met] *tr* légitimer

legit'imate dra'ma *s* théâtre *m* régulier

legitimize [lɪ'dʒɪtɪ,maɪz] *tr* légitimer

leg' of lamb' *s* gigot *m* d'agneau

leg' of mut'ton *s* gigot *m*

leg'-of-mut'ton sleeve' *s* manche *f* gigot

legume ['legjum], [lɪ'gjum] *s* (pod) légume *m*; (bot) légumineuse *f*

leisure ['liʒər], ['leʒər] *s* loisir *m*; at leisure à loisir; in leisure moments à temps perdu

lei'sure class' *s* désœuvrés *mpl*, rentiers *mpl*

lei'sure hours' *spl* heures *fpl* de loisir

leisurely ['liʒərli], ['leʒərli] *adj* tranquille, posé || *adv* posément, sans hâte

lemon ['lemən] *s* citron *m*; *(e.g., worthless car)* (coll) clou *m*

lemonade [,lemə'ned] *s* citronnade *f*

lem'on squeez'er *s* presse-citron *m*

lem'on tree' *s* citronnier *m*

lem'on verbe'na [vər'binə] *s* verveine *f* citronnelle

lend [lend] *v* (pret & pp lent [lent]) *tr* prêter

lender ['lendər] *s* prêteur *m*

lend'ing li'brary *s* bibliothèque *f* de prêt

length [leŋθ] *s* longueur *f*; *(e.g., of string)* bout *m*, morceau *m*; *(of time)* durée *f*; at length longuement, en détail; *(finally)* enfin, à la fin; in length de longueur; to go to any length to ne reculer devant rien pour; to keep at arm's length tenir à distance

lengthen ['lɛŋθən] *tr* allonger, rallonger ‖ *intr* s'allonger

length/wise/ *adj* longitudinal ‖ *adv* en longueur, dans le sens de la longueur

length·y ['lɛŋθɪ] *adj* (*comp* -ier; *super* -iest) prolongé, assez long

leniency ['linɪ·ənsɪ] *s* douceur *f*, clémence *f*

lenient ['linɪ·ənt] *adj* doux, clément

lens [lɛnz] *s* lentille *f*; (anat) cristallin *m*

Lent [lɛnt] *s* le Carême

Lenten ['lɛntən] *adj* de carême

lentil ['lɛntəl] *s* lentille *f*

leopard ['lɛpərd] *s* léopard *m*

leper ['lɛpər] *s* lépreux *m*

lep'er house' *s* léproserie *f*

leprosy ['lɛprəsɪ] *s* lèpre *f*

leprous ['lɛprəs] *adj* lépreux

lesbian ['lɛzbɪ·ən] *adj* érotique; Lesbian lesbien *f*; *s* (*female homosexual*) lesbienne *f*; **Lesbian** Lesbien *m*

lesbianism ['lɛzbɪ·ə‚nɪzəm] *s* saphisme *m*

lese majesty ['liz'mædʒɪstɪ] *s* crime *m* de lèse-majesté

lesion ['liʒən] *s* lésion *f*

less [lɛs] *adj* *comp* moindre §91 ‖ *s* moins *m* ‖ *adv comp* moins §91; **less and less** de moins en moins; **less than** moins que; (*followed by numeral*) moins de; **the less . . . the less** (or **the more**) moins . . . moins (or **plus**)

lessee [lɛs'i] *s* preneur *m*; (*e.g., of house*) locataire *mf*; (*e.g., of gasoline station*) concessionnaire *mf*

lessen ['lɛsən] *tr* diminuer, amoindrir ‖ *intr* se diminuer, s'amoindrir

lesser ['lɛsər] *adj comp* moindre §91

lesson ['lɛsən] *s* leçon *f*

lessor ['lɛsər] *s* bailleur *m*

lest [lɛst] *conj* de peur que, de crainte que

let [lɛt] *v* (*pret & pp* let; *ger* letting) *tr* laisser; (*to rent*) louer; **let** + *inf* que + *subj*, e.g., **let him come in** qu'il entre; **let alone** sans parler de, sans compter; **let well enough alone** le mieux est souvent l'ennemi du bien; **let us eat, work, etc.** mangeons, travaillons, etc.; **to be let off with** en être quitte pour; **to let** à louer, e.g., **house to be let** maison à louer; **to let alone**, **to let be** laisser tranquille; **to let by** laisser passer; **to let down** baisser, descendre; (*one's hair*) dénouer, défaire; (*e.g., a garment*) allonger; (*to leave in the lurch*) laisser en panne, faire faux bond à; **to let fly** décocher; **to let go** laisser partir; **to let have** laisser, e.g., **he let Robert have it for three dollars** il l'a laissé à Robert pour trois dollars; **to let in** laisser entrer; **to let in the clutch** (aut) embrayer; **to let into** admettre dans; **to let loose** lâcher; **to let off** laisser partir; (*e.g., steam from a boiler*) laisser échapper, lâcher; (*e.g., a culprit*) pardonner à; **to let oneself go** se laisser aller; **to let on that** (coll) faire croire que; **to let out** faire or laisser sortir; (*e.g., a dress*) élargir; (*a cry; a secret; a prisoner*) laisser échapper; (*to reveal*) révéler, divulguer; **to let out on bail** relâcher sous caution; **to let out the clutch** débrayer; **to let slip** laisser tomber; **to let s.o.** + *inf* permettre à qn de + *inf*; laisser qn + *inf*, e.g., **he let Mary go to the theater** il a laissé Marie aller au théâtre; **to let s.o. in on** (*a secret*) (coll) confier à qn; (*e.g., a racing tip*) (coll) tuyauter qn sur; **to let s.o. know s.th.** faire savoir q.ch. à qn, mettre qn au courant de q.ch.; **to let s.o. off with** faire grâce à qn de; **to let stand** laisser, e.g., **he let the errors stand** il a laissé les fautes; **to let s.th. go for** (*a low price*) laisser q.ch. pour; **to let through** laisser passer; **to let up** laisser monter ‖ *intr* (*said of house, apartment, etc.*) se louer; **to let down** (coll) ralentir; **to let go of** lâcher prise de; **to let out** (*said of class, school, etc.*) finir, se terminer; **to let up** (coll) ralentir, diminuer; (*on discipline; on a person*) devenir moins sévère

let/down/ *s* diminution *f*; (*disappointment*) déception *f*

lethal ['liθəl] *adj* mortel; (*weapon*) meurtrier

lethargic [lɪ'θɑrdʒɪk] *adj* léthargique

lethar·gy ['lɛθərdʒɪ] *s* (*pl* -gies) léthargie *f*

Lett [lɛt] *s* Letton *m*

letter ['lɛtər] *s* lettre *f*; **to the letter** à la lettre, au pied de la lettre ‖ *tr* marquer, avec des lettres

let'ter box' *s* boîte *f* aux lettres

let'ter car'rier *s* facteur *m*

let'ter drop' *s* passe-lettres *f*, fente *f* (dans la porte pour le courrier)

lettered *adj* (*person*) lettré

let'ter file' *s* classeur *m* de lettres

let'ter·head' *s* en-tête *m*

lettering ['lɛtərɪŋ] *s* (*action*) lettrage *m*; (*title*) inscription *f*

let'ter of cred'it *s* lettre *f* de crédit

let'ter o'pener *s* coupe-papier *m*

let'ter pa'per *s* papier *m* à lettres

let'ter-per'fect *adj* correct; sûr

let'ter press' *s* presse *f* à copier

let'ter-press' *s* impression *f* typographique; (*in distinction to illustrations*) texte *m*

let'ter scales' *spl* pèse-lettre *m*

let'ter-word' *s* sigle *m*

Lettish ['lɛtɪʃ] *adj & s* letton *m*

lettuce ['lɛtɪs] *s* laitue *f*

let'up' *s* accalmie *f*, pause *f*; **without letup** sans relâche

leucorrhea [‚lukə'ri·ə] *s* leucorrhée *f*

leukemia [lu'kimɪ·ə] *s* leucémie *f*

Levant [lɪ'vænt] *s* Levant *m*

Levantine ['lɛvən‚tin], [lɪ'væntin] *adj* levantin ‖ *s* Levantin *m*

levee ['lɛvɪ] *s* (*embankment*) levée *f*, digue *f*; réception *f* royale

lev·el ['lɛvəl] *adj* de niveau; (*flat*) égal, uni; (*spoonful*) arasé; **level with** de niveau avec, à fleur de ‖ *s* niveau *m*; **on a level with** au niveau de; **to be**

on the level (coll) être de bonne foi; to find one's level trouver son niveau ‖ v (pret & pp -eled or -elled; ger -eling or -elling) tr niveler; (to smooth, flatten out) aplanir, araser; (to bring down) raser; (a gun) braquer; (accusations, sarcasm) lancer, diriger; to level out égaliser; to level up (aer) redresser ‖ intr (aer) redresser; to level with (coll) parler franchement à

lev'el•head'ed adj équilibré, pondéré

lev'eling rod' s (surv) jalon-mire m, jalon m d'arpentage

lever ['lɪvər], ['lɛvər] s levier m ‖ tr soulever or ouvrir au moyen d'un levier

leverage ['lɪvərɪdʒ], ['lɛvərɪdʒ] s puissance f or force f de levier; (fig) influence f, avantage m

leviathan [lɪ'vaɪ·əθən] s léviathan m

levitation [,lɛvɪ'teʃən] s lévitation f

levi•ty ['lɛvɪti] s (pl -ties) légèreté f

lev•y ['lɛvi] s (pl -ies) levée f ‖ v (pret & pp -ied) tr lever; (a fine) imposer

lewd [lud] adj luxurieux, lubrique

lewdness ['ludnɪs] s luxure f, lubricité f

lexical ['lɛksɪkəl] adj lexical

lexicographer [,lɛksɪ'kɑgrəfər] s lexicographe mf

lexicographic(al) [,lɛksɪkə'græfɪk(əl)] adj lexicographique

lexicography [,lɛksɪ'kɑgrəfi] s lexicographie f

lexicology [,lɛksɪ'kɑlədʒi] s lexicologie f

lexicon ['lɛksɪkən] s lexique m

liabil•i•ty [,laɪ·ə'brlɪti] s (pl -ties) responsabilité f; (e.g., to disease) prédisposition f; liabilities obligations fpl, dettes fpl

liabil'ity insur'ance f assurance f tous risques

liable ['laɪ·əbəl] adj sujet; liable for (a debt, fine, etc.) passible de, responsable de; we (you, etc.) are liable to + inf (coll) ils ne peut que nous (vous, etc.) + pres subj; (coll) il est probable que nous (vous, etc.) + pres ind

liaison ['li·ə ,zɑn], [li'ezən] s liaison f

liar ['laɪ·ər] s menteur m

libation [laɪ'beʃən] s libation f

li•bel ['laɪbəl] s diffamation f, calomnie f; (in writing) écrit m diffamatoire ‖ v (pret & pp -beled or -belled; ger -beling or -belling) tr diffamer, calomnier

libelous ['laɪbələs] adj diffamatoire, calomnieux

liberal ['lɪbərəl] adj libéral; (share, supply, etc.) libéral, généreux, copieux; (ideas) large ‖ s libéral m

liberali•ty [,lɪbə'rælɪti] s (pl -ties) libéralité f; (breadth of mind) largeur f de vues

lib'er•al-mind'ed adj tolérant

liberate ['lɪbə ,ret] tr libérer

liberation [,lɪbə'reʃən] s libération f

liberator ['lɪbə ,retər] s libérateur m

libertine ['lɪbər ,tin] adj & s libertin m

liber•ty ['lɪbərti] s (pl -ties) liberté f; at liberty en liberté; at liberty to libre de; to take the liberty to se permettre de, prendre la liberté de

libidinous [lɪ'brdɪnəs] adj libidineux

libido [lɪ'bido], [lɪ'bardo] s libido f

librarian [laɪ'brɛrɪ·ən] s bibliothécaire mf

librar•y ['laɪ ,brɛri], ['laɪbrəri] s (pl -ies) bibliothèque f

li'brary num'ber s cote f

libret•to [lɪ'brɛto] s (pl -tos) livret m, libretto m

license ['laɪsəns] s permis m, licence f; (to drive) permis de conduire ‖ tr accorder un permis à, autoriser

li'cense num'ber s numéro m d'immatriculation; (aut) numéro minéralogique

li'cense plate' or tag' s plaque f d'immatriculation, plaque minéralogique

licentious [laɪ'sɛn/əs] adj licencieux

lichen ['laɪkən] s lichen m

lick [lɪk] s coup m de langue; (salt lick) terrain m salifère; (blow) (coll) coup m; at full lick (coll) à plein gaz; to give a lick and a promise to (coll) nettoyer à la six-quatre-deux; (coll) faire un brin de toilette à ‖ tr lécher; (e.g., the fingers) se lécher; (to beat, thrash) (coll) enfoncer les côtes à, rosser; (to beat, surpass, e.g., in a sporting event) (coll) battre, enfoncer; (e.g., a problem) (coll) venir à bout de; to lick into shape (coll) dégrossir; to lick up lécher

licking ['lɪkɪŋ] s léchage m; (drubbing) (coll) raclée f

licorice ['lɪkərɪs] s réglisse f

lid [lɪd] s couvercle m; (eyelid) paupière f; (hat) (slang) couvre-chef m

lie [laɪ] s mensonge m; to give the lie to donner le démenti à ‖ v (pret & pp lied; ger lying) tr—to lie one's way out se tirer d'affaire par des mensonges ‖ intr mentir ‖ v (pret lay; pp lain [len]; ger lying) intr être couché; (to be located) se trouver; (e.g., in the grave) gésir, e.g., here lies ci-gît; to lie down se coucher

lie' detec'tor s détecteur m de mensonges

lien [lin], ['li·ən] s privilège m, droit m de rétention

lieu [lu] s—in lieu of au lieu de

lieutenant [lu'tɛnənt] s lieutenant m; (nav) lieutenant m de vaisseau

lieuten'ant colo'nel s lieutenant-colonel m

lieuten'ant comman'der s (nav) capitaine m de corvette

lieuten'ant gov'ernor s (U.S.A.) vice-gouverneur m; (Brit) lieutenant-gouverneur m

lieuten'ant jun'ior grade' s (nav) enseigne m de première classe

life [laɪf] s (pl lives [laɪvz]) vie f; (of light bulb, lease, insurance policy) durée f; bigger than life plus grand que nature; for dear life de toutes ses forces; for life à vie, pour la vie, à perpétuité; **for the life of me!** (coll) de ma vie!; **lives lost** morts *mpl*; **long life** longévité *f*; **never in my life!**, **not on your life!** jamais de la vie!; **run for your life!** sauve qui peut!; **such is life!** c'est la vie!; **taken from life** pris sur le vif; **to come to life** revenir à la vie; **to depart this life** quitter ce monde; **to risk life and limb** risquer sa peau

life′ annu′ity *s* rente *f* viagère

life′ belt′ *s* ceinture *f* de sauvetage

life′blood′ *s* sang *m*; (fig) vie *f*

life′boat′ *s* chaloupe *f* de sauvetage; (*for shore-based rescue services*) canot *m* de sauvetage

life′ buoy′ *s* bouée *f* de sauvetage

life′ float′ *s* radeau *m* de sauvetage

life′ guard′ *s* (mil) garde *f* du corps

life′ guard′ *s* sauveteur *m*, maître nageur *m*

life′ impris′onment *s* emprisonnement *m* à vie

life′ insur′ance *s* assurance *f* sur la vie, assurance-vie *f*

life′ jack′et *s* gilet *m* de sauvetage

lifeless [′laɪflɪs] *adj* sans vie, inanimé; (*colors*) embu, terne

life′like′ *adj* vivant, ressemblant

life′ line′ *s* ligne *f* or corde *f* de sauvetage

life′long′ *adj* de toute la vie, perpétuel

life′ mem′ber *s* membre *m* à vie

life′ of lei′sure *s* vie *f* de château

life′ of Ri′ley [′raɪli] *s* (slang) joyeuse vie *f*, vie oisive

life′ of the par′ty *s* (coll) boute-entrain *m*

life′ preserv′er [prɪ′zɜrvər] *s* appareil *m* de sauvetage

lifer [′laɪfər] *s* (slang) condamné *m* à perpétuité

life′ raft′ *s* radeau *m* de sauvetage

lifesaver [′laɪf,sevər] *s* sauveteur *m*; (fig) planche *f* de salut

life′sav′ing *s* sauvetage *m*

life′ sen′tence *s* condamnation *f* à perpétuité

life′-size′ *adj* de grandeur nature

life′time′ *adj* à vie || *s* vie *f*, toute une vie; **in his lifetime** de son vivant

life′work′ *s* travail *m* de toute une vie

lift [lɪft] *s* haussement *m*, levée *f*; aide *f*; (aer) poussée *f*; (Brit) ascenseur *m*; (*of dumbbell or weight*) (sports) arraché *m*; **to give a lift to** (*by offering a ride*) conduire d'un coup de voiture, faire monter dans la voiture; (*to aid*) donner un coup de main à; ranimer || *tr* lever, soulever; (*heart*, *mind, etc.*) élever, ranimer; (*a sail*) soulager; (*an embargo*) lever; (*e.g.*, *passages from a book*) démarquer, plagier; (*to rob*) (slang) dérober; **to lift up** (*the hands*) lever; (*the head*) relever; (*the voice*) élever || *intr* se lever, se soulever; (*said of clouds*, *fog, etc.*) se lever, se dissiper

lift′ bridge′ *s* pont *m* levant, pont-levis *m*

lift′off′ *s* (rok) montée verticale, chandelle *f*

lift′ truck′ *s* chariot *m* élévateur

ligament [′lɪgəmənt] *s* ligament *m*

ligature [′lɪgət∫ər] *s* ligature *f*

light [laɪt] *adj* léger; (*having illumination*) éclairé; (*color, complexion, hair*) clair; (*beer*) blond; (*wine*) léger; **to make light of** faire peu de cas de || *s* lumière *f*; (*to control traffic*) feu *m*; (*window or other opening in a wall*) jour *m*; (*example, shining figure*) lumière; (*headlight of automobile*) phare *m*; du feu, e.g., **do you have a light?** (*e.g., to light a cigarette*) avez-vous du feu?; **according to one's lights** selon ses lumières, dans la mesure de son intelligence; **against the light** à contre-jour; **in a false light** sous un faux jour; **in a new light** sous un jour nouveau; **in the same light** sous le même aspect; **it is light** (*out*) il fait jour; **lights** (*navigation lights, parking lights*) feux *mpl*; (*of sheep, calf, etc.*) mou *m*; **lights out** (mil) l'extinction *f* des feux; **to bring to light** mettre au jour; **to come to light** se révéler; **to shed or throw light on** éclairer; **to strike a light** allumer || *adv* à vide; **to run light** (*said of engine*) aller haut le pied || *v* (*pret & pp* **lighted** *or* **lit** [lɪt]) *tr* (*to furnish with illumination*) éclairer, illuminer; (*to set afire, ignite*) allumer; **to light the way for** éclairer; **to light up** illuminer || *intr* s'éclairer, s'illuminer; allumer; (*to perch*) se poser; **to light from or off** (*an auto, carriage, etc.*) descendre de; **to light into** (*to attack; to berate*) (slang) tomber sur; **to light out** (*to skedaddle*) (slang) décamper; **to light up** s'éclairer, s'illuminer; **to light upon** (*by happenstance*) tomber sur, trouver par hasard

light′ bulb′ *s* ampoule *f* électrique, lampe *f* électrique

light′ complex′ion *s* teint *m* clair

lighten [′laɪtən] *tr* (*to make lighter in weight*) alléger, soulager; (*to provide more light*) éclairer, illuminer; (*to give a lighter or brighter hue to*) éclaircir; (*grief, punishment, etc.*) adoucir || *intr* (*to become less dark or sorrowful*) s'éclairer; (*to give off flashes of lightning*) faire des éclairs; (*to becomes less weighty*) s'alléger

lighter [′laɪtər] *s* (*to light cigarette*) briquet *m*; (*flat-bottomed barge*) chaland *m*, péniche *f*

light′-fin′gered *adj* à doigts agiles

light′-foot′ed *adj* au pied léger

light′-head′ed *adj* étourdi

light′-heart′ed *adj* joyeux, allègre, au cœur léger

light′house′ *s* phare *m*

lighting [′laɪtɪŋ] *s* allumage *m*, éclairage *m*

light′ing fix′tures *spl* appareils *mpl* d'éclairage

light′ me′ter *s* posemètre *m*

lightness [′laɪtnɪs] *s* (*in weight*) légèreté *f*; (*in illumination; of complexion*) clarté *f*

light·ning ['laɪtnɪŋ] *s* (*electric discharge*) foudre *f*; (*light produced by this discharge*) éclairs *mpl* ‖ *v* (*ger -ning*) *intr* faire des éclairs

light′ning arrest′er [ə‚rɛstər] *s* parafoudre *m*

light′ning bug′ *s* luciole *f*

light′ning rod′ *s* paratonnerre *m*

light′ op′era *s* opérette *f*

light′ read′ing *s* livres *mpl* d'agrément; lecture *f* légère or amusante

light′ship′ *s* bateau-feu *m*

light-struck ['laɪt‚strʌk] *adj* (phot) voilé

light′ wave′ *s* onde *f* lumineuse

light′weight′ *adj* léger ‖ *s* (sports) poids *m* léger

light′weight coat′ *s* surtout *m* de demi-saison

light′-year′ *s* année-lumière *f*

likable ['laɪkəbəl] *adj* sympathique

like [laɪk] *adj* (*alike*) pareils, semblables; pareil à, semblable à; (*typical of*) caractéristique de; (*poles of a magnet*) (elec) de même nom; **like father like son** tel le père tel fils; **that is like him** il n'en fait pas d'autres ‖ *s* pareil *m*, semblable *m*; **likes** (*desires*) goût *m*, inclinations *fpl*; **the likes of him** son pareil ‖ *adv*—**like enough** probablement; **like mad** comme un fou ‖ *prep* comme; **like that** de la sorte ‖ *conj* (coll) de la même manière que, comme ‖ *tr* aimer, aimer bien, trouver bon; plaire (with *dat*), e.g., **I like milk** le lait me plaît; se plaire, e.g., **I like it in the country** je me plais à la campagne ‖ *intr* vouloir; **as you like** comme vous voudrez; **if you like so** si vous voulez

likelihood ['laɪklɪ‚hʊd] *s* probabilité *f*, vraisemblance *f*

like·ly ['laɪklɪ] *adj* (*comp* **-lier**; *super* **-liest**) probable, vraisemblable; **to be likely to** + *inf* être probable que + *ind*, e.g., **Mary is likely to come to see us tomorrow** il est probable que Marie viendra nous voir demain ‖ *adv* probablement, vraisemblablement

like′-mind′ed *adj* du même avis

liken ['laɪkən] *tr* comparer, assimiler

likeness ['laɪknɪs] *s* (*picture or image*) portrait *m*; (*similarity*) ressemblance *f*

like′wise′ *adv* également, de même; **to do likewise** en faire autant

liking ['laɪkɪŋ] *s* sympathie *f*, penchant *m*; **to one's liking** à souhait; **to take a liking to** (*a thing*) accueillir avec sympathie; (*a person*) montrer de la sympathie à, se prendre d'amitié pour

lilac ['laɪlək] *adj* & *s* lilas *m*

Lilliputian [‚lɪlɪ'pjuʃən] *adj* & *s* lilliputien *m*

lilt [lɪlt] *s* cadence *f*

lil·y ['lɪlɪ] *s* (*pl* **-ies**) lis *m*, lis blanc; (*royal arms of France*) fleur *f* de lis; **to gild the lily** orner la beauté même

lil′y of the val′ley *s* muguet *m*

lil′y pad′ *s* feuille *f* de nénuphar

lil′y-white′ *adj* blanc comme le lis, lilial

Li′ma bean′ ['laɪmə] *s* (*Phaseolus limensis*) haricot *m* de Lima

limb [lɪm] *s* (*arm or leg*) membre *m*; (*of a tree*) branche *f*; (*of a cross; of the sea*) bras *m*; (astr, bot) limbe *m*; **to be out on a limb** (coll) être sur la corde raide

limber ['lɪmbər] *adj* souple, flexible ‖ *intr*—**to limber up** se dégourdir

lim·bo ['lɪmbo] *s* (*pl* **-bos**) limbes *mpl*

lime [laɪm] *s* (*calcium oxide*) chaux *f*; (*linden tree*) tilleul *m*; (*Citrus aurantifolia*) citron *m*; **sweet lime** (*Citrus limetta*) lime *f*

lime′kiln′ *s* four *m* à chaux

lime′light′ *s*—**to be in the limelight** être sous les feux de la rampe

limerick ['lɪmərɪk] *s* poème *m* humoristique en cinq vers

lime′stone′ *adj* calcaire ‖ *s* calcaire *m*, pierre *f* à chaux

limit ['lɪmɪt] *s* limite *f*, borne *f*; **to be the limit** (*to be exasperating*) (coll) être le comble; (*to be bizarre*) (coll) être impayable; **to go the limit** aller jusqu'au bout ‖ *tr* limiter, borner

limitation [‚lɪmɪ'teʃən] *s* limitation *f*

lim′ited-ac′cess high′way *s* autoroute *f*

lim′ited mon′archy *s* monarchie *f* constitutionnelle

limitless ['lɪmɪtlɪs] *adj* sans bornes, illimité

limousine ['lɪmə‚zin], [‚lɪmə'zin] *s* (aut) limousine *f*

limp [lɪmp] *adj* mou, flasque, souple ‖ *s* boiterie *f* ‖ *intr* boiter

limpid ['lɪmpɪd] *adj* limpide

linchpin ['lɪntʃ‚pɪn] *s* cheville *f* d'essieu, esse *f*

linden ['lɪndən] *s* tilleul *m*

line [laɪn] *s* ligne *f*; (*of poetry*) vers *m*; (*rope, string*) cordage *m*, corde *f*; (*wrinkle*) ride *f*; (*dash*) trait *m*; (*bar*) barre *f*; (*lineage*) lignée *f*; (*trade*) métier *m*; (*of merchandise*) article *m*; (*of traffic*) file *f*; (mil) rang *m*; (*the spectrum*) (phys) raie *f*; **hold the line!** (telp) ne quittez pas!; **in line** aligné, en rang; **in line with** conforme à, d'accord avec; **on the line** (telp) au bout du fil; **out of line** désaligné; en désaccord; **to bring into line with** mettre d'accord avec; **to drop s.o. a line** envoyer un mot à qn; **to fall into line** se mettre en ligne, s'aligner; **to hand s.o. a line** (slang) faire du baratin à qn, bourrer le crâne de qn; **to have a line on** (coll) se tuyauter sur; **to learn one's lines** apprendre son texte or rôle; **to read between the lines** lire entre les lignes; **to stand or wait in line** faire la queue; **to toe the line** se mettre au pas ‖ *tr* aligner; (*a face*) rider; (*a suit, coat, etc.*) doubler; (*brakes*) fourrer; **to be lined with** (e.g., *trees*) être bordé de ‖ *intr*—**to line up** s'aligner, se mettre en ligne; faire la queue

lineage ['lɪnɪ·ɪdʒ] *s* lignée *f*, race *f*

lineal ['lɪnɪ-əl] adj linéal; (succession) en ligne directe

lineaments ['lɪnɪ-əmənts] spl linéaments mpl

linear ['lɪnɪ-ər] adj linéaire

lined' pa'per s papier m rayé

line'man s (pl -men) (elec) poseur m de lignes; (rr) garde-ligne m

linen ['lɪnən] adj de lin ‖ s (fabric) toile f de lin; (yarn) fil m de lin; (sheets, tablecloths, underclothes, etc.) linge m, lingerie f; **pure linen** pur fil

lin'en clos'et s lingerie f

line' of fire' s (mil) ligne f de tir

line' of sight' s ligne f de mire

liner ['laɪnər] s (naut) paquebot m

line'-up' s mise f en rang; personnel m; (arrangement) disposition f; (of prisoners) défilé m de détenus, alignement m de suspects; (sports) composition f

linger ['lɪŋgər] intr s'attarder; (said of hope, doubt, etc.) persister; **to linger on** traîner; **to linger over** s'attarder sur

lingerie [,læn3ə'ri] s lingerie f fine pour dames, lingerie de dame

lingering ['lɪŋgərɪŋ] adj prolongé, lent

lingual ['lɪŋgwəl] adj lingual ‖ s (consonant) linguale f

linguist ['lɪŋgwɪst] s (person skilled in several languages) polyglotte mf; (specialist in linguistics) linguiste mf

linguistic [lɪŋ'gwɪstɪk] adj linguistique ‖ **linguistics** s linguistique f

liniment ['lɪnɪmənt] s liniment m

lining ['laɪnɪŋ] s (of a coat) doublure f; (of a hat) coiffe f; (of auto brake) garniture f; (of furnace, wall, etc.) revêtement m

link [lɪŋk] s maillon m, chaînon m; (fig) lien m; **links** terrain m de golf ‖ tr enchaîner; lier ‖ intr—**to link in, on, or up** se lier

linnet ['lɪnɪt] s (orn) linotte f

linoleum [lɪ'nolɪ-əm] s linoléum m

linotype ['laɪnə,taɪp] (trademark) s linotype f ‖ tr & intr composer à la lino

lin'otype op'erator s linotypiste mf

linseed ['lɪn,sid] s linette f, graine f de lin

lin'seed oil' s huile f de lin

lint [lɪnt] s bourre f, filasse f; (used to dress wounds) charpie f

lintel ['lɪntəl] s linteau m

lion ['laɪ-ən] s lion m; (fig) lion; **to put one's head in the lion's mouth** se fourrer dans la gueule du loup or du lion

lioness ['laɪ-ənɪs] s lionne f

li'on-heart'ed adj au cœur de lion

lionize ['laɪ-ə,naɪz] tr faire une célébrité de, traiter en vedette

li'ons' den' s (Bib) fosse f aux lions

li'on's share' s part f du lion

lip [lɪp] s lèvre f; (edge) bord m; (slang) impertinence f; **to hang on the lips of** être suspendu aux lèvres de; **to smack one's lips** se lécher les babines

lip'read' v (pret & pp -read [,red]) tr & intr lire sur les lèvres

lip' read'ing s lecture f sur les lèvres

lip' serv'ice s dévotion f des lèvres

lip'stick' s bâton m de rouge à lèvres

lique•fy ['lɪkwɪ,faɪ] v (pret & pp -fied) tr liquéfier

liqueur [lɪ'kɜr] s liqueur f

liquid ['lɪkwɪd] adj liquide ‖ s liquide m; (consonant) liquide f

liq'uid as'sets spl valeurs fpl disponibles

liquidate ['lɪkwɪ,det] tr & intr liquider

liquidity [lɪ'kwɪdɪti] s liquidité f

liquor ['lɪkər] s boisson f alcoolique, spiritueux m; (culin) jus m, bouillon m

Lisbon ['lɪzbən] s Lisbonne f

lisle [laɪl] s fil m d'Écosse, fil retors de coton

lisp [lɪsp] s zézayement m, blésement m ‖ intr zézayer, bléser

lissome ['lɪsəm] adj souple, flexible; (nimble) agile, leste

list [lɪst] s liste f; (selvage) lisière f; (naut) bande f; **to enter the lists** entrer en lice; **to have a list** (naut) donner de la bande ‖ tr cataloguer, enregistrer ‖ intr (naut) donner de la bande

listen ['lɪsən] intr écouter; **to listen in** rester à l'écoute; **to listen to** écouter; **to listen to reason** entendre raison

listener ['lɪsənər] s auditeur m; (educ) auditeur libre

listening ['lɪsənɪŋ] s écoute f

lis'tening post' s poste m d'écoute

listless ['lɪstlɪs] adj apathique, inattentif

list' price' s prix m courant, cote f

litany ['lɪtəni] s (pl -nies) litanie f

liter ['litər] s litre m

literal ['lɪtərəl] adj littéral; (person) prosaïque

literary ['lɪtə,rɛri] adj littéraire

literate ['lɪtərɪt] adj qui sait lire et écrire; (well-read) lettré ‖ s personne f qui sait lire et écrire; lettré m, érudit m

literati [,lɪtə'rati] spl littérateurs mpl

literature ['lɪtərət∫ər] s littérature f; (com) documentation f

lithe [laɪð] adj souple, flexible

lithia ['lɪθɪ-ə] s (chem) lithine f

lithium ['lɪθɪ-əm] s (chem) lithium m

lithograph ['lɪθə,græf], ['lɪθə,graf] s lithographie f ‖ tr lithographier

lithographer [lɪ'θagrəfər] s lithographe mf

lithography [lɪ'θagrəfi] s lithographie f

Lithuania [,lɪθʊ'enɪ-ə] s Lituanie f; la Lituanie

Lithuanian [,lɪθʊ'enɪ-ən] adj lituanien ‖ s (language) lituanien m; (person) Lituanien m

litigant ['lɪtɪgənt] adj plaidant ‖ s plaideur m

litigate ['lɪtɪ,get] tr mettre en litige ‖ intr plaider

litigation [,lɪtɪ'ge∫ən] s litige m

lit′mus pa′per [′lɪtməs] s papier m de tournesol

litter [′lɪtər] s fouillis m; (*things strewn about*) jonchée f; (*scattered rubbish*) ordures fpl; (*young brought forth at one birth*) portée f; (*bedding for animals*) litière f; (*vehicle carried by men or animals*) palanquin m; (*stretcher*) civière f || tr joncher || intr (*to bring forth young*) mettre bas

lit′ter-bug′ s souillon m, malpropre m, personne f qui dépose des ordures et des papiers dans la rue

littering [′lɪtərɪŋ] s—**no littering** (*public sign*) défense de déposer des ordures

little [′lɪtəl] adj petit; (*in amount*) peu de, e.g., **little money** peu d'argent; **a little** un peu de, e.g., **a little money** un peu d'argent || s peu m; **a little** un peu; **to make little of**, **to think little of** faire peu de cas de; **wait a little** attendez un petit moment, attendez quelques instants || adv peu §91; ne . . . guère §90, e.g., **she little thinks that** elle ne se doute guère que; **little by little** peu à peu, petit à petit

Lit′tle Bear′ s Petite Ourse f

Lit′tle Dip′per s Petit Chariot m

lit′tle fin′ger s petit doigt m, auriculaire m; **to twist around one's little finger** mener par le bout du nez

lit′tle-neck′ s coque f de Vénus

littleness [′lɪtəlnɪs] s petitesse f

lit′tle owl′ (*Athene noctua*) chouette f chevêche, chevêche f

lit′tle peo′ple spl (*fairies*) fées fpl; (*common people*) menu peuple m

Lit′tle Red Rid′ing-hood′ s le Petit Chaperon rouge

lit′tle slam′ s (bridge) petit chelem m

liturgic(al) [lɪ′tʌrdʒɪk(əl)] adj liturgique

litur-gy [′lɪtərdʒi] s (pl -gies) liturgie f

livable [′lɪvəbəl] adj (*house*) habitable; (*life, person*) supportable

live [laɪv] adj vivant, vif; (*coals; flame*) ardent; (*elec*) sous tension; (telv) en direct § [lɪv] tr vivre; **to live down** faire oublier || intr vivre; (*in a certain locality*) demeurer, habiter; **live and learn** qui vivra verra; **to live high** mener grand train; **to live in** (e.g., *a city*) habiter; **to live on** continuer à vivre; (e.g., *meat*) vivre de; (*a benefactor*) vivre aux crochets de; (*one's capital*) manger; **to live up to** (e.g., *one's reputation*) faire honneur à

live′ coal′ [laɪv] s charbon m ardent

livelihood [′laɪvlɪ,hʊd] s vie f; **to earn one's livelihood** gagner sa vie

livelong [′lɪv,lɒŋ], [′lɪv,lɑŋ] adj—**all the livelong day** toute la sainte journée

live·ly [′laɪvli] adj (comp -lier; super -liest) animé, vivant, plein d'entrain; (*merry*) enjoué, gai; (*active, keen*) vif; (*resilient*) élastique

liven [′laɪvən] tr animer || intr s'animer

liver [′lɪvər] s vivant m; (e.g., *in cities*) habitant m; (anat) foie m

liver·y [′lɪvəri] s (pl -ies) livrée f

liv′ery-man s (pl -men) loueur m de chevaux

liv′ery sta′ble s écurie f de louage

live′ show′ [laɪv] s (telv) prise f de vues en direct

live′stock′ [laɪv] s bétail m, bestiaux mpl, cheptel m

live′ tel′evision broad′cast [laɪv] s prise f de vues en direct

live′ wire′ [laɪv] s fil m sous tension; (slang) type m dynamique

livid [′lɪvɪd] adj livide

living [′lɪvɪŋ] adj vivant, en vie || s vie f; **to earn** or **to make a living** gagner sa vie

liv′ing quar′ters spl appartements mpl, habitations fpl

liv′ing room′ s salle f de séjour, salon m

liv′ing space′ s espace m vital

liv′ing wage′ s salaire m suffisant pour vivre, salaire de base

lizard [′lɪzərd] s lézard m

load [lod] s charge f; **loads** (**of**) (coll) énormément (de); **to get a load of** (slang) observer, écouter; **to have a load on** (slang) avoir son compte || tr charger || intr charger; **se charger**

loaded adj chargé; (*very drunk*) (slang) soûl; (*very rich*) (slang) huppé

load′ed dice′ spl dés mpl pipés

load′stone′ s pierre f d'aimant; (fig) aimant m

loaf [lof] s (pl **loaves** [lovz]) pain m || intr flâner

loafer [′lofər] s flâneur m

loam [lom] s terre f franche, glaise f; (*mixture used in making molds*) potée f

loamy [′lomi] adj franc, glaiseux

loan [lon] s prêt m, emprunt m || tr prêter

loan′ shark′ s usurier m

loan′ word′ s mot m d'emprunt

loath [loθ] adj—**loath to** peu enclin à

loathe [loð] tr détester

loathing [′loðɪŋ] s dégoût m

loathsome [′loðsəm] adj dégoûtant

lob [lab] s (tennis) lob m || v (pret & pp lobbed; ger lobbing) tr frapper en hauteur, lober

lob·by [′labi] s (pl -bies) vestibule m; (e.g., *in a theater*) foyer m; (*pressure group*) groupe m de pression, lobby m || v (pret & pp -bied) intr faire les couloirs

lobbying [′labɪ,ɪŋ] s intrigues fpl de couloir

lobbyist [′labɪ·ɪst] s intrigant m de couloir

lobe [lob] s lobe m

lobster [′labstər] s (spiny lobster) langouste f; (*Homarus*) homard m

lob′ster pot′ s casier m à homards

local [′lokəl] adj local || s (*of labor union*) succursale f; (journ) informations fpl régionales; (rr) train m omnibus

locale [lo′kæl] s lieu m, milieu m; scène f

locali•ty [lo'kælɪti] s (pl **-ties**) localité f
localize ['loka,laɪz] tr localiser
lo'cal supply' cir'cuit s secteur m
locate [lo'ket], ['loket] tr (to discover the location of) localiser; (to place, to settle) placer, installer; (to ascribe a particular location to) situer; **to be located** se trouver || intr se fixer, s'établir
location [lo'ke/ən] s (place, position) situation f, emplacement m; (act of placing) établissement m; (act of finding) localisation f, détermination f; (of a railroad line) tracé m; **on location** (mov) en extérieur
loca'tion shot' s (mov) extérieur m
lock [lak] s serrure f; (of a canal) écluse f; (of hair) mèche f, boucle f; (of a firearm) platine f; (wrestling) clef f; **lock, stock, and barrel** tout le bataclan, tout le fourbi; **under lock and key** sous clé || tr fermer à clef; (to key) caler, bloquer; (a boat) écluser, sasser; (a switch) (rr) verrouiller; **to be locked in each other's arms** être enlacés; **to lock in** enfermer à clef; **to lock out** fermer la porte à ou sur; (workers) fermer les ateliers contre; **to lock up** fermer à clef, mettre sous clé; (e.g., a prisoner) boucler, enfermer; (a form) (typ) serrer || intr (said of door) fermer à clef; (said of brake, wheel, etc.) se bloquer; **to lock into** s'engrener dans
locker ['lakər] s armoire f, coffre m de sûreté (in a station) compartiment m individuel
lock'er room' s vestiaire m à cases individuelles
locket ['lakɪt] s médaillon m
lock'jaw' s trisme m
lock' nut' s contre-écrou m
lock'out' s lock-out m
lock'smith' s serrurier m
lock' step' s—to march in lock step emboîter le pas
lock' stitch' s point m indécousable
lock'ten'der s éclusier m
lock'up' s (prison) (coll) bloc m, violon m
lock' wash'er s rondelle f Grower, rondelle à ressort
locomotive [,loka'motɪv] s locomotive f
lo•cus ['lokəs] s (pl **-ci** [saɪ]) lieu m; (math) lieu géométrique
locust ['lokəst] s (Pachytylus) (ent) criquet m migrateur, locuste f; (Cicada) (ent) cigale f; (bot) faux acacia m
lode [lod] s filon m, veine f
lode'star' s (astr) étoile f polaire; (fig) pôle m d'attraction
lodge [ladʒ] s (of gatekeeper; of animal; of Mason) loge f; (residence, e.g., for hunting) pavillon m; (hotel) relais m, hostellerie f || tr loger; **to lodge a complaint with** porter plainte auprès de || intr loger; (said of arrow, bullet) se loger

lodger ['ladʒər] s locataire mf, pensionnaire mf
lodging ['ladʒɪŋ] s logement m; (of a complaint) déposition f
loft [lɔft], [laft] s (attic) grenier m, soupente f; (hayloft) fenil m; (in theater or church) tribune f; (in store or office building) atelier m
loft•y ['lɔfti], ['lafti] adj (comp **-ier**; super **-iest**) (towering; sublime) élevé, exalté; (haughty) hautain
log [lɔg], [lag] s bûche f, rondin m; (record book) registre m de travail; (aer) livre m de vol; (record book) (naut) journal m de bord; (chip log) (naut) loch m; (rad) carnet m d'écoute; **to sleep like a log** dormir comme une souche || v (pret & pp logged; ger logging) tr (wood) tronçonner; (an event) porter au journal; (a certain distance) (naut) filer || intr (to cut wood) couper dès rondins
logarithm ['lɔgə,rɪðəm], ['lagə,rɪðəm] s logarithme m
log'book' s (aer) livre m de vol; (naut) journal m de bord, livre de loch
log' cab'in s cabane f en rondins
log' chip' s (naut) flotteur m de loch
log' driv'er s flotteur m
log' driv'ing s flottage m
logger ['lɔgər], ['lagər] s bûcheron m; (loader) (mach) grue f de chargement; (mach) tracteur m
log'ger-head' s tête f de bois; **at loggerheads** en bisbille, aux prises
logic ['ladʒɪk] s logique f
logical ['ladʒɪkəl] adj logique
logician [lo'dʒɪ/ən] s logicien m
logistic(al) [lo'dʒɪstɪk(əl)] adj logistique
logistics [lo'dʒɪstɪks] s logistique f
log'jam' s embâcle m de bûches; (fig) bouchon m, embouteillage m
log' line' s (naut) ligne f de loch
log'roll' intr faire trafic de faveurs politiques
log'wood' s bois m de campêche; (tree) campêche m
loin [lɔɪn] s (of beef) aloyau m; (of veal) longe f; (of pork) échine f; **to gird up one's loins** se ceindre les reins
loin'cloth' s pagne m
loiter ['lɔɪtər] tr—**to loiter away** perdre en flânant || intr flâner
loiterer ['lɔɪtərər] s flâneur m
loll [lall] intr se prélasser, s'allonger, s'affaler
lollipop ['lali,pap] s sucette f
Lom'bardy pop'lar ['lambərdi] s peuplier m noir
London ['lʌndən] adj londonien || s Londres m
Londoner ['lʌndənər] s Londonien m
lone [lon] adj solitaire, seul; (sole, single) unique
loneliness ['lonlɪnɪs] s solitude f
lone•ly ['lonli] adj (comp **-lier**; super **-liest**) solitaire, isolé
lonesome ['lonsəm] adj solitaire, seul
lone' wolf' s (fig) solitaire mf, ours m
long [lɔŋ], [laŋ] (comp **longer** ['lɔŋ-

gər], ['laŋgər]; *super* **longest** ['loŋgɪst'], ['laŋgɪst]) *adj* long; de long, de longueur, e.g., **two meters long** deux mètres de long or de longueur ‖ *adv* longtemps; **as long as** aussi longtemps que; *(provided that)* tant que; **before long** sous peu; **how long?** combien de temps?, depuis combien de temps?, depuis quand?; **long ago** il y a longtemps; **long before** longtemps avant; **longer** plus long; **long since** depuis longtemps; **no longer** ne . . . plus longtemps; ne . . . plus, e.g., **I could no longer see him** je ne pouvais plus le voir; **so long!** (coll) à bientôt!; **so long as** tant que; **to be long in** tarder à ‖ *intr*—**to long for** soupirer pour or après

long'boat' s chaloupe f

long' dis'tance s (telp) l'interurbain m; **to call s.o. long distance** appeler qn par l'interurbain

long'-dis'tance call' s (telp) appel m interurbain

long'-dis'tance flight' s (aer) vol m au long cours, raid m aérien

long'-drawn'-out' *adj* prolongé; *(story)* délayé

longevity [lan'dʒɛvɪti] s longévité f

long' face' s (coll) triste figure f

long'hair' *adj* & s intellectuel m; fanatique mf de la musique classique

long'hand' s écriture f ordinaire; **in longhand** à la main

longing ['loŋɪŋ], ['laŋɪŋ] *adj* ardent; s désir m ardent

longitude ['landʒɪ,t(j)ud] s longitude f

long' jump' s saut m en longueur

long-lived ['loŋ'laɪvd], ['laŋ'laɪvd], ['loŋ'laɪvd], ['laŋ'lɪvd] *adj* à longue vie; persistant

long'-play'ing rec'ord s disque m de longue durée

long' prim'er ['prɪmər] s (typ) philosophie f

long'-range' *adj* à longue portée; *(e.g., plan)* à long terme

long'shore'man s (pl -men) arrimeur m, débardeur m

long'-stand'ing *adj* de longue date

long'-suf'fering *adj* patient, endurant

long' suit' s (cards) couleur f longue, longue f; (fig) fort m

long'-term' *adj* à longue échéance

long'-wind'ed ['wɪndɪd] *adj* interminable; *(person)* intarissable

look [luk] s *(appearance)* aspect m; *(glance)* regard m; **looks** apparence f, mine f; **to take a look at** jeter un coup d'œil sur or à ‖ *tr* regarder; *(e.g., one's age)* paraître; **to look daggers at** lancer un regard furieux à; **to look the part** avoir le physique de l'emploi; **to look up** *(e.g., in a dictionary)* chercher, rechercher; *(to visit)* aller voir, venir voir ‖ *intr* regarder; *(to seek)* chercher; **it looks like rain** le temps est à la pluie; **look here!** dites donc!; **look out!** gare!, attention!; **to look after** s'occuper de; *(e.g., an invalid)* soigner; **to look at** regarder; **to look away** détourner

les yeux; **to look back** regarder en arrière; **to look down on** mépriser; **to look for** chercher; *(to expect)* s'attendre à; **to look forward to** s'attendre à, attendre avec impatience; **to look ill** avoir mauvaise mine; **to look in on** passer voir; **to look into** examiner, vérifier; **to look like** *(s.o. or s.th.)* ressembler à; *(to give promise of)* avoir l'air de; **to look out** faire attention; *(e.g., the window)* regarder par; **to look out on** donner sur; **to look through** *(a window)* regarder par; *(a telescope)* regarder dans; *(a book)* feuilleter; **to look toward** regarder du côté de; **to look up** lever les yeux; **to look up to** respecter; **to look well** avoir bonne mine

looker-on [,lukər'an], [,lukər'ɒn] s (pl lookers-on) spectateur m, assistant m

look'ing glass' s miroir m

look'out' s guet m; *(person)* guetteur m; *(place)* poste m d'observation; *(person or place)* (naut) vigie f; **that's his lookout** (coll) ça, c'est son affaire; **to be on the lookout for** être à l'affût de

loom [lum] s métier m ‖ *intr* apparaître indistinctement; s'élever; menacer, paraître imminent

loon [lun] s lourdaud m, sot m; (orn) plongeon m

loon·y ['luni] *adj* (comp -ier; super -iest) (slang) toqué ‖ s (pl -ies) (slang) toqué m

loop [lup] s boucle f; *(for fastening a button)* bride f; *(circular route)* boulevard m périphérique; *(in skating)* croisé m; **to loop the loop** (aer) boucler la boucle ‖ *tr* & *intr* boucler

loop'hole' s meurtrière f; (fig) échappatoire f

loop'-the-loop' s looping m

loose [lus] *adj* lâche; *(stone, tooth)* branlant; *(screw)* desserré; *(pulley, wheel)* fou; *(rope)* mou, détendu; *(coat, dress)* vague, ample; *(earth, soil)* meuble, friable; *(bowels)* relâché; *(style)* décousu; *(translation)* libre, peu exact; *(life, morals)* relâché, dissolu; *(woman)* facile; *(unpackaged)* en vrac; *(unbound, e.g., pages)* détaché; **to become loose** se détacher; **to break loose** *(from captivity)* s'évader; (fig) se déchaîner; **to let loose** lâcher, lâcher la bride à ‖ s—**to be on the loose** *(to debauch)* (coll) courir la prétentaine; *(to be out of work)* (coll) être sans occupation ‖ *tr* lâcher; *(to untie)* détacher

loose' end' s (fig) affaire f pendante; **at loose ends** désœuvré, indécis

loose'-leaf note'book s cahier m à feuilles mobiles

loosen ['lusən] *tr* lâcher, relâcher; *(a screw)* desserrer ‖ *intr* se relâcher

looseness ['lusnɪs] s relâchement m; *(of garment)* ampleur f; *(play of screw)* jeu m, desserrage m

loose'strife' s *(common yellow type)*

chasse-bosse *f*, grande lysimaque *f*; (*spiked-purple type*) salicaire *f*

loose'-tongued' *adj*—to be loose-tongued avoir la langue déliée

loot [lut] *s* butin *m*, pillage *m* || *tr* piller, saccager

lop [lɑp] *v* (*pret & pp* lopped; *ger* lopping) *tr*—to lop off abattre, trancher; (*a tree, a branch*) élaguer || *intr* pendre

lope [lop] *s* galop *m* lent || *intr*—to lope along aller doucement

lop'sid'ed *adj* déjeté, bancal

loquacious [lo'kweʃəs] *adj* loquace

lord [lɔrd] *s* seigneur *m*; (hum & poetic) époux *m*; (Brit) lord *m* || *tr*—to lord it over dominer despotiquement

lord·ly ['lɔrdli] *adj* (*comp* -lier; *super* -liest) de grand seigneur, majestueux; (*arrogant*) hautain, altier

Lord's' Day' *s* jour *m* du Seigneur

lordship ['lɔrdʃɪp] *s* seigneurie *f*

Lord's' Prayer' *s* oraison *f* dominicale

Lord's' Sup'per *s* communion *f*, cène *f*; Cène

lore [lor] *s* savoir *m*, science *f*; tradition *f* populaire

lorgnette [lɔrn'jɛt] *s* (*eyeglasses*) face-à-main *m*; (*opera glasses*) lorgnette *f*

lor·ry ['lɑri], ['lɔri] *s* (*pl* -ries) lorry *m*, wagonnet *m*; (*truck*) (Brit) camion *m*; (*wagon*) (Brit) fardier *m*

lose [luz] *v* (*pret & pp* lost [lɔst], [lɑst]) *tr* perdre; (*a patient who dies*) ne pas réussir à sauver; (*several minutes, as a timepiece does*) retarder de; to lose oneself in s'absorber dans; to lose one's way s'égarer || *intr* perdre; (*said of timepiece*) retarder

loser ['luzər] *s* perdant *m*

losing ['luzɪŋ] *adj* perdant || **losings** *spl* pertes *fpl*

loss [lɔs], [lɑs] *s* perte *f*; to be at a loss ne savoir que faire; to be at a loss to avoir de la peine à, être bien embarrassé pour; to sell at a loss vendre à perte

loss' of face' *s* perte *f* de prestige

lost [lɔst], [lɑst] *adj* perdu; lost in thought perdu or absorbé dans ses pensées; lost to perdu pour

lost'-and-found' depart'ment *s* bureau *m* des objets trouvés

lost' sheep' *s* brebis *f* perdue, brebis égarée

lot [lɑt] *s* lot *m*; (*for building*) lotissement *m*, lot; (*fate*) sort *m*, lot; a bad lot (coll) un mauvais sujet, de la mauvaise graine; a lot of or lots of (coll) un tas de; a queer lot (coll) un drôle de numéro; in a lot en bloc; to cast or to throw in one's lot with tenter la fortune avec; to draw or to cast lots tirer au sort; such a lot of tellement de; what a lot of . . . ! que de . . . !

lotion ['loʃən] *s* lotion *f*

lotter·y ['lɑtəri] *s* (*pl* -ies) loterie *f*

lotto ['lɑto] *s* loto *m*

lotus ['lotəs] *s* lotus *m*

loud [laud] *adj* haut, fort; (*noisy*) bruyant; (*voice*) fort; (*showy*) voyant || *adv* fort; (*noisily*) bruyamment; out loud à haute voix

loud-mouthed ['laud,mauθt], ['laud,mauðd] *adj* au verbe haut

loud'speak'er *s* haut-parleur *m*

Louisiana [lu,izi'ænə] *s* Louisiane *f*; la Louisiane

lounge [laundʒ] *s* divan *m*, sofa *m*; (*room*) petit salon *m*, salle *f* de repos; (*in a hotel*) hall *m* || *intr* flâner; (*e.g., in a chair*) se vautrer

lounge' liz'ard *s* (slang) gigolo *m*

louse [laus] *s* (*pl* lice [lais]) pou *m*; (slang) salaud *m* || *tr*—to louse up (slang) bâcler

lous·y ['lauzi] *adj* (*comp* -ier; *super* -iest) pouilleux; (*mean; ugly*) (coll) moche; (*bungling*) (coll) maladroit, gauche; lousy with (slang) chargé de

lout [laut] *s* lourdaud *m*, balourd *m*

louver ['luvər] *s* abat-vent *m*; (aut) auvent *m*

lovable ['lʌvəbəl] *adj* aimable, sympathique

love [lʌv] *s* amour *m*; affection *f*; (tennis) zéro *m*; in love with amoureux de; love at first sight le coup de foudre; love to all! vives amitiés à tous!; not for love or money pour rien au monde; to make love to faire la cour à; with much love! avec mes affectueuses pensées! || *tr & intr* aimer

love' affair' *s* affaire *f* de cœur

love'birds' *spl* inséparables *mpl*; nouveaux mariés *mpl*

love' child' *s* enfant *mf* de l'amour

love' feast' *s* (eccl) agape *f*

love' game' *s* (tennis) jeu *m* blanc

love' knot' *s* lacs *m* d'amour

loveless ['lʌvlis] *adj* sans amour; (*feeling no love*) insensible à l'amour

love' let'ter *s* billet *m* doux

lovelorn ['lʌv,lɔrn] *adj* délaissé d'amour; éperdu d'amour

love·ly ['lʌvli] *adj* (*comp* -lier; *super* -liest) beau; (*adorable*) charmant, gracieux; (*enjoyable*) (coll) agréable, aimable

love' match' *s* mariage *m* d'amour

love' po'tion *s* philtre *m* d'amour

lover ['lʌvər] *s* amoureux *m*, amant *m*; (*of hunting, sports, music, etc.*) amateur *m*, fanatique *mf*

love' seat' *s* causeuse *f*

love'sick' *adj* féru d'amour

love'sick'ness *s* mal *m* d'amour

love' song' *s* romance *f*, chanson *f* d'amour

loving ['lʌvɪŋ] *adj* aimant, affectueux; affectionné, e.g., your loving daughter votre fille affectionnée

lov'ing cup' *s* coupe *f* de l'amitié; trophée *m*

lov'ing-kind'ness *s* bonté *f* d'âme

low [lo] *adj* bas; (*speed; price*) bas; (*speed; price; number; light*) faible; (*opinion*) défavorable; (*dress*) décolleté; (*sound, note*) bas, grave; (*fever*) lent; (*bow*) profond; to lay low étendre, terrasser; **to lie low** se tenir coi || *s* bas *m*; (*moo of cow*) meuglement *m*; (aut) première vitesse *f*; (meteo) dépression *f* || *adv* bas; **to speak low** parler à voix basse || *intr* (*said of cow*) meugler

low/born/ *adj* de basse naissance

low/boy/ *s* commode *f* basse

low/brow/ *adj* (coll) peu intellectuel || *s* (coll) ignorant *m*

low/-cost/ hous/ing *s* habitations *fpl* à loyer modéré or à bon marché

Low/ Coun/tries *spl* Pays-Bas *mpl*

low/-down/ *adj* (coll) bas, vil || **low/-down/** *s* (slang) faits *mpl* véritables; **to give s.o. the low-down on** (slang) tuyauter qn sur

lower ['lo·ər] *adj* inférieur, bas || *tr* & *intr* baisser || ['lau·ər] *intr* se renfrogner, regarder de travers

low/er berth/ ['lo·ər] *s* couchette *f* inférieure

low/er case/ ['lo·ər] *s* (typ) bas *m* de casse

lower mid/dle class/ ['lo·ər] *s* petite bourgeoisie *f*

lowermost ['lo·ər,most] *adj* (le) plus bas

low/-fre/quency *adj* à basse fréquence

low/ gear/ *s* première vitesse *f*

lowland ['lolənd] *s* plaine *f* basse; **Lowlands** (*in Scotland*) Basse-Écosse *f*

low-ly ['loli] *adj* (*comp* **-lier**; *super* **-liest**) humble, modeste; (*in growth or position*) bas, infime

Low/ Mass/ *s* messe basse *f*, petite messe

low/-mind/ed *adj* d'esprit vulgaire

low/ neck/ *s* décolleté *m*

low/-necked/ *adj* décolleté

low/-pitched/ *adj* (*sound*) grave; (*roof*) à faible inclinaison

low/-pres/sure *adj* à basse pression

low/-priced/ *adj* à bas prix

low/ shoe/ *s* soulier *m* bas

low/-speed/ *adj* à petite vitesse

low/ spir/ited *adj* abattu

low/ spir/its *spl* abattement *m*, accablement *m*

low/ tide/ *s* marée *f* basse

low/ vis/ibil/ity *s* (aer) mauvaise visibilité *f*

low/-warp/ *adj* (tex) de basse lice

low/ wa/ter *s* (*of river*) étiage *m*; (*of sea*) niveau *m* des basses eaux; marée *f* basse

loyal ['lɔɪ·əl] *adj* loyal

loyalist ['lɔɪ·əlɪst] *s* loyaliste *mf*

loyal-ty ['lɔɪ·əlti] *s* (*pl* **-ties**) loyauté *f*

lozenge ['lazındʒ] *s* (*candy cough drop*) pastille *f*; (geom) losange *m*

LP ['el'pi] *s* (letterword) (trademark) (**long-playing**) disque *m* de longue durée

lubricant ['lubrıkənt] *adj* & *s* lubrifiant *m*

lubricate ['lubrı,ket] *tr* lubrifier

lubricous ['lubrıkəs] *adj* (*slippery*) glissant; (*lewd*) lubrique; inconstant

lucerne [lu'sʌrn] *s* luzerne *f*

lucid ['lusıd] *adj* lucide

luck [lʌk] *s* (*good or bad*) chance *f*;

(*good*) chance, bonne chance; **to be down on one's luck, to be out of luck** avoir de la malchance, être dans la déveine; **to be in luck** avoir de la chance, avoir de la veine; **to bring luck** porter bonheur; **to try one's luck** tenter la fortune, tenter l'aventure; **worse luck!** tant pis!, pas de chance!

luckily ['lʌkıli] *adv* heureusement, par bonheur

luckless ['lʌklıs] *adj* malheureux, malchanceux

luck-y ['lʌki] *adj* (*comp* **-ier**; *super* **-iest**) heureux, fortuné; (*supposed to bring luck*) porte-bonheur; **how lucky!** quelle chance!; **to be lucky** avoir de la chance

luck/y charm/ *s* porte-bonheur *m*

luck/y find/ *s* (coll) trouvaille *f*

luck/y hit/ *s* (coll) coup *m* de bonheur

lucrative ['lukrətıv] *adj* lucratif

ludicrous ['ludıkrəs] *adj* ridicule, risible

lug [lʌg] *s* oreille *f*; (*pull, tug*) saccade *f* || *v* (*pret* & *pp* **lugged**; *ger* **lugging**) *tr* traîner, tirer; (*to bring up irrelevantly*) (coll) ressortir, amener de force

luggage ['lʌgıdʒ] *s* bagages *mpl*

lug/gage car/rier *s* porte-bagages *m*

lugubrious [lu'g(j)ubrı·əs] *adj* lugubre

lukewarm ['luk,wɔrm] *adj* tiède

lull [lʌl] *s* accalmie *f* || *tr* bercer, endormir, calmer

lulla·by ['lʌlə,baɪ] *s* (*pl* **-bies**) berceuse *f*

lumbago [lʌm'bego] *s* lumbago *m*

lumber ['lʌmbər] *s* bois *m* de charpente, bois de construction || *intr* se traîner lourdement

lum/ber·jack/ *s* bûcheron *m*

lum/ber jack/et *s* canadienne *f*

lum/ber·man *s* (*pl* **-men**) (*dealer*) exploitant *m* forestier, propriétaire *m* forestier; (*man who cuts down lumber*) bûcheron *m*

lum/ber raft/ *s* train *m* de flottage

lum/ber room/ *s* fourre-tout *m*, débarras *m*

lum/ber·yard/ *s* chantier *m* de bois, dépôt *m* de bois de charpente

luminar-y ['lumı,neri] *s* (*pl* **-ies**) corps *m* lumineux; (astr) luminaire *m*; (*person*) (fig) lumière *f*

luminescent [,lumı'nesənt] *adj* luminescent

luminous ['lumınəs] *adj* lumineux

lummox ['lʌmaks] *s* (coll) lourdaud *m*

lump [lʌmp] *s* masse *f*; (*of earth*) motte *f*; (*of sugar*) morceau *m*; (*of salt, flour, porridge, etc.*) grumeau *m*; (*swelling*) bosse *f*; (*of ice, stone, etc.*) bloc *m*; **in the lump** en bloc; **to get a lump in one's throat** avoir un serrement de gorge || *tr* réunir; **to lump together** prendre en bloc, englober || *intr*—**to lump along** marcher d'un pas lourd

lumpish ['lʌmpıʃ] *adj* balourd

lump/ sug/ar *s* sucre *m* en morceaux

lump/ sum/ *s* somme *f* globale

lump·y ['lʌmpi] *adj* (*comp* **-ier**; *super* **-iest**) grumeleux; (*covered with lumps*) couvert de bosses; (*sea*) clapoteux

luna·cy ['lunəsi] *s* (*pl* **-cies**) folie *f*

lu'nar land'ing *s* alunissage *m*

lu'nar mod'ule *s* (rok) module *m* lunaire

lunatic ['lunətɪk] *adj* & *s* fou *m*

lu'natic asy'lum *s* maison *f* de fous

lu'natic fringe' *s* minorité *f* fanatique

lunch [lʌntʃ] *s* (*midday meal*) déjeuner *m*; (*light meal*) collation *f*, petit repas *m* || *intr* déjeuner; (*to snack*) casser la croûte, manger sur le pouce

lunch' bas'ket *s* panier *m* à provisions

lunch' cloth' *s* nappe *f* à thé

lunch' coun'ter *s* snack *m*, buffet *m*

luncheon ['lʌntʃən] *s* déjeuner *m*

luncheonette [,lʌntʃə'nɛt] *s* brasserie *f*, café-restaurant *m*

lunch'room' *s* brasserie *f*, café-restaurant *m*

lunch'time' *s* heure *f* du déjeuner

lung [lʌŋ] *s* poumon *m*

lunge [lʌndʒ] *s* mouvement *m* en avant; (*with a sword*) botte' *f* || *intr* se précipiter en avant; (*with a sword*) se fendre; to lunge at porter une botte à

lurch [lʌrtʃ] *s* embardée *f*; (*of person*) secousse *f*; to leave in the lurch laisser en plan || *intr* faire une embardée; (*said of person*) vaciller

lure [lur] *s* (*decoy*) leurre *m*, amorce *f*; (fig) attrait *m* || *tr* leurrer; to lure away détourner

lurid ['lurid] *adj* sensationnel; (*gruesome*) terrible, macabre; (*fiery*) rougeoyant; (*livid*) blafard

lurk [lʌrk] *intr* se cacher; (*to prowl*) rôder

luscious ['lʌʃəs] *adj* délicieux, succulent; luxueux, somptueux

lush [lʌʃ] *adj* plein de sève; (*abundant*) luxuriant; opulent, luxueux

lust [lʌst] *s* désir *m* ardent; (*greed*) convoitise *f*, soif *f*; (*strong sexual appetite*) luxure *f*

luster ['lʌstər] *s* lustre *m*

lus'ter·ware' *s* poterie *f* lustrée, poterie à reflets métalliques

lustful ['lʌstfəl] *adj* luxurieux, lascif

lustrous ['lʌstrəs] *adj* lustré, chatoyant

lust·y ['lʌsti] *adj* (*comp* **-ier**; *super* **-iest**) robuste, vigoureux

lute [lut] *s* (mus) luth *m*; (*substance used to close or seal a joint*) (chem) lut *m*

Lutheran ['luθərən] *adj* luthérien || *s* Luthérien *m*

Luxemburg ['lʌksəm,bʌrg] *s* le Luxembourg

luxuriant [lʌg'ʒurɪ-ənt], [lʌk'ʃurɪ-ənt] *adj* luxuriant; (*overornamented*) surchargé

luxurious [lʌg'ʒurɪ-əs], [lʌk'ʃurɪ-əs] *adj* luxueux, somptueux

luxu·ry ['lʌkʃəri], ['lʌgʒəri] *s* (*pl* **-ries**) luxe *m*

lux'ury i'tem *s* produit *m* de luxe

lux'ury tax' *s* impôt *m* somptuaire

lyceum [laɪ'si-əm] *s* lycée *m*

lye [laɪ] *s* lessive *f*

lying ['laɪ-ɪŋ] *adj* menteur || *s* le mensonge

ly'ing-in' hos'pital *s* maternité *f*, clinique *f* d'accouchement

lymph [lɪmf] *s* lymphe *f*

lymphatic [lɪm'fætɪk] *adj* lymphatique

lynch [lɪntʃ] *tr* lyncher

lynching ['lɪntʃɪŋ] *s* lynchage *m*

lynx [lɪŋks] *s* lynx *m*

Lyons ['laɪ-ənz] *s* Lyon *m*

lyre [laɪr] *s* (mus) lyre *f*

lyric ['lɪrɪk] *adj* lyrique || *s* poème *m* lyrique; **lyrics** (*of song*) paroles *fpl*; (theat) chansons *fpl* du livret

lyrical ['lɪrɪkəl] *adj* lyrique

lyricism ['lɪrɪ,sɪzəm] *s* lyrisme *m*

lyricist ['lɪrɪsɪst] *s* poète *m* lyrique; (*writer of words for songs*) parolier *m*

M

M, m [ɛm] XIII⁰ lettre de l'alphabet

ma'am [mæm], [mɑm] *s* (coll) madame *f*

macadam [mə'kædəm] *s* macadam *m*

macadamize [mə'kædə,maɪz] *tr* macadamiser

macaroon [,mækə'run] *s* macaron *m*

macaw [mə'kɔ] *s* (orn) ara *m*

mace [mes] *s* masse *f*

mace'bear'er *s* massier *m*

machination [,mækɪ'neʃən] *s* machination *f*

machine [mə'ʃin] *s* machine *f*; (*of a political party*) noyau *m* directeur, leviers *mpl* de commande || *tr* usiner, façonner

machine' gun' *s* mitrailleuse *f*

ma·chine'-gun' *v* (*pret* & *pp* **-gunned**; *ger* **-gunning**) *tr* mitrailler

ma·chine'-made' *adj* fait à la machine

machiner·y [mə'ʃinəri] *s* (*pl* **-ies**) machinerie *f*, machines *fpl*; (*of a watch*; *of government*) mécanisme *m*; (*in literature*) merveilleux *m*

machine' screw' *s* vis *f* à métaux

machine' shop' *s* atelier *m* d'usinage

machine' tool' *s* machine-outil *f*

machine' transla'tion *s* traduction *f* automatique

machinist [mə'ʃinɪst] *s* mécanicien *m*

mackerel ['mækərəl] *s* maquereau *m*

mack'erel sky' *s* ciel *m* pommelé or moutonné

mad [mæd] *adj* (*comp* **madder**; *super*

maddest) fou; (*dog*) enragé; (coll) fâché, irrité; **as mad as a hatter** fou à lier; **like mad** (coll) comme un fou, éperdument; **to be mad about** (coll) être fou or passionné de; **to drive mad** rendre fou

madam ['mædəm] *s* madame *f*; (*of a brothel*) (slang) tenancière *f*

mad'cap' *adj & s* écervelé *m*, étourdi *m*

madden ['mædən] *tr* rendre fou ‖ *intr* devenir fou

made-to-order ['medtə'ɔrdər] *adj* fait sur demande; (*clothing*) fait sur mesure

made'-up' *adj* inventé; (*artificial*) postiche; (*face*) maquillé

mad'house' *s* maison *f* de fous

mad'man' *s* (*pl* -**men**) fou *m*

madness ['mædnɪs] *s* folie *f*; (*of dog*) rage *f*

Madonna [mə'dɑnə] *s* madone *f*; (eccl) Madone

maelstrom ['melstrəm] *s* maelstrom *m*, tourbillon *m*

magazine ['mægə,zin], [,mægə'zin] *s* (*periodical*) revue *f*, magazine *m*; (*warehouse; for cartridges of gun or camera; for munitions or powder*) magasin *m*; (naut) soute *f*

mag'azine' rack' *s* casier *m* à revues

Magdalen ['mægdələn] *s* Madeleine *f*

Maggie ['mægi] *s* (coll) Margot *f*

maggot ['mægət] *s* asticot *m*

Magi ['medʒaɪ] *spl* mages *mpl*

magic ['mædʒɪk] *adj* magique ‖ *s* magie *f*; **as if by magic** comme par enchantement

magician [mə'dʒɪʃən] *s* magicien *m*

magisterial [,mædʒɪs'tɪrɪ-əl] *adj* magistral

magistrate ['mædʒɪs,tret] *s* magistrat *m*

Magna Charta ['mægnə'kɑrtə] *s* la Grande Charte *f*

magnanimous [mæg'nænɪməs] *adj* magnanime

magnate ['mægnet] *s* magnat *m*

magnesium [mæg'niʃɪ-əm], [mæg'niʒɪ-əm] *s* magnésium *m*

magnet ['mægnɪt] *s* aimant *m*

magnetic [mæg'netɪk] *adj* magnétique; (fig) attrayant, séduisant

magnetism ['mægnɪ,tɪzəm] *s* magnétisme *m*

magnetize ['mægnɪ,taɪz] *tr* aimanter

magne-to [mæg'nito] *s* (*pl* -**tos**) magnéto *f*

magnificent [mæg'nɪfɪsənt] *adj* magnifique

magni-fy ['mægnɪ,faɪ] *v* (*pret & pp* -**fied**) *tr* grossir; (opt) grossir

mag'nifying glass' *s* loupe *f*

magnitude ['mægnɪ,t(j)ud] *s* grandeur *f*; (astr) magnitude *f*

magpie ['mæg,paɪ] *s* (orn, fig) pie *f*

mahlstick ['mɑl,stɪk], ['mɔl,stɪk] *s* appui-main *m*

mahoga-ny [mə'hɑgəni] *s* (*pl* -**nies**) acajou *m*

Mahomet [mə'hɑmɪt] *s* Mahomet *m*

mahout [mə'haʊt] *s* cornac *m*

maid [med] *s* (*servant*) bonne *f*; (*young girl*) jeune fille *f*, demoiselle *f*

maiden ['medən] *s* jeune fille *f*, demoiselle *f*

maid'en·hair' *s* (bot) capillaire *m*

maid'en·head' *s* hymen *m*

maid'en·hood' *s* virginité *f*

maid'en la'dy *s* demoiselle *f*, célibataire *f*

maidenly ['medənli] *adj* virginal, de jeune fille

maid'en name' *s* nom *m* de jeune fille

maid'en voy'age *s* premier voyage *m*

maid'-in-wait'ing *s* (*pl* maids-in-waiting) fille *f* d'honneur, dame *f* d'honneur

maid' of hon'or *s* demoiselle *f* d'honneur

maid'serv'ant *s* fille *f* de service, servante *f*

mail [mel] *adj* postal ‖ *s* courrier *m*; (*system*) poste *f*; (*armor*) mailles *fpl*, cotte *f* de mailles; **by return mail** par retour du courrier; **mails** poste *f* ‖ *tr* mettre à la poste, envoyer par la poste

mail'bag' *s* sac *m* postal

mail'boat' *s* paquebot *m*, bateau-poste *m*

mail'box' *s* boîte *f* aux lettres

mail' car' *s* fourgon *m* postal, bureau *m* ambulant, wagon-poste *m*

mail' car'rier *s* facteur *m*

mail' clerk' *s* postier *m*; (mil, nav) vaguemestre *m*; (rr) convoyeur *m* des postes

mailing ['melɪŋ] *s* envoi *m*

mail'ing list' *s* liste *f* d'adresses; (*of subscribers*) liste d'abonnés

mail'ing per'mit *s* (label on envelopes) dispense du timbrage

mail'man' *s* (*pl* -**men**) facteur *m*

mail' or'der *s* commande *f* par la poste

mail'-order house' *s* établissement *m* de vente par correspondance or de vente sur catalogue; comptoir *m* postal (Canad)

mail'-order sell'ing *s* vente *f* par correspondance

mail'plane' *s* avion *m* postal

mail' train' *s* train-poste *m*

maim [mem] *tr* mutiler, estropier

main [men] *adj* principal ‖ *s* égout *m* collecteur, canalisation *f* or conduite *f* principale; **in the main** en général, pour la plupart

main' clause' *s* proposition *f* principale

main' course' *s* (culin) plat *m* principal, pièce *f* de résistance

main' deck' *s* pont *m* principal

main' floor' *s* rez-de-chaussée *m*

mainland ['men,lænd], ['menlənd] *s* terre *f* ferme, continent *m*

main' line' *s* (rr) grande ligne *f*

mainly ['menli] *adv* principalement

mainmast ['menmæst], ['men,mæst], ['men,məst] *s* grand mât *m*

mainsail ['mensəl], ['men,sel] *s* grand-voile *f*

main'spring' *s* (*of watch*) ressort *m* moteur, grand ressort; (fig) mobile *m* essentiel, principe *m*

main'stay' *s* (naut) étai *m* de grand mât; (fig) point *m* d'appui

main′ street′ *s* rue *f* principale

maintain [men′ten] *tr* maintenir; (*e.g.*, *a family*) entretenir, faire subsister

maintenance ['mentɪnəns] *s* entretien *m*, maintien *m*; (*department entrusted with upkeep*) services *mpl* d'entretien, maintenance *f*

maître d'hôtel [,metərdo′tel] *s* maître *m* d'hôtel

maize [mez] *s* maïs *m*

majestic [mə′dʒɛstɪk] *adj* majestueux

majes·ty ['mædʒɪsti] *s* (*pl* **-ties**) majesté *f*

major ['medʒər] *adj* majeur || *s* (*person of full legal age*) majeur *m*; (*educ*) spécialisation *f*; (*mil*) commandant *m* || *intr* (*educ*) se spécialiser

Majorca [mə′dʒɔrkə] *s* Majorque *f*; île *f* de Majorque

Majorcan [mə′dʒɔrkən] *adj* majorquin || *s* Majorquin *m*

ma′jor gen′eral *s* général *m* de division

majori·ty [mə′dʒɑrɪti], [mə′dʒɔrɪti] *adj* majoritaire || *s* (*pl* **-ties**) majorité *f*; (*mil*) grade *m* de commandant; **the majority of** la plupart de

major′ity vote′ *s* scrutin *m* majoritaire

make [mek] *s* fabrication *f*; (*brand name*) marque *f*; modèle *m* || *v* (*pret & pp* **made** [med]) *tr* faire; rendre, *e.g.*, **to make sick** rendre malade; (*money*) gagner; (*the cards*) battre; (*a train*) attraper; **to make into** transformer en; **to make known** faire savoir; **to make out** déchiffrer, distinguer; (*a bill, receipt, check*) écrire; (*a list*) dresser; **to make s.o.** + *inf* faire + *inf* + qn, *e.g.*, **I will make my uncle talk** je ferai parler mon oncle || *intr* être, *e.g.*, **to make sure** être sûr; **to make believe** feindre; **to make good** réussir; **to make off** filer, décamper

make′-believe′ *adj* simulé || *s* faux-semblant *m*, feinte *f*

maker ['mekər] *s* fabricant *m*

make′shift′ *adj* de fortune, de circonstance || *s* expédient *m*; (*person*) bouche-trou *m*

make′-up′ *s* arrangement *m*, composition *f*; (*cosmetic*) maquillage *m*; (*typ*) mise *f* en pages, imposition *f*

make′-up man′ *s* (*theat*) maquilleur *m*; (*typ*) metteur *m* en pages, imposeur *m*

make′weight′ *s* complément *m* de poids

making ['mekɪŋ] *s* fabrication *f*; (*of a dress; of a cooked dish*) confection *f*; **makings** éléments *mpl* constitutifs; (*money*) recettes *fpl*; **to have the makings of** avoir l'étoffe de

maladjusted [,mælə′dʒʌstɪd] *adj* inadapté

maladjustment [,mælə′dʒʌstmənt] *s* inadaptation *f*

mala·dy ['mælədi] *s* (*pl* **-dies**) maladie *f*

malaise [mæ′lez] *s* malaise *m*

malaria [mə′lɛrɪ·ə] *s* malaria *f*, paludisme *m*

Malay ['mele], [mə′le] *adj* malais || *s* (*language*) malais *m*; (*person*) Malais *m*

Malaya [mə′le·ə] *s* Malaisie *f*; la Malaisie

malcontent ['mælkən,tent] *adj & s* mécontent *m*

male [mel] *adj & s* mâle *m*

malediction [,mælɪ′dɪkʃən] *s* malédiction *f*

malefactor ['mælɪ,fæktər] *s* malfaiteur *m*

male′ nurse′ *s* infirmier *m*

malevolent [mə′levələnt] *adj* malveillant

malfeasance [,mæl′fizəns] *s* prévarication *f*, trafic *m*

malice ['mælɪs] *s* méchanceté *f*

malicious [mə′lɪʃəs] *adj* méchant

malign [mə′laɪn] *adj* pernicieux; malveillant || *tr* calomnier

malignan·cy [mə′lɪɡnənsi] *s* (*pl* **-cies**) malignité *f*

malignant [mə′lɪɡnənt] *adj* méchant, malin

malinger [mə′lɪŋɡər] *intr* faire le malade

malingerer [mə′lɪŋɡərər] *s* simulateur *m*

mall [mɔl], [mæl] *s* mail *m*

mallard ['mælərd] *s* (*orn*) col-vert *m*

malleable ['mælɪ·əbəl] *adj* malléable

mallet ['mælɪt] *s* maillet *m*

mallow ['mælo] *s* (*bot*) mauve *f*

malnutrition [,mæln(j)u′trɪʃən] *s* sous-alimentation *f*, malnutrition *f*

malodorous [mæl′odərəs] *adj* malodorant

malpractice [mæl′præktɪs] *s* incurie *f*; méfait *m*

malt [mɔlt] *s* malt *m*

maltreat [mæl′trit] *tr* maltraiter

mamma ['mɑmə], [mə′mɑ] *s* maman *f*

mammal ['mæməl] *s* mammifère *m*

mammalian [mæ′melɪ·ən] *adj & s* mammifère *m*

mammoth ['mæməθ] *adj* énorme, colossal || *s* mammouth *m*

man [mæn] *s* (*pl* **men** [men]) *s* homme *m*; (*servant*) domestique *m*; (*worker*) ouvrier *m*, employé *m*; (*checkers*) pion *m*; (*chess*) pièce *f*; **a man on,** *e.g.*, **what can a man do?** qu'est-ce qu'on peut faire?; **every man for himself!** sauve qui peut!; **man alive!** (*coll*) tiens!; fichtre!; **man and wife** mari et femme; **men at work** (*public sign*) travaux en cours || *v* (*pret & pp* **manned;** *ger* **manning**) *tr* (*a ship*) équiper; (*a fort*) garnir; (*a cannon, the pumps, etc.*) armer; (*a battery*) servir

man′ about town′ *s* boulevardier *m*, coureur *m* de cabarets

manacle ['mænəkəl] *s* manilla *f*; **manacles** menottes *fpl* || *tr* mettre les menottes à

manage ['mænɪdʒ] *tr* gérer, diriger; (*to handle*) manier || *intr* se débrouiller; **how did you manage to . . . ?** comment avez-vous fait pour . . . ?; **to manage to** s'arranger pour

manageable ['mænɪdʒəbəl] *adj* maniable

management ['mænɪdʒmənt] s direction f, gérance f; (group who manage) direction, administration f; (in contrast to labor) patronat m; under new management (public sign) changement de propriétaire

manager ['mænədʒər] s directeur m, gérant m; (e.g., of a department) chef m; (impresario) manager m

managerial [,mænə'dʒɪrɪ-əl] adj patronal

man'aging ed'itor s rédacteur m gérant

Manchuria [mæn't'ʊrɪ-ə] s Mandchourie f; la Mandchourie

man'darin or'ange ['mændərɪn] s mandarine f

mandate ['mændet] s mandat m || tr placer sous le mandat de

mandatory ['mændə,torɪ] adj obligatoire

mandolin ['mændəlɪn] s mandoline f

mandrake ['mændrek] s mandragore f

mane [men] s crinière f

maneuver [mə'nuvər] s manœuvre m || tr & intr manœuvrer

manful ['mænfəl] adj viril, hardi

manganese ['mæŋgə,nis], ['mæŋgə,niz] s manganèse m

mange [mendʒ] s gale f

manger ['mendʒər] s mangeoire f, crèche f

mangle ['mæŋgəl] s calandre f || tr lacérer, mutiler; (to press) calandrer

man-gy ['mendʒɪ] adj (comp -gier; super -giest) galeux; (dirty, squalid) miteux

man'han'dle tr malmener

man'hole' s trou m d'homme, regard m

manhood ['mænhʊd] s virilité f; humanité f

man'hunt' s chasse f à l'homme; chasse au mari

mania ['menɪ-ə] s manie f

maniac ['menɪ,æk] adj & s maniaque mf

maniacal [mə'naɪ-əkəl] adj maniaque

manicure ['mænɪ,kjʊr] s soins mpl esthétiques des mains et des ongles; (person) manucure mf || tr manucurer

manicurist ['mænɪ,kjʊrɪst] s manucure mf

manifest ['mænɪ,fest] adj manifeste || s (naut) manifeste m || tr & intr manifester

manifestation [,mænɪfes'teʃən] s manifestation f

manifes-to [,mænɪ'festo] s (pl -toes) manifeste m

manifold ['mænɪ,fold] adj multiple, nombreux || s (aut) tuyauterie f, collecteur m

manikin ['mænɪkɪn] s mannequin m; (dwarf) nabot m

man' in the moon' s homme m dans la lune

man' in the street' s homme m de la rue

manipulate [mə'nɪpjə,let] tr manipuler

man'kind' s le genre humain, l'humanité f || man'kind' s le sexe fort, les hommes mpl

manliness ['mænlɪnɪs] s virilité f

man-ly ['mænlɪ] adj (comp -lier; super -liest) viril, masculin

manna ['mænə] s manne f

manned' space'craft s vaisseau m spatial habité

mannequin ['mænɪkɪn] s mannequin m

manner ['mænər] s manière f; by all manner of means certainement; by no manner of means en aucune manière; in a manner of speaking pour ainsi dire; in the manner of à la, e.g., in the manner of the French, in the French manner à la manière française, à la française; manners manières; manners of the time mœurs fpl de l'époque; to the manner born créé et mis au monde pour ça

mannerism ['mænə,rɪzm] s maniérisme m

mannish ['mænɪʃ] adj hommasse

man' of let'ters s homme m de lettres, bel esprit m

man' of parts' s homme m de talent

man' of straw' s homme m de paille

man' of the world' s homme m du monde

man-of-war [,mænəv'wər] s (pl men-of-war) navire m de guerre

manor ['mænər] s seigneurie f

man'or house' s château m, manoir m

man'overboard' interj un homme à la mer!

man'pow'er s main-d'œuvre f; (mil) effectifs mpl

manse [mæns] s maison f du pasteur

man'serv'ant s (pl men'serv'ants) valet m

mansion ['mænʃən] s hôtel m particulier; château m, manoir m

man'slaugh'ter s (law) homicide m involontaire

mantel ['mæntəl] s manteau m de cheminée

man'tel-piece' s manteau m de cheminée; dessus m de cheminée

mantilla [mæn'tɪlə] s mantille f

mantle ['mæntəl] s manteau m de mante f; (of gaslight) manchon m || tr envelopper d'une mante; couvrir, revêtir; (to hide) voiler || intr (said of face) rougir

manual ['mænjʊ-əl] adj manuel || s (book) manuel m; (of arms) (mil) maniement m; (mus) clavier m d'orgue

man'ual dexter'ity s habileté f manuelle

man'ual train'ing s apprentissage m manuel

manufacture [,mænjə'fæktʃər] s fabrication f; (thing manufactured) produit m fabriqué || tr fabriquer

manufacturer [,mænjə'fæktʃərər] s fabricant m

manure [mə'n(j)ʊr] s fumier m || tr fumer

manuscript ['mænjə,skrɪpt] adj & s manuscrit m

many ['menɪ] adj beaucoup de; a good many bien des, maintes; how many combien de; many another bien d'autres; many more beaucoup d'autres;

so many tant de; **too many** trop de; **twice as many** deux fois autant de || *pron* beaucoup; **as many as** autant de; jusqu'à, e.g., **as many as twenty** jusqu'à vingt; **how many** combien; **many a** maint; **many another** bien d'autres; **many more** beaucoup d'autres; **so many** tant; **too many** trop; **twice as many** deux fois autant

man'y-sid'ed *adj* polygonal; *(having many interests or capabilities)* complexe

map [mæp] *s* carte *f*; *(of a city)* plan *m* || *v (pret & pp* **mapped**; *ger* **mapping)** *tr* faire la carte de; **to map out** tracer le plan de; **to put on the map** *(coll)* faire connaître, mettre en vedette

maple ['mepəl] *s* érable *m*

ma'ple sug'ar *s* sucre *m* d'érable

mar [mɑr] *v (pret & pp* **marred**; *ger* **marring)** *tr* défigurer, gâcher

marathon ['mærə,θɑn] *s* marathon *m*

maraud [mə'rɔd] *tr* piller || *intr* marauder

marauder [mə'rɔdər] *s* maraudeur *m*

marauding [mə'rɔdɪŋ] *adj* maraudeur || *s* maraude *f*

marble ['mɑrbəl] *s* marbre *m*; *(little ball of glass)* bille *f*; **marbles** *(game)* jeu *m* de billes || *tr* marbrer; *(the edge of a book)* jasper

march [mɑrtʃ] *s* marche *f*; **March** mars *m*; **to steal a march on** prendre de l'avance sur || *tr* faire marcher || *intr* marcher

marchioness ['mɑrʃənɪs] *s* marquise *f*

mare [mer] *s (female horse)* jument *m*; *(female donkey)* ânesse *f*

Margaret ['mɑrgərɪt] *s* Marguerite *f*

margarine ['mɑrdʒərɪn] *s* margarine *f*

margin ['mɑrdʒɪn] *s* marge *f*; *(border)* bord *m*; *(com)* acompte *m*

marginal ['mɑrdʒɪnəl] *adj* marginal

mar'gin release' *s* déclenche-marge *f*

mar'gin stop' *s* margeur *m*

marigold ['mærɪ,gold] *s (Calendula)* souci *m*; *(Tagetes)* œillet *m* d'Inde

marihuana or **marijuana** [,mɑrɪ-'hwɑnə] *s* marihuana *f* or marijuana *f*

marinate ['mærɪ,net] *tr* mariner

marine [mə'rin] *adj* marin, maritime || *s* flotte *f*; *(nav)* fusilier *m* marin; **tell it to the marines!** *(coll)* à d'autres!

Marine' Corps' *s* infanterie *f* de marine

mariner ['mærɪnər] *s* marin *m*

marionette [,mærɪ.ə'nɛt] *s* marionnette *f*

marital ['mærɪtəl] *adj* matrimonial

mar'ital sta'tus *s* état *m* civil

maritime ['mærɪ,taɪm] *adj* maritime

marjoram ['mɑrdʒərəm] *s* marjolaine *f*; origan *m*

mark [mɑrk] *s* marque *f*, signe *m*; *(of punctuation)* point *m*; *(in an examination)* note *f*; *(spot, stain)* tache *f*, marque; *(monetary unit)* mark *m*; *(starting point in a race)* ligne *f* de départ; **as a mark of** en témoignage de; **Mark Marc** *m*; **on your mark!** à vos marques!; **to hit the mark** mettre dans le mille, atteindre le but; **to**

leave one's mark laisser son empreinte; **to make one's mark** se faire un nom, marquer; **to miss the mark** manquer le but; **to toe the mark** se conformer au mot d'ordre || *tr* marquer; *(a student; an exam)* donner une note à; *(e.g., one's approval)* témoigner; **to mark down** noter; *(com)* démarquer; **to mark off** distinguer; **to mark up** (com) majorer

mark'down' *s* rabais *m*

marker ['mɑrkər] *s* marqueur *m*; *(of boundary)* borne *f*; *(landmark)* repère *m*

market ['mɑrkɪt] *s* marché *m*; **to bear the market** jouer à la baisse; **to bull the market** jouer à la hausse; **to play the market** jouer à la bourse; **to put on the market** lancer, vendre, or mettre sur le marché || *tr* commercialiser

marketable ['mɑrkɪtəbəl] *adj* vendable

mar'ket bas'ket *s* panier *m* à provisions

marketing ['mɑrkɪtɪŋ] *s* marché *m*; *(of a product)* commercialisation *f*, exploitation *f*

mar'ket-place' *s* place *f* du marché

mar'ket price' *s* cours *m* du marché, prix *m* courant

mark'ing gauge' *s* trusquin *m*

marks·man ['mɑrksmən] *s (pl* **-men)** tireur *m*

marks'man·ship' *s* habileté *f* au tir, adresse *f* au tir

mark'up' *s (profit)* marge *f* bénéficiaire; *(price increase)* majoration *f* de prix

marl [mɑrl] *s* marne *f* || *tr* marner

marmalade ['mɑrmə,led] *s* marmelade *f*

maroon [mə'run] *adj & s (color)* lie *f* de vin, rouge *m* violacé || *tr* abandonner, isoler

marquee [mɑr'ki] *s* marquise *f*

marquis ['mɑrkwɪs] *s* marquis *m*

marquise [mɑr'kiz] *s* marquise *f*

marriage ['mærɪdʒ] *s* mariage *m*

marriageable ['mærɪdʒəbəl] *adj* mariable

mar'riage certif'icate *s* acte *m* de mariage

mar'riage por'tion *s* dot *f*

mar'riage rate' *s* taux *m* de nuptialité

mar'ried life' ['mærɪd] *s* vie *f* conjugale

marrow ['mæro] *s* moelle *f*

mar·ry ['mærɪ] *v (pret & pp* **-ried)** *tr (to join in wedlock)* marier; *(to take in marriage)* se marier avec; **to get married to** se marier avec; **to marry off** marier || *intr* se marier

Mars [mɑrz] *s* Mars *m*

Marseilles [mɑr'selz] *s* Marseille *f*

marsh [mɑrʃ] *s* marais *m*, marécage *m*

mar·shal ['mɑrʃəl] *s* maître *m* des cérémonies; *(policeman)* shérif *m*; *(mil)* maréchal *m* || *v (pret & pp* **-shaled** or **-shalled**; *ger* **-shaling** or **-shalling)** *tr* conduire; *(one's reasons, arguments, etc.)* ranger, rassembler

marsh' mal'low *s* (bot) guimauve *f*

marsh'mal'low *s (candy)* pâte *f* de guimauve; bonbon *m* à la guimauve

marsh·y ['marʃi] adj (comp **-ier;** super **-iest**) marécageux

mart [mart] s marché m, foire f

marten ['martən] s (pine marten) martre f; (beech marten) fouine f

Martha ['marθə] s Marthe f

martial ['marʃəl] adj martial

mar/tial law/ s loi f martiale

martin ['martɪn] s (orn) martinet m

martinet [,martɪ'nɛt], ['martɪ,nɛt] s pètesec m

martyr ['martər] s martyr m || tr martyriser

martyrdom ['martərdəm] s martyre m

mar·vel ['marvəl] s merveille f || v (pret & pp **-veled** or **-velled;** ger **-veling** or **-velling**) intr s'émerveiller; **to marvel at** s'émerveiller de

marvelous ['marvələs] adj merveilleux

Marxist ['marksɪst] adj & s marxiste mf

Maryland ['mɛrələnd] s le Maryland

marzipan ['marzɪ,pæn] s massepain m

mascara [mæs'kærə] s rimmel m

mascot ['mæskət] s mascotte f

masculine ['mæskjəlɪn] adj & s masculin m

mash [mæʃ] s (crushed mass) bouillie f; (to form wort) fardeau m || tr écraser; (malt, in brewing) brasser

mashed/ pota/toes spl purée f de pommes de terre

masher ['mæʃər] s (device) broyeur m; (slang) tombeur m

mask [mæsk], [mask] s masque m; (phot) cache m || tr masquer; (phot) poser un cache à || intr se masquer

masked/ ball/ s bal m masqué

mason ['mesən] s maçon m; Mason Maçon

mason·ry ['mesənri] s (pl **-ries**) maçonnerie f; Masonry Maçonnerie

masquerade [,mæskə'red], [,maskə-'red] s mascarade f || intr se déguiser; **to masquerade as** se faire passer pour

mass [mæs] s masse f; (eccl) messe f || tr masser || intr se masser

massacre ['mæsəkər] s massacre m || tr massacrer

massage [mə'saʒ] s massage m || tr masser

mass/ arrest/ s rafle f

masseur [mə'sʌr] s masseur m

masseuse [mə'suz] s masseuse f

massive ['mæsɪv] adj massif

mass/ me/dia ['midɪə] spl communication f de masse

mass/ meet/ing s meeting m monstre, rassemblement m

mass/ produc/tion s fabrication f en série

mast [mæst], [mast] s mât m; (food for swine) gland m, faîne f; **before the mast** comme simple matelot

master ['mæstər], ['mastər] s maître m; (employer) chef m, patron m; (male head of household) maître de maison; (title of respect) Monsieur m; (naut) commandant m || tr maîtriser; (a subject) connaître à fond, posséder

mas/ter bed/room s chambre f du maître

mas/ter build/er s entrepreneur m de bâtiments

masterful ['mæstərfəl], ['mastərfəl] adj magistral, expert; impérieux, en maître

mas/ter key/ s passe-partout m

masterly ['mæstərli], ['mastərli] adj magistral, de maître || adv magistralement

mas/ter mechan/ic s maître m mécanicien

mas/ter·mind/ s organisateur m, cerveau m || tr organiser, diriger

mas/ter of cer/emonies s maître m des cérémonies; (in a night club, on television, etc.) animateur m

mas/ter·piece/ s chef-d'œuvre m

mas/ter stroke/ s coup m de maître

mas/ter·work/ s chef-d'œuvre m

master·y ['mæstəri], ['mastəri] s (pl **-ies**) maîtrise f

mast/head/ s (of a newspaper) en-tête m; (naut) tête f de mât

masticate ['mæstɪ,ket] tr mastiquer

mastiff ['mæstɪf], ['mastɪf] s mâtin m

masturbate ['mæstər,bet] tr masturber || intr se masturber

mat [mæt] s (for floor) natte f; (for a cup, vase, etc.) dessous m de plat; (before a door) paillasson m || v (pret & pp **matted;** ger **matting**) tr (to cover with matting) couvrir de nattes; (h air) emmêler; (with blood) coller || intr s'emmêler

match [mæt͡ʃ] s allumette f; (wick) mèche f; (counterpart) égal m, pair m; (suitable partner in marriage) parti m; (suitably associated pair) assortiment m; (game, contest) match m, partie f; **to be a match for** être de la force de, être à la hauteur de; **to meet one's match** trouver son pareil || tr égaler; (objects) faire pendant à, assortir || intr s'assortir

match/box/ s boîte f d'allumettes, porte-allumettes m

matchless ['mæt͡ʃlɪs] adj incomparable, sans pareil

match/mak/er s marieur m

mate [met] s compagnon m; (husband) conjoint m; (wife) conjointe f; (to a female) mâle m; (to a male) femelle f; (check-mate) mat m; (naut) officier m en second, second maître m || tr marier; (zool) accoupler || intr se marier; s'accoupler

material [mə'tɪrɪ·əl] adj matériel; important || s matériel m; (what a thing is made of) matière f; (cloth, fabric) étoffe f; (archit) matériau m; **materials** matériaux mpl

materialist [mə'tɪrɪ·əlɪst] s matérialiste mf

materialistic [mə,tɪrɪ·ə'lɪstɪk] adj matérialiste, matériel

materialize [mə'tɪrɪ·ə,laɪz] intr se matérialiser; (to be realized) se réaliser

matériel [mə,tɪrɪ'ɛl] s matériel m

maternal [mə'tʌrnəl] adj maternel

maternity [məˈtʌrnɪtɪ] s maternité f

mater′nity hos′pital s maternité f

mater′nity room′ s salle f d'accouchement

mater′nity ward′ s salle f des accouchées

math [mæθ] s (coll) math fpl

mathematical [ˌmæθɪˈmætɪkəl] adj mathématique

mathematician [ˌmæθɪməˈtɪʃən] s mathématicien m

mathematics [ˌmæθɪˈmætɪks] s mathématiques fpl

matinée [ˌmætɪˈne] s matinée f

mat′ing sea′son s saison f des amours

matins [ˈmætɪnz] spl matines fpl

matriarch [ˈmetrɪˌɑrk] s matrone f

matriar·chy [ˈmetrɪˌɑrkɪ] s (pl -chies) matriarcat m

matricide [ˈmetrɪˌsaɪd], [ˈmætrɪˌsaɪd] s (person) matricide mf; (action) matricide m

matriculate [məˈtrɪkjəˌlet] tr immatriculer || intr s'inscrire à l'université, prendre ses inscriptions

matriculation [məˌtrɪkjəˈleʃən] s inscription f, immatriculation f

matrimonial [ˌmætrɪˈmonɪ·əl] adj matrimonial

matrimo·ny [ˈmætrɪˌmonɪ] s (pl -nies) mariage m, vie f conjugale

ma·trix [ˈmetrɪks], [ˈmætrɪks] s (pl -trices [trɪˌsiz] or -trixes) matrice f

matron [ˈmetrən] s (woman no longer young, and of good standing) matrone f; intendante f, surveillante f

matronly [ˈmetrənlɪ] adj de matrone, digne, respectable

matter [ˈmætər] s matière f; (pathol) pus m; a matter of affaire de, une question de; for that matter à vrai dire; it doesn't matter cela ne fait rien; no matter n'importe, pas d'importance; no matter when n'importe quand; no matter where n'importe où; no matter who n'importe qui; what is the matter? qu'y a-t-il?; what is the matter with you? qu'avez-vous? || intr importer

mat′ter of course′ s chose f qui va de soi

mat′ter of fact′ s—as a matter of fact en réalité, effectivement, de fait

matter-of-fact [ˈmætərəvˌfækt] adj prosaïque, terre à terre

mattock [ˈmætək] s pioche f

mattress [ˈmætrɪs] s matelas m

mature [məˈtʃur], [məˈtur] adj mûr; (due) échu || tr faire mûrir || intr mûrir; (to become due) échoir

maturity [məˈtʃurɪtɪ], [məˈturɪtɪ] s maturité f; (com) échéance f

maudlin [ˈmodlɪn] adj larmoyant

maul [mol] tr malmener; (to split) fendre au coin

maulstick [ˈmolˌstɪk] s appui-main m

Maun′dy Thurs′day [ˈmondɪ] s jeudi m saint

mausole·um [ˌmosəˈli·əm] s (pl -ums or -a [ə]) mausolée m

maw [mo] s (of birds) jabot m; (of fish) poche f d'air

mawkish [ˈmokɪʃ] adj à l'eau de rose; (sickening) écœurant

maxim [ˈmæksɪm] s maxime f

maximum [ˈmæksɪməm] adj & s maximum m

May [me] s mai m || (l.c.) v (pret & cond might [maɪt]) aux—it may be il ne peut; may I? vous permettez?; may I + inf puis-je + inf, est-ce que je peux + inf; may I (may we, etc.) + inf peut-on + inf; may you be happy! puissiez-vous être heureux!

maybe [ˈmebɪ] adv peut-être

May′ Day′ s le premier mai m

mayhem [ˈmehem], [ˈme·əm] s mutilation f

mayonnaise [ˌme·əˈnez] s mayonnaise f

mayor [ˈme·ər], [mer] s maire m

May′pole′ s mai m

May′ queen′ s reine f du premier mai

maze [mez] s labyrinthe m, dédale m

me [mi] pron moi §85, §87; me §87

meadow [ˈmedo] s prairie f, pré m

mead′ow·land′ s herbage m, prairie f

meager [ˈmigər] adj maigre

meal [mil] s repas m; (grain) farine f; to miss a meal serrer la ceinture d'un cran

meal′ tick′et s ticket-repas m; (job) gagne-pain m

meal′time′ s heure f du repas

meal·y [ˈmilɪ] adj (comp -ier; super -iest) farineux

mean [min] adj (intermediate) moyen; (low in station or rank) bas, humble; (shabby) vil, misérable; (stingy) mesquin; (small-minded) bas, vilain, méprisable; (vicious) sauvage, mal intentionné; no mean fameux, excellent || s milieu m, moyen terme m; (math) moyenne f; by all means de toute façon, je vous en prie; by means of au moyen de; by no means en aucune façon; means ressources fpl, fortune f; (agency) moyen m; means to an end moyens d'arriver à ses fins; not by any means! jamais de la vie! || v (pret & pp meant [ment]) tr vouloir dire, signifier; (to intend) entendre; (to entail) entraîner; to mean s.th. for s.o. destiner q.ch. à qn; to mean to avoir l'intention de, compter || intr—to mean well avoir de bonnes intentions

meander [mɪˈændər] s méandre m || intr faire des méandres

meaning [ˈminɪŋ] s signification f, sens m; intention f

meaningful [ˈminɪŋfəl] adj significatif

meaningless [ˈminɪŋlɪs] adj sans signification, dénué de sens

meanness [ˈminnɪs] s bassesse f, vilenie f; (stinginess) mesquinerie f

mean′time′ s—in the meantime dans l'intervalle, sur ces entrefaites || adv entre-temps, en attendant

mean′while′ s & adv var of meantime

measles [ˈmizəlz] s rougeole f; (German measles) rubéole f

mea·sly [ˈmizlɪ] adj (comp -slier; super -sliest) rougeoleux; (slang) piètre, insignifiant

measurable ['mɛʒərəbəl] *adj* mesurable
measure ['mɛʒər] *s* mesure *f*; (*step, procedure*) mesure, démarche *f*; (*legislative bill*) projet *m* de loi; (*mus, poetic*) mesure; **in a large measure** en grande partie; **in a measure** dans une certaine mesure; **to take measures to** prendre des mesures pour; **to take s.o.'s measure** (fig) prendre la mesure de qn || *tr* mesurer; **to measure out** mesurer, distribuer || *intr* mesurer
measurement ['mɛʒərmənt] *s* mesure *f*; **to take s.o.'s measurements** prendre les mesures de qn
meas'uring cup' *s* verre *m* gradué
meat [mit] *s* viande *f*; (*food in general*) nourriture *f*; (*gist*) moelle *f*, substance *f*
meat'ball' *s* boulette *f* de viande
meat'hook' *s* croc *m*, allonge *f*
meat' mar'ket *s* boucherie *f*
meat' pie' *s* tourte *f* à la viande, pâté *m* en croûte
meat·y ['miti] *adj* (*comp* -ier; *super* -iest) charnu; (fig) plein de substance, étoffé
Mecca ['mɛkə] *s* La Mecque
mechanic [mə'kænɪk] *s* mécanicien *m*; **mechanics** mécanique *f*
mechanical [mə'kænɪkəl] *adj* mécanique; (fig) mécanique, machinal
mechan'ical draw'ing *s* dessin *m* industriel
mechan'ical engineer' *s* ingénieur *m* mécanicien
mechan'ical toy' *s* jouet *m* mécanique
mechanics [mɪ'kænɪks] *s* mécanique *f*
mechanism ['mɛkə,nɪzəm] *s* mécanisme *m*
mechanize ['mɛkə,naɪz] *tr* mécaniser
medal ['mɛdəl] *s* médaille *f*
medallion [mɪ'dæljən] *s* médaillon *m*
meddle ['mɛdəl] *intr* s'ingérer; **to meddle in** or **with** se mêler de, s'immiscer dans
meddler ['mɛdlər] *s* intrigant *m*, touche-à-tout *m*
meddlesome ['mɛdəlsəm] *adj* intrigant
median ['midɪən] *adj* médian || *s* médiane *f*
me'dian strip' *s* bande *f* médiane
mediate ['midɪ,et] *tr* procurer par médiation, négocier || *intr* s'entremettre, s'interposer
mediation [,midɪ'eʃən] *s* médiation *f*
mediator ['midɪ,etər] *s* médiateur *m*
medical ['mɛdɪkəl] *adj* médical
med'ical stu'dent *s* étudiant *m* en médecine
medicinal [mə'dɪsɪnəl] *adj* médicinal
medicine ['mɛdɪsɪn] *s* (*science and art*) médecine *f*; (*pharm*) médicament *m*
med'icine cab'inet *s* armoire *f* à pharmacie
med'icine kit' *s* pharmacie *f* portative
med'icine man' *s* (*pl* **men'**) sorcier *m* indien; (*mountebank*) charlatan *m*
medi·co ['mɛdɪ,ko] *s* (*pl* **-cos**) (slang) carabin *m*, morticole *m*
medieval [,midɪ'ivəl], [,mɛdɪ'ivəl] *adj* médiéval

medievalist [,midɪ'ivəlɪst], [,mɛdɪ'ivəlɪst] *s* médiéviste *mf*
mediocre ['midɪ,okər], [,midɪ'okər] *adj* médiocre
mediocri·ty [,midɪ'ɑkrɪti] *s* (*pl* **-ties**) médiocrité *f*
meditate ['mɛdɪ,tet] *tr & intr* méditer
meditation [,mɛdɪ'teʃən] *s* méditation *f*
Mediterranean [,mɛdɪtə'renɪ-ən] *adj* méditerranéen || *s* Méditerranée *f*
medi·um ['midɪ-əm] *adj* moyen; (culin) à point || *s* (*pl* **-ums** or **-a** [ə]) milieu *m*; (*means*) moyen *m*; (*in spiritualism*) médium *m*; (journ) organe *m*; **through the medium of** par l'intermédiaire de
me'dium of exchange' *s* agent *m* monétaire
me'dium-range' *adj* à portée moyenne
me'dium-sized' *adj* de grandeur moyenne
medlar ['mɛdlər] *s* (*fruit*) nèfle *f*; (*tree*) néflier *m*
medley ['mɛdli] *s* mélange *m*; (mus) pot-pourri *m*
medul·la [mɪ'dʌlə] *s* (*pl* **-lae** [li]) moelle *f*
Medusa [mə'duzə] *s* Méduse *f*
meek [mik] *adj* doux, humble
meekness ['miknɪs] *s* douceur *f*, humilité *f*
meerschaum ['mɪrʃəm], ['mɪrʃɔm] *s* écume *f* de mer; pipe *f* d'écume de mer
meet [mit] *adj*—**it is meet that** il convient que || *s* (sports) meeting *m* || *v* (*pret & pp* **met** [mɛt]) *tr* rencontrer; (*to make the acquaintance of*) faire la connaissance de; (*to go to meet*) aller au-devant de; (*a car in the street; a person on the sidewalk*) croiser; (*by appointment*) retrouver, rejoindre; (*difficulties; expenses*) faire face à; (*one's debts*) honorer; (*one's death*) trouver; (*a need*) satisfaire à; (*an objection*) réfuter; (*the ear*) frapper; **meet my wife (my friend, etc.)** je vous présente ma femme (mon ami, etc.) || *intr* se rencontrer; se retrouver, se rejoindre; (*to assemble*) se réunir; (*to join, touch*) se joindre, se toucher; (*said of rivers*) confluer; (*said of roads; said of cars, persons, etc.*) se croiser; **till we meet again** au revoir; **to meet with** se rencontrer avec, rencontrer; (*difficulties, an affront, etc.*) subir
meeting ['mitɪŋ] *s* rencontre *f*; (*session*) séance *f*; (*assemblage*) réunion *f*, assemblée *f*; (*of two rivers*) confluent *m*; (*of two cars; of two roads*) croisement *m*
meet'ing of the minds' *s* bonne entente *f*
meet'ing place' *s* rendez-vous *m*
megacycle ['mɛgə,saɪkəl] *s* mégacycle *m*
megaphone ['mɛgə,fon] *s* mégaphone *m*, porte-voix *m*
megohm ['mɛg,om] *s* mégohm *m*

melancholia [,melən'kolı·ə] *s* mélancolie *f*

melanchol·y ['melən,kali] *adj* mélancolique || *s* (*pl* -ies) mélancolie *f*

melee ['mele], ['mele] *s* mêlée *f*

mellow ['melo] *adj* moelleux; enjoué, débonnaire; (*ripe*) mûr || *tr* rendre moelleux, mûrir

melodic [mɪ'ladɪk] *adj* mélodique

melodious [mɪ'lodɪ·əs] *adj* mélodieux

melodramatic [,melədrə'mætɪk] *adj* mélodramatique

melo·dy ['melədi] *s* (*pl* -dies) mélodie *f*

melon ['melən] *s* melon *m*

melt [melt] *tr* & *intr* fondre; to melt into (*e.g.*, *tears*) fondre en

melt'ing pot' *s* creuset *m*

member ['membər] *s* membre *m*

mem'ber·ship' *s* membres *mpl*; (*in a club, etc.*) association *f*

membrane ['membren] *s* membrane *f*

memen·to [mɪ'mento] *s* (*pl* -tos or -toes) mémento *m*

mem·o ['memo] *s* (*pl* -os) (coll) note *f*, rappel *m*

mem'o book' *s* calepin *m*, mémento *m*

memoir ['memwar] *s* biographie *f*; memoirs mémoires *mpl*

mem'o pad' *s* bloc-notes *m*, bloc *m*

memoran·dum [,memə'rændəm] *s* (*pl* -dums or -da [də]) memorandum *m*; note *f*, rappel *m*

memorial [mɪ'morı·əl] *adj* commémoratif || *s* mémorial *m*; pétition *f*, mémoire *m*

memo'rial arch' *s* arc *m* de triomphe

Memo'rial Day' *s* la journée du Souvenir

memorialize [mɪ'morı·ə ,laɪz] *tr* commémorer

memorize ['memə ,raɪz] *tr* apprendre par cœur

memo·ry ['meməri] *s* (*pl* -ries) mémoire *f*; from memory de mémoire; in memory of en souvenir de, à la mémoire de

menace ['menɪs] *s* menace *f* || *tr* & *intr* menacer

menagerie [mə'næʒəri], [mə'nædʒəri] *s* ménagerie *f*

mend [mend] *s* raccommodage *m*, reprise *f* || *tr* réparer; (*to patch*) raccommoder; (*stockings*) repriser; (*to reform*) améliorer || *intr* s'améliorer, s'amender

mendacious [men'deʃəs] *adj* mensonger

mendicant ['mendɪkənt] *adj* & *s* mendiant *m*

mending ['mendɪŋ] *s* raccommodage *m*; (*of stockings*) reprisage *m*

menfolk ['men,fok] *spl* hommes *mpl*

menial ['minɪ·əl] *adj* servile || *s* domestique *mf*

menses ['mensiz] *spl* menstrues *fpl*

men's' fur'nishings *spl* confection *f* pour hommes

men's' room' *s* toilettes *fpl* pour hommes, lavabos *mpl* pour messieurs

menstruate ['menstru ,et] *intr* avoir ses règles

mental ['mentəl] *adj* mental

men'tal arith'metic *s* calcul *m* mental

men'tal defec'tive *s* débile *mf*

men'tal ill'ness *s* maladie *f* mentale

mentali·ty [men'tælɪti] *s* (*pl* -ties) mentalité *f*

men'tal reserva'tion *s* arrière-pensée *f*

men'tal test' *s* test *m* psychologique

mention ['menʃən] *s* mention *f* || *tr* mentionner; don't mention it il n'y a pas de quoi, je vous en prie

menu ['menju], ['menju] *s* menu *m*, carte *f*

meow [mɪ'au] *s* miaou *m* || *intr* miauler

Mephistophelian [,mefɪstə'filı·ən] *adj* méphistophélique

mercantile ['mʌrkən,til], ['mʌrkən ,taɪl] *adj* commercial, commerçant

mercenar·y ['mʌrsə,neri] *adj* mercenaire || *s* (*pl* -ies) mercenaire *mf*

merchandise ['mʌrtʃən ,daɪz] *s* marchandise *f*

merchant ['mʌrtʃənt] *adj* & *s* marchand *m*

mer'chant-man *s* (*pl* -men) navire *m* marchand

mer'chant marine' *s* marine *f* marchande

mer'chant ves'sel *s* navire *m* marchand

merciful ['mʌrsɪfəl] *adj* miséricordieux

merciless ['mʌrsɪlɪs] *adj* impitoyable

mercurial [mer'kjurı·əl] *adj* inconstant, versatile; (*lively*) vif

mercu·ry ['mʌrkjəri] *s* (*pl* -ries) mercure *m*

mer·cy ['mʌrsi] *s* (*pl* -cies) miséricorde *f*, pitié *f*; at the mercy of à la merci de

mere [mɪr] *adj* simple, pur; seul, e.g., at the mere thought of it à la seule pensée de cela; rien que, e.g., to shudder at the mere thought of it frissonner rien que d'y penser

meretricious [,merɪ'trɪʃəs] *adj* factice, postiche; de courtisane

merge [mʌrdʒ] *tr* fusionner || *intr* fusionner; (*said of two roads*) converger; to merge into se fondre dans

merger ['mʌrdʒər] *s* fusion *f*

meridian [mə'rɪdı·ən] *adj* & *s* méridien *m*

meringue [mə'ræŋ] *s* meringue *f*

merit ['merɪt] *s* mérite *m* || *tr* mériter

meritorious [,merə'torı·əs] *adj* méritoire; (*person*) méritant

merlin ['mʌrlɪn] *s* (orn) émerillon *m*

mermaid ['mʌr ,med] *s* sirène *f*

merriment ['merɪmənt] *s* gaieté *f*, réjouissance *f*

mer·ry ['meri] *adj* (*comp* -rier; *super* -riest) gai, joyeux; to make merry se divertir

Mer'ry Christ'mas *s* Joyeux Noël *m*

mer'ry-go-round' *s* chevaux *mpl* de bois, manège *m* forain

mer'ry-mak'er *s* noceur *m*, fêtard *m*

mesh [meʃ] *s* (*network*) réseau *m*; (*each open space of net*) maille *f*; (*net*) filet *m*; (*engagement of gears*) engrenage *m*; meshes rets *m*, filets *mpl* || *tr* (mach) engrener || *intr* s'engrener

mesmerize ['mesmə‚raɪz] *tr* magnétiser

mess [mes] *s* gâchis *m*; (*refuse*) saleté *f*; (*meal*) (mil) ordinaire *m*; (*for officers*) (mil) mess *m*; **to get into a mess** se mettre dans le pétrin; **to make a mess of gâcher** || *tr*—**to mess up** (*to botch*) gâcher; (*to dirty*) salir || *intr*—**to mess around** (*to putter*) (coll) bricoler; (*to waste time*) (coll) lambiner

message ['mesɪdʒ] *s* message *m*

messenger ['mesəndʒər] *s* messager *m*; (*one who goes on errands*) commissionnaire *m*

mess' hall' *s* cantine *f*; (*for officers*) mess *m*

Messiah [mə'saɪ‚ə] *s* Messie *m*

mess' kit' *s* gamelle *f*

mess'mate' *s* camarade *mf* de table; (nav) camarade de plat

mess' of pot'tage ['pɑtɪdʒ] *s* (Bib) plat *m* de lentilles

Messrs. ['mesərz] *pl* of Mr.

mess•y ['mesɪ] *adj* (*comp* **-ier**; *super* **-iest**) en désordre; (*dirty*) sale, poisseux

metal ['metəl] *s* métal *m*

metallic [mɪ'tælɪk] *adj* métallique

metallurgy ['metə‚lʌrdʒɪ] *s* métallurgie *f*

met'al pol'ish *s* brillant *m* à métaux

met'al-work' *s* serrurerie *f*, travail *m* des métaux

metamorpho•sis [‚metə'mɔrfəsɪs] *s* (*pl* **-ses** [‚siz]) métamorphose *f*

metaphony [mə'tæfənɪ] *s* métaphonie *f*, inflexion *f*

metaphor ['metəfər] *s* métaphore *f*

metaphorical [‚metə'fɑrɪkəl], [‚metə'fɔrɪkəl] *adj* métaphorique

metathe•sis [mɪ'tæθɪsɪs] *s* (*pl* **-ses** [‚siz]) métathèse *f*

mete [mit] *tr*—**to mete out** distribuer

meteor ['mitɪ‚ər] *s* étoile *f* filante; (*atmospheric phenomenon*) météore *m*

meteoric [‚mitɪ'ɑrɪk], [‚mitɪ'ɔrɪk] *adj* météorique; (fig) fulgurant

meteorite ['mitɪ‚ə‚raɪt] *s* météorite *m* & *f*

meteorology [‚mitɪ‚ə'rɑlədʒɪ] *s* météorologie *f*

meter ['mitər] *s* (*unit of measurement; verse*) mètre *m*; (*instrument for measuring gas, electricity, water*) compteur *m*; (mus) mesure *f*

me'ter read'er *s* releveur *m* de compteurs

methane ['meθen] *s* méthane *m*

method ['meθəd] *s* méthode *f*

methodic(al) [mɪ'θɑdɪk(əl)] *adj* méthodique

Methodist ['meθədɪst] *adj* & *s* méthodiste *mf*

Methuselah [mɪ'θuzələ] *s* Mathusalem *m*

meticulous [mɪ'tɪkjələs] *adj* méticuleux

metric(al) ['metrɪk(əl)] *adj* métrique

metrics ['metrɪks] *s* métrique *f*

metronome ['metrə‚nom] *s* métronome *m*

metropolis [mɪ'trɑpəlɪs] *s* métropole *f*

metropolitan [‚metrə'pɑlɪtən] *adj* & *s* métropolitain *m*

mettle ['metəl] *s* ardeur *f*, fougue *f*; **to be on one's mettle** se piquer au jeu

mettlesome ['metəlsəm] *adj* ardent, vif, fougueux

mew [mju] *s* miaulement *m* || *intr* miauler

Mexican ['meksɪkən] *adj* mexicain || *s* Mexicain *m*

Mexico ['meksɪ‚ko] *s* le Mexique

Mex'ico Cit'y *s* Mexico

mezzanine ['mezə‚nin] *s* entresol *m*; (theat) mezzanine *m* & *f*, corbeille *f*

mica ['maɪkə] *s* mica *m*

microbe ['maɪkrob] *s* microbe *m*

microbiology [‚maɪkrəbaɪ'ɑlədʒɪ] *s* microbiologie *f*

microfilm ['maɪkrə‚fɪlm] *s* microfilm *m* || *tr* microfilmer

microgroove ['maɪkrə‚gruv] *adj* & *s* microsillon *m*

mi'crogroove rec'ord *s* disque *m* à microsillons

microphone ['maɪkrə‚fon] *s* microphone *m*

microscope ['maɪkrə‚skop] *s* microscope *m*

microscopic [‚maɪkrə'skɑpɪk] *adj* microscopique

microwave ['maɪkrə‚wev] *s* micro-onde *f*

mid [mɪd] *adj*—**in mid course** à mi-chemin

mid'day' *s* midi *m*

middle ['mɪdəl] *adj* moyen, du milieu || *s* milieu *m*; **in the middle of** au milieu de

mid'dle age' *s* âge *m* moyen; **Middle Ages** moyen-âge *m*

middle-aged ['mɪdəl‚edʒd] *adj* d'un âge moyen

mid'dle class' *s* classe *f* moyenne, bourgeoisie *f*

mid'dle-class' *adj* bourgeois

Mid'dle East' *s* Moyen-Orient *m*

Mid'dle Eng'lish *s* moyen anglais *m*

mid'dle fin'ger *s* majeur *m*, doigt *m* du milieu

mid'dle-man' *s* (*pl* **-men'**) intermédiaire *mf*

middling ['mɪdlɪŋ] *adj* moyen, assez bien, passable || *adv* (coll) assez bien, passablement

mid•dy ['mɪdɪ] *s* (*pl* **-dies**) (coll) aspirant *m*

mid'dy blouse' *s* marinière *f*

midget ['mɪdʒɪt] *s* nain *m*, nabot *m*

midland ['mɪdlənd] *adj* de l'intérieur || *s* centre *m* du pays

mid'night' *adj* de minuit; **to burn the midnight oil** pâlir sur les livres, se crever les livres || *s* minuit *m*

midriff ['mɪdrɪf] *s* diaphragme *m*

mid'ship'man *s* (*pl* **-men**) aspirant *m*

midst [mɪdst] *s* centre *m*; **in our** (**your**, **etc.**) **midst** parmi nous (vous, etc.); **in the midst of** au milieu de

mid'stream' s—**in midstream** au milieu du courant

mid'sum'mer s milieu m de l'été

mid'way' adj & adv à mi-chemin || **mid'way'** s fête f foraine

mid'week' s milieu m de la semaine

mid'wife' s (pl -wives') sage-femme f

mid'win'ter s milieu m de l'hiver

mid'year' s mi-année f

mien [min] s mine f, aspect m

miff [mɪf] s (coll) fâcherie f || tr (coll) fâcher

might [maɪt] s puissance f, force f; **with might and main, with all one's might** de toute sa force || aux used to form the potential mood, e.g., **she might not be able to come** il se pourrait qu'elle ne puisse pas venir

mightily [ˈmaɪtɪli] adv puissamment; (coll) énormément

mighty [ˈmaɪti] adj (comp -ier; super -iest) puissant; (of great size) grand, vaste || adv (coll) rudement, diablement

mignonette [ˌmɪnjəˈnɛt] s réséda m

migraine [ˈmaɪɡren] s migraine f

migrate [ˈmaɪɡret] intr émigrer

migratory [ˈmaɪɡrəˌtori] adj migratoire

milch [mɪltʃ] adj laitier

mild [maɪld] adj doux

mildew [ˈmɪlˌd(j)u] s moisissure f; (on vine) mildiou m, blanc m

mildness [ˈmaɪldnɪs] s douceur f

mile [maɪl] s mille m

mileage [ˈmaɪlɪdʒ] s distance f en milles; (charge) tarif m au mille

mile'post' s borne f milliaire

mile'stone' s borne f milliaire; (fig) jalon m

militancy [ˈmɪlɪtənsi] s esprit m militant

militant [ˈmɪlɪtənt] adj & s militant m

militarism [ˈmɪlɪtəˌrɪzəm] s militarisme m

militarize [ˈmɪlɪtəˌraɪz] tr militariser

military [ˈmɪlɪˌtɛri] adj & s militaire m

mil'itary police'man s (pl -men) agent m de la police militaire

militate [ˈmɪlɪˌtet] intr militer

militia [mɪˈlɪʃə] s milice f

mili'tia-man s (pl -men) milicien m

milk [mɪlk] adj laitier || s lait m || tr traire; abuser de, exploiter; **to milk s.th. from s.o.** soutirer q.ch. à qn

milk'can' s pot m à lait, berthe f

milk' car'ton s boîte f de lait, berlingot m

milk' di'et s régime m lacté

milk'maid' s laitière f

milk'man' s (pl -men') laitier m, crémier m

milk' pail' s seau m à lait

milk'sop' s poule f mouillée

milk' tooth' s dent f de lait

milk'weed' s laiteron m

milk•y [ˈmɪlki] adj (comp -ier; super -iest) laiteux

Milk'y Way' s Voie f Lactée

mill [mɪl] s moulin m; (factory) fabrique f, usine f; millième m de dollar; **to put through the mill** (coll)

faire passer au laminoir || tr moudre, broyer; (a coin) créneler; (gears) fraiser; (steel) laminer; (ore) bocarder; (chocolate) faire mousser || intr—**to mill around** circuler

millennial [mɪˈlɛnɪəl] adj millénaire

millenni•um [mɪˈlɛnɪəm] s (pl -ums or -a [ə]) millénaire m

miller [ˈmɪlər] s meunier m

millet [ˈmɪlɪt] s millet m

milligram [ˈmɪlɪˌɡræm] s milligramme m

millimeter [ˈmɪlɪˌmitər] s millimètre m

milliner [ˈmɪlɪnər] s modiste f

mil'linery shop' [ˈmɪlɪˌnɛri], [ˈmɪlɪnəri] s boutique f de modiste

milling [ˈmɪlɪŋ] s (of grain) mouture f

mill'ing machine' s fraiseuse f

million [ˈmɪljən] adj million de || s million m

millionaire [ˌmɪljənˈɛr] s millionnaire mf

millionth [ˈmɪljənθ] adj & pron millionième (masc, fem) || s millionième m

mill'pond' s retenue f, réservoir m

mill'race' s bief m

mill'stone' s meule f; (fig) boulet m

mill' wheel' s roue f de moulin

mill'work' s ouvrage m de menuiserie

mime [maɪm] s mime mf || tr & intr mimer

mimeograph [ˈmɪmɪəˌɡræf], [ˈmɪmɪəˌɡraf] s ronéo f || tr ronéocopier, ronéotyper

mim•ic [ˈmɪmɪk] s mime mf, imitateur m || v (pret & pp -icked; ger -icking) tr mimer, imiter

mimic•ry [ˈmɪmɪkri] s (pl -ries) mimique f, imitation f

minaret [ˌmɪnəˈrɛt], [ˈmɪnəˌrɛt] s minaret m

mince [mɪns] tr (meat) hacher menu || intr minauder

mince'meat' s hachis m de viande et de fruits aromatisés; **to make mincemeat of** (coll) mettre en marmelade

mind [maɪnd] s esprit m; **to be of one mind** être d'accord; **to change one's mind** changer d'avis; **to have a mind to** avoir envie de; **to have in mind** avoir en vue; **to lose one's mind** perdre la raison; **to make up one's mind** prendre le parti de; **to slip one's mind** échapper à qn; **to speak one's mind** donner son avis || tr (to take care of) garder; (to obey) obéir (with dat); (to be troubled by) s'inquiéter de; (e.g., one's manners) faire attention à; (e.g., a dangerous step) prendre garde à; **mind your own business!** occupez-vous de vos affaires! || intr—**do you mind?** cela ne vous ennuie pas?, cela ne vous gêne pas?; **if you don't mind** si cela ne vous fait rien, si cela vous est égal; **never mind!** n'importe!

mindful [ˈmaɪndfəl] adj attentif; **mindful of** attentif à, soigneux de

mind' read'er s liseur m de la pensée

mind' read'ing s lecture f de la pensée

mine [maɪn] s mine f || pron poss le mien §89; à moi §85 A, 10 || tr (coal, m minerals, etc.) extraire; (to under-mine; to lay mines in) miner

mine/field/ s champ m de mines

mine/lay/er s poseur m de mines

miner ['mainər] s mineur m

mineral ['minərəl] adj & s minéral m

mineralogy [ˌminəˈrɑlədʒi] s minéralo-gie f

min/eral wool/ s laine f minérale, laine de scories

mine/sweep/er s dragueur m de mines

mingle ['miŋgəl] tr mêler, mélanger || intr se mêler, se mélanger

miniature ['mini·ətʃər], ['minitʃər] s miniature f

miniaturization [ˌmini·ətʃəriˈzeʃən], [ˌminitʃəriˈzeʃən] s miniaturisation f

miniaturize ['mini·ətʃəˌraiz], ['minitʃəˌraiz] tr miniaturiser

minimal ['miniməl] adj minimum

minimize ['miniˌmaiz] tr minimiser

minimum ['miniməm] adj minimum; (temperature) minimal || s minimum m

min/imum wage/ s salaire m minimum, minimum m vital

mining ['mainiŋ] adj minier || s exploi-tation f des mines; (nav) pose f de mines

minion ['minjən] s favori m; (hench-man) séide m

miniskirt ['miniˌskʌrt] s minijupe f

minister ['ministər] s ministre m; (eccl) pasteur m || intr—to minister to (the needs of) subvenir à; (a person) soigner; (a parish) desservir

ministerial [ˌminisˈtiri·əl] adj ministé-riel

minis·try ['ministri] s (pl -tries) minis-tère m; (eccl) clergé m; (eccl) pasto-rat m

mink [miŋk] s vison m

minnow ['mino] s vairon m

minor ['mainər] adj & s mineur m

Minorca [miˈnɔrkə] s Minorque f; île f de Minorque

minori·ty [miˈnɔriti], [maiˈnɔriti] adj minoritaire || s (pl -ties) minorité f

minstrel ['minstrəl] s (in a minstrel show) interprète m de chants nègres; (hist) ménestrel m

mint [mint] s hôtel m des Monnaies, Monnaie f; (bot) menthe f; (fig) mine f || tr frapper, monnayer; (fig) forger

minuet [ˌminjuˈet] s menuet m

minus ['mainəs] adj négatif || s moins m || prep moins; (coll) sans, dé-pourvu de

minute [maiˈn(j)ut] adj (tiny) minime; (meticulous) minutieux || ['minit] s minute f; **minutes** compte m rendu, procès-verbal m de séance; (often omitted in expressions of time), e.g., **ten after two**, ten minutes after two deux heures dix; **up to the minute** à la dernière heure; à la dernière mode; au courant

min/ute hand/ ['minit] s grande aiguil-le f

min/ute steak/ ['minit] s entrecôte f minute

minutiae [miˈn(j)uʃi·ˌi] spl minuties fpl

minx [miŋks] s effrontée f

miracle ['mirəkəl] s miracle m

mir/acle play/ s miracle m

miraculous [miˈrækjələs] adj miracu-leux

mirage [miˈrɑʒ] s mirage m

mire [mair] s fange f

mirror ['mirər] s miroir m, glace f || tr refléter

mirth [mʌrθ] s joie f, gaieté f

mir·y ['mairi] adj (comp -ier; super -iest) fangeux

misadventure [ˌmisədˈventʃər] s mésa-venture f

misanthrope ['misənˌθrop] s misan-thrope mf

misapprehension [ˌmisæpriˈhenʃən] s fausse idée f, malentendu m

misappropriation [ˌmisəˌpropriˈeʃən] s détournement m de fonds

misbehave [ˌmisbiˈhev] intr se con-duire mal

misbehavior [ˌmisbiˈhevi·ər] s mau-vaise conduite f

miscalculation [ˌmiskælkjəˈleʃən] s mécompte m

miscarriage [misˈkærɪdʒ] s fausse couche f; (e.g., of letter) perte f; (of justice) déni m, mal-jugé m; (fig) avortement m, insuccès m

miscar·ry [misˈkæri] v (pret & pp -ried) intr faire une fausse couche; (said, e.g., of letter) s'égarer; (fig) avorter, échouer

miscellaneous [ˌmisəˈleni·əs] adj di-vers, mélangé

miscella·ny [ˈmisəˌleni] s (pl -nies) miscellanées fpl

mischief ['mistʃif] s (harm) tort m; (disposition to annoy) méchanceté f; (prankishness) espièglerie f

mis/chief-mak/er s brandon m de dis-corde

mischievous ['mistʃivəs] adj (harmful) nuisible; (mean) méchant; (prankish) espiègle

misconception [ˌmiskənˈsepʃən] s con-ception f erronée

misconduct [misˈkɑndʌkt] s inconduite f; (e.g., of a business) mauvaise ad-ministration f || [ˌmiskənˈdʌkt] tr mal administrer; **to misconduct one-self** se conduire mal

misconstrue [ˌmiskənˈstru], [misˈkɑn-stru] tr mal interpréter

miscount [misˈkaunt] s erreur f de calcul || tr & intr mal compter

miscue [misˈkju] s fausse queue f; (blunder) bévue f || intr faire fausse queue; (theat) se tromper de réplique

mis·deal ['misˌdil] s maldonne f, mau-vaise donne f || [misˈdil] v (pret & pp -dealt) tr mal distribuer || intr faire maldonne

misdeed [misˈdid], ['misˌdid] s mé-fait m

misdemeanor [ˌmisdiˈminər] s mau-vaise conduite f; (law) délit m cor-rectionnel

misdirect [,mɪsdɪˈrekt], [,mɪsdaɪˈrekt] *tr* mal diriger

misdoing [mɪsˈduːɪŋ] *s* méfait *m*

miser [ˈmaɪzər] *s* avare *mf*

miserable [ˈmɪzərəbəl] *adj* misérable

miserly [ˈmaɪzərli] *adj* avare

miser·y [ˈmɪzəri] *s* (*pl* **-ies**) misère *f*, détresse *f*

misfeasance [mɪsˈfiːzəns] *s* (law) abus *m* de pouvoir

misfire [mɪsˈfaɪr] *s* raté *m* || *intr* rater

mis·fit [ˈmɪsˌfɪt] *s* (*clothing*) vêtement *m* manqué; (*thing*) laissé-pour-compte *m*; (fig) inadapté *m* || [mɪsˈfɪt] *v* (*pret & pp* **-fitted**; *ger* **-fitting**) *tr* mal aller (with *dat*) || *intr* mal aller

misfortune [mɪsˈfɔrtʃən] *s* infortune *f*, malheur *m*

misgiving [mɪsˈgɪvɪŋ] *s* pressentiment *m*, appréhension *f*, soupçon *m*

misgovern [mɪsˈgʌvərn] *tr* mal gouverner

misguidance [mɪsˈgaɪdəns] *s* mauvais conseils *mpl*

misguided [mɪsˈgaɪdɪd] *adj* mal placé, hors de propos; (*e.g., youth*) dévoyé

mishap [ˈmɪshæp], [mɪsˈhæp] *s* contretemps *m*, mésaventure *f*

misinform [,mɪsɪnˈfɔrm] *tr* mal renseigner

misinterpret [,mɪsɪnˈtʌrprɪt] *tr* mal interpréter

misjudge [mɪsˈdʒʌdʒ] *tr & intr* mal juger

mis·lay [mɪsˈle] *v* (*pret & pp* **-laid**) *tr* égarer, perdre

mis·lead [mɪsˈlid] *v* (*pret & pp* **-led**) *tr* égarer; corrompre

misleading [mɪsˈlidɪŋ] *adj* trompeur

mismanagement [mɪsˈmænɪdʒmənt] *s* mauvaise administration *f*

misnomer [mɪsˈnomər] *s* faux nom *m*

misplace [mɪsˈples] *tr* mal placer; (*to mislay*) (coll) égarer, perdre

misprint [ˈmɪsˌprɪnt] *s* erreur *f* typographique, coquille *f* || [mɪsˈprɪnt] *tr* imprimer incorrectement

mispronounce [,mɪsprəˈnaʊns] *tr* mal prononcer

misquote [mɪsˈkwot] *tr* citer à faux, citer inexactement

misrepresent [,mɪsreprɪˈzent] *tr* représenter sous un faux jour; (*e.g., facts*) dénaturer, travestir

miss [mɪs] *s* coup *m* manqué; **Miss** Mademoiselle *f*, Mlle; (*winner of beauty contest*) Miss *f* || *tr* manquer; (*to feel the absence of*) regretter; (*not to run into*) ne pas voir, ne pas rencontrer; (*e.g., one's way*) se tromper de; **he misses you very much** vous lui manquez beaucoup || *intr* manquer

missal [ˈmɪsəl] *s* missel *m*

misshapen [mɪsˈʃepən] *adj* difforme, contrefait

missile [ˈmɪsɪl] *s* projectile *m*; (*guided missile*) missile *m*

mis·sile launch·er *s* lance-fusées *m*

missing [ˈmɪsɪŋ] *adj* manquant, absent;

perdu; **missing in action** (mil) porté disparu; **to be missing** manquer, e.g., **three are missing** il en manque trois

miss·ing per·sons *spl* disparus *mpl*

mission [ˈmɪʃən] *s* mission *f*

missionar·y [ˈmɪʃənˌeri] *adj* missionnaire || *s* (*pl* **-ies**) missionnaire *m*

missis [ˈmɪsɪz] *s*—**the missis** (coll) votre femme *f*

missive [ˈmɪsɪv] *adj & s* missive *f*

mis·spell [mɪsˈspel] *v* (*pret & pp* **-spelled** or **-spelt**) *tr & intr* écrire incorrectement

misspelling [mɪsˈspelɪŋ] *s* faute *f* d'orthographe

misspent [mɪsˈspent] *adj* gaspillé; dissipé

misstatement [mɪsˈstetmənt] *s* rapport *m* inexact, erreur *f* de fait

misstep [mɪsˈstep] *s* faux pas *m*

miss·y [ˈmɪsi] *s* (*pl* **-ies**) (coll) mademoiselle *f*

mist [mɪst] *s* brume *f*, buée *f*; (*fine spray*) vapeur *f*; (*of tears*) voile *m*

mis·take [mɪsˈtek] *s* faute *f*, erreur *f*; **by mistake** par erreur, par méprise; **to make a mistake** se tromper || *v* (*pret* **-took**; *pp* **-taken**) *tr* (*to misunderstand*) mal comprendre; (*to be wrong about*) se tromper de; **to mistake s.o. for s.o. else** prendre qn pour qn d'autre

mistaken [mɪsˈtekən] *adj* erroné, faux; (*person*) dans l'erreur

mistak·en iden·tity *s* erreur *f* d'identité, erreur sur la personne

mistakenly [mɪsˈtekənli] *adv* par erreur

mister [ˈmɪstər] *s*—**the mister** (coll) votre mari *m* || *interj* (slang & pej) Jules!, mon petit bonhomme!

mistletoe [ˈmɪsəlˌto] *s* gui *m*

mistreat [mɪsˈtrit] *tr* maltraiter

mistreatment [mɪsˈtritmənt] *s* mauvais traitement *m*

mistress [ˈmɪstrɪs] *s* maîtresse *f*

mistrial [mɪsˈtraɪəl] *s* (law) procès *m* entaché de nullité

mistrust [mɪsˈtrʌst] *s* méfiance *f* || *tr* se méfier de || *intr* se méfier

mistrustful [mɪsˈtrʌstfəl] *adj* méfiant

mist·y [ˈmɪsti] *adj* (*comp* **-ier**; *super* **-iest**) brumeux; vague, indistinct

misunderstand [,mɪsʌndərˈstænd] *v* (*pret & pp* **-stood**) *tr* mal comprendre

misunderstanding [,mɪsʌndərˈstændɪŋ] *s* malentendu *m*

misuse [mɪsˈjus] *s* mauvais usage *m*, abus *m*; (*of words*) emploi *m* abusif || [mɪsˈjuz] *tr* faire mauvais usage de, abuser de; (*a person*) maltraiter

misword [mɪsˈwʌrd] *tr* mal rédiger, mal exprimer

mite [maɪt] *s* (*small contribution*) obole *f*; (*small amount*) brin *m*, bagatelle *f*; (ent) mite *f*

miter [ˈmaɪtər] *s* (carpentry) onglet *m*; (eccl) mitre *f* || *tr* tailler à onglet

mi·ter box· *s* boîte *f* à onglets

mitigate [ˈmɪtɪˌget] *tr* adoucir, atténuer

mitt [mɪt] *s* (*fingerless glove*) mitaine *f*; (*mitten*) moufle *f*; (baseball) gant *m* de prise; (*hand*) (slang) main *f*

mitten ['mɪtən] *s* moufle *f*

mix [mɪks] *tr* mélanger, mêler; *(cement; a cake)* malaxer; *(the cards; the salad)* touiller; **to mix up** *(to confuse)* confondre ‖ *intr* se mélanger, se mêler; **to mix with** s'associer à or avec

mixed *adj* mélangé; *(races; style; colors)* mêlé; *(feelings; marriage; school; doubles)* mixte; *(candy)* assorti; *(salad, vegetables, etc.)* panaché; *(number)* fractionnaire

mixed' drink' *s* boisson *f* mélangée

mixer ['mɪksər] *s (device)* mélangeur *m*; *(for, e.g., concrete)* malaxeur *m*; **to be a good mixer** (coll) avoir le don de plaire

mix'ing fau'cet *s* robinet *m* mélangeur

mixture ['mɪkstʃər] *s* mélange *m*

mix'-up' *s* embrouillage *m*

mizzen ['mɪzən] *s* artimon *m*

moan [mon] *s* gémissement *m* ‖ *intr* gémir

moat [mot] *s* fossé *m*

mob [mɑb] *s (mob)* populace *f*; *(crush of people)* cohue *f*; *(crowd bent on violence)* foule *f* en colère, ameutement *m* ‖ *v (pret & pp* **mobbed;** *ger* **mobbing)** *tr* s'attrouper autour de; fondre sur, assaillir

mobile ['mobɪl], ['mobɪl] *adj & s* mobile *m*

mobility [mo'bɪlɪti] *s* mobilité *f*

mobilization [,mobɪlɪ'zeʃən] *s* mobilisation *f*

mobilize ['mobɪ,laɪz] *tr & intr* mobiliser

mob' rule' *s* loi *f* de la populace

mobster ['mɑbstər] *s* (slang) gangster *m*

moccasin ['mɑkəsɪn] *s* mocassin *m*

Mo'cha cof'fee ['mokə] *s* moka *m*

mock [mɑk] *adj* simulé, contrefait ‖ *s* moquerie *f* ‖ *tr* se moquer de, moquer; *(to imitate)* contrefaire, singer; *(to deceive)* tromper ‖ *intr* se moquer; **to mock at** se moquer de; **to mock up** construire une maquette de

mock' elec'tion *s* élection *f* blanche

mocker•y ['mɑkəri] *s (pl -ies)* moquerie *f*; *(subject of derision)* objet *m* de risée; *(poor imitation)* parodie *f*; *(e.g., of justice)* simulacre *m*

mockingbird ['mɑkɪŋ,bʌrd] *s* moqueur *m*, oiseau *m* moqueur

mock' or'ange *s* seringa *m*

mock' tur'tle soup' *s* potage *m* à la tête de veau

mock'-up' *s* maquette *f*

mode [mod] *s (kind)* mode *m*; *(fashion)* mode *f*; *(gram, mus)* mode *m*

mod•el ['mɑdəl] *adj* modèle ‖ *s* modèle *m*; *(for dressmaker or artist; at a fashion show)* mannequin *m*; *(of a statue)* maquette *f* ‖ *v (pret & pp* **-eled** or **-elled;** *ger* **-eling** or **-elling)** *tr* modeler ‖ *intr* dessiner des modèles; servir de modèle, poser

mod'el air'plane *s* aéromodèle *m*

mod'el-air'plane build'er *s* aéromodéliste *mf*

mod'el-air'plane build'ing *s* aéromodélisme *m*

moderate ['mɑdərɪt] *adj* modéré ‖ ['mɑdə,ret] *tr* modérer; *(a meeting)* présider ‖ *intr* se modérer

moderator ['mɑdə,retər] *s (over an assembly)* président *m*; *(mediator; substance used for slowing down neutrons)* modérateur *m*

modern ['mɑdərn] *adj* moderne

modernize ['mɑdər,naɪz] *tr* moderniser

mod'ern lan'guages *spl* langues *fpl* vivantes

modest ['mɑdɪst] *adj* modeste

modes•ty ['mɑdɪsti] *s (pl -ties)* modestie *f*

modicum ['mɑdɪkəm] *s* petite quantité *f*

modifier ['mɑdɪ,faɪ·ər] *s* (gram) modificateur *m*

modi•fy ['mɑdɪ,faɪ] *v (pret & pp -fied)* *tr* modifier

modish ['modɪʃ] *adj* à la mode, élégant

modulate ['mɑdʒə,let] *tr & intr* moduler

modulation [,mɑdʒə'leʃən] *s* modulation *f*

mohair ['mo,her] *s* mohair *m*

Mohammedan [mo'hæmɪdən] *adj* mahométan ‖ *s* mahométan *m*

Mohammedanism [mo'hæmɪdə,nɪzəm] *s* mahométisme *m*

moist [mɔɪst] *adj* humide; *(e.g., skin)* moite

moisten ['mɔɪsən] *tr* humecter ‖ *intr* s'humecter

moisture ['mɔɪstʃər] *s* humidité *f*

molar ['molər] *adj & s* molaire *f*

molasses [mə'læsɪz] *s* mélasse *f*

mold [mold] *s* moule *m*; *(fungus)* moisi *m*, moisissure *f*; *(agr)* humus *m*, terreau *m*; *(fig)* trempe *f* ‖ *tr* mouler; *(to make moldy)* moisir ‖ *tr* moisir, se moisir

molder ['moldər] *s* mouleur *m* ‖ *intr* tomber en poussière

molding ['moldɪŋ] *s* moulage *m*; *(cornice, shaped strip of wood, etc.)* moulure *f*

mold•y ['moldi] *adj (comp* **-ier;** *super* **-iest)** moisi

mole [mol] *s (breakwater)* môle *m*; *(inner harbor)* bassin *m*; *(spot on skin)* grain *m* de beauté; *(small mammal)* taupe *f*

molecule ['mɑlɪ,kjul] *s* molécule *f*

mole'hill' *s* taupinière *f*

mole'skin' *s (fur)* taupe *f*; *(fabric)* moleskine *f*

molest [mə'lest] *tr* déranger, inquiéter; molester, rudoyer

moll [mɑl] *s* (slang) femme *f* du Milieu

molli•fy ['mɑlɪ,faɪ] *v (pret & pp* **-fied)** *tr* apaiser, adoucir

mollusk ['mɑləsk] *s* mollusque *m*

mollycoddle ['mɑlɪ,kɑdəl] *s* poule *f* mouillée ‖ *tr* dorloter

molt [molt] *s* mue *f* ‖ *intr* muer

molten ['moltən] *adj* fondu

molybdenum [mə'lɪbdɪnəm], [,mɑlɪb-'dinəm] *s* molybdène *m*

moment ['momənt] *s* moment *m*; **at**

any **moment** d'un moment à l'autre; **at that moment** à ce moment-là; **at this moment** en ce moment; **in a moment** dans un instant; **of great moment** d'une grande importance; **one moment please!** (telp) ne quittez pas!

momentary ['momən‚teri] *adj* momentané

momentous [mo'mentəs] *adj* important, d'importance

momen·tum [mo'mentəm] *s* (*pl* **-tums** or **-ta** [tə]) élan *m*; (mech) force *f* d'impulsion, quantité *f* de mouvement

monarch ['manərk] *s* monarque *m*

monarchic(al) [mə'narkɪk(əl)] *adj* monarchique

monar·chy ['manərki] *s* (*pl* **-chies**) monarchie *f*

monaster·y ['manes‚teri] *s* (*pl* **-ies**) monastère *m*

monastic [mə'næstɪk] *adj* monastique

monasticism [mə'næstɪ‚sɪzəm] *s* monachisme *m*

Monday ['mʌndi] *s* lundi *m*

monetary ['manɪ‚teri] *adj* (*pertaining to coinage*) monétaire; (*pertaining to money*) pécuniaire

money ['mʌni] *s* argent *m*; (*legal tender of a country*) monnaie *f*; **to get one's money's worth** en avoir pour son argent; **to make money** gagner de l'argent

mon'ey·bag' *s* sacoche *f*; **moneybags** (*wealth*) (coll) sac *m*; (*wealthy person*) (coll) richard *m*

mon'ey belt' *s* ceinture *f* porte-monnaie

moneychanger ['mʌni‚t/endʒər] *s* changeur *m*, cambiste *m*

moneyed ['mʌnid] *adj* possédant

mon'ey-lend'er *s* bailleur *m* de fonds

mon'ey-mak'er *s* amasseur *m* d'argent; (fig) source *f* de gain

mon'ey or'der *s* mandat *m* postal

Mongol ['maŋgol], ['maŋgal] *adj* mongol *f* ǁ *s* (*language*) mongol *m*; (*person*) Mongol *m*

mon·goose ['maŋgus] *s* (*pl* **-gooses**) mangouste *f*

mongrel ['mʌŋgrəl], ['maŋgrəl] *adj & s* métis *m*

monitor ['manɪtər] *s* contrôleur *m*; (*at school*) pion *m*, moniteur *m* ǁ *tr* contrôler; (rad) écouter

monk [mʌŋk] *s* moine *m*

monkey ['mʌŋki] *s* singe *m*; (*female*) guenon *f*; **to make a monkey of** tourner en ridicule ǁ *intr*—**to monkey around** tripoter; **to monkey around with** tripoter; **to monkey with** (*to tamper with*) tripatouiller

mon'key-shine' *s* (slang) singerie *f*

mon'key wrench' *s* clé *f* anglaise

monks'hood *s* (bot) napel *m*

monocle ['manəkəl] *s* monocle *m*

monogamy [mə'nagəmi] *s* monogamie *f*

monogram ['manə‚græm] *s* monogramme *m*

monograph ['manə‚græf], ['manə‚graf] *s* monographie *f*

monolithic [‚manə'lɪθɪk] *adj* monolithique

monologue ['manə‚lɔg], ['manə‚lag] *s* monologue *m*

monomania [‚manə'menɪ‚ə] *s* monomanie *f*

monomial [mə'nomɪ‚əl] *s* monôme *m*

monoplane ['manə‚plen] *s* monoplan *m*

monopolize [mə'napə‚laɪz] *tr* monopoliser

monopo·ly [mə'napəli] *s* (*pl* **-lies**) monopole *m*

monorail ['manə‚rel] *s* monorail *m*

monosyllable ['manə‚sɪləbəl] *s* monosyllabe *m*

monotheist ['manə‚θi·ɪst] *adj & s* monothéiste *mf*

monotonous [mə'natənəs] *adj* monotone

monotony [mə'natəni] *s* monotonie *f*

monotype ['manə‚taɪp] *s* monotype *m*; (*machine to set type*) monotype *f*

monoxide [mə'naksaɪd] *s* oxyde *m*, e.g., **carbon monoxide** oxyde *m* de carbone

monsignor [man'sinjər] *s* (*pl* **monsignors** or **monsignori** [‚mansi·njo'ri]) (eccl) monseigneur *m*

monsoon [man'sun] *s* mousson *f*

monster ['manstər] *adj & s* monstre *m*

monstrance ['manstrəns] *s* ostensoir *m*

monstrous ['manstrəs] *adj* monstrueux

month [mʌnθ] *s* mois *m*

month·ly ['mʌnθli] *adj* mensuel ǁ *s* (*pl* **-lies**) revue *f* mensuelle; **monthlies** (coll) règles *fpl* ǁ *adv* mensuellement

monument ['manjəmənt] *s* monument *m*

moo [mu] *s* meuglement *m* ǁ *intr* meugler

mood [mud] *s* humeur *f*, disposition *f*; (gram) mode *m*; **moods** accès *mpl* de mauvaise humeur

mood·y ['mudi] *adj* (*comp* **-ier**; *super* **-iest**) d'humeur changeante; (*melancholy*) maussade

moon [mun] *s* lune *f* ǁ *intr*—**to moon about** musarder; (*to daydream about*) rêver à

moon'beam' *s* rayon *m* de lune

moon'light' *s* clair *m* de lune

moon'light'ing *s* deuxième emploi *m*

moon'shine' *s* clair *m* de lune; (*idle talk*) baliverne *f*; (coll) alcool *m* de contrebande

moon' shot' *s* tir *m* à la lune

moor [mur] *s* lande *f*, bruyère *f*; **Moor** Maure *m* ǁ *tr* amarrer ǁ *intr* s'amarrer

Moorish ['murɪʃ] *adj* mauresque

moose [mus] *s* (*pl* **moose**) élan *m* du Canada, orignal *m*; (*European elk*) élan *m*

moot [mut] *adj* discutable

mop [map] *s* balai *m* à franges; (*of hair*) tignasse *f* ǁ *v* (*pret & pp* **mopped;** *ger* **mopping**) *tr* nettoyer avec un balai à franges; (e.g., *one's brow*) s'essuyer; **to mop up** (mil) nettoyer

mope [mop] *intr* avoir le cafard

moral ['marəl], ['mɔrəl] *adj* moral ǁ *s* (*of a fable*) morale *f*; **morals** mœurs *fpl*

morale [mə'ræl], [mə'ral] s moral m

morali·ty [mə'ræliti] s (pl -ties) moralité f

morass [mə'ræs] s marais m

moratori·um [,mɔrə'tori-əm], [,marə-'tori-əm] s (pl -ums or -a [ə]) moratoire m, moratorium m

morbid ['mɔrbid] adj morbide

mordacious [mɔr'de/əs] adj mordant

mordant ['mɔrdənt] adj & s mordant m

more [mor] adj comp plus de §91; plus nombreux; de plus, e.g., one minute more une minute de plus; more than plus que; (followed by numeral) plus de || s plus m; all the more so d'autant plus; what is more qui plus est; what more do you need? que vous faut-il de plus? || pron indef plus, davantage || adv comp plus §91; davantage; more and more de plus en plus; more or less plus ou moins; more than plus que, davantage que; (followed by numeral) plus de; neither more nor less ni plus ni moins; never more jamais plus, plus jamais; no more ne . . . plus §90; once more une fois de plus; the more . . . the more (or the less) plus . . . plus (or moins)

more·o'ver adv de plus, du reste

Moresque [mo'resk] adj mauresque

morgue [mɔrg] s institut m médico-légal, morgue f; (journ) archives fpl

Mormon ['mɔrmən] adj & s mormon m

morning ['mɔrniŋ] adj matinal, du matin || s matin m; (time between sunrise and noon) matinée f, matin; in the morning le matin; the morning after le lendemain matin; (coll) le lendemain de bombe

morn'ing coat' s jaquette f

morn'ing-glo'ry s (pl -ries) belle-de-jour f

morn'ing sick'ness s des nausées fpl

morn'ing star' s étoile f du matin

Moroccan [mə'rakən] adj marocain || s Marocain m

morocco [mə'rako] s (leather) maroquin m; Morocco le Maroc

moron ['mɔran] s arriéré m; (coll) minus mf, minus habens mf

morose [mə'ros] adj morose

morphine ['mɔrfin] s morphine f

morphology [mɔr'faledʒi] s morphologie f

morrow ['maro], ['mɔro] s—on the morrow (of) le lendemain (de)

Morse' code' [mɔrs] s alphabet m morse

morsel ['mɔrsəl] s morceau m

mortal ['mɔrtəl] adj & s mortel m

mortality [mɔr'tæliti] s mortalité f

mortar ['mɔrtər] s mortier m

mor'tar-board' s bonnet m carré; (of mason) taloche f

mortgage ['mɔrgidʒ] s hypothèque f || tr hypothéquer

mortgagee [,mɔrgi'dʒi] s créancier m hypothécaire

mortgagor ['mɔrgidʒər] s débiteur m hypothécaire

mortician [mɔr'ti/ən] s entrepreneur m de pompes funèbres

morti·fy ['mɔrti,fai] v (pret & pp -fied) tr mortifier

mortise ['mɔrtis] s mortaise f || tr mortaiser

mortuar·y ['mɔrt/u,eri] adj mortuaire || s (pl -ies) morgue f; chapelle f mortuaire

mosaic [mo'ze-ik] adj & s mosaïque f

Moscow ['maskau], ['masko] s Moscou m

Moses ['moziz], ['mozis] s Moïse m

Mos·lem ['mazləm], ['masləm] adj musulman || s (pl -lems or -lem) musulman m

mosque [mask] s mosquée f

mosqui·to [məs'kito] s (pl -toes or -tos) moustique m

mosqui'to net' s moustiquaire f

moss [mɔs], [mas] s mousse f

moss·y ['mɔsi], ['masi] adj (comp -ier; super -iest) moussu

most [most] adj super (le) plus de §91, (la) plupart de; for the most part pour la plupart || s (le) plus, (la) plupart; at the most au plus, tout au plus; most of la plupart de; to make the most of tirer le meilleur parti possible de || pron indef la plupart || adv super (le) plus §91, e.g., what I like (the) most ce que j'aime le plus; the (or his, etc.) most + adj le (or son, etc.) plus + adj || adv très, bien, fort, des plus

mostly ['mostli] adv pour la plupart, principalement

motel [mo'tel] s motel m

moth [mɔθ], [maθ] s teigne f, papillon m nocturne; (clothes moth) mite f

moth'ball' s boule f antimite, boule de naphtaline

moth-eaten ['mɔθ,itən], ['maθ,itən] adj mité

mother ['mʌðər] s mère f || tr servir de mère à; (to coddle) dorloter

moth'er coun'try s mère patrie f

Moth'er Goos'e's Nurs'ery Rhymes' spl les Contes de ma mère l'oie

moth'er-hood' s maternité f

moth'er-in-law' s (pl mothers-in-law) belle-mère f

motherless ['mʌðərlis] adj orphelin de mère

motherly ['mʌðərli] adj maternel

mother-of-pearl ['mʌðərəv'pʌrl] adj de nacre, en nacre || s nacre f

Moth'er's Day' s fête f des mères

moth'er supe'rior s mère f supérieure

moth'er tongue' s langue f maternelle

moth'er wit' s bon sens m, esprit m

moth' hole' s trou m de mite

moth'proof' adj antimite || tr rendre antimite

moth·y ['mɔθi], ['maθi] adj (comp -ier; super -iest) mité, plein de mites

motif [mo'tif] s motif m

motion ['mo/ən] s mouvement m; (gesture) geste m; (in a deliberating assembly) motion f, proposition f || intr —to motion to faire signe à

motionless ['mo/ənlis] adj immobile

mo'tion pic'ture s film m; motion pictures cinéma m

mo'tion-pic'ture *adj* cinématographique

mo'tion-pic'ture the'ater *s* cinéma *m*

motivate ['motɪ ,vet] *tr* motiver

motive ['motɪv] *adj* moteur ‖ *s* mobile *m*, motif *m*

mo'tive pow'er *s* force *f* motrice

motley ['motlɪ] *adj* bigarré; (*mixed*) mélangé

motor ['motər] *adj* & *s* moteur *m* ‖ *intr* aller en voiture

mo'tor-bike' *s* vélomoteur *m*

mo'tor-boat' *s* canot *m* automobile

mo'tor-bus' *s* autocar *m*

motorcade ['motər,ked] *s* défilé *m* de voitures

mo'tor-car' *s* automobile *f*

mo'tor-cy'cle *s* moto *f*

motorist ['motərɪst] *s* automobiliste *mf*

motorize ['motə,raɪz] *tr* motoriser

mo'tor launch' *s* chaloupe *f* à moteur

mo'tor-man *s* (*pl* -men) conducteur *m*, wattman *m*

mo'tor pool' *s* parc *m* automobile

mo'tor scoot'er *s* scooter *m*

mo'tor ship' *s* navire *m* à moteurs

mo'tor truck' *s* camion *m* automobile

mo'tor ve'hicle *s* véhicule *m* automobile

mottle ['motəl] *tr* marbrer, tacheter

mot-to ['moto] *s* (*pl* -toes or -tos) devise *f*

mound [maʊnd] *s* monticule *m*

mount [maʊnt] *s* montage *m*; (*hill, mountain*) mont *m*; (*horse for riding*) monture *f* ‖ *tr* & *intr* monter

mountain ['maʊntən] *s* montagne *f*

moun'tain climb'ing *s* alpinisme *m*

mountaineer [,maʊntə'nɪr] *s* montagnard *m*; (*climber*) alpiniste *mf*

mountainous ['maʊntənəs] *adj* montagneux

moun'tain range' *s* chaîne *f* de montagnes

mountebank ['maʊntɪ,bæŋk] *s* saltimbanque *mf*

mounting ['maʊntɪŋ] *s* montage *m*

mourn [morn] *tr* & *intr* pleurer

mourner ['mornər] *s* affligé *m*; (*woman hired as mourner*) pleureuse *f*; pénitent *m*; mourners deuil *m*

mourn'er's bench' *s* banc *m* des pénitents

mournful ['mornfəl] *adj* lugubre

mourning ['mornɪŋ] *s* deuil *m*

mouse [maʊs] *s* (*pl* mice [maɪs]) souris *f*

mouse'hole' *s* trou *m* de souris

mouser ['maʊzər] *s* souricier *m*

mouse'trap' *s* souricière *f*

moustache [məs'tæʃ], [məs'taʃ] *s* moustache *f*

mouth [maʊθ] *s* (*pl* mouths [maʊðz]) bouche *f*; (*of gun; of, e.g., wolf*) gueule *f*; (*of river*) embouchure *f*; by mouth par voie buccale; to make s.o.'s mouth water faire venir l'eau à la bouche à qn

mouthful ['maʊθ,fʊl] *s* bouchée *f*

mouth' or'gan *s* harmonica *m*

mouth'piece' *s* embouchure *f*; (*person*) porte-parole *m*

mouth'wash' *s* rince-bouche *m*, eau *f* dentifrice

movable ['muvəbəl] *adj* mobile

move [muv] *s* mouvement *m*; démarche *f*; (*from one house to another*) déménagement *m*; on the move en mouvement ‖ *tr* remuer; (*to excite the feelings of*) émouvoir; to move that (*parl*) proposer que; to move up (*a date*) avancer ‖ *intr* remuer; (*to stir*) bouger; (*said of traffic, crowd, etc.*) circuler; (*e.g., to another city*) déménager; don't move! ne bougez pas!; to move away or off s'éloigner; to move back reculer; to move in emménager

movement ['muvmənt] *s* mouvement *m*

movie ['muvɪ] *s* (*coll*) film *m*; movies (*coll*) cinéma *m*

mov'ie cam'era *s* caméra *f*

movie-goer ['muvɪ,go.ər] *s* (*coll*) amateur *m* de cinéma

mov'ie house' *s* (*coll*) cinéma *m*, salle *f* de spectacles

moving ['muvɪŋ] *adj* mouvant, en marche; (*touching*) émouvant; (*force*) moteur ‖ *s* mouvement *m*; (*from one house to another*) déménagement *m*

mov'ing pic'ture *s* film *m*; moving pictures cinéma *m*

mov'ing-pic'ture the'ater *s* cinéma *m*

mov'ing spir'it *s* âme *f*

mov'ing stair'way *s* escalier *m* mécanique, escalier roulant

mov'ing van' *s* voiture *f* de déménagement

mow [mo] *v* (*pret* mowed; *pp* mowed or mown) *tr* faucher; (*a lawn*) tondre; to mow down faucher

mower ['mo.ər] *s* faucheur *m*; (*mach*) faucheuse *f*; (*for lawns*) (*mach*) tondeuse *f*

m.p.h. ['em'pi'etʃ] *spl* (letterword) (miles per hour—six tenths of a mile equaling approximately one kilometer) km/h

Mr. ['mɪstər] *s* Monsieur *m*, M.

Mrs. ['mɪsɪz] *s* Madame *f*, Mme

much [mʌtʃ] *adj* beaucoup de, e.g., much time beaucoup de temps; bien de + *art*, e.g., much trouble bien du mal ‖ *pron indef* beaucoup; too much trop ‖ *adv* beaucoup, bien §91; however much pour autant que; how much combien; much less encore moins; too much trop; very much beaucoup

mucilage ['mjusɪlɪdʒ] *s* colle *f* de bureau; (*gummy secretion in plants*) mucilage *m*

muck [mʌk] *s* fange *f*

muck'rake' *intr* (coll) dévoiler des scandales

mucous ['mjukəs] *adj* muqueux

mu'cous lin'ing *s* (anat) muqueuse *f*

mucus ['mjukəs] *s* mucus *m*, mucosité *f*

mud [mʌd] *s* boue *f*; to sling mud at couvrir de boue

muddle ['mʌdəl] *s* confusion *f*, fouillis *m* ‖ *tr* embrouiller ‖ *intr*—to muddle through se débrouiller

mud'dle-head' s brouillon m

mud-dy ['mʌdi] adj (comp -dier; super -diest) boueux; (clothes) crotté ‖ v (pret & pp -died) tr salir; (clothes) crotter; (a liquid) troubler; (fig) embrouiller

mud'guard' s garde-boue m

mud'hole' s bourbier m

mudslinger ['mʌd,slɪŋər] s (fig) calomniateur m

muff [mʌf] s manchon m; (failure) coup m raté ‖ tr rater, louper

muffin ['mʌfɪn] s petit pain m rond, muffin m

muffle ['mʌfəl] tr (a sound) assourdir; (the face) emmitoufler

muffler ['mʌflər] s (scarf) cache-nez m; (aut) pot m d'échappement, silencieux m

mufti ['mʌfti] s vêtement m civil; in mufti en civil, en pékin, en bourgeois

mug [mʌg] s timbale f, gobelet m; (tankard) chope f; (slang) gueule f, museau m ‖ v (pret & pp mugged; ger mugging) tr (e.g., a suspect) (slang) photographier; (a victim) (slang) saisir à la gorge ‖ intr (slang) faire des grimaces

mug-gy ['mʌgi] adj (comp -gier; super -giest) lourd, étouffant

mulat-to [mju'læto], [mə'læto] s (pl -toes) mulâtre m

mulber-ry ['mʌl,beri] s (pl -ries) mûre f; (tree) mûrier m

mulct [mʌlkt] tr (a person) priver, dépouiller; (money) carotter, extorquer

mule [mjul] s (female mule; slipper) mule f; (male mule) mulet m

muleteer ['mjulə'tɪr] s muletier m

mulish ['mjulɪʃ] adj têtu, entêté

mull [mʌl] tr chauffer avec des épices; (to muddle) embrouiller ‖ intr—to mull over réfléchir sur, remâcher

mullion ['mʌljən] s meneau m

multigraph ['mʌlti,græf], ['mʌlti,graf] s (trademark) ronéo f ‖ tr ronéotyper, polycopier

multilateral [,mʌlti'lætərəl] adj multilatéral

multiple ['mʌltɪpəl] adj & s multiple m

multiplici-ty [,mʌlti'plɪsɪti] s (pl -ties) multiplicité f

multi-ply ['mʌlti,plaɪ] v (pret & pp -plied) tr multiplier ‖ intr se multiplier

multitude ['mʌlti,t(j)ud] s multitude f

mum [mʌm] adj silencieux; **mum's the word!** motus!, bouche cousue!; **to keep mum about** ne souffler mot de

mumble ['mʌmbəl] tr & intr marmotter

mummer-y ['mʌməri] s (pl -ies) momerie f

mum-my ['mʌmi] s (pl -mies) momie f; (slang) maman f

mumps [mʌmps] s oreillons mpl

munch [mʌntʃ] tr mâchonner

mundane ['mʌnden] adj mondain

municipal [mju'nɪsɪpəl] adj municipal

municipali-ty [mju,nɪsɪ'pælɪti] s (pl -ties) municipalité f

munificent [mju'nɪfɪsənt] adj munificent

munition [mju'nɪʃən] s munition f ‖ tr approvisionner de munitions

muni'tion dump' s dépôt m de munitions

mural ['mjurəl] adj mural ‖ s peinture f murale

murder ['mʌrdər] s assassinat m, meurtre m ‖ tr assassiner; (a language, proper names, etc.) (coll) estropier, écorcher

murderer ['mʌrdərər] s meurtrier m, assassin m

murderess ['mʌrdərɪs] s meurtrière f

murderous ['mʌrdərəs] adj meurtrier

murk-y ['mʌrki] adj (comp -ier; super -iest) ténébreux, nébuleux

murmur ['mʌrmər] s murmure m ‖ tr & intr murmurer

muscle ['mʌsəl] s muscle m

muscular ['mʌskjələr] adj musclé, musculeux; (system, tissue, etc.) musculaire

muse [mjuz] s muse f; **the Muses** les Muses ‖ intr méditer; **to muse on** méditer

museum [mju'zi·əm] s musée m

muse'um piece' s pièce f de musée

mush [mʌʃ] s bouillie f; (coll) sentimentalité f de guimauve

mush'room' s champignon m ‖ intr pousser comme un champignon

mush'room cloud' s champignon m atomique

mush-y ['mʌʃi] adj (comp -ier; super -iest) mou; (ground) détrempé; (coll) à la guimauve, sentimental

music ['mjuzɪk] s musique f; **to face the music** (coll) affronter les opposants; **to set to music** mettre en musique

musical ['mjuzɪkəl] adj musical

mu'sical com'edy s comédie f musicale

musicale [,mjuzi'kæl] s soirée f musicale; matinée f musicale

mu'sic box' s boîte f à musique

mu'sic cab'inet s casier m à musique

mu'sic hall' s salle f de musique; (Brit) music-hall m

musician [mju'zɪʃən] s musicien m

mu'sic lov'er s mélomane mf

musicology [,mjuzi'kaləʤi] s musicologie f

mu'sic rack' or **mu'sic stand'** s pupitre m à musique

musk [mʌsk] s musc m

musk' deer' s porte-musc m

musketeer [,mʌski'tɪr] s mousquetaire m

musk'mel'on s melon m; cantaloup m

musk'rat' s rat m musqué, ondatra m

Mus-lim ['mʌzlɪm] adj musulman ‖ s (pl -lims or -lim) musulman m

muslin ['mʌzlɪn] s mousseline f

muss [mʌs] tr (the hair) ébouriffer; (the clothing) froisser

Mussulman ['mʌsəlmən] adj & s musulman m

muss-y ['mʌsi] adj (comp -ier; super -iest) en désordre, froissé

must [mʌst] s moût m; nécessité f absolue ‖ aux used to express 1) necessity, e.g., **he must go away** il doit s'en aller; 2) conjecture, e.g., **he must be ill** il doit être malade; **he must have been ill** il a dû être malade

mustache [məs'tæʃ], [məs'taʃ], ['mʌs-tæʃ] *s* moustache *f*

mustard ['mʌstərd] *s* moutarde *f*

mus'tard plas'ter *s* sinapisme *m*

muster ['mʌstər] *s* rassemblement *m*; (mil) revue *f*; **to pass muster** être porté à l'appel; (fig) être acceptable ‖ *tr* rassembler; **to muster in** enrôler; **to muster out** démobiliser; **to muster up courage** prendre son courage à deux mains

mus'ter roll' *s* feuille *f* d'appel

mus·ty ['mʌsti] *adj* (*comp* **-tier;** *super* **-tiest**) (*moldy*) moisi; (*stale*) renfermé; (*antiquated*) désuet

mutation [mju'teʃən] *s* mutation *f*

mute [mjut] *adj* muet ‖ *s* muet *m*; (mus) sourdine *f* ‖ *tr* amortir; (mus) mettre une sourdine à

mutilate ['mjutɪˌlet] *tr* mutiler

mutineer [ˌmjutɪ'nɪr] *s* mutin *m*

mutinous ['mjutɪnəs] *adj* mutiné

muti·ny ['mjutɪni] *s* (*pl* **-nies**) mutinerie *f* ‖ *v* (*pret* & *pp* **-nied**) *intr* se mutiner

mutt [mʌt] *s* (*dog*) (slang) cabot *m*; (*person*) (slang) nigaud *m*

mutter ['mʌtər] *tr* & *intr* marmonner

mutton ['mʌtən] *s* mouton *m*

mut'ton·chop' *s* côtelette *f* de mouton; **muttonchops** favoris *mpl* en côtelette

mutual ['mjut/ʊ·əl] *adj* mutuel

mu'tual aid' *s* entraide *f*

mu'tual fund' *s* mutuelle *f*

muzzle ['mʌzəl] *s* (*projecting part of head of animal*) museau *m*; (*device to keep animal from biting*) muselière *f*; (*of firearm*) gueule *f* ‖ *tr* museler

my [maɪ] *adj* poss mon §88

myriad ['mɪrɪ·əd] *adj* innombrable ‖ *s* myriade *f*

myrrh [mɪr] *s* myrrhe *f*

myrtle ['mʌrtəl] *s* myrte *m*; (*periwinkle*) pervenche *f*

my·self' *pron pers* moi §85; moi-même §86; me §87

mysterious [mɪs'tɪrɪ·əs] *adj* mystérieux

myster·y ['mɪstəri] *s* (*pl* **-ies**) mystère *m*

mystic ['mɪstɪk] *adj* & *s* mystique *mf*

mystical ['mɪstɪkəl] *adj* mystique

mysticism ['mɪstɪˌsɪzəm] *s* mysticisme *m*

mystification [ˌmɪstɪfɪ'keʃən] *s* mystification *f*

mysti·fy ['mɪstɪˌfaɪ] *v* (*pret* & *pp* **-fied**) *tr* mystifier

myth [mɪθ] *s* mythe *m*

mythical ['mɪθɪkəl] *adj* mythique

mythological [ˌmɪθə'lɑdʒɪkəl] *adj* mythologique

mytholo·gy [mɪ'θɑlədʒi] *s* (*pl* **-gies**) mythologie *f*

N

N, n [ɛn] *s* XIVe lettre de l'alphabet

nab [næb] *v* (*pret* & *pp* **nabbed;** *ger* **nabbing**) *tr* (slang) happer; (*to arrest*) (slang) pincer, harponner

nag [næg] *s* bidet *m* ‖ *v* (*pret* & *pp* **nagged;** *ger* **nagging**) *tr* & *intr* gronder constamment; **to nag at** gronder constamment

nail [nel] *s* (*of finger*) ongle *m*; (*to be hammered*) clou *m*; **to bite one's nails** se ronger les ongles; **to hit the nail on the head** mettre le doigt dessus, frapper juste ‖ *tr* clouer; (*a lie*) mettre à découvert; (coll) saisir, attraper

nail'brush' *s* brosse *f* à ongles

nail' clip'pers *spl* coupe-ongles *m*

nail' file' *s* lime *f* à ongles

nail' pol'ish *s* vernis *m* à ongles

nail' scis'sors *s* & *spl* ciseaux *mpl* à ongles

nail' set' *s* chasse-clou *m*

naïve [nɑ'iv] *adj* naïf

naked ['nekɪd] *adj* nu; **to strip naked** se mettre tout nu; mettre tout nu; **with the naked eye** à l'œil nu

namby-pamby ['næmbi'pæmbi] *adj* minaudier

name [nem] *s* nom *m*; (*reputation*) renom *m*; **by name** de nom; **by the** **name of** sous le nom de; **to call names** traiter de tous les noms; **what is your name?** comment vous appelez-vous? ‖ *tr* nommer; (*a price*) fixer, indiquer

name' day' *s* fête *f*

nameless ['nemlɪs] *adj* sans nom, anonyme; (*horrid*) odieux

namely ['nemli] *adv* à savoir, nommément

name'sake' *s* homonyme *m*

nan·ny ['næni] *s* (*pl* **-nies**) nounou *f*

nan'ny goat' *s* (coll) chèvre *f*, bique *f*

nap [næp] *s* (*short sleep*) somme *m*, sieste *f*; (*of cloth*) poil *m*, duvet *m*; **to take a nap** faire un petit somme ‖ *v* (*pret* & *pp* **napped;** *ger* **napping**) *intr* faire un somme; manquer de vigilance; **to catch napping** prendre au dépourvu

napalm ['nepɑm] *s* (mil) napalm *m*

nape [nep] *s* nuque *f*

naphtha ['næfθə] *s* naphte *m*

napkin ['næpkɪn] *s* serviette *f*

nap'kin ring' *s* rond *m* de serviette

Napoleonic [nəˌpoʊlɪ'ɑnɪk] *adj* napoléonien

narcissus [nɑr'sɪsəs] *s* narcisse *m*; **Narcissus** Narcisse

narcotic [nɑr'kɑtɪk] adj & s narcotique m

narrate [næ'ret] tr narrer, raconter

narration [næ're∫ən] s narration f

narrative ['nærətɪv] adj narratif ǁ s narration f, récit m

narrator [næ'retər] s narrateur m

narrow ['næro] adj étroit; (e.g., margin of votes) faible ǁ **narrows** spl détroit m, goulet m ǁ tr rétrécir ǁ intr se rétrécir

nar'row escape' s—to have a narrow escape l'échapper belle

nar'row gauge' s voie f étroite

nar'row-mind'ed adj à l'esprit étroit, intolérant

nasal ['nezəl] adj nasal; (sound, voice) nasillard ǁ s (phonet) nasale f

nasalize ['nezə,laɪz] tr & intr nasaliser

nasturtium [nə'stʌr∫əm] s capucine f

nas•ty ['næsti], ['nɑsti] adj (comp -tier; super -tiest) mauvais, sale, dégoûtant; (color) féroce, farouche; désagréable

nation ['ne∫ən] s nation f

national ['næ∫ənəl] adj & s national m

na'tional an'them s hymne m national

nationalism ['næ∫ənə,lɪzəm] s nationalisme m

national•ty [,næ∫ən'ælɪti] s (pl -ties) nationalité f

nationalize ['næ∫ənə,laɪz] tr nationaliser, étatiser

na'tion-wide' adj de toute la nation

native ['netɪv] adj natif (land, language) natal; **native of** originaire de ǁ s natif m; (original inhabitant) naturel m, indigène mf, autochtone mf

na'tive land' s pays m natal

nativi•ty [nə'tɪvɪti] s (pl -ties) naissance f; (astrol) nativité f; **Nativity** Nativité f

NATO ['neto] s (acronym) (North Atlantic Treaty Organization) l'O.T.A.N. f, l'OTAN f

nat•ty ['næti] adj (comp -tier; super -tiest) coquet, élégant, soigné

natural ['næt∫ərəl] adj naturel ǁ s (mus) bécarre m; (mus) touche f blanche; **a natural** (coll) juste ce qu'il faut

naturalism ['næt∫ərə,lɪzəm] s naturalisme m

naturalist ['næt∫ərəlɪst] s naturaliste mf

naturalization [,næt∫ərəlɪ'ze∫ən] s naturalisation f

naturaliza'tion pa'pers spl déclaration f de naturalisation

naturalize ['næt∫ərə,laɪz] tr naturaliser

nature ['net∫ər] s nature f

naught [nɔt] s zéro m; rien m; **to come to naught** n'aboutir à rien

naugh•ty ['nɔti] adj (comp -tier; super -tiest) méchant, vilain; (story) risqué

nausea ['nɔ/ɪ•ə], ['nɔsɪ•ə] s nausée f

nauseate ['nɔ/ɪ,et], ['nɔsɪ,et] tr donner la nausée à ǁ intr avoir des nausées

nauseating ['nɔ/ɪ,etɪŋ], ['nɔsɪ,etɪŋ] adj nauséabond

nauseous ['nɔ/ɪ•əs], ['nɔsɪ•əs] adj nauséeux

nautical ['nɔtɪkəl] adj nautique; naval, marin

naval ['nevəl] adj naval

na'val acad'emy s école f navale

na'val of'ficer s officier m de marine

na'val sta'tion s station f navale

nave [nev] s (of a church) nef f, vaisseau m; (of a wheel) moyeu m

navel ['nevəl] s nombril m

na'vel or'ange s orange f navel

navigable ['nævɪgəbəl] adj (river) navigable; (aircraft) dirigeable; (ship) bon marcheur

navigate ['nævɪ,get] tr gouverner, conduire; (the sea) naviguer sur ǁ intr naviguer

navigation [,nævɪ'ge∫ən] s navigation f

navigator ['nævɪ,getər] s navigateur m

na•vy ['nevi] adj bleu marine ǁ s (pl -vies) marine f militaire, marine de guerre; (color) bleu m marine

na'vy bean' s haricot m blanc

na'vy blue' s bleu m marine

na'vy yard' s chantier m naval

nay [ne] adv non; voire, même ǁ s non m; (parl) vote m négatif

Nazarene [,næzə'rin] adj nazaréen ǁ s (person) Nazaréen m

Nazi ['nɑtsi], ['nætsi] adj & s nazi m

n.d. abbr (no date) s.d.

Ne'apol'itan ice' cream' [,ni•ə'pɑlɪtən] s glace f panachée

neap' tide' [nip] s morte-eau f

near [nɪr] adj proche, prochain; d'imitation; **near at hand** tout près; **near side** (of horse) côté m de montoir ǁ adv près, de près; presque; **to come near** s'approcher ǁ prep près de; auprès de ǁ tr s'approcher de

near'by' adj proche ǁ adv tout près

Near' East' s—the Near East le Proche Orient

nearly ['nɪrli] adv presque, de près; faillir, manquer de, e.g., **I nearly fell** j'ai failli tomber

near'-sight'ed adj myope

near'-sight'edness s myopie f

neat [nit] adj soigné, rangé; concis; (clever) adroit; (liquor) nature; (slang) chouette

neat's'-foot oil' s huile f de pied de bœuf

nebu•la ['nebjələ] s (pl -lae [,li] or -las) nébuleuse f

nebulous ['nebjələs] adj nébuleux

necessarily [,nesɪ'serɪli] adv nécessairement, forcément

necessary ['nesɪ,seri] adj nécessaire

necessitate [nɪ'sesɪ,tet] tr nécessiter, exiger

necessi•ty [nɪ'sesɪti] s (pl -ties) nécessité f

neck [nek] s cou m; (of bottle) col m, goulot m; (of land) cap m; (of tooth) collet m; (of violin) manche m, collet; (strait) étroit m; **neck and neck** manche à manche; **to break one's neck** (coll) se rompre le cou; **to stick one's neck out** prêter le flanc; **to win**

by a **neck** gagner par une encolure ‖ *intr* (slang) se peloter
neck′band′ *s* tour *m* de cou
neckerchief [′nekərt∫if] *s* foulard *m*
necking [′nekiŋ] *s* (slang) pelotage *m*
necklace [′neklis] *s* collier *m*
neck′piece′ *s* col *m* de fourrure
neck′tie′ *s* cravate *f*
neck′tie pin′ *s* épingle *f* de cravate
necrolo·gy [ne′kralədʒi] *s* (*pl* -**gies**) nécrologie *f*
nectar [′nektər] *s* nectar *m*
nectarine [ˌnektə′rin] *s* brugnon *m*
nee [ne] *adj* née
need [nid] *s* besoin *m*; (*want, poverty*) besoin, indigence *f*, nécessité *f*; **if need be** au besoin, s'il le faut ‖ *tr* avoir besoin de, falloir, e.g., **he needs money** il a besoin d'argent, il lui faut de l'argent; demander, e.g., **the motor needs oil** le moteur demande de l'huile ‖ *aux* devoir
needful [′nidfəl] *adj* nécessaire
needle [′nidəl] *s* aiguille *f* ‖ *tr* (*to prod*) aiguillonner; (coll) taquiner; (*a drink*) (coll) corser
nee′dle-point′ *s* broderie *f* sur canevas; (*lace*) dentelle *f* à l'aiguille
needless [′nidlis] *adj* inutile
nee′dle-work′ *s* ouvrage *m* à l'aiguille
need·y [′nidi] *adj* (*comp* -**ier**; *super* -**iest**) nécessiteux ‖ *s*—**the needy** les nécessiteux
ne′er-do-well [′nerdu‚wel] *adj* propre à rien ‖ *s* vaurien *m*
nefarious [ni′feri·əs] *adj* scélérat
negate [′neget], [ni′get] *tr* invalider; nier
negation [ni′ge∫ən] *s* négation *f*
negative [′negətiv] *adj* négatif ‖ *s* (*opinion*) négative *f*; (gram) négation *f*; (phot) négatif *m*
neglect [ni′glekt] *s* négligence *f* ‖ *tr* négliger; **to neglect to** négliger de
négligée or **negligee** [ˌnegli′ʒe] *s* négligé *m*, robe *f* de chambre
negligence [′neglidʒəns] *s* négligence *f*
negligent [′neglidʒənt] *adj* négligent
negligible [′neglidʒibəl] *adj* négligeable
negotiable [ni′go∫i·əbəl] *adj* négociable
negotiate [ni′go∫i·et] *tr* & *intr* négocier
negotiation [ni‚go∫i′e∫ən] *s* négociation *f*
negotiator [ni′go∫i‚etər] *s* négociateur *m*
Ne·gro [′nigro] *adj* noir, nègre ‖ *s* (*pl* -**groes**) noir *m*, nègre *m*
neigh [ne] *s* hennissement *m* ‖ *intr* hennir
neighbor [′nebər] *adj* voisin ‖ *s* voisin *m*; (fig) prochain *m* ‖ *tr* avoisiner ‖ *intr* être voisin
neigh′bor·hood′ *s* voisinage *m*; **in the neighborhood of** aux environs de; (*approximately, about*) (coll) environ
neighborliness [′nebərlinis] *s* bon voisinage *m*
neighborly [′nebərli] *adj* bon voisin
neither [′niðər], [′naiðər] *adj indef* ni, e.g., **neither one of us** ni l'un ni l'autre ‖ *pron indef* ni, e.g., **neither ni l'un ni l'autre ‖ *conj* ni; ni . . . non plus, e.g., **neither do I** ni moi non plus; **neither . . . nor** ni . . . ni
neme·sis [′nemisis] *s* (*pl* -**ses** [ˌsiz]) juste châtiment *m*; **Nemesis** Némésis *f*
neologism [ni′alə‚dʒizəm] *s* néologisme *m*
neon [′ni·an] *s* néon *m*
ne′on lamp′ *s* lampe *f* au néon
ne′on sign′ *s* réclame *f* lumineuse
neophyte [′ni·ə‚fait] *s* néophyte *mf*
nephew [′nefju], [′nevju] *s* neveu *m*
neptunium [nep′t(j)uni·əm] *s* neptunium *m*
Nero [′niro] *s* Néron *m*
nerve [nʌrv] *adj* nerveux ‖ *s* nerf *m*; audace *f*; **to get on s.o.'s nerves** porter sur les nerfs à qn; **to have a lot of nerve** avoir du toupet; **nerves of steel** avoir du nerf; **to lose one's nerve** avoir le trac
nerve′ cen′ter *s* nœud *m* vital; (anat) centre *m* nerveux
nerve′-rack′ing *adj* énervant, agaçant
nervous [′nʌrvəs] *adj* nerveux
ner′vous break′down *s* épuisement *m* nerveux, dépression *f* nerveuse
nerv·y [′nʌrvi] *adj* (*comp* -**ier**; *super* -**iest**) nerveux, musclé; (coll) audacieux, culotté; (slang) dévergondé
nest [nest] *s* nid *m*; (*set of things fitting together*) jeu *m* ‖ *intr* se nicher
nest′ egg′ *s* nichet *m*; (fig) boursicot *m*, bas *m* de laine
nestle [′nesəl] *intr* se blottir, se nicher
nest′ of ta′bles *s* table *f* gigogne
net [net] *adj* net ‖ *s* filet *m*; (*for fishing; for catching birds*) nappe *f*; (tex) tulle *m* ‖ *v* (*pret* & *pp* **netted**; *ger* **netting**) *tr* (*a profit*) réaliser
Netherlander [′neðər‚lændər], [′neðərləndər] *s* Néerlandais *m*
Netherlands [′neðərləndz] *s*—**The Netherlands** les Pays-Bas *mpl*
nettle [′netəl] *s* ortie *f* ‖ *tr* piquer au vif
net′work′ *s* réseau *m*; (rad, telv) chaîne *f*, réseau
neuralgia [n(j)u′rældʒə] *s* névralgie *f*
neuro·sis [n(j)u′rosis] *s* (*pl* -**ses** [siz]) névrose *f*
neurotic [n(j)u′ratik] *adj* & *s* névrosé *m*
neuter [′n(j)utər] *adj* & *s* neutre *m*
neutral [′n(j)utrəl] *adj* neutre ‖ *s* neutre *m*; (gear) point *m* mort
neutrality [n(j)u′træliti] *s* neutralité *f*
neutralize [′n(j)utrə‚laiz] *tr* neutraliser
neutron [′n(j)utran] *s* neutron *m*
neu′tron bomb′ *s* bombe *f* à neutrons
never [′nevər] *adv* jamais §90B; ne . . . jamais §90, e.g., **he never talks** il ne parle jamais
nev′er-more′ *adv* ne . . . plus jamais ‖ *interj* jamais plus!, plus jamais!
nev′er-the-less′ *adv* néanmoins
new [n(j)u] *adj* (*unused*) neuf; (*other, additional, different*) nouveau (before noun); (*recent*) nouveau (after noun); (*inexperienced*) novice; (*wine*)

jeune; **what's new?** quoi de nouveau?, quoi de neuf?

new′born′ adj nouveau-né

new′born child′ s nouveau-né m

New′cas′tle s—**to carry coals to Newcastle** porter de l'eau à la rivière

newcomer ['n(j)u‚kʌmər] s nouveau venu m

New′ Cov′enant s (Bib) nouvelle alliance f

newel ['n(j)u‚əl] s (of winding stairs) noyau m; (post at end of stair rail) pilastre m

New′ Eng′land s Nouvelle-Angleterre f; la Nouvelle-Angleterre

newfangled ['n(j)u‚fæŋgəld] adj à la dernière mode, du dernier cri

Newfoundland ['n(j)ufənd‚lænd] s Terre-Neuve f; **in** or **to Newfoundland** à Terre-Neuve || [n(j)u′faʊndlənd] s (dog) terre-neuve m

newly ['n(j)uli] adv nouvellement

new′ly-wed′ s nouveau marié m

new′ moon′ s nouvelle lune f

newness ['n(j)unɪs] s nouveauté f

New′ Or′leans ['ɔrli‚ənz] s la Nouvelle-Orléans

news [n(j)uz] s nouvelles fpl; **a news item** un fait-divers; **a piece of news** une nouvelle

news′ a′gency s agence f d'information, agence de presse; agence à journaux

news′beat′ s exclusivité f

news′boy′ s vendeur m de journaux

news′ bul′letin s bulletin m d'actualités

news′cast′ s journal m parlé; journal télévisé

news′cast′er s reporter m de la radio

news′ con′ference s conférence f de presse

news′ cov′erage s reportage m

news′deal′er s marchand m de journaux

news′ ed′itor s rédacteur m publicitaire

news′let′ter s circulaire f publicitaire

news′man′ s (pl -men′) journaliste m; (dealer) marchand m de journaux

New′ South′ Wales′ s la Nouvelle-Galles du Sud

news′pa′per adj journalistique || s journal m

news′paper clip′ping s coupure f de presse

news′paper-man′ s (pl -men′) journaliste m; (dealer) marchand m de journaux

news′paper rack′ s casier m à journaux

news′paper se′rial s feuilleton m

news′print′ s papier m journal

news′reel′ s actualités fpl

news′room′ s salle f de rédaction

news′stand′ s kiosque m

news′week′ly s (pl -lies) hebdomadaire m

news′wor′thy adj d'actualité

New′ Tes′tament s Nouveau Testament m

New′ Year′s′ Day′ s le jour de l'an

New′ Year′s′ Eve′ s la Saint-Sylvestre

New′ Year′s′ greet′ings spl souhaits mpl de nouvel An

New′ Year′s′ resolu′tion s résolution f de nouvel An

New′ York′ [jɔrk] adj newyorkais || s New York m

New′ York′er ['jɔrkər] s newyorkais m

next [nɛkst] adj (in time) prochain, suivant; (in place) voisin; (first in the period which follows) prochain (before noun), e.g., **the next time** la prochaine fois; (following the present time) prochain (after noun), e.g., **next week** la semaine prochaine; **next to** à côté de || adv après, ensuite; la prochaine fois; **who comes next?** à qui le tour? || interj au premier de ces messieurs!, au suivant!

next′-door′ adj d'à côté, voisin || **next′-door′** adv à côté; **next-door to** à côté de; à côté de chez

next′ of kin′ s (pl **next of kin**) proche parent m

Niag′ara Falls′ [naɪ'ægərə] s la Cataracte du Niagara

nib [nɪb] s pointe f; (of pen) bec m

nibble ['nɪbəl] s grignotement m; (on fish line) touche f; (fig) morceau m || tr & intr grignoter

nice [naɪs] adj agréable, gentil, aimable; (distinction) subtil, fin; (weather) beau; **nice and . . .** (coll) très; **not nice** (coll) vilain

nicely ['naɪsli] adv bien; avec délicatesse

nice·ty ['naɪsəti] s (pl -ties) précision f; (subtlety) finesse f

niche [nɪtʃ] s niche f; (job, position) place f, poste m

nick [nɪk] s (e.g., on china) brèche f; **in the nick of time** à point nommé, à pic || tr ébrécher; (for money, favors) (slang) cramponner

nickel ['nɪkəl] s (metal) nickel m; (coin) pièce f de cinq sous || tr nickeler

nick′el plate′ s nickelure f

nick′el-plate′ tr nickeler

nicknack ['nɪk‚næk] s colifichet m

nick′name′ s sobriquet m, surnom m || tr donner un sobriquet à, surnommer

nicotine ['nɪkə‚tin] s nicotine f

niece [nis] s nièce f

nif·ty ['nɪfti] adj (comp -tier; super -tiest) (slang) coquet, pimpant

niggard ['nɪgərd] adj & s avare mf

night [naɪt] s nuit f; (evening) soir m; **last night** (night that has just passed) cette nuit; (last evening) hier soir; **night before last** avant-hier soir

night′cap′ s bonnet m de nuit, casque m à mèche; (drink) posset m

night′ club′ s boîte f de nuit

night′fall′ s tombée f de la nuit

night′gown′ s chemise f de nuit

night′hawk′ s noctambule mf; (orn) engoulevent m

nightingale ['naɪtən‚gel] s rossignol m

night′latch′ s serrure f à ressort

night′ light′ s veilleuse f

night′long′ adj de toute la nuit || adv pendant toute la nuit

nightly ['naɪtli] adj nocturne; de chaque nuit || *adv* nocturnement; chaque nuit

night'mare' *s* cauchemar *m*

nightmarish ['naɪt,merɪʃ] *adj* (coll) cauchemardeux

night' owl' *s* (coll) noctambule *mf*

night' school' *s* cours *mpl* du soir

night'shade' *s* morelle *f*

night' shift' *s* équipe *f* de nuit

night' watch'man *s* (*pl* -men) veilleur *m* de nuit

nihilism ['naɪ·ɪ,lɪzəm] *s* nihilisme *m*

nil [nɪl] *s* rien *m*

Nile [naɪl] *s* Nil *m*

nimble ['nɪmbəl] *adj* agile, leste; (*mind*) délié

nim·bus ['nɪmbəs] *s* (*pl* -buses or -bi [baɪ]) nimbe *m*, auréole *f*; (meteo) nimbus *m*

nincompoop ['nɪnkəm,pup] *s* nigaud *m*

nine [naɪn] *adj & pron* neuf || *s* neuf *m*; **nine o'clock** neuf heures

nine'pins' *s* quilles *fpl*

nineteen ['naɪn'tin] *adj, pron, & s* dix-neuf *m*

nineteenth ['naɪn'tinθ] *adj & pron* dix-neuvième (*masc, fem*); **the Nineteenth** dix-neuf, e.g., **John the Nineteenth** Jean dix-neuf || *s* dix-neuvième *m*; **the nineteenth** (*in dates*) le dix-neuf

ninetieth ['naɪntɪ·ɪθ] *adj & pron* quatre-vingt-dixième (*masc, fem*) || *s* quatre-vingt-dixième *m*

nine·ty ['naɪntɪ] *adj & pron* quatre-vingt-dix || *s* (*pl* -ties) quatre-vingt-dix *m*

nine'ty-first' *adj & pron* quatre-vingt-onzième (*masc, fem*) || *s* quatre-vingt-onzième *m*

nine'ty-one' *adj, pron, & s* quatre-vingt-onze *m*

ninth [naɪnθ] *adj & pron* neuvième (*masc, fem*); **the Ninth** neuf, e.g., **John the Ninth** Jean neuf || *s* neuvième *m*; **the ninth** (*in dates*) le neuf

nip [nɪp] *s* pincement *m*, petite morsure *f*; (*of cold weather*) morsure; (*of liquor*) goutte *f* || *v* (*pret & pp* **nipped**; *ger* **nipping**) *tr* pincer, donner une petite morsure à; **to nip in the bud** tuer dans l'œuf || *intr* (coll) biberonner, picoler

nipple ['nɪpəl] *s* mamelon *m*; (*of nursing bottle*) tétine *f*; (mach) raccord *m*

nip·py ['nɪpɪ] *adj* (*comp* -pier; *super* -piest) piquant; (*cold*) vif; (Brit) leste, rapide

nirvana [nɪr'vɑnə] *s* le nirvâna

nit [nɪt] *s* pou *m*; (*egg*) lente *f*

niter ['naɪtər] *s* nitrate *m* de potasse; nitrate de soude

nitrate ['naɪtret] *s* azotate *m*, nitrate *m*; (*fertilizer*) engrais *m* nitraté || *tr* nitrater

nitric ['naɪtrɪk] *adj* azotique, nitrique

nitrogen ['naɪtrədʒən] *s* azote *m*

nitroglycerin [,naɪtrə'glɪsərɪn] *s* nitroglycérine *f*

nitrous ['naɪtrəs] *adj* azoteux

ni'trous ox'ide *s* oxyde *m* azoteux, protoxyde *m* d'azote

nit'wit' *s* (coll) imbécile *mf*

no [no] *adj indef* aucun, nul, pas de §90B; **no admittance** entrée *f* interdite; **no answer** pas de réponse; **no comment!** rien à dire!; **no go** or **no soap** (coll) pas mèche *f*; **no kidding** (coll) blague *f* à part; **no littering** défense *f* de déposer les ordures; **no loitering** vagabondage *m* interdit; **no parking** stationnement *m* interdit; **no place** nulle part; **no place else** nulle part ailleurs; **no shooting** chasse *f* réservée; **no smoking** défense de fumer; **no thoroughfare** circulation *f* interdite, passage *m* interdit; **no use** inutile; **with no sans** || *s* non *m* || *adv* non; **no good** vil; **no longer** ne . . . plus §90, e.g., **he no longer works here** il ne travaille plus ici; **no more** ne . . . plus §90, e.g., **he has no more** il n'en a plus; **no more** . . . (or *comp* in -er) **than** ne . . . pas plus . . . que, e.g., **she is no happier than he** elle n'est pas plus heureuse que lui

No'ah's Ark' ['no·əz] *s* l'arche *f* de Noé

nobili·ty [no'bɪlɪtɪ] *s* (*pl* -ties) noblesse *f*

noble ['nobəl] *adj & s* noble *mf*

no'ble·man *s* (*pl* -men) noble *m*

nobleness ['nobəlnɪs] *s* noblesse *f*

nobod·y ['no,bɑdɪ], ['nobədɪ] *s* (*pl* -ies) nullité *f* || *pron indef* personne; **ne** . . . **personne** §90, e.g., **I see nobody there** je n'y vois personne; personne ne, nul ne §90, e.g., **nobody knows it** personne ne le sait, nul ne le sait

nocturnal [nɑk'tʌrnəl] *adj* nocturne

nocturne ['nɑktʌrn] *s* nocturne *m*

nod [nɑd] *s* signe *m* de tête; (*greeting*) inclination *f* de tête || *v* (*pret & pp* **nodded**; *ger* **nodding**) *tr* (*the head*) incliner; **to nod assent** faire un signe d'assentiment || *intr* (*with sleep*) dodeliner de la tête; (*to greet*) incliner la tête

node [nod] *s* nœud *m*

noise [nɔɪz] *s* bruit *m* || *tr* (*a rumor*) ébruiter

noiseless ['nɔɪzlɪs] *adj* silencieux

nois·y ['nɔɪzɪ] *adj* (*comp* -ier; *super* -iest) bruyant

nomad ['nomæd] *adj & s* nomade *mf*

no' man's' land' *s* région *f* désolée; (mil) zone *f* neutre

nominal ['nɑmɪnəl] *adj* nominal

nominate ['nɑmɪ,net] *tr* désigner; (*to appoint*) nommer

nomination [,nɑmɪ'neʃən] *s* désignation *f*, investiture *f*

nominative ['nɑmɪnətɪv] *adj & s* nominatif *m*

nominee [,nɑmɪ'ni] *s* désigné *m*, candidat *m*

nonbelligerent [,nɑnbə'lɪdʒərənt] *adj & s* non-belligérant *m*

nonbreakable [nɑn'brekəbəl] *adj* incassable

nonchalant ['nɑnʃələnt], (,nɑnʃə'lɑnt) adj nonchalant

noncom ['nɑn,kʌm] s (coll) sous-off m

noncombatant [nɑn'kɑmbətənt] adj & s non-combattant m

noncommissioned [,nɑnkə'mɪʃənd] adj non breveté

non'commis'sioned of'ficer s sous-officier m

noncommittal [,nɑnkə'mɪtəl] adj évasif, réticent

nonconductor [,nɑnkən'dʌktər] s non-conducteur m, mauvais conducteur m

nonconformist [,nɑnkən'fɔrmɪst] adj & s non-conformiste mf

nondenominational [,nɑndɪ,nɑmɪ'neʃənəl] adj indépendant, qui ne fait partie d'aucune secte religieuse; (school) laïque

nondescript ['nɑndɪ,skrɪpt] adj indéfinissable, inclassable

none [nʌn] pron indef aucun §90B; (nobody) personne, nul §90B; ne . . . aucun, ne . . . nul §90; n'en ai pas, e.g., I have none je n'en ai pas; (as a response on the blank of an official form) néant || adv—to be none the wiser ne pas en être plus sage

nonentity [nɑn'entɪti] s (pl -ties) nullité f

none'such' s nonpareil m; (apple) nonpareille f; (bot) lupuline f, minette f

nonfiction [nɑn'fɪkʃən] s littérature f autre que le roman

nonfulfillment [,nɑnfʊl'fɪlmənt] s inaccomplissement m

nonintervention [,nɑnɪntər'venʃən] s non-intervention f

nonmetal ['nɑn,metəl] s métalloïde m

nonpartisan [nɑn'pɑrtɪzən] adj neutre, indépendant

nonpayment [nɑn'pemənt] s non-paiement m

non-plus ['nɑnplʌs], [nɑn'plʌs] s perplexité f || v (pret & pp -plused or -plussed) ger -plusing or -plussing) tr déconcerter, dérouter

nonresident [nɑn'rezɪdənt] adj & s non-résident m

nonresidential [nɑn,rezɪ'denʃəl] adj commercial

nonreturnable [,nɑnrɪ'tʌrnəbəl] adj (bottle) perdu

nonscientific [nɑn,saɪ-ən'tɪfɪk] adj anti-scientifique

nonsectarian [,nɑnsək'terɪ-ən] adj non-sectaire; qui ne fait partie d'aucune secte religieuse; (education) laïque

nonsense ['nɑnsens] s bêtise f, non-sens m

nonskid ['nɑn'skɪd] adj antidérapant

nonstop ['nɑn'stɑp] adj & adv sans arrêt; sans escale

nonviolence [nɑn'vaɪ-ələns] s non-violence f

noodle ['nudəl] s nouille f; (fool) (slang) niais m; (head) (slang) tronche f

nook [nʊk] s coin m, recoin m

noon [nun] s midi m

no' one' or no'-one' pron indef personne §90B; ne . . personne §90, e.g., no one there je n'y vois personne; personne ne, nul ne §90B, e.g., no one knows it personne ne le sait, nul ne le sait; no one else personne d'autre

noon'time' s midi m

noose [nus] s nœud m coulant; (for hanging) corde f, hart f

nor [nɔr] conj ni

norm [nɔrm] s norme f

normal ['nɔrməl] adj normal

Norman ['nɔrmən] adj normand || s (dialect) normand m; (person) Normand m

Normandy ['nɔrməndi] s Normandie f; la Normandie

Norse [nɔrs] adj & s norrois m

Norse'man s (pl -men) Norrois m

north [nɔrθ] adj & s nord m || adv au nord, vers le nord

North' Af'rican adj nord-africain || s Nord-Africain m

north'east' adj & s nord-est m

north'east'er s vent m du nord-est

northern ['nɔrðərn] adj septentrional, du nord

North' Kore'a s Corée f du Nord; la Corée du Nord

North' Kore'an adj nord-coréen || s (person) Nord-Coréen m

North' Pole' s pôle m Nord

northward ['nɔrθwərd] adv vers le nord

north'west' adj & s nord-ouest m

north' wind' s bise f

Norway ['nɔrwe] s Norvège f; la Norvège

Norwegian [nɔr'widʒən] adj norvégien || s (language) norvégien m; (person) Norvégien m

nose [noz] s nez m; (of certain animals) museau m; to blow one's nose se moucher; to have a nose for avoir le flair de; to keep one's nose to the grindstone travailler sans relâche, buriner; to lead by the nose mener par le bout du nez; to look down one's nose at faire un nez à; to thumb one's nose at faire un pied de nez à; to turn up one's nose at faire la nique à; under the nose of à la barbe de || tr flairer, sentir; to nose out flairer, dépister || intr—to nose about fouiner; to nose over capoter

nose' bag' s musette f

nose'bleed' s saignement m de nez

nose' cone' s ogive f

nose' dive' s piqué m

nose'-dive' intr descendre en piqué

nose' drops' spl instillations fpl nasales

nose'gay' s bouquet m

nose' glass'es spl pince-nez m

nostalgia [nɑ'stældʒə] s nostalgie f

nostalgic [nɑ'stældʒɪk] adj nostalgique

nostril ['nɑstrɪl] s narine f; (of horse, cow, etc.) naseau m

nostrum ['nɑstrəm] s (quack and his medicine) orviétan m; panacée f

nosy ['nozi] adj (comp -ier; super -iest) fureteur, indiscret

not [nɑt] *adv* ne §87, §90C; ne . . . pas §90, e.g., **he is not here** il n'est pas ici; non, non pas; **not at all** pas du tout; **not much** peu de chose; **not one** pas un; **not that** non pas que; **not yet** pas encore; **to think not** croire que non

notable ['notəbəl] *adj* & *s* notable *m*

notarize ['notə,raɪz] *tr* authentiquer

notarized *adj* authentique

nota·ry ['notəri] *s* (*pl* **-ries**) notaire *m*

notation [no'teʃən] *s* notation *f*

notch [nɑtʃ] *s* coche *f*, entaille *f*; (*of a belt*) cran *m*; (*of a wheel*) dent *f*; (*gap in a mountain*) brèche *f* ‖ *tr* encocher, entailler

note [not] *s* note *f*; (*short letter*) billet *m*; **notes** commentaires *mpl*; (*of a speech*) feuillets *mpl*; **note to the reader** avis *m* au lecteur ‖ *tr* noter; **to note down** prendre note de

note′book′ *s* cahier *m*; (*bill book, memo pad*, etc.) carnet *m*, calepin *m*

note′book cov′er *s* protège-cahier *m*

noted ['notɪd] *adj* éminent, distingué, connu

note′ pad′ *s* bloc-notes *m*

note′wor′thy *adj* notable, remarquable

nothing ['nʌθɪŋ] *s* rien *m* ‖ *pron indef* rien §90B; ne . . . rien §90, e.g., **I have nothing** je n'ai rien; **nothing at all** rien du tout; **nothing doing!** (slang) pas mèche! ‖ *adv*—**nothing less than** rien moins que

nothingness ['nʌθɪŋnɪs] *s* néant *m*

notice ['notɪs] *s* (*warning; advertisement*) avis *m*; (*in a newspaper*) annonce *f*; (*observation*) attention *f*; (*of dismissal*) congé *m*; **at short notice** à bref délai; **to take notice of** faire attention à; **until further notice** jusqu'à nouvel ordre ‖ *tr* s'apercevoir de, remarquer

noticeable ['notɪsəbəl] *adj* apparent, perceptible

notification [,notɪfɪ'keʃən] *s* notification *f*, avertissement *m*

noti·fy ['notɪ,faɪ] *v* (*pret* & *pp* **-fied**) *tr* aviser, avertir

notion ['noʃən] *s* notion *f*; intention *f*; **notions** mercerie *f*; **to have a notion to** avoir dans l'idée, avoir envie de

notorie·ty [,notə'raɪ·ɪti] *s* (*pl* **-ties**) renom *m* déshonorant, triste notoriété *f*

notorious [no'tori·əs] *adj* insigne, mal famé; (*person*) d'une triste notoriété

no′-trump′ *adj* & *s* sans-atout *m*

notwithstanding [,nɑtwɪð'stændɪŋ], [,nɑtwɪθ'stændɪŋ] *adv* nonobstant, néanmoins ‖ *prep* malgré ‖ *conj* quoique

nought [nɔt] *s* var of **naught**

noun [naʊn] *s* nom *m*

nourish ['nʌrɪʃ] *tr* nourrir

nourishment ['nʌrɪʃmənt] *s* nourriture *f*, alimentation *f*

Nova Scotia ['novə'skoʃə] *s* Nouvelle-Écosse *f*; la Nouvelle-Écosse

novel ['nɑvəl] *adj* nouveau; original, bizarre ‖ *s* roman *m*

novelette [,nɑvəl'ɛt] *s* nouvelle *f*, bluette *f*

novelist ['nɑvəlɪst] *s* romancier *m*

novel·ty ['nɑvəlti] *s* (*pl* **-ties**) nouveauté *f*; **novelties** bibelots *mpl*, souvenirs *mpl*

November [no'vembər] *s* novembre *m*

novice ['nɑvɪs] *s* novice *mf*

novitiate [no'vɪʃɪ·ɪt] *s* noviciat *m*

novocaine ['novə,ken] *s* novocaïne *f*

now [naʊ] *adv* maintenant; **just now** tout à l'heure, naguère; **now and again** de temps en temps ‖ *interj* allez-y!

nowadays ['naʊ·ə,dez] *adv* de nos jours

no′way′ or **no′ways′** *adv* en aucune façon

no′where′ *adv* nulle part; ne . . . nulle part; **nowhere else** nulle autre part, nulle part ailleurs

noxious ['nɑkʃəs] *adj* nocif

nozzle ['nɑzəl] *s* (*of hose*) ajutage *m*; (*of fire hose*) lance *f*; (*of sprinkling can*) pomme *f*; (*of candlestick*) douille *f*; (*of pitcher; of gas burner*) bec *m*; (*of carburetor*) buse *f*; (*of vacuum cleaner*) suceur *m*; (*nose*) (slang) museau *m*

nth [enθ] *adj* énième, nième; **for the nth time** pour la énième fois; **the nth power** la énième puissance

nuance [nju'ɑns], ['nju·ɑns] *s* nuance *f*

nub [nʌb] *s* protubérance *f*; (*piece*) petit morceau *m*; (slang) nœud *m*

nuclear ['n(j)uklɪ·ər] *adj* nucléaire

nu′clear pow′er plant′ *s* centrale *f* nucléaire

nu′clear test′ ban′ *s* interdiction *f* des essais nucléaires

nucleolus [n(j)u'kli·ələs] *s* nucléole *m*

nucleon ['n(j)ukli·ɑn] *s* nucléon *m*

nucle·us ['n(j)uklɪ·əs] *s* (*pl* **-i** [,aɪ] or **-uses**) noyau *m*

nude [n(j)ud] *adj* nu ‖ *s* nu *m*; **in the nude** nu, sans vêtements

nudge [nʌdʒ] *s* coup *m* de coude ‖ *tr* pousser du coude

nudist ['n(j)udɪst] *adj* & *s* nudiste *mf*

nudity ['n(j)udti] *s* nudité *f*

nugget ['nʌgɪt] *s* pépite *f*

nuisance ['n(j)usəns] *s* ennui *m*; (*person*) peste *f*

null [nʌl] *adj indef* nul

null′ and void′ *adj* nul et non avenu

nulli·fy ['nʌlɪ,faɪ] *v* (*pret* & *pp* **-fied**) *tr* annuler

numb [nʌm] *adj* engourdi; **to grow numb** s'engourdir ‖ *tr* engourdir

number ['nʌmbər] *s* numéro *m*, chiffre *m*; (*quantity*) nombre *m*; **wrong number** faux numéro ‖ *tr* numéroter; nombrer; (*to amount to*) s'élever à, compter; **to number among** compter parmi

numberless ['nʌmbərlɪs] *adj* innombrable

numbness ['nʌmnɪs] *s* engourdissement *m*

numeral ['n(j)umərəl] *adj* numéral ‖ *s* numéro *m*, chiffre *m*

numeration [‚n(j)uməˈreʃən] s numération f

numerical [n(j)uˈmerɪkəl] adj numérique

numerous [ˈn(j)umərəs] adj nombreux

numismatic [‚n(j)umɪzˈmætɪk] adj numismatique || **numismatics** s numismatique f

numskull [ˈnʌm‚skʌl] s (coll) sot m

nun [nʌn] s religieuse f, nonne f

nunci·o [ˈnʌn/ɪ‚o] s (pl -os) nonce m

nuptial [ˈnʌp/əl] adj nuptial || **nuptials** spl noces fpl

nurse [nʌrs] s infirmière f; (male nurse) infirmier m; (wet nurse) nourrice f; (practical nurse) garde-malade mf; (children's nurse) bonne f d'enfant, nurse f || tr soigner; (hopes; plants; a baby) nourrir

nurse′maid′ s bonne f d'enfant

nurser·y [ˈnʌrsəri] s (pl -ies) chambre f des enfants; (for day care) crèche f, pouponnière f; (hort) pépinière f

nurs′ery·man s (pl -men) pépiniériste m

nurs′ery school′ s maternelle f

nursing [ˈnʌrsɪŋ] s soins mpl; (profession) métier m d'infirmière; (by mother) nourriture f

nurs′ing bot′tle s biberon m

nurs′ing home′ s maison f de repos, maison de santé

nursling [ˈnʌrslɪŋ] s nourrisson m

nurture [ˈnʌrt/ər] s éducation f; nourriture f || tr élever; (to nurse) nourrir

nut [nʌt] s noix f, e.g., **Brazil nut** noix du Brésil; (of walnut tree) noix; (of filbert) noisette f; (to screw on a bolt) écrou m; (slang) extravagant m; **to be nuts about** (slang) être follement épris de

nut′crack′er s casse-noisettes m, casse-noix m; (orn) casse-noix

nut′hatch′ s sittelle f

nut′meat′ s graine f de fruit sec, graine de noix

nutmeg [ˈnʌt‚meg] s (seed or spice) noix f muscade, muscade f; (tree) muscadier m

nutriment [ˈn(j)utrɪmənt] s nourriture f

nutrition [n(j)uˈtrɪʃən] s nutrition f

nutritious [n(j)uˈtrɪʃəs] adj nutritif

nut′shell′ s coquille f de noix; **in a nutshell** en un mot

nut·ty [ˈnʌti] adj (comp -tier; super -tiest) à goût de noisette, à goût de noix; (slang) cinglé

nuzzle [ˈnʌzəl] tr fouiller du groin || intr fouiller du groin; s'envelopper chaudement; **to nuzzle up to** se pelotonner contre

nylon [ˈnaɪlən] s nylon m; **nylons** bas mpl de nylon, bas nylon

nymph [nɪmf] s nymphe f

O

O, o [o] s XVᵉ lettre de l'alphabet

oaf [of] s lourdaud m, rustre m

oak [ok] s chêne m

oaken [ˈokən] adj de chêne, en chêne

oakum [ˈokəm] s étoupe f

oar [or], [ɔr] s rame f, aviron m

oar′lock′ s tolet m

oars′man′ s (pl -men) rameur m

oa·sis [oˈesɪs] s (pl -ses [siz]) oasis f

oat [ot] s avoine f; **oats** (edible grain) avoine; **to feel one's oats** être imbu de sa personne; **to sow one's wild oats** (coll) jeter sa gourme

oath [oθ] s (pl oaths [oðz]) serment m; (swearword) juron m; **to administer an oath to** (law) faire prêter serment à; **to take an oath** prêter serment

oat′meal′ s farine f d'avoine; (breakfast food) flocons mpl d'avoine

obbligato [‚abɪˈgato] s accompagnement m à volonté

obdurate [ˈabdjərɪt] adj obstiné, endurci

obedience [oˈbidɪ·əns] s obéissance f

obedient [oˈbidɪ·ənt] adj obéissant

obeisance [oˈbesəns], [oˈbisəns] s hommage m; (greeting) révérence f

obelisk [ˈabəlɪsk] s obélisque m

obese [oˈbis] adj obèse

obesity [oˈbisɪti] s obésité f

obey [əˈbe] tr obéir (with dat); **to be obeyed** être obéi || intr obéir

obfuscate [abˈfʌsket], [ˈabfəs‚ket] tr offusquer

obituar·y [oˈbɪt/ʊ‚eri] adj nécrologique || s (pl -ies) nécrologie f

object [ˈabdʒɪkt] s objet m || [abˈdʒekt] tr objecter, rétorquer || intr faire des objections; **to object to** s'opposer à, avoir des objections contre

objection [abˈdʒek/ən] s objection f

objectionable [abˈdʒek/ənəbəl] adj répréhensible; répugnant, désagréable

objective [abˈdʒektɪv] adj & s objectif m

obligate [ˈablɪ‚get] tr obliger

obligation [‚ablɪˈgeʃən] s obligation f

obligatory [ˈablɪgə‚tori], [əˈblɪgə‚tori] adj obligatoire

oblige [əˈblaɪdʒ] tr obliger; **much obliged** bien obligé, très reconnaissant; **to be obliged to** être obligé de

obliging [əˈblaɪdʒɪŋ] adj accommodant, obligeant

oblique [əˈblik], [əˈblaɪk] adj oblique

obliterate [əˈblɪtə‚ret] tr effacer, oblitérer

oblivion [əˈblɪvɪ·ən] s oubli m

oblivious [əˈblɪvɪ·əs] adj oublieux

oblong [ˈablɔŋ], [ˈablɑŋ] adj oblong

obnoxious [əbˈnɑkʃəs] *adj* odieux, désagréable

oboe [ˈobo] *s* hautbois *m*

oboist [ˈobo·ɪst] *s* hautboïste *mf*

obscene [abˈsin] *adj* obscène

obsceni·ty [abˈsenɪti], [abˈsɪnɪti] *s* (*pl* -ties) obscénité *f*

obscure [əbˈskjur] *adj* obscur; (*vowel*) relâché, neutre

obscuri·ty [əbˈskjurɪti] *s* (*pl* -ties) obscurité *f*

obsequies [ˈabsɪkwiz] *spl* obsèques *fpl*

obsequious [əbˈsikwɪ·əs] *adj* obséquieux

observance [əbˈzʌrvəns] *s* observance *f*

observant [əbˈzʌrvənt] *adj* observateur

observation [ˌabzərˈveʃən] *s* observation *f*

observato·ry [əbˈzʌrvə ˌtori] *s* (*pl* -ries) observatoire *m*

observe [əbˈzʌrv] *tr* observer; (*silence*) garder; (*a holiday*) célébrer; dire, remarquer

observer [əbˈzʌrvər] *s* observateur *m*

obsess [əbˈses] *tr* obséder

obsession [əbˈseʃən] *s* obsession *f*

obsolescent [ˌabsəˈlesənt] *adj* vieillissant

obsolete [ˈabsəlit] *adj* désuet, vieilli; (*gram*) obsolète

obstacle [ˈabstəkəl] *s* obstacle *m*

ob'stacle course' *s* champ *m* d'obstacles, piste *f* d'obstacles

obstetrical [abˈstetrɪkəl] *adj* obstétrique

obstetrics [abˈstetrɪks] *spl* obstétrique *f*

obstina·cy [ˈabstɪnasi] *s* (*pl* -cies) obstination *f*, entêtement *m*

obstinate [ˈabstɪnɪt] *adj* obstiné

obstreperous [əbˈstrepərəs] *adj* turbulent

obstruct [əbˈstrʌkt] *tr* obstruer; (*movements*) empêcher, entraver

obstruction [əbˈstrʌkʃən] *s* obstruction *f*; (*on railroad tracks*) obstacle *m*; (*to movement*) empêchement *m*, entrave *f*

obtain [əbˈten] *tr* obtenir, se procurer ‖ *intr* prévaloir

obtrusive [əbˈtrusɪv] *adj* importun, intrus

obtuse [əbˈt(j)us] *adj* obtus

obviate [ˈabvɪ ˌet] *tr* obvier (with *dat*)

obvious [ˈabvɪ·əs] *adj* évident

occasion [əˈkeʒən] *s* occasion *f*; **on occasion** en de différentes occasions ‖ *tr* occasionner

occasional [əˈkeʒənəl] *adj* fortuit, occasionnel; (*verses*) de circonstance; (*showers*) épars; (*chair*) volant

occasionally [əˈkeʒənəli] *adv* de temps en temps, occasionnellement

occident [ˈaksɪdənt] *s* occident *m*

occidental [ˌaksəˈdentəl] *adj & s* occidental *m*

occlusion [əˈkluʒən] *s* occlusion *f*

occlusive [əˈklusɪv] *adj* occlusif ‖ *s* occlusive *f*

occult [əˈkʌlt] [ˈakʌlt] *adj* occulte

occupancy [ˈakjəpənsi] *s* occupation *f*, habitation *f*

occupant [ˈakjəpənt] *s* occupant *m*

occupation [ˌakjəˈpeʃən] *s* occupation *f*

occupational [ˌakjəˈpeʃənəl] *adj* professionnel; de métier

oc'cupa'tional ther'apy *s* thérapie *f* rééducative, réadaptation *f* fonctionnelle

occu·py [ˈakjə ˌpaɪ] *v* (*pret & pp* -pied) *tr* occuper; **to be occupied with** s'occuper de

oc·cur [əˈkʌr] *v* (*pret & pp* -curred; *ger* -curring) *intr* arriver, avoir lieu; (*to be found*; *to come to mind*) se présenter; **it occurs to me that** il me vient à l'esprit que

occurrence [əˈkʌrəns] *s* événement *m*; cas *m*, exemple *m*; **everyday occurrence** fait *m* journalier

ocean [ˈoʃən] *s* océan *m*

oceanic [ˌoʃɪˈænɪk] *adj* océanique

o'cean lin'er *s* paquebot *m* transocéanique

ocher [ˈokər] *s* ocre *f*

o'clock [əˈklak] *adv*—**it is one o'clock** il est une heure; **it is two o'clock** il est deux heures

octane [ˈakten] *s* octane *m*

oc'tane num'ber *s* indice *m* d'octane

octave [ˈaktɪv] [ˈaktev] *s* octave *f*

October [akˈtobər] *s* octobre *m*

octo·pus [ˈaktəpəs] *s* (*pl* -puses or -pi [ˌpaɪ]) pieuvre *f*, poulpe *m*

octoroon [ˌaktəˈrun] *s* octavon *m*

ocular [ˈakjələr] *adj & s* oculaire *m*

oculist [ˈakjəlɪst] *s* oculiste *mf*

odd [ad] *adj* (*number*) impair; (*that doesn't match*) dépareillé, déparié; (*queer*) bizarre, étrange; (*occasional*) divers; quelque, quelque; **three hundred odd horses** quelque trois cents chevaux; et quelques ‖ **odds** *spl* chances *fpl*; (*disparity*) inégalité *f*; (*on a horse*) cote *f*; **at odds** en désaccord, en bisbille; **by all odds** sans aucun doute; **to be at odds with** être mal avec; **to give odds to** donner de l'avance à; **to set at odds** brouiller

oddi·ty [ˈadɪti] *s* (*pl* -ties) bizarrerie *f*

odd' jobs' *spl* bricolage *m*, petits travaux *mpl*

odd' man' out' *s*—**to be odd man out** être en trop

odds' and ends' *spl* petits bouts *mpl*, bribes *fpl*; (*trinkets*) bibelots *mpl*; (*food*) restes *mpl*

ode [od] *s* ode *f*

odious [ˈodɪ·əs] *adj* odieux

odor [ˈodər] *s* odeur *f*; **to be in bad odor** être mal vu

odorless [ˈodərlɪs] *adj* inodore

Odyssey [ˈadɪsi] *s* Odyssée *f*

Oedipus [ˈedɪpəs], [ˈidəpəs] *s* Œdipe *m*

of [av], [ʌv], [ə] *prep* de; à, e.g., **to think of** penser à; e.g., **to ask s.th. of s.o.** demander q.ch. à qn; en, e.g., **a doctor of medicine** un docteur en médecine; moins, e.g., **a quarter of two** deux heures moins le quart; entre, e.g., **he of all people** lui entre tous; d'entre, e.g., **five of them** cinq d'entre eux; par, e.g., **of necessity** par nécessité; en or de, e.g., **made of**

wood en bois, de bois; (not translated), e.g., **the fifth of March** le cinq mars; (*morning*) nous la voyons souvent le matin

off [ɔf], [ɑf] *adj* mauvais, e.g., **off day** (*bad day*) mauvaise journée; libre, e.g., **off day** journée libre; de congé, e.g., **off day** jour de congé; (*account, sum*) inexact; (*meat*) avancé; (*electric current*) coupé; (*light*) éteint; (*radio; faucet*) fermé; (*street*) secondaire, transversal; (*distant*) éloigné, écarté || *adv* loin; à . . . de distance, e.g., **three kilometers off** à trois kilomètres de distance; parti, e.g., **they're off!** les voilà partis!; bas, e.g., **hats off!** chapeaux bas!; (naut) au large; (theat) à la cantonade || *prep* de; (*at a distance from*) éloigné de, écarté de; (naut) au large de, à la hauteur de; **from off** de dessous de

offal ['ɑfəl], ['ɔfəl] *s* (*of butchered meat*) abats *mpl*; (*refuse*) ordures *fpl*

off' and on' *adv* de temps en temps, par intervalles

off'beat' *adj* (slang) insolite, rare

off' chance' *s* chance *f* improbable

off'-col'or *adj* décoloré; (e.g., *story*) grivois, vert

offend [ə'fɛnd] *tr* offenser; **to be offended** s'offenser || *intr*—**to offend against** enfreindre

offender [ə'fɛndər] *s* offenseur *m*; (*criminal*) délinquant *m*, coupable *mf*

offense [ə'fɛns] *s* offense *f*; (law) délit *m*; **to take offense** (at) s'offenser (de)

offensive [ə'fɛnsɪv] *adj* offensant, blessant; (mil) offensif || *s* offensive *f*

offer ['ɔfər], ['ɑfər] *s* offre *f* || *tr* offrir; (*excuses; best wishes*) présenter; (*prayers*) adresser || *intr*—**to offer to** faire l'offre de; faire mine de, e.g., **he offered to fight** il a fait mine de se battre

offering ['ɔfərɪŋ], ['ɑfərɪŋ] *s* offre *f*; (eccl) offrande *f*

off'hand' *adj* improvisé; brusque || *adv* au pied levé; brusquement

office ['ɔfɪs], ['ɑfɪs] *s* fonction *f*, office *m*; (*in business, school, government*) bureau *m*; (*national agency*) office *m*; (*of lawyer*) étude *f*; (*of doctor*) cabinet *m*; **elective office** poste *m* électif; **good offices** bons offices; **to run for office** se présenter aux élections

of'fice boy' *s* coursier *m*, commissionnaire *m* de bureau

of'fice desk' *s* bureau *m* ministre

of'fice-hold'er *s* fonctionnaire *mf*

of'fice hours' *spl* heures *fpl* de bureau; (*of doctor, counselor, etc.*) heures de consultation

officer ['ɔfɪsər], ['ɑfɪsər] *s* (*of a company*) administrateur *m*, dirigeant *m*; (*of army, an order, a society, etc.*) officier *m*; (*police officer*) agent *m* de police, officier de police; **officer of the day** (mil) officier de service

of'ficer can'didate *s* élève-officier *m*

of'fice seek'er *s* solliciteur *m*

of'fice supplies' *spl* fournitures *fpl* de bureau, articles *mpl* de bureau

of'fice-supply' store' *s* papeterie *f*

of'fice work' *s* travail *m* de bureau

official [ə'fɪʃəl] *adj* officiel; (*stationery*) réglementaire || *s* fonctionnaire *mf*, officiel *m*; **officials** cadres *mpl*; (*executives*) dirigeants *mpl*

officialese [ə,fɪʃə'liz] *s* jargon *m* administratif

of'ficial board' *s* comité *m* directeur

officiate [ə'fɪʃɪ,et] *intr* (eccl) officier; **to officiate as** exercer les fonctions de

officious [ə'fɪʃəs] *adj* trop empressé; **to be officious** faire l'officieux

offing ['ɔfɪŋ], ['ɑfɪŋ] *s*—**in the offing** au large; (fig) en perspective

off'-lim'its *adj* défendu; (public sign) défense d'entrer, entrée interdite; (mil) interdit aux troupes

off'-peak heat'er *s* thermosiphon *m* à accumulation

off'print' *s* tiré *m* à part

off'-seas'on *s* morte-saison *f*

off'set' *s* compensation *f*; (typ) offset *m* || **off'set'** *v* (*pret & pp* **-set**; *ger* **-setting**) *tr* compenser

off'shoot' *s* rejeton *m*

off'shore' *adj* éloigné de la côte, du côté de la terre; (*wind*) de terre || *adv* au large, vers la haute mer

off'side' *adv* (sports) hors jeu

off'spring' *s* descendance *f*; (*descendant*) rejeton *m*, enfant *mf*; (*result*) conséquence *f*

off'stage' *adj* dans les coulisses || *adv* à la cantonade

off'-the-cuff' *adj* (coll) impromptu

off'-the-rec'ord *adj* confidentiel

often ['ɔfən], ['ɑfən] *adv* souvent; **how often?** combien de fois?; **as often as** combien de fois?; **tous les combien?**; **not often** rarement; **once too often** une fois de trop

ogive ['odʒaɪv], [o'dʒaɪv] *s* ogive *f*

ogle ['ogəl] *tr* lancer une œillade à; (*to stare at*) dévisager

ogre ['ogər] *s* ogre *m*

ohm [om] *s* ohm *m*

oil [ɔɪl] *s* huile *f*; (*painting*) huile, peinture *f* à l'huile; **holy oil** huile sainte, saintes huiles; **to pour oil on troubled waters** calmer la tempête, verser de l'huile sur les plaies de qn; **to smell of midnight oil** sentir l'huile; **to strike oil** atteindre une nappe pétrolifère; (fig) trouver le filon || *tr* huiler; (*to bribe*) graisser la patte à || *intr* (naut) faire le plein de mazout

oil' burn'er *s* réchaud *m* à pétrole

oil'can' *s* bidon *m* d'huile, burette *f* d'huile

oil'cloth' *s* toile *f* cirée

oil' com'pany *s* société *f* pétrolière

oil'cup' *s* (mach) godet *m* graisseur

oil' drum' *s* bidon *m* d'huile

oil' field' *s* gisement *m* pétrolifère

oil' gauge' *s* jauge *f* de niveau d'huile

oil′ lamp′ s lampe f à huile, lampe à pétrole

oil′man′ s (pl **-men′**) (retailer) huilier m; (operator) pétrolier m

oil′ pump′ s pompe f à huile

oil′ stove′ s poêle m à mazout, fourneau m à pétrole

oil′ tank′er s pétrolier m, tanker m

oil′ well′ s puits m à pétrole

oil‧y [′ɔɪlɪ] adj (comp **-ier**; super **-iest**) huileux, oléagineux; (fig) onctueux

ointment [′ɔɪntmənt] s onguent m, pommade f

O.K. [′oʹke] (letterword) adj (coll) très bien, parfait ‖ s (coll) approbation f ‖ adv (coll) très bien ‖ v (pret & pp **O.K.′d**; ger **O.K.′ing**) tr (coll) approuver ‖ interj O.K.!, ça colle!

okra [′okrə] s gombo m, ketmie f comestible

old [old] adj vieux; (of former times) ancien; (wine) vieux; **any old** n′importe, e.g., **any old time** n′importe quand; quelconque, e.g., **any old book** un livre quelconque; **at . . . years old** à l'âge de . . . ans; **how old is . . . ?** quel âge a . . . ?; **of old** d'autrefois, de jadis; **to be . . . years old** avoir . . . ans

old′ age′ s vieillesse f, âge m avancé

old′-clothes′man′ s (pl **-men′**) fripier m

old′ coun′try s mère patrie f

Old′ Cov′enant s (Bib) ancienne alliance f

old′-fash′ioned adj démodé, suranné; (literary style) vieillot

old′ fo′gey or **old′ fo′gy** [′fogi] s (pl **-gies**) vieux bonhomme m, grime m

Old′ French′ s ancien français m

Old′ Glo′ry s le drapeau des États-Unis

old′ hag′ s vieille fée f

old′ hand′ s vieux routier m

old′ lad′y s vieille dame f; (coll) grand-mère f

old′ maid′ s vieille fille f

old′ mas′ter s grand maître m; œuvre f d'un grand maître

old′ moon′ s Lune f à son décours

old′ peo′ple's home′ s hospice m de vieillards

old′ salt′ s loup m de mer

old′ school′ s vieille école f, vieille roche f

oldster [′oldstər] s vieillard m, vieux m

Old′ Tes′tament s Ancien Testament m

old′-time′ adj du temps jadis, d'autrefois

old′-tim′er s (coll) vieux m de la vieille, vieux routier m

old′ wives′ tale′ s conte m de bonne femme

Old Wom′an who lived′ in a shoe′ s mère f Gigogne

Old′ World′ s vieux monde m

old′-world′ adj de l'ancien monde; du vieux monde

oleander [‚olɪ′ændər] s laurier-rose m

olfactory [ɑl′fæktərɪ] adj olfactif

oligar‧chy [′ɑlɪ‚gɑrkɪ] s (pl **-chies**) oligarchie f

olive [′ɑlɪv] adj olive; (complexion) olivâtre ‖ s olive f; (tree) olivier m

ol′ive branch′ s rameau m d'olivier

ol′ive grove′ s olivaie f

ol′ive oil′ s huile f d'olive

Oliver [′ɑlɪvər] s Olivier m

ol′ive tree′ s olivier m

olympiad [o′lɪmpɪ‚æd] s olympiade f

Olympian [o′lɪmpɪ‧ən] adj olympien

Olympic [o′lɪmpɪk] adj olympique ‖ **Olympics** spl jeux mpl olympiques

omelet [′amə‚let], [′amlɪt] s omelette f

omen [′omən] s augure m, présage m

ominous [′amɪnəs] adj de mauvais augure

omission [o′mɪʃən] s omission f

omit [o′mɪt] v (pret & pp **omitted**; ger **omitting**) tr omettre

omnibus [′amnɪ‚bʌs], [′amnɪbəs] adj & s omnibus m

omnipotent [am′nɪpətənt] adj omnipotent

omniscient [am′nɪʃənt] adj omniscient

omnivorous [am′nɪvərəs] adj omnivore

on [ɑn], [ɔn] adj (light, radio) allumé; (faucet) ouvert; (machine, motor) en marche; (electrical appliance) branché; (brake) serré; (steak, chops, etc.) dans la poêle; (game, program, etc.) commencé ‖ adv—**and so on** et ainsi de suite; **come on!** (coll) allons donc!; **farther on** plus loin; **from this day on** à dater de ce jour; **later on** plus tard; **move on!** circulez!; **to be on** (theat) être en scène; **to be on to s.o.** (coll) voir clair dans le jeu de qn; **to have on** être vêtu de, porter; **to . . . on** continuer à + inf, e.g., **to sing on** continuer à chanter; **well on** avancé, e.g., **well on in years** d'un âge avancé ‖ prep sur; (at the time of) lors de; à, e.g., **on foot** à pied; e.g., **on my arrival** à mon arrivée; e.g., **on page three** à la page trois; e.g., **on the first floor** au rez-de-chaussée; e.g., **on the right** à droite; en, à, e.g., **on a journey** en voyage; e.g., **on arriving** en arrivant; e.g., **on fire** en feu; e.g., **on sale** en vente; e.g., **on the or an average** en moyenne; e.g., **on the top of** en dessus de; dans, e.g., **on a farm** dans une ferme; e.g., **on the jury** dans le jury; e.g., **on the street** dans la rue; e.g., **on the train** dans le train; par, e.g., **he came on the train** il est venu par le train; e.g., **on a fine day** par un beau jour; de, e.g., **on good authority** de source certaine, de bonne part; e.g., **on the north du** côté du nord; e.g., **on the one hand . . . on the other hand** d'une part . . . d'autre part; e.g., **on this side of** de ce côté-ci; e.g., **to have pity on** avoir pitié de; e.g., **to live on bread and water** vivre de pain et d'eau; sous, e.g., **on a charge of** sous l'inculpation de; e.g., **on pain of** death sous peine de mort; (not translated), e.g., **on Tuesday** mardi; e.g., **on Tuesdays** le mardi, tous les mardis; e.g., **on July fourteenth** le quatorze juillet; contre, e.g., **an attack on** une attaque contre; **it's on me** (*it's my turn to pay*) (coll) c'est ma tournée; **it's on the house** (coll) c'est la tournée du patron; **on examination** après examen; **on it** y, e.g., **there is the shelf; put the book on it** voilà l'étagère; mettez-y le livre; **on or about** (*a certain date*) aux environs de; **on or after** (*a certain date*) à partir de; **on tap** en perce, à la pression; **on the spot** (*immediately*) sur-le-champ; (*there*) sur place; (slang) en danger imminent; **to be on the committee** faire partie du comité; **to march on a city** marcher sur une ville

on' and **on'** adv continuellement, sans fin

once [wʌns] s—**this once** pour cette fois-ci ‖ adv une fois; (*formerly*) autrefois; **all at once** (*all together*) tous à la fois; (*suddenly*) tout à coup; **at once** tout de suite, sur-le-champ; (*at the same time*) à la fois, en même temps; **for once** pour une fois; **once and for all** une bonne fois, une fois pour toutes; **once in a while** de temps en temps; **once more** encore une fois; **once or twice** une ou deux fois; **once upon a time there was** il était une fois ‖ conj une fois que, dès que

once'-o'ver s (slang) examen m rapide; travail m hâtif; **to give the once-over to** (slang) jeter un coup d'œil à

one [wʌn] adj & pron un; un certain, e.g., **one Dupont** un certain Dupont; un seul, e.g., **with one voice** d'une seule voix; unique, e.g., **one price** prix unique; (*not translated when preceded by an adjective*), e.g., **the red pencil and the blue one** le crayon rouge et le bleu; **not one** pas un; **one and all** tous; **one and only** unique, e.g., **the one and only closet in the house** l'armoire unique de la maison; seul et unique, e.g., **my one and only umbrella** mon seul et unique parapluie; **one another** l'un l'autre; les uns les autres; **one by one** un à un; **that one** celui-là; **the one that** celui que, celui qui; **this one** celui-ci; **to become one** s'unir, se marier ‖ s un m; **one o'clock** une heure ‖ pron indef on §87, e.g., **one cannot go there alone** on ne peut pas y aller seul; **one's son**, e.g., **one's son** son fils

one'-horse' adj à un cheval; (coll) provincial, insignifiant

onerous ['ɑnərəs] adj onéreux

one-self' pron soi §85; soi-même §86; se §87, e.g., **to cut oneself** se couper; **to be oneself** se conduire sans affectation

one'-sid'ed adj à un côté, à une face; (*e.g., decision*) unilatéral; (*unfair*) partial, injuste

one'-track' adj à une voie; (coll) routinier

one'-way' adj à sens unique

one'-way tick'et s billet m d'aller, billet simple

onion ['ʌnjən] s oignon m; **to know one's onions** (coll) connaître son affaire

on'ion-skin' s papier m pelure

on'look'er s assistant m, spectateur m

only ['onli] adj seul, unique; (*child*) unique ‖ adv seulement; ne . . . que, e.g., **I have only two** je n'en ai que deux; réservé, e.g., **staff only** (*public sign*) réservé au personnel ‖ conj mais, si ce n'était que

on'rush' s ruée f

on'set' s attaque f; **at the onset** de prime abord, au premier abord

onslaught ['ɑn,slɔt], ['ɔn,slɔt] s assaut m

on'-the-job' adj (*training*) en stage; (coll) alerte

onus ['onəs] s charge f, fardeau m

onward ['ɑnwərd] or **onwards** ['ɑnwərdz] adv en avant

onyx ['ɑnɪks] s onyx m

ooze [uz] s suintement m; (*mud*) vase f, limon m ‖ tr filtrer ‖ intr suinter, filtrer; **to ooze out** s'écouler

opal ['opəl] s opale f

opaque [o'pek] adj opaque; (*style*) obscur

open ['opən] adj ouvert; (*personality*) franc, sincère; (*job, position*) vacant; (*hour*) libre; (*automobile*) découvert; (*market, trial*) public; (*question*) pendant, indécis; (*wound*) béant; (*to attack, to criticism, etc.*) exposé; (sports) international; **to break or crack open** éventrer; **to throw open the door** ouvrir la porte toute grande ‖ s ouverture f; (*in the woods*) clairière f; **in the open** au grand air, à ciel ouvert; (*in the open country*) en rase campagne; (*in the open sea*) en pleine mer; (*without being hidden*) découvert; (*openly*) ouvertement ‖ tr ouvrir; (*a canal lock*) lâcher; **to open fire** déclencher le feu ‖ intr ouvrir, s'ouvrir; (*said, e.g., of a play*) commencer, débuter; **to open into** aboutir à, déboucher sur; **to open on** donner sur; **to open up** s'épanouir, s'ouvrir

o'pen-air' adj en plein air, au grand air

o'pen-eyed' adj les yeux écarquillés

o'pen-hand'ed adj libéral, la main ouverte

o'pen-heart'ed adj ouvert, franc

o'pen-heart' sur'gery s chirurgie f à cœur ouvert

o'pen house' s journée f d'accueil; **to keep open house** tenir table ouverte

opening ['opənɪŋ] s ouverture f; (*in the woods*) clairière f; (*vacancy*) vacance f, poste m vacant; (*chance to say something*) occasion f favorable

o'pening night' s première f

o'pening num'ber s ouverture f

o'pening price' s cours m de début

o'pen-mind'ed adj à l'esprit ouvert, sans parti pris

o'pen se'cret s secret m de Polichinelle

o'pen shop' s atelier m ouvert aux non-syndiqués

o'pen‑work' s ouvrage m à jour, ajours mpl

opera ['apərə] s opéra m

op'era glass'es spl jumelles fpl de spectacle

op'era hat' s claque m, gibus m

op'era house' s opéra m

operate ['apə,ret] tr actionner, faire marcher; exploiter ‖ intr fonctionner; s'opérer; (surg) opérer; to operate on (surg) opérer

operatic [,apə'rætɪk] adj d'opéra

opera'ting expen'ses spl (overhead) frais mpl généraux, frais d'exploitation

op'erating room' s salle f d'opération

op'erating ta'ble s table f d'opération, billard m

operation [,apə're∫ən] s opération f; (of a business, of a machine, etc.) fonctionnement m; (med) intervention f chirurgicale, opération

operative ['apə,retɪv], ['apərətɪv] adj opératif; (surg) opératoire ‖ s (workman) ouvrier m; (spy) agent m, espion m

operator ['apə,retər] s opérateur m; (e.g., of a mine) propriétaire m exploitant; (of an automobile) conducteur m; téléphoniste mf, standardiste mf; (slang) chevalier m d'industrie, aigrefin m

operetta [,apə'retə] s opérette f

opiate ['opɪ,ɪt], ['opɪ,et] adj opiacé ‖ s médicament m opiacé; (coll) narcotique m

opinion [ə'pɪnjən] s opinion f; in my opinion à mon avis

opinionated [ə'pɪnjə,netɪd] adj fier de ses opinions, dogmatique

opium ['opɪəm] s opium m

o'pium den' s fumerie f

o'pium pop'py s œillette f

opossum [ə'pasəm] s opossum m, sarigue f

opponent [ə'ponənt] s adversaire mf, opposant m

opportune [,apər't(j)un] adj opportun, convenable

opportunist [,apər't(j)unɪst] s opportuniste mf

opportuni‑ty [,apər't(j)unɪti] s (pl ‑ties) occasion f; chance f

oppose [ə'poz] tr s'opposer à

opposite ['apəzɪt] adj opposé, contraire; d'en face, e.g., the house opposite la maison d'en face ‖ s opposé m, contraire m ‖ adv en face, vis-à-vis ‖ prep en face de, à l'opposite de

op'posite num'ber s (fig) homologue mf

opposition [,apə'zɪ∫ən] s opposition f

oppress [ə'pres] tr opprimer; (to weigh heavily upon) oppresser

oppression [ə'pre∫ən] s oppression f

oppressive [ə'presɪv] adj oppressif; (stifling) étouffant, accablant

oppressor [ə'presər] s oppresseur m

opprobrious [ə'probrɪ‑əs] adj infamant, injurieux, honteux

opprobrium [ə'probrɪ‑əm] s opprobre m

optic ['aptɪk] adj optique ‖ optics s optique f

optical ['aptɪkəl] adj optique

op'tical illu'sion s illusion f d'optique

optician [ap'tɪ∫ən] s opticien m

optimism ['aptɪ,mɪzəm] s optimisme m

optimist ['aptɪmɪst] s optimiste mf

optimistic [,aptɪ'mɪstɪk] adj optimiste

option ['ap∫ən] s option f

optional ['ap∫ənəl] adj facultatif

optometrist [ap'tamɪtrɪst] s opticien m; optométriste mf (Canad)

opulent ['apjələnt] adj opulent

or [ər] conj ou

oracle ['arəkəl], ['ɔrəkəl] s oracle m

oracular [o'rækjələr] adj d'oracle; dogmatique, sentencieux; (ambiguous) équivoque

oral ['orəl] adj oral

orange ['arɪndʒ], ['ɔrɪndʒ] adj orangé, orange ‖ s (color) orangé m, orange m; (fruit) orange f

orangeade [,arɪndʒ'ed], [,ɔrɪndʒ'ed] s orangeade f

or'ange blos'som s fleur f d'oranger

or'ange grove' s orangeraie f

or'ange juice' s jus m d'orange

or'ange squeez'er s presse-fruits m

or'ange tree' s oranger m

orang-outang [o'ræŋu,tæŋ] s orang-outan m

oration [o're∫ən] s discours m

orator ['arətər], ['ɔrətər] s orateur m

oratorical [,arə'tarɪkəl], [,ɔrə'tɔrɪkəl] adj oratoire

oratori‑o [,arə'torɪ,o], [,ɔrə'torɪ,o] s (pl ‑os) oratorio m

orato‑ry ['arə,tori], ['ɔrə,tori] s (pl ‑ries) art m oratoire; (eccl) oratoire m

orb [ɔrb] s orbe m

orbit ['ɔrbɪt] s orbite f; in orbit sur orbite ‖ tr (e.g., the sun) tourner autour de; (e.g., a rocket) mettre en orbite, satelliser ‖ intr se mettre en orbite

orchard ['ɔrt∫ərd] s verger m

orchestra ['ɔrkɪstrə] s orchestre m

orchestrate ['ɔrkɪ,stret] tr orchestrer

orchid ['ɔrkɪd] s orchidée f

ordain [or'den] tr destiner; (eccl) ordonner; to be ordained (eccl) recevoir les ordres

ordeal [or'dil], [or'di‑əl] s épreuve f; (hist) ordalie f

order ['ɔrdər] s ordre m; (of words) ordonnance f; (for merchandise, a meal, etc.) commande f; (military formation) ordre; (law) arrêt m, arrêté m; in order en ordre; in order of appearance (theat) dans l'ordre d'entrée en scène; in order that pour que, afin que; in order to + inf pour + inf, afin de + inf; on order en commande, commandé; order! à l'ordre!; orders (eccl) les ordres; (mil) la consigne; pay to the order of (com) payez à l'ordre de; to get s.th. out of order détraquer q.ch.; to put in order mettre en règle ‖ tr ordonner; (com) commander; to order around faire aller et venir; **to order s.o. to +** *inf* ordonner à qn de + *inf*

or′der blank′ s bon m de commande, bulletin m de commande

order•ly ['ɔrdərli] *adj* ordonné; *(life)* réglé; **to be orderly** avoir de l'ordre || s (pl -lies) (med) ambulancier m, infirmier m; (mil) planton m

ordinal ['ɔrdɪnəl] *adj & s* ordinal m

ordinance ['ɔrdɪnəns] s ordonnance f

ordinary ['ɔrdɪn‚ɛri] *adj* ordinaire; **out of the ordinary** exceptionnel

ordination [‚ɔrdɪn'eʃən] s ordination f

ordnance ['ɔrdnəns] s artillerie f; *(branch of an army)* service m du matériel

ore [or] s minerai m

oregano [ə'regə‚no] s origan m

organ ['ɔrgən] s (anat, journ) organe m; (mus) orgue m

organdy ['ɔrgəndi] s organdi m

or′gan grind′er s joueur m d'orgue

organic [ɔr'gænɪk] *adj* organique

organism ['ɔrgə‚nɪzəm] s organisme m

organist ['ɔrgənɪst] s organiste mf

organization [‚ɔrgənɪ'zeʃən] s organisation f

organize ['ɔrgə‚naɪz] *tr* organiser

organizer ['ɔrgə‚naɪzər] s organisateur m

or′gan loft′ s tribune f d'orgue

orgasm ['ɔrgæzəm] s orgasme m

or•gy ['ɔrdʒi] s (pl -gies) orgie f

orient ['ɔri‚ɛnt] s orient m; **Orient Orient** || ['ɔri‚ɛnt] *tr* orienter

oriental [‚ɔri'ɛntəl] *adj* oriental || (cap) s Oriental m

orientate ['ɔri‚ɛn‚tet] *tr* orienter

orientation [‚ɔri‚ɛn'teʃən] s orientation f

orifice ['ɑrɪfɪs], ['ɔrɪfɪs] s orifice m

origin ['ɑrədʒɪn], ['ɔrədʒɪn] s origine f

original [ə'rɪdʒɪnəl] *adj* (new, not copied; inventive) original; (earliest) originel, primitif; (first) originaire, premier || s original m

originality [ə‚rɪdʒɪ'nælɪti] s originalité f

originate [ə'rɪdʒə‚net] *tr* faire naître, créer || *intr* prendre naissance; **to originate from** provenir de

oriole ['ɔri‚ol], ['ɔri‚ol] s loriot m

ormolu ['ɔrmə‚lu] s bronze m doré; *(powdered gold for gilding)* or m moulu; *(alloy of zinc and copper)* similor m

ornament ['ɔrnəmənt] s ornement m || ['ɔrnə‚ment] *tr* ornementer, orner

ornamental [‚ɔrnə'mentəl] *adj* ornemental

ornate [ɔr'net], ['ɔrnet] *adj* orné, fleuri

ornery ['ɔrnəri] *adj* (coll) acariâtre, intraitable

ornithology [‚ɔrnɪ'θɑlədʒi] f ornithologie f

orphan ['ɔrfən] *adj & s* orphelin m

orphanage ['ɔrfənɪdʒ] s (asylum) orphelinat m; (orphanhood) orphelinage m

Orpheus ['ɔrfjus], ['ɔrfi‚əs] s Orphée m

orthodox ['ɔrθə‚dɑks] *adj* orthodoxe

orthogra•phy [ɔr'θɑgrəfi] s (pl -phies) orthographe f

oscillate ['ɑsɪ‚let] *intr* osciller

osier ['oʒər] s osier m

osmosis [ɑz'mosɪs], [ɑs'mosɪs] s osmose f

osprey ['ɑspri] s aigle m pêcheur

ossi•fy ['ɑsɪ‚faɪ] v (pret & pp -fied) *tr* ossifier || *intr* s'ossifier

ostensible [ɑs'tɛnsɪbəl] *adj* prétendu, apparent, soi-disant

ostentatious [‚ɑstɛn'teʃəs] *adj* ostentatoire, fastueux

osteopathy [‚ɑstɪ'ɑpəθi] s ostéopathie f

ostracism ['ɑstrə‚sɪzəm] s ostracisme m

ostracize ['ɑstrə‚saɪz] *tr* frapper d'ostracisme

ostrich ['ɑstrɪtʃ] s autruche f

other ['ʌðər] *adj* autre; **every other day** tous les deux jours; **every other one** un sur deux || *pron indef* autre || *adv*—**other than** autrement que

otherwise ['ʌðər‚waɪz] *adv* autrement, à part cela || *conj* sinon, e.g., **come at once, otherwise it will be too late** venez tout de suite, sinon il sera trop tard; sans cela, e.g., **thanks, otherwise I'd have forgotten** merci, sans cela j'aurais oublié

otter ['ɑtər] s loutre f

Ottoman ['ɑtəmən] *adj* ottoman || (l.c.) s (corded fabric) ottoman m; (divan) ottomane f; (footstool) pouf m; **Ottoman** (person) Ottoman m

ouch [aʊtʃ] *interj* aïe!

ought [ɔt] s zéro m; **for ought I know** pour autant que je sache || *aux* used to express obligation, e.g., **he ought to go away** il devrait s'en aller; e.g., **he ought to have gone away** il aurait dû s'en aller

ounce [aʊns] s once f

our [aʊr] *adj poss* notre §88

ours [aʊrz] *pron poss* le nôtre §89

our•selves′ *pron pers* nous-mêmes §86; nous §85, §87

oust [aʊst] *tr* évincer, chasser

out [aʊt] *adj* extérieur; absent; (fire) éteint; (secret) divulgué; (tide) bas; (flower) épanoui; (rope) filé; (lease) expiré; (gear) débrayé; (unconscious person) évanoui; (boxer) knockouté; (book, magazine, etc.) paru, publié; (out of print, out of stock) épuisé; (a ball) (sports) hors jeu; (a player) (sports) éliminé || s (pretext) échappatoire f; **to be on the outs with** être brouillé avec || *adv* dehors, au dehors; (outdoors) en plein air; **out and out** complètement; **out for** en quête de; **out for lunch** parti déjeuner; **out of** (cash) démuni de; (a glass, cup, etc.) dans; (a bottle) à; (the window, curiosity, friendship, respect, etc.) par; (range, sight) hors de; de, e.g., **to cry out of joy** pleurer de joie; e.g., **made out of fait** de; tas, e.g., **nine times out of ten** neuf fois sur dix; **out with it!** allez, dites-le; **to be out** (to be absent) être sorti; faire, e.g., **the sun is out** il fait du soleil; **to be out**

of bounds (sports) être hors jeu ‖ *prep* par ‖ *interj* hors d'ici!, ouste!

out′ and away′ *adv* de beaucoup, de loin

out′-and-out′ *adj* vrai; *(fanatic)* intransigeant; *(liar)* achevé

out′-and-out′er *s* (coll) intransigeant *m*

out′bid′ *v* (pret **-bid**; pp **-bid** or **-bidden**; ger **-bidding**) *tr* enchérir sur; (fig) renchérir sur ‖ *intr* surenchérir

out′board mo′tor *s* moteur *m* horsbord

out′break′ *s* déchaînement *m*; *(of hives; of anger; etc.)* éruption *f*; *(of epidemic)* manifestation *f*; *(insurrection)* révolte *f*

out′build′ing *s* annexe *f*, dépendance *f*

out′burst′ *s* explosion *f*; *(of anger)* accès *m*; *(of laughter)* éclat *m*; *(e.g., of generosity)* élan *m*

out′cast′ *adj & s* banni *m*, proscrit *m*

out′caste′ *adj* hors caste ‖ *s* hors-caste *mf*

out′come′ *s* résultat *m*, dénouement *m*

out′cry′ *s* (pl **-cries**) clameur *f*; *(of indignation)* levée *f* de boucliers

out-dat′ed *adj* démodé, suranné

out′dis′tance *tr* dépasser; (sports) distancer

out′do′ *v* (pret **-did**; pp **-done**) *tr* surpasser, l'emporter sur; **to outdo oneself** se surpasser

out′door′ *adj* au grand air; (sports) de plein air

out′door grill′ *s* rôtisserie *f* en plein air

out′doors′ *s* rase campagne *f*, plein air *m* ‖ *adv* au grand air, en plein air; en plein air; *(outside of the house)* hors de la maison; *(at night)* à la belle étoile

out′door swim′ming pool *s* piscine *f* à ciel ouvert

outer [ˈaʊtər] *adj* extérieur, externe

out′er space′ *s* cosmos *m*, espace *m* cosmique

out′field′ *s* *(baseball)* grand champ *m*

out′fit′ *s* équipement *m*, attirail *m*; *(caseful of implements)* trousse *f*, nécessaire *m*; *(ensemble)* costume et accessoires *mpl*; *(of a bride)* trousseau *m*; *(team)* équipe *f*; *(group of soldiers)* unité *f*; (com) compagnie *f* ‖ *v* (pret & pp **-fitted**; ger **-fitting**) *tr* équiper

out′go′ing *adj* en partance, partant; *(officeholder)* sortant; *(friendly)* communicatif, sympathique

out′grow′ *v* (pret **-grew**; pp **-grown**) *tr* devenir plus grand que; *(e.g., childhood clothes, activities, etc.)* devenir trop grand pour; abandonner, se défaire de

out′growth′ *s* excroissance *f*; (fig) résultat *m*, conséquence *f*

outing [ˈaʊtɪŋ] *s* excursion *f*, sortie *f*

outlandish [aʊtˈlændɪʃ] *adj* bizarre, baroque

out′last′ *tr* durer plus longtemps que; survivre (with *dat*)

out′law′ *s* hors-la-loi *m*, proscrit *m* ‖ *tr* mettre hors la loi, proscrire

out′lay′ *s* débours *mpl*, dépenses *fpl*

out′lay′ *v* (pret & pp **-laid**) *tr* débourser, dépenser

out′let′ *s* sortie *f*, issue *f*; *(escape valve)* déversoir *m*; *(for, e.g., pent-up emotions)* exutoire *m*; (com) débouché *m*; (elec) prise *f* de courant; **no outlet** (public sign) rue sans issue

out′line′ *s* *(profile)* contour *m*; *(sketch)* esquisse *f*; *(summary)* aperçu *m*; *(of a work in preparation)* plan *m*; *(main points)* grandes lignes *fpl* ‖ *tr* esquisser; *(a work in preparation)* ébaucher

out′live′ *tr* survivre (with *dat*)

out′lived′ *adj* caduc, désuet

out′look′ *s* perspective *f*, point *m* de vue

out′ly′ing *adj* éloigné, écarté, isolé

outmoded [ˌaʊtˈmodɪd] *adj* démodé

out′num′ber *tr* surpasser en nombre

out′-of-date′ *adj* démodé, suranné

out′-of-door′ *adj* au grand air

out′-of-doors′ *adj* au grand air ‖ *s* rase campagne *f*, plein air *m* ‖ *adv* au grand air, hors de la maison

out′ of or′der *adj* en panne; **to be out of order** *(to be out of sequence)* ne pas être dans l'ordre

out′ of print′ *adj* épuisé

out′ of tune′ *adj* désaccordé ‖ *adv* faux, e.g., **to sing out of tune** chanter faux

out′ of work′ *adj* en chômage

out′pa′tient *s* malade *mf* de consultation externe

out′patient clin′ic *s* consultation *f* externe

out′post′ *s* avant-poste *m*, antenne *f*

out′put′ *s* rendement *m*, débit *m*; *(of a mine; of a worker)* production *f*

out′rage *s* outrage *m*; *(wanton violence)* atrocité *f*, attentat *m* honteux ‖ *tr* faire outrage à, outrager; *(a woman)* violer

outrageous [aʊtˈredʒəs] *adj* outrageux; *(intolerable)* insupportable

out′rank′ *tr* dépasser en grade, dépasser en rang

out′rid′er *s* explorateur *m*; cow-boy *m*; *(mounted attendant)* piqueur *m*

outrigger [ˈaʊtˌrɪgər] *s* *(outboard framework)* balancier *m*; *(oar support)* porte-en-dehors *m*

out′right′ *adj* pur, absolu; *(e.g., manner)* franc, direct ‖ **out′right′** *adv* complètement; *(frankly)* franchement; *(at once)* sur le coup

out′set′ *s* début *m*, commencement *m*

out′side′ *adj* du dehors, d'extérieur ‖ **out′side′** *s* dehors *m*, extérieur *m*, surface *f*; **at the outside** tout au plus, au maximum ‖ **out′side′** *adv* dehors, à l'extérieur; *(outdoors)* en plein air; **outside of** en dehors de, à l'extérieur de; *(except for)* sauf ‖ **out′side′** or **out′side′** *prep* en dehors de, à l'extérieur de

outsider [ˌaʊtˈsaɪdər] *s* étranger *m*; *(intruder)* intrus *m*; *(uninitiated)* profane *mf*; *(dark horse)* outsider *m*

out′size′ *adj* hors série

out/skirts/ spl approches fpl, périphérie f

out/spo/ken adj franc; **to be outspoken** avoir son franc-parler

out/stand/ing adj saillant; (eminent) hors pair, hors ligne; (debts) à recouvrer, impayé

outward ['autwərd] adj extérieur; (apparent) superficiel; (direction) en dehors || adv au dehors, vers le dehors

out/weigh/ tr peser plus que; (in value) l'emporter en valeur sur

out/wit/ v (pret & pp -witted; ger -witting) tr duper, déjouer; (a pursuer) dépister

oval ['ovəl] adj & s ovale m

ova•ry ['ovəri] s (pl -ries) ovaire m

ovation [o've/ən] s ovation f

oven ['ʌvən] s four m; (fig) fournaise f

over ['ovər] adj fini, passé; (additional) en plus; (excessive) en excès; plus, e.g., **eight and over** huit et plus || adv au-dessus, dessus; (on the other side) de l'autre côté; (again) de nouveau; (on the reverse side of sheet of paper) au verso; (finished) passé, achevé; **all over** (everywhere) partout; (finished) fini; (completely) jusqu'au bout des ongles; **I'll be right over** (coll) j'arrive tout de suite; **over!** (turn the page!) voir au verso!, tournez!; (rad) à vous!; **over again** de nouveau, encore une fois; **over against** en face de; (compared to) auprès de; **over and above** en plus de; **over and out!** (rad) terminé!; **over and over** à coups répétés, à plusieurs reprises; **over here** ici, de ce côté; **over there** là-bas; **to be over** (an illness) s'être remis de; **to hand over** remettre || prep au-dessus de; (on top of) sur, par-dessus; (with motion) par-dessus, e.g., **to jump over a fence** sauter par-dessus une barrière; (a period of time) pendant, au cours de; (near) près de; (a certain number or amount) plus de, audessus de; (concerning) à propos de, au sujet de; (on the other side of) au delà de, de l'autre côté de; à, e.g., **over the telephone** au téléphone; (while doing s.th.) tout en prenant, e.g., **over a cup of coffee** tout en prenant une tasse de café; **all over** répandu sur; **over and above** en sus de, en plus de; **to fall over** (e.g., a cliff) tomber du haut de; **to reign over** régner sur

o/ver-all/ adj hors tout, complet; général, total || **overalls** spl combinaison f d'homme, cotte f, salopette f

o/ver-awe/ tr impressionner, intimider

o/ver-bear/ing adj impérieux, tranchant, autoritaire

o/ver-board/ adv par-dessus bord; **man overboard!** un homme à la mer!; **to throw overboard** jeter par-dessus le bord; (fig) abandonner

o/ver-cast/ adj obscurci, nuageux || s ciel m couvert || v (pret & pp -cast) tr obscurcir, couvrir

o/ver-charge/ s prix m excessif, majoration f excessive; (elec) surcharge f || **o/ver-charge/** tr majorer; (elec) surcharger; **to overcharge s.o. for s.th.** faire payer trop cher q.ch. à qn

o/ver-coat/ s pardessus m

o/ver-come/ v (pret -came; pp -come) tr vaincre; (difficulties) surmonter

o/ver-con/fidence s témérité f, confiance f exagérée

o/ver-con/fident adj téméraire, excessivement confiant

o/ver-cooked/ adj trop cuit

o/ver-crowd/ tr bonder; (a town, region, etc.) surpeupler

o/ver-do/ v (pret -did; pp -done) tr exagérer; **overdone** (culin) trop cuit || intr se surmener

o/ver-dose/ s dose f excessive

o/ver-draft/ s découvert m, solde m débiteur

o/ver-draw/ v (pret -drew; pp -drawn) tr tirer à découvert || intr excéder son crédit

o/ver-drive/ s (aut) surmultiplication f

o/ver-due/ adj en retard; (com) échu, arriéré

o/ver-eat/ v (pret -ate; pp -eaten) tr & intr trop manger

o/ver-exer/tion s surmenage m

o/ver-expose/ tr surexposer

o/ver-expo/sure s surexposition f

o/ver-flow/ s débordement m; (pipe) trop-plein m || **o/ver-flow/** tr & intr déborder

o/ver-fly/ v (pret -flew; pp -flown) tr survoler

o/ver-grown/ adj démesuré; (e.g., child) trop grand pour son âge; **overgrown with** (e.g., weeds) envahi par, recouvert de

o/ver-hang/ v (pret & pp -hung) tr surplomber, faire saillie au-dessus de; (to threaten) menacer || intr (to jut out) faire saillie

o/ver-haul/ s remise f en état || **o/ver-haul/** tr remettre en état; (to catch up to) rattraper

o/ver-head/ adj élevé; aérien, surélevé || s (overpass) pont-route m; (com) frais mpl généraux || **o/ver-head/** adv au-dessus de la tête, en haut

o/ver-head valve/ s soupape f en tête

o/ver-hear/ v (pret & pp -heard) tr entendre par hasard; (a conversation) surprendre

o/ver-heat/ tr surchauffer

overjoyed [,ovər'dʒɔɪd] adj ravi, transporté de joie

overland ['ovər,lænd], ['ovərlənd] adj & adv par terre, par voie de terre

o/ver-lap/ v (pret & pp -lapped; ger -lapping) tr enchevaucher || intr chevaucher

o/ver-lap/ping s recouvrement m, chevauchement m; (of functions, offices, etc.) double emploi m

o/ver-load/ s surcharge f; **sudden overload** (elec) coup m de collier || **o/ver-load/** tr surcharger o'ver·look' tr donner sur, avoir vue sur; (to ignore) fermer les yeux sur, passer sous silence; (to neglect) oublier, négliger

o'ver·lord' s suzerain m || o'ver·lord' tr dominer, tyranniser

overly ['ovərli] adv trop, à l'excès

o'ver·night' adv toute la nuit; du jour au lendemain; to stay overnight passer la nuit

o'ver·night' bag' s sac m de nuit

o'ver·pass' s passage m supérieur, pont-route m

o'ver·pay'ment s surpaye f, rétribution f excessive

o'ver·pop'u·la'tion s surpeuplement m, surpopulation f

o'ver·pow'er tr maîtriser; overpowered with grief accablé de douleur

o'ver·pow'er·ing adj accablant, irrésistible

o'ver·produc'tion s surproduction f

o'ver·rate' tr surestimer

o'ver·reach' tr dépasser

o'ver·ripe' adj blet, trop mûr

o'ver·rule' tr décider contre; (to set aside) annuler, casser

o'ver·run' v (pret -ran; pp -run; ger -running) tr envahir; (to flood) inonder; (limits, boundaries, etc.) dépasser || intr déborder

o'ver·sea' or o'ver·seas' adj d'outremer || o'ver·sea' or o'ver·seas' adv outre-mer

o'ver·see' v (pret -saw; pp -seen) tr surveiller

o'ver·se'er s surveillant m, inspecteur m

o'ver·shad'ow tr ombrager; (fig) éclipser

o'ver·shoes' spl caoutchoucs mpl

o'ver·sight' s inadvertance f, étourderie f

o'ver·sleep' v (pret & pp -slept) intr dormir trop longtemps

o'ver·step' v (pret & pp -stepped; ger -stepping) tr dépasser, outrepasser

o'ver·stock' tr surapprovisionner

o'ver·stuffed' adj rembourré

o'ver·sup·ply' s (pl -plies) excédent m, abondance f || o'ver·sup·ply' v (pret & pp -plied) tr approvisionner avec excès

overt ['ovərt], [o'vʌrt] adj ouvert, manifeste; (intentional) prémédité

o'ver·take' v (pret -took; pp -taken) tr rattraper; (a runner) dépasser; (an automobile) doubler; (to surprise) surprendre

o'ver·tax' tr surtaxer; (to tire) surmener, excéder

o'ver-the-coun'ter adj vendu directement à l'acheteur

o'ver·throw' s renversement m || o'ver·throw' v (pret -threw; pp -thrown) tr renverser

o'ver·time' adj & adv en heures supplémentaires || s heures fpl supplémentaires

o'ver·tone' s (mus) harmonique m; (fig) signification f, sous-entendu m

o'ver·trump' tr surcouper

overture ['ovərtʃər] s ouverture f

o'ver·turn' tr renverser, chavirer || intr chavirer; (aer, aut) capoter

overweening [,ovər'winɪŋ] adj arrogant, outrecuidant

o'ver·weight' adj au-dessus du poids normal; (fat) obèse || s excédent m de poids

overwhelm [,ovər'hwelm] tr accabler, écraser; (with favors, gifts, etc.) combler

o'ver·work' s surmenage m, excès m de travail || o'ver·work' tr surmener, surcharger; abuser de, trop employer || intr se surmener

Ovid ['ɑvɪd] s Ovide m

ow [au] interj aïe!

owe [o] tr devoir || intr avoir des dettes; to owe for avoir à payer, devoir

owing ['o·ɪŋ] adj dû, redû; owing to à cause de, en raison de

owl [aul] s (Asio) hibou m; (Strix) chouette f, hulotte f; (Tyto alba) effraie f

own [on] adj propre, e.g., my own brother mon propre frère || s—all its own spécial, authentique, e.g., an aroma all its own un parfum spécial, un parfum authentique; my own (your own, etc.) le mien (le vôtre, etc.) §89; of my own (of their own, etc.) bien à moi (bien à eux, etc.); on one's own à son propre compte, de son propre chef; to come into one's own entrer en possession de son bien; (to win out) obtenir des succès; (to receive due praise) recevoir les honneurs qu'on mérite; to hold one's own se maintenir, se défendre || tr posséder; être propriétaire de; (to acknowledge) reconnaître || intr—to own to convenir de, reconnaître; to own up (coll) faire des aveux; to own up to (coll) faire l'aveu de, avouer

owner ['onər] s propriétaire mf, possesseur m

ownership ['onər,ʃɪp] s propriété f, possession f

own'er's li'cense s carte f grise

ox [ɑks] s (pl oxen ['ɑksən]) bœuf m

ox'cart' s char m à bœufs

oxfords ['ɑksfərdz] spl richelieus mpl

oxide ['ɑksaɪd] s oxyde m

oxidize ['ɑksɪ,daɪz] tr oxyder || intr s'oxyder

oxygen ['ɑksɪdʒən] s oxygène m

oxygenate ['ɑksɪdʒə,net] tr oxygéner

ox'ygen tent' s tente f à oxygène

oxytone ['ɑksɪ,ton] adj & s oxyton m

oyster ['ɔɪstər] adj huîtrier || s huître f

oys'ter bed' s huîtrière f, banc m d'huîtres

oys'ter cock'tail s huîtres fpl écaillées aux condiments

oys'ter farm' s parc m à huîtres, clayère f

oys'ter fork' s fourchette f à huîtres

oys'ter knife' s couteau m à huîtres

oys'ter·man s (pl -men) écailler m
oys'ter op'ener s (person) écailler m; (implement) ouvre-huîtres m
oys'ter plant' s salsifis m

oys'ter shell' s coquille f d'huître
oys'ter stew' s soupe f à huîtres
ozone ['ozon] s ozone m; (coll) air m frais

P

P, p [pi] s XVIᵉ lettre de l'alphabet
pace [pes] s pas m; to keep pace with marcher de pair avec; to put through one's paces mettre à l'épreuve; to set the pace mener le train ‖ tr arpenter; to pace off mesurer au pas ‖ intr aller au pas
pace'mak'er s meneur m de train
pacific [pə'sɪfɪk] adj pacifique ‖ Pacific adj & s Pacifique m
pacifier ['pæsɪ,far·ər] s pacificateur m; (teething ring) sucette f
pacifism ['pæsɪ,fɪzəm] s pacifisme m
pacifist ['pæsɪfɪst] adj & s pacifiste mf
paci·fy ['pæsɪ,faɪ] v (pret & pp -fied) tr pacifier
pack [pæk] s paquet m; (of peddler) ballot m; (of soldier) paquetage m, sac m; (of beast of burden) bât m; (of hounds) meute f; (of evildoers; of wolves) bande f; (of lies) tissu m; (of playing cards) jeu m; (of cigarettes) paquet m; (of floating ice) banquise f; (of troubles) foule f; (of fools) tas m; (med) enveloppement m ‖ tr emballer, empaqueter; mettre en boîte; (e.g., earth) tasser; (to stuff) bourrer; to send packing (coll) envoyer promener ‖ intr faire ses bagages
package ['pækɪdʒ] s paquet m ‖ tr empaqueter
pack'age plan' s voyage m à forfait
pack' an'imal s bête f de somme
packet ['pækɪt] s paquet m; (naut) paquebot m; (pharm) sachet m
pack'ing box' or **case'** s caisse f d'emballage
pack'ing house' s conserverie f
pack'sad'dle s bât m
pack'thread' s ficelle f
pack'train' s convoi m de bêtes de somme
pact [pækt] s pacte m
pad [pæd] s bourrelet m; (of writing paper) bloc m; (for inking) tampon m; (of an aquatic plant) feuille f; (for launching a rocket) rampe f; (sound of footsteps) pas m ‖ v (pret & pp padded; ger padding) tr rembourrer; (to expand unnecessarily) délayer ‖ intr aller à pied
pad'ded cell' s cellule f matelassée, cabanon m
paddle ['pædəl] s (of a canoe) pagaie f; (for table tennis) raquette f; (of a wheel) aube f; (for beating) palette f ‖ tr pagayer; (to spank) fesser ‖ intr pagayer; (to splash) barboter
pad'dle wheel' s roue f à aubes

paddock ['pædək] s enclos m; (at race track) paddock m
pad'dy wag'on ['pædɪ] s (slang) panier m à salade
pad'lock' s cadenas m ‖ tr cadenasser
pagan ['pegən] adj & s païen m
paganism ['pegə,nɪzəm] s paganisme m
page [pedʒ] s (of a book) page f; (boy attendant) page m; (in a hotel or club) chasseur m ‖ tr (a book) paginer; appeler, demander, e.g., you are being paged on vous demande
pageant ['pædʒənt] s parade f à grand spectacle
pageant·ry ['pædʒəntrɪ] s (pl -ries) grand apparat m; vaines pompes fpl
page' proof' s seconde épreuve f; (journ) morasse f
paginate ['pædʒɪ,net] tr paginer
paging ['pedʒɪŋ] s mise f en pages
paid' in full' [ped] adj (formula stamped on bill) pour acquit
paid' vaca'tion s congé m payé
pail [pel] s seau m
pain [pen] s douleur f; on pain of sous peine de; to take pains se donner de la peine ‖ tr faire mal (with dat); it pains me to il me coûte de ‖ intr faire mal
painful ['penfəl] adj douloureux
pain'kil'ler s (coll) calmant m
painless ['penlɪs] adj sans douleur
pains'tak'ing adj soigneux; (work) soigné
paint [pent] s peinture f; wet paint peinture fraîche; (public sign) attention à la peinture! ‖ tr & intr peindre
paint'box' s boîte f de couleurs
paint'brush' s pinceau m
paint' buck'et s camion m
painter ['pentər] s peintre mf
painting ['pentɪŋ] s peinture f
paint' remov'er s décapant m
pair [per] s paire f; (of people) couple m ‖ tr accoupler ‖ intr s'accoupler
pair' of scis'sors s ciseaux mpl
pair' of trou'sers s pantalon m
pajamas [pə'dʒaməz], [pə'dʒæməz] spl pyjama m, pyjamas
Pakistan [,pɑkɪ'stɑn] s le Pakistan
Pakista·ni [,pɑkɪ'stɑni] adj pakistanais ‖ s (pl -nis) Pakistanais m
pal [pæl] s copain m ‖ v (pret & pp palled; ger palling) intr (coll) être de bons copains; to pal with être copain de
palace ['pælɪs] s palais m
palatable ['pælətəbəl] adj savoureux; (acceptable) agréable

palatal ['pælətəl] *adj* palatal ǁ *s* palatale *f*

palate ['pælɪt] *s* palais *m*

pale [pel] *adj* pâle ǁ *s* pieux *m*; limites *fpl* ǁ *intr* pâlir

pale'face' *s* visage *m* pâle

palette ['pælɪt] *s* palette *f*

palfrey ['pɔlfri] *s* palefroi *m*

palisade [‚pælɪ'sed] *s* palissade *f*; (*line of cliffs*) falaise *f*

pall [pɔl] *s* poêle *m*, drap *m* mortuaire; (*to cover chalice*) pale *f*; (*vestment*) pallium *m* ǁ *intr* devenir fade; **to pall on** rassasier

pall'bear'er *s* porteur *m* d'un cordon du poêle

pallet ['pælɪt] *s* grabat *m*

palliate ['pælɪ‚et] *tr* pallier

pallid ['pælɪd] *adj* pâle, blême

pallor ['pælər] *s* pâleur *f*

palm [pɑm] *s* (*of the hand*) paume *f*; (*measure*) palme *f*; (*leaf*) palme *f*; (*tree*) palmier *m*; **to carry off the palm** remporter la palme; **to grease the palm of** (slang) graisser la patte à ǁ *tr* (*a card*) escamoter; **to palm off s.th. on s.o.** refiler q.ch. à qn

palmet·to [pæl'meto] *s* (*pl* **-tos** or **-toes**) palmier *m* nain

palmist ['pɑmɪst] *s* chiromancien *m*

palmistry ['pɑmɪstri] *s* chiromancie *f*

palm' leaf' *s* palme *f*

palm' oil' *s* huile *f* de palme

Palm' Sun'day *s* le dimanche des Rameaux

palm' tree' *s* palmier *m*

palpable ['pælpəbəl] *adj* palpable

palpitate ['pælpɪ‚tet] *intr* palpiter

pal·sy ['pɔlzi] *s* (*pl* **-sies**) paralysie *f* ǁ *v* (*pret & pp* **-sied**) *tr* paralyser

pal·try ['pɔltri] *adj* (*comp* **-trier**; *super* **-triest**) misérable

pamper ['pæmpər] *tr* choyer, gâter

pamphlet ['pæmflɪt] *s* brochure *f*

pan [pæn] *s* casserole *f*; (*basin; scale of a balance*) bassin *m*; (slang) binette *f*; **Pan** Pan *m* ǁ *v* (*pret & pp* **panned**; *ger* **panning**) *tr* (*gold*) laver à la batée; (coll) débiner, éreinter ǁ *intr* laver à la batée; (mov) panoramiquer; **to pan out well** (coll) réussir

panacea [‚pænə'si‚ə] *s* panacée *f*

Panama ['pænə‚mɑ], [‚pænə'mɑ] *s* le Panama

Pan'ama Canal' *s* canal *m* de Panama

Pan'ama Canal' Zone' *s* zone *f* canal du Panama

Pan'ama hat' *s* panama *m*

Pan-American [‚pænə'merɪkən] *adj* panaméricain

pan'cake' *s* crêpe *f* ǁ *intr* (aer) descendre à plat, se plaquer

pan'cake land'ing *s* atterrissage *m* plaqué, sur le ventre, or à plat

panchromatic [‚pænkro'mætɪk] *adj* panchromatique

pancreas ['pænkrɪ‚əs] *s* pancréas *m*

pander ['pændər] *s* entremetteur *m* ǁ *intr* servir d'entremetteur; **to pander to** se prêter à; encourager

pane [pen] *s* carreau *m*, vitre *f*

pan·el ['pænəl] *s* panneau *m*; (*on wall*) lambris *m*; liste *f*, tableau *m*; groupe *m* de discussion ǁ *v* (*pret & pp* **-eled** or **-elled**; *ger* **-eling** or **-elling**) *tr* (*a room*) garnir de boiseries; (*a wall*) lambrisser

pan'·el discus'sion *s* colloque *m*

panelist ['pænəlɪst] *s* membre *m* d'un groupe de discussion

pang [pæŋ] *s* élancement *m*, angoisse *f*

pan'han'dle *s* queue *f* de la poêle; (geog) projection *f* d'un territoire dans un autre ǁ *intr* (slang) mendigoter

pan'han'dler *s* (slang) mendigot *m*

pan·ic ['pænɪk] *adj & s* panique *f* ǁ *v* (*pret & pp* **-icked**; *ger* **-icking**) *tr* semer la panique dans ǁ *intr* être pris de panique

pan'ic-strick'en *adj* pris de panique

pano·ply ['pænəpli] *s* (*pl* **-plies**) panoplie *f*

panorama [‚pænə'ræmə], [‚pænə'rɑmə] *s* panorama *m*

pan·sy ['pænzi] *s* (*pl* **-sies**) pensée *f*; (slang) tapette *f*

pant [pænt] *s* halètement *m*; **pants** pantalon *m*; **to wear the pants** (coll) porter la culotte ǁ *intr* haleter, panteler

pantheism ['pænθɪ‚ɪzəm] *s* panthéisme *m*

pantheon ['pænθɪ‚ɑn], ['pænθɪ·ən] *s* panthéon *m*

panther ['pænθər] *s* panthère *f*

panties ['pæntiz] *spl* culotte *f*

pantomime ['pæntə‚maɪm] *s* pantomime *f*

pan·try ['pæntri] *s* (*pl* **-tries**) office *m & f*, dépense *f*

pap [pæp] *s* bouillie *f*

papa ['pɑpə], [pə'pɑ] *s* papa *m*

papa·cy ['pepəsi] *s* (*pl* **-cies**) papauté *f*

paper ['pepər] *s* papier *m*; (*newspaper*) journal *m*; (*of needles*) carte *f* ǁ *tr* tapisser

pa'per·back' *s* livre *m* broché; (*pocketbook*) livre de poche

pa'per·boy' *s* vendeur *m* de journaux

pa'per clip' *s* attache *f*, trombone *m*

pa'per cone' *s* cornet *m* de papier

pa'per cup' *s* verre *m* en carton, gobelet *m* de papier

pa'per cut'ter *s* coupe-papier *m*

pa'per hand'kerchief *s* mouchoir *m* à jeter, mouchoir en papier

pa'per-hang'er *s* tapissier *m*

pa'per knife' *s* coupe-papier *m*

pa'per mill' *s* papeterie *f*

pa'per mon'ey *s* papier-monnaie *m*

pa'per nap'kin *s* serviette *f* en papier

pa'per plate' *s* assiette *f* en carton, assiette de papier

pa'p·r tape' *s* bande *f* de papier

pa'per tow'el *s* serviette *f* de toilette en papier

pa'per·weight' *s* presse-papiers *m*

pa'per work' *s* travail *m* de bureau

papier-mâché [‚pepərmə'ʃe] *s* papier-pierre *m*, papier *m* mâché

paprika [pæ'prikə], ['pæprɪkə] *s* paprika *m*

papy·rus [pə'paɪrəs] s (pl **-ri** [raɪ]) papyrus m

par [pɑr] s pair m; (golf) normale f du parcours; **at par** au pair; **to be on a par with** aller de pair avec

parable ['pærəbəl] s parabole f

parabola [pə'ræbələ] s parabole f

parachute ['pærə‚ʃut] s parachute m || tr & intr parachuter

par'achute jump' s saut m en parachute

parachutist ['pærə‚ʃutɪst] s parachutiste mf

parade [pə'red] s défilé m; (ostentation) parade f; (mil) parade || tr faire parade de || intr défiler; parader

paradise ['pærə‚daɪs] s paradis m

paradox ['pærə‚dɑks] s paradoxe m

paradoxical [‚pærə'dɑksɪkəl] adj paradoxal

paraffin ['pærəfɪn] s paraffine f || tr paraffiner

paragon ['pærə‚gɑn] s parangon m

paragraph ['pærə‚græf], ['pærə‚grɑf] s paragraphe m

Paraguay ['pærə‚gwe], ['pærə‚gwaɪ] s le Paraguay

Paraguayan [‚pærə'gwe·ən], [‚pærə'gwaɪ·ən] adj paraguayen || s Paraguayen m

parakeet ['pærə‚kit] s perruche f

paral·lel ['pærə‚lɛl] adj parallèle || s (line) parallèle f; (latitude; declination; comparison) parallèle m; **without parallels** (typ) barres fpl; **without parallel** sans pareil || v (pret & pp -leled or -lelled; ger -leling or -lelling) tr mettre en parallèle; entrer en parallèle avec, égaler

par'allel bars' spl barres fpl parallèles

paraly·sis [pə'rælɪsɪs] s (pl -ses [‚siz]) paralysie f

paralytic [‚pærə'lɪtɪk] adj & s paralytique mf

paralyze ['pærə‚laɪz] tr paralyser

paramount ['pærə‚maunt] adj suprême, capital

paranoiac [‚pærə'nɔɪ·æk] adj & s paranoïaque mf

parapet ['pærə‚pɛt] s parapet m

paraphernalia [‚pærəfər'nelɪ·ə] spl effets mpl personnels; attirail m

paraphrase ['pærə‚frez] s remaniement m || tr remanier

parasite ['pærə‚saɪt] s parasite m

parasitic(al) [‚pærə'sɪtɪk(əl)] adj parasite

parasol ['pærə‚sɔl], ['pærə‚sɑl] s parasol m, ombrelle f

paratrooper ['pærə‚trupər] s parachutiste m

parboil ['pɑr‚bɔɪl] tr faire cuire légèrement; (vegetables) blanchir

par·cel ['pɑrsəl] s colis m, paquet m || v (pret & pp -celed or -celled; ger -celing or -celling) tr morceler; **to parcel out** répartir

par'cel post' s colis mpl postaux

parch [pɑrtʃ] tr dessécher; (beans, grain, etc.) griller

parchment ['pɑrtʃmənt] s parchemin m

pardon ['pɑrdən] s pardon m; (remis-

sion of penalty by the state) grâce f; **I beg your pardon** je vous demande pardon || tr pardonner; pardonner (with dat); (a criminal) grâcier; **to pardon s.o. for s.th.** pardonner q.ch. à qn

pardonable ['pɑrdənəbəl] adj pardonnable

pare [per] tr (potatoes, fruit, etc.) éplucher; (the nails) rogner; (costs) réduire

parent ['perənt] s père m or mère f; origine f, base f; **parents** parents mpl, père et mère

parentage ['perəntɪdʒ] s paternité f or maternité f; naissance f, origine f

parenthe·sis [pə'rɛnθɪsɪs] s (pl -ses [‚siz]) parenthèse f; **in parentheses** entre parenthèses

parenthood ['perənt‚hud] s paternité f or maternité f

pariah [pə'raɪ·ə], ['pɑrɪ·ə] s paria m

par'ing knife' s couteau m à éplucher

Paris ['pærɪs] s Paris m

parish ['pærɪʃ] s paroisse f || s paroisse f

parishioner [pə'rɪʃənər] s paroissien m

Parisian [pə'rɪʒən], [pə'rɪʒən] adj & s parisien m

parity ['pærɪti] s parité f

park [pɑrk] s parc m || tr garer, parquer || intr stationner

parked adj en stationnement

parking ['pɑrkɪŋ] s parcage m; (e.g., in a city street) stationnement m; **no parking** (public sign) stationnement interdit

park'ing lights' spl (aut) feux mpl de stationnement, feux de position

park'ing lot' s parking m, parc m à autos

park'ing me'ter s parcomètre m

park'ing tick'et s contravention f, papillon m

park'way' s route f panoramique; (turnpike) autoroute f

parley ['pɑrli] s pourparlers mpl || intr parlementer

parliament ['pɑrlɪmənt] s parlement m

parliamentarian [‚pɑrlɪmɛn'tɛrɪ·ən] s expert m en usages parlementaires

parlor ['pɑrlər] s salon m; (in an institution) parloir m

par'lor car' s (rr) wagon-salon m

par'lor game' s jeu m de société

Parnassus [pɑr'næsəs] s le Parnasse

parochial [pə'rokɪ·əl] adj paroissial; (attitude) provincial

paro'chial school' s école f confessionnelle, école libre

paro·dy ['pærədi] s (pl -dies) parodie f || v (pret & pp -died) tr parodier

parole [pə'rol] s parole f d'honneur; liberté f sur parole || tr libérer sur parole

par·quet [pɑr'ke], [pɑr'kɛt] s parquet m; (theat) premiers rangs mpl du parterre || v (pret & pp -queted ['ked], ['kɛtɪd]; ger -queting ['ke·ɪŋ], ['kɛtɪŋ]) tr parqueter

parricide ['pærɪ‚saɪd] s (act) parricide m; (person) parricide mf

parrot ['pærət] *s* perroquet *m* || *tr* répéter or imiter comme un perroquet

par•ry ['pærɪ] *s* (*pl* -ries) parade *f* || *v* (*pret & pp* -ried) *tr* parer; (*a question*) éluder

parse [pɑrs] *tr* faire l'analyse grammaticale de

parsimonious [,pɑrsɪ'monɪ-əs] *adj* parcimonieux, regardant

parsley ['pɑrslɪ] *s* persil *m*

parsnip ['pɑrsnɪp] *s* panais *m*

parson ['pɑrsən] *s* curé *m*; pasteur *m* protestant

parsonage ['pɑrsənɪdʒ] *s* presbytère *m*

part [pɑrt] *s* partie *f*; (*share*) part *f*; (*of a machine*) organe *m*, pièce *f*; (*of the hair*) raie *f*; (*theat*) rôle *m*; **for my part** pour ma part; **for the most part** pour la plupart; **in part** en partie; **in these parts** dans ces parages; **on the part of** de la part de; **parts** qualités *fpl*; **parties** (*génitales*) *fpl*; **to be or form part of** faire partie de; **to be part and parcel of** faire partie intégrante de; **to do one's part** faire son devoir; **to live a part** (theat) entrer dans la peau d'un personnage; **to look the part** avoir le physique de l'emploi; **to take part in** prendre part à; **to take the part of** prendre parti pour; jouer le rôle de || *adv* partiellement, en partie; **part . . . part** moitié . . . moitié || *tr* séparer; **to part the hair** se faire une raie || *intr* se séparer; (*said, e.g., of road*) diverger; (*to break*) rompre; **to part with** se défaire de; se dessaisir de

par•take [pɑr'tek] *v* (*pret* -took; *pp* -taken) *intr*—**to partake in** participer à; **to partake of** (*e.g., a meal*) prendre; (*e.g., joy*) participer de

partial ['pɑrʃəl] *adj* partiel; (*prejudiced*) partial

participant [pɑr'tɪsɪpənt] *adj & s* participant *m*

participate [pɑr'tɪsɪ,pet] *intr* participer

participation [pɑr,tɪsɪ'peʃən] *s* participation *f*

participle ['pɑrtɪ,sɪpəl] *s* participe *m*

particle ['pɑrtɪkəl] *s* particule *f*

particular [pər'tɪkjələr] *adj* particulier; difficile, exigeant; méticuleux; **a particular . . . un certain . . .** || *s* détail *m*

particularize [pər'tɪkjələ,raɪz] *tr & intr* individualiser, particulariser

parting ['pɑrtɪŋ] *s* séparation *f*

partisan ['pɑrtɪzən] *adj & s* partisan *m*

partition [pɑr'tɪʃən] *s* partage *m*; (*wall*) paroi *f*, cloison *f* || *tr* partager; **to partition off** séparer par des cloisons

partner ['pɑrtnər] *s* partenaire *mf*; (*husband*) conjoint *m*; (*wife*) conjointe *f*; (*in a dance*) cavalier *m*; (*in business*) associé *m*

part'ner•ship' *s* association *f*; (com) société *f*

part' of speech' *s* partie *f* du discours

part' own'er *s* copropriétaire *mf*

partridge ['pɑrtrɪdʒ] *s* perdrix *f*

part'-time' *adj & adv* à mi-temps

par•ty ['pɑrtɪ] *adj* de gala || *s* (*pl* -ties) fête *f*, soirée *f*; (*diversion of a group of persons; individual named in contract or lawsuit*) partie *f*; (*with whom one is conversing*) interlocuteur *m*; (mil) détachement *m*, peloton *m*; (pol) parti *m*; (telp) correspondant *m*; (coll) individu *m*; **to be a party to** être complice de

party-goer ['pɑrtɪ,go·ər] *s* invité *m*; (*nightlifer*) noceur *m*

par'ty line' *s* (*between two properties*) limite *f*; (telp) ligne *f* à postes groupés || **par'ty line'** *s* ligne du parti; (*of communist party*) directives *fpl* du parti

par'ty pol'itics *s* politique *f* de parti

par'ty wall' *s* mur *m* mitoyen

pass [pæs], [pɑs] *s* (*navigable channel; movement of hands of magician; in sports*) passe *f*; (*straits*) pas *m*; (*in mountains*) col *m*, passage *m*; (*document*) laissez-passer *m*; difficulté *f*; (mil) permission *f*; (rr) permis *m* de circulation; (theat) billet *m* de faveur || *tr* passer; (*an exam*) réussir à; (*e.g., a student*) recevoir; (*a law*) adopter, voter; (*a red light*) brûler; (*to get ahead of*) dépasser; (*a car going in the same direction*) doubler; (*s.o. or s.th. coming toward one*) croiser; (*a certain place*) passer devant; **to pass around** faire circuler; **to pass oneself off as** se faire passer pour; **to pass out** distribuer; **to pass over** passer sous silence; (*to hand over*) transmettre; **to pass s.th. off on s.o.** repasser or refiler qch. à qn || *intr* passer; (educ) être reçu; **to bring to pass** réaliser; **to come to pass** se passer; **to pass as or for** passer pour; **to pass away** disparaître; (*to die out*) s'éteindre; (*to die*) mourir; **to pass by** passer devant; **to pass out** sortir; (slang) s'évanouir; **to pass over** passer sur; (*an obstacle*) franchir; (*said of storm*) s'éloigner; (*to pass through*) traverser; **to pass over to** (*e.g., the enemy*) passer à

passable ['pæsəbəl], ['pɑsəbəl] *adj* passable; (*road, river, etc.*) franchissable

passage ['pæsɪdʒ] *s* passage *m*; (*of time*) cours *m*; (*of a law*) adoption *f*

pass'book' *s* carnet *m* de banque

passenger ['pæsəndʒər] *adj* (e.g., *train*) de voyageurs; (*e.g., pigeon*) de passage || *s* voyageur *m*, passager *m*

passer-by ['pæsər'baɪ], ['pɑsər'baɪ] *s* (*pl* passers-by) passant *m*

passing ['pæsɪŋ], ['pɑsɪŋ] *adj* passager *m*; (*act of passing*) dépassement *m*; (*death*) trépas *m*; (*of time*) écoulement *m*; (*of a law*) adoption *f*; (*in an examination*) la moyenne; une mention passable

passion ['pæʃən] *s* passion *f*

passionate ['pæʃənɪt] *adj* passionné

passive ['pæsɪv] *adj & s* passif *m*

pass'key' *s* passe-partout *m*

pass'-out' check' *s* contremarque *f*

Pass/o/ver s Pâque f
pass/port/ s passeport m
pass/word/ s mot m de passe
past [pæst], [past] adj passé, dernier; (e.g., president) ancien ǁ s passé m ǁ prep au-delà de, passé; plus de; hors de, e.g., **past all understanding** hors de toute compréhension; **it's twenty past five** il est cinq heures vingt; **it's past three o'clock** il est trois heures passées
paste [pest] s (glue) colle f de pâte; (jewelry) strass m; (culin) pâte f ǁ tr coller
paste/board/ s carton m
pastel [pæs'tel] adj & s pastel m
pasteurize ['pæstə,raɪz] tr pasteuriser
pastime ['pæs,taɪm], ['pas,taɪm] s passe-temps m
past/ mas/ter s expert m en la matière, passé maître
pastor ['pæstər], ['pastər] s pasteur m
pastoral ['pæstərəl], ['pastərəl] adj pastoral ǁ s pastorale f
pastorate ['pæstərɪt], ['pastərɪt] s pastorat m
pas/try ['pestrɪ] s (pl -tries) pâtisserie f
pas/try cook/ s pâtissier m
pas/try shop/ s pâtisserie f
pasture ['pæstʃər], ['pastʃər] s pâturage m, pâture f ǁ tr faire paître ǁ intr paître
past/y ['pestɪ] adj (comp -ier; super -iest) pâteux; (face) terreux
pat [pæt] adj à propos; (e.g., excuse) tout prêt ǁ s petite tape f; caresse f; (of butter) coquille f ǁ v (pret & pp patted; ger patting) tr tapoter; caresser; **to pat on the back** encourager, complimenter
patch [pætʃ] s (e.g., of cloth) pièce f, raccommodage m; (of land) parcelle f; (of ice) plaque f; (of inner tube) rustine f; (e.g., of color) tache f; (beauty spot) mouche f ǁ tr rapiécer; **to patch up** rapetasser; (e.g., a quarrel) arranger, raccommoder
patent ['petənt] adj patent ǁ ['pætənt] adj breveté ǁ s brevet m d'invention; **patent applied for** une demande de brevet a été déposée ǁ tr breveter
pat/ent leath/er ['pætənt] s cuir m verni
pat/ent med/icine ['pætənt] s spécialité f pharmaceutique
pat/ent rights/ ['pætənt] spl propriété f industrielle
paternal [pə'tʌrnəl] adj paternel
paternity [pə'tʌrnɪti] s paternité f
path [pæθ], [paθ] s sentier m; (in garden) allée f; (of bullet, heavenly body, etc.) trajectoire f; (for, e.g., riding horses) piste f; **to beat a path** frayer un chemin
pathetic [pə'θɛtɪk] adj pathétique
path/find/er s pionnier m
pathology [pə'θɑlədʒi] s pathologie f
pathos ['peθɑs] s pathétique m
path/way/ s sentier m; (fig) voie f
patience ['peʃəns] s patience f
patient ['peʃənt] adj patient ǁ s malade mf; (undergoing surgery) patient m

pati-o ['pɑtɪ,o] s (pl -os) patio m
patriarch ['petrɪ,ark] s patriarche m
patrician [pə'trɪʃən] adj & s patricien m
patricide ['pætrɪ,saɪd] s (act) parricide m; (person) parricide mf
Patrick ['pætrɪk] s Patrice m
patrimo-ny ['pætrɪ,moni] s (pl -nies) patrimoine m
patriot ['petrɪ.ət], ['pætrɪ.ət] s patriote mf
patriotic [,petrɪ'ɑtɪk], [,pætrɪ'ɑtɪk] adj patriotique, patriote
patriotism ['petrɪ-ə,tɪzəm], ['pætrɪ-ə-,tɪzəm] s patriotisme m
pa-trol [pə'trol] s patrouille f ǁ v (pret & pp -trolled; ger -trolling) tr faire la patrouille dans ǁ intr patrouiller
patrol/man s (pl -men) s agent m de police
patrol/ wag/on s voiture f cellulaire
patron ['petrən], ['pætrən] adj patron ǁ s protecteur m; (com) client m
patronage ['petrənɪdʒ], ['pætrənɪdʒ] s patronage m, clientèle f
patronize ['petrə,naɪz], ['pætrə,naɪz] tr patronner, protéger; traiter avec condescendance; (com) acheter chez
pa/tron saint/ s patron m
patter ['pætər] s petit bruit m; (of rain) fouettement m; (of magician, peddler, etc.) boniment m ǁ intr (said of rain) fouetter; (said of little feet) trottiner
pattern ['pætərn] s patron m; modèle m
pat-ty ['pæti] s (pl -ties) petit pâté m
paucity ['positi] s rareté f; manque m, disette f
paunch [pɔntʃ] s panse f
paunch-y ['pɔntʃi] adj (comp -ier; super -iest) ventru
pauper ['pɔpər] s indigent m
pause [pɔz] s pause f; (mus) point m d'orgue; **to give pause to** faire hésiter ǁ intr faire une pause; hésiter
pave [pev] tr paver
pavement ['pevmənt] s pavé m; (surface) chaussée f
pavilion [pə'vɪljən] s pavillon m
paw [pɔ] s patte f; (coll) main f ǁ tr donner un coup de patte à ǁ intr (said of horse) piaffer
pawl [pɔl] s cliquet m d'arrêt
pawn [pɔn] s (in chess) pion m; (security, pledge) gage m; (tool of another person) jouet m ǁ tr mettre en gage; **to pawn s.th. off on s.o.** (coll) refiler q.ch. à qn
pawn/bro/ker s prêteur m sur gages
pawn/shop/ s mont-de-piété m, crédit m municipal
pawn/ tick/et s reconnaissance f du mont-de-piété
pay [pe] s paye f; (mil) solde f ǁ v (pret & pp paid [ped]) tr payer; (mil) solder; (a compliment; a visit; attention) faire; **to pay back** payer de retour; **to pay down** payer comptant; **to pay off** (a debt) acquitter; (a mortgage) purger; (a creditor) rembourser; **to pay s.o. for s.th.**

payer qn de q.ch., payer q.ch. à qn ‖ *intr* payer, rapporter; **to pay for** payer; **to pay off** (coll) avoir du succès; **to pay up** se libérer par un paiement

payable ['pe·əbəl] *adj* payable

pay' boost' *s* augmentation *f*

pay' check' *s* paye *f*

pay' day' *s* jour *m* de paye

pay' dirt' *s* alluvion *f* exploitable; (coll) source *f* d'argent

payee [pe'i] *s* bénéficiaire *mf*

pay' en'velope *s* sachet *m* de paye; paye *f*

payer ['pe·ər] *s* payeur *m*

pay' load' *s* charge *f* payante; (aer) poids *m* utile

pay'mas'ter *s* payeur *m*

payment ['pemənt] *m* paiement *m*; (*installment, deposit, etc.*) versement *m*

pay' phone' *s* taxiphone *m*

pay'roll' *s* bulletin *m* de paye; (*for officers*) état *m* de solde; (*for enlisted men*) feuille *f* de prêt

pay' sta'tion *s* téléphone *m* public

pea [pi] *s* pois *m*; **green peas** petits pois

peace [pis] *s* paix *f*

peaceable ['pisəbəl] *adj* pacifique

peaceful ['pisfəl] *adj* paisible, pacifique

peace'mak'er *s* pacificateur *m*

peace' of mind' *s* tranquillité *f* d'esprit

peace' pipe' *s* calumet *m* de paix

peach [pitʃ] *s* pêche *f*; (slang) bijou *m*

peach' tree' *s* pêcher *m*

peach·y ['pitʃi] *adj* (*comp* **-ier;** *super* **-iest**) (slang) chouette

pea'coat' *s* (naut) caban *m*

pea'cock' *s* paon *m*

pea'hen' *s* paonne *f*

peak [pik] *s* cime *f*, sommet *m*; (*mountain; mountain top*) pic *m*; (*of beard*) pointe *f*; (*of a cap*) visière *f*; (elec) pointe

peak' hour' *s* heure *f* de pointe

peak' load' *s* (elec) charge *f* maximum

peak' vol'tage *s* tension *f* de crête

peal [pil] *s* retentissement *m*; (*of bells*) carillon *m* ‖ *intr* carillonner

peal' of laugh'ter *s* éclat *m* de rire

peal' of thun'der *s* coup *m* de tonnerre

pea'nut' *s* cacahuète *f*; (bot) arachide *f*

pea'nut but'ter *s* beurre *m* de cacahuètes or d'arachide

pear [per] *s* poire *f*

pearl [pʌrl] *s* perle *f*

pearl' oys'ter *s* huître *f* perlière

pear' tree' *s* poirier *m*

peasant ['pezənt] *adj* & *s* paysan *m*

pea'shoot'er *s* sarbacane *f*

pea' soup' *s* (culin, fig) purée *f* de pois

peat [pit] *s* tourbe *f*

pebble ['pebəl] *s* caillou *m*; (*on seashore*) galet *m*

pebbled *adj* (*leather*) grenu

peck [pek] *s* coup *m* de bec; (*eight quarts*) picotin *m*; (*kiss*) (coll) baiser *m* d'oiseau, bécot *m*; (coll) tas *m* ‖ *tr* becqueter ‖ *intr* picorer; **to peck at** picorer; (*food*) pignocher

peculation [ˌpekjə'leʃən] *s* péculat *m*, détournement *m* de fonds

peculiar [pɪ'kjuljər] *adj* particulier; (*strange*) bizarre

pedagogue ['pedəˌgɑg] *s* pédagogue *mf*

pedagogy ['pedəˌgodʒi], ['pedəˌgɑdʒi] *s* pédagogie *f*

ped·al ['pedəl] *s* pédale *f* ‖ *v* (*pret* & *pp* **-aled** or **-alled;** *ger* **-aling** or **-alling**) *tr* actionner les pédales de ‖ *intr* pédaler

pedant ['pedənt] *s* pédant *m*

pedantic [pɪ'dæntɪk] *adj* pédant

pedant·ry ['pedəntri] *s* (*pl* **-ries**) pédanterie *f*

peddle ['pedəl] *tr* & *intr* colporter

peddler ['pedlər] *s* colporteur *m*

pedestal ['pedɪstəl] *s* piédestal *m*

pedestrian [pɪ'destrɪ·ən] *adj* (*style*) prosaïque ‖ *s* piéton *m*

pediatrics [ˌpidɪ'ætrɪks], [ˌpedɪ'ætrɪks] *s* pédiatrie *f*

pedigree ['pedɪˌgri] *s* généalogie *f*; (*table*) arbre *m* généalogique; (*of animal*) pedigree *m*

pediment ['pedɪmənt] *s* fronton *m*

peek [pik] *s* coup *m* d'œil furtif ‖ *intr* —**to peek at** regarder furtivement

peel [pil] *s* pelure *f*; (*of lemon*) zeste *m* ‖ *tr* peler; **to peel off** enlever ‖ *intr* se peler; (*said of paint*) s'écailler

peep [pip] *s* regard *m* furtif; (*of, e.g., chickens*) piaulement *m* ‖ *intr* piauler; **to peep at** regarder furtivement

peep'hole' *s* judas *m*

peer [pɪr] *s* pair *m* ‖ *intr* regarder avec attention; **to peer at** or **into** scruter

peerless ['pɪrlɪs] *adj* sans pareil

peeve [piv] *s* (coll) embêtement *m* ‖ *tr* (coll) irriter, embêter, fâcher

peevish ['pivɪʃ] *adj* maussade

peg [peg] *s* cheville *f*; (*for tent*) piquet *m*; **to take down a peg** (coll) rabattre le caquet de ‖ *v* (*pret* & *pp* **pegged;** *ger* **pegging**) *tr* cheviller; (*e.g., prices*) indexer, fixer; (*points*) marquer ‖ *intr* piocher; **to peg away** to travailler ferme à

Pegasus ['pegəsəs] *s* Pégase *m*

peg' leg' *s* jambe *f* de bois

peg' top' *s* toupie *f*; **peg tops** pantalon *m* fuseau

Pekin·ese [ˌpikɪ'niz] *adj* pékinois ‖ *s* (*pl* **-ese**) Pékinois *m*

Peking ['pi'kɪŋ] *s* Pékin *m*

pelf [pelf] *s* (pej) lucre *m*

pelican ['pelɪkən] *s* pélican *m*

pellet ['pelɪt] *s* boulette *f*; (*bullet*) grain *m* de plomb; (pharm) pilule *f*

pell-mell ['pel'mel] *adj* confus ‖ *adv* pêle-mêle

pelt [pelt] *s* peau *m*; coup *m* violent; (*of stones, insults, etc.*) grêle *f* ‖ *tr* cribler; (*e.g., stones*) lancer ‖ *intr* tomber à verse

pen [pen] *s* plume *f*; (*fountain pen*) stylo *m*; (*corral*) enclos *m*; (fig) plume; (*prison*) (slang) bloc *m* ‖ *v* (*pret* & *pp* **penned;** *ger* **penning**) *tr* écrire ‖ *v* (*pret* & *pp* **penned** or **pent** [pent]; *ger* **penning**) *tr* parquer

penalize ['pinəˌlaɪz] *tr* (*an action*) sanctionner; (*a person*) punir; (sports) pénaliser

penal·ty ['penəlti] s (pl **-ties**) peine f; (for late payment; in a game) pénalité f; **under penalty of** sous peine de

penance ['penəns] s pénitence f

penchant ['pen/ənt] s penchant m

pen·cil ['pensəl] s crayon m; (of light) faisceau m || v (pret & pp **-ciled** or **-cilled**) ger **-ciling** or **-cilling**) tr crayonner

pen'cil sharp'ener s taille-crayon m

pendent ['pendənt] adj pendant || s pendant m, pendentif m; (of chandelier) pendeloque f

pending ['pendɪŋ] adj pendant || prep en attendant

pendulum ['pendʒələm] s pendule f

pen'dulum bob' s lentille f & intr pénétrer

penetrate ['penɪˌtret] tr & intr pénétrer

penguin ['pengwɪn] s manchot m

pen'hold'er s porte-plume m; (rack) pose-plumes m

penicillin [ˌpenɪ'sɪlɪn] s pénicilline f

peninsula [pə'nɪnsələ] s presqu'île f; (large peninsula like Spain or Italy) péninsule f

peninsular [pə'nɪnsələr] adj péninsulaire

penitence ['penɪtəns] s pénitence f

penitent ['penɪtənt] adj & s pénitent m

pen'knife' s (pl **-knives**) canif m

penmanship ['penmənˌʃɪp] s calligraphie f; (person's handwriting) écriture f

pen' name' s pseudonyme m

pennant ['penənt] s flamme f; (sports) banderole f du championnat

penniless ['penɪlɪs] adj sans le sou

pen·ny ['penɪ] s (pl **-nies**) (U.S.A.) centime m; **not a penny** pas un sou || s (pl **pence** [pens]) (Brit) penny m

pen'ny-pinch'ing adj regardant

pen'ny-weight' s poids m de 24 grains

pen' pal' s (coll) correspondant m

pen'point' s bec m de plume

pension ['pen/ən] s pension f || tr pensionner

pensioner ['pen/ənər] s pensionné m

pensive ['pensɪv] adj pensif

Pentagon ['pentəˌgɑn] s Pentagone m

Pentecost ['pentɪˌkɔst], ['pentɪˌkɑst] s la Pentecôte

penthouse ['pentˌhaʊs] s toit m en auvent, appentis m; appartement m sur toit, maison f à terrasse

pent-up ['pentˌʌp] adj renfermé, refoulé

penult ['pinʌlt] s pénultième f

penum·bra [pɪ'nʌmbrə] s (pl **-brae** [bri] or **-bras**) pénombre f

penurious [pɪ'nurɪ·əs] adj (stingy) mesquin, parcimonieux; (poor) pauvre

penury ['penjərɪ] s indigence f, misère f

pen'wip'er s essuie-plume m

peo·ny ['pi·ənɪ] s (pl **-nies**) pivoine f

people ['pipəl] spl gens mpl, personnes fpl; **many people** beaucoup de monde; **my people** ma famille, mes parents; **people say** on dit || s (pl **peoples**) peuple m, nation f || tr peupler

pep [pep] s (coll) allant m || v (pret & pp **pepped**; ger **pepping**) tr—**to pep up** (coll) animer

pepper ['pepər] s (spice) poivre m; (fruit) grain m de poivre; (plant) poivrier m; (plant or fruit of the hot or red pepper) piment m rouge; (plant or fruit of the sweet or green pepper) piment doux, poivron m vert || tr poivrer; (e.g., with bullets) cribler

pep'per·box' s poivrière f

pep'per mill' s moulin m à poivre

pep'per·mint' s menthe f poivrée; (lozenge) pastille f de menthe

per [pʌr] prep par; **as per** suivant

perambulator [pər'æmbjəˌletər] s voiture f d'enfant

per capita [pər'kæpɪtə] par tête, par personne

perceive [pər'siv] tr (by the senses) apercevoir; (by understanding) percevoir

per cent or **percent** [pər'sent] pour cent

percentage [pər'sentɪdʒ] s pourcentage m; **to get a percentage** (slang) avoir part au gâteau

perceptible [pər'septəbəl] adj perceptible, sensible, appréciable

perception [pər'sep/ən] s perception f; compréhension f, pénétration f

perch [pʌrtʃ] s perchoir m; (ichth) perche f || tr percher || intr percher, se percher

percolate ['pʌrkəˌlet] tr & intr filtrer

percolator ['pʌrkəˌletər] s cafetière f à filtre

percussion [pər'kʌʃən] s percussion f

percus'sion cap' s capsule f fulminante

per diem [pər'daɪ·əm] par jour

perdition [pər'dɪʃən] s perdition f

perennial [pə'renɪ·əl] adj perpétuel; (bot) vivace || s plante f vivace

perfect ['pʌrfɪkt] adj & s parfait m || [pər'fekt] tr perfectionner

perfidious [pər'fɪdɪ·əs] adj perfide

perfi·dy ['pʌrfɪdɪ] s (pl **-dies**) perfidie f

perforate ['pʌrfəˌret] tr perforer

per'forated line' s pointillé m

perforation [ˌpʌrfə're/ən] s perforation f; (of postage stamp) dentelure f

perforce [pər'fors] adv forcément

perform [pər'form] tr exécuter; (surg) faire; (theat) représenter || intr jouer; (said of machine) fonctionner

performance [pər'forməns] s exécution f; (production) rendement m; (of a machine) fonctionnement m; (sports) performance f; (theat) représentation f

performer [pər'formər] s artiste mf

perform'ing arts' spl arts mpl du spectacle

perfume ['pʌrfjum] s parfum m || [pər'fjum] tr parfumer

perfunctory [pər'fʌŋktərɪ] adj superficiel; négligent

perhaps [pər'hæps] adv peut-être; **perhaps not** peut-être que non

per hour' à l'heure

peril ['perəl] s péril m
perilous ['perɪləs] adj périlleux
period ['pɪrɪ.əd] s période f; (in school) heure f de cours; (gram) point m; (sports) division f
pe'riod cos'tume s costume m d'époque
pe'riod fur'niture s meubles d'époque
periodic |,pɪrɪ'ɑdɪk| adj périodique
periodical L,pɪrɪ'ɑdɪkəl| adj périodique || s publication f périodique
peripheral [pə'rɪfərəl] adj périphérique
peripher·y [pə'rɪfəri] s (pl -ies) périphérie f
periscope l'perɪ,skop] s périscope m
perish l'perɪʃ] intr périr
perishable ['perɪ/əbəl] adj périssable
perjure ['pʌrdʒər] tr—to perjure oneself se parjurer
perju·ry l'pʌrdʒəri] s (pl -ries) parjure m
perk [pʌrk] tr—to perk up (the head) redresser; (the ears) dresser; (the appetite) ravigoter || intr—to perk up se ranimer
permanence ['pʌrmənəns] s permanence f
permanent ['pʌrmənənt] adj permanent || s permanente f
per'manent address' s domicile m fixe
per'manent ten'ure s inamovibilité f
per'manent wave' s ondulation f permanente
per'manent way' s (rr) matériel m fixe
permeate l'pʌrmɪ,et] tr & intr pénétrer
permissible [pər'mɪsɪbəl] adj permis
permission [pər'mɪ/ən] s permission f
per·mit l'pʌrmɪt] s permis m; (com) passavant m || [pər'mɪt] v (pret & pp -mitted; ger -mitting) tr permettre; to permit s.o. to permettre à qn de
permute [pər'mjut] tr permuter
pernicious [pər'nɪ/əs] adj pernicieux
pernickety [pər'nɪkɪti] adj (coll) pointilleux
perox'ide blonde' [pər'ɑksaɪd] s blonde f décolorée
perpendicular [,pʌrpən'dɪkjələr] adj & s perpendiculaire f
perpetrate l'pʌrpɪ,tret] tr perpétrer
perpetual [pər'pet/ʊ-əl] adj perpétuel
perpetuate [pər'pet/ʊ,et] tr perpétuer
perplex [pər'pleks] tr rendre perplexe
perplexed [pər'plekst] adj perplexe
perplexi·ty [pər'pleksɪti] s (pl -ties) perplexité f
persecute ['pʌrsɪ,kjut] tr persécuter
persecution [,pʌrsɪ'kju/ən] s persécution f
persevere [,pʌrsɪ'vɪr] intr persévérer
Persian ['pʌrʒən] adj persan || s (language) persan m; (person) Persan m
Per'sian blind' s persienne f
Per'sian Gulf' s Golfe m Persique
Per'sian rug' s tapis m de Perse
persimmon [pər'sɪmən] s plaquemine f; (tree) plaqueminier m
persist [pər'sɪst], [pər'zɪst] intr persister; to persist in persister dans; + ger persister à + inf
persistent [pər'sɪstənt], [pər'zɪstənt] adj persistant

person ['pʌrsən] s personne f; no person personne; per person par personne, chacun
personage ['pʌrsənɪdʒ] s personnage m
personal ['pʌrsənəl] adj personnel || s (journ) note f dans la chronique mondaine
personali·ty [,pʌrsə'nælɪti] s (pl -ties) personnalité f
per'sonal prop'erty s biens mpl mobiliers
personi·fy [pər'sɑnɪ,faɪ] v (pret & pp -fied) tr personnifier
personnel [,pʌrsə'nel] s personnel m
per'son-to-per'son tel'ephone call' s communication f avec préavis
perspective [pər'spektɪv] s perspective f
perspicacious [,pʌrspɪ'ke/əs] adj perspicace
perspiration [,pʌrspɪ're/ən] s transpiration f
perspire [pər'spaɪr] intr transpirer
persuade [pər'swed] tr persuader; to persuade s.o. of s.th. persuader q.ch. à qn, persuader qn de q.ch.; to persuade s.o. to persuader à qn de
persuasion [pər'sweʒən] s persuasion f; (faith) (coll) croyance f
pert [pʌrt] adj effronté; (sprightly) animé
pertain [pər'ten] intr—to pertain to avoir rapport à
pertinacious [,pʌrtɪ'ne/əs] adj obstiné, persévérant
pertinent ['pʌrtɪnənt] adj pertinent
perturb [pər'tʌrb] tr perturber
Peru [pə'ru] s le Pérou
peruse [pə'ruz] tr lire; lire attentivement
Peruvian [pə'ruvɪ·ən] adj péruvien || s Péruvien m
pervade [pər'ved] tr pénétrer, s'infiltrer dans
perverse [pər'vʌrs] adj pervers; obstiné; capricieux
perversion [pər'vʌrʒən] s perversion f
perversi·ty [pər'vʌrsɪti] s (pl -ties) perversité f; obstination f
pervert ['pʌrvərt] s pervers m, perverti m || [pər'vʌrt] tr pervertir
pes·ky ['peski] adj (comp -kier; super -kiest) (coll) importun
pessimism ['pesɪ,mɪzəm] s pessimisme m
pessimist ['pesɪmɪst] s pessimiste mf
pessimistic [,pesɪ'mɪstɪk] adj pessimiste
pest [pest] s insecte m nuisible; (pestilence) peste f; (annoying person) raseur m
pester ['pestər] tr casser la tête à, importuner
pest'house' s lazaret m
pesticide ['pestɪ,saɪd] s pesticide m
pestiferous [pes'tɪfərəs] adj pestiféré; (coll) ennuyeux
pestilence ['pestɪləns] s pestilence f
pestle ['pesəl] s pilon m
pet [pet] s animal m favori; familial m; (child) enfant m gâté; (anger) accès m de mauvaise humeur || v (pret &

pp petted; *ger* petting) *tr* choyer; (*e.g., an animal's fur*) caresser ‖ *intr* (slang) se bécoter

petal ['pɛtəl] *s* pétale *m*

pet'cock' *s* robinet *m* de purge

Peter ['pitər] *s* Pierre *m*; **to rob Peter to pay Paul** découvrir saint Pierre pour habiller saint Paul ‖ (*l.c.*) *intr* —**to peter out** (coll) s'épuiser, s'en aller en fumée

petition [pɪ'tɪʃən] *s* pétition *f* ‖ *tr* adresser *or* présenter une pétition à

pet' name' *s* mot *m* doux, nom *m* d'amitié

Petrarch ['pitrɑrk] *s* Pétrarque *m*

petri·fy ['pɛtrɪ,faɪ] *v* (*pret & pp* -**fied**) *tr* pétrifier ‖ *intr* se pétrifier

petrol ['pɛtrəl] *s* (Brit) essence *f*

petroleum [pɪ'trolɪ·əm] *s* pétrole *m*

pet' shop' *s* boutique *f* aux petites bêtes; (*for birds*) oisellerie *f*

petticoat ['pɛtɪ,kot] *s* jupon *m*

pet·ty ['pɛtɪ] *adj* (*comp* -**tier**; *super* -**tiest**) insignifiant, petit; (*narrow*) mesquin; intolérant

pet'ty cash' *s* petite caisse *f*

pet'ty expen'ses *s* menus frais *mpl*

pet'ty lar'ceny *s* vol *m* simple

pet'ty of'ficer *s* (naut) officier *m* marinier

petulant ['pɛtjələnt] *adj* irritable, boudeur

pew [pju] *s* banc *m* d'église

pewter ['pjutər] *s* étain *m*

Pfc. ['pi'ɛf'si] *s* (letterword) (**private first class**) soldat *m* de première classe

phalanx ['fɛlæŋks], ['fælæŋks] *s* phalange *f*

phantasm ['fæntæzəm] *s* fantasme *m*

phantom ['fæntəm] *s* fantôme *m*

Pharaoh ['fɛro] *s* Pharaon *m*

pharisee ['fɛrɪ,si] *s* pharisien *m*; **Pharisee** Pharisien *m*

pharmaceutical [,fɑrmə'sutɪkəl] *adj* pharmaceutique

pharmacist ['fɑrməsɪst] *s* pharmacien *m*

pharma·cy ['fɑrməsi] *s* (*pl* -**cies**) pharmacie *f*

pharynx ['færɪŋks] *s* pharynx *m*

phase [fez] *s* phase *f*; **out of phase** (*said of motor*) décalé ‖ *tr* mettre en phase; développer en phases successives; (coll) inquiéter; **to phase out** faire disparaître peu à peu

pheasant ['fɛzənt] *s* faisan *m*

phenobarbital [,fino'bɑrbɪ,tæl] *s* phénobarbital *m*

phenomenal [fɪ'nɑmɪ,nəl] *adj* phénoménal

phenome·non [fɪ'nɑmɪ,nɑn] *s* (*pl* -**na** [nə]) phénomène *m*

phial ['faɪ·əl] *s* fiole *f*

philanderer [fɪ'lændərər] *s* coureur *m*, galant *m*

philanthropist [fɪ'lænθrəpɪst] *s* philanthrope *mf*

philanthro·py [fɪ'lænθrəpi] *s* (*pl* -**pies**) philanthropie *f*

philatelist [fɪ'lætəlɪst] *s* philatéliste *mf*

philately [fɪ'lætəli] *s* philatélie *f*

Philippine ['fɪlɪ,pin] *adj* philippin ‖ **Philippines** *spl* Philippines *fpl*

Philistine [fɪ'lɪstin], ['fɪlɪ,stin], ['fɪlɪ,staɪn] *adj & s* philistin *m*

philologist [fɪ'lɑlədʒɪst] *s* philologue *mf*

philology [fɪ'lɑlədʒi] *s* philologie *f*

philosopher [fɪ'lɑsəfər] *s* philosophe *mf*

philosophic(al) [,fɪlə'sɑfɪk(əl)] *adj* philosophique

philoso·phy [fɪ'lɑsəfi] *s* (*pl* -**phies**) philosophie *f*

philter ['fɪltər] *s* philtre *m*

phlebitis [flɪ'baɪtɪs] *s* phlébite *f*

phlegm [flɛm] *s* flegme *m*; **to cough up phlegm** cracher des glaires, tousser gras

phlegmatic(al) [flɛg'mætɪk(əl)] *adj* flegmatique

phobia ['fobɪ·ə] *s* phobie *f*

Phoebe ['fibi] *s* Phébé *f*

Phoenicia [fɪ'nɪʃə], [fɪ'nɪʃə] *s* Phénicie *f*; la Phénicie

Phoenician [fɪ'nɪʃən], [fɪ'nɪʃən] *adj* phénicien *s* Phénicien *m*

phoenix ['finɪks] *s* phénix *m*

phone [fon] *s* (coll) téléphone *m* ‖ *tr & intr* (coll) téléphoner

phone' call' *s* coup *m* de téléphone, coup *m* de fil

phonetic [fo'nɛtɪk] *adj* phonétique ‖ **phonetics** *s* phonétique *f*

phonograph ['fonə,græf], ['fonə,grɑf] *s* phonographe *m*

phonology [fə'nɑlədʒi] *s* phonologie *f*

pho·ny ['foni] *adj* (*comp* -**nier**; *super* -**niest**) faux, truqué ‖ *s* (*pl* -**nies**) charlatan *m*

pho'ny war' *s* drôle *f* de guerre

phosphate ['fɑsfet] *s* phosphate *m*

phosphorescent [,fɑsfə'rɛsənt] *adj* phosphorescent

phospho·rus ['fɑsfərəs] *s* (*pl* -**ri** [,raɪ]) phosphore *m*

pho·to ['foto] *s* (*pl* -**tos**) (coll) photo *f*

photoengraving [,foto·ɛn'grevɪŋ] *s* photogravure *f*

pho'to fin'ish *s* photo-finish *f*

photogenic [,foto'dʒɛnɪk] *adj* photogénique

photograph ['fotə,græf], ['fotə,grɑf] *s* photographie *f* ‖ *tr* photographier ‖ *intr*—**to photograph well** être photogénique

photographer [fə'tɑgrəfər] *s* photographe *mf*

photography [fə'tɑgrəfi] *s* photographie *f*

photostat ['fotə,stæt] *s* (trademark) photostat *m* ‖ *tr & intr* photocopier

phrase [frez] *s* locution *f*, expression *f*; (mus) phrase *f* ‖ *tr* exprimer, rédiger; (mus) phraser

phrenology [frɪ'nɑlədʒi] *s* phrénologie *f*

phys·ic ['fɪzɪk] *s* médicament *m*; (*laxative*) purgatif *m* ‖ *v* (*pret & pp* -**icked**; *ger* -**icking**) *tr* purger

physical ['fɪzɪkəl] *adj* physique

phys'ical de'fect *s* vice *m* de conformation

physician [fɪ'zɪʃən] *s* médecin *m*

physicist ['fɪzɪsɪst] *s* physicien *m*

physics ['fɪzɪks] *s* physique *f*
physiogno·my [,fɪzɪ'ɑgnəmi], [,fɪzɪ-'ɑnəmi] *s* (*pl* -mies) physionomie *f*
physiological [,fɪzɪ·ə'lɑdʒɪkəl] *adj* physiologique
physiology [,fɪzɪ'ɑlədʒɪ] *s* physiologie *f*
physique [fɪ'zik] *s* physique *m*
pi [paɪ] *s* (math) pi *m*; (typ) pâté *m* || *v* (*pret & pp* **pied**; *ger* **piing**) *tr* (typ) mettre en pâte
pianist [pɪ'ænɪst], ['pi·ənɪst] *s* pianiste *mf*
pian·o [pɪ'æno] *s* (*pl* -os) piano *m*
pian'o stool' *s* tabouret *m* de piano
picayune [,pɪkə'jun] *adj* mesquin
picco·lo ['pɪkəlo] *s* (*pl* -los) piccolo *m*
pick [pɪk] *s* (*tool*) pic *m*, pioche *f*; (*choice*) choix *m*; (*choicest*) élite *f*, fleur *f* || *tr* choisir; (*flowers*) cueillir; (*fibers*) effiler; (*e.g., one's teeth, nose, etc.*) se curer; (*a scab*) gratter; (*a fowl*) plumer; (*a bone*) ronger; (*a lock*) crocheter; (*the ground*) piocher; (*e.g., guitar strings*) toucher; (*a quarrel; flaws*) chercher; **to pick off** enlever; (*to shoot*) descendre; **to pick out** trier; **to pick pockets** voler à la tire; **to pick to pieces** (coll) éplucher; **to pick up** ramasser; (*one's strength*) reprendre; (*speed*) accroître; (*a passenger*) prendre; (*a man overboard*) recueillir; (*an anchor; a stitch; a fallen child*) relever; (*information; a language*) apprendre; (*the scent*) retrouver; (rad) capter || *intr* (said of birds) picorer; **to pick at** (*to scold*) (coll) gronder; **to pick at one's food** manger du bout des dents; **to pick on** choisir; (coll) gronder; **to pick up** (coll) se rétablir
pick'ax' *s* pioche *f*
picket ['pɪkɪt] *s* (*stake, pale*) pieu *m*; (*of strikers; of soldiers*) piquet *m* || *tr* entourer de piquets de grève || *intr* faire le piquet
pick'et fence' *s* palis *m*
pick'et line' *s* piquet *m* de grève
pickle ['pɪkəl] *s* cornichon *m*; (*brine*) marinade *f*, saumure *f*; (coll) gâchis *m* || *tr* conserver dans du vinaigre
pick'lock' *s* crochet *m*; (*person*) crocheteur *m*
pick'-me-up' *s* (coll) remontant *m*
pick'pock'et *s* voleur *m* à la tire
pick'up' *s* chargement *m*; passager *m*; (*of a motor*) reprise *f*; (*truck; phonograph cartridge*) pick-up *m*; (*woman*) (coll) racoleuse *f*
pick'up arm' *s* bras *m* de pick-up
pick'up truck' *s* camionnette *f*
pic·nic ['pɪknɪk] *s* pique-nique *m* || *v* (*pret & pp* **-nicked**; *ger* **-nicking**) *intr* pique-niquer
pictorial [pɪk'torɪ·əl] *adj & s* illustré *m*
picture ['pɪktʃər] *s* tableau *m*; image *f*; photographie *f*; (*painting*) peinture *f*; (*engraving*) gravure *f*; (mov) film *m*; (*screen*) (mov, telv) écran *m*; **the very picture of** le portrait de, l'image de; **to receive the picture** (telv) capter l'image || *tr* dépeindre, représenter; **to picture to oneself** s'imaginer

pic'ture gal'lery *s* musée *m* de peinture
pic'ture post' card' *s* carte *f* postale illustrée
pic'ture show' *s* exhibition *f* de peinture; (mov) cinéma *m*
pic'ture sig'nal *s* signal *m* vidéo
picturesque [,pɪktʃə'resk] *adj* pittoresque
pic'ture tube' *s* tube *m* de l'image
pic'ture win'dow *s* fenêtre *f* panoramique
piddling ['pɪdlɪŋ] *adj* insignifiant
pie [paɪ] *s* pâté *m*; (*dessert*) tarte *f*; (*bird*) pie *f*
piece [pis] *s* (*of music; of bread*) morceau *m*; (*cannon, coin, chessman, pastry, clothing*) pièce *f*; (*of land*) parcelle *f*; (*e.g., of glass*) éclat *m*; **a piece of advice** un conseil; **a piece of furniture** un meuble; **to break into pieces** mettre en pièces, mettre en morceaux; **to give s.o. a piece of one's mind** (coll) dire son fait à qn; **to go to pieces** se désagréger; (*to be hysterical*) avoir ses nerfs; **to pick to pieces** (coll) éplucher || *tr* rapiécer; **to piece together** rassembler, coordonner
piece'meal' *adv* pièce à pièce
piece'work' *s* travail *m* à la tâche
piece'work'er *s* ouvrier *m* à la tâche
pied [paɪd] *adj* bigarré, panaché; (typ) tombé en pâté
pier [pɪr] *s* quai *m*; (*of a bridge*) pile *f*; (*of a harbor*) jetée *f*; **wall between two openings** (archit) trumeau *m*
pierce [pɪrs] *tr & intr* percer
piercing ['pɪrsɪŋ] *adj* perçant; (*sharp*) aigu
pier' glass' *s* grand miroir *m*
pie·ty ['par·əti] *s* (*pl* -ties) piété *f*
piffle ['pɪfəl] *s* (coll) futilités *fpl*, sottises *fpl*
pig [pɪg] *s* cochon *m*, porc *m*
pigeon ['pɪdʒən] *s* pigeon *m*
pi'geon·hole' *s* boulin *m*; (*in desk*) case *f* || *tr* caser; mettre au rancart
pi'geon house' *s* pigeonnier *m*
piggish ['pɪgɪʃ] *adj* goinfre
piggyback ['pɪgɪ,bæk] *adv* sur le dos, sur les épaules; en auto-couchette
pig'gy bank' ['pɪgɪ] *s* tirelire *f*, grenouille *f*
pig'-head'ed *adj* cabochard, têtu
pig' i'ron *s* gueuse *f*
piglet ['pɪglɪt] *s* cochonnet *m*
pigment ['pɪgmənt] *s* pigment *m*
pig'pen' *s* porcherie *f*
pig'skin' *s* peau *f* de porc; (coll) ballon *m* du football
pig'sty' *s* (*pl* -sties) porcherie *f*
pig'tail' *s* queue *f*, natte *f*; (*of tobacco*) carotte *f*
pike [paɪk] *s* pique *f*; autoroute *f* à péage; (*fish*) brochet *m*
piker ['paɪkər] *s* (slang) rat *m*
pile [paɪl] *s* tas *m*; (*stake*) pieu *m*; (*of rug*) poil *m*; (*of building*) masse *f*; (elec, phys) pile *f*; (coll) fortune *f*; **piles** (pathol) hémorroïdes *fpl* || *tr* empiler || *intr* s'empiler
pile' dri'ver *s* sonnette *f*

pilfer ['pɪlfər] *tr & intr* chaparder
pilgrim ['pɪlɡrɪm] *s* pèlerin *m*
pilgrimage ['pɪlɡrɪmɪdʒ] *s* pèlerinage *m*
pill [pɪl] *s* pilule *f*; (*something unpleasant*) pilule; (coll) casse-pieds *m*
pillage ['pɪlɪdʒ] *s* pillage *m* || *tr & intr* piller
pillar ['pɪlər] *s* pilier *m*
pillo·ry ['pɪlərɪ] *s* (*pl* -ries) pilori *m* || *v* (*pret & pp* -ried) *tr* clouer au pilori
pillow ['pɪlo] *s* oreiller *m*
pil/low-case/ or **pil/low-slip/** *s* taie *f* d'oreiller
pilot ['paɪlət] *s* pilote *m*; (*of gas range*) veilleuse *f* || *tr* piloter
pi/lot en/gine *s* locomotive-pilote *f*
pi/lot light/ *s* veilleuse *f*
pimp [pɪmp] *s* entremetteur *m*
pimple ['pɪmpəl] *s* bouton *m*
pim·ply ['pɪmplɪ] *adj* (*comp* -plier; *super* -pliest) boutonneux
pin [pɪn] *s* épingle *f*; (*of wearing apparel*) agrafe *f*; (*bowling*) quille *f*; (mach) clavette *f*, cheville *f*, goupille *f*; **to be on pins and needles** être sur les chardons ardents || *v* (*pret & pp* **pinned**; *ger* **pinning**) *tr* épingler; (mach) cheviller, goupiller; **to pin down** fixer, clouer
pinafore ['pɪnə,for] *s* tablier *m* d'enfant
pin/ball/ *s* billard *m* américain
pincers ['pɪnsərz] *s & spl* pinces *fpl*
pinch [pɪntʃ] *s* pinçade *f*; (*of salt*) pincée *f*; (*of tobacco*) prise *f*; (*of hunger*) morsure *f*; (*trying time*) moment *m* critique; (slang) arrestation *f*; **in a pinch** au besoin || *tr* pincer; (*to press tightly on*) serrer; (*e.g., one's finger in a door*) se prendre; (*to arrest*) (slang) pincer; (*to steal*) (slang) chiper || *intr* (said, *e.g., of shoe*) gêner; (*to save*) lésiner
pinchers ['pɪntʃərz] *s & spl* pinces *fpl*
pin/cush/ion *s* pelote *f* d'épingles
pine [paɪn] *s* pin *m* || *intr* languir; **to pine for** soupirer après
pine/ap/ple *s* ananas *m*
pine/ cone/ *s* pomme *f* de pin
pine/ nee/dle *s* aiguille *f* de pin
ping [pɪŋ] *s* sifflement *m*; (*in a motor*) cognement *m* || *intr* siffler; cogner
pin/head/ *s* tête *f* d'épingle; (coll) crétin *m*
pink [pɪŋk] *adj* rose || *s* rose *m*; (bot) œillet *m*; **to be in the pink** se porter à merveille
pin/ mon/ey *s* argent *m* de poche
pinnacle ['pɪnəkəl] *s* pinacle *m*
pin/point/ *adj* exact || *tr* situer avec précision
pin/prick/ *s* piqûre *f* d'épingle
pint [paɪnt] *s* chopine *f*
pin/up girl/ *s* pin up *f*
pin/wheel/ *s* (*fireworks*) soleil *m*; (*child's toy*) moulinet *m*
pioneer [,paɪə'nɪr] *s* pionnier *m* || *tr* défricher || *intr* faire œuvre de pionnier
pious ['paɪəs] *adj* pieux, dévot
pip [pɪp] *s* (*in fruit*) pépin *m*; (*on*

cards, dice, etc.) point *m*; (rad) top *m*; (vet) pépie *f*
pipe [paɪp] *s* tuyau *m*, tube *m*, conduit *m*; (*to smoke tobacco*) pipe *f*; (*of an organ*) tuyau; (mus) chalumeau *m* || *tr* canaliser || *intr* jouer du chalumeau; **pipe down!** (slang) boucle-la!
pipe/ clean/er *s* cure-pipe *m*
pipe/ dream/ *s* rêve *m*, projet *m* illusoire
pipe/ line/ *s* pipe-line *m*; (*of information*) tuyau *m*
pipe/ or/gan *s* grandes orgues *fpl*
piper ['paɪpər] *s* joueur *m* de chalumeau; (*bagpiper*) cornemuseur *m*; **to pay the piper** payer les violons
pipe/ wrench/ *s* clef *f* à tubes
piping ['paɪpɪŋ] *s* tuyauterie *f*; (sewing) passepoil *m*
pippin ['pɪpɪn] *s* (*apple*) reinette *f*; (*highly admired person or thing*) bijou *m*
piquancy ['pikənsɪ] *s* piquant *m*
piquant ['pikənt] *adj* piquant
pique [pik] *s* pique *f* || *tr* piquer; **to pique oneself on** se piquer de
pira·cy ['paɪrəsɪ] *s* (*pl* -cies) piraterie *f*
Piraeus [paɪ'ri·əs] *s* Le Pirée
pirate ['paɪrɪt] *s* pirate *m* || *tr* piller || *intr* pirater
pirouette [,pɪru'et] *s* pirouette *f* || *intr* pirouetter
pistol ['pɪstəl] *s* pistolet *m*
piston ['pɪstən] *s* piston *m*
pis/ton ring/ *s* segment *m* de piston
pis/ton rod/ *s* tige *f* de piston
pis/ton stroke/ *s* course *f* de piston
pit [pɪt] *s* fosse *f*, trou *m*; (*in the skin*) marque *f*; (*of certain fruit*) noyau *m*; (*for cockfights, etc.*) arène *f*; (*of the stomach*) creux *m*; (min) puits *m*; (theat) fauteuils *mpl* d'orchestre derrière les musiciens || *v* (*pret & pp* **pitted**; *ger* **pitting**) *tr* trouer; (*the face*) grêler; (*fruit*) dénoyauter; **to pit oneself against** se mesurer contre
pitch [pɪtʃ] *s* (*black sticky substance*) poix *f*; (*throw*) lancement *m*, jet *m*; (*of a boat*) tangage *m*; (*of a roof*) degré *m* de pente; (*of, e.g., a screw*) pas *m*; (*of a tone, of the voice, etc.*) hauteur *f*; (coll) boniment *m*, tam-tam *m*; **to such a pitch that** à tel point que || *tr* lancer, jeter; (*hay*) fourcher; (*a tent*) dresser; enduire de poix; (mus) donner le ton de || *intr* (*said of boat*) tanguer; **to pitch in** (coll) se mettre à la besogne; **to pitch into** s'attaquer à
pitch/ ac/cent *s* accent *m* de hauteur
pitcher ['pɪtʃər] *s* broc *m*, cruche *f*; (baseball) lanceur *m*
pitch/fork/ *s* fourche *f*; **to rain pitchforks** pleuvoir à torrents
pitch/ pipe/ *s* diapason *m* de bouche
pit/fall/ *s* trappe *f*; (fig) écueil *m*, pierre *f* d'écueil
pith [pɪθ] *s* moelle *f*; (fig) suc *m*
pith·y ['pɪθɪ] *adj* (*comp* -ier; *super* -iest) moelleux; (fig) plein de suc
pitiful ['pɪtɪfəl] *adj* pitoyable

pitiless ['pɪtɪlɪs] *adj* impitoyable

pit·y ['pɪti] *s* (*pl* **-ies**) pitié *f*; **for pity's sake!** par pitié!; **what a pity!** quel dommage! || *v* (*pret* & *pp* **-ied**) *tr* avoir pitié de, plaindre

pivot ['pɪvət] *s* pivot *m* || *tr* faire pivoter || *intr* pivoter

placard ['plækərd] *s* placard *m*, affiche *f* || *tr* placarder

placate ['pleket] *tr* apaiser

place [ples] *s* endroit *m*; (*job*) poste *m*, emploi *m*; (*seat*) place *f*; (*rank*) rang *m*; **everything in its place** chaque chose à sa place; **in no place** nulle part; **in place of** au lieu de; **in your place** à votre place; **out of place** déplacé; **to change places** changer de place; **to keep one's place** (fig) tenir ses distances; **to take place** avoir lieu || *tr* mettre, placer; (*to find a job for; to invest*) placer; (*to recall*) remettre, se rappeler; (*to set down*) poser || *intr* (turf) finir placé

place·bo [plə'sibo] *s* (*pl* **-bos** or **-boes**) remède *m* factice

place' card' *s* marque-place *f*, carton *m* marque-place

place' mat' *s* garde-nappe *m*

place'ment ['plesmənt] *s* placement *m*; (*location*) emplacement *m*

place'ment exam' *s* examen *m* probatoire

place'-name' *s* nom *m* de lieu, toponyme *m*

placid ['plæsɪd] *adj* placide

plagiarism ['pledʒə,rɪzəm] *s* plagiat *m*

plagiarize ['pledʒə,raɪz] *tr* plagier

plague [pleg] *s* peste *f*; (*great public calamity*) fléau *m* || *tr* tourmenter

plaid [plæd] *s* plaid *m*

plain [plen] *adj* clair; simple; (*e.g., answer*) franc; (*color*) uni; (*ugly*) sans attraits || *s* plaine *f*

plain' clothes' *spl*—**in plain clothes** en civil, en bourgeois

plain'clothes'man *s* (*pl* **-men'**) agent *m* en civil

plain' cook'ing *s* cuisine *f* bourgeoise

plain' om'elet *s* omelette *f* nature

plain' speech' *s* franc-parler *m*

plaintiff ['plentɪf] *s* (law) demandeur *m*, plaignant *m*

plaintive ['plentɪv] *adj* plaintif

plan [plæn] *s* plan *m*, projet *m*; (*drawing, diagram*) plan, dessein *m* || *v* (*pret* & *pp* **planned**; *ger* **planning**) *tr* projeter; **to plan to** se proposer de || *intr* faire des projets

plane [plen] *adj* plan, plat || *s* (aer) avion *m*; (bot) platane *m*; (carpentry) rabot *m*; (geom) plan *m* || *tr* raboter

plane' sick'ness *s* mal *m* de l'air

planet ['plænɪt] *s* planète *f*

plane' tree' *s* platane *m*

plan'ing mill' *s* atelier *m* de rabotage

plank [plæŋk] *s* planche *f*; (pol) article *m* d'une plate-forme électorale

plant [plænt], [plɑnt] *s* (*factory*) usine *f*; (*building and equipment*) installation *f*; (bot) plante *f* || *tr* planter

plantation [plæn'teʃən] *s* plantation *f*

planter ['plæntər] *s* planteur *m*

plant' louse' *s* puceron *m*

plasma ['plæzmə] *s* plasma *m*

plaster ['plæstər], ['plɑstər] *s* plâtre *m*; (*poultice*) emplâtre *m* || *tr* plâtrer; (*a bill, poster*) coller; (slang) griser

plas'ter cast' *s* plâtre *m*

plas'ter of Par'is *s* plâtre *m* à mouler

plastic ['plæstɪk] *adj* plastique || *s* (*substance*) plastique *m*; (*art*) plastique *f*

plas'tic bomb' *s* plastic *m*

plas'tic sur'gery *s* chirurgie *f* esthétique, chirurgie plastique

plate [plet] *s* (*dish*) assiette *f*; (*platter*) plateau *m*; (*sheet of metal*) tôle *f*, plaque *f*; vaisselle *f* d'or or d'argent; (anat, elec, phot, rad, zool) plaque; (typ) planche *f* || *tr* plaquer; (elec) galvaniser; (typ) clicher

plateau [plæ'to] *s* plateau *m*, massif *m*

plate' glass' *s* verre *m* cylindré

platen ['plætən] *s* rouleau *m*

platform ['plæt,form] *s* plate-forme *f*; (*for arrivals and departures*) quai *m*; (*of a speaker*) estrade *f*; (*political program*) plate-forme

plat'form car' *s* (rr) plate-forme *f*

platinum ['plætɪnəm] *s* platine *m*

plat'inum blonde' *s* blonde *f* platinée

platitude ['plætɪ,t(j)ud] *s* platitude *f*

Plato ['pleto] *s* Platon *m*

platoon [plə'tun] *s* section *f*

platter ['plætər] *s* plat *m*; (slang) disque *m*

plausible ['plɔzɪbəl] *adj* plausible

play [ple] *s* jeu *m*; (*drama*) pièce *f*; (*mach*) jeu; **to give full play to** donner libre cours à || *tr* jouer; (*e.g., the fool*) faire; (*cards; e.g., football*) jouer à; (*an instrument*) jouer de; **to play back** (*a tape*) faire repasser; **to play down** diminuer; **to play hooky** faire l'école buissonnière; **to play off** (sports) rejouer; **to play up** accentuer || *intr* jouer; **to play out** s'épuiser; **to play safe** prendre des précautions; **to play sick** faire semblant d'être malade; **to play up to** passer de la pommade à

play'back' *s* (*device*) lecteur *m*; (*reproduction*) lecture *f*

play'back head' *s* tête *f* de lecture

play'bill' *s* programme *m*; (*poster*) affiche *f*

play'er pian'o ['ple·ər] *s* piano *m* mécanique

playful ['plefəl] *adj* enjoué, badin

playgoer ['ple,go·ər] *s* amateur *m* de théâtre

play'ground' *s* terrain *m* de jeu

play'house' *s* théâtre *m*; (*dollhouse*) maison *f* de poupée

play'ing card' *s* carte *f* à jouer

play'ing field' *s* terrain *m* de sports

play'mate' *s* compagnon *m* de jeu

play'-off' *s* finale *f*, match *m* d'appui

play' on words' *s* jeu *m* de mots

play'pen' *s* parc *m* d'enfants

play'room' *s* salle *f* de jeux

play'thing' *s* jouet *m*

play'time' s récréation f
playwright ['ple ,raɪt] s auteur m dramatique, dramaturge mf
play'writ'ing s dramaturgie f
plea [pli] s requête f, appel m; prétexte m; (law) défense f
plead [plid] v (pret & pp pleaded or pled [pled]) tr & intr plaider; to plead not guilty plaider non coupable
pleasant ['plezənt] adj agréable
pleasant•ry ['plezəntri] s (pl -ries) plaisanterie f
please [pliz] tr plaire (with dat); it pleases him to il lui plaît de; please + inf veuillez + inf; to be pleased with être content or satisfait de || intr plaire; as you please comme vous voulez; if you please s'il vous plaît
pleasing ['plizɪŋ] adj agréable
pleasure ['plɛʒər] s plaisir m; at the pleasure of au gré de; what is your pleasure? qu'y a-t-il pour votre service?, que puis-je faire pour vous?
pleas'ure car' s voiture f de tourisme
pleas'ure trip' s voyage m d'agrément
pleat [plit] s pli m || tr plisser
plebe [plib] s élève m de première année
plebeian [plɪ'bi·ən] adj & s plébéien m
plebiscite ['plɛbɪ ,saɪt] s plébiscite m
pledge [plɛdʒ] s gage m; engagement m d'honneur, promesse f || tr mettre en gage; (one's word) engager
plentiful ['plentɪfəl] adj abondant
plenty ['plenti] s abondance f; plenty of beaucoup de || adv (coll) largement
pleurisy ['plʊrɪsi] s pleurésie f
pliable ['plaɪ·əbəl] adj pliable; docile, maniable
pliers ['plaɪ·ərz] s & spl pinces fpl, tenailles fpl
plight [plaɪt] s embarras m; (promise) engagement m || tr engager; to plight one's troth promettre fidélité
plod [plad] v (pret & pp plodded; ger plodding) tr parcourir lourdement et péniblement || intr cheminer; travailler laborieusement
plot [plat] s complot m; (of a play or novel) intrigue f; (of ground) lopin m, parcelle f; (map) tracé m, plan m; (of vegetables) carré m || v (pret & pp plotted; ger plotting) tr comploter, tramer; (a tract of land) faire le plan de; (a point) relever; (lines) tracer || intr comploter; to plot to + inf comploter de + inf
plough [plaʊ] s, tr & intr var of plow
plover ['plʌvər] s pluvier m
plow [plaʊ] s charrue f; (for snow) chasse-neige m || tr labourer; (the sea; the forehead) sillonner; (snow) déblayer; to plow back (com) affecter aux investissements || intr labourer; to plow through avancer péniblement dans
plow'man s (pl -men) laboureur m
plow'share' s soc m de charrue
pluck [plʌk] s cran m; (tug) saccade f || tr arracher; (flowers) cueillir; (a fowl) plumer; (one's eyebrows)

épiler; (e.g., the strings of a guitar) pincer || intr—to pluck at arracher d'un coup sec; to pluck up reprendre courage
pluck•y ['plʌki] adj (comp -ier; super -iest) courageux, crâne
plug [plʌg] s tampon m, bouchon m; (of sink, bathtub, etc.) bonde f; (of tobacco) chique f; (aut) bougie f; (on wall) (elec) prise f; (prongs) (elec) fiche f, prise; (old horse) (coll) rosse f; (hat) (slang) haut-de-forme m; (slang) annonce f publicitaire || v (pret & pp plugged; ger plugging) tr boucher; (a melon) entamer; to plug in (elec) brancher || intr—to plug away (coll) persévérer
plum [plʌm] s prune f; (tree) prunier m; (slang) fromage m
plumage ['plumɪdʒ] s plumage m
plumb [plʌm] adj d'aplomb; (coll) pur || s plomb m; out of plumb hors d'aplomb || adv d'aplomb; (coll) en plein; (coll) complètement || tr sonder
plumb' bob' s plomb m
plumber ['plʌmər] s plombier m
plumbing ['plʌmɪŋ] s plomberie f
plumb' line' s fil m à plomb
plume [plum] s aigrette f; (of a hat, of smoke, etc.) panache m || tr orner de plumes; (feathers) lisser; to plume oneself on se piquer de
plummet ['plʌmɪt] s plomb m || intr tomber d'aplomb, se précipiter
plump [plʌmp] adj grassouillet, potelé, dodu; brusque || s (coll) chute f lourde; (coll) bruit m sourd || adv en plein; brusquement || tr jeter brusquement; to plump oneself down s'affaler || intr tomber lourdement
plunder ['plʌndər] s pillage m; (booty) butin m || tr piller
plunge [plʌndʒ] s plongeon m; (pitching movement) tangage m || tr plonger || intr plonger; se précipiter; (fig) se plonger; (naut) tanguer; (slang) risquer de grosses sommes
plunger ['plʌndʒər] s plongeur m; (slang) risque-tout m
plunk [plʌŋk] adv d'un coup sec; (squarely) carrément || tr jeter bruyamment || intr tomber raide
plural ['plʊrəl] adj & s pluriel m
plus [plʌs] adj positif || s (sign) plus m; quantité f positive || prep plus
plush [plʌʃ] adj en peluche; (coll) rupin || s peluche f
plush•y ['plʌʃi] adj (comp -ier; super -iest) pelucheux; (coll) rupin
plus' sign' s signe m plus
Plutarch ['plutark] s Plutarque m
Pluto ['pluto] s Pluton m
plutonium [plu'toni·əm] s plutonium m
ply [plaɪ] s (pl plies) (e.g., of a cloth) pli m; (of rope, wool, etc.) brin m || v (pret & pp plied) tr manier; (a trade) exercer; to ply s.o. with presser qn de || intr faire la navette
ply'wood' s bois m de placage, contreplaqué m

P.M. ['pi'em] *adv* (letterword) (*post meridiem*) de l'après-midi, du soir
pneumatic [n(j)u'mætɪk] *adj* pneumatique
pneumat'ic drill' *s* foreuse *f* à air comprimé
pneumonia [n(j)u'monɪ'ə] *s* pneumonie *f*
P.O. ['pi'o] *s* (letterword) (*post office*) poste *f*
poach [potʃ] *tr* (eggs) pocher ‖ *intr* (hunting) braconner
poached' egg' *s* œuf *m* poché
poacher ['potʃər] *s* braconnier *m*
pock [pak] *s* pustule *f*
pocket ['pakɪt] *s* poche *f*; (billiards) blouse *f*; (aer) trou *m* d'air ‖ *tr* empocher; (*a billiard ball*) blouser; (*insults*) avaler
pock'et-book' *s* portefeuille *m*; (*small book*) livre *m* de poche
pock'et hand'kerchief *s* mouchoir de poche
pock'et-knife' *s* (*pl* **-knives**) couteau *m* de poche, canif *m*
pock'et mon'ey *s* argent *m* de poche
pock'mark' *s* marque *f* de la petite vérole
pock'marked' *adj* grêlé
pod [pad] *s* cosse *f*, gousse *f*
poem ['po·ɪm] *s* poème *m*
poet ['po·ɪt] *s* poète *m*
poetess ['po·ɪtɪs] *s* poétesse *f*
poetic [po'etɪk] *adj* poétique ‖ **poetics** *s* poétique *f*
poetry ['po·ɪtri] *s* poésie *f*
pogrom ['pogrəm] *s* pogrom *m*
poignancy ['pɔɪnənsi] *s* piquant *m*
poignant ['pɔɪnənt] *adj* poignant
point [pɔɪnt] *s* (*spot, dot, score, etc.*) point *m*; (*tip*) pointe *f*; (*of pen*) bec *m*; (*of conscience*) cas *m*; (*of a star*) rayon *m*; (*of a joke*) piquant *m*; (*of, e.g., grammar*) question *f*; (geog, naut) pointe; (typ) point; **beside the point, off the point** hors de propos; **on the point of** sur le point de; (*death*) à l'article de; **on this point** à cet égard, à ce propos; **point of a compass** aire *f* de vent; **point of order** rappel *m* au règlement; **points** (aut) vis *f* platinées; **to carry one's point** avoir gain de cause; **to come to the point** venir au fait; **to have one's good points** avoir ses qualités; **to make a point of** se faire un devoir de ‖ *tr* (*a gun, telescope, etc.*) braquer, pointer; (*a finger*) tendre; (*the way*) indiquer; (*a wall*) jointoyer; (*to sharpen*) tailler en point; **to point out** signaler, faire remarquer ‖ *intr* pointer; (*said of hunting dog*) tomber en arrêt; **to point at** montrer du doigt
point'-blank' *adj* & *adv* (*fired straight at the mark*) à bout portant; (*straightforward*) à brûle-pourpoint
pointed *adj* pointu; (*remark*) mordant
pointer ['pɔɪntər] *s* (*stick*) baguette *f*; (*of a dial*) aiguille *f*; (*dog*) chien *m* d'arrêt, pointer *m*
poise [pɔɪz] *s* équilibre *m*; (*assurance*)

aplomb *m* ‖ *tr* tenir en équilibre ‖ *intr* être en équilibre; (*in the air*) planer
poison ['pɔɪzən] *s* poison *m* ‖ *tr* empoisonner
poi'son gas' *s* gaz *m* asphyxiant
poi'son i'vy *s* sumac *m* vénéneux
poisonous ['pɔɪzənəs] *adj* toxique; (*plant*) vénéneux; (*snake*) venimeux
poke [pok] *s* poussée *f*; (*with elbow*) coup *m* de coude; (coll) traînard *m* ‖ *tr* pousser; (*the fire*) tisonner; **to poke fun at** se moquer de; **to poke one's nose into** (coll) fourrer son nez dans; **to poke s.th. into** fourrer q.ch. dans ‖ *intr* aller sans se presser; **to poke about** fureter
poker ['pokər] *s* tisonnier *m*; (cards) poker *m*
pok'er face' *s* visage *m* impassible
pok·y ['poki] *adj* (*comp* **-ier;** *super* **-lest**) (coll) lambin, lent
Poland ['poland] *s* Pologne *f*; la Pologne
polar ['polər] *adj* polaire
po'lar bear' *s* ours *m* blanc
polarize ['polə,raɪz] *tr* polariser
pole [pol] *s* (*long rod or, staff*) perche *f*; (*of flag*) hampe *f*; (*upright support*) poteau *m*; (astr, biol, elec, geog, math) pôle *m*; **Pole** (*person*) Polonais *m* ‖ *tr* pousser à la perche
pole'cat' *s* putois *m*
pole'star' *s* étoile *f* polaire
pole' vault' *s* saut *m* à la perche
police [pə'lis] *s* police *f* ‖ *tr* maintenir l'ordre dans
police' brutal'ity *s* brutalité *f* policière
police' commis'sioner *s* préfet *m* de police
police'man *s* (*pl* **-men**) agent *m* de police
police' pre'cinct *s* commissariat *m* de police
police' state' *s* régime *m* policier
police' sta'tion *s* poste *m* de police, commissariat *m*
police'wom'an *s* (*pl* **-wom'en**) femme *f* agent
pol·icy ['palɪsi] *s* (*pl* **-cies**) politique *f*; (ins) police *f*
polio ['polɪ,o] *s* (coll) polio *f*
polish ['palɪʃ] *s* poli *m*; (*for household uses*) cire *f*; (*for shoes*) cirage *m*; (fig) politesse *f*, vernis *m* ‖ *tr* polir; (*shoes, floor, etc.*) cirer; (*one's nails*) vernir; **to polish off** (coll) expédier; (*e.g., a meal*) (slang) engloutir ‖ **Polish** ['polɪʃ] *adj* & *s* polonais *m*
polite [pə'laɪt] *adj* poli
politeness [pə'laɪtnɪs] *s* politesse *f*
politic ['palɪtɪk] *adj* (*prudent*) diplomatique, politique; (*shrewd*) rusé
political [pə'lɪtɪkəl] *adj* politique
politician [,palɪ'tɪʃən] *s* politicien *m*
politics ['palɪtɪks] *s* & *spl* politique *f*
poll [pol] *s* liste *f* électorale; (*vote*) scrutin *m*; (*head*) tête *f*; sondage *m* d'opinion; **to go to the polls** aller aux urnes; **to take a poll** faire une enquête par sondage ‖ *tr* (*e.g., a dele-*

gation) dépouiller le scrutin de; (*a certain number of votes*) recevoir

pollen ['palən] *s* pollen *m*

poll'ing booth' /'polɪŋ/ *s* isoloir *m*

polliwog ['palɪ ,wag] *s* têtard *m*

pol'liwog initia'tion *s* baptême *m* de la ligne

poll' tax' *s* taxe *f* par tête

pollute [pə'lut] *tr* polluer

pollution [pə'luʃən] *s* pollution *f*

polo ['polo] *s* polo *m*

polonium [pə'lonɪəm] *s* polonium *m*

polygamist [pə'lɪgəmɪst] *s* polygame *mf*

polygamous [pə'lɪgəməs] *adj* polygame

polyglot ['palɪ ,glat] *adj & s* polyglotte *mf*

polygon ['palɪ ,gan] *s* polygone *m*

polynomial [,palɪ'nomɪ-əl] *s* polynôme *m*

polyp ['palɪp] *s* polype *m*

polytheist ['palɪ ,θi-ɪst] *s* polythéiste *mf*

polytheistic [,palɪθi'ɪstɪk] *adj* polythéiste

pomade [pə'med], [pə'mad] *s* pommade *f*

pomegranate ['pam ,grænɪt] *s* (*shrub*) grenadier *m*; (*fruit*) grenade *f*

pom-mel ['pʌməl], ['paməl] *s* pommeau *m* || *v* (*pret & pp* -meled *or* -melled; *ger* -meling *or* -melling) *tr* rosser

pomp [pamp] *s* pompe *f*

pompous ['pampəs] *adj* pompeux

pon-cho ['pant/o] *s* (*pl* -chos) poncho *m*

pond [pand] *s* étang *m*, mare *f*

ponder ['pandər] *tr* peser || *intr* méditer; **to ponder over** réfléchir sur

ponderous ['pandərəs] *adj* pesant

poniard ['panjərd] *s* poignard *m* || *tr* poignarder

pontiff ['pantɪf] *s* pontife *m*

pontifical [pan'tɪfɪkəl] *adj* (*e.g., air*) de pontife

pontoon [pan'tun] *s* ponton *m*

po-ny ['ponɪ] *s* (*pl* -nies) poney *m*; (*for drinking liquor*) petit verre *m*; (*coll*) aide-mémoire *m* illicite

poodle ['pudəl] *s* caniche *m*

pool [pul] *s* (*small puddle*) mare *f*; (*for swimming*) piscine *f*; (*game*) billard *m*; (*in certain games*) poule *f*; (*of workers*) équipe *f*; (*combine*) pool *m*; (*com*) fonds *m* commun || *tr* mettre en commun

pool'room' *s* salle *f* de billard

pool' ta'ble *s* table *f* de billard

poop [pup] *s* poupe *f*; (*deck*) dunette *f* || *tr* (slang) casser la tête à

poor [pur] *adj* pauvre; (*mediocre*) piètre; (*unfortunate*) pauvre (before noun); (*without money*) pauvre (after noun)

poor' box' *s* tronc *m* des pauvres

poor'house' *s* asile *m* des indigents

poorly ['purlɪ] *adj* souffrant || *adv* mal

pop [pap] *s* bruit *m* sec; (*soda*) boisson *f* gazeuse || *v* (*pret & pp* popped; *ger* popping) *tr* (*corn*) faire éclater || *intr*

(*said, e.g., of balloon*) crever; (*said of cork*) sauter

pop'corn' *s* maïs *m* éclaté, grains *mpl* de maïs soufflés, pop-corn *m*

pope [pop] *s* pape *m*

pop'eyed' *adj* aux yeux saillants

pop'gun' *s* canonnière *f*

poplar ['paplər] *s* peuplier *m*

pop-py ['papɪ] *s* (*pl* -pies) pavot *m*; (*corn poppy*) coquelicot *m*

pop'py-cock' *s* (coll) fadaises *fpl*

populace ['papjələs] *s* peuple *m*, populace *f*

popular ['papjələr] *adj* populaire

popularize ['papjələ ,raɪz] *tr* populariser, vulgariser

populate ['papjə ,let] *tr* peupler

population [,papjə'leʃən] *s* population *f*

populous ['papjələs] *adj* populeux

porcelain ['pɔrsəlɪn], ['pɔrslɪn] *s* porcelaine *f*

porch [pɔrt/] *s* (*portico*) porche *m*; (*enclosed*) véranda *f*

porcupine ['pɔrkjə ,paɪn] *s* porc-épic *m*

pore [por] *s* pore *m* || *intr*—**to pore over** examiner avec attention, s'absorber dans

pork [pork] *s* porc *m*

pork' and beans' *spl* fèves *fpl* au lard

pork'chop' *s* côtelette *f* de porc

pornography [pɔr'nagrəfi] *s* pornographie *f*

porous ['porəs] *adj* poreux

porphy-ry ['pɔrfɪrɪ] *s* (*pl* -ries) porphyre *m*

porpoise ['pɔrpəs] *s* marsouin *m*

porridge ['parɪdʒ], ['pɔrɪdʒ] *s* bouillie *f*, porridge *m*

port [port] *s* port *m*; (*opening in ship's side*) hublot *m*, sabord *m*; (*left side of ship or airplane*) bâbord *m*; (*wine*) porto *m*; (*mach*) orifice *m*

portable ['portəbəl] *adj* portatif

portage ['portɪdʒ] *s* transport *m*; portage *m*

portal ['portəl] *s* portail *m*

portcullis [port'kʌlɪs] *s* herse *f*

portend [por'tend] *tr* présager

portent ['portent] *s* présage *m*

portentous [por'tentəs] *adj* extraordinaire; de mauvais augure

porter ['portər] *s* (*doorkeeper*) portier *m*, concierge *m*; (*in hotels and trains*) porteur *m*

portfoli-o [port'folɪ ,o] *s* (*pl* -os) portefeuille *m*

port'hole' *s* hublot *m*

porti-co ['portɪ ,ko] *s* (*pl* -coes *or* -cos) portique *m*

portion ['porʃən] *s* portion *f*; (*dowry*) dot *f* || *tr*—**to portion out** partager, répartir

port-ly ['portlɪ] *adj* (*comp* -lier; *super* -liest) corpulent

port' of call' *s* port *m* d'escale

portrait ['portret], ['portrɪt] *s* portrait *m*; **to sit for one's portrait** se faire faire son portrait

portray [por'tre] *tr* faire le portrait de; dépeindre, décrire; (*theat*) jouer le rôle de portrayal [por'tre·əl] s représentation f; description f

Portugal ['port/əgəl] s le Portugal

Portu·guese ['port/ə,giz] adj portugais || s (language) portugais m || s (pl -guese) (person) Portugais m

port' wine' s porto m

pose [poz] s pose f || tr & intr poser; to pose as se poser comme

posh [paʃ] adj (slang) chic, élégant

position [pə'zɪʃən] s position f; (job) poste m; in position en place; in your position à votre place

positive ['pazɪtɪv] adj & s positif m

possess [pə'zes] tr posséder

possession [pə'zeʃən] s possession f; to take possession of s'emparer de

possible ['pasɪbəl] adj possible

possum ['pasəm] s opossum m; to play possum (coll) faire le mort

post [post] s (upright) poteau m; (job, position) poste m; (post office) poste f; (mil) poste m || tr (a notice, placard, etc.) afficher, placarder; (a letter) poster, mettre à la poste; (a sentinel) poster; (with news) tenir au courant; post no bills (public sign) défense d'afficher

postage ['postɪdʒ] s port m, affranchissement m

post'age due' s port m dû, affranchissement m insuffisant

post'age me'ter s affranchisseuse f à compteur

post'age stamp' s timbre-poste m

postal ['postəl] adj postal

post'al card' s carte f postale

post'al clerk' s postier m

post'al mon'ey or'der s mandat-poste m

post'al per'mit s franchise f postale, dispensé m du timbrage

post'al sav'ings bank' s caisse f d'épargne postale

post' card' s carte f postale

post'date' s postdate || post'date' tr postdater

poster ['postər] s affiche f

posterity [pas'terɪti] s postérité f

postern ['postərn] s poterne f

post'haste' adv en toute hâte

posthumous ['past/uməs] adj posthume

post'man s (pl -men) facteur m

post'mark' s cachet m d'oblitération, timbre m || tr timbrer

post'mas'ter s receveur m des postes, administrateur m du bureau de postes

post'master gen'eral s ministre m des Postes et Télécommunications

post-mortem [,post'mortəm] adj après décès, (fig) après le fait || s autopsie f; discussion f après le fait

post' of'fice s bureau m de poste

post'-office box' s case f postale, boîte f postale

post'paid' adv port payé, franc de port, franco de port

postpone [post'pon] tr remettre, différer; (a meeting) ajourner

postponement [post'ponmənt] s remise f, ajournement m

postscript ['post,skrɪpt] s post-scriptum m

posture ['pastʃər] s posture f || intr prendre une posture

post'war' adj d'après-guerre

po·sy ['pozi] s (pl -sies) fleur f; bouquet m

pot [pat] s pot m; (in gambling) mise f; to go to pot (slang) s'en aller à vau-l'eau

potash ['pat,æʃ] s potasse f

potassium [pə'tæsɪəm] s potassium m

pota·to [pə'teto] s (pl -toes) pomme f de terre; (sweet potato) patate f

pota'to chips' spl pommes fpl chips; croustelle f (Canad)

potbellied ['pat,belɪd] adj ventru

poten·cy ['potənsi] s (pl -cies) puissance f; virilité f

potent ['potənt] adj puissant, fort; (effective) efficace

potentate ['potən,tet] s potentat m

potential [pə'tenʃəl] adj & s potentiel (ielle)

pot'hang'er s crémaillère f

pot'herb' s herbe f potagère

pot'hold'er s poignée f

pot'hole' s nid m de poule

pot'hook' s croc m

potion ['poʃən] s potion f

pot'luck' s—to take potluck manger à la fortune du pot

pot' shot' s coup m tiré à courte distance

potter ['patər] s potier m || intr—to potter around s'occuper de bagatelles, bricoler

pot'ter's clay' s terre f à potier

pot'ter's field' s fosse f commune,

pot'ter's wheel' s roue f or tour m de potier

potter·y ['patəri] s (pl -ies) poterie f

pouch [pautʃ] s poche f, petit sac m; (of kangaroo) poche f ventrale; (for tobacco) blague f

poultice ['poltɪs] s cataplasme m

poultry ['poltri] s volaille f

poul'try·man s (pl -men) éleveur m de volailles; (dealer) volailleur m

pounce [pauns] intr—to pounce on fondre sur, s'abattre sur

pound [paund] s (weight) livre f; (for automobiles, stray animals, etc.) fourrière f || tr battre; (to pulverize) piler, broyer; (to bombard) pilonner; (e.g., an animal) mettre en fourrière; (e.g., the sidewalk) (fig) battre || intr battre

pound' ster'ling s livre f sterling

pour [por] tr verser; (tea) servir; to pour off décanter || intr écouler; (said of rain) tomber à verse; to pour out of sortir à flots

pout [paut] s moue f || intr faire la moue

poverty ['pavərti] s pauvreté f

POW ['pi'o'dʌbl,ju] s (letterword) (prisoner of war) P.G.

powder ['paudər] s poudre f || tr réduire en poudre; (to sprinkle with powder) poudrer || intr se poudrer

pow'dered sug'ar s sucre m de confiseur

pow'der puff' s houppe f

pow'der room' s toilettes fpl pour dames

powdery ['pavdəri] adj (like powder) poudreux; (sprinkled with powder) poussiéreux; (crumbly) friable

power ['pau·ər] s pouvoir m; (influential nation; energy, force, strength; of a machine, microscope, number) puissance f; (talent, capacity, etc.) faculté f; **the powers that be** les autorités fpl; **to seize power** saisir le pouvoir || tr actionner

pow'er brake' s (aut) servo-frein m

pow'er dive' s piqué m à plein gaz

pow'er-dive' intr piquer à plein gaz

powerful ['pau·ərfəl] adj puissant

pow'er-house' s usine f centrale; (coll) foyer m d'énergie

pow'er lawn'mower s tondeuse f à gazon à moteur

powerless ['pau·ərlɪs] adj impuissant

pow'er line' s secteur m de distribution

pow'er mow'er s tondeuse f à gazon à moteur; motofaucheuse f

pow'er of attor'ney s procuration f, mandat m

pow'er pack' s (rad) unité f d'alimentation

pow'er plant' s (powerhouse) centrale f électrique; (aer, aut) groupe m motopropulseur

pow'er steer'ing s (aut) servo-direction f

practicable ['præktɪkəbəl] adj praticable

practical ['præktɪkəl] adj pratique

prac'tical joke' s farce f, attrape f

prac'tical jok'er s fumiste m

practically ['præktɪkəli] adv pratiquement; (more or less) à peu près

prac'tical nurse' s garde-malade m

practice ['præktɪs] s pratique f; (of a profession) exercice m; (of a doctor) clientèle f; **in practice** en pratique, pratiquement; (well-trained) en forme; **out of practice** rouillé || tr pratiquer; (a profession) exercer, pratiquer; (e.g., the violin) s'exercer à; **to practice what one preaches** prêcher d'exemple || intr faire des exercices, s'exercer; (said of doctor, lawyer, etc.) exercer

practiced adj expert

practitioner [præk'tɪ/ənər] s praticien m

prairie ['preri] s steppes fpl; **the prairie** les Prairies fpl

praise [prez] s louange f || tr louer

praise'wor'thy adj louable

pram [præm] s voiture f d'enfant

prance [præns], [prɑns] intr caracoler, cabrioler

prank [præŋk] s espièglerie f

prate [pret] intr bavarder, papoter

prattle ['prætəl] s bavardage m, papotage m || intr bavarder, papoter; (said of children) babiller

prawn [prɔn] s crevette f rose, bouquet m

pray [pre] tr & intr prier

prayer [prer] s prière f

prayer' book' s livre m de prières

pray'ing man'tis ['mæntɪs] s mante f religieuse

preach [prit/] tr & intr prêcher

preacher ['prit/ər] s prédicateur m

preamble ['pri,æmbəl] s préambule m

precarious [prɪ'kerɪ·əs] adj précaire

precaution [prɪ'kɔ/ən] s précaution f

precede [prɪ'sid] tr & intr précéder

precedent ['presɪdənt] s précédent m

precept ['prisept] s précepte m

precinct ['prisɪŋkt] s enceinte f; circonscription f électorale

precious ['pre/əs] adj précieux || adv— **precious little** (coll) très peu

precipice ['presɪpɪs] s précipice m

precipitate [prɪ'sɪpɪ,tet] adj & s précipité m || tr précipiter || intr se précipiter

precipitous [prɪ'sɪpɪtəs] adj escarpé; (hurried) précipité

precise [prɪ'saɪs] adj précis

precision [prɪ'sɪʒən] s précision f

preclude [prɪ'klud] tr empêcher

precocious [prɪ'ko/əs] adj précoce

preconceived [,prikən'sivd] adj préconçu

predatory ['predə,tori] adj rapace; (zool) prédateur

predicament [prɪ'dɪkəmənt] s situation f difficile

predict [prɪ'dɪkt] tr prédire

prediction [prɪ'dɪk/ən] s prédiction f

predispose [,prɪdɪs'poz] tr prédisposer

predominant [prɪ'dɑmɪnənt] adj prédominant

preeminent [prɪ'emɪnənt] adj prééminent

preempt [prɪ'empt] tr s'approprier

preen [prin] tr lisser; **to preen oneself** se bichonner; être fier, se piquer

prefabricated [pri'fæbrɪ,ketɪd] adj préfabriqué

preface ['prefɪs] s préface f || tr préfacer

pre-fer [prɪ'fʌr] v (pret & pp -ferred; ger -ferring) tr préférer

preferable ['prefərəbəl] adj préférable

preference ['prefərəns] s préférence f

preferred' stock' s actions f privilégiées

prefix ['prifɪks] s préfixe m || tr préfixer

pregnan·cy ['pregnənsi] s (pl -cies) grossesse f

pregnant ['pregnənt] adj enceinte, grosse; (fig) gros

prehistoric [,prihɪs'tɑrɪk], [,prihɪs'tɔrɪk] adj préhistorique

prejudice ['predʒədɪs] s préjugé m; (detriment) préjudice m || tr prévenir, prédisposer; (to harm) porter préjudice à

prejudicial [,predʒə'dɪ/əl] adj préjudiciable

prelate ['prelɪt] s prélat m

preliminar·y [prɪ'lɪmɪ,neri] adj préliminaire || s (pl -ies) préliminaire m

prelude ['preljud], ['prilud] s prélude m || tr introduire; préluder à; (a piece of music) préluder par

premature [,prɪmə't(j)ur] adj prématuré; (plant) hâtif

premeditate [prɪ'medɪ,tet] tr préméditer

premier [prɪˈmɪr], [ˈprimɪ·ər] *s* premier ministre *m*

première [prəˈmjer], [prɪˈmɪr] *s* première *f*; (*actress*) vedette *f*

premise [ˈprɛmɪs] *s* prémisse *f*; **on the premises** sur les lieux; **premises** local *m*, locaux *mpl*

premium [ˈprimɪ·əm] *s* prime *f*

premonition [ˌpriməˈnɪʃən] *s* prémonition *f*

preoccupation [priˌɑkjəˈpeʃən] *s* préoccupation *f*

preoccu·py [priˈɑkjəˌpaɪ] *v* (*pret & pp -pied*) *tr* préoccuper

prepaid [priˈped] *adj* payé d'avance; (*letter*) affranchi

preparation [ˌprɛpəˈreʃən] *s* préparation *f*; **preparations** (*for a trip; for war*) préparatifs *mpl*

preparatory [prɪˈpærəˌtori] *adj* préparatoire

prepare [prɪˈper] *tr* préparer ǁ *intr* se préparer

preparedness [prɪˈperɪdnɪs], [prɪˈperdnɪs] *s* préparation *f*; armement *m* préventif

pre·pay [priˈpe] *v* (*pret & pp -paid*) *tr* payer d'avance

preponderant [prɪˈpɑndərənt] *adj* prépondérant

preposition [ˌprɛpəˈzɪʃən] *s* préposition *f*

prepossessing [ˌpripəˈzɛsɪŋ] *adj* avenant, agréable

preposterous [prɪˈpɑstərəs] *adj* absurde, extravagant

prep′ school′ [prɛp] *s* école *f* préparatoire

prerecorded [ˌpririˈkɔrdɪd] *adj* (*rad, telv*) différé

prerequisite [priˈrɛkwɪzɪt] *s* préalable *m*; (*educ*) cours *m* préalable

prerogative [prɪˈrɑgətɪv] *s* prérogative *f*

presage [ˈprɛsɪdʒ] *s* présage *m*; (*foreboding*) pressentiment *m* ǁ [prɪˈsedʒ] *tr* présager; pressentir

Presbyterian [ˌprɛzbɪˈtɪrɪ·ən] *adj & s* presbytérien *m*

prescribe [prɪˈskraɪb] *tr* prescrire ǁ *intr* faire une ordonnance

prescription [prɪˈskrɪpʃən] *s* prescription *f*; (*pharm*) ordonnance *f*

presence [ˈprɛzəns] *s* présence *f*

present [ˈprɛzənt] *adj* (*at this time*) actuel; (*at this place or time*) présent; **to be present at** assister à ǁ *s* cadeau *m*, présent *m*; (*present time or tense*) présent; **at present** à présent ǁ [prɪˈzɛnt] *tr* présenter

presentable [prɪˈzɛntəbəl] *adj* présentable, sortable

presentation [ˌprɛzənˈteʃən], [ˌprizənˈteʃən] *s* présentation *f*

presenta′tion cop′y *s* exemplaire *m* offert à titre d'hommage

presentiment [prɪˈzɛntɪmənt] *s* pressentiment *m*

presently [ˈprɛzəntli] *adv* tout à l'heure; (*now*) à présent

preserve [prɪˈzʌrv] *s* confiture *f*; (*for game*) chasse *f* gardée ǁ *tr* préserver, conserver; (*to can*) conserver

pre-shrunk [priˈʃrʌŋk] *adj* irrétrécissable

preside [prɪˈzaɪd] *intr* présider; **to preside over** présider

presiden·cy [ˈprɛzɪdənsi] *s* (*pl -cies*) présidence *f*

president [ˈprɛzɪdənt] *s* président *m*; (*of a university*) recteur *m*

presidential [ˌprɛzɪˈdɛnʃəl] *adj* présidentiel

press [prɛs] *s* presse *f*; (*e.g., for wine*) pressoir *m*; (*pressure*) pression *f*; (*for clothes*) armoire *f*; (*in weight lifting*) développé *m*; **in press** (*said of clothes*) lisse et net; (*said of book being published*) sous presse; **to go to press** être mis sous presse ǁ *tr* presser; (*e.g., a button*) appuyer sur, presser; (*clothes*) donner un coup de fer à, repasser ǁ *intr* presser; **to press against** se serrer contre; **to press forward, to press on** presser le pas

press′ a′gent *s* agent *m* de publicité

press′ box′ *s* tribune *f* des journalistes

press′ card′ *s* coupe-file *m* d'un journaliste

press′ con′ference *s* conférence *f* de presse

press′ gal′lery *s* tribune *f* de la presse

pressing [ˈprɛsɪŋ] *adj* pressé, pressant

press′ release′ *s* communiqué *m* de presse

pressure [ˈprɛʃər] *s* pression *f*

pres′sure cook′er *s* autocuiseur *m*, cocotte *f* minute

pressurize [ˈprɛʃəˌraɪz] *tr* pressuriser

prestige [prɛsˈtiʒ], [ˈprɛstɪdʒ] *s* prestige *m*

presumably [prɪˈz(j)uməbli] *adv* probablement

presume [prɪˈz(j)um] *tr* présumer; **to presume to** présumer ǁ *intr* présumer; **to presume on** or **upon** abuser de

presumption [prɪˈzʌmpʃən] *s* présomption *f*

presumptuous [prɪˈzʌmptʃʊ·əs] *adj* présomptueux

presuppose [ˌprisəˈpoz] *tr* présupposer

pretend [prɪˈtɛnd] *tr* feindre; **to pretend to** + *inf* feindre de + *inf* ǁ *intr* feindre; **to pretend to** (*e.g., the throne*) prétendre à

pretender [prɪˈtɛndər] *s* prétendant *m*; (*imposter*) simulateur *m*

pretense [prɪˈtɛns], [ˈpritɛns] *s* prétention *f*; feinte *f*; **under false pretenses** par des moyens frauduleux; **under pretense of** sous prétexte de

pretension [prɪˈtɛnʃən] *s* prétention *f*

pretentious [prɪˈtɛnʃəs] *adj* prétentieux

pretext [ˈpritɛkst] *s* prétexte *m*

pretonic [priˈtɑnɪk] *adj* prétonique

pret·ty [ˈprɪti] *adj* (*comp -tier; super -tiest*) joli; (*coll*) considérable ǁ *adv* assez; très

prevail [prɪˈvel] *intr* prévaloir, régner; **to prevail on** or **upon** persuader

prevailing [prɪˈvelɪŋ] *adj* prédominant; (*wind*) dominant; (*fashion*) en vogue

prevalent [ˈprɛvələnt] *adj* commun, courant

prevaricate [prɪ'værɪˌket] *intr* mentir

prevent [prɪ'vent] *tr* empêcher

prevention [prɪ'venʃən] *s* empêchement *m*; (e.g., of accidents) prévention *f*

preventive [prɪ'ventɪv] *adj* & *s* préventif *m*

preview ['priˌvju] *s* (of something to come) amorce *f*; (private showing) (mov) avant-première *f*; (show of brief scenes for advertising) film *m* annonce

previous ['privɪ·əs] *adj* précédent, antérieur; (notice) préalable; (coll) pressé || *adv*—previous to antérieurement à

prewar ['priˌwɔr] *adj* d'avant-guerre

prey [pre] *s* proie *f*; to be a prey to être en proie à || *intr*—to prey on or upon faire sa proie de; (e.g., a seacoast) piller; (e.g., the mind) ronger, miner

price [praɪs] *s* prix *m* || *tr* mettre un prix à, tarifer; s'informer du prix de

price' control' *s* contrôle *m* des prix

price' cut'ting *s* rabais *m*, remise *f*

price' fix'ing *s* stabilisation *f* des prix

price' freez'ing *s* blocage *m* des prix

priceless ['praɪslɪs] *adj* sans prix; (coll) impayable, absurde

price' list' *s* liste *f* de prix, tarif *m*

price' war' *s* guerre *f* des prix

prick [prɪk] *s* piqûre *f*; (spur; sting of conscience) aiguillon *m* || *tr* piquer; to prick up (the ears) dresser

prick·ly ['prɪkli] *adj* (comp -lier; super -liest) épineux

prick'ly heat' *s* lichen *m* vésiculaire, miliaire *f*

prick'ly pear' *s* figue *f* de Barbarie; (plant) figuier *m* de Barbarie

pride [praɪd] *s* orgueil *m*; (satisfaction) fierté *f*; to take pride in être fier de || *tr*—to pride oneself on or upon s'enorgueillir de

priest [prist] *s* prêtre *m*

priestess ['pristɪs] *s* prêtresse *f*

priesthood ['pristˌhud] *s* sacerdoce *m*

priest·ly ['pristli] *adj* (comp -lier; super -liest) sacerdotal

prig [prɪg] *s* poseur *m*, pédant *m*

prim [prɪm] *adj* (comp primmer; super primmest) compassé, guindé

prima·ry ['praɪˌmeri], ['praɪməri] *adj* primaire || *s* (pl -ries) élection *f* primaire; (elec) primaire *m*

primate ['praɪmet] *s* (eccl) primat *m*; (zool) primate *m*

prime [praɪm] *adj* premier, principal; (of the best quality) de première qualité, (le) meilleur; (math) prime || *s* fleur *f*, perfection *f*; commencement *m*, premiers jours *mpl*; prime of life fleur or force de l'âge || *tr* amorcer; (a surface to be painted) appliquer une couche de fond à; (to supply with information) mettre au courant

prime' min'ister *s* premier ministre *m*

primer ['prɪmər] *s* premier livre *m* de lecture; manuel *m* élémentaire || ['praɪmər] *s* (for paint) couche *f* de fond, impression *f*; (mach) amorce *f*

primeval [praɪ'mivəl] *adj* primitif

primitive ['prɪmɪtɪv] *adj* & *s* primitif *m*

primordial [praɪ'mɔrdɪ·əl] *adj* primordial

primp [prɪmp] *tr* bichonner, pomponner || *intr* se bichonner, se pomponner

prim'rose' *s* primevère *f*

prim'rose path' *s* chemin *m* de velours

prince [prɪns] *s* prince *m*

prince·ly ['prɪnsli] *adj* (comp -lier; super -liest) princier

Prince' of Wales' *s* prince *m* de Galles

princess ['prɪnsɪs] *s* princesse *f*

principal ['prɪnsɪpəl] *adj* & *s* principal *m*

principali·ty [ˌprɪnsɪ'pælɪti] *s* (pl -ties) principauté *f*

principle ['prɪnsɪpəl] *s* principe *m*

print [prɪnt] *s* empreinte *f*; (printed cloth) imprimé *m*; (design in printed cloth) estampe *f*; (lettering) lettres *fpl* moulées; (act of printing) impression *f*; (phot) épreuve *f*; out of print épuisé; small print petits caractères *mpl* || *tr* imprimer; écrire en lettres moulées; publier; (an edition; a photographic negative) tirer

print'ed mat'ter *s* imprimés *mpl*

printer ['prɪntər] *s* imprimeur *m*

prin'ter's dev'il *s* apprenti *m* imprimeur

prin'ter's er'ror *s* faute *f* d'impression, coquille *f*

prin'ter's ink' *s* encre *f* d'imprimerie

prin'ter's mark' *s* nom *m* de l'imprimeur

printing ['prɪntɪŋ] *s* imprimerie *f*; (act) impression *f*; (by hand) écriture *f* en caractères d'imprimerie; édition *f*; tirage *m*; (phot) tirage

print'ing frame' *s* (phot) châssis-presse *m*

print'ing of'fice *s* imprimerie *f*

prior ['praɪ·ər] *adj* antérieur || *s* prieur *m* || *adv* antérieurement; prior to avant; avant de

priori·ty [praɪ'ɔrɪti], [praɪ'ɔrɪti] *s* (pl -ties) priorité *f*

prism ['prɪzəm] *s* prisme *m*

prison ['prɪzən] *s* prison *f* || *tr* emprisonner

prisoner ['prɪzənər], ['prɪznər] *s* prisonnier *m*

pris'on van' *s* voiture *f* cellulaire

pris·sy ['prɪsi] *adj* (comp -sier; super -siest) (coll) bégueule

priva·cy ['praɪvəsi] *s* (pl -cies) intimité *f*; secret *m*

private ['praɪvɪt] *adj* privé, particulier; confidentiel, secret; (public sign) défense d'entrer || *s* simple soldat *m*; in private dans l'intimité, en particulier; privates parties *fpl*

pri'vate cit'izen *s* simple particulier *m*, simple citoyen *m*

pri'vate first' class' *s* soldat *m* de première

pri'vate hos'pital *s* clinique *f*

pri'vate sec'retary *s* secrétaire *m* particulier

privet ['prɪvɪt] *s* troène *m*

privilege ['prɪvɪlɪdʒ] s privilège m

priv·y ['prɪvi] adj privé; **privy to** averti de || s (pl **-ies**) cabinets mpl au fond du jardin

prize [praɪz] s prix m; (something captured) prise f || tr faire cas de, estimer

prize' fight' s match m de boxe

prize' fight'er s boxeur m professionnel

prize' ring' s ring m

prize' win'ner s lauréat m; **prizewinners** (list) palmarès m

pro [pro] s (pl **pros**) vote m affirmatif; (professional) (coll) pro m; **the pros and the cons** le pour et le contre || prep en faveur de

probabil·ity [ˌprabə'bɪlɪti] s (pl **-ties**) probabilité f

probable ['prabəbəl] adj probable

probably ['prabəbli] adv probablement

probate ['probet] s homologation f || tr homologuer

probation [pro'beʃən] s liberté f surveillée; (on a job) stage m

probe [prob] s sondage m; (instrument) sonde f; (rok) échos mpl; (rok) engin m exploratoire || tr sonder

problem ['prabləm] s problème m

prob'lem child' s enfant mf terrible

procedure [pro'sidʒər] s procédé m

proceed [pro'sid] s—**proceeds** produit m, bénéfices mpl || [pro'sid] intr avancer, continuer; continuer à parler; **to proceed from** procéder de; **to proceed to** se mettre à; (to go to) se diriger à

proceeding [pro'sidɪŋ] s procédé m; **proceedings** actes mpl

process ['prases] s (technique) procédé m; (development) processus m; **in the process of** en train de || tr soumettre à un procédé, traiter

procession [pro'seʃən] s cortège m, défilé m, procession f

pro'cess serv'er s huissier m exploitant

proclaim [pro'klem] tr proclamer

proclitic [pro'klɪtɪk] adj & s proclitique m

procommunist [pro'kamjənɪst] adj & s procommuniste mf

procrastinate [pro'kræstɪˌnet] tr différer || intr remettre les affaires à plus tard

proctor ['praktər] s surveillant m

procure [pro'kjur] tr obtenir, se procurer; (a woman) entraîner à la prostitution || intr faire du proxénétisme

procurement [pro'kjurmənt] s obtention f, acquisition f

procurer [pro'kjurər] s proxénète mf

prod [prad] s poussée f; (stick) aiguillon m || v (pret & pp **prodded**; ger **prodding**) tr aiguillonner

prodigal ['pradɪgəl] adj & s prodigue mf

prodigious [pro'dɪdʒəs] adj prodigieux

prodi·gy ['pradɪdʒi] s (pl **-gies**) prodige m

produce ['pradjus] s produit m; (eatables) denrées fpl || [pro'djus] tr produire; (a play) mettre en scène; (geom) prolonger

producer [pro'd(j)usər] s producteur m

product ['pradəkt] s produit m

production [pro'dʌkʃən] s production f

profane [pro'fen] adj profane; (language) impie, blasphématoire || s profane mf; impie mf || tr profaner

profani·ty [pro'fænɪti] s (pl **-ties**) blasphème m

profess [pro'fes] tr professer

profession [pro'feʃən] s profession f

professor [pro'fesər] s professeur m

proffer ['prafər] s offre f || tr offrir, tendre

proficient [pro'fɪʃənt] adj compétent expert

profile ['profaɪl] s profil m; courte biographie f || tr profiler; **to be profiled against** se profiler sur

profit ['prafɪt] s bénéfice m, profit m || tr profiter (with dat) || intr profiter; **to profit from** profiter à, de, on en

profitable ['prafɪtəbəl] adj profitable

prof'it-and-loss' account' s compte m de profits et pertes

profiteer [ˌprafɪ'tɪr] s profiteur m || intr faire des bénéfices excessifs

prof'it tak'ing s prise f de bénéfices

profligate ['praflɪgɪt] adj & s débauché m

pro' for'ma in'voice [ˌpro'fɔrmə] s facture f simulée

profound [pro'faund] adj profond

pro-French' adj francophile

profuse [prə'fjuz] adj abondant; (extravagant) prodigue

proge·ny ['pradʒəni] s (pl **-nies**) progéniture f

progno·sis [prag'nosɪs] s (pl **-ses** [siz]) pronostic m

prognosticate [prag'nastɪˌket] tr pronostiquer

pro·gram ['progræm] s programme m || v (pret & pp **-gramed** or **-grammed**; ger **-graming** or **-gramming**) tr programmer

programmer ['progræmər] s (comp) programmeur m; (mov, rad, telv) programmateur m

programming ['progræmɪŋ] s programmation f

progress ['pragres] s progrès m; cours m, e.g., **work in progress** travaux en cours; **to make progress** faire des progrès || [prə'gres] intr progresser

progressive [prə'gresɪv] adj progressif; (pol) progressiste || s (pol) progressiste mf

prohibit [pro'hɪbɪt] tr prohiber, interdire

prohibition [ˌpro·ə'bɪʃən] s prohibition f

project ['pradʒekt] s projet m || [prə'dʒekt] tr projeter || intr (to jut out) saillir; (theat) passer la rampe

projectile [prə'dʒektɪl] s projectile m

projection [prə'dʒekʃən] s projection f; (something jutting out) saillie f

projec'tion booth' s (mov) cabine f de projection

projector [prə'dʒektər] s projecteur m

proletarian [‚proli'tɛri·ən] *adj* prolétarien || *s* prolétaire *m*

proletariat [‚proli'tɛri·ət] *s* prolétariat *m*

proliferate [prə'lifə‚ret] *intr* proliférer

prolific [prə'lifik] *adj* prolifique

prolix ['prolıks], [pro'lıks] *adj* prolixe

prologue ['prolɔg], ['prolag] *s* prologue *m*

prolong [pro'lɔŋ], [pro'laŋ] *tr* prolonger

promenade [‚pramı'ned], [‚pramı-'nad] *s* promenade *f*; bal *m* d'apparat; (theat) promenoir *m* || *intr* se promener

prom'enade' deck' *s* (naut) pont-promenade *m*

prominent ['pramınənt] *adj* proéminent; (well-known) éminent

promiscuity [‚pramıs'kju·əti] *s* promiscuité *f*

promise ['pramıs] *s* promesse *f* || *tr & intr* promettre; **to promise s.o. to** promettre à qn de; **to promise s.th. to s.o.** promettre q.ch. à qn

prom'issory note' ['pramı‚sori] *m* billet *m* à ordre

promonto·ry ['pramən‚tori] *s* (pl -ries) promontoire *m*

promote [prə'mot] *tr* promouvoir

promoter [prə'motər] *s* promoteur *m*

promotion [prə'moʃən] *s* promotion *f*

prompt [prampt] *adj* prompt; (theat) souffler son rôle à || *tr* inciter; (theat) souffler son rôle à

prompter ['pramptər] *s* (theat) souffleur *m*

promp'ter's box' *s* (theat) trou *m* du souffleur

promptness ['pramptnıs] *s* promptitude *f*

promulgate ['praməl‚get], [pro'mʌl-get] *tr* promulguer

prone [pron] *adj* à plat ventre, prostré; **prone to** enclin à

prong [prɔŋ] *s* dent *f*

pronoun ['pronaun] *s* pronom *m*

pronounce [prə'nauns] *tr* prononcer

pronouncement [prə'naunsmənt] *s* déclaration *f*

pronunciation [prə‚nʌnsı'e/ən], [prə-‚nʌn/ı'e/ən] *s* prononciation *f*

proof [pruf] *adj*—**proof against** à l'épreuve de, résistant à || *s* preuve *f*; (phot, typ) épreuve *f*; **to read proof** corriger les épreuves

proof'read'er *s* correcteur *m*

prop [prap] *s* appui *m*; (to hold up a plant) tuteur *m*; **props** (theat) accessoires *mpl* || *v* (pret & pp propped; ger propping) *tr* appuyer; (hort) tuteur

propaganda [‚prapə'gændə] *s* propagande *f*

propagate ['prapə‚get] *tr* propager

pro·pel [prə'pel] *v* (pret & pp -pelled; ger -pelling) *tr* propulser

propeller [prə'pelər] *s* hélice *f*

propensi·ty [prə'pensıti] *s* (pl -ties) propension *f*

proper ['prapər] *adj* propre; (fitting, correct) convenable, comme il faut

proper·ty ['prapərti] *s* (pl -ties) propriété *f*; **properties** (theat) accessoires *mpl*

prop'erty own'er *s* propriétaire *mf*

prop'erty tax' *s* impôt *m* foncier

prophe·cy ['prafisi] *s* (pl -cies) prophétie *f*

prophe·sy ['prafi‚sai] *v* (pret & pp -sied) *tr* prophétiser

prophet ['prafit] *s* prophète *m*

prophetess ['prafitıs] *s* prophétesse *f*

prophylactic [‚prafi'læktık] *adj* prophylactique || *s* médicament *m* prophylactique

propitiate [prə'pıʃı‚et] *tr* apaiser

propitious [prə'pıʃəs] *adj* propice

prop'jet' *s* turbopropulseur *m*

proportion [prə'porʃən] *s* proportion *f*; **in proportion as** à mesure que; **in proportion to** en proportion de, en raison de; **out of proportion** hors de proportion || *tr* proportionner

proportionate [prə'porʃənit] *adj* proportionné

proposal [prə'pozəl] *s* proposition *f*; demande *f* en mariage

propose [prə'poz] *tr* proposer || *intr* faire sa déclaration; **to propose to** demander sa main à; (to decide to) se proposer de

proposition [‚prapə'zıʃən] *s* proposition *f* || *tr* faire des propositions malhonnêtes à

propound [prə'paund] *tr* proposer

proprietor [prə'praı·ətər] *s* propriétaire *mf*

proprietress [prə'praı·ətrıs] *s* propriétaire *f*

proprie·ty [prə'praı·əti] *s* (pl -ties) propriété *f*; (of conduct) bienséance *f*; **proprieties** convenances *fpl*

propulsion [prə'pʌlʃən] *s* propulsion *f*

prorate [pro'ret] *tr* partager au prorata

prosaic [pro'ze·ık] *adj* prosaïque

proscenium [pro'sını·əm] *s* avant-scène *f*

proscribe [pro'skraib] *tr* proscrire

prose [proz] *adj* en prose || *s* prose *f*

prosecute ['prası‚kjut] *tr* poursuivre

prosecutor ['prası‚kjutər] *s* (lawyer) procureur *m*; (plaintiff) plaignant *m*

proselyte ['prası‚lait] *s* prosélyte *mf*

prose' writ'er *s* prosateur *m*

prosody ['prasədi] *s* prosodie *f*

prospect ['praspekt] *s* perspective *f*; (future) avenir *m*; (com) client *m* éventuel || *tr & intr* prospecter; **to prospect for** (e.g., gold) chercher

prospector ['praspektər] *s* prospecteur *m*

prospectus [prə'spektəs] *s* prospectus *m*

prosper ['praspər] *intr* prospérer

prosperity [pras'pɛrıti] *s* prospérité *f*

prosperous ['praspərəs] *adj* prospère

prostitute ['prası‚t(j)ut] *s* prostituée *f* || *tr* prostituer

prostrate ['prastret] *adj* prosterné; (exhausted) prostré || *tr* abattre; **to prostrate oneself** se prosterner

prostration [pras'treʃən] *s* prostration *f*; (abasement) prosternation *f*

protagonist [pro'tægənɪst] s protagoniste m

protect [prə'tekt] tr protéger

protection [prə'tek/ən] s protection f

protein ['proti·ɪn], ['protin] s protéine f

pro-tempore [pro'tempə,ri] adj intérimaire, par intérim

protest ['protest] s protestation f || [pro'test] tr protester de; protester || intr protester

Protestant ['pratɪstənt] adj & s protestant m

protocol ['protə,kal] s protocole m

proton ['protan] s proton m

protoplasm ['protə,plæzəm] s protoplasme m

prototype ['protə,taɪp] s prototype m

protozoan [,protə'zo·ən] s protozoaire m

protract [pro'trækt] tr prolonger

protrude [pro'trud] intr saillir

protuberance [pro't(j)ubərəns] s protubérance f

proud [praud] adj fier; (vain) orgueilleux

proud' flesh' s chair f fongueuse

prove [pruv] v (pret proved; pp proved or proven ['pruvən]) tr prouver; (to put to the test) éprouver || intr se montrer, se trouver; to prove to be se révéler, s'avérer

proverb ['pravərb] s proverbe m

provide [prə'vaɪd] tr pourvoir, fournir; to provide s.th. for s.o. fournir q.ch. à qn || intr—to provide for pourvoir à; (e.g., future needs) prévoir

provided conj pourvu que, à condition que

providence ['pravɪdəns] s providence f; (prudence) prévoyance f

providential [,pravɪ'den/əl] adj providentiel

providing [prə'vaɪdɪŋ] conj pourvu que, à condition que

province ['pravɪns] s province f; (sphere) compétence f

prov'ing ground' s terrain m d'essai

provision [prə'vɪʒən] s (supplying) fourniture f; clause f; provisions provisions fpl

proviso [prə'vaɪzo] s (pl -sos or -soes) condition f, stipulation f

provocative [prə'vakətɪv] adj provocant

provoke [prə'vok] tr provoquer; fâcher, contrarier

provoking [prə'vokɪŋ] adj contrariant

prow [prau] s proue f

prowess ['prau·ɪs] s prouesse f

prowl [praul] intr rôder

prowler ['praulər] s rôdeur m

proximity [prak'sɪmɪti] s proximité f

prox·y ['praksi] s (pl -ies) mandat m; (agent) mandataire mf; by proxy par procuration

prude [prud] s prude mf

prudence ['prudəns] s prudence f

prudent ['prudənt] adj prudent

pruder·y ['prudəri] s (pl -ies) pruderie f

prudish ['prudɪ/] adj prude

prune [prun] s pruneau m || tr élaguer

Prussian ['prʌ/ən] adj prussien || s Prussien m

pry [praɪ] v (pret & pp pried) tr—to pry open forcer avec un levier; to pry s.th. out of s.o. extorquer, soutirer q.ch. à qn || intr fureter; to pry into fourrer son nez dans

P.S. ['pi'es] s (letterword) (postscript) P.-S.

psalm [sam] s psaume m

Psalter ['soltər] s psautier m

pseudo ['s(j)udo] adj faux, supposé, feint, factice

pseudonym ['s(j)udənɪm] s pseudonyme m

psyche ['saɪki] s psyché f

psychiatrist [saɪ'kaɪ·ətrɪst] s psychiatre mf

psychiatry [saɪ'kaɪ·ətri] s psychiatrie f

psychic ['saɪkɪk] adj psychique; médiumnique || s médium m

psychoanalysis [,saɪko·ə'nælɪsɪs] s psychanalyse f

psychoanalyze [,saɪko'ænə,laɪz] tr psychanalyser

psychologic(al) [,saɪko'ladʒɪk(əl)] adj psychologique

psychologist [saɪ'kalədʒɪst] s psychologue mf

psychology [saɪ'kalədʒi] s psychologie f

psychopath ['saɪkə,pæθ] s psychopathe m

psycho·sis [saɪ'kosɪs] s (pl -ses [siz]) psychose f

psychotic [saɪ'katɪk] adj & s psychotique mf

ptomaine ['tomen] s ptomaïne f

pub [pʌb] s (Brit) bistrot m, café m

puberty ['pjubərti] s puberté f

public ['pʌblɪk] adj & s public m

publication [,pʌblɪ'ke/ən] s publication f

publicity [pʌb'lɪsɪti] s publicité f

public'ity stunt' s canard m publicitaire

publicize ['pʌblɪ,saɪz] tr publier

pub'lic li'brary s bibliothèque f municipale

pub'lic-opin'ion poll' s sondage m de l'opinion, enquête f par sondage

pub'lic school' s (U.S.A.) école f primaire; (Brit) école privée

pub'lic serv'ant s fonctionnaire mf

pub'lic speak'ing s art m oratoire, éloquence f

pub'lic toi'let s chalet m de nécessité

pub'lic util'ity s entreprise f de service public; public utilities actions fpl émises par les entreprises de service public

publish ['pʌblɪ/] tr publier

publisher ['pʌblɪ/ər] s éditeur m

pub'lishing house' s maison f d'édition

puck [pʌk] s palet m

pucker ['pʌkər] s fronce m, faux pli m || tr froncer || intr se froncer

pudding ['pudɪŋ] s entremets m sucré au lait, crème f

puddle ['pʌdəl] s flaque f || tr puddler

pudg·y ['pʌdʒi] adj (comp -ier; super -iest) bouffi, rondouillard

puerile ['pju·ərɪl] adj puéril

puerili·ty [ˌpjuˑəˈrɪlɪti] s (pl -ties) puérilité f

Puerto Rican [ˈpwertoˈrikən] adj portoricain ‖ s Portoricain m

puff [pʌf] s souffle m; (of smoke) bouffée f; (in clothing) bouillon m; (in sleeve) bouffant m; (for powder) houppette f; (swelling) bouffissure f; (praise) battage m; (culin) moule m de pâte feuilletée fourré à la crème, à la confiture, etc. ‖ tr lancer des bouffées de; to puff oneself up se rengorger; to puff out souffler; to puff up gonfler ‖ intr souffler; (to swell) gonfler, se gonfler; to puff at or on (a pipe) tirer sur

puff' paste' s pâte f feuilletée

pugilism [ˈpjudʒɪˌlɪzəm] s science f pugilistique, boxe f

pugilist [ˈpjudʒɪlɪst] s pugiliste m

pugnacious [pʌgˈneʃəs] adj pugnace

pug'-nosed' adj camus

puke [pjuk] s (slang) dégobillage m ‖ tr & intr (slang) dégobiller

pull [pul] s secousse f, coup m; (handle of door) poignée f; (slang) piston m, appuis mpl ‖ tr tirer; (a muscle) tordre; (the trigger) appuyer sur; (a proof) (typ) tirer; to pull about tirailler; to pull away arracher; to pull down baisser; (e.g., a house) abattre; (to degrade) abaisser; to pull in rentrer; to pull off enlever; (fig) réussir; to pull on (a garment) mettre; to pull oneself together se ressaisir; to pull out sortir; (a tooth) arracher ‖ intr tirer; bouger lentement, bouger avec effort; to pull at tirer sur; to pull for (slang) plaider en faveur de; to pull in rentrer; (said of train) entrer en gare; to pull out partir; (said of train) sortir de la gare; to pull through se tirer d'affaire; (to get well) se remettre

pull' chain' s chasse f d'eau

pullet [ˈpulɪt] s poulette f

pulley [ˈpuli] s poulie f

pulmonary [ˈpʌlməˌneri] adj pulmonaire

pulp [pʌlp] s pulpe f; (to make paper) pâte f; (of tooth) bulbe m; to beat to a pulp (coll) mettre en bouillie

pulp' fic'tion s romans mpl à sensation; le roman de la concierge

pulpit [ˈpulpɪt] s chaire f

pulsate [ˈpʌlset] intr palpiter; vibrer

pulsation [pʌlˈseʃən] s pulsation f

pulse [pʌls] s pouls m; to feel or take the pulse of tâter le pouls à

pulverize [ˈpʌlvəˌraɪz] tr pulvériser

pu'mice stone' [ˈpʌmɪs] s pierre f ponce

pum·mel [ˈpʌməl] v (pret & pp -meled or -melled; ger -meling or -melling) tr bourrer de coups

pump [pʌmp] s pompe f; (slipperlike shoe) escarpin m ‖ tr pomper; (coll) tirer les vers du nez à; to pump up pomper; (a tire) gonfler ‖ intr pomper

pump'han'dle s bras m de pompe

pumpkin [ˈpʌmpkɪn], [ˈpʌŋkɪn] s citrouille f, potiron m

pun [pʌn] s calembour m, jeu m de mots ‖ v (pret & pp punned; ger punning) intr faire des jeux de mots

punch [pʌntʃ] s coup m de poing; (to pierce metal) mandrin m; (to drive a nail or bolt) poinçon m; (for tickets) pince f, emporte-pièce m; (drink; blow) punch m; (mach) poinçonneuse f; (energy) (coll) allant m, punch; to pull no punches parler carrément ‖ tr donner un coup de poing à; poinçonner

punch' bowl' s bol m à punch

punch' card' s carte f perforée

punch' clock' s horloge f de pointage

punch'-drunk' adj abruti de coups; (coll) abruti, étourdi

punched' tape' s bande f enregistreuse perforée

punch'ing bag' s punching-ball m; (fig) tête f de Turc

punch' line' s point m final, phrase f clé

punctilious [pʌŋkˈtɪlɪˑəs] adj pointilleux, minutieux

punctual [ˈpʌŋktʃuˑəl] adj ponctuel

punctuate [ˈpʌŋktʃuˌet] tr & intr ponctuer

punctuation [ˌpʌŋktʃuˈeʃən] s ponctuation f

punctua'tion mark' s signe m de ponctuation

puncture [ˈpʌŋktʃər] s perforation f; (of a tire) crevaison f; (med) ponction f ‖ tr perforer; (a tire) crever; (med) ponctionner

punc'ture-proof' adj increvable

pundit [ˈpʌndɪt] s pandit m; (savant) mandarin m; (pej) pontife m

pungent [ˈpʌndʒənt] adj piquant

punish [ˈpʌnɪʃ] tr & intr punir

punishment [ˈpʌnɪʃmənt] s punition f; (for a crime) peine f; (severe handling) mauvais traitements mpl

punk [pʌŋk] adj (slang) moche, fichu; to feel punk (slang) être mal fichu ‖ s amadou m; mèche f d'amadou; (decayed wood) bois m pourri; (slang) voyou m, mauvais sujet m

punster [ˈpʌnstər] s faiseur m de calembours

pu·ny [ˈpjuni] adj (comp -nier; super -niest) chétif, malingre

pup [pʌp] s chiot m

pupil [ˈpjupəl] s élève mf; (of the eye) pupille f, prunelle f

puppet [ˈpʌpɪt] s marionnette f; (person controlled by another) fantoche m, pantin m

pup'pet gov'ernment s gouvernement m fantoche

pup'pet show' s spectacle m de marionnettes, marionnettes fpl

pup·py [ˈpʌpi] s (pl -pies) petit chien m

pup'py love' s premières amours fpl

pup' tent' s tente-abri f

purchase [ˈpʌrtʃəs] s achat m; (leverage) point m d'appui, prise f ‖ tr acheter

pur'chasing pow'er s pouvoir m d'achat

pure [pjur] *adj* pur

purgative ['pʌrgətɪv] *adj & s* purgatif *m*

purgato·ry ['pʌrgə‚torɪ] *s* (*pl* -ries) purgatoire *m*

purge [pʌrdʒ] *s* purge *f* || *tr* purger

puri·fy ['pjurɪ‚faɪ] *v* (*pret & pp* -fied) *tr* purifier

puritan ['pjurɪtən] *adj & s* puritain *m*; **Puritan** puritain

purity ['pjurɪtɪ] *s* pureté *f*

purloin [pər'lɔɪn] *tr & intr* voler

purple ['pʌrpəl] *adj* pourpre || *s* (*violescent*) pourpre *m*; (*deep red, crimson*) pourpre *f*; **born to the purple** né dans la pourpre

purport ['pʌrport] *s* sens *m*, teneur *f*; (*intention*) but *m*, objet *m* || [pər'port] *tr* signifier, vouloir dire

purpose ['pʌrpəs] *s* intention *f*, dessein *m*; (*goal*) but *m*, objet *m*, fin *f*; **for all purposes** à tous usages; pratiquement; **for the purpose of**, **with the purpose of** dans le dessein de, dans le but de; **for this purpose** à cet effet; **for what purpose?** à quoi bon?, à quelle fin?; **on purpose** exprès, à dessein; **to good purpose** utilement; **to some purpose** à qch; **to no purpose** vainement; **to serve the purpose** faire l'affaire

purposely ['pʌrpəslɪ] *adv* exprès, à dessein, de propos délibéré

purr [pʌr] *s* ronron *m* || *intr* ronronner

purse [pʌrs] *s* bourse *f*, porte-monnaie *m*; (*handbag*) sac *m* à main || *tr* (*one's lips*) pincer

purser ['pʌrsər] *s* commissaire *m*

purse' snatch'er ['snætʃər] *s* voleur *m* à la tire

purse' strings' *spl* cordons *mpl* de bourse

pursue [pər's(j)u] *tr* poursuivre; (*a profession*) suivre

pursuit [pər's(j)ut] *s* poursuite *f*; profession *f*

pursuit' plane' *s* chasseur *m*, avion *m* de chasse

purvey [pər've] *tr* fournir

pus [pʌs] *s* pus *m*

push [pu/] *s* poussée *f* || *tr* pousser; (*a button*) appuyer sur, presser; **to push around** (coll) rudoyer; **to push aside** écarter; **to push away** or **back** repousser; **to push in** enfoncer; **to push over** faire tomber; **to push through** amener à bonne fin; (*a resolution, bill, etc.*) faire adopter || *intr* pousser; **to push forward** or **on** avancer; **to push off** se mettre en route; (naut) pousser au large

push' but'ton *s* bouton *m* électrique, poussoir *m*

push'-but'ton war'fare *s* guerre *f* presse-bouton

push'cart' *s* voiture *f* à bras

pushing ['pu/ɪŋ] *adj* entreprenant; indiscret; agressif

pusillanimous [‚pjusɪ'lænɪməs] *adj* pusillanime

puss [pus] *s* minet *m*; (slang) gueule *f*; **sly puss** (*girl*) (coll) futée *f* || *interj* minet!

Puss' in Boots' *s* Chat *m* botté

puss' in the cor'ner *s* les quatre coins *mpl*

puss·y ['pusi] *s* (*pl* -ies) *s* minet *m* || *interj* minet!

puss'y wil'low *s* saule *m* nord-américain aux chatons très soyeux

put [put] *v* (*pret & pp* put; *ger* putting) *tr* mettre, placer; (*to throw*) lancer; (*a question*) poser; **to put across** passer; faire accepter; **to put aside** mettre de côté; **to put away** ranger; (*to jail*) mettre en prison; **to put back** remettre; retarder; **to put down** poser; (*e.g., a name*) noter; (*a revolution*) réprimer; (*to lower*) baisser; **to put off** renvoyer; (*to mislead*) dérouter; **to put on** (*clothes*) mettre; (*a play*) mettre en scène, monter; (*a brake*) serrer; (*a light, radio, etc.*) allumer; (*to feign*) feindre, simuler; **to put oneself out** se déranger; **to put on sale** mettre en vente; mettre en solde; **to put out** (*the hand*) étendre; (*the fire, light, etc.*) éteindre; (*s.o.'s eyes*) crever; (*e.g., a book*) publier; (*to show to the door*) mettre dehors; (*to vex*) contrarier; **to put over** (coll) faire accepter; **to put s.o. through s.th.** faire subir q.ch. à qn; **to put through** passer; (*a resolution, bill, etc.*) faire adopter; **to put up** lever; (*a house*) construire, faire construire; (*one's collar, hair, etc.*) relever; (*a picture*) accrocher; (*a notice*) afficher; (*a tent*) dresser; (*an umbrella*) ouvrir; (*the price*) augmenter; (*money as an investment*) fournir; (*resistance*) offrir; (*an overnight guest*) loger; (*fruit, vegetables, etc.*) conserver; (coll) pousser, inciter || *intr* se diriger; **to put on** feindre; **to put up** loger; **to put up with** tolérer

put'-out' *adj* ennuyeux, fâcheux

putrid ['pjutrɪd] *adj* putride

putter ['pʌtər] *intr* —**to putter around** s'occuper de bagatelles

put·ty ['pʌti] *s* (*pl* -ties) mastic *m* || *v* (*pret & pp* -tied) *tr* mastiquer

put'ty knife' *s* (*pl* knives) couteau *m* à mastiquer

put'-up' *adj* (coll) machiné à l'avance, monté

puzzle ['pʌzəl] *s* énigme *f* || *tr* intriguer; **to puzzle out** déchiffrer || *intr* —**to puzzle over** se creuser la tête pour comprendre

puzzler ['pʌzlər] *s* énigme *f*, colle *f*

puzzling ['pʌzlɪŋ] *adj* énigmatique

PW ['pi'dʌbəl‚ju] *s* (letterword) (**prisoner of war**) P.G.

pyg·my ['pɪgmi] *adj* pygméen || *s* (*pl* -mies) pygmée *m*

pylon ['paɪlɑn] *s* pylône *m*

pyramid ['pɪrəmɪd] *s* pyramide *f* ǁ *tr* augmenter graduellement ǁ *intr* pyramider

pyre [paɪr] *s* bûcher *m* funéraire

Pyrenees ['pɪrɪ ,niz] *spl* Pyrénées *fpl*

pyrites [paɪ'raɪtiz], ['paɪraɪts] *s* pyrite *f*

pyrotechnical [,paɪrə'teknɪkəl] *adj* pyrotechnique

pyrotechnics [,paɪrə'teknɪks] *spl* pyrotechnie *f*

python ['paɪθən], ['paɪθɛn] *s* python *m*

pythoness ['paɪθɛnɪs] *s* pythonisse *f*

pyx [pɪks] *s* (eccl) ciboire *m*; (for carrying Eucharist to sick) (eccl) pyxide *f*; (at a mint) boîte *f* des monnaies

Q

Q, q [kju] *s* XVII⁰ lettre de l'alphabet

quack [kwæk] *adj* frauduleux, de charlatan ǁ *s* charlatan *m* ǁ *intr* cancaner, faire couin-couin

quacker·y ['kwækəri] *s* (*pl* -ies) charlatanisme *m*

quadrangle ['kwad,ræŋgəl] *s* plan *m* quadrangulaire; cour *f* carrée

quadrant ['kwadrənt] *s* (*instrument*) quart *m* de cercle, secteur *m*; (math) quadrant *m*

quadroon [kwad'run] *s* quarteron *m*

quadruped ['kwadrə ,ped] *adj & s* quadrupède *m*

quadruple ['kwadrupəl] or [kwad'rupəl] *adj & s* quadruple *m* ǁ *tr & intr* quadrupler

quadruplets ['kwadru ,plets], [kwad'ruplets] *spl* quadruplés *mpl*

quaff [kwaf], [kwæf] *s* lampée *f* ǁ *tr & intr* boire à longs traits

quagmire ['kwæg,maɪr] *s* bourbier *m*, fondrière *f*

quail [kwel] *s* caille *f* ǁ *intr* fléchir

quaint [kwent] *adj* pittoresque, bizarre

quake [kwek] *s* tremblement *m*; (earthquake) tremblement de terre ǁ *intr* trembler

Quaker ['kwekər] *adj & s* quaker *m*

Quak'er meet'ing *s* réunion *f* de quakers; (coll) réunion où il y a très peu de conversation

quali·fy ['kwalɪ ,faɪ] *v* (*pret & pp* -fied*) tr* qualifier; (e.g., a recommendation) apporter des réserves à, modifier; to qualify oneself for se préparer à, se rendre apte à ǁ *intr* se qualifier

quali·ty ['kwalɪti] *s* (*pl* -ties) qualité *f*; (of a sound) timbre *m*

qualm [kwam] *s* scrupule *m*; (remorse) remords *m*; (nausea) soulèvement *m* de cœur

quanda·ry ['kwandəri] *s* (*pl* -ries) incertitude *f*, impasse *f*

quanti·ty ['kwantɪti] *s* (*pl* -ties) quantité *f*

quan·tum ['kwantəm] *adj* quantique ǁ *s* (*pl* -ta [tə]) quantum *m*

quan'tum the'ory *s* théorie *f* des quanta

quarantine ['kwarən ,tin], ['kwɔrən ,tin] *s* quarantaine *f* ǁ *tr* mettre en quarantaine

quar·rel ['kwarəl], ['kwɔrəl] *s* querelle *f*, dispute *f*; to have no quarrel with n'avoir rien à redire à; to pick a quarrel with chercher querelle à ǁ *v* (pret & pp -reled or -relled; ger -reling or -relling) intr se quereller, se disputer; to quarrel over contester sur, se disputer

quarrelsome ['kwarəlsəm], ['kwɔrəlsəm] *adj* querelleur

quar·ry ['kwari], ['kwɔri] *s* (*pl* -ries) carrière *f*; (hunted animal) proie *f* ǁ *v* (pret & pp -ried) tr extraire ǁ *intr* exploiter une carrière

quart [kwɔrt] *s* quart *m* de gallon, pinte *f*

quarter ['kwɔrtər] *s* quart *m*; (American coin) vingt-cinq cents *mpl*; (of a year) trimestre *m*; (of town; of beef; of moon; of shield) quartier *m*; a quarter after one une heure et quart; a quarter of an hour un quart d'heure; a quarter to one une heure moins le quart; at close quarters corps à corps; quarters (mil) quartiers *mpl*, cantonnement *m* ǁ *tr & intr* (mil) loger, cantonner

quar'ter-deck' *s* gaillard *m* d'arrière

quar'ter-hour' *s* quart *m* d'heure; every quarter-hour on the quarter-hour tous les quarts d'heure au quart d'heure juste

quarter·ly ['kwɔrtərli] *adj* trimestriel ǁ *s* (*pl* -lies) publication *f* or revue *f* trimestrielle ǁ *adv* trimestriellement, par trimestre

quar'ter-mas'ter *s* (mil) quartier-maître *m*, intendant *m* militaire

Quar'ter-master Corps' *s* Intendance *f*, service *m* de l'Intendance

quar'ter note' *s* (mus) noire *f*

quar'ter rest' *s* (mus) soupir *m*

quar'ter tone' *s* (mus) quart *m* de ton

quartet [kwɔr'tet] *s* quatuor *m*

quartz [kwɔrts] *s* quartz *m*

quasar ['kwesar] *s* (astr) quasar *m*

quash [kwaʃ] *tr* étouffer; (to set aside) annuler, invalider

quatrain ['kwatren] *s* quatrain *m*

quaver ['kwevər] *s* tremblement *m*; (in the singing voice) trémolo *m*; (mus) croche *f* ǁ *intr* trembloter

quay [ki] *s* quai *m*, débarcadère *m*

queen [kwin] *s* reine *f*; (cards, chess) reine

queen' bee' s reine f des abeilles

queen' dow'ager s reine f douairière

queen·ly ['kwinli] adj (comp -lier; super -liest) de reine, digne d'une reine

queen' moth'er s reine f mère

queen' post' s faux poinçon m

queer [kwɪr] adj bizarre, drôle; (suspicious) (coll) suspect; (homosexual) (coll) pervers, inverti; **to feel queer** (coll) se sentir indisposé || s excentrique mf; (homosexual) (coll) tapette f, inverti m || tr (slang) faire échouer, déranger

quell [kwɛl] tr étouffer, réprimer; (pain, sorrow, etc.) calmer

quench [kwɛnt/] tr (the thirst) étancher; (a rebellion) étouffer; (a fire) éteindre

que·ry ['kwɪri] s (pl -ries) question f; doute m; (question mark) point m d'interrogation || v (pret & pp -ried) tr questionner; mettre en doute; (to affix a question mark) marquer d'un point d'interrogation

quest [kwɛst] s quête f; **in quest of** en quête de

question ['kwɛst/ən] s question f; doute m; **beyond question** indiscutable, incontestable; **it is a question of** il s'agit de; **out of the question** impossible, impensable; **to ask s.o. a question** poser une question à qn; **to beg the question** faire une pétition de principe; **to call into question** mettre en question; **to move the previous question** (parl) demander la question préalable; **without question** sans aucun doute || tr interroger, questionner; (to cast doubt upon) douter de, contester

questionable ['kwɛst/ənəbəl] adj discutable, douteux

ques'tion mark' s point m d'interrogation

questionnaire [,kwɛst/ən'ɛr] s questionnaire m

queue [kju] s queue f || intr—to queue up faire la queue

quibble ['kwɪbəl] intr chicaner, ergoter

quibbling ['kwɪblɪŋ] s chicane f

quick [kwɪk] adj rapide, vif || s—the quick and the dead les vivants et les morts; **to cut to the quick** piquer au vif

quicken ['kwɪkən] tr accélérer; (e.g., the imagination) animer || intr s'accélérer; s'animer

quick'lime' s chaux f vive

quick' lunch' s casse-croûte m, repas m léger

quickly ['kwɪkli] adv vite, rapidement

quick'sand' s sable m mouvant

quick'sil'ver s vif-argent m, mercure m

quick'-tem'pered adj coléreux

quiet ['kwaɪ·ət] adj (still) tranquille, silencieux; (person) modeste, discret; (market) (com) calme; **be quiet!** taisez-vous!; **to keep quiet** rester tranquille; (to not speak) se taire || s tranquillité f; (rest) repos m; **on the quiet** en douce, à la dérobée ||

tr calmer, tranquilliser; (a child) faire taire || intr—**to quiet down** se calmer

quill [kwɪl] s plume f d'oie; (hollow part) tuyau m (de plume); (of hedgehog, porcupine) piquant m

quilt [kwɪlt] s courtepointe f || tr piquer

quince [kwɪns] s coing m; (tree) cognassier m

quinine ['kwaɪnaɪn] s quinine f

quinsy ['kwɪnzi] s angine f

quintessence [kwɪn'tɛsəns] s quintessence f

quintet [kwɪn'tɛt] s quintette m

quintuplets ['kwɪntu,plɛts], [kwɪn'tʌplɛts], [kwɪn't(j)uplɛts] spl quintuplés mpl

quip [kwɪp] s raillerie f, quolibet m || v (pret & pp quipped; ger quipping) tr dire sur un ton railleur || intr railler

quire [kwaɪr] s main f

quirk [kwʌrk] s excentricité f; (subterfuge) faux-fuyant m; **quirk of fate** caprice m du sort

quit [kwɪt] adj quitte; **to be quits** être quitte; **to call it quits** cesser, s'y renoncer; **we are quits** nous voilà quittes || v (pret & pp quit or quitted; ger quitting) tr (e.g., a city) quitter; (one's work, a payment, etc.) cesser; **to quit + ger** s'arrêter de + inf || intr partir; (coll) lâcher la partie

quite [kwaɪt] adv tout à fait; **quite a story** (coll) toute une histoire

quitter ['kwɪtər] s défaitiste m, lâcheur m

quiver ['kwɪvər] s tremblement m; (to hold arrows) carquois m || intr trembler

quixotic [kwɪks'atɪk] adj de don Quichotte; visionnaire, exalté

quiz [kwɪz] s (pl quizzes) interrogation f, colle f || v (pret & pp quizzed; ger quizzing) tr examiner, interroger

quiz' sec'tion s classe f d'exercices

quiz' show' s émission-questionnaire f

quizzical ['kwɪzɪkəl] adj curieux; (laughable) risible; (mocking) railleur

quoin [kɔɪn], [kwɔɪn] s angle m; (cornerstone) pierre f d'angle; (wedge) coin m, cale f || tr coincer, caler

quoit [kwɔɪt], [kɔɪt] s palet m; **to play quoits** jouer au palet

quondam ['kwandæm] adj ci-devant, d'autrefois

quorum ['kworəm] s quorum m

quota ['kwotə] s quote-part f; (e.g., of immigration) quota m, contingent m

quotation [kwo'te/ən] s (from a book) citation f; (of prices) cours m, cote f

quota'tion marks' spl guillemets mpl

quote [kwot] s (from a book) citation f; (of prices) cours m, cote f; **in quotes** (coll) entre guillemets || tr (from a book) citer; (values) coter || intr tirer des citations; **to quote out of context** citer hors contexte || interj je cite

quotient ['kwo/ənt] s quotient m

R

R, r [ɑr] s XVIIIᵉ lettre de l'alphabet

rabbet ['ræbɪt] s feuillure f || tr feuiller

rab·bi ['ræbaɪ] s (pl -bis or -bies) rabbin m

rabbit ['ræbɪt] s lapin m

rab'bit stew' s lapin m en civet

rabble ['ræbəl] s canaille f

rab'ble-rous'er s fomentateur m, agitateur m

rabies ['rebiz], ['rebɪ‚iz] s rage f

raccoon [ræ'kun] s raton m laveur

race [res] s race f; (contest) course f; (channel to lead water) bief m; (rapid current) raz m || tr lutter de vitesse avec; (e.g., a horse) faire courir; (a motor) emballer || intr faire une course, courir; (said of motor) s'emballer

race' horse' s cheval m de course

race' ri'ot s émeute f raciale

race' track' s champ m de courses, hippodrome m

racial ['reʃəl] adj racial

rac'ing car' s automobile f de course

rac'ing odds' spl cote f

rack [ræk] s (shelf) étagère f; (to hang clothes) portemanteau m; (for baggage) porte-bagages m; (for guns; for fodder) râtelier m; (for torture) chevalet m; (bar made to gear with a pinion) crémaillère f; **to go to rack and ruin** aller à vau-l'eau || tr (with hunger, remorse, etc.) tenailler; (one's brains) se creuser

racket ['rækɪt] s raquette f; (noise) vacarme m; (slang) racket m; **to make a racket** faire du tapage

racketeer [‚rækɪ'tɪr] s racketter m || intr pratiquer l'escroquerie

rack' rail'way s chemin m de fer à crémaillère

rac·y ['resi] adj (comp -ier; super -iest) plein de verve, vigoureux; parfumé; (off-color) sale, grivois

radar ['redɑr] s (acronym) (**radio detecting and ranging**) radar m

ra'dar sta'tion s poste m radar

radiant ['redɪ·ənt] adj radieux, rayonnant; (astr & phys) radiant

radiate ['redɪ‚et] tr rayonner; (e.g., happiness) répandre || intr rayonner

radiation [‚redɪ'eʃən] s rayonnement m, radiation f

radia'tion sick'ness s mal m des rayons

radiator ['redɪ‚etər] s radiateur m

ra'diator cap' s bouchon m de radiateur

radical ['rædɪkəl] adj & s radical m

radi·o ['redɪ‚o] s (pl -os) radio f || tr radiodiffuser

radioactive [‚redɪ·o'æktɪv] adj radioactif

ra'dioac'tive fall'out s retombées fpl radioactives

ra'dio am'ateur s sans-filiste mf

ra'dio announ'cer s speaker m

ra'dio-broad'cast'ing s radiodiffusion f

ra'dio-fre'quency s radiofréquence f

radiogram ['redɪ·o‚græm] s radiogramme m

ra'dio lis'tener s auditeur m de la radio

radiology [‚redɪ'ɑlədʒi] s radiologie f

ra'dio net'work s chaîne f de radiodiffusion

ra'dio news'cast s journal m parlé, radio-journal m

ra'dio receiv'er s récepteur m de radio

radioscopy [‚redɪ'ɑskəpi] s radioscopie f

ra'dio set' s poste m de radio

ra'dio sta'tion s poste m émetteur

ra'dio tube' s lampe f de radio

radish ['rædɪʃ] s radis m

radium ['redɪ·əm] s radium m

radi·us ['redɪ·əs] s (pl -i [‚aɪ] or -uses) rayon m; (anat) radius m; **within a radius of** dans un rayon de, à . . . à la ronde

raffish ['ræfɪʃ] adj bravache; (flashy) criard

raffle ['ræfəl] s tombola f || tr mettre en tombola

raft [ræft], [rɑft] s radeau m; **a raft of** (coll) un tas de

rafter ['ræftər], ['rɑftər] s chevron m

rag [ræg] s chiffon m; **in rags** en haillons; **to chew the rag** (slang) tailler une bavette

ragamuffin ['rægə‚mʌfɪn] s gueux m, va-nu-pieds m; (urchin) gamin m

rag' doll' s poupée f de chiffon

rage [redʒ] s rage f; **to be all the rage** faire fureur; **to fly into a rage** entrer en fureur || intr faire rage

rag' fair' s marché m aux puces

ragged ['rægɪd] adj en haillons; (edge) hérissé

ragpicker ['ræg‚pɪkər] s chiffonnier m

rag'time' s rythme m syncopé du jazz; musique f syncopée du jazz

rag'weed' s ambroisie f

ragwort ['ræg‚wʌrt] s (Senecio vulgaris) séneçon m; (S. jacobaea) jacobée f

raid [red] s incursion f, razzia f; (by police) descente f; (mil) raid m || tr razzier; faire une descente dans

rail [rel] s rail m; (railing) balustrade f; (of stairway) rampe f; (of, e.g., a bridge) garde-fou m; (orn) râle m; **by rail** par chemin de fer || intr invectiver; **to rail at** invectiver

rail' fence' s palissade f à claire-voie

rail'head' s tête f de ligne

railing ['relɪŋ] s balustrade f

rail'road' adj ferroviaire || s chemin m de fer || tr (a bill) faire voter en vitesse; (coll) emprisonner à tort

rail'road cros'sing s passage m à niveau

railroader ['rel‚rodər] s cheminot m

rail'road sta'tion s gare f

rail'way' adj ferroviaire || s chemin m de fer

raiment ['remənt] s habillement m

rain [ren] s pluie f; **in the rain** sous la pluie || tr faire pleuvoir || intr pleuvoir; **it is raining cats and dogs** il pleut à seaux

rainbow ['ren‚bo] *s* arc-en-ciel *m*

rain'coat' *s* imperméable *m*

rain'fall' *s* chute *f* de pluie

rain'proof' *adj* imperméable

rain' wa'ter *s* eau *f* de pluie

rain·y ['reni] *adj* (*comp* **-ier**; *super* **-iest**) pluvieux

raise [rez] *s* augmentation *f*; (*in poker*) relance *f* || *tr* augmenter; (*plants, animals, children; one's voice; a number to a certain power*) élever; (*an army, a camp, a siege; anchor; game*) lever; (*an objection, questions, etc.*) soulever; (*doubts; a hope; a storm*) faire naître; (*a window*) relever; (*one's head, one's voice; prices; the land*) hausser; (*a flag*) arborer; (*the dead*) ressusciter; (*money*) se procurer; (*the ante*) relancer; **to raise up** soulever, dresser

raisin ['rezən] *s* raisin *m* sec, grain *m* de raisin sec

rake [rek] *s* râteau *m*; (*person*) débauché *m* || *tr* ratisser; **to rake together** râteler

rake'-off' *s* (coll) gratte *f*

rakish ['rekɪʃ] *adj* gaillard; dissolu

ral·ly ['ræli] *s* (*pl* **-lies**) ralliement *m*; réunion *f* politique; (*in a game*) reprise *f*; (*auto race*) rallye *m* || *v* (*pret* & *pp* **-lied**) *tr* rallier || *intr* se rallier; (*from illness*) se remettre; (*sports*) reprendre; **to rally to the side of** se rallier à

ram [ræm] *s* bélier *m* || *v* (*pret* & *pp* **rammed**; *ger* **ramming**) *tr* tamponner; **to ram down** or **in** enfoncer || *intr* se tamponner; **to ram into** tamponner

ramble ['ræmbəl] *s* flânerie *f* || *intr* flâner, errer à l'aventure; (*to talk aimlessly*) divaguer

rami·fy ['ræmɪ‚faɪ] *v* (*pret* & *pp* **-fied**) *tr* ramifier || *intr* se ramifier

ramp [ræmp] *s* rampe *f*

rampage ['ræmped3] *s* tempête *f*; **to go on a rampage** se déchaîner

rampart ['ræmpart] *s* rempart *m*

ram'rod' *s* écouvillon *m*

ram'shack'le *adj* délabré

ranch [rænt∫] *s* ranch *m*, rancho *m*

rancid ['rænsɪd] *adj* rance

rancor ['ræŋkər] *s* rancœur *f*

random ['rændəm] *adj* fortuit; **at random** au hasard

range [rend3] *s* (*row*) rangée *f*; (*scope*) portée *f*; (*mountains*) chaîne *f*; (*stove*) cuisinière *f*; (*for rifle practice*) champ *m* de tir; (*of colors, musical notes, prices, speeds, etc.*) gamme *f*; (*of words*) répartition *f*; (*of voice*) tessiture *f*; (*of vision, of activity, etc.*) champ *m*; (*for pasture*) grand pâturage *m*; **within range of** à portée de || *tr* ranger || *intr* se ranger; **to range from** s'échelonner entre, varier entre; **to range over** parcourir

range'find'er *s* télémètre *m*

rank [ræŋk] *adj* fétide, rance; (*injustice*) criant; (*vegetation*) luxuriant ||

s rang *m* || *tr* ranger || *intr* occuper le premier rang; **to rank above** être supérieur à; **to rank with** aller de pair avec

rank' and file' *s* hommes *mpl* de troupe; commun *m* des mortels; (*of the party, union, etc.*) commun *m*

rankle ['ræŋkəl] *tr* ulcérer; irriter || *intr* s'ulcérer

ransack ['rænsæk] *tr* fouiller, fouiller dans; mettre à sac

ransom ['rænsəm] *s* rançon *f* || *tr* rançonner

rant [rænt] *intr* tempêter

rap [ræp] *s* tape *f*; (*noise*) petit coup *m* sec; (slang) éreintement *m*; **to not care a rap** (slang) s'en ficher; **to take the rap** (slang) se laisser châtier || *v* (*pret* & *pp* **rapped**; *ger* **rapping**) *tr* & *intr* frapper d'un coup sec

rapacious [rə'pe∫əs] *adj* rapace

rape [rep] *s* viol *m* || *tr* violer

rapid ['ræpɪd] *adj* rapide || **rapids** *spl* rapides *mpl*

rap'id-fire' *adj* à tir rapide

rapidity [rə'pɪdəti] *s* rapidité *f*

rapier ['repɪ‚ər] *s* rapière *f*

rapt [ræpt] *adj* ravi; absorbé

rapture ['ræpt∫ər] *s* ravissement *m*

rare [rer] *adj* rare; (*meat*) saignant; (*amusing*) (coll) impayable

rare' bird' *s* merle *m* blanc

rarely ['rerli] *adv* rarement

rascal ['ræskəl] *s* coquin *m*

rash [ræ∫] *adj* téméraire || *s* éruption *f*

rasp [ræsp], [rɑsp] *s* crissement *m*; (*tool*) râpe *f* || *tr* râper || *intr* crisser

raspber·ry ['ræz‚beri], ['rɑz‚beri] *s* (*pl* **-ries**) framboise *f*

rasp'berry bush' *s* framboisier *m*

rat [ræt] *s* rat *m*; (*false hair*) (coll) postiche *f*; (*deserter*) (slang) lâcheur *m*; (*informer*) (slang) mouchard *m*; (*scoundrel*) (slang) cochon *m*; **rats!** zut!; **to smell a rat** (coll) soupçonner anguille sous roche

ratchet ['ræt∫ɪt] *s* encliquetage *m*

rate [ret] *s* taux *m*; (*for freight, mail, a subscription*) tarif *m*; **at any rate** en tout cas; **at the rate of** à raison de || *tr* évaluer; mériter || *intr* (coll) être favori

rate' of exchange' *s* cours *m*

rather ['ræðər], ['rɑðər] *adv* plutôt; (*fairly*) assez; **rather than** plutôt que || *interj* je vous crois!

rathskeller ['ræts‚kelər] *s* caveau *m*

rati·fy ['rætɪ‚faɪ] *v* (*pret* & *pp* **-fied**) *tr* ratifier

rating ['retɪŋ] *s* classement *m*, cote *f*

ra·tio ['re∫o], ['re∫ɪ‚o] *s* (*pl* **-tios**) raison *f*, rapport *m*

ration ['re∫ən], ['ræ∫ən] *s* ration *f* || *tr* rationner

rational ['ræ∫ənəl] *adj* rationnel

ra'tion book' *s* tickets *mpl* de rationnement

ra'tion card' *s* carte *f* de ravitaillement

rat' poi'son *s* mort *m* aux rats

rat'-tail file' *s* queue-de-rat *f*

rattan [ræ'tæn] *s* rotin *m*

rattle ['rætəl] s (number of short, sharp sounds) bruit m de ferraille, cliquetis m; (noisemaking device) crécelle f; (child's toy) hochet m; (in the throat) râle m || tr agiter; (to confuse) (coll) affoler; **to rattle off** débiter comme un moulin || intr cliqueter; (said of windows) trembler

rat'tle-snake' s serpent m à sonnettes

rat'trap' s ratière f

raucous ['rɔkəs] adj rauque

ravage ['rævɪdʒ] s ravage m; **ravages** (of time) injure f || tr ravager

rave [rev] s (coll) éloge m enthousiaste || intr délirer; **to rave about** or **over** s'extasier devant ou sur

raven ['revən] s corbeau m

ravenous ['rævənəs] adj vorace

rave' review' s article m dithyrambique

ravine [rə'vin] s ravin m

ravish ['rævɪʃ] tr ravir

ravishing ['rævɪʃɪŋ] adj ravissant

raw [rɔ] adj cru; (sugar, metal) brut; (silk) grège; (wound) vif; (wind) aigre; (weather) humide et froid; novice, inexpérimenté

raw'-boned' adj décharné

raw' deal' s (slang) mauvais tour m

raw'hide' s cuir m vert

raw' mate'rial s matière f première, matières premières, matière brute

ray [re] s (of light) rayon m; (fish) raie f

rayon ['re·ɑn] s rayonne f

raze [rez] tr raser

razor ['rezər] s rasoir m

ra'zor blade' s lame f de rasoir

ra'zor strop' s cuir m à rasoir

razz [ræz] tr (slang) mettre en boîte

reach [ritʃ] s portée f; **out of reach (of)** hors d'atteinte (de), hors de portée (de); **within reach of** à portée de || tr atteindre; arriver à; **to reach out** (a hand) tendre; (an arm) allonger || intr s'étendre

react [rɪ'ækt] intr réagir

reaction [rɪ'ækʃən] s réaction f

reactionar·y [rɪ'ækʃən‚erɪ] adj réactionnaire || s (pl -ies) réactionnaire mf

reactor [rɪ'æktər] s réacteur m

read [rid] v (pret & pp read [rɛd]) tr lire; **to read over** parcourir || intr lire; (said of passage, description, etc.) se lire; (said, e.g., of thermometer) marquer; **to read on** continuer à lire; **to read up on** étudier

reader ['ridər] s lecteur m; livre m de lecture

readily ['rɛdɪlɪ] adv (willingly) volontiers; (easily) facilement

reading ['ridɪŋ] s lecture f

read'ing desk' s pupitre m

read'ing glass' s loupe f; **reading glasses** lunettes fpl pour lire

read'ing lamp' s lampe f de bureau

read'ing room' s salle f de lecture

read·y ['rɛdɪ] adj (comp -ier; super -iest) prêt; (quick) vif; (money) comptant || v (pret & pp -ied) tr préparer || intr se préparer

read'y cash' s argent m comptant

read'y-made' suit' s (for men) complet m de confection; (for women) costume m de confection

ready-to-eat ['rɛditə'it] adj prêt à servir

ready-to-wear ['rɛditə'wɛr] adj prêt à porter || s prêt-à-porter m

reaffirm [‚ri·ə'fʌrm] tr réaffirmer

reagent [rɪ'edʒənt] s (chem) réactif m

real ['ri·əl] adj vrai, réel

re'al estate' s biens mpl immobiliers

re'al-estate' adj immobilier

realism ['ri·ə‚lɪzəm] s réalisme m

realist ['ri·əlɪst] s réaliste mf

realistic [‚ri·ə'lɪstɪk] adj réaliste

real·ty [rɪ'ælɪtɪ] s (pl -ties) réalité f

realize ['ri·ə‚laɪz] tr se rendre compte de, s'apercevoir de; (hopes, profits, etc.) réaliser

really ['ri·əlɪ] adv vraiment

realm [rɛlm] s royaume m; (field) domaine m

realtor ['ri·əl‚tɔr], ['ri·əltər] s agent m immobilier

ream [rim] s rame f; **reams** (coll) masses fpl || tr aléser

reap [rip] tr moissonner; (to gather) recueillir

reaper ['ripər] s moissonneur m; (mach) moissonneuse f

reappear [‚ri·ə'pɪr] intr réapparaître

reappearance [‚ri·ə'pɪrəns] s réapparition f

reapportionment [‚ri·ə'pɔrʃənmənt] s nouvelle répartition f

rear [rɪr] adj arrière, d'arrière, de derrière || s derrière m; (of a car, ship, etc.; of an army) arrière m; (of a row) queue f; **to the rear!** (mil) demitour à droite! || tr élever || intr (said of animal) se cabrer

rear' ad'miral s contre-amiral m

rear'-axle assem'bly s (pl -blies) pont m arrière

rear' drive' s traction f arrière

rearmament [rɪ'ɑrməmənt] s réarmement m

rearrange [‚ri·ə'rendʒ] tr arranger de nouveau

rear'-view mir'ror s rétroviseur m

rear' win'dow s (aut) lunette f arrière

reason ['rizən] s raison f; **by reason of** à cause de; **for good reason** pour cause; **to listen to reason** entendre raison; **to stand to reason** être de toute évidence || tr & intr raisonner

reasonable ['rizənəbəl] adj raisonnable

reassessment [‚ri·ə'sɛsmənt] s réévaluation f

reassure [‚ri·ə'ʃʊr] tr rassurer

reawaken [‚ri·ə'wekən] tr réveiller || intr se réveiller

rebate ['ribet], [rɪ'bet] s rabais m, escompte m; ristourne f, bonification f || tr faire un rabais sur

rebel ['rɛbəl] adj & s rebelle mf || **rebel** [rɪ'bɛl] v (pret & pp -belled; ger -belling) intr se rebeller

rebellion [rɪ'bɛljən] s rébellion f

rebellious [rɪ'bɛljəs] adj rebelle

re-bind [rɪ'baɪnd] v (pret & pp -bound) tr (bb) relier à neuf

rebirth ['ribʌrθ] s renaissance f

rebore [ri'bor] tr rectifier

rebound [ri'baʊnd], [ri'baʊnd] s rebondissement m || [ri'baʊnd] intr rebondir

rebroad·cast [ri'brɔd,kæst], [ri'brɔd,kɑst] s retransmission f || v (pret & pp -cast or -casted) tr retransmettre

rebuff [ri'bʌf] s rebuffade f || tr mal accueillir

re·build [ri'bɪld] v (pret & pp -built) tr reconstruire

rebuke [ri'bjuk] s réprimande f || tr réprimander

re·but [ri'bʌt] v (pret & pp -butted; ger -butting) tr réfuter, repousser

rebuttal [ri'bʌtəl] s réfutation f

recall [ri'kɔl], ['rikɔl] s rappel m || [ri'kɔl] tr rappeler; se rappeler de

recant [ri'kænt] tr rétracter || intr se rétracter

re·cap ['ri,kæp], [ri'kæp] v (pret & pp -capped; ger -capping) tr rechaper

recapitulation [,rikə,pɪtʃə'leʃən] s récapitulation f

re·cast ['ri,kæst], ['ri,kɑst] s refonte f || [ri'kæst], [ri'kɑst] v (pret & pp -cast) tr refondre; (metal; a play, novel, etc.) refondre; (the actors of a play) redistribuer

recede [ri'sid] intr reculer; (said of forehead, chin, etc.) fuir; (said of sea) se retirer

receipt [ri'sit] s (for goods) récépissé m; (for money) récépissé, reçu m; (recipe) recette f; **receipts** recettes; to acknowledge receipt of accuser réception de || tr acquitter

receive [ri'siv] tr recevoir; (stolen goods) receler; (a station) (rad) capter; **received payment** pour acquit || intr recevoir

receiver [ri'sivər] s (of letter) destinataire m; (in bankruptcy) syndic m, liquidateur m; (telp) récepteur m

receiv'ing set' s poste m récepteur

recent ['risənt] adj récent

recently ['risəntli] adv récemment

receptacle [ri'septəkəl] s récipient m; (elec) prise f femelle

reception [ri'sepʃən] s réception f; (welcome) accueil m

recep'tion desk' s réception f

receptionist [ri'sepʃənɪst] s préposé m à la réception

receptive [ri'septɪv] adj réceptif

recess [ri'ses], ['rises] s (of court, legislature, etc.) ajournement m; (at school) récréation f; (in a wall) niche f || [ri'ses] tr ajourner; (s.th., e.g., in a wall) encastrer || intr s'ajourner

recession [ri'seʃən] s récession f

recipe ['resɪ,pi] s recette f

recipient [ri'sɪpi·ənt] s (person) bénéficiaire mf; (of a degree, honor, etc.) récipiendaire m; (of blood) receveur m

reciprocal [ri'sɪprəkəl] adj réciproque

reciprocity [,resɪ'prɑsɪti] s réciprocité f

recital [ri'saɪtəl] s récit m; (of music or poetry) récital m

recite [ri'saɪt] tr réciter; narrer

reckless ['reklɪs] adj téméraire, imprudent, insouciant

reckon ['rekən] tr calculer; considérer; (coll) supposer, imaginer || intr calculer; **to reckon on** compter sur; **to reckon with** tenir compte de

reclaim [ri'klem] tr récupérer; (e.g., waste land) mettre en valeur; (a person) réformer

reclamation [,reklə'meʃən] s récupération f; (e.g., of waste land) mise f en valeur; (of a person) réforme f

recline [ri'klaɪn] tr appuyer, reposer || intr s'appuyer, se reposer

recluse [ri'klus], ['reklus] adj & s reclus m

recognition [,rekəg'nɪʃən] s reconnaissance f

recognize ['rekəg,naɪz] tr reconnaître; (parl) donner la parole à

recoil [ri'kɔɪl] s répugnance f; (of, e.g., firearm) recul m || intr reculer

recollect [,rekə'lekt] tr se rappeler

recollection [,rekə'lekʃən] s souvenir m

recommend [,rekə'mend] tr recommander

recompense ['rekəm,pens] s récompense f || tr récompenser

reconcile ['rekən,saɪl] tr réconcilier; **to reconcile oneself to** se résigner à

reconnaissance [ri'kɑnɪsəns] s reconnaissance f

reconnoiter [,rekə'nɔɪtər], [,rikə'nɔɪtər] tr & intr reconnaître

reconquer [ri'kɑŋkər] tr reconquérir

reconquest [ri'kɑŋkwest] s reconquête f

reconsider [,rikən'sɪdər] tr reconsidérer

reconstruct [,rikən'strʌkt] tr reconstruire; (a crime) reconstituer

reconversion [,rikən'vʌrʒən], [,rikən'vʌrʃən] s reconversion f

record ['rekərd] s enregistrement m, registre m; (to play on the phonograph) disque m; (mil) état m de service; (sports) record m; **off the record** en confidence; **records** archives fpl; **to break the record** battre le record; **to have a good record** être bien noté; (at school) avoir de bonnes notes || [ri'kɔrd] tr enregistrer

rec'ord chang'er s tourne-disque m automatique

recorder [ri'kɔrdər] s appareil m enregistreur; (law) greffier m; (mus) flûte f à bec

rec'ord hold'er s recordman m

recording [ri'kɔrdɪŋ] adj enregistreur || s enregistrement m

record'ing tape' s ruban m magnétique

rec'ord li'brary s discothèque f

rec'ord play'er s électrophone m

recount ['ri,kaʊnt] s nouveau dépouillement m du scrutin || [ri'kaʊnt] tr (to count again) recompter || [ri'kaʊnt] tr (to tell) raconter

recoup [ri'kup] tr recouvrer; **to recoup s.o. for** dédommager qn de

recourse [ri'kors], ['rikors] s recours m; **to have recourse to** recourir à

recover [ri'kʌvər] tr (to get back) recouvrir; (to cover again) recouvrir ‖ intr (to get well) se rétablir

recover·y [rɪ'kʌvəri] s (pl -ies) récupération f, recouvrement m; (e.g., of health) rétablissement m

recreant ['rekrɪ·ənt] adj & s lâche mf; traître m; apostat m

recreation [,rekrɪ'eʃən] s récréation f

recruit [rɪ'krut] s recrue f ‖ tr recruter; **to be recruited** se recruter

rectangle ['rek,tæŋgəl] s rectangle m

rectifier ['rektə,faɪər] s rectificateur m; (elec) redresseur m

recti·fy ['rektɪ,faɪ] v (pret & pp -fied) tr rectifier; (elec) redresser

rec·tum ['rektəm] s (pl -ta [tə]) rectum m

recumbent [rɪ'kʌmbənt] adj couché

recuperate [rɪ'kjupə,ret] tr & intr récupérer

re·cur [rɪ'kʌr] v (pret & pp -curred; ger -curring) intr revenir, se reproduire; revenir à la mémoire de

recurrent [rɪ'kʌrənt] adj récurrent

red [red] adj (comp redder; super reddest) rouge ‖ s (color) rouge m; **in the red** en déficit; **Red** (communist) rouge mf; (nickname) Rouquin m

red'bait' tr taxer de communiste

red'bird' s cardinal m d'Amérique, tangara m

red'-blood'ed adj vigoureux

red'breast' s rouge-gorge m

red'cap' s porteur m; (Brit) soldat m de la police militaire

red' cell' s globule m rouge

Red' Cross' s Croix-Rouge f

redden ['redən] tr & intr rougir

redeem [rɪ'dim] tr racheter; (a pawned article) dégager; (a promise) remplir; (a debt) s'acquitter de, acquitter

redeemer [rɪ'dimər] s rédempteur m

redemption [rɪ'dempʃən] s rachat m; (rel) rédemption f

red'-haired' adj roux

red'hand'ed adj & adv sur le fait, en flagrant délit

red'head' s (woman) rousse f

red' her'ring s hareng m saur; (fig) faux-fuyant m

red'-hot' adj chauffé au rouge; ardent; (news) tout frais

rediscount [ri'dɪskaunt] s réescompte m ‖ tr réescompter

rediscover [,rɪdɪs'kʌvər] tr redécouvrir

red'-let'ter day' s jour m mémorable

red' light' s feu m rouge; **to go through a red light** brûler un feu rouge

red'-light' dis'trict s quartier m réservé

red' man' s (pl men') Peau-Rouge m

re·do [ri'du] v (pret -did; pp -done) tr refaire

redolent ['redələnt] adj parfumé; redolent of exhalant une senteur de; qui fait penser à

redoubt [rɪ'daut] s redoute f

redound [rɪ'daund] intr contribuer; to redound to tourner à

red' pep'per s piment m rouge

redress [rɪ'dres], ['ridrəs] s redressement m ‖ [rɪ'dres] tr redresser

Red' Rid'ing-hood' s Chaperon rouge m

red'skin' s Peau-Rouge mf

red' tape' s paperasserie f, chinoiseries fpl administratives

reduce [rɪ'd(j)us] tr réduire ‖ intr maigrir

reduc'ing ex'ercises spl exercices mpl amaigrissants

reduction [rɪ'dʌkʃən] s réduction f

redundant [rɪ'dʌndənt] adj redondant

red' wine' s vin m rouge

red'wing' s (orn) mauvis m

red'wood' s séquoia m

reed [rid] s (of instrument) anche f; (bot) roseau m; **reeds** (mus) instruments mpl à anche

reedit [ri'edɪt] tr rééditer

reef [rif] s récif m; (of sail) ris m ‖ tr (naut) prendre un ris dans

reefer ['rifər] s caban m; (slang) cigarette f à marijuana

reek [rik] intr fumer; **to reek of** or **with** empester, puer

reel [ril] s bobine f; (of film) rouleau m, bobine; (of fishing·rod) moulinet m; (sway) balancement m; **off the reel** (coll) d'affilée ‖ tr bobiner; **to reel off** dévider; (coll) réciter d'un trait ‖ intr chanceler

reelection [,ri·ɪ'lekʃən] s réélection f

reenlist [,ri·en'lɪst] tr rengager ‖ intr rengager, se rengager

reenlistment [,ri·en'lɪstmənt] s rengagement m; (person) rengagé m

reen·try [rɪ'entrɪ] s (pl -tries) rentrée f; (rok) retour m à la Terre

reexamination [,ri·eg,zæmɪ'neʃən] s réexamen m

re·fer [rɪ'fʌr] v (pret & pp -ferred; ger -ferring) tr renvoyer ‖ intr—**to refer to** se référer à

referee [,refə'ri] s arbitre m ‖ tr & intr arbitrer

reference ['refərəns] s référence f

ref'erence room' s bibliothèque f de consultation

referen·dum [,refə'rendəm] s (pl -da [də]) référendum m

refill ['rifɪl] s recharge f ‖ [ri'fɪl] tr remplir à nouveau

refine [rɪ'faɪn] tr raffiner

refinement [rɪ'faɪnmənt] s raffinage m; (e.g., of manners) raffinement m

refiner·y [rɪ'faɪnərɪ] s (pl -ies) raffinerie f

reflect [rɪ'flekt] tr réfléchir ‖ intr (to meditate) réfléchir; **to reflect on** or **upon** réfléchir à or sur; nuire à la réputation de

reflection [rɪ'flekʃən] s (e.g., of light; thought) réflexion f; (reflected light; image) reflet m; **to cast reflections on** faire des réflexions à

reflex ['rifleks] adj & s réflexe m

reforestation [,rifɔrɪs'teʃən], [,rifɔrɪs'teʃən] s reboisement m

reform [rɪ'fɔrm] s réforme f ‖ tr réformer ‖ intr se réformer

reformation [,refər'meʃən] s réformation f; **the Reformation** la Réforme

reformato•ry [rɪˈfɔrmə͵torɪ] *s* (*pl* **-ries**) maison *f* de correction

reformer [rɪˈfɔrmər] *s* réformateur *m*

reform' school' *s* maison *f* de correction

refraction [rɪˈfrækʃən] *s* réfraction *f*

refrain [rɪˈfren] *s* refrain *m* ‖ *intr* s'abstenir

refresh [rɪˈfreʃ] *tr* rafraîchir ‖ *intr* se rafraîchir

refreshing [rɪˈfreʃɪŋ] *adj* rafraîchissant

refreshment [rɪˈfreʃmənt] *s* rafraîchissement *m*

refresh'ment bar' *s* buvette *f*

refrigerate [rɪˈfrɪdʒə͵ret] *tr* réfrigérer

refrigerator [rɪˈfrɪdʒə͵retər] *s* (*icebox*) glacière; réfrigérateur *m*; (*condenser*) congélateur *m*

refrig'erator car' *s* (rr) wagon *m* frigorifique

re•fuel [riˈfjul] *v* (*pret & pp* **-fueled** or **-fuelled**; *ger* **-fueling** or **-fuelling**) *tr* ravitailler en carburant ‖ *intr* se ravitailler en carburant

refuge [ˈrefjudʒ] *s* refuge *m*; **to take refuge (in)** se réfugier (dans)

refugee [͵refjuˈdʒi] *s* réfugié *m*

refund [ˈrifʌnd] *s* remboursement *m* ‖ [rɪˈfʌnd] *tr* (*to pay back*) rembourser ‖ [riˈfʌnd] *tr* (*to fund again*) consolider

refurnish [riˈfʌrnɪʃ] *tr* remeubler

refusal [rɪˈfjuzəl] *s* refus *m*

refuse [ˈrefjus] *s* ordures *fpl*, détritus *mpl* ‖ [rɪˈfjuz] *tr & intr* refuser

refute [rɪˈfjut] *tr* réfuter

regain [riˈgen] *tr* regagner; (*consciousness*) reprendre

regal [ˈrigəl] *adj* royal

regale [rɪˈgel] *tr* régaler

regalia [rɪˈgelɪ·ə] *spl* atours *mpl*, ornements *mpl*; (*of an office*) insignes *mpl*

regard [rɪˈgard] *s* considération *f*; (*esteem*) respect *m*; (*look*) regard *m*; **in** or **with regard to** à l'égard de; **regards** ses amitiés *fpl* ‖ *tr* considérer, estimer; **as regards** quant à

regarding [rɪˈgardɪŋ] *prep* au sujet de, touchant

regardless [rɪˈgardlɪs] *adj* inattentif ‖ *adv* (coll) coûte que coûte; **regardless of** sans tenir compte de

regatta [rɪˈgætə] *s* régates *fpl*

regen•cy [ˈridʒənsɪ] *s* (*pl* **-cies**) régence *f*

regenerate [rɪˈdʒenə͵ret] *tr* régénérer ‖ *intr* se régénérer

regent [ˈridʒənt] *s* régent *m*

regicide [ˈredʒɪ͵saɪd] *s* (*act*) régicide *m*; (*person*) régicide *mf*

regime [reˈʒim] *s* régime *m*

regiment [ˈredʒɪmənt] *s* régiment *m* ‖ [ˈredʒɪ͵ment] *tr* enrégimenter, régenter

regimental [͵redʒɪˈmentəl] *adj* régimentaire ‖ **regimentals** *spl* tenue *f* militaire

region [ˈridʒən] *s* région *f*

register [ˈredʒɪstər] *s* registre *m* ‖ *tr* enregistrer; (*a student; an automobile*) immatriculer; (*a letter*) recommander ‖ *intr* s'inscrire

reg'istered let'ter *s* lettre *f* recommandée

reg'istered mail' *s* envoi *m* en recommandé

reg'istered nurse' *s* infirmière *f* diplômée

registrar [ˈredʒɪs͵trɑr] *s* archiviste *mf*, secrétaire *mf*

registration [͵redʒɪsˈtreʃən] *s* enregistrement *m*; immatriculation *f*, inscription *f*; (*of mail*) recommandation *f*

registra'tion blank' *s* fiche *f* d'inscription

registra'tion fee' *s* frais *mpl* d'inscription

registra'tion num'ber *s* (*of soldier or student*) numéro *m* matricule

re•gret [rɪˈgret] *s* regret *m*; **regrets** excuses *fpl* ‖ *v* (*pret & pp* **-gretted**; *ger* **-gretting**) *tr* regretter

regrettable [rɪˈgretəbəl] *adj* regrettable

regular [ˈregjələr] *adj & s* régulier *m*

reg'ular fel'low *s* (coll) chic type *m*

regularity [͵regjəˈlærɪtɪ] *s* régularité *f*

regularize [ˈregjələ͵raɪz] *tr* régulariser

regulate [ˈregjə͵let] *tr* régler; (*to control*) réglementer

regulation [͵regjəˈleʃən] *s* régulation *f*; (*rule*) règlement *m*

rehabilitate [͵rihəˈbɪlɪ͵tet] *tr* réadapter; (*in reputation, standing, etc.*) réhabiliter

rehearsal [rɪˈhʌrsəl] *s* répétition *f*

rehearse [rɪˈhʌrs] *tr & intr* répéter

reign [ren] *s* règne *m* ‖ *intr* régner

reimburse [͵ri·ɪmˈbʌrs] *tr* rembourser

rein [ren] *s* rêne *f*; **to give free rein to** donner libre cours à ‖ *tr* contenir, freiner

reincarnation [͵ri·ɪnkarˈneʃən] *s* réincarnation *f*

rein'deer' *s* renne *m*

reinforce [͵ri·ɪnˈfors] *tr* renforcer; (*concrete*) armer

reinforcement [͵ri·ɪnˈforsmənt] *s* renforcement *m*

reinstate [͵ri·ɪnˈstet] *tr* rétablir

reiterate [riˈɪtə͵ret] *tr* réitérer

reject [ˈridʒekt] *s* pièce *f* or article *m* de rebut; **rejects** rebuts *mpl* ‖ [rɪˈdʒekt] *tr* rejeter

rejection [rɪˈdʒekʃən] *s* rejet *m*, refus *m*

rejoice [rɪˈdʒɔɪs] *intr* se réjouir

rejoin [riˈdʒɔɪn] *tr* rejoindre

rejoinder [rɪˈdʒɔɪndər] *s* réplique *f*; (law) réponse *f* à une réplique

rejuvenation [rɪ͵dʒuvɪˈneʃən] *s* rajeunissement *m*

rekindle [riˈkɪndəl] *tr* rallumer

relapse [rɪˈlæps] *s* rechute *f* ‖ *intr* rechuter

relate [rɪˈlet] *tr* (*to narrate*) relater; (*e.g., two events*) établir un rapport entre; **to be related** être apparenté

relation [rɪˈleʃən] *s* relation *f*; récit *m*, relation; (*relative*) parent *m*; (*kinship*) parenté *f*; **in relation to** or **with** par rapport à; **relations** (*of a sexual nature*) rapports *mpl*

relationship [rɪˈleʃən͵ʃɪp] *s* (*connection*) rapport *m*; (*kinship*) parenté *f*

relative ['rɛlətɪv] *adj* relatif || *s* parent *m*

relativity [,rɛlə'tɪvəti] *s* relativité *f*

relax [rɪ'læks] *tr* détendre; **to be relaxed** être décontracté or détendu || *intr* se détendre

relaxation [,rilæks'e/ən] *s* détente *f*, délassement *m*

relaxing [rɪ'læksɪŋ] *adj* tranquillisant, apaisant; (*diverting*) délassant

relay ['rile], [rɪ'le] *s* relais *m* || *v* (*pret & pp* **-layed**) *tr* relayer; (rad, telg, telp, telv) retransmettre || [rɪ'le] *v* (*pret & pp* **-laid**) *tr* tendre de nouveau

re'lay race' [rɪ'lis] *s* course *f* de relais

release [rɪ'lis] *s* délivrance *f*; (*from jail*) mise *f* en liberté; (*permission*) autorisation *f*; (aer) lâchage *m*; (mach) déclenchement *m* || *tr* délivrer; (*from jail*) mettre en liberté; autoriser; (*a bomb*) lâcher

relegate ['rɛlɪ,get] *tr* reléguer

relent [rɪ'lɛnt] *intr* se laisser attendrir, s'adoucir

relentless [rɪ'lɛntlɪs] *adj* implacable

relevant ['rɛləvənt] *adj* pertinent

reliable [rɪ'laɪ-əbəl] *adj* digne de confiance, digne de foi

reliance [rɪ'laɪ-əns] *s* confiance *f*

relic ['rɛlɪk] *s* (rel) relique *f*; (fig) vestige *m*

relief [rɪ'lif] *s* soulagement *m*; (*projection of figures; elevation*) relief *m*; (*aid*) secours *m*; (*welfare program*) aide *f* sociale; (mil) relève *f*; **in relief** en relief

relieve [rɪ'liv] *tr* soulager; (*to aid*) secourir; (*to release from a post; to give variety to*) relever; (mil) relever

religion [rɪ'lɪdʒən] *s* religion *f*

religious [rɪ'lɪdʒəs] *adj* religieux

relinquish [rɪ'lɪŋkwɪʃ] *tr* abandonner

relish ['rɛlɪʃ] *s* goût *m*; (*condiment*) assaisonnement *m*; **relish for** penchant *m* pour || *tr* goûter, apprécier

reluctance [rɪ'lʌktəns] *s* répugnance *f*; **with reluctance** à contrecœur

reluctant [rɪ'lʌktənt] *adj* hésitant, peu disposé

re-ly [rɪ'laɪ] *v* (*pret & pp* **-lied**) *intr*—**to rely on** compter sur, se fier à

remain [rɪ'men] *s*—**remains** restes *mpl*; œuvres *fpl* posthumes || *intr* rester

remainder [rɪ'mendər] *s* reste *m*; **remainders** bouillons *mpl* || *tr* solder

re-make [rɪ'mek] *v* (*pret & pp* **-made**) *tr* refaire

remark [rɪ'mɑrk] *s* remarque *f*, observation *f* || *tr & intr* remarquer, observer; **to remark on** faire des remarques sur

remarkable [rɪ'mɑrkəbəl] *adj* remarquable

remar-ry [rɪ'mæri] *v* (*pret & pp* **-ried**) *tr* remarier; se remarier avec || *intr* se remarier

reme-dy ['rɛmɪdi] *s* (*pl* **-dies**) remède *m* || *v* (*pret & pp* **-died**) *tr* remédier (with *dat*)

remember [rɪ'mɛmbər] *tr* se souvenir de, se rappeler; **remember me to** rappelez-moi au bon souvenir de || *intr* se souvenir, se rappeler

remembrance [rɪ'mɛmbrəns] *s* souvenir *m*

remind [rɪ'maɪnd] *tr* rappeler

reminder [rɪ'maɪndər] *s* note *f* de rappel, mémento *m*

reminisce [,rɛmɪ'nɪs] *intr* se livrer au souvenir, raconter ses souvenirs

remiss [rɪ'mɪs] *adj* négligent

remission [rɪ'mɪʃən] *s* rémission *f*

re-mit [rɪ'mɪt] *v* (*pret & pp* **-mitted**; *ger* **-mitting**) *tr* remettre || *intr* se calmer

remittance [rɪ'mɪtəns] *s* remise *f*, envoi *m*

remnant ['rɛmnənt] *s* reste *m*; (*of cloth*) coupon *m*; (*at reduced price*) solde *m*

remod-el [rɪ'mɑdəl] *v* (*pret & pp* **-eled** or **-elled**; *ger* **-eling** or **-elling**) *tr* modeler de nouveau, remanier; (*a house*) transformer

remonstrance [rɪ'mɑnstrəns] *s* remontrance *f*

remonstrate [rɪ'mɑnstret] *intr* protester; **to remonstrate with** faire des remontrances à

remorse [rɪ'mɔrs] *s* remords *m*

remorseful [rɪ'mɔrsfəl] *adj* contrit, repentant, plein de remords

remote [rɪ'mot] *adj* éloigné

remote' control' *s* commande *f* à distance, télécommande *f*

removable [rɪ'muvəbəl] *adj* amovible

removal [rɪ'muvəl] *s* enlèvement *m*; (*from house*) déménagement *m*; (*dismissal*) révocation *f*

remove [rɪ'muv] *tr* enlever, ôter; éloigner; (*furniture*) déménager; (*to dismiss*) révoquer || *intr* se déplacer; déménager

remuneration [rɪ,mjunə're/ən] *s* rémunération *f*

renaissance [,rɛnə'sɑns], [rɪ'nesəns] *s* renaissance *f*

rend [rɛnd] *v* (*pret & pp* rent [rɛnt]) *tr* déchirer; (*to split*) fendre; (*the air; the heart*) fendre

render ['rɛndər] *tr* rendre; (*a piece of music*) interpréter; (*lard*) fondre

rendez-vous ['rɑndə,vu] *s* (*pl* **-vous** [,vuz]) rendez-vous *m* || *v* (*pret & pp* **-voused** [,vud]; *ger* **-vousing** [,vu-ɪŋ]) *intr* se rencontrer

rendition [rɛn'dɪʃən] *s* (*translation*) traduction *f*; (mus) interprétation *f*

renegade ['rɛnɪ,ged] *s* renégat *m*

renege [rɪ'nɪg] *s* renonce *f* || *intr* renoncer; (coll) se dédire, ne pas tenir sa parole

renew [rɪ'n(j)u] *tr* renouveler || *intr* se renouveler

renewable [rɪ'n(j)u-əbəl] *adj* renouvelable

renewal [rɪ'n(j)u-əl] *s* renouvellement *m*

renounce [rɪ'nauns] *s* renonce *f* || *tr* renoncer (with *dat*) || *intr* renoncer

renovate ['rɛnə,vet] *tr* renouveler; (*a room, a house, etc.*) mettre à neuf, rénover, transformer

renown [ri'naun] s renom m

renowned [ri'naund] adj renommé

rent [rent] adj déchiré || s loyer m, location f; (tear, slit) déchirure f; for rent à louer || tr louer || intr se louer

rental ['rentəl] s loyer m, location f

rent·al a·gen·cy s (pl -cies) agence f de location

rent·ed car' s voiture f de louage, voiture de location; (chauffeur-driven limousine) voiture de grande remise

renter ['rentər] s locataire mf

renunciation [rɪ,nʌnsɪ'eʃən] s renonciation f

reopen [ri'opən] tr & intr rouvrir

reopening [ri'opənɪŋ] s réouverture f; (of school) rentrée f

reorganize [ri'ɔrgə,naɪz] tr réorganiser || intr se réorganiser

repair [rɪ'per] s réparation f; in good repair en bon état || tr réparer || intr se rendre

repaper [ri'pepər] tr retapisser

reparation [,repə'reʃən] s réparation f

repartee [,repər'ti] s repartie f

repast [rɪ'pæst], [rɪ'pɑst] s repas m

repatriate [ri'petri,et] tr rapatrier

re·pay [rɪ'pe] v (pret & pp -paid) tr rembourser; récompenser

repayment [rɪ'pemənt] s remboursement m; récompense f

repeal [rɪ'pil] s révocation f, abrogation f || tr révoquer, abroger

repeat [rɪ'pit] s répétition f || tr & intr répéter

re·pel [rɪ'pel] v (pret & pp -pelled; ger -pelling) tr repousser; dégoûter

repent [rɪ'pent] tr se repentir de || intr se repentir

repentance [rɪ'pentəns] s repentir m

repentant [rɪ'pentənt] adj repentant

repercussion [,ripər'kʌʃən] s répercussion f, contrecoup m

reperto·ry ['repər,tori] s (pl -ries) répertoire m

repetition [,repɪ'tɪʃən] s répétition f

replace [rɪ'ples] tr (to put back) remettre en place; (to take the place of) remplacer

replaceable [rɪ'plesəbəl] adj remplaçable, amovible

replacement [rɪ'plesmənt] s replacement m; (substitution) remplacement m; (substitute part) pièce f de rechange; (person) remplaçant m

replenish [rɪ'plenɪʃ] tr réapprovisionner; remplir

replete [rɪ'plit] adj rempli, plein

replica ['replɪkə] s reproduction f, réplique f

re·ply [rɪ'plaɪ] s (pl -plies) réponse f, réplique f || v (pret & pp -plied) tr & intr répondre, répliquer

reply' cou'pon s coupon-réponse m

report [rɪ'port] s rapport m; (rumor) bruit m; (e.g., of firearm) détonation f || tr rapporter; dénoncer; it is reported that le bruit court que; reported missing porté manquant || intr faire un rapport; (to show up) se présenter

report' card' s bulletin m scolaire

reportedly [rɪ'portɪdli] adv au dire de tout le monde

reporter [rɪ'portər] s reporter m

reporting [rɪ'portɪŋ] s reportage m

repose [rɪ'poz] s repos m || tr reposer; (confidence) placer || intr reposer

reprehend [,reprɪ'hend] tr reprendre

represent [,reprɪ'zent] tr représenter

representation [,reprɪzen'teʃən] s représentation f

representative [,reprɪ'zentətɪv] adj représentatif || s représentant m

repress [rɪ'pres] tr réprimer; (psychoanal) refouler

repression [rɪ'preʃən] s répression f; (psychoanal) refoulement m

reprieve [rɪ'priv] s sursis m || tr surseoir à l'exécution de

reprimand ['reprɪ,mænd], ['reprɪ,mand] s réprimande f || tr réprimander

reprint ['rɪ,prɪnt] s (book) réimpression f; (offprint) tiré m à part || [rɪ'prɪnt] tr réimprimer

reprisal [rɪ'praɪzəl] s représailles fpl

reproach [rɪ'protʃ] s reproche m; opprobre m || tr reprocher; couvrir d'opprobre; to reproach s.o. for s.th. reprocher q.ch. à qn

reproduce [,riprə'd(j)us] tr reproduire || intr se reproduire

reproduction [,riprə'dʌkʃən] s reproduction f

reproof [rɪ'pruf] s reproche m

reprove [rɪ'pruv] tr réprimander

reptile ['reptɪl] s reptile m

republic [rɪ'pʌblɪk] s république f

republican [rɪ'pʌblɪkən] adj & s républicain m

repudiate [rɪ'pjudɪ,et] tr répudier

repugnant [rɪ'pʌgnənt] adj répugnant

repulse [rɪ'pʌls] s refus m; (setback) échec m || tr repousser

repulsive [rɪ'pʌlsɪv] adj répulsif

reputation [,repjə'teʃən] s réputation f

repute [rɪ'pjut] s réputation f; of ill repute mal famé || tr—to be reputed to be être réputé

reputedly [rɪ'pjutɪdli] adv suivant l'opinion commune

request [rɪ'kwest] s demande f; on request sur demande || tr demander

Requiem ['rikwɪ,em], ['rekwɪ,em] s Requiem m

require [rɪ'kwaɪr] tr exiger

requirement [rɪ'kwaɪrmənt] s exigence f; besoin m

requisite ['rekwɪzɪt] adj requis || s chose f nécessaire; condition f nécessaire

requisition [,rekwɪ'zɪʃən] s réquisition f || tr réquisitionner

requital [rɪ'kwaɪtəl] s récompense f; (retaliation) revanche f

requite [rɪ'kwaɪt] tr récompenser; (to avenge) venger

re·read [ri'rid] v (pret & pp -read ['red]) tr relire

resale ['ri,sel], [ri'sel] s revente f

rescind [rɪ'sɪnd] tr abroger

rescue ['reskju] s sauvetage m; to the

rescue au secours, à la rescousse || *tr* sauver, secourir

res′cue par′ty *s* équipe *f* de secours

research [rɪ'sʌrtʃ], ['rɪsʌrtʃ] *s* recherche *f* || *intr* faire des recherches

re•sell [ri'sel] *v* (*pret & pp* -sold) *tr* revendre

resemblance [rɪ'zembləns] *s* ressemblance *f*

resemble [rɪ'zembəl] *tr* ressembler (with *dat*); **to resemble one another** se ressembler

resent [rɪ'zent] *tr* s'offenser de

resentful [rɪ'zentfəl] *adj* offensé

resentment [rɪ'zentmənt] *s* ressentiment *m*

reservation [,rezər've/ən] *s* location *f*, réservation *f*; (*Indian land*) réserve *f*; **without reservation** sans réserve

reserve [rɪ'zʌrv] *s* réserve *f* || *tr* réserver

reservist [rɪ'zʌrvɪst] *s* réserviste *m*

reservoir ['rezər,vwɑr] *s* réservoir *m*

re•set [ri'set] *v* (*pret & pp* -set; *ger* -setting) *tr* remettre; (*a gem*) remonter

re•ship [ri'ʃɪp] *v* (*pret & pp* -shipped; *ger* -shipping) *tr* réexpédier; (*on a ship*) rembarquer || *intr* se rembarquer

reshipment [ri'ʃɪpmənt] *s* réexpédition *f*; (*on a ship*) rembarquement *m*

reside [rɪ'zaɪd] *intr* résider, demeurer

residence ['rezɪdəns] *s* résidence *f*, domicile *m*

resident ['rezɪdənt] *adj & s* habitant *m*

residential [,rezɪ'denʃəl] *adj* résidentiel

residue ['rezɪd(j)u] *s* résidu *m*

resign [rɪ'zaɪn] *tr* démissionner de, résigner; **to resign oneself to** se résigner à || *intr* démissionner; se résigner; **to resign from** démissionner de

resignation [,rezɪg'neʃən] *s* (*from a job, etc.*) démission *f*; (*submissive state*) résignation *f*

resin ['rezɪn] *s* résine *f*

resist [rɪ'zɪst] *tr* résister (with *dat*); **to resist** + *ger* s'empêcher de + *inf* || *intr* résister

resistance [rɪ'zɪstəns] *s* résistance *f*

resole [ri'sol] *tr* ressemeler

resolute ['rezə,lut] *adj* résolu

resolution [rezə'luʃən] *s* résolution *f*

resolve [rɪ'zɑlv] *s* résolution *f* || *tr* résoudre || *intr* résoudre, se résoudre

resonance ['rezənəns] *s* résonance *f*

resort [rɪ'zɔrt] *s* station *f*, e.g., **health resort** station climatique; (*for help or support*) recours *m*; **as a last resort** en dernier ressort || *intr*—**to resort to** recourir à

resound [rɪ'zaund] *intr* résonner

resource [rɪ'sors], ['risors] *s* ressource *f*

resourceful [rɪ'sorsfəl] *adj* débrouillard

respect [rɪ'spekt] *s* respect *m*; **in many respects** à bien des égards; **in this respect** sous ce rapport; **to pay one's respects (to)** présenter ses respects (à); **with respect to** par rapport à || *tr* respecter

respectable [rɪ'spektəbəl] *adj* respectable; considérable

respectful [rɪ'spektfəl] *adj* respectueux

respectfully [rɪ'spektfəli] *adj* respectueusement; **respectfully yours** (*complimentary close*) veuillez agréer l'assurance de mes sentiments très respectueux

respective [rɪ'spektɪv] *adj* respectif

res′piratory tract′ ['respɪrə,tori], [rɪ'spaɪrə,tori] *s* appareil *m* respiratoire

respite ['respɪt] *s* répit *m*; **without respite** sans relâche

resplendent [rɪ'splendənt] *adj* resplendissant

respond [rɪ'spɑnd] *intr* répondre

response [rɪ'spɑns] *s* réponse *f*

responsibili•ty [rɪ,spɑnsɪ'bɪlɪti] *s* (*pl* -ties) responsabilité *f*

responsible [rɪ'spɑnsɪbəl] *adj* responsable; (*person*) digne de confiance; (*job, position*) de confiance; **responsible for** responsable de; **responsible to** responsable envers

responsive [rɪ'spɑnsɪv] *adj* sensible, réceptif; **prompt to sympathize**

rest [rest] *s* repos *m*; (*lack of motion*) pause *f*; (*what remains*) reste *m*; (*mus*) silence *m*; **at rest** en repos; (*dead*) mort; **the rest les autres** (*the remainder*) le restant; **the rest of us** nous autres; **to come to rest** s'immobiliser; **to lay to rest** enterrer || *tr* reposer || *intr* reposer, se reposer; **to rest on** reposer sur, s'appuyer sur

restaurant ['restərənt], ['restə,rɑnt] *s* restaurant *m*

rest′ cure′ *s* cure *f* de repos

restful ['restfəl] *adj* reposant; (*calm*) tranquille, paisible

rest′ing place′ *s* lieu *m* de repos, gîte *m*; (*of the dead*) dernière demeure *f*

restitution [,restɪ't(j)uʃən] *s* restitution *f*

restive ['restɪv] *adj* rétif

restless ['restlɪs] *adj* agité, inquiet; sans repos

restock [ri'stɑk] *tr* réapprovisionner; (*with fish or game*) repeupler

restoration [,restə're/ən] *s* restauration *f*

restore [rɪ'stor] *tr* restaurer; (*health*) rétablir; (*to give back*) restituer

restrain [rɪ'stren] *tr* retenir, contenir

restraint [rɪ'strent] *s* restriction *f*, contrainte *f*

restrict [rɪ'strɪkt] *tr* restreindre

restriction [rɪ'strɪkʃən] *s* restriction *f*

rest′ room′ *s* cabinet *m* d'aisance

result [rɪ'zʌlt] *s* résultat *m*; **as a result of** par suite de || *intr* résulter; **to result in** aboutir à

resume [rɪ'z(j)um] *tr & intr* reprendre

résumé [,rezɪ'z(j)u'me] *s* résumé *m*

resumption [rɪ'zʌmpʃən] *s* reprise *f*

resurface [ri'sʌrfɪs] *tr* refaire le revêtement de || *intr* (*said of submarine*) faire surface

resurrect [,rezə'rekt] *tr & intr* ressusciter

resurrection [ˌrezəˈrekʃən] s résurrection f
resuscitate [rɪˈsʌsɪˌtet] tr & intr ressusciter
retail [ˈritel] adj & adv au détail ‖ s vente f au détail ‖ tr vendre au détail, détailler ‖ intr se vendre au détail
retailer [ˈritelər] s détaillant m
retain [rɪˈten] tr retenir; engager
retaliate [rɪˈtælɪˌet] intr prendre sa revanche, user de représailles
retaliation [rɪˌtælɪˈeʃən] s représailles fpl
retard [rɪˈtɑrd] s retard m ‖ tr retarder
retch [retʃ] tr vomir ‖ intr avoir un haut-le-cœur
retching [ˈretʃɪŋ] s haut-le-cœur m
reticence [ˈretɪsəns] s réserve f
reticent [ˈretɪsənt] adj réservé
retina [ˈretɪnə] s rétine f
retinue [ˈretɪˌn(j)u] s suite f, cortège m
retire [rɪˈtaɪr] tr mettre à la retraite ‖ intr se retirer
retired adj en retraite
retirement [rɪˈtaɪrmənt] s retraite f
retire′ment pro′gram s programme m de prévoyance
retiring [rɪˈtaɪrɪŋ] adj (shy) effacé; (e.g., congressman) sortant
retort [rɪˈtɔrt] s riposte f, réplique f; (chem) cornue f ‖ tr & intr riposter
retouch [riˈtʌtʃ] tr retoucher
retrace [riˈtres] tr retracer; (one's steps) revenir sur
retract [rɪˈtrækt] tr rétracter ‖ intr se rétracter
retractable [rɪˈtræktəbəl] adj (aer) escamotable
re-tread [ˈriˌtred] s pneu m rechapé ‖ [riˈtred] v (pret & pp -treaded) tr rechaper ‖ [riˈtred] v (pret -trod; pp -trod or -trodden) tr & intr repasser
retreat [rɪˈtrit] s retraite f; to beat a retreat battre en retraite ‖ intr se retirer
retrench [rɪˈtrentʃ] tr restreindre ‖ intr faire des économies
retribution [ˌretrɪˈbjuʃən] s rétribution f
retrieve [rɪˈtriv] tr retrouver, recouvrer; (a fortune, a reputation, etc.) rétablir; (game) rapporter ‖ intr (said of hunting dog) rapporter
retriever [rɪˈtrivər] s retriever m
retroactive [ˌretroˈæktɪv] adj rétroactif
retrogress [ˈretrəˌgres] intr rétrograder
retrorocket [ˈretroˌrɑkɪt] s rétrofusée f
retrospect [ˈretrəˌspekt] s—to consider in retrospect jeter un coup d'œil rétrospectif à
retrospective [ˌretrəˈspektɪv] adj rétrospectif
re-try [riˈtraɪ] v (pret & pp -tried) tr essayer de nouveau; (law) juger à nouveau
return [rɪˈtʌrn] s de retour; by return mail par retour du courrier ‖ s retour m; (profit) bénéfice m; (yield) rendement m; (unwanted merchandise) rendu m; (of ball) renvoi m; (of income tax) déclaration f; in return

(for) en retour (de); **returns** (profits) recettes fpl; (of an election) résultats mpl ‖ tr rendre; (to put back) remettre; (to bring back) rapporter; (e.g., a letter) retourner ‖ intr (to go back) retourner; (to come back) revenir; (to get back home) rentrer; **to return empty-handed** revenir bredouille
return′ address′ s adresse f de l'expéditeur
return′ bout′ s revanche f
return′ game′ or **match′** s match m retour
return′ tick′et s aller et retour m
return′ trip′ s voyage m de retour
reunification [riˌjunɪfɪˈkeʃən] s réunification f
reunion [riˈjunjən] s réunion f
reunite [ˌrijuˈnaɪt] tr réunir ‖ intr se réunir
rev [rev] s (coll) tour m ‖ v (pret & pp revved; ger revving) tr (coll) accélérer; (to race) (coll) emballer ‖ intr (coll) s'accélérer
revamp [riˈvæmp] tr refaire
reveal [rɪˈvil] tr révéler
reveille [ˈrevəli] s réveil m
rev-el [ˈrevəl] s fête f; **revels** ébats mpl, orgie f ‖ v (pret & pp -eled or -elled; ger -eling or -elling) intr faire la fête, faire la bombe; **to revel in** se délecter à
revelation [ˌrevəˈleʃən] s révélation f; **Revelation** (Bib) Apocalypse f
revel-ry [ˈrevəlri] s (pl -ries) réjouissances fpl, orgie f
revenge [rɪˈvendʒ] s vengeance f; **to take revenge on s.o. for s.th.** se venger de q.ch. sur qn ‖ tr venger
revengeful [rɪˈvendʒfəl] adj vindicatif
revenue [ˈrevəˌn(j)u] s revenu m
rev′enue cut′ter s garde-côte m, vedette f
rev′enue stamp′ s timbre m fiscal
reverberate [rɪˈvʌrbəˌret] intr résonner
revere [rɪˈvɪr] tr révérer
reverence [ˈrevərəns] s révérence f ‖ tr révérer
reverend [ˈrevərənd] adj & s révérend m
reverent [ˈrevərənt] adj révérenciel
reverie [ˈrevəri] s rêverie f
reversal [rɪˈvʌrsəl] s renversement m
reverse [rɪˈvʌrs] adj contraire ‖ s contraire m; (of medal; of fortune) revers m; (of page) verso m; (aut) marche f arrière ‖ tr renverser; (a sentence) (law) révoquer ‖ intr renverser; (said of motor) faire machine arrière; (aut) faire marche arrière
reverse′ lev′er s levier m de renvoi
reverse′ side′ s revers m, dos m
reversible [rɪˈvʌrsɪbəl] adj réversible
revert [rɪˈvʌrt] intr revenir, faire retour
review [rɪˈvju] s revue f; (of a book) compte m rendu; (of a lesson) révision f ‖ tr revoir; (a book) faire la critique de; (a lesson) réviser, revoir; (past events; troops) passer en revue ‖ intr faire des révisions
revile [rɪˈvaɪl] tr injurier, outrager
revise [rɪˈvaɪz] s révision f; (typ)

épreuve *f* de révision || *tr* réviser; (*a book*) revoir

revised/ edi/tion *s* édition *f* revue et corrigée

revision [rɪ'vɪʒən] *s* révision *f*

revisionist [rɪ'vɪʒənɪst] *adj* & *s* révisionniste *mf*

revival [rɪ'vaɪvəl] *s* retour *m* à la vie; (*of learning*) renaissance *f*; (rel) réveil *m*; (theat) reprise *f*

revival/ meet/ings *spl* (rel) réveils *mpl*

revive [rɪ'vaɪv] *tr* ranimer; (*a victim*) ressusciter; (*a memory*) réveiller; (*a play*) reprendre || *intr* reprendre; se ranimer

revoke [rɪ'vok] *tr* révoquer

revolt [rɪ'volt] *s* révolte *f* || *tr* révolter || *intr* se révolter

revolting [rɪ'voltɪŋ] *adj* dégoûtant, repoussant; rebelle, révolté

revolution [ˌrevə'luʃən] *s* révolution *f*

revolutionar-y [ˌrevə'luʃəˌneri] *adj* révolutionnaire || *s* (*pl* **-ies**) révolutionnaire *mf*

revolve [rɪ'valv] *tr* faire tourner; (*in one's mind*) retourner || *intr* tourner

revolver [rɪ'valvər] *s* revolver *m*

revolv/ing book/case *s* bibliothèque *f* tournante

revolv/ing door/ *s* porte *f* à tambour, tambour *m* cylindrique

revolv/ing fund/ *s* fonds *m* de roulement

revolv/ing stage/ *s* scène *f* tournante

revue [rɪ'vju] *s* (theat) revue *f*

revulsion [rɪ'vʌlʃən] *s* aversion *f*, répugnance *f*; (*change of feeling*) revirement *m*

reward [rɪ'word] *s* récompense *f* || *tr* récompenser

rewarding [rɪ'wordɪŋ] *adj* rémunérateur; (*experience*) enrichissant

re-wind [rɪ'waɪnd] *v* (*pret* & *pp* **-wound**) *tr* (*film, tape, etc.*) renverser la marche de; (*a typewriter ribbon*) embobiner de nouveau; (*a clock*) remonter

rewire [rɪ'waɪr] *tr* (*a building*) refaire l'installation électrique dans

re-write [rɪ'raɪt] *v* (*pret* **-wrote**; *pp* **-written**) *tr* récrire

rhapso-dy ['ræpsədi] *s* (*pl* **-dies**) *s* rhapsodie *f*

rheostat ['riˌəˌstæt] *s* rhéostat *m*

rhetoric ['retərɪk] *s* rhétorique *f*

rhetorical [rɪ'tarɪkəl], [rɪ'tɔrɪkəl] *adj* rhétorique

rheumatic [ru'mætɪk] *adj* rhumatismal; (*person*) rhumatisant || *s* rhumatisant *m*

rheumatism ['rumə,tɪzəm] *s* rhumatisme *m*

Rhine [raɪn] *s* Rhin *m*

Rhineland ['raɪn,lænd] *s* Rhénanie *f*

rhine/stone/ *s* faux diamant *m*

rhinoceros [raɪ'nasərəs] *s* rhinocéros *m*

rhubarb ['rubarb] *s* rhubarbe *f*

rhyme [raɪm] *s* rime *f*; in rhyme en vers || *tr* & *intr* rimer

rhythm ['rɪðəm] *s* rythme *m*

rhythmic(al) ['rɪðmɪk(əl)] *adj* rythmique

rib [rɪb] *s* côte *f*; (*of umbrella*) baleine *f*; (archit, biol, mach) nervure *f* || *v* (*pret* & *pp* **ribbed**; *ger* **ribbing**) *tr* garnir de nervures; (slang) taquiner

ribald ['rɪbəld] *adj* grivois

ribbon ['rɪbən] *s* ruban *m*

rice [raɪs] *s* riz *m*

rice/ field/ *s* rizière *f*

rice/ pud/ding *s* riz *m* au lait

rich [rɪtʃ] *adj* riche; (*voice*) sonore; (*wine*) généreux; (*funny*) (coll) impayable; (coll) ridicule; **to get rich** s'enrichir; **to strike it rich** trouver le bon filon || *riches spl* richesses *fpl*

rickets ['rɪkɪts] *s* rachitisme *m*

rickety ['rɪkɪti] *adj* (*object*) boiteux, délabré; (*person*) chancelant; (*suffering from rickets*) rachitique

rickshaw ['rɪk,ʃɔ] *s* pousse-pousse *m*

rid [rɪd] *v* (*pret* & *pp* **rid**; *ger* **ridding**) *tr* débarrasser; **to get rid of** se débarrasser de

riddance ['rɪdəns] *s* débarras *m*; **good riddance!** bon débarras!

riddle ['rɪdəl] *s* devinette *f*, énigme *f* || *tr*—**to riddle with** cribler de

ride [raɪd] *s* promenade *f*; **to take a ride** faire une promenade (en auto, à cheval, à motocyclette, etc.); **to take s.o. for a ride** (to dupe s.o.) (slang) faire marcher qn; (to murder s.o.) (slang) descendre qn || *v* (*pret* **rode** [rod]; *pp* **ridden** ['rɪdən]) *tr* monter à; (coll) se moquer de; **ridden** dominé; **to ride out** (*e.g., a storm*) étaler || *intr* monter à cheval (à bicyclette, etc.); **to let ride** (coll) laisser courir

rider ['raɪdər] *s* (*on horseback*) cavalier *m*; (*on a bicycle*) cycliste *mf*; (*in a vehicle*) voyageur *m*; (*to a document*) annexe *f*

ridge [rɪdʒ] *s* arête *f*, crête *f*; (*of a fabric*) grain *m*

ridge/pole/ *s* faîtage *m*

ridicule ['rɪdɪ,kjul] *s* ridicule *m* || *tr* ridiculiser

ridiculous [rɪ'dɪkjələs] *adj* ridicule

rid/ing acad/emy *s* école *f* d'équitation

rid/ing boot/ *s* botte *f* de cheval, botte à l'écuyère

rid/ing hab/it *s* habit *m* d'amazone

rife [raɪf] *adj* répandu; **rife with** abondant en

riffraff ['rɪf,ræf] *s* racaille *f*

rifle ['raɪfəl] *s* fusil *m*; (*spiral groove*) rayure *f* || *tr* piller; (*a gun barrel*) rayer

rift [rɪft] *s* fente *f*, crevasse *f*; (*disagreement*) désaccord *m*

rig [rɪg] *s* équipement *m*; (*carriage*) équipage *m*; (naut) gréement *m*; (getup) (coll) accoutrement *m* || *v* (*pret* & *pp* **rigged**; *ger* **rigging**) *tr* équiper; (to falsify) truquer; (naut) gréer; **to rig out with** (coll) accoutrer de

rigging ['rɪgɪŋ] *s* gréement *m*; (fraud) truquage *m*

right [raɪt] *adj* droit; (*change, time, etc.*) exact; (*statement, answer, etc.*) correct; (*conclusion, word, etc.*)

juste; (*name*) vrai; (*moment, house, road, etc.*) bon, e.g., **it's not the right road** ce n'est pas la bonne route; qu'il faut, e.g., **it's not the right village** (spot, boy, etc.) ce n'est pas le village (endroit, garçon, etc.) qu'il faut; **to be all right** aller très bien; **to be right** avoir raison || *s* (*justice*) droit *m*; (*reason*) raison *f*; (*right hand*) droite *f*; (*fist or blow in boxing*) droit; **all rights reserved** tous droits réservés; **by right of** à titre de; **by rights** de plein droit; **by the right!** (mil) guide à droite!; **on the right** à droite; **right and wrong** le bien et le mal; **rights** droits; **to be in the right** avoir raison || *adv* directement; correctement; complètement; bien, en bon état; (*to the right*) à droite; (coll) très; même, e.g., **right here** ici même; **all right!** d'accord!; **right and left** à droite et à gauche; **right away** tout de suite; **to put right** mettre bon ordre à, mettre en état || *tr* faire droit à; (*to correct*) corriger; (*to set up-right*) redresser || *intr* se redresser || *interj* parfait!

right' about' face' *s* volte-face *f* || *interj* (mil) demi-tour à droite!

righteous ['raɪtʃəs] *adj* juste; vertueux

right' field' *s* (baseball) champ *m* droit

rightful ['raɪtfəl] *adj* légitime

right'-hand drive' *s* conduite *f* à droite

right-hander ['raɪt'hændər] *s* droitier *m*

right'-hand man' *s* bras *m* droit

rightist ['raɪtɪst] *adj & s* droitier *m*

rightly ['raɪtli] *adv* à bon droit, à juste titre; correctement, avec sagesse; **rightly or wrongly** à tort ou à raison

right' of assem'bly *s* liberté *f* de réunion

right' of way' *s* droit *m* de passage; **to yield the right of way** céder le pas

rights' of man' *spl* droits *mpl* de l'homme

right to work ['raɪttə'wʌrk] *s* liberté *f* du travail des ouvriers non syndiqués

right'-wing' *adj* de droite

right-winger ['raɪt'wɪŋər] *s* (coll) droitier *m*

rigid ['rɪdʒɪd] *adj* rigide

rigmarole ['rɪgmə,rol] *s* galimatias *m*

rigor ['rɪgər] *s* rigueur *f*; (pathol) rigidité *f*

rigorous ['rɪgərəs] *adj* rigoureux

rile [raɪl] *tr* (coll) exaspérer

rill [rɪl] *s* ruisselet *m*

rim [rɪm] *s* bord *m*, rebord *m*; (*of spectacles*) monture *f*; (*of wheel*) jante *f*

rind [raɪnd] *s* écorce *f*; (*of cheese*) croûte *f*; (*of bacon*) couenne *f*

ring [rɪŋ] *s* anneau *m*; (*for the finger*) bague *f*, anneau; (*for some sport or exhibition*) piste *f*; (*for boxing*) ring *m*; (*for bullfight*) arène *f*; (*of a group of people*) cercle *m*; (*of evildoers*) gang *m*; (*under the eyes*) cerne *m*; (*sound*) son *m*; (*of bell, clock, telephone, etc.*) sonnerie *f*; (*of a small bell; in the ears; of the glass of glassware*) tintement *m*; (*to summon a person*) coup *m* de sonnette; (*quality*) timbre *m*; (telp) coup de téléphone || *v* (*pret & pp* ringed) *tr* cerner || *intr* décrire des cercles || *v* (*pret* rang [ræŋ]; *pp* rung [rʌŋ]) *tr* sonner; **to ring up** (telp) donner un coup de téléphone à || *intr* sonner; (said, e.g., *of ears*) tinter; **to ring out** résonner

ring'bolt' *s* piton *m*

ring'dove' *s* (orn) ramier *m*

ring' fin'ger *s* annulaire *m*

ringing ['rɪŋɪŋ] *adj* résonnant, retentissant *s* sonnerie *f*; (*in the ears*) tintement *m*

ring'lead'er *s* meneur *m*

ringlet ['rɪŋlɪt] *s* bouclette *f*

ring'mas'ter *s* maître *m* de manège, chef *m* de piste

ring'side' *s* premier rang *m*

ring'snake' *s* (*Tropidonotus natrix*) couleuvre *f* à collier

ring'worm' *s* teigne *f*

rink [rɪŋk] *s* patinoire *f*

rinse [rɪns] *s* rinçage *m* || *tr* rincer

riot ['raɪ·ət] *s* émeute *f*; (*of colors*) orgie *f*; **to run riot** se déchaîner; (said *of plants or vines*) pulluler || *intr* s'ameuter

rioter ['raɪ·ətər] *s* émeutier *m*

rip [rɪp] *s* déchirure *f* || *v* (*pret & pp* ripped; *ger* ripping) *tr* déchirer; **to rip away or off** arracher; **to rip open or up** découdre; (*a letter, package, etc.*) ouvrir en le déchirant || *intr* se déchirer

rip' cord' *s* (*of parachute*) cordelette *f* de déclenchement

ripe [raɪp] *adj* mûr; (*cheese*) fait; (*olive*) noir

ripen ['raɪpən] *tr & intr* mûrir

ripple ['rɪpəl] *s* ride *f*; (*sound*) murmure *m* || *tr* rider || *intr* se rider; murmurer

rise [raɪz] *s* hausse *f*, augmentation *f*; (*of ground; of the voice*) élévation *f*; (*of a heavenly body; of the curtain*) lever *m*; (*in one's employment, in one's fortunes*) ascension *f*; (*of water*) montée *f*; (*of a source of water*) naissance *f*; **to get a rise out of** (slang) se payer la tête de; **to give rise to** donner naissance à || *v* (*pret* rose [roz]; *pp* risen ['rɪzən]) *intr* s'élever, monter; (*to get out of bed; to stand up; to ascend in the heavens*) se lever; (*to revolt*) se soulever; (said, e.g., *of a danger*) se montrer; (said *of a fluid*) jaillir; (*in someone's esteem*) grandir; (said *of river*) prendre sa source; **to rise above** dépasser; (*unfortunate events, insults, etc.*) se montrer supérieur à; **to rise to** (e.g., *the occasion*) se montrer à la hauteur de

riser ['raɪzər] *s* (*of staircase*) contre-marche *f*; (*of gas or water*) colonne *f* montante; **to be a late riser** faire la grasse matinée; **to be an early riser** être matinal

risk [rɪsk] *s* risque *m* || *tr* risquer

risk·y ['rɪski] *adj* (*comp* -ier; *super* -iest*) dangereux, hasardeux, risqué

risqué [rɪsˈke] adj risqué, osé
rite [raɪt] s rite m; **last rites** derniers sacrements mpl
ritual [ˈrɪt/ʊ·əl] adj & s rituel m
ri·val [ˈraɪvəl] adj & s rival m || v (pret & pp -valed or -valled; ger -valing or -valling) tr rivaliser avec
rival·ry [ˈraɪvəlrɪ] s (pl -ries) rivalité f
river [ˈrɪvər] adj fluvial || s fleuve m; (tributary) rivière f; (stream) cours m d'eau; **down the river** en aval; **up the river** en amont
riv'er bas'in s bassin m fluvial
riv'er·bed' s lit m de rivière
riv'er-front' s rive f d'un fleuve
riv'er·side' adj riverain || s rive f
rivet [ˈrɪvɪt] s rivet m || tr river
riv'et gun' s riveuse f pneumatique
rivulet [ˈrɪvjəlɪt] s ruisselet m
R.N. [ˈɑrˈɛn] s (letterword) (registered nurse) infirmière f diplômée
roach [rotʃ] s (ent) blatte f, cafard m; (ichth) gardon m
road [rod] s route f, chemin m; (naut) rade f; **road under construction** (public sign) travaux
road'bed' s assiette f; (rr) infrastructure f
road'block' s barrage m
road' hog' s écraseur m, chauffard m
road'house' s guinguette f au bord de la route
road' map' s carte f routière
road' serv'ice s secours m routier
road'side' s bord m de la route
road' sign' s poteau m indicateur
road'stead' s rade f
road'way' s chaussée f
roam [rom] tr parcourir; (the seas) sillonner || intr errer, rôder
roar [ror] s rugissement m; (of cannon, engine, etc.) grondement m; (of crowd) hurlement m; (of laughter) éclat m || intr rugir; gronder; hurler
roast [rost] s rôti m; (of coffee) torréfaction f || tr rôtir; (coffee) torréfier; (chestnuts) griller || intr se rôtir; torréfier
roast' beef' s rosbif m, rôti m de bœuf
roaster [ˈrostər] s (appliance) rôtissoire f; (for coffee) brûloir m; (fowl) volaille f à rôtir
roast' pork' s porc m rôti
rob [rab] v (pret & pp robbed; ger robbing) tr & intr voler; **to rob s.o. of s.th.** voler q.ch. à qn
robber [ˈrabər] s voleur m
robber·y [ˈrabərɪ] s (pl -ies) vol m
robe [rob] s robe f; (of a professor, judge, etc.) toge f; (dressing gown) robe f de chambre; (for lap in a carriage) couverture f || tr revêtir d'une robe || intr revêtir sa robe
robin [ˈrabɪn] s (Erithacus rubecula) rouge-gorge m; (Turdus migratorius) grive f migratoire
robot [ˈrobat] s robot m
robust [roˈbʌst] adj robuste
rock [rak] s roche f; (eminence) roc m, rocher m; (sticking out of water) rocher; (one that is thrown) pierre f; (slang) diamant m; **on the rocks**

(coll) fauché, à sec; (said of liquor) (coll) sur glace || tr balancer; (to rock to sleep) bercer || intr se balancer; se bercer
rock'-bot'tom adj (le) plus bas || s (le) fin fond m
rock' can'dy s candi m
rock' crys'tal s cristal m de roche
rocker [ˈrakər] s bascule f; (chair) chaise f à bascule; **to go off one's rocker** (slang) perdre la boussole
rock'er arm' s culbuteur m
rocket [ˈrakɪt] s fusée f; (arti, bot) roquette f || intr monter en chandelle; (said of prices) monter en flèche
rock'et bomb' s bombe f volante, fusée f
rock'et launch'er s lance-fusées m; (arti) lance-roquettes m
rock'et ship' s fusée f interplanétaire, fusée interstellaire
rock' gar'den s jardin m de rocaille
rock'ing chair' s fauteuil m à bascule
rock'ing horse' s cheval m à bascule
Rock' of Gibral'tar [dʒɪˈbrɔltər] s rocher m de Gibraltar
rock' salt' s sel m gemme
rock' wool' s laine f minérale, laine de verre
rock·y [ˈrakɪ] adj (comp -ier; super -iest) rocheux, rocailleux
Rock'y Moun'tains spl Montagnes fpl Rocheuses
rod [rad] s baguette f; (for punishment) verge f; (of the retina; elongated microorganism) bâtonnet m; (of authority) main f; (of curtain) tringle f; (for fishing) canne f; (Bib) lignée f, race f; (mach) bielle f; (surv) jalon m; (revolver) (slang) pétard m; **rod and gun** la chasse et la pêche
rodent [ˈrodənt] adj & s rongeur m
roe [ro] s (deer) chevreuil m; (of fish) œufs mpl
roger [ˈradʒər] interj O.K.!; (rad) message reçu
rogue [rog] s coquin m
rogues'' gal'lery s fichier m de la police de portraits de criminels
roguish [ˈrogɪʃ] adj espiègle, coquin
roister [ˈrɔɪstər] intr faire du tapage
role or rôle [rol] s rôle m
roll [rol] s rouleau m; (of thunder, drums, etc.) roulement m; (roll call) appel m; (list) rôle m; (of film) rouleau; (of paper money) liasse f; (of dice) coup m; (of a boat) roulis m; (of fat) bourrelet m; (culin) petit pain m; **to call the roll** faire l'appel || tr rouler; **to roll over** retourner; **to roll up** enrouler || intr rouler; (said of thunder) gronder; (to sway) se balancer; (to overturn) faire panache; (said of ship) rouler; **to roll over** se retourner; **to roll up** se rouler
roll'back' s repoussement m; (com) baisse f de prix
roll' call' s appel m; (vote) appel nominal
roller [ˈrolər] s rouleau m; (of a skate) roulette f; (wave) lame f de houle

roll'er bear'ing s coussinet m à rouleaux

roll'er coast'er s montagnes fpl russes

roll'er skate' s patin m à roulettes

roll'er-skate' intr patiner sur des roulettes

roll'er-skating rink' s skating m

roll'er tow'el s essuie-mains m à rouleau, serviette f sans fin

roll'ing mill' s usine f de laminage; (set of rollers) laminoir m

roll'ing pin' s rouleau m

roll'ing stock' s (rr) matériel m roulant

roll'-top desk' s bureau m à cylindre

roly-poly ['roli'poli] adj rondelet

romaine [ro'men] s romaine f

roman ['romən] adj & s (typ) romain m; **Roman** Romain m

Ro'man can'dle s chandelle f romaine

Ro'man Cath'olic adj & s catholique mf

Romance ['romæns], [ro'mæns] adj roman || (l.c.) [ro'mæns], ['romæns] s roman m de chevalerie; (made-up story) conte m bleu; (love affair) idylle f; (mus) romance f || (l.c.) [ro'mæns] intr exagérer, broder

Romanesque [,romən'esk] adj & s roman m

Ro'man nose' s nez m aquilin

Ro'man nu'meral s chiffre m romain

romantic [ro'mæntɪk] adj (genre; literature; scenery) romantique; (imagination) romanesque

romanticism [ro'mæntɪ,sɪzəm] s romantisme m

romanticist [ro'mæntɪsɪst] s romantique mf

romp [ramp] intr s'ébattre

rompers ['rampərz] spl barboteuse f

roof [ruf], [rʊf] s toit m; (of the mouth) palais m; **to raise the roof** (slang) faire un boucan de tous les diables

roofer ['rufər], ['rʊfər] s couvreur m

roof' gar'den s terrasse f avec jardin, pergola f

rook [rʊk] s (chess) tour f; (orn) freux m, corneille f || tr (coll) rouler; **to rook s.o. out of s.th.** (coll) filouter q.ch. à qn

rookie ['rʊkɪ] s (slang) bleu m

room [rum], [rʊm] s pièce f; (especially bedroom) chambre f; (where people congregate) salle f; (space) place f; **to make room for** faire place à || intr vivre en garni; **to room with** partager une chambre avec

room' and board' s le vivre et le couvert

room' clerk' s employé m à la réception

roomer ['rumər], ['rʊmər] s locataire mf

roomette [ru'met] s chambrette f de sleeping

room'ing house' s maison f meublée, maison garnie

room'mate' s camarade mf de chambre

room·y ['rumi], ['rʊmi] adj (comp -ier; super -iest) spacieux, ample

roost [rust] s perchoir m; (coll) logis

m, demeure f; **to rule the roost** (coll) faire la loi || intr se percher, percher

rooster ['rustər] s coq m

root [rut], [rʊt] s racine f; **to get to the root of** approfondir; **to take root** prendre racine || tr fouiller; **to root out** déraciner || intr s'enraciner; **to root around in** fouiller dans; **to root for** (coll) applaudir, encourager

rooter ['rutər], ['rʊtər] s (coll) fanatique mf, fana mf

rope [rop] s corde f; (lasso) corde à nœud coulant; **to jump rope** sauter à la corde; **to know the ropes** (slang) connaître les ficelles || tr corder; (cattle) prendre au lasso; **to rope in** (slang) entraîner

rope' lad'der s échelle f de corde

rope' walk'er s funambule mf, danseur m de corde

rosa·ry ['rozəri] s (pl -ries) rosaire m

rose [roz] adj rose || s (color) rose m; (bot) rose f

rose' bee'tle s cétoine f dorée

rose'bud' s bouton m de rose

rose'bush' s rosier m

rose'-col'ored adj rosé, couleur de rose; **to see everything through rose-colored glasses** voir tout en rose

rose' gar'den s roseraie f

rosemar·y ['roz,meri] s (pl -ies) romarin m

rose' of Shar'on ['ʃerən] s rose f de Saron

rosette [ro'zet] s rosette f; (archit, elec) rosace f

rose' win'dow s rosace f, rose f

rose'wood' s bois m de rose, palissandre m

rosin ['razɪn] s colophane f

roster ['rastər] s liste f, appel m; (educ) heures fpl de classe; (mil) tableau m de service; (naut) rôle m

rostrum ['rastrəm] s tribune f

ros·y ['rozi] adj (comp -ier; super -iest) rosé; (complexion) vermeil; (fig) riant

rot [rat] s pourriture f; (slang) sottise f || v (pret & pp rotted; ger rotting) tr & intr pourrir

ro'tary press' ['rotəri] s rotative f

rotate ['rotet], [ro'tet] tr & intr tourner; (agr) alterner

rotation [ro'teʃən] s rotation f; **in rotation** à tour de rôle

rote [rot] s routine f; **by rote** par cœur, machinalement

rot'gut' s (slang) tord-boyaux m

rotisserie [ro'tɪsəri] s rôtissoire f

rotogravure [,rotəgrə'vjʊr], [,rotə'grevjʊr] s rotogravure f

rotten ['ratən] adj pourri

rotund [ro'tʌnd] adj rond, arrondi; (e.g., language) ampoulé

rotunda [ro'tʌndə] s rotonde f

rouge [ruʒ] s fard m, rouge m || tr farder || intr se farder, se mettre du rouge

rough [rʌf] adj rude; (uneven) inégal; (coarse) grossier; (unfinished) brut; (road) raboteux; (game) brutal; (sea) agité; (guess) approximatif || tr—**to**

rough it faire du camping, coucher sur la dure; to rough up malmener

rough' draft' s ébauche f, avant-projet m, brouillon m

rough'house' s boucan m, chahut m || intr faire du boucan, chahuter

rough' ide'a s aperçu m

roughly ['rʌflɪ] adv grossièrement; brutalement; approximativement

rough'neck' s (coll) canaille f

roulette [ru'lɛt] s roulette f

round [raund] adj rond; (rounded) arrondi; rond; (e.g., shoulders) voûté; three (four, etc.) feet round trois (quatre, etc.) pieds de tour || s rond m; (inspection) ronde f; (of golf; of drinks; of postman, doctor, etc.) tournée f; (of applause) salve f; (of ammunition) cartouche f; (of veal) noix f; (boxing) round m; to go the rounds faire le tour || adv à la ronde; round about aux alentours; the year round pendant toute l'année; to pass round faire circuler, passer à la ronde || prep autour de || tr (to make round) arrondir; (e.g., a corner) tourner, prendre; (a cape) doubler; to round off or out arrondir; (to finish) achever; to round up rassembler; (suspects) cueillir || intr s'arrondir

roundabout ['raundə‚baut] adj indirect || s détour m; (carrousel) (Brit) manège m; (traffic circle) (Brit) rond-point m

rounder ['raundər] s (coll) fêtard m

round'house' s (rr) rotonde f

round'-shoul'dered adj voûté

round' steak' s gîte m à la noix

round' ta'ble s table f ronde; Round Table Table ronde

round'-trip' tick'et s billet m d'aller et retour

round'up' s (of cattle) rassemblement m; (of suspects) rafle f

rouse [rauz] tr réveiller || intr se réveiller

rout [raut] s déroute f || tr mettre en déroute

route [rut], [raut] s route f; (of, e.g., bus) ligne f, parcours m || tr acheminer

routine [ru'tin] adj routinier || s routine f

rove [rov] intr errer, vagabonder

rover ['rovər] s vagabond m

row [rau] s (coll) altercation f, prise f de bec; to raise a row (coll) faire du boucan || [ro] s rang m; (of, e.g., houses) rangée f; (boat ride) promenade f en barque; in a row à la file; (without interruption) de suite; in rows par rangs || intr ramer

rowboat ['ro‚bot] s bateau m à rames, canot m

row•dy ['raudɪ] adj (comp -dier; super -diest) tapageur || s (pl -dies) tapageur m

rower ['ro‚ər] s rameur m

rowing ['ro‚ɪŋ] s nage f, canotage m, sport m de l'aviron

royal ['rɔɪəl] adj royal

royalist ['rɔɪəlɪst] adj & s royaliste mf

royal•ty ['rɔɪəltɪ] s (pl -ties) royauté f; droit m d'auteur; redevance f, droit d'inventeur

r.p.m. ['ar'pi'ɛm] spl (letterword) (revolutions per minute) tours mpl à la minute

rub [rʌb] s frottement m; there's the rub (coll) voilà le hic || v (pret & pp rubbed; ger rubbing) tr frotter; to rub elbows with coudoyer; to rub out effacer; (slang) descendre, liquider || intr se frotter; (said, e.g., of moving parts) frotter; to rub off s'enlever, disparaître

rubber ['rʌbər] s caoutchouc m; (eraser) gomme f à effacer; (in bridge) robre m; rubbers (overshoes) caoutchoucs

rub'ber band' s élastique m

rubberize ['rʌbə‚raɪz] tr caoutchouter

rub'ber•neck' s (coll) badaud m || intr (coll) badauder

rub'ber plant' s figuier m élastique, caoutchoutier m; (tree) arbre m à caoutchouc, hévéa m

rub'ber stamp' s tampon m; (coll) béni-oui-oui m

rub'ber-stamp' tr apposer le tampon sur; (with a person's signature) estampiller; (coll) approuver à tort et à travers

rub'bing al'cohol s alcool m pour les frictions

rubbish ['rʌbɪʃ] s détritus m, rebut m; (coll) imbécillités fpl

rubble ['rʌbəl] s (broken stone) décombres mpl; (used in masonry) moellons mpl

rub'down' s friction f

rubric ['rubrɪk] s rubrique f

ru•by ['rubɪ] adj (lips) vermeil || s (pl -bies) rubis m

rucksack ['rʌk‚sæk] s sac-à-dos m

rudder ['rʌdər] s gouvernail m

rud•dy ['rʌdɪ] adj (comp -dier; super -diest) rougeaud, coloré

rude [rud] adj (rough, rugged) rude; (discourteous) impoli, grossier

rudeness ['rudnɪs] s rudesse f; impolitesse f

rudiment ['rudɪmənt] s rudiment m

rue [ru] tr regretter amèrement

rueful ['rufəl] adj lamentable; triste

ruffian ['rʌfɪən] s brute f

ruffle ['rʌfəl] s (in water) rides fpl; (of drum) roulement m; (sewing) jabot m plissé || tr (to crease; to vex) froisser; (the water) rider; (its feathers) hérisser; (one's hair) ébouriffer

rug [rʌg] s tapis m, carpette f

rugged ['rʌgɪd] adj rude, sévère; (road, country, etc.) raboteux; (person) robuste; (e.g., machine) résistant à toute épreuve

ruin ['ru-ɪn] s ruine f || tr ruiner

rule [rul] s règle f; autorité f; (reign) règne m; (law) décision f; as a rule en général; by rule of thumb empiriquement, à vue de nez || tr gouverner; (to lead) diriger, guider; (one's passions) contenir; (with lines) régler; (law) décider; **to rule out** écarter, éliminer ‖ *intr* gouverner; (*to be the rule*) prévaloir; **to rule over** régner sur

ruler ['rulər] *s* dirigeant *m*; souverain *m*; (*for ruling lines*) règle *f*

ruling ['rulɪŋ] *adj* actuel; (*e.g., classes*) dirigeant; (*quality, trait, etc.*) dominant ‖ *s* (*of paper*) réglage *m*; (law) décision *f*

rum [rʌm] *s* rhum *m*

Rumanian [ru'menɪ-ən] *adj* roumain ‖ *s* (*language*) roumain *m*; (*person*) Roumain *m*

rumble ['rʌmbəl] *s* (*of thunder*) grondement *m*; (*of a cart*) roulement *m*; (*of intestines*) gargouillement *m*; (slang) rixe *f* entre gangs ‖ *intr* gronder, rouler

ruminate ['rumɪˌnet] *tr & intr* ruminer

rummage ['rʌmɪdʒ] *intr* fouiller

rum'mage sale' *s* vente *f* d'objets usagés

rumor ['rumər] *s* rumeur *f* ‖ *tr—it is rumored that* le bruit court que

rump [rʌmp] *s* (*of animal*) croupe *f*; (*of bird*) croupion *m*; (*cut of meat*) culotte *f*; (*buttocks*) postérieur *m*

rumple ['rʌmpəl] *s* faux pli *m* ‖ *tr* (*paper, cloth, etc.*) froisser, chiffonner; (*one's hair*) ébouriffer

rump' steak' *s* romsteck *m*

rumpus ['rʌmpəs] *s* (coll) chahut *m*; (*argument*) (coll) prise *f* de bec; **to raise a rumpus** (coll) déclencher un chahut; faire une scène violente

rum'pus room' *s* salle *f* de jeux

run [rʌn] *s* course *f*; (*e.g., of good or bad luck*) suite *f*; (*on a bank by depositors*) descente *f*; (*of salmon*) remonte *f*; (*of, e.g., a bus*) parcours *m*; (*in a stocking*) échelle *f*, démaillage *m*; (cards) séquence *f*; (mus) roulade *f*; **in the long run** à la longue; **on the run** à la débandade, en fuite; **run of bad luck** série *f* noire; **the general run** la généralité; **to give free run to** donner libre carrière à; **to give s.o. a run for his money** en donner à qn pour son argent; **to have a long run** (theat) tenir longtemps l'affiche; **to have the run of** avoir libre accès à or dans; **to keep s.o. on the run** ne laisser aucun répit à qn; **to make a run in** (*a stocking*) démailler ‖ *v* (*pret* ran [ræn]; *pp* run; *ger* running) *tr* (*the streets; a race; a risk*) courir; (*a motor, machine, etc.*) faire marcher; (*an organization, project, etc.*) diriger; (*a business, factory, etc.*) exploiter; (*a blockade*) forcer; (*a line*) tracer; (turf) faire courir; **to run aground** échouer; **to run down** (*to knock down*) renverser; (*to find*) dépister; (*game*) mettre aux abois; (*to disparage*) (coll) dénigrer; **to run in** (*a motor*) roder; **to run off** (*a liquid*) faire écouler; (*copies, pages, etc.*) tirer; **to run through** (*e.g., with a sword*) transpercer; **to run up** (*a flag*) hisser; (*a debt*) (coll) laisser accumuler ‖ *intr* courir; (*said, e.g., of water;*

said of fountain pen, nose, etc.) couler; (*said of stockings*) se démailler; (*said of salmon*) faire la montaison; (*said of colors*) s'étaler, se déteindre; (*said of sores*) suppurer; (*said of rumor, news, etc.*) circuler, courir; (*for office*) se présenter; (mach) fonctionner, marcher; (theat) rester à l'affiche, se jouer; **to run** [filez]; **to run across** (*to meet by chance*) rencontrer par hasard; **to run along** border, longer; (*to go*) s'en aller; **to run at** se jeter sur; **to run away** se sauver, s'enfuir; (*said of horse*) s'emballer, s'emporter; **to run away with** enlever; **to run down** (*e.g., a hill*) descendre en courant; (*said of spring*) se détendre; (*said of watch*) s'arrêter (faute d'être remonté); (*said of storage battery*) se décharger, s'épuiser; **to run for** (*an office*) poser sa candidature pour; **to run in the family** tenir de famille; **to run into** heurter; (*to meet*) (coll) rencontrer; **to run off** se sauver, s'enfuir; (*said of liquid*) s'écouler; **to run out** (*said of passport, lease, etc.*) expirer; **to run out of** être à court de; **to run over** (*said of a liquid*) déborder; (*an article, a text, etc.*) parcourir; (*s.th. in the road*) passer sur; (*e.g., a pedestrian*) écraser; **to run through** (*an article, text, etc.*) parcourir; (*a fortune*) gaspiller

run'away' *adj* fugitif; (*horse*) emballé ‖ *s* fugitif *m*; cheval *m* emballé

run'down' *s* compte rendu *m*, récit *m*

run'-down' *adj* délabré; (*person; battery*) épuisé, à plat; (*clock spring*) détendu

rung [rʌŋ] *s* (*of ladder or chair*) barreau *m*; (*of wheel*) rayon *m*

runner ['rʌnər] *s* (*person*) coureur *m*; (*messenger*) courrier *m*; (*of ice skate or sleigh*) patin *m*; (*narrow rug*) rampe *f* d'escalier; (*strip of cloth for table top*) chemin *m* de table; (*in stockings*) démaillage *m*; (bot) coulant *m*

run'ner-up' *s* (*pl* **runners-up**) bon second *m*, premier accessit *m*

running ['rʌnɪŋ] *adj* (*person; water; expenses*) courant; (*stream; knot; style*) coulant; (*sore*) suppurant; (*e.g., motor*) en marche ‖ *s* (*of man or animal*) course *f*; (*of water*) écoulement *m*; (*of machine*) fonctionnement *m*, marche *f*; (*of business*) direction *f*

run'ning board' *s* marchepied *m*

run'ning com'mentar'y *s* (*pl* **-ies**) (rad, telv) reportage *m* en direct

run'ning head' *s* titre *m* courant

run'ning start' *s* départ *m* lancé

run'off elec'tion *s* scrutin *m* de ballottage

run'proof' *adj* indémaillable

runt [rʌnt] *s* avorton *m*

run'way' *s* piste *f*, rampe *f*

rupture ['rʌptʃər] *s* rupture *f*; (pathol) hernie *f* ‖ *tr* rompre; (*a ligament,* *blood vessel, etc.*) se rompre || *intr* se rompre

rural ['rʊrəl] *adj* rural

ru′ral free′ deliv′ery *s* distribution *f* gratuite par le facteur rural

ru′ral police′man *s* garde *m* champêtre

ruse [ruz] *s* ruse *f*

rush [rʌʃ] *adj* urgent || *s* course *f* précipitée, ruée *f*; précipitation *f*; (bot) jonc *m*; (formula on envelope or letterhead) urgent; **to be in a rush to** être pressé de || *tr* pousser vivement; (*e.g., to the hospital*) transporter d'urgence; (*a piece of work*) exécuter d'urgence; (*e.g., a girl*) insister auprès de; **to rush through** (*e.g., a law*) faire passer à la hâte || *intr* se précipiter, se ruer; **to rush about** courir ça et là; **to rush headlong** foncer tête baissée; **to rush into** (*e.g., a room*) faire irruption dans; (*an affair*) se jeter dans; **to rush out** sortir précipitamment; **to rush through** (*one's lessons, prayers, etc.*) expédier; (*e.g., a town*) traverser à toute vitesse; (*a tourist attraction*) visiter au pas de course; (*a book*) lire à la hâte; **to rush to** s'empresser de; **to rush to** one's face (*said of blood*) monter au visage à qn

rush′-bot′tomed chair′ *s* chaise *f* à fond de paille

rush′ hours′ *spl* heures *fpl* d'affluence or de pointe

rush′ or′der *s* commande *f* urgente

russet ['rʌsɪt] *adj* roussâtre, roux

Russia ['rʌʃə] *s* Russie *f*; la Russie

Russian ['rʌʃən] *adj* russe || *s* (*language*) russe *m*; (*person*) Russe *mf*

rust [rʌst] *s* rouille *f* || *tr* rouiller || *intr* se rouiller

rustic ['rʌstɪk] *adj* rustique; simple, net; (pej) rustaud || *s* paysan *m*, villageois *m*

rustle ['rʌsəl] *s* bruissement *m*; (*of, e.g., a dress*) froufrou *m* || *tr* faire bruire; (*cattle*) (coll) voler || *intr* bruire; (*said, e.g., of a dress*) froufrouter; **to rustle around** (coll) se démener

rust′proof′ *adj* inoxydable

rust•y ['rʌstɪ] *adj* (*comp* -ier; *super* -iest*) rouillé

rut [rʌt] *s* ornière *f*; (zool) rut *m*

ruthless ['ruθlɪs] *adj* impitoyable

rye [raɪ] *s* seigle *m*; whisky *m* de seigle

S

S, s [ɛs] *s* XIXᵉ lettre de l'alphabet

Sabbath ['sæbəθ] *s* sabbat *m*; dimanche *m*

sabbat′ical year′ [sə'bætɪkəl] *s* année *f* de congé

saber ['sebər] *s* sabre *m* || *tr* sabrer

sable ['sebəl] *adj* noir || *s* (*animal, fur*) zibeline *f*; noir *m*; **sables** vêtements *mpl* de deuil

sabotage ['sæbə,taʒ] *s* sabotage *m* || *tr* & *intr* saboter

saccharin ['sækərɪn] *s* saccharine *f*

sachet [sæ'ʃe] *s* sachet *m* (à parfums)

sack [sæk] *s* sac *m*; (*wine*) xérès *m* || *tr* mettre en sac; (mil) saccager; (coll) saquer, congédier

sack′cloth′ *s* grosse toile *f* d'emballage, serpillière *f*; (*worn for penitence*) cilice *m*; **in sackcloth and ashes** sous le sac et la cendre

sacrament ['sækrəmənt] *s* sacrement *m*

sacramental [,sækrə'mɛntəl] *adj* sacramentel

sacred ['sekrɪd] *adj* sacré

sa′cred cow′ *s* (fig) monstre *m* sacré

sacrifice ['sækrɪ,faɪs] *s* sacrifice *m*; **at a sacrifice** à perte || *tr* & *intr* sacrifier

sacrilege ['sækrɪlɪdʒ] *s* sacrilège *m*

sacrilegious [,sækrɪ'lɪdʒəs], [,sækrɪ'lidʒəs] *adj* sacrilège

sacristan ['sækrɪstən] *s* sacristain *m*

sad [sæd] *adj* (*comp* sadder; *super* saddest) triste

sadden ['sædən] *tr* attrister || *intr* s'attrister

saddle ['sædəl] *s* selle *f* || *tr* seller; **to saddle with** charger de, encombrer de

sad′dle•bag′ *s* sacoche *f* (de selle)

saddlebow ['sædəl,bo] *s* arçon *m* de devant

saddler ['sædlər] *s* sellier *m*

sad′dle•tree′ *s* arçon *m*

sadist ['sædɪst], ['sedɪst] *s* sadique *mf*

sadistic [sæ'dɪstɪk], [se'dɪstɪk] *adj* sadique

sadness ['sædnɪs] *s* tristesse *f*

sad′ sack′ *s* (slang) bidasse *mf*

safe [sef] *adj* (*from danger*) sûr; (*unhurt*) sauf; (*margin*) certain; **safe and sound** sain et sauf; **safe from** à l'abri de || *s* coffre-fort *m*, caisse *f*

safe′-con′duct *s* sauf-conduit *m*

safe′-depos′it box′ *s* coffre *m* à la banque; coffret de sûreté (Canad)

safe′guard′ *s* sauvegarde *f* || *tr* sauvegarder

safe′keep′ing *s* bonne garde *f*

safe•ty ['sefti] *adj* de sûreté || *s* (*pl* -ties*) (*state of being safe*) sécurité *f*, sûreté *f*; (*avoidance of danger*) salut *m*

safe′ty belt′ *s* ceinture *f* de sécurité

safe′ty match′ *s* allumette *f* de sûreté

safe′ty pin′ *s* épingle *f* de sûreté

safe′ty ra′zor *s* rasoir *m* de sûreté

safe′ty valve′ *s* soupape *f* de sûreté

saffron ['sæfrən] *adj* safrané || *s* safran *m*

sag [sæg] *s* affaissement *m* || *v* (*pret* &

pp **sagged**; *ger* **sagging**) *intr* s'affaisser

sagacious [sə'geʃəs] *adj* sagace

sage [sedʒ] *adj* sage ‖ *s* sage *mf*; (*plant*) sauge *f*

sage'brush' *s* armoise *f*

sail [sel] *s* voile *f*; (*sails*) voilure *f*; (*of windmill*) aile *f*; **full sail** toutes voiles dehors; **to set sail** mettre les voiles; **to take a sail** faire une promenade à la voile; **to take in sail** baisser pavillon ‖ *tr* (*a ship*) gouverner, commander; (*to travel over*) naviguer sur ‖ *intr* naviguer; **to sail along the coast** côtoyer; **to sail into** (coll) assaillir

sail'boat' *s* bateau *m* à voiles

sail'cloth' *s* toile *f* à voile

sailing ['selɪŋ] *s* navigation *f*; (*working of ship*) manœuvre *f*; (*of pleasure craft*) voile *f*

sail'ing ves'sel *s* voilier *m*

sail'mak'er *s* voilier *m*

sailor ['selər] *s* marin *m*; (*simple crewman*) matelot *m*

saint [sent] *adj* & *s* saint *m*

saint'hood *s* sainteté *f*

saintliness ['sentlɪnɪs] *s* sainteté *f*

Saint' Vi'tus's dance' ['vaɪtəsəz] *s* (pathol) danse *f* de Saint-Guy

sake [sek] *s*—**for the sake of** pour l'amour de, dans l'intérêt de; **for your sake** pour vous

salable ['seləbəl] *adj* vendable

salacious [sə'leʃəs] *adj* lubrique

salad ['sæləd] *s* salade *f*

sal'ad bowl' *s* saladier *m*

salary ['sæləri] *s* (*pl* -ries) salaire *m*

sale [sel] *s* vente *f*; **for sale** en vente; **on sale** en solde, en réclame

sales' clerk' *s* vendeur *m*

sales'girl' *s* vendeuse *f*, demoiselle *f* de magasin

sales'la'dy *s* (*pl* -dies) vendeuse *f*

sales'man *s* (*pl* -men) vendeur *m*, commis *m*

sales'man·ship' *s* l'art *m* de vendre

sales' promo'tion *s* stimulation *f* de la vente

sales'room' *s* salle *f* de vente

sales' talk' *s* raisonnements *mpl* destinés à convaincre le client

sales' tax' *s* taxe *f* sur les ventes, impôt *m* indirect

saliva [sə'laɪvə] *s* salive *f*

sallow ['sælo] *adj* olivâtre

sal·ly ['sæli] *s* (*pl* -lies) saillie *f*; (mil) sortie *f* ‖ *v* (*pret* & *pp* -lied) *intr* faire une sortie

salmon ['sæmən] *adj* & *s* saumon *m*

saloon [sə'lun] *s* cabaret *m*, estaminet *m*, bistrot *m*; (naut) salon *m*

salt [sɔlt] *s* sel *m* ‖ *tr* saler; **to salt away** (coll) économiser, mettre de côté

salt'cel'lar *s* salière *f*

salt' lick' *s* terrain *m* salifère

salt'pe'ter *s* (*potassium nitrate*) salpêtre *m*; (*sodium nitrate*) nitrate *m* du Chili

salt' pork' *s* salé *m*

salt'sha'ker *s* salière *f*

salt·y ['sɔlti] *adj* (*comp* -ier; *super* -iest) salé

salute [sə'lut] *s* salut *m* ‖ *tr* saluer

salvage ['sælvɪdʒ] *s* sauvetage *m*; biens *mpl* sauvés ‖ *tr* sauver; récupérer

salvation [sæl've/ən] *s* salut *m*

Salva'tion Ar'my *s* Armée *f* du Salut

salve [sæv], [sav] *s* onguent *m*, pommade *f*; baume *m* ‖ *tr* appliquer un onguent sur; (fig) apaiser

sal·vo ['sælvo] *s* (*pl* -vos or -voes) salve *f*

Samaritan [sə'mærɪtən] *adj* samaritain ‖ *s* Samaritain *m*

same [sem] *adj* & *pron indef* même (before noun); **at the same time** en même temps, au même moment, à la fois; **it's all the same to me** ça m'est égal; **just the same, all the same** malgré tout, quand même; **the same ... as** le même ... que

sameness ['semnɪs] *s* monotonie *f*

sample ['sæmpəl] *s* échantillon *m* ‖ *tr* échantillonner; essayer

sam'ple cop'y *s* (*pl* -ies) numéro *m* spécimen

sancti·fy ['sæŋktɪ,faɪ] *v* (*pret* & *pp* -fied) *tr* sanctifier

sanctimonious [,sæŋktɪ'monɪ·əs] *adj* papelard, bigot

sanction ['sæŋkʃən] *s* sanction *f* ‖ *tr* sanctionner

sanctu·ary ['sæŋktʃu,eri] *s* (*pl* -ies) sanctuaire *m*; refuge *m*, asile *m*

sand [sænd] *s* sable *m* ‖ *tr* sablonner

sandal ['sændəl] *s* sandale *f*

san'dal·wood' *s* santal *m*

sand'bag' *s* sac *m* de sable

sand' bar' *s* banc *m* de sable

sand'blast' *s* jet *m* de sable; (*apparatus*) sableuse *f* ‖ *tr* sabler

sand'box' *s* (rr) sablière *f*

sand'glass' *s* sablier *m*

sand'pa'per *s* papier *m* de verre ‖ *tr* polir au papier de verre

sand'pi'per *s* bécasseau *m*

sand'stone' *s* grès *m*

sand'storm' *s* tempête *f* de sable

sandwich ['sændwɪtʃ] *s* sandwich *m* ‖ *tr* intercaler

sand'wich man' *s* homme-affiche *m*

sand·y ['sændi] *adj* (*comp* -ier; *super* -iest) sablonneux; (*hair*) blond roux

sane [sen] *adj* sain, équilibré; (*principles*) raisonnable

sanguine ['sæŋgwɪn] *adj* confiant, optimiste; (*countenance*) sanguin

sanitary ['sænɪ,teri] *adj* sanitaire

san'itary nap'kin *s* serviette *f* hygiénique

sanitation [,sænɪ'teʃən] *s* hygiène *f*, salubrité *f*; (*drainage*) assainissement *m*

sanity ['sænɪti] *s* santé *f* mentale; bon sens *m*

Santa Claus ['sæntə,klɔz] *s* le père Noël

sap [sæp] *s* sève *f*; (mil) sape *f*; (coll) poire *f*, nigaud *m* ‖ *v* (*pret* & *pp* sapped; *ger* sapping) *tr* tirer la sève de; (*to weaken*) affaiblir; (mil) saper

sapling ['sæplɪŋ] s jeune arbre m; jeune homme m

sapphire ['sæfaɪr] s saphir m

Saracen ['særəsən] adj sarrasin || s Sarrasin m

sarcasm ['sɑrkæzəm] s sarcasme m

sardine [sɑr'din] s sardine f; **packed in like sardines** serrés comme des harengs

Sardinia [sɑr'dɪnɪ-ə] s Sardaigne; la Sardaigne

Sardinian [sɑr'dɪnɪ-ən] adj sarde || s (language) sarde m; (person) Sarde mf

sarsaparilla [ˌsɑrsəpə'rɪlə] s salsepareille f

sash [sæʃ] s ceinture f; (of window) châssis m

sash/ win/dow s fenêtre f à guillotine

sas·sy ['sæsi] adj (comp -sier; super -siest) (coll) impudent, effronté

satchel ['sætʃəl] s sacoche f; (of schoolboy) carton m

sate [set] tr soûler

sateen [sæ'tin] s satinette f

satellite ['sætəˌlaɪt] adj & s satellite m

sat/ellite coun/try s pays m satellite

satiate ['seʃɪˌet] adj rassasié || tr rassasier

satin ['sætɪn] s satin m

satire ['sætaɪr] s satire f

satiric(al) [sə'tɪrɪk(əl)] adj satirique

satirize ['sætɪˌraɪz] tr satiriser

satisfaction [ˌsætɪs'fækʃən] s satisfaction f

satisfactory [ˌsætɪs'fæktəri] adj satisfaisant

satis·fy ['sætɪsˌfaɪ] v (pret & pp -fied) tr satisfaire; (a requirement, need, etc.) satisfaire (with dat) || intr satisfaire

saturate ['sætʃəˌret] tr saturer

Saturday ['sætərdi] s samedi m

Saturn ['sætərn] s Saturne m

sauce [sɔs] s sauce f; (coll) insolence f, toupet m || tr assaisonner || [sɔs], [sæs] tr (coll) parler avec impudence à

sauce/pan/ s casserole f

saucer ['sɔsər] s soucoupe f

sau·cy ['sɔsi] adj (comp -cier; super -ciest) impudent, effronté

sauerkraut ['saʊrˌkraʊt] s choucroute f

saunter ['sɔntər] s flânerie f || intr flâner

sausage ['sɔsɪdʒ] s saucisse f, saucisson m

sauté [so'te] tr sauter, faire sauter

savage ['sævɪdʒ] adj & s sauvage mf

savant ['sævənt] s savant m, érudit m

save [sev] prep sauf, excepté f || tr sauver; (money) épargner; (time) gagner || intr économiser

saving ['sevɪŋ] adj économe || **savings** spl épargne f, économies fpl

sav/ings account/ s dépôt m d'épargne

sav/ings and loan/ associa/tion s caisse f d'épargne et de prêt

sav/ings bank/ s caisse f d'épargne

sav/ings book/ s livret m de caisse d'épargne

savior ['sevjər] s sauveur m

Saviour ['sevjər] s Sauveur m

savor ['sevər] s saveur f || tr savourer || intr—**to savor of** avoir un goût de

savor·y ['sevəri] adj (comp -ier; super -iest) (taste) savoureux; (smell) odorant || s (pl -ies) (bot) sariette f

saw [sɔ] s scie f; (proverb) dicton m || tr scier

saw/dust/ s sciure f de bois

saw/horse/ s chevalet m

saw/mill/ s scierie f

Saxon ['sæksən] adj saxon || s (language) saxon m; (person) Saxon m

saxophone ['sæksəˌfon] s saxophone m

say [se] s mot m; **to have one's say** avoir son mot à dire || v (pret & pp said [sed]) tr dire; **I should say not!** absolument pas!; **I should say so!** je crois bien!; **it is said** on dit; **no sooner said than done** sitôt dit, sitôt fait; **that is to say** c'est-à-dire; **to go without saying** aller sans dire; **you said it!** (coll) et comment!, tu parles!

saying ['se·ɪŋ] s proverbe m

scab [skæb] s croûte f; (strikebreaker) jaune m; canaille f

scabbard ['skæbərd] s fourreau m

scab·by ['skæbi] adj (comp -bier; super -biest) croûteux; (coll) vil

scabrous ['skæbrəs] adj scabreux; (uneven) rugueux

scads [skædz] spl (slang) des tas mpl

scaffold ['skæfəld] s échafaud m; (used in construction) échafaudage m

scaffolding ['skæfəldɪŋ] s échafaudage m

scald [skɔld] tr échauder

scale [skel] s (of thermometer, map, salaries, etc.) échelle f; (for weighing) plateau m; (incrustation) tartre m; (bot, zool) écaille f; (mus) échelle; **on a large scale** sur une grande échelle; **scales** balance f; **to tip the scales** faire pencher la balance || tr escalader; **to scale down** réduire à l'échelle de

scallop ['skɑləp] s coquille f Saint-Jacques, peigne m, pétoncle m; (thin slice of meat) escalope f; (on edge of cloth) feston m || tr (the edges) denteler, découper; (culin) gratiner et cuire au four et à la crème

scalp [skælp] s cuir m chevelu; (Indian trophy) scalp m || tr scalper; (tickets) (coll) faire le trafic de; (to hoodwink) (slang) abuser de

scalpel ['skælpəl] s scalpel m

scal·y ['skeli] adj (comp -ier; super -iest) écailleux

scamp [skæmp] s garnement m

scamper ['skæmpər] intr courir allégrement; **to scamper away** or **off** détaler

scan [skæn] v (pret & pp scanned; ger scanning) tr scruter; (e.g., a page) jeter un coup d'œil sur; (verses) scander; (telv) balayer

scandal ['skændəl] s scandale m

scandalize ['skændəˌlaɪz] tr scandaliser

scandalous ['skændələs] adj scandaleux

Scandinavian [ˌskændɪ'nevɪ-ən] adj

scandinave ‖ s (*language*) scandinave m; (*person*) Scandinave mf

scanning ['skænɪŋ] s (telv) balayage m

scant [skænt] adj maigre; (*attire*) léger, sommaire ‖ tr réduire; lésiner sur

scant·y ['skænti] adj (comp -ier; super -iest) rare, maigre; léger

scapegoat ['skep,got] s bouc m émissaire

scar [skɑr] s cicatrice f; (*on face*) balafre f ‖ v (pret & pp scarred; ger scarring) tr balafrer

scarce [skers] adj rare, peu abondant

scarcely ['skersli] adv à peine, presque pas; ne ... guère §90; scarcely ever rarement

scarci·ty ['skersɪti] s (pl -ties) manque m, pénurie f

scare [sker] s panique f, effroi m ‖ tr épouvanter, effrayer; to scare away or off effaroucher; to scare up (coll) procurer ‖ intr s'effaroucher

scare'crow' s épouvantail m

scarf [skɑrf] s (pl scarfs or scarves [skɑrvz]) foulard m, écharpe f

scarlet ['skɑrlɪt] adj s & écarlate f

scar'let fe'ver s scarlatine f

scar·y ['skeri] adj (comp -ier; super -iest) (*easily frightened*) (coll) peureux, ombrageux; (*causing fright*) (coll) effrayant

scathing ['skeðɪŋ] adj cinglant

scatter ['skætər] tr éparpiller; (*a mob*) disperser ‖ intr se disperser

scat'ter-brained' adj (coll) étourdi

scenari·o [sɪ'neri,o], [sɪ'nɑri,o] s (pl -os) scénario m

scene [sin] s scène f; (*landscape*) paysage m; behind the scenes dans les coulisses; to make a scene faire une scène

scener·y ['sinəri] s (pl -ies) paysage m; (theat) décor m, décors

sceneshifter ['sin,ʃɪftər] s (theat) machiniste m

scenic ['sinɪk], ['senɪk] adj pittoresque; spectaculaire; (theat) scénique

sce'nic rail'way s chemin m de fer en miniature des parcs d'attraction

scent [sent] s odeur f; parfum m; (*trail*) piste f ‖ tr parfumer; (*an odor*) renifler; (*game as a dog does; a trap*) flairer

scepter ['septər] s sceptre m

sceptic ['skeptɪk] adj & s sceptique mf

sceptical ['skeptɪkəl] adj sceptique

scepticism ['skeptɪ,sɪzəm] s scepticisme m

schedule ['skedjʊl] s (*of work*) plan m; (*of things to do*) emploi m du temps; (*of prices*) barème m; (rr) horaire m; on schedule selon l'horaire; selon les prévisions ‖ tr classer; inscrire au programme, à l'horaire, etc.; scheduled to speak prévu comme orateur

scheme [skim] s projet m; machination f, truc m ‖ tr projeter ‖ intr ruser

schemer ['skimər] s faiseur m de projets; intrigant m

schism ['sɪzəm] s schisme m, scission f

scholar ['skɑlər] s (*pupil*) écolier m;

(*learned person*) érudit m, savant m; (*holder of scholarship*) boursier m

scholarly ['skɑlərli] adj érudit, savant ‖ adv savamment

schol'ar·ship' s érudition f; (*award*) bourse f

scholasticism [skə'læstɪ,sɪzəm] s scolastique f

school [skul] adj scolaire; school zone (public sign) ralentir école ‖ s école f; (*of a university*) faculté f; (*of fish*) banc m ‖ tr instruire, discipliner

school' board' s conseil m de l'instruction publique

school'book' s livre m de classe, livre scolaire

school'boy' s écolier m

school'girl' s écolière f

school'house' s maison f d'école

schooling ['skulɪŋ] s instruction f, enseignement m; discipline f; frais mpl de l'éducation

schoolmarm ['skul,mɑrm] s maîtresse f d'école, institutrice f

school'mas'ter s maître m d'école, instituteur m

school'mate' s camarade mf d'école, condisciple m

school'room' s classe f, salle f de classe

school'teach'er s enseignant m, instituteur m

school'yard' s cour f de récréation

school' year' s année f scolaire

schooner ['skunər] s schooner m, goélette f

sciatica [saɪ'ætɪkə] s (pathol) sciatique f

science ['saɪəns] s science f

sci'ence fic'tion s science-fiction f

scientific [,saɪən'tɪfɪk] adj scientifique

scientist ['saɪəntɪst] s homme m de science, savant m

scimitar ['sɪmɪtər] s cimeterre m

scintillate ['sɪntɪ,let] intr scintiller, étinceler

scion ['saɪən] s héritier m; (hort) scion m

scissors ['sɪzərz] s & spl ciseaux mpl

scis'sors-grind'er s rémouleur m; (orn) engoulevent m

scoff [skɔf], [skɑf] s raillerie f ‖ intr —to scoff at se moquer de

scold [skold] s harpie f ‖ tr & intr gronder

scolding ['skoldɪŋ] s gronderie f

scoop [skup] s pelle f à main; (*for coal*) seau m; (*kitchen utensil*) louche f; (*of dredge*) godet m; (journ) nouvelle f sensationnelle; (naut) écope f ‖ tr creuser; to scoop out excaver à la pelle; (*water*) écoper

scoot [skut] intr (coll) détaler

scooter ['skuter] s trottinette f, patinette f

scope [skop] s (*field*) domaine m, étendue f; (*reach*) portée f, envergure f; to give free scope to donner libre carrière à

scorch [skɔrtʃ] tr roussir; flétrir, dessécher

scorched'-earth' pol'icy s politique f de la terre brûlée

scorching ['skɔrtʃɪŋ] adj brûlant; caustique, mordant

score [skor] s compte m, total m; (twenty) vingtaine f; (notch) entaille f; (on metal) rayure f, éraflure f; (mus) partition f; (sports) score m, marque f; **on that score** à cet égard; **to keep score** compter les points || tr (to notch) entailler; (to criticize) blâmer; (metal) rayer, érafler; (a success) remporter; (e.g., a goal) marquer; (mus) orchestrer

score'board' s tableau m

score'keep'er s marqueur m

scorn [skɔrn] s mépris m, dédain m || tr mépriser, dédaigner || intr—**to scorn** to dédaigner de

scorpion ['skɔrpɪ-ən] s scorpion m

Scot [skɑt] s Écossais m

Scotch [skɑtʃ] adj écossais; (slang) avare, chiche || s (dialect) écossais m; whisky m écossais; **the Scotch** les Écossais || (l.c.) s (wedge) cale f; (notch) entaille f || tr caler; entailler; (a rumor) étouffer

Scotch'man s (pl -men) Écossais m

Scotch' pine' s pin m sylvestre

Scotch' tape' s (trademark) ruban m cellulosique, adhésif m scotch

Scotland ['skɑtlənd] s Écosse f; l'Écosse

Scottish ['skɑtɪʃ] adj écossais || s (dialect) écossais m; **the Scottish** les Écossais

scoundrel ['skaundrəl] s coquin m, fripon m, canaille f

scour [skaur] tr récurer; (e.g., the countryside) parcourir

scourge [skʌrdʒ] s nerf m de bœuf, discipline f; (fig) fléau m || tr fouetter, flageller

scout [skaut] adj scout || s éclaireur m; (boy scout) scout m, éclaireur; a **good scout** (coll) un brave gars || tr reconnaître; (to scoff at) repousser avec dédain || intr aller en reconnaissance

scouting ['skautɪŋ] s scoutisme m

scout'ing par'ty s (pl -ties) (mil) détachement m de reconnaissance

scout'mas'ter s chef m de troupe

scowl [skaul] s renfrongnement m || intr se renfrogner

scram [skræm] v (pret & pp scrammed; ger scramming) intr (coll) ficher le camp; **scram!** (coll) fiche-moi le camp!

scramble ['skræmbəl] s bousculade f || tr brouiller || intr se disputer; grimper à quatre pattes

scram'bled eggs' spl œufs mpl brouillés

scrap [skræp] s ferraille f; (little bit) petit morceau m; (fight) (coll) chamaillerie f || v (pret & pp scrapped; ger scrapping) tr mettre au rebut || intr (coll) se chamailler

scrap'book' s album m de découpures

scrape [skrep] s grincement m; (coll) mauvaise affaire f || tr gratter, râcler

scrap' heap' s tas m de rebut

scrap' i'ron s ferraille f

scrap' pa'per s bloc-notes m; (refuse) papier m de rebut

scratch [skrætʃ] s égratignure f; **to start from scratch** partir de rien || tr gratter, égratigner

scratch' pad' s bloc-notes m, brouillon m

scratch' pa'per s bloc-notes m

scrawl [skrɔl] s griffonnage m || tr & intr griffonner

scraw-ny ['skrɔnɪ] adj (comp -nier; super -niest) décharné, mince

scream [skrim] s cri m perçant; (slang) personne f ridicule; (slang) chose f ridicule || tr & intr pousser des cris, crier

screech [skritʃ] s cri m perçant || intr jeter des cris perçants

screech' owl' s chat-huant m; (barn owl) effraie f

screen [skrin] s écran m; grillage m en fil de fer, treillis m métallique; (for sifting) crible m || tr abriter; (candidates) trier; (mov) porter à l'écran

screen' grid' s (electron) grille f blindée

screen'play' s scénario m; drame m filmé

screen' test' s bout m d'essai

screw [skru] s vis f; (naut) hélice f; **to have a screw loose** (coll) être toqué || tr visser; **to screw off** dévisser; **to screw tight** visser à bloc; **to screw up** (one's courage) rassembler || intr se visser

screw'ball' adj & s (slang) extravagant m, loufoque m

screw'driv'er s tournevis m

screw' eye' s vis f à œil

screw' press' s cric m à vis

screw' pro'pel'ler s hélice f

screw-y ['skru-i] adj (comp -ier; super -iest) (slang) loufoque

scrib'al er'ror ['skraɪbəl] s faute f de copiste

scribble ['skrɪbəl] s griffonnage m || tr & intr griffonner

scribe [skraɪb] s scribe m

scrimmage ['skrɪmɪdʒ] s mêlée f

scrimp [skrɪmp] tr lésiner sur || intr lésiner

scrip [skrɪp] s monnaie f scripturale, script m

script [skrɪpt] s manuscrit m, original m; (handwriting) écriture f; (mov) scénario m; (typ) script m

scriptural ['skrɪptʃərəl] adj biblique

scripture ['skrɪptʃər] s citation f tirée de l'Écriture; **Scripture** l'Écriture f; **the Scriptures** les Écritures

script'writ'er s scénariste mf

scrofula ['skrɑfjələ] s scrofule f

scroll [skrol] s rouleau m; (archit) volute f

scroll'work' s ornementation f en volute

scro-tum ['skrotəm] s (pl -ta [tə] or -tums) scrotum m, bourses fpl

scrub [skrʌb] adj rabougri || s arbuste m rabougri; personne f malingre; (sports) joueur m novice || v (pret &

pp scrubbed; *ger* scrubbing) *tr* frotter, nettoyer, récurer

scrub/bing brush/ *s* brosse *f* de chiendent

scrub/wom/an *s* (*pl* -wom/en) nettoyeuse *f*

scruff [skrʌf] *s* nuque *f*

scruple ['skrupəl] *s* scrupule *f*

scrupulous ['skrupjələs] *adj* scrupuleux

scrutinize ['skrutɪˌnaɪz] *tr* scruter

scruti-ny ['skrutɪnɪ] *s* (*pl* -nies) examen *m* minutieux

scuff [skʌf] *s* usure *f* || *tr* érafler

scuffle ['skʌfəl] *s* bagarre *f* || *intr* se bagarrer

scull [skʌl] *s* (*stern oar*) godille *f*; aviron *m* de couple || *tr* godiller || *intr* ramer en couple

sculler-y ['skʌlərɪ] *s* (*pl* -ies) arrière-cuisine *f*

scul/lery maid/ *s* laveuse *f* de vaisselle

scullion ['skʌljən] *s* marmiton *m*

sculptor ['skʌlptər] *s* sculpteur *m*

sculptress ['skʌlptrɪs] *s* femme *f* sculpteur

sculpture ['skʌlptʃər] *s* sculpture *f* || *tr & intr* sculpter

scum [skʌm] *s* écume *f*; (*of society*) canaille *f* || *v* (*pret & pp* scummed; *ger* scumming) *tr & intr* écumer

scum-my ['skʌmɪ] *adj* (*comp* -mier; *super* -miest) écumeux; (fig) vil

scurrilous ['skʌrɪləs] *adj* injurieux, grossier, outrageant

scur-ry ['skʌrɪ] *v* (*pret & pp* -ried) *intr* —to scurry around galoper; to scurry away or off déguerpir

scur-vy ['skʌrvɪ] *adj* (*comp* -vier; *super* -viest) méprisable, vil || *s* scorbut *m*

scuttle ['skʌtəl] *s* (*bucket for coal*) seau *m* à charbon; (*trap door*) trappe *f*; (*run*) course *f* précipitée; (naut) écoutillon *m* || *tr* saborder || *intr* filer, déguerpir

scut/tle-butt/ *s* (coll) on-dit *m*

scythe [saɪð] *s* faux *f*

sea [si] *s* mer *f*; at sea en mer; (fig) désorienté; by the sea au bord de la mer; to put to sea prendre le large

sea/board/ *s* littoral *m*

sea/ breeze/ *s* brise *f* de mer

sea/coast/ *s* côte *f*, littoral *m*

seafarer ['siˌfɛrər] *s* marin *m*; voyageur *m* par mer

sea/food/ *s* fruits *mpl* de mer, marée *f*

seagoing ['siˌgo-ɪŋ] *adj* de haute mer, au long cours

sea/ gull/ *s* mouette *f*, goéland *m*

seal [sil] *s* sceau *m*; (zool) phoque *m* || *tr* sceller

sea/ legs/ *spl* pied *m* marin

sea/ lev/el *s* niveau *m* de la mer

seal/ing wax/ *s* cire *f* à cacheter

seal/skin/ *s* peau *f* de phoque

seam [sim] *s* couture *f*; (*of metal*) joint *m*; (geol) fissure *f*; (min) couche *f*

sea/man *s* (*pl* -men) marin *m*

sea/ mile/ *s* mille *m* marin

seamless ['simlɪs] *adj* sans couture; (mach) sans soudure

seamstress ['simstrɪs] *s* couturière *f*

seam-y ['simɪ] *adj* (*comp* -ier; *super* -iest) plein de coutures; vil, vilain

séance ['se-ɑns] *s* séance *f* de spiritisme

sea/plane/ *s* hydravion *m*

sea/port/ *s* port *m* de mer

sea/ pow/er *s* puissance *f* maritime

sear [sɪr] *adj* desséché || *s* cicatrice *f* de brûlure || *tr* dessécher; marquer au fer rouge

search [sʌrtʃ] *s* recherche *f*; in search of à la recherche de || *tr & intr* fouiller; to search for chercher

searching ['sʌrtʃɪŋ] *adj* pénétrant, scrutateur

search/light/ *s* projecteur *m*

search/ war/rant *s* mandat *m* de perquisition

seascape ['siˌskep] *s* panorama *m* marin; (*painting*) marine *f*

sea/ shell/ *s* coquille *f* de mer

sea/shore/ *s* bord *m* de la mer

sea/sick/ *adj* —to be seasick avoir le mal de mer

sea/sick/ness *s* mal *m* de mer

season ['sizən] *s* saison *f* || *tr* assaisonner; (*troops*) aguerrir; (*wood*) sécher

seasonal ['sizənəl] *adj* saisonnier

seasoning ['sizənɪŋ] *s* assaisonnement *m*

sea/son's greet/ings *spl* meilleurs souhaits *mpl*, tous mes vœux *mpl*

sea/son tick/et *s* carte *f* d'abonnement

seat [sit] *s* place *f*, siège *m*; (*of trousers*) fond *m*; have a seat asseyez-vous donc; keep your seat restez assis || *tr* asseoir; (*a number of persons*) contenir; to be seated (*to sit down*) s'asseoir; (*to be in sitting posture*) être assis

seat/ belt/ *s* ceinture *f* de sécurité

seat/ cov/er *s* (aut) housse *f*

SEATO ['sito] *s* (acronym) (Southeast Asia Treaty Organization) OTASE *f*

sea/ wall/ *s* digue *f*

sea/way/ *s* voie *f* maritime; (*of ship*) sillage *m*; (*rough sea*) mer *f* dure

sea/weed/ *s* algue *f* marine; plante *f* marine

sea/wor/thy *adj* en état de naviguer

secede [sɪˈsid] *intr* se séparer, faire sécession

secession [sɪˈsɛʃən] *s* sécession *f*

seclude [sɪˈklud] *tr* tenir éloigné; (*to shut up*) enfermer

secluded *adj* retiré, écarté

seclusion [sɪˈkluʒən] *s* retraite *f*

second ['sekənd] *adj & pron* deuxième (*masc, fem*); second; the Second deux, e.g., John the Second Jean deux; to be second in command commander en second; to be second to none ne le céder à personne || *s* deuxième *m*, second *m*; (*in time; musical interval; of angle*) seconde *f*; (*in a duel*) témoin *m*, second *m*; (com) article *m* de deuxième qualité; the second (*in dates*) le deux || *adv* en second lieu || *tr* affirmer; (*to back up*) seconder

secondar-y ['sekənˌderɪ] *adj* secondaire || *s* (*pl* -ies) (elec) secondaire *m*

sec'ond best' s pis-aller m

sec'ond-best' adj (everyday) de tous les jours; **to come off second-best** être battu

sec'ond-class' adj de second ordre; (rr) de seconde classe

sec'ond-hand' s trotteuse f

sec'ond-hand' adj d'occasion, de seconde main

sec'ond-hand book'dealer s bouquiniste mf

sec'ond lieuten'ant s sous-lieutenant m

sec'ond mate' s (naut) second maître m

sec'ond-rate' adj de second ordre

sec'ond sight' s seconde vue f

sec'ond wind' s—**to get one's second wind** reprendre haleine

secre-cy ['sikrəsi] s (pl -cies) secret m; **in secrecy** en secret

secret ['sikrɪt] adj & s secret m; **in secret** en secret

secretar-y ['sekrɪ,teri] s (pl -ies) secrétaire mf; (desk) secrétaire m

se'cret bal'lot s scrutin m secret

secrete [sɪ'krit] tr cacher; (physiol) sécréter

secretive [sɪ'kritɪv] adj cachottier

se'cret serv'ice s deuxième bureau m

sect [sekt] s secte f

sectarian [sek'terɪ·ən] adj sectaire; (school) confessionnel || sectaire mf

section ['sekʃən] s section f

sectionalism ['sekʃənə,lɪzəm] s régionalisme m

sec'tion hand' s cantonnier m

sector ['sektər] s secteur m; (instrument) compas m de proportion

secular ['sekjələr] adj (worldly, of this world) séculier; (century-old) séculaire || s séculier m

secularism ['sekjələ,rɪzəm] s laïcisme m, mondanité f

secure [sɪ'kjur] adj sûr || tr obtenir; (to make fast) fixer

securi-ty [sɪ'kjuriti] s (pl -ties) sécurité f; (pledge) garantie f; (person) garant m; **securities** valeurs fpl

sedan [sɪ'dæn] s (aut) conduite f intérieure

sedan' chair' s chaise f à porteurs

sedate [sɪ'det] adj calme, discret

sedation [sɪ'deʃən] s sédation f

sedative ['sedətɪv] adj & s sédatif m

sedentary ['sedən,teri] adj sédentaire

sedge [sedʒ] s (Carex) laîche f

sediment ['sedɪmənt] s sédiment m

sedition [sɪ'dɪʃən] s sédition f

seditious [sɪ'dɪʃəs] adj séditieux

seduce [sɪ'd(j)us] tr séduire

seducer [sɪ'd(j)usər] s séducteur m

seduction [sɪ'dʌkʃən] s séduction f

seductive [sɪ'dʌktɪv] adj séduisant

sedulous ['sedʒələs] adj assidu

see [si] s (eccl) siège m || v (pret **saw** [sɔ]; pp **seen** [sin]) tr voir; **see other side** (turn the page) voir au dos; **to see s.o. play, to see s.o. playing** voir jouer qn, voir qn qui joue; **to see s.th. played** voir jouer q.ch. || intr voir; **to see through s.o.** (fig) voir venir qn

seed [sid] s graine f, semence f; sperme

m; (in fruit) pépin m; (fig) germe m; **to go to seed** monter en graine || tr semer, ensemencer

seed'bed' s semis m

seeder ['sidər] s (mach) semeuse f

seedling ['sidlɪŋ] s semis m

seed-y ['sidi] adj (comp -ier; super -iest) (coll) râpé, miteux

seeing ['si·ɪŋ] adj voyant || s vue f || conj vu que

See'ing Eye' dog' s chien m d'aveugle

seek [sik] v (pret & pp **sought** [sɔt]) tr chercher || intr chercher; **to seek after** rechercher; **to seek to** chercher à

seem [sim] intr sembler

seemingly ['simɪŋli] adv en apparence

seem-ly ['simli] adj (comp -lier; super -liest) gracieux; (correct) bienséant

seep [sip] intr suinter

seer [sɪr] s prophète m, voyant m

see'saw' s balançoire f, bascule f; (motion) va-et-vient m || intr basculer, balancer

seethe [sið] intr bouillonner

segment ['segmənt] s segment m

segregate ['segrɪ,get] tr mettre à part, isoler

segregation [,segrɪ'geʃən] s ségrégation f

segregationist [,segrɪ'geʃənɪst] s ségrégationniste mf

seismograph ['saɪzmə,græf], ['saɪzmə,graf] s sismographe m

seismology [saɪz'malədʒi] s sismologie f

seize [siz] tr saisir

seizure ['siʒər] s prise f; (law) saisie f; (pathol) attaque f

seldom ['seldəm] adv rarement

select [sɪ'lekt] adj choisi || tr choisir, sélectionner

selection [sɪ'lekʃən] s sélection f

selective [sɪ'lektɪv] adj sélectif

self [self] adj de même || s (pl **selves** [selvz]) moi m, être m; **all by one's self** tout seul; **one's better self** son meilleur côté m || pron—**payable to self** payable à moi-même

self'-addressed' en'velope s enveloppe f adressée à l'envoyeur

self'-cen'tered adj égocentrique

self'-con'fidence s confiance f en soi

self'-con'fident adj sûr de soi

self'-con'scious adj gêné, embarrassé

self'-control' s sang-froid m, maîtrise f de soi

self'-defense' s autodéfense f; **in self-defense** en légitime défense

self'-deni'al s abnégation f

self'-deter'mina'tion s autodétermination f

self'-dis'cipline s discipline f personnelle

self'-ed'ucated adj autodidacte

self'-employed' adj indépendant

self'-esteem' s amour-propre m

self'-ev'ident adj évident aux yeux de tout le monde

self'-explan'ator'y adj qui s'explique de soi-même

self'-gov'ernment s autonomie f; maîtrise f de soi

self'-impor'tant *adj* suffisant, présomptueux

self'-indul'gence *s* faiblesse *f* envers soi-même, intempérance *f*

self'-in'terest *s* intérêt *m* personnel

selfish ['sɛlfɪʃ] *adj* égoïste

selfishness ['sɛlfɪnɪs] *s* égoïsme *m*

selfless ['sɛlflɪs] *adj* désintéressé

self'-love' *s* égoïsme *m*

self'-made man' *s* (*pl* men') fils *m* de ses œuvres

self'-por'trait *s* autoportrait *m*

self'-possessed' *adj* maître de soi

self'-pres'erva'tion *s* conservation *f* de soi-même

self'-reli'ant *adj* sûr de soi, assuré

self'-respect'ing *adj* correct, honorable

self'-right'eous *adj* pharisaïque

self'-sac'rifice' *s* abnégation *f*

self'same' *adj* identique

self'-sat'isfied' *adj* content de soi

self'-seek'ing *adj* égoïste, intéressé

self'-serv'ice *s* libre-service *m*

self'-serv'ice laun'dry *s* (*pl* -dries) laverie *f* libre-service, laverie automatique

self'-start'er *s* démarreur *m* automatique

self'-styled' *adj* soi-disant

self'-taught' *adj* autodidacte

self'-tim'er *s* (phot) retardateur *m*

self'-willed' *adj* obstiné, entêté

self'-wind'ing *adj* à remontage automatique

sell [sɛl] *v* (pret & pp **sold** [sold]) *tr* vendre; **to sell out** solder; (*to betray*) vendre || *intr* vendre; **to sell for** (*e.g.*, ten dollars) se vendre à

seller ['sɛlər] *s* vendeur *m*

Selt'zer wa'ter ['sɛltsər] *s* eau *f* de Seltz

selvage ['sɛlvɪdʒ] *s* (*of fabric*) lisière *f*; (*of lock*) gâche *f*

semantic [sɪ'mæntɪk] *adj* sémantique || **semantics** *s* sémantique *f*

semaphore ['sɛmə ˌfor] *s* sémaphore *m*

semblance ['sɛmbləns] *s* semblant *m*

semen ['simən] *s* sperme *m*, semence *f*

semester [sɪ'mɛstər] *adj* semestriel || *s* semestre *m*

semicircle ['sɛmɪ ˌsʌrkəl] *s* demi-cercle *m*

semicolon ['sɛmɪ ˌkolən] *s* point-virgule *m*

semiconductor [ˌsɛmɪkən'dʌktər] *s* semi-conducteur *m*

semiconscious [ˌsɛmɪ'kɑnʃəs] *adj* à demi conscient

semifinal [ˌsɛmɪ'faɪnəl] *adj* avant-dernière || *s* demi-finale *f*

semilearned [ˌsɛmɪ'lʌrnɪd] *adj* à moitié savant

seminar ['sɛmɪ ˌnɑr] *s* séminaire *m*

seminary ['sɛmɪ ˌnɛri] *s* (*pl* -ies) séminaire *m*

semiprecious [ˌsɛmɪ'prɛʃəs] *adj* fin, semi-précieux

Semite ['sɛmaɪt], ['simaɪt] *s* Sémite *mf*

Semitic [sɪ'mɪtɪk] *adj* (*e.g.*, language) sémitique; (*person*) sémite

semitrailer ['sɛmɪ ˌtrelər] *s* semi-remorque *f*

senate ['sɛnɪt] *s* sénat *m*

senator ['sɛnətər] *s* sénateur *m*

send [sɛnd] *v* (pret & pp **sent** [sɛnt]) *tr* envoyer; (rad, telv) émettre; **to send back** renvoyer; **to send out** envoyer; **to send s.o.** for s.th. or s.o. envoyer qn chercher q.ch. or qn; **to send s.o. to** + *inf* envoyer qn + *inf* || *intr* (rad, telv) émettre; **to send for** envoyer chercher

sender ['sɛndər] *s* expéditeur *m*; (telg) transmetteur *m*

send'-off' *s* manifestation *f* d'adieu

senile ['sinaɪl], ['sɪnɪl] *adj* sénile

senility [sɪ'nɪlɪti] *s* sénilité *f*

senior ['sinjər] *adj* aîné; (*clerk, partner, etc.*) principal; (*rank*) supérieur; père, *e.g.*, **Maurice Laporte, Senior** Maurice Laporte père || *s* aîné *m*, doyen *m*; (*U.S. upperclassman*) étudiant *m* de dernière année

sen'ior cit'izens *spl* les vieilles gens *fpl*

seniority [sin'jɑrɪti], [sin'jɔrɪti] *s* ancienneté *f*, doyenneté *f*

sen'ior staff' *s* personnel *m* hors classe

sensation [sɛn'seʃən] *s* sensation *f*

sensational [sɛn'seʃənəl] *adj* sensationnel

sense [sɛns] *s* sens *m*; (*wisdom*) bon sens; (*e.g.*, *of pain*) sensation *f*; **to make sense out of** arriver à comprendre || *tr* percevoir, sentir

senseless ['sɛnslɪs] *adj* (lacking perception) insensible; (*unconscious*) sans connaissance; (*unreasonable*) insensé

sense' of guilt' *s* remords *m*

sense' or'gans *spl* organes *mpl* des sens

sensibility [ˌsɛnsɪ'brlɪti] *s* (*pl* -ties) sensibilité *f*; susceptibilité *f*

sensible ['sɛnsɪbəl] *adj* sensible; (endowed with good sense) sensé, raisonnable

sensitive ['sɛnsɪtɪv] *adj* sensible; (*touchy*) susceptible, sensitif

sensitize ['sɛnsɪ ˌtaɪz] *tr* sensibiliser

sensory ['sɛnsəri] *adj* sensoriel

sensual ['sɛn/ʊ-əl] *adj* sensuel

sensuous ['sɛn/ʊ-əs] *adj* sensuel

sentence ['sɛntəns] *s* (gram) phrase *f*; (law) sentence *f* || *tr* condamner

sentiment ['sɛntɪmənt] *s* sentiment *m*

sentimental [ˌsɛntɪ'mɛntəl] *adj* sentimental

sentinel ['sɛntɪnəl] *s* sentinelle *f*; **to stand sentinel** être en sentinelle

sentry ['sɛntri] *s* (*pl* -tries) sentinelle *f*

sen'try box' *s* guérite *f*

separate ['sɛpərɪt] *adj* séparé || ['sɛpə ˌret] *tr* séparer || *intr* se séparer

separation [ˌsɛpə're/ən] *s* séparation *f*

September [sɛp'tɛmbər] *s* septembre *m*

septic ['sɛptɪk] *adj* septique

sepulcher ['sɛpəlkər] *s* sépulcre *m*

sequel ['sikwəl] *s* conséquence *f*; (*something following*) suite *f*

sequence ['sikwəns] *s* succession *f*, ordre *m*; (cards, mov) séquence *f*; (*of tenses*) (gram) concordance *f*

sequester [sɪ'kwɛstər] *tr* séquestrer

sequin ['sikwɪn] *s* paillette *f*

ser-aph ['serəf] *s* (*pl* -aphs or -aphim [əfɪm]) séraphin *m*

Serb [sʌrb] *adj* serbe ‖ *s* Serbe *mf*

sere [sɪr] *adj* sec, desséché

serenade [ˌserə'ned] *s* sérénade *f* ‖ *tr* donner une sérénade à ‖ *intr* donner des sérénades

serene [sɪ'rin] *adj* serein

serenity [sɪ'rɛnɪti] *s* sérénité *f*

serf [sʌrf] *s* serf *m*

serfdom ['sʌrfdəm] *s* servage *m*

serge [sʌrdʒ] *s* serge *f*

sergeant ['sɑrdʒənt] *s* sergent *m*

ser'geant-at-arms' *s* (*pl* sergeants-at-arms) huissier *m*, sergent *m* d'armes

ser'geant ma'jor *s* (*pl* sergeant majors) sergent-major *m*

serial ['sɪrɪ-əl] *adj* de série ‖ *s* roman-feuilleton *m*

serially ['sɪrɪ-əli] *adv* en série; (*in installments*) en feuilleton

se'rial num'ber *s* numéro *m* d'ordre; (*mil*) numéro *m* matricule

se-ries ['sɪriz] *s* (*pl* -ries) série *f*; **in series** en série

serious ['sɪrɪ-əs] *adj* sérieux

seriousness ['sɪrɪ-əsnɪs] *s* sérieux *m*, gravité *f*

sermon ['sʌrmən] *s* sermon *m*

sermonize ['sʌrmə,naɪz] *tr* & *intr* sermonner

serpent ['sʌrpənt] *s* serpent *m*

se-rum ['sɪrəm] *s* (*pl* -rums or -ra [rə]) sérum *m*

servant ['sʌrvənt] *s* domestique *mf*; (*civil servant*) fonctionnaire *mf*; (*housemaid*) bonne *f*; (*humble servant*) (fig) serviteur *m*

serv'ant girl' *s* servante *f*

serv'ant prob'lem *s* crise *f* domestique

serve [sʌrv] *tr* servir; **to serve s.o. as** servir à qn de; **to serve time** purger une peine ‖ *intr* servir; **to serve as** (*to function as*) servir de; (*to be useful for*) servir à

service ['sʌrvɪs] *s* service *m*; (eccl) office *m*; **the services** (mil) les forces *fpl* armées ‖ *tr* entretenir, réparer

serviceable ['sʌrvɪsəbəl] *adj* utile, pratique; résistant

serv'ice club' *s* foyer *m* du soldat

serv'ice-man' *s* (*pl* -men') réparateur *m*; (mil) militaire *m*

serv'ice rec'ord *s* état *m* de service

serv'ice sta'tion *s* station-service *f*

serv'ice stripe' *s* chevron *m*, galon *m*

servile ['sʌrvɪl] *adj* servile

servitude ['sʌrvɪ,t(j)ud] *s* servitude *f*

sesame ['sɛsəmɪ] *s* sésame *m*; **open sesame!** sésame, ouvre-toi!

session ['sɛʃən] *s* session *f*; **to be in session** siéger

set [set] *adj* (*rule*) établi; (*price*) fixe; (*time*) fixé; (*smile*; *locution*) figé ‖ *s* ensemble *m*; (*of dishes, linen, etc.*) assortiment *m*; (*of dishes*) service *m*; (*of kitchen utensils*) batterie *f*; (*of pans*; *of weights*; *of tickets*) série *f*; (*of tools, chessmen, oars, etc.*) jeu *m*; (*of books*) collection *f*; (*of diamonds*) parure *f*; (*of tennis*)

set *m*; (*of cement*) prise *f*; (*of a garment*) tournure *f*; (*group of persons*) coterie *f*; (mov) plateau *m*; (rad) poste *m*; (theat) mise *f* en scène; **set of false teeth** dentier *m*; **set of teeth** denture *f* ‖ *v* (*pret* & *pp* set; *ger* setting) *tr* mettre, placer, poser; (*a date, price, etc.*) fixer; (*a gem*) monter; (*a trap*) tendre; (*a timepiece*) mettre à l'heure, régler; (*the hair*) mettre en plis; (*a bone*) remettre; **to set aside** mettre de côté; annuler; **to set going** mettre en marche; **to set off** mettre en valeur; (*e.g., a rocket*) lancer, tirer ‖ *intr* se figer; (*said of sun, moon, etc.*) se coucher; (*said of hen*) couver; (*said of garment*) tomber; **to set about, to set out** to se mettre à; **to set upon** attaquer

set'back' *s* revers *m*, échec *m*

set'screw' *s* vis *f* de pression

settee [se'ti] *s* canapé *m*; (*for two*) canapé à deux places, causeuse *f*

setting ['setɪŋ] *s* cadre *m*; (*of a gem*) monture *f*; (*of cement*) prise *f*; (*of sun*) coucher *m*; (*of a bone*) recollement *m*; (*of a watch*) réglage *m*; (*adjustment*) ajustage *m*; (theat) mise *f* en scène

set'ting-up' ex'er**cises** *spl* gymnastique *f* rythmique, gymnastique suédoise

settle ['setəl] *tr* établir; (*a region*) coloniser; (*a dispute, account, debt, etc.*) régler; (*a problem*) résoudre; (*doubts, fears, etc.*) calmer ‖ *intr* se coloniser; se calmer; (*said of weather*) se mettre au beau; (*said of building*) se tasser; (*said of sediment, dust, etc.*) se déposer; (*said of liquid*) se clarifier; **to settle down** s'établir; (*to be less wild*) se ranger; **to settle down to** (*a task*) s'appliquer à; **to settle on** se décider pour

settlement ['setəlmənt] *s* établissement *m*, colonie *f*; (*of an account, dispute, etc.*) règlement *m*; (*of a debt*) liquidation *f*; (*settlement house*) œuvre *f* sociale

settler ['setlər] *s* colon *m*

set'up' *s* port *m*, maintien *m*; (*of the parts of a machine*) installation *f*; (coll) organisation *f*

seven ['sevən] *adj* & *pron* sept ‖ *s* sept *m*; **seven o'clock** sept heures

seventeen ['sevən'tin] *adj, pron,* & *s* dix-sept *m*

seventeenth ['sevən'tinθ] *adj* & *pron* dix-septième (*masc, fem*); **the Seventeenth** dix-sept, e.g., **John the Seventeenth** Jean dix-sept ‖ *s* dix-septième *m*; **the seventeenth** (*in dates*) le dix-sept

seventh ['sevənθ] *adj* & *pron* septième (*masc, fem*); **the Seventh** sept, e.g., **John the Seventh** Jean sept ‖ *s* septième *m*; **the seventh** (*in dates*) le sept

seventieth ['sevəntɪ-ɪθ] *adj* & *pron* soixante-dixième (*masc, fem*) ‖ *s* soixante-dixième *m*

seven-ty ['sevənti] *adj* & *pron* soixante-dix ‖ *s* (*pl* -ties) soixante-dix *m*

sev'enty-first' adj & pron soixante et onzième (masc, fem) || s soixante et onzième m

sev'enty-one' adj, pron, & s soixante et onze m

sever ['sevər] tr séparer; (relations) rompre || intr se séparer

several ['sevərəl] adj & pron indef plusieurs

severance ['sevərəns] s séparation f; (of relations) rupture f; (of communications) interruption f

sev'erance pay' s indemnité f pour cause de renvoi

severe [sɪ'vɪr] adj sévère; (weather) rigoureux; (pain) aigu; (illness) grave

sew [so] v (pret sewed; pp sewed or sewn) tr & intr coudre

sewage ['s(j)u·ɪdʒ] s eaux fpl d'égouts

sewer ['s(j)u·ər] s égout m || ['so·ər] s (one who sews) couseur m

sewerage ['s(j)u·ərɪdʒ] s (removal) vidange f; (system) système m d'égouts; (sewage) eaux fpl d'égouts

sew'ing bas'ket s nécessaire m de couture

sew'ing machine' s machine f à coudre

sex [sɛks] s sexe m; the fair sex le beau sexe; the sterner sex le sexe fort; to have sex with (coll) avoir des rapports avec

sex' appeal' s sex-appeal m

sextant ['sɛkstənt] s sextant m

sextet [sɛks'tɛt] s sextuor m

sexton ['sɛkstən] s sacristain m

sexual ['sɛkʃu·əl] adj sexuel

sex·y ['sɛksi] adj (comp -ier; super -iest) (slang) aguichant, grivois; (story) érotique

sh [ʃ] interj chut!

shab·by ['ʃæbi] adj (comp -bier; super -biest) râpé, usé; (mean) mesquin; (house) délabré

shack [ʃæk] s cabane f, case f

shackle ['ʃækəl] s boucle f; shackles entraves fpl || tr entraver

shad [ʃæd] s alose f

shade [ʃed] s ombre f; (of lamp) abat-jour m; (of window) store m; (hue; slight difference) nuance f; (little bit) soupçon m || tr ombrager; (to make gradual changes in) nuancer

shadow ['ʃædo] s ombre f || tr ombrager; (to spy on) filer, pister

shad'ow gov'ernment s gouvernement m fantôme

shadowy ['ʃædo·i] adj ombreux, sombre; (fig) vague, obscur

shad·y ['ʃedi] adj (comp -ier; super -iest) ombreux, ombragé; (coll) louche

shaft [ʃæft], [ʃɑft] s (of mine; of elevator) puits m; (of feather) tige f; (of arrow) bois m; (of column) fût m, tige; (of flag) mât m; (of wagon) brancard m, limon m; (of motor) arbre m; (of light) rayon m; (to make fun of s.o.) trait m

shag·gy ['ʃægi] adj (comp -gier; super -giest) poilu, à longs poils

shag'gy dog' sto'ry s (pl -ries) histoire f sans queue ni tête

shake [ʃek] s secousse f || v (pret shook [ʃʊk]; pp shaken) tr secouer; (the head) hocher, secouer; (one's hand) serrer; to shake down faire tomber; (a thermometer) secouer; (slang) escroquer; to shake off secouer; (to get rid of) se débarrasser de; to shake up (a liquid) agiter, (fig) ébranler || intr trembler

shake'down' s (slang) exaction f, concussion f

shaker ['ʃekər] s (for salt) salière f; (for cocktails) shaker m

shake'up' s bouleversement m; (reorganization) remaniement m

shak·y ['ʃeki] adj (comp -ier; super -iest) tremblant, chancelant; (hand; writing) tremblé; (voice) tremblotant

shall [ʃæl] v (cond should [ʃʊd]) aux used to express 1) the future indicative, e.g., I shall arrive j'arriverai; 2) the future perfect indicative, e.g., I shall have arrived je serai arrivé; 3) the potential mood, e.g., what shall he do? que doit-il faire?

shallow ['ʃælo] adj peu profond; (dish) plat; (fig) creux, superficiel || shallows spl haut-fond m

sham [ʃæm] adj feint, simulé || s feinte f, simulacre m; (person) imposteur m || v (pret & pp shammed) ger shamming) tr feindre, simuler

sham' bat'tle s combat m simulé

shambles ['ʃæmbəlz] spl boucherie f; ravage m, ruine f; (disorder) pagaille f

shame [ʃem] s honte f; shame on you!, for shame! quelle honte!; what a shame! quel dommage! || tr faire honte à

shame'faced' adj penaud

shameful ['ʃemfəl] adj honteux

shameless ['ʃemlɪs] adj éhonté

shampoo [ʃæm'pu] s shampooing m || tr (the hair) laver; (a person) faire un shampooing à

shamrock ['ʃæmrɑk] s trèfle m d'Irlande

Shanghai ['ʃæŋhaɪ], [ʃæŋ'haɪ] s Changhaï m (l.c.) tr (coll) racoler

Shangri-la [ˌʃæŋgrɪ'lɑ] s le pays de Cocagne

shank [ʃæŋk] s jambe f, tibia m; (of horse) canon m; (of anchor) verge f; (culin) manche m; (of a column) fût m

shan·ty ['ʃænti] s (pl -ties) masure f, bicoque f

shan'ty·town' s bidonville m

shape [ʃep] s forme f; in bad shape (coll) mal en point; out of shape déformé || tr former || intr se former; to shape up prendre forme; avancer

shapeless ['ʃeplɪs] adj informe

shape·ly ['ʃepli] adj (comp -lier; super -liest) bien proportionné, bien fait, svelte

share [ʃɛr] s part f; (of stock in a company) action f || tr partager || intr to share in prendre part à, participer à

sharecropper ['ʃɛr ˌkrɑpər] s métayer m

share'hold'er s actionnaire mf

shark [ʃɑrk] *s* requin *m*; (*swindler*) escroc *m*; (slang) as *m*, expert *m*

sharp [ʃɑrp] *adj* aigu; (*wind, cold, pain, fight, criticism, edge, trot, mind*) vif; (*knife*) tranchant; (*point; tongue*) acéré; (*slope*) raide; (*curve*) prononcé; (*turn*) brusque; (*photograph*) net; (*hearing*) fin; (*step, gait*) rapide; (*taste*) piquant; (*reprimand*) vert; (*keen*) éveillé; (*cunning*) rusé, fin; (*mus*) dièse; (*stylish*) (coll) chic; **sharp features** traits *mpl* accentués || *adv* vivement; brusquement; précis, sonnant, tapant, e.g., **at four o'clock sharp** à quatre heures précises, sonnantes, or tapantes; **to stop short** s'arrêter net ou pile || *s* (mus) dièse *m* || *tr* (mus) diéser

sharpen [ʃɑrpən] *tr* aiguiser; (*a pencil*) tailler || *intr* s'aiguiser

sharpener [ʃɑrpənər] *s* aiguisoir *m*

sharper [ʃɑrpər] *s* filou *m*, tricheur *m*

sharp'shoot'er *s* tireur *m* d'élite

shatter [ʃætər] *tr* fracasser, briser || *intr* se fracasser, se briser

shat'ter-proof' *adj* de sécurité

shave [ʃev] *s*—**to get a shave** se faire raser, se faire faire la barbe; **to have a close shave** (coll) l'échapper belle || *tr* (*hair, beard, etc.*) raser; (*a person*) faire la barbe à, raser; (*e.g., wood*) doler; (*e.g., expenses*) rogner || *intr* se raser, se faire la barbe

shaving [ʃevɪŋ] *s* rasage *m*; **shavings** rognures *fpl*, copeaux *mpl*

shav'ing brush' *s* blaireau *m*

shav'ing soap' *s* savon *m* à barbe

shawl [ʃɔl] *s* châle *m*, fichu *m*

she [ʃi] *s* femelle *f* || *pron pers* elle §85, §87; ce §82B; **she who** celle qui §83

sheaf [ʃif] *s* (*pl* **sheaves** [ʃivz]) gerbe *f*; (*of papers*) liasse *f*

shear [ʃɪr] *s* lame *f* de ciseau; **shears** ciseaux *mpl*; (*to cut metal*) cisaille *f* || *v* (*pret* **sheared**; *pp* **sheared** or **shorn** [ʃɔrn]) *tr* (*sheep*) tondre; (*velvet*) ciseler; (*metal*) cisailler; **to shear off** couper

sheath [ʃiθ] *s* (*pl* **sheaths** [ʃiðz]) gaine *f*, fourreau *m*

sheathe [ʃið] *tr* envelopper; (*a sword*) rengainer

shed [ʃɛd] *s* hangar *m*; (*for, e.g., tools*) remise *f*; (*line from which water flows in two directions*) ligne *f* de faîte || *v* (*pret* & *pp* **shed**; *ger* **shedding**) *tr* répandre, verser; (*e.g., leaves*) perdre; (*e.g., light; skin*) jeter

sheen [ʃin] *s* lustre *m*, brillant *m*

sheep [ʃip] *s* (*pl* **sheep**) mouton *m*; (*ewe*) brebis *f*

sheep'dog' *s* chien *m* de berger

sheep'fold' *s* bergerie *f*

sheepish [ʃipɪʃ] *adj* penaud; timide

sheep'skin' *s* (*undressed*) peau *f* de mouton; (*dressed*) basane *f*; (*diploma*) (coll) peau d'âne

sheep'skin jack'et *s* canadienne *f*

sheer [ʃɪr] *adj* transparent; léger; (*stocking*) extra-fin; (*steep*) à pic; (fig) pur; (fig) vif, e.g., **by sheer**

---

force de vive force || *intr* faire une embardée

sheet [ʃit] *s* (*e.g., for the bed*) drap *m*; (*of paper*) feuille *f*; (*of metal*) tôle *f*, lame *f*; (*of water*) nappe *f*; (*of ice*) couche *f*; (naut) écoute *f*; **white as a sheet** blanc comme un linge

sheet' light'ning *s* fulguration *f*, éclairs *mpl* en nappe

sheet' met'al *s* tôle *f*

sheet' mu'sic *s* morceaux *mpl* de musique

sheik [ʃik] *s* cheik *m*; (coll) tombeur *m* de femmes

shelf [ʃɛlf] *s* (*pl* **shelves** [ʃɛlvz]) tablette *f*, planche *f*; (*of cupboard; of library*) rayon *m*; (geog) plateau *m*; **on the shelf** au rancart, laissé à l'écart

shell [ʃɛl] *s* coque *f*, coquille *f*; (*of nut*) écale *f*, coque; (*of pea*) cosse *f*; (*of oyster, clam, etc.*) écaille *f*; (*of building, ship, etc.*) carcasse *f*; (cartridge) cartouche *f*; (*projectile*) obus *m*; (*long, narrow racing boat*) yole *f* || *tr* écaler, écosser; (mil) bombarder, pilonner; **to shell out** (coll) débourser || *intr*—**to shell out** (coll) casquer

shel·lac [ʃəˈlæk] *s* laque *f*, gomme *f* laque || *v* (*pret* & *pp* **-lacked**; *ger* **-lacking**) *tr* laquer; (slang) tabasser

shell'fish' *s* fruits *mpl* de mer, coquillages *mpl*

shell' hole' *s* entonnoir *m*, trou *m* d'obus

shell' shock' *s* commotion *f* cérébrale

shelter [ʃɛltər] *s* abri *m* || *tr* abriter

shelve [ʃɛlv] *tr* (*a book*) ranger; (*merchandise*) entreposer; (*a project, a question, etc., by putting it aside*) enterrer, classer; (*to provide with shelves*) garnir de tablettes, rayons, or planches

shepherd [ʃɛpərd] *s* berger *m*; (fig) pasteur *m* || *tr* veiller sur, guider

shep'herd dog' *s* berger *m*, chien *m* de berger

shepherdess [ʃɛpərdɪs] *s* bergère *f*

sherbet [ʃɑrbət] *s* sorbet *m*

sheriff [ʃɛrɪf] *s* shérif *m*

sher·ry [ʃɛri] *s* (*pl* **-ries**) xérès *m*

shield [ʃild] *s* bouclier *m*; (elec) blindage *m*; (heral, hist) écu *m*, écusson *m* || *tr* protéger; (elec) blinder

shift [ʃɪft] *s* changement *m*; (*in wind, temperature, etc.*) saute *f*; (*group of workmen*) équipe *f* de relais; (fig) expédient *m* || *tr* changer; (*the blame, the guilt, etc.*) rejeter; **to shift gears** changer de vitesse || *intr* changer; changer de place; changer de direction; **to shift for oneself** se débrouiller tout seul

shift' key' *s* touche *f* majuscules

shiftless [ʃɪftlɪs] *adj* mollasse, peu débrouillard

shift·y [ʃɪfti] *adj* (*comp* **-ier**; *super* **-iest**) roublard; (*look*) chafouin; (*eye*) fuyant

shimmer [ʃɪmər] *s* chatoiement *m*, miroitement *m* || *intr* chatoyer, miroiter

shin [ʃɪn] *s* tibia *m*; (culin) jarret *m* ‖ *v* (*pret & pp* **shinned**; *ger* **shinning**) *intr*—to shin up grimper

shin'bone' *s* tibia *m*

shine [ʃaɪn] *s* brillant *m*; (*of cloth, clothing, etc.*) luisant *m*; (*on shoes*) coup *m* de cirage; **to take a shine to** (slang) s'enticher de ‖ *v* (*pret & pp* **shined**) *tr* faire briller, faire reluire; (*shoes*) cirer ‖ *v* (*pret & pp* **shone** [ʃon]) *intr* briller, reluire

shiner [ʃaɪnər] *s* (slang) œil *m* poché

shingle [ʃɪŋgəl] *s* bardeau *m*; (*of doctor, lawyer, etc.*) enseigne *f*; **shingles** (pathol) zona *m*

shining [ʃaɪnɪŋ] *adj* brillant, luisant

shin-y [ʃaɪni] *adj* (*comp* -**ier**; *super* -**iest**) brillant, reluisant; (*from much wear*) lustré

ship [ʃɪp] *s* navire *m*; (*steamer, liner*) paquebot *m*; (*aér*) appareil *m*; (nav) bâtiment *m* ‖ *v* (*pret & pp* **shipped**; *ger* **shipping**) *tr* expédier; (*a cargo; water*) embarquer; (*oars*) armer, rentrer ‖ *intr* s'embarquer

ship'board' *s* bord *m*; **on shipboard** à bord

ship'build'er *s* constructeur *m* de navires

ship'build'ing *s* construction *f* navale

ship'mate' *s* compagnon *m* de bord

shipment [ʃɪpmənt] *s* expédition *f*; (*goods shipped*) chargement *m*

ship'own'er *s* armateur *m*

shipper [ʃɪpər] *s* expéditeur *m*

shipping [ʃɪpɪŋ] *s* embarquement *m*, expédition *f*; (naut) transport *m* maritime

ship'ping clerk' *s* expéditionnaire *mf*

ship'ping mem'o *s* connaissement *m*

ship'ping room' *s* salle *f* d'expédition

ship'shape' *adj & adv* en bon ordre

ship's' pa'pers *spl* papiers *mpl* de bord

ship's' time' *s* heure *f* locale du navire

ship'-to-shore' ra'di•o [ʃɪptə'ʃor] *s* (*pl* -os) liaison *f* radio maritime

ship'wreck' *s* naufrage *m* ‖ *tr* faire naufrager ‖ *intr* faire naufrage

ship'yard' *s* chantier *m* de construction navale or maritime

shirk [ʃʌrk] *tr* manquer à, esquiver ‖ *intr* négliger son devoir

shirred' eggs' [ʃʌrd] *spl* œufs *mpl* pochés à la crème

shirt [ʃʌrt] *s* chemise *f*; **keep your shirt on!** (slang) ne vous emballez pas!; **to lose one's shirt** perdre jusqu'à son dernier sou

shirt'band' *s* encolure *f*

shirt'front' *s* plastron *m* de chemise

shirt'sleeve' *s* manche *f* de chemise; **in shirt sleeves** en bras de chemise

shirt'tails' *spl* pans *mpl* de chemise

shirt'waist' *s* chemisier *m*

shiver [ʃɪvər] *s* frisson *m* ‖ *intr* frissonner

shoal [ʃol] *s* banc *m*, bas-fond *m*

shock [ʃɑk] *s* (*bump, clash*) choc *m*, heurt *m*; (*upset, misfortune, earthquake tremor*) secousse *f*; (*of grain*) gerbe *f*, moyette *f*; (*of hair*) tignasse *f*; (elec) commotion *f*, choc; **to die of**

shock mourir de saisissement ‖ *tr* choquer; (elec) commotionner, choquer

shock' absorb'er [æb,sɔrbər] *s* amortisseur *m*

shocking [ʃɑkɪŋ] *adj* choquant, scandaleux

shock' troops' *spl* troupes *fpl* de choc

shod-dy [ʃɑdi] *adj* (*comp* -**dier**; *super* -**diest**) inférieur, de pacotille

shoe [ʃu] *s* soulier *m*; **to be in the shoes of** être dans la peau de; **to put one's shoes on** se chausser; **to take one's shoes off** se déchausser ‖ *v* (*pret & pp* **shod** [ʃɑd]) *tr* chausser; (*a horse*) ferrer

shoe'black' *s* cireur *m* de bottes

shoe'horn' *s* chausse-pied *m*

shoe'lace' *s* lacet *m*, cordon *m* de soulier

shoe'mak'er *s* cordonnier *m*

shoe' pol'ish *s* cirage *m* de chaussures

shoe'shine' *s* cirage *m* de

shoe' store' *s* magasin *m* de chaussures

shoe'string' *s* lacet *m*, cordon *m* de soulier; **on a shoestring** avec de minces capitaux

shoe'tree' *s* embauchoir *m*, forme *f*

shoo [ʃu] *tr* chasser ‖ *interj* ch!, filez!

shoot [ʃut] *s* (*sprout, twig*) rejeton *m*, pousse *f*; (*for grain, sand, etc.*) goulotte *f*; (*contest*) concours *m* de tir; (*hunting party*) partie *f* de chasse ‖ *v* (*pret & pp* **shot** [ʃɑt]) *tr* tirer; (*a person*) tuer d'un coup de fusil; (*to execute with a discharge of rifles*) fusiller; (*with a camera*) photographier; (*a scene; a motion picture*) tourner, roder; (*the sun*) prendre la hauteur de; (*dice*) jeter; **to shoot down** abattre; **to shoot up** (slang) cribler de balles ‖ *intr* tirer; s'élancer, se précipiter; (*said of pain*) lanciner; (*said of star*) filer; **to shoot at** faire feu sur; (*to strive for*) viser; **to shoot up** (*said of plant*) pousser; (*said of plant*) pousser; (*said of flame*) jaillir; (*said of prices*) augmenter

shooting [ʃutɪŋ] *s* tir *m*; (phot) prise *f* de vues

shoot'ing gal'ler•y *s* (*pl* -**ies**) stand *m* de tir, tir *m*

shoot'ing match' *s* concours *m* de tir

shoot'ing script' *s* découpage *m*

shoot'ing star' *s* étoile *f* filante

shop [ʃɑp] *s* (*store*) boutique *f*; (*workshop*) atelier *m*; **to talk shop** parler boutique, parler affaires ‖ *v* (*pret & pp* **shopped**; *ger* **shopping**) *intr* faire des emplettes, faire des courses; magasiner (Canad); **to go shopping** faire des emplettes, faire des courses; **to shop around** être à l'affût de bonnes occasions; **to shop for** chercher à acheter

shop'girl' *s* vendeuse *f*

shop'keep'er *s* boutiquier *m*

shoplifter [ʃɑp,lɪftər] *s* voleur *m* à l'étalage

shopper [ʃɑpər] *s* acheteur *m*

shopping [ʃɑpɪŋ] *s* achat *m*; (*purchases*) achats *mpl*, emplettes *fpl*

shop'ping bag' *s* sac *m* à provisions
shop'ping cen'ter *s* centre *m* commercial
shop'ping dis'trict *s* quartier *m* commerçant
shop' stew'ard *s* délégué *m* d'atelier
shop' win'dow *s* vitrine *f*, devanture *f*
shop'worn' *adj* défraîchi
shore [ʃor] *s* rivage *m*, rive *f*, bord *m*; (*sandy beach*) plage *f*; **shores** (*poetic*) pays *m* || *tr*—**to shore up** étayer
shore' din'ner *s* dîner *m* de marée
shore' leave' *s* (*nav*) descente *f* à terre
shore'line' *s* ligne *f* de côte
shore' patrol' *s* patrouille *f* de garde-côte; (*police*) (*nav*) police *f* militaire de la marine
short [ʃort] *adj* court; (*person*) petit; (*temper*) brusque; (*phonet*) bref; **in short** en somme; **short of breath** poussif; **to be short for** (coll) être le diminutif de; **to be short of** être à court de || *s* (elec) court-circuit *m*; (mov) court-métrage *m*; **shorts** culotte *f* courte, culotte de sport || *adv* court, de court; **to run short of** être à court de, manquer de; **to sell short** (com) vendre à découvert; **to stop short** s'arrêter net || *tr* (elec) court-circuiter || *intr* (elec) se mettre en court-circuit
shortage [ˈʃortɪdʒ] *s* manque *m*, pénurie *f*; crise *f*, e.g., **housing shortage** crise du logement; (com) déficit *m*; **shortages** manquants *mpl*
short'cake' *s* gâteau *m* recouvert de fruits frais *m*
short'-change' *tr* ne pas rendre assez de monnaie à; (*to cheat*) (coll) rouler
short' cir'cuit *s* court-circuit *m*
short'-cir'cuit *tr* court-circuiter
short'com'ing *s* défaut *m*
short'cut' *s* raccourci *m*
shorten [ˈʃortən] *tr* raccourcir || *intr* se raccourcir
shortening [ˈʃortənɪŋ] *s* raccourcissement *m*; (culin) saindoux *m*
short'hand' *adj* sténographique || *s* sténographie *f*; **to take down in shorthand** sténographier
short'hand notes' *spl* sténogramme *m*
short'hand typ'ist *s* sténodactylo *mf*
short-lived [ˈʃortˈlaɪvd], [ˈʃortˈlɪvd] *adj* de courte durée, bref
shortly [ˈʃortli] *adv* tantôt, sous peu; brièvement; (*curtly*) sèchement; **shortly after** peu après
short'-range' *adj* à courte portée
short' sale' *s* vente *f* à découvert
short'-sight'ed *adj* myope; **to be short-sighted** (fig) avoir la vue courte
short' sto'ry *s* nouvelle *f*, conte *m*
short'-tem'pered *adj* vif, emporté
short'-term' *adj* à court terme
short'wave' *adj* aux petites ondes, aux ondes courtes || *s* petite onde *f*, onde courte
short' weight' *s* poids *m* insuffisant
shot [ʃɑt] *adj* (*silk*) changeant; (*e.g., chances*) (coll) réduit à zéro; (*drunk*) (slang) paf || *s* coup *m* de feu, décharge *f*; (*marksman*) tireur *m*; (*pel-*

lets) petits plombs *mpl*; (*of a rocket into space*) lancement *m*, tir *m*; (*in certain games*) shoot *m*; (*snapshot*) instantané *m*; (mov) plan *m*; (*hypodermic injection*) (coll) piqûre *f*; (*drink of liquor*) (slang) verre *m* d'alcool; **a long shot** un gros risque, une chance sur mille; **to fire a shot** at tirer sur; **to start like a shot** partir comme un trait
shot'gun' *s* fusil *m* de chasse
shot'-put' *s* (sports) lancement *m* du poids
should [ʃʊd] *aux* used to express 1) the present conditional, e.g., **if I waited for him, I should miss the train** si je l'attendais, je manquerais le train; 2) the past conditional, e.g., **if I had waited for him, I should have missed the train** si je l'avais attendu, j'aurais manqué le train; 3) the potential mood, e.g., **he should go at once** il devrait aller aussitôt; e.g., **he should have gone at once** il aurait dû aller aussitôt; 4) a softened affirmation, e.g., **I should like a drink** je prendrais bien quelque chose à boire; e.g., **I should have thought that you would have known better** j'aurais cru que vous auriez été plus avisé
shoulder [ˈʃoldər] *s* épaule *f*; (*of a road*) accotement *m*; **across the shoulder** en bandoulière, en écharpe; **shoulders** (*of a garment*) carrure *f* || *tr* (*a gun*) mettre sur l'épaule; **to shoulder aside** pousser de l'épaule
shoul'der blade' *s* omoplate *f*
shoul'der strap' *s* (*of underwear*) épaulette *f*; (mil) bandoulière *f*
shout [ʃaʊt] *s* cri *m* || *tr* crier; **to shout down** huer || *intr* crier
shove [ʃʌv] *s* poussée *f* || *tr* pousser, bousculer || *intr* pousser; **to shove off** pousser au large; (slang) filer, décamper
shov-el [ˈʃʌvəl] *s* pelle *f* || *v* (*pret & pp* -eled *or* -elled; *ger* -eling *or* -elling) *tr* pelleter; (*e.g., snow*) balayer
show [ʃo] *s* exposition *f*; apparence *f*; (*display*) étalage *m*; (*of hands*) levée *f*; (*each performance*) séance *f*; (mov) film *m*; (theat) spectacle *m*; **to make a show of** faire parade de || *v* (*pret* showed; *pp* shown [ʃon] *or* showed) *tr* montrer; (*one's passport*) présenter; (*a film*) projeter; (*e.g., to the door*) conduire; **to show off** faire étalage de; **to show up** (coll) démasquer || *intr* se montrer; **to show through** transparaître; **to show up** (*against a background*) ressortir; (coll) faire son apparition
show' bill' *s* affiche *f*
show'boat' *s* bateau-théâtre *m*
show' bus'iness *s* l'industrie *f* du spectacle
show'case' *s* vitrine *f*
show'down' *s* cartes *fpl* sur table, moment *m* critique; **to come to a showdown** en venir au fait
shower [ˈʃaʊər] *s* averse *f*, ondée *f*; (*of blows, bullets, kisses, etc.*) pluie

f; (*bath*) douche *f* || *tr* faire pleuvoir; to shower with combler de || *intr* pleuvoir à verse

show'er bath' *s* douche *f*

show' girl' *s* girl *f*

show'man *s* (*pl* -men) impresario *m*; he's a great showman c'est un as pour la mise en scène

show'-off' *s* (coll) m'as-tu-vu *m*

show'piece' *s* pièce *f* maîtresse

show'place' *s* lieu *m* célèbre

show'room' *s* salon *m* d'exposition

show' win'dow *s* vitrine *f*

show•y ['∫'o-i] *adj* (*comp* -ier; *super* -iest) fastueux; (*gaudy*) voyant

shrapnel ['∫ræpnəl] *s* shrapnel *m*, obus *m* à mitraille; éclat *m* d'obus

shred [∫red] *s* morceau *m*, lambeau *m*; not a shred of pas l'ombre de; to tear to shreds mettre en lambeaux || *v* (*pret & pp* shredded or shred; *ger* shredding) *tr* mettre en lambeaux, déchiqueter

shrew [∫ru] *s* (*nagging woman*) mégère *f*; (zool) musaraigne *f*

shrewd [∫rud] *adj* sagace, fin

shriek [∫rik] *s* cri *m* perçant || *intr* pousser un cri perçant

shrike [∫raɪk] *s* pie-grièche *f*

shrill [∫rɪl] *adj* aigu, perçant

shrimp [∫rɪmp] *s* crevette *f*; (*insignificant person*) gringalet *m*

shrine [∫raɪn] *s* tombeau *m* de saint; (*reliquary*) châsse *f*; (*holy place*) lieu *m* saint, sanctuaire *m*

shrink [∫rɪŋk] *v* (*pret* shrank [∫ræŋk] or shrunk [∫rʌŋk]; *pp* shrunk or shrunken) *tr* rétrécir || *intr* se rétrécir; to shrink away or back from reculer devant

shrinkage ['∫rɪŋkɪdʒ] *s* rétrécissement *m*

shriv•el ['∫rɪvəl] *v* (*pret & pp* -eled or -elled; *ger* -eling or -elling) *tr* ratatiner, recroqueviller || *intr* se ratatiner, se recroqueviller

shroud [∫raʊd] *s* linceul *m*; (*veil*) voile *m*; shrouds (naut) haubans *mpl* || *tr* ensevelir; voiler

Shrove' Tues'day [∫rov] *s* mardi *m* gras

shrub [∫rʌb] *s* arbuste *m*

shrubber•y ['∫rʌbəri] *s* (*pl* -ies) bosquet *m*

shrug [∫rʌg] *s* haussement *m* d'épaules || *v* (*pret & pp* shrugged; *ger* shrugging) *tr* (*one's shoulders*) hausser; to shrug off minimiser; ne tenir aucun compte de || *intr* hausser les épaules

shudder ['∫ʌdər] *s* frisson *m*, frémissement *m* || *intr* frissonner, frémir

shuffle ['∫ʌfəl] *s* (*of cards*) battement *m*, mélange *m*; (*of feet*) frottement *m*; (*change of place*) déplacement *m* || *tr* (*cards*) battre; (*the feet*) traîner; (*to mix up*) mêler, brouiller || *intr* battre les cartes; traîner les pieds

shuf'fle-board' *s* jeu *m* de palets

shun [∫ʌn] *v* (*pret & pp* shunned; *ger* shunning) *tr* éviter, fuir

shunt [∫ʌnt] *tr* garer, manœuvrer; (elec) shunter, dériver

shut [∫ʌt] *adj* fermé || *v* (*pret & pp* shut; *ger* shutting) *tr* fermer; to shut in enfermer; to shut off couper; to shut up enfermer; (coll) faire taire || *intr* se fermer; shut up! (slang) tais-toi!, ferme-la!

shut'down' *s* fermeture *f*

shutter ['∫ʌtər] *s* volet *m*, contrevent *m*; (*over store window*) rideau *m*; (phot) obturateur *m*

shuttle ['∫ʌtəl] *s* navette *f* || *intr* faire la navette

shut'tle train' *s* navette *f*

shy [∫aɪ] *adj* (*comp* shyer or shier; *super* shyest or shiest) timide, sauvage; (*said of horse*) ombrageux; I am shy a dollar il me faut un dollar; to be shy of se méfier de || *v* (*pret & pp* shied) *intr* (*said of horse*) faire un écart; to shy away from éviter

shyster ['∫aɪstər] *s* (coll) avocat *m* marron

Sia•mese [‚saɪ·ə'miz] *adj* siamois || *s* (*pl* -mese) Siamois *m*

Si'amese twins' *spl* frères *mpl* siamois

Siberian [saɪ'bɪrɪ·ən] *adj* sibérien || *s* Sibérien *m*

sibyl ['sɪbɪl] *s* sibylle *f*

sic [sɪk], [sɪk] *adv* sic || [sɪk] *v* (*pret & pp* sicked; *ger* sicking) *tr*—sic 'em! (coll) pille!; to sic on lancer après

Sicilian [sɪ'sɪljən] *adj* sicilien || *s* Sicilien *m*

Sicily ['sɪsɪli] *s* Sicile *f*; la Sicile

sick [sɪk] *adj* malade; to be sick and tired of (coll) en avoir plein le dos de, en avoir marre de; to be sick at or to one's stomach avoir mal au cœur, avoir des nausées; to take sick tomber malade

sick'bed' *s* lit *m* de malade

sicken ['sɪkən] *tr* rendre malade || *intr* tomber malade; (*to be disgusted*) être écœuré

sickening ['sɪkənɪŋ] *adj* écœurant, dégoûtant

sick' head'ache *s* migraine *f* avec nausées

sickle ['sɪkəl] *s* faucille *f*

sick' leave' *s* congé *m* de maladie

sick•ly ['sɪkli] *adj* (*comp* -lier; *super* -liest) maladif, débile

sickness ['sɪknɪs] *s* maladie *f*; nausée *f*

side [saɪd] *adj* latéral, de côté || *s* côté *m*; (*of phonograph*) face *f*; (*of team, government, etc.*) camp *m*, parti *m*, côté; this side up (*on package*) haut || *intr*—to side with prendre le parti de

side' arms' *spl* armes *fpl* de ceinturon

side'board' *s* buffet *m*, desserte *f*

side'burns' *spl* favoris *mpl*

side' dish' *s* plat *m* d'accompagnement

side' door' *s* porte *f* latérale, porte *f* de service

side' effect' *s* effet *m* secondaire

side' en'trance *s* entrée *f* latérale

side' glance' *s* regard *m* de côté

side' is'sue *s* question *f* d'intérêt secondaire

side'line' *s* occupation *f* secondaire; on the sidelines sans y prendre part

sidereal [saɪ'dɪrɪ-əl] adj sidéral
side' road' s chemin m de traverse
side' sad'dle adv en amazone
side' show' s spectacle m forain; (fig) événement m secondaire
side' slip' s glissade f sur l'aile
side' split'ting adj désopilant
side' step' s écart m
side'-step' v (pret & pp -stepped; ger -stepping) tr éviter || intr faire un pas de côté
side' stroke' s nage f sur le côté
side'track' s voie f de garage || tr écarter, dévier; (rr) aiguiller sur une voie de garage
side' view' s vue f de profil
side'walk' s trottoir m
side'walk café' s terrasse f de café
sideward ['saɪdwərd] adj latéral || adv latéralement, de côté
side'ways' adj latéral || adv latéralement, de côté
side' whisk'ers spl favoris mpl
side'wise' adj latéral || adv latéralement, de côté
siding ['saɪdɪŋ] s (rr) voie f d'évitement, voie de garage
sidle ['saɪdəl] intr avancer de biais; to sidle up to se couler auprès de
siege [sidʒ] s siège m; to lay siege to mettre le siège devant
siesta [si'estə] s sieste f; to take a siesta faire la sieste
sieve [sɪv] s crible m, tamis m || tr passer au crible, au tamis
sift [sɪft] tr passer au crible, passer au tamis; (flour) tamiser; (fig) examiner soigneusement
sigh [saɪ] s soupir m || intr soupirer
sight [saɪt] s vue f; (of firearm) mire f; (of telescope, camera, etc.) viseur m; chose f digne d'être vue; a sight of (coll) énormément de; at sight de vue; à livre ouvert; by sight de vue; in sight of à la vue de; sad sight spectacle m navrant; sights curiosités fpl; to catch sight of apercevoir; what a sight you are! comme vous voilà fait! || tr & intr viser
sight' draft' s (com) effet m à vue
sight'-read' v (pret & pp -read [ˌred]) tr & intr lire à livre ouvert; (mus) déchiffrer
sight' read'er s déchiffreur m
sight'see'ing s tourisme m; to go sightseeing visiter les curiosités
sightseer ['saɪtˌsi·ər] s touriste mf, excursionniste mf
sign [saɪn] s signe m; (on a store) enseigne f || tr signer; to sign up engager, embaucher || intr signer; to sign off (rad) terminer l'émission; to sign up for (coll) s'inscrire à
sig·nal ['sɪgnəl] adj signalé, insigne || s signal m || v (pret & pp -naled or -nalled; ger -naling or -nalling) tr faire signe à, signaler || intr faire des signaux
sig'nal tow'er s tour f de signalisation
signature ['sɪgnətʃər] s signature f; (mus) armature f; (rad) indicatif m
sign'board' s panneau m d'affichage

signer ['saɪnər] s signataire mf
sig'net ring' ['sɪgnɪt] s chevalière f
significance [sɪg'nɪfɪkəns] s importance f; (meaning) signification f
significant [sɪg'nɪfɪkənt] adj important; significatif
signi·fy ['sɪgnɪˌfaɪ] v (pret & pp -fied) tr signifier
sign'post' s poteau m indicateur
silence ['saɪləns] s silence m || tr faire taire, réduire au silence
silent ['saɪlənt] adj silencieux
si'lent mov'ie s film m muet
silhouette [ˌsɪlu'et] s silhouette f || tr silhouetter
silicon ['sɪlɪkən] s silicium m
silicone ['sɪlɪˌkon] s silicone f
silk [sɪlk] s soie f
silk'-cotton tree' s fromager m
silken ['sɪlkən] adj soyeux
silk' hat' s haut-de-forme m
silk'-stock'ing adj aristocratique || s aristocrate mf
silk'worm' s ver m à soie
silk·y ['sɪlki] adj (comp -ier; super -iest) soyeux
sill [sɪl] s (of window) rebord m; (of door) seuil m; (of walls) sablière f
sil·ly ['sɪli] adj (comp -lier; super -liest) sot, niais
si·lo ['saɪlo] s (pl -los) silo m || tr ensiler
silt [sɪlt] s vase f
silver ['sɪlvər] s argent m || tr argenter; (a mirror) étamer
sil'ver-fish' s (ent) poisson m d'argent
sil'ver foil' s feuille f d'argent
sil'ver lin'ing s beau côté m, côté brillant
sil'ver plate' s argenterie f
sil'ver screen' s écran m
sil'ver-smith' s orfèvre m
sil'ver spoon' s—born with a silver spoon in one's mouth né coiffé
sil'ver-tongued' adj à la langue dorée, éloquent
sil'ver-ware' s argenterie f
similar ['sɪmɪlər] adj semblable
similari·ty [ˌsɪmɪ'lærɪti] s (pl -ties) ressemblance f, similitude f
simile ['sɪmɪli] s comparaison f
simmer ['sɪmər] tr mijoter || intr mijoter; to simmer down s'apaiser
Simon ['saɪmən] s Simon m; Simon says ... (game) Caporal a dit ...
simper ['sɪmpər] s sourire m niais || intr sourire bêtement
simple ['sɪmpəl] adj & s simple m
sim'ple-mind'ed adj simple, naïf; niais
simpleton ['sɪmpəltən] s niais m
simpli·fy ['sɪmplɪˌfaɪ] v (pret & pp -fied) tr simplifier
simulate ['sɪmjəˌlet] tr simuler
simultaneous [ˌsaɪməl'teni·əs], [ˌsɪməl'teni·əs] adj simultané
sin [sɪn] s péché m || v (pret & pp sinned; ger sinning) intr pécher
since [sɪns] adv & prep depuis || conj depuis que; (inasmuch as) puisque
sincere [sɪn'sɪr] adj sincère
sincerity [sɪn'serɪti] s sincérité f
sine [saɪn] s (trig) sinus m

sinecure ['saɪnɪ,kjur], ['sɪnɪ,kjur] *s* sinécure *f*

sinew ['sɪnju] *s* tendon *m*; (*fig*) nerf *m*, force *f*

sinful ['sɪnfəl] *adj* (*person*) pécheur; (*act, intention*) coupable

sing [sɪŋ] *v* (*pret* sang [sæŋ] *or* sung [sʌŋ]; *pp* sung) *tr & intr* chanter

singe [sɪndʒ] *v* (*ger* singeing) *tr* roussir; (*poultry*) flamber

singer ['sɪŋər] *s* chanteur *m*

single ['sɪŋgəl] *adj* seul, unique; (*unmarried*) célibataire; (*e.g., room in a hotel*) à un lit; (*bed*) à une place; (*e.g., devotion*) simple, honnête || *tr* —to single out distinguer, choisir

sin'gle bless'edness ['blesɪdnɪs] *s* le bonheur *m* du célibat

sin'gle-breast'ed *adj* droit

sin'gle-en'try *adj* (*bk*) en partie simple

sin'gle-en'try book'keeping *s* comptabilité *f* simple

sin'gle file' *s*—in single file en file indienne, à la file

sin'gle-hand'ed *adj* sans aide, tout seul

sin'gle life' *s* vie *f* de célibataire

sin'gle room' *s* chambre *f* à un lit

sin'gle-track' *adj* (*rr*) à voie unique; (*coll*) d'une portée limitée

sing'song' *adj* monotone || *s* mélopée *f*

singular ['sɪŋgjələr] *adj & s* singulier *m*

sinister ['sɪnɪstər] *adj* sinistre

sink [sɪŋk] *s* évier *m*; (*drain*) égout *m* || *v* (*pret* sank [sæŋk] *or* sunk [sʌŋk]; *pp* sunk) *tr* enfoncer; (*a ship*) couler, faire sombrer; (*a well*) creuser; (*money*) immobiliser || *intr* s'enfoncer, s'affaisser; (*under the water*) couler, sombrer; (*said of heart*) se serrer; (*said of health, prices, sun, etc.*) baisser; to sink into plonger dans; (*an armchair*) s'effondrer dans

sink'ing fund' *s* caisse *f* d'amortissement

sinless ['sɪnlɪs] *adj* sans péché

sinner ['sɪnər] *s* pécheur *m*

sintering ['sɪntərɪŋ] *s* (*metallurgy*) frittage *m*

sinuous ['sɪnju-əs] *adj* sinueux

sinus ['saɪnəs] *s* sinus *m*

sip [sɪp] *s* petite gorgée *f*, petit coup *m* || *v* (*pret & pp* sipped); *ger* sipping) *tr* boire à petits coups, siroter

siphon ['saɪfən] *s* siphon *m* || *tr* siphonner

si'phon bot'tle *s* siphon *m*

sir [sʌr] *s* monsieur *m*; (*British title*) Sir *m*; Dear Sir Monsieur

sire [saɪr] *s* sire *m*; (*of a quadruped*) père *m* || *tr* engendrer

siren ['saɪrən] *s* sirène *f*

sirloin ['sʌrlɔɪn] *s* aloyau *m*

sirup ['sɪrəp], ['sʌrəp] *s* sirop *m*

sis-sy ['sɪsi] *s* (*pl* -sies) efféminé *m*; fillette *f*; (*cowardly fellow*) poule *f* mouillée

sister ['sɪstər] *adj* (*fig*) jumeau || *s* sœur *f*

sis'ter-in-law' *s* (*pl* sisters-in-law) belle-sœur *f*

sit [sɪt] *v* (*pret & pp* sat [sæt]; *ger* sitting) *intr* s'asseoir; être assis; (*said of hen on eggs*) couver; (*for a portrait*) poser; (*said of legislature, court, etc.*) siéger; to sit down s'asseoir; to sit still ne pas bouger; to sit up se redresser; se tenir droit; to sit up and beg (*said of dog*) faire le beau

sit'-down strike' *s* grève *f* sur le tas

site [saɪt] *s* site *m*

sitting ['sɪtɪŋ] *s* séance *f*

sit'ting duck' *s* (*coll*) cible *f* facile

sit'ting room' *s* salon *m*

situate ['sɪtʃu,et] *tr* situer

situation [,sɪtʃu'e/ən] *s* situation *f*; poste *m*, emploi *m*

sitz' bath' [sɪts] *s* bain *m* de siège

six [sɪks] *adj & pron* six || *s* six *m*; at sixes and sevens de travers, en désaccord; six o'clock six heures

sixteen ['sɪks'tin] *adj*, *pron*, *& s* seize *m*

sixteenth ['sɪks'tinθ] *adj & pron* seizième (*masc, fem*); the Sixteenth seize, e.g., John the Sixteenth Jean seize || *s* seizième *m*; the sixteenth (*in dates*) le seize

sixth [sɪksθ] *adj & pron* sixième (*masc, fem*); the Sixth six, e.g., John the Sixth Jean six || *s* sixième *m*; the sixth (*in dates*) le six

sixtieth ['sɪkstɪ-ɪθ] *adj & pron* soixantième (*masc, fem*) || *s* soixantième *m*

six-ty ['sɪksti] *adj & pron* soixante; about sixty une soixantaine de || *s* (*pl* -ties) soixante *m*; (*age of*) soixantaine *f*

sizable ['saɪzəbəl] *adj* assez grand, considérable

size [saɪz] *s* grandeur *f*; dimensions *fpl*; (*of a person or garment*) taille *f*; (*of a shoe, glove, or hat*) pointure *f*; (*of a shirt collar*) encolure *f*; (*of a book or box*) format *m*; (*to fill a porous surface*) apprêt *m*; what size hat do you wear? du combien coiffez-vous?; what size shoes do you wear? du combien chaussez-vous? || *tr* classer; (*wood to be painted*) coller; to size up juger

sizzle ['sɪzəl] *s* grésillement *m* || *intr* grésiller

skate [sket] *s* patin *m*; (*ichth*) raie *f*; good skate (*slang*) brave homme *m* || *intr* patiner; to go skating faire du patin

skat'ing rink' *s* patinoire *f*

skein [sken] *s* écheveau *m*

skeleton ['skelɪtən] *s* squelette *m*

skel'eton key' *s* crochet *m*

skeptic ['skeptɪk] *adj & s* sceptique *mf*

skeptical ['skeptɪkəl] *adj* sceptique

skepticism ['skeptɪ,sɪzəm] *s* scepticisme *m*

sketch [sketʃ] *s* esquisse *f*; (*pen or pencil drawing*) croquis *m*, esquisse; (*lit*) aperçu *m*; (*theat*) sketch *m* || *tr* esquisser || *intr* croquer

sketch'book' *s* album *m* de croquis

skew [skju] *adj & s* biais *m* || *intr* biaiser

skewer ['skju-ər] *s* brochette *f* || *tr* embrocher

ski [ski] *s* ski *m* || *intr* skier; to go skiing faire du ski

ski′ boots′ *spl* chaussures *fpl* de ski

skid [skɪd] *s* (*sidewise*) dérapage *m*; (*forward*) patinage *m*; (*of wheel*) sabot *m*, patin *m* ‖ *v* (*pret & pp* **skidded**; *ger* **skidding**) *tr* enrayer, bloquer ‖ *intr* (*sidewise*) déraper; (*forward*) patiner

skid′ row′ [ro] *s* quartier *m* mal famé

skier [′ski-ər] *s* skieur *m*

skiff [skɪf] *s* skiff *m*, esquif *m*

skiing [′ski-ɪŋ] *s* ski *m*

ski′ jack′et *s* anorak *m*

ski′ jump′ *s* (*place to jump*) tremplin *m*; (*act of jumping*) saut *m* en skis

ski′ lift′ *s* remonte-pente *m*, téléski *m*

skill [skɪl] *s* habilité *f*, adresse *f*; (*job*) métier *m*

skilled *adj* habile, adroit

skillet [′skɪlɪt] *s* casserole *f*; (*frying pan*) poêle *f*

skillful [′skɪlfəl] *adj* habile, expert

skim [skɪm] *v* (*pret & pp* **skimmed**; *ger* **skimming**) *tr* (*milk*) écrémer; (*molten metal*) écumer; (*to graze*) raser ‖ *intr* —**to skim over** passer légèrement sur

ski′ mask′ *s* passe-montagne *m*

skimmer [′skɪmər] *s* écumoire *f*; (*straw hat*) canotier *m*

skim′ milk′ *s* lait *m* écrémé

skimp [skɪmp] *tr* bâcler ‖ *intr* lésiner; **to skimp on** lésiner sur

skimp·y [′skɪmpi] *adj* (*comp* -**ler**; *super* -**lest**) maigre; (*garment*) étriqué, avare, mesquin

skin [skɪn] *s* peau *f*; **by the skin of one's teeth** de justesse, par un cheveu; **soaked to the skin** trempé jusqu'aux os; **to strip to the skin** se mettre à poil ‖ *v* (*pret & pp* **skinned**; *ger* **skinning**) *tr* écorcher, dépouiller; (*e.g., an elbow*) s'écorcher; **to skin alive** (*coll*) écorcher vif

skin′-deep′ *adj* superficiel; (*beauty*) à fleur de peau

skin′ div′er *s* plongeur *m* autonome

skin′flint′ *s* grippe-sou *m*

skin′ game′ *s* (*slang*) escroquerie *f*

skin′ graft′ing *s* greffe *f* cutanée, autoplastie *f*

skin·ny [′skɪni] *adj* (*comp* -**nier**; *super* -**niest**) maigre, décharné

skip [skɪp] *s* saut *m* ‖ *v* (*pret & pp* **skipped**; *ger* **skipping**) *tr* sauter; **skip it!** ça suffit!, laisse tomber! ; **to skip rope** sauter à la corde ‖ *intr* sauter; **to skip out** *or* **off** filer

ski′ pole′ *s* bâton *m* de skis

skipper [′skɪpər] *s* patron *m* ‖ *tr* commander, conduire

skirmish [′skɑrmɪʃ] *s* escarmouche *f* ‖ *intr* escarmoucher

skirt [skɑrt] *s* jupe *f*; (*woman*) (slang) jupe *f* ‖ *tr* côtoyer, longer; éviter

ski′ run′ *s* descente *f* en skis

ski′ stick′ *s* bâton *m* de skis

skit [skɪt] *s* sketch *m*

skittish [′skɪtɪʃ] *adj* capricieux; timide; (*e.g., horse*) ombrageux

skulduggery [skʌl′dʌgəri] *s* (*coll*) fourberie *f*, ruse *f*, cuisine *f*

skull [skʌl] *s* crâne *m*

skull′ and cross′bones *s* tibias *mpl* croisés et tête *f* de mort

skull′cap′ *s* calotte *f*

skunk [skʌŋk] *s* mouffette *f*; (*person*) (coll) salaud *m*

sky [skaɪ] *s* (*pl* **skies**) ciel *m*; **to praise to the skies** porter aux nues

sky′div′er *s* parachutiste *mf*

sky′div′ing *s* parachutisme *m*, saut *m* en chute libre

sky′lark′ *s* (*Alauda arvensis*) alouette *f*, alouette des champs ‖ *intr* (coll) batifoler

sky′light′ *s* lucarne *f*

sky′line′ *s* ligne *m* d'horizon; (*of city*) profil *m*

sky′rock′et *s* fusée *f* volante ‖ *intr* monter en flèche

sky′scrap′er *s* gratte-ciel *m*

slab [slæb] *s* (*of stone*) dalle *f*; (*slice*) tranche *f*

slack [slæk] *adj* lâche, mou; négligent ‖ *s* mou *m*; (*slowdown*) ralentissement *m*; **slacks** pantalon *m* ‖ *tr* relâcher; (*lime*) éteindre; **to slack off** larguer ‖ *intr*—**to slack off** *or* **up** se relâcher

slacken [′slækən] *tr* relâcher; (*to slow down*) ralentir ‖ *intr* se relâcher; se ralentir

slacker [′slækər] *s* flemmard *m*; (*mil*) tire-au-flanc *m*, embusqué *m*

slack′ hours′ *spl* heures *fpl* creuses

slag [slæg] *s* scorie *f*

slake [slek] *tr* apaiser, étancher; (*lime*) éteindre

slalom [′slaləm] *s* slalom *m*

slam [slæm] *s* claquement *m*; (*cards*) chelem *m*; (*coll*) critique *f* sévère ‖ *v* (*pret & pp* **slammed**; *ger* **slamming**) *tr* claquer; (*coll*) éreinter; **to slam down** *or* flanquer sur ‖ *intr* claquer

slander [′slændər] *s* calomnie *f* ‖ *tr* calomnier

slanderous [′slændərəs] *adj* calomnieux

slang [slæŋ] *s* argot *m*

slant [slænt] *s* pente *f*; (*bias*) point *m* de vue ‖ *tr* mettre en pente, incliner; donner un biais spécial à ‖ *intr* être en pente, s'incliner

slap [slæp] *s* tape *f*, claque *f*; (*in the face*) soufflet *m*, gifle *f* ‖ *v* (*pret & pp* **slapped**; *ger* **slapping**) *tr* taper, gifler

slap′dash′ *adj*—**in a slapdash manner** à la va-comme-je-te-pousse ‖ *adv* à la six-quatre-deux

slap′stick′ *adj* bouffon ‖ *s* bouffonnerie *f*

slash [slæʃ] *s* entaille *f* ‖ *tr* taillader; (*e.g., prices*) réduire beaucoup

slat [slæt] *s* latte *f*

slate [slet] *s* ardoise *f*; (*of candidates*) liste *f* ‖ *tr* couvrir d'ardoises; inscrire sur la liste, désigner

slate′ pen′cil *s* crayon *m* d'ardoise

slate′ roof′ *s* toit *m* d'ardoises

slattern [′slætərn] *s* (*slovenly woman*) marie-salope *f*; (*slut*) voyoute *f*, gueuse *f*

slaughter [′slɔtər] *s* boucherie *f* ‖ *tr* abattre; massacrer

slaught'er-house' s abattoir m

Slav [slɑv], [slæv] adj slave || s (language) slave m; (person) Slave mf

slave [slev] adj & s esclave mf || intr besogner, trimer

slave' driv'er s (hist, fig) négrier m

slavery ['slevəri] s esclavage m; (institutition of keeping slaves) esclavagisme m

slave' ship' s négrier m

slave' trade' s traite f des noirs

Slavic ['slɑvɪk], ['slævɪk] adj & s slave m

slavish ['slevɪʃ] adj servile

slay [sle] v (pret slew [slu]; pp slain [slen]) tr tuer, massacrer

slayer ['sle-ər] s meurtrier m

sled [sled] s luge f || v (pret & pp sledded; ger sledding) intr faire de la luge, luger

sledge' ham'mer [sledʒ] s massette f, masse f

sleek [slik] adj lisse, luisant || tr lisser

sleep [slip] s sommeil m; to go to sleep s'endormir; to put to sleep endormir || v (pret & pp slept [slept]) tr—to sleep it over, to sleep on it prendre conseil de son oreiller; to sleep off (a hangover, headache, etc.) faire passer en dormant || intr dormir; (e.g., with a woman) coucher; to sleep late faire la grasse matinée; to sleep like a log dormir comme un loir

sleeper ['slipər] s dormeur m; (girder) poutre f horizontale; (tie) (rr) traverse f

sleep'ing bag' s sac m de couchage

sleep'ing car' s wagon-lit m

sleep'ing pill' s somnifère m

sleepless ['sliplɪs] adj sans sommeil

sleep'less night' s nuit f blanche

sleep'walk'er s somnambule mf

sleep-y ['slipi] adj (comp -ier; super -iest) endormi, somnolent; to be sleepy avoir sommeil

sleep'y-head' s endormi m, grand dormeur m

sleet [slit] s grésil m || intr grésiller

sleeve [sliv] s manche f; (mach) manchon m, douille f; to laugh in or up one's sleeve rire sous cape

sleigh [sle] s traîneau m || intr aller en traîneau

sleigh' bell' s grelot m

sleigh' ride' s promenade f en traîneau

sleight' of hand' [slaɪt] s prestidigitation f, tours mpl de passe-passe

slender ['slendər] adj svelte, mince, élancé; (resources) maigre

sleuth [sluθ] s limier m, détective m

slew [slu] s (coll) tas m, floppée f

slice [slaɪs] s tranche f || tr trancher

slick [slɪk] adj lisse; (appearance) élégant; (coll) rusé; s tache f, e.g., oil slick tache d'huile || tr lisser; to slick up (coll) mettre en ordre

slicker ['slɪkər] s ciré m, imper m; (coll) enjôleur m

slide [slaɪd] s (sliding) glissade f, glissement m; (sliding place) glissoire m; (of microscope) plaque f; (of trombone) coulisse f; (on a slide rule)

curseur m; (piece that slides) glissière f; (phot) diapositive f || v (pret & pp slid [slɪd]) tr glisser || intr glisser; to let slide ne faire aucun cas de, laisser aller

slide' fas'tener s fermeture f éclair

slide' rule' s règle f à calcul

slide' valve' s soupape f à tiroir

slid'ing con'tact s curseur m

slid'ing door' s porte f à coulisse

slid'ing scale' s échelle f mobile

slight [slaɪt] adj léger; (slender; insignificant) mince; (e.g., effort) faible || s affront m || tr faire peu de cas de, dédaigner; (a person) méconnaître

slim [slɪm] adj (comp slimmer; super slimmest) mince, svelte; (chance, excuse) mauvais; (resources) maigre

slime [slaɪm] s limon m, vase f; (of snakes, fish, etc.) bave f

slim-y ['slaɪmi] adj (comp -ier; super -iest) limoneux, vaseux

sling [slɪŋ] s (to shoot stones) fronde f; (to hold up a broken arm) écharpe f; (shoulder strap) bretelle f, bandoulière f || v (pret & pp slung [slʌŋ]) tr lancer; passer en bandoulière

sling'shot' s fronde f

slink [slɪŋk] v (pret & pp slunk [slʌŋk]) intr—to slink away s'esquiver

slip [slɪp] s glissade f, glissement m; bout m de papier; (for indexing, filing, etc.) fiche f; (cutting from plant) bouture f; (piece of underclothing) combinaison f; (blunder) faux pas m, bévue f; (naut) cale f; to give the slip to échapper à || v (pret & pp slipped; ger slipping) tr glisser; to slip off (a garment) enlever, ôter; to slip on (a garment, shoes, etc.) enfiler; to slip one's mind sortir de l'esprit, échapper à qn || intr glisser; (to blunder) faire un faux pas; to let slip laisser échapper; to slip away or off s'échapper, se dérober; to slip by s'échapper; (said of time) s'écouler; to slip up se tromper

slip'cov'er s housse f

slipper ['slɪpər] s pantoufle f

slippery ['slɪpəri] adj glissant; (deceitful) rusé

slip'-up' s (coll) erreur f, bévue f

slit [slɪt] s fente f, fissure f || v (pret & pp slit; ger slitting) tr fendre; (e.g., pages) couper; to slit the throat of égorger

slob [slɑb] s (slang) rustaud m

slobber ['slɑbər] s bave f; (fig) sentimentalité f || intr baver

sloe [slo] s (shrub) prunellier m; (fruit) prunelle f

slogan ['slogən] s mot m d'ordre, devise f; (com) slogan m

sloop [slup] s sloop m

slop [slɑp] s lavure f, rinçure f || v (pret & pp slopped; ger slopping) tr répandre || intr se répandre; to slop over déborder

slope [slop] s pente f; (of a roof) inclinaison f; (of a region, mountain, etc.) versant *m* ‖ *tr* pencher, incliner ‖ *intr* se pencher, s'incliner

slop-py ['slɑpi] *adj* (comp **-pier**; super **-piest**) mouillé; (*dress*) négligé, mal ajusté; (*work*) bâclé

slot [slɑt] *s* entaille *f*, rainure *f*; (*e.g., in a coin telephone*) fente *f*

sloth [sloθ], [slɔθ] *s* paresse *f*; (zool) paresseux *m*

slot' machine' *s* (*for gambling*) appareil *m* à sous; (*for vending*) distributeur *m* automatique

slouch [slautʃ] *s* démarche *f* lourde; (*person*) lourdaud *m* ‖ *intr* ne pas se tenir droit; (*e.g., in a chair*) se vautrer; **to slouch along** traîner le pas

slouch' hat' *s* chapeau *m* mou

slough [slau] *s* bourbier *m* ‖ [slʌf] (*of snake*) dépouille *f*; (pathol) escarre *f* ‖ *tr* **to slough off** se débarrasser de ‖ *intr* muer, se dépouiller

Slovak ['slovæk], ['slo'væk] *adj* slovaque ‖ *s* (*language*) slovaque *m*; (*person*) Slovaque *mf*

sloven-ly ['slʌvənli] *adj* (comp **-lier**; super **-liest**) négligé, malpropre

slow [slo] *adj* lent; (*sluggish*) traînard; (*clock, watch*) en retard; (*in understanding*) lourdaud ‖ *adv* lentement ‖ *tr & intr* ralentir; **SLOW** (public sign) ralentir; **to slow down** ralentir

slow'down' *s* grève *f* perlée

slow' mo'tion *s* ralenti *m*; **in slow motion** au ralenti, en ralenti

slow'poke' *s* (coll) lambin *m*, traînard *m*

slug [slʌg] *s* (*used as coin*) jeton *m*; (*of linotype*) ligne-bloc *f*; (zool) limace *f*; (*blow*) (coll) bon coup *m*; (*drink*) (coll) gorgée *f* ‖ *v* (pret & pp **slugged**; ger **slugging**) *tr* (coll) flanquer un coup à

sluggard ['slʌgərd] *s* paresseux *m*

sluggish ['slʌgɪʃ] *adj* traînard

sluice [slus] *s* canal *m*; (*floodgate*) écluse *f*; (*dam; flume*) bief *m*

sluice' gate' *s* vanne *f*

slum [slʌm] *s* bas quartiers *mpl* ‖ *v* (pret & pp **slummed**; ger **slumming**) *intr* **to go slumming** aller visiter les taudis

slumber ['slʌmbər] *s* sommeil *m*, assoupissement *m* ‖ *intr* sommeiller

slum' dwell'ing *s* taudis *m*

slump [slʌmp] *s* affaissement *m*; (com) crise *f*, baisse *f* ‖ *intr* s'affaisser; (*said of prices, stocks, etc.*) dégringoler, s'effondrer

slur [slʌr] *s* (*in pronunciation*) mauvaise articulation *f*; (*insult*) affront *m*; (mus) liaison *f*; **to cast a slur on** porter atteinte à ‖ *v* (pret & pp **slurred**; ger **slurring**) *tr* (*a sound, a syllable*) mal articuler; (*a person*) déprécier; (mus) lier; **to slur over** glisser sur

slush [slʌʃ] *s* fange *f*, boue *f* liquide; (*gush*) sensiblerie *f*

slut [slʌt] *s* chienne *f*; (*slovenly woman*) marie-salope *f*

sly [slaɪ] *adj* (comp **slyer** or **slier**; super **slyest** or **sliest**) rusé, sournois; (*mischievous*) espiègle, futé; **on the sly** furtivement, en cachette

smack [smæk] *s* claquement *m*; (*with the hand*) gifle *f*, claque *f*; (*trace, touch*) soupçon *m*; (*kiss*) (coll) gros baiser *m* ‖ *adv* en plein ‖ *tr* claquer ‖ *intr* **to smack of** sentir; avoir un goût de

small [smɔl] *adj* petit §91; (*income*) modique; (*short in stature*) court; (*petty*) mesquin; (typ) minuscule

small' arms' *spl* armes *fpl* portatives

small' beer' *s* petite bière *f*; (slang) petite bière

small' busi'ness *s* petite industrie *f*

small' cap'ital *s* (typ) petite capitale *f*

small' change' *s* petite monnaie *f*, menue monnaie

small' fry' *s* menu fretin *m*

small' intes'tine *s* intestin *m* grêle

small'-mind'ed *adj* mesquin, étriqué, étroit

smallpox ['smɔl,pɑks] *s* variole *f*

small' print' *s* petits caractères *mpl*

small' talk' *s* ragots *mpl*, papotage *m*

small'-time' *adj* de troisième ordre, insignifiant, petit

small'-town' *adj* provincial

smart [smɑrt] *adj* intelligent, éveillé; (*pace*) vif; (*person, clothes*) élégant, chic; (*pain*) cuisant; (*saucy*) impertinent ‖ *s* douleur *f* cuisante ‖ *intr* brûler, cuire; (*said of person with hurt feelings*) être cinglé

smart' al'eck ['ælɪk] *s* (coll) fat *m*, présomptueux *m*

smart' set' *s* monde *m* élégant, gens *mpl* chic

smash [smæʃ] *s* fracassement *m*, fracas *m*; (coll) succès *m* ‖ *tr* fracasser ‖ *intr* se fracasser; **to smash into** emboutir, écraser

smash' hit' *s* (coll) succès *m*, (coll) pièce *f* à succès

smash'-up' *s* collision *f*; débâcle *f*, culbute *f*

smattering ['smætərɪŋ] *s* légère connaissance *f*, teinture *f*

smear [smɪr] *s* tache *f*; (*vilification*) calomnie *f*; (med) frottis *m* ‖ *tr* tacher; calomnier; (*to coat*) enduire

smear' campaign' *s* campagne *f* de calomnies

smell [smɛl] *s* odeur *f*; (*aroma*) parfum *m*, senteur *f*; (*sense*) odorat *m* ‖ *v* (pret & pp **smelled** or **smelt** [smɛlt]) *tr & intr* sentir; **to smell of** sentir

smell'ing salts' *spl* sels *mpl* volatils

smell-y ['smɛli] *adj* (comp **-ier**; super **-iest**) malodorant, puant

smelt [smɛlt] *s* (*fish*) éperlan *m* ‖ *tr & intr* fondre

smile [smaɪl] *s* sourire *m* ‖ *intr* sourire; **to smile at** sourire à

smirk [smʌrk] *s* minauderie *f* ‖ *intr* minauder

smite [smaɪt] *v* (pret **smote** [smot]; pp **smitten** ['smɪtən] or **smit** [smɪt]) *tr* frapper; **to smite down** abattre

smith [smɪθ] *s* forgeron *m*

smith·y ['smɪθi] *s* (*pl* -ies) forge *f*

smitten [smɪtən] *adj* frappé, affligé; (coll) épris, amoureux

smock [smak] *s* blouse *f*; (*of artists*) sarrau *m*; (*buttoned in back*) tablier *m*

smock' frock' *s* sarrau *m*

smog [smag] *s* (coll) brouillard *m* fumeux

smoke [smok] *s* fumée *f*; (coll) cigarette *f*; **to go up in smoke** s'en aller en fumée || *tr* & *intr* fumer

smoked' glass'es *spl* verres *mpl* fumés

smoke'-filled room' *s* tabagie *f*

smoke'less pow'der ['smoklɪs] *s* poudre *f* sans fumée

smoker ['smokər] *s* fumeur *m*; (*room*) fumoir *m*; (*meeting*) réunion *f* de fumeurs; (rr) compartiment *m* pour fumeurs

smoke' rings' *spl* ronds *mpl* de fumée

smoke' screen' *s* rideau *m* de fumée

smoke'stack' *s* cheminée *f*

smoking ['smokɪŋ] *s* le fumer *m*; **no smoking** (public sign) défense de fumer

smok'ing car' *s* voiture *f* de fumeurs

smok'ing jack'et *s* veston *m* d'intérieur

smok'ing room' *s* fumoir *m*

smok·y ['smoki] *adj* (*comp* -ier; *super* -iest) fumeux, enfumé

smolder ['smoldər] *s* fumée *f* épaisse; feu *m* qui couve || *intr* brûler sans flamme; (*said of fire, anger, rebellion, etc.*) couver

smooch [smutʃ] *intr* (coll) se bécoter

smooth [smuð] *adj* uni, lisse; (*gentle, mellow*) doux, moelleux; (*operation*) doux, régulier; (*style*) facile || *tr* unir, lisser; **to smooth away** (*e.g., obstacles*) aplanir, enlever; **to smooth down** (*to calm*) apaiser, calmer; **to smooth out** défroisser

smooth'-faced' *adj* imberbe

smooth-shaven ['smuð'evən] *adj* rasé de près

smooth·y ['smuði] *s* (*pl* -ies) (coll) chattemite *f*, flagorneur *m*

smother ['smʌðər] *tr* suffoquer, étouffer; (culin) recouvrir

smudge [smʌdʒ] *s* tache *f*; (*smoke*) fumée *f* épaisse || *tr* tacher; (agr) fumiger

smudge' pot' *s* fumigène *m*

smug [smʌg] *adj* (*comp* smugger; *super* smuggest) fat, suffisant

smuggle ['smʌgəl] *tr* introduire en contrebande, faire la contrebande de || *intr* faire la contrebande

smuggler ['smʌglər] *s* contrebandier *m*

smuggling ['smʌglɪŋ] *s* contrebande *f*

smut [smʌt] *s* tache *f* de suie; (*obscenity*) ordure *f*; (agr) nielle *f*

smut·ty ['smʌti] *adj* (*comp* -tier; *super* -tiest) taché de suie, noirci; (*obscene*) ordurier; (agr) niellé

snack [snæk] *s* casse-croûte *m*; **to have a snack** casser la croûte

snack' bar' *s* snack-bar *m*, snack *m*

snag [snæg] *s* (*of tree; of tooth*) chicot *m*; **to hit a snag** se heurter à un obs-

tacle || *v* (*pret* & *pp* snagged; *ger* snagging) *tr* (*a stocking*) faire un accroc à

snail [snel] *s* escargot *m*; **at a snail's pace** à pas de tortue, comme un escargot

snake [snek] *s* serpent *m* || *intr* serpenter

snake' in the grass' *s* serpent *m* caché sous les fleurs; ami *m* perfide, traître *m*, individu *m* louche

snap [snæp] *s* (*breaking*) cassure *f*; (*crackling sound*) bruit *m* sec; (*of the fingers*) chiquenaude *f*; (*bite*) coup *m* de dents; (*cookie*) biscuit *m* croquant; (*catch or fastener*) bouton-pression *m*, fermoir *m*; (phot) instantané *m*; (slang) jeu *m* d'enfant, coup facile; **cold snap** coup *m* de froid; **it's a snap** (slang) c'est du tout cuit! || *v* (*pret* & *pp* snapped; *ger* snapping) *tr* casser net; (*one's fingers, a whip, etc.*) faire claquer; (*a picture, a scene*) prendre un instantané de; **to snap up** happer, saisir || *intr* casser net; faire un bruit sec; (*from fatigue*) s'effondrer; **to snap at** donner un coup de dents à; (*to speak sharply to*) rembarrer; (*an opportunity*) saisir; **to snap out of it** (slang) se secouer; **to snap shut** se fermer avec un bruit sec

snap' course' *s* (slang) cours *m* tout mâché

snap'drag'on *s* (bot) gueule-de-loup *f*

snap' fas'tener *s* bouton-pression *m*

snap' judg'ment *s* décision *f* prise sans réflexion

snap·py ['snæpi] *adj* (*comp* -pier; *super* -piest) mordant, acariâtre; (*quick, sudden*) vif; **make it snappy!** (slang) grouillez-vous!

snap'shot' *s* instantané *m*

snare [snɛr] *s* collet *m*; (*trap*) piège *m*; (*of a drum*) timbre *m*, corde *f* de timbre || *tr* prendre au collet, prendre au piège

snare' drum' *s* caisse *f* claire

snarl [snarl] *s* (*sound*) grognement *m*; (*intertwining*) enchevêtrement *m* || *tr* dire en grognant; enchevêtrer || *intr* grogner; s'enchevêtrer

snatch [snætʃ] *s* arrachement *m*; petit moment *m*; (*bit, scrap*) bribe *f*, fragment *m*; (*in weight lifting*) arraché *m* || *tr* saisir brusquement, arracher; **to snatch from** arracher à; **to snatch up** ramasser vivement || *intr*—**to snatch at** saisir au vol

sneak [snik] *adj* furtif || *s* chipeur *m*, mauvais type *m* || *tr* (*e.g., a drink*) prendre à la dérobée; glisser furtivement; (coll) chiper || *intr* se glisser furtivement; **to sneak into** se faufiler dans; **to sneak out** s'esquiver

sneaker ['snikər] *s* espadrille *f*

sneak' thief' *s* chipeur *m*, voleur *m* à la tire

sneak·y ['sniki] *adj* (*comp* -ier; *super* -iest) furtif, sournois

sneer [snɪr] *s* ricanement *m* || *intr* ricaner; **to sneer at** se moquer de

sneeze [sniz] *s* éternuement *m* || *intr* éternuer; **it's not to be sneezed at** (coll) il ne faut pas cracher dessus

snicker ['snɪkər] *s* rire *m* bête; (*in response to smut*) petit rire grivois || *intr* rire bêtement; **to snicker at** se moquer de

sniff [snɪf] *s* reniflement *m*; (*odor*) parfum *m*; (*e.g., of air*) bouffée *f* || *tr* renifler; (*e.g., fresh air*) humer; (*e.g., a scandal*) flairer; **to sniff up** renifler || *intr* renifler; **to sniff at** flairer; (*to disdain*) cracher sur

sniffle ['snɪfəl] *s* reniflement *m*; **to have the sniffles** être enchifrené || *intr* renifler

snip [snɪp] *s* (*e.g., of cloth*) petit bout *m*; (*cut*) coup *m* de ciseaux; (coll) personne *f* insignifiante || *v* (*pret & pp* snipped; *ger* snipping) *tr* couper; **to snip off** enlever, détacher

snipe [snaɪp] *s* (orn) bécassine *f* || *intr* —**to snipe at** canarder

sniper ['snaɪpər] *s* tireur *m* embusqué

snippet ['snɪpɪt] *s* petit bout *m*, bribe *f*; personne *f* insignifiante

snip-py ['snɪpɪ] *adj* (*comp* -pier; *super* -piest) hautain, brusque

snitch [snɪtʃ] *tr* (coll) chaparder || *intr* (coll) moucharder; **to snitch on** (coll) moucharder

sniv-el ['snɪvəl] *s* pleurnicherie *f*; (*mucus*) morve *f* || *v* (*pret & pp* -eled or -elled; *ger* -eling or -elling) *intr* pleurnicher; (*to have a runny nose*) être morveux

snob [snɑb] *s* snob *m*

snobbery ['snɑbərɪ] *s* snobisme *m*

snobbish ['snɑbɪʃ] *adj* snob

snoop [snup] *s* (coll) curieux *m* || *intr* (coll) fouiner, fureter

snoop-y ['snupɪ] *adj* (*comp* -ier; *super* -iest) (coll) curieux

snoot [snut] *s* (slang) nez *m*

snoot-y ['snutɪ] *adj* (*comp* -ier; *super* -iest) (slang) snob, hautain

snooze [snuz] *s* (coll) petit somme *m* || *intr* (coll) sommeiller

snore [snɔr] *s* ronflement *m* || *intr* ronfler

snort [snɔrt] *s* ébrouement *m*; (*of person, horse, etc.*) reniflement *m* || *tr* dire en reniflant, grogner || *intr* s'ébrouer, renifler bruyamment

snot [snɑt] *s* (slang) morve *f*

snot-ty ['snɑtɪ] *adj* (*comp* -tier; *super* -tiest) (coll) morveux; (slang) snob, hautain

snout [snaut] *s* museau *m*; (*of pig*) groin *m*; (*of bull*) mufle *m*; (*something shaped like the snout of an animal*) bec *m*, tuyère *f*

snow [sno] *s* neige *f* || *intr* neiger; **it is snowing** il neige; **to shovel snow** balayer la neige

snow'ball' *s* boule *f* de neige || *tr* lancer des boules de neige à || *intr* faire boule de neige

snow' blind'ness *s* cécité *f* des neiges

snow'-capped' *adj* couronné de neige

snow'-clad' *adj* enneigé

snow'drift' *s* congère *f*

snow'fall' *s* chute *f* de neige; (*amount*) enneigement *m*

snow'flake' *s* flocon *m* de neige

snow' flur'ry *s* (*pl* -ries) bouffée *f* de neige

snow' line' *s* limite *f* des neiges éternelles

snow'man' *s* (*pl* -men') bonhomme *m* de neige

snow'plow' *s* chasse-neige *m*

snow'shoe' *s* raquette *f*

snow'slide' *s* avalanche *f*

snow'storm' *s* tempête *f* de neige

snow' tire' *s* pneu *m* à neige

snow'white' *adj* blanc comme la neige || Snowwhite *s* Blanche-Neige *f*

snow-y ['sno·ɪ] *adj* (*comp* -ier; *super* -iest) neigeux

snow'y owl' *s* chouette *f* blanche

snub [snʌb] *s* affront *m*, rebuffade *f* || *v* (*pret & pp* snubbed; *ger* snubbing) *tr* traiter avec froideur, rabrouer

snub-by ['snʌbɪ] *adj* (*comp* -bier; *super* -biest) trapu; (*nose*) camus

snub'-nosed' *adj* camard

snuff [snʌf] *s* tabac *m* à priser; (*of a candlewick*) mouchure *f*; **to be up to snuff** (*to be shrewd*) (slang) être dessalé; (*to be up to par*) (slang) être dégourdi || *tr* priser; (*a candle*) moucher; **to snuff out** éteindre

snuff'box' *s* tabatière *f*

snuffers ['snʌfərz] *spl* mouchettes *fpl*

snug [snʌg] *adj* (*comp* snugger; *super* snuggest) confortable; (*garment*) bien ajusté; (*bed*) douillet; (*sheltered*) abrité; (*hidden*) caché; **snug and warm** bien au chaud; **snug as a bug in a rug** comme un poisson dans l'eau

snuggle ['snʌgəl] *tr* serrer dans ses bras || *intr* se pelotonner; **to snuggle up to** se serrer tout près de

so [so] *adv* si, tellement; ainsi; donc, par conséquent, aussi; or so plus ou moins; **so as to** afin de, pour; **so far** jusqu'ici; **so long!** (coll) à bientôt!; **so many** tant; tant de; **so much** tant; tant de; **so that** pour que, afin que; de sorte que; **so to speak** pour ainsi dire; **so what?** (slang) et alors?; **to hope so** espérer bien; **to think so** croire que oui || *conj* (coll) de sorte que

soak [sok] *s* trempage *m*; (slang) sac *m* à vin, soûlard *m* || *tr* tremper; (*to swindle*) (slang) estamper; **to soak to the skin** tremper jusqu'aux os || *intr* tremper

so'-and-so' *s* (*pl* -sos) (pej) triste individu *m*, mauvais sujet *m*; **Mr. So-and-so** Monsieur un tel

soap [sop] *s* savon *m* || *tr* savonner

soap'box' *s* caisse *f* à savon; (fig) plateforme *f*

soap'box or'ator *s* orateur *m* de carrefour

soap' bub'ble *s* bulle *f* de savon

soap' dish' *s* plateau *m* à savon

soap' fac'to·ry *s* (*pl* -ries) savonnerie *f*

soap' flakes' *spl* savon *m* en paillettes

soap' op'era *s* mélo *m*

soap' pow'der *s* savon *m* en poudre

soap'stone' s pierre f de savon; craie f de tailleur

soap'suds' spl mousse f de savon, eau f de savon

soap·y ['sopi] adj (comp -ier; super -iest) savonneux

soar [sor] intr planer dans les airs; prendre l'essor, monter subitement

sob [sab] s sanglot m || v (pret & pp sobbed; ger sobbing) intr sangloter

sober ['sobər] adj sobre; (expression) grave; (truth) simple; (not drunk) pas ivre; (no longer drunk) dégrisé || tr calmer; to sober up dégriser || intr—to sober up se dégriser

sobriety [so'braiəti] s sobriété f

sob' sis'ter s (slang) journaliste f larmoyante

sob' sto'ry s (pl -ries) (slang) lamentation f, jérémiade f

so'-called' adj dit; soi-disant, prétendu; ainsi nommé

soccer ['sakər] s football m

sociable ['so/əbəl] adj sociable

social ['so/əl] adj social || s réunion f sans cérémonie

so'cial climb'er s parvenu m, arriviste mf

so'cial events' spl mondanités fpl

socialism ['so/ə,lizəm] s socialisme m

socialist ['so/əlist] s socialiste mf

socialite ['so/ə,lait] s (coll) membre m de la haute société

so'cial reg'ister s annuaire m de la haute société

so'cial secu'rity s sécurité f sociale, assistance f familiale

so'cial serv'ice s assistance f sociale, aide f sociale, aide familiale

so'cial stra'ta [ˌstretə], [ˌstrætə] spl couches fpl sociales

so'cial work'er s assistant m social, travailleuse f familiale

socie·ty [sə'sai·əti] s (pl -ties) société f

soci'ety col'umn s carnet m mondain

soci'ety ed'itor s chroniqueur m mondain

sociology [ˌsosiˈalədʒi], [ˌso/iˈalədʒi] s sociologie f

sock [sak] s chaussette f; (slang) coup m de poing || tr (slang) donner un coup de poing à

socket ['sakit] s (of bone) cavité f, glène f; (of candlestick) tube m; (of caster) sabot m; (of eye) orbite f; (of tooth) alvéole m; (elec) douille f

sock'et joint' s joint m à rotule

sock'et wrench' s clé f à tube

sod [sad] s gazon m; motte f de gazon || v (pret & pp sodded; ger sodding) tr gazonner

soda ['sodə] s (soda water) soda m; (chem) soude f

so'da crack'er s biscuit m soda

so'da wa'ter s soda m

sodium ['sodi·əm] s sodium m

sofa ['sofə] s canapé m, sofa m

soft [soft], [saft] adj (yielding) mou; (mild) doux; (weak in character) faible; to go soft (coll) perdre la boule

soft'-boiled egg' s œuf m à la coque

soft' coal' s houille f grasse

soft' drink' s boisson f non-alcoolisée

soften ['sofən], ['safən] tr amollir; (e.g., noise) atténuer; (one's voice) adoucir; (one's moral fiber) affaiblir; to soften up amollir || intr s'amollir; s'adoucir; s'affaiblir

soft' land'ing s (rok) arrivée f en douceur

soft' ped'al s (mus) pédale f sourde

soft-ped'al v (pret & pp -aled or -alled; ger -aling or -alling) tr (coll) atténuer, modérer

soft' soap' s savon m mou, savon noir; (coll) pommade f

soft'-soap' tr (coll) passer de la pommade à

sog·gy ['sagi] adj (comp -gier; super -giest) saturé, détrempé

soil [sɔil] s sol m, terroir m || tr salir, souiller || intr se salir

soil' pipe' s tuyau m de descente

sojourn ['sodʒʌrn] s séjour m || ['so-dʒʌrn], [soˈdʒʌrn] intr séjourner

solace ['salis] s consolation f || tr consoler

solar ['solər] adj solaire

so'lar bat'tery s photopile f

sold [sold] adj—sold out (no more room) complet; (no more merchandise) épuisé; to be sold on (coll) raffoler de || interj (to the highest bidder) adjugé!

solder ['sadər] s soudure f || tr souder

sol'dering i'ron s fer m à souder

soldier ['soldʒər] s soldat m

sole [sol] adj seul, unique || s (of shoe) semelle f; (of foot) plante f; (fish) sole f || tr ressemeler

solemn ['saləm] adj sérieux, grave; (ceremony) solennel

solicit [sə'lisit] tr solliciter || intr quêter; (with immoral intentions) racoler

solicitor [sə'lisitər] s solliciteur m; agent m, représentant m; (com) démarcheur m; (law) procureur m; (Brit) avoué m

solicitous [sə'lisitəs] adj soucieux

solid ['salid] adj solide; (clouds) dense; (gold) massif; (opinion) unanime; (color) uni; (hour, day, week) entier; (e.g., three days) d'affilée || s solide m

sol'id geom'etry s géométrie f dans l'espace

solidity [sə'liditi] s solidité f, consistance f

soliloquy [sə'liləkwi] s (pl -quies) soliloque m

solitaire ['sali ˌter] s solitaire m; (cards) patience f, réussite f; to play solitaire faire une réussite

solitar·y ['sali ˌteri] adj solitaire || s (pl -ies) solitaire m

solitude ['sali ˌt(j)ud] s solitude f

so·lo ['solo] s (pl -los) solo m

soloist ['solo·ist] s soliste mf

solstice ['salstis] s solstice m

soluble ['saljəbəl] adj soluble

solution [sə'luʃən] s solution f

solvable ['sɑlvəbəl] adj soluble

solve [sɑlv] tr résoudre

solvency ['sɑlvənsı] s solvabilité f

solvent ['sɑlvənt] adj (substance) solubilisant; (person or business) solvable || s (of a substance) solvant m

somber ['sɑmbər] adj sombre

some [sʌm] adj indef quelque, du; **some way or other** d'une manière ou d'une autre || pron indef certains, quelques-uns §81; en §87 || adv un peu, passablement, assez; environ; quelque, e.g., **some two hundred soldiers** quelque deux cents soldats

some'body' pron indef quelqu'un §81; **somebody else** quelqu'un d'autre || s (pl -ies) quelqu'un m

some'day' adv un jour

some'how' adv dans un sens, je ne sais comment; **somehow or other** d'une manière ou d'une autre

some'one' pron indef quelqu'un §81

somersault ['sʌmər‚sɔlt] s saut m périlleux

some'thing s (coll) quelque chose m || pron indef quelque chose (masc) || adv quelque peu, un peu

some'time' adj ancien, ci-devant || adv un jour; un de ces jours

some'times adv quelquefois, de temps en temps; **sometimes . . . sometimes** tantôt . . . tantôt

some'way' adv d'une manière ou d'une autre

some'what' adv un peu, assez

some'where' adv quelque part; **somewhere else** ailleurs, autre part

somnambulist [sɑm'næmbjəlɪst] s somnambule mf

somnolent ['sɑmnələnt] adj somnolent

son [sʌn] s fils m

sonata [sə'nɑtə] s sonate f

song [sɔŋ], [sɑŋ] s chanson f; (of praise) hymne m; **to buy for a song** (coll) acheter pour une bouchée de pain

song'bird' s oiseau m chanteur

song' book' s recueil m de chansons

Song' of Songs' s (Bib) Cantique m des Cantiques

song' thrush' s grive f musicienne

song'writ'er s chansonnier m

sonic ['sɑnık] adj sonique

son'ic boom' s double bang m

son'-in-law' s (pl sons-in-law) gendre m, beau fils m

sonnet ['sɑnɪt] s sonnet m

son-ny ['sʌnı] s (pl -nies) fiston m

soon [sun] adv bientôt; (early) tôt; **as soon as** aussitôt que, dès que, sitôt que; **as soon as possible** le plus tôt possible; **how soon** quand; **no sooner said than done** sitôt dit sitôt fait; **soon after** tôt après; **sooner** plus tôt; (rather) (coll) plutôt; **sooner or later** tôt ou tard; **so soon** si tôt; **too soon** trop tôt

soot [sʊt], [sut] s suie f || tr—**to soot up** encrasser de suie || intr s'encrasser

soothe [suð] tr calmer, apaiser; flatter

soothsayer ['suθ‚se·ər] s devin m

soot-y ['sʊtı], ['sutı] adj (comp -ier; super -iest) (color; flame) fuligineux; couvert de suie

sop [sɑp] s morceaux m trempé; (fig) os m à ronger, cadeau m || v (pret & pp sopped; ger sopping) tr tremper, faire tremper; **to sop up** absorber

sophisticated [sə'fɪstɪ‚ketɪd] adj mondain, sceptique; complexe

sophistication [sə‚fɪstɪ'keʃən] s mondanité f

sophomore ['sɑfə‚mor] s étudiant m de deuxième année

sophomoric [‚sɑfə'morɪk] adj naïf, suffisant, présomptueux

sopping ['sɑpɪŋ] adj détrempé, trempé || adv—**sopping wet** trempé comme une soupe

soprano [sə'præno], [sə'prɑno] adj de soprano || s (pl -os) soprano f; (boy) soprano m

sorcerer ['sɔrsərər] s sorcier m

sorceress ['sɔrsərɪs] s sorcière f

sorcer-y ['sɔrsərı] s (pl -ies) sorcellerie f

sordid ['sɔrdɪd] adj sordide

sore [sor] adj douloureux, enflammé; (coll) fâché || s plaie f, ulcère m

sore'head' s (coll) rouspéteur m, grincheux m

sorely ['sorlı] adv gravement, grièvement; cruellement

soreness ['sornɪs] s douleur f, sensibilité f

sore' throat' s—**to have a sore throat** avoir mal à la gorge

sorori-ty [sə'rɑrɪtı], [sə'rɔrɪtı] s (pl -ties) club m d'étudiantes universitaires

sorrow ['sɑro], ['sɔro] s chagrin m, peine f, affliction f, tristesse f || intr s'affliger, avoir du chagrin; être en deuil; **to sorrow for** s'affliger de

sorrowful ['sɑrəfəl], ['sɔrəfəl] adj (person) affligé, attristé; (news) affligeant

sor-ry ['sɑrı], ['sɔrı] adj (comp -rier; super -riest) désolé, navré, fâché; (appearance) piteux, misérable; (situation) triste; **to be or feel sorry** regretter; **to be or feel sorry for** regretter (q.ch.); plaindre (qn); **to be sorry to** + inf regretter de + inf || interj pardon!

sort [sɔrt] s sorte f, espèce f, genre m; **a sort of** une espèce de; **out of sorts** de mauvaise humeur || tr classer; **to sort out** trier

so'-so' adj (coll) assez bon, passable, supportable || adv assez bien, comme ci comme ça

sot [sɑt] s ivrogne mf

soul [sol] s âme f; **not a soul** (coll) pas un chat; **upon my soul!** par ma foi!

sound [saʊnd] adj sain; solide, en bon état; (sleep) profond || s son m; (probe) sonde f; (geog) goulet m, détroit m, bras m de mer || adv (asleep) profondément || tr sonner; (to take a sounding of) sonder; **to sound out** sonder; **to sound the horn** klaxonner, corner || intr sonner; sonder; **to sound off** parler haut; **to sound strange** sembler bizarre

sound' bar'rier s mur m du son

sound' film' s film m sonore

sound' hole' s (of a violin) ouïe f

soundly ['saundli] adj sainement; profondément; (hard) bien

sound'proof' adj insonorisé, insonore || tr insonoriser

sound' track' s piste f sonore

sound' wave' s onde f sonore

soup [sup] s potage m, bouillon m; (with vegetables) soupe f; **in the soup** (coll) dans le pétrin or la mélasse

soup' kitch'en s soupe f populaire

soup' spoon' s cuiller f à soupe

soup' tureen' s soupière f

sour [saur] adj aigre; (grapes) vert; (apples) sur; (milk) tourné || tr rendre aigre || intr tourner, s'aigrir

source [sors] s source f

source' lan'guage s langue f source

source' mate'rial s sources fpl originales

sour' cher'ry s (pl -ries) griotte f; (tree) griottier m

sour' grapes' interj ils sont trop verts!

sour'puss' s (slang) grincheux m

south [sauθ] adj & s sud m; **the South** (of France, Italy, etc.) le Midi; (of U.S.A.) le Sud || adv au sud, vers le sud

South' Af'rica s la République sud-africaine

South' Amer'ica s Amérique f du Sud; l'Amérique du Sud

South' Amer'ican adj sud-américain || s (person) Sud-Américain m

south'east' adj & s sud-est m

southern ['sʌðərn] adj du sud, méridional

southerner ['sʌðərnər] s Méridional m; (U.S.A.) sudiste m

South' Kore'a s Corée f du Sud; la Corée du Sud

South' Kore'an adj sud-coréen || s (person) Sud-Coréen m

south'paw' adj & s (coll) gaucher m

South' Pole' s pôle m Sud

South' Vietnam'ese' [vɪ‚etnə'miz] adj sud-vietnamien || s (pl -ese) Sud-Vietnamien m

southward ['sauθwərd] adv vers le sud

south'west' adj & s sud-ouest m

souvenir [‚suvə'nɪr] s souvenir m

sovereign ['savrɪn], ['sʌvrɪn] adj souverain || s (king; coin) souverain m; (queen) souveraine f

sovereign•ty ['savrɪnti], ['sʌvrɪnti] s (pl -ties) souveraineté f

soviet ['sovɪ‚et], [‚sovɪ'et] adj soviétique || s soviet m; **Soviet** (person) Soviétique mf

So'viet Rus'sia s la Russie f soviétique

So'viet Un'ion s Union f soviétique

sow [sau] s truie f || [so] v (pret sowed; pp sown or sowed) tr (seed; a field) semer; (a field) ensemencer

soybean ['sɔɪ‚bin] s soya m, soja m

spa [spa] s ville f d'eau, station f thermale, bains mpl

space [spes] s espace m; (typ) espace f || tr espacer

space' age' s âge m de l'exploration spatiale

space'craft' s astronef f

space' flight' s voyage m spatial, vol m spatial

space' heat'er s chaufferette f

space' hel'met s casque m de cosmonaute

space'man or **space'man** s (pl -men' or -men) homme m de l'espace, astronaute m, cosmonaute m

space' probe' s coup m de sonde dans l'espace; (rocket) fusée f sonde

spacer ['spesər] s (of typewriter) barre f d'espacement

space'ship' s vaisseau m spatial, astronef m

space' sta'tion s station f orbitale

space' suit' s (rok) scaphandre m des cosmonautes

space' walk' s promenade f dans l'espace

spacious ['spe/əs] adj spacieux

spade [sped] s bêche f; (cards) pique m; **to call a spade a spade** (coll) appeler un chat un chat

spade'work' s gros travail m, défrichage m

spaghetti [spə'geti] s spaghetti m

Spain [spen] s Espagne f; l'Espagne

span [spæn] s portée f; (of time) durée f; (of hand) empan m; (of wing) envergure f; (of bridge) travée f || v (pret & pp spanned; ger spanning) tr couvrir, traverser

spangle ['spæŋgəl] s paillette f || tr orner de paillettes

Spaniard ['spænjərd] s Espagnol m

spaniel ['spænjəl] s épagneul m

Spanish ['spænɪ/] adj espagnol || s (language) espagnol m; **the Spanish** (persons) les Espagnols mpl

Span'ish-Amer'ican adj hispano-américain || s Hispano-Américain m

Span'ish broom' s genêt m d'Espagne

Span'ish fly' s cantharide f

Span'ish Main' s Terre f ferme; mer f des Antilles

Span'ish moss' s tillandsie f

spank [spæŋk] tr fesser

spanking ['spæŋkɪŋ] adj (Brit) de premier ordre; **at a spanking pace** à toute vitesse || s fessée f

spar [spar] s (mineral) spath m; (naut) espar m || v (pret & pp sparred; ger sparring) intr s'entraîner à la boxe; se battre

spare [sper] adj (thin) maigre; (available) disponible; (interchangeable) de rechange; (left over) en surnombre || tr (to save) épargner, économiser; (one's efforts) ménager; (a person) faire grâce à, traiter avec indulgence; (time, money, etc.) disposer de; (something) se passer de

spare' parts' spl pièces fpl détachées, pièces de rechange

spare'rib' s côte f découverte de porc, plat m de côtes

spare/ room/ s chambre f d'ami
spare/ tire/ s pneu m de rechange
spare/ wheel/ s roue f de secours
sparing ['spɛrɪŋ] adj économe, frugal
spark [spark] s étincelle f
spark/ coil/ s bobine f d'allumage
spark/ gap/ s (of induction coil) éclateur m; (of spark plug) entrefer m
sparkle ['sparkəl] s étincellement m, éclat m ‖ intr étinceler
sparkling ['sparklɪŋ] adj étincelant; (wine) mousseux; (soft drink) gazeux
spark/ plug/ s bougie f
sparrow ['spæro] s moineau m
spar/row hawk/ s épervier m
sparse [spars] adj clairsemé, rare; peu nombreux
Spartan ['spartən] adj spartiate ‖ s Spartiate mf
spasm ['spæzəm] s spasme m
spasmodic [spæz'madɪk] adj intermittent, irrégulier; (pathol) spasmodique
spastic ['spæstɪk] adj spasmodique
spat [spæt] s (coll) dispute f, prise f de bec; spats demi-guêtres fpl ‖ v (pret & pp spatted; ger spatting) intr se disputer
spatial ['speʃəl] adj spatial, de l'espace
spatter ['spætər] s éclaboussure f ‖ tr éclabousser
spatula ['spætʃələ] s spatule f
spawn [spɔn] s frai m ‖ tr engendrer ‖ intr frayer
spay [spe] tr châtrer
speak [spik] v (pret spoke [spok]; pp spoken) tr (a word, one's mind, the truth) dire; (a language) parler ‖ intr parler; so to speak pour ainsi dire; speaking! à l'appareil!; to speak out or up parler plus haut, élever la voix; (fig) parler franc
speak/-eas/y s (pl -ies) bar m clandestin
speaker ['spikər] s parleur m; (person addressing a group) conférencier m; (presiding officer) speaker m, président m; (rad) haut-parleur m
spear [spɪr] s lance f ‖ tr percer d'un coup de lance
spear/head/ s fer m de lance; (mil) pointe f, avancée f ‖ tr (e.g., a campaign) diriger
spear/mint/ s menthe f verte
special ['speʃəl] adj spécial, particulier ‖ s train m spécial
spe/cial-deliv/ery let/ter s lettre f exprès
specialist ['speʃəlɪst] s spécialiste mf
specialize ['speʃə,laɪz] tr spécialiser ‖ intr se spécialiser
special-ty ['speʃəlti] s (pl -ties) spécialité f
specie ['spisi] s—in specie en espèces
spe-cies ['spisiz] s (pl -cies) espèce f
specific [spɪ'sɪfɪk] adj & s spécifique m
specif'ic grav'ity s poids m spécifique
speci-fy ['spesɪ,faɪ] v (pret & pp -fied) tr spécifier
specimen ['spesɪmən] s spécimen m; (coll) drôle m de type
specious ['spiʃəs] adj spécieux
speck [spek] s (on fruit, face, etc.) tache f; (in the distance) point m;

(small quantity) brin m, grain m, atome m ‖ tr tacheter
speckle ['spekəl] s petite tache f ‖ tr tacheter, moucheter
spectacle ['spektəkəl] s spectacle m; spectacles lunettes fpl
spec/tacle case/ s étui m à lunettes
spectator ['spekteɾər], [spek'teɾər] s spectateur m
specter ['spektər] s spectre m
spec-trum ['spektrəm] s (pl -tra [trə] or -trums) spectre m
speculate ['spekjə,let] intr spéculer
speculator ['spekjə,leɾər] s spéculateur m, boursicotier m
speech [spitʃ] s discours m; (language) langage m; (of a people or region) parler m; (power of speech) parole f; (theat) tirade f; to make a speech prononcer un discours
speech/ clin/ic s centre m de rééducation de la parole
speech/ correc/tion s rééducation f de la parole
speechless ['spitʃlɪs] adj sans parole, muet; (fig) sidéré, stupéfié
speed [spid] s vitesse f; at full speed à toute vitesse ‖ v (pret & pp speeded or sped [sped]) tr dépêcher, hâter ‖ intr se dépêcher; to speed up aller plus vite
speeding ['spidɪŋ] s excès m de vitesse
speed/ king/ s as m du volant
speed/ lim/it s vitesse f maximum
speedometer [spi'damɪtər] s indicateur m de vitesse
speed/ rec/ord s record m de vitesse
speed/-up/ s accélération f
speed/way/ s (racetrack) piste f d'autos; (highway) autoroute f
speed-y ['spidi] adj (comp -ier; super -iest) rapide, vite, prompt
speed/ zone/ s zone f de vitesse surveillée
spell [spel] s sortilège m; intervalle m; (attack) accès m ‖ v (pret & pp spelled or spelt [spelt]) tr (orally) épeler; (in writing) orthographier, écrire; to spell out (coll) expliquer en détail ‖ v (pret & pp spelled) tr (to relieve) remplacer, relever, relayer
spell/bind/er s orateur m fascinant, orateur entraînant
spell/bound/ adj fasciné
spelling ['spelɪŋ] s orthographe f
spell/ing bee/ s concours m d'orthographe
spelunker [spɪ'lʌŋkər] s spéléo m
spend [spend] v (pret & pp spent [spent]) tr dépenser; (a period of time) passer
spender ['spendər] s dépensier m
spend/ing mon/ey s argent m de poche pour les menues dépenses
spend/thrift/ s prodigue mf, grand dépensier m
sperm [spʌrm] s sperme m
sperm/ whale/ s cachalot m
spew [spju] tr & intr vomir
sphere [sfɪr] s sphère f; corps m céleste
spherical ['sferɪkəl] adj sphérique

sphinx [sfɪŋks] s (pl **sphinxes** or **sphinges** [ˈsfɪndʒiz]) sphinx m

spice [spaɪs] s épice f; (fig) sel m, piquant m || tr épicer

spick-and-span [ˈspɪkəndˈspæn] adj brillant comme un sou neuf; tiré à quatre épingles

spic·y [ˈspaɪsi] adj (comp **-ier**; super **-iest**) épicé, aromatique; (e.g., gravy) relevé; (conversation, story, etc.) épicé, salé, piquant, grivois

spider [ˈspaɪdər] s araignée f

spi'der-web' s toile f d'araignée

spiff·y [ˈspɪfi] adj (comp **-ier**; super **-iest**) (slang) épatant, élégant

spigot [ˈspɪgət] s robinet m

spike [spaɪk] s pointe f; (nail) clou m à large tête; (bot) épi m; (rr) crampon m || tr clouer; ruiner, supprimer; (a drink) (coll) corser à l'alcool || intr (bot) former des épis

spill [spɪl] s chute f, culbute f || v (pret & pp **spilled** or **spilt** [spɪlt]) tr renverser; (a liquid) répandre; (a rider) désarçonner; (passengers) verser || intr se répandre, s'écouler

spill'way' s déversoir m

spin [spɪn] s tournoiement m, rotation f; (on a ball) effet m; (aer) vrille f; to go for a spin (coll) se balader en voiture; to go into a spin (aer) descendre en vrille || v (pret & pp **spun** [spʌn]; ger **spinning**) tr filer; faire tournoyer || intr filer; tournoyer

spinach [ˈspɪnɪtʃ], [ˈspɪnɪdʒ] s épinard m; (leaves used as food) des épinards

spinal [ˈspaɪnəl] adj spinal

spi'nal col'umn s colonne f vertébrale

spi'nal cord' s moelle f épinière

spindle [ˈspɪndəl] s fuseau m

spin'-dri'er s essoreuse f

spin'-dry' v (pret & pp **-dried**) tr essorer

spine [spaɪn] s épine f dorsale, échine f; (quill, fin) épine f; (ridge) arête f; (of book) dos m; (fig) courage m

spineless [ˈspaɪnlɪs] adj sans épines; (weak) mou; to be spineless (fig) avoir l'échine souple

spinet [ˈspɪnɪt] s épinette f

spinner [ˈspɪnər] s fileur m; machine f à filer

spinning [ˈspɪnɪŋ] adj tournoyant || s (act) filage m; (art) filature f

spin'ning wheel' s rouet m

spinster [ˈspɪnstər] s célibataire f, vieille fille f

spiraea [spaɪˈri·ə] s spirée f

spi·ral [ˈspaɪrəl] adj spiral, en spirale || s spirale f || v (pret & pp **-raled** or **-ralled**; ger **-raling** or **-ralling**) intr tourner en spirale; (aer) vriller

spi'ral stair'case s escalier m en colimaçon

spire [spaɪr] s aiguille f; (of clock tower) flèche f

spirit [ˈspɪrɪt] s esprit m; (enthusiasm) feu m; (temper, genius) génie m; (ghost) esprit, revenant m; **high spirits** joie f, abandon m; **spirits** (alcoholic liquor) esprit m, spiritueux m; **to raise the spirits of** remonter le

courage de || tr—**to spirit away** enlever, faire disparaître mystérieusement

spirited adj animé, vigoureux

spiritless [ˈspɪrɪtlɪs] adj sans force, abattu, déprimé

spir'it lev'el s niveau m à bulle

spiritual [ˈspɪrɪt/u·əl] adj spirituel || s chant m religieux populaire

spiritualism [ˈspɪrɪt/u·ə̩lɪzəm] s spiritisme m

spiritualist [ˈspɪrɪt/u·əlɪst] s spirite mf; (philos) spiritualiste mf

spir'ituous bev'erages [ˈspɪrɪt/u·əs] spl boissons fpl spiritueuses

spit [spɪt] s salive f; (culin) broche f || v (pret & pp **spat** [spæt] or **spit**; ger **spitting**) tr & intr cracher

spite [spaɪt] s dépit m, rancune f; **in spite of** en dépit de, malgré || tr dépiter, contrarier

spiteful [ˈspaɪtfəl] adj rancunier

spit'fire' s mégère f

spit'ting im'age s (coll) portrait m craché

spittoon [spɪˈtun] s crachoir m

splash [splæʃ] s éclaboussure f; (of waves) clapotis m; **to make a splash** (coll) faire sensation || tr & intr éclabousser

splash'down' s (rok) amerrissage m

spleen [splin] s rate f; (fig) maussaderie f, mauvaise humeur f; **to vent one's spleen on** décharger sa bile sur

splendid [ˈsplɛndɪd] adj splendide; (coll) admirable, superbe

splendor [ˈsplɛndər] s splendeur f

splice [splaɪs] s (in rope) épissure f; (in wood) enture f || tr (rope) épisser; (wood) enter; (film) réparer, coller; (slang) marier

splint [splɪnt] s éclisse f || tr éclisser

splinter [ˈsplɪntər] s éclat m, éclisse f; (lodged under the skin) écharde f || tr briser en éclats || intr voler en éclats

splin'ter group' s minorité f dissidente, groupe m fragmentaire

split [splɪt] adj fendu; (pea) cassé; (skirt) déchiré s fente f, fissure f; (quarrel) rupture f; (one's share) part f; (bottle) quart m, demi m; (gymnastics) grand écart m || v (pret & pp **split**; ger **splitting**) tr fendre; (money; work; ticket) partager; (in two) couper; (a hide) dédoubler; **to split hairs** couper les cheveux en quatre; **to split one's sides laughing** se tenir les côtes de rire; **to split the difference** couper la poire en deux || intr se fendre; **to split away (from)** se séparer (de)

split' fee' s (between doctors) dichotomie f

split' personal'ity s personnalité f dédoublée

split' tick'et s (pol) panachage m

splitting [ˈsplɪtɪŋ] adj violent; (headache) atroce || s fendage m; (of the atom) désintégration f; (of the personality) dédoublement m

splotch [splɑtʃ] s tache f || tr tacher, barbouiller

splurge [splʌrdʒ] *s* (coll) épate *f* ‖ *intr* (coll) se payer une fête; (*to show off*) (coll) faire de l'épate

splutter ['splʌtər] *s* crachement *m* ‖ *tr* —**to splutter out** bredouiller ‖ *intr* crachoter; (*said of candle, grease, etc.*) grésiller

spoil [spɔɪl] *s* (*object of plunder*) prise *f*, proie *f*; **spoils** (*booty*) butin *m*, dépouilles *fpl*; (*emoluments, especially of public office*) assiette *f* au beurre, part *f* du gâteau ‖ *v* (*pret & pp* **spoiled** or **spoilt** [spɔɪlt]) *tr* gâter, abîmer ‖ *intr* se gâter, s'abîmer; **to be spoiling for** (coll) brûler du désir de

spoilage ['spɔɪlɪdʒ] *s* déchet *m*

spoiled *adj* gâté

spoil'sport' *s* rabat-joie *m*

spoils' sys'tem *s* système *m* des postes aux petits copains

spoke [spok] *s* rai *m*, rayon *m*; (*of a ladder*) échelon *m*

spokes'man *s* (*pl* -men) porte-parole *m*

sponge [spʌndʒ] *s* éponge *f* ‖ *tr* éponger; (*a meal*) (coll) écornifler ‖ *intr* (coll) écornifler; **to sponge on** (coll) vivre aux crochets de

sponge' cake' *s* gâteau *m* de Savoie, gâteau mousseline

sponger ['spʌndʒər] *s* écornifleur *m*, pique-assiette *mf*

sponge' rub'ber *s* caoutchouc *m* mousse

spon-gy ['spʌndʒi] *adj* (*comp* -gier; *super* -giest) spongieux

sponsor ['spʌnsər] *s* patron *m*; (*godfather*) parrain *m*; (*godmother*) marraine *f*; (*law*) garant *m*; (*rad, telv*) commanditaire *m* ‖ *tr* patronner; (*law*) se porter garant de; (*rad, telv*) commanditer

spon'sor-ship' *s* patronnage *m*

spontaneous [spɑn'teni·əs] *adj* spontané

spoof [spuf] *s* (slang) mystification *f*; (slang) parodie *f* ‖ *tr* (slang) mystifier; (slang) blaguer ‖ *intr* (slang) blaguer

spook [spuk] *s* (coll) revenant *m*, spectre *m*

spool [spul] *s* bobine *f*

spoon [spun] *s* cuiller *f*; **to be born with a silver spoon in one's mouth** (coll) être né coiffé ‖ *tr* prendre dans une cuiller; **to spoon off** enlever avec la cuiller ‖ *intr* (coll) se faire des mamours

spooner ['spunər] *s* (coll) peloteur *m*

spoonerism ['spunə‚rɪzəm] *s* contrepèterie *f*

spoon'-feed' *v* (*pret & pp* -fed) *tr* nourrir à la cuiller; (*an industry*) subventionner; (coll) mâcher la besogne à

spoonful ['spun‚ful] *s* cuillerée *f*

spoon-y ['spuni] *adj* (*comp* -ier; *super* -iest) (coll) peloteur

sporadic(al) [spə'rædɪk(əl)] *adj* sporadique

spore [spor] *s* spore *f*

sport [sport] *adj* sportif, de sport ‖ *s* sport *m*; amusement *m*, jeu *m*; (biol) mutation *f*; (coll) chic type *m*; **a good**

sport un bon copain; (*a good loser*) un beau joueur; **in sport** par plaisanterie; **to make sport of** tourner en ridicule ‖ *tr* faire parade de, arborer ‖ *intr* s'amuser, jouer

sport' clothes' *spl* vêtements *mpl* de sport

sport'ing goods' *spl* articles *mpl* de sport

sports'cast'er *s* radioreporter *m* sportif

sports' ed'itor *s* rédacteur *m* sportif

sports' fan' *s* fanatique *mf*, enragé *m* des sports

sports'man *s* (*pl* -men) sportif *m*

sports'man-like' *adj* sportif

sports'man-ship' *s* sportivité *f*

sports'wear' *s* vêtements *mpl* sport

sports'writ'er *s* reporter *m* sportif

sport-y ['sporti] *adj* (*comp* -ier; *super* -iest) (coll) sportif; (*smart in dress*) (coll) chic; (*flashy*) (coll) criard, voyant; (coll) dissolu, libertin

spot [spɑt] *s* tache *f*; (*place*) endroit *m*, lieu *m*; **on the spot** sur place; (slang) dans le pétrin; **spots** (*before eyes*) mouches *fpl* ‖ *v* (*pret & pp* spotted; *ger* spotting) *tr* tacher; (coll) repérer, détecter ‖ *intr* se tacher

spot' cash' *s* argent *m* comptant

spot' check' *s* échantillonnage *m*

spot'-check' *tr* échantillonner

spotless ['spɑtlɪs] *adj* sans tache

spot'light' *s* spot *m*; (aut) projecteur *m* auxiliaire orientable; **to hold the spotlight** (fig) être en vedette ‖ *tr* diriger les projecteurs sur; (fig) mettre en vedette

spot' remov'er [rɪ'muvər] *s* détachant *m*

spot' weld'ing *s* soudage *m* par points

spouse [spauz], [spaus] *s* (*man*) époux *m*, conjoint *m*; (*woman*) épouse *f*, conjointe *f*

spout [spaut] *s* tuyau *m* de décharge; (*e.g., of teapot*) bec *m*; (*of sprinkling can*) col *m*, queue *f*; (*of water*) jet *m* ‖ *tr* faire jaillir; (*e.g., insults*) (coll) déclamer ‖ *intr* jaillir; **to spout off** (coll) déclamer

sprain [spren] *s* foulure *f*, entorse *f* ‖ *tr* fouler, se fouler

sprawl [sprɔl] *intr* s'étaler, se carrer

spray [spre] *s* (*of ocean*) embruns *mpl*; (*branch*) rameau *m*; (*for insects*) liquide *m* insecticide; (*for weeds*) produit *m* herbicide; (*for spraying insects or weeds*) pulvérisateur *m*; (*for spraying perfume*) vaporisateur *m* ‖ *tr* pulvériser; (*with a vaporizer*) vaporiser; (hort) désinfecter par pulvérisation d'insecticide; **to spray paint on** peindre au pistolet ‖ *intr*— **to spray out** gicler

sprayer ['spre·ər] *s* vaporisateur *m*, pulvérisateur *m*

spray' gun' *s* pulvérisateur *m*; (*for paint*) pistolet *m*; (hort) seringue *f*

spread [spred] *adj* étendu, écarté, ouvert ‖ *s* étendue *f*, rayonnement *m*; (*on bed*) dessus-de-lit *m*, couvre-lit *m*; (*on sandwich*) pâte *f*; (*buffet lunch*) collation *f* ‖ *v* (*pret & pp* spread) *tr* étendre, étaler; (*news*) répandre; (*disease*) propager; (*the wings*) déployer; (*a piece of bread*) tartiner ‖ *intr* s'étendre, s'étaler; se répandre, rayonner

spree [sprī] *s* bombance *f*, orgie *f*; to go on a spree (coll) faire la bombe

sprig [sprīg] *s* brin *m*, brindille *f*

spright·ly ['spraītlī] *adj* (*comp* -lier; *super* -liest) vif, enjoué

spring [sprīŋ] *adj* printanier ‖ *s* (*of water*) source *f*; (*season*) printemps *m*; (*jump*) saut *m*, bond *m*; (*elastic device*) ressort *m*; (*quality*) élasticité *f* ‖ *v* (*pret* sprang [spræŋ] or sprung [sprʌŋ]; *pp* sprung) *tr* (*the frame of a car*) faire déjeter; (*a lock*) faire jouer; (*a leak*) contracter; (*a question*) proposer à l'improviste; (*a prisoner*) (coll) faire sortir de prison ‖ *intr* sauter, bondir; (*said of oil, water, etc.*) jaillir; to spring up se lever; naître

spring'-and-fall' *adj* (*coat*) de demi-saison

spring'board' *s* tremplin *m*

spring' fe'ver *s* (hum) malaise *m* des premières chaleurs, flemme *f*

spring'like' *adj* printanier

spring'time' *s* printemps *m*

sprinkle ['sprīŋkəl] *s* pluie *f* fine; (culin) pincée *f* ‖ *tr* (*with water*) asperger, arroser; (*with powder*) saupoudrer; (*to strew*) parsemer ‖ *intr* tomber en pluie fine

sprinkler ['sprīŋklər] *s* arrosoir *m*

sprinkling ['sprīŋklīŋ] *s* aspersion *f*, arrosage *m*; (*with holy water*) aspersion; (*with powder*) saupoudrage *m*; (*of knowledge*) bribes *fpl*, notions *fpl*; (*of persons*) petit nombre *m*

sprin'kling can' *s* arrosoir *m*

sprint [sprīnt] *s* course *f* de vitesse, sprint *m* ‖ *intr* faire une course de vitesse, courir à toute vitesse

sprite [spraīt] *s* lutin *m*

sprocket ['sprakīt] *s* dent *f* de pignon; (*wheel*) pignon *m* de chaîne

sprock'et wheel' *s* pignon *m* de chaîne

sprout [spraūt] *s* pousse *f*, rejeton *m*; (*of seed*) germe *m* ‖ *intr* (*said of plant*) pousser, pointer; (*said of seed*) germer

spruce [sprūs] *adj* pimpant, tiré à quatre épingles ‖ *s* sapin *m*; (*Norway spruce*) épicéa *m* commun ‖ *intr* —to spruce up se faire beau, se pomponner

spry [spraī] *adj* (*comp* spryer or sprier; *super* spryest or spriest) vif, alerte

spud [spʌd] *s* (*chisel*) bédane *f*; (agr) arrache-racines *m*; (coll) pomme *f* de terre, patate *f*

spun' glass' [spʌn] *s* coton *m* de verre

spunk [spʌŋk] *s* (coll) cran *m*, courage *m*

spur [spʌr] *s* éperon *m*; (*of rooster*) ergot *m*; (*stimulant*) aiguillon *m*, stimulant *m*; (rr) embranchement *m*; on the spur of the moment sous l'impulsion du moment ‖ *v* (*pret* & *pp*

spurred; *ger* spurring) *tr* éperonner; to spur on aiguillonner, stimuler

spurious ['spjūrī·əs] *adj* faux; (*sentiments*) simulé, feint; (*document*) apocryphe

spurn [spʌrn] *tr* repousser avec mépris, faire fi de

spurt [spʌrt] *s* jaillissement *m*, giclée *f*, jet *m*; (*of enthusiasm*) élan *m*; effort *m* soudain ‖ *intr* jaillir; to spurt out gicler

sputnik ['sputnīk], ['spʌtnīk] *s* spoutnik *m*

sputter ['spʌtər] *s* (*manner of speaking*) bredouillement *m*; (*of candle*) grésillement *m*; (*of fire*) crachement *m* ‖ *tr* (*words*) débiter en lançant des postillons ‖ *intr* postillonner; (*said of candle*) grésiller; (*said of fire*) cracher, pétiller

spu·tum ['spjūtəm] *s* (*pl* -ta [tə]) crachat *m*

spy [spaī] *s* (*pl* spies) espion *m* ‖ *v* (*pret* & *pp* spied) *tr* (*to catch sight of*) entrevoir; to spy out découvrir par ruse ‖ *intr* espionner; to spy on épier, guetter

spy'glass' *s* longue-vue *f*

spying ['spaī·īŋ] *s* espionnage *m*

spy' ring' *s* réseau *m* d'espionnage

squabble ['skwabəl] *s* chamaillerie *f* ‖ *intr* se chamailler

squad [skwad] *s* escouade *f*, peloton *m*; (*of detectives*) brigade *f*

squadron ['skwadrən] *s* (aer) escadrille *f*; (mil) escadron *m*; (nav) escadre *f*

squalid ['skwalīd] *adj* sordide

squall [skwɔl] *s* bourrasque *f*, rafale *f*; (*cry*) braillement *m*; (coll) grabuge *m* ‖ *intr* souffler en bourrasque; brailler

squalor ['skwalər] *s* saleté *f*; misère *f*

squander ['skwandər] *tr* gaspiller

square [skwer] *adj* carré; (*honest*) loyal, franc; (*real*) véritable; (*conventional*) (slang) formaliste; nine (ten, etc.) inches square de neuf (dix, etc.) pouces en carré; nine (ten, etc.) square inches neuf (dix, etc.) pouces carrés; to get square with (coll) régler ses comptes avec; we'll call it square (coll) nous sommes quittes ‖ *s* carré *m*; (*of checkerboard or chessboard*) case *f*; (*city block*) pâté *m* de maisons; (*open area in town or city*) place *f*; (*of carpenter*) équerre *f*; to be on the square (coll) jouer franc jeu ‖ *adv* carrément ‖ *tr* carrer; (*a number*) élever au carré; (*wood, marble, etc.*) équarrir; (*a debt*) régler; (bk) balancer ‖ *intr*—to square off (coll) se mettre en posture de combat; to square with (*to tally with*) s'accorder avec; régler ses comptes avec

square' dance' *s* quadrille *m* américain

square' deal' *s* (coll) procédé *m* loyal

square' meal' *s* repas *m* copieux

square' root' *s* racine *f* carrée

squash [skwaʃ] *s* écrasement *m*; (bot) courge *f*; (sports) squash *m* ‖ *tr* écraser ‖ *intr* s'écraser

squash·y ['skwɑʃi] adj (comp **-ier**; super **-iest**) mou et humide; (fruit) à pulpe molle

squat [skwɑt] adj accroupi; (heavyset) trapu, ramassé || s position f accroupie || v (pret & pp squatted; ger squatting) intr s'accroupir; (to settle) s'installer sans titre légal

squatter ['skwɑtər] s squatter m

squaw [skwɔ] s femme f peau-rouge

squawk [skwɔk] s cri m rauque; (slang) protestation f, piaillerie f || intr pousser un cri rauque; (slang) protester, piailler

squeak [skwik] s grincement m; (of living being) couic m, petit cri m || intr grincer; pousser des petits cris, couiner

squeal [skwil] s cri m aigu || intr piailler; (slang) manger le morceau; to squeal on (slang) moucharder

squealer ['skwilər] s (coll) cafard m

squeamish ['skwimɪʃ] adj trop scrupuleux; prude; sujet aux nausées

squeeze [skwiz] s pression f; (coll) extorsion f; it's a tight squeeze (coll) ça tient tout juste || tr serrer; (fruit) presser; to squeeze from faire extorquer à; to squeeze into faire entrer de force dans || intr se blottir; to squeeze through se frayer un passage à travers

squeezer ['skwizər] s presse f, presse-fruits m

squelch [skwɛltʃ] s (coll) remarque f écrasante || tr écraser, réprimer

squid [skwɪd] s calmar m

squill [skwɪl] s (bot) scille f; (zool) squille f

squint [skwɪnt] s coup m d'œil furtif; (pathol) strabisme m || tr fermer à moitié || intr loucher; to squint at regarder furtivement

squint'-eyed' adj bigle, strabique; malveillant

squire [skwaɪr] s écuyer m; (lady's escort) cavalier m servant; (property owner) propriétaire m terrien; juge m de paix || tr escorter

squirm [skwʌrm] s tortillement m || intr se tortiller; to squirm out of se tirer de

squirrel ['skwʌrəl] s écureuil m

squirt [skwʌrt] s giclée f, jet m; (syringe) seringue f; (coll) morveux m || tr faire gicler || intr gicler, jaillir

stab [stæb] s coup m de poignard, de couteau; (wound) estafilade f; (coll) coup d'essai; to make a stab at (coll) s'essayer à || v (pret & pp stabbed; ger stabbing) tr poignarder

stabilize ['stebəl‚aɪz] tr stabiliser

stab' in the back' s coup m de Jarnac, coup de traître

stable ['stebəl] adj stable || s (for cows) étable f; (for horses) écurie f

stack [stæk] s tas m, pile f; (of hay, straw, etc.) meule f; (of sheaves) gerbier m; (e.g., of rifles) faisceau m; (of ship or locomotive) cheminée f; (of fireplace) souche f; stacks (in library) rayons mpl || tr entasser, empiler; mettre en meule, en gerbier, or en faisceau; (a deck of cards) truquer, donner un coup de pouce à; to stack arms former les faisceaux

stadi·um ['stedɪ‚əm] s (pl **-ums** or **-a** [ə]) stade m

staff [stæf], [staf] s bâton m; (of pilgrim) bourdon m; (of flag) hampe f; (of newspaper) rédaction f; (employees) personnel m; (servants) domestiques mfpl; (support) soutien m; (mil) état-major m; (mus) portée f || tr fournir, pourvoir de personnel; nommer le personnel pour

staff' head'quarters spl (mil) état-major m

staff' of'ficer s officier m d'état-major

stag [stæg] adj exclusivement masculin; to go stag aller sans compagne f homme m; (male deer) cerf m

stage [stedʒ] s stade m, étape f, phase f; (of rocket) étage m; (stagecoach) diligence f; (scene) champ m d'action, scène f; (staging) échafaudage m; (platform) estrade f; (of microscope) platine f; (theat) scène f; by easy stages par petites étapes; by successive stages par échelons; to go on the stage monter sur les planches || tr (a play, demonstration, riot, etc.) monter; (a play) mettre en scène

stage'coach' s diligence f, coche m

stage'craft' s technique f de la scène

stage' door' s entrée f des artistes

stage'-door John'ny s (pl **-nies**) coureur m de girls

stage' effect' s effet m scénique

stage' fright' s trac m

stage'hand' s machiniste m

stage' left' s côté m jardin

stage' man'ager s régisseur m

stage' name' s nom m de théâtre

stage' prop'erties spl accessoires mpl

stage' right' s côté m cour

stage'-struck' [strʌk] adj entiché de théâtre

stage' whis'per s aparté m

stagger ['stægər] tr ébranler; (to surprise) étonner; (to arrange) disposer en chicane, en zigzag; (hours of work, train schedules, etc.) échelonner || intr chanceler, tituber

staggering ['stægərɪŋ] adj chancelant; (amazing) étonnant

staging ['stedʒɪŋ] s échafaudage m; (theat) mise f en scène

stagnant ['stægnənt] adj stagnant

stag' par'ty s (pl **-ties**) (coll) réunion f entre hommes, réunion d'hommes seuls

staid [sted] adj posé, sérieux

stain [sten] s tache f, souillure f || tr tacher, souiller; (to tint) teindre || intr se tacher

stained' glass' s vitre f de couleur

stained'-glass win'dow s vitrail m

stain'less steel' ['stenlɪs] s acier m inoxydable

stair [ster] s escalier m; (step of a series) marche f, degré m; **stairs** escalier m

stair'case' s escalier m

stair′way′ s escalier m

stair′well′ s cage f d'escalier

stake [stek] s pieu m, poteau m; (of tent) piquet m; (marker) jalon m; (for burning condemned persons) bûcher m; (in a game of chance) mise f, enjeu m; at stake en jeu; to pull up stakes (coll) déménager || tr (a road) bornoyer; (plants) échalasser, ramer; (money) risquer; (to back financially) (slang) fournir aux besoins de; to stake all mettre tout en jeu; to stake off or out jalonner, piqueter

stale [stel] adj (bread) rassis; (wine or beer) éventé; (air) confiné; (joke) vieux; (check) proscrit; (subject) rabattu; (news) défloré, défraîchi; to smell stale (said of room) sentir le renfermé

stale′mate′ s (chess) pat m; (fig) impasse f; in stalemate pat || tr (chess) faire pat; (fig) paralyser

stalk [stɔk] s tige f; (of flower or leaf) queue f || tr traquer, suivre à la piste || intr marcher fièrement, marcher à grandes enjambées

stall [stɔl] s stalle f; (at a market) étal m, échoppe f; (slang) prétexte m || tr mettre dans une stalle; (a car) caler; (an airplane) mettre en perte de vitesse; to stall off (coll) différer sous prétexte || intr (said of motor) se bloquer; to stall for time (slang) temporiser

stallion [ˈstæljən] s étalon m

stalwart [ˈstɔlwərt] adj robuste; vaillant || s partisan m loyal

stamen [ˈstemən] s étamine f

stamina [ˈstæmɪnə] s vigueur f, résistance f

stammer [ˈstæmər] s bégaiement m, balbutiement m || tr & intr bégayer, balbutier

stammerer [ˈstæmərər] s bègue mf

stamp [stæmp] s empreinte f; (for postage) timbre m; (for stamping) poinçon m || tr (mail) affranchir; (money; leather; a medal) frapper, estamper; (a document) timbrer; (a passport) viser; to stamp one's feet trépigner; to stamp one's foot frapper du pied; to stamp out (e.g., a rebellion) écraser, étouffer

stampede [stæmˈpid] s débandade f; (rush) ruée f; (of people) sauve-qui-peut m || tr provoquer la ruée de || intr se débander

stamped′ self′-addressed′ en′velope s enveloppe f timbrée par l'expéditeur

stamp′ing grounds′ spl—to be on one's stamping grounds (slang) être sur son terrain, être dans son domaine

stamp′ pad′ s tampon m encreur

stamp′-vend′ing machine′ s distributeur m automatique de timbres-poste

stance [stæns] s attitude f, posture f

stanch [stɑntʃ] adj ferme, solide; vrai, loyal; (watertight) étanche || tr étancher

stand [stænd] s résistance f; position f; (of a merchant) étal m, éventaire m; (of a speaker) tribune f, estrade f; (of a horse) aplombs mpl; (piece of furniture) guéridon m, console f; (to hold music, papers) pupitre m; stands tribune f, stand m || v (pret & pp stood [stud]) tr mettre, placer, poser; (the cold) supporter; (a shock; an attack) soutenir; (a round of drinks) (coll) payer; to stand off repousser; to stand up (to keep waiting) (coll) poser un lapin à || intr se lever, se mettre debout; se tenir debout, être debout; en être, e.g., how does it stand? où en est-il?; to stand aloof or aside se tenir à l'écart; to stand by se tenir prêt; (e.g., a friend) rester fidèle à; to stand fast tenir bon; to stand for (to mean) signifier; (to affirm) soutenir; (to allow) tolérer; to stand in for doubler, remplacer; to stand in line faire la queue; to stand out sortir, saillir; to stand up se lever, se mettre debout; se tenir debout, être debout; to stand up against or to tenir tête à; to stand up for prendre fait et cause pour

standard [ˈstændərd] adj (product, part, unit) standard, de série, normal; (current) courant; (author, book, work) classique; (edition) définitif; (keyboard of typewriter) universel; (coinage) au titre || s norme f, mesure f, règle f, pratique f; (of quantity, weight, value) standard m; (banner) étendard m; (of lamp) support m; (of wires) pylône m; (of coinage) titre m; (for a monetary system) étalon m; (fig) degré m, niveau m; standards critères mpl; up to standard suivant la norme

stand′ard-bear′er s porte-drapeau m

stand′ard gauge′ s voie f normale

standardize [ˈstændər‚daɪz] tr standardiser

stand′ard of liv′ing s niveau m de vie

stand′ard time′ s heure f légale

standee [stænˈdi] s voyageur m debout; (theat) spectateur m debout

stand′-in′ s (mov, theat) doublure f, remplaçant m; (coll) appuis mpl, piston m

standing [ˈstændɪŋ] adj (upright) debout; (statue) en pied; (water) stagnant; (army; committee) permanent; (price; rule; rope) fixe; (custom) établi, courant; (jump) à pieds joints || s standing m, position f, importance f; in good standing estimé, accrédité; of long standing de longue date

stand′ing ar′my s armée f permanente

stand′ing room′ s places fpl debout

stand′ing vote′ s vote m par assis et levé

stand′pat′ adj & s (coll) immobiliste mf

stand′pat′ter s (coll) immobiliste mf

stand′point′ s point m de vue

stand′still′ s arrêt m, immobilisation f; to come to a standstill s'arrêter court

stanza [ˈstænzə] s strophe f

staple [ˈstepəl] adj principal || s (product) produit m principal; (for hold-

ing papers together) agrafe *f*; (bb) broche *f*; **staples** denrées *fpl* principales ‖ *tr* agrafer; (*books*) brocher

stapler ['steplər] *s* agrafeuse *f*; (bb) brocheuse *f*

star [star] *s* astre *m*; (*heavenly body except sun and moon*; *figure that represents a star*) étoile *f*; (*of stage or screen*) vedette *f* ‖ *v* (*pret & pp* **starred**; *ger* **starring**) *tr* étoiler, consteller; (mov, rad, telv, theat) mettre en vedette; (typ) marquer d'un astérisque ‖ *intr* apparaître comme vedette

starboard ['starbərd], ['star,bord] *adj* de tribord ‖ *s* tribord *m* ‖ *adv* à tribord

star′ board′er *s* (coll) pensionnaire *mf* de prédilection

starch [start/] *s* amidon *m*; (*for fabrics*) empois *m*; (*formality*) raideur *f*; (bot, culin) fécule *f*; (coll) force *f*, vigueur *f* ‖ *tr* empeser

starch·y ['start/i] *adj* (*comp* **-ier**; *super* **-iest**) empesé *m*; (*foods*) féculent; (*manner*) raide, guindé

stare [ster] *s* regard *m* fixe ‖ *tr*—**to stare s.o. in the face** dévisager qn; (*to be obvious to s.o.*) sauter aux yeux de qn ‖ *intr* regarder fixement; **to stare at** regarder fixement, dévisager

star′fish′ *s* étoile *f* de mer

star′gaze′ *intr* regarder les étoiles; rêvasser, être dans la lune

stark [stark] *adj* pur; rigide; désert, solitaire ‖ *adv* entièrement

stark′-na′ked *adj* tout nu

star′light′ *s* lumière *f* des étoiles

starling ['starlɪŋ] *s* étourneau *m*

star·ry ['stari] *adj* (*comp* **-rier**; *super* **-riest**) étoilé

Stars′ and Stripes′ *spl* bannière *f* étoilée

Star′-Spangled Ban′ner *s* bannière *f* étoilée

start [start] *s* commencement *m*, début *m*; (*sudden start*) sursaut *m*, haut-le-corps *m* ‖ *tr* commencer; (*a car, a motor, etc.*) mettre en marche, démarrer; (*a conversation*) entamer; (*a hare*) lever; (*a deer*) lancer; **to start** + *ger* se mettre à + *inf* ‖ *intr* commencer, débuter; démarrer; (*to be startled*) sursauter; **starting from** or **with** à partir de; **to start after** sortir à la recherche de; **to start out** se mettre en route

starter ['startər] *s* initiateur *m*; (aut) démarreur *m*; (sports) starter *m*

start′ing point′ *s* point *m* de départ

startle ['startəl] *tr* faire tressaillir ‖ *intr* tressaillir

startling ['startlɪŋ] *adj* effrayant; (*event*) sensationnel; (*resemblance*) saisissant

starvation [star′ve/ən] *s* inanition *f*, famine *f*

starva′tion di′et *s* diète *f* absolue

starva′tion wag′es *spl* salaire *m* de famine

starve [starv] *tr* affamer; faire mourir

de faim; **to starve out** réduire par la faim ‖ *intr* être affamé; être dans la misère; mourir de faim; (coll) mourir de faim

state [stet] *s* état *m*; (*pomp*) apparat *m*; **to lie in state** être exposé solennellement ‖ *tr* affirmer, déclarer; (*an hour or date*) régler, fixer; (*a problem*) poser

stateless ['stetlɪs] *adj* apatride

state·ly ['stetli] *adj* (*comp* **-lier**; *super* **-liest**) majestueux, imposant

statement ['stetmənt] *s* énoncé *m*, exposé *m*; (*account, report*) compte rendu *m*, rapport *m*; (*of an account*) (com) relevé *m*

state′ of mind′ *s* état *m* d'esprit, état d'âme

state′room′ *s* (naut) cabine *f*; (rr) compartiment *m*

states′man *s* (*pl* **-men**) homme *m* d'État

static ['stætɪk] *adj* statique; (rad) parasite ‖ *s* (rad) parasites *mpl*

station ['ste/ən] *s* station *f*; (*for police; for selling gasoline; for broadcasting*) poste *m*; (*of bus, subway, rail line, taxi; for observation*) station; (rr) gare *f* ‖ *tr* poster, placer

sta′tion a′gent *s* chef *m* de gare

stationary ['ste/ən,eri] *adj* stationnaire

sta′tion break′ *s* (rad) pause *f*

stationer ['ste/ənər] *s* papetier *m*

stationery ['ste/ən,eri] *s* papeterie *f*, fournitures *fpl* de bureau

sta′tionery store′ *s* papeterie *f*

sta′tion house′ *s* commissariat *m* de police

sta′tion identifica′tion *s* (rad) indicatif *m*

sta′tion-mas′ter *s* chef *m* de gare

sta′tion wag′on *s* familiale *f*, break *m*

statistical [stə′tɪstɪkəl] *adj* statistique

statistician [,stætɪs′tɪ/ən] *s* statisticien *m*

statistics [stə′tɪstɪks] *s* (*science*) statistique *f* ‖ *spl* (*data*) statistique, statistiques

statue ['stæt/u] *s* statue *f*

Stat′ue of Lib′erty *s* Liberté *f* éclairant le monde

statuesque [,stæt/u′esk] *adj* sculptural

stature ['stæt/ər] *s* stature *f*, taille *f*; caractère *m*, stature

status ['stetəs] *s* condition *f*; rang *m*, standing *m*

sta′tus quo′ [kwo] *s* statu quo *m*

sta′tus seek′er *s* obsédé *m* du standing

sta′tus sym′bol *s* symbole *m* du rang social

statute ['stæt/ut] *s* statut *m*

statutory ['stæt/u,tori] *adj* statutaire

staunch [stont/], [stant/] *adj & tr* var of **stanch**

stave [stev] *s* bâton *m*; (*of barrel*) douve *f*; (*of ladder*) échelon *m*; (mus) portée *f* ‖ *v* (*pret & pp* **staved** or **stove** [stov]) *tr*—**to stave in** défoncer, crever; **to stave off** détourner, éloigner

stay [ste] *s* (*visit*) séjour *m*; (*prop*) étai *m*; (*of a corset*) baleine *f*; (*of execution*) sursis *m*; (fig) soutien *m* ‖

tr arrêter ‖ *intr* rester; séjourner; (*at a hotel*) descendre; **to stay put** ne pas bouger; **to stay up** veiller

stay'-at-home' *adj* & *s* casanier *m*

stead [sted] *s*—**in s.o.'s stead** à la place de qn; **to stand s.o. in good stead** être fort utile à qn

stead'fast' *adj* ferme; constant

stead·y ['stedɪ] *adj* (*comp* -ier; *super* -iest) ferme, solide; régulier; (*market*) soutenu ‖ *v* (*pret* & *pp* -ied) *tr* raffermir ‖ *intr* se raffermir

steak [stek] *s* (*slice*) tranche *f*; bifteck *m*

steal [stil] *s* (coll) vol *m*; (*bargain*) (coll) occasion *f* ‖ *v* (*pret* **stole** [stol]; *pp* **stolen**) *tr* voler; **to steal s.th. from s.o.** voler q.ch. à qn ‖ *intr* voler; **to steal away** se dérober; **to steal into** se glisser dans; **to steal upon** s'approcher en tapinois

stealth [stelθ] *s*—**by stealth** en tapinois, à la dérobée

steam [stim] *s* vapeur *f*; (e.g., *on a window*) buée *f*; **full steam ahead!** en avant à toute vapeur!; **to get up steam** faire monter la pression; **to let off steam** lâcher la vapeur; (fig) s'épancher ‖ *tr* passer à la vapeur; (culin) cuire à la vapeur; **to steam up** (e.g., *a window*) embuer ‖ *intr* dégager de la vapeur, fumer; **to evaporer;** **to steam ahead** avancer à la vapeur; (fig) faire des progrès rapides; **to steam up** s'embuer

steam'boat' *s* vapeur *m*

steam' chest' *s* boîte *f* à vapeur

steam' en'gine *s* machine *f* à vapeur

steamer ['stimər] *s* vapeur *m*

steam' heat' *s* chauffage *m* à la vapeur

steam' roll'er *s* rouleau *m* compresseur; (fig) force *f* irrésistible

steam'ship' *s* vapeur *m*

steam' shov'el *s* pelle *f* à vapeur

steam' ta'ble *s* table *f* à compartiments chauffés à la vapeur

steed [stid] *s* coursier *m*

steel [stil] *s* acier *m*; (industry) sidérurgique ‖ *s* acier *m*; (*for striking fire from flint*) briquet *m*; (*for sharpening knives*) fusil *m* ‖ *tr* aciérer; **to steel oneself against** se cuirasser contre

steel' wool' *s* laine *f* d'acier, paille *f* de fer

steel'works' *spl* aciérie *f*

steelyard ['stil,jard], ['stiljərd] *s* romaine *f*

steep [stip] *adj* raide, abrupt; (*cliff*) escarpé; (*price*) (coll) exorbitant ‖ *tr* tremper; (e.g., *tea*) infuser; **steeped in** saturé de; (*ignorance*) pétri de; (*the classics*) nourri de

steeple ['stipəl] *s* clocher *m*; (*spire*) flèche *f*

stee'ple-chase' *s* course *f* d'obstacles

steer [stɪr] *s* bouvillon *m* ‖ *tr* diriger, conduire; (naut) gouverner ‖ *intr* se diriger; (naut) se gouverner; **to steer clear of** (coll) éviter

steerage ['stɪrɪdʒ] *s* entrepont *m*

steer'age pas'senger *s* passager *m* d'entrepont

steer'ing wheel' *s* volant *m*; (naut) roue *f* de gouvernail

stellar ['stelər] *adj* stellaire; (*rôle*) de vedette

stem [stem] *s* (*of plant; of key*) tige *f*; (*of column; of tree*) fût *m*, tige; (*of fruit*) queue *f*; (*of pipe; of feather*) tuyau *m*; (*of goblet*) pied *m*; (*of watch*) remontoir *m*; (*of word*) radical *m*, thème *m*; (naut) étrave *f*; **from stem to stern** de l'étrave à l'étambot, d'un bout à l'autre ‖ *v* (*pret* & *pp* **stemmed**; *ger* **stemming**) *tr* (e.g., *grapes*) égrapper; (e.g., *the flow of blood*) étancher; (*the tide*) lutter contre, refouler; (*to check*) arrêter, endiguer ‖ *intr*—**to stem from** provenir de

stem'-wind'er *s* montre *f* à remontoir

stench [stentʃ] *s* puanteur *f*

sten·cil ['stensəl] *s* pochoir *m*; (*work produced by it*) travail *m* au pochoir; (*for reproducing typewriting*) stencil *m* ‖ *v* (*pret* & *pp* **-ciled** or **-cilled**; *ger* **-ciling** or **-cilling**) *tr* passer au pochoir; tirer au stencil

stenographer [stə'nagrəfər] *s* sténo *f*, sténographe *mf*

stenography [stə'nagrəfɪ] *s* sténographie *f*

step [step] *s* pas *m*; (*of staircase*) marche *f*, degré *m*; (*footprint*) trace *f*; (*of carriage*) marchepied *m*; (*of ladder*) échelon *m*; (*procedure*) démarche *f*; **in step with** au pas avec; **step by step** pas à pas; **watch your step!** prenez garde de tomber!; (fig) évitez tout faux pas! ‖ *v* (*pret* & *pp* **stepped**; *ger* **stepping**) *tr* échelonner; **to step off** mesurer au pas ‖ *intr* faire un pas; marcher; (coll) aller en toute hâte; **to step aside** s'écarter; **to step back** reculer; **to step in** entrer; **to step on it** (coll) mettre tous les gaz; **to step on the starter** appuyer sur le démarreur

step'broth'er *s* demi-frère *m*

step'child' *s* (*pl* -**chil'dren**) beau-fils *m*; belle-fille *f*

step'daugh'ter *s* belle-fille *f*

step'fa'ther *s* beau-père *m*

step'lad'der *s* échelle *f* double, marchepied *m*, escabeau *m*

step'moth'er *s* belle-mère *f*

steppe [step] *s* steppe *f*

step'ping stone' *s* pierre *f* de passage; (fig) marchepied *m*

step'sis'ter *s* demi-sœur *f*

step'son' *s* beau-fils *m*

stere·o ['stɛri,o], ['stɪri,o] *adj* (coll) stéréo, stéréophonique; (coll) stéréoscopique ‖ *s* (*pl* -os) (coll) disque *m* stéréo; (coll) émission *f* en stéréophonique; (coll) photographie *f* stéréoscopique

stereotyped ['stɛrɪ-ə,taɪpt], ['stɪrɪ-ə,taɪpt] *adj* stéréotypé

sterile ['stɛrɪl] *adj* stérile

sterilize ['stɛrɪ,laɪz] *tr* stériliser

sterling ['stʌrlɪŋ] *adj* de bon aloi ‖ *s* livres *fpl* sterling; argent *m* au titre; vaisselle *f* d'argent

stern [stʌrn] *adj* sévère, austère; *(look)* rébarbatif ‖ *s* poupe *f*

stethoscope ['steθə ˌskop] *s* stéthoscope *m*

stevedore ['stivə ˌdor] *s* arrimeur *m*

stew [st(j)u] *s* ragoût *m* ‖ *tr* mettre en ragoût ‖ *intr* (coll) être dans tous ses états

steward ['st(j)uərd] *s* régisseur *m*, intendant *m*; maître *m* d'hôtel; (aer, naut) steward *m*

stewardess ['st(j)uərdɪs] *s* (aer) hôtesse *f* de l'air; (naut) stewardesse *f*

stewed′ fruit′ *s* compote *f*

stewed′ toma′toes *spl* purée *f* de tomates

stick [stɪk] *s* bâtonnet *m*, bâton *m*; *(rod)* verge *f*; *(wand; drumstick)* baguette *f*; *(of chewing gum; of dynamite)* bâton; *(firewood)* bois *m* sec; *(walking stick)* canne *f*; (naut) mât *m*; (typ) compositeur *m* ‖ *v* (pret & pp **stuck** [stʌk]) *tr* piquer, enfoncer; *(to fasten in position)* clouer, ficher, planter; *(to glue)* coller; *(a pig)* saigner; (coll) confondre; **stick 'em up!** (slang) haut les mains!; **to be stuck** être pris; *(e.g., in the mud)* s'enliser; *(to be unable to continue)* (coll) être en panne; **to stick it out** (coll) tenir jusqu'au bout; **to stick out** *(one's tongue)* tirer; *(one's head)* passer; *(one's chest)* bomber; **to stick up** *(in order to rob)* (slang) voler à main armée ‖ *intr* se piquer, s'enfoncer; se ficher, se planter; *(to be jammed)* être pris, se coincer; *(to adhere)* coller; *(to remain)* continuer, rester; **to stick out** saillir, dépasser; *(to be evident)* sauter aux yeux; **to stick up for** (coll) prendre la défense de

sticker ['stɪkər] *s* étiquette *f* gommée; *(difficult question)* (coll) colle *f*

stick′pin′ *s* épingle *f* de cravate

stick′-up′ *s* (slang) attaque *f* à main armée, hold-up *m*

stick·y ['stɪki] *adj* (comp -ier; super -iest) gluant, collant; *(hands)* poisseux; *(weather)* étouffant; *(question)* épineux; *(unaccommodating)* tatillon

stiff [stɪf] *adj* raide; difficile, ardu; *(joint)* ankylosé; *(brush; batter)* dur; *(style, manner)* guindé, empesé; *(drink)* fort; *(price)* (coll) salé, exagéré ‖ *s* *(corpse)* (slang) macchabée *m*

stiff′ col′lar *s* col *m* empesé

stiffen ['stɪfən] *tr* raidir, tendre; (culin) épaissir ‖ *intr* se raidir

stiff′ neck′ *s* torticolis *m*

stiff′-necked′ *adj* obstiné, entêté

stiff′ shirt′ *s* chemise *f* empesée, chemise à plastron

stifle ['staɪfəl] *tr* & *intr* étouffer

stig·ma ['stɪgmə] *s* (pl -mas or -mata [mətə]) stigmate *m*

stigmatize ['stɪgmə ˌtaɪz] *tr* stigmatiser

stilet·to [stɪ'leto] *s* (pl -tos) stylet *m*

still [stɪl] *adj* tranquille, calme, immobile; silencieux; *(wine)* non mousseux ‖ *s* alambic *m*; (phot) image *f*; (mov)

photogramme *m*; (poetic) silence *m* ‖ *adv* (yet) encore, toujours; *conj* cependant, pourtant ‖ *tr* calmer, apaiser; *(to silence)* faire taire ‖ *intr* se calmer, s'apaiser; se taire

still′born′ *adj* mort-né

still′ life′ *s* (pl **still lifes** or **still lives**) nature *f* morte

stilt [stɪlt] *s* échasse *f*; *(in the water)* pilotis *m*

stilted *adj* guindé; (archit) surhaussé

stimulant ['stɪmjələnt] *adj* & *s* stimulant *m*

stimulate ['stɪmjə ˌlet] *tr* stimuler

stimu·lus ['stɪmjələs] *s* (pl -li [ˌlaɪ]) stimulant *m*, aiguillon *m*; (physiol) stimulus *m*

sting [stɪŋ] *s* piqûre *f*; *(stinging organ)* aiguillon *m*, dard *m* ‖ *v* (pret & pp **stung** [stʌŋ]) *tr* & *intr* piquer

stin·gy ['stɪndʒi] *adj* (comp -gier; super -giest) avare, pingre

stink [stɪŋk] *s* puanteur *f* ‖ *v* (pret **stank** [stæŋk]; pp **stunk** [stʌŋk]) *tr* —**to stink up** empester, empuantir ‖ *intr* puer, empester; **to stink of** puer, empester

stinker ['stɪŋkər] *s* (slang) peau *f* de vache, chameau *m*

stint [stɪnt] *s* tâche *f*, besogne *f*; **without stint** sans réserve, sans limite ‖ *tr* limiter, réduire; **to stint oneself** se priver ‖ *intr* lésiner, être chiche

stipend ['staɪpɛnd] *s* traitement *m*, honoraires *mpl*

stipulate ['stɪpjə ˌlet] *tr* stipuler

stir [stʌr] *s* remuement *m*, agitation *f*; *(prison)* (slang) bloc *m*; **to create a stir** faire sensation ‖ *v* (pret & pp **stirred**; *ger* **stirring**) *tr* remuer, agiter; **to stir up** *(trouble)* fomenter ‖ *intr* remuer, s'agiter, bouger

stirring ['stʌrɪŋ] *adj* entraînant

stirrup ['stʌrəp], ['stɪrəp] *s* étrier *m*

stitch [stɪtʃ] *s* point *m*; *(in knitting)* maille *f*; (surg) point de suture; **not a stitch of** (coll) pas un brin de; **stitch in the side** point de côté; **to be in stitches** (coll) se tenir les côtes ‖ *tr* coudre; (bb) brocher; (surg) suturer ‖ *intr* coudre

stock [stak] *s* approvisionnement *m*, stock *m*; *(assortment)* assortiment *m*, capital *m*, fonds *m*; *(shares)* valeurs *fpl*, actions *fpl*; *(of meat)* bouillon *m*; *(of a tree)* tronc *m*; *(on an anvil)* billot *m*; *(of a rifle)* crosse *f*; *(of a tree; of a family)* souche *f*; *(live-stock)* bétail *m*, bestiaux *mpl*; *(handle)* poignée *f*; *(for dies)* tourne-à-gauche *m*; (hort) ente *f*; **in stock** en magasin; **on the stocks** (fig) sur le métier; **out of stock** épuisé; **stocks** *(for punishment)* pilori *m*; (naut) chantier *m*; **to take stock** faire le point; **to take stock in** (coll) faire grand cas de; **to take stock of** faire l'inventaire de ‖ *tr* approvisionner; garder en magasin; *(a forest or lake)* peupler; *(a farm)* monter en bétail; *(a pool)* empoissonner stockade [stɑ'ked] s palanque f, palissade f ‖ tr palissader

stock'breed'er s éleveur m de bestiaux

stock'breed'ing s élevage m

stock'bro'ker s agent m de change, courtier m de bourse

stock' car' s (aut) voiture f de série; (rr) wagon m à bestiaux

stock' com'pany s (com) société f à anonyme; (theat) troupe f à demeure

stock' div'idend s action f gratuite

stock' exchange' s bourse f

stock'hold'er s actionnaire mf

stocking ['stɑkɪŋ] s bas m

stock' mar'ket s bourse f, marché m des valeurs; to play the stock market jouer à la bourse

stock'pile' s stocks mpl de réserve ‖ tr & intr stocker

stock' rais'ing s élevage m

stock'room' s magasin m

stock-y ['stɑki] adj (comp -ier; super -iest) trapu, costaud

stock'yard' s parc m à bétail

stoic ['sto·ɪk] adj & s stoïque; Stoic stoïcien m

stoke [stok] tr (a fire) attiser; (a furnace) alimenter, charger

stoker ['stokər] s chauffeur m; (mach) stoker m

stolid ['stɑlɪd] adj flegmatique, impassible, lourd

stomach ['stʌmək] s estomac m ‖ tr digérer; (coll) digérer, avaler

stom'ach ache' s mal m d'estomac

stone [ston] s pierre f; (of fruit) noyau m; (pathol) calcul m; (typ) marbre m ‖ tr lapider; (fruit) dénoyauter

stone'-broke' adj (coll) complètement fauché, raide

stone'-deaf' adj sourd comme un pot

stone'ma'son s maçon m

stone's' quar'ry s (pl -ries) carrière f

stone's' throw' s—within a stone's throw à un jet de pierre

ston-y ['stoni] adj (comp -ier; super -iest) pierreux; (fig) dur, endurci

stooge [studʒ] s (theat) compère m; (slang) homme m de paille, acolyte m

stool [stul] s tabouret m, escabeau m; (bowel movement) selles fpl

stool' pi'geon s appeau m; (slang) mouchard m, mouton m

stoop [stup] s courbure f, inclinaison f; (porch) véranda f ‖ intr se pencher; se tenir voûté; (to debase oneself) s'abaisser

stoop'-shoul'dered adj voûté

stop [stɑp] s arrêt m; (in telegrams) stop m; (full stop) point m; (of a guitar) touche f; (mus) jeu m d'orgue; (public stop) stop; to put a stop to mettre fin à ‖ v (pret & pp stopped; ger stopping) tr arrêter; (a check) faire opposition à; to stop up boucher ‖ intr s'arrêter, arrêter; to stop + ger cesser de + inf, s'arrêter de + inf; to stop off descendre en passant; to stop off at s'arrêter un moment à; to stop over (aer, naut) faire escale

stop'cock' s robinet m d'arrêt

stop'gap' adj provisoire ‖ s bouche-trou m

stop'light' s signal m lumineux; (aut) feu m stop, stop m

stop'o'ver s arrêt m en cours de route, étape f

stoppage ['stɑpɪdʒ] s arrêt m; (of payments) suspension f; (of wages) retenue f; obstruction f; (pathol) occlusion f

stopper ['stɑpər] s bouchon m, tampon m

stop' sign' s signal m d'arrêt

stop' thief' interj au voleur!

stop'watch' s chronomètre m à déclic, compte-secondes m

storage ['storɪdʒ] s emmagasinage m, entreposage m; to put in storage entreposer

stor'age bat'ter·y s (pl -ies) (elec) accumulateur m, accu m

store [stor] s magasin m, boutique f; approvisionnement m; (warehouse) (Brit) entrepôt m; stores matériel m; vivres mpl; to set great store by faire grand cas de ‖ tr emmagasiner; (to warehouse) entreposer; (to supply or stock) approvisionner; to store away or up accumuler

store'house' s magasin m, entrepôt m; (of information) mine f

store'keep'er s boutiquier m

store'room' s dépense f, office f; (for furniture) garde-meuble m; (naut) soute f

stork [stork] s cigogne f

storm [storm] s orage m; (mil) assaut m; (fig) tempête f; to take by storm prendre d'assaut ‖ tr livrer l'assaut à ‖ intr faire de l'orage; (fig) tempêter

storm' cloud' s nuage m orageux; (fig) nuage noir

storm' door' s contre-porte f

storm' pet'rel ['petrəl] s oiseau m des tempêtes

storm' sash' s contre-fenêtre f

storm' troops' spl troupes fpl d'assaut

storm' win'dow s contre-fenêtre f

storm-y ['stormi] adj (comp -ier; super -iest) orageux

sto·ry ['stori] s (pl -ries) histoire f; (tale) conte m; (plot) intrigue f; (floor) étage m; (coll) mensonge m, histoire

sto'ry·tel'ler s conteur m; (fibber) menteur m

stout [staut] adj corpulent, gros; vaillant; ferme, résolu; (strong) fort ‖ s stout m

stout'-heart'ed adj au cœur vaillant

stove [stov] s (for heating a house or room) poêle m; (for cooking) fourneau m de cuisine, cuisinière f

stove'pipe' s tuyau m de poêle; (hat) (coll) huit-reflets m, tuyau de poêle

stow [sto] tr mettre en place, ranger; (naut) arrimer; to stow with remplir de ‖ intr—to stow away s'embarquer clandestinement

stowage ['sto·ɪdʒ] s arrimage m; (costs) frais mpl d'arrimage

stow'away' s passager m clandestin

straddle ['strædəl] *tr* enfourcher, chevaucher || *intr* se mettre à califourchon; (coll) répondre en normand

strafe [straf], [stref] *s* (slang) bombardement *m*, marmitage *m* || *tr* (slang) bombarder, marmiter

straggle ['strægəl] *intr* traîner; (*to be scattered*) s'éparpiller; **to straggle along** marcher sans ordre

straggler ['stræglər] *s* traînard *m*

straight [stret] *adj* droit; direct; loyal, honnête; correct, en ordre; (*hair*) raide; (*whiskey*) sec; (*candid*) franc; (*hanging straight*) d'aplomb; **to set s.o. straight** faire la leçon à qn || *s* (poker) séquence *f* || *adv* droit; directement; loyalement, honnêtement; (*without interruption*) de suite; **straight ahead** tout droit; **straight out** franchement, sans detours; **straight through** de part en part; d'un bout à l'autre; **to go straight** (coll) vivre honnêtement

straighten ['stretən] *tr* redresser; mettre en ordre || *intr* se redresser

straight' face' *s*—**to keep a straight face** montrer un front sérieux

straight'for'ward *adj* franc, direct; loyal

straight' off' *adv* sur-le-champ, d'emblée

straight' ra'zor *s* rasoir *m* à main

straight'way' *adv* sur-le-champ, d'emblée

strain [stren] *s* tension *f*; (*of a muscle*) foulure *f*; (*descendants*) lignée *f*; (*ancestry; type of virus*) souche *f*; (*trait*) héritage *m*, tendance *f*; (*vein*) ton *m*, sens *m*; (*bit*) trace *f*; (coll) grand effort *m*; **mental strain** surmenage *m* intellectuel; **strains** (*of, e.g., the Marseillaise*) accents *mpl*; **sweet strains** doux accords *mpl* || *tr* forcer; (*e.g., a wrist*) se fouler; (*e.g., one's eyes*) se fatiguer; (*e.g., part of a machine*) déformer; (*e.g., a liquid*) filtrer, tamiser; **to strain oneself** se surmener || *intr* s'efforcer; filtrer, tamiser; (*to trickle*) suinter; (*said of beam, ship, motor, etc.*) fatiguer; **to strain at** (*a leash, rope, etc.*) tirer sur; (*to balk at*) reculer devant

strained *adj* (*smile*) forcé; (*friendship*) tendu

strainer ['strenər] *s* passoire *f*, filtre *m*

strait [stret] *s* détroit *m*; **straits** détroit; **to be in dire straits** être dans la plus grande gêne

strait' jack'et *s* camisole *f* de force

strait'-laced' *adj* prude, collet monté, puritain

Straits' of Do'ver *spl* Pas *m* de Calais

strand [strænd] *s* (*beach*) plage *f*, grève *f*; (*of rope or cable*) toron *m*; (*of thread*) brin *m*; (*of pearls*) collier *m*; (*of hair*) cheveu *m* || *tr* toronner; (*to undo strands of*) décorder; (*a ship*) échouer

stranded *adj* abandonné; (*lost*) égaré; (*ship*) échoué; (*rope or cable*) à torons; **to leave s.o. stranded** laisser qn en plan

strange [strendʒ] *adj* étrange; (*unfa-* *miliar*) inconnu, étranger; (*unaccustomed*) inhabituel

stranger ['strendʒər] *s* étranger *m*; visiteur *m*

strangle ['stræŋgəl] *tr* étrangler, étouffer || *intr* s'étrangler

strap [stræp] *s* (*of leather, rubber, etc.*) courroie *f*; (*of cloth, metal, leather, etc.*) bande *f*; (*to sharpen a razor*) cuir *m* à rasoir; (*of, e.g., a harness*) sangle *f* || *v* (*pret & pp* **strapped**; *ger* **strapping**) *tr* attacher avec une courroie, sangler; (*a razor*) repasser sur le cuir

strap'hang'er *s* (coll) voyageur *m* debout

strapping ['stræpɪŋ] *adj* bien découplé, robuste; (coll) énorme, gros

stratagem ['strætədʒəm] *s* stratagème *m*

strategic(al) [strə'tidʒɪk(əl)] *adj* stratégique

strategist ['strætɪdʒɪst] *s* stratège *m*

strate-gy ['strætɪdʒɪ] *s* (*pl* **-gies**) stratégie *f*

strati-fy ['stræti,faɪ] *v* (*pret & pp* **-fied**) *tr* stratifier || *intr* se stratifier

stratosphere ['strætə,sfɪr], ['strætə-,sfɪr] *s* stratosphère *f*

stra-tum ['stretəm], ['strætəm] *s* (*pl* **-ta** [tə] *or* **-tums**) couche *f*; (*e.g., of society*) classe *f*, couche

straw [strɔ] *s* paille *f*; (*for drinking*) chalumeau *m*, paille; **it's the last straw!** c'est le bouquet!

straw'ber'ry *s* (*pl* **-ries**) fraise *f*; (*plant*) fraisier *m*

straw' hat' *s* chapeau *m* de paille; (*skimmer*) canotier *m*

straw' man' *s* (*pl* **men'**) (*figurehead*) homme *m* de paille; (*scarecrow*) épouvantail *m*; (*red herring*) canard *m*, diversion *f*

straw' mat'tress *s* paillasse *f*

straw' vote' *s* vote *m* d'essai

stray [stre] *adj* égaré; (*bullet*) perdu; (*scattered*) épars || *s* animal *m* égaré || *intr* s'égarer

streak [strik] *s* raie *f*, rayure *f*, bande *f*; (*of light*) trait *m*, filet *m*; (*of lightning*) éclair *m*; (*layer*) veine *f*; (*bit*) trace *f*; **like a streak** comme un éclair; **streak of luck** filon *m* || *tr* rayer, strier, zébrer || *intr* faire des raies; passer comme un éclair

stream [strim] *s* ruisseau *m*; (*steady flow of current*) courant *m*; (*of people, abuse, light, etc.*) flot *m*; (*of, e.g., automobiles*) défilé *m* || *intr* couler; (*said of blood*) ruisseler; (*said of light*) jaillir; (*said of flag*) flotter; **to stream out** sortir à flots

streamer ['strimər] *s* banderole *f*

stream'lined' *adj* aérodynamique, caréné; (fig) abrégé, concis

stream'lin'er *s* train *m* caréné de luxe

street [strit] *s* rue *f*; (*surface of the street*) chaussée *f*

street' Ar'ab *s* gamin *m* des rues

street'car' *s* tramway *m*

street' clean'er *s* balayeur *m*; (mach) balayeuse *f*

street′ clothes′ *spl* vêtements *mpl* de ville

street′ floor′ *s* rez-de-chaussée *m*

street′light′ *s* réverbère *m*

street′ sprink′ler *s* arroseuse *f*

street′ u′rinal *s* vespasienne *f*, édicule *m*, urinoir *m*

street′walk′er *s* racoleuse *f*, fille *f* des rues

strength [strɛŋθ] *s* force *f*; intensité *f*; (*of a fabric*) solidité *f*; (*of spirituous liquors*) degré *m*, titre *m*; (*com*) tendance *f* à la hausse; (*mil*) effectif *m*; **on the strength of** sur la foi de

strengthen [ˈstrɛŋθən] *tr* fortifier, renforcer; consolider ‖ *intr* se fortifier, se renforcer

strenuous [ˈstrɛnjuˌəs] *adj* actif, énergique; (*work*) ardu; (*effort*) acharné; (*objection*) vigoureux

stress [strɛs] *s* tension *f*, force *f*; (*mach*) stress *m*, tension; (*phonet*) accent *m* d'intensité; **to lay stress on** insister sur ‖ *tr* (*e.g., a beam*) charger; (*a syllable*) accentuer; insister sur, appuyer sur

stress′ ac′cent *s* accent *m* d'intensité

stretch [strɛtʃ] *s* allongement *m*; (*of the arm; of the meaning*) extension *f*; (*of the imagination*) effort *m*; (*distance in time or space*) intervalle *m*; (*section of road*) section *f*; (*section of country, water, etc.*) étendue *f*; **at a stretch** d'un trait; **in one stretch** d'une seule traite; **to do a stretch** (*slang*) faire de la taule ‖ *tr* tendre; (*the sense of a word*) forcer; (*a sauce*) allonger; **to stretch oneself** s'étirer; **to stretch out** allonger, étendre; (*the hand*) tendre ‖ *intr* s'étirer; (*said of shoes, gloves, etc.*) s'élargir; **to stretch out** s'allonger, s'étendre

stretcher [ˈstrɛtʃər] *s* (*for gloves, trousers, etc.*) tendeur *m*; (*for a painting*) châssis *m*; (*to carry sick or wounded*) civière *f*, brancard *m*

stretch′er-bear′er *s* brancardier *m*

strew [stru] *v* (*pret* strewed; *pp* strewed or strewn) *tr* semer, éparpiller; (*e.g., with flowers*) joncher, parsemer

stricken [ˈstrɪkən] *adj* frappé; (*e.g., with grief*) affligé; (*crossed out*) rayé; **stricken with** atteint de

strict [strɪkt] *adj* strict; (*exacting*) sévère

stricture [ˈstrɪktʃər] *s* critique *f* sévère; (*pathol*) rétrécissement *m*

stride [straɪd] *s* enjambée *f*; **to hit one's stride** attraper la cadence; **to make great (or rapid) strides** avancer à grands pas; **to take in one's stride** faire sans le moindre effort ‖ *v* (*pret* strode [strod]; *pp* stridden [ˈstrɪdən]) *tr* parcourir à grandes enjambées; (*to straddle*) enfourcher ‖ *intr* —**to stride across or over** enjamber; **to stride along** marcher à grandes enjambées

strident [ˈstraɪdənt] *adj* strident

strife [straɪf] *s* lutte *f*

strike [straɪk] *s* (*blow*) coup *m*; (*stopping of work*) grève *f*; (*discovery of* ore, oil, etc.) rencontre *f*; (*baseball*) coup du batteur; **to go on strike** se mettre en grève ‖ *v* (*pret* & *pp* struck [strʌk]) *tr* frapper; (*coins*) frapper; (*a match*) frotter; (*a bargain*) conclure; (*camp*) lever; (*the sails; the colors*) amener; (*the hour*) sonner; (*root; a pose*) prendre; **how does he strike you?** quelle impression vous fait-il?; **to strike it rich** trouver le filon; **to strike out** rayer; **to strike up** (*a song, piece of music, etc.*) attaquer, entonner; (*an acquaintance, conversation, etc.*) lier ‖ *intr* frapper; (*said of clock*) sonner; (*said of workers*) faire la grève; (*mil*) donner l'assaut; **to strike out** se mettre en route

strike′break′er *s* briseur *m* de grève, jaune *m*

striker [ˈstraɪkər] *s* frappeur *m*; (*on door*) marteau *m*; (*worker on strike*) gréviste *mf*

striking [ˈstraɪkɪŋ] *adj* frappant, saisissant; (*workers*) en grève

strik′ing pow′er *s* force *f* de frappe

string [strɪŋ] *s* ficelle *f*; (*of onions or garlic; of islands; of pearls; of abuse*) chapelet *m*; (*of words, insults*) enfilade *f*, kyrielle *f*; (*e.g., of cars*) file *f*; (*of beans*) fil *m*; (*for shoes*) lacet *m*; (*mus*) corde *f*; **strings** instruments *mpl* à cordes; **to pull strings** (fig) tirer les ficelles; **with no strings attached** (coll) sans restriction ‖ *v* (*pret* & *pp* strung [strʌŋ]) *tr* mettre une ficelle à, garnir de cordes; (*e.g., a violin*) mettre les cordes à; (*a bow*) bander; (*a tennis racket*) corder; (*beads, sentences, etc.*) enfiler; (*a cord, a thread, a wire, etc.*) tendre; (*to tune*) monter; **to string along** (slang) lanterner, faire marcher; **to string up** (coll) pendre ‖ *intr* —**to string along with** (slang) collaborer avec, suivre

string′ bean′ *s* haricot *m* vert

stringed in′strument *s* instrument *m* à cordes

stringent [ˈstrɪndʒənt] *adj* rigoureux; (*tight*) tendu; (*convincing*) convaincant

string′ quartet′ *s* quatuor *m* à cordes

string-y [ˈstrɪŋi] *adj* (*comp* -ier; *super* -iest) fibreux, filandreux

strip [strɪp] *s* (*of paper, cloth, land*) bande *f*; (*of metal*) lame *f*, ruban *m* ‖ *v* (*pret* & *pp* stripped; *ger* stripping) *tr* dépouiller; (*to strip bare*) mettre à nu; (*the bed*) défaire; (*a screw*) arracher le filet de, faire foirer; (*tobacco*) écoter; **to strip down** (*e.g., a motor*) démonter; **to strip off** enlever; (*e.g., bark*) écorcer ‖ *intr* se déshabiller

stripe [straɪp] *s* raie *f*, bande *f*; (*on cloth*) rayure *f*; (*flesh wound*) marque *f*; (*mil, nav*) chevron *m*, galon *m*; **to win one's stripes** gagner ses galons ‖ *tr* rayer

strip′ min′ing *s* exploitation *f* minière à ciel ouvert

strip'tease' s strip-tease m, déshabillage m suggestif

stripteaser ['strɪp ,tizər] s effeuilleuse f, strip-teaseuse f

strive [straɪv] v (pret **strove** [strov]; pp **striven** ['strɪvən]) intr s'efforcer; **to strive after** rechercher; **to strive against** lutter contre; **to strive to** s'efforcer à, s'évertuer à

stroke [strok] s coup m; (of pen; of wit) trait m; (of arms in swimming) brassée f; (caress with hand) caresse f de la main; (of a piston) course f; (of lightning) foudre f; (pathol) attaque f d'apoplexie; **at the stroke of** sonnant, e.g., **at the stroke of five** à cinq heures sonnantes; **to not do a stroke of work** ne pas en ficher une ramée || tr caresser de la main

stroll [strol] s promenade f; **to take a stroll** aller faire un tour || intr se promener

stroller ['strolər] s promeneur m; (for babies) poussette f

strong [strɔŋ], [straŋ] adj (comp **stronger** ['strɔŋgər], ['straŋgər]; super **strongest** ['strɔŋgɪst], ['straŋgɪst]) fort; (stock market) ferme; (musical beat) marqué; (spicy) piquant; (rancid) rance

strong'box' s coffre-fort m

strong' drink' s boissons fpl spiritueuses

strong'hold' s place f forte

strong' man' s (pl men') (e.g., in a circus) hercule m forain; (leader, good planner) animateur m; (dictator) chef m autoritaire

strong'-mind'ed adj résolu, décidé; (woman) hommasse

strontium ['strɑn/ɪ-əm] s strontium m

strop [strɑp] s cuir m à rasoir || v (pret & pp **stropped**; ger **stropping**) tr repasser sur le cuir

strophe ['strofi] s strophe f

structure ['strʌkt/ər] s structure f; (building) édifice m

struggle ['strʌgəl] s lutte f || intr lutter; **to struggle along** avancer péniblement

strug'gle for exist'ence s lutte f pour la vie

strum [strʌm] v (pret & pp **strummed**; ger **strumming**) tr (an instrument) gratter de; (a tune) tapoter || intr jouailler; **to strum on** plaquer des arpèges sur

strumpet ['strʌmpɪt] s putain f

strut [strʌt] s (brace, prop) étai m, support m, entretoise f; démarche f orgueilleuse f || v (pret & pp **strutted**; ger **strutting**) intr se pavaner

strychnine ['strɪknaɪn], ['strɪknɪn] s strychnine f

stub [stʌb] s (fragment) tronçon m; (of a tree) souche f; (of a pencil; of a cigar, cigarette) bout m; (of a check) talon m, souche || v (pret & pp **stubbed**; ger **stubbing**) tr—**to stub one's toe** se cogner le bout du pied

stubble ['stʌbəl] s éteule f, chaume m; (of beard) poil m court et raide

stubborn ['stʌbərn] adj obstiné; (head-strong) têtu; (resolute) acharné; (fever) rebelle; (soil) ingrat

stuc·co ['stʌko] s (pl -coes or -cos) stuc m || tr stuquer

stuck [stʌk] adj coincé, pris; (glued) collé; (unable to continue) en panne; **stuck on** (coll) entiché de

stuck'-up' adj (coll) hautain, prétentieux

stud [stʌd] s clou m à grosse tête; (ornament) clou doré; (on shirt) bouton m; (studhorse) étalon m; (horse farm) haras m; (bolt) goujon m; (archit) montant m || v (pret & pp **studded**; ger **studding**) tr clouter; **studded with** jonché de, parsemé de

stud' bolt' s goujon m

student ['st(j)udənt] adj estudiantin || s étudiant m; (researcher) chercheur m

stu'dent bod'y s étudiants mpl

stu'dent cen'ter s foyer m d'étudiants, centre m social des étudiants

stu'dent nurse' s élève f infirmière

stud' farm' s haras m

stud' horse' s étalon m

studied ['stʌdid] adj prémédité; recherché

studi·o ['st(j)udɪ ,o] s (pl -os) studio m, atelier m

studious ['st(j)udɪ-əs] adj studieux, appliqué

stud·y ['stʌdi] s (pl -ies) étude f; rêverie f; cabinet m || v (pret & pp -ied) tr & intr étudier

stuff [stʌf] s matière f; chose f; **to know one's stuff** (coll) s'y connaître || tr bourrer; (with food) gaver; (furniture) rembourrer; (an animal) empailler; (culin) farcir; **to stuff up** boucher || intr se gaver

stuffed' shirt' s collet m monté

stuffing ['stʌfɪŋ] s rembourrage m; (culin) farce f

stuff·y ['stʌfi] adj (comp -ier; super -iest) mal ventilé; (tedious) ennuyeux; (pompous) collet monté; **to smell stuffy** sentir le renfermé

stumble ['stʌmbəl] intr trébucher; (in speaking) hésiter

stum'bling block' s pierre f d'achoppement

stump [stʌmp] s (of tree) souche f; (e.g., of arm) moignon m; (of tooth) chicot m || tr (a design) estomper; (coll) embarrasser, coller; (a state, district, region) (coll) faire une tournée électorale en, dans, or à || intr clopiner

stump' speak'er s orateur m de carrefour

stump' speech' s harangue f électorale improvisée

stun [stʌn] v (pret & pp **stunned**; ger **stunning**) tr étourdir

stunning ['stʌnɪŋ] adj (coll) étourdissant, épatant

stunt [stʌnt] s atrophie f; (underdeveloped creature) avorton m; (coll) tour m de force, acrobatie f || tr atrophier || intr (coll) faire des acrobaties

stunted *adj* rabougri

stunt' fly'ing *s* vol *m* de virtuosité, acrobatie *f* aérienne

stunt' man' *s* (*pl* **men'**) cascadeur *m*, doublure *f*

stupe·fy ['st(j)upɪ,faɪ] *v* (*pret & pp* **-fied**) *tr* stupéfier

stupendous [st(j)u'pɛndəs] *adj* prodigieux, formidable

stupid ['st(j)upɪd] *adj* stupide

stupor ['st(j)upər] *s* stupeur *f*

stur·dy ['stʌrdɪ] *adj* (*comp* **-dier**; *super* **-diest**) robuste, vigoureux; (*resolute*) ferme, hardi

sturgeon ['stʌrdʒən] *s* esturgeon *m*

stutter ['stʌtər] *s* bégaiement *m* || *tr & intr* bégayer

sty [staɪ] *s* (*pl* **sties**) porcherie *f*; (*pathol*) orgelet *m*

style [staɪl] *s* style *m*; (*fashion*) mode *f*; (*elegance*) ton *m*, chic *m*; **to live in great style** mener grand train || *tr* appeler, dénommer; **to style oneself** s'intituler

stylish ['staɪlɪʃ] *adj* à la mode, élégant, chic

sty·mie ['staɪmi] *v* (*pret & pp* **-mied**; *ger* **-mieing**) *tr* contrecarrer

styp'tic pen'cil ['stɪptɪk] *s* crayon *m* styptique

suave [swɑv], [swev] *adj* suave; (*person*) affable; (*manners*) doucereux

sub [sʌb] *s* (coll) sous-marin *m*

subconscious [sʌb'kɑnʃəs] *adj & s* subconscient *m*

sub'divide' or **sub·divide'** *tr* subdiviser || *intr* se subdiviser

subdue [səb'd(j)u] *tr* subjuguer, vaincre, asservir; (*color, light, sound*) adoucir, amortir; (*passions, feelings*) dompter

sub'head' *s* sous-titre *m*

subject ['sʌbdʒɪkt] *adj* sujet, assujetti, soumis || *s* sujet *m*; (*e.g., in school*) matière *f* || [səb'dʒɛkt] *tr* assujettir, soumettre

subjection [səb'dʒɛkʃən] *s* sujétion *f*, soumission *f*

subjective [səb'dʒɛktɪv] *adj* subjectif

sub'ject mat'ter *s* matière *f*

subjugate ['sʌbdʒə,get] *tr* subjuguer

subjunctive [səb'dʒʌŋktɪv] *adj & s* subjonctif *m*

sub'lease' *s* sous-location *f* || **sub'lease'** *tr* sous-louer

sub·let [səb'lɛt], ['sʌb,lɛt] *v* (*pret & pp* **-let**; *ger* **-letting**) *tr* sous-louer

sub'machine' gun' *s* mitraillette *f*

sub'marine' *adj & s* sous-marin *m*

sub'marine chas'er *s* chasseur *m* de sous-marins

submerge [səb'mʌrdʒ] *tr* submerger || *intr* (*said of submarine*) plonger

submersion [səb'mʌrʒən], [səb'mʌr-ʃən] *s* submersion *f*

submission [səb'mɪʃən] *s* soumission *f*; (*delivery*) présentation *f*

submissive [səb'mɪsɪv] *adj* soumis

sub·mit [səb'mɪt] *v* (*pret & pp* **-mitted**; *ger* **-mitting**) *tr* soumettre || *intr* se soumettre

subordinate [səb'ɔrdɪnɪt] *adj & s*

subordonné *m* || [səb'ɔrdɪ,net] *tr* subordonner

subpoena [sʌb'pinə], [sə'pinə] *s* assignation *f*, citation *f* || *tr* citer

subscribe [səb'skraɪb] *tr* souscrire || *intr*—**to subscribe to** (*an opinion*; *a charity*; *a loan*; *a newspaper*) souscrire à; (*a newspaper*) s'abonner à

subscriber [səb'skraɪbər] *s* abonné *m*

subscription [səb'skrɪpʃən] *s* souscription *f*; (*to newspaper or magazine*) abonnement *m*; (*to club*) cotisation *f*; **to take out a subscription for s.o.** abonner qn; **to take out a subscription to** s'abonner à

subsequent ['sʌbsɪkwənt] *adj* subséquent, suivant

subservient [səb'sʌrvɪ·ənt] *adj* asservi, subordonné

subside [səb'saɪd] *intr* (*said of water, ground, etc.*) s'abaisser; (*said of storm, excitement, etc.*) s'apaiser

subsidiar·y [səb'sɪdɪ,ɛri] *adj* subsidiaire || *s* (*pl* **-ies**) filiale *f*

subsidize ['sʌbsɪ,daɪz] *tr* subventionner; suborner

subsi·dy ['sʌbsɪdi] *s* (*pl* **-dies**) subside *m*, subvention *f*

subsist [səb'sɪst] *intr* subsister

subsistence [səb'sɪstəns] *s* (*supplies*) subsistance *f*; existence *f*

sub'soil' *s* sous-sol *m*

substance ['sʌbstəns] *s* substance *f*

sub·stand'ard *adj* inférieur au niveau normal

substantial [səb'stænʃəl] *adj* substantiel; (*wealthy*) aisé, cossu

substantiate [səb'stænʃɪ,et] *tr* établir, vérifier

substantive ['sʌbstəntɪv] *adj & s* substantif *m*

sub'sta'tion *s* (*of post office*) bureau *m* auxiliaire; (elec) sous-station *f*

substitute ['sʌbstɪ,t(j)ut] *s* (*person*) remplaçant *m*, suppléant *m*, substitut *m*; (*e.g., for coffee*) succédané *m* || *tr* remplacer, e.g., **they substituted copper for silver** ils ont remplacé l'argent par le cuivre; substituer, e.g., **a hind was substituted for Iphigenia** une biche fut substituée à Iphigénie || *intr* servir de remplaçant; **to substitute for** remplacer, suppléer

substitution [,sʌbstɪ't(j)uʃən] *s* substitution *f*

sub'stra'tum *s* (*pl* **-ta** [tə] or **-tums**) substrat *m*

subterfuge ['sʌbtər,fjudʒ] *s* subterfuge *m*, faux-fuyant *m*

subterranean [,sʌbtə'reni·ən] *adj* souterrain

sub'ti'tle *s* sous-titre *m*

subtle ['sʌtəl] *adj* subtil

subtle·ty ['sʌtəlti] *s* (*pl* **-ties**) subtilité *f*

subtract [səb'trækt] *tr* soustraire

subtraction [səb'trækʃən] *s* soustraction *f*

suburb ['sʌbʌrb] *s* ville *f* de la banlieue; **the suburbs** la banlieue

suburban [sə'bʌrbən] *adj* suburbain

suburbanite [sə'bʌrbə,naɪt] *s* banlieusard *m*

subvention [səb'vɛnʃən] s subvention f || tr subventionner

subversive [səb'vʌrsɪv] adj subversif || s factieux m

subvert [səb'vʌrt] tr corrompre; renverser

sub'way s métro m; (tunnel for pedestrians) souterrain m

sub'way car' s voiture f de métro

sub'way sta'tion s station f de métro

succeed [sək'sid] tr succéder (with dat); to succeed one another se succéder || intr réussir; to succeed in + ger réussir à + inf; to succeed to (the throne; a fortune) succéder à

success [sək'sɛs] s succès m, réussite f; to be a success avoir du succès

successful [sək'sɛsfəl] adj réussi; heureux, prospère

succession [sək'sɛʃən] s succession f; in succession de suite

successive [sək'sɛsɪv] adj successif

succor ['sʌkər] s secours m || tr secourir

succotash ['sʌkə,tæʃ] s plat m de fèves et de maïs

succumb [sə'kʌm] intr succomber

such [sʌtʃ] adj & pron indef tel, pareil, semblable; such a un tel; such and such tel et tel; such as tel que

suck [sʌk] s—to give suck to allaiter || tr sucer; (a nipple) téter; to suck in aspirer; (to absorb) sucer || intr sucer; téter

sucker ['sʌkər] s suceur m; (sucking organ) suçoir m, ventouse f; (bot) drageon m; (ichth) rémora m; (gullible person) (coll) gogo m; (lollipop) (coll) sucette f

suckle ['sʌkəl] tr allaiter

suck'ling pig' s cochon m de lait

suction ['sʌkʃən] s succion f

suc'tion cup' s ventouse f

suc'tion pump' s pompe f aspirante

sudden ['sʌdən] adj brusque, soudain; all of a sudden tout à coup

suddenly ['sʌdənli] adv tout à coup

suds [sʌdz] spl eau f savonneuse; mousse f de savon

sue [s(j)u] tr poursuivre en justice || intr intenter un procès

suede [swed] s suède m; (for shoes) daim m

suet ['s(j)uɪt] s graisse f de rognon

suffer ['sʌfər] tr souffrir; (to allow) permettre; (a defeat) essuyer, subir || intr souffrir

sufferance ['sʌfərəns] s tolérance f

suffering ['sʌfərɪŋ] adj souffrant || s souffrance f

suffice [sə'faɪs] tr suffire (with dat) || intr suffire; it suffices to + inf il suffit de + inf

sufficient [sə'fɪʃənt] adj suffisant

suffix ['sʌfɪks] s suffixe m

suffocate ['sʌfə,ket] tr & intr suffoquer, étouffer

suffrage ['sʌfrɪdʒ] s suffrage m

suffragist ['sʌfrədʒɪst] s partisan m du droit de vote des femmes

suffuse [sə'fjuz] tr baigner, saturer

sugar ['ʃugər] s sucre m || tr sucrer;

(a cake) saupoudrer de sucre; (a pill) recouvrir de sucre || intr former du sucre

sug'ar beet' s betterave f sucrière, betterave à sucre

sug'ar bowl' s sucrier m

sug'ar cane' s canne f à sucre

sug'ar-coat' tr dragéifier; (fig) dorer

sug'ar dad'dy s (pl -dies) papa m gâteau

sug'ar ma'ple s érable m à sucre

sug'ar pea' s mange-tout m

sug'ar tongs' spl pince f à sucre

sugary ['ʃugəri] adj sucré; (fig) doucereux

suggest [səg'dʒɛst] tr suggérer

suggestion [səg'dʒɛstʃən] s suggestion f; nuance f, pointe f, soupçon m

suggestive [səg'dʒɛstɪv] adj suggestif

suicidal ['s(j)uɪ'saɪdəl] adj suicidaire

suicide ['s(j)uɪ,saɪd] s (act) suicide m; (person) suicidé m; to commit suicide se suicider

suit [s(j)ut] s costume m; (men's) complet m, costume; (women's) costume tailleur, tailleur m; (lawsuit) procès m; (plea) requête f; (cards) couleur f; to follow suit jouer la couleur; (fig) en faire autant || tr adapter; convenir (with dat), e.g., does that suit him? cela lui convient?; aller (with dat), seoir (with dat), e.g., the dress suits her well la robe lui va bien, la robe lui sied bien || intr convenir, aller

suitable ['s(j)utəbəl] adj convenable, à propos; compétent

suit'case' s valise f

suite [swit] s suite f || [s(j)ut] s (of furniture) ameublement m, mobilier m

suiting ['s(j)utɪŋ] s étoffe f pour complets

suit' of clothes' s complet-veston m

suitor ['s(j)utər] s prétendant m, soupirant m

sul'fa drugs' ['sʌlfə] spl sulfamides mpl

sulfide ['sʌlfaɪd] s sulfure m

sulfur ['sʌlfər] adj soufré || s soufre m || tr soufrer

sulfuric [sʌl'fjurɪk] adj sulfurique

sul'fur mine' s soufrière f

sulk [sʌlk] s bouderie f || intr bouder

sulk·y ['sʌlki] adj (comp -ier; super -iest) boudeur, maussade

sullen ['sʌlən] adj maussade, rébarbatif

sul·ly ['sʌli] v (pret & pp -lied) tr souiller

sulphur ['sʌlfər] adj, s & tr var of sulfur

sultan ['sʌltən] s sultan m

sul·try ['sʌltri] adj (comp -trier; super -triest) étouffant, suffocant

sum [sʌm] s somme f; tout m, total m; in sum somme toute || v (pret & pp summed; ger summing) tr—to sum up résumer

sumac or **sumach** ['ʃumæk], ['sumæk] s sumac m

summarize ['sʌmə,raɪz] tr résumer

summa·ry ['sʌməri] adj sommaire || s (pl -ries) sommaire m

summer ['sʌmər] *adj* estival || *s* été *m* || *intr* passer l'été

sum'mer resort' *s* station *f* estivale

sum'mer school' *s* cours *m* d'été, cours de vacances

summery ['sʌməri] *adj* estival, d'été

summit ['sʌmɪt] *s* sommet *m*

sum'mit con'ference *s* conférence *f* au sommet

summon ['sʌmən] *tr* appeler, convoquer; (law) sommer, citer, assigner

summons ['sʌmənz] *s* appel *m*; (law) citation *f*, assignation *f*, exploit *m*

sumptuous ['sʌmptʃu-əs] *adj* somptueux

sun [sʌn] *s* soleil *m* || *v* (pret & pp **sunned**; ger **sunning**) *tr* exposer au soleil || *intr* prendre le soleil

sun' bath' *s* bain *m* de soleil

sun'beam' *s* rayon *m* de soleil

sun'bon'net *s* capeline *f*

sun'burn' *s* coup *m* de soleil || *v* (pret & pp **-burned** or **-burnt**) *tr* hâler, basaner || *intr* se basaner

sun'burned' *adj* brûlé par le soleil

sundae ['sʌndi] *s* coupe *f* de glace garnie de fruits

Sunday ['sʌndi] *adj* dominical || *s* dimanche *m*

Sun'day best' *s* (coll) habits *mpl* du dimanche

Sun'day driv'er *s* chauffeur *m* du dimanche

Sun'day school' *s* école *f* du dimanche

sunder ['sʌndər] *tr* séparer, rompre

sun'di'al *s* cadran *m* solaire, gnomon *m*

sun'down' *s* coucher *m* du soleil

sundries ['sʌndriz] *spl* articles *mpl* divers

sundry ['sʌndri] *adj* divers

sun'fish' *s* poisson-lune *m*

sun'flow'er *s* soleil *m*, tournesol *m*

sun'glass'es *spl* lunettes *fpl* de soleil, verres *mpl* fumés

sunken ['sʌŋkən] *adj* creux, enfoncé; (rock) noyé; (ship) sous-marin

sun' lamp' *s* lampe *f* à rayons ultra-violets

sun'light' *s* lumière *f* du soleil

sun-ny ['sʌni] *adj* (comp **-nier**; super **-niest**) ensoleillé; (happy) enjoué; **it is sunny** il fait du soleil

sun'ny side' *s* côté *m* exposé au soleil; (fig) bon côté

sun' par'lor *s* véranda *f*

sun'rise' *s* lever *m* du soleil

sun'set' *s* coucher *m* du soleil

sun'shade' *s* (over door) banne *f*; parasol *m*; abat-jour *m*, visière *f*

sun'shine' *s* clarté *f* du soleil, soleil *m*; (fig) gaieté *f* rayonnante; **in the sunshine** en plein soleil

sun'spot' *s* tache *f* solaire

sun'stroke' *s* insolation *f*

sun' tan' *s* hâle *m*

sun'-tan oil' *s* huile *f* solaire

sun'up' *s* lever *m* du soleil

sun' vi'sor *s* abat-jour *m*

sup [sʌp] *v* (pret & pp **supped**; ger **supping**) *intr* souper

super ['supər] *adj* (slang) superbe, for-

midable || *s* (theat) figurant *m*; (slang) concierge *mf*

su'per-abun'dant *adj* surabondant

superannuated [,supər'ænju,etɪd] *adj* (person) retraité; (thing) suranné

superb [su'pʌrb], [sə'pʌrb] *adj* superbe

su'per-car'go *s* (pl **-goes** or **-gos**) subrécargue *m*

su'per-charge' *s* surcompression *f* || *tr* surcomprimer

supercilious [,supər'sɪlɪ-əs] *adj* sourcilleux, hautain, arrogant

superficial [,supər'fɪʃəl] *adj* superficiel

superfluous [su'pʌrflu-əs] *adj* superflu

su'per-high'way' *s* autoroute *f*

su'per-hu'man *adj* surhumain

su'per-impose' *tr* superposer

su'per-intend' *tr* surveiller; diriger

superintendent [,supərin'tendənt] *s* directeur *m*, directeur en chef; (of a building) concierge *mf*

superior [sə'pɪrɪ-ər], [su'pɪrɪ-ər] *adj* & *s* supérieur *m*

superiority [sə,pɪrɪ'arɪti], [su,pɪrɪ-'arɪti] *s* supériorité *f*

superlative [sə'pʌrlətɪv], [su'pʌrlətɪv] *adj* & *s* superlatif *m*

su'per-man' *s* (pl **-men'**) surhomme *m*

su'per-mar'ket *s* supermarché *m*

su'per-nat'ural *adj* & *s* surnaturel *m*

supersede [,supər'sid] *tr* remplacer

su'per-sen'sitive *adj* hypersensible

su'per-son'ic *adj* supersonique

superstition [,supər'stɪʃən] *s* superstition *f*

superstitious [,supər'stɪʃəs] *adj* superstitieux

supervene [,supər'vin] *intr* survenir

supervise ['supər,vaɪz] *tr* surveiller; diriger

supervision [,supər'vɪʒən] *s* surveillance *f*; direction *f*

supervisor ['supər,vaɪzər] *s* surveillant *m*, inspecteur *m*; directeur *m*

supper ['sʌpər] *s* souper *m*

sup'per-time' *s* heure *f* du souper

supplant [sə'plænt] *tr* supplanter

supple ['sʌpəl] *adj* souple, flexible

supplement ['sʌpləmənt] *s* supplément *m* || ['sʌplɪ,ment] *tr* ajouter à

suppliant ['sʌplɪ-ənt] *adj* & *s* suppliant *m*

supplicant ['sʌplɪkənt] *s* suppliant *m*

supplicate ['sʌplɪ,ket] *tr* supplier

supplier [sə'plaɪ-ər] *s* fournisseur *m*, pourvoyeur *m*

sup-ply [sə'plaɪ] *s* (pl **-plies**) fourniture *f*, provision *f*; (mil) approvisionnement *m*; **supplies** fournitures; (of food) vivres *mpl* || *v* (pret & pp **-plied**) *tr* fournir; (a person, a city, a fort) pourvoir, munir; (a need) répondre à; (what is lacking) suppléer; (mil) approvisionner

supply' and demand' *spl* l'offre *f* et la demande

support [sə'port] *s* soutien *m*, appui *m*; ressources *fpl*, de quoi vivre *m*; (pillar) support *m* || *tr* soutenir, appuyer; (e.g., a wife) entretenir, soutenir; (to hold up; to corroborate; to tolerate) supporter; to support oneself gagner sa vie

supporter [sə'portər] s partisan m, supporter m; (for part of body) suspensoir m

suppose [sə'poz] tr supposer; s'imaginer; I suppose so probablement, je pose that . . . à supposer que . . .; suppose we take a walk? si nous faisions une promenade?; to be supposed to + inf devoir + inf; (to be considered to be) être censé + inf

supposedly [sə'pozidli] adv censément

supposition [,sʌpə'zɪʃən] s supposition f

supposito·ry [sə'pazɪ,tori] s (pl -ries) suppositoire m

suppress [sə'pres] tr supprimer; (rebellion; anger) réprimer, contenir; (a yawn) étouffer, empêcher

suppression [sə'preʃən] s suppression f; (of a rebellion) subjugation f, répression f; (of a yawn) empêchement m

suppurate [′sʌpjə,ret] intr suppurer

supreme [sə'prim], [su'prim] adj suprême

supreme′ court′ s cour f de cassation

surcharge [′sʌr,tʃardʒ] s surcharge f || [,sʌr′tʃardʒ], [′sʌr,tʃardʒ] tr surcharger

sure [ʃur] adj sûr, certain; (e.g., hand) ferme; for sure à coup sûr, pour sûr; to be sure to + inf ne pas manquer de + inf; to make sure s'assurer || adv (coll) certainement, assurément; sure enough (coll) effectivement, assurément || interj (slang) mais oui!, bien sûr!, entendu!

sure′-foot′ed adj au pied sûr

sure·ty [′ʃurti], [′ʃuriti] s (pl -ties) sûreté f

surf [sʌrf] s barre f, ressac m, brisants mpl

surface [′sʌrfɪs] adj superficiel f || s surface f; (area) superficie f; on the surface à la surface, en apparence; to float under the surface nager entre deux eaux || tr polir la surface de; (a road) recouvrir, revêtir || intr (said of submarine) faire surface

sur′face mail′ s courrier m par voie ordinaire

surf′board′ s planche f pour le surf, surfboard m

surfeit [′sʌrfɪt] s satiété f || tr rassasier || intr se rassasier

surf′rid′ing s surfing m, planking m

surge [sʌrdʒ] s houle f; (elec) surtension f || intr être houleux; se répandre; to surge up s'enfler, s'élever

surgeon [′sʌrdʒən] s chirurgien m

surger·y [′sʌrdʒəri] s (pl -ies) chirurgie f; salle f d'opération

surgical [′sʌrdʒɪkəl] adj chirurgical

sur·ly [′sʌrli] adj (comp -lier; super -liest) hargneux, maussade, bourru

surmise [sər'maɪz], [′sʌrmaɪz] s conjecture f || [sər'maɪz] tr & intr conjecturer

surmount [sər'maunt] tr surmonter

surname [′sʌr,nem] s nom m de famil-

le; surnom m || tr donner un nom de famille à; surnommer

surpass [sər'pæs], [sər'pas] tr surpasser

surplice [′sʌrplɪs] s surplis m

surplus [′sʌrplʌs] adj excédent, excédentaire, en excédent || s surplus m, excédent m

sur′plus bag′gage s excédent m de bagages

surprise [sər'praɪz] adj à l'improviste, brusqué, inopiné || s surprise f, étonnement m; to take by surprise prendre à l'improviste, prendre au dépourvu || tr surprendre; to be surprised at être surpris de

surprise′ attack′ s attaque f brusquée

surprise′ pack′age s surprise f, pochette f surprise

surprise′ par′ty s (pl -ties) réunion f à l'improviste

surprising [sər'praɪzɪŋ] adj surprenant

surrealism [sə'ri·ə,lɪzəm] s surréalisme m

surrender [sə'rendər] s reddition f, soumission f; (e.g., of prisoners, goods) remise f; (e.g., of rights, property) cession f || tr rendre, céder || intr se rendre

surren′der val′ue s valeur f de rachat

surreptitious [,sʌrep'tɪʃəs] adj subreptice

surround [sə'raund] tr entourer

surrounding [sə'raundɪŋ] adj entourant, environnant || **surroundings** spl environs mpl, alentours mpl; entourage m, milieu m

surtax [′sʌr,tæks] s surtaxe f || tr surtaxer

surveillance [sər'vel(j)əns] s surveillance f

survey [′sʌrve] s (for verification) contrôle m; (for evaluation) appréciation f, évaluation f; (report) expertise f, aperçu m; (of a whole) vue f d'ensemble, tour m d'horizon; (measured plan or drawing) levé m, plan m; (surv) lever m or levé des plans; to make a survey (to map out) lever un plan; (to poll) effectuer un contrôle par sondage || [sʌr've], [′sʌrve] tr contrôler; apprécier, évaluer, faire l'expertise de; (as a whole) jeter un coup d'œil sur; (to poll) sonder; (e.g., a farm) arpenter, faire l'arpentage de; (e.g., a city) faire le levé de

sur′vey course′ s cours m général

surveying [sʌr've·ɪŋ] s arpentage m, géodésie f, levé m des plans

surveyor [sər've·ər] s arpenteur m

survival [sər'vaɪvəl] s survivance f; (after death) survie f

survive [sər'vaɪv] tr survivre (with dat) || intr survivre

surviving [sər'vaɪvɪŋ] adj survivant

survivor [sər'vaɪvər] s survivant m

survivorship [sər'vaɪvər,ʃɪp] s (law) survie f

susceptible [sə'septɪbəl] adj (capable) susceptible; (liable, subject) sensible; (to love) facilement amoureux

suspect [′sʌspekt], [səs'pekt] adj & s

suspect m ‖ [səs'pɛkt] tr soupçonner ‖ intr s'en douter

suspend [səs'pɛnd] tr suspendre

suspenders [səs'pɛndərz] spl bretelles fpl

suspense [səs'pɛns] s suspens m

suspension [səs'pɛnʃən] s suspension f; **suspension of driver's license** retrait m de permis

suspen'sion bridge' s pont m suspendu

suspicion [səs'pɪʃən] s soupçon m

suspicious [səs'pɪʃəs] adj (inclined to suspect) soupçonneux; (subject to suspicion) suspect

sustain [səs'ten] tr soutenir; (a loss, injury, etc.) éprouver

sustenance ['sʌstɪnəns] s subsistance f; (food) nourriture f

swab [swab] s écouvillon m; (naut) faubert m; (surg) tampon m ‖ v (pret & pp swabbed; ger swabbing) tr écouvillonner

swaddle ['swadəl] tr emmailloter

swad'dling clothes' spl maillot m

swagger ['swægər] s fanfaronnade f ‖ intr faire des fanfaronnades

swain [swen] s garçon m; jeune berger m; soupirant m

swallow ['swalo] s gorgée f; (orn) hirondelle f ‖ tr & intr avaler

swal'low-tailed coat' s frac m

swamp [swamp] s marécage m ‖ tr submerger, inonder

swamp·y ['swampi] adj (comp -ier; super -iest) marécageux

swan [swan] s cygne m

swan' dive' s saut m de l'ange

swank [swæŋk] adj (slang) élégant, chic

swan' knight' s chevalier m au cygne

swan's'-down' s cygne m, duvet m de cygne

swan' song' s chant m du cygne

swap [swap] s (coll) troc m ‖ v (pret & pp swapped; ger swapping) tr & intr troquer

swarm [swɔrm] s essaim m ‖ intr essaimer; (fig) fourmiller

swarth·y ['swɔrði], ['swɔrθi] adj (comp -ier; super -iest) basané, brun, noiraud

swashbuckler ['swɑʃ,bʌklər] s rodomont m, bretteur m

swat [swat] s (coll) coup m violent ‖ v (pret & pp swatted; ger swatting) tr (coll) frapper; (a fly) (coll) écraser

sway [swe] s balancement m; (domination) empire m ‖ tr balancer ‖ intr se balancer; (to hesitate) balancer

swear [swer] v (pret swore [swor]; pp sworn [sworn]) tr jurer; **to swear in** faire prêter serment à; **to swear off** jurer de renoncer à ‖ intr jurer; **to swear by** (e.g., a remedy) préconiser; **to swear to** déclarer sous serment; jurer de + inf

swear' words' spl gros mots mpl

sweat [swet] s sueur f ‖ v (pret & pp sweat or sweated) tr (e.g., blood) suer; (slang) faire suer; **to sweat it out** (slang) en baver jusqu'à la fin ‖ intr suer

sweater ['swetər] s chandail m

sweat' shirt' s maillot m de sport

sweat·y ['sweti] adj (comp -ier; super -iest) suant

Swede [swid] s Suédois m

Sweden ['swidən] s Suède f; la Suède

Swedish ['swidɪʃ] adj & s suédois m

sweep [swip] s balayage m; étendue f; (curve) courbe f; (of wind) souffle m; (of well) chadouf m; **at one sweep** d'un seul coup; **to make a clean sweep of** faire table rase de; (to win all of) rafler ‖ v (pret & pp swept [swept]) tr balayer; (the chimney) ramoner; (for mines) draguer ‖ intr balayer; s'étendre

sweeper ['swipər] s balayeur m; (mach) balai m mécanique

sweeping ['swipɪŋ] adj (movement) vigoureux; (statement) catégorique ‖ s balayage m; **sweepings** balayures fpl

sweep'-sec'ond s trotteuse f centrale

sweep'stake' s or spl loterie f; (turf) sweepstake m

sweet [swit] adj doux; sucré; (perfume, music, etc.) suave; (sound) mélodieux; (milk) frais; (person) charmant, gentil; (dear) cher; **to be sweet on** (coll) avoir un béguin pour; **to smell sweet** sentir bon ‖ **sweets** spl sucreries fpl

sweet'bread' s ris m de veau

sweet'bri'er s églantier m

sweeten ['switən] tr sucrer; purifier; (fig) adoucir ‖ intr s'adoucir

sweet'heart' s petite amie f, chérie f; **sweethearts** amoureux mpl

sweet' mar'joram s marjolaine f

sweet'meats' spl sucreries fpl

sweet' pea' s gesse f odorante, pois m de senteur

sweet' pep'per s piment m doux, poivron m

sweet' pota'to s patate f douce

sweet'-scent'ed adj parfumé

sweet'-toothed' adj friand de sucreries

sweet' wil'liam s œillet m de poète

swell [swel] adj (coll) élégant; (slang) épatant ‖ s gonflement m; (of sea) houle f; (mus) crescendo m; (pathol) enflure f; (coll) rupin m ‖ v (pret swelled; pp swelled or swollen ['swolən]) tr gonfler, enfler ‖ intr se gonfler, s'enfler; (said of sea) se soulever; (fig) augmenter

swell/head'ed adj suffisant, vaniteux

swelter ['sweltər] intr étouffer de chaleur

swept'back wing' s aile f en flèche

swerve [swʌrv] s écart m, déviation f; (aut) embardée f ‖ tr faire dévier ‖ intr écarter, dévier; (aut) faire une embardée

swift [swift] adj rapide ‖ adv vite ‖ s (orn) martinet m

swig [swig] s (coll) lampée f, trait m ‖ v (pret & pp swigged; ger swigging) tr & intr lamper

swill [swil] s eaux fpl grasses, ordures fpl; (drink) lampée f ‖ tr & intr lamper

swim [swɪm] *s* nage *f*; **to be in the swim** (coll) être dans le train ‖ *v* (pret **swam** [swæm]; pp **swum** [swʌm]; ger **swimming**) *tr* nager ‖ *intr* nager; (*said of head*) tourner; **to swim across** traverser à la nage; **to swim under water** nager entre deux eaux

swimmer ['swɪmər] *s* nageur *m*

swimming ['swɪmɪŋ] *s* natation *f*, nage *f*

swim'ming pool' *s* piscine *f*

swim'ming suit' *s* maillot *m* de bain

swim'ming trunks' *spl* slip *m* de bain

swindle ['swɪndəl] *s* escroquerie *f* ‖ *tr* escroquer

swine [swaɪn] *s* (*pl* **swine**) cochon *m*, pourceau *m*, porc *m*

swing [swɪŋ] *s* balancement *m*, oscillation *f*; (*device used for recreation*) escarpolette *f*; (*trip*) tournée *f*; (*boxing, mus*) swing *m*; **in full swing** en pleine marche ‖ *v* (pret & pp **swung** [swʌŋ]) *tr* balancer, faire osciller; (*the arms*) agiter; (*a sword*) brandir; (*e.g., an election*) mener à bien ‖ *intr* se balancer; (*said of pendulum*) osciller; (*said of door*) pivoter; (*said of bell*) branler; **to swing open** s'ouvrir tout d'un coup

swing'ing door' *s* porte *f* va-et-vient

swinish ['swaɪnɪʃ] *adj* cochon

swipe [swaɪp] *s* (coll) coup *m* à toute volée ‖ *tr* (coll) frapper à toute volée; (*to steal*) (slang) chiper

swirl [swʌrl] *s* remous *m*, tourbillon *m* ‖ *tr* faire tourbillonner ‖ *intr* tourbillonner

swish [swɪʃ] *s* (*e.g., of a whip*) sifflement *m*; (*of a dress*) froufrou *m*; (*e.g., of water*) susurrement *m* ‖ *tr* (*a whip*) faire siffler; (*its tail*) battre ‖ *intr* siffler; froufrouter; susurrer

Swiss [swɪs] *adj* suisse ‖ *s* Suisse *m*; **the Swiss** les Suisses *mpl*

Swiss' chard' [tʃɑrd] *s* bette *f*, poirée *f*

Swiss' cheese' *s* emmenthal *m*, gruyère *m*

Swiss' Guard' *s* suisse *m*

switch [swɪtʃ] *s* (*stick*) badine *f*; (*exchange*) échange *m*; (*hairpiece*) postiche *m*; (elec) interrupteur *m*; (rr) aiguille *f* ‖ *tr* cingler; (*places*) échanger; (rr) aiguiller; **to switch off** couper; (*a light*) éteindre; **to switch on** mettre en circuit; (*a light*) allumer ‖ *intr* changer de place

switch'back' *s* chemin *m* en lacet

switch'board' *s* tableau *m* de distribution; standard *m* téléphonique

switch'board op'erator *s* standardiste *mf*

switch'ing en'gine *s* locomotive *f* de manœuvre

switch'man *s* (*pl* **-men**) aiguilleur *m*

switch' tow'er *s* poste *m* d'aiguillage

switch'yard' *s* gare *f* de triage

Switzerland ['swɪtsərlənd] *s* Suisse *f*; la Suisse

swiv-el ['swɪvəl] *s* pivot *m*; (*link*) émerillon *m* ‖ *v* (pret & pp **-eled** or **-elled**; ger **-eling** or **-elling**) *tr* faire pivoter ‖ *intr* pivoter

swiv'el chair' *s* fauteuil *m* tournant

swoon [swun] *s* évanouissement *m* ‖ *intr* s'évanouir

swoop [swup] *s* attaque *f* brusque; **at one fell swoop** d'un seul coup ‖ *intr* foncer, fondre; **to swoop down on** s'abattre sur

sword [sord] *s* épée *f*; **to cross swords with** croiser le fer avec; **to put to the sword** passer au fil de l'épée

sword' belt' *s* ceinturon *m*

sword'fish' *s* espadon *m*

swords'man *s* (*pl* **-men**) épéiste *m*

sword' swal'lower ['swalo-ər] *s* avaleur *m* de sabres

sword' thrust' *s* coup *m* de pointe, coup d'épée

sworn [sworn] *adj* (*enemy*) juré; **sworn in** assermenté

sycophant ['sɪkəfənt] *s* flagorneur *m*

syllable ['sɪləbəl] *s* syllabe *f*

sylla-bus ['sɪləbəs] *s* (*pl* **-bi** [,baɪ] or **-buses**) programme *m*

syllogism ['sɪlə,dʒɪzəm] *s* syllogisme *m*

sylph [sɪlf] *s* sylphe *m*

sylvan ['sɪlvən] *adj* sylvestre

symbol ['sɪmbəl] *s* symbole *m*

symbolic(al) [sɪm'balɪk(əl)] *adj* symbolique

symbolism ['sɪmbə,lɪzm] *s* symbolisme *m*

symbolize ['sɪmbə,laɪz] *tr* symboliser

symmetric(al) [sɪ'metrɪk(əl)] *adj* symétrique

symme-try ['sɪmɪtrɪ] *s* (*pl* **-tries**) symétrie *f*

sympathetic [,sɪmpə'θetɪk] *adj* compatissant; bien disposé; (anat, physiol) sympathique

sympathize ['sɪmpə,θaɪz] *intr*—**to sympathize with** compatir à; comprendre

sympa-thy ['sɪmpəθɪ] *s* (*pl* **-thies**) sympathie *f*; (*shared sorrow*) compassion *f*; **to be in sympathy with** être en sympathie avec; **to extend one's sympathy** to offrir ses condoléances à

sym'pathy strike' *s* grève *f* de solidarité

sympho-ny ['sɪmfənɪ] *s* (*pl* **-nies**) symphonie *f*

symposi-um [sɪm'pozɪ-əm] *s* (*pl* **-a** [ə]) colloque *m*, symposium *m*

symptom ['sɪmptəm] *s* symptôme *m*

synagogue ['sɪnə,gɔg], ['sɪnə,gag] *s* synagogue *f*

synchronize ['sɪŋkrə,naɪz] *tr* synchroniser

synchronous ['sɪŋkrənəs] *adj* synchrone

syncopation [,sɪŋkə'peʃən] *s* syncope *f*

syncope ['sɪŋkə,pi] *s* syncope *f*

syndicate ['sɪndɪkɪt] *s* syndicat *m* ‖ ['sɪndɪ,ket] *tr* syndiquer ‖ *intr* se syndiquer

synonym ['sɪnənɪm] *s* synonyme *m*

synonymous [sɪ'nanɪməs] *adj* synonyme

synop-sis [sɪ'napsɪs] *s* (*pl* **-ses** [siz]) abrégé *m*, résumé *m*; (mov) synopsis *m* & *f*

syntax ['sɪntæks] *s* syntaxe *f*

synthe-sis ['sɪnθɪsɪs] *s* (*pl* **-ses** [,siz]) synthèse *f*

synthesize ['sɪnθɪ,saɪz] *tr* synthétiser

synthetic(al) [sɪn'θetɪk(əl)] *adj* synthétique
syphilis ['sɪfɪlɪs] *s* syphilis *f*
Syria ['sɪrɪ-ə] *s* Syrie *f*; la Syrie
Syrian ['sɪrɪ-ən] *adj* syrien || *s* (*language*) syrien *m*; (*person*) Syrien *m*
syringe [sɪ'rɪndʒ], ['sɪrɪndʒ] *s* seringue *f* || *tr* seringuer

syrup ['sɪrəp], ['sʌrəp] *s* sirop *m*
system ['sɪstəm] *s* système *m*; (*of lines, wires, pipes, roads*) réseau *m*
systematic(al) [,sɪstə'mætɪk(əl)] *adj* systématique
systematize ['sɪstəmə,taɪz] *tr* systématiser
systole ['sɪstəli] *s* systole *f*

T

T, t [ti] *s* XXᵉ lettre de l'alphabet
tab [tæb] *s* patte *f*; (*label*) étiquette *f*;
to keep tab on (coll) garder à l'œil;
to pick up the tab (coll) payer l'addition
tab·by ['tæbi] *s* (*pl* **-bies**) chat *m* moucheté; (*female cat*) chatte *f*; (*old maid*) vieille fille *f*; (*spiteful female*) vieille chipie *f*
tabernacle ['tæbər,nækəl] *s* tabernacle *m*
table ['tebəl] *s* table *f*; (*tableland*) plateau *m*; (*list, chart*) tableau *m*, table; to clear the table ôter le couvert; to set the table mettre le couvert || *tr* ajourner la discussion de
tab·leau ['tæblo] *s* (*pl* **-leaus** or **-leaux** [loz]) tableau *m* vivant
ta/ble·cloth/ *s* nappe *f*
table d'hôte ['tabəl'dot] *s* repas *m* à prix fixe
ta/ble·land/ *s* plateau *m*
ta/ble lin/en *s* nappage *m*, linge *m* de table
ta/ble man/ners *spl*—to have good table manners bien se tenir à table
tab/le·mate/ *s* commensal *m*
ta/ble of con/tents *s* table *f* des matières
ta/ble·spoon/ *s* cuiller *f* à bouche
tablespoonful ['tebəl,spun,ful] *s* cuillerée *f* à soupe or à bouche
tablet ['tæblɪt] *s* (*writing pad*) blocnotes *m*, bloc *m*; (*lozenge*) pastille *f*, comprimé *m*; plaque *f* commémorative
ta/ble talk/ *s* propos *mpl* de table
ta/ble ten/nis *s* tennis *m* de table
ta/ble·top/ *s* dessus *m* de table
ta/ble·ware/ *s* ustensiles *mpl* de table
ta/ble wine/ *s* vin *m* ordinaire
tabloid ['tæblɔɪd] *adj* (*press, article, etc.*) à sensation || *s* journal *m* de petit format à l'affût du sensationnel
taboo [tə'bu] *adj & s* tabou *m* || *tr* déclarer tabou
tabular ['tæbjələr] *adj* tabulaire
tabulate ['tæbjə,let] *tr* disposer en forme de table or en tableaux, dresser un tableau de, aligner en colonnes
tabulator ['tæbjə,letər] *s* tabulateur *m*
tacit ['tæsɪt] *adj* tacite
taciturn ['tæsɪtɜrn] *adj* taciturne
tack [tæk] *s* (*nail*) semence *f*; (*plan*) voie *f*, tactique *f*; (*of sail*) amure *f*; (*naut*) bordée *f*; (*sewing*) point *m* de

bâti || *tr* clouer; (*sewing*) bâtir || *intr* louvoyer
tackle ['tækəl] *s* attirail *m*; (*for lifting*) treuil *m*; (*football*) plaquage *m*; (*naut*) palan *m* || *tr* empoigner, saisir; (*a problem, job, etc.*) chercher à résoudre, attaquer; (*football*) plaquer
tack·y ['tæki] *adj* (*comp* **-ier**; *super* **-iest**) collant; (coll) râpé, minable
tact [tækt] *s* tact *m*
tactful ['tæktfəl] *adj* plein de tact; to be tactful avoir du tact
tactical ['tæktɪkəl] *adj* tactique
tactician [tæk'tɪʃən] *s* tacticien *m*
tactics ['tæktɪks] *spl* tactique *f*
tactless ['tæktlɪs] *adj* sans tact
tadpole ['tæd,pol] *s* têtard *m*
taffeta ['tæfɪtə] *s* taffetas *m*
taffy ['tæfi] *s* pâte *f* à berlingots; (coll) flagornerie *f*
tag [tæg] *s* (*label*) étiquette *f*; (*of shoelace*) ferret *m*; (*game*) chat *m* perché || *v* (*pret & pp* **tagged**; *ger* **tagging**) *tr* étiqueter; (*in the game of tag*) attraper || *intr* (coll) suivre de près; to tag along behind s.o. (coll) traîner derrière qn
tag/ day/ *s* jour *m* de collecte publique
tag/ end/ *s* queue *f*; (*remnant*) coupon *m*
Tagus ['tegəs] *s* Tage *m*
tail [tel] *s* queue *f*; (*of shirt*) pan *m*; tails (*of a coin*) pile *f*; (coll) frac *m*; to turn tail tourner les talons || *tr* (coll) suivre de tout près || *intr*—to tail after marcher sur les talons de; to tail off s'éteindre, disparaître
tail/ assem/bly *s* (*pl* **-blies**) (aer) empennage *m*
tail/ end/ *s* queue *f*, fin *f*
tail/light/ *s* feu *m* arrière
tailor ['telər] *s* tailleur *m* || *tr* (*a suit*) faire || *intr* être tailleur
tailoring ['telərɪŋ] *s* métier *m* de tailleur
tai/lor-made suit/ *s* (*men's*) costume *m* sur mesure, complet *m* sur mesure; (*women's*) costume tailleur, tailleur *m*
tai/lor shop/ *s* boutique *f* de tailleur
tail/piece/ *s* queue *f*; (*of stringed instrument*) cordier *m*
tail/race/ *s* canal *m* de fuite
tail/spin/ *s* chute *f* en vrille
tail/wind/ *s* (aer) vent *m* arrière; (naut) vent en poupe

taint [tent] s tache f ∥ tr tacher; (*food*) gâter

take [tek] s prise f; (*mov*) prise de vues; (*slang*) recette f ∥ v (*pret* took [tuk]; *pp* taken) tr prendre; (*a walk; a trip*) faire; (*a course; advice*) suivre; (*an examination*) passer; (*a person on a trip*) emmener; (*the occasion*) profiter de; (*a photograph*) prendre; (*a newspaper*) être abonné à; (*a purchase*) garder; (*a certain amount of time*) falloir, e.g., **it takes an hour to walk there** il faut une heure pour y aller à pied; (*to lead*) conduire, mener; (*to tolerate, stand*) supporter; (*a seat*) prendre, occuper, e.g., **this seat is taken** cette place est prise ou occupée; **do you take that to be important?** tenez-vous cela pour important?; **I take it that** je suppose que; **take it easy!** (coll) allez-y doucement!; **to be taken ill** tomber malade; **to take amiss** prendre mal; **to take away** enlever; emmener; (*to subtract*) soustraire, retrancher; **to take down** descendre; (*a building*) démolir; (*in writing*) noter; **to take in** (*a roomer*) recevoir; (*laundry*) prendre à faire à la maison; (*the harvest*) rentrer; (*a seam*) reprendre; (*to include*) embrasser; (*to deceive*) (coll) duper; **to take off** ôter, enlever; (*from the price*) rabattre; (*to imitate*) (coll) singer; **to take on** (*passengers*) prendre; (*a responsibility*) prendre sur soi; (*workers*) embaucher, prendre; **to take out** sortir; (*a bullet from a wound; a passage from a text; an element from a compound*) extraire; (*public sign*) à emporter; **to take place** avoir lieu; **to take s.th. from s.o.** enlever, ôter, ou prendre q.ch. à qn; **to take up** (*to carry up*) monter; (*to remove*) enlever; (*a dress*) raccourcir; (*an idea, method, etc.*) adopter; (*a profession*) embrasser, prendre; (*a question, a study, etc.*) aborder ∥ intr prendre; **to not take to** (*a person*) prendre en grippe; **to take after** ressembler à; (*to chase*) poursuivre; **to take off** s'en aller; (aer) décoller; **to take to** (*flight; the woods*) prendre; (*a bad habit*) se livrer à; (*a person*) se prendre d'amitié avec; (*to like*) s'adonner à; **to take to** + *ger* se mettre à + *inf*; **to take up with** s.o. (coll) se lier avec qn

take′-off′ s (aer) décollage m; (coll) caricature f

tal′cum pow′der [ˈtælkəm] s poudre f de talc

tale [tel] s conte m; mensonge m; (*gossip*) racontar m, histoire f

tale′bear′er s rapporteur m

talent [ˈtælənt] s talent m; gens mpl de talent

talented [ˈtæləntɪd] adj doué, talentueux

tal′ent scout′ s dénicheur m de vedettes

tal′ent show′ s crochet m radiophonique, radio-crochet m

talk [tɔk] s paroles fpl; (*gossip*) racon-

tars mpl, dires mpl; (*lecture*) conférence f, causerie f; **to cause talk** défrayer la chronique; **to have a talk with** s'entretenir avec ∥ tr parler; **to talk over** discuter; **to talk up** vanter ∥ intr parler; (*to chatter, gossip, etc.*) bavarder, jaser; **to talk back** répliquer; **to talk on** continuer à parler

talkative [ˈtɔkətɪv] adj bavard

talker [ˈtɔkər] s parleur m; **a great talker** (coll) un causeur, un hâbleur

talkie [ˈtɔki] s (coll) film m parlant

talk′ing doll′ [ˈtɔkɪŋ] s poupée f parlante

talk′ing pic′ture s film m parlant

tall [tɔl] adj haut, élevé; (*person*) grand; (coll) exagéré

tallow [ˈtælo] s suif m

tal•ly [ˈtæli] s (pl -lies) compte m, pointage m ∥ v (*pret & pp* -lied) tr pointer, contrôler ∥ intr s'accorder

tallyho [ˈtælɪ ˌho] interj taïaut!

tal′ly sheet′ s feuille f de pointage, bordereau m

talon [ˈtælən] s serre f

tamarack [ˈtæmə ˌræk] s mélèze m d'Amérique

tambourine [ˌtæmbəˈrin] s tambour m de basque

tame [tem] adj apprivoisé; (e.g., *lion*) dompté; (e.g., *style*) fade, terne ∥ tr apprivoiser; (e.g., *a lion*) dompter

tamp [tæmp] tr bourrer; (e.g., *a hole in the ground*) damer

tamper [ˈtæmpər] intr—**to tamper with** se mêler de; (*a lock*) fausser; (*a document*) falsifier; (*a witness*) suborner

tampon [ˈtæmpɑn] s (surg) tampon m ∥ tr (surg) tamponner

tan [tæn] adj jaune; (e.g., *skin*) bronzé, hâlé ∥ v (*pret & pp* tanned; *ger* tanning) tr tanner; (e.g., *the skin*) bronzer, hâler ∥ intr se hâler

tandem [ˈtændəm] adj & adv en tandem, en flèche ∥ s tandem m

tang [tæŋ] s goût m vif, saveur f; (*ringing sound*) tintement m

tangent [ˈtændʒənt] adj tangent ∥ s tangente f; **to fly off at or on a tangent** changer brusquement de sujet

tangerine [ˌtændʒəˈrin] s mandarine f

tangible [ˈtændʒɪbəl] adj tangible

Tangier [tænˈdʒɪr] s Tanger m

tangle [ˈtæŋgəl] s enchevêtrement m ∥ tr enchevêtrer ∥ intr s'enchevêtrer

tank [tæŋk] s réservoir m; (mil) char m

tank′ car′ s (rr) wagon-citerne m

tanker [ˈtæŋkər] s (ship) bateau-citerne m; (*truck*) camion-citerne m; (*plane*) ravitailleur m

tank′ truck′ s camion-citerne m

tanner [ˈtænər] s tanneur m

tanner•y [ˈtænəri] s (pl -ies) tannerie f

tantalize [ˈtæntə ˌlaɪz] tr tenter, allécher

tantamount [ˈtæntə ˌmaʊnt] adj équivalent

tantrum [ˈtæntrəm] s accès m de colère; **in a tantrum** en rogne

tap [tæp] s petit coup m; (*faucet*) robinet m; (elec) prise f; (mach) taraud m; **on tap** au tonneau, en perce;

(available) (coll) disponible; **taps** (mil) l'extinction *f* des feux ‖ *v (pret & pp* **tapped;** *ger* **tapping)** *tr* taper; *(a cask)* mettre en perce; *(a tree)* entailler; *(a telephone)* passer à la table d'écoute; *(a nut)* tarauder; *(resources, talent, etc.)* drainer; (elec) brancher sur ‖ *intr* taper

tap′ dance′ *s* danse *f* à claquettes

tap′-dance′ *intr* danser les claquettes, faire les claquettes

tap′ dan′cer *s* danseur *m* à claquettes

tape [tep] *s* ruban *m* ‖ *tr (an electric wire)* guiper; *(land)* mesurer au cordeau; *(to tape-record)* enregistrer sur ruban

tape′ meas′ure *s* mètre-ruban *m*, centimètre *m*

taper ['tepər] *s (for lighting candles)* allumette-bougie *f*; (eccl) cierge *m* ‖ *tr* effiler ‖ *intr* s'effiler

tape′-record′ *tr* enregistrer sur ruban magnétique ou au magnétophone

tape′ record′er *s* magnétophone *m*

tapes·try ['tæpɪstrɪ] *s (pl* **-tries)** tapisserie *f* ‖ *v (pret & pp* **-tried)** *tr* tapisser

tape′worm′ *s* ver *m* solitaire

tappet ['tæpɪt] *s* (mach) taquet *m*

tap′room′ *s* débit *m* de boissons, buvette *f*

tap′ wa′ter *s* eau *f* du robinet

tap′ wrench′ *s* taraudeuse *f*

tar [tar] *s* goudron *m*; (coll) marin *m* ‖ *v (pret & pp* **tarred;** *ger* **tarring)** *tr* goudronner; **to tar and feather** enduire de goudron et de plumes

tar·dy ['tardɪ] *adj (comp* **-dier;** *super* **-diest)** lent; retardataire, en retard

tare [ter] *s (weight)* tare *f*; (Bib) ivraie *f* ‖ *tr* tarer

target ['targɪt] *s* cible *f*; *(goal)* but *m*; (mil) objectif *m*; *(butt)* (fig) cible

tar′get ar′ea *s* zone *f* de tir

tar′get lan′guage *s* langue *f* cible

tar′get prac′tice *s* tir *m* à la cible

tariff ['tærɪf] *s (duties)* droits *mpl* de douane; *(tariffs in general)* tarif *m*

tarnish ['tarnɪʃ] *s* ternissure *f* ‖ *tr* ternir ‖ *intr* se ternir

tar′ pa′per *s* papier *m* goudronné

tarpaulin [tar'pɔlɪn] *s* bâche *f*, prélart *m*

tarragon ['tærəgən] *s* estragon *m*

tar·ry ['tarɪ] *adj (comp* **-rier;** *super* **-riest)** goudronneux ‖ ['tærɪ] *v (pret & pp* **-ried)** *intr* tarder; *(to stay)* rester, demeurer

tart [tart] *adj* aigrelet; *(reply)* mordant ‖ *s* tarte *f*; (slang) grue *f*, poule *f*

tartar ['tartər] *adj (sauce)* tartare; **Tartar** tartare ‖ *s (on teeth)* tartre *m*; **Tartar** Tartare *mf*

task [tæsk], [task] *s* tâche *f*; **to bring** or **take to task** prendre à partie

task′ force′ *s* (mil) groupement *m* stratégique mixte

task′mas′ter *s* chef *m* de corvée; (fig) tyran *m*

tassel ['tæsəl] *s* gland *m*; *(on corn)* barbe *f*; *(on nightcap)* mèche *f*; (bot) aigrette *f*

taste [test] *s* goût *m*, saveur *f*; *(sense of what is fitting)* goût, bon goût ‖ *tr* goûter; *(to sample)* goûter à; *(to try out)* goûter de ‖ *intr* goûter; **to taste like** avoir le goût de; **to taste of** avoir un goût de

taste′ bud′ *s* papille *f* gustative

tasteless ['testlɪs] *adj* sans saveur, fade; *(in bad taste)* de mauvais goût

tast·y ['testɪ] *adj (comp* **-ier;** *super* **-iest)** (coll) savoureux; (coll) de bon goût

tatter ['tætər] *s* lambeau *m* ‖ *tr* mettre en lambeaux

tatterdemalion [,tætərdɪ'meljən], [,tætərdɪ'mæljən] *s* loqueteux *m*

tattered *adj* en lambeaux, en loques

tattle ['tætəl] *s* bavardage *m*; *(gossip)* cancan *m* ‖ *intr* bavarder; cancaner

tat′tle-tale′ *adj* révélateur ‖ *s* rapporteur *m*, cancanier *m*

tattoo [tæ'tu] *s* tatouage *m*; (mil) retraite *f* ‖ *tr* tatouer

taunt [tɔnt], [tant] *s* sarcasme *m* ‖ *tr* bafouer

taut [tɔt] *adj* tendu

tavern ['tævərn] *s* café *m*, bar *m*, bistrot *m*; *(inn)* taverne *f*

taw·dry ['tɔdrɪ] *adj (comp* **-drier;** *super* **-driest)** criard, voyant

taw·ny ['tɔnɪ] *adj (comp* **-nier;** *super* **-niest)** fauve; *(skin)* basané

tax [tæks] *s* impôt *m*; **to reduce the tax on** dégrever ‖ *tr* imposer; *(e.g., one's patience)* mettre à l'épreuve; **to tax s.o. with** *(e.g., laziness)* taxer qn de

taxable ['tæksəbəl] *adj* imposable

taxation [tæk'seʃən] *s* imposition *f*; charges *fpl* fiscales, impôts *mpl*

tax′ collec′tor *s* percepteur *m*

tax′ cut′ *s* dégrèvement *m* d'impôt

tax′ eva′sion *s* fraude *f* fiscale

tax′-exempt′ *adj* net d'impôt, exempt d'impôts

tax·i ['tæksɪ] *s (pl* **-is)** taxi *m* ‖ *v (pret & pp* **-ied;** *ger* **-iing** or **-ying)** *tr* (aer) rouler au sol ‖ *intr* aller en taxi; (aer) rouler au sol ‖ *interj* hep taxi!

tax′i-cab′ *s* taxi *m*

tax′i danc′er *s* taxi-girl *f*

taxidermy ['tæksɪ,dʌrmɪ] *s* taxidermie *f*

tax′i driv′er *s* chauffeur *m* de taxi

tax′i-plane′ *s* avion-taxi *m*

tax′i stand′ *s* station *f* de taxis

tax′pay′er *s* contribuable *mf*

tax′ rate′ *s* taux *m* de l'impôt

tea [ti] *s* thé *m*; *(medicinal infusion)* tisane *f*

tea′ bag′ *s* sachet *m* de thé

tea′ ball′ *s* boule *f* à thé

tea′cart′ *s* table *f* roulante

teach [titʃ] *v (pret & pp* **taught** [tɔt]) *tr* enseigner; **to teach s.o. s.th.** enseigner q.ch. à qn; **to teach s.o. to** + *inf* enseigner à qn à + *inf* ‖ *intr* enseigner

teacher ['titʃər] *s* instituteur *m*, enseignant *m*; *(such as adversity)* (fig) maître *m*

teach′er's pet′ *s* élève *m* gâté

teaching ['titʃɪŋ] *s* enseignement *m*

teach′ing aids′ *spl* matériel *m* auxiliaire d'enseignement

teach′ing staff′ *s* corps *m* enseignant

tea′cup′ *s* tasse *f* à thé

tea′ dance′ *s* thé *m* dansant

teak [tik] *s* teck *m*

tea′ket′tle *s* bouilloire *f*

team [tim] *s* (*of horses, oxen, etc.*) attelage *m*; (sports) équipe *f* ‖ *tr* atteler ‖ *intr*—**to team up with** faire équipe avec

team′mate′ *s* équipier *m*

teamster ['timstər] *s* (*of horses*) charretier *m*; (*of a truck*) camionneur *m*

team′work′ *s* travail *m* en équipe; (*spirit*) esprit *m* d'équipe

tea′pot′ *s* théière *f*

tear [tɪr] *s* larme *f*; **to burst into tears** fondre en larmes ‖ [ter] *s* déchirure *f* ‖ [ter] *v* (*pret* **tore** [tor]; *pp* **torn** [torn]) *tr* déchirer; **to tear away, down, off,** or **out** arracher; **to tear up** (*e.g., a letter*) déchirer ‖ *intr* se déchirer; **to tear along** filer précipitamment, aller à fond de train

tear′ bomb′ [tɪr] *s* bombe *f* lacrymogène

tear′ duct′ [tɪr] *s* conduit *m* lacrymal

tearful ['tɪrfəl] *adj* larmoyant, éploré

tear′ gas′ [tɪr] *s* gaz *m* lacrymogène

tear-jerker ['tɪr‚dʒʌrkər] *s* (slang) comédie *f* larmoyante

tea′room′ *s* salon *m* de thé

tease [tiz] *tr* taquiner

tea′spoon′ *s* cuiller *f* à café

teaspoonful ['ti‚spun‚ful] *s* cuillerée *f* à café

teat [tit] *s* tétine *f*

tea′time′ *s* l'heure *f* du thé

technical ['tɛknɪkəl] *adj*

technicali-ty [‚tɛknɪ'kælɪti] *s* (*pl* -**ties**) technicité *f*; (*fine point*) subtilité *f*

technician [tɛk'nɪʃən] *s* technicien *m*

technique [tɛk'nik] *s* technique *f*

ted′dy bear′ ['tɛdi] *s* ours *m* en peluche

tedious ['tidɪəs], ['tidʒəs] *adj* ennuyeux, fatigant

teem [tim] *intr* fourmiller; **to teem with** abonder en, fourmiller de

teeming ['timɪŋ] *adj* fourmillant; (*rain*) torrentiel

teen-ager ['tin‚edʒər] *s* adolescent *m* de 13 à 19 ans

teens [tinz] *spl* numéros anglais qui se terminent en -teen (de 13 à 19); adolescence *f* de 13 à 19 ans; **to be in one's teens** être adolescent

tee-ny ['tini] *adj* (*comp* -**nier**; *super* -**niest**) (coll) minuscule, tout petit

teeter ['titər] *s* branlement *m*; balançoire *f* ‖ *intr* se balancer, chanceler

teethe [tið] *intr* faire ses dents

teething ['tiðɪŋ] *s* dentition *f*

teeth′ing ring′ *s* sucette *f*

teetotaler [ti'totələr] *s* antialcoolique *mf* (*qui s'abstient totalement de boissons alcooliques*)

tele·cast ['tɛlɪ‚kæst], ['tɛlɪ‚kɑst] *s* émission *f* télévisée ‖ *v* (*pret & pp* -**cast** or -**casted**) *tr & intr* téléviser

telegram ['tɛlɪ‚græm] *s* télégramme *m*

telegraph ['tɛlɪ‚græf], ['tɛlɪ‚grɑf] *s* télégraphe *m* ‖ *tr & intr* télégraphier

telegrapher [tɪ'lɛgrəfər] *s* télégraphiste *mf*

tel′egraph pole′ *s* poteau *m* télégraphique

telemeter [tɪ'lɛmɪtər] *s* télémètre *m*

telepathy [tɪ'lɛpəθi] *s* télépathie *f*

telephone ['tɛlɪ‚fon] *s* téléphone *m* ‖ *tr & intr* téléphoner

tel′ephone booth′ *s* cabine *f* téléphonique

tel′ephone call′ *s* appel *m* téléphonique

tel′ephone direc′tory *s* annuaire *m* du téléphone

tel′ephone exchange′ *s* central *m* téléphonique

tel′ephone op′erator *s* standardiste *mf*, téléphoniste *mf*

tel′ephone receiv′er *s* récepteur *m* de téléphone

tel′ephoto lens′ ['tɛlɪ‚foto] *s* téléobjectif *m*

teleprinter ['tɛlɪ‚prɪntər] *s* téléimprimeur *m*

telescope ['tɛlɪ‚skop] *s* télescope *m* ‖ *tr* télescoper ‖ *intr* se télescoper

telescopic [‚tɛlɪ'skɑpɪk] *adj* télescopique

teletype ['tɛlɪ‚taɪp] *s* (trademark) télétype *m*

tel′etype′writ′er *s* téléscripteur *m*

teleview ['tɛlɪ‚vju] *tr & intr* voir à la télévision

televiewer ['tɛlɪ‚vju‚ər] *s* téléspectateur *m*

televise ['tɛlɪ‚vaɪz] *tr* téléviser

television ['tɛlɪ‚vɪʒən] *adj* télévisuel ‖ *s* télévision *f*

tel′evision screen′ *s* écran *m* de télévision, petit écran

tel′evision set′ *s* téléviseur *m*

tell [tɛl] *v* (*pret & pp* **told** [told]) *tr* dire; (*a story*) raconter; (*to count*) compter; (*to recognize as distinct*) distinguer; **tell me another!** (coll) à d'autres!; **to tell off** compter; (coll) dire son fait à; **to tell s.o. to** + *inf* dire à qn de + *inf* ‖ *intr* produire un effet; **do tell!** (coll) vraiment!; **to tell on** influer sur; (coll) dénoncer; **who can tell?** qui sait?

teller ['tɛlər] *s* narrateur *m*; (*of a bank*) caissier *m*; (*of votes*) scrutateur *m*

temper ['tɛmpər] *s* humeur *f*, caractère *m*; (*of steel, glass, etc.*) trempe *f*; **to keep one's temper** retenir sa colère; **to lose one's temper** se mettre en colère ‖ *tr* tremper ‖ *intr* se tremper

temperament ['tɛmpərəmənt] *s* tempérament *m*

temperamental [‚tɛmpərə'mɛntəl] *adj* constitutionnel; capricieux, instable

temperance ['tɛmpərəns] *s* tempérance *f*

temperate ['tɛmpərɪt] *adj* tempéré; (*in food or drink*) tempérant

temperature ['tɛmpərət/ər] *s* température *f*

tempest ['tɛmpɪst] *s* tempête *f*; **tempest in a teapot** tempête dans un verre d'eau

tempestuous [tem'pestʃʊ‑əs] *adj* tempétueux

temple ['tempəl] *s* temple *m*; (*side of forehead*) tempe *f*; (*of spectacles*) branche *f*

templet ['templɪt] *s* gabarit *m*

tem‑po ['tempo] *s* (*pl* ‑pos *or* ‑pi [pi]) tempo *m*

temporal ['tempərəl] *adj* temporel; (*anat*) temporal

temporary ['tempə‚reri] *adj* temporaire

temporize ['tempə‚raɪz] *intr* temporiser

tempt [tempt] *tr* tenter

temptation [temp'teʃən] *s* tentation *f*

tempter ['temptər] *s* tentateur *m*

tempting ['temptɪŋ] *adj* tentant

ten [ten] *adj & pron* dix; **about ten** une dizaine de ‖ *s* dix *m*; **ten o'clock** dix heures

tenable ['tenəbəl] *adj* soutenable

tenacious [tɪ'neʃəs] *adj* tenace

tenacity [tɪ'næsɪti] *s* ténacité *f*

tenant ['tenənt] *s* locataire *mf*

ten′ant farm′er *s* métayer *m*

tend [tend] *tr* soigner; (*sheep*) garder; (*a machine*) surveiller ‖ *intr*—**to tend to** (*to be disposed to*) tendre à; (*to attend to*) vaquer à; **to tend towards** tendre vers or à

tenden‑cy ['tendənsɪ] *s* (*pl* ‑cies) tendance *f*

tender ['tendər] *adj* tendre ‖ *s* offre *f*; (aer, naut) ravitailleur *m*; (rr) tender *m* ‖ *tr* offrir

ten′der‑heart′ed *adj* au cœur tendre

ten′der‑loin′ *s* filet *m*

tenderness ['tendərnɪs] *s* tendresse *f*; (*of, e.g., the skin*) sensibilité *f*; (*of, e.g., meat*) tendreté *f*

tendon ['tendən] *s* tendon *m*

tendril ['tendrɪl] *s* vrille *f*

tenement ['tenɪmənt] *s* maison *f* d'habitation

ten′ement house′ *s* maison *f* de rapport; (*in the slums*) taudis *m*

tenet ['tenɪt] *s* doctrine *f*, principe *m*

tennis ['tenɪs] *s* tennis *m*

ten′nis court′ *s* court *m* de tennis

tenor ['tenər] *s* teneur *f*, cours *m*; (mus) ténor *m*

tense [tens] *adj* tendu ‖ *s* (gram) temps *m*

tension ['tenʃən] *s* tension *f*

tent [tent] *s* tente *f*

tentacle ['tentəkəl] *s* tentacule *m*

tentative ['tentətɪv] *adj* provisoire; (*hesitant*) timide

tenth [tenθ] *adj & pron* dixième (*masc, fem*); **the Tenth** dix, e.g., **John the Tenth Jean dix** ‖ *s* dixième *m*; **the tenth** (*in dates*) le dix

tent′ pole′ *s* montant *m* de tente

tenuous ['tenjʊ‑əs] *adj* ténu

tenure ['tenjər] *s* (*possession*) tenure *f*; (*of an office*) occupation *f*; (*protection from dismissal*) inamovibilité *f*

tepid ['tepɪd] *adj* tiède

term [tʌrm] *s* terme *m*; (*of imprisonment*) temps *m*; (*of office*) mandat *m*; (*of the school year*) semestre *m*; **terms** conditions *fpl* ‖ *tr* appeler, qualifier

termagant ['tʌrməgənt] *s* mégère *f*

terminal ['tʌrmɪnəl] *adj* terminal ‖ *s* (elec) borne *f*; (rr) terminus *m*

terminate ['tʌrmɪ‚net] *tr* terminer ‖ *intr* se terminer

termination [‚tʌrmɪ'neʃən] *s* conclusion *f*; (*extremity*) bout *m*; (*of word*) désinence *f*

terminus ['tʌrmɪnəs] *s* bout *m*, extrémité *f*; (*boundary*) borne *f*; (rr) terminus *m*

termite ['tʌrmaɪt] *s* termite *m*

term′ pa′per *s* dissertation *f*

terrace ['terəs] *s* terrasse *f* ‖ *tr* disposer en terrasse

terra firma ['terə'fʌrmə] *s* terre *f* ferme

terrain [te'ren] *s* terrain *m*

terrestrial [tə'restrɪ‑əl] *adj* terrestre

terrible ['terɪbəl] *adj* terrible; (*extremely bad*) atroce

terrific [tə'rɪfɪk] *adj* terrible, terrifiant; (coll) formidable

terri‑fy ['terɪ‚faɪ] *v* (*pret & pp* ‑fied) *tr* terrifier

territo‑ry ['terɪ‚tori] *s* (*pl* ‑ries) territoire *m*

terror ['terər] *s* terreur *f*

terrorize ['terə‚raɪz] *tr* terroriser

ter′ry cloth′ ['teri] *s* tissu‑éponge *m*

terse [tʌrs] *adj* concis, succinct

tertiary ['tʌrʃɪ‚eri], ['tʌrʃəri] *adj* tertiaire

test [test] *s* épreuve *f*; (*exam*) examen *m*; (*trial*) essai *m*; (*e.g., of intelligence*) test *m* ‖ *tr* éprouver, mettre à l'épreuve; examiner, tester

testament ['testəmənt] *s* testament *m*

test′ ban′ *s* interdiction *f* des essais nucléaires

test′ flight′ *s* vol *m* d'essai

testicle ['testɪkəl] *s* testicule *m*

testi‑fy ['testɪ‚faɪ] *v* (*pret & pp* ‑fied) *tr* déclarer ‖ *intr* déposer; **to testify to** témoigner de

testimonial [‚testɪ'monɪ‑əl] *s* attestation *m*

testimo‑ny ['testɪ‚moni] *s* (*pl* ‑nies) témoignage *m*

test′ pat′tern *s* (telv) mire *f*

test′ pi′lot *s* pilote *m* d'essai

test′ tube′ *s* éprouvette *f*

tes‑ty ['testi] *adj* (*comp* ‑tier; *super* ‑tiest) susceptible

tetanus ['tetənəs] *s* tétanos *m*

tether ['teðər] *s* attache *f*; **at the end of one's tether** à bout de ressources ‖ *tr* mettre à l'attache

tetter ['tetər] *s* (pathol) dartre *f*

text [tekst] *s* texte *m*

text′book′ *s* manuel *m* scolaire, livre *m* de classe

textile ['tekstɪl], ['tekstaɪl] *adj & s* textile *m*

textual ['tekstʃʊ‑əl] *adj* textuel

texture ['tekstʃər] *s* texture *f*; (*woven fabric*) tissu *m*

Thai ['tɑ‑i], [taɪ] *adj* thaï, thaïlandais ‖ *s* (*language*) thaï *m*; (*person*)

Thaïlandais *m*; the Thai les Thaïlandais

Thailand ['tarlənd] *s* Thaïlande *f*; la Thaïlande

Thames [temz] *s* Tamise *f*

than [ðæn] *conj* que; (*before a numeral*) de, e.g., more than three plus de trois

thank [θæŋk] *adj* (e.g., *offering*) de reconnaissance || thanks *spl* remerciements *mpl*; thanks to grâce à || thanks *interj* merci!; no thanks! merci! || thank *tr* remercier; thank you je vous remercie; thank you for merci de or pour; thank you for + *ger* merci de + *inf*; to thank s.o. for remercier qn de or pour; to thank s.o. for + *ger* remercier qn de + *inf*

thankful ['θæŋkfəl] *adj* reconnaissant

thankless ['θæŋklıs] *adj* ingrat

Thanksgiv'ing Day' *s* le jour d'action de grâces

that [ðæt] *adj dem* (*pl* those) ce §82; that one celui-là §84 || *pron dem* (*pl* those) celui §83; celui-là §84 || *pron rel* qui; que || *pron neut* cela, ça; that is c'est-à-dire; that's all voilà tout; that will do cela suffit || *adv* tellement, si, aussi; that far si loin, aussi loin; that much, that many tant || *conj* que; (*in order that*) pour que, afin que; in that en ce que

thatch [θæt∫] *s* chaume *m* || *tr* couvrir de chaume

thatched' cot'tage *s* chaumière *f*

thaw [θɔ] *s* dégel *m* || *tr* & *intr* dégeler

the [ðə], [ðı], [ðı] *art def* le §77 || *adv* d'autant plus, e.g., she will be the happier for it elle en sera d'autant plus heureuse; the more . . . the more plus . . . plus

theater ['θiːətər] *s* théâtre *m*

the'ater club' *s* association *f* des spectateurs

the'ater-go'er *s* habitué *m* du théâtre

the'ater page' *s* chronique *f* théâtrale

theatrical [θı'ætrıkəl] *adj* théâtral

thee [ðı] *pron pers* (*archaic, poetic, Bib*) toi §85; te §87

theft [θeft] *s* vol *m*

their [ðer] *adj poss* leur §88

theirs [ðerz] *pron poss* le leur §89

them [ðem] *pron pers* eux §85; les §87; leur §87; of them en §87; to them leur §87; y §87

theme [θim] *s* thème *m*; (*essay*) composition *f*; (*mus*) thème

theme' song' *s* leitmotiv *m*; (*rad*) indicatif *m*

them·selves' *pron pers* soi §85; eux-mêmes §86; se §87; eux §85

then [ðen] *adv* alors; (*next*) ensuite, puis; (*therefore*) donc; by then d'ici là; from then on, since then depuis lors, dès lors; then and there séance tenante; till then jusque-là; what then? et après?

thence [ðens] *adv* de là; (*from that fact*) pour cette raison

thence'forth' *adv* dès lors

theol·o·gy [θi'alədʒi] *s* (*pl* -gies) théologie *f*

theorem ['θiːərəm] *s* théorème *m*

theoretical [ˌθiːə'retıkəl] *adj* théorique

theo·ry ['θiːəri] *s* (*pl* -ries) théorie *f*

therapeutic [ˌθerə'pjutık] *adj* thérapeutique || therapeutics *spl* thérapeutique *f*

thera·py ['θerəpi] *s* (*pl* -pies) thérapie *f*

there [ðer] *adv* là; y §87; down there, over there là-bas; from there de là; en §87; in there là-dedans; on there là-dessus; there is or there are il y a; (*pointing out*) voilà; under there là-dessous; up there là-haut

there'abouts' *adv* aux environs, près de là; (*approximately*) à peu près

there'af'ter *adv* par la suite

there'by' *adv* par là; de cette manière

therefore ['ðer‚fɔr] *adv* par conséquent, donc

there'in' *adv* dedans, là-dedans

there'of' *adv* de cela; en §87

there'upon' *adv* là-dessus §85A; sur ce

there'with' *adv* avec cela

thermal ['θʌrməl] *adj* (*waters*) thermal; (*capacity*) thermique

thermocouple ['θʌrmo‚kʌpəl] *s* thermocouple *m*

thermodynamic [ˌθʌrmodaı'næmık] *adj* thermodynamique || thermodynamics *spl* thermodynamique *f*

thermometer [θər'mamıtər] *s* thermomètre *m*

thermonuclear [ˌθʌrmo'n(j)uklı·ər] *adj* thermonucléaire

Thermopylae [θər'mapı‚li] *s* les Thermopyles *pl*

ther'mos bot'tle ['θʌrməs] *s* thermos *m* & *f*, bouteille *f* thermos

thermostat ['θʌrmə‚stæt] *s* thermostat *m*

thesau·rus [θı'sɔrəs] *s* (*pl* -ri [raı]) trésor *m*; dictionnaire *m* analogique

these [ðiz] *adj dem* *pl* ces §82 || *pron dem pl* ces §83; ceux-ci §84

the·sis ['θisıs] *s* (*pl* -ses [siz]) thèse *f*

they [ðe] *pron pers* ils §87; eux §85; on §87, e.g., they say on dit; ce §82B

thick [θık] *adj* épais; (*pipe, rod, etc.*) gros; (*forest, eyebrows, etc.*) touffu; (*grass, grain, etc.*) dru; (*voice*) pâteux; (*gravy*) court; (*coll*) stupide, obtus; (*coll*) intime || *s* (*of thumb, leg, etc.*) gras *m*; the thick of (e.g., *a crowd*) le milieu de; (*e.g., a battle*) le fort de; through thick and thin contre vents et marées

thicken ['θıkən] *tr* épaissir || *intr* s'épaissir; (*said, e.g., of plot*) se corser

thicket ['θıkıt] *s* fourré *m*, maquis *m*

thick'-head'ed *adj* à la tête dure

thick'-lipped' *adj* lippu

thick'-set' *adj* trapu

thief [θif] *s* (*pl* thieves [θivz]) voleur *m*

thieve [θiv] *intr* voler

thiever·y ['θivəri] *s* (*pl* -ies) volerie *f*

thigh [θaı] *s* cuisse *f*

thigh'bone' *s* fémur *m*

thimble ['θımbəl] *s* dé *m*

thin [θın] *adj* (*comp* thinner; *super* thinnest) mince; (*person*) élancé, maigre; (*hair*) rare; (*soup*) clair;

(*gravy*) long; (*voice*) grêle; (*excuse*) fai̶‖ v ‖ (*pret & pp* thinned; *ger* thinning) *tr* amincir; (*colors*) délayer; **to thin out** éclaircir ‖ *intr* s'amincir; **to thin out** s'éclaircir

thine [ðaɪn] *adj poss* (archaic, poetic, Bib) ton §88 ‖ *pron poss* (archaic, poetic, Bib) le tien §89

thing [θɪŋ] *s* chose *f*; **for another thing** d'autre part; **for one thing** en premier lieu; **of all things!** par exemple!; **to be the thing** être le dernier cri; **to see things** avoir des hallucinations

thingumbob [ˈθɪŋəmˌbʌb] *s* (coll) truc *m*, machin *m*

think [θɪŋk] *v* (*pret & pp* thought [θɔt]) *tr* penser; (*to deem, consider*) estimer; **to think of** (*to have as an opinion of*) penser de ‖ *intr* penser, songer; **to think fast** avoir l'esprit alerte; **to think of** (*to direct one's thoughts toward*) penser à, songer à; **to think of it or them** y penser, y songer; **to think so** croire que oui

thinker [ˈθɪŋkər] *s* penseur *m*

third [θʌrd] *adj & pron* troisième (*masc, fem*); **the Third** trois, e.g., **John the Third** Jean trois ‖ *s* troisième *m*; (*in fractions*) tiers *m*; **the third** (*in dates*) le trois

third' degree' *s* (coll) passage *m* à tabac, cuisinage *m*

third' fin'ger *s* annulaire *m*

third' rail' *s* (rr) rail *m* de contact; rail conducteur

third'-rate' *adj* de troisième ordre

thirst [θʌrst] *s* soif *f* ‖ *intr* avoir soif; **to thirst for** avoir soif de

thirst'-quench'ing *adj* désaltérant

thirst-y [ˈθʌrsti] *adj* (*comp* -ier; *super* -iest) altéré, assoiffé; **to be thirsty** avoir soif

thirteen [ˈθʌrˈtin] *adj, pron, & s* treize *m*

thirteenth [ˈθʌrˈtinθ] *adj & pron* treizième (*masc, fem*); **the Thirteenth** treize, e.g., **John the Thirteenth** Jean treize ‖ *s* treizième *m*; **the thirteenth** (*in dates*) le treize

thirtieth [ˈθʌrtɪ-ɪθ] *adj & pron* trentième (*masc, fem*) ‖ *s* trentième *m*; **the thirtieth** (*in dates*) trente

thir-ty [ˈθʌrti] *adj & pron* trente; **about thirty** une trentaine de ‖ *s* (*pl* -ties) trente *m*; **the thirties** les années *fpl* trente

this [ðɪs] *adj dem* (*pl* these) ce §82; **this one** celui-ci §84 ‖ *pron dem* (*pl* these) celui §83; celui-ci §84 ‖ *pron neut* ceci ‖ *adv* tellement, si, aussi; **this far** si loin, aussi loin; **this much,** **this many** tant

thistle [ˈθɪsəl] *s* chardon *m*

thither [ˈθɪðər], [ˈðɪðər] *adv* là, de ce côté là

thong [θɔŋ], [θɑŋ] *s* courroie *f*

tho-rax [ˈθoræks] *s* (*pl* -raxes or -races [rəˌsiz]) thorax *m*

thorn [θɔrn] *s* épine *f*

thorn-y [ˈθɔrni] *adj* (*comp* -ier; *super* -iest) épineux

thorough [ˈθʌro] *adj* approfondi, complet; consciencieux, minutieux

thor'ough-bred' *adj* de race, racé; (*horse*) pur sang ‖ *s* personne *f* racée; (*horse*) pur-sang *m*

thor'ough-fare' *s* voie *f* de communication; **no thoroughfare** (public sign) rue barrée

thor'ough-go'ing *adj* parfait; consciencieux

thoroughly [ˈθʌroli] *adv* à fond

those [ðoz] *adj dem pl* ces §82 ‖ *pron dem pl* ceux §83; ceux-là §84

thou [ðau] *pron pers* (archaic, poetic, Bib) tu §87 ‖ *tr & intr* tutoyer

though [ðo] *adv* cependant ‖ *conj* (*although*) bien que, quoique; (*even if*) même si; **as though** comme si

thought [θɔt] *s* pensée *f*

thought' control' *s* asservissement *m* des consciences

thoughtful [ˈθɔtfəl] *adj* pensif; (*considerate*) prévenant, attentif; (*serious*) profond

thoughtless [ˈθɔtlɪs] *adj* étourdi, négligent; inconsidéré

thousand [ˈθauzənd] *adj & pron* mille, mil, e.g., **the year one thousand nineteen hundred and eighty-one** l'an mil neuf cent quatre-vingt-un ‖ *s* mille *m*; **a thousand un** millier de, mille

thousandth [ˈθauzəndθ] *adj & pron* millième (*masc, fem*) ‖ *s* millième *m*

thrash [θræʃ] *tr* rosser; (agr) battre; **to thrash out** débattre ‖ *intr* s'agiter; (agr) battre le blé

thread [θred] *s* fil *m*; (bot) filament *m*; (mach) filet *m*; **to hang by a thread** ne tenir qu'à un fil; **to lose the thread of** perdre le fil de ‖ *tr* enfiler; (mach) fileter

thread'bare' *adj* élimé, râpé; (*tire*) usé jusqu'à la corde

threat [θret] *s* menace *f*

threaten [ˈθretən] *tr & intr* menacer

threatening [ˈθretənɪŋ] *adj* menaçant

three [θri] *adj & pron* trois ‖ *s* trois *m*; **three o'clock** trois heures; **three of a kind** (cards) un fredon

three'-cor'nered *adj* triangulaire; (*hat*) tricorne

three'-ply' *adj* à trois épaisseurs; (*e.g., wool*) à trois fils

three' R's' [ɑrz] *spl* la lecture, l'écriture et l'arithmétique, premières notions *fpl*

three'score' *adj* soixante

threno-dy [ˈθrenədi] *s* (*pl* -dies) thrène *m*

thresh [θreʃ] *tr* (agr) battre; **to thresh out** (*a problem*) débattre ‖ *intr* s'agiter; (agr) battre le blé

thresh'ing floor' *s* aire *f*

thresh'ing machine' *s* batteuse *f*

threshold [ˈθreʃold] *s* seuil *m*; **to cross the threshold** franchir le seuil

thrice [θraɪs] *adv* trois fois

thrift [θrɪft] *s* économie *f*, épargne *f*

thrift-y [ˈθrɪfti] *adj* (*comp* -ier; *super* -iest) économe, ménager, frugal; prospère

thrill [θrɪl] s frisson m || tr faire frémir || intr frémir

thriller ['θrɪlər] s roman m, film m, or pièce f à sensation

thrilling ['θrɪlɪŋ] adj émouvant, passionnant

thrive [θraɪv] v (pret **thrived** or **throve** [θrov]; pp **thrived** or **thriven** ['θrɪvən]) intr prospérer; (said of child, plant, etc.) croître, se développer

throat [θrot] s gorge f; **to clear one's throat** s'éclaircir le gosier; **to have a sore throat** avoir mal à la gorge

throb [θrɑb] s palpitation f, battement m; (of motor) vrombissement m || v (pret & pp **throbbed**; ger **throbbing**) intr palpiter, battre fort; (said of motor) vrombir

throes [θroz] spl (of childbirth) douleurs fpl; (of death) affres fpl; **in the throes of** luttant avec

throne [θron] s trône m

throng [θrɑŋ], [θrɔŋ] s foule f, affluence f || intr affluer

throttle ['θrɑtəl] s (of steam engine) régulateur m; (aut) étrangleur m || tr régler; étrangler

through [θru] adj direct; (finished) fini; (traffic) prioritaire || adv à travers; complètement || prep au travers de, par; grâce à, par le canal de

through-out adv d'un bout à l'autre || prep d'un bout à l'autre de; (during) pendant tout

through' street' s rue f à circulation prioritaire

through'way' s autoroute f

throw [θro] s jet m, lancement m; (scarf) châle m || v (pret **threw** [θru]; pp **thrown**) tr jeter, lancer; (a glance; the dice) jeter; (e.g., a baseball) lancer; (e.g., a shadow) projeter; (blame; responsibility) rejeter; (a rider) désarçonner; (a game, career, etc.) perdre à dessein; **to throw away** jeter; **to throw back** renvoyer; **to throw in** ajouter; **to throw out** expulser, chasser; (e.g., an odor) répandre; (one's chest) bomber; **to throw over** abandonner; **to throw up** jeter en l'air; vomir; (one's hands) lever; (e.g., one's claims) renoncer à || intr jeter, lancer; jeter des dés; **to throw up** vomir

throw'back' s recul m; (setback) échec m; (reversion) retour m atavique

thrum [θrʌm] s v (pret & pp **thrummed**; ger **thrumming**) intr pianoter

thrush [θrʌʃ] s grive f

thrust [θrʌst] s poussée f; (with a weapon) coup m de pointe; (with a sword) coup d'estoc; (jibe) trait m; (rok) poussée f; **thrust and parry** la botte et la parade || v (pret & pp **thrust**) tr pousser; (e.g., a dagger) enfoncer; **to thrust oneself on** s'imposer à

thud [θʌd] s bruit m sourd || v (pret & pp **thudded**; ger **thudding**) tr & intr frapper avec un son mat

thug [θʌg] s bandit m, assassin m

thumb [θʌm] s pouce m; **all thumbs**

(coll) maladroit; **to twiddle one's thumbs** se tourner les pouces; **under the thumb of** sous la coupe de || tr tripoter; (a book) feuilleter; **to thumb a ride** faire de l'auto-stop; **to thumb one's nose at** (coll) faire un pied de nez à

thumb' in'dex s onglet m, encoche f

thumb'print' s marque f de pouce

thumb'screw' s papillon m, vis f à ailettes

thumb'tack' s punaise f

thump [θʌmp] s coup m violent || tr cogner || intr tomber avec un bruit sourd; (said, e.g., of marching feet) sonner lourdement; (said of heart) battre fort

thumping ['θʌmpɪŋ] adj (coll) énorme

thunder ['θʌndər] s tonnerre m || tr fulminer || intr tonner; **to thunder at** tonner contre, tempêter contre

thun'der-bolt' s foudre f; (disaster) coup m de foudre

thun'der-clap' s coup m de tonnerre

thunderous ['θʌndərəs] adj orageux; (voice; applause) tonnant

thun'der-show'er s pluie f d'orage

thun'der-storm' s orage m

thunderstruck ['θʌndər‚strʌk] adj foudroyé

Thursday ['θʌrzdi] s jeudi m

thus [ðʌs] adv ainsi; (therefore) donc; **thus far** jusqu'ici

thwack [θwæk] s coup m || tr flanquer un coup à

thwart [θwɔrt] adj transversal || adv en travers || tr déjouer, frustrer

thy [ðaɪ] adj poss (archaic, poetic, Bib) ton §88

thyme [taɪm] s thym m

thyroid ['θaɪrɔɪd] s thyroïde f; (pharm) extrait m thyroïde

thyself [ðaɪ'self] pron (archaic, poetic, Bib) toi-même §86; te §87

tiara [taɪ'ærə], [taɪ'erə] s tiare f; (woman's headdress) diadème m

tic [tɪk] s (pathol) tic m

tick [tɪk] s tic-tac m; (e.g., of pillow) taie f; (e.g., of mattress) housse f de coutil; (ent) tique f; **on tick** à crédit || tr—**to tick off** (to check off) pointer || intr tictaquer; (said of heart) battre

ticker ['tɪkər] s téléimprimeur m; (watch) (slang) toquante f; (heart) (slang) cœur m

tick'er tape' s bande f de téléimprimeur

ticket ['tɪkɪt] s billet m; (of bus, subway, etc.) ticket m; (of baggage checkroom) bulletin m; (of cloakroom) numéro m; (for boat trip) passage m; (of a political party) liste f électorale; (for violation) (coll) papillon m de procès-verbal, contravention f; **that's the ticket** (coll) c'est bien ça, à la bonne heure; **tickets, please!** vos places, s'il vous plaît!

tick'et a'gent s guichetier m

tick'et collec'tor s contrôleur m

tick'et of'fice s guichet m; (theat) bureau m de location

tick′et scalp′er [ˌskælpər] s trafiquant m de billets de théâtre

tick′et win′dow s guichet m

ticking [ˈtɪkɪŋ] s coutil m

tickle [ˈtɪkəl] s chatouillement m ‖ tr chatouiller; amuser; plaire (with dat) ‖ intr chatouiller

ticklish [ˈtɪklɪʃ] adj chatouilleux; (touchy) susceptible; (subject, question) épineux, délicat

tick′-tack-toe′ s morpion m

ticktock [ˈtɪkˌtɑk] s tic-tac m ‖ intr faire tic-tac

tid′al wave′ [ˈtaɪdəl] s raz m de marée; (e.g., of popular indignation) vague f

tidbit [ˈtɪdˌbɪt] s bon morceau m

tiddlywinks [ˈtɪdliˌwɪŋks] s jeu m de puce

tide [taɪd] s marée f; **against the tide** à contre-marée; **to go with the tide** suivre le courant ‖ tr—**to tide over** dépanner, remettre à flot; (a difficulty) venir à bout de

tide′land′ s terres fpl inondées aux grandes marées

tide′wa′ter s eaux fpl de marée; bord m de la mer

tide′water pow′er plant′ s usine f marémotrice

tidings [ˈtaɪdɪŋz] spl nouvelles fpl

ti·dy [ˈtaɪdi] adj (comp -dier; super -diest) propre, net, bien tenu; (considerable) (coll) joli, fameux ‖ s (pl -dies) voile m de fauteuil ‖ v (pret & pp -died) tr mettre en ordre, nettoyer ‖ intr—**to tidy up** faire un brin de toilette

tie [taɪ] s lien m, attache f; (knot) nœud m; (necktie) cravate f; (in games) match m nul; (mus) liaison f; (rr) traverse f ‖ v (pret & pp tied; ger tying) tr lier; (a knot, a necktie, etc.) nouer; (shoelaces; a knot; one's apron) attacher; (an artery) ligaturer; (a competitor) être à égalité avec; (mus) lier; **tied up** (busy) occupé; **to tie down** assujettir; **to tie up** attacher; (a package) ficeler; (a person) ligoter; (a wound) bander; (funds) immobiliser; (traffic, a telephone line) embouteiller ‖ intr (sports) faire match nul, égaliser

tie′back′ s embrasse f

tie′pin′ s épingle f de cravate

tier [tɪr] s étage m; (of stadium) gradin m

tiger [ˈtaɪgər] s tigre m

ti′ger lil′y s lis m tigré

tight [taɪt] adj serré, juste; (e.g., rope) tendu; (clothes) ajusté; (container) étanche; (game) serré; (money) rare; (miserly) (coll) chiche; (drunk) (coll) rond, noir ‖ **tights** spl collant m, maillot m ‖ adv fermement, bien; **to hold tight** tenir serré; se tenir, se cramponner; **to sit tight** (coll) tenir bon

tighten [ˈtaɪtən] tr (a knot, a bolt) serrer, resserrer; (e.g., a rope) tendre ‖ intr se serrer; se tendre

tight-fisted [ˈtaɪtˈfɪstɪd] adj dur à la détente, serré

tight′-fit′ting adj collant, ajusté

tight′rope′ s corde f raide

tight′rope walk′er s funambule mf

tight′ squeeze′ s (coll) situation f difficile, embarras m

tight′wad′ s (coll) grippe-sou m

tigress [ˈtaɪgrɪs] s tigresse f

tile [taɪl] s (for roof) tuile f; (for floor) carreau m ‖ tr (e.g., a house) couvrir de tuiles; (a floor) carreler

tile′ roof′ s toit m de tuiles

till [tɪl] s tiroir-caisse m ‖ prep jusqu'à ‖ conj jusqu'à ce que ‖ tr labourer

tilt [tɪlt] s pente f, inclinaison f; (contest) joute f; **full tilt** à fond de train ‖ tr pencher, incliner; **to tilt back** renverser en arrière; **to tilt up** redresser ‖ intr se pencher, s'incliner; (with lance) jouter; (naut) donner de la bande; **to tilt at** attaquer, critiquer; **to tilt back** se renverser en arrière

timber [ˈtɪmbər] s bois m de construction; (trees) bois m de haute futaie; (rafter) poutre f

tim′ber-land′ s bois m pour exploitation forestière

tim′ber line′ s limite f de la végétation forestière

timbre [ˈtɪmbər] s (phonet, phys) timbre m

time [taɪm] s temps m; heure f, e.g., **what time is it?** quelle heure est-il?; fois, e.g., **five times** cinq fois; e.g., **five times two is ten** cinq fois deux font dix; (period of payment) délai m; (phot) temps d'exposition; **at that time** à ce moment-là; à cette époque; **at the present time** à l'heure actuelle; **at the same time** en même temps; **at times** parfois; **behind the times** en retard sur son époque; **between times** entre-temps; **full time** plein temps; **in due time** en temps et lieu; **in no time** en moins de rien; **on time** à l'heure, à temps; **several times** à plusieurs reprises; **time and time again** maintes fois; **to beat time** (mus) battre la mesure; **to do time** (coll) faire son temps; **to have a good time** s'amuser bien, se divertir; **to lose time** (said o. timepiece) retarder; **to mark time** marquer le pas; **to play for time** (coll) chercher à gagner du temps ‖ tr mesurer la durée de; (sports) chronométrer

time′ bomb′ s bombe f à retardement

time′ card′ s registre m de présence

time′ clock′ s horloge f enregistreuse

time′ expo′sure s (phot) pose f

time′ fuse′ s fusée f fusante

time′-hon′ored adj consacré par l'usage

time′keep′er s pointeur m, chronométreur m; pendule f; montre f

timeless [ˈtaɪmlɪs] adj sans fin, éternel

time·ly [ˈtaɪmli] adj (comp -lier; super -liest) opportun, à propos

time′piece′ s pendule f; montre f

timer [ˈtaɪmər] s (person) chronométreur m; (of an electrical appliance) minuterie f

time′ sheet′ s feuille f de présence

time′ sig′nal s signal m horaire

time′ta′ble s horaire m; (rr) indicateur m

time′work′ s travail m à l'heure

time′worn′ adj usé par le temps; (venerable) séculaire

time′ zone′ s fuseau m horaire

timid ['tɪmɪd] adj timide

timing ['taɪmɪŋ] s chronométrage m; choix m du moment propice; (of an electrical appliance) minuterie f; (aut, mach) réglage m; (sports) chronométrage m; (theat) tempo m

tim′ing gears′ spl engrenage m de distribution

timorous ['tɪmərəs] adj timoré, peureux

tin [tɪn] s (element) étain m; (tin plate) fer-blanc m; (cup, box, etc.) boîte f || v (pret & pp tinned; ger tinning) tr étamer; (to can) (Brit) mettre en boîte

tin′ can′ s boîte f en fer-blanc, boîte de conserve

tincture ['tɪŋktʃər] s teinture f

tin′ cup′ s timbale f

tinder ['tɪndər] s amadou m

tin′der-box′ s briquet m à amadou; (fig) foyer m de l'effervescence

tin′ foil′ s feuille f d'étain, papier m d'argent

ting-a-ling ['tɪŋə,lɪŋ] s drelin m

tinge [tɪndʒ] s teinte f, nuance f || v (ger tingeing or tinging) tr teinter, nuancer

tingle ['tɪŋɡəl] s picotement m, fourmillement m || intr picoter, fourmiller; (e.g., with enthusiasm) tressaillir

tin′ hat′ s (coll) casque m en acier

tinker ['tɪŋkər] s chaudronnier m ambulant; (bungler) bousilleur m || tr bricoler; to tinker with tripatouiller

tinkle ['tɪŋkəl] s tintement m || tr faire tinter || intr tinter

tin′ plate′ s fer-blanc m

tin′-plate′ tr étamer

tin′ roof′ s toit m de fer-blanc

tinsel ['tɪnsəl] s clinquant m; (for a Christmas tree) paillettes fpl, guirlandes fpl clinquantes

tin′smith′ s ferblantier m

tin′ sol′dier s soldat m de plomb

tint [tɪnt] s teinte f || tr teinter

tin′type′ s ferrotypie f

tin′ware′ s ferblanterie f

ti-ny ['taɪnɪ] adj (comp -nier; super -niest) minuscule

tip [tɪp] s bout m, pointe f; (slant) inclinaison f; (fee to a waiter) pourboire m; (secret information) (slang) tuyau m || v (pret & pp tipped; ger tipping) tr incliner; (the scales) faire pencher; (a waiter) donner un pourboire à, donner la pièce à; to tip off (slang) tuyauter; to tip over renverser || intr se renverser; donner un pourboire

tip′cart′ s tombereau m

tip′-in′ s (bb) hors-texte m

tip′-off′ s (coll) tuyau m

tipped′-in′ adj (bb) hors texte

tipple ['tɪpəl] intr biberonner

tip′staff′ s verge f d'huissier; huissier m à verge

tip-sy ['tɪpsɪ] adj (comp -sier; super -siest) gris, grisé

tip′toe′ s pointe f des pieds || v (pret & pp -toed; ger -toeing) intr marcher sur la pointe des pieds

tirade ['taɪred] s diatribe f

tire [taɪr] s pneu m || tr fatiguer || intr se fatiguer

tire′ chain′ s chaîne f antidérapante

tired [taɪrd] adj fatigué, las

tire′ gauge′ s manomètre m

tire′ i′ron s démonte-pneu m

tireless ['taɪrlɪs] adj infatigable

tire′ pres′sure s pression f des pneus

tire′ pump′ s gonfleur m pour pneus

tiresome ['taɪrsəm] adj fatigant, ennuyeux

tissue ['tɪʃju] s tissu m; (thin paper) papier m de soie; (toilet tissue) papier hygiénique; (paper handkerchief) mouchoir m à jeter

tis′sue pa′per s papier m de soie

tit [tɪt] s téton m; (orn) mésange f; **tit for tat** à bon chat bon rat

titanium [taɪ′tenɪ·əm], [tɪ′tenɪ·əm] s titane m

tithe [taɪð] s dixième m; (rel) dîme f || tr soumettre à la dîme; payer la dîme sur

Titian ['tɪʃən] s le Titien m

Ti′tian red′ s blond m vénitien

title ['taɪtəl] s titre m || tr intituler

ti′tle deed′ s titre m de propriété

ti′tle-hold′er s tenant m du titre

ti′tle page′ s page f de titre

ti′tle role′ s rôle m principal

tit′mouse′ s (pl -mice) (orn) mésange f

titter ['tɪtər] s rire m étouffé || intr rire en catimini

titular ['tɪtʃələr] adj titulaire

to [tu], [tʊ], [tə] adv—**to and fro** de long en large || prep à; (towards) vers; (in order to) afin de, pour; envers, pour, e.g., **good to her** bon envers elle, bon pour elle; jusqu'à, e.g., **to this day** jusqu'à ce jour; e.g., **to count to a hundred** compter jusqu'à cent; moins, e.g., **a quarter to eight** huit heures moins le quart; contre, e.g., **seven to one** sept contre un; dans, e.g., **to a certain extent** dans une certaine mesure; en, e.g., **from door to door** de porte en porte; e.g., **I am going to France** je vais en France; de, e.g., **to try to** + inf essayer de + inf; **to him** lui §87

toad [tod] s crapaud m

toad′stool′ s agaric m; champignon m vénéneux

to-and-fro ['tu·ənd′fro] adj de va-et-vient

toast [tost] s pain m grillé; (with a drink) toast m || tr griller; porter un toast à, boire à la santé de

toaster ['tostər] s grille-pain m

toast′mas′ter s préposé m aux toasts

tobac-co [tə′bæko] s (pl -cos) tabac m

tobac′co pouch′ s blague f

toboggan [tə′bɑɡən] s toboggan m

tocsin ['taksɪn] s tocsin m; (bell) cloche f qui sonne le tocsin

today [tu'de] s & adv aujourd'hui m

toddle ['tadəl] s allure f chancelante || intr marcher à petits pas chancelants

toddler ['tadlər] s tout-petit m

tod·dy ['tadi] s (pl -dies) grog m

to-do [tə'du] s (pl -dos) embarras mpl, chichis mpl, façons fpl

toe [to] s doigt m du pied, orteil m; (of shoe, of stocking) bout m || v (pret & pp toed; ger toeing) tr—to toe the line or the mark s'aligner, se mettre au pas

toe'nail' s ongle m du pied

tog [tag] v (pret & pp togged; ger togging) tr—to tog out or up attifer, fringuer || togs spl fringues fpl

together [tu'geðər] adv ensemble; (at the same time) en même temps, à la fois

tog'gle switch' ['tagəl] s (elec) interrupteur m à culbuteur or à bascule

toil [tɔɪl] s travail m dur; toils filet m, piège m || intr travailler dur

toilet ['tɔɪlɪt] s toilette f; (rest room) cabinet m de toilette

toi'let ar'ticles spl objets mpl de toilette

toi'let bowl' s cuvette f

toi'let pa'per s papier m hygiénique

toi'let seat' s siège m des toilettes

toi'let set' s nécessaire m de toilette

toi'let soap' s savonnette f

toi'let wa'ter s eaux fpl de toilette

token ['tokən] adj symbolique || s signe m, marque f; (keepsake) souvenir m; (used as money) jeton m; by the same token de plus; in token of en témoignage de

tolerance ['talərəns] s tolérance f

tolerate ['talə,ret] tr tolérer

toll [tol] s (of bells) glas m; (payment) droit m de passage, péage m; (number of victims) mortalité f; (telp) tarif m || tr tinter; (to ring the knell for) sonner le glas de || intr sonner le glas

toll' bridge' s pont m à péage

toll' call' s appel m interurbain

toll'gate' s barrière f à péage

toll' road' s autoroute f à péage

toma·to [tə'meto], [tə'mato] s (pl -toes) tomate f

tomb [tum] s tombeau m

tomboy ['tam,bɔɪ] s garçon m manqué

tomb'stone' s pierre f tombale

tomcat ['tam,kæt] s matou m

tome [tom] s tome m

tomorrow [tu'maro], [tu'mɔro] adj, s, & adv demain m; tomorrow morning demain matin; until tomorrow à demain

tom-tom ['tam,tam] s tam-tam m

ton [tʌn] s tonne f

tone [ton] s ton m || tr accorder; to tone down atténuer; to tone up renforcer; (e.g., the muscles) tonifier || intr—to tone down se modérer

tone' po'em s poème m symphonique

tongs [tɑŋz], [tɔŋz] spl pincettes fpl; (e.g., for sugar) pince f; (of blacksmith) tenailles fpl

tongue [tʌŋ] s (language; part of body) langue f; (of wagon) timon m; (of buckle) ardillon m; (of shoe) languette f; to hold one's tongue se mordre la langue

tongue-tied ['tʌŋ,taɪd] adj bouche cousue

tongue' twist'er s phrase f à décrocher la mâchoire

tonic ['tanɪk] adj & s tonique m

tonight [tu'naɪt] adj & s ce soir

tonsil ['tansəl] s amygdale f

tonsillitis [,tansɪ'laɪtɪs] s amygdalite f

ton·y ['toni] adj (comp -ier; super -iest) (slang) élégant, chic

too [tu] adv (also) aussi; (more than enough) trop; (moreover) d'ailleurs; I did too! mais si!; too bad! c'est dommage!; too many, too much trop, trop de

tool [tul] s outil || tr (a piece of metal) usiner; (leather) repousser; (bb) dorer || intr—to tool along rouler; to tool up s'outiller

tool'box' s trousse f à outils

tool'mak'er s taillandier m

toot [tut] s son m du cor; (of auto) coup m de klaxon; (of locomotive) coup de sifflet || tr sonner || intr corner; (aut) klaxonner

tooth [tuθ] s (pl teeth [tiθ]) dent f; to grit, grind, or gnash the teeth grincer des dents, crisser des dents

tooth'ache' s mal m de dents

tooth'brush' s brosse f à dents

toothless ['tuθlɪs] adj édenté

tooth'paste' s pâte f dentifrice

tooth'pick' s cure-dent m

tooth' pow'der s poudre f dentifrice

top [tap] adj premier, de tête || s sommet m, cime f, faîte m; (of a barrel, table, etc.) dessus m; (of a page) haut m; (of a box) couvercle m; (of a carriage or auto) capote f; (toy) toupie f; (naut) hune f; at the top of en haut de; (e.g., one's class) à la tête de; at the top of one's voice à tue-tête; from top to bottom de haut en bas, de fond en comble; on top of sur; (in addition to) en plus de; tops (e.g., of carrots) fanes fpl; to sleep like a top dormir comme un sabot || v (pret & pp topped; ger topping) tr couronner, surmonter; (to surpass) dépasser; (a tree, plant, etc.) écimer

topaz ['topæz] s topaze f

top' bill'ing s tête f d'affiche

top'coat' s surtout m de demi-saison

toper ['topər] s soiffard m

top' hat' s haut-de-forme m

top'-heav'y adj trop lourd du haut

topic ['tapɪk] s sujet m

top'knot' s chignon m

top'mast' s mât m de hune

top'most' adj (le) plus haut

top'notch' adj (coll) d'élite

topogra·phy [tə'pagrafi] s (pl -phies) topographie f

topple ['tapəl] tr & intr culbuter

topsail ['tapsəl], ['tap,sel] s (naut) hunier m

top'soil' s couche f arable

topsy-turvy ['tɑpsɪ'tʌrvɪ] *adj* & *adv* sens dessus dessous

torch [tɔrtʃ] *s* torche *f*, flambeau *m*; (Brit) lampe *f* torche; **to carry the torch for** (slang) avoir un amour sans retour pour

torch/bear/er *s* porte-flambeau *m*; (fig) défenseur *m*

torch/light/ *s* lueur *f* des flambeaux

torch/light proces/sion *s* défilé *m* aux flambeaux

torch/ song/ *s* chanson *f* de l'amour non partagé

torment ['tɔrment] *s* tourment *m* || [tɔr'ment] *tr* tourmenter

torna-do [tɔr'nedo] *s* (*pl* -**does** or -**dos**) tornade *f*

torpe-do [tɔr'pido] *s* (*pl* -**does**) torpille *f* || *tr* torpiller

torpe/do-boat destroy/er *s* contre-torpilleur *m*

torpid ['tɔrpɪd] *adj* engourdi

torque [tɔrk] *s* effort *m* de torsion, couple *m* de torsion

torrent ['tarənt], ['tɔrənt] *s* torrent *m*

torrid ['tarɪd], ['tɔrɪd] *adj* torride

tor-so ['tɔrso] *s* (*pl* -**sos**) torse *m*

tort [tɔrt] *s* (law) acte *m* dommageable sauf rupture de contrat ou abus de confiance

tortoise ['tɔrtəs] *s* tortue *f*

tor/toise shell/ *s* écaille *f*

torture ['tɔrtʃər] *s* torture *f* || *tr* torturer

toss [tɔs], [tɑs] *s* lancement *m*; (*of the head*) mouvement *m* dédaigneux || *tr* lancer; (*one's head*) relever dédaigneusement; (*a rider*) démonter; (*a coin*) jouer à pile et face avec; **to toss about** agiter, ballotter; **to toss off** (*e.g., work*) expédier; (*in one gulp*) lamper; **to toss up** jeter en l'air || *intr* s'agiter; **to toss and turn** se tourner et retourner

toss/up/ *s* (coll) coup *m* de pile ou face; chances *fpl* égales

tot [tat] *s* bambin *m*, tout petit *m* || *v* (*pret* & *pp* **totted**; *ger* **totting**) *tr*—**to tot up** additionner

to-tal ['totəl] *adj* & *s* total *m*; **as a total** au total || *v* (*pret* & *pp* -**taled** or -**talled**; *ger* -**taling** or -**talling**) *tr* additionner, totaliser; (*to amount to*) s'élever à

totalitarian [to,tælɪ'terɪ-ən] *adj* & *mf* totalitaire

totem ['totem] *s* totem *m*

totter ['tatər] *intr* chanceler

touch [tʌtʃ] *s* (*act*) attouchement *m*; (*e.g., of color; with a brush*) touche *f*; (*sense; of pianist*) toucher *m*; (*of typist*) frappe *f*; (*little bit*) pointe *f*, brin *m*; **in touch** en communication; **to get in touch with** prendre contact avec || *tr* toucher; (*for a loan*) (slang) taper; **to touch off** déclencher; **to touch up** retoucher || *intr* se toucher; **to touch on** toucher à

touched *adj* touché; (*crazy*) timbré

touching ['tʌtʃɪŋ] *adj* touchant, émouvant || *prep* touchant, concernant

touch-y ['tʌtʃi] *adj* (*comp* -**ier**; *super* -**iest**) susceptible, irritable

tough [tʌf] *adj* dur, coriace; (*tenacious*) résistant; (*task*) difficile || *s* voyou *m*

toughen ['tʌfən] *tr* endurcir || *intr* s'endurcir

tough/ luck/ *s* déveine *f*

tour [tur] *s* tour *m*; (*e.g., of inspection*) tournée *f*; **on tour** en tournée || *tr* faire le tour de; (*e.g., a country*) voyager en; (theat) faire une tournée de, en, or dans || *intr* voyager

tour/ing car/ *s* voiture *f* de tourisme

tourist ['turɪst] *adj* & *s* touriste *mf*

tournament ['turnəmənt], ['tʌrnəmənt] *s* tournoi *m*

tourney ['turnɪ], ['tʌrnɪ] *s* tournoi *m* || *intr* tournoyer

tourniquet ['turnɪ,ket], ['tʌrnɪ,ke] *s* (surg) garrot *m*, tourniquet *m*

tousle ['tauzəl] *tr* ébouriffer; tirailler, maltraiter

tow [to] *s* remorque *f*; (*e.g., of hemp*) filasse *f*; **to take in tow** prendre en remorque; (fig) se charger de || *tr* remorquer

towage ['to-ɪdʒ] *s* remorquage *m*; droits *mpl* de remorquage

toward(s) [tord(z)], [tə'word(z)] *prep* vers; (*in regard to*) envers

tow/boat/ *s* remorqueur *m*

tow-el ['tau-əl] *s* serviette *f*, essuie-main *m* || *v* (*pret* & *pp* -**eled** or -**elled**; *ger* -**eling** or -**elling**) *tr* essuyer avec une serviette

tow/el rack/ *s* porte-serviettes *m*

tower ['tau-ər] *s* tour *f* || *intr* s'élever

towering ['tau-ərɪŋ] *adj* élevé, géant; (*e.g., ambition*) sans bornes

tow/er-man *s* (*pl* -**men**) (aer, rr) aiguilleur *m*

tow/ing serv/ice ['to-ɪŋ] *s* service *m* de dépannage

tow/line/ *s* câble *m* de remorque

town [taun] *s* ville *f*; **in town** en ville

town/ clerk/ *s* secrétaire *m* de mairie

town/ coun/cil *s* conseil *m* municipal

town/ cri/er *s* crieur *m* public

town/ hall/ *s* hôtel *m* de ville

town/ plan/ning *s* urbanisme *m*

towns/folk/ *spl* citadins *mpl*

town/ship *s* commune *f*; (U.S.A.) circonscription *f* administrative de six milles carrés

towns/man ['taunzmən] *s* (*pl* -**men**) citadin *m*

towns/peo/ple *spl* citadins *mpl*

town/ talk/ *s* sujet *m* du jour

tow/path/ *s* chemin *m* de halage

tow/rope/ *s* corde *f* de remorque

tow/ truck/ *s* dépanneuse *f*, voiture *f* de dépannage

toxic ['taksɪk] *adj* & *s* toxique *m*

toy [tɔɪ] *adj* petit; d'enfant || *s* jouet *m*, joujou *m*; (*trifle*) bagatelle *f* || *intr* jouer, s'amuser; **to toy with** (*a person*) badiner avec; (*an idea*) caresser

toy/ dog/ *s* chien *m* de manchon

toy/ sol/dier *s* soldat *m* de plomb

trace [tres] *s* trace *f*; (*of harness*) trait *m* || *tr* tracer; (*the whereabouts of* s.o. or s.th.) pister; (e.g., an influence) retrouver les traces de; (a design seen through thin paper) calquer; **to trace back** remonter jusqu'à l'origine de

tracer ['tresər] s traceur m

trac'er bul'let s balle f traçante

trache•a ['trekɪ-ə] s (pl -ae [,i]) trachée f

tracing ['tresɪŋ] s tracé m

trac'ing tape' s cordeau m

track [træk] s (of foot or vehicle) trace f; (of an animal; in a stadium) piste f; (of a boat) sillage m; (of a railroad) voie f; (of an airplane, of a hurricane) trajet m; (of a tractor) chenille f; (course followed) chemin m tracé; (sports) la course et le saut de barrières; (sports) athlétisme m; **off the beaten track** hors des sentiers battus; **on the right track** sur la bonne voie; **to be on the wrong track** faire fausse route; **to have an inside track** tenir la corde; **to keep track of** ne pas perdre de vue; **to make tracks** (coll) filer || tr traquer; laisser des traces de pas dans; **to track down** dépister

tracking ['trækɪŋ] s (of spaceship) repérage m

track'ing sta'tion s poste m de repérage

track'less trol'ley s trolleybus m

track' meet' s concours m de courses et de sauts, épreuve f d'athlétisme

track'walk'er s garde-voie m

tract [trækt] s (of land) étendue f; (leaflet) tract m; (anat) voie f

traction ['trækʃən] s traction f

trac'tion com'pany s entreprise f de transports urbains

tractor ['træktər] s tracteur m

trade [tred] s commerce m, négoce m; clientèle f; (calling, job) métier m; (exchange) échange m; (in slaves) traite f; **to take in trade** reprendre en compte || tr échanger; **to trade in** (e.g., a used car) donner en reprise || intr commercer; **to trade in** faire le commerce de; **to trade on** exploiter

trade'-in' s reprise f

trade'mark' s marque f déposée

trade' name' s raison f sociale

trader ['tredər] s commerçant m

trade' school' s école f des arts et métiers

trades'man s (pl -men) commerçant m; (shopkeeper) boutiquier m; (Brit) artisan m

trades' un'ion or **trade' un'ion** s syndicat m ouvrier

trade' winds' spl vents mpl alizés

trad'ing post' ['tredɪŋ] s factorerie f

trad'ing stamp' s timbre-prime m

tradition [trə'dɪʃən] s tradition f

traditional [trə'dɪʃənəl] adj traditionnel

traf•fic ['træfɪk] s (commerce) négoce m; (in the street) circulation f; (illegal) trafic m; (in, e.g., slaves) traite f; (naut, rr) trafic || v (pret & pp -ficked; ger -ficking) intr trafiquer

traf'fic cir'cle s rond-point m

traf'fic cop' s agent m de la circulation

traf'fic court' s tribunal m de simple police (pour les contraventions au code de la route)

traf'fic jam' s embouteillage m

traf'fic light' s feu m de circulation

traf'fic sign' s panneau m de signalisation, poteau m indicateur

traf'fic sig'nal s signal m routier

traf'fic tick'et s contravention f

traf'fic vi'olator s contrevenant m

tragedian [trə'dʒidɪ-ən] s tragédien m

trage•dy ['trædʒɪdi] s (pl -dies) tragédie f

tragic ['trædʒɪk] adj tragique

trail [trel] s trace f, piste f; (e.g., of smoke) traînée f || tr traîner; (to look for) pister || intr traîner; (said of a plant) grimper; **to trail off** se perdre

trailer ['trelər] s remorque f; (for vacationing) remorque de plaisance, caravane f; (mov) film-annonce m

trail'er court' s camp m pour caravanes

trail'er home' s caravane f

train [tren] s (of railway cars) train m; (of dress) traîne f; (of thought) enchaînement m; (streak) traînée f || tr entraîner, former; (plants) palisser; (a gun; a telescope) pointer || intr s'entraîner

trained' an'imals spl animaux mpl savants

trained' nurse' s infirmière f diplômée

trainer ['trenər] s (of animals) dresseur m; (sports) entraîneur m

training ['trenɪŋ] s entraînement m; instruction f; (of animals) dressage m

train'ing school' s école f technique; (reformatory) maison f de correction

train'ing ship' s navire-école m

trait [tret] s trait m

traitor ['tretər] s traître m

traitress ['tretrɪs] s traîtresse f

trajecto•ry [trə'dʒɛktəri] s (pl -ries) trajectoire f

tramp [træmp] s vagabond m; bruit m de pas lourds || tr parcourir à pied; (the street) battre || intr vagabonder; marcher lourdement; **to tramp on** marcher sur

trample ['træmpəl] tr fouler, piétiner || intr—**to trample on** or **upon** fouler, piétiner

trampoline ['træmpə,lin] s tremplin m de gymnase

tramp' steam'er s tramp m

trance [træns], [trɑns] s transe f; **in a trance** en transe

tranquil ['træŋkwɪl] adj tranquille

tranquilize ['træŋkwɪ,laɪz] tr tranquilliser

tranquilizer ['træŋkwɪ,laɪzər] s tranquillisant m

tranquillity [træn'kwɪlɪti] s tranquillité f

transact [træn'zækt], [træns'ækt] tr traiter, négocier || intr faire des affaires

transaction [træn'zækʃən], [træns'ækʃən] s transaction f; (of business) conduite *f*; **transactions** (*of a society*) actes *mpl*

transatlantic [ˌtrænsət'læntɪk] *adj & s* transatlantique *m*

transcend [træn'send] *tr* transcender ‖ *intr* se transcender

transcribe [træn'skraɪb] *tr* transcrire

transcript ['trænskrɪpt] *s* copie *f*; (*of a meeting*) procès-verbal *m*; (*educ*) livret *m* scolaire

transcription [træn'skrɪpʃən] *s* transcription *f*

transept ['trænsept] *s* transept *m*

trans·fer ['trænsfər] *s* (*e.g., of stock, property, etc.*) transfert *m*; (*from one place to the other*) translation *f*; (*from one job to the other*) mutation *f*; (*of a design*) décalque *m*; (*for bus or subway*) billet *m* de correspondance; (*public sign*) correspondance ‖ [træns'fʌr], ['trænsfər] *v* (*pret & pp* -ferred; *ger* -ferring) *tr* transférer; transporter; (*e.g., a civil servant*) déplacer; (*a design*) décalquer ‖ *intr* se déplacer; changer de train (de l'autobus, etc.)

transfix [træns'fɪks] *tr* transpercer

transform [træns'fɔrm] *tr* transformer ‖ *intr* se transformer

transformer [træns'fɔrmər] *s* transformateur *m*

transfusion [træns'fjuʒən] *s* transfusion *f*

transgress [træns'gres] *tr & intr* transgresser

transgression [træns'greʃən] *s* transgression *f*

transient ['trænʃənt] *adj* transitoire, passager; (*e.g., guest*) de passage ‖ *s* hôte *mf* de passage

transistor [træn'sɪstər] *s* transistor *m*

transit ['trænsɪt], ['trænzɪt] *s* transit *m*

transition [træn'zɪʃən] *s* transition *f*

transitional [træn'zɪʃənəl] *adj* transitoire, de transition

transitive ['trænsɪtɪv] *adj* transitif ‖ *s* verbe *m* transitif

transitory ['trænsɪˌtori] *adj* transitoire

translate [træns'let], ['trænslet] *tr* traduire

translation [træns'leʃən] *s* traduction *f*; (*transfer*) translation *f*

translator [træns'letər] *s* traducteur *m*

transliterate [træns'lɪtəˌret] *tr* translitérer

translucent [træns'lusənt] *adj* translucide, diaphane

transmission [træns'mɪʃən] *s* transmission *f*; (*gear change*) changement *m* de vitesse; (*housing for gears*) boîte *f* de vitesses

transmis'sion-gear' box' *s* boîte *f* de vitesses

trans·mit [træns'mɪt] *v* (*pret & pp* -mitted; *ger* -mitting) *tr & intr* transmettre; (*rad*) émettre

transmitter [træns'mɪtər] *s* (telg, telp) transmetteur *m*; (rad) émetteur *m*

transmit'ting sta'tion *s* poste *m* émetteur

transmute [træns'mjut] *tr* transmuer

transom ['trænsəm] *s* (*crosspiece*) lin-teau *m*; (*window over door*) imposte *f*, vasistas *m*; (*of ship*) barre *f* d'arcasse

transparen·cy [træns'perənsi] *s* (*pl* -cies) transparence *f*; (phot) diapositive *f*

transparent [træns'perənt] *adj* transparent

transpire [træns'paɪr] *intr* se passer; (*to leak out*) transpirer

transplant ['træns.plænt], ['træns-ˌplænt] *s* (*organ or tissue*) greffon *m*; (*operation*) greffe *f* ‖ [træns-'plænt], [træns'plænt] *tr* transplanter; (*e.g., a heart*) greffer

transport ['trænsport] *s* transport *m* ‖ [træns'port] *tr* transporter

transportation [ˌtrænspor'teʃən] *s* transport *m*; billet *m* de train, de bateau, or d'avion; (*deportation*) transportation *f*

transport'er bridge' [træns'portər] *s* transbordeur *m*

trans'port work'er *s* employé *m* des entreprises de transport

transpose [træns'poz] *tr* transposer

trans·ship [træns'ʃɪp] *v* (*pret & pp* -shipped; *ger* -shipping) *tr* transborder

transshipment [træns'ʃɪpmənt] *s* transbordement *m*

trap [træp] *s* piège *m*; (*pitfall*) trappe *f*; (*double-curved pipe*) siphon *m*; **traps** (mus) batterie *f* de jazz ‖ *v* (*pret & pp* trapped; *ger* trapping) *tr* prendre au piège, attraper

trap' door' *s* trappe *f*

trapeze [træ'piz] *s* trapèze *m*

trapezoid ['træpɪˌzɔɪd] *s* trapèze *m*

trapper ['træpər] *s* trappeur *m*

trappings ['træpɪŋz] *spl* (*adornments*) atours *mpl*; (*of horse's harness*) harmachement *m*

trap'shoot'ing *s* tir *m* au pigeon

trash [træ] *s* déchets *mpl*, rebuts *mpl*; (*junk*) camelote *f*; (*nonsense*) ineptie *f*; (*worthless people*) racaille *f*

trash' can' *s* poubelle *f*

travail [trə'vel] *s* labeur *m*; douleur *f* de l'enfantement

trav·el ['trævəl] *s* voyages *mpl*; (mach) course *f* ‖ *v* (*pret & pp* -eled or -elled; *ger* -eling or -elling) *tr* parcourir ‖ *intr* voyager; (mach) se déplacer

trav'el bu'reau *s* agence *f* de voyages

traveler ['trævələr] *s* voyageur *m*

trav'eler's check' *s* chèque *m* de voyage

trav'eling expen'ses *spl* frais *mpl* de voyage

trav'eling sales'man *s* (*pl* -men) commis *m* voyageur

traverse [trə'vʌrs] *tr* parcourir, traverser

traves·ty ['trævɪsti] *s* (*pl* -ties) *s* travestissement *m* ‖ *v* (*pret & pp* -tied) *tr* travestir

trawl [trɔl] *s* chalut *m* ‖ *tr* traîner ‖ *intr* pêcher au chalut

trawler ['trɔlər] *s* chalutier *m*

tray [tre] *s* plateau *m*; (*of refrigerator*) bac *f*; (chem, phot) cuvette *f*

treacherous ['tretʃərəs] *adj* traître

treacher·y ['tretʃəri] *s* (*pl* -ies) trahison *f*

tread [tred] *s* (*step; sound of steps*) pas *m*; (*gait*) allure *f*; (*of stairs*) giron *m*; (*of tire*) chape *f*; (*of shoe*) semelle *f*; (*of egg*) cicatricule *f* || *v* (*pret* **trod** [trɑd]; *pp* **trodden** ['trɑdən] *or* **trod**) *tr* marcher sur, piétiner || *intr* marcher

treadle ['tredəl] *s* pédale *f*

tread/mill/ *s* trépigneuse *f*; (*futile drudgery*) besogne *f* ingrate

treason ['trizən] *s* trahison *f*

treasonable ['trizənəbəl] *adj* traître

treasure ['treʒər] *s* trésor *m* || *tr* garder soigneusement; (*to prize*) tenir beaucoup à

treasurer ['treʒərər] *s* trésorier *m*

treasur·y ['treʒəri] *s* (*pl* -ies) trésorerie *f*; trésor *m*

treat [trit] *s* régal *m*, plaisir *m* || *tr* traiter; régaler; (*to a drink*) payer à boire à || *intr* traiter

treatise ['tritɪs] *s* traité *m*

treatment ['tritmənt] *s* traitement *m*

trea·ty ['triti] *s* (*pl* -ties) traité *m*

treble ['trebəl] *adj* (*threefold*) triple; (*mus*) de soprano *f* soprano *m*; (*voice*) soprano *m* || *tr & intr* tripler

tre/ble clef/ [klef] *s* clef *f* de sol

tree [tri] *s* arbre *m*

tree/ farm/ *s* taillis *m*

treeless ['trilɪs] *adj* sans arbres

tree/top/ *s* cime *f* d'un arbre

trellis ['trelɪs] *s* treillis *m*, treillage *m*; (*summerhouse*) tonnelle *f* || *tr* treillager

tremble ['trembəl] *s* tremblement *m* || *intr* trembler

tremendous [trɪ'mendəs] *adj* terrible; (*coll*) formidable

tremor ['tremər], ['trimər] *s* tremblement *m*

trench [trentʃ] *s* tranchée *f*

trenchant ['trentʃənt] *adj* tranchant

trench/ mor/tar *s* lance-bombes *m*

trend [trend] *s* tendance *f*, cours *m*

trespass ['trespəs] *s* entrée *f* sans permission; délit *m*, offense *f* || *tr* entrer sans permission; **no trespassing** (public sign) défense d'entrer; **to trespass against** offenser; **to trespass on** empiéter sur; (*s.o.'s patience*) abuser de

trespasser ['trespəsər] *s* intrus *m*

tress [tres] *s* tresse *f*; **tresses** chevelure *f*

trestle ['tresəl] *s* tréteau *m*; (*bridge*) pont *m* en treillis

trial ['traɪ·əl] *s* essai *m*; (*difficulty*) épreuve *f*; (*law*) procès *m*; **on trial** à titre d'essai; (*law*) en jugement; **to bring to trial** faire passer en jugement

tri/al and er/ror *s*—**by trial and error** par tâtonnements

tri/al balloon/ *s* ballon *m* d'essai

tri/al by ju/ry *s* jugement *m* par jury

tri/al ju/ry *s* jury *m* de jugement

tri/al or/der *s* commande *f* d'essai

tri/al run/ *s* course *f* d'essai

triangle ['traɪˌæŋgəl] *s* triangle *m*

tribe [traɪb] *s* tribu *f*

tribunal [trɪ'bjunəl], [traɪ'bjunəl] *s* tribunal *m*

tribune ['trɪbjun] *s* tribune *f*

tributar·y ['trɪbjəˌteri] *adj* tributaire || *s* (*pl* -ies) tributaire *m*

tribute ['trɪbjut] *s* tribut *m*; éloge *m*, compliment *m*; **to pay tribute to** (*e.g., merit*) rendre hommage à

trice [traɪs] *s*—**in a trice** en un clin d'œil

trick [trɪk] *s* tour *m*; (*prank*) farce *f*; (*artifice*) ruse *f*; (*cards in one round*) levée *f*; (*habit*) manie *f*; (*girl*) (coll) belle *f*; **to be up to one's old tricks again** faire encore des siennes; **to play a dirty trick on** faire un vilain tour à; **tricks of the trade** trucs *mpl* du métier || *tr* duper

tricker·y ['trɪkəri] *s* (*pl* -ies) tromperie *f*

trickle ['trɪkəl] *s* filet *m* || *intr* dégoutter

trickster ['trɪkstər] *s* fourbe *mf*

trick·y ['trɪki] *adj* (*comp* -ier; *super* -iest) rusé; (*difficult*) compliqué, délicat

tricolor ['traɪˌkʌlər] *adj & s* tricolore *m*

tried [traɪd] *adj* loyal, éprouvé

trifle ['traɪfəl] *s* bagatelle *f* || *tr*—**to trifle away** gaspiller || *intr* badiner

trifling ['traɪflɪŋ] *adj* frivole; insignifiant

trifocals [traɪ'fokəlz] *spl* lunettes *fpl* à trois foyers

trigger ['trɪgər] *s* (*of gun*) détente *f*; (*of any device*) déclencheur *m*; **to pull the trigger** appuyer sur la détente || *tr* déclencher

trig/ger-hap/py *adj*—**to be trigger-happy** (coll) avoir la gâchette facile

trigonometry [ˌtrɪgə'nɑmɪtri] *s* trigonométrie *f*

trill [trɪl] *s* trille *m* || *tr & intr* triller

trillion ['trɪljən] *s* (U.S.A.) billion *m*; (Brit) trillion *m*

trilo·gy ['trɪlədʒi] *s* (*pl* -gies) trilogie *f*

trim [trɪm] *adj* (*comp* **trimmer**; *super* **trimmest**) ordonné, coquet || *s* état *m*; ornement *m*; (*of sails*) orientation *f* || *v* (*pret & pp* **trimmed**; *ger* **trimming**) *tr* enguirlander; (*a Christmas tree*) orner; (*hat, dress, etc.*) garnir; (*the hair*) rafraîchir; (*a candle or lamp*) moucher; (*trees, plants*) tailler; (*the edges of a book*) rogner; (*the sails*) orienter; (coll) battre

trimming ['trɪmɪŋ] *s* (*of clothes, hat, etc.*) garniture *f*; (*of hedges*) taille *f*; (*of sails*) orientation *f*; **to get a trimming** (coll) essuyer une défaite

trini·ty ['trɪnɪti] *s* (*pl* -ties) trinité *f*; **Trinity** Trinité

trinket ['trɪŋkɪt] *s* colifichet *m*; (*trifle*) babiole *f*

tri·o ['tri·o] *s* (*pl* -os) trio *m*

trip [trɪp] *s* voyage *m*, trajet *m*, parcours *m*; (*stumble; blunder*) faux pas *m*; (*act of causing a person to stumble*) croc-en-jambe *m* || *v* (*pret & pp* **tripped**; *ger* **tripping**) *tr* faire trébucher; **to trip up** donner un croc-en-jambe à; prendre en défaut || *intr* trébucher

tripartite [traɪˈpɑrtaɪt] *adj* tripartite

tripe [traɪp] *s* tripe *f*; (*slang*) fatras *m*

trip/ham/mer *s* marteau *m* à bascule

triple [ˈtrɪpəl] *adj & s* triple *m* || *tr & intr* tripler

triplet [ˈtrɪplɪt] *s* (*offspring*) triplet *m*; (*stanza*) tercet *m*; (*mus*) triolet *m*; **triplets** (*offspring*) triplés *mpl*

triplicate [ˈtrɪplɪkɪt] *adj* triple || **tri-plicata** *m*; **in triplicate** en trois exemplaires

tripod [ˈtraɪpɒd] *s* trépied *m*

triptych [ˈtrɪptɪk] *s* triptyque *m*

trite [traɪt] *adj* banal, rebattu

triumph [ˈtraɪ-əmf] *s* triomphe *m* || *intr* triompher; **to triumph over** triompher de

trium/phal arch/ [traɪˈʌmfəl] *s* arc *m* de triomphe

triumphant [traɪˈʌmfənt] *adj* triomphant

trivia [ˈtrɪvɪ-ə] *spl* vétilles *fpl*

trivial [ˈtrɪvɪ-əl] *adj* trivial, insignifiant

triviali•ty [ˌtrɪvɪˈælɪti] *s* (*pl* -ties) trivialité *f*, insignifiance *f*

Trojan [ˈtrodʒən] *adj* troyen || *s* Troyen *m*

Tro/jan Horse/ *s* cheval *m* de Troie

Tro/jan war/ *s* guerre *f* de Troie

troll [trol] *tr & intr* pêcher à la cuiller

trolley [ˈtrɑli] *s* trolley *m*; (*streetcar*) tramway *m*

trol/ley car/ *s* tramway *m*

trol/ley pole/ *s* perche *f*

trolling [ˈtrolɪŋ] *s* pêche *f* à la cuiller

trollop [ˈtrɑləp] *s* souillon *f*; (*prostitute*) traînée *f*

trombone [ˈtrɑmbon] *s* trombone *m*

troop [trup] *s* troupe *f*; **troops** (mil) troupes *fpl* || *tr* (*the colors*) présenter || *intr* s'attrouper

trooper [ˈtrupər] *s* cavalier *m*; membre *m* de la police montée; **to swear like a trooper** jurer comme un charretier

tro•phy [ˈtrofi] *s* (*pl* -phies) trophée *m*; (sports) coupe *f*

tropic [ˈtrɑpɪk] *adj & s* tropique *m*; **tropics** tropiques, zone *f* tropicale

tropical [ˈtrɑpɪkəl] *adj* tropical

trot [trɑt] *s* trot *m* || *v* (*pret & pp* trotted; *ger* trotting) *tr* faire trotter; **to trot out** (slang) exhiber || *intr* trotter

troth [troθ], [troθ] *s* foi *f*; **in troth** en vérité; **to plight one's troth** promettre fidélité; donner sa promesse de mariage

trouble [ˈtrʌbəl] *s* dérangement *m*; (*illness*) trouble *m*; **that's not worth the trouble** cela ne vaut pas la peine; **that's the trouble** voilà le hic; **the trouble is that . . .** la difficulté c'est que . . . ; **to be in trouble** avoir des ennuis; (*said of a woman*) (coll) faire Pâques avant les Rameaux; **to be looking for trouble** chercher querelle; **to get into trouble** se créer des ennuis, s'attirer une mauvaise affaire;

to take the trouble to se donner la peine de; **with very little trouble** à peu de frais || *tr* déranger; affliger; **to be troubled about** se tourmenter au sujet de; **to trouble oneself** s'inquiéter || *intr* se déranger; **to trouble** to se donner la peine de

trou/ble light/ *s* lampe *f* de secours

trou/ble-mak/er *s* fomentateur *m*, perturbateur *m*

troubleshooter [ˈtrʌbəlˌʃutər] *s* dépanneur *m*; (*in disputes*) arbitre *m*

trou/ble-shoot/ing *s* dépannage *m*; (*of disputes*) composition *f*, arbitrage *m*

troublesome [ˈtrʌbəlsəm] *adj* ennuyeux

trou/ble spot/ *s* foyer *m* de conflit

trough [trɔf], [trɑf] *s* (*e.g., to knead bread*) pétrin *m*; (*for water for animals*) abreuvoir *m*; (*for feeding animals*) auge *f*; (*under the eaves*) chéneau *m*; (*between two waves*) creux *m*

troupe [trup] *s* troupe *f*

trouper [ˈtrupər] *s* membre *m* de la troupe; vieil acteur *m*; vieux routier *m*

trousers [ˈtraʊzərz] *spl* pantalon *m*

trous•seau [truˈso], [ˈtruso] *s* (*pl* -seaux *or* -seaus) trousseau *m*

trout [traʊt] *s* truite *f*

trowel [ˈtraʊ-əl] *s* truelle *f*; (*for gardening*) déplantoir *m*

Troy [trɔɪ] *s* Troie *f*

truant [ˈtru-ənt] *s*—**to play truant** faire l'école buissonnière

truce [trus] *s* trêve *f*

truck [trʌk] *s* camion *m*, poids *m* lourd; (*for baggage*) diable *m*; légumes *mpl*; (coll) rapports *mpl* || *tr* camionner

truck/driv/er *s* camionneur *m*

truck/ farm/ing *s* culture *f* maraîchère

truck/ gar/den *s* jardin *m* maraîcher

trucking [ˈtrʌkɪŋ] *s* camionnage *m*

truculent [ˈtrʌkjələnt], [ˈtrukjələnt] *adj* truculent

trudge [trʌdʒ] *intr* cheminer

true [tru] *adj* vrai; loyal; (*exact*) juste; (*copy*) conforme; **to come true** se réaliser || *tr* rectifier, dégauchir

true/ cop/y *s* (*pl* -ies) copie *f* conforme

true/-heart/ed *adj* au cœur sincère

true/love/ *s* bien-aimé *m*

truffle [ˈtrʌfəl], [ˈtrufəl] *s* truffe *f*

truism [ˈtru-ɪzm] *s* truisme *m*

truly [ˈtruli] *adv* vraiment; sincèrement; **yours truly** (*complimentary close*) veuillez agréer, Monsieur (Madame, etc.), l'assurance de mes sentiments distingués

trump [trʌmp] *s* atout *m*; brave garçon *m*, brave fille *f*; **no trump** sans atout || *tr* couper; **to trump up** inventer || *intr* couper

trumpet [ˈtrʌmpɪt] *s* trompette *f* || *tr & intr* trompeter

trumpeter [ˈtrʌmpətər] *s* trompette *m*

truncheon [ˈtrʌntʃən] *s* matraque *f*; (*of policeman*) bâton *m*

trunk [trʌŋk] *s* tronc *m*; (*chest for clothes*) malle *f*; (*of elephant*) trompe *f*; (aut) coffre *m*; trunks slip *m*

truss [trʌs] *s* (*framework*) armature *f*; (med) bandage *m* herniaire || *tr* armer; (culin) trousser

trust [trʌst] *s* confiance *f*; *(hope)* espoir *m*; *(duty)* charge *f*; *(safekeeping)* dépôt *m*; *(com)* trust *m*, cartel *m* || *tr* se fier à; *(to entrust)* confier; *(com)* faire crédit à || *intr* espérer; **to trust in** avoir confiance en

trust′ com′pany *s* crédit *m*, société *f* de banque

trustee [trʌs′ti] *s* administrateur *m*; *(of a university)* régent *m*; *(of an estate)* fidéicommissaire *mf*

trusteeship [trʌs′ti/ɪp] *s* tutelle *f*

trustful [′trʌstfəl] *adj* confiant

trust′wor′thy *adj* digne de confiance

trust·y [′trʌsti] *adj* *(comp* -ier; *super* -lest)* sûr, loyal || *s* *(pl* -les) forçat *m* bien noté

truth [truθ] *s* vérité *f*; **in truth** en vérité

truthful [′truθfəl] *adj* véridique

try [trɑɪ] *s* *(pl* tries) essai *m* || *v* *(pret & pp* tried) *tr* mettre à l'épreuve; *(law)* juger; **to try on or out** essayer || *intr* essayer; **to try to** essayer de

trying [′trɑɪ·ɪŋ] *adj* pénible

tryst [trɪst], [trɑɪst] *s* rendez-vous *m*

T′-shirt′ *s* gilet *m* de peau avec manches

tub [tʌb] *s* cuvier *m*, baquet *m*; *(clumsy boat)* *(coll)* rafiot *m*

tube [t(j)ub] *s* tube *m*; tunnel *m*; *(aut)* chambre *f* à air; *(subway)* *(Brit)* métro *m*

tuber [′t(j)ubər] *s* tubercule *m*

tubercle [′t(j)ubərkəl] *s* tubercule *m*

tuberculosis [t(j)u,bɑrkjə′losɪs] *s* tuberculose *f*

tuck [tʌk] *s* pli *m*, rempli *m* || *tr* plisser, remplier; **to tuck away** reléguer; **to tuck in** rentrer; **to tuck in bed** border; **to tuck up** retrousser

tucker [′tʌkər] *tr*—**to tucker out** *(coll)* fatiguer

Tuesday [′t(j)uzdi] *s* mardi *m*

tuft [tʌft] *s* touffe *f* || *tr* garnir de touffes || *intr* former une touffe

tug [tʌg] *s* tiraillement *m*, effort *m*; *(boat)* remorqueur *m* || *v* *(pret & pp* tugged; *ger* tugging) *tr* tirer fort; *(a boat)* remorquer || *intr* tirer fort

tug′boat′ *s* remorqueur *m*

tug′ of war′ *s* lutte *f* à la corde (de traction)

tuition [t(j)u′ɪʃən] *s* enseignement *m*; *(fees)* frais *mpl* de scolarité

tulip [′t(j)ulɪp] *s* tulipe *f*

tumble [′tʌmbəl] *s* chute *f*; *(sports)* culbute *f* || *tr* culbuter || *intr* tomber, culbuter; *(sports)* faire des culbutes; *(to catch on)* *(slang)* comprendre; **to tumble down** dégringoler

tum′ble·down′ *adj* croulant, délabré

tumbler [′tʌmblər] *s* gobelet *m*, verre *m*; acrobate *m*; *(self-righting toy)* poussah *m*, ramponneau *m*

tumor [′t(j)umər] *s* tumeur *f*

tumult [′t(j)umʌlt] *s* tumulte *m*

tun [tʌn] *s* tonne *f*

tuna [′tunə] *s* thon *m*

tune [t(j)un] *s* air *m*; *(manner of acting or speaking)* ton *m*; **in tune** *(mus)* accordé; *(rad)* en syntonie; **out of tune** *(mus)* désaccordé; **to change**

one's tune *(coll)* changer de disque || *tr* accorder; *(a radio or television set)* régler; **to tune in** *(rad)* syntoniser; **to tune up** régler

tungsten [′tʌŋstən] *s* tungstène *m*

tunic [′t(j)unɪk] *s* tunique *f*

tuning [′t(j)unɪŋ] *s* réglage *m*; *(rad)* syntonisation *f*

tun′ing coil′ *s* bobine *f* de syntonisation

tun′ing fork′ *s* diapason *m*

tun·nel [′tʌnəl] *s* tunnel *m*; *(min)* galerie *f* || *v* *(pret & pp* -neled or -nelled; *ger* -neling or -nelling) *tr* percer un tunnel dans or sous

turban [′tʌrbən] *s* turban *m*

turbid [′tʌrbɪd] *adj* trouble

turbine [′tʌrbɪn], [′tʌrbaɪn] *s* turbine *f*

turbojet [′tʌrbo,dʒɛt] *s* turboréacteur *m*; avion *m* à turboréacteur

turboprop [′tʌrbo,prɑp] *s* turbopropulseur *m*; avion *m* à turbopropulseur

turbulent [′tʌrbjələnt] *adj* turbulent

tureen [t(j)u′rin] *s* soupière *f*

turf [tʌrf] *s* gazon *m*; *(sod)* motte *f* de gazon; *(peat)* tourbe *f*; **the turf** le turf

turf′man *s* *(pl* -men) turfiste *mf*

Turk [tʌrk] *s* Turc *m*

turkey [′tʌrki] *s* dindon *m*; *(culin)* dinde *f*; *(flop)* *(slang)* four *m*; **Turkey** Turquie *f*; **la Turquie**

tur′key vul′ture *s* urubu *m*

Turkish [′tʌrkɪʃ] *adj & s* turc *m*

Turk′ish delight′ *s* loukoum *m*

Turk′ish tow′el *s* serviette *f* éponge

turmoil [′tʌrmɔɪl] *s* agitation *f*

turn [tʌrn] *s* tour *m*; *(change of direction)* virage *m*; *(bend)* tournant *m*; *(of events; of an expression)* tournure *f*; *(in a wire)* spire *f*; *(coll)* coup *m*, choc *m*; **at every turn** à tout propos; **by turns** tour à tour; **in turn** à tour de rôle; **to a turn** *(culin)* à point; **to do a good turn** rendre un service; **to take turns** alterner; **to wait one's turn** prendre son tour; **whose turn is it?** à qui le tour? || *tr* tourner; **to turn about or around** retourner; **to turn aside or away** détourner; **to turn back** renvoyer; *(an attack)* repousser; *(a clock)* retarder; **to turn down** *(a collar)* rabattre; *(e.g., the gas)* baisser; *(an offer)* refuser; **to turn from** détourner de; **to turn in** replier; *(a wrongdoer)* dénoncer; **to turn into** changer en; **to turn off** *(the water, the gas, etc.)* fermer; *(the light, the radio, etc.)* éteindre; *(a road)* quitter; **to turn on** *(the water, the gas, etc.)* ouvrir; *(the light, the radio, the gas, etc.)* allumer; **to turn out** mettre dehors; *(to manufacture)* produire; *(e.g., the light)* éteindre; **to turn over and over** tourner et retourner; **to turn up** *(a collar)* relever; *(one's sleeves)* retrousser; *(to unearth)* déterrer || *intr* tourner; se tourner; *(said of milk)* tourner; *(to toss and turn)* se retourner; *(to be dizzy)* tourner, e.g., **his head is turning** la tête lui tourne; **to turn about or around** se retourner, se tourner; **to turn aside or away** se détourner; **to turn back** rebrousser chemin; **to turn down** se rabattre; **to turn in** (coll) aller se coucher; **to turn into** tourner à or en; **to turn on** se jeter sur; (*to depend on*) dépendre de; **to turn out to be** se trouver être; **to turn out well** tourner bien; **to turn over** se retourner; (*said of auto*) capoter; **to turn up** se relever; se présenter, arriver

turn′coat′ s transfuge m

turn′down′ adj rabattu ‖ s refus m

turn′ing point′ s moment m décisif

turnip [′tʌrnɪp] s navet m; (*big watch*) (slang) bassinoire f; (slang) tête f de bois

turn′key′ s geôlier m

turn′ of life′ s retour m d'âge

turn′ of mind′ s inclination f naturelle

turn′out′ s (*gathering*) assistance f; (*output*) rendement m; (*equipment*) attelage m

turn′o′ver s renversement m; (com) chiffre m d'affaires

turn′pike′ s autoroute f à péage

turn′spit′ s tournebroche m

turnstile [′tʌrn‚staɪl] s tourniquet m

turn′stone′ s (orn) tourne-pierre m

turn′ta′ble s (*of phonograph*) plateau m porte-disque; (rr) plaque f tournante

turpentine [′tʌrpən‚taɪn] s térébenthine f

turpitude [′tʌrpɪ‚t(j)ud] s turpitude f

turquoise [′tʌrkɔɪz], [′tʌrkwɔɪz] s turquoise f

turret [′tʌrɪt] s tourelle f

turtle [′tʌrtəl] s tortue f

tur′tle·dove′ s tourterelle f

tur′tle·neck′ s col m roulé; chandail m à col roulé

Tuscan [′tʌskən] adj & s toscan m

Tuscany [′tʌskəni] s Toscane f; la Toscane

tusk [tʌsk] s défense f

tussle [′tʌsəl] s bagarre f ‖ intr se bagarrer

tutor [′t(j)utər] s précepteur m, répétiteur m ‖ tr donner des leçons particulières à ‖ intr donner des leçons particulières

tuxe·do [tʌk′sido] s (pl -dos) smoking m

TV [′ti′vi] s (letterword) (television) tévé f, télé f

twaddle [′twadəl] s fadaises fpl ‖ intr dire des fadaises

twang [twæŋ] s (*of musical instrument*) son m vibrant; (*of voice*) ton m nasillard ‖ tr faire résonner; dire en nasillant ‖ intr nasiller

twang·y [′twæŋi] adj (comp -ier; super -iest) (nasal) nasillard; (resonant) vibrant

tweed [twid] s tweed m

tweet [twit] s pépiement m ‖ intr pépier

tweeter [′twitər] s (rad) tweeter m

tweezers [′twizərz] spl brucelles fpl; pince f à épiler

twelfth [twelfθ] adj & pron douzième (masc, fem); **the Twelfth** douze, e.g., **John the Twelfth** Jean douze ‖ s

douzième m; **the twelfth** (*in dates*) le douze

twelve [twelv] adj & pron douze; **about twelve** une douzaine de ‖ s douze m; **twelve o'clock** (*noon*) midi m; (*midnight*) minuit m

twentieth [′twentɪ·ɪθ] adj & pron vingtième (masc, fem); **the Twentieth** vingt, e.g., **John the Twentieth** Jean vingt ‖ s vingt m; **the twentieth** (*in dates*) le vingt

twen·ty [′twenti] adj & pron vingt; **about twenty** une vingtaine de ‖ s (pl -ties) vingt m; **the twenties** les années fpl vingt

twen′ty-first′ adj & pron vingt et unième (masc, fem); **the Twenty-first** vingt et un, e.g., **John the Twenty-first** Jean vingt et un ‖ s vingt et unième m; **the twenty-first** (*in dates*) le vingt et un

twen′ty-one′ adj & pron vingt et un ‖ s vingt et un m; (cards) vingt-et-un

twen′ty-sec′ond adj & pron vingt-deuxième (masc, fem); **the Twenty-second** vingt-deux, e.g., **John the Twenty-second** Jean vingt-deux ‖ s vingt-deuxième m; **the twenty-second** (*in dates*) le vingt-deux

twen′ty-two′ adj, pron, & s vingt-deux m

twice [twaɪs] adv deux fois; **twice over** à deux reprises

twiddle [′twɪdəl] tr tourner, jouer avec; (e.g., one's moustache) tortiller

twig [twɪg] s brindille f

twilight [′twaɪ‚laɪt] adj crépusculaire ‖ s crépuscule m

twill [twɪl] s croisé m ‖ tr croiser

twin [twɪn] adj & s jumeau m ‖ v (pret & pp twinned; ger twinning) tr jumeler

twin′ beds′ spl lits mpl jumeaux

twine [twaɪn] s ficelle f ‖ tr enrouler ‖ intr s'enrouler

twinge [twɪndʒ] s élancement m ‖ intr élancer

twin′jet′ plane′ s biréacteur m

twinkle [′twɪŋkəl] s scintillement m; (*of the eye*) clignotement m ‖ intr scintiller; clignoter

twin′-screw′ adj à hélices jumelles

twirl [twʌrl] s tournoiement m ‖ tr faire tournoyer; (e.g., a cane) faire des moulinets avec ‖ intr tournoyer

twist [twɪst] s torsion f; (strand) cordon m; (*of the wrist, of rope, etc.*) tour m; (*of the road, river, etc.*) coude m; (*of tobacco*) rouleau m; (*of the ankle*) entorse f; (*of mind or disposition*) prédisposition f ‖ tr tordre, tortiller ‖ intr se tordre, se tortiller; **to twist and turn** (said, e.g., of road) serpenter; (*said of sleeper*) se tourner et se retourner

twister [′twɪstər] s (coll) tornade f

twit [twɪt] v (pret & pp twitted; ger twitting) tr taquiner

twitch [twɪtʃ] s crispation f ‖ intr se crisper

twitter [′twɪtər] s gazouillement m ‖ intr gazouiller

two [tu] *adj & pron* deux ‖ *s* deux *m*; to put two and two together raisonner juste; two o'clock deux heures

two'-cy'cle *adj* (mach) à deux temps

two'-cyl'inder *adj* (mach) à deux cylindres

two'-edged' *adj* à deux tranchants

two' hun'dred *adj, pron, & s* deux cents *m*

twosome ['tusəm] *s* paire *f*; jeu *m* à deux joueurs

two'-time' *tr* (slang) tromper

tycoon [taɪ'kun] *s* (coll) magnat *m*

type [taɪp] *s* type *m* ‖ *tr* typer; (to typewrite) taper; (a sample of blood) chercher le groupe sanguin sur ‖ *intr* taper

type'face' *s* œil *m*

type'script' *s* manuscrit *m* dactylographié

typesetter ['taɪp,sɛtər] *s* compositeur *m*, typographe *mf*; machine *f* à composer

type'write' *v* (pret -wrote; pp -written) *tr & intr* taper à la machine

type'writ'er *s* machine *f* à écrire

type'writer rib'bon *s* ruban *m* encreur

type'writ'ing *s* dactylographie *f*

ty'phoid fe'ver ['taɪfɔɪd] *s* fièvre *f* typhoïde

typhoon [taɪ'fun] *s* typhon *m*

typical ['tɪpɪkəl] *adj* typique

typi-fy ['tɪpɪ,faɪ] *v* (pret & pp -fied) *tr* symboliser; être le type de

typ'ing er'ror *s* faute *f* de frappe

typist ['taɪpɪst] *s* dactylo *f*

typographic(al) [,taɪpə'græfɪk(əl)] *adj* typographique

typograph'ical er'ror *s* erreur *f* typographique

typography [taɪ'pɑgrəfɪ] *s* typographie *f*

tyrannic(al) [tɪ'rænɪk(əl)], [taɪ'rænɪk(əl)] *adj* tyrannique

tyran-ny ['tɪrənɪ] *s* (pl -nies) tyrannie *f*

tyrant ['taɪrənt] *s* tyran *m*

ty-ro ['taɪro] *s* (pl -ros) novice *mf*

U

U, u [ju] *s* XXIᵉ lettre de l'alphabet

ubiquitous [ju'bɪkwɪtəs] *adj* ubiquiste, omniprésent

udder ['ʌdər] *s* pis *m*

ugliness ['ʌglɪnɪs] *s* laideur *f*

ug-ly ['ʌglɪ] *adj* (comp -lier; super -liest) laid; (disagreeable; mean) vilain

Ukraine ['jukren], [ju'kren] *s* Ukraine *f*; l'Ukraine

Ukrainian [ju'krenɪ·ən] *adj* ukrainien ‖ *s* (language) ukrainien *m*; (person) Ukrainien *m*

ulcer ['ʌlsər] *s* ulcère *m*

ulcerate ['ʌlsə,ret] *tr* ulcérer ‖ *intr* s'ulcérer

ulterior [ʌl'tɪrɪ·ər] *adj* ultérieur; secret, inavoué

ultimate ['ʌltɪmɪt] *adj* ultime, final, définitif

ultima-tum [,ʌltɪ'metəm] *s* (pl -tums or -ta [tə]) ultimatum *m*

ultrashort [,ʌltrə'ʃɔrt] *adj* (electron) ultra-court

ultraviolet [,ʌltrə'vaɪ·əlɪt] *adj & s* ultraviolet *m*

umbil'ical cord' [ʌm'bɪlɪkəl] *s* cordon *m* ombilical

umbrage ['ʌmbrɪdʒ] *s*—to take umbrage at prendre ombrage de

umbrella [ʌm'brɛlə] *s* parapluie *m*; (mil) ombrelle *f* de protection

umbrel'la stand' *s* porte-parapluies *m*

umlaut ['umlaut] *s* métaphonie *f*, inflexion *f* vocalique; (mark) tréma *m* ‖ *tr* changer le timbre de; écrire avec un tréma

umpire ['ʌmpaɪr] *s* arbitre *m* ‖ *tr & intr* arbitrer

UN ['ju'ɛn] *s* (letterword) (United Nations) ONU *f*

unable [ʌn'ebəl] *adj* incapable; to be unable to être incapable de

unabridged [,ʌnə'brɪdʒd] *adj* intégral

unaccented [,ʌn'æksɛntɪd], [,ʌnæk'sɛntɪd] *adj* inaccentué

unacceptable [,ʌnək'sɛptəbəl] *adj* inacceptable

unaccountable [,ʌnə'kauntəbəl] *adj* inexplicable; irresponsable

unaccounted-for [,ʌnə'kauntɪd,fɔr] *adj* inexpliqué, pas retrouvé

unaccustomed [,ʌnə'kʌstəmd] *adj* inaccoutumé

unafraid [,ʌnə'fred] *adj* sans peur

unaligned [,ʌnə'laɪnd] *adj* non-engagé

unanimity [,junə'nɪmɪtɪ] *s* unanimité *f*

unanimous [ju'nænɪməs] *adj* unanime

unanswerable [ʌn'ænsərəbəl] *adj* incontestable, sans réplique; (argument) irréfutable

unappreciative [,ʌnə'priʃɪ,etɪv] *adj* ingrat, peu reconnaissant

unapproachable [,ʌnə'protʃəbəl] *adj* inabordable; (fig) incomparable

unarmed [ʌn'armd] *adj* sans armes

unascertainable [,ʌn,æsər'tenəbəl] *adj* non vérifiable

unasked [ʌn'æskt], [ʌn'askt] *adj* non invité; to do s.th. unasked faire q.ch. spontanément

unassembled [,ʌnə'sɛmbəld] *adj* démonté

unassuming [,ʌnə's(j)umɪŋ] *adj* modeste, sans prétentions

unattached [,ʌnə'tæt/t] *adj* indépendant; (loose) détaché; (not engaged to be married) seul; (mil, nav) en disponibilité unattainable [ˌʌnəˈtenəbəl] adj inaccessible

unattractive [ˌʌnəˈtræktɪv] adj peu attrayant, peu séduisant

unavailable [ˌʌnəˈveləbəl] adj non disponible

unavailing [ˌʌnəˈvelɪŋ] adj inutile

unavoidable [ˌʌnəˈvɔɪdəbəl] adj inévitable

unaware [ˌʌnəˈwer] adj ignorant; **to be unaware of** ignorer || adv à l'improviste; à mon (son, etc.) insu

unawares [ˌʌnəˈwerz] adv (*unexpectedly*) à l'improviste; (*unknowingly*) à mon (son, etc.) insu

unbalanced [ʌnˈbælənst] adj non équilibré; (*mind*) déséquilibré; (*bank account*) non soldé

unbandage [ʌnˈbændɪdʒ] tr débander

un·bar [ʌnˈbɑr] v (pret & pp -barred; ger -barring) tr débarrer

unbearable [ʌnˈberəbəl] adj insupportable

unbeatable [ʌnˈbitəbəl] adj imbattable

unbecoming [ˌʌnbɪˈkʌmɪŋ] adj déplacé, inconvenant; (*dress*) peu seyant

unbelievable [ˌʌnbɪˈlivəbəl] adj incroyable

unbeliever [ˌʌnbɪˈlivər] s incroyant m

unbending [ʌnˈbendɪŋ] adj inflexible

unbiased [ʌnˈbɑr·əst] adj impartial

un·bind [ʌnˈbaɪnd] v (pret & pp -bound) tr délier

unbleached [ʌnˈblitʃt] adj écru

unbolt [ʌnˈbolt] tr (a gun; a door) déverrouiller; (a machine) déboulonner

unborn [ʌnˈbɔrn] adj à naître, futur

unbosom [ʌnˈbuzəm] tr découvrir; **to unbosom oneself** ouvrir son cœur

unbound [ʌnˈbaund] adj non relié

unbreakable [ʌnˈbrekəbəl] adj incassable

unbroken [ʌnˈbrokən] adj intact; ininterrompu; (*spirit*) indompté; (*horse*) non rompu

unbuckle [ʌnˈbʌkəl] tr déboucler

unburden [ʌnˈbʌrdən] tr alléger; **to unburden oneself** of se soulager de

unburied [ʌnˈberid] adj non enseveli

unbutton [ʌnˈbʌtən] tr déboutonner

uncalled-for [ʌnˈkɔld ˌfɔr] adj déplacé; (e.g., *insult*) gratuit

uncanny [ʌnˈkæni] adj inquiétant, mystérieux; rare, remarquable

uncared-for [ʌnˈkerd ˌfɔr] adj négligé; peu soignée

unceasing [ʌnˈsisɪŋ] adj incessant

unceremonious [ˌʌnserɪˈmoni·əs] adj sans façon

uncertain [ʌnˈsɑrtən] adj incertain

uncertain·ty [ʌnˈsɑrtənti] s (pl -ties) incertitude f

unchain [ʌnˈtʃen] tr désenchaîner

unchangeable [ʌnˈtʃendʒəbəl] adj immuable

uncharted [ʌnˈtʃɑrtɪd] adj inexploré

unchecked [ʌnˈtʃekt] adj sans frein, non contenu; non vérifié

uncivilized [ʌnˈsɪvɪˌlaɪzd] adj incivilisé

unclad [ʌnˈklæd] adj déshabillé

unclaimed [ʌnˈklemd] adj non réclamé; (*mail*) au rebut

unclasp [ʌnˈklæsp], [ʌnˈklɑsp] tr dégrafer; (*one's hands*) desserrer

unclassified [ʌnˈklæsɪˌfaɪd] adj non classé; (*documents, information, etc.*) pas secret

uncle [ˈʌŋkəl] s oncle m

unclean [ʌnˈklin] adj sale, immonde

un·clog [ʌnˈklɑg] v (pret & pp -clogged; ger -clogging) tr dégager, désobstruer

unclouded [ʌnˈklaudɪd] adj clair, dégagé

uncollectible [ˌʌnkəˈlektɪbəl] adj irrécouvrable

uncomfortable [ʌnˈkʌmfərtəbəl] adj (*causing discomfort*) inconfortable; (*feeling discomfort*) mal à l'aise

uncommitted [ˌʌnkəˈmɪtɪd] adj non engagé

uncommon [ʌnˈkɑmən] adj peu commun

uncompromising [ʌnˈkɑmprəˌmaɪzɪŋ] adj intransigeant

unconcerned [ˌʌnkənˈsʌrnd] adj indifférent

unconditional [ˌʌnkənˈdɪʃənəl] adj inconditionnel

uncongenial [ˌʌnkənˈdʒini·əl] adj peu sympathique; incompatible; désagréable

unconquerable [ʌnˈkɑŋkərəbəl] adj invincible

unconquered [ʌnˈkɑŋkərd] adj invaincu, indompté

unconscious [ʌnˈkɑnʃəs] adj inconscient; (*temporarily deprived of consciousness*) sans connaissance || s— **the unconscious** l'inconscient m

unconsciousness [ʌnˈkɑnʃəsnɪs] s inconscience f; perte f de connaissance, évanouissement m

unconstitutional [ˌʌnkɑnstɪˈt(j)uʃənəl] adj inconstitutionnel

uncontrollable [ˌʌnkənˈtroləbəl] adj ingouvernable; (e.g., *desires*) irrésistible; (e.g., *laughter*) inextinguible

unconventional [ˌʌnkənˈvenʃənəl] adj original, peu conventionnel; (*person*) non-conformiste

uncork [ʌnˈkɔrk] tr déboucher

uncouple [ʌnˈkʌpəl] tr désaccoupler

uncouth [ʌnˈkuθ] adj gauche, sauvage; (*language*) grossier

uncover [ʌnˈkʌvər] tr découvrir

unction [ˈʌŋkˈən] s onction f

unctuous [ˈʌŋktˈu·əs] adj onctueux

uncultivated [ʌnˈkʌltɪˌvetɪd] adj inculte

uncultured [ʌnˈkʌltʃərd] adj inculte, sans culture

uncut [ʌnˈkʌt] adj non coupé; (*stone, diamond*) brut; (*crops*) sur pied; (*book*) non rogné

undamaged [ʌnˈdæmɪdʒd] adj indemne

undaunted [ʌnˈdɔntɪd] adj pas découragé; sans peur

undecided [ˌʌndɪˈsaɪdɪd] adj indécis

undefeated [ˌʌndɪˈfitɪd] adj invaincu

undefended [ˌʌndɪˈfendɪd] adj sans défense

undefiled [ˌʌndɪˈfaɪld] adj sans tache

undeniable [ˌʌndɪˈnaɪ.əbəl] adj indéniable

under [ˈʌndər] adj (lower) inférieur; (underneath) de dessous || adv dessous; to go under sombrer; to keep under tenir dans la soumission || prep sous, au-dessous de, dessous; moins de, e.g., under forty moins de quarante ans; dans, e.g., under the circumstances dans les circonstances; en, e.g., under treatment en traitement; e.g., under repair en voie de réparation; à, e.g., under the microscope au microscope; e.g., under examination à l'examen; e.g., under the terms of aux termes de; e.g., under the word (in dictionary) au mot; to serve under servir sous les ordres de

un'der·age' adj mineur

un'der·arm pad' s dessous-de-bras m

un'der·bid' v (pret & pp -bid; ger -bidding) tr offrir moins que

un'der·brush' s broussailles fpl

un'der·car'riage s (aer) train m d'atterrissage; (aut) dessous m

un'der·clothes' spl sous-vêtements mpl

un'der·consump'tion s sous-consommation f

un'der·cov'er adj secret

un'der·cur'rent s courant m de fond; (fig) vague f de fond

un'der·devel'oped adj sous-développé

un'der·dog' s opprimé m; (sports) parti m non favori, outsider m

underdone [ˈʌndərˌdʌn] adj pas assez cuit

un'der·es'timate tr sous-estimer

un'der·gar'ment s sous-vêtement m

un'der·go' v (pret -went; pp -gone) tr subir, éprouver, souffrir

un'der·grad'uate adj & s non diplômé m

un'der·ground' adj souterrain; (fig) clandestin || s (subway) métro m; résistance f, maquis m || adv sous terre; to go underground (fig) entrer dans la clandestinité, prendre le maquis

un'der·growth' s sous-bois m; (underbrush) broussailles fpl

un'der·hand'ed adj sournois, dissimulé

un'der·line' or un'der·line' tr souligner

underling [ˈʌndərlɪŋ] s sous-ordre m, sous-fifre m

un'der·mine' tr miner, saper

underneath [ˌʌndərˈniθ] adj de dessous; (lower) inférieur || s dessous m || adv dessous, en dessous || prep sous, au-dessous de

un'der·nour'ished adj sous-alimenté

un'der·nour'ishment s sous-alimentation f

underpaid [ˌʌndərˈped] adj mal rétribué

un'der·pass' s passage m souterrain

un'der·pin' v (pret & pp -pinned; ger -pinning) tr étayer

un'der·priv'ileged adj déshérité

un'der·rate' tr sous-estimer

un'der·score' tr souligner

un'der·sea' adj sous-marin || un'der·sea' adv sous la surface de la mer

un'der·sec'retar'y s (pl -ies) sous-secrétaire m

un'der·sell' v (pret & pp -sold) tr vendre à meilleur marché que; (for less than the actual value) solder

un'der·shirt' s gilet m, maillot m de corps

un'der·signed' adj soussigné

un'der·skirt' s jupon m

un'der·stand' v (pret & pp -stood) tr & intr comprendre, entendre

understandable [ˌʌndərˈstændəbəl] adj compréhensible; that's understandable cela se comprend

un'der·stand'ing adj compréhensif || s compréhension f; (intellectual faculty, mind) entendement m; (agreement) accord m, entente f; on the understanding that à condition que; to come to an understanding arriver à un accord

un'der·stud'y s (pl -ies) doublure f || v (pret & pp -ied) tr (an actor) doubler

un'der·take' v (pret -took; pp -taken) tr entreprendre; (to agree to perform) s'engager à faire; to undertake to s'engager à

undertaker [ˈʌndərˌtekər] s (mortician) entrepreneur m de pompes funèbres

undertaking [ˌʌndərˈtekɪŋ] s entreprise f; (commitment) engagement m || [ˈʌndərˌtekɪŋ] s service m des pompes funèbres

un'der·tone' s ton m atténué; (background sound) fond m obscur; in an undertone à voix basse

un'der·tow' s (countercurrent below surface) courant m de fond; (on beach) ressac m

un'der·wear' s sous-vêtements mpl

un'der·world' s (criminal world) basfonds mpl, pègre f; (pagan world of the dead) enfers mpl

un'der·write' or un'der·write' v (pret -wrote; pp -written) tr souscrire; (ins) assurer

un'der·writ'er s souscripteur m; (ins) assureur m

undeserved [ˌʌndɪˈzɜrvd] adj immérité

undesirable [ˌʌndɪˈzaɪrəbəl] adj peu désirable; (e.g., alien) indésirable || s indésirable mf

undetachable [ˌʌndɪˈtætʃəbəl] adj inséparable

undeveloped [ˌʌndɪˈvɛləpt] adj (land) inexploité; (country) sous-développé

undigested [ˌʌndɪˈdʒɛstɪd] adj indigeste

undignified [ʌnˈdɪgnɪˌfaɪd] adj sans dignité, peu digne

undiscernible [ˌʌndɪˈzɜrnɪbəl], [ˌʌndɪˈsɜrnəbəl] adj imperceptible

undisputed [ˌʌndɪsˈpjutɪd] adj incontesté

undo [ʌnˈdu] v (pret -did; pp -done) tr défaire; (fig) ruiner

undoing [ʌnˈduˌɪŋ] s perte f, ruine f

undone [ʌnˈdʌn] adj défait; (omitted) inaccompli; to come undone se défaire; to leave nothing undone ne rien négliger undoubtedly [ʌn'dautɪdlɪ] *adv* sans aucun doute, incontestablement

undramatic [ˌʌndrə'mætɪk] *adj* peu dramatique

undress ['ʌn‿ˌdres], [ʌn'dres] *s* déshabillé *m*; (*scanty dress*) petite tenue *f* || [ʌn'dres] *tr* déshabiller || *intr* se déshabiller

undrinkable [ʌn'drɪŋkəbəl] *adj* imbuvable

undue [ʌn'd(j)u] *adj* indu

undulate ['ʌndjə‿let] *intr* onduler

unduly [ʌn'd(j)ulɪ] *adv* indûment

undying [ʌn'daɪ‿ɪŋ] *adj* impérissable

un'earned in'come ['ʌnˌɑrnd] *s* rente *f*, revenu *m* d'un bien

un'earned in'crement *s* plus-value *f*

unearth [ʌn'ʌrθ] *tr* déterrer

unearthly [ʌn'ʌrθlɪ] *adj* surnaturel, spectral; bizarre; (*hour*) indu

uneasy [ʌn'izɪ] *adj* inquiet; contraint, gêné

uneatable [ʌn'itəbəl] *adj* immangeable

uneconomic(al) [ˌʌnikə'nɑmɪk(əl)], [ˌʌnekə'nɑmɪk(əl)] *adj* peu économique; (*person*) peu économe

uneducated [ʌn'edjə‿ketɪd] *adj* ignorant, sans instruction

unemployed [ˌʌnem'plɔɪd] *adj* en chômage, sans travail || *spl* chômeurs *mpl*, sans-travail *mfpl*

unemployment [ˌʌnem'plɔɪmənt] *s* chômage *m*

un'employ'ment insur'ance *s* assurance-chômage *f*

unending [ʌn'endɪŋ] *adj* interminable

unequal [ʌn'ikwəl] *adj* inégal; to be unequal to (*a task*) ne pas être à la hauteur de

unequaled or unequalled [ʌn'ikwəld] *adj* sans égal, sans pareil

unerring [ʌn'ʌrɪŋ], [ʌn'erɪŋ] *adj* infaillible

UNESCO [ju'nesko] *s* (acronym) (United Nations Educational, Scientific, and Cultural Organization) l'Unesco *f*

unessential [ˌʌne'senʃəl] *adj* non essentiel

uneven [ʌn'ivən] *adj* inégal; (*number*) impair

uneventful [ˌʌnɪ'ventfəl] *adj* sans incident, peu mouvementé

unexceptionable [ˌʌnek'sepʃənəbəl] *adj* irréprochable

unexpected [ˌʌnek'spektɪd] *adj* inattendu, imprévu

unexplained [ˌʌnek'splend] *adj* inexpliqué

unexplored [ˌʌnek'splord] *adj* inexploré

unexposed [ˌʌnek'spozd] *adj* (phot) vierge

unfading [ʌn'fedɪŋ] *adj* immarcescible

unfailing [ʌn'felɪŋ] *adj* infaillible; (*inexhaustible*) intarissable

unfair [ʌn'fer] *adj* injuste, déloyal

unfaithful [ʌn'feθfəl] *adj* infidèle

unfamiliar [ˌʌnfə'mɪljər] *adj* étranger, peu familier

unfasten [ʌn'fæsən], [ʌn'fɑsən] *tr* défaire, détacher

unfathomable [ʌn'fæðəməbəl] *adj* insondable

unfavorable [ʌn'fevərəbəl] *adj* défavorable

unfeeling [ʌn'filɪŋ] *adj* insensible

unfilled [ʌn'fɪld] *adj* vide; (*post*) vacant

unfinished [ʌn'fɪnɪʃt] *adj* inachevé

unfit [ʌn'fɪt] *adj* impropre, inapte

unfold [ʌn'fold] *tr* déplier || *intr* se déplier

unforeseeable [ˌʌnfor'si‿əbəl] *adj* imprévisible

unforeseen [ˌʌnfor'sin] *adj* imprévu

unforgettable [ˌʌnfər'getəbəl] *adj* inoubliable

unforgivable [ˌʌnfər'grɪvəbəl] *adj* impardonnable

unfortunate [ʌn'fortʃənɪt] *adj* & *s* malheureux *m*

un-freeze [ʌn'friz] *v* (*pret* -froze; *pp* -frozen) *tr* dégeler

unfriend·ly [ʌn'frendlɪ] *adj* (*comp* -lier; *super* -liest) inamical

unfruitful [ʌn'frutfəl] *adj* infructueux

unfulfilled [ˌʌnfəl'frld] *adj* inaccompli

unfurl [ʌn'fʌrl] *tr* déployer

unfurnished [ʌn'fʌrnɪʃt] *adj* non meublé

ungain·ly [ʌn'genlɪ] *adj* gauche, disgracieux

ungentlemanly [ʌn'dʒentəlmənlɪ] *adj* mal élevé, impoli

ungird [ʌn'gɑrd] *tr* déceindre

ungodly [ʌn'gɑdlɪ] *adj* impie; (*dreadful*) (coll) atroce

ungracious [ʌn'greʃəs] *adj* malgracieux

ungrammatical [ˌʌngrə'mætɪkəl] *adj* peu grammatical

ungrateful [ʌn'gretfəl] *adj* ingrat

ungrudgingly [ʌn'grʌdʒɪŋlɪ] *adj* de bon cœur, libéralement

unguarded [ʌn'gɑrdɪd] *adj* sans défense; (*moment*) d'inattention; (*card*) sec

unguent ['ʌŋgwənt] *s* onguent *m*

unhandy [ʌn'hændɪ] *adj* maladroit; (*e.g.*, *tool*) incommode, pas maniable

unhap·py [ʌn'hæpɪ] *adj* (*comp* -pier; *super* -piest) malheureux, triste; (*unlucky*) malheureux, malencontreux; (*fateful*) funeste

unharmed [ʌn'hɑrmd] *adj* indemne

unharness [ʌn'hɑrnɪs] *tr* dételer

unheal·thy [ʌn'helθɪ] *adj* (*comp* -thier; *super* -thiest) malsain; (*person*) maladif

unheard-of [ʌn'hʌrd‿ˌɑv] *adj* inouï

unhinge [ʌn'hɪndʒ] *tr* (fig) détraquer

unhitch [ʌn'hɪtʃ] *tr* décrocher; (*e.g.*, *horse*) dételer

unho·ly [ʌn'holɪ] *adj* (*comp* -lier; *super* -liest) profane; (coll) affreux

unhook [ʌn'huk] *tr* décrocher; (*e.g.*, *a dress*) dégrafer

unhoped-for [ʌn'hopt‿for] *adj* inespéré

unhorse [ʌn'hors] *tr* désarçonner

unhurt [ʌn'hʌrt] *adj* indemne

unicorn ['junɪˌkorn] *s* unicorne *m*

unification [ˌjunɪfɪ'keʃən] *s* unification *f*

uniform ['junɪˌform] *adj* & *s* uniforme

m || *tr* uniformiser; vêtir d'un uniforme

uniformi•ty [ˌjunɪˈfɔrmɪti] *s* (*pl* -ties) uniformité *f*

uni•fy [ˈjunɪˌfaɪ] *v* (*pret & pp* -fied) unifier

unilateral [ˌjunɪˈlætərəl] *adj* unilatéral

unimpeachable [ˌʌnɪmˈpitʃəbəl] *adj* irrécusable

unimportant [ˌʌnɪmˈpɔrtənt] *adj* peu important, sans importance

uninhabited [ˌʌnɪnˈhæbɪtɪd] *adj* inhabité

uninspired [ˌʌnɪnˈspaɪrd] *adj* sans inspiration, sans vigueur

unintelligent [ˌʌnɪnˈtelɪdʒənt] *adj* inintelligent

unintelligible [ˌʌnɪnˈtelɪdʒɪbəl] *adj* inintelligible

uninterested [ʌnˈɪntrɪstɪd], [ʌnˈɪntəˌrestɪd] *adj* indifférent

uninteresting [ʌnˈɪntrɪstɪŋ], [ʌnˈɪntəˌrestɪŋ] *adj* peu intéressant

uninterrupted [ˌʌnɪntəˈrʌptɪd] *adj* ininterrompu

union [ˈjunjən] *adj* (*leader, scale, card, etc.*) syndical || *s* union *f*; (*of workmen*) syndicat *m*

unionize [ˈjunjəˌnaɪz] *tr* syndiquer || *intr* se syndiquer

un′ion shop′ *s* atelier *m* syndical

un′ion suit′ *s* sous-vêtement *m* d'une seule pièce

unique [juˈnik] *adj* unique

unison [ˈjunɪsən], [ˈjunɪzən] *s* unisson *m*; **in unison (with)** à l'unisson (de)

unit [ˈjunɪt] *adj* unitaire || *s* unité *f*; (elec, mach) groupe *m*

unite [juˈnaɪt] *tr* unir || *intr* s'unir

united [juˈnaɪtɪd] *adj* uni

Unit′ed King′dom *s* Royaume-Uni *m*

Unit′ed Na′tions *spl* Nations *fpl* Unies

Unit′ed States′ *spl* des États-Unis, américain || *s*—the United States les États-Unis

uni•ty [ˈjunɪti] *s* (*pl* -ties) unité *f*

universal [ˌjunɪˈvʌrsəl] *adj & s* universel *m*

u′niversal joint′ *s* joint *m* articulé, cardan *m*

universe [ˈjunɪˌvʌrs] *s* univers *m*

universi•ty [ˌjunɪˈvʌrsɪti] *adj* universitaire || *s* (*pl* -ties) université *f*

unjust [ʌnˈdʒʌst] *adj* injuste

unjustified [ʌnˈdʒʌstɪˌfaɪd] *adj* injustifié

unkempt [ʌnˈkempt] *adj* dépeigné; mal tenu, négligé

unkind [ʌnˈkaɪnd] *adj* désobligeant; (*pitiless*) impitoyable, dur

unknowable [ʌnˈno·əbəl] *adj* inconnaissable

unknowingly [ʌnˈno·ɪŋli] *adv* inconsciemment

unknown [ʌnˈnon] *adj* inconnu; (*not yet revealed*) inédit; **unknown to** à l'insu de || *s* inconnu *m*; (math) inconnue *f*

un′known quan′tity *s* (math, fig) inconnue *f*

Un′known Sol′dier *s* Soldat *m* inconnu

unlace [ʌnˈles] *tr* délacer

unlatch [ʌnˈlætʃ] *tr* lever le loquet de

unlawful [ʌnˈlɔfəl] *adj* illégal, illicite

unleash [ʌnˈliʃ] *tr* lâcher

unleavened [ʌnˈlevənd] *adj* azyme

unless [ʌnˈles] *prep* sauf || *conj* à moins que

unlettered [ʌnˈletərd] *adj* illettré

unlike [ʌnˈlaɪk] *adj* (*not alike*) dissemblables; différent de; (*not typical of*) pas caractéristique de; (*poles of a magnet*) (elec) de noms contraires || *prep* (*contrary to*) à la différence de

unlikely [ʌnˈlaɪkli] *adj* peu probable

unlimited [ʌnˈlɪmɪtɪd] *adj* illimité

unlined [ʌnˈlaɪnd] *adj* (*coat*) non fourré; (*paper*) non rayé; (*face*) sans rides

unload [ʌnˈlod] *tr* décharger; (*a gun*) désarmer; (coll) se décharger de || *intr* décharger

unloading [ʌnˈlodɪŋ] *s* déchargement *m*

unlock [ʌnˈlak] *tr* ouvrir; (*a bolted door*) déverrouiller; (*the jaws*) desserrer

unloose [ʌnˈlus] *tr* lâcher; (*to undo*) délier; (*a mighty force*) déchaîner

unloved [ʌnˈlʌvd] *adj* peu aimé, haï

unlovely [ʌnˈlʌvli] *adj* disgracieux

unluck•y [ʌnˈlʌki] *adj* (*comp* -ier; *super* -iest) malchanceux, malheureux

un•make [ʌnˈmek] *v* (*pret & pp* -made) *tr* défaire

unmanageable [ʌnˈmænɪdʒəbəl] *adj* difficile à manier, ingouvernable

unmanly [ʌnˈmænli] *adj* indigne d'un homme, poltron; efféminé

unmannerly [ʌnˈmænərli] *adj* impoli, mal élevé

unmarketable [ʌnˈmɑrkɪtəbəl] *adj* invendable

unmarriageable [ʌnˈmærɪdʒəbəl] *adj* non mariable

unmarried [ʌnˈmærɪd] *adj* célibataire

unmask [ʌnˈmæsk], [ʌnˈmɑsk] *tr* démasquer || *intr* se démasquer

unmatched [ʌnˈmætʃt] *adj* sans égal, incomparable; (*unpaired*) désassorti, dépareillé

unmerciful [ʌnˈmʌrsɪfəl] *adj* impitoyable

unmesh [ʌnˈmeʃ] *tr* (mach) désengrener || *intr* (mach) se désengrener

unmindful [ʌnˈmaɪndfəl] *adj* oublieux

unmistakable [ˌʌnmɪsˈtekəbəl] *adj* évident, facilement reconnaissable

unmitigated [ʌnˈmɪtɪˌgetɪd] *adj* parfait, fieffé

unmixed [ʌnˈmɪkst] *adj* sans mélange

unmoor [ʌnˈmur] *tr* désamarrer

unmoved [ʌnˈmuvd] *adj* impassible

unmuzzle [ʌnˈmʌzəl] *tr* démuseler

unnatural [ʌnˈnætʃərəl] *adj* anormal, dénaturé; maniéré; artificiel

unnecessary [ʌnˈnesəˌseri] *adj* inutile

unnerve [ʌnˈnʌrv] *tr* démonter, décontenancer, bouleverser

unnoticeable [ʌnˈnotɪsəbəl] *adj* imperceptible

unnoticed [ʌnˈnotɪst] *adj* inaperçu

unobserved [ˌʌnəbˈzʌrvd] *adj* inobservé, inaperçu

unobtainable [ˌʌnəb'tenəbəl] *adj* introuvable

unobtrusive [ˌʌnəb'trusɪv] *adj* discret, effacé

unoccupied [ʌn'ukjə,paɪd] *adj* libre, inoccupé

unofficial [ˌʌnə'fɪʃəl] *adj* officieux, non officiel

unopened [ʌn'opənd] *adj* fermé; (*letter*) non décacheté

unopposed [ˌʌnə'pozd] *adj* sans opposition; (*candidate*) unique

unorthodox [ʌn'ɔrθə,daks] *adj* peu orthodox

unpack [ʌn'pæk] *tr* déballer

unpalatable [ʌn'pælətəbəl] *adj* fade, insipide

unparalleled [ʌn'pærə,leld] *adj* sans précédent, sans pareil

unpardonable [ʌn'pardənəbəl] *adj* impardonnable

unpatriotic [ˌʌnpetrɪ'atɪk], [ˌʌnpætrɪ'atɪk] *adj* antipatriotique

unperceived [ˌʌnpər'sivd] *adj* inaperçu

unperturbable [ˌʌnpər'tʌrbəbəl] *adj* imperturbable

unpleasant [ʌn'plɛzənt] *adj* désagréable, déplaisant

unpopular [ʌn'papjələr] *adj* impopulaire

unpopularity [ʌn,papjə'lærɪti] *s* impopularité *f*

unprecedented [ʌn'prɛsɪ,dɛntɪd] *adj* sans précédent, inédit

unprejudiced [ʌn'prɛdʒədɪst] *adj* sans préjugés, impartial

unpremeditated [ˌʌnprɪ'mɛdɪ,tetɪd] *adj* non prémédité

unprepared [ˌʌnprɪ'perd] *adj* sans préparation; (*e.g., speech*) improvisé

unprepossessing [ˌʌnpripə'zɛsɪŋ] *adj* peu engageant

unpresentable [ˌʌnprɪ'zɛntəbəl] *adj* peu présentable

unpretentious [ˌʌnprɪ'tɛnʃəs] *adj* sans prétentions, modeste

unprincipled [ʌn'prɪnsɪpəld] *adj* sans principes, sans scrupules

unproductive [ˌʌnprə'dʌktɪv] *adj* improductif

unprofitable [ʌn'prafɪtəbəl] *adj* peu profitable, inutile

unpronounceable [ˌʌnprə'naunsəbəl] *adj* imprononçable

unpropitious [ˌʌnprə'pɪʃəs] *adj* défavorable

unpublished [ʌn'pʌblɪʃt] *adj* inédit

unpunished [ʌn'pʌnɪʃt] *adj* impuni

unqualified [ʌn'kwalə,faɪd] *adj* incompétent; parfait, fieffé

unquenchable [ʌn'kwɛntʃəbəl] *adj* inextinguible

unquestionable [ʌn'kwɛstʃənəbəl] *adj* indiscutable

unravel [ʌn'rævəl] *v* (*pret & pp* -eled or -elled; *ger* -eling or -elling) *tr* effiler; (fig) débrouiller ‖ *intr* s'effiler; (fig) se débrouiller

unreachable [ʌn'ritʃəbəl] *adj* inaccessible

unreal [ʌn'ri·əl] *adj* irréel

unreali·ty [ˌʌnrɪ'ælɪti] *s* (*pl* -ties) irréalité *f*

unreasonable [ʌn'rizənəbəl] *adj* déraisonnable

unrecognizable [ʌn'rɛkəg,naɪzəbəl] *adj* méconnaissable

unreel [ʌn'ril] *tr* dérouler ‖ *intr* se dérouler

unrelenting [ˌʌnrɪ'lɛntɪŋ] *adj* implacable

unreliable [ˌʌnrɪ'laɪ·əbəl] *adj* peu fidèle, instable, sujet à caution

unremitting [ˌʌnrɪ'mɪtɪŋ] *adj* incessant, infatigable

unrented [ʌn'rɛntɪd] *adj* libre, sans locataires

unrepentant [ˌʌnrɪ'pɛntənt] *adj* impénitent

un'requit'ed love' [ˌʌnrɪ'kwaɪtɪd] *s* amour *m* non partagé

unresponsive [ˌʌnrɪ'spansɪv] *adj* peu sensible, froid, détaché

unrest [ʌn'rɛst] *s* agitation *f*, trouble *m*; inquiétude *f*

un·rig [ʌn'rɪg] *v* (*pret & pp* -rigged; *ger* -rigging) *tr* (naut) dégréer

unrighteous [ʌn'raɪt/əs] *adj* inique, injuste

unripe [ʌn'raɪp] *adj* vert, pas mûr; précoce

unrivaled or **unrivalled** [ʌn'raɪvəld] *adj* sans rival

unroll [ʌn'rol] *tr* dérouler ‖ *intr* se dérouler

unromantic [ˌʌnro'mæntɪk] *adj* peu romanesque, terre à terre

unruffled [ʌn'rʌfəld] *adj* calme, serein

unruly [ʌn'ruli] *adj* indiscipliné, ingouvernable

unsaddle [ʌn'sædəl] *tr* (*a horse*) desseller; (*a horseman*) désarçonner

unsafe [ʌn'sef] *adj* dangereux

unsaid [ʌn'sɛd] *adj*—**to leave unsaid** passer sous silence

unsalable [ʌn'seləbəl] *adj* invendable

unsanitary [ʌn'sænɪ,tɛri] *adj* peu hygiénique

unsatisfactory [ʌn,sætɪs'fæktəri] *adj* peu satisfaisant

unsatisfied [ʌn'sætɪs,faɪd] *adj* insatisfait, inassouvi

unsavory [ʌn'severi] *adj* désagréable; (fig) équivoque, louche

unscathed [ʌn'skeðd] *adj* indemne

unscientific [ˌʌnsaɪ·ən'tɪfɪk] *adj* antiscientifique

unscrew [ʌn'skru] *tr* dévisser

unscrupulous [ʌn'skrupjələs] *adj* sans scrupules

unseal [ʌn'sil] *tr* desceller

unsealed *adj* (*mail*) non clos

unseasonable [ʌn'sizənəbəl] *adj* hors de saison; (*untimely*) inopportun

unseemly [ʌn'simli] *adj* inconvenant

unseen [ʌn'sin] *adj* invisible

unselfish [ʌn'sɛlfɪʃ] *adj* désintéressé

unsettled [ʌn'sɛtəld] *adj* instable; (*region*) non colonisé; (*question*) en suspens; (*weather*) variable; (*bills*) non réglé

unshackle [ʌn'ʃækəl] *tr* désentraver

unshaken [ʌn'ʃekən] *adj* inébranlé

unshapely [ʌn'ʃepli] *adj* difforme, informe
unshaven [ʌn'ʃevən] *adj* non rasé
unsheathe [ʌn'ʃið] *tr* dégainer
unshod [ʌn'ʃɑd] *adj* déchaussé; (*horse*) déferré
unshrinkable [ʌn'ʃrɪŋkəbəl] *adj* irrétrécissable
unsightly [ʌn'saɪtli] *adj* laid, hideux
unsinkable [ʌn'sɪŋkəbəl] *adj* insubmersible
unskilled [ʌn'skɪld] *adj* inexpérimenté; de manœuvre
un'skilled la'borer *s* manœuvre *m*
unskillful [ʌn'skɪlfəl] *adj* maladroit
unsnarl [ʌn'snɑrl] *tr* débrouiller
unsociable [ʌn'soʃəbəl] *adj* insociable
unsold [ʌn'sold] *adj* invendu
unsolder [ʌn'sɑdər] *tr* dessouder
unsophisticated [,ʌnsə'fɪstɪ,ketɪd] *adj* ingénu, naïf, simple
unsound [ʌn'saʊnd] *adj* peu solide; (*false*) faux; (*decayed*) gâté; (*mind*) dérangé; (*sleep*) léger
unspeakable [ʌn'spikəbəl] *adj* indicible; (*disgusting*) sans nom
unsportsmanlike [ʌn'sportsmən,laɪk] *adj* antisportif
unstable [ʌn'stebəl] *adj* instable
unsteady [ʌn'stedi] *adj* chancelant, tremblant, vacillant
unstinted [ʌn'stɪntɪd] *adj* abondant, sans bornes
unstitch [ʌn'stɪtʃ] *tr* découdre
un·stop [ʌn'stɑp] *v* (*pret & pp* **-stopped;** *ger* **-stopping**) *tr* déboucher
unstressed [ʌn'strest] *adj* inaccentué
unstrung [ʌn'strʌŋ] *adj* détraqué; (*necklace*) défilé; (*mus*) sans cordes
unsuccessful [,ʌnsək'sesfəl] *adj* non réussi; **to be unsuccessful** ne pas réussir
unsuitable [ʌn's(j)utəbəl] *adj* impropre; (*time*) inopportun; **unsuitable for** peu fait pour, inapte à
unsuspected [,ʌnsəs'pektɪd] *adj* insoupçonné
unswerving [ʌn'swɜrvɪŋ] *adj* ferme, inébranlable
unsympathetic [,ʌnsɪmpə'θetɪk] *adj* peu compatissant
unsystematic(al [,ʌnsɪstə'mætɪk(əl)] *adj* non systématique, sans méthode
untactful [ʌn'tæktfəl] *adj* indiscret, indélicat
untamed [ʌn'temd] *adj* indompté
untangle [ʌn'tæŋgəl] *tr* démêler, débrouiller
untenable [ʌn'tenəbəl] *adj* insoutenable
unthankful [ʌn'θæŋkfəl] *adj* ingrat
unthinkable [ʌn'θɪŋkəbəl] *adj* impensable
unthinking [ʌn'θɪŋkɪŋ] *adj* irréfléchi
untidy [ʌn'taɪdi] *adj* désordonné, débraillé
un·tie [ʌn'taɪ] *v* (*pret & pp* **-tied;** *ger* **-tying**) *tr* délier, dénouer
until [ʌn'tɪl] *prep* jusqu'à || *conj* jusqu'à ce que, en attendant jusqu'à ce que
untimely [ʌn'taɪmli] *adj* inopportun; (*premature*) prématuré
untiring [ʌn'taɪrɪŋ] *adj* infatigable

untold [ʌn'told] *adj* incalculable; (*suffering*) inouï; (*joy*) indicible; (*tale*) non raconté
untouchable [ʌn'tʌtʃəbəl] *adj & s* intouchable *mf*
untouched [ʌn'tʌtʃt] *adj* intact; indifférent; non mentionné
untoward [ʌn'tord] *adj* malencontreux
untrained [ʌn'trend] *adj* inexpérimenté; (*animal*) non dressé
untrammeled or **untrammelled** [ʌn'træməld] *adj* sans entraves
untried [ʌn'traɪd] *adj* inéprouvé
untroubled [ʌn'trʌbəld] *adj* calme, insoucieux
untrue [ʌn'tru] *adj* faux; infidèle
untrustworthy [ʌn'trʌst,wɜrði] *adj* indigne de confiance
untruth [ʌn'truθ] *s* mensonge *m*
untruthful [ʌn'truθfəl] *adj* mensonger
untwist [ʌn'twɪst] *tr* détordre || *intr* se détordre
unused [ʌn'juzd] *adj* inutilisé, inemployé; **unused to** [ʌn'juzdtu], [ʌn-'justu] peu accoutumé à
unusual [ʌn'juʒu·əl] *adj* insolite, inusité, inhabituel
unutterable [ʌn'ʌtərəbəl] *adj* indicible, inexprimable
unvanquished [ʌn'væŋkwɪʃt] *adj* invaincu
unvarnished [ʌn'vɑrnɪʃt] *adj* non verni; (fig) sans fard, simple
unveil [ʌn'vel] *tr* dévoiler; (*e.g., a statue*) inaugurer || *intr* se dévoiler
unveiling [ʌn'velɪŋ] *s* dévoilement *m*
unventilated [ʌn'ventɪ,letɪd] *adj* sans aération
unvoice [ʌn'vɔɪs] *tr* dévoiser, assourdir
unwanted [ʌn'wɑntɪd] *adj* non voulu
unwarranted [ʌn'wɑrəntɪd] *adj* injustifié; sans garantie
unwary [ʌn'weri] *adj* imprudent
unwavering [ʌn'wevərɪŋ] *adj* constant, ferme, résolu
unwelcome [ʌn'welkəm] *adj* (*e.g., visitor*) importun; (*e.g., news*) fâcheux
unwell [ʌn'wel] *adj* indisposé, souffrant; (*menstruating*) indisposée
unwholesome [ʌn'holsəm] *adj* malsain, insalubre
unwieldy [ʌn'wildi] *adj* peu maniable
unwilling [ʌn'wɪlɪŋ] *adj* peu disposé
unwillingly [ʌn'wɪlɪŋli] *adv* à contre-cœur
un·wind [ʌn'waɪnd] *v* (*pret & pp* **-wound**) *tr* dérouler || *intr* se dérouler
unwise [ʌn'waɪz] *adj* peu judicieux, malavisé
unwished-for [ʌn'wɪʃt,fɔr] *adj* non souhaité
unwittingly [ʌn'wɪtɪŋli] *adv* inconsciemment, sans le savoir
unwonted [ʌn'wʌntɪd] *adj* inaccoutumé, peu commun
unworldly [ʌn'wɜrldli] *adj* peu mondain; simple, naïf
unworthy [ʌn'wɜrði] *adj* indigne
un·wrap [ʌn'ræp] *v* (*pret & pp* **-wrapped;** *ger* **-wrapping**) *tr* dépaqueter, désenvelopper

un·wrinkled [ʌn'rɪŋkəld] *adj* uni, lisse, sans rides

unwritten [ʌn'rɪtən] *adj* non écrit; oral; (*blank*) vierge, blanc

unwrit'ten law' *s* droit *m* coutumier

un·yielding [ʌn'jildɪŋ] *adj* ferme, solide; inébranlable

unyoke [ʌn'jok] *tr* dételer

up [ʌp] *adj* montant, ascendant; (*raised*) levé; (*standing*) debout; (*time*) expiré; (*blinds*) relevé; **up in arms** soulevé, indigné || *adv* haut, en haut; **to be up against** se heurter à; **to be up against it** avoir la déveine; **to be up to** être capable de, être à la hauteur de; être à, e.g., **to be up to you (me, etc.)** être à vous (moi, etc.); **up and down** de haut en bas; (*back and forth*) de long en large; **up there** là-haut; **up to** jusqu'à; (*at the level of*) au niveau de, à la hauteur de; **up to and including** jusques et y compris; **what's up?** qu'est-ce qui se passe?; for expressions like **to go up** monter and **to get up** se lever, see the verb || *prep* en haut de, vers le haut de; (*a stream*) en montant || *v* (*pret & pp* **upped;** *ger* **upping**) (*coll*) faire monter; (*prices, wages*) (*coll*) élever || *interj* debout!

up-and-coming [ˌʌpən'kʌmɪŋ] *adj* (coll) entreprenant

up-and-doing [ˌʌpən'duɪŋ] *adj* (coll) entreprenant, alerte, énergique

up-and-up [ˌʌpən'ʌp] *s*—**to be on the up-and-up** (coll) être en bonne voie; (coll) être honnête

up·braid' *tr* réprimander, reprendre

upbringing [ˈʌpˌbrɪŋɪŋ] *s* éducation *f*

up'coun'try *adv* (coll) à l'intérieur du pays || *s* (coll) intérieur *m* du pays

up·date' *tr* mettre à jour

upheaval [ʌp'hivəl] *s* soulèvement *m*

up'hill' *adj* montant; difficile, pénible || **up·hill'** *adv* en montant

up·hold' *v* (*pret & pp* **-held**) *tr* soutenir, maintenir

upholster [ʌp'holstər] *tr* tapisser

upholsterer [ʌp'holstərər] *s* tapissier *m*

upholster·y [ʌp'holstəri] *s* (*pl* **-les**) tapisserie *f*

up'keep' *s* entretien *m*; (*expenses*) frais *mpl* d'entretien

upland [ˈʌplənd], [ˈʌpˌlænd] *adj* élevé || *s* région *f* montagneuse; **uplands** hautes terres *fpl*

up'lift' *s* élévation *f*; (*moral improvement*) édification *f* || **up·lift'** *tr* soulever, élever

upon [ə'pɑn] *prep* sur; à, e.g., **upon my arrival** à mon arrivée; **upon + ger** en + ger, e.g., **upon arriving** en arrivant

upper [ˈʌpər] *adj* supérieur; haut; (*first*) premier || *s* (*of shoe*) empeigne *f*

up'per berth' *s* couchette *f* du haut, couchette supérieure

up'per-case' *adj* (typ) du haut de casse

up'per clas'ses *spl* hautes classes *fpl*

up'per hand' *s* dessus *m*, haute main *f*

up'per mid'dle class' *s* haute bourgeoisie *f*

up'per·most *adj* (le) plus haut, (le) plus élevé; (le) premier || *adv* en dessus

uppish [ˈʌpɪʃ] *adj* (coll) suffisant, arrogant

up·raise' *tr* lever

up'right' *adj & adv* droit || *s* montant *m*

uprising [ʌp'raɪzɪŋ], [ˈʌpˌraɪzɪŋ] *s* soulèvement *m*, insurrection *f*

up'roar' *s* tumulte *m*, vacarme *m*

uproarious [ʌp'rorɪ·əs] *adj* tumultueux; (*funny*) comique, impayable

up·root' *tr* déraciner

ups' and downs' *spl* vicissitudes *fpl*

up·set' or **up'set'** *adj* (*overturned*) renversé; (*disturbed*) bouleversé; (*stomach*) dérangé || **up'set'** *s* (*overturn*) renversement *m*; (*of emotions*) bouleversement *m* || **up·set'** *v* (*pret & pp* **-set;** *ger* **-setting**) *tr* renverser; bouleverser || *intr* se renverser

up'set price' *s* prix *m* de départ

upsetting [ʌp'setɪŋ] *adj* bouleversant, inquiétant

up'shot' *s* résultat *m*; point *m* essentiel

up'side down' *adv* sens dessus dessous; **to turn upside down** renverser; se renverser; (*said of carriage*) verser

up'stage' *adj & adv* au second plan, à l'arrière-plan; **to go upstage** remonter || *s* arrière-plan *m* || **up'stage'** *tr* (coll) prendre un air dédaigneux envers

up'stairs' *adj* d'en haut || *s* l'étage *m* supérieur || *adv* en haut; **to go upstairs** monter, monter en haut

up·stand'ing *adj* droit; (*vigorous*) gaillard; (*sincere*) honnête, probe

up'start' *adj & s* parvenu *m*

up'stream' *adj & adv* en amont

up'stroke' *s* (*in writing*) délié *m*; (mach) course *f* ascendante

up'surge' *s* poussée *f*

up'swing' *s* mouvement *m* de montée; (com) amélioration *f*

up-to-date [ˈʌptə'det] *adj* à la page; (*e.g., account books*) mis à jour

up-to-the-minute [ˈʌptəðə'mɪnɪt] *adj* de la dernière heure

up'trend' *s* tendance *f* à la hausse

up'turn' *s* hausse *f*, amélioration *f*

up'turned' *adj* (*e.g., eyes*) levé; (*part of clothing*) relevé; (*nose*) retroussé

upward [ˈʌpwərd] *adj* ascendant || *adv* vers le haut; **upward of** plus de

Ural [ˈjurəl] *adj* Ouralien || *s* Oural *m*; **Urals** Oural

uranium [ju'renɪ·əm] *s* uranium *m*

urban [ˈʌrbən] *adj* urbain

urbane [ʌr'ben] *adj* urbain, courtois

urbanite [ˈʌrbəˌnaɪt] *s* citadin *m*, habitant *m* d'une ville

urbanity [ʌr'bænɪt] *s* urbanité *f*

urbanize [ˈʌrbəˌnaɪz] *tr* urbaniser

ur'ban renew'al *s* renouveau *m* urbain

urchin [ˈʌrtʃɪn] *s* gamin *m*, galopin *m*

ure·thra [ju'riθrə] *s* (*pl* **-thras** or **-thrae** [θri]) urètre *m*

urge [ʌrdʒ] *s* impulsion *f* || *tr & intr* presser

urgen·cy [ˈʌrdʒənsɪ] *s* (*pl* **-cies**) urgence *f*; insistance *f*, sollicitation *f*

urgent ['ʌrdʒənt] *adj* urgent, pressant; (*insistent*) pressant, importun

urinal ['jurɪnəl] *s* (*small building or convenience for men*) urinoir *m*, vespasienne *f*; (*for bed*) urinal *m*

urinary ['jurɪ,neri] *adj* urinaire

urinate ['jurɪ,net] *tr & intr* uriner; pisser (coll)

urine ['jurɪn] *s* urine *f*

urn [ʌrn] *s* urne *f*; (*for tea, coffee, etc.*) fontaine *f*

urology [jʊ'rɑlədʒi] *s* urologie *f*

us [ʌs] *pron pers* nous §85, §87

U.S.A. ['ju'es'e] *s* (letterword) (**United States of America**) E.-U.A. *mpl* or U.S.A. *mpl*

usable ['juzəbəl] *adj* utilisable

usage ['jusɪdʒ], ['juzɪdʒ] *s* usage *m*

use [jus] *s* emploi *m*, usage *m*; (*usefulness*) utilité *f*; in use occupé; of what use is it? à quoi cela sert-il?; out of use hors de service; to be of no use ne servir à rien; to have no use for s.o. tenir qn en mauvaise estime; to make use of se servir de; what's the use? à quoi bon? ‖ [juz] *tr* employer, se servir de, user de; to use up épuiser, user ‖ *intr*—I used to visit my friend every evening je visitais mon ami tous les soirs

used [juzd] *adj* usagé, usé; d'occasion, e.g., used car voiture *f* d'occasion; to be used (*to be put into use*) être usité, être employé; to be used as servir de; to be used to (*to be useful for*) servir à; used to ['justʊ] accoutumé à; used up épuisé

useful ['jusfəl] *adj* utile

usefulness ['jusfəlnɪs] *s* utilité *f*

useless ['juslɪs] *adj* inutile

user ['juzər] *s* usager *m*; (*of a machine, of gas, etc.*) utilisateur *m*

usher ['ʌʃər] *s* placeur *m*; ouvreuse *f*; (*doorkeeper*) huissier *m* ‖ *tr*—to usher in inaugurer; (*a person*) introduire

U.S.S.R. ['ju'es'es'ɑr] *s* (letterword) (**Union of Soviet Socialist Republics**) U.R.S.S. *f*

usual ['juʒu·əl] *adj* usuel; as usual comme d'habitude

usually ['juʒu·əli] *adv* usuellement, d'habitude, d'ordinaire

usurp [ju'zʌrp] *tr* usurper

usu·ry ['juʒəri] *s* (*pl* -ries) usure *f*

utensil [ju'tensɪl] *s* ustensile *m*

uter·us ['jutərəs] *s* (*pl* -i [,aɪ]) utérus *m*

utilitarian [,jutɪlɪ'tɛri·ən] *adj* utilitaire

utili·ty [ju'tɪlɪti] *s* (*pl* -ties) utilité *f*; service *m* public; utilities services en commun (*gaz, transports, etc.*)

utilize ['jutɪ,laɪz] *tr* utiliser

utmost ['ʌt,most] *adj* extrême; plus grand; plus éloigné ‖ *s*—the utmost l'extrême *m*, le comble *m*; to do one's utmost faire tout son possible; to the utmost jusqu'au dernier point

utopia [ju'topɪ·ə] *s* utopie *f*

utopian [ju'topɪ·ən] *adj* utopique ‖ *s* utopiste *m f*

utter ['ʌtər] *adj* complet, total, absolu ‖ *tr* proférer, émettre; (*a cry*) pousser

utterance ['ʌtərəns] *s* expression *f*, émission *f*; (gram) énoncé *m*; to give utterance to exprimer

utterly ['ʌtərli] *adv* complètement, tout à fait, totalement

---

V

V, v [vi] *s* XXIIe lettre de l'alphabet

vacan·cy ['vekənsi] *s* (*pl* -cies) (*emptiness; gap, opening*) vacance *f*; (*unfilled position or job*) vacance *f*; (*in a building*) appartement *m* disponible; (*in a hotel*) chambre *f* de libre; no vacancy (public sign) complet

vacant ['vekənt] *adj* (*empty*) vide; (*having no occupant; untenanted*) vacant, libre, disponible; (*expression, look*) distrait, vague

va'cant lot' *s* terrain *m* vague

vacate ['veket] *tr* quitter, évacuer ‖ *intr* (*to move out*) déménager

vacation [ve'keʃən] *s* vacances *fpl*; on vacation en vacances ‖ *intr* prendre ses vacances, passer ses vacances

vacationist [ve'keʃənɪst] *s* vacancier *m*

vaca'tion with pay' *s* congé *m* payé

vaccinate ['væksɪ,net] *tr* vacciner

vaccination [,væksɪ'neʃən] *s* vaccination *f*

vaccine [væk'sin] *s* vaccin *m*

vacillate ['væsɪ,let] *intr* vaciller

vacu·ity [væ'kju·ɪti] *s* (*pl* -ties) vacuité *f*

vacu·um ['vækju·əm] *s* (*pl* -ums or -a [ə]) vacuum *m*, vide *m* ‖ *tr* passer à l'aspirateur, dépoussiérer

vac'uum clean'er *s* aspirateur *m*

vac'uum pump' *s* pompe *f* à vide

vac'uum tube' *s* tube *m* à vide

vagabond ['vægə,bɑnd] *adj & s* vagabond *m*

vagar·y ['və'geri] *s* (*pl* -ies) caprice *m*

vagran·cy ['vegrənsi] *s* (*pl* -cies) vagabondage *m*

vague [veg] *adj* vague

vain [ven] *adj* vain; in vain en vain

vainglorious [ven'glorɪ·əs] *adj* vaniteux

valance ['væləns] *s* cantonnière *f*, lambrequin *m*

vale [vel] *s* vallon *m*

valedicto·ry [,vælɪ'dɪktəri] *s* (*pl* -ries) discours *m* d'adieu

valence ['veləns] *s* (chem) valence *f*

valentine ['vælən,taɪn] *s* (*sweetheart*)

valentin m; (card) carte f de la Saint-Valentin

Val'entine Day' s la Saint-Valentin
vale' of tears' s vallée f de larmes
valet ['vælɪt], ['væle] s valet m
valiant ['væljənt] adj vaillant
valid ['vælɪd] adj valable, valide
validate ['vælɪ‚det] tr valider; (sports) homologuer
validation [‚vælɪ'deʃən] s validation f; (sports) homologation f
valid·i·ty [və'lɪdɪti] s (pl -ties) validité f
valise [və'lis] s mallette f
valley ['væli] s vallée f, vallon m; (of roof) cornière f
valor ['vælər] s valeur f, vaillance f
valorous ['vælərəs] adj valeureux
valuable ['væljuˌəbəl], ['væljəbəl] adj précieux, de valeur || **valuables** spl objets mpl de valeur
value ['vælju] s valeur f; (bargain) affaire f, occasion f; to set a value on estimer, évaluer || tr (to think highly of) priser, estimer; (to set a price for) estimer, évaluer; if you value your life si vous tenez à la vie
val'ue-added tax' s taxe f à la valeur ajoutée, T.V.A.
valueless ['væljulɪs] adj sans valeur
valve [vælv] s soupape f; (of mollusk; of fruit; of tire) valve f; (of heart) valvule f; (mus) clé f
valve' cap' s chapeau m, bouchon m
valve' gear' spl (of gas engine) engrenages mpl de distribution; (of steam engine) mécanisme m de distribution
valve'-in-head' en'gine s moteur m à soupapes en tête, moteur à culbuteurs
valve' seat' s siège m de soupape
valve' spring' s ressort m de soupape
valve' stem' s tige f de soupape
vamp [væmp] s (of shoe) empeigne f; (patchwork) rapiéçage m; (woman who preys on man) (coll) femme f fatale, vamp f || tr (a shoe) mettre une empeigne à; (to set together) rapiécer; (a susceptible man) (coll) vamper; (an accompaniment) (coll) improviser
vampire ['væmpaɪr] s vampire m; femme f fatale, vamp f
van [væn] s camion m, voiture f de déménagement; (mil, fig) avant-garde f; (railway car) (Brit) fourgon m
vandal ['vændəl] adj & s vandale m || (cap) adj vandale || (cap) s Vandale m
vandalism ['vændə‚lɪzəm] s vandalisme m
vane [ven] s (weathervane) girouette f; (of windmill) aile f; (of propeller or turbine) ailette f; (of feather) lame f
vanguard ['væn‚gard] s (mil, fig) avant-garde f; in the vanguard à l'avant-garde
vanilla [və'nɪlə] s vanille f
vanish ['vænɪʃ] intr s'évanouir, disparaître
van'ishing cream' s crème f de jour
vani·ty ['vænɪti] s (pl -ties) vanité f; (dressing table) table f de toilette, coiffeuse f; (vanity case) poudrier m

van'ity case' s poudrier m, nécessaire m de toilette
vanquish ['væŋkwɪʃ] tr vaincre
van'tage point' ['væntɪdʒ] s position f avantageuse
vapid ['væpɪd] adj insipide
vapor ['vepər] s vapeur f
vaporize ['vepə‚raɪz] tr vaporiser || intr se vaporiser
va'por trail' s (aer) sillage m de fumée
variable ['vɛrɪ‚əbl] adj & s variable f
variance ['vɛrɪ‚əns] s différence f, variation f; at variance with en désaccord avec
variant ['vɛrɪ‚ənt] adj variant || s variante f
variation [‚vɛrɪ'eʃən] s variation f
varicose ['vɛrɪ‚kos] adj variqueux
var'icose veins' spl (pathol) varice f
varied ['vɛrɪd] adj varié
variegated ['vɛrɪ‚ə‚getɪd], ['vɛrɪ‚ge‚tɪd] adj varié; (spotted) bigarré, bariolé
varie·ty [və'raɪ‚ɪti] s (pl -ties) variété f
vari'ety show' s spectacle m de variétés
various ['vɛrɪ‚əs] adj divers, différent; (several) plusieurs; (variegated) bigarré
varnish ['varnɪʃ] s vernis m || tr vernir; (e.g., the truth) farder, embellir
varsi·ty ['varsɪti] adj (sports) universitaire || s (pl -ties) (sports) équipe f universitaire principale
var·y ['vɛri] v (pret & pp -ied) tr & intr varier
vase [ves], [vez] s vase m
vaseline ['væsə‚lin] s (trademark) vaseline f
vassal ['væsəl] adj & s vassal m
vast [væst], [vɑst] adj vaste
vastness ['væstnɪs], ['vɑstnɪs] s vaste étendue f, immensité f
vat [væt] s cuve f, bac m
Vatican ['vætɪkən] adj vaticane || s Vatican m
vaudeville ['vodvɪl], ['vodəvɪl] s spectacle m de variétés, music-hall m; (light theatrical piece interspersed with songs) vaudeville m
vault [volt] s (underground chamber) souterrain m; (of a bank) chambre f forte; (burial chamber) caveau m; (leap) saut m; (anat, archit) voûte f || tr & intr sauter
vaunt [vont], [vɑnt] s vantardise f || tr vanter || intr se vanter
veal [vil] s veau m
veal' chop' s côtelette f de veau
veal' cut'let s escalope f de veau
veer [vɪr] s virage m || tr faire virer || intr virer
vegetable ['vedʒɪtəbəl] adj végétal || s (plant) végétal m; (edible part of plant) légume m
veg'etable gar'den s potager m
veg'etable soup' s potage m aux légumes
vegetarian [‚vedʒɪ'tɛrɪ‚ən] adj & s végétarien m
vegetate ['vedʒɪ‚tet] intr végéter
vehemence ['vi·ɪməns] s véhémence f
vehement ['vi·ɪmənt] adj véhément

vehicle ['vi·ɪkəl] *s* véhicule *m*

veil [vel] *s* voile *m*; **to take the veil** prendre le voile ‖ *tr* voiler ‖ *intr* se voiler

vein [ven] *s* veine *f* ‖ *tr* veiner

velar ['vilər] *adj & s* vélaire *f*

vellum ['vɛləm] *s* vélin *m*; papier *m* vélin

veloci·ty [vɪ'lɑsɪti] *s* (*pl* -ties) vitesse *f*

velvet ['vɛlvɪt] *s* velours *m*

velveteen [,vɛlvɪ'tin] *s* velvet *m*

velvety ['vɛlvɪti] *adj* velouté

vend [vɛnd] *tr* vendre, colporter

vend/ing machine/ *s* distributeur *m* automatique

vendor ['vɛndər] *s* vendeur *m*

veneer [və'nɪr] *s* placage *m*; (fig) vernis *m* ‖ *tr* plaquer

venerable ['vɛnərəbəl] *adj* vénérable

venerate ['vɛnə,ret] *tr* vénérer

venereal [vɪ'nɪrɪ·əl] *adj* vénérien

Venetian [vɪ'niʃən] *adj* vénitien ‖ *s* Vénitien *m*

Vene/tian blind/ *s* jalousie *f*, store *m* vénitien

vengeance ['vɛndʒəns] *s* vengeance *f*; **with a vengeance** furieusement, à outrance; (*to the utmost limit*) tant que ça peut

vengeful ['vɛndʒfəl] *adj* vengeur

Venice ['vɛnɪs] *s* Venise *f*

venison ['vɛnɪsən], ['vɛnɪzən] *s* venaison *f*

venom ['vɛnəm] *s* venin *m*

venomous ['vɛnəməs] *adj* venimeux

vent [vɛnt] *s* orifice *m*; (*for air*) ventouse *f*; **to give vent to** donner libre cours à ‖ *tr* décharger

ventilate ['vɛntɪ,let] *tr* ventiler

ventilator ['vɛntɪ,letər] *s* ventilateur *m*

ventricle ['vɛntrɪkəl] *s* ventricule *m*

ventriloquism [vɛn'trɪlə,kwɪzəm] *s* ventriloquie *f*

ventriloquist [vɛn'trɪləkwɪst] *s* ventriloque *mf*

venture ['vɛnt/ər] *s* entreprise *f* risquée; **at a venture** à l'aventure ‖ *tr* aventurer ‖ *intr* s'aventurer; **to venture on** hasarder

venturesome ['vɛnt/ərsəm] *adj* aventureux

venturous ['vɛnt/ərəs] *adj* aventureux

venue ['vɛnju] *s* (law) lieu *m* du jugement; **change of venue** (law) renvoi *m*

Venus ['vinəs] *s* Vénus *f*

veracious [vɪ're/əs] *adj* véridique

veraci·ty [vɪ'ræsɪti] *s* (*pl* -ties) véracité *f*

veranda or **verandah** [və'rændə] *s* véranda *f*

verb [vʌrb] *adj* verbal ‖ *s* verbe *m*

verbalize ['vʌrbə,laɪz] *tr* exprimer par des mots; (gram) changer en verbe ‖ *intr* être verbeux

verbatim [vər'betɪm] *adj* textuel ‖ *adv* textuellement

verbiage ['vʌrbɪ·ɪdʒ] *s* verbiage *m*

verbose [vər'bos] *adj* verbeux

verdant ['vʌrdənt] *adj* vert; naïf, candide

verdict ['vʌrdɪkt] *s* verdict *m*

verdigris ['vʌrdɪ,grɪs] *s* vert-de-gris *m*

verdure ['vʌrdʒər] *s* verdure *f*

verge [vʌrdʒ] *s* bord *m*, limite *f*; **on the verge of** sur le point de ‖ *intr*—**to verge on** or **upon** toucher à; (*bad faith; the age of forty; etc.*) friser

verification [,vɛrɪfɪ'ke/ən] *s* vérification *f*

veri·fy ['vɛrɪ,faɪ] *v* (*pret & pp* -fied) *tr* vérifier

verily ['vɛrɪli] *adv* en vérité

veritable ['vɛrɪtəbəl] *adj* véritable

vermilion [vər'mɪljən] *adj & s* vermillon *m*

vermin ['vʌrmɪn] *s* (*objectionable person*) vermine *f* ‖ *spl* (*objectionable animals or persons*) vermine

vermouth [vər'muθ], ['vʌrmuθ] *s* vermout *m*

vernacular [vər'nækjələr] *adj* vernaculaire ‖ *s* langue *f* vernaculaire; (*everyday language*) langage *m* vulgaire; (*language peculiar to a class or profession*) jargon *m*

versatile ['vʌrsətɪl] *adj* aux talents variés; (*e.g., mind*) universel, souple

verse [vʌrs] *s* vers *mpl*; (*stanza*) strophe *f*; (Bib) verset *m*

versed [vʌrst] *adj*—**versed in** versé dans; spécialiste de

versification [,vʌrsɪfɪ'ke/ən] *s* versification *f*

versi·fy ['vʌrsɪ,faɪ] *v* (*pret & pp* -fied) *tr & intr* versifier

version ['vʌrʒən] *s* version *f*

ver·so ['vʌrso] *s* (*pl* -sos) (*e.g., of a coin*) revers *m*; (typ) verso *m*

versus ['vʌrsəs] *prep* contre

verte·bra ['vʌrtɪbrə] *s* (*pl* -brae [,bri] or -bras) vertèbre *f*

vertebrate ['vʌrtɪ,bret] *adj & s* vertébré *m*

ver·tex ['vʌrtɛks] *s* (*pl* -texes or -tices [tɪ,siz]) sommet *m*

vertical ['vʌrtɪkəl] *adj* vertical ‖ *s* verticale *f*

ver/tical hold/ *s* (telv) commande *f* de stabilité verticale

ver/tical rud/der *s* gouvernail *m* de direction

verti·go ['vʌrtɪ,go] *s* (*pl* -gos or -goes) vertige *m*

very ['vɛrɪ] *adj* véritable; même, e.g., **at this very moment** à cet instant même ‖ *adv* très, e.g., **I am very hungry** j'ai très faim; bien, e.g., **you are very nice** vous êtes bien gentil; tout, e.g., **the very first** le tout premier; e.g., **my very best** tout mon possible; **for my very own** pour moi tout seul; **very much** beaucoup

vesicle ['vɛsɪkəl] *s* vésicule *f*

vespers ['vɛspərz] *spl* vêpres *fpl*

vessel ['vɛsəl] *s* bâtiment *m*, navire *m*; (*container*) vase *m*; (anat, bot, zool) vaisseau *m*

vest [vɛst] *s* gilet *m*; **to play it close to the vest** (coll) jouer serré ‖ *tr* revêtir; **to vest with** investir de, revêtir de

vest/ed in/terests *spl* classes *fpl* dirigeantes

vestibule ['vɛstɪ,bjul] *s* vestibule *m*

ves'tibule car' s (rr) wagon m à soufflets

vestige ['vestɪdʒ] s vestige m

vestment ['vestmənt] s vêtement m sacerdotal

vest'-pock'et adj de poche, de petit format

ves•try ['vestri] s (pl -tries) sacristie f; (committee) conseil m paroissial

ves'try•man s (pl -men) marguillier m

Vesuvius [vɪˈs(j)uvɪ•əs] s le Vésuve

vetch [vetʃ] s vesce f; (Lathyrus sativus) gesse f

veteran ['vetərən] s vétéran m

veterinarian [ˌvetərɪˈnerɪ•ən] s vétérinaire mf

veterinar•y ['vetərɪˌneri] adj vétérinaire || s (pl -ies) vétérinaire mf

ve•to ['vito] s (pl -toes) veto m || tr mettre son veto à

vex [veks] tr vexer, contrarier

vexation [vekˈseʃən] s vexation f

via ['vaɪ•ə] prep via

viaduct ['vaɪ•əˌdʌkt] s viaduc m

vial ['vaɪ•əl] s fiole f

viand ['vaɪ•ənd] s mets m

vibrate ['vaɪbret] intr vibrer

vibration [vaɪˈbreʃən] s vibration f

vicar ['vɪkər] s vicaire m; (in Church of England) curé m

vicarage ['vɪkərɪdʒ] s presbytère m; (duties of vicar) cure f

vicarious [vaɪˈkerɪ•əs], [vɪˈkerɪ•əs] adj substitut; (punishment) souffert pour autrui; (power, authority) délégué; (enjoyment) partagé

vice [vaɪs] s vice m; (device) étau m

vice'-ad'miral s vice-amiral m

vice'-pres'ident s vice-président m

viceroy ['vaɪsrɔɪ] s vice-roi m

vice' squad' s brigade f des mœurs

vice versa ['vaɪsəˈvʌrsə], ['vaɪsˈvʌrsə] adv vice versa

vicini•ty [vɪˈsɪnɪti] s (pl -ties) voisinage m; environs mpl, e.g., New York and vicinity New York et ses environs

vicious ['vɪʃ•əs] adj vicieux; (mean) méchant; (ferocious) féroce

vicissitude [vɪˈsɪsɪˌt(j)ud] s vicissitude f

victim ['vɪktɪm] s victime f; (e.g., of a collision, fire) accidenté m

victimize ['vɪktɪˌmaɪz] tr prendre pour victime; (to swindle) duper

victor ['vɪktər] s vainqueur m

victorious [vɪkˈtorɪ•əs] adj victorieux

victo•ry ['vɪktəri] s (pl -ries) victoire f

victuals ['vɪtəlz] spl victuailles fpl

vid'eo sig'nal ['vɪdɪ•o] s signal m d'image

vid'eo tape' s bande f magnétique vidéo

vid'eo tape' record'er s magnétoscope m

vid'eo tape' record'ing s magnétoscope m

vie [vaɪ] v (pret & pp vied; ger vying) intr rivaliser, lutter

Vienna [vɪˈenə] s Vienne f

Vien•nese [ˌvi•əˈniz] adj viennois || s (pl -nese) Viennois m

Vietnam [ˌvi•etˈnɑm] s le Vietnam

Vietnam•ese [vɪˌetnɑˈmiz] adj vietnamien || s (pl -ese) Vietnamien m

view [vju] s vue f; in my view à mon avis, selon mon opinion; in view en vue; in view of étant donné, vu; on view exposé; with a view to en vue de || tr voir, regarder; considérer, examiner

viewer ['vju•ər] s spectateur m; (for film, slides, etc.) visionneuse f; (telv) téléspectateur m

view'find'er s viseur m

view'point' s point m de vue

vigil ['vɪdʒɪl] s veille f; (eccl) vigile f; to keep a vigil veiller

vigilance ['vɪdʒɪləns] s vigilance f

vigilant ['vɪdʒɪlənt] adj vigilant

vignette [vɪnˈjet] s vignette f

vigor ['vɪgər] s vigueur f

vigorous ['vɪgərəs] adj vigoureux

vile [vaɪl] adj vil; (smell) infect; (weather) sale; (disgusting) détestable

vili•fy ['vɪlɪˌfaɪ] v (pret & pp -fied) tr diffamer, dénigrer

villa ['vɪlə] s villa f

village ['vɪlɪdʒ] s village m

villager ['vɪlɪdʒər] s villageois m

villain ['vɪlən] s scélérat m; (of a play) traître m

villainous ['vɪlənəs] adj vil, infame

villain•y ['vɪləni] s (pl -ies) vilenie f, infamie f

vim [vɪm] s énergie f, vigueur f

vinaigrette' sauce' [ˌvɪnəˈgret] s vinaigrette f

vindicate ['vɪndɪˌket] tr justifier, défendre

vindictive [vɪnˈdɪktɪv] adj vindicatif

vine [vaɪn] s plante f grimpante; (grape plant) vigne f

vinegar ['vɪnɪgər] s vinaigre m

vinegary ['vɪnɪgəri] adj aigre; acariâtre

vine'grow'er [ˌgro•ər] s viticulteur m

vine' stock' s cep m

vineyard ['vɪnjərd] s vignoble m, vigne f

vintage ['vɪntɪdʒ] s vendange f; (year) année f, cru m; (coll) classe f, catégorie f

vin'tage wine' s bon cru m

vin'tage year' s grande année f

vintner ['vɪntnər] s négociant m en vins; (person who makes wine) vigneron m

vinyl ['vaɪnɪl], ['vɪnɪl] s vinyle m

viola [vaɪˈolə], [vɪˈolə] s alto m

violate ['vaɪ•ə‚let] tr violer

violation [ˌvaɪ•əˈleʃən] s violation f

violence ['vaɪ•ələns] s violence f

violent ['vaɪ•ələnt] adj violent

violet ['vaɪ•əlɪt] adj violet || s (color) violet m; (bot) violette f

violin [ˌvaɪ•əˈlɪn] s violon m

violinist [ˌvaɪ•əˈlɪnɪst] s violoniste mf

violoncel•lo [ˌvaɪ•ələnˈtʃelo], [ˌvi•ələn-ˈtʃelo] s (pl -los) violoncelle m

viper ['vaɪpər] s vipère f

vira•go [vɪˈrego] s (pl -goes or -gos) mégère f

virgin ['vʌrdʒɪn] adj vierge || s vierge f; (male virgin) puceau m

Virgin'ia creep'er [vərˈdʒɪnɪ•ə] s vigne f vierge

virginity [vər'dʒɪnɪti] s virginité f
virility [vɪ'rɪlɪti] s virilité f
virology [vaɪ'rɑlədʒi] s virologie f
virtual ['vʌrtʃu·əl] adj véritable, effectif; (mech, opt, phys) virtuel
virtue ['vʌrtʃu] s vertu f; mérite m, avantage m
virtuosi•ty [,vʌrtʃu'ɑsɪti] s (pl -ties) virtuosité f
virtuo•so [,vʌrtʃu'oso] s (pl -sos or -si [si]) virtuose mf
virtuous ['vʌrtʃu·əs] adj vertueux
virulence ['vɪrjələns] s virulence f
virulent ['vɪrjələnt] adj virulent
virus ['vaɪrəs] s virus m
visa ['vizə] s visa m || tr viser
visage ['vɪzɪdʒ] s visage m
vis-à-vis [,vizə'vi] adj face à face || s & adv vis-à-vis m || prep vis-à-vis de, vis-à-vis
viscera ['vɪsərə] spl viscères mpl
viscount ['vaɪkaunt] s vicomte m
viscountess ['vaɪkauntɪs] s vicomtesse f
viscous ['vɪskəs] adj visqueux
vise [vaɪs] s étau m
visible ['vɪzɪbəl] adj visible
vision ['vɪʒən] s vision f
visionar•y ['vɪʒə,neri] adj visionnaire || s (pl -ies) visionnaire mf
visit ['vɪzɪt] s visite f || tr visiter; (e.g., a person) rendre visite à || intr faire des visites
visitation [,vɪzɪ'teʃən] s visite f; justice f du ciel; clémence f du ciel; (e.g., in a séance) apparition f; Visitation (eccl) Visitation f
vis'iting card' s carte f de visite
vis'iting hours' spl heures fpl de visite
vis'iting nurse' s infirmière f visiteuse
vis'iting profes'sor s visiteur m
visitor ['vɪzɪtər] s visiteur m
visor ['vaɪzər] s visière f
vista ['vɪstə] s perspective f
visual ['vɪʒu·əl] adj visuel
visualize ['vɪʒu·ə,laɪz] tr (in one's mind) se faire une image mentale de, se représenter; (to make visible) visualiser
vital ['vaɪtəl] adj vital || vitals spl organes mpl vitaux
vitality [vaɪ'tælɪti] s vitalité f
vitalize ['vaɪtə,laɪz] tr vitaliser
vitamin ['vaɪtəmɪn] s vitamine f
vitiate ['vɪʃɪ,et] tr vicier
vitreous ['vɪtrɪ·əs] adj vitreux
vitriolic [,vɪtrɪ'alɪk] adj (chem) vitriolique; (fig) trempé dans du vitriol
vituperate [vaɪ't(j)upə,ret] tr vitupérer
viva ['vivə] s vivat m || interj vive!
vivacious [vɪ'veʃəs], [vaɪ'veʃəs] adj vif, animé
vivaci•ty [vɪ'væsɪti], [vaɪ'væsɪti] s (pl -ties) vivacité f
viva voce ['vaɪvə'vosi] adv de vive voix
vivid ['vɪvɪd] adj vif; (description) vivant; (recollection) vivace
vivi•fy ['vɪvɪ,faɪ] v (pret & pp -fied) tr vivifier
vivisection [,vɪvɪ'sekʃən] s vivisection f

vixen ['vɪksən] s mégère f; (zool) renarde f
viz. abbr (Lat: videlicet namely, to wit) c.-à-d., à savoir
vizier [vɪ'zɪr], ['vɪzjər] s vizir m
vocabular•y [vo'kæbjə,leri] s (pl -ies) vocabulaire m
vocal ['vokəl] adj vocal; (inclined to express oneself freely) communicatif, démonstratif
vocalist ['vokəlɪst] s chanteur m
vocalize ['vokə,laɪz] tr vocaliser || intr vocaliser; (phonet) se vocaliser
vocation [vo'keʃən] s vocation f; profession f, métier m
voca'tional guid'ance [vo'keʃənəl] s orientation f professionnelle
voca'tional school' s école f professionnelle
vocative ['vakətɪv] s vocatif m
vociferate [vo'sɪfə,ret] intr vociférer
vociferous [vo'sɪfərəs] adj vociférant, criard
vogue [vog] s vogue f; in vogue en vogue
voice [vɔɪs] s voix f; in a loud voice à voix haute; in a low voice à voix basse; with one voice unanimement || tr exprimer; (a consonant) voiser, sonoriser || intr se voiser
voiced adj (phonet) voisé, sonore
voiceless ['vɔɪslɪs] adj sans voix; (consonant) sourd
void [vɔɪd] adj vide; (law) nul; void of dénué de || s vide m || tr vider; (the bowels) évacuer; (law) rendre nul || intr évacuer, excréter
voile [vɔɪl] s voile m
volatile ['valətɪl] adj (solvent) volatil; (disposition) volage; (temper) vif
volatilize ['valətə,laɪz] tr volatiliser || intr se volatiliser
volcanic [val'kænɪk] adj volcanique
volca•no [val'keno] s (pl -noes or -nos) volcan m
volition [və'lɪʃən] s volition f, volonté f; of one's own volition de son propre gré
volley ['vali] s volée f || tr lancer à la volée; (sports) reprendre de volée || intr lancer une volée
vol'ley-ball' s volley-ball m
volplane ['val,plen] s vol m plané || intr descendre en vol plané
volt [volt] s volt m
voltage ['voltɪdʒ] s voltage m; high voltage haute tension f
volt'age drop' s perte f de charge
volte-face [vɔlt'fas] s volte-face f
volt'me'ter s voltmètre m
voluble ['valjəbəl] adj volubile
volume ['valjəm] s volume m; to speak volumes en dire long
vol'ume num'ber s tomaison f
voluminous [və'lumɪnəs] adj volumineux
voluntar•y ['valən,teri] adj volontaire || s (pl -ies) (mus) morceau m d'orgue improvisé
volunteer [,valən'tɪr] adj & s volontaire mf || tr offrir volontairement ||

intr (mil) s'engager; **to volunteer to** + *inf* s'offrir à + *inf*

voluptuar‧y [vəˈlʌpt/u,eri] *adj* voluptuaire ‖ *s* (*pl* -ies) voluptueux *m*

voluptuous [vəˈlʌpt/u-əs] *adj* voluptueux

vomit [ˈvɑmɪt] *s* vomissure *f* ‖ *tr* & *intr* vomir

voodoo [ˈvudu] *adj* & *s* vaudou *m*

voracious [vəˈreʃəs] *adj* vorace

voraci‧ty [vəˈræsɪti] *s* (*pl* -ties) voracité *f*

vor‧tex [ˈvɔrteks] *s* (*pl* -texes or -tices [tɪ,siz]) vortex *m*, tourbillon *m*

vota‧ry [ˈvotəri] *s* (*pl* -ries) fidèle *mf*

vote [vot] *s* vote *m*; **by popular vote** au suffrage universel; **to put to the vote** mettre aux voix; **to tally the votes** dépouiller le scrutin; **vote by show of hands** vote à main levée ‖ *tr* voter; **to vote down** repousser; **to vote in** élire ‖ *intr* voter; **to vote for** voter; **to vote on** passer au vote

voter [ˈvotər] *s* votant *m*, électeur *m*

vot′ing booth′ *s* isoloir *m*

vot′ing machine′ *s* machine *f* électorale

votive [ˈvotɪv] *adj* votif

vouch [vaut/] *tr* affirmer, garantir ‖ *intr*—**to vouch for** répondre de

voucher [ˈvaut/ər] *s* garant *m*; (*certificate*) récépissé *m*, pièce *f* comptable

vouch‧safe′ *tr* octroyer ‖ *intr*—**to vouchsafe to** + *inf* daigner + *inf*

vow [vau] *s* vœu *m*; **to take vows** entrer en religion ‖ *tr* (e.g., *revenge*) jurer ‖ *intr* faire un vœu; **to vow to** faire vœu de

vowel [ˈvau-əl] *s* voyelle *f*

voyage [ˈvɔɪ-ɪdʒ] *s* (*by air or sea*) traversée *f*; (*any journey*) voyage *m* ‖ *tr* traverser ‖ *intr* voyager

voyager [ˈvɔɪ-ɪdʒər] *s* voyageur *m*

vs. *abbr* (*versus*) contre

vulcanize [ˈvʌlkə,naɪz] *tr* vulcaniser

vulgar [ˈvʌlgər] *adj* grossier; (*popular, common; vernacular*) vulgaire

vulgari‧ty [vʌlˈgærɪti] *s* (*pl* -ties) grossièreté *f*, vulgarité *f*

Vul′gar Lat′in *s* latin *m* vulgaire

vulnerable [ˈvʌlnərəbəl] *adj* vulnérable

vulture [ˈvʌlt/ər] *s* vautour *m*

W

W, w [ˈdʌbəl,ju] *s* XXIIIᵉ lettre de l'alphabet

wad [wɑd] *s* (*of cotton*) tampon *m*; (*of papers*) liasse *f*; (*in a gun*) bourre *f* ‖ *v* (*pret & pp* **wadded**; *ger* **wadding**) *tr* bourrer

waddle [ˈwɑdəl] *s* dandinement *m* ‖ *intr* se dandiner

wade [wed] *tr* traverser à gué ‖ *intr* marcher dans l'eau, patauger; **to wade into** (coll) s'attaquer à; **to wade through** (coll) avancer péniblement dans

wad′ing bird′ *s* (orn) échassier *m*

wafer [ˈwefər] *s* (*thin, crisp cake*) gaufrette *f*; (*pill*) cachet *m*; (*for sealing letters*) pain *m* à cacheter; (eccl) hostie *f*

waffle [ˈwɑfəl] *s* gaufre *f*

waf′fle i′ron *s* gaufrier *m*

waft [wæft], [wɑft] *tr* porter; (*a kiss*) envoyer ‖ *intr* flotter

wag [wæg] *s* (*of head*) hochement *m*; (*of tail*) frétillement *m*; (*jester*) farceur *m* ‖ *v* (*pret & pp* **wagged**; *ger* **wagging**) *tr* (*the head*) hocher; (*the tail*) remuer ‖ *intr* frétiller

wage [wedʒ] *s* salaire *m*; **wages** gages *mpl*, salaire *m*; (fig) salaire, récompense *f* ‖ *tr*—**to wage war** faire la guerre

wage′ earn′er [,ʌrnər] *s* salarié *m*

wage′-price′ freeze′ *s* blocage *m* des prix et des salaires

wager [ˈwedʒər] *s* pari *m*; **to lay a wager** faire un pari ‖ *tr* & *intr* parier

wage′work′er *s* salarié *m*

waggish [ˈwægɪʃ] *adj* plaisant, facétieux

wagon [ˈwægən] *s* charrette *f*; (*Conestoga wagon; plaything*) chariot *m*; (mil) fourgon *m*; **to be on the wagon** (slang) s'abstenir de boissons alcooliques

wag′tail′ *s* hochequeue *m*, bergeronnette *f*

waif [wef] *s* (*foundling*) enfant *m* trouvé; animal *m* égaré or abandonné; (*stray child*) voyou *m*

wail [wel] *s* lamentation *f*, plainte *f* ‖ *intr* se lamenter, gémir

wain‧scot [ˈwenskət], [ˈwenskat] *s* lambris *m* ‖ *v* (*pret & pp* -scoted or -scotted; *ger* -scoting or -scotting) *tr* lambrisser

waist [west] *s* (*of human body; corresponding part of garment*) taille *f*, ceinture *f*; (*garment*) corsage *m*, blouse *f*

waist′band′ *s* ceinture *f*

waist′cloth′ *s* pagne *m*

waistcoat [ˈwest,kot], [ˈweskət] *s* gilet *m*

waist′-deep′ *adj* jusqu'à la ceinture

waist′line′ *s* taille *f*, ceinture *f*; **to keep** or **watch one's waistline** garder or soigner sa ligne

wait [wet] *s* attente *f*; **to lie in wait for** guetter ‖ *tr*—**to wait one's turn** attendre son tour ‖ *intr* attendre; **to wait for** attendre; **to wait on** (*customers; dinner guests*) servir

wait′-and-see′ pol′icy *s* attentisme *m*

waiter [ˈwetər] *s* garçon *m*; (*tray*) plateau *m*

wait′ing list′ *s* liste *f* d'attente

wait'ing room' s salle f d'attente; (of a doctor) antichambre f

waitress ['wetrɪs] s serveuse f; **wait-ress!** mademoiselle!

waive [wev] tr renoncer (with dat); (to defer) différer

waiver ['wevər] s renonciation f, abandon m

wake [wek] s (watch by the body of a dead person) veillée f mortuaire; (of a boat or other moving object) sillage m; **in the wake of** dans le sillage de, à la suite de || v (pret **waked** or **woke** [wok]; pp **waked**) tr réveiller || intr —**to wake to** se rendre compte de; **to wake up** se réveiller

wakeful ['wekfəl] adj éveillé

wakefulness ['wekfəlnɪs] s veille f

waken ['wekən] tr éveiller, réveiller || intr s'éveiller, se réveiller

wale [wel] s zébrure f || tr zébrer

Wales [welz] s le pays de Galles

walk [wɔk] s (act) promenade f; (distance) marche f; (way of walking, bearing) démarche f; (of a garden) allée f; (calling) métier m; **to fall into a walk** (said of horse) se mettre au pas; **to go for a walk** faire une promenade || tr promener; (a horse) promener au pas || intr aller à pied, marcher; (to stroll) se promener; **to walk away** s'en aller à pied; **to walk off with** (a prize) gagner; (a stolen object) décamper avec; **to walk out** sortir, partir subitement; (to go on strike) se mettre en grève; **to walk out on** abandonner; quitter en colère

walk'away' s (coll) victoire f facile

walker ['wɔkər] s marcheur m, promeneur m; (pedestrian) piéton m; (go-cart) chariot m d'enfant

walkie-talkie ['wɔkɪ'tɔkɪ] s (rad) émetteur-récepteur m portatif, parle-en-marche m

walk'ing pa'pers spl—**to give s.o. his walking papers** (coll) congédier qn

walk'ing stick' s canne f

walk'-on' s (actor) figurant m, comparse mf; (role) figuration f

walk'out' s (coll) grève f improvisée

walk'o'ver s (coll) victoire f dans un fauteuil

walk'-up' s appartement m sans ascenseur

wall [wɔl] s mur m; (between rooms; of a pipe, boiler, etc.) paroi f; (of a fortification) muraille f; **to go to the wall** succomber; perdre la partie || tr entourer de murs; **to wall up** murer

wall'board' s panneau m or carreau m de revêtement

wall' clock' s pendule f murale

wallet ['wɑlɪt] s portefeuille m

wall'flow'er s (bot) ravenelle f, giroflée f; **to be a wallflower** (coll) faire tapisserie

wall' lamp' s applique f

wall' map' s carte f murale

Walloon [wɑ'lun] adj wallon || s (dialect) wallon m; (person) Wallon m

wallop ['wɑləp] s (coll) coup m, gnon m; **with a wallop** (fig) à grand fracas || tr (coll) tanner le cuir à, rosser; (a ball) (coll) frapper raide; (to defeat) (coll) battre

wallow ['wɑlo] s souille f || intr se vautrer; (e.g., in wealth) nager

wall'pa'per s papier m peint || tr tapisser

walnut ['wɔlnət] s noix f; (tree and wood) noyer m

walrus ['wɔlrəs], ['wɑlrəs] s morse m

Walter ['wɔltər] s Gautier m

waltz [wɔlts] s valse f || tr & intr valser

wan [wɑn] adj (comp **wanner**; super **wannest**) pâle, blême; (weak) faible

wand [wɑnd] s baguette f; (emblem of authority) bâton m, verge f

wander ['wɑndər] tr vagabonder sur, parcourir || intr errer, vaguer; (said of one's mind) vagabonder

wanderer ['wɑndərər] s vagabond m

wan'der-lust' s manie f des voyages, bougeotte f

wane [wen] s déclin m; (of moon) décours m || intr décliner; (said of moon) décroître

wangle ['wæŋɡəl] tr (to obtain by scheming) (coll) resquiller; (accounts) (coll) cuisiner; (e.g., a leave of absence) (coll) carotter; **to wangle one's way out of** (coll) se débrouiller de || intr (coll) pratiquer le système D

want [wɑnt], [wɔnt] s (need; misery) besoin m; (lack) manque m; **for want of** faute de, à défaut de; **to be in want** être dans la gêne || tr vouloir; (to need) avoir besoin de; **to want s.o. to** + inf vouloir que qn + subj; **to want to** + inf avoir envie de + inf, vouloir + inf || intr être dans le besoin; **to be wanting** manquer

want' ads' spl petites annonces fpl

wanton ['wɑntən] adj déréglé; (e.g., cruelty) gratuit; (e.g., child) espiègle; (e.g., woman) impudique

war [wɔr] s guerre f; **to go to war** se mettre en guerre; (as a soldier) aller à la guerre; **to wage war** faire la guerre || v (pret & pp **warred**; ger **warring**) intr faire la guerre; **to war on** faire la guerre contre

warble ['wɔrbəl] s gazouillement m || intr gazouiller

warbler ['wɔrblər] s (orn) fauvette f

war' cloud' s menace f de guerre

war' correspon'dent s correspondant m de guerre

war' cry' s (pl **cries**) cri m de guerre

ward [wɔrd] s (person, usually a minor under protection of another) pupille mf; (guardianship) tutelle f; (of a city) circonscription f électorale, quartier m; (of a hospital) salle f; (of a lock) gardes fpl || tr—**to ward off** parer

war' dance' s danse f guerrière

warden ['wɔrdən] s gardien m; (of a jail) directeur m; (of a church) marguillier m; (gamekeeper) garde-chasse m

ward' heel'er s politicailleur m servile

ward'robe' s garde-robe f

ward'robe trunk' s malle-armoire f

ward'room' s (nav) carré m des officiers

ware [wer] s faïence f; **wares** articles mpl de vente, marchandises fpl

ware'house' s entrepôt m

ware'house'man s (pl -men) gardemagasin m, magasinier m

war'fare' s guerre f

war'head' s charge f creuse

war'-horse' s cheval m de bataille; (coll) vétéran m

warily ['werɪlɪ] adv prudemment

war'like' adj guerrier

war' loan' s emprunt m de guerre

war' lord' s seigneur m de la guerre

warm [wɔrm] adj chaud; (welcome, thanks, friend, etc.) chaleureux; (heart) généreux; **it is warm** (said of weather) il fait chaud; **to be warm** (said of person) avoir chaud; **to keep s.th. warm** tenir q.ch. au chaud; **you're getting warm!** (you've almost found it!) vous brûlez! || tr chauffer, faire chauffer; **to warm up** réchauffer || intr se réchauffer; **to warm up** se réchauffer, chauffer, se chauffer; (said of speaker, discussion, etc.) s'animer, s'échauffer

warm'-blood'ed adj passionné, ardent; (animals) à sang chaud

war' memor'ial s monument m aux morts de la guerre

warmer ['wɔrmər] s (culin) réchaud m

warm'-heart'ed adj au cœur généreux

warm'ing pan' s bassinoire f

warmonger ['wɔr,mʌŋgər] s belliciste mf

war' moth'er s marraine f de guerre

warmth [wɔrmθ] s chaleur f

warm'-up' s exercices mpl d'assouplissement; mise f en condition

warn [wɔrn] tr prévenir; **to warn s.o. to** avertir qn de

warning ['wɔrnɪŋ] s avertissement m; **without warning** par surprise

warn'ing shot' s coup m de semonce

war' of attri'tion s guerre f d'usure

warp [wɔrp] s (of a fabric) chaîne f; (of a board) gauchissement m; (naut) touée f || tr gauchir; (the mind, judgment, etc.) fausser; (naut) touer || intr se gauchir; (naut) se touer

war'path' s—**to be on the warpath** être sur le sentier de la guerre; (to be out of sorts) (coll) être d'une humeur de dogue

war'plane' s avion m de guerre

warrant ['wɔrənt], ['wɑrənt] s garantie f; certificat m; (for arrest) mandat m d'arrêt || tr garantir; certifier; justifier

war'rant of'ficer s (mil) sous-officier m breveté; (nav) premier maître m

warran·ty ['wɔrəntɪ], ['wɑrəntɪ] s (pl -ties) garantie f; autorisation f

warren ['wɔrən], ['wɑrən] s garenne f

warrior ['wɔrjər], ['wɑrjər] s guerrier m

Warsaw ['wɔrsɔ] s Varsovie f

war'ship' s navire m de guerre

wart [wɔrt] s verrue f

war'time' s temps m de guerre

war'-torn' adj dévasté par la guerre

war·y ['werɪ] adj (comp -ier; super -iest) prudent, avisé

wash [wɑʃ], [wɔʃ] s lavage m; (clothes washed or to be washed) lessive f; (dirty water) lavure f; (place where the surf breaks; broken water behind a moving ship) remous m; (aer) souffle m || tr laver; (one's hands, face, etc.) se laver; (dishes, laundry, etc.) faire; (e.g., a seacoast) baigner; **to wash away** enlever; (e.g., a bank) affouiller, ronger || intr se laver; faire la lessive

washable ['wɑʃəbəl], ['wɔʃəbəl] adj lavable

wash'-and-wear' adj de repassage superflu, de séchage rapide

wash'ba'sin s (basin) cuvette f; (fixture) lavabo m

wash'bas'ket s corbeille f à linge

wash'board' s planche f à laver

wash'bowl' s (basin) cuvette f; (fixture) lavabo m

wash'cloth' s gant m de toilette

wash'day' s jour m de lessive

washed'-out' adj délavé, déteint; (coll) flapi, vanné

washed'-up' adj (coll) hors de combat, ruiné

washer ['wɑʃər], ['wɔʃər] s laveur m; (machine) laveuse f, lessiveuse f; (ring of metal) rondelle f; (ring of rubber) rondelle de robinet

wash'er·wom'an s (pl -wom'en) blanchisseuse f

wash' goods' spl tissus mpl grand teint

washing ['wɑʃɪŋ], ['wɔʃɪŋ] s lavage m; (act of washing clothes) blanchissage m; (clothes washed or to be washed) lessive f; **washings** lavures fpl

wash'ing machine' s machine f à laver, laveuse f automatique

wash'ing so'da s cristaux mpl de soude

wash'out' s affouillement m; (person) (coll) raté m; **to be a washout** (coll) faire fiasco, faire four

wash'rag' s gant m de toilette, torchon m

wash'room' s cabinet m de toilette, lavabo m

wash' sale' s (com) lavage m des titres

wash'stand' s lavabo m

wash'tub' s baquet m, cuvier m

wash' wa'ter s lavure f

wasp [wɑsp] s guêpe f

wasp' waist' s taille f de guêpe

waste [west] adj (land) inculte; (material) de rebut || s gaspillage m; (garbage) déchets mpl; (wild region) région f inculte; (of time) perte f; (for wiping machinery) chiffons mpl de nettoyage, effiloche f de coton; **to lay waste** dévaster; **wastes** déchets; excrément m || tr gaspiller, perdre || intr—**to waste away** dépérir, maigrir

waste'bas'ket s corbeille f à papier

wasteful ['westfəl] adj gaspilleur

waste'pa'per s papier m de rebut

waste′ pipe′ s tuyau m d'écoulement, vidange f

waste′ prod′ucts spl déchets mpl

wastrel ['westrəl] s gaspilleur m, prodigue mf

watch [wɑt∫] s montre f; (lookout) garde f, guet m; (naut) quart m; to be on the watch for guetter; to be on watch (naut) être de quart; to keep watch over surveiller || tr (to look at) observer; (to oversee) surveiller || intr être aux aguets; (to keep awake) veiller; to watch for guetter; to watch out faire attention; to watch out for faire attention à; to watch over surveiller; watch out! attention!, gare!

watch′ case′ s boîtier m de montre

watch′ chain′ s chaîne f de montre

watch′ charm′ s breloque f

watch′ crys′tal s verre m de montre

watch′ dog′ s chien m de garde; gardien m vigilant

watch′ dog′ commit′tee s comité m de surveillance

watchful ['wɑt∫fəl] adj vigilant

watchfulness ['wɑt∫fɪnɪs] s vigilance f

watch′mak′er s horloger m

watch′man s (pl -men) gardien m

watch′ night′ s réveillon m du jour de l'an

watch′ pock′et s gousset m

watch′ strap′ s bracelet m d'une montre

watch′tow′er s tour f de guet

watch′word′ s mot m d'ordre, mot de passe; devise f

water ['wɔtər], ['wɑtər] s eau f; of the first water de premier ordre; (diamond) de première eau; to back water (naut) culer; reculer; to be in hot water (coll) être dans le pétrin; to fish in troubled waters pêcher en eau trouble; to hold water (coll) tenir debout, être bien fondé; to make water (to urinate) uriner; (naut) faire eau; to pour or throw cold water on (fig) jeter une douche froide sur, refroidir; to swim under water nager entre deux eaux; to tread water nager debout || tr (e.g., plants) arroser; (horses, cattle, etc.) abreuver; (wine) couper; to water down atténuer || intr (said of horses, cattle, etc.) s'abreuver; (said of locomotive, ship, etc.) faire de l'eau; (said of eyes) se mouiller, larmoyer

wa′ter buf′fa·lo s (pl -loes or -los) buffle m

wa′ter car′rier s porteur m d'eau

wa′ter clos′et s water-closet m, waters mpl

wa·ter·col′or s aquarelle f

wa·ter-cooled′ adj à refroidissement d'eau

wa·ter·course′ s cours m d'eau; (of a stream) lit m

wa′ter·cress′ s cresson m de fontaine

wa′ter cure′ s cure f des eaux

wa′ter·fall′ s chute f d'eau

wa′ter·front′ s terrain m sur la rive

wa′ter gap′ s percée f, trouée f, gorge f

wa′ter ham′mer s (in pipe) coup m de bélier

wa′ter heat′er s chauffe-eau m, chauffe-bain m

wa′ter ice′ s boisson f à demi glacée

wa′ter·ing can′ s arrosoir m

wa′ter·ing place′ s (for cattle) abreuvoir m; (for tourists) ville f d'eau

wa′ter·ing pot′ s arrosoir m

wa′ter·ing trough′ s abreuvoir m

wa′ter jack′et s chemise f d'eau

wa′ter lil′y s nénuphar m

wa′ter line′ s ligne f de flottaison; niveau m d'eau

wa·ter·logged′ adj détrempé

wa′ter main′ s conduite f principale

wa′ter·mark′ s (in paper) filigrane m; (naut) laisse f

wa′ter·mel′on s pastèque f, melon m d'eau

wa′ter me′ter s compteur m à eau

wa′ter pipe′ s conduite f d'eau

wa′ter po′lo s water-polo m

wa′ter pow′er s force f hydraulique, houille f blanche

wa·ter·proof′ adj & s imperméable m

wa′ter rights′ spl droits mpl de captation d'eau, droits d'irrigation

wa′ter·shed′ s ligne f de partage des eaux

wa′ter ski′ing s ski m nautique

wa′ter span′iel s (zool) barbet m

wa′ter·spout′ s descente f d'eau, gouttière f; (funnel of wet air) trombe f

wa′ter-supply′ sys′tem s service m des eaux; réseau m de conduites d'eau

wa′ter ta′ble s (geol) nappe f phréatique

wa′ter-tight′ adj étanche; (argument) inattaquable; (law) sans clause échappatoire

wa′ter tow′er s château m d'eau

wa′ter wag′on s—to be on the water wagon (coll) s'abstenir de boissons alcooliques

wa′ter·way′ s voie f navigable

wa′ter wheel′ s roue f hydraulique; roue à aubes or à palettes; roue-turbine f

wa′ter wings′ spl flotteur m de natation

wa′ter·works′ s (system) canalisations fpl d'eau; (pumping station) usine f de distribution des eaux

watery ['wɔtərɪ], ['wɑtərɪ] adj aqueux; (eyes) larmoyant; (food) insipide, fade

watt [wɑt] s watt m

wattage ['wɑtɪdʒ] s puissance f en watts

watt′-hour′ s (pl watt-hours) watt-heure m

wattle ['wɑtəl] s (of bird) caroncule f; (of fish) barbillon m

watt′me′ter s wattmètre m

wave [wev] s onde f, vague f; (in hair) ondulation f; geste m de la main; (of heat or cold; of people; of the future) vague f; (phys) onde f || tr (a handkerchief) agiter; (the hair) onduler; (a hat, newspaper, cane) brandir; to wave aside écarter d'un geste;

to **wave good-bye** faire un signe d'adieu; **to wave one's hand** faire un geste de la main ‖ *intr* s'agiter; *(said of a flag)* ondoyer; **to wave to** faire signe à

wave/length/ *s* longueur *f* d'onde

wave/ mo'tion *s* mouvement *m* ondula-toire

waver ['wevər] *intr* vaciller

wav·y ['wevi] *adj (comp* **-ier;** *super* **-iest)** onduleux, ondoyant; *(hair; road surface)* ondulé; *(line)* tremblé, onduleux

wax [wæks] *s* cire *f* ‖ *tr* cirer ‖ *intr*— **to wax and wane** croître et décroître; **to wax indignant** s'indigner

wax/ bean/ *s* haricot *m* beurre

wax/ pa/per *s* papier *m* paraffiné

wax/ ta/per *s* allumette-bougie *f*

wax/wing/ *s* (orn) jaseur *m*

wax/works/ *s* musée *m* de cire

way [we] *s* voie *f*; *(road)* chemin *m*; *(direction)* côté *m*, sens *m*; *(manner)* façon *f*, manière *f*; *(means)* moyen *m*; *(habit, custom)* manière, habitude *f*, usage *m*; **across the way** en face; **all the way** jusqu'au bout; **by the way** à propos; **by way of** par; comme; **get out of the way!** ôter-vous de là!; **in a way** en un certain sens; **in every way** à tous les égards; **in my (his, etc.) own way** à ma (sa, etc.) façon or manière; **in no way** en au-cune façon; **in some ways** par cer-tains côtés; **in such a way that** de sorte que; **in that way** de la sorte; **in this way** de cette façon; **on the way** chemin faisant; **on the way to** en route pour; **out of the way** écarté; **that way** par là; **the wrong way** le mauvais sens, la mauvaise route; *(the wrong manner)* la mauvaise fa-çon; *(when brushing hair)* à contre-poil; **this way** par ici; **to be in the way** être encombrant; **to feel one's way** avancer à tâtons; **to get out of the way** s'écarter; **to get (s.th. or s.o.) out of the way** se débarrasser de *(q.ch. or qn)*; **to give way** céder; **to go one's own way** faire route bande à part; **to go one's way** passer son chemin; **to go out of one's way** faire un détour; (fig) se déranger; **to have one's way** avoir le dernier mot, l'emporter; **to keep out of s.o.'s way** se tenir à l'écart de qn; **to know one's way around** connaître son affaire, être à la coule; **to lead the way** montrer le chemin; **to make one's way** se frayer un chemin; **to make way for** faire place à; **to mend one's ways** s'amen-der; **to see one's way to** trouver moyen de; **to stand in the way of** barrer le chemin à; **under way** en marche, en cours; **way down** descen-te *f*; **way in** entrée *f*; **way out** sortie *f*; **ways** *(for launching a ship)* couette *f*, anguilles *fpl*; **way through** passage *m*; **way up** montée *f*; **which way?** par où?

way/bill/ *s* feuille *f* de route, lettre *f* de voiture

wayfarer ['we,ferər] *s* voyageur *m*, vagabond *m*

way/lay/ *v (pret & pp* **-laid)** *tr* em-busquer; *(to buttonhole)* arrêter au passage

way/ of life/ *s* mode *f* de vivre, genre *m* de vie, train *m* de vie

way/side/ *s* bord *m* de la route; **to fall by the wayside** rester en chemin

wayward ['wewərd] *adj* capricieux; re-belle

we [wi] *pron pers* nous §85, §87; nous autres, e.g., **we Americans** nous au-tres américains

weak [wik] *adj* faible

weaken ['wikən] *tr* affaiblir ‖ *intr* fai-blir, s'affaiblir

weakling ['wiklɪŋ] *s* chétif *m*, ma-lingre *mf*; *(in character)* mou *m*

weak/-mind/ed *adj* irrésolu, d'esprit faible; *(feeble-minded)* débile

weakness ['wiknɪs] *s* faiblesse *f*

weal [wil] *s* papule *f*; *(archaic)* bien *m*

wealth [wɛlθ] *s* richesse *f*

wealth·y ['wɛlθi] *adj (comp* **-ier;** *super* **-iest)** riche, opulent

wean [win] *tr* sevrer; **to wean away from** détacher de

weapon ['wɛpən] *s* arme *f*

weaponry ['wɛpənri] *s* armement *m*

wear [wer] *s (use)* usage *m*; *(wasting away from use)* usure *f*; *(clothing)* vêtements *mpl*, articles *mpl* d'habille-ment; **for evening wear** pour le soir; **for everyday wear** pour tous les jours ‖ *v (pret* **wore** [wor]; *pp* **worn** [worn])* *tr* porter; *(to put on)* met-tre; **to wear down or out** user; *(e.g., one's patience)* épuiser ‖ *intr* s'user; **to wear off** s'effacer; **to wear on** s'écouler, s'avancer; **to wear out** s'user; **to wear well** durer

wearable ['werəbəl] *adj* mettable

wear/ and tear/ [ter] *s* usure *f*

weariness ['wɪrɪnɪs] *s* lassitude *f*, fa-tigue *f*; ennui *m*

wear/ing appar/el ['werɪŋ] *s* vêtements *mpl*, habits *mpl*

wearisome ['wɪrɪsəm] *adj* lassant, en-nuyeux

wea·ry ['wɪri] *adj (comp* **-rier;** *super* **-riest)** las ‖ *v (pret & pp* **-ried)** *tr* lasser ‖ *intr* se lasser

weasel ['wizəl] *s* (zool) belette *f*; (slang) mouchard *m*

wea/sel words/ *spl* mots *mpl* ambigus

weather ['wɛðər] *s* temps *m*; **to be un-der the weather** (coll) se sentir pa-traque; *(from drinking)* (coll) avoir mal aux cheveux; **what's the weather like?** quel temps fait-il? ‖ *tr* altérer; *(e.g., difficulties)* survivre à, étaler ‖ *intr* s'altérer

weath/er balloon/ *s* ballon *m* atmosphé-rique

weath/er-beat/en *adj* usé par les in-tempéries

weath/er bu/reau *s* bureau *m* météoro-logique, météo *f*

weath/er-cock/ *s* girouette *f*; (fig) girouette, caméléon *m* weath'er fore'cast *s* bulletin *m* météorologique

weath'er fore'casting *s* prévision *f* du temps

weath'er-man' *s* (*pl* -men') météorologue *mf*, météorologiste *mf*

weath'er report' *s* bulletin *m* de la météo

weath'er strip'ping *s* bourrelet *m*

weath'er vane' *s* girouette *f*

weave [wiːv] *v* (*pret* wove [wov] or weaved; *pp* wove or woven ['wovən]) *tr* tisser; (to weave one's way through se faufiler à travers, se faufiler entre || *intr* tisser; serpenter, zigzaguer

weaver ['wivər] *s* tisserand *m*

web [web] *s* (piece of cloth) tissu *m*; (roll of newsprint) rouleau *m*; (of spider) toile *f*; (between toes of birds and other animals) palmure *f*; (of an iron rail) âme *f*; (fig) trame *f*

web'-foot'ed *adj* palmé, palmipède

wed [wed] *v* (*pret* & *pp* wed or wedded; *ger* wedding) *tr* (to join in wedlock) marier; (to take in marriage) épouser || *intr* épouser, se marier

wedding ['wedɪŋ] *adj* nuptial || *s* mariage *m*, noces *fpl*

wed'ding ban'quet *s* repas *m* de noce

wed'ding cake' *s* gâteau *m* de mariage

wed'ding cer'emo·ny *s* (*pl* -nies) cérémonie *f* nuptiale

wed'ding day' *s* jour *m* des noces; anniversaire *m* du mariage

wed'ding dress' *s* robe *f* nuptiale, robe de noce

wed'ding march' *s* marche *f* nuptiale

wed'ding night' *s* nuit *f* de noces

wed'ding pres'ent *s* cadeau *m* de mariage; wedding presents corbeille *f* de mariage

wed'ding ring' *s* anneau *m* nuptial, alliance *f*

wedge [wedʒ] *s* coin *m* || *tr* coincer

wedlock ['wedlɑk] *s* mariage *m*

Wednesday ['wenzdi] *s* mercredi *m*

wee [wi] *adj* tout petit

weed [wid] *s* mauvaise herbe *f*; the weed (coll) le tabac; weeds vêtements *mpl* de deuil || *tr* & *intr* désherber, sarcler; to weed out éliminer, extirper

weed'ing hoe' *s* sarcloir *m*

weed' kill'er *s* herbicide *m*

week [wik] *s* semaine *f*; a week from today d'aujourd'hui en huit; week in week out d'un bout de la semaine à l'autre

week'day' *s* jour *m* de semaine, jour ouvrable

week'end' *s* fin *f* de semaine, week-end *m* || *intr* passer le week-end

week·ly ['wikli] *adj* hebdomadaire || *s* (*pl* -lies) hebdomadaire *m* || *adv* tous les huit jours

weep [wip] *v* (*pret* & *pp* wept [wept]) *tr* pleurer || *intr* pleurer; (to drip) suinter; to weep for pleurer; (joy) pleurer de

weep'ing wil'low *s* saule *m* pleureur

weep·y ['wipi] *adj* (*comp* -ier; *super* -iest) (coll) pleurnicheur

weevil ['wivəl] *s* charançon *m*

weft [weft] *s* (yarns running across warp) trame *f*; (fabric) tissu *m*

weigh [we] *tr* peser; (anchor) lever; to weigh down faire pencher; to weigh in one's hand soupeser || *intr* peser; to weigh heavily with avoir du poids auprès de; to weigh in (sports) se faire peser

weight [wet] *s* poids *m*; to gain weight prendre du poids; to lift weights faire des haltères; to lose weight perdre du poids; to throw one's weight around (coll) s'imposer || *tr* charger; (statistically) pondérer; to weight down alourdir

weightless ['wetlɪs] *adj* sans pesanteur

weightlessness ['wetlɪsnɪs] *s* apesanteur *f*

weight' lift'er *s* (sports) haltérophile *m*

weight' lift'ing *s* poids et haltères *mpl*

weight·y ['weti] *adj* (*comp* -ier; *super* -iest) pesant, lourd; (troublesome) grave; important, puissant

weir [wɪr] *s* (dam) barrage *m*; (trap) filet *m* à poissons

weird [wɪrd] *adj* surnaturel; étrange

welcome ['welkəm] *adj* bienvenu; (change, news, etc.) agréable; to be welcome to + *inf* être libre de + *inf*; you are welcome! (i.e., gladly received) soyez le bienvenu!; (in response to thanks) de rien!, je vous en prie!, il n'y a pas de quoi!; you are welcome to it c'est à votre disposition; (ironically) je ne vous envie pas || *s* bienvenue *f*, bon accueil *m* || *tr* souhaiter la bienvenue à, faire bon accueil à, accueillir; to welcome coldly faire mauvais accueil à, accueillir froidement

weld [weld] *s* soudure *f* autogène; (bot) gaude *f*, réséda *m* || *tr* souder à l'autogène

welder ['weldər] *s* soudeur *m*; (mach) soudeuse *f*

welding ['weldɪŋ] *s* soudure *f* autogène

welfare ['wel,fer] *s* bien-être *m*; (for underprivileged) aide *f* sociale

wel'fare state' *s* état-providence *m*

wel'fare work' *s* assistance *f* sociale

well [wel] *adj* bien (enjoying good health) bien, bien portant; all's well tout est bien; it would be just as well to il serait bon de; to be well aller bien || *s* puits *m*; (natural source of water) source *f*, fontaine *f*; (of stairway) cage *f* || *adv* bien; as well aussi; as well as aussi bien que; well and good! à la bonne heure! || *intr*—to well up jaillir || *interj* alors!, tiens!

well'-behaved' *adj* de bonne conduite; (child) sage

well'-be'ing *s* bien-être *m*

well'born' *adj* bien né

well-bred ['wel'bred] *adj* bien élevé

well'-disposed' *adj* bien disposé

well-done ['wel'dʌn] *adj* bien fait; (culin) bien cuit

well'-dressed' *adj* bien vêtu

well'-fixed' *adj* (coll) bien renté, riche

well'-formed' *adj* bien conformé

well'-found'ed *adj* bien fondé

well'-groomed' *adj* paré, soigné

well'-heeled' *adj* (coll) huppé, riche

well'-informed' *adj* bien informé

well'-inten'tioned *adj* bien intentionné

well-kept ['wel'kept] *adj* bien tenu; *(secret)* bien gardé

well-known ['wel'non] *adj* bien connu, notoire

well'-matched' *adj* bien assortis

well'-mean'ing *adj* bien intentionné

well'-nigh' *adv* presque

well'-off' *adj* fortuné, prospère

well'-preserved' *adj* bien conservé

well-read ['wel'red] *adj* qui a beaucoup de lecture

well-spent ['wel'spent] *adj* bien employé

well'-spring' *s* source *f*, source intarissable

well' sweep' *s* chadouf *m*

well'-thought'-of' *adj* de bonne réputation

well'-timed' *adj* opportun

well-to-do ['welta'du] *adj* aisé, cossu

well-wisher ['wel'wɪʃər] *s* partisan *m*, ami *m* fidèle

well'-worn' *adj* usé; *(subject)* rebattu

Welsh [welʃ] *adj* gallois || *s (language)* gallois *m*; the Welsh les Gallois *mpl* || *(l.c.) intr* (slang) manquer à sa parole, manquer à ses obligations; to welsh on s.o. (slang) manquer à qn

Welsh'man *s (pl* -men) Gallois *m*

Welsh' rab'bit or rare'bit ['rerbɪt] *s* fondue *f* au fromage et à la bière sur canapé

welt [welt] *s* zébrure *f*; *(border)* bordure *f*; *(of shoe)* trépointe *f*

welter ['weltər] *s* confusion *f*, fouillis *m* || *intr* se vautrer

wel'ter-weight' *s (boxing)* poids *m* mi-moyen

wen [wen] *s* kyste *m* sébacé, loupe *f*

wench [wentʃ] *s* jeune fille *f*, jeune femme *f*

wend [wend] *tr*—to wend one's way (to) diriger ses pas (vers)

west [west] *adj* & *s* ouest *m* || *adv* à l'ouest, vers l'ouest

western ['westərn] *adj* occidental, de l'ouest || *s* (mov) western *m*

westerner ['westərnər] *s* habitant *m* de l'ouest, Occidental *m*

West' Ger'many *s* Allemagne *f* de l'Ouest; l'Allemagne de l'Ouest

West' In'dies ['ɪndiz] *spl* Indes *fpl* occidentales, Antilles *fpl*

westward ['westwərd] *adv* vers l'ouest

wet [wet] *adj (comp* wetter; *super* wettest) mouillé; *(damp)* humide; *(rainy)* pluvieux; *(paint)* frais; (coll) antiprohibitionniste; all wet (slang) fichu, erroné || *s* antiprohibitionniste *mf* || *v (pret & pp* wet or wetted; *ger* wetting) *tr* mouiller || *intr* se mouiller

wet' bat'ter-y *s (pl* -ies) pile *f* à liquide

wet' blan'ket *s* trouble-fête *mf*, rabat-joie *m*

wet' nurse' *s* nourrice *f*

wet' paint' *s* peinture *f* fraîche; (public sign) attention à la peinture

whack [hwæk] *s* (coll) coup *m*, gnon *m*; *(try)* (coll) tentative *f*; to have a whack at (coll) s'attaquer à || *tr* (coll) cogner

whale [hwel] *s* baleine *f*; *(sperm whale)* cachalot *m*; to have a whale of a time (coll) s'amuser follement || *tr* (coll) rosser

whale'bone' *s* baleine *f*, fanon *m* de baleine

whaler ['hwelər] *s* baleinier *m*

wharf [hwɔrf] *s (pl* wharves [hwɔrvz] or wharfs) quai *m*, débarcadère *m*

what [hwɑt] *adj interr* quel §80, e.g., what time is it? quelle heure est-il?; e.g., what is his occupation? quel est son métier? || *adj rel* ce qui, e.g., I'll give you what water I have left je vous donnerai ce qui me reste d'eau; ce que, e.g., I know what drink you want je sais ce que vous voulez comme boisson || *pron interr* qu'est-ce qui, e.g., what happened? qu'est-ce qui s'est passé?; que, e.g., what are you doing? que faites-vous?; qu'est-ce que, e.g., what are you doing? qu'est-ce que vous faites?; comment, e.g., what is he like? comment est-il?; combien, e.g., what is two and two? combien font deux et deux?; what (did you say)? comment?; what else? quoi d'autre?, quoi encore; what for? pourquoi donc?; what if si, e.g., what if I were to die? si je venais à mourir?; what if I did?, what of it?, so what? qu'importe?, what is it? qu'est-ce que c'est?, qu'est-ce qu'il y a?; what now? alors?; what's that? qu'est-ce que c'est que cela?; what then? et après? || *pron rel* ce qui, ce que; ce dont §79, e.g., I have what you need j'ai ce dont vous avez besoin; ce à quoi, e.g., I know what you are thinking of je sais ce à quoi vous pensez; (sometimes untranslated), e.g., he asked them what time it was il leur a demandé l'heure; to know what's what (coll) s'y connaître, être au courant || *interj* comment!; what a que de, e.g., what a lot of people! que de monde!; quel §80, e.g., what a pity! quel dommage!

what-ev'er *adj* quel que §80; moindre or quelconque, e.g., is there any hope whatever? y a-t-il le moindre espoir?, y a-t-il un espoir quelconque? || *pron* tout ce qui; tout ce que, e.g., tell him whatever you like dites-lui tout ce que vous voudrez; quoi que, e.g., whatever you do quoi que vous fassiez; whatever comes à tout hasard

what'not' *s* étagère *f*

what's'-his-name' *s* (coll) Monsieur un tel

wheal [wil] *s* papule *f*

wheat [hwit] *s* blé *m*

wheedle ['hwidəl] *tr* enjôler

wheel [hwil] *s* roue *f*; **at the wheel** au volant || *tr* (*to turn*) faire pivoter; (*a wheelbarrow, table, etc.*) rouler || *intr* pivoter; (*said, e.g., of birds in the sky*) tournoyer; **to wheel about** or **around** faire demi-tour

wheelbarrow ['hwil,bæro] *s* brouette *f*

wheel/base/ *s* (aut) empattement *m*

wheel/chair/ *s* fauteuil *m* roulant pour malade, voiture *f* d'infirme

wheel/ horse/ *s* (*horse*) timonier *m*; (*person*) bûcheur *m*

wheelwright ['hwil ,rait] *s* charron *m*

wheeze [hwiz] *s* respiration *f* sifflante; (pathol) cornage *m* || *intr* respirer avec peine, souffler

whelp [hwelp] *s* petit *m* || *tr* & *intr* mettre bas

when [hwen] *adv* quand || *conj* quand, lorsque; (*on which, in which*) où; (*whereas*) alors que

whence [hwens] *adv* & *conj* d'où

when•ev/er *conj* chaque fois que, quand

where [hwer] *adv* & *conj* où; **from where** d'où

whereabouts ['hwerə ,bauts] *s*—**the whereabouts of** l'endroit où se trouve || *adv* & *conj* où donc

whereas [hwer'æz] *conj* tandis que, attendu que || *s* considérant *m*

where•by/ *conj* par lequel

wherefore ['hwerfor] *s* & *adv* pourquoi *m* || *conj* à cause de quoi

where•from/ *adv* d'où

where•in/ *adv* d'où; en quoi || *conj* où

where•of/ *adv* de quoi || *conj* dont §79

where/up•on/ *adv* sur quoi, sur ce

wherever [hwer'evər] *conj* partout où; où que, n'importe où

wherewithal ['hwerwɪð ,ɔl] *s* ressources *fpl*, moyens *mpl*

whet [hwet] *v* (*pret* & *pp* **whetted**; *ger* **whetting**) *tr* aiguiser

whether ['weðər] *conj* si; que, e.g., **it is doubtful whether you can finish** il est douteux que vous puissiez finir; e.g., **whether he is rich or poor** qu'il soit riche ou qu'il soit pauvre; **whether or no** de toute façon; **whether or not** qu'il en soit ainsi ou non

whet/stone/ *s* pierre *f* à aiguiser

whew [hwju] *interj* ouf!

whey [hwe] *s* petit lait *m*

which [hwɪtʃ] *adj interr* quel §80, e.g., **which university do you prefer?** quelle université préférez-vous?; **which one?** lequel? || *adj rel* le . . . que, e.g., **choose which road you prefer** choisissez le chemin que vous préférez || *pron interr* lequel §78; **which is which?** lequel des deux est-ce?; **which of them?** lequel d'entre eux? || *pron rel* qui; que; dont §79

which•ev/er *adj rel* n'importe quel || *pron rel* n'importe lequel

whiff [hwɪf] *s* bouffée *f*; **to get a whiff of** flairer

while [hwaɪl] *s* temps *m*, moment *m*; **a**

long while longtemps; **a (little) while ago** tout à l'heure; **in a little while** sous peu, tout à l'heure || *conj* pendant que; (*as long as*) tant que; (*although*) quoique || *tr*—**to while away** tuer, faire passer

whim [hwɪm] *s* caprice *m*, lubie *f*

whimper ['hwɪmpər] *s* pleurnicherie *f* || *tr* dire en pleurnichant || *intr* pleurnicher

whimsical ['hwɪmzɪkəl] *adj* capricieux, lunatique

whine [hwaɪn] *s* geignement *m*; (*of siren*) hurlement *m* || *intr* geindre; (*said of siren*) hurler

whin•ny ['hwɪni] *s* (*pl* -**nies**) hennissement *m* || *v* (*pret* & *pp* -**nied**) *intr* hennir

whip [hwɪp] *s* fouet *m* || *v* (*pret* & *pp* **whipped** or **whipt**; *ger* **whipping**) *tr* fouetter; (*to defeat*) battre; (*the end of a rope*) surlier; **to whip out** (*e.g., a gun*) sortir brusquement; **to whip up** (*e.g., a supper*) (coll) préparer à l'improviste; (*e.g., enthusiasm*) (coll) stimuler

whip/cord/ *s* corde *f* à fouet

whip/ hand/ *s* main *f* du fouet; (*upper hand*) avantage *m*, dessus *m*

whip/lash/ *s* mèche *f* de fouet

whipped/ cream/ *s* crème *f* fouettée, chantilly *m*

whipper-snapper ['hwɪpər,snæpər] *s* freluquet *m*, paltoquet *m*

whip/ping boy/ *s* tête *f* de Turc

whip/ping post/ *s* poteau *m* des condamnés au fouet

whippoorwill [,hwɪpər'wɪl] *s* (*Caprimulgus vociferus*) engoulevent *m* américain

whir [hwʌr] *s* ronflement *m* || *v* (*pret* & *pp* **whirred**; *ger* **whirring**) *intr* ronfler

whirl [hwʌrl] *s* tourbillon *m*; (*of events, parties, etc.*) succession *f* ininterrompue || *tr* faire tourbillonner || *intr* tourbillonner; **his head whirls** la tête lui tourne

whirligig ['hwʌrlɪ ,gɪg] *s* tourniquet *m*; (ent) gyrin *m*, tourniquet

whirl/pool/ *s* tourbillon *m*, remous *m*

whirl/wind/ *s* tourbillon *m*

whirlybird ['hwʌrlɪ,bʌrd] *s* (coll) hélicoptère *m*

whisk [hwɪsk] *s* coup *m* léger; (*broom*) époussette *f*; (culin) fouet *m* || *tr* balayer; (culin) fouetter; **to whisk out of sight** escamoter || *intr* aller comme un trait

whisk/ broom/ *s* époussette *f*

whiskers ['hwɪskərz] *spl* barbe *f*, poils *mpl* de barbe; (*on side of face*) favoris *mpl*; (*of cat*) moustaches *fpl*

whiskey ['hwɪski] *s* whisky *m*

whisper ['hwɪspər] *s* chuchotement *m* || *tr* chuchoter, dire à l'oreille || *intr* chuchoter

whispering ['hwɪspərɪŋ] *s* chuchotement *m*

whist [hwɪst] *s* whist *m*

whistle ['hwɪsəl] *s* (*sound*) sifflement

m; (*device*) sifflet *m*; **to wet one's whistle** (coll) s'humecter le gosier ‖ *tr* siffler, siffloter ‖ *intr* siffler; **to whistle for** siffler; attendre en vain, se voir obligé de se passer de

whis′tle stop′ *s* arrêt *m* facultatif

whit [hwɪt] *s*—not a whit pas un brin; **to not care a whit** s'en moquer

white [hwaɪt] *adj* blanc ‖ *s* blanc *m*; blanc d'œuf; **whites** (pathol) pertes *fpl* blanches

white′caps′ *spl* moutons *mpl*

white′ coal′ *s* houille *f* blanche

white′-col′lar *adj* de bureau

white′ feath′er *s*—**to show the white feather** lâcher pied, flancher, caner

white′fish′ *s* poisson *m* blanc, merlan *m*

white′ goods′ *spl* vêtements *mpl* blancs; tissus *mpl* de coton, cotonnade *f*; (*appliances*) appareils *mpl* électroménagers

white′-haired′ *adj* aux cheveux blancs, chenu; (coll) favori

white′-hot′ *adj* chauffé à blanc

white′ lead′ [lɛd] *s* céruse *f*, blanc *m* de céruse

white′ lie′ *s* mensonge *m* pieux

white′ meat′ *s* blanc *m*

whiten [′hwaɪtən] *tr & intr* blanchir

whiteness [′hwaɪtnɪs] *s* blancheur *f*

white′ slav′ery *s* traite *f* des blanches

white′ tie′ *s* cravate *f* blanche; tenue *f* de soirée

white′wash′ *s* blanc *m* de chaux, badigeon *m*; (*cover-up*) couverture *f* ‖ *tr* blanchir à la chaux; (*e.g., a guilty person, a scandal*) blanchir

whither [′hwɪðər] *adv & conj* où, là où

whitish [′hwaɪtɪʃ] *adj* blanchâtre

whitlow [′hwɪtlo] *s* panaris *m*

Whitsuntide [′hwɪtsən,taɪd] *s* saison *f* de la Pentecôte

whittle [′hwɪtəl] *tr* tailler au couteau; **to whittle away** or **down** amenuiser

whiz or **whizz** [hwɪz] *s* sifflement *m*; (slang) prodige *m* ‖ *v* (pret & pp **whizzed**) *intr*—**to whiz by** passer en sifflant, passer comme le vent

who [hu] *pron interr* qui; quel §80; **who else?** qui d'autre?; qui encore?; **who is there?** (mil) qui vive? ‖ *pron rel* qui; celui qui §83

whoa [hwo] *interj* holà!, doucement!

who•ev′er *pron rel* quiconque; celui qui §83; qui que, e.g., **whoever you are** qui que vous soyez

whole [hol] *adj* entier ‖ *s* tout *m*, totalité *f*, ensemble *m*; **on the whole** somme toute, à tout prendre

whole′heart′ed *adj* sincère, de bon cœur

whole′ note′ *s* (mus) ronde *f*

whole′ rest′ *s* (mus) pause *f*

whole′sale′ *adj & adv* en gros; (*e.g., slaughter*) en masse ‖ *s* gros *m*, vente *f* en gros ‖ *tr & intr* vendre en gros

whole′sale price′ *s* prix *m* de gros

wholesaler [′hol,selər] *s* commerçant *m* en gros, grossiste *mf*

whole′sale trade′ *s* commerce *m* de gros

wholesome [′holsəm] *adj* sain

wholly [′holi] *adv* entièrement

whom [hum] *pron interr* qui ‖ *pron rel* que; lequel §78; celui que §83; **of whom** dont, de qui §79

whom•ev′er *pron rel* celui que §83; tous ceux que; (*with a preposition*) quiconque

whoop [hup], [hwup] *s* huée *f*; (*cough*) quinte *f* ‖ *tr*—**to whoop it up** (slang) pousser des cris ‖ *intr* huer

whoop′ing cough′ [′hupɪŋ], [′hupɪŋ] *s* coqueluche *f*

whopper [′hwapər] *s* (coll) chose *f* énorme; (*lie*) (coll) gros mensonge *m*

whopping [′hwapɪŋ] *adj* (coll) énorme

whore [hor] *s* putain *f* ‖ *intr*—**to whore around** courir la gueuse

whortleberry [′hwʌrtəl,beri] *s* (*pl -ries*) myrtille *f*

whose [huz] *pron interr* à qui, e.g., **whose pen is that?** à qui est ce stylo? ‖ *pron rel* dont, de qui §79; duquel §78

why [hwaɪ] *s* (*pl* whys [hwaɪz]) pourquoi *m*; **the why and the wherefore** le pourquoi et le comment ‖ *adv* pourquoi; **why not?** pourquoi pas? ‖ *interj* tiens!; **why, certainly!** mais bien sûr!; **why, yes!** mais oui!

wick [wɪk] *s* mèche *f*

wicked [′wɪkɪd] *adj* méchant, mauvais

wicker [′wɪkər] *adj* en osier ‖ *s* osier *m*

wicket [′wɪkɪt] *s* guichet *m*; (croquet) arceau *m*

wide [waɪd] *adj* large; (*range*) vaste, étendu; (*spread, angle, etc.*) grand; large de, e.g., **eight feet wide** large de huit pieds ‖ *adv* loin, partout; **open wide!** ouvrez bien!

wide′-an′gle *adj* grand-angulaire

wide′-awake′ *adj* bien éveillé

widen [′waɪdən] *tr* élargir ‖ *intr* s'élargir

wide′-o′pen *adj* grand ouvert

wide′spread′ *adj* (*arms, wings*) étendu; répandu, universel

widow [′wɪdo] *s* veuve *f* ‖ *tr*—**to be widowed** devenir veuf

widower [′wɪdo•ər] *s* veuf *m*

widowhood [′wɪdo,hud] *s* veuvage *m*

wid′ow's mite′ *s* obole *f*

wid′ow's weeds′ *spl* deuil *m* de veuve

width [wɪdθ] *s* largeur *f*; (*of cloth*) lé *m*

wield [wild] *tr* (*sword, pen*) manier; (*power*) exercer

wife [waɪf] *s* (*pl* wives [waɪvz]) femme *f*, épouse *f*

wig [wɪg] *s* perruque *f*

wiggle [′wɪgəl] *s* tortillement *m* ‖ *tr* agiter ‖ *intr* tortiller, se tortiller

wig′wag′ *s* télégraphie *f* optique ‖ *v* (pret & pp **-wagged**; ger **-wagging**) *tr* transmettre à bras avec fanions ‖ *intr* signaler à bras avec fanions

wigwam [′wɪgwam] *s* wigwam *m*

wild [waɪld] *adj* sauvage; (*untamed*) sauvage, fauve; (*frantic, mad*) frénétique; (*hair; dance; dream*) échevelé; (*passion; torrent; night*) tumultueux;

, plan) insensé, extravagant; *z)* déréglé; *(blows, bullet, shot)* perdu; **wild about** or **for** fou de || **wilds** *spl* régions *fpl* sauvages || *adv* —**to run wild** dépasser toutes les bornes; *(said of plants)* pousser librement

wild/ boar/ *s* sanglier *m*

wild/ card/ *s* mistigri *m*

wild/cat/ *s* chat *m* sauvage; lynx *m*; *(well)* sondage *m* d'exploration

wild/cat strike/ *s* grève *f* sauvage, grève spontanée

wild/ cher/ry *s (pl* -ries) merise *f*; *(tree)* merisier *m*

wilderness ['wɪldərnɪs] *s* désert *m*

wild/fire/ *s* feu *m* grégeois; feu *m* follet; éclairs *mpl* en nappe; **like wildfire** comme une traînée de poudre

wild/ flow/er *s* fleur *f* des champs

wild/ goose/ *s* oie *f* sauvage

wild/-goose/ chase/ *s*—**to go on a wild-goose chase** faire buisson creux

wild/life/ *s* animaux *mpl* sauvages

wild/ oats/ *spl*—**to sow one's wild oats** jeter sa gourme

wile [waɪl] *s* ruse *f* || *tr*—**to wile away** tuer, faire passer

will [wɪl] *s* volonté *f*; *(law)* testament *m*; **against one's will** à contre-cœur; **at will** à volonté; **with a will** de bon cœur || *tr* vouloir; *(to bequeath)* léguer || *intr* vouloir; **do as you will** faites comme vous voudrez || *(pret & cond* **would** [wʊd]) *aux* used to express 1) the future indicative, e.g., **he will arrive early** il arrivera de bonne heure; 2) the future perfect indicative, e.g., **he will have arrived before I leave** il sera arrivé avant que je parte; 3) the present indicative denoting habit or custom, e.g., **after breakfast he will go out for a walk every morning** après le petit déjeuner il fait une promenade tous les matins

willful ['wɪlfəl] *adj* volontaire; *(stubborn)* obstiné

willfulness ['wɪlfəlnɪs] *s* entêtement *m*

William ['wɪljəm] *s* Guillaume *m*

willing ['wɪlɪŋ] *adj* disposé, prêt; **to be willing** to vouloir bien; **willing or unwilling** bon gré mal gré

willingly ['wɪlɪŋli] *adv* volontiers

willingness ['wɪlɪŋnɪs] *s* bonne volonté *f*, consentement *m*

will-o'-the-wisp ['wɪləðə'wɪsp] *s* feu *m* follet; *(fig)* chimère *f*

willow ['wɪlo] *s* saule *m*

willowy ['wɪlo-i] *adj* souple, agile; svelte, élancé; couvert de saules

will/ pow/er *s* force *f* de volonté

willy-nilly ['wɪlɪ'nɪli] *adv* bon gré mal gré

wilt [wɪlt] *tr* flétrir || *intr* se flétrir

wil·y ['waɪli] *adj (comp* -ier; *super* -iest) rusé, astucieux

wimple ['wɪmpəl] *s* guimpe *f*

win [wɪn] *s (coll)* victoire *f* || *v (pret & pp* **won** [wʌn]; *ger* **winning**) *tr* gagner; *(a victory, a prize)* remporter; **to win back** regagner; **to win over** gagner, convaincre || *intr* ga-

gner; convaincre; **to win out** *(coll)* réussir

wince [wɪns] *s*—**without a wince** sans sourciller || *intr* tressailler

winch [wɪntʃ] *s* treuil *m*; *(handle, crank)* manivelle *f*

wind [wɪnd] *s* vent *m*; *(breath)* haleine *f*, souffle *m*; **to break wind** lâcher un vent, faire un pet; **to get wind of** avoir vent de; **to sail close to the wind** courir au plus près; **to sail into the wind** aller au lof, venir au lof || *tr* faire perdre le souffle à || *intr* flairer le gibier || [waɪnd] *v (pret & pp* **wound** [waʊnd]) *tr* enrouler; *(a timepiece)* remonter; *(yarn, thread, etc.)* pelotonner; **to wind up** enrouler; remonter; *(to finish)* (coll) terminer, régler || *intr* serpenter

windbag ['wɪnd,bæg] *s (of bagpipe)* outre *f*; (coll) moulin *m* à paroles

windbreak ['wɪnd,brek] *s* abrivent *m*

wind/ cone/ [wɪnd] *s* (aer) manche *f* à air

winded ['wɪndɪd] *adj* essoufflé

windfall ['wɪnd,fɔl] *s (fig)* aubaine *f*

wind/ing road/ ['waɪndɪŋ] *s* route *f* en lacet

wind/ing sheet/ *s* linceul *m*

wind/ing stairs/ *spl* escalier *m* en colimaçon

wind/ in/strument [wɪnd] *s* (mus) instrument *m* à vent

windlass ['wɪndləs] *s* treuil *m*

windmill ['wɪnd,mɪl] *s* moulin *m* à vent; *(on a modern farm)* aéromoteur *m*; **to tilt at windmills** se battre contre des moulins à vent

window ['wɪndo] *s* fenêtre *f*; *(of ticket office)* guichet *m*; *(of store)* vitrine *f*; *(aut)* glace *f*

win/dow dress/er *s* étalagiste *mf*

win/dow dress/ing *s* art *m* de l'étalage; (coll) façade *f*

win/dow en/velope *s* enveloppe *f* à fenêtre

win/dow frame/ *s* châssis *m*, dormant *m*

win/dow-pane/ *s* vitre *f*, carreau *m*

win/dow screen/ *s* grillage *m*

win/dow shade/ *s* store *m*

win/dow-shop/ *v (pret & pp* -shopped; *ger* -shopping) *intr* faire du lèche-vitrines, lécher les vitrines

win/dow shut/ter *s* volet *m*

win/dow sill/ *s* rebord *m* de fenêtre

windpipe ['wɪnd,paɪp] *s* trachée-artère *f*

windshield ['wɪnd,ʃild] *s* pare-brise *m*

wind/shield wash/er *s* lave-glace *m*

wind/shield wip/er *s* essuie-glace *m*

windsock ['wɪnd,sɑk] *s* manche *f* à air

windstorm ['wɪnd,stɔrm] *s* tempête *f* de vent

wind/ tun/nel [wɪnd] *s* tunnel *m* aérodynamique

wind-up ['waɪnd,ʌp] *s* conclusion *f*, fin *f*

windward ['wɪndwərd] *adj & adv* au vent || *s* côté *m* du vent; **to turn to windward** louvoyer

wind·y ['wɪndi] adj (comp -ier; super -iest) venteux; (verbose) verbeux; **it is windy** il fait du vent

wine [waɪn] s vin m || tr—**to wine and dine s.o.** fêter qn

wine' cel'lar s cave f

wine' glass' s verre m à vin

winegrower ['waɪn,gro·ər] s viticulteur m

winegrowing ['waɪn,gro·ɪŋ] s viticulture f

wine' list' s carte f des vins

wine' press' s pressoir m

winer·y ['waɪnəri] s (pl -ies) pressoir m

wine' skin' s outre f à vin

wine' stew'ard s sommelier m; (of prince, king) bouteiller m

winetaster ['waɪn,testər] s (person) dégustateur m; (pipette) taste-vin m

wing [wɪŋ] s aile f; (e.g., of hospital) pavillon m; (pol) parti m, faction f; **in the wings** (theat) dans la coulisse; **on the wing** au vol; **to take wing** prendre son essor || tr (to wound) blesser; **to wing one's way** voler

wing' chair' s fauteuil m à oreilles

wing' col'lar s col m rabattu

wing' load' s (aer) charge f alaire

wing' nut' s écrou m ailé

wing' spread' s envergure f

wink [wɪŋk] s clin m d'œil; **to not sleep a wink** ne pas fermer l'œil; **to take forty winks** (coll) piquer un roupillon || tr cligner || intr cligner des yeux; **to wink at** cligner de l'œil à; (e.g., an abuse) fermer les yeux sur

winner ['wɪnər] s gagnant m, vainqueur m

winning ['wɪnɪŋ] adj gagnant; (attractive) séduisant || **winnings** spl gains mpl

winnow ['wɪno] tr vanner, sasser; (e.g., the evidence) passer au crible

winsome ['wɪnsəm] adj séduisant

winter ['wɪntər] s hiver m || intr passer l'hiver; (said of animals, troops, etc.) hiverner

win'ter·green' s (oil) wintergreen m; (bot) gaulthérie f

win·try ['wɪntri] adj (comp -trier; super -triest) hivernal, froid

wipe [waɪp] tr essuyer; **to wipe away** essuyer; **to wipe off or out** effacer; (to annihilate) anéantir; **to wipe up** nettoyer

wiper ['waɪpər] s torchon m; (elec) contact m glissant; (mach) came f

wire [waɪr] s fil m; télégramme m; **hold the wire!** (telp) restez à l'écoute!; **on the wire** (telp) au bout du fil; **reply by wire** réponse f télégraphique; **to get in under the wire** arriver juste à temps; terminer juste à temps; **to pull wires** (coll) tirer les ficelles || tr attacher avec du fil de fer; (a message) télégraphier; (a house) canaliser || intr télégraphier

wire' cut'ter s coupe-fil m

wire' draw' v (pret -drew; pp -drawn) tr tréfiler

wire' entan'glement s réseau m de barbelés

wire' gauge' s calibre m or jauge f pour fils métalliques

wire'-haired' adj à poil dur

wireless ['waɪrlɪs] adj sans fil

wire' nail' s clou m de Paris

wire'pho'to s (pl -tos) (trademark) (device) bélinographe m; (photo) bélinogramme m

wire'pull'ing s (coll) influences fpl secrètes, piston m

wire' record'er s magnétophone m à fil d'acier

wire'tap' s (device) table f d'écoute || v (pret & pp -tapped; ger -tapping) tr passer à la table d'écoute

wiring ['waɪrɪŋ] s (e.g., of house) canalisation f; (e.g., of radio) montage m

wir·y ['waɪri] adj (comp -ier; super -iest) nerveux; (hair) raide

wisdom ['wɪzdəm] s sagesse f

wis'dom tooth' s dent f de sagesse

wise [waɪz] adj sage; (step, decision) judicieux, prudent; **to be wise to** (slang) voir clair dans le jeu de, percer le jeu de; **to get wise** (coll) se mettre au courant || s—**in no wise** en aucune manière || tr—**to wise up** (slang) avertir, désabuser

wiseacre ['waɪz,ekər] s fat m, fierot m

wise'crack' s (coll) blague f, plaisanterie f || intr (coll) blaguer, plaisanter

wise' guy' s (slang) type m goguenard

wish [wɪʃ] s souhait m, désir m; **best wishes** meilleurs vœux mpl; (formula used to close a letter) amitiés; **last wishes** dernières volontés fpl; **to make a wish** faire un vœu || tr souhaiter, désirer; **to wish s.o. s.th.** souhaiter q.ch. à qn; **to wish s.o. to** + inf souhaiter que qn + subj; **to wish to** + inf vouloir + inf

wish'bone' s fourchette f

wishful ['wɪʃfəl] adj désireux

wish'ful think'ing s optimisme m à outrance; **to indulge in wishful thinking** se forger des chimères

wish'ing well' s puits m aux souhaits

wistful ['wɪstfəl] adj pensif, rêveur

wit [wɪt] s esprit m; (person) homme m d'esprit; **to be at one's wits' end** ne plus savoir que faire; **to keep one's wits about one** conserver toute sa présence d'esprit; **to live by one's wits** vivre d'expédients

witch [wɪtʃ] s sorcière f

witch'craft' s sorcellerie f

witch' doc'tor s sorcier m guérisseur

witch'es' Sab'bath s sabbat m

witch' ha'zel s teinture f d'hamamélis; (bot) hamamélis m

witch' hunt' s chasse f aux sorcières

with [wɪð], [wɪθ] prep avec; (at the home of; in the case of) chez; (in spite of) malgré; à, e.g., **the girl with the blue eyes** la jeune fille aux yeux bleus; e.g., **coffee with milk** café au lait; e.g., **with open arms** à bras ouverts; e.g., **with these words . . . à ces mots . . .** ; de, e.g., **with a loud**

voice d'une voix forte; e.g., **with all his strength** de toutes ses forces; e.g., **to be satisfied with** être satisfait de; e.g., **to fill with** remplir de

with·draw' v (pret **-drew**; pp **-drawn**) tr retirer || intr se retirer

withdrawal [wɪð'drɔ·əl], [wɪθ'drɔ·əl] s retrait m

wither ['wɪðər] tr faner || intr se faner

with·hold' v (pret & pp **-held**) tr (money, taxes, etc.) retenir; (permission) refuser; (the truth) cacher

with·hold'ing tax' s impôt m retenu à la source

with·in' adv à l'intérieur; là-dedans §85A || prep à l'intérieur de; (in less than) en moins de; (within the limits of) dans; (in the bosom of) au sein de; (not exceeding a margin of error of) à . . . près, e.g., **I can tell you what time it is within five minutes** je peux vous dire l'heure à cinq minutes près; à portée de, e.g., **with·in reach** à portée de la main

with·out' adv au-dehors, dehors || prep au dehors de; (lacking, not with) sans; **to do without** se passer de; **without** + ger sans + inf, e.g., **he left without seeing me** il est parti sans me voir; sans que + subj, e.g., **he left without anyone seeing him** il est parti sans que personne ne le voie

with·stand' v (pret & pp **-stood**) tr résister à

witness ['wɪtnɪs] s témoin m; **in witness whereof** en foi de quoi; **to bear witness** rendre témoignage || tr (to be present at) être témoin de, assister à; (to attest) témoigner; (e.g., a contract) signer

wit'ness stand' s barre f des témoins

witticism ['wɪtɪˌsɪzəm] s trait m d'esprit

wittingly ['wɪtɪŋli] adv sciemment

wit·ty ['wɪti] adj (comp **-tier**; super **-tiest**) spirituel

wizard ['wɪzərd] s sorcier m

wizardry ['wɪzərdri] s sorcellerie f

wizened ['wɪzənd] adj desséché

woad [wod] s guède f

wobble ['wɑbəl] intr chanceler; (said of table) branler; (said of voice) chevroter; vaciller

wob·bly ['wɑbli] adj (comp **-blier**; super **-bliest**) vacillant

woe [wo] s malheur m, affliction f; **woe is me!** pauvre de moi!

woebegone ['wobɪˌgɔn], ['wobɪˌgɑn] adj navré, abattu, désolé

woeful ['wofəl] adj triste, désolé; très mauvais

wolf [wʊlf] s (pl **wolves** [wʊlvz]) loup m; galant m, tombeur m de femmes; **to cry wolf** crier au loup; **to keep the wolf from the door** se mettre à l'abri du besoin, joindre les deux bouts || tr & intr engloutir

wolf' cub' s louveteau m

wolf'hound' s chien-loup m

wolf' pack' s bande f de loups

wolfram ['wʊlfrəm] s (element) tungstène m; (mineral) wolfram m

wolf's'-bane' or **wolfs'bane'** s tue-loup m, aconit m, napel m

woman ['wʊmən] s (pl **women** ['wɪmɪn]) femme f

wom'an doc'tor s femme f médecin, doctoresse f

womanhood ['wʊmənˌhʊd] s le sexe féminin; les femmes fpl

womanish ['wʊmənɪʃ] adj féminin; (effeminate) efféminé

wom'an·kind' s le sexe féminin

wom'an la'borer s femme f manœuvre

woman·ly ['wʊmənli] adj (comp **-lier**; super **-liest**) féminin, femme

wom'an preach'er s femme f pasteur

womb [wum] s utérus m, matrice f; (fig) sein m

wonder ['wʌndər] s merveille f; (feeling of surprise) émerveillement m; (something strange) miracle m; **for a wonder** chose étonnante; **no wonder that** . . . rien d'étonnant que . . . ; **to work wonders** faire des merveilles || tr—**to wonder that** s'étonner que; **to wonder why, if, whether** se demander pourquoi, si || intr—**to wonder at** s'émerveiller de, s'étonner de

won'der drug' s remède m miracle

wonderful ['wʌndərfəl] adj merveilleux, étonnant

won'der·land' s pays m des merveilles

wonderment ['wʌndərmənt] s étonnement m

wont [wʌnt], [wɔnt] adj—**to be wont to** avoir l'habitude de || s—**his wont** son habitude

wonted adj habituel, accoutumé

woo [wu] tr courtiser

wood [wʊd] s bois m; (for wine) fût m; **out of the woods** (coll) hors de danger, hors d'affaire; **to take to the woods** se sauver dans la nature; **woods** bois m or mpl

woodbine ['wʊdˌbaɪn] s (honeysuckle) chèvrefeuille m; (Virginia creeper) vigne f vierge

wood' carv'ing s sculpture f sur bois

wood'chuck' s marmotte f d'Amérique

wood'cock' s bécasse f

wood'cut' s (typ) gravure f sur bois

wood'cut'ter s bûcheron m

wooded ['wʊdɪd] adj boisé

wooden ['wʊdən] adj en bois; (style, manners) guindé, raide

wood' engrav'ing s (typ) gravure f sur bois

wood'en-head'ed adj (coll) stupide, obtus

wood'en leg' s jambe f en bois

wood'en shoe' s sabot m

wood' grouse' s grand tétras m, grand coq m de bruyère

woodland ['wʊdlənd] adj sylvestre || s pays m boisé

wood'land scene' s (painting) paysage m boisé

wood'man s (pl **-men**) bûcheron m

woodpecker ['wʊdˌpɛkər] s pic m; (green woodpecker) pivert m, pic-vert m

wood' pig'eon s (orn) ramier m

wood'pile' s tas m de bois

wood' screw' *s* vis *f* à bois

wood'shed' *s* bûcher *m*

woods'man *s* (*pl* **-men**) bûcheron *m*; (*trapper*) trappeur *m*, chasseur *m*

wood' tick' *s* vrillette *f*

wood'winds' *spl* (mus) bois *mpl*

wood'work' *s* (*working in wood*) menuiserie *f*; (*things made of wood*) boiseries *fpl*

wood'work'er *s* menuisier *m*

wood'worm' *s* (ent) artison *m*

wood·y ['wudi] *adj* (*comp* **-ier**; *super* **-iest**) boisé; (*like wood*) ligneux

wooer ['wu·ər] *s* prétendant *m*

woof [wuf] *s* trame *f*; (*fabric*) tissu *m*

woofer ['wufər] *s* (rad) boomer *m*, woofer *m*

wool [wul] *s* laine *f*

woolen ['wulən] *adj* de laine ‖ *s* tissu *m* de laine; **woolens** lainage *m*

wool'gath'ering *s* rêvasserie *f*

woolgrower ['wul‚gro·ər] *s* éleveur *m* des bêtes à laine

wool·ly ['wuli] *adj* (*comp* **-lier**; *super* **-liest**) laineux

word [wʌrd] *s* mot *m*; (*promise, assurance*) parole *f*; **in other words** autrement dit; **in your own words** en vous propres termes; **my word!** ça alors!; **not a word!** motus!; **the Word** (eccl) le Verbe; **to break one's word** manquer à sa parole; **to have words with** échanger des propos désagréables avec; **to make s.o. eat his words** faire ravaler ses paroles à qn; **to put in a word** placer un mot; **to take s.o. at his word** prendre qn au mot, croire qn sur parole; **upon my word!** ma foi!; **without a word** sans mot dire; **words** (*e.g., of song*) paroles ‖ *tr* formuler, rédiger

word'-forma'tion *s* formation *f* des mots

wording ['wʌrdɪŋ] *s* langage *m*

word' or'der *s* ordre *m* des mots

word'-stock' *s* vocabulaire *m*

word·y ['wʌrdi] *adj* (*comp* **-ier**; *super* **-iest**) verbeux

work [wʌrk] *s* travail *m*, ouvrage *m*; (*production, deed*) œuvre *f*, ouvrage; **at work** en œuvre; (*not at home*) au travail, au bureau, à l'usine; **out of work** sans travail, en chômage; **to shoot the works** (slang) mettre le paquet; **works** œuvres; mécanisme *m*; (*of clock*) mouvement *m* ‖ *tr* faire travailler; (*to operate*) faire fonctionner, faire marcher; (*wood, iron*) travailler; (*mine*) exploiter; **to work out** élaborer, résoudre; **to work up** préparer; stimuler ‖ *intr* travailler; (*said of motor, machine, etc.*) fonctionner, marcher; (*said of remedy*) faire de l'effet; (*said of wine, beer*) fermenter; **how will things work out?** à quoi tout cela aboutira-t-il?; **to work hard** travailler dur; **to work loose** se desserrer; **to work out** (sports) s'entraîner; **to work too hard** se surmener

workable ['wʌrkəbəl] *adj* (*feasible*) réalisable; (*that can be worked*) ouvrable

work'bas'ket *s* corbeille *f* à ouvrage

work'bench' *s* établi *m*

work'book' *s* manuel *m*; (*notebook*) carnet *m*; (*for student*) cahier *m* de devoirs

work'box' *s* boîte *f* à ouvrage; (*for needlework*) coffret *m* de travail

work'day' *adj* de tous les jours; prosaïque, ordinaire ‖ *s* jour *m* ouvrable; (*part of day devoted to work*) journée *f*

worked'-up' *adj* préparé, ouvré; (*excited*) agité, emballé

worker ['wʌrkər] *s* travailleur *m*, ouvrier *m*, employé *m*

work' force' *s* main-d'œuvre *f*; personnel *m*

work'horse' *s* cheval *m* de charge; (*tireless worker*) vrai cheval *m* de labour

work'house' *s* maison *f* de correction; (Brit) asile *m* des pauvres

work'ing class' *s* classe *f* ouvrière

work'ing day' *s* jour *m* ouvrable; (*daily hours for work*) journée *f*

work'ing-girl' *s* jeune ouvrière *f*

work'ing hours' *spl* heures *fpl* de travail

work'ing-man' *s* (*pl* **-men'**) travailleur *m*

work'ing-wom'an *s* (*pl* **-wom'en**) ouvrière *f*

work'man *s* (*pl* **-men**) ouvrier *m*

workmanship ['wʌrkmən‚ʃɪp] *s* habileté *f*, professionnelle, facture *f*; (*work executed*) travail *m*

work' of art' *s* œuvre *f* d'art

work'out' *s* essai *m*, épreuve *f*; (*physical exercise*) séance *f* d'entraînement

work'room' *s* atelier *m*; (*for study*) cabinet *m* de travail, cabinet d'études

work'shop' *s* atelier *m*

work' stop'page *s* arrêt *m* du travail

world [wʌrld] *adj* mondial ‖ *s* monde *m*; **a world of** énormément de; **for all the world** à tous les égards, exactement; **not for all the world** pour rien au monde; **since the world began** depuis que le monde est monde; **the other world** l'autre monde; **to bring into the world** mettre au monde; **to go around the world** faire le tour du monde; **to see the world** voir du pays; **to think the world of** estimer énormément, avoir une très haute opinion de

world' affairs' *spl* affaires *fpl* internationales

world'-fa'mous *adj* de renommée mondiale

world' his'tory *s* histoire *f* universelle

world·ly ['wʌrldli] *adj* (*comp* **-lier**; *super* **-liest**) mondain

world'ly-wise' *adj*—**to be worldly-wise** savoir ce que c'est que la vie

world' map' *s* mappemonde *f*

World' Se'ries *s* championnat *m* mondial

world's' fair' *s* exposition *f* universelle

world' war' *s* guerre *f* mondiale

world'-wide' adj mondial, universel

worm [wʌrm] s ver m || tr enlever les vers de; (a secret, money, etc.) soutirer; **to worm it out of him** lui tirer les vers du nez || intr se faufiler

worm-eaten ['wʌrm,itən] adj vermoulu

worm' gear' s engrenage m à vis sans fin

worm'wood' s (Artemisia) armoise f; (Artemisia absinthium) armoise absinthe; (something grievous) (fig) absinthe f

worm·y ['wʌrmɪ] adj (comp -ier; super -iest) véreux

worn [worn] adj usé, fatigué

worn'-out' adj épuisé, usé; éreinté

worrisome ['wʌrɪsəm] adj inquiétant; inquiet, anxieux

wor·ry ['wʌrɪ] s (pl -ries) souci m, inquiétude f; (cause of anxiety) ennui m, tracas m || v (pret & pp -ried) tr inquiéter; (to harass, pester) ennuyer, tracasser; **to be worried s'in-**quiéter || intr s'inquiéter; **don't worry!** ne vous en faites pas!

worse [wʌrs] adj comp pire, plus mauvais §91; and **to make matters worse** et par surcroît de malheur; **so much the worse** tant pis; **to make or get worse** empirer; **what's worse** qui pis est; **worse and worse** de pis en pis || adv comp pis, plus mal §91

worsen ['wʌrsən] tr & intr empirer

wor·ship ['wʌr/ɪp] s culte m, adoration f || v (pret & pp -shiped or -shipped; ger -shiping or -shipping) tr adorer || intr prier; (to go to church) aller au culte

worshiper or **worshipper** ['wʌr/ɪpər] s adorateur m, fidèle mf

worst [wʌrst] adj super pire §91; pis || s (le) pire, (le) pis; **to the hurt the worst** être le plus gravement atteint (blessé, etc.); **to get the worst of it** avoir le dessous || adv super pis §91

worsted ['wʊstɪd] adj de laine peignée || s peigné m, tissu m de laine peignée

wort [wʌrt] s (of beer) moût m

worth [wʌrθ] adj digne de; valant, e.g., **book worth three dollars** livre valant trois dollars; **to be worth** valoir; avoir une fortune de; **to be worth +** ger valoir la peine de + inf; **to be worth while** valoir la peine || s valeur f; **a dollar's worth of** pour un dollar de

worthless ['wʌrθlɪs] adj sans valeur; (person) bon à rien, indigne

worth'while' adj utile, de valeur

wor·thy ['wʌrðɪ] adj (comp -thier; super -thiest) digne || s (pl -thies) notable mf; (hum, ironical) personnage m

would [wʊd] aux used to express 1) the past future, e.g., **he said he would come** il a dit qu'il viendrait; 2) the present conditional, e.g., **he would come if he could** il viendrait s'il pouvait; 3) the past conditional, e.g., **he would have come if he had been able (to)** il serait venu s'il avait pu; 4) the

potential mood, e.g., **would that I knew it!** plût à Dieu que je le sache!, je voudrais le savoir!; 5) the past indicative denoting habit or custom in the past, e.g., **he would visit us every day** il nous visitait tous les jours

would'-be' adj prétendu

wound [wund] s blessure f || tr blesser

wounded ['wundɪd] adj blessé || s— **the wounded** les blessés mpl

wow [wau] s (e.g., of phonograph record) distorsion f; (slang) succès m formidable || tr (slang) enthousiasmer || interj (slang) formidable!

wrack [ræk] s vestige m; (ruin) naufrage m; (bot) varech m

wraith [reθ] s apparition f

wrangle ['ræŋgəl] s querelle f || intr se quereller

wrap [ræp] s couverture f; (coat) manteau m || v (pret & pp wrapped; ger wrapping) tr envelopper, emballer

wrap'around wind'shield s pare-brise m panoramique

wrapper ['ræpər] s saut-de-lit m; (of newspaper or magazine) bande f; (of tobacco) robe f

wrap'ping pa'per s papier m d'emballage

wrath [ræθ], [rɑθ] s colère f

wrathful ['ræθfəl], ['rɑθfəl] adj courroucé, en colère

wreak [rik] tr assouvir

wreath [riθ] s (pl wreaths [riðz]) couronne f; (of smoke) volute f, panache m

wreathe [rið] tr enguirlander; (e.g., flowers) entrelacer || intr (said of smoke) s'élever en volutes

wreck [rek] s (shipwreck) naufrage m; (debris at sea or elsewhere) épave f; (of train) déraillement m; (of airplane) écrasement m; (of auto) accident m; (of one's hopes) naufrage; **to be a wreck** être une ruine || tr (a ship, one's hopes) faire échouer; (a train) faire dérailler; (one's health) ruiner

wreckage ['rekɪdʒ] s débris mpl, décombres mpl, ruines fpl

wrecker ['rekər] s (tow truck) dépanneuse f; (person) dépanneur m

wreck'ing car' s voiture f de dépannage

wreck'ing crane' s grue f de dépannage

wren [ren] s (orn) troglodyte m; (kinglet) (orn) roitelet m

wrench [rent/] s clef f; (pull) secousse f; (twist of a joint) foulure f || tr (e.g., one's ankle) se fouler; (to twist) tordre

wrest [rest] tr arracher violemment

wrestle ['resəl] s lutte f || intr lutter

wrestling ['reslɪŋ] s (sports) lutte f, catch m

wres'tling match' s rencontre f de catch

wretch [ret/] s misérable mf

wretched ['ret/ɪd] adj misérable

wriggle ['rɪgəl] s tortillement m || tr tortiller || intr se tortiller; **to wriggle out of** esquiver adroitement

wrig‧gly ['rɪgli] *adj* (*comp* **-glier;** *super* **-gliest**) frétillant; évasif

wring [rɪŋ] *v* (*pret & pp* **wrung** [rʌŋ]) *tr* tordre; (*one's hands*) se tordre; (*s.o.'s hand*) serrer fortement; **to wring out** (*clothes*) essorer; (*money, a secret, etc.*) arracher

wringer ['rɪŋər] *s* essoreuse *f*

wrinkle ['rɪŋkəl] *s* (*in skin*) ride *f*; (*in clothes*) pli *m*, faux pli; (*clever idea or trick*) (coll) truc *m* ‖ *tr* plisser ‖ *intr* se plisser

wrin‧kly ['rɪŋkli] *adj* (*comp* **-klier;** *super* **-kliest**) ridé, chiffonné

wrist [rɪst] *s* poignet *m*

wrist′band′ *s* poignet *m*

wrist′ watch′ *s* montre-bracelet *f*

writ [rɪt] *s* (eccl) écriture *f*; (law) acte *m* judiciaire

write [raɪt] *v* (*pret* **wrote** [rot]; *pp* **written** ['rɪtən]) *tr* écrire; **to write down** consigner par écrit; baisser le prix de; **to write in** insérer; **to write off** (*a debt*) passer aux profits et pertes; to write up rédiger un compte rendu de; (*to ballyhoo*) faire l'éloge de ‖ *intr* écrire; **to write back** répondre par écrit

writer ['raɪtər] *s* écrivain *m*

writ′er's cramp′ *s* crampe *f* des écrivains

write′-up′ *s* compte *m* rendu; (*ballyhoo*) battage *m*; (com) surestimation *f*

writhe [raɪð] *intr* se tordre

writing ['raɪtɪŋ] *s* écriture *f*; (*something written*) écrit *m*, œuvre *f*; (*profession*) métier *m* d'écrivain; **at this writing** au moment où j'écris; **to put in writing** mettre par écrit

writ′ing desk′ *s* bureau *m*, écritoire *f*; (*in schoolroom*) pupitre *m*

writ′ing pa′per *s* papier *m* à lettres

wrong [rɔŋ], [rʌŋ] *adj* (*unjust*) injuste; (*incorrect*) erroné; (*road, address, side, place, etc.*) mauvais; **ne pas . . . qu'il faut,** e.g., **I arrived at the wrong city** je ne suis pas arrivé à la ville qu'il fallait; (*word*) impropre; **qui ne marche pas,** e.g., **something is wrong with the motor** il y a quelque chose qui ne marche pas dans le moteur; **to be wrong** (*i.e., in error*) avoir tort; (*i.e., to blame*) être le coupable ‖ *s* mal *m*; injustice *f*; **to be in the wrong** être dans son tort, avoir tort; **to do wrong** faire du mal, faire du tort ‖ *adv* mal; **to go wrong** faire fausse route; (*said, e.g., of a plan*) ne pas marcher; (*said of one falling into evil ways*) se dévoyer; **to guess wrong** se tromper ‖ *tr* faire du tort à, être injuste envers

wrongdoer ['rɔŋ‚du‧ər], ['rʌŋ‚du‧ər] *s* malfaiteur *m*

wrong′do′ing *s* mal *m*, tort *m*; (*misdeeds*) méfaits *mpl*

wrong′ num′ber *s* (telp) mauvais numéro *m*; **you have the wrong number** vous vous trompez de numéro

wrong′ side′ *s* (*e.g., of material*) revers *m*, envers *m*; (*of the street*) mauvais côté *m*; **to drive on the wrong side** circuler à contre-voie; **to get out of bed on the wrong side** se lever du pied gauche; **wrong side out** à l'envers; **wrong side up** sens dessus dessous

wrought′ i′ron [rɔt] *s* fer *m* forgé

wrought′-up′ *adj* excité, agité

wry [raɪ] *adj* (*comp* **wrier;** *super* **wriest**) tordu, de travers; forcé, ironique

wry′neck′ *s* (orn) torcol *m*; (pathol) torticolis *m*

X

X, x [eks] *s* XXIVᵉ lettre de l'alphabet

Xavier ['zævɪ‧ər], ['zevɪ‧ər] *s* Xavier *m*

xenophobe ['zenə‚fob] *s* xénophobe *mf*

Xerxes ['zɑrksiz] *s* Xerxès *m*

Xmas ['krɪsməs] *adj* de Noël ‖ *s* Noël *m*

X′ ray′ *s* (*photograph*) radiographie *f*; **to have an X ray** passer à la radio; **X rays** rayons *mpl* X

X′-ray′ *adj* radiographique ‖ **X′-ray′** *tr* radiographier

X′-ray treat′ment *s* radiothérapie *f*

xylophone ['zaɪlə‚fon] *s* xylophone *m*

Y

Y, y [waɪ] *s* XXVᵉ lettre de l'alphabet

yacht [jɑt] *s* yacht *m*

yacht′ club′ *s* yacht-club *m*

yah [jɑ] *interj* (*in disgust*) pouah!; (*in derision*) oh là là!

yam [jæm] *s* igname *f*; (*sweet potato*) patate *f* douce

yank [jæŋk] *s* (coll) secousse *f* ‖ *tr* (coll) tirer d'un coup sec

Yankee ['jæŋki] *adj & s* yankee *mf*

yap [jæp] s jappement m; (slang) criaillerie f ‖ v (pret & pp yapped; ger yapping) intr japper; (slang) criailler; (slang) dégoiser

yard [jɑrd] s cour f; (for lumber, for repairs, etc.) chantier m; (measure) yard m; (naut) vergue f; (rr) gare f de triage

yard′arm′ s (naut) bout m de vergue

yard′mas′ter s (rr) chef m de dépôt

yard′stick′ s yard m en bois (en métal, etc.); (fig) unité f de comparaison

yarn [jɑrn] s fil m, filé m; (coll) histoire f

yarrow ['jæro] s mille-feuille f

yaw [jɔ] s (naut) embardée f; yaws (pathol) pian m ‖ intr faire des embardées

yawl [jɔl] s yole f

yawn [jɔn] s bâillement m ‖ intr bâiller; être béant

ye (old spelling of the [ðə]) art le, e.g., **ye olde shoppe** la vieille boutique ‖ [ji] pron (obs) vous

yea [je] s oui m; vote m affirmatif ‖ adv oui, voire

yeah [je] adv (coll) oui; **oh yeah?** (coll) de quoi?; **oh yeah!** (coll) ouais!

yean [jin] intr (said of ewe) agneler; (said of goat) chevreter

year [jɪr] s an m, année f; **to be . . . years old** avoir . . . ans; **year in year out** bon an mal an

year′book′ s annuaire m

yearling ['jɪrlɪŋ] s animal m d'un an; (horse) yearling m

yearly ['jɪrli] adj annuel ‖ adv annuellement

yearn [jɑrn] intr—**to yearn for** soupirer après; **to yearn to** brûler de

yearning ['jɑrnɪŋ] s désir m ardent

yeast [jist] s levure f

yell [jɛl] s hurlement m; (school yell) cri m de ralliement ‖ tr & intr hurler

yellow ['jɛlo] adj jaune; (cowardly) (coll) froussard; (e.g., press) à sensation; **to turn yellow** jaunir; (coll) avoir la frousse ‖ s jaune m ‖ tr & intr jaunir

yel′low-ham′mer s (orn) bruant m jaune

yellowish ['jɛlo·ɪʃ] adj jaunâtre

yel′low-jack′et s (ent) frelon m

yel′low streak′ s (coll) trait m de lâcheté

yelp [jɛlp] s glapissement m, jappement m ‖ intr glapir, japper

yen [jɛn] s—**to have a yen to or for** (coll) avoir envie de

yeo·man ['jomən] s (pl -men) yeoman m; (clerical worker) (nav) commis m aux écritures

yeo′man of the guard′ s (Brit) hallebardier m de la garde du corps

yeo′man's serv′ice s effort m précieux

yes [jɛs] s oui m ‖ adv oui; (to contradict a negative statement or question) si or pardon, e.g., "**You didn't know.**" "**Yes, I did!**" "Vous ne le saviez pas." "Si!" ‖ v (pret & pp yessed; ger yessing) tr dire oui à ‖ intr dire oui

yes′ man′ s (pl men′) (coll) M. Toujours; **to be a yes man** opiner du bonnet; **yes men** (coll) béni-oui-oui mpl

yesterday ['jɛstərdi], ['jɛstər‚de] adj, s, & adv hier m; **yesterday morning** hier matin

yet [jɛt] adv encore; **as yet** jusqu'à présent; **not yet** pas encore ‖ conj cependant

yew′ tree′ [ju] s if m

Yiddish ['jɪdɪʃ] adj & s yiddish m

yield [jild] s rendement m; (crop) produit m; (income produced) rapport m, revenu m ‖ tr rendre, produire; (a profit; a crop) rapporter; (to surrender) céder ‖ intr produire, rapporter; céder, se rendre; (public sign) priorité (à droite; à gauche)

YMCA ['waɪ'ɛm'si'e] s (letterword) (Young Men's Christian Association) Association f des jeunesses chrétiennes

yo·del ['jodəl] s tyrolienne f ‖ v (pret & pp -deled or -delled; ger -deling or -delling) tr & intr jodler

yogurt ['jogurt] s yogourt m

yoke [jok] s (pair of draft animals) paire f; (device to join a pair of draft animals) joug m; (of a shirt) empiècement m; (elec) culasse f; (fig) joug; **to throw off the yoke** secouer le joug ‖ tr accoupler

yokel ['jokəl] s rustaud m, manant m

yolk [jok] s jaune m d'œuf

yonder ['jɑndər] adj ce . . . -là là-bas ‖ adv là-bas

yore [jor] s—**of yore** d'antan

you [ju] pron pers vous, tu §85; vous, tu §87; vous, te §87 ‖ pron indef (coll) on §87, e.g., **you go in this way** on entre par ici

young [jʌŋ] adj (comp younger ['jʌŋgər]; super youngest ['jʌŋgɪst]) jeune ‖ **the young** les jeunes; (of animal) les petits mpl; **to be with young** (said of animal) être pleine; **young and old** les grands et les petits

young′ la′dy s (pl -dies) jeune fille f; (married) jeune femme f; **young ladies** jeunes personnes fpl

young′ man′ s (pl men′) jeune homme m; **young men** jeunes gens mpl

young′ peo′ple spl jeunes gens mpl

youngster ['jʌŋstər] s gosse mf

your [jur] adj poss votre, ton §88

yours [jurz] pron poss le vôtre, le tien §89; **a friend of yours** un de vos amis; **cordially yours** (complimentary close) amitiés; **yours truly or sincerely yours** (complimentary close) veuillez agréer, Monsieur, l'expression de mes sentiments distingués

your·self [jur'sɛlf] pron pers (pl -selves ['sɛlvz]) vous-même, toi-même §86; vous, te §87; vous, toi §85

youth [juθ] s (pl youths [juðs], [juðz]) jeunesse f; (person) jeune homme m; **youths** jeunes mpl

youthful ['juθfəl] *adj* jeune, juvénile
yowl [jaul] *s* hurlement *m* ‖ *intr* hurler
Yugoslav ['jugo'slɑv] *adj* yougoslave ‖ *s* Yougoslave *mf*

Yugoslavia ['jugo'slɑvɪ-ə] *s* Yougoslavie *f*; la Yougoslavie
Yule' log' [jul] *s* bûche *f* de Noël
Yule'tide' *s* les fêtes *fpl* de Noël

Z

Z, z [zi] or [zɛd] (Brit) *s* XXVIᵉ lettre de l'alphabet
za·ny ['zeni] *adj* (*comp* **-nier;** *super* **-niest**) bouffon, toqué ‖ *s* (*pl* **-nies**) bouffon *m*
zeal [zil] *s* zèle *m*
zealot ['zɛlət] *s* zélateur *m*, adepte *mf*
zealotry ['zɛlɛtri] *s* fanatisme *m*
zealous ['zɛləs] *adj* zélé
zebra ['zibrə] *s* zèbre *m*
zenith ['zinɪθ] *s* zénith *m*
zephyr ['zɛfər] *s* zéphyr *m*
zeppelin ['zɛpəlɪn] *s* zeppelin *m*
ze·ro ['zɪro] *s* (*pl* **-ros** or **-roes**) zéro *m* ‖ *intr*—**to zero in** (in (mil) régler la ligne de mire
ze'ro hour' *s* heure *f* H
zest [zɛst] *s* enthousiasme *m*; (*agreeable and piquant flavor*) saveur *f*, piquant *m*
Zeus [zus] *s* Zeus *m*
zig·zag ['zɪg͵zæg] *adj* & *adv* en zigzag ‖ *s* zigzag *m* ‖ *v* (*pret* & *pp* **-zagged;** *ger* **-zagging**) *intr* zigzaguer

zinc [zɪŋk] *s* zinc *m*
Zionism ['zaɪ-ə͵nɪzəm] *s* sionisme *m*
zip [zɪp] *s* (coll) sifflement *m*; (coll) énergie *f* ‖ *v* (*pret* & *pp* **zipped;** *ger* **zipping**) *tr* fermer à fermeture éclair ‖ *intr* siffler; **to zip by** (coll) passer comme un éclair
zipper ['zɪpər] *s* fermeture *f* éclair
zither ['zɪθər] *s* cithare *f*
zodiac ['zodɪ͵æk] *s* zodiaque *m*
zone [zon] *s* zone *f*
zon'ing or'dinance *s* réglementation *f* urbaine
zoo [zu] *s* zoo *m*
zoologic(al) [͵zo-ə'lɑdʒɪk(əl)] *adj* zoologique
zoology [zo'ɑlədʒi] *s* zoologie *f*
zoom [zum] *s* vrombissement *m*; (aer) montée *f* en chandelle ‖ *intr* vrombir; **to zoom up** monter en chandelle
zoot' suit' [zut] *s* costume *m* zazou
Zu·lu ['zulu] *adj* zoulou ‖ *s* (*pl* **-lus**) Zoulou *m*

Speak any language
as easily as you speak your own!

FRENCH

☐ 12860   **FRENCH STORIES**   Wallace Fowlie, ed. $2.50

☐ 14890   **THE BANTAM NEW COLLEGE FRENCH &** $2.75
            ENGLISH DICTIONARY   Roger J. Steiner

☐ 14168   **READ, WRITE, SPEAK FRENCH** $2.95
            Mendor Brunetti

HEBREW

☐ 14420   **THE NEW BANTAM-MEGIDDO HEBREW &** $2.95
            ENGLISH DICTIONARY   Reuben Sivan &
            Edward A. Levenston

ITALIAN

☐ 14210   **THE BANTAM NEW COLLEGE ITALIAN &** $2.50
            ENGLISH DICTIONARY   Robert Melzi

LATIN

☐ 13252   **THE NEW COLLEGE LATIN & ENGLISH** $2.50
            DICTIONARY John Traupman

SPANISH

☐ 12936   **SPANISH STORIES**   Angel Flores, ed. $2.25

☐ 13718   **THE BANTAM NEW COLLEGE SPANISH &** $2.50
            ENGLISH DICTIONARY   Edwin B. Williams

☐ 14386   **FIRST SPANISH READER**   Angel Flores, ed. $2.25

Buy them at your local bookstore or use this handy coupon for ordering:

Bantam Books, Inc., Dept. EDC, 414 East Golf Road, Des Plaines, Ill. 60016

Please send me the books I have checked above. I am enclosing $_____
(please add $1.00 to cover postage and handling). Send check or money order
—no cash or C.O.D.'s please.

Mr/Mrs/Miss_____

Address_____

City_____State/Zip_____

                                                      EDC—2/81
Please allow four to six weeks for delivery. This offer expires 7/81.

THE NAMES THAT SPELL
GREAT LITERATURE

Choose from today's most renowned world authors—every one
an important addition to your personal library.

Hermann Hesse

☐	13956	MAGISTER LUDI	$2.95
☐	13523	DEMIAN	$2.25
☐	14305	THE JOURNEY TO THE EAST	$2.25
☐	13855	SIDDHARTHA	$2.50
☐	14563	BENEATH THE WHEEL	$2.95
☐	14445	NARCISSUS AND GOLDMUND	$2.95
☐	14462	STEPPENWOLF	$2.75
☐	11510	ROSSHALDE	$1.95

Alexander Solzhenitsyn

☐	10111	THE FIRST CIRCLE	$2.50
☐	13441	ONE DAY IN THE LIFE OF IVAN DENISOVICH	$2.50
☐	13720	CANCER WARD	$3.95

Jerzy Kosinski

☐	14117	STEPS	$2.50
☐	14489	THE PAINTED BIRD	$2.75
☐	2613	COCKPIT	$2.25
☐	14661	BLIND DATE	$2.95
☐	13843	BEING THERE	$2.50
☐	14577	THE DEVIL TREE	$2.50

Doris Lessing

☐	13433	THE SUMMER BEFORE THE DARK	$2.95
☐	13675	THE GOLDEN NOTEBOOK	$3.95
☐	13967	THE FOUR-GATED CITY	$3.95
☐	14398	BRIEFING FOR A DESCENT INTO HELL	$2.95
☐	12581	MEMOIRS OF A SURVIVOR	$2.50

Buy them at your local bookstore or use this handy coupon for ordering

The Inquisitive Mind

Bantam/Britannica Books were created for those with a desire to learn. Compacted from the vast Britannica files, each book gives an indepth treatment of a particular facet of science, world events, or politics. These accessible, introductory volumes are ideal for the student and for the intellectually curious who want to know more about the world around them.

Bantam Book Catalog

Here's your up-to-the-minute listing of over 1,400 titles by your favorite authors.

This illustrated, large format catalog gives a description of each title. For your convenience, it is divided into categories in fiction and non-fiction—gothics, science fiction, westerns, mysteries, cookbooks, mysticism and occult, biographies, history, family living, health, psychology, art.

So don't delay—take advantage of this special opportunity to increase your reading pleasure.

Just send us your name and address and 50¢ (to help defray postage and handling costs).